WINSTON S. CI
1941

THE CHURCHILL BIOGRAPHY IS COMPLETE IN EIGHT VOLUMES

Volume I. Youth, 1874–1900 *by Randolph S. Churchill*
  Volume I. Companion (in two parts)
Volume II. Young Statesman, 1900–1914 *by Randolph S. Churchill*
  Volume II. Companion (in three parts)
Volume III. 1914–1916 *by Martin Gilbert*
  Volume III. Companion (in two parts)
Volume IV. 1917–1922 *by Martin Gilbert*
  Volume IV. Companion (in three parts)
Volume V.1922–1939 *by Martin Gilbert*
  Volume V. Companion 'The Exchequer Years' 1922–1929
  Volume V. Companion 'The Wilderness Years' 1929–1935
  Volume V. Companion 'The Coming of War' 1936–1939
Volume VI. 1939–1941, 'Finest Hour' *by Martin Gilbert*
  The Churchill War Papers: Volume I 'At the Admiralty'
Volume VII. 1941–1945, 'Road to Victory' *by Martin Gilbert*
Volume VIII. 1945–1965, 'Never Despair' *by Martin Gilbert*

Churchill – A Life *by Martin Gilbert*

OTHER BOOKS BY MARTIN GILBERT

The Appeasers (*with Richard Gott*)
The European Powers, 1900–1945
The Roots of Appeasement
Recent History Atlas, 1860–1960
British History Atlas
American History Atlas
Jewish History Atlas
First World War Atlas
Russian Imperial History Atlas
Soviet History Atlas
The Arab–Israeli Conflict, Its History in Maps
Sir Horace Rumbold, Portrait of a Diplomat
Churchill, A Photographic Portrait
Jerusalem Illustrated History Atlas
Jerusalem, Rebirth of a City
Exile and Return, The Struggle for Jewish Statehood
Children's Illustrated Bible Atlas
Auschwitz and the Allies
Atlas of the Holocaust
The Jews of Hope, the Plight of Soviet Jewry Today
Shcharansky, Hero of our Time
The Holocaust, the Jewish Tragedy
First World War
Second World War
In Search of Churchill
History of the Twentieth Century (*in three volumes*)

Editions of documents
Britain and Germany Between the Wars
Plough My Own Furrow, the Life of Lord Allen of Hurtwood
Servant of India, Diaries of the Viceroy's Private Secretary, 1905–1910

THE CHURCHILL WAR PAPERS

VOLUME III

The Ever-Widening War

1941

MARTIN GILBERT

W. W. NORTON & COMPANY
New York London

First American edition 2001

Printed in the United States of America

The text of this book is composed in Monotype Baskerville
Manufacturing by The Courier Companies, Inc.

Library of Congress Catalog Card Number: 92-44367

ISBN 0-393-01959-4

W. W. Norton & Company, Inc., 500 Fifth Avenue, New York, N.Y. 10110
www.wwnorton.com

W.W. Norton & Company Ltd., 10 Coptic Street, London WC1A 1PU

1 2 3 4 5 6 7 8 9 0

The Churchill War Papers are
dedicated to the memory of
Emery Reves
who helped to carry the books
of Sir Winston Churchill
to the world

The Ever-Widening War is dedicated to those
members of Churchill's wartime Private Office
and personal staff
who
over the years
have helped me with recollections, materials, advice
and encouragement

Sir John Colville
Kathleen Hill
General Sir Ian Jacob
Patrick Kinna
Sir John Martin
Elizabeth Nel
Sir John Peck
Sir Richard Pim
Sir Leslie Rowan

and to two of those without whose work on the Churchill papers
half a century ago
mine would have been all but impossible

Sir William Deakin
Denis Kelly

Contents

Preface

1941 was a testing time for Britain: the second full year of war, but the first year in which the battles were fought from the start without hesitation. No 'phoney war' marked the opening months. The Blitz which had been intense during the last months of 1940 continued; the Battle of the Atlantic intensified; the struggle in North Africa was unremitting.

This volume of the Churchill War Papers, for the year 1941, covers several turning points of the war, each of which added to the burdens of war direction. Among these were the British decision at the beginning of the year to send troops to Greece, the German invasion of Yugoslavia and Greece in April, Rashid Ali's revolt in Iraq during April and May, the military confrontation with Vichy France in Syria in May, the German invasion of the Soviet Union in June, British aid to the Soviet Union throughout the rest of the year, the British occupation of Iran in September, and, in December, the Japanese attack on the United States, Britain and the Dutch East Indies. A persistent need throughout the year was the maintenance of Britain's transatlantic lifeline, and the despatch and use of British troops in North Africa. The volume follows Churchill's daily concerns, inquiries, presentations of war policy, and search for improved means of both defence and attack.

The year 1941 'opens in storm', Churchill wrote to President Roosevelt on New Year's Day. It was typical of Churchill that he would send one of his first messages of the year to the President of the United States. His many messages to Roosevelt during 1941, published here in their entirety, were a crucial vehicle for British war policy. Churchill worked hard throughout the year to sustain and enhance American support, while commenting wryly that the American 'love of doing business may lead them to denude us of all our realizable resources before they show any inclination to be Good Samaritan'. (*January 1*) In his second message of the year to

Roosevelt, on the following day, Churchill sent a reasoned appeal for Britain to be able to pay for the goods it needed without being in danger of having 'to default or be stripped bare of our last resources', an outcome, he stressed, that was 'full of danger and causes us profound anxiety'. Roosevelt's agreement that British warships could use American ports 'delighted' him. (*January 11*) The emergence of Lend Lease was 'a draught of life'. (*March 8*) It told the British people 'by an ocean-borne trumpet that we are no longer alone'. (*March 18*)

At every opportunity Churchill stressed the crucial nature of co-operation between Britain and the United States. Without such co-operation and 'identity of purpose', he told an Anglo-American gathering in London, 'the chance of setting the march of mankind clearly and surely along the highroads of human progress would be lost and might never return'. (*January 9*)

Although Churchill's wish to fly to Bermuda to meet Roosevelt in February was opposed by King George VI for fear of Churchill's personal security (*26 February*), the links with Roosevelt were persistently maintained. Joint naval co-operation was a predominant theme (*as on March 19 and 22*). Roosevelt's emissaries were made particularly welcome, predominant among them, after Harry Hopkins had returned to Washington, being Averell Harriman. 'I am all for trusting Mr Harriman fully and working with him on the most intimate terms', Churchill told the Cabinet Secretary. (*March 26*) The extension of American naval patrols in the Atlantic as far west as the 25th Meridian was, Churchill told Roosevelt, 'a long step towards salvation'. (*April 13*) Concerns with regard to the Battle of the Atlantic often surfaced in Churchill's letters to Roosevelt (*as on April 24 and 25, and July 7*).

Churchill saw a major role in United States policy, even while neutral, 'to deter the wavering nations, such as Vichy France, Spain etc'. (*April 28*) Scrutinizing the British government's departmental contacts with the United States, he was alert to any tone which he felt might create ill-will. 'A negative answer like this,' he wrote on one occasion, 'is chilling and ill-suited to our present purpose.' (*April 29*) That purpose was to take fullest advantage of the many pro-British initiatives that Roosevelt had taken. A British Admiral who had, in Churchill's view, cast a 'cold douche' on that purpose was swiftly rebuked. (*April 30, May 1*) Whoever was responsible for starting the idea that Britain would like 'their destroyer forces to operate on their side of the Atlantic rather than ours' should be 'immediately removed from all American contacts . . . No question of Naval strategy in the Atlantic is comparable with the importance of drawing the Americans to this side.' (*June 28*)

As the war widened and Britain's position worsened – following the defeat of the British forces in Greece, setbacks in the Middle East and continued sinkings at sea – there was a note almost of desperation in Churchill's telegram to Roosevelt setting out the dangers of the situation. The 'one decisive counterweight', Churchill wrote, to the 'growing pessimism' in Turkey, the Near East and Spain about Britain's chances 'would be if United States were immediately to range herself with us a belligerent power'. Were she to do so 'I have little doubt that we could hold the situation in the Mediterranean until the weight of your munitions gained the day.' (*May 4*)

No such United States declaration of war was forthcoming, although further American help included American merchant ships and tankers put at Britain's disposal. In his telegram of May 4 Churchill thanked Roosevelt for 'all your generous and bold assistance to us and to the common cause'. Monitoring American help and making sure that it was as effective as possible was for Churchill a daily task (*as on May 4 and 10*). As battle began in Crete, and the sinkings in the Atlantic continued, Churchill set out his 'anxiety' to Roosevelt. 'We are at a climacteric of the war, when enormous crystallizations are in suspense but imminent.' Yet the United States was still neutral, a fact Churchill did not have to labour. 'Whatever happens,' Churchill added, 'you may be sure we shall fight on, and I am sure we can at least save ourselves. But what is the good of that?' (*May 21*) A draft telegram to Wendell Willkie that day, which Churchill did not send, but which he sent to Roosevelt, put the danger even more starkly. The 'immense burden and danger to be borne by someone before Hitler is beat' was increasing. 'How easy now – how hard a year hence will be the task.'

Every few days as the Battle of the Atlantic intensified, Churchill sent Roosevelt an account of the war at sea, always praising such help as the United States Navy was giving. (*May 22*) The sinking of the *Bismarck* was cause for rejoicing. (*May 29*) But the continuing neutrality of the United States was always a burden for Churchill. As he wrote to his son Randolph, who was then in the Western Desert: 'The United States are giving us more help every day, and longing for an opportunity to take the plunge. Whether they will do so or not remains an inscrutable mystery of American politics. The longer they wait, the longer and the more costly the job will be which they will have to do.' (*June 8*)

Churchill's broadcast speech to the University of Rochester – 'Divided, the dark age returns. United, we can save and guide the world' – was a clarion call to the United States. (*June 16*) Three days later he was able to report to the War Cabinet on further American initiatives, conveyed to him by Roosevelt, which would ease the burden on Britain in the Atlantic. The correspondence between Prime Minister and President revolved around every aspect of warmaking. Concerns about tank design led to a direct appeal by Churchill to Roosevelt. (*June 26*) His meeting with Roosevelt in August, off Newfoundland, was a high point in his advocacy of the closest possible Anglo-American co-operation. While it was being planned, Churchill sent Roosevelt an outline of his war policies. (*July 25*) From the first day of the meeting, a closer relationship was created, and a joint Anglo-American Declaration of Principles was under discussion. (*August 10*) Extraordinary progress over many areas of common policy was made on the following day (*August 11*) and a joint telegram sent to Stalin about 'how best our two countries can help your country'. (*August 12*)

On his return to London, Churchill gave the War Cabinet a full account of the discussions with Roosevelt and what the two of them had decided. (*August 19*) To his government Ministers, Churchill transmitted his optimism as a result of his Atlantic meeting. Of Roosevelt's attitude to the Americans and the European war, Churchill told his colleagues: 'He was obviously determined that they should come in.' In the Atlantic, American policy was clear: 'Everything was to be done to force an incident.' (*August 19*) A week later Churchill told the same colleagues: 'The President is a tremendous friend of ours and will do all he can, both to help us win the war and to consolidate peace afterwards.' Churchill's own postwar intention, he added, was to make Germany 'fat but impotent'. (*August 26*)

Churchill was also able to express in the strict secrecy of the War Cabinet the doubts that sometimes assailed him. As the minutes of one meeting recorded – written as always in the third person: 'He sometimes wondered whether the President realized the risk that the United States were running by keeping out of the war. If Germany beat Russia to a standstill and the United States had made no further advance towards entry into the war, there was a great danger that the war might take a turn against us.' (*August 25*) Reflecting on the Newfoundland meeting, Churchill revealed one of his innermost concerns when he told his son Randolph that he was 'deeply perplexed to know how the deadlock is to be broken and the United States brought boldly and honourably into the war. There is a very dangerous feeling in America that they need not worry now as all will be well.' (*August 29*) A day later Churchill told one of his Private Secretaries that without an American declaration of war on Germany, 'though we cannot now be defeated, the war might drag on for another four or five years, and civilization and culture would be wiped out.' (*August 30*)

Churchill did not reveal his concern about this when he spoke in the House of Commons of the Atlantic Charter, the course of the war, and 'perils which have been overcome'. (*September 9*) When the South African leader, General Smuts, urged Churchill in early November to press Roosevelt for an American declaration of war, Churchill recalled a remark that Roosevelt had made to him during the Newfoundland meeting: 'I shall never declare war; I shall make war. If I were to ask Congress to declare war they might argue about it for three months.' (*November 9*)

Churchill's letters to Roosevelt gave full vent to the seriousness of the situation, and tried to warn Roosevelt of America's vulnerability. Reflecting on Hitler's intentions, Churchill wrote to the President: 'One may well suppose his programme to be: 1939 – Poland; 1940 – France; 1941 – Russia; 1942 – England; 1943 —— ?' Britain 'must be prepared to meet a supreme onslaught from March 1942 onward.' (*October 20*)

A major public declaration to come out of the first Churchill–Roosevelt meeting was the Atlantic Charter, pledging that after the war there would be 'no territorial changes that do not accord with the freely expressed wishes of the people concerned'. (*August 10*) Churchill had reservations with regard to the application of the Atlantic Charter to Britain's colonial subjects. The principles enunciated 'would only arise in those cases where transference of territory or sovereignty arose'. (*August 20*) He had no qualms, however, about the words in the Charter about the 'final destruction of Nazi tyranny', believing that it was of 'great importance' that Roosevelt should have agreed to that. (*August 24*) In a radio broadcast, Churchill set the meeting with Roosevelt in the context of an intensified war against Germany, based upon 'the deep underlying unities which stir, and at decisive moments rule, the English-speaking peoples throughout the world'. (*August 24*)

Churchill's concern for secrecy, for the security of documents and the secrecy of military operations, was frequently expressed. In a note on the first day of the year to the head of the Cabinet Office and the head of his Defence Staff, he insisted that 'a new, intense drive must be made to secure greater secrecy in all matters relating to the conduct of the war', and set out twelve points for their consideration and implementation. (*January 1*) At the end of that month he removed the Dominion High Commissioners from the list of recipients of secret summaries prepared by the Air Staff and Air Ministry. (*January 27*) He was constantly trying to restrict the circulation of secret material, noting on one occasion, of a document he felt had been too widely distributed: 'The copies circulated are to be destroyed by fire.' (*February 17*) With regard to the transfer of British secrets to Roosevelt, however, he was 'willing to give the President at any time any information on special points'. (*March 31*)

Another matter of security – the insecurity of those telephone lines that were without scramblers – led Churchill to advise 'care always being taken that the conversation would not be intelligible to anyone not in the swim'. (*April 22*) A month later he set out detailed suggestions for the protection of secret papers, with a covering note: 'I ask each Minister to see that the arrangements in his Department are reviewed on the lines indicated, and I propose to arrange for a report to be submitted to me . . .'. (*May 27*) An option for 'burning' or 'returning' documents did not impress him. (*October 6*)

Side by side with secrecy came the art of deception, which Churchill also addressed, writing with regard to convoy secrecy, that 'the continued fabrication and dissemination of false information is a necessary part of security'. (*April 30*) A month later, in a detailed paper for the War Cabinet, he set out the ministerial and departmental responsibilities with regard to secret documents and the 'special precautions' that had to be taken with them, as well as with access to offices, secret waste paper, maps and wall charts, telephone conversations, code words, gossip, and the selection of staff ('a negative check, i.e. that nothing is known against a man or woman, is of very little value'). (*May 27*)

Honours was another topic on which Churchill felt strongly. 'It is such a pity to give Honours in a sort of automatic, routine way . . .' (*February 16*) He warned Attlee of the 'very serious criticism' that would arise if 'it could be suggested' that a certain admiral had been 'induced to join the Labour Party by the prospect of a Peerage'. (*October 13*) The fair distribution of Honours nationwide led him to assure the 'King of Lancashire' that, in the distribution of Honours, 'the great merits of the good people of Lancashire' have not been unrewarded'. (*November 13*) As for the knighthood for 'that grand old minstrel' Harry Lauder, 'no honour was better deserved'. (*December 30*) Few things irritated Churchill more than what he called the 'jealousy and cliquism' with which the Air Ministry treated the former head of Fighter Command, Sir Hugh Dowding. The omission of Dowding's name from an Air Ministry booklet on the Battle of Britain was something that 'nine out of ten men would unhesitatingly condemn'. (*April 12*)

Dishonour was another theme. When Churchill's former friend and colleague, Lloyd George, the Prime Minister who had presided over the victory in 1918, expressed his doubts as to the efficacy of Britain's war effort, Churchill told the House of Commons: 'It was the sort of speech with which, I imagine, the illustrious and venerable Marshal Pétain might well have enlivened the closing days of M. Reynaud's Cabinet.' (*May 7*) Reflecting on past mistakes was a consistent, painful theme. 'It is but a few years ago,' Churchill told the American people during his first wartime broadcast to the United States – while America was still neutral – 'since one united gesture by the peoples, great and small, who are now broken in the dust, would have warded off from mankind the fearful ordeal it has had to undergo. But there was no unity. There was no vision. The nations were pulled down one by one while the others gaped and chattered.' (*June 16*) Six days later, when he broadcast to both the British and the Russian people, he spoke of the 'follies of countries and governments which have allowed themselves to be struck down one by one, when by united action they could have saved themselves and saved the world from the catastrophe'. (*June 22*)

While deeply involved in the daily details of war policy, Churchill also kept continually in mind the wider strategic picture. An example of this is the survey which he sent at the start of the year to the Chiefs of Staff Committee examining the likely developments in Libya, East Africa, Spain, North Africa and the Balkans: 'The attitude of Yugoslavia may well be determined by the support we give to Greece . . .' But the defence of Britain came first: 'the task of preventing Invasion, of feeding the island, and of speeding our armament production must in no way be compromised for the sake of any other objective whatsoever'. (*January 7*) Three days later, at a meeting of the Defence Committee, Churchill raised questions about how a German invasion would be met, telling the Chiefs of Staff that 'we should almost certainly exact a heavy penalty from the Germans should they attempt to invade this island, but an attitude of undue confidence might court disaster'. To dwell on 'shortfalls of equipment' was not enough, he warned General Brooke. There was an 'immense mass of new equipment' with which to seek to repel an invader, and among the troops a 'steady inculcation of the offensive spirit', in which Brooke himself was 'so rightly engaged'. (*January 11*) Nine days later Churchill wrote to Brooke about the need for plans to hunt down German amphibious tanks if they got ashore. He approved Home Guard exercises in Britain to face a simulated German invasion, but warned that 'it will be some time before there is a rifle for every man in the Home Guard'. (*February 14*) A day later he raised the question of the vulnerability of Whitehall to an intensified air attack. He also pressed for the evacuation 'right now' of the population in the coastal zones where an invading force might come ashore. (*February 15*)

The defence of aerodromes in Britain against parachute or glider troops led Churchill to lay down as a rule to be followed: 'It must be understood by all ranks that they are expected to fight and die in defence of their airfields' and 'every man must have a weapon of some kind, be it only a mace or a pike . . . Let me also see some patterns of maces and pikes'. (*June 29*) This was written a week after the German invasion of Russia. Churchill assumed, as did most well-informed observers, that Russia would be defeated within three or four months. Taking steps to prepare Britain for invasion, he told Roosevelt: 'I am asking that everything here shall be at concert pitch for invasion from September 1.' (*July 1*) Ten days later, Churchill's thoughts on invasion focused on the possibility of German parachute landings 'at or near the centre of government'. (*July 10*) The Air Defence of Great Britain remained a concern throughout the year, and must be 'as flexible as possible'. The maximum number of anti-aircraft guns should be 'in mobile form'. (*October 8, 9*) Units of the Home Guard should be turned into 'mobile formations for Home Defence in emergency'. (*October 21*) Not only how to meet a German invasion of Britain, but how British troops could be sent to meet a German invasion of Ireland, was among Churchill's concerns. 'Let me see the exact programme,' he asked his advisers. (*February 4*) But he did regard such a German attack as constituting 'a deadly thrust against us'. (*February 17*)

The need for action was a frequent call in Churchill's minutes and telegrams. His enthusiasm for an expeditionary force against either Sicily or Sardinia arose from his hopes that such an attack would divert German resources from the battle which General Wavell was about to launch in the Western Desert. (*January 21*) Inaction was anathema to him, and could produce sarcasm, as when he enquired, with regard to the naval Commander-in-Chief, Mediterranean, who had been told of the movement of German supply ships: 'Please ask specifically what if anything he is going to do. We are still at war.' (*August 24*) Calls for action were frequent, and intended to encourage as well as to goad. To the military Commander-in-Chief, Middle East, Churchill telegraphed as the day of battle drew near: 'The only thing that matters is to beat the life out of Rommel and Co.' (*December 4*)

The continuing German air attacks on Britain from the start of the year led to Churchill's close scrutiny of defence measures through the Night Air Defence Committee of the War Cabinet, which discussed measures to combat incoming bomber attacks. (*February 10*) The Atlantic sinkings and the means to combat them were under regular scrutiny during his chairmanship of meetings of the Import Executive, and of the Battle of the Atlantic Committee, and were the subject of a Directive in which he set out the needs and priorities. (*March 6*) 'The sinkings are bad,' Churchill confided to Roosevelt four days later, 'and the strain is increasing at sea.' When one of his Private Secretaries said, of the daily losses in the Atlantic, 'It is distressing', Churchill replied: 'Distressing, it is terrifying. If it goes on it will be the end of us.' (*February 26*) A constant vigilance with regard to the import of food and munitions marked Churchill's daily scrutiny of the charts which were prepared for him. (*March 26*) The improvement of air raid shelters – 'more security, warmth, light, and amenities for all' – was another concern. (*March 29*) The availability and serviceability of tanks, especially in the Middle East, was a source of continual vigilance (*for example, April 20 and 22; May 8 and 13*), as were the troop and armoured vehicle reinforcements being sent to the Western Desert. (*June 3*)

Watching experiments, including those of anti-tank weapons, led Churchill to propose for 'good anti-tank weapons and plenty of them' (*April 23*) and the establishment of a 'Tank Parliament' over which Churchill presided. (*May 5, May 13, June 19*) The pace and nature of aircraft production was the subject of his repeated scrutiny: a 'static' condition was not enough. (*July 12*) Torpedo supplies were another area of scrutiny (*July 13*) as was munitions production. (*July 23*) A 'Sunday holiday' was not acceptable for Fighter Command. (*July 13*) Reading a report of delays in aircraft production, Churchill began his reply: 'This is a melancholy story.' (*August 16*) The details of naval construction had been a concern of his since his first appointment as First Lord in 1911. 'I am greatly interested in the proposed design . . . I understand and hope . . . I should very much like to see . . . Pray let me have your views.' (*August 16*) Within two weeks he had further, detailed thoughts to impart. 'It is surely a false disposition . . . The best use that could be made . . .' (*August 29*)

Churchill was alert to any falling off in productive capacity, or what he considered wrong priorities with regard to manpower and raw materials, seeking 'the utmost economy' in Service requirements. (*August 26*) Less than two weeks later he was 'deeply concerned at the slow expansion of the production of heavy and medium bombers'. (*September 7*) Military manpower needs for the defence of Britain were continually monitored. Waste of manpower was 'an abuse'. (*September 15*) Troops had to be 'all ready like fighting cocks'. (*October 5*) Army lectures on current affairs must not provide 'opportunities for the professional grouser and agitator with a glib tongue'. (*October 6*) The powers of the Production Executive over the Supply Departments should be examined: they had become 'inquisitorial and discretionary' (*November 4*) in a way not intended when the Production Executive had been set up. The campaign for directing women into the munitions industries 'should be pressed forward'. (*November 6*)

The rationalization of building programmes, to make the best use of the limited manpower available, remained a concern throughout the year. 'Departments must exercise the greatest possible economy of building labour . . .' (*November 27*) Five days later, in the House of Commons, Churchill called for 'a further degree of sacrifice and exertion', as the 'crisis of manpower and womanpower is at hand'. The need to provide 'tanks, aeroplanes and other weapons of war or war commodities to Russia' added to the tasks in hand. The age limit for compulsory military service would be raised from forty-one to fifty-one. Men over the age of forty-one 'will set free fighting men already in the Services for active mobile jobs'. The lower age of military service would be reduced from nineteen to eighteen-and-a-half. Women would play a larger part in the Service structure: more than 100,000 were required for the Air Defence forces. 'The technical apparatus of modern warfare gives extraordinary opportunities to women.' Single women between the ages of twenty and thirty would be conscripted under new compulsory powers. 'Such are the new burdens which the hard course of our fortunes compels us to invite the nation to assume.' (*December 2*)

Two weeks later Churchill was seeking the best way to 'co-ordinate labour policy' between the different Departments concerned. (*December 18*) It was a constant effort of vigilance, imagination and, above all, experience. As Minister of Munitions in the First World War he had held considerable powers, and understood the mechanisms and conflicts of production.

As part of his refusal to accept that any adverse situation for Britain was not capable of improvement, Churchill made several attempts to detach Vichy France from the Axis, offering General Weygand six British divisions in North Africa if Germany tried to occupy Vichy French territory there. (*January 11 and 14*) The offer was in vain: 'No scrap of nobility or courage has been shown by these people so far,' Churchill noted on February 12; a week later the Vichy leaders were 'this grovelling crowd'. Admiral Darlan was 'a bad man, with a narrow outlook and a shifty eye'. (*March 15*) British policy towards Syria (*May 19, 20*) involved the first military confrontation with Vichy since the attack on the French warships at Oran almost a year earlier.

Throughout the year, Churchill made persistent and successful efforts to encourage Spain to remain neutral. British gold played its part in this, as did the skills of the ambassador, Sir Samuel Hoare, and Churchill's own agent, Captain Hillgarth. Churchill explained to a colleague with regard to British plans to drive the Germans from North Africa, and the resultant possibility of a German advance through Spain to Gibraltar: 'We are led to believe that the Spaniards will resent and resist any invasion of their country by the Germans, who are hated by the morose and hungry Spanish people.' (*October 25*)

In search of initiatives against the Germans and Italians, Churchill sought the exploration of many different schemes, including the invasion of Sardinia. (*January 20*) But no scheme which the Chiefs of Staff opposed was ever carried out: he always deferred to their collective judgment; indeed, there was no way that he could not do so. Priorities were a daily problem throughout 1941; Churchill's ability to sift, arrange and drive those priorities was central to his war direction. North Africa versus Greece had been one from the first week of the year. 'We shall soon be, as usual, torn between conflicting needs', Churchill explained – that of 'sustaining' the Greek struggle against the Italians on Albanian soil, and against the threat of a German advance into the Balkans, 'becomes an object of prime importance'. (*January 6*) Concern that the invasion of Britain remained Hitler's ultimate aim, and would be pursued by him even after 'the defeat of Russia', made anti-invasion preparations another priority, always high on the list of things to be watched and sustained. (*January 7*) A note to Anthony Eden set out the conflicting claims of the Balkan, North African and East African theatres. (*February 12*) A note to Wavell that same day explained the Greek priority.

The War Cabinet's decision to send British troops to Greece was discussed at length before being approved. Churchill felt strongly the moral imperative to go to the aid of Greece. But he was keenly aware of the military aspect, telling Anthony Eden and General Wavell, who were in Athens: 'Do not consider yourself obligated to a Greek enterprise if in your hearts you feel it will only be another Norwegian fiasco.' (*February 20*) At the crucial War Cabinet, the minutes recorded: 'The views expressed were, without exception, in favour of sending military assistance to Greece.' (*February 24*) From that moment, help for Greece became one of the priorities of Churchill's questioning and proposals.

Not only policies but personalities provided cause for concern. Churchill found General de Gaulle 'very remarkable, having regard to the heartbreaking difficulties of his position'. (*February 14*) Five days later he wrote to the Chiefs of Staff: 'It would be a serious step to forbid de Gaulle to act as he wishes.' To Eden, Churchill wrote about de Gaulle: 'We recognize no other chief or rival'. (*February 23*) To de Gaulle himself, Churchill wrote: '. . . you embody the hope of millions of Frenchmen and Frenchwomen who do not despair of the future of France and the French Empire'. (*April 3*) As the battle for Syria began, and Free French forces were about to be in combat against the forces of Vichy France, Churchill wrote to de Gaulle: 'At this hour when Vichy touches fresh depths of ignominy, the loyalty and courage of the free French save the glory of France.' (*June 6*). Difficulties with de Gaulle arose after an interview with an American journalist in which the general expressed his 'unfriendly expressions about England'. (*August 27*) This had been 'very disturbing'. (*August 28*) De Gaulle quickly disavowed the interview and was, in Churchill's words, 'returning I think with his tail between his legs'. (*August 30*) He would be asked, nevertheless, 'for explanations of his unfriendly conduct and absurd statements'. (*September 1*) Churchill also sought de Gaulle's personal rebuttal of his 'unfriendly attitude by speech and action'. (*September 2*) At a face-to-face meeting the grievances were fully aired on both sides and much was resolved. 'The Prime Minister said that he had a double object in view: to encourage General de Gaulle's supporters in France, and therefore to do nothing which would diminish General de Gaulle's stature as the champion of continued resistance to the enemy; and at the same time to improve relations between His Majesty's Government and the Free French Movement by giving the latter a broader basis.' De Gaulle promised to give 'the utmost weight' to this. (*September 12*) Churchill pressed for a Council of French anti-Vichy leaders whereby de Gaulle could be advised, guided, and in some way controlled. (*September 23*) A year earlier it was Churchill's friend General Louis Spears – then Churchill's emissary with de Gaulle, who had said that the heaviest cross he had to bear was the Cross of Lorraine. But reconciliation was always possible: a telegram which de Gaulle sent on the eve of Churchill's birthday spoke of that birthday becoming 'une fête de la victoire'. (*November 29*) Churchill at once acknowledged 'your charming message . . . read with the greatest pleasure'. (*December 1*)

A personality whose appearance in Britain created a brief flurry of amazement was that of Hitler's deputy, Rudolf Hess. It emerged that he had no mission from Hitler, and no real purpose relevant to the war, but his arrival was a momentary distraction. (*May 11–16*) Churchill sent Roosevelt a full account of the Hess interviews and of the impression Hess had made, commenting: 'no ordinary signs of insanity can be detected'. (*May 16*)

For Hitler himself there was to be no compromise: 'we were not prepared to negotiate with Hitler at any time on any subject'. (*July 7*) Churchill's policy with regard to peace overtures reaching Britain was 'absolute silence . . . I am absolutely opposed to the slightest contact'. (*September 10*) Two months later Churchill repeated this pledge publicly. Britain would 'never enter into any negotiations with Hitler or any party in Germany which represents the Nazi regime.' The fact that there was talk of negotiations showed 'that the guilty men who have let Hell loose upon the world are hoping to escape with their fleeting triumphs and ill-gotten plunders, from the closing net of doom'. (*November 10*)

Enigma decrypts, derived from Britain's ability to tap into Germany's most secret method of radio communication, revealed German preparations on many fronts, giving Churchill and those closest to him a clear picture of the developments they would have to face. The index entry for 'Enigma' enables the extent of this source of information to be followed throughout the year. Based on his daily reading of Enigma, Churchill was able to explain to Wavell that German preparatory moves against the Balkans were not a 'bluff to cause dispersion of forces' but preparations for an invasion of the Balkans 'of deadly quality'. (*January 11*) In Churchill's view, and that of his War Cabinet, such an invading force would have to be stopped: hence the British diversion of forces, including air forces, from North Africa to Greece. Once Tobruk was secured, Churchill explained to Wavell, 'all operations in Libya are subordinated to aiding Greece'. To the leader of the Yugoslav coup, General Simovic, Churchill sent information, derived from Enigma, about the advance of German troops towards Yugoslavia, and suggested an immediate Yugoslav attack on the 'demoralized and rotten' Italian troops in Albania, seizing their equipment. (*April 4*)

While the Soviet Union was still allied with Germany, Churchill sent Stalin a message – disguised as if it came from 'a trusted agent' – of the movement of German troops towards the Polish-Soviet border in southern Poland. These troop movements, Churchill noted, had only been countermanded as a result of the Serbian revolution. 'Your Excellency will readily appreciate the significance of these facts.' (*April 3*) This was the first of several messages giving Stalin information, in fact derived from top secret Enigma intercepts, about German intentions against the Soviet Union. The fate of this particular message was much on Churchill's mind in later months. (*October 14*) A detailed Enigma-based account of German forces concentrating along the Soviet borders was sent to Stalin. (*June 10*) Once Hitler had invaded the Soviet Union, further detailed Enigma-based information, crucial to Soviet defences, was sent regularly, the first within forty-eight hours of the German attack. (*June 24*) Churchill took care to ensure that the origin of such messages would not be 'imperilled'. (*July 17*) To his own military Commander-in-Chief in the Middle East, Churchill was prepared to send an actual, as opposed to a paraphrased, Enigma message, to make clear beyond doubt what military moves the German High Command was planning in North Africa, hoping that this information would reinforce his exhortation that soon 'it will be a moment to do and dare'. (*May 7*)

A crisis regarding the use of Enigma came on the eve of the battle for Crete, when the question of maintaining the secrecy of this crucial source of information was at the centre of how the battle should be conducted. (*May 10, 12*) The battle itself – 'a desperate, grim battle' – was a source of considerable anxiety for Churchill. (*May 20–24, May 26–27*) But after the evacuation of Crete, he lost no time in seeking a military post mortem – 'a number of questions which should be enquired into'. (*June 2*) Many of these he addressed, and answered, eight days later in the House of Commons. But when further details of the battle reached him, he had further questions. (*June 14, July 3*)

The protection of Enigma was always in Churchill's mind; he wanted all Enigma-based messages that were being sent to him by air for his meeting with Roosevelt off Newfoundland to be 'put in a weighted case, so that they will sink in the sea if anything happens to the airplane'. (*August 3*) Lord Beaverbrook was warned on his mission to Moscow that 'no one in Russia', including the British Ambassador or other members of the mission, 'must know about our special sources of information'. (*September 25*) During the 'Crusader' offensive in the Western Desert, Churchill expressed to the Commander-in-Chief his 'anxiety' about the security of 'our special stuff'. (*November 23*)

Churchill monitored all possible threats to national morale, and sought to sustain it. On the very first day of the year he conveyed his concern that John Masefield's book on the Dunkirk evacuation might lead to conclusions drawn that were 'disparaging' to the High Command. Harry Hopkins was with Churchill on the night when news came in that a British cruiser had been sunk by German dive bombers in the Mediterranean, and a new aircraft carrier badly damaged. Recalling Churchill's mood that night, Hopkins wrote to Roosevelt: 'he never falters or displays the least despondence – till four o'clock he paced the floor telling me of his offensive and defensive plans'. (*January 11*)

In his broadcasts, Churchill sought to inspire the captive nations of Europe. 'The tunnel may be dark and long, but at the end there is light . . . Keep your soul clean from all contact with the Nazis; make them feel even in their fleeting hour of brutish triumph that they are the moral outcasts of mankind. Help is coming; mighty forces are arming on your behalf.' (*August 24*) Through his parliamentary speeches and broadcasts, Churchill conveyed his sense of purpose to the British people: all his 1941 speeches and broadcasts are printed in full in this volume. Among those which made a considerable impact was the one in which, after ranging over every aspect of the war, he warned his listeners that 'next to cowardice and treachery, over-confidence, leading to neglect or slothfulness, is the worst of martial crimes'. Preparations against a possible German invasion had to be maintained. This broadcast ended with Churchill's answer – 'in your name' – to words of encouragement he had received from Roosevelt. Churchill said he would tell the President in reply: 'We shall not fail or falter; we shall not weaken or tire. Neither the sudden shock of battle, nor the long-drawn trials of vigilance and exertion will wear us down. Give us the tools and we will finish the job.' (*February 9*)

To the Canadians, Churchill spoke of how Canada was 'the linchpin of the English-speaking world'. (*September 4*) He had earlier spoken of traditions which British and Canadians shared, and of the tradition they shared with the people of France 'of valour and faith', which Canada kept 'alive in these dark days, and which we are confident will in the end bring back to life France itself'. (June 1) British help for the French resistance was part of that process, as was help to the Yugoslav resistance, where it could be carried out. (*August 27, 28; October 26*) To this end, 'Everything in human power should be done.' (*November 28*)

With the Atlantic Ocean as Britain's lifeline, for food and munitions,

Churchill studied the daily convoy situation with great care. A collision between two convoys at sea led him to stress 'the gravity of the loss' of munitions. (*January 3*) Three days later his concerns for convoy losses led him to warn General Wavell not to ask for excessive numbers of non-combatant troops to be sent to the Middle East using the convoy route around the Cape of Good Hope: 'I beg you to convince me that you will continually comb, scrub and purge all rearward services in a hard, unrelenting manner, as Kitchener did.' Naval policy in the Mediterranean held Churchill's persistent gaze, as seen in his message to the First Lord and First Sea Lord beginning 'I am distressed . . .' (*April 12*) and in his eleven-point Directive two days later. The passage of convoys through the Mediterranean from Gibraltar to Malta, to bring relief to the besieged island, and to bring urgently needed war supplies to Egypt, was an unceasing burden. (*April 30*)

Many details caused Churchill concern: his Statistical Department prepared for him on a weekly basis State of Readiness diagrams which he studied, and as a result of which he took action, monitoring the production and distribution of rifles, guns and ammunition (*for example on January 19 and February 15*), and the distribution and future use of Britain's ever-stretched military manpower. (*January 29*) He was concerned, while contemplating the possibility of a German invasion in 1941, that training against gas attack should be brought 'up to full efficiency' and civilian masks overhauled. 'Very few people carry gas masks nowadays.' (*January 19*) Churchill also expressed his dissatisfaction with preparations for offensive chemical warfare, 'should this be forced upon us by the actions of the enemy'. (*April 15*) The fall in production of gas containers was 'shocking and absolutely contrary to the express instructions of the Cabinet over many months'. (*July 17*) The restrictions on the production of mustard gas was 'alarming'. (*August 20*) Breakdowns and delay in the production of fuzes was 'continual'. (*September 8*) The manufacture of every type of weaponry and war machinery came under Churchill's scrutiny: in anticipation of an eventual amphibious landing in Europe, he put considerable effort into securing landing craft of the most effective design, both for troops and for tanks. (*September 8*)

Churchill examined everything that was put before him, from the charts of his Statistical Department, to items in the newspapers, all of which he looked through daily. His own travels about Britain, were also a source of many subsequent initiatives. In a typical one week period he asked questions and gave instructions with regard to coal deliveries in London (*January 21*), people made homeless as a result of German air attack (*also January 21*), merchant shipping losses (*January 23*), and the installation of gun batteries at Dover (*January 26*). He also concerned himself (*as on February 15*) with the wording of leaflets and the local preparations to meet a German invasion. Were the Germans to invade, he confided early in the year, and he had to make a radio broadcast, he would end it with the words: 'The hour has come; kill the Hun.' (*January 25*). A variant on this was: 'Let every one, Kill a Hun'. (*June 29*). This spirit, Churchill wrote to his senior military advisers, 'must be inculcated ceaselessly into all ranks . . .' (*June 29*)

Evacuation of civilians from the coastal area had also to be constantly under review: 'A scheme must be prepared . . .' (*October 10*). In studying a report of Britain's vulnerability to invasion, Churchill doubted however that the author recognized just how much warning would be given, as a result of aerial reconnaissance of the ports in which the invasion barges were being made ready, how the air force would be able to subject the barges to 'the heaviest bombing during what might be a fortnight or more', and how strong would be Britain's naval resistance to the invading fleet. Churchill then asked for details of each phase of the planned reaction. (*November 23*) He also discussed the role of the Home Guard in the event of an invasion alert, and of 'the great mass of hefty manhood now in reserved occupations who may not join the Army but who have volunteered for the Home Guard'. (*November 23*)

Churchill focused at all times on the need to challenge and eventually defeat Germany. How to prevent Germany obtaining the supplies of copper she needed for her war industries was a question he put to Hugh Dalton, the head of the Special Operations Executive, for clandestine activity in Axis lands. (*February 1*) The fate of munitions cargoes was raised three days later. Britain's own production of alloy steel was another concern. (*February 10*) The unloading of munitions at British ports always attracted his careful attention. (*as on February 11 and February 28*) The need 'for effecting a purge and reduction' of government committees also elicited his initiative. (*March 14*) Fuelling at sea was another concern (*as on March 21 and April 4*) as was the reduction of hours being worked by machine tools in munitions factories. (*April 8*) Studying charts of munitions production, he noted 'Northern Ireland does not appear to be making its utmost contribution to the war effort', although one-eighth of the working population was out of work. (*May 5*) A case which highlighted inequalities in the pensions paid to servicemen's widows caught his attention; it led to a pertinent query to the Cabinet Minister concerned. (*May 10, 16*) To his statistical adviser, Lord Cherwell, his request was a succinct one: 'Do your best to find the solid truth.' (*July 17*)

Rationing was something about which Churchill continually sought amelioration, as when he learned of plans to reduce the petrol ration which was intended to come into effect during the August Bank Holiday. Many people might be getting leave that August, he wrote, 'for the first time' since the start of the war. 'Could you not arrange to begin the experiment in October?' (*June 14*) That same day he addressed the question of the meat ration: 'you should make further efforts to open out your meat supplies'. Three weeks later he was looking to the United States for substantially increased food imports. (*July 7*) A 'flexible coupon system' was one of his proposals, in an attempt to make 'a variety of alternative goods available'. (*July 27*)

Learning of a new sanction with regard to petrol rationing, Churchill was not convinced that it was wise. 'I understand,' he wrote to the Minister concerned, 'that there is a proposal to make it a penal offence for any motorist who gets a supplementary ration of petrol not to keep a log book in which every journey is recorded. To create and multiply offences which are not condemned by public opinion, which are difficult to detect and can only be punished in a capricious manner is impolitic.' (*August 9*) Hearing complaints 'from many quarters' about the Egg Distribution Scheme, Churchill found time amid the growing crisis in the Far East to pass the complaints on to the Minister of Food. 'The scarcity of eggs is palpable.' (*December 6*) Two days after Pearl Harbor and the Japanese attack on Malaya, Churchill was trying to prevent the imposition of rationing for sweets and chocolate. (*December 9*) That day he also set out his ideas for replanting trees where trees had to be cut down: 'Surely you are replanting two or three trees for every large one you cut down.' Egg rationing problems emerged again while Churchill was on his way across the Atlantic to see Roosevelt. 'Backyard fowls use up a lot of scrap and so save cereals', Churchill pointed out. (*December 22*)

Among Churchill's military worries was the 'lamentable' decision of the Australian government to withdraw its troops from Tobruk. (*September 15, 17*) But all 'personal feelings' had to be 'subordinated to appearance of unity'. (*September 18*) That day Churchill telegraphed to the British Commander-in-Chief in the Middle East: 'Any public controversy would injure foundations of Empire and be disastrous to our general position in the war. Everything must be borne with patience, and in the end all will come right.'

Churchill continually urged caution before enterprises or attitudes that he felt might be exaggerated or injudicious, as when he opposed specific offensive actions against the Norwegian coast (*January 3*), the Italian Dodecanese islands (*January 13*) or Pantellaria Island off Sicily (*January 18*), or told the Government's Senior Diplomatic Adviser of his intention 'to talk rather more about the Nazis and rather less about the Germans', adding words of advice: 'We must not let our vision be darkened by hatred.' (*January 7*)

Belief that there was a single predominant strategy to win the war did not convince him. Early in the year he pointed out that in the first days of the war the Air Ministry had believed that a bombing attack on the Ruhr could shatter German industry. 'Careful calculations had shown that this could be done. After anxious thought, the attack was eventually made when the Germans invaded the Low Countries, but there had only been a fractional interruption of work in the industries of the Ruhr.' (*January 13*) Nevertheless, the bombing would continue, and 'our power to strike him will increase'. (*February 2*) It was 'very disputable', however, 'whether bombing by itself will be a decisive factor in the present war. On the contrary, all that we have learned since the war began shows that its effects, both physical and moral, are greatly exaggerated.' The most that could be said, Churchill told the Chief of the Air Staff, was that 'it will be a heavy and, I trust, a seriously increasing annoyance'. (*September 27*) But his caveat remained. 'Even if all the towns of Germany were rendered largely uninhabitable, it does not follow that the military control would be weakened or even that war industry could not be carried on.' (*October 7*)

Churchill was always ready to acknowledge and encourage bravery and achievement. To the people of Dover he sent a message on their 'courage and resourcefulness' under bomb and shell fire. (*January 1*) Three days later he wrote to the Australian Prime Minister of the 'magnificent manner' in which the Australian offensive in the Western Desert had opened. Progress in protecting oil storage tanks in Britain drew forth a letter of praise to the Minister responsible. (*January 5*) That same day he wrote to General Wavell to congratulate him 'on your second brilliant victory, so profoundly helpful at this turning point to the whole cause'. A day later he urged the War Cabinet and the Ministry of Information to lay stress on 'the brilliance of the tactics adopted by General Wavell', while at the same time not belittling what the Australians had done 'by laying too much stress on the fact that there had not been too much fighting'. Reading daily accounts of the German air bombardment of Malta, he sent a message to the garrisons, citizens and Royal Air Force personnel on their 'magnificent and ever-memorable defence'. (*January 21*) Two days later he sent Wavell and all those under him a further message on victories in the Western Desert that 'will long be regarded as models of the military art'. After a visit to Glasgow he wrote to the Lord Provost about the 'loyal and alert public spirit of which I saw so many signs'. He was sure that were the full force of the German air attack to be turned upon Glasgow, 'her citizens will endure and surmount it'. (*January 28*)

Churchill did not hesitate to make his praises public. General Wilson's forces in Syria had shown 'skill and tenacity'. (*July 14*) Admiral Somerville's troop convoy escort work in the Mediterranean had been carried out with 'skill and resolution'. (*August 3*) The civil defence forces in Britain had 'acquitted themselves with distinction'. (*July 14*) Churchill also recalled that day the height of the 1940 Blitz against London:

> The courage, the unconquerable grit and stamina of the Londoners showed itself from the very outset. Without that all would have failed. Upon that rock, all stood unshakable. All the public services were carried on, and all the intricate arrangements, far-reaching details, involving the daily lives of so many millions, were carried out, improvised, elaborated, and perfected in the very teeth of the cruel and devastating storm.

To the bomber crews who were attacking targets in Germany and German shipping in ports throughout German-occupied Europe, Churchill recalled the Crimean War of almost a century earlier when he wrote: 'The Charge of the Light Brigade at Balaklava is eclipsed in brightness by these almost daily deeds of fame'. (*August 30*) To the commander of the naval force attacking German troop and supply ships seeking to reinforce the Western Desert during the 'Crusader' offensive, Churchill wrote: 'all concerned may be proud to have been a real help to Britain and our cause'. (*November 27*)

Courage, perseverance and endurance were always to be recognized. Churchill was angered by delays in issuing rewards for gallantry. (*January 11*) To the Polish Commander-in-Chief in exile, Churchill wrote of 'the great Polish nation, whose homes have been broken and whose monuments have been shattered, but whose free spirit will never crumble like bricks or stone'. (*January 13*)

The Egyptian Government and elite met with less praise, Churchill telling Eden that he trusted the time would come when the interests of the Egyptian peasantry, the Fellaheen, would be 'cherished' by the British government, 'even if some of the rich pashas and landowners and other pretended nationalists have to pay the same kind of taxes as are paid by wealthy people in Britain'. Churchill added: 'A little of the radical, democratic sledge-hammer is needed in the Delta, where so many fat, insolent class and party interests have grown up under our tolerant protection.' (*January 20*) This minute impressed one of Churchill's Private Secretary's as showing 'the PM's genuine love of democracy'. (*January 22*)

Warnings could be issued even to royalty: the Duke of Windsor, then in the Bahamas, was told not to say things that 'will certainly be interpreted as defeatist and pro-Nazi' (*March 17*) or could be exploited by the Isolationists. (*March 20*) Churchill also sought a press attaché for the Duke who could tell him what he ought not to say. (*June 11*) Three months later Churchill warned the Duke and Duchess not to be exploited or misrepresented during their forthcoming visit to the United States and Canada. 'Our dearest wish and greatest need in this country is to have the United States enter the war. It is no use pressing them, but, on the other hand, no word should ever be spoken inconsistent with this object.' (*September 13*) Churchill also sent the Duke of Windsor speech notes as a guide for when he was in the United States. 'You would naturally ask the President whether anything in this would embarrass him.' (*September 22*)

Terror in the lands under German occupation stirred Churchill's fiercest anger. Told of the imminent slaughter of Jews in Roumania, he suggested holding the Roumanian dictator and his immediate circle 'personally responsible in life and limb if such a vile act is perpetrated'. (*February 1*) Churchill referred to the German treatment of civilians under Hitler's rule and that of 'his Nazi gang' when he broadcast to the Polish people of how 'Every week his firing parties are busy in a dozen lands. Monday he shoots Dutchmen; Tuesday Norwegians; Wednesday French or Belgians stand against the wall; Thursday it is the Czechs who must suffer. And now there are the Serbs and the Greeks to fill his repulsive bill of executions. But always, all the days, there are the Poles.' (*May 3*)

Churchill elaborated on the fate of the captive nations – 'hounded, terrorized, exploited' – when he spoke to their governments in exile in London. (*June 12*). He wanted 'more stir' made after the Germans had executed two Norwegian Trade Union leaders. (*September 13*) The 'Nazi butcheries in France' were the subject of one of the few Press statements issued by Churchill during the war. 'These cold-blooded executions of innocent people will only recoil upon the savages who order and execute them.' The German atrocities throughout Europe 'and above all behind the German front in Russia, surpass anything that has been known since the darkest and most bestial ages of mankind'. Not only denunciation, but 'Retribution for those crimes' must, in Churchill's words, 'henceforward take its place among the major purposes of the war.' (*October 25*)

In a speech at the Mansion House two weeks later, Churchill elaborated on the killings in Europe, where 'Hitler's firing parties are busy every day in a dozen countries'. Norwegians, Belgians, Frenchmen, Dutch, Poles, Czechs, Serbs, Croats, Slovenes, Greeks and 'above all in scale' Russians, 'are being butchered by thousands and by tens of thousands after they have surrendered'. Individual and 'mass executions' had become 'a part of the regular German routine'. All these victims 'of the Nazi executioner in so many lands, who are labelled Communists and Jews – we must regard them just as if they were brave soldiers who die for their country on the field of battle.' A 'river of blood' was flowing: 'It is not the hot blood of battle where good blows are given and returned. It is the cold blood of the execution yard and the scaffold, which leaves a stain indelible for generations and for centuries.'(*November 10*)

The atrocities in Russia included the mass murder of many

thousands of Jews. Details of these killings reached Churchill through Enigma, where the phrase 'Communists and Jews' was often attached to a report of the murder of hundreds and even thousands of people in a single day. Churchill made a public statement drawing attention to the enormity of the killings: 'The Jew bore the brunt of the Nazis' first onslaughts upon the citadels of human dignity and freedom. He has borne and continued to bear a burden that might have seemed to be beyond endurance.' In the day of victory 'the Jew's sufferings and his part in the struggle will not be forgotten.' (*November 14*) Churchill had already suggested to the War Cabinet that after the war an 'autonomous Jewish State should be set up in Palestine, 'with reasonable room for expansion'. (*September 24*)

In the House of Commons, Churchill had repeatedly to set the tone and answer criticism. Parliamentary debates, he said in his first Commons speech of 1941, 'are of the very greatest value to the life-thrust of the nation'. (*January 22*) To Eden he had confided a day earlier that he was 'fatalistic about the House' and maintained that the 'bulk of Tories' hated him. His speech was a thorough explanation of the workings of his war administration. It ended with the powerful assertion that he would be failing 'in my duty were I to suggest that the future, with all its horrors, contains any element which justifies lassitude, despondency or despair'. He had no doubt that the House of Commons would wish 'to give its tribute of encouragement as well as its dose of correction, and will lend the heave of its own loyal strength to the forward surges which have now begun'.

The relationship between the House of Commons and the conduct of the war, including the direct participation of Members of Parliament in the war – 'an extremely high form of public duty' – was the theme of another speech. (*February 27*) Among his major presentations of the course of the war and of British war policy was that following the German invasion of Yugoslavia and Greece. In that presentation the Battle of the Atlantic was central; as was the contribution of the United States to that battle, most recently – 'I am now authorized to state' – through ten fast naval vessels, former anti-prohibition revenue cutters which 'will now serve an even higher purpose'. (*April 9*)

Criticism following the evacuation of Greece led Churchill to call for a Vote of Confidence in the House of Commons, and in defence of Britain's war policy to present a major Parliamentary survey of the German victories in the Balkans, the situation in the Mediterranean, the Rashid Ali revolt in Iraq – soon to be crushed – North Africa, the Battle of the Atlantic, and the war as conducted from Downing Street. The difficulty, Churchill said in answer to one criticism, was not 'to have more breaks put on the wheels; the difficulty is to get more impetus and speed behind it'. And he went on, in an impassioned yet realistic appeal:

> I ask you to witness, Mr Speaker, that I have never promised anything or offered anything but blood, tears, toil and sweat, to which I will now add our fair share of mistakes, shortcomings and disappointments, and also that this may go on for a very long time, at the end of which I firmly believe – though it is not a promise or a guarantee, only a profession of faith – that there will be complete, absolute and final victory.

It was almost a year since Churchill had become Prime Minister. 'When I look back on the perils which have been overcome,' he said, 'upon the great mountain waves in which the gallant ship has driven, when I remember all that has gone wrong, and remember also all that has gone right, I feel sure that we have no need to fear the tempest. Let it roar, let it rage. We shall come through.' (*May 7*)

A month later, in another survey of the war following the evacuation of Crete, Churchill answered criticisms and set out the course and nature of the battle that had been lost, and spoke also of the success in Iraq, of the 'unbroken' front in the Western Desert, and of the battle that was then in progress in Syria and about to be won. 'I think it would be most unfair and wrong, and very silly in the midst of a defence which has so far been crowned with remarkable success, to select the loss of the Crete salient as an excuse and pretext for branding with failure or taunt the great campaign for the defence of the Middle East, which has so far prospered beyond all expectation, and is now entering upon an even more intense and critical phase.' (*June 10*)

In Secret Session, Churchill gave the Commons a full account of the Battle of the Atlantic, not minimizing any of the dangers. 'Let us not forget,' he concluded, 'that the enemy has difficulties of his own; that some of these difficulties are obvious; that there may be others which are more apparent to him than to us; and that all the great struggles of history have been won by superior will power wresting victory in the teeth of odds or upon the narrowest of margins.' (*June 25*) Just over two months later Churchill gave the House of Commons a full account, ranging over every theatre of war, pointing to much 'solid improvement' along what he called 'the terrible road we chose at the call of duty'. (*September 9*) In a second survey of the war that month, Churchill told Members of Parliament: 'We have climbed from the pit of peril on to a fairly broad plateau. We can see before us the difficult and dangerous onward path which we must tread. But we can also feel the parallel movements or convergence of the two mighty nations . . . Russia and the United States.' (*September 30*)

That winter, in a survey of the war in which he stressed both the naval improvements in the Atlantic and the agricultural improvements in Britain, Churchill also gave personal advice: 'The process of self-improvement is, of course, continuous, and every man and woman throughout the land, in office or out of office, in Parliament or in the cities and municipalities of our country – everyone great and small, should try himself by his conscience every day to make sure he is giving his utmost effort to the common cause.' (*November 12*)

Churchill certainly did this himself, and had no hesitation in giving a lead with regard to unstinting effort. King George VI's reference to 'all your arduous work' was not misplaced. (*January 2*) Eight days later, the first message from Roosevelt's emissary Harry Hopkins reported that 'Everyone tells me that he works fifteen hours a day and I can well believe it.' The Australian Prime Minister, Robert Menzies, was struck by his 'amazing grasp of detail'. (*March 2*) On seeing Churchill at work for the first time, during the Lend Lease negotiations, the American Ambassador, John Winant, was 'deeply impressed not only with his grasp of the values involved and his appreciation of the defence needs of the United States but also with his knowledge of the details of the negotiations, with which he had familiarized himself on such short notice'. (*March 5*) To his secretary Elizabeth Layton, Churchill said: 'We must go on and on, like the gun-horses, till we drop.' (*July 29*)

Churchill's Private Office was critical of some aspects of his activity. 'He supplies drive and initiative,' John Colville wrote after a talk with his fellow Private Secretary, John Peck, 'but he often meddles where he would better leave things alone, and the operational side of the war might profit if he gave it a respite, and turned to grapple with Labour and Production.' (*June 19*) In defence of his method, Churchill told a Secret Session of the House of Commons:

> Do not let anyone suppose that inside this enormous government we are a mutual-admiration society. I do not think, and my colleagues will bear me witness, any expression of scorn or severity which I have heard used by our critics has come anywhere near the language I have been myself accustomed to use, not only orally, but in a continued stream of written minutes.
>
> In fact, I wonder that a great many of my colleagues are on speaking terms with me. They would not be if I had not complained of and criticized all evenly and alike. But, bound together as we are by a common purpose, the men who have joined hands in this affair put up with a lot, and I hope they will put up with a lot more.

'It is the duty of the Prime Minister', Churchill added, 'to use the power which Parliament and the nation have given him to drive others, and in war like this that power has to be used irrespective of anyone's feelings. If we win, nobody will care. If we lose there will be nobody to care.' (*June 25*) Six months later he wrote to Clement Attlee from Ottawa that, in his absence, 'a very firm attitude' should be adopted in the House of Commons 'to snarlers and naggers who are trying to make trouble . . .' (*December 30*)

Labour and Production, which in June both Colville and Peck hoped Churchill would turn his attention to, were the subject of one of his most important Parliamentary presentations of the year. (*July 29*) There were many other aspects of the war other than the operational side with which he was continually engaged. Information and propaganda were the theme of one memorandum earlier that summer. (*July 2*) That day, the amelioration of rationing and an increase in meat supplies was again one of Churchill's concerns: he had authorized 'pressure on the United States to increase her pork outlet', and ten days later noted that American pork supplies 'can be rapidly expanded'. (*July 12*)

Among the anxieties confronting Churchill in 1941 was the search for the *Bismarck*, and the loss of the *Hood* during the chase. His son-in-law Vic Oliver was a witness to that anxiety, as were John Colville and Sir Alexander Cadogan. (*May 24–26*) It was shortly after his account to the House of Commons about the search for the *Bismarck* that Churchill was able – while discussing the question of conscription for Northern Ireland – to break off his own remarks to announce that the *Bismarck* had been sunk. (*May 27*).

The Battle of the Atlantic sinkings continued, so much so that Churchill opposed publication of the losses, as publication 'might have a discouraging effect on public opinion in this country'. (*June 16*)

Churchill's dislikes were openly aired. He was reluctant to see too great a focus on post-war planning, writing to the Cabinet Secretary with regard to the Committee on the Reconstruction of Town and Country: 'We must be very careful not to allow these remote post-war problems to absorb energy which is required, maybe for several years, for the prosecution of the war.' (*January 4*) Stressing the urgent need to repair windows of houses in bomb-damaged areas, Churchill told the Minister for Works and Buildings that same day: 'Do not let spacious plans for a new world divert your energies in saving what is left of the old.' To make damaged houses habitable was 'your No. 1 war task.' But he was not without plans for the post-war world, expressing the hope, while talking to Harry Hopkins, that a National Government would continue for two or three years after the war so that, as John Colville, one of his Private Secretaries recorded, 'the country might be undivided in its efforts to put into effect certain principles – or rather measures – of reconstruction'. (*January 11*) Churchill also expressed his desire that day for a future United States of Europe: 'it should be built by the English; if the Russians built it there would be Communism and squalour; if the Germans built it there would be tyranny and brute force.' To a Conservative Party gathering he stressed the need for national unity not only in war, but in the 'practical measures of reconstruction' once the war was won. (*March 27*)

Appeasement, when revealed as the reaction of the weak, always vexed Churchill. The decision of Prince Paul of Yugoslavia to seek German goodwill, he told Eden, 'looks like that of an unfortunate man in the cage with the tiger, hoping not to provoke him while steadily dinner-time approaches'. (*January 14*) In an attempt to persuade Yugoslavia not to ally itself with Germany in the impending German attack on Greece, Churchill wrote directly to the Yugoslav Prime Minister. His letter began: 'Your Excellency, the eventual total defeat of Hitler and Mussolini is certain. No prudent and far-seeing man can doubt this in view of the respective declared resolves of the British and American democracies.' (*March 22*) The United States was then, of course, still neutral.

To a diplomat whose work in Belgrade he admired, Churchill telegraphed as Yugoslavia's decision hung in the balance: 'Continue to pester, nag and bite. Demand audiences. Don't take no for an answer. Cling on them . . .' (*March 26*) Learning of the dramatic Yugoslav challenge to the Germans on the following day, he declared: 'This patriotic movement arises from the wrath of a valiant and warlike race at the betrayal of their country by the weakness of their rulers and the foul intrigues of the Axis powers.' The Yugoslav nation had 'found its soul'. (*March 27*) A new war zone had opened, in both Yugoslavia and Greece, with all the additional strains on Britain's resources, but creating a renewed impetus to resist German tyranny. Both countries were overrun by Germany, but the battles had shown that a German advance could be challenged by fighting troops, even if it could not be halted.

In June another war zone opened, when Germany invaded the Soviet Union. Churchill was at Chequers when the attack began. (*June 22*) That same night he made one of the most important of all his wartime broadcasts: 'Any man or State who fights on against Nazidom will have our aid.' If Hitler were able to defeat Russia, he would then turn westward and attempt to invade Britain. 'The Russian danger is therefore our danger . . . We shall give whatever help we can to Russia and the Russian people. We shall appeal to our friends and allies in every part of the world to take the same course and pursue it, as we shall, faithfully and steadfastly to the end.'

From the morning after Churchill's speech, aid to the Soviet Union from Britain assumed as great a part on Churchill's daily agenda as did aid to Britain from the United States. Often, it was aid to Britain from the United States – including aircraft – that was sent on, even without being uncrated, to the Soviet Union. Within a month of the German invasion, Churchill explained to Stalin that 'anything sensible and effective that we can do to help will be done' and gave the Soviet leader details of what was proposed. (*the first four on July 20, 25, 28 and 31*). He was 'most anxious', Churchill told the War Cabinet, 'that we should do all we could to help the Russians'. (*July 24*) A month later he sent Stalin details of war materials, including aircraft, that was already on the way to Russia, explaining that 'I have been searching for any way to give you help . . .' (*August 28*) One of those ways was to use the sea and overland route through Persia, for which Churchill sought help from Roosevelt as Britain could not 'find the whole of the shipping by ourselves'. (*September 1*) A 'cry for help' from Stalin was answered during two days of deliberations, amid fears that the Soviet leader might be seeking a separate peace with Germany. (*September 4, 5*)

Following this discussion, Churchill informed Stalin that considerable quantities of aluminium would be coming to him from Canada. (*September 9*) A programme of monthly deliveries of a wide range of supplies requested by Stalin was being worked out by a joint Anglo-American mission that was in London, and would soon be on its way to Moscow. President Roosevelt envisaged the first plan going on to the end of June 1942, 'but naturally we shall go on with you until victory', Churchill assured Stalin. (*September 18*) Considerable discussion on aid to Russia, including the possibility of sending British troops to the Caucasus, ensued. (*September 19*) That day, an eye-witness of the discussion recalled Churchill's technique to make sure that the decision to send substantial aid to Russia was 'safe and firm'. Stalin was quickly informed, Churchill telling him that 'the American proposals have not yet gone beyond the end of June 1942, but I have no doubt that considerably larger quotas can be furnished by both countries thereafter ' All the quotas up to June 1942, Churchill pointed out, 'are supplied almost entirely out of British production, or production which the United States would have given us under our own purchases or under the Lend Lease Bill'. (*September 21*)

A special Directive from Churchill examined the scale and implications of aid to Russia, including the possibility of a British amphibious landing in Europe, possibly against German-occupied Norway. (*September 22*) To the House of Commons, Churchill explained that the British and American Missions that had gone to Moscow were instructed 'to provide really effective quantities of British and American supplies' to Russia, including tanks 'for which we have waited so long' and large quantities of raw materials 'vital to modern war'. (*September 30*). A week later Churchill sent Stalin details of the 'continuous convoys' that would be leaving British ports 'every ten days' with tanks, aircraft, guns and ammunition. (*October 6*) As supplies to Russia continued to flow, Churchill set out the organizational chain of command and responsibility. (*October 15*) The plan to help Russia by means of a British military expedition against German-occupied Norway was put to the experts, and turned down, but not until after Churchill had pressed it, General Brooke later recalled, by a series of questions 'interspersed with sarcasm and criticism'. (*October 12*) Churchill was also critical of the delay in sending Royal Air Force units to Russia: 'I am not content with the arrangements ' (*October 24*). 'He wished that a larger force had been sent.' The despatch of British troops to fight in the Caucasus was considered, but rejected, as they 'would be certain in the end to be overwhelmed'. Any sent to South Russia 'would not be of a size which would in any way affect the march of events on the Eastern Front, and the Russians would not think much of so small a reinforcement'. (*October 27*)

When the British Ambassador to Russia pressed for British troops to be sent to Russia, as Stalin had asked, Churchill replied robustly. 'They certainly have no right to reproach us . . . We have done our very best to help them at the cost of deranging all our plans for rearmament and exposing ourselves to heavy risks when the spring invasion season comes . . . We will do anything more in our power that is sensible, but it would be silly to send two or three British or British-Indian divisions into the heart of Russia to be surrounded and cut to pieces as a symbolic sacrifice.' (*October 28*) Writing direct to Stalin, Churchill offered to send Wavell to Moscow 'or wherever you will' to explain this. (*November 4*)

One method of helping Stalin which Churchill suggested was to base British bomber squadrons in Northern Persia 'to aid the Russians in the defence of the Caucasus'. If Baku were to fall to the Germans, these bombers could strike at the oilfields there 'and try to set the ground alight'. (*November 5*) The possibility of sending ground troops to Russia remained on the agenda of possibilities until the end of the year, 'provided always that Stalin prefers troops to supplies'. (*December 3*)

Enigma-based information continued to be sent to Stalin as the Germans advanced on Moscow. 'Are you warning the Russians of the developing concentration?' Churchill asked the head of the Secret Intelligence Service, Brigadier Menzies ('C'), when he saw in the Enigma material details of a particular impending German attack. (*October 2*) Stalin's complaints about British aid were strident. (*November 11*) In a letter to the British ambassador in Moscow, Sir Stafford Cripps, Churchill pointed out: 'we have wrecked our Air and Tank programmes for their sake, and in our effort to hold German Air power in the west we have lost more than double the pilots and machines lost in the Battle of Britain last year.' (*November 15*) As the German forces continued to drive towards Moscow, Britain's 'Crusader' offensive in the Western Desert began. (*November 18*) Within three weeks it had forced the Germans to divert air forces, troops and troop transport aircraft from the Russian front. (*December 5*)

While making great efforts to send aid to Russia, Churchill was vexed when Stalin protested about the quality of the aid and called for Britain to launch a 'second front somewhere in the Balkans or France' (*September 4*). He was even more vexed when the British Ambassador to Russia, Sir Stafford Cripps, endorsed Stalin's complaints. 'No one wants to recriminate,' Churchill told the ambassador, with a reference to the Nazi-Soviet pact of August 1939, 'but it is not our fault that Hitler was enabled to destroy Poland before turning his forces against France, or to destroy France before turning them against Russia.' (*September 5*)

In the immediate aftermath of the German invasion of the Soviet Union, Churchill sought to initiate offensive action in northern Europe, including increased British air attacks and a 'large raid' of 25 to 30,000 men – including Canadians – on the coast of northern France. This was the genesis of the Dieppe raid of the following year. 'Now the enemy is busy in Russia is the time to "make hell while the sun shines".' (*June 23*) Four days later, after watching a practice exercise for future British amphibious attacks, Churchill set out a series of questions and suggestions, and asked for a progress report 'in one week'. He also congratulated those on the exercise for their 'efficiency and keenness'. (*June 28*)

From June to December the Russian dimension was a daily concern, and burden, for Churchill. His plan to send a British naval squadron to the Arctic was linked in his mind with the possibility that 'Russia could keep the field and go on with the war . . . As long as they go on, it does not matter so much where the front lies. These people have shown themselves worth backing, and we must make sacrifices and take risks even at inconvenience, which I recognize, to maintain their morale.' (*July 10*)

To Stalin, Churchill declared in his first message since the German attack on Russia, that Britain would 'do everything to help you that time, geography and our growing resources allow'. Heavy bombing raids on Germany had been carried out 'both day and night'. Almost 250 bombers had been in action the previous night. 'This will go on. Thus we hope to force Hitler to bring back some of his air power to the West and gradually take some of the strain off you.'. Churchill's message ended: 'We have only to go on fighting to beat the life out of these villains.' (*July 7*) That same day he told the Chief of the Air Staff: 'One of our great aims is the delivery on German towns of the largest quantity of bombs per night.'

Bombing policy had far wider implications than the Russian front. 'We live in a terrible epoch of human history,' Churchill told Londoners. (*July 14*)

> But we believe there is a broad and sure justice running through its theme. It is time that the Germans should be made to suffer in their own homeland and cities something of the torment they have twice in our lifetime let loose upon their neighbours and upon the world.
>
> We have now intensified for a month past our systematic, scientific, methodical bombing on a large scale of the German cities, seaports, industries, and other military objectives.
>
> We believe it to be in our power to keep this process going, on a steadily rising tide, month after month, year after year, until the Nazi regime is either extirpated by us or, better still, torn to pieces by the German people themselves.

Weaknesses in bombing policy found Churchill ever inventive. When he learned that as many as three-quarters of all bombs dropped on Germany 'go astray', he put up two ideas to try to remedy this. (*September 15*) He elaborated on one of these a week later in a note to the Chief of the Air Staff: 'All this should be pursued night and day by your people.' (*September 22*)

Churchill had a number of pet dislikes. When confronted by a request that the word 'British' should be used instead of 'English', he wrote to a Scottish Member of Parliament: 'I get a little nettled sometimes by the very small clique who write indignant letters if the word England is ever mentioned. I do not believe that clique expresses at all the opinions of the Scottish people, who are too sure of themselves to be so petty.' (*February 15*) Belgium was a country that could rouse Churchill's ire: 'After the war had begun,' he wrote nine months after Belgium's surrender, 'the King's attitude and that of his Government in treating Germany and Britain (with its 600,000 graves on Belgian soil) as if they were "six of one and half-a-dozen of the other", was an ineffaceable blot on the Belgian name.' (*February 16*) Finland also stirred anger; the attitude of its government was 'obnoxious and aggressive'. The Finnish ambassador in London 'should be made to feel his position acutely. One cannot be on two sides at once.' (*July 16*)

Churchill always preferred using the older 'well-known' forms of place names, with which he was familiar. 'I should like Livorno to be called in English – Leghorn', he wrote to Eden; adding that 'of course . . . if at any time you are conversing agreeably with Mussolini in Italian, Livorno would be correct.' (*January 18*) As acting Foreign Secretary in Eden's absence he promised himself 'a treat': in all Foreign Office prints Istanbul was to have Constantinople printed after it in brackets, and after Thailand, Siam. (*February 16*). Later in the year he wanted to see the word Persia used, not Iran, as 'dangerous mistakes may easily occur' by confusing Iran and Iraq. (*August 2*). Iceland had to be 'Iceland (C)' so as not to confuse it with Ireland.

The length of Foreign Office telegrams was always a cause of vexation. It was 'an evil which ought to be checked' he wrote. 'It is sheer laziness not compressing thought into a reasonable space.' (*January 11*) A diplomat should not 'pour out upon us over these congested wires all the contradictory gossip which he hears'. (*February 17*). Of a diplomat alleged to have been 'unsympathetic, slack and unhelpful' to the British community in Marseilles, Churchill asked for a report. (*April 10*)

Lack of information always upset Churchill. Not having received reports of the fighting in Greece for several days from General Wavell or General Wilson, Churchill telegraphed to Wavell: 'This is not the way His Majesty's Government should be treated. It is also detrimental to the Service, as many decisions have to be taken here . . .' (*April 19*) He was scathing, too, when presented with assessments that he considered exaggerated, as when a practice exercise to meet a German invasion concluded that the Germans would be able rapidly to put a substantial army ashore. 'It would be of the greatest advantage,' Churchill wrote, 'if officers who believe it is so easy to land large forces with their vehicles, ammunition and stores, in a few hours on open beaches, would make a plan for a British landing of the force in question either on the Dutch or the French coasts.' (*April 23*)

To his son Randolph, Churchill wrote: 'The Admirals, Generals and Air Marshals chant their stately hymn of "Safety First". The Shinwells, Wintertons and Hore Belishas do their best to keep us up to the mark. In the midst of this I have to restrain my natural pugnacity by sitting on my own head. How bloody!' (*October 30*) To General Wavell, on the eve of his summer offensive in the Western Desert, Churchill had given a broad hint at what had been a past and might be a future criticism. 'I venture once again to emphasize,' he wrote, 'that the objective is not the reaching of particular positions but the destruction by fighting of the armed force of the enemy wherever it may be found.' (*June 9*) After the failure of Wavell's offensive in the Western Desert a week later, Churchill resisted the general's proposal to go on the defensive for three months, asking the Chiefs of Staff: 'Have we really got to accept this?' (*June 20*)

General Ismay, the head of Churchill's Defence Office, recalled after the war that 'there was a very general impression in Whitehall that Wavell was very tired'. He was replaced by General Auchinleck, whose 'great zeal and character' in Iraq had much impressed Churchill. (*June 30*) At the same time, a civilian Minister of State was sent out to Cairo to supervise the massive task of supply. (*July 5*) Three days later Auchinleck was rebuked for speaking to journalists about British needs for American manpower. 'It is a mistake,' Churchill told him, 'for Generals in High Command to make speeches or give interviews to Press correspondents . . . Now that you have broken the ice with war correspondents, I trust you will not find it necessary to make any further public statements on political or strategic issues, or that if you wish to do so you will consult me beforehand.' (*July 8*)

To Eden, Churchill complained that the senior British diplomat in Iran 'does not seem to be at all at the level of events'. (*September 6*) There could be praise however for those by whose actions Churchill was impressed, as when he wrote of one senior airman: 'I watched his work here very closely . . . He embodies offensive warfare'. (*May 16*). A paper by General Paget setting out measures for maintaining anti-invasion vigilance so impressed him that he minuted: 'I agree with every word of it', and promised the general whatever support he needed. (*December 20*) There was also potential praise of someone as yet unknown: 'Renown awaits the Commander who first in this war restores Artillery to its prime importance upon the battlefield . . .' (*October 7*) Churchill hoped that this commander would be Auchinleck, to whom he sent a series of messages and exhortations about the renewed offensive in the Western Desert. (*October 14, 16*) But Churchill's hopes were not fulfilled: 'I am disquieted' (*October 17*). 'My apprehensions' (*October 18*). 'No choice but to accept your new proposal . . . while disappointed and alarmed by retardation I fully accept your new arrangements.' (*October 21*) Churchill added, hoping to encourage Auchinleck: 'Enemy is now ripe for sickle.' (*October 24*)

To Roosevelt, Churchill had sent a full account 'For yourself alone' of the impending offensive, before it was postponed, and of its importance for the future of the war, including future amphibious landings 'on the beaches of three or four countries ripe for revolt'. (*October 20*) Postponement was galling to Churchill, who wrote, when it came, to Oliver Lyttelton, his Minister Resident in the Middle East: 'All here were astonished.' (*October 21*) But he soon found himself pressing for the postponed plan to be pursued with vigour at its new date, determined to secure air bases from which British bombing attacks could be made on Italy – 'the weaker partner in the Axis' (*October 25*) – or advantage taken of a much-hoped-for offer by General Weygand for British forces to enter French North Africa. (*October 28*) Having been told by an emissary of Auchinleck's detailed plans, Churchill sent words of encouragement 'of the way in which you are concentrating all your power upon the destruction of the enemy's armour and of his armed forces generally'. (*October 30*)

Following the success of 'Crusader', of which Churchill sent Roosevelt up-to-the-minute reports, Churchill planned a further forward move in the Western Desert, as well as a move to get French North Africa 'in our hands'. To this end he sought to enlist Roosevelt's support. (*November 24*) That day he also wrote to the Chiefs of Staff about future offensive plans, commenting: 'it is prudent to take a forward view on assumption of success'. To Auchinleck, he exhorted further efforts to ensure that 'Crusader' did succeed: 'Close grip upon the enemy by all units will choke the life out of him.' (*November 25*)

In a speech to the boys of his old school, Harrow, Churchill set out what he saw as the lesson of the ten months when Britain was alone and under heavy German aerial bombardment:

> Never give in, never give in, never, never, never, never – in nothing, great or small, large or petty – never give in except to convictions of honour and good sense. Never yield to force; never yield to the apparently overwhelming might of the enemy. We stood alone a year ago, and to many countries it seemed that our account was closed, and that we were finished . . .

'Very different is the mood today,' Churchill told the schoolboys. 'We now find ourselves in a position where I can say that we can be sure that we only have to persevere to conquer.' (*October 29*)

Many diarists recorded Churchill's table talk. John Colville's diary is a regular source of insight into life at Downing Street and Chequers. Oliver Harvey provides a Foreign Office perspective and Harold Nicolson a parliamentary one. The journalist Charles Eade had three luncheon encounters in 1941, of each of which he made a note. (*March 6, July 24, November 19*). Several of those who saw Churchill at close quarters recorded personal aspects of his moods and behaviour. Sir Alexander Cadogan recorded Churchill saying: 'I'm not afraid of the air, I'm not afraid of invasion, I'm less afraid of the Balkans – but – I am anxious about the Atlantic.' (*March 20*) Visiting Swansea with her father after a heavy German air raid, Churchill's daughter Mary wrote in her diary: 'It is rather frightening how terribly they depend on him'. (*April 11*)

One result of Churchill's visit to Swansea, and to Bristol on the following day, was the allocation of more foodstuffs to the civilian population. (*April 12*) Churchill was encouraged by his visits to the blitzed towns. When in the House of Commons, he was asked about public 'uneasiness' with regard to the conduct of the war, he replied: 'The public are showing all those qualities of stability and phlegm, when things are not going well, that have made us what we are and have carried us thus far.' (*April 22*) Five days later Churchill addressed these concerns in a radio broadcast in which he surveyed the whole spectrum of British war policy. Two hundred million people in the British Empire and the United States were 'determined', he said, 'that the cause of freedom shall not be trampled down, nor the tide of world progress turned backwards, by the criminal Dictators'; and he ended with William Clough's poem and its concluding line, full of anticipation of America's increased support: 'But westward, look, the land is bright.'

The war in Europe was never overshadowed by the storm clouds in the Far East, yet the possibility of a Japanese attack on British possessions in Malaya, Burma and even India, as well as Hong Kong, was present throughout the year, and was raised at the War Cabinet early in the year. (*February 6, 15*) At this second meeting there was reference to 'many drifting straws'. That day Churchill wrote to Roosevelt at length about the prospects and dangers of war with Japan. Nine days later he saw the Japanese ambassador in London, telling him: 'I had confidence that the Japanese did not wish to embark upon such a tremendous struggle as would be inevitable if they went to war with the British and Americans.' (*February 24*) A letter which Churchill wrote to the Japanese Foreign Minister set out the reasons why Japan could not win a war against Britain and the United States (*April 2*).

Preparations for a possible attack by Japan touched on the defence of Malaya, Singapore and Australia. But priorities were such that 'it would be foolish to send further reinforcements to Malaya in the near future'. (*April 9*) The same was true of Singapore. (*April 10*) Four months later, the despatch of at least one 'modern ship' to the Far East was under discussion, proposed by Clement Attlee. (*August 19*) Britain was committed to go to war against Japan, Churchill told the War Cabinet, 'if Japan was at war with the United States. But if Japan declared war on Russia, Britain ought not to declare war on Japan, even if pressed by Russia to do so, unless the United States was also at war with Japan. (*October 16*) To Roosevelt, Churchill wrote, in an unprecedented pledge, that should the United States 'become at war with Japan, you may be sure that a British declaration of war upon Japan will follow within the hour'. (*October 20*)

The issue of naval reinforcements to the Far East intensified in the autumn. 'No time should now be lost in sending the *Prince of Wales*.' (*October 17*) Churchill agreed with the Australian government that this modern battleship – on which he had crossed the Atlantic for his meeting with Roosevelt – was 'the best possible deterrent' to Japan.

(*October 25*) But he reserved the right to bring the ship back into the Atlantic once she reached the Cape of Good Hope, should she be needed against German warships there. When the decision was made to send her, Roosevelt was told. 'This ought to serve as a deterrent on Japan,' Churchill wrote. 'There is nothing like having something that can catch and kill anything. I am very glad we can spare her at this juncture The firmer your attitude and ours the less chance of their taking the plunge.' (*November 1*) That plunge was only five weeks away. Japan had become a daily concern, the War Cabinet frequently discussing Japanese intentions (*as on November 3*). Confidently, Churchill told Stalin that the *Prince of Wales* 'can catch and kill any Japanese ship'. (*November 4*)

Churchill hoped to find a deterrent to Japanese action, envisaged as imminent against the Chinese in Yunnan, to cut the Burma Road supply route. The Chinese had appealed to Britain for help to prevent the route being cut. Churchill suggested to Roosevelt that a 'formidable' warning by the United States was needed. Britain would be 'ready to make a similar communication' and would 'stand with you and do our utmost to back you in whatever course you choose'. (*November 5*) In a public appeal to the Japanese five days later, Churchill said, after recalling his own vote in favour of the Anglo-Japanese Alliance of 1902, and his always having been 'a sentimental well-wisher' of the Japanese: 'Viewing the vast sombre scene as dispassionately as possible, it would seem a very hazardous adventure for the Japanese people to plunge quite needlessly into a world struggle in which they may well find themselves opposed in the Pacific by States whose population comprises nearly three-quarters of the human race.' Then, turning to a practical consideration which he had raised seven months earlier with the Japanese Foreign Minister, he asked: 'If steel is a basic foundation of modern war, it would be rather dangerous for a power like Japan, whose steel production is only about seven million tons a year, to provoke quite gratuitously a struggle with the United States, whose steel production is now about ninety millions . . .' (*November 10*)

Neither Churchill's warnings – nor his public statement at the Mansion House on November 10, 'that should the United States become involved in war with Japan, the British declaration will follow within the hour', echoing his October 20 pledge to Roosevelt – seemed able to deter Japan. On the last day of November a Japanese attack on Thailand seemed imminent. This would involve the advance of Japanese troops in the Kra Isthmus, along the border with Malaya, which would be both 'an obvious threat to Singapore', and would in itself foreshadow the prospect of 'a clash which might involve us in war'. (*November 30*)

In the first week of December Britain decided, as Churchill informed the Australian Prime Minister, to take 'forestalling action at Kra Isthmus if necessary', and also to 'assure Dutch that we will help them at once if they are attacked'. (*December 5*) On the following day, as information reached him that a Japanese 'armada' was moving westward from Indochina, Churchill put an 'Action this Day' label on his orders to deny the Japanese the use of the Miri oil plant in Borneo. (*December 6*) Once the United States was at war with Japan, Churchill told Averell Harriman that day, Britain would declare war on Japan 'not within the hour but within the minute'. Meanwhile, three British declarations of war were issued in connection with the war in Europe, against three States that were engaged in the German offensive against Russia: Roumania, Hungary and Finland. Churchill's personal appeal to the Finnish leader, Marshal Mannerheim, to halt his troops, had been in vain. (*November 28, December 4*) The three declarations of war were issued at midnight on December 5.

In the early evening of Saturday December 6, Churchill telegraphed to General Auchinleck, whose troops were then in action in the Western Desert, that Roosevelt 'has now definitely said that the United States will regard it as hostile act if Japanese invade Siam, Malaya, Burma or the Dutch East Indies, and he is warning Japan this week, probably Wednesday'. The coming Wednesday was December 10. Events superceded Roosevelt's intention. Churchill, meanwhile, was worried lest Britain would be attacked by Japan, and be at war with both Germany and Japan, but that no Japanese attack would be made on the United States, and Congress would not be willing to declare war on Japan.

On the morning of Sunday December 7, as more reports of Japanese naval movements reached him, Churchill telegraphed to the Prime Minister of Thailand that an 'imminent Japanese invasion' of his country was possible. Churchill added: 'The preservation of the full independence and sovereignty of Thailand is a British interest, and we shall regard an attack on you as an attack on ourselves.'

That night, Averell Harriman found Churchill 'tired and depressed'; during dinner at Chequers he was 'immersed in his thoughts, with his head in his hands part of the time'. Then, at nine o'clock, came news over the BBC of the Japanese attack on Pearl Harbor. Churchill at once telephoned Roosevelt, who confirmed the news. British territory had also been attacked by Japan, simultaneously. Britain and the United States both declared war on Japan. That day Churchill prepared to set off for the United States to confer with Roosevelt, proposing to go by sea – an eight day journey – to one of the ports on the eastern seaboard. One reason for his journey was to make sure, he explained to the King, 'that our share of munitions and other aid does not suffer more than is, I fear, inevitable'. (*December 8*) Churchill's hopes of being with Roosevelt within ten days of Pearl Harbor were to be disappointed, but he was in Washington before 1941 came to an end.

Four days after Pearl Harbor, Germany declared war on the United States. The war had become a World War. Churchill told the House of Commons: 'We have at least four-fifths of the population of the globe upon our side. We are responsible for their safety and for their future. In the past we have had a light which flickered, in the present we have a light which flames, and in the future there will be a light which shines over all the land and sea.' (*December 8*)

The immediate future was filled with setbacks, starting with the sinking of the *Prince of Wales* and the *Repulse*. (*December 10*) On the following day Churchill gave an account of the war to the House of Commons in which he began with encouraging news from the Western Desert, where the troops had fought 'in every circumstance of fatigue and hardship with one sincere, insatiable desire, to engage the enemy and destroy him . . .' In the Battle of the Atlantic, merchant shipping losses were less than a fifth of what they had been in the summer. In the war in Russia, by the very fact of making war Hitler had committed 'one of the outstanding blunders of history'. The sufferings of the German troops were 'indescribable'. Their losses had been 'immense'. For its part, despite the widening war, Britain would 'faithfully and punctually fulfil the very serious undertakings we have made to Russia'. In the Far East, the loss of life on the two warships had been 'most melancholy'. He could not discuss the resulting situation. 'It may well be that we shall have to suffer considerable punishment'. No one should underrate 'the length of time it will take to create, marshal and mount the great force in the Far East which will be necessary to achieve absolute victory'. (*December 11*)

Churchill had to make new plans; to Wavell, who had become Commander-in-Chief in India, he gave instructions to 'resist Japanese advance towards Burma and India and try to cut their communications down the Malay Peninsula'. (*December 12*) To the defenders of Hong Kong he telegraphed that day: 'Every day of your resistance brings nearer our certain final victory.' Churchill also made plans to visit Roosevelt, it being explained as a matter of security that he was going to Scotland to see Lord Beaverbrook off to the United States. (*December 12*) As the journey began, measures were taken to strengthen Britain's position in the Indian Ocean (*December 13, 15*) and for the defence of Singapore. (*December 15, 19*)

Churchill used the sea voyage to the United States to set out his views on the future conduct of the war in four substantial memoranda. The first two concerned the war in 1942 both in the Atlantic and Europe (*December 16*) and in the Pacific. (*December 17*) The third looked at plans for 1943, which would include preparations 'for the liberation of the captive countries of Western and Southern Europe by landing at suitable points, successively or simultaneously, of British and American armies strong enough to enable the conquered populations to revolt'. (*December 18*) The fourth memorandum looked at the future conduct of the war in the Pacific, its premise being 'The resources of Japan are a wasting factor.' (*December 20*) During the transatlantic voyage Churchill also set out his suggestions for the meeting with Roosevelt. 'Joint strategy must be settled and agreed . . .' (*December 20*)

From mid-Atlantic, Churchill sent an exhortation to Hong Kong on the defence of the island. It included the sentence 'There must, however, be no thought of surrender.' (*December 20*) That day Churchill sent a survey of the war to his wife, who was in London. Hong Kong seemed 'on the verge of surrender after only a fortnight's struggle'. But the entry of the United States into the war 'is worth all the losses in the East many times over. Still these losses are very painful to endure and will be very hard to repair.'

The talks with Roosevelt were pivotal to the future conduct of the war. At a Press conference on the day of his arrival Churchill told the assembled journalists: 'I can't describe the feelings of relief with which I find Russia victorious, and the United States and Great

Britain standing side by side.' (*December 23*) Russian forces had begun to push the German troops back from the outskirts of Moscow.

When Churchill reached the White House, Roosevelt handed him a draft Declaration of Common Purpose, under which all the Allied governments would agree to co-ordinate their military effort and resources, and to continue the war until the Axis powers had been 'finally' defeated. At this first Washington meeting, Roosevelt agreed to Churchill's request to send four air squadrons 'for immediate bombing attacks on Germany'. (*December 23*) The intensity of the war against Germany would not be reduced because of the war against Japan.

At dinner that evening in the White House, a guest recalled that Churchill and Roosevelt discussed the Boer War; then the powdered eggs being sent from the United States to Britain; then unhappy childhoods. Churchill also used one of his favourite phrases: 'There is no use having a dog and barking yourself.' (*December 23*) After dinner the President and Prime Minister discussed the North African situation and the need to forestall the Germans in French Morocco, and in the Spanish and Portuguese Atlantic Islands. Churchill sent a detailed account of this discussion to the War Cabinet and the Chiefs of Staff on the following morning. (*December 24*) To his wife, Churchill confided, on Christmas Eve: 'The Americans are magnificent in their breadth of view.' In a broadcast to the American people that night Churchill remarked: 'This is a strange Christmas Eve. Almost the whole world is locked in deadly struggle, and, with the most terrible weapons which science can devise, the nations advance upon each other.'

That day, General Auchinleck reported to Churchill that British forces had occupied Benghazi. The following day, Japanese forces overran Hong Kong. Addressing a Joint Session of Congress, Churchill spoke of how, in Washington, 'I have found an Olympian fortitude which, far from being based upon complacency, is only the mask of an inflexible purpose and the sure proof of a sure and well-grounded confidence in the final outcome.' It would be 'a long and hard war', but 'now that our two considerable nations, each in perfect unity, have joined all their life energies in a common resolve, a new scene opens, upon which a steady light will glow and brighten'. Churchill then looked back to the years when he had been in the political wilderness, his call unheeded for the redress of the grievances of the vanquished. 'Five or six years ago it would have been easy, without shedding a drop of blood, for the United States and Great Britain to have insisted on fulfilment of the disarmament clauses of the treaties which Germany signed after the Great War, that also would have been the opportunity for assuring to Germany those raw materials which we declared in the Atlantic Charter should not be denied to any nation, victor or vanquished. The chance has passed. It is gone. Prodigious hammer-strokes have been needed to bring us together again . . .' In days to come, 'the British and American peoples will for their own safety and for the good of all walk together side by side in majesty, in justice, and in peace'. (*December 26*)

It was not only to the United States Congress that Churchill referred to the mistakes of the past. Three months earlier, in the House of Commons, he had expressed the hope that some of his critics would 'reflect a little on their own records in the past, and by searching their hearts and memories will realize the fate which awaits nations and individuals who take an easy or popular course, or who are guided in defence matters by the shifting winds of well-meaning public opinion'. (*September 29*)

During the fifth day of Churchill's sojourn in Washington he telegraphed to Auchinleck with congratulations on his most recent successes in the Western Desert, suggestions for future moves, and news of the extent of the American commitment both to the European and North African war theatres. Against French North Africa, he reported, 'Highly trained American divisions may be thrown into the scales'. (*December 27*)

That night, at the White House, Churchill had a mild heart attack. His doctor decided to tell him that it was no more than 'sluggish' circulation. (*December 27*) Work continued, including the second of two morning confrontations with Roosevelt when Churchill was in his bath. (*December 24, 28*) A final set of decisions concerned the war in the Pacific. A British general would be Supreme Commander of all the Allied land forces in the South-West Pacific – Churchill proposed and Roosevelt accepted General Wavell for the task – and an American admiral would command all the naval forces. The United States would be responsible for the Pacific Ocean east of the Philippines. (*December 28*)

On December 28 Churchill went by train to Ottawa, where he spent three days. At dinner on the second day, according to an eye-witness, 'He grumbled about having to make another oration in Parliament on the morrow and said that he was not a hen to lay an unlimited number of eggs'. (*December 29*) In his address to a joint session of the Canadian parliament he praised the Canadian contribution to the war effort, including the Empire pilot-training scheme and the shipyard building of corvettes and merchant ships. Recalling that the French generals had warned at the time of the battle for France in May 1940, 'In three weeks England will have her neck wrung like a chicken', Churchill commented: 'Some chicken!' and, amid the laughter, 'Some neck!' (*December 30*)

It was immediately after this speech that Churchill was photographed by Yousuf Karsh, who took two photographs, the famous 'frowner' and the less known 'smiler' (which is on the jacket of this volume). That day Churchill called for 'no weakness or pandering' to Australia, after reading an article critical of Britain by the Australian Prime Minister, but Churchill added: 'at the same time we will do all in human power to come to their aid.'

On the following afternoon, December 31, Churchill left Ottawa by train. He was in the train, travelling southward towards Washington, as the New Year began.

There could be moments of light relief even during a dark and dangerous year. Reading in the newspaper of senior officers taking part in a seven-mile cross country run with their men, Churchill commented: 'Who is the general of this division, and does he run the seven miles himself? If so, he may be more useful for football than war. Could Napoleon have run seven miles before Austerlitz. Perhaps it was the other fellow he made run.' (*February 4*) Asked in a Royal Air Force officers' mess if he would like some tea, Churchill replied: 'Good God no, my wife drinks that, I'll have a brandy.' (*September 25*) On the following day, after Churchill gave one of his famous 'V for Victory' signs, one of his Private Secretaries noted in his diary: 'The PM will give the V-sign with two fingers in spite of the representations repeatedly made to him that this gesture has quite another significance.' (*September 26*)

Churchill's moods during 1941 were reflected in the diaries of those who worked closest to him. Elizabeth Layton, his secretary from 1941 to 1945, noted during a difficult period of the war in 1941: 'He was in a bad mood all this week and every time I went to him he used a new and worse swear word. However, he usually rounded it off by beaming goodnight at me, so one can't bear any malice or even let it worry one.' (*July 18*) A week later, Miss Layton wrote to her parents: 'You might think that seeing such a person at close quarters might lessen one's admiration and respect, or make him seem more commonplace. But not so in this case; he is just as amazing and terrific and full of character in his private life as he is over the radio or in the House of Commons. He bullies his servants, but then completely makes up by giving a really charming smile. On the rare occasions when a brave soul has expostulated at his treatment he has been told "Oh don't mind me, it's only my way".' (*July 25*)

'Anger', Churchill told one lunchtime visitor, 'is a waste of energy. Steam which is used to blow off a safety valve would be better used to drive an engine'. (*July 24*)

During what was for Britain one of the most dangerous periods of 1941 – while the battle for Crete was raging, the pro-German Rashid Ali still ruler of Baghdad, the Battle of the Atlantic a scene of daily sinkings, and the *Bismarck* still evading its pursuers – Anthony Eden wrote to Churchill: 'This is a bad day; but tomorrow – Baghdad will be entered, *Bismarck* sunk. On some date the war will be won, and you will have done more than any man in history to win it.' (*May 26*) On the following day General Sir Alan Brooke, whose often critical approach to Churchill was a noted feature of his private comments, wrote in his diary:

> It is surprising how he maintains a light-hearted exterior in spite of the vast burden he is bearing. He is quite the most wonderful man I have ever met, and it is a source of never-ending interest, studying him and getting to realize that occasionally such human beings make their appearance on this earth – human beings who stand out head and shoulders above all others.

Martin Gilbert
Merton College, Oxford
16 July 1999

Acknowledgements

Fifty years ago Winston Churchill's literary assistant, Bill (later Sir William) Deakin, DSO, was entrusted by Churchill with the task of combing the official records of Churchill's premiership, and of preparing several thousand documents in printed form for Churchill's use in his forthcoming war memoirs. Each document which Deakin selected was printed in booklet form, the booklets marked 'Most Secret' and given the added designation: 'To be kept under lock and key: it is requested that special care be taken to ensure the secrecy of this document'. One of these sets, in which the first document in this volume appears, consisted of Churchill's personal telegrams. Another, which includes the second document published in this volume, contains Churchill's personal minutes. Since the opening of the Public Records for the war years, each of these telegrams and minutes is available in its original form. But the work that Deakin did, the fruits of which are now available for all researchers at the Archive Centre at Churchill College, Cambridge, not only formed the basis of Churchill's own memoirs, but remains of great benefit to the work of all historians seeking to understand Churchill's premiership.

Among those who helped Churchill arrange the mass of material in his archive was Denis Kelly, whose subsequent friendship and encouragement meant a great deal to me. It has been both strange and pleasing to come across his handwriting from time to time, as on Churchill's copy of his letter to King George VI of 22 September 1941, on which Kelly had noted: 'Not published in War Memoirs'.

My own researches relevant to this volume of documents date back to my correspondence in 1964 with Percy Chubb (who was present at the first dinner given by President Roosevelt to Churchill at the White House in 1941) and with Lady Asquith of Yarnbury (the former Violet Bonham Carter). Important material relating to the Enigma decrypts of German top secret radio messages came from my correspondence with Edward Thomas, one of the contributing authors of Professor Sir Harry Hinsley's multi-volume *British Intelligence in the Second World War*.

The family of Churchill's first wartime Principal Private Secretary, Sir Eric Seal, made available to me his private papers and manuscript recollections. Churchill's Principal Private Secretary for the years 1941 to 1945, Sir John Martin, gave me access to his wartime notes. Sir John Colville gave me access to his wartime diary; for this volume as for its two predeccesors this diary has proved an important source of material not available in other documents. Sir John Peck, another member of Churchill's wartime Private Office, was generous with archival material and historical guidance, as well as giving me access to his manuscript memoirs, 'Bull and Benediction'. General Sir Ian Jacob, a member of the wartime Defence Secretariat, let me see his account of Churchill's visit to Washington in December 1941. Patrick Kinna and Sir Richard Pim, both of whom served Churchill during the war years, provided me with archival material and recollections for the year 1941.

Churchill's secretary Elizabeth Nel (formerly Elizabeth Layton) has helped me on many points of detail, both with her own recollections, and by letting me use the letters she sent from London to her parents. Kathleen Hill recalled the moment when Churchill learned of the sinking of the *Prince of Wales* and *Repulse*. I have also received material from participants in the events described from Joan Bright Astley, Peregrine Churchill, Michael Clark, Sir Arthur Harris, Colonel Harvie-Watt, Squadron-Leader Ronald E. Ladbrook, Helen Robbins Millbank (Helen Kirkpatrick) and Michael Stuart. Lord Balfour of Inchyra let me use his diary of the Anglo-American Mission to Moscow.

Many archivists, librarians and their staffs have helped me to track down material, especially for the annotations in this volume. I am particularly grateful to the Royal Archives, BBC Resources (Written Archives Centre), the Contemporary Medical Archives Centre, the Ministry of Defence Air Historical Branch, the Polish Institute and Sikorski Museum Archive, the Public Record Office, the Imperial War Museum, and the Roosevelt Archive.

I have also made use of material from the archives of Lord Beaverbrook, Lord Camrose, Lord Cherwell (Professor Lindemann), Corder Catchpool, Neville Laski, Robert Menzies, Captain Stephen Roskill, Lady Soames, Baroness Spencer-

Churchill, G. R. Storry, Commander C.R. Thompson, Dr Chaim Weizmann, and Baron Wedgwood; as well as from the Harrow School Archive; from the published diaries of Henry Channon, Hugh Dalton, Lord Harvey of Tasburgh and Sir Harold Nicolson; and from the published memoirs of the Earl of Avon (Anthony Eden) and Lord Ismay.

I have also received documentary material from Piers Brendon, (Keeper of the Archives, Churchill Archives Centre, Churchill College Cambridge), and from Lady Soames. For permision to quote individual letters I am grateful to Her Majesty the Queen, and to Her Majesty Queen Elizabeth The Queen Mother.

Peter Halban, who was present when I began work on the first document in this volume, drew my attention to several points of interest which I was able to follow up. I have been helped on many points of detail by:

Petrína Bachmann (Attaché, Embassy of Iceland), Lady de Bellaigue (Registrar, Royal Archives, Windsor), Caroline Buttle (Club Administrator, The Jockey Club),

Diana Coffey (Air Historical Branch, Minitry of Defence), Lord Campbell of Croy, David Cesarani (The Wiener Library), Julian Challis, Michael Chapman (Chief Librarian, subsequently Head of Customer Services, Ministry of Defence, Whitehall Library), Diana Coffey (Air Historical Branch, Ministry of Defence), Ronald L. Cohen, His Excellency Kjell Colding (Royal Norwegian Embassy), Robert Craig,

Hugo Deadman (House of Lords Library), Eamon Dyas (Group Records Manager, News International), Barbara Donnelly (Librarian, Naval War College Library, Newport, Rhode Island),

Ian Easton (Personal Assistant to the Lord Provost of Glasgow); P.J.V. Elliott (Senior Keeper, Department of Research and Information Services, Royal Air Force Museum), Alexandra Erskine (Librarian, the *Daily Telegraph)*, Oliver Everett (Assistant Keeper of the Royal Archives),

Professor M.R.D. Foot,

Rita Gibbs (Archivist, Harrow School), Anna Girvan (Reference Center Assistant, United States Information Service, London),

Grace Hamblin, Jo Hanford (Assistant Librarian, Royal Naval Museum), Sara Hawkins (Stanbridge Earls School, Romsey), J. H. Holroyd (10 Downing Street), Steingrímur Hermannsson (Governor, Central Bank of Iceland), Sir Peter Hutchison

(Chairman, Forestry Commission), Jack Hyde (Librarian, Confederation of British Industry),

Sir Martin Jacomb (The British Council), Morwen Johnson (London Library),

Sally Keeley (Public Information Office, House of Commons), Louise King (Churchill Archives Centre), Susan Knowles (Senior Document Assistant, BBC Written Archives Centre, Caversham),

Penelope Lisles (Australian High Commission), Major C.J. Louch (Coldstream Guards),

Dr. Denis MacShane, MP, Len Mader (Department of External Affairs, Ottawa), Morris Massel, Dr Alastair Massie (Archives Department, National Army Museum), Lieutenant Colonel Anthony Mather (Central Chancery of the Orders of Knighthood), Annele Melas (Press Office, Embassy of Finland), Keith Miller (Head of the Department of Weapons, Equipment and Vehicles, National Army Museum). Piers Morgan (Editor, the *Daily Mirror*), Ros Morris, Masatoshi Muto, Director (Japan Information and Cultural Centre, Embassy of Japan),

Verne W. Newton (Director, Franklin D. Roosevelt Library),

Geoffrey W. Oxley (City Archivist, Kingston Upon Hull),

Maria Padmore (City Council, Kingston upon Hull), Professor Ben Pimlott (Warden, Goldsmiths College), Stephen Plant (Churchill Archives Centre)

His Excellency Vidhya Rayananonda (Royal Thai Embassy), Phil Reed (Curator, Cabinet War Rooms), David M. Reel (Assistant Curator, The Forbes Magazine Collection), His Excellency J.H.R.D. van Roijen (Royal Netherlands Embassy).

Chris Sadowski (Assistant Editor, International Whitaker's Almanac), James R Sewell (City Archivist, Corporation of London Records Office), Julia G.A. Sheppard (Archivist, Contemporary Medical Archives Centre, Wellcome Institute for the History of Medicine), Graham Snelling (Curator, The National Horseracing Museum), Keith Southey (Public Relations Manager, Dover Harbour Board), Mike Spick (Development Officer, Sheffield Local Studies Library), Andrzej Suchcitz, Keeper of Archives, Polish Institute and Sikorski Museum, London,

Suha Tanyeri (Defence Attaché, Turkish Embassy), Paul Thorpe (Foreign and Commonwealth Office Library).

Jeff Walden (Senior Document Assistant, BBC Resources), Fiona

Wilkes (Merton College Library), and His Excellency Lode Willems (Embassy of Belgium).

The staffs of the British Library Newspaper Library, Colindale; the London Library; and the Public Record Office, Kew, have always eased the task of compiling these volumes, since I began work on them thirty years ago.

The sorting of the documentary material for 1941, without which I could not have begun detailed work on it, was a formidable task, undertaken at different times since I began work two decades ago on the material in this volume by William Sturge, Taffy Sassoon, Larry Arnn and Abe Eisenstat. The archival work at the Public Record Office, Kew, as well as much of the sorting of the documents in the Churchill papers, was shared from the first days with my wife Susie, who, during the work on Volume Six of the biography – which included the year 1941 – helped track down many elusive archival details.

Richard Langworth, of the International Churchill Society, has been a source of encouragement throughout the work on the War Papers. Without his tenacity in securing funds they could not have been published. The principal financial help came from Wendy Reves, whose generosity, and determination to see these volumes continued with, is a source of continual and much-appreciated encouragement. Further considerable help was given by The Leverhulme Trust, to whose patience and generosity I am extremely grateful; by Conrad Black and the Telegraph Newspapers; and by Annenberg Foundation, through the Churchill Centre, Washington DC.

Kay Thomson helped me from the first day with correspondence and the massive task of organising and collating, and with innumerable enquiries.

Tony Whittome of Random House undertook to see this volume through the press with skill and dedication. He and I were both helped considerably in this task by the eagle eye of Myra Jones. The skills of the typesetters Michael T. Harrington and Allan Ticehurst made an indispensable contribution.

Sources and Bibliography

In the course of compiling this volume I have used material from the following collections of public and private papers:

The private papers of Robert Barrington-Ward, Lord Beaverbrook, Lord Camrose, Corder Catchpool, Sir John Colville, Charles Eade, Philip Guedalla, Colonel George Harvie-Watt, Sir Ian Jacob, Neville Laski QC, Lady Lytton (Pamela Plowden), Sir John Martin, Elizabeth Nel, Sir John Peck, Sir Richard Pim, Sir Eric Seal, Lady Soames, Commander C.R. (Tommy) Thompson papers and Baron Wedgwood (Josiah Wedgwood).

Letters to the author from Percy Chubb (1 March 1977), Peregrine Churchill (10 March 1998), Michael Clark (25 May 1999), Dr. Michael Dunnill (15 October 1984), Squadron-Leader Gillam (20 January 1983), Patrick Kinna (24 August 1982 and 10 October 1984), Squadron-Leader Ronald Ladbrook (27 December 1968), Sir John Martin (15 August 1982), Elizabeth Nel (20 November 1997), Garrison Norton (27 December 1964), Sir John Peck (18 August 1982) and Michael Stuart (22 May 1999); conversations with the author, Baroness Asquith of Yarnbury (25 August 1964); Kathleen Hill (15 October 1982).

The principal archival collection used in this volume is the Churchill papers, which I worked on at the Bodleian Library, Oxford, and which are now permanently housed at Churchill College, Cambridge. I have also been given access to material in the following collections: Royal Archives, BBC Written Archives Centre, Cherwell papers (Nuffield College, Oxford), Harrow School Archive, Robert Menzies papers, Forbes Magazine Collection (Churchill engagement cards), Franklin D. Roosevelt papers, Public Record Office, Kew (Admiralty, Air Ministry, Cabinet, Foreign Office, Premier, Secret Intelligence Service, and War Office papers), Captain Stephen Roskill papers (Churchill College, Cambridge),

General Sikorski papers (Polish Institute and Sikorski Museum), Baroness Spencer-Churchill papers (Churchill College, Cambridge) and the Weizmann Archive.

I have drawn documentary and historical material the following published works:

The Earl of Avon, *The Eden Memoirs, The Reckoning*, London, 1965.

Lord Balfour of Inchrye, *Wings over Westminster*, London, 1973.

Ralph Bennett, *Ultra and Mediterranean Strategy, 1941–1945*, London, 1989.

Michael Bloch, *The Duke of Windsor's War*, London, 1982.

Arthur Bryant, *The Turn of the Tide, 1939-1943: A Sudy Based on the Diaries and Autobiographical Notes of Field Marshal The Viscount Alanbrooke, KG, OM*, London, 1957.

Alan Campbell-Johnson, *The Life of Lord Halifax*, London, 1941.

Lord Chandos, *The Memoirs of Lord Chandos*, London, 1962.

Winston S. Churchill, *The Second World War*, Volume 2, London 1949.

Winston S. Churchill, *The Second World War*, Volume 3, London 1950.

Winston S. Churchill, *His Father's Son: The Life of Randolph Churchill*, London, 1996.

John Colville, *The Fringes of Power: Downing Street Diaries, 1939-1955*, London, 1985.

Joan Comay, *The Diaspora Story, The Epic of the Jewish People Among the Nations*, London, 1981 (facsimile document)

David Dilks (editor), *The Diaries of Sir Alexander Cadogan, OM, 1938-1945*, London, 1971.

James Douglas-Hamilton, *The Truth About Rudolf Hess*, Edinburgh, 1993.

Charles Eade (editor), *The Unrelenting Struggle: War Speeches of the Right Hon. Winston S. Churchill, CH, MP*, London, 1942.

Charles Eade (compiler), *Secret Session Speeches by the Rt Honorable Winston Churchill OM, CH, MP*, London, 1946.

Charles de Gaulle, *The Call to Honour, 1940-1942, Documents*, London, 1955.

W. Averell Harriman and Elie Abel, *Special Envoy to Churchill and Stalin, 1941-1946*, London, 1976.

John Harvey (editor), *The War Diaries of Oliver Harvey*, London, 1978.

G.S. Harvey-Watt, *Most of My Life*, London, 1980.

Harry Hinsley and others, *British Intelligence in the Second World War*, London, 1976.

The Memoirs of General the Lord Ismay, London, 1960.

Warren Kimball, *Churchill and Roosevelt, the Complete Correspondence*, Princeton, New Jersey, 1984.

Lord Moran, *Winston Churchill, The struggle for survival, 1940-1965*, London, 1966.

Jean Nicol, *Meet me at the Savoy*, London, 1955.

Nigel Nicolson (editor). *Harold Nicolson, Diaries and Letters, 1939-1945*, London, 1967.

Vic Oliver, *Mr Showbusiness*, London, 1954.

Alan Palmer, *Who's Who in Modern History, 1860-1960*, London, 1980.

Ben Pimlott (editor), *The Second World War Diary of Hugh Dalton*, London, 1986.

Paul Preston, *Franco: A Biography*, London, 1993.

Alfred Price, *Blitz on Britain, 1939-1945*, London, 1977.

Robert Rhodes James (editor), *Chips: The Diaries of Sir Henry Channon*, London, 1967.

Robert Rhodes James, *Victor Cazalet: A Portrait*, London, 1976.

Robert E. Sherwood, *The White House Papers of Harry L. Hopkins*, 2 volumes, London, 1948.

David Stafford, *Churchill and Secret Service*, London, 1997.

Charles Stuart (editor), *The Reith Diaries*, London, 1975.

V.E., Tarrant, *King George V Class Battleships*, London, 1991.

A.J.P. Taylor, *Beaverbrook*, London, London, 1972.

John G. Winant, *A Letter from Grosvenor Square*, London, 1947.

Frederick Woods, *A Bibliography of the Works of Sir Winston Churchill, KG, OM, CH*, London,1969.

Evelyn Wrench, *Geoffrey Dawson and Our Times*, London, 1955.

B.D. Zevin (editor), *Nothing to Fear, The Selected Addresses of Franklin Delano Roosevelt, 1932-1945*, London, 1947.

Hansard (Parliamentary Debates)

Newspapers: *Canberra Times, Daily Mirror, Daily Telegraph, Evening Standard, Jewish Chronicle, The Listener, Manchester Guardian, National Review, Sunday Dispatch*, and *The Times*.

Gramophone records: His Master's Voice, ALP 1554, 1556

January 1941

Winston S. Churchill to President Franklin D. Roosevelt[1]

(*Premier papers, 3/468*)

1 January 1941
2.20 a.m.

At this moment when the New Year opens in storm, I feel it my duty on behalf of the British Government, and indeed of the whole British Empire, to tell you, Mr President, how lively is our sense of gratitude and admiration for the memorable declaration which you made to the American people and to the lovers of freedom in all the Continents on Sunday last.[2]

We cannot tell what lies before us but with this trumpet call we march forward heartened and fortified, and with the confidence which you have expressed that in the end all will be well for the English speaking peoples and those who share their ideals.

[1] Franklin Delano Roosevelt, 1882–1945. United States Assistant Secretary of the Navy, 1913–20. Governor of New York State, 1929–33. President of the United States, 1933–45. Churchill's support for Roosevelt was frequently repeated in his articles in both Britain and America. 'I am,' he wrote in *Colliers* magazine in the first year of Roosevelt's presidency, 'though a foreigner, an ardent admirer of the main drift and impulse which President Roosevelt has given to the economic and financial policy of the United States.' When, at Oxford, an undergraduate echoed the prevailing anti-American feeling by asking Churchill if he approved Roosevelt's policy 'of neglecting the affairs of the rest of the world for the especial benefit of the United States', Churchill replied with feeling: 'The President is a bold fellow, I like his spirit' (*G. R. Storry papers*, note of 23 February 1934).

[2] Roosevelt's nationwide broadcast of 29 December 1940, in which he declared: 'We must be the arsenal of the democracies.'

Winston S. Churchill to Anthony Eden[1]
(*Premier papers, 3/126/1*)

1 January 1941

I understand that Mdlle Curie[2] received from Monsieur Dupuy[3] the account which she repeated at Ditchley in the presence of an American woman journalist Helen Kirkpatrick,[4] and that this American journalist transmitted the information to the Chicago newspaper which she represents over her own signature.[5] If these facts are correct Mr Dupuy is at fault for talking indiscreetly to Mdlle Curie. Mademoiselle Curie, who is a woman of distinction, should have had the good sense not to gossip about it at a country house party. Miss Helen Kirkpatrick has betrayed the confidence for journalistic profit. Both these women should be questioned by MI5 at the

[1] Pierre Dupuy, 1896–1969. A French Canadian. First Secretary, Canadian Legation, Paris, 1928–40. Canadian Minister in Vichy, 1940. Canadian Chargé d'Affaires for Belgium, the Netherlands and France, 1940–3. CMG, 1943. Canadian Ambassador in The Hague, 1947–52; in Rome, 1952–8; in Paris, 1958–63.

[2] Eve Curie, 1904– . Born in Paris, the daughter of Marie Curie. A pianist, she gave her first concert in Paris in 1925. Musical critic of *Candide*. After her mother's death in 1934, she collected and classified all her papers, and wrote her biography (published in 1937; translated into 32 languages). Co-ordinator of Women's War Activities, Paris, 1939–40. Returned to Paris from a lecture tour in the United States, 2 May 1940. Went to London June 1940. Deprived of her French citizenship by the Vichy Government, April 1941. War Correspondent, Libya, Russia, Burma and China, 1941–3. Enlisted as a Private in the Fighting French Corps; received her basic training in England; First Lieutenant, 1944. Co-publisher of *Paris-Presse*, an evening paper in Paris, 1944–9. Special Adviser to the Secretary-General of NATO (in Paris), 1952–4.

[3] Robert Anthony Eden, 1897–1977. Educated at Eton and Christ Church, Oxford. Served on the Western Front, 1915–18, when he was awarded the Military Cross. Conservative MP, 1923–57. Parliamentary Under-Secretary, Foreign Office, 1931–3. Lord Privy Seal, 1934–5. Minister for League of Nations Affairs, 1935. Foreign Secretary, 1935–8. Secretary of State for Dominion Affairs, September 1939 to May 1940. Foreign Secretary, May 1940 to July 1945 and October 1951 to April 1955. Knight of the Garter, 1954. Prime Minister, 1955–7. Created Earl of Avon, 1961. One of his brothers was killed near Ypres in October 1914; another in 1916 at the battle of Jutland. His elder son was killed in action in Burma on 23 June 1945, aged 20.

[4] Helen P. Kirkpatrick, 1909– . Born in Rochester, New York (Lady Randolph Churchill's birthplace). Educated at Smith College, Massachusetts, and at the University of Geneva. Joined the Foreign Policy Association, Geneva, 1935. Editor of *Geneva*, a monthly magazine on international affairs, 1935–7. A free-lance journalist writing from Geneva for the *Manchester Guardian*, *Daily Telegraph*, *News Chronicle* and *New York Herald Tribune*, 1936–7. Co-founder in 1937 of *The Whitehall News Letter*, (with V. Gordon Lennox), a weekly bulletin on international affairs, to which Churchill was a subscriber. Resident in London, 1937–9; London Correspondent of the Paris daily *L'Oeuvre*, 1937–9. Author of *This Terrible Peace* (about the Munich agreements), 1938, and *Under the British Umbrella*, 1939. Foreign and War Correspondent of the *Chicago Daily News*, 1939–45, in London, North Africa, Italy and France; Paris Bureau Chief, 1944–6. European Diplomatic Correspondent of the *New York Post*, 1946–9. Worked for the US Department of State, and Economic Cooperation Administration, Washington and Paris, 1949–53. Assistant to the President, Smith College, 1953–5. In 1954 she married Robbins Milbank.

[5] On 24 December 1940 Helen Kirkpatrick telegraphed to the *Chicago Daily News*: 'Great Britain has reason to feel confident today that the Vichy government will not lend itself, or the remaining units of the French fleet, to any German action against this country. There is not the same confidence that

earliest moment, and their explanations obtained. If these bear out the facts as you imparted them to me, Mr Dupuy should be made aware of the channel by which the leakage occurred. It would appear in any case to be necessary that Miss Helen Kirkpatrick should be shipped out of the country at the earliest moment. It is very undesirable to have a person of this kind scouting about private houses for copy regardless of British interests.

I have referred your Minute to Mr Bracken[1] for his comments. I do not gather that you are making any suggestion that he was responsible for the leakage, but this is not quite clear from your Minute.

Winston S. Churchill to Admiral Pound[2]
(*Churchill papers, 20/36*)

1 January 1941

Some talk was used the other day about the probability of the Italians having flash-less powder at Workshop[3] thus making the operation more difficult. Pray therefore ascertain whether they are using flash-less powder at Bardia. They are as likely to have it at one as at the other.

WSC[4]

unoccupied France will not be taken over by the Germans in the relatively near future. Aside from reports from Vichy that Fernand de Brinon, general delegate to the occupational authorities in Paris, has informed the German government of Vichy's refusal to give military co-operation or to reinstate Pierre Laval as foreign minister, Chief of State Marshal Henri Pétain has assured the British government that he will not consider assisting the Germans in any way. M. Rouget, a businessman from Vichy, once again has been in London and has conveyed the determination of the Vichy government both to live up to its obligations under the armistice and not to give any military assistance to Germany. Further confirmatory messages were brought back from Vichy by P. Dupuy, former first secretary of the Canadian legation in Paris, whose appointment as Canadian observer in Vichy was announced on December 14. Dupuy arrived in London early this week and is reported to have brought with him a personal message from Marshal Pétain and from Admiral Darlan, his secretary of state for navy.'

[1] Brendan Bracken, 1901–1958. Educated in Australia and at Sedbergh School. Journalist and financier. Conservative MP for North Paddington, 1929–45; for Bournemouth, 1950–1. Elected to the Other Club, 1932. Chairman of the *Financial News*. Managing Director of the *Economist*. Chairman of the *Financial Times*. Parliamentary Private Secretary to the Prime Minister (Churchill), 1940–1. Privy Councillor, 1940. Minister of Information, 1941–5. First Lord of the Admiralty, 1945. Created Viscount, 1952.

[2] Alfred Dudley Pickman Rogers Pound, 1877–1943. Entered the Royal Navy, 1891. Torpedo Lieutenant, 1902. Captain, 1914. Second Naval Assistant to Lord Fisher, December 1914 to May 1915. Flag Captain, HMS *Colossus*, 1915–17. Took part in the Battle of Jutland. Served on the Admiralty Staff, 1917–19. Director of Plans Division, 1922. Commanded the Battle Cruiser Squadron, 1929–32. Knighted, 1933. Second Sea Lord, 1932–5. Commander-in-Chief, Mediterranean, 1936–9. Admiral of the Fleet, 1939. First Sea Lord and Chief of the Naval Staff, 1939–43. He declined a peerage in 1943. Order of Merit, 1943.

[3] The proposed capture of Pantellaria Island, between Cape Bon (Tunisia) and Sicily.

[4] All Churchill's minutes were initialled 'WSC', usually in red ink. Signatures other than WSC are included wherever they exist on the archival version cited in this volume.

Winston S. Churchill to Sir Archibald Sinclair[1] *and Air Chief Marshal Sir Charles Portal*[2]
(*Churchill papers, 20/36*)

1 January 1941

What is the story behind this article[3] which appears in a great many papers and deals with all kinds of matters of a secret nature. Who is Mr Engel and what facilities was he given over here?

Winston S. Churchill to Sir Edward Bridges,[4] *General Ismay*[5] *and Eric Seal*[1]
(*Churchill papers, 20/36*)

1 January 1941

With the beginning of the New Year, a new intense drive must be made to secure greater secrecy in all matters relating to the conduct of the war; and the

[1] Archibald Henry Macdonald Sinclair, 1890–1970. Educated at Eton and Sandhurst. Entered Army, 1910. 4th Baronet, 1912. Captain, 1915. 2nd in Command of the 6th Royal Scots Fusiliers, while Churchill was in command, January–May 1916. Squadron-Commander, 2nd Life Guards, 1916–18. Elected to the Other Club, 1917. Major, Guards Machine Gun Regiment, 1918. Private Secretary to Churchill, Ministry of Munitions, 1918–19. Churchill's personal Military Secretary, War Office, 1919–21. Churchill's Private Secretary, Colonial Office, 1921–2. Liberal MP for Caithness and Sutherland, 1922–45. Secretary of State for Scotland, 1931–3. Leader of the Parliamentary Liberal Party, 1935–45. Secretary of State for Air in Churchill's wartime Coalition, 1940–5. Knight of the Thistle, 1941. Created Viscount Thurso, 1952.

[2] Charles Frederick Algernon Portal, 1893–1971. Known as 'Peter'. On active service, 1914–18 (despatches, DSO and bar; Military Cross). As a 2nd Lieutenant, Royal Engineers, he was in both the advance to and the retreat from Mons in 1914. Seconded to the Royal Flying Corps, 1915. Major, commanding 16 Squadron, 1917 (working for the Canadian Corps, then carrying out night bombing tasks). Air Ministry (Directorate of Operations and Intelligence), 1923. Commanded the British Forces in Aden, 1934–5. Instructor, Imperial Defence College, 1936–7. Director of Organization, Air Ministry, 1937–8. Air Member for Personnel, Air Council, 1939–40. Air Officer Commanding-in-Chief, Bomber Command, April–October 1940. Knighted, July 1940. Chief of the Air Staff, October 1940–November 1945. Created Baron, 1945; Viscount, 1946. Order of Merit, 1946. Knight of the Garter, 1946. Controller, Atomic Energy, Ministry of Supply, 1946–51. Chairman, British Aircraft Corporation, 1960–8.

[3] A reference in *The Times* and other British papers to an article on new British aircraft: the article by Leonard Engel had been published in an American technical journal *Flying and Popular Aviation*.

[4] Edward Bridges, 1892–1969. Son of the poet laureate Robert Bridges. On active service, 1914–18 (Military Cross). Served in the Treasury, 1919–39. Secretary to the Cabinet, 1938–46. Knighted, 1939. Permanent Secretary, Treasury, 1945–56. Created Baron, 1957. Knight of the Garter, 1965.

[5] Hastings Lionel Ismay, 1887–1965. Educated at Charterhouse and Sandhurst. 2nd Lieutenant, 1905; Captain, 1914. On active service in India, 1908 and the Somaliland, 1914–20 (DSO). Staff College, Quetta, 1922. Assistant Secretary, Committee of Imperial Defence, 1925–30. Military Secretary to the Viceroy of India (Lord Willingdon), 1931–3. Colonel, 1932. Deputy Secretary,

following points should have your attention. You should consider them together and report to me:

1. Renewal of the cautions issued a year ago against gossip and talk about Service matters. Probably a new set of posters is required to attract attention.

2. Renewal of the orders which were then issued to all Departments.

3. Severe further restrictions on the circulation of secret papers; especially those relating to operations, strength of the armed forces, foreign policy, &c. Every Department should be asked to submit proposals for restricting the circulation of papers. This is all the more important on account of the ever-increasing elaboration of Government Departments and Whitehall population.

4. The use of boxes with snap locks is to be enforced for all documents of a secret character. Ministers and their Private Secretaries should have snap-lock boxes on their desks, and should never leave confidential documents in trays when they are out of the room.

5. Boxes should always be snapped to when not immediately in use. Access to rooms in which confidential secretaries and Ministers are working should be restricted wherever possible, and ante-rooms provided into which visitors can be shown.

6 A small red star label should be devised to be placed on most secret papers, i.e, those dealing with operations and the strength of the armed forces. It is not necessary for all the Private Secretaries in the office to read these starred documents. They should always be circulated in locked boxes, and transferred immediately to other locked boxes for my use and for the use of Ministers.

7. A restriction of telegrams relating to future operations is to be made. Sometimes lately I have received an account of future operations where the name of the place is mentioned as well as its future code-word. This happened in the case of 'Influx'[2] yesterday. All such documents which contain the name of the place and the code-word should be collected and either destroyed by fire or put in a safe.

Committee of Imperial Defence, 1936–8; Secretary (in succession to Sir Maurice Hankey), 1938. Major-General, 1939. Chief of Staff to the Minister of Defence (Churchill), 1940–5. Knighted, 1940. Deputy Secretary (military) to the War Cabinet, 1940–5. Lieutenant-General, 1942. General, 1944. Chief of Staff to the Viceroy of India (Lord Mountbatten,) 1947. Created Baron, 1947. Secretary of State for Commonwealth Relations, 1951–2. Secretary-General of NATO, 1952–7. Knight of the Garter, 1957. He published his memoirs in 1960.

[1] Eric Arthur Seal, 1898–1972. Served in Royal Air Force, 1918. Entered the Patent Office, 1921; the Admiralty, 1925. Principal Private Secretary to the First Lord, 1938–40 (Lord Stanhope, then Churchill); to the Prime Minister (Churchill), 1940–1. Deputy Secretary of the Admiralty (North America), 1941–3. Member of the British Supply Council, Washington, 1943. Under-Secretary of the Admiralty (London), 1943–5. Director-General of Building Materials, Ministry of Works, 1947–8. Deputy Under-Secretary of State, Foreign Office (German Section), 1948–51. Deputy-Secretary, Ministry of Works, 1951–9. Knighted, 1955.

[2] The planned invasion of Sicily (not carried out until July 1943).

8. Ministers should be requested to restrict as far as possible the circle within which it is necessary to discuss secret matters. It is not necessary for Parliamentary Private Secretaries (unless Privy Councillors) to be informed more than is necessary for the discharge of their Parliamentary and political duties.

9. We are having trouble through the activities of foreign correspondents of both sexes. The disclosures of Engel[1] published in today's papers are a capital example. Proposals should be made for restricting the facilities accorded to them in obtaining confidential information. It must be remembered that everything said to America is instantly communicated to Germany and that we have no redress.

10. The wide circulation of Intelligence Reports and the general tendency to multiply reports of all kinds must be curtailed. Each Department connected with the war should be asked to submit a report showing what further restrictions and curtailments they propose to introduce in the New Year. Some time ago the late Cabinet decided that Ministers not in the War Cabinet should submit beforehand speeches on the war, or references in speeches to the war, to the Minister of Information. This has apparently fallen into disuse. Let me have a report as to what is happening. A more convenient method might be that Ministers wishing to refer to these subjects should consult General Ismay as representing the Minister of Defence beforehand. No officials who have, for instance, been on Missions abroad should make public statements concerning their work without previous Ministerial approval.

11. I have already dealt with the circulation of secret information to friendly attachés – especially Americans – and we have restricted the character of the information. This process should continue – the bulk of the documents circulated being made up by interesting padding such as might well appear in the newspapers.

12. The newspapers repeatedly publish – mostly with innocent intentions – facts about the war and policy which are detrimental. Where these have not been censored beforehand, a complaint should be made afterwards in every case. The Ministry of Information should report what they are doing.

Pray consider all these matters and let me know of any others that occur to you; and advise me on how these points are to be made and through what channels to the various authorities affected.

[1] Leonard Engel, 1916-1964. Born in New York. Author of more than four hundred articles on science and medicine for fifty American magazines, including *Colliers, Harpers* and *The Scientific American*. Writer on military affairs for the newspaper *PM*, 1940-45. Editor of a book of essays, *New Worlds of Modern Science*.

Winston S. Churchill to the Cecil Byford[1]
(*Churchill papers, 20/21*)

1 January 1941

My dear Sir,

Please tell the staff of the Dover Harbour Board how much I appreciated the good wishes which you sent me on their behalf and your own. This expression of their confidence and sympathy gave me very great pleasure.

The people of Dover had much to endure in 1940. They were attacked not only by bomb but also by shell-fire, and they saw the enemy installed in positions not far distant from their own White Cliffs. They have faced these dangers in a manner worthy of Dover's great traditions, and I know that whatever 1941 may bring their courage and resourcefulness will not be found wanting.

Yours vy faithfully
Winston S. Churchill

David Margesson[2] *to John Masefield*[3]
(*Churchill papers, 20/27*)

1 January 1941

Dear Mr Masefield,

I am writing this letter by direction of the Prime Minister. It relates to your book, *Twenty-five Days.*

The book was recently considered by my predecessor, Mr Eden, and the Army Council, who decided that the subject matter gave a picture of the operations leading up to the Dunkirk evacuation which was incomplete in itself and, moreover, liable to be misinterpreted by many readers.

[1] General Manager, Dover Harbour Board, 1938–65.

[2] Henry David Reginald Margesson, 1890–1965. Educated at Harrow and Magdalene College, Cambridge. On active service, 1914–18 (Military Cross). Captain, 1918. Conservative MP for Upton, 1922–3; for Rugby, 1924–42. Assistant Government Whip, 1924. Junior Lord of the Treasury, 1926, 1926–9 and 1931. Chief Government Whip, 1931–40. Privy Councillor, 1933. Secretary of State for War, 1940–2. Created Viscount, 1942.

[3] John Masefield, Poet Laureate from 1930 until his death in 1967. Order of Merit, 1935. His account of Dunkirk, *The Nine Days Wonder*, was published in 1941. Masefield's only son, Lewis, a Private in the Royal Army Medical Corps, was killed in action in the Western Desert, twenty-five miles from Tobruk, on 29 May 1942, aged thirty-one.

The vivid diary form in which you have cast the narrative has made it seem that the operations which resulted in the withdrawal of the BEF[1] were disjointed and without plan, since it is impossible for a narrative in that form to describe the foresight which was shown in anticipating enemy action and disposing troops to meet it before it occurred. Yet that is the essence of the military feat performed by the leaders of the BEF, which would have been annihilated but for their grip of a rapidly changing situation and skilled resourcefulness in dealing with it. The general effect of the narrative is therefore to deprive the Army leaders of the credit and confidence which were due to them, and to transfer that credit to the Navy and the Air Force. Both these Services cooperated splendidly, but they would be the first to say that the success of the retreat to Dunkirk was due in the main to the military qualities of the Commander and of his subordinates and staff in all formations.

The Prime Minister considers it most unfortunate that it should be possible for conclusions disparaging to the High Command to be drawn from the writings of such a high authority as yourself, at a time like this, when our Libyan successes have done so much to establish the confidence of the Army in itself and its leaders. He, therefore, with great reluctance, directs that the book be withdrawn. This he is entitled to do, since you asked for, and were granted, special facilities.

I need not say how sorry I am personally that the care and thought which you have devoted to your work should for the moment be brought to nothing. I suggest, however, that we need only regard the present situation in the light of a postponement. Fuller and further information regarding the operations in Flanders is now available here, and I shall be happy to arrange for you to have access to this, in order to recast those passages in the book which deal with the part played by the Army.

If you are agreeable to this course, I will endeavour to save you as much labour as possible by supplying you with a full and continuous narrative of the actual campaign. This you could, of course, rewrite in your own way. I am sure that the combination of the two should furnish a record of the highest historic value. Despite the additional labour involved, I hope you will feel able to accede to my request.

I should only like to add that reasonable compensation will be paid to your publishers, both here and in the United States, and of course to yourself, for the actual nugatory expenditure which has been incurred.

Yours sincerely
David Margesson

[1] The British Expeditionary Force, commanded by Field Marshal Lord Gort.

John Colville[1]*: diary*
(*Colville papers*)

1 January 1941

The PM has circulated a minute about preserving the secrecy of documents which suddenly makes me feel rather conscious-stricken about this diary. I haven't the heart to destroy it and shall compromise by keeping it locked up here, even more strictly than hitherto.

As the PM went off to Chartwell, I was able to linger over lunch . . .

This evening the PM met his Waterloo when inspecting the girders and constructions above the CWR.[2] He would not wait for me to return with an effective light, and using only the torch in the handle of his walking-stick sank up to his ankles in thick liquid cement!

Desmond[3] told us of MI5's discovery that Muselier[4] and several of his staff were traitors, agents of the Vichy Government who had betrayed our intentions at Dakar (we have documents to prove it). When he told the PM, the latter gave orders that they should be arrested tonight and de Gaulle[5] informed by special messenger.

I stayed on duty late, until the PM in the early hours ascended to the roof

[1] John Rupert Colville, 1915–87. A grandson of the Earl of Crewe. Page of Honour to King George V, 1927–31. Educated at Harrow and Trinity College, Cambridge. Entered the Diplomatic Service, 1937. Assistant Private Secretary to Neville Chamberlain, 1939–40; to Churchill, 1940–1. Royal Air Force Volunteer Reserve, 1941–3. Assistant Private Secretary to Churchill, 1943–5; to Clement Attlee, 1945. Private Secretary to Princess Elizabeth, 1947–9. CVO, 1949. Joint Principal Private Secretary to Churchill 1951–5. CB, 1955. Active in the development of Churchill College, Cambridge. Knighted, 1974. Author of a number of volumes of recollections and history, as well as *The Fringes of Power, Downing Street Diaries* (1985). Five years before publication, Sir John Colville gave me access to these diaries, from which I made the transcripts published in this volume.

[2] The Central War Room, or Cabinet War Room, in the basement of the Board of Trade building in Whitehall. It has been open to the public since 1984. In the year 1998/99 it had 280,000 visitors, its largest number since opening.

[3] Desmond Morton, 1891–1971. 2nd Lieutenant, Royal Artillery 1911. Converted to Roman Catholicism shortly before the First World War. Shot through the heart while commanding a Field Battery at the Battle of Arras, April 1917, but survived the wound. Later awarded the Military Cross. ADC to Sir Douglas Haig, 1917–18. Seconded to the Foreign Office, 1919. Head of the Committee of Imperial Defence's Industrial Intelligence Centre, January 1929–September 1939; its terms of reference were 'To discover and report the plans for manufacture of armaments and war stores in foreign countries.' A member of the Committee of Imperial Defence sub-committee on Economic Warfare, 1930–9. Principal Assistant Secretary, Ministry of Economic Warfare, 1939. Personal Assistant to Churchill throughout the Second World War. Knighted, 1945. Economic Survey Mission, Middle East, 1949. Seconded to the Ministry of Civil Aviation, 1950–3.

[4] Emile Henry Muselier, 1882–1965. Entered the French Navy, 1902. Captain, 1918. Admiral Commanding the Navy and Defences of Marseilles, 1938–40. Joined General de Gaulle, July 1940. Commander-in-Chief of the Free French Naval Forces, 1940–2; of the Free French Air Forces, 1940–1. Chief of the French Naval Delegation, Military Mission for German Affairs, 1944–5. Honorary British knighthood, 1946.

[5] General Charles de Gaulle, see page 53, note 1.

to look at the stars and the new moon. Eden and Kingsley Wood[1] spent much of the evening here discussing the question of financial assistance from America. I sat in the room while the PM drafted a forceful telegram to Roosevelt, not hiding from him the dangerous drain on our resources. Sombre though the telegram was, with its warning that only by American financial help could Hitlerism be 'extirpated from Europe, Africa and Asia', the PM seemed to enjoy drafting it and his *obiter dicta* to Kingsley Wood who sat perched on the edge of his armchair, were not particularly depressing. But he obviously fears that the Americans' love of doing good business may lead them to denude us of all our realisable resources before they show any inclination to be the Good Samaritan.

MI5 went off to arrest Muselier, another Frenchman and two French ladies. One of the ladies was found in bed with a doctor attached to the Free French forces. In the house of the other was found the 2nd Secretary of the Brazilian Embassy, stark naked! It was through the Brazilian Embassy that information was passed to Vichy. The Admiral himself was found to be in possession of dangerous drugs.

Anthony Eden: recollection
(*'The Eden Memoirs, The Reckoning'*)

1 January 1941

On New Year's night I was in the Foreign Office after dinner, when the Prime Minister summoned me to discuss a telegram to President Roosevelt. Kingsley Wood and Beaverbrook[2] were also there. When we had done our

[1] Kingsley Wood, 1881–1943. Member of the London County Council, 1911–19. Chairman, London Insurance Committee, 1917–18. Conservative MP for Woolwich West, 1918–43. Knighted, 1918. Parliamentary Private Secretary to the Minister of Health, 1919–22. Parliamentary Secretary, Ministry of Health, 1924–9 (when Neville Chamberlain was Minister); Board of Education, 1931. Privy Councillor, 1928. Chairman, Executive Committee of the National Conservative and Unionist Association, 1930–2. Postmaster-General, 1931–5. Minister of Health, 1935–8. Secretary of State for Air, 1938–40. Lord Privy Seal, April–May 1940. Chancellor of the Exchequer from May 1940 until his death.

[2] William Maxwell Aitken, 1879–1964. A Canadian financier. Conservative MP, 1910–16. Knighted, 1911. Elected to the Other Club, 1912. Canadian Expeditionary Force Eye-Witness in France, May–August 1915; Canadian Government Representative at the Front, September 1915–16. Newspaper proprietor: bought the *Daily Express*, his largest circulation newspaper, in December 1916. Created Baron Beaverbrook, 1917. Chancellor of the Duchy of Lancaster and Minister of Information, 1918. Minister for Aircraft Production, 1940–1. Minister of State, 1941. Minister of Supply, 1941–2. Lord Privy Seal, 1943–5. Known as 'Max'. On 28 May 1915, when Churchill's fortunes were at their lowest ebb following his removal as First Lord of the Admiralty at the height of the Gallipoli campaign, Beaverbrook (then Sir Max Aitken) had written, in an article commissioned by Lord Northcliffe but never published: 'Nor need Mr Churchill despair of his future. It will undoubtedly be high and even splendid, for he possesses many qualities which no other public man can claim. If his future were as dark as I believe it to be bright he would I think encounter it with the same composure'. (*Churchill papers: 2/237*)

work and the others had gone, Churchill took me out to the roof. It was raining and the firing that evening was slight. I could not help wondering what fate would have in store for us before the next New Year's day came around.

Winston S. Churchill to President Franklin D. Roosevelt
(*Churchill papers, 20/49*)

2 January 1941
Personal and Secret

I agree with your proposal to stave off our difficulties by sending a warship to Capetown to collect the gold at our disposal there, amounting, I believe, to about thirty millions sterling. I ought to let you know this transaction will almost certainly become known to the world with varying reactions.

Meanwhile I learned with pleasure from Mr Purvis[1] of his talk with you and Morgenthau[2] on Monday. Instructions have been given to furnish you with any further figures about our requirements which you may seek.

We are deeply grateful for all your understanding of the problems which will be thrown up in the interval before Congress approves your proposals. It is not only a question of total amounts but of how we are to live through a period which may extend to February 15th. What would be the effect upon the world situation if we had to default in payments to your contractors who have their workmen to pay? The idea that in the interval we shall either have to default or be stripped bare of our last resources is full of danger and causes us profound anxiety. I feel sure this will be ever in your thoughts.

Furthermore, apart from the general totals and the interim period there arises a group of problems about the scope of your plan after being approved by Congress. What is to be done about the immense heavy payments still due to be made under existing orders before delivery is completed? Substantial advance payments on these same orders have already denuded our resources.

[1] Arthur Blaikie Purvis, 1890–1941. Born in London. Worked for the Nobel Explosives Company, Glasgow, 1910–24. Moved to Canada, becoming President of Canadian Industries Ltd (manufacturers of chemicals). A leading industrialist in Canada between the wars; Chairman of the National Employment Commission, 1936–8. Director-General of the British Purchasing Commission (New York and Washington), 1939–40. Chairman of the Anglo-French Purchasing Board, Washington, December 1939 to June 1940. Privy Councillor, 1940. Chairman of the British Supply Council in North America, 1941. Killed in an air crash, 14 August 1941.

[2] Henry Morgenthau Junior, 1891–1967. A gentleman farmer in New York State before the First World War. Lieutenant, United States Navy, 1918. A neighbour and early supporter of Governor (later President) Roosevelt. New York State Conservation Commissioner, 1931. Chairman of the Federal Farm Board, 1933. Secretary of the Treasury, 1934–45. A strong supporter of active American defence preparations, and of Lend-Lease. His plan in 1944 to reduce post-war Germany to a pastoral condition, with almost no industry, was rejected by President Truman, who would not take him to the Potsdam Conference, whereupon he resigned.

We have unceasing need for various American commodities not definitely weapons: for instance raw materials and oil. Canada and other Dominions, Greece and also Poland and Czecho-Slovakia have clamant dollar needs to keep their war effort alive. I do not seek to know immediately how you will solve these later questions. We shall be entirely ready for our part to lay bare to you all our resources and liabilities around the world and we shall seek no more help than the common cause demands. We naturally wish to feel sure that the powers with which you propose to arm yourself will be sufficiently wide to deal with these larger matters subject to all proper consideration. Without the prompt and effective solution of these problems Hitlerism cannot be extirpated from Europe, Africa and Asia.

War Cabinet: minutes
(*Cabinet papers, 65/17*)

2 January 1941 — 10 Downing Street
11.30 a.m.

The Prime Minister said that, when the Eire Government was informed of what we proposed to do, it should be emphasized that this step was taken in no vindictive spirit and only necessity forced us into such a step.

Winston S. Churchill to General Ismay
(*Churchill papers, 20/36*)

2 January 1941

Let me have the whole series of my telegrams to General Wavell,[1] C-in-C, Mediterranean, and Air Marshal Longmore,[2] from the beginning of November to the present date. They should be collected in a file, which should include all the Private and Personal telegrams.

[1] Archibald Percival Wavell, 1883–1950. On active service in South Africa, 1901, and on the Western Front, 1914–16 (wounded, Military Cross). Military Attaché with the Russian Army in the Caucasus, 1916–17, and with the Egyptian Expeditionary Force, Palestine, 1917–18. CMG, 1919. Commanded the troops in Palestine and Transjordan, 1937–8. General Officer Commanding-in-Chief, Southern Command, 1938–9. Knighted, 1939. Commander-in-Chief, Middle East, 1940–1; India, 1941–3. Field Marshal, 1943. Created Earl, 1947. Biographer of Field Marshal Allenby.

[2] Arthur Murray Longmore, 1885–1970. Lieutenant-Commander, Royal Navy, on active service 1914–18, including the Battle of Jutland (despatches, DSO). Royal Air Force, 1919. Air Officer Commanding Coastal Command, 1933–6. Knighted, 1935. Air Officer Commanding-in-Chief, Training Command, 1939. Air Officer Commanding-in-Chief, Middle East, 1940–1. Inspector-General of the Royal Air Force, 1941. Retired list, 1942. One of his three sons was killed in action in 1943.

King George VI[1] *to Winston S. Churchill*
(*Churchill papers, 20/20*)

2 January 1941 Sandringham

My dear Prime Minister,

I must send you my best wishes for a happier New Year, & may we see the end of this conflict in sight during the coming year. I am already feeling better for my sojourn here; it is doing me good, & the change of scene and outdoor exercise is acting as a good tonic. But I feel that it is wrong for me to be away from my place of duty, when everybody else is carrying on. However, I must look upon it as a medicine & hope to come back refreshed in mind & body, for renewed efforts against the enemy.

I do hope & trust you were able to have a little relaxation at Christmas with all your arduous work. I have so much admired all you have done during the last seven months as my Prime Minister, and I have so enjoyed our talks together during our weekly luncheons. I hope they will continue on my return, as I do look forward to them so much.

I hope to pay a visit to Sheffield next Monday. I can do it from here in the day.[2] It was indeed kind of you to help me with my broadcast on Xmas day, & very many thanks for the Siren Suit. The shelter is finished & already for use now.

With renewed good wishes,

I remain,
Yours very sincerely,
George R.I.

Winston S. Churchill to President Franklin D. Roosevelt
(*Churchill papers, 20/49*)

3 January 1941

I have received your message of December 31st on the subject of the supply of milk and vitamin concentrates for children in Unoccupied France, and we

[1] Albert Frederick Arthur George, 1895–1952. Second son of King George V. Educated at Royal Naval Colleges Osborne and Dartmouth; Lieutenant, 1918. Succeeded his brother as King, December 1936. Crowned (as George VI), May 1937.

[2] On the evening of 12 December 1940 the Germans launched Operation Crucible, an attempt to bring steel production to a halt in Sheffield. The attack lasted for nine hours. The centre of the city was badly damaged, but almost all the steel-producing capacity was intact. When a building in the city centre collapsed on its basement in which seventy-five people were sheltering only seven survived.

have been greatly impressed by your arguments in favour of this proposal. The anxiety which we have always felt about this project is that it would lead to similar demands on behalf of our German-occupied allies. We are indeed sure to be hard pressed by these unhappy people, and it is therefore important that we should maintain the distinction which you draw so clearly between German-occupied territories and those not in actual occupation. I feel sure that I can count upon your help to maintain this distinction, for otherwise the whole fabric of our blockade would be fatally undermined, and I need not stress to you what this would mean in terms of final victory.

2. We are prepared to agree at once to the despatch of the first ship to Seville, Barcelona and Marseilles, as you propose, subject to the following arrangements as regards safeguards, which seem to us to meet the case:

(1) Relief goods to be confined to medical supplies in the strict sense (excluding cod and halibut liver oil), vitamin concentrates, dried or tinned milk and children's clothing.

(2) Distribution to be effected solely by the American Red Cross either direct to their own depots or, under strict supervision, to children's hospitals and clinics.

(3) Assurances to be secured from the Vichy Government that the press shall be allowed to publish periodical accounts of the relief work undertaken, such accounts to include reference to the co-operation of His Majesty's Government in allowing passage through the blockade.

(4) Further shipments to be stopped if there should be any evidence that these conditions are not being fulfilled.

3. There is one point over which you can help us greatly. In any announcement of the scheme which is made in America we should like our part in the transaction to be presented in as favourable a light as possible. While it would be made clear that this step had been taken on your initiative, we would like it stated that the relief goods are available only by goodwill of His Majesty's Government. The impression which we should like to see created is that of Anglo-American cooperation for humanitarian ends.

Winston S. Churchill to Viscount Cranborne[1]
(*Churchill papers, 20/36*)

3 January 1941

I wish to keep the Tuesday meetings exclusive for the War Cabinet, who alone bear responsibility for policy apart from its execution. But you would, of course, come on the other days, and indeed on that day if there were any need.

It would certainly not be possible to consult the Dominions before breaking off an action such as that at Dakar,[2] nor indeed about any direct military operation, even where their own troops were liable to be engaged, as is perhaps now the case. The safety of the troops themselves requires unity and secrecy in the command. I think you should read more thoroughly the papers about Dakar, and especially my reply to Mr Menzies's[3] hectoring telegram inspired by Bruce[4] and Menzies' apology. I could not for a moment admit the right of the Dominions to have a representative at every meeting of the War Cabinet, or, to reverse the statement, that His Majesty's Servants may never meet without supervision. I cannot add to the numbers of the War Cabinet. As you know, I am under criticism that they have already grown to eight.

I trust the arrangements I have indicated will be satisfactory to you, even with the added burden you have been good enough to accept.

[1] Robert Arthur James Gascoyne-Cecil, Viscount Cranborne, 1893–1972. Eldest son of the 4th Marquess of Salisbury. Known as 'Bobbety'. Conservative MP for South Dorset, 1929–41. Parliamentary Secretary of State for Foreign Affairs, 1935–8; resigned with Anthony Eden, February 1938. Paymaster-General, 1940. Privy Councillor, 1940. Summoned to the House of Lords in his father's barony of Cecil of Essendon, 1941. Secretary of State for Dominion Affairs, 1940–2 and 1943–5; for the Colonies, 1942. Leader of the House of Lords, 1942–5. Knight of the Garter, 1946. Succeeded his father as 5th Marquess, 1947. Lord Privy Seal, 1951–2. Secretary of State for Commonwealth Relations, 1952. Lord President of the Council, 1952–7. Leader of the House of Lords, 1951–7. In 1937 he was elected to the Other Club.

[2] A reference to the unsuccessful attack on the Vichy French garrison at Dakar by British and Free French Forces in September 1940. Churchill telegraphed his explanation of the episode to the Dominion Prime Ministers, including Menzies, on 27 September 1940 (Volume Two of the Churchill War Papers, page 878). Churchill replied to Menzies' criticism on 2 October 1940 (Volume Two, pages 894–6).

[3] Robert Gordon Menzies, 1894–1978. Prime Minister of Australia, 1939–41. Minister for Co-ordination of Defence, 1939–42. Minister for Information and Minister for Munitions, 1940. Leader of the Opposition, 1943–9. Prime Minister, 1949–66. Knight of the Garter, 1963.

[4] Stanley Melbourne Bruce, 1883–1967. Born in Melbourne, Australia. On active service, Europe, 1914–17 (twice wounded, despatches, Military Cross). Prime Minister of Australia and Minister for External Affairs, 1923–29. Minister without Portfolio, 1932–33. Australian Representative at the League of Nations, 1932–38. President of the Council of the League of Nations, 1936. High Commissioner for Australia in London, 1933–45. Representative of Australia in the British War Cabinet, and on the Pacific War Council, 1942. Minister for Australia to the Netherlands Government in Exile, London, 1942–45. Created Viscount (Bruce of Melbourne), 1947. Chairman of the World Food Council, 1947–51.

Winston S. Churchill to Admiral Pound
(*Churchill papers, 20/36*)

3 January 1941

Even half a dozen 'Martlets'[1] would be an invaluable addition to the equipment of *Illustrious* and *Formidable*, and might easily teach enemy bombers at sea lessons which would greatly add to the security of His Majesty's Ships in the Mediterranean.

I am very glad to hear about the 'Brewsters'.[2]

Winston S. Churchill to Viscount Cranborne, Sir Kingsley Wood and Ronald Cross[3]
(*Churchill papers, 20/36*)

3 January 1941

I am relying upon you, the Minister of Shipping and the Chancellor of the Exchequer to give me reports every few days as to how the screw is being applied to Southern Ireland.

[1] An American-built fighter flown by the Fleet Air Arm. First used in the Western Desert, the Martlet (the Grumman Martlet) had a maximum speed of 310 m.p.h. and an effective range of 390 miles. Armed with four machine guns, it was of particular service on convoy escort duties.

[2] Nicknamed the Buffalo, the Brewster was the United States Navy's first monoplane fighter. It had a range of 965 miles, with a maximum speed of 321 miles an hour (cruising speed 161 mph).

[3] Robert Hibbert Cross, 1896–1968. Served in the Royal Flying Corps, 1914–18. A merchant banker. Conservative MP, 1931–45 and 1950–1. Minister of Economic Warfare, 1939–40. Minister of Shipping, 1940–1. Created Baronet, 1941. High Commissioner in Australia, 1941–5. Governor of Tasmania, 1951–58.

Winston S. Churchill to A.V. Alexander,[1] *Admiral Pound, Ronald Cross and Sir Andrew Duncan*[2]
(*Churchill papers, 20/36*)

3 January 1941

1. I was greatly distressed at the loss of the cargo of the *City of Bedford*. It is the heaviest munition loss we have sustained. Seven and a half million cartridges is a grievous blow. It would be better to disperse these cargoes among more ships.

2. I presume you have inquired into the causes of this collision, and of the two in-coming, out-going convoys being routed so close together. I must again emphasize the gravity of the loss.

Winston S. Churchill to Admiral Pound
(*Churchill papers, 20/36*)

3 January 1941

C-in-C[3] is not at all forthcoming on this,[4] and I do not quite understand the words underlined in para. 2. As you know, I do not wish to disturb the Norwegian coast for a trifle like this. I think you would do well to drop it.

[1] Albert Victor Alexander, 1885–1965. Educated at an elementary school, and technical classes, in Bristol. Labour (Co-operative) MP for Hillsborough, 1922–31 and 1935–50. Parliamentary Secretary, Board of Trade, 1924. First Lord of the Admiralty in Ramsay MacDonald's second Labour Government, 1929–31; in Churchill's war-time Coalition Government, 1940–45; and in Attlee's Labour Government, 1945–6. Member of the Cabinet Delegation to India, 1946. Minister of Defence, 1947–50. Created Viscount, 1950. Chancellor of the Duchy of Lancaster, 1950–1. Leader of the Labour Peers in the House of Lords, 1955–65. Created Earl, 1963. Knight of the Garter, 1964.

[2] Andrew Rae Duncan, 1884–1952. Coal Controller, 1919–20. Chairman of the Advisory Committee of the Mines Department, 1920–9. Vice-President, Shipbuilding Employers' Federation, 1920–7. Knighted, 1921. Chairman of the Central Electricity Board, 1927–35. A director of the Bank of England, 1929–40. Chairman of the Executive Committee of the British Iron and Steel Federations, 1935–40 and 1945–52. MP for the City of London, 1940–50. President of the Board of Trade, 1940 and 1941. Minster of Supply, 1940–1 and 1942–5. A Director of Imperial Chemical Industries, and of the Dunlop Rubber Company. One of his two sons was killed in action in the Second World War.

[3] John Cronyn Tovey, 1885–1971. On active service as a destroyer-captain, 1914–18 (despatches, DSO). Appointed Commander after the Battle of Jutland, 1916, for 'the persistent and determined manner in which he attacked enemy ships'. Rear-Admiral, Destroyers, Mediterranean, 1938–40. Vice-Admiral Second-in-Command, Mediterranean Fleet, 1940. Commander-in-Chief, Home Fleet, 1940–3 (his responsibilities included the Murmansk and Archangel convoys). Knighted, 1941. Admiral of the Fleet, 1943. Commander-in-Chief, the Nore, 1943–6. Created Baron, 1946.

[4] The Cabinet had decided, at the request of the Chancellor of the Exchequer and the First Lord of the Admiralty, to 'cease to provide Eire with any facilities for obtaining shipping'. The Cabinet also agreed that 'the policy in regard to the regulation of food supplies to Eire should be one of gradual diminution. Thus we should not cut off all supplies of tea at once, but should continue to supply Eire with small quantities for the present.'

Winston S. Churchill to Colonel Jacob[1]
('War Memoirs', volume 3, pages 636–7)

3 January 1941

I presume that this corps will be most carefully scrubbed and re-scrubbed to make sure no Nazi cells develop in it. I am very much in favour of recruiting friendly Germans and keeping them under strict discipline, instead of remaining useless in concentration camps, but we must be doubly careful we do not get any of the wrong breed.

Winston S. Churchill to General Ismay
(Cabinet papers, 120/413)

3 January 1941

Let me have a list of all the code-names of operations now in force. You need not put the translations opposite them, as I probably know them all and in any event I can ask you verbally.

Winston S. Churchill to Herbert Morrison[2] *and Malcolm MacDonald*[3]
('War Memoirs', Volume 3, page 638)

4 January 1941

What happens in the case where a shelter is not safe, but is nevertheless occupied, as many are? The ruling should be, I think, that every shelter that is occupied, whether safe or not, must be under the responsibility of the Minister of Health for its internal arrangements, and that there should be no distinction

[1] Edward Ian Claud Jacob, 1899–1993. Second Lieutenant, Royal Engineers, 1918. Military Assistant Secretary, Committee of Imperial Defence, 1938. Lieutenant-Colonel, 1939. Military Assistant Secretary to the War Cabinet, 1939–45. CBE, 1942. Retired from the Army, 1946, with the rank of Lieutenant-General. Controller, European Services, BBC, 1946. Knighted, 1946. Chief Staff Officer to the Minister of Defence, and Deputy Secretary to the Cabinet, 1952. Director-General of the BBC, 1952–60.

[2] Herbert Stanley Morrison, 1888–1965. Began work as an errand boy at the age of fourteen. Secretary to the London Labour Party, 1915–40. Mayor of Hackney, 1920–1. Member of the London County Council, 1922. Labour MP for South Hackney, 1923–4, 1929–31 and 1935–59. Minister of Transport, 1929–31. Instrumental in winning the London County Council for Labour, 1934. Minister of Supply, May–October 1940. Home Secretary and Minister of Home Security, 1940–5 (Member of the War Cabinet, 1942–5). Lord President of the Council (responsible for economic planning and co-ordination) and Leader of the House of Commons, 1945–51. Organizer of the Festival of Britain, 1951 (in 1999 his grandson Peter Mandelson, Secretary of State for Trade and Industry, had responsibility for the Millennium Dome). Created a Life Peer, 1959.

[3] Malcolm John MacDonald, 1901–1981. Son of Ramsay MacDonald. Educated at Bedales and Queen's College, Oxford. Labour MP for Bassetlaw, 1929–31 (National Labour 1931–5); for Ross and

between approved and unapproved shelters. The Minister of Health must *act* whenever the shelter is used. On the other hand, as shelter accommodation increases and improves the Minister of Home Security would naturally be closing the most unsafe ones.

Pray let me know that this view is correct.

Winston S. Churchill to Rear Admiral Bonham-Carter[1]
(*Churchill papers, 2/416*)

4 January 1941

I am delighted to hear of the honour which has been conferred on my one-time Naval Secretary.

Winston S. Churchill

Winston S. Churchill to Captain Lord Louis Mountbatten[2]
(*Churchill papers, 2/416*)

4 January 1941

Many congratulations on the distinction awarded to you, well deserved after ~~trials and~~ tribulations and achievements.[3]

Cromarty, 1936–45. Parliamentary Under-Secretary, Dominions Office, 1931–5. Privy Councillor, 1935. Secretary of State for Dominion Affairs, 1935–8 and 1938–9; Colonial Secretary, 1935 and 1938–40. Minister of Health, 1940–1. High Commissioner, Canada, 1941–6. Governor-General of Malaya, Singapore and British Borneo, 1946–8. Commissioner General for South-East Asia, 1948–55. High Commissioner, India, 1955–60. Governor-General of Kenya, 1963–4; High Commissioner, 1964–5. British Special Representative in East and Central Africa, 1965–6; in Africa, 1966–9. Order of Merit, 1969.

[1] Stuart Sumner Bonham-Carter, 1889–1972. On active service, 1914–18 (despatches, Distinguished Service Order); commanded HMS *Intrepid* at Zeebrugge. Assistant Director of Naval Equipment, 1932–34. Commodore, Royal Naval Barracks, Chatham, 1937–39. Naval Secretary to the First Lord of the Admiralty (Churchill), 1939. Rear-Admiral, 3rd Battle Squadron, 1940. CB, 1941. Vice-Admiral, Malta, 1943. Knighted, 1943. Rear-Admiral, 18th Cruiser Squadron, 1944.

[2] Prince Louis Francis Albert Victor Nicholas of Battenberg, 1900–79. Second son of Prince Louis of Battenberg. A naval cadet, 1913–15. Midshipman, 1916. His father was created Marquess of Milford Haven, and assumed the surname Mountbatten in 1917. Commander, 1932. Naval Air Division, Admiralty, 1936. Captain, 1937. Commanded HMS *Kelly*, 1939 (despatches twice). Chief of Combined Operations, 1942–3. Supreme Allied Commander, South-East Asia, 1943–6. Created Viscount Mountbatten of Burma, 1946. Viceroy of India, 1947. Created Earl, 1947. Governor-General of India, 1947–8. First Sea Lord, 1955–9. Admiral of the Fleet, 1956. Chief of the Defence Staff, 1959–65. Murdered by Irish terrorists of the Irish Republican Army (IRA), 27 August 1979, at Mullaghmore in the Irish Republic. Also murdered in the same explosion were his daughter's mother-in-law (aged eighty-two), his grandson Nicholas (aged fourteen), and a seventeen-year-old boatman. On the same day, eighteen British soldiers were killed in a landmine explosion in County Down, Northern Ireland.

[3] Churchill deleted the words 'trials and' after he was given the draft telegram to sign, and added the words: 'and achievements'. In the margin of a draft telegram of congratulations to the C-in-C Home Fleet, Admiral Tovey, he wrote in the margin, after crossing out the telegram: 'I hardly know him'.

Winston S. Churchill to Sir Edward Bridges
(*Churchill papers, 20/36*)

4 January 1941

Make now a good plan in print of the existing High Committees by which the main action of the Government, both on its civil and military side, is regulated, and show it to me. I intend to have it printed.

Winston S. Churchill to Sir Edward Bridges
(*Cabinet papers, 21/1350*)

4 January 1941

Let me have a list of all Committees of a Ministerial character forming part of the Central Government, with any offshoots there may be.

2. Ask each Department to furnish a list of all the Committees of a Departmental nature which exist at the present time.

3. This information is the prelude to a New Year's effort to cut down the number of such Committees.

Winston S. Churchill to Sir Edward Bridges
(*Churchill papers, 20/36*)

4 January 1941

1. The Committee on War Aims has largely completed its work in the draft Statement which it has drawn up and which should now be circulated to the Cabinet. In any case, War Aims is quite a different matter from the reconstruction of this country, which is entrusted to the Minister without Portfolio.[1] The functions which The Lord Privy Seal[2] meant to give up to him

[1] Arthur Greenwood, 1880–1954. Lecturer in Economics, Leeds University, and Chairman of the Yorkshire District Workers' Educational Association. Assistant Secretary, Ministry of Reconstruction, 1917–19. Labour MP for Nelson and Colne, 1922–31; for Wakefield, 1932–54. Parliamentary Secretary, Ministry of Health, 1924. Minister of Health, 1929–31. Privy Councillor, 1929; Deputy Leader of the Labour Party, 1935. Member of the War Cabinet, as Minister without Portfolio, 1940–2. Lord Privy Seal, 1945–7. Chairman of the Labour Party, 1952.

[2] Clement Richard Attlee, 1883–1967. Educated at Haileybury and University College, Oxford. Called to the Bar, 1906. Tutor and lecturer, London School of Economics, 1913–23. On active service at Gallipoli, Mesopotamia (wounded) and France, 1914–19; Major, 1917. First Labour Mayor of Stepney, 1919, 1920; Alderman, 1920–7. Labour MP for Limehouse, 1922–50; for West Walthamstow, 1950–5. Parliamentary Private Secretary to Ramsay MacDonald, 1922–4. Under-Secretary of State for War, 1924. Chancellor of the Duchy of Lancaster, 1930–1. Postmaster-General, 1931. Deputy Leader of the Labour Party in the House of Commons, 1931–45. Leader of the

were not concerned with War Aims, but with the definite problems of reconstruction; at least that is my understanding of the matter.

You had better talk with the Lord Privy Seal upon this point.

2. I do not consider that the kind of Committee for Post-War Reconstruction is at all filled by the personnel of the Committee on War Aims.

3. It is quite natural to put the Minister without Portfolio at the head of the Committee on the Reconstruction of Town and Country, to which the Minister of Works and Buildings[1] already belongs. I do not think it is necessary to add the two Ministers mentioned by the Chancellor of the Exchequer, and a letter should be drafted by you for him fms[2] accordingly. We must be very careful not to allow these remote post-war problems to absorb energy which is required, maybe for several years, for the prosecution of the war.

Winston S. Churchill to General Ismay, for General Loch[3] and others concerned
(*Churchill papers, 20/36*)

4 January 1941
Action this Day

In the PE fuze[4] the greatest interest attaches to high-altitude work against machines flying over 10,000 feet which are not dive-bombing but trying to hit HM ships or land targets, perhaps with improved bomb-sights. It is desired to be able to burst salvoes of 8 or more in close proximity to the EA[5] with fatal results. Even if this could be achieved only in clear, good weather, it would be of the highest advantage, as important operations would be arranged to seek that weather.

Opposition, 1935–40. Lord Privy Seal, 1940–2. Deputy Prime Minister, 1942–5. Lord President of the Council, 1943–5. Prime Minister, 1945–51 (Minister of Defence, 1945–6). Leader of the Opposition, 1951–5. Created Earl, 1955.

[1] John Charles Walsham Reith, 1889–1971. Educated Royal Technical College, Glasgow. Engineer's apprentice; then joined S. Pearson & Son Ltd, as an engineer, 1913. On active service, Royal Engineers, 1914–15 (seriously wounded in the head). Major, 1915. Mission to America, for munitions contracts, 1916–17. Admiralty Engineer-in-Chief's Department, 1918. In charge of liquidation of munitions engineering contracts, 1919. First General Manager, BBC, 1922; Managing Director, 1923; Director-General, 1927–38. Knighted, 1927. Chairman, BOAC, 1939–40. Minister of Information, 1939–40. Minister of Transport, 1940. National MP for Southampton, 1940. Created Baron, 1940. Minister of Works, 1940–2. Lieutenant-Commander, RNVR, 1942. Director of Combined Operations, Material Department, Admiralty, 1943–5. Member, Commonwealth Telecommunications Board, 1946–50.

[2] For my signature.

[3] Kenneth Morley Loch, 1890–1961. Entered the Army, 1910. On active service, 1914–18, including the retreat from Mons and the Battle of the Aisne (despatches twice, MC). Director, Anti-Aircraft and Coastal Defence, War Office, 1939–41. Master General of Ordnance, India, 1944–7. Knighted, 1946. British Control Commission, Germany, 1948–9.

[4] An anti-aircraft device, for ground fire against attacking aircraft.

[5] Enemy aircraft.

2. Is this high-altitude work being pressed to the full, both in the manufacture and in the Research-Training sphere? Are the officers concerned fully apprised? Defence against dive-bombing was the original purpose, and this may well be achieved both by PE and AD,[1] but the emphasis must now be placed upon high-altitude work.

3. This also applies to the AD fuze firing the aerial mines at the highest altitudes of all. It is in this direction that the highest tactical and operational results will be achieved.

Winston S. Churchill to Anthony Eden
(*Churchill papers, 20/36*)

4 January 1941

Why should he[2] go to the United States to make mischief there? He should be returned to this country, and made to feel such weight of displeasure as can be brought to bear. Anyhow, creatures like this should not be favoured with seats on the Clipper across the Atlantic.

Winston S. Churchill to A. V. Alexander and Admiral Pound
(*Churchill papers, 20/36*)

4 January 1941

Does not a torpedo seaplane require about a thousand yards to run its torpedo? Would it not be possible to moor lines of nets so as to shield to a large extent the ships lying at anchor from this form of attack? It would be like putting up a kind of movable breakwater.

I should think it very likely that they will have a go at you one of these days.

Winston S. Churchill to Sir Archibald Sinclair and Air Chief Marshal Sir Charles Portal
(*Churchill papers, 20/36*)

4 January 1941

I note also that the current returns show 100 more Bomber aircraft serviceable than there are crews. Evidently it is the crews which are the limiting factor at the moment.

[1] I have omitted the name of the person concerned.
[2] Anti-aircraft ammunition.

Winston S. Churchill to Air Chief Marshal Sir Charles Portal
(*Churchill papers, 20/36*)

4 January 1941

I asked Air Marshal Peirse[1] for a note on the possible acceleration of the expansion of the Bomber Command. Perhaps you will kindly read this, so that we can talk about it tomorrow night. Pray treat it as personal and private, and not official.

Winston S. Churchill to Ronald Cross
(*Churchill papers, 20/36*)

4 January 1941

The Import Executive will explore the whole of this situation, the development of which was one of the reasons for calling the said Executive into being. I shall myself keep in the closest touch with the Import Executive, and will endeavour to give the necessary decisions. It is hoped that by the more efficient use of our shipping, its turn round, port and labour resources, the tonnage available may be increased beyond the 33,000,000 tons which is all you can at present foresee. The Ministry of Shipping and the Ministry of Transport, together with the Ministry of Labour, will cooperate actively with the Import Executive, and their work will be effectively concerted by the Executive. In addition to this, the Admiralty will be asked to concentrate more effort upon the repair of ships, even to some extent to the detriment of new merchant shipbuilding. We hope American aid will be forthcoming, and that greater security will be achieved by our convoys as the nights shorten, and our main reinforcements of escorting craft come into service..

Winston S. Churchill to Sir John Reith
(*Premier papers, 3/181/1*)

4 January 1941
Action this Day

The great increase in the destruction and damage to house property makes it all the more necessary that you should regard emergency first-aid work to

[1] Richard Edmund Charles Peirse, 1892–1970. A pilot in the Royal Naval Air Service, 1913–14, and one of Churchill's flying instructors at that time. On active service, 1914–18 (DSO, AFC). Deputy Director of Operations and Intelligence, Air Ministry, 1930–3. Air Officer Commanding British Forces, Palestine and Transjordan, 1933–6. Deputy Chief of the Air Staff, 1937–40. Knighted 1940. Vice-Chief of the Air Staff, 1940. Air Officer Commanding-in-Chief, Bomber Command, 1940–2; India, 1942–3; Allied Air Commander-in-Chief, South-East Asia, 1943–4.

buildings slightly damaged as the most important task. Please let me have a weekly report of what you are doing in this respect. I continue to see great numbers of houses where the walls and roofs are all right, but the windows have not been repaired, and which are consequently uninhabitable. At present I regard this as your No. 1 war task. Do not let spacious plans for a new world divert your energies in saving what is left of the old.

Winston S. Churchill to Robert Menzies
(*Churchill papers, 20/49*)

4 January 1941

I send you the heartiest congratulations from all friends here upon the magnificent manner in which the Australian offensive against Bardia has opened.

The piercing of the western sector and the capture of at least 5,000 prisoners in itself constitutes a fine feat of arms, and is, I trust and believe, the prelude to even greater success.

Winston S. Churchill to King George VI
(*Royal Archives*)

5 January 1941

Sir,

I am honoured by Your Majesty's most gracious letter. The kindness with which Your Majesty and the Queen[1] have treated me since I became First Lord and still more since I became Prime Minister has been a continuous source of strength and encouragement during the vicissitudes of this fierce struggle for life. I have already served Your Majesty's father and grandfather[2] for a good many years as a Minister of the Crown, and my father and grandfather[3] served Queen Victoria, but Your Majesty's treatment of me has been intimate and generous to a degree that I had never deemed possible.

[1] Lady Elizabeth Bowes-Lyon, 1900– . Daughter of the 14th Earl of Strathmore. In 1923 she married the Duke of York, who succeeded his brother (King Edward VIII) as King George VI in 1936, when she became Queen Elizabeth. On the accession to the throne of her daughter Elizabeth as Queen Elizabeth II in 1952, she was styled Her Majesty Queen Elizabeth The Queen Mother.

[2] King George V and King Edward VII.

[3] Lord Randolph Churchill (as Secretary of State for India, and Chancellor of the Exchequer) and the 7th Duke of Marlborough (Lord President of the Council and Lord Lieutenant of Ireland).

Indeed, Sir, we have passed through days and weeks as trying and as momentous as any in the history of the English Monarchy, and even now there stretches before us a long, forbidding road. I have been greatly cheered by our weekly luncheons in poor old bomb-battered Buckingham Palace, and to feel that in Your Majesty and the Queen there flames the spirit that will never be daunted by peril, nor wearied by unrelenting toil. This war has drawn the Throne and the people more closely together than was ever before recorded, and Your Majesties are more beloved by all classes and conditions than any of the princes of the past. I am indeed proud that it should have fallen to my lot and duty to stand at Your Majesty's side as First Minister in such a climax of the British story, and it is not without good and sure hope and confidence in the future that I sign myself, 'on Bardia day', when the gallant Australians are gathering another twenty thousand Italian prisoners,

Your Majesty's faithful and devoted
servant and subject,
Winston S. Churchill

Winston S. Churchill to Viscount Cranborne
(*Churchill papers, 20/36*)

5 January 1941

I like all this[1] except the despatch of so many invaluable aircraft at a time when the danger of war with Japan has receded. In particular the PBYs[2] are urgently needed for the North-Western Approaches where vital war operations are in progress. The Air needs may be met later in the year, but not so early as April. Preparations may, however, be made for the reception of these aircraft, so that their transference could be rapid should the occasion arise.

I do not take an alarmist view about the defence of Singapore, at the present time.

[1] A draft telegram to Australia and New Zealand, summarizing the Appreciation of the Commander-in-Chief, Far East, Air Chief Marshal Sir Robert Brooke-Popham, and the conclusions on it of the military advisers.

[2] Catalina flying-boats.

Winston S. Churchill to Geoffrey Lloyd[1]
(*Churchill papers, 20/36*)

5 January 1941

I am glad to see the progress made in protecting our oil storage tanks and to hear of the success of the device. Pray press on with this in so far as prior demands for materials and labour allow and so save dollars and ships.

Winston S. Churchill to Anthony Eden and Hugh Dalton[2]
(*Churchill papers, 20/36*)

5 January 1941

I have read Sir Robert Vansittart's[3] dated 30.12.40. My message to Italy was deliberately designed to separate the Italian people from the Fascist régime and from Mussolini; and, now that France is out of the war, I certainly intend to talk rather more about the Nazis and rather less about the Germans. I do not agree with Sir Robert Vansittart's line on this. We must not let our vision be darkened by hatred or be obscured by sentiment.

A much more fruitful line is to try to separate the Prussians from the South Germans. I do not remember that the word 'Prussia' has been used much

[1] Geoffrey William Geoffrey-Lloyd, 1902–1984. Conservative Member of Parliament for Birmingham Ladywood, 1931–41. Parliamentary Private Secretary to Stanley Baldwin, 1931–35. Under-Secretary, Home Office, 1935–39. Secretary for Mines, 1939–40. Chairman of the Oil Control Board, 1939–45. Secretary for Petroleum, 1940–42. Minister in charge of the Petroleum Warfare Department, 1940–45. Parliamentary Secretary (Petroleum), Ministry of Fuel and Power, 1942–45. Minister of Information, 1945. A Governor of the BBC, 1946–49. Conservative Member of Parliament for Birmingham King's Norton, 1950–55; for Sutton Coldfield, 1955–74. Minister of Fuel and Power, 1951–55. Minister of Education, 1957–59. Created Baron, as Lord Geoffrey-Lloyd, 1974.

[2] Edward Hugh John Neale Dalton, 1887–1962. Educated at Eton and King's College, Cambridge. Barrister, 1914. On active service in France and Italy, 1914–18. Lecturer, London School of Economics, 1919. Reader in Commerce, University of London, 1920–5; Reader in Economics, 1925–6. Labour MP for Camberwell, 1924–9; for Bishop Auckland, 1929–31 and 1935–59. Parliamentary Under-Secretary, Foreign Office, 1929–31. Chairman, National Executive of the Labour Party, 1936–7. Minister of Economic Warfare, 1940–2. President of the Board of Trade, 1942–5. Chancellor of the Exchequer, 1945–7; resigned over a Budget leak, 1947. Minister of Town and Country Planning, 1950–1. Created Baron, 1960.

[3] Robert Gilbert Vansittart, 1881–1957. Educated at Eton. Entered the Diplomatic Service, 1902. Assistant Clerk, Foreign Office, 1914; 1st Secretary, 1918; Counsellor, 1920. Secretary to Lord Curzon, 1920–4. Principal Private Secretary to Ramsay MacDonald, 1928–30. Knighted, 1929. Permanent Under-Secretary of State for Foreign Affairs, 1930–8. Elected to the Other Club, 1933. Chief Diplomatic Adviser to the Foreign Secretary, 1938–41. Privy Councillor, 1940. Created Baron, 1941. His autobiography, *The Mist Procession*, was published posthumously, in 1958. His brother Arnold was killed in action in 1915.

lately. The expressions to which I attach importance and intend to give emphasis are 'Nazi tyranny' and 'Prussian militarism'.[1]

Winston S. Churchill to General Ismay for the Chiefs of Staff Committee
(Premier papers, 3/222/5)

5 January 1941

PREPARATION OF THE OBSTRUCTION OF AGRICULTURAL LAND TO PREVENT LANDING OF TROOP-CARRYING AIRCRAFT

Before any action is taken, Home Forces should confer with the minister of Agriculture in order that measures can be taken which give the most benefit to the one and do the least harm to the other. When this process is complete, let me know what is the total estimated food loss to agriculture entailed.

Remember food is a part of our war and also the present denudation of the German Air in the west. It is becoming increasingly serious to hamper agriculture.

Winston S. Churchill to General Wavell
(Churchill papers, 20/49)

5 January 1941
Personal and Secret

Hearty congratulations on your second brilliant victory, so profoundly helpful at this turning-point to the whole cause. You knocked and it was opened. I have now verified the Walt Whitman quotation. Authentic text is as follows: 'Now understand me well – it is provided in the essence of things that from any fruition of success, no matter what, shall come forth something to make a greater struggle necessary.'

Time may be short. I cannot believe Hitler will not intervene soon. I cabled your message about the Corps Commanders and the Bishop textually to President Roosevelt under strict secrecy, hoping it will buck him up before his inaugural address tomorrow, 6th.

I see you did not understand my reference to Great St Bernard, which I was

[1] Two days later, Churchill wrote direct to Sir Robert Vansittart about Vansittart's criticisms, see page 38.

told was General Wilson's[1] pet name for Freyberg.[2] Am sending you in the next few days long appeals about purging rearward services. Strain of putting shipping round the Cape is definitely affecting feeding arrangements here and transport of munitions, airplanes and pilots across the Atlantic. I am counting upon you to make every man in ME[3] row his weight in the boat. Tell Longmore nothing shall stop remounting his men on the best ponies. Am sending him a telegram tomorrow. RAF have played up splendidly in this God-granted series of successes. Once more, every good wish.

Winston S. Churchill to President Franklin D. Roosevelt
(*Churchill papers, 20/49*)

6 January 1941
Personal and Secret

I dare say you will like to know our latest war news. Following just received from General Wavell:

(Most Secret.)

'Bardia operations proceeding satisfactorily. News is scarce, but refers to mopping up. Indicates enemy resistance only in isolated places.

'Prisoners may exceed 25,000, including definitely 2 Corps Commanders, 4 Divisional Commanders and rumoured 1 Bishop accompanied by 3 Nuns.'

The General has now telegraphed that all resistance has ceased. Every good wish for tomorrow's momentous statement.

[1] Henry Maitland Wilson, 1881–1964. Known as 'Jumbo'. On active service in South Africa, 1899–1902; on the Western Front, 1914–17 (despatches, DSO). General Officer Commanding-in-Chief, Egypt, 1939; in Cyrenaica, 1940; in Greece, 1941; in Palestine and Transjordan, 1941. Knighted, 1940. Commander-in-Chief, Allied Forces in Syria, 1941; Persia-Iraq Command, 1942–3; Middle East, 1943. Supreme Allied Commander, Mediterranean Theatre, 1944. Field Marshal, 1944. Head of the British Joint Staff Mission, Washington, 1945–7. Created Baron, 1946.

[2] Bernard Freyberg, 1889–1963. Born in London. Educated in New Zealand. Sub-Lieutenant, Royal Naval Division, 1914. On active service at Antwerp, 1914, the Dardanelles, 1915 and in France, 1916–18 (despatches six times, wounded nine times, DSO and two bars, Victoria Cross). He won the Victoria Cross for 'conspicuous bravery and brilliant leadership' at Beaumont Hamel, during the Battle of the Somme, 1916. General Staff Officer, War Office, 1933–4. Posted to India, 1937, but after a breakdown of his health, invalided out of the army. Passed fit for general service, September 1939. General Officer Commanding Salisbury Plain Area, October 1939. General Officer Commanding the New Zealand Forces from November 1939 until the end of the war. Commander-in-Chief, Allied Forces in Crete, 1941. Knighted, 1942. Awarded the third bar to his DSO, Italy, 1944. Governor General of New Zealand, 1946–52. Created Baron, 1951.

[3] Middle East.

Winston S. Churchill to Sir Ian Hamilton[1]
(*Churchill papers, 2/419*)

6 January 1941

I am thinking of you and Wagon Hill[2] when another January sixth brings news of a fine feat of arms.

Winston

War Cabinet: minutes
(*Cabinet papers, 55/17*)

6 January 1941
12.30 p.m.

There had been no further news beyond that already published regarding the capture of Bardia. 25,000 prisoners had been taken including 2 Corps Commanders and 4 Senior Generals.

The Prime Minister said that this operation had been brilliantly executed, and our total of 400 casualties was extraordinarily small. In a broadcast that morning a BBC spokesman had stressed the pitiful condition of the Italian forces. It was undesirable to belittle what the Australians had done by laying too much emphasis on the fact that there had not been much fighting. The line to take was that the Italians, normally excellent soldiers, had not on this occasion fought with their accustomed bravery owing to their being out of sympathy with the cause for which they were fighting. Stress should be laid on the great weight of our bombardment, and on the brilliance of the tactics adopted by General Wavell.

The War Cabinet –

Invited the Minister of Information after consultation with the War Office to make a personal broadcast that evening bringing out these points.

[1] Ian Standish Monteith Hamilton, 1853–1947. Entered Army, 1872. Major-General, 1900. Knighted, 1900. Chief of Staff to Lord Kitchener, 1901–02. General, 1914. Commander of the Central Force, responsible for the defence of England in the event of invasion, August 1914–March 1915. Commanded the Mediterranean Expeditionary Force at Gallipoli, March–October 1915, after which he received no further military command.

[2] A ridge near Ladysmith, fortified by the British as part of the defence of Ladysmith. A Boer attack on it was repulsed on 6 January 1900.

Winston S. Churchill to General Ismay, for the Chiefs of Staff Committee
(Churchill papers, 20/36)

6 January 1941

I am concerned about the mobile naval base plan. It has swollen unchecked to 5,800 men, and is a tremendous inroad on WS 6.[1] In the present strategic situation, do we really want to have this mobile base out of reach and out of action till the middle of March or probably with reloading, &c., till the beginning of April? How would this bear on 'Influx' supposing we had to do something there in a hurry? How would it affect a Benghazi occupation, supposing we got there in February? Not only is it eating up convoy space unpurged, but it will be unavailable during a very critical period.

I should be glad if the COS[2] would weigh this and also consider, if time permits, what could be sent instead.

Winston S. Churchill to David Margesson and General Sir John Dill[3]
(Churchill papers, 20/36)

6 January 1941

1. WS 5A has already started and B starts immediately. There is therefore no question about them. They contain together 55,000 men, of which 12,000 are for India, &c., and 43,000 for ME. Of the 43,000 ME, about 22,000 are for fighting units and drafts, and 21,000 technical, L of C, base, &c., of which about 4,000 are Navy and RAF. Thus the army in ME receives 22,000 fighting and 17,000 other men.

2. The present composition of the army in the Middle East (excluding Kenya and Aden nearly 70,000) reveals 150,000 fighting troops. Behind this are 40,000 L of C and 20,000 base establishments and details, i.e., 150,000 to 60,000. To this will now be added WS 5A and B 22,000 fighting and 17,000 L of C base, &c., making a total of 172,000 fighting and 77,000 rearward services.

[1] Convoys from Britain to Egypt that went via the Cape of Good Hope used the prefix WS. Unable to use the Mediterranean, they had to travel south along the African Atlantic coast and north through the Indian Ocean to the Red Sea and Suez City (at the southern end of the Suez Canal).

[2] The Chief of the Naval Staff, Admiral Pound.

[3] John Greer Dill, 1881–1944. Born in Northern Ireland. Entered the Army, 1901. On active service, 1914–18 (DSO). Commanded the British Forces in Palestine, 1936–7. Knighted, 1937. General Officer Commanding Aldershot Command, 1937–9. Commanded the 1st Army Corps, France, 1939–40. Chief of the Imperial General Staff, 1940–1. Head of the British Joint Staff Mission, Washington, from 1941 until his death.

3. Convoy WS 6 now being loaded contains 8,500 fighting troops, plus fighting share of 4,000 drafts – say 2,500 – equals total fighting troops 11,000. Excluding the mobile Naval base 5,300 (of which later)[1] and the RAF (including training school to Capetown) and RN 7,000, 2,000 Free French and about 9,000 base and other details. Upon the arrival of this convoy the total figure for the Middle East will stand at fighting troops 183,000 and 86,000 rearward units, i.e., 15 to 7. The progressive deterioration in the proportion between fighting troops and rearward services must be noted.

4. But the category 'fighting troops' requires further searching analysis. We are told, for example, that the 7th Australian Division 14,800 is untrained and largely unequipped and there is the Cavalry Division 8,500 whose mechanization has not yet made progress and who cannot really be called fighting troops except for local order. There are several other units I could specify which are similarly not fighting troops in the effective mobile sense – say 6,000. Thus 29,000 should properly be subtracted from the fighting total, reducing it from 183,000 to 154,000 and added to the rearward services and non-effective, raising them from 86,000 to 115,000. The condition of the army of the Middle East (excluding the 70,000 in Kenya and Aden) is therefore represented by 154,000 fighting troops and 115,000 rearward and non-effective (except for immediate local security). The proportion of non-effectives seems much too high. It must be remembered that further great reductions could be made from the effective fighting troops, since every Division or Brigade Group has its own First-Line transport and is supposed to be a self-contained military unit. Further it should not be forgotten that in order to supply all this rearward and unorganized or non-effective strength the rations of the British people have had to be severely reduced, and further cuts are in prospect, and that every man and every ton of stores has to be carried and transported at heavy risk from enemy U-Boat, air and raider attacks round the Cape of Good Hope by ships whose there-and-back voyage occupies, with turn-round, not less than four months. It is therefore incumbent upon all loyal persons whether at home or in ME to try to increase the fighting troops and to keep at the lowest possible the rearward and non-effective services. In this lies a great opportunity for brilliant administrative exertion which might produce results in war economy equal to those gained by a considerable victory in the field.

5. If I could be assured that the plethora of rearward services contained in the aforesaid convoys WS 5A and B and WS 6 would animate and render effective the 29,000 non-effective fighting men mentioned in paragraph 4

[1] Printed, as the previous document, on page 30, to be circulated by General Ismay.

above, I should be content. For instance, will the 7th Australian Division gain the ancillary services necessary to fit it for other than local action?

Will the 8,500 Cavalry Division become a mechanized unit capable of acting in Brigades or at least Regiments against the enemy? Then although the proportions of non-fighting troops now crowding our convoys would still be a very hard measure, at any rate the army in the ME would grow markedly in fighting strength, and the delay in sending the 50th Division would be tolerable. It may be that some consoling information will be forthcoming about this.

The question of whether it would be better to send the First Brigade of the 50th Division instead of the mobile Naval base in WS 6 is nicely balanced, but preparations may have advanced too far for a convenient change of plan. This must be considered tomorrow (7th) by COS Committee observing that it will be out of action for nearly three months.

6. It is otherwise necessary to approve the despatch of WS 6 (reduced to 34,000 or less) as now proposed. I deeply regret the resultant composition of the Army in the ME. When all these convoys have arrived its total will amount to 240,000 plus 43,000, plus 20,000 – total 300,000, to which must be added 70,000 in Aden and Kenya – total 370,000 men, on pay and ration strength. From this enormous force the only recognizable fighting military units are the following:

6th Australian Division.
1 New Zealand Division, comprising 2 Brigade Groups.
4th Indian Division.
5th Indian Division.
16th Infantry Brigade.
2nd Armoured Division.
7th Armoured Division (Incomplete).
6th British Division (Incomplete).

and such fighting units as have been formed from the 70,000 men in Kenya and Aden, *e.g.*, 2 South African Brigades, 2 West African brigades and local East African forces. It is hoped that to these will soon be added (a) the completion of the above incomplete units; (b) a seventh British Division formed out of the unclassified and by combing the rearward services

the 7th Australian Division
and a mechanized Cavalry Division.

This will amount to about ten Divisions, Infantry, Armoured and Cavalry, plus say 1 Division from Kenya – total 11 Divisions. Even this would be a very small crop to gather from so vast a field.

Winston S. Churchill to Mrs Bertram Cartland[1]
(*Churchill papers, 2/417*)

6 January 1941

Dear Mrs Cartland

It is with great sorrow that I have heard that you have received news that Ronald[2] was killed in action in May last. Pray accept my deepest sympathy in the loss of so brilliant and splendid a son, whose exceptional abilities would have carried him far had he not proudly given his life for his country.

Yours sincerely,
Winston S. Churchill

Winston S. Churchill to General Ismay, for the Chiefs of Staff Committee
(*Churchill papers, 20/36*)

6 January 1941

Please see the attached from the Foreign Secretary.[3] In spite of the evident need to pursue the Italians along the Libyan coast while the going is good, we shall have to consider the despatch of 4 or 5 more squadrons RAF to Greece, and possibly the diversion of the part of the second armoured division.

I cannot look beyond Benghazi at the present time, and if Tobruk is taken there will be very few Italian troops, and by no means their best, east of Benghazi.

Although perhaps by luck and daring and through the poor fighting qualities of the Italians we may collect comparatively easily most delectable prizes on the Libyan shore, the massive importance of taking Valona and keeping the Greek front in being must weigh hourly with us.

[1] Mother of Barbara Cartland, the author and playwright, born 1904, and of Ronald and Anthony Cartland, both killed in action on successive days in 1940. Her husband Major Bertram Cartland, had been killed in action on the Western Front on 27 May 1918.

[2] John Ronald Hamilton Cartland, 1907–40. Educated at Charterhouse. Worked at Conservative Central Office, 1927–35. Conservative MP for King's Norton, 1935–40. Captain, 53rd Anti-Tank Regiment, Royal Artillery, British Expeditionary Force, 1940. Killed in action in France, 30 May 1940. Churchill wrote of him, on 7 November 1941 (in the preface to Barbara Cartland's book *Ronald Cartland*): 'At a time when our political life had become feckless and dull, he spoke fearlessly for Britain. His words and acts were instinct with the sense of our country's traditions and duty. His courage and bearing inspired those who met him or heard him.' Ronald Cartland's brother Anthony had been killed in action on the previous day, 29 May 1940.

[3] Eden had sent Churchill a minute about the possibility of a German attack on Greece through Bulgaria.

Winston S. Churchill to A.V. Alexander and Admiral Pound
(*Churchill papers, 20/36*)

6 January 1941
Action this Day
Secret

I consider it absolutely necessary to press on with the process of remounting Longmore's Airmen upon the best machines.

I see *Furious* has already delivered her second consignment at Freetown. Nothing ought to stand in the way of her carrying a third as fast as possible. There is no way in which our Air power can be so rapidly increased as by giving this mass of good pilots in the Middle East machines worthy of their quality and experience. Everything goes to show that they may soon have to operate in Greece and Turkey against the Germans.

I hope the Admiralty will be able to help our general interests in this all-important matter.

Winston S. Churchill to Air Chief Marshal Longmore
(*Churchill papers, 20/49*)

6 January 1941
Personal and Private

Greatly admire your brilliant support of army operations, and congratulate you upon a victory over enemy air force achieved against heavy numerical odds. Let your people know how much we appreciate what they have done at this juncture so important and possibly cardinal for our affairs. We shall soon be, as usual, torn between conflicting needs. Sustaining of Greek battle thus keeping in the field their quite large army becomes an objective of prime importance. You are no doubt thinking of this. Am asking Admiralty to send third consignment via Takoradi at fastest. Will advise you definitely tomorrow. Probably four or five squadrons will be required for Greece, and yet you will have to carry army forward in Libya. You may count on being thoroughly remounted, but all your rearward services must be searchingly combed. All good wishes.

Winston S. Churchill to Lord Beaverbrook
(*Churchill papers, 20/20*)

6 January 1941 10 Downing Street

My dear Max,

I have not the slightest intention of letting you go. I sh'd feel myself struck a most cruel blow if you were to persist in so morbid & unworthy an intention. You w'd deprive me and the Government of services wh are irreplaceable, & as I said in my last letter the public w'd regard y'r act as desertion of duty. You have no right in the height of a war like this to put yr burdens on me. You are in the collar & you have got to go on. No one knows better than you how much I depend on you for counsel & comfort. I cannot believe that you will do such a thing. If y'r health requires it, take a few weeks rest. But abandon the ship now – never!

Yours always
Winston S. Churchill

Winston S. Churchill to Lord Beaverbrook
(*Churchill papers, 20/20*)

no date

My dear Max,

I am very sorry to receive your letter. Your resignation would be quite unjustified and would be regarded as desertion. It would in one day destroy all the reputation that you have gained and turn the gratitude and goodwill of millions of people to anger. It is a step you would regret all your life. No Minister has ever received the support which I have given you, and you know well the burden which will be added to my others by your refusal to undertake the great commission with which I sought to entrust you. It is not possible in this nor would I agree to it even if it were, to entrust any one Minister with the dictatorial powers over the vast area covered by the Import and Production programme. But the arrangement which I have made would give you effective power to render a very great service to the British nation in its days of trial.

If I am to accept as final your refusal to take the Chairmanship of the Imports Executive which all its members wish to accord you, I will myself take your place and will return to London tomorrow for the purpose of holding the first meeting.

If in addition to refusing these urgent duties you propose to give up the Ministry of Aircraft Production and retire from the War Cabinet, that will be an additional offence from which I am sure you will not escape without grievous public censure. I can only hope that your better nature will prevail and that you will once again rise to the height of the great events in which you have played so honourable a part.

John Colville: diary
(*Colville papers*)

6 January 1941

I was at No. 10 from 2 p.m. till 8.15 and had an exhausting time what with the issues of press communiques about the new Production Executive etc., and wrangles with Lord Beaverbrook. The PM had his sleep and while he was dressing treated me to a discourse on the siege of Ladysmith and why he always remembered January 6th.[1] On the way over to the Annex for dinner, he said: 'I think Anthony is putting his hand on the Foreign Office. I see a different touch in the telegrams'.

I was on duty after dinner when an encouraging telegram came which makes it look as if Tobruk may fall close after Bardia. Then we shall have to make a decision: whether to press on to Benghazi or whether to stop and divert our striking force elsewhere. The threat of a German advance into the Balkans, and the slowing up of the Greek offensive in Albania in the face of more determined resistance, give cause to think. It would be disastrous to let the Greek triumph end in defeat, as did the victories of the Finnish army last winter.

The PM worked intensively until 2 a.m. and sent yet another eloquent note to Lord Beaverbrook, ending 'Danton, no weakness'.[2] Then he went to bed and, as he snuggled beneath the bed clothes, smiling at the thought of Bardia and, he hopes soon, Tobruk, he had the grace for once to apologize for keeping me up so late!

[1] On 6 January 1900, having escaped from the Boer prisoner-of-war camp in Pretoria, Churchill was commissioned in the British forces, changing his status back from journalist to soldier. On February 28 he was entered Ladysmith with the liberating forces.

[2] The last words of Georges Danton (1759–1794) addressed to himself a few moments before he was guillotined – at the age of 35.

Winston S. Churchill to Lord Beaverbrook
(*Churchill papers, 20/20*)

Private
7 January 1941
Midnight 10 Downing Street

My dear Max,

You must not forget in the face of petty vexations the vast scale of events and the brightly-lighted stage of history upon which we stand.

I understand all that you have done for us; and perhaps I shall live to tell the tale.

'Danton no weakness'.

Yours always
W

War Cabinet: minutes
(*Cabinet papers, 65/17*)

7 January 1941 10 Downing Street
12.30 p.m.

The Prime Minister informed the War Cabinet that he had invited the Chiefs of Staff to consider whether we could now afford some further assistance to Greece, more particularly by reinforcing our air detachment in that country.

Winston S. Churchill to General Wavell
(*Churchill papers, 20/49*)

7 January 1941
Private and Personal

I am sorry to spoil the hour of your splendid victory by awkward matters of housekeeping. If your demands for non-fighting services are maintained on the present scale the whole scope and character of our effort in the Middle East will have to be reviewed. Shipping has now become the dominant factor and will remain so certainly for the next six months. Rations of heavy munition workers are being cut down to levels of which British armies, except in actual operations, have never dreamed. Severe stringency in human rations and slaughter of cattle through lack of feeding-stuffs lie before us. Transport of vital munitions, aeroplanes, trained pilots, raw materials for munition factories, now offered from across the Atlantic, is endangered. The main war effort of the nation may be compromised. The voyage round the Cape imposes an almost prohibitive burden. It is quite certain that all the convoys will have to be severely cut.

2. I think you will admit that I have done my utmost to reinforce and nourish the ME armies and we have not only made sacrifices but have run grave risks to do so. Therefore I feel I have a right to ask you to make sure that the rearward services do not trench too largely upon the effective fighting strength, that you have less fat and more muscle, that you have a smaller tail and larger teeth. You have well over 350,000 troops on your ration strength, and the number of units which are fighting or capable of fighting appears to me disproportionately small. It is distressing to see convoys sent by the heart's blood of the nation's effort consisting so largely of rearward services of all kinds.

3. I am well aware of all the arguments which can be deployed in favour of every rearward establishment. I do not dispute their validity: the question is one of emphasis and proportion. This is no time for ideal establishments to be drawn up by staff officers and pushed out to us as essential minima. I beg you to convince me that you will continually comb, scrub and purge all rearward services in a hard unrelenting manner, as Kitchener did. This conviction will enable me to impose the severe sacrifices required upon the British nation, and to secure for the campaign of 1941 in the Middle East the opportunities which may await it under your direction.

Winston S. Churchill to Sir Robert Vansittart
(*Churchill papers, 20/36*)

7 January 1941
Private. Secret.

My message to Italy, of which you approved, was deliberately designed to separate the Italian people from the Fascist régime and from Mussolini. Now that France is out of the war, I certainly intend, quite contrary to your second paragraph on page 2, to talk rather more about the Nazis and rather less about the Germans. I definitely disagree with your line on this.[1] We must not let our vision be darkened by hatred or obscured by sentiment. If your policy means anything, it means the extermination of 40 or 50 million people. This is silly. A much more fruitful line is to try to separate the Prussians from the South Germans. I do not remember that you have used the word 'Prussia' lately. The expressions to which I attach importance and intend to give emphasis are 'Nazi tyranny' and 'Prussian militarism'.

[1] Vansittart had denounced what he called the 'myth' of two Germanys, one good and one bad, and characterized all Germans as 'evil'.

I heard from many quarters that the line you took in your broadcast could not possibly be sustained by united public opinion here.[1]

Winston S. Churchill to General Ismay, for the Chiefs of Staff Committee
(Churchill papers, 20/36)

7 January 1941

1. The speedy destruction of the Italian armed forces in North-East Africa must be our prime major overseas objective in the opening months of 1941. Once the Italian army in Cyrenaica has been destroyed, the Army of the Nile becomes free for other tasks. We cannot yet tell what these will be.

2. The fall of Bardia should enable an advanced base to be established there for the capture of Tobruk. With Bardia and Tobruk in our hands, it should be possible to drop the land communications with Alexandria almost entirely, and to rely upon sea transport for our farther westward advance. Every plan should be made now to use Tobruk to its utmost capacity.

3. The striking force to be maintained west of Bardia and Tobruk need not be large. The Second and Seventh Armoured Divisions, the Sixth Australian Division, the New Zealand Brigade Group, soon to become a Division, with perhaps one or two British Brigades comprising not more than 40,000 to 45,000 men, should suffice to overpower the remaining Italian resistance, and to take Benghazi. The distance from Tobruk to Benghazi by the coastal road is not much above 250 miles, compared with about 370 from Alexandria to Tobruk. Thus, once Tobruk is established as a base, and our land communications begin from there, no greater strain should be thrown upon the land transport than at present, and it should be possible to start fresh from Tobruk as if Tobruk were Alexandria, and to maintain the moderate but adequate striking force required. With the capture of Benghazi, this phase of the Libyan campaign would be ended.

4. The question is, how long will it take? Having regard to the very heavy Italian losses in their best troops and in their vehicles and equipment, and to the fact that we have the command of the sea, the collapse in Cyrenaica might be very rapid. Indeed, all might go with a run at any time. The need for haste is obvious. It would, however, suffice for our general strategy if Benghazi and everything east of it were effectively in our possession, and occupied as a military and naval base at any time during March.

[1] On 6 March 1941 Churchill wrote to Alfred Duff Cooper, the Minister of Information: 'When I demurred to Sir Robert Vansittart making a broadcast the other day, I had not realized it was in French to the French people. I see no objection to Sir Robert making broadcast to the French people for whom his particular views have a real attraction and value'. (*Churchill papers, 20/30*)

5. The aforesaid Libyan operations need not therefore at all affect the simultaneous pushing of the campaign against the Italians in Abyssinia. General Wavell has already withdrawn the 4th Italian Division. The 5th Indian Division is also available, and it should be possible to carry out the Kassala Operation and to spread the revolt in Abyssinia, while at the same time the Kenyan forces press northwards by Lake Rudolf. At any time we may receive armistice proposals from the cut-off Italian garrison in Abyssinia. This army must have been buoyed up with hopes of an Italian conquest of the Delta and of the Canal, enabling communications to be restored and supplies to reach them by the Nile and the Red Sea. These hopes are already dead. On the other hand, the vast size of Abyssinia, the lack of all communications, especially sea communications, and the impossibility of nourishing large forces, may bring about an indefinite delay. It is, however, not an unreasonable hope that by the end of April the Italian Army in Abyssinia will have submitted or been broken up.

6. The moment that this is apparent, the northward movement of all the effective forces in Kenya, as well as those in the Sudan and Abyssinia, will become possible. These forces will thenceforward become a reserve available for operations in the Eastern Mediterranean. If we take the present total strength of the Armies in the Middle East at about 370,000 (including WS 5 and 6), it might be reasonably expected that the equivalent of 10 Divisions would stand in the Nile valley, together with 2 additional Divisions from home, a total of 12, after providing the necessary garrisons and security troops for Abyssinia, Cyrenaica, Egypt and Palestine. These 12 Divisions should thus be free (apart from new distractions) by the end of April.

II

7. To invade and force a way through Spain to the Straits of Gibraltar against the will of the Spanish people and Government, especially at this season, is a most dangerous and questionable enterprise for Germany to undertake, and it is no wonder that Hitler, with so many sullen populations to hold down, has so far shrunk from it. With the permission of the Spanish Government, it would of course be a short and easy matter for the Germans to gain control of Lisbon and of the Algeciras and Ceuta batteries, together with appropriate Air fields. According to Captain Hillgarth, RN,[1] who has

[1] Alan Hugh Hillgarth, 1899–1978. Entered the Royal Navy as a cadet at the Osborne Naval College at the age of eight. Wounded at the Dardanelles, 1915. Vice-Consul, Palma, Majorca, 1932–37; Consul, 1937–39. Naval Attaché, Madrid, 1939–43. Chief of Intelligence Staff, Eastern Fleet, 1943–44; Chief of British Naval Intelligence, Eastern Theatre, 1944–46. For five years after the Second World War he was Churchill's principal informant on Intelligence matters (a full account of which is in David Stafford, *Churchill and Secret Service*, London, 1997).

lived long in Spain and is fresh from contact with our Ambassador,[1] it is becoming increasingly unlikely that the Spanish Government will give Hitler passage or join the war against us. General Wavell's victories in Libya have played and will play an important part in Spanish opinion. If they are refused permission, it is most unlikely that the Germans will try to force their way into and through Spain before the month of April. From every point of view, this delay is helpful to us. We have the use of Gibraltar; we have the time for our strength in the Middle East to accomplish its task there, and again to become free; above all, there is the possibility of events taking a favourable turn in France and at Vichy.

8. We must now be most careful not to precipitate matters in Spain, or set the Spanish Government against us more than it is already, or provoke Herr Hitler to a violent course towards Spain. The operations 'Brisk'[2] and 'Shrapnel'[3] cannot be contemplated unless or until Spain offers passage to Germany, or Germany begins to force one. Having regard to the winter season, it would seem that both these Operations, hitherto held at 48 hours' notice, might have some relaxation. All these matters are highly speculative. There can be no certainty about them. But the fact that Hitler has not acted through Spain as we feared, when conditions, both political and climatic, were more favourable to him, makes it on the whole a reasonable working assumption that any German adventure in Spain will at least wait for the Spring.

III

9. The probabilities of delay in Spain until the Spring give rise to the hope that the Vichy Government, under German pressure or actual German incursion, may either proceed to North Africa and resume the war from there, or authorise General Weygand[4] to do so. If such an event could be brought

[1] Samuel John Gurney Hoare, 1880–1959. Educated at Harrow and New College, Oxford. Conservative MP for Chelsea, 1910–44. Succeeded his father as 2nd Baronet, 1915. Lieutenant-Colonel, British Military Mission to Russia, 1916–17 and to Italy, 1917–18. Deputy High Commissioner, League of Nations, for care of Russian refugees, 1921. Secretary of State for Air, October 1922–January1924 and 1924–9. Secretary of State for India, 1931–5; for Foreign Affairs, 1935. First Lord of the Admiralty, 1936–7; Home Secretary, 1937–9; Lord Privy Seal, 1939–40; Secretary of State for Air, April–May 1940. Ambassador to Spain, 1940–4. Created Viscount Templewood, 1944.

[2] British plan to take the Portuguese Azores islands to provide air and naval bases for closing the 'Atlantic gap' in which German U-boats could operate with little threat of British air attack.

[3] The plan to seize the Cape Verde Islands from Portugal.

[4] Maxime Weygand, 1867–1965. Chief of Staff to Marshal Foch, 1914–23. Honorary British knighthood, 1918. French High Commissioner for Syria, 1923–4. Commander-in-Chief of the French Army, 1931–5. Chief of the General Staff of National Defence and Commander-in-Chief (for the second time) from 19 May 1940, in place of General Gamelin, until the armistice a month later. Governor-General of Algeria and Delegate-General of the Vichy Government in French Africa, 1941. A prisoner of the Germans in Germany, 1942–5; a prisoner of the French in France, 1945–6. The third volume of his memoirs was published in English as *Recalled to Service*.

about before the Straits of Gibraltar fell into German control, we should have a very good chance of resisting a German attempt against the Straits indefinitely. We could move troops into Morocco by the Atlantic ports; we should have the use of the French Air bases in North Africa. The whole situation in the Mediterranean would be completely revolutionized in our favour. The position of any Italian forces remaining in Tripoli would become impossible. We might well be able to open the Mediterranean for supplies and reinforcements for the Middle East.

10. We have therefore thought it right to assure Marshal Pétain[1] and General Weygand that we will assist them with up to 6 Divisions, substantial Air forces and the necessary Naval power from the moment they feel able to take the all-important step we so greatly desire. We have also impressed upon them the danger of delaying their action until the Germans have made their way through Spain and become masters of the Straits and of Northern Morocco. We can but wait and see what Vichy will do. Meanwhile, we enforce the blockade of France fitfully and as naval convenience offers, partly to assert the principle, partly to provide a 'smoke-screen' of Anglo-French friction, and especially not to let the Vichy Government feel that life will be tolerable for them so far as we are concerned if they do nothing. It is greatly to our interest that events should develop rapidly in France. Presumably Herr Hitler realizes this. Nevertheless, the probabilities are that the French climax will come about before anything decisive happens in Spain.

IV

11. We must continually expect that Hitler will soon strike some heavy blow, and that he is now making preparations on a vast scale with customary German thoroughness. We can, of course, easily come down through Italy and establish an Air power in Sicily. Perhaps this is already taking place.

The Chiefs of the Staff Committee are requested to press on with their study of 'Influx',[2] which may conceivably require emergency treatment. It is not seen, however, how 'Influx' can be accorded priority over the operations in Libya; certainly not, whatever happens, until Tobruk has been taken and a good forward base made there – if not farther west – to protect Egypt.

[1] Henri Philippe Pétain, 1856–1951. Entered the French Army, 1878. Colonel, August 1914. Commanded the 6th Division of Infantry at the Battle of the Marne. Commanded the 2nd Army, 1915. In charge of the defence of Verdun, 1916. General-in-Chief, 1917–18; he impressed Churchill in April 1918 by his determination to throw back the German onslaught. Marshal of France, 1918. Inspector-General of the French Army, 1922–31. Minister of War, 1934. Ambassador to Spain, March 1939 to May 1940. Minister of State and Vice-President of the Council, May–June 1940. Chief of the French State (with the seat of government at Vichy), June 1940 to June 1944. Detained by the Germans after he tried to cross into France in the summer of 1944. Brought to trial in France in 1945 and sentenced to death; his sentence having been commuted to life imprisonment, he died in prison six years later.

[2] The occupation of Sicily.

V

12. All the foregoing shows that nothing would suit our interest better than that any German advance in the Balkans should be delayed till the Spring. For this very reason one must apprehend that it will begin earlier. The exploits of the Greek army have been an enormous help to us. They have expressed themselves generously about the extremely modest aid in the Air which was all we could give. But should their success be followed by a check or a deadlock, we must expect immediate demands for more aid. The only aid we can give quickly is four or five more squadrons from the Middle East, perhaps some artillery regiments, and some or all of the tanks of the Second Armoured Division now arrived and working up in leisurely fashion in Egypt.

Furious has reached Takoradi, and forty Hurricanes, &c., will soon raise Air Marshal Longmore's strength to well over a hundred Hurricane fighters. His losses in the offensive have been singularly small. His action in withdrawing squadrons from Aden and the Sudan has been vindicated. Tobruk may soon be in our hands, and thereafter it would seem that a strong reinforcement of Air power for Greece should be provided. This should include Hurricane Squadrons. Have the aerodromes in Greece been lengthened and adapted to them? Has the airfield in Crete yet been made suitable for their landing on passage? The call when it comes may be very urgent. Everything must be set in train now. We must know also how long it would take to move the Second Armoured Division to the Piraeus, and what numbers are involved.

13. All accounts go to show that a Greek failure to take Valona will have very bad consequences. It may be possible for General Wavell, with no more than the forces he is now using in the Western Desert, and in spite of some reduction in his Air Force, to conquer the Cyrenaica province and establish himself at Benghazi; but it would not be right for the sake of Benghazi to lose the chance of the Greeks taking Valona and thus to dispirit and anger them, and perhaps make them in the mood for a separate peace with Italy. Therefore the prospect must be faced that after Tobruk the further Westward advance of the Army of the Nile may be seriously cramped. It is quite clear to me that supporting Greece must have priority after the Western flank of Egypt has been made secure.

VI

14. The attitude of Yugoslavia may well be determined by the support we give to Greece and by their fortunes before Valona. While it is impossible to dogmatize, it would be more natural for the Germans to press on through Roumania to the Black Sea and to press down through their old ally Bulgaria to Salonika, rather than to force their way through Yugoslavia. Many troop movements and many more rumours would seem to point to this. Evidently there is a great building-up of German strength, and improvement of German communications towards the South-East. We must so act as to make it certain

that if the enemy enters Bulgaria, Turkey will come into the war. If Yugoslavia stands firm and is not molested, if the Greeks take Valona and maintain themselves in Albania, if Turkey becomes an active ally, the attitude of Russia may be affected favourably. Anyone can see how obnoxious and indeed deadly a German advance to the Black Sea or through Bulgaria to the Aegean must be to Russia. Fear only will restrain Russia from war, and perhaps a strong allied front in the Balkans with the growing prestige of the British Army and Sea and Air power may lessen that fear. But we must not count on this.

VII

15. Last, but dominating all our war effort, is the threat of Invasion, the Air warfare and its effects on production, and the grievous pressure upon our Western ports and North-Western communications. One cannot doubt that Herr Hitler's need to starve or crush Great Britain is stronger than it has ever been. A great campaign in the East of Europe, the defeat of Russia, the conquest of the Ukraine, and advance from the Black Sea to the Caspian, would none of them separately nor all together bring him victorious peace while the British Air power grew ever stronger behind him and he had to hold down a whole Continent of sullen, starving peoples. Therefore, the task of preventing Invasion, of feeding the island, and of speeding our armament production must in no way be compromised for the sake of any other objective whatsoever.

Winston S. Churchill to General Ismay
(*Churchill papers, 20/36*)

7 January 1941

This is all wrong.[1] If Japan goes to war with us there is not the slightest chance of holding Hong Kong or relieving it. It is most unwise to increase the loss we shall suffer there. Instead of increasing the Garrison it ought to be reduced to a symbolical scale. Any trouble arising there must be dealt with at the Peace Conference after the war. We must avoid frittering away our resources on untenable positions. Japan will think long before declaring war on the British Empire, and whether there are two or six battalions at Hong Kong will make no difference to her choice. I wish we had fewer troops there, but to move any would be noticeable and dangerous.

[1] Two weeks later Churchill received, in a sealed envelope, a list of the code names allotted to him, as Minister of Defence, by the Inter-Services Security Board. There were thirty-two names on the list, which Churchill was welcome to use at random for any future operation needing a code name. The fourth name on the list was 'Battleaxe'. ('Code Names Allotted to the Minister of Defence', 22 January 1941: *Cabinet Papers 120/413*). The code name 'Battleaxe' was eventually given to Wavell's offensive against Rommel in the Western Desert, launched on 15 June 1941.

Winston S. Churchill to General Ismay
(Cabinet papers, 120/413)

7 January 1941

CODE NAMES

I am glad to see that the matter is being organized so well. It is essential that there should be no book. Each section may have its own small circle, but only one list of the whole should be kept, and that in the office of the Minister of Defence. Whatever you do, do not let the official printing presses go and blether out these secrets, as they do so many others.

The subordinate class of names used for convoys, movements, warnings, &c., stand in a wholly different position from the comparatively small number of names used by the Supreme Command for special or considerable operations. You should assume the responsibility of classification and let me see it.[1]

Winston S. Churchill to Sir Archibald Sinclair
(Churchill papers, 20/36)

7 January 1941

1. I am very glad to hear of the approach of the American volunteers. This is a project I have long cherished and I cordially approve the response you propose to make.

2. For many reasons I am sorry about what you say in the first part of your paper.[2]

Winston S. Churchill to William Mackenzie King[3]
(Churchill papers, 20/49)

7 January 1941
Personal and Most Secret

I am as distressed as you are at indiscretions regarding M. Dupuy's mission.[4]

[1] Telegrams to the Air Ministry from the Commander-in-Chief, Far East, sent on 6 January 1941, about the Defence of Hong Kong.

[2] The shortage of advanced trainer aircraft.

[3] William Lyon Mackenzie King, 1874–1950. Born in Ontario. First entered the Canadian Government as Minister of Labour, Canada, 1909. Leader of the Liberal Party of Canada, 1919. Leader of the Opposition, 1919–21 and 1930–5. Prime Minister of Canada, 1921–30 and 1935–48. Secretary of State for External Affairs, 1935–46. Order of Merit, 1947.

[4] The leakage through Helen Kirkpatrick about Pierre Dupuy's mission to Vichy, see pages 2–3.

Careful enquiry has been instituted here, but it has been impossible to fix definite responsibility. Journalists are of course always careful to safeguard their sources, and we have been unable to obtain from the correspondent who sent the message a clear indication of the manner in which she obtained the news.

Her message should in any case have been referred to higher authority by the Censor, and I can only regret that he failed to do so.

The reason why I am approaching you in this matter is that I am most anxious that you should agree that M. Dupuy may return to Vichy to resume his mission, which is, I am sure, of the utmost value to our cause.

In proof of this I send you in my immediately following telegram for your personal and most secret information the text of a message which I have been able to send to Marshal Pétain, thanks to the contacts which M. Dupuy established during his visit to Vichy. I am anxious that this message should also reach General Weygand with the least possible delay, and I was therefore glad to learn from M. Dupuy that if he returned to Vichy he would propose to travel by way of North Africa. This would enable him to see General Weygand and to carry out a further piece of work for us, the importance of which I do not need to emphasise to you.

Winston S. Churchill to Geoffrey Dawson[1]
(*Churchill papers, 20/21*)

7 January 1941
Private

My dear Dawson,

I have been reading your leading article today and have been wondering what it all amounts to.[2] I wish you would let me know privately precisely what it is you think should be done. If you could give me a few short headings I would study them with attention.

Yours very sincerely,
Winston S. Churchill

[1] George Geoffrey Robinson, 1874–1944. Educated at Eton and Magdalen College, Oxford. Fellow of All Souls, 1896. Private Secretary to Milner in South Africa, 1901–5. Editor of the *Johannesburg Star*, 1905–10. Editor of *The Times*, 1912–19 and 1923–41. Took the surname Dawson, 1917.

[2] In a leading article entitled 'Unused Resources', commenting on the establishment of a Production Executive and an Import Executive to allocate priority of materials and 'animate and regulate' production and imports, *The Times* commented on 'a growing exasperation over what is felt to be the excessive dependence of Ministers upon appeals to the public in matters where they have, at their own request, been given power to take whatever action may be necessary. Worst of all the impression has been created that on the whole economic side of the war the Government are still fumbling without any comprehensive policy.'

Winston S. Churchill to A. V. Alexander
(*Churchill papers, 20/36*)

8 January 1941

It would seem that there should be a thorough purge of Naval Officers serving at the Admiralty. The lists which have been sent from your office show that over a quarter of the Active List Captains and Commanders are serving at the Admiralty in London or Bath. When the other Active List Officers holding shore appointments are added, it seems that a number within measurable distance of half of the Captains and Commanders on the Active List are ashore.

Taking Active and Retired Lists together, there are 545 Executive Officers in the Admiralty, including 30 Commanders in the Naval Intelligence Division alone. All told, the Naval Staff of this Division amounts to 77.

I have recently been calling for severe reductions in the rearward services for the army in the Middle East, very largely in order to ease the shipping situation. It is hardly fair to call for these reductions while such conditions prevail here in London.

I am told that officers fitted to take command of HM ships in war are in short supply. Naval Officers have received a very elaborate and lengthy training to fit them for this, their proper function. They ought only to be employed ashore where it can be shown that the need for their services at a desk is greater than the need for them afloat.

An examination was made by Admiral Kennedy-Purvis's[1] Committee when I was First Lord. But the figures which have now been furnished show clearly that another and far more drastic purge is required. It is not sufficient to consider whether each officer is fully employed. I am sure they all want to go to sea and that they are all working hard ashore. Work always tends to increase with the increase of staff.

I hope you will cope with this problem. The most direct way to reduce work is to make an arbitrary all-round cut in the staff of, say, 25 per cent., to be effective in six weeks' time. In the meantime, all appeals against this cut to be carefully examined by a competent committee in the light of the general considerations I have advanced above, and only admitted if good cause can be

[1] Charles Edward Kennedy-Purvis, –1946. Commanded the First Cruiser Squadron, Mediterranean Fleet, 1936–38. President of the Royal Naval College, Greenwich, and Vice-Admiral Commanding the Royal Naval War College, 1938–40. Knighted, 1939. Commander-in-Chief, America and West Indies, 1940–42. Deputy First Sea Lord, 1942–46.

shown. Care should, of course, be taken not to change key men and important Chiefs who have accumulated a mass of special knowledge. But this does not affect the main proposition.[1]

Winston S. Churchill to Anthony Eden
(*Churchill papers, 20/36*)

8 January 1941
5.40 p.m.
Action this Day

I have only this moment (5.40 pm) received the attached,[2] which you will see arrived here 5.20 pm on January 5. I should be so much obliged if you would have a special inquiry made into the causes of the delay. This is a message which particularly affected me. If it had not been for Mr. Bracken hearing through private sources of Mr Hopkins'[3] movements, I should not have been able to arrange for him and Commander Thompson[4] to go down and meet Mr Hopkins on his arrival, so that he may receive an invitation to spend Sunday night at Ditchley. It seems to me extraordinary that I should not receive this message for 48 hours after it came here.

[1] On 23 March 1941 Churchill minuted to A.V. Alexander: 'I am very sorry indeed to receive your answer to my minute of January 8 which tells me that after two and a half months' enquiry practically nothing can be done. Both the Air Ministry and the War Office have instituted severe combs of the younger combatant officers. I must press for further consideration to the request which I have made. Meanwhile, will you kindly have prepared for me a complete list of the employment of these officers in the different Departments, showing the numbers of each rank. Names are not necessary.'

[2] Telegram from the British Embassy in the United States, No. 49 (Departmental No. 2).

[3] Harry Hopkins, 1890–1946. Director of the (New Deal) Works Progress Administration, 1935–8; Secretary of Commerce, 1938–40; Administrator of Lend-Lease, 1941–45; President Roosevelt's closest aide, he lived at the White House when he was not on wartime missions to London or Moscow, or in hospital (in 1937 he underwent surgery for cancer of the stomach). Travelled to Moscow on a mission for President Truman, May 1945.

[4] Charles Ralfe Thompson, 1894–1966. Midshipman, 1911. Served mainly in submarines, 1915–31. Flag Lieutenant and Flag Commander to the Board of Admiralty, 1936–40. OBE, 1938. Retired with the rank of Commander, 1939. Personal Assistant to the Minister of Defence (Churchill), 1940–5. CMG, 1945. Known as 'Tommy' Thompson.

Defence Committee (Operations): minutes
(Cabinet papers, 69/2)

8 January 1941
9.30 p.m.
Secret

ASSISTANCE TO GREECE[1]

The Prime Minister said that all information pointed to an early advance by the German Army, which was massing in Roumania, with the object of invading Greece via Bulgaria. It seemed likely that the advance might start about 20th January, and would be carried out with a compact force of two Armoured Divisons backed up by about 200 dive bombers. The Bulgarians would connive at the German action. The Greek Army, which was fully engaged in Albania, would find itself in a hopeless position. The Russian attitude was unknown. A German advance was against her interests, as there was no doubt that the Germans' ultimate objective would be the oil at Baku. Russia would be much encouraged by Turkish resistance to Germany, and this in turn would depend upon the manner in which we could support the Greeks. They would be likely to see whether yet again one of our friends was to be trampled down without our being able to prevent their fate. It was true that the weather at this time of year did not favour an advance through Bulgaria, but the Norwegian campaign had shown that Germany was not deterred by snow; and just because we hoped that the Germans would put off their action until the Spring, it was all the more likely that they would act now. It might be that the help which we could bring to the Greeks in the time available would not be enough to save them. Nevertheless, there was no other course open to us but to make certain that we had spared no effort to help the Greeks, who had shown themselves so worthy.

Mr Eden emphasized the importance of our action in Greece as a deciding factor in the attitude of Turkey. Furthermore, the Greeks were a temperamental race, and we must do something to maintain their morale, which showed signs of sagging now that their advance had slowed down.

There was some discussion upon the effect of trying to help Greece on the

[1] Those present for this discussion, which gained its urgency from the Enigma decrypts of German Signals Intelligence, were all privy to the Enigma secret. They were: Churchill, Eden (Secretary of State for Foreign Affairs), A.V. Alexander (First Lord of the Admiralty), David Margesson (Secretary of State for War), Sir Archibald Sinclair (Secretary of State for Air), Sir Dudley Pound (First Sea Lord and Chief of the Naval Staff), General Sir John Dill (Chief of the Imperial General Staff), Air Chief Marshal Sir Charles Portal (Chief of the Air Staff) and Major General Sir Hastings Ismay (Office of the War Cabinet). The only member of the War Cabinet Secretariat present was Lieutenant-Colonel E.I.C. Jacob.

Egyptian campaign, and on the amount of help that we should subsequently be able to give to Turkey.

The Prime Minister said that the prosecution of the campaign in Libya must now take second place. We should naturally continue to advance if resistance was feeble, and if it could be overcome with the small forces now operating. From the political point of view, it was imperative to help the Greeks against the Germans, and a decision as to what could be done must be taken forthwith.

The Committee agreed:

(a) That in view of the probability of an early German advance into Greece through Bulgaria, it was of the first importance, from the political point of view, that we should do everything possible, by hook or by crook, to send at once to Greece the fullest support within our power.

(b) That a decision on the form and extent of our assistance should be taken within the next 48 hours at latest.

(c) That in the light of (a) and (b) above, the Chiefs of Staff should submit their recommendations as to the instructions to be sent to the Commanders-in-Chief, in time for them to be considered by the Defence Committee at a meeting which had been arranged for 9.30 pm on 9th January.

Winston S. Churchill: speech[1]

(*'The Times', 10 January 1941.*)

9 January 1941 — Pilgrims' Society Luncheon

It is no exaggeration to say that the future of the whole world and the hopes of a broadening civilization upon Christian ethics depend upon the relations between the British Empire or Commonwealth of Nations and the USA.

The identity of purpose and persistence of resolve prevailing throughout the English-speaking world will, more than any other single fact, determine the way of life which will be open to the generations, and perhaps to the centuries, which follow our own.

If the co-operation between the United States and the British Empire in the task of extirpating the spirit and regime of totalitarian intolerance, wherever it may be found, were to fail, the British Empire, rugged and embattled, might indeed hew its way through and preserve the life and strength of our own country and our own Empire for the inevitable renewal of the conflict on worse terms, after an uneasy truce.

[1] In honour of Lord Halifax, who was shortly to leave for the United States as British Ambassador, following the death of Lord Lothian.

But the chance of setting the march of mankind clearly and surely along the highroads of human progress would be lost and might never return.

Therefore we stand, all of us, upon the watch towers of history, and have offered to us the glory of making the supreme sacrifices and exertions needed by a cause which it may not be irrelevant to call sublime.

I have always taken the view that the fortunes of mankind in its tremendous journey are principally decided for good or ill – but mainly for good, for the path is upward – by its greatest men and its greatest episodes.

I therefore hail it as a most fortunate occurrence that at this awe-striking climax in world affairs there should stand at the head of the American Republic a famous statesman, long versed and experienced in the work of government and administration, in whose heart there burns the fire of resistance to aggression and oppression, and whose sympathies and nature make him the sincere and undoubted champion of justice and of freedom, and of the victims of wrongdoing wherever they may dwell.

And not less – for I may say it now that the party struggle in the United States is over – do I rejoice that this pre-eminent figure should newly have received the unprecedented honor of being called for the third time to lead the American democracies in days of stress and storm.

His Majesty's Government had placed in Washington an Ambassador, Lord Lothian,[1] whose character and qualities were outstanding and had gained him the trust and friendship of President Roosevelt. Suddenly and unexpectedly Lord Lothian was struck down by death.

A link was broken, a gap was opened, and a loss of the highest consequence was sustained at a very grave moment in the annals of the British and American peoples, and for those generous and wide causes which they have in their different ways and in their different situations so resolutely espoused.

We therefore thought it our duty to restore this link, to fill this gap, to repair this loss by sending without regard to the derangement of our forces and circle here, the best we could find, without regard to any other consideration whatsoever.

We chose our Foreign Secretary,[2] who had himself chosen Lord Lothian, to

[1] Philip Henry Kerr, 1882–1940. Educated at the Oratory School, Birmingham and New College, Oxford. Worked as a civil servant in South Africa, 1905–8. Editor, *The Round Table*, 1910–16. Secretary to Lloyd George, 1916–21. Secretary of the Rhodes Trust, 1925–39. Succeeded his cousin as 11th Marquess of Lothian, 1930. Chancellor of the Duchy of Lancaster, 1931. Chairman of the Indian Franchise Committee, 1932. Ambassador in Washington from 1939 until his death.

[2] Edward Frederick Lindley Wood, 1881–1959. Educated at Eton and Christ Church, Oxford. Conservative MP for Ripon, 1910–25. Parliamentary Under-Secretary of State for the Colonies, 1921–2. President of the Board of Education, 1922–4. Minister of Agriculture, 1924–5. Created Baron Irwin, 1925. Viceroy of India, 1926–31. President of the Board of Education, 1931–4. Succeeded his father as 3rd Viscount Halifax, 1934. Secretary of State for War, 1935. Lord Privy Seal, 1935–7. Lord President of the Council, 1937–8. Foreign Secretary, 1938–40. Ambassador in Washington, 1941–6. Order of Merit, 1946. One of his three sons was killed in action in Egypt in October 1942.

fill Lord Lothian's place. Our choice was most agreeable to the President, and it commands the full confidence of nearly all of those in this country who mean to persevere in our righteous cause until its certain victorious end is reached.

In Edward Halifax we have a man of light and leading, whose company is a treat and whose friendship it is an honour to enjoy.

I have often disagreed with him in the twenty years I have known him in the rough and tumble of British politics, but I have always respected him and his actions, because I know that courage and fidelity are the essence of his being, and that, whether as a soldier with his regiment in the last war, or as the ruler of, and trustee for, four hundred millions in India, he has never swerved from the path of duty as he saw it shining out before him.

As a man of deep but unparaded and unaffected religious convictions, and as for many years an ardent lover of the chase, he has known how to get the best out of both worlds.

Like all members of the present National Government in Great Britain, most of whom seem to be gathered around this board today, he has vowed himself to prosecute this war against the Nazi tyranny at whatever cost until its last vestiges are destroyed.

We send the United States an envoy who comes from the very centre of our counsels and knows all our secrets.

Although, while Lord Halifax is serving as Ambassador out of this country he cannot be a member of the War Cabinet, he will be, if I may borrow a military term not wholly inappropriate to the times in which we live, as it were seconded from it.

He still attends all our meetings, and will continue to do so during the weeks before his departure, and should he be able to return here for consultation at any time in the summer, as I hope may be possible, he will resume his full functions and responsibilities as a Minister of the Crown.

We now bid him, and his brilliant and devoted wife,[1] God-speed and all good fortune, and it is our fervent hope that he may prosper in a mission as momentous as any that the Monarchy has entrusted to an Englishman in the lifetime of the oldest of us here.

[1] Lady Dorothy Onslow, daughter of the 4th Earl of Onslow. She married Lord Halifax in 1909.

John Colville: diary
(*Colville papers*)

9 January 1941

I was at No. 10 from 4 p.m. till dinner-time, the main preoccupation being with General de Gaulle,[1] since it has now been discovered that the documents incriminating Admiral Muselier were false and had been forged by two disgruntled officers of the Free French forces. The PM was greatly pleased because De Gaulle 'behaved like a Gentleman', was not at all cantankerous about the episode, and said that his only interest was to see that honour and justice were satisfied.

James Stuart[2] came to No. 10 and was offered, and accepted, the post of Chief Whip.

Defence Committee (Operations): minutes
(*Cabinet papers, 69/2*)

9 January 1941 Cabinet War Room
9.45 p.m.
Secret

The general conclusions of the discussion were as follows:

(i) The first priority should be accorded to the capture of Tobruk. After that operations in Libya should be limited to what can be done without great loss, and without engaging appreciable numbers of fresh troops. The operation against Kassala should be pushed ahead as rapidly as possible. The proposed telegram to Commanders-in-Chief should be amended to make this policy clear.

(ii) After Tobruk had been dealt with, assistance to Greece would assume first priority. Decisions as to the form this should take would have to await the

[1] Charles de Gaulle, 1890–1970. On active service on the Western Front, 1914–16 (three times wounded, mentioned in despatches). Prisoner of war, 1916–18 (he made five attempts to escape). An advocate between the wars of armoured divisions as an essential part of warfare. Commanded the 4th Armoured Brigade, 5th Army, September 1939; the 4th Armoured Division, May 1940. Under-Secretary for War and National Defence, 6 June 1940. Chief of the Free French (later President of the French National Committee), London and Brazzaville, 1940–2. President of the French Committee of National Liberation, Algiers, 1943. President of the Provisional Government of the French Republic, and head of its armed forces, November 1943 to January 1946. Prime Minister, June 1958 to January 1959. President, December 1958 to June 1969.

[2] James Gray Stuart, 1897–1971. Third son of the 17th Earl of Moray. Educated at Eton. On active service, 1914–18 (Military Cross and bar). Conservative MP for Moray and Nairn, 1923–59. Entered the Whips' Office, 1935; Deputy Chief Whip, 1938–41; Government Chief Whip, 1941–5; Chief Opposition Whip 1945–8. Privy Councillor, 1939. Secretary of State for Scotland, 1951–7. Created Viscount Stuart of Findhorn, 1959.

receipt of the advice which would be given by the Commanders-in-Chief after they had received the Chiefs' of Staff telegram, and had conferred with General Metaxas[1].

(iii) In principle, the better class aircraft should be employed in Greece against the Germans, leaving the less modern to deal with the Italians.

(iv) Every effort should be made to pass the 34 'I' tanks, which had lagged from Convoy WS 5, through the Mediterranean to Greece during February.

(v) It would be advisable to tell the Turks in general terms that we were disposed to give considerable assistance to the Greeks in the event of a German attack, which appeared imminent, and that their support would be of great value, and would have a favourable effect on Russia. They should exert their influence to stimulate the Yugoslavs to adopt a firm attitude in the face of German threats. HM Ambassadors in Greece and Yugoslavia[2] should also be informed of the objects of the proposed visit of the Commanders-in-Chief to Athens.

Winston S. Churchill to Anthony Eden
(*Churchill papers, 20/36*)

9 January 1941

I have read both these papers.[3] The Greek Minister's request should, of course, go to the Chiefs of Staff. Major Morton minutes that General Wavell has been authorized on the recommendation of the Chiefs of Staff and of his Committee to enter into negotiations immediately for the purchase from Syria through Turkey of 1,000 motor lorries. Wavell should certainly send more of the captured Italian lorries.

If you will let me know when Mittelman[4] is to go back to Africa I will certainly give him a letter to Weygand. Meanwhile, it is most important that a copy of my telegram to Pétain should reach Weygand by any channel, and not necessarily wait for Mittelman to deliver it.

[1] Yanni Mextaxas, 1870–1941. Fought in the Greek Army against the Turks, 1897. Chief of the General Staff, 1913. A rival and opponent of Venizelos, he was against the entry of Greece into the war, on the side of Britain and France, in 1915. Formed the Party of Free Opinion, 1923. Deputy Prime Minister, 1935. Prime Minister, 1936, at the head of a Cabinet of ex-army officers and non-politicians. Ruled Greece as an autocrat from 1936 until his death.

[2] Sir Michael Palairet (in Greece) and Sir Ronald Campbell (in Yugoslavia).

[3] Accounts of Anthony Eden's interviews with the Greek Minister to London on 7 January 1941 (Greece's appeal for lorries), and Operation 'Lancelot' the visit of a senior Vichy officer, Colonel Mittelman, to London.

[4] Colonel Mittelman, codename 'Lancelot', who had come from Weygand's headquarters in Algiers.

Defence Committee (Operations): minutes
(*Cabinet papers, 69/2*)

10 January 1941
10.30 a.m.
Secret

INVASION

The Prime Minister asked what action was proposed should the Germans succeed in making a lodgement in East Anglia and attempt to bring across supply ships, under cover of their heavy Naval forces?

Sir Charles Portal suggested that the best way of dealing with this threat would be to attack the roots of the lodgement with our bombers and sink the store ships while they were unloading.

Admiral Phillips[1] said that it was not proposed to order the Home Fleet South of the Tyne unless Hitler threw in his own heavy forces in an effort to obtain temporary mastery of the narrow seas. The Fleet would not be ordered South for a feint by the German Navy. The minefield off the East Coast would give some protection against sporadic German Naval activity in this area although a gap some 15 miles broad had been left for the operations of the Nore Command.

Sir Reginald Drax[2] doubted the effectiveness of this Eastern mine-barrier, which had been reduced in extent by wastage in spite of recent attempts to thicken it. The gap had been necessary earlier in the war but was now of much less value.

The Prime Minister thought that the employment of the Home Fleet in narrow waters should be further considered by the Naval Staff. It could not be laid down that our modern capital ships would in no circumstances be required to operate in the narrow seas, but we must be wary of German tactics designed to draw our heavy ships into these perilous waters. The Naval Staff should also consider whether it was desirable to close the gap in the Eastern minefield.

[1] Tom Spencer Vaughan Phillips, 1888–1941. Entered the Royal Navy, 1903. Director of Plans, Admiralty, 1935–8. Commodore Commanding the Home Fleet Destroyer Flotillas, 1938–9. Rear-Admiral, 1939. Vice-Chief of the Naval Staff, 1939–41. Knighted, 1941. Commander-in-Chief of the Eastern Fleet, 1941. Drowned when his flagship, the *Prince of Wales*, was sunk by Japanese torpedo bombers on 10 December 1941.

[2] Reginald Aylmer Plunkett-Ernle-Erle-Drax, 1880–1967. Entered the Royal Navy, 1896. Present at the Battles of Heligoland Bright, Dogger Bank and Jutland, 1914–16 (despatches). DSO, 1918. Commander-in-Chief, America and West Indies Station, 1932–4. Knighted, 1934. Commander-in-Chief, Plymouth, 1935–8. Admiral, 1936. Commander-in-Chief, The Nore, 1939–41. Commodore of Ocean Convoys, 1943–5.

Sir Charles Forbes[1] thought that the chances of invasion being successful were so remote and the consequences of failure were likely to be so serious for Hitler that we should do all we could to persuade the Germans to attempt invasion. He suggested that the Prime Minister should cease to warn the public of these dangers and should try to give the impression that we were living in a fool's paradise.

The Prime Minister agreed that we should almost certainly exact a heavy penalty from the Germans should they attempt to invade this island, but an attitude of undue confidence might court disaster. Home Forces were keyed up to a pitch of efficiency by a realisation of the danger and any relaxation of our precautions would affect the morale of the Army as well as inducing a dangerous relaxation throughout the country as a whole.

HOME DEFENCE

Sir Alan Brooke[2] said that the events of the last few months appeared to have had the following effect on Home Defence:-

(i) The series of reverses suffered by Italy at sea, on land and in the air, had reduced the scope of enemy offensive operations in Africa and in the Mediterranean; the danger of invasion had therefore increased.

(ii) Recent operations by the Germans against our sea communications, ports and armament industry had exercised a direct bearing on the power of this country to resist invasion, since Naval forces had been withdrawn from an anti-invasion role and the army re-equipment programme had been delayed.

(iii) The withdrawal of formations for despatch overseas had repercussions on the efficiency of our defences, as all reinforcements for other theatres were made up in equipment prior to departure at the expense of other units and formations of Home Forces.

Continuing, Sir Alan Brooke emphasized the continued shortage of equipment, weapons and ammunition and quoted figures of the more important deficiencies. Shortage of ammunition had a serious effect on training and large numbers of troops had had no practice with tracer ammunition nor with the anti-tank rifle . . .

In conclusion, Sir Alan Brooke suggested that the man power situation

[1] Charles Morton Forbes, 1880–1960. Entered the Royal Navy, 1894. Served at Jutland, 1916 (DSO). Director of Naval Ordnance, 1925–8. Third Sea Lord and Controller of the Navy, 1932–4. Vice-Admiral, 1st Battle Squadron, 1934–6. Knighted, 1935. Commander-in-Chief, Home Fleet, 1938–40; Plymouth, 1941–3.

[2] Alan Francis Brooke, 1883–1963. Entered the Army, 1902. On active service, 1914–18 (DSO and bar, despatches six times). General Officer Commanding-in-Chief, Anti-Aircraft Command, 1939. Commanded the 2nd Army Corps, British Expeditionary Force, 1939–40. Knighted, 1940. General Officer Commanding-in-Chief, Home Forces, 1940–1. Chief of the Imperial General Staff, 1941–6. Field Marshal, 1944. Created Baron, 1945; Viscount Alanbrooke, 1946. Order of Merit, 1946. Master Gunner, St James's Park, 1946–56. His statue in Whitehall was unveiled by the Queen in 1993.

should be reviewed and that the allotment of equipment to Home Forces should be increased from the present figure of 40 per cent.

The Prime Minister said that a shortage of ships imposed a check on the rate at which we could despatch reinforcements overseas. The programme of sending 1 Division per month could not now be adhered to. The man power situation was already under review but the Commander-in-Chief, Home Forces, would do well to scrutinize his rearward Services and make all possible economies. A constant watch was maintained on the equipment and ammunition situation, particularly small arms ammunition, and energetic measures were being taken to accelerate production. The present bottle-neck in artillery ammunition was the rate of filling shells and fuzes.

DEFENCE OF THE DOVER PROMONTORY

Sir Bertram Ramsay[1] said that there had been delays in the programme for installing coast defence equipments in the Dover area, and some of the 6-inch equipments already installed could not yet operate through lack of the necessary fire control apparatus. Some of the 9.2-inch equipments which had been expected, had been diverted elsewhere.

The Prime Minister stressed the importance of completing the coast defences of the Dover area as soon as possible, and directed that Weekly Progress Reports should be prepared and submitted to him. The diversion of 9.2-inch equipments from Dover to Freetown had been ordered as a counter measure against the possibility of betrayal to Germany of the powerful units of the French Fleet.

BOMBER COMMAND

The Prime Minister said that he had been much concerned by the slow rate of expansion of our Bomber Force, and had under examination a series of proposals for speeding it up.

ORKNEYS AND SHETLANDS

The Prime Minister said that he hoped to visit Scapa some time in the near future and see for himself the improvements in the defences. He hoped that full use was being made of the VLA balloon.[2]

[1] Bertram Home Ramsay, 1883–1945. Entered the Royal Navy, 1898; commanded Monitor 25, Dover Patrol, 1915; HMA *Broke*, 1916–18. Chief of Staff, China Station, 1929–31. On the Staff of the Imperial Defence College, 1931–33. Commanded HMS *Royal Sovereign*, 1933–5. Rear-Admiral and Chief of Staff, Home Fleet, 1935. Retired, 1938. Recalled, 1939. Flag Officer, Dover, 1939–42. Knighted, 1940. Naval Commander, Eastern Task Force, Mediterranean, 1943. Allied Naval Commander-in-Chief, Expeditionary Force, 1944–5. Killed in an aeroplane accident in France, January 1945. His 'finest hour' was as the naval officer in command of 'Operation Dynamo', the evacuation of the Dunkirk beachhead, in June 1940.

[2] Very Large Array barrage balloons which, under the War Office's Q Plan of 1939, formed part of the integrated defences at Scapa Flow (in conjunction with heavy and light anti-aircraft guns, and searchlights). In 1941 the eighty-one balloons in the barrage at that time, double the number in 1939, became 960 Squadron.

NAVAL REPAIRS

The First Lord of the Admiralty said that the Supply Departments were pressing for a diversion of skilled labour from naval repair and modification work to the repair of merchant vessels.

The Prime Minister said that if more men were required for the repair of merchant ships they should be taken off new merchant ship construction and not from naval repair and modification work.

Winston S. Churchill: recollection
(*'War Memoirs', Volume 3, pages 20-1*)

[10 January 1941]

On January 10 a gentleman arrived to see me at Downing Street with the highest credentials. Telegrams had been received from Washington stating that he was the closest confidant and personal agent of the President. I therefore arranged that he should be met by Mr Brendan Bracken on his arrival at Poole Airport, and that we should lunch together alone the next day. Thus I met Harry Hopkins, that extraordinary man, who played, and was to play, a sometimes decisive part in the whole movement of the war. His was a soul that flamed out of a frail and failing body. He was a crumbling lighthouse from which there shone the beams that led great fleets to harbour. He had also a gift of sardonic humour. I always enjoyed his company, especially when things went ill. He could also be very disagreeable and say hard and sour things. My experiences were teaching me to be able to do this too, if need be.

At our first meeting we were about three hours together, and I soon comprehended his personal dynamism and the outstanding importance of his mission. This was the height of the London bombing, and many local worries imposed themselves upon us. But it was evident to me that here was an envoy from the President of supreme importance to our life. With gleaming eye and quiet, constrained passion he said:

'The President is determined that we shall win the war together. Make no mistake about it.

'He has sent me here to tell you that at all costs and by all means he will carry you through, no matter what happens to him – there is nothing that he will not do so far as he has human power.'

Harry Hopkins to President Franklin D. Roosevelt
(*'The White House Papers of Harry L. Hopkins'*)

10 January 1941

Number 10 Downing St is a bit down at the heels because the Treasury next door has been bombed more than a bit. The Prime Minister is no longer permitted to sleep here and I understand sleeps across the street. He told me they are building a real shelter for him so that he can sleep in peace nearby. Everyone tells me that he works fifteen hours a day and I can well believe it. His man Friday – Brendan Bracken – met me at the door – showed me about the old and delightful house that has been home of Prime Ministers of the Empire for two hundred years. Most of the windows are out – workmen over the place repairing the damage – Churchill told me it wouldn't stand a healthy bomb.

Bracken led me to a little dining-room in the basement – poured me some sherry and left me to wait for the Prime Minster. A rotund – smiling – red-faced gentleman appeared – extended a fat but none the less convincing hand and wished me welcome to England. A short black coat – striped trousers – a clear eye and a mushy voice was the impression of England's leader as he showed me with obvious pride the photographs of his beautiful daughter-in-law and grandchild.[1]

The lunch was simple but good – served by a very plain woman who seemed to be an old family servant. Soup – cold beef – (I didn't take enough jelly to suit the PM and he gave me some more) – green salad – cheese and coffee – a light wine and port. He took snuff from a little silver box – he liked it.

I told him the President was anxious to see him in April – he expressed regret that Bermuda would not be the place – the climate was nice – he would bring a small staff – go on a cruiser and by accident meet the President at the appointed place – and discuss our problems at leisure. He talked of remaining as long as two weeks and seemed very anxious to meet the President face to face. We discussed the difficulty of communication with the President at long range – there is no question but that he wants to meet the President – the sooner the better.

I told him there was a feeling in some quarters that he, Churchill, did not like America, Americans or Roosevelt. This set him off on a bitter though fairly constrained attack on Ambassador Kennedy,[2] whom he believes is

[1] Pamela Churchill and Winston Churchill (later a Conservative Member of Parliament).

[2] Joseph Patrick Kennedy, 1888–1969. Born in Boston. Graduated from Harvard, 1912. Assistant General Manager, Fore River Plant, Bethlehem Shipbuilding Corporation, 1917–19. Investment banker. Chairman of the Securities Exchange Commission, 1934–5 and of the US Maritime Commission, 1937. Ambassador to London, 1937–41. Of his four sons, Joseph was killed in action in 1944; John (President of the United States) was assassinated in 1963; and Robert (a Senator) was assassinated in 1968.

responsible for this impression. He denied it vigorously – sent for a secretary to show me a telegram which he had sent to the President immediately after his election in which he expressed his warm delight at the President's re-election.

I told of my mission – he seemed pleased – and several times assured me that he would make every detail of information and opinion available to me and hoped that I would not leave England until I was fully satisfied of the exact state of England's need and the urgent necessity of the exact material assistance Britain requires to win the war.

He reviewed with obvious pride his own part in the war to date – he didn't *know* that England could withstand the onslaught after France fell – but he felt sure that it could – it did – and it will withstand the next one – he thinks the invasion will not come, but if they gain a foothold in England with 100,000 men 'we shall drive them out' – beside its excellent coast defences Britain has twenty-five well-trained and equipped divisions – trained only in offensive warfare which will drive Germany's army into the sea. Germany cannot invade Britain successfully. He thinks Hitler may use poison gas, but if they do England will reply in kind killing man for man – 'for we too have the deadliest gases in the world' – but under no circumstances will they be used unless the Germans release gas first. He said he believed Hitler would not strike at Spain now, because the population is starving and Hitler does not want sullen people around his armies – he has enough of that already – but the spring might tell a different story – and left me the impression that Spain would be overrun in the spring.

He thinks Greece is lost – although he is now reinforcing the Greeks – and weakening his African Army – he believes Hitler will permit Mussolini to go only so far downhill – and is 'now preparing for the attack which must bring its inevitable result.' He knows this will be a blow to British prestige and is obviously considering ways and means of preparing the British public for it. He realizes it will have a profound and disappointing effect in America as well. Churchill, too, thinks Turkey will stay put and probably be in the war when Germany moves through Bulgaria. This Churchill thinks will be the route.

This debacle in Greece will be overcome in part by what he considers to be the sure defeat of the Italians in Africa. He feels England can bring great military pressure on Italy – and fully intends to – Britain will control the Mediterranean and the Suez against Germany. He has offered Weygand six divisions – if the former strikes – he is in close touch with Pétain on this point – he spoke with no great assurance about it – but it is clear Churchill intends to hold Africa – clean out the Italians and cooperate with Weygand if the opportunity permits. He expressed the hope that we would not go too far in feeding any of the dominated countries. He feels that tough as it is that one of Hitler's great weaknesses is to be in control of territory inhabited by a dejected and despairing people.

Churchill said that while Germany's bombers were at the ratio of 2½ to 1 at the present time – that would be soon reduced to 1½ to 1 – and then he felt they could hold their own in the air – indeed, he looks forward with our help to mastery in the air and then Germany with all her armies will be finished. He believes that this war will never see great forces massed against one another.

He took me up to the Cabinet Room, where there was 'a better fire' – and showed me on the map where the convoys are coming through to Liverpool and Glasgow – and of the route the German bombers are taking from France to Norway to intercept the ships.

John Colville: diary

(*Colville papers*)

10 January 1941

The President's envoy, Mr Hopkins, was lunching with the PM and they were so greatly impressed with each other that their tête-à-tête did not break up till nearly 4. Then we left for Ditchley (the moon is full and Chequers an obvious target) . . .

Before dinner we drank and thawed while Winston pointed out, in reply to Mrs Tree,[1] that Wavell had done very well but that the Italians were the sort of enemy against whom any general should be only too happy to be matched!

Dinner was an exquisite meal at which I sat next to Mrs Tree. Afterwards Winston smoked the biggest cigar in history and became very mellow. There was an interlude in which I talked to the exceptionally pleasant Dinah,[2] after which Winston retired to bed with a very full box and in an excellent temper while I whiled away the time arranging the box in my beautiful working room below.

After the drafting of a long and intricate telegram to Wavell, for consideration by the Chiefs of Staff, we went to bed at about 1.30. The point of the telegram was that in view of the imminence of a German attack in the Balkans we must relax our effort in Libya, once Tobruk has fallen, and divert a part of our forces to the aid of Greece. The army authorities in the Middle East are in despair at this; they believe the Balkan threat is only a bluff.

Tobruk is proving a tougher nut to crack than we had supposed. It may take a week, the PM says.

[1] Nancy Parkins of Richmond, Virginia; a niece of Nancy Astor, and widow of Henry Field of Chicago. She married Ronald Tree in 1920. Their marriage was dissolved in 1947. She later married again, becoming Nancy Lancaster.

[2] Dinah Brand, born 1920. Daughter of Robert (later Baron Brand). Economist and Treasury adviser. In 1943 she married Lyttelton Fox, and in 1953 Christopher Bridge.

Winston S. Churchill to David Margesson and General Sir John Dill
(*Churchill papers, 20/36*)

11 January 1941

I should be glad if you would convey to Sir Alan Brooke my feeling that his contribution yesterday did not seem to be at the level of the discussion. Merely to bring a list of shortfalls in equipment from the establishment scale, all of which deficiencies he knows I am well aware of from the diagrams which are made for me, was not very illuminating. One would have hoped he would also have stated something about how he proposed to use the mobile force of 25 Divisions and about 2,000 guns with its immense mass of new equipment in offensive counter-attack should any lodgment be made upon these shores. At the very least he should have acknowledged the substantial weekly improvement made in the equipment of his growing Command. He might also have mentioned the great improvement in training, the extremely high quality of the new beach brigades, the doubling of the practice ammunition, and the steady inculcation of the offensive spirit upon which he is so rightly engaged. I do not think the picture he gave to the other Commanders-in-Chief represented either the actual position or its great improvement.

Winston S. Churchill to the Import Executive, and Sir Andrew Duncan
(*Churchill papers, 20/36*)

11 January 1941

Mr Hopkins spoke to me about the President being told that we had a great mass of shipping plying between non-British ports, and also foreign shipping, and unless he had the means to answer this there was an obstacle to America making exertions with her own shipping. The Ministry of Shipping have been very sticky about this and no doubt the vested interests of various shipping companies clog their action. We must be able to show that we are doing our best, both for the sake of the direct advantage and to procure the largest American assistance.

Mr Hopkins said that the condition that the Americans should guarantee not to operate on such routes after the war would be an obstacle to the President, whereas in fact no such condition was needed as the US could not possibly live against our competition on such routes in practice.

Winston S. Churchill to Anthony Eden
(*Churchill papers, 20/36*)

11 January 1941

You spoke to me the other day about the length of telegrams. I feel that this is an evil which ought to be checked. Ministers and Ambassadors abroad seem to think that the bigger the volume of their reports home the better is their task discharged. All kinds of gossip and rumours are sent regardless of credibility. The idea seems to be to keep up a continued chat which no one ever tries to shorten. I suggest that you should issue a general injunction, but that in addition telegrams which are unduly verbose or trivial should be criticized as such, and their authors told 'this telegram was needlessly long.' It is sheer laziness not compressing thought into a reasonable space. I try to read all these telegrams, and I think the volume grows from day to day. Please let me know what you think can be done.

Winston S. Churchill to John Moore-Brabazon[1]
(*Churchill papers, 20/36*)

11 January 1941

I very much regret to learn that your recommendations for awards for gallantry during the September raids on the London docks have only now, January 7, reached Lord Chatfield.[2] It is most unfortunate that this long delay should have intervened, obstructing the distribution of the George Medal, to which so much importance attaches. Will you kindly convey my regrets to those responsible, and will you let me know what measures will be taken in future to prevent any such breakdown occurring again.

[1] John Theodore Cuthbert Moore-Brabazon, 1884–1964. Educated at Harrow and Trinity College, Cambridge. Pioneer motorist and aviator; holder of pilot's Certificate No. 1. Won the *Daily Mail* £1,000 for flying a circular mile, 1909. Lieutenant-Colonel in charge of the Royal Flying Corps Photographic Section, 1914–18 (Military Cross, despatches thrice). Conservative MP for Chatham, 1918–29; for Wallasey, 1931–42. Chairman, Air Mails Committee, 1923. Elected to the Other Club, 1936. Parliamentary Private Secretary to the Lord Privy Seal, 1939–40. Minister of Transport, 1940–1. Minister of Aircraft Production, 1941–2. Created Baron, 1942. He published *The Brabazon Story* in 1956.

[2] Alfred Ernie Montacute Chatfield, 1873–1967. Entered Navy, 1886. Served at the battles of Heligoland (1914), Dogger Bank (1915) and Jutland (1916). Fourth Sea Lord, 1919–20. Knighted, 1919. Rear-Admiral, 1920. Assistant Chief of the Naval Staff, 1920–2. Third Sea Lord, 1925–8. Commander-in-Chief, Atlantic Fleet, 1929–31. Vice-Admiral, 1930. Commander-in-Chief, Mediterranean, 1931–2. First Sea Lord, January 1933 to September 1938. Admiral of the Fleet, 1935. Created Baron, 1937. Privy Councillor, 1939. Minister for Co-ordination of Defence, 1939–40 (with a seat in the War Cabinet). Chairman, Civil Defence Honours Committee, 1940–6. Author of *The Navy and Defence* (1942), and *It Might Happen Again* (1947). In 1937 he was elected to the Other Club.

Winston S. Churchill to David Margesson
(*Churchill papers, 20/36*)

11 January 1941

Today's article in the *Daily Mirror* seems to me to be intended to obstruct the National Defence, and you should not hesitate if you think it necessary to bring it before the Cabinet.[1]

Winston S. Churchill to President Franklin D. Roosevelt
(*Churchill papers, 20/49*)

11 January 1941

You will doubtless have been informed by State Department of the delivery to Marshal Pétain of a personal message which I sent the latter.

It seems, from the report on this subject of your Chargé d'Affaires in Vichy, that the Marshal may not have realized that the message was one from myself and that it involved considerably more than a suggestion of assistance in the event of the French Government deciding to cross to North Africa. The Marshal was no doubt too much embarrassed by the presence of M Flandin[2] to give as much attention to it as he might otherwise have done.

Would you think it possible and desirable to instruct your Ambassador at Vichy to convey again the substance of the message to the Marshal if he gains the impression that the latter had not grasped its full import, and make it quite clear to him that the message came from myself? I do not want to press Marshal Pétain to cross to North Africa; I would not press him for any further answer: I only want to be sure that there has been no misunderstanding and that the Marshal should be fully aware of the nature and origin of the message.

[1] A leading article headed 'More Men!' in the *Daily Mirror* of 11 January 1941 began: 'The old cry of massacring Brass Hats in the last war! "More men" for the trenches and for slaughter. Do we still hear the banshee bellowing? Today men in the highest age group at present conscripted for military service are to register. These are the "36's".' The article continued 'This incessant call-up is also disquieting because it appears to be indiscriminate . . . To take only one instance. Can the government seriously propose to comb out more agricultural workers – men whose labour saves shipping space and helps us to beat the threat of Hitler's blockade? Are we to sacrifice the vital need for food supplies to this military mania for clapping men into battle dress?'

[2] Pierre Etienne Flandin, 1889–1958. Chef de Cabinet to the Prime Minister (Millerand), 1913–14. Entered the Chamber of Deputies, 1914. Director of the Allied Aeronautical Service, 1917. Under-Secretary for Air, 1920. President of the First International Conference on Aerial Navigation, 1921. Minister for Commerce, June 1924. November 1929 and March 1930. After 1930 he suffered constant pain from a broken arm which never properly healed. Minister for Finance, 1931 and 1932. Leader of the Right Centre group of Deputies, 1932. Prime Minister, November 1934–June 1935. Minister for Foreign Affairs, January–June 1936. After his visit to Germany in 1937, Blum's Government issued a communiqué declaring that he went as a private individual only. Arrested by the Allies in North Africa, 1943. Tried by the French Government, 1946, but acquitted of the charge of collaboration with the Germans (Randolph Churchill spoke in Flandin's defence at the trial, on his father's behalf). Following the trial Flandin was declared ineligible for Parliament.

Winston S. Churchill to General Wavell and Air Chief Marshal Longmore
(*Churchill papers, 20/49*)

11 January 1941

Our information contradicts idea that German concentration in Roumania is merely 'move in war of nerves' or 'bluff to cause dispersion of force.' We have a mass of detail showing continual passage of troops to Roumania, selection and occupation of aerodromes in Roumania, movements of Signals and other advance agents into Bulgaria, and that a large-scale movement may begin on or soon after 20th March. Most probable subsequent development is early establishment of armoured force and strong air force in Bulgaria, followed by rapid advance aiming at Salonika.[1] Hostile forces to be employed in aforesaid invasion would not be large but of deadly quality. One, perhaps two, Armoured Divisions with probably two Mountain Divisions, over 100 dive-bombers supported by fighters and some parachute troops, seem to be all that could cross the Bulgarian-Greek frontier up till the middle of February.

2. But this force, if not stopped, may play exactly the same part in Greece as German army's break-through on the Meuse played in France. All Greek divisions in Albania will be fatally affected. These are the facts and implications which arise from our information in which we have good reason to believe. And is this not also the very thing the Germans ought to do to harm us most? Destruction of Greece will eclipse victories you have gained in Libya and might affect decisively Turkish attitude, especially if we had shown ourselves callous of fate of Allies. You must now therefore conform your plans to larger interests at stake.

3. Nothing must hamper capture of Tobruk, but thereafter all operations in Libya are subordinated to aiding Greece, and all preparations must be made from the receipt of this telegram for the immediate succour of Greece up to the limits prescribed by CAS and CIGS.[2] These matters have been earnestly weighed by Defence Committee of Cabinet and General Smuts[3] has independently cabled almost identic views.

[1] Daily Enigma decrypts gave a series of clues to the German plan. A crucial Enigma decrypt on January 9 gave the news that German Air Force personnel were moving into Bulgaria to lay down telephone and teleprinter lines to the Bulgarian-Greek border along the main axis of advance towards Salonika. (F.H. Hinsley and others, *British Intelligence in the Second World War, Its Influence on Strategy and Operations*, Volume l, London, 1979, page 353.)

[2] The Chief of the Air Staff, Air Chief Marshal Sir Charles Portal, and the Chief of the Imperial General Staff, General Sir Charles Dill.

[3] Jan Christian Smuts, 1870–1950. Born in Cape Colony. General, commanding Boer Commando Forces, Cape Colony, 1901. Colonial Secretary, Transvaal, 1907. Minister of Defence, Union of South Africa, 1910–20. Second-in-Command of the South African forces that defeated the Germans in South-West Africa, July 1915. Honorary Lieutenant-General commanding the Imperial forces in East Africa, 1916–17. South African Representative at the Imperial War Cabinet, 1917 and 1918. Prime Minister of South Africa, 1919–24. Minister of Justice, 1933–9. Prime Minister, 1939–48. Field-Marshal, 1941. OM, 1947. In 1917 he was made an honorary member of the Other Club. One of Churchill's last public speeches was at the unveiling of Smuts' statue in Parliament Square in 1956.

4. We expect and require prompt and active compliance with our decisions, for which we bear full responsibility. Your joint visit to Athens will enable you to contrive the best method of giving effect to the above decisions. It should not be delayed.

John Colville: diary
(*Colville papers*)

11 January 1941 Ditchley

Very annoyed at being disturbed early by the PM.

He is delighted by the new American bill to assist us, which allows British warships the use of American ports and contains wide powers for the President in every sphere of assistance to us. He says this is tantamount to a declaration of war by the United States. At any rate it is an open challenge to Germany to declare war if she dares. In view of this bill it will be more difficult for us to resist the American tendency – which Kingsley Wood lamented to me yesterday – to strip us of everything we possess in payment for what we are about to receive.

. . . Mr Hopkins arrived with Tommy Thompson and his quiet charm and dignity held the table. He said that the new Presidential bill would arouse loud controversy, but he felt sure it would succeed. He told us of the Duke of Windsor's[1] recent visit to the President on his yacht when the former spoke very charmingly of the King (a fact which touched Winston), and he said that the Duke's entourage was very bad. Moreover HRH's recent yachting trip with a violently pro-Nazi Swede[2] did not create a very good impression. It was the astounding success of the King and Queen's visit to the US which had made America give up its partizanship of the Windsors.

[1] Edward Albert Christian George Andrew Patrick David, 1894–1972. Entered the Royal Navy as a Cadet, 1907. Prince of Wales, 1910–36. 2nd Lieutenant, Grenadier Guards, August 1914. Attached to Sir John French's Staff, November 1914. Served in France and Italy, 1914–18. Major, 1918. Succeeded his father as King, January 1936. Abdicated, December 1936. Duke of Windsor, 1936. In 1937 he married Wallis Simpson, who became Duchess of Windsor. Resident in France, 1937–40. Governor General and Commander-in-Chief, Bahamas, 1940–5. Returned to France in 1945, and lived there until his death.

[2] Axel Wenner-Gren, 1881–1961. A Swedish engineer-industrialist. Founder of the Electrolux Company, 1919. Visited Goering in 1936 with a view to bringing the Nazis and their international critics together. Published *An Appeal to Everyman* in 1937 calling for international disarmament, the establishment everywhere of democratic government, and the abolition of trade barriers. In May 1939 he tried to initiate Anglo-German discussions, to which end he again saw Goering, and also Neville Chamberlain. On 28 August 1939 he offered his yacht *Southern Cross* to the British and Germans, as a place on which negotiations could take place aimed at persuading the Polish Government to make concessions to Germany, with a view to averting war. Resident in the Bahamas during the Second World War; at the end of 1940 the Duke of Windsor travelled to the United States with him on board his yacht; after the visit (to Miami) they cruised in the western Bahamas together, where Wenner-Gren had fishery interests. In 1940 he gave $25,000 to the University of Toronto for research.

Winston expressed the opinion, forcibly, that Socialism was bad, that jingoism was worse, and that the two combined, in a kind of debased Italian fascism, was the worst creed ever designed by man.

Brendan, who had taken Hopkins over to Blenheim, said that Hopkins had told him his mission was to see what we needed so that we might get it – even if it meant transferring to us armaments belonging to the US forces. The President was resolved that we should have the means of survival and of victory.

The PM has been troubled by *The Times'* attack on his new Production Executive etc., and indeed the criticisms voiced there reflect a widely felt complaint. So he has taken the trouble to write a full explanation to Geoffrey Dawson, and at dinner he expounded his views, emphasizing that he had no use for Committees in a purely advisory capacity but that there was no one man today who could be an economic dictator or maintain a position similar to his, on the military side, as Minister of Defence. His exercise of his office was only made possible by the power which he possessed as Prime Minister.

When the ladies had gone, Mr Hopkins paid a graceful tribute to the PM's speeches which had, he said produced the most stirring and revolutionary effect on all classes and districts in America. At an American Cabinet meeting the President had had a wireless set brought in so that all might listen to the Prime Minister. The PM was touched and gratified. He said that he hardly knew what he said in his speeches last summer; he had just been imbued with the feeling that 'it would be better for us to be destroyed than to see the triumph of such an impostor'. When, at the time of Dunkirk, he had addressed a meeting of Ministers 'below the line' he had realized that there was only one thing they wanted to hear him say: that whatever happened to our army we should still go on. He had said it.

The PM said that after the war he could never lead a party Government against the Opposition leaders who had cooperated so loyally. He hoped a national Government would continue for two or three years after the war so that the country might be undivided in its efforts to put into effect certain principles – or rather measures – of reconstruction. He then proceeded to give – after saying that the text of the American Bill that morning had made him feel that a new world had come into being – a graphic description of the future, as he visualized it, from an international point of view. He began by saying that there must be a United States of Europe and he believed it should be built by the English: if the Russians built it, there would be communism and squalor; if the Germans built it, there would be tyranny and brute force. He then outlined his ideas, which I have related before, in the quick unhesitating manner which means he has really warmed to his subject. He asked Hopkins what he thought, and the reply, slow, deliberate, halting was a remarkable contrast to the ceaseless flow of eloquence to which we had listened. Hopkins said that there were two kinds of men: those who talked and those who acted. The President, like the Prime Minister, was one of the latter. Although Hopkins had heard him sketch out an idea very similar to the PM's, Roosevelt refused to listen to those who talked so much of war aims and was intent only upon one end: the destruction of Hitler. Winston hastily explained that he had been speaking very freely and was just anxious to let Hopkins realize that we were not all devoid of thoughts of the future: he would be the first to agree that the destruction of 'those foul swine' was the primary and overriding objective.

Oliver Lyttelton:[1] *recollection*
(*'The Memoirs of Lord Chandos'*)

11 January 1941

When the ladies had left the table, Winston sprang into a majestic monologue, tracing the origins and course of the war up to that date. If it had been taken down, it would have been recognized as the substance of his first two volumes of the Second World War. His sonorous eloquence, his sense of history, of man's destiny and Great Britain's part in it were enthralling. He turned at the last to our war aims. 'We seek no treasure, we seek no territorial gains, we seek only the right of man to be free; we seek his right to worship his God, to lead his life in his own way, secure from persecution. As the humble labourer returns from his work when the day is done, and sees the smoke curling upwards from his cottage home in the serene evening sky, we wish him to know that no rat-a-tat-tat' – here he rapped on the table – 'of the secret police upon his door will disturb his leisure or interrupt his rest. We seek government with the consent of the people, man's freedom to say what he will, and when he thinks himself injured, to find himself equal in the eyes of the law. But war aims other than these we have none.'

He paused. 'What will the President say to all this?' Harry Hopkins did not reply for the best part of a minute – and how long that seems – and then,

[1] Oliver Lyttelton, 1893–1972. The son of Alfred Lyttelton, Balfour's Colonial Secretary. Educated at Eton and Trinity College, Cambridge. 2nd Lieutenant, Grenadier Guards, December 1914; on active service on the Western Front, 1915–18 (Military Cross, DSO, despatches three times, wounded April 1918). Entered merchant banking, 1919. Joined the British Metal Corporation, 1920; later managing director. Elected to the Other Club at the beginning of 1939. Appointed Controller of Non-Ferrous Metals, September 1939. President of the Board of Trade, and Privy Councillor, July 1940. Conservative MP for Aldershot, 1940–54. Minister of State, Middle East (based in Cairo), and Member of the War Cabinet, June 1941. Minister of Production, March 1942–May 1945. Chairman of Associated Electrical Industries, 1945–51 and 1954–63. Secretary of State for Colonial Affairs, 1951–4. Created Viscount Chandos, 1954. Chairman of the National Theatre Board, 1962; Life President, 1971. Knight of the Garter, 1970. One of his three sons was killed on active service in Italy in 1944. The second of the Royal National Theatre's three auditoria bears his name.

exaggerating his American drawl, he said, 'Well, Mr Prime Minister, I don't think the President will give a dam' for all that.' Heavens alive, it's gone wrong, thought I. There was another pause, and then Harry said, 'You see, we're only interested in seeing that that Goddam sonofabitch, Hitler, gets licked'.

There was loud laughter, and at that moment a friendship was cemented which no convulsion ever undermined.

Winston S. Churchill to General Smuts
(*Churchill papers, 20/49*)

12 January 1941
Most Secret and Personal

Your No. 32 arrived when we had reached certain definite conclusions after three or four days' thought. I read it to Defence Committee, three Chiefs of Staff, three Service Ministers,[1] Attlee, Eden, myself. All struck by complete coincidence of view. Only point of difference is we think northward advance from Kenya with large forces would involve long delay through transport shortage. Rebellion making good headway, Emperor[2] enters soon. Advance Kassala–Agordat cuts tap root. Force you mention already on the way. Pressure from Kenya to be maintained at utmost, but we cannot carry too many troops on this line. Please send Division at earliest. Perhaps by time it approaches can land it in Red Sea. Better keep as fluid as possible in view of Imponderabilia. Come though please now.

Fully agreed pay no heavy price beyond Tobruk, where very likely 25,000 Wops in net. Go on while the going is good so as to make as far-thrown a western flank for Egypt as possible, meanwhile shifting all useful elements to impending war-front Bulgarian-Greek frontier. Naturally Wavell and Co. heart-set on chase, but Wavell going Monday or Tuesday Athens concert reinforcements with Greeks. I send you herewith copy of my telegram to Wavell approved by COS Committee. It speaks for itself. Cannot guarantee success, can only make what we think best arrangements. Weather, mountains, Danube crossing, fortified Greek-Bulgarian frontier, all helpful factors. Turkey, Yugoslavia, Russia, all perhaps favourably influenced by evidences of British support of Greece.

Whatever happens in Balkans, Italian army Abyssinia probably

[1] A. V. Alexander (First Lord of Admiralty), Sir Archibald Sinclair (Secretary of State of Air) and David Margesson (Secretary of State for War).

[2] Ras Tafari Makonnen, 1892–1975. Made Regent of Ethiopia after the death of his cousin King Menelek II, 1916. Crowned Emperor, 1930, taking his baptismal name Haile Selassie. Driven out by the Italians, 1936. Resident in Jerusalem, 1938–40. Re-entered Addis Ababa, May 1941. Deposed by a coup led by some of his Army officers, 1974. Died in his former palace less than a year later.

destroyable. If this should come off everything useful from Kenya forward to Mediterranean. Hope Army of South African Union will be there for summer fighting. Very large reinforcements coming continually round Cape. Most grateful for all your help and above all for your sure-footed judgment which marches with our laboriously reached conclusions.

Winston S. Churchill to David Margesson and Sir John Dill
(*Churchill papers, 20/36*)

12 January 1941

MECHANIZATION OF THE CAVALRY DIVISION IN PALESTINE

1. This is a distressing story. These troops have been carried out with their horses and maintained at great expense in the Middle East since the early months of the war. Several months ago it was decided by the War Office they should be mechanized. I gladly approved. Now I learn, as the result of one of my own inquiries, that nothing has been done about this, that the whole Division is to be carted back again home – presumably without their horses – and that this is not to begin until June 1. After that there will be a further seven or eight months before they will be of any use. Thus 8,500 officers and men, including some of our finest Regular and Yeomanry Regiments, will, except for security work, have been kept out of action at immense expense for two years and five months of war.

2. Let me have a calculation of the cost involved in –

(a) sending these troops to the Middle East;
(b) maintaining them with rations, pay and allowances from the beginning of the War to the beginning of March 1942;
(c) transporting them home again.

3. There must be many better uses to which these troops could be put in the Middle East. Having regard to their high intrinsic quality they should very quickly acquire new additional training. It is not necessary that the organization and establishment should follow exactly the same patterns approved for Mechanized or Armoured formations at home. The establishments of the independent motorized brigade groups here might be more suitable than those of a division. The Household Cavalry in the Spring of 1918 or Autumn of 1917 were very rapidly converted into a machine-gun regiment, and achieved their training in a couple of months at Etaples. I cannot understand why the Cavalry Division should not train in Palestine, where at any rate they count as local security troops. One would have thought it was the very country.

4. Some of the captured Italian tank equipment might be taken over by these highly competent regular or quasi-regular units. Alternatively, or in

partial substitute, we have a good supply of Bren-gun carriers, 200 of which could certainly be sent out.

5. There are various other solutions. They might be converted into an Infantry Division, as several Cavalry Divisions were in the last War or formed, perhaps, into independent brigade groups. In this case they would be drafted up to full strength as Infantry Battalions. If this is not acceptable, they could be sent to India to liberate an equal number of Regulars in Battalions serving there: say, 8 Battalions. Or again, they might form the kernel of a force to dominate Iraq. One thing is certain: now that we are starving ourselves to send men to the East with ever-dwindling shipping, there can be no question of bringing this large body of men and these invaluable cadres home, especially perhaps at the very moment when the fighting in the Middle East is at its height.

Winston S. Churchill to Sir Archibald Sinclair and Air Chief Marshal Sir Charles Portal
(*Churchill papers, 20/36*)

12 January 1941

Must the operational reports from the Middle East be of their present inordinate length and detail? It surely is not necessary to describe minutely what happened in every individual raid of a dozen aircraft over the enemy's lines and encypher and decypher all this at each end, and cable it, thus congesting the lines.

I suggest that the average weekly wordage of these routine telegrams should be calculated for the last two months and Air Marshal Longmore asked to reduce them to say, one-third their present length.

The Foreign Office are also asking for condensation of their messages.

Winston S. Churchill to Herbert Morrison
(*Churchill papers, 20/36*)

12 January 1941

This kind of propaganda[1] ought not to be allowed, as it is directly contrary to the will of Parliament and hampers our maintenance of resistance to the

[1] A Communist circular addressed to all active working men and women.

enemy. I do not see why if Mosley[1] is confined, subversives and Communists like D. M. Pritt[2] and the other signatories should not be equally confined. The Law and the regulations ought to be enforced against those who hamper our war effort, whether from the extreme Right or the extreme Left. That is the position which the Conservative Party adopt, and I think it is a very strong one and one of which the country as a whole would approve. I know it is your wish to enforce an even justice, and if you bring the matter before the Cabinet I am sure you will receive full support. 'Sauce for the goose is sauce for the gander!'

Winston S. Churchill to the Import Executive
(*Churchill papers, 20/36*)

12 January 1941

I have had the following figures[3] prepared for me. They show that 30 per cent. deduction from gross imports of steel is made for 'shipping lag' and 10 per cent. for sinkings (despite the fact that the Imports programme itself allows for sinkings), and that a further 15 per cent. of the imported steel will not be of use to industry as it will accumulate as dead stock and working stock. No doubt in practice we get what we get, and as our consuming power is also lagging in time considerable surpluses are liable to accumulate. One of the objects in forming the Import Executive and Production Executive was to make sure that allowances for lag, losses, &c., were not counted several times over, each Department making its own allowance as the material passed through its control. I hope, therefore, you will review the steel import programme so as not to present an inflated figure which might prejudice general calculations of what we can do in 1941 on the import tonnage available for all commodities. As you know I am all for importing steel. But let us have a true idea of what we are doing. These cumulative safety margins distort all efforts to plan the future.

[1] Oswald Ernald Mosley, 1896–1980. Educated at Sandhurst. On active service, 1917–18. A Conservative MP, 1918–22, he sat as an Independent, 1922–4 and as a Labour member, 1924 and 1926–31. Succeeded his father as 6th baronet, 1928. Labour Chancellor of the Duchy of Lancaster, 1929–30. Founded the British Union of Fascists, 1932. Imprisoned, 1940–5. He published his autobiography, *My Life*, in 1968. Mosley was married to Clementine Churchill's cousin Diana Mitford.

[2] Denis Nowell Pritt, 1887–1972. Called to the Bar, 1909; practised until 1960. King's Counsel, 1927. Member of Parliament (Socialist) for North Hammersmith, 1935–50. Published his pro-Soviet *Light on Moscow*, 1939; *USSR Our Ally*, 1941. President of the Society for Cultural Relations with the USSR. His criticisms of United States policy appeared in *Star-Spangled Shadow*, 1947 and *The State Department and the Cold War*, 1948. Lenin Peace Prize, 1954. Professor of Law, University of Ghana, 1965–66.

[3] On the steel supply position for the first quarter of 1941.

Winston S. Churchill to the Earl of Selborne[1]
(*Churchill papers, 20/29*)

12 January 1941
Confidential

My dear Selborne,

Thank you so much for your very kind letter. Wavell and Wilson (who actually fought the battle) have done splendidly. We took a big risk here in July, August and September in sending out so many troops, tanks and guns in spite of the threat of invasion. Now we are much stronger. That bad man may as you say try Ireland and the mad policy of de Valera[2] makes it difficult to ward off the first lodgment. However we are watching very carefully and will do our best.

Yours very sincerely,
Winston S. Churchill

Winston S. Churchill to Commander Thompson
(*Churchill papers, 20/32*)

12 January 1941 10 Downing Street

AIR RAID SHELTER FOR CHARTWELL

Commander Thompson.

You should look into this. These people make everything impossible. I think it will be better just to do without.[3]

[1] Roundell Cecil Palmer, Viscount Wolmer, 1887-1971. A Conservative Member of Parliament (as Viscount Wolmer) from 1910 until October 1940, when he succeeded to the Earldom. Assistant Director of War Trade, 1916-18. Assistant Postmaster General, 1924-29. Privy Councillor, 1929. From 1940 to 1942 he was Director of Cement, Ministry of Works and Buildings; and from 1942 to 1945 Minister of Economic Warfare. Companion of Honour, 1945. President of the Church Army, 1949-61.

[2] Eamon de Valera, 1882–1975. Born in New York. A leading figure in the Easter Rebellion, 1916. Sentenced to death; sentence commuted to life penal servitude on account of his American birth. Released under the general amnesty, June 1917. President of the Sinn Fein, 1917–26. Elected to Parliament as a Sinn Fein MP, 1918. Imprisoned with other Sinn Fein leaders, 1918; escaped from Lincoln Jail, February 1919. 'President of the Irish Republic, 1919–22. Rejected the Irish Treaty and fought with the Irregulars against the Free State Army, 1922–3. President of Fianna Fail, 1926–59. Leader of the Opposition in the Free State Parliament, 1927–32. Prime Minister and Minister for External Affairs, 1932–48. Prime Minister for a second and third time, 1951–4 and 1957–9. President of the Republic of Ireland, 1959–73.

[3] Churchill was upset by the Office of Works estimate of £700 for a blast-proof bomb shelter at Chartwell. When Commander Thompson confirmed the estimate, Churchill minuted 'Too costly. We must chance it.'

John Colville: diary
(*Colville papers*)

12 January 1941 Ditchley

The PM asked what the Americans would do when they had accumulated all the gold in the world and the other countries then decided that gold was of no value except for filling teeth. 'Well,' said Mr Hopkins, 'We shall be able to make use of our unemployed in guarding it!'

We saw several films including *Night Train to Munich*,[1] which I had seen before. In the middle the telephone rang and I was told that HMS *Southampton* had been destroyed by dive-bombers in the Mediterranean.[2] When I took the PM aside afterwards and broke the news to him, he was less upset than I expected, though he bitterly regretted that he had been dissuaded from allowing Operation Workshop[3] to go through. 'I flinched,' he said, 'and now I have cause to regret it.'

From midnight till 2.0 a.m. the PM, smoking a phenomenally large cigar, paced about in front of the fire at the far end of the Library and gave, for Hopkins' benefit, an appreciation of the war up to date.[4] Ronnie Tree,[5] Oliver

[1] Also known as 'Gestapo' and 'Night Train'. Made in 1940, directed by Carol Reed. When the Germans march into Prague in March 1939, armour-plating inventor Dr Bomasch flees to England. His daughter Anna (played by Margaret Lockwood) escapes from arrest to join him but the Gestapo kidnap them both back to Berlin. A British secret service agent Gus Bennett (Rex Harrison) follows the kidnappers, disguised as a senior German army officer, pretending to woo Anna to the German cause.

[2] This was the first German naval appearance in the Mediterranean, and had been known to the Air Ministry in advance through Intelligence sources, partly Enigma and partly low-grade. By mischance, however, the information never reached either the Admiralty or Churchill.

[3] The proposed capture of the Italian island of Pantellaria, off Sicily.

[4] Unknown to Colville, Hopkins, or Churchill's other listeners, during January 12 Churchill had received encouraging news concerning Germany's plans for invasion. For on that day an Enigma decrypt revealed that German wireless stations on the circuit of the air formation headquarters responsible for German Air Force equipment in Belgium and Northern France were 'no longer to be manned as from 10 January'. At the same time, firing practices which could not be completed 'owing to frost' were to be transferred to southern France. This seemed clearly to reduce, at least until the frosts in northern France and Belgium were 'less severe', the prospect of an imminent invasion. 'Officer Only', 'Most Secret', 'Invasion of Britain', MI 14, 12 January 1941: *War Office Papers, 199/911A*.

[5] Ronald Tree, 1897–1976. Son of Arthur Tree and Countess Beatty. Educated at Winchester. On active service in France and Italy, 1917–18. Managing Editor of *Forum* magazine, New York, 1922–6. Joint Master of the Pytchley Hounds, 1927–33. Conservative MP for Harborough, 1933–45. Parliamentary Private Secretary to Robert Hudson, 1936–8; to Sir John Reith, 1940; to Alfred Duff Cooper; 1940–1 and to Brendan Bracken, 1941–3. Parliamentary Secretary, Ministry of Town and Country Planning, 1945. During the Second World War, at times of a full moon, Churchill would spend his weekends at Tree's home, Ditchley, instead of at Chequers, because of the danger of air attack.

Lyttelton, Prof.,[1] Tommie Thompson and I sat and goggled, while Hopkins occasionally made some short comment. He began by discussing the future. The question of populations was important. Germany had 60 millions on whom she could count; the remainder were at least a drag and potentially a danger. The British Empire had more white inhabitants than that, and if the US were with us – as he seemed in this discourse to assume they actively would be – there would be another 120 millions. So we were not outmatched in numbers any more than we were in courage and resolution. He did not believe that Japan would come in against the threat of Anglo-American armed resistance and he thought it more than probable that the Germans would be obliged to occupy the whole of France, thus driving the French to take up arms again in North Africa (He later said he believed that if he had gone to Bordeaux in those last fateful days he would have been able to tip the balance in favour of further resistance overseas).

Turning to the past, he sketched the whole history of the war, Norway, the trap when we marched our men right up into Belgium, his visits to France, the air battles, Libya, and, above all, the threat of invasion. He believed that Oran had been the turning-point in our fortunes: it made the world realize that we were in earnest in our intentions to carry on. He sketched the possibilities of invasion, of 'lodgements', of the use of gas, but he said he now felt quite confident, even though it was wrong to say that we should actually welcome invasion as so many people were now feeling. I think Hopkins must have been impressed.

[1] Frederick Alexander Lindemann, 1886–1957. Born at Baden Baden (where his mother was taking the cure); son of Alsatian father who had emigrated to Britain in the early 1870s, and an American mother. Educated at Blair Lodge, Scotland; Darmstadt 1902–5, and Berlin University 1906–10. Doctor of Philosophy, Berlin, 1910. Studied physical chemistry in Paris, 1912–14. Worked at the Physical Laboratory, RAF, 1915–18, when he helped to organize the kite balloon barrage. Learned to fly, 1916. Personally investigated the aerodynamic effects of aircraft spin. Professor of Experimental Philosophy (physics), Oxford, 1919–56. Student of Christ Church (where he subsequently resided), 1921. Elected to the Other Club, 1927. Published his *Physical Significance of the Quantum Theory*, 1932. Member of the Expert Committee on Air Defence Research, Committee of Imperial Defence, 1935–9. Unsuccessful by-election candidate, Oxford University, 1937. Personal Assistant to the Prime Minister (Churchill), 1940–1; in 1953 Churchill's Private Secretary, John Martin, wrote to him, about the war years: 'Those without experience in the inner circle will never know the size of Winston's debt to you and how much stimulus and inspiration of ideas flowed from your office.' Created Baron Cherwell, 1941. Paymaster-General, 1942–5 and 1951–3. Privy Councillor, 1943. Viscount, 1956. His brother-in-law, Lieutenant Noel Musgrave Vickers (a barrister, born 1880, who had married Linda Lindemann in 1910) was killed in action on 24 March 1918, leaving a two-year-old son.

Harry Hopkins to President Franklin D. Roosevelt
(*'The White House Papers of Harry L. Hopkins'*)

12 January 1941

Dear Mr President:

These notes are sent by Col Lee,[1] who is returning with Halifax. Will you save them for me until I get back, when I shall try to put them into readable form.

The people here are amazing from Churchill down, and if courage alone can win – the result will be inevitable. But they need our help desperately, and I am sure you will permit nothing to stand in the way. Some of the ministers and underlings are a bit trying, but no more than some I have seen.

Churchill is the gov't. in every sense of the word – he controls the grand strategy and often the details – labour trusts him – the army, navy, air force are behind him to a man. The politicians and upper crust pretend to like him. I cannot emphasize too strongly that he is the one and only person over here with whom you need to have a full meeting of minds.

Churchill wants to see you – the sooner the better – but I have told him of your problem until the bill is passed. I am convinced this meeting between you and Churchill is essential – and soon – for the battering continues and Hitler does not wait for Congress.

I was with Churchill at 2 a.m. Sunday night when he got word of the loss of the *Southampton* – the serious damage to the new aircraft carrier (*Illustrious*) – a second cruiser knocked about – but he never falters or displays the least despondence – till four o'clock he paced the floor telling me of his offensive and defensive plans.

I cannot believe that it is true that Churchill dislikes either you or America – it just doesn't make sense.

Churchill is prepared for a setback in Greece – the African campaign will proceed favourably – German bombers in the Mediterranean make the fleet's operation more difficult – convoys must all go around the Cape. An invasion, they feel sure, can be repelled – Churchill thinks it will not come soon, but Beaverbrook and others think it will come and soon.

This island needs our help now, Mr President, with everything we can give them.

There is no time to be out of London, so I am staying here – the bombs aren't nice and seem to be quite impersonal. I have been offered a so-called

[1] Raymond E. Lee, United States Military Attaché to London; later, as Brigadier-General, a participant in the August 1941 Churchill-Roosevelt meeting off Newfoundland.

bombproof apartment by Churchill – a tin hat and gas mask have been delivered – the best I can say for the hat is that it looks worse than my own and doesn't fit – the gas mask I can't get on – so I am all right.

There is much to tell but it will have to wait – for I must be off to Charing Cross.

Harry

Harry Hopkins to President Franklin D. Roosevelt
(*'The White House Papers of Harry L. Hopkins'*)

12 January 1941

In the two weeks since my arrival in England I have spent twelve evenings with Mr Churchill and I have explored every aspect of our mutual problems with him. I have also had extended conferences with all the Cabinet Ministers and most of the Undersecretaries. I have had long and detailed conferences with the Chief of the Imperial General Staff, Sir John Dill, and with the First Sea Lord, Admiral Pound, and with the Chief of the Air Staff, Sir Charles Portal, and with the Chiefs of the Fighter[1] and Bomber[2] Commands. I have visited Scapa Flow and the Coast Defences at Dover and various cities and towns and airfields. They have given me complete access to all confidential material which is concerned with my mission here. I believe that insofar as it is possible to get a picture of the situation here in a short time, I have got a reasonably clear perception not only of the physical defences of Britain, but of the opinions of the men who are directing the forces of this nation. Your 'former Navy person' is not only the Prime Minister, he is the directing force behind the strategy and the conduct of the war in all its essentials. He has an amazing hold on the British people of all classes and groups. He has particular strength both with the military establishments and the working people. The most important single observation I have to make is that most of the Cabinet and all of the military leaders here believe that invasion is imminent. They are straining every effort night and day to meet this. They believe that it may come at any moment, but not later than May 1. They believe that it will certainly be an all-out attack, including the use of poison gas and perhaps some other new weapons that Germany may have developed. The spirit of

[1] William Sholto Douglas, 1893–1969. On active service, 1914–18 (despatches thrice, Military Cross, DFC). Commanded Nos. 43 and 85 (fighter) squadrons, 1917–18. Assistant Chief of the Air Staff, 1938–40. Deputy Chief of the Air Staff, 1940. Air Officer Commanding-in-Chief, Fighter Command, 1940–2; Middle East Command, 1943–4; Coastal Command, 1944–5. Knighted, 1941. Commanding the British Air Forces of Occupation, Germany, 1945–6. Governor, British Zone of Germany, 1946–7. Created Baron, 1948. Chairman, British European Airways, 1949–64.

[2] Air Marshal Sir Richard Peirse, see page 23, note 1.

this people and their determination to resist invasion is beyond praise. No matter how fierce the attack may be you can be sure that they will resist it, and effectively. The Germans will have to do more than kill a few hundred thousand people here before they can defeat Britain. I therefore cannot urge too strongly that any action you may take to meet the immediate needs here must be based on the assumption that invasion will come before May 1. If Germany fails to win this invasion then I believe her sun is set. I am convinced that if we act boldly and promptly on a few major fronts we can get enough material to Britain within the next few weeks to give her the additional strength she needs to turn back Hitler.

Winston S. Churchill to President Franklin D. Roosevelt

(*Churchill papers, 20/49*)

13 January 1941
Personal and Private

Hopkins and I spent the weekend together and he is coming along with me on a short tour of fleet bases, so we shall have plenty of time to cover all points at leisure. I am most grateful to you for sending so remarkable an envoy who enjoys so high a measure of your intimacy and confidence.

Winston S. Churchill to Sir Edward Bridges

(*Premier papers, 4/25/3*)

13 January 1941

During his stay over here Mr Hopkins will see various Ministers and discuss Departmental matters with them. Will you kindly impress upon these Ministers that Mr Hopkins does not desire that any account of these interviews should be cabled Departmentally to our corresponding Departments in the United States. Mr Hopkins' relations are with the President alone, and he does not want them complicated by an appearance of doing business on the Departmental level. Should it be necessary in spite of the above to make any reference, I should be glad to be acquainted beforehand and see the draft telegrams.

John Colville to C. G. Eastwood[1]
(*Churchill papers, 20/31*)

13 January 1941
Most Secret

My dear Eastwood,

Mr Hopkins, President Roosevelt's Envoy, has been staying with the Prime Minister for the weekend, and during that time, the conversation at one moment turned to the Duke of Windsor.

Mr Hopkins mentioned the deplorable effect which the Duke's recent cruise with Mr Wenner-Gren had had in America, and he afterwards told me that he thought Lord Lloyd[2] ought to know that any claim by Mr Wenner-Gren to intimacy or friendship with members of the United States Administration was quite unfounded. He was considered a dangerous pro-Nazi and all his activities were closely watched. Sometimes he was received by people in touch with the United States Government but it was, as Mr Hopkins put it, only 'to let him talk'.

I do not know if Lord Lloyd will wish to bring this to the Duke of Windsor's notice, nor am I quite sure whether Mr Hopkins told it to me with this intention, but in any case I feel sure he would not wish his name dragged into the matter.

Mr Churchill has dictated a note to Lord Lloyd in reply to his minute about Mr Wenner-Gren, and you have doubtless already seen this.

[1] Christopher Gilbert Eastwood, 1905–1983. Entered the Home Civil Service, 1927. Private Secretary, High Commissioner for Palestine, 1932–34. Private Secretary to the Secretary of State for the Colonies (Lord Lloyd and Lord Moyne), 1940–41. Principal Assistant Secretary, Cabinet Office, 1945–47. Assistant Under-Secretary of State, Colonial Office, 1947–52 and 1954–66.

[2] George Ambrose Lloyd, 1879–1941. Educated at Eton and Cambridge. Travelled widely in the East as a young man. Honorary Attaché, Constantinople Embassy, 1905. Special Trade Commissioner to Turkey, including Mesopotamia, 1907. Conservative MP for West Staffordshire, 1910–18. A director of Lloyds Bank, 1911–18. Captain, 1914. On active service in Gallipoli, Mesopotamia and the Hedjaz; he accompanied T. E. Lawrence on one of his desert raids. Present at the capture of Gaza, 1917. Knighted, 1918. Governor of Bombay, 1918–23. Conservative MP for Eastbourne, 1924–5. Privy Councillor, 1924. Created Baron, 1925. High Commissioner for Egypt and the Sudan, 1925–9. One of the Vice-Presidents (with Churchill) of the India Defence League, 1933–5. Chairman, British Council, 1936. Elected to the Other Club, 1936. Secretary of State for the Colonies, 1940–1. His son, Alexander David Frederick Lloyd, was on active service in Palestine, the Middle East, and Europe, 1939–45; Parliamentary Under Secretary of State, Home Office, 1952–4; Colonial Office, 1954–7; then President of the Commonwealth and British Empire Chambers of Commerce.

Winston S. Churchill to Lord Lloyd
(*Churchill papers, 20/36*)

13 January 1941

What reply do you propose to make to the Duke's answer to your warning? I think he should certainly know the passage marked 'A.'[1]

Winston S. Churchill to Arthur Greenwood
(*Churchill papers, 20/21*)

13 January 1941

My dear Arthur Greenwood,

I am in cordial agreement with your paper especially that part of it which refers to war-time needs. Prompt first-aid to lightly wounded houses, immediate restoration of glass or other material to keep out the weather, seem to be vital duties for the Minister of Works and Buildings and have marked precedence over attractive plans for the post-war period.

Yours v sincerely,
Winston S. Churchill

Winston S. Churchill to General Sikorski[2]
(*Churchill papers, 20/21*)

13 January 1941

Dear General Sikorski,

I am most deeply touched by your letter of January 1 and your gift of £450, as the first instalment of a collection which is being made by Polish serving officers and men and civilians in this country towards the rebuilding of the Guildhall.

This is a moving token, which will stir the hearts of everyone in this city and

[1] The passage marked 'A' was an extract from a letter to Axel Wenner-Gren from a friend in Rio to the effect that Wenner-Gren would find in Nassau a new and interesting family with whom he would doubtless become very friendly, and that this family had sympathetic understanding with totalitarian ideas.

[2] Wladyslaw Sikorski, 1881–1943. Organizer of pre-1914 Polish Military Organization, 1909. Lieutenant-Colonel, Polish Legions, 1914–18. Commanded two Army corps in the defence of Poland against the Bolsheviks, 1920. Prime Minister of Poland, 1922–3. Minister of Military Affairs, 1923–5. Commander, Lwow Army Region (which he had defended against the Ukrainians in 1919), 1926–8. On half-pay, 1928–39. Recalled to service, 1939. Prime Minister of the Polish Government in exile (first in Paris, then in London) and Commander-in-Chief of the Polish Army, from the fall of Poland until his death in an air crash at Gibraltar on 4 July 1943.

Empire. We see in it a symbol of the friendship of the great Polish nation, whose homes have been broken and whose monuments have been shattered, but whose free spirit will never crumble like bricks or stone.

I have sent your cheque to the Lord Mayor,[1] who will shortly be writing to you to express his gratitude. I understand that for the moment no plans have been made for the rebuilding of the Guildhall, but it is suggested that until a decision is reached your gift should be set aside for a special purpose, perhaps for a window, which may stand as a record of the generosity of your countrymen and as a reminder of our common trials and common sacrifice.

Winston S. Churchill to General Ismay, for the Chiefs of Staff Committee
(*Premier papers, 3/124/2*)

13 January 1941

DODECANESE ISLANDS

I do not think it would be wise to attack these smaller islands. They are no use in themselves, they are not necessary for the attack upon the larger islands now that we hold Crete. Stirring up this quarter will put the enemy on their guard, and will bring about the disagreement between Greece and Turkey which has become only too apparent as we have explored tentatively this subject. The Defence Committee have not approved these operations.

Winston S. Churchill to General Ismay, for the Chiefs of Staff Committee
(*Churchill papers, 20/36*)

13 January 1941

AIR REINFORCEMENTS TO THE FAR EAST

I do not remember to have given my approval to these very large diversions of Force. On the contrary, if my Minutes are collected they will be seen to have an opposite tendency. The political situation in the Far East does not seem to require, and the strength of our Air Force by no means warrants, the maintenance of such large forces in the Far East at this time.

[1] George Henry Wilkinson, 1885–1967. Alderman, City of London, 1933–59. Chairman, Ministry of Home Security London Deep Shelter Committee, 1940–44. Chairman, National Greek Relief, 1941–7. Lord Mayor of London, 1940–1. Created Baronet, 1941. Chairman and Treasurer, Lord Mayor's National Air Raid Distress Fund, 1941–5.

Winston S. Churchill to General Ismay, for the Chiefs of Staff Committee
(*Churchill papers, 20/36*)

13 January 1941
Action this Day

1. The effective arrival of German aviation in Sicily may be the beginning of evil developments in the Central Mediterranean. The successful dive-bombing attacks upon *Illustrious* and the two cruisers show the need for having these ships fitted with aerial mine throwers. I do not know why *Illustrious* could not have had a couple. The improved naval pattern of aerial mine should be pressed on with at the utmost. Surely we ought to try to put half a dozen Grummans on *Formidable* before she goes into the Mediterranean. The need for high-speed aircraft to catch dive-bombers out at sea seems very great.

2. I am very apprehensive of the Germans establishing themselves in 'Workshop',[1] in which case, with a strong force of dive-bombers, they will close the Narrows. I fear this may be another example of the adage 'a stitch in time saves nine'. I am satisfied, however, that the training and preparation of the Commandos had not reached a degree which would have allowed them to be used at the time of 'Excess'.[2]

3. It is necessary now that 'Workshop' should be reviewed. It has become far more urgent and also at the same time more difficult, and once the Germans are installed there it will become more difficult still. I should be glad if revised and perfected plans could be ready by today week. Plans should also be made to find an opportunity at the earliest moment. The question of whether to try it or not can only be settled after these matters of method and timing have been satisfactorily disposed of.

4. I remain completely of opinion that 'Workshop' is cardinal.

Winston S. Churchill to Anthony Eden
(*Churchill papers, 20/36*)

13 January 1941

You spoke about a French officer who was shortly returning to Morocco and would have access to Weygand. I cannot see him before I leave tomorrow, Tuesday, January 14, but if you wish I will write a letter to Weygand which he can carry.

[1] Sicily.
[2] A naval convoy bringing troops for Malta and aircraft for Alexandria, from Gibraltar through the Mediterranean.

Winston S. Churchill to Sir Alexander Cadogan[1]
(*Churchill papers, 20/36*)

13 January 1941

I have found it difficult to follow the Thailand story. Will you kindly have its essentials put down for me on one sheet of paper?

Winston S. Churchill to Professor Lindemann
(*Churchill papers, 20/36*)

13 January 1941

. . . what is the good of multiplying anti-tank rifles ahead of ammunition supply. Draft a minute asking about this, and also inquire into the delay in formulating the larger demands, and, finally, why was this very much larger demand not submitted to me before? I expect to be consulted on all important changes of demand and establishment.

War Cabinet: minutes
(*Cabinet papers, 65/21*)

13 January 1941
6 p.m.

The Minister of Information informed the War Cabinet that the view of many of the leading newspaper editors would be against the suppression of the *Daily Worker*. The suggestion was also made that the right course would be to take action against the Communist Party as such.

The Prime Minister emphasized the importance of acting in a way which would convince public opinion that we were meting out even-handed justice to those who fomented opposition to the successful prosecution of the war, whether Fascists or Communists.

[1] Alexander George Montagu Cadogan, 1884–1968. Seventh son of the 5th Earl Cadogan. Educated at Eton and Balliol College, Oxford. Attaché Diplomatic Service, 1908. British Minister to China, 1933–5; Ambassador, 1935–6. Knighted, 1934. Deputy Under-Secretary of State for Foreign Affairs, 1936–7; Permanent Under-Secretary, January 1938–February 1946. Permanent British Representative at the United Nations, 1946–50. Government Director, Suez Canal Company, 1951–7. Chairman of the BBC, 1952–7. One brother, William George Sydney Cadogan, born in 1879, was killed in action in France on 14 November 1914. Another brother, Edward Cecil George Cadogan, was a Conservative MP from 1922 to 1945 and largely responsible for the abolition of judicial corporal punishment.

Defence Committee (Operations): minutes
(Cabinet papers, 69/2)

13 January 1941
9.30 p.m.

BOMBING OF GERMANY

Mr Eden thought that we should not overlook the importance of attacking the German people. The reason the Germans were attacking our people was probably because it was this type of attack which they themselves most feared.

The Prime Minister said that he was sceptical of these cut and dried calculations which showed infallibly how the war could be won. In the early days of the war it had been said that if the Royal Air Force were allowed to launch an attack upon the Ruhr, they would, with preciseness and certitude, shatter the German industry. Careful calculations had been made to show that this could be done. After anxious thought, the attack was eventually made when the Germans invaded the Low Countries, but there had only been a fractional interruption of work in the industries of the Ruhr.

Sir Charles Portal pointed out that the Ruhr proposal had been based on low bombing in daylight, and the plan had been to eliminate the power stations. In the event, it had not proved possible to undertake day bombing over Germany, and the day bombers had all been used in support of the land battle. He did not think that the two plans were comparable, since the present one was based on actual experience of night bombing, and the forecasts made were not unduly optimistic.

SABOTAGE

Some discussion took place on the possibility of effective sabotage, and Mr Dalton explained various schemes which he had under consideration, and which were set out in his Memorandum (COS (41) 3 (0)).

The Prime Minister drew attention to the lack of success which had attended all our efforts at sabotage in the past, and doubted whether any appreciable results would be achieved.

Mr Dalton said that if certain conditions were satisfied, he hoped to be able to do a good deal.

GERMAN OIL INSTALLATIONS

Sir Charles Portal pointed out that if the Germans launched a campaign in the Balkans, they would be unable to receive the full volume of supplies from Roumania, which was an added reason for doing everything possible to limit the amount of oil which they could produce from their own resources.

Captain Margesson thought that it was essential to concentrate our efforts, and he had come to the conclusion that oil presented the most favourable target.

The Prime Minister thought that there would be no harm in trying the policy advocated by the Chiefs of Staff, though he doubted whether it would be possible to stick to it. The strength of the defences round the oil plants would greatly increase, and the pressure of events would force us to divert efforts elsewhere.

PANTELLARIA ISLAND

The Prime Minister said that German dive bombers were now established in Sicily, and might soon be operating from Pantellaria. If we could take that place, and put two or three squadrons of fighters there, a lane could be kept clear for our shipping to use.

The Prime Minister said that we were open to very grave reproach for not having taken Pantellaria while we still had an opportunity. This, he felt, would be classed as one of the capital errors of the war. Pantellaria was a priceless strategic rock, and had been held by a garrison of Italians, who, from their very long isolation, would not have been as formidable as even the garrison of Bardia. We had missed the chance, and now we should find that the Germans would occupy the island, and probably a position on the African coast, and we should find the Mediterranean closed to us. The fate of Malta itself might be sealed. We ought now to see whether we could not still take the island. If we did not fight for the central Mediterranean, we should certainly not be able to use it.

Some discussion took place as to whether, if German dive bombers were established in Sicily, it would be possible to carry out the operation against Pantellaria; or if the island were captured, whether we could possibly maintain our garrison.

It was pointed out that the ships taking part in the operation would be in danger of dive bombing attack for about 50 miles before dark on the evening of the attack, and again the following morning after they had withdrawn.

The view was expressed by Vice-Admiral Phillips and Sir Charles Portal that the Germans could control the Channel with bombers from Sicily just as easily as from Pantellaria; but the Prime Minister observed that their control would be exercized much more easily if they had a number of positions from which they could operate their bombers. Pantellaria could be compared with Heligoland.

Sir Charles Portal said that Pantellaria would be of more value to us than to the Germans, though the latter would naturally wish to deny it to us.

DODECANESE

The importance of taking the Dodecanese was also emphasized, since the Germans could fly dive bombers to the islands from Bulgaria.

The Prime Minister said that he was not against taking the Dodecanese, but he was averse from operations against the smaller islands, which would only stir up the area without destroying the danger. In any case, the operations could not be carried out until March or April. The urgent matter now was to overhaul operation 'Workshop' and to see whether by some means it could be carried out.

John Martin:[1] *letter*
(*Martin papers*)

14 January 1941

We set out from King's Cross in a 'Special' on Tuesday[2] and woke up next day in Caithness in the middle of a deserted heath, the ground white with snow and a blizzard howling at the windows. There had been a derailment in front of us and it was some time before this was cleared away and we could get on to Thurso. There was much discussion as to what we should do, for the sea was stormy and my master had a bad cold.

Charles Peake:[3] *diary*
(*'The Life of Lord Halifax', page 471*)

14 January 1941 Outside Thurso

He [Churchill] came beaming into the breakfast car where he consumed a large glass of brandy and then said hoarsely: 'I'll go and get my Mothersills.' After a bit the PM began to talk about a new anti-aircraft device we were going to see, and which he said he was going to fire: 'It costs about £100 a minute to fire it,' the Captain of the Fleet said rather drily. The smile faded from the PM's lips and the corners of his mouth turned down like a baby.

[1] John Miller Martin, 1904–91. Entered the Dominions Office, 1927. Seconded to the Malayan Civil Service, 1931–4. Secretary, Palestine Royal Commission, 1936–7. Private Secretary to the Prime Minister (Winston Churchill), 1940–1; Principal Private Secretary, 1941–5. Assistant Under-Secretary of State, Colonial Office, 1945–56. Deputy Under-Secretary, 1956–65. Knighted, 1952. High Commissioner, Malta, 1965–7. His memoir, *Downing Street, The War Years*, was published shortly after his death in 1991.

[2] Churchill was travelling by train with Lord Halifax (who was on his way to the United States as Ambassador) and Harry Hopkins (who was returning to Washington). The train was stopped for three hours outside Thurso because of a derailed truck.

[3] Charles Brinsley Pemberton Peake, 1897–1958. Captain, Leicestershire Regiment; on active service, 1915–18 (despatches, Military Cross). Entered Diplomatic Service, 1922. Head of the News Department, Foreign Office, and Chief Press Adviser, Ministry of Information, 1939. Personal Assistant to Lord Halifax in Washington, 1941. British Representative to the French National Committee, 1942–44. Political Adviser to General Eisenhower, Supreme Commander, Allied Expeditionary Force, 1944–45. Consul-General, Tangier, 1945–46. Ambassador at Belgrade, 1946–51. Knighted, 1948. Ambassador at Athens, 1951–57.

'What, not fire it?' 'Yes, darling,' Mrs Churchill[1] added quickly, 'you may fire it just once.' 'Yes, that's right, I'll fire it just once. Only once. That couldn't be bad.' Nobody had the heart to say that it would be bad, and he was soon beaming again.[2]

Winston S. Churchill to Anthony Eden
(*Churchill papers, 20/36*)

14 January 1941

The Cabinet today should consider the telegrams from Belgrade about Prince Paul's[3] views. They leave me unchanged. It is for the Greeks to say whether they want Wavell to visit Athens or not. It is the Greeks who must be the judges of the German reactions.

Secondly, if the Germans are coming south they will not require pretexts. They are, it would seem, already acting in pursuance of a carefully-thought-out plan which one can hardly assume will be hurried or delayed in consequence of any minor movements of ours. The evidence in our possession of the German movements seems overwhelming. In the face of it Prince Paul's attitude looks like that of an unfortunate man in the cage with a tiger, hoping not to provoke him while steadily dinner-time approaches.

[1] Clementine Hozier, 1885–1977. Daughter of Lady Blanche Ogilvy (eldest daughter of the 10th Earl of Airlie) and Colonel Henry Hozier, soldier, war correspondent and (from 1874) Secretary to the Corporation of Lloyds of London, insurance under-writers. She married Churchill in 1908; they had five children, Diana (born 1909), Randolph (born 1911), Sarah (born 1914), Marigold (born 1919) and Mary (born 1922). In the First World War Clementine Churchill was active providing, through the YWCA, canteens for munitions workers; in the Second World War she presided over the Red Cross Aid to Russia Fund and the Fulmer Chase Maternity Home. From 1941 to 1947 she was also President of the YWCA War and National Fund, and from 1949 to 1951, Chairman of the YWCA National Hostels Committee. Created Baroness Spencer-Churchill, 1965; she took her seat on the cross benches, and not only attended the House of Lords thirteen times in seven months, but voted in favour of the abolition of the death penalty on 20 July 1965. A Trustee of Lord Attlee's Memorial Foundation, 1966. President of the National Benevolent Fund for the Aged, 1972. For a comprehensive account of her life, see Mary Soames, *Clementine Churchill*, London, 1976.

[2] Six days later, John Colville listened to John Martin's account of the Scottish trip, which, Colville wrote in his diary, 'seems to have been almost farcical at times, especially when the UP weapon was fired in the PM's honour and all but ended in exploding on top of the whole party'.

[3] Paul Karageorgevic, 1893–1976. Regent for his nephew King Peter of Yugoslavia, 1934–41. Signed a secret pact with the Axis, 25 March 1941. Deposed two days later (when Peter was proclaimed King). Fled to Greece. In exile, first in Kenya, then in Paris, until his death.

Winston S. Churchill to Sir Samuel Hoare
(*Churchill papers, 20/49*)

14 January 1941
Personal and Secret

I have had long and excellent talks with Hillgarth, who has greatly impressed us with the work you are doing. I brought him before the Defence Committee, where he produced a great effect. My hope is that the Germans will not go through Spain by favour ever, or by force until at least the Spring; and that in this interval the Pétain Government will be so maltreated by Germany that they will allow Weygand to reopen the war in Africa.

2. This would be strategically and politically more important to us than anything that could happen in Spain. If, however, we send troops to help Weygand via Casablanca or other West Atlantic ports, we should be in a position to press the French authorities to give some satisfaction to the Spanish claims in Morocco contingent on the Spaniards playing straight. It ought therefore to be possible to reconcile the conflicting interests to which you have drawn attention.

Winston S. Churchill to Professor Lindemann and Sir Edward Bridges
(*Churchill papers, 20/36*)

15 January 1941

DEPARTMENTAL REQUIREMENTS FROM THE UNITED STATES

Get a good dossier ready by the end of the week. Keep to a few broad simple points. Endeavour particularly to find out what it is the Departments want most in the next five months.

John Martin: diary
(*John Martin papers*)

16 January 1941

Morning in HMS *Nelson*. Returned through stormy seas to Thurso and left for the South.

John Martin: letter
(*Martin papers*)

17 January 1941

Then down through the night to Inverkeithing, for a visit to the dockyards, where the PM was received with immense enthusiasm. Thence to Edinburgh, where we picked up the Regional Commissioner, Tom Johnston,[1] and his principal officer, Norman Duke,[2] and gave them lunch in our train on the way to Glasgow. The visit was supposed to be a secret; but a mob of hundreds if not thousands was waiting at Queen Street Station and we had quite to fight our way to our cars and then into the City Chambers. The PM had been asked to meet the Councillors and Baillies and say a few words to them; but to our horror we found a crowd of about 200, a platform and press reporters. The PM rose to the occasion however, though he had no prepared speech, and made a full length oration, which went down very well.

Winston S. Churchill: speech
(*Churchill papers, 9/150*)

17 January 1941

City Chambers
Glasgow

I can hold out no hopes of an easy passage. Before us lie dangers – I hardly like to say as great as those through which we have passed, but, at any rate, dangers which, if we neglect anything, might be fatal, mortal. Before us lie many months of having to endure bombardment of our cities and industrial areas without the power to make equal reply. Before us lie sufferings and tribulations. I am not one of those who pretend that smooth courses are open to us or that our experiences during this year are going to be deprived of terrible characteristics.

But what the end will be – about that I cannot have the slightest doubt. The

[1] Thomas Johnston, 1881–1965. Founder and Editor of the radical magazine *Forward.* Labour Member of Parliament for West Stirlingshire, 1922–24; Dundee, 1924–29; West Stirlingshire, 1929–31 and 1931–45. Lord Privy Seal, 1931. Regional Commissioner, Scottish Civil Defence Region, 1939–41. Secretary of State for Scotland, 1941–45. Chairman of the Scottish National Forestry Commissioners 1945–48. Chairman of the Scottish Tourist Board, until 1959. Companion of Honour, 1953. Director of the Independent Television Authority in North-East Scotland, 1960–65.

[2] Robert Norman Duke, 1893–1969. On active service, France and Flanders, 1914–18. (Distinguished Service Order, Military Cross, despatches thrice). Brigade Major, 1918. Entered the Civil Service (Scottish Office), 1919; Principal Assistant Secretary, 1937–39; Secretary, Scottish Home Department, 1939; Principal Officer to the Regional Commissioner for the Scottish Civil Defence Region, 1939–41; additional Deputy Under-Secretary of State, Air Ministry, 1942–43; Joint Deputy Secretary, Ministry of Fuel and Power (in charge of the Petroleum Division), 1944–45. Knighted, 1945. Chairman, South East Scotland Electricity Board, 1948–55.

two dictators are always endeavouring to feed their people with every kind of optimistic tale, but here we have made up our minds; here we look at facts with unillusioned eyes, because we are conscious of the rightness of our cause and because we are determined that at whatever cost, whatever suffering, we will not fail mankind at this turning point in its fortunes.

Mr Harry Hopkins has come in order to put himself in the closest relation with things here. He will soon return to report to his famous chief the impressions he has gathered in our islands. We do not require in 1941 large armies from oversea. What we do require are weapons, ships, and aeroplanes.

All that we can pay for we will pay for, but we require far more than we shall be able to pay for. And I watch with deep emotion the stirring processes by which the Democracy of the Great American Republic is establishing its laws and formulating its decisions in order to make sure that the British Commonwealth of Nations is able to maintain, as it is maintaining at the present time, the front line of civilization and of progress.

My one aim is to extirpate Hitlerism from Europe. The question is such a simple one. Are we to move steadily forward and have freedom, or are we to be put back into the Middle Ages by a totalitarian system that crushes all forms of individual life and has for its aim little less than the subjugation of Europe and little more than the gratification of gangster appetites?

Do not suppose that we are at the end of the road. Yet, though long and hard it may be, I have absolutely no doubt that we shall win a complete and decisive victory over the forces of evil, and that victory itself will be only a stimulus to further efforts to conquer ourselves and to make our country as worthy in the days of peace as it is proving itself in the hours of war.

Sir Charles Wilson:[1] *diary*
(*'Winston Churchill, The Struggle for Survival 1940-1965'*)

17 January 1941 Station Hotel, Glasgow

DINNER

I sat next to Harry Hopkins, an unkempt figure. After a time he got up and, turning to the PM, said:

'I suppose you wish to know what I am going to say to President Roosevelt on my return. Well, I'm going to quote you one verse from the Book of Books

[1] Charles McMoran Wilson, 1882–1977. A physician. On active service as a Medical Officer, 1914–18; Major, Royal Army Medical Corps (Military Cross, despatches twice). Dean of St Mary's Hospital Medical School, 1920–45. Knighted, 1938. Churchill's doctor for fifteen years, from 1940–1955. President of the Royal College of Physicians, 1941–50. Created Baron Moran, 1943. In 1965, immediately after Churchill's death, he published *Winston Churchill, The Struggle for Survival.*

in the truth of which Mr Johnston's mother and my own Scottish mother were brought up: "Whither thou goest, I will go; and where thou lodgest, I will lodge: thy people shall be my people, and thy God my God."'[1] Then he added very quietly: 'Even to the end.'

I was surprised to find the PM in tears. He knew what it meant.

Even to us, the words seemed like a rope thrown to a drowning man.

Winston S. Churchill to Viscount Cranborne
(*Premier papers, 3/127/3A*)

17 January 1941

I have read these two documents[2] which do not seem to me to add very much to what we already know or what is obvious in the existing Southern Irish situation. The strategic position has been repeatedly examined and the Admiralty have a paper on the urgent need for the Irish bases as well as for air fields on the south and west coasts. I am asking General Ismay to see that this information is placed before you.

I do not consider that it is at present true to say that possession of these bases is vital to our survival. The lack of them is a grievous injury and impediment to us. More than that it would not at present be true to say. I could not, however, give the assurance suggested by Mr Dillon[3] that in no circumstances should we 'violate Irish neutrality'. I do not personally recognise Irish neutrality as a legal act. Southern Ireland having repudiated the Treaty, and we not having recognized Southern Ireland as a Sovereign State, that country is now in an anomalous position. Should the danger to our war effort through the denial of the Irish bases threaten to become mortal, which is not the case at present, we should have to act in accordance with our own self-preservation and that of our cause. Meanwhile the policy which we recently decided on should be carried out as you are doing, and the influence of the United States must be invoked by every means open to us. It is possible that Mr Hopkins, with whom I have had long talks, will himself visit Ireland, and I am of opinion that his visit might be useful. I do not think the time is ripe yet for you to visit Ireland, unless you receive a direct invitation from Mr de Valera. It would be better to see how the economic and shipping pressures work. At any time the slow movements of events in Ireland may be violently interrupted by a German descent, in which case with or without an invitation we should have

[1] From the Book of Ruth, chapter 1, verse 16.

[2] A report of a visit to Ireland by R.J.H. Shaw of *The Times*, and a memorandum by Sir J. Maffey of a recent interview with De Valera.

[3] Thomas Dillon, 1884–1971. Member of the Executive Council of Sinn Fein, 1917–22. Professor of Chemistry, University of Galway, 1919–54.

to go to turn out the invaders. For the present therefore I see no policy other than the one we have recently adopted.

I do not at all wonder that Mr de Valera regrets the disappearance from power of Mr Chamberlain,[1] who gave him the Irish bases and a good many other things for nothing.[2]

Winston S. Churchill to Anthony Eden
(*Churchill papers, 20/36*)

18 January 1941

If you approve I should like Livorno to be called in the English – Leghorn; and Istanbul in English – Constantinople. Of course when speaking or writing Turkish we can use the Turkish name; and if at any time you are conversing agreeably with Mussolini in Italian, Livorno would be correct.

And why is Siam buried under the name of Thailand?

Winston S. Churchill to General Metaxas
(*Churchill papers, 20/49*)

18 January 1941

I warmly thank your Excellency for your congratulations on the capture of Bardia. It gives me the greatest pleasure to be able to reply congratulating you equally on the continued success of the Greek Army, in spite of the most difficult weather conditions, which now present a more serious obstacle to your victorious advance than the dispirited enemy. I have telegraphed your message to the Prime Minister of the Commonwealth of Australia, to whom I know it will give the greatest satisfaction.

[1] Arthur Neville Chamberlain, 1869–1940. Son of Joseph Chamberlain, his mother died in childbirth in 1875. Educated at Rugby and Mason College, Birmingham. In business in the Bahamas, 1890–7. Lord Mayor of Birmingham, 1915–16. Director-General of National Service, 1916–17 (when his cousin Norman, to whom he was devoted, was killed in action on the western front). Conservative MP for Ladywood, 1918–29; for Edgbaston, 1929–40. Postmaster-General, 1922–3. Paymaster-General, 1923. Minister of Health, 1923, 1924–9 and 1931. Chancellor of the Exchequer, 1923–4 and 1931–7. Leader of the Conservative Party, 1937. Prime Minister, 1937–40. Lord President of the Council, May–November 1940.

[2] In April 1938 Chamberlain's government had agreed with the Government of Eire to give up all British naval rights at Queenstown, Berehaven and Lough Swilly. These rights had been secured as part of the Irish Treaty of 1922, at which time Churchill, as one of the principal negotiators, had placed the highest importance on Britain retaining control of these three naval bases. On 5 May 1938, during a debate in the House of Commons, he attacked the decision as 'an improvident example of appeasement', comparable to the abandonment of Gibraltar or Malta. The House of Commons listened to him with what he later described as 'a patient air of scepticism'. There were frequent, angry interruptions, and his criticisms of Chamberlain were widely resented by his fellow Conservative MPs. Bitterly he told them: 'You are casting away real and important means of security and survival for vain shadows and for ease.'

Winston S. Churchill: recollections
('The Second World War', Volume Three, pages 52-3)

18 January 1941 Chequers

THE ATTACK ON PANTELLARIA ISLAND

All agreements were obtained, but with our other affairs we could not meet the date at the end of January at which we had aimed. At a conference at Chequers on the morning of January 18 I agreed with the First Sea Lord and the other Chiefs of Staff to put it off for a month. I think I could have turned the decision the other way, but like the others I was constrained by the pressure of larger business, and also by talk about the Commandos not being yet fully trained. Keyes,[1] who was not present, was bitterly disappointed. The delay proved fatal to the plan. Long before the month had passed the German Air Force arrived in Sicily, and all wore a very different complexion. There is no doubt about the value of the prize we did not gain. Had we been in occupation of Pantellaria in 1942 many fine ships that were lost in our convoys, which we then fought through to Malta, might have been saved, and the enemy communications with Tripoli still further impaired. On the other hand, we might well have been overpowered by German air attack, lost our vantage and complicated our defence of Malta in the interval.

I felt acutely the need of Pantellaria. But our hour had passed. Too much was upon us from many quarters. It was not till May 1943, after the destruction of the German and Italian armies in Tunis, that, under a heavy bombardment, Pantellaria was taken by a British landing force at the order of General Eisenhower. We were then all-powerful in this theatre, and though the task was deemed very serious beforehand there was no loss.

[1] Roger John Brownlow Keyes, 1872–1945. Entered the Royal Navy, 1885, Naval Attaché, Athens and Constantinople, 1905–7. Commodore in charge of submarines, North Sea and adjacent waters, August 1914–February 1915. Chief of Staff, Eastern Mediterranean Squadron (Dardanelles), 1915. Director of Plans, Admiralty, 1917. Vice-Admiral in Command of the Dover Patrol (and Zeebrugge raid), 1918. Knighted, 1918. Created Baronet, 1919. Deputy Chief of the Naval Staff, 1921–5. Commander-in-Chief, Mediterranean, 1925–8; Portsmouth, 1929–31. Admiral of the Fleet, 1930. Elected to the Other Club, 1930. National Conservative MP, 1934–43. Director of Combined Operations, 1940–1. Created Baron, 1943. Churchill wrote the forward to his memoirs, *Adventures Ashore & Afloat* (1939). His elder son was killed in action in Libya, leading a raid on Rommel's headquarters, 18 November 1941.

Winston S. Churchill to James Stuart
(Churchill papers, 20/36)

18 January 1941

Please see attached[1] from the Lord Privy Seal and my notes thereupon. Mr Bevin[2] is sending me a copy of his speech. I think it will be better for me to let the House make its criticisms upon the new arrangement of Committees, and to deal with these for the first time when I wind up on the Tuesday. It is surely better for me to keep my powder and shot till the criticisms have been made. I do not think, therefore, that I should make a statement at the beginning, and I do not wish anyone else to make a statement upon these Ministerial arrangements except myself. I think I have a very good account to give the House, and I would rather keep it for the wind up. I do not think it would be possible to take the Boothby[3] case on Wednesday. It would be better to fix that for the Tuesday following, which gives time for the report and his evidence to be digested, and also for opinions to form. This was the view of the Lord Privy Seal.

Winston S. Churchill to Ernest Bevin
(Churchill papers, 20/21)

19 January 1941

My dear Bevin,

I have made a few notes upon your excellent statement which you will see as you look through it. You want about ten lines at the end, which I think might well express the determination of the working people of this country to eradicate the curse of Hitlerism from Europe, and the way in which they mean

[1] A memorandum from Clement Attlee on the forthcoming debate on Production.

[2] Ernest Bevin, 1881–1951. National Organizer, Dockers Union, 1910–21. General Secretary, Transport and General Workers' Union, 1921–40. Member of the Trades Union Congress General Council, 1925–40. Labour MP for Central Wandsworth, 1940–50; for East Woolwich, 1950–1. Minister of Labour and National Service, 1940–5. Privy Councillor, 1940. Secretary of State for Foreign Affairs, 1945–51. Lord Privy Seal, 1951.

[3] Robert John Graham Boothby, 1900–86. Educated at Eton and Magdalen College, Oxford. Conservative MP for East Aberdeenshire, 1924–58. Parliamentary Private Secretary to the Chancellor of the Exchequer (Churchill), 1926–9. Elected to the Other Club, 1928. Parliamentary Secretary, Ministry of Food, 1940–1. A British Delegate to the Consultative Assembly, Council of Europe, 1949–57. Knighted, on Churchill's recommendation, 1953. Created Baron, 1958. President of the Anglo-Israel Association. Rector of St Andrews University, 1958–61. Chairman, Royal Philharmonic Orchestra, 1961–3. Published *The New Economy* (1943), *I Fight to Live* (1947), *My Yesterday, Your Tomorrow* (1962) and *Recollections of a Rebel* (1978).

to go on whatever it cost. I am assuming that Max[1] is satisfied with the references to MAP.[2]

I was not quite clear about the point at the top of page 53, but no doubt you will settle that with the others.

Page 41, the word 'turnover' is not quite clear. What I suppose is meant is chaotic inflow and outflow and unsettled conditions generally.

Page 40. I think you should tell them a little more about this 'Limitation of supply order'. Two or three lines would do. I did not feel I understood quite what was happening.

I will lie back till the next day and pick up any pieces that may be on the ground. I think your statement will be most effective.

Yours very sincerely
Winston S. Churchill

Winston S. Churchill to Sir John Reith
(*Premier papers, 3/18/1*)

19 January 1941

NUMBERS AVAILABLE TO REPAIR HOUSES: 3,085 MEN

Press on. If double the numbers were available it w'd be too little.

Winston S. Churchill to David Margesson and General Sir John Dill
(*Churchill papers, 20/36*)

19 January 1941

ANTI-TANK RIFLES AND AMMUNITION

Although the 55-division programme was agreed in Autumn 1939 the Ministry of Supply appear only to have had the demand for the increased number of rifles in April 1940. It is quite true that higher figures than the original 31 thousand appeared in the Military Co-ordination Committee papers, but there seems to have been considerable delay in putting forward a definite requirement for 74 thousand.

Is there really any use in pressing for an increase in the number of rifles when the ammunition supply is so deplorably short? We appear to have enough anti-tank rifles for unit equipment of about 35 divisions, but we only have 120 rounds per rifle and are only making 13 rounds per rifle per month.

I have instructed my statistical section to prepare you a copy of my State of Readiness diagrams.[3]

[1] Lord Beaverbrook.
[2] The Ministry of Aircraft Production, of which Lord Beaverbrook was the head.
[3] These diagrams were prepared for Churchill under the supervision of Professor Lindemann.

Winston S. Churchill to President Franklin D. Roosevelt
(*Churchill papers, 20/49*)

19 January 1941

You probably know that Halifax will arrive at Annapolis in our new battleship HMS *King George V*. She cannot, of course, stay more than twenty-four hours. I don't know whether you would be interested to see her. We should be proud to show her to you, or to any of your high naval authorities, if you could arrange that. She is due at entrance of Chesapeake Bay at 7.00 am on 24th January. If you will communicate to me any suggestions or wishes we will do our best to meet them.

Winston S. Churchill to General Ismay, for the Chiefs of Staff Committee, and to Herbert Morrison
(*Churchill papers, 20/36*)

19 January 1941
Action this Day
Secret

1. Many and increasing indications point to the early use of gas against us. The Armed Forces have been kept fully abreast of these possibilities, and are accustomed to use their masks and eye-shields. It would be well, however, to issue renewed instructions to all Commands, and also to consider whether any new filter is required for possible new toxic gases.

Let me have a report on this (one page).

2. But what is the condition of the masks in the hands of the civil population? Have they been overhauled regularly? Very few people carry masks nowadays. Is there any active system of gas training? It appears that the whole of this has become extremely urgent. Let me have an early report of the present position, and what is being done to bring it up to full efficiency. This report should also cover the decontamination system, and staffs.

3. Finally, it is important that nothing should appear in the newspapers, or be spoken on the BBC, which suggests that we are making a fuss about anti-gas arrangements, because the enemy will only use this as part of his excuse, saying that we are about to use it on him. I am of opinion, nevertheless, that a nation-wide effort must be made.

Winston S. Churchill to Air Chief Marshal Sir Charles Portal
(*Churchill papers, 20/36*)

19 January 1941

STATE OF THE METROPOLITAN AIR FORCE

The new form of return certainly looks more encouraging than the old and I approve the principles on which it is based. Will you, however, explain to me how it is that the Fighter Command has 1,318 crews fully operational and only 1,181 serviceable aircraft, when there are at least 700 serviceable aircraft of fighter types in the ASUs.[1] Why should these machines not be moved up into the Squadrons? At any rate, up to the level of their initial equipment, viz., 1,218.

The effect of the return would make anyone suppose that you were short of fighter aircraft, whereas you have a plethora with which to form new squadrons.

Eric Seal: letter
(*Seal papers*)

19 January 1941 Chequers

We have had staying with us over the weekend one Harry Hopkins, an American, who is a close confidant of the President's. He is really a very charming & interesting man. Winston has taken to him tremendously. Tonight (this is for your ears only) we rang up the President – & the Prime Minister spoke to him. He started off 'Mr President – it's me – Winston speaking'!!

Winston S. Churchill to A. V. Alexander
(*Churchill papers, 20/36*)

20 January 1941

The First Sea Lord told me last night when he came to Chequers that you were thinking of relieving Admiral Drax and replacing him by Admiral Lyon.[2] I did not demur to this. But I was surprised this morning to see from the announcement that it had already been decided before I was consulted in any

[1] Air Storage Units, aircraft in storage.

[2] George Hamilton D'Oyly Lyon, 1883–1947. Played rugby football for England, 1908. Served in HMS *Monarch* throughout the First World War; present at the Battle of Jutland, 1916. Rear-Admiral Commanding the Third Cruiser Squadron, 1935–8. Commander-in-Chief, South Atlantic, 1938–40; The Nore, 1941–3. Knighted, 1940. One of his three sons was killed in action near Dunkirk in May 1940.

way. As the change-over does not take place till April, there surely would have been plenty of time for you to tell me about it beforehand.

2. I am glad to learn from the First Sea Lord that the letter relieving Admiral Somerville[1] has not yet gone. In view of all the circumstances, I think the question might be reviewed.

Winston S. Churchill to Anthony Eden
(*Churchill papers, 20/36*)

20 January 1941
Secret

I saw the other day a claim put forward that we should be grateful to Egypt for the help she was giving us. I was very glad to read your answering telegram. But for our exertions, Egypt would now be incorporated in the Italian Empire. I do not think they deserve any thanks at all. On the contrary, chidings should be administered to make them redeem their character now that the main danger has been passed. Surely they should be reminded that they owe their immunity and independence entirely to British arms, and they should feel that Great Britain, having faithfully discharged her obligations under the Treaty, has claims upon them of a different order to any asserted of late years.

History will regard Egypt (if such an individuality exists) as having been shamed by the pusillanimous, cowardly manner in which she allowed her frontiers to be invaded and her cities bombed, without ever daring to make a declaration of war against the aggressor.

I do hope we are not going to have any false pussyfoot sentiments about these people, whom we have rescued from a horrible fate, and who lie in the hollow of our hands. I trust the time will come when the interests of the Fellaheen will be cherished by His Majesty's Government, even if some of the rich pashas and landowners and other pretended nationalists have to pay the same kind of taxes as are paid by wealthy people in Britain. A little of the radical, democratic sledge-hammer is needed in the Delta, where so many fat, insolent class and party interests have grown up under our tolerant protection.

Excuse my striking this note thus early.

[1] James Fownes Somerville, 1882–1949. Entered the Royal Navy, 1898. On active service at the Dardanelles, 1915 (despatches, DSO). Commanding the Destroyer Flotillas, Mediterranean Fleet, 1936–8. Commander-in-Chief, East Indies, 1938–9. Retired list, 1939. Knighted, 1939. Officer Commanding Force H, 1940–42. Commander-in-Chief, Eastern Fleet, 1942–4. Head of the British Admiralty Delegation, Washington, 1944–5. Admiral of the Fleet, 1945.

Winston S. Churchill to General Sir Alan Brooke
(*Churchill papers, 20/36*)

20 January 1941
Secret

How would you propose to deal with a limited number of large amphibian Tanks which got ashore and roamed about? Am I right in supposing that your light forces would surround them and follow them about at the closest quarters, preventing the crews from refuelling or getting food and sleep, or from ever leaving the armour of their vehicles? If, say, not more than 40 of these Tanks came ashore, would they be followed and hunted to death in this manner, apart from anything that artillery, mines and Tank traps could do?

Anyhow, please let me know what would be your plan.

War Cabinet: minutes
(*Cabinet papers, 65/21*)

20 January 1941
5 p.m.
Most Secret

GREECE

The Prime Minister said that it seemed clear that Prince Paul had told the Greek Government that if they allowed any British land forces to enter Greece, the Yugoslav Government would allow the Germans to attack Greece through Yugoslavia. No doubt he had then tried to curry favour with the Germans by telling them that he had kept British units out of Greece. He hoped that, if he had not already done so, the Foreign Secretary would make it quite clear to the Yugoslav Government that there had never been any question of our forcing help on Greece. That country must decide its own fate.

VICHY FRANCE

The Prime Minister said that he conceived Marshal Pétain's main object to be to keep the Germans out of Unoccupied France by threatening that if they came in, the Fleet, and North Africa would join this country. It remained to be seen how long he could keep the Germans in play.

MALTA

The Prime Minister emphasized the importance of maintaining a strong air defence at Malta. Adequate fighter reinforcements must be sent. He asked the Chief of the Imperial General Staff to ascertain the state of the AA[1] ammunition reserve.

[1] Anti-aircraft.

Winston S. Churchill to Anthony Eden
(*Churchill papers, 20/36*)

20 January 1941

I presume you are keeping your eye upon all this.[1] Your predecessor[2] was entirely misled in December 1939. Our attitude towards all such inquiries or suggestions should be absolute silence. It may well be that a new peace offensive will open upon us as an alternative to threats of invasion and poison gas.

John Colville: diary
(*Colville papers*)

20 January 1941

The Cabinet was at 5 at the CWR, as always on Mondays, and afterwards the PM was feeling very polite. He even went so far as to say (after I had fetched him his red ink pen and much else besides): 'Will you add yet another to all the kindnesses you have been heaping on my head by turning out the electric fire?', which is not the way he usually asks for things!

Anthony Eden: diary
(*'The Reckoning'*)

20 January 1941

Dined with Winston and Clemmie alone. W in very good form and clearly encouraged by his most successful Clyde trip. He had been through all three ILP[3] seats and warmly welcomed everywhere.

He was pleased I was at Foreign Office and asked me to confess I was also. I did so. 'For,' said W, 'it is like moving up from fourth form to the sixth.'

We had long meeting of Defence Committee . . . W was reluctant to give up a certain favourite project of his[4] I talked to him of this again after the meeting.

[1] Two telegrams from the British Minister in Berne, Switzerland, reporting an interview between Field Marshal Goering and a Swedish courier, Baron Carl Barde, on the subject of peace moves.

[2] Lord Halifax.

[3] The Independent Labour Party.

[4] The capture of Pantellaria Island.

He admits it cannot now be carried out, but is very irritated against Chiefs of Staff for not having done it sooner.

News of Italian withdrawal from Kassala came in during evening. Winston maintained at dinner that this was 'Anthony's strategy'. Which, of course, is nonsense, but I did have to struggle with him to prevent him forbidding Wavell to move 4th Indian Division south, as we had planned. Anyway if we can advance to Agordat this should be important contribution to finishing up Italian East African resistance.

Defence Committee (Operations): minutes
(Cabinet papers, 69/2)

20 January 1941
9.30 p.m.

Sir Dudley Pound said that the Chiefs of Staff had reviewed the Mediterranean situation in the light of two new factors:

(a) The Greeks had made it clear that they did not wish for assistance from our land forces in the immediate future.

(b) German aircraft had established themselves in Sicily – thus gaining a temporary control of the centre of the Mediterranean.

Under these conditions, the Chiefs of Staff were of the opinion that we should make certain of our hold of the Eastern Mediterranean, so as to ensure the safety of the main fleet base at Alexandria; and to enable us, should it become necessary, to send forces to help the Greeks or the Turks. To carry out this policy, we must first of all clear Cyrenaica, and secure Benghazi. This would deprive the Italians and the Germans of all the first class aerodromes in North Africa within striking distance of Alexandria. Moreover, Cyrenaica could then be held with a comparatively small force, thus freeing the greater part of the Army of the Nile, and our air forces in the Middle East, for action elsewhere. Secondly, in order to diminish the threat to our lines of communication to Greece or to Smyrna, we must clear the Dodecanese. Having achieved these two objectives, we could build up a strategical reserve in the Middle East, which could be used, possibly to help the Greeks at Salonika, or on the line of the lakes, or more probably to assist the Turks.

The Chiefs of Staff had considered what action could be taken in the central and Western Mediterranean. They had come to the conclusion that even if it were possible to capture Pantellaria, we should not be enabled by its use to control the passage through the Narrows. The Germans had at their disposal seven good aerodromes in Sicily. The passage of the Narrows could not be carried out completely in darkness, and ships would be exposed to heavy dive bombing attack at one end or the other, from which the scale of fighter defence which could be provided from Malta, Pantellaria, and aircraft carriers, would not be sufficient protection. The Chiefs of Staff had given preliminary investigation to an operation against Sardinia, but they found that in attempting to take the island, they would be faced with conditions very similar to those which had led to failure in Norway. It would be impossible for us to provide any depth to our air support, which, until we managed to get fighters ashore, would have to be provided entirely from carriers. The inadequacy of such support against a strong shore-based air force had been clearly demonstrated in Norway. An operation against Sicily would be open to very nearly the same objections, though we would have a better starting point in Malta. The only conditions which could hold out a real chance of success to operations against either Sicily or Sardinia would be the use of French bases in Tunisia. Our land and air forces could move forward step by step from the Atlantic coast to Tunis, and could then operate on fairly even terms with the enemy.

In the present situation, the Chiefs of Staff strongly urged that the three Glen ships,[1] and the commandos at present earmarked for operation 'Workshop' should be sailed forthwith to the Middle East via the Cape. The capture of the Dodecanese was becoming of vital importance, and the Commanders-in-Chief in the Middle East had constantly pressed for the Glen ships, and the landing craft which they carried, to be sent out, so as to enable decisive operations against the islands to be undertaken. There were sufficient landing craft on the Glen ships to enable a large force to be thrown ashore in the first flight; and to attempt a combined operation against a strongly held island without the proper landing craft would result in much heavier casualties, and might jeopardize success.

The Prime Minister said that he had read the Chiefs of Staff Report with considerable concern, since it seemed to lead to the minimum of aggressive action. We had lost the chance of capturing Pantellaria, and the changes which had taken place in the central Mediterranean meant that it might never recur. As a set-off to this, the Chiefs of Staff in their report suggested that we should not lose sight of the importance of occupying Sicily. He entirely agreed with this sentiment, and would support any practicable plan which could be proposed, but no-one could suggest that we were in a position to carry out so large an operation, which would be rendered specially difficult by the fact that the German army could pour down through Italy and across the Straits of Messina to oppose us. We had not the forces for the great battle which would result. This kind of action being denied to us, all that the Chiefs of Staff could recommend was the capture of Benghazi and of the Dodecanese.

While, he entirely favoured both of these operations, he was not prepared to agree that they were a satisfying object for the great forces now gathered in

[1] Converted Glen Line passenger ships, being used as fast troop carriers. Three of them were adapted as Landing Ships Infantry Large – LSI(L)s – each capable of holding three assault battalions during amphibious landings.

the Middle East. The Army of the Nile should be able to take Benghazi with quite a small force. The port should then be turned into a strong base, supplies should be collected there, and guns installed: and a strong defensive flank thus prepared for Egypt. No great forces would be required on the line of communication, and the main army would be free for other work. Meanwhile, it was proposed to await the arrival of the Glen ships, which would have to go all round the Cape before attacking the Dodecanese.

He was firmly opposed to sending the Special Troops away to the Middle East, where they would pass out of our control. During the passage they would be removed from the scene of activity in both theatres of war. Surely it ought to be possible for the Army of the Nile to capture the Dodecanese with the resources now at their disposal. All that the Commanders-in-Chief had so far wished to attempt was the landing of small forces on unimportant islands. It was wrong to advertise your intentions before the means were ready to take decisive action. All that such raids would have done would have been to have aroused the garrisons, and stimulated the Germans to hurry to their assistance. Political difficulties between the Greeks and the Turks would have been needlessly provoked. It was essential, when the Dodecanese were to be attacked, that they should be dealt with decisively.

Turning to the situation in the Balkans, the Prime Minister said that we could not force the Greeks to receive our help. We were open to no reproach in the matter, and he did not regret the offer we had made; but he could not believe that General Metaxas was right in his theory that the Germans were limiting themselves to defensive action in the Balkans. All our information showed that preparations were well under way for the occupation of Bulgaria, with the connivance of the Bulgarian authorities.[1] There would be no invasion; the country would be sapped from within like Roumania. The Turks would probably remain quiescent, and the Germans would gain a dominating position from which to threaten Salonika.

Under these conditions, it was hopeless for us to imagine that we could fight for Salonika.

DODECANESE

Some discussion then took place upon the likelihood of the Germans establishing themselves in the Dodecanese.

Sir Charles Portal thought that the Germans would have considerable difficulty in operating any large number of aircraft from the Islands without several weeks' preparation. A large number of transport aircraft would have

[1] An Enigma decrypt of January 18 showed German Air Force hutments being sent to Bulgaria. A decrypt of 20 January 1941 showed that the German Air Force mission in Roumania was discussing long-term arrangements for the supply of German Air Force fuel to depots in Bulgaria (CX/JQ 603 and 605 quoted in F.H. Hinsley and others, *British Intelligence in the Second World War, Its Influence on Strategy and Operations*, Volume l, London, 1979, page 355).

to be used and, at present, unless they fly over Greece, these could only reach the Islands via Italy and Benghazi. A considerable quantity of men and stores would have to be transported and the Germans would find it difficult to maintain any high rate of serviceability among their aircraft with such extemporised arrangements.

The Prime Minister thought that the presence of German aircraft in the Islands, under these conditions, would not constitute a great danger, nor greatly prejudice our attack; but the garrisons might be stimulated to give a higher degree of resistance.

Discussion then turned upon the date on which an attack might be launched against the Dodecanese.

The Prime Minister said that he was anxious to give the war a more active scope in the Mediterranean. We were being attacked at Malta (and one of the first charges on our resources must be to keep the Island supplied with fighters so that it could continue the highly successful resistance which it was putting up), and we should no doubt see the Germans arrive at Salonika. Greece might be ruined. We would find it difficult, if not impossible, to parry these blows and therefore, we must take steps to counter them by aggressive action at some other point.

SARDINIA

The Prime Minister said that he had asked for a plan to capture Sardinia to be examined. The enemy could not bring large land forces to Sardinia, nor could bombers from Italy or Sicily operate there with Fighter escort. Its capture by us would open up prospects of attacking the whole of Italy from the air from good bases. The Island lay in close relation to Corsica, which might be convenient if the French in North Africa continued the struggle. There was only one Italian corps in the Island. Preliminary study showed that an operation might be done with one corps and some special service troops.

Sir Charles Portal pointed out that, if we succeeded in getting ashore in Sardinia, we should still have to maintain our forces there under a very heavy scale of bomber attack from Sicily and Italy. Our experience in Norway had shown the difficulty of doing this.

The Prime Minister summing up the discussion, said that there was general agreement that Benghazi and the Dodecanese must be cleared up as soon as possible and that the Army of the Nile should immediately set to work to constitute a mobile reserve which would be ready to proceed as required, either to Greece or Turkey, or for other operations in the Mediterranean. With regard to other projects, and to the disposal of the Glen ships and commandos, he would prefer to take further time for consideration and would draft a minute setting out his conclusions the following morning.

Winston S. Churchill to General Ismay, for the Chiefs of Staff Committee
(*Cabinet papers, 69/2*)

21 January 1941

The following decisions arise from our discussion last night:

1. Three Glen ships with full complement of landing craft and with the commandos assigned to those ships on board, less one Commando (which General Wavell already has), should sail at earliest round the Cape to Suez.

2. There will remain behind –

(a) The Commando redundant through one being already in Egypt.
(b) The Commando troops embarked on *Karanja*.
(c) The rest of the Commando force in this country. This should be made up immediately to the full strength of 5,000 and fully equipped and should continue their training at full speed. If this is not done we shall have lost an essential weapon of offence needed to man and use the new landing craft which are coming out steadily now from the builders. It will be necessary for DCO[1] to remain at home to reorganize and rebuild this force up to its full 5,000.

Pray let me have a plan to implement paras. 1 and 2 during the day (21st).

3. General Wavell should be told that his plans for advancing to Benghazi are approved. Unless this presents altogether unexpected difficulties he should at the same time be able to prepare in the Delta a force sufficient to take the principal Mandibles[2] when the landing craft and the commandos arrive. In the meanwhile he is to make all preparations in order that the attack may be delivered at the earliest moment. He should be asked to report on the above assumption when he could do this and what main units he would use. It is hoped that the attack would be delivered not later than March 1.

4. General Wavell should also begin immediately to build up in the Delta a strategic reserve to be used in Greece or Turkey as occasion may require. Having established themselves strongly at Benghazi with a field force and an armoured Division based on that port he could drop the overland line of communication and thus save both men and transport.

Benghazi, if captured, should be made a strongly defended Naval and Air base, guns, &c., being drawn as may be necessary both from Alexandria and intermediate ports or posts on the line of communication. He ought therefore to be able to create a strategic striking force (of which the troops for Mandibles will form a first instalment) in the next two months. It is hoped that this force may soon attain the equivalent of four Divisions, though probably Brigade group organization would be preferable.

[1] The Director of Combined Operations, Admiral of the Fleet Sir Roger Keyes, MP.

[2] The seizure of the Italian Dodecanese Islands (in the eastern Mediterranean). The largest of these islands is Rhodes. On the evening of 27 January 1941 Churchill went to the underground Central War Room to 'inspect' models of the islands of Leros and Rhodes (Churchill Engagement Book: *Forbes Magazine Collection*).

5. The Air disposition must conform to the above subject to the commitments we have already made to Greece. The first duty of the AOC-in-C ME[1] is none the less to sustain the resistance of Malta by a proper flow of fighter reinforcements. To enable these tasks to be performed *Furious* will make another voyage with a third consignment of forty Hurricanes.

6. An expeditionary force of two Divisions plus certain Corps units and the Commandos when reorganized, should be prepared for action in the Western Mediterranean whether for 'Influx' or 'Yorker'[2] to aid General Wavell as circumstances may suggest. Both these plans are to be studied and perfected – 'Yorker' being the more probable. A Commander should be appointed and an attempt made to be ready to act after March 1. The impingement of the above on later convoys to ME must be examined and reported.

Anthony Eden: diary

(*'The Eden Memoirs, The Reckoning', page 318*)

21 January 1941

Winston was tired and depressed, for him. His cold is heavy on him. He was inclined to be fatalistic about the House, maintained that bulk of Tories hated him, that Malaya, Australian Government's intransigence and 'nagging' in House was more than any man could be expected to endure.

Winston S. Churchill: Oral Answers

(*Hansard*)

21 January 1941 House of Commons

WAR AND PEACE AIMS.

Mr Mander[3] asked the Prime Minister whether he is now able to make a statement with reference to the war and peace aims of the Government?

The Prime Minister (Mr Churchill): Most right-minded people here and abroad, and especially in the United States, already fully understand the causes and principles for which we are waging war upon the Nazi tyranny. His Majesty's Government are always on the look-out for any opportunity of making a statement that would be helpful to our victory and to the liberation

[1] The Air Office Commanding-in-Chief, Middle East (Air Vice-Marshal Longmore).

[2] Influx: proposed British occupation of Sicily. Yorker: the proposed capture of Sardinia.

[3] Geoffrey Le Mesurier Mander, 1882–1962. Head of Mander Bros, paint and varnish manufacturers. Liberal MP, 1929–45. A leading Parliamentary critic of the Munich agreement, 1938. Parliamentary Private Secretary to the Secretary of State for Air (Sir Archibald Sinclair), 1942–5. Knighted, 1945. Joined the Labour Party, 1948.

of the nations now ground down under the German yoke. I am not, however, able to add anything at the present time to previous answers on this subject.

Mr Mander: Has not the appetite of the public been considerably whetted by various speeches made recently by Ministers, in which they spoke of some statement on the subject to be made shortly, and cannot that appetite be satisfied shortly?

Mr Stephen:[1] Is the right hon. Gentleman not unduly optimistic about how well aware people in other countries are?

The Prime Minister: I happened to be visiting the hon. Member's constituency recently, and the people there seemed fully aware of it.

Mr Stephen: Yes, but is the right hon. Gentleman aware that people in other countries may not be so well aware?

The Prime Minister: As I have said, when a good opportunity presents itself, I or other Ministers will certainly be on the look-out to turn that opportunity to the best advantage.

QUESTIONS TO MINISTERS.

Mr Tinker[2] asked the Prime Minister whether he is aware that Members are concerned with replies which they get from Departments on matters that they feel would not be to the public good if followed by Questions on the Order Paper; and will he give consideration to see what way they can be dealt with?

The Prime Minister: My hon. Friend may be assured that Ministers are always anxious to answer the inquiries of hon. Members as fully as circumstances permit. If he has any particular instance in mind, I would suggest that he should approach the Minister concerned, who will, I am sure, supply him with as detailed a reply as possible.

Mr Tinker: That is just the point. I have written to Ministers because I have not got satisfaction about the matters on which I have put Questions to them, and I wonder what steps I ought to take to get the matters further ventilated. When it is a question that might affect the security of the State, what other means have we of getting redress? That is the question.

The Prime Minister: I think the hon. Member should wrestle with the Minister concerned, in as good an accord as is possible. I am sure every effort would be made to give him all possible information, because naturally he would not wish to put a Question on the Paper which would do harm.

[1] Campbell Stephen, 1884–1947. An 'ardent Socialist' (according to his *Who's Who* entry), and a Barrister-at-Law. Teacher of science and mathematics, 1919–22. Labour MP, 1922–31 and from 1935 until his death.

[2] John Joseph Tinker, 1875–1957. A miners' agent in Lancashire. Labour MP, 1923–45. Parliamentary Private Secretary to the Secretary of State for War, 1924.

BRITISH BROADCASTING CORPORATION (CHARTER).

Mr De la Bère[1] asked the Prime Minister whether he will consider taking steps to amend the charter of the British Broadcasting Corporation, which was renewed on 1st January, 1937, for 10 years, so as to allow of a more elastic administration throughout the war period?

The Prime Minister: I do not think it is necessary to amend the charter of the British Broadcasting Corporation in order to secure administration suitable for war conditions.

Mr De la Bère: Can my right hon. Friend tell me whether, in matters of policy, the BBC are always voicing the views of the Government? Is he not aware that the general public are certainly under the impression that they are, whether the Government like it or not?

The Prime Minister: No, Sir. The British Broadcasting Corporation give, I believe, considerable latitude to expressions of opinion which are not injurious to the war effort, and I should be very sorry to think that Ministers were in any way to be held responsible for all statements by the BBC.

Mr Granville:[2] Is it not a fact that the Minister of Information has absolute control with regard to certain matters affecting the BBC?

The Prime Minister: Yes, Sir, he has effective control in matters which are of high consequence, but that control would not be used in such a way as to allow only expressions of opinion such as would be used by Ministers upon the wireless.

PRODUCTION EXECUTIVE.

Mr Craven-Ellis[3] asked the Prime Minister whether consideration was given to the present full time and heavy responsibilities of the members of the new Production Executive when their appointments were made; and as to whether a greater contribution to the organisation of total war would have been for the members of this executive to devote their full time to the important matter of production?

The Prime Minister: These matters will no doubt be referred to in the course of the Debate.

[1] Rupert De la Bère, 1893–1978. Captain, East Surrey Regiment; on active service, 1914–18 (including Mesopotamia). Seconded to Royal Air Force, 1918. Conservative Member of Parliament for Evesham, 1935–50; for South Worcestershire, 1950–55. Sheriff of the City of London, 1941–42. Lord Mayor of London, 1952–53. Knighted, 1952.

[2] Edgar Louis Granville, 1899–1998. Served with the Australian Infantry Force, Gallipoli, Egypt and France, 1915–18. A Liberal MP, 1929–31; National Liberal, 1931–42; Liberal, 1942–51. Parliamentary Private Secretary to Herbert Samuel, 1931; to Sir John Simon, 1931–6. Captain, Royal Artillery, 1939–40. Created Baron Granville of Eye, 1967. He sat in the Lords as an independent.

[3] William Craven-Ellis, –1959. A director of several investment and property companies. Conservative MP, 1931–45. Chairman of the Parliamentary and Monetary Committee of the House of Commons, 1934–44.

Mr Craven-Ellis: Is the right hon. Gentleman aware that the country is not satisfied with having this Committee as a part-time body? As we are organising total war, does he not consider that it should be a whole-time Committee?

The Prime Minister: No, Sir, I have strong views on this matter and have had some experience on which to form them, and I should certainly be ready to discuss the matter in debate; but it would be very foolish, as we are to have a two-days' Debate, to begin dabbling with the subject by means of questions and answers.

Winston S. Churchill to Sir John Anderson[1]
(Churchill papers, 20/36)

21 January 1941

I see that deliveries of coal to London during recent weeks have been running at 250,000 tons per week. It appears, if the Mines Department's estimates of requirements are correct, that there will be a shortage unless 410,000 tons a week are delivered from now until the end of March.

I should be glad to know whether you agree with the estimates of the Mines Department, and, if so, what steps you propose to take to increase deliveries by the required amount. I find it hard to understand why deliveries by rail during the last three months should have fallen to only three-fifths of last year's figure.

Winston S. Churchill to Malcolm MacDonald
(Churchill papers, 20/36)

21 January 1941

Is it not possible to reduce more rapidly the number of homeless people in the London rest centres? I am hoping that this week will show that they have practically all been dispersed. One cannot tell when another heavy attack may not be made upon us, and a quiet week should be a precious gain.

[1] John Anderson, 1882–1958. Educated at Edinburgh and Leipzig Universities. Entered the Colonial Office, 1905; Secretary, Northern Nigeria Lands Committee, 1909. Secretary to the Insurance Commissioners, London, 1913. Secretary, Ministry of Shipping, 1917–19. Knighted, 1919. Chairman of the Board of Inland Revenue, 1919–20. Joint Under-Secretary of State in the Government of Ireland, 1920. Permanent Under-Secretary of State, Home Office, 1922–32. Governor of Bengal, 1932–7. MP for the Scottish Universities, 1928–50. Lord Privy Seal, 1938–9. Home Secretary and Minister of Home Security, 1939–40. Lord President of the Council, 1940–3. Chancellor of the Exchequer, 1943–5. Chairman of the Port of London Authority, 1946–58. Created Viscount Waverley, 1952. Order of Merit, 1957. Member of the BBC General Advisory Council.

Winston S. Churchill to General Dobbie[1]
(*Churchill papers, 20/49*)

21 January 1941

I send you, on behalf of the War Cabinet, our heartfelt congratulations upon the magnificent and ever-memorable defence which your heroic garrison and citizens, aided by the Navy and above all by the Royal Air Force, are making against Italian and German attacks. The eyes of all Britain, and indeed of the whole British Empire, are watching Malta in her struggle day by day, and we are sure that success as well as glory will reward your efforts.

Winston S. Churchill to President Franklin D. Roosevelt
(*Churchill papers, 20/49*)

21 January 1941

I am grateful for your message of the 13th January and the instructions which you have sent to Admiral Leahy.[2]

We have been considering other means of encouraging Marshal Pétain, and it occurs to us that it might help him to know that we would give every facility for the mobilisation and departure from Alexandria of the units of the French fleet there in the event of the resumption by the French North African Empire of hostilities against Germany and Italy. Such a message would make clear to Marshal Pétain that we should be prepared, if and when the time comes, to take certain definite action at Alexandria which otherwise he might not assume. It would, in fact, give him a basis on which to make further plans.

We feel that this message would come well from Admiral Leahy in continuation of my message to the Marshal, which you have already instructed your Ambassador to deliver.

[1] William George Sheddon Dobbie, 1879–1964. On active service in South Africa, 1899–1902, and on the Western Front, 1914–18 (despatches seven times, Mons ribbon, DSO). Inspector of the Royal Engineers, 1930–35. General Officer Commanding Malaya, 1935–9. Governor and Commander-in-Chief, Malta, 1940–2. Lieutenant-General, 1940. Knighted, 1941. One of his two sons was killed in action in the Second World War.

[2] William D. Leahy, 1875–1959. Commissioned in the United States Navy, 1899. Admiral, 1936. Chief of Naval Operations, 1937. Governor of Puerto Rico, 1939. American Ambassador to Vichy France, 1940–41. Chief of Staff to the President and to the Joint Chiefs of Staff, 1942–49. Honorary knighthood, 1945. In 1950 he published his memoirs, *I Was There*.

Robert Boothby to Winston S. Churchill
(*Churchill papers, 20/34*)

21 January 1941

Dear Prime Minister,

I beg herewith to tender you my resignation as Parliamentary Secretary to the Ministry of Food.

This decision is not dictated by the findings of the Select Committee.[1] I have felt for some time that it would be my duty to resign even if the Committee had exonerated me. For I consider that the way in which the case against me was prepared and presented is without parallel or precedent in Parliamentary history. My only regret is that the way in which I have been treated has prevented my rendering service to a cause for which I have fought as long as you have yourself.

I reserve all further comment on these matters for my constituents and for the House of Commons. I profoundly deplore this interruption of an association with you which I have deeply and sincerely valued.

Yours sincerely,
Robert Boothby

Winston S. Churchill to Robert Boothby
(*Churchill papers, 20/21*)

21 January 1941

My dear Boothby,

I have received your letter of today resigning your office in the Government with very great regret on personal and on public grounds. No other course was however possible in view of the report of the Select Committee to which you refer.

I take this opportunity of thanking you for the industry and ability with which you discharged your duties while a member of the Administration.

Yours sincerely,
Winston S. Churchill

[1] The Select Committee found that Boothby had acted improperly in connection with the Czech assets in Britain. He thereupon resigned as Parliamentary Secretary at the Ministry of Food, and was never to be in government again. Boothby's sense of grievance against Churchill became more vocal with the passing of time, although he was later, at Churchill's recommendation, knighted, made a British delegate to the Consultative Assembly of the Council of Europe, and made a Peer. Despite his and his biographer's protestations that Churchill could have protected him against censure, it is not clear to me that this could have been done without impropriety on Churchill's part.

Winston S. Churchill: Oral Answers
(*Hansard*)

22 January 1941 House of Commons

CONDUCT OF A MEMBER.

Mr Lees-Smith[1] (by Private Notice) asked the Prime Minister whether he has any statement to make in regard to the report from the Select Committee on the Conduct of a Member?

The Prime Minister: The report came into our hands only yesterday afternoon, and I am sure that the House will require time to consider it, before any question of debate arises. If a Debate is desire, arrangements will be made for it to take place on an early date. As the House is aware, my hon. Friend the Member for East Aberdeen (Mr Boothby) has resigned his office as Parliamentary Secretary to the Ministry of Food.

Winston S. Churchill to General Ismay, for the Chiefs of Staff Committee
(*Churchill papers, 20/36*)

22 January 1941

LOFOTEN ISLANDS[2]

I should like to feel sure that the Chiefs of the Staff have carefully considered whether this Operation is likely to stir up the Norwegian coast and lead to reinforcements of the German forces in the Peninsula. It seems to me that as the attack is on Islands and obviously connected with blockade measures, this danger is obviated. There would be no need to go on the mainland as I understand the Operation.

Pray advise me.

[1] Hastings Bertrand Lees-Smith, 1878–1941. Labour MP, 1910–18 and 1920–3, 1924–31 and from 1935 until his death. Postmaster-General, 1929–31. President of the Board of Education, 1931. Privy Councillor, 1931. Acting Chairman of the Parliamentary Labour Party, 1940–1.

[2] Proposed by Hugh Dalton and approved by Churchill and the Chiefs-of-Staff, the Lofoten Islands raid (Operation Claymore) was said publicly to have been for the destruction of the fish processing plant there, the most important source by which Germany obtained vitamins A and D. The actual aim, which was achieved, was to capture a German Enigma machine used by the German navy, the code keys of which had been proving virtually impossible to break. One such Enigma machine was on board the *Krebs*; its commander, Lieutenant Hans Küpfinger, had managed to throw his machines overboard before he was killed. He had insufficient time, however, to destroy other elements of the Enigma message procedure, including his coding documents, so that after three weeks' intensive work at Bletchley, it became possible for British Intelligence to read all German naval traffic in home waters for the last week of April and much of May, with only a relatively short delay of between three and seven days. The Norwegians were to suffer for the Lofoten Islands raid, Josef Terboven setting up at once, as Goebbels wrote in his diary five days later, 'a punitive court of the harshest kind'.

John Colville: diary
(*Colville papers*)

22 January 1941

I lunched with Eric Seal at the House, and then we both went into the box to hear the PM wind up the debate. He did so extremely well, explaining his reasons for the new Committee machinery (which has been much criticized) with the utmost clearness and cogency. The House was much entertained by his quips and his mastery of the art of anti-climax. He expounded the little understood facts about the slowness of changing from Peace to War production and the increased need of man-power, in industry rather than the forces, as that transfer takes place. He answered the demand for a Dictator on the Home Front, to correspond with the Minister of Defence on the military side, by disparaging dictators in general and by pointing out that he could only maintain his ascendancy as Minister of Defence because he was also Prime Minister. In general he welcomed criticism even when, for the sake of emphasis, it parted company with reality!

Tobruk fell.

I am continually impressed by the PM's genuine love of democracy; viz. a recent minute to the Foreign Secretary about Egypt.[1]

Winston S. Churchill: speech
(*Hansard*)

22 January 1941 House of Commons

The Prime Minister (Mr Churchill): Let me begin by offering my apologies to the House and asking for its indulgence, because I am winding up a Debate of which I have been able to hear only a portion. I have carefully read the parts of the Debate to which I was not able to listen, but I have addressed my mind to the large general issues which led to the fixing of the Debate. I hope that hon. Members who have spoken when I was not present will accept my apology on account of the other calls which I have upon me. I think I have said before that to try to carry on a war, a tremendous war, without the aid and guidance of the House of Commons would be a super-human task. I have never taken the view that the Debates and criticisms of this House are a drag and a burden. Far from it. I may not agree with all the criticism – I may be stunned by it, and I may resent it; I may even retort – but at any rate, Debates on these large issues are of the very greatest value to the life-thrust of the nation, and they are of great assistance to His Majesty's Government.

[1] See above, 20 January 1941.

Therefore, when, as we gathered, there was a wish to have a day's discussion of large questions connected with the Home Front – man-power, priorities, supply and so forth – I offered not only one day, but two days. I think two are better than one, because sometimes, when there is only one day's Debate, especially under our rather restricted conditions of meeting, one may find that the Minister makes a long statement and that afterwards there is nothing in the Debate but the criticism; whereas, after two day's Debate, it is possible to perceive the main character of the criticism and to endeavour, as far as possible, to reassure the House upon the points which have most been called into question.

I want to begin by communicating to the House the main ideas which I have formed, with much thought and some experience, upon the machinery for conducting war. I have reached the conclusion that in the present circumstances a War Cabinet composed of four or five men free from Departmental duties would not give the best results. It may be submitted that that is a very arguable proposition. Some may say that that system assisted to carry us to victory in the last war. I saw the system at close quarters, and I do not think that it was in practice altogether what it was represented to be in theory. The War Cabinet of those days was largely an instrument designed to give the great man who then conducted our affairs wide powers to deal with matters over the whole field, and in practice the meetings of that body, theoretically so eclectic, were attended by very much larger numbers than those who now grace our council board.

Personally, I have formed the view that it is better that there should be in the responsible directing centres of Government some, at any rate, of the key Ministers. There is the Minister for Foreign Affairs, who always attended in the last war. There is the Chancellor of the Exchequer, because, after all, one must not forget that the Chancellor of the Exchequer has a function. There is the Minister of Labour, because, as we have been reminded in the excellent speech which the hon. Member for East Stirling (Mr Woodburn)[1] has just delivered, the spontaneous, sustained, good will effort of the labouring masses of this country is the sole foundation upon which we can escape from our present difficulties. Then there is the Minister of Aircraft Production, because aircraft production is the key to survival, and, if I may say so, the Minister of Aircraft Production, who was described by the hon. Member who has just sat down as an old sea raider, which is a euphemistic method of describing a pirate, is a man of altogether exceptional force and genius, who is at his very best when things are at their very worst. Then there are the Defence Ministers,

[1] Arthur Woodburn, 1890–1978. An engineer (ironfoundry) administrator, author and economist. Labour MP for Clackmannan and East Stirling, 1939–70. Member of the Select Committee on National Expenditure, 1939–45. Parliamentary Private Secretary to the Secretary of State for Scotland, 1941–5. Secretary of State for Scotland, 1947–50.

the three Service Ministers. But, as the Prime Minister under this arrangement, which the House has approved, is also the Minister of Defence, he represents those Departments in the War Cabinet. We make altogether eight, and yet we hold a great many of the key offices in our body. I think it is better to work in that way than to have five Ministers entirely divorced from their Departments, because that means that when a discussion has taken place in the Cabinet, the leaders of these Departments have to be summoned, and the whole business has to be gone over again in order to learn what it is they think they can do and to persuade them and convince them that it is necessary to do what has been decided upon.

The House must not under-rate the power of these great Departments of State. I have served over 20 years in Cabinets, in peace and war, and I can assure the House that the power of these great Departments is in many cases irresistible because it is based on knowledge and on systematized and organised currents of opinion. You must have machinery which carries to the Cabinet with the least possible friction the consent and allegiance of these great Departments. It is not a question of loyalty. It is a question of honest differences of opinion which arise, and there are many matters to be settled and decided which would not arise in the ordinary Departmental mind. There are great difficulties in dealing with Departments of State unless the key Departments are brought into the discussion in the early stages and, as it were, take part in the original formation and initiation of our designs.

I said the Minister of Defence represents the Service Ministers in the War Cabinet, and he, in the name of the War Cabinet and subject to its accord, directs the conduct of the war. Why then, it is asked, have we not got on the civil side another similar Minister? That, I think, was the point raised by my hon. Friend the Member for Montgomery (Mr C. Davies).[1] Why should there not be another similar Minister who would equally direct and concert the whole home front or a great part of it? The answer is this: The Minister of Defence is also Prime Minister, and he can therefore exercise his general function of superintendence and direction without impinging upon the constitutional responsibilities of the Service Ministers. If, however, a Minister of Defence were appointed who was not the Prime Minister – and I am discussing this matter quite impersonally – he would not have any real authority except, of course, a co-ordinating and conciliatory power over the three great Service Ministries and their responsible heads. The First Lord of the Admiralty and the Secretaries of State for War and Air could at any time appeal against him to the War Cabinet, and the whole matter in dispute would

[1] Clement Davies, 1884–1962. An expert on agricultural law. Liberal MP for Montgomeryshire from 1929 until his death. President of the Welsh Liberal Federation, 1945–8. President of the Parliamentary Association for World Government, 1951. One of his two sons and his only daughter were killed in action in the Second World War.

then have to be argued out there once more. If at any time it becomes necessary to appoint a Minister of Defence who is not also Prime Minister, then I tell the House plainly that the Minister will have to be in fact First Lord of the Admiralty and Secretary of State for War and Air, and hold the seals or letters patent of those Departments, otherwise he will have no more power than the various Ministers for the Co-ordination of Defence have had in the years before the war and in the six months at the beginning of the war.

Let me now apply these considerations to the civil side. Here also the Departments have very strong characteristics, and the Ministers at their head have definite constitutional responsibilities to Crown and Parliament. Here also are immense volumes of specialised and organized knowledge. Where am I to find a man who, without himself being Prime Minister, would have the personal ascendancy in his nature to govern and concert the action of all those Ministers and Departments on the civil side, and drive in a happy and docile team the Minister of Supply, the Minster of Labour, and the Minister of Aircraft Production, to say nothing of the Ministers of Transport, Shipping, Agriculture, Food and Trade? I doubt if such a man exists. Certainly I do not know him. We do not live in a dictator country, where people can be brutally overruled. That is our merit. We do not want a dictator. We live in a country where His Majesty's Cabinet governs subject to the continual superintendence, correction and authority of Parliament. In the last resort, only the Cabinet can exert the necessary authority over all these Departments I have mentioned on the civil side. How, then, is this process to be achieved, with the maximum of action and the minimum of pressure? There is the problem for which I ventured, very respectfully, to offer a solution in the recent announcement of the formation of the Government Committees.

Let me, at this point, make a brief diversion upon the uses and abuses of committees and the possibility of administrative action by them. Four years ago I criticised the pre-war Administration for their reliance upon an elaborate network of committees. I was answered by a quotation from my own account of the organization which I set up in the Ministry of Munitions in 1917. In this quotation I was represented to have said, quite accurately, that practically all the work of the Ministry of Munitions was done by a council of committees. That seemed a very good answer in those days, when I had not the advantage of so much support in this House as I have today. Let me make plain to the House the difference between the Council Committees of the old Ministry of Munitions and ordinary advisory inter-departmental committees. The Council Committees were exclusively composed of men who had under their direct control the executive and administrative branches concerned in the problem, and who bore the great responsibility for executing any agreement or any decision reached among them. That is the fact. They were like chieftains, each arriving with so many of his clan, and when the clans were joined together the Highland army was complete. The ordinary consultative and advisory committee is attended by representatives of many branches and Departments – and everyone likes to have his representative on any committee that may be going; they try to agree upon forms of words for a report; and then, too often, they are inclined to pass the buck to some other futile body, equally respectable. The difference between these two kinds of committees is the difference between cheese and chalk – and cheese is much the scarcer and the more nourishing of the two.

Every British Cabinet in the last 30 or 40 years has conducted a large part of its work by Cabinet Committees. Instead of the whole Cabinet sitting there hour after hour, they appoint four or five Ministers to go into this or that particular matter, to hammer it out among themselves, and then to come back and advise the parent body. Such Committees are often based upon the Ministers, the co-ordination of whose Departments is essential to the solution of the problem. They have the strongest incentive to agree, because they are all colleagues: honourable men working for a common object; and if they do agree, they can make their Departments carry out their decisions, and carry them out with alacrity and good will. This was the system which I applied at the Ministry of Munitions in August, 1917. It was certainly generally considered to be a very great improvement and easement in organization upon what had gone before, and this is the system which, *mutatis mutandis*, I have applied now to the two extraordinarily difficult and vital spheres of our life which are covered by the Import Executive and the Production Executive.

The Import Executive consists of the five great importers from these five Departments – the Ministry of Supply, the Ministry of Aircraft Production, the Controllers' Department at the Admiralty, represented by the First Lord, the Food Ministry, and the Board of Trade, which also represents the minor importers. If the men at the head of these Departments, who are among the leading and most active Ministers in the administration, could not settle among themselves how to bring in the greatest volume of imports in which we are all vitally interested, I should be very much disappointed, and indeed, surprised. In order that control may be effective, the handling Departments, that is to say, the Ministry of Transport and the Ministry of Shipping, the Department responsible for shipbuilding and repairs, and in this connection the Ministry of Labour, whose Minister is in the Chair on the other Committee – these Departments serve them and carry out their policy. Take all this business of the docks under the attack which is being made upon them, problems of labour and transport, of turning ships round and so forth. This group of men have everything in their hands. If they can agree – and at their service are the great Departments – they can execute the policy which they put forward.

Similar principles inspired the creation of the Production Executive, the kernel of which consists of the three same supply Ministers who are on the Import Executive and who also constitute the Committee regulating purchases in the United States. Here are these three Supply Ministers at the root of our war production business, and naturally you meet them in all these organisms of Government. This then, is the instrumentation which, I believe, will produce the most effective and rapid action. I am entitled to an opinion in the matter, because, after all, the House has laid on me the responsibility, and I have the right to be judged by the results. So far as the results have gone up to the present, they have given satisfaction to all concerned, and a number of very important and practical decisions have been taken by the complete and unanimous agreement of the parties concerned, followed by immediate action in the Departments concerned.

I see – and I am endeavouring to address myself to the pith of the argument which has been adduced – that some critics have asked, 'Are you not overburdening these Ministers, each with his own Department, by making this one chairman, and these others members of this Imports or Production Executive? If they have to do all this work on these Executives, how are they going to do their own work?' But this is exactly their own work. This is the particular work they have to do. The management of these affairs and its interplay with other Departments constitutes the major problem before each one of them.

I saw that someone wrote in a newspaper that this was a policy of thrusting executives upon overburdened Ministries. Well, that is like saying you are thrusting the Stock Exchange upon stockbrokers or thrusting upon general managers of railways, at a time when railway action had to be concerted, frequent or occasional meetings together. This is the very process by which our business will be discharged. As to the Chairman of this Committee, he is not *facile princeps* but *primus inter pares*, which, for the benefit of any old Etonians present, I should, if very severely pressed, venture to translate. At any rate, all these Ministries have equal and direct responsibilities. But it is asked, 'Why should you not choose less busy men for these tasks?' It surely would not be any help to these busy men to burden them with the task of explaining over and over again their business to others who cannot know a tithe of what they know about it themselves and then, when inevitable differences arise, of having to carry them up to the Cabinet and fight all over again there.

The way to help busy men is to help them to come to a decision together by agreement and to give them power to make this decision promptly effective through all parts of the Government machinery at their disposal. I have my views about this, having served in so many capacities and relationships, and I can assure the House that there is no more formidable and effective organization of power than a unit of four or five consenting minds, each of which has at its disposal full and necessary powers for the discharge of the business entrusted to them. It is not for these executives to decide how many men shall be allotted to the Army, Navy or Air Force, or how much shipping shall be used to bring in food or materials, or carry troops to this campaign or that. These particular blockings-in belong in the main to the War Cabinet, and I accept the responsibility of making sure that the general policy determined by the War Cabinet is interpreted correctly by the executives. In the event of differences I hope to adjust them, and if I fail the matter must be settled, in the last resort, by the Cabinet. In no other way can business in war-time proceed with the necessary despatch. However, it is most desirable that the Cabinet itself shall not be overburdened with business. Ministers must be free when they will to stand away from the intricate machinery of government and the routine of daily work and together survey the stormy skies. Therefore, in order to diminish the number of occasions on which it is necessary to have recourse to the Cabinet, we have this Steering or Planning Committee, over which the Lord President of the Council presides, which deals with the larger issues, and also deals with questions of adjustment. It is fitted to do so, because, although it is not exactly the Cabinet, it contains a very large proportion of its members. The chairmen of the two Executive Committees, the Chancellor of the Exchequer, who at this point – having, of course, already approved departmental purchases as a matter of routine – comes in on general policy, the Minister charged with reconstruction, and the Ministers at the head of the Security and Home Departments, should be able to settle most things there without its being necessary to bring these matters to the Cabinet presided over by the Prime Minister. In this way I hope my own work, which is considerable, will be reduced and more effectively devolved.

I must say a word about the functions of the Minister charged with the study of post-war problems and reconstruction. It is not his task to make a new world, comprising a new Heaven, a new earth, and no doubt a new hell (as I am sure that would be necessary in any balanced system). It is not his duty to set up a new order or to create a new heart in the human breast. These tasks must be undertaken by other agencies. The task of my right hon. Friend is to plan in advance a number of large practical steps which it is indispensable to take if our society is to move forward, as it must, which steps can be far larger and taken far more smoothly if they are made with something of the same kind of national unity as has been achieved under the pressure of this present struggle for life. The scope of my right hon. Friend's task is practical and has regard to national unity, on the one hand, and about three years as a time limit on the other. There certainly will be four or five great spheres of action in which practical and immediate advance may be made if we can continue on the morrow of the victory to act with the unity which we shall have used to bring that victory. I feel my right hon. Friend is very well fitted for this great task, and it gives him a grand and a growing opportunity of historic national service.

Now, I leave these matters of Governmental machinery, and I turn to the larger issues. We had forceful speeches yesterday from the Noble Lord the Minister for Horsham – [Hon. Members: 'Member'] – certainly, it would be no unworthy department – the Noble Lord the Member for Horsham (Earl

Winterton),[1] and from my hon. Friend the Member for Seaham (Mr Shinwell),[2] and today we have had a speech from my hon. and learned friend the Member for Montgomery (Mr Clement Davies), of which I heard only a portion, but which I gather from this sample was an exhaustive treatment of the subject in all its branches and in all its aspects, which had for its characteristic the aim of saying all that was true on both sides of the different aspects dealt with, and sought for the best of both worlds during a prolonged tour through the universe. I ask myself whether our affairs are in fact as badly managed at the present time as these speeches suggest. I am sure there are an awful lot of things which could be done better, and I do not at all resent criticism, even when, for the sake of emphasis, it for a time parts company with reality.

But are my hon. Friend and my Noble Friend right in thinking that things are being so very ill done here, and so much less effectively done here, than they are in the great dictator countries? Let us look into this. At the root of all questions of man-power lies the size of the Army. The Navy and Air Force make gigantic demands upon us, but the great customers for man-power are the Army and the industries which sustain the Army. The size of the Army was settled within a few weeks of the outbreak of war. We have not altered that decision except to the extent of providing for the equipment of 10 more divisions. The scale of the Army is the scale which was settled in November, 1939. I am not going to say how many divisions it amounts to; but it is a very large and formidable force, both in connection with sea power and amphibious power, and of course for the defence of these islands. Counting the Home Guard we have round about 4,000,000 armed and uniformed men who would all play their part in defence of our hearths and homes. But naturally the armies which could be put into the field and taken overseas in formed military units would be measured by quite different standards – the principal standard would be fixed by shipping tonnage available. At the time when the scale of the Army was settled, in 1939, a vast series of factories, plants and establishments were set on foot, sufficient to provide this Army with all

[1] Edward Turnour, 1883–1962. Educated at Eton and New College, Oxford. Conservative MP, 1904–18, 1918–40 and 1940–51. Succeeded his father as 6th Earl Winterton, 1907. As an Irish peer, he continued to sit in the House of Commons. An original member of the Other Club, 1911. Served at Gallipoli, in Palestine and in Arabia, 1915–18. Under-Secretary of State for India, 1922–4 and 1924–9. Chancellor of the Duchy of Lancaster, 1937–9. Paymaster-General, 1939. Chairman, Inter-Governmental Committee for Refugees, 1938–45.

[2] Emanuel Shinwell, 1884–1986. Unsuccessful Labour candidate for Linlithgowshire, 1918; elected, 1922; re-elected, 1923. Defeated, 1924; re-elected at a by-election in April 1928 and again at the general election of 1929. Defeated in 1931. Parliamentary Secretary, Mines Department, 1924 and 1931. Financial Secretary, War Office, 1929–30. Labour MP for Linlithgow, 1928–31; for Seaham, 1935–50; for Easington, 1950–70. Minister of Fuel and Power, 1945–7. Secretary of State for War, 1947–50. Minister of Defence, 1950–1. Chairman of the Parliamentary Labour Party, 1964–7. Created Baron (Life Peer), 1970.

that it would require in continuous action on the Continent of Europe against the German enemy. The bulk of these new plants are only just beginning to come into production, and many of them are still structurally incomplete. We have a very large number of plants which are all simultaneously three-quarters or four-fifths finished. That is what happens at this period in any war when you change from peace production to war production. As these plants come into operation, the construction services – the builders and those who lay on the water, light and power and make the communications – will depart and the munition workers will have to be assembled. All this takes time and you cannot go faster than a certain speed. Perhaps we might go a little faster; by all means let us try, but the stages cannot be omitted. The Noble Lord was very scornful yesterday about the Minister of Labour because he said that we had more people now employed in munitions and aircraft than we had in 1918. I was astonished that my Noble Friend, who has some experience of Government, should show himself so unaware of the slow and gradual process of munition production, because he said he had been my follower in the re-armament agitation, and I have repeatedly explained to the House in the last three or four years how lengthy and gradual this process must inevitably be.

Earl Winterton rose –

The Prime Minister: I have only a few minutes.

Earl Winterton: It is a very unfair quotation.

The Prime Minister: I have the quotation here:

'I want to say a word about production and what was really a calamitous statement of the right hon. Gentleman. He said, as if it were satisfactory to the whole House, that munition production today was greater than it had been in June, 1918. If I did not wish to be polite to the right hon. Gentleman I should say that it was a fatuous comparison.' – [Official Report, 21st January, 1941; col.107, Vol.368.]

It is not possible to make a warship go to sea and fight against the enemy until the fires have been lighted under the boilers, and have got hold, until the water has got tepid, and has got warm, and finally until steam and vast power has been generated. Whilst this is going on there is no use rushing about uttering alarming cries. This is not a very good thing to do if you happen to be one of the people who did not start to warm up the boilers in good time.

I was Minister of Munitions in July, 1918, and I am therefore able to measure more or less the intensity of the effort of munitions production which was then going on. I was greatly encouraged to learn some weeks ago that in the sixteenth month of this war we had already surpassed by several hundred thousand workers the number of persons employed in munitions and aircraft production in the forty-eighth month of the last war, and it was mentioned from the Labour benches that the productivity of one pair of human hands has greatly increased in the interval. I have kept myself constantly informed of the great tide of new factories which are rising to a productive level. In the next six months we shall have for the first time an intense demand upon our man-power and woman-power. This is the problem that lies before us. We are now about to enter, for the first time in this war, the period of man-power stringency, because for the first time we are going to have the apparatus and layout which this man-power and woman-power will be required to handle. That is the reason for the very far-reaching declaration of which the Minister of Labour thought it necessary to apprise the House and the country in his statement yesterday.

Now is the time when the full war effort will gradually be able to be realized as the plants come into being. It is true that we have not so many women employed as we had in 1918 but there are two reasons, one, which was given, that so many more were employed already before the war situation began – that is a reason which is very important – and also the shell filling factories are only gradually coming into being. They were only constructed after the outbreak of war.

I am, of course, aware that a mechanized army makes an enormous additional drain upon the administrative and tactical branches which lie behind the fighting vehicles. I have thought, nevertheless, for some time that the Army and the Air Force – the Navy not so much – have a great need to comb their tails in order to magnify their teeth. I have felt for some time that there was considerable scope for saving of man-power on the rearward and preparatory services in order to develop the highest economy and the highest manifestation of fighting power. I look to very considerable combings and scrapings in the Air Force and Army, particularly the Army, not in order to cut these Forces down, but in order to reduce their demands upon the man-power market as far as possible during the coming stringent months so that we shall be able to man the new factories and shipyards and to till the new fields which are coming into production. Both these fighting Departments are engaged in this process at the present time, and the Army in particular are making very great savings from their rearward services in order to promote the forward sharpening and expansion which is necessary.

In all this the Army problem has been greatly eased because, in the mercy of God, we have had no slaughter or wastage comparable to the last war. It is, indeed, amazing that after 16 months of war between the greatest States armed with the most deadly weapons not more than 60,000 British folk, nearly half of whom are civilians, have lost their lives by enemy action. It is a terrible figure, but it is far less than in a single protracted battle on the Western Front in 1916, 1917 or 1918. Therefore, while our Army is growing every week in power, strength, efficiency and equipment, and while a decisive expansion of the Air Force is in progress, it is the munitions factories and agriculture rather than the fighting Services which will in the next five or six months make the chief demand for man-power upon the public. It is to these problems and tasks that we are now addressing ourselves.

Criticism is easy; achievement is more difficult. I do not pretend that there is no room for improvement and for acceleration, even apart from the methodical expansion which is going on. It is certain that the peak of our war effort has not yet been reached. It cannot be reached until the plants are all working, but my mind goes back, not to what has been said here, but to what I read outside a few weeks ago, when our critics were crying out about our inaction against Italy and wondering whose was the hidden hand that was shielding Mussolini from British wrath. At that time I endured the taunts in silence because I knew that the large and daring measures had already been taken which have since rendered possible the splendid victories in Libya – Sidi Barrani, Bardia, and it may well be that while I am speaking Tobruk and all it contains are in our hands. Apart from the Libyan victories, extremely important developments are taking place on both frontiers of Abyssinia and in Eritrea which may themselves be productive and fruitful of pregnant results.

Far be it from me to paint a rosy picture of the future. Indeed, I do not think we should be justified in using any but the more sombre tones and colours while our people, our Empire and indeed the whole English-speaking world are passing through a dark and deadly valley. But I should be failing in my duty if, on the other side, I were not to convey to the House the true impression, namely, that this great nation is getting into its war stride. It is accomplishing the transition from the days of peace and comfort to those of supreme, organised, indomitable exertion. Still more should I fail in my duty were I to suggest that the future, with all its horrors, contains any element which justifies lassitude, despondency or despair. His Majesty's Government welcome the stimulus that the House of Commons and the Press and the public of this island give to us in driving forward our war effort, and in trying to gain an earlier inch or a more fruitful hour, wherever it may be possible; but I have no doubt that the House, in its overwhelming majority, nay almost unanimously, will wish also to give its tribute of encouragement as well as its dose of correction, and will lend the heave of its own loyal strength to the forward surges which have now begun.

Winston S. Churchill to General Wavell
(*Churchill papers, 20/49*)

23 January 1941
Personal and Secret

I again send you my most heartfelt congratulations on the third of the brilliant victories which have in little more than six weeks transformed the situation in the Middle East, and have also sensibly affected the movement of the whole war.[1] The daring and scope of the original conception, the perfection of Staff work and execution have raised the reputation of the British and Australian army and its leadership, and will long be regarded as models of the military art. Will you please convey these expressions in which the War Cabinet, and, I doubt not, Parliament, would most cordially associate themselves, to Air Chief Marshal Longmore and Air Commodore Collishaw,[2] and to Generals Wilson, O'Connor,[3] MacKay[4] and Creagh.[5] I shall be making a further statement on these lines before long.

Winston S. Churchill to Air Chief Marshal Sir Charles Portal and Admiral Sir Dudley Pound
(*Churchill papers, 20/36*)

23 January 1941
Action this Day

I wish to draw your attention to the prime importance of arranging as speedily as possible for a dozen or more Grumman Martlets or converted

[1] In the first days following the entry into Tobruk by British and Australian troops, fifty Italian tanks had been captured, and more than 25,000 Italian soldiers had been taken prisoner.

[2] Raymond Collishaw, 1893–1976. Born in Canada. Royal Canadian Navy, Fishery Protection Service, 1908–14. On active service in France, Royal Naval Air Service, 1915–18. Reached second place (with total of sixty) in records for pilots of British Empire on number of hostile aircraft destroyed (despatches four times, Distinguished Service Order and bar). Commanded RAF Detachment, South Russian Expedition, 1919–20 (despatches) North Persia, 1920. Served in Iraq, 1921–23 (despatches). Air Officer Commanding Egypt Group, RAF, 1939–43.

[3] Richard Nugent O'Connor, 1889–1981. The son of a sergeant-majorOn active service in France and Italy (despatches nine times, Military Cross, Distinguished Service Order and bar). Military Governor of Jerusalem, 1938–39. Commanded the Western Desert Forces in Libya, 1940–41. Knighted, 1941. Taken prisoner of war by the Germans. Escaped in 1944 while in captivity in Italy. After three and a half months in hiding, managed to cross the German lines. A Corps Commander in France, 1944 (despatches). General Officer Commanding-in-Chief, Western Army, India, 1945–46. Adjutant-General to the Forces, 1946–47. Retired, 1948. Commandant, Army Cadet Force Scotland, 1948–59. 2nd High Commissioner, Church of Scotland General Assembly, 1964. A Justice of the Peace for Ross and Cromarty. Knight of the Thistle, 1971.

[4] Iven Giffard MacKay, 1882–1966. Born and educated in Australia, the son of a Scottish Presbyterian Minister schoolmaster. On active service, Gallipoli, 1915 (wounded on Lone Pine). Commanded 1st Australian Machine Gun Battalion in France, June 1918; lst Australian Infantry Brigade, October 1918. Studied at the Cavendish Laboratory, Cambridge, 1919. Headmaster, Cranbrook School, Sydney, 1933–40. General Officer Commanding the 2nd Division, Commonwealth Military Forces, 1940. 6th Division, Australian Imperial Forces, 1940–41 (Western Desert, Libya, Greece, Crete). Knighted, 1941. General Officer Commanding-in-Chief, Home Forces, Australia, 1941–42, General Officer Commanding New Guinea Forces, 1943. High Commissioner for Australia in India, 1944–48.

[5] Michael O'Moore Creagh, 1892–1970. Entered the Army, 1911. On active service, 1914–18 (despatches, Military Cross). Major-General, 1940. Knighted, 1941. Retired, 1944. United Nations Relief and Rehabilitation Agency (UNRRA), 1944–46. Chief of the Emergency Supply, United European Regional Office (active in post-war help for Europe, especially Greece).

Brewsters being embarked upon aircraft-carriers operating in the Mediterranean. I have pressed for this for some time, and now the C-in-C, Mediterranean,[1] 824, says quite definitely that 'Fulmars[2] are really not fast enough.' It is absolutely necessary to have a comparatively small number of really fast Fighter aircraft on our carriers. Without these the entire movement of our ships is hampered. I am well aware of the difficulties of non-folding wings, absence of arresting hooks, &c., but I cannot easily believe that they cannot be solved before April.

I beg that you will give your earnest consideration to ante-dating this. Even if only a small number could be supplied, you would gain an important relief and advantage. Surely a few dozen could be converted to folding wings by hand-labour as a special job.

I am not satisfied that the urgency and significance of this comparatively small change is realised.

Winston S. Churchill to the Import Executive
(*Churchill papers, 20/36*)

23 January 1941

REPLACEMENT OF LOSSES OF MERCHANT SHIPS

I request that you will not consider yourselves bound by the estimate of losses put forward by the Ministry of Shipping, or take that as the foundation for future calculations. The Ministry of Shipping have reached a total of 5¼ million tons per annum by taking as their basis the period since the collapse of France, including the quite exceptional losses of the Norwegian and French evacuations. A better alternative method of calculation would be to take the monthly rate for the whole year 1940, which is 4¼ million tons; or, again, for the whole war, which is between 3¾ and 4 million tons provided the extraordinary evacuation losses are deducted.

2. It is probably prudent to assume that this rate will continue. It does not follow, however, that it will not be reduced, as our improved methods come into play and the additional destroyers reach the Fleet. Bearing this in mind, I think it would be safe to work on the monthly average since the beginning of the war.

[1] The Commander-in-Chief, Mediterranean, Admiral Sir Andrew Cunningham, see page 194, note 1.

[2] The Fulmar was a British two-seater fighter, built by Fairey, and flown by the Fighter Air Arm. It was the first British fighter to carry eight machine guns. It had a range of 625 miles, with a maximum speed of 253 miles an hour (cruising speed 228 mph). It was first in action in Malta in January 1941.

Winston S. Churchill to Sir Kingsley Wood
(*Churchill papers, 20/36*)

23 January 1941
Action this Day

FINANCIAL ASSISTANCE FOR AIR RAID DAMAGE AT MALTA

Surely they should be allowed to come into our scheme on exactly the same terms as our own people, and in retrospective effect.

They are under siege.

Your answer is pretty frigid.

Winston S. Churchill to Sir Kingsley Wood
(*Churchill papers, 20/36*)

24 January 1941

FINANCIAL ASSISTANCE FOR AIR RAID DAMAGE AT MALTA

Frankly, I do not think the conventional phrases about 'urgent consideration' and 'sympathy and support' are good enough at this time for these people, who have so loyally espoused our cause, and are under constant attack.

A more detailed statement should be made in the sense of your paragraph 2.

Winston S. Churchill to General Sir John Dill
(*Churchill papers, 20/36*)

24 January 1941
Secret

You told me Lord Gort[1] was going to Gibraltar. Has he started? Where is he? Such a visit by him should afford an opportunity for the discussion for which the Ambassador[2] asks. We shall have to make up our minds upon the degree of assistance which could be afforded to a friendly Spain.

[1] John Standish Surtees Prendergast Vereker, 1886–1946. Succeeded his father as 6th Viscount Gort, 1902. Educated at Harrow and Sandhurst. 2nd Lieutenant, 1905; Captain, 1914. On active service, 1914–18 (despatches nine times, Victoria Cross, Military Cross, DSO and 2 bars). General, 1937. Chief of the Imperial General Staff, 1937–9. Commander-in-Chief of the British Field Force, 1939–40. Inspector-General to the Forces for Training, 1940. Governor and Commander-in-Chief, Gibraltar, 1941–2; Malta, 1942–4. High Commissioner and Commander-in-Chief, Palestine, 1944–5. In 1938 he became a member of the Other Club.

[2] The British Ambassador to Spain, Sir Samuel Hoare.

When I assented to General Montgomery[1] as a Corps Commander taking over the study of the Tangier proposition, or of the aid to General Weygand, I by no means excluded Lord Gort should the proportions of the expedition be larger than a Corps.

I feel very doubtful of our ability to fight the Germans anywhere on the mainland of Europe.

Winston S. Churchill to General Ismay
(*Churchill papers, 20/36*)

24 January 1941

Let me have on a single sheet of paper the Units now on the seas for the Middle East – all, that is to say, who have not yet landed.

John Colville: diary
(*Colville papers*)

24 January 1941

The PM took Mr Hopkins off to see the batteries at Dover.

John Colville: diary
(*Colville papers*)

24 January 1941 Chequers

. . . the PM and Harry Hopkins arrived about 7.00.

At dinner Hopkins said how impressed he had been to see, when dining with Bevin, Morrison and Sir Andrew Duncan, on what friendly and familiar terms a great industrialist could be with Labour leaders. Such a thing could not happen in America.

Hopkins told the PM that during the afternoon at Dover he had heard one workman say to another, as Winston passed, 'There goes the bloody British Empire'. Winston's face wreathed itself in smiles and turning to me he lisped: '<u>Very</u> nice'. I don't think anything has given him such pleasure for a long time.

[1] Bernard Law Montgomery, 1887–1976. Entered the Army, 1903. On active service, 1914–18. Major-General, 1938. Commanded the 3rd Division, 1939–40; the 5th Corps, 1940; the 12th Corps, 1941. Knighted, 1942. Commanded the Eighth Army (including the Battle of El Alamein), 1942–3; the 21st Army Group (including the Normandy Landings), 1944–5. Field Marshal, 1944. Created Viscount, 1946. Knight of the Garter, 1946. Chief of the Imperial General Staff, 1946–8. Deputy Supreme Allied Commander, Europe, 1951–8.

The PM said he did not now see how invasion could be successful and he now woke up in the mornings, as he nearly always had, feeling as if he had a bottle of champagne inside him and glad that another day had come. In May and June, however, he had been sorry when the nights were over and he had often thought about death, not, he said, 'that I much believe in personal survival after death, at least not of the memory'. He was not, he said, much worried by the chance of being bombed – in this connection he is fond of quoting M. Poincaré's statement, 'I take refuge beneath the impenetrable arch of probability'.

Jack Churchill[1] asked when we were going to recapture British Somaliland. The PM replied that we must concentrate on the major operation. As Napoleon said, *Frappez la masse et la reste vient par surcroit.*

Hopkins thought that a statement to the effect that any move by Japan against American interests in the East would be considered an unfriendly act by Great Britain, would have a most important effect in the US. The PM was delighted and promised to say this as soon as the President let him know the time was ripe.

After dinner I read to the CIGS on the 'Scrambler' (our new telephonic secrecy device) a long telegram from the PM to Wavell protesting against the latter's enormous demand for rearward services. Wavell had well over 300,000 men in North Africa but could only put 45,000 into the field. The CIGS didn't like this telegram and subsequently I had to ring him up again so that he and the PM might wrangle about it. Eventually the PM agreed to tone down the wording, but said that plain-speaking was necessary in War and he didn't see why Wavell should want still more YMCAs etc. behind the lines!

At midnight the PM and Harry Hopkins came into my office and talked. The PM was much impressed by the fact that there are 200,000 white civilians in Abyssinia and he is a little worried about their fate when 'those savage warriors, who have been burned with poison gas' get among them. If the Duke of Aosta[2] will surrender in time, the PM thinks we might be able to hold the Abyssinians back.

'Never give in,' said the PM, 'and you will never regret it.' A negotiated

[1] John Strange Spencer Churchill, 1880–1947. Churchill's younger brother, known as 'Jack'. Educated at Harrow. On active service in South Africa, 1900 (wounded). Major Queen's Own Oxfordshire Hussars, 1914–18. Served at Dunkirk, 1914; on Sir John French's staff, Flanders, 1914–15; on Sir Ian Hamilton's staff at the Dardanelles, 1915; on General Birdwood's staff, France, 1916–18. A stockbroker, he served as a partner with the City firm of Vickers da Costa, 1918–40. In 1931 he was elected to the Other Club; asked once why he so enjoyed his brother's company, Churchill is said to have replied: 'Jack is unborable'.

[2] Amadeo, Duke of Aosta, 1898–1942. A cousin of the King of Italy. Governor of Italian East Africa, and Commander-in-Chief of the Italian armies in Eritrea and Ethiopia, 1937–41. Undertook the invasion of British Somaliland, August 1940. Surrendered to the British with the remnants of the Italian East African Army (including five generals and 7,000 men), May 1941; died while a prisoner of war in Nairobi, 1942.

Peace would be a German victory and would leave open the way for another and final 'spring of the Tiger' in a few years time. Hopkins agreed and said that Lindbergh,[1] and others in America who favoured a negotiated Peace, really desired a German victory. The PM wound up by saying that after the last war he had been asked to provide an inscription for a French War Memorial. His suggestion, which was rejected, had been; 'In war fury, in defeat defiance, in victory magnanimity, in peace goodwill'.

The PM summoned me into his bedroom and, as he undressed, said very nicely that he didn't think there was much point in his letting me join up in the Guards, though there was every point in my wanting to do so . . . .

Winston S. Churchill to Admiral of the Fleet Sir Roger Keyes
(*Churchill papers, 20/21*)

24 January 1941
Personal and Private

My dear Roger,

I do not think you ought to write me letters of this kind[2] on matters which affect those under whom you are serving.

It is not possible for me to argue out with you privately, either by letter or in conversation, every decision of the Defence Committee which affects your Command. My burdens would become intolerable if I were to attempt such a thing.

You and your Commandos will have to obey orders like other people. And that is all there is to be said about it.

I am very sorry if you are not pleased. I do my best.

Yours ever

[1] Charles Augustus Lindbergh, 1902–1974. Born in Detroit. Educated at the University of Wisconsin. Enrolled in flying school, 1922, becoming an air mail line pilot at St Louis. Flew alone from New York to Paris, 1927 (the first solo trans-Atlantic non-stop flight). Flew from the United States to Denmark via Greenland, Ireland, and the Shetland Islands, with a view to establishing a trans-Atlantic air route, 1933. In 1932, following the kidnapping and murder of his son, the Press agreed not to pursue him for stories. A leading isolationist; subsequently, from April 1939, recalled to service as Special Adviser on technical matters to the Office of the Chief of the Air Corps, charged with making a survey of United States' aviation facilities. Brigadier-General, 1940. Awarded the Pulitzer Prize for his book *The Spirit of Saint Louis* (1953).

[2] Keyes' letter is not in the Churchill papers: on 5 February 1941 Churchill wrote again, returning a second letter from the Admiral: 'My dear Roger, It is quite impossible for me to receive a letter of this character. I am sure it would do you a great deal of harm if it fell into unsympathetic hands. I therefore return it to you with its enclosures. If you wish to write on matters affecting the Commandos, pray do so to General Ismay. (Churchill papers, 20/21A)

John Colville: diary
(*Colville papers*)

25 January 1941
afternoon Chequers

The PM, alarmed by the number of papers in his box, worked all the afternoon in bed.

A considerable amount of work was done, including a letter to the editor of the *Daily Mirror*, protesting against that newspaper's Fifth Column attitude, and an enormous memorandum to David Margesson about man-power, the Army's excessive dependence on rearward services, and the distribution of the 37 divisions we now have available.[1]

Winston S. Churchill to Sir Archibald Sinclair and Lord Beaverbrook
(*Churchill papers, 20/36*)

25 January 1941

RANK OF RAF OFFICERS SERVING IN THE MINISTRY OF AIRCRAFT PRODUCTION

This difficulty arises when Army officers are required for positions in the Ministry of Supply, and it has usually been settled amicably between sister Departments. Positions of a certain consequence in the Ministry of Supply have carried with them a certain rank, and this rank has been conferred temporarily, locally, and for the purpose of the appointment, upon the officers selected. This rank, of course, is not a substantive rank but only a kind of brevet or acting rank. Therefore it in no way interferes with the permanent flow of promotion in the Regular Army. It lapses with the appointment, not even persisting as Brevets do. The War Office made no objection when I asked that Lt-Colonel Asquith[2] should be appointed Brigadier on becoming Director of Trench Warfare in 1918, in fact, they tried all they could to help me in my work, which was supplying them with all they needed. All the arguments on page 2 of the Secretary of State for Air's letter completely ignore the temporary and *ex officio* character of the rank, which I thought was very clearly recognized in our conversation. Naturally there should be friendly consultations between the Departments, but it is the duty of the Air Ministry to try to meet the legitimate needs of the Minister of Aircraft Production in

[1] The letter to Margesson was sent on 29 January 1941 and is reproduced here under that date.

[2] Arthur Melland Asquith, 1883–1939. Known as 'Oc'. Sudan Civil Service, 1906–11. In business, 1911–14. Enlisted in the Royal Naval Volunteer Reserve, 1914. Served in the Royal Naval Division at Antwerp, Dardanelles and western front, 1914–16. Four times wounded. Served in the Ministry of Munitions, 1918; in the Ministry of Labour, 1919. Company director.

regard to the ranks held by officers definitely seconded to his side of the Service. On the other hand, it would never do for MAP to lay down, for instance, the rule that posts with ranks assigned to them could be created ad *lib.* without any regard to the character of the posts or of the effects produced in the Air Force Service. None of these matters would raise difficulties if they were dealt with in the spirit of goodwill and co-operation. I could not give an unlimited right to the Minister of Aircraft Production such as is suggested in his letter. On the other hand, it would be a very serious thing for the Air Ministry to refuse a reasonable request made in any specific case. All disputed cases are to be referred to me as Minister of Defence.

Winston S. Churchill to Anthony Eden and Herbert Morrison
(*Churchill papers, 20/36*)

25 January 1941
Secret

These two communications[1] cause me concern. I have heard from various quarters that the witch-finding activities of MI5 are becoming an actual impediment to the more important work of the Department. I am carefully considering certain changes, not only in MI5 but in the Intelligence and Secret Service control. In the meanwhile, I should be very glad if you would both consult together on these two letters. It would be a great pity if Lord Lytton's[2] resignation had to be accepted. He is a man of the very highest capacity and patriotism, and it seems to me altogether wrong that his judgement and that of his Committee should not have been made effective in the great majority of cases. Lord Beaverbrook's complaint is from quite another angle. I have no doubt there is a certain amount of risk that some bad people may get loose, but our dangers are so much less now than they were in May and June. The whole organization of the country, the Home Guard and so forth, is so much more efficient against Fifth Column activities that I am sure a more rapid and general process of release from internment should be adopted.

[1] Letters from Lord Lytton and Lord Beaverbrook about the release of aliens from internment.

[2] Victor Alexander George Robert Lytton, 1876–1947. Educated at Eton and Trinity College, Cambridge. Succeeded his father as 2nd Earl of Lytton, 1891. Civil Lord of the Admiralty, 1916; Additional Parliamentary Secretary, Admiralty, 1917; British Commissioner for Propaganda in France, 1918; Civil Lord of the Admiralty, 1919–20. Under-Secretary of State for India, 1920–2. Governor of Bengal, 1922–7; Acting Viceroy of India, April–August 1925. Head of the League of Nations' Mission to Manchuria, 1932. Chairman, Secret Service Committee, 1939–45. Chairman of Palestine Potash Ltd, Central London Electricity Ltd, the London Power Company, and the Hampstead Garden Suburb Trust Ltd.

Winston S. Churchill to Sir John Anderson and Lord Beaverbrook
(*Churchill papers, 20/36*)

25 January 1941

CONTROL OF FACTORY AND STORAGE ACCOMMODATION

1. I should deprecate bringing this matter before the Cabinet. The survey of the country should be conducted by the Lord President and under the authority of his Committee. Extreme priority is to be given to meeting the needs of MAP when any factory has been bombed out of action.

2. I should be glad to be informed of any case in which a delay of more than 48 hours occurs in finding new premises. It ought, indeed, to be possible, once a general survey has been made, for MAP to specify in advance the buildings they would require in various localities, stating the order of preference. These buildings could not, of course, be kept vacant, if they were urgently needed by others, but other alternatives could be put on the list. I hope this view may be accepted by the two Ministers to whom this minute is addressed.

Winston S. Churchill to General Ismay, for the Chiefs of Staff Committee
(*Premier papers, 3/234*)

25 January 1941

PROPOSED CAPTURE OF SICILY

Surely this is burdening the Middle East Command with too much. Wavell will have to use all his spare strength help Turkey and/or Greece. How can he possibly develop a large-scale Operation of this character. I do not think this telegram should have been sent without previous reference to me, and I would then have decided whether reference to the Defence Committee were necessary.

John Colville: diary
(*Colville papers*)

25 January 1941 Chequers
evening

Over the brandy Hopkins showed the PM and Dill the details of the American rearmament programme, which I had already perused. It is clear that gigantic efforts are being made, but the PM warned Hopkins that the results could not be expected for about 18 months. Our own war factories were only just beginning their full production (e.g. last week our ammunition output doubled). Then the CIGS produced the papers about 'Operation Victor', a military exercise which has been taking place during the last few days as practice against invasion.[1] The papers include an able appreciation of the advantages and tactics of invasion written, as if by the German Staff, by General Weeks[2] of the War Office. It is very comprehensive and sensible, much impressed the PM, and would certainly do great credit to the Germans if genuine. I was asked to read this out aloud, and afterwards an account of the first stages of the exercise. This account contained, as an appendix, a broadcast by the PM on the beginning of invasion! I read this out aloud and its language caused much amusement, though the PM promised he would produce a far better one in the event and said that the sham one was a good example of the mistake of using conventional adjectives, attached to conventional nouns, merely for the sake of effect. If he did have to make such a speech he would end it: 'The hour has come; kill the Hun.'

There was some discussion about Eire, Dill putting forward the theory that the Germans would invade Ireland as a diversion, like they did Norway, before the main attack materialised.

The rest of the evening was spent in the Great Hall, where the gramophone played and the PM, in the intervals of discoursing to Hopkins or Dill, tripped a little measure. Hopkins seems a little doubtful whether we shall have any warning of invasion, but the PM and Dill seem confident that complete surprise is impossible.

[1] Four days later, General Brooke wrote to Churchill: 'I think that all the Services and Departments engaged have derived great value from the exercise by way of improving plans for Home Defence. Conferences are now being held to distil the main lessons . . .' On February l, Brooke sent Churchill a detailed account of the exercise during which the 'German' invading forces had been checked after fifteen separate landings (the main ones on the Norfolk, Suffolk and Kent coasts). In London, two 'German' brigades and thirty light tanks were 'landed' by parachute. They succeeded in seizing Neasden power station and the Metropolitan Water Works. Action was in progress against all parachute parties at the end of the exercise (HF3978/Ops, General Headquarters, Home Forces, 1 February 1941: *Premier papers, 3/4696/2, folios 2 16*).

[2] Ronald Morce Weeks, 1890–1960. Joined Pilkington Brothers, 1912. On active service, 1914–18 (despatches thrice, Distinguished Service Order, Military Cross and bar). Retired from the army 1919. Joined Pilkington Brothers; Director, 1926; Chairman, 1939. Rejoined army, 1939. Chief of Staff, Territorial Division, 1939. Brigadier, General Staff, Home Forces, 1940. Major-General, Director of Army Equipment, 1941. Lieutenant-General, Deputy Chief of the Imperial General Staff, 1942–45. Knighted, 1943. Deputy Military Governor and Chief of Staff, British Zone, Control Commission of Germany, 1945. Retired from the Army, 1945. Chairman, British Scientific Instrument Research Association, 1946–51. National Advisory Council on Education for Industry and Commerce, 1948–56. Created Baron, 1956. British Government Representative on the Board of British Petroleum, 1956–60.

Winston S. Churchill to General Ismay, for the Chiefs of Staff Committee
(*Churchill papers, 20/36*)

26 January 1941
Secret

I was much concerned when I visited Dover on Friday to find the slow and halting progress in the installation of the latest and best Batteries.

(1) Some guns which are ready mounted cannot be brought into action because ancillary material, such as sights and control instruments, has not been delivered. A suggestion of the Controller[1] indicated that these guns could be brought into action quickly by the intelligent improvisation of simple means of control workable, although not so technically satisfying as those to be supplied eventually.

(2) Some guns cannot be completed for action owing to delay in the work involved in anchoring the mountings. Reasons given for this being lack of shuttering timbers for concreting, inefficient labour and the weather.

As regards (1), the attached Progress Report shows the situation, and it is difficult to escape the conclusion that there is a lack of initiative on the spot when such a bald statement as 'no dates given for delivery' is accepted.

As regards (2), the lack of the necessary facilities for progress seems to demand some immediate action, while the labour position might be referred to the Ministry of Labour.

I was informed that all the causes of delay had been reported through the 'usual channels', but as far as those on the spot were aware nothing very much seems to have happened. It would seem best, therefore, to start from the other end of the 'usual channels' and sound backwards to find where the delay in dealing with the matter has occurred.

I gathered from Admiral Ramsay that in his opinion the lack of drive behind this work was due to the fact that no one senior Officer seemed to regard the whole matter as his personal interest, although several, somewhat less senior, were active in their own particular spheres.

The Controller said that he could deal with the two points raised about deficiencies in ammunition, i.e., shortages of 5.5″ fuses and 6″ cartridges, but the report of this, too, seems to have grounded in mid 'usual channels.'

The completion of these Batteries is of the utmost urgency, and I request the Chiefs of the Staff to give all the necessary instructions and to call for a weekly report to be forwarded to me.

[1] Bruce Austin Fraser, 1888–1981. Third Sea Lord and Controller of the Navy, 1939–42. Knighted 1941. Second-in-Command, Home Fleet, 1942. Commander-in-Chief, Home Fleet, 1943–4. Commander-in-Chief, Eastern Fleet, 1944. Commander-in-Chief, British Pacific Fleet, 1944–5. Admiral 1944. Created Baron Fraser of North Cape, 1946. First Sea Lord and Chief of the Naval Staff, 1948–51.

Winston S. Churchill to Alfred Duff Cooper[1]
(*Churchill papers, 20/36*)

26 January 1941

Who was responsible for arranging the broadcast of the Minister of Shipping to the United States? It is altogether wrong that a junior Minister should make a statement of this high consequence at a time when everything is so critical there. The moment I heard the summary of the broadcast, I was sure that this preaching tone would be most unhelpful at this very delicate moment.

I find Mr Hopkins here was affected in the same way. I cannot allow these extremely sensitive, and at the same time momentous, relationships to be handled in this fashion. This is the second time Mr Cross has intervened, the first occasion being about seizing the Danish ships. Did you see a transcript of his broadcast before it was delivered?

For the future, no Ministerial broadcasts, other than by Members of the War Cabinet, are to be allowed without my approval of the occasion and your report to me on the proposed matter.

Winston S. Churchill to General Wavell
(*Churchill papers, 20/49*)

26 January 1941
Private and Personal

You will have by now received the Chiefs of Staff telegram sent by my direction after a meeting of the Defence Committee about future operations. The apparition of the German aircraft in the Central Mediterranean has forced me for the time being to abandon the hopes I had formed of opening and picketing the way through the Narrows, thus enabling troop convoys to pass regularly. Unless this situation can be rectified during the early months of this year the lack of shipping and the distance round the Cape will undoubtedly affect the scale to which I had hoped to raise the Army of the Nile and the strength of your Command. It pained me very much to find the convoys sent at so much cost and risk round the Cape should so largely consist of rearward services and make so small an addition to our organized Fighting Units. I shall try my utmost to support you in every way, and I must ask in return that you convince me that every man in the Middle East is turned to the highest possible use and that the largest number of organized Divisional or perhaps preferably Brigade Units are formed. The soldiers in the rearward Services and Establishments should play an effective part in internal security.

[1] Minister of Information: for his biographical note, see page 174, note 1.

2. I was perplexed by your telegram No.0/36796 cypher 21/1. I thought you wanted to have a large strategic reserve in the Delta, and this is in accordance with the directions we have given from here. Certainly there is no need to send another South African Division to swell the 70,000 troops of various kinds who are now virtually out of action in Kenya. I asked General Smuts, and he has agreed, to keep the destination of the new Division fluid, as I thought that by the time transport, &c., could be arranged he might be willing for them to come north to join the Army of the Nile. How can you expect me to face the tremendous strain upon our shipping, affecting as it does all our food and import of munitions, in order to carry more Divisions from this country to the Middle East, when you seem opposed to taking a South African Division which would only have less than half the distance to come. I hope indeed that both the South African Divisions now in Kenya will in a few months be moved to the Delta and that the West African Brigade will be sent as promised back to Freetown. On no account must General Smuts be discouraged from his bold and sound policy of gradually working South African Forces into the main theatre.

3. The information reaching me from every quarter leaves me no doubt that the Germans are now already establishing themselves upon the Bulgarian aerodromes, and making every preparation for action against Greece. This infiltration may, indeed almost certainly will, attain decisive proportions before any clear cut issue of invasion has been presented to the Turks, who will then be told to keep out or have Constantinople bombed. We must expect a series of very heavy, disastrous blows in the Balkans, and possibly a general submission there to German aims. The stronger the strategic reserve which you can build up in the Delta, and the more advanced your preparations to transfer it to the European shores, the better will be the chances of securing a favourable crystallization.

Winston S. Churchill to Colonel Jacob

(*Churchill papers, 20/36*)

26 January 1941

1. I wanted to know also the Units going to India, especially the Artillery Units. Pray let me have this.

2. Let me have the order of battle of the troops in the Middle East in a simplified form, showing what Divisions or Brigade Groups there are actually formed, and what they are short of in establishment after the convoys now on the sea have arrived.

Winston S. Churchill to General Smuts
(*Churchill papers, 20/49*)

26 January 1941
Most Secret and Personal

My colleagues and I have most carefully considered your views concerning our policy towards Abyssinia and Italian East Africa. If I now send you this personal message it is in the hope that after studying its contents you will agree with us that, in view of the operations now taking place in East Africa, we can no longer delay a Parliamentary announcement.

As to the question of Abyssinia as an independent State, you will note that we do not commit ourselves to any boundaries or other details. And the fact that guidance in political and economic affairs is an essential part of the arrangement leaves the relations of the Powers to Abyssinia entirely open for decision by the Peace Conference.

As to the recognition of the Emperor, you will recall that within two weeks of Italy's entry into the war we facilitated the Emperor Haile Selassie's return to Africa. In taking this action, we were careful to avoid assuming any commitment towards Haile Selassie personally, since at that time it was not clear to what extent he would enjoy the support even of those chieftains who, for some time, had been conducting guerrilla warfare against the Italians. We were also aware that a certain opposition to the Emperor was believed to exist amongst the Galla and other minority tribes. During the last six months, however, while General Wavell and the Sudan authorities were preparing the Eritrean and other operations, which are now starting, and, in co-operation with the Emperor, were concurrently fomenting internal disturbances in Abyssinia, it has become apparent that Haile Selassie stands out as the only possible candidate for the throne of a new Abyssinia. The Emperor is, in all probability, the only enlightened Abyssinian Prince, and has already asked for advisers who will help him to establish his eventual Government. He recognises that one of the immediate and major responsibilities of that Government would be to prevent the return of abuses such as slavery and Amharic persecution of tribal minorities, evils against which he was endeavouring to fight when the Italian crisis of 1935–36 supervened. Moreover, we understand that not only has the Emperor secured the allegiance of the Amhara chieftains, but also that the reports which we have received as to the hostility of the Galla towards him are exaggerated. It is certain that many Galla tribesmen are in revolt against the Italians. Furthermore, the Emperor's proclamation, which has been disseminated widely throughout the country, has caused a profound impression. There is every reason to suppose that in regard to minorities and in other directions the Emperor will be prepared, with assistance, to co-operate when the time comes.

In addition to the foregoing, we are already virtually committed to the

Emperor by the answer given to a Parliamentary question here on the 11th July, 1940, the text of which is contained in my immediately following telegram. It has also already been announced that we have no territorial ambitions in Abyssinia, which we would wish to see free and independent, and that we are according every assistance possible to those Abyssinians who have taken up arms against the common enemy. The battle has now been joined, and the Emperor has actually crossed the border to lead in person the native forces fighting the Italians. I greatly fear that if, for any reason, His Majesty's Government were to display reluctance to announce not only their intention to afford him all possible military and other support, but also their ultimate aim of enabling him to regain his throne, once victory has been achieved, the political repercussions both here and overseas – particularly in India and USA – would be unfortunate in the extreme. Public opinion, especially in the Liberal and Labour parties, would be affronted, and discouragement would be felt by other refugee princes in our midst.

In studying your message under reply, we gave particular thought to your suggestion that our announcement on the lines contemplated might be calculated to prolong the Italian resistance. On reflection, however, I am sure you will appreciate that the Italians are already fully aware of the support we are actually giving the Emperor. We believe here that the Italians have for long discounted at any rate the temporary loss of their East African Empire, and have realised that if they were defeated they would lose Abyssinia, whose Emperor would no doubt be restored. In the circumstances, my own feeling is that our announcement would not have any marked effect upon Italian morale one way or another.

There remains the general objection to making promises and declarations in advance of peace similar to those which proved so embarrassing to us in certain cases after the last war. But those embarrassments arose largely out of (1) our making apparently conflicting promises to different parties, and (2) the conflicting claims of our allies at the Peace Conference. Neither of these difficulties should arise in the present case.

We greatly value your counsel in this matter, and the War Cabinet have carefully reviewed the whole question in the light of your message. We keenly appreciate the importance of doing everything on this occasion to avoid repeating the errors of the past. We feel, however, that this form of recognition of the Ethiopian State and Emperor, subject to the safeguards set out in the latter part of paragraph 6 of telegram Z.25, is the right course, and we hope very much that in the light of these explanations you will agree with our view that an announcement should be made in the following terms:

'His Majesty's Government would welcome the reappearance of Abyssinia as an independent State and are prepared to recognize the Emperor Haile Selassie's claim to the restoration of his throne. The Emperor has intimated to His Majesty's Government that he will need outside assistance in the restored

Ethiopian State, and His Majesty's Government would welcome the granting of such assistance on an international basis.

'I take this opportunity to reaffirm that His Majesty's Government have themselves no territorial ambitions in Abyssinia.'

John Colville: diary
(*Colville papers*)

26 January 1941
afternoon
Chequers

In thanking the PM for his tribute to him in the House the other day, Beaverbrook writes: 'You have given me a certificate of character which will carry me through my days. And that is good for me. Because there is a difference between us. You will be talked of even more widely after you are dead than during your lifetime. But I am talked of while I live, and save for my association with you, I will be forgotten thereafter.' Lord B knows how to lay it on – and also how to forward his own cause in his unceasing struggles with the Air Ministry, of which the PM said to me on Friday that he was heartily sick.

Sir Charles and Lady Portal arrived at tea-time and as Mrs C was still out, the PM escorted them up to the Long Gallery for tea, together with Hopkins and Prof, who came today. We started talking about the Classics, Portal being a Wykhamist and thus presumably learned, and the PM said that the use of the new pronunciation in Latin was one of the few things he felt passionate about. Latin spoken in the old way was beautiful to hear; the new way was not only ugly but by hiding the resemblance between English and Latin words removed one of the first utilitarian arguments in favour of the Classics.

We got on to the House of Lords and the PM said that in England our architecture produced our manner of living and not vice versa. Thus the two-party system owed its supremacy here partly to the shape of the Houses of Parliament. You had to be on one side or the other and it was difficult to cross the floor. He had done it and he knew. Indeed he had re-done it, which everybody said was impossible. They had said you could rat but you couldn't re-rat.

John Colville: diary
(*Colville papers*)

26 January 1941
evening
Chequers

When the women had gone to bed, I listened in the Great Hall to as interesting a discussion as I ever hope to hear. We sat in a circle, Portal,

Hopkins, Jack Churchill, myself and Prof, while the PM stood with his back against the mantelpiece, a cigar between his teeth, his hands in the armpits of his waistcoat. Every few seconds he would start forward, trip over the marble grate, walk four or five paces, turn abruptly and resume his position against the mantelpiece. All the while a torrent of eloquence flowed from his lips, and he would fix one or another of us with his eye as he drove home some point. He talked of the past, the present and the future, and the subject matter of his talk was roughly as follows:

In recent history two men had been the most harmful influence in English politics, Joseph Chamberlain[1] and Baldwin.[2] The first had pushed us into the Boer War and, by setting Europe against us, had stimulated the Germans to build a fleet. The second had dominated the scene for 15 years. He had pushed out of public life the men with the greatest experience, LG,[3] Birkenhead[4] etc; and he had made possible the resurgence of Germany and the decay of our own strength. He was just sufficiently good to be suffering now acutely for what he had done. This led to a digression about the

[1] Joseph Chamberlain, 1836–1914. A leading radical reformer and imperial statesman. Colonial Secretary, 1895–1903. Left the Conservative Government in order to oppose Free Trade, 1903. Churchill recalled, a quarter of a century after Chamberlain's death: '. . . after he had split the Conservative Party and convulsed the country by raising the Protectionist issue, I had my last important conversation with him. I was writing my father's life, and wrote to him asking for copies of letters in his possession. We were at that time in full political battle, and although I was of small consequence I had attacked him with all the ferocity of youth, face to face in Parliament and throughout the country. I was one of those younger Conservatives most prominent in resisting the policy on which he had set his heart and the last efforts of his life. To my surprise he replied to my letter by suggesting that I should come and stay with him for a night at Highbury to see the documents. So I went, not without some trepidation. We dined alone. With the dessert a bottle of '34 port was opened. Only the briefest reference was made to current controversies. "I think you are quite right," he said, "feeling as you do, to join the Liberals." You must expect to have the same sort of abuse flung at you as I have endured. But if a man is sure of himself, it only sharpens him and makes him more effective." Apart from this our talk lay in the controversies and personalities of twenty years before.' (*Great Contemporaries*, London, 1937, pages 73–4)

[2] Stanley Baldwin, 1867–1947. Educated at Harrow and Trinity College, Cambridge. Conservative MP for Bewdley, 1908–37. Financial Secretary to the Treasury, 1917–21. President of the Board of Trade, 1921–2. Chancellor of the Exchequer, 1922–3. Prime Minister, 1923–4 and 1924–9. Lord President of the Council, 1931–5. Prime Minister (for the third time), 1935–7. Created Earl, and Knight of the Garter, 1937.

[3] David Lloyd George, 1863–1945. Educated at a Welsh Church school. Solicitor, 1884. Liberal MP for Caernarvon, 1890–1931. President of the Board of Trade, 1905–8. Privy Councillor, 1905. Chancellor of the Exchequer, 1908–15. An original member of the Other Club (founded by Churchill and F. E. Smith), 1911. Minister of Munitions, May 1915–July 1916. Secretary of State for War, July–December 1916. Prime Minister, December 1916-October 1922. Order of Merit, 1919. Independent Liberal MP, 1931–45. Created Earl, 1945.

[4] Frederick Edwin Smith, 1872–1930. Known as 'F.E.'. Conservative MP, 1906–19. With Churchill, he founded the Other Club in 1911. Head of the Press Bureau, August 1914; resigned, October 1914. Lieutenant-Colonel, attached to the Indian Corps in France, 1914–15. Solicitor-General, May 1915. Knighted, 1915. Attorney-General, November 1915 to 1919. Created Baron Birkenhead, 1919. Lord Chancellor, 1920–2. Created Viscount, 1921. Created Earl, 1922. Secretary of State for India, 1924–8.

'Carthaginian peace' of Versailles: we had exacted a thousand millions in reparations; we and the US had contributed 2000 millions in loans to set Germany on her feet again and rebuild her power. It was possible that in some 20 months we and the US would again have to make a peace settlement and there would once more be those who wished to help Germany on to her feet. 'Only one thing in history is certain: that mankind is unteachable.'

There was some discussion of currency problems, the PM coming out strongly in favour of 'the commodity dollar', the rate of which would be fixed by the prices of a number of selected commodities. He compared the currency problem to that of daylight saving; by a little tampering with the clock great benefits could be reaped; but by overdoing it in either direction all advantage must be lost. Hopkins agreed that the present financial system was unsatisfactory, and said that the President was in favour of some such scheme as the PM had outlined; but the opposition of Wall Street had been intense. However in favour of the financiers, the PM pointed out that today everybody wanted Credit but nobody had any patience with creditors!

The PM said that when the war was over there would be a short lull during which we had the opportunity to establish a few basic principles, of justice, of respect for the rights and property of other nations, and indeed of respect for private property so long as its owner was honest and its scope moderate. We could find nothing better than Christian Ethics on which to build and the more closely we followed the Sermon on the Mount, the more likely we were to succeed in our endeavours. But all this talk about war aims was absurd at the present time: the Cabinet Committee to examine the question had produced a vague paper, 4/5 of which was from the Sermon on the Mount and the remainder an Election Address!

Japan and the US was the next topic, and Hopkins expressed the belief that if America came into the war the incident would be with Japan. The PM said that the advantage of America as an ally to the disadvantage of Japan as an enemy was as 10 to 1. Why, look at their respective power of steel production – and 'modern war is waged with steel'. Besides Japan must have been greatly affected by the fate of the Italian navy, which on paper had been so strong. 'Fate holds terrible forfeits for those who gamble on certainties'.

The PM sat down heavily on the sofa, said he had talked too much, and asked Hopkins for his views. Speaking slowly but very emphatically, Hopkins stated that the President was not much concerned with the future. His preoccupation was with the next few months. As far as war aims were concerned, there were only very few people in America, liberal intellectuals, who cared about the matter; and they were nearly all on our side. He believed the same to be true of people in this country. All he would say of the future was that he believed the Anglo-Saxon peoples would have to do the rearrangement: the other nations would not be ripe for co-operation for a long time. He thought the problems of reconstruction would be very great, greater than the PM had implied; and we should have to send men to the conference table who were tough and not sentimental.

As far as the present was concerned, there were four divisions of public opinion in America: a small group of Nazis and Communists, sheltering behind Lindbergh, who declared for a negotiated peace and wanted a German victory; a group, represented by Joe Kennedy, which said 'Help Britain, but make damn sure you don't get into any danger of war'; a majority group which supported the President's determination to send the maximum assistance at whatever risk; and about 10% or 15% of the country, including Knox,[1] Stimson[2] and most of the armed forces, who were in favour of immediate war.

The important element in the situation was the boldness of the President, who would lead opinion and not follow it, who was convinced that if England lost, America too, would be encircled and beaten. He would use his powers if necessary; he would not scruple to interpret existing laws for the furtherance of his aim; he would make people gape with surprise, as the British Foreign Office must have gasped when it saw the terms of the Lease and Lend Bill. The boldness of the President was a striking factor in the situation. He did not want war, indeed he looked upon America as an Arsenal which should provide the weapons for the conflict and not count the cost; but he would not shrink from war.

I talked to the PM as he went to bed and found him most communicative and benign. Nobody is more loveable than he when he is in this frame of mind. He recounted to me the difficulties in the way of an invader whose lines of communication would be cut and who could not dominate the air during the day-time. But, I said, the Germans must know this as well as we do and surely the implication is that they will not invade. 'To tell you the truth,' he said, 'that is what I think, and so does Portal. But the others don't think so.' He said he would not feel so confident, remembering as he did Neville Chamberlain's conviction a year ago that Germany would not invade Holland and Belgium, were it not for the fact that we had air superiority in the day and that we were not pinning our faith in the Maginot Line, 'a great China Wall', but in our

[1] W. Frank Knox, 1874–1944. Republican who supported the Allied war effort. Roosevelt appointed him Secretary of the Navy in June 1940, (he had been the Republican Vice-Presidential candidate in 1936). Co-head of the Office of Production Management (to establish Lend-Lease), 1940–41. An advocate of increased American naval participation in the Atlantic convoys, 1941. He died in April 1944.

[2] Henry Lewis Stimson, 1867–1950. Born in New York City. Admitted to the Bar, 1891. Secretary of War, 1911–13 (under President Taft). Colonel, American Expeditionary Force, France, 1917–18. Governor-General of the Philippines, 1927–9 (under Coolidge). Secretary of State, 1929–32 (under Hoover). Member of Panel, Permanent Court of Arbitration, The Hague, 1938–48. Secretary of War (under Roosevelt), 1940–5. No other politician has served in the Cabinets of two Republican and two Democratic presidents.

troops behind the beaches who would attack any lodgment and make each separate one into a Sidi Barrani, a Bardia or a Tobruk.

He snuggled down beneath the bedclothes, I gave him his *Boswell's Tour of the Hebrides*, and smiling sweetly he wished me good-night.

John Colville: diary
(*Colville papers*)

27 January 1941

The PM worked in bed till eleven and then went up to London, while I got into my car and drove to Ardley. It has been a particularly agreeable week-end, interesting and not too hectic, and the PM has throughout been at his most entertaining and shewn the sunniest side of his disposition. He has been extremely friendly and has even taken to calling me by my Christian name. He said last night at dinner that he hated nobody and didn't feel he had any enemies – except the Huns, and that was professional! Few men are as good-natured, and it is an interesting spot-light on No. 10 last winter that he should have been regarded with such dislike and mistrust.

Winston S. Churchill to Viscount Cranborne
(*Churchill papers, 20/36*)

27 January 1941

I cannot agree to the Dominion High Commissioners receiving the Most Secret Air Staff Daily Operational Summary and the Air Ministry Daily Summary of reports of enemy action against the United Kingdom. The former contains information on operational matters of the most secret character. You must explain to the Dominion High Commissioners that our rule (which does not, of course, imply any want of confidence) is that very secret matters must only be made known to those who must know them in order to do their job.

The Dominion High Commissioners cannot possibly feel any sense of grievance in not being shown a copy of a document which is not, in fact, circulated to any member of the War Cabinet.

As regards information on air-raid damage, I see no purpose in giving the High Commissioners a detailed daily statement. It is well known that the first reports of air-raid damage are always exaggerated, and that after a serious raid the position cannot be appraised for two or three days. It is much better to give them a weekly document, when it has been possible to assess the position accurately.

A good deal of information on air-raid damage is, I believe, contained in the

Weekly Résumé of Operational Information furnished to the Dominion High Commissioners. If it is necessary to give them more information on air-raid damage, arrangements might be made to let them have a weekly report on this matter which is prepared by the Ministry of Home Security, provided that the Minister (whom I have not consulted) agrees.

Winston S. Churchill to Sir Archibald Sinclair and Hugh Dalton
(*Churchill papers, 20/36*)

27 January 1941

There must be a very great deal of railway traffic from Germany to Italy; coal alone should account for nearly 200,000 tons a week averaged over the year. It is obviously most important that this should be impeded in every way. In view of the mountainous nature of the country through which the railways run, this should be feasible. Please let me have a report on what has been done and is being done.

President Franklin D. Roosevelt to Winston S. Churchill
(*Facsimile, 'The Second World War', Volume Three, page 25*)

20 January 1941[1]

The White House
Washington

Dear Churchill

Wendell Willkie[1] will give you this. He is truly helping to keep politics out over here.

[1] Wendell Willkie handed Churchill this letter when they lunched together in London on 27 January 1941. It had been written on 20 January 1941.

[2] Wendell Lewis Willkie, 1892–1944. Born in Indiana. A lawyer and a Democrat. Became a Republican in opposition to Roosevelt's New Deal. Unlike many Republicans, he was not an isolationist. Won the Republican Party nomination for the Presidency, 1940. Lost, but gained a larger Republican popular vote than any previous contender (a vote eventually exceeded by Eisenhower in 1952). Visited Britain, Russia and China as Roosevelt's personal emissary, 1940–1.

I think this verse applies to your people as it does to us:

'Sail on, O ship of State!
Sail on, O Union, strong and great!
Humanity with all its fears,
With all the hopes of future years,
Is hanging breathless on thy fate.'[1]

As ever yours,
Franklin D. Roosevelt

Winston S. Churchill to President Franklin D. Roosevelt
(*Churchill papers, 20/49*)

28 January 1941
Personal and Secret

I received Willkie yesterday and was deeply moved by the verse of Longfellow's which you had quoted. I shall have it framed as a souvenir of these tremendous days and as a mark of our friendly relations which have been built up telegraphically but also telepathically under all the stresses.

All my information shows that the Germans are persevering in their preparations to invade this country and we are getting ready to give them a reception worthy of the occasion. On the other hand, the news from the East shows that a large army and air force are being established in Roumania and that the advance parties of the German air force have already to the extent of several thousands infiltrated themselves into Bulgarian aerodromes with the full connivance of the Bulgarian Government. It would be natural for Hitler to make a strong threat against the British Isles in order to occupy us here and cover his Eastern designs. The forces at his disposal are, however, so large that he could carry out both offensives at the same time. You may be sure we shall do our best in both quarters.

I am most grateful to you for your splendid reception of Halifax and for all you are doing to secure us timely help.[2] It has been a great pleasure to me to make friends with Hopkins, who has been a great comfort and encouragement

[1] Longfellow wrote 'hopes' in the fourth line, and opened the stanza: 'Thou too, sail on, O Ship of State.' (*Building of the Ship*).

[2] On the previous day, 27 January 1941, Staff Conversations had opened in Washington, authorized by Churchill and Roosevelt to determine 'the best methods by which the armed forces of the United States and British Commonwealth, with its present Allies, could defeat Germany and the Powers allied with her, should the United States be compelled to resort to war', and to seek agreement on the methods and nature of Anglo-American military cooperation, strategy, strength of forces and eventual 'unit of field command in cases of strategic or tactical joint operations.' ('United States British Staff Conversations, Report', 27 March 1941, 'Secret', ABC-1: *Premier papers 3/489/2, folios 8–13*). The British delegation consisted of Rear-Admirals Bellairs and Danckwerts, Major-General Morris, Air Vice-Marshal Slessor and Captain A.W. Clarke, RN. The American delegation included Major-General S.D. Embick and Rear-Admiral Ghormley. (ABC = American British Conversations)

to everyone he has met. One can easily see why he is so close to you. Colonel Donovan[1] also has done fine work in the Middle East.

All my respects and kindest regards. I hope you are already better.

Robert Boothby: statement
(Hansard)

28 January 1941 House of Commons

. . . I am very sorry to leave the Ministry of Food, where I was exceptionally fortunate in having an opportunity of studying at first hand the methods of so great an administrator as Lord Woolton.[2] I am still more sorry that I have had to sever my association with the Prime Minister, in whom I have always had such great faith, and whose star – now, fortunately for this country, in the ascendant – I have followed for many years.

With regard to my future action, I want only to say this at present. The true picture of events is still so clear before my eyes that I am quite unable to comprehend how an interpretation could have been put on them which could make me seem unworthy of membership of this House. It is not true that I suddenly took an interest in Czecho-Slovakian affairs because I was given a financial interest. I helped the Czechs because I did not want them to be robbed by the Germans, not because I wanted to rob them myself. It is not true that I pressed the claims in which I might be held to have had an interest as against others. On the contrary, I pressed in this House that the small claims, in which no one suggests that I had an interest, should be met in full. It is not true that I deliberately deceived the Chancellor or the House. When

[1] William Joseph Donovan, 1883–1959. A United States lawyer. On active service, France, 1917–18 (Congressional Medal of Honour). Assistant to the Attorney General of the United States, 1924–29. Chairman, Boulder Dam Canyon Project Commission, 1934–39. Unofficial observer in Britain for the Secretary of the Navy, 1940. Sent by President Roosevelt on missions to south-east Europe and the Middle East to observe resistance movements, 1940–41. Co-ordinator of Information (Intelligence), 1941–42. Head of the OSS (Office of Strategic Services), from 13 June 1942 to 1 October 1945, recruiting agents in Europe, North Africa and Burma. Brigadier-General 1943; Major-General, 1944. Assistant to Judge Jackson at the Nuremberg Trials, 1945–46. Ambassador to Thailand, 1953–59.

[2] Frederick James Marquis, 1883–1964. A successful businessman, statistician and economist. Chairman of Lewis's Investment Trust. Knighted, 1935. Director-General of Equipment and Stores, Ministry of Supply, 1939–40. Created Baron Woolton, 1939. Privy Councillor, 1940. Minister of Food, 1940–3. Companion of Honour, 1942. Member of the War Cabinet, and Minister of Reconstruction, 1943–5. Chairman of the Conservative and Unionist Central Office, 1946–55. Chancellor of the Duchy of Lancaster, 1952–5. Viscount, 1953. Earl, 1956.

I disclaimed any financial interest to the Chancellor, I was answering his charge that I and my Committee were working for payment, and that I was being paid as Chairman. It is not true that I advocated any case on account of personal interest. I challenge denial that everything I said or advocated was in the national interest.

Finally, it is not true that I have received one single penny for anything I said or did with regard to the Czech claims. Knowing all this, I cannot, of my own free will, take any action that might even imply an acknowledgment of guilt on my part. Folly I have admitted; guilt I cannot admit. In face of the issues which confront us all my own plight fades into insignificance. Whatever happens, I intend to serve the country to the best of my ability in some capacity. There is only one objective for anyone today and that is to win the war. What else matters? In accordance with precedent, Mr Speaker, I now propose to withdraw from the Chamber.

The hon. Member then withdrew from the chamber.

Question,

'That the report of the Select Committee on the Conduct of a Member be now considered.'

put, and agreed to.

Report considered accordingly.

Winston S. Churchill: speech

(*Hansard*)

28 January 1941 House of Commons

The Prime Minister: I beg to move,

'That this House doth agree with the Report of the Committee.'

We cannot, I think, with any advantage attempt to re-try a matter to which the Committee have devoted so many days and so much thought and attention. The House, as a whole, cannot, in the nature of things, deal with these complicated matters except by the practice which is settled and has been so long adopted of referring them to a Committee of the House. It would be, I venture to think, fatal to the whole of that practice if the House were to disregard the opinion of the Committee unless something had been brought to their notice which showed that the Committee had been misinformed, or unless they had reason to doubt the competence or the impartiality of their Committee. Therefore, I do not propose to enter upon the arguments, and I am bound to say that I do not believe any great advantage will be derived if that should be done in other quarters.

The Committee commended itself to the House by its composition and its high character. It has discharged its distasteful task with efficiency and expedition, and it came unanimously to the conclusions which are contained in the Report. The Chairman of the Committee, one of the oldest Members in the House, is well known to all of us, and it is a tribute to our system and to him that all parties in the House should have agreed in appointing him. The task was an unenviable one, but everybody will agree that it has been discharged to the satisfaction of the House. I do not think that any choice was open to the head of the Government, when the evidence came into our possession by somewhat unusual events connected with war-time conditions, but to bring the matter before a Select Committee and to ask the House to concur in that course. My hon. Friend was a Minister, and the reputation of the Government as well as the House might have been seriously affected if we had neglected to take any further step.

I shall not attempt to add anything to the Report or comment on it in any way. It sets a very high standard, but we have to set a very high standard for the House of Commons, and we have to try to live up to that standard. The fault of my hon. Friend may have been serious. The penalty is most severe. It is at least the interruption of a career of high Parliamentary promise. It causes pain to all. I am sure that the House has been quite exceptionally distressed by this affair and all that is connected with it; and especially it is a source of great pain to me because, over a good many years, my hon. Friend, as he has reminded the House, has been one of my personal friends, often a supporter at lonely and difficult moments, and I have always entertained a warm personal regard for him. If it is painful to us, it is also a loss to all. It is a loss to His Majesty's Government, who lose a highly competent and industrious Minister, one of the few of that generation who has attained advancement and who has discharged his tasks with admitted and recognised distinction. It is also a loss to the House. We are none too fertile in talents of the order that have just been displayed to us. Altogether it is a heartbreaking business. The popularity of my hon. Friend, his abilities, and the manner in which during his short tenure of office he conducted himself, all add to the poignancy of our feelings, but I do not think they can influence our course of action. There we must leave this matter. We should accept the Report of the Committee, and that is all we have to do. As for my hon. Friend, one can only say that there are paths of service open in war time which are not open in times of peace; and some of these paths may be paths to honour.[1]

[1] Boothby joined the Royal Air Force Volunteer Reserve. In 1944 he was Liaison Officer to General Le Gentilhomme, of the Free French Forces.

Winston S. Churchill to Randolph S. Churchill[1]
(*Churchill papers, 1/362*)

28 January 1941

I send you two letters of introduction to the persons I mentioned.[2] They are in a sealed envelope not to be opened till you get to sea, in order that your destination may not become apparent.

The Boothby Debate passed over as painlessly as possible. His speech was a remarkable parliamentary performance, and perceptibly affected the opinion of the House. I do not think he will have to resign his Seat.

Winston S. Churchill to General Smuts
(*Churchill papers, 2/422*)

28 January 1941

My dear Friend,

This letter should be handed to you by my son Randolph, who is going out with his Commando to the Middle East. I do not know whether his ship will stop long enough at Capetown, or whether he will be able to get leave to come ashore. If this should be possible, it would give me great pleasure to feel that you and he had had a talk, and that I had presented him to you.

Believe me,
Yours ever,
Winston S. Churchill

[1] Randolph Frederick Edward Spencer Churchill, 1911–1968. Churchill's only son. His godfathers were F.E. Smith and Sir Edward Grey. Educated at Eton and Christ Church, Oxford. On leaving Oxford in 1932, without taking his degree, he worked briefly for the Imperial Chemical Industries as assistant editor of their house magazine. Joined the staff of the *Sunday Graphic*, 1932; wrote subsequently for many newspapers, including the *Evening Standard* (1937–9). Reported during Hitler's election campaign of 1932, the Chaco War of 1935 and Spanish Civil War; accompanied the Duke of Windsor on his tour of Germany, 1937. Unsuccessful Parliamentary candidate 1935 (twice), 1936, 1945, 1950 and 1951. Conservative MP for Preston, 1940–5. On active service, North Africa and Italy, 1941–3. Major, British mission to the Yugoslav Army of National Liberation, 1943–4 (MBE Military, 1944). Historian; editor of several volumes of his father's speeches, and author of the first two volumes of this biography, and of the first two sets of document volumes.

[2] General Smuts and General Wavell: Randolph was on his way to Cairo, via Capetown.

Winston S. Churchill to General Wavell
(*Churchill papers, 2/423*)

28 January 1941

My dear Wavell,

This letter should be handed to you by my son Randolph, who is going with his Commando to join your Army in the Middle East. I do not know whether he will be able to get leave to come to your Headquarters, or whether you will be there when he can. Assuming, however, that these difficulties do not make it impossible, it would be a pleasure to me to make him known to you personally, and I shall be grateful for any kindness you can show him agreeably with the Service.

Believe me,
Yours very sincerely,
Winston S. Churchill

Winston S. Churchill to Sir John Anderson
(*Churchill papers, 20/36*)

28 January 1941

While the Import and Production Executives necessarily are concerned with the practical handling of the business committed to them, it is essential that the larger issues of Economic policy should be dealt with by your Committee, and primarily by you. This is in accordance with the drift of well-informed public opinion. You should, therefore, not hesitate to take the initiative over the whole field. You should summon economists like Keynes[1] to give their views to you personally. You should ask for any assistance or staff you require, utilising, of course, the Statistical Department. Professor Lindemann and his Branch will assist you in any way you wish, and will also act as liaison between you and me. I wish you to take the lead prominently and vigorously in this Committee, and it should certainly meet at least once a week, if not more often.

Will you consult with Sir Edward Bridges on the above, and let me know how you propose to implement it?

[1] John Maynard Keynes, 1883–1946. Educated at Eton and King's College Cambridge. Economist. Editor of the *Economic Journal*, 1911–44. Served at the India Office, 1906–08; the Treasury, 1915–19. Principal Treasury Representative at the Paris Peace Conference, 1919. Created Baron, 1942. Leader of the British Delegation to Washington to negotiate the American Loan, 1945. Among his publications were *The Economic Consequences of the Peace* (1919) and *The Economic Consequences of Mr Churchill* (July 1925).

Winston S. Churchill to Sir Archibald Sinclair
(*Churchill papers, 20/36*)

28 January 1941

The understanding which I hoped would be reached the other night was that you would make your concessions on the equipment side in return for receiving back Ferry organizations. Without the slightest reference to what you were to give, you proceed to claim all you were to get. I do not wonder, therefore, that misunderstanding and friction has arisen.

I do not wish this matter to be discussed in the Cabinet at the present time, or until I have first made a further effort to adjust the unhappy differences between you and MAP by which my labours are greatly increased.

It is for me to decide the division of functions between the Air Ministry and MAP, and I propose to do this in the next few days.[1]

Winston S. Churchill to Sir Patrick Dollan[2]
(*Churchill papers, 20/21*)

28 January 1941

My dear Lord Provost,

Thank you so much for your letter and may I once more express the thanks of Mrs Churchill and myself for the kindness of our reception in Glasgow. We were indeed touched by the warmth of the welcome we received.

I was struck by the evident keenness and efficiency of the various Civil Defence services, and came away fortified by the assurance that, if the full force of the enemy's attack should be turned upon Glasgow, as upon so many cities in the South, her citizens will endure and surmount it. The decision of the Transport employees, to which you refer, is a true expression of the loyal and alert public spirit of which I saw so many signs.

Yours sincerely,
Winston S. Churchill

[1] Two days later Churchill wrote to the Chief of the Air Staff, Sir Charles Portal: 'It was a great mistake to go and make a demand for the Ferry pools, saying that this was settled at our dinner, without making any proposal about Equipment Depots. This only made more trouble for me and yourselves. I shall certainly not reach any decision about delimiting the functions of the two Ministries without talking it over with you.' (Prime Minister's Personal Minute M 100/1, *Premier papers, 3/9*)

[2] Patrick Joseph Dollan, –1963. A rope worker, grocery apprentice; miner (for eight years). Member of the Glasgow Corporation, 1913–46. Glasgow and Scottish Chairman, Independent Labour Party, 1920–31. Lord Provost of Glasgow, 1938–41. Knighted, 1941.

Winston S. Churchill to Alfred Duff Cooper
(*Churchill papers, 20/36*)

29 January 1941
Action this Day

MINISTER OF INFORMATION

I do not think that a busy Minister like the Minister of Shipping,[1] whose Department is now under special strain and scrutiny, should attempt to give weekly broadcasts. I am assured that this particular broadcast contains nothing but harmless abuse of the Germans, but the fewer Ministers who broadcast the better.

2. I am very sorry you have got Mr. J. B. Priestley[2] back, and that his first broadcast should have been an argument utterly contrary to my known views. How many more has he got to do? Have you any control over what he says? He is far from friendly to the Government, and I should not be too sure about him on larger issues.

Winston S. Churchill to David Margesson
(*Churchill papers, 20/36*)

29 January 1941

I am very much obliged to you for the considerable effort you have made to meet my views and reduce Army demands upon the man-power of Great Britain.

2. I still do not understand how a Division supposed to be complete with 15,000 men of all arms, requires 35,000 men, or 20,000 extra. Perhaps it will be simpler to take a Corps of 3 divisions, which on your calculations would require 105,000 men, of which 45,000 only would be included in Field Units. Let me have a table showing how the remaining 60,000 are divided between:

(a) Corps troops.
(b) Share of Army troops.
(c) Lines of communication troops.

3. Neither do I understand the scale on which the line of communication troops are calculated. The troops in Great Britain lie in the midst of their base of supplies and of the most highly developed railway network in the world. They have roads innumerable and of high quality. In the event of invasion, the advances they would have to make are in the nature of 70-100 miles at the outside, although, of course, a larger lateral movement by rail from South to

[1] Ronald Cross.

[2] John Boynton Priestley, 1894–1984. Of radical, non-conformist, North Country stock. On active service, 1914–18. Author, dramatist and literary critic. Member of the National Theatre Board, 1966–67. Order of Merit, 1977.

North, or vice versa, might be required. Such conditions are not comparable at all with those prevailing in France, where, owing to our choosing to base ourselves on St Nazaire, &c., we had a 500-mile line of communication, mainly by road, to maintain. What are the differences in the scale of L of C troops provided for the first 10 Divisions in France this time last year, and those you now propose for the troops retained in Great Britain for defence?

4. The problem will not be solved without taking a view forward of what is likely to happen in the next twelve months. We shall certainly have to keep not less than 15 British Divisions behind the beaches to guard against invasion. For the bulk of these a scale much less than the French scale (BEF) should suffice. The Forces in the Middle East, now that the Mediterranean is closed, can only be built up at a reduced rate. But we ought to assume that by July there will be in the Delta or up the Nile 4 Australian, 1 New Zealand, 1[1] + 1 South African, 6 out of 8 Indian and 3 British Divisions, or their equivalents in Brigade groups. In addition, there will be in Africa the 4 African Colonial Divisions. These last, surely, are not Divisions in the ordinary sense, i.e., capable of being used as integral tactical Units in the field? Are they not, in fact, the garrisons of East and West Africa and the Sudan, requiring only small complements of artillery and technical troops, and with lines of communication provided locally? Let me know what scale of Corps troops, share of Army troops and L of C troops you contemplate for these 4 sedentary or localized so-called 'Divisions'. Is it not a mistake to call them Divisions in any sense?

5. Returning to the Army of the Nile, with its 16 Divisions, it must be observed that, once Benghazi has been taken and strongly fortified with a Field Force based upon it, the conditions in Egypt should be such as to enable internal order to be maintained by Indian Divisions, who will, in fact, be living very close to the possible centres of disturbance, and who will not have to take the field like a British Division acting in France or Flanders, or even a British Division at home. What scale of L of C troops are you providing for these? Do you think it necessary to organize them in Corps, and supply them with the European quota of medium and heavy artillery, &c.?

6. We must, however, contemplate as our main objective in this theatre the bringing into heavy action of the largest possible Force from the Army of the Nile to fight in aid of Greece or Turkey, or both. How many Divisions, or their equivalent, do you contemplate being available by July for action in south-east Europe? I should have thought that the 4 Australian, 1 New Zealand, one of the 2 South Africans, the 3 British, and 3 of the six Indian Divisions should be available, total 12. These troops must be equipped on the highest scale, for it is Germans they will have to fight. On the other hand, they will come into

[1] Churchill noted here: 'Extra to original 57'.

action only gradually. Probably 4 Divisions by the end of March, and the rest as shipping and equipment becomes available. The problem, therefore, is for a first-class scale for 12 Divisions against the Germans, a very much reduced second-class scale against the disorders in Egypt, or to take charge of conquered Italian territory, and a still lower scale for the so-called African Colonial Division. I hope that with this picture, which the General Staff should consider carefully, your problem may be more precisely defined, viz., 5 British Divisions at home at highest mobility; 10 at secondary; working up to 12 from the Middle East in action against the Germans in Greece or Turkey on the highest scale, 4 in Egypt, Sudan, &c., on a moderate scale, and 4 African Colonials according to local conditions, total 35, to which must be added 2 Indian Divisions, for service in Malaya, total 37, leaving from your total of 58[1] – 21 Divisions. Of these 9 are Armoured Divisions, leaving 12 British Infantry Divisions to be accounted for.

7. What is the picture and forecast for these 12 British Divisions? Up to 6 they have to go at very short notice to French North Africa, or alternatively perhaps to work with a friendly Spain. We cannot do both. These 6 Divisions will come into operation in 2 Corps of 3 Divisions each, but owing to shipping exigencies they can only come gradually into operation. In so far as they come into action at all, it will be against the Germans. Therefore, whatever is thought to be the most appropriate scale must be provided. It must, however, be observed that neither of these theatres offer opportunities for the use of heavy or much medium artillery, and that in the Spanish alternative the war might well take a guerrilla form.

8. We cannot hope to arm the remaining 6 Divisions to the full scale for many months to come, but if they were brought to the anti-German scale for oversea operations by the end of August, it would be satisfactory.

9. Nine armoured Divisions are comprised in the total number of 58. What is the distribution contemplated for these? At first sight, 4 at home, 2 available for amphibious action in the West, and 3 in the Middle East or Balkan theatre, would seem appropriate. It is clear that the rearward and repair services of any of these Divisions sent abroad require to be on a larger scale than those which lie handy to all the great workshops of Great Britain. Have these differentiations been allowed for?

10. Battle wastage at 8,500 a month is not excessive as a theoretical forecast. In practice, however, it does not seem likely that, apart from invasion, action on this scale will begin for several months. It might be safe as a working arrangement to bring this monthly figure of 8,500 into account only from July 1, 1941. This would save 60,000 men.

[1] One South African division extra to the original fifty-seven divisions.

11. The wastage from normal causes of 18,750 a month, or 243,750 a year, appears a high figure, and one wonders whether it may not be reduced as better accommodation and more settled conditions are established in Great Britain, and as the men themselves become more seasoned, and the result of weeding-out weaklings through discharge. I should like to know how many of these men discharged from the Army are unfit for any other form of war work. What is the number of deaths per month, the total incapacitated, those fit for lighter duties, and those fit for munitions work? I should expect that at least 10,000 a month would be capable of some other form of employment. This point is important for the War Office, as in stating the man-power demand which is to be made upon the nation the Army should credit itself with any men who are yielded up who are still capable of civilian service. This, of course, does not affect the problem, but only the statement of the problem; none the less, it is important.

12. I regard ADGB[1] as a source which may well at some future date yield economies because of new methods and our increasing ascendancy in the air. It is astonishing how great are the numbers of men required per gun. Careful study should make it possible to reduce the numbers in many localities, and to accept a slightly lower scale of immediate preparedness. Even a small percentage of saving under these heads would enable the additional guns and searchlights now coming into action to be manned with a smaller demand upon man-power.

13. I hope I am not to infer from the expression 'Beach Battalions' that any body of young, physically fit, efficiently-trained men would be relegated to a particular function. It is indispensable that a continuous rotation should take place, all Brigades taking their place on the Beaches in turn, or coming into the back areas for service in the mobile Divisions.

14. Generally speaking, I do not consider that a demand by the Army for 900,000 men, less 60,000, less 150,000 (paragraphs 10 and 11) = 690,000 net up to October 1, 1942, is excessive. The Training process must be maintained; wastage must be made good. Once the Army is heavily engaged, it would be more natural to draw large numbers from the public and to comb the Munitions and ARP[2] Services. It is the demand in the next six months, while military operations are at a minimum, that I am anxious to keep within limits.

15. I await the further information which I ask for in this paper, but meanwhile, I should greatly regret to see 20 Medium regiments or 480 guns retrenched for a mere saving of 18,000 men out of the enormous totals presented; and similarly, 7 Field Regiments of 168 guns for the sake of saving 5,600 men. It is essential to strengthen the Army in fighting troops, and it is

[1] Air Defence of Great Britain.
[2] Air Raid Precautions.

better to take some risks in theoretical calculations of wastage, even if these should be falsified at a later date, than to fail at this moment to produce the proper quota of artillery.

Winston S. Churchill to Anthony Eden
(*Churchill papers, 20/36*)

29 January 1941

ITALIAN NON-COMBATANTS IN EAST AFRICA

The end of para. 2 appears to be somewhat dangerous.[1] The burden of feeding the 200,000 civilians is an important part of the war strain operating on the Duke of Aosta. I do not feel that he should be relieved of this strain except as part of a capitulation, by which he could withdraw with his people to assigned places within Eritrea pending the post-war settlement. We should have to feed them there.

Winston S. Churchill to General Smuts
(*Churchill papers, 20/49*)

29 January 1941
Most Secret and Personal

Thank you for your helpful message of 28th January, which has this evening been considered by the Cabinet. In the light of your views we now suggest that terms of announcement should be as follows:

'His Majesty's Government would welcome the reappearance of any independent Ethiopian State and recognize the claim of the Emperor Haile Selassie to the throne. The Emperor has intimated to His Majesty's Government that he will need outside assistance and guidance. His Majesty's Government agree with this view and consider that any such assistance and guidance in economic and political matters should be the subject of international arrangement at the conclusion of peace. They reaffirm that they have themselves no territorial ambitions in Abyssinia.

'In the meanwhile the conduct of military operations by Imperial forces in parts of Abyssinia will require temporary measures of military guidance and control. These will be carried out in consultation with the Emperor, and will be brought to an end as soon as the situation permits.'

You will see that the first paragraph embodies your draft subject to minor

[1] Telegram No. 282 from the Foreign Office to Cairo.

verbal changes and to insertion of 'independent' before 'Ethiopian State.' We feel that in view of the terms of the Parliamentary Question and Answer of the 11th July we cannot omit the word 'independent', but this is qualified by the remainder of the paragraph, which closely follows your text.

We trust that in the light of the above you will see no objection to the adoption of the announcement in its revised form. It is now proposed that announcement should be made in Parliament here on Tuesday, 4th February, and we should therefore be grateful for an early reply.

Winston S. Churchill to General Wavell
(Churchill papers, 20/49)

29 January 1941
Personal and Secret

Your 0/37805.

1. I thank you for your assurance in paragraph 1. I quite understand that your rearward services must be specially maintained because of the great distances and the absence of local reserves and repair facilities such as we have here. No doubt also an operation like the Libyan campaign, with desert conditions, distances and speed, makes extraordinary demands, but you must not mind my sending you a further analysis which I am preparing of the ration and fighting strength of the Armies in ME. Please remember I have many interests to consider here at the centre, and I must count on you to help in every way possible.

2. Smuts's position is that he can send troops anywhere in Africa, but would have to get another Resolution from the South African House before going beyond Africa. There is no hurry in taking the Division, and I do not want it to come till it can disembark in Egypt.

3. Your 0/37843. We will consider the whole position in the next few days, and try to send you first what you need most. We are also considering general strategic issues raised in paragraphs 7, 8, 9 and 10, arising out of the probable early arrival of German Air Force on and in Aegean, and possible collapse of Greece and abstention of Turkey.

4. I hope you received my telegram of congratulations sent on 23rd.

Winston S. Churchill to Viscount Halifax
(Churchill papers, 20/49)

30 January 1941

I must congratulate you upon the manner in which your Embassage has opened. Everyone is very pleased here.

Winston S. Churchill to Colonel Donovan
(*Churchill papers, 20/49*)

30 January 1941

Many congratulations upon all you are doing.

John Colville: diary
(*Colville papers*)

30 January 1941

As a result of last night's meeting, the PM drafted at No. 10 a telegram to the Turkish President[1] asking that in view of the certainty of a German move through Bulgaria we should be allowed to base a number of squadrons on Turkey. From every source news comes that Germany's intentions in the Balkans are serious, and from whatever angle the Chiefs of Staff regard the matter it remains evident that Turkey is the key to the situation. Hence the PM's telegram.

Winston S. Churchill to President Inönü
(*Churchill papers, 20/49*)

31 January 1941

The rapidly growing danger to Turkey and to British interests leads me, Mr President, to address you directly. I have sure information that the Germans are already establishing themselves upon Bulgarian aerodromes. Hutments are being prepared, and advance servicing personnel numbering several thousands have arrived. This has been done with the full connivance of the Royal Bulgarian Air Force and undoubtedly of the Bulgarian Government. Very soon, perhaps in a few weeks, the movement into Bulgaria of German troops and Air Squadrons will begin. The Air Squadrons will only have to fly from their stations in Roumania to the bases they are preparing in Bulgaria, and will immediately be able to come into action. Then, unless you promise the Germans not to march against Bulgaria or against their troops passing through Bulgaria, they will bomb Istanbul and Adrianople the same night, and also dive-bomb your troops in Thrace. No doubt they would hope either

[1] Ismet Inönü, 1884–1974. Born in Smyrna. Served in the Ottoman army, 1904–1918. Active in the defence of Gallipoli, 1915. Chief of Staff to Mustapha Kemal, 1920; defeated the Greeks near the village of Inönü (1921) from which he took his surname. Prime Minister of Turkey, 1924–38; President, 1938–50. Leader of the parliamentary opposition, 1950–61. Prime Minister, 1961–65. Leader of the parliamentary opposition for a second time, 1965–72.

to reach Salonika unopposed or to compel the Greeks to make peace with Italy and yield them Air bases in Greece and in the Islands, thus endangering the communications between our Armies in Egypt and the Turkish Army. They would deny the use of Smyrna to our Navy, they would completely control the exits from the Dardanelles, and thus complete the encirclement of Turkey in Europe on three sides. This would also facilitate their attacks upon Alexandria and Egypt generally.

Of course, I know, Mr President, that, confronted with these mortal dangers, Turkey would declare war. But why is it necessary to hand over to the enemy the enormous advantage of being able to secure the mastery of the Bulgarian airfields without a shot being fired or a word being said?

Germany is, in fact, preparing to repeat on the frontiers of Turkey the same manoeuvre as she accomplished on the frontiers of France in April and May 1940. But in this case, instead of having hesitating and terrified neutrals like Denmark, Holland and Belgium, she has in Bulgaria a confederate and former ally who has, beyond all doubt, abandoned the will, and never had the power, to resist. All this, I repeat, may fall upon us in February or in March, and will be open to the Germans even without moving any large masses of troops from the moment when the Bulgarian airfields have been fitted to receive the German Air Force and are occupied by the advanced aircraft personnel and ground staff. Do we propose to sit still with folded hands and watch the steady preparation of this deadly stroke?

It seems to me that we should be held gravely blameworthy by our respective nations if we were to fail in ordinary prudence and foresight. Even now, we have waited too long.

I therefore propose to you, Mr President, that you and I should repeat in defence of Turkey the same kind of measures which the Germans are taking on the Bulgarian airfields. My Government wish to send to Turkey at the earliest moment when accommodation can be provided at least ten Squadrons of Fighter and Bomber aircraft in, apart from the five now in action in, Greece. If Greece should surrender or be beaten down, we will transfer these other five air squadrons to Turkish airfields and, further, we will fight the air war from Turkish bases with ever-increasing air forces of the highest quality. Thus we shall help to give the Turkish Army the additional air support which they need to sustain their famous military qualities.

But, more than that, we shall place Turkey in a position, once our Squadrons are on the Turkish airfields, to threaten to bombard the Roumanian oilfields if any German advance is made into Bulgaria, or if the air personnel already in Bulgaria is not speedily withdrawn. We will undertake not to take such action from Turkish airfields except by agreement with you.

There is more to come. The attitude of Russia is uncertain and it is our hope it may remain loyal and friendly. Nothing will more restrain Russia from aiding Germany, even indirectly, than the presence of powerful British bombing forces, which could (from Turkey) attack the oilfields of Baku. Russia is dependent upon the supply from these oilfields for a very large part of her agriculture, and far-reaching famine would follow their destruction. We are assured that the whole soil around the oilwells is impregnated with petroleum, making it possible to start a conflagration on a scale not hitherto witnessed in the world.

Thus Turkey, once defended by air power, would have the means perhaps of deterring Germany from overrunning Bulgaria and quelling Greece, and of counterbalancing the Russian fear of the German Armies. If this decisive position is to be saved, there is not an hour to lose, and on receipt of your assent His Majesty's Government will immediately give the necessary orders for our advanced personnel, either in uniform or in plain clothes, as you prefer, to start at once for Turkey.

Further, we are prepared to send you a hundred AA guns, which are now either in or on their way to Egypt. These would be complete with personnel, either in uniform, if you so desire, or in the guise of instructors.

All other measures which have been discussed with Marshal Chakmak,[1] and also the naval measures, will, at the right moment, be brought into operation.

The victories we have gained in Libya will enable us to give a far more direct and immediate measure of aid to Turkey in the event of our two countries becoming allied in war, and we will make common cause with you and use our growing strength to aid your valiant Armies.

Winston S. Churchill to the Chiefs of Staff Committee
(Churchill papers, 20/36)

31 January 1941
Action this Day
Secret

We must not overlook the decision we have conveyed to General Wavell that once Tobruk was taken the Greek-Turkish situation must have priority. The advance to Benghazi is most desirable, and has been emphasized in later

[1] Fevzi Chakmak, 1876–1950. Born in Constantinople. Lieutenant, Ottoman Army, 1895. Fought in the Balkan Wars, 1912–13. General commanding the Turkish troops at the Dardanelles (1915), in the Caucasus (1916–17) and in Syria (1918). Chief of the Turkish General Staff, 1918. Minister of War in the Sultan's Government, 1920. Resigned, to join Mustafa Kemel (Atatürk). Prime Minister and Minister of War, Grand National Assembly, Ankara, 1921–22. Chief of Staff of the Turkish Army, 1922–44. In February 1941, during Anglo-Turkish talks Marshal Chakmak and his officers explained that the would not declare war on Germany, if Germany attacked Greece – which should have been a Turkish obligation – because, lacking modern weapons, the Turks would be a liability. Elected to the Assembly as an independent opposition member, 1946–8. Died in Istanbul.

telegrams. Nevertheless, only Forces which do not conflict with European needs can be employed. As the forecast is now that Benghazi cannot be captured till the end of February, it is necessary that this should be impressed upon General Wavell. For instance, the Air support promised to Turkey cannot be delayed till then. It may, however, be possible to reconcile both objectives.

Winston S. Churchill to Alfred Duff Cooper
(*Churchill papers, 20/36*)

31 January 1941

Mr Priestley's broadcasts. Is he paid for them? If so, there is no reason at all why we should subsidise hampering criticism. In view of the fact that you undertake to vet his drafts, and of what you say truly about martyrisation, I agree that he should finish the present series, provided that no fee is paid. The Chief Whip[1] spoke to me of the offence given to the Party by Mr Priestley coming back on the broadcasts, and some attention ought to be paid to Conservative opinion.

Winston S. Churchill to Alfred Duff Cooper and the Foreign Office
(*Churchill papers, 20/36*)

31 January 1941

I see no reason to deal with this matter[2] in the House of Commons. I have repeatedly characterized Mr Griffin's statement as a malicious lie. This should be stated as often as possible on the American radio.

Winston S. Churchill to Viscount Cranborne
(*Churchill papers, 20/36*)

31 January 1941

I agree with the general line of your talk.[3] I could in no circumstances give the guarantee asked for, and for the reasons you state.

About arms. If we were assured that it was Southern Ireland's intention to enter the war, we would, of course, if possible beforehand share our anti-

[1] James Stuart.

[2] A statement which Churchill was alleged to have made in 1936, and which was being circulated in America by supporters of isolation, that America ought not to have come into the First World War.

[3] With J.W. Dulanty, the Irish High Commissioner in London (in 1917 he had been Principal Assistant Secretary at the Ministry of Munitions, when Churchill was Minister).

aircraft weapons with them, and make secretly with them all possible necessary arrangements for their defence. Until we are so satisfied, we do not wish them to have further arms, and certainly will not give them ourselves.

The concession about Lough Swilly is important and shows the way things are moving. No attempt should be made to conceal from Mr De Valera the depth and intensity of feeling against the policy of Irish neutrality. We have tolerated and acquiesced in it, but juridically we have never recognized that Southern Ireland is an independent sovereign State, and she herself has repudiated Dominion Status. Her international status is undefined and anomalous. Should the present situation last till the end of the war, which is unlikely, a gulf will have opened between Northern and Southern Ireland, which it will be impossible to bridge in this generation.

Let me have a further report on economic pressure.

Winston S. Churchill: speech
('The Times', 1 February 1941)

31 January 1941 Portsmouth

I have thought about you and your friends in Southampton a good deal when we knew how heavily you were being attacked, and I am glad to find an afternoon to come and see you to wish you good luck and offer you the thanks and congratulations of the Government for the manner in which you are standing up to these onslaughts of the enemy. We see that the enemy has been decisively defeated by the RAF and he was not able last autumn to invade our country. We see that our friends across the ocean are taking a very warm interest in the struggle for freedom here. The great American democracy has pledged itself to give us its aid. We have here Mr Hopkins, the envoy and friend of President Roosevelt, that great statesman and friend of freedom and democracy. One cannot help feeling enormously encouraged by the spirit of the ever-growing movement of aid to Britain which we see laying hold of the mighty masses of the United States.

Lastly, what has happened to Italy? She with her crafty and calculating chief thought she could win a very cheap and easy victory by stabbing France in the back. The tables have been turned in a most remarkable fashion by the brilliant operation of General Wavell and General Wilson and the splendid effort made by the Greeks in repelling invasion of their native land. These two events, one in Africa and the other in Europe, have together shown the rottenness and weakness of the Nazi-fascist régime so far as Italy is concerned. Instead of marching on in triumph to Athens and Cairo they are now forced to bring in the Germans to rescue and rule them.

All this gives us encouragement to face the long and hard ordeals which lie before us but to which we shall not be found unequal. We shall come through. We cannot tell when, we cannot tell how, but we shall come through. We have none of us any doubt whatever, nor is there much doubt among lovers of freedom in other countries throughout the world that we shall come through with triumph. When we have done so, we shall have the right to say we live in an age which, in all the long history of Britain, was most filled with glorious achievement and most graced by duties done.

We have a powerful army in this Island. We have strongly fortified defences all around our coasts. These defences are well manned, and behind them are large mobile armies capable of advance and counter-attack upon any forces which might gain temporary lodgment on our shores.

Nevertheless I do not feel that it would be right for any of those who are responsible, or for the people of this country generally, to dismiss from their minds the possibility of an invasion.

We in this island stand four-square in the path of European dictators. Their threats will not appal us. It is certain that if Herr Hitler found the invasion of this island difficult in July, he found it more difficult in September, and if he found it difficult in September, it will not have become easier by February or March or April.

That bad man has never had so great a need as he has now to strike Great Britain from his path. He is master of a great part of Europe. His armies can move almost where they will upon the Continent. He holds down eight or ten countries by force, by the secret police, and the still more odious local Quislings. But every day that this occupation of Austria, Czechoslovakia, Poland, Norway, Denmark, Holland, Belgium, and France – and presently perhaps Italy – lasts, there is built up a volume of hatred for the Nazi creed and for the German name which generations, and perhaps centuries, will hardly efface.

Therefore it is for Herr Hitler a matter of supreme consequence to break down the resistance of Great Britain and thus rivet effectively the shackles he has prepared for the people of Europe. But it is one thing to have a need, and another to be able to satisfy that need.

But remember that the price is eternal vigilance. The reason why one feels a confidence that this man's concentrated hatred will not be effective against our island is because every one of us is up and doing, because there will be ceaseless attention paid by all our forces to every sign of enemy preparations, and because we know that we now have millions of armed men and scores of well-equipped units capable of meeting a landing force and of engaging them with good prospects of success.

The offensive in the Middle East has succeeded beyond our dreams. Now that nearly 80,000 prisoners have been taken – and perhaps there are more to come – now that eight or nine divisions of well-equipped Italian troops have been dashed out of existence with inconceivably small losses, people may be inclined to underrate the merit of the achievement. It was a task of the greatest hazard, but it was a risk well run. The maintenance of our Island and the turning of the table in Egypt and Libya are very important in the history of the war. They give us an opportunity to address ourselves to the problem of the perils of 1941 with far greater advantage than was at our disposal six or eight months ago. We are still a partly-armed nation, but as 1941 moves along its course, we shall gradually become a well-armed nation, and the fight will then be conducted on more equal terms.

I hope that by the end of this year or the beginning of next year we may, in the air and on the land, be at no disadvantage so far as equipment is concerned with the German foe.

My one aim is to extirpate Hitlerism from Europe. The question is such a simple one. Are we to move steadily forward and have freedom, or are we to be put back into the Middle Ages by a totalitarian system that crushes all forms of individual life and has for its aim little less than the subjugation of Europe and little more than the gratification of gangster appetites?

Do not suppose that we are at the end of the road. Yet, though long and hard it may be, I have absolutely no doubt that we shall win a complete and decisive victory over the forces of evil, and that victory itself will be only a stimulus to further efforts to conquer ourselves and to make our country as worthy in the days of peace as it is proving itself in the hours of war.[1]

Eric Seal: letter to his wife

(*Seal papers*)

31 January 1941

On Friday we went off to Southampton & Portsmouth, to look at the damage. It is a dismal sight, particularly at Portsmouth, where one whole street we went along has just ceased to exist. There is nothing but stacks of debris on either side of the road. It is comparable only to the damage one saw in France in the last war. We did not see anything quite so bad at Southampton; but they say that it is even worse there in places. This damage is however surprisingly local – you go along a devastated street, & then suddenly find yourself in a normal town. It looks very odd to see quite unconcerned people out shopping walking along the pavement, with nothing behind them but piles of brick & rubbish, with notice boards saying that this was so & so's shop, & that they have moved to a new address.

[1] Churchill's last two paragraphs were those with which he had ended his speech in Glasgow on 17 January 1941 (see pages 89–90).

Eric Seal: letter to his wife
(Seal papers)

31 January 1941 Chequers

We came straight back here by special train, Hopkins came with us all the way, & spent the night. It was quite a small party – PM, Mrs C, Hopkins, General Ismay, Commander Thompson (Tommy) & myself. PM was in great form. He gets on like a house afire with Hopkins, who is a dear, & is universally liked. As you know, he lives in the White House with Roosevelt, & is very much in his confidence.

After dinner Hopkins produced a big box of gramophone records, all American tunes or ones with an Anglo-American significance. We had these until well after midnight the PM walking about, sometimes dancing a *pas seul*, in time with the music. We all got a bit sentimental & Anglo-American, under the influence of the good dinner & the music. The PM kept on stopping in his walk, & commenting on the situation – what a remarkable thing that the two nations should be drawing so much together at this critical time, how much we had in common etc. He feels a great bond of sympathy for America, & in particular for Roosevelt. He had an American mother,[1] as you know. I feel sure that great things may come of this extraordinary feeling of close relationship. It was at the time very pleasant & satisfying – but difficult to convey in words, especially within the confines of a letter. Everyone present knew & liked each other – it is quite extraordinary how Hopkins has endeared himself to everyone here he has met.

Sir John Reith: diary
('The Reith Diaries')

31 January 1941

DINNER WITH GENERAL DILL

He said the PM dealt far too much with detail and seemed often unable to appreciate or understand major issues. One minute out of ten was perhaps useful – occasionally very good. A great part of the time of responsible ministers was taken up in dealing with silly minutes from the PM. He himself was continually having to argue with him. I asked if on balance the PM did more harm than good – i.e. more nuisance and upset to those running the war than benefit from public opinion of him. He thought it a very moot point – in fact if I hadn't switched off that point I am sure he would have said more harm than good which is what I feel.

[1] Jennie Jerome, 1854–1921. Daughter of Leonard Jerome of New York. Married Lord Randolph Churchill, 1874. Mother of Winston and Jack Churchill. Editor of the *Anglo-Saxon Review*, 1899–1901. Married George Cornwallis-West, 1900; marriage dissolved, 1913. Married Montagu Porch, 1918.

February 1941

Winston S. Churchill to David Margesson

(*Churchill papers, 20/36*)

1 February 1941

1. I am astonished that you should consider the Memorandum marked 'C',[1] which consists almost entirely of generalities with which I am acquainted, should be any answer to my minute No. 29/1. I had expected that due attention would be paid paragraph by paragraph and point by point to this long and careful minute upon which I spent many hours, in conjunction with the Officers of the Office of Minister of Defence. Take, for instance, the points in paras. 4, 5 and 6, none of which are referred to in the agreeable essay tabbed 'C'. This paper 'C' in fact amounts to a complete refusal to make any detailed examination into the rearward services of the Army in the Middle East, or by implication into those upon which I have sent you other minutes in respect of the Armies at home. I could not feel I was discharging my responsibilities as Minister of Defence if I allowed this matter to be blocked in this way. There will have to be an impartial inquiry, perhaps even a Parliamentary inquiry, unless I can feel I have the loyal assistance of the War Office in endeavouring to put their house into better order.

2. It is evident that the proportions between teeth and tail in the Middle East and the character of the reinforcements from this country must take into account the fact that we have to supply the rearward services of the Australian, New Zealand and other divisions in addition to our own. None the less, every effort should be made to secure the highest economy, and deductions drawn from the peculiar conditions of the fighting, and the rapid advance made in Libya do not necessarily apply to a campaign in Thrace or behind the Bosphorus.

3. I am also awaiting your reply to my comments and queries about your 'Army and Man Power' paper of January 23.

[1] A memorandum by David Margesson dated 23 January 1941.

4. Coming to the Memorandum 'C,' there are two specific points where the figures are clearly erroneous. Para. 11, the 3 African Colonial Divisions are treated on the same scale of rearward services as the British or Australian Divisions. But surely this is not so, and still more surely, it ought not to be so. Thus a factor of 17 is reached, to be divided into the total man power, whereas in fact 14, or at the outside 15, would suffice for this particular illustration. See also para. 16. Germany is credited with 6,500,000 under arms, out of which 205 Divisions have been formed, giving a total for a gross Division of say 30,000 men. If we followed the same method with the British Forces, as set out in your paper of January 23, we should have to divide the present state of the Army, namely, 2,085,000, by the formed Divisions, say 35, adding say 10 for the Beach Battalions, &c., this would give a total per British Division, not of the already challengeable figure of 35,000 but of 46,000.

5. I could not possibly agree to accept as final the calculations of the War Office as set out by the Field Force Committee. This work must be subject to scrutiny like any other data. It is quite certain that nothing but advantage can arise by a careful re-examination in the light not of war in general but of the particular operations in which we shall almost certainly be engaged in the next twelve months. I earnestly hope you will help me in this and endeavour to save man-power for the Army as well as for Munitions work.

6. You say in your minute to me of the 23rd that public comments on the size of the Army and the ratio of its Administration Services are irritating to the Commands, and you ask me to make some reference to this in any broadcast I may make. Unless I feel I am being helped in my effort to keep the rearward services within reasonable and necessary bounds, and to purge them of redundancy, I should certainly not be able to testify in the sense you desire. On the contrary, it may become my duty to emphasize the need for a searching overhaul of the Administrative Staffs and Services in the interests of the strength of the Army itself.

Winston S. Churchill to Lord Beaverbrook

(A. J. P. Taylor, 'Beaverbrook', page 429)

1 February 1941

MINISTRY OF AIRCRAFT PRODUCTION

It cannot be admitted that any one Department can peg out claims for itself all over the country, even if it most obligingly hands over the premises and waives its rights whenever a case is shown.

I think it would be a great pity to bring this before the Cabinet. I could not support you, and everyone else would vote against your having a privilege or monopoly. I do not see how it can be any satisfaction to you to put yourself and me in this position. On the merits I cannot feel you are right, and with anyone else but you I should long ago have settled it by a stroke of the pen.

Winston S. Churchill to Anthony Eden
(*Churchill papers, 20/36*)

1 February 1941

ALLEGED IMPENDING ROUMANIAN SLAUGHTER OF JEWS

Would it not be well to tell General Antonescu[1] that we will hold him and his immediate circle personally responsible in life and limb if such a vile act is perpetrated?

Perhaps you may think of something more diplomatic than this.

Winston S. Churchill to A. V Alexander
(*Churchill papers, 20/36*)

1 February 1941
Most Secret

Thank you for your further report on progress in researches on measures to impede enemy RDF[2] methods.

As you say, the matter is of vital urgency. We need results quickly. I imagine that no fruits are to be expected from the bigger researches for some time. Are you satisfied, therefore, that the results with small floats are so disappointing as to warrant abandoning this line of research? I infer from your minute of December 17 that you were envisaging only dipoles on stationary floats. If the difficulty has been that the enemy could quickly detect their immobility, should we not try simple means of making them move? Could they not be towed, e.g., on low kites, behind destroyers or fast escort vessels? A set of dipoles hanging from the kite cable should, I am told, give an echo very like a ship.

I should be glad if you would look into this matter again, and let me have a further report as soon as possible.

We should have something, however imperfect, in service before the Spring.

[1] Ion Antonescu, 1882–1946. Chief of the Roumanian General Staff, 1937. Minister of War, 1939–40. Dictator of Roumania, 1940–44. Allied Roumania with the Axis Powers, 1941. Annexed south-west Ukraine, 1941. Renamed Odessa 'Antonescu'. Arrested, 23 August 1944, by the 23-year-old King Michael. Charged with war crimes, May 1946; found guilty and shot, 1 June 1946.

[2] Radio Direction Finding; later known as Radar.

Winston S. Churchill to Hugh Dalton
(*Churchill papers, 20/36*)

1 February 1941
Secret

You have no doubt been considering what we can do to prevent Germany obtaining supplies of copper, in view of the fact that although she may be able to substitute aluminium, she may well become subject to a severe stringency in the two metals taken together.

I understand that considerable excess capacity exists in the South American copper mines. I am told that we have no evidence that copper has proceeded from South America to Germany; but that last year South America exported about 70,000 tons to Russia and 150,000 tons to Japan, whose stocks are estimated at a year's consumption. As soon as Germany exhausts her stocks, it is obvious that she will make every effort to obtain South American copper, and it is vital to take measures in advance to prevent Japan and Russia building stocks and to prevent Germany obtaining access to the surplus capacity which exists in Chile.

Apparently we are importing about 600,000 tons of copper from Canada, Rhodesia, South Africa and the Belgian Congo. As these sources are under our control, we should be able to divert purchases to South America without danger that Germany would obtain supplies from the sources we gave up.

I understand that you have been giving consideration to this problem, and that the Treasury is doubtful if the expenditure of dollars on pre-emptive purchase is justifiable. Will you let me have a report on your plans?

Winston S. Churchill to Alexandros Korizis[1]
(*Churchill papers, 20/49*)

1 February 1941

I was much gratified by the message which your Excellency was good enough to send me on the occasion of your assumption of the office of President of the Council.

I grieve at the tragic loss which you and your country have suffered in the death of your great leader.[1] I am glad that your Excellency has been called to high office as his successor. In wishing you all strength and success in your task,

[1] Alexandros Korizis. President of the Council (Prime Minister) of Greece from 29 January 1941 until his suicide on 18 April 1941.

[2] Metaxas had died suddenly on 29 January 1941, 'leaving the Greek kingdom without any experienced "strong man" to meet the challenge of war' (Alan Palmer, *Who's Who in Modern History, 1860–1960*, Holt, Rinehart and Winston, New York, 1980, page 230).

I look forward to the same intimate collaboration between our Allied Governments in the energetic prosecution of the war against the common enemy until final victory is achieved.

General Sir Alan Brooke: diary
('Turn of the Tide')

2 February 1941

Had to leave at 6 p.m. to go over to Chequers where I was due for the night. Party consisted of PM, Mrs Churchill and daughter, Anthony Eden and wife, Attlee, Professor Lindemann, and secretary. After dinner epidiascope was produced and I had to give a lecture on our recent Home Defence Exercise. They were all three very interested in it and the PM very flattering about the defensive measures that had been taken. But he would not acknowledge that an invasion of this country on that scale was possible in the face of partial sea-control and local air-control.

Anthony Eden: diary
('Eden Memoirs', page 254)

2 February 1941

We all sallied forth for a short walk in afternoon, Winston protesting mildly, but eager to show us Happy Valley, into which he wishes to pour a waterfall, electrically driven!

Winston S. Churchill to General Ismay
(Churchill papers, 20/36)

2 February 1941
Secret

'Marie'[1] might be an operation of the greatest value. The Senegalese should not be sent into Abyssinia, but should be kept till the Foreign Legion Battalion arrives. Where would they be kept, and how?

One must consider that at any moment Weygand might move our way, in which case the Free French troops could go into Jibuti to animate the converted garrison, and even begin operations against the Italians.

Another favourable situation might be reached if, as a consequence of our

[1] A Free French operation to take Jibuti from Vichy France.

advance in Eritrea, the British forces were able to get into touch with the French Colony at Jibuti. Anyhow, with these favourable possibilities in the wind, it would be a great pity not to keep our Free French force in hand. As for the political consequences, they can only be judged a few days before launching operations.

Winston S. Churchill to Sir Percy Hurd[1]
(*Churchill papers, 20/21*)

2 February 1941
Private

Dear Sir Percy Hurd,

As you may imagine, these questions are constantly discussed in the Defence Committee. We have in fact made many heavy attacks on German cities, particularly Mannheim, Bremen and Hamburg, in which most severe damage was done. I do not think a declaration of the kind you have in mind would deter the enemy from bombing us. He knows already that we are doing our utmost, and that our power to strike him will increase.

Yours sincerely,
Winston S. Churchill

P.S. I am glad you did not put your Question down. Thank you.

Winston S. Churchill to Queen Elizabeth
(*Churchill papers, 20/29*)

3 February 1941

Madam,

I am very glad that Your Majesty found Fowlers' Dictionary entertaining. He is a real master of his subject, always sensible, lucid and practical, and above all never a pedant. He liberated me from many errors and doubts e.g. 'I should have liked to have been there' instead of the simple 'I sh'd have liked to be there'.

We are both looking forward to lunching tomorrow with Your Majesties.

Your faithful servant,
Winston S. Churchill

[1] Percy Angier Hurd, –1950. Editor and Managing Director of *The Outlook*, 1898–1904. London editor of the *Montreal Star*. Editor, *Canadian Gazette*. Delegate to the Devastated Regions of France. Allied Relief Committee of the Royal Agricultural Society, 1915–18. Conservative Member of Parliament for Frome, 1918–23; for Devizes, 1924–45. President of the Rural District Councils Association, 1925–45. Knighted, 1932. Author of several books, including *Canada: Past, Present and Future* and *The Fighting Territorials* (2 volumes).

Winston S. Churchill to Air Chief Marshal Sir Charles Portal
(*Churchill papers, 20/36*)

3 February 1941
Secret
Action this Day

1. I have been deeply interested in your Statement and figures attached, and I spent a long time last night discussing them with the Lord Privy Seal, the Foreign Secretary and the C-in-C, Home Forces.

2. It is evident that much turns upon the relative Fighter strength of the two Air Forces. One must therefore try to be sure, as far as is humanly possible. You do not state what is your data for thinking that only 50 per cent, of the GAF[1] is serviceable on any given day (or is this average serviceability for any given week? It is very much the same thing). But are you basing yourself entirely upon the facts about the two Gruppen which have come to our notice? If so, should we not be generalizing too much from the particular?

3. I am so anxious to have simple, agreed figures on which we can work together. It only queers the pitch if you add in the handful of Beaufighters and Blenheims with the Coastal Command, and thus make the figures you now give me different from those in the current weekly return.

4. I should like also to know what the corresponding figures would be of relative Fighter strength GAF and RAF, if on the same basis as your new figures we went back to August or September. I imagine it would show that we were then much weaker relatively, and are now definitely stronger. If so, the fact is cardinal.

I do not want you to be bothered with these detail adjustments, and I shall be glad if you will let Professor Lindemann come round and reach conclusions, which have your assent, with your people.

War Cabinet: minutes
(*Cabinet papers, 65/21*)

3 February 1941
5 p.m.

The Prime Minister informed the War Cabinet of certain recent developments of policy.

(1) The evidence in our possession showed that the Bulgarian Government were conniving at the German infiltration into their country. Aerodromes were being constructed and hutments were going up, and it was only a question of a

[1] German Air Force.

short time before Germany would be in a position to compel Turkey to fall in with her wishes, under threat of the bombing of Istanbul and Adrianople.

(2) The Chief of the Air Staff had argued strongly in favour of a simultaneous infiltration by British air units into Turkish territory, as the only effective means of stiffening the Turkish resistance.

(3) A message had been sent to the President offering the co-operation of ten squadrons of the Royal Air Force. In his absence the message was delivered to the Turkish Foreign Minister[1]. The Turkish Foreign Minister had viewed our offer with some dismay and had said that he could give no final answer without consulting the Turkish President and Prime Minister.[2] He affected to regard as exaggerated the reports of the German penetration into Bulgaria. He had also argued that the acceptance of our offer would be tantamount to a declaration of war on Germany, for which his country was not ready.

(4) If the German plan was allowed to develop unhindered, there was every prospect that South Eastern Europe would witness this spring a repetition of last spring's events in Scandinavia and the Low Countries.

The message was now being communicated to the Turkish President.

John Colville: diary
(*Colville papers*)

3 February 1941

On Late Duty, but the PM obligingly thought of going to bed at 11.30.

Winston S. Churchill to David Margesson
(*Churchill papers, 20/36*)

4 February 1941

Please see *The Times* of February 4, page 2, column 5, last paragraph. Is it really true that a 7-mile cross-country run is enforced upon all in this Division from Generals to Privates? Does the Army Council think this a good idea? It looks to me rather excessive. A Colonel or a General ought not to exhaust himself in trying to compete with young boys running across country 7 miles at a time. The duty of Officers is no doubt to keep themselves fit, but still more to think for their men, and to take decisions affecting their safety or comfort. Who is the General of this division, and does he run the 7 miles himself? If so, he may be more useful for football than war. Could Napoleon have run 7

[1] Shukri Sarajoglu, Turkish Foreign Minister from November 1938 to August 1942, when he became Prime Minister (until August 1946).

[2] President Ismet Inönü and Prime Minister Dr Refik Saydam (Prime Minister from February 1939 to July 1942).

miles across country at Austerlitz? Perhaps it was the other fellow he made run. In my experience, based on many years' observation, officers with high athletic qualifications are not usually successful in the higher ranks.

Winston S. Churchill to Alfred Duff Cooper[1]
(*Churchill papers, 20/36*)

4 February 1941

Every statement in this[2] is a pure invention, both in substance and in fact. It bears no resemblance to anything I have ever said or thought. If it is published it should be denied categorically and in the most effective manner possible.

2. I do not see why, if the *Daily Mail* is asked not to publish it, the rest of our Censorship should not be employed. Otherwise the paper which behaved well is penalized for those which wish to behave badly. As far as the United States is concerned, we can do nothing but denounce it as the lie it is.

3. The matter has a graver significance, because this is the kind of propaganda on gas that the Germans would use as a prelude to its employment. The Secret Service should endeavour to probe the matter. It looks to me as if it were a very significant German portent.

Winston S. Churchill to General Ismay, for David Margesson and General Dill
(*Churchill papers, 20/36*)

4 February 1941

The statement that one Division could not be transferred from Great Britain to Ireland in less than eleven days, no matter how great the emergency,

[1] Alfred Duff Cooper, 1890–1954. Known as 'Duff'. Educated at Eton and New College, Oxford. Entered the Foreign Office as a Clerk, 1913. On active service, Grenadier Guards, 1917–18 (DSO, despatches). Conservative MP for Oldham (Churchill's first constituency), 1924–9. Financial Secretary, War Office, 1928–9 and 1931–4. MP for St Georges Westminster, 1931–45. Financial Secretary, Treasury, 1934–5. Privy Councillor, 1935. Secretary of State for War, 1935–7. First Lord of the Admiralty, 1937–8. Minister of Information, 1940–1. British Representative, Singapore, 1941. Chancellor of the Duchy of Lancaster, 1941–3. British Representative, French Committee of National Liberation, 1943–4. Ambassador to France, 1944–7. Knighted, 1948. Created Viscount Norwich, 1952. In 1919 he married Lady Diana Manners. In 1928 he was elected to the Other Club.

[2] Churchill's views on gas had been expressed in a minute to General Ismay on 26 December 1940, in which Churchill wrote: 'I am deeply anxious that gas warfare should not be adopted at the present time. For this very reason I fear the enemy may have it in mind, and perhaps it may be imminent. Every precaution must be kept in order and every effort made to increase retaliatory power. Sometimes I have wondered whether it would be any deterrent on the enemy if I were to say that we should never use gas ourselves unless it had first been used against us, but that we had actually in store many thousands of tons of various types of deadly gas with their necessary containers, and that we should immediately retaliate upon Germany. On the whole, I think it is perhaps better to say nothing unless or until we have evidence that the attack is imminent.' (*Churchill papers, 20/13*)

nor how careful the previous preparations, is one which deserves your earnest attention. When we remember the enormous numbers which were moved from Dunkirk to Dover and the Thames in May under continued enemy attack, it is clear that the movement of personnel cannot be the limiting factor. The problem is, therefore, one of the movement of the artillery and vehicles. This surely deserves special study. Let me see the exact programme which occupies the eleven days, showing the order in which men, guns and vehicles will embark. This would show perhaps that say nine-tenths of the Division might come into action in much less than eleven days. Or again a portion of the mechanical transport, stores and even some of the artillery, including Bren-gun carriers, might be found from reserves in this country and sent to Ireland in advance where they would be none the less a reserve for us, assuming no need in Ireland arose. Surely now that we have the time some ingenuity might be shown in shortening this period of eleven days to move 15,000 fighting men from one well-equipped port to another – the voyage taking only a few hours. If necessary some revision of the scale of approved establishments might be made in order to achieve the high tactical object of a more rapid transference and deployment.

We must remember that in the recent exercise 'Victor', five German Divisions, two of which were armoured and one motorized, were landed in about forty-eight hours in the teeth of strenuous opposition, not at a port with quays and cranes, but on the open beaches. If we assume that the Germans can do this, or even half of it, we must contrast this with the statement of the eleven days required to shift one Division from the Clyde to Belfast. We have also the statement of the Chiefs of the Staff Committee that it would take thirty days to land one British Division unopposed alongside the quays and piers of Tangier. Perhaps the officers who worked out the landings of the Germans under 'Victor' could make some suggestion for moving this Division into Ireland via Belfast without taking eleven days about it. Who are the officers who worked out the details that this move will take eleven days? Would it not be wise to bring them into contact with the other officers who landed these vast numbers of Germans on our beaches so swiftly and enabled whole armoured Divisions and motorized troops to come into full action in forty-eight hours.

Evidently it would be wiser to keep open the option of moving this Division as long as possible, and in order to do this we must have the best plan worked out to bring the largest possible portion of the Division into action in Ireland in the shortest possible time. I am not prepared to approve the transfer of the Division until this enquiry has been made. There must be an effort to reconcile the evident discrepancies as between what we assume the enemy can do and what, in fact, we can do ourselves.

Winston S. Churchill to Alfred Duff Cooper
(*Churchill papers, 20/36*)

4 February 1941

The activities of Foreign Correspondents are giving a good deal of trouble. See, for example, the disclosures of Engel, published in the newspapers of the 1st January.

Steps should be taken to restrict the facilities accorded to Foreign Correspondents for obtaining confidential information, bearing in mind that everything sent to America is instantly communicated to Germany.

Pray consider this matter, in consultation with the Ministers concerned, and report to me.

Winston S. Churchill to Alfred Duff Cooper
(*Churchill papers, 20/36*)

4 February 1941

The newspapers continue to publish – mostly with innocent intentions – facts about the war and our policy which should not be disclosed. Where this happens, and the information published has not previously been submitted to the Censorship, a complaint should, in my view, be lodged with the newspaper in question in each case.

Pray report what action you are taking at the present time to deal with this type of case.

Winston S. Churchill to Alfred Duff Cooper
(*Churchill papers, 20/36*)

4 February 1941

On the 11th October, 1939, the War Cabinet appointed a Committee to consider, among other matters, the advisability of the issue to the general public, by the Ministry of Information, of warnings against mentioning matters of a confidential character in public, and of the display on hoardings and elsewhere of similar notices.

The Report of this Committee (W.P.(G)(39)87) was approved by the War Cabinet on the 15th November, 1939, when it was laid down that the Ministry of Information should be recognized as the Department primarily responsible for warning the public against discussion of confidential matters in the public places, and that they should periodically hold Departmental Conferences to review the results of policy and submit reports as necessary to the War Cabinet.

Pray consider, in discharge of this responsibility, whether the time has come for a fresh drive in this matter, including the provision of a new set of posters to attract public attention.

Winston S. Churchill to Arthur Greenwood
(*Churchill papers, 20/21*)

4 February 1941

My dear Minister without Portfolio,

I have not been able till now to deal with your letter of January 6, and its accompanying Memorandum.

I have given much thought to the composition of your Committee. It will not be possible for any of the Ministers in charge of Departments mainly concerned with the conduct of the war, to pay real attention to post-war reconstruction. To those Ministers I must reluctantly add myself, though I shall be very glad to hear from time to time how you are progressing. I do not think that a high level Ministerial Committee with a balance of the political Parties, such as you seem to favour, could really relieve the Cabinet of its responsibilities for giving guidance on main questions of principle. I should therefore prefer that in the first phase of your labours you should be assisted by a Working Committee to thrash out schemes within the ambit of the general principles approved by the Cabinet, which Committee would be composed, in part at least, of representatives of Departments with a major interest in reconstruction, regard being also paid to the representation of the political Parties. I therefore suggest to you the following Committee:-

The Minister without Portfolio (Chairman)[1]

The Lord Privy Seal[2]

The Chancellor of the Exchequer[3]

The Minister of Works and Public Buildings[4] (by virtue of the special responsibility assigned to him for matters of physical reconstruction of town and country after the war)

The Secretary of State for Dominion Affairs[5] (as a Conservative Minister who could probably spare time for this work)

[1] Arthur Greenwood.
[2] Clement Attlee.
[3] Sir Kingsley Wood.
[4] Sir John Reith.
[5] Viscount Cranborne.

The Minister of Agriculture[1] or the Minister of Transport[2] (either of whom would attend when the business in hand so required)

The Minister of Health[3] (or the Parliamentary Secretary) (since the Ministry of Health is the Department more concerned than any other in such matters as planning the location of industries, insurance schemes, and the like)

The Secretary, Department of Overseas Trade[4] plus, say, two Under-Secretaries. I suggest the Parliamentary Secretary to the Foreign Office and the Parliamentary Secretary, the Board of Trade.[5]

Your Memorandum on the work of reconstruction had better be submitted to this Committee. Should the need for a decision in principle arise (either on this Memorandum or on some other point), this could be taken either by the Steering Committee, or preferably, by the War Cabinet. I suggest that your Terms of Reference should be those assigned to the War Aims Committee, but amended as shown on the annexed sheet, to give rather greater prominence to the domestic side of the work.

I should hope that, acting on this general reference, you will be able to carry the work forward yourself, with the help of your Committee, and that it will not be necessary to come to the War Cabinet until after the next few critical months are over; by which time you should have accumulated a considerable volume of material, and surveyed the entire field.

Yours very sincerely,
Winston S. Churchill

TERMS OF REFERENCE

(1) To arrange for the preparation of practical schemes of reconstruction, to which effect can be given in a period of, say, three years after the war. These plans should have as their general aim the perpetuation of the national unity achieved in this country during the war, through a social and economic structure designed to secure equality of opportunity and service among all classes of the community.

(2) To prepare a scheme for a post-war European and world system, with particular regard to the economic needs of the various nations, and to the problem of adjusting the free life of small countries in a durable international order.

[1] Robert Spear Hudson, 1886–1957. Educated at Eton and Magdalen College, Oxford. Attaché, Diplomatic Service, 1911; First Secretary, 1920–3. Conservative MP for Whitehaven, 1924–9; for Southport, 1931–52. Parliamentary Secretary, Ministry of Labour, 1931–5. Minister of Pensions, 1935–6. Secretary, Department of Overseas Trade, 1937–40. Privy Councillor, 1938. Minister of Shipping, April–May 1940. Minister of Agriculture and Fisheries, 1940–5. Created Viscount, 1952.

[2] John Moore-Brabazon, see page 240, n.1.

[3] Malcolm MacDonald, who four days later was succeeded as Minister of Health by Ernest Brown. Their Parliamentary Secretary was Florence Horsbrugh.

[4] Harcourt Johnstone, see page 1123, n.1.

[5] R. A. Butler and Gwyllim Lloyd George respectively. Four days later Gwyllim Lloyd George was succeeded by Charles Waterhouse as Parliamentary Secretary at the Board of Trade.

Winston S. Churchill to Cecil King[1]
(*Churchill papers, 20/21*)

5 February 1941

Dear Mr King,

Thank you very much for your letter and I was glad we had a talk.[2] All this fine thought about the rising generation ought not to lead you into using your able writers to try to discredit and hamper the Government in a period of extreme danger and difficulty. Nor ought it to lead you to try to set class against class and generally 'rock the boat' at such a time. Finally I think it is no defence for such activities to say that your papers specialize in 'vitriolic' writing. Indeed throwing vitriol is thought to be one of the worst of crimes. No man who is affected with 'vitriolism' is worthy to shape the future, or likely to have much chance of doing so in our decent country.

There is no reason why you should not advocate a statement of war aims. I wonder that you do not draw one up in detail and see what it looks like. I see that Mr Mander has tabled his war aims which seem to me to bear out what I ventured to say in the House, namely 'that most right-minded people are well aware of what we are fighting for'. Such a task would be well-suited to the present lull.

Yours sincerely,
Winston S. Churchill

Winston S. Churchill to A.V. Alexander and Admiral Pound
(*Churchill papers, 20/36*)

4 February 1941
Secret
Action this Day

1. A number of convoys with most important munition cargoes are now approaching. I know what your stresses are and I feel sure you will make every effort possible.

2. We have now the gift announced of 250,000 more rifles and 50 million rounds – .300. To get this here quickly and safely is a prime object. Pray go

[1] Cecil Harmsworth King, 1901–1987. Newspaper proprietor. Director, *Daily Mirror*, 1929. Deputy Chairman, *Sunday Pictorial*, 1942. Chairman Daily Mirror Newspapers Ltd and Sunday Pictorial Newspapers Ltd, 1951–63; International Publishing Corporation, 1963–68. Director of Reuters, 1953–59. Chairman of the Newspaper Proprietors' Association, 1961–68. A Director of the Bank of England, 1965–68. Part-time member, National Coal Board, 1966–69.

[2] Churchill had invited Cecil King to lunch on the previous day, 4 February 1941.

into the matter with others concerned and let me know what is possible. I cannot bear to see more than 50,000 rifles or 10 million rounds in any one ship. Less if possible.

Winston S. Churchill to William Mackenzie King[1]

(*Churchill papers, 20/49*)

5 February 1941

Your message about visit of Ralston[1] and Howe[2] greatly appreciated here. We are of course delighted to have such opportunities of personal discussion with Canadian Ministers, who never fail to bring with them and leave with us a sense of renewed energy and confidence. I like to think how close together we stand against the common enemy.

War Cabinet: minutes

(*Cabinet papers, 65/21*)

5 February 1941
12.30 p.m.

The Prime Minister said that the First Lord of the Admiralty had informed him that Italian convoys had recently been crossing the Sicilian Channel and proceeding down the Tunisian coast in French territorial waters. The Admiralty already had authority to intercept French merchant ships in French territorial waters in the Gibraltar area. It was important that the Admiralty should have authority to sink enemy ships in French territorial waters South of Latitude 35°46' North. The Foreign Secretary was in agreement with this view, and instructions had been given in this sense. He hoped that the War Cabinet would approve this action.

The War Cabinet endorsed the action taken.

[1] James Layton Ralston, 1881–1948. Commanded a Canadian battalion in the First World War. Representative of the interests of the Maritime Provinces in the Canadian Parliament. Minister of National Defence, 1926–30 and 1940–44. Served briefly as Minister of Finance, 1939–40.

[2] Clarence Howe, 1886–1960. Minister of Railways and Canals, 1935 responsible for the launching of the Canadian Broadcasting Corporation (CBC) and devising the first Canadian trans-continental airline systems. Minister of Munitions and Supply, 1940–48; of Reconstruction, 1944–48. In December 1940 he survived the torpedoing of the liner *Western Prince* in the Atlantic, while on his way to Britain (spending eight hours in an open boat with his companions before being rescued). Minister of Trade and Commerce, 1948–51; of Defence Production, 1951–60.

Winston S. Churchill to Sir Thomas Barnes[1]
(*Churchill papers, 2/431*)

6 February 1941

I am not prepared to agree to pay, or have paid, any expenses incurred by Mr Griffin in bringing this blackmailing suit for political purposes, after he has broken every rule of decent confidence, and has fastened on me mischievous suggestions in the German interest. If Mr Griffin goes on with this suit, which is unlikely in view of the changed opinion of the United States, I think he should be met in the Courts. I have no objection to giving evidence in this country on commission.

I understood when I was First Lord that the Treasury Solicitors would fight this case. I am quite sure they will not have to go very far before the other side are tired of it. Let the rascal pay his own costs.

War Cabinet: minutes
(*Cabinet papers, 65/17*)

6 February 1941
12.15 p.m.

Prime Minister's Room
House of Commons

LEASE OF BRITISH BASES[2]

The Secretary of State for Dominion Affairs[3]

It was hard to imagine any dispute arising over the bases which could not be settled in a spirit of goodwill in direct negotiation between London and Washington, assuming that attempts to settle it locally had failed.

The United States negotiators had made it plain that they had no authority to discuss Defence questions, including the system of command in the areas affected; they had suggested that these might be reserved for examination at a later date in staff conversations.

The Dominions Secretary handed round the following formula which had been drafted to meet the difficulties of the United States negotiators:

It is recognized that the defence of the Leased Areas and the Territories in which they lie is of mutual interest and concern to the United States and His Majesty's Government, and questions of mutual defence shall be the subject of agreement between the two parties, due regard being given to the position

[1] Thomas James Barnes, 1888–1964. Assistant Solicitor, Board of Inland Revenue, 1919. Legal Adviser, Ministry of Shipping, 1918–20. Solicitor, Board of Trade, 1920–33. Knighted, 1927. Procurator-General and Treasury Solicitor, 1934–53. Member of the Monopolies and Restrictive Practices Commission.

[2] The British bases to be leased to the United States (originally as part of the 'Destroyers for Bases' arrangement) were in Newfoundland, Bermuda, the Bahamas, Antigua, St. Lucia, Trinidad and British Guiana.

[3] Viscount Cranborne.

of the Governors of the Territories as representatives of His Majesty. When the United States is engaged in war or in time of other emergency, it shall have all such rights in the territory and the surrounding waters and air spaces as may be necessary for conducting military operations.

It was understood that the United States negotiators would accept this formula.

The Prime Minister thought that the formula was in substance unobjectionable and could fairly be accepted. The United States had now openly espoused our cause, and had virtually promised us financial help of incalculable value. We must do what we could to meet American difficulties. The last sentence could operate in one of three sets of circumstances –

(a) War between the United States and ourselves. This was unthinkable.
(b) A state in which we were both at war on the same side. We should then gladly give them what they wanted.
(c) A state in which they were at war and we were neutral. In such a position the United States would not antagonize us by unreasonable demands. They would be anxious to win our favour, just as we were now anxious to win theirs.

He attached great importance to the conception of Sovereignty, from the point of view that there must be no suggestion that the West Indian peoples were being driven out of the British Empire or compelled to become American citizens. But on all points bearing on this aspect of the matter the United States negotiators had met us.

War Cabinet: minutes
(*Cabinet papers, 65/21*)

6 February 1941
12.15 p.m.

The Secretary of State for Foreign Affairs said that on the previous day most secret information had been received that Japan had warned her Embassy staff in London to reduce their contacts with the British authorities to a minimum, and to be prepared to leave the country at short notice. He had sent a telegram to Washington containing this information. The Viceroy of India[1] had also been informed.

[1] Victor Alexander John Hope, 1887–1952. Earl of Hopetoun until 1908. Known as 'Hopey'. Educated at Eton. Succeeded his father as 2nd Marquess of Linlithgow, 1908. On active service, 1914–18 (despatches). Commanded the Border Armoured Car Company, 1920–6. Civil Lord of Admiralty, 1922–4. Deputy Chairman of the Conservative Party Organization, 1924–6. Chairman, Royal Commission on Indian Agriculture, 1926–8. Chairman, Joint Select Committee on Indian Constitutional Reform, 1933–34. Chairman, Medical Research Council, 1934–36. Privy Councillor, 1935. Viceroy of India, 1936–43. Knight of the Garter, 1943. Chairman of the Midland Bank. His country seat was Hopetoun House, South Queensferry, two miles west of the Forth Bridge.

On the following day he proposed to see the Japanese Ambassador[1] and give him a frank review of the present position as we saw it. The Secretary of State added that he had seen the Chinese Ambassador[2] on the previous day and had formed the opinion that the internal situation in China was far from satisfactory.

The Prime Minister said that the Foreign Secretary's information was of a serious character. He hoped that India and Burma would be ready to take action should the need arise.

Referring to the dropping of mines by the Germans in the Suez Canal, which might result in the closing of the Canal for some 15 days, the Prime Minister said that this might have been done by Germany as an indication to Japan of what she could accomplish in preventing us sending reinforcements to the Far East.

Winston S. Churchill: tribute

(*Hansard*)

6 February 1941 House of Commons

THE LATE LORD LLOYD

The Prime Minister: The House will have learned with sorrow of the loss, not only that His Majesty's Government, but our country and the whole Empire, have sustained in the sudden and unexpected death of the Secretary of State for the Colonies and newly-chosen Leader of the House of Lords. To

[1] Mamoru Shigemitsu, 1881–1957. Japanese Minister to China, 1930–36 (when he lost a leg to a Korean terrorist's bomb, an injury that was painful to him for the rest of his life). Ambassador to the Soviet Union 1936–38; to Britain, 1938–41. Appointed Ambassador to the Nanking (puppet) Government two days after Pearl Harbor. Ambassador to France, 1942. Foreign Minister, 1943–5. One of the two Japanese who participated in the Japanese surrender on board USS *Missouri*, 1945. Imprisoned for war crimes. Subsequently Deputy Prime Minister and Foreign Minister, 1954–56.

[2] Vi Kyuin Wellington Koo, 1888–1985. Doctor of Philosophy, Columbia University, New York. Chinese Minister to the United States, 1915. Member (and later head) of the Chinese Delegation to the Paris Peace Conference, 1919. Represented China on the Council of the League of Nations, Geneva, 1920–22. Minister of Foreign Affairs, Peking, 1922–24; Finance Minister, 1926; Prime Minister and Minister of Foreign Affairs, 1921–27; Minister of Ambassador in London, 1941–46; Ambassador in Washington, 1946–56. Judge of the International Court of Justice, 1957–67 (Vice-President, 1964–67).

me the loss is particularly painful. Lord Lloyd and I have been friends for many years and close political associates during the last 12 years. We championed several causes together which did not command the applause of large majorities; but it is just in that kind of cause, where one is swimming against the stream, that one learns the worth and quality of a comrade and friend.

The late Lord Lloyd was a man of high ability. He had energy, he had industry; and these were spurred throughout his life by a consuming desire to serve the country and uphold the British name. He had travelled far and had acquired an immense mass of special knowledge, particularly knowledge of Egypt, East Africa, Arabia and India. He was deeply versed in the affairs of the unhappy countries in the South-East of Europe, which now lie under the shadow of approaching danger and misery. In all these spheres, his opinion and advice were of the highest value. Having served under Lawrence in the Desert War, he had acquired a great love for the Arab race, and he devoted a large part of his life to their interest. His name is known and his death will be mourned in wide circles of the Moslem world. When we remember that the King-Emperor is the ruler of incomparably more Mohammedan subjects than any other Prince of Islam, we may, from this angle, measure the serious nature of the loss we have sustained.

George Lloyd fought for his country on land and in the air. As honorary commodore of an air squadron, he learned to fly a Hurricane aeroplane and obtained a pilot's certificate when almost 60 years of age, thus proving that it is possible for a man to maintain in very high efficiency eye and hand, even after a lifetime of keen intellectual work. He was a very good friend of the Royal Air Force, and, in recent years, was President of the Navy League. His was the voice which, as far back as 1934, moved a resolution at the National Union of Conservative Associations which led that body to urge upon the then Government a policy of immediate rearmament. Although an Imperialist and, in some ways, an authoritarian, he had a profound, instinctive aversion from Nazism. He foresaw from the beginning the danger of Hitler's rise to power and above all to armed power, and he lived and acted during the last four or five years under a sense of the rapidly growing danger to this country.

For two long and critical periods, covering together nearly 10 years, he represented the Crown, as Governor of Bombay, or as High Commissioner in Egypt. His administration of the Bombay Presidency was at once firm and progressive, and the Lloyd reservoir across the Indus River in Sind, which is the base of the largest irrigation scheme in the world and irrigates an area, formerly a wilderness, about the size of Wales – this great barrage, the Lloyd barrage, as it is called, is a monument which will link his name to the prosperity of millions yet unborn, who will see around them villages, townships, temples and fertile fields where all was formerly naught but savage scrub and sand. Lord Lloyd took over the High Commissionership of Egypt in the dark hour after the murder of Sir Lee Stack.[1] He restored, during his tenure, a very great measure of stability and tranquillity to the Nile Valley, and he achieved this without violence or bloodshed. He gained the good will of important elements in Egypt without sacrificing British interests and our relations with Egypt have progressively improved since those days, though other hands and other points of view have played their part in that. If he, like other British statesmen, promised to protect the people of the Egyptian Delta from foreign aggression, he lived long enough to see all the obligations and undertakings of Great Britain to the Egyptian people brilliantly vindicated by the decisions of war.

When I was called upon to form the present Administration, in the heat of the great battle in France, it was a comfort to me to be able to reach out to so trusted a friend. Although his views, like perhaps some of mine, were very often opposed to the Labour party, I say, with the full assent of all his Labour colleagues, that he gained their respect and confidence and their regard in all those trying months, and that they found many deep points of agreement with him of which they had not previously been aware. The departure of Lord Halifax to the United States made it necessary to choose a new Leader for the House of Lords on behalf of the Government, and Lord Lloyd was selected for that important task. This gave him a great deal of satisfaction, and in the evening, two hours before his death, he conversed with others of his friends about the future work which lay before him in an expanding field and spoke with hopefulness and satisfaction about his ability to discharge it. Then, very suddenly, he was removed from us by death.

I would like to think, as one likes to think of every man in this House and elsewhere, that he died at the apex, at the summit, of his career. It is sometimes said that good men are scarce. It is perhaps because the spate of events with which we attempt to cope and strive to control have far exceeded, in this modern age, the old bounds, that they have been swollen up to giant proportions, while, all the time, the stature and intellect of man remained unchanged. All the more, therefore, do we feel the loss of this high-minded and exceptionally gifted and experienced public servant. I feel I shall only be discharging my duties to the House when I express, in their name, our sympathy for his widow, who has shared so many of his journeys and all the ups and downs of his active life, and who, in her grief, may have the comfort of knowing what men and women of all parties think and feel about the good and faithful servant we have lost.

[1] Major-General Sir Lee Oliver Fitzmaurice Stack, Governor-General of the Sudan and Sirdar of the Egyptian Army from 1919, had been assassinated in Cairo by Egyptian nationalist fanatics on 20 November 1924.

Parliamentary Questions: Oral Answers
(*Hansard*)

6 February 1941 House of Commons

NEWSPAPER ACTIVITIES

The following Question stood upon the Order Paper:

Mr Mander, – To ask the Prime Minister on what dates, and in what circumstances, representatives of the *Daily Mirror* and *Sunday Pictorial* were officially interviewed and warned about the political attitude they were adopting; what was the precise objection taken to their attitude; and whether any other papers, apart from those recently suppressed, have received warnings?

The Lord Privy Seal (Mr Attlee): As the Prime Minister is unavoidably detained, though he will be present a little later, will you, Sir, allow this Question to be repeated at the end of Questions?

Mr Speaker: I can take that course under the Standing Orders.

Later:

The Prime Minister (Mr Churchill): Sir, I am not prepared to give any information about confidential communications passing between His Majesty's Government and those who control or conduct newspapers. I must ask the House to support His Majesty's Government in this decision, which is necessary for the effective prosecution of the war.

Mr Mander: Is it not the case that unofficial representations were made through certain newspaper proprietors to the *Daily Mirror*, on the strength of which it obtained an interview with the Lord Privy Seal and was told that its activities were subversive, but when asked in what way they were subversive, the Lord Privy Seal was unable to give any information? Is it not reasonable that a newspaper should be told in what way its activities are considered prejudicial to the public interest?

The Prime Minister: I do not at all accept this one-sided account of what was undoubtedly a confidential conversation. I do not accept it. But who has ever heard of its being suggested that the Government are not entitled to have confidential conversations with persons connected with the newspaper Press or almost any other form of legitimate activity?

Mr Bevan:[1] On the other hand, is it not extremely undesirable that the

[1] Aneurin Bevan, 1897–1960. A coal miner from the age of thirteen. Miners' disputes agent, 1926. Labour MP from 1929 until his death. Forced in 1944 to give the Labour Party a written assurance of loyalty or be expelled (he gave the assurance). Minister of Health, 1945–51 (when he introduced the National Health Service). Minister of Labour and National Service, 1951: resigned in protest against defence spending and National Health Service charges (also resigning was the President of the Board of Trade, Harold Wilson, later Prime Minister). Treasurer of the Labour Party, and Deputy Leader of the Opposition, from 1956 until his death. His often acerbic manner (he was reported to have called the Conservatives 'lower than vermin') caused Churchill to dub him a 'merchant of discourtesy'.

editors of any newspapers should be under a misapprehension as to where they offend? Is not the main complaint here the ambiguity of the charge brought by the Government against the newspapers? If the Government think the newspapers are behaving improperly, why do they not prosecute on specific charges, so that the newspapers may know where they are, and not use this weapon of secret terror?

The Prime Minister: I do not at all accept the version which has been given. As far as I can make out from the hon. Gentleman's Supplementary Question, the Government would only be entitled to prosecute newspapers, and would never be entitled to have, even unofficially, confidential conversations with their owners or controllers. Such an idea is altogether foolish and has no relation whatever to the way in which affairs are conducted in this country.

Mr Shinwell: But does not this make the position of the Press somewhat uncertain, because they are unaware whether their contents are pleasing to the Government or not, and are only made aware when they receive a friendly visit, not from the police, who are directly responsible, but from others?

The Prime Minister: I think that contention is utterly absurd. Persons, whether Ministers or otherwise, are fully entitled to talk to newspaper people, and very considerable latitude should be allowed on such occasions.

John Colville: diary

(*Colville papers*)

6 February 1941

In the evening the PM got busy with the appointment of large numbers of Under-Secretaries and Ministers. Lord Moyne[1] succeeds Lloyd, and Ernest

[1] Walter Edward Guinness, 1880–1944. 3rd son of the 1st Earl of Iveagh. Educated at Eton. Wounded while on active service in South Africa, 1900–1. Conservative MP for Bury St Edmunds, 1907–31. On active service, 1914–18 (despatches thrice). Under-Secretary of State for War, 1922–3. Financial Secretary, Treasury, 1923–4 and 1924–5. Minister of Agriculture and Fisheries, 1925–9. Created Baron Moyne, 1932. A director of Arthur Guinness, Son, and Company, brewers. Elected to the Other Club, 1934. Secretary of State for the Colonies, 1941–2. Minister Resident, Cairo 1944 (where he was murdered by Jewish terrorists).

Brown[1] becomes Minister of Health instead of Malcolm MacDonald,[2] and Tom Johnston S of S for Scotland. The PM told me he was delighted with 'the lay-out' which includes the Editor of *Forward* (Tom Johnston) and the premier Duke (Under Sec. For Agriculture)[3] and thus shows the breadth of the Administration.

Sir Alexander Cadogan: diary
('The Diaries of Sir Alexander Cadogan, OM, 1938-1945')

6 February 1941

Some more very bad-looking Jap telephone conversations, from which it appears they have decided to attack us. A.[4] was seeing Hopkins and I went in and guardedly gave them the news. We then went over to see PM, about 6.50. Found he had been 'Cabinet-making' – consequent on poor G. Lloyd's death. A. sympathized at this extra burden, but PM said he liked it – as he evidently did. Showed us the list, and asked what we thought of Bernard Norfolk. I thought it very good. A. asked how he had thought of it. WSC said he had been through a list of Dukes – Buccleuch, Westminster, Bedford, Manchester – we didn't stop to hear the rest!

Winston S. Churchill to General Ismay, for the Chiefs of Staff Committee
(Churchill papers, 20/36)

6 February 1941
Action this Day

REINFORCEMENTS FOR MALTA

I cordially approve the attached draft[5] which seems of the highest urgency.

2. Although, of course, the difficulties of assaulting Malta are enormously

[1] Ernest Brown, 1881–1962. A Baptist lay preacher. On active service in Italy, 1916–18 (Military Cross). Liberal MP for Leith, 1927–31; Liberal National, 1931–45. Parliamentary Secretary, Ministry of Health, 1931–2. Secretary to the Mines Department, 1932–5. Privy Councillor, 1935; Minister of Labour, 1935–40 (and National Service May, 1939–May 1940). Secretary for Scotland, 1940–1. Minister of Health, 1941–43. Chancellor of the Duchy of Lancaster, 1943–5. Minister of Aircraft Production, 1945. Companion of Honour, 1945.

[2] Malcolm MacDonald was appointed High Commissioner to Canada.

[3] Bernard Marmaduke Fitzalan-Howard, 16th Duke of Norfolk, 1908–1975. Succeeded his father as Duke, 1917. Parliamentary Under-Secretary for Agriculture, 8 February 1941–23 May 1945; Parliamentary Secretary, Secretary, Ministry of Agriculture and Fisheries May–July 1945. President of the Council for the Protection of Rural England, 1945–71. Manager, Middlesex Cricket Club team to Australia and New Zealand, 1962–63. Vice-Chairman of the Turf Board, 1965–68. President of the Territorial and Army Volunteer Reserve Association, 1970–75.

[4] Anthony Eden.

[5] Not printed.

increased by the British fuelling base in Suda Bay, nevertheless, I shall be glad to see a second Battalion sent there, at the earliest opportunity, making seven British Battalions in all. Considering that in view of the Italian rout there should be no great difficulty in sparing this seventh Battalion from Egypt, and that the trouble is carrying them there by the Fleet, one must ask whether it is not as easy to carry two as it is to carry one. It seems a pity to let the baker's cart go with only one loaf, when the journey is so expensive and the loaf available, and that it might as easily carry two. Pray consider this. But no delay.

Winston S. Churchill to Anthony Eden
(Churchill papers, 20/36)

6 February 1941
action this day

I really cannot take interest in the Tangier quarrel, considering where we stand in other matters and the proportion of events. Do you not think you could let Ambassador Hoare round it all up and get it out of the way?

Winston S. Churchill to Air Chief Marshal Sir Charles Portal
(Premier papers, 3/205)

6 February 1941
Private, Secret.

Some time ago we asked Greece to prepare airfields for 14 Squadrons, and this work is still going on. Then, after various interchanges, you proposed sending 10 Squadrons to Turkey, which the Turks have not yet accepted, but which they may accept. The President has cut short his journey on my message. Suppose they do accept, and after that Greece demands further aid beyond the 5 Squadrons allotted, what are you going to do? I am afraid you have got to look at this very seriously. I am in it with you up to the neck. But have we not, in fact, promised to sell the same pig to two customers? We might have a legal quibble about the word 'promise'. But I think we have got to look into this matter rather more deeply than that. Let me know what you feel about it and what you think can be done.

Nothing was said about time or priority, so we have that to veer and haul on.

Winston S. Churchill to Alfred Duff Cooper
(*Churchill papers, 20/36*)

6 February 1941

The Secretary of State for War told me that the Military Adviser would be relieved of his duties in consequence of his gross lapse[1]. I request, therefore, that similar strictness should be used in respect of others who have failed or shown themselves unfitted for their functions. It is very hard to conduct military operations when, in the teeth of General Wavell's request and a Cabinet decision made effective by your own minute, we still have the BBC proclaiming the route by which our soldiers are about to advance against the enemy. It may be that in this case no serious loss of life will occur. Now, therefore, is the moment to clean up your arrangements and tone up your men.

Winston S. Churchill to Lord Beaverbrook
(*Churchill papers, 20/36*)

6 February 1941

Since our whole programme of arms output depends on the execution of training, up-grading and dilution of labour on a greatly increased scale, it is essential that the War Cabinet should have a statistical report at regular intervals showing clearly the progress achieved.

Whether a report covering the whole field should be made by the Production Executive or separate reports be submitted by each of the Producing Departments, you will no doubt wish to decide among yourselves.

I am sending a copy of this minute to the Chairman of the Production Executive.

[1] The release to the newspapers of information about the short route to Benghazi (the officer concerned had spoken of a 'short cut').

Eric Seal: letter
(*Seal papers*)

7 February 1941 10 Downing Street

In the middle of dinner we arranged with masterly skill for the PM at Chequers to speak to a passenger on a train at Coatbridge in Scotland! The passenger was warned at the station before, & the train held up whilst he talked. It was quite a stunt – you would have laughed to see us juggling with the telephones. All this in connection with the reconstruction of the Govt which is coming out tomorrow.[1]

Harry Hopkins to Winston S. Churchill
(*Premier papers, 4/25/3*)

8 February 1941 Chequers

My dear Mr Prime Minister, I shall never forget these days with you – your supreme confidence and will to victory – Britain I have ever liked – I like it the more.

As I leave for America tonight I wish you great and good luck – confusion to your enemies – victory for Britain.

Ever so cordially, Harry Hopkins.

On Saturday, 8 February 1941, General O'Connor's troops entered the border town of Agheila, completing the conquest of Cyrenaica.

John Martin: letter
(*Martin papers*)

9 February 1941

I have been busy, among other things, with the preparation for today's broadcast, which looks as if it ought to be a very effective and enheartening speech. We had a rather hectic search for a passenger from the north to whom the PM wanted to speak the other evening. After a long hunt in Perth station, where his supposed train was then standing, we found a hotel porter who had seen him leave by an earlier train. We managed to get a message to it at Larbert and held it up at Coatbridge, where the man was brought to the station-master's office. It was a race against the express to get the calls through in time.

[1] The passenger was H.J. Scrymgeour-Wedderburn (later Earl of Dundee), who was appointed a Parliamentary Under Secretary in the Scottish Office.

Winston S. Churchill: broadcast
(*His Master's Voice, ALP 1554*)

9 February 1941

The whole British Empire has been proud of the Mother Country, and they long to be with us over here in even larger numbers. We have been deeply conscious of the love for us which has flowed from the Dominions of the Crown across the broad ocean spaces. There is the first of our war aims: to be worthy of that love, and to preserve it.

All through these dark winter months the enemy has had the power to drop three or four tons of bombs upon us for every ton we could send to Germany in return. We are arranging so that presently this will be rather the other way round; but, meanwhile, London and our big cities have had to stand their pounding. They remind me of the British squares at Waterloo. They are not squares of soldiers; they do not wear scarlet coats. They are just ordinary English, Scottish and Welsh folk – men, women and children – standing steadfastly together. But their spirit is the same, their glory is the same; and, in the end, their victory will be greater than far-famed Waterloo.

All honour to the Civil Defence Services of all kinds – emergency and regular, volunteer and professional – who have helped our people through this formidable ordeal, the like of which no civilized community has ever been called upon to undergo. If I mention only one of these services here, namely the Police, it is because many tributes have been paid already to the others. But the Police have been in it everywhere, all the time, and as a working woman wrote to me: 'What gentlemen they are!'

More than two-thirds of the winter has now gone, and so far we have had no serious epidemic; indeed, there is no increase of illness in spite of the improvised conditions of the shelters. That is most creditable to our local, medical and sanitary authorities, to our devoted nursing staff, and to the Ministry of Health, whose head, Mr Malcolm MacDonald, is now going to Canada in the important office of High Commissioner.

There is another thing which surprised me when I asked about it. In spite of all these new war-time offences and prosecutions of all kinds; in spite of all the opportunities for looting and disorder, there has been less crime this winter and there are now fewer prisoners in our jails than in the years of peace.

We have broken the back of the winter. The daylight grows. The Royal Air Force grows, and is already certainly master of the daylight air. The attacks may be sharper, but they will be shorter; there will be more opportunities for work and service of all kinds; more opportunities for life. So, if our first victory was the repulse of the invader, our second was the frustration of his acts of terror and torture against our people at home.

Meanwhile, abroad, in October, a wonderful thing happened. One of the two Dictators – the crafty, cold-blooded, blackhearted Italian, who had thought to gain an Empire on the cheap by stabbing fallen France in the back – got into trouble. Without the slightest provocation, spurred on by lust of power and brutish greed, Mussolini attacked and invaded Greece, only to be hurled back ignominiously by the heroic Greek Army; who, I will say, with your consent, have revived before our eyes the glories which, from the classic age, gild their native land. While Signor Mussolini was writhing and smarting under the Greek lash in Albania, Generals Wavell and Wilson, who were charged with the defence of Egypt and of the Suez Canal in accordance with our treaty obligations, whose task seemed at one time so difficult, had received very powerful reinforcements of men, cannon, equipment and above all, tanks, which we had sent from our Island in spite of the invasion threat. Large numbers of troops from India, Australia and New Zealand have also reached them. Forthwith began that series of victories in Libya which have broken irretrievably the Italian military power on the African Continent. We have all been entertained, and I trust edified, by the exposure and humiliation of another of what Byron called

> Those Pagod things of sabre sway
> With fronts of brass and feet of clay.

Here then, in Libya, is the third considerable event upon which we may dwell with some satisfaction. It is just exactly two months ago, to a day, that I was waiting anxiously, but also eagerly, for the news of the great counter-stroke which had been planned against the Italian invaders of Egypt. The secret had been well kept. The preparations had been well made. But to leap across those seventy miles of desert, and attack an army of ten or eleven divisions, equipped with all the appliances of modern war, who had been fortifying themselves for three months – that was a most hazardous adventure.

When the brilliant decisive victory at Sidi Barrani, with its tens of thousands of prisoners, proved that we had quality, manoeuvring power and weapons superior to the enemy, who had boasted so much of his virility and his military virtues, it was evident that all the other Italian forces in eastern Libya were in great danger. They could not easily beat a retreat along the coastal road without running the risk of being caught in the open of our armoured divisions and brigades ranging far out into the desert in tremendous swoops and scoops. They had to expose themselves to being attacked piecemeal.

General Wavell – nay, all our leaders, and all their lithe, active, ardent men, British, Australian, Indian, in the Imperial Army – saw their opportunity. At that time I ventured to draw General Wavell's attention to the seventh chapter of the Gospel of St Matthew, at the seventh verse, where, as you all know – or ought to know – it is written: 'Ask, and it shall be given; seek, and ye shall find; knock, and it shall be opened unto you.' The Army of the Nile has asked, and it was given; they sought, and they have found; they knocked, and it has been opened unto them. In barely eight weeks, by a campaign which will long be studied as a model of the military art, an advance of over 400 miles has been made. The whole Italian Army in the east of Libya, which was reputed to exceed 150,000 men, has been captured or destroyed. The entire province of Cyrenaica – nearly as big as England and Wales – has been conquered. The unhappy Arab tribes, who have for thirty years suffered from the cruelty of Italian rule, carried in some cases to the point of methodical extermination, these Bedouin survivors have at last seen their oppressors in disorderly flight, or led off in endless droves as prisoners of war.

Egypt and the Suez Canal are safe, and the port, the base and the airfields of Benghazi constitute a strategic point of high consequence to the whole of the war in the Eastern Mediterranean.

This is the time, I think, to speak of the leaders who, at the head of their brave troops, have rendered this distinguished service to the King. The first and foremost General Wavell, Commander-in-Chief of all the Armies in the Middle East has proved himself a master of war, sage, painstaking, daring and tireless. But General Wavell has repeatedly asked that others should share his fame.

General Wilson, who actually commands the Army of the Nile, was reputed to be one of our finest tacticians – and few will now deny that quality. General O'Connor, commanding the 13th Corps, with General MacKay, commanding the splendid Australians, and General Creagh, who trained and commanded the various armoured divisions which were employed – these three men executed the complicated and astoundingly rapid movements which were made, and fought the actions which occurred. I have just seen a telegram from General Wavell in which he says that the success at Benghazi was due to the outstanding leadership and resolution of O'Connor and Creagh, ably backed by Wilson.

I must not forget here to point out the amazing mechanical feats of the British tanks, whose design and workmanship have beaten all records and stood up to all trials; and show us how closely and directly the work in the factories at home is linked with the victories abroad.

Of course, none of our plans would have succeeded had not our pilots, under Air Chief Marshal Longmore, wrested the control of the air from a far more numerous enemy. Nor would the campaign itself have been possible if the British Mediterranean Fleet, under Admiral Cunningham,[1] had not chased the Italian navy into its harbours and sustained every forward surge of the Army with all the flexible resources of sea power. How far-reaching these

[1] Andrew Browne Cunningham, 1883–1963. Entered the Royal Navy, 1898. On active service, 1914–18 (DSO and two bars). Vice-Admiral Commanding the Battle Cruiser Squadron, 1937–8. Deputy Chief of the Naval Staff, 1938–9. Knighted, 1939. Commander-in-Chief, Mediterranean, 1939–42. Head of the British Admiralty Delegation, Washington, 1942. Naval Commander-in-Chief, Expeditionary Force, North Africa, 1942. Commander-in-Chief, Mediterranean, 1943. Admiral of the Fleet, 1943. First Sea Lord and Chief of the Naval Staff, 1943–6. Created Baron, 1945; Viscount, 1946. In 1951 he published his memoirs, *A Sailor's Odyssey*.

resources are we can see from what happened at dawn this morning, when our Western Mediterranean Fleet, under Admiral Somerville, entered the Gulf of Genoa and bombarded in a shattering manner the naval base from which perhaps a Nazi German expedition might soon have sailed to attack General Weygand in Algeria or Tunis. It is right that the Italian people should be made to feel the sorry plight into which they have been dragged by Dictator Mussolini; and if the cannonade of Genoa, rolling along the coast, reverberating in the mountains, reached the ears of our French comrades in their grief and misery, it might cheer them with the feeling that friends – active friends – are near and that Britannia rules the waves.

The events in Libya are only part of the story: they are only part of the story of the decline and fall of the Italian Empire, that will not take a future Gibbon so long to write as the original work. Fifteen hundred miles away to the southward a strong British and Indian army, having driven the invaders out of the Sudan, is marching steadily forward through the Italian Colony of Eritrea, thus seeking to complete the isolation of all the Italian troops in Abyssinia. Other British forces are entering Abyssinia from the west, while the army gathered in Kenya – in the van of which we may discern the powerful forces of the Union of South Africa, organized by General Smuts – is striking northward along the whole enormous front. Lastly, the Ethiopian patriots, whose independence was stolen five years ago, have risen in arms; and their Emperor, so recently an exile in England, is in their midst to fight for their freedom and his throne. Here, then, we see the beginnings of a process of reparation, and the chastisement of wrongdoing, which reminds us that, though the mills of God grind slowly, they grind exceeding small.

While these auspicious events have been carrying us stride by stride from what many people thought a forlorn position, and was certainly a very grave position in May and June, to one which permits us to speak with sober confidence of our power to discharge our duty, heavy though it be in the future – while this has been happening, a mighty tide of sympathy, of good will and of effective aid, has begun to flow across the Atlantic in support of the world cause which is at stake. Distinguished Americans have come over to see things here at the front, and to find out how the United States can help us best and soonest. In Mr Hopkins who has been my frequent companion during the last three weeks, we have the Envoy of the President, a President who has been newly re-elected to his august office. In Mr Wendell Willkie we have welcomed the champion of the great Republican Party. We may be sure that they will both tell the truth about what they have seen over here, and more than that we do not ask. The rest we leave with good confidence to the judgment of the President, the Congress and the people of the United States.

I have been so very careful, since I have been Prime Minister, not to encourage false hopes or prophesy smooth and easy things, and yet the tale that I have to tell today is one which must justly and rightly give us cause for deep thankfulness, and also, I think, for strong comfort and even rejoicing. But now I must dwell upon the more serious, darker and more dangerous aspects of the vast scene of the war. We must all of us have been asking ourselves: What has that wicked man whose crime-stained regime and system are at bay and in the toils – what has he been preparing during these winter months? What new devilry is he planning? What new small country will he overrun or strike down? What fresh form of assault will he make upon our Island home and fortress; which – let there be no mistake about it – is all that stands between him and the dominion of the world?

We may be sure that the war is soon going to enter upon a phase of greater violence. Hitler's confederate, Mussolini, has reeled back in Albania, but the Nazis – having absorbed Hungary and driven Roumania into a frightful internal convulsion – are now already upon the Black Sea. A considerable Nazi German army and air force is being built up in Roumania, and its forward tentacles have already penetrated Bulgaria. With – we must suppose – the acquiescence of the Bulgarian Government, airfields are being occupied by German ground personnel numbering thousands, so as to enable the German air force to come into action from Bulgaria. Many preparations have been made for the movement of German troops into or through Bulgaria, and perhaps this southward movement has already begun.

We saw what happened last May in the Low Countries, how they hoped for the best; how they clung to their neutrality; how woefully they were deceived, over-whelmed, plundered, enslaved and since starved. We know how we and the French suffered when, at the last moment, at the urgent belated appeal of the King of the Belgians,[1] we went to his aid. Of course, if all the Balkan people stood together and acted together, aided by Britain and Turkey, it would be many months before a German army and air force of sufficient strength to overcome them could be assembled in the southeast of Europe. And in those months much might happen. Much will certainly happen as American aid becomes effective, as our air power grows, as we become a well-armed nation, and as our armies in the East increase in strength. But nothing is more certain than that, if the countries of southeastern Europe allow themselves to be pulled to pieces one by one, they will share the fate of

[1] Léopold, 1901–1983. Married, 1926, Princess Astrid of Sweden. Succeeded his father (King Albert) as King of the Belgians in 1934 as Léopold III. Queen Astrid was killed in a car crash in Switzerland in 1935. In September 1939 Léopold reasserted Belgian neutrality. On the German invasion, 10 May 1940, he assumed command of the Belgian Army. surrendered, 28 May 1940. Detained by the Germans, as a technical prisoner of war, with his mother, Queen Elisabeth, in the royal palace of Laeken, 1940–4. Twice travelled to Germany to urge Hitler to improve the lot of the Belgians. Deported to Germany on 7 June 1944, the day after the Normandy Landings. Prevented from returning to the throne in 1945, he lived in Switzerland. In 1950 he returned to Belgium after a referendum voted by 5 to 3 for him to do so. The Socialist government resigned in protest, and rioting followed. A year later, in 1951, he abdicated in favour of his son King Baudouin.

Denmark, Holland and Belgium. And none can tell how long it will be before the hour of their deliverance strikes.

One of our difficulties is to convince some of these neutral countries in Europe that we are going to win. We think it astonishing that they should be so dense as not to see it as clearly as we do ourselves. I remember in the last war, in July, 1915, we began to think that Bulgaria was going wrong, so Mr Lloyd George, Mr Bonar Law, Sir F. E. Smith and I, asked the Bulgarian Minister to dinner to explain to him what a fool King Ferdinand would make of himself if he were to go in on the losing side. It was no use. The poor man simply could not believe it, or could not make his Government believe it. So Bulgaria, against the wishes of her peasant population, against all her interests, fell in at the Kaiser's tail and got sadly carved up and punished when the victory was won. I trust that Bulgaria is not going to make the same mistake again. If they do, the Bulgarian peasantry and people, for whom there has been much regard, both in Great Britain and in the United States, will for the third time in thirty years have been made to embark upon a needless and disastrous war.

In the central Mediterranean the Italian Quisling, who is called Mussolini, and the French Quisling, commonly called Laval,[1] are both in their different ways trying to make their countries into doormats for Hitler and his New Order, in the hope of being able to keep, or get the Nazi Gestapo and Prussian bayonets to enforce, their rule upon their fellow-countrymen. I cannot tell how the matter will go, but at any rate we shall do our best to fight for the Central Mediterranean.

I dare say you will have noticed the very significant air action which was fought over Malta a fortnight ago. The Germans sent an entire *Geschwader* of dive-bombers to Sicily. They seriously injured our new aircraft-carrier *Illustrious*, and then, as this wounded ship was sheltering in Malta harbour, they concentrated upon her all their force so as to beat her to pieces. But they were met by the batteries of Malta which is one of the strongest defended fortresses in the world against air attack; they were met by the Fleet Air Arm and by the Royal Air Force, and in two or three days, they had lost, out of a hundred and fifty dive-bombers, upwards of ninety, fifty of which were destroyed in the air and forty on the ground. Although the *Illustrious*, in her damaged condition, was one of the great prizes of the air and naval war, the

[1] Pierre Laval, 1883–1945. A lawyer. Socialist Deputy for the Seine, 1914–19 and (as an Independent) 1924–7. Independent Senator, 1927–44. Minister of Public Works, 1925; of Justice, 1926; of Labour, 1930 and 1932. Prime Minister and Foreign Minister, 1931–2 and 1935–6. Foreign Minister, 1934–5. Deputy Prime Minister and Minister of Information (under Pétain), July–December 1940. Prime Minister (under Pétain), April 1942 to August 1944 (also Foreign Minister, Minister of the Interior, and Minister of Information and Propaganda). Arrested by the Gestapo, 1944, and interned, 1944–5. Tried in Paris for treason, his trial began on 4 October 1945; he was sentenced to death on 10 October and executed on 15 October.

German *Geschwader* accepted the defeat; they would not come any more. All the necessary repairs were made to the *Illustrious* in Malta harbour, and she steamed safely off to Alexandria under her own power at 23 knots. I dwell upon this incident, not at all because I think it disposes of the danger in the Central Mediterranean, but in order to show you that there, as elsewhere, we intend to give a good account of ourselves.

But after all, the fate of this war is going to be settled by what happens on the oceans, in the air, and – above all – in this island. It seems now to be certain that the Government and people of the United States intend to supply us with all that is necessary for victory. In the last war the United States sent two million men across the Atlantic. But this is not a war of vast armies, firing immense masses of shells at one another. We do not need the gallant armies which are forming throughout the American Union. We do not need them this year, nor next year; nor any year that I can foresee. But we do need most urgently an immense and continuous supply of war materials and technical apparatus of all kinds. We need them here and we need to bring them here. We shall need a great mass of shipping in 1942, far more than we can build ourselves, if we are to maintain and augment our war effort in the West and in the East.

These facts are, of course, all well known to the enemy, and we must therefore expect that Herr Hitler will do his utmost to prey upon our shipping and to reduce the volume of American supplies entering these islands. Having conquered France and Norway, his clutching fingers reach out on both sides of us into the ocean. I have never underrated this danger, and you know I have never concealed it from you. Therefore, I hope you will believe me when I say that I have complete confidence in the Royal Navy, aided by the Air Force of the Coastal Command, and that in one way or another I am sure they will be able to meet every changing phase of this truly mortal struggle, and that sustained by the courage of our merchant seamen, and of the dockers and workmen of all our ports, we shall outwit, outmanoeuvre, outfight and outlast the worst that the enemy's malice and ingenuity can contrive.

I have left the greatest issue to the end. You will have seen that Sir John Dill, our principal military adviser, the Chief of the Imperial General Staff, has warned us all that Hitler may be forced, by the strategic, economic and political stresses in Europe, to try to invade these islands in the near future. That is a warning which no one should disregard. Naturally, we are working night and day to have everything ready. Of course, we are far stronger than we ever were before, incomparably stronger than we were in July, August and September. Our Navy is more powerful, our flotillas are more numerous; we are far stronger, actually and relatively, in the air above these islands, than we were when our Fighter Command beat off and beat down the Nazi attack last autumn. Our Army is more numerous, more mobile and far better equipped and trained than in September, and still more than in July.

I have the greatest confidence in our Commander-in-Chief, General Brooke, and in the generals of proved ability who, under him, guard the different quarters of our land. But most of all I put my faith in the simple unaffected resolve to conquer or die which will animate and inspire nearly four million Britons with serviceable weapons in their hands. It is not an easy military operation to invade an island like Great Britain, without the command of the sea and without the command of the air, and then to face what will be waiting for the invader here. But I must drop one word of caution; for next to cowardice and treachery, over-confidence, leading to neglect or slothfulness, is the worst of martial crimes. Therefore, I drop one word of caution. A Nazi invasion of Great Britain last autumn would have been a more or less improvised affair. Hitler took it for granted that when France gave in we should give in; but we did not give in. And he had to think again. An invasion now will be supported by a much more carefully prepared tackle and equipment of landing craft and other apparatus, all of which will have been planned and manufactured in the winter months. We must all be prepared to meet gas attacks, parachute attacks, and glider attacks, with constancy, forethought and practised skill.

I must again emphasize what General Dill has said, and what I pointed out myself last year. In order to win the war Hitler must destroy Great Britain. He may carry havoc into the Balkan States; he may tear great provinces out of Russia; he may march to the Caspian; he may march to the gates of India. All this will avail him nothing. It may spread his curse more widely throughout Europe and Asia, but it will not avert his doom. With every month that passes the many proud and once happy countries he is now holding down by brute force and vile intrigue are learning to hate the Prussian yoke and the Nazi name as nothing has ever been hated so fiercely and so widely among men before. And all the time, masters of the sea and air, the British Empire – nay, in a certain sense, the whole English-speaking world – will be on his track, bearing with them the swords of justice.

The other day, President Roosevelt gave his opponent in the late Presidential Election a letter of introduction to me, and in it he wrote out a verse, in his own handwriting, from Longfellow, which he said, 'applies to you people as it does to us'. Here is the verse:

. . . Sail on, O Ship of State!
Sail on, O Union, strong and great!
Humanity with all its fears,
With all the hopes of future years,
Is hanging breathless on thy fate!

What is the answer that I shall give, in your name, to this great man, the thrice-chosen head of a nation of a hundred and thirty millions? Here is the answer which I will give to President Roosevelt: Put your confidence in us. Give us your faith and your blessing, and, under Providence, all will be well.

We shall not fail or falter; we shall not weaken or tire. Neither the sudden shock of battle, nor the long-drawn trials of vigilance and exertion will wear us down. Give us the tools, and we will finish the job.[1]

Defence Committee (Operations): minutes
(*Cabinet papers, 69/2*)

10 February 1941 Cabinet War Room
9.30 a.m.
Secret

Mr Eden argued that the best way of ensuring that Turkey would fight would be to give effective help to the Greeks. If we failed in this, we should lose all hope of facing Germany with the Balkan front, we should probably lose our safe communications with Turkey, and we should lose Yugoslavia. He thought the Greeks were anxious to know what we were prepared to do, so that they could make their plan. If we could say to them that we were prepared to provide forces of a certain strength, then we could discuss with them where these forces could best be used, and agree upon our joint action. If we held back, and allowed the Greeks to be crushed, it was almost certain that the Turks would not fight.

The Prime Minister thought it would be wrong to abandon the Greeks, who were putting up a magnificent fight, and who were prepared to fight the Germans, so that we could later help Turkey, who was shirking her responsibilities, and taking no action to prevent the Germans establishing themselves in a threatening position in Bulgaria. We could not blame the Greeks if they bowed to the superior force of the Germans, if we refused them help. We were not bound to the Turks. They had not accepted our offer, and it would suit us to have a genuinely neutral Turkey blocking our right flank. He did not think that it was necessarily impossible for the Greeks and ourselves to hold the Germans, who would be advancing down the Struma valley. The Greeks might be able to disengage a few Divisions in time, and if we could support them with air and mechanized forces, we might delay them long enough to encourage the Turks, and possibly the Yugoslavs, to join in the battle.

There was considerable further discussion, in the course of which the view

[1] General Smuts, who heard Churchill's speech on the radio in South Africa, telegraphed: 'Each broadcast is a battle'. Twenty-two years later, on 9 April 1963, in proclaiming Churchill an honorary citizen of the United States, President John F. Kennedy declared: 'He mobilized the English language and sent it into battle.'

was generally expressed that it was essential for us to come to the assistance of the Greeks, if they would have us. It was realized that the time factor was of great importance. The Germans might be ready to move by 10th March, which did not allow much time for the movement of forces from Egypt. Immediate steps should therefore be taken to concert measures with the Greeks, and to make a common plan. If the Greeks would not agree to British forces being sent to their country forthwith, it might then be necessary to consider whether the advance on Tripoli was justified as an alternative.

Night Air Defence Committee of the War Cabinet: minutes
(*Cabinet Papers, 81/22*)

10 February 1941
11.30 a.m.

FREE BALLOON BARRAGE

The Prime Minister said that he had been very disturbed at learning that the secret of the aerial mine had got out as a result of some of our free balloons drifting over to Occupied France. He had understood that we had provided against this danger by making the balloons self-destroying. Now that the secret was out it was reasonable to anticipate that the enemy would fit wire cutters to his bombers.

Vice Admiral Fraser[1] explained that though self-destroying mechanism had been fitted, some failures were inevitable. He was emphatic that the most promising antidote to night bombing was to fill the path of the enemy bomber with obstructions, and on this principle urged most strongly that the development of the free balloon barrage should be given the highest priority. He argued that the very fact that these balloons created such difficulties for our own aircraft was a proof of their deterrent value. He questioned whether the enemy could fit cutters quickly enough and in sufficient numbers to deal with the problem for several months.

PE FUZES[2]

It was reported that 5,000 PE Fuzes would shortly be ready for issue to the Army.

[1] The Controller of the Navy.

[2] Photo-electric proximity fuse. In 1941 it was handed over to the United States where it was mass produced. In 1944 it played a crucial part in shooting down the Vl rocket.

The Prime Minister directed:

(a) That the 5,000 PE Fuzes should not be dispersed, but concentrated for the defence of one or two important targets where dive-bombing attacks might be expected: and that special arrangements should be made for the study of their behaviour when in action by skilled scientists, who should be attached to the UP[1] Batteries concerned.

(b) That the War Office should reconsider the question of the use of UPs for the defence of Malta.

(c) That the Admiralty should examine the possible advantages of fitting UPs on ships for defence against dive-bombers.

SEARCHLIGHTS

A new searchlight 'carpet' in clusters of three had been completed, but in many cases these clusters had not been linked by telephone with the Battery Headquarters.

The Prime Minister directed:

That, taking into account the various priorities involved, Air Marshal Joubert[2] should take such steps as might be possible with the General Post Office to complete the provision of telephone communications for the new searchlight layout.

BLIND LANDING

Air Marshal Joubert reported that every effort was being made to press on with the equipping of night interception aerodromes with Lorenz apparatus.[3] Meanwhile Mr Watson Watt[4] was exploring an alternative method of blind landing by means of Very High Frequency.

The Prime Minister directed:

That all facilities should be given for the development of blind landing by means of Very High Frequency.

[1] Unrotated Projectile: an anti-aircraft rocket.

[2] Philip Bennet Joubert de la Ferté, 1887–1965. Joined the Royal Field Artillery, 1907; the Royal Flying Corps, 1913. On active service in France, Egypt and Italy, 1914–18 (despatches six times, DSO). Air Officer Commanding-in-Chief, Royal Air Force, India, 1937–9. Knighted, 1938. Assistant Chief of the Air Staff, 1939–40. In charge of radar and radar counter-measures, 1939–40. Adviser to the Admiralty on Combined Operations, 1940. Officer Commanding-in-Chief, Coastal Command, 1941–3. Inspector General of the Royal Air Force, 1943. Director of Public Relations, Air Ministry, 1946–7.

[3] A blind-landing system developed before the war by a German scientist, Dr Hans Plendl, and used by many civil airlines.

[4] Robert Watson-Watt, 1892–1973. Engineer and inventor. Educated at St Andrews University. Joined the staff of the Meteorological Office, London, 1915, where he did successful research into the radio location of thunderstorms. Superintendent of the radio research stations at Aldershot and Slough, 1921; subsequently Superintendent of the radio department of the National Physical Laboratory. His radio wave experiments for detecting aircraft were sponsored by the Air Ministry in 1935. Superintendent at Bawdsey, 1936–8. Director of Communications Development, Air Ministry, 1938–40. After Pearl Harbor (December 1941) he advised the United States on radar defence. Knighted, 1942. After the war he received £50,000 for his contribution to radar development.

General Sir Alan Brooke: diary
(*'Turn of the Tide', page 251*)

10 February 1941

... the Prime Minister and 'Pug' Ismay came to lunch with us. He was in great form and did a complete tour of my Headquarters after lunch, visiting every single department. He finished up by inviting me to see his new flat in the building, and we visited his study, sitting-room, dining-room, Mrs Churchill's bedroom, bathroom, his own, kitchen, scullery, etc.[1]

Winston S. Churchill to Admiral Somerville
(*Premier papers, 3/370*)

10 February 1941 — 10 Downing Street

I congratulate you on the success of the enterprise against Genoa, which I was very glad to see you proposed yourself.

Winston S. Churchill to Sir Andrew Duncan
(*Churchill papers, 20/36*)

10 February 1941

I am disturbed to hear of the heavy fall in the output of alloy steel during the five weeks ended January 18th. No doubt the low figure for the first week can be explained by the raids on Sheffield, but output in the next four weeks averaged only three-fifths of normal, and the recovery has been disappointingly slow. Please let me know what the prospects for an increase in output are.

According to CPD (P&M)[2] 66th Meeting, the Steel Control claim that it takes 6 weeks to get the steel from the ports to the works. No doubt the Import Executive will take steps to diminish this delay. The Steel Control also state that deliveries from America are limited by lack of shipping. This is surprising in view of the relatively small tonnage involved.

[1] This was No. 10 Annexe, Churchill's set of rooms above the Cabinet War Rooms, facing St James's Park.
[2] Committee for Projectile Development (Projected and Manufactured).

Winston S. Churchill to Brendan Bracken
(*Churchill papers, 20/36*)

10 February 1941

I am much surprised to read the enclosed[1] by your Under-Secretary[2]. What is the meaning of the passage at B? What are the 'drastic concessions about our Colonies which we should make within the next few months'? What are the 'material advantages of the Hitlerian system'? Considering that we can only with the greatest difficulty supply ourselves on strict rations, how is it that we can 'offer immediate supplies of foodstuffs' to any country which is able to liberate itself, &c. On what authority does Mr Nicolson say that we are offering a New 'World Government' or a 'Federation'? All these statements are devoid of any practical foundation at the present time. It is most improper that an Under-Secretary should attempt to declare the policy of the Government on the gravest matters, especially when I have on several occasions deprecated any attempt to declare war aims.

Will you please ask Mr Nicolson for his explanation?

Winston S. Churchill to General Ismay for the Chiefs of Staff Committee
(*Churchill papers, 20/36*)

11 February 1941

I see no reason why you should not consider raising an Anti-Mussolini or Free-Italian force in Cyrenaica. Volunteers might be called for from the hundred thousand prisoners we have taken. There must be a great many who hate fascism. We might even rule Cyrenaica under the Free-Italian flag and treat it in the same way as de Gaulle's colonies are being treated, subject to our military control. Anyhow, I wish Cyrenaica to be petted and made extremely comfortable and prosperous, more money being spent upon them than they are intrinsically worth. Can we not make this place a base for starting a real split in Italy and the source of anti-Mussolini propaganda? We might make it a model of British rule, hold it in trust for the Italian people, and have four or five thousand Italian troops sworn to the liberation of Italy from the German and Mussolini yoke. This could be run as world propaganda. The matter raises wide political considerations and I am sending a copy of this minute to the Foreign Secretary.

[1] A speech by Harold Nicolson reported in the *Manchester Guardian* on 3 February 1941.

[2] Harold George Nicolson, 1886–1968. Son of Sir Arthur Nicolson (1st Baron Carnock). Educated at Wellington and Balliol College, Oxford. Entered Foreign Office, 1909; Counsellor, 1925. Served at the Paris Peace Conference, 1919. Teheran, 1925–7 and Berlin, 1927–9. On editorial staff of *Evening Standard*, 1930. National Labour MP for West Leicester, 1935–45. Parliamentary Secretary, Ministry of Information, 1940–1. A Governor of the BBC, 1941–6. Joined the Labour Party, 1947. Author and biographer. Knighted, 1953.

Winston S. Churchill to Ronald Cross
(*Churchill papers, 20/36*)

11 February 1941
Action this Day

Is it true that the steamship *New Toronto*, which arrived at Liverpool, was ordered to proceed northabout to London; and is it true that this order was only cancelled as a result of the protest of the Captain, who pointed out the enormous value of the cargo, which contained *inter alia* 19,677 sub-machine guns, and 2,456,000 cartridges? The arrival of these ships with large consignments of invaluable munitions ought to receive your personal attention in every case.

Pray give me a report. I attach my copy of the expected arrivals on which I always follow the movements of these important cargoes. The ship referred to is on page 5.

Winston S. Churchill: minute[1]
(*Churchill papers, 20/36*)

11 February 1941
Confidential

1. In all questions of propaganda in Belgium, whether by broadcast or by the dropping of leaflets, the view of the recognized Belgian Government should normally prevail. It is only when there is a clash between the approved policy of the Cabinet and the Belgian view that any question of restraint should arise. In such an event the Foreign Secretary will decide.

2. A ticklish point would be the King of the Belgians and the attitude to be adopted towards him is evidently one of high policy which the Foreign Office alone can advise the Cabinet.

3. The principles thus enunciated in the Belgian case should be made applicable generally and, subject to such modifications as may be desirable, to the other countries who have recognized Governments now resident in Great Britain.

[1] This minute was addressed to Anthony Eden, Hugh Dalton, Alfred Duff Cooper, Sir Robert Vansittart and Major Morton.

Defence Committee (Operations): minutes
(*Cabinet papers, 69/2*)

11 February 1941
6 p.m.
Secret

Sir John Dill thought that it would be difficult for General Wavell to find 4 Divisions in the immediate future to send to Greece. Except for the 2nd Armoured Division, and the New Zealand Division, and the 6th British Division which was forming, all his trained and equipped formations were already engaged in operations.

The Prime Minister said that we would have to intervene with at least 4 Divisions, rising to 6 or 10 in the summer. Out of the large mass of men accumulated in the Middle East, great efforts must be made to produce more mobile formations. As much use as possible should be made of Yeomanry, and other troops not fully trained or equipped, to relieve the best troops of garrison duty. The Poles should be available to fight in Europe. It was necessary to press on with Mandibles,[1] and, when captured, they should not require mobile troops to hold them. The main operation should start within 48 hours of the arrival of the Glen ships in the Middle East.

CYRENAICA

The Prime Minister said that he had been turning over in his mind the possibility that we might make out of Cyrenaica the beginning of a Free Italy, on the lines of Free France. We might proclaim to the world that we were holding it in trust for Italy, and call upon Italian volunteers to join our efforts to overthrow Fascist tyranny.

Mr Eden said that at first sight he was inclined to favour the idea of raising a Free Italian Army, but he was not so sure that it would be wise to nail the Italian flag to the mast of Cyrenaica. It was clearly a matter which would require considerable thought.

GREECE

The Prime Minister said that it would be necessary to make an offer of assistance to the Greeks, and guns withdrawn from the Army would very rapidly be replaced from new production. It would take two or three weeks to load the guns and ammunition, by which time there might have been developments in the situation. He thought that 100 75 mm. guns with 1,200 rounds per gun should be sent.

AIRCRAFT FOR THE GREEK FORCES

The Committee then considered a proposal by the Chief of the Air Staff that the Greeks should be given enough Tomahawks to equip and maintain

[1] The plan to seize the Dodecanese Islands from Italy.

one Squadron of 12 aircraft, with an immediate reserve of six, provided that this would not interfere with the passage of our urgent needs in Hurricanes and Glenn Martins along the Takoradi route. These Tomahawks would be found from the number which had arrived at Takoradi, and would be sent as soon as they were in a fit condition for war.

The Prime Minister said that the fundamental principle for the disposal of aircraft to the Middle East should be that the equipment of British Squadrons with the best possible aircraft should have absolute priority. Since satisfactory numbers of Hurricanes were arriving in the Middle East, he thought it would be reasonable to part with Tomahawks for the Greek Air Force.

The Committee:

Approved the proposal put forward by the Chief of the Air Staff to allot sufficient Tomahawks to the Greeks to permit the equipment and subsequent maintenance of one Squadron of 12 aircraft, with an immediate reserve of six aircraft.

On 12 February 1941 a German General, Erwin Rommel, arrived in Tripoli with his personal staff to take command of the growing German forces in Tripolitania. By chance, also on February 12, Anthony Eden and General Sir John Dill prepared to set out for Cairo and Athens.

Winston S. Churchill: Oral Answers
(*Hansard*)

12 February 1941 House of Commons

WAR AND PEACE AIMS

Mr Martin[1] asked the Prime Minister whether consultations on peace aims and reconstruction have taken place with the Government of the United States of America; and whether he can give the House an assurance that, before any statement is made outside this country, His Majesty's Government will inform Parliament of their policy?

The Prime Minister (Mr Churchill): There is such a thorough comprehension in the United States of what we are fighting for and what we stand for that I can recall no occasion when the question of peace aims or reconstruction has been mentioned by any of the representatives of the American Government I have seen or corresponded with. I can certainly give the House no assurance about statements which may be made about war aims

[1] John Hanbury Martin, 1892–1983. On active service 1914–18 (wounded). Founder and Chairman, Southwark Housing Association, 1930. Member of the London Insurance Committee, 1936–45. Labour Member of Parliament for Central Southwark, 1939–48. Secretary of the Franco-British Parliamentary Association.

outside this country, or indeed inside this country outside the ranks of the Government. Statements of British policy will be made by His Majesty's Ministers on such occasions as seem agreeable to the public interest.

Mr G. Griffiths:[1] Can the Prime Minister make the statement at Nine o'Clock on Sunday night? It would be a very good job if he did.

The Prime Minister: I think I must be allowed to be the judge.

Winston S. Churchill to the Foreign Office
(*Churchill papers, 20/36*)

12 February 1941

We have made Weygand great offers, to which we have had no reply. It is clear that he will be actuated only by forces set in motion by pressure of Nazis on Vichy. Our attitude at the present time should not be one of appeal to him. Until he has answered through some channel or other the telegram I sent him, he ought not to be given supplies. Not one scrap of nobility or courage has been shown by these people so far, and they had better go on short commons till they come to their senses.

The policy of occasional blockade should be enforced as Naval means are available.

Winston S. Churchill to Foreign Office
(*Churchill papers, 20/36*)

12 February 1941

In Spain we must not worry too much about Tangier and tiresome claims and legalities. We do not know what will come of the Franco-Musso[2] talks; but, assuming Ambassador Hoare and Attaché Hillgarth are right about their Generals and Spain refuses to give Hitler passage or join Axis immediately, it becomes of the utmost importance to crash in food, i.e., wheat, as much as we can, and persuade the President of the USA to act similarly. The few weeks remaining before the snows melt in the Pyrenees are of extreme importance. The more food we can bring in the better. This will give the best chance of a favourable reaction when the German invasion comes on Spain. Don't boggle, but feed.

Pray take this as a general directive.

[1] George Arthur Griffiths, 1880–1945. Educated at a Church of England School. A colliery worker. Member of the South Yorkshire Miners Welfare Committee. Member of the Coalowners and Workmen Joint Board. Member of the Royston Urban District Council, 1910–45 (Chairman seven times). Labour Member of Parliament for the Hemsworth Division of Yorkshire from 1934 until his death.

[2] Franco, absolute ruler of Spain since 1939, refused all pressure from both Mussolini and Hitler to take an active part in the war on the side of the Axis.

John Colville: diary
(*Colville papers*)

12 February 1941

Desmond Morton told me that there was great opposition to the PM's decision not to press on to Tripoli but to divert our effort to Greece and Turkey. In continuing our African campaign we had the practical certainty of winning all North Africa and holding an impregnable position. In forming a bridgehead in Greece we ran the risk of another Dunkirk. The CIGS[1] felt so strongly about it that he was almost thinking of resigning, and the military were making a determined effort to get Wavell to intervene. There was no constitutional means of forcing Wavell to obey; c.f. the old controversy between Haig and Lloyd George. Desmond pointed out that this was the vital decision of the first stage of the war.

Winston S. Churchill: Note for Anthony Eden
(*Churchill papers, 20/36*)

12 February 1941

1. During his visit to the Mediterranean theatre the Foreign Secretary will represent His Majesty's Government in all matters diplomatic and military. He will report whenever necessary to the War Cabinet through the Prime Minister.

2. His principal object will be the sending of speedy succour to Greece. For this purpose he will initiate any action as he may think necessary with the C-in-C of the Middle East, with the Egyptian Government and with the Governments of Greece, Yugoslavia and Turkey. He will, of course, keep the Foreign Office informed and he will himself be informed by the Foreign Office or the Prime Minister of all changes of plan or view occurring at home.

3. The CIGS will advise on the military aspect and the Foreign Secretary will make sure that in case of any difference his views are also placed before His Majesty's Government.

4. The following points require particular attention:

(a) What is the minimum garrison that can hold the western frontier of Libya, and Benghazi, and what measures should be taken to make Benghazi a principal garrison and air base. The extreme importance is emphasized of dropping the overland communications at the earliest moment.

(b) The régime and policy to be enforced in Cyrenaica, having regard to our desire to separate the Italian nation from the Mussolini system.

[1] The Chief of the Imperial General Staff, General Sir John Dill.

(c) The execution of the operation Mandibles[1] at the earliest moment (including, if necessary, repacking of the commandos at Capetown), having regard, however, to its not becoming an impediment to the main issue.

(d) The formation in the Delta of the strongest and best equipped force in divisional or brigade organisations which can be despatched to Greece at the earliest moment.

(e) The drain to be made upon our resources for the purpose of finishing up in Eritrea and breaking down the Italian positions in Abyssinia. The former is urgent; the latter, though desirable, must not conflict with major issues. It may be necessary to leave it to rot by itself.

(f) The great mass of troops, over 70,000, now engaged in the Kenya theatre must be severely scrutinized in order particularly to liberate the South African divisions for service in Egypt. Any communication with General Smuts had better pass through the Prime Minister. A further conference between the Foreign Secretary and General Smuts might well be convenient.

(g) The Foreign Secretary, when visiting Athens with the CIGS, General Wavell and any other officers, is fully empowered to formulate with the Greek government the best arrangement possible in the circumstances. He will at the same time try to keep HMG informed or seek their aid as far as possible. In an emergency he must act as he thinks best.

(h) He will communicate direct with the Governments of Yugoslavia and Turkey, duplicating his messages to the Foreign Office. The object will be to make them both fight at the same time or do the best they can. For this purpose he should summon the Minister at Belgrade or the Ambassador in Turkey[2] to meet him as may be convenient. He will bear in mind that while it is our duty to fight, and, if need be, suffer with Greece, the interests of Turkey in the second stage are no less important to us than those of Greece. It should be possible to reconcile the Greek and Turkish claims for air and munitions support.

(i) The Foreign Secretary will address himself to the problem of securing the highest form of war economy in the armies and air forces of the Middle East for all the above purposes, and to making sure that the many valuable military units in that theatre all fit in to a coherent scheme and are immediately pulling their weight.

(j) He should advivse HMG through the Prime Minister upon the selection of commanders for all the different purposes in view. In this he will no doubt consult with General Wavell, who enjoys so large a measure of the confidence of HMG. The selection of the General who commands

[1] The seizure of the Dodecanese Islands from Italy.

[2] Sir Ronald Campbell (Belgrade) and Sir Hughe Knatchbull-Hugessen (Ankara).

in Greece is of the highest consequence, and it is hoped that an agreed recommendation may be made on this point.

(k) Air Chief Marshal Longmore will be required to give effect to the wishes and decisions of the Foreign Secretary in accordance with the general scope of the policy here set out. But here again in the event of any difference the Foreign Secretary will transmit the Air Chief Marshal's views through the War Cabinet to the Prime Minister. The duty of the Air Force in the Middle East is to provide the maximum air effort in Greece and Turkey agreeable with the nourishing of operations in the Sudan and Abyssinia and the maintenance of Benghazi.

(l) The Foreign Secretary will consult with Admiral Cunningham upon naval operations necessary for all the above purposes, and will ask HMG for any further support either by transports or warships which may seem necessary.

(m) He will propose to HMG any policy concerning Iraq, Palestine or Arabia which may harmonize with the above purposes. He may communicate direct with these countries and with the Government of India, though not in a mandatory sense. The India Office must be kept informed.

(n) He will report upon the whole position at Gibraltar, Malta, and if possible on return at Takoradi.

(o) In short, he is to gather together all the threads, and propose continuously the best solutions for our difficulties, and not be deterred from acting upon his own authority if the urgency is too great to allow reference home.

Winston S. Churchill to Sir John Anderson

(*Churchill papers, 20/36*)

12 February 1941

There is too much truth in what Dr Burgin[1] says for him to be put off by the usual official grimace. I suggest that you see him and deal with the proposition at 'A'.[2] I hear a great many cases where the Government absolutely fail to pay individuals what is admittedly their due. It seems to me that Dr Burgin's letter might prove a very good peg for you to hang a real stirring-up of these

[1] Edward Leslie Burgin, 1887–1945. Educated in Lausanne and Paris. Solicitor. Intelligence Officer, 1916–18 (on active service in Italy, despatches). Liberal MP for Luton, 1929–45 (Liberal National since 1931). Charity Commissioner, 1931–32. Parliamentary Secretary, Board of Trade, 1932–37. Privy Councillor, 1937. Minister of Transport, 1937–39. Minister of Supply, 1939–40.

[2] Leslie Burgin had complained about the Government's indifference with regard to problems besetting employers.

Departments upon. When one is in Office one has no idea how damnable things can feel to the ordinary rank and file of the public. Dr Burgin is a very able man and has experience. Could you not draw him out and see what suggestions he has to make, and also what examples he has to give of the shortcomings which I fear with too much justice he alleges?

Winston S. Churchill to Sir Michael Palairet[1] *and General Wavell*

(*Churchill papers, 20/49*)

12 February 1941

VISIT OF ANTHONY EDEN AND GENERAL DILL TO THE MIDDLE EAST

Request you will take all possible precautions for safety of our two Envoys having regard to nasty habits of Wops and Huns.

Winston S. Churchill to General Wavell

(*Cabinet papers, 69/2*)

12 February 1941
Most Secret and Personal

1. Accept my heartfelt congratulations on this latest admirable victory, and on the unexpected speed with which Cyrenaica has been conquered. I have carried out your wishes in mentioning Generals O'Connor and Creagh.

2. Defence Committee considered whole situation last night, comprising extremely favourable developments in United States supplies. Second, increasingly menacing attitude of Japan and plain possibility she may attack us in the near future. Third, undoubted serious probability of attempt invasion here. In this general setting we must settle Mediterranean plans.

3. We should have been content with making a safe flank for Egypt at Tobruk, and we told you that thereafter Greece and/or Turkey must have priority, but that if you could get Benghazi easily and without prejudice to European calls so much the better. We are delighted that you have got this prize three weeks ahead of expectation, but this does not alter, indeed it rather confirms, our previous directive, namely, that your major effort must now be to aid Greece and/or Turkey. This rules out any serious effort against Tripoli, although minor demonstrations thitherwards would be a useful feint. You should therefore make yourself secure in Benghazi and concentrate all available forces in the Delta in preparation for movement to Europe.

[1] Michael Palairet, 1882–1956. Entered the Diplomatic Service, 1905. Minister to Roumania, 1929–35; to Sweden, 1935–7; to Austria, 1937–8; to Greece, 1939–42. Knighted, 1938. Assistant Under-Secretary of State, Foreign Office, 1943–5.

4. Both Greece and Turkey have hitherto refused our offers of technical Units, because they say these are too small to solve their main problem, but conspicuous enough to provoke German intervention. However, this intervention becomes more certain and imminent every day, and may begin at any time now. If Turkey and Yugoslavia would tell Bulgaria they will attack her unless she joins them in resisting a German advance southward, this might create a barrier requiring much larger German forces than are now available in Roumania. But I fear they will not do this, and will fool away their chances of combined resistance, as was done in the Low Countries.

5. Our first thoughts must be for our ally Greece, which His actually fighting so well. If Greece is trampled down or forced to make a separate peace with Italy, yielding also Air and Naval strategic points against us to Germany, effect on Turkey will be very bad. But if Greece, with British aid, can hold up for some months German advance, chances of Turkish intervention will be favoured. Therefore, it would seem that we should try to get in a position to offer the Greeks the transfer to Greece of the fighting portion of the Army which has hitherto defended Egypt, and make every plan for sending and reinforcing it to the limit with men and material.

6. We do not know what Greece will say to a great offer of this kind. We do not know what are her means of resisting an invasion from Bulgaria by German forces. It is reasonable to assume that they have a plan to move troops from Albania to hold the Passes and lines of defence already built along or near the Bulgarian frontier. They cannot surely have pursued their advantage in Albania without any thought of this mortal danger to their right and almost rear. If they have a good plan it would be worth our while to back it with all our strength, and fight the Germans in Greece, hoping thereby to draw in both Turks and Yugoslavs. You should begin forthwith plans and timetables, as well as any preparatory movements of shipping.

7. It is not intended that you should delay Mandibles, which we regard as most urgent.

8. In order to give the very best chance to concerting all possible measures; both diplomatic and military, against the Germans in the Balkans, we are sending the Foreign Secretary and CIGS to join you in Cairo. They will leave on the 12th February and should reach you 14th or 15th February. Having surveyed the whole position in Cairo and got all preparatory measures on the move, you would no doubt go to Athens with them, and thereafter, if convenient, to Angora. It is hoped that at least four divisions, including one armoured division, and whatever additional air forces the Greek airfields are ready for, together with all available munitions, may be offered in the best possible way and in the shortest time.

9. We can form no opinion here as to what ports of Greece we should use or what front we should try to hold or try to get them to hold. That can only be settled on the spot with the Greek Command.

10. In the event of it proving impossible to reach any good agreement with the Greeks, and work out a practical military plan, then we must try to save as much from the wreck as possible. We must, at all costs, keep Crete and take any Greek islands which are of use as air bases. We could also reconsider the advance on Tripoli. But these will only be consolation prizes after the classic race has been lost. There will, of course, always remain the support of Turkey.

11. You will, of course, show this to Longmore and give him my best regards.

12. Operative orders are being sent by the Chiefs of Staff.

Winston S. Churchill to L. S. Amery[1]
(*Churchill papers, 20/21*)

12 February 1941
Midnight

My dear Leo,

I agree with what you say in your letter of February 10,[2] and if wishes were acts we could rejoice together. You will see in a day or two what we have done. Pray remember however how limited are our resources and how inexorable the obstacles of time and space.

Yours very sincerely,
Winston S. Churchill

Winston S. Churchill to David Margesson
(*Churchill papers, 20/36*)

13 February 1941
Action this Day

Major Kermit Roosevelt[3] has been to me in great distress, because although his own doctors and his Regimental doctor have said he was quite fit, the

[1] Leopold Charles Maurice Stennett Amery, 1873–1955. A contemporary of Churchill at Harrow. Fellow of All Souls College, Oxford, 1897. *Manchester Guardian* correspondent in the Balkans and Turkey, 1897–9. Served on the editorial staff of *The Times*, 1899–1909. Conservative MP, 1911–45. Intelligence Officer in the Balkans and eastern Mediterranean, 1915–16. Assistant Secretary, War Cabinet Secretariat, 1917–18. Parliamentary Under-Secretary, Colonial Office, 1919–21. First Lord of the Admiralty, 1922–4. Colonial Secretary, 1924–9. Secretary of State for India and Burma, 1940–5. Known as 'Leo'.

[2] About the need to advance through Libya.

[3] Kermit Roosevelt, –1943. Son of President Theodore Roosevelt. Commissioned in the British Army, 1915; on active service in Mesopotamia (Military Cross). Captain, Motor Machine Guns. Transferred to the American Army, 1916; on active service commanding an artillery battery, 1917–18. Major, British Army, September 1939 to March 1940 and June 1940 to May 1941.

Millbank doctors have marked him 'E' this morning, thus putting him out of the Army. When he came originally to me at the Admiralty in October 1939, I considered it a matter of political consequence that his wish to serve with us in the fight should be granted. I thought it symbolic. I still think that he should not be treated as an ordinary case, and if he wishes to go on with us he should be allowed to do so.

Will you very kindly look into the matter. His morale is very high, and he is very unhappy at the idea of being invalided out now.

Winston S. Churchill to General Ismay, for the Chiefs of Staff Committee
(*Churchill papers, 20/36*)

13 February 1941
Secret
Action this Day

I do not approve the composition of this convoy, which in its 42,000 men includes only a small proportion of fighting troops, apart from passive defence like CD.[1] Only one Regular Battalion is included. We have not at present in ME a single organized British Division, and General Wavell is trying to scrape together enough to form the 6th Division, the only one in sight.

Let me have a proposal to send instead of some of these non-combatant details, one complete Infantry Division from this country. How many ships will it require?

We have also been told repeatedly that the 7th Australian Division cannot be considered available for lack of equipment. We should, therefore, send out the necessary fighting equipment in store-ships.

This convoy, as at present composed, would give General Wavell well over 400,000 men out of which surprisingly few tactical fighting Units can apparently be organized.

It must be remembered that the whole character of the problem is altered by the fall of Benghazi, and the almost certain decision not to advance into Tripoli. The Services which have hitherto borne the strain of the desert fighting, can in large part now be diverted to any operation undertaken elsewhere. Have all these proposals been reviewed in the light of these important strategic changes?

I will go through the details with the War Office this evening at 9.30. Let everything be prepared, and warn the necessary Officers to attend.

[1] Coastal Defence.

Winston S. Churchill to Colonel Hollis[1]
(*Churchill papers, 20/36*)

13 February 1941

Why is it necessary to send 16 25-pounder guns to India, when they are so urgently needed here and in the Middle East? Pray let me know whether there are any more to go, and what the programme is.

Winston S. Churchill to General Wavell
(*Churchill papers, 20/49*)

13 February 1941

You know by now who are coming and when.[2] Meanwhile, proceed as in paragraph 4[3] and get all convenient things moving in that direction.

Winston S. Churchill to General Wavell
(*Churchill papers, 20/49*)

14 February 1941

Our friends are unhappily held up 48 hours at Plymouth by bad weather, but you will no doubt be making arrangements to facilitate decisions being taken rapidly when they arrive. War Office have sent you a telegram which resulted from a long day's work on composition of WS 7.[4] I am trying to get another 8 MT ships[5] out of the Import Executive, which would allow me to send you 50th Division complete without depriving you of the most essential details for which you have asked. The situation having been changed by your victories, a new view of desert communications requirements may be taken. I should feel more comfortable about the Army of the Nile if it had two good British Divisions.

[1] Leslie Chasemore Hollis, 1897–1963. Joined the Royal Marine Light Infantry, 1914. Served with the Grand Fleet and Harwich Force, 1915–18, including the Battle of Jutland. Assistant Secretary, Committee of Imperial Defence, 1936–9. Lieutenant-Colonel, 1937. Senior Assistant Secretary in the office of the War Cabinet, 1939–46. CBE, 1942. Major-General, 1943. Sole representative of the Defence Office with Churchill, during the Prime Minister's illness at Carthage and recuperation at Marrakech, 1943–4. Knighted, 1946. Chief Staff Officer to the Minister of Defence, 1947–9. Commandant General, Royal Marines, 1949–52. Author of *One Marine's Tale* (1956) and *War at the Top* (1959).

[2] The visit of Anthony Eden and General Sir John Dill to Athens.

[3] The proposal to instruct Eden and Dill to examine with the Greek General Staff the problem of British help for Greece.

[4] The seventh convoy from Britain to Egypt via the Cape of Good Hope.

[5] Motor transport ship.

Winston S. Churchill to Sir Andrew Duncan, for the Import Executive
(*Churchill papers, 20/36*)

14 February 1941
Most Secret

I am very anxious to send a complete infantry division with their guns and essential vehicles to the Middle East in Convoy WS 7. The men can be fitted in by displacing others, but the guns and vehicles will require extra ships. I am told that 8 MT ships will be wanted over and above those required to carry the 450 vehicles which the War Office already wish to send in the Convoy.

I understand that loading would have to start about 21st February if these ships are to arrive in Egypt at the same time or shortly after the Convoy. Pray consider how these 8 ships could be found and let me have a report of what can be done and at what cost in imports, but take no action in the meanwhile.

Winston S. Churchill to A. V. Alexander
(*Churchill papers, 20/36*)

14 February 1941

I enclose a copy of Mr Justice Oliver's[1] Report on the Convoy question. The main proposals in the Report for future action fall under four heads:

(1) Trade Convoys.

Paragraph 4 states that a very detailed examination would be necessary before anything but the most cursory conclusion could be reached on Trade Convoys. In paragraph 5 it is suggested that attention should be concentrated on the most stringent safeguarding of the route to be followed.

Is it your view that the more detailed enquiry suggested in paragraph 4 is called for?

(2) War Convoys.

Paragraphs 6 to 18 deal mainly with the production of Most Secret documents dealing with convoys and with the procedure for handling such documents.

Most of the suggestions made in the Report cover much the same ground as the general Memorandum on Security Matters which, by my directions, was recently circulated to Departments for their comments before issue. The

[1] Roland Giffard Oliver, 1882–1967. On active service, 1914–18 (Military Cross). Recorder of Folkestone, 1926–38. Member of the Budget Enquiry Committee, 1936. Chairman of the Committee on Court Martial Procedure, 1938. Knighted, 1938. Judge of the High Court of Justice, King's Bench Division, 1938–57. Chairman of the Prison and Detention Barracks Enquiry, 1943.

Report, however, contains one new and very important suggestion, namely, the use for very Secret matters of coloured paper, each sheet of which would be numbered and accounted for.

I wish to be furnished with a report showing the steps taken by the Departments concerned to limit the amount of information circulated in regard to war convoys. The most drastic reduction should be made in the number of persons who are given detailed information with a clear bearing on our future military plans. The arrangements made on this matter must conform to the general principle that information of Most Secret matters is only conveyed to those who must know it in order to perform their job.

The general application of the precautions suggested by Mr Justice Oliver for dealing with Most Secret Papers will be taken up as part of the general drive on Security matters referred to above.

(3) Closely connected with (2) is the suggestion in paragraph 11 that the question of war convoys should be handled as a whole in a single office.

I should be glad of the views on this suggestion of the three Service Ministers and the Minister of Shipping.

(4) Paragraphs 19 to 22 deal with the possible sources of leakage of information on war convoys through persons outside the Service. In paragraph 20 Mr Justice Oliver says that he feels baffled by the problem, which he suggests should be handled by those who have technical knowledge which he does not possess.

I should be grateful for your views and those of your colleagues as to how this part of the field had best be tackled.

I am sending a copy of this Minute, and of Mr Justice Oliver's Report, to the Secretaries of State for War and Air, and to the Minister of Shipping.

Winston S. Churchill to Brendan Bracken

(*Churchill papers, 20/36*)

14 February 1941

I doubt very much whether you are right in supposing that the Allied Governments here are entirely content with the propaganda issued from the BBC to their respective countries. Many complaints reach me. I doubt whether they have sufficient opportunities of consultation with the Ministry of Information. After all they must know more about their own countries than we do, and it is to our interest to give them the best possible chance of keeping alive under increasingly difficult circumstances.

Winston S. Churchill to General Wavell
(*Churchill papers, 20/49*)

14 February 1941

About Catroux,[1] &c CIGS has told you what I have ascertained here, namely, that Catroux had ample warning of Gentilhomme's[2] arrival, and that he would be put under your orders. General de Gaulle does not think that Catroux will persist in his resignation. He certainly has no grounds for doing so in my opinion. I consider de Gaulle a bigger man than Catroux. Indeed I find him very remarkable, having regard to the heartbreaking difficulties of his position. His authority should be respected by Catroux, and it is the only Free French authority recognized by His Majesty's Government. As to 'Marie',[3] we all thought here it would be a very useful step, though it would have to be timed and taken in relation to larger situations. There is no need to come to any decision about it at the present time.

Winston S. Churchill to Sir John Squire[4]
(*Churchill papers, 20/21*)

14 February 1941
Private and Confidential

Dear Sir John

Thank you for your letter of January 30 about the equipment and state of readiness of the Home Guard. I am afraid it will be some time before there is a rifle for every man in the Home Guard. The additional supplies we have asked for from the United States are not yet available.

[1] Georges Catroux, 1877–1969. A professional soldier, he spent most his career in Syria, where in 1930 a young staff officer, Captain de Gaulle, was much impressed by his ability to rouse local sympathy and respect. As Governor-General of Indo-China in 1940, he was the only French proconsul and the only Général d'Armée to join de Gaulle, for which he was condemned to death by Vichy. In 1941 he was appointed by de Gaulle to Command the Free French forces against the Vichy forces in the Syrian campaign. Free French representative in Algeria, 1943. Ambassador to Moscow, 1945–8. Honorary British knighthood, 1946. Governor-General of Algeria, 1956.

[2] General Paul-Louis Le Gentilhomme. Commanding the French troops on the Somali coast, 1940, with his headquarters at Jibuti. He was one of only two commanders and Governors-General (the other being General Catroux in Indo-China) who maintained their opposition to Vichy. He was unable to persuade his subordinates to remain in the war. In April 1941 he led seven battalions of Free French troops against the Vichy forces in Syria, when, despite being severely wounded, he continued in action. A member of the Free French National Committee, 1941, in charge of the War Department.

[3] The proposed capture of Jibuti by Free French Forces, with British support.

[4] John Collings Squire, 1884–1958. Poet and literary critic. Educated at Blundell's and St John's College, Cambridge. Literary Editor of the *New Statesman*, 1913; acting Editor, 1917–18. Unsuccessful Parliamentary Candidate (Labour), 1918 and 1924. Editor of the *London Mercury*, 1919–34. Knighted, 1933. Author of more than forty volumes of poetry and essays.

I have recently called for the issue of orders to overhaul the local defence schemes now Spring is in sight, and to make sure that every man in the Home Guard knows where to go and what to do when the alarm is given. In back areas it may be that in the early stages of an invasion there would be little to do but keep a look out and an inlying piquet ready to deal with parachutists and the like. On the other hand, if there were an airborne landing on a considerable scale, Home Guards might well find themselves involved in their defence duties almost at once. The former duty however will be none the less important because it may involve long periods of watching without anything happening.

The idea of a dress rehearsal is one of which I entirely approve and in fact orders have already been issued in certain Commands for it to be carried out. Care has to be taken however not to interfere unduly with work of national importance.

Yours vy truly
Winston S. Churchill

Winston S. Churchill to Foreign Office and Chiefs of Staff Committee
(*Churchill papers, 20/36*)

15 February 1941

Would it not be well for me to ask President Roosevelt to instruct Admiral Leahy to make representations to Marshal Pétain about the anxiety which we feel at the predominating influence of Admiral Darlan.[1] It should be pointed out that Admiral Darlan nourishes abnormal and professional resentment against this country, and that he is believed to have advocated declaration of war with us on several occasions. Such a representation would probably draw disclaimers both from Pétain and the Admiral, and Admiral Leahy would no doubt have talks with Admiral Darlan, and might bring him round and rally him to his duty. In fact, I think that Admiral Leahy might try to be the means of improving Darlan as far as possible, and anyhow finding out how we stand with him.

The matter is very serious in the light of the stories that Pétain at 84 is going to have an operation for prostate gland, which might well carry him off.

[1] Jean Louis Xavier Francois Darlan, 1881–1942. Entered the French Navy, 1899. On active service, 1914–18 (three citations). Admiral, 1933. Commander-in-Chief of the French Navy from April 1939 to June 1940. Minister of Marine (under the Vichy Government) from June 1940 to April 1942. Distrusted by the Germans. He was in North Africa visiting his sick son when the Allies landed on 8 November 1942. Chief of State in French North Africa (with General Eisenhower's approval) from 11 November 1942 until his assassination on 24 December 1942.

Winston S. Churchill to General Ismay
(Churchill papers, 20/36)

15 February 1941

I do not remember having been consulted in any way upon the proposal to land parachute troops in Italy. I remember hearing about the project to land men from a submarine to attack bridges from the coast. The use of parachute troops was a serious step to take, in view of the invasion aspect here, and I would rather not have opened this chapter, raising as it does all sorts of questions about the status and uniform of these troops.

Let me have a report as soon as possible upon the preparation and execution of this plan, showing exactly what authorities were consulted. Make sure that for the future my initial is obtained to all projects of this character.

Winston S. Churchill to General Macready[1]
(Churchill papers, 20/36)

15 February 1941

DOVER DEFENCES

From your account one would think that everything was going on splendidly and that no ground for complaint existed. But this was certainly not the opinion of the responsible Officers I met on the spot. I was distressed by the vigour of their complaints, and the evident feeling behind them. Let me have a report each week from the Commander of the Corps Coast Artillery, and let it pass through your office with any comments you may wish to make.

Winston S. Churchill: minute[2]
(Churchill papers, 20/36)

15 February 1941

The keeping open of the Suez Canal must be regarded as a prime task. For this purpose it is necessary that trustworthy watchers should be stationed

[1] Gordon Nevil Macready, 1891–1956. Only son of General Sir Nevil Macready (one of Churchill's senior advisers at the War Office in 1919). On active service, 1914–18 (despatches six times). Special Mission (to organize a police force) in Poland, 1919. Chief of the British Military Mission to the Egyptian Army, 1938. Assistant Chief of the Imperial General Staff, 1940–2. Chief of the British Army Staff at Washington, 1942. Knighted, 1945. Regional Commissioner for Lower Saxony, 1946–7. Colonel-Commandant, Royal Engineers, 1946–56. Economic Adviser to the UK High Commissioner in Germany, 1949–51.

[2] This minute (Prime Minister's Personal Minute, M.170/1) was sent to General Ismay for the Chiefs of Staff Committee, and also to A.V. Alexander (First Lord of the Admiralty), Admiral Pound (First Sea Lord), David Margesson (Secretary of State for War) and the Assistant Chief of the Imperial General Staff (General MacCready).

constantly every hundred yards or so to spot the fall of mines from aircraft. It would be a pity to use tactical formations for this at a time when, as we are repeatedly told by the War Office and by the Command in the Middle East, we have very large numbers of trustworthy men for whom we have neither equipment nor cadres suited to tactical action in Divisions. The Yeomanry Division, the drafts waiting to replace casualties, the non-Divisional personnel waiting behind the 7th Australian Division not yet equipped or trained, should enable such a watch to be established without hindering the progress of tactical units.

Pray let a scheme be worked out for consideration here and subsequent transmission as a suggestion to ME Command.

Winston S. Churchill to Lord Woolton
(*Churchill papers, 20/36*)

15 February 1941

Will you kindly let me know whether you have anything in mind on the lines indicated in the attached cutting.[1] Some of the proposals here set out seem to me to be extremely foolish, likely to lead to waste of food-stuffs and cause far more trouble and dislocation than they are worth.

Let me know where this kind of tendentious propaganda comes from.

Please make no large departure without consulting the Cabinet beforehand.

Winston S. Churchill to James Stuart
(*Churchill papers, 20/36*)

15 February 1941

CHAIRMANSHIP OF THE BRITISH COUNCIL

This would be all right from a Departmental or Service point of view. May there not, however, be trouble with the Conservative party if one post after another of this kind goes to our Socialist Colleagues who are now well up on recent changes? Can you think of a good Conservative?[2]

[1] An article in *The Times* on 15 February 1941 headed 'New Rationing Schemes' which stated that a 'general ration for all was under consideration'. According to the article 'the consumer who selected the prime cut of meat, for instance, would have to be satisfied with less than one who chose a cheaper cut. Those so minded would be free to spend their money on partridge or fresh salmon or caviare, always provided they did not exceed the limit of expenditure laid down for any one week. Alternative schemes are under consideration, but all have this in common, that they would equalize expenditure on food, with every one being given a similar chance of obtaining equal rations of the essential foods and no more.

[2] Lord Lloyd's successor as Chairman of the British Council was the Rt Hon. Sir Malcolm Robertson, a former Ambassador to Argentina (1927–29), a Conservative Member of Parliament from 1940 to 1945.

Winston S. Churchill to Sir Edward Bridges
(*Churchill papers, 20/36*)

15 February 1941

I should like to see the arguments for maintaining the British Council set out shortly on one sheet of paper. I should have thought that with MEW on one side and M of I on the other[1] there was very little place for it. However, I have no doubt that the people working in this Department would like to state quarters on the British public. I have no doubt they do their work extremely well, but I have to think of the public. What is the staff of the British Council, and how much does it cost in one way or another per annum?

The matter cannot be settled before the Debate on Tuesday. We must not let ourselves be hustled.

Winston S. Churchill to General Ismay
(*Churchill papers, 20/36*)

15 February 1941
Secret

The Chiefs of the Staff should consider today (Saturday) the possibilities of attacking Mogadishu. Now that Kismayu has fallen so easily into our hands, one can see how much enemy resistance in this Kenya theatre was overrated. It may well be that by pushing northward rapidly, Mogadishu will fall an easy prey.

Winston S. Churchill to General Ismay
(*Churchill papers, 20/36*)

15 February 1941
Secret

Let me have the file of telegrams showing my efforts to have the attack made on Kismayu, at an early date, and the decision taken by the local General to put it off till May, with subsequent decision to strike earlier. Also General Smuts telegram of disappointment that it was put off. Let me have these as soon as possible. They can be printed later. I want to refresh my mind with the whole 4-monthly story. It all seems very discreditable to the Kenya Command, who have devoured troops from all directions and on all pretexts,

[1] The Ministry of Economic Warfare (under Hugh Dalton) and the Ministry of Information (under Brendan Bracken).

and who have done but patrol warfare and skirmishes, and only screwed up courage to take Kismayu after the rottenness of the Italians became apparent.

Let me have the telegrams by Monday.

Winston S. Churchill to General Smuts
(*Churchill papers, 20/49*)

15 February 1941
Most Secret and Personal

Joyful acceleration capture Benghazi, Cyrenaica, gives us secure flank for Egypt. Kismayu is also good. We must now try help Greeks and spur Turks to resist forthcoming German offensive towards Aegean. Cannot guarantee good results on mainland of Europe, but we must do our best and save what islands we can from the wreck should our utmost efforts prove vain. We have therefore sent Foreign Secretary and CIGS to Cairo, thereafter visiting Athens and Angora, in order to concert strongest possible front. They will probably be three weeks in ME. Pray consider whether you could meet them. Please duplicate to me through United Kingdom High Commissioner any messages you send to them.

Winston S. Churchill to Sir Edward Bridges
(*Premier papers, 4/69/1*)

15 February 1941

VULNERABILITY OF WHITEHALL TO AIR ATTACK[1]

We went through all this last September and came to the conclusion that we could fight it out in London. Meanwhile many improvements have been made although the buildings are far from secure. The difficulties of movement are very great indeed, but certainly the alternative citadels should be brought to a live state of readiness by the 1st March. I have been concerned that there is no kind of protection for GHQ, Home Forces, except that afforded by the fairly strong structure of the building in which they live.

How many bombs have been thrown within a thousand yards of the Central War Room?[2] I do not myself agree that no serious attempt has been made, but we should certainly be prepared for a new assault with two thousand and even five thousand pound bombs.

More speed and energy should be put into covering GHQ.

[1] Churchill noted on this minute: 'Circulate to War Cabinet and Service Ministers only, by my special directions'.

[2] From the outbreak of war until February 1941, there had been forty bombing attacks on the Whitehall area; 146 High Explosive bombs had fallen within a thousand yards of the Cenotaph.

Winston S. Churchill to Colonel Jacob
(*Churchill papers, 20/36*)

15 February 1941

Considering the demand for 25-pounders here to repulse invasion, I am of opinion that no more should go to India for the next three months. If they are only for training purposes, the 40 already there should be sufficient to enable gunners already skilled in handling the 18-pounder to acquire proficiency with the 25-pounder.

Winston S. Churchill to General Ismay
(*Churchill papers, 20/36*)

15 February 1941

PREPARATION OF THE PUBLIC MIND FOR INVASION

. . . the point I was after was what is to be the signal or signals, because that was asked in the Questions and I have undertaken responsibility that it is all right. On the general issue I do not believe the Vice-Chiefs are any better prophets than anyone else. I do not wish leaflets and propaganda to be put out till I have seen them. There is an M of I leaflet about 'staying put', which is mentioned today in the papers, and does not seem very good. It is most important that the directions should be considered as a whole, and not put out piecemeal in little pamphlets and penny numbers.

I have become increasingly convinced that the reduction in the population in the coastal zones should begin now. I am told there are 25,000 more people in Brighton than is usual at this time of year. We must begin persuading the people to go away, and at the same time Officers should go round and explain to those who wish to stay what is the safest place in their houses, and that they will not be able to leave after the flag falls. Pray get this on the move, and report to me.

Winston S. Churchill to Professor Lindemann
(*Churchill papers, 20/36*)

15 February 1941

NOTIFICATIONS OF INFECTIOUS DISEASES

It seems to me that the Scotch are much worse than the English, but that on the whole, especially in England, we are better than in 1939. It is astonishing that pneumonia and diphtheria should be so much less than in peace time. Pray let me have any comments from a statistical point of view.

Winston S. Churchill to F.W. Pethick-Lawrence, MP[1]
(*Churchill papers, 20/21*)

15 February 1941
Private

Dear Mr Pethick-Lawrence,

The remarkable representation which the Scottish people have in the high positions both at Home and abroad in the British Government and in the armies, should I think be borne in mind. Care is always taken to use the word British in dealing with the actions of the State. I could not however accept the view that the word English is never to be used.

We are a very humble folk, bearing many burdens, but we have also our small place on the pages of history. I have taken very great pains, as you can see from recent appointments, to meet Scottish Nationalist sentiment; but I get a little nettled sometimes by the very small clique who write indignant letters if ever the word England is mentioned. I do not believe that clique expresses at all the opinions of the Scottish people, who are too sure of themselves to be so petty.

Yours very faithfully,
Winston S. Churchill

Winston S. Churchill to Sir Andrew Duncan
(*Churchill papers, 20/36*)

15 February 1941

OPERATION 'RUBBLE'[2]

You told me Binney[3] did the whole thing, and, therefore, I do not see why he should not have an exceptional honour. I do not see why he should be embarrassed. However, if you abandon Binney I cannot fight for him.

[1] Frederick William Pethick-Lawrence, 1871–1961. Educated at Eton and Trinity College, Cambridge. Opposed the South Africa War. Editor, *The Echo*, 1902–05. Editor, *Labour Record and Review*, 1905–07; Joint-Editor, *Votes for Women*, 1907–14. Sentenced to nine months in prison for conspiracy in connection with a military suffragette demonstration, 1912. Unsuccessful Peace Negotiation candidate for South Aberdeen, 1917. Labour Member of Parliament, West Leicester, 1923–31; East Edinburgh, 1935–45. Financial Secretary to the Treasury, 1929–31. Secretary of State for India and Burma, 1945–47. Created Baron, 1945. Member of the Political Honours Scrutiny Committee, 1949–61.

[2] Norwegian merchant ships running the German naval blockade from the Swedish port of Gothenburg, escorted by the Royal Navy.

[3] Thomas Hugh Binney, 1883–1953. Gunnery Officer, *Queen Elizabeth*, 1914–18 (Distinguished Service Order, 1919). Deputy Director, Plans Division, Admiralty, 1925–27. Director Tactical School, 1931–32. Commanded HMS *Hood*, 1932–33. Rear-Admiral, First Battle Squadron, 1936–38. Commandant, Imperial Defence College, 1939. Admiral Commanding Orkneys and Shetlands, 1939–42. Knighted, 1940. Governor of Tasmania, 1945–51. Despite Churchill's suggestion he received no 'exceptional honour'.

Winston S. Churchill to Jonkheer E. Michiels van Verduynen[1]
(*Churchill papers, 20/21*)

15 February 1941

My dear Excellency,

I was so pleased by the large box of cigars from Java which Your Excellency sent me on Thursday. Will you be good enough to tell those who so kindly gave them that I am delighted not only by the excellence of the cigars themselves but also by the spirit in which they were given. I have, as you know, the greatest admiration for the courage and defiance shown by the Dutch people in the trials they have had to face. They have proved that the tradition of William the Silent still lives. Whatever the future may hold, I know that their fellow countrymen in the East Indies will be no less worthy of their heritage.

Yours sincerely,
Winston S. Churchill

Winston S. Churchill to President Franklin D. Roosevelt
(*Churchill papers, 20/49*)

15 February 1941
Secret and Personal

Many drifting straws seem to indicate Japanese intention to make war on us or do something that would force us to make war on them in the next few weeks or months. I am not myself convinced that this is not a war of nerves designed to cover Japanese encroachments in Siam and Indo-China. However, I think I ought to let you know that the weight of the Japanese Navy, if thrown against us, would confront us with situations beyond the scope of our naval resources. I do not myself think that the Japanese would be likely to send the large military expedition necessary to lay siege to Singapore. The Japanese would no doubt occupy whatever strategic points and oilfields in the Dutch East Indies and thereabouts that they covet, and thus get into a far better position for a full-scale attack on Singapore later on. They would also raid Australian and New Zealand ports and coasts, causing deep anxiety in those

[1] Edgar Michiels van Verduynen, 1885–1952. A Dutch diplomat, he had been Minister in Prague before the war. Minister (later Ambassador) in London, 1939–52. Foreign Office Minister without Portfolio, Dutch Government in Exile in London, 1942–45.

Dominions, which have already sent all their best-trained fighting men to the Middle East. But the attack which I fear the most would be by raiders, including possibly battle-cruisers, upon our trade routes and communications across the Pacific and Indian Oceans. We could by courting disaster elsewhere send a few strong ships into these vast waters, but all the trade would have to go into convoy and escorts would be few and far between. Not only would this be a most grievous additional restriction and derangement of our whole war economy, but it would bring altogether to an end all reinforcements of the Armies we had planned to build up in the Middle East from Australasian and Indian sources. Any threat of a major invasion of Australia or New Zealand would, of course, force us to withdraw our Fleet from the Eastern Mediterranean with disastrous military possibilities there, the certainty that Turkey would have to make some accommodation, or re-opening of the German trade and oil supplies from the Black Sea. You will therefore see, Mr President, the awful enfeeblement of our war effort that would result merely from the sending out by Japan of her battle-cruisers and her twelve 8-inch gun cruisers into the Eastern Oceans, and still more from any serious invasion threat against the two Australasian Democracies in the Southern Pacific.

Some believe that Japan in her present mood would not hesitate to court or attempt to wage war both against Great Britain and the United States. Personally I think the odds are definitely against that, but no one can tell. Everything that you can do to inspire the Japanese with the fear of a double war may avert the danger. If, however, they come in against us and we are alone, the grave character of the consequences cannot easily be overstated.

Winston S. Churchill to Sir Alexander Cadogan

(*Churchill papers, 20/36*)

16 February 1941

JAPANESE DIPLOMATIC INTERCEPTS

These conversations and the delayed telegram have the air of being true, and make one feel the earlier conversations were real. If so, there is a decided easement, and the danger for the moment seems to have passed. The delayed telegram strongly favours this, as naturally, if they were not going to act, they would try to make amends to the Germans and Italians by sending their man on a diplomatic demonstration. Altogether I must feel very considerably reassured. I have always been doubtful they would face it.

No doubt you saw my telegram yesterday to Roosevelt. It will do no harm, I think, although the situation has somewhat changed.

Winston S. Churchill to the Ministry of Economic Warfare
(*Churchill papers, 20/36*)

16 February 1941

BRITISH PROPAGANDA TO FRANCE AND BELGIUM

I agree about co-ordinated leaflets, but all depends upon an intimate liaison between you and M of I on the one hand, and De Gaulle on the other. We must not tie De Gaulle up too tightly. We have never received the slightest good treatment or even courtesy from Vichy, and the Free French movement remains our dominant policy. I am sure if you consult with De Gaulle or his people, all will be satisfactory. I think he is much the best Frenchman now in the arena, and I want him taken care of as much as possible.

Winston S. Churchill to Sir Alexander Cadogan
(*Churchill papers, 20/36*)

16 February 1941

Please make sure that Mr Eden receives on arrival at Cairo an effective summary of all the dominating telegrams from the Balkans which are now coming in. The summary should not exceed four pages.

Winston S. Churchill to Sir Alexander Cadogan
(*Churchill papers, 20/36*)

16 February 1941

I am going to give myself a treat while I am in charge of the Foreign Office.[1] Will you please give directions that all well-known names like Constantinople, Adrianople, Smyrna, Siam, &c., which have undergone recent changes, are to be printed in all domestic Foreign Office publications, printed or typed, as follows:

Istanbul (Constantinople).

Thailand (Siam).

Report to me what names you will treat in this way.

[1] In Anthony Eden's absence.

Winston S. Churchill to A. V. Alexander
(*Churchill papers, 20/36*)

16 February 1941

SHIPPING FIGURES, TO BE SENT TO HARRY HOPKINS

I think it would be better not to send these additional figures at the present time, but to wait until the proper Statistical Branches on each side are in operation. Nothing causes more friction than statistics emanating from different authorities, which are discordant through being based on slightly different data.

I hope you agree.

Winston S. Churchill to David Margesson
(*Churchill papers, 20/36*)

16 February 1941

POSSIBLE HONOUR FOR GENERAL CREAGH

I think it such a pity to give Honours in a sort of automatic routine way, like all our Civil Servants receive them in due course, and everyone gets their K and G.[1] A brilliant action should be recognized in a striking and exceptional fashion.[2] It will be all the better if it makes a stir. I see no reason to consult General Wavell.

I was very doubtful whether the Admiral should have a GCB. But it would have been invidious to leave him out.

Winston S. Churchill to Sir Alexander Cadogan
(*Premier papers, 3/69A*)

16 February 1941
Secret

I thought this letter[3] from Pierlot[4] pretty good cheek. The behaviour of Belgium before the war constituted an act of scandalous ingratitude, as well as

[1] K: the Knighthood of an Order of Chivalry; G: the Grand Cross of the Order, the highest rank.

[2] General Creagh got his 'K' (a KBE, Knighthood of the Order of the British Empire). It is not clear what 'striking and exceptional' honour Churchill had in mind.

[3] Protesting against Churchill's reference in his recent broadcast to Belgian foreign policy before the war.

[4] Hubert Pierlot, Prime Minister of Belgium, February 1939 to February 1945 (also Foreign Minister, April to September 1939). Headed the Belgian Government in exile in London from June 1940. Two of his sons were killed in a railway accident in Britain in April 1941.

of purblind folly, now proved. After the war had begun, the King's attitude and that of his Government in treating Germany and Britain (with its 600,000 graves on Belgian soil) as if they were 'six of one and half-a-dozen of the other', was an ineffaceable blot on the Belgian name. In addition, their frantic appeal for our help at the last moment, and their desertion at the first moment, are terrible deeds.

Remembering all this, I wonder whether my answer is not sufficiently stiff. If not, pray amend it. One must always remember that they are down and out, and have no hope but from the England they deserted and cruelly injured.

On 17 February 1941 a War Office communiqué stated: 'No Italians remain on the soil of Egypt, the Sudan or Kenya except as prisoners.'

Winston S. Churchill to Viscount Halifax
(*Churchill papers, 20/49*)

17 February 1941

In the light of this telegram and of other reports which we have received about Admiral Darlan, we feel great anxiety at the predominant influence which he now exercises at Vichy. He nourishes abnormal and professional resentment against this country, and we have even been told that he has advocated action which would be tantamount to a declaration of war on us. The matter is now very serious in view of a report which has reached us that Marshal Pétain is to have a prostate operation which may well carry him off, in which case, as matters now stand, Darlan would succeed him.

2. I should be grateful if President Roosevelt were able to instruct Admiral Leahy to talk to Marshal Pétain about our anxieties on this score. Such a representation would probably draw disclaimers both from Marshal Pétain and Admiral Dalan, but Admiral Leahy would no doubt also talk to Admiral Darlan and might bring him round and rally him to his duty. In fact, Admiral Leahy might be the means of improving Darlan as much as possible, and anyhow of finding out how we stand with him.

Winston S. Churchill to Foreign Office
(*Churchill papers, 20/36*)

17 February 1941
Secret

POSSIBLE APPOINTMENT OF ADMIRAL DARLAN AS SUCCESSOR TO MARSHAL PÉTAIN

I regard these developments with misgiving and distrust. We have received nothing but ill-treatment from Vichy. It would have been better to have had Laval, from our point of view, than Darlan, who is a dangerous, bitter, ambitious man without the odium which attaches to Laval. I think it is important at the moment to be stiff with these people, and to assert the blockade whenever our ships are available. In the meantime, an end should be put to the cold-shouldering of General de Gaulle and the Free French movement, who are the only people who have done anything for us, and to whom we have made very solemn engagements. The emphasis should be somewhat shifted.

Please also see in this connection my telegram to the President.

Winston S. Churchill to the War Office[1]
(*Churchill papers, 20/36*)

17 February 1941

General Wavell has 31 British Regular Battalions of which, as far as I can make out, only about 15 are incorporated in divisional formations. Pray correct me if I am wrong. It is indeed astonishing that he should be put to these straits to find a few Battalions for Crete and Malta. If the West African Brigade were transferred from Kenya to Freetown, two British Battalions now degenerating there could come forward to the Nile Army.

The use of three Battalions to escort prisoners to India, the whole Yeomanry and Regular Cavalry Division unemployed in Palestine, large numbers of Australian troops for which we are told there is no equipment on the regular scale of establishment, the Polish Brigade, the drafts awaiting incorporation in Units which have not yet suffered any casualties – all these are large resources if ingeniously and economically used.

Are there any British Battalions in East Africa?

Please give me your aid in the study of these aspects.

[1] This minute was addressed to the Vice-Chief of the Imperial General Staff (General Haining) and the Director of Military Operations (General Kennedy).

Winston S. Churchill: minute[1]
(Churchill papers, 20/36)

17 February 1941

POSSIBLE GUARANTEE TO THE NETHERLANDS EAST INDIES

This matter is not immediately urgent, and I doubt myself whether the issue will present itself in this particular form. The American attitude is all-important, and it would not be wise to raise the matter again with them until after the Lease and Lend Bill is through, when the President will have a much freer hand. Bring up again thereafter.

Winston S. Churchill to David Margesson and General Sir Robert Haining[1]
(Churchill papers, 20/36)

17 February 1941
Action this Day

TRANSFER OF A DIVISION TO NORTHERN IRELAND

1. I do not think it is desirable to move this Division, especially in view of the possibilities of our sending the Fiftieth away.

2. Meanwhile, plans should be worked out to procure the necessary acceleration should a move become indispensable. These plans should include (a) a reconsideration of the Admiralty objections to using the Mersey as well as the Clyde. Are there no smaller ports from which embarkation could be made? (b) Would it not be possible to arrange the move on the basis of a precautionary period of four days in which additional MT ships could be assembled? (c) The objections about moving part of the vehicles deserve further study. For instance, the troops might have issued to them an additional quantity of transport while in England to break it in, and then either this or the old could be sent to Ireland. I cannot believe that there is no floating reserve of transport capable of providing for such a small need as this. A little combing out and tightening up of the Mechanical Transport Depots, Slough, &c., would certainly yield what is required.

3. We must not be content with anything less than a saving of five days out of the eleven during which the Division will be out of action on both sides of the Channel. This period must be shortened to six days, but a reasonable precautionary notice might be expected.

[1] This minute was addressed to the Foreign Office, and to General Ismay for the Chiefs of Staff Committee.

[2] Robert Hadden Haining, 1882–1959. 2nd Lieutenant, 1901; Major, 1915. On active service, 1914–18 (despatches six times, DSO); Major-General, 1934. Commandant, Imperial Defence College, 1935–6. Deputy Director of Military Operations and Intelligence, War Office, 1936–8. General Officer Commanding the British Forces in Palestine and Transjordan, 1938–9. Knighted, 1940. Vice-Chief of the Imperial General Staff, 1940–1. Intendant-General, Middle East, 1941–2.

Winston S. Churchill to David Margesson
(*Churchill papers, 20/36*)

17 February 1941

BRITISH CAVALRY DIVISION IN PALESTINE

I deeply regret the whole story of this fine body of men, and that the War Office can devise nothing better than to bring them all home in June to begin a training which will keep them so long out of effective action.

What exactly does the CIGS mean by 'late autumn' in paragraph 3?

Meanwhile the Division will have to render whatever service is necessary in guarding the Suez Canal, maintaining order, &c., or, if necessary, escorting prisoners, so as to liberate British battalions for active service.[1]

Winston S. Churchill to Sir Alexander Cadogan
(*Churchill papers, 20/36*)

17 February 1941

Please draw attention again to Mr Eden's injunction against the length of telegrams sent to the Foreign Office by their representatives abroad.

The zeal and efficiency of a diplomatic representative is measured by the quality, and not by the quantity, of the information he supplies. He is expected to do a good deal of filtering for himself, and not simply to pour out upon us over these congested wires all the contradictory gossip which he hears. So much is sent that no true picture can be obtained. One cannot see the wood for the trees. There is no harm in sending 'background' on by Bag.

Winston S. Churchill to A. V. Alexander and Admiral Pound
(*Churchill papers, 20/36*)

17 February 1941
Secret

This appreciation[2] is far too long, and ought never to have been telegraphed in its present form.

[1] The Cavalry Division in Palestine was not an armoured but a horsed division. Owing to the difficult terrain it was sent into action against the Vichy French in Syria in 1941.

[2] A telegram from the British Embassy in Washington (No. 8 Gleam) concerning Naval Staff Conversations with the United States.

I very much deplore Admiral Bellairs[1] spreading himself in this way, and using such extreme arguments as those contained in the last sentence of paragraph 6. I trust the appreciation has not been sent in, and that a short and simple expression of our views may take its place without the need to employ all this redundancy of argument and repetition of facts, which, apart from their proportions, are present in the minds of anyone who has thought about the subject.

What has been the use of all this battling? Anyone could have seen that the United States would not base a battle-fleet on Singapore and divide their naval forces, enabling the Japanese to fight an action on even terms with either one of them. They said so weeks ago, and I particularly deprecated the raising of this controversy. Our object is to get the Americans into the war, and the proper strategic dispositions will soon emerge when they are up against reality, and not trying to enter into hypothetical paper accords beforehand.

I think we should say:

'We loyally accept the United States Navy dispositions for the Pacific. We think it is unlikely that Japan will enter the war against Great Britain and the United States. It is still more unlikely that they would attempt any serious land operations in Malaya, entailing movements of a large army and the maintenance of its communications, while a United States Fleet of adequate strength remains at Hawaii. It would, however, be a wise precaution, in our opinion, if the American Asiatic Fleet were somewhat reinforced with cruisers. Perhaps as the war develops, some enterprise with aircraft-carriers strongly supported by fast ships against the Japanese homeland towns might be attempted; but this is a matter better settled on any actual contact with the event. In the meanwhile, apart from the admirable dispositions proposed by the United States for the Atlantic, we should be glad of assistance in convoys through the Pacific and Indian Oceans against individual Japanese raiding cruisers.'

The first thing is to get the United States into the war. We can then best settle how to fight it afterwards. Admiral Bellairs is making such heavy weather over all this that he may easily turn the United States Navy Board into a hindrance and not a help to the main object, namely, the entry of the United States.

I do not see why, even if Singapore were captured, we could not protect Australia by basing a fleet on Australian ports. This would effectively prevent invasion.

[1] Roger Mowbray Bellairs, 1884–1959. Entered the Royal Navy, 1900. War Staff Officer, Grand Fleet, 1914–16 (despatches). CB, 1930. Retired with the rank of Rear-Admiral, 1932. Admiralty Representative, League of Nations Permanent Advisory Commission, 1932–9. Admiralty (including mission to USA), 1939–46; Head of the Admiralty Historical Section, 1948–56.

As for India, if the Japanese were to invade it would make the Indians loyal to the King-Emperor for a hundred years. But why would they be such fools as to get tied up there with vastly superior, unbeaten naval forces on the high seas?

Winston S. Churchill to General Ismay
(*Churchill papers, 20/36*)

17 February 1941

What are the arrangements in British Columbia for dealing with the Japanese colony there should Japan attack? The matter is, of course, one for the Canadian Government, but it would be interesting to know whether adequate forces are available in that part of the Dominion. About thirty years ago, when there were anti-Japanese riots, the Japanese showed themselves so strong and so well organised as to be able to take complete control.

Winston S. Churchill to Viscount Cranborne and Sir Kingsley Wood
(*Premier papers, 3/128*)

17 February 1941
Secret

ECONOMIC SANCTIONS AGAINST SOUTHERN IRELAND

I hope we shall not fall into the error of becoming too tender-footed in this policy.

The intention was to make Southern Ireland realize how great a wrong they were doing to the cause of freedom by their denial of the ports. We must expect they will make some complaints from time to time. A stern mood should prevail in view of the ordeals to which the British nation is exposed.

Winston S. Churchill to General Ismay, for the Chiefs of Staff Committee
(*Churchill papers, 20/36*)

17 February 1941
Secret

Although a preliminary movement on Ireland may well be a part of the German invasion plan, with a view specially to drawing off forces from this country, I cannot myself feel it would be a very deadly thrust at us. It would put the Irish against the Germans, and give us an immediate pretext, invited or not invited, to march in from the North, and also to attack the German detachments at the landing places. Any shipping used on the Irish adventure would certainly be destroyed, and would therefore be a deduction from the main invasion facilities. We should surely be able to reinforce Ireland, having the command of the sea and being so much nearer, better than would the Germans. The German Air Force could fight nowhere at so great a disadvantage as from the improvised and undefended Irish aerodromes. It is not seen why they should, at great risk and cost, cart bombs to Ireland in order to cart them back to England, when all the time they could come direct from France or Belgium. If Ireland and Great Britain were invaded simultaneously, the decision in Great Britain would govern the Irish case.

For all these reasons, I think we should feel inclined to hold ourselves loose and free in regard to such a menace, while making every scheme of which military and naval ingenuity are capable to move more troops across the Irish Channel. The more closely these moves are studied beforehand and the shorter the time they take, the better will be the options open to us.

I shall be glad to know your views.

Winston S. Churchill to General Ismay and Sir Edward Bridges
(*Cabinet papers, 120/744*)

17 February 1941
Secret

There was no need to circulate the details in para. 2[1] to anyone. The whole of the information necessary for distribution is contained in paras. 1, 3 and 4.

Let me know to whom this SR 41/10 was circulated, how many copies were struck, in what Department is the duplicating machine which struck it off, and who gave the orders for it to go in this form. Meanwhile, withdraw every copy and substitute the amended version. The copies circulated are to be destroyed by fire under the supervision of the Defence Office.

This is a very good example of what not to do.

Winston S. Churchill: minute[2]
(*Churchill papers, 20/36*)

17 February 1941

The term 'Division' must not become a stumbling block. A Division is a tactical unit of all arms for use in its integrity against the enemy. Divisions are

[1] Details relating to the movement of the Japanese Foreign Minister: those details had been acquired from diplomatic decrypts, the existence of which was a matter of the utmost secrecy.

[2] This minute was circulated to the Chiefs of Staff Committee, the Secretary of State for War, David Margesson, and the Vice Chief of the Imperial General Staff, General Haining (as Churchill's Defence Minute D.57 of 1941).

joined together to form Corps, Armies and groups of Armies, with appropriate troops for the larger formations. These characteristics do not arise where there is no prospect of using a Division in its integrity, or as a part of a larger formation. Although for administrative purposes a Divisional Command may be bestowed upon a number of troops equal to a division, who have special duties assigned to them, this should not mislead us.

2. We speak, for instance, of a 'Division' in Iceland, but it would be absurd to treat this Division as similar to those which would operate against the Germans. We now know what this Division has got to do, and how it is distributed. It is divided into the garrisons of several posts at landing places in a considerable country, and no doubt should have a number of mobile columns which can rapidly proceed to any threatened spot. Its artillery and extra Divisional troops and lines of communication services should be organized and accounted for on a scale suited to the actual task of these troops in Iceland. It should properly be called 'the Iceland Force,' and would in no way resemble the conventional establishment of a Division. It might want more of one thing and less of another.

3. The African Colonial Divisions ought not surely to be called Divisions at all. No one contemplates them standing in the line against a European army. They comprise a large body of West and East African riflemen organized in Battalions, and here and there largely for administrative purposes, in Brigades. We can now expect that the Italians will, in a few months, be liquidated in North-East Africa. What enemy, then, will oppose these three African Colonial Divisions? Anyone who knows these vast countries can see that these African 'Divisions' will be distributed in small posts and garrisons, with a number of mobile columns comprising armoured cars, &c. The idea of their being supplied with Divisional and Corps artillery, together with a share of the line of communication troops on the British scale, is not sensible. They cannot be used so far north as Libya on account of the cold. We cannot contemplate holding down Abyssinia once it has been 'liberated'. Indeed, one imagines the whole of North-East Africa returning very rapidly to peace-time conditions. Therefore I cannot accept these three African Colonial Divisions as such. They are, indeed, only miscellaneous units of the African Defence Force.

Winston S. Churchill to Lady Desborough[1]
(*Churchill papers, 20/21*)

17 February 1941

Dearest Ettie,

Thank you so much for sending me the Memoir on Evan.[2] It was so kind of you to send it to me. What a charming friend he was, and what a splendid man.

Am I right in thinking that 'Into Battle' was the title of Julian's poem engraved on the monument at Taplow? If so, I hope you will forgive me if I have trespassed upon it without asking you beforehand. I did not myself search for the title, which was merely submitted to me by Randolph among several others. Could you send me a copy of the poem? It begins: 'The fighting man shall from the sun . . .'

Yrs affec
W

Winston S. Churchill: Written Answers
(*Hansard*)

18 February 1941

Major Lloyd[3] asked the Prime Minister whether, in view of the length of speeches in proportion to the curtailment of the normal hours of sitting of the House, he will consider either extending the time of the daily sitting or adding to the number of the sittings of the House each week and thus provide greater facilities for more Members of the House to speak than exist at present or alternatively, enlist the co-operation of honourable Members by inviting them to accept a self-denying ordinance in this respect?

The Prime Minister: The question of limiting the length of speeches has been considered on many occasions but no satisfactory remedy has so far been

[1] Ethel Anne Priscilla Fane, 1867–1952. Known as 'Ettie'. Married, 1887, William Henry Grenfell, 1st Baron Desborough. Their homes at Taplow Court in Buckinghamshire, and at Panshanger in Hertfordshire, were two of the great social houses of the pre-1914 and post-war decades. Lady Desborough was a Lady of the Bedchamber to Queen Mary, 1911–36. Two of her sons, including the poet Julian Grenfell, were killed in action on the western front (in May and July 1915). Her third son died in 1926 as a result of a motor car accident.

[2] Evan Edward Charteris, 1864–1940. Sixth son of the tenth Earl of Wemyss. Barrister; King's Counsel, 1919. On active service, 1916–18 (Royal Flying Corps, Tank Corps). Chairman of the National Portrait Gallery from 1928 until his death. Knighted, 1932. A Trustee of the National Gallery, 1922–39. Biographer of John Sargent (1927) and Sir Edmund Gosse (1931). He died on 16 November 1940.

[3] Ernest Guy Richard Lloyd, 1890–1987. On active service, 1914–17 (despatches, Distinguished Service Order). On active service in France, 1939–40. Conservative Member of Parliament for East Renfrewshire, 1940–59. Knighted, 1953. Created Baronet, 1960.

found. The solution rests with hon. Members themselves and any voluntary arrangement which would allow a greater number to give expression to their views on important Debates within the time allotted would undoubtedly be to the general advantage. My hon. and gallant Friend will appreciate that the length and the number of sittings must depend primarily upon the progress of urgent and essential Government business, and I would remind him that the length of the sitting was recently extended.

Winston S. Churchill to John Moore-Brabazon[1]
(*Churchill papers, 20/36*)

18 February 1941

I am shocked to learn that those who had to take the decision to unload or divert the *New Toronto* were ignorant of the cargo which she carried. I always keep check myself personally of the approaching ships which are carrying large consignments of munitions. Do you not get these lists in good time, and do you not yourself personally watch over the fate of these vitally important cargoes? If not, please make arrangements to do so, and report to me when these arrangements are made and what they are.

Winston S. Churchill to General Ismay, for the Chiefs of Staff Committee
(*Churchill papers, 20/36*)

19 February 1941

BRITISH OFFERS TO GENERAL WEYGAND

Pray see Major Morton's letter,[2] which I fear is only too true. It is impossible to base a policy upon this grovelling crowd. Events may move them, but they have not the slightest concern for us. We have made very great offers to Weygand and I expect these may have been exploited to our enemies. For the present our attitude should remain reserved and indeterminate.

[1] John Theodore Cuthbert Moore-Brabazon, 1884–1964. Educated at Harrow and Trinity College, Cambridge. Pioneer motorist and aviator; holder of Pilot's Certificate No. 1. Won the *Daily Mail* £1,000 for flying a circular mile. 1909. Lieutenant-Colonel in charge of the Royal Flying Corps Photographic Section, 1914–18 (Military Cross, despatches thrice). Conservative MP for Chatham, 1918–29; for Wallasey, 1931–42. Chairman, Air Mails Committee, 1923. Elected to the Other Club, 1936. Parliamentary Private Secretary to the Lord Privy Seal, 1939–40. Minister of Transport, 1940–1. Minister of Aircraft Production, 1941–2. Created Baron, 1942. He published *The Brabazon Story* in 1956.

[2] Of 17 February 1941, critical of the efficacy of British contacts with General Weygand.

Winston S. Churchill to General Ismay, for the Chiefs of Staff Committee
(*Churchill papers, 20/36*)

19 February 1941

Pray give further consideration to this[1]. They must not forget our obligations to de Gaulle. We are not getting anything out of Vichy, Weygand and Co. We are in no relation with them. We have to pursue this difficult policy of making and breaking contacts. It would be a serious step to forbid de Gaulle to act as he wishes.

Winston S. Churchill to Viscount Cranborne
(*Churchill papers, 20/36*)

19 February 1941

PROPOSED VISIT BY LORD CRANBORNE TO EIRE

This matter will have to be decided by the Cabinet. Would you not find difficulties in repelling the charge that our action was 'a deliberate attempt by Great Britain to squeeze Ireland'? I have a great dislike myself of dealing in humbug, especially with a nation like the Irish. You might easily have to make some inconvenient admissions or else say what is not true. You would leave behind you a trail of courtesies, comforts and reassurances which ill consorts with the hard policy which it is our duty to pursue. I do not see what you could learn that you do not know already, only too well. We always make the mistake of not following through a policy. What can you say that would alter the situation? The time may come, but I do not feel that it has come yet.

However, if you wish to raise it in Cabinet, pray do so.

Winston S. Churchill to Herbert Morrison
(*Churchill papers, 20/36*)

19 February 1941

Surely we cannot let this matter[2] rest here? I have for a long time wondered why this ill-disposed person[3] is not given the same measure of justice as Sir Oswald Mosley. The fact that he is a Duke should make it the more necessary to treat him with severity.

[1] A note by Major Morton giving General de Gaulle's view on the future of Réunion and Madagascar.

[2] A leaflet, *Have Britons Brains*, thought to have been written by the Duke of Bedford.

[3] Hastings William Sackville Russell, Marquess of Tavistock, 1888–1953. Succeeded his father, as 12th Duke of Bedford, 1940.

Winston S. Churchill to Sir Alexander Cadogan
(*Churchill papers, 20/36*)

19 February 1941

It is impossible to make a serious advance upon Tripoli across 300 miles of desert without drawing upon our air and naval forces in such a way as to render it impossible for us to offer any effective aid to Greece or Turkey. Therefore we have sent the Foreign Secretary and CIGS to Cairo to discuss the situation on the spot with all concerned. All the points which you have made have been considered by the Chiefs of Staff and me, and their force is not denied. It may well be that neither Turkey nor Greece could accept our aid, judging it the offer of a 6-foot plank to bridge a 10-foot stream.

If, however, Greece resolves to resist the German advance we shall have to help them with whatever troops we can get there in time. They will not, I fear, be very numerous. The alternative is to invite Greece to make a separate peace with Italy at German dictation with the consequences of the German occupation of all Greek airfields. Should this happen we must save what we can from the wreck, and the other idea you favour will again become open. It may well happen.

I have read all these telegrams[1] already. Meanwhile I cordially approve of 1,2,3 marked A on page 3 of your minute.

This is the whole issue now to be discussed in Cairo. Our envoys have been delayed for five days by weather.

Winston S. Churchill to A.V. Alexander
(*Churchill papers, 20/36*)

19 February 1941
Action this Day

1. I must record in writing what I said to you yesterday, namely, that the rapid improvement of the repair of damaged ships has become one of the first objectives and needs of our National life.

2. About the *Siamese Prince*.[2] Considering the enormous importance of the cargo of this vessel, I do not understand why destroyers were not sent out to escort her in. That there were three destroyers available was shown by the fact that they were immediately sent out when it was too late. Moreover, four destroyers or more were protecting the laying of the mine-fields to the North, which, after all, is a very fantastic project and only devised as a means of using up mines made for a perfectly different purpose.

[1] From Washington and Tangier, about German infiltration into Morocco.

[2] The *Siamese Prince* was torpedoed and sunk on 17 February 1941 in the North Atlantic between Scotland and Iceland: it was one of four British merchant ships sunk that day.

Winston S. Churchill to Admiral Pound
(*Churchill papers, 20/36*)

19 February 1941
Action this Day

I should like to see the Naval dispositions set forth in Part I[1] put out on our big war map in the Admiralty war-room. At the same time the corresponding British dispositions might be considered, and we might put them on after studying the American lay-out. I do not know if you have a map free for this. If, however, it does not take too much trouble, I should like to see this at five o'clock this evening, when I would come over. We could thus survey the whole world disposition of the combined Fleets. It is a great help to me to be able to take a general view ocularly.

War Cabinet: minutes
(*Cabinet papers, 65/17*)

20 February 1941 Prime Minister's Room
12 noon House of Commons
Secret

The Prime Minister said that he had received a personal telegram from Lord Halifax stating that it was of the utmost importance that we should without delay hand over to America our remaining financial resources in that country. We should have to resign ourselves to meeting American wishes. A few weeks ago he had doubted the wisdom of this course; but he no longer did so, since it was clear that we should receive from America far more than we could possibly give. He proposed, however, to send a private telegram to the President, asking him to ensure that our securities were not taken over at knock-down prices.[2]

The Prime Minister said that the Secretary of State for Foreign Affairs and the Chief of the Imperial General Staff had now arrived at Cairo on their way to Athens and Angora. The object of this visit was to see what help could be given to the Greeks and the Turks in the event of a German advance south

[1] Of Telegram No. 11, Gleam, from Washington, reporting on the progress of the Naval Staff Conversations with the United States.

[2] After Churchill had spoken, Sir Kingsley Wood, (the Chancellor of the Exchequer) told the War Cabinet 'that this matter concerned the direct investments owned in the United States by the Insurance Companies and such firms as Courtaulds. Unless the transaction was very carefully handled, we might lose large sums. Sir Walter Peacock and others were already in the United States endeavouring to arrange for an orderly liquidation. But there was a fringe of people in America who hoped to make sums of money out of the transaction. Lord Halifax, Mr Purvis, and Sir F. Phillips all held that we must do what was asked, and he feared that we had no alternative in the matter.'

through Bulgaria and to ascertain how the diplomatic situation in that part of the world could be made to conform to the military; and what the prospects were of inducing Yugoslavia and Turkey to take action.

If the Greeks decided to oppose a German advance into their country, we should have to help them to the full extent of our power and Mr Eden would inform them of what help we could give. It might well be that a German thrust toward Salonika would be irresistible; but if the Greeks decided to fight, we should do what we could. It was possible, of course, that before making their advance the Germans would offer the Greeks such attractive terms that they would feel bound to make peace. In that case we could not very well blame them, nor should we take such a decision on the part of the Greeks too tragically. We should have done our duty and should then have to content ourselves by making our position in the Greek Islands as strong as possible. From these Islands we could wage air war against Germany, which might eventually turn in our favour.

The Prime Minister, continuing, said that the first phase of our air reinforcement of Egypt was a highly economical one. Our pilots in the Middle East, an extremely experienced body of men, were now being remounted with the best machines. Should we have to face the fact that Greece was in the enemy's hands and Turkey an honest neutral (the latter being the least we could expect) it would remain for consideration what we should do with our strong forces now in the Delta. In that event, the question of advancing into Tripoli would again arise. He hoped we should not have to put any large part of our army into Greece. In fact it was unlikely that it would be possible for a large British force to get there before the Germans.

The Prime Minister then read to the War Cabinet the instructions which had been issued to the Secretary of State for Foreign Affairs before his departure,[1] which were generally endorsed by the War Cabinet.

Winston S. Churchill to Anthony Eden
(*Churchill papers, 20/49*)

20 February 1941
Personal and Secret

Thankful you have arrived safely. I was making great exertions to carry 50th Division to you and had wrung additional shipping from Shipping Ministry with generous contribution by Admiralty. Am baffled by reply. Clearly HQ, ME, is not accurately informed about composition of convoys. For instance, Wavell believed WO were sending 11,000 drafts, whereas actual

[1] Churchill's Note to Anthony Eden of 12 February 1941.

figure was only 7,500. Also he complained of needing 3,000 signallers to make him up to about 10,000 ditto, but 3,300 signallers are in WS 5, WS 6, and in WO revised version of WS 7. Hope you will be able to clear all this up. Essential that exact details of convoys and field states should be known at both ends. My impression is one of enormous jumbles of ration strength troops in ME, with many half-baked tactical formations. 6th British Division and 7th Australian Division both seem likely to be imperfect for some time. Find out what we can send to make these effective fighting units. Some local improvisation by transfer from other half-baked units should surely be possible. Establishments are not sacrosanct if practical results obtainable on different basis. Latest Middle East ration strength return shows increase of nearly 50,000 between 31st December and 31st January. Does nothing emerge in the shape of fighting units from this reinforcement? If fighting formations are so few compared to ration strength, and in addition movement of these few formations to another theatre is so lengthy and nothing can be done to improve matters we must recognize limits of our power to act on mainland and indeed whole Middle East proposition must be relegated to secondary sphere.

2. Am concerned at check developing at Keren. Abyssinia might be left to rot but we had hopes Eritrea would be cleaned up. Try to include this in your disposition of Air and other forces.

3. Do not consider yourselves obligated to a Greek enterprise if in your hearts you feel it will only be another Norwegian fiasco. If no good plan can be made please say so. But of course you know how valuable success would be.

Winston S. Churchill to Ernest Bevin

(*Churchill papers, 20/36*)

20 February 1941

We are very short of ammunition. Production is held up entirely on account of filling, which, in turn, is held up on account of labour. With our present factories we could increase the ammunition output two and a half-fold by mid-May if we could provide the labour to run them.

The additional labour required is:

	By March 31	By Mid-May
Skilled Males	340	940
Other males	9,100	20,100
Females	22,500	40,900
Total	32,000	62,000

Please inform me what difficulties stand in the way of providing this labour and what measures are being taken to overcome them.

Winston S. Churchill to Sir Andrew Duncan
(*Churchill papers, 20/36*)

20 February 1941

It is satisfactory that arrangements have now been made to link the shipping figures more closely to those on which plans for consumption will be based.

Meanwhile, it appears that the rate of delivery of steel to consumers during the first 5 weeks of the current quarter has been no higher than during the last three quarters despite the greater need.

I understand that imports of steel during the last 7 months have been equivalent to 2.3 million finished tons and output to 5.1 million finished tons, while deliveries to consumers have been only 6.1 million finished tons. Would not the position be greatly relieved if some of this apparent excess of 1.3 million tons could be made available for consumption?

I see that imports of iron ore continue ahead of programme, while steel and other commodities lag behind. This seems strange in view of the shipping situation.

Winston S. Churchill to Franklin D. Roosevelt
(*Churchill papers, 20/49*)

20 February 1941
Secret

I have better news about Japan. Apparently Matsuoka[1] is visiting Berlin, Rome and Moscow in the near future. This may well be diplomatic sop to cover absence of action against Great Britain. If Japanese attack which seemed imminent is now postponed, this is largely due to fear of United States. The more these fears can be played upon the better, but I understand thoroughly your difficulties pending passage Bill on which our hopes depend. Appreciation given in my last Personal and Secret of naval consequences following Japanese aggression against Great Britain holds good in all circumstances.

[1] Yosuke Matsuoka, 1880–1946. Japanese delegate to the League of Nations, 1932–3; staged a dramatic walk-out when Japan was censored for its invasion of Manchuria. Foreign Minister, September 1940 to July 1941. Completed the Tripartite Pact with Germany and Italy, 23 September 1940. Signed a Neutrality Pact with Molotov, Moscow, 13 April 1940. Forced to resign because this Pact was considered by the Japanese government to be unacceptable 'direct action' on Matsuoka's part, signing an agreement with Japan's traditional enemy. In retirement, 1941–45. Tried by the Allies for his part in initiating the war, and executed.

Winston S. Churchill to Herbert Morrison
(*Churchill papers, 20/36*)

21 February 1941

You should cause careful enquiry to be made into the allegations in this letter.[1] If they were true it would be a grave reflection on the Department of the Home Office which deals with aliens. There have been other complaints of delays in dealing with these cases and of failure to acknowledge correspondence. I should like to be assured that all these cases are being dealt with as expeditiously as possible, and that no correspondence about them is left unduly long without answer or acknowledgment.

Pray let me know the result of your enquiries.

Winston S. Churchill to the Geoffrey Lloyd
(*Churchill papers, 20/36*)

21 February 1941

The very low imports of oil previously reported for the week ended the 11th January have remained low, amounting to only half what they were in January last year, and covering only half the consumption.

I trust steps are being taken to draw as much oil as possible from America, thus avoiding the long haul from the Persian Gulf round the Cape. It should be possible to arrange with the American producers for their customers in the East to be supplied from the Persian Gulf, Burma and the Netherlands East Indies in return for a corresponding amount of oil being delivered to us, some arrangement being made to retain good will.

Winston S. Churchill to Herbert Morrison and Sir Edward Bridges
(*Churchill papers, 20/36*)

21 February 1941
Action this Day

By what authority or charter does Lord Ashfield[2] give a London Transport medal for bravery? The Crown is the fountain of honour in this country, and

[1] In fact two letters, dated 11 and 16 February 1941, from a wife about the internment of her husband.

[2] Albert Henry Stanley, 1874–1948. Son of Henry Stanley of Detroit. Educated in the United States. General Manager, American Electric Railways, 1895–1907. General Manager, Metropolitan District Railway and Tube Railways in London, 1907. Managing Director of the Underground Group of Companies, 1912. Knighted, 1914. Director-General of Mechanical Transport, 1916. Conservative MP, Ashton-under-Lyne, 1916–20. President of the Board of Trade, 1916–19. Created Baron Ashfield, 1920. Chairman, Underground Group of Companies, 1919–33. Chairman, London Passenger Transport Board, 1933–47.

no-one except with special permission (as I believe in the case of the Merchant Service), has a right to assume such power. If this goes on we shall have every private firm in the country giving medals to their employees. I have no doubt all these men deserve the George Medal. The Ashfield process will have to be cancelled and the National reward substituted. We shall have the brewers giving a medal to their chuckers-out if we go on like this.

Winston S. Churchill to General Smuts
(*Churchill papers, 20/49*)

21 February 1941
Personal and Secret

I share your misgivings. I fear Russian attitude[1] has undermined Turks, and it may be that they will do no more than maintain an honest neutrality. Whole Greek position must be considered now by our Envoys at Cairo. Will keep you informed.

Winston S. Churchill to William Mackenzie King
(*Churchill papers, 20/49*)

21 February 1941

I was delighted to read your speech in the Canadian House of Commons on 17th February. You are quite right to prepare men's minds for a coming shock of extreme severity. It is a comfort to think how much better prepared we are than in the autumn.

Let me also tell you how encouraged everyone here was by the strong array of facts which you brought together when broadcasting on 2nd February. Your ships and planes are doing great work here. The Air training scheme is one of the major, and possibly the decisive, factor in the war. Your plans for the Army are of enormous help. I lunched with McNaughten[2] last week and had very good talks with him and his principal officers about the Canadian Corps. They lie in the key positions of our National Defence. The Secretary

[1] The Soviet Union was then allied to Germany (through the Ribbentrop-Molotov, or Nazi-Soviet, Pact of August 1939).

[1] Andrew George Latta McNaughten, 1887–1966. Born in Canada. On active service, 1914–18 (wounded twice, despatches thrice). Chief of the Canadian General Staff, 1929–35. Commanded the 1st Division, Canadian Overseas Force, 1939–40. Lieutenant-General, 1940. General Officer Commanding the Canadian Corps, 1940–2. General Officer Commanding-in-Chief, the First Canadian Army, 1942–4. General, 1944. President, Canadian Atomic Energy Control Board, 1946–9. His younger son, a Squadron Leader, Royal Canadian Air Force, was killed in action over Germany in 1942.

of State for War, who is with me now, wishes to endorse all this and sends his kindest regards.

What a pleasure it is to see the whole Empire pulling as one man, and believe me, my friend, I understand the reasons for your success in marshalling the great war effort of Canada.

Winston S. Churchill to Sir Alexander Cadogan
(*Churchill papers, 20/36*)

21 February 1941
Action this Day

Let me have by return the digest of the conversations[1] which are to be sent to President Roosevelt. The passage marked A in the attached is essential to the story. Be careful in making the digest you do not lose the snappiness of the dialogues. If I can have these tomorrow I will send them with a covering note. I thought about 2,000 words might be necessary for the digest.

Winston S. Churchill to Anthony Eden
(*Churchill papers, 20/49*)

21 February 1941

I have always felt it essential you should see Greeks before Angora, otherwise commitments might have been made to Angora which would tie your hands about Greeks, who are actually fighting. Therefore, am in complete agreement with procedure you propose.

Winston S. Churchill to Harry Hopkins
(*Churchill papers, 20/49*)

21 February 1941

Because of representations that have reached us, we are authorizing our Ambassador to express to the President our willingness to put the realization of all our direct investments, i.e., businesses, &c., owned by us, into the hands of a joint United States and British Board. Is this really necessary? It will place us in great difficulties here and will, we think, create embarrassments on your side.

[1] An intercepted telephone conversation between General Shingha, Nepalese Minister in London, and Vimolnart, Thai Minister in London; and an intercepted telephone conversation from Vimolnart and Iwasaki, of the Japanese Embassy, about Japanese-German plans in the Far East.

Winston S. Churchill to Hubert Pierlot
(*Premier Papers, 3/69A*)

21 February 1941

My dear Prime Minister,

I am very sorry if anything I said should have been embarrassing to you. It was far from my wish, and quite frankly, the reaction of which you speak in your letter was not one which at all occurred to me.

I cannot conceal from you my own personal belief that if Belgium had adhered to the Allied cause at the outbreak of the war, the whole movement of the French armies and the whole course of events might have taken an entirely different turn. But as you know, my policy is to look forwards and not to look back, and I am sure that any British Government which emerges successfully from this war will do its utmost to right the wrongs which Belgium has suffered.

I should like to assure you also that I thoroughly understand the extraordinary difficulties in which the Governments of small countries are placed when they lie in the midst of the great quarrels of the world; and that I by no means excuse the British Governments of the years before the war for the ambiguous and uncertain lead they gave to Europe, thus aggravating the difficulties of the smaller Powers.

I hope, therefore, you will feel full confidence in the resolve of His Majesty's Government and of the British nation to liberate Belgium once again from the oppressor, and to work with you and your Government in closest accord.

Yours very sincerely,
Winston S. Churchill

Winston S. Churchill to Air Chief Marshal Sir Charles Portal
(*Churchill papers, 20/36*)

22 February 1941
Action this Day

I do not like the tone of this telegram.[1] ACM Longmore has shown himself very unappreciative of the immense efforts we are making to support him and to increase his forces. At every stage throughout this Libyan affair we have had to press him forward beyond his judgment or inclination, with results which should be very satisfactory to him as well as to the public interest.

As you know, I have long been more than doubtful whether he is making

[1] From Air Chief Marshal Longmore, commanding the air forces in the Middle East, to the Air Ministry (in which, as well as criticisms of the air supply to the Middle East, Anthony Eden was referred to as 'Anthony' and General Sir John Dill as 'John').

efficient and effective use of the enormous Air personnel now at his disposal. He has been most pessimistic and unduly cautious at every stage. The programme of Squadrons with which he proposes to support any action in Greece and/or Turkey is far below what is necessary.

Pray let me see the answer you propose to send before it goes. It is not customary to speak of the Foreign Secretary and CIGS by their Christian names in this way, and a hint to this effect might well be given.

Winston S. Churchill to A.V. Alexander and Admiral Pound
(*Churchill papers, 20/36*)

22 February 1941
Action this Day

PROPOSED BRITISH GUARANTEE TO THE NETHERLANDS EAST INDIES

Decision on this may await the passage of the 'Lease and Lend' Bill, after which we will state our case frankly to the United States. Subject to further discussion. I am of opinion that we should now guarantee the Dutch the maintenance or return of their possessions at the end of the war, and that we will fight on till this is achieved, but that the actual method by which we achieve this, i.e., at what point we should declare war upon Japan, must rest with us, and that, meanwhile, Staff conversations should proceed without our being committed.

Winston S. Churchill to Sir Andrew Duncan
(*Churchill papers, 20/36*)

22 February 1941
Action this Day

The Prime Minister would be glad if you would bring the attached notes and diagrams[1] to the attention of the Import Executive. They have been prepared under the Prime Minister's personal direction by Professor Lindemann. They disclose a most grave and as yet unexplained tendency, which, if it is not corrected, will hazard the life of Britain and paralyse her war effort.

The Prime Minister does not understand how it is that, when the sinkings are less (although very serious) and the volume of tonnage (apart from its routeing) very little diminished, there should be such a frightful fall in imports.

He draws particular attention to Diagram D, which is most alarming. He is

[1] Charts prepared by Professor Lindemann showing merchant ship sinkings and tonnage; Lindemann also drafted this letter to the Minister of Supply.

very glad to see that according to Diagram A there is a sharp recovery in the last two weeks, and he hopes this may be the first fruits of the Import Executive.

The Prime Minister will be glad to see the Import Executive Committee at 5 p.m. on Tuesday, with a view to learning from them whether they have any further measures to propose to avert a potentially mortal danger.

Winston S. Churchill to David Margesson
(*Churchill papers, 20/36*)

22 February 1941
Secret

The approved scale of the Army is 55 Divisions plus 1 additional South African Division and minus, in my opinion, 3 African Colonial Divisions; total Tactical Divisional Units = 53, of which 11 are to be Armoured. I see no reason to alter this target at the present time.

2. During the next six months, only 130,000 men are required by the Army, and the Minister of Labour is ready to supply 150,000. Would it not be prudent to take a decision governing the six months only, and review the position in four months' time, when we shall know more of the scale and character of the fighting?

3. Will you kindly give me your views upon the Minister of Labour's paper WP (G) (41) 22, and also some notes prepared for me by Professor Lindemann which are to be treated as private. I am very much inclined to a greater development of Armoured Divisions than we have at present, but it is not necessary to take a decision at the present time, as Tanks and Tank Guns, not personnel, are the bottle-neck.

4. You may count on me to sustain the Army in every possible way, provided I am convinced that it will comb itself.

Winston S. Churchill to Sir Kingsley Wood and James Stuart
(*Churchill papers, 20/36*)

22 February 1941
Action this Day

PAYMENT OF MEMBERS OF BOTH HOUSES OF PARLIAMENT SERVING IN HM FORCES OR ASSISTING HM GOVERNMENT IN A CIVIL CAPACITY

A man who receives a salary must be returned as paid. If he draws expenses only, he may be returned as honorary. This would not apply to the Ambassadors, who should be shown as 'Expenses of representation', but may also be classed as honorary where no salary is drawn. The Regional

Commissioners should certainly be shown, and described 'paid' or 'honorary' according to circumstances. I will take the opinion of the Cabinet on Tuesday or Wednesday as to whether we cannot hold the position of not disclosing the amounts in any case. I think we should and can do so. People who do a good work and are necessary to the war effort are entitled to be paid what is regarded as sufficient for their needs and work. Each case must be judged separately. The same applies about drawing the salary of an MP while drawing other pay. This is a matter for the individual to decide, and it would be invidious to disclose his decision. I think we should ask the House to support us in the above. The whole matter is plainly one of confidence in His Majesty's Government. It might, however, also be considered whether disclosure might not be made in confidence to a Select Committee, which would be free to report any case of impropriety to the House; but I should deprecate this.

Pray let me have your advice.

Winston S. Churchill to Alfred Duff Cooper
(*Churchill papers, 20/30*)

22 February 1941

PROPOSED FURTHER BROADCASTS
BY SIR ROBERT VANSITTART TO FRANCE

Minister of Information,

I think we have had enough of this. I do not agree with Sir RV's views, and they do not represent the policy either of HMG or the USA. I have covered all this so far – but now Stop.

Hugh Dalton: diary
(*'Second World War Diary of Hugh Dalton, 1940-45'*)

22 February 1941

I tell Morton that I should like the PM to see some of the chaps in my London show.[1] It is this which leads him to say that the PM now sees fewer and fewer people and many Ministers hardly ever.

He says the PM, when he made his fateful decision not to send more fighter planes to France in the summer, said, 'I won't throw any more snowballs into hell.'

[1] As Minister of Economic Warfare, Hugh Dalton was also in charge of the Special Operations Executive (SOE) carrying out sabotage activities and liaison with partisan groups in German-occupied territory.

Winston S. Churchill to Sir Alexander Cadogan
(*Churchill papers, 20/36*)

23 February 1941

INTERCEPTS CONCERNING VICHY FRANCE AND GERMANY

All this goes to show that we should continue to give increasing support to General de Gaulle. I cannot believe that the French nation will give their loyalty to anyone who reaches the head of the State because he is thought well of by the Germans. We should reason patiently with Washington against giving any food to unoccupied France or North Africa. For this purpose, all the unsatisfactory feeling of the Vichy–Weygand scene should be in the hands of our Ambassador in Washington. I am sure Darlan is an ambitious crook. His exposure and Weygand's weakness will both, as they become apparent, inure to the credit of De Gaulle.

Winston S. Churchill to Anthony Eden
(*Churchill papers, 20/49*)

23 February 1941

FREE FRENCH INTRIGUE IN EGYPT

Have sent Morton to de Gaulle with gist of your 364 from Cairo. At the same time, I hope you will bear in mind that de Gaulle is the sole Free French authority with whom His Majesty's Government have entered into agreements and that we recognize no other chief or rival.[1]

Winston S. Churchill to Ronald Cross
(*Churchill papers, 20/21*)

23 February 1941

My dear Cross,

The kind of Press criticism of which you have sent me a specimen, and the articles which I noticed in the *Daily Mail*, will not have any effect upon your Ministerial position, and I should advise you to pay no attention to them. Everybody can see how very serious are the problems of our imports, and I have addressed a special memorandum to the Import Executive upon them.

[1] A day later, on 24 February 1941, Churchill warned Eden that Catroux's wife, who was in Cairo with her husband, 'plays a mischievous part' (Personal and Secret, *Churchill papers, 20/49*).

But I know well that only one section of these problems is under the control of the Ministry of Shipping, and that it would be most unfair to lay upon you a burden for which many Departments have been responsible.

Yours sincerely,
Winston S. Churchill

Winston S. Churchill to Anthony Eden
(*Churchill papers, 20/49*)

23 February 1941

Do not act on Cripps'[1] suggestion Stalin[2] without further reference here. Best way of gaining Russians is a good throw in Balkans. A mere visit would do no good. They might simply trade it off to Germany. I would hardly trust them for your personal safety or liberty. Of course, if they thought we would win, all would be well, but then your visit would be unnecessary and they would come to us. It is no good running after these people. Events alone will convince them and they would be glad to be convinced. If Stalin likes to invite you to meet him at Odessa that is a serious proposition, but why should he do that while odds seem heavily against us in Greece. Am deeply impressed by CIGS's telegram 0/43125. Anxiously awaiting results of your conference in Greece. Half-measures are vain.

War Cabinet: minutes
(*Cabinet papers, 65/21*)

24 February 1941
5 p.m.

The Prime Minister said that the War Cabinet had to reach a most important decision, namely, whether to open a new theatre of war in Greece.

[1] Richard Stafford Cripps, 1889–1952. Educated at Winchester. Barrister, 1913. Red Cross, France, 1914. Assistant Superintendent, Queen's Ferry Munitions Factory, 1915–18 (when his work much impressed Churchill). Labour MP, 1931–50. Solicitor-General, 1930–1. Knighted, 1930. Ambassador to Moscow, 1940–2.

[2] Josef Vissarionovich Djugashvili, 1879–1953. Born in Georgia. A Bolshevik revolutionary, he took the name Stalin (man of steel). In exile in the Siberian Arctic, 1913–16. Active in Petrograd during the October revolution, 1917. Commissar for Nationalities, 1917–18. General Secretary of the Central Committee of the Communist Party, 1922. Effective ruler of Russia from 1923. Purged his opponents with show trials, 1936–8, murdering without compunction opponents and critics, and ordinary citizens who had committed no crime. Authorized the Nazi-Soviet Pact, August 1939. Succeeded Molotov as Head of Government, May 1941. Became a Marshal of the Soviet Union, May 1943. Buried beside Lenin in the Lenin Mausoleum, 1953. 'Downgraded' to the Kremlin Wall, 1960. In 1989 Mikhail Gorbachev began the official process inside the Soviet Union of denouncing Stalin's crimes.

Among the telegrams contained in WP (41) 38 he would draw particular attention to one from himself to Mr Eden, in which he said that if it was considered that the Greek enterprise would only be another Norwegian fiasco he should say so. In spite of this telegram the Foreign Secretary, the Chief of the Imperial General Staff and General Wavell had recommended that we should send armed forces to Greece to help the Greeks meet a German advance through Bulgaria. The telegrams received on the question were impressive. General Wavell was in favour of the operation, although he was inclined to understatement, and so far had always promised less than he had performed, and was a man who wished to be better than his word. He (the Prime Minister) could imagine that General Wavell's first wish would be to complete the successful campaign in North East Africa, and clear the Italians entirely from that part of the world. General Wavell's opinion therefore in favour of action in Greece must have considerable weight. The Chief of the Imperial General Staff had, he thought, always doubted whether Germany could be successfully resisted on the mainland, and had always taken a restrained view about our going into Greece. He had now sent a remarkable telegram to the Vice Chief of Staff from the Chief of the Imperial General Staff saying that he considered by sending or forces to Greece we had a reasonable chance of resisting a German advance. Further the Chiefs of Staff had reported that, on balance, they considered that the enterprise should go forward. The Prime Minister added that, pending a decision of the Cabinet, he had given instructions for preparations for the operation to proceed. He, himself, was in favour of going to the rescue of Greece, one of the results of which might be to bring in Turkey and Yugoslavia, and to force the Germans to bring more troops from Germany. The reaction of the United States would also be favourable.

On the other hand, the difficulties of maintaining an army on land must not be under-rated, for it would have to be supplied by ships going round the Cape of Good Hope. He felt, however, that if the Greeks were to fight the Germans we must fight and suffer with them. If any of his colleagues had misgivings about the enterprise they should express them now.

Mr Menzies[1] said that before an Australian force could be employed in a new theatre of war, he would have to communicate with his colleagues. The question was clearly one of balancing risks, but there were one or two points on which he would like to be reassured. How long, for instance, would it take to put our troops into Greece, in order to take up a defensive position. Could our shipping maintain the strain of the operation? He was also a little uneasy regarding the equipment of the 7th Australian Division which was to be employed in this theatre, and which was now in Palestine, and equipped on the training scale. What were the prospects of giving full equipment to this

[1] Robert Menzies, the Prime Minister of Australia.

division? If these questions could be answered favourably, it would remove certain doubts in the minds of his colleagues in Australia.

The Prime Minister said that he did not anticipate that the German advance would take place until about the 12-15th March, and our troops should arrive at their positions at about the same time.

The Vice Chief of the Imperial General Staff said that the 7th Australian Division was fully equipped, except for divisional artillery and certain motor transport. He gave particulars of the number of 25-pounders which had been despatched to Egypt, and he had no doubt that the deficiences would be made good out of equipment already on the spot. It was practically certain that General Blamey[1] would have been called into consultation on this question. He thought that Mr Menzies could rest assured that no Australian Division would be put into line without a full establishment of the necessary weapons.

The Chief of the Air Staff, in answer to a question as to our air position in Greece, said that at the moment we had 7 squadrons in the country, but the Air Officer Commanding hoped to raise this number to 14, and possibly 16, during March. In his opinion Germany would take some little time to develop the full weight of her air effort from Bulgaria. The total strength of the German Air Force in Roumania was between 430-450 machines, but 120 of these were co-operational aircraft. We should have about 250 machines.

Mr Menzies asked whether if the enterprise failed, the price of failure would be confined to the loss of the equipment of an armoured division.

The Prime Minister said that if we should be pressed back, our troops might well have to be evacuated; but that we ought to be able to evacuate safely all but the wounded.

Mr Menzies said that the justification for the enterprise rested on the prospect of our being able to put up a good fight. If the enterprise was only a forlorn hope, it had better not be undertaken. Could he say to his colleagues in Australia that the venture had a substantial chance of success?

The Prime Minister said that in the last resort this was a question which the Australian Cabinet must assess for themselves on Mr Menzies' advice. In his (the Prime Minister's) opinion, the enterprise was a risk which we must undertake. At the worst he thought that the bulk of the men could be got back to Egypt, where new equipment could by then be provided. The war turned in his opinion on our –

(1) holding England
(2) holding Egypt
(3) retaining command of the sea
(4) obtaining command of the air and
(5) being able to keep open the American arsenals.

[1] General Sir Thomas Blamey, commanding the 1st Australian Corps in the Western Desert, see page 522, note 1.

The enterprise in Greece was an advance position which we could try to hold, without jeopardizing our main position.

The Prime Minister said that the courage of the Serb race must not be forgotten. The Yugoslav Government was trembling, but the effect of our helping the Greeks might stiffen the resistance of the Balkan peoples to German aggression.

It was recalled that Colonel Donovan had stressed in a telegram to the President the importance of the formation of a Balkan front. If we now forsook Greece it would have a bad effect in the United States.

Mention was also made of the effect of our action on Russia and of a suggestion that the Foreign Secretary should see Stalin.

The Prime Minister said that he had telegraphed to Mr Eden saying that he did not think he should see Stalin unless he received a very positive invitation to do so. The position of Russia was not an enviable one, Germany was now on the Black Sea at Constanza, where she would soon have a flotilla and she would be in a position to obtain oil from Baku and Batoum. He thought the Russian attitude was one of making concessions to Germany in order to gain time.

The Minister of Aircraft Production[1] thought that the enterprise would involve a serious strain on our shipping, particularly if it should prove necessary to withdraw our forces from Greece, in which event the enterprise would, he thought, go a long way towards reducing essential imports to this country. He thought that the effect of the enterprise on our shipping resources should be closely examined.

The Prime Minister then invited all the Ministers present to express their views.

The views expressed were, without exception, in favour of sending military assistance to Greece.

Winston S. Churchill to Anthony Eden
(*Churchill papers, 20/49*)

24 February 1941

The Chiefs of Staff having endorsed action on lines proposed in your telegrams Nos 355 and 358 from Cairo, and No. 262 from Athens, I brought whole question before War Cabinet this evening, Mr Menzies being present. Decision was unanimous in the sense you desire, but, of course, Mr Menzies must telegraph home. Presume, also, you have settled with New Zealand Government about their troops. No need anticipate difficulties in either quarter. Therefore, while being under no illusions, we all send you the order 'Full Steam Ahead'.

[1] Lord Beaverbrook.

Winston S. Churchill to Sir Robert Craigie[1]
(*Cabinet papers, 21/952*)

24 February 1941
Confidential

Sir,

I have the honour to transmit to your Excellency the enclosed record of a conversation which I had on the 24th February with the Japanese Ambassador.[2]

RECORD OF A CONVERSATION BETWEEN THE PRIME MINISTER AND THE JAPANESE AMBASSADOR

Before handing the Japanese Ambassador the attached aide-mémoire, we had some conversation. I dwelt upon the long and friendly relations of the two countries, my own feelings ever since the Japanese Alliance of 1902, and the great desire that we all felt here not to sunder the relations between the two countries. Japan could not expect us to view with approval what was going on in China, but we had maintained a correct attitude of neutrality, and indeed a very different kind of neutrality to that which we had shown when we had helped them in their war against Russia.

I assured the Ambassador that we had not the slightest intention of attacking Japan, and had no wish to see her other than prosperous and peaceful, and I said what a pity it would be if at this stage, when she already had China on her hands, she got into a war with Great Britain and the United States. This would mean not only a spreading of the conflict, but the prolongation of the war.

I then referred to a hint which Mr Matsuoka had given that Japan might mediate between Great Britain and Germany, and made clear the points set forth in the aide-mémoire.

The Ambassador said that he quite understood about mediation, and that it had only been put forward as a part of their general attitude. He then proceeded to say that Japan had no intention of attacking us or the United States, and had no desire to become involved in a war with either Power. They would not attempt to attack Singapore or Australia, and he repeated several times that they would not attempt to gain a footing or make encroachments in the Dutch East Indies. The only complaint which Japan had, he said, was our attitude to China, which was encouraging China and adding to their

[1] Robert Leslie Craigie, 1883–1959. Entered the Foreign Office, 1907. British Representative, Inter-Allied Blockade Committee, 1916–18. First Secretary, Washington, 1920–3; transferred to the Foreign Office, 1923; Counsellor, 1928; Assistant Under-Secretary of State, 1934–7. Knighted, 1936. Privy Councillor, 1937. Ambassador to Japan, 1937–41. UK Representative to the United Nations War Crimes Commission, 1945–8.

[2] Mamoru Shigemitsu, see page 183, note 1.

difficulties. It might be they had made mistakes in entering into China, but even we made mistakes sometimes, and it was our attitude of partisanship for the Chinese which had led to some estrangement between Britain and Japan.

I pointed out that the military measures we had taken were all of a defensive character, and that Singapore was also a purely defensive point, designed only to enable us to join hands with Australasia, who was dear to us. He did not contest the defensive character of Singapore, or that our military measures had been purely defensive, but he expressed regret at the Press campaign launched against Japan recently. I said we had nothing to do with this campaign. It was not started by the Government, and simply arose out of the situation developing in the Far East and the utterances of Japanese statesmen. I said I thought it had done good and cleared the air, because instead of the grave dangers of war becoming apparent only to the small military circles who largely control the Japanese Government, the whole Japanese nation knew what was going on and the dangers lying ahead, and I had confidence that the Japanese did not wish to embark upon such a tremendous struggle as would be inevitable if they went to war with the British and Americans.

The Ambassador renewed his protestations that they never had had any intention of so doing, and that all they wanted was to preserve the peace of the Pacific.

I felt bound to remain him of the Triple Pact which they had made with the Axis Powers, and that this naturally was ever in our minds. One could not believe that a Pact so much in favour of Germany and so little in favour of Japan, had not got some secret provisions, and at any rate Japan had left us in doubt as to what interpretation she would put upon it in certain eventualities. The Ambassador said that they had made explanations at the time, and that their object was to limit the conflict, &c. I told him the Axis Pact had been a very great mistake for Japan. Nothing had done them more harm in their relations with the United States, and nothing had brought Great Britain and the United States closer together.

I then renewed my friendly assurances, and gave him the note which follows. His whole attitude throughout was most friendly and deprecatory, and we have no doubt where he stands in these matters.

MEMORANDUM HANDED BY THE PRIME MINISTER TO THE JAPANESE AMBASSADOR

The note from His Imperial Japanese Majesty's Minister for Foreign Affairs containing a message to His Britannic Majesty's Secretary of State for Foreign Affairs has been laid before the Prime Minister.

The Prime Minister is gratified to observe that Mr Matsuoka sees no reason to apprehend any untoward developments in East Asia, and notes with satisfaction his assurances about the peaceful intentions of the Imperial Japanese Government.

Since Mr Matsuoka, for his part, makes reference to 'movements of the British and American Governments in their attempt to expedite and enlarge warlike preparations', the Prime Minister would allow himself to offer certain observations which he hopes may remove any misunderstanding of the position of His Majesty's Government.

There is no question of His Majesty's Government making any attack upon or committing any act of aggression against Japan; and the Prime Minister is sure that this also represents the intentions of the United States, though, of course, he cannot claim to speak for them. All the preparations which are being made in oriental regions by Great Britain and the United States are of a purely defensive character. Incidentally, the Prime Minister would wish to assure Mr Matsuoka that the concern which Mr Eden expressed to the Japanese Ambassador was not based exclusively on reports from His Majesty's Ambassador in Tokyo, but on the course of events in the Far East and on a study of the speeches of the Japanese Minister for Foreign Affairs himself.

Turning now to the war in progress in Europe between Great Britain and Germany, it will be within Mr Matsuoka's recollection that, before the outbreak of the war, His Majesty's Government made every effort, by concession and reasonable dealing, to avert hostilities. That is recognized throughout the world, and, indeed, the Government of the day in this country were severely criticized for having travelled too far along this road. Their efforts were unavailing, and the German Government, by attacking Poland after so many breaches of faith and of treaties, chose the arbitrament of war.

His Majesty's Government, having thus been forced to enter upon this grievous quarrel, have no thought but to carry it to a victorious conclusion. Naturally, it takes some time for the peaceful communities which compose the British Empire to overtake the military preparations of countries which have long been exulting in their martial might, and adapting their industries to war production. But even now His Majesty's Government feel well assured of their ability to maintain themselves against all comers, and they have every reason to hope that within a few months they will, with the rapidly increasing supply of materials which is coming from the United States, be overwhelmingly strong.

Mr Matsuoka makes allusion to the help which this country is receiving from the United States of America. The Prime Minister would observe that that help is being given for the very reason that the battle which this country is waging is for the overthrow of the system of lawlessness and violence abroad and cold, cruel tyranny at home which constitutes the German Nazi régime.

It is this system that the peoples of the British Empire, with the sympathy and support of the whole English-speaking world, are resolved to extirpate from the Continent of Europe. His Majesty's Government have no designs upon the integrity or independence of any other country, and they seek no advantage for themselves except the satisfaction of having rid the earth of a hateful terror and of restoring freedom to the many insulted and enslaved nations of the European Continent. This they would regard as the greatest honour that could reward them, and the crowning episode in what, for the Western World, is a long continuity of history.

Mr Matsuoka, with the loftiest motives, has hinted at his readiness to act as the mediator between the belligerents. The Prime Minister is sure that, in the light of what he has said and upon further reflection, Mr Matsuoka will understand that in a cause of this kind, not in any way concerned with territory, trade or material gains, but affecting the whole future of humanity, there can be no question of compromise or parley.

It would be a matter of profoundest regret to His Majesty's Government if by any circumstances Japan and this country were to become embroiled, and this not only because of their recollection of the years during which the two countries were happily united in alliance, but also because such a melancholy event would both spread and prolong the war without, however, in the opinion of His Majesty's Government, altering its conclusion.

Winston S. Churchill to the Import Executive
(*Churchill papers, 20/36*)

25 February 1941

ADMIRALTY SALVAGE ORGANIZATION

I learn that the salvage organization has recently made as great a contribution to the maintenance of our shipping capacity as new construction, about 370,000 gross tons having been salved in the last five months of 1940, as against 340,000 tons built, while the number of ships being dealt with by the salvage organisation has increased very rapidly, from 10 in August to about 30 now.

They are to be congratulated on this, and I feel sure that, if anything can be done to assist in the expansion of their equipment and finding of suitable officers, your Executive will see that such measures are taken.

Meanwhile, we cannot take full advantage of these results, owing to shortage of repairing capacity. I have no doubt that your Executive is planning an increase of this capacity, and, meanwhile, is making use of facilities overseas in the case of all vessels capable of doing one more voyage before repair.

Winston S. Churchill to Sir Alexander Cadogan
(*Churchill papers, 20/36*)

25 February 1941
Secret

General Sikorski, in conversation with me a week ago, expressed a desire to pay a visit to the United States and Canada, for the purpose *inter alia* of working up sentiment in the large American-Polish community, of encouraging a stream of recruits to go to Canada, and of arranging in Canada a training camp. In this way we shall obtain a stream of recruits for the Polish Corps, which is already a very fine body of men. I promised to find out what the President and Mr Mackenzie King would think of such a visit. Will you please draft a telegram accordingly for my consideration.

Winston S. Churchill to General Ismay
(*Churchill papers, 20/36*)

25 February 1941

Find out from the Chiefs of the Staff whether they think I may now draft a telegram on the Greek situation and our decision for the secret information of the President, or should we wait a little?

Winston S. Churchill to General Wavell
(*Churchill papers, 20/49*)

25 February 1941

Secrecy. Every effort will be made here but Australian and New Zealand Governments have already been informed as was necessary. Can easily keep Sikorski waiting a week but you must say when I should tell him. Am proposing tell President Roosevelt quite soon as most important enlist his interest early.

It is essential you should give me rough timetable of movements, observing that impact of your advanced parties in Greece will certainly be reported. Therefore it seems desirable to compress movement as much as possible.

Canal. Most important for us to know where the Roumanian oil project fits in to timetable as this will certainly open the ball. Chiefs of Staff will examine reinforcement of Wellingtons today and hope to accelerate. Evidently Greeks will have final word on this operation.

We have great anxiety about closing of Canal, particularly on account of

Mandibles, which assumes ever-growing urgency. Glens expected arrive 8th. Surely you want about three thousand trustworthy white men watching Canal, but with your large numbers of personnel not incorporated in tactical formations this should present no difficulty. Canal problem must be mastered at all costs.

Delighted at capture of Mogadishu. Second South African Division should come north at earliest. You will no doubt raise this with General Smuts.

Am expecting to hear from you about sending 50th Division and use of 6th British Division after Mandibles. Most necessary in Imperial interests that British units should participate.

Winston S. Churchill: minute[1]

(*Churchill papers, 20/36*)

25 February 1941
Secret

I am not satisfied that sufficient efforts are being made to press on with the development of the UP weapon in multi-barrel form for engaging high-flying targets, and with the production of ammunition. We must not be satisfied with engaging targets at 18,000 feet; and I see no reason why research and development in this direction should not proceed without detriment to the production of the weapons and ammunition of the type already established. I hear that trials with an eleven-barrelled projector on a 3.7-inch mounting were highly satisfactory, and that it is proposed to construct similar projectors on a 3-inch mounting. Let me have weekly reports of progress.

2. I am told that we have at present in the field more projectors than rounds. It is said that future production of ammunition will be much increased, and that there will soon be a satisfactory supply, but last August I was told that 5,000 projectiles would be ready by the middle of that month, and 10,000 about the beginning of September. I hope the present forecasts will prove to be better founded than the optimistic statements made then. Let me have a weekly report of production.

3. I should like to know what production of minefields is planned. It is not certain which form, e.g., free balloon minefields or UP minefields will be successful; and demands for mines must not be allowed to get out of proportion – especially as I understand that they will interfere with the production of ordinary UP ammunition. Let me have a report, to show their effect upon each other.

[1] This minute was sent to General Ismay (for the Minister of Supply), to the Secretary of State for War, and to the First Lord of the Admiralty.

4. I should like to discuss all these matters at an early meeting of the Defence Committee (Supply).

Winston S. Churchill to General Ismay
(Churchill papers, 20/36)

25 February 1941

We have already about forty 4,000-lb. bombs, though the attachments are not yet quite complete. The Commander-in-Chief, Bomber Command, should be asked for his ideas on how to turn these to the best effect.[1]

Winston S. Churchill to A. V. Alexander, Admiral Pound and General Ismay
(Churchill papers, 20/36)

25 February 1941

In view of Herr Hitler's threats about intensified U-boat attacks, and also of recent losses even in escorted convoy, I wish to have a meeting after dinner tonight at 9.30 upon the subject.

Pray bring whatever Officers you please to the Central War Room.

Winston S. Churchill to Lord Woolton
(Churchill papers, 20/21)

25 February 1941

EVENING STANDARD HEADLINE: 'PRISON IF YOU EAT MEAT AND FISH, EGG OR CHEESE[2]

My dear Woolton,

I must say I do not like all this rather dictatorial publicity. I do not think anyone ought to be sent to prison merely for making mistakes, but only if it

[1] The 4,000-pound bomb was so large that it could just be squeezed into a Wellington bomber. It resembled 'two dustbins joined end to end' (Norman Longmate, *The Bombers*), and could not be aimed. The first to be dropped on Germany was during a raid on Emden at the end of May 1941. Subsequently the size of British bombs dropped on Germany steadily increased, culminating in the 22,000-pounder in 1945.

[2] In the *Evening Standard* on 25 February 1941 an article headed 'Gaol if you eat meat *and* fish or eggs' gave details of what it called Lord Woolton's 'long awaited order limiting restaurant and hotel meals to one course of fish, meat, poultry, eggs or cheese'. The *Evening Standard* commented: 'The order comes into force on March 10. Breach of it by either the catering establishment or the customer will involve fines and/or imprisonment for both. Under the Order you may eat mixtures of certain items; for example, bacon and sausage, bacon and kidney, veal and ham, egg and bacon. You must not have more than one egg with your bacon. You will still be allowed to eat steak and kidney pie, but you will not be able to have poultry accompanied by a slice of fried bacon or cold chicken and ham at one meal. Cheese may be used for flavouring without making it a dish in the controlled categories.'

was clear there was some steady consistent purpose to break the regulations. To say that anybody can eat as much as they can get of one staple food, but that they have committed a crime if they eat a lesser quantity of two foods is scarcely logical.

The manufacture of novel and artificial crimes is much to be deprecated. So also is the effect of these kinds of declarations when repeated, as they no doubt will be, upon the enemy radio.

I could have wished that this class of announcement should be referred to the Cabinet before it was made public.

Yours vy sincerely
Winston S. Churchill

Winston S. Churchill to Air Chief Marshal Sir Charles Portal
(*Churchill papers, 20/36*)

26 February 1941

It is extraordinary that Middle East should have received no more than 12 aircraft during the whole week.[1] There must be a hold-up at Takoradi.

2. The figures are difficult to understand. Lost and seriously damaged amount to 17, receipts to 12, and yet we are shown a net loss of 15. Will you kindly have this explained.

3. Paper B should be re-drafted to show numbers of aircraft in Greece as well as in Egypt and the Sudan.

It seems frightfully difficult to get any improvement. When does the *Furious* start with her next consignment?

Import Executive: minutes
(*Cabinet papers, 86/1*)

26 February 1941 10 Downing Street
5 p.m.
Secret

Present: The Right Hon. W. S. Churchill, Prime Minister (In the Chair)

The right Hon. Sir Andrew Duncan, Minister of Supply and Chairman of the Import Executive

[1] Return dated 24 February 1941 of receipts and losses of aircraft in the Middle East.

The Right Hon. A. V. Alexander, First Lord of the Admiralty
The Right Hon. O. Lyttelton, President of the Board of Trade
The Right Hon. Lord Woolton, Minister of Food
The Right Hon. J.T.C. Moore-Brabazon, Minister of Transport
The Right Hon. R. H. Cross, Minister of Shipping
Professor Lindemann

A preliminary discussion took place, in the course of which the following points were made which required immediate investigation:

(1) The First Lord of the Admiralty should prepare a scheme which would effect a progressive reduction of at least 100,000 tons a month in the total tonnage of shipping under repair, provided that the present rate of damage did not increase. For this purpose he should submit a scheme showing the effect of taking 5,000 men from new construction of Naval vessels, and 5,000 men from the new construction of merchant ships.

(2) The Minister of Labour and National Service should also submit his proposals for increasing the total labour force available at the shipyards.

(3) The Minister of Shipping should report on the steps which might be taken to ensure that shipowners should have the same incentive to get their ships rapidly to sea where they had been damaged by enemy action as they already had in the case of ships damaged by other causes.

(4) The Ministers of Shipping and Transport should prepare a scheme to effect an immediate reduction of at least 15% in the time taken to turn round at ports, and a progressive improvement thereafter. The following points should be considered in this connection:-

(a) The introduction of improved and centrally-controlled lighting at the ports:

(b) The question should be further pursued of using the existing lighting system at the Clyde until an Alert was sounded. Any difference of opinion should be submitted to higher authority.

(c) The employment of labour on two shifts.

(d) The reduction of the time spent in 'waiting'.

(5) The First Lord of the Admiralty should report on the possibility of saving time on degaussing[1] by accepting a lower standard of efficiency and by accepting further risks.

(6) An analysis and explanation should be submitted by the First Lord of the Admiralty and the Minister of Shipping, of the long time at present taken on voyages across the Atlantic.

(7) The attention of the Secretary of State for War and the Secretary of State for Air should at once be drawn to the proposals for defence of shipping against U-Boat and air attack made at the meeting held on 25th February; viz:

[1] The principal protection against magnetic mines, in use since the early months of 1940.

(a) additional military personnel and machine guns;
(b) a squadron of Wellingtons for immediate employment with convoys, and a second Wellington squadron (to relieve the first) to be fitted with ASV[1] and the crews trained to work with Coastal Command.
(c) as soon as possible 4 Stirlings to be allocated to Coastal Command.

(8) The First Lord of the Admiralty should examine further the possibility of arranging for omitting the call of northabout convoys at Oban.

This suggestion should be brought to the notice of the Secretary of State for War.

(9) The Minister of Shipping was invited to prepare a draft telegram for the Prime Minister to send to President Roosevelt, asking for his assistance in obtaining the use of enemy shipping in USA ports and in particular of Danish ships.

(10) Note was taken that the following points were being examined but were not yet ripe for discussion with the Prime Minister:

(a) The President of the Board of Trade was proposing to see the Prime Minister of the Commonwealth of Australia with a view to the imposition by the Commonwealth Government of restriction of consumption which would free shipping at present employed on importing goods to Australia.
(b) The Minister of Shipping was examining the possibility of obtaining control of certain Dutch and Norwegian ships which were not at present employed on bringing goods to this country.
(c) The Minister of Shipping was discussing with the Minister of Labour and the National Maritime Board the steps necessary to provide for the continued employment of seamen, so as to build up the necessary reserve.
(d) The Minister of Shipping hoped to discuss shortly with representatives of the USA Maritime Commission the employment of USA ships outside the danger zone so as to relieve the burden on British shipping.

John Colville: diary
(*Colville papers*)

26 February 1941

After dinner the PM dictated his speech, which was full of historical allusions and legal intricacies, on the Disqualification of Members Bill, which has been occasioned by the appointment of Malcolm MacDonald as High Commissioner for Canada. The PM will get away with it of course, but I think

[1] ASV sets: an airborne radar device.

he is unwise to use his personal influence with the House in an instance which is of little immediate importance. By so doing he may weaken his power on an occasion when it is really necessary. He is a great House of Commons man and loves to make use of his parliamentary art; but I believe his prestige in the House would be even greater if he only appeared there on rare and solemn occasions.

In the early hours news came from the Admiralty of another serious disaster to a convoy.[1] Brendan and I commented gloomily on the great threat to our life-line which is developing and will continue to develop. He suggested I should not tell the PM tonight as it would prevent him sleeping. But at 3.00 a.m. he asked me point-blank if there was any news from the Admiralty and I had to tell him. He became very pensive. 'It is very distressing,' I said weakly. 'Distressing!', he replied, 'it is terrifying. If it goes on it will be the end of us.'

King George VI to Winston S. Churchill
(*Churchill papers, 20/29*)

26 February 1941 Windsor Castle

My dear Prime Minister,

I have given a lot of anxious thought to your idea of going to Bermuda soon to meet President Roosevelt.

The advantage of your getting to know him personally is, I realize very great; in fact, if there was any question of a divergence of views between our two countries, it might be overwhelming.

Fortunately this is not the case, & I must confess that the more I think of this project, the more it disturbs me. If, by an unlucky chance, some misfortune were to befall you in the course of your journey, it would be a grave blow to the cause of the Empire & our Allies. In any case, it would I imagine, be impossible for the meeting to be kept secret until after your return, & I cannot help thinking that your absence from this country, for however short a time, during the next critical weeks would be as heavy an addition to the anxieties of the people as it would be to mine.

I do hope therefore that you will think carefully over these points before coming to any decision.

Believe me

Yours very sincerely
George R.I.

[1] Six merchant ships in convoy had been sunk on 22 February 1941 by the *Scharnhorst* or *Gneisenau*. Four more merchants ships were sunk on February 23 by German submarines, four on February 24, and three on February 26.

War Cabinet: minutes
(*Cabinet papers, 65/21*)

27 February 1941
5.30 p.m.

A further discussion took place on the decision to despatch military assistance to Greece.

The Prime Minister said that he felt no doubt that the decision taken at the last Meeting had been right. It had been taken in full knowledge of the many difficulties which would attend the opening of a new theatre of war in Greece, e.g:

(a) The necessity for supplying our forces by the long route round the Cape.
(b) The heavy attacks now being made on our shipping.
(c) The danger of the Suez Canal being blocked by enemy action.

On the other hand it had previously been our intention to maintain in the Middle East a larger force than we now contemplated sending to Greece. The slightly longer voyage to Greece was not in itself a formidable addition to our difficulties.

Mr Menzies informed the War Cabinet that he had received the Commonwealth Government's reply to the telegram which he had sent after the last meeting of the Cabinet. His colleagues had appreciated the need for an immediate decision and concurred in the proposed use of two Australian divisions in the forces initially contemplated for the Greek campaign. They had made it plain that, had more time been available, they would have sought advice on the following aspects of the plan.

(a) The small size of the force proposed, relative to the task before it. Would it not be possible to provide additional numbers, and also to augment them as equipment became available?

(b) They could not agree to Australian troops taking part in the campaign, unless they were equipped on the maximum establishment scale.

(c) Their consent to the participation of Australian forces was conditional on plans having been completed beforehand to ensure that evacuation (if it should become necessary) could be successfully undertaken.

Mr Menzies recalled that the Chief of the Imperial General Staff had been satisfied that the forces to be initially despatched to Greece were of adequate size. He intended to point this out to his colleagues in Australia.

The Dominions Secretary[1] said that the New Zealand Government had also telegraphed concurring in the course proposed, on the understanding that the New Zealand division would be fully equipped before leaving, and that it would be accompanied by an armoured brigade. In a separate telegram,

[1] Viscount Cranborne.

however, the New Zealand Government had asked for an assurance that the force proposed was, in fact, considered to be adequate for the hazardous operation to be undertaken. They also asked what arrangements were being made for providing support for the Australian and New Zealand forces, after operations had begun?

Mr Menzies said that the Governments of the Commonwealth of Australia and of New Zealand had both of them accepted the large political arguments in favour of the despatch of military assistance to Greece. It should be appreciated, however, that it was proposed to send to Greece two of the four Australian Divisions, and the one New Zealand Division. The issues involved were, therefore, of outstanding importance to both Australia and New Zealand.

The Prime Minister said that he was deeply moved by the messages from the Commonwealth and New Zealand Governments. They had responded magnificently to what was, perhaps, the most severe proposal ever put before Dominion Governments. It was quite natural that they should make the points raised which in no way detracted from the value of their response. Answers should be sent to the points raised by the Governments of Australia and New Zealand.

The political value of military steps now decided upon, must not be ignored. Thus:

(a) The course adopted was the policy best calculated to retain the military co-operation not only of the 18 Greek Divisions now in the field, but also to secure the 27 Turkish Divisions now in Thrace. Those forces, together with our own would be larger than any which the Germans could put into the field against us for several months.

(b) We must not dismiss the possibility of Yugoslavia coming in on our side.

(c) We should hope to be able to send considerable reinforcements. The 6th Division would probably be available in about 2 months' time, while it might be possible to send the 50th Division to Greece from the United Kingdom.

A considerable Empire force (including the South African Division) was now engaged in East Africa and might be available to proceed north after the Italian position had been liquidated.

A 2nd Division had been promised from South Africa. The Foreign Secretary and the Chief of the Imperial General Staff were to meet General Smuts in Egypt.

The Prime Minister said that he had not yet received General Wavell's report on the date by which the Divisions from the Middle East could take the field in Greece.

In order to limit the number of people in the secret, the new plan had not yet been communicated to the Canadian and Union Governments. For the same reason, President Roosevelt had not yet been informed. Probably the right moment for taking them into our confidence would be when we had seen General Wavell's time-table.

It would be a mistake to draw any pessimistic inferences from the recent encounter between British and German armoured fighting vehicles in Libya. The German force had been driven back; there were no indications that the Germans were preparing to attempt the considerable operation of an advance across the Libyan Desert. It was not known how many German mechanised formations had been ferried over to Libya.

House of Commons: Business of the House
(Hansard)

27 February 1941 House of Commons

Mr Shinwell: Has my right hon. Friend consulted the Prime Minister on the question of a Debate on shipping and ship-building?

Mr Attlee: I am afraid there will be no time for that.

Mr Shinwell: Is not the subject one of extreme importance to the whole war situation, and are we not to have an opportunity of discussing it in private or in public so that we may know how we stand and at the same time be afforded an opportunity of offering some constructive proposals?

The Prime Minister (Mr Churchill): The question of the time of the House must be considered. There is a great deal of Business that we must get through. If it is the desire of the House to have a Debate, obviously it can only take place in secret.

Earl Winterton: Would the right hon. Gentleman consider in connection with this matter whether the old method of arranging Business through the usual channels is not now completely out of date in view of the fact that there is no regular Opposition, and if, in respect to a matter like this, there is a general desire in different quarters of the House for a Debate, will he give prior consideration to it over other questions which may be put through the ordinary usual channels?

The Prime Minister: Of course, the Government is composed of all the political parties in the House, who have signified their loyalty to it. The focus of opposition has not yet become precisely defined. If a sufficient body of Gentlemen constituted themselves an Opposition, they could be definitely recognised as such, and we should know where and who they were, and special facilities would no doubt be extended.

Earl Winterton: Is it necessary to have an Opposition to do that? Surely if there is a general wish for a Debate, those who have that wish can express it without constituting themselves an Opposition.

The Prime Minister: The Whips of the different parties do endeavour to ascertain the opinion of the House as a whole and not merely of those who work on the basis of an Opposition. I am not aware that anything has arisen which renders their functions inoperative, but it might be in the event of the emergence of a definite Opposition that we would have to reconsider the present arrangements.

Mr Shinwell: If we might for a moment escape from the academic question of an Opposition, might we know the right hon. Gentleman's view on the subject of a Debate in secret, as he suggests, before Easter?

The Prime Minister: I shall have to go into the question of the Business that we have to get through before Easter. The House is aware that we have a lot of work to get through. The Debate could not possibly take place in public.

Sir I. Albery:[1] Will the right hon. Gentleman take into account the fact that articles appearing in the Press have stirred up public anxiety and therefore it is desirable to ventilate the subject, if necessary in Secret Session?

Mr Mander: With regard to the Business before us today, may I ask whether there is to be a free vote of all parties supporting the Government or is it to be a free vote for one party only?

The Prime Minister: The Government regard the Division on this Bill as a matter of confidence.

Mr Shinwell: Are we to understand that the right hon. Gentleman, having consulted the Lord Privy Seal and having been made aware of the decision of the Labour Party, regards this as a matter of confidence?

The Prime Minister: Yes, Sir, certainly. Those who have no confidence in the Government will have full liberty so to testify in the Lobby.

Mr Shinwell: Are we to understand that the right hon. Gentleman has elevated the question which has arisen out of the appointment of the right hon. Member for Ross and Cromarty (Mr M. MacDonald) as High Commissioner in Canada to a question which is to be regarded as a matter of confidence in the Government? May we not repose our confidence in the Government and at the same time be free to express our opinions on a matter of this kind?

The Prime Minister: If this Bill were not acceded to by the House, very great inconvenience would arise to the war effort of the country. [Hon. Members: 'No.'] That is my opinion. If there is a desire to bring matters to the test, the House is perfectly free to have every opportunity of expressing itself.

Sir Percy Harris:[2] Is it not one thing to have a free discussion, as we shall have today, and quite another thing to vote against the Government?

Mr A. Bevan: Would it not be desirable for the right hon. Gentleman to postpone his decision upon this matter until he has had an opportunity of

[1] Irving James Albery, 1879–1967. Member of the Stock Exchange, 1902–64. On active service in South Africa, 1900, and on the Western Front 1914–18 (Military Cross, despatches). Conservative MP, 1934–45. Knighted, 1936.

[2] Percy Alfred Harris, 1876–1952. Barrister. Member of the London County Council, 1907–34 and from 1946 until his death. Assistant Director, Volunteer Services, War Office, 1916. Liberal MP, 1916–18 and 1922–45. Created Baronet, 1932. Chief Whip, Liberal Parliamentary Party, 1935–45; Deputy Leader, 1940–5. Privy Councillor, 1940. Author of *Forty Years In and Out of Parliament.*

hearing the Debate? Will he consider this point also? I understand that the Debate is being opened by the Attorney-General.[1] Would it not have been more desirable for the House to have been put in possession of the Prime Minister's views at the beginning of the Debate?

The Prime Minister: I do not think it will be possible to postpone a decision whether the Government regard this as a vote of confidence or not until the Debate is reaching its conclusion. That would not be fair to hon. Gentlemen who are making up their minds what course they should take. With regard to the order of speakers in the Debate, it has always been the rule to allow the Government some latitude in the choice of those they put up.

Commander Sir Archibald Southby:[2] May I ask whether the reply given to me yesterday by the Lord Privy Seal that the Prime Minister has no intention of having a secret discussion on the question of the administration of the bases leased to the United States was based on the question of time, or whether there was any other reason? Has my right hon. Friend considered the point that in view of the fact that the House of Commons is the custodian of the Empire, it is right that no final decision should be come to until the House has been told exactly what the position is? I entirely support the right hon. Gentleman in arranging the leasing of these bases, but there is a feeling in the House and the country that the representatives of the people should be told what is being done with the British Empire when bases are being given to the United States.

The Prime Minister: I do not think it will be desirable to have a Debate on this subject at the present time. I must really emphasize the fact that there is a war on.

Winston S. Churchill: speech

(*Hansard*)

27 February 1941 House of Commons

The Prime Minister (Mr Churchill): I must again make apologies to the House if I have not been present during every speech that has been made in

[1] Donald Bradley Somervell, 1889–1960. Educated at Harrow and Magdalen College, Oxford. Fellow of All Souls College, Oxford. On active service, 1914–18. King's Counsel, 1929. Conservative MP for Crewe, 1931–45. Knighted, 1933. Solicitor-General, 1933–6. Attorney-General, 1936–45. Privy Councillor, 1938. Home Secretary, 1945. A Lord Justice of Appeal, 1946–54. Created Baron Somervell of Harrow, 1954. A Lord of Appeal in Ordinary, 1954–60. A member of the Other Club from 1939. His father was Churchill's English teacher at Harrow.

[2] Archibald Richard James Southby, 1886–1969. Entered the Royal Navy as a cadet, 1901; Lieutenant, 1908. Served in the Grand Fleet and on the North America and West Indian Station, 1913–18. Member of the Naval Armistice Commission, 1918–19; the Naval Inter-Allied Commission of Control, 1919–20; Commander, 1920. Conservative Member of Parliament for Epsom, 1928–47. Assistant Government Whip, 1931–35. Junior Lord of the Treasury, 1935–37. Created Baronet, 1937. Member of the Parliamentary Delegation to Buchenwald Concentration Camp, April 1945.

the course of this Debate, but when I have been able to be present I must say that I have experienced a sensation of relief at the air of detachment which prevails in this House, and which seems to me in such very sharp contrast to some of the grave realities which are proceeding out of doors.

I must ask the House to give His Majesty's Government the minor facilities and conveniences – for that is all they are – which are afforded to us in this Bill. I must make it a question of confidence, because it touches definitely our war effort, it arises directly out of the war, and it is concerned only with the period of the war. If there is a suggestion – it has not been pressed in any quarter in any unkind manner – that the government will abuse their powers under this Bill and proceed by mean and flagitious manoeuvres to perpetuate their tenure of power, if there were such suggestions, either tacit or spoken, obviously that also would be a matter of confidence.

My right hon. and learned Friend the Attorney-General has described the existing position and has shown, what every speaker has accepted, the confusion of accident and anomaly of legal fiction and Parliamentary circumnavigation into which we have fallen over generations, quite innocently and for good reasons, and in which we now lie. This now seems to have been brought to a head by the case of my right hon. Friend the Member for Ross and Cromarty (Mr M. MacDonald). But the need for the Bill had already become imperative, even if this particular appointment had not been made. My right hon. and gallant Friend the Member for Burton (Colonel Gretton)[1] spoke of this Measure as a Bill on a purely personal issue. He is really quite wrong; he is beside the mark in making such a statement. He said we were getting along quite well without it, but that is really not the case, as I shall venture to show the House during the course of my remarks.

Although this Bill is associated with a particular case, the circumstances which have rendered it necessary are far more general in their application, and I do not think it is possible to state a case against the Bill on grounds of high constitutional principle. My hon. Friend the Member for Cambridge University (Mr Pickthorn)[2] seemed to seek to do so, but I should warn the House against lending countenance to the constitutional doctrine which he has enunciated. He told us that the legislative functions of Parliament had

[1] John Gretton, 1867–1947. Educated at Harrow. Conservative MP for South Derbyshire, 1895–1906, for Rutland, 1907–18, and for Burton, 1918–43. Chairman of Bass, Ratcliff and Gretton Ltd, brewers. Colonel, Territorial Army, 1912. Privy Councillor, 1926. A leader of the 'die hards' over India, 1929–35. Created Baron, 1944. One of his brothers, a Captain in the Bedfordshire Regiment, was killed in action at Ypres on 18 December 1915.

[2] Kenneth William Murray Pickthorn, 1892–1975. Constitutional historian. Fellow of Corpus Christi College, Cambridge, from 1914. On active service in France and Macedonia, 1915–19. Dean, Tutor and subsequently President of Corpus Christi College, 1919–44. Conservative Member of Parliament for Cambridge, 1935–50; for Carlton (Nottinghamshire), 1950–66. Parliamentary Secretary, Ministry of Education, 1951–54. Created Baronet, 1959.

ceased to be important. He even said that the control of finance had ceased to be real or important, although that is a structure around which the whole of our procedure had been built. What he considered the function of the House of Commons to be – and I took the trouble to write down his words – was ' a market upon which the price of the Prime Minister's stock is based.'

I deprecate this squalid language of the bucket-shop as applied to the serious, responsible functions of the State, and I think it would be lamentable if the youth of a great centre of learning should be tempted to accept such slipshod and questionable guidance. The truth is that all the fundamental constitutional principles concerned with the holding of offices of profit and the vacation of seats – which was the real point behind this apparatus – have been blurred or effaced by decisions already taken by the House in this or previous Parliaments. Anomalies arise from the fact that positions under the Crown do or do not disqualify, according to the application or interpretation of words in old Statutes passed a long time ago in different circumstances and for different purposes.

These anomalies have continually been the target for Parliamentary attention and correction in recent years. Successive enactments have freed Ministers of the Crown from the need of re-election on appointment to office. This has been found convenient in practice, and I agree with my right hon. Friend the member for Newcastle-under-Lyme (Mr Wedgwood)[1] that we have lent ourselves, perhaps too readily, to those great changes. But they have been made, and made in modern times. It was a very important provision that Members, on appointment to high office, should submit themselves to re-election; it was a very important provision because it prevented a Government different from that which the electors had in mind at the time of the election from taking and holding office for a time, and filling up all its posts, without the country having a chance to challenge the matter, with different persons, of perhaps quite different policies from those the electorate had been led to contemplate, and from those that the country might wish. A Government so formed, even without a majority in the House, not daring to send a Minister that it had chosen to the process of by-election – saved from that by the legislation of the House – such a Government might take executive action which would have irrevocable consequences either in the direction of war or peace. It was a safeguard of immense consequence, but the House parted with it. It has been totally discarded by the House in my lifetime.

[1] Josiah Clement Wedgwood, 1872–1943. Naval architect, 1896–1900. On active service in South Africa, 1900. Liberal MP for Newcastle-under-Lyme, 1906–19. Commanded armoured cars in France, Antwerp, Gallipoli and East Africa, 1914–17 (DSO, wounded, despatches twice). Assistant Director, Trench Warfare Department, Ministry of Munitions, 1917. War Office Mission to Siberia, 1918. Elected to the Other Club, 1918 (resigned, 1930). Granted the Labour Whip, May 1919. Labour MP, 1919–42. Vice-Chairman of the Labour Party, 1921–4. Chancellor of the Duchy of Lancaster, 1924. Created Baron, 1942. Known as 'Josh'.

Mr Wedgwood: By the wish of the party leaders.

The Prime Minister: Surely the House is not going to shelter behind party leaders; surely, the right hon. Member will not try to get behind such a poor little ill-filled sandbag as that. Now that I have shown hon. Members the camel they have already swallowed, I hope they will address themselves with renewed sense of proportion to this somewhat inconsiderable gnat. An office of profit is, in my view – I do not speak as a lawyer – a term of art. It applies to many positions where there is not remuneration. A Junior Lord of the Treasury, unpaid, is an office of profit, but a special mission, though it may be very highly paid and may last for years, is not a disqualifying office of profit. A foreign Embassy, even though, as in the case of the right hon. and learned Member for East Bristol (Sir S. Cripps), it is a formal, definite, diplomatic appointment and not a special mission in any sense, has, according to the advice we have received, been held not to disqualify as an office of profit. That advice has not been challenged, or has not yet been challenged, by the House or by the common informer. [An Hon. Member: 'He takes no salary.'] That has nothing to do with it. That is one of the anomalies I am trying to bring out. It would make no difference if the right hon. and learned Member took a salary. He takes the fees of representation necessary to the discharge of these important duties. Even though it is a formal appointment, it has not been challenged, though I must say I should have thought it was a very doubtful case. If an office was in existence before 1705, it may be held by a Member of Parliament and profit drawn from it unless, of course, it comes under a special ban in some later Statutes, which are numerous and obscure. The High Commissionership of one of our great Dominions, not having been in existence in 1705, thus disqualifies, whereas an Embassy to a foreign country does not. I am only putting it forward to show the anomalies.

Then there is a distinction into which I shall not trouble to plunge too deeply, though it appeals, I believe, to legal and litigious minds – a distinction between an office of profit and a place of profit. Such a distinction would smite the holder of an unpaid office of profit, and would leave unscathed the paid holder of a place of profit. That is hardly a very satisfactory logical situation for us to have reached, although my right hon. Friend says that everything is going on very well. I have been assured that it would be possible to get out of what may be called the MacDonald difficulty in the following way: The High Commissionership in Canada would be left vacant, and the right hon. Gentleman the Member for Ross and Cromarty would be sent to Canada on a special mission, and his mission would be to discharge all the functions which would normally fall to be discharged by the High Commissioner. I am not going to play such a game as that with the House of Commons. I am sure it is very much better in this matter for the Government to come frankly to the House, tell the House their difficulties, and ask for the necessary assistance and relief. And that is what we are doing.

The House has already given to the Executive immense latitude during wartime. It allows and encourages officers in the Armed Forces to serve on full pay in any rank, and to combine their public duties with their military appointment. There is no limit except, of course, that of the general control of Parliament over the Executive. There is no legal limit at all upon the multiplication of military appointments, either at the front or the rear. Regional Commissioners, without limit of number, and deputy Regional Commissioners can, as we have been reminded, hold their duties and sit in Parliament by recent war-time legislation, without re-election, whether they are paid or unpaid. The power under the emergency legislation to create new offices and appoint additional Under-Secretaries is unlimited. There are many other facilities which have been given by the House. Why have all these facilities been accorded to the Government by the House? The reason is that the House in its wisdom does not wish the Executive to be hampered in the conduct of the war, and it is quite sure that it can by its inalienable ultimate authority correct any excess or abusive use of these immense discretionary powers. But let me say this: There never has been a Government which had less need to hire or suborn Members of Parliament to vote for them than this present Administration at this actual time.

Therefore I make these two submissions to the House: First, that the whole of this question of office and places of profit is in a state of great legal complexity and obscurity, and that the law may strike here or there by accident or caprice without any reference to any principle of logic, or reason or constitutional doctrine. That is my submission, and, I think, it is a subject which may well occupy the careful deliberations and study of a Select Committee, with a view to clarifying the whole position, with all due respect for tradition, and with proper regard to the interests of the modern State in times of peace or party warfare.

I am very glad that there should be a Select Committee, and I would very gladly myself, if invited, give evidence before it, when I have a little more time, upon the sound and healthy constitutional usages which should be defined, preserved and established. The terms of reference which we would suggest for this committee would be:

'To inquire into the existing Statutes which provide for disqualification of Members of the House of Commons by reason of their holding offices or places of profit under the Crown, and to make recommendations as to the proper principles on which future legislation in normal times of peace should be based.'

That is the reference which will in due course have to be submitted to the House.

If the committee completed its work before the Expiring Laws Continuance Bill came on, obviously the House would include the Measure in the Expiring Laws Continuance Bill, in the light of any report that the committee might make. If desired, the committee should not be wholly limited to the post-war period, but that is a matter which can well be discussed when the Motion for appointing the Select Committee and the terms of reference are before the House. [Interruption.] I think I should prefer to follow the course I have indicated, because I think it is the normal course. We have introduced the principle that the Bill should last only for a year, consequently the House can bring up the point on the Bill; or, if the reference is questioned, then again on the Motion for appointment of the committee it will be possible to raise the point, and I shall have a chance of giving it more consideration, and nothing will be lost in the meanwhile.

My second submission is this: The House has already given to a wicked and unworthy Executive, if such there were, immense powers of wrongdoing, so far as legality is concerned, which wrongdoing can only be corrected by turning the Government out by a hostile vote. I hope I may be allowed to leave the legal aspect and its tangles for the wider practical considerations which arise. I think we should be wise to leave it to our Select Committee to tidy up the present state of confusion and uncertainty and meanwhile get on with the war, because although one would hardly think it, there is a war on and life and liberties, and even wider causes, are hanging in the balance.

Let us, therefore, look at a few simple, non-legal issues which seem to me, as a layman, relevant to the subject and which also are involved in the practical needs of the hour. The first point is this: A Member of Parliament, when he gives service to the Crown at this time of mortal conflict, ought to be able to know whether he is doing right or not. In the White Paper which has been laid before the House there are a very large number of doubtful or borderline cases. The case of the hon. Member for Edgbaston (Sir P. Bennett)[1] stands out. Are we to regard my hon. Friend as a grand constitutional criminal or not? I fear that we must if this Bill is not passed. What is the crime that may be alleged against him? He is giving his highly competent service in the Ministry of Aircraft Production in an executive office as Director-General. He does not take any remuneration. He does not even draw out-of-pocket or travelling expenses. I am assured that his work is of real value in a sphere which we all know is of critical importance. Suddenly a constituency where my hon. Friend was well known and apparently well respected, with its eyes open to the office he held and to the ties which bound him to assist the Government, elected him, and he unwitting accepted the honour.

[1] Peter Frederick Blaker Bennett, 1880–1957. Joint Managing Director, Joseph Lucas Industries. Member of the Prime Minister's Panel of Industrial Advisers, 1938–39. Director General of Tanks and Transport, Ministry of Supply, 1939–40. Conservative Member of Parliament for Edgbaston, 1940–53. Director General of the Emergency Services Organization, Ministry of Aircraft Production, 1940–41. Knighted, 1941. Chairman, Automatic Gun Board, 1941–44. Parliamentary Secretary, Ministry of Labour, 1951–52. Created Baron, 1953. President of the British Productivity Council, 1955–57.

Mr Granville (Eye): He can come down to the House of Commons.

The Prime Minister: I will deal with all the facets of the argument in turn. I am assured that my hon. Friend the Member for Edgbaston might on the action of a common informer be mulcted in financial penalties, or upon a Motion in this House his election might be declared null and void. My hon. Friend is not alone. The hon. and gallant Member for Ormskirk (Commander King-Hall)[1] and the hon. Member for Rotherhithe (Mr Benjamin Smith)[2] are equally in this dangerous area, but worse may come. There may be a good many more fish in the net. My right hon. and gallant Friend the Member for Burton, in his comfortable, secure position in that constituency, has not realized that not everyone is in that position of impeccable political stability which he has so long enjoyed.

I took the trouble, working into the early hours this morning, to go through the White Paper with the Law Officers of the Crown, and I am sure that there are quite a lot of other cases, most disputable, or at any rate very doubtful and challengeable, where action might be taken by the common informer. Such action would proceed in the courts at the expense of the hon. Member concerned. It might be carried from court to court to his endless vexation and the detriment of his war work, and, possibly, to his heavy financial loss. I do not think any fair-minded man would expect a Government which had offered and sanctioned such appointments to permit this state of uncertainty to continue or to allow men who are giving valuable and faithful services to the State at the Government's request to lie under the menace and distress of potential persecution. I am asked why I make this a vote of confidence. This is why I felt bound to do so. If these men are to be censured, let us be censured too. If they are to be punished, let us share their misfortunes. If the House will not give to them and to us this relief, then I think the House will be taking upon its shoulders a more direct responsibility than it usually desires to do, in view of the burdens, not inconsiderable, of our present-day life. And so I put before the House, as the first of the practical objects of this Bill, fair play to individual Members, and I call upon the House to give their particular

[1] William Stephen Richard King-Hall, 1893–1966. On active service in the Royal Navy, 1914–18. Admiralty Naval Staff, 1919–20. China Squadron, 1921–23. Intelligence Officer, Mediterranean Fleet, 1925–26; Atlantic Fleet, 1927–28. Admiralty War Staff, 1928–29. Founded the K-H News-Letter Service, 1936. Independent Member of Parliament, Ormskirk Division of Lancashire, 1939–44. Ministry of Aircraft Production, 1940–42; Ministry of Fuel and Power, 1943–45. Founded the Hansard Society for Parliamentary Government, 1944; Chairman of Council 1944–62. Radio and television commentator on public events. Author of more than twenty historical and political books. Knighted, 1954. Created Baron (Life Peer), 1966.

[1] Ben Smith, 1879–1964. Joined the Merchant Navy as a boy. Later served in the Royal Navy for seven years. Left the Navy to become a hansom cab, and then a taxi cab, driver. An active member of the London Cab Drivers' Union. Organizer, Transport and General Workers' Union. Labour MP for Rotherhithe, 1923–31 and 1935–46. A Junior Labour Whip, 1925. Parliamentary Secretary, Ministry of Aircraft Production, 1942. Minister Resident in Washington for Supply, 1943–5. Knighted, 1945. Minister of Food, 1945–6.

attention to this aspect and ask them, in the name of the Government, to afford the relief and security to these men which are their due.

There is a second point which ought not to be overlooked. At this time, when we are fighting for our lives, surely it is in the interests of the country that the Government responsible for the safety of the people, and for the successful emergence of the British Empire from its perils, should have full freedom, as long as it retains the confidence of the House of Commons, to make the best appointments which it can devise. Let me illustrate this point by another case, that of my right hon. Friend the Member for Ross and Cromarty.[1] He has been chosen for the High Commissionership of one of our great Dominions, and he accepted the task as a war-time duty. He made no conditions, but he expressed the earnest hope and natural desire that he might remain a Member of the House of Commons. I agreed to this so far as it rested with me, and I promised to seek from Parliament any statutory powers that might be needed. It seemed to me that if the House accepted, and indeed highly approved, the sending of two of its Members as Ambassadors to Moscow and to Madrid,[2] no very serious, certainly no novel, constitutional issue would arise if it sent another of its Members to be High Commissioner in Canada. That was my feeling. I had never dreamed that between these two cases, the two Ambassadorships and the High Commissionership in Canada, all of which are out of this country, it could have been represented that there yawned and gaped this vast, hideous gulf of constitutional principle, and I take great shame myself for not having appreciated the point.

I would say a word on the merits of this appointment, which has been rather commented on by my right hon. Friend below the Gangway. I attach very great importance to these High Commissionerships in the Dominions. I am anxious that in this time of war we should fill vacancies which arise in the High Commissionerships so far as possible by men of outstanding political reputation who have long experience of the House of Commons and of Cabinet government. I must admit that I may be biased in favour of the House of Commons. I have lived all my life here, and I owe any part I have been able to take in public affairs entirely to the consideration with which I have been treated by the House. But making any allowances for this bias, discounting it, as I ought, I do not hesitate to say that 5 or 10 years' experience as a Member of this House is as fine an all-round education in public affairs as any man can obtain. Sometimes we see very able men in the great professions making public speeches which are odd and ill-judged, although they are most capable, upright men, probably possessing abilities above our average here. Why, only the other day there was a military officer with a very fine record much respected by all those with whom he worked, who wrote a letter for which he

[1] Malcolm MacDonald.
[2] Sir Stafford Cripps and Sir Samuel Hoare.

was properly censured, a letter most awkward and unhelpful to the very work on which he was engaged. Had that officer sat here even for the lifetime of a single Parliament, and rubbed shoulders with everyone, as we do, in the lobbies and elsewhere, he would never have made such a goose of himself. We get to know something about each other when we work together in this House. We see men with their qualities and defects.

In appointing a House of Commons man to a position of importance and delicacy, we are not, as it were, buying a – perhaps I had better say taking a leap in the dark, as too often has to be done, especially in time of war. Therefore, I was very glad to find in the right hon. Member for Ross and Cromarty, and also in Lord Harlech,[1] men of proved Parliamentary and Ministerial capacity and standing, and I am very glad to find that those appointments have given the greatest satisfaction both in Canada and South Africa, and have evoked the most cordial responses from those two outstanding Empire statesmen, Mr Mackenzie King and General Smuts. It would be a pity if, in this difficult process of selection, I should be forced to confine entirely to the House of Lords the area of my advice to the Crown. There are, no doubt, many capable men in the House of Lords with long Parliamentary experience, but I do not know why it should be considered essential to the moral and constitutional well-being of the House of Commons that choice should be confined solely to the Upper Chamber. We should take the best men at this time, those best fitted to hold appointments. There is no reason why the House of Commons should place itself under a particular ban on ability in this matter.

Now there arises the question of the rights and interest of constituents. It is a very serious question. A constituency chooses a Member to represent it in this House. The Member goes off, perhaps for a long period of time, to Moscow or Madrid or Ottawa, or it may be to Mogadishu or Benghazi. Here is a constituency, as it is said, disfranchised. Is not this a great constitutional misfortune? It certainly raises an important question, and we should look at it in some detail. It is not only in the field of service to the State that such issues arise. A sheaf of examples has been furnished to me. I will not quote names. A Member may fall a victim to a long illness which totally incapacitates him and as a result of which, after some years, he dies; or perhaps he lingers on. A

[1] William George Arthur Ormsby-Gore, 1885–1965. Educated at Eton and New College Oxford. Conservative MP, 1910–38. Intelligence Officer, Arab Bureau, Cairo, 1916. Assistant Secretary, War Cabinet, 1917–18. Member of the British Delegation (Middle East Section) to the Paris Peace Conference, 1919. British Official Representative on the Permanent Mandates Commission of the League of Nations, 1920. Under-Secretary of State for the Colonies, 1922–24, and 1924–29. Privy Councillor, 1927. First Commissioner of Works, 1932–36. Secretary of State for the Colonies, 1936–38. Succeeded his father as 4th Baron Harlech, 1938. High Commissioner, South Africa, 1941–44. Chairman of both the Midland Bank, and the Bank of West Africa. A Trustee of both the Tate and National Galleries.

Member may become mentally deranged or feeble-minded – I am not going to cite any particular instance – and so long as that Member is not actually certified a lunatic, he can hold his seat and draw his salary. A Member may be detained in prison under war-time regulations for an indefinite period – a most painful situation for any Government to become responsible for. Or he may be sent to prison by the courts for misdemeanour without the constituency having the slightest power to compel him to resign.

An even more irritating case than this, from the point of view of the constituency, is when a Member has been elected to support a particular party or a particular policy and, after being returned, circumstances arise which lead him, conscientiously or otherwise, to support a different party or the opposite policy. A Member again may obviously fail to represent his constituents. He may be entirely out of harmony with their views, and he may grossly misrepresent them without having the slightest intention to do so. These cases are not numerous, but they occur constantly, and a constituency has no redress. Of course, an honourable man actuated by good taste and good feeling would, as is the usual practice, submit himself voluntarily for re-election, but a constituency has no power whatever to make him do so. While we are on this question of Members employed abroad, let me say I have had a written message from my right hon. Friend the member for Ross and Cromarty, in which he says:

'I wrote on the day of the announcement of my impending appointment to Canada to the Chairman of the National Committee of my constituency, saying two things: (1) That I understood the Government were introducing legislation which, if passed, would enable me to retain my seat in the House.

(2) That, nevertheless, I would offer my resignation from Parliament to the National Committee in that constituency, and would resign forthwith if the general feeling in Ross and Cromarty was that they should have a Member of Parliament who was not absent oversea.'

Returning to the general theme of my argument, I have cited a whole set of cases which could easily be extended and of which many examples could be found within living memory, where the constituency for the time being is apparently disfranchised, and it is asked: 'Ought we not to provide for this?' I would not mind the Select Committee considering that aspect, but, speaking as a fairly old Parliamentarian, I am myself very doubtful whether a change in our long-established practice would be beneficial to the House of Commons. Of course, there are Parliaments like the Parliament in Soviet Russia, where the constituencies have the power of recall; that is to say, if a Member or a delegate makes speeches or asks questions or gives votes of a kind not desired by his constituency, or by the party machine, a kind of round-robin of electors can be signed, and he can be forced to submit himself for re-election.

This power of recall is contrary to the best interests and dignity of Parliament, and the whole Parliamentary tradition as built up in this country, which is at once the cradle and citadel of Parliamentary government, is adverse to it. I believe it would give a great deal more power to the executive Government and to the party machinery, which has in recent times often been considered to be too powerful and too efficient. The independence of all Members would be affected. They would not know whether, at any time, they might not be exposed to an agitation worked up in their constituencies and thus forced to fight a by-election on a bad wicket. We must be very careful not to take short or impulsive views on these questions when dealing with an institution of the antiquity and vitality of the House of Commons. Once we start on this business of recall for any of the reasons I have mentioned, you will find that one will lead on to another; once we start on this business of recall, we shall have altered in a degrading sense the character of the House of Commons and the status of its Members. In attempting to avoid an occasional anomaly, we might find that we had seriously affected the health and vigour of this famous, world-honoured institution. I believe it will be found on reflection far wiser to put up with these occasional hard cases than to be drawn on to the slippery slope which would lead to the promulgation of the doctrine of recall.

I have given the best reply that I can to my hon. Friend on the subject of the disfranchisement of a constituency. But there is another important Parliamentary lesson to be borne in mind by the House. It is none of our business to declare what constituencies think and wish. We learned that in the Wilkes case. In the cases of these three eminent Members who have been appointed Ambassadors or High Commissioner, from what I can hear in this time of war, when we are all working together – or are supposed to be – and are certainly in the utmost danger and also in a very great period of national history, these constituencies regard it as a very great honour that their Members have been chosen to render these high and distinguished services to our country and its cause. In the same way constituencies feel proud that their representatives should go to the front on active service and face, as many have done and are doing, the level as opposed to the vertical fire of the enemy. We shall see what view will be taken in Ross and Cromarty, but at any rate it is for them and not for us. The Members for constituencies neighbouring on those of men absent on active service or on public duty are nearly always found ready to look after local business and constituency correspondence, and the public Departments will be particularly careful in replying to such correspondence to make sure that the constituency does not suffer from the absence of its Member on what I must consider as an extremely high form of public duty.

There is, I am told, quite a lot of feeling in the country that we all ought to help as much as we can, and constituencies are glad to make a sacrifice in being inconvenienced if they think it conduces to the national advantage and safety. That is my answer to the question about the rights and interests of constituencies, and I hope that it also will be carefully considered by the House. Thus, there is the question of fair play to the individual Member, there is the question of the interest of the State in the freedom of choice and appointment, and there is the question of the alleged misfortunes to the constituency.

I come to the last issue which arises from this Bill. Is it in the interests of the House of Commons that its Members should play active, useful, and perhaps distinguished parts in the great struggle which is now going on, or ought they to confine themselves strictly to Parliamentary business and attendance upon this House? I may say that the House, or some of its Members, have shown themselves rather changeable upon this point. I remember my predecessor, the late Mr Neville Chamberlain, drawing a very strict line against the employment of Members of Parliament, and considerable offence being given, and his modifying that line to meet the wish of the House. For my own part, I have a very clear opinion, which I expressed in the Debate on the Address last November. Here is what I said – and it met, as I thought, with general approval –

'I entirely agree with what has been said about the desirability of Members of Parliament serving not only in the military forces but in all other forms of warfare and discharging their Parliamentary duties at the same time or in alternation. No doubt, difficulties arise, but I think they are well covered, and that the good sense of the House and of hon. Members will enable these dual and occasionally conflicting functions to be discharged.'

I went on to say – I abridge it a little – that the fact that

'this House should be a House of active living personalities, engaged to the hilt in the national struggle, each according to the full strength that he has to give, each according to the aptitudes which he possesses, is, I think, one of the sources of the strength of the Parliamentary institution.' – [Official Report, 21st November, 1940; cols. 31-2, Vol. 366.]

I think this policy commanded the entire approval of the House. And there are many traditions which justify the desire of the Government to find useful employment for hon. Members. In the days when the Parliamentary liberties we have gained were being fought for, Parliamentary figures, in and out of the Administration, were prominent in every field of public service and were hastening in, as they do now, from the battlefield to cast their votes and to give their counsel. It was so in the Marlborough wars, it was so under Lord Chatham, it was so in the wars against Napoleon. The Duke of Wellington, then Sir Arthur Wellesley, went out to the Army in the Peninsula while still holding the Irish Secretaryship; and when the Army went into winter quarters he returned home, and resumed his duties on the Treasury Bench. A great and respectable tradition has followed those lines. In earlier times, I must admit, in a mood of temporary and melancholy self-abasement, or under harsh external pressure, the House of Commons passed a self-denying ordinance. That was the prelude to the dictatorship of Oliver Cromwell. In the Act of Settlement, 1702, Parliament proposed to prevent every Member of the House of Commons from holding any kind of office under the Crown.

It is to the House of Lords, in the later Acts of 1705 and 1707, that we owe that immense assertion of democratic power and popular control which is secured by the presence of the principal Members of the Executive in the House of Commons, chosen mainly from its Members, and living its daily life in full intimacy and association. In the palmy days of Queen Victoria, great respect was paid to the position of a Member of Parliament. His status and authority were everywhere considered. He was much looked up to. Then there was an interlude. As the franchise became more democratic, it grew to be the fashion in certain social circles to speak with contempt about Members of Parliament as a class and as a type. They were represented as mere spouters and chatterboxes, the putters of awkward questions and the raisers of small points of procedure. Kipling wrote his poem:

'Paget, MP, was a liar and a fluent liar therewith.'

Altogether, there was a phase in which Members of Parliament were thought to be rather a poor lot. That period is over. This White Paper is a proof that it is over. What is this White Paper? I say it is a roll of honour.

Mr Bevan: Who are included in that roll of honour? It is an astounding doctrine that you are giving us now.

The Prime Minister: The roll is not by any means necessarily final. That is the answer I give to the hon. Gentleman, and if he will not reproach me with an endeavour to suborn him, I can only say that the roll is not necessarily complete. Many things have yet to happen. This White Paper records a process reached naturally and even inevitably under the conditions of these tremendous and terrible times, and which, while it serves the interest of the nation at war, dignifies and enhances the character and quality of Parliamentary representation.

It is the policy of this present Government to raise and sustain the personal status of Members of Parliament in every possible manner. It is my deliberate policy, as Leader of the House, to do so and always to watch very carefully – as indeed I have done – over the safety and dignity of the House and keep it alive and effective under conditions in which it has never before been attempted to carry on Parliamentary Government in any civilized State. I am sure that, when the war is over, this institution which we cherish and serve will have gained by having in its ranks large numbers of Members who have played an important part in the great days through which we shall have passed, and who will have their share in winning the victory, the fruits of which we and other Parliaments will then enjoy.

Victor Cazalet:[1] *diary*
(Robert Rhodes James, 'Victor Cazalet, a Portrait', pages 254-5)

27 February 1941

To hear Winston – 55 mins. I saw him in Smoking Room afterwards. He was exhausted. Tears in his eyes. He had worked till 3 a.m. to prepare it. He makes a mistake at end, and his peroration was badly interrupted by Aneurin Bevan. How difficult to say anything not to upset him in this mood!

Eric Seal: letter to his wife
(Seal papers)

27 February 1941 10 Downing Street

It's just striking midnight. We have had an interesting day, if a strenuous one. I have been down at the House nearly all day, preparing for the PM's speech on the bill to enable Malcolm Macdonald to retain his seat. As I told you, there was a good deal of feeling about it. The PM nevertheless scored a resounding Parliamentary success – with far greater knowledge of his subject & depth of argument than any of his opponents. It sounds ridiculous that we should do such a thing in the middle of a war – but it was really a sort of holiday for him, & he was quite braced up as a result, like anyone who can do something supremely well, & enjoys the sensation of a perfect piece of work!

[1] Victor Alexander Cazalet, 1896–1943. Educated at Eton and Christ Church, Oxford. Oxford half blue for tennis, racquets and squash, 1915. Served on the Western Front, 1915–18), when he won the Military Cross. A member of General Knox's staff in Siberia, 1918–19. Conservative Member of Parliament for Chippenham from 1924 until his death. Parliamentary Secretary, Board of Trade, 1924–6. Political Liaison Officer to General Sikorski, 1940–3. Killed in the air crash in which Sikorski died. His sister, Thelma Cazalet-Keir, was Conservative Member of Parliament for Islington East from 1931 to 1945.

Winston S. Churchill to Harry Hopkins
(*Premier papers, 4/17/2*)

28 February 1941
Personal and Secret

The packet of rifles and ammunition which we owe to your intercession has safely arrived, and is a great addition to our security.[1] I am, however, increasingly anxious about high rate of shipping losses in North-Western Approaches and shrinkage in tonnage entering Britain. This has darkened since I saw you. Let me know when Bill[2] will be through. The strain is growing here.

Winston S. Churchill to A. V. Alexander and Admiral Pound
(*Churchill papers, 20/36*)

28 February 1941
Action this Day

City of Calcutta, due Loch Ewe the 2nd March, is reported to be going to Hull, arriving the 9th March. This ship must on no account be sent to the East coast. It contains 1,700 machine guns, 44 aeroplane engines, and no fewer than 14,000,000 cartridges. These cartridges are absolutely vital to the defence of Great Britain, which has been so largely confided by the Navy to the Army and the Air. That it should be proposed to send such a ship round to the East coast with all the additional risk, is abominable. I am sending a copy of this minute to the Minster of Transport.

Another ship now of great importance is the *Euriades*, due Liverpool the 3rd March. She has over 9,000,000 cartridges.

I shall be glad to receive special reports as to what will be done about both these ships.

Winston S. Churchill to A.V. Alexander and Admiral Pound
(*Churchill papers, 20/36*)

28 February 1941

MERCHANT SHIP LOSSES IN THE ATLANTIC

I am quite content with the form in which you propose to give the figures. Analysis of your table seems to show the following results:

[1] The packet was 250,000 rifles and fifty million rounds of ammunition. It had reached Britain with a Canadian troop convoy.

2 The Lend-Lease Bill.

(1) In the North-Western Approaches the risk on the inward voyage (nearly 5 in 100) is far greater than on the outward voyage (under 2 in 100).

(2) Too few ships sail outward independently to allow a valid statistical average.

(3) Among inward-bound ships there does not seem to be much difference in risk between those which started in convoy (including the stragglers) and the fast, larger ships sailing independently.

While I am personally convinced of the soundness of the convoy system, I nevertheless wish that it should be continually subjected to unprejudiced judgment in the light of ascertained facts. The question of lowering the speed-limit for ships routed independently is, as you know, being raised by the Import Executive.

Winston S. Churchill to David Margesson and Sir Edward Bridges
(*Churchill papers, 20/36*)

28 February 1941

I am very doubtful about this.[1] It will raise many complications in security, and there is still unemployment here. I should have thought they would be employed on works, roads, &c., in the Middle East or in India. It would be new mouths to feed here.

The matter should certainly come again before the War Cabinet.

Winston S. Churchill to Sir Archibald Sinclair
(*Churchill papers, 20/36*)

28 February 1941
Secret

BOMBING OF ROME

This matter is not pressing at the present time. If we should decide later on to do it, I hope we shall not confine ourselves to the targets shown in (b), but let them have a good dose where it will hurt them most.

[1] A War Office proposal to employ Italian prisoners-of-war as workshop mechanics, in addition to those to be employed on land-reclamation work.

Winston S. Churchill to General Smuts
(*Churchill papers, 20/49*)

28 February 1941
Personal and Secret

I am so glad you are going to meet Eden and Dill. We have taken a grave and hazardous decision to sustain the Greeks and to try and make a Balkan front. I look forward to receiving your personal views upon this after your Conference. This decision make it most necessary to reinforce Egypt and Libya, and I hope you will arrange with Wavell and Dill to bring *Acanthus* forward to the Mediterranean at the earliest moment, asking me about shipping difficulties, which are great. Our affairs are helped by rapid successes gained in East Africa. It is only a few weeks ago they were telling us they could not move on Kismayu till May. Now we have Mogadishu and the whole place in our hands. Kindest regards.

Import Executive: minutes
(*Cabinet papers, 86/1*)

28 February 1941 — 10 Downing Street
10 a.m.
Secret

The meeting[1] had before them reports on a number of points referred for immediate investigation at the meeting on February 26th. The following decisions were reached:

(1) Arrangements should be made for daily meetings of representatives of the Admiralty (Trade Division) and the Ministries of Transport and Shipping so that immediate decisions could be given when concerted action was required for resolving difficulties and delays that were holding up shipping in our ports.

(2) Efficiency was being impaired as a result of the rule requiring all merchant ships to keep up steam in their boilers while in port in this country, so that they could be moved rapidly in the event of invasion. The Chiefs of Staff Committee should consider as a matter of urgency whether this requirement could be relaxed for all ports other than London.

(3) Representatives of the Admiralty and the Ministry of Shipping, with the assistance of Professor Lindemann, should prepare for submission early in the

[1] With Churchill again in the Chair, as on 26 February 1941. Those present were the same as on February 26, with the exception of Sir Cyril Hurcomb, Director-General, Ministry of Shipping (who came in place of his Minister, Ronald Cross).

following week a detailed analysis and explanation of the time at present taken on the voyage across the Atlantic.

(4) The First Lord of the Admiralty was invited to work out with the naval staff a plan for direct convoys that would omit the call at Oban or Loch Ewe, and to submit it to the Prime Minister by Monday, March 3rd. It was appreciated that unless additional escort vessels could be made available, this would involve a reduced scale of escort. But it might be necessary to run additional risks in order to maintain our importing capacity.

(5) The Import Executive should consult with the expert advisers of the Admiralty early in the following week with a view to:

(a) reach agreement on the independent sailing of ships of between 12 and 13 knots; and

(b) a preliminary discussion on general convoy policy.

Any proposals for a radical change in general convoy policy would, of course, require to be considered by the Defence Committee or the War Cabinet before being adopted.

(ii) An estimate was given of the additional shipping required for military purposes.

The Prime Minister gave directions that these additional demands should be the subject of the most thorough scrutiny by the Ministry of Shipping and War Office.

March
1941

Winston S. Churchill to Viscount Halifax
(*Churchill papers, 20/49*)

1 March 1941

COMMENTS ON A DRAFT SPEECH TO BE DELIVERED
BY LORD HALIFAX ON WAR AIMS

You will no doubt have seen the President's remarks to Mr Winant[1] about war aims, in which he emphasized that his war aim was to win the war. Personally, I like paragraphs 3, 4 and 5 much better than 12, 13, 14 and 15. I do not know what is meant by the last four lines of paragraph 14 so far as they affect the individual. Do you contemplate the abolition of private property, especially in the forms of rent and interest, unless related to some form of service to the State? If so, this will carry very far, unless, of course, you count managing one's own estate and hunting foxes as such service, in which case the passage means nothing. Is conducting a private business for private profit service to the State? In paragraph 15 I do not understand how the whole world can be compelled to join together to bring the world back to health. We may call a conference of sixty or seventy nations, but it is very probable that most of them will be thinking of their own interests. All the thought in these four paragraphs suffers from being both hackneyed and loose. There is no teeth in it anywhere. I should strongly advise recasting on less ambitious lines. It is a pretty tough job to reshape human society in an after-dinner speech. Pray forgive me striking this note of caution, but of course, I have no doubt the speech will work out all right. All good wishes.

[1] John Gilbert Winant (known as Gil), 1889–1947. On active service in France, 1917–18. Governor of New Hampshire, 1925–27, 1931–35. Chairman of the Social Security Board, 1935–37 (an integral part of Roosevelt's New Deal). United States Ambassador in London, 1941–46. Order of Merit, 1946. Author of *A Letter from Grosvenor Square* (1947) and his wartime speeches, *Our Greatest Harvest* (published posthumously, 1950).

Winston S. Churchill to General Ismay, for the Chiefs of Staff Committee
(*Churchill papers, 20/36*)

1 March 1941

The responsibilities of the Director of Combined Operations were laid down in a directive issued to Lieut.-General A. G. B. Bourne[1] by the Chiefs of Staff in June 1940. In view of the changes which have taken place since that date it is desirable that these responsibilities should be re-defined.

At the same time, it is to be recognized that the division of responsibility between the Director of Combined Operations on the one hand and the Joint Planning Staff on the other is not capable of precise definition. There must always be border-line cases which will have to be settled as they arise by mutual consultation.

General Scope of DCO's Responsibilities.

2. The Director of Combined Operations is responsible, under the general direction of the Minister of Defence and the Chiefs of Staff, for:-

(a) The command and training in irregular warfare generally, and in landing operations in particular, of the troops specially organized for this purpose, i.e., the Special Service Troops.

(b) The supervision of the technical training in landing operations of such other troops as may from time to time be earmarked for enterprises which call for this particular type of training.

(c) The development, including experiment, research and trial, of all forms of special equipment and craft required for opposed landings.

(d) The initiation, within the general policy prescribed, and the planning and execution of operations by the Special Service Troops, reinforced if necessary by small forces – naval, military and air – which are not normally under his command.

For the purpose of making plans he may have any assistance he requires from the Joint Planing Staff.

In this connexion, the Prime Minister has laid it down as a guide that the Director of Combined Operations should be responsible for the planning and execution of raiding operations which involve not more than 5,000 men.

(e) The provision of advice to the Chiefs of Staff and the Joint Planning Staff on the technical aspects of landing operations.

[1] Alan George Barwys Bourne, 1882–1967. Entered the Royal Marine Artillery, 1899. Served on HMS *Tiger*, 1915–17; in France, 1918 (DSO). Assistant Adjutant-General, Royal Marines, 1931–5. Colonel Commandant, Portsmouth Division, Royal Marines, 1935–8. Adjutant-General, 1939–43. Lieutenant-General, 1939. Knighted, 1941. General, 1942.

Administration

3. The routine administration of the Special Service Troops, including maintenance and movements, will be the responsibility of the War Office. The DCO is, however, responsible for advising the War Office as to how these units can be organized, armed, equipped and located, to meet his particular needs.

Special Equipment and Landing Craft

4. The Director of Combined Operations will have under his command and direction of Inter-Services Training and Development Centre.

Authority for Operations

5. The general policy for raiding operations will be laid down from time to time by the Chiefs of Staff in accordance with the direction of the Prime Minister and Minister of Defence.

Winston S. Churchill to Sir Archibald Sinclair,
Air Chief Marshal Sir Charles Portal and Lord Beaverbrook
(*Premier papers, 3/9*)

1 March 1941

MAP will continue to be responsible for the Atlantic Ferry Service.[1] The Air Ministry is to supply the desired personnel or their equipment.

By the end of the first week in March I wish to receive a report that this has been done in such a manner as to render the Ferry Service effective.

Winston S. Churchill to Sir Archibald Sinclair and Lord Beaverbrook
(*Churchill papers, 20/36*)

1 March 1941

1. All promotions of RAF Officers rest in the domain of the Air Ministry.

2. All appointments inside MAP including No. 41 Group and kindred establishments, belong to the Minister of Aircraft Production. If the Minister wishes to fill a vacancy with an RAF officer, but has no suitable officer available under his own control, he will ask the Air Ministry to submit a succession of names of suitable officers whom they can make available.

[1] The Ministry of Aircraft Production; Churchill was seeking to resolve the continuing dispute about respective areas of responsibility between the Secretary of State for Air (Sir Archibald Sinclair) and the Minister of Aircraft Production (Lord Beaverbrook).

3. Where RAF personnel is serving in MAP, the Air Ministry, before making any promotions, even by routine, will consult the Minister of Aircraft Production.

4. Seeing that certain specified posts in MAP carry with them a definite rank in the RAF, the Minister of Aircraft Production will consult the Air Ministry before making such appointments in order to avoid inconvenience in the Service.

5. The Air Ministry will consider it their duty as a general rule to meet the wishes of the Minister of Aircraft Production in the above matters, even though they may not agree with the course proposed.

6. In the event of disagreement arising in any particular case under paras. 3, 4 and 5, the matter is to be referred to me as Minister of Defence for decision.

7. A Branch will be established in the Office of the Minister of Defence in order to advise me upon the details of such disputed cases. General Ismay will make proposals to this end.

8. All superior officers of the Air Ministry and all high officials of MAP are hereby reminded that it is their duty to meet the wishes of the sister Department to the utmost possible extent. Failure to comply with this instruction will be regarded as disservice to the public in time of danger.

9. The above paragraphs will be brought to the notice of those concerned by the Secretary of State for Air and the Minister of Aircraft Production in their respective Departments.

Winston S. Churchill to David Margesson

(*Churchill papers, 20/36*)

1 March 1941

I am relieved to hear that the 250,000 rifles and the 50,000,000 rounds of ammunition have arrived safely with the Canadian troop convoy. When I raised the point of getting the Admiralty to give up the .303 rifles and take the American rifles in exchange it was proposed to me on other papers that a very much larger and better change was possible by giving the newly-arrived American rifles to the static troops in Great Britain, thus liberating 250,000 .303s for the Regular Army. I presume this will now be done. On the last occasion when we got the American rifles across we made a regular evolution of it, and had special trains waiting, and the like. I now hope you will make a rapid evolution of this new windfall, so that the weapons are in the hands of those who need them at the earliest moment.

Perhaps you will let me know what arrangements are being made.

Winston S. Churchill to Lord Moyne
(*Churchill papers, 20/36*)

1 March 1941

General Wavell, like most British military officers, is strongly pro-Arab. At the time of the licences to the ship-wrecked illegal immigrants being permitted, he sent a telegram not less strong than this, predicting widespread disaster in the Arab world, together with the loss of the Basra-Baghdad-Haifa route. The telegram should be looked up, and also my answer, in which I overruled the General and explained to him the reasons for the Cabinet decision. All went well, and not a dog barked.

It follows from the above that I am not in the least convinced by all this stuff. The Arabs, under the impression of recent victories, would not make any trouble now. However, in view of the Lustre[1] policy I do not wish General Wavell to be worried now by lengthy arguments about matters of no military consequence to the immediate situation. Therefore, Doctor Weizmann[2] should be told that the Jewish Army project must be put off for six months, but may be reconsidered again in four months. The sole reason given should be lack of equipment.

Winston S. Churchill to General Wavell
(*Premier papers, 3/288/5*)

1 March 1941

Hearty congratulations on the brilliant result of the campaign in Italian Somaliland.[3] Will you convey to General Cunningham[4] the thanks and appreciation of His Majesty's Government for the vigorous, daring and highly successful operations which he has conducted in command of his ardent, well-trained, well-organized Army? Will you ask him to convey this message to his troops? Publish as you find convenient.

You will no doubt discuss future operations with General Smuts on the 7th. As you know, I have always wanted the South African Divisions to come

[1] The decision to send British troops from Egypt to Greece.

[2] Chaim Weizmann, 1874–1952. Born in Russia, educated in Germany. Reader in Bio-chemistry, University of Manchester, 1906. Naturalized as a British subject, 1910. Director Admiralty Laboratories, 1916–19. President of the World Zionist Organization, and of the Jewish Agency for Palestine, 1921–31 and 1935–46. Chairman, Board of Governors, Hebrew University of Jerusalem, 1932–50. Adviser to the Ministry of Supply, London, 1939–45. First President of the State of Israel from 1949 until his death. His eldest son, Flight-Lieutenant Michael Weizmann, RAF, was killed in action in 1942.

[3] South African troops had entered Mogadishu, the capital of Italian Somaliland, on 25 February 1941. Three days later all the Italian forces still fighting surrendered.

[4] General Alan Cunningham, Commanding the East Africa Forces (see page 415 n.3).

forward to the Mediterranean shore, and you will certainly need them now. One would hope also that there would not be much difficulty in reclaiming British Somaliland. At present we seem to have swapped Somalilands with the enemy.

The capture of so many prisoners and arms is most satisfactory.

Winston S. Churchill to King George VI
(*Churchill papers, 20/29*)

1 March 1941

I am very grateful to Your Majesty for the kindness and consideration of Your Majesty's letter of February 26.

The situation has not yet reached a point where we need consider this matter at all with a view to decision. I have indeed been wondering whether President Roosevelt might not perhaps entertain the idea of a meeting in Iceland, which would be a very short journey for me. Moreover, this rendezvous could be kept entirely secret.

I am however deeply impressed with the weight of all the arguments which Your Majesty has been good enough to set out in terms so gracious and complimentary.

The danger of invasion must never be absent from our minds.

I remain,
Your Majesty's faithful and devoted servant,
Winston S. Churchill

Winston S. Churchill to Lady Oliphant[1]
(*Churchill papers, 20/28*)

1 March 1941 — 10 Downing Street

My dear Christine,

Forgive me for not answering earlier your letter of February 20. But I have had to have inquiry made into the whole affair. While this was in train, I am afraid we received discouraging news, as we have just heard from the United States Embassy that the Germans are unwilling to proceed 'at present' with the arrangements for the exchange, on the ground that the area through

[1] Christine McRae, the daughter of William Sinclair, and widow of Churchill's cousin, Victor, 1st Viscount Churchill. She married Sir Lancelot Oliphant in 1939. He was then Ambassador to Belgium and Minister to Luxembourg. He was captured in France while preceeding from Bruges to Le Havre to join the Belgian Gopvernment in exile in London. He was interned in Germany from 2 June 1940 until 27 September 1941. He resumed his ambassadorial duties in October 1941.

which the ship transporting the British and German officials would have to pass is a combat area and that they would be unable to ensure her safety. This is a sad blow, but it is clear that the German Admiralty who, I fancy, were never sincere in this matter, have effectively dispelled hope, at any rate for the time being, of the exchange going through. There is, I fear, nothing that I can do to get this decision reconsidered. We cannot retaliate, and though we intend to take steps to ensure that everybody shall see where the blame for the breakdown lies protests or remonstrances will not help. So I am afraid you must make up your mind to a further period of delay, while never giving up hope, as we shall not, that something may happen to get the scheme started again.

I have had careful inquiries made into the progress of these negotiations and I am satisfied that at no stage are the Prisoners of War Department to blame, either through sins of omission or commission, for the various delays that have occurred. Anyone who examines the course of the negotiations would see that Sir G. Warner[1] must have become 'sick and tired' of the obstruction and evasions of the German authorities, but they would also agree that he never relaxed his efforts, and I can assure you that we shall miss no opportunity to reopen the matter, and omit no action that might achieve a happy result.

Yours ever,
Winston S. Churchill

Winston S. Churchill to Anthony Eden
(*Churchill papers, 20/49*)

1 March 1941

I am perplexed and somewhat unsettled by accounts which have so far reached us about Castelorizzo.[2] We did not understand how this island or, indeed, Casos, was selected and timed so much in advance of main Mandibles. Story received about Casos seems to show lack of purpose and management, and difficult to believe enemy not disturbed. Story about Castelorizzo does not

[1] George Redston Warner, 1879–1978. Entered the Foreign Office, 1903. Served in Tangier and Oslo. Knighted, 1934. Minister at Berne, 1935–39. In charge of repatriation negotiations, London, 1940–45.

[2] On the night of 24 February 1941 a British raiding party of two hundred Commandos landed on the outlying Dodecanese island of Castelorizzo. This was the first phase of the operation 'Abstention'. Before the larger force waiting offshore could land, the Italians struck back, first by air and then by sea, causing havoc to the British plans. What was to have been a permanent occupation of the island was abruptly abandoned, and the expedition returned to Crete. 'No communiqué', Churchill was informed, 'has or will be issued.' The withdrawal must be treated 'as though the intention was to carry out a raid only' (Signal from C-in-C Mediterranean, 9.44 a.m., 28 February 1941: *Premier papers 3/124/1, folio 14*).

explain how many of our men landed; where they landed; how far they got; what they did; what prisoners they took; what losses they suffered. How was it that enemy could be reinforced by sea, observing we had supposed we had local control of the sea? What was the naval and military force which relieved and reinforced the enemy? Where did they come from; how did they get there? How was it that, after island reported captured, it was only discovered during evacuation that a considerable enemy ship was in the inner harbour? Did we ever take the inner harbour or the defences around it? Anxiety also arises from severity of air attack. Was this not foreseen? Where did it come from? Was it Italian or German? Please ascertain all details.

Importance of knowing these facts does not arise mainly through this particular operation, for evidently these same conditions may be present in aggravated form when larger Mandibles is attempted. Pray endeavour to reassure me on this.

Largest project must certainly be affected if enemy air dominance can be maintained in these waters. Without certainty that we can take and hold main Mandibles whole question of communications of largest scheme seems challenged.

For these reasons, vitally important we should understand whole sequence of plan as you and our military friends foresee it.

Winston S. Churchill to Anthony Eden
(Churchill papers, 20/49)

1 March 1941

Without in any way blaming Turks, I cannot see that you have got anything out of them. Obvious German move is to over-run Bulgaria,[1] further intimidate Turkey by threat of air attacks, force Greece out of the war, then turn on Yugoslavia, compelling her to obey; after which Turkey can be attacked or not, at their hostile convenience.

Your main appeal should now be made to Yugoslavia. We have not as yet received any answer to King's telegram to Palsy.[2] A sudden move south by Yugoslavia would produce an Italian disaster of the first magnitude, possibly decisive on whole Balkan situation. If at the same moment Turkey declared war, enemy could not gather sufficient forces for many months, during which our air strength will grow. I am absolutely ready to go in on a serious hazard if there is reasonable chance of success, at any rate for a few months, and all

[1] In fact, Bulgaria formally joined the German-Italian Axis that day (1 March 1941), and on the following day the Bulgarian Parliament approved, by 150 votes to 20, the presence of German troops in the Bulgarian capital, Sofia, and the principal Bulgarian Black Sea port, Varna.

[2] Prince Paul, the Yugoslav Regent.

preparations should go forward at fullest speed. But I should like you so to handle matters in Greece that if upon final consideration of all the factors, including Mandibles possibilities, you feel that there is not even a reasonable hope, you should still retain power to liberate Greeks from any bargain and at the same time liberate ourselves. Evidently you and we have a few days in which to make final decision. Meanwhile, all should proceed as arranged.

Robert Menzies: diary
(*'Canberra Times', 18 July 1982*)

1 March 1941

The PM in conversation will steep himself (and you) in gloom on some grim aspect of the war (tonight shipping losses to Focke Wulf planes and U-boats – the supreme menace of the war, and on which, with Dudley Pound, First Sea Lord, we have had much talk) only to proceed to fight his way out while he is pacing the floor with the light of battle in his eyes.

In every conversation he inevitably reaches a point where he positively enjoys the war: 'Bliss in that age it was to be alive'.[1]

'Why do people regard a period like this as years lost out of our lives when beyond question it is the most interesting period of them? Why do we regard history as of the past and forget we are making it?'

Hugh Dalton: diary
(*'The Second World War Diary of Hugh Dalton, 1940-45'*)

2 March 1941 — Chequers

Arrived at Chequers, I found only Menzies, several women – Mrs Churchill and, I think two daughters – various underlings, the Prof, Seal and Thompson. PM in great form. Complained that his beer was not cold enough. Spoke in praise of onions, of which we had a good supply. '*L'oignon fait la force*', that, he said, was Baldwin's idea of a joke. It appealed to his mediocre wit. He jeered a little at Halifax, and his draft on Peace Aims. There was 'no precision of mind in it regarding correlation of "rights and duties"'. What duties did a person living on idle investments perform? Yet did Halifax propose to confiscate all such property? Of course not. He then talked of Socialism, the Nationalization of the railways, and the old Liberal attitude against monopoly. But 'You can never go back and take away from people what they have.'

[1] William Wordsworth 'French Revolution, as it appeared to Enthusiasts':
Bliss was it in that dawn to be alive.
But to be young was very heaven!

Therefore you could not unnationalize the Post Office, even if you could prove that it would be more efficiently run by a private company. There must be a profit incentive and there must be a ladder. All this, I thought, was rather superficial. He has not been doing much new thinking on these subjects since the last war.

His mind was much on the sinkings.[1] He told Van yesterday that he was thinking of them all the time. A chart was put out on the floor before lunch. Not so bad as he had thought, in these last weeks, in which, however, most damage is being done from the air. The troops were eating too much. They could do with less rations. And they are using too much cotton and wool material.

Through lunch Menzies sat rather silent, a little over-awed, but he will tell the tale all right in Melbourne when he gets back. PM said, 'Hitler says that 16 million Jews ought to go and live in Australia. What do you say to that?' He had no good quick answer. PM also made the old joke about MEW and MUW of which he is very fond.[2]

After lunch I had three-quarters of an hour with him alone. I offered to send for Gladwyn,[3] whom I was keeping at the end of a telephone an hour away. No, he said, that is too far. I pressed very strongly my need for more aircraft, and read some notes on the present position. He asked me to write a short Minute on this and said he would do what he could to help. There is great competition for aircraft. I say that we are now ready for more tools. I say that in particular we are stuck for civil aircraft. He says, rather defensively, 'That is not Beaverbrook's fault.' Vansittart, he says, 'gets things a little out of proportion.' He asks whether we have not many Left-Wing elements at Woburn?[4] (with a slight chuckle). I say that I am accused by others of Fascist methods and getting rid of Reds and even Pinks at MEW. I say that our people are being sniped. I want him to be satisfied. He says, 'I am not dissatisfied. I know that you are a very able man.' (This would go all right in a headline, but not much warmth.) He goes on to say that Bracken may have been saying some things which he had no authority to say. Morton has denied saying what he is alleged, and adds, 'He read me a letter saying that he was much impressed with what he had seen.' PM adds that Attlee has spoken to him

[1] During February, seventy-five British merchant ships had been sunk, with a total of 315,304 tons.

[2] The Ministry of Ungentlemanly Warfare: also known, because of its Special Operations Executive responsibilities, as the Ministry of Dirty Tricks.

[3] Hubert Miles Gladwyn Jebb, 1900–1996. Entered the Foreign Office, 1924. Foreign policy adviser, Ministry of Economic Warfare, , 1940–41. Head of the Reconstruction Department of the Foreign Office, 1942. Acting Secretary-General, United Nations, 1945–46. United Kingdom Permanent Representative, United Nations, 1950–54. Knighted, 1954. Ambassador to France, 1954–60. Created Baron Gladwyn, 1960. Deputy Leader of the Liberal Party in the House of Lords from 1967. Member of the European Parliament from 1972, the year in which he published *Memoirs of Lord Gladwyn*.

[4] Woburn Abbey, Bedfordshire, the headquarters of Special Operations.

about all this. I press that the PM should see some of my chaps. I speak of some of them. I say that Nelson[1] was a friend of Lloyd and Alexander. When Tory MP for Stroud, he spoke against the Gold Standard. I sometimes wonder whether the PM remembers this against him. The PM says, 'No, I am not that kind of man.' Brigadier Gubbins[2] seems to register slightly, and of Hambro[3] he says, 'I want to give both him and —[4] a K.' At first he said, 'No, I see no one.' Then when pressed further, 'How many do you want me to see?'

Robert Menzies: diary

(*'Canberra Times, 18 July 1982'*)

2 March 1941

Churchill grows on me. He has amazing grasp of detail and by daily contact with the Services' HQs knows of dispositions and establishments quite accurately.

But I fear that (though experience of supreme office has clearly improved and steadied him) his real tyrant is the glittering phrase – so attractive to his mind that awkward facts have to give way. But this is the defect of this quality. Reasoning to a pre-determined point is mere advocacy, but it becomes something much better when the conclusion is that you are going to win the war and that you're damned if anything will stand in your way.

Churchill's course is set. There is no defeat in his heart.

[1] Frank Nelson, 1883–1966. Educated in Britain and Germany (Heidelberg). Chairman of the Bombay Chamber of Commerce, 1922–23. President, Associated Chambers of Commerce, India and Ceylon, 1923. Member of the Bombay Legislative Council, 1923. Knighted, 1924. Conservative Member of Parliament for Stroud, 1924–31. British Consul, Basel, 1939. Special Operations Executive, 1941–43; Head of SO2, dealing with sabotage. Wing Commander, Air Intelligence, Washington, 1944. In command of Air Force Intelligence, British Zone of Occupation, Germany, 1945–46.

[2] Colin McVean Gubbins, 1896–1976. On active service 1914–19 (France, Belgium, North Russia; wounded; Military Cross). War Office, 1935–39. Chief of Staff, British Military Mission to Poland, 1939. Raised and commanded independent Companies, later Commandos, France and Norway, 1940. Raised and commanded Auxiliary Units for special duties, Home Forces, June 1940; Special Operations Executive (SOE), November 1940–January 1946. Knighted, 1946. One of his two sons was killed in action in Italy, 1944.

[3] Charles Jocelyn Hambro, 1897–1963. On active service, Coldstream Guards, 1915–19 (Military Cross). Banker. Chairman of Hambros Bank. A Director of the Bank of England. Sheriff of the County of London, 1933. Deputy Head of SO2 (sabotage in Europe), 1940–42. Knighted 1941 Executive Director of SOE, May 1942 to September 1943. Head of the British Raw Materials Mission, Washington, 1944–45, and British Member of the Combined Raw Materials Board.

[4] Hugh Dalton left a blank at this point.

Winston S. Churchill to Alfred Duff Cooper
(*Churchill papers, 20/36*)

2 March 1941

This article[1] bears on its own face the reason why it should not be published. It shows the endeavours that are being made to keep this matter secret: 'Questions are parried with a smile,' &c.; 'Their job isn't one to be talked about.' With such a confession staring him in the face the Censor let the matter go through, thus prostrating the effort to keep secrecy. In these circumstances I cannot think that the officer in question is fit for his job. However, I defer to your view.

What is the name of the special correspondent concerned which you said you would obtain? If he had written this in a letter to a foreign country he would have brought himself in the range of the most severe penalty. As, however, his message is published in a newspaper, and thus conveyed to the enemy via Lisbon or New York, he is immune. What had MI5 to say about it?

Winston S. Churchill to Lord Woolton
(*Churchill papers, 20/21*)

2 March 1941
Private

My dear Woolton,

Thank you very much for your letter, and believe me, I realize all the difficulties with which you are manfully contending.

I still think that from the point of view of economy it would be better to allow and even encourage in the restaurants the eating up of scraps of all kinds through these being well and tastily cooked, rather than to compel people to plump for the solid, simple dishes.

When a person has the choice of having a piece of cheese or a slice of roast beef, most will choose the latter. They way not to get fish eaten is to put it into competition with game or meat. When I visited a restaurant on Saturday for the first time for some months, the proprietor told me that your regulations

[1] An article in the *Daily Mirror* of 14 February 1941, headed 'Spies Trap Nazi Code'. It began: 'Britain's radio spies are at work every night. During the day they work in factories, shops and offices. Colleagues wonder why they never go to cinemas or dances. But questions are parried with a smile – and silence. Their job isn't one to be talked about. Home from work, a quick meal, and the hush-hush men unlock the door of a room usually at the top of the house. There, until the small hours, they sit, head-phones on ears, taking down the Morse code messages which fill the air. To the layman these would be just a meaningless jumble of letters. But in the hands of code experts they might produce a message of vital importance to our Intelligence Service. No pay is given to the men who tap the air for these messages. They are drawn from the radio enthusiasts who operated their own short-wave transmitters before the war.'

would cause him no inconvenience, as there were many exceptions, i.e. oysters and whitebait. Apparently a lobster is all right, but not a crab.

I should also have thought that an exhortation not to leave anything on the plate, and to take small portions with, if necessary, a second helping, would be a wise step. However, these are only my personal views.

Perhaps before you have any other important announcement to make, you will consult the Cabinet, and then the Minister of Information will be able to make sure that the right emphasis is put on the orders before the news is given to the newspapers.

I am always at your disposal if you want to consult me.

Yours very sincerely
Winston S. Churchill

Eric Seal: letter to his wife
(*Seal papers*)

4 March 1941

We stayed on at Chequers over Monday night,[1] because Winston had a bit of a cold. His doctor[2] came down to see him, & spend the night, bringing with him a nasal specialist, who pronounced that the cold was due to snuff, wh. the PM was taking in the vain hope that it would ward off a cold!! Anyway, snuff has been eschewed, & the cold is much better.

Winston S. Churchill to Lord Moyne and Viscount Cranborne
(*Churchill papers, 20/36*)

4 March 1941
Secret

UNITED STATES BASES IN THE WESTERN HEMISPHERE

You can easily have a first-class row with the United States about these matters, and this will be particularly vexatious at a time when the Lease and Lend Bill is on its passage. I am anxious, therefore, by one means or another to keep this business as quiet as possible till the Bill is through. We shall then have only the President to deal with, and not be in danger of giving ammunition to our enemies in the Senate.

[1] Monday, 3 March 1941.
[2] Sir Charles Wilson.

War Cabinet: minutes
(*Cabinet papers, 65/18*)

4 March 1941
6.15 p.m.

BELGIUM

The Prime Minister said that he had just seen the Belgian Ministers and the Belgian Ambassador,[1] who had complained about the arrangements for the Belgian Government in this country communicating with the people of Belgium. The Belgian Government had been helpful to us and we should be accommodating to them in this matter.

JAPAN

The Prime Minister said that he had seen the Japanese Ambassador. The Japanese Minister for Foreign Affairs had sent his thanks for the Memorandum sent to him, and had said that Japan had never intended to offer mediation between this country and Germany. The Japanese Ambassador had made it clear that, under the Tripartite Pact, Japan was under no obligation to enter the war, except in circumstances of which she would be the judge. The Ambassador had also stressed Japan's desire not to get involved in war with us.

VICHY FRANCE

The Prime Minister thought we should adhere to our policy of not relaxing our blockade of Vichy-controlled territories, except in so far as we might be compelled to make concessions by the force of public opinion in America. All such concessions should be confined to the minimum.

This view met with general approval.

THE BALKANS[2]

The Prime Minister said that prospects in the Balkans were not promising. Bulgaria was now under German control. It looked as though Greece would have to fight for her life and as though Yugoslavia intended to take no action before she was surrounded.[3] If the Yugoslavs were to decide to act at once, their armies might well wipe out the Italian armies in Albania.

[1] Baron Cartier de Marchienne, 1871–1946. Entered the Belgian Diplomatic Service, 1892. Ambassador to the United States, 1920–27; to Britain, 1927–46. Honorary knighthood, 1934.

[2] Because of the particular secrecy of this item it was not recorded in the War Cabinet Minutes but retained in the Confidential Annex of the Cabinet Secretary's Standard File (*Cabinet papers, 65/22*).

[3] Unknown to Churchill, on 4 March 1941 the Regent of Yugoslavia, Prince Paul, while visiting Hitler at Berchtesgarten, promised orally to follow the example of Bulgaria and allow German troops and aircraft to be based in Yugoslavia.

No further telegram had yet been received from the Secretary of State for Foreign Affairs on military policy. No doubt he would report again as soon as he had returned to Egypt. The time table of movements was due to start that day, but no troops were due to arrive in Greece for another four days. If General Dill and General Wavell wished the movement to proceed, he (the Prime Minister) was most disinclined to issue countermanding orders. Nevertheless, he still thought the Cabinet might wish to take a final view of the whole position in the light of the information to be received in the next few days.

John Colville: diary
(*Colville papers*)

4 March 1941

The PM returned from Chequers at noon and saw Colonel Donovan, just back from the Balkans, where the stage is set and the curtain about to rise.

The PM had Herschel Johnson[1] and Winant[2] to dine and discussed with them the American bases problem. I had to rush away from the dinner table three times in order to procure various telegrams. It is very difficult to find what the PM wants because his descriptions are so elliptical.

Winston S. Churchill to Herbert Morrison
(*Churchill papers, 20/36*)

4 March 1941
Secret

Certain aerodromes are being built in Northern Ireland for the use of squadrons of the Royal Air Force operating in the North West Approaches. It is vital that these aerodromes should be completed without delay. Please take up with the Government of Northern Ireland, in the most effective manner possible, the question of giving the highest priority to supplying transport and hard core for their construction. The Air Ministry will let you know what exactly is required.

[1] Herschel V. Johnson, 1894–1956. Served in the United States Army in France, 1917–18. Entered the US Foreign Service, 1920. First Secretary and Counsellor of Embassy, London, 1934–41. Minister to Sweden, 1941–6; Ambassador to Brazil, 1948–53.

[2] The America Ambassador.

Winston S. Churchill to Ernest Bevin
(*Churchill papers, 20/36*)[1]

4 March 1941
Secret

In order to improve the efficiency of our air squadrons working in the North West Approaches, aerodromes at Stornoway, Benbecula and Tiree are being constructed. This work is of the very highest priority, though for geographical reasons labour is difficult to obtain. Please give this matter urgent attention, in consultation with the Secretary of State for Air.

2. I understand that about 250 to 400 men are required at each place, and nothing should be allowed to stand in the way of getting them.

John Colville: diary
(*Colville papers*)

5 March 1941

Johnson and Winant, the new US Ambassador, in the Cabinet room at No. 10, to discuss the vexed problem of the American bases in the West Indies, which we have given on lease for 99 years in return for 50 obsolete destroyers. The West Indian Colonies themselves, the oldest of the Crown, are resentful and their feelings are shared by many people here in view of the conditions which the Americans have demanded and which amount to Capitulations. Both sides are haggling and ill-feeling has arisen. Bridges thinks that if the Government accepted all the American desiderata they would be defeated in the House of Commons. The Colonial Office are frightened that in the heat of conflict we shall cede such that will afterwards be most regrettable. Lord Cranborne sees in the American attitude a dangerous emphasis on hemisphere defence: an inclination to make special concessions to Canada because she is an American nation; a tendency which might well lead to Western hemisphere isolationism after the war.

But the PM is ill-satisfied with the point of view expressed by his colleagues. He believes that the safety of the state is at stake, that America in providing us with credits will enable us to win the war which we could not otherwise do, and that we cannot afford to risk the major issue in order to maintain our pride and to preserve the dignity of a few small islands.

[1] Churchill wrote similar minutes to the Minister of Transport, for the completion of runways ('of the utmost urgency'), and to the Ministry of Shipping ('no delay in shipping material for these aerodromes from this country').

I think his view is statesmanlike, but America, if she persists, is going to arouse a lot of bitterness in England and set back the cause of Anglo-American unity.

While the PM was trying to reach a modus vivendi on this question, an alarming telegram arrived from Eden. It showed the Greek situation in a sombre light. Eden, Dill and Wavell have found General Papagos[1] discouraged and obviously weakened by the loss of Metaxas. They have accepted a strategic position which will mean that our troops will find themselves in a dangerous plight. Yugoslavia is weak and vacillating; Turkey is in no position to do anything but remain on the defensive. Eden says: 'This is as tough a proposition as even I have known.'

Last night David Margesson told me how much he disliked the whole venture upon which we are about to embark. Many others feel the same. It was thrust upon us partly because, in the first place, the PM felt that our prestige, in France, in Spain and in the US, could not stand our desertion of Greece; partly because Eden, Dill, Wavell[2] and Cunningham (who has now telegraphed to point out the extreme length to which his resources are stretched) recommended it so strongly. But the danger of another Norway, Dunkirk and Dakar rolled into one, looms threateningly before us.

More telegrams came. The PM went very late to lunch with Oliver Lyttelton, and I snatched ¼ of an hour for a quick mouthful. After his afternoon sleep, the PM, emerging from beneath the bedclothes and yawning, said, voicing his waking thought: 'The poor Chiefs of the Staff will get very much out of breath in their desire to run away'. I showed him a telegram from Eden urging that a high decoration for General Papagos would help matters. 'Too cheap,' he commented with a disgusted gesture.

The Cabinet met at 5.00 and afterwards the PM drafted a telegram to Eden urging that we should not be justified in preventing the Greeks from accepting German terms if they felt themselves unable to resist. If they wished to fight, well and good; we should have to do our utmost.

This telegram was discussed at 10.00 p.m. Defence Meeting.

[1] Alexander Papagos, 1883–1955. Born in Athens. In action during the Balkan Wars, 1912–13 (against the Bulgarians) and in Asia Minor, 1920 (against the Turks). Chief of the Army General Staff, 1936–40. Commander-in-Chief of the Greek Army, 1940–1. Held in various German concentration camps as a hostage from 1943 until his release by the Americans in 1945. In 1949 he was recalled to his position as Commander-in-Chief to wage war against the Communist guerrillas in Northern Greece. Refused to take power in Athens after a military coup in his favour, May 1951. Headed the Greek Rally Party in Parliament, August 1951. Prime Minister from November 1952 until his death.

[2] Colville noted at this point, while preparing his diary for publication after the war: 'Having been opposed to the whole scheme of intervention on behalf of Greece, he veered round and became its warmest exponent.'

John G. Winant: recollection
(*'A Letter from Grosvenor Square'*)

5 March 1941

I had never seen Mr Churchill at work before, and I was deeply impressed not only with his grasp of the values involved and his appreciation of the defence needs of the United States, but also with his knowledge of the detail of the negotiations with which he had familiarized himself on such short notice. I became quickly conscious of his vast experience in public matters which he had acquired during more than forty years of active participation in public life. There was no detail of the problem before us which was not alive to him and on which his knowledge of the past did not throw light as well as constructive criticism.

War Cabinet: minutes
(*Cabinet papers, 65/18*)

5 March 1941 10 Downing Street
5.30 p.m.

The Prime Minister said that over the week-end two new factors had come into play. First, the Castelorizzo operation had been a fiasco, and news had been received that the Mandibles Operation[1] could not be carried out until the movement of our forces to Greece was complete. This meant that we should not be able to concentrate all our available air forces against the German advance into Greece. Secondly, it had become evident that the air menace to the Suez Canal had in no way been mastered.

On the 3rd March he had sent a Personal telegram to the Foreign Secretary. [This was read to the War Cabinet.] The purport of this telegram was that the Foreign Secretary should conduct his negotiations on the basis that preparations for the despatch of troops to Greece should proceed. On this basis the Foreign Secretary would have a better chance of obtaining the co-operation of Turkey and Yugoslavia. The Foreign Secretary's main appeal should be addressed to the latter. If Yugoslavia could be persuaded to make a sudden move into Albania, this might well mean disaster to the Italian forces.

Although it had been decided that arrangements for the despatch of our forces should proceed, the situation in the Balkans had already deteriorated. The Prime Minister had therefore suggested to the Foreign Secretary that he should so handle matters that it would still remain open to us to take a final decision on the despatch of forces to Greece and to liberate the Greeks from their undertakings.

The Prime Minister then read a further Personal telegram received from

[1] The plan to seize the Dodecanese Islands, and in particular Rhodes.

the Foreign Secretary. The main points were that the Foreign Secretary saw no alternative between encouraging Greece to the best of our power to resist, and standing by and allowing her to collapse before German threats: while the proposition was a tough one, neither he nor his advisers saw any alternative to doing our best to see it through.

The Prime Minister added that if the Greeks had taken any action, or entered into any commitments, on the strength of undertakings received from us, then we should have no alternative but to go through with the plan. But, so far as we could see, they had taken no such action. Indeed, they had not taken the steps which we had expected in withdrawing divisions from the Albanian and Macedonian fronts. In his judgment it was still open to us, if on consideration this seemed the wisest course, to tell the Greeks that we would liberate them from any undertaking which they had given to us. It would follow, of course, that the Greeks would be free to make terms with Germany.

The Parliamentary Under-Secretary of State for Foreign Affairs[1] said that if we abandoned Greece, this might have a bad effect on the position in Spain which was uncertain, and in North Africa where German infiltration was increasing.

The Prime Minister thought that the effect in Spain and North Africa would be worse if we landed in Greece and were driven out, than if we remained masters of the Delta and seized the Dodecanese. General Papagos had said that it was quite impossible to make any withdrawals from the Albanian Front, since his troops there were exhausted and greatly outnumbered. Was the significance of this that his troops could not face being taken away from the Albanian campaign and being put up against German forces? Might not Greece collapse in the face of a German ultimatum?

Eric Seal: letter to his wife

(*Seal papers*)

5 March 1941 10 Downing Street

An amusing incident occurred. The meeting which is just over adjourned for a few minutes. The Secretary of State for Air called me, & said that Prime Minister wanted either me or the Chiefs of Staff. So I went in & asked. PM replied – 'I don't want you or the Chiefs of Staff, or the Secretary of State, but a marine with some whisky & soda!'

[1] Richard Austen Butler, 1902–82. Known as 'Rab'. President of the Cambridge Union, 1924. Conservative MP for Saffron Walden, 1929–65. Under-Secretary of State, India Office, 1932–7. Parliamentary Secretary, Ministry of Labour, 1937–8. Under-Secretary of State for Foreign Affairs, 1938–41. Privy Councillor, 1939. Minister of Education, 1941–5. Minister of Labour, 1945. Chancellor of the Exchequer, 1951–5. Lord Privy Seal, 1955–61. Home Secretary, 1957–62. Deputy Prime Minister, 1962–3. Secretary of State for Foreign Affairs, 1963–4. Created Baron Butler of Saffron Walden, 1965. Master of Trinity College, Cambridge, 1965–78.

Defence Committee (Operations): minutes
(Cabinet papers, 69/2)

5 March 1941 Cabinet War Room
10 p.m.

The Prime Minister expressed the view that in face of a German ultimatum, the Greeks would find it impossible to carry on the struggle. There was little or nothing which we could do to assist them in time. He thought the telegram should go, and that it should be followed up by the commentary prepared by the Chiefs of Staff.

Winston S. Churchill to Anthony Eden
(Cabinet papers, 65/22)

5 March 1941

Situation has indeed changed for worse. Following on their No. 54582 (MO5), to which reply has not yet been received, Chiefs of Staff have presented serious commentary, which follows in my next. Failure of Papagos to act as agreed with you on 21st February, obvious difficulty of his extricating his army from contact in Albania and timetable of our possible movements furnished by Wavell in his 0/45461 of 3rd March, together with other adverse factors recited by Chiefs of Staff, *e.g.*, postponement of Mandibles and closing of Canal,[1] make it difficult for Cabinet to believe that we now have any power to avert fate of Greece unless Turkey and/or Yugoslavia come in, which seems most improbable. We have done our best to promote Balkan combination against Germany. We must be careful not to urge Greece against her better judgment into a hopeless resistance alone when we have only handfuls of troops which can reach scene in time. Grave Imperial issues are raised by committing New Zealand and Australian troops to an enterprise which, as you say, has become even more hazardous. We are bound to lay before the Dominions Governments your 313 and Chiefs of Staff appreciation. Cannot forecast their assent to operation. We do not see any reasons for expecting success except that, of course, we attach great weight to opinions of Dill and Wavell.

We must, as indicated in my telegram No. 396 to Athens, liberate Greeks from feeling bound to reject a German ultimatum. If, on their own they resolve to fight, we must to some extent share their ordeal. But rapid German

[1] On 3 March 1941, the day on which the Suez Canal was to have been cleared of mines, the Germans managed to lay ten more mines in the Canal, with the result, as Churchill was informed, that the Canal was 'now completely closed' and not likely to be cleared until 11 March 1941. (Chiefs of Staff, Aide Memoire, 5 March 1941, *Cabinet Papers, 65/22*)

advance will probably prevent any appreciable British Imperial forces from being engaged.

Loss of Greece and Balkans by no means a major catastrophe for us, provided Turkey remains honest neutral. We could take Mandibles and consider plans for Influx or Tripoli. We are advised from many quarters that our ignominious ejection from Greece would do us more harm in Spain and Vichy than the fact of submission of Balkans, which with our scanty forces alone we have never been expected to prevent.

I send you this to prepare your mind for what, in the absence of facts very different from those now before us, will probably be expressed in Cabinet decision tomorrow.

Chiefs of Staff: Commentary[1]
(*Cabinet papers, 69/2*)

5 March 1941

1. Our envoys at their first interview with the King of Greece[2] and General Papagos reported that they were 'greatly impressed by the attitude and spirit' of Papagos. At their recent interview, they found him 'unaccommodating and defeatist', though he appears to have cheered up towards the end. This change of attitude on the part of Papagos was perhaps only to be expected in view of the German arrival on the Greco-Bulgar frontier and of the failure of any support from Yugoslavia or Turkey. Nevertheless, it is bound to react unfavourably on the fighting spirit of his Army.

2. The Greeks undertook on February 21st to begin withdrawing their advance troops to the line which we should have to hold if the Yugoslavs were not willing to come in, and to start work immediately on improving communications in Greece to facilitate the occupation of this line. Today (twelve days later) we learn that no withdrawal has commenced and we gather that no work has been done. In view of the paramount importance of the time factor, this is serious.

3. We were to have had 35 Greek Battalions to help us hold the line. We are now told that we are to have three Greek divisions and seven Battalions from Western Thrace but that these only amount to 23 battalions at most. With the exception of the 12th Division these are all newly formed and have not yet fought. One of the divisions can hardly have any guns, while the remainder

[1] Telegraphed by Churchill to Eden immediately after his own telegram.

[2] George II, 1889–1947. Became King of Greece in September 1922; deposed in April 1923. Returned as King in November 1935. Assumed the Premiership of Greece after the suicide of Korizis, 1941. In exile, 1941–5, first in Cairo, then in London. Negotiated a Lend-Lease agreement with the United States, 1943. Returned to Greece in 1946.

can only have captured Italian material. But, in addition to the 35 battalions for which we had hoped, we had contemplated that the Greeks would be able to withdraw some divisions from their Albanian front. General Papagos now says that this cannot be done as they are 'exhausted and outnumbered'.

4. We have always contemplated that 'Mandibles' would be captured before – or at least simultaneously with – the move to Greece. It now appears that 'Mandibles' cannot be undertaken until the movement to Greece has been completed. This means that instead of being able to concentrate all available air forces against the German advance, considerable air operations will have to be conducted against 'Mandibles' in order to protect our lines of communication to Greece.

5. The mining of the Suez Canal has become a more acute handicap. It was to have been open on 3rd March, but the Germans put in ten more mines that day. The Canal is now completely closed, and on past form may not be clear until 11th March. Only half of the MT ships required for the movement to Greece, are North of the Canal, and all personnel ships are South of it. Even if personnel for Greece are carried in men-of-war, the whole force cannot be dealt with in this manner.

THE TIME FACTOR

6. We have estimated that one armoured and three motorised divisions could reach the Bulgar-Greek frontier on the 5th March, and in addition an infantry division by 11th March. We further estimate that, assuming weak delaying action by the Greeks in the Rupel area, the Germans could have two divisions on the Alyakmon Line by about the 15th March, and concentrate the whole five divisions there by 22nd March.

7. We are now told that General Papagos intends to fight in the Rupel area with three divisions. Until we receive an answer to our telegram 64 we have no means of knowing how much delay will be imposed on a German advance, since much will depend on the strength of the position, the equipment and morale of the Greek troops, and on whether an effective scheme of demolitions has been prepared and can be executed. If the delay imposed is short, we should at the best have one armoured brigade and one New Zealand brigade to oppose the first two German divisions on the Alyakmon line.

CONCLUSION

8. Our conclusion is that the hazards of the enterprise have considerably increased. Nevertheless, despite our misgivings and our recognition of a worsening of the general situation we are not as yet in a position to question the military advice of those on the spot, who in their latest telegram, describe the enterprise as not by any means hopeless.

Eric Seal: letter to his wife
(*Seal papers*)

6 March 1941 10 Downing Street

Winston is very active, & not in too good a humour. I think his cold is getting him down a bit.

Winston S. Churchill: recollection
('*The Second World War*', *Volume Three*')

[6 March 1941]

SHIPPING LOSSES IN THE ATLANTIC

The pressure grew unceasingly, and our shipping losses were fearfully above our new construction. The vast resources of the United States were only slowly coming into action. We could not expect any further large windfalls of vessels such as those which had followed the overrunning of Norway, Denmark, and the Low Countries in the spring of 1940. Moreover, damaged shipping far exceeded our repairing resources, and every week our ports became more congested and we fell farther behind. At the beginning of March over 2,600,000 tons of damaged shipping had accumulated, of which about 930,000 tons were ships undergoing repair while loading cargoes, and nearly 1,700,000 tons were immobilized by the need of repairs. Indeed, it was to me almost a relief to turn from these deadly under-tides to the ill-starred but spirited enterprises in the military sphere. How willingly would I have exchanged a full-scale attempt at invasion for this shapeless, measureless peril, expressed in charts, curves, and statistics!

My thought had rested day and night upon this awe-striking problem. At this time my sole and sure hope of victory depended upon our ability to wage a long and indefinite war until overwhelming air superiority was gained, and probably other Great Powers were drawn in on our side. But this mortal danger to our life-lines gnawed my bowels. Early in March exceptionally heavy sinkings were reported by Admiral Pound to the War Cabinet. I had already seen the figures, and after our meeting, which was in the Prime Minister's room at the House of Commons, I said to Pound, 'We have got to lift this business to the highest plane, over everything else. I am going to proclaim "the Battle of the Atlantic".' This, like featuring 'the Battle of Britain' nine months earlier, was a signal intended to concentrate all minds and all departments concerned upon the U-boat war.

In order to follow this matter with the closest personal attention, and to give timely directions which would clear away difficulties and obstructions and force action upon the great number of departments and branches involved, I brought into being the Battle of the Atlantic Committee. The meetings of this committee were held weekly, and were attended by all Ministers and high functionaries concerned, both from the fighting services and from the civil side. They usually lasted not less than two and a half hours. The whole field was gone over and everything thrashed out; nothing was held up for want of decision.

Winston S. Churchill: Directive
(Churchill papers, 23/9)

6 March 1941
Most Secret

THE BATTLE OF THE ATLANTIC

DIRECTIVE BY THE MINISTER OF DEFENCE

In view of various German statements, we must assume that the Battle of the Atlantic has begun.

The next four months should enable us to defeat the attempt to strangle our food supplies and our connection with the United States. For this purpose –

1. We must take the offensive against the U-boat and the Focke Wulf wherever we can and whenever we can. The U-boat at sea must be hunted, the U-boat in the building yard or in dock must be bombed. The Focke Wulf, and other bombers employed against our shipping, must be attacked in the air and in their nests.

2. Extreme priority will be given to fitting out ships to catapult, or otherwise launch, fighter aircraft against bombers attacking our shipping. Proposals should be made within a week.

3. All the measures approved and now in train for the concentrations of the main strength of the Coastal Command upon the North-Western Approaches, and their assistance on the east coast by Fighter and Bomber Commands, will be pressed forward. It may be hoped that, with the growing daylight and the new routes to be followed, the U-boat menace will soon be reduced. All the more important is it that the Focke Wulf, and, if it comes, the Ju. 88, should be effectively grappled with.

4. In view of the great need for larger numbers of escorting destroyers, it is for consideration whether the American destroyers now in service should go into dock for their second scale of improvements until the critical period of this new battle has been passed.

5. The Admiralty will re-examine, in conjunction with the Ministry of Shipping, the question of liberating from convoys ships between 13 and 12 knots, and also whether this might not be tried experimentally for a while.

6. The Admiralty will have the first claim on all the short-range AA guns,

UP weapons and PAC.[1] that they can mount upon suitable merchant ships plying in the danger zone. Already 200 Bofors or their equivalents have been ordered to be made available by ADGB[2] and the factories. But these should be followed by a constant flow of guns, together with crews or nucleus crews, as and when they can be taken over by the Admiralty. A programme for three months should be made.

7. We must be ready to meet concentrated air attacks on the ports on which we specially rely (Mersey, Clyde and Bristol Channel). They must therefore be provided with a maximum defence. A report of what is being done should be made in a week.

8. A concerted attack by all Departments involved must be made upon the immense mass of damaged shipping now accumulated in our ports. By the end of June this mass must be reduced by not less than 400,000 tons net. For this purpose, a short view may for the time being be taken both on merchant and naval shipbuilding. Labour should be transferred from new merchant shipbuilding which cannot finish before September 1941, to repairs. The Admiralty have undertaken to provide from long-distance projects of warship building or warship repairs up to 5,000 men at the earliest moment, and another 5,000 should be transferred from long-distance merchant shipbuilding.

9. Every form of simplification and acceleration of repairs and degaussing, even at some risk, must be applied in order to reduce the terrible slowness of the turn-round of ships in British ports. A saving of 15 days in this process would in itself be equivalent to 5 million tons of imports, or a tonnage of 1¼ millions of the importing fleet saved. The Admiralty have already instructed their officers in all ports to aid this process, in which is involved the process of repairs, to the utmost. Further injunctions should be given from time to time, and the port officers should be asked to report what they have done and whether they have any recommendations to make. It might be desirable to have a conference of port officers, where all difficulties could be exposed and ideas interchanged.

10. The Minister of Labour has achieved agreement in his conference with employers and employed about the interchangeability of labour at the ports. This should result in a substantially effective addition to the total labour force. In one way or another, at least another 40,000 men must be drawn into ship repairing, shipbuilding and dock labour at the earliest moment. Strong propaganda should be run locally at the ports and yards, in order that all engaged may realize the vital consequences of their work. At the same time, it is not desirable that the Press or the broadcast should be used unduly, since this would only encourage the enemy to further exertions.

[1] Parachute and Cable device: an anti-aircraft rocket.
[2] Air Defence of Great Britain.

11. The Ministry of Transport will ensure that there is no congestion at the quays, and that all goods landed are immediately removed. For this purpose, the Minister will ask the Chairman of the Import Executive for any further assistance required. He should also report weekly to the Import Executive upon the progress made in improving the ports on which we specially rely by transference of cranes, &c., from other ports. He should also report on the progress made in preparing new facilities at minor ports, and whether further use can be made of lighterage to have more rapid loading or unloading.

12. A Standing Committee has been set up of representatives from the Admiralty Transport Department, the Ministry of Shipping and the Ministry of Transport, which will meet daily and report all hitches or difficulties encountered to the Chairman of the Imports Executive. The Imports Executive will concert the whole of these measures and report upon them to me every week, in order that I may seek Cabinet authority for any further steps.

13. In addition to what is being done at Home, every effort must be made to ensure a rapid turn-round at ports abroad. All concerned should receive special instructions on this point, and should be asked to report on the measures which they are taking to implement these instructions, and on any difficulties that may be encountered.

Winston S. Churchill: Directive
(*Churchill papers, 23/9*)

6 March 1941
Most Secret

ARMY SCALES

DIRECTIVE BY THE MINISTER OF DEFENCE

When in September 1939 the Cabinet approved the formation of a Field Army of 55 Divisions, it was not realized that a Division as contemplated by the War Office with its share of Corps, Army, GHQ and L of C formations would require 42,000 men, exclusive of all training establishments and of all garrisons, depots or troops not included in the Field Army. At that time also it was assumed that the bulk of our Army would stand in the line with the French under conditions comparable to those of the last War, whereas the bulk of our Army now has to stay at home and defend the Island against invasion. Thirdly, the shipping stringency makes it impossible to transport and maintain very large forces overseas, especially on the high scales which the War Office regard as necessary.

2. Out of the 55 Divisions (now become 57), 36 are British and 21 Overseas

troops. Of the 36 British Divisions, one (so-called) Division is in Iceland, and one (the 6th) is forming in Egypt, together with 2 Armoured Divisions there, total British Divisions now overseas = 4.

3. Twenty-five British Infantry Divisions and the equivalent of 7 Armoured Divisions in process of formation, total 32, are now included in the Home Forces Army. At 19,500 men apiece, these 25 British Infantry Divisions aggregate 487,500 men, and the 7 Armoured Divisions at 14,000 apiece aggregate 98,000, total 585,500. In addition to the Divisional organization, C-in-C, Home Forces, has 10 independent Brigades, including the Guards Brigades, 27 Beach Brigades, and 14 unbrigaded Battalions, all British. At an average of 3,500 men apiece, these 42 Brigades or equivalents account for about 150,000 men. Therefore the total number of British in tactical formations at home amounts to 735,500 men.

4. There are on our ration strength at home 1,800,000 British soldiers. 735,500 are accounted for in the above formations, leaving 1,064,500 to be explained as Corps, Army and GHQ troops and ADGB or as Training Establishments, depots, &c., and as part of the rearward services of the forces overseas.

5. It is upon this pool of 1,064,500 that the Army must live. By wise economies, by thrifty and ingenious use of man power, by altering establishments to fit resources, it should be possible to make a very great improvement in the fighting strength. Apart from this capital fund of man-power, the Army can count each year upon its 18's and 19's. It is only in the event of heavy casualties being sustained through many Divisions being simultaneously and continuously in action, which except in the case of invasion is extremely unlikely, that any further inroad can be allowed upon the man-power resources of Great Britain. In other words the Army can rely on being kept up to something like their present figure of about 2 million British, and they will be judged by the effective fighting use they make of it.

6. At the same time, it will be well to plan an eventual increase of Armoured formations to the equivalent of 14 Armoured Divisions (or 15 if the Australian Armoured Division materializes), in which would be included the Army Tank Brigades. A reduction of several Infantry Divisions would be required, and the British Army would then be composed of 14 Armoured Divisions (or their equivalent) and about 22 Infantry Divisions. The War Office and Ministry of Supply should work out proposals on these lines.

7. The 3 East African Divisions and the West African Division should not be organized in formations higher than Brigades or small mobile groups adapted to the duties they have to perform.

8. It will be impossible for us to maintain from Great Britain any large addition to our Army in the Middle East, because we have to go round the Cape. The main accretion of this Army must come from India, Australasia and South Africa, with later on munitions from the United States. Three or

four more British Divisions is the most we can hope to send and keep there. One must consider that General Weygand's silence has released us from any offer of helping him up to six Divisions, although, of course, we might act on our own volition. An amphibious striking force of eight or ten Divisions, mostly armoured, is the utmost that need be envisaged in the West. There can be no question of an advance in force against the German Armies on the mainland of Europe.

9. The above considerations and the situation as a whole make it impossible for the Army, except in resisting invasion, to play a primary role in the defeat of the enemy. That task can only be done by the staying power of the Navy, and above all by the effect of Air predominance. Very valuable and important services may be rendered Overseas by the Army in operations of a secondary order, and it is for these special operations that its organization and character should be adapted.

10. The reactions of the foregoing directive on manpower accommodation, ammunition, stores, &c., should be worked out.

Winston S. Churchill to Alfred Duff Cooper
(*Churchill papers, 20/36*)

6 March 1941

When I demurred to Sir Robert Vansittart making a broadcast the other day, I had not realized it was in French to the French people. I see no objection to Sir Robert making broadcast to the French people, for whom his particular views have a real attraction and value.

Winston S. Churchill to Sir Alexander Cadogan
(*Churchill papers, 20/36*)

6 March 1941

THE FUTURE OF KING CAROL OF ROUMANIA[1]

If Canada does not want him, he could certainly be offered accommodation in some of our numerous Islands. Anyhow, I think we should help him. What do you suggest?

[1] Carol II, 1893–1953. Married Princess Helen of Greece, 1921. Barred by his father from succession to the throne because of his liaison, after 1923, with Magda Lupescu, with whom he lived in Switzerland from 1925 to 1930. Returned to Roumania on his father's death and was proclaimed king. Established a royal dictatorship, 1937; banned all political Parties, 1938. Forced to cede Roumanian territory to Hungary, Bulgaria and the Soviet Union, June-August 1940. Abdicated, September 1940. Spent his remaining years in exile with Magda Lupescu.

Charles Eade:[1] *notes of a luncheon*
(*Charles Eade papers*)

6 March 1941

We lunched in a small room, strengthened by steel girders in the basement of No. 10. I was received by Mrs Churchill and had some sherry before lunch. She was wearing one of the scarves decorated with miniatures of posters of national slogans, such as 'Go to it', 'Lend to Defend' and similar phrases. There was no formality about the gathering, in fact, it was decided to start lunch without the Prime Minister. We were seated at the table, but had not been served with the first course, when he came in. We lunched at a small round table. I sat immediately facing Mr Churchill, with Mrs Churchill on my right and Professor Lindemann on my left. Winston kissed Lady Portarlington[2] on arrival, and she addressed him as Winston.

The lunch consisted of a fish patty, tornedos with mushrooms on top and braised celery and chipped potatoes, peaches and cheese to follow. The drinks were sherry before lunch, a light white wine (probably French) during lunch and port and brandy afterwards as well as coffee. Saccharin as well as sugar was on the coffee tray. Cigars and cigarettes were also handed round.

I had imagined that the conversation at such a small gathering would be very carefully kept away from anything to do with the war, but this was not so at all. The war was talked about all the time, and it seemed that the Prime Minister had not the slightest reluctance to discuss any aspect or problem of the war brought up by any of the guests. He talked with considerable satisfaction about the British raid on the Norwegian island of Lofoten, which is near Narvik. He said that the Germans had been making cod-liver oil there and that this would be used to make up the deficiency in vitamins from which the German population was suffering.[3]

We discussed the air raids, and Dr Conant[4] was told that perhaps he was taking a risk staying at Claridges Hotel, because it was not a steel construction. Mrs Churchill said that he ought to move to the Dorchester at which both she and Lady Portarlington laughed heartily, and it was explained to Dr Conant that although his life may be in greater danger at Claridges, his reputation may be

[1] Editor of the *Sunday Dispatch*; and editor of five volumes of Churchill's wartime speeches.

[2] Winnifreda Yuill. She married the 6th Earl of Portarlington in 1907. Their only son, Viscount Seymour, an Air Commodore, Auxiliary Air Force, was killed on active service in Europe in 1944.

[3] This was Operation Claymore. The account given by Churchill to his guests hid its more serious, and secret, purpose (see page 112, note 2).

[4] James Bryant Conant, 1893–1978. Instructor in Chemistry, Harvard University, 1916–17. Major, United States Chemical Warfare Service, 1918. Professor of Organic Chemistry, Harvard, 1928–33. President of Harvard, 1933–53. Chairman, National Defence Research Committee, and Deputy-Director Office of Scientific Research and Development, 1941–46. Steering Committee, Manhattan Project charged with the production of atomic bombs, 1942–45. United States High Commissioner (later Ambassador) to the Federal Republic of Germany, 1953–57.

in greater danger at the Dorchester. He then said that as an educationalist and President of Harvard, he would rather risk his life than his reputation.

Mr Churchill, talking of risks, made the remark that although it was always good to take a chance, you should never offer a 'sitter'.

I said that my experience was that the main thing must be to avoid glass and blast. At this, the Prime Minister barked across the table, 'But how do you avoid blast?' I said he was at that moment sitting in a position in that room in which he was exposed to blast if there was an air raid, because he was just in front of the window, and if bombs were dropping, it would be better to move to a corner. But his reply to that was that if there was an air raid, the butler immediately shuts the steel shutters, and thus that particular danger was removed.

We talked about the huge bomb which was dropped about three weeks ago at Hendon. Mr Churchill said that it weighed 4,000 lbs and killed about 80 people, injuring about 300 others. It swept away streets of small houses. I asked him whether it contained any new form of explosive, but he said that it did not. It was only the great size that was novel.

Another point mentioned was the absurdity of some Englishwomen who give cups of tea and cigarettes to German airmen brought down while raiding this country. Mrs Churchill commented on the inability of the English people to hate their enemies and Winston said that before this war was over, we should be hating our enemies all right.

We discussed the possibility of the Germans carrying out heavy raid on Athens. Churchill said he was sure that the Italians, fearful for the fate of Rome, would try to stop such raids. I suggested that the bombing of Athens would be a good thing from our point of view as it would shock American opinion. Churchill said that the Americans' sentiment was not a 'classical sentiment' and that such raids would not horrify Americans any more than any other raids on undefended cities.

Talking of bombing, I expressed the view that although our bombing was probably more effective bomb for bomb than the Germans, there was a very great desire in this country that the ordinary people of Germany should suffer the effects of the bombing, and I said that I knew wherever Mr Churchill had gone, he had been told by the people who greeted him that he must 'give it back to them'.

Mr Churchill replied with the remark he had made before that 'Duty must come before pleasure.'

Mrs Churchill roared with laughter at this, and said: 'You are bloodthirsty,' a remark which the Prime Minister did not quite get, and it had to be repeated several times for his benefit.

Frank as the conversation had been about the war and its problems, I was quite astonished when Mrs Churchill said: 'But, Winston, why don't we land a million men on the continent of Europe? I am sure that the French would rise up and help us.'

To this, the Prime Minister replied that you could not land a million men all at once and that the vanguards would almost certainly be shot down. Mr Churchill emphasized to Dr Conant that the passing of the Lend Lease Bill in America was of vital importance to us. He rejected very emphatically the idea that we did not want America in the war on our side because, as some people think, it would be better to have America's industrial help instead of seeing the main output go to America's own armed forces if she came into the conflict. Mr Churchill said that if America declared war on Germany, it would lead to such a vast increase in America output that it would be of great benefit to us, and, in any case, the possession of the America fleet would go a long way towards solving our problem of fighting the U-Boats.

Dr Conant told us about his own evidence before the Commission considering America's aid to Britain, and I said it was a pity his evidence had been given the same day as that by Mr Willkie and La Guardia, the Mayor of New York, as it did not receive all the publicity it should have done. Dr Conant said that it was unfortunate that so many people in America were anxious to keep America out of the war at any cost, because they took the view that 'nothing was worse than war'.

Lady Portarlington interjected a remark that that was true. I started to oppose that, but before I could get half a dozen words out, Churchill snapped in his best radio manner, 'Slavery is worse than war. Dishonour is worse than war.' Lady Portarlington hastened to agree.

Telling Dr Conant of the need for American help, Churchill laughingly repeated his wireless sentence, 'Give us the tools, and we will finish the job.'

Churchill had also said that although we did not need an American army to help us, we could make great use of American technicians, particularly wireless experts.

The Prime Minister also commented that Dr Conant looked a very young man to be president of a university. Conant is 48, but looks younger. He became president of Harvard at 40. We spoke of Mr Winant, the new US Ambassador, and I asked whether he was really as shy as he was reputed to be. Mr Churchill said that Winant had not seemed to him to be a shy man.

We also talked about the timidity of the Balkan States in the face of Nazi aggression, and Churchill said: 'It is difficult when you live in the cage with the tiger. Fortunately, we are outside the cage, protected by salt water bars.'

The Prime Minister, who drank quite a lot of port and brandy and smoked a big cigar which he lit at least 10 times, also spoke of the foolishness of the British in the past in allowing Germany to re-arm under Hitler. I asked whether it was not true that Germany had, in any case, been re-arming under its previous governments, and he agreed that this was so, but he thought that we could have stopped all that if we had taken not only a firm line about armaments, but done something to remove the Germans' grievances instead of goading them to Hitlerism. He reminded him of something I had never known before: that the German people twice rejected Hitler in free elections and the second time by a bigger majority than the first.

The Prime Minister said that one of the most unfortunate things that had ever happened in this country was the vote by members of the Oxford Union some years ago, saying that they would not in any circumstances fight for the defence of their own country. He said that this vote was exaggerated and misinterpreted abroad, giving the impression that we were a decadent people and that other countries could oppose us. He agreed with me that in any case, most of the young men who had voted in that debate, were now serving in the military forces.

Another point that the Prime Minister made was that no one could ever say that this war was won on the playing fields of Eton, although Eton, like all other schools, had played its part. He felt it a pity that so many boys from Eton went into the older services, rather than the Royal Air Force, and was interested when I told him that Bedford Grammar School had produced more air pilots than any other school in the country.

The Prime Minister also spoke about the people who were always asking him to declare his aim, and said that the aim was to win the war, and then deal afterwards with the question of peace. He seemed to feel for a moment, I thought, that perhaps that would be a problem for someone other than himself to solve.

'Perhaps,' he said with a laugh, 'Mr Mander.'

I explained to Conant that Mander was an MP who had made a reputation by asking lots of nuisance questions. Mrs Churchill ridiculed the idea that anyone but Winston would be handling after-war problems.

The Prime Minister showed us a letter that President Roosevelt had sent him by Wendell Wilkie, the defeated candidate in the recent United States Presidential election. He had it framed. The letter contains a quotation from Longfellow's poem which read: 'Sail on O ship of state! Sail on O Union, strong and great! Humanity, with all its fears, with all the hopes of future years! Is hanging breathless on thy fate!'

It was addressed to him as 'A Certain Naval Person.'[1] This, apparently, was a sort of code name used when Roosevelt telephoned Churchill.

One charming point illustrating the informality of the luncheon was that when he had finished his meat course, the Prime Minister got up from the table and took his own empty plate over to the sideboard without troubling to have it removed by the butler.

Apart from the war, there was a certain amount of leg-pulling at the expense of Professor Lindemann on the question of science versus religion. Apparently there are three fundamental scientific reasons which make religion

[1] In telegraphing to President Roosevelt, Churchill described himself as 'Former Naval Person'.

appear true, and Lindemann was asked to explain these. I did not quite grasp the full meaning of these three points, but each in its turn was rather impishly rejected and destroyed by the Prime Minister who looked quite mischievous and was obviously ragging Lindemann, who was addressed by Mr and Mrs Churchill as 'Prof'. So far as I could gather, the three points, roughly, were: 1) Heat tends to spread and equalize itself. The sun is much hotter than the earth, which shows that the earth must have been separately heated at a date much later than the sun, 2) Moving bodies, plants and stars etc. should, theoretically, have come together in one huge mass. What force has prevented their doing so? 3) Uranium is continually halving itself. Why is there any uranium left on earth?

While we were still sitting and talking after lunch, Mr Churchill's Parliamentary Private Secretary, Mr Brendan Bracken, came in and joined us for a cigar and a drink. I was rather surprised when he addressed the Prime Minister as 'Winston'. The lunch lasted from 1.35 until 3.20 and we then said goodbye to Mr and Mrs Churchill and Bracken showed Dr Conant and myself the Cabinet room before we left No. 10. Outside the Cabinet Room, there were a number of coathooks and I was amused to see that mine had been hung on the private hook of the Secretary of State for the Dominions.

On my way back to the office I sent a box of flowers to Mrs Churchill.

War Cabinet: minutes
(*Cabinet papers, 65/22*)

6 March 1941
6 p.m.

The Prime Minister said that the aspect of the situation which had caused him most anxiety was lest the Greeks might feel that we had put undue pressure on them and had persuaded them against their better judgment to put up a hopeless resistance against the Germans. It must be remembered that it was only possible to send small forces to Greece in the time available. We should only have one Infantry Brigade and one Armoured Brigade in Greece by the middle of the month, and only one complete Division by the end of the month. He did not wish us to expose ourselves to the charge that we had caused another small nation to be sacrificed without being able to afford effective help.

It was for this reason that he had inserted the words in Telegram 607 that 'we must liberate the Greeks from feeling bound to reject the German ultimatum.' If, however, the Greeks were really determined to fight knowing the limitations of the help which we could give them, then we had no choice but to carry out the agreement reached at Athens.

No decision could be reached until the War Cabinet had received the answer to the very searching questions put in Telegram 607. The Prime Minister felt fairly confident that Mr Eden and his military advisers would send an answer on the same lines as Telegram No. 327 from Athens. In this telegram Sir Michael Palairet had taken the line that there was no question of 'liberating the Greeks from feeling bound to reject the ultimatum'. They had decided to fight Germany, alone if necessary, and the question was whether we would help them or abandon them.

The Prime Minister also felt that the chances of success in this enterprise must be greater than would appear from Telegram 313 from Athens. It was inconceivable that the Chief of the Imperial General Staff[1] could have signed the Military Agreement with General Papagos if he regarded the chances of success in the operation as hopeless.

Summing up the discussion, the Prime Minister said that no decision was called for that evening, or, indeed, could be taken until a reply had been received from the Foreign Secretary. It would perhaps be as well, in order to avoid any risk of divided counsels, to send Mr Eden a telegram to make it clear that the War Cabinet could take no decision until a reply had been received to telegram No. 607.

The fact that a decision was deferred would not in any way imperil the operation, since action was proceeding and our troops were on the move; but the first flight would not reach Greece until the 8th March.

The Prime Minister said that his own view was clear, that we could not now go back on the agreement signed by General Dill and General Papagos, unless the Greeks themselves released us.

The proposition in its new aspect must, of course, be put to the Australian and New Zealand Governments. It would, however, be better to wait until a reply had been received from the Foreign Secretary and the matter could be seen in better perspective, before making these communications.

The War Cabinet:

(1) Authorized the despatch of a telegram to the Foreign Secretary, at Cairo, informing him that, with reference to the final paragraph of telegram 607, the War Cabinet would take no decision until they had received his reply to that telegram:

(2) Deferred a decision until the following day, when it was expected that the Foreign Secretary's reply would have been received.

[1] General Sir John Dill.

Winston S. Churchill to Anthony Eden
(*Cabinet papers, 65/22*)

6 March 1941
8 p.m.

War Cabinet are taking no decision until we receive your reply.

John Colville: diary
(*Colville papers*)

7 March 1941 10 Downing Street

Very anxious decisions have been in the air, making the PM impatient, the atmosphere electric and the pace tremendous.

Winston S. Churchill to Anthony Eden
(*Cabinet papers, 65/22*)

7 March 1941
2.55 a.m.
Most Secret and Personal

1. I will bring your measured and deliberate reply to my 607 contained in your 455 before Cabinet today.[1] Meanwhile, all preparations and movements should go forward at utmost speed.

2. I am deeply impressed with steadfast attitude maintained by you and your military advisers, Dill, Wavell and, I presume, Wilson, on the broad merits after full knowledge of local and technical situation and in view of the memo by the COS Committee.

3. Two points are dominant. First, we must not take on our shoulders responsibility of urging Greeks against their better judgment to fight a hopeless battle and involve their country in probable speedy ruin. If, however, knowing how little we can send at particular dates they resolve to fight to the death, obviously we must, as I have already said, share their ordeal. It must not be said and, on your showing, it cannot be said, that, having so little to give, we dragged them in by over-persuasion. I take it, from your attitude and Athens telegrams 89 and 90, that you are sure on this point.

[1] Eden and Dill had telegraphed to Churchill with the text of an agreement signed between Dill and General Papagos whereby three Greek divisions would remain in Macedonia to defend the northern frontier, on the Nestos-Rupel line. Three further divisions and seven battalions would concentrate on the Aliakhmon position. The British forces would be despatched to Piraeus and Volos 'as rapidly as shipping will permit', and 'will concentrate on Aliakhmon position on which it is intended the Graeco-British forces should be able to battle'. (Telegram No. 326, 'Immediate', 'Most Secret' (Eden and Dill to Churchill), despatched 1.50 a.m. received 7.10 a.m., 6 March 1941: *Cabinet papers, 65/22*).

4. Second point. It happens that most of the troops to be devoted to this solemn duty are the New Zealand Division and after March the Australians. We must be able to tell the New Zealand and Australian Governments faithfully that this hazard, from which they will not shrink, is undertaken, not because of any commitment entered into by a British Cabinet Minister at Athens and signed by CIGS, but because Dill, Wavell and other Commanders-in-Chief are convinced that there is a reasonable fighting chance. This I regard as implied by your positive reactions to our questioning telegrams.

5. Please remember in your stresses that, so far, you have given us few facts or reasons on their authority which can be presented to these Dominions as justifying the operation on any grounds but *noblesse oblige*. A precise military appreciation is indispensable.

6. You know how our hearts are with you and your great officers.

Winston S. Churchill to Air Chief Marshal Sir Charles Portal
(Churchill papers, 20/36)

7 March 1941

1. Having heard about the greatly improved qualities of the modified aircraft in question,[1] it occurred to me that it would be a pity, for the sake of using a few at a time, to take the enemy a present of the knowledge of our spring fashions, and that it would be better to wait until a really effective blow could be struck. In the last war the tanks were given away while we still had only a few. When I mentioned this matter to the AOC-in-C, Fighter Command,[2] he said he thought he would like to use some of them all the time. Hence my Minute.

2. I am much obliged to you for all the reasons you set out. I am not quite clear why there would be advantage in the enemy treating all our Spitfires 'with increased respect'. I thought your great need was to bring him to action, in spite of his evasive tactics. We should be very glad to know the kind of surprises which the Germans have in store for us in the spring, and also the limits of their potential changes. However, if you think it a good thing to do, I shall certainly not contest your opinion.

[1] The Spitfire Mark V, fitted with a Rolls Royce Merlin engine. More than 6000 were produced. They formed the main weapon of Fighter Command from mid-1941 and during 1942.

[2] Air Marshal W. Sholto Douglas.

Winston S. Churchill to Sir Archibald Sinclair
(*Churchill papers, 20/36*)

7 March 1941

RESEARCH AND DEVELOPMENT OF AIRCRAFT ENGINES

MAP has also asked to circulate a paper which contains a lot of secret stuff. I have no objection to this, provided that the circulation is confined to the Defence Committee and the War Cabinet, and that the copies are returned to the issuing Minister after perusal. The number of copies printed should be kept to a minimum, each should be numbered, and the issuing Department should be responsible for knowing where every one is.

Winston S. Churchill to Admiral J. C. Tovey
(*Churchill papers, 20/49*)

7 March 1941

LOFOTEN ISLANDS RAID

I am so glad you were able to find the means of executing 'Claymore'. This admirable raid has done serious injury to the enemy and has given an immense amount of innocent pleasure at home.

War Cabinet: minutes
(*Cabinet papers, 65/18*)

7 March 1941 — 10 Downing Street
12 noon

PROPOSED EXTENSION OF RATIONING

The Prime Minister thought that the proposal raised serious issues. The rationing of other commodities drove people to consume more bread, and a shortage of jam was therefore a serious matter. He contrasted the amount of the weekly ration per person (2 ozs.), with the rations in the Forces – 10 ozs. for a man and 14 for a woman. A very small reduction in the amount of wheat imported into the country would provide the extra tonnage required to import enough jam to maintain the present level of consumption. We must see to it that we imported sufficient delicacies to avoid an unduly austere diet. Attention should also be paid to bringing in articles in a less bulky form, so as to save shipping space.

VICHY FRANCE AND THE BRITISH BLOCKADE

The Prime Minister said that it had been clear to him for some time that we should not be able permanently to deny all supplies of foodstuffs to

Unoccupied France. His policy had been to maintain our blockade in its full rigour as long as possible, and then, at the latest possible date, to allow the least possible infraction of it. Admiral Darlan's threat to convoy supplies across the Atlantic called for a new move on our part.

GREECE

The Prime Minister said that a considered military appreciation was on the way home from Cairo that would supply the detailed arguments; but we knew the conclusions already. The time had now come for taking a decision. In his view it was our duty to go forward, making the necessary communications to the Dominions whose forces were to take part in the campaign.

GREEK REQUEST TO REFRAIN FROM BOMBING OPERATIONS OVER ROUMANIA AND BULGARIA

The Prime Minister said that it was very unfortunate that we should be deprived of the opportunity –

(a) To bomb the Roumanian Oil Fields

(b) To bomb the German communications and so delay their advance, while our concentration was being effected.

GERMAN INVASION OF GREECE

The Prime Minister said that the following considerations seemed to him to be of importance:

(a) We had a fair prospect of reaching the Aliakmon line in time to check the German advance. If so there might be a pause while the enemy brought up new forces.

(b) The Yugoslavs were adopting a cryptic attitude, but we need not despair entirely of their entry into the war on our side.

(c) If the Anglo-Greek forces were compelled to retire from the Aliakmon line, they would be retiring down a narrowing peninsula, which contained a number of strong defensive positions.

(d) We should shortly have strong air forces in Greece. They would be outnumbered by the enemy's air forces but the odds would not be greater than they had been on many occasions.

(e) Our policy had been so developed that nobody could represent us as having forced a hopeless resistance on the Greeks.

His own view was that we should go forward with a good heart.

Winston S. Churchill to Anthony Eden
(*Churchill papers, 20/49*)

7 March 1941

Cabinet this morning considered project in light of your telegrams 313, 314, 326 from Athens and 455 from Cairo, and my telegrams 607 and 608. Chiefs of Staff advised that, in view of steadfastly-expressed opinion of Commanders-in-Chief on the spot, of CIGS and Commanders of the Forces to be employed, it would be right to go on. Cabinet decided to authorize you to proceed with the operation, and by so doing Cabinet accepts for itself the fullest responsibility. We will communicate with Australian and New Zealand Governments accordingly.

John Colville: diary
(*Colville papers*)

7 March 1941 Chequers
evening

The PM was much happier. His mind is relieved now that a great decision has been irrevocably taken. He was witty and entertaining.

John Colville: diary
(*Colville papers*)

8 March 1941 Chequers

Mr Hopkins rang me up from New York at 3.00 a.m. to say the Lease and Lend Bill had passed.[1]

Winston S. Churchill to John G. Winant
(*Premier papers, 4/17/2*)

8 March 1941

My dear Ambassador,

Thank you so much for your letter of March 7, and for letting me know of the message you received from Harry Hopkins. What you say is certainly

[1] This was the vote in the Senate, where the Bill passed by 60 votes to 31. All that remained was the final vote in the House of Representatives, and Presidential assent.

encouraging, and I am particularly glad to hear of the arrangements which are being made to let us have the benefit of American technical assistance.

The news about the Bill is a draught of life.

Yours very sincerely
Winston S. Churchill

Winston S. Churchill to General Smuts
(*Churchill papers, 20/49*)

8 March 1941

Many thanks for your telegram, which confirms decision already taken here. On one trifling point I must advise you. Idea that Beaverbrook has a hoard of aeroplanes which he refuses to disgorge is pure nonsense. For the last four months, on the authority of the Defence Committee, every possible aircraft has been sent by every possible route, crated or flown, to the Middle East, and this process will continue by every means that can be devised. Hope you will not hurry back too soon to the Cape. I like to feel you so near, my old friend.

John Colville: diary
(*Colville papers*)

8 March 1941

At dinner this evening there were present, besides the Prime Minister, General de Gaulle, General Spears,[1] Mr Menzies (Prime Minister of Australia), Duncan and Diana Sandys,[2] Tommy Thompson and myself.

[1] Edward Louis Spears, 1886–1974. Joined the Kildare Militia, 1903. Captain, 11th Hussars, 1914. Four times wounded, 1914–15 (Military Cross). Liaison Officer with French 10th Army, 1915–16. Head of the British Military Mission to Paris, 1817–20. Brigadier-General, 1918. National Liberal MP for Loughborough, 1922–4.; Conservative MP for Carlisle, 1931–45. Churchill's Personal Representative with the French Prime Minister, May–June 1940. Head of British Mission to de Gaulle, 1940. Head of Mission to Syria and the Lebanon, 1941. First Minister to Syria and the Lebanon, 1942–4. Knighted, 1942; created Baronet, 1953. Elected to the Other Club, 1954. Chairman of Ashanti Goldfields. Chairman (later President) of the Institute of Directors.

[2] Duncan Edwin Sandys, 1908–87. Educated at Eton and Magdalen College, Oxford. 3rd Secretary, British Embassy, Berlin, 1930. Conservative MP for Norwood, 1935–45; for Streatham, 1950–74. Political columnist, *Sunday Chronicle*, 1937–9. Member of the National Executive of the Conservative Party, 1938–9. Elected to the Other Club, 1939. On active service in Norway, 1940 (disabled; Lieutenant-Colonel, 1941). Financial Secretary, War Office, 1941–3. Chairman, War Cabinet Committee for defence against flying bombs and rockets, 1943–5. Privy Councillor, 1944. Minister of Works, 1944–5; of Supply, 1951–4; of Housing and Local Government, 1954–7; of Defence, 1957–9; of Aviation, 1959–60. Secretary of State for Commonwealth Relations, 1960–4 (and for Colonies, 1962–4). Created Baron Duncan-Sandys, 1974. In 1935 he married Churchill's daughter Diana (marriage dissolved, 1960). Companion of Honour, 1973.

We talked of Germany and the Germans . . .

Duncan Sandys was very bloodthirsty. He wanted to destroy Germany by laying the country waste and burning towns and factories, so that for years the German people might be occupied in reconstruction. He wanted to destroy their books and libraries so that an illiterate generation might grow up.

Louis Spears replied that this would make the Germans more hardy and virile, while their western conquerors would be growing effete on the fruits of victory. In his view Richelieu was the greatest of modern European Statesmen. He had understood the Germans and at the Diet of Ratisbon he had so divided them that they took centuries to unite. The PM replied that this was not applicable to modern conditions, though Prussia must be separated from South Germany.

The PM said he was in no way moved by Duncan's words. He did not believe in pariah nations, and he saw no alternative to the acceptance of Germany as part of the family of Europe. In the event of invasion he would not even approve of the civil population murdering the Germans quartered on them. Still less would he condone actrocities against the German civil population if we were in a position to commit them. He cited an incident in Ancient Greece when the Athenians spared a city which had massacred some of their citizens, not because its inhabitants were men, but 'because of the nature of man'. This impressed Mr Menzies deeply.

The conversation turned to Rome and Carthage. The PM drew a comparison between this country and Carthage, but pointed out that the Carthaginians were vanquished because they lost command of the sea. Mr Menzies said that moreover they had not a Winston Churchill (forgetting Hannibal!). Anyhow, said the PM, the Almighty had given Carthage a raw deal last time, and might alter the outcome on this occasion.

Winston S. Churchill to President Franklin D. Roosevelt
(*Churchill papers, 20/49*)

9 March 1941

Our blessings from the whole British Empire go out to you and the American nation for this very present help in time of trouble.

Winston S. Churchill to Sir Alexander Cadogan
(*Premier papers, 4/17/2*)

9 March 1941

What is being done to ram in effect of passage of Lease and Lend Bill?

Winston S. Churchill to General Ismay
(*Churchill papers, 20/36*)

9 March 1941

OPERATION AGAINST CASTELORIZZO

I am thoroughly mystified about this Operation,[1] and I think it is the duty of the Chiefs of the Staff to have it probed properly. How was it that the Navy allowed these large reinforcements to be landed, when in an affair of this kind everything depended upon the Navy isolating the Island? It is necessary to clear this up, on account of impending and more important operations. One does not want to worry people who are doing so well for us in many ways and are at full extension, and yet it is indispensable for our success that muddles of this kind should not be repeated.

Winston S. Churchill to Anthony Eden
(*Churchill papers, 20/49*)

9 March 1941

1. I entirely agree with all your handling of the Balkan telegrams. There seems still a chance of Yugoslavia coming in, and more than a chance of her keeping the door shut.

2. While you are on the spot you should deal faithfully with Egyptian Prime Minister,[2] Farouk[3] and anyone else about our security requirements. It is

[1] Castelorizzo island lies midway between Rhodes and Cyprus. A British Commando occupied it on 25 February 1941 after slight opposition. The naval forces then withdrew to Cyprus. Heavy German air attacks developed after which the Germans landed reinforcements, unopposed by the British naval forces. The British forces then left the island.

[2] Nahas Pasha. Negotiated the Anglo-Egyptian Treaty of 1936 (with Anthony Eden). Eden later (after a meeting with Nahas Pasha and Churchill in 1943) wrote: 'He had proved himself a stalwart friend when troubles and dangers had thickened around us. One of his foibles, not unknown in politicians of other lands, was a conviction that he had never acted in error, nor, he explained to us solemnly, even once in contradiction to the dictates of his conscience. Mr Churchill looked at him for a moment with an expression in which incredulity and humour were mingled and replied: '*Moi, j'ai toujours traité ma conscience en bien camarade.*'

[3] Farouk, 1920–65. Born in Cairo. King of Egypt from 1936 to 1952. Overthrown after displaying for many years a politically fatal combination of corruption and incompetence. Died in exile in Rome.

intolerable that Roumanian Legation should become a nest of Hun spies, or that the Canal zone should be infested by enemy agents. I hope you will make these people realize that as we are fighting for our lives we shall stop at nothing to secure the safety of the Imperial Forces which are defending Egypt. I am relying on you to put a stop to all this ill-usage we are receiving at the hands of those we have saved.

3. Will you tell Smuts how glad I should be if now he is so near he could come and do a month's work in the War Cabinet as of old. If he likes the idea it will be indispensable to have two planes, and in any case I am insistent upon all possible precautions being taken for your return journey. Pray tell Longmore to submit a scheme to me by cable.

4. Hope you are looking into Castelorizzo business, which has done much harm outside and completely puzzles me. Do not overlook those parts of your instructions dealing with the economy of the Middle East Armies. Am relying on you to clean up, and to make sure that every man pulls his weight. A few days might well be devoted to this. Give my regards to Dill.

Winston S. Churchill to Viscount Halifax
(*Churchill papers, 20/49*)

9 March 1941
Personal and Secret

1. Many thanks for your letter of 21st and Parents' Institute enclosure. Am always deeply interested in your immense range of telegrams. I thank God the Bill is through, as the strain on naval and mercantile resources is growing.

2. Am sending today telegram through you to President about our decisions in Balkans. These have cost us much heart-searching, but the die is now cast.

3. There is still a chance that Yugoslavia will resist. All possible United States pressure should be put on her. Russian reaction should also make it easier for Turks to do their duty.

4. Your 1005 about Salter.[1] Am much in favour of this,[2] and propose he should remain Parliamentary Under-Secretary to Shipping while discharging this all-important mission which may well last the whole year. He is very keen,

[1] James Arthur Salter, 1881–1975. Transport Department, Admiralty, 1904. Chairman, Allied Maritime Transport Executive, 1918. Knighted, 1922. Director, Economic and Finance Section, League of Nations, 1919–20 and 1922–31. Professor of Political Theory and Institutions, Oxford, 1934–44. Independent MP for Oxford University, 1937–50. Parliamentary Secretary, Ministry of Shipping, 1939–41; Ministry of War Transport, 1941. Head of the British Merchant Shipping Mission, Washington, 1941–3. Privy Councillor, 1941. Chancellor of the Duchy of Lancaster, 1945. Conservative MP, 1951–3. Minister of State for Economic Affairs, 1951–2. Minister of Materials, 1952–3. Created Baron, 1953.

[2] The proposal for a British Shipping Mission to the United States.

and undoubtedly has most valuable contacts in United States. Winant spoke to me most earnestly about importance of sending him. To enhance his prestige I propose submitting his name for Privy Councillorship. He will of course be under your authority. Let me know immediately if you like these arrangements, as I want to put this through Monday. With much suffering and stringency we ought to get through this year in spite of heavy shipping losses, but there is little hope of victory and none of the United States being armed for her own security till the end of 1942, and we cannot get through 1942 without several million tons of United States new construction of merchant ships whether by Hog Island plan or some other. Salter will be excellent in keeping all this alive. You should rub it in all you can, drawing attention to what I wrote in my long letter sent to President at Lothian's request.[1]

5. Lastly, I am becoming ready to ease up about letting food into unoccupied France, provided and as long as they will prevent German infiltration into North Africa, and especially if they would send some more of their warships from Toulon to Atlantic Moroccan ports. Dupuy has telegraphed that he has better impressions of Darlan and Vichy generally than we have sustained. We are waiting for his return and expect to advise you soon of definite decision. It is most important that the United States should give Sam[2] the food he wants for Spain, but they ought not to link this question with the French supplies.

General Sir Alan Brooke: diary
(*Alanbrooke papers*)

9 March 1941

In the evening departed for Chequers at 6.15 p.m. arrived there at 7.45 p.m. House party consisting of PM, Mr Menzies (PM of Australia), Sandys and his wife, PM's youngest daughter,[3] Professor Lindemann, etc.

PM suffering from bronchitis, came down to dinner in his 'siren suit', a one-piece garment like a child's romper-suit of light blue. He was in great form and after dinner sent for his rifle to give me a demonstration of the 'long port'

[1] Churchill telegram to Roosevelt of 8 December 1940, published in Volume Two of the Churchill War Papers, *Never Surrender*, on pages 1189–1197.

[2] Sir Samuel Hoare, British Ambassador in Madrid.

[3] Mary Churchill, 1922– . Churchill's fifth and youngest child. Served with the Auxiliary Territorial Service, 1940–5; accompanied her father on several of his wartime journeys. In 1947 she married Captain Christopher Soames (later Lord Soames). They have five children. In 1978 her husband was created a Life Peer, and in 1979 she published *Clementine Churchill*, a biography of her mother. Created DBE, 1980, after her husband's term as Governor of Rhodesia. In 1982 she published *A Churchill Family Album*, in 1990, *Winston Churchill, His Life as a Painter*, and in 1999 *Speaking for Themselves: The Personal Letters of Winston and Clementine Churchill.* Chairman, Royal National Theatre Board, since 1989.

which he wanted to substitute for the 'slope'. He followed this up with some bayonet exercise![1]

Robert Menzies: diary
(Menzies papers)

9 March 1941

Winston is completely certain of America's full help, of her participation in a Japanese war, and of Roosevelt's passionate determination to stamp out the Nazi menace from the earth. Is he right? I cannot say. If the PM was a better listener and less disposed to dispense with all expert or local opinion, I might feel a little easier about it – he's a holy terror. I went to bed tired.

John Colville: diary
(Colville papers)

10 March 1941

The PM has been suffering from Bronchitis and is not going back to London. His capacity for work is totally unimpaired and his temper is scarcely ruffled. He came down to lunch with Mary, Tommy Thompson and me. Afterwards he told us about Robert Graves's book on the American War of Independence (*Serjeant Lamb*), which he is reading with particular enjoyment, and lamented the difficulties caused by the Bases Agreement.

Lord Moyne (S of S for the Colonies) and Sir Richard Peirse (C-in-C Bomber Command) came for the night. Big Bombs (the new 4000 pounder) alternated with West Indian bases as the main topic and I sat up late arranging the PM's complex papers about the latter.

Winston S. Churchill to President Franklin D. Roosevelt
(Premier papers, 4/25/5)

10 March 1941
Personal and Secret

I must now tell you what we have resolved about Greece. Although it was no doubt tempting to try to push on from Benghazi to Tripoli, and we may

[1] Alanbrooke later recalled, when re-reading his diary for publication: 'It was one of the first occasions on which I had seen Winston in one of his real light-hearted moods. I was convulsed watching him give this exhibition of bayonet exercises with his rifle, dressed in his siren-suit and standing in the ancestral hall of Chequers. I remember wondering what Hitler would have thought of this demonstration of skill at arms.'

still use considerable forces in this direction, we have felt it our duty to stand with the Greeks, who have declared to us their resolve, even alone, to resist the German invader. Our Generals Wavell and Dill, who have accompanied Mr Eden to Cairo, after heart-searching discussions with us, believe we have a good fighting chance. We are therefore sending the greater part of the Army of the Nile to Greece, and are reinforcing to the utmost possible in the air. Smuts is sending the South Africans to the Delta. Mr President, you can judge these hazards for yourself.

At this juncture the action of Yugoslavia is cardinal. No country ever had such a military chance. If they will fall on the Italian rear in Albania there is no measuring what might happen in a few weeks. The whole situation might be transformed, and the action of Turkey also decided in our favour. One has the feeling that Russia, though actuated mainly by fear, might at least give some reassurance to Turkey about not pressing her in the Caucasus or turning against her in the Black Sea. I need scarcely say that the concerted influence of your Ambassadors in Turkey, Russia, and above all in Yugoslavia, would be of enormous value at the moment, and indeed might possibly turn the scales.

In this connection I must thank you for magnificent work done by Donovan in his prolonged tour of Balkans and Middle East. He has carried with him throughout an animating, heart-warming flame.

I have been working steadily about the bases on turning the mountains back into molehills, but even so, the molehills remain to be disposed of. I hope to send you a cable Monday leaving very little that is not cleared away. Please lend a hand with the shovel if you can. Remember it is the inflexible policy of His Majesty's Government, with or without any reciprocal consideration, to make sure that the United States has full, effective military security both in war, and in the necessary peace-time preparations for war, in these Islands and areas. Give us the best chance you can to bring the local people along, for, after all, these Islands are their only home, and I want them to be your friends as well as ours.

The sinkings are bad and the strain is increasing at sea.

Winston S. Churchill: minute[1]
(*Churchill papers, 20/36*)

10 March 1941

It is of the utmost importance that a clear and consistent picture of our requirements should be presented to the United States administration, and

[1] This minute was sent, in various forms, to the Secretary of State for War, and the First Lord of the Admiralty, the Secretary of State for Air, the Minister of Supply, the Minister of Aircraft Production and the Foreign Office.

that their efforts on our behalf should not be hampered by any doubts as to our vital needs and their order of priority.

I had occasion to deal with one aspect of this matter recently, when I directed that all statistical statements relating to our war effort intended for the United States Government should be co-ordinated centrally here and despatched through our Ambassador at Washington.

Another aspect of the same question has now been brought to my notice. Mr Hopkins has reported that the Service Attachés at the American Embassy in London are in the habit of sending messages, based on contacts with subordinate officers in the Service and Supply Departments in London, which may well differ from the case which is being put to the Navy and Army Departments in Washington. He quoted a case in which the Navy Department were being pressed to allot destroyers to us, and found themselves confronted with an expression of opinion of some anonymous officer in one of the Service Departments in London, conveyed through a Service Attaché of the United States Embassy in London, to the effect that it was no good hoping to cope with submarines by destroyers until we had more long range fighters.

I should be glad if you would be good enough to take the necessary steps to ensure that all officers in your Department, who are brought into contact with the Staff of the American Embassy, and particularly with the Service Attachés, do not express opinions which are likely to conflict with the views which are being urged on our behalf in Washington. These officers may not perhaps be aware that the views which they happen to express casually are liable to be reported to Washington. It would also seem important that officers who are in contact with the United States Service Attachés should be acquainted in general terms with the nature of the requests which are being put from time to time to the United States Government in Washington, so that they may be on their guard against making remarks which would be inconsistent with those requests.

Winston S. Churchill to General Ismay
(*Churchill papers, 20/36*)

10 March 1941

Low-flying attack should only be a real danger on days of low cloud or mist, when our Fighters cannot find the enemy. The use of aerial mines hung from small balloons should be considered for the defence of factories. Only 20 lbs lift is required, so that quite a small balloon should be sufficient. When this proposal was put forward for defending estuaries, it was decided that a considerably greater altitude was required, so as to have a double-purpose defence, which has entailed the production of much larger balloons, which in turn require power winches, &c. We must be content with defence up to heights of 1,000 or 1,500 ft by smaller, simpler balloons without power winches. On windy days they could be replaced by kites.

This method of defence is not desirable for Aerodromes, since the balloons would all have to be hauled down when our own machines were taking off or landing. For the defence of Aerodromes, therefore, rockets carrying mines into the air seem particularly suited.

Winston S. Churchill to Air Chief Marshal Sir Charles Portal
(*Churchill papers, 20/36*)

10 March 1941
Action this Day

MIDDLE EAST REINFORCEMENTS: PROGRESS REPORT: WEEK ENDING 8 MARCH 1941

On these figures there is obviously a frightful hold up at Takoradi. One hundred and ninety-five machines are there in one condition or another. Twenty were received during the week, and only five were despatched. This is congestion – I had almost said constipation. What are you going to do about it? The *Furious* will be bearing down quite soon. It seems to me a very large scale effort should be made and the whole scale of the route doubled, together with proper fortification and defence of Takoradi. All this is absolutely vital.

Winston S. Churchill to Alfred Duff Cooper
(*Churchill papers, 20/36*)

10 March 1941
Action this Day

DRAFT INVASION LEAFLET

Obviously there are two conditions, districts where fighting is going on, and districts where it is not. The words 'stay put' are wholly inapplicable to the second class, which is by far the more numerous, probably 99/100ths of the country. For these districts the order should be 'Carry on'.

Neither is the expression 'Stay put' really applicable to the districts where fighting is going on. First of all, it is American slang; secondly, it does not express the fact. The people have not been 'put' anywhere. What is the matter with 'Stand fast' or 'Stand firm'? Of the two, I prefer the latter. This is an English expression, and it says exactly what is meant by paragraph 3.

Paragraphs 12 and 13 clearly apply only to the fighting areas. In the present context you might have a wholesale massacre of maps, motor-cars and bicycles throughout the country.

The great point of principle in paragraph 14 should once again be referred to the Cabinet. I should myself feel most reluctant to give an absolute negative. I should have thought paragraph 15 would be sufficient, especially with the addition of the last few words of paragraph 14.

You might begin like this: If this Island is seriously invaded, everyone in it will immediately receive orders either to 'Carry on' or to 'Stand firm'. In the vast majority of cases the order will be 'Carry on', as is set out in the first three paragraphs of the following paper. The order 'Stand firm' applies only to those districts where fighting is actually going on, and is intended to make sure that there will be no fugitives blocking the roads, and that everyone who has decided to stay in a likely area of attack, as, for instance, on the east and south coasts, will 'Stand firm' in his dwelling or shelter till the enemy in the neighbourhood have been destroyed or driven out.

Winston S. Churchill to Lord Woolton
(*Churchill papers, 20/36*)

10 March 1941

PROPOSED FOOD MISSION TO THE UNITED STATES

Would you kindly let me know what will be the objects and duties of the Food mission you propose to send to the United States. I am at this time actively considering sending Sir Arthur Salter there to expedite and animate the whole business of merchant shipbuilding. This is a process which requires continued effort and attention, as an enormous scheme of shipbuilding has to be set on foot in American yards. What has been done up to the present is less than half of what we need.

I do not, however, see food problems in the same plane as this. There is plenty of food in the United States, and with our dollar allocations we should be able to select wisely what to use in our tonnage. Why does this require a special mission?

I have been trying as much as possible to keep the missions to the United States as few as possible. However, I shall be very glad to hear what your reasons are.

John Colville: diary
(*Colville papers*)

11 March 1941

Early bedside conference with Lord Moyne. The PM decided to tackle the bases problem with the American Ambassador this afternoon.

His bronchitis is still bad, but in spite of everybody's wishes he insisted on returning to London in time for the usual Tuesday lunch with the King.

Clementine S. Churchill to Winston S. Churchill
(Churchill papers, 20/24)

11 March 1941 10 Downing Street

Prime Minister.

I have been thinking over the little plan which was sent to me by Jacques Balsan.[1] It has occurred to me that the house in which he says there are 450 German airmen might be used as a hospital in which case of course it could not be bombed. This thought occurred to me this morning and I am telling you about it at once.

CSC

Winston S. Churchill to Professor Lindemann
(Churchill papers, 20/36)

11 March 1941

I am expecting you to have ready for me tonight the general layout of the Imports programme under different heads, so that I can see where I can scrape off with a pencil another half-million tons for food.

Sir Alexander Cadogan: diary
('The Diaries of Sir Alexander Cadogan, OM, 1938-1945')

12 March 1941

PM sent for me about his telegram to Roosevelt about supplies to France and N. Africa. It's not a good message – rather woolly – not up to his form. After changing some detail, I suggested a change of shape. But he wouldn't have it![2]

[1] Colonel Jacques Balsan, Consuelo Vanderbilt's second husband, whom she married in 1921, the year after her marriage to the 9th Duke of Marlborough had been dissolved. A balloonist and aviator, in 1899 he had flown a balloon from France to Prussia, and in 1909 had received his aeroplane pilot's licence. On active service as a pilot in Morocco (1913–14; Captain, Legion d'Honneur), and in the First World War. He died in 1956.

[2] Admiral Darlan had threatened war with Britain if the British naval blockade of Vichy ports was not brought to an end.

Winston S. Churchill to President Franklin D. Roosevelt
(*Churchill papers, 20/49*)

12 March 1941
Personal and Secret

Admiral Darlan's declaration and threats make me wonder whether it would not be best for you to intervene as a friend of both sides and try to bring about a working agreement. We do not wish to push things to extremes and we naturally should be most reluctant in a thing like this to act against your judgment after you have weighed all the pros and cons. We fear very much the prolongation of the war and its miseries which would result from the breakdown of the blockade of Germany, and there are immense difficulties in preventing Germany from profiting directly or indirectly from anything imported into unoccupied France. Dealing with Darlan is dealing with Germany, for he will not be allowed to agree to anything they know about which does not suit their book. Also, there is the danger of rationing spreading to occupied France, Belgium, Holland and Norway. Perhaps, however, you might be able to devise a scheme under American supervision which would limit the leakage, and might also give you a number of agents in favourable positions in unoccupied France and in French Africa. It would be easier for you to talk to Vichy, with whom you are in regular diplomatic relations, than for us to negotiate via Madrid or by making speeches on the broadcast. Besides this, Darlan has old scores to pay out against us because of the dire action we were forced to take against his ships.

2. Would you therefore consider coming forward on the basis of how shocked you were at the idea of fighting breaking out between France and Great Britain, which would only help the common foe. Then you might be able to procure Vichy assent to a scheme for allowing a regular ration of food to go through, month by month, as long as other things were satisfactory. These other things might form the subject of a secret arrangement of which the Germans would not know, by which German infiltration into Morocco and French African ports would be limited to bare armistice terms, and by which an increasing number of French warships would gradually be moving from Toulon to Casablanca or Dakar.

3. I have asked the Foreign Office to telegraph to Lord Halifax all the sort of things we think should be taken care of, so that he can tell you about them, but the two I have mentioned are worth more to us than the disadvantages of a certain amount of leakage of food to the enemy. It would have to be made clear that the relief accorded was limited to stated quantities of food at agreed intervals, and did not extend to other goods. For instance, there is a French ship, the *Bangkok*, with 3,000 tons of rubber on board which is certainly not all for the teats of babies' bottles, and we have abundant cases of all kinds of valuable munition materials which are going straight to Germany or Italy.

Moreover, it would be a great pity if any large number of ships, which are all needed for our life and the war effort, were used up in food carrying. I do not want the people here, who, apart from heavy bombardment likely to be renewed soon, are having to tighten their belts and restrict their few remaining comforts, to feel that I am not doing my best against the enemy. Nevertheless, if it were not unwelcome I would gladly invite you to act as intermediary and make the best plan you can to beat Hitler. We have supreme confidence in you, and would receive with profound respect what you thought best to be done.

4. The bases question has, I think, been tidied up, and I hope to bring an agreed document before the Cabinet tomorrow (Thursday) afternoon. Will you let me know when you would like the announcement to be made? Does it matter if it comes on the morrow of the passing of the Lease-Lend Bill?

Winston S. Churchill: Oral Answer
(*Hansard*)

12 March 1941 House of Commons

UNITED STATES LEASE-LEND BILL[1]

Mr Lees-Smith (by Private Notice) asked the Prime Minister whether he can give the House any information about the Lease and Lend Bill?

The Prime Minister (Mr Churchill): The Lease-Lend Bill became law yesterday, when it received the signature of the President. I am sure the House would wish me to express on their behalf, and on behalf of the nation, our deep and respectful appreciation of this monument of generous and far-seeing statesmanship.

The most powerful democracy have, in effect, declared in solemn Statute that they will devote their overwhelming industrial and financial strength to ensuring the defeat of Nazism in order that nations, great and small, may live in security, tolerance and freedom. By so doing, the Government and people of the United States have in fact written a new Magna Carta, which not only

[1] On the previous day, 11 March 1941, the House of Representatives had approved the Lend-Lease Bill by 317 votes to 71, whereupon it was immediately signed by President Roosevelt. Under the Lend-Lease Act seven billion dollars were appropriated 'to carry out national policy of giving every possible material assistance to the countries resisting aggression'. The first appropriation, up to 31 August 1941, was set at 5,295 million US dollars, out of which Britain would be able to draw on 4,736 million. The second biggest sum, 320 million, was for China ('Second Report under the Act of March 11, 1941 – Lend-Lease Act', copy in *Cabinet papers, 115/436*).

has regard to the rights and laws upon which a healthy and advancing civilization can alone be erected, but also proclaims by precept and example the duty of free men and free nations, wherever they may be, to share the responsibility and burden of enforcing them.

In the name of His Majesty's Government and speaking, I am sure, for Parliament and for the whole country, and indeed, in the name of all freedom-loving peoples, I offer to the United States our gratitude for her inspiring act of faith.

Mr Granville: May I ask the Prime Minister, in view of the great importance of this statement whether he would consider making a broadcast to the United States of America in similar terms and on a wavelength which could be heard by the people of this country as well?

The Prime Minister: That is a matter in which a decision would have to be taken at the appropriate moment.[1]

John Colville: diary
(*Colville papers*)

12 March 1941

Went to the House with the PM and heard him sing a paean of praise to the US for having passed the Lease and Lend Bill. He described it as a second Magna Carta (using words suggested by Professor Whitehead[2] of the FO).[3]

He then saw the Bermudan delegates and spoke to them so charmingly about their losses over the Bases question that they told me they thought he felt it as keenly as they themselves.

[1] Six days later, on 18 March 1941, Churchill spoke to the (Anglo-American) Pilgrims Society. His speech, broadcast live from the Savoy Hotel, London, was transmitted to the United States.

[2] John Henry Constantine Whitehead, 1904–1960. Mathematician. Fellow and Tutor of Balliol College, Oxford, 1933–46. War Service with the Admiralty and the Foreign Office, 1941–45. Waynflete Professor of Pure Mathematics and Fellow of Magdalen College, Oxford, 1947–60. President, London Mathematical Society, 1953–55.

[3] While preparing his diary for publication, Colville noted at this point: 'The was the only occasion I remember during the war when Mr Churchill used somebody else's draft, or at any rate a portion of it, in making a speech to the House of Commons. In all other cases the text was entirely his own.'

Winston S. Churchill to Sir Arthur Salter
(*Churchill papers, 20/21*)

12 March 1941
Confidential

My dear Salter,

As you know we hope that, now the Lend-Lease Bill is through, the United States Administration will be prepared to give us assistance on a scale far surpassing anything which they have hitherto done. Of all our needs none is more pressing than that of obtaining from the United States the assistance which we require in the matter of merchant shipping. In order to convince the United States Administration of our needs it will be necessary for the general shipping problem in its widest aspects to be explained to and constantly kept before them. This can best be done by someone who, like yourself, can speak with authority and first-hand knowledge of the problems confronting us. I therefore invite you to undertake this supremely important task and I ask you to proceed to the United States as soon as this can be arranged.

It will be your task, under the general directions of His Majesty's Ambassador in Washington, to explain to the United States Administration our general import situation, to inform them of the measures we have taken and are taking to ensure that the fullest use is made of all the tonnage in the allied service, and to emphasize the various ways in which the United States Government can and should both add to the tonnage at our disposal, and help us to use that tonnage to the maximum advantage.

At the same time it will be your duty to supervise the handling of the technical questions arising from the programme of merchant shipbuilding on our behalf in the United States of America, which must be pressed forward with the utmost vigour. You will therefore be the head of our Mission which deals with these matters, and as such you will be a member of the British Supply Council in North America.

The battle of the Atlantic has begun. The issue may well depend on the speed with which our resources to combat the menace to our communications with the Western Hemisphere are supplemented by those of the United States of America. I look to you to bring this fact home to the United States Administration and to convince them that they must act accordingly.

Yours very sincerely,
Winston S. Churchill

Winston S. Churchill to Sir Walter Citrine[1]
(*Churchill papers, 20/25*)

12 March 1941
Private

PUBLICITY ABOUT GERMAN PARACHUTE MINES

My dear Citrine,

I don't think you are right on this matter. We do not want the subject of land mines with parachute attachments discussed in the public press. The newspapers reach Lisbon every few days and all that is militarily useful is telegraphed on by capable people to the Germans.

At the time when these big parachute mines began to come down about four months ago, we thought of making a great complaint about it, but after prolonged discussion it was decided to keep it all quiet. This was not done out of any spirit of tyranny or vain glorious exercise of authority but because being fallible human beings and placed in positions of some responsibility, we thought that we had better not show what was hurting us and rather to concentrate on other aspects.

This instruction was therefore given to the Censorship and there has been no discussion about land mines in the public press. If however any reference to the subject is made by any person of consequence like yourself, obviously the whole subject is thrown open and it will become very difficult to stop articles full of information being published which will, I have no hesitation in saying, hamper the conduct of the war and give the enemy a gratuitous advantage.

On several other occasions a particular topic has been banned and then, when once it was opened, an uncontrollable amount of stuff was printed giving a lot of information to the enemy.

I do not think there is any danger of this kind of ban on particular technical topics being applied to close people's mouths improperly, and I would not myself be responsible for an abuse of the reason 'military necessity'.

[1] Walter McLennan Citrine, 1887–1981. Secretary of the Electrical Trades Union, 1914–20; Assistant General Secretary, 1920–3. Assistant Secretary, Trades Union Congress, 1924–5; General Secretary, 1926–46. Director of the *Daily Herald*, 1929–46. Knighted, 1935. Visited Russia, 1936 and 1938. Privy Councillor, 1940. Member of the National Production Advisory Council, 1942–6, and 1949–57. Created Baron, 1946. Member of the National Coal Board, 1946–7. Chairman of the Central Electricity Authority, 1947–57. CBE, 1958. On 23 March 1941 Churchill wrote to Sir Archibald Sinclair: 'I have already seen Sir Walter Citrine and will take occasion to pay a compliment to him when I am the guest of the TUC at luncheon on Thursday. Meanwhile I think it would be a good thing if you asked him to come to see you, and you explained the technical points involved.You should mention that you do this at my desire.' (Prime Minister's Personal Minute No. 346 of 1941, *Churchill papers, 20/25*)

I heard of course at the Cabinet about this difference, but I was not aware you were going to make the matter public, and it was this making the matter public which I read in the newspapers.

When we next meet, which I hope will be soon, I will tell you all about the details which I cannot put on paper.

Yours v sincerely,
Winston S. Churchill

Dr Chaim Weizmann: note of a meeting[1]
(*Weizmann archive*)

12 March 1941 — 10 Downing Street

The meeting with the PM which took place on the 12th about 3.30 p.m. at 10 Downing Street came as a surprise. I was talking to Mr Brendan Bracken & then Martin[2] appeared and announced to me that the PM would see me for a few minutes . . .

At the end of our conversation the PM said that he was thinking of a settlement between us and the Arabs after the war. The man with whom we should come to an agreement is Ibn Saud.[3] He the PM would see to it and would use his good offices. IS would be made the Lord of the Arab countries, the 'Boss of the Bosses' as he put it. But 'he would have to agree with Weizmann' (he put it that way) with regard to Palestine. I will see you through the PM said. I swear to the truth of this statement.

Winston S. Churchill to Air Chief Marshal Sir Charles Portal
(*Churchill papers, 20/36*)

12 March 1941

I see accounts of Germans increasing their Aerodrome accommodation in Northern France. I suppose our Aerodromes in the south-east of the Island which we planned some time ago will now be coming steadily into use. Let me have a note on the augmentation which is in progress or has been achieved.

[1] This note was written on 15 March 1941.
[2] Churchill's Private Secretary, John Martin.
[3] Ibn Saud, 1880–1953. Born in Riyadh, a member of the Wahhabi dynasty. Exiled as a child by the Turks, Led a Bedouin revolt to regain Riyadh, 1902. King of Hejaz and Nejd, 1926–32; King of Saudi Arabia, 1932–53.

Winston S. Churchill to Peter Fraser[1]
(*Churchill papers, 20/49*)

12 March 1941
Secret

We are deeply moved by your reply,[2] which, whatever the fortunes of war may be, will shine in the history of New Zealand and be admired by future generations of free men in every quarter of the globe.

To make good the request and assumption at the end of your message shall be our faithful unremitting endeavour.

War Cabinet: minutes
(*Cabinet papers, 65/18*)

13 March 1941 10 Downing Street
5.30 p.m.

The Prime Minister reviewed the course of events since the first Agreement had been made for the lease of bases, in exchange for the grant of destroyers. This Agreement had greatly strengthened President Roosevelt's position. We should now soon receive immeasurable benefits under the Lease and Lend Act.

It was unfortunate that the United States authorities wished to have their rights set down in such precise legal terms. He would have preferred that the matter should be dealt with on more general lines.

It could be argued that in certain hypothetical events the terms of the Agreement would have very awkward consequences for us. But, if the matter was looked at from the point of view of the countries with which the United States was likely to be involved in war, the position was not nearly so alarming.

The strategic value of these bases was that they could be used by some other Power for attack on the United States. So long as the United States were in occupation of the leased areas there was no danger that they would permit the bases or the neighbouring British territories to be occupied by any third nation.

[1] Peter Fraser, 1884–1950. Born in Scotland. Joined the Independent Labour Party in London, 1908. Emigrated to New Zealand, 1910. Prominent in the New Zealand Labour Party. Prime Minister of New Zealand, 1940–9. Privy Councillor, 1940. Companion of Honour, 1945.

[2] Concurring in the decision to send Imperial forces to Greece and assenting to the employment of the New Zealand Division.

SALE OF GOVERNMENT-OWNED SHIPS

Summing up, the Prime Minister said that nothing must be done which would impede the full liberty of the Government to arrange for the construction of the types of ships best suited for war needs, or which would lead to delay. He sympathized, however, with the shipping lines which had lost a number of ships, and wished for some assurance that those losses would, so far as possible, be replaced, so as to enable the firms to continue in business after the war. This country had profited considerably by the enterprise of shipping firms. He saw no reason why an arrangement to earmark particular Government-built ships for transfer to private ownership at the end of the war in replacement of losses should result in the firms concerned receiving any more favourable financial terms in respect of those ships than if the ships remained in the Government ownership until the end of the war. The sort of arrangement he had in mind was one whereby ships were provisionally allocated for transfer to private firms in replacement of losses, but the transfer of ownership was put into cold storage until the date determined as the official end of war.

A solution on these lines would not prejudge any question of change in our social structure after the war. If the issue of nationalization was raised, it should be raised on its merits as a general issue, and not in regard to a single industry.

The War Cabinet –

(1) Agreed generally that the question of the sale of Government-owned ships to United Kingdom owners in replacement of vessels lost during the war should be settled on the lines indicated generally by the Prime Minister.

SOVIET DECLARATION TO REMAIN NEUTRAL IN THE EVENT OF AN ATTACK ON TURKEY[1]

The Prime Minister said that this message gave us a certain measure of reassurance. He had feared that Russia might seize the occasion of Turkey being invaded to send troops through the Caucasus into Asiatic Turkey.

The Yugoslav situation looked better than had seemed probable ten days previously.

[1] This declaration, made by the Soviet Union to Turkey, was transmitted in a conversation between Sir Stafford Cripps and Andrei Vyshinski on 10 March 1941, and reported to London by Cripps. 'The substance of the conversation', the War Cabinet were told, 'was that the Soviet Government's attitude to the Balkan question was far from corresponding with the stories which were going about. They had made a declaration to the Turkish Government that should Turkey be attacked by any foreign power, and should she be obliged to take up arms to defend her territory, she might count on the full understanding and neutrality of the Soviet Government.' (Moscow telegram No. 204)

Winston S. Churchill to the Foreign Office
(*Churchill papers, 20/36*)

14 March 1941

What are the reasons why King Carol should not come to England? It is true he has a mistress, Madame Lupescu, but since when have private morals been a bar to the right of asylum? Some of the many Revolutionaries who have sought shelter on our shores have had far from conventional private lives. Although it was well known that King Carol had a mistress and was separated from his wife, that did not prevent his being invited by the very respectable pre-War Government, being the guest of Their Majesties the King and Queen and receiving public welcome at a banquet in the Guildhall.

This wretched man has been chased and hunted. As far as I can make out he did his best for us. Although it may be extravagant eulogy, I believe it true to say he was the brightest spot in Roumania.

It may also be said that he is a King; but considering we have here the oldest and strongest monarchy in Europe, it is not quite seen where this comes in.

Evidently these are matters to be settled by personal opinion, and therefore the Cabinet must decide. Personally, I see no reason why King Carol should not come here and try to lead a new and better life.[1]

Winston S. Churchill to Air Chief Marshal Sir Charles Portal
(*Churchill papers, 20/36*)

14 March 1941
Action this Day

The Egg-layer[2] pulled off another success last night. Only one was up, but it got its prey. I cannot understand how there has been this frightful delay in devising and making the release-gear. More than three months seem to have been consumed upon a task so incomparably easier than many which are being solved. Failing any mechanical solution, why cannot a hole be cut in the floor of the aeroplane and a man lying on his stomach push by hand the eggs, which are about the size of a Stilton cheese, one after another through the hole? The spacing would not be absolutely regular, but it might be just as lucky. At any rate, I want to see this hold-up and hitch for myself. I could come

[1] King Carol was given asylum by the British in Bermuda. His subsequent places of exile included Mexico, Brazil, Spain, Switzerland and Portugal, where he died.

[2] Aerial mines had long been one of Churchill's special projects, both during his years in opposition (when he was a member of the Air Defence Research Sub-Committee of the Committee of the Imperial Defence) and at the Admiralty, where the mines had been given the code name 'Egglayer'.

to Northolt aerodrome at four o'clock this afternoon, Friday, if you can arrange to have the people concerned on the spot. It would be very nice if you would come, too, and spend the night at Chequers.

There is a new danger. Now that the Admiralty balloon barrage people have given away the idea of the aerial mine and its wire, parachute, &c., the cutter may soon be coming along, and when we are at last ready we may be too late.

Surely now, when they seem to be turning on to the Mersey and the Clyde and will have to be working up to those fixed points, now is the time of all others for the egg-layers to reap their harvest.[1]

Winston S. Churchill to Anthony Eden
(*Cabinet papers, 65/22*)

14 March 1941
Personal and Secret
To be decyphered by Mr Eden or his Personal Assistant

1. I have come to the conclusion that it is better for you to stay in Middle East until the opening phase of this crisis has matured. Your instructions give you the means of concerting the political and military action of all the factors involved. The attitude of Yugoslavia is still by no means hopeless and situation may at any moment arise which would enable you to go there. Turkey requires stimulus and guidance as events develop. No one but you can combine and concert the momentous policy which you have pressed upon us and which we have adopted. The War Cabinet needs a representative on the spot, and I need you there very much indeed.

2. I saw Sikorski this morning and asked for the Polish Brigade. He agreed in the most manly fashion, but he asked that this Brigade, which was one of the few remaining embodiments of Polish nationality, should not be lightly cast away or left to its fate. I promised full equipment and no greater risks than would be run by our own flesh and blood. He said you have millions of soldiers, we have only these few Units. I hope you appreciate what we are asking of these valiant strangers and that General Wavell will have this in his mind always.

[1] On 12 March 1941, in good visibility and with a full moon, 340 bombers dropped 300 tons of explosives and 64,000 incendiaries on Merseyside. A smaller but still heavy raid took place on the following night. In Birkenhead, 264 people were killed, at Wallesey 198 and in Liverpool 49. On the nights of 13/14 and 14/15 March there were two heavy raids on Clydeside. During the first, 200 aircraft dropped 272 tons of explosives and almost 60,000 fire bombs. At Yarrow's shipyard, a single bomb hit a shelter and 80 workers were killed. In the second raid, 83 people were killed when a parachute mine hit a four-storey tenement. In all, during the two nights of raids 55,000 people were made homeless, and 1,085 people killed.

3. I feel very much the fact that we are not using a single British Division. I am arranging to send the 50th Division with Convoy WS 8 leaving April 22. A special convoy would only have saved a week, and we cannot afford the extra escort.

4. We have not been told by Wavell whether Glens got through Canal, but presume this will be regarded as urgent in the highest degree. A source, of which you are aware, shows that preparations are being made to withdraw German personnel from the big Mandible in expectation of its British occupation. You ought not to be easily contented with delaying Mandibles indefinitely. We need to take it at earliest moment, and thereafter we need the 6th Division, whether things go well or ill. We must not be reproached with hazarding only other people's troops. You ought to press hard and long for taking Mandibles before the end of the month.

5. Can you tell me why Papagos does not draw three or four Divisions from Albania to strengthen his right front? Recent check which Italians are said to have received and fact that German advance has not yet begun may still give time for this. Present strategic layout of Greek Army looks to me most dangerous. Papagos must have good reasons, and if you have learned them pray let me know.

6. Of course, if Yugo came in, this would justify Greek strength in Albania. But this is not yet known. Presume you and Dill have studied carefully possibilities of a Yugo attack on Italians in Albania. Here they might win victory of the first order, and at the same time gain the vast mass of the equipment they need to preserve their independence and can never find elsewhere in time.

7. Do not let Lemnos be picked up by the Germans as an Air base for nothing. See Naval Attaché, Athens, telegram No. 1253/12.

8. It seems right to obtain a decision at Keren and open Appearance[1] before withdrawing Air Squadrons you have thereabouts.

9. Your 547 containing Longmore's complaints overlooks what is on the way. Fifteen cased Hurricanes reached Takoradi today. Sixteen more should be there in next few days. Forty flying Hurricanes in *Pageant* should land within the next two or three days. All these should reach Egypt before end of March. A further thirty-three cased Hurricanes are already at sea, total Hurricanes one hundred and four. Parts to complete twenty Tomahawks are in *Pageant* and in flying boat due to leave for Takoradi tonight. Arrival of these should enable flow of Tomahawks to begin. Parts to equip other Tomahawks have left this country. Every effort will be made to fly twenty-two Wellingtons to ME in next fortnight. Only weather will prevent.

10. Project of flying a Squadron of Hurricane IIs to Malta from the west is

[1] British landings east and west of Italian-held Berbera, British Somaliland.

full of danger, because approach of aircraft-carriers will be detected by German reconnaissance planes, and repetition *Illustrious* in a worse form by dive-bombers from Cagliari may occur. Admiralty are, however, still studying it. Gain over sending them via Takoradi is a fortnight to three weeks.

11. Lastly, publicity. Increasingly hard hold Press in view of American reports and many rumours here. We know from special source that German military attaché has telegraphed approximate size of expedition[1] correctly to Berlin, though he is in error in other respects. Am having gist of this telegram repeated to you. You need not feel under any obligation to issue communiqué at present. It would indeed be a diplomatic error to aid Hitler to found his aggression nominally upon an admission of this kind by us.

12. Fact that Longmore thinks you ought to come home via Lagos, in which view Portal concurs, is final reason for my wish for you and Dill to remain on scene. For otherwise, apart from larger considerations in my paragraph 1, you will both be out of action at either end during a most critical seven days. Everything is going quite quietly here, and we have begun to claw the Huns down in the moonlight to some purpose.[2] God bless you all.

Winston S. Churchill to Viscountess Byng of Vimy[3]

(*Churchill papers, 20/21*)[4]

14 March 1941

Julian[5] w'd have liked to see these days, & the greater ones that are dawning.

[1] Operation Lustre, British military support for Greece.

[2] German air raids on Merseyside on 12 March 1941 and on the Clyde the following day met strong opposition. At the same time, British bombers struck at Berlin, Hamburg and Bremen on March 12, and were to attack Düsseldorf on March 15. These British raids were part of Operation 'Abigail', a series of reprisal raids, but not publicly revealed as such, and including Düsseldorf, code name 'Delilah'; Bremen, code name 'Jezebel' and Mannheim, code name 'Rachel'. The Air Ministry's instructions to Bomber Command for these raids included the sentence: 'With object causing widespread uncontrollable fires suggest first ten sorties carry incendiary bombs only . . .' (Telegram X.629, 2 December 1940: *Air Ministry papers, 20/5195*).

[3] Viscountess Byng of Vimy: Marie Evelyn Moreton, daughter of Sir Richard Moreton. She married Julian Byng in 1902. She later published *Barriers* (1912) and *Anne of the Marshland* (1913). A Dame of Grace of the Order of St John of Jerusalem.

[4] Churchill wrote the words below in his own hand, as a postscript to a formal letter thanking Lady Byng for her 'generous contribution' of £5,000 for the purchase of a Spitfire.

[5] Julian Hedworth George Byng, 1862–1935. Entered Army, 1883. On active service in the Sudan, 1884; in South Africa, 1899–1902. Major-General, 1909. Commanded the Troops in Egypt, 1912–14. Commanded the 3rd Cavalry Division, 1914–15; the Cavalry Corps, 1915; the 9th Army Corps, 1915–16; the 17th Army Corps, 1916; the Canadian Corps, 1916–17, the 3rd Army, 1917–19. Knighted, 1915. General 1917. Created Baron, 1919, and granted £30,000 by Parliament for his war service. Governor-General of Canada, 1921–6. Created Viscount, 1926. Commissioner, Metropolitan Police, 1928–31. Field Marshal, 1932.

Winston S. Churchill: War Cabinet Paper
(Churchill papers, 23/9)

14 March 1941 10 Downing Street

COMMITTEES

NOTE BY THE PRIME MINISTER, ADDRESSED TO MINISTERS IN CHARGE OF DEPARTMENTS

I circulate herewith a note upon the inordinate and unchecked growth of Committees which now amount to 800 in the Central Government alone. This paper has been prepared by my directions, and suggests to all Departments methods for effecting a purge and reduction both of Committees and of the numbers upon them.

I ask each Minister to see that proposals are submitted to him without delay, having for their object a reduction in the number of Committees by 25 per cent., and a reduction in the number of persons attending these Committees by 25 per cent. I propose to arrange for a report to be submitted to me at a later date showing what action has been taken to give effect to the directive.

DIRECTIVE

The returns submitted by some thirty Departments in reply to the circular letter addressed to them on the 7th January showed about 800 Committees of the Central Government. This figure excludes some 2,600 Local Committees, mainly attached to the Ministries of Labour, Food and Information, designed to maintain essential local contacts.

Properly used, Committees are an invaluable aid to public business. Some differences cannot be resolved except by discussion face to face; and where several Departments are concerned a Committee, properly organized, will save much time and correspondence. But it is clear that the Committee system has been allowed to run riot, and that what should be a useful time-saving device is in danger, not only of wasting the time of officials and of delaying action, but of sapping the responsibility of those called upon to take decisions and to direct action.

An effort should now be made to reduce both the number of Committees and the time spent upon them, and to see that the work of the Committees retained is properly organized. In particular, attention should be paid to the following aspects:

Numbers attending Committees

(1) The prime evil is that far too many people attend Committee meetings. This growth in numbers is bad for Committee business in two ways: first, because officers have to spend time in listening to long discussions when they should be at their desks.

Secondly, because, while business can be transacted with efficiency and speed among five or six people, when twenty or thirty are present the proceedings become cumbrous, and frank speaking more difficult.

This increase in the numbers attending Committee meetings springs from two causes. First, the wish to ensure that every Department concerned is consulted before action is decided upon, has led to Departments being granted permanent representation on Committees however remote their interest in the business to be done. In future, Inter-Departmental Committees will comprise only the representatives of the Departments essentially concerned. Representatives of lesser or intermittent interests may be sent the relevant Papers, but such representatives will only be invited to attend meetings for particular items when necessary.

Secondly, a habit has grown up of Departmental representatives on Committees hunting in couples. Occasionally as many as six representatives of the same Department have attended a meeting.

The normal practice should be that, if several sections of a Department are concerned in a matter their representatives should meet beforehand to settle the line of action to be taken, and to select one of their number to attend the meeting. This representative should, save in matters of high policy, which require reference to Ministers, be in a position to answer for his Department.

Responsibilities of Chairmen

(2) Chairmen of Committees must accept responsibility for the orderly conduct of business. They must see that proper Agenda papers are issued; that, save in cases of great urgency, the issues to be discussed are set out concisely in writing and circulated before the meeting. Above all, they must see that discussion is kept to the point at issue and irrelevance curtailed; that the numbers attending meetings are reduced to the minimum (see (1) above); and that meetings are not held unless necessary. Again, every Chairman should in advance of the meeting, digest the papers and think out the tentative line or lines on which the issues to be determined can be resolved, and, if need be take preliminary soundings.

Chairmen should also discourage lengthy Minutes. Minutes must, of course, record the conclusions reached, with precise directions as to the action to be taken by each Department or Officer. The general rule should be to record, apart from the conclusions, only the briefest summary of any important points raised in discussion, a record of which is necessary for a clear understanding of the Committee's Conclusions.

Finally, Chairmen are responsible for ensuring that Secretaries, under their direction, follow up items not settled at meetings, and take steps either to get them disposed of outside the Committee or to have preliminary points discussed outside the Committee, in order that the question may be ripe for a decision when it is again put on the Agenda.

Advisory and Consultative Committees

(3) The Departments responsible for Agricultural, Trade and Industrial matters, Labour, Education and so forth, have appointed a large number of Central Committees to keep them in touch with outside interests coming within their sphere. While these contacts are no doubt advantageous, certain Departments have been over-ready to use this device, and to appoint new advisory bodies for each fresh development. One Sub-Department alone has no less than 29 such Advisory Committees. Departments needing advisory bodies should select people with all-round experience, who can give advice on a wider range of matters. Departments should overhaul their existing Advisory and Consultative Committees on these lines as opportunity offers. In future when advice is required on some fresh topic, this should be done by extending the reference to some existing body, rather than by creating a new body.

Scientific Advisory Committees

(4) The need for regular consultation with outside scientific or technical experts has led to a great increase since the war in the number of scientific advisory bodies. Further experience may well show that there is some overlapping between the various bodies established, and that the normal Committee procedure is not that best suited for the purpose in hand, and leads to some waste of effort, especially in the case of the larger bodies set up. But in many cases the practice of regular consultation with outside scientific experts has not been long established: and for the moment the present contacts should be allowed to develop freely.

Departmental Committees

(5) Another type of Committee is the Committee consisting solely of representatives of different Sections or Branches within a particular Department. While the officer charged with a particular branch of business should rightly make a habit of conferring with his subordinates, this should rarely imply a formal Committee. The habit of establishing formal Committees in a Department is, indeed, probably a sign that the Departmental organization is at fault and that there is no officer in effective charge of each main branch of the Department's functions.

Liaison Officers

(6) Yet another type of Committee is the Committee which rarely, if ever, meets, its members being, in effect, liaison officers in certain Departments, nominated on their behalf to deal with particular questions, who are consulted by the Chairman and Secretary as occasion demands. This is a useful administrative device; and it is not intended that a purge of the Committee system should lead to its extinction.

Ad hoc Inquiries

(7) An *ad hoc* inquiry into some particular question can often be carried out

more effectively and expeditiously, not by the appointment of a Committee, but by entrusting the matter to a single individual whose duty it will be to consult and seek advice from the various parties concerned.

Permanent Heads of Departments are responsible to Ministers for seeing that the Committee business of their Departments is overhauled on the general lines indicated in this note. In particular steps should be taken to see that only those persons who are able to manage Committee business effectively are appointed as Chairmen of Committees; that unnecessary Departmental Committees are abolished; that new Committees are not set up without due authority, and then only when no satisfactory alternative can be devised; and, finally, that the number of persons attending Committees is reduced to the minimum.

Averell Harriman:[1] *recollection*
(*'Special Envoy to Churchill and Stalin, 1941-1946'*)

15 March 1941

The Prime Minister welcomed me most warmly. He remembered our first meeting, when I called on him at Cannes in 1927 to get his advice about Russia, and he talked about our meeting in New York two years later, at the time of the Wall Street crash. He freely admitted having caught the speculative fever of the time and lost the money he had just received from the publication of a new book.

I was surprised to see how grateful Mrs Churchill was for a small bag of tangerines I had brought her from Lisbon. Her unfeigned delight brought home to me the restriction of the dreary British wartime diet, imposed by the sharp reduction of imports, even in the Prime Minister's house.

After dinner Churchill took me aside and began to describe in considerable detail the problems of the war and what the United States might do to help. I forgot all about presenting my letter from Roosevelt. There was no need for formal introductions. As soon as I could I explained to the Prime Minister that

[1] William Averell Harriman, 1891–1986. Vice President in Charge of Purchases and Supplies, Union Pacific Railroad, 1914–18. Chairman of the Board, Merchant Shipping Corporation, 1917–25. Chairman of the Board Union Pacific Railroad, 1932–46. Member Business Advisory Council, Department of Commerce, 1933–40. Division Administrator, National Recovery Administration, 1934. Roosevelt's emissary (Special Representative) London, to negotiate Lend-Lease arrangements, March 1941. Accompanied Lord Beaverbrook on his mission to Moscow, with the rank of Ambassador, September 1941. Served on The Combined Production and Resources Board, London, 1942. United States Ambassador to Moscow, 1943–46. Ambassador to Britain, 1946. United States Secretary of Commerce, 1946–48. Special Assistant to President Truman, 1950–51. Chairman, NATO Commission on Defence Plans, 1951. Assistant Secretary of State, Far Eastern Affairs, 1961–63. United States negotiator, Limited Test Ban Treaty, 1963; Vietnam Peace Talks, Paris, 1968–69. In 1971 he married Pamela Leland Hayward (Pamela Digby), Randolph Churchill's former wife.

Washington would need a lot more information about Britain's war plans and prospects if there was to be a large increase in assistance under the new Lend-Lease law. I warned him that the demands of our own Army and Navy were so great, and the immediately available resources so pitifully limited, that it would be a struggle unless our military chiefs were persuaded that Britain could make better use of the matériel.

My own usefulness in pleading Britain's case, I told him bluntly, would depend entirely upon the extent of my knowledge and understanding of her position and needs. I was greatly reassured by his response.

You shall be informed, Churchill said. We accept you as a friend. Nothing will be kept from you.

Winston S. Churchill to Admiral Fraser
(Churchill papers, 20/36)

15 March 1941
Action this Day

Give me a report on the progress of the ships to carry and disgorge Tanks. How many are there? What is their tonnage? How many Tanks can they take in a flight? When will each one be ready? Where are they being built? What Mark of Tank can they carry?

Winston S. Churchill to the Foreign Office
(Churchill papers, 20/36)

15 March 1941

Darlan is a bad man, with a narrow outlook and a shifty eye. A naval crook is usually a bad kind of crook. France has never been dominated by the Navy. I agree that it is by no means certain Darlan will succeed Pétain. His downfall would certainly be very welcome. He is more dangerous than Laval, because less odious to the French people. On the other hand, he will probably be a more timid politician, having waded to power through a different kind of mud, and unsure of his footing.

Winston S. Churchill to the Foreign Office
(Churchill papers, 20/36)

15 March 1941

Being a strong Monarchist, I am in principle in favour of Constitutional Monarchies as a barrier against Dictatorships, and for many other reasons. It would be a mistake for Great Britain to try to force her systems on other countries, and this would only create prejudice and opposition. The main policy of the Foreign Office should, however, be to view with a benevolent eye natural movements among the populations of different countries towards Monarchies. Certainly we should not hinder them, if we cannot help.

Winston S. Churchill to General Ismay and Sir Edward Bridges
(Premier papers, 3/9)

16 March 1941
Secret

DISPUTE BETWEEN THE AIR MINISTRY AND MINISTRY OF AIRCRAFT PRODUCTION ABOUT THE USE TO BE MADE OF BOEING CLIPPERS AND B24S

I am getting very tired of this, and someone must decide.

I therefore rule that:

1. The three Boeing Clippers are to go to the Takoradi route.

2. Of the six B24s, one, the first, is to help the Minister of Economic Warfare in his Scandinavian work, and the other five are to be employed on ferrying pilots across the Atlantic under MAP.

3. The turret development must wait till the seventh B24 is delivered, unless there is some better plan.

4. The Air Ministry must continue to assist to their utmost MAP in the process of ferrying.

Pray have this communicated to the Secretary of State for Air and Lord Beaverbrook. Sir Edward Bridges should consider whether it is necessary to bring this before the Cabinet, in view of previous discussions. If so, it must come up tomorrow (Monday).

Winston S. Churchill to Sir Horace Wilson[1] and Sir Edward Bridges
(Churchill papers, 20/36)

16 March 1941
Secret

Information received here shows that there is serious danger of Ministers or officials conversing freely with persons connected with the De Valera Government about war matters. It must be remembered that the German

[1] Horace John Wilson, 1882–1972. Entered the Civil Service, 1900; Permanent Secretary, Ministry of Labour, 1921–30. Knighted, 1924. Chief Industrial Adviser to the Government, 1930–9. Seconded to the Treasury for special service with Stanley Baldwin, 1935–7, and with Neville Chamberlain, 1937–40 (when he had a room at 10 Downing Street). Permanent Secretary to the Treasury and Head of the Civil Service, 1939–42.

Legation in Dublin is in close touch with several of the Southern Irish Ministers.

Will you consider how this warning can best be given discreetly to those concerned?

Winston S. Churchill to Sir Stafford Cripps
(*Churchill papers, 20/49*)

16 March 1941
Personal

I have read all your admirable telegrams. We are working on the Turks to our best ability, but they are unresponsive through fear.

Winston S. Churchill to Viscount Halifax
(*Premier papers, 4/17/2*)

16 March 1941
Personal and Secret

1. I do not think it would be a good thing for me to try to deal either directly or indirectly with one of the President's Departmental Chiefs. Ambassador Winant, who is with me here, agrees with this instinctive view of mine. There could be no objection, of course, to Chancellor of the Exchequer mentioning me in some telegram of his. I am not, however, prepared to send or sponsor any telegram about this financial wrangle.[1]

2. Ambassador Winant suggests that we have a talk on Monday with his Financial Adviser, Ben Cohen,[2] and we may be able to think of something better next week.

3. Anyhow, I am clear that this is no time for us to be driven from pillar to post. A breakdown, deadlock, or even local crash might clear the air. Gallup polls show President's popularity highest in consequence of aid to Britain. Remember that, although they may not all realize it, their lives are now in this business too. We cannot always be playing up to minor political exigencies of Congress politics. Morgenthau may have a bad time before his Committee, but Liverpool and Glasgow are having a bad time now. Much more evil is coming to us quite soon.

[1] Over Lend-Lease; Churchill knew that, two days earlier, at a White House Correspondents' Association dinner, Roosevelt had promised Britain and her Allies all the food, arms and other war materials they needed to defeat Hitler.

[2] Benjamin Victor Cohen, 1894-1983. A lawyer, born in the United States, the son of Jewish immigrants from Poland, he represented American Zionists at the Paris Peace Conference, 1919. A member of Roosevelt's 'Brain Trust' from 1933, he was a principal creator of the New Deal, the legislation for which he helped to draft. General Counsel, Public Works Administration, 1934-41.

4. Don't you think there has been too much telegraphing on the Treasury file, and that it would be good to make a break of two or three days and see what happens? As far as I am concerned, I refuse altogether to be hustled and rattled. God knows we are doing our bit. Chancellor of the Exchequer agrees.

Winston S. Churchill to President Franklin D. Roosevelt
(*Churchill papers, 20/49*)

17 March 1941

Pray accept my most sincere congratulations and grateful thanks on your magnificent speech.[1] It is a trumpet-call to free men all over the world, and will play a weighty part in drawing them together. I must also thank you for your most kind and complimentary reference to me.

Winston S. Churchill to the Duke of Windsor
(*Churchill papers, 20/49*)

17 March 1941
Private and Personal

After much consideration and inquiry, I have reached conclusion that your Royal Highness's proposed visit to United States would not be in the public interest, nor, indeed, in your own at the present time. I trust, therefore, that you will be willing to defer it until a less crucial stage in British and American relations has been reached.

2. There would be no objection and indeed advantage if your Royal Highness cared to make a cruise about the West Indian Islands. It would be impossible, however, for His Majesty's Government to approve the use of Mr Wenner-Gren's yacht for such a purpose. This gentleman is, according to the reports I have received, regarded as a pro-German international financier, with strong leanings towards appeasement, and suspected of being in communication with the enemy. Your Royal Highness may not, perhaps, realize the tensity of feeling in the United States about people of this kind and

[1] In a broadcast from Washington on 15 March 1941 Roosevelt pledged 'the fullest and ever-increasing aid' to Britain, Greece, China and all other governments in exile of occupied countries 'until total victory is won'. His address was broadcast in English, German, Italian, French, Turkish, Greek, Norwegian, Dutch, Spanish, Portuguese, Albanian, Serbian, Czech and Slovak. 'Let not the dictators of Europe and Asia doubt unanimity now,' he said. 'Our country is going to be what our people have proclaimed it must be – an Arsenal of Democracy. Today at last – at long last – ours is not a partial effort. It is a total effort, and that is the only way to guarantee ultimate victory . . . Every plane, every other instrument of war, old and new, which we can spare now we will send oversea. That is common sense strategy. But there must be speed in production as well. The need is now.'

the offence which is given to the Administration when any countenance is given to them.

3. Exception is taken also in the United States to your Royal Highness's interview recently published in *Liberty*, of which it is said that the language, whatever was meant, will certainly be interpreted as defeatist and pro-Nazi, and by implication approving of the isolationist aim to keep America out of the war.[1] I have obtained the best report possible of this interview, which has been republished here in the *Sunday Dispatch* of March 16, and I must say it seems to me that the views attributed to your Royal Highness have been unfortunately expressed by the journalist, Mr Oursler.[2] I could wish, indeed, that your Royal Highness would seek advice before making public statements of this kind. I should always be ready to help as I used to in the past.

Sir Alexander Cadogan: diary
(*'The Diaries of Sir Alexander Cadogan, OM, 1938-1945'*)

17 March 1941

Walking back from lunch at the Savoy, I found the PM and Seal getting out of a car to inspect the work on the 'fortress' which is being built on the old Whitehall Gardens site, and tacked myself on to them. The work being done is impressive, but not so much so as Winston's progress round the works, with his cigar, up and down ladders, puddling through half-set concrete, talking to workmen about their private affairs, putting to any sufficient audience the question 'Are we downhearted' and really enjoying himself thoroughly. And no doubt giving a good deal of pleasure.

[1] Quoting from the American magazine *Liberty*, the *Sunday Dispatch* of 16 March 1941 quoted an interview between the editor of *Liberty*, Fulton Oursler, and the Duke of Windsor in which the Duke told his interviewer about American aid to Britain: 'If the United States really believes in giving aid to Britain money is certainly needed.' Asked if it would ever be repaid, the Duke replied: 'Perhaps it never should be. You may feel that that is a strange thing for me to say, but look at it from another point of view. You have a friend, and he comes to borrow money which he needs desperately; he is out of a job. Say his wife needs an immediate operation and his pocket book is empty. If you can afford to help him you want to do so; if you are a wise man, however, and value his friendship, you don't lend him money, you give it to him. You may never get your money back, but you preserve his friendship. But the question of debt and bad feeling engendered by stupid people who call you Uncle Shylock are not the only obstacles to the friendship between our two countries.'

[2] Charles Fulton Oursler, 1893-1952. Journalist from 1910; from 1923 motion picture scriptwriter, novelist and short story writer. Editor, *Liberty*, 1931–42. Senior Editor, *Reader's Digest*, 1944. Creator of the radio series 'The Greatest Story Ever Told'.

War Cabinet: minutes
(*Cabinet papers, 65/18*)

17 March 1941 10 Downing Street
5 p.m.

The Prime Minister said that the position resulting from the present shipping losses presented a most formidable problem, and one which must be tackled by every means in our power. We were at the moment completely on the defensive at sea, and the Admiralty had had to disperse many important units from the Home Fleet for convoy duties and to hunt the raiders on the Atlantic routes. From the point of view of invasion, this detachment of forces would have to be carefully watched. A very heavy toll had been taken of our merchant shipping, and he thought that at the present time our Naval resources were at a fuller stretch than they had been at any time in the last war.

One method of relieving our difficulties would be if the United States would convoy ships West of the 30th meridian. Another way would be if the United States would allow some of their warships to cruise in the Atlantic and to pass on to us information obtained by them as to the whereabouts of German raiders. Such an act would be less un-neutral than the convoying of ships.

The Prime Minister, continuing, said that he had seen Mr Winant and Mr Harriman over the weekend, and had been greatly encouraged by their attitude. These two gentlemen were apparently longing for Germany to commit some overt act that would relieve the President of his election and pre-election declaration regarding keeping out of the war. Mr Harriman had said that the United States might be prepared to escort their own ships outside the prohibited area. He was working out a scheme whereby United States ships would take over the long hauls, leaving us with the short hauls. They were also planning a very big merchant shipbuilding programme, which would mature in 1942.

Continuing, the Prime Minister said that our shipping difficulties were the blackest cloud which we had to face. But we must remember that we had dealt with, and overcome, equal perils in the past.

John Colville: diary
(*Colville papers*)

18 March 1941

The PM made a speech at the Pilgrims' luncheon. Lunch was at 1.15: he was still dictating his speech at 1.30!

Winston S. Churchill: speech at the Pilgrims' Society Luncheon
(BBC Written Archives Centre)

18 March 1941 Savoy Hotel,
London

We are met here today under the strong impression and impact of the historic declaration made on Saturday last by the President of the United States, and where could there be a more fitting opportunity than at this gathering of the Pilgrims to greet the new American Ambassador for me to express on behalf of the British nation and Empire the sense of encouragement and fortification in our resolve which has come to us from across the ocean in those stirring, august, and fateful presidential words? You have come here, Mr Winant, to a community which is being tried and proved before mankind and history, and tried and proved to a degree and on a scale and under conditions which have not previously been known to human experience.

We have here a free society, governed through a Parliament which rests upon universal suffrage and upon the public opinion of the whole nation. We are being subjected to daily assaults which, if not effectively resisted and repelled would soon prove mortal. We have to call upon our whole people – men, women, and children alike – to stand up with composure and fortitude to the fire of the enemy, and to accept increasing privations while making increasing efforts. Nothing like this has ever been seen before.

We have our faults, and our social system has its faults, but we hope that, with God's help, we shall be able to prove for all time, or at any rate, for a long time, that a State or Commonwealth of Nations, founded on long-enjoyed freedom and steadily-evolved democracy, possesses amid the sharpest shocks the faculty of survival in a high and honourable and, indeed, in a glorious degree. At such a moment, and under such an ordeal, the words and the acts of the President and people of the United States come to us like a draught of life, and they tell us by an ocean-borne trumpet call that we are no longer alone.

We know that other hearts in millions and scores of millions beat with ours; that other voices proclaim the cause for which we strive; other strong hands wield the hammers and shape the weapons we need; other clear and gleaming eyes are fixed in hard conviction upon the tyrannies that must and shall be destroyed. We welcome you here, Mr Winant, at the moment when a great battle in which your Government and nation are deeply interested is developing its full scope and severity. The Battle of the Atlantic must be won in a decisive manner. It must be won beyond all doubt if the declared policies of the Government and people of the United States are not to be forcibly frustrated. Not only German U-boats, but German battle cruisers have crossed to the American side of the Atlantic and have already sunk some of our independently-routed ships not sailing in convoy. They have sunk these ships as far west as the 42nd meridian of longitude.

Over here upon the approaches to our island an intense and unrelenting struggle is being waged to bring in the endless stream of munitions and food without which our war effort here and in the Middle East – for that shall not be relaxed – cannot be maintained. Our losses have risen for the time being, and we are applying our fullest strength and resource, and all the skill and science we can command, in order to meet this potentially mortal challenge. And not only, I must remind you, does our shipping suffer by the attacks of the enemy, but also the fertility of its importing power is reduced by many of the precautions and measures which we must take to master and dominate the attacks which are made upon us.

But our strength is growing every week. The American destroyers which reached us in the autumn and winter are increasingly coming into action. Our flotillas are growing in number. Our air power over the island and over the seas is growing fast. We are striking back with increasing effect. Only yesterday I received the news of the certain destruction of three German U-boats. Not since October 13, 1939, had I been cheered by such delectable tidings of a triple event.[1]

It is my rule, as you know, not to conceal the gravity of the danger from our people, and therefore I have a right to be believed when I also proclaim our confidence that we shall overcome them. But anyone can see how bitter is the need of Hitler and his gang to cut the sea roads between Great Britain and the United States, and, having divided these mighty Powers, to destroy them one by one. Therefore we must regard this Battle of the Atlantic as one of the most momentous ever fought in all the annals of war. Therefore, Mr Winant, you come to us at a grand turning-point in the world's history. We rejoice to have you with us in these days of storm and trial, because we know we have a friend and a faithful comrade who will 'report us and our cause aright.' But no one who has met you can doubt that you hold, and embody in a strong and intense degree, the convictions and ideals which in the name of American democracy President Roosevelt has proclaimed.

In the last few months we have had a succession of eminent American citizens visiting these storm-beaten shores and finding them unconquered and unconquerable – Mr Hopkins, Mr Willkie, Colonel Donovan, and now today we have here Mr Harriman and yourself. I have dwelt with all these men in mind and spirit, and there is one thing I have discerned in them all – they would be ready to give their lives, nay, be proud to give their lives, rather than that the good cause should be trampled down and the darkness of barbarism again engulf mankind. Mr Ambassador, you share our purpose, you will share our dangers, you will share our anxieties, you shall share our secrets, and the day will come when the British Empire and the United States will share together the solemn but splendid duties which are the crown of victory.

[1] The reported sinking of three U-boats (subsequently proved false).

Winston S. Churchill to Viscount Halifax
(*Cabinet papers, 65/18*)

18 March 1941
2.35 p.m.

UNITED STATES OPPOSITION TO MAINTENANCE OF BRITISH BLOCKADE IN VICHY FRANCE[1]

This is very baffling. We cannot allow the blockade to lapse without anything to put in its place. I certainly understood that the United States Government felt quite strongly that grain should be allowed into France under a system of rationing, and that they would take a hand in this. Now that we accept their view, they recoil, and the only advice I get is in paragraph 6, 'we should be wise to be a little bit lighter on French shipping.' At the moment we are doing nothing to French ships, and convoys growing larger every day are passing in and out of the Straits, the most part with only nominal escorts. The policy of the Government is still that this traffic should be stopped, whenever we have the naval strength conveniently to hand, and that even if they are escorted we should not be deterred so long as we have ample superiority of force. A further operation of this kind was ordered for the end of last week, but we postponed it pending a fuller exposition of American views and wishes. It is now due to come along again quite soon. I cannot believe the United States Government would wish us to do simply nothing and have the war prolonged by our letting all these cargoes, containing not only food but rubber and other war materials, pass unhindered into Germany. We must know with some precision what the United States want and advise, or whether they would rather not be asked.

Winston S. Churchill to A. V. Alexander
(*Churchill papers, 20/36*)

19 March 1941
In a locked box
Private to First Lord alone

This is surely a pretty humble rôle for the Admiralty to play. I should like to know the reason why Potato Jones and his merchant seamen in a poor little tramp steamer are to carry our 12 Hurricanes, vitally needed by Malta, while the Royal Navy has to be kept far from these dangers. I never thought we should come to this.[2]

[1] American opposition had been expressed to Lord Halifax by the American Secretary of State, Cordell Hull.

[2] Churchill had just seen a telegram from the Admiralty to the Commander-in-Chief, Mediterranean, that twelve Hurricanes were to go to Malta on a merchant ship, S.S. *Parracombe*.

Battle of the Atlantic Committee: minutes[1]
(*Cabinet papers, 86/1*)

19 March 1941
5 p.m.
Secret

10 Downing Street

TURN-ROUND OF SHIPPING

The Prime Minister emphasized the vital need for reducing the time of the turn-round by, say, 15 days. Every effort must be directed to this end.

Winston S. Churchill to President Franklin D. Roosevelt
(*Churchill papers, 20/49*)

19 March 1941
Personal and Private

On 8th March German battle-cruisers *Scharnhorst* and *Gneisenau* approached one of our convoys north of Cape de Verde Islands, but on seeing our battleship escort retreated. On morning 15th our shipping which was returning independently to America was attacked by them at a point about 500 miles south-east of Newfoundland where, owing to fog on the Great Banks, shipping is at this season compelled to concentrate. Several ships were sunk by gunfire.

2. The attack was renewed on 16th near the same area, where three more ships were sunk. In the evening one enemy warship with a tanker in company was sighted by one of our battleships guarding a convoy just before dark, but was lost sight of as night fell. Presence of these battle-cruisers so far to the west of 30th meridian is latest phase in battle of Atlantic. While these powerful raiders are out the whole of our available battleship strength has to be employed on escorting convoys, but there are many ships on the seas with no protection.

3. The enemy appears to have based himself on the central areas of the north Atlantic, where he maintained his supply ships, and from thence he carried out raids against our various routes. This central area is almost unknown water to us today, because with the many calls on our limited resources for convoy escort we have no vessels to spare to round up hostile supply ships and search the areas. Moreover, against these two battle-cruisers our light forces would be thrown away.

[1] This was the first meeting of the War Cabinet's Battle of the Atlantic Committee. Churchill was in the Chair. The other Ministers present were Lord Beaverbrook (Minister of Aircraft Production), Ernest Bevin (Minister of Labour and Minister of National Service), A.V. Alexander (First Lord of the Admiralty), David Margesson (Secretary of State for War), Sir Archibald Sinclair (Secretary of State for Air), Sir Andrew Duncan (Minister of Supply), J.T.C. Moore-Brabazon (Minister of Transport), Lord Woolton (Minister of Food) and R.H. Cross (Minister of Shipping).

4. It would be a very great help if some American warships and aircraft could cruise about in this area, as they have a perfect right to do, without any prejudice to neutrality. Their mere presence might be decisive, as enemy would fear they might report what they saw and we could then despatch an adequate force to try to engage them. The more ships that go out to cruise and the sooner they go the greater the advantage.

5. I will report any further enemy movement of which we become aware.

Winston S. Churchill to Sir Samuel Hoare
(*Churchill papers, 20/49*)

19 March 1941

I have discussed your telegram No. 426 of the 9th March with the Chiefs of Staff. We fully agree with you as to what we should like to do, if we could, to encourage Spanish resistance. You know full well that for the moment we have a pretty heavy overdraft, and it is difficult to draw further on our capital. Nevertheless, we cannot tell yet how the ebb and flow of the war in the Atlantic and at our own front door, and further afield in the Balkans and Middle East, will affect what we may find ourselves able either to earmark or to send to Spain. Your views are most helpful, and I can assure you that we are not losing sight of the advice you have given us.

Winston S. Churchill to Anthony Eden
(*Churchill papers, 20/49*)

19 March 1941
Personal and Secret

Pray use your own judgment about when to return, but please act on Longmore's advice. Let me know what you decide. Try to bring Yugoslavia home in the bag.

John Colville: diary
(*Colville papers*)

19 March 1941

Back to London after tea. The PM had the American Biddle[1] (Ambassador to all our fugitive allies over here) and Harriman (President R's personal representative on shipping questions) to dinner and as there was a heavy raid[2] he took his guests and his whole private office up to the roof of the Air Ministry to watch the fun. He quoted to us Tennyson's prescient lines about aerial warfare.[3]

Eric Seal: letter to his wife
(*Seal papers*)

19 March 1941 10 Downing Street

There is a pretty bad Blitz on London tonight. The PM insisted on taking two Americans – Biddle (an Ambassador) & Harriman, onto the roof, & a fantastic climb it was – up ladders, a long circular stairway, & a tiny manhole right at the top of a tower. No bombs fell whilst we were up – although fire engines were continually passing, & the guns were firing all the time, with planes droning overhead.[4]

[1] Anthony J. Drexel Biddle, 1896–1961. On active service with the United States Army, 1917–18. United States Ambassador to Norway, 1935–37; to Poland 1937–40; to Poland, Belgium, the Netherlands, Luxembourg, Norway, Greece, Yugoslavia and Czechoslovakia (all in London), 1941–44. A senior official, with the rank of General, Supreme Headquarters Allied Expeditionary Force (SHAEF), 1945–8; at the Department of the Army, Washington, 1948–61. United States Ambassador to Spain, 1961.

[2] On the night of 19/20 March, known as 'The Wednesday', 500 German bombers attacked the London docks, in a raid lasting six hours. More than 122,000 incendiaries were dropped. Parachute mines destroyed rows of houses in West Ham, Poplar and Stepney and 200 fires started. Eight hospitals were hit. In a shelter in Poplar, 44 civilians died when a shelter was hit. In all, more than 500 people were killed, the highest yet recorded in a single night's raid. Ten days later the government announced that the total civilian deaths from air raids since the outbreak of war was 28,859. A further 5,000 soldiers had also been killed and more than 40,000 people seriously injured.

[3] Tennyson's lines were: 'Hear the heavens fill with shouting,
and there rain'd a ghastly dew
From the nations' airy navies
grappling in the central blue.'
(*Locksley Hall.*)

[4] On 23 March 1941 Anthony Biddle wrote to Churchill: 'On the roof I gained an impressive picture of the effective strides achieved here, both by the air and ground organizations (civil as well as military). It is a great tribute to your courageous intelligence and inspiring leadership and to the magnificent spirit of your brave countrymen. Then too I was so grateful for the opportunity of going with you "below" – for it was so interesting to see what you have done there, and to gain a "first-hand" clear perspective of the many activities as you so kindly pointed them out on the maps. It was grand being with you . . .' (*Churchill papers, 2/416*).

Sir Alexander Cadogan: diary
(*'The Diaries of Sir Alexander Cadogan, OM, 1938-1945'*)

20 March 1941

At end of Cabinet, PM said 'I'm not afraid of the air, I'm not afraid of invasion, I'm less afraid of the Balkans – but – I am anxious about the Atlantic'.[1]

War Cabinet: minutes
(*Cabinet papers, 65/18*)

20 March 1941
12 noon
Secret

Prime Minister's Room
House of Commons

BLOCKADE

The War Cabinet were informed of an exchange of telegrams about American plans for sending foodstuffs to Unoccupied France. The Prime Minister had since received a personal telegram from the President, which confirmed that our policy and that of the United States was in line on the matter.

The Prime Minister said that the United States were about to send two food ships to Unoccupied France. These must be let through the blockade unconditionally. But we must make it clear that we were not abandoning the blockade of France, and it was important that we should stop a convoy in the near future. After rummaging the vessels for such articles of contraband as rubber (which, if found, should be removed), it would probably be desirable to let them go. The presence with a convoy of a small French Naval escort ought not to deter us.

BALKANS

The War Cabinet were reminded that no official announcement had yet been made that any of our troops had landed in Greece.

The Prime Minister said there were strong reasons against making this announcement. First, Mr Eden and General Wavell were against it, and the Greeks also opposed it. Secondly, although the Germans knew that our troops had landed, they might make a public announcement on our part a pretext for launching their attack on Greece. Although the Press position was difficult to hold, he thought that we must accept the advice of those on the spot.

The War Cabinet accepted this view.

[1] Between 15 and 19 March 1941, eighteen British merchant ships were sunk, eleven by either the *Scharnhorst* or the *Gneisenau*.

GREECE

The Prime Minister said that he had seen General Sikorski, who had taken a very manly attitude in regard to the use of the Polish Brigade in Greece. The General had emphasized, however that he hoped this Brigade would not be put in a position where it might possibly be cut off, as these troops were all that Poland possessed.[1]

Winston S. Churchill to the Duke of Windsor
(*Churchill papers, 20/49*)

20 March 1941
Personal and Secret

SUGGESTION BY THE DUKE OF WINDSOR THAT HE SHOULD TOUR THE BAHAMA ISLANDS, AND THE DUKE'S INVOLVEMENT IN ANGLO-AMERICAN RELATIONS

Your telegram of 18th March, Para. 1. This will be quite satisfactory to His Majesty's Government. Para. 2. The question of providing Your Royal Highness with a Press representative will be immediately examined here, and I hope to make a proposal in a few days.

Para. 3. Your Royal Highness's appointment as Governor of the Bahamas is self-contained and is not specially concerned with Anglo-American relations. Anything, however, that Your Royal Highness has been able to do to improve these relations is warmly welcomed here. His Majesty's Government do not think that a visit to the United States would be helpful at the present time, and we have been so advised by very competent people on the spot. The appended passage from the article in *Liberty* which has not been repudiated by Your Royal Highness gives the impression and can indeed only bear the meaning of contemplating a negotiated peace with Hitler. That is not the policy of His Majesty's Government; nor is it that of the Government and vast majority of the people of the United States, where there is a very fierce and passionate feeling rising. It would be a thousand pities if the anti-Windsor propaganda, which I agree with you is contemptible, should get mixed up with the anti-Hitler propaganda which is strong and growing in America. Yet this might easily occur. The Isolationists would certainly exploit your words as much as possible. You would be beset by reporters, and if you handled them no more successfully than Mr Oursler you would be grievously embarrassed and harm would be done to British interests. On other grounds Lord Halifax has reported to me that your visit would become 'a rare show', and certainly I could not take the responsibility of recommending it at the present time.

[1] No Polish troops were sent to Greece.

Later on when the atmosphere is less electric, when the issues are more clear-cut and when perhaps Your Royal Highness's public utterances as they now stand are more in harmony with the dominant tides of British and American feeling, I think an agreeable visit for you both might well be arranged. Meanwhile, in this sad time of sacrifice and suffering it is not, I think, much to ask that deference should be shown to the advice and wishes of His Majesty's Government and of Your Royal Highness's friends, among whom I have always tried to bear my part.

Winston S. Churchill to Sir Kingsley Wood
(*Premier papers, 4/17/2*)

20 March 1941
Most Secret

What does all this mean?[1] Are we going to get our advances for building up factories in the United States repaid to us to enable us to finance our American affairs outside the Lease and Lend Bill provision? If not, how can we carry on? Anyhow, if we do not get any accommodation in this way, we must clearly hold on to all our remaining assets and gold yields. I am sure we shall have to come to a show-down; but I would precede it by a lie-down and appear dumb and immobile. Let the difficulties mount up, and let things have a small crash. As far as I can make out we are not only to be skinned, but flayed to the bone.[2] I would like to get them hooked a little firmer, but they are pretty well on now. The power of the debtor is in the ascendant, especially when he is doing all the fighting. Keep this to yourself, but let me have your views.

Winston S. Churchill to General Smuts
(*Churchill papers, 20/49*)

20 March 1941

Do you think it would be a good thing if Princess Juliana[3] and her children came to live in South Africa for the duration instead of the United States? How does this strike you? It is only one of my own ideas, and I do not know whether the parties concerned would like it.[4] All good wishes. I am sorry my

[1] Information in two telegrams (Nos.1231 and 1232) from Washington, sent by Sir Frederick Phillips, about payments to the United States.

[2] Churchill had originally written: 'As far as I can make out we are not only to be thin-skinned but super-skinned.'

[3] Princess Juliana of the Netherlands, a daughter of Queen Wilhelmina. In exile in London during the Second World War. She succeeded her mother as Queen in 1948. In 1980 she abdicated in favour of her eldest daughter, Beatrix.

[4] Princess Juliana and her children went, not to South Africa, but to Canada.

telegram missed you at Cairo. Hope is broadening in the Balkans. All good wishes.

Winston S. Churchill to Anthony Eden
(*Churchill papers, 20/49*)

20 March 1941

Am deeply impressed with message to Yugoslavia you have procured from Turks. Attitude of Yugo outweighs everything else. Position seems to have improved unexpectedly. Presume you will keep your teeth into this till decision one way or the other is pronounced. Greatly need you both at home, but this is the trophy.

Winston S. Churchill to Sir Alexander Cadogan
(*Churchill papers, 20/36*)

20 March 1941

Now that we are giving this food to Spain, surely we must demand as an essential condition of any further assistance that what we are doing should be published in Spanish newspapers.

Winston S. Churchill to General Ismay, for the Chiefs of Staff Committee
(*Churchill papers, 20/36*)

20 March 1941

I should be glad if the Chiefs of the Staff would review the Jibuti situation, including Marie,[1] in the light of all the new facts – our victories, our arrival in the neighbourhood, collapse of Italians who were going to dictate armistice terms to the French in the Colony, journey of De Gaulle, as well as attitude of Catroux and Co. What do we want from this place? What is its value once we have cut the railways to Addis Ababa and surrounded it on all sides? Is it any use to us at all if we have got Massawa? On the other hand, if an internal conversion could be promoted with a little outside Free French push, would not this tidy up the whole area and at the same time give a needed fillip to De Gaulle? What shipping is there in the harbour worth having? How does Jibuti live? We do not want to have any responsibility for feeding them except for a good *quid pro quo*.

[1] A Free French plan to take Jibuti from Vichy control.

I should like the COS to look at the matter as if we had never heard of the place till yesterday.

John Colville: diary
(*Colville papers*)

20 March 1941

At the House for Questions and the Cabinet. There was a scene over Boothby who is behaving idiotically and committing breaches of privilege. On the way home in the car the PM, speaking of this, said he would have no part in the matter; if there was one thing in the world he found odious, it was a man-hunt.

Our master having gone to dine at the Other Club,[1] we took the opportunity of playing noisy and childish games in the Mess, and were much excited by the news that the *Scharnhorst* and *Gneisenau* had been located in the Atlantic and might well be intercepted.

Winston S. Churchill: Oral Answers
(*Hansard*)

20 March 1941

BROADCASTING POLICY (ARTISTES AND TECHNICIANS)

Mr G. Strauss[2] asked (1) the Minister of Labour whether, in view of his appeal to local authorities not to dismiss employees who, in pursuance of the right granted to them by Parliament, have been exempted from military service on grounds of conscience, he will look into the cases of Mr F. W. T. Atkin and Mr J. Clapham, skilled technicians on the British Broadcasting Corporation, who have been dismissed for this reason; although, in Mr

[1] The Other Club had been founded in 1911. The then Liberal Party stalwart Churchill and his Conservative friend F.E. Smith (later Earl of Birkenhead) had been among the prime movers. The aim was to bring together, at fortnightly dinners while Parliament was in session, political and other figures who had been caught up in the current acerbity of party politics, at the time of the crisis over the power of the House of Lords, and to maintain convivial relations. The club's meetings were held in the Pinafore Room at the Savoy Hotel. Churchill attended his last meeting on 10 December 1964. The only engagement in his desk calendar for the month after his death was to the Other Club on 4 February 1965.

[2] George Russell Strauss, 1901–93. Labour MP, 1929–31 and 1934–79. Member of the London and Home Counties Traffic Advisory Committee, 1936. Parliamentary Secretary to the Minister of Aircraft Production (Sir Stafford Cripps), 1942–5. Minister of Transport, 1946–7. Privy Councillor, 1947. Minister of Supply, 1947–51. Introduced the Theatres Bill (for the abolition of stage censorship), 1968. 'Father of the House', 1974. Created Baron, 1979.

Clapham's case, he was granted total exemption on condition he continued his work at the British Broadcasting Corporation;

(2) asked the Prime Minister whether the Government have now looked into the matter of political discrimination by the British Broadcasting Corporation in regard to the employment of its artistes and technicians?

The Prime Minister (Mr Churchill): I will answer these two Questions together. The British Broadcasting Corporation have informed me that they have reconsidered the cases of those artistes who attended the People's Convention, and have decided that they shall not be debarred from giving performances on the broadcast in the normal way as opportunity arises. It is no part of the policy of His Majesty's Government to accord the special facilities of the microphone to persons whose words and actions are calculated to hamper the nation in its struggle for life. But the connection between this and musical and dramatic performances of all kinds, or the relation of such performance to political acts and opinions, are not apparent or worth while establishing.

In regard to Question No. 7, the rights which have been granted in this war and the last to conscientious objectors are well-known, and are a definite part of British policy. Anything in the nature of persecution, victimization, or man-hunting is odious to the British people. It is quite a different matter, however, to employ conscientious objectors in highly confidential and responsible technical work. This should be reserved for those who are fully in support of the national war effort. The decision in this case was for the British Broadcasting Corporation, but I cordially endorse it.

Mr Strauss: Arising out of that reply, part of which will give great satisfaction, might I ask whether we are to take it that a man who exercises the right given him by Parliament, and chooses to be a conscientious objector, will in future be allowed to broadcast music, or, if a technician employed in work not of a specially confidential nature, will be allowed to retain his employment?

The Prime Minister: If he were allowed to broadcast, it would be in his capacity as a musician, or a musical performer, and would not have any relation to his political or conscientious views. I think we should have to retain a certain amount of power in the selection of the music. Very spirited renderings of "Deutschland Uber Alles" would hardly be permissible.

Mr Bevan: Does the right hon. Gentleman appreciate that we are not asking that a person's music should not be broadcast because he is not sympathetic to the national effort? But, in the case of these technicians, the tribunals have very often granted them exemption on condition that they remain at their jobs, yet it seems that, after that, they are dismissed by authorities deriving their authority from Parliament. Is not that extremely undesirable?

The Prime Minister: I think that, on the whole, I have stated the view of the vast majority of people in this country.

Mr Neil Maclean:[1] Arising out of the first part of the Answer, dealing with the removal of the ban upon those who attended a People's Convention, I would like to ask the Prime Minister whether the removal of the ban is also going to apply to such individuals as, for example, the conductor of the Scottish Orpheus Orchestra, who has also been banned with his choir from giving a concert over the radio because he has pacifist views?

The Prime Minister: I see no reason to suppose that the holding of pacifist views would make him play flat.

Mr Maclean: Is not the Prime Minister aware that evidently the Governors of the BBC play flat, and will he give a direct answer to the question of whether it covers such cases as I have indicated?

The Prime Minister: My endeavour is to make them play up.

Winston S. Churchill to Professor Lindemann
(*Churchill papers, 20/36*)

21 March 1941

You must have all your figures about Imports, Munitions, Food, &c., down at Chequers tonight.

Winston S. Churchill to Lord Woolton
(*Churchill papers, 20/36*)

21 March 1941

I hope the term 'Communal Feeding Centres' is not going to be adopted. It is an odious expression suggestive of Communism and the workhouse. I suggest you call them 'British Restaurants.'[2] Everybody associates the word 'restaurant' with a good meal, and they may as well have the name if they cannot get anything else.

[1] Neil Maclean, 1876–1953. Apprenticed in an engineering workshop at the age of 12. Member of the national executive of the Workers' Union. MP for Glasgow Govan, 1915–50. Member of the 'Hands off Russia' committee, 1919; Chairman of the Anglo-Russian Parliamentary Committee, 1924. Scottish Whip of the Labour Party, 1918–23. Refused office in the first Labour Government. Chairman of the Parliamentary Labour Party, 1945–6.

[2] The name British Restaurants was the one adopted.

Winston S. Churchill to A. V. Alexander and Admiral Pound
(*Churchill papers, 20/36*)

21 March 1941
Action this Day

1. When I was at the Admiralty I repeatedly asked that more attention should be paid to the development of fuelling at sea. Now we find the German battle-cruisers are able to remain out for many weeks at a time without going into any base or harbour to replenish. If they can re-fuel at sea it is a scandal that we cannot do so. Again and again our ships have to be called off promising hunts in order to go back to fuel, six or seven hundred miles away. The argument that the Germans can send their tankers where they know they will find them, when we never know what is going to happen being on the defensive and not having the initiative, does not appeal to me. Arrangements should be made to have a few tankers in suitable positions off the usual routes so that if our ships are operating as they are now they could call one of these up and make a rendezvous. The neglect of this principle of fuelling at sea is a grievous drag on the power of the Fleet. It is the duty of the Admiralty to solve the problem.

2. Even more painful is the fact that we are not apparently able to fuel our destroyers in the comparatively calm waters off the African coast. The spectacle of this big convoy now coming up from Sierra Leone having one or two ships sunk every day by a trailing U-boat, and now the battleship escort herself also torpedoed, is most painful. Nothing can be more like 'asking for it' than to have a battleship escort waddling along with a six and a half knot convoy, without any effective AS[1] escort (other than the three corvettes). The Sierra Leone convoys will have to have destroyers with them. Ships sunk in these waters are just as great a loss to us, and just as much a part of the Battle of the Atlantic as if they are on the North-Western approaches. I am told that destroyers cannot go the distance. Why can they not be re-fuelled at sea, as has now been done, under pressure of events, for the corvettes? I am glad to hear about the air reinforcements. But destroyers are needed too. They must go all the way and be re-fuelled by the escort.

3. The whole question of the Cape Verde Islands being used as a German U-boat fuelling base must now be reviewed with a view to action being taken. I shall be glad to hear from you on all these points.

[1] Anti-submarine.

Winston S. Churchill to Sir Archibald Sinclair
(*Churchill papers, 20/36*)

21 March 1941
Personal

I have lately been putting a great deal of pressure upon the War Office to reduce their intake, and they are making efforts to meet my views. The Air Force, on the other hand, is rapidly expanding. All the more must every effort be made to practise economy in man and woman power. All experience shows that when the Services have a free hand in regard to Establishments, they give very little care to anything except making themselves safe and comfortable. The present ratio of Ground Services to First Line Air Strength is deplorable, and getting worse every day.

The suggestion in the enclosed paper seems worth considering. But in addition you should aim at combing off at least 50,000 personnel from the total demanded. I hope you will undertake to do this, and not simply send me long arguments to show that everything is perfect, and all criticism an intrusion. You must remember that there is practically no Treasury control on War Services demands, and that it is my responsibility as Minister of Defence to see that our limited man-power is used to the best advantage. I want proposals for 50,000 men to be combed off the total Establishment, and after this combing has been effected I want a substitution of 50,000 more women if they can be got, or as many as can be got, for the men demanded.

Having been in Office for so many years, I have entirely lost confidence in the Departments where their own interests are concerned unless a policy is enforced upon them by a competent politician at their head. This is what is meant by House of Commons control, of which you used to be the leading champion.

Winston S. Churchill to A. V. Alexander and Admiral Pound
(*Churchill papers, 20/36*)

21 March 1941

THE EVACUATION OF CASTELORIZZO

What disciplinary or other measures are going to be taken upon this deplorable piece of mis-management occurring after we have had already eighteen months' experience of war?

Winston S. Churchill to A. V. Alexander and Sir Archibald Sinclair
(Churchill papers, 20/36)

21 March 1941

The use of aeroplanes not only to attack our ships but also to direct the U-boats on to them is largely responsible for our losses in the North-Western approaches. No effort to destroy the Focke-Wulfs should be spared. If we could employ RDF[1] methods to find their positions and to direct long range fighters or shipborne aircraft to the attack we ought to be able to inflict serious casualties. Might it not be feasible to place a RDF station on Rockall? However inconvenient and unpleasant, the geographical position appears to be so good that it would be worth making a great effort to maintain a station there, at any rate during the summer months. The hills south of Lough Erne would also offer a valuable site. It might be even better if we could find ways and means of establishing stations on Tory Island or on one of the islands off the Kerry coast. These islands might be leased privately by some wealthy American friends. Please let me have a report from the technical point of view on the military results which could be expected if any of these things could be done and upon any other possibilities that have been or might be examined.

We should also study methods of disturbing the aircraft's communications with U-boats. I understand that the system is that the Focke-Wulf signals to Brest, whence directions are sent to the U-boat, the process taking about an hour and a half. Is it not practicable either to jam these communications or to confuse all concerned by a series of spurious messages? Presumably apparatus of the usual type for interfering with the Focke-Wulf's radio methods of navigation, which must be vital over the sea in bad weather, has not been neglected.

I assume that we DF[2] the signals he uses. If he uses ASV[3] it should be practicable to locate and home on him with suitable apparatus.

Winston S. Churchill to Sir Edward Bridges
(Churchill papers, 20/36)

21 March 1941

DELAY IN POSTAL AND TELEGRAPH CENSORSHIP
ON FREIGHT FOR IRELAND

To what Department or Departments should I address a Minute calling for precise explanations as to whom is responsible for this shocking delay? I have

[1] Radio Direction Finding.
[2] Direction Finding (tracing radio signals).
[3] ASV sets: air-to-surface vessel, an airborne radar device.

in mind the holding of another inquiry by Mr Justice Singleton,[1] with a view to inflicting disciplinary measures upon officials proved to have shown sloth and negligence.

I thought you had developed a follow-up department. It does not seem to have done much in this case.[2]

Kathleen Hill[3] *to Arthur Christiansen*[4]
(*Churchill papers, 2/417*)

21 March 1941
Private

Dear Sir,

The Prime Minister has asked me to send the enclosed cutting from today's *Daily Express*,[5] and to tell you that you are misleading the public when you suggest in the second paragraph that he 'promised' to drop four bombs on Germany for every one they drop here at any period in the near future. You ought to know perfectly well that nothing of this kind is possible for very many months to come.

[1] John Edward Singleton, 1885–1957. Called to the Bar, 1906. On active service, 1914–18; Captain, Royal Field Artillery. KC, 1922. Conservative MP, 1922–3. Recorder of Preston, 1928–34. Knighted, 1934. A Judge of the King's Bench Division, 1934–48. Headed two wartime inquiries, the first on bombsights, the second on German Air Force strength. Privy Councillor, 1949. A Lord Justice of Appeal from 1948 until his death.

[2] As Minister of Munitions in 1917–18, Churchill had created a Follow-Up Department at his Ministry which was noted for its effectiveness.

[3] Rose Ethel Kathleen Hill, 1900–1992. Chief Clerk, Automobile Association and Motor Union Insurance Company, Portsmouth, 1917–24, and a member of the Portsmouth Philharmonic Society (first violins), 1918–24. District Commissioner of Girl Guides, Bengal-Nagpur Railway, 1928–30. Secretary to the Chief Commissioner of Girl Guides for All-India, 1930–2. Broadcast as a solo violinist, Calcutta, Bombay and Delhi, 1935–6. Returned to England, 1937. Churchill's first Residential Secretary, July 1937; lived at Chartwell from July 1937 to September 1939. Churchill's Personal Private Secretary from 1939 to 1946. MBE, 1941. Curator of Chequers, 1946–69.

[4] Arthur Christiansen, 1904–1963. Educated at Wallasey Grammar School. Joined the *Wallasey Chronical*, 1920. News Editor of the *Sunday Express*, 1926–9; Assistant Editor, 1928–33. Editor of the *Daily Express*, 1933–57; Editorial Director, 1957–9. Director, Independent Television News, 1960–2. In 1961 he published his memoirs, *Headlines All My Life*.

[5] On 21 March 1941 the Opinion column in the *Daily Express*, headed 'Just a small force', declared: 'Londoners going to work early yesterday morning, after their fiercest raid this year, were distressed and angry at an Air Ministry announcement which said that 'a small force of bombers' made an attack on Cologne at the same time as the blitz on London. Why a 'small' force. Why can't we begin to implement the Prime Minister's promise that for every bomb the Germans drop on us we will rain four on them? they asked.'

Kathleen Hill to Arthur Christiansen
(*Churchill papers, 2/417*)

22 March 1941
Private and Confidential

Mr Churchill wishes me to add that the bad weather was the reason why only a small Bomber force was sent on this occasion, although much larger forces were eagerly awaiting their chance.

Winston S. Churchill to Edward Emerson[1]
(*Churchill papers, 20/21*)

22 March 1941

When Mr Penson[2] and you saw me on the 18 March you told me of the apprehensions which you felt as to some of the provisions in the proposed Agreement with the United States on Leased Bases.

I can assure you that both I and those of my colleagues who have been engaged in the negotiations have had fully in mind the great importance which is attached in Newfoundland to the matters dealt within the Agreement and I can readily appreciate the feeling which Mr Penson and you told me might arise that Newfoundland was being asked in this Agreement to give up much which she holds of value.

I need not say how sorry we in this country would be if this should be so. I would only ask the people of Newfoundland, of whose loyalty we have, in this testing time as throughout her long and eventful history, had ample proof, to bear in mind the wide issues which hang upon this Agreement.

The exchange of notes of last September providing for the lease of bases in British territories and the transfer of destroyers by the United States was hailed, and rightly so, not only as an act of the highest significance in itself but also as a symbol of co-operation between the great democracies in the defence of liberty and all that they hold dear. The fruits of that agreement in this wide sphere are already being made manifest, ever more and more as each day passes. During the last fortnight we have seen notable proofs of the profound

[1] Lewis Edward Emerson, 1890–1949. Admitted to the Bar, Newfoundland, 1912. Member of the Newfoundland Executive Council, 1924. Member of the House of Assembly, 1928. Minister of Justice and Attorney General, 1932–34. Commissioner for Justice and Attorney General, 1937–44. Commissioner for Defence, 1940–44. Knighted 1944. Chief Justice, Supreme Court of Newfoundland, 1944–49.

[2] John Hubert Penson, 1893–1979. On active service, 1916–19 (despatches, Military Cross and bar). Commissioner for Finance, Newfoundland, 1937–41. Secretary General, British Supply Mission in Washington, 1944–45. Attaché, British Embassy, Washington, 1947–53. Executive Secretary, International Materials Conference, Washington, 1953.

results flowing from it. The present Agreement, which gives effect in detail to the general arrangements embodied in the original exchange of notes, is not merely a contract. It is one more stage in the process of which the exchange of notes was the first step. Without this agreement it is impossible to say what would be the effects on the prosecution of the war and the whole future of the world. I have every confidence that all those who have to administer the provision of the instrument in practice will do so with regard not so much to the letter of the documents as to the spirit animating the Governments who have put their signature to them.

It is with these considerations in our minds that, recognizing to the full the considerable sacrifices made by Newfoundland to the cause which we all have at heart and her splendid contribution to the war effort, we ask her to accept the Agreement. It will be yet one more example of what she is ready to do for the sake of the Empire, of liberty and of the welfare of all mankind.

Yours vy faithfully
Winston S. Churchill

Sir Alexander Cadogan: diary
(*'The Diaries of Sir Alexander Cadogan'*)

22 March 1941

. . . there were telegrams from Belgrade suggesting message from King[1] to Prince Paul. And the PM with a crushing telegram to Tsvetkovitch.[2] PM was on the telephone all the morning from Chequers. And he had the idea of carrying out 'Shrapnel' and 'Brisk'.[3]

[1] Peter Karageorgevic, 1923–1970. Son of King Alexander of Yugoslavia, who was assassinated at Marseille in 1934. Ruled through his uncle, the Regent Paul, 1934–41. Brought to the throne after a *coup d'état* in his favour, 27 March 1941. Fled to Athens, April 1941. In exile, with his Government, in London, 1941–45. Signed an agreement with Marshal Tito to be represented in Yugoslavia through a Regency Council, 1 November 1944. On 29 November 1945 Tito declared a Republic. King Peter never returned to his country.

[2] Dragisa Cvetkovic. Prime Minister of Yugoslavia, February 1939 to March 1941. Reached agreement with the Croats in August 1939 whereby their leader (Macek) entered the Belgrade government. In December 1939 he signed a pact of friendship with Hungary. Summoned to Berchtesgaden, 14 February 1941, when Hitler offered not to march through Yugoslavia on his way to Greece if Yugoslavia agreed to join the Tripartite pact (the German-Italian-Japanese Axis). Cvetkovic refused Hitler's demand.

[3] Operation Shrapnel, a plan to seize the Cape Verde Islands from Portugal; Operation Brisk, a plan to seize the Azores from Portugal.

Winston S. Churchill to Dr Cvetkovic
(*Churchill papers, 20/49*)

22 March 1941

Your Excellency, the eventual total defeat of Hitler and Mussolini is certain. No prudent and far-seeing man can doubt this in view of the respective declared resolves of the British and American democracies. There are only 65,000,000 malignant Huns, most of whom are already engaged in holding down Austrians, Czechs, Poles and many other ancient races they now bully and pillage. The people of the British Empire and of the United States number nearly 200,000,000 in their homelands and British Dominions alone. We possess the unchallengeable command of the oceans, and with American help will soon obtain decisive superiority in the air. The British Empire and the United States have more wealth and more technical resources, and they make more steel than the whole of the rest of the world put together. They are determined that the cause of freedom shall not be trampled down nor the tide of world progress turned backwards by the criminal dictators, one of whom has already been irretrievably punctured. We know that the hearts of all true Serbs, Croats, and Slovenes, beat for the freedom, integrity and independence of their country, and that they share the forward outlook of the English-speaking world. If Yugoslavia were at this time to stoop to the fate of Roumania, or commit the crime of Bulgaria, and become accomplice in an attempted assassination of Greece, her ruin will be certain and irreparable. She will not escape, but only postpone the ordeal of war, and her brave armies will then fight alone after being surrounded and cut off from hope and succour. On the other hand, the history of war has seldom shown a finer opportunity than is open to the Yugoslav armies if they seize it while time remains. If Yugoslavia and Turkey stand together with Greece, and with all the aid which the British Empire can give, the German curse will be stayed and final victory will be won as surely and as decisively as it was last time. I trust your Excellency may rise to the height of world events.[1]

Winston S. Churchill to Anthony Eden
(*Churchill papers, 20/49*)

22 March 1941

To me it seems more important to get Yugoslavia into the war anyhow than to gain a few days on the Salonica front. Play the hand as you think best.

[1] On 24 March 1941, two days after Churchill's appeal Cvetkovic, and his Foreign Minister Dr Cincar-Markovic, travelled by train to Vienna and, to the alarm and anguish of many Yugoslav patriots, signed a pact with Hitler.

Winston S. Churchill to A.V. Alexander and Admiral Pound
(*Churchill papers, 20/36*)

22 March 1941
Most Secret
Action this Day

If the presence of the enemy battle-cruisers to a Biscayan port is confirmed, every effort by the Navy and the Air Force should be made to destroy them there, and for this purpose serious risks and sacrifices must be faced. If, however, unhappily they escape and resume their depredations, then action on the following lines would seem to be necessary, and should be considered even now:

1. In order to regain the initiative in the Atlantic, three hunting groups should be formed at earliest, namely: *Renown* and *Ark Royal, Hood* and *Furious, Repulse* and *Argus*. Each of these groups must have one or two Tankers, and every device is to be used to enable them to refuel at sea. The Tankers need not necessarily accompany the groups, but should be in positions where the groups could rendezvous with them.

2. The sea front from Iceland to Cape de Verde will be roughly divided into three sectors, in each of which one hunting group will normally be working. Although working independently of the convoys, they will give an additional measure of protection to convoys passing in their neighbourhood. These dispositions should be completed by the end of April, and will come into operation in instalments at earliest.

3. A plan will be made to replace *Furious* at earliest, by converting one or more ships as aircraft transports. At the same time, the Air Ministry will arrange for increased crating to Takoradi.

4. Considering how far we have carried the dispersal of the Fleet on escort duty, no objection could be taken to using *Nelson* in place of *Hood*.

5. A flotilla must be found for the Freetown convoys. This can be achieved out of the remaining 25 American destroyers which will have to work up in this southern area. Arrangements must be made to fuel the destroyers from the escort cruiser or battleships.

6. The evidences of German infiltration into the de Verde Islands, and the probability that they are being used to re-fuel U-boats, make it necessary to carry out Operation Brisk at the earliest date. Once we have got possession, we must make a good refuelling base there, and expel the enemy's U-boat tenders from these Islands. I will discuss separately the political pros and cons of this.

As many flying-boats as can be spared, up to 6, should be employed in the Freetown area, and will also work from the Islands when captured.

7. Pray let me have your thought on the above, together with all possible means of carrying it out.

Winston S. Churchill: minute[1]
(*Churchill papers, 20/36*)

22 March 1941
Most Secret

1. German infiltration has begun in the Cape de Verde Islands. It seems highly probable that 3 or 4 U-boats are working from there against our African trade route. A number of ships have been sunk in recent convoys, and the *Malaya* has been torpedoed while escorting the latest convoy. For six months we have kept valuable ships tethered and a Brigade of Marines ready at the shortest notice for the Operation Brisk. I am coming to the conclusion that this Operation must now be carried out.

2. We know from Sir Samuel Hoare's able telegrams how serious are the objections which he will urge. Obviously nothing can be said beforehand. The United States will be favourable to this operation, as they are much interested in the Islands. I will, however, consult the President beforehand. I do not believe that the German decision to overrun the Iberian Peninsula and to occupy Spain or Portugal, or both, will be dependent upon our doing Brisk. They know what they are going to do already. I do not believe that either Spain or Portugal will be more inclined to have the Germans on top of them because we are holding the Cape de Verde Islands.

Winston S. Churchill to A.V. Alexander and Admiral Pound
(*Churchill papers, 20/36*)

22 March 1941

Pray check this telegram to President, and unless there are any material alterations which you have to suggest, let it be dispatched through FO today.

This is the kind of stuff he likes on his cruise.

Winston S. Churchill to President D. Roosevelt
(*Churchill papers, 20/49*)

22 March 1941
Personal and Most Secret

1. On evening of 20th aircraft from one of our Carriers saw *Scharnhorst* and *Gneisenau* about the latitude of Bordeaux 600 miles out steering north. The light failed before a seaplane attack could be made. However, our dispositions

[1] This Minute (Churchill's Defence Minute D.100 of 1941), was addressed to General Ismay for the Chiefs of Staff Committee, Sir Alexander Cadogan and R.A. Butler.

were such that there were good hopes of an action Friday, 21st, had enemy continued northwards. We now have reason to believe that on being sighted by aircraft they turned east and are in one of the Biscay ports. If this is confirmed, we shall attempt to deal with them there by every means.

2. Presence of these two fast, strong ships in the Atlantic has forced us to disperse our whole battle fleet. As enemy knows this, it has its bearing on invasion. There are, however, no signs that this is imminent. Meanwhile, enemy has been headed off three convoys in succession. The strain on our resources is extreme.

3. It seems highly probable that 3 or 4 U-boats are working against our African trade route. A number of ships have been sunk in recent convoys, and the battleship *Malaya* has been torpedoed while escorting the latest convoy. We should be much obliged if she could be repaired in United States yard. She is now steaming thither at 14 knots.

Winston S. Churchill to General Ismay
(*Churchill papers, 20/36*)

23 March 1941
Action this Day

War Office and Middle East should be called upon for an exact account of all refrigerated meat ships they have requisitioned, and where and how these are at present employed. I have been told that some are used in the Middle East as depots for stores. Let me have a full list, distinguishing between vessels which have been heavily converted to troop carriers and those which could easily return to their normal duties.

Winston S. Churchill to General Ismay, for the Chiefs of Staff Committee and Admiralty
(*Churchill papers, 20/36*)

23 March 1941

Is it true that the War Office demanded provision for 8 gallons of water a day per man on a troopship, and that this has become a factor greatly reducing the numbers which can be taken? Has there been any impartial investigation of the War Office standards? I was much surprised to learn that only about 3,500 men were taken in the *Queen Elizabeth* and the *Queen Mary* each. This is hardly more than the numbers they carry when engaged in luxury passenger service. If I remember rightly, over 8,000 men were sent in the *Aquitania* or *Mauretania* to the Dardanelles in May 1915.

2. Could any saving in shipping be effected by transhipping personnel from the transports into the giant liners at Capetown? Now that the Red Sea will

soon be clear of enemy SMs and ACs,[1] it would seem attractive to organize a fast service from Capetown. The matter should at any rate be examined.

Winston S. Churchill to Colonel Hollis, for the Chiefs of Staff Committee
(*Churchill papers, 20/36*)

23 March 1941

COMPOSITION OF A CONVOY[2]

I approve the composition as set out, but I hope a substitute for the *Dominion Monarch* will be found, and she be turned over immediately to carrying meat in her refrigerated space. If necessary, 1,500 men will have to be left behind. They had better come out of the RAF than break the Divisional organization.

Winston S. Churchill to General Ismay
(*Churchill papers, 20/36*)

23 March 1941

SMALL BRITISH PORTS

Most of this is mere talk.[3] What is the use, for instance, of saying that no demand has been made for cranes at the smaller ports when these smaller ports have not been used and so do not feel the pinch? Surely we ought to have facilities prepared, both for unloading into lighters and coasters, and for removing traffic from the small ports by improved land communications by road or rail. Let me have a list of the ports which could so be used, and let me have proposals for a minute, which I will thereafter draft, to procure effective action as a vital insurance. We have far too much at stake in the Clyde and Mersey.

For the purposes of this, use any help you may require.

Winston S. Churchill to Hugh Dalton, A.V. Alexander and Sir Edward Bridges
(*Churchill papers, 20/36*)

23 March 1941

It is not intended to reach at the present time any decision to allow all food to pass freely into unoccupied France. On the other hand, if the French submit

[1] Submarines and Aircraft Carriers.

[2] This was Convoy WS 8, from Britain to the Middle East via the Atlantic Ocean, Cape of Good Hope, Indian Ocean and Red Sea.

[3] A note by the Minister of Transport on the lack of demand for the use of small ports in the British Isles.

to contraband control, a certain moderate ration of food might be allowed. At the present time I am leaving the initiative in the food negotiations to the United States, and it would not be a good thing to have another incident like the selling of the bananas at Algeciras. It is regretted that MEW[1] was not present when this matter cropped up unexpectedly. He is free to raise it if he desires during the week in Cabinet. A more precise definition of our attitude is required than appeared in the conversation of last week.

Winston S. Churchill to Air Chief Marshal Longmore
(*Churchill papers, 20/49*)

23 March 1941
Personal and Secret

I have been concerned to read your continual complaints of the numbers of aircraft which are sent you. Every conceivable effort has been made under my express direction to reinforce you by every route and method for the last five months. In order to do this, the Navy have been deprived of *Argus* and *Furious*, and are left without a single AC Carrier except occasionally *Ark Royal* to cope with the German battle-cruisers in the Atlantic. We are as fully informed as you of what you are getting. A weekly report is submitted to me of all movement via Takoradi. Therefore, when I read a telegram from General Smuts in which he refers to 'Beaverbrook being persuaded to disgorge from his hoard', or when I read the C-in-C, Mediterranean's,[2] telegram to First Sea Lord stating that 'Only one Hurricane was received during the month of March', and when I also read your A/442 which seeks to justify this absurd statement, I fear there must be some talk emanating from your Headquarters which is neither accurate nor helpful.

Winston S. Churchill to Sir Andrew Duncan
(*Churchill papers, 20/36*)

23 March 1941

You will have seen my directive about the Army, attached.[3] See also Secretary of State for War's note marked B.[4] I did not contemplate reducing in any way our orders in the United States. Everything will be late, and the more we have the better. At any time we may have Allies or neutrals to arm.

[1] The Minister of Economic Warfare, Hugh Dalton.
[2] Admiral Sir Andrew Cunningham.
[3] Churchill's Directive (as Minister of Defence) of 6 March 1941.
[4] Not printed. It concerned the need for additional arms purchases in the United States as a result of Churchill's Directive of 6 March 1941.

It is a question whether, in view of the change from ten (or eleven) Armoured Divisions to fifteen with corresponding reduction in ordinary Divisions, we should modify our demand upon the United States. There are great disadvantages in changing plans with them and flustering them with new proposals. If more Tanks are needed for extra Armoured Divisions, would it not be better to alter the incidence here, and leave the American programmes unaltered? Thus we should keep the matter in our own hands.

After considering this and the file, talk to me about your proposed telegram.[1]

Winston S. Churchill to William Mackenzie King
(Churchill papers, 20/49)

24 March 1941

We have been weighing very carefully the important questions raised in your messages Nos. 35 and 36 of the 2nd March and my immediately succeeding telegram sets out the views of our advisers on these matters.[2]

We think these views are sound. The position is bluntly that we have not all the equipment that would enable us to give complete protection on both sides of the Atlantic and the question is therefore how can we make the best use of the material we have having regard to what the enemy is trying to do and the probabilities as to his future course of action. The issue of the war will clearly depend on our being able to maintain the traffic across the Atlantic. All our advice is that our present dispositions afford the best means of achieving this. If we were to divert any substantial part of our forces from their present area of operations to cover wider areas where there is admittedly some risk of enemy action, we should only imperil the whole and play into his hands.

We are indeed most deeply appreciative of all that Canada has done and, in particular, how you have stripped yourselves of protection on your Atlantic coasts to help us. As soon as we get more ships, or should the dangers of enemy attack on the western side of the Atlantic become greater, we shall not hesitate to consider redispositions at once.

[1] Not Printed. Sir Andrew Duncan's telegram to Washington dealt with the requirement of the Ministry of Supply with regards to tanks and ordnance to be manufactured in the United States.

[2] Transatlantic seaborne trade and naval traffic.

Winston S. Churchill to William Mackenzie King
(*Churchill papers, 20/49*)

24 March 1941

His Majesty's Government in the United Kingdom have studied most carefully your views and are in fully sympathy with your anxieties and responsibilities regarding adequacy of Canadian defences. Military advisers have also examined your Chiefs of Staff analysis of the Canadian Home Defence position. The following summarizes our assessment of the situation and our ability to assist.

2. In weighing the possibility of assisting in the strengthening of those features of the Canadian home defence position to which the Canadian Chiefs of Staff have drawn attention, we have had to bear in mind most carefully the position here and in the other theatres where we are facing the enemy's attack. As you are aware, Germany is now making a supreme effort, both at sea and in the air, against our trade. We ourselves are making corresponding effort to defeat these attacks by assembling all the escort vessels we can lay our hands on, by transferring anti-aircraft weapons from our home defences to merchant shipping and by diverting still more air forces to defend our ships against the German long-range aircraft which attack our shipping in areas hitherto regarded as immune. At the same time, with improving weather conditions, we have to be ready to meet the increasing attacks of the German bomber force against objectives in this country. Finally, we have from now on to be fully prepared to meet a large-scale attempt at invasion. Our military advisers have just completed a detailed examination of the requirements necessary to meet these threats and it is clear that, if we are not to fall below the danger line, we have very little to spare from the forces immediately available at home. At the same time, the recent developments in the Balkans and Middle East theatres make it essential for us to maintain the flow of our reinforcements to the Middle East. We have the fullest confidence in our ability to defeat the threats to this country and to build up our growing offensive power, but you will appreciate that we are bound in the common interest, referred to in your Chiefs of Staff Appreciation, to weigh with the greatest care any additional withdrawals from the United Kingdom and its North-Western Approaches.

3. While we fully realisze the possibility of tip-and-run raids on the Canadian eastern seaboard, we are of the opinion that such raids are unlikely in view of the risk the raiders would run of air attack and possible shadowing. They are more likely to attack the shipping routes in the Western Atlantic. Moreover, an additional deterrent is the likelihood that operations against the Canadian seaboard must precipitate the entry of the United States of America into the war. This we feel is particularly the case in the neighbourhood of Newfoundland, where our enemies must realize the sensitiveness of the USA to operations in the area of her newly-acquired bases.

4. We note that the Canadian Chiefs of Staff make no specific reference to strengthening the anti-submarine protection of shipping near the Canadian coast. In view of indication that U-boat activity may be extending to the Western Atlantic, the question of strengthening the naval and air forces now available in Canada for A/S duties[1] is now under consideration between the Admiralty and NSHQ[2] Ottawa. We are of the opinion that the enemy will only adopt the less economical use of submarines in the Western Atlantic for the purpose of making us over-insure ourselves there at the expense of the decisive area of the North-Western Approaches. Every effort will be made to strike the right balance between providing essential A/S forces for the Canadian coast and maintaining our strength on this side of the Atlantic.

5. With regard to air attack, the threat of attack by German land-based aircraft is virtually non-existent, as no German aircraft is capable of making the Atlantic flight from existing air bases with any appreciable bomb load.

6. It is in this light that we have considered the request in the final paragraph of your telegram. We feel that, in view of the situation shown in paragraph 2 above, our present combined naval dispositions not only are best in the common interest, in existing circumstances, but are adequate to deal with the scale of attack which we think probable in the Western Atlantic. Nevertheless, you may rest assured that redisposition will be made if the situation there changes.

7. We agree that the four reconnaissance squadrons covering Canada's Atlantic approaches are hardly adequate for the area in question. In view, however, of the urgent and pressing need for this type of aircraft elsewhere, it is difficult at present to provide aircraft for the formation of additional squadrons. We are giving full consideration to your views on the expansion of the Royal Canadian Air Forces in the preparation of the revised air target programme.

Winston S. Churchill to General Ismay, for the Chiefs of Staff Committee
(*Churchill papers, 20/36*)

24 March 1941
Most Secret

POSSIBLE SEIZURE OF PORTUGESE ISLANDS IN THE ATLANTIC

1. How would it be for the United States to be asked to send a few ships to Madeira, or to cruise among the Islands? Report[3] does not deal with this.

[1] Anti-submarine duties.
[2] National Security Headquarters.
[3] A Report by the Chiefs of Staff, dated 23 March 1941, deprecating the seizure of Portugal's Atlantic Islands, or their attempted capture once Germany had secured them.

2. Surely if the Germans take over any of these Islands, we shall have to try to beat them out. It is curious that no attempt should be made to deal with this proposition. If it is so easy for the Germans to occupy Madeira or other Islands, and they would be quite safe and inexpugnable there, why don't they do it?

3. I am concerned at the suggestion in para. 8. This would be a supreme admission of failure and defeat at sea. The Admiralty must not suppose that such a policy would be accepted by Cabinet or Parliament. It would entail a fatal paralysis of our food supply and war effort.

War Cabinet, Night Air Defence Committee: minutes[1]

(*Cabinet papers, 81/22*)

24 March 1941
11.30 a.m.
Secret

FREE BALLOON BARRAGE

The free balloon barrage had met with no known success during the period under review. The limitations imposed by weather on the operation of this barrage were stressed, and it was also pointed out that the man-power involved was considerable, and that a large amount of transport was required to make the men and equipment sufficiently mobile.

The Prime Minister directed –

That the free balloon barrage should be operated for a further month in the Liverpool area, and that during this period production of free balloon barrage equipment should be maintained at its present level. After a month the matter should be brought before the Committee for a decision whether the free balloon barrage should be further proceeded with.

SUPPLY OF ANTI-AIRCRAFT GUNS

Vice Admiral Phillips said that the production of AA guns showed little increase since the outbreak of war. At the present time, the number of vital points to be defended at home and overseas was increasing at a rate in excess of output.

The Prime Minister directed:

That the Minister of Supply should be asked to submit a report on the production of 3.7-inch guns.

[1] Churchill was the Chairman of the War Cabinet's Night Air Defence Committee. The one other Cabinet Minister on the Committee was Sir Archibald Sinclair. The fifteen other members were mostly from the Air Ministry (including Robert Watson Watt), the Admiralty and the War Office. Professor Lindemann was also a member.

UP WEAPON[1]

Vice Admiral Phillips said that 6 ships were now being fitted with the UP weapon.

The Prime Minister directed –

That the production of this equipment should be pressed ahead since it would secure our shipping and vital centres against the dive-bomber.

The Prime Minister concluded the meeting by saying that it was clear our Night Fighters and AA guns were becoming increasingly effective. We now welcomed moonlight. Light in all its forms was now our ally.[2]

Winston S. Churchill to Anthony Eden
(*Churchill papers, 20/49*)

24 March 1941

Am being pressed about announcing move of our troops to Greece. It has been published in the United States. We know the Germans know, and it is odd they should have kept it quiet. You have told Campbell[3] he may tell the Serbs. The Press here have been very good and Parliament patient. I see an argument against our making the admission as Hitler would base his invasion upon it. On the other hand, it is very difficult defend denying British and Australasian public knowledge thus widely known. Let me know what you will do and your reasons.

War Cabinet: minutes
(*Cabinet papers, 65/18*)

24 March 1941
5 p.m.

The War Cabinet were reminded that no official announcement had been made that any of our troops had landed in Greece. The knowledge that our men were already in Greece might strengthen the hands of our friends in Yugoslavia.

[1] The Unrotated Projectile, an anti-aircraft rocket.

[2] Churchill and the War Cabinet were told later that day (at 5 p.m.), that the casualties in the German air raid against London on the night of 19/20 March had been 'heavier than at first reported', with 504 people killed and 1,511 injured. On the night of 21/22 March, in a German air raid on Plymouth 150 people had been killed and 250 seriously injured.

[3] Ronald Ian Campbell, 1890–1983. Entered the Diplomatic Service, 1914. Minister Plenipotentiary, Paris, 1938–39. Minister at Belgrade, 1939–41. Knighted, 1941. Minister in Washington, 1941–45. Ambassador to Egypt, 1946–50. Director of the Royal Bank of Scotland, 1950–65.

The Prime Minister said that the case in favour of an announcement was very strong. But it had been agreed that the decision when to make the announcement should be taken by the authorities in the Middle East. The decision must be left to the Foreign Secretary who was playing our hand with great skill.

The War Cabinet –

Invited the Prime Minister to telegraph to the Foreign Secretary suggesting that an announcement of the landing of our troops in Greece might influence opinion in Yugoslavia, but leaving the final decision to the Foreign Secretary.

The Prime Minister said that while the German Battle Cruisers *Scharnhorst* and *Gneisenau* were at large in the Atlantic, every important convoy had to be escorted by a big ship. The situation was so tight that, when the *Malaya* had been hit by a torpedo, the convoy which she was escorting had had to be re-routed by Trinidad and Iceland. The demands of Malta and the Middle East for aircraft involved the use of aircraft carriers (which would be very valuable for reconnaissance) to transport aircraft to Takoradi. All this meant that our Naval resources were stretched to the fullest extent. The Home Fleet was now dispersed, and no attempt was being made to assert our command of the North Sea. Fortunately at the moment there were no indications of immediate invasion, and the dispersed Naval units could be concentrated in Home Waters within about a week. On the credit side also were the facts that we had superior air power in daylight, and a powerful Army at home. By the end of that week more than 1,000 heavy tanks should be available.

While these aspects of the situation were undoubtedly serious, there was no cause for alarm.

Winston S. Churchill: Oral answers

(*Hansard*)

25 March 1941 House of Commons

REQUEST FOR A FURTHER DEBATE ON THE ROBERT BOOTHBY CENSURE

The Prime Minister: I hope I shall correctly interpret the general sense of the House if I move that this House does not feel itself called upon to proceed further in this matter. I think the hon. Member for East Aberdeen (Mr Boothby) has given us the feeling that he intended no kind of disrespect or reflection upon the fair fame and integrity of the House of Commons Committee, and in all the circumstances I believe that the House, having inquired with some particularity into it, would do well to let the matter drop.

Resolved,

'That, having heard the statement of Mr Boothby and a statement by the

Chairman of the Select Committee on the Conduct of a Member, this House does not desire to entertain the matter further.'

Winston S. Churchill to Major Kermit Roosevelt
(Churchill papers, 20/29)

25 March 1941

My dear Major Roosevelt,

In the letter which you wrote to me after I had regretfully told you that there could be no chance of your remaining on the active list you asked me whether you might be accepted for service in a minesweeper. While I have nothing but admiration for your anxiety to serve in any capacity that may be open to you, I am sorry that the medical reports on your case make it impossible for me to recommend you for anything of this kind.

I hate to disappoint you because I know how truly your heart is with us; but there is no alternative open to me.

Yours sincerely,
Winston S. Churchill

Winston S. Churchill to Viscount Cranborne
(Churchill papers, 20/36)

25 March 1941
Most Secret

What is the point of worrying the Dominions with all this questionable stuff?[1] Have they asked for such an appreciation? Surely the other side should be stated too, namely:

1. That even if they make their original landings the communications to these lodgments will be interrupted by the Fleet inside a week.

2. That we have every reason to believe that we can maintain the superiority in the British daylight air, and that our Bomber Force will therefore 'Namsos'[2] all the landings by day as well as by night.

3. That, apart from the Beaches, we have the equivalent of nearly 30 divisions with 1,000 Tanks at the 1st April, held in reserve to be hurled at the different invasion points.

[1] A draft telegram to all the Dominion Governments setting out the arguments for and against the likelihood of a German invasion of Britain.

[2] A reference to the British landing at Namsos, in Norway, in April 1940, which had to be abandoned as a result of German air superiority.

4. That we have 1,600,000 men in the Home Guard, of whom a million possess rifles or machine guns to deal with sporadic descents of parachutists, &c.

Frankly, however, I do not see the object of spouting all this stuff out – some of it injurious if it leaked – unless it is thought the Dominions require to be frightened into doing their duty.

Sir Alexander Cadogan: diary
(*'The Diaries of Sir Alexander Cadogan', OM, 1938-1945*)

25 March 1941

PM sent for me at 3.15. He showed me telegram from Roosevelt agreeing to *Illustrious* being repaired in US. Then he spoke to me about 'Son of a bitch', which I took to be Tsvetkovitch, but found he meant Stoyadinovitch.[1]

Winston S. Churchill to the Foreign Office
(*Churchill papers, 20/36*)

25 March 1941

WEST INDIAN BASES

The Americans should be told that I too have a Parliament to consider, and that the text of the Agreement should be available for Members at 5 p.m. instead of 6 p.m. on Thursday next. Publication in the newspapers here will not take place till the next day, but I must mention to Parliament early on Thursday that the papers will be laid at 5 p.m.

[1] Milan Stoyadinovitch, 1888–1961. Educated at the University of Belgrade, and subsequently in England, France and Germany. Entered the Accountancy Section of the Serbian Ministry of Finance, 1914; head of the section, 1917–19. Lecturer in Economics at Belgrade University, 1920–2. Yugoslav Minister of Finance, 1922–6. President of the Finance Committee of the Yugoslav National Assembly, 1927. Prime Minister of Yugoslavia, June 1935 to February 1939. As his own Foreign Minister from 1935 to 1939, he aligned Yugoslavia more closely with Germany and Italy. Narrowly escaped assassination at the hands of a fellow member of Parliament, who shot at him while he was speaking, 1936. Interned by the Yugoslav Government in April 1940. Handed over to the British, and held on the island of Mauritius, 1941–8. Emigrated to South America, 1948. Settled in Argentina, 1950, becoming editor of the economic weekly, *La Economista*. He died in Buenos Aires.

Winston S. Churchill to David Margesson
(*Churchill papers, 20/36*)

25 March 1941
Action this Day

1. Your letter and paper of March 23. The scope of my note of March 6 was limited to the end of the year 1942. I cannot at present look further than that. But even in 1943 I see grave reasons to doubt whether we shall have the power to invade the mass of the European Continent, and engage the 250 Divisions which Hitler may well be still maintaining there.

2. The requirements of the C-in-C, Home Forces, are noted. It is quite natural that every General should try to keep as many troops as possible in his own hands unless some other objective presents itself. But when I remember that Sir Alan Brooke was ready to send large numbers of troops and half our few Tanks out of the country in July, August and September last in order to defend the Nile Valley I am reassured as to what his attitude will be should other needs arise. I do not accept the view that only 2 Divisions can be spared from the immense force now gathered at home. We must not get too 'invasion-minded'. When real needs arise in other quarters, risks will be run with courage here, as they have been in the past. In the meanwhile, the question does not arise.

3. I agree that the figure of 'about 2 millions' should be interpreted as 2,195,000.

4. I also agree that for the 15 Armoured Divisions mentioned by me may be substituted 12 Armoured Divisions and 9 Army Tank Brigades; and that the target figure for the Imperial Army in March 1942 may be the 59⅓ equivalent Divisions set out in Appendix C.

5. Although the telegram sent by the Minister of Supply to Mr Purvis No. 204 Pursa has been approved by me for the sake of greater precision, it is clearly understood there is to be no diminution in our requests to the United States in respect of anything we really need, and in particular that the equipment for the ten extra Divisions must be maintained.

6. Finally, the Army will be maintained at the figure of 2,195,000. If the nineteens are not sufficient, additional reservations will be lifted to meet wastage. This also applies to casualties, when they begin on a large scale.

It would no doubt be ideal to have always in training all the drafts needed to supply the approved maximum wastage in battle, and finish the war up with our training depots full. Our resources do not allow such counsels of perfection, and in the circumstances it will be better to face a certain amount of temporary depletion in establishments should many of our Divisions be heavily engaged abroad simultaneously, than to make this further draft upon the public and keep it standing by indefinitely. Besides, according to C-in-C, Home Forces, everybody has got to stay at home.

Winston S. Churchill to James Stuart
(*Churchill papers, 20/36*)

26 March 1941
Secret

POSSIBLE LABOUR PEERS

The Lord Privy Seal gave me the attached list and I shall be glad if you will investigate the different claims and qualities. It is important that the Labour Party should be represented in the House of Lords and, owing to troubles about Lords Nathan[1] and Strabolgi,[2] they are very weak there. It is a good thing that the Labour Party should use the House of Lords instead of spurning it. I am prepared on grounds of high policy to make four Labour Peers in a batch and say why. I do not think The King would object. At present almost the only Labour Peers are the wretched Pacifists made by MacDonald.[3] I am assured that all on this list are sound on a fight to a finish.

Winston S. Churchill to Sir Edward Bridges
(*Churchill papers, 20/36*)

26 March 1941

I am all for trusting Mr Harriman fully and working with him on the most intimate terms. At the same time we must keep the power of private

[1] Harry Louis Nathan, 1889–1963. Solicitor. One of the original officers of the Territorial Force, 1908. On active service at Gallipoli, 1915 and in France (severely wounded). Liberal Member of Parliament, North-East Bethnal Green, 1929–35. Labour Member of Parliament, Central Wandsworth, 1937–40. Acting Commanding Welfare Officer, Eastern Command, 1939–41; London District, 1941–43. Member of Ministry of Pensions Central Advisory Committee, 1942–45. Created Baron, 1940. Parliamentary Under-Secretary of State for War, 1945–46. Minister of Civil Aviation, 1946–48. Chairman of the Committee on Charitable Trusts, 1950.

[2] Joseph Montague Kenworthy, 1886–1953. Entered the Royal Navy 1902; on active service, 1914–16; Admiralty War Staff, 1917. Commander, Royal Navy, 1918. Liberal Member of Parliament for Hull Central, 1919–26; Labour, 1926–31. President of the United Kingdom Pilots Association, 1922–25. Succeeded his father, as 10th Baron Strabolgi, 1934. Opposition Chief Whip, House of Lords, 1938–42. Lieutenant, Home Guard, 1940–46. Among his many publications were studies of the Narvik, Dunkirk, Singapore and Italian campaigns.

[3] James Ramsay MacDonald, 1866–1937. Labour MP for Leicester, 1906–18, for Aberavon, 1922–29 and for Seaham, 1929–31. Leader of the Labour Party, 1911–14. Prime Minister and Secretary of State for Foreign Affairs, January to November 1924. Prime Minister, 1929–35. National Labour MP, 1931–35. Lord President of the Council, 1935–37.

correspondence with Pursa.[1] It should not be difficult to devise methods for a secret series of this kind. Let me have proposals.

Otherwise, I approve.[2]

War Cabinet Battle of the Atlantic Committee: minutes
(*Cabinet papers, 86/1*)

26 March 1941 — 10 Downing Street
5 p.m.

The Minister of Shipping[3] gave a report of his recent talk with Mr Harriman.

77 fast cargo liners were due for launching in the United States of America this year and 50 next year and Mr Harriman thought that a considerable number of these might be handed over to us if a really strong case were presented. He had suggested that the best case would take the form of a suggestion that these ships could be used for carrying military equipment to the Middle East. These vessels could form part of the fast convoys and would thus save the time of a larger number of escorting craft and become the equivalent of a gift of destroyers and cruisers. A draft statement on these lines was being prepared.

The Minister of Shipping was invited to prepare a statement on these lines, to send to Mr Harriman, a copy of which should be sent to the Prime Minister.

Winston S. Churchill to General Wavell
(*Churchill papers, 20/49*)

26 March 1941
Personal and Secret

1. We are naturally concerned at rapid German advance to Agheila.[4] It is their habit to push on whenever they are not resisted. I presume you are only waiting for the tortoise to stick his head out far enough before chopping it off. It seems extremely important to give them an early taste of our quality. What is the state and location of 7th Armoured Division? Pray give me your

[1] The British Purchasing Commission in the United States, headed by Arthur Purvis.

[2] Of the proposal that a member of Averell Harriman's organization should work in close association with the North American Supply Committee, and have access to all its documents and telegrams.

[3] Ronald Cross.

[4] On 24 March 1941 German forces, using M.13 Tanks, occupied Fort Agheila, which had not previously been in British occupation. By evening they had advanced eighteen miles further east.

appreciation. I cordially approve your request to General Smuts for a Brigade of 1st South African Division. Everything must be done to accelerate movement of 2nd South African Division. 50th Division starts 22nd.

2. As soon as the Keren-Massawa region is cleared and Red Sea becomes safe we hope to induce America to deliver direct to Suez. We are doing everything in human power to keep you supplied with aircraft, but *Furious* will now be required to act against enemy battle-cruisers in Atlantic. I fully understand your difficulties.

Winston S. Churchill: Memorandum[1]

(*Churchill papers, 23/9*)

26 March 1941
Secret

THE IMPORT PROGRAMMES

1. We should assume an import of not less than 31 million tons in 1941. On this basis, food cannot be cut lower than 15 million tons, and a million is required for the Board of Trade. This leaves 15 millions for the Ministry of Supply, as against 19 millions to which they were working on the 35 million programme. A cut of 4 millions has, therefore, to be made by the Ministry of Supply, for which a revised programme should be framed. Ferrous materials, timber and pulp seem to offer the main field of reduction. As we can now buy steel freely in the United States, the keeping in being of the whole of the existing steel industry cannot be accepted as an indispensable factor. We must try to import in the most concentrated forms and over the shortest routes. This principle must also influence food imports.

2. Should our total imports fall below 31 millions, the deficit should for the present be met by the Ministry of Food and the Ministry of Supply on the basis of one ton cut in food to two tons in supply. Should the imports exceed 31 millions, the benefit will be shared in the same proportion. The position will be reviewed in the autumn, when this year's harvest is known.

3. I have received from the War Office a reply to my Notes about Army Scales, which they have had under consideration for three weeks. My notes did not look further ahead than 1942, and must be subject to review in the light of events. My figure of 'about 2 millions' may be interpreted as desired by the War Office at '2,195,000,' for which the arrangements are completed. The War Office proposal to substitute for my figure of 15 Armoured Divisions, 12 Armoured Divisions and 9 Army Tank Brigades, may be approved, and the target figure for the grand total of the Imperial Army in March 1942 of

[1] Printed for the War Cabinet as War Cabinet Paper WP 69 of 1941.

59⅓ 'equivalent Divisions,' may be accepted. The resultant saving on man-power intake from now to the end of 1942 is about 475,000. This saving, and the increase in armoured forces at the expense of infantry and artillery, should afford an important relief to the Ministry of Supply in hutments, clothing and projectiles.

4. The Purvis Programme, which was submitted to President Roosevelt in January to give him the general scale, may now be more precisely defined as the Ministry of Supply desire, and in so doing, if convenient, the adjustment may be made to cover the change in the proportion of Armoured Forces. However, it is important that no diminution should be made in anything we need and are likely to get from the United States; in particular, the equipment for the 10 extra Divisions should stand.

5. The Naval Programme is the subject of a separate note, but the following principles which have a bearing on imports may be stated here:

The remaining three King George V Class battleships must be completed at full speed. The construction of *Vanguard*, which is the only capital ship which can reach us in 1943 and before 1945, is most desirable. One new Monitor is also needed. No other heavy ships can be proceeded with at present, and no more armour-plate can be provided for other naval purposes for the next six months; nor should new armour-plate factories be laid down. This position will be reviewed on the 1st September in the light of –

(a) The Battle of the Atlantic

(b) The relationship of the United States to the war.

The requirements of the Admiralty for armour-plate must not exceed the 16,500 tons provided for 1941, nor the 25,000 tons for 1942. If these limits are observed, the Ministry of Supply should be able to execute the increased Tank Programme.

6. The Ministries of Food and Agriculture should, upon the basis of 15 million tons import in 1941, concert an 18 months' programme, drawing as may be necessary upon our meat reserves on the hoof to cover the next six months, but endeavouring to provide by concentrated imports the most varied dietary possible for the nation at war. By taking a period as long as 18 months, it should be possible to avoid hurried changes in policy, to use reserves as balancing factors, and to make the best use of the assigned tonnage.

7. The British Air power will continue to be developed to the utmost within the above limits and with the present priorities and assignments.

Winston S. Churchill to A.V. Alexander and Admiral Pound
(*Churchill papers, 20/36*)

26 March 1941
Action this Day

Pray give your full thought to this. The Germans have occupied Sicily. They are in Tripoli; they are in Cagliari. At any time they may occupy Pantellaria. We have thus been unable to prevent the closing of the Central Mediterranean and this may presently entail the loss of Malta.

2. Personally, I think we should study the capture of Sardinia, as at least giving us a foothold in this vital area, and I am having the plan re-examined. But . . .

3. . . . the only certain cure is to improve the AA armament of our ships. We must have a number of vessels which in these clear skies can kill the dive-bomber and often bring down the high-bomber. You know how hard I have been trying since the beginning of the war to find a method. If you can make the PE[1] work it will do it. There is also the LAM[2] fired from UP.[3]

4. We need to fit out special ships with decks covered with UP weapons firing the various fuzes – PE, LAM and AD.[4] It is a scandal that *Illustrious* has no protection against dive-bombers, and that *Formidable* has been sent out with nothing but the high-angle guns, which have been proved to fail. No doubt I shall be told everything is being done – all is going forward – but I am sure that if there were a real drive in the Admiralty from the top great results would be achieved.

5. Cannot floating platforms on tankers with batteries of UP be towed along behind warships and merchant ships through this area? You are not afraid of the U-boat. You are not afraid of the mines. You are simply driven out of the area by the Ju. 87s. Cannot some of the kind of effort that was put into beating the Magnetic Mine be turned on to beating the dive-bomber by fire?

6. Every day I have this feeling that ships could be equipped with fire-weapons that would protect them from close air attack and that this would solve our problem, but that the Admiralty treat the problem as if it were one of many and not almost the greatest form in which their duty is presented.

I beg for your help.

[1] PE fuzes: an anti-aircraft device for ground fire against attacking aircraft.

[2] The Long Aerial Mine for use against German bombers. It consisted of a bomb hanging from a parachute at the end of a long wire, the intention being to drop large numbers of LAMs above a German bomber fleet so that they would fall and catch in the bombers' propellers before being wound up and detonated. The wires were laid in the form of a curtain.

[3] UP: Unrotated Projectile, an anti-aircraft rocket.

[4] AD: anti-aircraft ammunition.

Winston S. Churchill to Ronald Campbell
(*Churchill papers, 20/49*)

26 March 1941

Do not let any gap grow up between you and S[1] or Ministers. Continue to pester, nag and bite. Demand audiences. Don't take no for an answer. Cling on to them, pointing out Germans are already taking the subjugation of the country for granted. This is no time for reproaches or dignified farewells. Meanwhile, at the same time, do not neglect any alternative to which we may have to resort if we find present Government have gone beyond recall. Greatly admire all you have done so far. Keep it up by every means that occur to you.

In the early hours of 27 March 1941, the day after Milan Stoyadinovitch and his Ministers travelled to Vienna to join the Tripartite Pact (Germany, Italy, Japan) the Stoyadinovitch government was overthrown by a coup d'état headed by General Simovitch, which put King Peter on the throne, and renounced the pro-German orientation of the previous government and the regent, Prince Paul.

Winston S. Churchill to Anthony Eden
(*Churchill papers, 20/49*)

27 March 1941

In view of *coup d'état* in Serbia, it would surely be well for you both to be on the spot in Cairo so as to concert events. Now surely is the chance to bring in Turkey and form a joint front in the Balkans. Can you now get a meeting in Cyprus or Athens of all concerned? When you know the situation, ought you not to go to Belgrade? Meanwhile, we are doing all possible and carrying on.

Winston S. Churchill to Ismet Inönü
(*Churchill papers, 20/49*)

27 March 1941

Your Excellency. The dramatic events which are occurring in Belgrade and throughout Yugoslavia may offer the best chance of preventing the German invasion of the Balkan Peninsula. Surely now is the time to make a common front which Germany will hardly dare assail. I have cabled to President

[1] Stoyadinovitch.

Roosevelt to ask him for American supplies to be extended to all Powers resisting German aggression in the East. I am asking Mr Eden and General Dill to concert all possible measures of common safety.

Sir Alexander Cadogan: diary
(*'The Diaries of Sir Alexander Cadogan'*)

27 March 1941

Good news on arriving at FO, of *coup d'état* in Belgrade. Went to see PM at 11.40. He due to make speech at 12. Gave him his phrase 'Yugoslav nation has found its soul', which was featured by evening papers.

Winston S. Churchill: speech
(*Charles Eade, editor, 'The Unrelenting Struggle', pages 83–8*)

27 March 1941 Conservative Association

I thank you for the great kindness and cordiality of your welcome. If I am a few minutes late, you will, I am sure, excuse me, because before I sit down I will tell you something which will perhaps explain that I have other business today to deal with.

The reason why His Majesty entrusted me in May last with the formation of a Government was because it was an almost universal opinion that national unity must be established in order to face the dangers by which we were encompassed.

You will remember how our leader, Mr Neville Chamberlain, the moment he felt that he could not command the unity of all parties, even though he stood at the head of a great Parliamentary majority and the great mass of the Conservative party – how he, with perfect self-abnegation which for ever will be an example to public men and will long be associated with his name, stepped aside and resigned his high office. He gave me all possible help, and I was able to form in a week – in the midst of a great battle which was raging in France and the Low Countries – a Government of national union, an all-party Government. That was a dark hour, but we got through it.

Then at a later stage Mr Chamberlain, whose work was of the greatest assistance to the new Government, who served under his former lieutenant with perfect loyalty, was stricken by illness and died. You then invited me to be the leader of the Conservative Party. I gave at the time my reasons for accepting this very great task. I believed, and I still believe, that it is possible to reconcile the duties of the leader of the Conservative Party with those of the Prime Minister of a National Government. And, indeed, I thought I could discharge the task more easily if I were able to address myself to it on the same basis and with the same status as the leaders of the two other parties also represented in the National Government.

Nearly a year has gone by since the new Government was formed. In these times one loses the measure of time; sometimes it feels as if it were ten years and sometimes as if it were only ten days. Anyhow, however you count it or reckon it in your mental picture, here we are still, never so strong or so hopeful as we are today. This is because the national unity has been preserved and fortified; because we have set an example to all countries in the hour of danger.

National unity requires sacrifices from all parties, and no party has sacrificed more than the Conservative Party with its large Parliamentary majority. Many eminent men have had their careers interrupted, many Ministers of promise have seen their prospects obscured, but none has thought of himself; all have made the sacrifices, and we are proud that the Conservative Party has made the greatest sacrifices. We shall continue to make these sacrifices, and we shall preserve national unity until we have finally beaten down Satan under our feet. I cannot tell you how and when this will come, but that it will come is certain. I cannot attempt to forecast the form or character of the victory, still less what the situation in Europe and in the world or what the mood in the minds of men may be when that victory has been won.

I hope, however, that there will be national unity in making the peace. I hope also that there will be national unity in certain practical measures of reconstruction and social advance to enable this country to recover from the war and, as one great family, get into its stride again. If this hope were not realized, if no common ground could be found on post-war policy between the parties, it would be a misfortune, because we should then have to ask the nation to decide upon the outstanding issues and party government would be the result.

I may say, however, that some of the ties and friendships which are being formed between members of the administration of all parties will not be very easy to tear asunder, and that the comradeship of dangers passed and toils endured in common will for ever exercise an influence upon British national politics far deeper than the shibboleths and slogans of competing partisans. We have found good, loyal, able comrades in our Labour and Liberal friends, and we work together with the single aim, so well expressed in your resolution today, of saving Europe and the world from the curse and tyranny of Nazism.

Anyone in any party who falls below the level of the high spirit of national unity which alone can give national salvation is blameworthy. I know it is provoking when speeches are made which seem to suggest that the whole structure of our decent British life and society, which we have built up so slowly and patiently across the centuries, will be swept away for some new order or other, the details of which are largely unannounced. The spirit sometimes tempts me to rejoinder, and no doubt there are many here who have experienced passing sensations of the same kind, but we must restrain those emotions; we must see things in their true proportion; we must put aside everything which hampers us in the speedy accomplishment of our common purpose.

Moreover, I do not believe that partisanship will benefit, after the war is over, those who indulge in it when the war is going on. The country will judge party men and women in every sphere of life, throughout the island, not by any partisan remarks or rejoinders they may have uttered, but by the contributions which they will have made to the common victory. There is an honourable competition in which we may all strive as parties and as individuals to win the prize. Therefore, the guidance which I offer to the Conservative Party as its leader is that we keep our party organization in good order by associating it at every point with the war effort, and that we concentrate all our thoughts and actions on the victory of the great cause we serve.

It is because of the interests of national unity that I have forborne to produce a catalogue of war aims or peace aims; every one knows quite well what we are fighting about, but if you try to set forth in a catalogue what will be the exact settlement of affairs in a period which, as I say, is unforeseeable; if you attempt to do that you will find that the moment you leave the sphere of pious platitude you will descend into the arena of heated controversy. That would militate against the efforts which we are making, and we could not in justice to our country take such a step.

I was very glad to see that the illustrious leader of the American people, President Roosevelt, is of the same opinion, though in our correspondence the topic has never been mentioned. In speaking of the mission of his new Ambassador to this country, Mr Winant, a worthy representative of a great nation at a crucial moment – in speaking of his mission, President Roosevelt, when he was asked what instructions were given to the Ambassador about peace aims, replied that he did not see much use in talking about peace aims until Hitler had been defeated. Without taking any final or irrevocable view of what may be desirable in these matters, I may say that I think that the simplest objects are the best. Life, which is so complicated and difficult in great matters, nearly always presents itself in simple terms. For the time being the defeat of Hitler and Hitlerism is a sufficient war aim, and will open the door to every worthy peace aim.

I said that the Government was formed in a dark hour and there was worse to come. But I cannot pretend to you, my friends and supporters, that I took up my task with any other feeling than that of invincible confidence. That is the feeling which inspires me here today. Since then we have had the deliverance of Dunkirk, which gave us back the core and fibre of our Regular Army. Since then we have had a series of notable victories.

First of all the frustration of Hitler's invasion plan by the brilliant exploits of the Royal Air Force; secondly, the frustration of his attempt to cow and terrorize the civil population of this country by ruthless air bombing. That has recoiled, futile and shameful, from the unflinching courage of the whole of our people. Thirdly, we have had the destruction of the Italian power and Empire in Africa by our Armies there, and although they were left unsupported by our French Ally, and although we were deprived of all the strategic points necessary to maintain direct contact through the Mediterranean, nevertheless we have been able not only to defend the Nile Valley, but to remove almost all – and the rest soon – the stains which Italian tyranny has wrought on African soil.

But there is another supreme event more blessed than victories – namely, the rising of the spirit of the great American nation and its ever more intimate association with the common cause. Much of that has been accomplished by the sentiment aroused in American breasts at the spectacle of courage and devotion shown by simple and ordinary folk of this country in standing up to the fire of the enemy.

Britain could, I believe, save herself for the time being, but it will take the combined efforts of the whole of the English-speaking world to save mankind and Europe from the menace of Hitlerism and to open again the paths of progress for the people. Therefore I say that if we look back on these five events, all of which have added to our strength and our means of survival and carried us forward on our journey to success, we must see that we have much to be thankful for.

Do not let us ever suppose that our troubles are ended. There is another matter. The Battle of the Atlantic must be won so that food supplies and munitions and every form of American aid may come to us in ever-growing volume. That battle is fought against the surface raider, against the aircraft which steal up from the French and Norwegian coasts right round our islands every day, and against the U-boats. It is fought by the Royal Navy, by the Merchant Marine, by the men who are working the docks and ports and harbours, and by the women who stand at their side in equal danger. That battle is being fought. It engages the deep interest of the great peoples on both sides of the ocean, and I cannot doubt that before many months are passed I shall be able to declare to you that it has been decisively won.

But there are other difficulties and dangers which beset us, and we cannot expect to have successes unchequered by reverses. We must be ready, as we have always been ready, to take the rough with the smooth. We must have spirits so constant that we can derive from misfortune added strength, and if we are cheered by victory, we are also inspired to greater efforts by rebuffs. We cannot tell how long the road will be. We only know that it will be stony, painful and uphill and that we shall march along it to the end.

And now, here at this moment, I have great news for you and the whole country. Early this morning the Yugoslav nation found its soul. A revolution has taken place in Belgrade and the Ministers who but yesterday signed away the honour and freedom of the country are reported to be under arrest. This patriotic movement arises from the wrath of a valiant and warlike race at the betrayal of their country by the weakness of their rulers and the foul intrigues of the Axis Powers.

We may therefore cherish the hope – I speak, of course, only on information which has reached me – that a Yugoslav Government will be formed worthy to defend the freedom and integrity of their country. Such a government in its brave endeavour will receive from the British Empire, and, I doubt not, in its own way from the United States, all possible aid and succour. The British Empire and its Allies will make common cause with the Yugoslav nation, and we shall continue to march and strive together until victory is won.

On 27 March 1941, in Washington, the United States – British Staff Conversations were concluded, culminating in Joint Basic War Plan Number One of the United States and the British Commonwealth 'for war against the Axis Powers'. This plan, which was comprehensive in its scope, covered the detailed disposition of the land, sea and air forces of both Britain and the United States, from the moment that America would enter the war.[1]

Winston S. Churchill: speech[2]
(*'Daily Telegraph and Morning Post', 28 March 1941*)

27 March 1941

It is a very striking thing, Mr Winant, that the strongest organizations of capital and labour in this country should have united to do you welcome. It is explained by the high position which the Ambassador of the United States has always held; it is explained also by the gravity of the struggle in which we are engaged; but most of all it is explained by your especial personality and the services you have rendered to the joint movements of labour and industry throughout the world. It is a great pleasure to see Mr Winant among us. He gives us the feeling that all President Roosevelt's men give me, that they would be shot stone dead rather than see this cause let down.

Now at this time we have brought into being a National Government, and a Government which rests as one of its main sources of strength upon the trade union organization of this country. In the United States during the presidency

[1] Britain-United States (J) No. 30 of 1941, 27 March 1941, 'Secret' (*Premier papers, 3/489/1*). Also known as 'Defence Plan No. l'.

[2] To members of the Trades Union Congress and the employers, gathered to honour Ambassador Winant.

of Mr Roosevelt enormous efforts have been made to broaden the whole basis of industry and society, and we watch them with the utmost interest and sympathy.

But I may say, and I know Mr Winant will not think it critical and invidious if I say, that we have been several generations broadening and developing the trade union movement in this country, and we have had some differences from time to time, but every one knows, and I have been taught it all my public life, that the employers of this country are deeply thankful there is in existence a strong organized trade union movement with which they can deal, and which keeps its bargains and which moves along a controlled and suitable path of policy.

The trade union movement has willingly accepted in this war the temporary suspension of privileges which have taken generations to win. They have been handed over to the custody and keeping of the State, and without that we should not be able to produce under the severe conditions of the enemy's fire the immense output of munitions of all kinds which is needed if we are to let our soldiers, sailors, and airmen meet the enemy on even terms of equipment. It is a matter of honour to the whole country that these privileges shall be restored and resumed when this crisis has passed away, unless some other better arrangements can be made.

As for the future, I have always been a bit shy of defining war aims but if these great communities, now struggling not only for their own lives but for the freedom and progress of the world, emerge victorious, there will be an electric atmosphere in the world which may render possible an advance towards a greater and broader social unity and justice than could otherwise have been achieved in peace-time in a score of years. We are not theorists or doctrinaires. Trade unionists are practical men aiming at practical results. I might say that our aim will be to build a society in which there will be wealth and culture, but where wealth shall not prey on commonwealth nor culture degenerate into class and pride.

Today I have good news. It was breaking all our hearts to see the gallant Serbian and Yugoslav people signing away their souls through weak and cowardly rulers to those who, once they had them in their grip, would have shaken the life and independence out of them. But I rejoiced when I heard an hour before this luncheon that a revolution had taken place at 2 o'clock this morning, and that the Ministers who went to sign have been arrested.

Though I don't know what will happen, and one cannot be sure of anything, I believe it is reasonable to expect that we shall have a Government in Yugoslavia which will repudiate the pact which was signed the day before yesterday, and will be ready to defend the honour and the frontiers of Yugoslavia against aggression. If that be so, Great Britain will recognize that Government, Great Britain will give all the aid in her power to those who are defending their native lands; to the heroic Greeks; to the Turks if they are attacked. We will give all the aid we can. We are not as strong as we shall be when the plants have delivered their fruit, when the great factories have produced the weapons, but still we get stronger every day.

We will give all the aid we can to those who are fighting to defend their freedom and their native land, and I am quite sure that the President of the United States will be actuated by the same generous impulse to sustain those who are fighting to be free, and that according to the laws and the constitution of the United States – for, after all, as a great democratic leader, he must move with the whole march of the nation – his sympathies and aid will also be extended in full measure to the Serbian people.

Therefore this is a time when we may have good hope of the results of this war. The final result is perhaps distant, but it may be much nearer than we suppose. You cannot tell. I lived through all the last War and survived many of its political vicissitudes, including the 12½ per cent., which, at any rate, you will admit was well meant.[1] I remember at the Ministry of Munitions being told that we were running short of this and that, that we were running out of bauxite and steel, and so forth; but we went on, and, in the end the only thing we ran short of was Huns. One fine morning we went down to our offices to get on with the work of preparing for the campaign of 1919, and found they had all surrendered.

We must prepare ourselves for long pilgrimages and voyages, yet relief may reward patient and resolute effort.

Eric Seal to his wife

(*Seal papers*)

27 March 1941 10 Downing Street

The PM had two speeches today – one at the Conservative Assoc, & the other at a luncheon to Winant, given by the TUC & the employers in conjunction. This latter I attended, as you will see by the card. I hope the seal assigned to your unworthy husband will give you much gratification!!

The PM made a very fine impromptu speech; & driving away in the car together I said to him that I thought he got on better with the Trades Union people than with the Tories – he said yes, – they have a certain native virility

[1] As Minister of Munitions, Churchill had awarded a 12½ per cent wage increase to munitions workers. This had led to widespread strikes in factories throughout the country, so that the increase had to be extended to cover all workers in war industries.

– although he found himself in sympathy with the Tories on theoretical matters like free enterprise & the rights of property. I said they (the Trade Unionists) were essentially conservative, & not much of the pale intellectual about them & he agreed.

When we got back to No 10, the Bases Agreement with the Americans was signed – in the glare of arc lights & cinemas. If you go to the flicks next week you'll probably see me!

Then we had a Cabinet in the Air Ministry – the idea being to hold a cinema show afterwards. This was the first time it has been held in another Govt office. The cinema show was quite interesting, including some pictures of every aircraft being shot down taken from fighter aircraft during actual combat. You could see them flying to bits in the most gratifying way!

War Cabinet: minutes
(*Cabinet papers, 65/18*)

27 March 1941
5 p.m.

2. The War Cabinet were informed that a military *coup d'état* had taken place in Yugoslavia in the small hours of that morning. The President of the Council[1] and a number of other Ministers, including the Minster of War,[2] had been placed under arrest. King Peter had issued a proclamation to the effect that he had taken the Royal authority into his hands, and had entrusted the Government to General Simovitch.[3] The repudiation of the Government which had signed the Three-Power Pact was a clear rebuff to our enemies.

The Prime Minister informed his colleagues that he had taken the following action:

(1) He had asked the Foreign Secretary and the Chief of the Imperial General Staff to return at once to Cairo to concert events.

(2) He had authorized the British Minister in Belgrade to inform the new Government that, on the basis that they were determined to denounce the Pact with Germany, and to help in the defence of Greece, we recognized them as the Government of Yugoslavia.

[1] Dragisha Cvetkovic.

[2] Petar Pesic (Peter Peshich). Yugoslav general. Minister of War from 7 November 1940 to 27 March 1941.

[3] Dusan Simovic (Dushan Simovitch), 1882–1962. Chief of the Army General Staff, Yugoslavia, 1939–40. Chief of the Air Force Staff, 1940–41. Opposed to the pro-German orientation of Prince Paul. Led a coup against Prince Paul's Government, 27 March 1941, became Head of the Government, and proclaimed Peter II as king. Fled to Greece at the end of April 1941. Prime Minister of the Royal Yugoslav Government in exile in London, 1941–42. Nominated by King Peter as head of his government in 1945, but rejected by Tito. Returned to Yugoslavia, 1946, living there until his death.

VICHY FRANCE AND THE NAVAL BLOCKADE

The Prime Minister said that our policy had been to maintain the blockade against the French, but not to a point which might sting them to violent action. There had been a movement in the United States in favour of victualling Unoccupied France; and we had suggested to President Roosevelt that he might make a working agreement for us with the French. So far, however, nothing had transpired. The reaction of the United States to the agreement made with the Germans by Admiral Darlan made it a good moment to enquire how these negotiations were progressing. The situation was a serious one, for the French were importing some 2½ million tons from North Africa and 1¾ million tons from West Africa. More than half of these cargoes found their way to Germany and this quantity of imports might be greatly increased. There was some reason to suppose that the French were negotiating to import cargoes from South America. If the public in this country felt that we were not taking a strong line in this matter, there would be a good deal of bitter feeling. If we allowed food into Unoccupied France, we might be asked to relax the blockade of enemy occupied countries.

War Cabinet, Defence Committee (Operations): minutes
(*Cabinet papers, 69/2*)

27 March 1941 Cabinet War Room
9.45 p.m.
Secret

OPERATION 'WINCH'[1]

The Prime Minister recapitulated the history of the discussions which had taken place as to the possibility of carrying out this Operation and drew the attention of the Committee to the urgent appeals which had been received from the Foreign Secretary, the Commanders-in-Chief in the Middle East, and the Governor of Malta[2] for the strengthening of the fighter defences of the Island. All kinds of objections had been raised. First of all it was said that HMS *Argus* could only do 17 knots and that there would only be one day in four when there would be enough wind to allow Hurricane IIs to fly off her deck. Then it had been suggested that the *Ark Royal* might be used on account of her superior speed, but it had been objected that she would be seriously endangered in the event of air attack if her decks were obstructed by Hurricanes. A counter proposal had been put up by the Admiralty to run a disguised merchant ship through to Malta, but the Commander-in-Chief,

[1] The despatch of fighter aircraft to Malta by aircraft carrier through the Mediterranean from Gibraltar.

[2] General Dobbie.

Mediterranean had given his opinion that such a ship would be certain to be discovered and intercepted. Then it was said that a solution to the difficulties with the *Ark Royal* had been found and he had thought that all was settled, and now the Admiralty said that on account of the battle-cruisers at Brest the Operation could not be carried out. Force H[1] must be kept hanging about in case they should come out. Force H would in any case have to go back to Gibraltar to refuel, and he had thought that advantage could be taken of this to carry out Operation 'Winch'. Meanwhile other arrangements could be made to watch the Bay of Biscay. In the old days we had found it possible to intercept ships at sea without the help of aircraft carriers, and he did not see why it could not be done now.

Mr Alexander said that the Admiralty could not be charged with not being helpful. Month after month they had been helping to reinforce the Middle East with aircraft. They had conveyed one hundred and ninety four aircraft at great cost to their own vital work in the Atlantic.

The Prime Minister agreed that HMS *Furious* had now done three voyages largely at his instigation, but he drew attention to the enormous efforts which the air forces in the Middle East had been and were being asked to make. They had certainly made wonderful use of the aircraft which had been given them. He thought the risk in the Bay of Biscay had been exaggerated. Force H would be absent for about eight days, during which time the watch would not be quite so good, though it could be maintained with other ships and with submarines. Against this must be weighed the arrival of twelve aircraft of the highest performance to Malta. This would enable twelve more aircraft to be spared for Greece.

Winston S. Churchill: Note[2]

(*Churchill papers, 23/9*)

27 March 1941

NAVAL PROGRAMME 1941

DIRECTIVE BY THE MINISTER OF DEFENCE

Naval programmes have been continuous throughout the war, all slips being filled as vacated. It is, nevertheless, convenient at this time of year that the admiralty should present their present needs of new construction in a general list and obtain Cabinet sanction for their policy.

[1] A British naval squadron, formed on 28 June 1940, commanded by Admiral James Somerville (later by Rear-Admiral E.N. Syfret, later still by Vice-Admiral Algernon Willis). Based at Gibraltar, and operating inside the Mediterranen, it was created to fill the vacuum left by the French fleet after the fall of France. It was disbanded in October 1943.

[2] This Note was printed as part of War Cabinet Paper WP 69 of 1941.

2. No one can doubt that the construction of small craft for anti-U-boat warfare, for minesweeping, for combating the E-boats, and for assault landings should proceed to the full extent of our resources. It is essential, however, that simplicity of design, speed of construction and the largest possible numbers should govern the whole of this small craft programme. The construction of destroyers should in no case exceed 15 months. I understand from the Controller that apart from enemy action or strikes he can guarantee this in respect of the 40 now projected.

3. We cannot at the present time contemplate any construction of heavy ships that cannot be completed in 1942. This rules out further progress upon the *Lion* and *Temeraire* and the laying-down of *Conqueror* and *Thunderer*. It also makes it impossible to begin the four heavy cruisers contemplated in the programme of 1940. Work will, therefore, be limited to completing the three remaining battleships of the King George V class and to building the three light cruisers of the 1941 programme, all of which it is understood can be completed before the end of 1942. An additional Monitor, for which the guns are already available, can also be completed before the end of 1942.

4. The need of concentrating labour on merchant repairs and on repairs to the fighting fleet, makes it impossible to begin any new aircraft-carriers after *Victorious, Indomitable* and *Indefatigable* have been completed. Such new aircraft-carriers could not in any case be ready until 1944.

5. The requirements of the Navy in armour-plate can on the above basis be adjusted to meet the needs of the Army tank programme and can be limited to 16,500 tons in 1941 and 25,000 tons in 1942. No new armour-plate plant need be erected at present.

6. The one exception to the above principles is the *Vanguard*, which can complete in 1943 and is the only capital ship we can by any means obtain before 1945. As we have the guns and turrets for the *Vanguard*, it is eminently desirable that this vessel should be pressed forward, provided that this can be done within the limits of the armour-plate provision in paragraph 5.

7. Nothing in the above should hinder the work on the drawings and designs of any of the postponed vessels, including especially the new aircraft-carrier.

8. In view of the need to concentrate on repairs, the output of new merchant ships may be reduced from 1,250,000 tons, which is the present target, to 1,100,000 in 1942, and we should not at the present time proceed with any merchant vessels which cannot be completed by the end of 1941. It is to the United States building that we must look for relief in 1942.

9. The whole of our heavy ship construction will be reviewed on the 1st September, 1941, in the light of –

(a) the Battle of the Atlantic, and
(b) the relation of the United States to the War.

Sir Charles Wilson to Kathleen Hill
(*Churchill papers, 2/420*)

27 March 1941

Dear Mrs Hill,

The Prime Minister asked me for the names of the four doctors whom he had seen, as I think he wanted to send them his *Marlborough.*

He reminded me that I had not done this.

The names are:[1]

Winston S. Churchill to General Wavell
(*Cabinet papers, 69/2*)

28 March 1941

Defence Committee desire me to convey to you their cordial congratulations on the double success at Keren and Harar and request that you will transmit their thanks to General Platt[2] and General Cunningham[3] and the forces under their command for the continued rapid execution of their memorable campaign.

[1] The doctors to whom Churchill's biography of the first Duke of Marlborough was sent were Sir Thomas Dunhill (who had seen Churchill at Chequers on 1 December 1940), C.P. Wilson (who had seen him at Chequers on 3 March 1941), Dr Frank Kellett (who had done a blood test on 3 December 1940) and Dr H Courtenay Gage (who had done an X-ray examination on 24 February 1941).

[2] William Platt, 1885–1975. On active service, North West Frontier of India, 1908 (despatches, Distinguished Service Order); in France and Belgium, 1914–18 (DSO). Major-General, commanding the troops in Sudan, and Commandant of the Sudan Defence Force, 1938-40. General Officer Commanding-in-Chief, 1941–45. A Free French detachment under his command captured Massawa on 8 April 1941. Knighted, 1941. Colonel of the Wiltshire Regiment, 1942–54.

[3] Alan Gordon Cunningham, 1887–1983. On active service, 1914–18 (Military Cross, DSO, despatches five times). Major-General, 1938. General Officer Commanding East Africa Forces, 1940–1; 8th Imperial Army, Middle East, 1941. Knighted, 1941. Lieutenant-General, 1943. General Officer Commanding Northern Ireland, 1943–4; Eastern Command, 1944–5. General, 1945. High Commissioner and Commander-in-Chief, Palestine, 1945–8 (and the last British officer to leave Palestine, from Haifa port, when the Mandate came to an end).

Winston S. Churchill to Harry Hopkins
(*Premier papers, 3/224/1*)

28 March 1941
4.30 p.m.
Personal and Private

Am delighted to see you in this great post.[1] Yesterday was a grand day, Belgrade, Keren, Harar. The strain at sea on our naval resources is too great for us to provide adequate hunting groups, and this leads to a continuance of heavy disastrous losses inflicted on our immense traffic and convoys. We simply have not got enough escorts to go round and fight at the same time. Am in closest touch with Harriman. Kindest regards from all here.

Winston S. Churchill to General Ismay and Sir Edward Bridges
(*Churchill papers, 20/36*)

28 March 1941

A small inter-Departmental Committee of Ministry of Shipping, Admiralty and War Office should prepare plan for the release by the end of May of 4 million cubic feet of refrigerated space from the Army and the Navy. The Committee should report to the Minister of Defence, showing what inconveniences such a withdrawal would entail. The 24 armed merchant-cruisers have not done much this war, and have suffered heavy losses from the enemy's warships. Why do 'ocean-boarding vessels' require refrigerated space? Can they not be reduced in number?

Let me have a fuller report on the depot and accommodation ships used by the Navy. Cannot they be replaced by other vessels without refrigeration plants? At least 2 millions will have to come off the Army troopships.

Propose me names for the Committee, after acquainting the Departments of my purpose. I will appoint an independent Chairman, and Professor Lindemann or Professor Roy Harrod[2] will represent me. Reports should be made in one week from today.

[1] Roosevelt had just appointed Hopkins to 'advise and assist' him on Lend-Lease, as 'bookkeeper'. Although never formally given the title of Administrator (which many ascribed to him), Hopkins performed that function. It was his first official government post since he had resigned seven months earlier as Secretary of Commerce. Robert Sherwood writes: 'The Lend Lease appointment brought Hopkins out of the shadows in which he had dwelt as a mysterious confidant, and made him, in one huge area of authority, the de facto Deputy President.' (*The White House Papers*, Volume one, page 267)

[2] Roy Forbes Harrod, 1900–1978. Economist. Oxford University Lecturer in Economics, 1929–37 and 1946–52; Reader in Economics, 1952–57. Served under Professor Lindemann (later Lord Cherwell) in Churchill's S (Statistical) Branch, 1940–42. Statistical Adviser to the Admiralty, 1943–45. Economic Adviser, International Monetary Fund, 1952–53. Knighted, 1959. Biographer of Keynes. Author of *The Prof (a Personal Memoir of Lord Cherwell)*, 1959.

Winston S. Churchill to Air Chief Marshal Longmore
(*Churchill papers, 20/49*)

28 March 1941
Personal

Many thanks for your telegram. Night and day I work to send you more by every route and every method. I hope liquidation of Keren may help you. Direct shipments from America are being vigorously pursued. Winch[1] is on.

Winston S. Churchill to General Wavell
(*Churchill papers, 20/49*)

28 March 1941
Most Secret

Many thanks for your 0/52146. War Office tell me they have sent 5 Cruiser Tanks in WS7 and are sending 20 more in WS 8, the whole unaccompanied. I am seeing whether we can send you in addition an Army Tank Brigade in WS 8. Infantry Tanks are now flowing well from the factories and even cruisers have begun to move. You say the 7th Armoured Division will not be fit again till 15th May. Does this exclude all of them from action? I hope that Keren and its consequences will soon give you another Infantry Division and release some Air Squadrons. Chiefs of Staff have agreed to send the big liners to Suez, which speeds both Australian and South African reinforcements. I realize how much we are piling on you, but events at Belgrade have made Lustre[2] into a great stroke of policy, quite apart from its purely military aspect.

2. I trust Mandibles[3] is being prepared with the utmost thoroughness, that there will be perfect unity between the Navy and Army, that one of your very finest officers will be put in charge, and that the date will be kept.

3. We highly admire here the exact measurements you made of the force needed for the Eritrean campaign. I am going to broadcast on Sunday, and should like to mention that the 4th Indian Division fought at Sidi Barrani and within three weeks were fighting at Kassala. Also, I think I ought to say: 'Considerable British and Imperial forces have arrived in Greece.' We know from sure sources that the Germans are well informed. It is very difficult to explain to Press and MPs why, when so much has been made public in US and enemy wireless show that they know, that no statement may be made in Britain or Australia.

[1] The transport of fighter aircraft to Malta by aircraft carrier.
[2] British military aid to Greece, including infantry divisions from Egypt.
[3] The capture of the Italian Dodecanese Islands (principally Rhodes and Kos).

Winston S. Churchill to the Foreign Office
(*Churchill papers, 20/36*)

28 March 1941

Monsieur Stoyadinovitch should be treated with formal courtesy, but kept under constant surveillance. The Governor[1] should be informed that he is a bad man, who was certainly financially corrupted by Germany in the years before the war, and was at this juncture undoubtedly a potential Serbian Quisling. It is not desirable that relations other than formal should spring up between him and the Governor or his household, or between him and people in the Island. Food and comfort should be appropriate to the scale of a Colonel.

Winston S. Churchill to Sir Alexander Cadogan and R.A. Butler
(*Churchill papers, 20/36*)

28 March 1941
Action this Day

AIR ASSISTANCE TO GREECE: GREEK REQUEST

We simply cannot get more Fighters out than we are sending by every method and route. We are flying out additional Bombers to bring our Squadrons up from 12 to 20. To send new Squadrons of Bombers would require additional servicing personnel to travel round the Cape, i.e., three months. If you like to dish up the 'sad' reply marked A, for the Greek Minister, with a little more agreeable sauce, by all means do so, adding everything useful from CAS's minute of 26.3.41. You do not need to refer to me again.

Sir Alexander Cadogan: diary
(*'The Diaries of Sir Alexander Cadogan*)

28 March 1941

About 6, PM sent for me and gave me, to read, draft of a long telegram to A[2] on strategy. Gist was – what do we want of Turkey? Turkey won't be drawn into an offensive, and perhaps shouldn't be. We ought to say to her 'After events in Belgrade, Germany may be shy of attacking Yugoslavia, may

[1] Bede Edmund Hugh Clifford, 1890–1969. Private and Military Secretary to the Governor-General of Australia, 1919–20; to the Governor-General of South Africa (Prince Arthur of Connaught) 1921–24. Governor and Commander-in-Chief, Bahamas, 1932–1937; Mauritius, 1937–42; Trinidad and Tobago, 1942–46. Knighted, 1933. Among his books were *Irrigation and Hydro-Electric Resources of Mauritius*, and an autobiography, *Proconsul*.

[2] Anthony Eden, who was then on his way from Malta to Athens.

pretend she never meant to attack Greece, and may turn her whole assault on you! Hadn't we, Greeks, Turks, Yugs better say if one is attacked all will defend: a strong defensive. Meanwhile, you Turks, don't get crumpled up in Thrace. Strategic retirement as a precaution. Then Hitler, with his 30 Divisions, may sheer off our 70. He may attack Soviet.' Told PM of our news of German armoured Divisions being rushed back to Cracow. This rather in line with his ideas.

Winston S. Churchill to Anthony Eden

(*Churchill papers, 20/49*)

28 March 1941
Personal and Secret

See my telegram No. 684 to Angora containing message to Turkish President and Hugessen's[1] telegrams Nos. 692, 686 and 540.

1. Though I am not impressed with Hugessen's arguments about 'mulishness', you should decide about the message as you think fit. Let us, however, visualize clearly what we want in the Balkans and from Turkey and work towards it as events serve.

2. Together Yugoslavia, Greece, Turkey and ourselves have 70 Divisions mobilized. Germans have not yet got more than 30 in this theatre. Therefore, the 70 could say to the 30 if you attack any of us you will be at war with all, the Germans would either attack in mountainous regions and with poor communications at heavy odds, or alternatively they would have to bring large reinforcements from Germany. But even this does not cure their difficulties, because first it will take some months to bring the reinforcements to the theatre, and secondly the theatre itself, and indeed the communications leading to it, are not strong enough to carry much larger forces without a prolonged process of communication improvement. Therefore, it is very likely that a triple note by the three Balkan Powers would lead to the maintenance of peace, or to a prolonged delay in the German advance. Perhaps advance could not be made for many months, and then they miss the season. Meanwhile, British reinforcements and British and American supplies will vastly increase resisting power of Allied armies. There is, therefore, a good prospect if the three Allies could be brought into line that no invasion southwards would be tried by the enemy. Here is what the Turks want.

[1] Hughe Montgomery Knatchbull-Hugessen, 1886–1971. Entered the Foreign Office, 1908. British Minister to the Baltic States, 1930–4; in Teheran, 1934–6. Knighted, 1936. Ambassador to China, 1936–7; to Turkey, 1939–44; to Brussels, 1944–7. In 1949 he published his memoirs *Diplomat in Peace and War*. Known, after secret documents in his possession had been stolen by the German Spy Cicero in Turkey, as 'Snatch'.

3. This is Turkey's best chance of avoiding war. For look at the alternative. If all three remain disunited the Germans may feel that it will be better to leave Greece and Yugoslavia alone and turn their whole striking force rapidly against Turkey in Thrace. There have been suggestions of this in various telegrams, and perhaps Turkish appreciation of this danger may have made her none too keen on getting Yugoslavia into the war. Thus, by doing nothing. Turkey runs the greatest danger of having everything concentrated upon her. One can hardly doubt that the mass of Turkish troops gathered in Thrace would soon be driven back in confusion upon the Chatalja and Bosphorus, without any obligation or opportunity on the part of Yugoslavia or Greece to take the pressure off by counter-attack, or by lengthening the fighting front.

4. The proper order for anyone to give who had the power would be (a) the diplomatic declaration of unity and demand to be let alone as set forth above, and (b) a simultaneous withdrawal of the bulk of the Turkish army to Chatalja and the Asiatic shore, leaving only strong covering troops and rearguards in Thrace. Such a policy of firm united declaration, coupled with sound strategic withdrawal, would prevent the Germans from gaining a decisive victory in Thrace, would not require any offensive from Turkey, and would, unless the Germans shied off, expose them to a stalemate front from, say, the lines of Chatalja through the Rupel–Nestos sector right up along the northern Serbian front. Even this could not develop for a long time. But what a dangerous and uninviting prospect for an enemy for whom quick successes are especially important. Surely this is the true Turkish interest if it can be brought about, and we ought to try to make them see it, however mulish they may be. The Turks' greatest danger is to be taken on alone jammed up in Thrace.

5. How does this above square with British interests? If Germany, notwithstanding the objections, attacks in the Balkans, we must play our part there with our full available strength. If, on the other hand, she pretends that she never wished to bring war into the Balkans, and leaves Greece, Yugoslavia and Turkey alone, then we might turn our forces to a strong summer and autumn campaign in the Central Mediterranean, including Tripoli, Sicily and the Italian toe. We should have a good pad in our right hand to protect our Middle Eastern interests, and take smart action on a medium scale with our left in the Central Mediterranean.

6. Is it not possible that if a united front were formed in the Balkan Peninsula, Germany might think it better business to take it out of Russia, observing that we have had many reports of heavy concentrations in Poland and intrigues in Sweden and Finland.

7. Pray consider these opinions for what they are worth.

John Colville: diary
(*Colville papers*)

28 March 1941

To Chequers, arriving just in time for dinner. Party consisted of PM, Sir John Anderson, Pug,[1] Tommy, Mary and Pamela.[2] Chief excitement was report of naval engagement with Italians off Crete – this time a true one. Talk ranged from foreign policy to home front. PM said people were very much happier in the war than might have been expected. Anderson went further and thought war might prove to have been a real blessing to the country. He is a pompous ass, but clever.

The PM, in praising Chamberlain's courage during his illness, said that he knew not the first thing about war, Europe or Foreign politics. Discourse on the Admiralty: found the best brain in the navy, though the most cautious. Alexander would have had to face much hostile criticism if he had not been a Labour man.

John Colville: diary
(*Colville papers*)

29 March 1941 Chequers

A family luncheon party after which the PM gave me a short lecture on the various invaders of Russia, especially Charles XII.[3]

Winston S. Churchill: Minute[4]
(*Churchill papers, 20/36*)

29 March 1941

Now is the time to begin a radical improvement in the shelters, so that by next winter there may be more safety, more comfort, warmth, light and amenities for all who use them. The Anderson shelters should be inspected, and those that are waterlogged should either be removed or their owners

[1] General Ismay.

[2] Pamela Digby, born 1920. Daughter of the 11th Baron Digby. In 1939 she married Randolph Churchill, from whom she obtained a divorce in 1946; their son Winston was born at Chequers in 1940. She subsequently married Leyland Hayward, and then Averell Harriman. United States Ambassador to Paris, from 1993 until her death in 1997.

[3] King Charles XII of Sweden invaded Russia in 1709, when he was defeated by Peter the Great at the Battle of Poltava (8 July 1709).

[4] This Minute (Prime Minister's Personal Minute No. 368 of 1941) was addressed to the Lord President of the Council (Sir John Anderson), the Home Secretary (Herbert Morrison) and the Minister of Health (Ernest Brown).

helped to give them a good foundation. As many people as possible should be encouraged to use the Andersons and the table shelters inside the house, which should soon be coming forward in large numbers. The basement shelters in London should be overhauled, strengthened and traversed, wherever possible. The pavement shelters should be made more attractive. They might well have another blast wall built round them and should of course be repaired or rebuilt where the materials were not satisfactory owing to the emergency. All the big shelters should be effectively traversed up. A regular campaign should be set on foot to get ready for the winter. There is plenty of time now, and I am prepared to help you with concrete and other materials.

Will you kindly let me have proposals for action.

Winston S. Churchill to Ernest Brown
(*Churchill papers, 20/36*)

29 March 1941

I would rather this[1] went to the Embassy, as I have to keep my requests to the President for very rare major occasions.

How are you getting on with the shelters? We must have a fine lay out for the next winter – more security, warmth, light and amenities for all. Now is the time to begin.

Winston S. Churchill to A.V. Alexander and Admiral Pound
(*Churchill papers, 20/36*)

29 March 1941
Secret

I know how much you have on hand. Nevertheless, it is most important to show Darlan that we have not abandoned the blockade. It would be very convenient if the situation after 'Winch' allowed another 'Ration'.[2] Pray bear this constantly in mind.

[1] A suggestion that Churchill appeal direct to Roosevelt for an extension of American Red Cross help to Britain.

[2] Operation Ration: ships with food for Vichy France which would be allowed through the British naval blockade.

Winston S. Churchill to President Franklin D. Roosevelt
(*Admiralty papers, 199/1928*)

29 March 1941
sent 8.20 p.m.
Personal and Secret

1. Since my telegram No. 1344 about feeding Unoccupied France, we have been confronted with agreement between Darlan and Berlin for the supply of large quantities of foodstuffs to Unoccupied France in exchange, naturally, for a *quid pro quo* to the occupied zone from which the German Army of Occupation is a heavy gainer. There are also press reports of Vichy trying to negotiate purchases of food-stuffs in Latin America. If we were to put up with this it would mean that the French ships, unhampered by the needs of convoy, would soon be doing a big trade and Germany would secure at least half of the import. This seems to put the matter in a new light.

2. Parliament and the public will ask me why, when we are ourselves suffering a grievous blockade and British rations are reduced week by week, the French and Germans should have these advantages, thus prolonging the war. Moreover, the Belgians, Dutch and Norwegians, whose privations and sufferings are far worse than those of Vichy France, may soon ask that their own ships in our service should carry food to the own countries. We ourselves in Britain need more ships and food more stringently every week in order to carry on the war with this present vigour.

3. I am therefore instructing the Admiralty to tighten up the blockade of Unoccupied France as far as our naval resources and opportunities allow, and I hope you will not think this is unwise or unreasonable. The two gift ships will, of course, be let through as agreed between us. We are cabling in detail through Lord Halifax.

John Colville: diary
(*Colville papers*)

30 March 1941 Chequers

The news of the great naval victory off Cape Matapan, for which we have been waiting, came through just after the Kents[1] had left and was greeted with

[1] Prince George Edward Alexander Edmund, 1902–1942. Fourth son of King George V. Served in the Royal Navy, 1921–7; on the staff of the Commander-in-Chief, Atlantic Fleet, 1927. Attached to the Foreign Office, 1929. Married Princess Marina of Greece, 1934. Created Duke of Kent, 1934. Privy Councillor, 1937. Group-Captain, Royal Air Force, 1937. Rear-Admiral, Major General and Air Vice-Marshal, 1939. Governor-General Designate of Australia, 1938, but the outbreak of war prevented him from taking up his post. Naval Intelligence Division, Admiralty, 1939–40. Air Commodore, Royal air Force, 1940. Killed in an air crash in Scotland while flying to Iceland to make a tour of inspection, 25 August 1942. His son Prince Michael of Kent was born on 4 July 1942, and nine weeks before his father's death.

yells of delight. 'How lucky the Italians came in,' said the PM.

'The tearing up of the paper fleet of Italy,' was Winston's comment on today's news.

Winston S. Churchill to President Franklin D. Roosevelt
(*Premier papers, 3/324/10*)

30 March 1941
Important
Personal and Secret

1. Yesterday's action in Mediterranean most successful. Commander-in-Chief has just signalled three Italian 8-inch cruisers, the very latest date, and two large destroyers sunk. One 6-inch doubtful. The Littorio battleship got away seriously damaged. Apart from casualties in aircraft already announced, British naval forces suffered no loss of any kind in ships or personnel.

2. I have now to acknowledge both your kind messages of March 25th and 29th. Once *Malaya* is in dock it might be well for this to be announced from your side. Naturally we should like it. The ten revenue cutters will be most welcome and *Malaya*'s personnel will be available. Admiralty are making arrangements with your authorities. Sinkings continue heavy and, in spite of all efforts, we are unable to limit them while maintaining vigorous fighting. I cannot conceal from you that rate of loss due to inadequate escorts is terribly costly. The ten cutters will be a Godsend.

3. The *Scharnhorst* and *Gneisenau* have been photographed in Brest. We are very glad to know where they are, and still more where they are not. We shall attack them by every means, but danger of air attack by day and difficulty of aiming by night make chances of decisive results doubtful.

4. In my long telegram about feeding Vichy France of March 12th I mentioned to you the *Bangkok*, a French ship with 3,000 tons of rubber on board. Today this ship passed the Straits of Gibraltar in French convoy escorted by French destroyer *Simoun*. We intercepted to enforce contraband control. French escort did not fire, but ships persisted on their course. A concealed French battery opened from the Moroccan shore upon our intercepting cruiser, and battery was severely mauled in return. *Bangkok* and other French vessels took refuge in French Moroccan port of Nemours while action with battery was in progress. We now learn that *Bangkok* had already discharged her rubber at Casablanca. All this rubber will, of course, be ferried across Mediterranean, and practically all of it will go to Germany. Enemy aew short of rubber and will want a lot for campaigns against Greece and Yugoslavia. I wonder whether you would feel inclined to say that delivery of the 10,000 tons of wheat in the two ships depends on your being satisfied that

this rubber is either (a) handed over, or (b) kept in France. Case seems a very good one, and it is sometimes easier to take steps on practical instances than on general principles.

5. We have here[1] Ambassador Winant and Harriman as well as Menzies, Commonwealth Premier, all of whom send their respects.

Winston S. Churchill to General Ismay, for the Chiefs of Staff Committee
(Churchill papers, 20/36)

30 March 1941

1. In the invasion exercise 'Victor' two armoured, one motorized, and two infantry divisions were assumed to be landed by the enemy on the Norfolk coast in the teeth of heavy opposition. They fought their way ashore, and were all assumed to be in action at the end of forty-eight hours.

2. I presume the details of this remarkable feat have been worked out by the staff concerned. Let me see them. For instance, how many ships and transports carried these five divisions? How many armoured vehicles did they comprise? How many motor lorries, how many guns, how much ammunition, how many men, how many tons of stores, how far did they advance in the first forty-eight hours, how many men and vehicles were assumed to have landed in the first twelve hours, what percentage of loss were they debited with? What happened to the transports and store-ships while the first forty-eight hours of fighting was going on? Had they completed emptying their cargoes, or were they still lying inshore off the beaches? What naval escort did they have? Was the landing at this point protected by superior enemy daylight fighter formations? How many fighter aeroplanes did the enemy have to employ, if so, to cover the landing-places?

All this data would be most valuable for our future offensive operations. I should be very glad if the same officers would work out a scheme for our landing an exactly similar force on the French coast at the same extreme range of our fighter protection, and assuming that the Germans have naval superiority in the Channel. Such an enterprise as this accomplished in forty-eight hours would make history, and if the staffs will commit themselves definitely to the adventure and can show how it is worked out in detail I should very much like to bring it before the Defence Committee for action at the earliest moment.

[1] At Chequers.

Winston S. Churchill to Arthur William Fadden[1]
(*Churchill papers, 20/49*)

30 March 1941
Most Secret

When a month ago we decided upon 'Lustre'[2] it looked a rather bleak military adventure dictated by *noblese oblige*. Thursday's events in Belgrade show far-reaching effects of this and other measures we have taken on whole Balkan situation. German plans have been upset and we may cherish renewed hopes of forming a Balkan front with Turkey comprising about 70 Allied divisions from the four Powers concerned. This is, of course, by no means certain yet. But even now it puts 'Lustre' in its true setting, not as an isolated military act, but as a prime mover in large design. Whatever outcome may be, everything that has happened since 'Lustre' decision taken justifies it. Delay also will enable full concentration to be made on Greek front instead of piecemeal engagement of our forces. Result unknowable, but prize has increased and risks have somewhat lessened. Am in closest touch with Menzies. Wish I could talk it over with you.

Sir Alexander Cadogan: diary
(*'The Diaries of Sir Alexander Cadogan'*)

30 March 1941

PM rang me up from Chequers to say French now bombing Gib. Drafted telegram for him to send to Vichy through Washington warning them that if this goes on we bomb Vichy, and pursue them everywhere! He approved it. Also on his instructions drafted telegram to Wavell to warn Italians that if they scuttle ships in Massawa we won't feed an Italian in Africa.

Winston S. Churchill to Alfred Duff Cooper
(*Churchill papers, 20/36*)

30 March 1941
Personal

I enclose a draft of a Minute which I am proposing to issue on the delay in dealing with the Control of Freights to Ireland.

[1] Arthur William Fadden, 1895–1973. Treasurer, Commonwealth of Australia, 1940–41 and 1949–58. Member of the Advisory War Council, 1940–45. Minister for Air and for Civil Aviation, August-October 1940. Acting Prime Minister of Australia while Robert Menzies was in Britain, February–May 1941; Prime Minister, August–October 1941. Leader of the Opposition, 1941–43. Acting Prime Minister eight times, 1950–56. Knighted, 1951.

[2] British military aid for Greece. The Australian Government had also agreed to commit troops.

I should be glad of any comments you may have before the Minute is issued to you and to the other Ministers concerned.

I learn that on the 21st August, 1940, a memorandum on the Control of Freights to Ireland was submitted to the Standing Inter-Departmental Committee on Censorship, by the Director of Postal and Telegraph Censorship.

This matter was one of great complication, with political reactions, on which divergent views were expressed by a number of Departments. After a scheme had been drawn up by the Departments concerned, considerable time elapsed before the Railway Executive Committee were in a position to comment on the scheme.

The new Control of Communications Order, necessary to give effect to the scheme, did not come before the Home Policy Committee until the 11th March, 1941; that is to say, nearly seven months after the matter had first been broached.

Even when allowance is made for the difficulties involved, and for the conflicting views expressed, there is no excuse for so much delay in bringing this matter to a conclusion. I have therefore decided that a full Inquiry should be made into the whole conduct of this matter by all those concerned, in order that responsibility for the delay may be brought home and disciplinary measures taken if sloth or negligence should be disclosed.

I understand that your Department is the one primarily concerned, but that a number of other Departments are also concerned. Copies of this Minute are accordingly being sent to:

The three Service Ministers,
The Minister of Transport,
The Chancellor of the Exchequer, who is responsible for –
  The Board of Customs and Excise,
  The Treasury Solicitor, and
  The Parliamentary Counsel Office,
The Secretary of the War Cabinet.

Winston S. Churchill to Anthony Eden[1]
(*Churchill papers, 20/49*)

30 March 1941
Most Secret

Your 542 and Angora No. 707 received, also Wavell's 0/52629. Have put off broadcast one week because Roosevelt speaking tonight and also expect situation clear then.

[1] Eden had just reached Athens from Cairo.

2. I told C[1] to send you substance of sure information lately received in his Nos. JQ/803/T1 and JQ/803/T2.[2] My reading is that the bad man concentrated very large armoured forces, &c., to overawe Yugoslavia and Greece, and hoped to get former or both without fighting. The moment he was sure Yugoslavia was in the Axis he moved three of the five panthers towards the Bear believing that what was left would be enough to finish the Greek affair. However, Belgrade revolution upset this picture and caused orders for northward move to be arrested in transit. This can only mean in my opinion intention to attack Yugoslavia at earliest or alternatively act against the Turk. It looks as if heavy forces will be used in Balkan Peninsula and that Bear will be kept waiting a bit. Furthermore, these orders and counter-orders in their relation to the Belgrade *coup* seem to reveal magnitude of design both towards south-east and east. This is the clearest indication we have had so far. Let me know in guarded terms whether you and Dill agree with my impressions.

Winston S. Churchill to Sir Alexander Cadogan
(*Premier papers, 3/252/2*)

31 March 1941

PROPOSED LETTER TO THE JAPANESE FOREIGN MINISTER

I propose to bring this up at the Cabinet this evening. I thought it would be a good thing to send it to Mr Matsuoka. (Private Office to check the points in question and fair copy.)

War Cabinet: minutes
(*Cabinet papers, 65/18*)

31 March 1941 10 Downing Street
5 p.m.

INTERCEPTION OF A FRENCH CONVOY OFF ALGIERS

The Prime Minister said that the Captain of the *Sheffield*[3] had sent a signal saying that he could only have prevented the convoy from escaping by

[1] Stewart Graham Menzies, 1890–1968. A nephew of Muriel Wilson, to whom Churchill had proposed marriage in the late 1890s. Educated at Eton. Served in the Grenadier Guards, 1909–10; the Life Guards, 1910–39. On active service, 1914–18, involved from 1915 in counter-espionage and security duties at General Headquarters, France (despatches, DSO, Military Cross). Lieutenant-Colonel, 1919. Chief of the War Office Secret Service, 1919 (under Churchill). Military Representative of the War Office, Secret Intelligence Service, 1919. Personal Assistant to the Head of the Secret Intelligence Service (Admiral Sir Hugh Sinclair) from 1923. Colonel, 1932. Head of the Secret Intelligence Service, November 1939 to May 1952. CB, 1942. Knighted, 1943.

[2] Enigma decrypts: details of German troop movements from the Polish-Soviet border to the Balkans.

[3] Captain Larcom, see page 428, note 1.

opening fire on the destroyer and the ships in the convoy; and that such action would have been contrary to International Law, and would have had bad political effects. In fact, however, such action would have been in harmony with International Law.

The First Lord of the Admiralty gave details of the instructions regarding the interception of merchant vessels laid down in the Prize Manual. These provided for firing two blank rounds; then for a shot across the bows. If this was disregarded, force could be used. The incident was being enquired into and, in the light of this experience, further instructions would be issued regarding the interception of convoys either east or west of Gibraltar.

The Prime Minister said that it might not be convenient for us to make a further interception in the near future. But it was vitally necessary not to allow a complete breach to be made in our blockade. He invited the First Lord of the Admiralty to arrange for plans to be prepared for a further interception, when forces were available, and to ensure that the instructions to be followed on this occasion as to the force to be used were quite definite.

JAPAN

The Prime Minister said that Mr Matsuoka[1] had sent a message asking Mr Shigemitsu[2] to meet him in France. On the whole he thought that the fact that Mr Shigemitsu was friendly to us and would testify to the strength and unity of this country out-weighed the arguments in favour of preventing him from making the journey.

He proposed to see Mr Shigemitsu before he started, and he wished to give Mr Shigemitsu a sealed letter to be delivered to Mr Matsuoka. His letter, which would be very frank, would set out a number of questions which the Japanese Government should answer, before embarking on war against us.

The War Cabinet –

(i) agreed that Mr Shigemitsu should be allowed to leave this country for the purpose of visiting Mr Matsuoka.

(ii) approved the text of the Prime Minister's letter to Mr Matsuoka subject to an omission in the first paragraph.

The Prime Minister urged the Service Ministers to do all in their power to curb the growth of establishments. A reduction of 50,000 should be aimed at in the Royal Air Force establishment. The Secretary of State for Air said the great difficulty in obtaining the type of man-power required was in itself a powerful incentive to economy.

The Minister of Food said that the revised programme (which would give him 14 million tons in the second year of war) gave him the prospect of providing the people of this country with an adequate and sufficiently varied diet.

1 The Japanese Foreign Minister.

2 The Japanese Ambassador to London.

The Prime Minister said that it was essential to import sufficient to maintain the staying-power of the people, even if this meant a somewhat slower development of our Service programmes. Nothing must interfere with the supplies necessary to maintain the stamina and resolution of the people of this country.

The Minister of Food said that the supply of meat depended mainly on sufficient refrigerated tonnage being available. The Prime Minister said that he had appointed a Committee to investigate this matter. The United States authorities should be asked whether they could fit up ships as troop-carriers and thus release some of our refrigerated space for carrying meat.

COMMITMENT TO THE NETHERLANDS EAST INDIES

The arguments on the other side were expressed by the Prime Minister and Sir Dudley Pound, as follows:

(a) Although we might decide to go to war with Japan if she attacked the Netherlands East Indies, it would be wrong to tie ourselves down to do so beforehand. There was little or no help which we could give to the Netherlands East Indies if the Americans did not join with us; and it might therefore pay us when the time came to delay a declaration of war until a more suitable moment.

(b) All our action must be judged from its effect on our power to win the war against Germany. If, when the moment came, the right way to win the war against Germany were thought to be to declare war on Japan, then we should do so. If, on the other hand, it appeared at the time that it would pay us to keep out of war with Japan, we should not hesitate to do so.

(c) We ought to wait to see what the United States of America would do. The Americans would be in a bad position to criticize us if they were to hang back when we, who already had our hands full with Germany and Italy, did not go to war with Japan.

Mr Butler[1] hoped that it might be possible to get something arranged in Washington in the way of a joint declaration. The Dutch were anxious to be associated with us in any approach to Washington. The Foreign Office were anxious also to make progress in the matter, because Staff Conversations in the Far East had been going ahead fast, and the Dutch were getting a little suspicious of the fact that these conversations were accompanied by no political gesture. If the Japanese suspected any break in the common front, they would be encouraged to undertake some adventure.

The Prime Minister said that he was prepared to enter into any declaration, or into any commitment, provided the Americans were in it with us.

[1] R. A. Butler, Parliamentary Under-Secretary of State for Foreign Affairs.

Winston S. Churchill to A. V. Alexander and Admiral Pound
(*Churchill papers, 20/36*)

31 March 1931
Action this Day

Surely *Sheffield*'s statement about 'unjustifiable in the international law' is not true? In fact, in your communiqué you have taken the opposite view. Moreover, why does the Captain[1] of the *Sheffield* state that the only alternative was to 'sink' (repeat 'sink') destroyers and convoys? Surely he could have fired shots across their bows, and then one or two shots into their bridges, so as to bring the Captains to their senses. What is the approved procedure for compelling a convoy or merchant ships to submit to contraband control?

There does not appear to have been much need for sending Telegram No. 506 from the Admiralty. This must be regarded as a very unsatisfactory episode, and we must know what the procedure is and tell our Officers before the next convoy is intercepted, as it ought to be. We cannot allow the whole of our rights at sea to be cast away. The political consequences must be weighted here.

Winston S. Churchill to Lord Moyne
(*Churchill papers, 20/36*)

31 March 1941

You should inform Sir B. Bourdillon[2] that General Spears has my full confidence, and that he and General de Gaulle are working satisfactorily together. You should tell him that the description of General Spears as 'an unscrupulous politician with no military knowledge at all' is highly offensive and untrue. Very few people saw more of the Great War from the High Staff and front line than General Spears.

[1] Charles Arthur Aiskew Larcom. Mentioned in despatches on 1 February 1941 for 'outstanding zeal, patience and cheerfulness, for never failing to set an example of whole-hearted devotion to duty, without which the high tradition of the Royal Navy would not be upheld'. On 14 October 1941 he received the Distinguished Service Order for his 'mastery, determination and skill' in the action against the *Bismarck* in May 1941. He retired from the Royal Navy in 1942.

[1] Bernard Henry Bourdillon, 1883–1948. Joined the Indian Civil Service, 1908. On active service, Iraq insurrection, 1920 (despatches). Acting High Commissioner, Iraq, 1925–26. Colonial and Chief Secretary, Ceylon, 1929–32. Knighted, 1931. Governor and Commander-in-Chief, Uganda, 1932–35; Nigeria, 1935–43. Chairman, British Empire Relief Association. Published *The Future of the Colonial Empire*, 1945.

Winston S. Churchill to Sir Archibald Sinclair
(*Churchill papers, 20/36*)

31 March 1941

DISCLOSURE OF SECRET INFORMATION TO THE UNITED STATES

I discussed this matter with the United States Ambassador. I told him that I did not like the spreading habit of daily routine returns of secret matters being put into widening lithographic circulation. Not only were daily returns precise and dangerous if they were left lying about or fell into wrong hands, but also that the fact of returns being made every day and circulated led to an immense amount of these papers being extant. Therefore I was not prepared to give the information daily as asked for. On the other hand, I saw less objections to giving the return asked for on a fortnightly basis, which would make it a more valuable and significant paper. In addition, I should be willing to give the President at any time any information on special points. The Ambassador said he would talk to the Naval Attaché.[1] I should greatly prefer to make the return monthly. In any case the most strict engagements must be entered into that the copy furnished is not to be multiplied and sent fooling around to a dozen American Departments. It is already bad enough to do this here.

Winston S. Churchill to Anthony Eden and General Wavell
(*Churchill papers, 20/49*)

31 March 1941

Now that our forces are advancing on Asmara and Massawa, we should inform the Duke of Aosta that if the ships in Massawa harbour, of which there are reported to be 35, are scuttled, we shall consider ourselves relieved of all responsibility for feeding the Italian population of Eritrea and Abyssinia in view of the great shortage of shipping in the world and our own requirements.

[1] Joseph Harold Wellings, Lieutenant Commander, United States Navy. In 1942 he was given command of the destroyer *Strong*, first on Atlantic convoy duty and then in the Pacific, where he was seriously injured when his ship was torpedoed. As an Admiral, he commanded from 1954 the Naval Task Force Group at the Eniwetok and Bikini Atoll nuclear tests.

Winston S. Churchill to A.V. Alexander and Admiral Pound
(*Cabinet papers, 120/713*)

31 March 1941
Action this Day

I saw somewhere a statement that we have told the Turks we could give them no naval aid in the Black Sea, and I minuted that we should at any rate give aid by means of a Submarine Flotilla. It is no use leaving the Black Sea entirely to the Turkish Navy, and should Turkey enter the war we must be ready to put a sufficient force to deal with any armed German craft that may appear and to arrest trade between Roumania and the Caucasus. We ought to tell the Turks that if they enter the war we will make sure they have the command of the Black Sea.

Winston S. Churchill to General Wavell
(*Churchill papers, 20/49*)

31 March 1941

The Duke of Kent came to see me yesterday expressing a keen desire to visit the Middle East as an Air Force Officer. HRH's manner of inspecting troops is very good and pleasing to the men. Let me known whether such a visit would be useful or agreeable to you. HRH is not at all a person to get in anybody's way when serious matters are afoot. Impression produced by his presence on outer world would be good, and especially with Australian public, in view of his being Governor-General designate for the Commonwealth.

April 1941

Winston S. Churchill to General Wavell

(Churchill papers, 20/37)

1 April 1941
sent 1.30 p.m.[1]
Personal

I have discussed your 1/52950, dated March 30 to VCIGS,[2] with Chiefs of Staff and Cadogan. We consider that you should follow policy laid down in Chiefs of Staff telegram No. 68 of March 25 as closely as possible, subject to any modification which may seem desirable after your discussions with General de Gaulle. In particular, the initial approach to French Somaliland should be made by Free French authorities, and there should be no hesitation in using the blockade weapon to the full. Do not worry about the susceptibilities of Weygand and Vichy. We will look after them at this end.

2. I hope that on this and similar matters you will feel able to give full weight to the views of General de Gaulle, to whom His Majesty's Government have given solemn engagements, and who has their full backing as leader of the Free French Movement.

3. There are indications that Syria may soon be ripe to come across, but for the present it should be allowed to simmer.

4. Please inform Secretary of State when you next see him.

[1] This telegram inaugurated a new series, Prime Minister's Personal Telegrams, of which it was given the serial number T.1.

[2] The Vice Chief of the Imperial General Staff, Lieutenant-General Sir Robert Haining.

John Colville: diary
(Colville papers)

1 April — 10 Downing Street

On late duty, but the PM, whose indigestion continues to afflict him, went to bed by midnight.

Winston S. Churchill: Oral Answers
(Hansard)

1 April 1941 — House of Commons

Mr Martin asked the Prime Minister whether the statement on war aims made by His Majesty's Ambassador in Washington at New York is to be regarded as officially expressing the views of His Majesty's Government?

The Prime Minister: His Majesty's Ambassador in Washington consulted me about the admirable speech which he made in New York on 25th March, which is in full accord with the general outlook of His Majesty's Government. But Lord Halifax said in his speech that it was not possible now to draw detailed plans for the future structure of the community of nations, and I myself have recently had occasion to say that it was not my intention to produce at the present time a catalogue of war aims and peace aims.

Harold Nicolson: diary
('Diaries and Letters, 1939-1945')

1 April 1941

In the smoking-room Winston sits down and has his glass of Bristol Milk and is prepared to answer questions. Members cluster round him rather ingratiatingly. 'How well you are looking, Prime Minister.' He does in fact look better than I have seen him look for years. All that puffy effect has gone and his face is almost lean, with the under-lip pouting defiance all the time. He says: 'Yes, I am well. I am in fine trim. More than I was this time last year. We are doing well. We have a real Army now. We have tanks – good tanks. We have guns. In the air our position is not merely absolutely, but relatively, stronger.' He talks of the battle of the Ionian Sea or whatever it will be called.[1] He says that the Italians displayed poor seamanship and violated 'those

[1] The battle, which had given Britain naval mastery in the Eastern Mediterranean, became known as the Battle of Cape Matapan.

elementary rules of strategy which are familiar to every Dartmouth cadet'. He speaks very bitterly of Darlan. 'I should like to break that man. Expressing gratitude to Germany, which has humbled his country in the dust.' He tells me to get out the *Völkischer Beobachter* statement that Germany's war aim is to reduce this country 'to degradation and poverty', and to placard it throughout the country. 'It should be on every wall', he says.

Winston S. Churchill to Sir Andrew Duncan and the Import Executive
(*Churchill papers, 20/36*)

1 April 1941

At the last meeting of the 'Battle of the Atlantic' Committee, the impression was conveyed that the great improvement in the turn-round of tankers was mainly due to improved methods of pumping. This is not so. The time has been reduced from 11.3 days to 3.3 days. The main proportion of this time saved was due to good and improved organization. This is shown in the subjoined table. Improved discharge accounts for less than a third of the total saving. Two-thirds of it is in more able organization.

You and your Committee should look into this and see how far the Ministry of Shipping can adopt the methods of the Petroleum Department.

Winston S. Churchill to Anthony Eden
(*Churchill papers, 20/37*)

1 April 1941
sent 1.45 p.m.

1. We are anxious to know what attitude the Greek Government may adopt towards the employment of British air forces from Greek aerodromes in the event of German attack against Yugoslavia and/or Turkey and not against Greece.

2. The basis of our plans must be to give full support to our own forces, but we must be prepared to assist our allies if they are attacked.

3. If Yugoslavia is attacked we are not anxious to move British air forces to Yugoslav aerodromes, since this course has the disadvantage that it might compromise our ability to give full support to the British Army if Greece were subsequently attacked and our forces were on the Aliakmon line. Similarly, if Turkey alone is attacked, and the Greeks are unwilling to allow us to operate from Greek bases, we should be compelled to transfer part of our air force to Turkey, with the consequent disadvantage that we might be unable to render full support subsequently to our own forces.

4. From every point of view it is desirable that the Greeks should afford us

full freedom of action to use their aerodromes to support either Yugoslavia or Turkey.

5. Will you therefore take up this question as a matter of urgency with the Greek Government and endeavour to persuade them to permit us the use of their aerodromes in any of the eventualities mentioned above.

Winston S. Churchill to Clement Attlee
(*Churchill papers, 20/21*)

1 April 1941
Private

My dear Attlee,

Your note about Privy Councillorships of March 26. We are not at present giving any political Honours and it is thought that a PC for Ammon[1] would fall into the political category. There is a case for David Grenfell[2] as he is a Minister, but I am advised that if he were sworn, other Ministers would have to receive consideration at the same time, for instance, Llewellin.[3] I will however bear it all carefully in mind when a suitable opportunity occurs.

I am studying the list of Peerages which you sent me and I will write to you about it soon. These would not be Political Honours, but Honours connected with the smooth working of our Parliamentary institution under conditions of Coalition Government.

Yours very sincerely,
Winston S. Churchill

[1] Charles George Ammon, 1873–1960. Educated at Public Elementary Schools. Worked for the Post Office for twenty-four years. A Methodist Local Preacher. Labour Member of Parliament, North Camberwell, 1922–31 and 1935–44. Parliamentary Secretary, Admiralty, 1924 and 1929–31. Member of the Select Committee on National Expenditure, 1939–44. Chairman of the Mission to Newfoundland, 1943. Chairman, National Dock Labour Corporation, 1944–47. Created Baron, 1944. Privy Councillor, 1945. A Deputy Speaker, House of Lords, 1945–58. Mayor of Camberwell, 1950–51.

[2] David Rhys Grenfell, 1881–1968. A coal miner (underground) from the age of twelve to the age of thirty-five, Miners' Agent, 1916. Labour MP, 1922–59. Member of the Forestry Commission, 1929–42. CBE, 1935. Secretary for Mines, 1940–2. Chairman, Welsh Tourist Board, 1948. Privy Councillor, 1951. 'Father of the House', 1953–9 (Churchill had first been elected 22 years earlier, in 1900, but had been out of the Commons from 1922 to 1924).

[3] John Jestyn Llewellin, 1893–1957. On active service, Royal Artillery, 1914–18. Colonel Commanding the Dorset Heavy Brigade. Called to the Bar, 1921. Conservative MP for Uxbridge, 1929–45. Civil Lord of the Admiralty, 1937–9. Parliamentary Secretary, Ministry of Supply, 1939–40. Parliamentary Secretary, Ministry of Aircraft Production, 1940–1. Parliamentary Secretary, Ministry of War Transport, 1941–2. President of the Board of Trade, 1942. Minister of Aircraft Production, 1942. Minister Resident in Washington for Supply, 1942–3. Minister of Food, 1943–5. Created Baron, 1945.

Winston S. Churchill to General Sir John Dill
(*Churchill papers, 20/37*)

1 April 1941

A variety of details show rapid re-grouping against Yugoslavia. To gain time against Huns is to lose it against Wops. Nothing should stop Yugo developing full strength against latter at earliest. By this alone can they gain far-reaching initial success and masses of equipment in good time.

Winston S. Churchill to A. V. Alexander
(*Churchill papers, 20/20*)

2 April 1941

My dear First Lord,

The War Cabinet, whom I consulted this evening were definitely of the opinion that it was the duty of the naval authorities to carry out the approved policy of the transference of men from other shipbuilding and ship-repairing tasks to merchant ship repair work. I hope I may have your assurance tomorrow that the Controller of the Admiralty will make this policy effective. I should greatly regret the issues which would arise in the event of a failure by any of the Naval Lords to comply with the decisions which have been taken by His Majesty's Government. You are at liberty to show this letter to any of your naval colleagues on the Board.

Yours vy sincerely,
Winston S. Churchill

Winston S. Churchill to A. V. Alexander and Admiral Pound
(*Churchill papers, 20/36*)

2 April 1941
Action this Day

It will be necessary to strengthen the blockade against unoccupied France and to assert effectively our rights of contraband control. Recently we have gone gently, largely to keep in touch with United States opinion. I now expect they will be willing to see us go a good deal farther. If the French note is received, a severe reply will be made to it. I shall be glad if the Admiralty will make sure they have the necessary ships at Gibraltar to arrest and overhaul all French ships, and that our officers there are fully apprised of their duties and of their rights under International Law.

Will you make me proposals accordingly which can be brought before the Cabinet either Thursday or Monday?

2. With regard to the *Bangkok*, she was allowed through the Straits of Malacca in virtue of some agreement with the French in the Far East, yet she was carrying deadly rubber to the enemy. Let me know what is this agreement and what we received in return for it. Also what is its usefulness at the present time. I presume it can be denounced by either party. Such an offence as sending the *Bangkok* with this rubber would afford a good occasion.

Winston S. Churchill to General Wavell
(*Churchill papers, 20/49*)

2 April 1941

It seems most desirable to chop the German advance against Cyrenaica. Any rebuff to the Germans would have far-reaching prestige effects. It would be all right to give up ground for the purposes of manoeuvre, but any serious withdrawal from Benghazi would appear most melancholy. I cannot understand how the enemy can have developed any considerable force at the end of this long, waterless coast-road. From the most secret messages sent you you will see that a squadron of JU 88s was stopped going to Tripoli because the operational focus had shifted. Therefore I cannot feel that there is at this moment a persistent weight behind the German attack on Cyrenaica. If this blob, which has come forward against you, could be cut off you might have a prolonged easement. Of course, if they succeed in wandering onwards they will gradually destroy the effect of your victories. Have you got a man like O'Connor or Creagh dealing with this frontier problem?

Winston S. Churchill to Yosuke Matsuoka
(*Churchill papers, 20/37*)

2 April 1941

I venture to suggest a few questions which it seems to me deserve the attention of the Imperial Japanese Government and people.

1. Will Germany, without the command of the sea or the command of the British daylight air, be able to invade and conquer Great Britain in the spring, summer, or autumn of 1941? Will Germany try to do so? Would it not be in the interests of Japan to wait until these questions have answered themselves?

2. Will the German attack on British shipping be strong enough to prevent American aid from reaching British shores, with Great Britain and the United States transforming their whole industry to war purposes?

3. Did Japan's accession to the Triple Pact make it more likely or less likely that the United States would come into the present war?

4. If the United States entered the war at the side of Great Britain, and

Japan ranged herself with the Axis Powers, would not the naval superiority of the two English-speaking nations enable them to dispose of the Axis Powers in Europe before turning their united strength upon Japan?

5. Is Italy a strength or a burden to Germany? Is the Italian Fleet as good at sea as on paper? Is it as good on paper as it used to be?

6. Will the British Air Force be stronger than the German Air Force before the end of 1941, and far stronger before the end of 1942?

7. Will the many countries which are being held down by the German army and Gestapo learn to like the Germans more or will they like them less as the years pass by?

8. Is it true that the production of steel in the United States during 1941 will be 75 million tons, and in Great Britain about 12½, making a total of nearly 90 million tons? If Germany should happen to be defeated, as she was last time, would not the 7 million tons steel production of Japan be inadequate for a single-handed war?

From the answers to these questions may spring the avoidance by Japan of a serious catastrophe, and a marked improvement in the relations between Japan and the two great sea-Powers of the West.[1]

Winston S. Churchill to President Franklin D. Roosevelt
(*Churchill papers, 20/49*)

2 April 1941

1. We have entirely authentic secret information[2] that Vichy Government have received 'permission' from Armistice Commission to transfer battleship *Dunquerque*,[3] with escort protection of the whole 'Strasburg' group, from Oran to Toulon for 'disarmament'. Transfer will begin on 4th April.

2. It seems certain that object of transfer is to effect repairs, and we must of course assume it is being done on German orders.

3. I do not need to point out to you the grave danger to which this exposes us. The menace from German surface raiders is already great enough. The addition of such a vessel to the raiding fleet would set us a hard problem indeed. If any value were to be attached to Admiral Darlan's word, it might be hoped that he would in the last resort order out of French metropolitan ports naval units ready for sea. But if *Dunquerque* is docked and immobilized for repairs, that gives the Germans time to swoop and gain possession of her.

[1] In his memoirs Churchill reflected on this telegram: 'I was rather pleased with this when I wrote it, and I don't mind the look of it now.'

[2] In 1948, in order not to reveal that Britain had been able to read Germany's most secret radio communications, the phrase 'authentic secret information' was altered in Churchill's war memoirs to read 'trustworthy information'.

[3] The *Dunquerque* had been severely damaged during the British bombardment of French warships at Oran in June 1940.

4. I fear this is a sinister confirmation of our worst suspicions of Darlan.

5. You have already, through your Ambassador in Vichy, indicated to the French Government that negotiations for the supply of grain to unoccupied France would be greatly facilitated if French warships in metropolitan ports were gradually transferred to North African Atlantic ports. Here we have Darlan not merely failing to comply with your wishes, but deliberately flying in the face of them.

6. I earnestly hope that you may at once indicate to Marshal Pétain that, if Darlan persists in this action, he will be cutting off relief from his country and finally forfeiting American sympathy. We ourselves in this situation could of course lend no assistance to the revictualling of France. There may be just a chance that Marshal Pétain may deter him from this action, but if not, the matter for us is so vital that we may, even in spite of all the dangerous implications, have to make an effort to intercept and sink this vessel. I should like to hear from you that you would understand the necessity for such a step.

7. It is, of course, of first importance that neither the French nor their masters should guess the source of the information or be made aware that we might take the drastic action mentioned in paragraph 6.

Winston S. Churchill to President Franklin D. Roosevelt
(*Churchill papers, 20/37*)

3 April 1941

1. I am most grateful for your message just received through the Ambassador about the shipping.

2. During the last few weeks we have been able to strengthen our escorts in Home North-Western Approaches, and in consequence have hit the U-boats hard. They have now moved further west, and this morning (April 3) sank four ships on the 29th Meridian one day before our escort could meet them.[1] Beating the U-boat is simply a question of destroyers and escorts, but we are so strained that to fill one gap is to open another. If we could get your ten cutters taken over and manned we would base them on Iceland, where their good radius would give protection to convoys right up to where they meet our British-based escorts. Another important factor in North-Western Approaches is long-distance aircraft. These are now coming in. Meanwhile, though our losses are increasingly serious, I hope we shall lessen the air menace when in a month or six weeks' time we have a good number of Hurricane fighters flying off merchant ships patrolling or escorting in the danger zone.

[1] By the end of the day, seven merchant ships had been sunk, five British, one Greek and one Norwegian. Their cargoes included oil, grain, wheat and steel.

War Cabinet: minutes
(*Cabinet papers, 65/22*)

3 April 1941 Prime Minister's Room
12 noon House of Commons

The Prime Minister informed the War Cabinet that secret information had been received that Admiral Darlan had obtained permission from the German Armistice Commission at Wiesbaden to take the *Dunquerque* across to Toulon. Once at Toulon, the ship would be, for all practical purposes, in German hands. This, of course, was the exact opposite of the course which we and President Roosevelt had asked the French to adopt in regard to their fleet.

The question at issue was whether we should give orders to two of our submarines, which were in the neighbourhood, to attack the *Dunquerque* on the way across. The Admiralty were anxious to take no action which might bring the French Fleet into the war against us. On the whole, however, the Prime Minister favoured ordering our submarines to take action. We should not however, adopt this course without knowing that it had the concurrence of President Roosevelt, to whom he had telegraphed on the previous day to ascertain his views.

If we decided to take action against this ship, he thought that it would not be safe to give any warning of our intended action, since the ship would certainly be escorted by French Naval vessels.

The First Sea Lord said that the Navy had its hands so full that they would be most reluctant to take any action which might bring the French Fleet in the war against us. The French Fleet was strong in submarines and destroyers, while the *Strasbourg* could be used with effect on the trade routes against us. The *Dunquerque* could only have been given temporary repairs, as she had remained in the anchorage at Oran. He thought, therefore, that from three to eight months work would be necessary before she could be fully repaired.

The Prime Minister said that his personal view was that the sinking of the *Dunquerque* would not enable the Vichy Government to bring the French people into the war against us. The matter, was, however, one on which we must clearly await President Roosevelt's views. He asked his colleagues to give consideration to the matter in the meantime.

BALKANS

The Prime Minister said that a further telegram had been received from General Wavell saying that he was most anxious that no public announcement should be made of the arrival of our troops in Greece. It was significant that, although the Italians had referred to the increase in our convoys to Greece, they had not mentioned that we had landed troops in Greece. Probably this was because this news would encourage the Yugoslavs. This in itself was a strong argument in favour of an announcement. But we must adhere to our decision to leave this matter to be settled by those on the spot.

Winston S. Churchill to A.V. Alexander
(*Churchill papers, 20/36*)

3 April

1. No attack should be made upon the *Dunquerque* unless or until an answer is received from President Roosevelt which expresses no objection. Absence of any reference to the topic in his answer may be taken as consent.

2. On this reply being received, the First Lord should, if possible, consult the Lord Privy Seal in my absence, and decide.

3. Personally, my bias is strongly in favour of making the attack. Alas, we cannot be sure of success. Perhaps it is ten to one against a successful attack on a ship properly escorted by destroyers. If, however, this unfinished, damaged, probably lightly-manned and possibly towed vessel were sunk neatly and cleanly (probably with little loss of life, as she will be sailing with ample escort), this would be regarded all over the world as a great score for the British Navy, and as showing our unrepentant continuity of purpose since Oran.[1] It would certainly be acclaimed like the *Altmark* episode in the United States.[1]

4. The reaction on Vichy would not, in my opinion, be serious. They would know they were found out doing a pro-Hun trick. So far as the French people are concerned, nothing would be easier than by repeated broadcasts to explain that this ship was being delivered over in a helpless condition into the German power, as in the event of a German descent she could not get away from the dock at Toulon like the mobilized Units of the French Fleet.

[1] When, on 3 July 1940, following the capitulation of France, British warships opened fire on French warships in the naval harbour at Mers-el-Kebir, following the French refusal to join the British, sail to a British port, or sail to a French port in the West Indies to be demilitarized or 'entrusted' to the United States. More than 1,250 Frenchmen were killed during the nine-minute action.

[2] On 16 February 1940 a British destroyer, *HMS Cossack*, had entered Josing Fjord, inside Norwegian territorial waters, and boarded the German raider and supply ship *Altmark*, which was holding 300 British merchant seamen, all of whom were liberated. Some of them had been held captive on the *Altmark* for four and a half months.

War Cabinet, Defence Committee (Operations)
(*Cabinet papers, 69/2*)

3 April 1941
10.30 p.m.

Cabinet War Rooms

The Prime Minister read to the Committee a telegram which he had sent to the President of the United States on the subject of the possible move of the French battleship, *Dunquerque*, from Oran to Toulon.

He had now received a reply which he read to the Committee. He enquired what the naval arrangements were to meet the situation.

Sir Dudley Pound said that two submarines would be in position by the following morning. They had been given orders to torpedo the ship without warning on receipt of an operative code word.

The Prime Minister said that the approach now being made by the American Ambassador to Marshal Pétain might cause the French to cancel the move of the ship, but in case it did not it was necessary now to decide whether the submarines should be given executive orders. He thought that the successful torpedoing of the ship would increase our prestige, and would be viewed as the natural sequel to our action at Oran last summer. He did not think for a minute that our action would cause the French to declare war. Admiral Darlan was always hostile to us, but he would be unable to make the French nation follow him in such an extreme step. Many Frenchmen would much dislike the idea of one of their battleships falling into the hands of the Germans. He thought that we should be right to give orders to the submarines to act. The French might bomb Gibraltar in revenge, in which case we could attack Vichy.

John Colville: diary
(*Colville papers*)

3 April 1941

We have been compelled to evacuate Benghazi in face of the German advance from Tripoli. The PM is greatly worried, but Pug refused to take it too tragically. However the proposed visit to Liverpool and Manchester this evening is cancelled.[1]

[1] Churchill had wanted to visit several towns that had recently been bombed. During March 1941 a total of 4,259 British civilians had been killed during German air raids.

Winston S. Churchill to Anthony Eden
(*Cabinet papers, 69/2*)

3 April 1941
Personal, private and secret

Evacuation Benghazi serious, as Germans, once established in Aerodromes thereabouts, will probably deny us use of Tobruk. Find out what is strategic and tactical plan to chop the enemy. Let me know to what point retirement is ordered. How does 9th Australian Division get back, and how far? Remember that in his 0/45279 of March 2 Wavell gave many cogent arguments for believing his Western flank secure.

2. Far more important than the loss of ground is the idea that we cannot face the Germans and that their appearance is enough to drive us back many scores of miles. This may react most evilly throughout Balkans and Turkey. Pray go back to Cairo and go into all this. Sooner or later we shall have to fight Huns. By all means make the best plan of manoeuvre, but anyhow fight. Can nothing be done to cut the coastal road by a seaborne descent behind them, even if it means putting off Mandibles?[1]

Winston S. Churchill to General de Gaulle
(*Churchill papers, 20/37*)

3 April 1941

We are very grateful for the help which the Free French Forces have given us in the victorious African campaign. But for the disaster of Bordeaux,[2] the whole Mediterranean would now be an Anglo-French lake and the whole African shore would be free and embattled in the cause of freedom. You, who have never faltered or failed in serving the common cause, possess the fullest confidence of His Majesty's Government, and you embody the hope of millions of Frenchmen and Frenchwomen who do not despair of the future of France and the French Empire.

[1] The seizure of the Dodecanese Islands from Italy.

[2] The agreement of the French government, at Bordeaux in June 1940, to seek an Armistice with Germany. De Gaulle had wanted to fight on, if necessary in Brittany.

Winston S. Churchill to Lord Beaverbrook
(*Churchill papers, 20/36*)

3 April 1941

ATLANTIC FERRY

I am afraid I have not the life or the strength, nor is it my duty, to carry this business further. Would it be agreeable to you that the matter should be decided by the Lord President's Committee? There are three possible alternatives: You must run the show and give satisfaction to your customers; the Air Ministry must run the show, and give satisfaction to you in moving the Ferry pilots; or thirdly, you and they must agree amicably on some division which will work.

Winston S. Churchill to Sir John Reith
(*Churchill papers, 20/36*)

3 April 1941

The First Lord of the Admiralty has represented to me that he would be greatly assisted in the protection of Admiralty oil tanks by additional bricklayers and labourers to assist in the building of the surrounding brick walls. The numbers he mentions are 150 more bricklayers and 625 more labourers, of which a good proportion should be bricklayers' labourers. More rapid delivery of materials would also be necessary.

I attach importance to the work of completing the protection of above-ground oil storage at the earliest possible date conformable with the essential requirements.

I should be grateful if you would consider, in consultation with the Admiralty and other Departments concerned, whether this additional aid can be furnished.

Winston S. Churchill to Sir Stafford Cripps
(*Premier papers, 3/170/1*)

3 April 1941

Following from me to M Stalin, provided it can be personally delivered by you:

I have sure information from a trusted agent[1] that when the Germans thought they had got Yugoslavia in the net, that is to say, after 20th March, they began to move 3 out of the 5 Panzer Divisions from Roumania to Southern Poland. The moment they heard of the Serbian revolution this movement was countermanded. Your Excellency will readily appreciate the significance of these facts.

Winston S. Churchill to Sir Stafford Cripps
(*Premier papers, 3/170/1*)

4 April 1941

My telegram No. 278 (of 3rd April: information to be conveyed to M Stalin).

If your reception gives you opportunity of developing the argument, you might point out that this change in German military dispositions surely implies that Hitler, through the action of Yugoslavia, has now postponed his previous plans for threatening Soviet Government. If so, it should be possible for Soviet Government to use this opportunity to strengthen their own position. This delay shows that the enemy forces are not unlimited, and illustrates the advantages that will follow anything like a united front.

2. Obvious way of Soviet Government strengthening its own position would be to furnish material help to Turkey and Greece and through latter to Yugoslavia. This help might so increase German difficulties in Balkans as still further to delay the German attack on Soviet Union, of which there are so many signs. If, however, opportunity is not now taken to put every possible spoke in the German wheel, danger might revive in a few months' time.

3. You would not, of course, imply that we ourselves required any assistance from Soviet Government or that they would be acting in any interests but their own. What we want them to realize, however, is that Hitler intends to attack them sooner or later, if he can; that the fact that he is in conflict with us is not

[1] There was no 'trusted agent': the information which Churchill sent Stalin derived entirely from the Germans' own most secret system of communications, the Enigma radio messages, which were being decrypted at Bletchley, and of which translations and summaries were sent to Churchill every day.

in itself sufficient to prevent him doing so if he is not also involved in some special embarrassment, such as now confronts him in Balkans, and that it is consequently in Soviet interests to take every possible step to ensure that he does not settle his Balkan problem in the way he wants.

Winston S. Churchill to A.V. Alexander and Admiral Pound

(*Churchill papers, 20/36*)[1]

4 April 1941

FUELLING AT SEA

Considering that the *Malaya* was escorting an 8-knot convoy, or perhaps even a 6-knot convoy, I do not see why the danger of her oiling a destroyer at 12 knots should be stressed. It is quite true that during the period of oiling the destroyer the battleship could not manoeuvre to avoid a torpedo. On the other hand, the advantages of having destroyers along with the convoy far more than repay this temporary disability. If four destroyers were taken along with the convoys, one would be oiling while the other three would be protecting. Anyhow, nothing could be worse than to have a battleship tethered to a 6 or 8-knot convoy without any anti-U-boat craft to protect her. This is what was done on the convoy in question.

Winston S. Churchill to General Wavell

(*Churchill papers, 20/37*)

4 April 1941

1. We are making an intense effort to reinforce you with aircraft and tanks at earliest. Chiefs of Staff are now drafting statement of decisions we have taken today. Feel sure you will be surprised as well as encouraged by all this.

2. Press and public have taken evacuation of Benghazi admirably; confidence in High Command is unshakeable. I warned the country a week ago that they must not expect continuance of unbroken successes and take the rough with the smooth. Therefore, be quite sure that we shall back you up in adversity even better than in good fortune.

3. I must return to need of telling public that we have sent strong forces to Greece. Minister of Information[2] is being hard pressed, especially by representatives of Dominions Papers. American Press is full of reports and Colonel Donovan has publicly praised courage of the British Government in

[1] This was Churchill's 400th Personal Minute of 1941.

[2] Alfred Duff Cooper.

sending troops to aid Greece. Resentment is caused by what seems to be unreasonable veto. Press here have played the game and handled Benghazi in exactly the right way, and it is unwise to provoke those of whose good offices we may have need. When on Wednesday I move Resolution of thanks to Middle Eastern Forces, I must refer to support given to Greece, but it would be a pity to wait so long. Pray draft me the form of announcement which you would think least harmful. It will be possible to prevent undue speculation or any statement going beyond general intimation of the move we have made.

Winston S. Churchill to President Franklin D. Roosevelt
(Churchill papers, 20/49)

4 April 1941

Count Sforza's[1] suggestion has been most attentively considered here. I beg you to realize our difficulties. Duke of Aosta might, indeed, be ready to yield Addis Ababa and march off into the mountains to carry on the war for some weeks or even months while leaving us with the whole responsibility for the health and safety of the civilian population numbering scores of thousands. We have no means of discharging such a task until the organized fighting ends. We do not even hold port Jibuti, the railway line is broken, every ounce of transport we possess is sustaining our troops in their long advance. Result might well be a lamentable breakdown, whole burden of which would be cast on us like the Concentration Camps in the old South African War. The moment the Duke brings the fighting to an end we will strain every nerve, and there might be prospects of success. Any prolongation of Italian resistance in Ethiopia delays our reinforcement of Libya, and you can see how urgent that has become. It is not merely a case of giving the enemy an immense military advantage, but undertaking a task in which we should fail.

Winston S. Churchill to General Simovitch
(Churchill papers, 20/49)

4 April 1941

From every quarter my information shows rapid heavy concentration and advance towards your country by German ground and air forces. Large

[1] Count Carlo Sforza, 1873–1952. An anti-Fascist Italian politician who fled to France in 1927, then moved to the United States in 1940. In 1943 he returned to Italy, refusing to join the Badoglio government unless King Victor Emmanuel (whom he called the 'Pétain of Italy') abdicated. Joined the Cabinet April 1944. President of Italy's preliminary parliamentary assembly, September 1945.

movements of air forces are reported to us from France by our agents there.[1] Bombers have even been withdrawn from Tripoli according to our African Army Intelligence. I cannot understand argument that you are gaining time. The one supreme stroke for victory and safety is to win a decisive forestalling victory in Albania, and collect the masses of equipment that would fall into your hands. When the four German mountain Divisions reported by your General Staff as entraining in the Tyrol reach Albania a very different resistance will confront you than could be offered by rear of the demoralized and rotten Italians.

Sir Alexander Cadogan: diary
(*'The Diaries of Sir Alexander Cadogan'*)

4 April 1941

PM sent for me about 7. Sat with him till 7.50 while he dictated – very slowly – some quite useful telegrams. He was going to Chequers. At 7.10 said 'make dinner at 9'. At 7.20 'I'll dine here and go down after'. At 7.30 'Put me through to Mrs Churchill: we can't go down tonight.'! Hope he won't have a meeting at midnight. Got away just before 8. PM told me he'd heard nothing of *Dunquerque* and thought it 10 to 1 against her moving. Told him I hoped he'd win his bet. As regards Libya, he said 'No news, good news'. I hope we shan't get any.

Winston S. Churchill to General Simovitch
(*Churchill papers, 20/37*)

5 April 1941

As this is the first time I have had the honour to address your Excellency[2] I send my heartiest good wishes for the success of your administration and for the safety and independence of the brave nation whose fortunes you guide.

[1] Although Churchill could not say so, the most important of 'my information' was not 'our agents' in France but was the German Air Force Enigma messages decrypted at Bletchley, in particular Enigma decrypts CX/JQ803, 808, 821, 825 and 849 (military movements) and 823 and 829 (air preparations), summarized in F.H. Hinsley and others, *British Intelligence in the Second World War, Its Influence on Strategy and Operations*, Volume l, London, 1979, page 371–2.

[2] Churchill sent this telegram to the British Embassy in Belgrade, to be added to his telegram of the previous evening to General Simovitch.

Winston S. Churchill to General Ismay, for the Chief of Staff Committee
(*Cabinet papers, 120/442*)

5 April 1941

OBSTRUCTION OF AGRICULTURAL LAND TO PREVENT LANDING OF ENEMY TROOP-CARRYING AIRCRAFT

Before any action is taken, Home Forces should confer with the Minister of Agriculture in order that measures can be taken which give the most benefit to the one and do the least harm to the other. When this process is complete, let me know what is the total estimated food loss to agriculture entailed.

Remember food is a part of our war, and also the present denudation of the German air in the west. It is becoming increasingly serious to hamper agriculture.

Winston S. Churchill to Sir Alexander Cadogan and R. A Butler
(*Churchill papers, 20/36*)

5 April 1941

Encourage Sir Miles Lampson[1] to take the stiffest line with the Egyptian Government in order to prevent espionage and tale-bearing for the benefit of our enemies by foreign and neutral diplomatists in Egypt.

Winston S. Churchill to Air Chief Marshal Sir Charles Portal
(*Churchill papers, 20/36*)

5 April 1941
Secret

AIR MARSHAL LONGMORE: RETURN OF RECEIPTS AND LOSSES OF AIRCRAFT MIDDLE EAST, AS OF 31 MARCH 1941

Two things are to me incredible:

1. That with a total personnel strength of 26,600 and a pilot strength of 1,175 and 1,044 aircraft on charge, we can only fight 292 aircraft against the enemy.

2. That with this immense personnel and mass of obsolete machines he

[1] Miles Wedderburn Lampson, 1880–1964. Entered the Foreign Office, 1903. British Minister to China, 1926–33. Knighted, 1927. High Commissioner for Egypt and the Sudan, 1934–6; Ambassador to Egypt and High Commissioner for the Sudan, 1936–46. Privy Councillor, 1941. Created Baron Killearn, 1943. Special Commissioner in South-East Asia, 1946–8.

cannot find the necessary servicing staff for the new aeroplanes as they arrive, but that large numbers have to be sent round the Cape, with resultant destructive delays.

I am sure there must be frightful mismanagement and futility.

Winston S. Churchill to Anthony Eden
(*Churchill papers, 20/49*)

5 April 1941

I am glad you feel able to take such a reassuring view of Libyan situation. From this end it looks serious. However, if you both feel you could do no good from Cairo you should return home, where we shall all be delighted to see you.

Winston S. Churchill to A. V. Alexander and Admiral Pound
(*Churchill papers, 20/36*)

5 April 1941

NAVAL VESSELS FROM THE UNITED STATES

See attached eminently satisfactory answer to our requests. If seven cutters are available at New York within a week, why not make an evolution of getting them manned and into action from Iceland a fortnight later? Anyhow, let me be assured that all is in train for manning and bringing into action these vessels at the earliest moment.

Winston S. Churchill to A. V. Alexander
(*Churchill papers, 20/36*)

5 April 1941
Private

Admiral Edward Collins[1] seems to be a great student of French and American politics, and we must bear him in mind for a diplomatic career should his tenderness towards French convoys render him unsuitable for his present employment.

[1] George Frederick Basset Edward-Collins, 1883–1958. Midshipman, HMS *Goliath*, Boxer War, China, 1900. Served in HMS *Superb* and *Tiger*, 1914–18. Rear-Admiral, 1935. Chief of Staff, Mediterranean Station, 1936–38. Commanded 2nd Cruiser Squadron, 1938–40 (despatches). Knighted, 1939. Second-in-Command, Home Fleet, 1940. Commanding the North Atlantic Station, 1941–43. Temporary Governor of Gibraltar, 1942. Admiral 1943. Retired, 1944. Flag Officer in charge, 1944–45.

Winston S. Churchill to King George VI
(*Churchill papers, 20/20*)

5 April 1941
Most Secret

Sir,

I have carefully considered Sir Alexander Hardinge's[1] letter of the 4th instant. It is certainly true that if the French declared war upon us, or handed over their fleet and bases to the Germans, an undue strain would be thrown upon our Navy, unless the United States came to our aid. But if we are to take the line that nothing must be done by us which gives Admiral Darlan a chance or pretext to take hostile action, the result could only be to destroy our whole policy of blockade, and make him entire master of our actions in relation to France. It would in fact be easier for him to carry Vichy into a declaration of war on the grounds that we were stopping food ships for the French people, than on the grounds that we had sunk a warship that was being taken back from Africa and put into the German power. Therefore the matter of the *Dunquerque* cannot be measured apart from the general principles involved.

As soon as I heard that the *Dunquerque* was to sail, I asked President Roosevelt to make the strongest possible representations and threats to Vichy. I thought and said it was ten to one that these representations would deter the French. If, however, they persisted, then it seemed to me that we were bound to try to sink her, or admit ourselves powerless. We could not be certain that we should succeed; but if we did succeed and the *Dunquerque* was sunk, the action would be the natural, logical sequel to our bombardment of Oran. The French did not declare war then, nor in my opinion would they declare war now. They did not declare war after Dakar, although two days' severe fighting occurred and a French submarine was sunk.

Since Oran many things have happened to make it much less likely they would declare war in consequence of such an incident. In war, risks have to be run, and one cannot give absolute guarantees. But, except in one respect, the risk is certainly very much less now than it was at the time of our attack on Oran, which, as Your Majesty will remember, was so generally acclaimed here and in the United States. Since Oran, the Italian Navy has been largely destroyed, and the remnant discredited and cowed. Since Oran, the attitude

[1] Alexander Henry Louis Hardinge, 1894–1960. Educated at Harrow and Trinity College, Cambridge. On active service, 1915–18 (wounded, Military Cross). Adjutant, Grenadier Guards, 1919–20. Assistant Private Secretary to King George V, 1920–36. Private Secretary to King Edward VIII, 1936; and to King George VI, 1936–43. Privy Councillor, 1936. Knighted, 1937. Succeeded his father as 2nd Baron Hardinge of Penshurst, 1944 (his elder brother having died of wounds received in action on 18 December 1914).

of the United States has changed in the marvellous manner which we all rejoice. Opinion in France has also changed enormously in our favour. There is, it is true, the character, malice and ambition of Admiral Darlan. From my knowledge of France and of the pressure the United States can bring to bear on France, I do not believe that Admiral Darlan could carry his country or even his Government into war; nor would they hand over the Fleet, and thus deprive themselves of their only bargaining power. This is a matter not of naval but of political judgment.

I hope therefore Your Majesty will feel easy in your mind about this *Dunquerque* matter, and let me bear the burden as I am ready to do. It is a comparatively small burden compared with some others which now weigh heavily.

As Your Majesty is no doubt already aware, the American Ambassador last night informed me that the French have given the President an assurance that the *Dunquerque* will not be moved for ten days. The orders for her sailing have therefore been countermanded, and the whole project is in suspense. I imagine that the ten days was a way of saving Darlan's face with his colleagues, and that he has experienced a decided check. During these ten days, the United States' pressure will no doubt be continued or even strengthened, and personally I doubt whether the project will be renewed. If it is, we must judge the issue as it appears at that time.

I remain
With my humble duty,
Your Majesty's devoted
servant and subject,
Winston S. Churchill

At dawn on Sunday 6 April 1941 – Palm Sunday – the Germans launched Operation Retribution, a massive air attack on the Yugoslav capital. After two days of intense bombardment, more than 17,000 citizens of Belgrade had been killed. Also on April 6, German warplanes struck at the Greek port of Piraeus, where at that very moment six units of the British Expeditionary Force were disembarking.

As German troops attacked Yugoslavia, they were joined by Hungarian units. Within twenty-four hours the Yugoslav border defences were broken.

Winston S. Churchill to President Franklin D. Roosevelt
(*Churchill papers, 20/49*)

6 April 1941

1. Most grateful for your spirited intervention about *Dunquerque.* It is quite true that Toulon could not repair her for from three to six months, but why do we want that hanging over our head anyway? Darlan's honour about her never falling into German hands is rooted in dishonour. A ship in dry-dock or under heavy repair could not possibly get away before the Germans could lay hold of Toulon. Their officers and agents are on the spot all the time, and remember how easy we found it to cop the French ships at Portsmouth and Plymouth. We ought to stick to our settled policy of resisting all transfers of French ships from African to German-controlled or potentially German-controlled French ports, and encourage all movement the other way. If Darlan gets *Dunquerque* to Toulon, why should he not ask for *Jean Bart* from Casa Blanca or *Richelieu* from Dakar. Therefore, I urge strong and stern continuance of utmost pressure you can exert. Evidently this is most powerful, as we have certain knowledge that they were to sail morning 4th and all preparations made. Pétain does not know half what this dirty Darlan does. It would be far better if your pressure deterred Darlan, as it has already, than that we should have to take rough action with all its dangers.

2. Question is whether timely publicity might not help deter. Do you mind if I say something like this on Wednesday in Commons: 'There was always the risk that Darlan might bring *Dunquerque* from Oran to Toulon in order to prepare her for war purposes. Such an act would affect the balances of naval power throughout the world, and would affect American interests besides our own. Representations have been made to Marshal Pétain by the United States Government which should have shown Vichy Government how undesirable this step would be from the point of view of French interests. His Majesty's Government would certainly be bound to regard it as a menacing act done at Hitler's instigation and as a step in Admiral Darlan's schemes for gaining personal control of France as the Germans' trusted agent. In these circumstances His Majesty's Government would hold themselves free to take any action which was suitable against this ship, either in passage or while under repair in Toulon harbour. They would greatly regret if such a situation arose, as they have no wish or policy toward France other than her liberation from the German yoke and the maintenance of the integrity of the French Empire.' Please let me know what you think of this, or whether you can get the matter settled behind the scenes.

3. The last convoy which was attacked in the Atlantic was attacked about the 29th Meridian before it met destroyer escort, and as the convoy would have been at the mercy of the U-boat for another 24 hours the Commodore in charge of the convoy rightly ordered it to scatter. However, before it was

scattered three ships were torpedoed, and after it had scattered eight further ships were torpedoed. When escort arrived as far west as endurance of vessels permitted, U-boat was hunted and destroyed, but only after the damage had been done and the valuable cargoes produced by American labour cast away. We have also had a DF signal, which indicates a U-boat as far west as the 36th Meridian. I report these facts to you, Mr President, so you may judge their significance.

4. We have a hard struggle before us both in Greece and Libya, but will do our best according to our resources.[1] You will be glad to learn that we have received the appended message from the Duke of Aosta: 'HRH Duke D'Aosta wishes to express his appreciation of the initiative taken by General Wavell and General Cunningham regarding the protection of women and children in Addis Ababa, demonstrating the strong bonds of humanity and race still existing between the Nations.'

5. It was very pleasant to hear your voice and receive your encouragement last night.[2]

Winston S. Churchill to Colonel Hollis

(*Churchill papers, 20/36*)

6 April 1941

OPERATIONS 'BALLAST' AND 'GOLDEN EYE'[3]

I am reluctant to close these prospects. It will dishearten Sir Samuel Hoare and those working with him. My position is unchanged from that expressed in No. 471. It would be better to let Golden Eye languish and shrink rather than knock it on the head. Let me therefore have an intermediate plan which involves the least possible waste of preparations already made, and show me what the remaining dimensions will be.

[1] That night, six Royal Air Force Wellington bombers struck at the railway yards in the Bulgarian capital, Sofia, in an attempt to delay the movement of German military supplies to the Yugoslav front. In Greece, the New Zealand Division, the 6th Australian Division and one armoured brigade were on their way to the Aliakhmon Line in northern Greece. In the Aegean, a battalion of British troops occupied the Greek Island of Lemnos, to deny it to the Germans and to safeguard shipping in the Aegean.

[2] No record has yet been found of this telephone conversation between Churchill and Roosevelt.

[3] Ballast was the British plan to establish a military force in Spanish North Africa as part of Operation Blackthorn (assistance to Spain in the event of a German occupation of Spain). Golden Eye (also Goldeneye) was the British Liaison Delegation at Gibraltar.

Winston S. Churchill to David Margesson
(*Churchill papers, 20/36*)

7 April 1941

It has been suggested that it might be useful in case of invasion to have ready a number of official-looking labels in German which could be used as required, e.g., to misdirect the troops, or mislead about mined bridges and contaminated petrol. Being in German they would not mislead our men. Some idea of the appearance of such labels could probably be obtained from people returned from France. C-in-C, Home Forces,[1] might consider this.

Winston S. Churchill to the Marquess of Linlithgow
(*Churchill papers, 20/37*)

7 April 1941

The whole Empire has been stirred by the achievement of the Indian forces in Eritrea. For me the story of the ardour and perseverance with which they scaled and finally conquered the precipitous heights of Keren recalls memories of the North-West Frontier of long years ago, and it is as one who has had the honour to serve in the field with Indian soldiers from all parts of Hindustan, as well as in the name of His Majesty's Government, that I ask Your Excellency to convey to them and to the whole Indian Army the pride and admiration with which we have followed their heroic exploits.

War Cabinet: minutes
(*Cabinet papers, 65/22*)

7 April 1941 — 10 Downing Street

The Prime Minister said that the situation had undergone a serious change since the War Cabinet had last met. He read to the War Cabinet the latest telegram from General Wavell. General Wavell reported that the position in the Western Desert had greatly deteriorated on the previous day, owing to the enemy moving on Mechili by the desert route, and to further vehicle losses of the 3rd Armoured Brigade, which had now little fighting value. The state of the Indian Motor Brigade was not known. The 9th Australian Division, less one Brigade in Tobruk, had been withdrawing on the previous night to the Gazala area, west of Tobruk, and did not appear to be pressed. A further Australian Infantry Brigade group and an improvised armoured unit were landing at Tobruk that day, and it was hoped to stabilize the front there.

[1] General Sir Alan Brooke.

A telegram had also been received from Mr Eden saying that the position was serious and that the Germans were advancing in greater strength and more rapidly than had been anticipated.

The Prime Minister said that this deterioration in the position was due to our relative weakness in armoured units, caused by the 7th Armoured Division having been sent back to Cairo to refit. He had not realized that this Division would be so completely out of action. The German forces opposed to us consisted of all or part of one armoured and two motorized Divisions.

Tobruk was a strongly fortified place, and the German force which had advanced so rapidly could hardly possess the necessary artillery to reduce it. If we could hold the advance at Tobruk, we could be well satisfied. But we must recognize that this might not be possible. Large reinforcements had, however, reached General Wavell in the last fortnight, and with events moving in our favour in Abyssinia it should be possible to move up units from this area in the near future.

The Prime Minister then read to the War Cabinet a telegram dated 2nd March, from General Wavell, in which he had given a hopeful appreciation of the situation in Cyrenaica and the scale of attack likely to be expected from the enemy. The War Cabinet decision regarding assistance to Greece had largely been founded on this appreciation.

Mr Menzies said that he had received a telegram from his colleagues in Australia expressing anxiety about the situation. They had stated quite clearly that he (Mr Menzies) when asking for consent to send Australian troops to Greece, had said that our military advisers discounted the likelihood of a thrust in Cyrenaica by the enemy. The possibility of a German advance had been underestimated by General Wavell and it had been perhaps unwise to attempt to hold Benghazi with only partly trained troops. The German advance in Cyrenaica would upset the plans made for sending further troops to Greece.

The Prime Minister agreed that this was so. It was also unfortunate that it would be impossible to proceed in the near future with plans for operations against the Dodecanese which would continue to be a threat against our sea communications with Greece. The loss of the *Northern Prince* in the Eastern Mediterranean was serious, as the ship had contained material badly needed by the Greek powder factory. The loss of shipping in the Piraeus and the damage to the port through air attack would also hamper us in sending reinforcements to Greece.[1] He thought we had no strategic error with which to reproach ourselves, although we had no doubt underestimated the likelihood of serious enemy attack in Cyrenaica.

[1] During German air attacks on Piraeus on 6 April 1941, six merchant ships with military cargoes were sunk. The port itself was then badly damaged when a British merchant ship, *Clan Fraser*, with 200 tons of high explosives on board, was hit by German bombs and blew up.

Winston S. Churchill to General Wavell
(*Churchill papers, 20/49*)

7 April 1941

You should surely be able to hold Tobruk with its permanent Italian defences at least until or unless the enemy brings up strong artillery forces. It seems difficult to believe that he can do this for some weeks. He would run great risks in masking Tobruk and advancing upon Egypt, observing that we can reinforce from the sea and would menace his communications. Tobruk therefore seems to be a place to be held to the death without thought of retirement. I should be glad to hear of your intentions.

2. Inconvenience is caused by your issue from Cairo of communiqués which sometimes reverse what we have been told to say here, and which in other cases have not struck the right note for our public. London is the place where opinion has to be held. Actually there is more complaint today about Cairo communiqué belittling the value of Benghazi than about its loss. I wish you therefore to send your communiqués to the War Office in plain language and let us handle them ourselves for all concerned, including Egypt and Australia. Slight delay must be accepted. Please ask Cunningham and Longmore to conform as regards naval and air communiqués, Cunningham using cypher when necessary.

War Cabinet: minutes
(*Cabinet papers, 65/18*)

8 April 1941 Cabinet War Room
9.30 p.m.

The War Cabinet were given the latest information as to the military situation in the Balkans and Middle East.

In Cyrenaica it was believed that our infantry formations had completed their withdrawal to the Tobruk area. The Prime Minister thought that there were signs that the rush of the enemy's advance was exhausting itself and that the situation gave less cause for anxiety. Particulars were given as to the dispositions of our troops.

In the Balkans the Greek troops were holding out at the Roupel Pass and on the Nestos Line. To the west of the Roupel Pass the position was rather confused, but it seemed that the Yugoslav troops had given ground on the Strumica Valley. The German forces advancing via Kumanovo had captured Skoplje. The Yugoslav forces which had entered Albania might be taken in the rear by this force.

Winston S. Churchill to General Ismay
(*Churchill papers, 20/36*)

8 April 1941

We must have the fullest information about Tobruk. Let a large-scale plan be prepared, and as soon as possible a model, comprising not only Tobruk but the El Adem area. Let me have meanwhile the best photographs available both from the air and from the ground.

Winston S. Churchill to Sir Andrew Duncan
(*Churchill papers, 20/36*)

8 April 1941

I observe with some concern from the census of machine tools that there was a reduction in the average hours worked by production machine tools from 66 to 58 hours per week, between June and November 1940. It is, of course, not possible to reach such perfect balance between different machines that all machines are fully exploited. But the hours actually worked seem lower than might have been hoped. A small loss (1½ hours per week) is attributed directly to air raids. Some further loss is presumably due to the tendency to close factories during hours of darkness. Perhaps you would let me know the number of shifts that are being worked in the factories.

It will be extremely difficult to make a case for the urgent delivery of machine tools from America if we cannot employ those we have to better advantage.

I am addressing similar minutes to the Minister of Aircraft Production and the First Lord.

Winston S. Churchill to Sir Edward Bridges
(*Churchill papers, 20/36*)

8 April 1941

It is very important not to have a serious break in the work at Easter. The normal Monday meeting should be at 5 p.m. Ministers are responsible for being available on the telephone at the shortest notice. It is much better for Ministers to take their holidays in rotation.

Let me have a list of who will go and who will stay. I am told that Easter is a very good time for invasion.[1]

[1] Germany had bombed Belgrade the previous Palm Sunday; on Good Friday two years earlier (7 April 1939) Italian forces had invaded Albania.

John Colville: diary
(*Colville papers*)

8 April 1941

The PM spent all the afternoon composing his speech for tomorrow. After dinner I took part of it round to the American Embassy to show Winant. He made four pertinent observations in respect of the effect on US opinion and I was deeply impressed by his unassertive shrewdness and wisdom. I afterwards explained these points to the PM who accepted them.

Winston S. Churchill to A. V. Alexander
(*Churchill papers, 20/36*)

9 April 1941
Action this Day

Was it very wise to have published the fact that you have captured no more than 50 officers and 400 men from the German U-boats during the whole war? This would actually amount to the crews of 5 or 6 U-boats. Most people reading the figures would take them as a confession of marked failure. Who is the authority who put this out at this time?

Winston S. Churchill: Speech
(*Hansard*)

9 April 1941 House of Commons

WAR SITUATION.

MIDDLE EAST VICTORIES.

THANKS OF THE HOUSE.

The Prime Minister (Mr Churchill): I beg to move,

'That this House on the occasion of the recent victories by sea, land and air in North Africa, Greece and the Mediterranean, records with gratitude its high appreciation of the services of all ranks of His Majesty's Forces in those brilliant operations, and also of those who by their labours and fortitude at home have furnished the means which made these successes possible.'

We are now able and indeed required to take a more general view of the war than when this Resolution of thanks was first conceived. The loss of Benghazi and the withdrawal imposed upon us by the incursion into Cyrenaica are injurious chiefly on account of the valuable airfields around Benghazi which have now passed into the enemy's hands. Apart from this important aspect, we should have been content, in view of the danger which was growing in the Balkans, to have halted our original advance at Tobruk. The rout of the Italians, however, made it possible to gain a good deal of ground easily and cheaply, and it was thought worth while to do this, although, in consequence of other obligations already beginning to descend upon us, only comparatively light forces could be employed to hold what was won. The movement of the German air forces and armoured troops from Italy and Sicily into Tripoli had begun even before we took Benghazi, and our submarines and aircraft have taken a steady toll of the transport-carrying German troops and vehicles. But that has not prevented – and could not prevent – their building of a strong armoured force on the African shore. With this force they have made a rapid attack in greater strength than our commanders expected at so early a date, and we have fallen back upon stronger positions and more defensible country. I cannot attempt to forecast what the course of the fighting in Cyrenaica will be. It is clear, however, that military considerations alone must guide our generals and that these problems must in no way be complicated by what are called prestige values or by consideration of public opinion. Now that the Germans are using their armoured strength in Cyrenaica we must expect much hard and severe fighting, not only for the defence of Cyrenaica, but for the defence of Egypt.

It is fortunate, therefore, that the Italian collapse in Eritrea and Ethiopia, and in British and Italian Somaliland, is liberating progressively very substantial forces and masses of transport to reinforce the Army of the Nile. This sudden darkening of the scene in Cyrenaica in no way detracts from the merit of the brilliant campaigns which have destroyed the Italian Empire in North East Africa, nor does it in any way diminish our gratitude to the troops or our confidence in the commanders who have led them. On the contrary, we shall show that we are no fair-weather friends and that our hearts go out to our Armies even more warmly when they are in hard action than when they are sailing forward on the flowing tide of success. I took occasion a fortnight ago to warn the public that an unbroken continuance of success could not be hoped for, that reverses as well as victories must be expected, that we must be ready, as indeed we always are ready, to take the rough with the smooth. Since I used this language other notable episodes have been added to those that have gone before. Keren was stormed after hard fighting, which cost us about 4,000 casualties, and the main resistance of the Italian army in Eritrea was overcome. Foremost in all this fighting in Eritrea have been our Indian troops, who have at all points and on all occasions sustained the martial reputation of the sons of Hindustan.

After the fall of Keren the Army advanced. Asmara has surrendered and the port of Massawa[1] is in our hands. The Red Sea has been virtually cleared

[1] The principal port of Italian Eritrea. More than 10,000 Italian soldiers were taken prisoner in the port.

of enemy warships, which is a matter of considerable and even far-reaching convenience. Harar has fallen, and our troops have entered and taken charge of Addis Ababa itself. The Duke of Aosta's army has retreated into the mountains, where it is being attended upon by the patriot forces of Ethiopia. The complete destruction or capture of all Italian forces in Abyssinia, with a corresponding immediate relief to our operations elsewhere, may reasonably be expected. Besides these land operations, the Royal Navy under Admiral Cunningham, splendidly aided by the Fleet Air Arm and the Royal Air Force, have gained the important sea battle of Matapan, decisively breaking the Italian naval power in the Mediterranean. When we look back upon the forlorn position in which we were left in the Middle East by the French collapse, when we remember that not only were our Forces in the Nile Valley out-numbered by four or five to one by the Italian armies, that we could not contemplate without anxiety the defence of Nairobi, Khartoum, Cairo, Alexandria, Jerusalem and the Suez Canal, and that this situation has been marvellously transformed, that we have taken more Italian prisoners than we have troops in the country, that the British Empire has stood alone and conquered alone, except for the aid of the gallant Free French and Belgian Forces, who, although few in number, have borne their part – when all this recalls itself to our minds amid the unrelenting pressure of events, I feel confident that I can commend this Resolution to the House and that it will be most heartily and enthusiastically acclaimed.

I now turn from Cyrenaica and Abyssinia to the formidable struggle which has followed the German invasion of the Balkan Peninsula, with all its attendant savagery and science. For some months past we have witnessed and watched with growing concern the German absorption of Hungary, the occupation of Roumania and the seduction and occupation of Bulgaria. Step by step we have seen this movement of the German military power to the South and South-East of Europe. A remorseless accumulation of German armoured and motorized divisions, and of aircraft, has been in progress in all these three countries for months, and at length we find that the Greeks and the Southern Slavs, nations and States which never wished to take part in the war and neither of which was capable of doing the slightest injury to Germany, must now fight to the death for their freedom and for the lands of their fathers.

Until Greece was treacherously and suddenly invaded in November last at the behest of the base Italian dictator, she had observed a meticulous neutrality. It may be that the sentiments of her people, like those of all free and honourable men in every country, were on our side but nothing could have been more correct than the behaviour of her Government in diplomatic conduct and relations. We had no contacts or engagements of a military character with the Greek Government. Although there were islands like Crete, of the highest consequence to us and although we had given Greece our guarantee against aggression, we abstained from the slightest intrusion upon her. It was only when she appealed to us for aid against the Italian invader that we gave whatever support in the air and in the matter of supplies was possible.

All this time, the Germans continued to lavish friendly assurances upon Greece and to toy with the idea of a commercial treaty. German high officials, both in Athens and Berlin, expressed their disapproval of the Italian invasion and offered their sympathy to Greece. Meanwhile, since the beginning of December the movements of German forces through Hungary and Roumania towards Bulgaria became apparent to all. More than two months ago, by the traitorous connivance of the Bulgarian King and Government, the advance parties of the German Air Force, in plain clothes, were gradually admitted to Bulgaria and took possession of the Bulgarian airfields. Many thousands of German airmen, soldiers and political police had already percolated into Bulgaria and were ensconced in key positions before the actual announcement of the accession of Bulgaria to the Axis was made. German troops then began to pour openly into Bulgaria in very large numbers. One of the direct objectives of these forces was, plainly, Salonika, which I may mention, they have entered at 4 o'clock this morning.

It has never been our policy or our interest to see the war carried into the Balkan Peninsula. In the middle of February, we sent our Foreign Secretary and the Chief of the Imperial General Staff to the Middle East, in order to see whether anything could be done to form a united defensive front in the Balkans. They went to Athens. They went to Ankara. They would have gone to Belgrade, but they were refused permission by the government of Prince Paul. Of course, if these three threatened States had stood together they could have had at their disposal 60 or 70 divisions which, if a good combined plan had been made and if prompt united action had been taken in time, might have confronted the Germans with a project of resistance which might well have deterred them altogether and must, in any case, have long delayed them, having regard to the mountainous and broken character of the country to be defended and the limits of the communications available in the various countries through which the German armies had forced or intrigued their way.

Although we were most anxious to promote such a defensive front by which alone the peace of the Balkans could be maintained, we were determined not to urge the Greeks, already at grips with the Italians, upon any course contrary to their desires or judgment. The support which we can give to the peoples who are fighting, or are ready to fight, for freedom in the Balkans and in Turkey, is necessarily limited at the present time, and we did not wish to take the responsibility of pressing the Greeks to engage in a conflict with the new and terrible foe gathering upon their frontiers. However, on the first occasion when the Foreign Secretary and the Chief of the Imperial General Staff met the Greek King and Prime Minister, the Prime Minister declared spontaneously on behalf of the Government that Greece was resolved, at all costs, to defend her freedom and native soil against any aggressor, and that even if they were left wholly unsupported by Great Britain, or by their neighbours Turkey and Yugoslavia, they would, nevertheless, remain faithful to their alliance with Great Britain, which came into play at the opening of the Italian invasion, and that they would fight to the death against both Italy and Germany.

This being so, it seemed that our duty was clear. We were bound in honour to give them all the aid in our power. If they were resolved to face the might and fury of the Huns, we had no doubts but that we should share their ordeal and that the soldiers of the British Empire must stand in the line with them. We were advised by our generals on the spot, the Chief of the Imperial General Staff, and Generals Wavell and Papagos, both victorious commanders-in-chief, that a sound military plan, giving good prospects of success, could be made. Of course, in all these matters there is hazard and in this case, as anyone can see, without particularizing unduly, there was for us a double hazard. It remains to be seen how well those opposing risks and duties have been judged, but of this I am sure, that there is no less likely way of winning a war than to adhere pedantically to the maxim of 'Safety first'. Therefore, in the first weeks of March we entered into a military agreement with the Greeks, and the considerable movement of British and Imperial troops and supplies which has since developed began to take place. The House would very rightly reprove me if I entered into any details, or if while this widespread battle is going on I attempted in any way to discuss either the situation or its prospects.

I therefore turn to the story of Yugoslavia. This valiant, steadfast people, whose history for centuries has been a struggle for life, and who owe their survival to their mountains and to their fighting qualities, made every endeavour to placate the Nazi monster. If they had made common cause with the Greeks when the Greeks, having been attacked by Italy, hurled back the invaders, the complete destruction of the Italian armies in Albania could certainly and swiftly have been achieved long before the German forces could have reached the theatre of war. And even in January and February of this year, this extraordinary military opportunity was still open. But the Government of Prince Paul, untaught by the fate of so many of the smaller countries of Europe, not only observed the strictest neutrality and refused even to enter into effective Staff conversations with Greece or with Turkey or with us, but hugged the delusion that they could preserve their independence by patching up some sort of pact or compromise with Hitler. Once again we saw the odious German poisoning technique employed. In this case, however, it was to the Government rather than to the nation that the doses and the inoculations were administered. The process was not hurried. Why should it have been? All the time the German armies and air force were massing in Bulgaria. From a few handfuls of tourists, admiring the beauties of the Bulgarian landscape in the wintry weather, the German forces grew to 7, 12,

20 and finally to 25 divisions. Presently, the weak and unfortunate Prince, and afterwards his Ministers, were summoned, like others before them, to Herr Hitler's footstool, and a pact was signed which would have given Germany complete control not only over the body but over the soul of the Slav nation. Then at last the people of Yugoslavia saw their peril, and with a universal spasm of revolt and national resurgence very similar to that which in 1808 convulsed and glorified the people of Spain, they swept from power those who were leading them into a shameful tutelage, and resolved at the eleventh hour to guard their freedom and their honour with their lives. All this happened only a fortnight ago.

A boa constrictor who had already covered his prey with his foul saliva and then had it suddenly wrested from his coils, would be in an amiable mood compared with Hitler, Goering, Ribbentrop and the rest of the Nazi gang when they experienced this bitter disappointment. A frightful vengeance was vowed against the Southern Slavs. Rapid, perhaps hurried, redispositions were made of the German forces and German diplomacy. Hungary was offered large territorial gains to become the accomplice in the assault upon a friendly neighbour with whom she had just signed a solemn pact of friendship and non-aggression. Count Teleki[1] preferred to take his own life rather than join in such a deed of shame. A heavy forward movement of the German armies already gathered in and dominating Austria was set in motion through Hungary to the Northern frontier of Yugoslavia. A ferocious howl of hatred from the supreme miscreant was the signal for the actual invasion. The open city of Belgrade was laid in ashes, and at the same time a tremendous drive by the German armoured forces which had been so improvidently allowed to gather in Bulgaria was launched Westward into Southern Serbia. And it no longer being worth while to keep up the farce of love for Greece, other powerful forces rolled forward into Greece, where they were at once unflinchingly encountered and have already sustained more than one bloody repulse at the hands of that heroic Army. The British and Imperial troops have not up to the present been engaged. Further than this I cannot attempt to carry the tale.

Therefore, I turn for a few moments to the larger aspects of the war. I must first speak of France and of the French people, to whom in their sorrows we are united not only by memories but by living ties. I welcome cordially the declaration of Marshal Pétain that France could never act against her former Ally or go to war with her former Ally. Such a course so insensate, so unnatural and, on lower grounds, so improvident, might we – though, of course, it is not for me to speak for any Government but our own – alienate from France for long years the sympathies and support of the American

[1] Prime Minister of Hungary from 16 February 1939 until his death on 3 April 1941.

democracy. I am sure that the French nation would, with whatever means of expression are left to them, repudiate such a shameful deed. We must, however, realize that the Government of Vichy is in a great many matters, though happily not in all, in the hands of Herr Hitler acting daily through the Armistice Commission at Wiesbaden. Two million Frenchmen are prisoners in German hands. A great part of the food supply of France has been seized by Germany. Both prisoners and food can be doled out month by month in return for hostile propaganda or unfriendly action against Great Britain. Or again, the cost of the German occupation of France, for which a cruel and exorbitant toll is exacted, may be raised still further as a punishment for any manifestations of sympathy with us. Admiral Darlan tells us that the Germans have been generous in their treatment of France. All the information which we receive both from occupied and unoccupied France, makes me very doubtful whether the mass of the French people would endorse that strange and somewhat sinister tribute. However, the generosity of the German treatment of France is a matter for Frenchmen to judge.

But I wish to make it clear that we must maintain our blockade against Germany and those rights of contraband control at sea, which have never been disputed or denied to any belligerent, and which a year ago France was exercising to the full with us. Some time ago we were ready to enter upon economic negotiations with the French. But any chance of fruitful negotiation was nipped in the bud by the generous Germans, and imperative orders were given from Wiesbaden to the Government of Vichy to break off all contact with us. Nevertheless, we have in practice allowed very considerable quantities of food to go into France out of our sincere desire to spare the French people every hardship in our power. When, however, it comes to thousands of tons of rubber and other vital war materials which pass, as we know, directly to the German armies, we are bound, even at the risk of collisions with French warships at sea, to enforce our rights as recognized by international law. There is one other form of action into which the Vichy Government might be led by the dictation of Germany, namely, the sending of powerful war vessels, which are unfinished or damaged, back from the French African ports to ports in Metropolitan France which are either under the control of the Germans, or may at very short notice fall under their control. Such movements of French war vessels from Africa to France would alter the balance of naval power, and would thus prejudice the interests of the United States as well as our own. Therefore, I trust that such incidents will be avoided, or, if they cannot be avoided, that the consequences which follow from them will be understood and fairly judged by the French nation, for whose cause we are contending no less than for our own.

I am glad to be able to report to the House a continued and marked improvement in the relative strength of the Royal Air Force as compared with that of Germany; also I draw attention to the remarkable increase in its actual strength and in its bomb-dropping capacity, and to the marked augmentation in the power and size of the bombs which we shall be using in even greater numbers. The sorties which we are now accustomed to make upon German harbours and cities are increasing in numbers of aircraft employed and in the weight of the discharge with every month that passes, and in some cases we have already in our raids exceeded in severity anything which any single town has in a single night experienced over here. At the same time, there is a sensible improvement in our means of dealing with German raids upon this Island,[1] and a very great measure of security has been given to this country in day-time – and we are glad that the days are lengthening. But now the moonlight periods are also looked forward to by the Royal Air Force as an opportunity for inflicting severe deterrent losses upon the raiders, as well as for striking hard at the enemy in his own territory. The fact that our technical advisers welcome the light – daylight, moonlight, starlight – and that we do not rely for our protection on darkness, clouds and mists, as would have been the case some time ago, is pregnant with hope and meaning. But, of course, all these tendencies are only in their early stages, and I forbear to enlarge upon them.

But, after all, everything turns upon the Battle of the Atlantic, which is proceeding with growing intensity on both sides. Our losses in ships and tonnage are very heavy, and vast as are the shipping resources which we control, these losses could not continue indefinitely without seriously affecting our war effort and our means of subsistence. It is no answer to say that we have inflicted upon the Germans and Italians a far higher proportion of loss compared with the size of their merchant fleets and the fleeting opportunities they offer us, than they have upon us, with our world-wide traffic continually maintained. We have, in fact, sunk, captured or seen scuttled over 2,300,000 tons of German and Italian shipping. But we have ourselves lost since the beginning of the war nearly 4,000,000 tons of British tonnage. As against that, we have gained under the British flag over 3,000,000 of foreign or newly-constructed tonnage, not counting the considerable foreign tonnage which has also come under our control. Therefore, at the moment our enormous fleets sail the seas without any serious or obvious diminution, as far as the number of ships is concerned.

[1] There had been considerable progress, though of course Churchill could not say so, in the use of decoy fires. In March German bombers had struck for up to six hours at decoy sites near Cardiff and Bristol. At Portsmouth on April 17 more than 75 per cent of the bombs dropped were to fall on the decoy area. (Reports by Sir Archibald Sinclair to Churchill of 25 March 1941 and 23 April 1941: *Premier papers, 3/118, folios 3, 6 and 7*). On 8 April 1941, however, serious damage had been done to three aircraft factories in Coventry, and, as Lord Beaverbrook wrote to Churchill, at Daimler No. 1 Shadow Factory all magnesium, raw materials, steel and aluminium had been destroyed in ten bays. But, Beaverbrook added, 'we will escape complete disaster by reason of the dispersal plans which were carried out last year'. (Minute of 9 April 1941: *Premier papers, 3/18/2, folio 98*). On the day of Churchill's speech (9 April 1941) it was announced that 29,856 British citizens had been killed as a result of air bombardment since the outbreak of war.

But what is to happen in the future if these losses continue at the present rate? Where are we to find another three or four million tons to fill the gap which is being created and carry us on through 1942? We are building merchant ships upon a very considerable scale and to the utmost of our ability, having regard to other calls upon our labour. We are also making a most strenuous effort to make ready for sea the large number of vessels which have been damaged by the enemy and the still larger number which have been damaged by the winter gales. We are doing our utmost to accelerate the turn-round of our ships, remembering – this is a striking figure – that even 10 days' saving on turn-round on our immense fleets is equal to a reinforcement of 5,000,000 tons of imports in a single year. I can assure the House that all the energy and contrivance of which we are capable have been and will continue to be devoted to these purposes, and we are already conscious of substantial results. But, when all is said and done, the only way in which we can get through the year 1942 without a very sensible contraction of our war effort is by another gigantic building of merchant ships in the United States similar to that prodigy of output accomplished by the Americans in 1918. All this has been in train in the United States for many months past. There has now been a very large extension of the programmes, and we have the assurance that several millions of tons of American new-built shipping will be available for the common struggle during the course of the next year. Here, then, is the assurance upon which we may count for the staying power without which it will not be possible to save the world from the criminals who assail its future.

The Battle of the Atlantic must, however, be won, not only in the factories and shipyards, but upon the blue water. I am confident that we shall succeed in coping with the air attacks which are made upon the shipping in the Western and North-Western approaches. I hope that eventually the inhabitants of the sister Island may realize that it is as much in their interest as in ours that their ports and air fields should be available for the naval and air forces which must operate ever further into the Atlantic. But, while I am hopeful that we shall gain mastery over the air attack upon our shipping, the U-boats and the surface raiders, ranging ever farther to the Westward, ever nearer to the shores of the United States, constitute a menace which must be overcome if the life of Britain is not to be endangered and if the purposes to which the Government and people of the United States have devoted themselves are not to be frustrated. We shall, of course, make every effort in our power. The defeat of the U-boats and of the surface raiders has been proved to be entirely a question of adequate escorts for our convoys. It would be indeed disastrous if the great masses of weapons, munitions and instruments of war of all kinds, made with the toil and skill of American hands, at the cost of the United States, and loaned to us under the Aid to Britain Act, were to sink into the depths of the ocean and never reach the hard-pressed fighting line. That would be a result lamentable to us over here, and I cannot believe that it would be found acceptable to the proud and resolute people of the United States. Indeed, I am now authorized to state that 10 United States Revenue cutters, fast vessels of about 2,000 tons displacement, with a fine armament and a very wide range of endurance, have already been placed at our disposal by the United States Government and will soon be in action. These vessels, originally designed to enforce prohibition, will now serve an even higher purpose.

It is, of course, very hazardous to try to forecast in what direction or directions Hitler will employ his military machine in the present year. He may at any time attempt the invasion of this Island. That is an ordeal from which we shall not shrink. At the present moment he is driving South and South-East through the Balkans, and at any moment he may turn upon Turkey. But there are many signs which point to a Nazi attempt to secure the granary of the Ukraine and the oil fields of the Caucasus as a German means of gaining the resources wherewith to wear down the English-speaking world. All this is speculation. I will say only one thing more. Once we have gained the Battle of the Atlantic and are certain of the constant flow of American supplies which is being prepared for us, then, however far Hitler may go, or whatever new millions and scores of millions he may lap in misery, he may be sure that, armed with the sword of retributive justice, we shall be on his track.

Harold Nicolson: diary

(*'Diaries and Letters 1939-1945'*)

9 April 1941

I go down to the House to hear Winston make his statement. It had been devised as a motion congratulating the fighting services on their victories, and I remember a few days ago how Winston promised that he would say to us, 'Fly your flags in celebration'. These victories are now dust and ashes.

The PM comes in at 11.56 and is greeted with cheers. He sits between Greenwood and Attlee, scowls at the notes in his hand, pulls out a gold pencil and scribbles an addition to the last sheet. He than gets up to speak in a grim and obstinate voice. He throws out news incidentally. We have taken Massawa. The Germans entered Salonika at 4 a.m. this morning. At this news there is a silent wince of pain throughout the House. He discloses that the USA have given us their revenue cutters. His peroration implies that we are done without American help. He indulges in a few flights of oratory. There is a little joke about the boa-constrictor, and a little joke about the revenue cutters having previously been used for prohibition. But he evidently feels that even graver news is ahead of us. The House is sad and glum.

Geoffrey Dawson: diary
('Geoffrey Dawson and Our Times', page 438)

9 April 1941

Winston had made a great survey of the war in the House of Commons, a restrained but effective effort. The news from the Balkans was not good and he made no attempt to pretend that it was.

War Cabinet, Battle of the Atlantic Committee: minutes
(Cabinet papers, 86/1)

9 April 1941 10 Downing Street
5 p.m.
Secret

REPAIRS TO MERCHANT SHIPPING

The Prime Minister expressed himself as disappointed with the progress made in increasing the labour force on repair work, and asked for a further report in a week's time.

OVER-SIDE LOADING AND DISCHARGE

The Prime Minister referred to the need for making sure that sufficient barges and coasters were collected at the West Coast ports to deal with the position if one of the larger West Coast ports was put out of action.

Winston S. Churchill to Alexandros Korizis[1]
(Churchill papers, 20/37)

9 April 1941

I am much touched by Your Excellency's message of congratulation on the victory of Cape Matapan. I hope that this will mark the beginning of a series of naval victories by our joint forces. May I take this opportunity of again expressing to your Excellency my admiration of the gallant fight waged by the heroic Greek army during the past months and now against fresh hordes of savage invaders.

[1] The Greek Prime Minister (President of the Council of Ministers).

War Cabinet, Defence Committee (Operations): minutes
(*Cabinet papers, 69/2*)

9 April 1941
9.45 p.m.

Cabinet War Room

THE SITUATION IN IRAQ[1]

The Prime Minister said that the Committee were greatly indebted to the Viceroy[2] and to the Commander-in-Chief, India,[3] for the way in which they had responded immediately to the request for the despatch of a force to Iraq, as set out in the telegram from the Viceroy dated 9th April, 1941. Although the despatch of troops from India to Iraq entailed diverting these forces from Malaya, the situation could be accepted since there were indications that the Japanese Government had been given reason to pause, and the situation in the Far East was now less tense.

The Prime Minister suggested that the 'C' Class cruiser might land a small party immediately on arrival at Basra, and that subsequently with the landing of the main force from India, we could establish an effective bridgehead covering the port of Basra.

The Prime Minister emphasized the importance of Basra, a port of disembarkation for aircraft shipped direct from the USA for the Middle East. It was essential that a comprehensive scheme should be drawn up for organizing a large assembly park at Basra and that Mr Harriman should be identified with this scheme. He invited the Secretary of State for India[4] to preside over a Committee and to report within a week.

THE FAR EAST

The Prime Minister said that everything indicated a slackening of the tension in the Far East. It was most unlikely that the Japanese would enter the war in the next three or four months, and it would be foolish to send further reinforcements to Malaya in the near future. He quite appreciated Mr Menzies' anxiety, but the completion of the defences of Malaya must be subordinated to more pressing needs elsewhere.

[1] In March 1941 the pro-German Rashid Ali al-Gaylani, a former Prime Minister of Iraq, had seized power in Baghdad. The pro-British regent, Emir Abdullah, fled. The first British troops, which had been sent from India, reached Basra on April 18.

[2] Lord Linlithgow.

[3] Claude John Eyre Auchinleck, 1884–1981. On active service in Egypt and Aden, 1914–15; Mesopotamia, 1916–19 (DSO, 1917). On active service on the North-West Frontier of India, 1933 and 1935. CB, 1934. Deputy Chief of the General Staff, Army Headquarters, India, 1936. Member of the Expert Committee on the Defence of India, 1938. Knighted, 1940. Commander-in-Chief, Southern Command, 1940. Commander-in-Chief, India, 1941. Commander-in-Chief, Middle East, 1941–2. Commander-in-Chief, India, 1943–7. Field-Marshal.

[4] L. S. Amery.

The Prime Minister thought it would be the height of folly to lay down in advance rigid dispositions which we should take up if Japan entered the war. First of all, this was a most unlikely event, unless we received some severe setbacks. Secondly, Mr Menzies' hypothesis was most unlikely to occur. The entry of Japan into the war would be a challenge to the USA, which he felt certain they would accept. He thought we should repeat to Mr Menzies the general promise already given, that in the event of a serious major attack, we would abandon everything to come to their help: but that did not mean that we would give up our great interests in the Middle East on account of a few raids by Japanese cruisers.

Mr Alexander said that he had had some discussion with Mr Menzies on this point. Mr Menzies had said that he could not be satisfied with general assurances. It would be necessary for the Australian public to feel that they were being properly protected. For this reason, Mr Menzies would like to take back with him a definite statement that we would send some specific help if danger threatened.

Some discussion took place as to the probable Japanese action in the event of war, and the difficulties which would confront a major expedition, either against Singapore or against Australia.

The Prime Minister expressed the view that far the most damaging action which the Japanese could take would be to loose twenty 8-inch cruisers on to our trade routes. We should be forced to send all our shipping in convoy with battleship escort, and this we could only do with the help of the USA.

Sir Dudley Pound agreed. He thought it unlikely that the Japanese would send the whole of their fleet South, as they were very nervous of the damage that might be done to their own cities, and would pay regard to the potential threat of the American fleet.

Mr Attlee thought it would be wrong to give Mr Menzies a worthless promise with which to delude his people. It should be the task of Mr Menzies to educate them.

The Prime Minister agreed. He thought it would be wrong to give up sound strategical ideas in order to satisfy the ignorance of the Australian Opposition.

The Committee agreed with this view.

The Prime Minister expressed the view that it would be most unwise to fritter away aircraft to Australia, where they would not come into action against the Germans, when we could not foresee how the battle would go in the vital areas.

After some further discussion The Prime Minister authorized the Secretary of State for Air to discuss this question with Mr Menzies the following day on the lines which he had proposed but, having regard to our own urgent needs, not to promise more than was absolutely necessary.

Averell Harriman to President Franklin D. Roosevelt
('Special Envoy to Churchill and Stalin, 1941-1946')

10 April 1941

England's strength is bleeding.[1] In our own interest, I trust that our Navy can be directly employed before our partner is too weak.

Winston S. Churchill to Sir Alexander Cadogan
(*Churchill papers, 20/36*)

10 April 1941

THE RT HON. J. C. WEDGWOOD

I should think he would do good in America as his fire and passion for democracy and freedom would appeal. If Lord Halifax himself has cabled for him, the Ministry of Information should facilitate his journey and his convenience in regard to the small sums of money required. Would it not be possible to arrange a passage on one of HM Ships going across on escort duty? Let the matter be studied sympathetically.

I will see him before he goes, when all is arranged. He is a splendid fellow.

Winston S. Churchill to Sir William Fraser[2]
(*Churchill papers, 20/21*)

10 April 1941

My dear Bill,

Thank you for your letter of April 2 about the courageous behaviour of certain survivors of the crew of S.S. *British Premier*.[1]

I have given directions that it should be brought to notice in the proper quarter for consideration with other acts of endurance and bravery performed by the Merchant Service.

Yours vy faithfully,
Winston S. Churchill

[1] In less than three days, 31,000 tons of British merchant shipping had been sunk (War Cabinet, 10 April 1941, 12 noon, *Cabinet papers 65/18*).

[1] William Jocelyn Ian Fraser, 1897–1974. On active service, 1915–16 (blinded in action). Conservative Member of Parliament, North Pancras, 1924–29 and 1931–36. Knighted 1934. A Governor of the BBC, 1937–39 and 1941–46. Conservative Member of Parliament for Lonsdale, 1940–50; for Morecambe and Lonsdale, 1950–58. Companion of Honour, 1953. National President of the British Legion, 1947–58. Created Baron (Fraser of Lonsdale), 1958. President of the International Congress of War Blinded, 1973.

War Cabinet: minutes
(*Cabinet papers, 65/18*)

10 April 1941 10 Downing Street

BATTLE OF DERNA

The Secretary of State for War said that the German High Command had broadcast a communiqué stating that they had taken prisoner 6 British generals, 2 colonels and 2,000 troops at Derna. We should have to issue a communiqué. Should we admit that Generals O'Connor, Neame[1] and Gambier-Parry[2] were missing?

The Prime Minister thought that the names of these three generals should appear in the communiqué, which should state that part of our rear-guard had been cut off, and that our main force was now in the Tobruk area.

POSSIBLE APPROACH TO PRESIDENT ROOSEVELT WITH REGARD TO NAVAL BASE FACILITIES IN EIRE

The Prime Minister thought that it would be better to await developments before making this further approach. If the time came when the United States were prepared to escort convoys to this country, they would then almost certainly be ready to bring strong pressure to bear on the Eire Government.

The War Cabinet decided against a further approach to President Roosevelt at this stage.

Winston S. Churchill to General Ismay, for the Chiefs of Staff Committee
(*Churchill papers, 20/36*)

10 April 1941

DEFENCE OF MALAYA

There is no objection in principle to preparing the necessary plans for holding this forward position in the north, but we must not tie up a lot of troops in these regions which we can so readily and rapidly reinforce from

[1] Philip Neame, 1888–1978. Entered the Army, 1908. On active service, 1914–18 (Victoria Cross; despatches five times). Published *German Strategy in the Great War*, 1923. Gold Medal, British Olympic Sporting Rifle Team, France, 1924. Served in India, 1924–38; member of the political-military mission to Lhasa, Tibet, 1936. Commandant, Royal Military Academy, Woolwich, 1938–39. Deputy Chief of the General Staff, British Expeditionary Force, France, 1939–40. Commander of the 4th Indian Division, Western Desert 1940. Military Governor, Cyrenaica, 1941. Commanded the British, Australian and Indian forces against Rommel's first attack in Cyrenaica, March-April 1941. Prisoner of war, 1941. Escaped (from Italy), 1943. Lieutenant-Governor and Commander-in-Chief, Channel Islands, 1945–53. Knighted, 1946.

[2] Michael Denman Gambier-Parry, 1891–1976. Entered the army in 1911. On active service at Gallipoli and Mesopotamia (despatches six times). Military Cross, 1916. Royal Tank Corps, 1924. Head of the Military Mission to the Greek Army, 1940. General Officer Commanding 2nd Armoured Division, Western Desert, 1941. Prisoner of war in Italy, 1941–43.

India. We are not now attempting to defend Singapore at Singapore, but from nearly 500 miles away. I view with great reluctance the continued diversion of troops, aircraft and supplies to a theatre which it is improbable will be lighted up unless we are heavily beaten elsewhere.

Winston S. Churchill to L. S. Amery
(*Churchill papers, 20/36*)

10 April 1941
Action this Day

Thank you very much for prompt and efficient action which you took yesterday. I shall be greatly interested to see the plan you will make in the next few days for making Basra a great American assembly point. Naturally, you will plan your scheme in stages so that we can have the use of it as it develops progressively. A widespread defence scheme against Air attack must also be prepared. The necessary RDF stations to enable our fighters to get into the air in good time must be provided. Ask the Military for plenty of photographs of the place, and send them forward with your report. Try to keep the report very short.

Winston S. Churchill to A. V. Alexander
(*Churchill papers, 20/36*)

10 April 1941

I saw yesterday an officer[1] of the Coldstream who had escaped, after serious wounds and many adventures, from Germany to France. He complained to me bitterly of the unsympathetic treatment meted out to him and others in his plight by Paymaster Commander Muir, OBE,[2] at Gibraltar. I should be glad if you would look into this and see whether there is any foundation for what I am told. Apparently Muir is in a position where he can be very rough with the soldiers.

[1] Lieutenant J.M. Langley, Coldstream Guards. In 1941 he was working in MI6. The Secretary of State for War, David Margesson, wrote to Churchill on 22 May 1941: 'He is the Liaison Officer between MI6 and the War Office, whose duty it is to co-ordinate all arrangements to facilitate escapes by our prisoners of war from enemy occupied countries. He is well suited to this work by virtue of his own experience, and is doing it excellently. He is shortly leaving for Barcelona to co-ordinate arrangements there and in Spain generally'. (*Churchill papers, 20/27*)

[2] Gerald Robin Muir. Paymaster Lieutenant, Royal Navy. Stationed at Gibraltar. He had been appointed to the Military Division of the Order of the British Empire in January 1941.

Winston S. Churchill to Sir Alexander Cadogan
(*Churchill papers, 20/36*)

10 April 1941

I do not hear very good reports about Major J.H.Dodds, CMG,[1] who was Consul-General at Nice until the French collapsed, and since then has been working unofficially with the American Consulate at Marseilles, looking after the British community there. He is alleged to be unsympathetic, slack and unhelpful.

I should be glad of a report.

Winston S. Churchill and Chiefs of Staff to General Wavell
(*Churchill papers, 20/49*)

10 April 1941

We await your full appreciation. Meanwhile, you should know how the problem looks to us. From here it seems unthinkable that the fortress of Tobruk should be abandoned without offering the most prolonged resistance. We have a secure sea-line of communication. The enemy's line is long and should be vulnerable provided he is not given time to organize at leisure. So long as Tobruk is held and its garrison includes even a few armoured vehicles which can lick out at his communications, nothing but a raid dare go past Tobruk. If you leave Tobruk and go 260 miles back to Mersa Matruh, may you not find yourself faced with something like the same problem? We are convinced you should fight it out at Tobruk.

Winston S. Churchill to General Wavell
(*Churchill papers, 20/37*)

10 April 1941

We all cordially endorse your decision to hold Tobruk and will do all in our power to bring you aid.

[1] James Hugh Hamilton Dodds, 1880–1956. On active service, South Africa, 1901–02; Somaliland, 1908–10. Consul and Chargé d'Affaires, Addis Ababa, Abyssinia, 1911–24; Tripoli, 1924–28; Palermo, 1928–36. Consul-General, Nice, 1936–40. Attached to the United States Consulate, Marseille, 1940–41. Retired, 1941. Assumed the surname Dodds Crewe, 1945.

John Colville: diary
(*Colville papers*)

10 April 1941

The PM was terribly upset by a serious motor smash to Duncan Sandys.

Left for a tour of the South West with the PM, Winant, Harriman, Mrs Churchill, Mary, Ismay, Tommy and a batch of officers connected with the new technical inventions. We all slept on the train.

Mary Churchill: diary
(*Lady Soames papers*)

10 April 1941

We are now on our way to Swansea.[1]

Have just read Papa's speech verbatim – EXCELLENT. So clear and explicit.

Derna evacuated. Many prisoners taken.

John Colville: diary
(*Colville papers*)

11 April 1941

Good Friday. Reached Swansea at 8.00 a.m. and spent the morning among the City's battered ruins and inspecting detachments of Civil Defence Workers. The centre of the town has not a house standing. I was amazed by the eagerness and cheerfulness of the population. W had a great reception.

We went on by train to Cardigan and motored from there to Aberporth on Cardigan Bay, where we saw a noisy but interesting display of rockets, UP projectors, etc., such as would have delighted the Prof's heart if he had not been laid up with a chill at Marlow. The firing of the rockets was bad and at the first display a childishly easy target was repeatedly missed; but the multiple projectors seemed promising; so did the aerial mines descending with parachutes.

We slept on the train at a wayside station called Whitland.

[1] Churchill was accompanied on this journey by his wife, his daughter Mary, two Americans, John G. Winant and Averell Harriman, Admiral Fraser, and Sir Frederick Pile.

Mary Churchill: diary
(*Lady Soames papers*)

11 April 1941

The devastation in parts of the town is ghastly.

Never have I seen such courage – love – cheerfulness and confidence expressed as by the people today.

Wherever he went they swarmed around Papa – clasping his hand – patting him on the back – shouting his name.

Not just fair weather friends these – he through many years earned their gratitude – won their confidence – been rewarded with their love.

It is rather frightening how terribly they depend on him.

It was wonderful their spirit 'grim and gay'.

The triumph of the Spirit of Man above the fear and squalor of material sorrows.

News today –

Hungary stabs Yugoslavia in the back.

John Colville: diary
(*Colville papers*)

12 April 1941

Arrived early at Bristol. Bathed and breakfasted with the PM and Harriman at the Grand Hotel. The rest of the party joined us from the train and led by the Lord Mayor[1] we walked and motored through devastation such as I had never thought possible. Swansea is mild in comparison. There had been a bad raid during the night and many of the ruins were still smoking. The people looked bewildered but, as at Swansea, were brave and were thrilled by the sight of Winston who drove about sitting on the hood of an open car and waving his hat.

At the university the PM, as Chancellor, conferred honorary degrees on Winant and Menzies and made an excellent impromptu speech in which he likened the fortitude of Bristol to that which we are accustomed 'to associate with Ancient Rome and modern Greece'. The gowns and pageantry were a strange contrast to the smoking ruins just outside.

[1] Thomas Underdown, 1872–1953. Schoolmaster. President of the National Union of Teachers, 1917–18. Chairman of the Bristol South Liberal Association, 1928–33. Alderman, Bristol, from 1938. Lord Mayor, 1940–41. Author of *Bristol under Blitz*, 1942.

General Ismay: recollection[1]
(*Churchill papers, 4/198*)

[12 April 1941]

You went to Bristol on 12 April 1941 to confer Degrees on Winant and Menzies. The train was parked just outside Bristol on the previous night and it was clear that Bristol was getting it hot. We went straight to the Hotel from the station and you then did a tour of the stricken areas. People were still being dug out, but there was no sign of faltering anywhere. Only efficiency and resolution. At one of the rest centres at which you called, there was a poor old woman who had lost all her belongings sobbing her heart out. But as you entered, she took her handkerchief from her eyes and waved it madly shouting 'Hooray, hooray.'

Averell Harriman to President Franklin D. Roosevelt
(*'Special Envoy to Churchill and Stalin, 1941-1946'*)

12 April 1941

The PM inspected the damaged area, walking among the people and visiting the reception centres. A grim, determined people, but I talked to many of them. They wanted him to see they had no complaints and were ready for the next one.

Winston S. Churchill: speech
(*'The Unrelenting Struggle', pages 103–4*)

12 April 1941 Bristol

Here we are gathered in academic robes to go through a ceremonial and repeat formulas associated with the giving of university degrees. Many of those here today have been all night at their posts, and all have been under the fire of the enemy in heavy and protracted bombardment. That you should gather in this way is a mark of fortitude and phlegm, of a courage and detachment from material affairs worthy of all that we have learned to believe of Ancient Rome or of modern Greece.

I go about the country whenever I can escape for a few hours or for a day from my duty at headquarters, and I see the damage done by the enemy attacks; but I also see side by side with the devastation and amid the ruins

[1] General Ismay set down this recollection of Churchill on 28 November 1946, when Churchill was preparing his war memoirs.

quiet, confident, bright, and smiling eyes, beaming with a consciousness of being associated with a cause far higher and wider than any human or personal issue. I see the spirit of an unconquerable people. I see a spirit bred in freedom, nursed in a tradition which has come down to us through the centuries, and which will surely at this moment, this turning-point in the history of the world, enable us to bear our part in such a way that none of our race who come after us will have any reason to cast reproach upon their sires.

Mr Winant is the interpreter of the great Republic to us, and he is our interpreter and friend, sending back his messages across the ocean to them. Through him and other distinguished representatives of the United States who are with us today, including Mr Harriman, we make another tie with the illustrious President of the United States, and with the executive of that vast community, at a time when great matters of consequence to all the world are being resolved. It has been to me an honour which will stand out in my twelve years' tenure of office as your Chancellor to confer this degree upon Mr Winant.

In Dr Conant, who is, much to his regret, not with us today, we have a figure widely and deeply respected throughout the United States, and particularly among the youth who attend Harvard University, holding up a clear beacon light for young men of honour and courage.

Mr Menzies brings with him the strong assurance of the Australian Commonwealth that they will, with us, go through this long, fierce, dire struggle to the victorious end. It is, indeed, a marvellous fact that Australia and New Zealand, who are separated from us and from Europe, with all its passions and quarrels, by the great ocean spaces, should send their manhood and scatter their wealth upon this world cause. No law, no constitution, no bond or treaty pledges them to spend a shilling or send a man.

We welcome Mr Menzies here. He has sat with us in Cabinet. He has seen every aspect of our life at home. And he is going back presently by the United States to Australia. Much will have happened by the time he returns there. Australian and New Zealand troops may well be in contact with the enemy today. There, to the classic scenes of the ancient lands of Greece, they will bring the valour of the sons of the Southern Cross.

Winston S. Churchill: recollection
('The Second World War, Volume Three')

[12 April 1941] Bristol

The ceremony went forward as planned. I spent an hour driving round the worst hit places and then repaired to the University. Everything proceeded with strict formality, but the large building next to the University was still burning and the bright academic robes of some of the principal actors did not conceal the soaked and grimy uniforms of their night's toil. The whole scene was moving.

John G. Winant: recollection
(*'A Letter from Grosvenor Square'*)

12 April 1941

ON THE TRAIN

Quite suddenly he turned to me and said: 'I am going to see to it that the necessary tonnage is allotted for foodstuffs to protect them (the civil population) from the strain and stresses that they may be subjected to in this period of great emergency.'

In allotting more tonnage for foodstuffs I realized that Mr Churchill had been deeply moved by what he had seen on this trip of the people's needs. At this desperate time there was always the temptation to cut down on food because of the compelling need for steel and armaments. When I wrote to the President of the Prime Minister's few words on the train I told him that I felt deeply that this policy of protection was necessary. I knew that he would fully understand.

John Colville: diary
(*Colville papers*)

12 April 1941

Reached Chequers for dinner. Mr and Mrs Eden and Sir J. Dill came. A hectic night starting in gloom and ending in glad momentous news from the USA – Winant received a telegram for the PM from Roosevelt announcing America's intention to extend her patrol area as far west as the 25th Meridian.

Winston S. Churchill to General Wavell
(*Churchill papers, 20/49*)

12 April 1941 Chequers

We are working night and day here to aid you especially by Navy and Air action on Tripoli and communications. Hope signal you tomorrow large-scale decisions. Following is personal from me: Tobruk (please spell with a 'K') seems an invaluable bridgehead for offensive punches against all by-passers. One has the hope that our fellows will establish unit ascendancy in minor combats and that incursion of small raiding parties will not be allowed to deflect the general lay-out. Foreign Secretary and CIGS are with me here and we all send you our assurance of complete confidence and every wish for good fortune. This is one of the crucial fights in the history of the British Army.

Winston S. Churchill to Sir Archibald Sinclair
(*Churchill papers, 20/36*)

12 April 1941
Private

This is not a good story.[1] The jealousies and cliquism which have led to the committing of this offence are a discredit to the Air Ministry, and I do not think any other Service Department would have been guilty of such a piece of work. What would have been said if the War Office had produced the story of the Battle of Libya and had managed to exclude General Wavell's name, or if the Admiralty had told the tale of Trafalgar and left Lord Nelson out of it? It grieves me very much that you should associate yourself with such behaviour. I am sure you were not consulted beforehand on the point, and your natural loyalty to everything done in your Department can alone have led you to condone what nine out of ten men would unhesitatingly condemn.

Winston S. Churchill to A.V. Alexander and Admiral Pound
(*Churchill papers, 20/36*)

12 April 1941
Action this Day

1. I am distressed at C-in-C, Mediterranean's,[2] No. 1444, which begins by pointing out vital consequences of stopping German reinforcements via Tripoli, and reaches the very easy conclusion that, in spite of the numerous difficulties about Malta, the Air Force must do it. In my view, a heavy risk should be run by the Royal Navy to break up Tripoli and cut the communications. Not only should destroyers and light cruisers from Malta prey on the convoys, aided by our submarines, but a strong assault should be made by capital ships. We are letting ourselves be placed in dire disaster and even, according to the Admiral, Alexandria may be lost and the Fleet driven away, because of a hundred or so of Ju 87s. This is really too easy for the enemy. Air bombardment is a small thing compared to the fire of 15-inch or 16-inch guns.

[1] The non-mention of the name of Air Chief Marshal Sir Hugh Dowding in the Air Ministry booklet *The Battle of Britain*. Dowding had been Air Officer Commanding-in-Chief, Fighter Command, throughout the battle.

[2] Admiral Sir Andrew Cunningham.

2. Why do you not consider the following: In conjunction with Double Winch[1] on the 23rd send *Nelson* and *Rodney* through to join Cunningham, instructing him to use these ships, fuelling with his own from Suda Bay, to smash Tripoli to pieces. Two or three of the Didos might go with them, and he would, of course, use his armoured Carrier *Formidable*.

3. I doubt very much whether his plan of sending heavy Bombers to Egypt is feasible, and even so, they have seven or eight hundred miles to go before they can reach Tripoli.

4. At the present time the whole situation in the Nile Valley is compromised by the failure of the Navy to close the passage from Italy to Libya, or to break up the port facilities at Tripoli, and it is really not fair to throw it on to the Air, who, with the limited flying grounds of Malta and the shorter nights for movement from Great Britain, are not strong enough to do the work.

5. Please see especially the telegram marked A by me, although apparently unnumbered, and also the telegram marked B beginning 'my 1444, Part II'. Why should not the naval attacks be continued, or at any rate be continuously intermittent after fuelling at Crete?

6. Pray let me know how you propose to deal with the situation which C-in-C, Mediterranean, rightly describes as vital. We must be prepared to face some losses at sea, instead of the Navy sitting passive and leaving it to the Air. But, of course, the Air should act to the full as well. It is the duty of the Navy, assisted by the Air, to cut the communications between Italy and Tripoli.

Winston S. Churchill to Anthony Eden

(*Churchill papers, 20/36*)

12 April 1941
Action this Day

VICHY GOVERNMENT COMPLAINT ABOUT INTERCEPTION OF A FRENCH CONVOY OFF THE COAST OF ALGERIA

Reply should surely emphasize the following points:

1. That a mere notification by the French to the British Admiralty that they have extended their territorial waters from 3 to 20 miles has no validity.

2. That the *Bangkok* had been full of rubber, 3,000 tons, which rubber was landed at Casablanca to be conveyed to the German Army by Admiral Darlan in little ships across the Mediterranean as opportunity served, while the *Bangkok* went round to the Straits of Gibraltar ready to assume an air of injured innocence.

[1] Aircraft taken by carrier in convoy through the Mediterranean, from Gibraltar to a point from which they could fly more safely to Malta, Suda Bay (Crete) and Alexandria (Egypt).

3. Anyway, the French shore batteries had no right to resist the ordinary right of search under international law for the purpose of ascertaining whether contraband or war materials were or were not on the four ships in the convoy. In fact, their firing upon us would have justified our firing upon the convoy, and if need be sinking them. But for the sake of humanity, and because the Captain in Command was a Pussyfoot, we let them all go. This matter is still being enquired into by the Admiralty, and I have not yet had the report.

Winston S. Churchill to A.V. Alexander
(*Churchill papers, 20/36*)

12 April 1941

MANNING OF UNITED STATES' COAST GUARD CUTTERS

This is a great pity, and I am very sorry to hear of these delays. Considering the vital character of the Battle of the Atlantic, I am surprised that the Admiralty take such an easy-going view of their responsibilities. In a few months things may be much easier, and it may be possible to give more leave. Remember that our merchant seamen are to be drowned and their ships sunk in the interval. I am entirely out of sympathy with these kind of proposals.

Winston S. Churchill to Anthony Eden
(*Churchill papers, 20/36*)

12 April 1941
Action this Day

BRITAIN, THE UNITED STATES, AND VICHY FRANCE

I should give the following answer to Mr Hull:[1]

1. On the whole I think it a good thing that the two flour ships should go. In any case, we will do whatever the United States Government wish.

2. We want to hold on to the 110 ships, as we need them very much.

3. On the general question of the *Dunquerque*, etc., my proposal is the following: If Admiral Darlan tries to carry her from Africa to Toulon, we shall, if convenient, try to sink her on the way, though this need not be mentioned as it would make it harder to do. If *Dunquerque* or *a fortiori, Richelieu* or *Jean Bart* reached Toulon, we should bomb them in Toulon harbour exactly as we are bombing *Scharnhorst* and *Gneisenau* in Brest. No more, no less. If the French retaliated on Gibraltar, we should super-retaliate on Vichy, ton for ton.

[1] Cordell Hull, 1871–1955. Elected to the United States Congress for Tennessee, 1907–21 and 1923–31; Senator, 1931–3. Secretary of State, 1933–44. Nobel Peace Prize, 1945. He published *The Memoirs of Cordell Hull* (two volumes) in 1948.

Moreover, I think it a very good thing to let the French know beforehand what the tariff would be, and perhaps the Americans would be the best medium through which to convey the gentle idea.

Pray talk to me about this when we meet, but in the meantime do nothing inconsistent therewith.

Winston S. Churchill to President Franklin D. Roosevelt
(*Foreign Office papers, 954/29*)

13 April 1941
Secret and Personal

Deeply grateful for your momentous cable[1] just handed me by Ambassador Winant. Will cable tomorrow at greater length, but have no doubt that 25th Meridian is a long step towards salvation. All your wishes about handling the matter, publicity, etc., will, of course, be respected.

2. Your message about Rochat's note.[2] We are delighted that *Dunquerque* is not to be moved without your agreement or at least notice being given you. It is remarkable how they have conformed to your representations. This eases the position for the immediate future. You will not, I am sure, expect us to let the French extort our agreement to abandon our rights of contraband control, even over food-stuffs, just because they do not send *Dunquerque* back to Toulon, observing we could probably sink this ship in transit, or, failing that, bomb her

[1] Roosevelt's telegram of 11 April 1941, extending the American patrol zone in the North Atlantic to all waters 'west of about West longitude 25 degrees'. The telegram began: 'We propose immediately to take the following steps in relation to the security of the Western Hemisphere, which steps will favorably affect your shipping problem. It is important for domestic political reasons which you will readily understand that this action be taken by us unilaterally and not after diplomatic conversations between you and us. Therefore before taking this unilateral action I want to tell you about the proposal. This Government proposes to extend the present so-called security zone and patrol areas which have been in effect since very early in the War to a line covering all North Atlantic waters west of about west longitude 25 degrees. We propose to utilize aircraft and naval vessels working from Greenland, Newfoundland, Nova Scotia, the United States, Bermuda and West Indies, with possible later extension to Brazil if this can be arranged. We will want in great secrecy notification of movement of convoys so our patrol units can seek out any ships or planes or aggressor nations operating west of the new line of the security zone. We will immediately make public to you position aggressor ships or planes when located in our patrol area west of West longitude 25 degrees.'

[2] Charles A. Rochat, Acting Secretary-General of the Vichy Ministry for Foreign Affairs, had given a note to the American Embassy in Vichy, promising not to move the French battleship *Dunquerque* from Oran to Toulon, in return for a guarantee by Britain not to interfere with shipments of goods to French colonies and to (unoccupied) Vichy France. The United States had informed Vichy on 4 April 1941 that 'Should such a transfer take place the Government of the United States could no longer envisage the continuation of the policy which it desire to pursue for the supplying, as far as possible, of its indispensable aid to unoccupied France, to say nothing of other acts of cooperation envisaged.' (Warren F. Kimball, *Churchill & Roosevelt, The Complete Correspondence*, Volume One, page 167.)

nightly in Toulon harbour as we are bombing *Scharnhorst* and *Gneisenau* in Brest.

3. Your declaration about the Red Sea area.[1] We are, of course, going all out to fight for the Nile Valley. No other conclusion is physically possible. We have half a million men there or on the way and mountains of stores. All questions of cutting the loss are ruled out. Tobruk must be held not as a defensive position, but as an invaluable bridgehead on the flank of any serious by-pass advance on Egypt. Our Air and Navy must cut or impede enemy communications across Central Mediterranean. Matter has to be fought out and must in any case take some time. Enemy's difficulties in land communication, over 800 miles long, must make attack in heavy force a matter of months. Even if Tobruk had to be evacuated from the sea, which we command, there are other strong fighting positions already organized. I personally feel that this situation is not only manageable but hopeful. Dill and Eden, who have just come back, concur.

4. I need scarcely say, Mr President, that paragraphs 2 and 3 deal with minor issues[2] compared to the tremendous decision announced in your No. 1 and once again I express on behalf of the British Commonwealth of Nations our profound gratitude.

On 13 April 1941, German troops entered Belgrade. In northern Greece, soldiers from Britain, Australia and New Zealand stood alongside Greek troops preparing to defend the Aliakhmon line. In Iraq, the pro-German *coup d'état* by Rashid Ali threatened Britain's oil and strategic supply lines throughout the Middle East. In Libya, Rommel's forces had captured Bardia and were encircling Tobruk.

[1] Under his 'Red Sea Order' of 10 April 1941, Roosevelt, in a proclamation issued in Washington, rescinded an earlier Order making the Red Sea a combat zone. The new Order thus ended the prohibition on American merchant ships entering the Red Sea. American merchant ships could therefore take supplies through the Indian Ocean and the Red Sea to the Suez Canal, for use by the British in Egypt and North Africa. American aircraft were also permitted to use a Red Sea flight path to Egypt.

[2] Paragraph 2 dealt with the utilization of United States aircraft and naval vessels in the extended security zone, 'working from Greenland Newfoundland, Nova Scotia, the United States, Bermuda and the West Indies, with possible later extension to Brazil if this can be arranged'. Paragraph 3 dealt with refuelling at sea 'wherever advisable', and with the declaration that the Red Sea area was 'no longer a combat zone'.

War Cabinet, Defence Committee (Operations): minutes
(*Cabinet papers, 69/2*)

13 April 1941 Chequers
11.15 a.m.

MOVEMENTS OF THE GREEK ARMY

The Prime Minister suggested that a telegram should be sent to Sir Michael Palairet for communication to General Wilson, instructing him to impress upon General Papagos in the strongest possible terms the necessity for closing the gap between the Greek Western Army and the British Expeditionary Force.

It was agreed that the Prime Minister should telegraph accordingly.

The Prime Minister expressed the view that 'I' tanks[1] would be extremely useful in the Middle East for such duties as guarding aerodromes, attacking enemy aerodromes, defeating the attacks of lighter tanks on such places as Tobruk, and for guarding the Delta. Both infantry and cruiser tanks were now coming out in considerable quantities, and the number of the former that we were despatching to the Middle East would be more than replaced in a very short time. So far as invasion was concerned, the risk of this detachment seemed infinitely less than it had been when the decision was taken to send the 7th Armoured Division to the Middle East. Apart from anything else, we were now immeasurably stronger in the air. Accordingly, the Prime Minister directed that the order for the despatch of the four tank battalions in the next convoy should standt.

THE GERMAN ADVANCE ON EGYPT

The Prime Minister referred to the gravity of the situation that had developed in Cyrenaica. The enemy's armoured forces were advancing on Egypt without meeting any serious resistance, but they had little or nothing behind them at present. If, however, immediate and drastic steps were not taken to cut the communications between Italy and Tripoli and to block the port of Tripoli itself, the enemy's strength would progressively increase, and we should find ourselves driven out of Egypt altogether. It was true that even if the Canal were lost, the Mediterranean Fleet, together with such merchant shipping as happened to be in the Mediterranean at the time, would undoubtedly fight its way out westwards, but we should lose our whole army of about half a million men and all their equipment. This would not mean

[1] 'I' Tanks: Infantry tanks designed to provide close support for infantry during an advance. The Infantry Tank Mark II, the Matilda, was slow but heavily armoured. It had given a good account of itself in the battle for France in 1940, and in the early campaigns in North Africa, but was withdrawn in 1942 after proving vulnerable to the latest German anti-tank weapons. It had a speed of fifteen miles an hour, carried a crew of four, and was armed with a two-pounder gun and a machine gun. Nearly 3,000 were produced.

losing the war, but it was unthinkable that we should suffer a disaster of such magnitude without making a supreme effort to avert it.

Turning to the suggestion that the *Rodney* and *Nelson* should be sent to Sir Andrew Cunningham, the First Sea Lord said that these ships were unsuitable for work in the Mediterranean. He thought the better plan would be to let Sir Andrew Cunningham do the bombardment of Tripoli with the ships already at his disposal, together with the *Queen Elizabeth* which would be sent to him round the Cape. Continuing, he said that the loss of one or two capital ships would be a very serious matter at the present time, when the attitude of Japan was in the balance.

The Prime Minister said that he had no fear of Japan coming in against us at the moment. In any event, she was far more likely to do so if the Germans were to overrun Egypt and kill or capture the whole of our vast army there.

Continuing, he said that we ought to combine action against the enemy's sea communications with amphibious operations against his land communications. The Commandos were available in the Middle East, as were the Glen ship and special landing craft, and we ought to be able to put forces ashore at places such as Sirte and El Misurata, and interrupt the enemy's communications at these points. There was no reason to suppose that we should necessarily lose the Glen ships and landing craft in these operations: but even if this were to happen, the price would be well worth paying, if the result was an appreciable delay in the enemy's advance.

Winston S. Churchill: broadcast[1]
(*BBC Written Archives Centre*)

13 April 1941

To the people of Yugoslavia, to the Serbs, the Croats, and the Slovenes, I send my greetings. You have been wantonly attacked by a ruthless and barbarous aggressor. Your capital has been bombed, your women and children brutally murdered. Our cities in England, too, have been bombed by the same insensate foe. Our women and children have been murdered. Our sympathy for you therefore is heartfelt, for we are sharing the same sufferings. But as we have faith in our victory, so we have faith in yours. Do not regret the staunch courage which has brought on you this furious onslaught. Your courage will shine out in the pages of history and will, too, reap a more immediate reward. Whatever you may lose in the present, you have saved the future.

You are making an heroic resistance against formidable odds, and in doing

[1] This broadcast was relayed to Yugoslavia in Serbo-Croat.

so you are proving true to your great traditions. Serbs, we know you. You were our allies in the last War, and your arms are covered with glory. Croats and Slovenes, we know your military history. For centuries you were the bulwark of Christianity. Your fame as warriors spread far and wide on the Continent. One of the finest incidents in the history of Croatia is the one when, in the sixteenth century, long before the French Revolution, the peasants rose to defend the rights of man, and fought for those principles which centuries later gave the world democracy.

Yugoslavs, you are fighting for those principles today. The British Empire is fighting with you, and behind us is the great democracy of the United States, with its vast and ever-increasing resources. However hard the fight, our victory is assured.

Winston S. Churchill to Ronald Campbell[1]
(*Churchill papers, 20/37*)

13 April 1941
Most Immediate
Secret
sent 9.15 p.m.

It will not be possible at any time to send British surface warships, or British or American merchant ships, or transports up the Adriatic north of Valona. The reason for this is the Air, which did not exist effectively in the last war. The ships would only be sunk and that would help no one. All the aircraft we can allot to the Yugoslav theatre is already at the service of the Yugoslav General Staff, through Air Marshal D'Albiac.[2] There are no more at present. You must remember Yugoslavs have given us no chance to help them and refused to make a common plan, but there is no use in recriminations and you must use your own judgment how much of this bad news you impart to them.

2. We do not see why the King or Government should leave the country, which is vast, mountainous and full of armed men. German tanks can no doubt move along the roads and tracks, but to conquer the Serbian armies they must bring up infantry. Then will be the chance to kill them. Surely, the young King and the Ministers should play their part in this. However, if at any time the King and a few personal attendants are forced to leave the country

[1] Ronald Campbell was then with the retreating Serbian forces at Vrnjaska Banja.
[2] John Henry D'Albiac, 1894–1963. On active service, 1914–18 (France). Distinguished Service Order, 1916. Entered Royal Air Force, 1918. Air Officer Commanding, Palestine, 1939; Greece, 1940; Iraq, 1941; Ceylon 1942; Tactical Air Force, 1943–44. Deputy Commander, Mediterranean Allied Tactical Air Force, 1944. Director-General of Personnel, Air Ministry, 1945–46. Knighted, 1946. Retired, 1946. Commandant, London Airport, 1947–57.

and no aeroplanes can be provided, a British submarine could be sent to Cattaro (Kotor) or some other neighbouring place.

3. Apart from the successful defence of mountain regions, the only way in which any portion of the Serbian army can get in touch with our supplies by land is through establishing contact with Greeks in Albania and Monastir. They could then share in the defence of Greece and in the common pool of supplies, and if all fails every effort will be made to evacuate as many fighting men as possible to islands or to Egypt.

4. You should continue to do your utmost to uphold the fighting spirit of the Yugoslav Government and army, reminding them how the war in Serbia ebbed and flowed back and forth last time.

Winston S. Churchill to General Wilson[1]
(*Cabinet papers, 69/2*)

13 April 1941
sent 7.30 p.m.

Glad to see movement of 20th Greek and Cavalry Division to close the gap between the Greek Western Army and your army. It is glaringly obvious that a German advance southwards through this gap will not only turn your Aliakmon position, but far more decisively round up the whole of the Greek army in Albania. It is impossible for me to understand why the Greek Western Army does not make sure of its retreat into Greece. Chief of the Imperial General Staff states that these points have been put vainly time after time. All good wishes to you in this memorable hour.

2. Also glad to hear that King is not leaving Greece at present. He has a great opportunity of leaving a name in history. If, however, he or any part of the Greek army are forced to leave Greece, every facility will be afforded them in Cyprus, and we will do our best to carry them there. The garrisoning of Crete by a strong Greek force would also be highly beneficial, observing that Crete can be fed by sea.

1 General Wilson was then at Athens.

Winston S. Churchill to A.V. Alexander and Admiral Pound
(*Churchill papers, 20/36*)

14 April 1941
Action this Day

GERMAN CONVOY REACHES NORTH AFRICA

This is a serious Naval failure. Another deadly convoy has got through. We have a right to ask why did not the Navy stop them. It is the duty of the Navy to stop them.

Winston S. Churchill to Alfred Duff Cooper
(*Churchill papers, 20/36*)

14 April 1941

SHIPPING LOSSES TO BE PUBLISHED MONTHLY INSTEAD OF WEEKLY

There is no good making heavy weather about this. The publication of the weekly sinkings is to be discontinued henceforward, i.e., no more, no publication next Tuesday. When the Press ask why have the week's figures not come out, the answer will be they are to be published monthly instead of weekly. When the comment is made that we are afraid to publish weekly because, as you say, we 'desire to cover up the size of our most recent shipping losses,' the answer should be: 'Well, that is what we are going to do anyway.' Friends and enemies will no doubt put on their own interpretation. But only the facts will decide. We shall have a lot of worse things than that to put up with in the near future.

I will answer any question on the subject myself in the House.

Winston S. Churchill to General Wavell
(*Cabinet papers, 69/2*)

14 April 1941

Your 0/56699 on Tobruk action early morning 14th April. Convey heartiest congratulations from War Cabinet to all engaged in most successful fight. Bravo Tobruk. We feel it vital that Tobruk should be regarded as sally-port and not please as excrescence. Can you not find good troops who are without transport to help hold perimeter, thus freeing at least one, if not two, Australian Brigade Groups to act as General Fortress Reserve and potential striking force.

Winston S. Churchill to the Dominion Prime Ministers[1]
(*Churchill papers, 20/49*)

14 April 1941

1. I am sure you are anxious to know how we view present situation in the Middle East, and the following will supplement my remarks in the House of Commons on Wednesday.

2. Of the two main attacks, that in Cyrenaica appears secondary to that in the Balkans, but the former has achieved unexpected success, and reports indicate that the Germans are moving more land forces to exploit it, but are at present unable to spare additional air forces. Should they be able to do so we may be faced later with the threat of the development of a large-scale attack on Egypt. The deciding factors here are our power to hamper or cut his communications from Italy and Sicily to Tripoli, the speed with which we can reinforce with tanks, anti-tank guns and aircraft, and the enemy's ability to maintain his forces. This will be no easy task for him, as Benghazi will be unusable for some time, and his road L of C[1] will be a long one. The Germans are also making trouble for us in Iraq and are attempting to do so in Syria. They do not appear to intend to attack Turkey at present.

3. As ever, our vital strategic requirement in the Middle East remains the security of our main base of operations in Egypt, and so we are faced with the problem as to how far we can maintain our forces in Greece and at the same time safeguard the security of Egypt.

4. However the present situation may have developed, we still consider the decision we made in sending our forces to Greece strategically correct. The situation in the Balkans is so fluid that it is not possible at present to give a considered appreciation, but even with the rapid German advance into Yugoslavia, the picture is better than that which seemed possible before the Yugoslavian *coup d'état*. There can, therefore, be no question of withdrawing those forces now, quite apart from what we have said and undertaken *vis-à-vis* Greece and Yugoslavia. As long as our forces continue to operate in Greece, they compel the enemy to fight, contain his forces and prevent him re-establishing normal economic conditions in the Balkans.

5. At the same time, as all other available forces are required for the defence of the Egyptian frontier, we have decided we must hold up for the present the despatch of the second Australian division to Greece, and limit our commitments in Greece to maintaining the forces which have already arrived there.

(To The Prime Minister of New Zealand only.)

[1] The Prime Ministers of Canada, Newfoundland, Australia and New Zealand.
[2] Lines of Communication.

This means that 'Lustre'[1] will be short by one division and the Polish brigade of the strength that we put before you when you generously agreed to the inclusion of the New Zealand division in that force, but I am sure you will appreciate the over-riding factors which have since intervened.

(To all.)

6. We have taken various steps which will accelerate considerably the arrival in the Middle East of additional aircraft, tanks, anti-tank guns and other reinforcements. These measures include reinforcements for our air forces in Egypt by squadrons withdrawn from Aden and East Africa, and of our fleet in the Eastern Mediterranean by destroyers from the Red Sea. Our aim will be to re-establish ourselves in Cyrenaica at the first opportunity. In the meantime, we propose to act strongly against the enemy's lines of communication in Tripoli and from Tripoli forward.

Winston S. Churchill to Arthur William Fadden

(*Churchill papers, 20/37*)

14 April 1941

We should all be grateful here if Menzies' stay could be prolonged to cover immediate crisis in Balkans and Libya. It is a great advantage to have him with us in War Cabinet and Defence Committee while your troops are so much to the fore. I have therefore urged him to put off his departure for at least another fortnight.

I cannot tell how things will go in Greece, but feel hopeful German thrust through Libya will be broken. Tobruk is all-important as our offensive sally-port, observing that we have command of the sea and at least equality in the air.

You will be glad to hear that German penetration of Tobruk early this morning was repulsed with loss of 6 tanks out of 20 and between 200 and 300 German prisoners captured. These prisoners stated that they were short of food and water, were much shaken by Australian artillery and wept at repulse of their comrades. Dive-bombing attacks at dawn by 50 Ju 87s did no damage and we clawed 12 down.

The movements of United States towards us are increasingly favourable. We are doing all we can. All good wishes to you and your colleagues.

[1] The Allied Forces in Greece.

War Cabinet: minutes
(*Cabinet papers, 65/18*)

14 April 1941
5 p.m.

10 Downing Street

MERCHANT SHIPPING

The Prime Minister said that it was for serious consideration whether the Admiralty should not release a considerable number of the vessels now employed as Armed Merchant Cruisers, and which would be very valuable for our import programme.

RISK OF WEDGE BETWEEN GREEK AND ALBANIAN ARMIES

The War Cabinet were reminded of the constant efforts which had been made to induce the Greeks to bring back part of their main Army from Albania, or to withdraw the right flank of their main forces, so as to avoid this very danger.

The Prime Minister said that we should be in no way responsible for the consequences, seeing that we had continuously pressed upon the Greeks that it was necessary to take steps to meet this danger.

EGYPT

The Prime Minister said that in his view things in Egypt were serious but not desperate. There was no cause for the alarm such as had already shown itself in certain elements in the United States. The enemy were using a line of communication several hundreds of miles long to maintain a small but highly mechanized force. Provided we could cut the German column from its bases, it was within our power to turn defeat into victory.

Continuing, the Prime Minister said that it was absolutely vital that steps should be taken to cut the enemy's communications from Italy and Sicily with Tripoli. Unless these communications were cut, the enemy could bring superior armed forces to bear against us, with most serious consequences. The stakes were high, and the Navy must be prepared to suffer heavy losses in order to cut the enemy line of communication.

War Cabinet, Defence Committee (Operations): minutes
(*Cabinet papers, 69/2*)

14 April 1941
9.45 p.m.

Cabinet War Room

LIBYA

The Prime Minister handed round copies of the directive on the war in the Mediterranean which he had read out to the War Cabinet that evening. He suggested that this directive, accompanied by any observations which the Chiefs of Staff might consider desirable, should be telegraphed to the Commanders-in-Chief, Mediterranean and Middle East for their guidance.

Continuing, he said that it was essential that Tobruk should be held not just with the idea of denying the port to the enemy, but as an active threat to his farther advance. If, say, 5,000 more men could be introduced into the fortress to hold the pill-boxes, and thus free troops to form a reserve, and possibly to carry out sorties, the enemy would be forced to lay siege to the place, and this would hamper all their operations.

THE ISSUE OF COMMUNIQUES

The Prime Minister said that he was quite prepared to agree to the ordinary day-to-day communiqués being issued by the Commanders-in-Chief on the spot, provided that they would refer home before issuing statements on serious or exceptional matters, about which it was important to give the public correct guidance.

Winston S. Churchill: Directive
(*Cabinet papers, 120/10*)

14 April 1941

THE WAR IN THE MEDITERRANEAN

If the Germans can continue to nourish their invasion of Cyrenaica and Egypt through the port of Tripoli and along the coastal road, they can certainly bring superior armoured forces to bear upon us with consequences of the most serious character. If, on the other hand, their communications from Italy and Sicily with Tripoli are cut, and those along the coastal road between Tripoli and Agheila constantly harassed, there is no reason why they should not themselves sustain a major defeat.

2. It becomes the prime duty of the British Mediterranean Fleet under Admiral Cunningham to stop all sea-borne traffic between Italy and Africa by the fullest use of surface craft, aided so far as possible by aircraft and submarines. For this all-important objective, heavy losses in battleships, cruisers and destroyers, must if necessary be accepted. The harbour at Tripoli must be rendered unusable by recurrent bombardment, and/or by blocking and mining, care being taken that the mining does not impede the blocking or bombardments. Enemy convoys passing to and from Africa must be attacked by our cruisers, destroyers and submarines, aided by the Fleet Air Arm and the Royal Air Force. Every convoy which gets through must be considered a serious naval failure. The reputation of the Royal Navy is engaged in stopping this traffic.

3. Admiral Cunningham's Fleet must be strengthened for the above purposes to whatever extent is necessary. The *Nelson* and *Rodney*, with their heavily-armoured decks, are especially suitable for resisting attacks from the German dive-bombers, of which undue fears must not be entertained. Other reinforcements of cruisers, minelayers and destroyers must be sent from the west as opportunity serves. The use of the *Centurion* as a blockship should be studied, but the effectual blocking of Tripoli harbour would be well worth a battleship upon the active list.

4. When Admiral Cunningham's Fleet has been reinforced, he should be able to form two bombarding squadrons, which may in turn at intervals bombard the port of Tripoli, especially when shipping or convoys are known to be in the harbour.[1]

5. In order to control the sea communications across the Mediterranean, sufficient suitable naval forces must be based on Malta, and protection must be afforded to these naval forces by the Air Force at Malta, which must be kept at the highest strength in Fighters of the latest and best quality that the Malta Aerodromes can contain. The duty of affording Fighter protection to the naval forces holding Malta should have priority over the use of the Aerodromes by Bombers engaged in attacking Tripoli.

6. Every endeavour should be made to defend Malta harbour by the UP weapon in its various developments, especially by the LAM fired by the improved naval method.

7. Next in importance after the port at Tripoli comes the 400-mile coastal road between Tripoli and Agheila. This road should be subjected to continuous harassing attacks by forces landed from the Glen ships in the special landing craft. The Commandos and other forces gathered in Egypt should be freely used for this purpose. The seizure of particular points from the sea should be studied, and the best ones chosen for prompt action. Here, again, losses must be faced, but small forces may be used in this harassing warfare, being withdrawn, if possible, after a while. If even a few light or medium Tanks could be landed, these could rip along the road, destroying very quickly convoys far exceeding their own value. Every feasible method of harassing constantly this section of the route is to be attempted, the necessary losses being faced.

8. In all the above paragraphs, the urgency is extreme, because the enemy will grow continually stronger in the Air than he is now, and especially should

[1] British naval forces bombarded Tripoli at dawn on 21 April 1941. The British force, Churchill told the House of Commons on 22 April 1941, 'was not seriously molested and suffered no loss in ships'. (*Hansard*, 22 April 1941). On 22 April 1941 Admiral Cunningham informed the Admiralty that he did not wish to repeat the attack as he doubted if he could achieve surprise again, and that in carrying out the attack the Fleet had already run 'unjustifiable risks'. (Signal 118, 'Hush Most Secret', 2.36 p.m., 22 April 1941: *Churchill papers, 4/351B*)

his attack on Greece and Yugoslavia be successful, as may be apprehended. Admiral Cunningham should not, therefore, await the arrival of battleship reinforcements, nor should the use of the Glen ships be withheld for the sake of 'Mandibles'.

9. It has been decided that Tobruk is to be defended with all possible strength. But Tobruk must not be regarded as a defensive operation, but rather as an invaluable bridgehead or sally-port on the communications of the enemy. It should be reinforced as may be necessary both with infantry and by armoured fighting vehicles, to enable active and continuous raiding of the enemy's flanks and rear. If part of the defences of the perimeter can be taken over by troops improvised with transport, this should permit the organization of a mobile force both for the future reserve and for striking at the enemy. It would be a great advantage should the enemy be drawn into anything like a siege of Tobruk and compelled to transport and feed the heavy artillery forces for that purpose.

10. It is above all necessary that General Wavell should regain Unit ascendancy over the enemy and destroy his small raiding parties, instead of our being harassed and hunted by them. Enemy patrols must be attacked on every occasion, and our own patrols should be used with audacity. Small British parties in armoured cars, or mounted on motorcycles, or, if occasion offers, infantry, should not hesitate to attack individual tanks with bombs and bombards as is planned for the defence of Britain. It is important to engage the enemy even in small affairs in order to make him fire off his gun ammunition, of which the supply must be very difficult.

11. The use of the Royal Air Force against the enemy's communications, or concentrations of fighting vehicles, is sufficiently obvious not to require mention.

Winston S. Churchill to Sir Archibald Sinclair

(*Churchill papers, 20/36*)

15 April 1941

I remain far from satisfied with the state of our preparations for offensive chemical warfare, should this be forced upon us by the actions of the enemy.

I have before me a Report on this matter by the Inter-Service Committee on Chemical Warfare (COS (41) 143), together with a commentary thereon by the Ministry of Supply (COS (41) 200). From these two documents the following special points emerge:

1. The deficiency of gas shell is still serious. Although the production of 6-inch and 5.5-inch gas shell was due to start in February, none has yet been produced. I understand that the shortage of 25-pdr gas-filled shell is due to the lack of empty shell cases.

2. The production of 30-lb. LC bomb, Mark I,[1] will not keep pace with the production of the 5-in UP weapon, the new mobile projector for use with the Army. Indeed, supplies will be insufficient even for training purposes.

3. The production of phosgene gas is inadequate. The output from the plant is now about 65 per cent of capacity, having previously been only 50 per cent, over a period of some months.

I propose to examine the whole position at an early meeting of the Defence Committee (Supply).

In order that this examination may be as complete as possible, I shall be glad to receive from the Minister of Aircraft Production and the Minister of Supply, for circulation in advance of the meeting, brief comprehensive statements of the position so far as each is concerned, showing in respect of each of the main gas weapons and components (including gases):

1. Total requirements notified to them, with dates.
2. Stocks of components in the custody of each on the 1st April.
3. Supplies delivered by 1st April to RAF or Army authorities.
4. Estimated output during each of the next six months.

I shall be glad if these statements can be submitted within a week. They should be addressed to Sir Edward Bridges.

I am addressing similar minutes to the Secretary of State for War, the Minister of Supply, and the Minister of Aircraft Production.

Winston S. Churchill to Air Marshal Longmore

(*Churchill papers, 20/37*)

15 April 1941

All your vigorous reactions give us here greatest pleasure. Have feeling the enemy in Libya hard pressed after bold effort. Now is the time to strike. Compliment squadrons in Tobruk for clawing down dive-bombers. We are crowding everything we can out to you and stream is now beginning to flow. Whereas you have received only 370 from November till now, 528 more are on the way, and a further 880 will start before end of May.

[1] A Light Case (thin casing) bomb. Its fuse blew off the back, so that the contents could escape. During the Phoney War (September 1939 to April 1940) it had been used for leaflet dropping over Germany. It could also be used for gas.

Winston S. Churchill to Anthony Eden
(*Churchill papers, 20/36*)

15 April 1941
Secret

I presume that all possible precautions are taken to prevent King Farouk levanting in his aeroplanes. Please let me know what has been done about this.

Winston S. Churchill to General Sir John Dill
(*Churchill Papers, 20/36*)

15 April 1941

TANKS IN THE HANDS OF TROOPS IN THE UNITED KINGDOM

By this return, which I study every week, you will see that you have 1,169 heavy Tanks in this country in the hands of troops. The monthly production of over 200 is going to increase in the near future. If the training of the men has not kept pace with the already much-retarded deliveries of the Tanks, that is the responsibility of the War Office. I do not wonder that difficulties are encountered in training when 238 cruiser Tanks are given to one armoured division, and only 38 to another. Perhaps if the 11th Armoured Division had a few more I Tanks it would come along quicker.

Personally, I am not convinced that it is right to make each division entirely homogeneous. A judicious mixture of weapons, albeit of varied speeds, should be possible in the division. Moreover, some of these armoured vehicles ought to carry field artillery, and even one or two large guns or mortars. Let me have a report on what the Germans do.

Winston S. Churchill to Anthony Eden
(*Churchill papers, 20/36*)

15 April 1941

INTERCEPTION OF FRENCH SHIPS

I should be much obliged if you would convene a meeting of the Admiralty and MEW,[1] and formulate some clarifying proposals. Evidently the subject divides itself into two parts. First, the policy and principles we follow. Are we to take French ships because we lack tonnage? Are we to send all French ships in for contraband examination, or search them ourselves on the high seas? Are we to let food ships go freely provided they submit themselves to examination? There are other variants of the problem which arise.

[1] Ministry of Economic Warfare.

The second part is the enforcement of our policy. Here it is evident that our resources may not enable us to carry into full effect the principles we adopt. The Admiralty have not the strength to maintain a strict, continuous blockade. We must do the best we can as occasion serves. It would be a great help if the principles could be defined.

Winston S. Churchill to Sir Samuel Hoare
(*Churchill papers, 20/37*)

15 April 1941

As regards Portuguese conversations, Colonel Rodrigues[1] is fully in Salazar's[2] confidence and made a good impression here. We went some way to meet Portuguese requirements in material, considering all the other channels, e.g., Greek, Yugoslav, Turkish. But we could not definitely commit ourselves to putting a force on mainland. Problem of the islands has been further considered and we intend to concert defence measures with Portuguese, if they will play.

I shall await your recommendations, on improving liaison with the Portuguese, after Torr's[3] visit to Gibraltar.

Winston S. Churchill to Colonel Jacob
(*Churchill papers, 20/36*)

16 April 1941

Let me have on one sheet of paper lists showing at present time and in September last the strength of British Home Forces in (A) Rifles and SAA.[4] (B) Artillery – including all types of field and medium guns under one head, and also coast-defence batteries, and also AA, both heavy and light. (C) Number of I Tanks and cruiser tanks in the hands of the troops. (D) Ration and rifle

[1] José Filipe de Barros Rodriques, born 1890. An artillery commander with the Portuguese Expeditionary Force on the Western Front, 1915–18. Head of the Portuguese Army Cartographic Services, 1936–43. Chief of the Portuguese General Staff Observer Military Mission, Spain, 1937–38. In charge of Politico-military negotiations with Britain, 1941. General, 1943. Permanent Inspector, Cartographic Services of the Army, 1945–55. Head of the Mission inaugurating Portugal's entry into NATO, 1949.

[2] Antonio de Oliveira Salazar, 1889–1970. Portuguese Minister of Finance, 1928–32. Prime Minister, and dictator, of Portugal, 1932–68. Served as his own Foreign Minister, 1936–47 and his own War Minister, 1936–44. Incapacitated by a stroke, 1968.

[3] William Wyndham Terre Torr, 1890–1963. Entered the Army, 1910. Adjutant, Albanian Gendarmerie, Scutari, 1913. On active service in France, 1915–18 (despatches four times, Military Cross, Distinguished Service Order). Member of the Thoroughbred Breeders Association; Master of the Staff College Hunt, 1921–22. Military Attaché, Madrid and Lisbon, 1925–28; Washington and Central American Republics, 1934–38; Colonel, 1935. Military Attaché, Spain, 1939–46.

[4] Small Arms Ammunition.

strength of the fighting formations. (E) Number of Divisions and Brigade groups (a) on the beaches, (b) behind the beaches in Army or GHQ Reserve or otherwise. (F) Strength of fighter aircraft available for action at the two dates. (G) Strength and weight of discharge of bomber aircraft at the two dates. (H) Strength of the flotillas in Home Waters at the two dates. Very general and round figures will do. Don't go too much into details.

Winston S. Churchill to Anthony Eden

(*Churchill papers, 20/36*)

16 April 1941

PLACE FOR YUGOSLAV GOVERNMENT AND KING TO ESTABLISH THEMSELVES

The Colonial Secretary demurs to Cyprus on the same grounds as concerned the Greeks. He points out there is practically no AA protection there. He suggests Palestine, which is safe and handy to Egypt, and where the assembly of Yugoslav Military refugees would be valuable from the point of view of local order.

Winston S. Churchill to Anthony Eden

(*Churchill papers, 23/9*)

16 April 1941

I set special importance on the delivery of this personal message from me to Stalin.[1] I cannot understand why it should be resisted. The Ambassador is not alive to the military significance of the facts. Pray oblige me.

Winston S. Churchill to President Franklin D. Roosevelt

(*Churchill papers, 20/37*)

16 April 1941
Most Secret

1. I had intended to cable you more fully on your momentous message about the Atlantic. Admiralty received the news with the greatest relief and satisfaction and have prepared a technical paper. They wonder whether, since

[1] This was the message sent through Sir Stafford Cripps on April 3. Not knowing that Churchill's source was the German Air Force's own most secret radio communications, decrypted at Bletchley, Cripps feared that the message was an attempt to alarm Stalin unduly, and to cast unsubstantiated suspicions on the neutrality provisions of the Nazi-Soviet Pact.

Admiral Ghormley[1] arrives here in about two days, it would be better to discuss this with him before despatch. I do not know whether he is apprised or not. The matter is certainly of highest urgency and consequence. There are about fifteen U-boats now operating on the 30th Meridian and, of course, United States Flying-boats working from Greenland would be a most useful immediate measure.

2. I cannot tell what will happen in Greece, and we have never under-rated the enormous power of the German military machine on the mainland of Europe. We are not able to send ships to Cattaro to bring away Yugoslav refugees, because of even more clamant commitments and of the Air and Naval strength of the enemy in the Adriatic.

3. I am personally not unduly anxious about the Libyan-Egyptian position. We estimate Germans have one Colonial Armoured Division and perhaps the whole of one ordinary Armoured Division, comprising, say, 600 to 650 tanks, of which a good many have already been destroyed or have broken down. There are no German Infantry yet in Cyrenaica except the few battalions comprised in the German Armoured Divisions. Difficulties of supply of petrol, food, water and ammunition must be severe, and we know from prisoners of the strain under which these audacious formations are working. We are naturally trying to bring our own Armoured forces, which were largely refitting at the time of the attack, into action and are reinforcing Egypt from all parts of the Middle East, where we have nearly half a million men. Tobruk I regard as an invaluable bridge-head or sally-port. We do not feel at all out-matched at present in the Air and are growing stronger constantly. The whole power of the Mediterranean Fleet, which is being strongly reinforced, will be used to cut the sea and coastal communications. There are, of course, Italian forces besides the Germans, and we believe the Germans are now sending, or trying to send, a third Armoured Division from Sicily.

4. The repulse of the German attacks on Tobruk on the 14th/15th seems to me important, as this small, fierce fight, in which the enemy lost prisoners, killed and tanks, together with aircraft, out of all proportion to our losses, is the first time they have tasted defeat and they are working on very small margins. Meanwhile, our efforts to turn off the tap have met with a noteworthy success in the Central Mediterranean. Four destroyers from Malta in the early hours of this morning, 16th, caught a German-Italian convoy of five large ships loaded with ammunition and mechanical transport

[1] Robert Lee Ghormley, 1883–1958. Graduated from the United States Naval Academy, 1906. On active service, Atlantic, 1916–18. Commanded the battleship *Nevada*, 1935. Rear-Admiral, 1938. Director of War Plans, Navy Department, 1938. Assistant Chief of Naval Operations, 1939. Special Naval Observer, London, England, 1940-41. Vice-Admiral, 1941. Commander, South Pacific Forces and South Pacific Area, 1942. Commander, Hawaiian Sea Frontier, 1943–44. Commander, United States Naval Forces in Germany, 1944–45. Chairman, General Board, Navy Department, Washington, 1946.

and escorted by three Italian destroyers. The whole convoy and all its escort were sunk. We lost one destroyer in the fight.[1] We are keeping the strength of our forces secret for the present.

War Cabinet, Battle of the Atlantic Committee: minutes
(*Cabinet papers, 86/1*)

16 April 1941 10 Downing Street
5 p.m.

TURN-ROUND SHIPPING

The Prime Minister said that he had been supplied with figures which showed a considerable improvement in the rate of discharge of bulk cargoes in February as compared with January, 1941. The Minister of Supply said that a representative of Mr Harriman, who had been visiting the ports, had reported a considerable improvement in recent weeks.

The Prime Minister drew attention to the savings that could be secured on the round voyage of liners if –

(a) the time occupied by loading in this country were cut out, exports being sacrificed; and
(b) liners were to sail as soon as they were ready instead of waiting for fixed sailing dates.

PETROL IMPORTS

The Prime Minister emphasized the need for a considerable economy in the use of petrol, by the public as well as by the Services.

Winston S. Churchill to Admiral Sir Andrew Cunningham
(*Churchill papers, 20/37*)

16 April 1941
Personal and Most Secret

I was very pleased to read your report of today showing the excellent work done by your light forces along the Libyan coast, in preventing any serious

[1] The destroyer that was sunk was the *Mohawk*. The German and Italian supply ships were carrying units of the 15 Panzer Division to North Africa. The engagement constituted the first significant victory for the German Air Force Enigma decrypts in the Mediterranean shipping war, and took the cutting edge off the knife of danger on which Churchill's directive had focused. Henceforth, and with increasing impact, German and Italian high grade decrypts were to contribute significantly to the sinking of Axis supply ships. (F.H. Hinsley and others, *British Intelligence in the Second World War, Its Influence on Strategy and Operations*, Volume l, London, 1979, pages 394 and 400). This Enigma success, one of the official historians, Edward Thomas, has written, 'set the pattern for a most important development', the setting up of 'Force K'. As Thomas noted, Churchill had 'immediately grasped the significance' of this Enigma success (Edward Thomas, notes for the author, 3 December 1982).

landing of stores east of Benghazi and the magnificent success of the division of destroyers under Captain D 14, of which we have just heard. This is certainly one of the keys to victory. It is very difficult to see how a force of any size can be kept in ammunition, apart from other essentials, if it is dependent upon the long road from Tripoli, and at the same time is actively engaged by our land and air forces.

2. I am, however, a little concerned at your 2355 of 13th instant, about what is to happen to the French ships if a heavy scale of bombing attack is developed against Alexandria. Even if you thought it desirable to withdraw some of your ships to Port Said or Haifa, you would no doubt leave others to operate from Alexandria, and the French ships would have to take their chance with these. Indeed, they would help to dilute the risk.

3. If the worst happened, the only alternatives which should be offered to the French would be to join us or for their ships to be rendered permanently unserviceable under our supervision. There could be no question of allowing them to stay in Alexandria after we had left or to go to French or African ports or pass through the Canal and escape into the Indian Ocean. The United States would never forgive us if we allowed such a disturbance of the Naval balance of power. In no circumstances could these ships be allowed to fall into German hands or get loose in the world, where they might be used against us by a French Government entirely under German control. I hope and believe, however, that none of these unpleasant questions will arise.

4. It is necessary now for you, among your many other cares, to prepare plans for bringing off from Greece the maximum British and Imperial personnel and also as many Greeks as possible in the event of a collapse there. The more Greeks who can arrive in Crete and the more British and Imperial troops who can get back to Egypt the better. Here again, however, one hopes that a good battle has yet to be fought.

5. Chiefs of Staff concur.

War Cabinet, Defence Committee (Operations): minutes
(*Cabinet papers, 69/2*)

16 April 1941
9.45 p.m.
Secret

THE MIDDLE EAST AND GREECE: THE AIR SITUATION

The Prime Minister drew attention to Telegram No. ML 491 of the 16th April from the Air Officer Commanding-in-Chief, Middle East,[1] in which it was said that two fighter squadrons were being withdrawn from Greece to Crete. He thought it would be necessary to consider whether in the critical

[1] Air Marshal Sir Arthur Longmore.

battles which might now be taking place we could possibly allow the army to fight without air support.

Sir Charles Portal said that it had been hoped to get 8 fighter squadrons to Greece, but for various reasons only 3 were there. This was not a sufficient number to provide adequate cover to their own aerodromes in addition to taking part in the battle. They were operating from advanced landing grounds without full repair facilities and thus they could not deal with the damage done to the aircraft by low-flying attacks. The strength of the squadrons was reduced to about a third. He was convinced that it would be better to get such aircraft as they could away to Crete where they would be able to give some cover to an evacuation rather than to remain where they were and lose them all on the ground. It would in any case be too late to countermand the orders issued by the Air Officer Commanding-in-Chief.

The Prime Minister said that this might very well be the right thing to do but it was most important that all possible air support should be given particularly to the Australian and New Zealand troops. The next fortnight's fighting in the air in Libya would be most important. He would like to know what the probable rate of German reinforcement in Libya would be and how our own strength would increase.

Sir Charles Portal undertook to provide the Prime Minister with an estimate on these lines.

THE ATTITUDE OF THE PRESS

Sir Walter Monckton[1] said that the Press appeared more immediately concerned with the situation in Greece than with that in Egypt, and he was being asked whether we were evacuating the country or whether our troops were likely to be cut off.

The Prime Minister said that it should be explained to the Press that we were in a dilemma. If we said that everything was going well and then more or less without warning had to announce bad news, we were accused of concealing the truth; if, on the other hand we said the position was very serious and likely to deteriorate we should greatly discourage those taking part in the operations and particularly the Greeks. The Press might be told that there had been no alternative to our giving assistance to the Greeks, and that there had been every chance that we should, by our action, persuade the Yugoslavs and the Turks to fight. In this we had been partially successful. Emphasis should be laid on the heroic struggle of the Greeks and of the great

[1] Walter Turner Monckton, 1891–1965. Educated at Harrow and Balliol College, Oxford. President of the Oxford Union Society, 1913. On active service, 1915–19 (Military Cross). Called to the Bar, 1919. King's Counsel, 1930. Attorney-General to the Prince of Wales, 1932–6. Knighted, 1937. Director-General of the Press Censorship Bureau, 1939–40. Director-General, Ministry of Information, 1940–1; of British Propaganda and Information Services, Cairo, 1941–2. Solicitor-General, 1945. Conservative MP for Bristol West, 1951–7. Minister of Labour and National Service, 1951–5. Minister of Defence, 1955–6. Paymaster-General, 1956–7. Created Viscount, 1957.

sufferings they had endured for the cause. The note to strike about Egypt was subdued confidence. The enemy had superiority in armoured vehicles but his administrative difficulties were very great. The Press must not lose sight of the fact that the Battle of the Atlantic and the attitude of the United States of America were the decisive factors in the war.

Winston S. Churchill to General Wavell
(*Cabinet papers, 69/2*)

16 April 1941

We have no news from you of what has happened on Imperial Front in Greece.

2. We cannot remain in Greece against wish of Greek Commander-in-Chief and thus expose country to devastation. Wilson or Palairet should obtain endorsement by Greek Government of Papagos's request. Consequent upon this assent, evacuation should proceed, without, however, prejudicing any withdrawal to Thermopylae position[1] in co-operation with the Greek Army. In the meantime, all your proposed preparations for evacuation should proceed, and you will naturally try to save as much material as possible.

3. Crete must be held in force, and you should provide for this in the redistribution of your forces. It is important that strong elements of Greek army should establish themselves in Crete together with King and Government. We shall aid and maintain defence of Crete to the utmost.

On the night of 16–17 April 1941 there was a heavy air raid on London, with 450 German aircraft taking part. It was one of the heaviest raids of the war. During the raid, St Paul's Cathedral was damaged, and bombs fell on the Admiralty. In Greece, German troops continued their advance.

[1] The Thermopylae position, to which the Greeks and their Allies fell back after April 18, having being unable to hold the Aliakhmon line further north. The defence of Thermopylae by British, Australian and New Zealand units made possible the mass evacuation of Allied troops from ports to the south-west. On April 25 the troops holding Thermopylae themselves withdrew, to be evacuated.

Sir Alexander Cadogan: diary
(*'The Diaries of Sir Alexander Cadogan'*)

17 April 1941

Awful Blitz last night (450 machines). Couldn't sleep till all clear at 4.30. Fine morning and warm. Walked by devious way to FO. Area Piccadilly, St James' Street, Pall Mall, Lower Regent Street pretty well devastated. Cabinet 11.30. Admiralty hit. From his place at Cabinet table, Winston observed this gave him a better view of Nelson Column. Quite true. Papagos has asked us to evacuate and we agree to try. No one knows what happened. N. Africa looks a bit better. Winston says it's all right, referring to tenuity of enemy forces. But then how the hell did they get there?

War Cabinet: minutes
(*Cabinet papers, 65/22*)

17 April 1941 — 10 Downing Street
12 noon

The Prime Minister read to the War Cabinet a telegram received from General Wavell late on the previous night. This telegram repeated a message received from General Wilson. The latter had just had a conversation with General Papagos who said that the Greek Army was severely pressed, and agreed to withdraw to the Thermopylae position. General Papagos had also suggested to General Wilson that 'as things might become critical in future, he should re-embark British troops and save Greece devastation'. General Wavell asked for instructions on General Papagos's suggestion that we should embark our forces. In the meantime, arrangements to this end were being made.

The Prime Minister said that the clear implication of General Papagos's statement was that the Greeks might be unable to continue the struggle. We had always taken the view that we should not go to help the Greeks unless they wanted us to do so. If the Greeks now decided that they did not wish to continue the struggle on the mainland, we should fall in with their views. This view was reinforced by the fact that Air Vice-Marshal D'Albiac had reported that the aerodromes we occupied in Eastern Greece had been shot up and that he was withdrawing some of his squadrons to Crete.

The Prime Minister said that the Defence Committee which had been meeting the previous night when the telegram had been received, had decided to despatch a reply to the effect that if the Greek Government endorsed General Papagos's request, evacuation should proceed, without, however, prejudicing withdrawal from the Thermopylae position in co-operation with the Greek Army. In the meantime, preparations for evacuation should proceed. In this telegram, General Wavell had also been informed that Crete must be held in force, and that it was important that strong elements of the Greek Army should establish themselves in Crete, together with the King and Government.

The War Cabinet expressed their agreement with the line taken in this telegram.

Discussion followed as to the prospects of withdrawing our forces.

The Prime Minister said that we had 59,000 men in Greece. He was afraid that we should lose most of our artillery and tanks in Greece, but he hoped that the anti-tank guns could be taken off.

The Prime Minister read to the War Cabinet a telegram from the Commander-in-Chief, Middle East, giving particulars of the distribution of enemy forces in the forward area, i.e., between Tobruk and Sollum.

The Prime Minister thought that the situation in Libya was considerably better than it had appeared a week ago. There were, however, reports of a further German Armoured Division, which might be concentrated either in Tripoli or near Benghazi, waiting for supplies to move forward. Nevertheless, the German thrust seemed to be of manageable proportions, and there was a good chance that it might be liquidated.

The sinking of five enemy supply ships on the previous day had been most opportune, and reconnaissance reports by our Fleet, from the air, showed no enemy supply ships between Bardia and Sollum.

The Prime Minister said that he had asked General Wavell to telegraph home his communiqués before they were issued. This scheme, however, had not worked well, and he had now authorized General Wavell to issue factual communiqué s on his own responsibility, but to telegraph home for approval the text of any communiqués which gave general appraisements of the situation.

There would, no doubt, be criticism, both in Parliament and in the Press, of the failure of our military effort in the Balkans. But it was reasonable to assume that both Parliament and the public would behave worthily of the situation.

Winston S. Churchill to Air Chief Marshal Sir Charles Portal
(*Churchill papers, 20/36*)

17 April 1941
Action this Day

1. It must be recognized that the inability of the Bomber Command to hit the enemy cruisers in Brest constitutes a very definite failure of this arm. No serious low-level daylight attack has been attempted. The policy of the Air Ministry in neglecting the dive-bomber type of aircraft is shown by all

experience to have been a very grievous error, and one for which we are paying dearly both in lack of offensive power and by the fear of injury which is so prevalent afloat.

2. The German battle cruisers are two of the most important vessels in the war, as we have nothing that can both catch and kill them. I have never asked that you should try to fight weather at the same time as the enemy, but good weather may increasingly be expected. I do not think this target ought to be abandoned. On the contrary, efforts ought to be made to overcome the causes of failure. Let the following be examined with the Admiralty:

Take *Victorious* in her unworked-up condition and let her mount 20 Hurricane fighters on her upper deck. Would this degree of fighter protection suffice to enable a dawn attack to be made by daylight by, say, a dozen bombers with the best-aiming bomb-sight we have been able to develop? Let this be studied forthwith and a report made to me.

3. Naturally, I sympathize with the desire to attack Germany, to use the heaviest bombs and to give Berlin a severe dose; and I agree that the bulk of the Bomber Command should be used against German targets; but PRUs[1] should be taken every day of the battle cruisers and frequent attacks made upon them, by smaller numbers when weather is suitable or by larger forces when any movement is observable, during dark hours, apart altogether from the special daylight operations suggested above.[2]

Winston S. Churchill to General Wavell

(*Churchill papers, 20/37*)

17 April 1941

I like the look of your situation very much. Hope 7th Division or part of it will soon be in action again. Meanwhile, the more the enemy can be kept moving and firing, the better. Tobruk is your offensive hook and has called their bluff to some purpose already. All our best information shows they are

[1] Photographic Reconnaissance Unit flights.

[2] Churchill noted at this point in his war memoirs: 'The *Gneisenau* had in fact been torpedoed in Brest harbour on April 6 by an aircraft of Coastal Command. In this gallant attack the aircraft and all the crew were lost. The pilot was awarded a posthumous VC. A few days later Bomber Command aircraft scored four hits on the same ship with bombs. These successes were not known to us at the time. In July 1941 the *Scharnhorst* moved from Brest to La Pallice, in the Bay of Biscay, for trials and sea training, but three days later she was successfully bombed in harbour there and severely damaged. She returned to Brest for further extensive repairs.

frightfully short of everything. It would be a fine thing to cop the lot. This is certainly possible if we can cut off their supplies and wear them down. All good wishes. Thank you for your letter about R.[1]

On 17 April 1941 the Yugoslav army surrendered to the overwhelmingly stronger German attackers. King Peter was flown to safety, and to exile, by a Royal Air Force flying boat which picked him up on the Dalmatian coast. On the following day, the Greek Prime Minister, Alexandros Korizis, committed suicide.

John Colville: diary
(*Colville papers*)

18 April 1941

The PM saw the Press editors to prepare their minds for grave possibilities in Greece. At 6.0 he left for Ditchley.

War Cabinet, Defence Committee (Operations): minutes
(*Cabinet papers, 120/300*)

18 April 1941 10 Downing Street
4.45 p.m.
Secret

BOMBING POLICY

The Prime Minister asked for the Committee's approval to a statement being published in the Press and broadcast by the BBC to the effect that if Athens and Cairo were bombed, we should begin the systematic bombing of Rome.

There was general agreement to the communiqué which was issued for publication subject to certain minor amendments.[2]

[1] General Wavell had written to Churchill to say that his son Randolph was in Cairo, doing well. Randolph Churchill was then serving in North Africa as a member of No. 8 Commando (B Battalion) of Layforce, the commando force commanded by Lieutenant-Colonel Robert Laycock, with its headquarters near Alexandria. In June the headquarters was moved to Mersa Matruh, with advance parties at Tobruk. Another member of the battalion was the novelist Evelyn Waugh.

[2] One of the amendments, for which Churchill was responsible, was the statement: 'The greatest care will be taken not to bomb the Vatican City, and the strictest orders to that effect have been issued' (Telephoned to the BBC, 5.20 p.m., 18 April 1941 (*Premier papers, 3/14/3, folios 451-2*).

Sir Charles Portal said he hoped it was understood that the bombing of Rome would mean diverting some of our bombers from more important military objectives in Libya and possibly Greece.

The Prime Minister said that we should naturally implement our undertaking in accordance with the requirements of the circumstances prevailing at the time.

The Committee –

Instructed the Secretary to arrange for the publication of the statement and for it to be broadcast on the 6 p.m. news that evening.

Winston S. Churchill to Anthony Eden
(*Churchill papers, 20/36*)

18 April 1941

Has Sir Stafford Cripps yet delivered my personal message of warning about the German danger to Stalin? I am very much surprised that so much delay should have occurred, considering the importance I attach to this extremely pregnant piece of information.[1]

Winston S. Churchill to Air Chief Marshal Longmore
(*Churchill papers, 20/37*)

18 April 1941

It is not possible to lay down precise sequence and priority between interests none of which can be wholly ignored, but the following may be a guide. The extrication of New Zealand, Australian and British troops from Greece affects the whole Empire. It ought to be possible to arrange shipping in and out of Tobruk either before or after the evacuation crisis, observing Tobruk has two months' supplies. You must divide between protecting evacuation and sustaining battle of Libya. But if these clash, which may be avoidable, emphasis must be given to victory in Libya. Don't worry about Iraq for the present. It looks like going smoothly. Crete will at first only be a receptacle of whatever can get there from Greece. Its fuller defence must be organized later. In the meanwhile, all forces there must protect themselves from air bombing by dispersion and use their bayonets against parachutists or air-borne

[1] Without referring to the earlier delays, Eden wrote to Churchill later on April 18: 'I much regret the delay in the despatch of this message, which was – quite unnecessarily – held up owing to my visit to Sandringham. The telegram has now gone off.'

intruders, if any. Subject to the above general remarks, victory in Libya counts first, evacuation of troops from Greece second. Tobruk shipping, unless indispensable to victory, must be fitted in as convenient, Iraq can be ignored and Crete worked up later.

Winston S. Churchill to Sir Michael Palairet
(*Churchill papers, 20/37*)

18 April 1941

Your No. 738 to Foreign Office.

Your paragraph 1. When the above telegram was despatched, such situation reports as had been received from Greece were very meagre, and a report had just reached London from a good source that German troops had broken through on our right flank, and an official report had arrived from d'Albiac that he was withdrawing the bulk of our Air Force.

Your paragraph 2. General Wilson's message to General Wavell was quite clear. General Papagos had specifically suggested that 'as things may become critical in the future, we should re-embark British troops and save Greece from devastation' (repeat 'save Greece from devastation').

The specific endorsement of this suggestion by the King of Greece and/or Greek Government is necessary before we can commit ourselves to re-embarkation. Is this endorsement freely forthcoming? Do they adopt General Papagos's words 'to save Greece from devastation'? Please approach King or Government immediately and seek their view.

Your paragraph 3. I do not understand the inference that General Wilson would or could have proposed re-embarkation of British forces as 'sound tactics' if General Papagos had not himself suggested it.

Reference paragraph 4. I much appreciate the generous attitude of the President of the Council, and I approve the language you held. The British Forces had, and have, but one rôle to play in Greece, and this is to render the maximum assistance for as long as possible to the heroic Greek Army and Nation.

Winston S. Churchill to General Sir John Dill
(*Churchill papers, 20/36*)

18 April 1941
Secret
Action this Day

1. After the capture of Benghazi on February 6 the 7th Armoured Division, which had done so much good hard service, was ordered back to Cairo to refit.

This involved a journey of over 400 miles, and must have completed the wearing out of the tracks of many of the Tanks. It was an act of improvidence to send the whole Division all this way back, in view of the fact that German elements were already reported in Tripoli. The whole of the Tanks in this division could not have been all simultaneously in a condition of needing prolonged heavy repairs. Workshops should have been improvised at the front for lighter repairs, and servicing personnel sent forward. Thus, besides the 3rd Armoured Brigade, there would have been a considerable proportion of the Armoured Brigade in the 7th Division. General Wavell and his officers seem, however, to have thought that no trouble could arise before the end of May. This was a very serious miscalculation, from which vexatious consequences have flowed.

2. After their journey back, at least 114 cruisers and 48 infantry Tanks, total 162, entered the workshops in Egypt, and are still there, and are not expected to come out faster than 40 by May 15 and 41 by May 30. It seems incredible that machines that could have made their journey back under their own power should all have taken this enormous time, and that only the handful of Tanks in Tobruk have emerged from the workshops. Let me have a return showing exactly what dates the cruiser and infantry tanks entered the Egyptian workshops, and which dates any came out and the rest are expected to come out. There seems to be a degree of slackness and mismanagement about this repair work which is serious.

3. What exactly are the 60 cruisers M3, said to be arriving from the United States by the end of April? We have not heard about these so far.

Winston S. Churchill to General Wavell
(*Churchill papers, 20/37*)

19 April 1941
Secret

So far His Majesty's Government have not received from General Wilson or from you any account of the fighting in Greece, although heavy and prolonged actions have been in progress for several days, and lengthy newspaper reports of a confused character have been telegraphed home. This is not the way His Majesty's Government should be treated. It is also detrimental to the Service, as many decisions have to be taken here, and we are in constant relation with the Dominions and with foreign countries. I wish you to make sure that this state of things ends at once, and that a short daily report of what is happening on the Front of the British and Imperial Army is sent direct from our Headquarters in Greece at least every twenty-four hours.

Winston S. Churchill to Viscount Cranborne
(*Churchill papers, 20/36*)

19 April 1941
Action this Day

There can be no question of the Australians being separately withdrawn from the fighting line. I have been assuming that Mr Menzies keeps his Government acquainted with the position and I do not think we need very much to interfere. You should consult with him before replying. Mr Bruce is not good when things are bad.

Winston S. Churchill to Alfred Duff Cooper
(*Churchill papers, 20/21*)

19 April 1941

My dear Duff,

Yours of April 17. I think it would be a very great mistake for you to make plans for being so much out of London at this period. Even before I needed you the other night, I heard that it was already being said that you 'were trying to run the Ministry of Information from Bognor'.

When I was at the Admiralty, nearly all the difficult Press questions arose late in the evening. Besides this, you surely have great opportunities in the evening of keeping in touch with the many personalities who come within your sphere. As a general rule, all Ministers when not away on duty should be in London all the week, and weekends should only be taken warily.

Yours ever,
Winston S. Churchill

John Martin: private letter
(*Martin papers*)

19 April 1941 Ditchley

I did have an afternoon off, going with the PM on an inspection of Czech forces with President Benes[1] and their Prime Minister, Monseigneur Sramek.[2] I thought it rather moving – all those poor exiles, the tiny remnant of an army and they were so pleased to be visited and eager in their welcome. We had tea in the officers' mess – a band, a singer, their own special cakes and neat whiskey handed round in small glasses. As the PM left a choir of soldiers sang 'Rule Britannia' with great enthusiasm. We also had that sad National Anthem.[3] They showered on the Churchills all sorts of gifts of their own making – drawings, coloured woodwork, embroidery etc.

It is again quite an American party, with three of Roosevelt's envoys.[4] We also have the Chief of the Air Staff (Sir Charles Portal) and Lord Rothermere.[5]

Winston S. Churchill to Anthony Eden
(*Churchill papers, 20/36*)

20 April 1941

REQUEST FOR FULL BRITISH RECOGNITION
OF CZECHOSLOVAK GOVERNMENT

President Benes handed me the attached yesterday. I see no reason why we should not give the Czechs the same recognition as we have given the Poles, and encourage the Americans to follow our example. In neither case should we be committed to territorial frontiers.

[1] Eduard Beneš, 1884–1948. Born in Bohemia, the son of a farmer. Educated in Prague, Berlin and London. A leading member of the Czechoslovak National Council, Paris, 1917–18. Czech Minister for Foreign Affairs, 1918–35; Prime Minister, 1921–2. President of the Czechoslovak Republic, 1935–8. In exile, 1939–45; President of the Czechoslovak National Committee in London, 1939–45. Re-elected as President of the Republic, Prague, 1945. Resigned, 1948. Author of many books and pamphlets on the Czech question.

[2] Jan Sramek, 1870–1956. Born in the Austro-Hungarian province of Moravia. Ordained a priest, 1892; founded the Christian Social Workers' Organization; Member of the Moravian Provincial Parliament, 1906; the Viennese Parliament, 1907. Joined the Czechoslovak Government (as leader of the People's Party) shortly after independence in 1918. Held several Ministerial portfolios, 1920–38, including Health, Social Welfare and Unification. Prime Minister of Czechoslovakia from December 1927 to February 1929, and (in exile) from July 1940 to April 1945.

[3] 'Where is my Motherland' (in 1999 the National Anthem of the Czech Republic).

[4] John G. Winant, the United States Ambassador; Averell Harriman and Dr Conant.

[5] Esmond Cecil Harmsworth, 1898–1978. Captain, Royal Marine Artillery, 1918; his two older brothers had already been killed in action on the Western Front. ADC to Lloyd George at the Paris Peace Conference, 1919. Conservative MP for the Isle of Thanet, 1919–29. Chairman of the Newspaper Proprietors' Association, 1934–61. Member of the Advisory Council, Ministry of Information, 1939. Succeeded his father as 2nd Viscount Rothermere, 1940.

Winston S. Churchill to Lord Moyne
(*Churchill papers, 20/36*)

20 April 1941

LEASE OF BASE IN TRINIDAD TO THE UNITED STATES GOVERNMENT

I hope you will not let Governor Young[1] cause trouble and make minor difficulties over this matter. We certainly don't want him in Washington.

Winston S. Churchill to David Margesson
(*Churchill papers, 20/36*)

20 April 1941

In Libya some German tanks are now in our possession. Even if these were damaged, we should take all possible steps to get them examined by a skilful designer of British tanks or some other suitable engineering expert.

If circumstances permit, a German tank, or suitable parts of one, could be sent home in due course. Meanwhile, if there is no adequate expert already in the Middle East, one should be sent out immediately to conduct an examination on the spot.

I am sending a similar minute to the Minister of Supply.

Winston S. Churchill to Anthony Eden
(*Churchill papers, 20/36*)

20 April 1941
Action this Day

I am increasingly of the opinion that if the Generals on the spot think they can hold on in the T[2] position for a fortnight or three weeks, and can keep the

[1] Hubert Winthrop Young, 1885–1950. 2nd Lieutenant, Royal Artillery, 1904. Transferred to the Indian Army, 1908. Adjutant, 116th Mahrattas, 1913. Assistant Political Officer, Mesopotamia, 1915. Deputy Director, Local Resources Department, Mesopotamia, 1917. Transferred to the Hedjaz operations at the request of T. E. Lawrence, March 1918, where he organized transport and supplies for the Arab forces. President of the Local Resources Board, Damascus, 1918. Major, 1919. Member of the Eastern Department of the Foreign Office, 1919–21. Assistant Secretary, Middle East Department, Colonial Office, 1921–6. Colonial Secretary, Gibraltar, 1926–9. Counsellor for the High Commissioner, Iraq, 1929–32. Knighted, 1932. Minister to Baghdad, 1932. Governor and Commander-in-Chief, Nyasaland, 1932–4; Northern Rhodesia, 1934–8; Trinidad and Tobago, 1938–42. Unsuccessful Liberal candidate at the 1945 election. In 1933 he published *The Independent Arab*.

[2] The Thermopylae position.

Greek Army fighting, or enough of it, we should certainly support them if the Dominions will agree. I do not believe the difficulty of evacuation will increase, if the enemy suffers heavy losses. On the other hand, every day the German Air Force is detained in Greece, enables the Libyan situation to be stabilized, and may enable us to bring in the extra Tanks. If this is accomplished safely and the T position holds, we might even feel strong enough to reinforce from Egypt. I am most reluctant to see us quit, and if the troops were British only and the matter could be decided on military grounds alone, I would urge Wilson to fight if he thought it possible. Anyhow, before we commit ourselves to evacuation, the case must be put squarely to the Dominions after tomorrow's Cabinet. Of course, I do not know the conditions in which our retreating forces will reach the new key position.

Winston S. Churchill to General Ismay
(*Churchill papers, 20/36*)

20 April 1941

Let me have the best possible map of the Thermopylae line.

Winston S. Churchill to General Ismay
(*Cabinet papers, 120/52*)

20 April 1941

I wish to have a conference on Tank questions and future developments, to which the Commanders of the Tank Divisions should be invited, as well as representatives of the Ministry of Supply. This conference should be fixed for Monday week, i.e., the 5th May.

The officers of the Tank forces should be encouraged to prepare papers of suggestions, and are to be free to express their views. An Agenda should be prepared in the same way as is done for the conferences of Commanders-in-Chief.

Pray put this all in train, and let me have a minute in a suitable form to send to the War Office.

Winston S. Churchill: Minute[1]
(*Churchill papers, 20/36*)

20 April 1941
Most Secret

Troops should be sent to Basra as fast as possible. At least the 3 Brigades originally promised should be hurried there, but if General Auchinleck[2] can find suitable Units, let him do so.

Future dispositions can be settled when we are established.

Winston S. Churchill to Anthony Eden
(*Churchill papers, 20/36*)

20 April 1941
Action this Day

It should be made clear to Sir K. Cornwallis[2] that our chief interest in sending troops to Iraq is the covering and establishment of a great assembly base at Basra, and that what happens up-country, except at Habbaniya, is at the present time on an altogether lower priority. Our rights under the Treaty were invoked to cover this disembarkation and to avoid bloodshed, but force would have been used to the utmost limit to secure the disembarkation, if necessary. Our position at Basra, therefore, does not rest solely on the Treaty, but also on a new event arising out of the war. No undertakings can be given that troops will be sent to Baghdad or moved through to Palestine, and the right to require such undertakings should not be recognized in respect of a Government which has in itself usurped power by a *coup d'état*, or in a country where our Treaty rights have so long been frustrated in the spirit. Sir K. Cornwallis should not, however, entangle himself by explanations.

There would be no objection to his giving a broadcast on the lines of 354. This is all that Rashid Ali was promised and all he ought to get.

[1] This Minute was addressed to General Ismay, for the Chiefs of Staff Committee, the Secretary of State for India (L.S. Amery) 'and all concerned'.

[2] Kinahan Cornwallis, 1883–1959. President, Oxford University Athletic Club, 1904–06. Sudan Civil Service, 1906–14; Egyptian Civil Service, 1914–24. Director of the Arab Bureau, Cairo, 1916–20. On active service with the Arab Revolt, 1916–18 (despatches). Seconded to the Iraq Government, 1921. Adviser to the Minister of the Interior, Iraq, 1921–35. Knighted, 1929. Retired, 1935. Served in the Foreign Office, 1939–41. Ambassador in Baghdad, 1941–45. Chairman, Middle East Committee, Foreign Office, 1945–46. His younger son was killed in action in 1945.

Winston S. Churchill to General Ismay, for the Chiefs of Staff Committee
(*Cabinet papers, 120/10*)

20 April 1941
Most Secret

1. See General Wavell's 0/57776 and SD57777. The fate of the war in the Middle East, the loss of the Suez Canal, the frustration or confusion of the enormous forces we have built up in Egypt, the closing of all prospects of American co-operation through the Red Sea – all may turn on a few hundred armoured vehicles. They must be carried there if possible at all costs.

2. I will preside at noon tomorrow (Monday), 21st, at a meeting of COS and Service Ministers, and any necessary action or collection of information must proceed forthwith.

3. The only way in which this great purpose can be achieved is by sending the fast mechanical transport ships of the fast section of WS 7 through the Mediterranean. Para. 3 of General Wavell's SD57777 shows that machines, not men, are needed. The risk of losing the vehicles, or part of them, must be accepted. Even if half got through, the situation would be restored.[1] The 5 MT ships carry 250 Tanks, all but 14 of which are I Tanks. Every endeavour should be made to increase the numbers of Cruiser Tanks in this consignment. I am told 20 more can be loaded at a delay of perhaps twenty-four hours, i.e., MT convoy would sail on the morning of April 23.

4. The personnel will go by the Cape with the WS convoy, subject to any modifications which the CIGS may desire.

5. I have asked the Ministry of Shipping to try to find two other MT ships of equal speed, without regard to other interests, by the date mentioned. If these are found, an additional 100 Cruiser Tanks should be taken from the 1st Armoured Division, assuming that they are fitted for tropical warfare, apart altogether from the special desert-worthy fitting.

6. The Admiralty and Air Ministry will consider and prepare this day a plan for carrying this vital convoy through the Mediterranean. Of course, we must accept the risk, and no guarantee can be expected. Malta, however, should have been reinforced by then as the result of Double Winch. The Mountbatten destroyers[2] and other naval reinforcements should have reached there (or else be with the convoy). The enemy's dive-bombers have many other objectives, and they will not know what the convoy contains.

7. Speed is vital. Every day's delay must be avoided. Let me have timetable of what is possible, observing that at 16 knots the distance is only about 8 days, say 10 from the date of sailing, viz., April 23. This would give General Wavell

[1] Of the 295 tanks sent through the Mediterranean during May, under Operation Tiger, 238 reached Wavell safely.

[2] The 5th Destroyer Flotilla, of which Mountbatten was Captain.

effective support during the first week in May. Secrecy is of the highest importance, and no one outside the highest circles need know of the intention to turn off at Gibraltar. Everyone on board the convoys must think they are going round the Cape.

General Ismay: recollection
(*Churchill papers, 4/351A*)

[20 April 1941][1]

At about 11 a.m. on April 20th, you summoned me to Ditchley and read out the minute in question, which you had only just dictated. You told me to take it straight up to London and summon the Chiefs of Staff to discuss it at once. As it was a Sunday, the Chiefs of Staff had to be collected from their country residences, and it was not until 6 p.m. that we got round the table.

Although it is not recorded in the minutes of the meeting, I distinctly remember that the first reactions were –

(a) That the tanks were not available in this country: and
(b) That, even if they were available, the chances of their getting through the Mediterranean were remote, since on the day before entering the Narrows[2] and on the morning after passing Malta they would be liable to dive-bombing attack out of range of our shore-based fighters.

However, after a very long meeting, opposition petered out, and the Chiefs of Staff were able to report to you at 12 noon the following day the ways and means by which Operation 'Tiger' could be carried out.

War Cabinet: minutes
(*Cabinet papers, 65/22*)

21 April 1941 10 Downing Street
5 p.m.

General Wavell had asked the King of Greece whether the Greek Army could give effective aid to the left flank of the Thermopylae position, since without this the British forces could not hold the position indefinitely; in fact, possibly not for very long. The King had agreed that the time factor made it impossible for any organized Greek forces to support the British left flank on the Thermopylae position before the enemy could attack; and agreed that it was General Wavell's duty to take immediate steps for the re-embarkation of

[1] General Ismay set down these recollections for Churchill in a letter of 11 November 1946, while Churchill was in the early stages of preparing his war memoirs.
2 The Sicilian Channel between Sicily and Tunisia.

such portion of his Army as he could. The King had spoken with deep regret on having been the means of placing the British forces in such a position. The need had been impressed on the King and his Ministers for absolute secrecy, and for all measures to be taken which would make the re-embarkation possible.

The Prime Minister said that General Blamey's[1] Corps had fought with distinction a rearguard battle against heavy odds in the most depressing form of action for soldiers. They had added one more glorious page to the history of the Anzacs. They had borne the main brunt of the fighting and must have inflicted serious losses on the enemy. They could not hope to defend the Thermopylae position successfully with their left flank in the air. It looked as though they would shortly have to meet the renewed onset of three German armoured divisions.

The RAF in Greece were outmatched in numbers.

If the War Cabinet had been asked to decide the course of action to be taken, he thought that they would certainly have decided that the British Imperial Force must be evacuated. That decision had already been taken at the meeting that morning of General Wavell, General Wilson and Sir Michael Palairet with the King of Greece.

The War Cabinet agreed that the decision taken in Athens that morning must stand.

The Prime Minister said that it should be made plain to the Commanders-in-Chief that the main thing was to get the men away, and that we should not worry about saving vehicles.

The Prime Minister commented on the fact that he had received no adequate situation reports from Greece reporting any of the heavy fighting of the last ten days.

A short discussion followed as to the need for a statement in Parliament that week. The Prime Minister hoped that there was no need for making any statement during the next day or so. In any case, public discussion in Parliament was to be deprecated at this stage. He hoped to give a broadcast when more material was available.

The Lord Privy Seal[2] suggested that a steadying statement later in the week might be desirable.

[1] Thomas Albert Blamey, 1884–1951. Born in New South Wales. On active service, 1914–18 (despatches seven times, Distinguished Service Order). Chief of Staff, Australian Corps, 1918; Australian Imperial Force, 1919. Chief Commissioner of Police, Victoria, 1925–37. Knighted, 1935. Chairman of the Australian Man Power Committee, 1939–40. General Officer Commanding 6th Australian Division, Australian Imperial Force, 1939–40; lst Australian Corps, 1940–41; Australian Imperial Force, Middle East, 1941. Deputy Chief of Staff, Middle East, 1941. 1st Class Military Cross of Greece, 1941. Commander-in-Chief, Allied Land Forces, South-West Pacific Area, 1942–45. Field Marshal, 1950.

[2] Clement Attlee.

War Cabinet, Defence Committee (Operations): minutes
(*Churchill papers, 4/55*)

21 April 1941
11 p.m.

OPERATION 'TIGER'

The First Sea Lord agreed with the plan to pass the convoy through the Mediterranean.

The Chief of the Air Staff said he would try to arrange for a Beaufighter Squadron to give additional protection from Malta.

The Prime Minister asked the Committee to consider sending 100 additional cruiser tanks with the convoy – this would have a profound effect on operations in Libya.

In discussion it was stated that this would involve a delay of two days in sailing (to 26th April).

The Chief of the Imperial General Staff opposed the despatch of additional tanks in view of the shortage for Home Defence.

The Committee agreed:

1. That Operation 'Tiger' should proceed.

2. That a sixth ship should be added to the convoy, to include 67 Mark VI tanks.

Winston S. Churchill to General Wavell
(*Churchill papers, 20/49*)

22 April 1941
Personal and Most Secret
To be deciphered by the Personal Assistant of C-in-C

1. I have been working hard for you in the last few days and you will, I am sure, be glad to know that we are sending 307 of our best tanks through the Mediterranean, hoping they will reach you around May 10. Of these, 99 are cruisers Mark IV and Mark VI with the necessary spare parts for the latter and 180 I tanks.

2. In your SD57777, para. 3, you said you had the trained personnel for six regiments. We are therefore sending only the vehicles to you by the short cut. The men go round the Cape as already arranged subject to some adjustments.

3. You will receive through the regular channels (a) full details of the tanks which are being sent and of the spare parts which fit in with what you have got already, and (b) directions as to various fittings you have to make for desert service. I hope you will immediately set to work on all preparations so that a real evolution can be made of this job and the famous 7th Armoured Division,

whose absence was so unexpected to us, will resume under Creagh its victorious career.

4. On the receipt of the detailed information you should furnish us with your plan for bringing these vehicles into action at the very earliest moment. If this consignment gets through the hazards of the passage, which, of course, cannot be guaranteed, the boot will be on the other leg and no German should remain in Cyrenaica by the end of the month of June.

5. In making your preparations for bringing these vehicles into action you should pretend that they are coming round the Cape as secrecy is most important, and very few here have been told. Thus when you get them the chance of surprise may be offered. All good wishes.

Winston S. Churchill to General Wavell

(*Churchill papers, 20/37*)

22 April 1941
Personal and Secret

EVACUATION FROM GREECE

In the execution of this policy you will no doubt not worry about vehicles or stores, but get the men away. We can re-arm them later.

Winston S. Churchill to General Ismay and Sir Edward Bridges

(*Churchill papers, 20/36*)

22 April 1941
Action this Day
Please implement

1. Attention is directed to the fact that the Green Line cannot be considered absolutely safe. It ought not to be used for any precise discussion about very secret matters, especially future operations. Should this become indispensable, guard terms and synonyms should be used, care always being taken that the conversation would not be intelligible to anyone not in the swim.

2. The use of the 'scrambler' which is 'safe' should be developed in the secret circle and widened thereafter. At present it works unhandily, but those concerned must get used to it. It must be made to work easily and effectively. The Postmaster-General[1] should be furnished with a list of those to whom it should be supplied. Pray, therefore, draw up such a list for my consideration.

[1] W. S. Morrison, see page 714, note 1.

Winston S. Churchill: Oral Answers
(*Hansard*)

22 April 1941 Church House[1]

Mr Wedgwood: Is not our representation by the right hon. Member for Chelsea (Sir S. Hoare) in Spain a little too expensive?

The Prime Minister: Many people thought in July of last year that Spain would enter the war against us, and I think that it is very largely due to the brilliant discharge of his duties in Spain that our relations with that country have tended to improve and not to deteriorate at this critical time.

Mr A. Bevan: Is the right hon. Gentleman aware that the handing-over of this money to Spain is causing deep anxiety throughout the country and a great deal of unrest and that the public cannot see in the newspapers of Spain and in the public utterances of Spanish statesmen any gratitude or recognition whatever of this country; and are we to wait for another *fait accompli* from Spain?

The Prime Minister: I do not know what is meant by the last remark about another *fait accompli* at all. This policy has been most carefully considered, and the state of our affairs in every part of the world does not allow matters of this kind to be handled in a rough and reckless or debonair fashion. We do not wish to do anything which would give any excuse for a breach at the present time between us and the Spanish Government; and I certainly consider that the starving condition of the people of Spain fully justifies assistance being given by Great Britain, and by the United States, if she chooses so to act, irrespective of whether any expressions of gratitude are forthcoming or not.

WORD 'BILLION' (MEANING)

Sir Percy Hurd asked the Prime Minister whether he is aware of the confusion arising from differences of meaning of the word 'billion' on the two sides of the Atlantic; and whether in view of our new economic intimacy, he will confer with the Government of the United States of America and Canada, so as to obtain uniformity in this matter.

The Prime Minister: The word 'billion' has, it is true, different, or alternative, meanings on the opposite sides of the Atlantic, but I do not think this has led to any difficulties in accounting. For all practical financial purposes a billion represents one thousand millions, especially in the case of anything we owe.

[1] Following the severe damage to the Debating Chamber of the House of Commons, and to many other parts of the Palace of Westminster, the Commons assembled on April 22 in its new home, Church House, Westminster.

BUSINESS OF THE HOUSE (WAR SITUATION)

Mr Lees-Smith (by Private Notice) asked the Prime Minister whether he has any statement to make on the war situation?

The Prime Minister: Might I be allowed to preface my remarks by expressing to you, Mr Speaker,[1] the very great satisfaction of every part of the House at your return after your indisposition, and also our satisfaction that your indisposition kept you out of your official residence on a recent occasion.[2]

I have no statement which could be usefully made to the House today, beyond what I said before we separated or what has appeared since in the newspapers. Operations of many kinds are going on, and we have others to think of besides ourselves. I should deprecate any proposal for a Debate at the present time, and I hope the House will once again show its forbearance to those who are charged with the conduct of the war, and will display to the world those qualities of poise and steadiness which have been its characteristic on so many difficult and anxious occasions.

The only piece of news I have for the House which has not yet been published, is that the Mediterranean Battle Fleet, under Admiral Cunningham, at daybreak yesterday, bombarded Tripoli harbour for 42 minutes, inflicting very heavy damage both on the port and on the shipping in the harbour, the extent of which is not at present fully known.[3] On the way there, our aircraft of the Fleet Air Arm intercepted five German troop-carrying planes, and shot down four in flames. I have not yet heard whether they were full or empty. The Fleet was not seriously molested and suffered no loss in ships.

Mr Hore-Belisha:[4] The House will, of course, show all the forbearance which the Government think necessary in this situation and particularly

[1] Edward Algernon Fitzroy, 1869–1943. Son of the 3rd Baron Southampton. Educated at Eton and Sandhurst. A page of honour to Queen Victoria. Conservative MP for Daventry, 1900–6 and 1910–43. Captain, 1st Life Guards, 1914 (wounded at the first battle of Ypres). Commanded the mounted troops of the Guards Division, 1915–16. Deputy Chairman of Committees, House of Commons, 1922–8. Privy Councillor, 1924. Speaker of the House of Commons from 1928 until his death. His widow was created Viscountess Daventry in 1943. Their son Michael (born 1895) was killed in action on 15 April 1915.

[2] When the Speaker's House was bombed; and with it the Chamber of the House of Commons.

[3] In his diary for 22 April 1941, Henry 'Chips' Channon, a Conservative MP and frequent critic of Churchill, noted: 'Winston announced that the Navy had bombarded Tripoli and he did it deftly, thus disarming a somewhat hostile house'.

[4] Leslie Hore-Belisha, 1893–1957. His father, an Army officer, died when Hore-Belisha was nine months old. Known, on account of his Jewish origins, as 'Horeb Elisha'. Educated at Clifton and St John's College, Oxford. On active service in France, 1915–16 and at Salonika, 1916–18. President of the Oxford Union, 1919. Liberal MP for Plymouth Devonport, 1923–42 (National Liberal from 1931; Independent from 1942–5. Parliamentary Secretary, Board of Trade, 1931–2. Financial Secretary, Treasury, 1932–4. Minister of Transport, 1934–7 (with a seat in the Cabinet from October 1936). Privy Councillor, 1935. Secretary of State for War, 1937–40 (Member of the War Cabinet, 1939–40). Minister of National Insurance, 1945. Created Baron, 1954.

desires not to embarrass the operation of our troops in any way. Would my right hon. Friend bear in mind, however, the absolute necessity for a proximate Debate on this subject as soon as it can possibly be held? He will be aware of the anxiety expressed in Australia at the lack of authentic news and that Parliament there has been called together for the purpose of hearing a statement. May I also ask whether it would be convenient – because it would cause far less embarrassment – for the Foreign Secretary to make a statement, in any conditions that the Government might think appropriate, upon his recent visits? Finally, may I ask my right hon. Friend – who has just told us good news, or at least comparatively good news – whether it is true that the Germans have occupied Samothrace?

The Prime Minister: I should think it not unlikely, but I have not at the moment direct confirmation of that. With regard to a Debate, it is quite obvious that once the situation reaches temporary arrest a full statement should be made to the House as to what has happened in the past. As to scanty information being given, I must frankly say that we have had the very greatest difficulty in obtaining fuller accounts, or accurate accounts, of the difficult and intricate movement of our Forces in Greece. They have been of the most complicated character and have been carried out with extraordinary skill, but we have not received from day to day – even the Government – full information from the Commanders engaged. But that has not been any hindrance to the course of the action or operation, and I have asked that we may in the future receive fuller reports, if possible without prejudice to the interests on the spot. With regard to a statement by the Foreign Secretary on his tour, either in public or in Secret Session, I should deprecate that at the present time because I do not think that the materials are available for the necessary presentation of the Government's case to the House.

Earl Winterton: May I ask my right hon. Friend whether he realizes the fact that the Foreign Secretary has been abroad on a most important mission presumably – because he is one of the key members of the Government – for no less than six weeks or two months, and that there are questions, such as the position of Iraq in relation to the British Empire and the position of Spain, about which there is most calamitous news this morning ? Surely he does not wish to deprive the House of its right, if it wishes to do so, of having a full statement from the Foreign Secretary, either in private or in public, about the result of his visit?

The Prime Minister: No, Sir, if there is a desire to have a statement on foreign affairs, that is one question, but to have a statement on the recent tour by the Foreign Secretary would not in my opinion, be convenient at the present time, either to the House or in the public interest.

Commander Sir Archibald Southby: In view of my right hon. Friend's remarks about the difficulty of obtaining news from Greece, which I quite understand, does the same difficulty apply to getting authentic news as to what is going on in Libya? The public are very exercised in their minds about what is going on there and ought to be reassured if possible.

The Prime Minister: I think one is very accurately informed of what is going on in Libya –

Mr Wedgwood: Greece is much more important.

The Prime Minister: I do not think we must embark upon comparison of the different classes of dangerous duties which are set to His Majesty's Forces. In reply to my hon. and gallant Friend the Member for Epsom (Sir A. Southby), I do not think any statement on the subject of Libya would be appropriate at the present time and, indeed it may be, for a little while to come.

Mr Shinwell: Is my right hon. Friend aware that the public are very uneasy about the situation, and that a statement, in secret obviously, by the Foreign Secretary might remove some of the uneasiness?

The Prime Minister: As to the uneasiness of the public, I am bound to say that I have not formed that view. The public are showing all those qualities of stability and phlegm, when things are not going well, that have made us what we are and have carried us thus far.

Winston S. Churchill to Peter Fraser[1]

(*Churchill papers, 20/38*)

22 April 1941
Most Secret

I am very grateful for your message, and for its generous and courageous terms. We have been kept very short of information ourselves, but apparently these complicated operations were most difficult to follow as the various Brigades were working independently and moving fast. The Anzacs[2] and New Zealanders acquitted themselves in a glorious manner, and have hit the enemy far harder than he has hit them. Our troops are now on the Thermopylae position, but I have no doubt that early re-embarkation will be necessary. For this operation all plans were made some time ago and have only to be applied to the existing circumstances. The three Commanders-in-Chief[3] are reuniting at Cairo in order to concert the highest possible action. You may be sure that the safe withdrawal of the men will have precedence over any other consideration except that of honour. We cannot, however, endanger the battle

[1] Prime Minister of New Zealand.

[2] Churchill is using the word Anzacs – originally the Australian and New Zealand forces serving in the First World War – for the Australians alone.

[3] General Wavell, Admiral Cunningham and Air Marshal Longmore.

in Libya by withdrawing too much of our Air Force from there. I have so greatly admired the grandeur of the attitude of your Government, and my thoughts turn many times a day to the fortunes of your one splendid New Zealand Division and of my heroic friend Freyberg. Undoubtedly a phase of acute anxiety lies before us in the Greek theatre, but the highly competent officers of the spot seem to feel good confidence in their ability to solve its problems.

Winston S. Churchill to A.V. Alexander and Admiral Pound

(*Churchill papers 20/36*)

22 April 1941

COMMENTS ON AN ADMIRALTY MEMORANDUM

Para. 2. It was a pity to spoil the observation of the Fleet by this bombardment from the Air.[1] Did the Commander-in-Chief order it, or not?

Para. 3. This throws an instructive light upon our fears about 'Workshop'[2] and all its batteries, bristling with guns, as we were told.

Para. 5. I presume that, as the policy of bombardment has not achieved the object we had in view, the other project will now be revived.

Para. 6. I shall be glad to know whether they were north-bound or south-bound.

Winston S. Churchill to Air Chief Marshal Sir Charles Portal

(*Churchill papers 20/36*)

22 April 1941

MIDDLE EAST REINFORCEMENTS

PROGRESS REPORT FOR WEEK ENDING 18 APRIL 1941

This Return shows a frightful congestion at Takoradi of 285, a run-off of only 25 in the current week and a proposed despatch of only 38 more next week. I apprised you some time ago of my misgivings about the capacity of Takoradi, and you were good enough to reassure me, but this looks as if we were going to get into a thorough jam there. Let me know your projected arrivals there in the next six weeks, for, if you cannot clear them by more than 40 a week, we shall be open to serious criticism.

[1] The bombardment of Tripoli, see page 545.

[2] The capture of Pantellaria Island.

Winston S. Churchill to General Sir John Dill
(*Churchill papers, 20/36*)

22 April 1941
Action this Day

I have examined the Tank situation with General Crawford.[1] After the 67 Cruiser Tanks and their spares have gone, deliveries in the next three months should be over 288. Deliveries of I Tank may reach 500, and we shall almost certainly have in May and June a good delivery of the A22s. It appears that the spare parts of the Mark IV's and the Mark VI's are largely identical except for the steering gear and one or two minor points. The engines are identical, and there is a good supply of spares already in the Middle East on which the Mark VI can draw. Therefore, we only have to send the parts which are not identical.

Your trouble in the next three months is going to be finding properly trained Units for the Tanks which will reach you.

2. I should be very glad if you would yourself look into the question of not wearing out too rapidly in training the 1,100 Tanks now in the hands of troops. We do not want to be told all of a sudden that the Tanks of a whole Division on which we are counting have to go in for a long refit, like those of the 7th Armoured Division, just at the moment we need them most. It seems to me that training should be divided into two parts: (a) training in the use of the Tank, for which even in Divisions not yet fully supplied model Tanks must be provided; and (b) tactical training. In this field everything possible should be done to spare the movement of masses of Tanks. A great number of exercises can surely be carried out with Bren gun carriers driven at the corresponding speed of the Tanks, and only now and again should the Tanks themselves be made to wear out their tracks. The principle of the 'cover act' being ridden till you get to the Meet should commend itself to Cavalry Officers.

Pray give me a report of this.

[1] John Scott Crawford, 1889–1978. Royal Army Service Corps, 1915–28. Royal Army Ordnance Corps, 1928–39. Director of Mechanisation, Ministry of Supply, 1939; Deputy Director-General of Tanks and Transport, 1940–43. Deputy Director–General of Armaments Production, 1943–45.

Winston S. Churchill to Air Chief Marshal Sir Charles Portal
(*Churchill papers, 20/36*)

22 April 1941

NUMBER OF SERVICEABLE AIRCRAFT AS COMPARED WITH OPERATIONAL CREWS

I have sent you other minutes bearing on this subject in the last day or two, but the point is that you are not expanding your Fighter Force in Squadrons sufficiently to carry the very great mass of aircraft with which Beaverbrook, aided by the United States, is now going to bombard you. You are quite right when you say in paragraph 4 that Air Marshal Sholto Douglas is more concerned about his crew position. That was exactly the point I wished to make. Why do you not start another 10 Squadrons and cut into this surplus of Spitfires and Hurricanes? However, deal with this please when you answer my other minutes.

Winston S. Churchill to General Sir John Dill
(*Churchill papers, 20/36*)

22 April1941

PLANS FOR THE DEFENCE OF TOBRUK

All this seems very sound and very practical but we must not forget that the besieged are four or five times as strong as the besiegers. There is no objection to their making themselves comfortable, but they must be very careful not to let themselves be ringed in by a smaller force, and consequently lose their offensive power upon the enemy's communications. Twenty-five thousand men with 100 guns and ample supplies are expected to be able to hold a highly fortified zone against 4,500 men at the end of 700 miles of communications, even though those men be Germans; in this case some of them are Italians. The figures which I have used are those which have been furnished to me by the War Office. We must not put our standards too low in relation to the enemy.

Winston S. Churchill to General Ismay
(*Churchill papers 20/36*)

22 April 1941
Most Secret

Make sure all this is put in train, and that all who come are apprised of the experiment and the conditions under which it takes place. Let us have also a target suspended from a balloon about 6,000 feet high at least, or, alternatively, if the balloon could be got up to 10,000 feet we could fire at the balloon itself. Let great attention be paid to the aiming of the projector and the training of the crew.

2. I propose to spend a whole day at Shoeburyness, beginning early, lunching in my train, so that every kind of experiment should be added to the programme. In particular I wish to see a discharge simultaneously of 20 or 30 of the 2-inch parachute and aerial mine projectors (? Queen Bee). We are also to see the 3-inch projectors for this, fired at 22,000 feet. Could not some kind of smoke device be substituted for the mine charge, so as to make the tackle visible at this great height?

3. I wish to see the Bombards, &c., firing at armour-plate, and further trials of the sticky bombs, the Smith guns,[1] &c.

4. I expect to see, finally, A22 manoeuvre under severe conditions. The three Chiefs of Staff will, it is hoped, be able to attend.

War Cabinet, Battle of the Atlantic Committee: minutes
(*Cabinet papers, 86/1*)

23 April 1941 10 Downing Street
5 p.m.

The Prime Minister asked whether the adoption of various measures would enable us to transfer tonnage from the import of oil to the import of food. Could anything more be done by transferring tankers from the Abadan route to the Gulf route?

FITTING OUT SHIPS WITH CATAPULT AIRCRAFT

The fitting-out of merchant ships was proceeding in accordance with schedule and 29 ships had now been earmarked for this purpose. One was expected to be completed by the end of April, 8 during May, 11 in June and 6 in July. It had been assumed that the importing capacity of these ships could not be sacrificed and it had, therefore, been intended that, while the 5 White Ensign ships would patrol continuously in the danger area, the merchant ships when fitted to carry catapult aircraft should be employed on ordinary importing service on the short transatlantic voyage.

The Prime Minister pointed out that on this plan they would only spend about 30 days in the year in the area where protection against air attack was needed. This would be a very uneconomical use of specially fitted ships and Hurricane aircraft. At any rate the first 10 merchant ships fitted to catapult

[1] The Smith gun was an anti-tank weapon, invented by Major William H. Smith, and produced for use by the Home Guard. In 1941 Major Smith was Managing Director of Triang Toys. As many as 4,000 were produced. An expert comments that it was 'a bit of a suicide weapon because you had to get very close in order to hit a tank' (which the Home Guard never had to do in anger).

aircraft should be made available for continuous patrolling in the danger area and should be continued on this service if they were found to be successful. It was a matter for consideration whether, if they were to be continuously so employed, smaller ships should be fitted out for this service than those which had been already earmarked. It might be possible to use smaller ships for continuous patrolling and to employ the bigger ships on the Freetown run, as had been originally intended. The Beaufighters at present assigned for work on the North-Western approaches were urgently required for other duties.

Winston S. Churchill to General Ismay
(Churchill papers, 20/36)

23 April 1941

MOVEMENT OF TROOPS FROM INDIA TO IRAQ

Surely the second week in May is a very distant date for the 2nd Brigade to start from India? Why cannot the 3rd Brigade mobilize at the same time and start with them? Go into this matter with the India Office and War Office, and let me have a very considerable improvement, especially for the 2nd Brigade. Explain to me what is holding up the movement.

Winston S. Churchill to General Ismay, for Chiefs of Staff Committee
(Churchill papers, 20/36)

23 April 1941

ANALYSIS OF INVASION EXERCISE 'VICTOR'

1. I find it very difficult to believe that these figures and facts have any relation to reality. They should be compared with the rate at which we were able to land troops in Greece over a sea of which we had the command, and in the absence of opposition, and with all the facilities of the Piraeus at our disposal. In about six weeks we were able to send only 7 Brigades, including one Armoured Brigade. It is, of course, quite reasonable for assumptions of this character to be made as a foundation for a military exercise. It would be indeed darkening counsel to make them the foundation of serious military thought.

2. How is it also that our Fighters could only on the 24th January and the 25th January make 432 sorties as against 1,500 sorties by the Germans, whose Fighter strength is not superior to ours, and who have to come a longer distance? The CAS[1] should report upon this, both as respects the 24th and 25th January, and the present time. The Air Ministry should also state what,

[1] The Chief of the Air Staff, Air Chief Marshal Sir Charles Portal.

in fact, were the average number of sorties per diem in August and September 1940 by the British and German Fighters when the German defeat was so pronounced and the German fighter strength relatively so much greater.

3. C-in-C, Home Forces,[1] should explain what is the Cabinet decision to which he refers at the bottom of page 2 of his letter to General Haining. Sir Edward Bridges should furnish the record of the Cabinet proceeding at which it was decided that 'ample supplies' for the enemy should be provided locally. I was not aware of any such decision as the confinement of the matter to GHQ; nor has the Cabinet been informed until now of the anxiety felt by C-in-C, Home Forces, on this point.

4. In para. 7 on page 4 it is assumed that the Germans will have at the outset superior strength in destroyers. In the case of invasion, it is admitted that some notice will be available beforehand, and I should like to be informed by the Admiralty what force of destroyers, cruisers and battleships they can have available in the Channel and the southern part of the North Sea on the 5th, 6th and 7th days respectively after the warning.

5. It would be the greatest advantage if officers who believe that it is so easy to land large forces with their vehicles, ammunition and stores, in a few hours on open beaches, would make a plan for a British landing of the force in question either on the Dutch or the French coasts.

Winston S. Churchill to General Sir John Dill
(*Cabinet papers, 120/52*)

23 April 1941

I fancy your trouble in the near future is going to be a plethora of tanks. In your para.2 you speak of the speed and range of these vehicles. In practice things do not work out like that. It is only very rarely that a large homogeneous force has to make a prolonged advance or manoeuvre. Most times there are many hours wasted in each action when everyone is standing about and only a few can get on. Thus there is far more to be said for a mixed grill, and I cannot think of anything more foolish than stripping 5 Divisions of cruiser tanks in order to have one all of a kind. This is one of the matters which must be discussed at the Tank Parliament about which I am sending you a note. A meeting must be held in the near future. In England there are very short distances and enclosed country, and the differences between cruiser and I tanks will tend to diminish almost to vanishing point. Uniform organizations ought not to be higher than a Brigade. The tanks ought to be more evenly distributed between the units in this lull.

[1] General Sir Alan Brooke, to whom Churchill also sent a copy of this minute.

Winston S. Churchill to David Margesson
(*Churchill papers, 20/36*)

23 April 1941

All the lessons of this war emphasize the necessity for good anti-tank weapons and plenty of them. The number of anti-tank guns that can be produced is necessarily limited: all the more need therefore to press forward with whatever substitutes can do the trick.

I thought that the bombard was distinctly hopeful and I was told that you had decided to order 2,000 of these with 300,000 anti-tank projectiles and 600,000 anti-personnel projectiles. When can we expect these weapons to be in the hands of the troops? And at what rate? Pray let me have a programme.

Winston S. Churchill to David Margesson
(*Churchill papers, 20/36*)

23 April 1941

There are persistent rumours that the Germans are constructing tanks with very thick armour – figures of 4″–6″ are mentioned. Such armour would be impervious to any existing anti-tank gun or indeed any mobile gun; the tracks and other vulnerable parts are very small targets.

Tests have shown that plastic explosive applied to armour plate, as for instance in the bombard developed by Colonel Blacker[1] and Colonel Jefferis,[2] has very great cutting power and this may be a solution to the problem. In any event we must not be caught napping. I feel sure that the War Office are alive to the threat of the very thick-skinned tank, and have an antidote in mind. Pray let me have a report.

[1] Latham Valentine Stewart Blacker, –1964. Aviator, soldier, explorer and inventor. On active service, North-West Frontier of India, 1908. Aeroplane pilot, 1911. Flying Officer, Royal Flying Corps, France and Flanders, 1915–16 (wounded). Staff Captain, Aeronautics, War Office, 1916. On active service, Royal Flying Corps, 1917–17 (very severely wounded). On active service against the Bolsheviks in Central Asia, 1918–20; in the Third Afghan War, 1919; on the Turkestan Frontier, 1920 (OBE). Acting Lieutenant-Colonel, 1919–20. Exploring in Central Asia, 1920–23). On active service, Indian frontier, 1923 and 1930–31. Took part in the 1933 Mount Everest flight. Inventor of the Blacker Bombard, the Hedgehog (anti-submarine device), and the Petard (anti-armoured vehicle device). Author of *On Secret Patrol in High Asia* (1921) and *Tales from Turkestan* (1924).

[2] Millis Rowland Jefferis, 1899–1963. Joined the Royal Engineers, 1918. Major, 1937. Commanded the 1st Field Squadron, Royal Engineers, 1937–9. Served in Norway, 1940 (despatches). A designer of bombs, mines, mortars and anti-tank rockets, he worked directly under Churchill (as Minister of Defence) at an experimental establishment at Whitchurch near Chequers, 1940–5. CBE, 1942. Brigadier, 1942. Knighted, 1945. Major-General, 1945. Deputy Engineer-in-Chief, India, 1946. Engineer-in-Chief, Pakistan, 1947–50. Chief Superintendent, Military Engineering Experimental Establishment, 1950–3.

Princess Elizabeth[1] *to Winston S. Churchill*
(*Churchill papers, 20/29*)

23 April 1941 Windsor Castle

Dear Mr Churchill,

I want to thank you and Mrs Churchill so very much for the lovely roses you sent me for my birthday.[2] It was so kind of you to think of me when I know how very busy you are and I appreciate such a lovely present very much indeed.

I am afraid you have been having a very worrying time lately, but I am sure things will begin to look up again soon.

With again so many thanks.

Yours sincerely

Elizabeth

War Cabinet: minutes
(*Cabinet papers, 65/18*)

24 April 1941 Prime Minister's Room
12 noon Houses of Commons Annexe

MIDDLE EAST

The Prime Minister asked the Chief of the Air Staff to let him have the material for a telegram to the Commander-in-Chief, Mediterranean, explaining the measures which had been taken to reinforce our air forces in the Middle East.

ROYAL NAVY

The Prime Minister said that the deck armour on the new monitor included in the 1941 programme must be thick enough to meet air attack.

THE BALKANS AND THE MIDDLE EAST[3]

Mr Menzies said that he was uneasy as to whether our forces in Greece, in view of immediate operations, would be given sufficient protection from the air.

[1] Elizabeth, elder daughter of the Duke and Duchess of York (later King George VI and Queen Elizabeth). Born in 1926. Made her first wartime radio broadcast on 13 October 1940, on *Children's Hour*, telling the Commonwealth: 'We know, every one of us, that in the end all will be well'. Colonel, Grenadier Guards, 1942. Counsellor of State from 1944, first acting in this capacity on 22 July 1944 when the King was visiting the Italian battlefields. Joined the Auxiliary Transport Service (ATS), 24 February 1945; qualified as a driver, 14 April 1945; promoted Junior Commander, 27 July 1945. Married Lieutenant Philip Mountbatten RN, 1947. Became Queen (as Elizabeth II) on the death of her father, 6 February 1952.

[2] Princess Elizabeth had celebrated her 15th birthday on 21 April 1941.

[3] This 'Most Secret' section of the War Cabinet's discussion was recorded in the War Cabinet Confidential Annex (*Cabinet papers, 65/22*).

The Prime Minister said that a telegram had been sent to the Commanders-in-Chief, Middle East, giving the priority in which our forces in the Middle East would be used. He had been told that it was not possible to lay down a precise sequence of priority between the various objectives. Our resources must be divided between protecting evacuation and sustaining battle in Libya, but if these clashed, emphasis must be given to victory in Libya.

The Prime Minister said that, in order to relieve Mr Menzies' anxiety, he would send a further telegram stating that the Prime Minister of Australia had expressed anxiety on this question, and asking Air Marshal Longmore without prejudice to the immediate safety of Libya, to spare all the aircraft he could for Greece during the immediately critical days.

The War Cabinet approved this suggestion.

Winston S. Churchill: Business of the House
(*Hansard*)

24 April 1941 — Church House

Mr Lees-Smith: May I ask the Prime Minister whether he has any statement to make on the future Business of the House?

The Prime Minister (Mr Churchill): Yes, Sir.

On the first Sitting Day – Motions to approve the Determination of Needs Regulations, and the Timber (Charges) (No. 3) Order.

The second Sitting Day will be the fifth Allotted Supply Day, when a Debate will take place on Food Distribution on the Ministry of Food Vote.

On the third Sitting Day – Second Reading of the Public and other Schools (War Conditions) Bill (Lords)

I am aware that the House expects a Debate on the war situation at an early date, and consequently the Business which I have announced may have to be altered. The House will realize, however, that any question of a Debate must depend upon the situation prevailing at the time. I venture to suggest that the precise moment is one for the Government to decide, and I am confident that the House will be willing to leave the matter in our hands. Members may rest assured that they will be given full information as soon as I am in a position to give it, but a serious responsibility rests upon His Majesty's Government not to take any course, or make any statement, which will prejudice the safety and success of the British, Australian, New Zealand and Greek soldiers who at this time are in close contact with the enemy.

Mr Hore-Belisha: The House, of course, appreciates the conditions upon which a Debate would be possible. While entirely accepting what has been laid down by my right hon. Friend, and the understanding that a Debate is to take place as early as possible, may I ask whether, with regard to a statement by my right hon. Friend the Foreign Secretary, the Prime Minister can say whether the material has now been assembled? It would be normal to expect a statement from my right hon. Friend on his recent tour so that we may have the basis for a proper judgment upon these matters. If my right hon. Friend thought it was undesirable for the Foreign Secretary to make such a statement in Open Session, I am sure the house would be ready to hear it in Secret Session. I am not asking for a Debate but merely to hear a statement from my right hon. Friend the Foreign Secretary as soon as that is possible.

The Prime Minister: I think that the circumstances connected with the tour of my right hon. Friend the Foreign Secretary are intimately interwoven with the main matters which the House wishes to discuss, and which I shall see they have the fullest opportunity of discussing, either in public or private, as may be thought best, on an occasion which is found, at the earliest moment, to be compatible with the public interests and which, at the earliest moment, enables the Government to give a full and reasonable account of what has taken place.

Earl Winterton: May I ask one question which arises in this connection? Will my right hon. Friend see that His Majesty's Government in Great Britain, so far as is possible, concert with His Majesty's Government in Australia, so that any Debate which takes place shall take place, as far as is possible, simultaneously in this House and in the Australian House of Representatives? It would be most unfortunate if information was given in another country which was not available in this country.

The Prime Minister: Of course, it would be an innovation for us to adopt the position that if a Debate took place in Australia, we must necessarily have a Debate on the same day here. It would in a sense be an intrusion on their perfectly separate and independent rights of government under the Statute of Westminster. At the same time there would be obvious inconveniences in Debates on these matters taking place piecemeal. We are in the very closest touch with the Dominion Ministers and Governments, not only in Australia, but in New Zealand, and also in Canada and South Africa. Certainly an effort will be made, as far as possible, without the slightest prejudice to independent and separate action, to arrange these Debates. I asked when the Australian Parliament was likely to meet, and, according to information I received just before I came into the House, it is unlikely to assemble before the first week in May, and, of course, the Debate would not take place until the end of that week. I give that information under all reserve.

Mr Granville: In view of the statement of the Australian Prime Minister two days ago, is there any reason, as people in this country also have a great interest in that theatre of war, why a similar statement should not be made here?

The Prime Minister: I have been considering whether I might not make some statement of a general character, but I have been anxious to make sure, if I were to do so, that I should not be treating the House with disrespect if I suggested that a Debate on the matter should be postponed to a later occasion. If I could say anything helpful on the matter in the interval, not, of course, going into the controversial aspect, I feel that perhaps the House would give me that latitude.

Commander Sir Archibald Southby: Will the right hon. Gentleman bear in mind that, in view of the gravity of recent events, the public would prefer that a Debate should take place in Public rather than in Secret Session?

The Prime Minister: Yes, but do not let us lose our sense of proportion about the gravity of recent events.

John Colville: diary
(*Colville papers*)

24 April 1941

With PM in Upper War Room, Admiralty, most of the afternoon. We walked back down Whitehall and he expatiated on the beauty of the Banqueting Hall, saying he could not think why it had not been copied for Government offices. He told me that today New Zealand troops were fully engaged at Thermopylae – an historic event which he had been certain would happen.

Winston S. Churchill to David Margesson and Sir Andrew Duncan
(*Churchill papers, 20/36*)

24 April 1941
Secret

I propose to hold periodical meetings to consider tank and anti-tank questions, the first of which will be at 10 Downing Street on Monday, the 5th May, at 11 a.m. These meetings would be attended by yourselves, accompanied by appropriate officers. From the War Office I would propose that the CIGS, ACIGS[1] and General Pope[2] should come, and General Martel[3] and his

[1] The Chief of the Imperial General Staff, General Sir John Dill, and the Assistant Chief of the Imperial General Staff, General Sir Robert Haining.

[2] Vivian Vavasour Pope, 1891–1941. Entered the Army, 1912. On active service, 1914–18 (wounded thrice, despatches five times, Distinguished Service Order, Military Cross); North Russia, 1919 (despatches). Brigadier, General Staff, Southern Command, 1938; Director of Armoured Fighting Vehicles, War Office, 1939–41.

[3] Giffard Le Quesne Martel, 1889–1958. On active service 1914–18 (despatches five times, Distinguished Service Order, Military Cross). Assistant Director of Mechanization, War Office, 1936–38; Deputy Director, 1938–39. Commander, Royal Armoured Corps, 1940–41. Head of the British Military Mission to Moscow, 1943. Knighted 1943. Chairman, Royal Cancer Hospital, 1945–50. He published his memoirs, *An Outspoken Soldier*, in 1949, and several other books among them *East Versus West*, 1952.

Armoured Divisional Commanders should also be invited. On the Supply side, I should like Mr Burton,[1] Admiral Brown[2] and General Crawford to be present.

2. I am particularly anxious that all officers attending the meeting should be encouraged to send in their suggestions as to the points which should be discussed, and to express their individual views with complete freedom. I contemplate, in fact, a 'Tank Parliament'.

3. An agenda will be prepared for each meeting by my Defence Officer, and it will include any points which you wish to place upon it, and any suggestions or questions which the Tank Commanders wish to put forward. I myself should like to discuss the organization of Armoured Divisions, and the present state of their mechanical efficiency, as well as the larger questions which govern 1943.

Winston S. Churchill to President Franklin D. Roosevelt

(*Churchill papers, 20/38*)

24 April 1941
sent at 2.45 p.m.

1. I now reply in detail to your message of 11th April. The delay has been caused by waiting for Admiral Ghormley, whose arrival was uncertain. The First Sea Lord has had long discussions with Ghormley, as the result of which I am advised as follows:

2. In the Battle of the Atlantic we have two main problems to deal with in addition to the menace from aircraft round our coast. These problems are those of the U-boats and the raiders.

3. As regards the U-boats, we have had considerable success in dealing with these pests when they were working somewhere in the longitude of 22° West in the North-Western Approaches. Whether it was because of our success or for some other reason, they are now working in about 30° West.

4. We have, however, been able gradually to strengthen our escorting forces, thanks to the United States destroyers which were sent us, and by the use of Iceland as a refuelling base for the escorts.

[1] Geoffrey Duke Burton, 1893–1954. Royal Engineers. Served at Gallipoli, in Egypt and in Palestine (despatches twice). Managing Director, Birmingham Small Arms Company, 1933–44. Director-General of Tanks and Transport, 1940–45. Knighted, 1942.

[2] Harold Arthur Brown, 1878–1968. Educated at the Royal Naval Engineers College. Entered Navy, 1894. In 1912, when Churchill was First Lord of the Admiralty, Brown was the Engineer-Lieutenant on board the destroyer *Cameleon*. Vice-Admiral, 1932. Engineer-in-Chief of the Fleet, Admiralty, 1932–6. Knighted, 1934. Retired, 1936. Director-General of Munitions Production, Army Council, 1936–9. Director-General of Munitions Production, Ministry of Supply, 1939–40. Controller-General of Munitions Production, 1941–2. Chairman of the Armament Development Board, Ministry of Supply, 1942–6. Chairman of the Fuel Research Board, 1947–50.

5. It may be expected that the enemy's reaction to this will be to send his U-boats still further west, and, as most of them are based on either Lorient or Bordeaux, they can do this without operating further from their bases than they are at the present time.

6. It is quite likely, therefore, that the area to the westward of 35° West and to the southward of Greenland will be the next danger area, and it is one which it is difficult for us to deal with. Aerial reconnaissance which could be carried out from Greenland to cover this area would therefore be of the greatest value, as if a U-boat were located, we should be able to re-route our convoys by signal so as to pass clear of the danger.

7. Another area in which we are having considerable trouble is that from Freetown up through Cape Verdes to the Azores. We cannot route our convoys very far to the west owing to the endurance of the vessels on this run. In fact, it is only by reducing their cargo and taking in extra fuel that they can make the passage. We are providing such escorts for these convoys as we are able, but it is quite inadequate, and it would be of the greatest help if air reconnaissance by one of the United States carriers would cover the water some distance in advance of the convoys.

8. There will be no difficulty in giving the American naval authorities notification of the movement of convoys.

9. As regard raiders, one great danger-point is off Newfoundland, as we have a very large amount of shipping proceeding independently through this area. This was the area in which the *Scharnhorst* and *Gneisenau* made such a bag. Any additional long-range air reconnaissance which could be carried out from Newfoundland or Nova Scotia would be of the greatest assistance.

10. We hope to station a powerful capital ship in either Nova Scotia or Newfoundland which would be able to take advantage of any information which we receive regarding the activities of raiders.

11. There are various areas on our trade routes in which the enemy is liable to operate and which are west of the longitude 25° West. There are also certain areas in the North and South Atlantic off the trade routes in which the enemy maintain their supply ships and where they go to refuel. Up to the present time we have been unable to search out these areas, as we have not had the ships to do it with. If we knew that reconnaissance was going to take place over any given area, we would endeavour to have in the vicinity a force which would be capable of dealing with any raider which was located. Apart from any information which your ships were able to broadcast, the mere fact of air reconnaissance taking place over these areas would give the enemy a great feeling of uneasiness.

12. It is understood that arrangements have already been made for secret intercommunication between British and United States warships.

13. For yourself alone. There is another matter closely connected with above which is causing me and the Naval Staff increasing anxiety. The

capacity of Spain and Portugal to resist the increasing German pressure may at any time collapse, and the anchorage at Gibraltar be rendered unusable. To effect this the Germans would not need to move a large army through Spain, but merely to get hold of the batteries which molest the anchorage, for which a few thousand artillerists and technicians might be sufficient. They have already done some of their usual preliminary penetration into Tangier, and thus both sides of the Straits might quickly pass into the hands of expert hostile gunners.

14. Of course, the moment Spain gives way or is attacked we shall despatch two expeditions which we have long been holding in readiness, one from Britain to one of the islands in the Azores, and subsequently to a second island, and the second expedition to the same in the Cape de Verde. But these operations will take eight days from the signal being given, and one can never tell that the Germans may not have forestalling plans on foot. With our other naval burdens we have not the forces to maintain a continuous watch. It would be a very great advantage if you could send an American squadron for a friendly cruise in these regions at the earliest moment. This would probably warn Nazi raiders off, and would keep the place warm for us as well as giving us invaluable information.

15. I have had long talks with Mr Forrestal,[1] and am taking him and Harriman with me tomorrow night to study the position in the Mersey area, so important to the North-Western Approaches.

Winston S. Churchill to General Wavell

(*Churchill papers, 20/38*)

24 April 1941
sent at 3.30 p.m.

1. Would not smoke screens used from different directions, according to wind, give considerable immunity to ships in Tobruk harbour? Have you the necessary materials and appliances?

2. We should be glad to have details about the German Tanks recently captured by the Tobruk garrison. In particular, are they tropicalized, desert-worthy, and fitted for use in the very hot weather?

[1] James V. Forrestal, 1892–1949. Under-Secretary, United States Navy Department (the position held by Franklin D. Roosevelt in the First World War), 1940–44. Established a Controlled Materials Plan, to establish priorities with regard to materials. Sent to London to negotiate Lend-Lease arrangements, 1941. Acting Secretary of the Navy, 1944. An eye-witness of the Allied landings in the South of France 1944 (as was Churchill). Recommended the unification of all three services into a Department of Defence. Opposed too rapid a demobilization, 1945.

3. We still await news of the actions at Agheila and Mechili which resulted in the loss of the 3rd Armoured Brigade and the best part of a Motorized Cavalry Brigade. Evidently there was a severe defeat, and it is essential to our comprehension of your difficulties, as well as of our own, that we should know broadly what happened, and why. Were the troops outnumbered, outmanoeuvred or outfought, or was there some mistake, as is alleged, about premature destruction of petrol store. Surely the reports of the survivors should have made it possible to give us a coherent story of this key action. I cannot help you if you do not tell me.

4. While I recognize the difficulties of giving information of the fighting in Greece set out in your telegram, I cannot feel that the explanation is complete. General Wilson must have known every night something about the position of the troops whose retreat he was concerting with so much skill, and whether any particular Brigade groups were engaged or not during the day. He ought to have sent a short report every night, and could, if necessary, have employed a Staff Officer for this purpose. As it was, we did not know for eight days even that fighting was going on.

John Colville: diary
(*Colville papers*)

24 April 1941

The PM left for a tour of Liverpool and Manchester.

During the nights of 24 and 25 April 1941, 17,000 troops were evacuated from the coves and beaches of Greece.

Winston S. Churchill to President Franklin D. Roosevelt
(*Churchill papers, 20/38*)

25 April 1941
Personal and Secret
sent at 3.30 p.m.

Greatly cheered by the news about 'Navy Western Hemisphere Defence Plan No. 2'. It almost entirely covers the points made in my cable to you which crossed the official communication. We are deeply impressed by the rapidity with which it is being brought into play. We have just received a report which indicates that a surface raider is operating in a position about 300 miles south-east of Bermuda. Everything will be done to tell the Commander-in-Chief of the United States Fleet about our convoys and other matters. Admiral Ghormley is in the closest touch with the Admiralty and the necessary Staff arrangements will be perfected.

2. The route taken by British shipping to and from the Cape is dependent on the areas in which U-boats are suspected, but a route west of 26° West is being used at the present time, and will be used whenever possible.

3. We welcome the energetic steps the United States Navy are taking to prepare bases in the North-Western Approaches.

4. The Anzacs have been fighting all day in the Pass of Thermopylae; but, Mr President, you will long ago have foreseen the conclusion of these particular Greek affairs. I wish we could have done more. I am sure we were bound to do our utmost.

I am, as I told you in my last, not at all discontented with Libya. The magnet of Tobruk is exercising its powerful attractive influence, and we are hoping both to reinforce our Army from the south and to harry, if not cut, hostile communication across the Mediterranean. In this theatre we shall, I think, come through.

5. But how small is this compared with the Battle of the Atlantic, which the action you have just taken may well decide in a favourable sense.

6. We are, of course, observing the strictest secrecy. You will, I am sure, however, realize that if it were possible for you to make any kind of disclosure of declaration on these lines it might powerfully influence the attitude both of Turkey and Spain at a cardinal moment.

Winston S. Churchill to William Mackenzie King

(*Churchill papers, 20/49*)

25 April 1941

I am most grateful to you for your message. Please accept my warmest thanks for this personal account of your conversations with President Roosevelt and others during your visit to the United States, and my congratulations on the results achieved. Like yourself, I have always attached the highest importance to dovetailing Canada's war effort in production and finance with the effort of the United States to aid us both. I well know the part Canada, under your leadership, can play in uniting the effort of the Empire and of the United States. It was good of you to take the initiative on this occasion, and I thank you for this new service to our common interests.

Winston S. Churchill to Admiral Sir Andrew Cunningham
(*Churchill papers, 20/38*)

26 April 1941
Personal and Secret

1. I am somewhat concerned at your 118. There can be no departure from the principle that it is the prime responsibility of the Mediterranean Fleet to sever all communication between Italy with Africa.

2. I am sorry that the haze caused by the aircraft attack hampered your firing at Tripoli. We ought to have foreseen this, but it is no use repining, and after all results were substantial and achieved without casualties in ships or men. Personally, I was not surprised at this immunity, and certainly the fact that the main batteries of the principal enemy base in Africa, although under German control, were at twenty minutes' notice, show that enemy cannot be always ready everywhere at the same time. I suppose there is no doubt that the blocking plan would, in these circumstances, have come off.

3. About your air support: you should obtain accurate information, because no judgment can be formed without it. CAS tells me that the same weight of bombs as you fired of shells into Tripoli in 42 minutes, viz., 530 tons, might have been dropped –

(a) by one Wellington Squadron from Malta in 10½ weeks,
or
(b) by one Stirling Squadron from Egypt in about 30 weeks.

The latter figure is theoretical, since the Stirling has not been operated at extreme range, nor is it suitable for operations under Middle East conditions, which is not the case. I am advised that it would not be practicable to operate Stirlings, &c., from Egypt now. All this new class of heavy bombers of which you speak so confidently are still suffering from the normal 'teething troubles' common to all types when first brought into service. In fact, of the 70 new heavy bombers on the strength of Bomber Command yesterday (23rd), 68 were unserviceable from one cause or another. You can imagine what would happen to this class of aircraft if they were separated from the parent workshops in their present stage.

4. Your remarks in paragraph C about our withholding the Beauforts from Malta show that you do not appreciate the fact that the primary aim of the air force in Malta is to defend the naval base against air attack, in order that your surface craft may operate against enemy convoys with their decisive power as so successfully demonstrated. This policy may be right or wrong, it may prove too costly in ships, but we think it ought to be tried. For the purposes of Tiger, apart from what comes from Double Winch, we are sending 15 Beaufighters to Malta, and also to supplement the efforts of the surface forces to interrupt ships between Italy and Tripoli, we are sending out today 6 of the specially trained Blenheim bombers which have been doing so well against coastal shipping here.

5. The first paragraph of your C is really not justified. The main disposition of forces between the various theatres rests with the Defence Committee, over which I preside, and not with the Air Ministry, who execute our decisions. Ever since November I have tried by every method and every route to pump aircraft into the Middle East. Great risks have been run and sacrifices made, especially when two-thirds of one whole fighter squadron were drowned in trying to fly to Malta, and when *Furious* was taken off her Atlantic duties to make three voyages to Takoradi. I always try hard here to sustain you in every way and acclaim your repeated successes, and I earnestly hope you will also believe that we at the centre try to take sound and bold decisions amid our many difficulties.

6. At my request CAS will forward to you, through the AOC, C-in-C,[1] a detailed technical note on the above points.

7. In the last paragraph of your B you wonder how I could have suggested that *Nelson* and/or *Rodney* should be spared from the Atlantic to join the Mediterranean Fleet. I thought they were specially suitable because of their deck armour and the apprehensions entertained of the dive-bomber attacks. Whether they could be spared or not depends upon the situation in the Atlantic. About this, in view of your high position, I will now inform you. I have been for a long time in constant intimate communication with President Roosevelt. He has now begun to take over a great part of the patrolling west of the 26th Meridian West. The whole American Atlantic Fleet, with numerous flying boats, entered into action in the first phase of this plan at midnight, 24th, GMT. United States warships will cruise along our convoy routes, shadow, or as they call it 'trail' all raiders or U-boats observed, and broadcast their positions in plain language to the world at four-hourly intervals, or oftener if needed. It is desired that this shall not be announced suddenly, but become apparent as it develops. The matter is therefore confided to you in the highest secrecy. The easement and advantage of it to the Admiralty is enormous, and, of course, it may easily produce even more decisive events. Therefore, you do not need at this moment to be unduly concerned about the Atlantic, and can devote your resources, which we are increasing in so many ways, to the cutting off of enemy communication with Africa, whether by Tripoli or Cyrenaica. On this depends the battle of Egypt.

8. I have taken the pains to give you this full account out of my admiration for the successes you have achieved, your many cares, my sympathy for you in the many risks your fleet has to run, and because of the commanding importance of the duty you have to discharge.

[1] The Chief of the Air Staff, Sir Charles Portal, and the Air Officer Commanding-in-Chief, Middle East, Air Marshal Longmore.

Winston S. Churchill to Ivan Subotić[1]
(*Churchill papers, 20/21*)

26 April 1941

My dear Excellency,

In your letter of 21 April you drew my attention to the great importance your Government and people attached to the evacuation from Greece of the Yugoslav officers, soldiers and civilians who have been able to pass through the enemy's line and to reach the Imperial and Greek forces in that country. Your Prime Minister has also expressed to us through His Majesty's Ambassador in Cairo his anxiety that these people should leave as soon as possible for Palestine.

I am glad to be able to inform Your Excellency that instructions had already been sent to His Majesty's Minister in Athens to do all he could in consultation with the Greek and our own military authorities to evacuate Yugoslav personnel, and that these instructions have since been renewed. We have also explained to Sir Michael Palairet that we fully agree as to the political importance of getting as many Yugoslavs away as possible.

I think however that I must warn you that it may be by no means easy to evacuate the Yugoslavs concerned and that we ourselves have no knowledge of the precise number of your nationals in Greece. Nevertheless you may rest assured that His Majesty's Government will do their best.

With much sympathy,
Believe me
Yours very truly
Winston S. Churchill

On the night of 26–27 April 1941 more than 19,000 troops were evacuated from the Greek beaches, under intense air bombardment. In a series of German dive-bomber attacks, 700 survivors of the sunken transport *Slamat*, who had been rescued by the destroyers *Diamond* and *Wryneck*, were again dive-bombed, and 650 of them were killed. By April 30 more than 50,000 soldiers and airmen had been evacuated: Britons, Australians, New Zealanders, Cypriots, Greeks, Yugoslavs and Palestinian Jews. But more than 11,500 men had been taken prisoner.

During the course of the week-long evacuation, twenty-six Allied ships were sunk by air attack, including five hospital ships.

[1] Ivan Subotic (Soubbotitch). Yugoslav Minister in London, 1939-41.

John Colville: diary
(Colville papers)

27 April 1941

Winston spoke on the wireless, less vividly than usual, but painting a sombre picture of the position in the east and bidding us turn our eyes westwards.

Winston S. Churchill: broadcast
(BBC Written Archives Centre)

27 April 1941

I was asked last week whether I was aware of some uneasiness which it was said existed in the country on account of the gravity, as it was described, of the war situation. So I thought it would be a good thing to go and see for myself what this 'uneasiness' amounted to, and I went to some of our great cities and seaports which had been most heavily bombed, and to some of the places where the poorest people had got it worst. I have come back not only reassured, but refreshed. To leave the offices in Whitehall with their ceaseless hum of activity and stress, and to go out to the front, by which I mean the streets and wharves of London or Liverpool, Manchester, Cardiff, Swansea or Bristol, is like going out of a hothouse on to the bridge of a fighting ship. It is a tonic which I should recommend any who are suffering from fretfulness to take in strong doses when they have need of it.

It is quite true that I have seen many painful scenes of havoc, and of fine buildings and acres of cottage homes blasted into rubble-heaps of ruin. But it is just in those very places where the malice of the savage enemy has done its worst, and where the ordeal of the men, women and children has been most severe, that I found their morale most high and splendid. Indeed, I felt encompassed by an exaltation of spirit in the people which seemed to lift mankind and its troubles above the level of material facts into that joyous serenity we think belongs to a better world than this.

Of their kindness to me I cannot speak, because I have never sought it or dreamed of it, and can never deserve it. I can only assure you that I and my colleagues, or comrades rather – for that is what they are – will toil with every scrap of life and strength, according to the lights that are granted to us, not to fail these people or be wholly unworthy of their faithful and generous regard. The British nation is stirred and moved as it has never been at any time in its long, eventful, famous history, and it is no hackneyed trope of speech to say that they mean to conquer or to die.

What a triumph the life of these battered cities is, over the worst that fire and bomb can do. What a vindication of the civilized and decent way of living we have been trying to work for and work towards in our Island. What a proof of the virtues of free institutions. What a test of the quality of our local authorities, and of institutions and customs and societies so steadily built. This ordeal by fire has even in a certain sense exhilarated the manhood and womanhood of Britain. The sublime but also terrible and sombre experiences and emotions of the battlefield which for centuries had been reserved for the soldiers and sailors, are now shared, for good or ill, by the entire population. All are proud to be under the fire of the enemy. Old men, little children, the crippled veterans of former wars, aged women, the ordinary hard-pressed citizen or subject of the King, as he likes to call himself, the sturdy workmen who swing the hammers or load the ships; skilful craftsmen; the members of every kind of ARP service, are proud to feel that they stand in the line together with our fighting men, when one of the greatest of causes is being fought out, as fought out it will be, to the end. This is indeed the grand heroic period of our history, and the light of glory shines on all.

You may imagine how deeply I feel my own responsibility to all these people; my responsibility to bear my part in bringing them safely out of this long, stern, scowling valley through which we are marching, and not to demand from them their sacrifices and exertions in vain.

I have thought in this difficult period, when so much fighting and so many critical and complicated manoeuvres are going on, that it is above all things important that our policy and conduct should be upon the highest level, and that honour should be our guide. Very few people realize how small were the forces with which General Wavell, that fine Commander whom we cheered in good days and will back through bad – how small were the forces which took the bulk of the Italian masses in Libya prisoners. In none of his successive victories could General Wavell maintain in the desert or bring into action more than two divisions, or about 30,000 men. When we reached Benghazi, and what was left of Mussolini's legions scurried back along the dusty road to Tripoli, a call was made upon us which we could not resist. Let me tell you about that call.

You will remember how in November the Italian Dictator fell upon the unoffending Greeks, and without reason and without warning invaded their country, and how the Greek nation, reviving their classic fame, hurled his armies back at the double-quick. Meanwhile Hitler, who had been creeping and worming his way steadily forward, doping and poisoning and pinioning, one after the other, Hungary, Roumania and Bulgaria, suddenly made it clear that he would come to the rescue of his fellow-criminal. The lack of unity among the Balkan States had enabled him to build up a mighty army in their midst. While nearly all the Greek troops were busy beating the Italians, the tremendous German military machine suddenly towered up on their other frontier. In their mortal peril the Greeks turned to us for succour. Strained as were our own resources, we could not say them nay. By solemn guarantee given before the war, Great Britain had promised them her help. They declared they would fight for their native soil even if neither of their neighbours made common cause with them, and even if we left them to their fate. But we could not do that. There are rules against that kind of thing; and to break those rules would be fatal to the honour of the British Empire, without which we could neither hope nor deserve to win this hard war. Military defeat or miscalculation can be redeemed. The fortunes of war are fickle and changing. But an act of shame would deprive us of the respect which we now enjoy throughout the world, and this would sap the vitals of our strength.

During the last year we have gained by our bearing and conduct a potent hold upon the sentiments of the people of the United States. Never, never in our history, have we been held in such admiration and regard across the Atlantic Ocean. In that great Republic, now in much travail and stress of soul, it is customary to use all the many valid, solid arguments about American interests and American safety, which depend upon the destruction of Hitler and his foul gang and even fouler doctrines. But in the long run – believe me, for I know – the action of the United States will be dictated, not by methodical calculations of profit and loss, but by moral sentiment, and by that gleaming flash of resolve which lifts the hearts of men and nations, and springs from the spiritual foundations of human life itself.

We, for our part, were of course bound to hearken to the Greek appeal to the utmost limit of our strength. We put the case to the Dominions of Australia and New Zealand, and their Governments, without in any way ignoring the hazards, told us that they felt the same as we did. So an important part of the mobile portion of the Army of the Nile was sent to Greece in fulfilment of our pledge. It happened that the divisions available and best suited to this task were from New Zealand and Australia, and that only about half the troops who took part in this dangerous expedition came from the Mother Country. I see the German propaganda is trying to make bad blood between us and Australia by making out that we have used them to do what we would not have asked of the British Army. I shall leave it to Australia to deal with that taunt.

Let us see what has happened. We knew, of course, that the forces we could send to Greece would not by themselves alone be sufficient to stem the German tide of invasion. But there was a very real hope that the neighbours of Greece would by our intervention be drawn to stand in the line together with her while time remained. How nearly that came off will be known some day. The tragedy of Yugoslavia has been that these brave people had a government who hoped to purchase an ignoble immunity by submission to the Nazi will. Thus when at last the people of Yugoslavia found out where they were being taken, and rose in one spontaneous surge of revolt, they saved the soul and future of their country: but it was already too late to save its territory. They had no time to mobilize their armies. They were struck down by the ruthless and highly-mechanized Hun before they could even bring their armies into the field. Great disasters have occurred in the Balkans. Yugoslavia has been beaten down. Only in the mountains can she continue her resistance. The Greeks have been overwhelmed. Their victorious Albanian army has been cut off and forced to surrender, and it has been left to the Anzacs and their British comrades to fight their way back to the sea, leaving their mark on all who hindered them.

I turn aside from the stony path we have to tread, to indulge a moment of lighter relief. I daresay you have read in the newspapers that, by a special proclamation, the Italian Dictator has congratulated the Italian army in Albania on the glorious laurels they have gained by their victory over the Greeks. Here surely is the world's record in the domain of the ridiculous and the contemptible. This whipped jackal, Mussolini, who to save his own skin has made all Italy a vassal state of Hitler's Empire, comes frisking up at the side of the German tiger with yelpings not only of appetite – that can be understood – but even of triumph. Different things strike different people in different ways. But I am sure there are a great many millions in the British Empire and in the United States, who will find a new object in life in making sure that when we come to the final reckoning this absurd impostor will be abandoned to public justice and universal scorn.

While these grievous events were taking place in the Balkan Peninsula and in Greece, our forces in Libya have sustained a vexatious and damaging defeat. The Germans advanced sooner and in greater strength than we or our Generals expected. The bulk of our armoured troops, which had played such a decisive part in beating the Italians, had to be refitted, and the single armoured brigade which had been judged sufficient to hold the frontier till about the middle of May was worsted and its vehicles largely destroyed by a somewhat stronger German armoured force. Our Infantry, which had not exceeded one division, had to fall back upon the very large Imperial armies that have been assembled and can be nourished and maintained in the fertile delta of the Nile.

Tobruk – the fortress of Tobruk – which flanks any German advance on Egypt, we hold strongly. There we have repulsed many attacks, causing the enemy heavy losses and taking many prisoners. That is how the matter stands in Egypt and on the Libyan front.

We must now expect the war in the Mediterranean on the sea, in the desert, and above all in the air, to become very fierce, varied and widespread. We had cleaned the Italians out of Cyrenaica, and it now lies with us to purge that province of the Germans. That will be a harder task, and we cannot expect to do it at once. You know I never try to make out that defeats are victories. I have never underrated the German as a warrior. Indeed I told you a month ago that the swift, unbroken course of victories which we had gained over the Italians could not possibly continue, and that misfortunes must be expected. There is only one thing certain about war, that it is full of disappointments and also full of mistakes. It remains to be seen, however, whether it is the Germans who have made the mistake in trampling down the Balkan States and in making a river of blood and hate between themselves and the Greek and Yugoslav peoples. It remains also to be seen whether they have made a mistake in their attempt to invade Egypt with the forces and means of supply which they have now got. Taught by experience, I make it a rule not to prophesy about battles which have yet to be fought out. This, however, I will venture to say, that I should be very sorry to see the tasks of the combatants in the Middle East exchanged, and that General Wavell's armies should be in the position of the German invaders. That is only a personal opinion, and I can well understand you may take a different view. It is certain that fresh dangers besides those which threaten Egypt may come upon us in the Mediterranean. The war may spread to Spain and Morocco. It may spread eastward to Turkey and Russia. The Huns may lay their hands for a time upon the granaries of the Ukraine and the oil-wells of the Caucasus. They may dominate the Black Sea. They may dominate the Caspian. Who can tell? We shall do our best to meet them and fight them wherever they go. But there is one thing which is certain. There is one thing which rises out of the vast welter which is sure and solid, and which no one in his senses can mistake. Hitler cannot find safety from avenging justice in the East, in the Middle East, or in the Far East. In order to win this war, he must either conquer this Island by invasion, or he must cut the ocean life-line which joins us to the United States.

Let us look into these alternatives, if you will bear with me for a few minutes longer. When I spoke to you last, early in February, many people believed the Nazi boastings that the invasion of Britain was about to begin. It has not begun yet, and with every week that passes we grow stronger on the sea, in the air, and in the numbers, quality, training and equipment of the great Armies that now guard our Island. When I compare the position at home as it is today with what it was in the summer of last year, even after making allowance for a much more elaborate mechanical preparation on the part of the enemy, I feel that we have very much to be thankful for, and I believe that provided our exertions and our vigilance are not relaxed even for a moment, we may be confident that we shall give a very good account of ourselves. More than that it would be boastful to say. Less than that it would be foolish to believe.

But how about our life-line across the Atlantic? What is to happen if so many of our merchant ships are sunk that we cannot bring in the food we need to nourish our brave people? What if the supplies of war materials and war weapons which the United States are seeking to send us in such enormous quantities should in large part be sunk on the way? What is to happen then? In February, as you may remember, that bad man in one of his raving outbursts threatened us with a terrifying increase in the numbers and activities of his U-boats and in his air attack – not only on our Island but, thanks to his use of French and Norwegian harbours, and thanks to the denial to us of the

Irish bases – upon our shipping far out into the Atlantic. We have taken and are taking all possible measures to meet this deadly attack, and we are now fighting against it with might and main. That is what is called the Battle of the Atlantic, which in order to survive we have got to win on salt water just as decisively as we had to win the Battle of Britain last August and September in the air.

Wonderful exertions have been made by our Navy and Air Force; by the hundreds of mine-sweeping vessels which with their marvellous appliances keep our ports clear in spite of all the enemy can do; by the men who build and repair our immense fleets of merchant ships; by the men who load and unload them; and need I say by the officers and men of the Merchant Navy who go out in all weathers and in the teeth of all dangers to fight for the life of their native land and for a cause they comprehend and serve. Still, when you think how easy it is to sink ships at sea and how hard it is to build them and protect them, and when you remember that we have never less than two thousand ships afloat and three or four hundred in the danger zone; when you think of the great armies we are maintaining and reinforcing in the East, and of the world-wide traffic we have to carry on – when you remember all this, can you wonder that it is the Battle of the Atlantic which holds the first place in the thoughts of those upon whom rests the responsibility for procuring the victory?

It was therefore with indescribable relief that I learned of the tremendous decisions lately taken by the President and people of the United States. The American Fleet and flying boats have been ordered to patrol the wide waters of the Western Hemisphere, and to warn the peaceful shipping of all nations outside the combat zone of the presence of lurking U-boats or raiding cruisers belonging to the two aggressor nations. We British shall therefore be able to concentrate our protecting forces far more upon the routes nearer home, and to take a far heavier toll of the U-boats there. I have felt for some time that something like this was bound to happen. The President and Congress of the United States, having newly fortified themselves by contact with their electors, have solemnly pledged their aid to Britain in this war because they deem our cause just, and because they know their own interests and safety would be endangered if we were destroyed. They are taxing themselves heavily. They have passed great legislation. They have turned a large part of their gigantic industry to making the munitions which we need. They have even given us or lent us valuable weapons of their own. I could not believe that they would allow the high purposes to which they have set themselves to be frustrated and the products of their skill and labour sunk to the bottom of the sea. U-boat warfare as conducted by Germany is entirely contrary to international agreements freely subscribed to by Germany only a few years ago. There is no effective blockade, but only a merciless murder and marauding over wide, indiscriminate areas utterly beyond the control of the German seapower.

When I said ten weeks ago: 'Give us the tools and we will finish the job,' I meant, give them to us: put them within our reach – and that is what it now seems the Americans are going to do. And that is why I feel a very strong conviction that though the Battle of the Atlantic will be long and hard, and its issue is by no means yet determined, it has entered upon a more grim but at the same time a far more favourable phase. When you come to think of it, the United States are very closely bound up with us now, and have engaged themselves deeply in giving us moral, material, and, within the limits I have mentioned, naval support.

It is worth while therefore to take a look on both sides of the ocean at the forces which are facing each other in this awful struggle, from which there can be no drawing back.

No prudent and far-seeing man can doubt that the eventual and total defeat of Hitler and Mussolini is certain, in view of the respective declared resolves of the British and American democracies. There are less than seventy million malignant Huns – some of whom are curable and others killable[1] – many of whom are already engaged in holding down Austrians, Czechs, Poles, French and the many other ancient races they now bully and pillage.

The peoples of the British Empire and of the United States number nearly two hundred millions in their homelands and in the British Dominions alone. They possess the unchallengeable command of the oceans, and will soon obtain decisive superiority in the air. They have more wealth, more technical resources, and they make more steel, than the whole of the rest of the world put together. They are determined that the cause of freedom shall not be trampled down, nor the tide of world progress turned backwards, by the criminal Dictators.

While therefore we naturally view with sorrow and anxiety much that is happening in Europe and in Africa, and may happen in Asia, we must not lose our sense of proportion and thus become discouraged or alarmed. When we face with a steady eye the difficulties which lie before us, we may derive new confidence from remembering those we have already overcome. Nothing that is happening now is comparable in gravity with the dangers through which we passed last year. Nothing that can happen in the East is comparable with what is happening in the West.

Last time I spoke to you I quoted the lines of Longfellow which President Roosevelt had written out for me in his own hand. I have some other lines

[1] This phrase from 'malignant Huns' to 'killable', led Corder Catchpool, a veteran pacifist and First World War conscientious objector, to publish an open letter to Churchill in which he declared: 'I think that such a wholesale indictment is not in accordance with truth, and that the spirit it breathes is a pagan spirit, the opposite of what Jesus taught as to the Christian attitude towards sinful mankind. I make bold to prophesy that if this spirit predominates in the minds of our Government and People, then the present generation will pass away without any hope of realizing that new and better world for which men are agonizing now.' (Letter dated 3 May 1941: *Catchpool papers*)

which are less well known but which seem apt and appropriate to our fortunes to-night, and I believe they will be so judged wherever the English language is spoken or the flag of freedom flies:

For while the tired waves, vainly breaking,
Seem here no painful inch to gain,
Far back, through creeks and inlets making,
Comes silent, flooding in, the main.
And not by eastern windows only,
When daylight comes, comes in the light;
In front the sun climbs slow, how slowly!
But westward, look, the land is bright.[1]

General Sir Alan Brooke: diary
(*'Turn of the Tide'*)

27 April 1941 Chequers

PM was broadcasting at 9 p.m., so we had to wait for dinner till 9.50 p.m. He was in great form after his broadcast and kept us up till 3.30 a.m.

General Sir Alan Brooke to Winston S. Churchill
(*Churchill papers., 20/24*)

28 April 1941 10 Downing Street

Dear Prime Minister,

This is just a short line to thank you again for your great kindness in inviting me periodically to Chequers, and of thus giving me an opportunity of discussing the problems of the defence of this country with you, and of putting some of my difficulties before you.

These informal talks are of the very greatest help to me, & I do hope you realize how grateful I am to you for your kindness.

With my many thanks.

Yrs v sincerely
A. F. Brooke

[1] Immediately after his broadcast, Churchill telephoned Violet Bonham Carter and to her amazement asked: 'Did you hear my broadcast?' 'Of course I did, Winston,' she replied, 'Everybody in England listens when you speak.' 'Did you not recognize the poem?' he went on to ask her. Violet Bonham Carter did; thirty-five years earlier she had read it to him, noticing then how struck he had been by it, and staggered now that he should not only remember that poetry reading of so long ago, but also telephone her about it. (Baroness Asquith of Yarnbury, conversation with the author, 25 August 1964). The poem was *Say Not The Struggle Naught Availeth* by Arthur Hugh Clough.

Winston S. Churchill: War Cabinet Directive
(*Cabinet papers, 120/10*)

28 April 1941
Most Secret

Japan is unlikely to enter the war unless the Germans make a successful invasion of Great Britain, and even a major disaster like the loss of the Middle East would not necessarily make her come in, because the liberation of the British Mediterranean Fleet which might be expected, and also any troops evacuated from the Middle East to Singapore would not weaken the British war-making strength in Malaya. It is very unlikely, moreover, that Japan will enter the war either if the United States have come in, or if Japan thinks that they would come in consequent upon a Japanese declaration of war. Finally, it may be taken as almost certain that the entry of Japan into the war would be followed by the immediate entry of the United States on our side.

These conditions are to be accepted by the Service Departments as a guide for all plans and actions. Should they cease to hold good, it will be the responsibility of Ministers to notify the Service Staffs in good time.

2. The loss of Egypt and the Middle East would be a disaster of the first magnitude to Great Britain, second only to successful invasion and final conquest. Every effort is to be made to reinforce General Wavell with military and Air forces, and if Admiral Cunningham requires more ships, the Admiralty will make proposals for supplying them. It is to be impressed upon all ranks, especially the highest, that the life and honour of Great Britain depends upon the successful defence of Egypt. It is not to be expected that the British forces of the land, sea and Air in the Mediterranean would wish to survive so vast and shameful a defeat as would be entailed by our expulsion from Egypt, having regard to the difficulties of the enemy and his comparatively small numbers. Not only must Egypt be defended, but the Germans have to be beaten and thrown out of Cyrenaica. This offensive objective must be set before the troops.

3. All plans for evacuation of Egypt or for closing or destroying the Suez Canal are to be called in and kept under the strict personal control of Headquarters. No whisper of such plans is to be allowed. No surrenders by officers and men will be considered tolerable unless at least 50 per cent. casualties are sustained by the Unit or force in question. According to Napoleon's maxim, 'when a man is caught alone and unarmed, a surrender may be made.' But Generals and Staff Officers surprised by the enemy are to use their pistols in self-defence. The honour of a wounded man is safe. Anyone who can kill a Hun or even an Italian has rendered good service.

4. The Army of the Nile is to fight with no thought of retreat or withdrawal. This task is enforced upon it by physical facts, for it will be utterly impossible to find the shipping for moving a tithe of the immense

masses of men and stores which have been gathered in the Nile Valley.

5. In considering reinforcements for the Middle East, the question of the defence of Great Britain against invasion does not arise, as the available shipping would be far less than the ships which would contain the number of troops who could be safely sent.

6. Should 'Tiger' succeed, the empty ships should be returned by the short cut, keeping their deck armaments for this purpose. It must be remembered that General Wavell has, with the troops returned from Greece, a trained personnel of 8 or 9 Tank Regiments, for which the Tanks now sent or in his possession are barely sufficient. Moreover, the personnel of the Tank Corps now going round the Cape will require other Tanks besides those already provided to await them on their arrival. Therefore we must contemplate a repetition of 'Tiger' at the earliest moment. The situation, however, must be judged when and if the MT ships return.

7. 'Double Winch' having succeeded again, should be repeated with the utmost speed, all preparations being made to the aircraft in the meanwhile.

8. There is no need at the present time to make any further dispositions for the defence of Malaya and Singapore, beyond those modest arrangements which are in progress, until or unless the conditions set out in paragraph 1 are modified.

Winston S. Churchill to Sir Edward Bridges and General Ismay
(Churchill papers, 20/36)

28 April 1941

FOR THE WAR CABINET BATTLE OF THE ATLANTIC COMMITTEE

1. It is not intended to use the catapult ships as ordinary freighters; nor can a number like 200, which has been mentioned, be at any time contemplated.

2. There are at present five catapult patrol vessels working like the *Pegasus*. These should be joined at the earliest moment by the first ten catapult-fitted merchant ships, and from these fifteen vessels there must be found a regular patrol covering or accompanying the convoys in the Focke-Wulf zone.

3. As some of these vessels are probably heavier, faster and more valuable MV's[1] than are required for this patrolling service, they are to be replaced at earliest by other smaller vessels which the Ministry of Shipping can better spare. The large ones already fitted, having been relieved, may ply on the Freetown–Britain route, as they will have the opportunity of going through two danger zones in each voyage, and the catapult Hurricanes will thus have adequate opportunities of fighting.

[1] Merchant Vessels.

4. If the fifteen ships devoted to the North-Western Approaches patrol are proved to be a success and it is thought necessary to increase their numbers, a proposal should be put forward. At the same time, the Beaufighter aircraft now employed on patrol duties should be returned to the Fighter Command, where they are most urgently needed for night-fighting.

Winston S. Churchill to General Ismay

(*Churchill papers, 20/36*)

28 April 1941
Secret

1. Let me have this day the minute which I wrote in the summer of last year directing that 5,000 Parachute Troops were to be prepared, together with all the minutes of the Departments concerned which led to my afterwards agreeing to reduce this number to 500. I shall expect to receive the office files before midnight.

2. Let me have all the present proposals for increasing the Parachute and Glider Force, together with a time-table of expected results.

Winston S. Churchill to General Ismay, for the Chiefs of Staff Committee

(*Churchill papers, 20/36*)

28 April 1941
Secret

This evening I wish to discuss the impending developments of the war in the Mediterranean. It seems probable that the Germans will

(a) attack Crete,
(b attack Malta, for which their aircraft are already moving to Foggia, and
(c) make a move through Spain on Morocco.

it is necessary to survey this position, and in particular to consider what steps can be taken, apart from 'Puma', &c.,[1] to resist or counter German penetration of Morocco or Tangier.

[1] The plan to seize the Spanish Canary Islands, and the Portuguese Cape Verde Islands, off the Atlantic coast of Africa, in the event of a German move against Spain and Portugal.

Winston S. Churchill to General Ismay, for the Chiefs of Staff Committee
(*Churchill papers, 20/36*)

28 April 1941

I see a statement that the Italians shot all the Free French prisoners they took at Tobruk. If this is true, it raises the question of reprisals. You should consider the following proposal: Hand over 1,000 Italian officers to the Free French in Central Africa as working capital, and announce that for every Free Frenchmen shot by the Italians, two (or three (?)) Italian officers would be executed. The question is whether an announcement of this kind might not be advantageous. However, in view of the fact that the Huns have 50,000 of our men in their hands, and of the great importance of not starting a massacre of prisoners, the matter requires very careful consideration so far as policy and publicity are concerned. On the whole, I think we should give the Italians to de Gaulle and let him say what he likes about it. This is a matter upon which I have reached no final conclusion.

Winston S. Churchill to General Sir John Dill
(*Churchill papers, 20/36*)

28 April 1941
Most Secret

The DMO[1] yesterday spoke of plans which had been prepared in certain eventualities for the evacuation of Egypt.

Let me see these plans, and any material bearing upon them.

Winston S. Churchill to A.V. Alexander and Admiral Pound
(*Churchill papers, 20/36*)

28 April 1941

ITALIAN SHIPS SAILING TO BENGHAZI FROM TRIPOLI

The C-in-C Mediterranean,[2] has been fully occupied in the successful conduct of the evacuation, but now he must resume his efforts to blockade Cyrenaican ports and to catch these ships or as many of them as possible. It ought to be far easier to blockade Cyrenaican ports than Tripoli. Both must be attempted, but failure to achieve the second would be specially lamentable.

[1] The Director of Military Operations, General Kennedy (see page 566, note 1).
[2] Admiral Sir Andrew Cunningham.

Winston S. Churchill to General Wavell
(*Premier papers, 3/109*)

28 April 1941
telephoned from Chequers, 11.30 a.m.

It seems clear from our information[1] that a heavy airborne attack by German troops and bombers will soon be made on Crete. Let me know what Forces you have in the island and what your plans are. It ought to be a fine opportunity for killing the parachute troops. The island must be stubbornly defended.

Winston S. Churchill to General Wavell
(*Churchill papers, 20/38*)

28 April 1941

Thank you very much for your general outline of what occurred on the Western frontier. We seem to have had rather bad luck. I expect we shall get this back later. Every good wish.

Winston S. Churchill to General Auchinleck
(*Churchill papers, 20/38*)

28 April 1941

REINFORCEMENTS FROM INDIA TO IRAQ

We are greatly obliged to you for the alacrity with which you have improved on your previous arrangements.

John Colville: diary
(*Colville papers*)

28 April 1941

Back at No.10 there is a tense feeling as the evacuation of our troops from Greece is now taking place.

The PM's speech has been well received though there is inevitably some disillusionment after the brilliant successes of the last few months. Many people think too much emphasis has been laid on the part played by Anzacs and New Zealanders. From the papers one would hardly suppose British

[1] This information was the German Air Force's own most secret radio signal system, decrypted at Bletchley under the general designation of 'Enigma' (later 'Ultra').

troops had been fighting in Greece or Africa at all. It was, of course, the same at Gallipoli in the last war.

There is some consolation in the fact that our successes in Abyssinia and East Africa proceed undiminished.

Winston S. Churchill to Viscount Halifax

(*Foreign Office papers, 954/29*)

28 April 1941
Secret and Personal
sent 4.55 p.m.

Do not discourage the President from posing his questions direct to me or allow any of the Naval Staff to do so. My personal relations with him are of importance, and it would be a pity if they were superseded by ordinary staff routine.

War Cabinet: minutes

(*Cabinet papers, 65/18*)

28 April 1941
5 p.m.

10 Downing Street

PARLIAMENT

The Prime Minister said that in view of the progress of events he saw no reason why there should not now be a public debate in the House of Commons. The critics of the Government were few, but vocal; but they had succeeded in spreading reports of dissatisfaction which, he believed, were entirely false. His impression from going about the country was of complete national unity. Parliamentary government depended on voting and not merely on debate. He proposed therefore, that on the occasion of the debate, which might be on the following Thursday, the Government should put down a Resolution and make it a matter of confidence.

This view met with acceptance, but it was felt that the terms of the Resolution would require a good deal of thought. The Prime Minister said that he would speak himself and would prefer to open the debate.

SHIPPING LOSSES

The Prime Minister thought that if unexpectedly low figures were now published, this might give a handle to American Isolationists at a crucial moment. He therefore thought that the publication of the April shipping losses, due to be made at the end of the month should be deferred for the present. Publication of these figures might perhaps be put on a quarterly basis.

INFORMATION

Mr Menzies said that journalists and Press in the United States were strongly pro-British, but that the bulk of their news came from German sources because we did not provide them with adequate news. He thought that the dissatisfaction of Australian opinion had also been due to the dearth of news. Generally, he thought that we underestimated the propaganda value of news service.

In discussion, considerable support was expressed for this view.

The Prime Minister pointed out that in regard to the operations in Greece it would have been impossible for us to give more information since for a period of several critical days we had been without any information ourselves. He had sent a telegram of protest to General Wavell. In conditions such as prevailed in this war, he thought that there must necessarily be periods when virtually nothing could be said about the progress of operations. But later a time would come when a full account could be given. As, for example, in the debate which had now been arranged

WARNING THE VICHY GOVERNMENT

The Prime Minister thought that the most effective course would be if His Majesty's Government were to tell the Vichy Government through the United States Government, that they would be doing a great wrong if they agreed to German troops landing in Syria, or Morocco or passing through unoccupied France.

TURKEY

The Prime Minister thought that we must acquiesce in the view that Turkey's role would be a passive one; but as a neutral she might protect our flank. As regards supplies to Turkey, he saw no reason to reach any far-reaching decision that day. Events were likely to develop quickly in the Middle East. Our policy should be based on the fact that no useful purpose would be served by putting strong pressure on Turkey. Equally it would be wrong at this moment to discontinue furnishing supplies to Turkey. We should therefore continue to send supplies, but the volume should not be increased. Indeed it might be a wise precaution to diminish the despatch of articles which would have little or no value to our own forces in the Middle East if circumstances were to prevent their delivery to Turkey. The Prime Minister thought that if events should be so managed that the enemy forces did not march through Turkey, we should have derived a great benefit from the Turkish alliance. The factor which was most likely to be effective in persuading Turkey to remain faithful to the alliance would be a still further advance on the part of the United States towards the attitude of belligerent alliance.

THE EVACUATION FROM GREECE, AND ITS AFTERMATH[1]

The Prime Minister thought that we could congratulate ourselves on the number of troops evacuated from Greece. It might well be that our total losses, killed, wounded and prisoners, would be between 5,000 and 10,000. The concluding stages of the Greek campaign had been a glorious episode in the history of British arms. The losses we had inflicted on the German troops had almost certainly exceeded our own: this notwithstanding that the withdrawal had been effected almost without air support.

He felt no regret over the decision to send troops to Greece. Had we not done so, Yugoslavia would not now be an open enemy of Germany. Further, the Greek war had caused a marked change in the attitude of the United States.

The Prime Minister said that we must now expect a period of great enemy activity in the Mediterranean. Attacks would be made on Crete and Malta, and probably West Africa and Gibraltar. The enemy's plan was, no doubt, to base strong air forces on Crete and Rhodes, which would be used to attack our surface forces off the Libyan coast. If the enemy could prevent our surface forces from operating in the Eastern Mediterranean, they could hope to use the ports in Cyrenaica sufficiently to build up heavy forces for an attack on Egypt. The air menace was the greatest menace which we had to face.

The Chief of the Air Staff gave particulars of our air squadrons at present in Egypt. We had 3 Hurricane squadrons, 3 Blenheim squadrons, 4 Wellington squadrons, 1 Wellesley squadron, 2 squadrons for army co-operation. In addition, 2 Tomahawk and 4 Maryland squadrons were forming. 23 Hurricanes had recently reached Malta by a special operation.

The Prime Minister said that since the previous November we had used every possible means to send air reinforcements out to the Middle East. Until the beginning of November the position in this country had not enabled us to send forces away from the home front.

Reference was made to the fact that since the 19th April, 13 ships were reported to have sailed for Benghazi from Tripoli.

The Prime Minister said that while the Navy had been engaged in the evacuation of our forces from Greece, it had not been possible to stop the enemy convoys. But now that evacuation was over, the Navy would be in a position to devote more attention to this essential activity.

The War Cabinet were informed that Benghazi harbour was too wide to block. We had destroyed all the cranes there, but the enemy was, no doubt, discharging from lighters. The reason why we had not been able to retain Benghazi harbour had been that we had not sufficient AA defence to protect that port as well as Tobruk.

[1] In view of the particular secrecy of this discussion, it was not recorded in the War Cabinet minutes but in the Confidential Annex (*Cabinet papers, 65/22*).

Reference was made to the position of Crete, and particulars were given of our forces.

The Prime Minister said that he had sent a telegram to General Wavell to tell him that he thought an attack on Crete was imminent, and to ask what were his plans. He (the Prime Minister) was somewhat doubtful of our ability to hold Crete against a prolonged attack.

In reply to a question, the Prime Minister said that the battalion which had landed on Lemnos had been withdrawn when the Germans had taken Salonika. There had no longer been any purpose in holding Lemnos once the Germans were free to launch air attack from Salonika. The Germans were now occupying other islands in the Aegean. We had not the strength to hold these islands against the air attack which could be directed against them.

John Colville: diary
(*Colville papers*)

28 April 1941

On late duty. Most of the time the PM spent at a Defence Committee considering urgent problems arising out of the Mediterranean situation and in particular operations 'Tiger' and 'Jaguar'.[1] To these Defence meetings came the Lord Privy Seal, the Foreign Secretary, the three Service Ministers, the Chiefs of Staff, and Ismay, Hollis and Jacob.

War Cabinet, Defence Committee (operations): minutes
(*Cabinet papers, 69/2*)

28 April 1941
9.30 p.m.

THE ATTITUDE OF THE FRENCH

The Prime Minister said that he would address a telegram to the President, emphasizing the need for a powerful demarche on the part of the American Government to deter the wavering nations, such as Vichy France, Spain, etc. If the Amercians proposed eventually to enter the war, now was the time to exercise their influence in order to shorten the struggle.

EGYPT

The Prime Minister emphasized the necessity for fighting every inch of the way in Egypt. He had formed the impression that our comparatively easy successes against the Italians, followed as they had been by a sudden reverse

[1] Tank and aircraft reinforcements to Egypt through the Mediterranean.

at the hands of the Germans, had not been a good preparation for the Army for what was now confronting them. It was necessary to impress on them that they must hold on at all costs. Nothing would be more ignominious than to be driven out of Egypt by an inferior Army operating at the end of a long, precarious, line of communications. He did not like to see the way in which the Tobruk garrison seemed to be allowing itself to be hemmed in. The war was now in a grim phase, and the Chief of the Imperial General Staff should take steps to impress on the Commander-in-Chief in the Middle East the need for hard fighting, and bold action.

Sir John Dill said that the garrison at Tobruk were by no means inactive, and had done several very successful raids, and had captured a large number of prisoners. With the number of tanks which they had in Tobruk. It was not possible for them to raid deeply enough to cut the line of communications of the forward German troops. The Infantry Tank was slow, and had a short radius of action. Our soldiers were in no way inferior to the Germans, but they were at present suffering from an inferiority in equipment. In desert fighting, everything depended upon tanks. When the tank situation had improved, he felt certain that the Commander-in-Chief would not be lacking in action. In the meantime, he probably felt that he must husband his resources.

The Prime Minister said that he noticed that Air Marshal Longmore had removed his fighters from Tobruk. This might be a right decision, but it was essential that Tobruk should be used as an advanced landing ground. He was amazed to hear that in the Western Desert the Royal Air Force only had fourteen serviceable Hurricanes

Lord Beaverbrook said that the great problem which faced mechanized forces of tanks or aircraft was maintaining serviceability. When he had taken over the Ministry of Aircraft Production, he had found that this work had been much neglected, and there were about 1,700 aircraft awaiting repair. He questioned whether the repair and maintenance organization in Egypt was efficient. He suggested that a really good Service expert should be sent out there to see whether matters could not be improved.

Sir Charles Portal said that he was certain that there could be no grounds for criticism in the forward areas, where the ground staffs of squadrons showed the utmost resource in keeping their aircraft in the air. It might be possible to find grounds for criticism further back, but he had a very good man in charge of administration in Egypt, and he doubted whether anyone else going out to strange conditions would produce better results.

The Prime Minister said he would like the Chief of the Air Staff to consider the situation, as it would be very mortifying if the Royal Air Force in Egypt, working from their own long-established bases, could not do better than the Germans, who suffered from many disadvantages. He was not satisfied with conditions at Takoradi, where large numbers of aircraft seemed to be piling up.

Sir Charles Portal pointed out that six weeks were saved by the Takoradi route. There were limits to the number which could be received in Egypt in cases, for assembly there.

The Prime Minister referred to remarks made by the Commander-in-Chief, Mediterranean, in recent signals, which showed that he was under the impression that only small numbers of aircraft were being sent to the Middle East. He felt that the Commander-in-Chief was not being given proper information on the subject. It was easy for anyone to suggest that greater numbers should be sent, but it was not easy to find any method by which it could be done.

CRETE

The Prime Minister said that all information pointed to an early German attack upon Crete. There seemed to be preparations for an airborne landing.

The Prime Minister suggested that twelve Hurricanes might be sent from Malta to Crete to strengthen the fighter defence.

SPAIN

The Prime Minister enquired what action we could take if the Germans obtained permission from the Spaniards to move through their country to attack Gibraltar, and possibly to penetrate Morocco and Tangier. We were going to do our best to bring pressure on the French to resist any move into North Africa, and it might be that they would enquire what help we could give them. If we had nothing prepared, we would be too late to seize the opportunity. He thought that preparations should be made for the landing of at any rate one Division in the case of a French invitation.

General Kennedy[1] *to Winston S. Churchill*

(*Churchill papers, 20/26*)

28 April 1941

My dear Prime Minister,

I address this note to you with a realization of considerable temerity.

But I cannot get out of my mind that you may still think I was being defeatist in my discussion with you last night. I would rather give up my post than hold it upon such a basis.

[1] John Noble Kennedy, 1893–1970. Royal Navy, 1911. Royal Artillery, 1915. On active service, 1915–18 (despatches, Military Cross); South Russian campaign, 1919 (despatches). Deputy Director of Military Operations, War Office, 1938; Director of Plans, 1939. Commander, Royal Artillery, 52nd Division, France, 1940. Director of Military Operations, War Office, 1940–3. Assistant Chief of the Imperial General Staff (Operations and Intelligence), 1943–5. Knighted, 1945. Governor of Southern Rhodesia, 1946–54. Chairman, National Convention of Southern Rhodesia, 1960. In 1959 he published his memoirs, *The Business of War.*

I have never believed, and never will, that we can lose this war. No one under your leadership could believe such a thing.

Surely you cannot think it wrong that I should hold firm views – and that they should remain firm in this particular instance even after the overwhelming onslaught to which you subjected them?

It is after all my duty to look as clear sightedly as I can at all possibilities – even unpleasant possibilities – and to form opinions and to give them frankly to you when you think it worth while to hear them.

In all I said I was merely endeavouring to lay before you evidence to be weighed in reaching grave decisions. I do not believe the position in the Middle East to be hopeless. I agree that we may yet achieve a great victory there.

But I do believe that there is a limit to the price we can safely pay for such a victory and that the assessment of that price is a problem which should now be solved.

I hope you will forgive me for writing this note to you. But I am far from happy in thinking over what you said to me.

I yield to no one in my devotion to you and it was hard indeed to say to you things that provoked your anger.

Very sincerely yours
J. N. Kennedy

Winston S. Churchill to General Kennedy
(*Churchill papers, 20/26*)

29 April 1941

My dear General,

Our conversation was purely informal and private. I am very glad to read what you say about it. I do not agree with your views, but you were perfectly entitled to express them.

Yours v truly,
Winston S. Churchill

Winston S. Churchill to President Franklin D. Roosevelt
(*Premier papers, 3/187*)

29 April 1941

At this moment much hangs in the balance. We must expect dangerous demands will be made upon Turkey. They will try their best to have themselves let alone and may go a long way to meet German wishes short of actually giving passage to large quantities of German troops. It is of the utmost importance to stiffen them, for I do not think the Germans wish to attack them. We should be content if Turkey remained an unmolested pad protecting, albeit passively, our Eastern flank in Egypt.

2. Syria is a far more imminent danger. The German airborne troops may land there, refuelling at Rhodes. Our naval forces are fully engaged in trying to cut the enemy communications between Sicily and Libya, on which the decision in the Nile Valley largely depends. We have also to fight for Crete, which may, according to our information, soon be attacked. We could not therefore be sure of preventing a small sea-borne expedition to Syria from slipping through. If the German air force and troop-carrier planes get installed in Syria they will soon penetrate and poison both Iraq and Iran and threaten Palestine.

3. Meanwhile, at the western end of the Mediterranean, I must regard the Spanish situation as most critical. Hitler may easily be able to get control of the batteries which would deny us the use of Gibraltar harbour or even the batteries on the African shore. The infiltration into Tangier is continuous, and both Morocco and Algeria may soon be infected. Once the German air force is well established in Morocco it will not be long before Dakar becomes a German U-boat base.

4. All this comes back to Vichy. We have sent official telegrams through Lord Halifax and the State Department about this, saying precisely what we should like the United States to do and, of course, we shall be guided by your action and support it in every way. Now is the time when very large and important areas may be lost, and if at a later period the United States becomes a belligerent we should all have a much longer journey to take. I trust therefore you will be able to put the most extreme pressure upon Vichy to break with the Germans if they violate Syria, Morocco, Algeria or Tunis. I feel Hitler may quite easily now gain vast advantages very cheaply, and we are so fully engaged that we can do little or nothing to stop him spreading himself.

Winston S. Churchill to Air Chief Marshal Longmore

(*Churchill papers, 20/49*)

29 April 1941

It has been decided to repeat as soon as possible, and on a much larger scale, the recent operations for flying Hurricanes off aircraft-carriers to Malta. Intention is to despatch by this means up to 140 Hurricanes, as well as 18 Fulmars. It is impossible to give firm dates at this stage, but we hope that 64 Hurricanes and 9 Fulmars will arrive in Middle East by the 25th May.

2. Twenty-five fighter pilots leave the 3rd May for Takoradi to hasten ferrying of Hurricanes and Tomahawks.

3. Capacity of route to Egypt via Takoradi freed by above use of carriers will be employed to increase flow of Tomahawks and bombers. Greatest possible increase in Blenheim shipments will be made.

Winston S. Churchill to Anthony Eden

(*Churchill papers, 20/36*)

29 April 1941

We do not often bring in outsiders to talk to the Cabinet and, indeed, so many are there already that the gathering is unwieldy.

The basis of Captain Hillgarth's policy is of the most secret character, and cannot possibly be mentioned.[1] Yet without it, his assurances would not carry conviction. In your absence I got him to attend a meeting of the Defence Committee, and this could be repeated if you desire. Meanwhile, I am asking him to luncheon.

Winston S. Churchill to Admiral Pound

(*Premier papers, 3/109*)

29 April 1941

SIGNAL FROM THE ADMIRALTY TO THE NAVAL COMMANDER-IN-CHIEF, MEDITERRANEAN

This is not at all what was meant last night. You are giving him the strongest lead to abandon Crete. I thought our view was that Crete should be held at all reasonable cost.

Your para. 2 presupposes the recapture of Benghazi. What grounds are there for assuming this?

I am much disturbed by the tenor of this signal.

[1] Hillgarth had been personally charged by Churchill, at the end of May 1940, with the task of keeping Spain out of the war. To this end Churchill had allocated \$10 million (to be held in the United States) for the necessary payments to Spanish officials, primarily senior army officers. The principal recipient was General Antonio Aranda Mata, commander of the Spanish War College, who received at least \$2 million. Returning to London in January 1941, Hillgarth again saw Churchill, before returning to Spain as supervisor of SOE Operations there. In May 1941 Churchill provided Hillgarth with extra funds for his task.

Winston S. Churchill to A.V. Alexander and Admiral Pound
(*Churchill papers, 20/36*)

29 April 1941

BRITISH TROOPS WHO HAVE MADE THEIR WAY TO THE GREEK COAST

Mind we don't despair too soon about the people at Kalamati or other points along the coast. It seems hard to believe Germans can have got there already in greater force than our men who are trying to escape. Fighting may break out or our people may go to some other part of the shore and signal your boats. Do not let them do this in vain. Please send something to Cunningham on these lines by the most urgent method.

Winston S. Churchill to General Ismay, for the Chiefs of Staff Committee
(*Churchill papers, 20/36*)

29 April 1941

NOTE BY PROFESSOR LINDEMANN ON DESTRUCTION OF IRAQ OIL WELLS

I agree with the attached memorandum, for which I called.

If any preparations are made, they would have to be made secretly, and at the same time we should have to have a substantial armed force in plain clothes on the spot. We must expect that, if the Shah falls under the German influence or menace, he will soon be looking after his wells for them. What has been done about this?

Winston S. Churchill to General Ismay, for the Chiefs of Staff Committee
(*Churchill papers, 20/36*)

29 April 1941

Is it not rather strange that, when we announced that the port of Benghazi while in our occupation was of no use, and, secondly, that on our evacuation we had completely blocked it, the enemy are using it freely?

Winston S. Churchill to General Ismay
(*Churchill papers, 20/36*)

29 April 1941

I noticed that the parachutists who landed on Saturday several times had their knuckles terribly cut. Has the question of protecting their hands and kneecaps been considered?

Winston S. Churchill to Anthony Eden, A.V. Alexander and David Margesson
(*Premier papers, 3/230/1*)

29 April 1941

I would rather that telegrams of this kind[1] should not be sent without my seeing them first. What does the convenience of our shipping mean compared to engaging the Americans in the war? A negative answer like this is chilling and ill-suited to our present purpose.

John Colville: diary
(*Colville papers*)

29 April 1941

To the House for Questions. The PM had three tiresome ones (about War Aims, smaller War Cabinet etc.) and gave the same answer to all three in succession: 'No, Sir.'

Winston S. Churchill: Oral Answers
(*Hansard*)

29 April 1941

House of Commons
Church House

BRITISH WAR AND PEACE AIMS

Mr Mander asked the Prime Minister whether he will provide facilities for discussing the Motion in the name of the hon. Member for East Wolverhampton approving the declarations of British war and peace aims, made in March by His Majesty's Ambassador to the United States in New York, since published as a White Paper?

The Prime Minister (Mr Churchill): No, Sir.

WAR CABINET

Mr Granville asked the Prime Minister whether, in view of the enormous responsibilities involved in decisions on policy in the prosecution of the war, he will consider appointing a small supreme War Cabinet of Ministers without Departmental responsibility and irrespective of party considerations; and whether he will consider inviting statesmen of the calibre of Mr Menzies to join such a War Cabinet?

The Prime Minister: No, Sir.

[1] Telegram No. 2275 from the Foreign Office to Washington replying to an American request for British troopships to transport United States Forces to Iceland in the event of the United States entering the war.

Mr Granville: Is the Prime Minister satisfied that it is still possible for busy and overworked Ministers to run great Departments of State and attend War Cabinet meetings for the purpose of giving vital decisions on war policy? Further, as the whole British Empire is involved in this war, does he not think the time has come to invite Empire statesmen to join an Empire War Cabinet, or an Imperial War Cabinet similar to that established in the last war?

The Prime Minister: We had a Debate about this some time ago, when it was very fully discussed and when I gave a very full explanation to the House. I have nothing to add to that.

Sir Henry Morris-Jones:[1] Is the Prime Minister himself alone responsible for strategy to the country and to the House?

The Prime Minister: In the statement which I made – I think it was 2½ months ago – I gave a very full account of how the machinery of government was run.

Mr Granville: Is it the intention to call a meeting of the Imperial War Conference?

The Prime Minister: At the present time there is no such intention.

WAR PROPAGANDA

Mr Granville asked the Prime Minister whether, in view of the vital importance of propaganda to the total war effort, he will now consider the creation of an adequate Ministry of Propaganda, presided over by a Minister with a seat in the War Cabinet, instead of merely attending its meetings?

The Prime Minister: No, Sir.

Mr Granville: Is the Prime Minister aware that we were told during a broadcast by the Director-General of the Ministry of Information that the Ministry of Information had no powers to release certain news from Service Departments, and does he not think that this is a matter which should receive the attention of the War Cabinet from time to time?

Mr Lawson:[2] Would not the Minister for Propaganda have less time to attend to propaganda if he were a member of the War Cabinet?

The Prime Minister: The House has several times shown a desire to limit as

[1] John Henry Morris-Jones, 1884–1972. On active service, 1914–18, serving as a doctor at Wimereux (Military Cross). A medical practitioner for twenty years. Liberal MP, 1929–31: Liberal National, 1931–50. Assistant Government Whip, 1932–5. A Lord Commissioner of the Treasury, 1935–7. Knighted, 1937. Chairman of the Welsh Parliamentary Party, 1941–2. Member of the Parliamentary Delegation to Buchenwald concentration camp, April 1945. Author of *Doctor in the Whips' Room*, 1955.

[2] John James Lawson, 1881–1965. Began work in a coalmine at the age of twelve. Labour Member of Parliament for Chester-le-Street, 1919–49. Financial Secretary to the War Office, 1924; Parliamentary Secretary, Ministry of Labour, 1929–31. Member of the Imperial War Graves Commission 1930–47. Deputy Regional Commissioner, Civil Defence, Northern Region, 1939–44. Vice-Chairman, British Council, 1944. Secretary of State for War, 1945–46. Vice-Chairman, National Parks Commission, 1949–57. Created Baron, 1950.

much as possible the membership of the War Cabinet. But the Minister of Information, by an entirely novel departure which was taken when the present Government was formed, is present at Cabinet meetings in order that he may be fully informed of what is going on, and, as he is present at the Cabinet, he naturally expresses his opinion when he thinks it desirable, or when he is asked for it.

Mr Granville: If the Prime Minister is unable to take action with regard to this, will he see that the country gets more news on the war situation?

The Prime Minister: I hope the country will always get all possible news on the war situation, but I hope, in fact I am sure, the country will not wish to receive news on the war situation which adds to the dangers of our troops, while delicate, dangerous and critical operations are being successfully carried out.

Commander Locker-Lampson:[1] Is it not much better to wait and trust the Prime Minister?

WAR SITUATION

Mr Lees-Smith (by Private Notice) asked the Prime Minister when a Debate on the war situation will take place?

The Prime Minister: Although a statement on Business will be made at the usual time later in the week, it may be for the convenience of the House if I say now that on the first Sitting Day after this week we propose to make arrangements for a general Debate on the progress of the war, and for that purpose we shall place on the Paper the following Motion:

'That this House approves the policy of His Majesty's Government in sending help to Greece, and declares its confidence that our operations in the Middle East and in all other theatres of war will be pursued by the Government with the utmost vigour.'

Mr Lees-Smith: Can the Debate on that motion, if the House so desires, be extended over two days?

The Prime Minister: Yes, if the House wishes, it can take place on the first and second days.

Mr Shinwell: Apart from the Motion which the government will place on the Paper, and which the House will no doubt accept, will there be an opportunity to discuss the general conduct of the war, questions of economic policy and the like, as well as strategy?

The Prime Minister: The conduct of the war embraces a very wide field, and the Motion is not intended to have any restrictive effect.

[1] Oliver Stillingfleet Locker-Lampson, 1881–1954. Educated at Eton and Trinity College Cambridge. Editor of *Granta*, 1900. Called to the Bar, 1907. Conservative MP, 1910–45. Lieutenant-Commander, Royal Naval Air Service, December 1914; Commander, July 1915. Commanded the British Armoured Car detachment in Russia, 1916–17. Parliamentary Private Secretary to Austen Chamberlain, 1919–21. Churchill's Private Secretary, 1926.

Mr Lawson: Is it the intention of the Government that the whole Debate shall be held in public?

The Prime Minister: Yes, I think so.

John Colville: diary
(*Colville papers*)

29 April 1941

An afternoon of busy operational discussions: we must save Egypt and Suez at all costs. The evacuation of Greece seems to have been fairly successful and we have got over 40,000 away out of 55,000 all told. The Germans are crowing, but are furious about Winston's speech yesterday.

War Cabinet, Defence Committee (Operations)
(*Cabinet papers, 69/2*)

29 April 1941 10 Downing Street
5 p.m.

The Secretary of State for war informed the committee that he had that morning attended trials of a number of anti-tank weapons, of which the Bombard,[1] the anti-tank rifle grenade, and the ST grenade[2] had proved outstandingly successful. The Bombard was a very formidable anti-tank weapon, and he hoped that 2,500 would be produced by August. ICI[3] said that they could manufacture 25,000 bombs per week, without interfering with other ammunition capacity.

The Prime Minister said that it was six or seven months since he had first seen the Bombard tried out, and he was astonished to hear that the War Office

[1] The Bombard, privately invented by Colonel L.V.S. Blacker, and subsequently developed and modified by Brigadier Jefferis at the Ministry of Defence Establishment at Whitchurch near Chequers, was an anti-tank mortar bomb, of which 19,000 were produced for the Home Guard by the end of 1943. Fired from the shoulder, it was also called the PIAT gun (Projectile Infantry Anti-Tank).

[2] A Sticky Type Bomb: another anti-tank grenade.

[3] Imperial Chemical Industries.

had been so slow in grasping its possibilities, and pressing on its production. The development of the sticky bomb had also been opposed at every step.

Sir John Dill said that he was unaware that the Bombard had been in existence all that time. He undertook to have a full enquiry made on the subject, and to report to the Prime Minister.

The Prime Minister said that Hispano Suiza cannon[1] must be regarded as aircraft armament, and could only be lent for other purposes until they were required. The 102 which had been received by the Admiralty would have to be returned when needed. The Admiralty must press on with the production of other weapons, including rocket devices.

War Cabinet, Defence Committee (Operations): minutes
(Cabinet papers, 69/2)

29 April 1941
5 p.m.

In the course of a full discussion, the Prime Minister stated his views as to the attitude of Japan. First of all, they would not enter the war, unless a successful invasion of this country took place. The events in the Middle East would not make them more likely to come in, as they would feel that we should be free to send further reinforcements to the Far East. Secondly, they would be most unlikely to come in if they thought that by doing so they would bring in the United States of America. Finally, if the Japanese did come in, he felt sure the United States would declare war.

Various possible contingencies in the Middle East were discussed, and the Prime Minister said that all efforts must be concentrated on winning the battle, and driving the Germans out of Libya. He did not think it would be right to place on paper ideas which might tend to distract the minds of those conducting the battle to a consideration of their line of retreat; and he suggested that the best plan would be for the Chiefs of Staff to have a further discussion with Mr Menzies, at which the method of meeting various contingencies could be touched upon, without proceeding to the length of drawing up a Staff study of possible plans.

[1] The Hispano-Suiza gun, which fired a high-velocity shell, was the standard British fighter armament for the greater part of the Second World War. It was introduced in the summer of 1940 after many design and manufacturing difficulties had been overcome. It achieved impressive results in Hurricanes and Spitfires, as well as in Typhoons, Mosquitoes and Beaufighters.

Winston S. Churchill: minute[1]
(*Churchill papers, 20/36*)

30 April 1941
Most Secret

1. We have provided to the utmost for the support of the army in ME so far as AFVs[2] are concerned. But even if our plans in this matter do not miscarry, victory will not be obtained without a similar operation with the Air Force.

2. 'Winch' and 'Double Winch' have succeeded, and 'Triple Winch' is in preparation, but this is not enough to get us out of the accusation of 'driblets'. An operation similar to 'Tiger' must be planned for the Air.

3. Accordingly, arrangements should be made to add to 'Triple Winch' which carries 30 fighters, *Furious* which should carry 50, and *Victorious* which may carry 60. But say, in all, 130.

4. The operation presents itself in principle as *Argus, Furious* and *Victorious* carrying 130 (either in one or two movements) under the protection of *Renown* and *Ark Royal*, &c., to the point of discharge, whence they can fly via Malta and Suda Bay to Alexandria. *Ark Royal* will be kept free for air protection of *Argus, Furious* and *Victorious*, the two last of whom can steam at least 25 knots and thus throw off effectively.

5. It would be far better to carry out this operation in one, even if, in order to avoid congestion at Malta, it were necessary to steam back on the course for 12 or 24 hours. However, the dates of readiness of the three aircraft-carriers (protected by *Ark Royal*, &c.) depend upon various factors, e.g., when can *Argus* get home, when will *Furious* be ready, when will *Victorious* have her propellors and rudder fixed. This should be carefully studied and report made to the Defence Committee tomorrow night. It would be helpful if all three *carrying* aircraft-carriers could sail from Great Britain not later than 12th May. If this date can be improved upon it may be of inestimable importance.

6. It is not much to ask of *Victorious* to do this great service while working up, and the Admiralty are invited to forgo filling her up with her own special aircraft for ocean work for the short time needed.

7. The Air Ministry and MAP (who have already been advised verbally) will report at the same time as the Admiralty upon the possibility of completing at least 130 Hurricanes and Spitfires with the long-distance tank and the special tropical equipment. The latter, if not completed in time, must not delay the operation.

[1] Churchill addressed this minute to General Ismay for the Chiefs of Staff Committee; the Minister of Aircraft Production (Lord Beaverbrook), the First Lord of the Admiralty, A.V. Alexander, and the First Sea Lord, Admiral Pound.

[2] Armoured Fighting Vehicles.

8. The crated machines of the six fighter squadrons and their maintenance personnel due for WS 9[1] will go as arranged, and the machines will be available for replacements when they arrive. Their pilots will take the short cut.

9. Let all this be concerted and synchronized this day, 30th April. General Ismay is charged with this task.

10. All concerned are reminded that we have in the Middle East an army of nearly half a million men, whose whole fighting value may be frustrated and even destroyed by a temporary hostile superiority in tanks and aircraft. The failure to win the battle of Egypt would be a disaster of the first magnitude to Great Britain. It might well determine the decisions of Turkey, Spain and Vichy. It might strike the United States the wrong way, i.e., they might think we are no good. Thus a true sense of proportion must rule, and the necessary accommodations must be made and the inevitable risks run.

Winston S. Churchill to Hubert Pierlot
(*Churchill papers, 20/28*)

30 April 1941

My dear Excellency,

The official burdens on your shoulders are indeed heavy. I write to tell you how deeply I sympathize with you in having to bear this new burden of personal loss and sorrow.[2]

Yours sincerely
Winston S. Churchill

War Cabinet, Battle of the Atlantic Committee: minutes
(*Cabinet papers, 86/1*)

30 April 1941 — 10 Downing Street
5 p.m.

It was reported that after a period of very few sinkings in the North-West Approaches there had been a successful submarine attack on a convoy in

[1] The ninth convoy from Britain to the Middle East via the Atlantic Coast of Africa, the Cape of Good Hope, the Indian Ocean, and the Red Sea.

[2] Two of the Belgian Prime Minister's sons, while on their way back to school, had been killed two days earlier in a railway accident, when a coach on the London to Newcastle express train caught fire near Claypole, Lincolnshire. The coach had been specially reserved for sixty-four boys from Ampleforth College, Yorkshire. In all, six boys were killed.

daylight on the previous day.[1] This was the first attack in daylight on an escorted convoy for six months. One ship sailing independently had also been sunk. Detailed reports of the convoy attack had not yet been received.

The First Lord of the Admiralty was invited to report to the Prime Minister on this attack as soon as full information was available.

The Prime Minister drew special attention to the satisfactory increase in the number of workers employed on merchant repairs.

The First Lord of the Admiralty urged that greater effort should be made to provide short-range cannon guns for the defence of ships against aircraft rather than that reliance should be placed on machine guns, even with dual or quadruple mounting.

The Prime Minister said that efforts should rather be concentrated on the use of the UP weapon,[2] the production of which would not conflict with that of guns. He asked the First Lord of the Admiralty to submit a report to the meeting the following week, setting out plans for supplementing by the use of the UP weapon the existing proposals for the defence of ships. The report should show in what forms this weapon could be fitted to ships, should give a forecast of deliveries and should include suggestions for increasing production. The Minister of Supply would no doubt co-operate as regards ammunition supply for the UP weapon.

Winston S. Churchill to Anthony Eden
(*Churchill papers, 20/36*)

30 April 1941

When did Sir Stafford Cripps deliver my message to M. Stalin? Will you very kindly ask him to report.

Winston S. Churchill: minute[3]
(*Churchill papers, 20/36*)

30 April 1941

Further to my Minute of this date on convoy secrecy. Nothing will prevent very large numbers of people knowing that ships are assembled constantly for convoy. Nor can the kind of Cargoes they are carrying be kept secret. There

[1] HX 12 (a convoy leaving Halifax, Nova Scotia, for British ports) had been attacked in the North Atlantic 23 degrees west of Iceland.

[2] The Unrotated Projectile, anti-aircraft rocket.

[3] Churchill addressed this minute (Prime Minister's Personal Minute, M.491/1) to the First Sea Lord (Admiral Pound), the Secretary of State for War (David Margesson), the Secretary of State for Air (Sir Archibald Sinclair) and the Minister of Shipping, Ronald Cross.

is an immense amount of talk at all the shipowners' offices and at the ports. By all means let every effort be made as proposed by MI5 and in my previous Minute. In such a case, however, where so much is visible and must be known, the continued fabrication and dissemination of false information is a necessary part of security. All kinds of Münchhausen tales can be spread about to confuse and baffle the truth. Sun helmets or winter clothing should be hawked about and calculated leakages made of false and sometimes true intentions. For this purpose a small group of lively officers should be formed working under the daily Ports Committee or under the MI5 as may be thought desirable. Perhaps FOP[1] could help.

Winston S. Churchill: minute[2]
(*Churchill papers, 20/36*)

30 April 1941

I have considered the Minutes which you and your Service colleagues and the Minister of Shipping sent me in reply to my Minute of the 14th February.

The replies show a wide measure of agreement as to how this matter should be handled, and moreover, that a great deal has already been done for the better security of war convoys. This, however, needs continual vigilance, and I therefore ask:

(1) That the Security Officers in the Service Departments and in the Ministry of Shipping should keep a watchful eye on the domestic arrangements in each of the Departments concerned, and should meet periodically to pool their experience.

(2) That the security aspect of convoys should be made a feature of the daily meetings of the Priority of Movements Committee. I should like a report showing what has been done in, say, two months' time.

(3) I should also like a report at the same time of the activities of the Security Investigation Committee on Shipping, established in February.

[1] The Future Operations Planning section of the Joint Planning Staff.

[2] The Prime Minister addressed this minute (Prime Minister's Personal Minute M.492/1) to the same recipients as the previous minute.

Winston S. Churchill to Air Vice Marshal William Sholto Douglas
(*Churchill papers, 20/36*)

30 April 1941

I am much obliged for your full account of the 'Mutton'[1] operations, and hope that when everyone has got used to the drill it will prove as effective as it did in the preliminary trials. I was much interested in many of the items mentioned in your paper, which we could not discuss as the Interception Meeting had to be postponed. I am especially glad to note that you are pressing on with the use of light to make the final kill. It seems possible that this will enable us to make bags in the dark period as heavy as those we can get on the best moonlight nights.

Winston S. Churchill to General Ismay, for the Chiefs of Staff Committee
(*Churchill papers, 20/36*)

30 April 1941

I see it announced in the German Press that Crete is to be the next object of attack. Although our evidence points the other way, we must not exclude the possibility that Crete is a blind, and Syria or Cyprus the quarry.

Winston S. Churchill: Oral Answers
(*Hansard*)

30 April 1941

House of Commons
Church House

Mr Lees-Smith: May I ask the Prime Minister whether he has any statement to make with regard to the withdrawal of our Forces from Greece?

The Prime Minister (Mr Churchill): As I am most anxious to give the House, the nation and the Empire information at the earliest possible moment, and also in view of the extravagant claims made by the enemy, I think it right now to give the figures, so far as they are known, of the evacuation of the Empire Forces from Greece. Up to the time when evacuation was seen to be inevitable, we had landed about 60,000 men in Greece, including one New Zealand and one Australian division. Of these at least 45,000 have been evacuated, and considering that our Air Force was,

[1] The Long Aerial Mine (see page 402 n.2).

through the superiority of the enemy, forced to leave the air-fields from which it could alone effectively cover the retreat of our troops, and that only a small portion of it could cover the points of embarkation, this must be considered remarkable. The conduct of the troops and especially the rearguards in fighting their way to the sea merits the highest praise. This is the first instance where air bombing, prolonged day after day, has failed to break the discipline and order of the marching columns who, besides being thus assailed from the air, were pursued by no less than three German armoured divisions as well as by the whole strength of the German mechanized forces which could be brought to bear. In the actual fighting, principally on Mount Olympus, around Grevena and at Thermopylae, about 3,000 casualties, killed and wounded, are reported to have been suffered by our troops. This was a very small part of the losses inflicted on the Germans, who on several occasions, sometimes for two days at a time, were brought to a standstill by forces one-fifth of their number. Nor, of course, does it take any account of German losses incurred in their assaults on the Greek and Yugoslav Armies.

It will, I dare say, be possible to give a fuller account in the Debate next week, but I think I have said enough to show the House that, painful as are our losses, we have much to be thankful for and the Empire Forces have much to be proud of.

Sir Hugh O'Neill:[1] When the right hon. Gentleman says that 45,000 men have been evacuated, does he mean that they successfully reached their bases without mishap?

The Prime Minster: I believe that is so; indeed I think I am well within the figure, but, as I say, I have given the information in the terms in which it was given to me.

Mr Garro-Jones:[2] Does the Prime Minister feel able to make any general statement about the evacuation, or alternatively the destruction, of the heavy equipment of the Forces?

The Prime Minister: The heavy equipment could not, of course, be removed, but the Germans are not short of heavy equipment.

[1] Robert William Hugh O'Neill, 1883–1982. Ulster Unionist Member of Parliament for Mid-Antrim, 1915–22. County Antrim, 1922–50; North Antrim, 1950–52. On active service, France and Palestine, 1915–18. Created Baronet 1929. First Speaker of the House of Commons for Northern Ireland, 1921–29 and Member of Parliament for County Antrim in the Parliament of Northern Ireland, 1921–29. Parliamentary Under-Secretary of State for India and Burma, 1939–40. Created Baron Rathcavan, 1953. His son Con O'Neill, a diplomat was one of those who interrogated Rudolf Hess in 1941.

[2] George Morgan Garro-Jones, 1894–1960. On active service, Royal Flying Corps, 1915–17. Advisory Officer to the United States Air Service, 1918. London editor, *Daily Dispatch*, 1922–4. Liberal MP, South Hackney, 1924–9. Labour MP for Aberdeen from 1935 until his death.

Mr Benson:[1] May I ask whether 45,000 is the maximum number we can expect to be evacuated?

The Prime Minister: I think I said 'at least 45,000.' Supposing anything else were going forward, I naturally could not refer to it.

Henry Channon[2]: diary
(*'Chips'*)

30 April 1941

Winston made a statement to the House about the evacuation from Greece: it has been less of a disaster than we feared, for over 45,000 men have got away. The House, whilst restive, was relieved.

Sir Alexander Cadogan: diary
(*'The Diaries of Sir Alexander Cadogan, OM, 1938-1945'*)

30 April 1941

These dirty Iraquis are attacking us at Habbaniya. We have authorized bombing.

Met PM who said 'So you've got another war on your hands tonight!'

War Cabinet, Defence Committee (Operations): minutes
(*Cabinet papers, 69/2*)

30 April 1941 Cabinet War Room
10 p.m.

The Prime Minister said that he was not happy with the situation in Libya where it appeared that sufficiently vigorous steps were not being taken by any of the three Services to strike the Germans before they became stronger and to prevent the arrival of reinforcements and stores. He recognized that the

[1] George Benson, 1889–1973. Estate agent and valuer. Labour Member of Parliament for Chesterfield, 1929–31, 1935–50 and 1950–64. Knighted, 1958. Author of a *History of Socialism.*

[2] Henry Channon, 1897–1958. An American by birth. Educated privately, and at Christ Church, Oxford. In 1933 he married Lady Honor Guinness, elder daughter of the 2nd Earl of Iveagh. Conservative MP for Southend-on-Sea, 1935–50; for Southend on Sea (West), 1950–8. Parliamentary Private Secretary to the Under Secretary of State for Foreign Affairs (R.A. Butler) 1938–41. Knighted, 1957. Known as 'Chips'.

navy had been fully engaged on the evacuation of troops from Greece, but now that this was over it was imperative that they should put a stop to the arrival of enemy ships in the Ports of Cyrenaica.

Sir Dudley Pound said that the Commander-in-Chief fully realized the vital necessity of stopping this traffic and now that his forces were to some extent freed from their preoccupations in Greece, he would no doubt take appropriate steps.

The Prime Minister enquired whether it was known what General Wavell proposed to do. The Army appeared to be adopting a supine attitude and he would like to be reassured that this would only continue while forces were being gathered together. He noticed from the latest tank return that there were now at least one hundred cruiser and infantry tanks effective in Egypt and it ought to be possible to do something with these. The anti-tank gun situation had also very greatly improved.

THE DISPOSITION OF THE AMERICAN FLEET

The Prime Minister drew attention to Telegram No. Gleam 42 in which it was stated that Colonel Knox and Mr Stimson had approached Admiral Danckwerts[1] with the proposal that a large part of the American Pacific Fleet should now be moved into the Atlantic. He was horrified to read in the Telegram that Admiral Danckwerts had poured cold water on the suggestion. While there might be something to be said for the views expressed by Admiral Danckwerts on the grounds of pure strategy, the over-riding consideration was that a move of such great psychological importance should not have been given a cold reception. Admiral Danckwerts should have refrained from expressing his opinion, and should have referred the matter for consideration by the Government.

[1] Victor Hilary Danckwerts. Served in the Royal Navy from 1904. On active service at the Battle of the Falkland Islands, 1914. Captain, 1930. CMG, 1936. Director of Plans, Admiralty, 1938–40; Naval Representative, Washington, 1940–2.

May 1941

Winston S. Churchill to Sir Edward Bridges, Sir Horace Wilson and Eric Seal
(*Churchill papers, 20/36*)

1 May 1941

I have decided to take action immediately as follows:

1. Lord Beaverbrook to be appointed Minister of State. The new title distinguishes him from the Minister without Portfolio,[1] thus avoiding confusion. No public statement will be made of his duties, but by a minute to the Cabinet he will be assigned supervisory and referee functions in regard to priorities. Let this be drafted for my signature.

2. I propose to invite Colonel Moore-Brabazon to become Minister of Aircraft Production in succession to Lord Beaverbrook.

3. Mr Ronald Cross will be invited to become High Commissioner to the Commonwealth of Australia.

4. Mr Leathers[2] will be appointed Minister for Shipping and Transport with a seat in the Lords. The amalgamation of the two departments for the purposes of the war will be effected forthwith. The details of this process will be worked out by a Cabinet Committee under the Lord President of the Council or the Lord Privy Seal[3] as speedily as may be, assisted by the new Minister; and certain functions of the Ministry of Transport which are only remotely connected with Communications will be, if desirable, transferred to the Board of Trade or other departments. When the process is complete, the

[1] Arthur Greenwood, a senior Labour Party figure, who served as Minister without Portfolio, and a Member of the War Cabinet, from May 1940 to February 1942.

[2] Frederick James Leathers, 1883–1965. Shipowner and company director. Served at the Ministry of Shipping, 1915–18. Chairman of William Cory and Son Ltd; Mann, George and Co Ltd; R. and J. H. Rea Ltd; and the Steamship Owners' Coal Association Ltd. A director of several steamship companies. Adviser to the Ministry of Shipping on all matters relating to Coal, 1940–1. Created Baron, 1941. Minister of War Transport, 1941–5. Companion of Honour, 1943. Secretary of State for the Co-ordination of Transport, Fuel and Power, 1951–3. Created Viscount, 1954.

[3] Sir John Anderson or Clement Attlee.

combined Ministry will become the Ministry of Communications, or perhaps the Ministry of War-time Communications.

5. Mr Llewellin will be invited to become additional Parliamentary Secretary to the Ministries of Shipping and Transport in the House of Commons pending the completion of a Ministry of War-time Communications. A submission will be made for conferring a Privy Councillorship upon Mr Llewellin.

6. The Under-Secretaryship at the Ministry of Aircraft Production will be filled by Mr Montague,[1] non-official arrangements being made for the department to be answered for in the House of Lords.

7. It is proposed to make these submissions to The King tomorrow and publish Friday or Saturday.

8. Let all necessary steps be taken to implement the above

(a) by drafting the minute assigning Lord Beaverbrook his Cabinet duties in respect of Priorities;
(b) by preparing the necessary submissions to The King;
(c) by preparing the necessary public announcements;
(d) Sir Horace Wilson will confer with Mr Leathers upon the financial arrangements which may be necessitated by his relinquishing the 50 or 60 companies of which he is Director or mainspring; and also upon any adjustment of income tax or super-tax consequent upon cessation of his present occupation.

9. There will be no alteration in the composition or functions of the Import and Production Executives, except that Colonel Moore-Brabazon as MAP will succeed Lord Beaverbrook on the Production Committee.

10. I hope all the above may be settled before I leave London for Plymouth tonight.

War Cabinet: minutes
(*Cabinet papers, 65/18*)

1 May 1941 House of Commons Annexe
12 noon

The Minister of Home Security said that Plymouth had suffered from air attacks five nights running. The last attack (night the 29th/30th April) had

[1] Frederick Montague, 1876–1966. Newsboy, shop assistant, freelance journalist, copy-editor. Parliamentary Agent, Labour Party. Served as a Lieutenant (served in France and Palestine; full Lieutenant, Commercial Subjects, Egyptian Military Schools, 1917-18). Alderman, Islington Borough Council, 1919–25. Labour Member of Parliament for West Islington, 1923–31, 1935–45. Under-Secretary of State for Air, 1929–31. Parliamentary Secretary, Ministry of Transport, 1940–41; Ministry of Aircraft Production, 1940–42. Created Baron Amwell, 1947.

been less severe than some earlier attacks. One disturbing feature was that the Press had drawn attention to an unofficial nightly exodus from Plymouth into surrounding districts.

The Secretary of State for Foreign Affairs gave the War Cabinet the latest information about the situation in Iraq. Troops of the Iraqi Army had taken up positions on the hills surrounding Habbaniya aerodrome.

With the Prime Minister's authority, a telegram had been sent authorizing such measures being taken as were necessary to restore the position, including if need be, the use of our air forces against the Iraq Army.

PUBLICATION OF SHIPPING LOSSES MOVING FROM MONTHLY TO QUARTERLY FIGURES

The Prime Minister said that the object he had in mind was not that the publication of losses should necessarily be withheld, but that we should get out of the position in which we were committed to automatic publication of the figures, whether or not it suited us to publish them. As, however, the first monthly statement was not due until the 15th May, there was time for further reflection.

HOME DEFENCE, EVACUATION OF COASTAL AREAS

The Prime Minister informed the War Cabinet that this matter had been considered by the Defence Committee, who had recommended:-

(a) That until definite signs of preparations for invasion began to be observed, there should be no extension of the ban on visitors to the coastal belt.

(b) That the Chiefs of Staff should keep a close watch on the situation and warn the War Cabinet when the first signs were observed, so that the extension of the ban could be considered among the first of the precautionary steps to be taken.

The War Cabinet endorsed these recommendations.

ROBERT MENZIES

The Prime Minister said that this was the last occasion on which Mr Menzies would attend the War Cabinet on this visit. He wished to say how much he and his colleagues had appreciated having Mr Menzies with them and how much they had valued his counsel, and looked forward to having him among them again. He had won an outstanding place in the esteem of the British people, and would take back to Australia the admiration and affection of all.

War Cabinet, Defence Committee (Operations), minutes
(Cabinet papers, 69/2)

1 May 1941 House of Commons Annexe
1 p.m.

The Prime Minister said that this matter had been discussed towards the end of a Meeting of the Defence Committee held the previous night which had lasted until after midnight. He had been most disturbed at Admiral Danckwerts' reception of the proposition which had been put to him by Colonel Knox. Our chance of victory was almost certainly bound up with American participation; and within the last two or three days he had thought it right to send a personal telegram to Mr Roosevelt begging him to do his utmost to get the United States of America into the war as soon as possible. It was therefore disturbing to find that when two of the President's principal colleagues had suggested an advance into the Atlantic, the suggestion had been received with a cold douche. This movement of the fleet would have a tremendous effect on public opinion in the United States, and, in his judgment could not be interpreted in any way as leaving Australia and New Zealand in the lurch. On the contrary, there was no greater deterrent to Japan than the prospect of fighting the British and American fleets. If he himself had thought it more likely that the proposed move would increase the chances of Japanese intervention, he would have unhesitatingly advised against it. As it was he had thought it absolutely essential to apprise the Americans at once that the advice tendered by Admiral Danckwerts was not endorsed by His Majesty's Government, who were entirely in favour of the move to the Atlantic. It was for this reason that he had authorized the despatch of telegram Boxes No. 36. After the Meeting it had been brought to his notice that he (Mr. Menzies) should be consulted in this matter, and he had given directions that the telegram should be brought to his attention the first thing that morning.

Winston S. Churchill to Viscount Halifax
(Cabinet papers, 69/2)

1 May 1941

Please instruct Military Mission to take no action on this telegram until further orders. Admiral Danckwerts should have referred to London the issues raised in Gleam 42 before entering into detailed discussions.

2. Naturally, we ourselves are greatly impressed with the proposition, and our opinion remains as expressed in my telegram under reference.

3. It is, however, of great consequence that, before any answer is given on a matter of this kind, the Dominions of Australia and New Zealand, whose position is directly affected, should be consulted.

4. The Dominions of Australia and New Zealand are being consulted at once, and we will telegraph as soon as we can. In the meantime, you should arrange for an informal indication of the position, as set out in this telegram, to be given to the United States Government, emphasizing, of course, that the final decision will clearly rest with them.

Winston S. Churchill to Admiral Sir Andrew Cunningham
(Churchill papers, 20/38)

1 May 1941
sent 8.26 p.m.

We are making extreme exertions to reinforce you from the Air. It has been decided to repeat as soon as possible and on a much larger scale the recent operations Winch and Dunlop.[1] *Ark Royal, Argus, Furious* and *Victorious* will all be used to carry up to 140 additional Hurricanes, as well as 18 Fulmars, with pilots. We hope that 64 Hurricanes and 9 Fulmars will arrive in Middle East by the 25th May. Meanwhile, 25 Fighter pilots leave the 23rd May for Takoradi to hasten ferrying of Hurricanes and Tomahawks. Capacity of route to Egypt via Takoradi freed by above use of Carriers will be employed to increase flow of Tomahawks and Hurricanes. Greatest possible shipment of Blenheims will be made at the same time. I may have more to signal about Bomber reinforcements later.

2. I also congratulate you upon the brilliant and highly successful manner in which the Navy have once again succoured the Army and brought off four-fifths of the entire force.

3. It is now necessary to fight hard for Crete, which seems soon to be attacked heavily, and for Malta as a base for flotilla action against the enemy's communications with Libya. Constantly improving attitude of United States and their naval co-operation justifies risks involved. Your plans for Tiger are excellent and give good chances.

4. But, above all, we look to you to cut off sea-borne supplies from the Cyrenaican ports and to beat them up to the utmost. It is in our power to give you information of priceless value about enemy transport movements to these ports. It causes grief here whenever we learn of the arrival of precious aviation spirit in one ship after another. This great battle for Egypt is what the Duke of Wellington called 'A close-run thing', but if we can reinforce you and Wavell, as proposed by Operations Tiger and Jaguar, and you can cut off the tap of inflow, our immense armies in the Middle East will soon resume their ascendancy. All good wishes.

[1] Reinforcements for the Middle East, through the Mediterranean.

Winston S. Churchill to General Wavell
(*Churchill papers, 20/49*)

1 May 1941

Please see my signal to Admiral Cunningham appended. I congratulate you upon successful evacuation. We have paid our debt of honour with far less loss than I feared. Feel sure you are waiting to strike a blow. Enemy's difficulties must be immense. Am looking forward to hear from you, but best of all by events.

Winston S. Churchill to Air Marshal Longmore
(*Churchill papers, 20/38*)

1 May 1941
Personal and Secret
sent 9.35 p.m.

It has been decided to repeat as soon as possible and on a much larger scale the recent operations for flying Hurricanes off aircraft carriers to Malta. Intention is to despatch by this means up to 140 Hurricanes as well as 18 Fulmars. It is impossible to give firm dates at this stage but we hope that 64 Hurricanes and 9 Fulmars will arrive in Middle East by 25 May.[1]

2. 25 fighter pilots leave May 3 for Takoradi to hasten ferrying of Hurricanes and Tomahawks.

3. Capacity of route to Egypt via Takoradi freed by above use of carriers will be employed to increase flow of Tomahawks and bombers. Greatest possible increase in Blenheim shipments will be made.

John Colville: diary
(*Colville papers*)

1 May 1941

Left for a tour of Plymouth after dinner with the PM, Mrs Churchill, First Sea Lord, his Secretary (Brockman),[2] Averell Harriman, Pug and Tommy. Plymouth has been cruelly laid waste in the last fortnight.

[1] This was Operation Jaguar, the successor to Operation Tiger.

[2] Ronald Vernon Brockman, 1909– . Entered the Royal Navy, 1927. Assistant Secretary to the First Sea Lord (Admiral Backhouse), 1938–39. Secretary to the First Sea Lord (Admiral Pound), 1939–43. Secretary to the Supreme Allied Commander, South-East Asia (Lord Mountbatten), 1943–45.

On the way to Paddington in the car, the PM told me that Leathers was entirely his own choice and that he hoped great things of his experience and tried ability.

Eric Seal: letter to his wife
(*Seal papers*)

2 May 1941 10 Downing Street

When I woke up yesterday morning, & discovered that Winston had made up his mind to go forward with his plans for reconstructing the Govt. I felt so strongly that some of his proposals were inadvisable that I sat down in my dressing gown & wrote him a note. I then went off to dress, telling Martin to wait until I had my trousers on before giving it to him! I felt that I would be able to stand the blast much better then!! But there was no violent reaction until I was in the car with him going to lunch – when he suddenly detonated & said I knew nothing about it. That is always the first phase. But as the thing was virtually settled I didn't think it worth while arguing with him. Strictly between ourselves, I don't like the layout at all. One of my difficulties on these occasions is that I am never ultimately quite sure whether these moves of his are really bad, or whether they are strokes of genius! Judged by ordinary standards, they are often bad, but in his hands they often turn out to produce astounding results. He has a wonderful knack for handling public opinion, & of course an unrivalled experience of public affairs. A civil servant inevitably has a more parochial view, of administrative efficiency, & not of the political results as a whole.

John Colville: diary
(*Colville papers*)

2 May 1941

We awoke in the train which was stationary on the line somewhere in Devonshire between banks of primroses and violets. At 9.30 we drew into Plymouth where we were greeted by the two MPs Lady Astor[1] (also Lady

[1] Nancy Witcher Langhorne, 1879–1964. Born in Virginia. Married first, in 1897, Robert Gould Shaw (divorced, 1903); second, in 1906, the 2nd Viscount Astor. Conservative MP for Plymouth Sutton, 1919–45 (the first woman to take her seat in the Westminster Parliament). Companion of Honour, 1937.

Mayoress) and Mrs Rathbone[1] who squabbled like two she-cats until the PM, who was still shaving when we arrived, emerged on to the platform.

The whole party – PM and Mrs Churchill, Harriman, First Sea Lord, his Secretary (Brockman), Pug, Tommy and I – went to Admiralty House, Devonport, to meet the new C-in-C, Sir Charles Forbes. Then began the morning's tour of the dockyard. Brockman and I did not go to Mountbatten, but waited to get the news and then proceeded to the North Yard where we looked at the melancholy ruins of a terrace of lovely houses in which Brockman's had been. The PM arrived in a launch and we then walked for miles, along quays, through workshops, over ships. We saw *Centurion*, now a decoy ship made to look like one of the KGV class. Just before lunch we reached the RN barracks, where bombs had killed a number of sailors. There was a gruesome sight in the Gymnasium: beds in which some 40 slightly injured men lay, separated only by a low curtain from some coffins which were being nailed down. The hammering must have been horrible to the injured men, but such has been the damage that there was nowhere else it could be done.

The men lunched in the barracks, in a room decorated with a frieze of wooden ships representing the Armada, designed by Wylie. We had a revolting lunch (tepid brown Windsor Soup, etc.!) and then returned to Admiralty House so that the PM might sleep.

At 3.30 we drove round Plymouth. It has suffered five heavy raids in nine nights and scarcely a house seems to be habitable. It is far worse than Bristol: the whole City is wrecked except, characteristically, the important parts of the naval establishment. Mount Edgecombe, where we used to land from the sea, is burnt out as well. In Plymouth itself I saw a bus which had been carried bodily, by the force of an explosion, on to the roof of a building some 150 yards from where it had been standing.

We had tea at Lady Astor's house, where I had a long talk with the wife of the Regional Commissioner, Lady Elles.[2]

At 6.30 we left the scene of horror and desolation on the return journey to Chequers, where we arrived at midnight.

There was news to make the PM gravely depressed. A long telegram from Roosevelt explaining that the US could not co-operate with us in preventing Germany from seizing the Azores and Cape Verde Islands; news that one of the ships containing many tanks for the reinforcement of Wavell (Operation

[1] Eleanor Rathbone, 1872–1946. Educated Kensington High School and Somerville College, Oxford. The first woman member of the Liverpool City Council, 1909–34. Independent MP for the Combined English Universities, 1929–46. Chairman, Children's Nutrition Council and National Joint Committee for Spanish Relief. Secretary, Parliamentary Committee for Refugees. Vice-Chairman, National Committee for Rescue from Nazi Terror.

[2] Lady Elles: Mrs A. H. Du Boulay, whom General Elles married in 1939 (having earlier been twice a widower).

Tiger) had developed serious engine trouble; a signal that HMS *Jersey*, one of Lord Louis Mountbatten's destroyers, had sunk at Malta blocking the Grand Harbour; and finally the fact that the Iraqis, who opened fire on our troops this morning (two hours before we had intended firing on them!) were fighting well and were not proving to be the rabble we expected.

So the PM, in worse gloom than I had ever seen him, dictated a telegram to the President drawing a sombre picture of what a collapse in the Middle East would entail.[1] Then he sketched to Harriman, Pug and me a world in which Hitler dominated all Europe, Asia and Africa and left the US and ourselves no option but an unwilling peace.

It is clear that Spain, Vichy and Turkey are waiting on the result of the issue in North Africa, where Tobruk still resists valiantly. If Suez were to fall the Middle East would be lost, and Hitler's robot new order would receive the inspiration which might give it real life (JRC not WSC!).

In a less dark mood the PM said that this moment is decisive: it is being established not whether we shall win or lose, but whether the duration of the war will be long or short. With Hitler in control of Iraq oil and Ukrainian wheat, not all the staunchness of 'our Plymouth brethren' will shorten the ordeal.

I think it is largely Plymouth that has caused him such melancholy – he keeps on repeating: 'I've never seen the like.'[2]

Winston S. Churchill to Anthony Eden
(*Churchill papers, 20/36*)

2 May 1941

Pray look at these two documents[3] of moment and examine them with your advisers. If you think necessary, come down this afternoon, Saturday, or for lunch and discuss with me. It seems to me as if there has been a considerable recession across the Atlantic, and that quite unconsciously we are being left very much to our fate. At any rate whatever may be the final stages of the war this fateful moment is likely to be lost.

[1] This telegram was sent to Washington on 4 May 1941 (*pages 599–600*).

[2] At a Civil Defence Committee meeting in the Cabinet Offices five days later (on 7 May 1941), Harold Nicolson, who was present, noted that Herbert Morrison 'worried about the effect of the provincial raids on morale. He keeps on underlining the fact that the people cannot stand this intensive bombing indefinitely and that sooner or later the morale of other towns will go, even as Plymouth's has gone.' (*Harold Nicolson, Diaries and letters, 1939-1945*)

[3] The exchange of telegrams between President Roosevelt and Churchill about the future of the Portuguese Atlantic Islands.

Winston S. Churchill to Anthony Eden
(*Churchill papers, 20/36*)

2 May 1941

RELAXATION OF BRITISH NAVAL BLOCKADE OF VICHY FRANCE

I do not understand Lord Halifax's attitude about this, and I cannot think it is inspired from here. The fact that a few wheat ships reach unoccupied France from the United States is of very little importance, and the advantage of having United States controllers in unoccupied France is important. If Admiral Leahy is to have influence at Vichy, he must have something to bargain with. He must have friendly relations with Vichy, and be in a position to have something to take away and give, as well as merely to threaten. I have for some time not felt keen about stopping food ships so long as we could get adequate contraband control. Anyhow, ships are passing freely through the Straits, and we are too busy to intercept them. Why, then, this frightful fuss with Mr Hull, which seems out of all proportion to the consequences?

I do not like paragraph 8 at all, nor do I understand why this statement should be a 'bombshell' – see paragraph 5. Considering the vast issues at stake, I am very sorry that this conversation was so stiffly conducted.

Please let me know whether anything has been sent from the Foreign Office which would have stimulated the Ambassador to such unexpected vehemence.

Winston S. Churchill to General Freyberg
(*Premier papers, 3/109*)

2 May 1941

Congratulate you on your vitally important Command.[1] Feel confident your fine troops will destroy parachutists man to man at close quarters. Every good wish.

John Colville: diary
(*Colville papers*)

3 May 1941

Too little sleep made the PM irritable all the morning and morose at lunch, when he discovered that Mrs C had used some of his favourite honey, sent from Queensland, to sweeten the rhubarb.

[1] General Freyberg, the Commander of the New Zealand Division, had been appointed commander of the mixed British, Commonwealth and Greek forces on Crete.

Winston S. Churchill to General Ismay
(*Churchill papers, 20/36*)

3 May 1941

DESTRUCTION OF IRAQ OIL WELLS

I certainly do not think we should begin at once destroying the wells, but the pipelines should stand on a different footing. At any rate the personnel should be provided, and every preparation should be made. So far as the pipelines are concerned I am agreeable for the people on the spot having the power to destroy the necessary machinery forthwith if they consider there is danger of German seizure.

Winston S. Churchill to Peter Fraser[1]
(*Premier papers, 3/109*)

3 May 1941

I am very glad that the exigencies of evacuation should have carried in New Zealand Division, after its brilliant fighting in Greece, in such good order to Crete. Naturally, every effort will be made to re-equip them, and in particular artillery, in which General Wavell is already strong, is being sent. The successful defence of Crete is one of the most important factors in the defence of Egypt. I am very glad that General Wavell has accepted my suggestion to put Freyberg in command of the whole island. You may be sure we shall sustain him in every way possible.

2. Our information points to an airborne attack being delivered in the near future, with possibly an attempt at sea-borne attack. The Navy will certainly do their utmost to prevent the latter, and it is unlikely to succeed on any large scale. So far as airborne attack is concerned, this ought to suit the New Zealanders down to the ground, for they will be able to come to close quarters, man to man, with the enemy, who will not have the advantage of tanks and artillery, on which he so largely relies. Should the enemy get a landing in Crete that will be the beginning, and not the end, of embarrassments for him. The island is mountainous and wooded, giving peculiar scope to the qualities of your troops. We can reinforce it far more easily than the enemy, and there are over 30,000 men there already.

3. It may be however that the enemy is only feinting at Crete, and will be going farther east. We have to consider all contingencies in the employment of our scanty and overpressed Air Force. Why is it scanty and overpressed? Not because we do not possess ever-growing resources and reserves here. Not

[1] The Prime Minister of New Zealand, who had just arrived in Cairo on his way to England.

because we have not done everything in human power to reinforce the Middle East with air. It is simply because of the physical difficulties of getting aircraft and their servicing personnel to the spot by the various routes and methods open to us. You may be sure we shall try our best to reinforce our air-power, and we are at this moment making very far-reaching but hazardous efforts. The disposition between competing needs of such air forces as are in the East must be left to the Commanders-in-Chief. I am not without hope that things will be better in the Middle East in a month or so.

4. Everyone here admires the dignity and stoicism of New Zealand in enduring the agonizing suspense of the evacuation. Its successful conclusion, after inflicting so much loss upon the enemy and paying our debt of honour to Greece, is an inexpressible relief to the Empire.

Winston S. Churchill to Captain Peto[1]
(*Churchill papers, 2/428*)

3 May 1941

Dear Captain Peto,

King's Norton had in Ronald Cartland a young member of high promise who was loved by all who knew him for his great personal charm and respected by friends and opponents alike for his courage and intellectual integrity. His death on the field of battle has left a sad gap in our ranks and it is only fitting that his successor at King's Norton should be like him a serving officer who supports the war policy pursued by the Government and generally approved by the nation.

I am confident that I can rely upon the electors to make clear by the majority they accord to you that this is their view and that they are not the people to be duped by well-meaning extremists into the illusion that victory or peace can be reached by any easy short cut. By giving you their vote they will show their confidence in me and my colleagues from all the political parties to make the best possible strategic use of the ever-increasing resources at our disposal.

Those who are sincerely convinced that Hitler and Hitlerism must be extirpated from Europe should regard it as part of their duty in defending their country to go to the poll and record their vote. They must remember that every enemy of Britain will look to the voting in King's Norton to see if there

[1] Basil Arthur John Peto, 1900–1954. Joined the Royal Artillery, 1924. King's Dragoon Guards, 1926. Aide-de-Camp to the Governor of Bombay, 1929–31. Captain, 1932. Served in Egypt, 1932–35. Retired from the Army 1939. Rejoined on the outbreak of war. Conservative Member of Parliament for King's Norton, 1941–45. Parliamentary Private Secretary to the Chairman of the Oil Board (Geoffrey Lloyd), December 1941–February 1945.

is any weakening in the national resolve. No one should commit the act of negligence involved in staying at home just because the seat is in no danger of being lost. Every vote counts.

Yours very truly,
Winston S. Churchill

Winston S. Churchill to Air Chief Marshal Sir Charles Portal and John Moore-Brabazon[1]
(*Churchill papers, 20/36*)

3 May 1941

Why is this Squadron[2] not made up to its IE[3] of 18? How is it that only 7 are available for supply in view of the fact that they are hardly ever allowed to go up into the Air? Why is a town like Plymouth left to be subjected to five raids on successive nights, or almost successive, without this device being used; and why is no attempt made to lay LAMs[4] across the beams when they are pointed on Liverpool or London? I do not feel this device is yet free from the many years of obstruction which have hampered its perfection. Recent action by the Air Force against the night raider has flagged sadly, and you cannot afford to neglect a method which for the number of times it has been used has produced an extraordinarily high percentage of results. Let me have a programme for increasing the numbers employed.

Winston S. Churchill: broadcast
(*'The Listener', 8 May 1941*)[5]

3 May 1941

Tonight I am speaking to the Polish people all over the world. This is the hundred-and-fiftieth anniversary of the adoption by your Parliament of the Constitution.

[1] The new Minister of Aircraft Production.
[2] No. 93 Squadron. Churchill was commenting on the squadron's Returns of Daily State of Minelaying Aircraft for 30 April and 2 May 1941.
[3] Initial Equipments, for Royal Air Force crews.
[4] The Long Aerial Mine.
[5] Kathleen Hill noted: 'The text published in *The Listener* was checked at No.10 with the copy from which the PM spoke, including the slight alterations he made.'

You are right to keep this day as a national holiday, because your Constitution of 1791 was a pattern, when it was framed, of enlightened political thought. Your neighbours in those bygone days saw in the adoption of this system the beginning of the regeneration of Poland. They hastened to perpetrate the partition of your country before the Polish nation could consolidate its position.

The same tragedy, the same crime, was repeated in 1939. The Germans became alarmed at the success achieved by the Polish nation in setting its house in order. They saw that their aggressive designs would be thwarted by the growth of a strong, independent Polish State. At the time of the brutal German attack in September, 1939, your country had in the face of tremendous difficulties achieved notable progress during the twenty years of its revived national existence.

To complete this work of national reconstruction, you needed, and you hoped for, a similar period of peaceful development. When the call came, Poland did not hesitate. She did not hesitate to risk all the progress she had made rather than compromise her national honour; and she showed in the spontaneous response of her sons and daughters that spirit of national unity and of self-sacrifice which has maintained her among the great nations of Europe through all her many trials and tribulations.

I know from talks I have had with Poles now in this country how magnificently the mass of the Polish nation answered the appeal to duty in the hour of need. I have been deeply moved by what I have heard of the inhabitants of Warsaw during the three weeks of the siege, and of their continued strenuous resistance to the alien oppressor who now occupies their city.

We in this country who are conscious that our strength is built on the broad masses of the British nation appreciate and admire the Polish nation for its noble attitude since the outbreak of the war. Mainly for geographical reasons personal contacts between our two peoples have been restricted in the past; and fighting as we are at opposite ends of Europe against our common foe this war has not yet provided an opportunity for such personal contacts on any large scale between you and my own countrymen.

The fortunes of war have, however, brought to these shores your President, your Government and many thousands of brave Polish soldiers, airmen, sailors and merchant seamen. Their bearing has won them universal admiration in this country and cast further lustre, if that were possible, upon the proud, heroic traditions of Poland.

It has been my privilege to come to know your Prime Minister and Commander-in-Chief, General Sikorski, whose leadership, energy and unfaltering confidence is a source of great encouragement to all who meet him. I have visited your soldiers in Scotland while they were waiting to repel the invader; and while they are longing in their hearts above all to carry back the flag of freedom to their fellow-countrymen at home.

I have seen your pilots, who have by their prowess played a glorious part in the repulse of the German air hordes. Meanwhile, your soldiers have been earning the respect and high regard of their comrades in the Royal Navy and Merchant Marine, with whom they are sharing the tasks of maintaining these contacts with America and with the outside world through which will come the liberation of your country. The presence here of your Government and armed forces has enabled us to get to know each other better and to build a foundation for Anglo-Polish relations after our common victory and the restoration of your freedom.

Our thoughts go out tonight not only to those valiant exiled Poles whom we have learned to like and respect in the British Islands and who stand armed in the ranks of the armies of liberation, but even more to those who are gripped at home in the merciless oppression of the Hun.

All over Europe, races and States whose culture and history made them a part of the general life of Christendom in centuries when the Prussians were no better than a barbarous tribe, and the German Empire no more than an agglomeration of pumpernickel principalities, are now prostrate under the dark, cruel yoke of Hitler and his Nazi gang. Every week his firing parties are busy in a dozen lands. Monday he shoots Dutchmen; Tuesday Norwegians; Wednesday, French or Belgians stand against the wall; Thursday it is the Czechs who must suffer. And now there are the Serbs and the Greeks to fill his repulsive bill of executions. But always, all the days, there are the Poles. The atrocities committed by Hitler upon the Poles, the ravaging of their country, the scattering of their homes, the affronts to their religion, the enslavement of their man-power, exceed in severity and in scale the villainies perpetrated by Hitler in any other conquered land.

It is to you Poles, in Poland, who bear the full brunt of the Nazi oppression – at once pitiless and venal – that the hearts of the British and American Democracies go out in full and generous tide. We send you our message of hope and encouragement tonight, knowing that the Poles will never despair and that the soul of Poland will remain unconquerable.

This war against the mechanized barbarians, who, slave-hearted themselves, are fitted only to carry their curse to others – this war will be long and hard. But the end is sure; the end will reward all toil, all disappointments, all suffering in those who faithfully serve the cause of European and world freedom. A day will dawn, perhaps sooner than we now have a right to hope, when the insane attempt to found a Prussian domination on racial hatred, on the armoured vehicle, on the secret police, on the alien overseer and on still more filthy Quislings, will pass like a monstrous dream. And in that morning of hope and freedom, not only the embattled and at last well-armed Democracies but all that is noble and fearless in the New World as well as in the Old, will salute the rise of Poland to be a nation once again.

John Colville: diary
(*Colville papers*)

4 May 1941 Chequers

. . . The PM, tempted by the warmth, sat in the garden working and glancing at me with suspicion from time to time in the (unwarranted) belief that I was trying to read the contents of his special buff boxes.[1]

The C-in-C Bomber Command (Peirse) came to dine and sleep.

Winston S. Churchill to President Franklin D. Roosevelt
(*Churchill papers, 20/38*)

4 May 1941

Your friendly message assures me that no temporary reverses, however heavy, can shake your resolution to support us until we gain the final victory. I quite see your difficulties about paragraph 1 so far as visits are concerned, but the consequences reflect themselves upon paragraph 2.

2. The conditions in your first sentence of this paragraph (paragraph 2) make it almost certain that we shall be forestalled. We ourselves are deeply impressed with those conditions, but, on the other hand, how are we to deal with German penetration by tourists and agents ready for some fine day when a German armed expedition will arrive, finding all prepared for them beforehand? The terror which Germany exercises on the Governments of Portugal and Spain forces them to take no notice of infiltration in these islands, lest worse befall them at home. You may be sure that they will try to synchronize any decisive move from Spain on Portugal with a stroke on the Islands. We have taken no decision yet, but I am sure you would not wish to prescribe our remaining passive if we feel we have to act in advance of the conditions set forth in the first sentence of your paragraph 2.

3. Should we decide to move against these islands, not only would we declare that they are occupied only for the purpose of British defence, and not for permanent occupation, and that we will restore the islands to Portuguese sovereignty at the close of the war if Portugal is restored as an independent nation, but we should be perfectly ready that the United States should stand guarantor for the execution of such an engagement. We are far from wishing to add to our territory, but only to preserve our life, and perhaps yours.

[1] The locked boxes, to which Churchill had the key, contained material derived from the Bletchley Park reading of top secret German radio signals.

4. Your paragraph 3. We must not be too sure that the consequences of the loss of Egypt and the Middle East would not be grave. It would seriously increase the hazards of the Atlantic and the Pacific, and could hardly fail to prolong the war, with all the suffering and military dangers that this would entail. We shall fight on whatever happens, but please remember that the attitude of Spain, Vichy, Turkey and Japan may be finally determined by the outcome of the struggle in this theatre of war. I cannot take the view that the loss of Egypt and the Middle East would be a mere preliminary to the successful maintenance of a prolonged oceanic war. If all Europe, the greater part of Asia and Africa became, either by conquest or agreement under duress, a part of the Axis system a war maintained by the British Isles, United States, Canada and Australia against this mighty agglomeration would be a hard, long and bleak proposition. Therefore, if you cannot take more advanced positions now, or very soon, the vast balances may be tilted heavily to our disadvantage. Mr President, I am sure that you will not misunderstand me if I speak to you exactly what is in my mind. The one decisive counterweight I can see to balance the growing pessimism in Turkey, the Near East and in Spain would be if United States were immediately to range herself with us as a belligerent Power. If this were possible I have little doubt that we could hold the situation in the Mediterranean until the weight of your munitions gained the day.

5. We are determined to fight to the last inch and ounce for Egypt, including its outposts of Tobruk and Crete. Very considerable risks are being run by us for that, and personally I think we shall win, in spite of the physical difficulties of reinforcing by tanks and air. But I adjure you, Mr President, not to under-rate the gravity of the consequences which may follow from a Middle Eastern collapse; in this war every post is a winning-post, and how many more are we going to lose?

6. With regard to Vichy, we are more than willing that you should take the lead, and work out how to get the best from them by threats or favours. You alone can forestall the Germans in Morocco. If they are once installed it will not be necessary for them to go overland, they will soon get air-borne troops to Dakar.

7. I shall await with deep anxiety the new broadcast which you contemplate. It may be the supreme turning point.

8. Let me thank you for the splendid help in shipping and tankers which we owe to your action, and for all your generous and bold assistance to us and to the common cause.

Winston S. Churchill to General Ismay
(*Premier papers, 3/156/6*)

4 May 1941

Let me have a report on the efficiency of the gunners and personnel managing the 15-inch batteries and searchlights at Singapore. Are they fitted with RDF?[1]

Winston S. Churchill to General Wavell
(*Churchill papers, 20/38*)

4 May 1941

Your 0/61343 and 0/64713. Have you read OL211 of 4th instant? Presume you realize authoritative character of this information?[2] Actual text more impressive than paraphrase showing enemy 'thoroughly exhausted', unable, pending arrival 15th Panzer Division and of reinforcements, to do more than hold ground gained at Tobruk, and assigning as main task of Africa Corps retention of Cyrenaica with or without Tobruk, Sollum, Bardia. Also definitely forbidding any advance beyond Sollum, except for reconnaissance, without permission.

2. This condition of enemy only bears out what you believed would be brought upon him by supply difficulty and his premature audacious advance. Severe fighting which has attended his attacks on Tobruk imposes utmost strain on troops in this plight. It would seem to me, judging from here, most important not to allow fighting round Tobruk to die down, but to compel enemy to fire his ammunition and use up his strength by counter-attack. For this purpose trust you will consider reinforcing Tobruk as well as harrying enemy about Sollum. It seems to me that if you leave him quiet he will gather supplies and strength for a forward move. But if continuously engaged now, his recovery will be delayed and perhaps prevented.

3. In a week from now we shall know whether Tiger[3] has passed narrows, and you would surely be justified then in running greater risks and possibly reinforcing Tobruk with some of your I and Cruiser Tanks. In this way a great opportunity might be created.

[1] Radio Direction Finding, later known as Radar and still secret. The existence of radar was not revealed until 18 June 1941, when Air Chief Marshal Sir Philip Joubert de la Ferté described publicly how the device performed, while stressing that 'for security reasons the operational methods of the weapon are still a close secret'. The headline in the Toronto *Globe and Mail* was succinct: 'Radio Secret Dooms German Raiders.'

[2] Based on Enigma decrypts of Germany's own top secret radio signals. Wavell had been told the nature of this source of British knowledge.

[3] The passage of two warships through the Straits of Gibraltar with military supplies to Egypt, including anti-tank weapons.

4. Tobruk has marvellously served its purpose owing to the splendid way in which it has been and is being defended. I trust no respite will be given to enemy there.

5. You have not yet told me how if Tiger gets through you propose to handle precious supplies it brings, nor how long it will take to arm each Regiment with the new weapons. Have you made plans to bring the new weapons into the field at earliest moment? If you wait till you are quite ready, enemy may well be ready too, and victory which is not now far off may recede indefinitely.

6. I feel entitled to put these views before you because in my sphere I am running risks and making exertions to secure you Tiger and Jaguar. If they succeed I shall try to repeat them at once.

7. Success of Salient[1] should by now have brought you a large reinforcement of AT guns, in addition to arrival of an AT Regiment in WS 6.[2]

8. I concur fully in the Staff telegram about the Iraq trouble. According to my returns you have close upon half a million men under your Command, and I do not believe there are more than 25,000 Germans in Africa. The success of Demon[3] should make you easier.

9. I should be grateful if you would pass the following message to General Morshead[4] at Tobruk: 'The whole Empire is watching your steadfast and spirited defence of this important outpost of Egypt with gratitude and admiration.'

Winston S. Churchill to Anthony Eden

(*Churchill papers, 20/36*)

4 May 1941

I was also a little disturbed at the telegram[5] already beginning to make such good arrangements for the further flight of the King of Greece from Crete. Although this was no doubt done as a matter of routine, we must not let it be thought that we do not intend to fight long and bitterly for Crete, or that we do not have good hopes of holding it.

[1] The passage of two ships through the Mediterranean to Egypt.

[2] An Anti-Tank Regiment was on board convoy WS 6 (from Britain to the Middle East via the Cape of Good Hope).

[3] The evacuation of Greece.

[4] Leslie James Morshead, 1889–1959. On active service with the Australian Imperial Forces, 1914–18 (Gallipoli and France, despatches six times, Distinguished Service Order). Commanded the 18th Australian Infantry Brigade, Middle East, 1941–42; Commandant, Tobruk Garrison, 1941. General Officer Commanding the Australian Imperial Force, Middle East, 1942–43. Commonwealth 9th Australian Division at El Alamein, 1942. Knighted 1943. General Officer Commanding New Guinea Force, 1944. Task Force Commander, Borneo operations, 1945 (despatches thrice).

[5] From the Foreign Office in London to the Foreign Office representative in Canea, Crete.

Winston S. Churchill to Sir Hughe Knatchbull-Hugessen
(*Churchill papers, 20/49*)

4 May 1941

General Wavell has under his command nearly 500,000 men, but these are spread out over the enormous territories with the defence of which he is charged. The collapse of the Italian resistance in the south is enabling much stronger concentrations to be made in the desert.

2. Forces operating in the desert were limited not by the numbers at the General's disposal, but by the conditions of supply in the desert.

3. We were sending men to Greece as fast as the shipping allowed up to the 100,000 when the progress of the enemy's invasion made it useless to continue.

4. All supplies of Tanks and aircraft in the Middle East are limited, not by the quantities available in Great Britain, but by the rate at which they can be transported.

The above may assist you with the Turks.

Winston S. Churchill to Viscount Halifax
(*Churchill papers, 20/49*)

4 May 1941

We have been trying to provide crews for additional USA destroyers as follows: 10 on April 1, 10 on May 1, 10 on June 1. The 10 cutters which we are now manning absorbed the crews of the 10 destroyers allowed for April 1. This is about our limit in the time mentioned. Of course, if we could get new destroyers which could come into action forthwith and stand up to the severe service, we could give them the crews now provided for some of the original 50, of which only 30 are as yet in service. Any of the new destroyers sent over here could be worked unaltered in their American fittings, and would be held ready to be turned over to the US Navy on entering the war.

2. Are you sure that Knox is not pressing for still more vigorous action, *i.e.*, convoys, and perhaps Hull, with diplomatic caution, is not feeling his way to half-measures? This would explain the '2 or 3 months' remark and also his wish that American Embassy should not know of his *démarche*. Such complications are found in many Governments. I should be inclined to go a little slow on this till the reactions following on the reverses in the Middle East are more clear.

Winston S. Churchill to General Ismay, for the Chiefs of Staff Committee
(Churchill papers, 20/36)

4 May 1941

DRAFT MIDDLE EAST APPRECIATION FOR PRESIDENT ROOSEVELT

1. It seems very lucky that this appreciation was not sent off as soon as it was completed, because, obviously, the situation has entirely changed. Moreover, until Tiger is completed, it is not possible to take a true view. Meanwhile, it would be a good thing if the Staff brought their appreciation up to date, noting –

(a) The evacuation of the Army in Greece and consequent reinforcement by 45,000 men.
(b) The arrival of WS 6 with artillery and anti-Tank rifles.
(c) See Operation Salient successfully finished with important AT reinforcements.
(d) Operation in Iraq.
(e) Approach of reinforcements from the south.
(f) Concentration of Air forces from the south.
(g) Stubborn resistance of Tobruk, and difficulty of enemy's communications.
(h) Strong forces now available in Crete. The Operations Tiger and Jaguar must not be mentioned.
(i) The expression '3 <u>weak</u> armoured regiments' does not quite give the right idea. It is better to give the number of good serviceable Tanks in each, or in all three.

2. Paragraph 26 is not correct. It may be true that the war 'can only be lost in and around the United Kingdom.' It is not true it can only be won there. We are not told how it is to be won unless Air bombing on a large scale is intended.

3. Lastly, shipping shortage will ensure that the United Kingdom is not unduly denuded.

4. I do not think the document as it stands, even when brought up to date, is suitable for transmission to the President. There is too much detail and the broad picture does not emerge. However, if the changes I have suggested are made, I will myself consider sending him a message, based upon the facts after we know what happens to Tiger.

John Colville: diary
(Colville papers)

4 May 1941 Chequers

The PM worked until after 2 a.m. in bed, almost emptying a very full box while the Prof sat in his bedroom acting as a waste-paper basket and I stood at the foot of the bed collecting those papers with which he had dealt.

War Cabinet: minutes
(Cabinet papers, 65/18)

5 May 1941 10 Downing Street
5 p.m.

The Minister for Economic Warfare[1] reminded the War Cabinet that we had resisted proposal made by the United States State Department in February last to send food to unoccupied France. On the 4th March they had returned to the charge, and we had agreed to the sailing of two wheat ships, subject to assurances that the entry of further Germans into French Africa should be forbidden, the activities of the Armistice Commission limited, and certain British Consular Officers allowed to return.

On the 30th April our Ambassador[2] had been informed by the State Department that they had agreed in principle with a proposal of the French Government that two further wheat ships should be sent to unoccupied France as soon as possible, by early July at the latest, and that the United States Government should have complete control of the disposal of the wheat and facilities for appointing controllers.

Looked at from the blockade point of view, we had made concessions without any substantial *quid pro quo*. The attitude of the State Department in making this arrangement without prior consultation with us was hardly consistent with the previous negotiations on the matter.

On the other hand, the Prime Minister pointed out that, owing to other demands on our Naval forces, we were not maintaining an effective blockade of unoccupied France.

[1] Hugh Dalton.
[2] Lord Halifax.

War Cabinet, Tank Parliament[1]
(Cabinet papers, 120/52)

5 May 1941 10 Downing Street
11.15 a.m.

The Prime Minister said that he had wished to make a general examination of the present position and prospects of armoured formations, and for this reason had decided to set up a 'Tank Parliament', at which there could be free discussion and exchange of views.

It was necessary to consider not only 1941 and 1942, but also 1943. Reviewing the progress of events since the last war, and the experiences of the present day, when we saw large armies paralysed by comparatively small forces of armoured fighting vehicles, it was evident that our tank programme was a matter of the greatest importance. Last summer, when we had so little, it had been necessary to concentrate on existing types; but at the same time, the A22 had been designed, and this would be the staple article for late 1941, and possibly for 1942. We should have to go better than that for 1943. Looking at the broad strategy of the war, we might have to reckon with a break eastwards by the Germans, with the object of nullifying the blockade. This would cause a steady drain on their resources, and we should do our best to pulverize them by our air bombardment. This might not, however, be decisive, and we must therefore come back to consideration of what could be done on land. We must look ahead to the utilization of the large resources of ourselves and the United States of America, and fashion the means to win.

In a recent Directive, he had set as the aim for 1942 the equivalent of 15 Armoured Divisions. For 1943, we must aim perhaps at 25. People spoke of creating a balanced Army, but if we could land at various places in the enemy's enormous coast-line really powerful forces of tanks, we could reckon on the uprising populations to assist us. Our ultimate programme must therefore be examined, and with it must go a programme for all the vessels which would be required for overseas operations. With this end in view, he would like to discuss, at successive meetings, all aspects of armoured warfare, with a view to framing decisions for the future.

ORGANIZATION OF THE ARMOURED DIVISION

The Prime Minister said that he had been struck by the fact that armoured Divisions were at present organized throughout with one type of tank. It seemed to him that there was a good case for a mixture of fast and slower tanks

[1] This was the first meeting of a Cabinet Committee known as the Tank Parliament. Churchill was in the Chair. The other Ministers present were Lord Beaverbrook (Minister of State), Sir Andrew Duncan (Minister of Supply) and David Margesson (Secretary of State for War), together with their officials, and with Professor Lindemann. Lieutenant Colonel E.I.C. Jacob was the Tank Parliament Secretary.

within the Division – the fast ones to go ahead and seize important ground, or manoeuvre against the enemy; the slower tanks coming up to relieve them, or to administer a blow. A fleet at sea was composed of battleships, cruisers, destroyers, etc., each with their different task, but each forming part of the whole. He would like to hear the arguments.

Lieut.-General Martel said that much thought had been given to this subject, and many different organizations had been tried out during recent years. Originally, tank units had been composed of a mixture of light and medium tanks, but eventually it had been found better to make units homogeneous. The main objection to the mixture was that the different tanks had different march speeds, and they had to refuel at different intervals. This caused great difficulties in the movement of formations.

Major-General McCreery[1] favoured the composite unit. It would not be sufficient to have a brigade of two Infantry tank regiments, and one Cruiser tank regiment, as with such an arrangement, the fast unit would get worked night and day. This was shown in Egypt, where the armoured cars had been badly overworked.

The Prime Minister said that in their advance on Calais and Boulogne, it certainly had seemed that the Germans employed mixed detachments containing everything from the motor-cycle to the heavy tank and the 6-inch Howitzer.

The Prime Minister enquired whether we were still making light tanks, and was informed that a new light tank was being developed, rather on the model of the German 9-ton tank. It would have 1¾-inch armour, and a 2-pdr gun, and its uses would be for transport by air; for use in difficult country; or on combined operations. This would not be in full production this year. In the meantime, a few of the older pattern were still being made.

[1] Richard London McCreery, 1898–1967. On active service in France, 1914–18 (Military Cross); 1940 (Distinguished Service Order). Commander, 8th Armoured Division (Middle East, 1941–42, Tunisia, 1943). Chief of General Staff, Middle East, 1942. Knighted, 1943. Commanding the Eighth Army in Italy, 1944–45. General Officer Commanding-in-Chief, British Forces of Occupation in Austria, and British Representative as the Allied High Commissioner for Austria, 1945–46. General Officer Commanding-in-Chief, British Army of Occupation on the Rhine (BAOR), 1946–48. British Army Representative, Military Staff Committee, United Nations, 1948–49. Retired, 1949. Colonel Commandant, Royal Armoured Corps, 1947–56.

Winston S. Churchill to Sir Edward Bridges
(Churchill papers, 20/36)

5 May 1941

What arrangement is it proposed to make to provide Lord Beaverbrook with suitable office accommodation and a secretarial staff and assistance?

It would be convenient if this could be found in the Annexe, perhaps on the floor above that which I occupy with the staff of No. 10.[1]

Winston S. Churchill to Herbert Morrison
(Churchill papers, 20/36)

5 May 1941

Northern Ireland does not appear to be making its utmost contribution to the war effort. I am informed by the Chairman of the Production Executive[2] that one-eighth of the insured population is out of work, and that, when certain constructional work is complete, more will be thrown out. About a third of the unemployed are linen trade workers, who should be adaptable for semi-skilled work in munitions production.

I understand that there are the usual difficulties, shortage of certain types of skilled labour, and of machine tools, although there is some doubt whether the machine tools are used to capacity, and that the power supply is concentrated in one vulnerable station.

Mr Bevin reports that steps are being taken to overcome these difficulties, that his contacts with the Northern Irish Government are satisfactory and that our Supply Departments are making as much use as possible of the resources of Northern Ireland. But he adds that 'it is now up to Northern Ireland to display some initiative on their own if they wish to make a fuller contribution.'

Please give consideration to what steps might be taken to stimulate this initiative.

It is desirable that arrangements for dilution be concluded at once and that fuller information on the machine tool situation be obtained. Meanwhile, could not another experiment in the loan of surplus man-power to this country be made?

[1] Churchill's suite of rooms was directly above the Cabinet War Rooms, with a view over St James's Park. It was known as 'No. 10 Annexe'.

[2] Ernest Bevin.

Winston S. Churchill to Air Chief Marshal Sir Charles Portal
(*Churchill papers, 20/36*)

5 May 1941
Most Secret

The future relative Air strength in the Middle East. I sent you back your paper last night, asking for it to be amended in the light of repeated Jaguars. I must, however, add that I am most deeply concerned at the prospect which you unfold. If at the present time, when we have a superiority, we can only just hold our own, what will be our position in June, when, according to you and the present layout, the enemy will have, or may have, nearly double our strength?

If I had not asked for this forecast, I should have been left unaware of what we are marching into. I cannot understand how this prospect was not laid bare by the Air Ministry and the Chiefs of the Staff at an earlier date.

I do not know of any new facts which have come to hand, for personally I never expected the Greek venture to succeed, unless Turkey and Yugoslavia both came in.

It is indispensable that we should maintain parity in the Middle East, and you should without delay submit proposals up to the maximum humanly possible, assuming you have full use of all the A/C Carriers up to the throwing-off point.

You have not yet shown me what you propose to do in Bombers. How did you get the Beaufighters into Malta? Can they fly direct?

Winston S. Churchill to General Ismay, for the Chiefs of Staff Committee
(*Churchill papers, 20/36*)

6 May 1941

This 0/61872 from General Wavell and 5197 G from C-in-C India,[1] should be considered forthwith, and a report made to me at the House of Commons before luncheon today.

(1) Why should the force mentioned in para. 1, which seems considerable, be deemed insufficient to deal with the Iraq Army? What do you say about this? Fancy having kept this Cavalry Division in Palestine all this time without having the rudiments of a mobile column organized!

(2) Why should the troops at Habbaniya give in before 12th May? Their losses have been nominal as so far reported. Their infantry made a successful

[1] General Auchinleck.

sortie last night, and we are told that the bombardment stops whenever our aircraft appear. Great efforts should be made by the Air Force to aid and encourage Habbaniya. Surely some additional infantry can be flown there as reinforcements from Egypt. The most strenuous orders should be given to the Officer Commanding to hold out.

How can a settlement be negotiated, as General Wavell suggests? Suppose the Iraqis, under German instigation, insist upon our evacuating Basra, or moving in small detachments at their mercy across the country to Palestine. The opinion of the SNO, Basra,[1] is that a collapse or surrender here would be disastrous. This is also the opinion of India. I am deeply disturbed at General Wavell's attitude. He seems to have been taken as much by surprise on his eastern as he was on his western flank, and in spite of the enormous number of men at his disposal, and the great convoys reaching him, he seems to be hard up for battalions and companies. He gives me the impression of being tired out.

The proposals of C-in-C, India, for reinforcing Basra seem to deserve most favourable consideration.

War Cabinet, Defence Committee (Operations): minutes

(*Cabinet papers, 69/2*)

6 May 1941
12.30 p.m.

House of Commons

IRAQ

The Prime Minister referred to a telegram No. 0/61872 from General Wavell.

He said that two serious military points were raised in this telegram. First, General Wavell seemed doubtful whether the mobile column which he was assembling would prove strong enough to relieve Habbaniya. Secondly, General Wavell expressed doubts as to whether Habbaniya could hold out. He had therefore addressed a Minute to the Chiefs of Staff, asking them to consider this telegram, and to advise the Defence Committee.

In reply to an enquiry by the Prime Minister, Sir Charles Portal said that German long-range bombers could fly from Rhodes to Baghdad, but they would have to rely entirely upon Iraqi resources for stores and maintenance, unless they were able to refuel in Syria, and use transport aircraft.

[1] Ralph Leatham, 1886-1954. Entered the Royal Navy as a cadet, 1900. Rear-Admiral, First Battle Squadron, 1938-39. Commander-in-Chief, East Indies Station (and Senior Naval Officer, Basra), 1939-41. Knighted, 1942. Flag Officer in Charge, Malta, 1942-43; Deputy Governor of Malta, 1943. Commander-in-Chief, Plymouth, 1943-45. Governor and Commander-in-Chief, Bermuda, 1946-49.

The Prime Minister saw no advantage in negotiations. Rashid Ali has planned the whole of his present action, but we had forestalled him by arriving at Basra, and had forced him to go ahead before he could be effectively supported by the Axis. We should treat the present situation like a rebellion.

Winston S. Churchill to General Ismay, for the Chiefs of Staff Committee
(Churchill papers, 20/36)

6 May 1941

Surely I gave directions that the C-in-C was to have full liberty to capture enemy hospital ships in retaliation for their brutality. Let me see the correspondence.

Winston S. Churchill to Air Chief Marshal Sir Charles Portal
(Churchill papers, 20/36)

6 May 1941
Action this Day

RETURN DATED 4 MAY 1941 OF RECEIPTS AND LOSSES OF AIRCRAFT IN THE MIDDLE EAST

Here is another shocking week at Takoradi. Only 18 aircraft have been despatched, whereas I think a programme of nearly double the number was promised. I am afraid it must be realized that this is a very great failure and breakdown in our arrangements, which may play its part in a disastrous result to the great battle proceeding in the Nile Valley. In spite of all my warnings and appeals, we are actually doing worse than we did six or eight weeks ago. Leaving the American machines out for the moment, about which there is obviously a complete breakdown, I cannot understand why the 18 Hurricanes and 36 Blenheims, which are so sorely needed, cannot be sent immediately, and why the arrangements for the return of ferry pilots to Takoradi are not made. I asked you two months ago to send an officer out to report upon the breakdown. But I have not heard anything of his work.

Winston S. Churchill to General Sir John Dill
(Churchill papers, 20/36)

6 May 1941

Inquiries should be made whether the troops in Crete have a sufficiency of good maps. Otherwise we shall soon find that any German arrivals will be better informed about the island than our men.

Winston S. Churchill to Admiral Pound
(*Churchill papers, 20/36*)

6 May 1941

MOBILE NAVAL BASE DEFENCE ORGANIZATION FOR SUDA BAY, CRETE

How was it this took 12 weeks on passage, and why was the equipment packed without any relation to its employment? One would have thought a mobile naval base plant would, above all other things, have been stowed, so that it could have been taken out and employed.

It seems to me an inquiry should be held into this lapse of Staff work.

Winston S. Churchill: message
(*Churchill papers, 20/49*)

7 May 1941

TO BE READ AT THE ANNUAL BANQUET OF AMERICAN BOOKSELLERS[1]

Your calling has been well described as the mighty power of the spirit in the word.

This power has been taken away from many nations by Nazi tyrants. Not easily will it be taken from English-speaking peoples, who from writers living and dead gather courage and constancy to strengthen us in the trials we must undergo.

When the minds of nations can be cowed by the will of one man, civilization is broken irreparably. You, who have measured the strength of the Nazi conspiracy against the world, need no reminder that the means by which nations are raised to greatness are the virtues bred by freedom of speech and writing.

A one-man State is no State. It is an enslavement of the soul, the mind, the body of mankind. The brute will of Germany's fleeting dictator has exiled or imprisoned the best of her writers. This remorseless despot now complains against the freedom of American writers. Their fault is that they stand for a free way of life. It is a life that is death to meteoric tyrants. So be it. And so it will be.

[1] Churchill sent this message to Lord Halifax as Prime Minister's Personal Telegram T. 142 of 5 May 1941. It was read out by Lord Halifax at the banquet.

Winston S. Churchill: Oral Answers
(Hansard)

7 May 1941 House of Commons

MEMBERS OF PARLIAMENT (GOVERNMENT APPOINTMENTS)

Mr De la Bère asked the Prime Minister whether, in view of the increasing growth of patronage and Government appointments which have been secured by a large number of Members of the present House of Commons, he will introduce legislation to limit the number of these so as not to exceed 50 per cent. of the sitting Members, and thus ensure that the House of Commons remains representative of the electorate?

The Prime Minister (Mr Churchill): As my hon. Friend is aware, certificates which would prevent the extension of disqualification applying are required under the House of Commons Disqualification (Temporary Provisions) Act, 1941, to be signed by the First Lord of the Treasury, and a copy laid before the House of Commons. Any change in the law dealing with this matter ought, I think, to await the recommendations of the Select Committee now considering the position.

Mr De la Bère: Is the right hon. Gentleman aware that power always corrupts and that absolute power corrupts absolutely? Can he not see the danger of the power given to this group being utilized for intrigue or other purposes, and is it not absolutely anti-democratic?

The Prime Minister: I do not think that the general principle can be stated in such absolute terms. Power exercised under the vigorous and vigilant supervision of a properly elected Parliamentary Assembly has frequently been found to be compatible with a very high standard of public life.

POST-WAR RECONSTRUCTION (SCOTLAND)

Mr Mathers[1] asked the Prime Minister what Minister will be responsible for co-ordinating the work of the Ministry of Works and Buildings and the Minister without Portfolio in respect of the comprehensive planning of Scotland for post-war development?

The Prime Minister: The co-ordination of the preparatory work on all reconstruction problems is carried out by the Ministerial Committee under the chairmanship of my right hon. Friend the Minister without Portfolio. The various Departments concerned are represented at meetings of the Committee.

[1] George Mathers, 1886–1965. A railway clerk, 1899. Active in the Trade Union Movement from 1908. President of the Carlisle Trades Council and Labour Party, 1917–20. Chairman, Edinburgh Central Independent Labour Party. Labour Member of Parliament, West Edinburgh, 1929–31; Linlithgowshire, 1935–50; West Lothian, 1950–51. Parliamentary Private Secretary to the Parliamentary Under-Secretary of State for India, 1929. Scottish Labour Whip, 1935–45. Deputy Chief Whip 1945–46. Lord High Commissioner, General Assembly of the Church of Scotland, 1946–48, 1951. Created Baron, 1951. Knight of the Thistle, 1956.

Mr Mathers: Does that mean that there is special oversight of the Scottish side of this business?

The Prime Minister: Yes, Sir, I am sure that that course is provided for. At the same time we have met the principle of not disclosing the actual membership and composition of committees. It is a very old rule.

Mr Mathers: Will the right hon. Gentleman keep in mind what he already knows as to the trend of Scottish susceptibilities?

The Prime Minister: Yes, indeed, having been a Member for a Scottish constituency for 15 years.[1]

MINISTER OF STATE

44. Major Vyvyan Adams[2] asked the Prime Minister whether it is intended to introduce legislation to legalize the new office of Minister of State?

The Prime Minister: No legislation is necessary for this purpose.

Major Adams: Is not this office a wholly novel one in our Constitution?

The Prime Minister: No, Sir, His Majesty has from time immemorial appointed what Ministers he thinks desirable to whatever office he thinks appropriate. Legislation is only necessary where it is desired that the holder of a newly created office should sit in the House of Commons. The Minister of State lately appointed sits, of course, in the other place, but no fresh legislation would be required even if it were desired to appoint a Minister of State who is a Member of this House, because provision has already been made by Section 2 of the Re-election of Ministers Act, 1919, whereby a member of the Privy Council may be appointed a Minister of the Crown at a salary and may sit and vote in this House, provided that not more than three such Ministers are so appointed at the same time.

Mr Maxton:[3] Will the Prime Minister let us know what is the distinction between a Minister without Portfolio and a Minister of State?

The Prime Minister: The advantage in the new term lies not so much in the distinction as in the difference.

Mr Thorne:[4] Have they got the same power and authority?

The Prime Minister: Certainly. They are both members of the War Cabinet

[1] Churchill represented Dundee as Liberal Member of Parliament from 1908 until 1922 (when he was defeated by a Prohibitionist, and was then out of Parliament for two years).

[2] Samuel Vyvyan Trerice Adams, 1900–51. Educated at Haileybury and King's College, Cambridge. Called to the Bar, 1927. Conservative MP for West Leeds, 1931–45. Member of the Executive of the League of Nation's Union, 1933–46. On active service, 1939–45 (major, Duke of Cornwall's Light Infantry). In 1940, under the pen name 'Watchman', he published *Churchill: Architect of Victory*. Political researcher, 1946–51.

[3] James Maxton, 1885–1946. Known as 'Jimmy'. A leading Scottish radical. Labour MP for Glasgow (Bridgeton) from 1922 until his death. Chairman of the Independent Labour Party (ILP), 1926–31 and 1934–39. Biographer of Lenin.

[4] Will Thorne, 1857–1946. Began work at the age of six, in a barber's shop. A founder member of the National Union of General and Municipal Workers, 1889; General Secretary, 1889–1934. CBE, 1930. A member of the West Ham Town Council from 1890 until his death. Labour MP for West Ham, 1906–45. Privy Councillor, 1945.

and have both general and particular spheres of duty assigned to them.

Mr Mander: Can the right hon. Gentleman state the salary which will be paid to the Minister of State?

The Prime Minister: It would be the salary of the other members of the War Cabinet, but I do not know whether he takes it or not. I have not been told.

Parliamentary Debate: War Situation, Assistance to Greece
(Hansard)

7 May 1941 House of Commons

Mr Lloyd George: . . . I sat one night listening to the six o'clock news on the wireless, giving the story of the Battle of Mount Olympus. I was thrilled by the account that we were holding our own and flinging back our enemies with great loss, and then at the end of it there was this sentence: 'The German communiqué claims that Mount Olympus has been captured and that the Germans are in Larissa.' That was all the news that we had. There was no contradiction of the German claim. Then, somebody who was there said, 'There must be something wrong about that; we will listen to the nine o'clock news.' Well, we listened to the nine o'clock news, and there was just a repetition of the German claim. That is not the way to treat a decent, honest, brave public that is willing to make any sacrifice for what it thinks is right.

The Prime Minister (Mr Churchill): I am sure that we had not at that time any information on the subject. During seven days of fighting we received no information. The circumstances were peculiar, and I complained about it, but there is no question on our part of withholding information. If we had known that Larissa had been occupied, we should certainly have said so.

Mr Lloyd George: I do not know who is to blame, whether the Government or anybody else, but surely the distance from the respective battle fronts to their headquarters was pretty nearly the same, and we ought to have known. The result was that the whole story, right up to the end, had to be gathered from the German communiqués and not from ours. If the Prime Minister says that the Government were not responsible, I accept that at once, but I feel that they ought to have been informed.

The Prime Minister: Certainly.

Winston S. Churchill: speech
(Hansard)

7 May 1941 House of Commons

The Prime Minister (Mr Churchill): This debate, as I think will be agreed on all hands, has been marked by a high sense of discretion and a high degree of responsibility in all who have taken part in it. If there were any speech I could single out especially for praise, it would, I think, be the last, to which we have just listened. My hon. Friend the Member for Derby (Mr Noel-Baker)[1] is a great devotee of the Greek cause, and all that he has said has shown how deeply he has studied the articulation of their defences and, of course, their fortunes. If there were any speech which I felt was not particularly exhilarating, it was the speech of my right hon. Friend the Member for Carnarvon Boroughs (Mr Lloyd George), who honoured us by one of his always deeply important and much valued appearances in the House. My right hon. Friend made complaints, first of all, of the speech of the Foreign Secretary yesterday because he did not refer to Spain, Russia, Vichy and Turkey. But this was not a Debate on foreign policy, although no doubt such might well be arranged, in public or in private, and I do not think the speech of the Foreign Secretary can be judged entirely by what he said. Rather might it be judged by what he did not say. If he did not refer to Spain, it was not because we have not plenty of information about Spain or because there are not a lot of things that could be said about Spain.

I am not sure how those things which could be said about Spain could be couched in a vein which would be helpful to our affairs. Again, much might be said about Russia, but I am not quite sure that we should gain any advantage by saying it, and I am not quite certain we should receive any thanks from the Soviet Government. It would be possible for one to dilate at length upon the sad and sorry and squalid tale of what is going on at Vichy, but I really do not think we should profit ourselves well if we tarried very long to examine and dissect that tragic spectacle. With regard to Turkey, I thank my right hon. Friend for the great restraint with which he spoke about that country, whose relations are so highly valued by us, and whose part to play in this great world conflict is of the greatest importance. But there are two points on which I think I can a little relieve my right hon. Friend's fears and anxieties about Turkey. First of all, he said they had allowed ships which carried the German troops to the Greek Islands to come through the Dardanelles. They had no right to stop them. While at peace, they had no right whatever to stop them. That would be a decision to quit their neutrality. Article 4 of the Convention reads as follows:

'In time of war, Turkey not being belligerent, merchant vessels under any flag or with any kind of cargo shall enjoy freedom of transit and navigation in the Straits.'

[1] Philip John Noel-Baker, 1889–1982. A Quaker; First Commandant, Friends Ambulance Unit, France, 1914–15 (subsequently on the Italian front). League of Nations Secretariat, 1919–22; active in publicising and supporting the work of the League of Nations. Labour MP, 1929–31 (for Coventry) and 1936–70 (for Derby). Parliamentary Secretary, Ministry of War Transport, 1942–5. Secretary of State for Air, 1946–7; for Commonwealth Relations, 1947–50. British delegate to the United Nations Preparatory Commission, 1945; member of the British Delegation to the UN General Assembly, 1946–7. Minister of Fuel and Power, 1950–1. Nobel Peace Prize, 1959. Created Baron, 1977.

It is evident that a decision by Turkey to stop these vessels would have been of very great consequence to her. [Interruption.] I said merchant vessels. I believe that one of them may have been used in the occupation of the Islands, but there were other vessels in possession of the Germans and Italians which may equally have been used for that purpose. At any rate, the question of the interpretation of their neutrality is a matter obviously of supreme consequence to Turkey. I do not think we should make a reproach upon that subject. Nor did my right hon. Friend do so. He merely put the case.

Then my right hon. Friend the Member for Carnarvon Boroughs said that he had read how Turkey had made some agreement with the Iraqi Government, and he asked about that. I always thought it was a most unfortunate and most tiresome thing when both Persia and Mesopotamia changed their names at about the same time to two names which were so much alike – Iran and Iraq. I have endeavoured myself in the domestic sphere to avoid such risks by naming the new Minister a Minister of State in order that there should be no confusion between him and the Minister without Portfolio. That unfortunate procedure on the part of these two neighbouring States has led my right hon. Friend into needless anxiety. I am very happy to be able to relieve him. It appears that the arrangement is between Turkey and Persia, and that it relates to measures to strengthen the Turco-Persian borders, which we knew all about, which have been prepared for some time, and which are now put into force as from 4th May, 1941. I hope I have relieved my right hon. Friend's anxiety on that score, which indeed was entirely excusable owing to the unhappy similarity of the names of these two countries.

I must, however, say that I did not think the speech of my right hon. Friend was particularly helpful at a period of what he himself called discouragement and disheartenment. It was not the sort of speech which one would have expected from the great war leader of former days, who was accustomed to brush aside despondency and alarm, and push on irresistibly towards the final goal. It was the sort of speech with which, I imagine, the illustrious and venerable Marshal Pétain might well have enlivened the closing days of M. Reynaud's Cabinet. But in one respect I am grateful to my right hon. Friend for the note which he struck, because if anything could make it clearer that we ought to close our Debate by a Vote of Confidence, it is the kind of speech which he delivered, and the kind of speeches we have heard from some of the ablest and most eminent Members of the House. I think the Government were right to put down a Motion of confidence, because after our reverses and disappointments in the field, His Majesty's Government have a right to know where they stand with the House of Commons, and where the House of Commons stands with the country. Still more is this knowledge important for the sake of foreign nations, especially nations which are balancing their policy at the present time, and who ought to be left in no doubt about the stability or otherwise of this resolved and obstinate war Government. Questions are asked, conversations take place in the Lobbies, paragraphs are written in the political columns of the newspapers, and before you know where you are, you hear in all the Embassies with which we are in relation queries, 'Will the Government last? – Are they going to break up? – Will there be a change of administration and a change of policy?'

I think it is essential, considering the tremendous issues which are at stake, and, not to exaggerate, the frightful risks we are all going to run, and are running, that we should have certitude on these matters. In enemy countries they take a lively interest in our proceedings, and I flatter myself that high hopes are entertained that all will not go well with His Majesty's present advisers. The only way in which these doubts can be removed and these expectations disappointed is by a full Debate followed by a Division, and the Government are entitled to ask that such a Vote shall express itself in unmistakable terms. I see that one of the newspapers, which is described as a supporter of the Government, and which supports us by being the most active in keeping us up to the mark – like the Noble Lord the Member for Horsham (Earl Winterton), now relieved from all necessity of keeping himself up to the mark – has deplored the fact of this Motion of Confidence being proposed, because such a procedure might lead some Members to make speeches in favour of the Government, whereas it would be much more useful if the Debate consisted entirely of informative criticism. I am not one, and I should be the last, unduly to resent even unfair criticism, or even fair criticism, which is so much more searching. I have been a critic myself – I cannot at all see how I should have stood the test of being a mere spectator in the drama which is now passing. But there is a kind of criticism which is a little irritating. It is like that of a bystander who, when he sees a team of horses dragging a heavy wagon painfully up a hill, cuts a switch from the fence, and there are many switches, and belabours them lustily. He may well be animated by a benevolent purpose, and who shall say the horses may not benefit from his efforts, and the wagon get quicker to the top of the hill?

I think that it would be a pity if this important and critical Debate, at this moment which my right hon. Friend describes as disheartening and discouraging, consisted solely of critical and condemnatory speeches, because, apart from the inartistic monotony, it would tend to give a distorted impression to many important and interested foreign observers who are not very well acquainted with our Parliamentary or political affairs. Therefore I ask the House for a Vote of Confidence. I hope that those, if such there be, who sincerely in their hearts believe that we are not doing our best and that they could do much better, I hope that they will carry their opinion to its logical and ultimate conclusion in the Lobby. Here I must point out, only for the benefit it is admitted of foreign countries, that they would run no risk in doing so. They are answerable only to their consciences and to their constituents. It is a free Parliament in a free country. We have succeeded in maintaining under difficulties which are unprecedented, and in dangers which, in some cases, might well be mortal, the whole process and reality of Parliamentary institutions. I am proud of this. It is one of the things for which we are fighting. Moreover, I cannot imagine that any man would want to bear, or consent to bear, the kind of burden which falls upon the principal Ministers in the Government, or upon the head of the Government in this terrible war, unless he were sustained, and continually sustained, by strong convinced support, not only of the House of Commons, but of the nation to whom the House of Commons is itself responsible.

It is very natural that the House should not be entirely satisfied with the recent turn of events in the Middle East, and that some Members should be acutely disappointed that we have not been able to defend Greece successfully against the Italian or German armies, and that we should have been unable to keep or extend our conquests in Libya. This sudden darkening of the landscape, after we had been cheered by a long succession of victories over the Italians, is particularly painful. For myself, I must confess that I watched the fate of Greece after her repulse of the Italian invader, with agony. The only relief I feel is that everything in human power was done by us and that our honour as a nation is clear. If anything could add a pang to this emotion, it would be the knowledge we had of the approaching and impending outrage, with so little power to avert from this heroic and famous people a fate so hideous and so undeserved. My right hon. Friend the Member for Devonport (Mr Hore-Belisha) and some others, have spoken of the importance in war of full and accurate Intelligence of the movements and intentions of the enemy. That is one of those glimpses of the obvious and of the obsolete with which his powerful speech abounded.

So far as the German invasion of the Balkans is concerned, we had long and ample forewarning of what was in prospect. It is three months since I stated publicly in a broadcast that the Bulgarian air-fields were being occupied with the knowledge of the Bulgarian Government by the advance parties and agents of the German air force. Talk of our diplomacy being idle – our diplomacy has never ceased for one moment to try to apprise countries of the dangers and perils that were coming on them, and urging them to common action by which their own security and safety could only be maintained. Every week one watched the remorseless movement of vast German forces through Hungary, through Roumania and into Bulgaria, or towards the Croatian frontier of Yugoslavia, until at last no fewer than 40 German divisions, five of which were armoured, were massed upon the scene. Hitler has told us that it was a crime in such circumstances on our part to go to the aid of the Greeks. I do not wish to enter into arguments with experts. This is not a kind of crime of which he is a good judge. When the first request for a Debate began to be made about a fortnight ago, I understood that our critics wished to argue that we were wrong to go to Greece, especially in view of what happened in Libya. Therefore, we put the question of aid to Greece in the forefront of this Motion of Confidence. However, apart perhaps from some echoes in the speech of my right hon. Friend the Member for Devonport, no one, as far as I can make out, has challenged our action in this respect.

Mr Hore-Belisha (Devonport): I never challenged that.

The Prime Minister: We cannot judge our aid to Greece without the consequential effect on the position in Libya, and on that my right hon. Friend made a charge, if my memory serves me aright. Looking back on the sad course of events, I can only feel, as the Prime Minister of New Zealand has so nobly declared, that if we had again to tread that stony path, even with the knowledge we possess today, I for one would do the same thing again, and that is the view of all my colleagues in the War Cabinet and on the Defence Committee, and I believe that view is almost universally sustained by the House. After all, military operations must be judged by the success which attends them rather than by the sentiments which inspired them, though these, too, may play their part in the verdict of history and in the survival of races. It remains to be seen whether the Italian dictator, in invading Greece, and the German dictator, in coming to his rescue and trampling them into a bloody welter, will in fact have gained an advantage or suffered a loss when the full story of the war is completed.

Even from a strictly military point of view the addition of the whole of the Balkan peoples to the number of ancient and independent States and Sovereignties which have now fallen under the Nazi yoke, and which have to be held down by force or by intrigue, may by no means prove a source of strength to the German Army. This vast machine, which was so improvidently allowed to build itself up again during the last eight years, has now spread from the Arctic to the Aegean and from the Atlantic Ocean to the Black Sea. That is no source of strength, and, returning from the military to the political aspect, nothing can more surely debar the Germans from establishing and shaping the new Europe – and one will certainly emerge – than the fact that the German name and the German race have become and are becoming more universally and more intensely hated among all the people in all the lands than any name or any race of which history bears record.

Some have compared Hitler's conquests with those of Napoleon. It may be that Spain and Russia will shortly furnish new chapters to that theme. It must be remembered, however, that Napoleon's armies carried with them the fierce, liberating and equalitarian winds of the French Revolution, whereas Hitler's Empire has nothing behind it but racial self-assertion, espionage, pillage, corruption and the Prussian boot. Yet Napoleon's Empire, with all its faults, and all its glories, fell and flashed away like snow at Easter till nothing remained but His Majesty's ship *Bellerophon*, which awaited its suppliant refugee. So I derive confidence that the will-power of the British nation, expressing itself through a stern, steadfast, unyielding House of Commons, once again will perform its liberating function and humbly exercise and execute a high purpose among men, and I say this with the more confidence because we are no longer a small Island lost in the Northern mists, but around us gather in proud array all the free nations of the British Empire, and this time from across the Atlantic Ocean the mighty Republic of the United States proclaims itself on our side, or at our side, or, at any rate, near our side.

I do not intend today to discuss the large, complicated questions of munitions or food production. On a future occasion, probably in Secret Session, the Minister of Supply will make a considerable statement to the House. My right hon. Friend the Member for Devonport, who is so far-seeing now that we have lost his services, and who told us at the end of November, 1939, that we were comfortably winning the war, had the temerity yesterday to raise the subject of our admitted shortage of tanks. There is one very simple point about tanks, which I think he might have mentioned to us, in the years preceding the war when he was at the head of the War Office and had the opportunity of the highest technical advice. In the last war, tanks were built to go three or four miles an hour and to stand up to rifle or machine-gun bullets. In the interval the process of mechanical science had advanced so much that it became possible to make a tank which could go 15, 20 and 25 miles an hour and stand up to cannon fire. That was a great revolution, by which Hitler has profited. That is a simple fact which was perfectly well known to the military and technical services three or four years before the war. It did not spring from German brains. It sprang from British brains, and from brains like those of General de Gaulle in France, and it has been exploited and turned to our grievous injury by the uninventive but highly competent and imitative Germans. The British Tank Corps knew all about it and wrote it down, but apparently my right hon. Friend did not take it in – at any rate, he did not mention it to us in those simple terms, and, indeed, it may be that the point may not have struck him until now. It would have been a very valuable contribution to our pre-war preparations. My right hon. Friend played a worthy part in bringing in compulsory service.

Earl Winterton (Horsham and Worthing): Hear, hear. Did the Home Secretary?

The Prime Minister: He was not a member of the Government.

Earl Winterton: He opposed it.

The Prime Minister: I have often noticed a difference in the note taken by my Noble Friend on the occasions when he has been in and out of office.

Earl Winterton: I was one of your few supporters.

The Prime Minister: I am not too sure that the change of note did not depend entirely on the amount of information my Noble Friend was able to receive. To return to the point, I was saying that my right hon. Friend played a worthy part in bringing in compulsory service. I should not have referred to this matter if he had not endeavoured to give the House a sort of idea of his super-prevision and super-efficiency and shown himself so aggressive when, I think, with all good will, he sometimes stands in need of some humility in regard to the past.

Mr Hore-Belisha: I think that what the right hon. Gentleman is doing in indulging in petty recriminations is quite unworthy of the great purpose that we have in common. I made no reproach whatever against the Government for any lack of tanks. I suggested, and I think the House concurred with me, that the same priority that has been given to air-craft should now be given to tanks, because the Germans achieved their victory in Libya without air superiority. If I am responsible for the present tank position, I willingly accept, although I would never claim some part in the credit of the advances of General Wavell. I have never claimed that at all. The point is that my right hon. Friend has been in office for 20 months. I have been out of office for 16 months. During that period he has enjoyed unprecedented powers. With the abrogation of trade union regulations, with the full support of every party, which I never enjoyed, and indeed some of those supporting him now were opposing me, in my own proposals, and to reproach one who has been out of office 16 months is irrelevant.

The Prime Minister: I thought my right hon. Friend rose to correct me on some point, and not to renew or elaborate the speech which he delivered yesterday.

Mr Hore-Belisha: Let us get on with the war.

The Prime Minister: My right hon. Friend must restrain himself. Let me tell my right hon. Friend that we are now making every month as many heavy tanks as there existed in the whole British Army at the time he left the War Office – and that we shall very soon, before the end of this year, be producing nearly double that number. This takes no account of the immense productive efforts in the United States. I only say this to him by way of reassuring him that the good work which he did, the foundations which he laid, have not been left to stand where they were when he went out of office. He must learn to 'forgive us our trespasses as we forgive them that trespass against us'.

My right hon. Friend the Member for Carnarvon Boroughs[1] made his usual criticisms about the composition and character of the Government, of the war control and of the War Cabinet, and the House is entitled to know, has a right to know, who are responsible for the conduct of the war. The War Cabinet consists of eight members, five of whom have no regular Departments, and three of whom represent the main organisms of the State, to wit, Foreign Affairs, Finance and Labour, which in their different ways come into every great question that has to be settled. That is the body which gives its broad

[1] David Lloyd George.

sanction to the main policy and conduct of the war. Under their authority, the Chiefs of Staff of the three Services sit each day together, and I, as Prime Minister and Minister of Defence, convene them and preside over them when I think it necessary, inviting, when business requires it, the three Service Ministers. All large issues of military policy are brought before the Defence Committee, which has for several months consisted of the three Chiefs of Staff, the three Service Ministers and four members of the War Cabinet, namely, myself, the Lord Privy Seal, who has no Department, the Foreign Secretary and Lord Beaverbrook. This is the body, this is the machine; it works easily and flexibly at the present time, and I do not propose to make any changes in it until further advised.

My right hon. Friend spoke of the great importance of my being surrounded by people who would stand up to me and say, 'No, No, No.' Why, good gracious, has he no idea how strong the negative principle is in the constitution and working of the British war-making machine? The difficulty is not, I assure him, to have more brakes put on the wheels; the difficulty is to get more impetus and speed behind it. At one moment we are asked to emulate the Germans in their audacity and vigour, and the next moment the Prime Minister is to be assisted by being surrounded by a number of 'No-men' to resist me at every point and prevent me from making anything in the nature of a speedy, rapid and, above all, positive constructive decision.

However, I must say that, in this whole business of Libya and Greece, I can assure the House that no violence has been done to expert military opinion, either in the Chiefs of Staff Committee at home or in the generals commanding in the field. All decisions have been taken unitedly and freely and in good will, in response to the hard pressure of events. I would make it clear, however, that, in certain circumstances or emergencies, the responsible political Minister representing the Government of the country would not hesitate to assume responsibility for decisions which might have to be taken, and I, personally, as head of the Government, obviously assume that responsibility in the most direct personal form. It follows, therefore, when all is said and done, that I am the one whose head should be cut off if we do not win the war. I am very ready that this should be so, because, as my hon. Friend the Member of Seaham (Mr Shinwell) feelingly reminded us yesterday, most of the Members of the House would probably experience an even more unpleasant fate at the hands of the triumphant Hun.

I notice a tendency in some quarters, especially abroad, to talk about the Middle East as if we could afford to lose our position there and yet carry on the war to victory on the oceans and in the air. Stated as an academic and strategic fact, that may be true, but do not let anyone underrate the gravity of the issues which are being fought for in the Nile Valley. The loss of the Nile Valley and the Suez Canal and the loss of our position in the Mediterranean, as well as the loss of Malta, would be among the heaviest blows which we could sustain. We are determined to fight for them with all the resources of the British Empire, and we have every reason to believe that we shall be successful. General Wavell has under his orders at the present moment nearly 500,000 men. A continual flow of equipment has been in progress from this country during the last 10 months, and, now that the Italian resistance in Abyssinia, East Africa and the Somalilands is collapsing, a steady concentration Northwards of all these Forces is possible, and, indeed, it has been for many weeks rapidly proceeding; and General Smuts has ordered the splendid South African Army forward to the Mediterranean shores.

Warfare in the Western Desert or, indeed, in all the deserts which surround Egypt, can only be conducted by comparatively small numbers of highly equipped troops. Here, the fortunes of war are subject to violent oscillation, and mere numbers do not count. On the contrary, the movement in the desert of large numbers would, if things went wrong, lead only to disaster on a larger scale. That is what happened to the Italians. For many months last year a steady flow of Italian troops moved forward day by day from West to East along the coastal roads of Libya, in order to build up an army for the invasion of Egypt. In December those masses were ripe for the sickle; 180,000 men lay along the North African shore, from Benghazi to the Egyptian frontier. Once the head of this force was chopped and broken, it was not physically possible for this great army to retreat. It had been built up bit by bit. It could not retreat all at once; the single coastal road could not carry it, and the transport available could not feed it on the move. The victory of Sidi Barrani, as I told the House some months ago, settled the fate of the troops in Cyrenaica. They did not possess command of the sea, they were beaten in the air, and no course was open to them but to be pinned against the sea and destroyed in detail at Bardia, Tobruk and Benghazi.

The same thing, with important modifications, might well have happened to us when the German armoured forces defeated, dispersed and largely destroyed our single armoured brigade which was guarding the advanced frontier of the Province of Cyrenaica. There are no exact accounts of what happened at Agedabia and Mechili. The generals have been taken prisoner through running undue risks in their personal movements, risks which they could run against the Italians, but not against the Germans. The remnants of the armoured brigade are now fighting in Tobruk. Events are moving so fast, people have so much to do and the intensity of the war is such, that there is not much time to be spared to dwell upon the past. But there are certain broad features which will interest the House. It may surprise the House to learn that the German armoured force was not much larger than our own. But tactical mistakes were committed and mischances occurred, and with very little fighting our armoured force became disorganized. However, the troops we had in Benghazi only amounted to a division, and this division, by a rapid retreat, gained the fortress of Tobruk in good order and unmolested, and there joined the large garrison. There, a month ago, it stood at bay, and there it stands at bay today.

The Germans, as we now know from the examination of prisoners, had no expectation of proceeding beyond Agedabia. They meant to engage our armoured troops and create a diversion to prevent the despatch of reinforcements to Greece, while they were bringing over larger forces from Italy and Sicily and building up their supplies and communications, but when they won their surprising success, they exploited it with that organized, enterprising audacity which ranks so high in the military art. They pushed on into the blue – I might say into the yellow ochre – of the desert, profiting by their easy victory as they have done in so many countries, and for the morrow they took, in this case, little thought either what they should eat or what they should drink. They pushed on until they came up against Tobruk. There they met their prop, a hard and heavy prop, not the less important because, like all these desert operations, it was on a small scale. They pushed on until they came in contact also with the large forces which guard the frontiers of Egypt and which lie there securely based on the road, railway and sea communications. There, for the present moment, they stop.

I shall not attempt to carry the story further this afternoon. To do so would be foolish and might be harmful, but this I will say, that so long as the enemy have a superiority in armoured vehicles they will have an advantage in desert warfare, even though at the present time the air forces are about equal. But, as I said, this desert warfare must be conducted only by small forces. Thirty or forty thousand men is the most who can be supplied in the desert, and it is very doubtful whether even this number can be attained. For the invasion of Egypt, for an invasion in main force such as the Italians contemplated last autumn, enormous preparations would be required, great supplies would have to be built up and maintained, a pipeline might have to be made to carry an artificial river forward with the troops. We, on the other hand, lying back on our fertile delta, which incidentally is the worst ground in the world for armoured vehicles, and enjoying the command of the sea, confront the enemy with problems far more difficult, because on a far larger scale than any he has yet solved in Africa. All the more true is this while we defend, as we intend to do to the death and without thought of retirement, the valuable and highly offensive outposts of Crete and Tobruk. Crete has not yet been attacked, but Tobruk has already been the scene of a most stubborn and spirited defence by the Australian and British troops gathered within these widespread fortified lines, under the command of the Australian General Morshead. The strategic significance of Tobruk was obvious from the first, and anyone can see now how irresistibly it has imposed itself as a magnet on the enemy. I have gone into all this military detail, not in order to burden the House with it, but in order to give Members an indication of what happened, and why, and what were the various factors.

I have gone into all these details because I want to make it clear that we intend to fight with all our strength for the Nile Valley and its surrounding country and for the command of the Mediterranean. We have every reason to believe that our troops and resources will give a good account of themselves. Let there be no feather-headed or defeatist talk about cutting our losses in the Middle East. I agree with my right hon. Friend the Member for Devonport in that. But, as I said early in December, when our situation in Egypt was far more critical than it is now, it is a case of deeds, not words. We must allow the story to unfold. My hon. and gallant Friend the Member for Petersfield (Sir G Jeffreys),[1] in a speech to which I listened with great interest, asked a very fair question: how was it that this very large number of Germans got across to Libya without our Intelligence or generals knowing about it? Perhaps they did know about it; or perhaps the numbers were not so very large, after all. It depends on what you call 'very large'. At any rate, our generals on the spot believed that no superior German force could advance as far across the desert towards Egypt, as soon or as effectively as they did; and, secondly, that if they did advance, they would not be able to nourish themselves. That was a mistake. But anyone who supposes that there will not be mistakes in war is very foolish. I draw a distinction between mistakes. There is a mistake which comes through daring, what I call a mistake towards the enemy in which you must always sustain your commanders, by sea, land or air. There are mistakes from the safety-first principle, mistakes of turning away from the enemy; and they require a far more acid consideration.

In the first belief to which I have just referred our generals were proved wrong; the second has not been decided. It has not yet been seen how the forces that advance will fare in the desert fighting, with all its chances and hazards, which still lie at no great distance before us. I will allow the speech of my hon. and gallant Friend the Member for Petersfield to detain me a moment longer on military issues, because it illustrates some of the points in the Debate. He reminded us of Frederick the Great's maxim, that it was pardonable to be defeated but that it was not pardonable to be surprised. On the other hand, when your enemy has five or six times as large a regular army as you have, much more amply equipped, and a good deal stronger in the air and far stronger in tanks; and when he lies in the centre of the war scene, and

[1] George Darell Jeffreys, 1878–1960. On active service with the Grenadier Guards, Nile Expedition, 1898 (including the Battle of Khartoum); South African War, 1900–02; France and Flanders, 1914–18 (including the retreat from Mons). Churchill's Commanding Officer when Churchill was in training with the 2nd Battalion Grenadier Guards, December 1915. Commanded the 19th Division (severely wounded), 1917–18 (despatches nine times). Major-General, 1922. Commanded London District, 1920–24. Knighted, 1924. General Officer Commanding-in-Chief, Southern Command, India, 1932–36. Chairman Hampshire County Council Civil Defence Committee, 1938–54. County Organizer, Hampshire Home Guard, 1940. Conservative Member of Parliament, Petersfield, 1941–51. Created Baron, 1952. Colonel, Grenadier Guards, 1952–60. His only son was killed in action in France, 1940.

can strike out in any one, two or three different directions simultaneously, out of a choice of seven or eight, it is evident that your problems become very difficult. It is also evident, I think, that you would not solve your problem, as Frederick the Great's maxim and his remarks seem to suggest, by being prepared at every point to resist not only what is probable but what is possible. In such circumstances, upon which there is no need to enlarge, it is not possible to avoid repeated rebuffs and misfortunes, and these, of course, we shall very likely have to go through for quite a long time. Therefore, the right hon. Gentleman the Member for Devonport, the hon. Member for Seaham and any others of our leading lights in the embryonic all-party Opposition to the Government are not likely to run short of opportunities where they will be able to point to our lack of foresight and to the failure of our Intelligence service, of which I will only say that it was thought to be the best in the world in the last war, and it is certainly not the worst in the world today.

Some have pointed to what has happened in Iraq as another instance of the failure of our Intelligence and our diplomacy. My hon. and gallant Friend the Member for Wycombe (Sir A. Knox),[1] though in a perfectly friendly way, has inquired about that. We have been told that the Foreign Office never knows anything that is going on in the world, and that our organization is quite unadapted to meet the present juncture. But we have known only too well what was going on in Iraq, and as long ago as last May, a year ago, the Foreign Office began to ask for troops to be sent there to guard the line of communications. We had not the troops. All that we could send had to go to the Nile Valley. In default of troops, it was very difficult to make head against the pronounced pro-Axis intrigues of Rashid Ali, who eventually, after his removal from power at our instance, staged a *coup d'état* against the Regent and the lawful Government of the country. Obviously, his object was to have everything ready for the Germans as soon as they could reach Iraq according to programme. However, in this case the ill-informed, slothful, kid-gloved British Government, as it has no doubt become since it has been deprived of the abilities of some valuable Members, actually forestalled this plot. Three weeks ago strong British forces, which are continually being reinforced from India, were landed at Basra, and they assumed control of that highly important bridge-head in the East for which we shall, no doubt, have to fight hard and long.

Mr Cocks[2] (Broxtowe): Could not they have gone there before?

[1] Alfred William Fortescue Knox, 1870–1964. 2nd Lieutenant, 1891. ADC to the Viceroy of India (Lord Curzon), 1899–1900 and 1902–3. Lieutenant-Colonel, 1911. Military Attaché, St Petersburg, 1911–18. Major-General, 1918. Chief of the British Military Mission to Siberia, 1918–20. Knighted, 1919. Conservative MP for Wycombe, 1924–45. Member of Council of the Indian Empire Society.

[2] Frederick Seymour Cocks, 1882–1953. In 1918 he published *The Secret Treaties*, denouncing British policy during the First World War. Labour MP from 1929 until his death. Member of the Joint Select Committee on Indian Constitutional Reform, 1933–4. Member of the All-Party Committee on Parliamentary Procedure, 1945–6. Leader of the All-Party Parliamentary Delegation to Greece, 1946. CBE, 1950.

The Prime Minister: Rashid Ali, having consented to the first stage of this action, was led into a more violent course. He attacked the British air cantonment at Habbaniya, and for several days we were very anxious about the people there. We are very anxious about them even yet. They had, however, been reinforced beforehand. Air Forces from Egypt and Palestine were able to give powerful assistance, and I am glad to inform the House that yesterday the garrison sallied out and attacked the besiegers, with the result that they completely routed them and put them to flight. Twenty-six Iraqi officers and 408 men were taken prisoners, and the total enemy casualties are estimated at 1,000. While this was going on, our Air Force attacked and largely destroyed the reinforcing convoy of lorries and ammunition which was on its way to the besiegers. Other operations are in progress, and I shall not predict their results. But we shall try to make headway against all our foes, wherever they present themselves and from whatever quarter they come. A combative spirit in all directions is essential. It may be that the Germans will arrive before we have crushed the revolt, in which case our task will become more difficult. It may be that the revolt went off at half-cock in consequence of our forestalling action in landing at Basra. I would, therefore, enjoin caution on some of our critics, who may perhaps find that they have been premature in saying that we were too tardy, and too soon in saying that we were too late. We are not at war with Iraq; we are dealing with a military dictator who attempted to subvert the constitutional Government, and we intend to assist the Iraqis to get rid of him and get rid of the military dictatorship at the earliest possible moment.

I ask you to witness, Mr Speaker, that I have never promised anything or offered anything but blood, tears, toil and sweat, to which I will now add our fair share of mistakes, shortcomings and disappointments and also that this may go on for a very long time, at the end of which I firmly believe – though it is not a promise or a guarantee, only a profession of faith – that there will be complete, absolute and final victory.

Now we come to the Battle of the Atlantic. It is a mistake to say that the Battle of the Atlantic is won. First of all, how is it won? It would be quite easy to reduce our losses at sea to vanishing point by the simple expedient of keeping our ships in harbour or to reduce them markedly by overloading them with precautions. The Admiralty, on whom the first burden rests, naturally measure their struggle by the ships which they bring safely into port, but that is not the test by which those responsible for the highest direction of the country have to be guided. Our test is the number of tons of imports brought into this island in a given quarter or a given year. At present we are maintaining great traffics, although with heavy losses. We try to meet these losses by building new ships, repairing damaged ships, by repairing them more speedily and by acceleration of the turn-round of our ships in our ports and in foreign ports. We have made great progress in these spheres since the beginning of the year, but there is much more to do in that field.

With the continued flow of assistance which has already been given to us by the United States, and promised to us, we can probably maintain our minimum essential traffic during 1941. As for 1942, we must look for an immense construction of merchant ships by the United States. This is already in full swing, and since I last mentioned this subject to the House a month ago, I have received assurances that the construction of merchant vessels by the United States, added to our own large programme of new building and repair, should see us through the year of 1942. It may be that 1943, if ever we have to endure it as a year of war, will present easier problems. The United States patrol, announced by President Roosevelt, on which the American Navy and Air Force are already engaged, takes a very considerable part of the Atlantic Ocean, in a certain degree, off our hands, but we need a good deal more help, and I expect we shall get a good deal more help in a great many ways. In fact, it has been declared that we are to have all the help that is necessary, but here I speak with very great caution, for it is not for a British Minister to forecast, still less to appear to prescribe, the policy of the United States. So far in our relations with that great Republic, which began so well under the auspices of Lord Lothian, I do not think we have made any serious mistakes. Neither by boasting nor by begging have we offended them. When a mighty democracy of 130,000,000 gets on the move, one can only await the full deployment of these vast psychological manifestations and their translation into the physical field. Anyone can see Hitler's fear of the United States from the fact that he has not long ago declared war upon them.

In some quarters of the House, or at any rate among some Members, there is a very acute realization of the gravity of our problems and of our dangers. I have never underrated them. I feel we are fighting for life and survival from day to day and from hour to hour. But, believe me, Herr Hitler has his problems, too, and if we only remain united and strive our utmost to increase our exertions, and work like one great family, standing together and helping each other, as 5,000,000 families in Britain are doing today under the fire of the enemy, I cannot conceive how anyone can doubt that victory will crown the good cause we serve. Government and Parliament alike have to be worthy of the undaunted and unconquerable people who give us their trust and who give their country their all.

It is a year almost to a day since, in the crash of the disastrous Battle of France, His Majesty's present Administration was formed. Men of all parties, duly authorized by their parties, joined hands together to fight this business to the end. That was a dark hour, and little did we know what storms and perils lay before us, and little did Herr Hitler know, when in June, 1940, he received the total capitulation of France and when he expected to be master of all Europe in a few weeks and the world in a few years, that 10 months later, in May, 1941, he would be appealing to the much-tried German people to prepare themselves for the war of 1942. When I look back on the perils which have been overcome, upon the great mountain waves in which the gallant ship has driven, when I remember all that has gone wrong, and remember also all that has gone right, I feel sure we have no need to fear the tempest. Let it roar, and let it rage. We shall come through.

Question put,

'That this House approves the policy of His Majesty's Government in sending help to Greece and declares its confidence that our operations in the Middle East and in all other theatres of war will be pursued by the Government with the utmost vigour.'

The House divided: Ayes, 447; Noes, 3.[1]

Harold Nicolson; diary
(*'Diaries and Letters, 1939-45'*)

7 May 1941

After lunch I return to the House. Winston is speaking as I enter. He holds the House from the very first moment. He stands there in his black conventional suit with the huge watch-chain. He is very amusing. He is very frank. At moments I have a nasty feeling that he is being a trifle too optimistic. He is very strong, for instance, about Egypt and our position in the Mediterranean. He attacks Hore-Belisha mercilessly. The vote of confidence is given 447 to 3. Pretty good. As Winston goes out of the Chamber towards the Members' Lobby, there is a spontaneous burst of cheering which is taken up outside. He looks pleased.

John Colville: diary
(*Colville papers*)

7 May 1941

The PM wound up a debate on the war in the House, scoring a great parliamentary success and utterly confounding LG and Hore-Belisha. I wished I had gone down to hear him, as I could have.

The PM went early to bed elated by his forensic successes. I pointed out to him that it was nearly a year since the debate in which Chamberlain fell.

[1] The three Members of Parliament who went into the Lobby against the Government were D.N. Pritt (North Hammersmith, Labour), Dr Alfred Salter (West Bermondsey, Labour) and William Gallacher (West Fife, Communist). The Independent Labour Party was not able to vote against the Government, as it had wished to do, as one of its members was ill and the other two, including their leader, James Maxton, had to act as tellers in the 'no' Lobby.

Tonight we shot down more night-raiders than ever before: at least 23 fell to guns and fighters.[1]

Winston S. Churchill to Air Vice-Marshal Smart[2]
(*Churchill papers, 20/38*)

7 May 1941
sent at 8.55 p.m.

Your vigorous and splendid action has largely restored the situation. We are all watching the grand fight you are making. All possible aid will be sent. Keep it up.

Winston S. Churchill to General Freyberg
(*Churchill papers, 20/38*)

7 May 1941
sent 11 p.m.

Everyone in Britain has watched with gratitude and admiration the grand fighting deeds of the New Zealand Division upon the ever-famous battlefields of Greece. It is only gradually that we have learned and are learning the full tale, and the more the accounts come in the more we realize the vital part you played in a task of honour and a deed of fame. Throughout the whole Empire and the English-speaking world the name of New Zealand is saluted. Our thoughts are with you now – God bless you all.

[1] The main German air attack that night was against Humberside.

[2] Churchill wrote in Volume Three of *The Second World War* (recalling 1941): 'On April 29, 230 British women and children had been flown to Habbaniya from Baghdad. The total number in the cantonment was just over 2,200 fighting men, with no fewer than 9,000 civilians. The Flying School thus became a point of grave importance. Air Vice-Marshal Smart, who commanded there, took bold and timely precautions to meet the mounting crisis. The Flying School had previously held only obsolescent or training types, but a few Gladiator fighters had arrived from Egypt, and eighty-two aircraft of all sorts were improvised into four squadrons.'

Winston S. Churchill to General Wavell
(*Churchill papers, 20/38*)

7 May 1941
sent 11.30 p.m.

I told them to send by Most Secret method the actual text of the OL message to which I referred in my 012 of 4/5.[1] You and your Generals alone can judge the tactical possibilities, whether at Sollum or Tobruk. But if Tiger comes through[2] it will be a moment to do and dare. I am asking for a rapid transfer from Malta of Hurricanes to your Command once the tiger's tail is clear. Those Hun people are far less dangerous once they lose the initiative. All our thoughts are with you.

2. It would seem that the Habbaniya show has greatly improved, and audacious action now against the Iraqis may crush the revolt before the Germans arrive. They can, of course, fly there direct in heavy bombers, but these would only have what they stand up in and could not operate long. We must forestall the moral effect of their arrival by a stunning blow. I presume that, if Rutba and Habbaniya are clear, column will take possession of Baghdad or otherwise exploit success to the full. Other telegrams are being sent to you about rousing the tribes and about Government policy.

Winston S. Churchill to Anthony Eden
(*Churchill papers, 20/36*)

7 May 1941

Will you consider whether it would not be a good thing to publish my letter to Matsuoka. I think it is important that the people of Japan generally and a circle wider than the Matsuoka military circle should be apprised of the direction in which they are moving.

[1] Churchill had arranged for Wavell to be sent the actual (translated) text of a German top secret Enigma message, as decrypted at Bletchley Park three days earlier. Normally only summaries or paraphrases of such translated messages were sent, in order to protect the source of the information. In this case, Churchill judged it to be of particular importance for Wavell to know precisely what it was that the Germans were planning in the Western Desert. OL (Orange Leonard) was a typical digraph as used in transmitting messages from an individual spy or agent: those who saw the code reference could assume that it was an agent and would be unaware of the true source. Churchill also proposed on May 7 that General Freyberg receive the actual texts of decrypts relating to German plans for a parachute landing at Maleme airport in Crete, but the Secret Intelligence Service informed Freyberg not to act on this information unless he had at least one other non-Enigma source for it: as a result of this caveat, Freyberg was unable to make the necessary dispositions to concentrate his defences at Maleme, which fell to the Germans the day after the landing.

[2] Tank reinforcements to be sent to Egypt through the Mediterranean (the tank personnel to be sent on the longer route via Cape of Good Hope).

Winston S. Churchill to James Stuart
(*Churchill papers, 20/29*)

8 May 1941

My dear James,

As yesterday was your first big day in the House,[1] I must thank you and congratulate you upon the most remarkable Lobby that resulted from your care and exertions. I am sure the country will be strengthened and its interests advanced by the remarkable vote of confidence at a moment when many things are difficult.

Winston S. Churchill to General Ismay, for the Chiefs of Staff Committee
(*Churchill papers, 20/36*)

8 May 1941

I must have the advice of the Staffs upon the Syrian business available for Cabinet this morning. A supreme effort must be made to prevent the Germans getting a footing in Syria with small forces and then using Syria as a jumping off ground for the air domination of Iraq and Persia. It is no use General Wavell being vexed at this disturbance on his eastern flanks . . . We ought to help in every way without minding what happens at Vichy.

I shall be most grateful if the Staff will see what is the most that can be done.

Winston S. Churchill to A.V. Alexander
(*Churchill papers, 20/36*)

8 May 1941
Action this Day

SHIPPING LOSSES

After what you told me yesterday of the high figures of losses for April, I think you should mention the matter at the Cabinet today. In view of the present state of American opinion and of Mr Vandenberg's efforts to belittle our losses (see *The Times* of today[2] and check his figures), I have come to the conclusion that we should publish. I am glad we kept the option.

[1] As Chief Whip.

[2] Senator Vandenberg of Michigan, a leading Isolationist, had stated that the number of ships sunk carrying supplies to Britain was not particularly high, and that the 'emergency' spoken of by the Secretary of War, Henry Stimson, in a speech on May 6 was 'not as grave' as had been asserted. Of the 159 merchant ships sunk by the Germans between January 1 and April 30, only twelve had been bound from United States ports and only eight had been carrying supplies to the United Kingdom. Vandenberg quoted these figures from a letter written to him by Admiral Land, Head of the United States Maritime Commission.

War Cabinet: minutes
(*Cabinet papers, 65/18*)

8 May 1941 Prime Minister's Room
12 noon House of Commons

The Prime Minister informed the War Cabinet that the figures of losses of munitions from the United States of America while crossing the Atlantic (which we had so far refused to publish) had become known to certain circles in the United States of America and were being used to our detriment.

He suggested that the announcement of the April Shipping losses should take the form of a table of shipping losses month by month from May 1940 up to and including April. The figure for the latter month should not distinguish between losses in the North-Western Approaches, in the Mediterranean or other theatres, though it should be stated that the global figure of April losses covered all theatres, including the Mediterranean.

The Prime Minister said that a most critical and anxious operation was now being carried out in the Mediterranean. Some 200-250 German heavy tanks together with a large number of light tanks were now in North Africa. General Wavell possessed only some 100 heavy tanks although 50 more were coming out of the workshops in Egypt at the end of this month. The dispatch of further tanks round the Cape would take a very long time. It had, therefore, been decided to run the great risk of sending tank reinforcements to General Wavell through the Mediterranean. These reinforcements consisted of 306 tanks, of which 87 were cruiser tanks, 49 light tanks and the balance I tanks. In addition we were sending out in the Convoy about 50 Hurricane aircraft, and considerable quantities of guns, vehicles, ammunition supplies and other stores. This valuable cargo was being carried in five ships, which steamed at the rate of 14½ knots. The convoy was at the present moment in the danger zone. The Admiralty and the Air Ministry had made most careful plans for the convoy's escort.

The Prime Minister continuing said that should the whole of these reinforcements succeed in reaching General Wavell, he would have over 400 heavy tanks at his disposal, a number far in excess of the German tank strength. With this force the military situation in North Africa might be turned to our advantage. No military personnel had been included in the convoy, but trained tank personnel was available in Egypt to man the tanks.

Referring to the military situation in the Western Desert, the Prime Minister said that it would seem as if the German advance had not only been held up but had for the moment come to a stand-still. From certain information it looked as if the enemy was short of ammunition, petrol and food, and was feeling the effects of the hard weather conditions. With good fortune the Battle of Egypt might well turn in our favour. The risks taken in this operation were very great; but the operation would justify itself if half this equipment could be got safely through to Egypt.

War Cabinet, Battle of the Atlantic Committee: minutes
(*Cabinet papers, 86/1*)

8 May 1941
5 p.m.

10 Downing Street

Reference was made to the effects of the recent air attacks on port areas. In the raid on Liverpool on May 3rd 17 ships of about 95,000 tons had been lost or damaged, a cold store had been demolished and other damage had been done in the dock area. At Belfast two ships had been sunk, three slightly damaged and one had been driven aground. The Harland and Wolff Works had also been seriously damaged. They were engaged on production work for all the Service Departments (in particular on building corvettes) but it was not yet possible to say how serious the effect on production would be. The ship repairing plant would be disorganized for ten days. Damage had also been done to shipping under construction at Greenock.

The Prime Minister said that all possible measures must be taken to increase the defences of the port areas against night air attacks. A number of different Departments were concerned besides the Admiralty and the Ministry of Shipping and he asked the Secretary to submit proposals to him as to the Ministers who should be invited to investigate this matter.

The Meeting had before them a table giving information up to 1st May, 1941, and also a progress report by the Minister of Labour and National Service showing the number of men transferred to the shipyards under the Industrial Registration Order.

The Prime Minister said that the former table showed a continued reduction in the gross tonnage undergoing or awaiting repair, particularly in the tonnage immobilized by repair. On the other hand, it was most unsatisfactory that there had been a fall in the number of men engaged on merchant repair work, notwithstanding increases in the numbers employed on new naval construction.

Sir James Lithgow[1] said that except in the Liverpool area all repair jobs were fully manned. More men could not be usefully employed on repair work except by the introduction of double shift working. The negotiations for the introduction of this system were not going very well.

[1] James Lithgow, 1883–1952. Shipbuilder. On active service, France, 1914–17, (wounded, despatches). Director of Shipbuilding Production, Admiralty, 1917. Created Baronet, 1925. Member of the Central Electricity Board, 1927–30. President of the Federation of British Industries, 1930–32. Chairman of the Scottish Development Council, 1931–39. Member of the Board of Admiralty, as Controller of Merchant Shipbuilding and Repairs, 1940–46.

The Minister of Labour and National Service[1] said that he wished to deal with the matter, not in general terms, but on the basis of particular areas and yards at which advantage would be obtained from double shift working.

The Prime Minister invited the Lord Privy Seal[2] to hold a meeting with the Minister of Labour, the Minister of Shipping, Sir James Lithgow and others concerned with a view to reporting on this matter to the next week's meeting. The investigation should take special account of the need for cutting down excessive hours of work and the report should submit recommendations on the question whether we should continue to try to secure double shift working; if so, in which areas and on which categories of work.

FITTING OUT SHIPS WITH CATAPULT AIRCRAFT

The Prime Minister said that he had received a report from the Minister of State[3] on the questions referred to him at the last Meeting. The report recommended that, in addition to 4 White Ensign ships, 35 merchant ships should be fitted out with catapult aircraft, and that these vessels should be employed on the ordinary cargo service on the Canadian and Sierra Leone routes. Each ship would have to carry two pilots. This plan would absorb all the merchant vessels fitted with catapults which would become available until the end of August. Until experience had been gained, no recommendation was made as to the fitting out or use of further vessels fitted with catapult aircraft.

These recommendations were approved.

The Prime Minister said that the defence of ships now had first priority. This, however, did not mean that all the weapons available should be allotted to that purpose. Under our present system priority and allocation went hand in hand.

War Cabinet, Defence Committee (Operations): minutes
(*Cabinet papers, 69/2*)

8 May 1941
9.45 p.m.

TAKORADI

The Prime Minister said that on many occasions in the last three months, he had addressed Minutes to the Secretary of State for Air and the Chief of the Air Staff, urging that greater efforts should be made to develop the Takoradi route on a big scale. There was a serious accumulation of aircraft at

[1] Ernest Bevin.
[2] Clement Attlee.
[3] Lord Beaverbrook (since 1 May 1941).

Takoradi, and it was evident that inadequate steps had been taken to secure American aid in erecting American aircraft. He could not believe that any Treasury objection could stand in the way of the maximum effort in such a vital matter.

The Prime Minister said that he must be furnished with material for a reply to the American Ambassador. It would be most unfortunate if the Americans had grounds for thinking that we are incompetent to make use of the resources they were putting at our disposal; and in his reply he would like to be able to make requests and proposals for American assistance on the Takoradi route.

IRAQ

The Prime Minister thought the time had passed for trying to liquidate matters by political settlements or promises to the Arabs. The immediate problem was to oppose the imminent German arrival. As we had no troops ourselves to do it with the right course seemed to be to give General Catroux the lorries he required for his troops and to tell him to go in and attempt to win the French over.

TELEGRAM TO HARRY HOPKINS

The Prime Minister read to the Committee a telegram which he had drafted for despatch to Mr Hopkins on the subject of our general shipping situation. The Committee expressed their agreement with the terms of the telegram.

Winston S. Churchill to Harry Hopkins

(*Churchill papers, 20/38*)

8 May 1941
Most Immediate
Most Secret

Our shipping losses for April amount to just under 500,000 tons sunk and 285,000 damaged. Of tonnage lost, over 300,000 were incurred in the Atlantic and the rest in the Mediterranean fighting. Besides the loss in ships sunk and damaged at sea we are losing very heavily in the bombing of our western ports when cargoes are destroyed or damaged.[1] I have had to take labour off long-

[1] German bombers had struck at Clydeside on 5 and 6 May 1941, and at Merseyside on May 7. On May 8, in a particularly successful effort at bending the German 'beam', German bombers striking as they thought at the Rolls-Royce works at Derby, dropped 235 high-explosive bombs on empty fields many miles away in the Vale of Belvoir. But the bombing raids still took a steady toll: at Hull, Manchester and Bristol 'serious fires' had been started on the night of May 7, with extensive damage to the Merseyside docks, already much damaged over the past four days. Thirteen merchant ships had been bombed and sunk at Liverpool docks on May 3, one on May 4, one on May 5, two on May 7 and three on May 8. In the raid on Clydeside, 57 civilians had been killed.

term new construction of merchant ships in order to keep pace with repairs. I send you the full list of monthly losses sunken since the beginning of the war, and also the last few months' monthly total of damaged ships under repair. Harriman, who attends my weekly meetings of the Battle of the Atlantic Committee, will tell you what efforts we are making, and with success, to reduce the arrears of repairs. It is this general aspect of our tonnage losses and enforced concentration on repairs which constitutes the crux of the Battle of the Atlantic. The case is not only the loss of particular cargoes of weapons, for these we can often guard specially, but also the loss of food cargoes and steel and the constant diminution of our available tonnage, and the still greater diminution of our importing capacity, which is now less than half what it was in peace. I am publishing on May 15 the losses of this very bad month. This rather than the sinking of specific American cargoes is the broad verity of the situation.

On 8 May 1941, Churchill established a Ministry of War Transport, bringing the Ministry of Shipping and the Ministry of Transport under a single Minister. He chose for this task Frederick Leathers, on whom a Peerage was conferred.[1]

Winston S. Churchill to General Wavell
(*Cabinet papers, 69/2*)

9 May 1941

The Defence Committee have considered your No. 0/62719 of 8th May about Iraq. Our information is that Rashid Ali and his partisans are in desperate straits. However this may be, you are to fight hard against them. The mobile column being prepared in Palestine should advance as you propose or earlier if possible and actively engage the enemy whether at Rutba or Habbaniya. Having joined the Habbaniya forces you should exploit the situation to the utmost, not hesitating to try to break into Baghdad even with quite small forces and running the same kind of risks as the Germans are accustomed to run and profit by.

[1] A major part of Leathers' work had been the building up of links with his American opposite number, Lewis Douglas, of the United States Shipping Board. Churchill wrote in his war memoirs: 'Leathers was an immense help to me in the conduct of the war. It was very rarely that he was unable to accomplish the hard tasks I set. Several times when all staff and departmental processes had failed to solve the problems of moving an extra division or trans-shipping it from British to American ships, or of meeting some other need, I made a personal appeal to him, and the difficulties seemed to disappear as if by magic.' (Winston S. Churchill, *The Second World War*, Volume 3, London, 1950, page 132)

2. There can be no question of negotiation with Rashid Ali unless he immediately accepts the terms in COS Telegram No. 96. Such negotiation would only lead to delay, during which the German Air Force will arrive. We do not think that any ground forces you may be able to divert to Iraq will affect your immediate problem in the Western Desert. The Air Force must do its best to cover both situations. Only in the event of you being actually engaged or about to engage in an offensive in the Western Desert should Tedder[1] deny the necessary Air support to the Iraq operations.

3. You will no doubt realize grievous danger of Syria being captured by a few thousand Germans transported by air, and our information leads us to believe that Admiral Darlan has probably made some bargain to help the Germans to get in there. In face of your evident feeling of lack of resources we can see no other course open than to furnish General Catroux with the necessary transport and let him and his Free French do their best at the moment they deem suitable, the RAF acting at the same time, if possible, with a few aircraft against German landing. Any improvement you can make on this would be welcome.

Winston S. Churchill to the Emperor Haile Selassie
(*Churchill papers, 20/49*)

9 May 1941

It is with deep and universal pleasure that the British nation and Empire have learned of Your Imperial Majesty's welcome home to your capital at Addis Ababa. Your Majesty was the first of the lawful sovereigns to be driven from his throne and country by the Fascist Nazi criminals, and is now the first to return in triumph. Your Majesty's thanks will be duly conveyed to the Commanders, Officers and men of the British and Empire forces who have aided the Ethiopian patriots in the total and final destruction of the Italian military usurpation. His Majesty's Government look forward to a long period of peace and progress in Ethiopia after the forces of evil have been finally overthrown.

War Cabinet, Defence Committee (Operations): minutes
(*Cabinet papers, 69/2*)

9 May 1941 — 10 Downing Street
12 noon

OPERATION 'PUMA'

Sir Roger Keyes said that he was in full agreement with the plan which he considered offered every prospect of success.

[1] Air Marshal A. W. Tedder, Air Officer Commanding-in-Chief, RAF Middle East (see page 662, note 1).

The Prime Minister then said that it would be necessary to consider the political situation in which this expedition might be launched. This might be:-

(a) A position where Spain agreed to allow the Germans to enter their country or where the Germans enter Spain and the Spaniards do not resist. In either case the Operation would have to be launched as soon as possible.

(b) If the Germans entered Spain and the Spaniards resisted, he presumed that the Operation would entail no fighting and the Spaniards would welcome our help.

(c) If the Spaniards yielded under protest to a German advance he thought that the resistance to our forces in this Operation would be slight.

(d) We might launch this expedition without waiting for adverse developments in Spain. He thought that such a course was undesirable and would have an unfortunate political effect.

Continuing, the Prime Minister asked whether the expedition could be held in readiness for an indefinite period and what the effect would be.

Rear Admiral Hamilton[1] and Major General Sturges[2] explained that in this case the forces would be employed on training for the Operation but they would have to be at seven days' notice. In the meantime the expedition was ready to sail on the 22nd May.

Winston S. Churchill to Admiral Pound
(*Premier papers, 3/432*)

9 May 1941
Action this Day
Secret

The Lord Privy Seal[3] mentioned to me the danger of Tiger when and if he gets to Alexandria. May he not be bombed in harbour? Ought not special arrangements for an umbrella to be made? In this connection I have wondered whether some of the Malta Hurricanes should not go on via Suda to Egypt and take part in affairs there.

[1] Louis Henry Keppel Hamilton, 1890–1957. On active service, Cameroons, 1915 (despatches, Distinguished Service Order). Naval Staff (Plans), 1940–42. Flag Officer-in-Charge, Malta, 1943–45. Knighted, 1944. First Naval Member, and Chief of Naval Staff, Commonwealth Naval Board, 1945–48. For his war service he was awarded a bar to his Distinguished Service Order, and the Norwegian War Cross.

[2] Robert Grice Sturges, 1891–1970. Entered the Royal Navy, 1908; transferred to the Royal Marine Light Infantry, 1912. On active service, 1914–18 (including Gallipoli). In command of operations in Iceland, 1940; Madagascar, 1942; Commando Group, 1943 (wounded, despatches twice, Distinguished Service Order). Lieutenant-General, 1945. Knighted, 1945.

[3] Clement Attlee.

John Colville: diary
(*Colville papers*)

9 May 1941

The PM went off to Ditchley very excited about operation Tiger. The convoy has passed through the narrows between Sicily and N. Africa and only one ship out of five, carrying a huge consignment of tanks for Wavell, has gone down. The PM thinks this will have far-reaching consequences on the war. He said to me: 'The poor Tiger has already lost one claw and another is damaged; but still I would close on what is left.'

Winston S. Churchill to Air Chief Marshal Sir Charles Portal
(*Churchill papers, 20/36*)

10 May 1941
Most Secret

To remind you of our conversation yesterday afternoon at Downing Street, I wish to receive your proposals for the maximum speedy reinforcement of ME, with medium and heavy bombers. Our forces in Egypt must be able to bomb Rhodes and the enemy-occupied islands, as well as Benghazi, Derna, &c., with increasing severity. Only in this way can we counteract the Fighter and Stuka superiority which the enemy is so clearly building up. Besides this, the sinking of small ships approaching Cyrenaica is vital. So also is the attack on convoys passing from Sicily to Tripoli, and upon Tripoli itself. However, for the special operation Scorcher[1] it would be right to move fighters both from Malta and Alexandria to the threatened islands when the time comes near.

Winston S. Churchill to Sir Edward Bridges
(*Churchill papers, 20/36*)

10 May 1941

I have decided that the Lord Privy Seal should have daylight accommodation in No. 11 Downing Street, and have discussed this with the Chancellor of the Exchequer. It was thought that the drawing-room floor might be available. This would give him a fine room for conferences. The Chancellor of the Exchequer would continue to use the ground floor.

It would be convenient if Lord Beaverbrook were accommodated in the

[1] British plans for the defence of Crete.

rooms vacated by the Whips in No. 12 Downing Street. Thus the whole Defence organization would be pretty close together so far as its Ministers were concerned.

Pray consult with the Chancellor of the Exchequer and Lord Beaverbrook, and make the necessary arrangements.

After-dark accommodation must still be provided in Great George Street, but I daresay rooms overlooking the Park would not be necessary, and the movement of Home Forces could thus be avoided.

Winston S. Churchill to General Ismay, for Admiral Pound, General Sir John Dill and Air Chief Marshal Sir Charles Portal
(*Premier papers, 3/109*)

10 May 1941
Most Secret

1. It is for consideration whether in respect of Scorcher the aerodromes in question should not be allowed easily to fall into the enemy's hands, and then when the glider landings or airborne landings have begun in force, tanks (of which surely there should be 20 I at least) and special assault parties in concealment nearby could advance and destroy the intruders.

2. So important do I consider all this aspect that it would be well to send a special officer by air to see General Freyberg and show him personally the actual texts of all the messages[1] bearing upon this subject. These messages could then be destroyed by fire. The officer would be answerable for their destruction in the event of engine failure *en route*. No one should be informed but the General, who would give his orders to his subordinates without explaining his full reasons.

3. It is specially important that the apparent success of the airborne landings should encourage the putting forth of the seaborne.

4. We must discuss the whole affair together this week.

Winston S. Churchill to David Margesson and General Sir John Dill
(*Churchill papers, 20/36*)

10 May 1941

1. Naturally, we all wish to make an end in Abyssinia. Let me have a short account of the position. How many troops have we still operating from the Sudan and Kenya in Abyssinia and on the L of C[2] –

[1] Enigma decrypts.
[2] Lines of Communication.

(a) ration strength
(b) fighting strength

setting forth the principal formation by brigades or columns. What is the total number of transport vehicles assigned to these forces? What is the Air Force strength in personnel, in Squadrons, and in effective machines? What is the number of troops and transport now being moved northwards? Where is the Duke of Aosta, and what is the number of troops under his control? What is their condition, and what are the prospects of reducing him? When can this be expected? When do the rains come, and how do they affect the problem?

2. What are the remaining forces in the Sudan and in Kenya that have not crossed the Abyssinian frontier (on similar lines to the above)?

3. Are we quite sure that we are not getting into the position where all our transport needed in the north will be tied up with Italian civilian personnel?

4. How is the evacuation of prisoners going on, both from Abyssinia to other parts of Africa and from all Africa overseas to India?

5. Above all, we must be careful not to waste men and strength in this area once the victory has been won. The Emperor, being restored, will govern the country, no doubt taking advice from us. We ought not to leave any large forces there, but assist him with food and money. There is no evidence of inhumanity towards the Italians. On the contrary, he has made a very good proclamation.

6. What proposals do you make for the garrisons of Kenya, Sudan, Abyssinia and Eritrea, after the Duke of Aosta is liquidated? What troops are being kept in British and Italian Somaliland? What is the present garrison of Aden? In the main, the African troops will, I suppose, be used, except for Aden, with only enough British units to ensure discipline. Above all, we must not fritter and disperse our resources, which will be needed in Palestine and in Iraq, as well as in Egypt. Once the main fighting is over, many of these long lines of communication can be dispensed with and the normal routes used. I expect you will find these lines of communication absolutely loaded with personnel. Every man must play his part. Pray let me have your active assistance. The cleansing of E. Africa of surplus forces in the shortest time is as good as a successful battle.

Winston S. Churchill to Viscount Cranborne
(*Churchill papers, 20/36*)

10 May 1941

I have always been most strongly in favour of making sure that the Jews have proper means of self-defence for their Colonies in Palestine. The more you can get done in this line, the safer we shall be.

Winston S. Churchill to Air Chief Marshal Sir Charles Portal
(*Churchill papers, 20/36*)

10 May 1941
Action this Day

BEAUFIGHTERS AT MALTA

Pray let me know what is the upshot of your discussions with the First Sea Lord. Surely we ought to have a policy of long-range Fighters fitted with extra tanks and self-priming pumps. The Germans are developing this night and day. No doubt a sacrifice in fighting efficiency is involved. They seem to think it worth while.

We may soon require the Beaufighters again for a special Operation.

Winston S. Churchill to Air Chief Marshal Sir Charles Portal
(*Churchill papers, 20/36*)

10 May 1941
Action this Day

The result of the Battle of Egypt now depends more upon the Air reinforcements than upon the Tanks. From every quarter and by every route, including repeated Jaguars, fighter aircraft must be sent. The Takoradi bottle-neck must be opened up and the congestion relieved. I have asked on other papers for a further large dispatch of Wellingtons, half-a-dozen additional Squadrons at the least. A regular flying-boat service should be established to bring back pilots which are accumulating in Egypt surplus to machines. Advantage should be taken of the presence of Air Chief Marshal Longmore in England to make a comprehensive plan of reinforcements. Speed is essential, as from every side one gets information of the efforts the enemy are making. I had not read your minute when I sent you my earlier one of this day's date.

Winston S. Churchill to Alfred Duff Cooper
(*Churchill papers, 20/36*)

10 May 1941

SOUTHERN IRISH PORTS

I am very sorry you committed yourself to this statement, which is contrary to the policy of HMG and differs widely from my own views. Eire has repudiated the status of a Dominion. We have not recognized in any Statutory or formal manner its present position, which is anomalous and undefined. You have heard me in Cabinet repeatedly refuse to give any guarantee to Mr De Valera's Government that we shall not take the ports by force in certain eventualities. On the contrary, I have often said that if it became a matter of life and death, we should do this. It may well be that force will have to be used. This principle was accepted even by the Chamberlain Government. I cannot see why you found it necessary to make a declaration of this kind. Did you consult the Dominions Secretary[1] before doing so?

Winston S. Churchill to Sir Kingsley Wood
(*Churchill papers, 20/36*)

10 May 1941

Do you think this distinction is justifiable?[2] Is there much money in it? I was told of a case of a sailor who was drunk on duty and drowned in consequence, his widow getting full pension; while another sailor on well-earned leave, killed by enemy action, was far worse treated in respect of his wife. I doubt very much whether treating leave earned by service as equivalent to service for these purposes would cost you much, and it would remove what seems to me to be a well-founded grievance.

Winston S. Churchill to President Franklin D. Roosevelt
(*Churchill papers, 20/38*)

10 May 1941

I expect you are now acquainted with the splendid offer which General Arnold[3] made to us of one-third of the rapidly expanding capacity for pilot training in the United States to be filled with pupils from here.[4] We have made active preparations and the first 550 of our young men are now ready to leave, as training was to have begun early next month. A second batch of 550 will follow on their heels. I now understand there are legal difficulties. I hope, Mr President, that these are not serious, as it would be very disappointing to us and would upset our arrangements if there were now to be delay. General Arnold's offer was an unexpected and very welcome addition to our training facilities. Such ready-made capacity of aircraft, airfields and instructors all in

[1] Viscount Cranborne.

[2] The differentiation as regards pension between the widow of a serviceman killed on duty and the widow of one killed by enemy action while on leave.

[3] Henry Marley Arnold, 1886–1950. Born in Pennsylvania. A pioneer airman, he learned to fly with Orville Wright. Chief of the United States Army Air Corps, 1938. Member of the United States Joint Chiefs of Staff, 1941–45. An advocate of the decisive influence of air power on strategy.

[4] On 21 May 1941 Churchill received a telegram from Roosevelt which read: 'All plans discussed with you by Arnold for training pilots have been approved here. There are no legal difficulties in the way and the training can begin promptly. We are rushing six additional small aircraft carriers for you. First three should be available in three or four months.' (*Churchill papers, 20/39*)

balance we could not obtain to the same extent and in the same time by any other means. It will greatly accelerate our effort in the air.

Winston S. Churchill to Hubert Pierlot[1]
(*Churchill papers, 20/38*)

10 May 1941

On the anniversary of the day when, in violation of the utmost solemn undertakings, the German Government, without cause or provocation, launched their armed forces against the territory of Belgium, I wish to acknowledge in the name of His Majesty's Government the effective help which the Belgian Government, the Belgian Empire, and the Belgian Armed Forces and merchant marine have given to the allied cause throughout the past year. We remember also your soldiers who resisted the invader in the battle of Belgium, and who now, in their homes, oppose the will of the invader. The sympathy and admiration of His Majesty's Government and of the British people go out in especial measure to the Belgian people now under the hateful Nazi tyranny, who, by their courage and endurance, daily contribute to the defence of freedom.

Anthony Eden: diary
(*'The Reckoning'*)

10 May 1941
midnight

He[2] was in favour of changing Auchinleck and Wavell about. Max[3] agreed as Amery had already done. The other three of us[4] were more doubtful. As I knew the men best, I found the advice not easy to give. I have no doubt that Archie has the better mind, but one does not know how he is bearing the strain and one cannot tell, though some of his recent reactions seem to indicate that he is flagging. In the end I weakly counselled delay and asked to wait for Crete result.

[1] The Belgian Prime Minister (in exile in London). Churchill sent similar messages to the Netherlands Prime Minister and the Luxembourg Minister for Foreign Affairs, both of whom were in London.

[2] Churchill.

[3] Beaverbrook.

[4] Attlee, Margesson and Eden: meeting with Churchill, Beaverbrook and Amery in Churchill's room at No. 10 Annexe, following a meeting of the Defence Committee.

On the night of 10–11 May 1941, a German air raid on London killed 1,436 people. The House of Commons debating chamber was destroyed, and serious damage done to the British Museum, Westminster School, the Royal Mint, the Law Courts, the Public Record Office, the Mansion House, St James's Palace, and more than 5,000 homes. In all, 12,000 people made homeless. As several German bomber units had already been transferred eastward, many of the bomber crews had to fly double sorties. In all 541 sorties were made. Only 14 bombers failed to return.

Josiah Wedgwood to Winston S. Churchill
(*Churchill papers 20/30*)

11 May 1941

My dear Winston,

Don't be distressed at the ruins. Such ruins are good assets: all round the globe, and especially in America! My impression is that they had better have hit the Acropolis. But, even if Dean's Yard is hit too, – do not move Parliament away from London.

Jos

John Colville: diary
(*Colville papers*)

11 May 1941

I stood on Westminster Bridge and thought ironically of Wordsworth and 1802. St Thomas' Hospital was ablaze, the livid colour of the sky extended from Lambeth to St Paul's, flames were visible all along the embankment, there was smoke rising thickly as far as the eye could see. After no previous raid has London looked so wounded next day.

I went to Church at St Martin's in the Field where the electricity had failed, the windows were blocked and only candles were burning. From outside came the intermittent ringing of fire-engines and ambulances.

After breakfast I rang up the PM at Ditchley and described what I had seen. He was very grieved that William Rufus's roof at Westminster Hall should have gone. He told me we had shot down 45 which, out of 380 operating, is a good result.[1]

[1] The correct figure, as eventually amended by the Air Ministry, was thirty-three.

Winston S. Churchill: recollection
('The Second World War', volume 3, page 43)

[11 May 1941]

On Sunday, May 11, I was spending the weekend at Ditchley. During the evening news kept coming in of the heavy air raid on London of the night before. There was nothing I could do about it, so I watched the Marx Brothers in a comic film which my hosts had arranged. I went out twice to inquire about the damage, and heard it was bad. The merry film clacked on, and I was glad of the diversion. Presently a secretary told me that somebody wanted to speak to me on the telephone on behalf of the Duke of Hamilton.[1] The Duke was a personal friend of mine, and was commanding a fighter-sector in the East of Scotland, but I could not think of any business he might have with me which could not wait till the morning. However, the caller pressed to speak with me, saying the matter was one of urgent Cabinet importance. I asked Mr Bracken to hear what he had to say. After a few minutes Mr Bracken told me that the Duke said he had an amazing piece of information to report. I therefore sent for him. On arrival he told me that a German prisoner whom he had interviewed alone said he was Rudolf Hess.[2] 'Hess in Scotland!' I thought this was fantastic. The report however was true.

John Martin: diary
(Martin papers)

11 May 1941 Ditchley

Arrival of Duke of Hamilton to report on arrival of Rudolf Hess. PM informed me that I am to succeed Seal as Principal Private Secretary.[3]

[1] Lord Douglas Douglas-Hamilton, 1903–1973. Conservative Member of Parliament for Renfrewshire, 1930–40. Chief Pilot, Mount Everest Flight Expedition, 1933. President of the British Air Lines Pilot's Association, 1937. Succeeded his father, as 14th Duke of Hamilton in 1940. Served in the Royal Air Force, 1939–45 (despatches). Lord High Commissioner to the General Assembly of the Church of Scotland, 1953–55 and 1958. President of the Air League, 1959–68.

[2] Rudolf Hess, 1894–1987. On active service in the Bavarian infantry at Ypres, 1915. Commissioned in the German Air Corps, 1916. Hitler's Political Secretary, 1920–31. Deputy Leader of the German Nazi Party, 1934–41. Flew from Germany to Britain, 10 May 1941, landing by parachute. Interned as a prisoner of war, 1941–45. Sentenced to life imprisonment by the Nuremberg Tribunal, 1946. Imprisoned in Spandau Prison, West Berlin, being from 1966 its sole detainee. He committed suicide there at the age of ninety-three.

[3] Eric Seal had been appointed Deputy Secretary of the Admiralty, North America, to be based in Washington. For his work as Churchill's Principal Private Secretary he was created CB (Companion of the Order of the Bath).

Winston S. Churchill to General Arnold
(*Churchill papers, 20/38*)

11 May 1941

I am much obliged for the information reported by your observer in Egypt. The Air Ministry tell me that we have recently sent out to Takoradi the best officers we can find but they are necessarily less familiar with American than with British types of aircraft and engines and welcome your offer of American experts. Details of numbers and grades desired will be sent to you by the Air Ministry as soon as possible.

2. In the climate of tropical West Africa no man can work as hard or as long as at home. We should like to work three shifts and are planning to use ships for additional living quarters.

3. We are sending to Africa one of our most energetic and competent senior technical officers who will be responsible to Commander-in-Chief for repair and maintenance in Egypt and for general control of Takoradi reinforcement route, sole responsibility for which lies with Air Ministry. Some decentralization of local control is necessary on a route which begins in British or American factories and ends in Egypt.

4. Criticism of technical inexperience of certain drafts to Takoradi is justified but there is now great dilution throughout RAF. We are now sending picked men. We gratefully accept your offer of loan of experts and MAP is being pressed to provide tools and equipment.

5. We agree about importance of BPC[1] inspection and I am passing your criticism to the MAP.

6. I am much obliged for the help already given and for your offer of skilled men. Assembly of aircraft is not sole bottleneck of deliveries from Takoradi. Any acceleration must be matched by corresponding increase in transport aircraft for ferry pilots. Can your promised deliveries of American transport aircraft to Africa be accelerated? Thank you so much for cabling direct to me.

Winston S. Churchill to Clement Attlee
(*Churchill papers, 20/36*)

11 May 1941

I am not including the four Labour Peers you required for additional representation in the House of Lords in the Birthday List, as I think they should appear separately in the near future as a measure of State policy. They will I think have to go before the Political Committee. The ones I would

[1] The British Purchasing Commission, Washington.

suggest are Mr Pethwick-Lawrence, Mr Wedgwood Benn[1] (if he will take it), Mr Mallon[2] of Toynbee Hall, and Jos. Wedgwood (if I can overcome the divorce objection, which I expect I can). How far would this meet your view? All these men would do credit to the Labour party in the House of Lords.[3]

I see you have recommended David Grenfell[4] for a Privy Councillorship, and I should be very ready to do this but for the trouble we have had recently with him. I have not heard how this was settled. Perhaps you would speak to me about this on Monday.

I have included Albert Victor Alexander in the Honours List for a CH.[5] He has had a very trying year and has stood up to it well, in his battered and much-tried Admiralty.

Winston S. Churchill to William Mackenzie King
(*Churchill papers, 20/38*)

11 May 1941
Private and Secret

I am delighted to hear that Mr Menzies' visit was so successful. He was with us here through times of peculiar stress, and we found him a staunch comrade. A meeting of the Imperial Conference about July or August for a month or six weeks would be most desirable if it could be arranged. I hope we shall give a good account of ourselves in the Middle East. It will not be for the want of trying. Every good wish. It is splendid the way you have carried Canada forward in such perfect unity.

[1] William Wedgwood Benn, 1877–1960. An aviator in the First World War, he had first entered Parliament as a Liberal in 1906, crossing to Labour in 1928. From 1929 to 1931 he was Secretary of State for India, and from 1945 to 1946 Secretary of State for Air. He did accept a peerage in 1941, becoming Viscount Stansgate. The oldest of his three sons was killed on air operations in 1944. His second son, Anthony Wedgwood Benn (Tony Benn) later renounced the peerage, having instigated the Act to make disclaimer possible.

[2] James Joseph Mallon, 1875–1961. Secretary of the National League to establish a Minimum Wage, 1906. Member of the first thirteen Trade Boards (established by Churchill under the Trade Boards Act), 1909. Warden of Toynbee Hall, 1919–54. Member of the Board of Governors of the BBC, 1937–9 and 1941–6. Companion of Honour, 1939. Adviser to the Ministry of Food on Feeding in Air Raid Shelters, 1940–5. Member of the National Assistance Board, 1948.

[3] Pethick-Lawrence became a Baron in 1945; Wedgwood became a Baron and J.J. Mallon declined all further Honours (he had been appointed Companion of Honour in 1939).

[4] David Rees Grenfell, 1881–1968. Worked underground in the coal mines from the age of twelve to the age of thirty-five. Miners' agent, 1916. Labour MP for Gower, 1922–59. Secretary for Mines, 1940–42. He became a Privy Councillor in 1951. Father of the House of Commons, 1953–59.

[5] Alexander, the First Lord of the Admiralty, was made a Companion of Honour (he had been a Privy Councillor since 1929, when he had been made First Lord in Ramsay MacDonald's second Labour Government).

Sir Alexander Cadogan: diary
(*'The Diaries of Sir Alexander Cadogan'*)

12 May 1941

We went to see PM in CWR.[1] He already had text of an announcement, which included remark that Hess had come here 'in the name of humanity'. This won't do – looks like a peace offer, and we may want to run the line that he has quarrelled with Hitler.

Queen Elizabeth to Winston S. Churchill
(*Churchill papers, 1/361*)

12 May 1941 Windsor Castle
The day of our Coronation

The Queen thanks Mr Churchill most gratefully for his kindness in sending news of the progress and safe arrival of Tiger. Even though he lacks a claw or two, it is to be hoped that he will still be able to chew up a few enemies.

Any risk was well worth taking.

The Queen is dreadfully sorry about the House of Commons, and the damage to Westminster Abbey.

Winston S. Churchill to Sir Archibald Sinclair
(*Churchill papers, 20/36*)

12 May 1941

THE AIR TRAINING SITUATION

I am sorry that you do not wish to give me the information on the points of fact mentioned in Lord Beaverbrook's minute to me of the 30th April. I was very tired at the time I wrote my minute of the 3rd May, or I would have embodied the points of fact in Lord Beaverbrook's note in a minute of my own. I hope you will overlook this lack of ceremony, and make sure the Service does not suffer thereby through my not being able to get the information I seek.

Is it really true, for instance, that no fewer than 1,186 Trainer aircraft, or 31 per cent., were unserviceable on the 18th April? That only one-third of those unserviceable were awaiting spares? That if the Tiger Moths were left out, only 309 machines were grounded for lack of spares? That there are 500 Tiger Moths in store? That in November, when the new programme was laid down, it was planned to turn out 4,008 pilots from the Flying Training Schools, whereas the actual output was 2,731?

[1] The Central War Room (also known as the Cabinet War Room).

It does not seem to me that more than a page would be required to furnish the actual figures, and this was all I asked for.

In suggesting a one-page reply, my only object was to relieve you of the necessity of making lengthy explanations, which I feared might be a burden to you and even, if you will forgive me, to me.

War Cabinet: minutes
(*Cabinet papers, 65/18*)

12 May 1941 10 Downing Street
5 p.m.

The Prime Minister said that Operation Tiger had now been successfully completed, with the exception of one ship (*Empire Song*) which had struck a mine and sunk. This ship had by no means had the most valuable cargo. He was sure that the War Cabinet would wish to congratulate the Navy and the RAF on the very successful arrangements which they had made for the escort of this convoy, which had been sighted by the enemy at an early stage in its voyage.

The result would be greatly to increase General Wavell's strength in heavy tanks, for which he already had ample personnel. As soon as the tanks had been 'run in', General Wavell would have a great opportunity, and for this reason it was essential to maintain the strictest secrecy as to the extent of the reinforcements in *matériel* which had been carried in this convoy.

During the movements of the Fleet to escort this convoy, Benghazi had been bombarded. Ships had been sunk in the harbour, and two ships on their way to Benghazi, including an ammunition ship, had been sunk.

The Prime Minister added that further operations were on foot regarding additional air reinforcements to the Middle East.

In Iraq, things were better, but progressing slowly. General Wavell was anxious to meet C-in-C, India,[1] and it was proposed that he should fly to Basra to meet him.

Winston S. Churchill to General Wavell
(*Cabinet papers, 69/2*)

12 May 1941
Personal and Secret

1. There is no objection to your going to Basra to meet C-in-C, India, if this can be arranged, but, of course, your presence in Cairo seems of first consequence in these next few days. I presume you are making sure personally that contents of Tiger, about which the utmost secrecy is being observed, are

[1] General Auchinleck, who later succeeded Wavell as Commander-in-Chief, Middle East.

placed in the hands of troops at the earliest moment, and that all the new possibilities of action will be turned to account. In this connection see 2nd Epistle to the Corinthians, Chapter VI, verse 2.[1] It seems to me you have a wonderful opportunity, which, if not seized, may never return.

2. Will you consider whether at least another dozen I Tanks with skilled personnel should not go to help Scorcher.

3. About Iraq – you do not need to bother too much about the long future. Your immediate task is to get a friendly Government set up in Baghdad, and to beat down Rashid Ali's forces with the utmost vigour. We do not wish to be involved at present in any large-scale advance up the river from Basra, nor have we prescribed occupation of Kirkuk or Mosul. We do not seek any change in the independent status of Iraq, and full instructions have been given in accordance with your own ideas upon this point. But what matters is action; namely, the swift advance of the mobile column to establish effective contact between Baghdad and Palestine. Every day counts, for the Germans may not be long. We hoped from your 61872 that column would be ready to move 10th, and would reach Habbaniya 12th, assuming Habbaniya could hold out, which they have done and a good deal more. We trust these dates have been kept, and that you will do your utmost to accelerate movement.

4. Movement eastward to Palestine of a brigade of the 4th Indian Division must not be at expense of offensive action in the decisive desert theatre. I am sure you have this in mind, remembering how very well balanced was your withdrawal of troops of this same Division for Abyssinia after your victory at Sidi Barrani.

War Cabinet, Defence Committee (Operations): minutes
(*Cabinet papers, 69/2*)

12 May 1941 10 Downing Street
5 p.m.

CRETE

The Prime Minister said that it was very desirable that certain OL messages should be seen in their original text by the officer who was to command Scorcher;[2] and he asked the Chiefs of Staff to consider as a matter of urgency how this could best be arranged.

[1] 'For he saith, I heard thee in a time accepted, and in the day of salvation have I succoured thee: behold, now is the accepted time: behold, now is the day of salvation.'

[2] Churchill wanted General Freyberg, the officer commanding the forces in Crete, to be shown the actual texts of German operational orders, as decrypted from Enigma at Bletchley.

IRAQ

The Prime Minister thought that the bombing of the Power Station would have a salutary effect on the Baghdadis.

The Committee invited the Chief of the Air Staff to inform the AOC-in-C, Middle East that he had authority to bomb the Power Station north-west of Baghdad if he so desired.

Winston S. Churchill: Oral Answers

(*Hansard*)

13 May 1941 House of Commons

SHIPPING LOSSES (PUBLICATION)

Rear-Admiral Beamish[1] asked the Prime Minister whether on the analogy of not publishing the damage by enemy action to shipyards, factories, warehouses, railways, roads, etc., he will discontinue the publication of shipping losses, while communicating them as necessary to friendly Powers?

The Prime Minister (Mr Churchill): In all these matters, a balance has to be struck between giving the utmost information to the public and the least possible helpful information to the enemy. At the present time we are publishing our shipping losses monthly, as this seems to meet both the aforesaid conditions most agreeably. But all these questions have to be kept under constant review in the light of changing circumstances.

Rear-Admiral Beamish: Is the right hon. Gentleman aware how often these figures are misinterpreted, unbacked as they are by great achievements and relevant facts?

The Prime Minister: If you have no great achievements, you will find that the absence of figures will not prevent misrepresentation and misinterpretation.

WAR WEAPONS PRODUCTION

Mr Granville asked the Prime Minister whether in order to standardize types of tanks, guns, ships and aircraft and to place the production of war weapons under single direction, he will give consideration to setting up an allied war production council, to include representatives of the British Commonwealth and the United States of America; and whether he will invite the United States Government to ask Mr Wendell Willkie and other eminent American industrial and political leaders to join such a body in order to give their services for an arms drive?

[1] Tufton Percy Hamilton Beamish, 1874–1951. Assistant Chief to the Chief of the Naval War Staff, Admiralty, 1912–13. Naval Assistant to the First Sea Lord, 1914. Commanded HMS *Invincible*, 1914–15 (including the Battle of the Falkland Islands); HMS *Cordelia*, 1915–17 (including the Battle of Jutland). CB, 1917. Rear-Admiral, retired, 1925. Conservative MP for Lewes, 1924–9 and 1936–45. One of his two sons was killed in action in 1945.

The Prime Minister: No, Sir. The machinery to co-ordinate the production of war weapons in the British Empire and the United States of America is working smoothly and is being constantly developed. I would not presume to advise the United States Government who should represent them on any joint organization which may be set up now or in the future as part of that machinery.

Mr Granville: Will the right hon. Gentleman take into consideration that the Allied single command was the turning point in the last war, and that the union of British and American production to beat Nazi mechanization may be the decisive factor in this; and as most experts seem to agree upon this, will not it be better to suggest it for consideration now rather than later?

The Prime Minister: I am not at all sure that these very large and discursive topics are well suited for treatment at Question time.

MINISTER OF STATE

Major V. Adams asked the Prime Minister what are the precise functions that will be discharged by the holder of the office of Minister of State?

The Prime Minister: The Minister of State will discharge general Cabinet duties and the special duties assigned to a Member of the Defence Committee of the War Cabinet. The Defence Committee works in two sections: the Defence Committee (Operations), and Defence Committee (Supply). In future, the Lord Privy Seal will act as Deputy Chairman of the former; and the Minister of State, of the latter body. The Minister of State will also act as Referee on priority questions.

Mr Shinwell: Will anybody be able to protect the Referee?

The Prime Minister: Yes, Sir, I shall always be at hand.

Sir H. Williams:[1] Will this Minister have a seal?

The Prime Minister: If in the course of the discharge of his important functions, it is found that the use of a seal will be helpful in the public interest, I have not the slightest doubt that timely measures will be taken to provide it.

RUDOLF HESS

Mr Lees-Smith (by Private Notice) asked the Prime Minister whether he has any further statement to make with regard to the announcement that Rudolf Hess, the Nazi leader, has landed in Scotland?

The Prime Minister: I have nothing to add at present to the statement issued last night by His Majesty's Government, but obviously a further statement will be made in the near future concerning the flight to this country of this very high and important Nazi leader.

Mr Lawson: In view of the German propaganda statement over the wireless that this gentleman was suffering from mental instability, has the Prime

[1] Sir Herbert Williams, MP for South Croydon (see page 670, note 1).

Minister any information to give us on that matter, or is that particular disease limited to the chief of the German propagandists?

The Prime Minister: Obviously, I have not any information at the moment, but after an examination has been made, I will make a further statement.

Sir Henry Morris-Jones: Will my right hon. Friend consider asking the Minister of Information, if necessary, to see that this piece of news is handled with skill and imagination?

The Prime Minister: I had an opportunity of being in the company of the Minister of Information till a very late hour last night, but I think this is one of these cases where imagination is somewhat baffled by the facts as they present themselves.

Major Vyvyan Adams: Will the Prime Minister bear in mind this 'gentleman's' record of devotion to the evil genius of Europe?

The Prime Minister indicated assent.

Captain Cunningham-Reid:[1] With regard to the Ministry of Information, which has been mentioned, does the Prime Minister consider that it was prudent to announce that Hess was in a Glasgow hospital? Was not that rather unfair on the people of Glasgow, who may now expect a rain of bombs?

The Prime Minister: Perhaps he will not always be in Glasgow.[2]

John Colville: diary
(*Colville papers*)

13 May 1941

The Hess story has, of course, made everyone gape. This morning, after returning from the House with the PM, I saw an account of H's interview with Kirkpatrick,[3] which is only being shown to Eden, Attlee and Beaverbrook. It is clear that Hess is no traitor but genuinely believes he can persuade us that we cannot win and that a compromise peace is obtainable. His essential pre-requisite is the fall of the Churchill Government. The poor Duke of Hamilton feels acutely the slur of being taken for a potential Quisling – which he certainly is not.

[1] Alec Stratford Cunningham-Reid, –1977. On active service with the Royal Engineers and Royal Flying Corps, 1914–18 (despatches, Distinguished Flying Cross). Conservative Member of Parliament for Warrington, 1922–23 and 1924–29; for St Marylebone, 1932–45 (sitting as an Independent, 1942–45).

[2] Hess was held in Maryhill Barracks, Glasgow. One of his first requests was that he should be moved out of Glasgow so as not to risk being killed in a German bombing raid on the city.

[3] Ivone Augustine Kirkpatrick, 1897–1964. On active service, 1914–18 (wounded, despatches twice). Diplomatic Service, 1919. First Secretary, Rome, 1930–2; Counsellor, Berlin, 1933–8. Director of the Foreign Division, Ministry of Information, 1940. Controller, European Services, BBC, 1941. Assistant Under-Secretary of State, Foreign Office, 1945; Deputy Under-Secretary, 1948. Permanent Under-Secretary (German Section), 1949; Permanent Under-Secretary of State, 1953–7. Knighted, 1948. Chairman of the Independent Television Authority, 1957–62.

Winston S. Churchill to Anthony Eden
(*Churchill papers, 20/36*)

13 May 1941

HESS

On the whole it will be more convenient to treat him as a prisoner of war, under WO and not HO[1]; but also as one against whom grave political charges may be preferred. This man, like other Nazi leaders, is potentially a war-criminal and he and his confederates may well be declared outlaws at the close of the war. In this case his repentance would stand him in good stead.

2. In the meanwhile he should be strictly isolated in a convenient house not too far from London, fitted by 'C'[2] with the necessary appliances, and every endeavour should be made to study his mentality and get anything worthwhile out of him.[3]

3. His health and comfort should be ensured; food, books, writing materials and recreation being provided for him. He should not have any contacts with the outer world or visitors except as prescribed by the Foreign Office. Special guardians should be appointed. He should see no newspapers and hear no wireless. He should be treated with dignity as if he were an important General who had fallen into our hands.

War Cabinet, Tank Parliament
(*Cabinet papers, 120/52*)

13 May 1941
12 noon

10 Downing Street

The Prime Minister said that no-one could disagree on the principle that the Army, and particularly the armoured divisions, must have air forces working in the closest co-operation with them. The question at issue was one of quantity, and of the impingement of Army requirements on other programmes.

The Prime Minister said that the main problem confronting the Army was the defence of this Island and the character of the operation could be foreseen. The enemy would probably gain several lodgments, and the armoured divisions would move up to counter-attack them. Their operations would thus be offensive, and would certainly require a proper quantity of aircraft to

1 Under the War Office and not the Home Office.

2 Stuart Menzies, head of the Secret Intelligence Services.

3 Desmond Morton later reported to Churchill, after several interrogations of Hess that summer: 'He firmly believes that the Government will one day wish to send him back to Germany with an offer of peace terms' (Minute of 28 July 1941, *Premier papers, 3/219/2*).

ensure that the armoured divisions would receive the support they required.

Sir Charles Portal said that the whole of the Bomber Command would be available to operate against the invaders.

The Prime Minister said that this strategic bombing by Bomber Command of ports, ships, beaches, etc., could not be regarded in the same light as close support of armoured formations. The armoured divisions would be moving forward perhaps over ground partly occupied by the enemy, and would need immediate air support under their own control. The Middle East was quite a different problem.

The Prime Minister enquired why no more than three squadrons could be immediately equipped, as so many Tomahawks were now in the country. It would not be necessary to wait for all the modifications. The important thing was that training should start at once.

The Prime Minister enquired why three squadrons could not now be equipped with Blenheims.

Air Commodore Goddard[1] said that Army Co-operation Squadrons had to be reduced for the benefit of Bomber Command, and what was left was insufficient to do the reconnaissance which the Army required.

Lord Beaverbrook said that if it were decided that Tomahawks should be issued in numbers for the Army Co-operation Squadrons, he felt sure that the Ministry of Aircraft Production would be able to do it, probably without affecting other programmes.

The Prime Minister said that he would like a scheme prepared to equip as early as possible fourteen Army Co-operation Squadrons, partly with Tomahawks, and partly with Blenheims. These would then be completely at the disposal of the Army. It would then be necessary to tackle the problem of the future. Next year, the Army must have a weapon perfectly adapted for their own use. In the meanwhile, the close association of squadrons with the Army, and their combined training, should be pressed forward throughout the summer.

At the request of the Prime Minister, Lord Beaverbrook undertook to examine, in consultation with the Ministers concerned, the question of suitably re-equipping the Army Co-operation Squadrons, and to report to the Prime Minister in time for the next meeting of the Committee, which would be held the following week.

[1] Robert Victor Goddard, 1897–1987. On active service with the Royal Navy, Royal Naval Air Service, Royal Flying Corps and Royal Air Force, 1914–19. Air Ministry, 1919; head of the German Intelligence Section, Air Ministry, 1936–8; Deputy-Director of Intelligence, 1938–9; Director of Military Co-operation, 1940–1. Chief of the Air Staff, New Zealand, 1941–3. Air Officer in charge of administration, Air Command, South East Asia, 1943–6. RAF Representative, Washington, 1946–8. Knighted, 1947. Member of the Air Council for Technical Services, 1948–51.

Winston S. Churchill to David Margesson and General Sir John Dill
(*Premier papers, 3/284/2*)

13 May 1941
Most Secret
Action this Day

1. It is just three weeks since it was decided to run the risks of Tiger. Its success may well have transformed the situation in ME. Equal efforts must be made for Jaguar.

2. General Wavell has already in Egypt the trained, experienced personnel to man 6 Tank Regiments. He probably has 3, certainly 2, more Tank Regiments' personnel evacuated without their Tanks from Greece. You have sent additional personnel for 4 Tank Regiments round the Cape. General Wavell has, therefore, the men for 12 or 13 Tank Regiments, additional to the existing Tank Units now formed at Tobruk and Mersa Matruh, which absorb perhaps 100 Tanks. The 250 Heavy Tanks which have come through in Tiger; the 50 expected from the Cairo workshops in May; the 25 or 30 expected in June; and the 60 American expected at the end of June will arm about 8 Regiments of personnel without allowing for wastage in Tanks. There are therefore 4 Regiments requiring to be armed, apart altogether from wastage.

3. It is much better to provide ample forces in war so as to achieve a swift result, rather than to budget for a continued flow of wastage over a long period of months. I am therefore of opinion that we should send all we can from here at the earliest moment.

4. You yourself propose to supply replacement Tanks at 50 a month, or 150 in the months of May, June and July. If these vehicles are to reach the scene in time to affect the issue, they will have to go through the Mediterranean, and for this purpose it will be necessary that the whole 150 should go in one convoy at one time. I hope this may not be later than the last ten days of June. I should be content with half Cruisers and half I tanks; but, of course, 100 Cruisers and 50 I Tanks would be better; or 100 Cruisers and 100 I Tanks, best of all.

5. I have asked the Admiralty to consider when another convoy can be provided. Perhaps the four fast MT ships should return home westward through the Mediterranean, keeping their deck armament, as soon as possible. But this may not be convenient to the Admiralty on account of the exigencies of their blockade and Scorcher.[1] Also it may be possible to find three or four suitable fast MT ships here. I hope to hear in the course of the day from the Admiralty.

6. It will be necessary that we should have 150 to 200 Tanks of both types,

[1] Code names for Crete (Colorado), and for the defence of Crete (Scorcher).

tropicalized and ready for despatch, between the 15th June and the 30th June. Preparations should be made for this at once.

7. The question of whether they should be sent through or not must be decided by the Defence Committee, who will make their recommendations to the Cabinet.

Winston S. Churchill to General Sir John Dill
(*War Office papers, 216/5*)

13 May 1941
Action this Day

1. There is a great deal in your paper of 6th May with which I agree. There are also many statements which leave me unconvinced. I thoroughly agree with you in para. 8 that our military advisers underrated the Germans in Norway, in Belgium, and in Libya. Of these, Belgium is the most remarkable. Yet I never remember hearing a single British soldier point to the weakness of the Sub-Maginot line or deprecate our occupation of Belgium. I only mention this to show that even the most expert professional opinion may sometimes err amid the many uncertainties of war.

2. Your para. 9 does not seem to me to put comparable alternatives. I gather you would be prepared to face the loss of Egypt and the Nile Valley, together with the surrender or ruin of the Army of half a million we have concentrated there, rather than lose Singapore. I do not take that view, nor do I think the alternative is likely to present itself. The defence of Singapore is an operation requiring only a very small fraction of the troops required to defend the Nile Valley against the Germans and Italians. I have already given you the political data upon which the military arrangements for the defence of Singapore should be based, namely, that should Japan enter the war the United States will in all probability come in on our side; and in any case Japan would not be likely to besiege Singapore at the outset, as this would be an operation far more dangerous to her and less harmful to us than spreading her cruisers and battle-cruisers on the Eastern trade routes.

3. While agreeing with most of your para. 8, I wonder whether the German action in the Balkans can be cited as an example of 'their capacity for overcoming the most formidable difficulties'. As a mere exercise in historical perspective, I should have thought the opposite was true. They were allowed to accumulate unresisted overwhelming forces to attack Yugoslavia before it was mobilized, and when it had been betrayed by its pre-war Government; Greece was exhausted and held by the Italian Army, and we were left

practically alone with only one-fifth the armoured vehicles, and practically no Air, to resist their overwhelming onslaught. The fact that with all these advantages, so cheaply gained, the Germans were unable to impede seriously the masterly extrication and re-embarkation of our forces, inspires me with confidence and not with apprehension.

4. The truisms set forth in para. 10 depend entirely upon their application to circumstances. But I hope the last sentence is not intended to have any relevance to the present position in Egypt.

5. In para. 3 I was not aware that the Chiefs of the Staff had themselves calculated the scale of attack upon this country, though I have no doubt the tactical exercise called Victor was concerned with such matters.

6. With regard to the training of the 5 Armoured Divisions and 2 Armoured Tank Brigades which are partly equipped in this country, this is a matter for which the War Office is responsible. They have quite enough equipment for training purposes if it is properly distributed and properly used. Tanks are coming forward in a good flow now, though I fear A 22 will only produce about half the 160 I had hoped for up to the end of July.

7. I am sending you another paper on the immediate steps required.

Winston S. Churchill to Sir John Reith
(Churchill papers, 20/36)

13 May 1941
Action this Day

I highly approve of your activities about providing an alternative to the House of Commons No. 2 now installed at the Church Building. It occurred to me, however, this morning, and I was asked some questions on the point, whether we could not <u>in addition</u> try to find some accommodation in the Palace of Westminster. We could leave the Lords in their present Chamber, and perhaps the Royal Gallery could be fitted for the House of Commons. There seem to be three or four fine, large empty rooms at that end of the building. Of course, if we could work there it would be far more convenient to the ordinary Member. The Smoking-Room, Writing-Rooms, Libraries, Dining-Room, &c., I believe are largely intact, and these make a great difference to Members. I should have thought you could have staged a very good House of Commons in the Royal Gallery. I do not think The King would object. Indeed, he seemed most anxious to help us in every way. Will you therefore get hold of the Chief Whip and have the possibilities explored.

Winston S. Churchill to Air Chief Marshal Sir Charles Portal
(*Churchill papers, 20/36*)

13 May 1941

A-M Tedder's[1] 417. Please tell him that I like very much his general layout and am glad to feel that he has the handling of the important and complicated operations which impend. I make a few general observations upon time-table and emphasis of possible events. A victory in Libya comes first both in time and importance. Its results would dominate Iraq. All values would be altered both in German and Iraqi minds. It would be a comfort if we could get a friendly Government reinstalled at Baghdad and he should help as much as he can. Nothing must, however, prejudice victory in the Western Desert over Germans. There are two operations in Western Desert: The smaller now going on and the larger when contents of Tiger are disgorged. Between these two may come hostile attack on Colorado and Scorcher.[2] It seems to me likely that Scorcher will be later than 17th because such complex arrangements nearly always lead to delays. But there is no authority for this. A new view may be possible after the smaller Western Desert operation is over. Anyhow, the Malta-Tripoli business may have to slow down pending decisions in the Desert and in Colorado. Jaguar is on the way and Malta may be milked of Hurricanes in anticipation of Jaguar arriving. 15 or 20 extra Hurricanes in the Desert may play a most important part, and Beaufighters should stay at Malta for ten days more. One clear-cut result is worth a dozen wise precautions. Longer views about Iraq and Syria can be taken later.

[1] Arthur William Tedder, 1890–1967. Educated at Whitgift and Magdalene College, Cambridge. Colonial Service (Fiji), 1914. On active service, Royal Flying Corps, France, 1915–17 and Egypt, 1918–19 (despatches thrice). Commanded 207 Squadron, Constantinople, 1922–3; Royal Naval Staff College, 1923–4; No 2 Flying Training School, 1924–6. Director, RAF Staff College, 1921–9. Director of Training, Air Ministry, 1934–6. Air Officer Commanding RAF Singapore, 1936–8. Director-General, Research and Development, Air Ministry, 1938–40. Deputy Air Officer Commander-in-Chief, RAF, Middle East, 1940–1; Air Officer Commander-in-Chief, RAF, Middle East, 1941–3. Knighted, 1942. Air Commander-in-Chief, Mediterranean Air Command, 1943. Deputy Supreme Commander (under General Eisenhower), 1943–5. Created Baron, 1946. Chief of the Air Staff, and First and Senior Air Member, Air Council, 1946–50. Chairman, British Joint Services Mission, Washington, 1950–1. Chancellor of the University of Cambridge from 1950 until his death.

[2] The British code names for the island of Crete, and for the defence of Crete.

Winston S. Churchill to Air Chief Marshal Sir Charles Portal
(*Churchill papers, 20/36*)

13 May 1941

Let me have a statement showing all aeroplanes of every type that you have now got moving, or propose to move during the present month, from here to the Middle East by every route and every method; showing also the expected arrivals.

Winston S. Churchill to General Auchinleck
(*Churchill papers, 20/38*)

13 May 1941

I am very glad you are going to meet Wavell at Basra. He will tell you about Tiger and Scorcher. A victory in Libya would alter all values in Iraq both in German and Iraqi minds.

2. We are most grateful to you for the energetic efforts you have made about Basra. The stronger the forces India can assemble there the better. But we have not yet felt able to commit ourselves to any advance (except with small parties when the going is good) northward towards Baghdad and still less to occupation in force of Kirkuk and/or Mosul. This cannot be contemplated until we see what happens about Tiger and Scorcher. We are therefore confined at the moment to trying to get a friendly Government installed in Baghdad and building up the largest possible bridgehead at Basra. Even less can we attempt to dominate Syria at the present time though the Free French may be allowed to do their best there. The defeat of the Germans in Libya is the commanding event, and larger and longer views cannot be taken till that is achieved and everything will be much easier then.

Winston S. Churchill to General Wavell
(*Churchill papers, 20/38*)

14 May 1941
Personal and Secret

All my information points to need for Scorcher any day after 17th. Everything seems to be moving in concert for that and with great elaboration. Hope you have got enough in Colorado and that those there have the needful in cannon, machine guns and AFVs. It may well be that in so large and complicated a plan zero date will be delayed. Therefore, reinforcements sent now might well arrive in time, and certainly for the second round, should enemy gain a footing. I should particularly welcome chance for our high-class troops to come to close grips with those people under conditions where enemy has not got his usual mechanical advantages, and where we can surely reinforce much easier than he can. I suppose Admiral is with you in every detail of this and that you and Tedder have concerted the best possible Air plan, having regard to other tasks. All good wishes.

Winston S. Churchill to A.V. Alexander and Admiral Pound
(*Premier papers, 3/432*)

14 May 1941
Action this Day

Further to my Tiger No.2, one would hope that it could be fitted in during the moonless period after about the middle of June. In order to give greater security it might be well to send *Victorious* right through, and thus give the C-in-C Mediterranean[1] what he longs for, namely, two armoured aircraft-carriers. For this purpose however it is most desirable that *Victorious*, and if possible the other aircraft-carriers who would be accompanying her, should have a proportion of the best and fastest fighters which can be thrown off a float. What happened to those American Martlet aircraft? I have not heard of them for some months, yet we were told they were so promising on account of their high speed. How is the unloading of Tiger going on?

Lord Beaverbrook to Sir Samuel Hoare
(*Beaverbrook papers*)

14 May 1941

I do not know whether this new job will work or not. It will, in large measure, depend on how much authority the Prime Minister is prepared to delegate.

His idea is that he will delegate a very great deal. But he is inclined to think in terms of Bridges and Seal and so on. I do not say this in criticism of Winston. It is part of the man's character, just one of the aspects of his temperament which must be accepted. And, indeed, it is a comment that has sometimes been made about me.

In the House of Commons' debate the other day, Winston at once brought the whole House under his control. If democracy means the sort of Parliament that he is handling, then in making war, there is no evil in democracy. But, in truth it is only a sham of a Parliament.

The Front Bench is part of the sham. There Attlee and Greenwood, a sparrow and a jackdaw, are perched on either side of the glittering bird of paradise.

[1] Admiral Sir Andrew Cunningham.

Winston S. Churchill to Lord Halifax
(*Churchill papers, 20/38*)

14 May 1941

I am very much honoured by the invitation which Rochester University has tendered me, coming as it does from the city where my Grandparents[1] spent so many happy years. I hope it may be possible for me to make a short speech to the University on June 16, and I will certainly try to do so.

Winston S. Churchill to President Franklin D. Roosevelt
(*Churchill papers, 20/38*)

14 May 1941
Personal and Secret

Thank you so much for your very kind message, and I hope you will soon be quite well again. I have good hopes that, in view of certain steps we have taken, the situation in Libya will be improved before long. It is therefore particularly important for you to go forward confidently with all your plans for supplying our Middle Eastern Armies by American ships to Suez. In Iraq, too, we are trying to regain control, and, anyhow, we are making a large strong bridgehead at Basra, where later on in the war American machines may be assembled and supplies unloaded. Syria is, however, a cause of great anxiety. There is no doubt that Darlan will sell the pass if he can, and German aircraft are already passing into Iraq. I have no means of action on that caitiff Government. The more Leahy can do the better. It is the only hope. We are also sure Vichy is letting transport, &c., go to Tripoli overland from Tunis. The Azores and Cape de Verde Islands are always liable to be jumped by the Germans at the same time as they break into Spain or seduce the Spanish Government. It will be very difficult for us to avoid being either too soon or too late. Finally, one of our armed merchant cruisers was torpedoed this morning between the 38th and 39th Meridians. I will send you a special report about Hess shortly.

[1] Leonard and Clara Jerome. Leonard Jerome (1818–91) was a successful stockbroker, financier and newspaper proprietor. His grandfather had fought for American independence in George Washington's army.

Winston S. Churchill to General de Gaulle
(*Cabinet papers, 69/2*)

14 May 1941

We had a meeting of the Defence Committee this afternoon, at which question of Jibuti was discussed.

We decided –

(a) to maintain the strict blockade of Jibuti;
(b) to ask you to allow General Catroux to remain in Palestine, where, indeed, he may already be acting;
(c) to send you a cordial invitation to go to Cairo if you feel that you can safely leave the guardianship of the Free French territories.

War Cabinet, Defence Committee (Operations): minutes
(*Cabinet papers, 69/2*)

14 May 1941
5 p.m.

SYRIA

The Prime Minister said that we must do everything possible to organize a force to go into Syria to support the air action and to exploit any success which might result from General Catroux's broadcast and a revulsion of feeling by some of the French in Syria against the German landings. He enquired whether Polish troops could be used.[1]

Sir John Dill said that he would send a telegram to General Wavell asking what possibility there was of moving the Poles to the Palestine frontier.

RELATIONS WITH VICHY

The Prime Minister said that it must be made clear to the Vichy Government how we regarded the situation. It was alleged that the French in Tunis had assisted the Germans by providing transport for their forces into Tripoli. It was now clear that the French authorities were conniving at German infiltration into Syria.

OPERATION PUMA[2]

The Prime Minister said that in view of the present situation he could not

[1] No Polish troops were used in the invasion of Syria. In opposing this, Sikorski telegraphed to General Kopanski, the Commander of the Independent Carpathian Rifle Brigade (then in Palestine): 'Armed conflict with France undesirable. She holds our gold and hundreds of thousands of Poles and tens of thousands of Polish soldiers as hostages. Avoid being called to Syria.' (*Polish Institute and Sikorski Museum*)

[2] The proposed British capture of the (Spanish) Canary islands, part of Operation Pilgrim, which included the seizure of all the Portuguese Cape Verde islands in the Atlantic, in the event of a German occupation of Spain and Portugal.

allow the Expedition to sail now. We should have to face the possibility that we might be forestalled in the Iberian Peninsula by German action.

OPERATION SCORCHER

The Prime Minister suggested that it might be well to let Admiral Cunningham know that we regarded Operation Scorcher as holding a higher priority even than the interruption of enemy supplies to Tripoli. He thought, however, that these two commitments need not clash.

Sir Dudley Pound said he would send a signal to the Commander-in-Chief, Mediterranean, drawing his attention to the supreme importance of Operation Scorcher.

Anthony Eden: diary
(*'The Eden Memoirs, The Reckoning'*)

14 May 1941

Winston rang me up late at night with text of statement he wants to make in House tomorrow about Hess, quoting trend of his statements. I protested, urging Germans must be kept in dark as to what Hess had said. Winston then demanded alternative draft and I struggled out of bed and produced it and telephoned it. A few minutes later Winston telephoned he did not like it and Duff was much upset. On the other hand Max agreed with me. Which was it to be, his original statement or no statement. I replied: 'no statement'. 'All right, no statement' (crossly!), and telephone was crashed down. Time 1.30 a.m.[1]

John Colville: diary
(*Colville papers*)

15 May 1941

The PM answered questions (inadvertently letting fall in answer to a supplementary that MEW were connected with propaganda) and then proposed a resolution thanking the House of Peers for their message of condolence on the loss of the Chamber of the House of Commons.

[1] Eden commented in his memoirs: 'A few days later the Prime Minister reverted to his projected statement about Hess, this time at the Cabinet, but nobody liked it, so that nothing came of it. Lord Beaverbrook told me afterwards that we might have to "strangle the infant" a third time, but fortunately it was not reborn.'

Winston S. Churchill: Oral Answers
(*Hansard*)

15 May 1941 House of Commons

BRITISH PROPAGANDA (ENEMY COUNTRIES)

Mr Maclean asked the Prime Minister which Department is responsible for British propaganda in enemy countries?

The Prime Minister: Several Departments assist in this important work, and His Majesty's Government take collective responsibility for their actions.

Mr Maclean: To whom can Questions with regard to this kind of propaganda be addressed?

The Prime Minister: If Questions are put down for the Minister of Information or the Minister of Economic Warfare, whichever of these Ministers felt himself particularly affected would give an answer.

Mr Maclean: But it is already the case that both Ministers referred to by the Prime Minister think they are not interested and not in charge of the propaganda indicated in the Question.

The Prime Minister: If nobody will take the Question, I will.

Mr Shinwell: Can the Prime Minister say who is responsible for this if the Minister of Information is not responsible? Why should my right hon. Friend deal with matters of this kind? Cannot he delegate them to another Minister?

The Prime Minister: Nothing would be simpler for me than to give a precise account of exactly how these matters are managed, but I do not think it would be advantageous.

Mr Shinwell: Does not the Prime Minister misunderstand me? To whom can Questions be addressed about this kind of propaganda? The Minister of Economic Warfare disclaims responsibility, and if it is not the task of the Minister of Information, whose task is it?

The Prime Minister: It is the task of the Minister of Information and of the Minister of Economic Warfare, certain aspects of which, obviously the economic aspect, are under his care, and if a Question is put down to either one of these Ministers, I will see that it is answered by the appropriate Minister. If it falls between the two, I shall be glad to serve the House.

WAR CABINET

Mr Mander asked the Prime Minister whether, with a view to giving the fullest expression to national unity, he will consider the advisability, when a suitable opportunity presents itself, of including representatives of all three parties in the War Cabinet?

The Prime Minister: If one of the Service Ministers were included in the War Cabinet, it would be necessary to include all three. This would be in direct contradiction of the principle which is so often urged upon us that the War Cabinet should be a small body of non-Departmental Ministers. In order that the leader of the Liberal party should be a member of the War Cabinet, it would be necessary that he should give up his office as Air Minister. I should greatly regret to lose the services of my right hon. Friend the Member for Caithness (Sir A. Sinclair) in this most important war post, and I am surprised that a member of the party he leads with so much distinction should in effect propose such a course. At the time of the formation of the Government it was announced that the leaders of the three parties participating in the Government, whether members of the War Cabinet or not, would be consulted when questions arose affecting the general character and aims of the Government, including conditions of peace. It would be a great pity to depart from it.

Sir Henry Morris-Jones: Would the Prime Minister bear in mind that the best way to win this war is to forget all parties and appoint the best men available?

The Prime Minister: Certainly, Sir, but the co-operation of all parties has, indeed, facilitated the selection of the best men.

RUDOLF HESS

Mr Granville: In view of the various and contradictory reports, and in view of the report regarding the Duke of Hamilton this morning, will the Prime Minister take the first opportunity of giving the House of Commons, the Parliament of the country, authentic news of this matter?

The Prime Minister: Yes, Sir, I will; but in selecting the opportunity, I must have regard to the public interest.

Major Adams: Does not my right hon. Friend consider that it was unfortunate that 48 hours were allowed to elapse, during which the enemy were enabled to issue an entirely deceitful version?

The Prime Minister: It was certainly not unfortunate, and if it had been unfortunate, it would have been unavoidable, because we had first of all to establish the identity of the German airman who had landed, and we only had evidence which, though it was very interesting, could not be considered conclusive. In view of the surprising character of the occurrence, I did not believe it, although I was very interested, when I was told in the course of Sunday; but I immediately sent up an officer who knew the Deputy Führer and who was able to speak with him in good and fluent German. While that was still proceeding, there came the German announcement of the insanity of the Deputy Führer and his flight to England. [Hon. Members: 'Scotland.'] Yes, Scotland. What had hitherto been a surmise built on increasing probability merged into definite certainty.

Mr Woodburn: Is there any truth in the inference given by the German wireless that they wished to impress upon Germany that Scotland was ready to make a separate peace with Germany?

The Prime Minister: Whatever delusions may exist, that is not among them.

WAR MANUFACTURE

Sir H. Williams:[1] Will the Minister of Supply be able to deal with questions of priority covering all branches of war manufacture?

The Prime Minister: No, Sir. I think we had better hear the speech the Minister makes and then any omissions from it can be the subject of fair comment.

Sir H. Williams: I put my supplementary question because it is now 10 months since the Select Committee on National Expenditure drew attention to the need for an efficient system of priority, and also to the confusion which existed in respect of priority.

The Prime Minister: I am sure it will be possible to show to the House that there has been a very great improvement made during that time. It is not really a question of priority, but of allocation.

Mr Bevan: In view of the fact that every day allegations are made on the part of national administrators concerning the failure of production in many cases, does the Prime Minister think that public anxiety in these matters will be effectively allayed by a Private Session of the House of Commons? Ought not an opportunity be given for public Debate, particularly in view of the fact that it is the desire of many of us to try and collect sufficient public pressure to force or persuade the Government to take certain action which we think is desirable? How can we be expected to do that if all our Debates on these matters take place in Secret Session?

Sir I. Albery: Are the Government asking the House to agree to a Secret Session because they have statements to make which cannot be made in public?

The Prime Minister: Yes, Sir. So far as the Government are concerned, we should welcome a Public Session, but unhappily if a Public Session were held, we should not be able to make any statements of the precise character which would be of interest to the House and which are important factors in the formation of the judgment of the House. What we have to do is to tell the House all that can be told on these matters in Secret Session, and then the House will, according to whether it feels confidence or the reverse, convey assurance or alarm to the country.

[1] Herbert Geraint Williams, 1884–1954. Educated at the University of Liverpool. Electrical and Marine Engineer. Secretary, Machine Tool Trades Association, 1911–28. Secretary, Machine Tool Department, Ministry of Munitions, 1917–18. Conservative MP for Reading, 1924–9; for South Croydon, 1932–45; for Croydon East, 1950–4. Parliamentary Secretary, Board of Trade, 1928–9. Knighted, 1939. Member of the House of Commons Select Committee on Expenditure, 1939–44. Chairman, London Conservative Union, 1939–48; National Union of Conservatives and Unionist Associations, 1948. Created Baronet, 1953.

Mr Bevan: Will the Prime Minister be good enough to reply to the point I have made? In view of the fact that hundreds of thousands of workmen do know the actual facts of the situation, and in view of the fact that newspapers have quite rightly been betraying a great deal of anxiety about this, ought we not to have a Public Session to allay the anxiety?

The Prime Minister: I do not know that there is so much anxiety. I hope it will be shown that very great progress has been made. Anything more foolish than publicly to give our facts and figures in detail, which will go in a few hours to Lisbon and then be telegraphed immediately to Germany, I cannot imagine. We really must leave some work for the German Intelligence.

Mr Gallacher:[1] The Prime Minister has just said, that in Secret Session Ministers would make a statement to the House and that on the basis of the information and the discussion which took place Members could then convey to the country whether there was a feeling of assurance or disquiet. Does that mean that after this Private Session we can go to the country and say what we have heard?

The Prime Minister: No, Sir, not at all. It would be quite impossible for Members to quote what had occurred or to give away any secret information imparted, but it would be equally impossible for them wholly to conceal their feelings whether of enthusiasm or the reverse.

BRITISH EMPIRE (NOMENCLATURE)

Mr Martin asked the Prime Minister whether, in view of certain undesirable associations of the word 'Imperial', he will consider with the Prime Ministers of the Dominions and the Government of India, the use of the word 'Commonwealth' in all references to co-operative activity between those States and ourselves?

The Prime Minister: The word 'Imperial' and the word 'Commonwealth' have both of them time-honoured associations in the minds of His Majesty's subjects. Some prefer the one and some the other, and like a great many British conventions they are not too rigidly or precisely or even logically applied. The roots of these ideas go far back into our history, which is the common inheritance of all subjects of the King-Emperor and members of the British Commonwealth of Nations, and this is no time to institute pedantic divisions about nomenclature.

[1] William Gallacher, 1881–1965. Began work as a grocer's delivery boy at the age of twelve. Chairman, Clyde Workers' Committee, 1914–18. Imprisoned four times for political activities, 1917, 1918, 1921 and 1925. Attended the 2nd Congress of the Communist International, Moscow, 1920 (where he met Lenin). Member of the Executive Committee of the Communist International, 1924, and again in 1935. Communist MP, 1935–50 (the only Communist MP 1935–45, then one of two). President of the Communist Party, 1953–63.

Winston S. Churchill to General Wavell[1]
(*Churchill papers, 20/49*)

15 May 1941
sent at 5.10 p.m.

I am increasingly impressed with the weight of the attack impending upon Colorado, especially from the Air. Trust all possible reinforcements have been sent.

War Cabinet, Defence Committee (Operations): minutes
(*Cabinet papers, 69/2*)

15 May 1941 Cabinet War Room
9.45 p.m.

The Prime Minister said that he did not believe the Japanese would attack the Netherlands East Indies unless they were sure that the United States would remain neutral, and unless they were prepared to go much further and to attack us. He did not believe that such a situation would arise. Why should the Japanese risk going to war with the Americans and ourselves when by waiting they could see whether the Germans were going to win the war. He agreed with the First Sea Lord that there was little we can do to help the Dutch and it was unpleasant in such circumstances to be committed to an automatic declaration of war. We were, however, in the war with the Dutch and it would be difficult to accept their declaration and to say nothing ourselves. He had observed that the Japanese always showed nervousness when either the United States or ourselves took a strong line, and a public declaration would be a deterrent. The Japanese would behave like the Italians. They would enter the war when they thought that we were on the point of defeat, so that they could gather the spoils without danger to themselves.

The Prime Minister said that he sympathized with the view expressed by the First Sea Lord[2] and it was clear that there could be no redistribution of naval forces to strengthen the Far East. Nevertheless he felt it was incumbent on us to make common cause with those who were attacked by aggressors.

[1] This telegram was also sent to the Naval and Air Commanders-in-Chief, Admiral Sir Andrew Cunningham and Air Vice Marshal Longmore.

[2] That 'we should be most unwise to commit ourselves further'.

Winston S. Churchill: statement
(*Hansard*)

15 May 1941

HOUSE OF COMMONS (DESTRUCTION OF CHAMBER)
LORDS MESSAGE OF SYMPATHY

I feel that the House would not wish this very kindly Message which we have received from the other branch of the Legislature to pass without formal recognition, so that the episode may take its place in the Journals of the House and be upon record for future generations. The House of Lords have themselves suffered personal loss in this last attack in the death of Captain Elliott,[1] so many years Custodian of the House of Lords, and of two police officers who, in the discharge of their duties, fell under the fire of the enemy.[2] We feel that the recognition we should give to the Resolution of the House of Peers should take the form of a Resolution of the House of Commons, and I therefore move this motion.

Winston S. Churchill to Sir Kingsley Wood
(*Churchill papers, 20/36*)

16 May 1941

I draw a clear distinction between deaths arising from the fire of the enemy and ordinary accidents. This is the line of demarcation which we have successfully maintained in the Bill dealing with compensation for war injuries. The Air attack on this country is novel and sporadic, and can also quite safely be kept in a compartment by itself. Therefore I reject the arguments about the concessions spreading to ordinary accidents, and from the Armed Forces to persons in employ on a part-time system, such as Air Raid wardens and the like. I consider that in a Regular service, persons bound by discipline on permanent engagement have a right to be considered when on leave as enjoying the same privileges in regard to pensions for their widows, &c., as when they are with their Units. Here again is a frontier which can be effectively maintained.

In a Regular disciplined force, leave is regarded as earned, and is part of the normal system of the Force, and it breeds contempt of the governing

[1] Captain Edward L.H. Elliott. Custodian of the House of Lords from 1928 until his death in May 1941.

[2] At 12.30 a.m. on the night of 10/11 May 1941 a High Explosive bomb which hit a Fire Watchers' Post at the south east corner of the Royal Gallery at the Palace of Westminster killed two fire watchers, War Reserve Police Constables Farrant and Stead. Fifteen minutes later a 50lb bomb penetrated the ARP storeroom where it killed Captain Elliott, who was in the room with his wife and two daughters.

machinery when one man's widow is left with half the pension of the other, merely because he was hit by the enemy's fire while on leave.

Let me know what would be the expense if the regulations were amended as I have here suggested.

Winston S. Churchill to General Dobbie[1]

(*Churchill papers, 20/38*)

16 May 1941

Am sure Stevenson[2] is your man. I watched his work here very closely. Since beginning of March he has revolutionized East and South coast Air fighting against German shipping. He embodies offensive warfare. Results have been extraordinary. Will keep on feeding you. All good wishes.

Winston S. Churchill to General Ismay

(*Churchill papers, 20/36*)

16 May 1941

What is the situation at Martinique? Are the 50 million pounds of gold still there? What French forces are there? What French vessels are in harbour? I have it in mind that the United States might take over Martinique to safeguard it from being used as a base for U-boats in view of Vichy collaboration.[3]

[1] The Governor of Malta (*see page 110, note 1*).

[2] Donald Fasken Stevenson, 1895–1964. On active service, 1914–18 (despatches, Military Cross with Bar, Distinguished Service Order). With the Royal Air Force in Palestine, 1936. Director of Home Operations, Air Ministry, 1938–41. Air Officer Commanding No.2 Bomber Group, 1941; Burma, 1942; Bengal, 1943; Northern Ireland, 1944. Commanding No.9 Fighter Group, 1944. British Commissioner, Allied Control Commission, Roumania, 1944–47.

[3] The French Caribbean territories of Martinique, Guadeloupe and French Guiana were under the overall rule of Vice-Admiral Georges Robert, who in June 1940 had declared for Vichy. A British naval blockade, which restricted trade with France and the United States, and prevented the movement of French warships and gold from Martinique, was taken over by the United States after it entered the war in December 1941. Local resistance groups forced Robert to resign in June 1943, when he was replaced first by a Giraudist and then by a Gaullist.

Winston S. Churchill to General Wavell
(*Churchill papers, 20/38*)

16 May 1941
Most Immediate
Personal

It will be serious risk and inconvenience to push this hundred extra tanks through Mediterranean. We shall be grateful if you can spare us this. But exigencies of the sustained battles you will have to fight must claim priority, and in view of heavy loss of I tanks on 15th May, victory may depend upon the last hundred. Do not please ask if you can do without them by the short route. Do not hesitate to ask if you think the sixteen days gained is vital to the decision of the battle, remembering always that perhaps they may be lost in transit.

Winston S. Churchill to General Smuts
(*Churchill papers, 20/29*)

16 May 1941
Absolutely Secret and Personal
To be decyphered only by General Smuts' most confidential secretary or staff officer

I am as usual in close sympathy and agreement with your military outlook. I recently had measures taken to reinforce Wavell in what he was weakest, and I have hopes that we shall be successful in heavy offensive fighting in the Western Desert during the next few weeks. We also expect a strong attack by the enemy on Crete almost immediately and have made all possible preparations for it. If favourable decisions are obtained at these two points, our problems in Syria and Iraq should be simplified. We are also reinforcing Middle East most powerfully from the Air by every conceivable method. I have good hopes that we shall win the campaign in the Eastern Mediterranean this summer, and maintain our hold upon the Nile Valley and the Suez Canal. President Roosevelt is pushing United States supplies towards Suez to the utmost. The South African Army will be very welcome on the Mediterranean shore.

The western end of the Mediterranean is more doubtful, but Spain has hitherto stood up well to German pressure. We shall let Darlan know at the proper time that if Vichy aircraft bomb Gibraltar, we shall not bomb France but the Vichy skunks wherever they may hide out. We have not overlooked the possibility of Gibraltar harbour becoming unusable and have made the best preparations open to us. Perhaps the United States may be willing to come more closely in to the West African business especially at Dakar.

Finally the Battle of the Atlantic is going fairly well. Instead of Hitler reaching a climax of blockade in May as he expected, we have just finished the best six weeks of convoys for many months. We shall certainly get increasing American help in the Atlantic and personally I feel confident our position will be strengthened in all essentials before the year is out. The Americans are making very great provision to replace shipping losses in 1942, and I feel they are being drawn nearer and nearer to their great decision. It is better however not to count too much on this.

It looks as if Hitler is massing against Russia. A ceaseless movement of troops, armoured forces and aircraft northwards from the Balkans and eastward from France and Germany is in progress. I should myself suppose his best chance was to attack the Ukraine and Caucasus thus making sure of corn and oil. Nobody can stop him doing this, but we hope to blast the Fatherland behind him pretty thoroughly as the year marches on. I am sure that with God's help we shall beat the life out of the Nazi regime.

The King tells me he is going to send you a special message for your birthday on May 24, so I will send my heartfelt good wishes now.[1]

Winston S. Churchill to Sir Alexander Cadogan
(*Churchill papers, 20/36*)

16 May 1941

1. Please make now a fairly full digest of the conversational parts of Hess's three interviews, stressing particularly the points mentioned by me in the statement I prepared but did not deliver. I will then send this to President Roosevelt with a covering telegram.

2. I approved the War Office proposal to bring Hess to the Tower by tonight pending his place of confinement being prepared at Aldershot.

3. His treatment will become less indulgent as time goes on. There need be no hurry about interviewing him, and I wish to be informed before any visitors are allowed. He is to be kept in the strictest seclusion, and those in charge of him should refrain from conversation. The public will not stand any pampering <u>except for intelligence purposes</u> with this notorious war criminal.

[1] At Churchill's suggestion, King George VI was about to appoint General Smuts an Honorary Field Marshal in the British Army.

Winston S. Churchill to President Franklin D. Roosevelt
(*Churchill papers, 20/38*)

16 May 1941

Foreign Office Representative[1] has had three interviews with Hess.

At first interview on night of May 11th–12th Hess was extremely voluble and made long statement with the aid of notes. First part recapitulated Anglo-German relations during past thirty years or so, and was designed to show that Germany had always been in the right and England in the wrong. Second part emphasized certainty of German victory due to development in combination of submarine and air weapon, steadiness of German morale and complete unity of German people behind Hitler. Third part outlined proposals for settlement. Hess said that the Führer had never entertained any designs against the British Empire, which would be left intact save for the return of former German colonies, in exchange for a free hand for him in Europe. But condition was attached that Hitler would not negotiate with present Government in England. This is the old invitation to us to desert all our friends in order to save temporarily the greater part of our skin.

Foreign Office Representative asked him whether when he spoke of Hitler having a free hand in Europe he included Russia in Europe or in Asia. He replied 'In Asia.' He added, however, that Germany had certain demands to make of Russia which would have to be satisfied, but denies rumours that attack on Russia was being planned.

Impression created by Hess was that he had made up his mind that Germany must win the war, but saw that it would last a long time and involve much loss of life and destruction. He seemed to feel that if he could persuade people in this country that there was a basis for a settlement that might bring the war to an end and avert unnecessary suffering.

At second interview on May 14th, Hess made two further points:

(1) In any peace settlement Germany would have to support Rashid Ali and secure eviction of British from Iraq.

(2) U-boat war with air co-operation would be carried on till all supplies to these islands cut off. Even if these islands capitulated and Empire continued the fight, blockade of Britain would continue, even if that meant that the last inhabitant of Britain died of starvation.

At third interview on May 15th nothing much emerged save incidentally some rather disparaging remarks about your country and the degree of assistance that you will be able to furnish to us. I am afraid, in particular, he is not sufficiently impressed by what he thinks he knows of your aircraft types and production.

[1] Ivone Kirkpatrick, who had known Hess before the war when Kirkpatrick was serving in the British Embassy in Berlin.

Hess seems in good health and not excited and no ordinary signs of insanity can be detected.

He declares that this escapade is his own idea and that Hitler was unaware of it beforehand.

If he is to be believed he expected to contact members of a 'peace movement' in England, whom he would help to oust present Government.

If he is honest and if he is sane this is an encouraging sign of ineptitude of German Intelligence Service.

He will not be ill-treated, but it is desirable that the Press should not romanticize him and his adventure. We must not forget that he shares responsibility for all Hitler's crimes and is a potential war criminal whose fate must ultimately depend upon the decision of the Allied Governments.

Mr President, all the above is for your own information. Here we think it best to let the Press have a good run for a bit and keep the Germans guessing. The German Officer prisoners of war here were greatly perturbed by the news, and I cannot doubt that there will be deep misgivings in the German Armed Forces about what he may say.

Winston S. Churchill to A. V. Alexander and Admiral Pound

(*Churchill papers, 20/36*)

17 May 1941

At the end of February the Admiralty seem to have had 40 ships of 10,000 tons and over employed as armed merchant cruisers, since when I believe about 3 have been sunk. We are so short of troop carriers now that I must ask for some of these ships to be surrendered. I suggest you hand over any you have left in excess of 30, *i.e.*, about 7, leaving them with their armaments, but with reduced naval crews and choosing those which will carry the largest number of troops. They will thus be able to defend themselves and the convoy of which they form a part.

The case of the *Scythia*, merchant ship, which it was proposed to bring home from the Cape unloaded on a 25-days' voyage through all the danger zones in order to serve as a troop carrier in Convoy WS 8B[1] shows the stringency under which we suffer.

I must really ask the Admiralty to do this with the utmost expedition.

[1] The second section of the eighth convoy from Britain to the Middle East via the Cape of Good Hope.

Winston S. Churchill to Admiral Pound
(*Churchill papers, 20/36*)

17 May 1941

CHART OF GROSS TONS OF MERCHANT SHIPPING SALVAGED

This chart of the immense work of the Salvage Department makes me anxious that you should convey to those in charge of that Branch a very high and express measure of commendation. Perhaps you would let me see a draft of what you propose.

Winston S. Churchill to General Wavell
(*Churchill papers, 20/38*)

17 May 1941
Most Immediate
Personal and Secret
sent at 10.30 p.m.

Results of action seem to us satisfactory. Without using tigercubs, you have taken the offensive, have advanced 30 miles, have captured Halfaya and Sollum, have taken 500 German prisoners and inflicted heavy losses in men and AFV's[1] upon the enemy. For this, 20 I tanks and 1,000 or 1,500 casualties do not seem to be at all too heavy cost.

2. News from Tobruk is also good, especially as enemy's loss is greater than ours. Enemy is certainly anxious about Tobruk and reports with apparent satisfaction when it is quiet. It seems of the utmost importance to keep on fighting at Tobruk.

3. Enemy is bringing up 'Axis reinforcements' and is seeking to re-establish the situation. We should surely welcome this as he may not be in a condition to stand severe continuous fighting. CIGS and I both feel confident of good results of sustained pressure, because the extremely worried state of the enemy is known to us. We feel sure you should keep at it both at Sollum and Tobruk. He cannot possibly fill the gap like you can. Presume you are using your powerful mechanized field artillery to the full at both places, compelling him to fire off ammunition of which we know he is short. We should also be grateful if, without burdening yourself personally, you could have some officer on your staff send a fuller report of the events and position as known at GHQ each evening. This is all the more desirable when operations of such outstanding importance for the world situation as those in the Western Desert are in progress.

[1] Armoured Fighting vehicles.

4. What are your dates for bringing tigercubs into action?

5. We would both also like to emphasize the vital importance of Habforce[1] acting with the greatest vigour and accepting all risks. General Clark[2] must take a leaf out of the book of our successful leaders in the Indian Mutiny, when they were never daunted by superior numbers and struck hard and decisively whatever the odds.

Winston S. Churchill to Anthony Eden
(*Churchill papers, 20/36*)

18 May 1941

CHAIRMANSHIP OF THE BRITISH COUNCIL

On personal grounds, what you propose would be very agreeable to me. But the name of Malcolm Robertson[3] has been brought to my notice. He is certainly a far abler and more experienced man; has great energy and is doing nothing; whereas the Duke of Devonshire[4] is already employed.

There are, however, several important matters about the British Council which must be settled before we can make these appointments. First, is it to go on? Many people consider that now we are at war and have a Ministry of Information it is redundant. It is certainly very expensive, and apart from junketings in South American States there are very few countries open to it. There are no doubt a number of influential people who have ensconced themselves in this organization. Full justification will have to be shown to the Cabinet by defining and explaining the reality of its work in the immediate future. On the whole, I am inclined to think that its usefulness ended with the death of Lord Lloyd.

A second point is its relations, if it is continued, with the Minister of Information. Parliament will certainly be entitled to know that our

[1] The British and Transjordanian military force seeking to relieve Habbaniya, which was besieged.

[2] John George Walters Clark, 1892–1948. Entered the Army, 1911. On active service in Flanders, 1914–18 (wounded, despatches thrice, Military Cross and clasp). Major-General, 1940. General Officer Commanding the lst Cavalry Division, 1939–42. Commanded Habforce, Iraq, May–June 1941. General Officer Commanding, Allied Forces Headquarters, 1942–43; Chief Administrative Officer, 1944. Head of the Allied Military Mission to Greece, 1945–47.

[3] Malcolm Arnold Robertson, 1877–1951. Entered the Foreign Office, 1898. British High Commissioner, Rhineland, 1920–1. Consul-General, Tangier, 1920–5. Knighted, 1924. Ambassador to the Argentine, 1927–9. Chairman of Spillers Ltd, 1930–47. Conservative candidate for Mitcham, Surrey, 1940, following the death of the sitting member; MP, 1940–5. Chairman of the British Council, 1941–5.

[4] Edward William Spencer Cavendish, 10th Duke of Devonshire 1895–1950. On active service (as Marquess of Hartington), Dardanelles and France (despatches twice). Member of the British Peace Delegation, Paris, 1919. Conservative Member of Parliament (before succeeding to the Dukedom) for West Derbyshire, 1923–38) Parliamentary Under-Secretary of State for Dominion Affairs, 1936–40; for India and Burma, 1940–42; for the Colonies, 1942–45.

propaganda is properly concerted. We have already the Ministry of Economic Warfare and the Ministry of Information in considerable dispute over their overlapping functions. Now we are to have the British Council. I fear this will not be thought to be a well-conceived solution. However, I should be very glad to know your views about it, and perhaps you will let me have a note on the points I have made before we take the matter to the Cabinet.

Winston S. Churchill to Viscount Cranborne, and General Ismay for the Chiefs of Staff Committee
(*Churchill papers, 20/36*)

18 May 1941

SUPPLY OF EQUIPMENT TO EIRE

I do not object to the ten Hector aircraft being given to Southern Ireland, nor to their purchasing the one Hurricane and one Hudson which are interned there. I do not like giving them Vickers guns, or all these demolition materials (items 3–10), because they are much more likely to be used against us if we march down from the North than against German invaders, of whose coming there is very little chance. I see no objections to items 11 and 12, nor perhaps item 2. In principle, however, it will be far better to await further developments in the United States.

I hope the small concessions made will serve as petty cash in the meanwhile.

Winston S. Churchill to Admiral Sir Andrew Cunningham
(*Premier papers, 3/109*)

18 May 1941
Personal
Most Secret
Sent 4.54 p.m.

Our success in Scorcher would, of course, affect whole world situation. May you have God's blessing in this memorable and fateful operation, which will react in every theatre of the war.

Winston S. Churchill to General Freyberg
(*Premier papers, 3/109*)

18 May 1941
sent 5.45 p.m.

All our thoughts are with you in these fateful days. We are glad to hear of the reinforcements which have reached you and the strong dispositions you have made. We are sure that you and your brave troops will perform a deed of lasting fame. Victory where you are would powerfully affect world situation. Navy will do its utmost.

War Cabinet: minutes
(*Cabinet papers, 65/18*)

19 May 1941 10 Downing Street
5 p.m.

Shipping casualties since the 15th May included 3 meat ships, totalling 26,000 tons, which had been torpedoed West of Freetown.

The Prime Minister said that he intended to bring the position in the Central Atlantic to the notice of President Roosevelt. He asked the First Sea Lord to prepare the draft of a telegram.

A number of vessels had also been damaged in Crete and one had been sunk in the North-Western Approaches.

In the recent operations round Sollum, Capuzzo and Halfaya Pass we had taken all our objectives, but Capuzzo had afterwards been lost to a counter-attack by at least 40 enemy tanks. The capture of 500 German prisoners was satisfactory, while our forces in Tobruk had also done well.

The Duke of Aosta had accepted terms of capitulation for the garrison of Amba Alagi, amounting to some 7,000 men. This meant the end of Italian resistance in the North of Abyssinia, but enemy forces were still resisting in the South and near Gondar.

The Prime Minister said that he had received a message from Mr Willkie to the effect that American opinion was in need of guidance as to the directions in which we required their help. The Prime Minister read to the War Cabinet a draft of the reply which would be sent after Mr Winant had consulted the President in regard to it.

SYRIA[1]

The Prime Minister said that he had prepared a first outline of his views as to the policy which we should adopt in regard to Syria, and was sending a copy

[1] The secrecy of this item was such that it was not printed in the Cabinet conclusions (themselves marked Secret) but only in the War Cabinet's Confidential Annex (*Cabinet papers, 65/22*).

to the Foreign Secretary for his observations. He thought that we might give the French one last chance of stopping the passage of the German air force through Syria. If they did not take this chance, we should proclaim Syria to be an independent Arab State. It was relevant that Syria was territory mandated to France by the League of Nations, and that France had ceased to be a member of the League.

War Cabinet, Defence Committee (Operations): minutes
(*Cabinet papers, 69/2*)

19 May 1941
9.45 p.m.

DRAFT TELEGRAM TO THE GOVERNMENTS OF AUSTRALIA AND NEW ZEALAND

The Prime Minister thought that the tone of the draft telegram was unduly depressing and seemed to take no account of the value of the American gesture in moving a large part of the Pacific Fleet into the Atlantic.

UNITED STATES' OPINION

. . . the view was put forward by the Prime Minister and Mr Alexander –

(a) that the Americans should be educated out of their present idea that they should only enter the war when we were at the last gasp;
(b) that nothing would be gained by piling on the agony of our shipping losses; throughout the war the Germans had consistently put out greatly exaggerated claims of our shipping losses and it would be wrong for us now to try and give the impression that the German propaganda was right after all;
(c) that if we began to give the Americans specific cases of the sinking of certain commodities, this would lead to a demand for information as to what proportion of our imports of those commodities these losses represented and then to a demand for information as to the resources available in this country. In this way we should be led on to exposing the whole of the facts about our situation to the great profit of the enemy.
(d) that if we emphasized to America the gloomy side of our situation, it would have a depressing effect on our own people; moreover, our gloomy attitude might well be quickly discredited when it was found that the May shipping losses in the Atlantic were not serious;
(e) that it was difficult to see in what precise way the Battle of the Atlantic could be dramatized or the facilities for American journalists improved. The latter had expressed themselves very satisfied at a recent conference with the First Lord of the Admiralty.

Winston S. Churchill to General Dobbie
(*Churchill papers, 20/38*)

19 May 1941

Alas Stevenson reported medically unfit, but CAS is sending another first-class officer. Everyone here appreciates splendid work Maynard[1] has done, working up from the very beginning, but it is felt that a change would be better now. Maynard will be well looked after here.

Winston S. Churchill to General Cunningham and General Platt
(*Churchill papers, 20/38*)

19 May 1941

Following for Generals Cunningham and Platt: I send you and your gallant armies my heartfelt congratulations and those of His Majesty's Government upon this timely and brilliant culmination of your memorable and strenuous campaign.

Pray make this known to your troops if you desire.

Winston S. Churchill to General Wavell
(*Churchill papers, 20/49*)

19 May 1941
Personal and Secret

1. I have asked in earlier telegrams during the past few weeks to be told programme of using tigercubs when they arrive and also that all preparations should be made beforehand to place them in the field with the minimum delay.

Tremendous risks were run to give you this aid, and I wish to be assured that not an hour will be lost in its becoming effective.

2. According to Admiralty information *Clan Chattan* should have been unloaded by May 15th, second ship May 17, third ship May 19 and fourth

[1] Forster Herbert Martin Maynard, 1893–1976. On active service, 1914–18. Royal Naval Division, Royal Naval Air Service and Royal Air Force. Commanded University of London Air Squadron, 1935–36. Air Officer Commanding RAF Malta, 1940–41. Air Vice-Marshal, 1941. Air Officer in charge of Administration, Coastal Command, United Kingdom, 1941–44. Air Officer Commanding 19th Group, 1944–45. Retired, 1945.

May 22. *Clan Chattan* alone contained 67 cruisers. Shall be obliged if you will tell me in detail what has happened since these cruisers were landed. Are they yet in hands of troops? Why does it take a fortnight to bring them into action? What work has to be done upon them? How are they to be moved to the front? I understood you would have the trained and experienced units all ready for them. Can I have a definite time-table in respect of the mobilization of the AFVs of all these four ships?

3. I regret prospect of loss of a fortnight more, *i.e.* 19 days from the date of arrival of convoy before vehicles can come into action. If it is physically inevitable, it must be borne, but to me it seems hard. I fear you will have a very different enemy in front of you in a fortnight hence from what you have now. Of course, I understand that we must not fritter tigercubs away piecemeal.

4. Please also state whether German 6-pdr gun is fired from their tanks or otherwise brought into action. If the former, how many vehicles does your intelligence estimate enemy possesses with this weapon?

5. Is it not possible to increase the number of tanks in Tobruk by nightly instalments so as to act offensively from this deadly position? Your last news from Tobruk is good and I also rejoice our casualties Sollum area were so much less than I expected. Sollum seems to have been a profitable operation.

Winston S. Churchill to William Mackenzie King

(*Churchill papers, 20/49*)

19 May 1941

Thank you for your telegram as regards French diplomatic representation in Canada. I appreciate and welcome your desire to give some mark of Canada's disapproval of the Vichy Government at the present time. Clearly there is nothing further to hope from Vichy. They have gone over into the German camp and will collaborate with Hitler to the utmost extent that French public opinion will allow. I do not therefore personally feel that there is any value in Canada continuing, any longer, diplomatic relations with Vichy, nor do I think it likely that there is any further useful work that Dupuy could do. I fully recognize however, that there may be considerations of an especially Canadian character which the Canadian Government may feel bound to take into account.

If you did not wish to go so far as a complete rupture of relations you might possibly like to consider depriving the French Legation of cypher and bag facilities which Dupuy did not enjoy in Vichy.

As there is also a French Legation at Pretoria would you care to repeat to General Smuts substance of your telegram to me and my reply.

Winston S. Churchill to Anthony Eden

(*Churchill papers, 20/36*)

19 May 1941

I think we should certainly keep Mr Dupuy at Vichy as long as possible, and consequently that the Canadian Government should allow their French representative to remain at Ottawa. I do not contemplate a breach of relations between the British and Vichy Governments, but only that we shall knock them about as much as may be necessary in the anomalous conditions prevailing while still preserving contacts which may be of value. It must be remembered that nothing like this relationship has ever been seen before in diplomatic history. Should we have to bomb Vichy, we should advise Canada in time for her to withdraw her man. I should be glad to discuss this with you if you disagree.

Winston S. Churchill: Note[1]

(*Cabinet papers, 120/10*)

19 May 1941

SYRIAN POLICY

PART I.

1. If we can hold our own in the Western Desert and in Crete, the invasion of Syria must take first place in our thoughts. For this, we must have an Arab policy. The French have forfeited all rights in Syria since they quitted the League of Nations, and we are entitled to argue that their Mandate has lapsed. Furthermore, none of our promises to de Gaulle cover mandated territories. Therefore it seems to me that we should give them one more chance, and only one.

2. If the French Army in Syria will come over to us and work with the Free French Forces till the end of the war, we should refrain from raising the question of the lapse of the Mandate, and France's claims in Syria would be adjudicated at the Peace Conference. If, however, they are going against us, or maintaining an attitude of malevolent passivity, we must get the Syrian Arabs on our side. For this purpose, we should proclaim that the French Mandate has lapsed; that France has no right to deliver the Syrians over to Germans or Italians; and that we proclaim an Independent Sovereign Arab State in Syria in permanent alliance with Turkey on the one side and Great Britain on the other. It would follow from this that the French in Syria would be disarmed and offered passage back to France, or else remain in easy

[1] Churchill commented, after the war, while preparing his war memoirs: 'No distribution was made of this memorandum, which should be considered as being in draft form only.'

internment during the war. Further, that the Free French Forces should not be employed in Syria, but should be moved to the Western Desert or some other theatre. The position would have to be put squarely to de Gaulle, but his reactions should not affect our course. All private and commercial property rights of French citizens would, of course, be respected and preserved.

3. I am not sufficiently acquainted with Syrian affairs to be able to formulate a plan for the creation of the Syrian State, but I cannot doubt that our Islamic experts can easily do so.

4. The effect of our Proclamation, if followed by a wise decision as to Arab personalities, might well gratify the Arab race and rally them to a strong Nationalist movement to expel all European masters, or would-be masters, from their country.

5. If we cannot get the French, we must have the Syrians. The question, however, arises whether, when and how a public offer, probably in the form of an ultimatum, should be made to the French Army in Syria.

6. As one of the principal objects is to join up with the Turks, they should be consulted, and it is possible that some restoration of territory might be made to them in the North of Syria, and the disputes which they have had with the French about Syria would be settled in a sense favourable to the Turks.

PART II.

7. I have for some time past thought that we should try to raise Ibn Saud to a general overlordship of Iraq and Transjordania.

I do not know whether this is possible, but the Islamic authorities should report. He is certainly the greatest living Arab, and has given long and solid proofs of fidelity. As the custodian of Mecca, his authority might well be acceptable. There would, therefore, be perhaps an Arab King in Syria and an Arab Caliph or other suitable title over Saudi Arabia, Iraq and Transjordania.

8. At the time of giving these very great advancements to the Arab world, we should, of course, negotiate with Ibn Saud a satisfactory settlement of the Jewish problem; and, if such a basis were reached, it is possible that the Jewish State of Western Palestine might form an independent Federal Unit in the Arab Caliphate. This Jewish State would have to have the fullest rights of self-government, including immigration and development, and provision for expansion in the desert regions to the southward, which they would gradually reclaim.

9. As soon as the enemy forces in Cyrenaica have been destroyed, as they should be, having regard to our large numerical superiority in troops, artillery and tanks and the Air reinforcements we are sending, and provided Crete is held, we should invade Syria in force unless in the meanwhile a favourable situation has been created by the internal action of the Syrian Arabs.

10. This note seeks only to outline the most favourable political basis for military action.

John Colville: diary
(*Colville papers*)

19 May 1941

Before going to bed the PM told me he expected the German attack on Crete to begin tomorrow.[1]

'British Workers' to Winston S. Churchill[2]
(*Churchill papers, 2/415*)

20 May 1941

May God grant you the very best of health and strength to carry us through our Greatest Ordeal in History to keep the British Empire free.

From British Workers

War Cabinet, Defence Committee (Operations): minutes
(*Cabinet papers, 69/2*)

20 May 1941 10 Downing Street
1 p.m.

SYRIA

The Prime Minister thought that General Catroux should be allowed to carry out his plan and should be supported to the best of our ability. His move into Syria would be more in the nature of a political coup rather than a military invasion. It was worth taking a chance which might come off, rather than watch the Germans establishing themselves in Syria without attempting to prevent them. If events turned in our favour at Baghdad and Crete, the effect on Syria might be very great and friendly forces would rally to us.

There was general agreement with the views expressed by the Prime Minister. It was also felt that the proclamation should be framed to appeal to the Syrians, rather than to the French.

[1] Enigma had provided the precise details. The first German air bombardment on Maleme and Heraklion airports began at 5.30 the following morning, 20 May 1941.

[2] This message was found on 20 May 1941 in the pocket of one of the siren-suits which had been made to order for Churchill.

Winston S. Churchill: Oral Answers
(*Hansard*)

20 May 1941 House of Commons

ORGANIZATION

Mr Lindsay[1] asked the Prime Minister whether, in view of the fact that air attack inevitably creates a number of novel problems, affecting the movement, housing and feeding of the people, the effective solution of which demands a staff and line organization on a national and regional basis, as in the case of fire, he will consider the advisability of appointing a Minister of Civil Defence or make such other appropriate changes in the national and regional organization as he thinks fit so that the courage of the people and the devotion of officials and voluntary workers is worthily matched and reinforced?

The Prime Minister (Mr Churchill): His Majesty's Government are naturally fully alive to the new problems created by air attack, and we do not hesitate to make changes in the national, regional and local organization of Civil Defence to meet new conditions. But I do not consider that a radical change in the present chain of responsibility is necessary or desirable in present circumstances.

Mr Lindsay: Without asking for any definite proposal, do I understand that the Prime Minister has not a word to say on this subject?

The Prime Minister: I hope I have not yet got to my last word.

PRODUCTION AND IMPORT EXECUTIVES

Mr Granville: In order to avoid the tragedy of 'too late and too little' in this vast question of mechanization, will the Prime Minister now place war production and priorities under single control and direction, and will he also take an opportunity of reading a leader in today's *Times* on this question?

The Prime Minister: I was not really aware that my hon. Friend should prescribe to me my light reading in the morning. I may say that on several occasions I have given to the House explanations of the flexible machinery which we have for conducting the war at the present time, and on a suitable occasion I should be prepared to add to the statements I have made, but I do not contemplate any decisive changes in policy, at any rate at the present time.

Mr Maxton: Does the Prime Minister refuse to read the *Times* articles?

The Prime Minister: Not when I agree with them.

[1] Kenneth Lindsay, 1897–1991. Educated at St Olave's school. On active service, 1916–18. At Worcester College, Oxford, 1921–2; President of the Oxford Union, 1922. Secretary, Political and Economic Planning (PEP), 1931–5. Independent National MP for Kilmarnock Burghs, 1933–45; Independent MP for the Combined English Universities, 1945–50. Civil Lord of the Admiralty, 1935–7. Parliamentary Secretary, Board of Education, 1937–40. Director of the Anglo-Israel Association, 1962–73. A Vice-President of the Educational Interchange Council (sometime Chairman), 1968–73.

Winston S. Churchill: statement
(*Hansard*)

20 May 1941 House of Commons

The Prime Minister: Since we last were together several important events have happened on which perhaps I might presume to say a few words to the House. The victory of Amba Alagi has resulted in the surrender of the Duke of Aosta and his whole remaining forces, and must be considered to bring major organized resistance by the Italians in Abyssinia to an end. No doubt other fighting will continue for some time in the South, but this certainly wears the aspect of the culmination of a campaign which I think is one of the most remarkable ever fought by British or Imperial arms. It reflects the utmost credit on Generals Cunningham and Platt, who discharged so well the task assigned to them by the Commander-in-Chief in the Middle East, Sir Archibald Wavell. When we look back to January, I find that the best expert opinion fixed the middle or end of May as the earliest date at which we could advance upon Kismayu, and anyone who has acquainted himself with the geography will see the enormous achievements, beyond anything that could have been hoped for, which have been accomplished by audacious action and by extraordinary competence in warfare in those desolate countries.

I take this opportunity of pointing out that in this campaign the South African Army, strong forces raised in the Union of South Africa, have played a most distinguished part. They were ordered by General Smuts to go forward, and, now that this theatre is closing down, they are to move northward to the Mediterranean. But also two British Indian divisions have gained laurels in the fighting at Kassala and all the way from Kassala to Keren and in the final event. These Indian divisions consist of six Indian and three British battalions. I am assured that the greatest admiration is felt at the extraordinary military qualities displayed by the Indian troops and that their dash, their ardour and their faithful endurance of all the hardships have won them the regard of their British comrades. Sometimes we have seen cases where not a single British officer remained and the battalion conducted itself in the most effective manner. Altogether this campaign is one which reflects very high honour upon the soldiers of India of all castes and creeds who were engaged. I feel that I could not refer to this matter without bringing it in a direct and emphatic manner to the attention of the House.

The second event which has occurred since we were last here is the sharp and well sustained action at Sollum. This is of interest because it was fought exclusively between British and German troops. It has not, I suppose, been found worth while to maintain Italian troops at the end of such a long and precarious line of communications. Fighting was severe but, of course, not on a very large scale. Several of our motorized brigades, supported by armoured brigades and strong artillery, advanced about 30 miles from the position where they had been deployed for some weeks past and attacked the enemy, taking Sollum, Halfaya Pass and Fort Capuzzo, and the armoured troops then got round the tanks and were very well situated about one o'clock on the 17th. The Germans launched a resolute counter-attack by about 40 tanks and recaptured Capuzzo. That entailed the withdrawal of the armoured brigade from the advantageous position which it had attained. The operation, therefore, was indecisive. The Germans claim 100 British prisoners, but we have 500 Germans in our hands, and the losses in tanks and in personnel on their side are certainly as heavy as, if not heavier than ours. These operations must be regarded on the background that for more than six weeks past the Germans have been proclaiming that they would shortly be in Suez and have been making much credit with the neutral world by spreading at large statements of this kind. It is, therefore, satisfactory for us to see that we have retained strong offensive power and that the fighting is being maintained, at any rate, on even terms in the advance areas of the approaches to Egypt.

The third matter is not yet known to the House. For the last few days our reconnoitring aeroplanes have noticed very heavy concentrations of German aircraft of all kinds on the aerodromes of Southern Greece. We have attacked them night after night, inflicting considerable damage. It is now clear that these concentrations were the prelude to an attack upon Crete. An airborne attack in great strength started this morning, and what cannot fail to be a serious battle has begun and is developing. Our troops there – British, New Zealand and Greek Forces – are under the command of General Freyberg, and we feel confident that most stern and resolute resistance will be offered to the enemy.

John Colville: diary

(*Colville papers*)

20 May 1941

At 5.00 the PM sped down to the House again and interrupted their business to give them the latest 'hot news' from Crete, clasping a dirty postcard on which I had scrawled the last signal.

Winston S. Churchill: statement

(*Hansard*)

20 May 1941 House of Commons

The Prime Minister (Mr Churchill): I must apologize to the House for having introduced a distraction into the keen and workmanlike discussion which has been proceeding upon the Bill before it, but, as I mentioned to the

House this morning that a serious attack had been begun upon the Island of Crete by airborne troops, I thought that the House would like to know, before it separated, what is the latest information in the possession of the Government. But I cannot pretend that the statement is of momentous importance. It is only because we are all together in this matter that I thought that the House would be most anxious to be kept fully informed, as it is my duty to do whenever possible. After a good deal of intense bombing of Suda Bay and the various aerodromes in the neighbourhood, about 1,500 enemy troops, wearing New Zealand battle-dress, landed by gliders, parachutes and troopcarriers in the Canea-Maleme area. This message was sent at 12 o'clock today, when the military reported that the situation was in hand. Apparently the capture of Maleme aerodrome was the enemy's object, and this has so far failed.

A later report at 3 o'clock says that there is continuous enemy reconnaissance, accompanied by sporadic bombing and machine-gunning, chiefly against anti-aircraft defence. The military hospital between Canea and Maleme, captured by the enemy, has now been recaptured. There is reported to be a fairly strong enemy party South of the Canea-Maleme Road, which has not yet been mopped up, but other parties are reported to be accounted for. Heraklion was bombed, but there has been no landing so far. I must apologize to the House for intruding on them, but I thought they would like to hear how the action has so far developed.

Winston S. Churchill to Viscount Halifax
(*Churchill papers, 20/38*)

21 May 1941

I have received through Consul-General at New York[1] a message from Wendell Willkie, text of which is contained in my immediately following telegram.[2] I drafted the reply shown in my telegram No. 202, which is pretty

[1] Godfrey Digby Napier Haggard, 1884–1969. Vice-Consul, Central America, 1908. Chargé d'Affaires, Havana, 1921. Consul-General, Brazil, 1924; Chicago, 1928–32; Paris, 1932–8; New York, 1938–44. Knighted, 1943. Director, American Forces Liaison Division, Ministry of Information, 1944–5.

[2] Wendell Willkie had written to Churchill: 'I send you this because of my great concern about American public opinion, which is hesitant and confused by present issue. I returned advocating destroyers for Britain after talk with you and Alexander. Donovan returned advocating convoys after talk with authorities in England. Forrestal now returns, presumably after similar conversations, saying that convoys not necessary and that bombers are sufficient. I am fearful that this policy places our friends outside Administration in untenable positions. Obviously, your policy must be flexible and constantly changing, but might there not be some method, through your representatives here, to keep your friends advised as to changes of needs? My affectionate and respectful regards.' (*Churchill papers, 20/39*)

stiff, and asked Mr Winant to submit it to the President beforehand so as to avoid any embarrassment or complaint. The President replied, as I had expected, strongly deprecating any such direct intercourse. I am therefore sending Willkie only the message contained in my telegram No. 203. (Most private.) This is in accordance with Winant's advice. Please seek occasion to get in touch with Willkie and without quoting actual text of my cancelled message tell him how the land lies. We want to gratify and stimulate Willkie without enabling it to be suggested that we have a separate line of communication with him, and above all without the slightest disloyalty to President or doing anything which would queer his pitch. Winant is likely to come over to see President, and will certainly do his best for us. Cable me if anything is not clear or requires amplifying.

Things are pretty good here.

Winston S. Churchill to President Franklin D. Roosevelt
(*Churchill papers, 20/49*)

21 May 1941
sent at 5.30 p.m.

You may be sure, Mr President, I would do nothing concerning the United States contrary to your guidance. I have therefore sent to Willkie, through Halifax, only a thankful acknowledgment of his kind message. This is in accordance with Winant's advice, which I follow.

I hope you will forgive me if I say there is anxiety here. We are at a climacteric of the war, when enormous crystallizations are in suspense but imminent. Battle for Crete has opened well. I had steps taken to reinforce Egypt in a manner which gives me good confidence about the Western Desert. Should Winant come home, he will explain to you what was done. We now have to launch out into Syria with the Free French in the name of Syrian and Lebanon independence. Spain, Vichy and Turkey are a riveted audience.

At heavy cost in other waters we have been doing better in Battle of the Atlantic lately, but as I send this message Admiralty tell me that eight ships have been sunk in a convoy as far out as the fortieth meridian west longitude. You will see from my cancelled message to Willkie how grievous I feel it that the United States should build 3 or 4 million tons of shipping and watch their equivalent being sunk beforehand.

Whatever happens, you may be sure we shall fight on, and I am sure we can at least save ourselves. But what is the good of that?

Let me once again express my gratitude and that of the British Empire for all you have done for us.

Winston S. Churchill to Wendell Willkie
(*Foreign Office papers, 954/29*)

21 May 1941

DRAFT TELEGRAM, SUBMITTED TO PRESIDENT ROOSEVELT, BUT THEN CANCELLED

1. There has been no change in our attitude. We want destroyers and long-range bombers, but far more we want effective convoy to farthest possible point. Feel sure Forrestal must have been mis-reported in saying anything contrary to this.

2. Total of American munitions sunk is no measure of the danger. Loss of tonnage is enormous, and any success we have in giving special protection to valuable convoys from United States is paid for by other losses in Atlantic, off Freetown or in other waters or by diminution of our war-effort in Mediterranean. I have never said that the British Empire cannot make its way out of this war without American belligerence, but no peace that is any use to you or which will liberate Europe can be obtained without American belligerence, towards which convoys is a decisive step. Every day's delay adds to the length of the war and the difficulties to be encountered. West Africa, Spain, Vichy, Turkey, the Arab world, all hang in the balance. Japan hangs in the balance. Wait three months and all this may be piled up against us in adverse sense, thus lengthening the war to periods no man can pretend to know about, and increasing immensely the danger and burden to be borne by someone before Hitler is beat. How easy now – how hard a year hence will be the task.

3. At present rate, in next twelve months we shall lose four and a half million tons of shipping. The United States, by a prodigy of generous constructive effort, will build perhaps three and a half and we build the other million. Where have we got to then? Just marking time and swimming level with the bank against the stream. Whereas co-operation of even a third of the American Navy would save at least one-half of the tonnage beforehand and give that mastery which alone can abridge the torments of mankind.

4. Most grateful to you for your cable.

Winston S. Churchill: statement
(*Hansard*)

21 May 1941 House of Commons

The Prime Minister: In the Suda Bay area further airborne attacks commenced at 4.30 yesterday. About 3,000 men were dropped. By 6.30 the greater part of these had been accounted for. Fighting continues, and the situation was reported to be in hand at 9 p.m. The method of attack was by

Stukas, that is, dive-bombers, and Messerschmitts, followed by gliders and parachutes. In the Heraklion and Retimo areas attacks began at 5.30 by parachutists. Troop-carrying aircraft, many of which crashed, also landed. There are no details yet. Of course, we must expect that fighting will continue and increase in severity.

Mr Molson:[1] Is there any confirmation of the report that the parachutists who were dropped were wearing New Zealand battle-dress?

The Prime Minister: Yes, and another report said that those who landed at Retimo were wearing English battle-dress. I see that the Germans have denied this.

Mr Molson: Will the men dressed in British uniform be dealt with according to international law.

The Prime Minister: I am not sufficiently informed of the exact circumstances. I think that we must leave a certain amount of discretion to those on the spot.

War Cabinet, Defence Committee (Operations): minutes
(*Cabinet papers, 69/2*)

21 May 1941 — 10 Downing Street
3 p.m.

The Prime Minister read out the latest telegrams on the situation in Crete and referred to earlier reinforcements to the Island.

Crete should be regarded as a key position in the Mediterranean. Not only would its capture by the Germans inflict upon us a severe loss in men and in prestige, but it would bring the German Air Force within effective range of our fleet at Alexandria with all that this entailed.

Referring to General Freyberg's telegram on the results of the first day's fighting, the Prime Minister said that he saw no reason why we should not retain our hold on the Island provided that General Wavell was able to land reinforcements on the southern side and that the Navy could prevent anything in the way of a German seaborne landing. With the forces available and with such reinforcements as could be rushed in, General Freyberg should be able to hold his own against airborne attack. It was against this background of a critical situation in Crete and the threat of a renewed German advance from Libya that the conduct of operations against Syria should be reviewed.

[1] Arthur Hugh Elsdale Molson, 1903–1991. President of the Oxford Union, 1925. Political Secretary, Association of Chambers of Commerce of India, 1926–29. Barrister-at-Law, Inner Temple, 1931. Conservative Member of Parliament for Doncaster, 1931–35; for the High Peak Division of Derbyshire, 1939–61. Served in the 36th Searchlight Regiment, 1939–41; Staff Captain, 11th Anti-Aircraft Division, 1941–42. Minister of Works, 1957–59. Created Baron, 1961. Chairman of the Council for the Protection of Rural England, 1968–71.

Winston S. Churchill to General Wavell
(*Churchill papers, 20/49*)

21 May 1941
sent 7.20 p.m.
To be handed personally to C-in-C
Personal and Secret

Reference your telegram No. 0/65982 of 21st May to CIGS, the following is decision to which Defence Committee has come today:

1. Nothing in Syria must detract at this moment from winning the battle of Crete, or in the Western Desert. Freyberg's No. 0/66006 declares he is hard pressed. No troops needed to sustain him can be diverted. Presume you are already reinforcing him to the utmost to master enemy airborne attack.

2. There is no objection to your mingling British troops with the Free French who are to enter Syria; but, as you have clearly shown, you have not the means to mount a regular military operation, and as you were instructed yesterday, all that can be done at present is to give the best possible chance to the kind of armed political inroad described in Chief of Staff No. 027 of 20.5.41, para. 3.

3. You are wrong in supposing that policy described in Chief of Staff No. 027 of 20th arose out of any representations made by the Free French Leaders or General Spears. It arises entirely from the view taken here by those who have the supreme direction of war and policy in all theatres. Our view is that if the Germans can pick up Syria and Iraq with petty air forces, tourists and local revolts we must not shrink from running equal small-scale military risks, and facing the possible aggravation of political dangers from failure. For this decision we, of course, take full responsibility, and should you find yourself unwilling to give effect to it, arrangements will be made to meet any wish you may express to be relieved of your Command.

Winston S. Churchill: message[1]
(*Churchill papers, 20/39*)

22 May 1941

Hearty greetings to the American Iron and Steel Institute. I well remember my harmonious relations with United States steel makers and the valuable contribution which they made to the successful outcome of the war of 1914–18. I recognize with gratitude the still greater efforts which they are now making in the cause of world-wide liberty.

[1] Churchill telegraphed this message to Lord Halifax on 21 May 1941 with a covering note: 'Will you ask Sir Gerald Campbell, who will be guest at the American Iron and Steel Institute Annual Dinner tomorrow, May 22nd, to give the Institute the following message from me.'

War Cabinet, Battle of the Atlantic Committee: minutes
(*Cabinet papers, 86/1*)

22 May 1941 10 Downing Street
5 p.m.

TURN ROUND OF SHIPPING: CARGO LINERS

The Prime Minister read out an analysis based on a typical sample of the time taken by cargo liners for the round trip to North America in peace-time and at present. The comparative figures were 39 and 86 days. The days in port or moving coastwise were 14 and 43 days respectively.

PORT FACILITIES: DOCK WORKERS' ACCOMMODATION

The Prime Minister asked the Minister of Labour and National Service as Chairman of the Production Executive to consult the Minister of Works and Buildings and the other Ministers concerned and to report to the next Meeting on the possibility of providing temporary living accommodation and transport facilities, so that dock workers could be housed at some distance from the dangerous port areas.

John Colville: diary
(*Colville papers*)

22 May 1941

The navy are having a heavy task off Crete and have lost a lot of ships, including *Gloucester* and *Fiji*. I expressed grief to the PM who replied: 'What do you think we build the ships for?' He deprecates the navy's way of treating ships as if they were too precious ever to risk.

Winston S. Churchill: statement
(*Hansard*)

22 May 1941 House of Commons

The Prime Minister (Mr Churchill): This is a somewhat indeterminate moment in the battle for Crete on which to make a statement, and I can only give a very provisional account. Fighting is continuing with intensity, and, although the situation is in hand, the Germans have gained some local successes, at heavy cost. They are using large numbers of airborne and parachute troops, and these are being increased daily. The position at Heraklion is that our troops are still holding the aerodrome, although the Germans are now in what is called occupation of the town, which probably means that they are ensconced in certain buildings in the town. In the Retimo district there is no report of any particular fighting, although an attempt by the enemy to attack an aerodrome early yesterday morning was successfully held. In the Canea-Suda Bay sector heavy enemy air attacks in the early morning of yesterday were followed, in the course of the day, by further parachute landings South-West of Canea, which were heavily engaged by our artillery and machine guns. At Maleme Aerodrome, 10 miles South-West of Canea, it appears that the enemy are now in occupation of the aerodrome and the area to the West of it, but the aerodrome is still under our fire. Elsewhere in this sector the coastal line remains in our hands.

The fighting is going on, deepening in intensity, and will certainly continue for some time. Last night the enemy began to try seaborne landings, but a convoy, making for Crete, was intercepted by our naval forces, and two transports and a number of caiques, Greek boats, which probably contained troops intended for landing operations, were sunk, and an enemy destroyer, which was escorting the convoy, was also sunk. But, during the course of today, very much larger attempts have been made by the enemy to carry an army into Crete, and a convoy of 30 vessels was discerned this morning by our forces, and was presumably attacked by them. My information is not complete to that point. The convoy turned away towards the Islands of the Archipelago, and was being attacked by our destroyers and light forces. I have not received any further information as to what happened, except that there has been a great deal of fighting during the day, with the enemy air forces attacking our ships, and we attacking the convoy. I am sorry to say that I have got no definite information as to the results, but I feel they can hardly be other than satisfactory, in view of the naval forces of which we dispose in the Mediterranean sphere.

Mr A. Bevan (Ebbw Vale): Will the Prime Minister use whatever methods are available to him to convey from the House of Commons, this Sitting Day, our admiration of and confidence in the defenders of Crete?

The Prime Minister: I certainly will. It is a most strange and grim battle that is being fought. Our side have no air, because they have no aerodromes, and not because they have no aeroplanes, and the other side have very little or no artillery or tanks. Neither side has any means of retreat. It is a desperate, grim battle. I certainly will send the good wishes of the House, and the encouragement and approval of the House, to these men who are fighting what is undoubtedly a most important battle which will affect the whole course of the campaign in the Mediterranean.

War Cabinet: minutes
(*Cabinet papers, 65/18*)

22 May 1941
12.30 p.m.

Prime Minister's Room
House of Commons Annexe

CONSCRIPTION FOR NORTHERN IRELAND

The Prime Minister said that he had seen Mr Dulanty[1] that morning. Mr Dulanty had used the usual arguments, and had said that the application of conscription to Northern Ireland might be expected to lead to trouble, or even to bloodshed. He had also argued that, since most of the Protestants in Northern Ireland were serving in the Home Guard, conscription would, in fact, apply to Catholics only. He (the Prime Minister) had said that this was a misapprehension, since conscription would be applied to those serving in the Home Guard.

Mr Dulanty had then enumerated the various ways in which Ireland was giving help to this country, including the facilities for the civil flying-boats at Foynes. He had, however, made it clear that the mention of these facilities was not intended as a threat of their withdrawal if conscription was applied to Northern Ireland.

The Prime Minister said that he had also indicated to Mr Dulanty that the feeling in this country about the attitude of Southern Ireland was very hard and bitter, and that, if that attitude was persisted in, it would lead to a permanent embitterment of feeling after the war. He had promised to report what Mr Dulanty had said to the War Cabinet, but he had not led him to think that the War Cabinet would be much influenced by these representations.

Winston S. Churchill to President Franklin D. Roosevelt
(*Churchill papers, 20/49*)

22 May 1941

1. The Admiralty have asked me to send you the two attached papers 'A' and 'B'. The first is technical, the second speaks for itself.

2. Battle in Crete is severe because, having no airfields within effective range, we cannot bring any Air Force into action either to aid defence or

[1] John Whelan Dulanty, 1883–1955. Secretary, Faculty of Technology, University of Manchester, 1908. Honorary Director of the Irish League of Great Britain (committed to Home Rule) before the First World War. An examiner, Board of Education, 1913. Principal Assistant Secretary, Minister of Munitions, 1917–19 (while Churchill was Minister). CBE, 1918. Assistant Secretary, Treasury, 1920. CB, 1920. Managing Director of Peter Jones, 1921–5. At the request of the Irish Government, became Irish Commissioner for Trade in Great Britain, 1926, and an Irish Delegate at the London Naval Conference, 1936. High Commissioner of the Irish Republic in London, 1930–50; Ambassador, 1950.

protect patrolling squadrons. Two of our cruisers and two destroyers sunk today. We are destroying many of highest-class German troops and have sunk at least one convoy.

3. Yesterday, 21st, *Bismarck, Prinz Eugen* and eight merchant ships located in Bergen. Low clouds prevented air attack. Tonight they have sailed. We have reason to believe that a formidable Atlantic raid is intended. Should we fail to catch them going out, your Navy should surely be able to mark them down for us. *King George V, Prince of Wales, Hood, Repulse* and Aircraft Carrier *Victorious* with ancillary vessels will be on their track. Give us the news and we will finish the job.

Annex A

1. Patrols at present being operated by United States Forces in Areas 1, 2 and 3 are considered to have been of great value. The situation has now, however, materially changed.

(a) U-boats have now started operations to the west of 40° W. in Area I.

(b) Attacks on our trade at an early date by heavy surface units are anticipated.

Area I

U-boat attack.

2. Hitherto our Halifax–United Kingdom convoys have only been escorted to 35° W. It will now be necessary to extend this escort over the whole route. This will entail a considerable reduction in the scale of defence which can be provided for each convoy.

Surface Raider Attack.

Our Battle Fleet is small and therefore the scale of protection we can afford to meet this form of attack is inadequate. It has hitherto been our policy to afford battleship protection to as many convoys as possible from Halifax to 40° W.

3. It would be of great help in meeting the above threats if United States forces operating in Area I could cover the area through which our trade normally passes with the object, firstly, of making Surface Raiders and U-boats feel insecure, secondly, of reporting the positions of enemy units sighted so that our merchant ships can be routed clear and our surface forces bring those of the enemy to action. Air reconnaissance in the vicinity of the convoy would be particularly valuable and generally, the closer the United States forces work to a convoy, the more effective will be their aid.

4. The area in which United States patrols would be of greatest value is Area X and secondary to that is Area Y, as given in attached note.

Area II.

5. In Area II the tracks being followed by United States Forces are being received. These cover the area excellently and a British cruiser has been stationed to follow along in the vicinity of United States forces to act as a killing force.

Area III.

6. This area has recently become very critical as U-boats have spread themselves on a line between Freetown and the N.E. corner of Brazil, and have recently taken heavy toll of our shipping. It is suspected that they receive assistance from the Italian Commercial Air Line, which flies between Brazil and the Cape Verde Islands. It is possible that enemy surface forces may also operate in this area, where there is a considerable amount of shipping.

7. The area in which United States forces would be of most assistance in fulfilling the above objects is Area Z given on attached note. It is intended shortly to station a cruiser as an attacking force in the vicinity of the United States forces in this area.[1]

War Cabinet, Defence Committee (Operations): minutes
(*Cabinet papers, 69/2*)

23 May 1941 10 Downing Street
12 noon

The Prime Minister read out the latest telegrams from Crete. The situation appeared to be in hand except for the Maleme area where the Germans had forced a lodgment and airborne landings were taking place. It was unfortunate that the defenders had not been able to stamp out the parachutists in this area and it was essential that the German lodgment west of Canea should be obliterated by vigorous counter-attacks as soon as possible. The Fleet could not protect the island indefinitely from seaborne landings and if the situation could be fully restored while the power of the Fleet lasted, then the enemy would be faced with the prospect of beginning all over again.

General Freyberg should throw in all the available reserves, including if necessary the reinforcements to be landed that night, in an effort to restore the situation at the western end of the island before it was too late.

The Prime Minister said that as the situation in the North-Western Approaches seemed easier he was in favour of the proposal to transfer a squadron of Beaufighters to the Middle East, whose primary task should be the protection of the Fleet when at sea.

[1] Annex 'B' was a list of ships sunk West of 26 degrees West between March 31 and May 20, thirty-four in all. Among their cargoes were oil, grain, wheat, steel and paper. On the Belgian merchantman *Ville de Liège*, sunk on April 12, 2,862,600 rounds of Small Arms Ammunition, 74 tons of trucks and 20 aero engines had been lost. On the *Darlington Court* (sunk with ten other merchant ships on May 20), five aircraft and a thousand machine guns had been lost.

UNITED STATES OPINION

The Prime Minister read out a telegram which he had sent to President Roosevelt with the object of bringing along American opinion.

The Committee expressed their approval of the terms of this telegram.

The Prime Minister then referred to a suggestion which had been made by Lord Beaverbrook that the Foreign Secretary and the Service Ministers should give weekly interviews to American Press Correspondents. He would like time to consider this suggestion, but thought that weekly conferences would impose a considerable strain on those Ministers. There would, moreover, be the danger that the American Correspondents would get varying impressions from these different interviews.

SYRIA

The Prime Minister read out General Wavell's reply to the telegram which had been sent after the discussion at a previous meeting of the Defence Committee. He was somewhat surprised to see that General Wavell referred to Crete as a 'commitment', when the island was, in reality, part of this outpost position in the Eastern Mediterranean.

Mr Eden referred to a telegram from General Smuts on the situation in Syria in which he expressed the view that the threat to Egypt from this direction was more dangerous than that from the Libyan desert where physical conditions were against a very large scale attack.

The Prime Minister said that he did not entirely agree with this view; the threat from Libya was imminent, whereas any threat from Syria would take some time to develop. The Germans could not build up a large army in Syria without the assistance, or at least the connivance, of the Turks.

Winston S. Churchill to General Wavell

(*Churchill papers, 20/49*)

23 May 1941

1. Your 0/66385. Many thanks for your telegram. These are very hard times and we must all do our best to help each other.

2. Crete battle must be won. Even if enemy secure good lodgments fighting must be maintained indefinitely in the island, thus keeping enemy main striking force tied down to the task. This will at least give you time to mobilize tigercubs and dominate situation Western Desert. While it lasts it also protects Cyprus. Hope you will reinforce Crete every night to fullest extent. Is it not possible to send more tanks and thus reconquer any captured aerodrome? Enemy's exercises and losses in highest class troops must be very severe. He cannot keep it up forever.

3. Syria. It is your views that weigh with us and not those of Free French. You had better have de Gaulle close to you. Let me know if I can help you with him. We cannot have Crete battle spoiled for the sake of Syria. Therefore inferior methods may be the only ones open at the moment.

4. Iraq. We hope Habforce[1] will soon enter Baghdad establishing Regent there.

5. Following for General Freyberg from me: 'The whole world is watching your splendid battle, on which great events turn.'

Winston S. Churchill to General Ismay, for Chiefs of Staff Committee
(*Churchill papers, 20/36*)

23 May 1941
Secret
Action this Day

Whatever arrangements were made between Admiral Cunningham and the French Admiral at Alexandria are superseded by Vichy action in destroying basis of Armistice terms. We should now seize the French ships by complete surprise, killing without hesitation all who withstand us. It should be possible to cut off a good many of the crews while on shore. Action must be carefully concerted, but should not be delayed beyond a few days. These vessels, with all their faults, will form indispensable replacement reserve for our Mediterranean fleet. No other way of repairing losses can be seen.

Please give this matter your consideration and report to me tomorrow.

Sir Alexander Cadogan: diary
(*'The Diaries of Sir Alexander Cadogan, OM, 1938-1945'*)

23 May 1941

I caught Defence Cttee as they were breaking up at 1 with a problem of whether to bomb a German raider slinking along N Spanish coast making for Bordeaux, within territorial waters. Thank Heaven, Winston decided it wasn't worth the risk.

[1] The British and Indian military force that had lifted the siege of Habbaniya, forty-five miles west of Baghdad.

John Colville: diary
(*Colville papers*)

23 May 1941

Drove my own car to Chequers. PM arrived later from a tank inspection, bringing with him David Margesson, Pownall[1] (the new VCIGS), Macready (ACIGS), Averell Harriman, Jack Churchill and Ismay.

An entirely male party. The PM laments very strongly that the tanks which he asked Wavell to send to Crete were not sent. They might have made the whole difference to the battle.

Winston S. Churchill: recollection
(*Churchill papers, 4/219*)

24 May 1941
3 a.m.

Chequers

THE SEARCH FOR THE 'BISMARCK'

There was however nothing for me to do and I went to bed, asking not to be called on the naval affair until I rang. I was so well tired out with other work that I slept soundly. I had complete confidence in the First Sea Lord, Admiral Pound, and liked the way he was playing the hand.

I awoke in peaceful Chequers about 9 a.m. with all that strange thrill which one feels at the beginning of a day in which great news is expected, good, or bad.

General Ismay: recollection
(*'Memoirs of General the Lord Ismay'*)

24 May 1941

The situation in Crete was critical, but the conversation at Chequers that night was confined almost exclusively to the impending clash at sea, and we sat up even later than usual, on the chance of getting some news. But none came, and at last we went to bed. I had only just dropped off to sleep – or so

[1] Henry Royds Pownall, 1887–1961. Entered the Army, 1906. On active service 1914–18 (DSO, Military Cross). Director of Military Operations and Intelligence, War Office, 1938–9. Chief of the General Staff, British Expeditionary Force, 1939–40. Knighted, 1940. Inspector-General of the Home Guard, 1940. General Officer Commanding the British Troops in Northern Ireland, 1940–1. Vice-Chief of the Imperial General Staff, 1941. Commander-in-Chief, Far East, 1941–2. General Officer Commanding the Forces in Ceylon, 1942–3. General Officer Commanding-in-Chief, Persia, 1943. Chief of Staff to the Supreme Allied Commander, South-East Asia (Lord Mountbatten), 1943–4. Chief Commissioner, St John's Ambulance Brigade, 1947–9. Chancellor, Order of St John, 1951. Churchill's principal helper on the military aspects of his war memoirs, 1945–55.

it seemed – when I heard the sounds of conversation in Averell's room, which was opposite mine. I jumped out of bed to see the Prime Minister's back view disappearing down the corridor. Averell's door was ajar and I went in. He looked puzzled. 'Winston has just been in and told me that the *Hood* has blown up but that he reckons we have got the *Bismarck* for certain.'

Vic Oliver:[1] *recollection*
('Mr Showbusiness')

24 May 1941 [Chequers]

Mr Churchill came down from his study looking inexpressibly grim. We guessed that yet another disaster had occurred, though we knew it was no use to ask him what it was. Mrs Churchill quietly poured him a glass of port, and, thinking it would relieve the tension, suggested I play something on the piano. I was about to start on *Lily of Laguna*, but immediately checked myself, feeling that a popular song would be out of place; so after a few seconds' reflection I decided on Beethoven's *Appassionata* sonata, but I had played only a few bars when Mr Churchill rose to his feet and thundered: 'Stop! Don't play that!'

We were all surprised, for it was the first time he had raised his voice to me. I turned round, puzzled, and asked: 'What's the trouble – don't you like it?'

'Nobody plays the *Dead March* in my house,' he said. We all laughed. 'It's not the *Dead March,*' I said. 'it's the *Appassionata* sonata.'

Mr Churchill was notoriously unmusical. He glowered again. 'You can say what you like,' he said, 'I know it's the funeral march.'

I turned back to the piano. 'But surely, sir, you can tell the difference between this . . .' and I struck a few chords of the *Appassionata*, 'and . . .'

Before I had time to finish, Mr Churchill thundered again: 'Stop it! Stop it! I want no *Dead March*, I tell you.'

Sarah rushed over to the piano and told me to play his favourite song instead. I did so, and the moment passed. Next day it was announced that HMS *Hood* had been sunk with heavy loss of life.[2]

[1] Victor Samek, 1898–1964. Born in Austria, the son of Baron Victor von Samek. Educated at the University of Vienna. Relinquished his father's title, 1922. A concert pianist, he worked in the United States from 1933 to 1935 under the stage name Vic Oliver; subsequently he worked on the stage and in revues in Britain and America. Married, as his third wife, Sarah Churchill, 1936 (from whom he obtained a divorce in 1945).

[2] At 6 a.m. on 24 May 1941 a shell from the *Bismarck* passed through the light armour of the *Hood* and exploded in the stern magazine. The ship blew up and sank almost immediately. Of the 1,419 men in ship's complement (95 officers and 1,324 ratings and Royal Marines) only three were saved.

Winston S. Churchill to Anthony Eden
(*Churchill papers, 20/36*)

24 May 1941

MEMORANDUM BY MAYNARD KEYNES ON BRITISH WAR AIMS

As you know, I am very doubtful about the utility of attempts to plan the peace before we have won the war, but there seems nothing in all this that will prejudice the future.

I fear that para. 13, though quite true, will not attract the Germans and will anger some of our own people. I should not have thought it was a very good moment to launch this economic manifesto when all our minds are concentrated, or ought to be concentrated, upon the struggle. I do not think anyone knows what will happen when we get to the end of the war, and personally I am holding myself uncommitted.

P.S. I thank you very much for showing it to me.

War Cabinet: minutes
(*Cabinet papers, 65/18*)

24 May 1941 Chequers
12 noon

APPLICATION OF CONSCRIPTION TO NORTHERN IRELAND

Mr Andrews[1] said that a successful Meeting of the Ulster Unionist Council had been held the previous day. The Council had been unanimously in favour of conscription in Northern Ireland. Although they appreciated that there were difficulties, they had given him (Mr Andrews) a free hand to tell Mr Churchill to do what His Majesty's Government in the United Kingdom thought was best for the Empire. They were anxious to help in every possible way.

Mr Churchill said that he was grateful for this approach to the subject. He suggested that discussion should proceed on the basis that it was the desire of the majority of the Parliament and the people of Northern Ireland that

[1] John Miller Andrews, 1871–1956. Member of the County Council of Down (Northern Ireland), 1917–37. Unionist Member of the Northern Ireland Parliament, 1921–53. President of the Ulster Unionist Labour Association. Minister of Labour in the Northern Ireland Cabinet, 1921–37. President of the Belfast Chamber of Commerce, 1936. Minister of Finance Northern Ireland, 1937–40. Prime Minister of Northern Ireland, 1940–43. Companion of Honour, 1943.

conscription should be applied to Northern Ireland, and that the difficulties inherent in this question should be examined on that basis.

The Prime Minister said that although we were not publicly committed to applying conscription to Northern Ireland, yet it was known that the matter had been under consideration, and any decision not to proceed with the matter would, he thought, be regarded as a recoil on our part, and was a serious matter. For the moment he did not wish to reach a decision whether or not any statement should be made in Parliament the following Thursday. The best course would be to defer taking any decision, and to await Sir John Maffey's[1] suggestions. In the meantime, it was of the utmost importance that no hint of the upshot of the afternoon's discussion should be allowed to become known.[2]

Winston S. Churchill to Sir Andrew Duncan
(*Churchill papers, 20/36*)

24 May 1941

Your minute of April 16 refers to the reduction in the average hours worked by production machine tools to 61 per week last December and mentions the prospect of an improvement with the increasing hours of daylight.

I trust that fully manned double-shifts have been or can now be introduced in a large number of your factories. The chief obstacle may presumably be the shortage of labour. If this is so perhaps you could discuss the matter with the Minister of Labour and report to me further.

I am sending a copy of this minute to the Minister of Labour and similar minutes to the First Lord and the Minister of Aircraft Production.

[1] John Loader Maffey, 1877–1969. Entered the Indian Civil Service, 1899. Private Secretary to the Viceroy, 1916. Chief Political Officer with the forces in Afghanistan, 1919. Knighted, 1921. Chief Commissioner, North-West Frontier Province, 1921–3. Governor-General of the Sudan, 1926–33. Permanent Under-Secretary of State at the Colonial Office, 1933–7) United Kingdom Representative in Eire, 1939–49. Created Baron Rugby, 1947.

[2] For political reasons – the Irish Republic remaining neutral – conscription was never introduced in Northern Ireland.

Winston S. Churchill to General Chiang Kai-shek[1]
(*Churchill papers, 20/39*)

24 May 1941

Your generous message gives me great personal encouragement[2] and I heartily reciprocate your good wishes.

My fellow-countrymen and I have followed not only with sympathy but with admiration the courageous struggle which the Chinese people have waged for so long. We realize how much their steadfastness owes to your dynamic personality and leadership. We know that they will endure, like ourselves, all perils and hardships till the object of these sacrifices is attained.

In our different spheres our two countries are both fighting in the ranks of freedom against tyranny and aggression. Your cause, too, is that of democracy. Have no doubt, therefore, that we shall do all we can to help China to maintain her independence.

The cause which inspires both our nations is just. We need not fear the outcome.

Winston S. Churchill to Peter Fraser
(*Premier papers, 3/109*)

24 May 1941
Most Immediate
Most Secret

I sympathize with and share your feelings of anxiety, but I cannot accept the implications of the final sentence of your telegram. Suggestion that we are

[1] Chiang Kai-shek, 1887–1975. Joined Sun Yat-sen's revolutionary party in 1907. A member of the revolutionary army, Shanghai, on the outbreak of the Chinese revolution, 1911. Served at Chinese General Headquarters, 1918–20. Visited the Soviet Union to study its military and social systems, 1923. Founder and Principal, Whampoa Military Academy, Canton, 1924. Member of the General Executive Committee of the Kuomintang, 1926. Commander-in-Chief, Northern Expeditionary Forces, 1926–8. Chairman of State, and Generalissimo of all fighting services, 1928–31. Resigned, 1931. Director-General of the Kuomintang Party, 1938. Chairman of the Supreme National Defence Council, 1939–47. President of the Republic of China, 1948. Retired, 1948. Formed a Government on behalf of the Chinese Nationalists in Formosa (Taiwan), 1949.

[2] In the course of his message, which was sent from Chungking, Chiang Kai-shek wrote: 'I should like to thank you warmly for your Government's good-will towards China as expressed by agreement recently signed at Washington for the establishment of stabilization fund. I am grateful also for other tangible evidences of Great Britain's wish to help China in her struggle against aggression. With the keenest interest I watch the battles now being fought out in the Atlantic and Mediterranean. Like you I have no doubts about their ultimate result, and I share to the full your undaunted confidence that the cause of the great democracies for which China has now been fighting for four years, will triumph. I feel great admiration for you, both as a statesman and a military strategist, and I firmly believe that under your staunch and fearless leadership the British Empire will be able not only to frustrate aggression in Europe but to bring permanent peace to Europe and Asia alike. This is indeed our common aim. We shall achieve it.' (Chungking telegram No. 244, sent 20 May 1941, *Churchill papers, 20/39*)

holding back air assistance for the sake of the United Kingdom is really quite unfounded. There are ample aircraft in the United Kingdom, and we have been sending them as fast as possible by every route and by every method. As far as the Navy is concerned, Admiral Cunningham has been directed by the Admiralty to give the strongest support to Crete, in spite of his losses. On the question of military reinforcements, you should address yourself to General Wavell, who has received similar instructions. I have done and will continue to do everything in my power. I hope soon to see you in England.

John Colville: diary
(*Colville papers*)

25 May 1941 Chequers

Bismarck has been lost during the hours of darkness. A day of fearful gloom ensured. The PM cannot understand why the *Prince of Wales* did not press home her attack yesterday and keeps on saying it is the worst thing since Trowbridge turned away from the *Goeben* in 1914.[1] He rated the First Lord and the First Sea Lord continuously, both on this account and because in the Mediterranean the Navy shows, he thinks, a tendency to shirk its task of preventing a seaborne landing in Crete since Cunningham fears severe losses from bombing. The PM's line is that Cunningham must be made to take every risk: the loss of half the Mediterranean fleet would be worth while in order to save Crete.

The PM cheered up at dinner, which was a family affair (by which I mean Ismay, Tommy, Jack Churchill, self and the Prof, who is soon to be a peer). He criticized Wavell very heavily about tanks for Crete and expressed amazement that W should have thought he could get reinforcements ashore after the fight had begun. He considered the Middle East had been very badly managed. If he could be put in command there he would gladly lay down his present office – yes and even renounce cigars and alcohol!

After dinner we had a film: *Western Union* (with Red Indians and all the Wild West trappings)[2] and the PM's favourite *March of Time*.[3]

[1] The German battle cruiser which, together with the light cruiser *Breslau*, evaded a naval search instituted by Churchill in August 1914 and reached the safety of the Black Sea where, under German command, but flying the Turkish colours, she bombarded several Russian Black Sea ports, precipitating Turkey's early entry into the war on the side of Germany.

[2] In this film outlaws attempt to thwart the Western Union in the last leg of their expansion westward in the 1860s. One outlaw goes straight and works for the telegraph company; his brother leads the renegades. Directed by Fritz Lang. Randolph Scott played the hero.

[3] The *March of Time* was a series of newsreels usually on a single subject lasting from sixteen to twenty minutes. The most famous, produced in 1938, *Inside Nazi Germany*, was the first commercially released anti-Nazi American picture. It began with genuine footage shot in Germany, but also contained several re-enactments (the Catholic nuns shown in prison were cleaners working in the film company's New York office).

With a final comment that these three days had been the worst yet, he went to bed at 2.15 a.m. There is, however, still a chance that the *Ark Royal* and the *Rodney* may catch the *Bismarck* before she reaches the French port for which she seems to be making.

Winston S, Churchill to Sir John Reith
(Churchill Papers, 20/36)

25 May 1941

REALLOCATION OF ACCOMMODATION IN THE PALACE OF WESTMINSTER

More than a week has passed and this matter must be settled on Monday (tomorrow) at latest.

Pray report to me what happens, and whether you require my assistance in expediting matters. What is it proposed to do with the House of Lords Chamber to fit it for the House of Commons? How long is the fitting of these two Chambers estimated to take? A week ago you talked of about a fortnight. Have all the plans been made? Has work on the fittings actually begun? I was hoping we could get in the week after next. Have all the necessary repairs been made to the libraries, dining-rooms, &c., at the House of Commons?

Winston S. Churchill to Herbert Morrison
(*Churchill papers, 20/36*)

25 May 1941

1. The quotation attached has no bearing on the present situation, except in so far as it favours decided action. We irritated the Irish, but did not push our plan through our fear of their objections. We must at all costs avoid having toyed with the subject and giving it up through weakness.[1]

2. Northern Ireland is a self-governing entity which has formally expressed its desire by a majority for the enactment of Conscription, and there is no question of enforcing it in Southern Ireland.

3. We have nearly 100,000 men in Northern Ireland now in order to defend Southern Ireland, and there will be no need to increase this number in consequence of Conscription.

Many thanks, however, for showing me the extract.

[1] On 23 March 1941 Churchill had minuted to the Dominions Secretary, Viscount Cranborne: 'I have given directions for the screw to be tightened steadily in accordance with the policy settled three months ago'. (*Premier papers, 3/127/2*) Confronted with further delays in intercepting freight to Ireland, 14 April 1941 Churchill minuted to Sir Edward Bridges: 'Naturally I am in favour of pursuing these matters and inflicting censure and punishment where negligence or laxity has occurred.' (Churchill Cabinet Office series minute, C.40/1, *Churchill papers, 20/36*)

Winston S. Churchill to Lord Beaverbrook
(*Premier papers, 3/298/2*)

25 May 1941

Will you kindly draw up a proposal for a large infusion of civilian management into the rearward services of the Middle East Army, both as affecting mechanical vehicles and aircraft; or are you satisfied that Air Marshal Dawson[1] will manage the aircraft part of it all right? In drawing up this project you should state the number of civilian experts you think should be employed, and also the names of the principal people. My idea is that General Haining, who is supposed to be very clever at military organization, should be a kind of Intendent-General at the back of the Middle East front, and should take this burden off the Commander-in-Chief. Do you know General Haining, and what do you think of him? As at present arranged, he will start next week, so that what has to be done must be done quickly.[2] Please speak to me after luncheon.

Winston S. Churchill to the Polish Ambassador[3]
(*Churchill papers, 20/21*)

25 May 1941

My dear Ambassador,

After my broadcast to the people of Poland I received the most gratifying letter from representatives of Polish cultural, social and professional organizations at present in Great Britain. I should be very grateful if Your Excellency would let the senders of this letter know how much I value their words.

[1] Grahame George Dawson, 1895-1944. A sapper, Royal Engineers, 1914. Sub-Lieutenant, Royal Naval Air Service, 1915 (Dunkirk, Dardanelles). Captain, Royal Air Force, 1918. An advanced engineering specialist. In charge of the RAF School of Aeronautical Engineering, 1934-38. Engineer, Staff Duties, Headquarters Fighter Command, 1939-40. Director of Canadian and American Production, Ministry of Aircraft Production, 1940-41, commanding the Atlantic Ferry Organization (ATFERO), 1940-41. Headquarters Staff, Middle East Command, 1941-43 (CBE for distinguished service); Mediterranean Command, 1943-44; Mediterranean Allied Air Forces, 1944 . Killed while on his way to the Far East in the air accident (in which Air Vice-Marshal Leigh Mallory died) on 14 November 1944.

[2] General Sir Robert Haining did become Intendant-General, Middle East, serving as such until his retirement from active service in 1942.

[3] Edward Raczyński, 1891–1993. Educated at Krakow and Leipzig Universities, and at the London School of Economics. Entered the Polish Ministry of Foreign Affairs, 1919. Polish Minister to the League of Nations and Polish Delegate to the Disarmament Conference, 1932–4; Ambassador to London, 1934–45. Acting Polish Minister for Foreign Affairs (in London), 1941–2; Minister of State for Foreign Affairs in General Sikorski's Cabinet, London, 1942–3. Chairman of the Polish Research Centre, London, 1940–67. President of the Polish Government in Exile from 1979 until his death.

I am happy to think that the sympathy and common purpose which now unite us in war will remain a lasting bond between our two countries in the brighter days to come.

Yrs sincerely
Winston S. Churchill

Hugh Dalton: diary
(*'The Second World War Diary of Hugh Dalton, 1940-45'*)

26 May 1941

At Cabinet the Beaver[1] makes a row about propaganda to America. We should give the US more news. General sense of gloom. A convoy has been sunk in the Atlantic; we have had heavy naval losses in the Mediterranean (two cruisers and four destroyers sunk and two battleships hit in the 'sea defile' north of Crete); the *Hood* sunk and the *Bismarck* still at large.

Thus, says the PM, the Germans have established a 'unit superiority' over us. This is the most injurious and distressing naval incident since we missed the *Goeben*.

John Colville: diary
(*Colville papers*)

26 May 1941

Left Chequers at 12.30, following the PM's cortege in my car at break-neck speed. The Cretan situation seems slightly better and at the PM's instigation the Chiefs of Staff have sent a signal to the C-in-C that no risk can be considered too heavy to win the battle.

Rowan,[2] our new Private Secretary from the Treasury, arrived.

[1] Lord Beaverbrook.

[2] Thomas Leslie Rowan, 1908–1972. Entered the Colonial Office, 1930; Treasury, 1933. Assistant Private Secretary to the Chancellor of the Exchequer (Neville Chamberlain), 1934–37. Captained England at Hockey, 1937, 1938 and 1947. Assistant (later Principal) Private Secretary to the Prime Minister (Churchill), 1941–45; to Clement Attlee, 1945–47. Second Secretary, Treasury, 1947–49 and 1951–58. Knighted, 1949. Economic Minister, British Embassy, Washington, 1949–51. Chairman, Vickers Ltd, 1967–71. Chairman of the British Council, 1971–72.

Anthony Eden to Winston S. Churchill
(*Churchill papers, 20/26*)

26 May 1941 Foreign Office

My dear Winston,

This is a bad day; but tomorrow – Baghdad will be entered, *Bismarck* sunk.[1]

On some date the war will be won, and you will have done more than any man in history to win it.

No answer

Yours
Anthony

War Cabinet: minutes
(*Cabinet papers, 65/18*)

26 May 1941 10 Downing Street
5 p.m.

UNITED STATES ECONOMIC ASSISTANCE TO THE VICHY GOVERNMENT

The Prime Minister doubted whether the consignments which the United States Government proposed to send were of great consequence. It had long been the policy of the United States Government to combine inducements to the Vichy Government with threats of more drastic action. On the whole, he was not disposed to take a very stiff line with the United States Government on this matter.

Winston S. Churchill to the Defence Committee
(*Churchill papers, 20/36*)

26 May 1941

ITALIAN COAST DEFENCES AT TOBRUK, BENGHAZI, BARDIA, MASSAWA AND KISMAYU[2]

It is interesting to see how very much exaggerated were the estimates formed by our Intelligence Service of the coastal defences of the various Italian ports that have now come into our hands. I have long suspected that the Italians, and probably the French also, like to have it thought that their

[1] The *Bismarck* was sunk on 27 May 1941; Rashid Ali fled from Baghdad four days later.

[2] Churchill circulated the figures which showed, port by port, an Intelligence estimate of 144 to 147 guns, as against a total of 84 reported after capture. The figures were: Tobruk (estimate, 26; after capture, 15), Benghazi (estimate, 37; after capture, 12), Bardia (estimate, 7 to 9; after capture 5), Massawa (estimate, 64; after capture 29), Kismayu (estimate, 10 to 11; after capture 23).

seaward defences are on a very heavy scale. We were told, for instance, that Massawa was defended by four 8-inch, ten large calibre, and sixteen 6-inch, total 30 high-powered guns. Not one existed. In the light of this exposure, the Intelligence Branches of the different Departments should carefully re-examine their scale of foreign coastal fortifications, which otherwise may prove to be a deterrent upon action.

Winston S. Churchill to William Morrison[1]

(*Churchill papers, 20/36*)

26 May 1941

COMMUNICATIONS WITH ADMIRALTY HOUSE, PLYMOUTH

It was not only the routes about which I complained, but the extraordinary difficulty in getting contacts, particularly on the Scrambler. The communications between the Admiralty and these naval ports ought to be kept in the highest order. Pray let me have a report of what you will do.

Winston S. Churchill to A. V. Alexander and Admiral Pound

(*Churchill papers, 20/36*)

26 May 1941

As soon as Jaguar[2] is completed, His Majesty's Government must be in a position if they think fit to intercept an escorted French convoy passing through the Straits of Gibraltar.

[1] William Shepherd Morrison, 1893–1961. Known as 'Shakes' Morrison. Served in the Royal Field Artillery, France, 1914–18 (wounded, Military Cross, despatches three times). Captain, 1919. President of the Edinburgh University Union, 1920. Called to the Bar, 1923. Conservative MP for Cirencester and Tewkesbury, 1929–59. King's Counsel, 1934. Financial Secretary to the Treasury, 1935–6. Privy Councillor, 1936. Minister of Agriculture and Fisheries, 1936–9. Chancellor of the Duchy of Lancaster and Minister of Food, 1939–40. Postmaster-General, 1940–3. Minister of Town and Country Planning, 1943–5. Speaker of the House of Commons, 1951–9. Created Viscount Dunrossil, 1959. Governor-General of Australia, 1960–1. A member of the Other Club from 1936. One of 'Shakes' Morrison's eight brothers, Alexander, had been killed in action at Loos in 1915.

[2] The transfer by aircraft carrier of 140 fighter aircraft through the Mediterranean to Malta and Egypt.

Sir Alexander Cadogan: diary
(*'The Diaries of Sir Alexander Cadogan'*)

26 May 1941

Cabinet at 5. Poor Winston very gloomy – due of course to *Hood* and Crete. In latter place things look black. Only ⅓rd of our Mediterranean Fleet undamaged, and once Germans start reinforcing by sea, we're done. Message came in that our carrier aircraft had been airborne from 3 till 5 without contacting *Bismarck*.

A tiresome and most acrimonious discussion about publication of figures of recent sinking of convoy. Cabinet (including A,[1] against my advice) in favour. Winston furious, and Cabinet climbed down to him. Then a discussion on conscription in Ulster. Cabinet again against Winston (rightly). He made passionate appeal: to back down now, in face of clamour, would show that the mainspring of resolution was broken &c., &c., That is all very well. But what he does is to jump to decisions – ill-considered – and then say that it shows weakness to recede. It shows stupidity to jump to them. A very gloomy and unpleasant Cabinet. Max was on edge and very pugnacious (on the surface). Bevin was almost the only supporter of the PM on Ulster. But he made a most timid and rambling statement. I wrote to A, 'Bevin's spiritual home is Delphi.' Poor Winston will recover all right if we get a bit of good news. Tonight he was almost throwing his hand in, but there is a bit of the histrionic art in that.

Winston S. Churchill to General Wavell
(*Churchill papers, 20/39*)

27 May 1941
sent 00.50 a.m.

Hope you are preparing your desert stroke and that Tobruk will not be idle.

Winston S. Churchill to General Freyberg
(*Churchill papers, 20/39*)

27 May 1941
sent 1.35 a.m.

Your glorious defence commands admiration in every land. We know enemy is hard pressed. All aid in our power is being sent.

[1] Anthony Eden.

Winston S. Churchill to General Wavell,
Admiral Cunningham and Air Chief Marshal Longmore
(*Premier papers, 3/109*)

27 May 1941
sent 2 a.m.

Victory in Crete essential at this turning point in the war. Keep hurling in all aid you can.

War Cabinet: minutes
(*Cabinet papers, 65/18*)

27 May 1941
10.30 a.m.

Prime Minister's Room
House of Commons Annexe

The Prime Minister informed the War Cabinet of the latest situation in regard to the *Bismarck*. She had received four hits from torpedoes, and was virtually stationary. Strong naval forces were near at hand. There was every hope that we should soon receive information that this enemy ship had been destroyed.

NORTHERN IRELAND: CONSCRIPTION

The Prime Minister said that, after the discussion at the last Meeting of the War Cabinet, he had come to the conclusion that the best plan would be to include in the statement which he was proposing to make that morning in the House on the naval battle and on the fighting in Crete, a short statement on the following lines: He would refer to the answer which he had given in the House on the 20th May that this question had for some time past engaged the attention of His Majesty's Government and that he hoped to make a statement about it in the present week; he would say that various enquiries had been made and that His Majesty's Government had now come to the conclusion that, although there could be no dispute about our rights, or about the merits, it would be more trouble than it was worth to apply conscription to Northern Ireland.

While he regretted that it should be necessary to reach this conclusion, he felt that it was best to dispose of the matter in this way.

The War Cabinet –

Approved the Prime Minister's suggestion to deal with the matter on these lines.

CRETE[1]

The Prime Minister read to the War Cabinet a telegram (No. 0/67710 dated 26th May) from General Wavell to the Chief of the Imperial General Staff in regard to the situation in Crete. This telegram stated that General Wavell had discussed the situation with Admiral Cunningham and Air Marshal Tedder and General Blamey, the New Zealand Prime Minister also being present. General Wavell said that the present programme of land reinforcements during the next few days could not be increased without inadmissable loss of warships. He had received a telegram from General Freyberg which stated that the limit of endurance had been reached by the troops and that the situation was hopeless. To this telegram General Wavell had replied making certain suggestions for holding the situation.

A further telegram (No. 0/67750) of the same date from General Wavell stated that our front on the west of Canea had broken and our troops were coming back in disorder. Casualties had been heavy. Efforts were being made to stabilize the position temporarily.

The Prime Minister said that all chances of winning the battle in Crete now appeared to have gone and we should have to face the prospect of the loss of most of our forces there. There was no action that we in this country could take in regard to the matter.

The Prime Minister added that our submarines in the Mediterranean had achieved some remarkable sinkings, the *Upholder* had claimed to have sunk the *Conti Grandi* and three other merchant ships whilst the *Urchin* and another submarine had accounted for 21,000 tons of enemy shipping.

The Prime Minister added that he proposed in his statement in the House that morning on the situation in Crete to say that hard fighting was continuing in Crete, and to emphasize the advantage which the enemy held by having command of the air.

The War Cabinet took note of the above statement.

Winston S. Churchill to President Franklin D. Roosevelt
(*Foreign Office papers, 954/29*)

27 May 1941
sent 2.15 p.m.

I have not yet thanked you for your message about General Arnold's training proposals and the provision of small aircraft-carriers. All this will be most helpful.

[1] Because of the particular secrecy of this item it was not recorded in the regular minutes of the meeting, but in the War Cabinet Confidential Annex (*Cabinet papers, 65/22*).

Winston S. Churchill: Oral Answers
(*Hansard*)

27 May 1941 House of Commons

Mr Gallacher asked the Prime Minister why Rudolf Hess is being treated as a prisoner of war in view of the fact that he has no rank or status in the German army?

The Prime Minister (Mr Churchill): The answer is because, in the opinion of His Majesty's Government, this is the most convenient and appropriate classification for the man in question at the present time.

Mr Gallacher: In view of all the circumstances surrounding this case, would it not be desirable to put this man on trial as an alien entering this country without a passport or as a German spy in a military uniform, or are the Government afraid to do that?

The Prime Minister: I think that we must be the judges of what is the best method to adopt. I think that the House, better than the hon. Gentleman, can judge whether we are afraid or not.

Winston S. Churchill: statement
(*Hansard*)

27 May 1941 House of Commons

WAR SITUATION

Mr Lees-Smith: May I ask the Prime Minister whether he has any statement to make on the course of the war?

The Prime Minister: Yes, Sir. The battle in Crete has now lasted for a week. During the whole of this time our troops have been subjected to an intense and continuous scale of air attack, to which, owing to the geographical conditions, our Air Forces have been able to make only a very limited, though very gallant, counterblast. The fighting has been most bitter and severe, and the enemy's losses up to the present have been much heavier than ours. We have not, however, been able to prevent further descents of airborne German reinforcements, and the enemy's attack and the weight of this attack has grown from day to day. The battle has swayed backwards and forwards with indescribable fury at Canea and equally fiercely, though on a smaller scale, at Retimo and Heraklion. Reinforcements of men and supplies have reached and are reaching General Freyberg's Forces, and at the moment at which I am speaking the issue of their magnificent resistance hangs in the balance.

So far, the Royal Navy have prevented any landing of a seaborne expedition, although a few shiploads of troops in caiques may have slipped through. Very heavy losses have been inflicted by our submarines, cruisers and destroyers upon the transports and the small Greek ships. It is not possible to state with accuracy how many thousands of enemy troops have been drowned, but the losses have been very heavy. The services rendered by the Navy in the defence of Crete have not been discharged without heavy losses to them. Our Fleet has been compelled to operate constantly without air protection within effective bombing range of the enemy airfields. Claims even more exaggerated than usual have been made by the German and Italian wireless, which it has hitherto not been thought expedient to contradict. I may state, however, that we have lost the cruisers *Gloucester* and *Fiji* and the destroyers *Juno, Greyhound, Kelly* and *Kashmir,* by far the greater part of their crews having been saved. Two battleships and several other cruisers have been damaged, though not seriously, either by hits or near misses, but all will soon be in action again, and some are already at sea. The Mediterranean Fleet is today relatively stronger, compared to the Italian Navy, than it was before the Battle of Cape Matapan. There is no question whatever of our naval position in the Eastern Mediterranean having been prejudicially affected. However the decision of the battle may go, the stubborn defence of Crete, one of the important outposts of Egypt, will always rank high in the military and naval annals of the British Empire.

In Iraq, our position has been largely re-established, and the prospects have greatly improved. There have been no further adverse developments in Syria. In Abyssinia, the daily Italian surrenders continue, many thousands of prisoners and masses of equipment being taken.

While this drama has been enacted in the Eastern Mediterranean, another episode of an arresting character has been in progress in the Northern waters of the Atlantic Ocean. On Wednesday of last week, 21st May, the new German battleship, the *Bismarck,* accompanied by the new eight-inch-gun cruiser *Prinz Eugen,* were discovered by our air reconnaisance at Bergen, and on Thursday, 22nd May, it was known that they had left. Many arrangements were made to intercept them should they attempt, as seemed probable, to break out into the Atlantic Ocean with a view to striking at our convoys from the United States. During the night of 23rd to 24th our cruisers got into visual contact with them as they were passing through the Denmark Strait between Iceland and Greenland. At dawn on Saturday morning the *Prince of Wales* and the *Hood* intercepted the two enemy vessels. I have no detailed account of the action, because events have been moving so rapidly, but the *Hood* was struck at about 23,000 yards by a shell which penetrated into one of her magazines, and blew up, leaving only very few survivors. This splendid vessel, designed 23 years ago, is a serious loss to the Royal Navy, and even more so is the loss of the men and officers who manned her.

During the whole of Saturday our ships remained in touch with the *Bismarck* and her consort. In the night aircraft of the Fleet Air Arm from the *Victorious* struck the *Bismarck* with a torpedo, and arrangements were made for effective battle at dawn yesterday morning, but as the night wore on the weather deteriorated, the visibility decreased, and the *Bismarck*, by making a sharp turn, shook off the pursuit. I do not know what has happened to the *Prinz Eugen*, but measures are being taken in respect of her. Yesterday, shortly before midday, a Catalina aircraft – one of the considerable number of these very far-ranging scouting aeroplanes which have been sent to us by the United States – picked up the *Bismarck*, and it was seen that she was apparently making for the French ports – Brest or Saint Nazaire. On this, further rapid dispositions were made by the Admiralty and by the Commander-in-Chief, and, of course, I may say that the moment the *Bismarck* was known to be at sea the whole apparatus of our ocean control came into play, very far-reaching combinations began to work, and from yesterday afternoon – I have not had time to prepare a detailed statement – Fleet Air Arm torpedo-carrying seaplanes from the *Ark Royal*, made a succession of attacks upon the *Bismarck*, which now appears to be alone and without her consort. About midnight we learned that the *Bismarck* had been struck by two torpedoes, one amidships and the other astern. This second torpedo apparently affected the steering of the ship, for not only was she reduced to a very slow speed, but she continued making uncontrollable circles in the sea. While in this condition, she was attacked by one of our flotillas, and hit by two more torpedoes, which brought her virtually to a standstill, far from help and far outside the range at which the enemy bomber aircraft from the French coast could have come upon the scene. This morning, at daylight or shortly after daylight, the *Bismarck* was attacked by the British pursuing battleships. I do not know what were the results of the bombardment; it appears, however, that the *Bismarck* was not sunk by gunfire, and she will now be dispatched by torpedo. It is thought that this is now proceeding, and it is also thought that there cannot be any lengthy delay in disposing of this vessel.

Great as is our loss in the *Hood*, the *Bismarck* must be regarded as the most powerful, as she is the newest battleship in the world, and this striking of her from the German Navy is a very definite simplification of the task of maintaining the effective mastery of the Northern seas and the maintenance of the Northern blockade. I daresay that in a few days it will be possible to give a much more detailed account, but the essentials are before the House and although there is shade as well as light in this picture I feel that we have every reason to be satisfied with the outcome of this fierce and memorable naval encounter.

Mr Garro Jones: May I ask the Prime Minister whether he can say what was the weight of the projectiles which were thrown on the *Bismarck* prior to the abandonment of the gun attack for torpedo attacks?

The Prime Minister: I naturally cannot. I only heard about five minutes before I came into the Chamber the latest information to reach the Admiralty, and, as I have said, I have no doubt we shall get further information in the course of the day.

NORTHERN IRELAND (CONSCRIPTION)

The Prime Minister: My right hon. Friend the Member for Antrim (Sir H. O'Neill) had a Question (No. 46) on the Order Paper about the application of conscription to Northern Ireland. I said a week ago that this matter had been engaging our attention. We have made a number of inquiries in various directions, with the result that we have come to the conclusion that at the present time, although there can be no dispute about our rights or about the merits, it would be more trouble than it is worth to enforce such a policy.

Sir Hugh O'Neill: Will it not make a rather bad impression throughout the Empire that, once again, the Government have had to burke this issue, obviously because of pressure from Southern Ireland?

The Prime Minister: I do not think that I can put it better than I have done. After a full survey we came to the decision which I have announced.

Sir H. O'Neill: There is one point which I think, in fairness, the Prime Minister would like to make clear. Was it not the view of the Government of Northern Ireland that conscription could be and should be applied?

The Prime Minister: Yes, Sir. That was the view of the Government of Northern Ireland, for whose loyal aid and continued and constant support of our cause, no words of praise can be too high.

Later –

The Prime Minister: I do not know whether I might venture, with great respect, to intervene for one moment. I have just received news that the *Bismarck* is sunk.

Sir John Peck:[1] *recollection*

(*Peck papers*)

27 May 1941

The tension snapped and the House was overjoyed.

Facing Winston sat the two most persistent critics of his conduct of the war – Emanuel Shinwell and Aneurin Bevan. Shinwell looked across and caught Winston's eye, grinned broadly and gave him a friendly and encouraging nod. Bevan sat with shoulders hunched and hands in pockets; a black scowl on his face, unable to conceal his chagrin that Churchill should have a victory to record.

[1] John Howard Peck, 1913–1995. Assistant Private Secretary to the First Lord of the Admiralty (Lord Stanhope), 1937–9; to the Minister for Co-ordination of Defence (Lord Chatfield), 1939–40; to the First Lord of the Admiralty (Churchill), April–May 1940; to the Prime Minister (Churchill), 1940–5. Transferred to the Foreign Service, 1946. Ambassador to Senegal, 1962–6 and Mauritania, 1962–5. Under-Secretary of State, 1966–70. Ambassador to the Republic of Ireland, 1970–3. Knighted, 1971. He published his memoirs, *Dublin from Downing Street*, in 1978.

Winston S. Churchill to General Ismay, for the Chiefs of Staff Committee
(*Churchill papers, 20/36*)

27 May 1941
Secret

1. This is a sad story, and I feel myself greatly to blame for allowing myself to be overborne by the resistances which were offered. One can see how wrongly based these resistances were when we read paragraph 6 of the Air Staff paper in the light of what is happening in Crete, and may soon be happening in Cyprus and in Syria.

2. See also my minute on gliders. This is exactly what has happened. The gliders have been produced on the smallest possible scale, and so we have practically now neither the parachutists nor the gliders except these 500.

3. Thus we are always found behind-hand by the enemy. We ought to have 5,000 parachutists and an Airborne Division on the German model, with any improvements which might suggest themselves from experience. We ought also to have a number of carrier-aircraft. These will all be necessary in the Mediterranean fighting of 1942, or earlier if possible. We shall have to try to retake some of these Islands which are being so easily occupied by the enemy. We may be forced to fight in the wide countries of the East, in Persia or Northern Iraq. A whole year has been lost, and I now invite the Chiefs of Staff to make proposals for trying, so far as is possible, to repair the misfortune.

The whole file is to be brought before the Chiefs of Staff this evening.

Winston S. Churchill to General Ismay, for the Chiefs of Staff Committee
(*Churchill papers, 20/36*)

27 May 1941

I am in general agreement with the appreciation of CIGS; but it is clear that priority and emphasis of the Operations must be prescribed from here.

I should be glad if the Chiefs of the Staff would consider forthwith the following proposed Directive:

(Secret.)

1. In view of General Wavell's latest messages, he should be ordered to evacuate Crete forthwith, saving as many men as possible without regard to material, and taking whatever measures, whether by reinforcement or otherwise, are best.

2. With the capture of Suda Bay or Kastelli on the south side, the enemy will be most eager to land a seaborne force. The Navy must not open their sea guard yet, and should try, in any case, to take the heaviest toll, thus getting some of our own back.

3. The defence of Egypt from the west and from the north under the increased weight of the Air attack from Crete presents the standard military problem of a central force resisting two attacks from opposite quarters. In this case the choice seems clearly dictated by the facts.

4. The attack through Turkey and/or through Syria cannot develop in great strength for a good many weeks, during which events may make it impossible.

5. In the Western Desert alone the opportunity for a decisive military success presents itself. Here the object must not be the pushing back of the enemy to any particular line or region, but the destruction of his armed force, or the bulk of it, in a decisive battle fought with our whole strength. It should be possible in the next fortnight to inflict a crushing defeat upon the Germans in Cyrenaica. General Wavell has upwards of 400 Heavy Tanks against 130 enemy Heavy Tanks, plus their 9-tonners, as well as light armoured forces upon both sides. He has a large plurality of other arms, particularly artillery. He has sure communications, ample supplies and much help from the sea. He should therefore strike with the utmost strength in the Western Desert against an enemy already in great difficulties for supplies and ammunition. Here is the only chance of producing a major military success, and nothing should stand in its way.

6. There is no objection meanwhile to the advance he proposes with the forces specified into Syria, and he may get the Aerodromes there before the Germans have recovered from the immense drain upon their Air power which the unexpectedly vigorous resistance of Freyberg's army has produced.

7. Forces should not be frittered away on Cyprus at this juncture. We cannot attempt to hold Cyprus unless we have the Aerodromes in Syria. When we have these, and if we have gained a decisive victory in Cyrenaica, an advance under adequate Air cover into Cyprus may become possible. We must not repeat in Cyprus the hard conditions of our fight in Crete.

8. For the above purposes, Jaguar must immediately be resumed and expanded. *Victorious* is now at liberty. The movement of all troops and transport from Abyssinia northward must be pressed to the utmost, observing that the 50th Division from England less one Brigade is also already approaching, together with other reinforcements.

9. To sum up, the orders should be:

(a) Evacuate Crete.

(b) Destroy the German force in Cyrenaica, thus disengaging Tobruk and securing the airfields to the westward.

(c) Endeavour to peg out claims in Syria for reinforcement after a Cyrenaican victory as in (b).

All these operations should be capable of completion before the middle of June.

War Cabinet, Defence Committee (Operations): minutes
(*Cabinet papers, 69/2*)

27 May 1941
9.45 p.m.

Cabinet War Room

CRETE

The Prime Minister said that events now necessitated the evacuation of our forces from Crete, and an order to this effect had been sent to General Wavell.

LIBYA, CYPRUS, SYRIA

Sir Dudley Pound explained the vital importance from the naval point of view of the recapture of Cyrenaica. Unless this could be done it would be difficult for the Mediterranean Fleet to keep open the line of communication to Malta or to interrupt the German line of communication from Greece to Cyrenaica.The Chiefs of Staff were not in favour of attempting to defend Cyprus. Adequate forces for both Cyprus and Syria could not be found, and the retention of Cyprus would be of little value if the Germans got into Syria. On the other hand they would have to fight the Germans in Syria sooner or later and it would be better to go in now before the Germans got any stronger. Once we were established in Syria we could do to the Germans in Cyprus what they had done to us in Crete.

The Prime Minister said that he entirely agreed with the Chiefs of Staff. The first essential was to defeat the German Army in Libya. Our second task would be to try to peg out claims in Syria with the small forces which could be made available without detracting from our effort in Libya. We might thus succeed in forestalling the Germans and in encouraging the Turks. The amount of air support which should be allotted to the Syrian operation would require careful consideration.

There was general agreement with the views expressed by the Prime Minister.

IRAQ

The Prime Minister said that he was unable to understand what was happening in Iraq. No information was being sent home about the situation and about what was being done at Ramadi and Falluja. He had expected for days now to hear that we were in Baghdad. He asked Sir John Dill to send off a telegram to enquire the position.

The Committee –

(a) Agreed that the policy to be followed in the Middle East should be as follows:-

(i) Our forces should be evacuated from Crete.

(ii) Every effort should be made to destroy the German Army in Cyrenaica.

(iii) General Wavell should be authorized to advance into Syria as soon as he was reasonably prepared in accordance with the plan outlined in his telegram No.067415 of 25th May.

(iv) The Turks should be invited to enter Syria at the same time and to occupy Aleppo. Our plans should be communicated to General de Gaulle but not to anyone else in the Free French forces.

MIDDLE EAST

The Prime Minister said that the sinking of the *Bismarck*[1] had greatly eased the naval position and he hoped that the Admiralty would therefore do what they could to help the struggle in the Middle East by further shipments of fighter aircraft on carriers to Malta.

Winston S. Churchill: War Cabinet Paper

(*Churchill papers, 23/9*)

27 May 1941 10 Downing Street
Secret

SECURITY

NOTE BY THE PRIME MINISTER ADDRESSED TO MINISTERS IN CHARGE OF DEPARTMENTS

An intense effort should be made to achieve greater security in matters where secrecy is of fundamental importance to the conduct of the war.

No detailed set of rules can be devised applicable to all Departments. The methods set out in the annexed Memorandum, which has been prepared under my directions, are based on the experience of Departments generally. They are intended to provide a guide by means of which the systems now in force will be tested; and they should not be departed from without good reason.

The Permanent Head of each Department is responsible to his Minister for reviewing from time to time the arrangements in his Department, taking this Memorandum as a guide. It is only by constant effort that, on the one hand, security can be ensured, and, on the other hand, the multiplicity of needless restrictions, which clog the progress of business, can be avoided.

I ask each Minister to see that the arrangements in his Department are reviewed on the lines indicated, and I propose to arrange for a report to be submitted to me at a later date showing what action has been taken to give effect to this Note.

[1] Earlier that day: of her crew of 2,222 only 115 were saved. She had been sighted by a Coastal Command Catalina flying boat flown by a United States pilot.

MEMORANDUM

DEFINITION OF 'HIGHLY SECRET' PAPERS

1. Reasons can be found for labelling as 'Secret' a very large proportion of the documents produced in Government Departments or circulating within the Fighting Services. But the attempt to apply rigid precautions to a very large volume of documents not only slows down the machine, but inevitably makes it impossible to apply the precautions effectively, and leads to their neglect.

2. The first essential in any sound security system is therefore to ensure a proper understanding of the limited class of documents to which really stringent precautions should be applied, and to cut out unnecessary precautions in regard to other documents.

3. There is at present no uniform practice in departments for designating the various degrees of secrecy applicable to different classes of documents. The stringent precautions described in this Memorandum are intended to apply to that strictly limited class to which the highest degree of secrecy is assigned. These are referred to below as 'highly secret' papers, though this may not necessarily be their actual marking.

4. The papers to be included in this class are not easy to specify, but they should be confined as far as possible to the following: –

(i) Plans of future operations.
(ii) Papers giving particulars of the disposition or impending movements of our forces, or of convoys, escorts and ships.
(iii) Particulars of the present and future strength of our forces, and rates of production of major munitions of war.
(iv) A small, but very important, class of political papers dealing with such matters as negotiations for alliances, and the like.
(v) Information, the disclosure of which would make known the methods relied on by our Intelligence Service, or would imperil our secret agents, and information about counter-espionage matters.
(vi) Information about new secret methods of warfare, including scientific and technical developments in connection therewith.

5. It must, of course, be understood that there are many documents which although they may contain some information bearing on the above matters, do not on that account qualify to belong to the 'highly secret' class. For example, the posting of an Officer to a particular regiment in a particular locality may disclose the location of that unit. But a document containing information of this kind is not in the same category of secrecy as a Paper which sets out the whole of our Order of Battle.

PRECAUTIONS TO BE OBSERVED IN RESPECT OF 'HIGHLY SECRET' PAPERS

6. One of the most obvious precautions, and one most often neglected, is to control the habit of compiling and putting into circulation comprehensive documents giving details on these very secret matters. Individual officers or

sections need usually only be given particulars of that part of the business which affects them.

7. No detailed code of rules can be devised which will be applicable to all Departments. The system in force must ensure:

(i) That every Paper dealing with highly Secret matters should be seen by as few people as possible.

(ii) That those who handle it at any stage in its production, distribution and subsequent use, can be identified and are known to be trustworthy.

8. The notes in the following paragraphs are intended to give effect to these two cardinal points, and are based on the general experience of Departments.

Production of 'Highly Secret' Papers

9. This must not be carried out in general typing sections, but in a special section of people of known reliability. The 'Copy-number' system must be employed for such Papers, and must be extended to cover all preliminary drafts circulated for approval.

10. The copy-number system cannot in itself prevent the purloining of loose sheets during the production of a document. The only safeguards against this are, first, the employment of persons of known reliability and, secondly, effective supervision throughout the time when such documents are being produced.

11. All rough drafts, dictation books and waste-paper containing any part of the document must be disposed of as secret waste (see paragraph 26).

Distribution

12. The number of copies of 'Highly Secret' Documents distributed should be as few as possible and the destination of each must be recorded. Each copy for distribution should be enclosed in a sealed envelope addressed to the recipient, and bearing instructions that it is to be opened only by the recipient. The envelope containing the document should be forwarded in a locked box. The contents of any such box and the time of its despatch must be recorded and the box should be signed for by the messenger who takes it to its destination in another department.

Reception

13. There must be a proper system in all Departments for the central reception of boxes containing 'Highly Secret' documents from other Departments. The receipt given by this central organization to the messenger who brings the box ends the responsibility of the issuing Department for that box. The rapid conveyance of the box to the person for whom it is intended is then the responsibility of the receiving Department.

Distribution and handling within the originating or receiving Department

14. All 'Highly Secret' documents are addressed to individuals. Some responsible person, deputed for the purpose, must be charged with ensuring that the document is not passed to any person who is not bound to see it in the course of his duty. Such documents are never to be copied by the recipients, but short extracts may be made and sent to officers required to take action

thereon. If further complete copies are required, these should be obtained from the Department issuing the document, where the additional distribution can be recorded. When a 'Highly Secret' document is passed for action to individuals other than the recipient, a check must be kept to ensure that the document is returned to the original holder.

Files containing 'Highly Secret' Papers

15. Any files on which 'Highly Secret' Papers are put must be specially marked and subject to special precautions. They should only be circulated in locked boxes, unless they are carried by responsible officials. The typing of minutes on these files must be carried out under special precautions, and their custody entrusted to special sections.

'HIGHLY SECRET' TELEGRAMS

16. Telegrams dealing with 'Highly Secret' matters cannot be dealt with in the same way as 'Highly Secret' documents generally. In the first place, speed is essential in the case of telegrams dealing with, e.g., operational matters, and it is often important that many Officers should receive copies at once. Again, these telegrams are often of passing importance only, and it is not as a rule necessary to record the destination of each copy or to take receipts. Nevertheless, the system in force should be sufficiently elastic to ensure that special precautions can be applied to the very small number of telegrams dealing with matters on which secrecy is absolutely vital, which are received from time to time. For example:

(i) Only persons of known reliability should be employed on cyphering, and on reproducing telegrams, and the staffing arrangements should permit of a real measure of supervision over the staff engaged in this work.

(ii) Continual effort must be made to keep the distribution down to the minimum. This can only be done by constant personal investigation by an officer charged with the task by the Head of the Department.

(iii) Highly Secret Telegrams should be circulated only in locked boxes, or by the hand of responsible officials.

(iv) Care must be taken to destroy superfluous drafts and copies.

PRECAUTIONS FOR DEALING WITH PAPERS OF A LESSER DEGREE OF SECRECY

17. It is not the purpose of these notes to prescribe what precautions should be applied to documents of a secret character other than those falling in the Highly Secret category as defined at the beginning of this note. It must be left to Departments to settle which of the above precautions should be adopted, either as they stand, or with modifications. All possible steps should be taken to exclude entirely from any secret category papers which are not really secret, since too great an insistence on secrecy not only hampers the work, but brings the whole system into discredit.

GENERAL SECURITY PRECAUTIONS

18. The following notes touch on security precautions in a number of matters of general office routine.

Rooms where Secret Papers are handled

19. 'Highly Secret' documents should never be left in trays or on desks except when they are being worked on. Where available, boxes with snap locks should be kept in each room in which documents can be placed when they are not locked up in a safe. Boxes containing 'Highly Secret' documents should not be left about in rooms at night, but should be placed in safes or steel presses.

20. Wall-maps, diagrams and charts on which dispositions, &c., are marked, should be covered, so that they cannot be seen by visitors or others entering the room.

Selection of Staff

21. Care should be taken to employ a staff of known reliability in the special sections for the production of 'Highly Secret' documents and for other key employments, such as cyphering staffs. A negative check, i.e., that nothing is known against a man or woman, is of very little value. What is required is personal recommendation from some person whose judgment can be relied on.

Code words

22. The code word for an operation should not be mentioned in the same document as any reference which might give a clue to the nature of the operation. Where this cannot be avoided the document must be included in the 'Highly Secret' class.

Gossip

23. General warnings have from time to time been issued on the dangers of gossip on confidential matters, and the discussion of such matters in public places. It is the duty of all who have knowledge of operations projected, or being carried out, to refrain from imparting their knowledge to anyone who is not bound in the course of his duty to be made aware of it.

Telephones

24. Staffs should constantly be reminded that, unless a 'privacy equipment' has been installed, no conversation on the telephone, even on the 'direct line' or 'federal' systems, can be regarded as secure. If it is necessary to deal with secret matters on the telephone, this should be done by allusions which would be understood by the two people carrying on the conversation, but not by anyone else.

Access to Offices

25. A system should be in force in all Government Departments directly concerned with the conduct of the war to ensure that no person can enter unless (i) he possesses a Pass issued by a Department; or (ii) a temporary Pass is issued to him. Visitors, even when provided with temporary Passes, must be

conducted to the officer whom they wish to see, by a messenger, and should not be allowed to wander about unescorted.

Secret Waste

26. Secret Waste, which includes spoilt copies of Secret documents of all kinds, recalled drafts and other superfluous Secret Papers, must be collected and burnt, under supervision. The only exception to this is where a shredding machine has been installed in the Department concerned and operated under supervision. A constant check must be kept to see that Secret waste does not go into the ordinary waste-paper basket to which unauthorized persons have access.

Locks, safes and keys

27. Departments are enjoined to review the security of the safes or locked presses in which highly Secret Papers are kept.

28. Boxes for the circulation of Secret Papers should not be left lying about unlocked, even if empty.

29. Officers should be encouraged not to take their keys out of the office, but to leave them in an office keybox opened by a combination lock.

General Sir Alan Brooke: diary[1]

(*'The Turn of the Tide'*)

27 May 1941

PM is in great form, and on the whole a very successful meeting. It is surprising how he maintains a light-hearted exterior in spite of the vast burden he is bearing. He is quite the most wonderful man I have ever met, and it is a source of never-ending interest, studying him and getting to realize that occasionally such human beings make their appearance on this earth – human beings who stand out head and shoulders above all others.

The evacuation of Crete was begun on 27 May 1941. Within four days, more than 16,000 men were embarked. The 5,000 who remained on the island were then authorized to surrender.

[1] This entry was written after a meeting of the Tank Parliament at which the need for greater tank production was urged.

Winston S. Churchill to General Wavell
(*Churchill papers, 20/39*)

28 May 1941
sent 8.30 p.m.
Personal

So long as there was hope of victory in Crete, it was right to make all efforts, but since you and Freyberg pronounced situation hopeless I have moved the Chiefs of Staff to send you the directive contained in their Nos. 118 and 119 with which I am in full accord.[1]

2. Everything must now be centred upon destroying the German forces in the Western Desert. Only by this deed will you gain the security on your Western flank which will enable you to keep the Germans out of Syria and yourself gain contact with Turkey. I hope therefore that the maximum possible forces will be thrown into what, unless you have a better name, may be called Tigercubs. For the first time it seems to me you have a definite superiority in numbers of AFVs, especially heavier types, as well as in mechanized infantry, artillery and supplies. The Tobruk sally-port also presents strategic opportunities of the highest order. In spite of Cretan losses, the air position in Libya has improved. Now, before the enemy has recovered from the violent exertions and heavy losses involved in his onslaught upon Crete, is the time to fight a decisive battle in Libya, and go on day after day facing all necessary losses until you have beaten the life out of General Rommel's army. In this way the loss of Crete will be more than repaired, and the future of the whole campaign in the Middle East will be opened out.

3. We were all very much puzzled when you sent Wilson to Palestine and appointed Beresford-Peirse[2] to the Western Desert. Although the latter is a good Divisional Commander, it is difficult to believe that he can compare with Wilson in military stature, reputation or experience of high command in desert warfare. As so much of our fortune hangs upon this impending battle, I ask you to consider whether there is still time for Wilson to be given the Command.

4. As I try to support you and your Army in every way, and especially in adversity, I feel sure that you will not resent these observations which I feel it my duty to make.

[1] Instructing Wavell to evacuate Crete.

[2] Noel Monson de la Poer Beresford-Peirce, 1887–1953. On active service, 1914–18 (Distinguished Service Order). Commander, 4 Indian Division, 1940–41. Commander, Western Desert Force, April-September 1941. Knighted, 1941. General Officer Commanding, Sudan, September 1941-April 1942. Commander, 15 Indian Corps, 1942. General Officer Commanding-in-Chief, Southern Army, India, 1942–45. Welfare General in India, 1945–47. Colonel Commandant, Royal Artillery, for 1944 until his death.

Winston S. Churchill to General Ismay, for the Chiefs of Staff Committee
(*Churchill papers, 20/36*)

28 May 1941

I regard it as a matter of State policy that the Yugoslavs shall be aided to the utmost possible to form Air Squadrons and also at least a Brigade Group, and that we should supply the equipment in both cases.

I should be glad to receive a scheme.

Winston S. Churchill to Averell Harriman
(*Churchill papers, 20/21*)

28 May 1941
Secret

My dear Harriman,

Thank you very much for your letter of May 26 about the delivery of six DC2's and fourteen Lockheed transports for Bathurst.

I am delighted to have this good news.

Yours sincerely,
Winston S. Churchill

Winston S. Churchill to A. V. Alexander and Admiral Pound
(*Churchill papers, 20/36*)

28 May 1941
Action this Day
Most Secret

The bringing into action of the *Prinz Eugen* and the search for her, raise questions of the highest importance. It is most desirable that the United States Navy should play a part in this. It would be far better, for instance, that she should be located by a United States ship, as this might tempt her to fire upon that ship, thus providing the incident for which the United States Government would be so thankful.

Pray let this matter be considered from this point of view, apart from its ordinary naval aspect. If we can only create a situation where the *Prinz Eugen* is being shadowed by an American vessel, we shall have gone a long way to solve the largest problem.

Pray let me know what is known about the *Prinz Eugen*.

Winston S. Churchill to President Franklin D. Roosevelt
(*Churchill papers, 20/39*)

29 May 1941
sent 4.05 p.m.

We are uplifted and fortified by your memorable declaration and by the far-reaching executive measures involved in the state of emergency you have proclaimed.[1] Pray accept, Mr President, my heartfelt thanks. It was very kind of you to let me know beforehand of the great advance you found it possible to make.

I have now also received your message about the impressive additional output you are sending to the Middle East in United States ships. Winant will tell you what I managed to send out there secretly, and the hopes I have of some good news coming to hand before long.

It seems most important to find the *Prinz Eugen* before she cuts into our convoys. The Admiralty and Ghormley are in the closest touch. But this is a new, very fast and powerful ship, and there is much danger while she is at large for any convoy unprotected by battleship escort.

I will send you later the inside story of the fighting with the *Bismarck*. She was a terrific ship and a masterpiece of naval construction. Her removal eases our battleship situation as we should have had to keep *KGV*, *Prince of Wales* and the two *Nelsons* practically tied to Scapa Flow to guard against a sortie of *Bismarck* and *Tirpitz*, as they could choose their moment and we should have to allow for one of our ships refitting. Now it is a different story. The effect upon the Japanese will be highly beneficial. I expect they are doing all their sums again.

Winston S. Churchill to General Ismay, for the Chiefs of Staff Committee
(*Churchill papers, 20/36*)

29 May 1941
Secret

SEIZING FRENCH SHIPS AT ALEXANDRIA

The plan must be carefully concerted and kept up to date, and the C-in-C should be warned that the moment may come when it will be required.

[1] In a broadcast on 27 May 1941, Roosevelt proclaimed a 'state of unlimited emergency', and he told the American people: 'We pledged material support to other democracies and we will fulfil that pledge.' United States armed forces were being placed 'in strategic military positions'. What had 'started as a European war has developed, as the Nazis always intended it should develop, into a world war for world domination'. Unless the 'advance of Hitlerism is forcibly checked now the Western Hemisphere will be within the range of Nazi weapons of destruction . . . We shall actively resist Hitler's every attempt to gain control of the seas . . . Our patrols help to ensure the delivery of supplies to Britain.'

The situation in relation to Vichy has for the moment become less tense than when my No. D167/1[1] was written.

The acquisition of these ships should be an important gain in spite of the delays before they could come into action. They ought not to be undervalued.

The moment for action must be chosen by the War Cabinet. We must wait at present to see how things go in Syria.

Winston S. Churchill to David Margesson

(*Churchill papers, 20/36*)

29 May 1941

ITALIAN PRISONERS OF WAR HELD IN EAST AFRICA

It occurs to me that we must now consider using these Italian white prisoners in Great Britain. A plan was set on foot to bring 2,000 over here for the Ministry of Agriculture. I was not myself attracted by this idea, as it seemed to be on such a small scale but raising all kinds of novel complications. However, it might be better to use these docile Italian prisoners of war instead of bringing in disaffected Irish, over whom we have nothing like the same control. It would be worth while to make a plan for bringing in, say, 25,000 of these Italians, and employing them as an organized mobile body upon the land.

Sir Edward Bridges is asked to arrange for a meeting under the Lord President, of Secretary of State for War, Minister of Labour, Minister of Agriculture, and Minister of War Transport. The report of this Committee could be brought before the Cabinet at the same time as your paper.

Winston S. Churchill to Robert Menzies

(*Churchill papers, 20/49*)

29 May 1941

Sincere congratulations on the powerful, moving addresses you have delivered in Canada, the United States and, above all, on your return home. These have been fully reported in England and have confirmed all the goodwill you gathered from our people. I thank you also for your very kindly

[1] Churchill minute of 23 May 1941, to General Ismay, for the Chiefs of Staff Committee, printed on pages 703 of this volume.

references to me. Reading the Australian despatches, I often think of Chatham's[1] famous invocation: 'Be one people!'

Best of luck.

Winston S. Churchill: Oral Answers
(Hansard)

29 May 1941 House of Commons

SOCIAL WELFARE (BOMBED AREAS)

Miss Ward[2] asked the Prime Minister whether, in view of certain problems which have arisen known to him, he will consider appointing a Minister of Social Welfare for severely-bombed areas?

The Prime Minister: No, Sir.[3] I do not think that there are circumstances which would justify the creation of a new Ministry for this purpose.

Miss Ward: In view of the fact that there is a fairly strong opinion on this matter, may I ask my right hon. Friend not to close his mind until after the Debate upon the Civil Defence services?

The Prime Minister: I will keep my mind ajar.

War Cabinet, Defence Committee (Operations): minutes
(Cabinet papers, 69/2)

29 May 1941 10 Downing Street
6 p.m.

The Prime Minister read out a personal telegram which he had just received from President Roosevelt.[4]

CRETE

With reference to the danger of German reprisals on the wounded and other troops that would of necessity be left behind, the Prime Minister suggested that an announcement should be made to the effect that we should treat all captured parachutists as honourable prisoners of war, provided they were wearing a uniform which clearly distinguished them from the defenders.

[1] William Pitt, 1st Earl of Chatham (Pitt the Elder). He made this remark during the Seven Years War (1756–1763).

[2] Irene Mary Bewick Ward, 1895–1980. Stood unsuccessfully as a Conservative candidate in 1924 and 1929. Conservative Member of Parliament for Wallsend-on-Tyne, 1931–45; for Tynemouth, 1950–74. Dame of the British Empire, 1955. Created Baroness (Life Peer), 1974. A wartime supporter of the First Aid Nursing Yeomanry (FANY), in 1955 she published *FANY Invicta*.

[3] Churchill was replying to Miss Ward through Mr Speaker.

[4] Offering to use American pilots to take aircraft from factories in the United States to their 'ultimate take off' across the Atlantic – usually Botwood, Newfoundland – thus freeing up British pilots, who would normally do this, for Atlantic Ferry duties.

Referring to the comment on the disappointing reception accorded in the British Press to President Roosevelt's speech, the Prime Minister directed that the Ministry of Information should arrange for a more enthusiastic line to be taken.

DEFENCE OF ALEXANDRIA AND THE SUEZ CANAL AGAINST AIR ATTACK

The Prime Minister suggested that in view of the increased scale of air attack which could now be expected to develop on Alexandria and on the Suez Canal, we should consider the despatch of some night fighters to Egypt, together with the necessary control equipment. It was most important that the Suez Canal zone should be adequately defended and that in the event of things going wrong in the Eastern Mediterranean, the Fleet should not find itself mined in, and be faced with the prospect of fighting its way out through the Straits of Gibraltar.

JIBUTI

The Prime Minister suggested that the Foreign Office should be prepared to take action in French Somaliland at the psychological moment of our entry into Syria, and that in the meanwhile a strict blockade should be maintained.

War Cabinet, Defence Committee (Operations): minutes
(*Cabinet papers, 69/2*)

29 May 1941
10 p.m.

Cabinet War Room

UNITED KINGDOM
SMOKE SCREENS FOR THE PROTECTION OF VULNERABLE POINTS

The Prime Minister said that he did not wish to prejudge the question but he could not contemplate the taking of any additional men for this purpose from the Army over and above the 8,000 already employed on smoke protection work.

John Colville: diary
(*Colville papers*)

29 May 1941

PM much upset by telegram from Wavell who shows some sign of defeatism. 'He sounds a tired and disheartened man,' said the PM.

Winston S. Churchill to Anthony Eden
(*Churchill papers, 20/36*)

30 May 1941

No encouragement should be given to these suggestions of treachery and bad faith on our part towards the Zionists.[1] Not much perspicacity was required from the United States Minister to enable him to find out that our Zionist policy is an impediment to our good relations with the Arabs. I am quite certain that we should lose in America far more than we should gain in the East. The political reactions here would be of the most formidable character. The Labour and Liberal Parties in the Government would resist, and I am in full accord with them.

Winston S. Churchill to General Ismay
(*Premier papers, 3/238/2*)

30 May 1941

DESTRUCTION OF IRAQI OIL FIELDS

The COS Committee should take into consideration the notes which Professor Lindemann has written. There will be a fierce and justifiable outcry if we fail to destroy these oil fields before they fall into enemy hands.

I should like a further report.

Winston S. Churchill to Sir Archibald Sinclair
(*Churchill papers, 20/36*)

30 May 1941

RE-EQUIPMENT OF ARMY CO-OPERATION SQUADRONS

The Army must be given the modest force they require, and I am satisfied that the 30 Blenheims should be handed over to them, so that some joint training can be achieved before the invasion season. It is not necessary to hand over the whole of the second 30 required for a reserve immediately. Losses up to that amount can be made good as they occur from the ASU[2] reserves.

[1] These suggestions were being made by the Revisionist Zionist Movement.
[2] Aircraft Storage Units, aircraft in storage.

Winston S. Churchill to General Wavell
(*Churchill papers, 20/39*)

30 May 1941
Secret and Personal

Jibuti. It will be convenient to have this place in the near future, and I shall be glad if you will consider what forces would be necessary to break the French resistance, and whether they could be found without prejudice to other needs. The time to strike depends, of course, upon events in Syria which may lead to a breach with Vichy, or alternatively to co-operation between the French Army in Syria and the Free French. Either way the seizure of Jibuti might be fitted in. Meanwhile the blockade should be maintained with the utmost strictness, and any preparatory concentrations on the Jibuti frontier which you think helpful may be made. In this way actual fighting may be avoided, as is greatly to be desired. The moment for action can only be fixed in consultation with us.

Winston S. Churchill to Robert Hudson[1] *and Tom Johnston*[2]
(*Churchill papers, 20/36*)

30 May 1941

I have been considering the minutes you sent me early in April concerning the production of sugar beet in Scotland. It seems to me agreed that it is desirable that in order to save shipping space the production of sugar beet should be maintained. I am also informed that the starch equivalent of beet products per acre is two-thirds greater than that of potatoes. But I infer from what you say that for financial reasons farmers prefer to produce potatoes, of which there is no shortage.

It seems clear therefore that measures should be taken to ensure that sufficient beet is produced, if necessary at the expense of potatoes. It ought to be possible to settle between the Ministries concerned whether the increase is to be made in Scotland or in Northern England, but it certainly appears that it would be most convenient to produce the additional quantity for the Cupar factory in Scotland.

If it is too late to obtain this extra output this year, steps should be taken to make sure that the shortage is not repeated in 1942. Indeed, since beet is apparently a very valuable crop in present circumstances, it should be considered whether a much larger acreage should not in future be devoted to it. Please report to me further on this at a later date.

I am sending a copy of this minute to the Minister of State.

[1] Minister of Agriculture and Fisheries.
[2] Secretary of State for Scotland.

Winston S. Churchill to President Franklin D. Roosevelt
(*Churchill papers, 20/39*)

30 May 1941
Most Immediate and Secret

1. We cordially welcome your taking over Iceland at the earliest possible moment, and will hold ourselves and all our resources there at your disposal as may be found convenient. It would liberate a British Division for defence against invasion or the Middle East. It would enable us to concentrate our flying boats now there on North-Western Approaches. If it could be done in the next three weeks or less, or even begun, it would have a moral effect even beyond its military importance. You have only to say the word and our staffs can get to work at once.

2. Spain and Portugal – At any time now Hitler may obtain Air bases in Southern Spain or in North Africa, Spanish or French, from which he can make Gibraltar harbour unusable by our Fleet. The moment this happens, or we are sure it is going to happen, we shall send our expeditions, which have long been prepared and are waiting beside their ships, to occupy the Grand Canary, the Cape Verde Islands and one of the Azores. The code names for these three expeditions will be cabled in a separate message. We cannot provide an army to defend Portugal on the mainland, and the same is true of Spain, though we would try to help a guerrilla there. Meanwhile, we were about to offer Portuguese anti-aircraft and other equipment to defend Azores and Cape Verde Islands, and were encouraging them to withdraw their Government there if overrun by the Nazis. If Salazar accepts our help and protection in the islands, he would, of course, welcome assistance of US support. As we are already discussing with Salazar help to Portugal, had we not better go ahead and try to obtain his approval of the idea of withdrawing to the islands? It is a matter of approach and method. These could be discussed forthwith between State Department and Foreign Office. Whatever Salazar's decision, we should in the event have to obtain control of the islands, for which US co-operation would be invaluable.

3. We should welcome collaboration with an American token force before, during or after occupation of Atlantic Islands, and, if you wish, would turn them over to you as a matter of mutual war convenience.

4. We should naturally welcome United States occupation of Dakar, and would afford all facilities in our power. We have some rather costly experience and knowledge of this place. Surest method is by landing Tanks from specially constructed vessels on neighbouring beaches. I suggest that immediate consultation between your officers and ours should be given to make a workable plan, and have it ready in case circumstances should require its use.

Winston S. Churchill to Robert Menzies
(*Churchill papers, 20/39*)

31 May 1941

Your 2649. Everything in human power has been and will be done to strengthen our Air Force in ME. First part of Jaguar operation already completed. Second part starts this morning. We hope to have reasonable Air superiority for first time in approaching operations in Western Desert. As you well know, difficulty of Air reinforcements in ME is not supply of aeroplanes here nor wish to send them, but the delay round the Cape and the limited capacity of the short cuts via T and M.[1] Nevertheless, in May well over one thousand were simultaneously moving along various routes thither. Process is continuing.

2. Difficulty of defending Crete did not arise so much through shortage of Aircraft, but from absence of well-defended Air fields within Fighter range.

3. Country you mention in fourth paragraph[2] will be occupied at earliest with such forces as we can find. It is only when we secured Air field there that an advance into Cyprus in strength will be possible, and by then it may well be too late. We can only do our best.

4. Evacuation of Crete is proceeding with success, over 11,000 having already reached Alexandria. Continuance of resistance there without Air support would have jeopardized naval position in Mediterranean. All the above is most secret.

Winston S. Churchill to the Marquess of Linlithgow
(*Churchill papers, 20/39*)

31 May 1941
Personal and Secret

Your 1029-8 of May 23. If the expansion you think of making in your Executive Council is required for the war effort, it would certainly be justified on that ground. But see your statement in para. 10: 'It will not enhance our war effort.' If, on the other hand, it is intended as an instalment of constitutional change, are you convinced that it will be worth while, in view of your statement in para. 10, that 'This scheme will not give real satisfaction and will be violently criticized as falling short of even moderate demands and as not conceding transfer of Defence or Finance, &c.' Is there any danger of these proposals being repudiated at once by the Parties, both Congress and the

[1] Takoradi and Monrovia.
[2] Syria.

Moslem League? Are you sure that Jinnah,[1] Sikandar[2] or Nazimuddin[3] will not be provoked and piqued, as apprehended by you in para. 6? Can you assure me that at this critical time in Iraq, Syria and throughout the Moslem world a positively bad effect may not be produced among them on the balance? Is there not a danger also that Gandhi[4] will point to this minor step as a renewed cause of offence? Is the aged Hydari[5] likely to prove an efficient counsellor, or has he been chosen merely because he is the least likely appointment to antagonize Jinnah and the Moslem League?

These changes, small though they be, will, of course, stir the embers of controversy, both in India and the House of Commons. Have you satisfied yourself that they are worth the trouble they involve? I shall be glad to have your answers upon these points before the matter is brought before the Cabinet, as I should propose on Monday, June 9.

[1] Mohammed Ali Jinnah, 1876–1948. Member of the Imperial Legislative Council from 1910; President of the all-India Muslim League 1916, 1920 and since 1934. 'Founder of Pakistan' and its first Governor-General, 1948.

[2] Sikander Hyat-Khan, 1892–1942. On active service, Third Afghan War, 1919: the first Indian to command a Company on active service. Revenue Member, Punjab Government, 1930–35 and 1937–37. Acting Governor of the Punjab, 1932, 1934. Knighted, 1933. Prime Minister of the Punjab from 1937 (and Deputy Governor of the Reserve Bank of India from 1935) until his death.

[3] Khwaja Nazimuddin, 1894–1964. A schoolboy in Aligarh and at Dunstable (England). A graduate of Trinity Hall, Cambridge. Chairman, Dacca Municipality, 1922–34. Minister of Education, Bengal, 1929–34. Knighted, 1934. Home Minister, 1937. Member of the Bengal Cabinet, 1937–41; resigned, December 1941. Leader of the Muslim League Parliamentary Party, Bengal, and Leader of the Opposition, Bengal Legislative Assembly, 1942–43. Chief Minister of Bengal, 1943–54. Food Delegate on behalf of India to the United States, 1945–46. Chief Minister of East Pakistan, 1947. Governor-General of Pakistan (in succession to Jinnah), 1948–51. Prime Minister of Pakistan 1951–58.

[4] Mohandas Karamchand Gandhi, 1869–1948. Born in India. Called to the Bar, London, 1889; practised as a barrister in South Africa, 1889–1908; gave up his practice in order to devote himself to championing the rights of Indian settlers in South Africa, 1908; leader of the Passive Resistance Campaign in South Africa, 1908–14; started the Non-Cooperation Movement in India, 1918; given sole authority to lead the national movement by the Indian National Congress, 1921; inaugurated the Civil Disobedience Campaign, 1930; frequently imprisoned; opposed the partition of India into Hindu and Muslim states; severely critical of the Hindu caste-system; assassinated by an orthodox Hindu in 1948, within a year of the creation of India and Pakistan as independent states.

[5] Akbar Hydari, 1869–1942. Joined the Indian Finance Department, 1888. Deputy Accountant-General, Bombay, 1897; Madras, 1901; Finance and Comptroller, Indian Treasuries, 1903. Finance and Railway Member, Hyderabad State Executive Council, 1921–37. Knighted, 1928. Chairman, Committee of Indian State Ministers, 1934–41. President, Hyderabad State Executive Council, 1937–41. Member for Information, Governor-General, Executive Council, India, 1941.

June 1941

Winston S. Churchill: speech
(BBC Written Archives Centre)

1 June 1941 — 10 Downing Street

I am glad to have an opportunity of speaking again to the people of Canada. Your comradeship in this mortal struggle cheers and fortifies the people of these islands. To Nazi tyrants and gangsters it must seem strange that Canada, free from all compulsion or pressure, so many thousands of miles away, should hasten forward into the van of the battle against the evil forces of the world. These wicked men cannot understand the deep currents of loyalty and tradition that flow between the different self-governing nations of the British Empire. The people of Great Britain are proud of the fact that the liberty of thought and action they have won in the course of their long, romantic history should have taken root throughout the length and breadth of a vast continent, from Halifax to Victoria.

But the Canadians are the heirs of another tradition: the true tradition of France, a tradition of valour and faith which they keep alive in these dark days and which we are confident will in the end bring back again to life France itself.

The people of this country know that the prayers, the toil and the anxious thought of all Canadians are with them in their severe ordeal. Canada has given abundant proofs of her purpose. Canadian troops are becoming a familiar sight in the towns and villages of England. I have met many men of the Canadian forces, and I have never seen a finer body of troops. It has not fallen to them as yet to be engaged with the enemy, but they have been allotted a task of vital importance, to play their part in the defence of the heart of the Empire, and to meet the enemy, should he venture to come, upon the very threshold of the land. And when the test comes and if the test comes – and come it may – I know they will prove that they are worthy sons of those who stormed the Vimy Ridge twenty-four years ago.

But this war will not be won by valour in action alone. It will be won also by a hard, persevering effort in field and in factory. It will not be won without a multitude of minor, prosaic, unnoticed sacrifices.

I have heard from your Prime Minister, my friend – my old friend, Mr Mackenzie King – of the remarkable organization which has been built up in Canada, to raise this, the greatest war loan in her history; and I am confident that this tremendous effort will be crowned by success.

I speak to you this afternoon from No. 10 Downing Street, here in the capital and the governing centre of this battered but indomitable city and island. Our people have been through much in the last few months. They have learned much – and some things they will never forget. But above all they have learned their own strength. They have tested their resolve under heavy hardship and danger. None of them, none of us, doubts that together, with the whole Empire together, with the Old World and the New World together – no one doubts that we can or that we shall see it through; and that when at length we march again back into the light of happier and easier days, Canada will play her just part in laying the foundations of a wider and a better world.

Winston S. Churchill to Viscount Halifax
(*Churchill papers, 20/39*)

1 June 1941

You are reported as having said that the problem of the night raider will be solved in a few weeks. I ought to let you know that although everything is coming along well this is far too sanguine a hope. A year would have been nearer the mark.

Winston S. Churchill to General Ismay, for the Chiefs of Staff Committee
(*Churchill papers, 20/36*)

1 June 1941
Most Secret

Although I hold most strongly that we should not fritter away our forces in defence of Cyprus, I do not wish to exclude the possibility of Air defence, even before we are masters of the Syrian airfields. If, as a result of a successful outcome of Tigercubs (or Bruiser[1]), it should be found possible to spare two or

[1] Operation in the Western Desert to relieve the siege of Tobruk (later named Operation Battleaxe). Operation Tiger was the despatch of tank reinforcements through the Straits of Gibraltar to Egypt: in their correspondence, Wavell and Churchill referred to these tanks as 'tigercubs'. In the second Tiger, on 6 May 1941, thirteen fast British merchant ships had carried 295 tanks and fifty fighter aircraft in their holds. One merchantman was sunk and fifty-seven tanks and seven fighters lost.

three Fighter Squadrons, these should be sent; and, anyhow, meanwhile preparations should be made to receive them at short notice in Cyprus. I do not know what is the position and state of the existing Aerodromes. I attach some notes written for me at my request by the C-in-C, Fighter Command.[1]

I should be glad if the whole subject could be reviewed by the staffs, so that we may take a new view after Bruiser is over.

Winston S. Churchill to General Ismay, for the Chiefs of Staff Committee
(*Churchill papers, 20/36*)

1 June 1941
Action this Day

Adverting to my wish that the West African Brigade should be returned from East Africa to Freetown forthwith, and that the captured Italian arms should be used to equip the Shadow Brigade now forming at Freetown or thereabouts, I have had a talk with General Giffard.[2] He says that the West African battalions require an average of 80 British officer and non-commissioned officer personnel, and that these will be lacking for the Shadow Brigade, and that even if supplied they would be better employed on handling any modern equipment we can find. It has been suggested to me that the great plethora of Polish officers in Polish divisions, amounting to several thousands, might be married up to this West African Shadow Brigade. I am sure that General Sikorski could easily be persuaded to find two or three hundred, and they would be very good.

Pray let this be examined and a plan made. General Giffard should be consulted, and I should like to have a report before he leaves the country, the object being the transfer of the West African Brigade from east to west, and the development of the Shadow Brigade on Italian equipment and Polish white infusion.[3]

[1] Air Vice Marshal Sir William Sholto Douglas.

[2] George James Giffard, 1886–1964. On active service 1914–18 (wounded, despatches four times). Inspector–General, African Colonial Forces, 1938–39. Military Secretary to the Secretary of State for War, War Office, 1939; General Officer Commanding, British Forces in Palestine and Transjordan, 1940: General Officer Commanding, West Africa, 1940–44; Knighted, 1941; General Officer Commanding-in-Chief, West Africa, 1941–42; Eastern Army, India, 1943; 11th Army Group, South-East Asia, 1943–44.

[3] The Poles accepted Churchill's suggestion.

War Cabinet: minutes
(*Cabinet papers, 65*)

2 June 1941 10 Downing Street
5 p.m.

The Prime Minister said that the tragic sequence of events in Crete had now reached their conclusion. Some 17,000 of our troops had been evacuated. The defence and evacuation of the island raised a number of questions which should be enquired into. For example, why had not long-range guns been fixed where they could fire on the aerodromes? Why had not the aerodromes been mined, and more tanks landed? Again, the public would ask why, if we had taken 17,000 men off, we could not have sent adequate reinforcements to hold the island. The answer was that, once we had lost the aerodromes, we no longer had it in our power to bring in reinforcements and supplies except at excessive cost to the Fleet.

As for the evacuation itself, after 5,000 men had been embarked on the first night, the Commander-in-Chief, Mediterranean, had telegraphed home emphasizing the serious losses the Fleet might suffer if further troops were removed. We had insisted, however, on the evacuation proceeding, and a further 12,000 had been got away without any further serious naval losses.

The First Sea Lord said that the Commander-in-Chief had made it clear that he was prepared to carry on with the evacuation until the last ship. But he had thought it his duty to inform the Government of the large Naval losses which the operation might entail, in view of its repercussions on our position in the Mediterranean generally.

The Prime Minister said that on Saturday night he had heard that it was proposed to abandon further evacuation and to leave 5,000 men on the beaches. He (the Prime Minister) and the First Sea Lord had taken the view that further efforts should be made to evacuate these men. But before the order could be given, General Weston[1] had reported that the men were exhausted, and ordered them to capitulate.

In discussion, there was some criticism that we had not prepared sufficient aerodromes in Crete, and a comparison was drawn between the speed with which the Germans made aerodromes available. It was pointed out that the Germans used what was, in effect, slave labour for this work. While we had been preparing aerodromes in Crete we had had to contend with winter conditions. We had also been making aerodromes in Turkey and only a limited number of engineers had been available.

The Chief of the Air Staff said that the loss of our aerodromes in Crete was basically due to our having insufficient light AA defences.

[1] Eric Culpeper Weston, 1888–1950. Entered Royal Marines, 1906. On active service, 1914–18. Colonel Commandant, Royal Marines, 1939. On active service, 1939–45 (Greece and Crete); Greek Military Cross, 1st class.

It was also urged that there was a risk that if our troops were repeatedly asked to undertake operations without adequate air protection, this might, in time, have a demoralizing effect on them.

Winston S. Churchill to President Franklin D. Roosevelt
(*Churchill papers, 20/39*)

2 June 1941
Secret

I am finding it necessary to build up a much stronger organization of the rearward Services in the Middle East to sustain the large forces now gathering in and about the Nile Valley. An important mission is going out by air, comprising high military and civilian experts. We must consider the formation of a well-equipped base, either at Port Sudan (as your son[1] suggested) or/and at Massawa, near which lies the town of Asmara with its fine buildings, in order to arrange for the reception of American materials which you are sending to us in increasing quantities. American tanks and American aircraft require a good sprinkling of American civilian volunteer personnel to instruct us in their use and help keep them serviceable. I should be grateful if you would allow Averell Harriman to go out with the mission as independent observer, taking with him one or two of his own assistants. He would then be able to advise upon the best measures to be taken to ensure the most efficient use of all that you are sending. He is quite willing to go; indeed, he would like it. The trip might take him six weeks, but it would be well worth it.

John Colville: diary
(*Colville papers*)

2 June 1941

Late in the afternoon I accompanied the PM and Mrs Churchill to Chartwell where they plan to have a few days' rest. I am sleeping in the cottage which the PM built with his own hands and have his very comfortable bedroom.

We dined in the cottage; the PM, Mrs C, Tommy, Miss Whyte[2] and I. Mrs C and I played backgammon; the PM professed extreme tiredness and at one

[1] Elliott Roosevelt, a Captain in the United States Army Air Corps, was in Britain discussing the ferrying of pilots to Britain.

[2] Maryott Whyte, 1895–1973. Known as 'Cousin Moppett' and 'Nana'. Clementine Churchill's first cousin. A 'Norland' nanny. She lived at Chartwell between the wars, and was Mary Churchill's nanny, as well as looking after Chartwell when Mrs Churchill was in London. During the Second World War, when Chartwell was closed, she lived in a cottage near the house to supervise the estate.

moment even lay prostrate on the dining-room floor while Mrs C and I continued to rattle the dice and Tommy sipped his brandy pensively.

After dinner the PM went up to the big house and worked till 1.30, dictating to Miss Layton[1] while I sat in his study, looked at his books, and plied him with papers when supplies ran short.

He is very much perturbed by the fact that the rearguard, consisting of Royal Marines, were left behind in Crete. He blames the Navy and went so far as to describe it as a shameful episode.

Winston S. Churchill to Anthony Eden

(*Churchill papers, 20/36*)

2 June 1941
Action this Day

THE FUTURE OF CYPRUS

It is much better to leave all questions of territorial readjustment to be settled after the war. Once we depart from this principle, many other difficult cases may arise. I do not think we ought to cede an inch of British territory during the war.

It does not follow that Cyprus will immediately be taken. If it is, the Germans will be able, if they choose, to give it nominally to the Greek Quisling Government while using it for military purposes themselves. This will not make much difference to what happens.

I have followed very closely all that has happened in Cyprus since I visited the Island and wrote a Memorandum on the Tribute at the end of 1907. I suppose you are aware there is a substantial Moslem population in Cyprus, who have been very loyal to us, and who would much resent being handed over to the Greeks.

[1] Elizabeth Layton. Born in Suffolk. Went with her parents to Canada, 1924, at the age of seven. Returned to Britain to attend a secretarial course, 1936. One of Churchill's two personal secretaries, 1941–45 (she began work at Downing Street on 5 May 1941). Accompanied Churchill on most of his overseas journeys, including Washington (1943), Cairo (1943), Moscow (1944), Athens (1944) and Yalta (1945). After the war she married Lieutenant Frans Nel, a South African army officer who had been captured at Tobruk and been a prisoner of war in Germany from 1942 to 1945. In 1958 Elizabeth Nel published one of the most charming of all the books of reflections about Churchill, *Mr Churchill's Secretary*.

Winston S. Churchill to Air Chief Marshal Sir Charles Portal
(*Churchill papers, 20/36*)

2 June 1941
Action this Day

LENGTHENING THE RANGE OF FIGHTER AIRCRAFT

I am glad you are pressing on with this vital business. Anyone can see you will have to pay in gunfire and manoeuvrability for the advantage of range, but this may be well worth while.

I do not regard your last sentence as exhaustive. Machines must be modified so as to enable us to fight at particular points in daylight, both by Bombers and Fighters. This is particularly true of the Aegean Archipelago, where we ought to be able to bomb the Cretan and Dodecanese Aerodromes by daylight under Fighter protection. We have got to adapt machines to the distances which have to be traversed. Again, now that so much of the German Air Force is moving East, and France is largely weakened, we ought to attempt daylight raids into Germany for bombing on a severe scale. For this the range of our Fighters must be extended. If this is not done, you will be helpless in the West and beaten in the East.

Winston S. Churchill to Sir Archibald Sinclair
(*Churchill papers, 20/36*)

2 June 1941
Action this Day
Secret

Sir Hugh Dowding[1] would clearly not be eligible for the United States ferry service.

It seems to me that the best arrangement would be to send Air Marshal Barratt[2] there, and replace him with Sir Hugh Dowding, who will give

[1] Hugh Caswall Tremenheere Dowding, 1882–1970. Educated at Winchester. Joined the Royal Artillery, 1900; Royal Flying Corps, 1914. On active service, 1914–19 (despatches). Director of Training, Air Ministry, 1926–9. Commanding the Fighting Area, Air Defence of Great Britain, 1929–30. Air Member for Research and Development, 1930–6. Knighted, 1933. Air Officer Commanding-in-Chief, Fighter Command, 1936–40. Mission to the USA for the Ministry of Aircraft Production, 1940–4. Created Baron, 1943.

[2] Arthur Sheridan Barratt, 1891–1966. Second Lieutenant, Royal Artillery, 1910. A pilot, Central Flying School, 1914. An air observer for the artillery, 1916–17 (Military Cross, despatches four times). Wing Commander, Royal Flying Corps, 1917. Director of Staff Duties, Air Ministry, 1935. Air Marshal, 1939. Principal RAF Liaison Officer with the French Air Force, September–December 1939. Air Officer Commanding-in-Chief, British Air Forces in France (BAAF), January–June 1940. Refused to leave the beaches at Dunkirk until he was certain that all his men had got away. Knighted, 1940. Air Officer Commanding-in-Chief, 1940–3. Air Officer Commanding-in-Chief, Technical Training Command, 1943–5. Air Chief Marshal, 1946.

confidence to the Army that they will have their interests fully represented. I hope you will find yourself able to do this, as I am sure nothing but good will come of it.

Winston S. Churchill to Sir Archibald Sinclair
(*Churchill papers, 20/21*)

2 June 1941
Private

My dear Archie,

You have sent me a very serious minute in answer to my request, and I am afraid I must tell you that I do not see how you can expect me to bear my responsibilities if my very clearly and courteously expressed wishes are not treated with proper respect and consideration. As Minister of Defence I am bound to take a direct part in all high appointments in the Fighting Services. No important appointment has been made by either of the other two Services during my tenure without my being consulted, and you yourself have always hitherto followed this practice.

I hope therefore that you will be willing to reconsider your minute, which I now return to you.[1]

John Colville: diary
(*Colville papers*)

3 June 1941 Chartwell

I had lunch alone with the PM and the Yellow Cat,[2] which sat in a chair on his right-hand side and attracted most of his attention. He was meditating deeply on the Middle East, where he is intent on reorganizing the rearward services, and on Lord Beaverbrook who is proving particularly troublesome. The PM said that Lord B just did not begin to understand how to get on with the military. While he brooded on these matters, he kept up a running conversation with the cat, cleaning its eyes with his napkin, offering it mutton and expressing regret that it could not have cream in wartime. Finally he said some very harsh things about Wavell, whose excessive caution and inclination to pessimism he finds very antipathetic.

[1] Sinclair's animosity to Dowding had already led to Churchill's anger when he saw an Air Ministry booklet on the Battle of Britain in which no mention was made of Dowding.

[2] This was Tango. Grace Hamblin writes: 'All cats were made much of, and ginger was the favoured colour – or – "tango" – "Tangerine colour" according to my dictionary!! Sir William Nicholson stayed at Chartwell a great deal before the war when he was painting the "Conversation Piece" which still hangs near the dining room, and "for fun" did a number of charming sketches of Tango.' (*Letter to the author, 22 December 1997*).

Kathleen Harriman[1] to her sister
('Special Envoy to Churchill and Stalin, 1941-1946')

3 June 1941

The PM is much smaller than I expected and a lot less fat. He wears RAF blue jaeger one-piece suits (the only way to keep warm in that house), and looks rather like a kindly teddy bear.

He expresses himself wonderfully – continually comes out with delightful statements. I'd expected an overpowering, rather terrifying man. He's quite the opposite: very gracious, has a wonderful smile and isn't at all hard to talk to.

Winston S. Churchill to General Wavell
(Churchill papers, 20/39)

3 June 1941
Private and Personal

1. Please telegraph exactly what ground and Air forces you are using for Exporter.[2] What are you doing with the Poles? It seems important to use and demonstrate as much Air-power as possible at the very outset, and even the older machines may play their part as they did so well in Iraq. Will it be possible to use some machines in the opening days of Exporter which can return to take part in Bruiser? Nothing must prejudice Bruiser.[3]

2. There is a storm of criticism about Crete, and I am being pressed for explanations on many points. Do not worry about this at all now. Simply keep your eye on Exporter, and, above all, Bruiser. These alone can supply the answers to criticisms just or unjust. The Air superiority available for Bruiser far exceeds anything you are likely to have for many months. As Napoleon said: 'La bataille répondra.' All good wishes.

Winston S. Churchill to General Ismay
(Churchill papers, 20/36)

3 June 1941

This interesting memo,[4] is worthy of the attention of COS Committee. I do not feel convinced by it. At any rate, either war or a show-down is near.

[1] Averell Harriman's daughter, who was with him in Britain.
[2] The codename for the Syrian campaign.
[3] The relief of Tobruk and capture of Cyrenaica.
[4] By General Sikorski, written on May 23, in which, while stating that Germany was ready militarily to attack the Soviet Union, Sikorski concluded that for political reasons 'a German attack on Russia does not seem to enter into consideration'.

Winston S. Churchill to General Ismay, for the Chiefs of Staff Committee
(*Churchill papers, 20/36*)

3 June 1941

DEFENCE OF TAKORADI

I feel very much concerned about this route. Even if the channel of information was irregular, that should not prevent us from facing the danger squarely. We are always being surprised by the Germans because, by their enterprise and audacity, they do things which we consider impossible. Owing to my anxiety, I asked on other papers quite independently of this that the matter might be re-examined.

A fighter force should certainly be organized at Takoradi out of the large surplus of machines which have accumulated there. Fort Lamy has also been pointed out to me as a very weak link.

Winston S. Churchill to General Wavell
(*Premier papers, 3/298/2*)

3 June 1941
Most Secret

I have for some time been considering means by which I could lighten the burden of administration which falls on your shoulders while you have four different campaigns to conduct and so much quasi-political and diplomatic business.

2. During the last nine months we have sent you close on 50 per cent. of our whole output here excepting tanks and less India's sub-share. You have, at the present moment, 530,000 soldiers on your ration strength, 500 field guns, 350 AA guns, 450 heavy tanks, and 350 anti-tank guns. In the months of January to May, upwards of 7,000 mechanical vehicles have reached you. In drafts alone, apart from units, we have sent since the beginning of the year, 13,000. The fighting in the south has for two months past enabled a northward movement to begin, yet you are evidently hard put to it to find a brigade or even a battalion, and in continual telegrams you complain of your shortage of transport, which you declare limits all your operations.

3. In order to help you to produce the best results, I wish to relieve you as much as possible of administration and thus leave you free to give your fullest thought to policy and operations. Here at home General Brooke has a very large Army to handle and train, but he has behind him the Departments of the War Office and the Ministry of Supply. Something like this separation of functions must be established in the Middle East, although in this case your ultimate authority as Commander-in-Chief will reign over the whole theatre.

4. What has been said above applies also *mutatis mutandis* to the Air Force and the Fleet Air Arm.

5. The shipping stringency has prevented the reinforcement of the Middle East to the scale which I had hoped some months ago, and the undoubted threat of invasion has in the last summer and autumn made the General Staff and the Home Forces Command most close-fisted. Nevertheless, it is hoped, depending on the situation, to send you in the next four months, that is to say, June, July, August and September, an additional Infantry Division besides the 50th, as well as a full supply of drafts, details and equipment of all kinds. Thus it should be possible to organize for the autumn and winter campaigns, which may well be very severe, the following mobile field forces:

4 Australian Divisions, 1 New Zealand Division, 2 British Indian Divisions (4th and 5th), 2 South African Divisions, The 6th British Infantry Division – to be organized on the spot, The 50th British Infantry Division, and The new Division (total British Divisions 3).

You have now ready or in process of construction the 7th and the 2nd Armoured Divisions, and you have got to make the best you can of the trained Cavalry Division which is being reconstituted as an Armoured force. Total 15 Divisions. This represents about 600,000 men, from which, without prejudice to the mobile divisions, internal security forces and rearward services must also be provided.

6. All future British Indian Divisions will go in at Basra, and I hope that Eritrea, Abyssinia, Kenya and the Somalilands can be left to native African forces (less one West African Brigade to be returned to West Africa) and armed white police.

7. The development and maintenance of the Army of the Nile operating in Cyrenaica and in Syria would require organization and workshops on a far larger scale than you have yet enjoyed. Not only must the Egyptian workshops be raised in strength and efficiency, but further bases, with adequate port facilities, will have to be built up, say, at Port Sudan and Massawa, using perhaps the town of Asmara, which has fine buildings, and also Jibuti, when we get it. At the same time developments on a great scale will be set on foot by the Government of India with our active aid, it being hoped that at least 6 or 7 divisions, with apparatus, may presently operate thence.

8. I therefore propose to set up under your general authority an organization under an Officer of high rank, who will be styled 'Intendant-General of the Army of the Middle East'. This Officer will be equipped with an ample staff drawn largely from your existing administration staff and with a powerful and growing civilian element to discharge for you, as mentioned above, many of the services rendered by the War Office and Ministry of Supply to General Brooke. His duties will include the supervision and control of rearward administrative services, including the military man-power not embodied in the tactical Units or employed in the active military zone.

9. President Roosevelt is now sending, in addition to the 30 ships under the American flag, another 44 vessels, which carry, among other things, 200 additional Light Tanks from the United States Army Production, and many other important items of which I will furnish you a list. It seems to me probable, and I am trying to arrange, that a great part of the supply of your armies shall come direct from the United States both by the Eastern and the Western routes.

10. Accordingly, we are sending out by air General Haining and Mr T. C. L. Westbrook[1] of the Ministry of Aircraft Production. General Haining will be appointed Intendant-General. The War Office are telegraphing to you separately instructions which are being issued to him. Under him, Mr Westbrook will take charge of the development of ports and transportation facilities and the reception, maintenance and repair of the whole of the armoured vehicles and mechanical transport. He will be accompanied by a number of consultants on specialized subjects, such as transportation, port development and workshops. He will collaborate with Air Marshal Dawson, who is in charge of the cognate activities of the Royal Air Force and Fleet Air Arm, with a view to pooling resources.

11. General Haining's duties in the first place will be to examine on the spot and to discuss with you the implementing and precise definition of the general directive and policy set forth in the preceding paragraphs which must be accepted as a decision of His Majesty's Government. After not more than a fortnight from the date of his arrival, the report must be telegraphed home. I hope it may be agreed, but any points of difference will be settled promptly by me. Moreover, I shall not allow the scheme to lose any of its force and scope in the detailed application which must now be given to it.

12. Because of the great mass and importance of the American supplies, and the fact that the war in the Middle East cannot be conducted at its needful scale without them, I have asked President Roosevelt to allow his envoy here, Mr Harriman, to proceed forthwith to the Middle East with the other members of the Mission. Mr Harriman enjoys my complete confidence and is in the most intimate relations with the President and with Mr Harry Hopkins. No one can do more for you. Mr Harriman will be accompanied by one or two of his own assistants who have shown great aptitude and ardour over here. It would be disastrous if large accumulations of American supplies arrived without efficient measures for their reception and without large-scale planning for the future. Besides this, it will be necessary that considerable numbers of American engineers and mechanics should come for the servicing and repair of their own types of aircraft, tanks, and MT.[2] I commend Mr Harriman to

[1] Trevor Cresswell Lawrence Westbrook, 1901–1978. General Manager, Vickers Supermarine, 1929–36; Vickers Aviation Section, 1937–40. Ministry of Aircraft Production, 1940. Director of Aircraft Repairs and all American aircraft purchases. Member of the Ministers' Council, 1941. Production Adviser to the Ministry of Supply, 1941–42. Mission to the United States, 1942. Production Controller, de Havilland Aircraft, 1942–45. Production Adviser, de Havilland's Canada.

[2] Motor Transport.

your most attentive consideration. He will report both to his own Government and to me as Minister of Defence.

Winston S. Churchill to A. V. Alexander
(*Churchill papers, 20/36*)

4 June 1941
Secret

RELEASE OF MINERS ENGAGED ON ADMIRALTY UNDERGROUND OIL STORAGE SCHEMES

1. It is a mistake in my view to go on with Lyness beyond the limited scheme agreed when I was at the Admiralty. The number of miners employed on the whole three schemes, Lyness, Invergordon and Portsmouth, is, as you say, very small. I think you should set an example by releasing them.

2. The fact that when your underground schemes are completed only 15 per cent. of Naval oil will be comprised, shows how very exiguous and elusive this form of protection is.

3. I do not know why you should assume that during an invasion the enemy will be able to make stronger attacks upon our oil depots than he can in ordinary times. One would suppose he would first of all be concerned in employing his limited Air Force upon the support of his major operations.

Sir Alexander Cadogan: diary
(*'The Diaries of Sir Alexander Cadogan'*)

5 June 1941

Defence Committee last night decided to go on with Syria. PM takes the cynical view that he has to face a debate on Crete on Tuesday. So we'd better begin the Syrian venture on Saturday and take the two together!

John Colville: diary
(*Colville papers*)

5 June 1941

New appointments are under consideration, connected with the establishment of a ministry of light, fuel, heat etc. Beaverbrook has refused an offer of Agriculture <u>and</u> Food. Brendan says that he takes up more of the PM's time than Hitler.

Winston S. Churchill to Lord Beaverbrook
(*Churchill papers, 20/24*)

5 June 1941 10 Downing Street

My dear Max,

It has been announced that a Ministry of Fuel, Power and Light will be created. If you would like to take charge of this while remaining a member of the War Cabinet, I will immediately go into the matter and see whether I can arrange it. It would not be possible for you to take coal alone and handle it in the executive manner which would be natural to you, and leave power and light where they are now. These three are intimately connected and form a command of their own.

Alternatively it might be possible to persuade Hudson to take Fuel, Power and Light, and for you to take Agriculture. Many people think that Agriculture and Food should be in one hand, but I am not in a position at present to make any such proposal to you, as it does not appear that Lord Woolton has any desire to relinquish his work at Food, – a difficult task which he does very well. I note also that in your letter of last night you say definitely that you would not wish to take on Food.

Here then are the only two proposals for direct executive authority which it is in my power at the present time to suggest to you.

I have always felt that your bent is for executive authority and your splendid achievements at MAP proved this was true. I must again remind you that at the time Chamberlain retired from the Government I made severe and intricate efforts to give you a much wider sphere than MAP, and to place you in the control of all those responsibilities which formed the old Ministry of Munitions, i.e. MAP plus M of S.[1] You were ill then, and you refused. Other arrangements have now become consolidated.

More recently you insisted upon leaving MAP. I regretted this very much because I felt your genius worked to full capacity there. But the state of your health was such that I could not press you further, and after resistance of over three weeks I met your wish.

There are two functions in war-time Government. The Executive and the Supervisory. The Parliamentary and Press mood stresses very strongly the need for men with no Executive office but a broad, instructed and reflective outlook on the war. It is not possible to combine this with vehement executive action in this or that particular topic or particular Department without destroying the responsibility of the Ministerial chiefs of those Departments. The Prime Minister, whoever he may be, is indeed accorded a certain right of incursion and as Minister of Defence I have wide powers. The Services and Departments will take from a Prime Minister what they will not take from

[1] Ministry of Aircraft Production and Ministry of Supply.

anyone else. I am in full agreement with you that the present arrangement is not working well. The alternative therefore is that you should either take an Executive Department while remaining a member of the War Cabinet or reconcile yourself to the higher but more indirect and remote forms of authority.[1]

War Cabinet: minutes
(*Cabinet papers, 65/18*)

5 June 1941
12 noon

10 Downing Street

CRETE

The Prime Minister said that a desire had been expressed that there should be a debate in the following week in the House of Commons on the operations in Crete. The debate must take place, although his own view was that it did not increase the prestige of the House that a debate should take place on what was no more than an isolated operation in the middle of a big campaign.

As regards procedure he proposed, in reply to a question, to indicate that no Government speech would be made at the opening of the debate, which would be held in public; but that a speech would be made by a Government spokesman at the close of the proceedings if the course of the debate made this necessary.

The War Cabinet approved generally the course proposed.

The Prime Minister then reviewed the strategy of the operations in Crete. He was satisfied that there had been overwhelming justification on military grounds for the course which had been adopted.

BRITISH BLOCKADE OF FRENCH NORTH AFRICA

The Prime Minister said that as the United States Government were showing interest in this part of the world, and thought that they could do something effective if they held out inducements to General Weygand, we should have to fall in with their views.

VICHY GOVERNMENT INTENTIONS[2]

The Prime Minister said that he thought we must now consider the contingency that the Vichy Government might take warlike action against us. He did not think that they would declare war on us, but that they might do everything short of that to help the Germans. Plans should be prepared on this

[1] Churchill prepared this letter for sending, then marked it 'Hold'. It was never sent.

[2] This section of the War Cabinet's discussion was recorded in the Confidential Annex (*Cabinet papers, 65/22*).

assumption. We ought to have ready at hand some form of effective action against this eventuality. Among the matters which should be considered were:

(a) The possibility of attacking Vichy and Toulon from the air.
(b) Unlimited submarine warfare against French shipping (unless provided with navicerts) in certain zones, which would be laid down.

The Prime Minister then read a telegram from the Commander-in-Chief, Mediterranean (2344C of 4th June) in regard to the French Fleet at Alexandria, asking for instructions as to the action which he should take if the situation developed as the result of our forces entering Syria.

The Prime Minister thought that no action should be taken *vis-à-vis* the French Fleet at Alexandria until we had marched into Syria, as there was a chance that Admiral Godefroi[1] would come over to our side. A reply to Admiral Cunningham should be drafted on these lines.

Winston S. Churchill to A. V. Alexander and Admiral Pound
(*Churchill papers, 20/36*)

5 June 1941

U-BOAT SINKINGS NEAR DAKAR

This must be regarded as a Naval disaster of the first order, and I must ask what measures you are taking to cope with this new situation?

I do not know why the Admiralty have decided to close their minds to the idea that the German U-boats are being succoured from Dakar. Nothing could be more helpful to bring in American aid than the statement that Dakar is being used; yet the Admiralty go out of their way to make out that Dakar is innocent.

War Cabinet, Battle of Atlantic Committee: minutes
(*Cabinet papers, 86/1*)

5 June 1941 10 Downing Street
6 p.m.

SHIPPING LOSSES: TAKORADI SUPPLY ROUTE

The Prime Minister referred to the recent heavy shipping losses off the West Coast of Africa. We had strong reasons for suspecting that enemy U-boats were operating from a base at Dakar, but this had not been definitely proved, as they might be using supply ships.

An account was given of the steps already taken and the further steps proposed for providing increased protection for our shipping in these waters.

[1] Commander of the French naval forces in the Eastern Mediterranean, 1940. It was his ships that the British had interned in Alexandria in June 1940.

Steps were also being taken to decrease, so far as possible, the volume of shipping calling at Freetown.

The Prime Minister referred to the heavy losses which we had been recently inflicting on enemy shipping and asked the First Lord of the Admiralty to submit a statement showing these losses as a proportion of the merchant shipping available for use by the enemy.

TURN-ROUND OF SHIPPING: UNITED KINGDOM

The Prime Minister said that he saw no reason why night-shifts should not be employed on loading and unloading cargoes, provided that splinter and blast proof protection was built near-by, where the dockers could take refuge if an alarm was given.

The Import Executive was invited to take this question up as a matter of urgency.

War Cabinet, Defence Committee (Operations): minutes

(*Cabinet papers, 69/2*)

5 June 1941 Cabinet War Room
9.30 p.m.

IRAQ OIL

The Prime Minister said that it would be better to destroy the oil facilities in Iraq too soon rather than to allow them to fall into the hands of the Germans. That would be a disaster.

Mr Geoffrey Lloyd[1] said that the main functions of the Haifa pipe line was to supply the Mediterranean Fleet with oil. If the Chiefs of Staff considered it strategically sound to destroy this line, he would not oppose that decision. He drew attention however to the shortage of oil tankers and to the fact that, if we destroyed the Haifa oil line, we should require the equivalent of another eight to eleven tankers.

In further discussion the danger was stressed that we might delay destroying the oil facilities until it was too late. This should be avoided at all costs.

In summing up the Prime Minister said that all preparations to destroy the oil facilities should go forward with the utmost despatch but that we should not take a decision to effect the destruction until we saw how the situation in Syria turned out.

[1] The Secretary for Petroleum.

Winston S. Churchill to Air Chief Marshal Sir Charles Portal
(*Churchill papers, 20/36*)

5 June 1941

Please see General Wavell's personal telegram to me today, stating Air Force available for Exporter and Battleaxe.[1] They seem terribly disappointing, especially the latter. Does Air Marshal Tedder realize the critical character of operation, and the need of a great effort? Have you not received any message from him yourself?

Winston S. Churchill to General Dobbie
(*Churchill papers, 20/39*)

6 June 1941

I am entirely in agreement with your general outlook. The War Office will deal in detail with all your points. It does not seem that an attack on Malta is likely within the next two or three weeks. Meanwhile, other events of importance will be decided enabling or compelling a new view to be taken. You may be sure we regard Malta as one of the master-keys of the British Empire. We are sure that you are the man to hold it, and we will do everything in human power to give you the means.

John Colville, diary
(*Colville papers*)

6 June 1941
midday

. . . today the PM is away at a demonstration near Cromer.[2]

[1] Exporter was the codename for the British military campaign to take Syria from Vichy control. Battleaxe was the planned British offensive in the Western Desert designed to pin the Axis forces in front of Sollum while a combined infantry and armoured force opened the way for a drive to relieve the garrison in beleaguered Tobruk.

[2] It was at Overstrand near Cromer that Churchill and his family had been holidaying on the eve of war in 1914.

John Colville: diary
(*Colville papers*)

6 June 1941
evening

The PM returned, instead of going straight on to Ditchley, on account of telegrams from Washington which show that Pétain and Weygand have both agreed to military cooperation with Germany, and of difficulties connected with the Free French, General Spears, Syria and innumerable complications related to matters of prestige and *amour propre*.

Winston S. Churchill to General de Gaulle
(*Churchill papers, 20/39*)

6 June 1941
Most Immediate
Secret

I wish to send you my best wishes for success of our joint enterprise in the Levant. I hope that you are satisfied that everything possible is being done to provide support to the arms of Free France. You will, I am sure, agree that this action, and indeed our whole future policy in the Middle East, must be conceived in terms of mutual trust and collaboration. Our policies towards the Arabs must run on parallel lines. You know that we have sought no special advantages in the French Empire, and have no intention of exploiting the tragic position of France for our own gain.

I welcome therefore your decision to promise independence to Syria and the Lebanon, and, as you know, I think it essential that we should lend to this promise the full weight of our guarantee. I agree that we must not in any settlement of the Syria question endanger the stability of the Middle East. But subject to this we must both do everything possible to meet Arab aspirations and susceptibilities. You will, I am sure, bear in mind the importance of this.

All our thoughts are with you and the soldiers of Free France. At this hour when Vichy touches fresh depths of ignominy, the loyalty and courage of the Free French save the glory of France.

Winston S. Churchill to General de Gaulle
(*Churchill papers, 20/49*)

6 June 1941

I must ask you in this grave hour not to insist on declaring Catroux High Commissioner of Syria.[1]

John Colville: diary
(*Colville papers*)

6 June 1941

On late duty. The PM dictated his speech for next Tuesday, rather cantankerous in tone and likely, unless substantially toned down, to cause a good deal of unfavourable comment. Pug says he thinks it is impossible to run a war efficiently if so much time has to be devoted to justifying one's actions in the House of Commons. At the risk of seeming smug he maintains that no error or misconception was made in the direction of the campaign from this end. General Freyberg specifically said he was not afraid of the air.

Went to bed exhausted at 2.30 a.m.

Henry Channon: diary
(*'Chips'*)

6 June 1941

On all sides one hears increasing criticism of Churchill. He is undergoing a noticeable slump in popularity and many of his enemies, long silenced by his personal popularity, are once more vocal. Crete has been a great blow to him.

John Colville: diary
(*Colville papers*)

7 June 1941

The Prime Minister saw the editors of the newspapers this morning with a view to damping down their criticism and explaining the position.

De Gaulle is showing himself highly-strung and quarrelsome. Desmond

[1] De Gaulle agreed that General Catroux would be called 'French Delegate and Plenipotentiary'. Two weeks later, on 19 June 1941 Churchill telegraphed to De Gaulle: 'You may be sure that I always cherish the interests of the Free French Movement so vital to the rebirth of France.' (Prime Minister's Personal Telegram, T.308, *Churchill papers, 20/40*).

Morton actually thinks he might go over to Vichy. Much will depend on events in the very near future.

The PM went off to Ditchley at tea-time . . .

Winston S. Churchill to President Franklin D. Roosevelt
(*Churchill papers, 20/39*)

7 June 1941
Personal and Secret

We enter Syria in some force tomorrow morning in order to prevent further German penetration. Success depends largely upon attitude of local French troops. De Gaulle's Free French outfit will be prominent but not in the van. He is issuing a proclamation to the Arabs offering, in the name of France, complete independence and opportunity to form either three or one or three in one free Arab States. Relations of these States with France will be fixed by treaty safeguarding established interests somewhat on the Anglo-Egyptian model. General Catroux is not to be called High Commissioner but French delegate and plenipotentiary.

2. I cannot tell how Vichy will react to what may happen. I do not myself think they will do much worse than they are now doing, but, of course, they may retaliate on Gibraltar or Freetown. I should be most grateful if you would keep your pressure up upon them. We have no political interests at all in Syria except to win the war.

3. Thank you so much for letting Harriman go to the Middle East. He is seeing your son tomorrow before leaving, and I shall see him myself, I hope, at luncheon on Monday.

Winston S. Churchill to John Moore-Brabazon
(*Churchill papers, 20/36*)

7 June 1941

I am informed that in the week ended 24th May a total of 23 of all types of American aircraft were assembled in this country, and in the week ended 31st May the figure was 34.[1]

These figures show that modification and assembly is proceeding at a rate far short of that at which aircraft are arriving in this country from the United States. On this basis, it is not likely that we will catch up on the American

[1] These figures, which were accurate, were sent to Churchill by the Minister of State, Lord Beaverbrook (Moore-Brabazon's predecessor as Minister of Aircraft Production).

aircraft, now numbering more than 1,000, which are awaiting modification and assembly.

A bigger basis of operations and a wider scale of conversions seems to be urgently required. Pray let me have your proposals.

Winston S. Churchill to General Sir John Dill
(*Churchill papers, 20/36*)

7 June 1941
Most Secret

OPERATIONS IN SYRIA

But surely if things go well and there is not any serious opposition, he will run on even with small columns of a few hundred men and occupy the airfields in the north, and take possession of the towns? As long as this is viewed as a purely military operation, these kind of plans are all right, but, supposing it turns out that the people are well disposed, we ought without hesitation to run great risks and overrun as much of the country as possible.

Latakia is a place which is worrying me a good deal. Possibly there may be a German landing there in force if the Navy fails to stop them.

I do not see how we shall be greatly benefited if we leave the fortified line of the Palestine frontier only for the defence of Damascus and Beirut, and if the enemy at his leisure occupies the airfields in the north. Please speak to me about this.

Winston S. Churchill to Robert Menzies
(*Churchill papers, 20/39*)

7 June 1941
sent 6.55 p.m.
Most secret and personal

It is all right your sending a telegram like your 344[1] to me through the High Commissioner, but if it is anything purely personal I would rather it came to me direct, and there are some things I must say to you in Australia that I should not care to mention to a single soul here beyond our limited circle. I think it important we should preserve a direct channel for exceptional messages. Such messages should begin Winch.[2] Does this suit you? Let me know.

2. We go into Syria tomorrow morning in considerable force. The other

[1] On the need for air reinforcements for both the defence of Cyprus and Malta.
[2] 'Winch' was to be the future prefix of all Menzies' secret telegrams.

plan about which you know will be a little later. I cannot guarantee results about Syria as it all depends upon which way the two French cats jump. Am more hopeful of the other business.

3. I feel very much for you in all your difficulties. I cannot help being hopeful about the future. Second part of Jaguar,[1] about 50 in all, got through last night.

Winston S. Churchill to General Sir John Dill
(*Churchill papers, 20/36*)

7 June 1941
Secret

As soon as we know the results of Battleaxe[2] we shall be able to come to a decision on this.

I agree with you it is impossible to meet General Wavell's requests. He would be very well advised 'to undertake large-scale offensive armoured operations' while his fleeting superiority remains. If he can destroy or cripple the armoured forces of the enemy and occupy the all-important airfields, the pressure of the enemy may be greatly retarded and reduced.

Winston S. Churchill to Professor Lindemann
(*Cherwell papers*)

7 June 1941
Action this Day
Secret

I have several times asked you to check up on German and British Air strengths as we left it at the end of Mr Justice Singleton's investigations.[3] Pray let me have this return by Monday at latest.

I should imagine that the enemy have lost a great many more aircraft than we have, but what is the new rate of construction which he has achieved? How do matters stand? It is over two months ago since I had a thorough check made.

[1] The despatch of fighter aircraft to Egypt through the Mediterranean, on board aircraft carriers.

[2] The planned offensive operations in the Sollum, Tobruk and Capuzzo area.

[3] Basing himself on the most secret source of British Signals Intelligence, Enigma, in April 1941 Judge Singleton had calculated the German Air Force front line strength at 4,420 as against a British front line strength of 3,485 (2,751 in the Metropolitan Air Force and 734. Lindemann noted on 10 June 1941 that the British air strength had increased by 217 since then.

Operation Exporter, the attack on Vichy French forces in Syria, began on the morning of 8 June 1941, with the capture of Beirut and Damascus as its objective.

Winston S. Churchill to Randolph Churchill
(*Churchill papers, 1/362*)

8 June 1941 Ditchley

Darling Randolph,

Averell Harriman is travelling out to the Middle East, and I take the opportunity of sending you a line. There is so much to say, one hardly knows where to begin.

Harriman's daughter, who is charming, and Pamela have made friends and are going to take a small house together while he is away. It seems a pity that the house that was furnished at Ickleford is not available. Still, you are getting a very good rent.

A gigantic 4,000 pound bomb fell just outside the building of your flat in Westminster Gardens, obliterating the fountain and cracking the whole structure on one side. Unluckily it is the wrong side for you. The CIGS who was sleeping quite close, in fact about twenty yards away, seems to have had a marvellous escape and is greatly exhilarated by the explosion. I am trying to get a similar stimulus applied in other quarters, but it is difficult to arrange.

The Annexe is now becoming a very strong place, but we have only once been below the armour during a raid. Your Mother is now insisting upon becoming a fire watcher on the roof, so it will look very odd if I take advantage of the securities provided. However, I suppose everybody must do their duty.

I sent you out an inquiry about the 60 men[1] because I heard a great deal of criticism here about these special troops surrendering in droves, and so on, and whatever other people may think, I am quite clear that these men ought to have fought till at least thirty per cent. were killed or wounded. Large, general capitulations are of a different character, but small parties are expected to put up a fight and not walk out of a cave with their hands up like a lot of ridiculous loons.

A young officer brought a letter from you hot-foot last week, but it was dated March 3, arriving June 6. Much your best chance would be to post letters at the Embassy, and I daresay they would stretch a point to oblige you.

[1] An incident which took place when Italian forces surprised the small British garrison on Castelorizzo Island, the most easterly of the Italian Dodecanese islands, off the southern coast of Turkey.

I see Pamela from time to time, and she gives me very good accounts of Winston.[1] I have not seen him as he is living in Max's domains.

The Air attack has greatly lessened, and the Air Force are very disappointed that this moon-phase should have been spoiled by clouds, as they were hoping to make an impression upon the raiders. On the whole, I think the attack will not be so successful as it has been in the past, and at the moment we are having very little of it. Anyhow, I think the Baby is quite safe where he is.

You know Duncan[2] had a frightful accident. He was going down in a car from London to Aberporth, and was lying down asleep with his shoes off. He had two drivers, but both fell asleep simultaneously. The car ran into a stone bridge which narrowed the road suddenly, and both his feet are smashed up, also some injury to his spine. For the time being he has had to give up his Command, but it is possible he may be able to return to his duties by hobbling about. He has done extraordinary good work, and had become a Colonel. If he breaks down, there is always the House of Commons.

Our old House of Commons has been blown to smithereens. You never saw such a sight. Not one scrap was left of the Chamber except a few of the outer walls. The Huns obligingly chose a time when none of us were there. Oddly enough, on the last day but one before it happened I had a most successful Debate and wound up amid a great demonstration. They all got up and cheered as I left. I shall always remember this last scene. Having lived so much of my forty years in this building, it seems very sad that its familiar aspect will not for a good many years be before me.[3] Luckily we have the other place in good working order, so that Parliamentary institutions can function 'undaunted amid the storms'. We are now going to try the experiment of using the House of Lords. The Peers have very kindly moved on into the big Robing Room, and handed over their Debating Chamber to us. In about a fortnight

[1] Winston Spencer Churchill, 1940– . Born 10 October 1940, the son of Randolph and Pamela Churchill. Educated at Eton and Christ Church Oxford. A newspaper correspondent from 1963 (Yemen, Congo, Angola). In 1964 he published *First Journey*. Author, with his father, of *The Six Day War* (1967). Conservative MP since 1967. Parliamentary Private Secretary to the Minister of Housing and Construction, 1970–2; to the Minister of State, Foreign and Commonwealth Office, 1972–3. Conservative Party front bench spokesman on defence, 1976–8. Author of *Defending the West*, 1981. Member of the Select Committee on Defence since 1983. A Governor of the English-Speaking Union, 1975–80. Published *Memories and Adventures*, 1989 and a biography of his father, *His Father's Son*, in 1996.

[2] Duncan Sandys, who was married to Churchill's daughter Diana.

[3] On 17 May 1941 the *Daily Telegraph* published an extract from a First World War reminiscence by A. MacCallum Scott, who had been in the House of Commons with Churchill one evening in March 1917. 'Just before we left the building,' MacCallum Scott recalled, 'he took me by the arm and steered me into the deserted Commons chamber. All was darkness, except for a ring of faint light from concealed lamps under the gallery. We could dimly discern the untidy litter of papers on the floor and the table, but the walls and the roof were invisible. "Look at it!" he said. "This little place is what makes the difference between us and Germany. It is in virtue of this that we muddle through to success, and for lack of this Germany's brilliant efficiency will lead her to final disaster. This little room is the shrine of the world's liberties."'

I expect we shall be there. I never thought to make speeches from those red benches, but I daresay I shall take to it all right.

An Opposition is being formed out of the left-outs – LG, Hore-Belisha, Shinwell, Winterton, and some small fry, mostly National Liberals. They do their best to abuse us whenever the war news gives them an opportunity, but there is not the slightest sign that the House as a whole, or still less the country, will swerve from their purpose. I expect next Tuesday when I have to speak on Crete, we shall have Horeb[1] descanting upon the shortage of anti-aircraft guns. I am going to remind him of the Privilege case,[2] and a few other things which occur to me.

I hope you will try to see Averell Harriman when he arrives. I have made great friends with him, and have the greatest regard for him. He does all he can to help us.

By the time you get this, all sorts of things will have happened which I cannot refer to on paper. At the present time I am hopeful that we shall retrieve and restore the position. Meanwhile, in the larger sphere, not only are we gaining mastery over the Air attack, but making good progress in the Battle of the Atlantic. The United States are giving us more help every day, and longing for an opportunity to take the plunge. Whether they will do so or not remains an inscrutable mystery of American politics. The longer they wait, the longer and the more costly the job will be which they will have to do.

I am sending with this a copy of *Into Battle*. It appears that this title was the name of Julian Grenfell's sonnet, and I got a note from Ettie Desborough saying how much she appreciated our having appropriated it. In order to put this right, I have, as you will see, had inserted in the new editions some of the best lines of his poem.[3]

[1] Leslie Hore-Belisha.

[2] On 17 June 1938 Duncan Sandys had sent Hore-Belisha the draft of a question which he wished to ask on London's air defences. As the question was clearly based on secret information, Hore-Belisha, with Churchill's approval, told Sandys to call on the Attorney-General, who told Sandys that unless he disclosed the name of his informant, he would be liable to prosecution under the Official Secrets Act. On June 29 Sandys informed the House that, in his capacity as a junior officer in the Territorial Army, he had received orders to appear in uniform before the Military Court of Inquiry. This he submitted, was a 'gross breach' of the privileges of the House. His submission was upheld, and a Committee of Privileges reported on the following day that a breach of privilege had indeed been committed. During the ensuing debate, Churchill commented caustically that an act devised to protect the national defence should not be used to shield Ministers who had neglected national defence.

[3] In the sixth printing (and subsequent printings) of *Into Battle*, Churchill quoted the second stanza of Julian Grenfell's poem:

> The fighting man shall from the sun
> Take warmth, and life from the glowing earth;
> Speed with the light-foot winds to run,
> And with the trees to newer birth;
> And find, when fighting shall be done,
> Great rest, and fullness after dearth.

We have a pleasant party here (Ditchley), and a very good film each night. I find this a great relief at weekends, as it takes one away for a couple of hours from the war mill. Oliver Lyttelton is here with his wife.[1] He had had a great success with a Bill to crush out all small businesses, and another to take all our clothes away from us. These very severe measures have proved extremely palatable to the nation, and the victims seem to have been all reduced to complacency. I also put, as you will have seen, Mr Leathers in a fine position. He is our Traffic Manager. Pray God he delivers the goods.

Mr Brabner[2] has just arrived with messages from you, and also news of the battle – fresh from Maleme Aerodrome; but as he left before the battle began, he was not quite so informative as I had hoped.

Everything is very solid here, and I feel more sure than ever that we shall beat the life out of Hitler and his Nazi gang. We are waiting with much interest to know what fortunes have attended our entry into Syria. No one can tell which way the Vichy French cat will jump, and how far the consequences of this action will extend. It looks to me more and more likely that Hitler will go for Stalin. I cannot help it. All my sympathies are already fully engaged.

I am having this letter left for you at the Embassy, Cairo, and am asking them to tell you that it has arrived. I do not want it to go up to the line, and after you have received it, you should not take it there. Leave it at the Embassy, or burn it. Do not show it to strangers. I am glad that Lampson and his wife[3] have been nice to you, and I am sure it is a comfort to have a good hot bath and a clean bed there when you come in from the Desert.

All good luck.
My very best wishes
Your loving father
Winston S. Churchill

P.S. I send you a cheque for £100 which I expect you can get cashed in Cairo. I am telling Lloyds to notify some Bank or other there in case they have not a Branch, and will send you full advice about it.

[1] Lady Moira Godolphin Osborne, fourth daughter of the tenth Duke of Leeds. One of their three sons was later killed in action.

[2] Rupert Arnold Brabner, 1911–1945. A merchant banker. Member of the London County Council, 1937. Conservative Member of Parliament for Hythe, 1939. Under-Secretary of State for Air, 1944. Missing, presumed dead, on a flight to Canada, when he was to have represented Britain at the formal ending of the Empire Air Training Scheme, March 1945. Churchill announced his death in the House of Commons on 28 March 1945.

[3] Jacqueline, daughter of Sir Aldo Castellani, a leading expert in tropical diseases. She married Lampson, as his second wife, in 1934.

Winston S. Churchill to President Franklin D. Roosevelt
(*Churchill papers, 20/39*)

8 June 1941

At the end of last year we were on the point of holding a meeting of the Representatives of the Dominions and Allied Governments in London. The meeting was to hear a statement from me on the war situation and was intended to be a symbol of our common determination to see the war through to a successful conclusion. The meeting was postponed as it proved impossible to persuade the Greek Government, who at that time were not at war with Germany, to send a representative.

2. We think this is a good moment to revive the proposal, and a meeting has indeed been suggested by two of our Allies. At a time when the Germans are trying to declare peace in Europe, it will be useful to show that the inhabitants of the occupied countries are still alive and vigorous, and that their lawful Governments are carrying on the war from overseas with all the resources at their command.

3. The meeting will be on June 12th. It will be quite brief. I shall make a statement and I have no doubt that the Allied Representatives will also speak. The meeting will be attended by the Dominion High Commissioners, and the Prime Ministers, Foreign Secretaries and other representatives of the Allied Governments. The Free French movement will be represented. The resolution, of which I am sending you a copy, has already been agreed with the Dominions and Allies.

4. I hope the meeting will provide a convincing demonstration of our common tenacity of purpose, but I need hardly say, Mr President, what an accession of strength it would be if the United States Government felt it possible to be associated in some form or another with the proceedings.

Winston S. Churchill to General Ismay, for the Chiefs of Staff Committee
(*Cabinet papers, 120/300*)

8 June 1941

LORD TRENCHARD'S[1] MEMORANDUM ON BOMBING POLICY

Is para. 5 (a)[2] to be interpreted as concentrating upon the marshalling yards business in contradistinction to oil, enemy warships, U-boats and aircraft factories and residential districts in large cities? If so, it seems to me a very bleak and restricted policy.

Generally speaking, I believe it will be found better to have a definite programme for each month and carry it out as far as possible, rather than trying to formulate a policy expressed in terms of principle. For this purpose, let me see, set out on three sheets of paper, the work of the Bomber Command in March, April and May, showing sorties each night, targets attacked, weight of bombs discharged and our losses.

Winston S. Churchill to A. V. Alexander and Admiral Pound
(*Churchill papers, 20/36*)

8 June 1941

FRENCH WARSHIPS AT ALEXANDRIA

We cannot give a guarantee not to use the ships ourselves during the war. On the contrary, our only interest in acquiring them is to use them. Otherwise they would be better scuttled. There must be no weakening on this point. On the other hand, assurances may be given that ships will be restored at the end of the war and compensation paid for any lost in the fighting.

Repatriation can of course be offered. If they will not agree, let them starve in strict isolation on their ships, till they come to their senses.

[1] Hugh Montague Trenchard, 1873–1956. Entered the Army, 1893. Active service, South Africa, 1899–1902 (dangerously wounded). Major, 1902. Assistant Commandant, Central Flying School, 1913–14. Lieutenant-Colonel, 1915. General Officer Commanding the Royal Flying Corps in the Field, 1915–17. Major-General, 1916. Knighted, 1918. Chief of the Air Staff, 1918–29. Air Marshal, 1919. Created Baronet, 1919. Air Chief Marshal, 1922. Marshal of the Royal Air Force, 1927. Created Baron, 1930. Commissioner, Metropolitan Police, 1931–5. Created Viscount, 1936. Trustee of the Imperial War Museum, 1937–45. A member of the Other Club from 1926. His elder son, and both his stepsons, were killed in action in the Second World War.

[2] Of a Chiefs of Staff Report (Chiefs of Staff Report No. 86, Operations, of 1941), commenting on Lord Trenchard's Memorandum on Bombing Policy.

Winston S. Churchill to Robert Menzies
(*Cabinet papers, 69/2*)

9 June 1941
Personal and Secret

It is not possible to hold Cyprus without having control of the Syrian airfields. We therefore thought it better to try to gain these, when we should be in a position to support Cyprus more effectively. In the meanwhile there is one Australian Divisional Mechanized Cavalry Regiment and one British Battalion with local troops and six Hurricanes. They are a deterrent on anything but a fairly substantial hostile scale of attack. If the enemy comes in force before we have got hold of Syria, the 1,500 men in Cyprus will have to take to the mountains, which are rugged and high, and there maintain a guerrilla as long as possible. If we cannot get control of Syria or the Germans defeat the guerrilla in the mountains, we shall probably get a good many away. Chiefs of Staff do not think this is an unfair task to set troops. There are many worse in war. No other course is open except immediate evacuation, inviting unopposed landing. I am anxious to help you in your difficulties, and, if you wish it, I will see that Australian troops are withdrawn from Cyprus with or without relief.

War Cabinet: minutes
(*Cabinet papers, 65/18*)

9 June 1941 10 Downing Street
5 p.m.

INDIA

The Prime Minister thought that it would be important, when the expansion of the Executive was announced, to base its justification on administration needs, and to emphasize that the changes did not, of course, provide any solution of the constitutional issue.

Winston S. Churchill to General Wavell
(*Premier papers, 3/287/1*)

9 June 1941

Your 0/70840.[1] Many thanks for this very full *exposé*. We notice that you do not mention the Air at all, in which we hoped you would have large superiority over the Germans. I was much concerned at your statement in an earlier

[1] A memorandum by General Wavell, 'Appreciation of the Situation in the Western Desert'.

telegram that you would have only 4 fighter and 4 bomber squadrons on date of Battleaxe. I presume you are in daily touch with Tedder and still more that your two staffs are working operationally in the closest combination. The CAS informs me that on the latest information from Tedder you should have 10 squadrons in Western Desert besides support from 3½ Wellington squadrons which can play a most important part. In addition, I hope that at least some elements of the 7 squadrons re-equipping and immobile may be used in the battle in view of its supreme importance. In fact, it is to be hoped that pilots and aircraft available from whatever source can be fed to the advanced units, which I realize are limited in number through losses of transport and equipment in Greece. This should enable you to make good your losses in a manner not possible to the enemy. You should therefore consider not only the number of squadrons available, but the number of aircraft which can be brought into action during the three or four days' intense fighting which may be necessary for a decision. I hope that, after the closest possible concert with Tedder, you will tell us how it is proposed to use the Air Force as one of the decisive and integral features of your plan.

2. I am very sorry to learn that you can employ no more than the 8 battalions mentioned in paragraph 6. I take it this is the usual transport shortage. Kindly state how many lorries are required per battalion, how many you are using for the whole operation, and how many you have on charge in Egypt.

3. Are we right in inferring from your 1 (b) that enemy may attack Tobruk before Battleaxe begins? If so, I presume you would welcome it.

4. I venture once again to emphasize that the objective is not the reaching of particular positions but the destruction by fighting of the armed force of the enemy wherever it may be found. As your force diminishes, so should his. He has a far longer line of communication than you and must be in greater difficulties about supply, especially of ammunition.

5. You do not state how many AT guns you propose to employ although they would seem to be necessary to protect the infantry and strong points gained against enemy Tank counter-attacks.

6. I am very glad to read your last paragraph of 0/70840 because this battle may well be the turning-point of the whole campaign.

I have also received your 0/70904 of 7/6 about Haining's mission and your actual strength. All this will be most carefully examined by the War Office. I fully recognize your grievous losses of MT in Greece.

Sir Alexander Cadogan: diary
(*'The Diaries of Sir Alexander Cadogan'*)

9 June 1941

Cabinet at 5. Can't make out what's happening in Syria. Wilson's technique – directly an operation begins – is to dry up completely and give *no* news at all. PM very angry at this, as he has to make statement to House tomorrow. He said 'it's damned bad manners'. He discussed course of debate tomorrow. He said: 'People criticize this Government, but its great strength – and I dare say it in this company – is that there's no alternative! I *don't* think it's a bad Government. Come to think of it, it's a very good one. I have *complete* confidence in it. In fact there never has been a government to which I have felt such sincere and whole-heated loyalty!'

During 10 June 1941, on Churchill's instructions, the Soviet Ambassador in London, Ivan Maisky, was given by Sir Alexander Cadogan a list of German troops concentrated on the Soviet borders, identifying all units. The Ambassador was not told this information derived from the British reading of German Enigma messages.

Winston S. Churchill to General Wavell
(*Churchill papers, 20/49*)

10 June 1941

There are some rumours in the newspapers here that we are deliberately going slow in Syria so as to avoid shedding French blood. This will cause adverse comments when Parliament meets on Tuesday, and I hope I may receive your assurances that military considerations alone rule.

War Cabinet, Defence Committee (Operations): minutes
(*Cabinet papers, 69/2*)

10 June 1941 Cabinet War Room
9.45 p.m.

AIR REINFORCEMENTS FOR IRAQ

The Prime Minister drew attention to Telegram No. 7146/G dated the 8th June from the Commander-in-Chief, India,[1] in which he pressed for some air

[1] General Auchinleck.

forces to be at the disposal of the Force Commander in Iraq.[1] He (the Prime Minister) had already questioned the decision of the Chiefs of Staff that No. 60 Squadron should not be brought back from Singapore as suggested by Commander-in-Chief, India. He thought it would be fulfilling a more useful function in Iraq than at Singapore. We could not afford to fritter away our resources by keeping squadrons far from the battle to meet unlikely eventualities.

Winston S. Churchill: speech
(*Hansard*)

10 June 1941 House of Commons

The Prime Minister (Mr Churchill): I do not think anyone, however Ministerially-minded, could possibly complain of the tone, temper and matter of this Debate. The kind of criticism we have had today, some of it very searching, is the kind of criticism that the Government not only accept but welcome. All the same, the House will permit me perhaps to point out that the way in which this Debate came about was calculated to give one the feeling of a challenge to the security of the Administration, and, from the point of view of the advantage to the country, that raises serious considerations. There were all kinds of paragraphs and reports which appeared in the papers about the grave uneasiness and unrest, stating that a Debate on Crete must take place. The parties were demanding it, the Labour party, the Liberal party and members of the Conservative party were demanding it, and there must be a full accounting, an inquest held, and so forth. That being so, one is bound to take a serious view because of the interests which are confided into our care.

I think that it would be a mistake if the House got into the habit of calling for explanations on the varying episodes of this dangerous and widespread struggle and asking for an account to be given of why any action was lost or any part of the front was beaten in. In the first place, no full explanations can possibly be given without revealing valuable information to the enemy, information not only about a particular operation which is over, but about the general position and also of the processes of thought which are followed, such as they may be, by our war direction and our high command. There is always a danger that a Minister in my position, in seeking to vindicate the course we have pursued, should inadvertently say something which may supply the enemy with some essential, with some seemingly innocent fact, about which the enemy is in doubt, and thus enable the enemy to construct a

[1] Major-General J. G. W. Clark (see page 680, note 2).

comprehensive and accurate picture of our state of mind and the way in which we are looking at things. The heads of the Dictator Governments are not under any similar pressure to explain or excuse any ill-success that may befall them. Far be it from me to compare myself or the office I hold or the functions I discharge with those of these pretentious and formidable potentates. I am only the servant of the Crown and Parliament and am always at the disposal of the House of Commons, where I have lived my life.

Still the House, and I think I may say also the country, have placed very considerable responsibilities upon me, and I am sure they would not wish any servant they have entrusted with such duties to be at a disadvantage against our antagonists. I have not heard, for instance, that Herr Hitler had to attend the Reichstag and tell them why he sent the *Bismarck* on her disastrous cruise, when by waiting for a few weeks, and choosing his opportunity, when perhaps our capital ships were dispersed on convoy duty, she might have gone out accompanied by the *Tirpitz*, another 45,000 ton ship, and offered a general sea battle. Neither have I heard any very convincing statement by Signor Mussolini of the reasons why the greater part of his African Empire has been conquered and more than 200,000 of his soldiers are prisoners in our hands.

I must say, quite frankly, to the House that I should feel myself under a needless disadvantage if it were understood that I should be obliged, in public Debate, to give an account, possibly a controversial account, of our operations irrespective of whether the times were suitable or not. It would, for instance, have been a nuisance if Parliament had demanded a Debate on the loss of the *Hood* before we had been in a position to explain what measures we had taken to secure the destruction of the *Bismarck*. I always take – and I am sure that what I say will be accepted – very great pains to serve the House, and on all occasions to associate the House in the fullest possible manner with the conduct of the war, but I think it would be better, and I submit it to the House, if in the future I were permitted on behalf of His Majesty's Government to choose the occasions for making statements about the war, which I am most anxious to do.

There is another general reason why I should have deprecated a Debate upon the Battle of Crete. It is only one part of the very important and complicated campaign which is being fought in the Middle East, and to select one particular sector of our widely extended front for Parliamentary Debate is a partial, lopsided and misleading method of examining the conduct of the war. A vast scene can only be surveyed as a whole, and it ought not to be exposed and debated piecemeal, especially at a time when operations which are all related to one another are wholly incomplete. Into the general survey of the war come all sorts of considerations about the gain and loss of time and its effect upon the future. There also comes into the picture the entire distribution of our available resources to meet the many calls that are made upon them. For instance, my hon. Friend the Member for Kidderminster (Sir

J. Wardlaw-Milne),[1] who has just spoken, asked why it was that when we had Crete in our possession for more than six months we had wasted all that time for constructing numerous airfields and placing them in the highest state of defence, and he reminded us how very efficiently the Germans would have done a work like that if Crete had fallen into their hands. Everyone will, I dare say, admit that it would have been a mistake to make a great number of airfields in Crete unless we could find the anti-aircraft guns, both of high and low ceiling, and the aircraft to defend those airfields, for that would simply have facilitated the descent of the enemy's airborne troops upon the island.

Why then, first of all, I must ask, were enough guns not provided for the two serviceable airfields which existed in Crete? To answer that question one would have to consider how many guns we have and whether we could afford to spare them for that purpose. That leads us to a wider sphere. All this time, the Battle of the Atlantic has been going on, and a great number of the guns which might have usefully been deployed in Crete have been, and are, being mounted in the merchant vessels to beat off the attacks of the Fokke Wulf and Heinkel aircraft, whose depredations have been notably lessened thereby.

Again, we must consider, on the subject of these guns, whether our airfields at home, our air factories or the ports and cities in our Islands, which are under heavy and dangerous attack, should have been further denuded or stinted of guns, in the last six or seven months, for the sake of the war in the Middle East. Further, it must be remembered – I did not notice that this was mentioned – that everything we send out to the Middle East is out of action for the best part of three months, as it has to go round the Cape. We have run very great risks and faced very serious maulings in this Island, in order to sustain the war in the Mediterranean, and no one, I venture to submit, can be a judge of whether we should have run more risks or exposed ourselves to heavier punishment at home, for the sake of fortifying and multiplying the Cretan airfields, without having full and intimate knowledge of all our resources and making a complete survey of the various claims upon them.

We did, however, from the moment that the Greek Government invited us into Crete, take steps to defend the anchorage of Suda Bay, as an important naval base, to develop the aerodrome nearby and to provide the base and the aerodrome with the largest quantity of high and low ceiling guns which we thought it fit to divert from other strategic points in the Mediterranean. We provided, in fact, a deterrent to the enemy attack sufficient to require a major effort on his part; but, of course, there are a great many islands and strategic

[1] John Wardlaw-Milne, –1967. Member of the Bombay Municipal Corporation, 1907–17. Lieutenant-Colonel commanding the 4th (Bombay) Artillery, Indian Defence Force, 1914–19. President, Government of India's War Shipping Advisory Committee, 1914–18. Conservative MP, 1922–45. Knighted, 1932. Chairman, House of Commons Committee on National Expenditure, 1939–45. Chairman, Conservative Foreign Affairs Committee, 1939–45 (also the India and Anglo-Egyptian Committees).

points in the seas, and to attempt to be safe everywhere is to make sure of being strong nowhere.

Therefore, it may well be that if the House were able to go into detail into these matters, which I am afraid is not possible, hon. Members would feel that a reasonable and right disposition of our Forces was made; but without going into the facts and figures, which I am sure no one would wish me to do, even in Secret Session, let alone in Public Session, it is quite impossible for the House, or even for the newspapers, to arrive at a justly proportioned and level judgment on this affair. There is, however, this much that I should like to say: A man must be a perfect fool who thinks that we have large quantities of anti-aircraft guns and aircraft lying about unused at the present time. I will speak about aircraft in a moment, but, so far as anti-aircraft guns are concerned, large and expanding as is our present production, every single gun is in action at some necessary point or other, and all future production for many months ahead is eagerly competed for by rival claimants with, very often, massive cases behind each one of them.

This goes back a long way, but four years ago, in March, 1937, I mentioned to the House that the Germans had already got 1,500 mobile anti-aircraft guns – mobile and formed in batteries – in addition to the whole of their static artillery of anti-aircraft defence. Since then they have been making them at a great rate, and they have also conquered more than all they want from the many countries they have overthrown, so that our position is very different from that. The right hon. Member for Devonport (Mr Hore-Belisha) has made today a very cogent and moderate, well-informed and thoughtful contribution to the Debate, but he used a different mood and tone in a speech which he recently delivered in the country, and that at any rate makes it necessary for me to say that the state in which our Army was left when the right hon. Gentleman had ended his two years and seven months' tenure of the War Office, during the greater part of which he was also responsible for production and supply, was lamentable. We were short of every essential supply, but most particularly of those modern weapons, those special classes of weapons, the anti-aircraft gun, the anti-tank gun and the tank itself, which have proved themselves the vital necessities of modern war, a fact which he is now prepared to suggest we are so purblind and out-dated as not to be able to comprehend.

Mr Hore-Belisha: I do not know why the right hon. Gentleman, for the purposes of Debate, should make a statement such as he has made, that I left the Army in a lamentable condition. It is quite out of accord with what he himself said after the retreat from Dunkirk, that we had lost the finest lot of equipment that had every left these shores, and that the Army had been fully equipped in almost ever particular. The French Ambassador stated that we had fully discharged our obligations to the French. Perhaps my right hon. Friend will be good enough to recall that up till very recently before the war the whole House and indeed the country were opposed to the creation of a Continental Army, which nevertheless I proceeded to try and create. I do not seek to be judged by my achievements, but by what I tried to do, and my right hon. Friend will realize that my obstacles were greater than his today.

The Prime Minister: I thought that I had misquoted my right hon. Friend in some way, but it appears he wished to continue the argument. I am dealing not with the particular equipment of the troops who went to France, who naturally drained the rest of our Forces, but the fact remains that the equipment of our Army at that time, and at the outbreak of war, was of the most meagre and deficient character, and that the deficiencies made themselves most marked – and still make themselves most marked – in the very type of weapons for which there is the greatest possible demand. I could give facts and figures upon this point if we were in private which would, I think, leave no dispute upon the subject. I am not throwing all the blame for this upon my right hon. Friend at all – certainly not – but I think it is only fair, when he himself comes forward and sets himself up as an arbiter and judge, and speaks so scornfully of the efforts of some others who have inherited his dismal legacy, I think when he speaks in this way – he has a great responsibility in the matter – it is only fair to point out to him that he is one of the last people in this country entitled to take that line.

Mr Granville (Eye): No recriminations.

The Prime Minister: The hon. Gentleman said something about no recriminations, but extremely violent and hostile speeches have been spread about, doing a great deal of harm, and about which I have received information from different countries and capitals, showing the uncertainty and disturbance which are caused by them, and certainly if we are attacked we shall counter-attack.

Mr Granville: We are dealing with the future, not with the past.

The Prime Minister: The hon. Member for Eye (Mr Granville) had better return to his lucubrations in constitutional experiment, which exercise his mind so much at present. So much for the difficulty in which we stand in the matter of the anti-aircraft guns. The output is at last rapidly expanding, but the fact remains that our outfits are incomparably inferior in numbers to those possessed by the Germans, and every claim has to be weighed against every other claim. Another general question which may fairly be asked is, 'Why have we not got much stronger and much larger air forces in the Middle East?' I can only say this: From the moment when the Battle of Britain was decided in our favour, in September and October of last year, by the victories of our fighters, we have been ceaselessly sending aircraft as fast as possible to the Middle East, by every route and by every method. During the present year, as our strength in the air has grown, we have not been hampered in this matter, as we were in the case of the anti-aircraft guns, by lack of aircraft. The problem has been to send them to the Eastern theatre of war.

Anyone can see how great are the Germans' advantages, and how easy it is for the Germans to move their Air Force from one side of Europe to another. They can fly along a line of permanent airfields. Wherever they need to alight and refuel, there are permanent airfields in the highest state of efficiency, and, as for the services and personnel and all the stores which go with them – without which the squadrons are quite useless – these can go by the grand continental expresses along the main railway lines of Europe. One has only to compare this process with the sending of aircraft packed in crates, then put on ships and sent on the great ocean spaces until they reach the Cape of Good Hope, then taken to Egypt, set up again, trued up and put in the air when they arrive, to see that the Germans can do in days what takes us weeks, or even more. This reflection, I say, has its bearing upon the possibility of a German movement back from the East to the West, which certainly could be executed very swiftly if they were to resolve upon an assault upon this country. I can give an assurance to the House that we have done, are doing, and will do, our utmost to build up the largest possible Air Force in the Middle East; and it is not aircraft, but solely transportation, which is –

Mr Shinwell: That is the whole trouble.

The Prime Minister: Not transportation in the sense of shipping tonnage, but in the sense of the time that it takes to transfer under the conditions of the present war. It is not aircraft, but transportation, which is the limiting factor at this end. I have dealt with anti-aircraft guns; I have dealt with aircraft. As to the disposition of our Air Force in the Middle East, it is primarily a matter for the Commanders-in-Chief in the Middle East, although His Majesty's Government share to the full their responsibility for whatever is done. I might refer again to what was said by my hon. and gallant Friend the Member for Lewes (Rear-Admiral Beamish) about the importance of co-ordination between the Services. It is carried to a very high pitch. The Chief Air Officer lives in the same house in Cairo as the Commander-in-Chief. They are there side by side. The Naval Commander-in-Chief has to be at sea very often. He has to be at Alexandria. But the very closest association exists between these branches. The idea that any one of these problems would be studied by one of these commanders only, without the closest association with the other two is quite an illusory idea, and I can really assure my hon. Friend on that point.

Major Milner[1] (Leeds, South East): Who has the final say?

The Prime Minister: It is not so much a question of the final say. No disagreement that I know of has arisen. Obviously, the Army is the main factor

[1] James Milner, 1889–1967. On active service, 1914–18 (wounded, despatches, Military Cross and bar). Chairman, Leeds City Labour Party, 1926. Labour MP, 1929–51. Member, Indian Franchise Committee, 1932. Founder, Solicitors' Group, House of Commons. Chairman, History of Parliament Trust. Chairman of the Fire Committee (Civil Defence of the Houses of Parliament), 1943–5. Deputy Speaker, 1943–5. Deputy Speaker, 1943–5 and 1945–51. Created Baron, 1951.

in that business, and the Fleet is preserving the security of the Army on the seas, and preserving the command of the seas, and the Air is assisting the Army and the Fleet in all their functions. But in the event of any differences, they can be settled in a few hours by reference here. These Commanders-in-Chief have to settle it among themselves, although we share to the full responsibility for whatever is done. It must not be forgotten that apart from the effort we made in Greece, which was very costly in aircraft, the situation in Iraq, in Palestine, and potentially in Syria, as well as the winding-up of the Abyssinian story, all made very heavy demands upon our aircraft, and the situation in the Western Desert had also to be considered. Before any rational judgment could be formed upon the disposition of our Air Force and the consequent failure to supply an adequate Air Force for Crete, it would be necessary, as in the case of the anti-aircraft guns, to know not only what are our whole resources, but also what is the situation in these other theatres, which were all, as my right hon. Friend the Member for Keighley (Mr Lees-Smith) pointed out, all intimately interrelated, and it is no use trying to judge these matters without full knowledge, and that full knowledge obviously cannot be made public, and ought not to be spread outside the narrowest circle compatible with the execution of operations.

I come to the next stage of my argument, because I am offering the House an argument, if they will bear with me as I unfold it. I have shown them the foundations upon which we started, and I now go a step forward. In March we decided to go to the aid of Greece in accordance with our Treaty obligations. This, of course, exposed us to the danger of being attacked in the Western Desert, and also to defeat by overwhelming numbers in Greece unless Yugoslavia played her part or unless the Greek Army could be extricated to hold some narrower line than that actually chosen. If Greece was overrun by the enemy, it seemed probable that Crete would be the next object of attack. The enemy, with his vast local superiority in air power, was able to drive our aircraft from the airfields of Greece, and adding this to his enormously superior anti-aircraft batteries, he was able to make those airfields rapidly available for his own use. Moreover, as the season was advancing, many more airfields became available to him as the weather improved and dried them up. It was evident, therefore, that the attack upon Crete, if it were made, would be primarily an airborne attack, for which, again, a vastly superior hostile air force would be available.

The question then arose as to whether we should try to defend Crete or yield it without a fight. No one who bears any responsibility for the decision to defend Crete was ignorant of the fact that conditions permitted of only the most meagre British air support to be provided for our troops in the island or for our Fleet operating round the island. It was not a fact that dawned upon the military and other authorities after the decision had been taken; it was the foundation of a difficult and harsh choice, as I shall show. The choice was:

Should Crete be defended without effective air support or should the Germans be permitted to occupy it without opposition? There are some, I see, who say that we should never fight without superior or at least ample air support and ask when will this lesson be learned? But suppose you cannot have it? The questions which have to be settled are not always questions between what is good and bad; very often it is a choice between two very terrible alternatives. Must you, if you cannot have this essential and desirable air support, yield important key points, one after another?

There are others who have said to me, and I have seen it in the newspapers, that you should defend no place that you cannot be sure you can hold. Then, one must ask, can one ever be sure how the battle will develop before it has ever been fought? If this principle of not defending any place you cannot be sure of holding were adopted, would not the enemy be able to make an unlimited number of valuable conquests without any fighting at all? Where would you make a stand and engage them with resolution? The further question arises as to what would happen if you allowed the enemy to advance and overrun, without cost to himself, the most precious and valuable strategic points? Suppose we had never gone to Greece and had never attempted to defend Crete? Where would the Germans be now? Suppose we had simply resigned territory and strategic islands to them without a fight? Might they not, at this early stage of the campaign in 1941, already be masters of Syria and Iraq and preparing themselves for an advance into Persia?

The Germans in this war have gained many victories. They have easily overrun great countries and beaten down strong Powers with little resistance offered to them. It is not only a question of the time that is gained by fighting strongly, even if at a disadvantage, for important points. There is also this vitally important principle of stubborn resistance to the will of the enemy. I merely throw out these considerations to the House in order that they may see that there are some arguments which deserve to be considered before you can adopt the rule that you have to have a certainty of winning at any point and that if you have not got it beforehand you must clear out. The whole history of war shows the fatal absurdity of such a doctrine. Again and again, it has been proved that fierce and stubborn resistance, even against heavy odds and under exceptional conditions of local disadvantage, is an essential element in victory. At any rate, the decision was taken to hold Crete. The decision to fight for Crete was taken with the full knowledge that air support would be at a minimum, as anyone can see – apart from the question of whether you have adequate supplies or not – who measures the distances from our airfields in Egypt and compares them with the distances from enemy airfields in Greece and who acquaints himself with the radius of action of dive-bombers and aircraft.

Of course, I take the fullest personal responsibility for that decision, but the Chiefs of Staff, the Defence Committee and General Wavell, the

Commander-in-Chief, all in turn and in their various situations not only thought that Crete ought to be defended in the circumstances, which were fully before them, but that, in spite of the lack of air support, we had a good chance of winning the battle. No one had any illusions about the scale of the enemy airborne attack. We knew it would be gigantic and intense. The reconnaissances over the Greek aerodromes showed the enormous mass of aircraft which were gathering there – many hundreds – and it turned out that the enemy was prepared to pay an almost unlimited price for this conquest, and his resources when concentrated upon any particular point may often be overwhelming at that point.

My right hon. Friend the Member for Devonport referred to the broadcasts which were given by the spokesman of the War Office, Major-General Collins,[1] and by the spokesman of the Air Ministry, Air-Commodore Goddard. I take no responsibility for those statements. I take no responsibility for those or any others that may be made. It is very convenient to bring them up in the course of Debate, but the officers who give these broadcasts are not acquainted with the control of affairs and with what is decided or thought or felt in the Chiefs of Staff Committee or the Defence Committee. How can they be? One does not spread things about in that way.

Mr Bellenger:[2] Stop the broadcasts.

The Prime Minister: I would have liked very much to have stopped them, and in some cases I have reduced them in number. I think it is a very risky thing to ask a professional officer, naval, military or air, to give a weekly expatiation on the war when, in the nature of things, although he may be very accomplished in his profession, he cannot know and ought not to know the facts as they are understood at the secret meetings.

Mr G. Griffiths: Everybody thinks he speaks for the Government.

The Prime Minister: I am very glad to see the feeling in the House on the subject, because, on the other side, one is appealed to ceaselessly to give more information, to make the war more interesting to the people, and to tell them more about what is going on. But it is not possible for the head of the Government or even for the Chiefs of Staff to vet – to use a slang term – beforehand these detailed weekly statements which are made. I think the

[1] Dudley Stuart Collins, 1881–1959. On active service, South Africa, 1901–02; European War, 1914–16 (despatches, Distinguished Service Order with bar). Chief Engineer, Southern Command, 1931–35. Director of Fortifications and Works, War Office, 1935–39. Deputy Quartermaster-General, 1939–41. Retired, with the honorary rank of Lieutenant-General, 1941. Spokesman, War Office, 1941–5.

[2] Frederick John Bellenger, 1894–1968. Started work as a tea-packer at the age of 14. Later a boy messenger in the Post Office. Enlisted, August 1914. On active service, Royal Artillery, 1914–18 (twice wounded). 2nd Lieutenant, 1916. A Conservative member of the Fulham Borough Council, 1922–8. Elected to Parliament for Labour, 1935. Captain, Royal Artillery, 1939–40 (including the retreat to Dunkirk). Financial Secretary, War Office, 1945–6. Secretary of State for War, 1946–7.

matter must certainly be reconsidered. [Hon. Members: 'Hear, hear.'] As I have said, no one had any illusions about the tremendous scale of the airborne attack, the greatest ever delivered in the world, or thought that we should resist it without any but the most restricted air support on our side. That is the fact. It is not a nice case, but it is the fact. Let us look at the anatomy of this battle of Crete which was undertaken in those bleak circumstances. We hoped that the 25,000 to 30,000 good troops – I am making it a little vague – with artillery and a proportion of tanks, aided by the Greek forces, would be able to destroy the parachute and glider landings of the enemy and prevent him from using the airfields or the harbours.

Our Army was to destroy the airborne attacks, while the Navy held off or destroyed the seaborne attacks. But there was a time limit. The action of the Navy in maintaining the Northern sea guard without adequate air defence was bound to be very costly. My hon. Friend has pointed out how serious were those losses. We could only stand a certain proportion of naval losses before the Northern sea guard of the Fleet would have to be withdrawn. If meanwhile the Army could succeed in biting off the head of the whole terrific apparatus of the airborne invasion before the naval time limit, or loss limit, was reached, then the enemy would have to begin all over again, and, having regard to the scale of the operation, the enormous, unprecedented scale of the operation, and the losses he would have to incur, he might well for the time being have at least broken it off – at any rate, there would have been a long delay before he could have mounted it again. That was the basis on which the decision was taken.

I wonder what would have been said by our critics if we had given up the island of Crete without firing a shot. We should have been told that this pusillanimous flight had surrendered to the enemy the key of the Eastern Mediterranean, that our communications with Malta and our power to interrupt the enemy's communications with Libya were grievously endangered. There is only too much truth in all that, although perhaps it will not in the end turn out so badly. Crete was an extremely important salient in our line of defence. It was like Fort Douaumont at Verdun in 1916; it was like Kemmel Hill in 1918. These were taken by the Germans, but in each case the Germans lost the battle and also the campaign, and in the end they lost the war. But can you be sure the same result would have been achieved if the Allies had not fought for Douaumont, and had not fought for Kemmel Hill? What would they have fought for if they had not fought for them? These battles can only be judged in their relation to the campaign as a whole.

I have been asked a lot of questions. My right hon. Friend the Member for Keighley[1] put them very clearly and precisely about the actual conduct of the

[1] Hastings Bertrand Lees-Smith.

battle of Crete. For instance, why were the Cretan airfields not mined beforehand? Or again, why were they not commanded by long-range gunfire, or why were not more tanks allotted to their defences? There are many other questions like that. I can give answers to these questions, but I do not propose to discuss tactics here, because I am sure it is quite impossible for us to fight battles in detail, either beforehand or afterwards, from Whitehall or from the House of Commons. His Majesty's Government in their responsibility to Parliament choose the best generals they can find, set before them the broad strategic objects of the campaign, offer them any advice or counsel that may seem fitting, ask searching questions which are very necessary in respect of particular plans and proposals, and then they support them to the best of their power in men and munitions, and also, so long as they retain their confidence, they support them with loyal comradeship in failure or success.

It is impossible to go into tactical details, and I never remember in the last war, in those great battles which cost something like 40,000, 50,000 or 70,000 men – I am talking of battles of a single day – in which sometimes there were very grave errors made, that they were often made the subject of the arraignment of the Government in the House of Commons. It is only where great strategic issues of policy come that it is fitting for us here to endeavour to form a final opinion. Defeat is bitter. There is no use in trying to explain defeat. People do not like defeat, and they do not like the explanations, however elaborate or plausible, which are given them. For defeat there is only one answer. The only answer to defeat is victory. If a Government in time of war gives the impression that it cannot in the long run procure victory, who cares for its explanations? It ought to go – that is to say, if you are quite sure you can find another which can do better. However, it must be remembered that no Government can conduct a war unless it stands on a solid, stable foundation, and knows it stands on that foundation and, like a great ship, can win through a period of storms into clearer weather. Unless there is a strong impression of solidarity and strength in a Government in time of war, that Government cannot give the support which is necessary to the fighting men and their commanders in the difficult periods, in the disheartening and disappointing periods. If the Government has always to be looking over its shoulder to see whether it is going to be stabbed in the back or not, it cannot possibly keep its eye on the enemy.

There is another point of some difficulty which presents itself to me whenever I am asked to make a statement to the House. Ought I to encourage good hopes of the successful outcome of particular operations, or ought I to prepare the public for serious disappointments? From the purely British standpoint, there is no doubt that the second of these courses is to be preferred, and this is the course that I have usually followed. It is the course which, no doubt, would commend itself to my noble Friend [Lord Winterton]. He has been urging us to look on the gloomy side of things – a kind of inverted Couéism.[1] When you get up in the morning you say to yourself, 'We can easily lose this war in the next four months,' and you say it with great emphasis and go on your daily task invigorated. I must point out to my noble Friend, and to the House generally, that the British nation is unique in this respect. They are the only people who like to be told how bad things are, who like to be told the worst, and like to be told that they are very likely to get much worse in the future and must prepare themselves for further reverses. But when you go to other countries – oddly enough I saw a message from the authorities who are most concerned with our Arab problem at present, urging that we should be careful not to indulge in too gloomy forecasts. The Arabs do not understand the British character of meeting trouble long before it comes, and they think it is much better to go on putting a bold face on things and then meet the disaster when it arrives. Any statements of a pessimistic character which are used here are calculated to discourage our friends and to spread alarm and despondency over wide regions, to affect the nicely balanced neutrals and to encourage the enemy, who, of course, seizes upon any phrase or any gloomy allusion and repeats it myriad-fold in his strident propaganda.

It is a nice question whether the increase in our war effort which would result from my noble Friend administering this austere mental treatment to himself in the mornings would counterbalance the undoubted harm which would be done when a phrase torn from its context, and probably with an alteration of the verb, is sent throughout the world – 'Admission in the House of Commons by an eminent nobleman and ex-Minister: We are going to lose the war,' or something like that. I am not blaming him at all. I feel just like him about it, and it is very much safer. It makes me feel very much whether Members of Parliament have not got to pick their words a little carefully. After all, in this deadly war in which we are gripped, with dangers which are measureless, as they are unprecedented, closing upon us in so many quarters, with so much to defend and such limited resources, so many chances which may turn ill against us – when we think of this position, it is a great pity if statements are made which add nothing to the informative criticism which is so valuable, but can be taken from their context and placarded all over the world as a sign that we are not united or that our case is much worse than it is.

There is one thing I regret very much and that is that the brunt of this fighting in the Middle East – I quite agree it is a very foolish expression 'in the Middle East' – or East should have fallen so heavily on the splendid Australian

[1] Couéism: a method of auto-suggestion devised by Emile Coué (1857–1926), a French pharmacist. At his clinic in Nancy he introduced a method of psychotherapy characterized by frequent repetition of the formula, 'Every day, and in every way, I am becoming better and better'. Coué regarded himself not primarily as a healer, but as one who taught others to heal themselves.

and New Zealand troops. I regret it for this reason among others, that the German propaganda is always reproaching us for fighting with other people's blood, and they mock us with the insulting taunt that England will fight to the last Australian or New Zealander. I was very glad to see that Mr Menzies, in his noble speech of Sunday night, dealt with this vile propaganda as it deserved. There have been, in fact, during 1941, almost as many British as there are Australian and New Zealand troops engaged in all the operations in the Western Desert, in Greece and in Crete. The losses during this year compared with the numbers engaged are slightly heavier for the British than for the Dominion troops.

In Crete also, the numbers were almost exactly equal, and the British loss again was slightly heavier. These figures include killed, wounded and missing. They exclude Indian or non-British troops. In order to turn the edge of this German propaganda, I have asked my right hon. and gallant Friend the Secretary of State for War to endeavour to have mentioned more frequently the names of British regiments, when this can be done without detriment to the operations. The following British regiments and units, for instance, fought in Crete: The Rangers, the Black Watch, the Argyle and Sutherland Highlanders, the Leicestershire Regiment, the Welch Regiment, the York and Lancaster Regiment, the Royal Artillery, the Royal Engineers and numbers of the Royal Marines, who formed the rearguard and suffered the most heavily of all. In fact, of 2,000 Royal Marines landed in Crete, 1,400 became casualties or prisoners. Naval losses of life in these operations exceeded 500 officers and men, and while this was going on, we also lost 1,300 men in the *Hood*. Out of 90,000 lives lost so far in this war at home and abroad, at least 85,000 come from the Mother Country. Therefore, I repel and repudiate the German taunt, both on behalf of the Mother Country and of the Dominions of Australia and New Zealand.

It might well be asked – I am trying to look at the questions which might fairly be asked – why, having begun the battle for Crete, did you not persist in the defence of the island? If you could bring off 17,000 men safely to return to Egypt, why could you not have reinforced with 17,000 men to carry on the battle? I have tried to explain in a simple way that the moment it was proved that we could not crush the airborne landings before the Fleet losses became too heavy to hold off longer a seaborne landing, Crete was lost, and it was necessary to save what was possible of the Army. It is one thing to take off 17,000 men as we did, with their side arms, and quite another to land them in a fighting condition with guns and materials. It is a wonderful thing that as many as 17,000 got away in face of the enemy's overwhelming command of the air.

I do not consider that we should regret the Battle of Crete. The fighting there attained a severity and fierceness which the Germans have not previously encountered in their walk through Europe. In killed, wounded, missing and prisoners we have lost about 15,000 men. This takes no account of the losses of the Greeks and Cretans, who fought with the utmost bravery and suffered so heavily. On the other hand, from the most careful and precise inquiries I have made, and which have been made by the Commanders-in-Chief on the spot, we believe that about 5,000 Germans were drowned in trying to cross the sea and at least 12,000 killed or wounded on the island itself. In addition, the air force the Germans employed sustained extraordinary losses, above 180 fighter and bomber aircraft being destroyed and at least 250 troop-carrying aeroplanes. This, at a time when our air strength is overtaking the enemy's, is important. I am sure it will be found that this sombre, ferocious battle, which was lost, and lost, I think, upon no great margin, was well worth fighting and that it will play an extremely important part in the whole defence of the Nile Valley throughout the present year. I do not think there are any who are responsible for it would not take the same decision again, although no doubt, like our critics, we should be wiser in many ways after the event.

It is asked, Will the lessons of Crete be learned, and how will they affect the defence of this Island? Officers who took part in the thickest of the fighting in responsible positions, including a New Zealand brigadier, are already approaching this country. At the same time, very full appreciations have been made by the Staff in the Middle East and are being made in a more lengthy form. All this material will be examined by the General Staff here and will be placed at the disposal of General Sir Alan Brooke, who commands the several millions of armed men we have in this Island, including, of course, the Home Guard. Every effort will be made to profit by it. There are, however, two facts to be borne in mind in comparing what happened in Crete with what might happen here. In the first place, we rely upon a strong superiority in air power and certainly upon a much greater air power, both actually and relatively, than was proved sufficient last autumn. This sustains not only the land defence but liberates again the power of the Navy from the thraldom in which it was held round Crete. In the second place, the scale of the effort required from the Germans in attack would have to be multiplied many times over from what was necessary in Crete, and it might be that this would be beyond the capacity of their resources or their schemes. Everything, however, will be done to meet an airborne and seaborne attack launched upon a vast scale and maintained with total disregard of losses.

We shall not be lulled by the two arguments I have put forward into any undue sense of security. An attack by parachute troops and gliders may be likened to an attack by incendiary bombs, which, if not quickly extinguished one by one, may lead not only to serious fires but to an enormous conflagration. We are making many improvements in the defence of our airfields and in the mobility of the forces which will be employed upon that and other tasks. Nothing will be stinted, and not a moment will be lost. Here I ought to say that it is not true that the Germans clothed their parachute troops who attacked Crete in New Zealand uniforms. I gave that report to the House as it reached me from the Commander-in-Chief in the Middle East, but he now informs me that the mistake arose from the fact that parachute troops, after landing at one point, drove a number of New Zealand walking wounded before them and along with them in their attack, and consequently the cry arose that they themselves were in New Zealand uniforms. There is no objection to the use of parachute troops in war so long as they are properly dressed in the uniform of their country and so long as that uniform is in itself distinctive. This kind of fighting is, however, bound to become very fierce as it breaks out behind the fronts and lines of the armies, and the civil population is almost immediately involved.

Now I come to the operations which have begun in Syria. I have been waiting all day to have further news of our advance, but at the time I got up to speak I had not received any advices that I could impart to the House.

Mr Hore-Belisha: Will the right hon. Gentleman say something about the Air Arm co-operation?

The Prime Minister: I certainly will. The right hon. Gentleman associated himself with a very strong movement there has been for a much greater development of the air force which is actually associated with the Army. Last year, when we were considering our affairs, the great need was to multiply fighters and bombers. It became an enormously important matter. Nevertheless, portions of the Army co-operation squadrons were associated with the military forces, but not on the scale which was desirable or to the extent which was desirable. I think it is of the utmost consequence that every division, especially every armoured division, should have a chance to live its daily life and training in a close and precise relationship with a particular number of aircraft that it knows and that it can call up at will and need.

Mr Bellenger: Under its own command?

The Prime Minister: Certainly, for the purposes of everything that is a tactical operation. It was not possible last year to provide it on a large scale without trenching on other domains which were more vital to our safety, but it is the intention to go forward upon that path immediately and to provide the Army with a larger number, a considerably larger number, of aeroplanes suited entirely to the work they have to do, and above all to the development of that wireless connection between the ground forces and the air which the Germans have carried to such an extraordinary point of perfection. If this had been done in Crete, it would not have made any difference to the event there, because the numbers there for the purpose of co-operating with the troops could not have altered the event.

My right hon. Friend the Member for Devonport[1] asked me who it was who

[1] Leslie Hore-Belisha.

decided that the Air Forces on the aerodromes in Crete were to be withdrawn. It was decided by the Commander-in-Chief of the Air Force in the Middle East, on the recommendation of General Freyberg, concurred in by the RAF officer commanding on the spot, Group-Captain Beamish. It was at that request. The numbers were small, and if they had not been withdrawn, they would have been blown off the aerodromes without having been able in the slightest degree to affect the course of events. I did overlook that point in my statement, and I am glad that my right hon. Friend has reminded me of it.

Now I come to the Syrian operation. Let me repeat that we have no territorial designs in Syria or anywhere else in French territory. We seek no Colonies or advantages of any kind for ourselves in this war. Let none of our French friends be deceived by the blatant German and Vichy propaganda. On the contrary, we shall do all in our power to restore the freedom, independence and rights of France. I have, in a letter which I wrote to General de Gaulle, said 'the rights and the greatness of France', we shall do all in our power to restore her freedom and her rights, but it will be for the French to aid us in restoring her greatness. There can be no doubt that General de Gaulle is a more zealous defender of France's interests than are the men of Vichy, whose policy is that of utter subservience to the German enemy.

It did not take much intelligence to see that the infiltration into Syria by the Germans and their intrigues in Iraq constituted very great dangers to the whole Eastern flank of our defence in the Nile Valley and the Suez Canal. The only choice before us in that theatre for some time has been whether to encourage the Free French to attempt a counter-penetration by themselves or whether, at heavy risk in delay, to prepare a considerable force, as we have done. It was also necessary to restore the position in Iraq before any serious advance in Syria could be made. Our relations with Vichy and the possibilities of an open breach with the Vichy Government evidently raised the military and strategic significance of these movements to the very highest point. Finally, and above all, the formidable menace of the invasion of Egypt by the German Army in Cyrenaica, supported by large Italian forces, with German stiffening, remains our chief pre-occupation in the Middle East.

The advance by the German army forces into Egypt has been threatened for the last two months, and there would not be much use in attempting to cope with the situation in Syria, if, at the same time, our defences in the Western Desert were beaten down and broken through. We had to take all these things into consideration, and I was very glad indeed when General Wavell reported that he was in a position to make the advance which began on Sunday morning, and which, so far as I have been informed up to the present, is progressing with very little opposition and favourably. This position in Syria was very nearly gone. The German poison was spreading through the country, and the revolt in Iraq, perhaps beginning prematurely, enabled us to take the necessary measures to correct the evil; but, as I say, we must not rejoice or give way to jubilation while we are engaged in operations of this difficulty and when the reaction of the Germans still remains to us obscure and unknown.

It is very easy, if I may say so, for critics, without troubling too much about our resources and even without a sense of the features of time and distance, to clamour for action now here and now there: 'Why do you not go here; what' as I think an hon. Member said, 'are you dithering about; why do you not go in there?' and so on. Indeed, one can see how many attractive strategic propositions there are, even with the most cursory examination of the atlas. But the House will, I am sure, best guard its own dignity and authority by refraining from taking sweeping or superficial views. Others have said that we must not follow a hand-to-mouth strategy, that we must regain the initiative and impart to all our operations that sense of mastery and design which the Germans so often display. No one agrees with that more than I do, but it is a good deal easier said than done, especially while the enemy possesses vastly superior resources and many important strategical advantages. For all those reasons I have never, as the House knows, encouraged any hope of a short or easy war.

None the less, it would be a mistake to go to the other extreme and to belittle the remarkable achievements of our country and its Armed Forces. There are many things for which we may be thankful. The air attack on this Island has not overwhelmed us; indeed, we have risen through it and from it strengthened and glorified. There is no truth in the statement of my right hon. Friend the Member for Devonport, which he made in his speech in the country, that productivity in our factories is falling off at an alarming rate. It may not be going as fast as we would like, and if anyone can do anything to make it go faster, or tell us how to do it, he will be rendering a great service. But it is not simply a question of giving very strident orders and demands. There is a great deal more than that in making the whole of our factories go properly, but it is certainly the exact reverse of the truth to say that productivity is falling off at an alarming rate. In guns and heavy tanks, for instance, the monthly average for the first quarter of 1941 was 50 per cent. greater than in the last quarter of 1940. The output for the month of May, a four-week month, was the highest yet reached and more than double the monthly rate for the last quarter of 1940.

Mr Hore-Belisha: Surely my right hon. Friend is confusing productivity and the production. Of course, there is an increase of production in certain articles, but with absenteeism, to which his attention was called by the Labour party conference, and by the Select Committee on Aircraft Production, the output per man cannot be what it was, and one can give many other illustrations.

Mr Benjamin Smith (Rotherhithe): It is not the men but the lack of materials.

Mr Hore-Belisha: I agree.

The Prime Minister: I read into the word the meaning most people read into it; when he said productivity was falling off, I took it to mean not the effort of each man but the general production. I felt I must contradict his statement today because it happens that I have heard from two foreign countries in the course of the morning of the very serious effect which this statement produced upon opinions there; how it was published rapidly throughout Spain, for instance, and given the greatest prominence coming as it did from an ex-Secretary of State. It was said to be exercising a bad effect.

Mr. Hore-Belisha: But the Minister of Labour the very same day had said that the building of factories and aerodromes was falling behind. Did that get circulated in Spain?

The Prime Minister: I do not see any difficulty in reconciling that. The Minister might be urging the men to make greater efforts, he might say that this particular lot of airfields were falling behind, what the programme actually was, but that is quite a different thing from saying that the productivity of our factories is falling off. I must say I do not think we are in a sufficiently safe position to allow ourselves the full luxuries of vehement statements upon these very grave matters. As I say, we have many things we may be thankful for. In the first place, we have not been overwhelmed by the air attack; and our production, far from being beaten down by the disorganization of that attack, has been increasing at a very high rate.

The Battle of the Atlantic is also being well maintained. In January, Herr Hitler mentioned March as the peak month of his effort against us on the sea. We were to be exposed to attacks on a scale never before dreamed of, and there were rumours of hundreds of U-boats and masses of aircraft to be used against us. These rumours were spread against us in the world, and a very alarming impression was produced. March has gone, April has gone, May has gone, and now we are in the middle of June. Apart from the losses incurred in the fighting in the Mediterranean – which were serious – the month of May was the best month we have had for some time on the Atlantic. Prodigious exertions were made to bring in the cargoes and to protect the ships, and these exertions have not failed. It is much easier to sink ships than to build them or to bring them safely across the ocean. We have lately been taking a stronger hand in this sinking process ourselves. It is a most astonishing fact that in the month of May we sank, captured or caused to be scuttled no less than 257,000 tons of enemy shipping, although they present us with a target which is perhaps one-tenth as great as we present to them. While they slink from port to port, under the protection of their air umbrella, and make short, furtive voyages from port to port across the seas, we maintain our whole world-wide traffic, with never less than 2,000 ships on the seas or less than 400 in the danger zones on any day. Yet the losses we inflicted upon them in the month of May were, I think, in the nature of three-quarters of the losses they inflicted upon us. This also has a bearing on the possibility of seaborne invasion, because the destruction of enemy tonnage is proceeding at a most rapid and satisfactory rate.

Nor need these solid grounds for thankfulness and confidence fall from us when we look at the aspect of the war in the Middle East. We have been at war for 21 months. Almost a year has passed since France deserted us and Italy came in against us. If anybody had said in June last that we should today hold every yard of the territories for which Great Britain is responsible in the Middle East; that we should have conquered the whole of the Italian Empire of Abyssinia, Eritrea and East Africa; that Egypt, Palestine and Iraq would have been successfully defended, he would have been thought a very foolish visionary. But that is the position at the moment. It is more than three months since the Germans gave out that they would be in Suez in a month and were telling the Spaniards that when Suez fell they would have to come into the war. Two months ago many people thought that we should be driven out of Tobruk, or forced to capitulate there. The last time we had a Debate on the war in this House so instructed a commentator as my hon. and gallant Friend the Member for Petersfield (Sir G. Jeffreys) warned us gravely of the danger of a German thrust at Assiout, at the head of the delta.

Six weeks ago all Iraq was aflame, and Habbaniya was declared to be in the direst jeopardy. Women and children were evacuated by air. It was reported from enemy quarters that a surrender would be forced. A hostile, insurgent Government ruled in Baghdad, in closest association with the Germans and the Italians. Our forces were pinned in Basra, having only just landed. Kirkuk and Mosul were in enemy hands. All has now been regained. We are advancing into Syria in force. Our front at Mersa Matruh in the Western Desert is unbroken and our defensive lines there are stronger than ever. The large forces which were occupied in the conquest of Abyssinia are now set free, with an immense mass of transport, and large numbers are on their way to, or have already reached, the Delta of the Nile.

I think it would be most unfair and wrong, and very silly in the midst of a defence which has so far been crowned with remarkable success, to select the loss of the Crete salient as an excuse and pretext for branding with failure or taunt the great campaign for the defence of the Middle East, which has so far prospered beyond all expectation, and is now entering upon an even more intense and critical phase.

I give no guarantee, I make no promise or prediction for the future. But if the next six months, during which we must expect even harder fighting and many disappointments, should find us in no worse position than that in which we stand today, if, after having fought so long alone, single-handed against the might of Germany and against Italy, and against the intrigues and treachery of Vichy, we should still be found the faithful and unbeaten guardians of the Nile Valley and of the regions that lie about it, then I say that a famous chapter will have been written in the martial history of the British Empire and Commonwealth of Nations.

Winston S. Churchill to Lord Moyne
(*Churchill papers, 20/31*)

11 June 1941
Secret

DUKE OF WINDSOR'S REQUEST FOR A PRESS ATTACHÉ

It is first necessary to find the man. I hear from various quarters of very unhelpful opinions being expressed both by the Duke and Duchess. What is wanted is a competent and important American publicist who would come down from time to time to Nassau, and try to instil sound ideas into that circle. It does not matter if there is a row. We want someone of sufficient character and standing to say, 'This sort of stuff you put out in your interview has done a great deal of harm. I can only tell you the opinion in the United States. It will affect your influence there.' Or again, 'Any language of this kind will cut you off from the great mass of the American people.'

I do not much like using an American journalist or editor for this purpose, but it might have more effect as he might gain influence with the Duke by showing him how to prepare the way for him to make an American visit, which would be utterly impossible while he expresses the kind of views attributed to him.

When we have found a good man, he had better fly over here, so that we can explain to him verbally the importance and character of his mission.

I was thinking of someone of the standing of Mr Chenery,[1] of *Collier's* Magazine. But there may well be more lively personalities.

Advise me how we can proceed in these directions, and talk to me about it. The less there is on paper, the better. There is no harm in sending the telegram.

[1] William Ludlow Chenery, 1884–1949. Born in Virginia. Educated at the University of Chicago. Reporter for the *Chicago Evening Post*, 1910–14. Edited the leader page of the *Rocky Mountain News*, 1914. Editorial writer on the *Chicago Herald*, 1914–18. Associate-editor of *The Survey*, 1919; the *New York Globe*, 1921–3. Editorial writer, *New York Herald*, 1923. Managing Editor, *New York Sun*, 1923. Editor, *New York Telegram-Mail*, 1924. Editor of *Collier's Weekly*, 1925–43. President, Pelham (New York) Board of Education, 1937. Publisher of *Collier's Weekly* from 1943 until his death.

Winston S. Churchill: Oral Answers
(*Hansard*)

11 June 1941 House of Commons

DOMINION REQUEST FOR A DOMINION WAR CABINET

Mr Granville: Would my right hon. Friend accept the assurance that there is a considerable public opinion which requires this, but which does not desire to bicker or to hinder the Prime Minister in the conduct of the war? Will he bear in mind that I am merely following the writings and the precepts of Winston Churchill.

The Prime Minister: I am afraid that at times that gentleman was very annoying.

John Colville: diary
(*Colville papers*)

11 June 1941

Shigemitsu, the lame Japanese Ambassador, came to say good-bye to the PM at No. 10. I suppose he is being recalled on account of his known anglophil views.

Winston S. Churchill to President Franklin D. Roosevelt
(*Churchill papers, 20/39*)

11 June 1941
Secret and Personal

I am looking forward to welcoming your son here. I have been told that he has a plan to take over, equip and defend an air base at Bathurst in Gambia as a staging and servicing point for heavy US bombers to be flown across the Atlantic to the Middle East. His idea is that USA should lease base and install naval, military and air defences. Bombers would be flown from USA via Pernambuco to be serviced Bathurst, then flown on by American ferry pilot organization to Egypt. Bathurst base all-American. We are whole-heartedly in favour of this proposal and would be prepared to give you a lease at Bathurst on similar terms to those already given for bases in the Western Atlantic. I had intended to postpone putting this proposal to you until I had talked it over with your son, but he has been delayed, and the matter is so urgent that I wanted to put it to you at once. If the proposal commends itself to you in principle, our Staffs over here could work out the details.

Winston S. Churchill to William Mackenzie King
(*Churchill papers, 20/39*)

11 June 1941
Most Secret and Personal

I am most grateful to you for your communications with regard to the proposed meeting of Dominion Prime Ministers. Let me assure you that I realize fully the difficulties which a Prime Minister must find in leaving his country in time of war, in view of the many problems which constantly crop up. The last thing I want to do is to cause embarrassment to you or the Prime Ministers of the other Dominions. On the other hand, there are powerful reasons in favour of such a meeting at an early date. The war has now been in progress for nearly two years, and it would be a great help to me to have your combined minds on the many strategic and other problems that we have to face. I am therefore reluctant to abandon the project, which I believe to be of considerable importance from the Empire point of view. I should be most grateful if you could consider the matter again in the light of this telegram. I hope, on further reflection, you may feel it possible to come to this country at any rate for a limited period of time. I would suggest, as a date, the end of July. This should be convenient to Mr Fraser, who is shortly due here and would, I hope, be able to arrange to stay on over the period of the meeting. Should your reply be favourable, I would then get into immediate touch with the other Prime Ministers.

Winston S. Churchill to Loyd Moyne and General Ismay
(*Churchill papers, 20/36*)

11 June 1941

Our policy is the strictest possible blockade of Jibuti. The fairest terms have been offered to these people. Nothing must be done to mitigate the severity of the blockade. It might, however, be possible to arrange that if a return were furnished of the number of new-born babies and young children, a very limited amount of nourishment might be allowed to pass into the town under the most strict restrictions and surveillance.

On no account must the Governor of Aden[1] take any action which will weaken the blockade, and no supplies of any kind are to move into the town without my approving the arrangements first.

[1] John Hathorn Hall, 1894–1979. On active service, 1914–18; awarded the Military Cross and the Belgian Croix de Guerre. Entered the Egyptian Civil Service (Ministry of Finance), 1919–20. Assistant Principal, Colonial Office (Middle East Department), 1921; Principal, 1927. Chief Secretary to the Government of Palestine, 1933–7. British Resident, Zanzibar, 1937–40. Governor and Commander-in-Chief, Aden, 1940–4. Knighted, 1944. Governor and Commander-in-Chief, Uganda, 1944–51.

In the Honours List published on 12 June 1941, Professor Lindemann received a barony (becoming Lord Cherwell) and Kathleen Hill received an MBE.

John Colville: diary
(*Colville papers*)

12 June 1941

At 12.00 began the meeting of Allied Representatives in the picture gallery at St James' Palace. I attended and sat at a table with Edward Bridges, Nicholas Lawford[1] and Roger Makins.[2] The PM made a powerful speech of invective against the enemy, which he enjoys and at which he excels. The representatives of ten nations sat round the long table and listened appreciatively, but the dignity of the scene was marred by such modern appliances as microphones, cinema apparatus and innumerable photographers. This did not disturb the PM who shook his finger at the microphone as if it had been the Führer himself that he was addressing. When he came to a passage in which he spoke of the stain on the German name which nothing would eradicate for hundreds of years, Van[3] (who today becomes Lord Van) became wreathed in appreciative smiles.

Winston S. Churchill: speech[4]
(*BBC Written Archives Centre*)

12 June 1941 St James's Palace

In the twenty-second month of the war against Nazism we meet here in this old Palace of St James's, itself not unscarred by the fire of the enemy, in order to proclaim the high purposes and resolves of the lawful constitutional Governments of Europe whose countries have been overrun; and we meet here also to cheer the hopes of free men and free peoples throughout the world. Here before us on the table lie the title-deeds of ten nations or States

[1] V. G. Lawford (known as Nicholas). Assistant Private Secretary to Anthony Eden at the Foreign Office, 1940–45.

[2] Roger Makins, 1904–1996. Entered the Foreign Office, 1928. Served in Washington, 1931–4. Acting First Secretary, 1939. Adviser on League of Nations Affairs, 1939. Acting Counsellor, 1940. Deputy Under-Secretary of State, Foreign Office, 1948–52. Knighted, 1949. Ambassador to the United States, 1953–6. Joint Permanent Secretary to the Treasury, 1956–9. Chairman, United Kingdom Atomic Energy Authority, 1960–4. Created Baron Sherfield, 1964.

[3] Sir Robert Vansittart.

[4] The speech notes from which Churchill read when delivering this paragraph are printed immediately following this text.

whose soil has been invaded and polluted, and whose men, women, and children lie prostrate or writhing under the Hitler yoke. But here also, duly authorized by the Parliament and democracy of Britain, are gathered the servants of the ancient British Monarchy and the accredited representatives of the British Dominions beyond the seas, of Canada, Australia, New Zealand, and South Africa, of the Empire of India, of Burma, and of our Colonies in every quarter of the globe. They have drawn their swords in this cause. They will never let them fall till life is gone or victory is won. Here we meet, while from across the Atlantic Ocean the hammers and lathes of the United States signal in a rising hum their message of encouragement and their promise of swift and ever-growing aid.

What tragedies, what horrors, what crimes have Hitler and all that Hitler stands for brought upon Europe and the world! The ruins of Warsaw, of Rotterdam, of Belgrade[1] are monuments which will long recall to future generations the outrage of the unopposed air-bombing applied with calculated scientific cruelty to helpless populations. Here in London and throughout the cities of our Island, and in Ireland, there may also be seen the marks of devastation. They are being repaid, and presently they will be more than repaid.

But far worse than these visible injuries is the misery of the conquered peoples. We see them hounded, terrorized, exploited. Their manhood by the million is forced to work under conditions indistinguishable in many cases from actual slavery. Their goods and chattels are pillaged, or filched for worthless money. Their homes, their daily life are pried into and spied upon by the all-pervading system of secret political police which, having reduced the Germans themselves to abject docility, now stalk the streets and byways of a dozen lands. Their religious faiths are affronted, persecuted, or oppressed in the interests of a fantastic paganism devised to perpetuate the worship and sustain the tyranny of one abominable creature. Their traditions, their culture, their laws, their institutions, social and political alike, are suppressed by force or undermined by subtle, coldly-planned intrigue.

The prisons of the Continent no longer suffice. The concentration camps are overcrowded. Every dawn the German volleys crack. Czechs, Poles, Dutchmen, Norwegians, Yugoslavs and Greeks, Frenchmen, Belgians, Luxembourgers, make the great sacrifice for faith and country. A vile race of quislings – to use the new word which will carry the scorn of mankind down the centuries – is hired to fawn upon the conqueror, to collaborate in his designs, and to enforce his rule upon their fellow-countrymen, while grovelling low themselves. Such is the plight of once glorious Europe, and such are the atrocities against which we are in arms.

[1] Warsaw was bombed in September 1939, Rotterdam in May 1940, and Belgrade in April 1941, each at the outbreak of hostilities, and with heavy civilian casualties.

It is upon this foundation that Hitler, with his tattered lackey Mussolini at his tail and Admiral Darlan frisking by his side, pretends to build out of hatred, appetite, and racial assertion of a new order for Europe. Never did so mocking a fantasy obsess the mind of mortal man. We cannot tell what the course of this fell war will be as it spreads remorselessly through ever-wider regions. We know it will be hard, we expect it will be long; we cannot predict or measure its episodes or its tribulations. But one thing is certain, one thing is sure, one thing stands out stark and undeniable, massive and unassailable, for all the world to see.

It will not be by German hands that the structure of Europe will be rebuilt or the union of the European family achieved. In every country into which the German armies and the Nazi police have broken there has sprung up from the soil a hatred of the German name and a contempt for the Nazi creed which the passage of hundreds of years will not efface from human memory. We cannot yet see how deliverance will come, or when it will come, but nothing is more certain than that every trace of Hitler's footsteps, every stain of his infected and corroding fingers will be sponged and purged and, if need be, blasted from the surface of the earth.

We are here to affirm and fortify our union in that ceaseless and unwearying effort which must be made if the captive peoples are to be set free. A year ago His Majesty's Government was left alone to face the storm, and to many of our friends and enemies alike it may have seemed that our days too were numbered, and that Britain and its institutions would sink for ever beneath the verge. But I may with some pride remind your Excellencies that, even in that dark hour when our Army was disorganized and almost weaponless, when scarcely a gun or a tank remained in Britain, when almost all our stores and ammunition had been lost in France, never for one moment did the British people dream of making peace with the Conqueror, and never for a moment did they despair of the common cause. On the contrary, we proclaimed at that very time to all men, not only to ourselves, our determination not to make peace until every one of the ravaged and enslaved countries was liberated and until the Nazi domination was broken and destroyed.

See how far we have travelled since those breathless days of June a year ago. Our solid, stubborn strength has stood the awful test. We are masters of our own air, and now reach out in ever-growing retribution upon the enemy. The Royal Navy holds the seas. The Italian fleet cowers diminished in harbour, the German Navy is largely crippled or sunk. The murderous raids upon our ports, cities, and factories have been powerless to quench the spirit of the British nation, to stop our national life, or check the immense expansion of our war industry. The food and arms from across the oceans are coming safely in. Full provision to replace all sunken tonnage is being made here, and still more by our friends in the United States. We are becoming an armed community. Our land forces are being perfected in equipment and training.

Hitler may turn and trample this way and that through tortured Europe. He may spread his course far and wide, and carry his curse with him: he may break into Africa or into Asia. But it is here, in this island fortress, that he will have to reckon in the end. We shall strive to resist by land and sea. We shall be on his track wherever he goes. Our air power will continue to teach the German homeland that war is not all loot and triumph.

We shall aid and stir the people of every conquered country to resistance and revolt. We shall break up and derange every effort which Hitler makes to systematize and consolidate his subjugation. He will find no peace, no rest, no halting-place, no parley. And if, driven to desperate hazards, he attempts the invasion of the British Isles, as well he may, we shall not flinch from the supreme trial. With the help of God, of which we must all feel daily conscious, we shall continue steadfast in faith and duty till our task is done.

This, then, is the message which we send forth today to all the States and nations, bond or free, to all the men in all the lands who care for freedom's cause, to our allies and well-wishers in Europe, to our American friends and helpers drawing ever closer in their might across the ocean: this is the message – Lift up your hearts. All will come right. Out of the depths of sorrow and sacrifice will be born again the glory of mankind.

Winston S. Churchill: speech notes[1]

(*Elizabeth Nel papers*)

12 June 1941

The prisons of the continent
no longer suffice.
The concentration camps are crowded.
Every dawn the G firing-parties
are at their work.
Czechs, Poles, Dutchmen, Norwegians,
Serbs and Greeks, Frenchmen, Belgians,
Yugoslavs,
make the final sacrifice
for faith and country.
A vile race of Quislings
– to use the new word wh will carry
the scorn of mankind
down the centuries –

[1] These notes are set out in the form Churchill used for almost all his speeches. Among his Private Office it was known as 'speech form' or 'Psalm form'. The notes reproduced here were kept by Elizabeth Layton (later Nel), who had begun work for Churchill ten days earlier, and was to remain his secretary until the end of the war. There were no Luxembourgers in the notes, only in the speech; and the 'crowded' concentration camps became 'overcrowded'.

is hired to fawn upon the conqueror,
to 'collaborate' in his designs
and to enforce his rule
upon their fellow-countrymen
while grovelling low themselves.
Such is the plight of once glorious Europe,
and such are the atrocities
against wh we are in arms.

War Cabinet: minutes
(*Cabinet papers, 65/18*)

12 June 1941 10 Downing Street
5 p.m.

The Prime Minister said that it was most important that no instructions should be issued which ran counter to the principle that we must stand fast and fight it out in Egypt.

John Colville: diary
(*Colville papers*)

12 June 1941

On late duty. The PM was much impressed by a photograph of today's conference, brought by a young man from the *Daily Sketch*, and said it was the most artistic grouping he had ever seen, better than any of the groups painted by Sargent, etc., on similar occasions and yet quite haphazard.

John Colville: diary
(*Colville papers*)

13 June 1941

The PM went off to see a demonstration at Shoeburyness before lunch.

Winston S. Churchill to Viscount Halifax
(*Churchill papers, 20/39*)

14 June 1941

Jos Wedgwood is lecturing or touring somewhere in the United States. Would you kindly convey the following message from me to him: 'In view of the fact we have a Government of all Parties, it is necessary to strengthen the representation of the Labour Party in the House of Lords, and I feel you are admirably suited to discharge this public duty at this serious time. It would give me great pleasure to submit your name, through the usual channels, to The King for a Barony of the United Kingdom, and I trust you will feel yourself able to comply with my wish. What about it? –

Winston'[1]

Winston S. Churchill to Sir John Anderson
(*Churchill papers, 20/36*)

14 June 1941

I learn that under the scheme for reducing the basic civilian ration of petrol by half once every three months the reduction is to be made for the first time this August.

Could not this be avoided? We have to think of Bank Holiday and of the fact that many people may be getting leave this August for the first time since the war. They are no doubt counting on having their cars full at the end of July and having also at their disposal the full ration for August.

Could you not arrange to begin the experiment in October? To make good the loss an extra half-ration month could be intercalated during the winter.

Winston S. Churchill to Lord Woolton
(*Churchill papers, 20/36*)

14 June 1941

I notice from your monthly report that requisitions under the Lend/Lease Act for food shipments from the United States amount to 122,000 tons for the three months May–July. The figures given in LE (41) 76[2] suggest an annual rate of ¾ million tons of food imports from the States over the next 20 months. These figures seem very low. Are we exploiting to the full the new possibilities under Lend/Lease? Pray let me see the figures of your most recent plans for food imports from the USA.

[1] Josiah Wedgwood accepted a Peerage.
[2] Import Executive paper No. 76 of 1941.

Winston S. Churchill to Lord Woolton and Robert Hudson
(*Churchill papers, 20/36*)

14 June 1941
Action this Day

1. I was very glad to hear from you that the 12 hens scheme would be abandoned in favour of 'No official food for more than 12 hens unless you come into the public pool.' 'Public chicken-food for public eggs.'

2. Have you done justice to rabbit production? Although rabbits are not by themselves nourishing, they are a pretty good mitigation of vegetarianism. They eat mainly grass and greenstuffs, so what is the harm in encouraging their multiplication in captivity?

3. I welcome your increase of the meat ration, but it would be a pity to cut this down in the winter, just when fresh vegetables will also drop. Can you not get in additional supplies of American corned beef, pork and bacon to bridge the winter gap? The more bread you force people to eat, the greater the demands on tonnage will be. Reliance on bread is an evil which exaggerates itself. It would seem that you should make further efforts to open out your meat supplies.

4. I view with great concern any massacre of sheep and oxen. The reserve on the hoof is our main standby.

5. I have sent you on another paper a minute about making more use of American supplies.

Winston S. Churchill to A.V. Alexander, Admiral Pound and Admiral Fraser
(*Churchill papers, 20/36*)

14 June 1941
Most Secret

The turn which the war has taken requires a review of our submarine programme. The enemy is committed to overseas operations in the Middle East. He has to hold many islands, and supply his African army. In view of his Air superiority, on which he depends for the maintenance of his lines of communication by sea, our surface ships will not be able to take their normal part fully. Submarines in large numbers will be wanted.

2.For the invasion of the United Kingdom also the enemy will rely upon his Air umbrella as much as possible, especially at a distance from our coasts. For this, submarine forces are required in larger numbers.

3. The Germans, the Italians, and soon perhaps the French will have to be subjected to unlimited submarine blockade by our forces, and for this increased submarine construction will be required.

4. If you concur in these general needs, I shall be glad if you will prepare an

additional submarine programme to be pushed forward with the utmost speed, subject to discussion of priorities. Numbers and speed of construction are the first factors, as these vessels will be for short-range work. Surface speed, size, number of torpedo tubes and modern complications and refinements must, where necessary, give way.

Pray let me have your thought about all this.

Winston S. Churchill to Alfred Duff Cooper, General Ismay and Sir Edward Bridges
(*Churchill papers, 20/36*)

14 June 1941

I see no reason why the military, naval and air force broadcast talks should not continue, provided that they are of a general and informative character and contain no expressions of opinion, either personal or official, about operations which are in progress or in prospect.

Winston S. Churchill to General Ismay, for the Chiefs of Staff Committee
(*Churchill papers, 20/36*)

14 June 1941
Most Secret

Brigadier Inglis,[1] with whom I had a long talk last night, gave a shocking account of the state of the troops in Crete before the battle. He stated that there were not above 10,000 men in the fighting units. None of the New Zealand battalions had been made up to strength or re-equipped after the Greek evacuation, except to a limited extent. Such transport and light tanks as were available had to be fished up out of a sunken ship. There were no Mills grenades. The RASC, RAOC,[2] and other rearward troops were quite unarmed, thoroughly disorganized, and represented *bouches inutiles*. Even the artillery and gunners had no personal arms. The only field guns available were Italian. The only well-equipped troops which reached the Island were some British troops and Royal marines, none of which took part in the battle until the retreat began.

2. If the above statements are correct, and they must be searchingly tested,

[1] Lindsay Merritt Inglis, 1894–1966. Born and educated in New Zealand. On active service in the Mediterranean, France and Flanders, 1914–18. A Barrister and Solicitor of the Supreme Court of New Zealand, 1920–39. On active service in Egypt, the Western Desert, Crete and Syria, 1940–42. Commander the 4th New Zealand Armoured Brigade, Egypt and Italy, 1943–44. Major-General, 1944. Chief Judge and President of the Court of Appeal, Control Commission Supreme Court, Germany. 1947–50.

[2] The Royal Army Service Corps and the Royal Army Ordnance Corps.

they contrast markedly with the statements made to us beforehand by General Wavell and General Freyberg, although in the latter's case a robust view of the task set him is creditable. On April 18, according to General Wavell, Crete was warned that an attack was likely, and our warnings in most precise detail from April 30 onwards are on record. I cannot feel that there was any real grip shown by Middle East HQ upon this operation of the defence of Crete. They regarded it as a tiresome commitment, while at the same time acquiescing in its strategic importance. No one in high authority seems to have sat down for two or three mornings together and endeavoured to take a full forward view of what would happen in the light of our information, so fully given, and the many telegrams sent by me and by the Chiefs of the Staff about Scorcher. No one seems to have said 'We have got to hold the place with practically no Air support. What then should be our policy about airfields and the counter-attacks of paratroops or other airborne landings? What supplies and equipment are necessary, and how do we get them in?' The food difficulty was not mentioned to us. The non-removal of the *bouches inutiles* was a great fault, although some I believe were taken off. It is true that some of the supplies were sunk *en route*. The slowness in acting upon the precise intelligence with which they were furnished, and the general evidence of lack of drive and precision filled me with disquiet about this Middle East Staff. It is evident that very far-reaching steps will have to be taken.

3. I am far from reassured about the tactical conduct of the defence by General Freyberg, although full allowance must be made for the many deficiencies noted above. There appears to have been no counter-attack of any kind in the Western sector until more than 36 hours after the airborne descents had begun. There was no attempt to form a mobile reserve of the best troops, be it only a couple of battalions. There was no attempt to obstruct the Maleme Aerodrome, although General Freyberg knew he would have no Air in the battle. The whole conception seems to have been of static defence of positions, instead of the rapid extirpation at all costs of the airborne landing parties. It was lucky, however, that the troops got away when they did, as there was no food in the island, and no means of bringing it there.

4. The situation of the German garrison will not be pleasant. Every effort should be made to intercept their supplies by our submarines. One or two should always be preying about the approaches to Suda Bay and other north coast ports of Crete. The enemy should be forced to keep his garrison at the lowest.

5. There will have to be a detailed inquiry into the Defence of Crete. We must, for our own information and future guidance, have all the facts established.

Winston S. Churchill to Robert Menzies
(*Churchill papers, 20/39*)

14 June 1941
Personal and Secret

Tiger and Jaguar having duly arrived, we attack in the West at dawn – Sunday – hoping to disengage your brave fellows in T.[1]

On 15 June 1941 General Wavell launched Operation Battleaxe against General Rommel's forces in the Western Desert.

Winston S. Churchill to General Sikorski
(*Churchill papers, 20/21*)

15 June 1941

My dear General,

I have under consideration a plan for the expansion of our forces in West Africa and feel that you may wish to play some part in it. The proposals involve the formation of additional mechanized reconnaissance units, anti-tank units, infantry, and a proportion of ancillary services.

I feel that we have in this an opportunity to make use of some of the very fine officer material which you have in this country which at the present time, owing to a shortage of other ranks, cannot be used to the full extent of their capabilities.

Our forces in West Africa consist of native troops with a cadre of Europeans to command and administer them. The Europeans are drawn from our Regular Army and, in peace-time, specially selected officers do a tour in West Africa of 18 months which can be extended to a limited period. I may say that service in West Africa has always proved very popular owing to the increased responsibilities borne by comparatively junior officers; moreover, the African native makes a loyal and efficient soldier whom the officer is proud to command.

I could accept for this expansion scheme up to a total of 400 Polish officers, and feel sure that this proposal will appeal to you and will provide an outlet for some of your very fine young officers.

[1] Tobruk.

Before making a decision, you may like to discuss the matter with the CIGS[1] who will be able to give full details of the work and conditions in West Africa. I shall be glad to hear in due course whether you are willing to help us in this way.

Yours sincerely,
Winston S. Churchill

Winston S. Churchill to President Franklin D. Roosevelt
(*Premier papers, 3/230/1*)

15 June 1941
Most Secret and Personal

I am much encouraged by Ghormley's letter about your marines taking over that cold place,[2] and I hope that once first instalments have arrived you will give full publicity to it. People must have hope to face the long haul that lies ahead. It would also produce the best effects in Spain, Vichy, France and Turkey.

2. I had hoped for quicker progress in Syria, but Vichy is so far putting up with what we are doing to them without taking warlike action elsewhere and I think it will be all right.

3. Winant will no doubt have told you about what I sent out to Egypt secretly to restore the balance there. This will be used tomorrow (Sunday), and as it will be the first occasion when we hope to have definite superiority in tackle, both on the ground and above it, I naturally attach the very greatest importance to this venture. The above is for your eye alone.

4. From every source at my disposal, including some most trustworthy,[3] it looks as if a vast German onslaught on Russia was imminent. Not only are the main German armies deployed from Finland to Roumania, but the final arrivals of air and armoured forces are being completed. The pocket battleship *Lutzow*, which put her nose out of the Skaggerak yesterday and was promptly torpedoed by our coastal aircraft, was very likely going north to give naval strength on the Arctic flank. Should this new war break out, we shall, of

[1] The Chief of the Imperial General Staff, General Sir John Dill.

[2] Iceland.

[3] On 12 June 1941 British Intelligence decrypted a message, which was dated June 4, sent from Berlin to Tokyo by the Japanese Ambassador to Germany. The Ambassador, Count Oshima, reported a conversation with Hitler, in which the Führer told him that Communist Russia must be 'eliminated'. Hitler added that if Japan 'lagged behind when Germany declared a state of war against Russia, it was quite open to her to do so'. Neither Hitler, nor Ribbentrop, who was also present at the discussion, gave any date for this 'state of war'. But the Ambassador reported that the atmosphere of urgency during the conversation suggested a German invasion of Russia was at hand (Joint Intelligence Committee Report No. 252 (O) of 1941, 12 June 1941: F.H. Hinsley and others, *British Intelligence in the Second World War, Its Influence on Strategy and Operations*, Volume l, page 478, London, 1979).

course, give all encouragement and any help we can spare to the Russians, following principle that Hitler is the foe we have to beat. I do not expect any class political reactions here and trust a German-Russian conflict will not cause you any embarrassment.

5. We must also take full advantage of a possible breather in the Middle East to get things in good shape there. I am looking forward to Harriman's report. Kindest regards, and every wish that your indisposition may soon pass.

Winston S. Churchill to Alexander Korda[1]
(*Churchill papers, 2/419*)

15 June 1941

Many congratulations upon your admirable film about Nelson.[2]

Winston Churchill

Winston S. Churchill to Colonel Sir Robert Williams[3]
(*Churchill papers, 20/30*)

16 June 1941

My dear Sir Robert,

Thank you so much for your encouraging message, which I greatly value from one who was so long in the House of Commons with me.

Do you remember our journey back from India in 1897 when a nice young MP, Sandys[4] by name, was on board? His son is now my son-in-law.

With kind regards,
Believe me,
Yours sincerely,

[1] Alexander Korda, 1893–1956. Born in Hungary. Educated at Budapest University. Film producer in Budapest, Vienna, Berlin, Hollywood and Paris. Founder and Chairman of London Film Productions Ltd, 1932. Became a British subject, 1936. Founded Alexander Korda Productions, 1939. Made 112 films, including *The Scarlet Pimpernel* (1934), *The Third Man* (1949) and *Richard III* (1956). Knighted 1942.

[2] The film was *That Hamilton Woman* (also known as *Lady Hamilton*). It quickly became Churchill's favourite film. One of the script writers was R.C. Sherriff. Laurence Olivier played Nelson, Vivien Leigh (whom Olivier had just married) was Lady Hamilton. While it was being filmed, Olivier insisted upon learning to fly. Set in 1804, the film has Big Ben chiming – some fifty years before Big Ben was built. Churchill knighted Korda in 1942.

[3] Robert Williams, 1848–1943. Conservative Member of Parliament for West Dorset, 1895–1922. Created Baronet, 1916. Landowner. A Director of William Deacon's Bank. He and Churchill had sat in the House of Commons together for twenty-one years.

[4] George John Sandys, 1875–1937. On active service, South Africa, 1899–1902. Conservative Member of Parliament for Wells, 1910–18. On active service, Western Front, 1914 (wounded at Ypres). Attaché British Legation, Berne, 1921–22; British Embassy, Paris, 1922–25.

War Cabinet: minutes
(*Cabinet papers, 65/18*)

16 June 1941 10 Downing Street
5 p.m.

TURKEY

The Prime Minister said that the central fact was that Turkey still remained a neutral. It was important that the Press should not heap abuse on Turkey when the signature of the agreement became known.[1]

SHIPPING LOSSES

The War Cabinet were informed that under present arrangements the shipping losses for the month of May were due to be published on the following day. The losses for May as at present known amounted to 461,000 tons. This figure included 54,000 tons in the Mediterranean, 155,000 tons in the North Atlantic, 186,000 tons in the Freetown area, and 61,000 tons in United Kingdom and coastal waters (this last figure included losses in ports in the United Kingdom). The losses in April, as published, had been 488,000 tons. To this figure must be added losses of 93,000 (largely in the Mediterranean) subsequently reported.

The Prime Minister emphasized the seriousness of these losses. He thought that their publication might have a discouraging effect on public opinion in this country. From the point of view of public opinion in the United States, publication might well have a beneficial effect. On the other hand, if we were to cease publication at this moment, this in itself would be somewhat of a shock to public opinion in the United States and might secure for us as much the same result.

The issue was evenly balanced, but, on the whole, the Prime Minister thought that it was important that we should not get into a position in which we were under an obligation to publish figures at regular monthly intervals.

The Prime Minister said that in the forthcoming Debate in the House of Commons on shipping matters he proposed to move the House into Secret Session and to make a full statement of the various measures which had been put in hand in connection with the Battle of the Atlantic. The House should know how serious the position was and what had already been done to meet it. It would be for consideration whether this speech should be made at the beginning of the Debate or in reply to it.

The War Cabinet took note with approval of this statement.

[1] The Turkish-German Treaty was signed on 18 June 1941. Three days later Turkey refused the passage of Vichy French troops across Turkey to Syria. Although the Turkish Government did allow the Germans, under the treaty, to move military equipment through Turkey to both Syria and Iraq, it did not permit German troops to make the passage.

Winston S. Churchill: broadcast[1]
(*BBC Written Archives Centre*)

16 June 1941

I am grateful, President Valentine[2] for the honour which you have conferred upon me in making me a Doctor of Laws of Rochester University in the State of New York. I am extremely complimented by the expressions of praise and commendation in which you have addressed me, not because I am or ever can be worthy of them, but because they are an expression of American confidence and affection which I shall ever strive to deserve.

But what touches me most in this ceremony is that sense of kinship and of unity which I feel exists between us this afternoon. As I speak from Downing Street[3] to Rochester University and through you to the people of the United States, I almost feel I have the right to do so, because my mother, as you have stated, was born in your city, and here my grandfather, Leonard Jerome, lived for so many years, conducting as a prominent and rising citizen a newspaper with the excellent eighteenth-century title of the *Plain Dealer*.

The great Burke has truly said, 'People will not look forward to posterity who never look backward to their ancestors,' and I feel it most agreeable to recall to you that the Jeromes were rooted for many generations in American soil, and fought in Washington's armies for the independence of the American Colonies and the foundation of the United States. I expect I was on both sides then. And I must say I feel on both sides of the Atlantic Ocean now.

At intervals during the last forty years I have addressed scores of great American audiences in almost every part of the Union. I have learnt to admire the courtesy of these audiences; their sense of fair play; their sovereign sense of humour, never minding the joke that is turned against themselves; their earnest, voracious desire to come to the root of the matter and to be well and truly informed on Old World affairs.

And now, in this time of world storm, when I have been called upon by King and Parliament and with the support of all parties in the State to bear the chief responsibility in Great Britain, and when I have had the supreme honour of speaking for the British nation in its most deadly danger and in its

[1] The full text of this broadcast was first printed on 28 June 1941 in the *Imperial Review* (No. 6, Volume VIII). It was later made available as a gramophone recording, the profits of which went to Clementine Churchill's Aid to Russia charity.

[2] Alan Valentine, 1901-1980. Olympic gold medallist, American rugby football team, Paris Olympics, 1924. A professor at Yale, he published *The English Novel* in 1927. President of the University of Rochester from 1935, one of the youngest men ever appointed to head a major university in the United States; under his presidency the university became a centre of research into the use of atomic energy. Chief of the Netherlands Mission of the Marshall Plan. First head of the Economic Stabilization Agency in the Truman administration. His wife, Lucia Garrison Norton, was a descendant of William Lloyd Garrison, the abolitionist.

[3] The broadcast was in fact made from the underground Central War Room (also known as the Cabinet War Room).

finest hour, it has given me comfort and inspiration to feel that I think as you do, that our hands are joined across the oceans, and that our pulses throb and beat as one. Indeed I will make so bold as to say that here at least, in my mother's birth city of Rochester,[1] I hold a latchkey to American hearts.

Strong tides of emotion, fierce surges of passion, sweep the broad expanses of the Union in this year of fate. In that prodigious travail there are many elemental forces, there is much heart-searching and self-questioning; some pangs, some sorrow, some conflict of voices, but no fear. The world is witnessing the birth throes of a sublime resolve. I shall presume to confess to you that I have no doubts what that resolve will be.

The destiny of mankind is not decided by material computation. When great causes are on the move in the world, stirring all men's souls, drawing them from their firesides, casting aside comfort, wealth and the pursuit of happiness in response to impulses at once awe-striking and irresistible, we learn that we are spirits, not animals, and that something is going on in space and time, and beyond space and time, which, whether we like it or not, spells duty.

A wonderful story is unfolding before our eyes. How it will end we are not allowed to know. But on both sides of the Atlantic we all feel, I repeat, all, that we are a part of it, that our future and that of many generations is at stake. We are sure that the character of human society will be shaped by the resolves we take and the deeds we do. We need not bewail the fact that we have been called upon to face such solemn responsibilities. We may be proud, and even rejoice amid our tribulations, that we have been born at this cardinal time for so great an age and so splendid an opportunity of service here below.

Wickedness, enormous, panoplied, embattled, seemingly triumphant, casts its shadow over Europe and Asia. Laws, customs and traditions are broken up. Justice is cast from her seat. The rights of the weak are trampled down. The grand freedoms of which the President of the United States has spoken so movingly are spurned and chained. The whole stature of man, his genius, his initiative and his nobility, is ground down under systems of mechanical barbarism and of organized and scheduled terror.

For more than a year we British have stood alone, uplifted by your sympathy and respect and sustained by our own unconquerable will-power and by the increasing growth and hopes of your massive aid. In these British Islands that look so small upon the map we stand, the faithful guardians of the rights and dearest hopes of a dozen States and nations now gripped and tormented in a base and cruel servitude. Whatever happens we shall endure to the end.

But what is the explanation of the enslavement of Europe by the German

[1] Churchill's mother was, in fact, born in Brooklyn, New York, but had spent much of her childhood in Rochester, New York State.

Nazi regime? How did they do it? It is but a few years ago since one united gesture by the peoples, great and small, who are now broken in the dust, would have warded off from mankind the fearful ordeal it has had to undergo. But there was no unity. There was no vision. The nations were pulled down one by one while the others gaped and chattered. One by one, each in his turn, they let themselves be caught. One after another they were felled by brutal violence or poisoned from within by subtle intrigue.

And now the old lion with her lion cubs at her side stands alone against hunters who are armed with deadly weapons and impelled by desperate and destructive rage. Is the tragedy to repeat itself once more? Ah no! This is not the end of the tale. The stars in their courses proclaim the deliverance of mankind. Not so easily shall the onward progress of the peoples be barred. Not so easily shall the lights of freedom die.

But time is short. Every month that passes adds to the length and to the perils of the journey that will have to be made. United we stand. Divided we fall. Divided, the dark age returns. United, we can save and guide the world.

War Cabinet, Defence Committee (Operations): minutes
(Cabinet papers, 69/2)

16 June 1941 Cabinet War Room
9.45 p.m.

BAKU

The Prime Minister drew attention to the paramount importance of denying the Baku oil supplies to the Germans. Every effort should be made to ensure that our preparations to this end should be completed as soon as possible.

An attack on the largest possible scale should be made on an oil target of the type of Gelsenkirchen.

INDIA

The Prime Minister said that it would take a considerable time for the enemy to develop an attack upon India and he was opposed to diverting any large quantity of material from active theatres of operation to India. He agreed, however, that the plan represented our ultimate aim.

War Cabinet, Defence Committee (Operations): minutes
(*Cabinet papers, 69/2*)

17 June 1941
12 noon

The Prime Minister gave the Commanders-in-Chief a general review of recent events and of the present situation.

2. Crete
We had sustained a heavy reverse in Crete. It had been thought that our troops there would be sufficient to deal with the airborne landings whilst the Fleet held off seaborne attacks. It now appeared that our troops, after their withdrawal from Greece, were not adequately equipped. The losses to the Fleet had been serious and we had been unable to continue naval operations without endangering our naval position in the Mediterranean.

There was no doubt that the Germans also had sustained heavy losses which they had not attempted to minimize. They had had to make a great air effort to capture Crete and the operations had contained enemy air forces which might have given us a lot of trouble elsewhere e.g. in Iraq.

3. Iraq
Here we had acted with promptitude and we were able to nip in the bud Rashid Ali's pro-Axis movement. The situation was now fairly good but there was still much feeling in the Iraq Army.

4. Syria
We had assembled the best possible force in the circumstances for operations in Syria but it was unfortunately deficient of armoured fighting vehicles. The resistance had been greater than was expected. However, hostilities with Vichy French had not spread and this was doubtless due to the forceful diplomacy of Admiral Leahy and to the strong anglophil feeling in France.

5. Libya
The Prime Minister outlined the position of our forces in the Middle East after the successful operations against the Italians. He gave details of the great efforts which we had made, and the serious risks which we had taken, to give the Commanders-in-Chief adequate reinforcements by operations Tiger and a succession of Jaguars.

By these means we had given the Commanders-in-Chief in the Middle East a superiority in number of weapons, tanks and aircraft which were so essential in present day war. For the first time we were in a position to face the Germans on a level footing.

The Prime Minister then gave details of Operation Battleaxe and explained that the object of this operation was to wipe out the enemy force in Libya and to seize the aerodromes in Cyrenaica from which the RAF could give fighter cover to the Mediterranean Fleet. With those aerodromes in our hands we would be in a position to interrupt seriously the enemy sea lines of communication to Tripoli.

He awaited with great anxiety the outcome of this important battle.

6. United Kingdom

The security of this country was vital to the successful prosecution of the war but risks had to be run to maintain our large armies in the Middle East. However, shipping would be one limiting factor to what we could send even if it were politically desirable to do so. He hoped however that, within the next three or four months, we should be able to spare another Division for the Middle East in addition to the drafts and large numbers of tanks required to keep our armoured forces up to strength. Our position in this country had undoubtedly improved greatly during the last year.

In the defence of this country, the adequate protection of fighter aerodromes was the key to the position. An investigation was being made regarding the defence of our aerodromes which should take into account the lessons learned from the Crete battle.

7. The Battle of the Atlantic

Although improvements had been made in the turn round of shipping and in the working of ports, the Battle of the Atlantic continued to cause anxiety. It was now necessary to convoy right across the Atlantic and we were incurring heavy attacks on shipping off the West coast of Africa.

He expected further forward action from the USA in the near future. With America's assistance we could sustain shipping losses up to 400,000 tons a month.

He referred to the successes which we had had against the German surface naval forces.

8. The Position in Europe

The whole of the mainland of Europe was virtually under the Nazi heel. The Germans were now concentrating against Russia. The acquisition of the Baku oil fields and the wheat from the Ukraine would ease their position considerably.

If the Russians fought, we must take every advantage which such a conflict offered. He considered that the war was tending to spread further eastwards.

9. The Future

The scale of our air attack upon Germany was increasing in weight and we should make every effort to attack the enemy during the day time. Ultimately there were possibilities in landing large numbers of tanks to assist the conquered nations to rise against the Germans.

Summing up, the Prime Minister said we must maintain our position in this

Island, and our forces in the Middle East and make every effort to strengthen our air forces.

The Prime Minister said that he was anxious that Commanders-in-Chief should be kept fully informed of the situation, but reluctant to increase the circulation list of highly secret papers. He had accordingly given General Ismay instructions to organize a special secret information centre in the Office of the Minister of Defence which Commanders-in-Chief could visit whenever they came to London. No trouble should be spared in organizing this centre which should start functioning by 1st July at latest.[1]

John Colville: diary
(*Colville papers*)

18 June 1941

Operation Battleaxe has obviously failed and we have to face the bitter fact of being beaten by the Germans on equal terms. Indeed we should have had great superiority were not Wavell so lavish with his rearward services and so cautious about using his full strength. The PM is gravely disappointed as he had placed great hopes on this operation for which Operation Tiger had been staged. Fortunately it will not appear as a major defeat as we merely return to our positions after a sharp and costly battle; but neither the general public nor the Germans know what hopes were set by the Cabinet (though not by Wavell or Dill) on a successful offensive.

John Martin: diary
(*Martin papers*)

18 June 1941

With PM to Weybourne[2] (Norfolk) to see demonstration of UP (rocket) against Queen Bees (unmanned aircraft).

[1] The Special Information Centre (SIC) was set up in the Cabinet Offices at Storeys Gate, just above Churchill's Annexe. Organized by Joan Bright, it eventually contained more than 800 secret files (Joan Bright Astley, *Inner Circle*, London, 1971).

[2] Pronounced 'Webburn', and the subject of a warning to any potential invader:

He who would England win
Must first at Weybourne Hook begin.

John Colville: diary
(Colville papers)

18 June 1941

When the PM came back he was in good spirits, less perturbed than I had expected by the fiasco of Battleaxe, and told me he was now busy considering where next we could take the offensive.

John Colville to Winston S. Churchill
(Churchill papers, 2/434)

18 June 1941

I attach below an extract from a letter from Lord Halifax about a gift of cigars from Mr Sam M. Kaplan of New York. These cigars have now arrived.

You will shortly be receiving another large consignment of cigars bought for you by subscribers to the Cuban newspaper *Bohemia* and also 2,400 cigars from the Cuban National Commission of Tobacco.

I have discussed with the Professor, and also with Lord Rothschild[1] of MI5, the question of security and they both insist that however reputable the source from which the cigars come it is impossible to ensure that they are safe. It would be perfectly possible to insert a grain of deadly poison in, say, one cigar in fifty, and although Lord Rothschild can and will arrange for those that arrive to be x-rayed, he would only guarantee them as safe after subjecting each one to a careful analysis. This could not be done without destroying the cigars.

The element of risk is slight in the case of Mr Kaplan's cigars and all those sent from Cuba. Sir G. Ogilvie Forbes[2] has vouched for the bona fides of the *Bohemia* and of the Cuban National Commission of Tobacco. Nevertheless,

[1] Nathaniel Mayer Victor Rothschild, 1910–1990. Educated at Harrow and Trinity College, Cambridge. Fellow of Trinity College, 1935–9. Succeeded his uncle as 3rd Baron Rothschild, 1937. On active service (Military Intelligence), 1939–45 (George Medal, American Legion of Merit, American Bronze Star). Director, British Overseas Airways Corporation, (BOAC), 1946–58. Chairman of the Agricultural Research Council, 1948–58. Assistant Director of Research, Department of Zoology, Cambridge University, 1950–70. Member of the BBC General Advisory Council, 1952–6. Vice-Chairman, Shell Research Limited, 1961–3; Chairman, 1963–70. Research Co-ordinator, Royal Dutch Shell Group, 1965–70. Director-General, and First Permanent Under-Secretary, Central Policy Review Staff (the 'Think Tank'), Cabinet Office, 1971–94. Chairman, N. M. Rothschild & Sons, 1975–6. In 1977 he published a volume of memoirs, *Meditations of a Broomstick*.

[2] George Arthur D. Ogilvie-Forbes, 1891–1954. On active service, Gallipoli (1915) and Mesopotamia, 1916–18) (wounded, despatches twice). General Staffing War Office, 1918. Entered the Diplomatic Service, 1919. Served in Stockholm, Copenhagen, Helsinki, Belgrade, Mexico City, the Vatican, Madrid, and Berlin (as Counsellor of Embassy, 1937–39). Knighted, 1937. Counsellor of Embassy, Oslo, 1939. British Minister, Havana, 1940–44; Ambassador to Venezuela, 1944–48. Member of Council, Catholic Union of Great Britain, 1949.

the proposal to make these gifts to you was (except in the case of Mr Kaplan) very widely advertised and an enemy agent might have been able to suborn one of the men engaged in the rolling or packing of the cigars. Professor Lindemann and Lord Rothschild were strongly of the opinion that you ought not to smoke any cigars received from overseas while the war lasts. The Professor thought however that you might like to let them accumulate in a safe and dry place until after the war, when you might feel justified in taking the risk involved in smoking them if you wished to do so.[1]

Winston S. Churchill to General Smuts
(*Premier papers, 3/287/2*)

18 June 1941
Most Secret

After our defeat at Agedabia Wavell's tank force was almost non-existent. One Brigade was dispersed at Agedabia, one lost all its vehicles in Greece, while 7th Armoured Division was sent back to Cairo for a mechanical overhaul which has kept it out of action till now. Enemy, on the other hand, commanded between 200 and 250 Medium and 9-ton Tanks. Position was one of grave anxiety. I therefore resolved to run heavy risks to reinforce him, and during the first week of May we dispatched over 300 of our latest Tanks from this country through the Mediterranean. One ship was mined, but favoured by weather the others got through, thus giving Wavell back a numerical superiority in AFVs.[2] I had hoped he could have taken the offensive in Libya by the end of May. However, it was not till June 15 that he could begin. By this time out of 450 Medium Tanks in his possession he had organized about 250 for battle, and the 7th Armoured Division was remounted. Meanwhile, by six successive operations we have strongly reinforced him in the Air, sending flights of about forty at a time from aircraft-carriers to fly to Malta and then on. This has involved diverting the aircraft-carriers of the Navy from protection against raiders and also a high risk to pilots. Nevertheless, it was the only way of rapid reinforcement. By this and other means we had in May alone upwards of a thousand aircraft *en route* for

[1] On 9 October 1941 Lord Rothschild wrote to Churchill's Private Office from MI5: 'Confirming our telephone conversation of the other day, about twenty-five of the cigars have been examined and are innocuous from both the toxicological and the bacteriological point of view. I am hoping to have the final report on the others in the very near future. There is one rather interesting point about cigars. That is that the substance normally in them, nicotine, is itself very poisonous indeed and there are only a few things which the smoking end of a cigar could be treated with which might be more harmful. The reason why one does not suffer from nicotine in a cigar is because as it burns, the nicotine is burnt away also.' (*Churchill papers, 2/434*)

[2] Armoured Fighting Vehicles.

ME and for the battle of the 15th we had substantial superiority in the air over Egypt and around it.

2. It was therefore with much hope that I awaited the result of the battle which began on Monday morning. For the first two days the operations prospered. This was the first occasion where we have fought the Germans without being at a great disadvantage in technical equipment. Had we succeeded, Tobruk would have been disengaged, and its garrison which still retains mobility, would have made a sortie upon the enemy's flank and rear. The third day's fighting, however, went heavily against us, and we are now withdrawing with the loss of at least 100 and perhaps 150 Tanks to our old position. The enemy losses also are heavy. At the present moment the troops seem to be getting clear all right, but for the time being we have little hope of regaining the initiative.

3. We are doing all we can in Syria, and now that we are once again on the defensive in the west, it may be possible to add weight to the Syrian effort.

4. I deeply regret that you do not feel able to fix a date for your arrival here, but I fully recognize the very strong reasons you give. Meanwhile, I will do my utmost to keep you informed. As you know I have sent you from time to time personal telegrams which like this one endeavour to place the inmost facts before you.

5. According to all the information I have been able to gather, Hitler is going to take what he wants from Russia, and the only question is whether Stalin will attempt a vain resistance. I have increasingly good hopes of the United States.

6. Thank you so much for your telegram about my speech. Kindest regards.

Winston S. Churchill to General Ismay, for the Chiefs of Staff Committee

(*Churchill papers, 20/36*)

18 June 1941
Most Secret

There is much force in the First Sea Lord's remark of last night, to the effect that as we are now forced back upon the defensive on the Libyan front we should switch over some Air, and perhaps a few surviving Tanks, to the Syrian front, and try to make a good job of that. The news from Syria in this morning's Situation Report wears a better complexion. Also, it seems that our people may get back in the west. Perhaps it would be better to wait for a few hours, or till tomorrow, in order to hear Wavell's final report. But there would be no harm in drafting a telegram for consideration meanwhile on the above lines.

Winston S. Churchill to Sir Archibald Sinclair and Air Chief Marshal Sir Charles Portal
(*Premier papers, 3/4/1*)

18 June 1941
Secret

1. I saw a statement in the papers the other day that the Air Force were calling for several thousand volunteers to defend their Aerodromes. What is the meaning of this? It was represented that this was a part of the application of the lessons of Crete. But many people have wondered why such a petty measure should have been paraded. Perhaps, however, it is all nonsense.

2. This gives me the opportunity to say that all Air Force ground personnel at Aerodromes have got to undergo sharp, effective and severe military training in the use of their weapons, and in all manoeuvres necessary for the defence of the Aerodromes. Every single man must be accounted for in the defence, and every effort should be made to reach a high standard of nimbleness and efficiency.

Will you kindly let me have a report on this?

Winston S. Churchill to General Sikorski
(*Churchill papers, 20/21*)

18 June 1941
Secret

My dear General,

The memoranda which you left with me on the 20 May are being considered by the Departments concerned, but I can give you a preliminary reply.

In your first memorandum you asked for the release of aircraft either from this country or from the USA to enable your Government to maintain communications with Poland. We all realize the great importance of maintaining these air communications, but you will understand that it is very difficult to do so during the short summer nights. Aircraft cannot make the return trip during the hours of darkness, and are very vulnerable to air attack on their homeward journey. But the Air Ministry will do everything in their power to assist you during the coming autumn and winter, when they hope to have the means of doing so.

In your second memorandum you suggested that the sum of £600,000 should be made available during the coming year for subversive work in the general Allied interest by Polish organizations in countries other than the USA. I understand that the Chancellor of the Exchequer will be able to provide the assistance in this matter which you desire and that Mr Dalton will be getting into touch with you with regard to details.

Your third proposal for making use of the Polish colonies in the USA and in Latin America raises some difficulties. Our information is that the US Government and public are now alive to the danger of Axis subversive activities and might resent any outside attempt to assist them in work which they regard as their own responsibility. Although the position is not quite the same in Latin America, the Governments there require rather delicate handling, and we should like to have a more detailed statement of the work which you think might be done by Polish communities before considering your suggestion further.

Yours very sincerely,
Winston S. Churchill

War Cabinet, Tank Parliament: minutes
(*Cabinet papers, 120/52*)

19 June 1941 10 Downing Street
5 p.m.

The Prime Minister gave an account of recent operations in Libya in which the 7th Armoured Division had been engaged. He said that arrangements were being made to fly home Officers of different ranks who had taken part in the battle as it was important that every aspect of the operation should be studied. He invited the Chief of the Imperial General Staff to form two groups for this study; one to investigate tactical and organizational matters, and the other to study technical matters.

The Prime Minister said that there were a number of points which he proposed to set before the Secretary of State for War on the subject of the organization and creation of Armoured Formations. Was it quite certain that the Division was the right organization, particularly for the more backward units? He was inclined to think that the Armoured Brigade Group might be more suitable. He had noticed in accounts of the operations in Libya, that there had been reference to the 7th Armoured Division 'less one Brigade' which, in effect, meant half the Division as there were only two Brigades. He was also anxious that, in forming the new Armoured Formations, a start should be made as early as possible by giving units a complete outfit of Bren Carriers which could gradually be replaced by tanks. The important point was to get the unit, at an early stage, conscious of its existence as a complete entity. At the same time the Signals should get going so that this most important part of the control organization would rapidly become efficient. If some such system were adopted, the Armoured Formations would have a tactical value at all stages of their evolution.

John Colville: diary
(*Colville papers*)

19 June 1940

John Peck and I agreed that the PM does not help the Government machine to run smoothly and his inconsiderate treatment of the Service Departments would cause trouble were it not for the great personal loyalty of the Service Ministers to himself. He supplies drive and initiative, but he often meddles where he would better leave things alone and the operational side of the war might profit if he gave it a respite and turned to grapple with Labour and Production.

Winston S. Churchill to Anthony Eden
(*Churchill papers, 20/36*)

19 June 1941

ARRIVAL OF UNITED STATES TROOPS IN ICELAND: PUBLICITY

The first consideration is the safety of the American troops in transit. Therefore until they have actually reached Iceland, or are on the point of doing so, no announcement should be made, nor any hint leak out, especially from our end.

2. As soon as the troops have arrived and begun to land, I should like the fullest publicity. See my telegram to the President on the subject. Primarily, the form of announcement must rest with the President. The substance of what I should like is as follows:

'Strong forces of United States Marines, complete with Tanks, artillery and aircraft, have landed in Iceland to reinforce the British troops holding the island.'

I do not see that it is necessary to tell the enemy any more than the above.

3. As to what we should tell the Icelanders, that should be agreed with the United States, and no doubt a form satisfactory to all parties can be drafted. It should not, however, be made public until the transports are in Reykjavik.

Winston S. Churchill to Ernest Bevin
(*Churchill papers, 20/36*)

19 June 1941
Secret

IMPORTATION OF IRISH LABOUR

It is not desirable to bring over large numbers of these hostile people to this island at a time when invasion must be considered more than likely.

If any are brought over, the more thoroughly they are organized the better. Let me know what numbers are contemplated and what kind of organization is proposed.

Winston S. Churchill: Oral Answers
(*Hansard*)

19 June 1941 House of Commons

HOUSE OF COMMONS
(RECONSTRUCTION)

Major Vyvyan Adams asked the Prime Minister whether before any decision is taken to reconstruct the Chamber of the House of Commons in its old form, to rebuild on the same site according to a different and more convenient design, or to take a wholly different site for a new Palace of Westminster, he will undertake to grant full facilities for a Debate in the House?

The Prime Minister: I cannot conceive that anyone would wish to make the slightest structural alteration in the House of Commons other than perhaps some improvement in the system of ventilation, or some minor readjustment of the accommodation in the Galleries not affecting the size, shape or character.

Mr Lees-Smith: With regard to the first Sitting Day, will the Prime Minister indicate what arrangements will be made for the Debate on shipping?

The Prime Minister: I have come to the conclusion, after careful reflection, that any Debate on the shipping situation ought to be in Private Session. [Hon. Members: 'No.'] I think that there might be serious danger to the public interests if the matter were discussed in public. If the Debate is in secret, I shall hope to be able to make a statement to the House. I should certainly not attempt to do so in public. I do not think I could do justice to the topic, every part of which is inter-related. I must remind the House that the Battle of the Atlantic is a continuous operation going on from day to day, and its seriousness has not by any means been removed by anything that has occurred as the year has advanced. So I hope the House will be willing to accept the judgment of the Government upon the matter, at any rate until after we have discussed it.

Mr Shinwell: May I beg my right hon. Friend to reconsider his decision?

The Prime Minister: I cannot feel that any justice could be done to this subject by partial statements on behalf of the Government. I feel that in order to deal with it there must be comprehensive statements going to the root of matters. I am sure they cannot be made in public. I therefore feel that a Debate which was conducted merely as it were from particular, detached angles would not be helpful to the House or informative to the public. I think the advantage of our discussing the matter in Secret Session will be to enable the House to see whether or not the argument set forth by the Government is a correct one. I certainly feel that it will be very difficult indeed to conduct the Debate in public. I have always taken the view, if the House wishes to make speeches on topics, that whenever possible and Business permits, the House should be given an opportunity to do so, but Government statements on this subject are extremely difficult to make, in fact impossible to make, except under the protection of a Secret Session.

The Prime Minister: I think I must really ask the House to be advised by His Majesty's Government upon this matter. I could go into it in great detail when we are together privately. It would be a great pity if we were forced to conduct discussions on these most grave matters with the enemy listening, every word reaching them quite soon. No justice can be done to the arguments; there can be no real freedom in argument. A statement can easily be made and will be made from time to time by the Government. It is said that the statement would be partial and one-sided. I thought we were all rather on one side now, but if there are two opinions about that, I still trust that the Government will receive the support of the House in this matter. No decision is final. We can have our Debate and see what the conclusions are among ourselves, and perhaps some statement may be made in public afterwards, because that would be quite possible. I do not feel that any justice could be done to this topic by a public Debate at present. As to the desire expressed by the right hon. Gentleman opposite that we should give a greater stimulus to the shipbuilding and ship repairing effort, it might well be that a Debate of that kind might take place after the House is in possession of the real facts.

Mr Shinwell: That is precisely what we want.

The Prime Minister: But it would be impossible to separate that from the general question of the Battle of the Atlantic.

Earl Winterton: I beg to give the right hon. Gentleman notice that I shall raise the matter on the Question of the rest of the proceedings being in Secret Session. I shall raise the point with you, Mr Speaker, whether there is anything to preclude the Press from publishing information contained in that Debate, since the House will not then have gone into Secret Session.

The Prime Minister: Nothing would be further from my wish than to deprive the noble Lord of any Parliamentary facilities of which he may desire to avail himself. On the contrary, I think we have achieved during this war and under this Government the greatest association of the representative institution with the Executive that has ever been attempted under such conditions. Personally, I labour constantly to secure the power, authority and prestige of the House of Commons. That shall always be my faithful effort and endeavour, because I think it would be a glorious thing if we came through this with all our Parliamentary faculties undiminished, nay, having, in fact, played a vital part in the struggle. I look upon the House as friends; we could not fight this through without them, and in that spirit I should wish this matter to be considered. If, after the Debate is over, when a new view may be taken on either side as to what should be done, the Noble Lord wishes to try conclusions with the Administration on any point, it may be a very convenient opportunity for seeing exactly who his friends and associates are.

Mr. A Bevan: Will an early opportunity be given to the House to discuss the general question of production, particularly in view of the fact that the whole atmosphere is being poisoned by charges of absenteeism directed against workers and by statements made by responsible labour leaders about slackness in the workshops and mismanagement? Does not the right hon. Gentleman think that it would be in the public interest to have a Debate on this matter in public at the earliest possible moment, because, as I say, the whole atmosphere is now being seriously poisoned?

The Prime Minister: I think it would be a very good thing to have such a Debate, and certainly it should be in public, but I hope that everyone, on both sides of the argument, will keep his attention constantly fixed upon the object, namely, improved production, and that we shall not get into a fight between capital and labour or between employers and working classes, each beginning to throw things at the other in a metaphorical sense. I am sure that that would give an altogether false impression abroad as to the real purpose which unites us all.

War Cabinet: minutes

(*Cabinet papers, 65/18*)

19 June 1941 Prime Minister's Room
12.30 p.m. House of Commons Annexe

PUBLICATION OF SHIPPING LOSSES

The Prime Minister said that he had further considered this matter since the last meeting. While he still attached importance to getting free of the obligation to publish these figures at regular monthly intervals, he thought that there was much to be said for publishing the figures for May and for June –

which would probably be a better month – and ceasing publication thereafter. It would be particularly difficult to deny publication of the May losses just before the Debate on shipping matters. Accordingly, he had not sent the proposed personal telegram to Mr Hopkins. No indication should be given to the Press at this stage of any intention to discontinue publication. But he proposed, in the Debate on shipping matters in the House of Commons, to inform the House in secret session of the argument put forward by the First Lord against monthly publication of these losses, namely, that it gave the enemy accurate information, which they could not otherwise obtain, as to the effect of changes in their submarine strategy.

USSR

The War Cabinet were informed that there was no change in the position between Russia and Germany. The question was raised what line should be taken in regard to publicity if war broke out between Germany and Russia.

The Prime Minister said that Germany should be represented as an insatiable tyrant, that had attacked Russia in order to obtain material for carrying on the war.

UNITED STATES OF AMERICA[1]

The Prime Minister informed his colleagues that he had received a telegram from President Roosevelt in regard to the proposal (originally made by Captain Roosevelt) that the United States should establish a base in West Africa, possibly at Bathurst.

The President said that the United States Army was studying the possibility of a ferry service from West African landing places, of which Bathurst might be one. This project would be gone into with the British Air Marshal in charge of the Atlantic ferry service.[2]

The President's message had ended on a very cordial note. He had referred to the steps taken to freeze German and Italian assets and to close German Consulates in the USA. He (the President) judged that the reaction in the United States was ninety per cent. favourable.

The Prime Minister also informed the War Cabinet that the United States were sending a force of Marines to Iceland to reinforce the British garrison. Later they proposed to send about 25,000 American soldiers, who would relieve the British garrison, which we should then be free to use elsewhere. It was, of course, of the utmost importance to preserve the secrecy of this matter until President Roosevelt made his announcement in regard to it. But when the news came out it was bound to create a great impression.

[1] This item of the War Cabinet's discussion was recorded only in the Confidential Annex (Cabinet papers, 65/22).

[2] The Atlantic Ferry Organisation (ATFERO) was commanded by Air Vice Marshal Grahame George Dawson.

Winston S. Churchill to Robert Menzies
(*Premier papers, 3/287/2*)

19 June 1941
Most Secret

1. General Wavell's attack in the Western Desert which began Sunday morning, prospered till the evening of the second day, but on the third day the German counter-attack caused him to yield up all his gains and we were glad to be able to get back to our original position without disaster. Number of armoured vehicles on each side about 200; we had a superiority in the Air. Forces employed on both sides represented an intense form of war effort.

2. Losses on both sides were severe; we lost at least 100 tanks, but enemy seemed in no condition to press the pursuit. Had these operations been successful and the enemy been pushed to the neighbourhood of Tobruk, substantial results might have been gained. As it is, our effort to regain the initiative has failed, and it may be some months before we can resume the offensive. There is no reason to suppose enemy possesses strength at present to force Mersa Matruh position, or that he is at all triumphant. On the other hand, situations at Tobruk and at Malta engage serious attention of the Staffs. We must fight hard.

3. I send you in a separate message (T 311) the answer to questions set out in your No. 363. These should dispose of suggestions that we do not regard defence of Middle East as second only to life of Britain.

4. No immediate crisis is expected on west of the Nile.

5. You will have had the telegram about the reported French request for an armistice in Syria. I hope the report is well founded, but the news tonight is that sharp Vichy French resistance at various points continues. Now that we are thrown back on the defensive in the West, Wavell may be able to reinforce the Syrian operation with more Air tanks and men. We have suggested this to him.

6. Little did we think this time last year that we should stand where we do today in the Middle East. Pray see our previous correspondence after the Dakar fiasco. We are certainly in a much better position to defend the Nile Valley than we were then, but I make no promises and give no guarantees, except that we will do our best.

John Colville: diary
(*Colville papers*)

20 June 1941

Departed at 9.15 for Dover with the PM and a large party. . . .[1]

We saw an 18-inch gun on a railway mounting, a formidable object with a brass plate 'HMG Boche-Buster'.

After telephoning to Ismay about the PM's latest project – the replacement of Wavell by Auchinleck – awaited the arrival of the party. The haze and heat made it impossible to see the coast of France, so the PM consoled himself by ordering the firing of rounds by the UP batteries.

Left the train with the PM at a small station and spent the afternoon at Chartwell. The garden was glorious. After a long sleep the PM, in a purple dressing-gown and grey felt hat, took me to see his goldfish. He was ruminating deeply about the fate of Tobruk since the failure of Battleaxe and contemplating means of resuming the offensive. He continued this train of thought in the cottage, conversing the while with the Yellow Cat and with Desmond about his garden.

Back in London an emissary from Marshal Pétain came to see the PM, sponsored by 'C'.

Winston S. Churchill to General Ismay
(*Premier papers, 3/4/1*)

20 June 1941

Please focus clearly in writing –

(a) The arrangements now proposed for more intimate association of the Army and the co-operating Air Force squadrons; and

(b) The responsibility for airfields in the United Kingdom in the event of invasion.

[1] Including Sir Archibald Sinclair, Sir Roger Keyes, General Sir John Dill and Desmond Morton.

Winston S. Churchill to Anthony Eden
(*Churchill papers, 20/36*)

20 June 1941

I agree with the First Lord's view[1] and suggest you telegraph in this sense to Lord Halifax. On no account should the figure of 30 millions or thereabouts be disclosed.[2] Wendell Willkie should be told from me:

'Please be careful, my friend, lest, in trying to galvanize American opinion, you disclose facts which dishearten our merchant seamen, who have to go repeatedly to sea in the teeth of many dangers, and at the same time lead the enemy to redouble his attacks. I am sure you will think of the effect on all the different audiences who will study your words. Kindest regards. – Winston Churchill.'

Winston S. Churchill to President Franklin D. Roosevelt
(*Churchill papers, 20/40*)

20 June 1941

1. In reply to your telegram of June 17, we should warmly welcome the proposed Ferry Service from Brazil to West Africa by American Army pilots and the establishment of American-manned staging posts with servicing facilities at the three places named. We are sending our Air Marshal all the information necessary to enable him to confer with the Army Air Corps Staff on this matter. At present the American aircraft we use and propose to use in the Middle East do not include heavy bombers and the question of range will therefore have to be examined. If the ferry can be used for heavy bombers only, we would examine the question of introducing those types into the Middle East so as to take advantage of the scheme proposed. Delays on our route between Takoradi and Egypt in the past have been mainly due to shortage of transport aircraft for bringing ferry pilots back to Takoradi. The generous provision of 20 American transport aircraft for this service will greatly ease our difficulty.

2. The hard fighting in the Western Desert failed to achieve our hopes of regaining the initiative. Forces and losses were about equal. There will be a good deal more fighting on this front and I see no reason why we should not maintain an active successful defensive. I hope the Syrian position will

[1] Of Wendell Willkie's disclosure of the estimate of cargo tonnage reaching Britain across the Atlantic.

[2] In May 1941 a total of 136,260 tons of Allied and neutral merchant shipping was sunk. In June, the tonnage sunk fell to 61,414. German U-boat successes in the Atlantic included the sinking of more than 30 million rounds of rifle ammunition.

improve, as we are now able to reinforce from the Western Desert to some extent. You will have received our reply to the reported request for Armistice terms. Today, however, the French have continued to offer sharp resistance.

3. Harriman is reported to be on the Takoradi route. I have for months been trying to improve the 'hopping stones'. His advice will be most valuable.

4. I was greatly cheered by your concluding paragraph. There will be no weakening here.

Winston S. Churchill to General Ismay, for the Chiefs of Staff Committee
(*Churchill papers, 4/55*)

20 June 1941

1. Pray examine the following:

A renewed attempt to regain the initiative in Libya and disengage Tobruk. For this purpose take advantage of the west and east Malta convoy, and send 100 cruiser tanks at the earliest moment. The time to do this is if and when the enemy is engaged against Russia. Exceptionally strong fighter protection must be provided from Malta, and also fighter protection, long range or other, from Mersa Matruh, refuelling at Tobruk – the Tobruk land-ground itself being protected by strong additional fighter patrols from Mersa during the refuelling. The battle should be fought the right way, i.e., strong offensive from Tobruk towards El Adem with their existing tank force reinforced by 30 or 40 more tanks. On the night of day two of this sortie an advance with the largest possible forces from Mersa Matruh positions should be made, and fight for a decision simultaneously on both fronts. W has at the present time in the field and workshops 450 tanks less losses, say 120 – equals 330. To these add 60 American which should be arriving now, the 100 despatched in the fast ships which should reach him early in July, the extra 100 mentioned above (if they get through) – total by August 1 say 590, of which about 200 are cruisers and 60 fast American lights, say 500 all types in action, of which 100 are from Tobruk and 400 from Mersa. Use (say) the troops that fought last time as convenient, plus two leading brigades of the 50th Division and one additional South African brigade or their equivalent. For all of these transport should be available from the great numbers of lorries arriving in June and July. Meanwhile finish off the Syrian affair and concentrate air force to the utmost in the West, the highest possible development of squadrons being made.

2. The alternative is to remain on the defensive as General Wavell proposes for the next three months, which means that Tobruk should be evacuated at the earliest moment with losses of 50 tanks, 100 guns, 1,000 vehicles and all stores, also the possibility of disaster. Still it might be done. Further consequences are that the enemy will reinforce very strongly and build up his army for a main offensive against Egypt as soon as the weather cools or

perhaps sooner. The Admiral has abandoned all hopes of blocking Tripoli and perhaps Benghazi also with *Anson*. Every single one of our plans has failed. The enemy has completely established himself in the Central Mediterranean. We are afraid of his dive-bombers at every point. Our ships cannot enforce any blockade between Italy and Cyrenaica or Greece and Cyrenaica, apart from submarines. The Air Force are plainly unable to stop them reinforcing.

Have we really got to accept this?

Winston S. Churchill to the Marquess of Linlithgow
(Churchill papers, 20/40)

20 June 1941
Most Urgent
Absolutely Secret and Personal

I have come to the conclusion that a change is needed in the command in the Middle East. Wavell has a glorious record, having completely destroyed the Italian Army and conquered the Italian Empire in Africa. He has also borne up well against the German attacks and has conducted war and policy in three or four directions simultaneously since the beginning of the struggle. I must regard him as our most distinguished General. Nevertheless, I feel he is tired, and that a fresh eye and an unstrained hand is needed. I wish therefore to bring about a change-over for temporary war time conditions between him and Auchinleck. I feel sure Auchinleck would infuse a new energy and precision into the defence of the Nile Valley, and that Wavell would make an admirable Commander-in-Chief in India, who would aid him in the whole of the great sphere which India is now assuming as our flank moves eastward. Anyone can see arguments against such an exchange, but I hope you will help me in bringing this about. I shall await your reply before communicating with either officer. This telegram is therefore for you alone.

General Ismay: recollection[1]
(Churchill papers, 4/220)

[20 June 1941]

The deciding episode that lives in my mind was that both Eden and Dill thought that Wavell had been tremendously affected by the breach of his desert flank by Rommel. His Intelligence had misinformed him and the thrust came as a complete surprise. I seem to remember Eden saying that Wavell had

[1] Ismay set down this recollection for Churchill in a letter of 13 December 1948, when Churchill was preparing his war memoirs.

'aged ten years in the night'. You yourself said that Rommel had torn the new won laurels from Wavell's brow and thrown them in the sand.

I think there was a very general impression in Whitehall that Wavell was very tired.

Some time ago you asked me whether I remembered the reasons that impelled you to replace Wavell by Auchinleck, and I replied that you and all of us in London got the feeling that Wavell was a tired man.

Ian Jacob reminded me last night[1] of an episode which confirmed this view, and which I now recollect very vividly. I can see you now, holding out both your hands as though you had a fishing rod in each of them, and you said: 'I feel that I have got a tired fish on this rod, and a very lively one on the other'.

You were very pleased with Auchinleck at that time because he had been so forward in the Iraq affair.

Winston S. Churchill to General Wavell
(*Churchill papers, 20/40*)

21 June 1941
Personal and Secret

I have come to the conclusion that the public interest will best be served by the appointment of General Auchinleck to relieve you in the Command of the armies of the Middle East. I have greatly admired your command and conduct of these armies both in success and adversity, and the victories which are associated with your name will be famous in the story of the British Army, and are an important contribution to our final success in this obstinate war. I feel, however, that after the long strain you have borne, a new eye and a new hand are required in this most seriously menaced theatre. I am sure that you are incomparably the best man and most distinguished officer to fill the vacancy of Commander-in-Chief in India. I have consulted the Viceroy upon the subject, and he assures me that your assumption of this great office and task will be warmly welcomed in India, and adds that he himself will be proud to work with one who bears in his own words so shining a record. I propose therefore to submit your name to His Majesty accordingly.

2. General Auchinleck is being ordered to proceed at once to Cairo, where you will make him acquainted with the whole situation and concert with him the future measures which you and he will take in common to meet the German drive to the East now clearly impending. I trust he may arrive by air within the next four or five days at latest. After you have settled everything up

[1] Ismay set down this recollection for Churchill in a letter of 2 February 1949.

with him you should proceed at your earliest convenience to India. No announcement will be made and the matter must be kept strictly secret until you are both at your posts.[1]

On Saturday, 21 June 1941, Churchill lunched at Downing Street with Lord Louis Mountbatten, who had just returned from Crete, where he had commanded the destroyer *Kelly*. Mountbatten gave Churchill an account, which he repeated to John Colville, of how when the *Kelly* had been sunk, 'the Germans machine-gunned him and his crew as they swam'. From Downing Street, Churchill drove to Chequers, for the rest of the weekend.

Anthony Eden: recollection
('*The Eden Memoirs, The Reckoning*')

21 June 1941

As our Intelligence had shown the German attack on Russia to be imminent, the Prime Minister asked me to come to Chequers on Saturday, June 21st, for the weekend. We had some talk after dinner about the consequences for us should the attack really take place. Our advisers were pessimistic about what the Russians could do. Cripps excused the Soviet appeasement of the Nazis on the grounds of their extreme weakness. Every day must count for them. He had told the War Cabinet on June 16th that the prevailing view in diplomatic circles in Moscow was that Russia could not hold out against Germany for more than three or four weeks. Dill, in conversation with me, hoped for a few weeks longer, but thought we should be unwise to count on more than six or seven.

When I went to bed that night I had no clear view on these matters, only the conviction that for the Germans to have to suffer losses in Russia, even for a spell, on a scale far exceeding those they were now enduring, must ease some of the strain upon us.

[1] General Wavell replied on 22 June 1941: 'I think you are wise to make change and get new ideas and action on many problems in Middle East and am sure Auchinleck will be successful choice. I appreciate your generous references to my work and am honoured that you should consider me fitted (?to) fill post of C-in-C India.' (*Churchill papers, 20/40*)

John Colville: diary
(*Colville papers*)

21 June 1941

To Chequers in time for dinner. Party consisted of PM and Mrs C, Mary, Judy Montagu,[1] Tommy, Mr and Mrs Winant, Mr and Mrs Eden, Edward Bridges.

During dinner the talk turned to the demand for an Imperial War Cabinet. 'Well,' said the PM, 'you can easily turn the War Cabinet into a museum of Imperial celebrities, but then you have to have another body to manage the war.'

The PM says a German attack on Russia is certain and Russia will assuredly be defeated. He thinks that Hitler is counting on enlisting capitalist and right-wing sympathies in this country and the US. PM says he is wrong; he will go all out to help Russia. Winant asserts that same will be true in US. After dinner, when I was walking on the lawn with the PM, he elaborated this and I said that for him, the arch anti-communist, this was bowing down in the House of Rimmon.[2] He replied that he had only one single purpose – the destruction of Hitler – and his life was much simplified thereby. If Hitler invaded Hell he would at least make a favourable reference to the Devil!

During dinner there was much talk on the US coming into the war and also on Pétain's emissary, who has made it clear that what was holding Frenchmen back from us was their uncertainty about our victory and about the US coming in.

When I was alone in the garden with the PM he said to me: 'You will live through many wars, but you will never have such an interesting time as you are having now – and you may get some fighting later on.' He then spoke of Wavell and Auchinleck and said it had been very difficult. I wondered if Wavell might not sulk and refuse India, but the PM said he had been afraid of just putting him on the shelf as that would excite much comment and attention. I suggested (as CIGS had) that W would use his pen after the war; the PM replied that he could use his too and would bet he sold more copies! He then said he thought David Margesson was very good at the WO.

[1] Judy Montagu, 1923–1972. Only child of Edwin Montagu and Venetia Stanley (Clementine Churchill's cousin), and a close friend of Churchill's daughter Mary. Her father died before she was two years old. In 1962 she married Milton Gendel. After the Second World War, when she served in the ATS, she was active in the work of the Invalid Children's Aid Association.

[2] '. . . when my master goeth into the house of Rimmon to worship there, and he leaneth on my hand, and I bow myself in the house of Rimmon: when I bow down in the house of Rimmon, the Lord pardon thy servant in this thing' (2 Kings 5, verse 18).

Winston S. Churchill: recollection
(*The Second World, Volume 3, page 330*)

[22 June 1941]

When I awoke on the morning of Sunday, the 22nd, the news was brought to me of Hitler's invasion of Russia. This changed conviction into certainty. I had not the slightest doubt where our duty and our policy lay. Nor indeed what to say. There only remained the task of composing it. I asked that notice should immediately be given that I would broadcast at 9 o'clock that night. Presently General Dill, who had hastened down from London, came into my bedroom with detailed news. The Germans had invaded Russia on an enormous front, had surprised a large portion of the Soviet Air Force grounded on the airfields, and seemed to be driving forward with great rapidity and violence. The Chief of the Imperial General Staff added, 'I suppose they will be rounded up in hordes.'

I spent the day composing my statement. There was not time to consult the War Cabinet, nor was it necessary. I knew that we all felt the same on this issue. Mr Eden, Lord Beaverbrook, and Sir Stafford Cripps – he had left Moscow on the 10th – were also with me during the day.

John Colville: diary
(*Colville papers*)

22 June 1941 Chequers

Awoken by the telephone with the news that Germany had attacked Russia. I went a round of the bedrooms breaking the news and produced a smile of satisfaction on the faces of the PM, Eden and Winant. Winant, however, suspects it may all be a put up job between Hitler and Stalin (Later the PM and Cripps laughed this to scorn).

Eden rushed off to the FO for the day; the PM decided to broadcast and actually came down to the Hawtrey Room at 11.00 a.m. to prepare it; Sir Stafford and Lady Cripps[1] motored over to discuss the situation and ended by staying to lunch and dine. Mr Fraser, the singularly unattractive and dull Labour Prime Minister of New Zealand, came to lunch and to stay the night, as did Cranborne and Beaverbrook.

[1] Isobel, 2nd daughter of Commander Harold Swithinbank. She married Cripps in 1911. They had one son and three daughters.

Lord Beaverbrook: recollection
(A.J.P. Taylor, 'Beaverbrook')

[22 June 1941]

Mr Churchill listened, questioned, considered, all through the day. Occasionally he sat in the garden in the hot sunshine. Then again he would stride to his office, restless to a degree. But though he was restless he had in fact early made up his mind. He would broadcast that night his determination that Russia should be given all the aid in Britain's power.

It was a decision taken without calling his Cabinet together. There was no time to summon his colleagues. It was a decision taken in the likelihood that it would arouse a measure of hostility, albeit unspoken, among sections of his own Party. Nor could he have any guarantee either of the attitude of the British newspapers.

Colonel Moore-Brabazon: recollection[1]
(Churchill papers, 20/24)

[22 June 1941]

You will remember that you rang me up the day the Germans marched on Russia about production matters and in concluding the talk, in that you were going to broadcast that night, you did say: 'Do you not think we ought to help?' And I said 'yes' enthusiastically.

John Colville: diary
(Colville papers)

22 June 1941 Chequers

The PM's broadcast was not ready till 20 minutes before he was due to deliver it and it gave me great anxiety, but even more so to Eden who wanted to vet the text and couldn't. But when it was made it impressed us all: it was dramatic and it gave a clear decision of policy – support for Russia.

[1] Colonel Moore-Brabazon, Beaverbrook's successor as Minister of Aircraft Production, set down these recollections in a letter to Churchill (marked 'Private') of 3 September 1941.

Winston S. Churchill: broadcast
('The Listener', 26 June 1941)[1]

22 June 1941 Chequers

I have taken occasion to speak to you tonight because we have reached one of the climacterics of the war. The first of these intense turning-points was a year ago when France fell prostrate under the German hammer, and when we had to face the storm alone. The second was when the Royal Air Force beat the Hun raiders out of the daylight air, and thus warded off the Nazi invasion of our island while we were still ill-armed and ill-prepared. The third turning-point was when the President and Congress of the United States passed the Lease-and-Lend enactment, devoting nearly 2,000 millions sterling of the wealth of the New World to help us to defend our liberties and their own. Those were the three climacterics. The fourth is now upon us.

At four o'clock this morning Hitler attacked and invaded Russia. All his usual formalities of perfidy were observed with scrupulous technique. A non-aggression treaty had been solemnly signed and was in force between the two countries. No complaint had been made by Germany of its non-fulfilment. Under its cloak of false confidence, the German armies drew up in immense strength along a line which stretches from the White Sea to the Black Sea; and their air fleets and armoured divisions slowly and methodically took their stations. Then suddenly, without declaration of war, without even an ultimatum, German bombs rained down from the air upon the Russian cities, the German troops violated the frontiers; and an hour later the German Ambassador,[2] who till the night before was lavishing his assurances of friendship, almost of alliance, upon the Russians, called upon the Russian Foreign Minister to tell him that a state of war existed between Germany and Russia.

Thus was repeated on a far larger scale the same kind of outrage against every form of signed compact and international faith which we have witnessed in Norway, Denmark, Holland and Belgium, and which Hitler's accomplice and jackal Mussolini so faithfully imitated in the case of Greece.

All this was no surprise to me. In fact I gave clear and precise warnings to Stalin of what was coming. I gave him warning as I have given warning to others before. I can only hope that this warning did not fall unheeded. All we know at present is that the Russian people are defending their native soil and that their leaders have called upon them to resist to the utmost.

Hitler is a monster of wickedness, insatiable in his lust for blood and plunder. Not content with having all Europe under his heel, or else terrorized into various forms of abject submission, he must now carry his work of

[1] This broadcast was also issued as a gramophone record, His Master's Voice, ALP 1556.
[2] Frederic Werner Schulenburg.

butchery and desolation among the vast multitudes of Russia and of Asia. The terrible military machine, which we and the rest of the civilized world so foolishly, so supinely, so insensately allowed the Nazi gangsters to build up year by year from almost nothing, cannot stand idle lest it rust or fall to pieces. It must be in continual motion, grinding up human lives and trampling down the homes and the rights of hundreds of millions of men. Moreover it must be fed, not only with flesh but with oil.

So now this bloodthirsty guttersnipe must launch his mechanized armies upon new fields of slaughter, pillage and devastation. Poor as are the Russian peasants, workmen and soldiers, he must steal from them their daily bread; he must devour their harvests; he must rob them of the oil which drives their ploughs; and thus produce a famine without example in human history. And even the carnage and ruin which his victory, should he gain it – he has not gained it yet – will bring upon the Russian people, will itself be only a stepping-stone to the attempt to plunge the four or five hundred millions who live in China, and the three hundred and fifty millions who live in India, into that bottomless pit of human degradation over which the diabolic emblem of the Swastika flaunts itself. It is not too much to say here this summer evening that the lives and happiness of a thousand million additional people are now menaced with brutal Nazi violence. That is enough to make us hold our breath. But presently I shall show you something else that lies behind; and something that touches very nearly the life of Britain and of the United States.

The Nazi regime is indistinguishable from the worst features of Communism. It is devoid of all theme and principle except appetite and racial domination. It excels all forms of human wickedness in the efficiency of its cruelty and ferocious aggression. No one has been a more consistent opponent of Communism than I have for the last twenty-five years. I will unsay no word that I have spoken about it. But all this fades away before the spectacle which now is unfolding. The past with its crimes, its follies and its tragedies flashes away. I see the Russian soldiers standing on the threshold of their native land, guarding the fields where their fathers have tilled from time immemorial. I see them guarding their homes where mothers and wives pray – ah yes, for there are times when all pray – for the safety of their loved ones, the return of the breadwinner, of their champion, or their protector. I see the ten thousand villages of Russia, where the means of existence was wrung so hardly from the soil, but where there are still primordial human joys, where maidens laugh and children play. I see advancing upon all this in hideous onslaught the Nazi war machine, with its clanking, heel-clicking, dandified Prussian officers, its crafty expert agents fresh from the cowing and tying down of a dozen countries. I see also the dull, drilled, docile, brutish masses of the Hun soldiery plodding on like a swarm of crawling locusts. I see the German bombers and fighters in the sky, still smarting from many a British whipping, delighted to find what they believe is an easier and a safer prey.

Behind all this glare, behind all this storm, I see that small group of villainous men who plan, organize and launch this cataract of horrors upon mankind. And then my mind goes back across the years to the days when the Russian armies were our allies against the same deadly foe; when they fought with so much valour and constancy, and helped to gain a victory from all share in which, alas, they were – through no fault of ours – utterly cut out. I have lived through all this and you will pardon me if I express my feelings and the stir of old memories.

But now I have to declare the decision of His Majesty's Government – and I feel sure it is a decision in which the great Dominions will, in due course, concur – for we must speak out now at once, without a day's delay. I have to make the declaration, but can you doubt what our policy will be? We have but one aim and one single, irrevocable purpose. We are resolved to destroy Hitler and every vestige of the Nazi regime. From this nothing will turn us – nothing. We will never parley, we will never negotiate with Hitler or any of his gang. We shall fight him by land, we shall fight him by sea, we shall fight him in the air, until with God's help we have rid the earth of his shadow and liberated its peoples from his yoke. Any man or state who fights on against Nazidom will have our aid. Any man or state who marches with Hitler is our foe. This applies not only to organized states but to all representatives of that vile race of Quislings who make themselves the tools and agents of the Nazi regime against their fellow-countrymen and the lands of their birth. They – these Quislings – like the Nazi leaders themselves, if not disposed of by their fellow-countrymen, which would save trouble, will be delivered by us on the morrow of victory to the justice of the Allied tribunals. That is our policy and that is our declaration. It follows, therefore, that we shall give whatever help we can to Russia and the Russian people. We shall appeal to all our friends and allies in every part of the world to take the same course and pursue it, as we shall, faithfully and steadfastly to the end.

We have offered the Government of Soviet Russia any technical or economic assistance which is in our power, and which is likely to be of service to them. We shall bomb Germany by day as well as by night in ever-increasing measure, casting upon them month by month a heavier discharge of bombs, and making the German people taste and gulp each month a sharper dose of the miseries they have showered upon mankind. It is noteworthy that only yesterday the Royal Air Force, fighting inland over French territory, cut down with very small loss to themselves 28 of the Hun fighting machines in the air above the French soil they have invaded, defiled and profess to hold. But this is only a beginning. From now forward the main expansion of our Air Force proceeds with gathering speed. In another six months the weight of the help we are receiving from the United States in war materials of all kinds, and especially in heavy bombers, will begin to tell.

This is no class war, but a war in which the whole British Empire and

Commonwealth of Nations is engaged without distinction of race, creed or party. It is not for me to speak of the action of the United States, but this I will say: if Hitler imagines that his attack on Soviet Russia will cause the slightest division of aims or slackening of effort in the great Democracies who are resolved upon his doom, he is woefully mistaken. On the contrary, we shall be fortified and encouraged in our efforts to rescue mankind from his tyranny. We shall be strengthened and not weakened in determination and in resources.

This is no time to moralize on the follies of countries and governments which have allowed themselves to be struck down one by one, when by united action they could have saved themselves and saved the world from this catastrophe. But when I spoke a few minutes ago of Hitler's blood-lust and the hateful appetites which have impelled or lured him on his Russian adventure, I said there was one deeper motive behind his outrage. He wishes to destroy the Russian power because he hopes that if he succeeds in this, he will be able to bring back the main strength of his army and air force from the East and hurl it upon this island, which he knows he must conquer or suffer the penalty of his crimes. His invasion of Russia is no more than a prelude to an attempted invasion of the British Isles. He hopes, no doubt, that all this may be accomplished before the winter comes, and that he can overwhelm Great Britain before the fleet and air power of the United States may intervene. He hopes that he may once again repeat upon a greater scale than ever before, that process of destroying his enemies one by one, by which he has so long thrived and prospered, and that then the scene will be clear for the final act, without which all his conquests would be in vain – namely, the subjugation of the Western Hemisphere to his will and to his system.

The Russian danger is therefore our danger, and the danger of the United States, just as the cause of any Russian fighting for his hearth and home is the cause of free men and free peoples in every quarter of the globe. Let us learn the lessons already taught by such cruel experience. Let us redouble our exertions and strike with united strength while life and power remain.

John Colville: diary

(*Colville papers*)

22 June 1941 Chequers

Later, the night being very warm, we all walked in the garden and I gossiped with Edward Bridges while the PM continued an onslaught, begun at dinner, on the people who had let us in for this most unnecessary of all wars. He was harsh about Chamberlain whom he called 'the narrowest, most ignorant, most ungenerous of men'. At dinner it had been Chatfield[1] whom he belaboured and the people at the Admiralty and elsewhere whose desire for 'absurd self-abasement had brought us to the verge of annihilation'.

On going to bed the PM kept on repeating how wonderful it was that Russia had come in against Germany when she might so easily have been with her. He is also very pleased with our daylight sorties by fighters which, today and yesterday, accounted for 58 enemy planes over France for the loss of 3 pilots. We seem to command the daylight air over enemy territory as well as our own.

Winston S. Churchill to Lord Moyne[2]
(Churchill papers, 20/21)

22 June 1941
Secret

My dear Moyne,

Their Lordships' House will have been informed of the following Resolution which was agreed to unanimously by the House of Commons on June 19:

'That this House desires to express its warm appreciation of the courtesy of the House of Peers in placing their Chamber at the disposal of this House.'

As this Resolution was moved in Secret Session there can be no record of the proceedings to supplement this unadorned statement. It was therefore the general wish of the House that I should write to you, as Leader of the House of Lords, asking you to inform their Lordships of the very real gratitude displayed by all Members in every quarter of the House.

Had it not been for this most generous gesture, most of the rooms and other facilities which will now become available again to Members of the House of Commons would have been lost to us, although standing almost unharmed, and it would have been impossible to provide for Members a great measure of comfort and convenience which will now be restored.

It has been, and will remain, my endeavour to secure the power, authority and prestige of Parliament. After nearly two years of war Parliament remains within the Palace of Westminster, and it would be a glorious thing to fight our

[1] Alfred Ernle Montacute Chatfield, 1873–1967. Entered the Royal Navy, 1886. Served at the battles of Heligoland (1914), Dogger Bank (1915) and Jutland (1916). Fourth Sea Lord, 1919–20. Knighted, 1919. Rear-Admiral, 1920. Assistant Chief of the Naval Staff, 1920–2. Third Sea Lord, 1925–8. Commander-in-Chief, Atlantic Fleet, 1929–31. Vice-Admiral, 1930. Commander-in-Chief, Mediterranean, 1931–2, First Sea Lord, January 1933 to September 1938. Admiral of the Fleet, 1935. Created Baron, 1937. Privy Councillor, 1939. Minister for Co-ordination of Defence, 1939–40 (with a seat in the War Cabinet). Chairman, Civil Defence Honours Committee, 1940–6. Author of *The Navy and Defence* (1942), and *It Might Happen Again* (1947). In 1937 he was elected to the Other Club.

[2] This letter was written to Lord Moyne (the Secretary of State for the Colonies) in his capacity as Leader of the House of Lords.

way through this war with our Parliamentary institutions not merely undiminished but enhanced.

No action on the part of their Lordships could be more helpful in bringing this about, and it is with nothing less than the greatest personal pleasure and gratitude that I ask you to convey to the members of the House of Lords this message of thanks, which has the unanimous and full approval of the Members of the House which I have the honour to lead.

I am aware that the new Chamber of the House of Lords in the King's Robing Room will not yet be complete. I hope however that the work is so far advanced as not to cause great inconvenience or discomfort to their Lordships in the discharge of their duties.

Winston S. Churchill to General Sir John Dill
(Churchill papers, 20/36)

22 June 1941

TANKS AT GENERAL WAVELL'S DISPOSAL

Kindly add how many he has got in the workshops, and how many fit for action. I make him 100 lost out of 200, plus 50 in Tobruk, leaving 150 in hand. To these must be added any subsequently received from the workshops. We ought to have a weekly Tank state showing the exact conditions, under three or four heads.

Winston S. Churchill to General Wavell
(Churchill papers, 20/40)

23 June 1941

Am most grateful to you for your telegram. I hope you will allow me to say that I feel a very high sense of comradeship with you after the ups and downs of this tremendous year in the Middle East. I should prefer you to go to India and take over, after which I should like you to come home for consultation on the whole problem, which would give you the chance of a rest. On the other hand, I see the advantages of early consultation and also sparing you the extra journey. I am therefore telegraphing to the Viceroy putting the point to him. I have not yet heard from Auchinleck when he will reach Cairo. Once I know he is there I shall make the announcement of both appointments, keeping your coming home, of course, quite secret until you arrive. I will cable again tomorrow.

Winston S. Churchill to General Ismay, for the Chiefs of Staff Committee
(*Churchill papers, 20/36*)

23 June 1941
Most Secret

1. The success which has attended the admirable offensive of the RAF over the Pas de Calais should encourage this to be pressed day after day as long as it proves profitable. The number of Bombers going by day should be increased as much as possible, so as to take full advantage by daylight of the various targets presented. For this purpose the Cabinet should be asked to agree to the bombing of any important factories which are being used on a large scale for the repair or manufacture of enemy aircraft; and any important objectives in the area dominated should be subjected to the heaviest daylight bombing and effectively destroyed. The French workmen should at the right moment be warned to keep away from the factories, though this should not prevent our beginning before they have notice.

2. On the assumption that our domination of the Air over this area will be successfully established, the Staffs should consider whether a serious operation in the form of a large raid should not be launched under full Air protection. I have in mind something of the scale of 25 to 30 thousand men – perhaps the Commandos plus one of the Canadian divisions. It would be necessary to create a force exactly adapted to the tactical plan rather than to adhere to the conventional establishments of divisions. As long as we can keep Air domination over the Channel and the Pas de Calais, it ought to be possible to achieve a considerable result.

3. Among the other objectives, the destruction of the guns and batteries, of all shipping (though there is not much there now), of all stores and the killing and capturing of a large number of Germans present themselves. The blocking of the harbours of Calais and Boulogne might also be attempted.

4. I should like to have a preliminary discussion this evening at 9.45 p.m., and if the principle is approved the plans should be perfected as soon as possible in case the Air domination should be achieved. Now the enemy is busy in Russia is the time to 'Make hell while the sun shines'.

Winston S. Churchill to Sir Archibald Sinclair and Air Chief Marshal Sir Charles Portal
(*Premier papers, 3/11/1*)

23 June 1941
Secret

What is the position about the bombing of the Black Forest this year? It ought to be possible to produce very fine results.[1]

Winston S. Churchill to Sir John Dill, and to General Ismay for the Chiefs of Staff Committee
(*Churchill papers, 20/36*)

23 June 1941
Secret

It would appear wise now to announce the date, say, 1st September, by which all our defences are to be brought to the very highest anti-invasion efficiency. It would be necessary to make it clear that meanwhile no vigilance is to be relaxed. On the contrary, a note of invasion alarm should be struck, and everybody set to work with redoubled energy.

This, however, must not prevent the despatch of necessary reinforcements to the Middle East.

War Cabinet: minutes
(*Cabinet papers, 65/18*)

23 June 1941 — 10 Downing Street
5 p.m.

The Prime Minister said that it had been necessary to act quickly, following on Germany's attack on Russia on Sunday morning. He hoped the War Cabinet would approve the line which he had taken in his broadcast the previous evening. The Debate on Shipping matters which had been due to take place on the following day, had been postponed. It had been arranged that the Foreign Secretary should make a statement on the position resulting from Germany's attack on Russia.

The Prime Minister thought it was important that the Labour members of the Cabinet, in any speeches which they might make, should continue to draw

[1] On 2 July 1941, Portal minuted to Churchill: 'crops will not burn, but forests will'. Bomber Command 'will therefore go for the forests'. What was needed, he explained, was 'a variant on the sticky bomb or Molotov Cocktail which will scatter an inflammable mixture on the trees themselves' as there was no undergrowth under pine trees for a standard incendiary bomb to set fire to. A new bomb was therefore to be devised (*Premier papers, 3/11/1, folio 12*).

a line of demarcation between the tenets of the Labour Party and those of Communism. (The Lord Privy Seal[1] said that he was proposing to emphasize this in a broadcast on the following evening.)

Winston S. Churchill: Oral Answers
(Hansard)

24 June 1941 House of Commons

PARLIAMENTARY PRIVATE SECRETARIES

Mr Mander asked the Prime Minister whether he will make a statement with a view to the removal of doubts as to the precise status of Parliamentary Private Secretaries; to what extent they are to be regarded as part of the Government with right to speak on its behalf without independence as to speaking or voting; or whether it is the intention that they should enjoy the freedom of Private Members in these respects?

The Prime Minister: Parliamentary Private Secretaries occupy a special position, which is not always understood by the general public, either at home or abroad. Parliamentary Private Secretaries are not members of the Government, and should not be spoken of as such. They are Private Members, and should therefore be afforded as much liberty of action as possible; but their close and confidential association with Ministers necessarily imposes certain obligations on them, and has led to the following generally accepted practice: That Parliamentary Private Secretaries should not make statements in the House or put Questions on matters affecting the Department with which they are connected. They should also exercise great discretion in any speeches or broadcasts which they make outside the House, bearing in mind that, however careful they may be to make it clear that they are speaking only as Private Members, they are nevertheless liable to be regarded as speaking with some of the knowledge and authority which attaches to a member of the Government.

Mr de Rothschild:[2] Is the Prime Minister aware that it is very disconcerting to find these gentlemen flitting from one side of the House to the other, and to

[1] Clement Attlee, who had been leader of the Labour Party since 1935, and a Labour Member of Parliament since 1922.

[2] James Armand de Rothschild, 1878–1957. Known as 'Jimmy'. Born in Paris, the son of Baron Edmond de Rothschild, (patron of Jewish agricultural enterprise in Palestine). Educated in Paris and at Trinity College, Cambridge. On active service, 1914–18, on the western front and in Palestine; Major, Royal Fusiliers, 1918. Liaison Officer with the Zionist Commission in Palestine, 1918. President of the Palestine Jewish Colonization Association, 1924. A Director of the Palestine Electric Corporation, and a patron of the Hebrew University of Jerusalem. A member of the Other Club from 1925. Liberal MP for the Isle of Ely, 1929–45. Trustee of the Wallace Collection, 1941–55. Joint Parliamentary Secretary, Ministry of Supply, 1945. An advocate of making Palestine a British colony, in order to preserve the rights of both Jews and Arabs. In 1946 he contributed £5,000 towards the purchase of Chartwell for the National Trust. He left his own country house at Waddesdon and its contents to the National Trust.

note that whereas on the one side they are replete with praise, on the other side they are voluble in their criticisms?

The Prime Minister: We have all done a bit of flitting in our time, and no doubt we have suited our conduct to our circumstances.

IMPERIAL WAR CONFERENCE

Mr Lees-Smith (by Private Notice) asked the Prime Minister whether he has any statement to make about the progress of the war.

The Prime Minister: I do not think that this would be a good occasion for me to make another statement on the war situation in the Middle East. I should prefer to leave a longer interval before recurring to the topics we discussed so fully a fortnight ago. There are quite serious disadvantages in reviewing too frequently the course of operations which are still in progress.

I was, however, asked to give information about the policy of His Majesty's Government in relation to an Imperial War Conference. As I told the House, we very much desire such a Conference and we had hoped that the end of July or the beginning of August might be a suitable occasion. I have now received replies to the inquiries I have made. Both General Smuts and Mr Mackenzie King regret that the exigencies of their work in their respective countries make it impossible for them to come here in the near future. Mr Menzies has only just returned to Australia, though I hope we shall see him here again before long. Mr Fraser, the Prime Minister of New Zealand, arrived last Saturday and is sitting with us constantly in our councils. He would not, however, be able to remain indefinitely. The House will readily understand that these Prime Ministers of important and powerful Governments, with the legislatures and the whole war effort of their peoples to guide, find great difficulties in meeting here simultaneously. I hope these difficulties may be resolved at some time in the future, but for the present I feel that it is impossible to fix a date.

THE TURKISH TREATY[1]

Earl Winterton: I do not wish to detain the House – and I have already answered the hon. Gentleman's point – but I am entitled to put this point of view and I shall be most agreeably surprised if in the next few weeks a great many Members of the House, including the Government, do not agree that what happened in connection with the signature of this treaty was a most serious blow to us.

The Prime Minister: I do not rise for the purpose of continuing the Debate on the lines to which it has been turned by the Noble Lord, because I am sure that it would not be at all in the public interest to continue on those lines. I rise rather to hope that the other aspects of the difficult foreign situation may

[1] The ten-year Pact of Friendship, signed between Germany and Turkey in Ankara on 18 June 1941.

engage the attention of the House and that we should not seek to probe and define too clearly the attitude of certain Powers who, surrounded by very great difficulties, may not wish, or may not be in a position, to declare themselves. All this pressing for a precise answer 'Yes' or 'No' may sometimes lead to getting an answer contrary to the one you expected, and I am bound to say that I hoped this fairly obvious point would have impressed itself even upon the Noble Lord. These excursions of his into foreign politics, which, I must say, he is less well fitted to discuss than some of the other numerous topics on which he assists us, will not, I trust, be too frequent. I find it very difficult to derive any principle of guidance if no reference is to be made to any country in which the Noble Lord has fought. It would be an altogether undue complication of the liberties of our speech. I trust that we shall drop the topic now, because it really is a case of 'least said, soonest mended'.

Winston S. Churchill to Brigadier Menzies[1]
(*'British Intelligence in the Second World War'*)

24 June 1941

Providing no risks are run.

John Martin: diary
(*Martin papers*)

24 June 1941

Late night (till 3.40 a.m.) on PM's shipping speech.

War Cabinet, Defence Committee (Operations): minutes
(*Cabinet papers, 69/2*)

25 June 1941
10 p.m. Cabinet War Room

IRAN AND THE PERSIAN GULF

The Prime Minster drew attention to the probability that the war in the Middle East might spread in the near future in the direction of Iran and the Persian Gulf. He thought that plans should now be made to enable a considerable air force to be built up at Basra, as otherwise, when the threat

[1] Who had asked Churchill about divulging Enigma secrets to Stalin (without revealing the true source).

developed, we might find ourselves without sufficient facilities in that area to enable us to meet it.

REINFORCEMENTS FOR MALTA

Sir Dudley Pound explained to the Committee a plan which had been prepared by the Chiefs of Staff for reinforcing Malta with troops, equipment and supplies – the full details of which had been communicated to the Prime Minister.

The Prime Minister said that he welcomed this plan, but that he wished further study to be given to the proposal which he had put to the Chiefs of Staff in his Minute of the 20th June (COS(41) 113 (0)), that the opportunity should be taken while running these reinforcements to Malta to pass 100 Cruiser Tanks through the Mediterranean to Egypt. It appeared that, as things now were, we could not undertake any offensive operation in Libya for three months. This meant that not only should we lose the present opportunity while the Germans were preoccupied elsewhere, but the garrison at Tobruk would be left in great jeopardy. We were much too inclined to play for safety until a great emergency arose, but we should now realize that, unless drastic steps were taken, there could hardly be any alternative but to evacuate Tobruk forthwith.

John Colville: diary
(*Colville papers*)

25 June 1941

In Secret Session the PM told the House of Commons the facts about the shipping position and the Battle of the Atlantic, which show real signs of improvement. Last weekend Winant told me America hoped next year to build 2,000,000 tons of shipping more than was scheduled.

On late duty. Finished *My Early Life*[1] while the PM discussed his new proposal for sending a Cabinet minister to take up permanent residence in the Middle East. This has been stimulated by a telegram from Randolph.[2] Oliver Lyttelton has been selected.

[1] Churchill's memoir of his childhood and soldiering days, first published in 1930. The American title was *A Roving Commission*.

[2] On 7 June 1941 Randolph Churchill had telegraphed to his father from Cairo (with the knowledge and encouragement of the British Ambassador to Egypt, Sir Miles Lampson): 'Do not see how we can start winning war out here until we have a competent civilian on the spot to provide day-to-day political and strategic direction. Why not send a member of the War Cabinet here to preside over whole war effort? Apart from small personal staff, he would need two outstanding men to co-ordinate supply and direct censorship, intelligence, and propaganda. Most thoughtful people here realize need for radical reform along these lines. No more shunting of personnel will suffice, and the present time seems particularly ripe and favourable for a change of system. Please forgive me troubling you, but consider present situation deplorable and urgent action vital to any prospects of success.'

Winston S. Churchill: speech

('Secret Session Speeches by the Rt. Hon. Winston S. Churchill, OM, CH, MP')

25 June 1941 House of Commons

SECRET SESSION

THE BATTLE OF THE ATLANTIC

From the beginning of the war to the end of 1940 the losses of British, Allied, and neutral merchant shipping from all causes amounted to about five million tons. But after allowing for our new building and the capture, purchase, and chartering of foreign vessels, the total amount of shipping serving us at the end of 1940 was only about one and one-half million tons less than at peacetime. The total tonnage serving us at the outbreak of war can be variously estimated from twenty-six millions to about twenty-two millions according to the classes of shipping included. Not all this tonnage, it is true, is available for importing service. Some four millions have been withdrawn for naval and military purposes. Some vessels are engaged in essential Empire trade; some are too small to cross the Atlantic; some are immobilized by damage. Tankers amounting to some four and one-half millions form a specialized class wholly absorbed by our oil requirements. We hope to maintain our oil imports fairly near the pre-war level, and in the figures which I shall presently give you for imports I shall therefore exclude oil. If the losses I have quoted are compared with the total fleet, they would amount to about five per cent. On so large a turnover that could not be considered dangerous for sixteen months of the kind of war we have been fighting.

There were, however, two important aggravations. First, there was no comparable windfall to set against the continuance in 1941 of losses at the rate sustained in 1940. Secondly, the protective measures of the Admiralty-convoy, diversion, degaussing, mine clearance, the closing of the Mediterranean, generally the lengthening of the voyages in time and distance, to all of which must be added delays at the ports through enemy action and the blackout – have reduced the operative fertility of our shipping to an extent even more serious than the actual loss. The Admiralty naturally think first of bringing the ships safely to port and judge their success by a minimum of sinkings. But the life and war effort of the country also depend directly upon the weight of imports safely landed.

In the best peace year we imported about sixty million tons. After France went out we could not look forward to an import in 1941 of much more than half this total. Since I went to the Admiralty at the beginning of the war, I have formed and developed a strong Statistical Department of my own under Professor Lindemann. In this way I receive every week a number of key diagrams which cover the entire field of our war effort, and reveal graphically all unfavourable or favourable tendencies. The increasing discrepancy between the comparatively small net loss of tonnage and the enormous fall in imports became more and more evident during the winter of 1940. Many measures were taken by the departments principally concerned, the Ministry of Supply, the Ministry of Food, and the Board of Trade. The imports had for some time past been strictly controlled and all luxuries had been eliminated. The programmes of these three importing departments were framed so as to give priority to articles which make the least demand on shipping space. Our export trade was concentrated on articles of a high exchange value. Ships were increasingly concentrated upon the short Atlantic haul. Drastic steps were taken to stimulate home production. I will not enter upon the question of home production of food, for that requires a debate of its own. But great savings have been made in the imports of timber, which stood at over ten million tons at the beginning of the war, at four and one-half million tons in 1940, and has at last been reduced for the current year to little more than one million tons, reduction being made good partly by economies, and partly by home felling, which has been done on a very large scale. Oil reserves have fallen from the high level at the beginning of the war; but our stocks in all essentials of raw materials have been maintained, and the food reserves stand this summer higher than they did a year ago. At the end of September, when the new harvest is in, they will be substantially better than when the first war harvest was garnered.

I must, however, try to bring home to the House the extraordinary difficulties of our strategic position arising from Hitler's mastery of the European coast. These difficulties far exceed anything that was experienced in the last war. In fact, if at the beginning of 1940 we had been told that the enemy would be in effectual command of all the Continental Atlantic ports, from Narvik to Bayonne, most of the high naval and air experts would have said that the problem of supplying Britain would become insoluble and hopeless.

I remember that in the last war an inquiry was made into the possibilities of feeding this island if the Port of London were closed, and the report was extremely pessimistic. The Port of London has now been reduced to one-quarter. The traffic of all the ports on the east coast is enormously shrunken. The traffic along the south coast is at a tithe of its normal. The English Channel, like the North Sea, is under the close air attack of the enemy. We have had to transfer our importing capacity increasingly to the west-coast ports, and as Southern Ireland is denied us as a base for our protecting flotillas and air squadrons, practically the whole of our traffic comes in through the North-Western Approaches between Ireland and Scotland, and is handled at the Clyde, the Mersey, and to a lesser extent at the ports of the Bristol Channel. All these ports are under frequent and sometimes long-repeated air attacks, and apart from the damage, there are all the restrictions caused by air-raid damage, delays, and blackout conditions.

During the winter months the U-boats developed a new technique of attacking by night. The losses mounted heavily, and the new year dawned upon us bleak and grim.

Besides the depredations of the U-boats, there was growing up a form of air attack upon our Western Approaches by means of long-range Focke Wulf machines. These aircraft – of which happily at the beginning there were only a few, but which might be expected to grow constantly in numbers – could sally out from Brest or Bordeaux, fly right round the British islands, refuel in Norway, and then make the return journey next day. On their way they would see far below them the very large convoys of fifty or sixty ships, to which we have been forced to resort through the scarcity of escorts. Moving inwards or outwards on their voyages, they could attack these convoys or individual ships with destructive bombs, or they could signal by modern perfected wireless to the waiting U-boats, advising them what course to steer in order to make interceptions.

The U-boats themselves could manoeuvre on the surface in the darkness at a greater speed than the convoys. By somewhat reducing the war heads of their torpedoes and somewhat increasing the compressed air bottle which drives them, they were able to fire volleys of torpedoes which ran through the array of the convoys, sometimes striking three or four ships at once. I went through as a Minister some of the worst periods of the U-boat attack in the last war. I have studied the conditions long and carefully, and have thought often about them in the intervening years. Nothing that happened then, nothing that we imagined in the interval, however alarming it seemed at the time, was comparable to the dangers and difficulties which now beset us. I repeat that every high authority that I know of, if asked in cold blood a year ago how we should get through, would have found it impossible to give a favourable answer. I have no doubt that the able experts who advise Hitler told him that our doom was certain.

We do not hear much about the mining now, yet almost every night thirty or forty enemy aeroplanes are casting these destructive engines in all the most likely spots to catch our shipping. We do not hear about it much because by the resources of British science and British organization it has been largely mastered. We do not hear much about it because twenty thousand men and a thousand ships toil ceaselessly with many strange varieties of apparatus to clear the ports and channels each morning of the deadly deposits of the night. We do not hear much about this work or about the men who do it or the men who plan it. It is taken as a matter of course, like the heroic, marvellous feats of the Salvage Service, which has recovered since the war, in every circumstance of storm and difficulty, upwards of a million tons of shipping, which would otherwise have been castaway. A few critical or scathing speeches, a stream of articles in the newspapers, showing how badly the war is managed and how incompetent are those who bear the responsibility – these obtain the fullest publicity; but the marvellous services of seamanship and devotion, and the organization behind them, which prove at every stage and step the soundness of our national life; the inconquerable, the inexhaustible adaptiveness and ingenuity of the British mind; the iron, unyielding, unwearying tenacity of the British character, by which we live, by which we shall certainly be saved – and save the world – these, though fully realized by our foes abroad, are sometimes overlooked by our friends at home.

But I must go back to the beginning of the present year. In January Hitler made a speech threatening us with ruin and pointing with confidence to that combination of air and sea power lapping us about on all sides, by which he hoped, and still hopes, to bring about our starvation and surrender.

In the spring our U-boat war will begin at sea, and they will notice that we have not been sleeping [shouts and cheers]. And the Air Force will play its part and the entire armed forces will force the decision by hook or by crook.

Early in January, as the House will remember, we formed the Import Executive, consisting of the principal importing departments under the Chairmanship of the Minister of Supply, and its sister executive, the Production Executive, under the Ministry of Labour. The principal object of the first of these bodies was to grapple with the import situation, to improve the organization of shipping and transport, and to solve the many intricate problems of labour and organization arising at the ports. There was also the division of our imports between the different importing departments to be settled.

At the beginning of March, after a heavy batch of sinkings, I thought it right to proclaim 'The Battle of the Atlantic'. I did this in order to focus the extreme attention and energies of all concerned upon this struggle for life, and to meet the increased severity of attack which Hitler threatened. I am going to read to the House, as we are in Secret Session, the actual directive which I issued, and which, with the approval of the War Cabinet, was issued on March 6 to all concerned. This is, of course, a most secret document and should on no account be quoted or referred to.

'In view of various German statements . . .'[1]

In order to follow this matter with the closest personal attention, and to give directions from day to day which clear away difficulties and obstructions, and force action upon the great number of departments and branches involved, I held a weekly meetings at which all the Ministers and many of the high functionaries concerned were present, both from the Fighting Services and on the civil side. At these meeting, of which there have been twelve, each lasting some two and one-half hours, the whole field was gone over, and everything thrashed out. Thus, nothing was held up for want of decisions. Presently Mr

[1] Churchill read out his Directive in full. It is published in this volume with the documents of 6 March 1941, pages 315–7.

Harriman, President Roosevelt's expediter of supplies, joined us and made his own invaluable contribution from the American end. These meetings reinforced the work of the Import Executive, and now as things have begun to run more smoothly, I have felt it possible to make the meetings fortnightly.

I was assisted in my work not only by Professor Lindemann's Statistical Department, but also by the Cabinet Secretariat. These two bodies analysed the weekly reports which came in from all departments, and directed my attention to the weak points and shortcomings. I tell the House all this because I am not sure that there is much good in long strings of complaints and criticism, in themselves often both well founded and well meant, made by Members who are quite unaware of the remedial steps which have been taken, in many cases long before they got to know of the evils. To have debates filled with all this when no comprehensive reply can be made without exposing to the enemy the whole of our inside arrangements, misgivings, and corrective measures is neither a healthy nor a helpful process. Presently I will show the House what have been the results of our exertions up to date.

Meanwhile there is another aspect which must be considered. All our war policy, the whole scale and maintenance of our armies abroad, the movement to the east of thirty or forty thousand men a month, as well as the conditions of life to be undergone by the people of this island – all this depends upon the tonnage imported and the number of ships we have afloat on the seas. We have, in fact, to make a budget of imports for the year 1941 exactly in the same way as the Chancellor of the Exchequer makes his Financial Budget for the year. By the end of March, all the studies and discussions of our ways and means were completed. In my capacity as Minister of Defence, I submitted to the War Cabinet my proposals for the size and character of the three branches of the Fighting Services, and also the quantity and character of the imports for which we should strive.

I will read the House the memorandum which sets forth what we hope to achieve in the present year, so far as imports are concerned. Here again I am going to read the actual words of my memorandum of March 26, because I am anxious to take the House fully into the confidence of the government. But I must again emphasize that the figures in this memorandum should not on any account be made public. In this way I shall answer the reproaches which are made here and out-of-doors that we are complacent and lacking in foresight and that there is no concerted plan which all departments are following.

As to complacency, let me say this. Do not let anyone suppose that inside this enormous government we are a mutual-admiration society. I do not think, and my colleagues will bear me witness, any expression of scorn or severity which I have heard used by our critics has come anywhere near the language I have been myself accustomed to use, not only orally, but in a continued stream of written minutes. In fact, I wonder that a great many of my colleagues are on speaking terms with me. They would not be if I had not complained of and criticized all evenly and alike. But, bound together as we are by a common purpose, the men who have joined hands in this affair put up with a lot, and I hope they will put up with a lot more. It is the duty of the Prime Minister to use the power which Parliament and the nation have given him to drive others, and in war like this that power has to be used irrespective of anyone's feelings. If we win, nobody will care. If we lose, there will be nobody to care.

Now I come to my memorandum of March 26:

'We should assume . . .'[1]

This programme requires an adjustment of our fighting forces. The air power will continue to be developed to the utmost within the limits fixed by import tonnage, and with the present priorities and assignments. The Admiralty ship-building programmes have been remodelled so as to ensure for the time being a pull forward of construction likely to be available in the present year, at the expense of long-term policies which, however necessary, must yield their priorities till we are through the present crisis. I had to make very severe demands upon the War Office, first to cut down their manpower requirement, and secondly to feed their growing formations by internal economies, in order, among other things, to provide for a very much larger proportion of armoured divisions and of the more highly technical units for which our increasing supply of modern weapons would be forthcoming.

The size and scale of our armies is wrapped in mystery, and I am not going to give any precise figure. I wish, however, here in secret, to correct exaggerated ideas. People talk of armies of four or five millions. If the Germans believe it, so much the better. Do not let us reassure them. In fact, however, the actual size is only about half the figure I mentioned. In addition, there is, however, the Home Guard of one and three-quarter millions and the Dominions, Indian, and Colonial armies, which are large and important and for which we provide many essential services.

In order to adjust the War Office need for manpower to the possibilities of tonnage, to the requirements of the Air Force and Navy, and to the vast sphere of munition production, I had to ask my right honourable friend the Secretary of State for War and the Army Council to accept a reduction of just under half a million men. They did so, and have recast their organization accordingly. But having done that, I must warn the House that I cannot and will not have the Army drained, mulcted, and knocked about any further. They will help in emergencies, but otherwise the soldiers must not be taken from their training. In a few months or even less we may be exposed to the most frightful invasion

[1] Churchill read out this memorandum in full; it is printed in this volume with the documents for 26 March 1941, on pages 400–1.

that the world has ever seen. We have a foe who, to wipe us out forever, would not hesitate to lose a million men; and if he tries to come we have got to take care that he loses that or better. For this purpose, military training must be carried to the highest degree. The men must be active, well disciplined, competent with their arms, practised in all the latest manoeuvres which our hard experience suggests. We cannot have men pulled out of their units, disturbing symmetry and order, on any large scale for any purpose.

The coal problem has been mentioned, and strenuous efforts are being made to solve it. Unless these efforts are successful, we shall have to shiver this winter. But it will be better to do that than starve our munition factories, or pull fifty thousand miners out of the army. They are grand fighting men, these miners, and I am only sorry we cannot allow any more to exchange the pick for the rifle, as they would be proud to do. I am satisfied that up to the present a good layout of our available forces has been made. But, of course, later on in the year, we must review the position. I have hopes that the growing ascendancy and power of our Air Force, and the ever-improving methods of night defence against air raiders, may enable us to get a further reinforcement for the Army to meet the normal wastage, apart from battle casualties, by a very considerable scrubbing of ADGB (Air Defence of Great Britain), which now claims nearly half a million men. One hundred and seventy thousand women are needed, and, if found, will liberate a corresponding number of men from the batteries, searchlights, and predictors. There are any amount of tasks of the highest importance and honour which women can do in ADGB, fighting alongside their menfolk under the fire of the enemy.

Now let me return to the shipping and tonnage problem, and let us see what are the results which have followed from my directive of March 6 and from the ceaseless efforts of all my colleagues in this field and along these lines. The sixteenth report of the Select Committee on National Expenditure, which was issued last week, bears witness to the fact that a considerable improvement in the conditions of the ports has already been effected (see paragraph 4). No one can, however, be satisfied with conditions as they are. Much more remains to be done, and much more must be done, if this part of our problem is to be solved. There could be no better subject for a public debate than the matter contained in this searching and well-balanced report. But I did not wish that debate to take place until the House had been put in possession of our general scheme and outlook, and could judge everything in its proper setting. A debate on what is called production could very well be centred around this report, and should also of course extend to the conditions prevailing in the mines and factories.

I take first the operational side. Three hundred Bofors and 100 Hispano Suiza guns have been installed in merchant ships and crews provided by the War Office to work them. Many hundred machine guns with other weapons of new types have also been mounted. A large scheme was instituted to improve the merchant seamen in the use of these weapons. Specially fitted onmibuses are provided in which practical training and instruction can be given. This is now beginning to yield results. The powerful reinforcements of long-range aircraft – the Hudsons and the Whitleys – which were sent in March and April to the Western Approaches are now active. We have received from the United States and have converted here for fighting purposes a considerable and growing number of those splendid long-range flying boats, the Catalinas, to aid our own Sunderland aircraft. It was a Catalina that first spotted the *Bismarck.* A number of special vessels carrying catapult Hurricane aircraft are employed on patrolling duties, and a much larger number of merchant ships are being fitted to carry one Hurricane each on their ordinary commercial voyages. The first of these are just beginning to come back with the convoys from the other side of the ocean. Soon every North Atlantic convoy or its escort will contain at least one vessel carrying a catapult fighter aircraft which can rise to attack, with very hopeful prospects, a prowling Focke Wulf.

New airfields in Northern Ireland, in the Hebrides, and in Iceland are being constructed with all possible speed. Iceland is a point of particular importance, and I hope to have more to tell you about this one of these days. Of course, up to the present only an instalment of these new measures has had time to take effect. But see how the losses due to the aircraft attack in the North Atlantic have declined. Here are the figures to the nearest thousand:

February	86,000 tons
March	69,000 "
April	59,000 "
May	21,000 "
June (to date)	18,000 "

Thus, this attack by aircraft, to which Hitler attached such importance and which seemed to be so loaded with menace, has not grown worse, but, on the contrary, at the present moment seems to have markedly dwindled away. The House should observe that the use of aircraft is not only defensive for our ships in convoy. It also tends to drive away the enemy aircraft and prevent them scouting for U-boats and guiding them to our ships. At the same time, our aircraft guide our own destroyers and corvettes to attack the U-boats themselves. Oppressed by these measures, the enemy has now been led to operate farther from our shores and he now ranges in the Western half of the Atlantic and in the South Atlantic. This drives him well into the zone in which the United States patrols are becoming increasingly effective. It also ruptures that deadly combination of the air and U-boat attack upon which Hitler had been encouraged by his advisers to build his hopes. Of course, I hope for very much greater aid from the United States, but this must come by itself, as I am sure it will do, in God's good time.

In the present phase we are much strained. The American patrol does not as yet give us full security in the zones the President has certified, and the U-boat danger is so pronounced as to make it necessary for us to convoy right across the ocean. With our limited number of anti U-boat vessels, this has meant halving the escorts, or something like it. But I hope this phase will pass. The rate of sinkings last winter led many people to doubt the value of the convoy system. Up to March, vessels over fifteen knots sailed independently, trusting to their speed and the size of the ocean spaces. The Admiralty, on whom in the last war the convoy system was forced, have now become its most strenuous advocates. We thought it right, however, to make the experiment of allowing ships which could steam thirteen knots or over, and then twelve knots or over, to sail independently. Experience seems to show that the convoy system is the best for anything except really fast ships, and in spite of the large convoys and the small escorts which our poverty forces upon us, it has now been decided to go back to the fifteen-knot limit below which nothing must sail independently. I should like the House to realize, however, that the whole question of convoy was not only re-examined but tested, and that both the Admiralty and the Ministry of Shipping, now merged in the Ministry of War Transport, are agreed about the fifteen-knot limit.

I shall have to recur in a few moments once again to the operational side, but I now turn to the position at the ports. At the beginning of March there were over 2,600,000 tons of damaged shipping accumulated in our ports, of which about 930,000 tons were ships undergoing repair while working cargo, and nearly 1,700,000 were immobilized by the need of repairs. The tonnage immobilized solely by repairs is the most injurious and obnoxious feature of the story. In my directive of March 6, which I read just now, I aimed at beating this down by 400,000 by July 1. But later on we became more ambitious, and we set ourselves as a target a reduction of 750,000 tons by the same date. We had a heavy blow as a result of the air attacks made on the Mersey and the Clyde at the beginning of May. These added many thousands of tons to the total of ship tonnage damaged at sea. We also had a windfall which added to the number of ships to be repaired. A number of ships given up as hopeless were rescued by our Salvage Service and added to the repair list. Nevertheless, in spite of these additions, unwelcome and welcome, the tonnage immobilized by reason of repair on June 12, the latest date for which I have figures, has been reduced to just under a million tons. This represents a gain, not yet indeed of the 750,000 tons at which we aimed, but of 700,000 tons, which is tolerably near it. Even although we remember, before we crow too much, that there is always a diminution in the summer weather of marine casualties, quite apart from enemy action, the figures I have mentioned should give rise not only to relief but to satisfaction.

Let us glance for a moment at some of the measures by which this result has been achieved. The first is, of course, the steady drive which is being made to increase the labour force on merchant-ship repairs. There are now in the private shipbuilding yards engaged on hull work, 11,000 more workers than at the end of January. There has also been a definite transfer from naval to merchant work. My right honourable friend the Minister of Labour has worked very hard at this.

Another economy in the turn-round has been effected by a simplification of degaussing. The brilliant and faithful servants who mastered the magnetic mine aspired naturally towards perfection in the degaussing system beyond what we can afford in these hard times. We have to balance risks against getting the ships quickly to sea. It is now very rare indeed for a ship to be delayed simply on account of degaussing repairs or improvements; either these are effected while the ship is discharging or loading or a certain amount of chance is taken. With Mr Harriman's aid a proportion of the more thorough and more permanent installations is being effected in the United States ports. There may well be a saving of two or three days in the turn-round on this process alone. Other savings have been effected by a more close concert of action between the naval and civil port authorities, and though I cannot put a precise figure on the total saving, it is certainly substantial and will be further increased. Never forget that the saving in the turn-round of a single day over the vast field of our traffic is worth a quarter of a million tons in effective imports during a year.

I have never allowed the excuse to be pleaded of congestion at our ports, because in spite of all our difficulties, we are in fact only handling and budgeting to handle about half the pre-war traffic. None the less, a great effort is being made. Inland sorting depots which enable the goods to be got away quickly from the air-raided quaysides into the country are commended by the Select Committee. Six of these are in process of construction to serve our west-coast ports. The first will come into partial operation in September. To get the best out of the South Wales ports we are quadrupling the railway line from Newport to the Severn Tunnel; part of the quadrupled line is already in operation. Some of the transport bottlenecks are found at inland junctions on the western side of the island because a greater strain is being cast upon them than they were constructed to bear. These are being opened up. A considerable development of overside discharge at suitable anchorages has been organized, not only as a relief but as an alternative in case of very heavy attack. A large expansion in our crane facilities is on foot, both to equip new emergency ports and to make existing port facilities more flexible under attack. In May alone, one hundred and thirty mobile cranes were delivered from British factories and from the United States as compared with the previous average of fifty in the last four months. I should trespass unduly upon the House if I were to describe this part of our struggle in any more detail.

I am now able to present some general conclusion. Our losses and those of our Allies by sinking in the last few months have been very heavy. In the last twelve months they amount to 4,600,000 tons. The enemy continually varies his form of attack in order to meet our counter-measures. We give him a hot time in the North-Western Approaches, he opens up off the banks of Newfoundland or even nearer to the American coast. We deploy our escorts and our flying boats more widely, the United States Navy advances into the conflict, and the enemy develops heavy and effective U-boat attack off Dakar and in the Cape Verde Islands area. Every move or new device on one side is met by a counter on the other.

It is because it is vital that the enemy should not know how much success attends these moves that we propose in the near future to stop the monthly publication of shipping losses. We have published the very heavy figures for May and also all the arrears which have come in later about the losses for April and March. The April and May figures were swollen by the severe fighting in the Mediterranean; it looks as if the June figures will be better, although, of course, at any moment a flock of U-boats getting into one of our convoys may upset our forecasts. At the present time, June 25, five days before the end of the month, we might hope to be within 300,000 tons. But then again there may be some arrears. Still, June in the middle of the summer will certainly show a better figure than February or March, those spring months in which Hitler boasted the fury of his attack would break upon us.

After June we do not propose to publish any more figures. It is giving too much help to the enemy to let him know each month the success or failure of his repeated variants of attack. He knows our figures are true; they are of the greatest value to him; I have no doubt the German Admiralty would pay £100,000 a month for the information we so meticulously compile and proclaim. We get nothing in return; he tells us nothing except extraordinary lies and exaggerations which have long since been discredited. Our task, our effort for survival, is surely hard enough without our becoming an effective branch of the German Intelligence Service. I have no doubt there will be a howl, not only from the Germans, but from some well-meaning patriots in this island. Let them howl. We have got to think of our sailors and merchant seamen, the lives of our countrymen, and of the life of our country, now quivering in the balance of mortal peril.

It would be a great mistake for us to ingeminate and emphasize our woes. I cannot share that sense of detachment which enables some people to feel they are rendering a public service by rubbing in the most dark and anxious part of our situation. Only the other day our great friend President Roosevelt stated some figures about our losses in relation to British and American new building in the most startling and alarming form. There was nothing very new about these figures and facts, and we gave our assent beforehand to the President's use of them. It certainly had a bad effect in all the balancing countries, in Spain, at Vichy, in Turkey, and in Japan.

The Japanese Ambassador, in taking leave the other day, a man most friendly to peace between our countries, inquired anxiously of me about Mr

Roosevelt's statement, which he evidently felt might be a factor in an adverse decision by Japan, which he hoped to avert. The House must not underrate the dangers of our plight. We cannot afford to give any advantages to the enemy in naval information, nor can we afford to paint our affairs in their darkest colours before the eyes of neutrals and to discourage our friends and encourage our foes all over the world.

I end upon this figure of 31,000,000 tons import in 1941, which I ask shall be kept most strictly secret. If we can bring this in, we can carry on our life at home and our war effort in the East without any further serious restrictions. If we fail to do it, we shall be definitely weakened in our struggle for existence and for the right to breathe the air of freedom. I believe we shall succeed, and it may even be there will be some improvement. This would become certain if we obtained more direct assistance from the flotillas and flying boats of the United States, and still more if the United States took the plunge in good time.

On the present showing, if we can resist or deter actual invasion this autumn, we ought to be able, on the present undertakings of the United States, to come through the year 1941. In 1942 we hope to be possessed of very definite air ascendancy, and to be able not only to carry our offensive bombing very heavily into Germany, but to redress to some extent the frightful strategic disadvantages we suffer from the present German control of the Atlantic seaports of Europe. If we can deny to the enemy or at least markedly neutralize the enemy-held Atlantic ports and airfields, there is no reason why the year 1942, in which the enormous American new building comes to hand, should not present us with less anxious ordeals than those we must now endure and come through.

I will add only one other word. Let us not forget that the enemy has difficulties of his own; that some of these difficulties are obvious; that there may be others which are more apparent to him than to us; and that all the great struggles of history have been won by superior will power wresting victory in the teeth of odds or upon the narrowest of margins.

War Cabinet: minutes

(*Cabinet papers, 65/18*)

25 June 1941 Prime Minister's Room
12.30 p.m. House of Commons

The Prime Minister said that at a Press Conference that morning he had informed the Press that we should cease publication of the figures of shipping losses after June. This had been accepted with a good grace.

John Colville: diary
(*Colville papers*)

26 June 1941

The PM departed to Scotland to see Sir R. Keyes' commandos and other 'special' organizations.

Winston S. Churchill to President Franklin D. Roosevelt
(*Churchill papers, 20/40*)

26 June 1941

I am concerned at the result which may follow from British and American tank design for the future proceeding on independent lines. Already the M3 American Medium Tank is being produced in three types to American, British and Canadian orders. These types, although basically identical, vary in several respects, particularly as regards main armament. You have retained the 75-mm. gun, whereas we and the Canadians are going for the 6-pdr. gun, with 75-mm. and 2-pdr weapons as interim steps.

It is obvious that nothing must be done to disturb production now in hand here or in North America. We want all the tanks we can get as soon as possible.

At the same time, I am impressed with the importance of strengthening the liaison between the USA and the British, and I suggest we should evolve machinery which will ensure that future designs in each class of tank are as similar as possible, thus eliminating unnecessary maintenance difficulties.

At the present moment tank design in the States is controlled by the United States Ordnance Board, whilst in England it is controlled by our Tank Board.

I would strongly suggest for your consideration that a joint Anglo-American Tank Board should be set up in America, to include Canadian as well as British representation, for the purpose of controlling and co-ordinating tank design and production as regards new types. You will remember that Baruch[1] and I set up an organization on similar lines to look after production at Châteauroux in 1917.

[1] Bernard Mannes Baruch, 1870–1965. Born in South Carolina, the son of a Jewish doctor who had emigrated from East Prussia in the 1850s. A self-made financier, he became a millionaire before he was thirty. As Chairman of the United States War Industries Board from 3 March 1918 until the end of the war eight months later he was in almost daily communication with Churchill (then Minister of Munitions). Accompanied President Wilson to the Paris Peace Conference, 1919. In 1929 and 1931 he was one of Churchill's hosts on his visits to the United States. From 1946 to 1951 he was United States Representative on the Atomic Energy Commission. When he presented his private archive to Princeton University in 1964 it contained 1,200 letters from nine Presidents, and 700 communications from Churchill.

The Tank Board in England will, of course, still be necessary to deal with current modifications and proposals for new types, and here also I suggest that American representation should be included, or a Board formed similar to that suggested above. The Boards here and in America would have to work in close liaison.

Our common aim, you will agree, must be to design much better tanks than the Nazis, to be ahead in the race guns versus armour, and to produce them quicker than they can. This, I feel sure, can only be achieved by the closest co-operation in design as well as in production, and I think there is already ample evidence that we can learn a lot from your technicians on the mechanical side, whilst we can possibly give you valuable advice, obtained by newly-bought experience, as to the fighting requirements.

If you agree, I would suggest that the detailed composition of the Board and your representation on our Board here might be discussed by your representatives with the British Army Staff and British Supply Council.

Winston S. Churchill to Harry Hopkins
(*Premier papers, 3/426/3*)

26 June 1941

I have sent a telegram in the following terms to the President:

There is another question in regard to tanks which troubles me. Is sufficient attention being paid to producing the largest possible number of tanks in the next 6 to 9 months, which may be so critical? There are two theatres of war in which, during that period, we may be forced to fight hard on land, namely, the Middle East and the United Kingdom. In the first of these we shall inevitably have to meet a great German effort to capture Egypt and the vital oil areas of Iraq and Persia. In the second, we may have to meet an invasion. A large number of tanks in both theatres is a necessity if we are successfully to overcome these dangers.

Our own production has grown rapidly, but it is not enough to cover these requirements. If we could be assured of 2,000 Medium Tanks from the USA before the end of 1941, and 300 Medium Tanks in each of the first six months of 1942 our fears that we will have to undertake land operations without adequate armoured forces will be set at rest.

We have all along stressed the importance of the aircraft and naval programmes, and I know that you are sparing no effort to produce heavy bombers in large numbers as soon as possible. We must not, however, lose sight of the immediate problem, which is to increase the delivery of tanks in the next 6 to 9 months without interfering with vital air and naval programmes.

I would like to be assured that this position is fully realized in the USA and that there is no risk of your maximum possible tank production being curtailed through lack of presentation of our necessities there.

The Joint Staff Mission is in possession of full information of our strategical needs, and I have instructed them to give your Chiefs of Staff further detailed information on the question should they require it.

John Martin: diary
(Martin papers)

27 June 1941

Landing exercises on Loch Fyne and visit to Combined Training Centre at Inveraray.

Winston S. Churchill to General Ismay, for the Chiefs of Staff Committee, and for Admiral Fraser
(Premier papers, 3/260/1)

27 June 1941
Report Progress in One Week

1. British amphibious attacks overseas are begun usually in the dark hours, during which it is hoped to get a certain number of Bofors guns ashore, but these will be quite inadequate to cover the landing places from the dive-bomber attack which must be expected almost anywhere at dawn or shortly after.[1] The guns will have taken up positions in the dark and cannot possibly have their predictors and combined control effective in so short a time.

2. To bridge the gap between the first landing and the seizure of airfields, with consequent establishment of British fighter squadrons and air protection, it is necessary that effective AA artillery support at least in low-ceiling fire should be provided. How is this to be done? It can only be done by the provision of floating batteries which can take their stations in the dark hours of the first attack and be ready to protect the landing places from daylight onwards.

3. 170 TLC[2] are now rapidly coming out month by month. At least one dozen of these should be fitted as floating batteries. They should be armed either with Bofors or with multiple UP projectors with AD or PE fuze.[3] The large size TLC are well suited to this. Let a plan be made of the best possible

[1] It was German dive-bombing attacks and the lack of adequate British anti-aircraft fire, that had led to the abandonment of Operation 'Abstention', the seizure of the Dodecanese island of Castelorizzo.

[2] Tank Landing Craft

[3] An anti-aircraft device, for ground-directed rocket fire against attacking aircraft.

arrangement of the guns or projectors, or both mixed. The best forms of fire control and the principle of the four-cornered ship, so as to fire at attacks from various quarters simultaneously, should be developed. This is a task for gunnery and UP experts, who should be given the dimensions of the deck place available, and should work out a full scheme in technical appliances and personnel required. The Controller should report what alterations would be necessary in the ships. One ship should be so fitted at once and a nucleus of officers trained in the fighting of a floating battery under these conditions. It would not be necessary to arm more than one ship at the present time, and it could be used for training and experimental purposes, but the remaining eleven should be got ready, with any improvements which may suggest themselves to receive their guns or projectors. All the base fittings should be made and built in so that the weapons can be rapidly mounted. Meanwhile the guns and projectors can continue to play their part in ADGB[1] the necessary number being earmarked for speedy transfer should an amphibious operation become imminent.

Pray let me have a report in one week, showing the proposed action and the time-table.[2]

Winston S. Churchill to David Margesson and General Sir John Dill

(*Churchill papers, 20/36*)

27 June 1941
Action this Day

Some time ago I formed the opinion that it would be far better to give names to the various marks of tanks. These could be kept readily in mind, and would avoid the confusing titles by marks and numbers. This idea did not find favour at the time, but it is evident that a real need for it exists, because the I Tank, Mark II, is widely known as Matilda, and one of the other Infantry tanks is called Valentine. Moreover, the existing denominations are changed and varied. A 22 has an alias, I think.[3] Pray therefore set out a list of the existing official titles of all the tanks by types and marks now existing or under construction or design in our service and in the American service, together with suggested names for them, in order that these may be considered and discussed.

[1] Air Defence of Great Britain.

[2] Churchill noted on this document, while preparing his war memoirs: 'This minute shows the genesis of the landing-craft flak (LCF), which was a converted tank landing-craft carrying a powerful battery of light anti-aircraft guns. It was used to provide close air defence to landing-craft during an assault. Six of these were in service by May 1942, and thereafter the numbers greatly increased.'

[3] The Churchill tank!

Winston S. Churchill to Admiral of the Fleet Sir Roger Keyes
(*Churchill papers, 20/36*)

28 June 1941

Will you please convey to the officers and men whom I inspected yesterday at exercises in Loch Fyne and on shore my congratulations on the high efficiency and keenness which were everywhere apparent?

For the success of the operations for which they are being trained, perfect co-operation between units of all three Services is essential, and to achieve this long, hard and patient training is inevitable. It was evident that this is cheerfully accepted and loyally carried out.

I hope that the opportunities which they are so eagerly awaiting will soon be made for them, and when the time comes I wish them all good success.

Winston S. Churchill to A. V. Alexander and Admiral Pound
(*Churchill papers, 20/36*)

28 June 1941
Action this Day

Please make the following signal from me to *Gladiolus*:
'Hearty congratulations to you and ship's Company on your right and left.'[1]

Winston S. Churchill to Anthony Eden
(*Churchill papers, 20/36*)

28 June 1941

It is very important that a flow of recruits should be obtained for the Polish Camp in Canada from the United States. We should aid General Sikorski in this and also guide him.

Winston S. Churchill to Sir Archibald Sinclair
(*Churchill papers, 20/36*)

28 June 1941

I understand that little or no provision is made for the defence of aerodromes between the date at which they are fit for operational use and the date at which they are actually taken over; and that this interval is often a long

[1] For the sinking of a German U-boat.

one, especially if some minor adjustments have to be made after the main work is completed. This appears to be a serious gap in our defences. Pray let me know what the position is.

Winston S. Churchill to Averell Harriman
(*Churchill papers, 20/40*)

28 June 1941

How are you getting on? I am most anxious to have a least at 500-words telegram from you. You can cable in perfect secrecy through the Embassy. Considerable changes are afoot in the Middle East and I hope you will be in Cairo in the first week of July. I will see that you have full and timely information. All good wishes.

Winston S. Churchill to John G. Winant
(*Churchill papers, 20/21*)

28 June 1941

My dear Ambassador,

I see in the Press this morning a report that the President has indicated his readiness to send Eire arms, if Eire would promise to defend herself against German attack.

Is this report correct? I should not, myself, place great confidence in such as assurance from the present Government of Eire, and should have hoped that the condition for the supply of arms would be their agreement to give us the use of the bases.

Yours v sincerely,
Winston S. Churchill

Winston S. Churchill to Anthony Eden, A.V. Alexander and Admiral Pound
(*Churchill papers, 20/36*)

28 June 1941
Action this Day

Who has been responsible for starting this idea[1] among the Americans, that we should like their destroyer forces to operate on their own side of the Atlantic rather than upon ours? Whoever has put this about has done great

[1] Reported in Telegram No. 2965 of 26 June 1941 from the British Embassy in Washington to the Foreign Office in London.

dis-service, and should be immediately removed from all American contacts. I am in entire agreement with Mr Stimson. No question of Naval strategy in the Atlantic is comparable with the importance of drawing the Americans to this side. May I ask that this should be accepted at once as a decision of policy, and that it should be referred, if necessary, to the Cabinet on Monday.

Winston S. Churchill to Lord Beaverbrook
(*Churchill papers, 20/21*)

28 June 1941
Personal

My dear Max,

I found your two letters awaiting me on my return from Scotland. I really cannot interfere in your relations with Duncan.[1] I merely reported to you that he had obtained the impression that you thought he was 'complacent'. Certainly you have repeatedly told me that all was not well with the Ministry of Supply, and that you thought he was inclined to be too easily satisfied. That at least is the impression I have sustained. There was nothing wrong in your saying this to me in view of our personal relations and the public interest.

I do not know what you mean by saying that you 'have been standing down since the beginning of June'. You insisted on leaving the Ministry of Aircraft Production, and ever since then I have been trying to find work for you of the kind that would be most agreeable to you and give the best results to the public. This I feel sure is in the executive sphere and I hope that as Minister of Supply you will recapture the immense measure of public acclamation which attended your handling of MAP in the crisis of last year.[2]

No one I am sure has ever taken more trouble to meet the wishes and suit the bent of a colleague than I have with you on account of my admiration for your qualities and our personal friendship.

With regard to your second note, I hope you will do your utmost to drive up production and that you will regard your work as urgent. This might have gone without saying in time of war. I always try to support all Ministers in their tasks, especially those who undertake the most hard and difficult tasks, and I do not read your letter in the sense of any exceptional or special conditions being required by you, other than those of goodwill and good friendship. You are quite welcome to stay in No.12 Downing Street and I am glad it is a convenience to you.

[1] Sir Andrew Duncan, Minister of Supply.

[2] On becoming Minister of Aircraft Production on 14 May 1940, Lord Beaverbrook had been responsible for the rapid increase in the production of fighter aircraft.

With regard to your wish to retire on January 1, that of course is a matter which rests with you, but I should think it would be better to judge when we see what the state of the war and the state of your health are at that date.

I have received the King's approval to the submissions which I made of yours and Duncan's appointments and of the vacation by Oliver Lyttelton of the Board of Trade. To meet your wishes his appointment as Minister of State will not be known until he reaches Cairo in a few days' time. I propose to publish the other appointments in time for Monday morning's papers and to with-hold them from the BBC meanwhile.

Yours ever
WSC

Winston S. Churchill: War Cabinet Paper
(*Cabinet papers, 120/250*)

28 June 1941
Secret

FUNCTIONS OF THE MINISTER OF STATE FOR THE MIDDLE EAST
MEMORANDUM BY THE PRIME MINSTER[1]

1. It is undesirable to detail in advance precisely the functions of the Minister of State when in the Middle East. It is sufficient to say that he will represent the War Cabinet on the spot and will carry out its policy and use its authority for that purpose.

2. To enable him to discharge these functions, he will be fully informed of the approved policy of His Majesty's Government on all major issues. If any question should arise on which he requires special guidance, he will, provided that there is time, refer the matter Home. He will in any case report constantly to His Majesty's Government. His official channel of communication with His Majesty's Government will be the Secretary of the War Cabinet, through the medium of the office of His Majesty's Ambassador in Cairo and the Foreign Office. He will also communicate directly with the Prime Minister and Minster of Defence by personal telegrams whenever convenient.

3. The principal task of the Minister of State will be to ensure a successful conduct of the operations in the Middle East by –

(a) relieving the Commanders-in-Chief as far as possible of those extraneous responsibilities with which they have hitherto been burdened; and

(b) giving Commanders-in-Chief that political guidance which has not hitherto been available locally;

[1] The genesis of this paper was a telegram which Randolph Churchill had sent to his father on 7 June 1941, from Cairo, suggesting, as a matter of urgency, the establishment of a unified Middle East authority with the necessary powers to provide 'day to day political and strategic direction'.

(c) settling promptly matters within the policy of His Majesty's Government but involving several local authorities.

4. Examples of (a) above are:

(i) Relations with the Free French.
(ii) Relations with the Emperor of Abyssinia.
(iii) The administration of occupied enemy territory.
(iv) Propaganda and subversive warfare.
(v) Finance and economic warfare.
(vi) General supervision over the activities of the Intendant-General, including all matters locally connected with supplies from the United States of America.
(vii) Disposal of prisoners of war.

On these matters the Minister of State will of course refer Home where necessary on important issues of policy and will receive from time to time directions from His Majesty's Government.

5. To enable him to discharge the functions in paragraph 3 (b) above, he will preside over meetings of the Commanders-in-Chief whenever they so desire or he has any point to raise.

6. On the diplomatic and political side he will co-ordinate so far as is necessary the policy of His Majesty's representatives in Egypt, the Sudan, Palestine and Trans-Jordan, Iraq (which will, however, remain for operational purposes under the Government of India), Abyssinia, British Somaliland, occupied enemy territories (Eritrea and Italian Somaliland), Syria (when occupied) and Cyprus. This instruction in no way detracts from the existing individual responsibilities of His Majesty's representatives in the above territories, or their official relationships with their respective departments at Home.

7. He will, as soon as he feels in a position to do so, submit reports to the Prime Minister on the above instructions and his requirements of staff to enable him to implement them.

Winston S. Churchill to Robert Menzies

(*Churchill papers, 20/40*)

28 June 1941

You will have seen that Lyttelton vacated Presidency, Board of Trade, being replaced by Andrew Duncan; and becomes the Minister of State in the War Cabinet, vice Lord Beaverbrook who will become Minister of Supply where a new impetus will be beneficial.

Lyttelton leaves by Air 30th and should reach Cairo 3rd with a small nucleus secretariat. He will represent the War Cabinet in the Middle East, and his principal duty will be to relieve the High Command of all extraneous burdens and to settle promptly on the spot in accordance with the policy of HMG many questions affecting several Departments which have hitherto required reference Home.

The instructions I have given Captain Lytteleton are appended. I send also a copy of my message to General Wavell on the mission and appointment of General Haining[1] as Intendant General to relieve the Commander in Chief of much of the work done in England for Sir Alan Brooke by the War Office and Ministry of Supply. General Haining has important civilian assistance, principally Mr Westbrook of MAP. The whole of the servicing arrangements for tanks, MTs and aircraft require improvement. A large-scale organization for the reception of American materials must be developed. Mr Harriman is already on the spot representing President Roosevelt.

2. It has been decided to relieve General Wavell of the Command of the Middle East, in order that he may become Commander in Chief in India. General Auchinleck from India will become Commander in Chief in the Middle East. I am sure this exchange of duties is in the general interests, and I look forward to the close co-operation of these two Commanders, who know the whole position thoroughly. The appointment of the Minister of State and his arrival at Cairo together with the appointments of the two Commanders in Chief, will be published in the newspapers of July 4, being confidentially released to them during July 3. Till then the utmost secrecy must be observed.

Winston S. Churchill to General Wavell
(*Churchill papers, 20/49*)

29 June 1941
Personal and Secret

The King has been pleased to appoint Captain Oliver Lyttelton, formerly President of the Board of Trade, to be Minister of State in the War Cabinet, *vice* Lord Beaverbrook, who becomes Minister of Supply. Captain Lyttelton leaves by Air 30th, and should reach Cairo 3rd, with a small nucleus

[1] Of General Haining, Randolph Churchill wrote to his father on 5 July 1941, from Alexandria: 'I have taken a great liking to your Intendant-General. He has struck me as incomparably the ablest General I have ever met. Even judged by normal standards, he would be remarkable. It is immensely refreshing to find one man with red tabs whom one can talk to on level terms as an ordinary human being. It is also refreshing to find a General who has a private secretary. It makes it quite a pleasure to do business with him. One of the handicaps that Military people suffer from is that the first 20 years of their life they are never in a position to learn how to run an office or even to dictate a letter. By the time that such amenities are in their power, they are too set in their ways to change; as a result of which you can see Generals wandering round GHQ looking for bits of string and sealing wax. My solution for "Muddle East", as it is widely known, is to sack half of the people in the office and provide half the remainder with competent shorthand typists. It would treble the efficiency of the Army.' (*Churchill papers, 20/33*).

secretariat. He will represent the War Cabinet in the Middle East, and his prime duty will be to relieve the High Command of all extraneous burdens, and to settle promptly on the spot, in accordance with the policy of HMG, many questions affecting several Departments or authorities which hitherto have required reference Home. This is largely in accordance with your telegram of the 18th April, No. 9275, but goes a good deal further. The instructions I am giving to Captain Lyttelton follow in my next, No.055 (T 356).

Please inform General Auchinleck when he arrives and Sir Miles Lampson. Complete secrecy should be observed about Captain Lyttelton's journey and mission till he has arrived.

The appointment of the Minister of State and his arrival at Cairo together with the appointments of the two Commanders-in-Chief will be published in the newspapers of the 4th July, being confidentially released to them during the 3rd July. Till then the utmost secrecy must be observed.

Winston S. Churchill to General Ismay, for the Chiefs of Staff Committee
(*Churchill papers, 20/36*)

29 June 1941

1. What are the sailing dates for WS 10 and WS 11 respectively?[1] How is it proposed to divide the troops between the different convoys?

2. Let me have a state of the Air Force in the Middle East, including Iraq, showing total ration strength there or already on the way, total airplanes on charge, total effective fighting strength by airplanes, pilots and crews. Let me have also the composition of the 15,000 additional and the number of additional first-line strength it is proposed to produce from them.

3. The Minister of Shipping should be asked to make proposals for carrying the whole of the forces involved in these two convoys, and for showing what the consequential reactions would be. Cannot we get a few big liners out of the United States, or from the ships of foreign countries interned by them?

4. Of course, if the Russians collapse very easily[2] we must consider the despatch of the 18th Division.

[1] Two more convoys from Britain to the Middle East that had to go via the Cape of Good Hope.

[2] In anticipation of a swift German victory, the Roumanian Army had joined the fighting in Russia on 27 June 1941, General Mannerheim had called upon the people of Finland to take part in a 'holy war' against Soviet Communism, and Hungary had declared war on the Soviet Union. On June 29, a week after the German invasion of the Soviet Union, two German armoured corps completed a vast encirclement in Byelorussia, cutting off tens of thousands of Russian troops in the area of Gorodishche. On the following day tens of thousands more Russian soldiers were captured in the encirclement of Bialystok; the cities of Bobruisk and Lvov were captured; and an attack was begun towards Kiev.

Winston S. Churchill to Sir Archibald Sinclair and Air Chief Marshal Sir Charles Portal
(*Churchill papers, 20/36*)

29 June 1941

1. Further to my Minute of 20th June, about the responsibility of the Air Force for the local and static defence of aerodromes. Every man in Air Force uniform ought to be armed with something, a rifle, a tommy gun, a pistol, a pike or a mace; and every one, without exception, should do at least one hour's drill and practice every day. Every airman should have his place in the defence scheme. At least once a week an alarm should be given as an exercise (stated clearly beforehand in the signal that it is an exercise) and every man should be at his post. 90 per cent. should be at their fighting stations in five minutes at the most. It must be understood by all ranks that they are expected to fight and die in the defence of their airfields. Every building which fits in with the scheme of defence should be prepared, so that each has to be conquered one by one by the enemy's parachute or glider troops. Each of these posts should have its leader appointed. In two or three hours the troops will arrive; meanwhile, every post should resist them and must be maintained – be it only a cottage or a mess – so that the enemy has to master each one. This is a slow and expensive process for him.

2. The enormous mass of non-combatant personnel who look after the very few heroic pilots, who alone in ordinary circumstances do all the fighting, is an inherent difficulty in the organization of the Air Force. Here is the chance for this great mass to add a fighting quality to the necessary services they perform. Every airfield should be a stronghold of fighting air-groundmen, and not the abode of uniformed civilians in the prime of life protected by detachments of soldiers.

3. In order that I may study this matter in detail, let me have the exact field state of Northolt aerodrome, showing every class of airman, the work he does, the weapons he has, and his part in the scheme of defence. We simply cannot afford to have the best part of half of a million uniformed men, with all the prestige of the Royal Air Force attaching to them, who have not got a definite fighting value quite apart from the indispensable services they perform for the pilots.

Winston S. Churchill to David Margesson and General Sir John Dill
(Churchill papers, 20/36)

29 June 1941

Pray see a copy of a Minute I have sent to Secretary of State for Air and CAS.[1] We have to contemplate the descent from the air of perhaps a quarter of a million parachutists, glider-borne or crash-landed airplane troops. Everyone in uniform, and anyone else who likes, must fall upon these wherever they find them and attack them with the utmost alacrity –

'Let every one
Kill a Hun.'

This spirit must be inculcated ceaselessly into all ranks of HM Forces – in particular military schools, training establishments, depôts; all the rearward services must develop a quality of stern, individual resistance. No building occupied by troops should be surrendered without having to be stormed. Every man must have a weapon of some kind, be it only a mace or a pike. The spirit of intense individual resistance to this new form of sporadic invasion is a fundamental necessity. I have no doubt a great deal is being done.

Please let me know exactly how many uniformed men you have on ration strength in this island, and how they are armed.

I should like Sir Alan Brooke to see this Minute and enclosure, and to give me his views about it. Let me also see some patterns of maces and pikes.

Elizabeth Layton: diary
(Elizabeth Nel papers)

30 June 1941

It was a surprise visit[2] to see how the men would take a sudden invasion scare, and they were fairly slow. He discovered some of them about half an hour later still in the canteen place, and sent them off with hives of bees in their bonnets.

[1] Churchill's minute to the Secretary of State for Air, Sir Archibald Sinclair and the Chief of the Air Staff, Air Chief Marshal Sir Charles Portal, printed as the previous document.

[2] To Northolt aerodrome.

John Colville: diary
(*Colville papers*)

30 June 1941

Finding the Annexe stuffy on these hot summer evenings the PM now proposes to dine and work at No. 10. I was on duty there until 1.30 while the terms of the Communiques about the new Middle East appointments, and the methods of announcing them were thrashed out.

Winston S. Churchill to General Smuts
(*Churchill papers, 20/49*)

30 June 1941

1. You will have seen the Ministerial changes announced on 30th. Besides this Lyttelton becomes Minister of State in the War Cabinet and proceeds at once to Cairo where he will represent the War Cabinet on the spot, will relieve the Commander in Chief of a great deal of extraneous work, and settle many questions affecting several authorities and Departments which otherwise would require reference here. See his instructions in my next. See also my telegram to Wavell about General Haining's mission, which he gladly accepted.

2. It has been decided to send Wavell to India as Commander in Chief, and Auchinleck who has shown great zeal and character to command in the Middle East. I am sure this exchange of duties is in the general interest. A new hand and a fresh eye is needed at Cairo.

3. No one can tell at present how long the Russians will hold out. It may be that the German spearhead will turn in a south-easterly direction far behind the southern front which has not yet been seriously attacked. One theory of German motive in attacking Russia is the need to reduce their army in order to increase munitions production and compete successfully with the increased British and American flow. However they will certainly have enough troops to attack in the East where numbers are limited by transport and remount a formidable invasion against us in the autumn. They are likely to be short in the Air but I am having everything set to concert pitch here from September 1 on.

4. The battle of Sollum was a great disappointment as we had superiority in the air and quite a good showing in tanks. The operation was so handled that the Tobruk garrison stood idle while our Sollum forces were driven back, all German tanks being moved from Tobruk to the Sollum battlefields. This appears contrary to the classical principles. The battle was hard and even and might easily have turned our way. The enemy lost heavily and was in no condition to pursue.

5. General Auchinleck will have to decide whether a further offensive in the desert can be renewed in the next month or six weeks. Tobruk is said to be supplied for two months apart from current supplies from the sea and in Wavell's opinion the enemy will find it difficult to mount a major attack before then. We have sent and are sending everything physically possible to the Middle East, including additionally the 18th Division. I also append the tank and Air reinforcements reaching Egypt or on the way. We cannot run more risks here.

6. If you could pay a visit to Cairo it would be much welcomed. Pray let me know if you receive this telegram. I had no acknowledgment of my last two Personal & Privates and it is a comfort to me to cable to you. All good wishes.

Winston S. Churchill to Robert Menzies
(*Churchill papers 20/49*)

30 June 1941
Personal, Secret and Private

I hope you will like the Ministerial changes which I have thought it necessary to make. Besides these, I feel Wavell will do admirably in India as the war drives eastward. It was necessary to have a new hand and a fresh eye in the Middle East. Auchinleck is thought by all to be the best man. He has shown great ardour and zeal in India's participation in Iraq fighting. He did well at Narvik, and effected immediate improvement in the Southern Command. He has always seemed to me a man of exceptional determination and energy. I am sure he will get on well with Blamey.

2. Of course, the vital decision in ME is whether the offensive can be resumed in the next month or six weeks, in which case Tobruk could be disengaged after playing an important part in the battle. Wavell does not consider Tobruk in danger during the next two months, as supplies are sufficient, and it will take enemy all their time to mount major attack. Advantages of fighting another battle in Western Desert while Tobruk can intervene are obvious. Last time our forces were engaged in detail and all enemy tanks from Tobruk were able to count-attack at Sollum. I must regard this as contrary to classical principles of war. A victory in the Western Desert would also have as its invaluable prize the airfields of eastern Cyrenaica, thus off-setting serious inconveniences of loss of Crete.

You will have seen from the tables I sent you what our tank and aircraft reinforcements will be. The new Commander must take a new view, which I will at once report to you.

3. I fully agree with what you say about taking advantage of German engagement with Russia. I do not know how long Russians will hold out. Germans are certainly advancing rapidly in central and northern sectors. If

they have not advanced on the southern sector, it is perhaps because they are not pressing, but it seems quite possible their main spearhead will point south-east.

4. Please remember that they have enough troops to push vigorously in the east and at the same time mount an enormous invasion of Britain, their only shortage being aircraft, which is, however, important. We must be prepared here for an extraordinary assault, and I am having everything brought to concert-pitch by September 1. I shall broadcast a warning next Sunday. We must not overlook the needs of the main front.

5. United States are going to garrison Iceland shortly, which is an immense advance towards the war, but hope deferred maketh the heart sick.

Winston S. Churchill to General Wavell
(*Churchill papers, 20/49*)

30 June 1941

Harriman should be told about all changes, and should await Lyttelton's arrival in Cairo so as to pool all information and settle arrangements for reception American supplies.

War Cabinet: minutes
(*Cabinet papers, 65/18*)

30 June 1941 10 Downing Street
5 p.m.

BOMBING OF GERMANY

The heavy losses in bombers on the nights of the 28th and 29th June[1] had been due to phenomenal light conditions.

The Prime Minister said that our attacks must continue. But the Chief of the Air Staff might inform the Commander-in-Chief, Bomber Command, that he had liberty to instruct our bombers to turn back if altogether exceptional weather conditions prevailed.

USSR: REPORT OF MILITARY SITUATION

Authentic news was scarce. But it looked as though the Russian forces had been concentrated too far forward and had been taken by surprise.

[1] On the night of 27/28 June 1941, 73 Wellington bombers and 35 Whitleys attacked Bremen. According to *Bomber Command War Diaries* (edited by Martin Middlebrook and Chris Everitt) 'they encountered storms, icing conditions and, reported for the first time in Bomber Command records, 'intense night-fighter attacks. 11 Whitleys – 31 per cent of the Whitleys dispatched – and 3 Wellingtons were lost, the heaviest night loss of the war so far. On the night of 29/30 June 1941, in another attack on Bremen, of 106 aircraft, seven were lost, while over Hamburg, of 28 bombers, 6 were lost.

North of the Pripet Marshes. – It seemed that the Germans had broken through on a wide front, both in North-East Poland and in Lithuania, and that the main weight of their mobile formations had reached the general line Minsk–Vilna.

Another German drive was developing on the front Vilna–Dvinsk.

South of the Pripet Marshes. – There had been hard fighting in the Luck–Lwow sector and the Germans appeared to have achieved a break-through.

In this sector the German aim might be to turn the line of Dniester.

The Russian military position appeared to be very grave, although German air and land losses had been considerable.

The War Cabinet took note of these statements.

APPOINTMENT OF INTENDANT-GENERAL, MIDDLE EAST

Copies of a Memorandum by the Prime Minister (WP (41) 148) as to the functions of the Minister of State for the Middle East were handed round.

The Prime Minister hoped that the appointment would afford considerable relief to the Commanders-in-Chief and would enable them to concentrate to a far greater degree on the operational side of their work. The Prime Minister of New Zealand had been made aware of this proposal, which had also been communicated to the Prime Ministers of the Commonwealth of Australia and the Union of South Africa.

In discussion on the organization in the Middle East, the Prime Minister said that General Haining (the Intendant-General) had asked for executive powers in regard to Army servicing and repairs. Air Vice-Marshal Dawson was examining the aircraft repair and servicing organization.

Mr Harriman was also in the Middle East, largely with the object of satisfying himself that proper arrangements existed for taking over the large supplies of American material now arriving in the Middle East.

Mr Fraser mentioned certain apparent defects in our orgainization which had come to his notice while in the Middle East.

The Prime Minister said that it would be very helpful if Mr Fraser could put on paper the impressions he had formed. This Paper might either be communicated to him (the Prime Minister) or circulated to the War Cabinet.

The Prime Minister also informed the War Cabinet that, as Minister of Defence, he had decided on an exchange of duties between General Wavell and General Auchinleck. Copies of the telegrams in regard to this change were being circulated to the War Cabinet.

The War Cabinet were informed that these changes would not be made public for another two days.

The War Cabinet –

Took note, with approval, of the above arrangements.

DEPARTMENTAL PUBLIC RELATIONS OFFICERS

The Prime Minister said that it was impossible to uproot from the Departments the organization of Departmental Publicity Officers which had grown up to meet a real need. It was essential, however, that the Public Relations Officers of Departments should meet together daily under the chairmanship of the Minister of Information. These officers would not, of course, be under the orders of the Minister of Information in the same sense that they were under the orders of their Departmental Ministers. But it would be their duty to work together with the Minister as members of a team. In this view, the real function of the Ministry lay in co-ordinating the work of these Publicity Officers so as to ensure a single consistent propaganda policy, and in bringing about a constant flow of good and interesting speeches.

HORSE RACING

The Minister of War Transport said that he would like to reduce the number of extra trains run in connection with races after September. At the present time it was stated publicly that no additional facilities would be provided, but in practice a number of relief trains were run. He also hoped that no races would be held on certain courses, e.g., Newbury, which were situated on railway lines on which there was great pressure.

The Prime Minister strongly deprecated any attempt to put a stop to horse racing, but welcomed an attempt to prevent a recurrence of large assemblies of motor-cars, such as had attended the recent Derby Meeting at Newmarket.

Winston S. Churchill to General Ismay, for the Chiefs of Staff Committee
(*Churchill papers, 20/36*)

30 June 1941

Although we take a heavy toll, very large enemy reinforcements are crossing to Africa continually. The Navy seem unable to do anything. The Air Force only stop perhaps a fifth. You are no doubt impressed with the full gravity of the situation.

Winston S. Churchill to Lord Beaverbrook[1]
(*Churchill papers, 20/36*)

30 June 1941
Most Secret
Action this Day

In the Secret Session on Sir Andrew Duncan's vote, questions were asked by Mr Shinwell and others about how we stood in 'Heavy Tanks'. We have hitherto regarded A22 as the heaviest we should make, though a great deal of work has been done, I think by Stern,[2] on a still larger type. I believe there is even a pilot model. Of course, our problem is different from the Russian or great Continental Powers because of shipment, although that is no final bar.

However, it now appears, on the highest authority, that the Russians have produced a very large Tank, said to be over 70 tons, against which the German A/T 6-pounder has proved useless. It seems to me that the question of a much heavier Tank has now come sharply to the front. The whole position must be reviewed, and we must know where we are – and that soon.[3]

Elizabeth Layton: diary
(*Elizabeth Nel papers*)

30 June 1941

Dictation that night, and he was most amiable. I had to sit for hours in the Cabinet Room opposite him, waiting (we are working at No. 10 at night now, he prefers it). General Ismay was there. It is funny to listen to old Big Ben chiming the quarters and hours, and the sound getting all mixed up with its own echo which comes across the Horse Guards from the Admiralty.

[1] Lord Beaverbrook had replaced Sir Andrew Duncan as Minister of Supply on the previous day, 29 June 1941. During Beaverbrook's tenure of the Ministry of Supply, the Minister was a Member of the War Cabinet.

[2] Albert Stern, 1878–1966. Lieutenant, Royal Naval Volunteer Reserve (Armoured Car Division), 1914. Secretary to the Landship Committee, Admiralty, 1916. Major, Machine Gun Corps, Heavy Branch, 1916. Head of the Tank Supply Committee, Ministry of Munitions, 1916; Director-General, Mechanical Warfare Department (rank of Lieutenant-Colonel), 1917; Commissioner, Mechanical Warfare, Overseas and Allies, 1918. Knighted, 1918. Member of the London Committee of the Ottoman Bank, 1921–64. Chairman, Special Vehicle Development Committee, Ministry of Supply, 1939–43.

[3] At seventy tons, the A22 (later known as the Churchill tank), was the heaviest British tank at that time. In 1942 it was used during the Dieppe raid. The A39 (the Tortoise) developed in 1944, weighed seventy-eight tons, and was the heaviest ever completed. The heaviest Russian tank to go into action was the KV1, which weighed forty tons. The more widely used Russian T34 was less heavy.

July 1941

On 1 July 1941, German forces captured Riga and continued their advance into Russia across the Beresina River. That day the Royal Air Force initiated a series of bombing raids on German port facilities at Brest, Cherbourg, Lorient, Le Havre and the Seine, followed by a series of night bombing raids on Bremen, Cologne, the Rhineland and the Ruhr.

Winston S. Churchill to General Ismay

(*Churchill papers, 20/36*)

1 July 1941

I will come and see the maps in the Central War Room of the movements on the Russian front. If necessary, in the interests of extreme secrecy, the maps can be put in the Chief of Staff's room. An officer from the War Office is to be charged with keeping it up to date for my special benefit.

The kind of maps I am getting now are no help.

Winston S. Churchill to General Auchinleck

(*Premier papers, 3/291/1*)

1 July 1941
Personal and Secret

You take up your great command at a period of crisis. After all the facts have been laid before you it will be for you to decide whether to renew the offensive in the Western Desert and if so when. You should have regard especially to the situation at Tobruk, the process of enemy reinforcement of Libya and the temporary German preoccupation in their invasion of Russia.

You should also consider the vexatious dangers of the operations in Syria flagging and the need for a decision on one or both of these fronts. You will decide whether and how these operations can be fitted in together. The urgency of these issues will naturally impress itself upon you. We shall be glad to hear from you at your earliest convenience.

Winston S. Churchill to General Wavell
(Churchill papers, 20/49)

1 July 1941

Far from postponing announcement it must now be made during evening July 1 for publication in papers July 2 as many people have had to be informed. You and Auchinleck should arrange between yourselves date of actual transfer of command. Make sure operations do not suffer.

Winston S. Churchill to Alfred Duff Cooper
(Churchill papers, 20/36)

1 July 1941

MIDDLE EAST APPOINTMENT OF MINISTER OF STATE
AND CHANGE OF COMMAND

Between the time that this statement is issued to the Press for release as proposed, all diplomatic and other cables must be held up. Otherwise we shall have some Swede passing this information to Germany, and it will come out for the first time on the German 10 o'clock broadcast. It is therefore for consideration whether a much later hour should not be fixed for the issue to the Press than 5.30 p.m. Much though I should like to give them the opportunity of writing their leading articles, &c., I cannot run the risk of the German wireless being the first to tell the tale. This would have a disastrous effect upon public confidence, and the explanation, although simple, would never overtake the initial impression.

If it is too difficult to save this tit-bit for the Press, we can, of course, give it on the 6 o'clock or 9 o'clock broadcast. This avoids all risks, and we may have to come to it.

Tell me what you propose.

Winston S. Churchill to King George II of Greece
(*Churchill papers, 20/40*)

1 July 1941
Personal and Secret

I have been thinking a great deal about Your Majesty in these months of stress, danger and sorrow, and I wish to tell you how much Your Majesty's bearing amid these vicissitudes has been admired by your many friends in England as well as by the nation at large. The warmest welcome awaits you here where all are resolved to conquer or to perish. It is my confident hope that when the good days come the glory which Greece has won will help to heal the memory of her present suffering.

Winston S. Churchill to A.V. Alexander and Admiral Pound
(*Churchill papers, 20/36*)

1 July 1941
Action this Day
Secret

I presume that effective arrangements have been made to prevent reinforcement of the Vichy forces in Syria by sea. How does this matter stand?

Winston S. Churchill to President Franklin D. Roosevelt
(*Churchill papers, 20/40*)

1 July 1941
Personal and Secret

I am most grateful for your telegram about American merchant shipbuilding programme. This vast expansion opens up the prospects of the future and assures the means of continuing the war in this vital sphere to a victorious conclusion. I know you will feel with me the pain that such vast masses of tonnage should have to be sunk before being replaced by colossal American efforts. Any increase in our escorts will produce an immediate saving in losses. Forgive me mentioning this when I know all you are doing. The last ten days have been very fruitful in enemy submarine destruction, four Germans, two Italians, and a hostile Vichy boat having been certainly disposed of. We are also getting very good results with our own submarines in the Mediterranean against enemy merchant vessels and by our Air attacks by bomb or torpedo upon them both in Home waters and the Mediterranean. I am asking that everything here shall be at concert pitch for invasion from September 1. I trust your health continues good.

Winston S. Churchill: speech
(BBC Written Archives Centre)

1 July 1941 10 Downing Street

I am much affected by the kindness of the message which Mr Mackenzie[1] brings and by the emblem which has been carried so far over the land, through the air, and over the sea. It represents another impulse of the great effort which Canada is making in all these months and years of storm. We are in this old house and garden, which has for hundreds of years been the centre from which the British Government has been conducted, on this sunshiny afternoon without any enemy aeroplanes daring to come within the range of our fighting Air Force.

I am proud to welcome the Canadian representatives[2] who have come all this way to encourage us in our fight and to add their own weighty contribution and to assure us – if, indeed, assurance is needed – that Canada will be with us to the end.

The end may be far off. We cannot tell. That depends on the enemy. How long he will resist we cannot say. How long that wicked man will torture and afflict nations or how often or in what directions he will set his murder machine in motion we cannot tell.

One thing we are assured of is that he and his villainous crew will be delivered to the doom and shame which is their due and that we, ourselves, will have the honour of having something to do with it.

1 Ian Alistair Mackenzie, born in Scotland in 1890, emigrated to British Columbia in 1914, after qualifying as a lawyer. Entered the Canadian House of Commons in 1930. Minister of National Defence, 1935–39. At the time of his mission to London he was Minister of National Pensions and Health.

2 The second of the two Canadian representatives (with both of whom Churchill lunched on 4 July 1941) was Charles Gavan Power, who had first entered the Canadian Cabinet in 1935 as Minister of Pensions and National Health. He became Postmaster-General of Canada in September 1939, and Minister of National Defence for Air in May 1940. In November 1940 he was made Associate Minister of National Defence.

Winston S. Churchill to Alexander Korda
(*Churchill papers, 2/419*)

1 July 1941 10 Downing Street
Private wire

Would not 'Emma' be a better title or Nelson's famous saying 'If there were more Emmas there w'd be more Nelsons.'[1]

Winston S. Churchill: Oral Answers
(*Hansard*)

2 July 1941 House of Commons

UNITED STATES TRADE WITH VICHY FRANCE

The Prime Minister (Mr Churchill): I think that we must in this important matter be guided to a very large extent by the opinion of the great and friendly country whose assistance is indispensable to our war effort.

Mr Shinwell: Yes, Sir, and although obviously the Government must be guided to some extent by the opinions of countries with whom we are in friendly relations, does not the right hon. Gentleman agree that the passage of these ships certainly requires some further explanation, in view of the fact that goods that we require in this country are being sent to what is, in fact, enemy country?

The Prime Minister: Yes, Sir. I think it would be a difficult question to thrash out in public, from various points of view. I think that there is a good deal to be said on both sides of the argument. On the whole I have become convinced that it is an advantage to the United States to have contacts which in our case no longer exist.

Sir Irving Albery: Would it not have been better if this Question had been answered by the Secretary of State for Foreign Affairs, who is responsible, and not the Minister of Economic Warfare?

The Prime Minister: A question of this kind begins over the matter of shipping or of economic warfare.

Mr Shinwell: Is this practice to be continued, or is this to be regarded as an isolated case?

[1] This telegram was sent to Alexander Korda at 1040 North Las Palmas Avenue, Hollywood. Korda replied on 4 July 1941: 'The title Emma was used for an American film stop Nelsons saying is too long stop how about quote more Emmas more Nelsons unquote or quote Nelsons Emma unquote or quote Emma Lady Hamilton unquote very grateful for your suggestion as dislike title intensely myself stop respectfully yours Alexander Korda.' In a second telegram on 12 July 1941 Korda told Churchill: 'Have just learnt from our London distributors that all publicity material already printed and bearing title Lady Hamilton so am frightfully sorry but it is now too late to change title stop may I still hope that my services can be used in the near future stop respectfully yours Alexander Korda.' (*Churchill papers, 2/419*)

The Prime Minister: I cannot possibly answer that question. Is the hon. Member discontented? Mr Shinwell: I am discontented.

The Prime Minister: Then, in that case, he should take the opportunity of raising this matter in Debate.

Mr Shinwell: The right hon. Gentleman did not want a Debate.

The Prime Minister: The whole tendency of this Question pays too little attention to the gravity of the situation.

Mr Shinwell: The right hon. Gentleman suggests that this matter can be raised in Debate. I understood him to say that it would be wrong to raise it in Debate. The Prime Minister: Perhaps if the Debate took a certain turn I should have to draw the attention of Mr Speaker to the fact that there were Strangers present.

Mr Hammersley:[1] Are the Government quite satisfied that proper safeguards have been taken to see that this oil does not release other oil which might be sent to enemy countries?

The Prime Minister: The whole matter has been most carefully discussed and is a matter of high policy. I am of the opinion that the views of the United States should be treated with the greatest respect. I am certain of this, that any action which may at this time be taken by the United States is conceived only with a sincere desire to aid the war effort of this country.

MINISTERIAL CHANGES

Mr Hore-Belisha: On Business, may I ask my right hon. Friend the Prime Minister whether he is going to make a statement in Parliament of the changes which have been announced this morning, and whether now, or at some date which may suit him better?

The Prime Minister: No, Sir. I do not think that I have any statement to make, certainly not at the present time, on the subject.

Mr Hore-Belisha: Would it not be showing a proper regard for Parliament to make a statement about a matter of this kind, which involves great constitutional changes? Does my right hon. Friend say that he declines to make such a statement or that it is inconvenient for him to make one now?

The Prime Minister: I do not think that precedents really would favour the view which the right hon. Gentleman is putting forward that all changes of this kind should be preceded by a statement in Parliament or announced in Parliament. That is certainly not the precedent according to my recollection and experience. I do not see any advantage to adding to the information

[1] Samuel Schofield Hammersley, 1892–1965. On active service as a Second Lieutenant, Gallipoli, 1915; as a Captain, Tank Corps, France, 1916–18. Chairman of several cotton-spinning companies. Conservative Member of Parliament for Stockport, 1924–35; for East Willesden, 1938–45. Parliamentary Private Secretary to the Financial Secretary to the Treasury, 1927. Textile Mission to India, 1933. Rejoined the Army, 1939. Worked on Tanks at the Ministry of Supply, 1940–43. Chairman of the Parliamentary Palestine Committee, 1943–45; of the Anglo-Israel Association, 1951–63. author of *Industrial Leadership* (1925).

already given at the present time, and I cannot foresee any time in the immediate future when it would be necessary for me to make a statement to the House on this subject.

Mr Hore-Belisha: My right hon. Friend has referred to precedents. Is there any precedent for appointing a Minister to occupy a station abroad, because it is the constitutional position that all Ministers are accountable directly to Parliament? [Hon. Members: 'What about Halifax?'] Lord Halifax is an Ambassador, but this is the Minister of State, and all Ministers are constitutionally responsible to Parliament. As this is a complete innovation, would it not be courteous to Parliament to give some further elucidation?

The Prime Minister: I am sure that the House will not accuse me of wanting in respect of deference in every effort to serve them, but if the right hon. Gentleman wishes to make a criticism of what is widely accepted as a highly useful and important step in the appointment of a member of the War Cabinet to be resident at the seat of the Middle Eastern war, I daresay some Parliamentary opportunity will occur. I have no doubt that some answer will be made to him although whether the answer will satisfy his wide-ranging curiosity I cannot tell.

War Cabinet, Battle of the Atlantic Committee: minutes
(*Cabinet papers, 86/1*)

2 July 1941 — 10 Downing Street
5 p.m.
Secret

The Prime Minister asked:

(1) That the First Lord of the Admiralty and the Secretary of State for Air should submit a joint report to the next meeting, showing the measures proposed to counter night air attacks on East Coast shipping.

(2) That a table should be prepared by the Admiralty for the next meeting, showing merchant ships lost by air attack during each of the months from February to June, 1941, separate figures being given for losses in coastal waters, elsewhere in the North Atlantic and in other waters.

The Prime Minister, who said it was clear that we should have to have night-work at the ports during the coming winter, invited the Lord Privy Seal to enquire into this matter, and to submit a report to the next meeting.

The Prime Minister asked what help had been derived from the United States patrols. The answer given was that some little help had been received in regard to raiders, but virtually none at all in regard to U-boats.

The Prime Minister invited the Admiralty to submit a report to him as to the working of the US Naval Patrols since they had been instituted. He had it in mind to invite the US Government to let us have a greater number of escort vessels.

THE IMPORT SITUATION

The Prime Minister, summing up the discussion, said that he did not think that the present situation could be regarded at all favourably. Notwithstanding the reduction in the time of discharge at the ports, the time taken on the round voyage was not being reduced.

Winston S. Churchill: Memorandum[1]

(*Churchill papers, 23/9*)

2 July 1941
Secret

INFORMATION AND PROPAGANDA

The main functions of the Ministry of Information are:

(a) to ensure that news regarding the progress of the war shall reach the public as fully and as quickly as is consistent with the interests of our national security; and

(b) to publicize and interpret Government policy in relation to the war, to help to sustain public morale and to stimulate the war effort, and to maintain a steady flow of facts and opinions calculated to further the policy of the Government in the prosecution of the war.

For the effective discharge of these functions, it is the duty of the Minister of Information to preserve intimate and cordial relations with the newspapers through their proprietors, editors and reporters; and to make the newspapers feel that the Ministry is their friend and the pump and channel by which information is collected from the various Departments.

The Government fully recognize the importance of an effective service of news and propaganda; and the arrangements outlined below have been made with the object of enabling such a service to be organized and maintained, while at the same time securing that the essential interests of national security are properly safeguarded.

NEWS AND CENSORSHIP

2. The issue of news and official communiqués will continue to be canalized through the Ministry of Information.

In the interests of national security, however, the publication of war news from the Fighting Departments, or from Civil Departments in their connection with the war, must be subject in the event of dispute to the veto of the Departmental Minister concerned.

The enable this security control to function speedily, the three Service Departments will maintain in the Ministry of Information an officer of

[1] War Cabinet Paper 149 of 1941, a revise of War Cabinet paper 142 of 1941, which had been discussed at the War Cabinet on 30 June 1941, and had been amended as a result of that discussion.

adequate seniority and standing who (except when matters of the highest policy are involved) can take final responsibility for passing any particular item of news for publication. These officers will be men who are capable of taking quick decisions and understand the importance of news service as part of our propaganda war.

The Service Ministers concerned will be readily accessible to determine important issues of policy which cannot be decided by their representative stationed in the Ministry of Information; and each of these Ministers will designate an official of the highest standing in his Department who will be empowered to take a final decision if he is not himself available.

The right of veto will not be exercised unreasonably, and it will be understood that a final decision must not be unduly delayed. Where the representative of a Service Department stationed in the Ministry of Information objects to the publication of a particular item of news, and persists in his objections after discussion with the Ministry of Information, then, if the Ministry of Information nevertheless think that there should be publication, it will be the duty of the representative of the Service Department to refer the matter to his Department where it will be considered forthwith and a decision taken.

It is to be understood that only the Service Minister or the official designated to take decisions on his behalf will be entitled to override the view of the Minister of Information in favour of the publication of a particular item of news.

3. It will be the duty of all Departmental Ministers, especially the Foreign Secretary and the Service Ministers, to keep the Minister of Information fully supplied with all the news and information at their disposal. The use and exploitation of this news will be regarded as primarily the responsibility of the Ministry of Information.

Operational communiqués issued as such by the Service Department or by Commanders on the war fronts must not be altered, even in form, without the consent of the Minister concerned. But the Minister of Information must be free to make the fullest use of the substance of such communiqués – e.g., in issuing summaries of the day's news – being himself responsible for ensuring that nothing issued under his authority is inconsistent with the terms of the communiqués themselves.

4. The general duty of censorship, like that of exploiting news, will remain a function of the Ministry of Information, who, armed with the general knowledge derived from their contact with the Departments and with the War Cabinet, will correct, prune or amplify the whole flood of news reaching them from every quarter.

Departmental Ministers will, however, retain their right to veto or require the publication of particular facts or statements where they think it necessary to do so in the interests of national security.

PUBLICITY: GENERAL

5. Departments which have Public Relations Branches and Press Officers will preserve their existing contacts with the Press on matters of a purely departmental nature.

Similarly, Departments will continue to be responsible for the issue of departmental publications and of directions to the public on departmental matters – the Ministry of Information continuing, as in the past, to help so far as may be mutually convenient.

6. On the other hand, the Ministry of Information will act, in co-operation with the Departments concerned, as the central agency for the conduct of all publicity which affects more than one Department or subserves the policy of the Government as a whole.

All organized propaganda carried out on behalf of one or more Departments through the medium of the Press, films, posters or radio will be conducted through the Ministry of Information. All paid-space advertising will be, not only placed, but planned and carried through at all stages, by the Ministry of Information in co-operation with the Departments concerned.

7. In carrying out his tasks the Minister of Information has a right to the loyal assistance of every officer and civil Department concerned.

All Ministers must therefore be held responsible for seeing that their Public Relations Officers collaborate fully and effectively with each other and with the Ministry of Information in the organization and conduct of propaganda relating to the prosecution of the war. In any inter-Departmental work they should function, not independently, but as members of a team under the Chairmanship of the Ministry of Information furthering the purposes and policy of that Ministry. Nothing in this plan need prevent the use of a Departmental organization for the execution of a particular project (e.g., the making of a film), where that is generally recognized to be the most convenient course, but this must not derogate from the responsibility of the Ministry of Information over the field of propaganda as a whole. Instructional films, such as those prepared by the War Office in connection with the training of troops, are on a different footing and should remain the responsibility of the Department.

The Treasury will be asked to consider with the Departments concerned what rearrangements of personnel may be entailed by this new alignment of functions and responsibilities.

BBC

8. The Ministry of Information will take full day-to-day editorial control of the BBC service of news and propaganda and will be responsible for both initiative and censorship. It will be the duty of the Minister of Information to carry with him, so far as possible, the Board of Governors, who stand as umpires and sureties to Parliament for the spirit in which the BBC is conducted.

SPEECHES

9. The Ministry of Information will also conduct, when necessary, speaking campaigns in the country with the object of maintaining public morale at a high level through the largest number of competent exponents.

10. Ministers who are members of the War Cabinet and those who regularly sit in with them, namely, the Service Ministers, the Home Secretary, the Secretary of State for Dominions, the Colonial Secretary, as the Leader of the House of Lords and the Minister of Information are free to make speeches expounding the policy of the War Cabinet. However, the making of speeches by many different Ministers in time of war is to be deprecated because of the danger of discrepancies occurring, which can be used to stultify the Administration. Ministers of Cabinet rank, in the pre-war sense, including the Service Ministers, should speak on their Departmental work when this is indispensable, but they would be well advised to consult the Minister of Information on any passage about which they may have doubt, especially if it lies outside their Departmental sphere. All Ministers should, of course, always consult the Foreign Office on any matter affecting our relations with foreign Powers, including, of course, any direct appeals to the public in foreign States. It is undesirable that, as a general practice, Ministers other than the War Cabinet Ministers should deal with military topics. Should they desire to do so, they are requested to consult General Ismay, representing the Minister of Defence, on any particular points outside broad and common knowledge. Ministers not of Cabinet rank and Under-Secretaries ought not to discuss the general policy of the war, apart from exhortations to zeal and the happy re-statement of the accepted commonplaces, without reference to the Minister of Information.

Winston S. Churchill to Colonel Jacob
(*Churchill papers, 20/36*)

2 July 1941

RETURN OF STRENGTH OF FORCES, AT HOME AND IN THE MIDDLE EAST

I do not think you ought to have omitted these 700 guns, a large proportion of which are still with the field batteries, and returned the total of only 1,863. The War Office ought not to advance figures which give an inaccurate account of the Field Army. First the '75's' are treated as negligible, though they are perfectly good guns for modern war. The next dodge will be to treat the converted 18/25-pounders as not worth counting and thus to present me with figures which are misleading. I quite understand the desire of the Home Forces and the War Office to make things out as bad as they possibly can, in the hopes of getting more, or stopping ME reinforcements. I hate the feeling of a case being made up against me, and now I wonder whether all the other figures are not similarly coloured. I rely on you to test these matters and make sure I derive a true impression.

Winston S. Churchill to Lord Woolton
(*Churchill papers, 20/36*)

2 July 1941

I am glad that the egg scheme attributed to you was not actually the scheme you had in mind. It is always difficult to hold the balance between the need for increasing total food supplies and the need to maintain a fair distribution. We should not be too hard on the private individual who increases his supplies by his own efforts.

It is satisfactory that the meat prospects are improving, and I hope that pressure on the United States to increase her pork outlet will soon enable us to raise the ration without risk of having subsequently to reduce it.

We do not wish to create a grievance amongst farmers by compelling them to slaughter beasts which they can fatten without imported feeding stuffs; on the other hand, of course, the country cannot go hungry because farmers do not choose to bring their beasts to market. It will no doubt be possible to arrange with the Minister of Agriculture, perhaps by a carefully worked out price policy, a scheme which will keep the meat supply as constant as possible without having regard to seasonal factors.

As to wheat, the point I had in mind was not so much our stock as the danger of getting into a vicious circle: people eat more bread owing to a shortage of meat and thereby compel you to import more wheat, thus reducing the shipping space available for bringing in other foods. I do not believe there is great danger of the harvest being destroyed by the enemy this year. We have found it very hard to burn crops, and if you will ask the Air Ministry, they will explain to you why the dew conditions in this country make it even harder here than on the continent.

Winston S. Churchill to Anthony Eden
(*Churchill papers, 20/36*)

2 July 1941
Action this Day

COMMENT ON A TELEGRAM FROM THE BRITISH AMBASSADOR TO TURKEY[1]

All this is very silly. Russia was our ally in the last war and owing to the Bolshevists making a separate peace she ranked with the defeated nations and not with the victors. She was, in fact, stripped of Finland, the Baltic States, a

[1] Sir Hughe Knatchbull-Hugessen.

large part of Poland, and (I think) Bessarabia.[1] That is what I meant by saying that she had no share in the victory. I never meant that she had no share in territorial gains, because we were not then, and are not now, fighting for territorial gains. It is quite true, however, that at the time of the Dardanelles in 1915 we did promise Russia Constantinople, but all that fell to the ground with the Bolshevik Revolution and the peace of Brest-Litovsk. Nothing was further from my mind than to revive it.

I should not worry too much about the Turks at the moment. They have a guilty conscience and the net is closing round them. It is natural they should shy at puddles. They ought not to be encouraged to do so. Our Ambassador there sends far too many telegrams and every telegram is far too long. He had better let them alone and let events take their course for the next few days.

If anyone supposes that Turkish doubts or misgivings about this remark of mine weigh one-millionth part of the events proceeding on the Russo-German front he ought to have a holiday. I see much too much Knatchbull-Hugessen in the telegrams. And not much result has come from all his fuss. There ought to be room in diplomacy for 'Les silences du Colonel Bramble'.[2]

Winston S. Churchill to Oliver Lyttelton
(*Churchill papers, 20/40*)

3 July 1941
Personal and Secret
Not to be decyphered till he arrives

As soon as the new Military Command is established you should procure answers to the questionnaire contained in my immediately following telegram, and cable them home at low priority. We should like to have the answers during the month of July.

Winston S. Churchill to Oliver Lyttelton
(*Churchill papers, 20/49*)

3 July 1941
Not to be decyphered till he arrives

My immediately preceding telegram (T366).

The following questionnaire to the Middle East has been drafted in the office of the Minister of Defence regarding the battle of Crete:

[1] Russian since 1812, Bessarabia joined Roumania in 1918. It was occupied by the Soviet Union following an ultimatum from Moscow on 26 June 1940.

[2] A week later, on reading a telegram from Sir Ronald Campbell, the British Ambassador in Lisbon, Churchill minuted: 'A terrible lot from Campbell! Zeal should not lead to such a spate. It defeats its own ends'. (Prime Minister's Personal Minute, 9 July 1941: *Churchill papers, 20/36*)

(1) What orders were issued by Middle East Command in November 1940, when Crete was first occupied, for the preparation of defences, the obstruction of possible landing grounds, the mining of aerodromes and the erection of barbed wire?

What work had been done in the period up to 18th April, 1941?

(2) When the evacuation of Greece took place, and it was realized the attack on Crete would be the sequel, what further orders were issued by Middle East Command, and what was the garrison which they were trying to build up by 17th May?

What additional work on defences was accomplished?

(3) How many infantry, artillery, engineer and signal units were there in Crete on 20th May, and what was –

(a) the establishment

(b) the strength, and

(c) the equipment position of each?

In cases where answers to the above questions disclose considerable deficiencies, either in personnel or equipment, reasons should be stated.

(4) What was the position as regards the following on the 20th May:

(a) Tanks – number and type.

(b) Field guns – number and type. (Is it a fact that there were no 25-pounders and that the French 75s had no sights or instruments?) Had the gunners any personal arms?

(c) AA guns – number and type.

(d) Ammunition for (b) and (c) above.

(e) Transport vehicles – number and type.

(5) What was the strength of the non-fighting formations, i.e., RASC, RAOC,[1] Provost, &c., and how far were these armed? How many of these were 'bouches inutiles' who 'found' themselves in Crete in the process of evacuation from Greece?

(6) Were there still any Italian prisoners in the Island, and, if so, how many?

(7) Statements have been made that –

(a) There was no ammunition for the Breda guns.[2]

(b) There were no Mills grenades.

(c) There was a serious shortage of digging tools and fieldworks stores.

To what extent are these statements correct? Reasons for any serious deficiencies should be given.

(8) What was the position as regards supplies of food, medical stores, &c., when the attack started?

(9) What orders were issued by the GOC in Crete during the period 17th April/20th May for the tactical conduct of the battle?

[1] Royal Army Service Corps and Royal Army Ordnance Corps.

[2] The Breda gun was the standard Italian machine gun during the Second World War. In 1999 'deactivated' examples could be purchased on the Internet at deactivated@firearms.ab.ca

Winston S. Churchill to Anthony Eden
(Churchill papers, 20/36)

3 July 1941
Action this Day
Secret

It was never our intention that the de Gaullists should virtually step into the places of the Dentz[1] administration, or that they should govern Syria in the name of France. Their losses and contribution have been only a small fraction of ours. They should be given a certain prominence in order to show that French interests in Syria are safeguarded against any other European Power,[2] and that we have no desire to supplant France in her privileged and favoured position in Syria. However, all this is but about one to four or five in our Syrian policy, which remains the independence of Syria and all its peoples. No French policy which conflicts with this major decision can be accepted. It is therefore for de Gaulle or Catroux to make the same kind of arrangements with Syria as we made in the case of Iraq, with the important difference that in the ultimate issue we have military force behind us and he has not, to any extent.

Winston S. Churchill to David Margesson and General Sir John Dill
(Churchill papers, 120/52)

3 July 1941

1. In forming a very large armoured force such as we contemplate, while at the same time carrying on the war, a large element of improvization is necessary, and this applies especially to the more backward formations. It is highly questionable whether the divisional organization is right for armoured troops. A system of self-contained Brigade Groups forming part of the Royal Tank Corps would be operationally and administratively better. One can see how ill-adapted the divisional system is when the 7th Armoured Division, one of our most highly-trained and armoured units, goes into action 'less one Brigade', it having in fact only two, with certain additional elements. However, where divisional formations have grown up and have been clothed with armed reality, the conditions of war do not permit the disturbance of a

[1] Henri Dentz, French High Commissioner for Syria, and Commander-in-Chief for the Vichy French Forces in Syria, 1940–41. Signed an armistice with the British, 10 July 1941. Arrested a few months later when it was discovered he had broken the terms of the armistice by sending Allied prisoners of war out of Syria after the armistice had been signed.

[2] Both phrases underlined here were underlined by Churchill before he sent this Minute to the Foreign Secretary.

change. With the more backward formations, the case is different. They should be brought into coherent existence as Brigade Groups armed with the best weapons available at the moment, and worked up gradually by increasing the proportion of the latest armoured vehicles. Care should be taken that in every phase of their working up, they should have a definite fighting value. It may not be possible to give all the armoured Brigade Groups the same equipment at the same time. They must take what is going, and make the best of it. For instance, in forming a new or backward armoured Brigade Group in this country, it should first of all receive a full complement of armoured cars or Bren gun carriers, and should immediately become 'Brigade conscious'. They should be trained in regimental and brigade exercises just as if they were a fully-equipped armoured formation. This is specially true in all WT services. In an emergency they would act as a Motor Machine Gun unit. As proper Tanks become available, these should be infused into the Regiments as a growing core, until finally the men are well used to looking after motor vehicles and well-trained in the manoeuvres of an armoured Brigade formation. They would then eventually receive their full equipment of whatever Tanks are available; these Tanks themselves being replaced by later models as they come to hand or are transferred to them from the more fully equipped formations. Thus at every stage there would be weeded out the non-Tank-minded personnel, there would be an expansion of instruction in Tank tactics, and a practical value in the event of emergency would be maintained.

2. Different conditions present themselves in the case of the Cavalry Division, which has so long been in Palestine ineffective as a military factor. This Cavalry Division should be re-organized as fast as emergency conditions of war permit, in two Brigade Groups, each of which should consist of 3 Tank Regiments, 12 motorized field guns, one motorized Machine Gun Regiment and ancillary services. The formation of these two armoured Brigade Groups should have a high priority, certainly one in advance of the more backward British armoured units. It would be a great convenience if these two Brigades could in the first instance be ripened from mere Motor Machine Gun units into Tank units by receiving the flow of Light Medium Tanks from the United States which has now begun. President Roosevelt has informed me that he has allocated (apart from the 60 already approaching and other orders) 200 Light Cruiser Tanks for shipment in American vessels to Suez in the next few months. Surely these additional 200 should form the main equipment of the two ex-Cavalry Armoured Brigade Groups. The balance of the various regiments would continue to use pro tem the armoured cars or Bren gun carriers which they had begun to work with. The marrying of these good troops to the windfall of 200 extra American Light Cruiser Tanks would bring into being two effective Armoured Brigade units extremely well adapted for Palestinian, Syrian and Iraqian warfare at a far earlier date than any equal fighting value could be achieved.

Winston S. Churchill to A. V. Alexander
(*Churchill papers, 20/36*)

3 July 1941

FORMATION OF GUNNERY AND ANTI-AIRCRAFT WARFARE DIVISION

I am very glad you are going to form this Division. You are quite right in thinking the weakness of the Fleet against Air attack is one of your greatest problems. Admiral Cunningham's demands for continuous Air support by standing patrols would practically ruin our Air Force in the Middle East. In fact the Fleet can only have such support when engaged on important operations. It will not I think be possible to form a Coastal Command (except with Fleet Air Arm pilots) in the Middle East. In these circumstances, gunnery is the chief line of advance, and you know how ceaselessly I have tried to persuade the authorities, military and naval, to take an interest in the varieties of UP weapons and fuzes. The radio fuze seems to be the most promising. I still find myself inclined to think that the floating UP platforms will have to be made and towed about with the Fleet.

See also my minute about floating batteries for landing operations.

I hope that the proposed increase of combatant personnel on shore may be met by pruning the existing staff.

War Cabinet, Defence Committee (Operations): minutes
(*Cabinet papers, 69/2*)

3 July 1941 Cabinet War Room
9.45 p.m.
Secret

The Prime Minister invited the First Sea Lord to provide him with a paper on the value of the present American system of patrols in the Atlantic, showing the number of escorts required to make our convoys safe and the extent to which these could be provided from our own resources. He thought he would take an opportunity to draw the attention of the Americans to the futility of a policy which, through lack of effective help, permitted sinkings to continue at a high rate and relied on making them good by future building.

The Prime Minister said that he very much deplored the fact that the 27,600 men, which it was proposed to send in Convoy WS 10, did not contain any new fighting formations. He had many times commented on the fact that, out of the large mass of men available in the Middle East, so few fighting formations could be produced for operations. He felt certain that there was mis-management and disorganization and he did not feel at all inclined to press for extra shipping to carry further additions to the rearward services which were already much too large.

The Prime Minister read to the Committee a telegram he had received from Mr Harriman, in which a number of criticisms were made of the arrangements in the Middle East, of the co-operation between the Services, and of the progress of port development. Mr Harriman said that he found an air of complacency in Cairo and no sense of urgency.

The Prime Minister said that it was essential to ensure that the Middle East Command should have a great superiority in Air Forces. No effort must be spared to achieve this object; it was therefore necessary for another aircraft carrier operation to be staged on the lines of Operation Railway.[1]

Winston S. Churchill to J. A. Spender[2]

(*Churchill papers, 20/29*)

3 July 1941
Private

My dear Spender,

Many thanks for your letter of June 18 which I have carefully considered and discussed with some of my colleagues. You will see that we have endeavoured to make some improvement in the Ministry of Information compatible with Military needs. I have also had two or three interviews with the Editors of the principal papers which I believe did good. I could not however undertake anything in the nature of weekly conferences on the American Presidential lines. You must remember that unlike the President I have to appear continuously before the legislature. Indeed I have had to give much more time to the House of Commons than I bargained for when the Ministry was formed.

I am much obliged to you however for your friendly letter. I am always glad to hear from you.

Yours v sincerely
Winston S Churchill

[1] The reinforcement of British aircraft to Malta through the Mediterranean via Gibraltar.

[2] J. Alfred Spender, 1862–1942. Journalist and author. Editor of the Hull *Eastern Morning News*, 1886–90. Editor of the *Westminster Gazette*, 1896–1922. Member of the Royal Commission on the Private Manufacture of Armaments, 1935. Companion of Honour, 1937. Biographer of two Liberal Prime Ministers, Campbell-Bannerman, and Asquith. His last two books, of seventeen, were *The Government of Mankind* (1938) and *New Lamps and Ancient Lights* (1940). He died on 21 June 1942.

War Cabinet, Defence Committee (Operations): minutes
(*Cabinet papers, 69/2*)

4 July 1941 10 Downing Street
10.50 a.m.
Secret

PROPOSED RAID ON A VILLAGE NEAR LE TOUQUET[1]

The Prime Minister said that he thought the proposed operation most inadequate and out of proportion in the general war situation. The results would be very small and might be achieved with disproportionate loss. The enemy would claim to have repulsed an attack and the general attitude throughout the world would probably be ridicule at the feeble efforts which were all that we could achieve to help the Russians. The whole affair would appear as a fiasco. He sympathized with the desire of the troops for action, but he saw no good reasons for pursuing such a plan.[2]

The Prime Minister drew attention to the statement reported in the *Daily Telegraph* that morning by Senator Wheeler,[3] that United States troops were going to embark for Iceland on July 23rd and 24th. He felt that this was a disgraceful disclosure which might, if it had been accurate, have gravely endangered the lives of American troops. He invited the First Sea Lord to give him some data to show the naval possibilities which might have resulted so that he could draw the attention of the President to the matter.

Winston S. Churchill to General Ismay, for the Chiefs of Staff Committee
(*Premier papers, 3/230/1*)

4 July 1941
Most Secret

The only thing that matters is for the United States to arrive in Iceland – as soon and as many as possible. Whether we stay or go, in whole or in part, is altogether secondary; and, indeed, I think it preferable that the two forces should be in the Island together for some time to come.

[1] Sir Roger Keyes, Director of Combined Operations, had proposed to the War Cabinet 'an outline plan for an operation which would involve the landing of 320 men and six tanks on the French coast not far from Le Touquet. The objective of the raid would be to clear a village of Germans, capturing prisoners, and subsequently to beat up an aerodrome nearby with tanks. The troops would be about one and a quarter hours on shore and would re-embark just before dawn. Strong fighter escort would then be provided and a good air battle might result. Given good conditions he thought that there was a reasonable chance of success'.

[2] This decision not to act was a great disappointment to Sir Roger Keyes, whose brainchild the raid (with 320 men and six tanks) was.

[3] Burton Kendall Wheeler, 1882–1975. Elected to the Montana Legislature, 1910. Senator for Montana, 1922–44.

Winston S. Churchill to General Ismay
(Churchill papers, 20/36)

4 July 1941

I am told that some of the Cadet OTCs[1] – boys of 13–14 years – are armed with .303 rifles. In one case 300 are in the Armoury.

Please find out about this, because the fighting troops must have priority over Cadet Corps at this time.

Winston S. Churchill to President D. Roosevelt
(Churchill papers, 20/40)

5 July 1941
1 a.m.

Following are considerations which weighed with us in deciding upon change in command in the Middle East. Wavell has a glorious record, having completely destroyed the Italian Army and conquered the Italian Empire in Africa. He has also borne up well against German attacks and has conducted war and policy in three or four directions simultaneously since the beginning of the struggle. I must regard him as our most distinguished General. Nevertheless, though this should not be stated publicly, we felt that, after the long strain he had borne, he was tired, and a fresh eye and an unstrained hand were needed in this most seriously menaced theatre. Incomparably the best and most distinguished officer to take his place was General Auchinleck, the Commander-in-Chief in India. We feel sure that Auchinleck will infuse a new energy and precision into the defence of the Nile Valley, while Wavell will make an admirable Commander-in-Chief in India who will aid him in the whole of the great sphere which India is now assuming, as our flank moves eastward. (As Commander-in-Chief, India, Wavell will have operations in Iraq under his control.)

Wavell has gracefully accepted this decision, saying that he thinks us wise to make the change and get new ideas and action on the many problems in the Middle East. The Viceroy has assured me that his shining achievements will secure him a very warm welcome in India from the army and public opinion.

The present lull in the German offensive in the Middle East has provided a convenient opportunity for change over. It coincides also with the appointment of Oliver Lyttelton as Minister of State to represent the War Cabinet in that theatre and relieve the Commanders-in-Chief of many non-operational

[1] Officers Training Corps.

functions which have hitherto greatly increased their burdens, such as relations with the Free French, relations with the Emperor of Abyssinia, the administration of occupied enemy territory, propaganda and economic warfare. The Minister of State will also exercise general supervision over the activities of the Intendant-General (another innovation), including all matters locally connected with supplies from the United States.

The Intendant-General (General Haining) will relieve the Army Commander-in-Chief of detailed control of rearward administrative services and supply arrangements.

All these changes will, I hope, result in a greatly increased vigour and drive in our effort in the Middle East and ensure that the fullest use is made of the formidable resources steadily accumulating there from the United Kingdom, the overseas Empire and the United States. Harriman will doubtless be reporting upon them. He is being asked to await Lyttelton's arrival in Cairo (now expected on July 5), so as to pool all information and settle arrangements for the reception of American supplies.

Winston S. Churchill to Sir Archibald Sinclair

(*Churchill papers, 20/36*)

5 July 1941
Secret

REQUEST FROM THE NEW ZEALAND PRIME MINISTER

We cannot afford to send Hudsons[1] away out of this country till the American deliveries reach 100 a month. As soon as they do, the 64 in question may be worked off to New Zealand at 10 a month, provided there is no falling back in the American supply, in which case 10 per cent. can be sent as convenient.

Winston S. Churchill to Anthony Eden

(*Churchill papers, 20/36*)

5 July 1941
Secret

The Finns, having definitely entered the war on Hitler's side, deserve severe treatment.

[1] Lockheed Hudsons, twin-engined American aircraft used by Coastal Command for maritime patrol, convoy and anti-submarine work. Armed with up to seven machine guns, and 750 pounds weight of bombs, they took an important part in the Battle of Atlantic, and were later used to fly agents to and from occupied Europe. It had a range of 2,160 miles and a maximum speed of 255 miles and hour.

I presume we have taken all their ships found at sea, and that the Finnish Minister[1] is deprived of all facilities, cipher and otherwise.

There is no need to declare war, but it seems to me they should have much the same treatment as if they were at war.

Winston S. Churchill to Admiral Pound
(*Churchill papers, 20/36*)

5 July 1941
Most Secret

GERMAN U-BOAT STRENGTH

It is disconcerting to have such a violent change introduced into the figures. That the Admiralty should be out by no less than 51 boats makes me desire to know more about the new evidence which has led to this most serious conclusion. I should be glad if you would allow Professor Lindemann to go into this new evidence with your Submarine Department, and explain to him, as convenient, the basis on which it rests, when these facts first dawned upon the Admiralty, and what are the future prospects.

I must say that I feel this very decisive change and aggravation of our dangers should have been reported to me as a major event, and not simply be elicited as a result of the inquiry I made on 2.7.41. I had been reassured by the figures as epitomized in your returns, but now feel very anxious indeed, especially if there are going to be any more surprises of this kind.

I should also like to know what the American calculation is. They must have had good facilities for finding out about German new building. This unexpected increase tallies with Hess' talk.

I presume you have also investigated the question of crews.

Further, what danger is there of the Germans getting hold of the Russian submarines in the Baltic?

Winston S. Churchill to Major Desmond Morton
(*Churchill papers, 20/36*)

6 July 1941
Most Secret

Please make sure that a list is kept of young Frenchmen who are sentenced by the Vichy Courts to imprisonment for de Gaullist sympathies in France or in Morocco, so that they may be looked after later on.

[1] George Achates Gripenberg, 1890–1975. Educated in Finland and at the London School of Economics. Entered the Finnish Foreign Service 1918. Minister to Brazil, Argentina and Chile, 1929–32; in London 1933–41; at the Holy See, 1942–43; in Stockholm, 1943–54. Finnish Ambassador to the United Nations, 1954–56; Permanent Finnish Delegate to the United Nations, 1956–59.

Winston S. Churchill to David Margesson
(*Churchill papers, 20/36*)

6 July 1941
Action this Day

Why have we not yet been told that the Blues, Life Guards and Essex Yeomanry took part in the capture of Palmyra? These Units have long ago been identified by contact, and there cannot be any military reasons for not disclosing this interesting piece of information to the British public.

It is the kind of abuse of Censorship, in the name of operational secrecy, that rightly irritates the House as well as the Press, and makes the more important positions more difficult to hold.

Winston S. Churchill to Herbert Morrison
(*Churchill papers, 20/36*)

6 July 1941
Secret

IRISH LABOURERS CROSSING TO BRITAIN

Obviously, the German Embassy in Dublin can work in any German agents they wish through this channel, and I personally feel serious anxiety about throwing open the door at the very time when we have to prepare for invasion on the most formidable scale from Germany. On the other hand, we want the labour, and there is, I fear, a pretty good leak anyhow.

Winston S. Churchill to General Sir John Dill
(*Churchill papers, 20/36*)

6 July 1941
Action this Day
Secret

1. It is nearly six months since you and Mr Eden went to Cairo, charged inter alia with the task of reporting on the interior economy of the Army in the Middle East. Yet today the condition is deplorable, and our detailed knowledge most defective. The War Office ought to have a full picture of the development of the fighting formations, and I certainly cannot discharge my responsibilities without it.

2. It is not much to ask a division or brigade group to send in a monthly return of their major items of equipment. I cannot imagine a competent Divisional General who would not know where he was in this matter from week to week, indeed almost from day to day.

3. I do not think the mock-up telegram is unduly lengthy for a monthly return considering the immense daily flow, including Air Force trivialities.

4. General Haining's organization ought to know the whole position, and there ought to be no difficulty in their telling us.

You are wrong in supposing that this return is needed for statistical purposes only. Without a clear up-to-date picture of the state of Middle East formations, no view or major decisions can be taken by the Defence Committee or the War Cabinet. The alternative is to continue in the state of ignorance and confusion which is leading us towards disaster.

While I should be ready to agree to some small simplification of details, if you will propose it to me, I must insist upon knowing all the essential facts.

Winston S. Churchill to General Auchinleck

(*Premier papers, 3/291/1*)

6 July 1941
11.20 p.m.
Personal and Secret

1. Your No. 1527 of 4/7. I agree about finishing off Syria and here we have always thought that holding Syria is the necessary foundation for holding or retaking Cyprus. One hopes that Syria may not be long now and that you will not be forestalled in Cyprus. The priority of both these operations over offensive action in Western Desert after what has happened is fully recognized.

2. Nevertheless Western Desert remains decisive theatre this autumn for defence of Nile Valley. Only by reconquering the lost airfields of Eastern Cyrenaica can Fleet and Air Force resume effective action against enemy sea-borne supplies.

3. In General Wavell's No. SD/57777 of 18th April he stated that he had six regiments of trained armoured personnel awaiting tanks. This was a main element in decision to send Tiger. Besides this, personnel for three additional Tank Regiments are now approaching round the Cape. Your need for armoured vehicles is therefore fully realized, in spite of the stress which Wavell and you both lay upon further training for these already-trained armoured units. We make out that you should have by end of July 500 cruiser, Infantry and American cruiser tanks if your workshops are properly organized, besides a large number of ill-conceived light tanks and armoured cars.

4. This cannot be improved upon in the months of July and August, except by certain American arrivals and a few replacements from Home. Even thereafter remember we have to be at concert pitch to resist invasion from September 1, and General Staff are naturally reluctant to send another substantial instalment of tanks round the Cape (now the only way), thus

putting them out of action till early October at either end. After October, American supplies should grow and our position here be easier, but much will have happened before then.

5. At present our Intelligence shows considerable Italian reinforcements of Libya, but little or no German. However, a Russian collapse might soon alter this to your detriment, without diminishing invasion menace here.

6. Scale of our air reinforcement has been laid before you. Air Staff are becoming anxious about our heavy struggle and are disinclined to repeat Railway. Even so, it seems probable that during July, August and part of September you should have decided air superiority; but then again, a Russian collapse would liberate considerable German air reinforcements for Africa, and if enemy do not attempt invasion, but merely pretend, they can obtain air superiority on your western front during September.

7. On top of this comes the question of Tobruk. We cannot judge from here what the offensive value of Tobruk will be in two months' time, or what may happen meanwhile. It would seem that reduction or complete penning-in of Tobruk by enemy is indispensable preliminary to serious invasion of Egypt.

8. From all these points of view it is difficult to see how your situation is going to be better after the middle of September than it is now, and it may well be worsened. I have no doubt you will maturely but swiftly consider the whole problem.

9. In the light of your decision, and as a part of it, please tell us if you desire any alteration in composition of convoys WS 10 and WS 11, bearing in mind reinforcements in man-power from Australia and the South which are already on their way. When I query, as I have during the last six months, the immense proportion of rearward services and non-combatant troops included in our convoys, I recognize the fact that we have to supply these services for the Australian and NZ man-power fighting units. Nevertheless, when I am told that you have 33 Field Artillery Regiments and three on the way, apart from AA Regiments, I wonder in what battle circumstances this mass of Artillery can be deployed. There is hardly time to alter composition of WS 10, which leaves at the end of this month, but I should like to know that it is what you most want.

10. Convoy WS 11 is still, however, in hand.

Over 75,000 men are earmarked for this convoy, although at present there is only shipping for under 30,000. It would be possible, by making costly sacrifices here, like bringing home ships from S. Africa without cargoes through the circuitous and dangerous routes which alone are open, and by some other measures, to make an effort to carry a much larger reinforcement in WS 11 than is now planned. On present showing Defence Committee do not think these sacrifices justifiable. But if you have plans which require special implementing you should ask for what you want and we will do our best.

11. About the air. I feel that for all major operational purposes your plans

must govern the employment of the whole air force throughout the Middle East, bearing in mind, of course, that the Air Force has its own dominant strategic rôle to play, and must not be frittered away in providing small umbrellas for the Army, as it seems to have been in the Sollum battle. In your No. 1527 you speak of aircraft supporting the Army and aircraft supporting the Navy and aircraft employed on independent strategic tasks. The question is, what are the proportions? These will have to be arranged from time to time by the Commanders-in-Chief in consultation. But nothing in these arrangements should mar the integrity of the Air Force contribution to any major scheme you have in hand. One cannot help feeling that in the Sollum fight our air superiority was wasted and that our force in Tobruk stood idle while all available enemy tanks were sent to defeat our desert offensive.

12. I shall be obliged if you will consider the foregoing points, consulting so far as necessary with Mr Lyttelton and General Haining, and thereafter let me know how we can best help you.

Winston S. Churchill to J. V. Stalin
(*Premier papers, 3/401/1*)

7 July 1941
4.30 p.m.
Personal and Most Secret

We are all very glad here the Russian armies are making such strong and spirited resistance to the utterly unprovoked and merciless invasion of the Nazis. There is general admiration of the bravery and tenacity of the soldiers and people. We shall do everything to help you that time, geography and our growing resources allow. The longer the war lasts the more help we can give. We are making very heavy attacks both day and night with our Air Force upon all German-occupied territory and all Germany within our reach. About 400 daylight sorties were made overseas yesterday. On Saturday night over 200 heavy bombers attacked German towns, some carrying three tons apiece, and last night nearly 250 heavy bombers were operating. This will go on. Thus we hope to force Hitler to bring back some of his Air power to the West and gradually take some of the strain off you. Besides this the Admiralty have at my desire prepared a serious operation to come off in the near future in the Arctic, after which I hope contact will be established between British and Russian Navies. Meanwhile, by sweeps along the Norwegian coast we have intercepted various supply ships which were moving north against you.

We welcome arrival of Russian Military Mission in order to concert future plans.

We have only got to go on fighting to beat the life out of these villains.

War Cabinet: minutes
(*Cabinet papers, 65/19*)

7 July 1941 10 Downing Street
6 p.m.

The Prime Minister said that the arrival of United States Marines in Iceland (C)[1] was expected that day. As soon as they had arrived, President Roosevelt would make an announcement to Congress.

The Prime Minister invited attention to the important declaration made by the Foreign Secretary in his speech at Leeds on the 5th July that we were not prepared to negotiate with Hitler at any time on any subject. While this statement expressed the opinion of the whole War Cabinet, it was perhaps the most explicit public declaration on the subject which had been made. Such a declaration had been necessary at this moment in order to forestall any peace offensive by Hitler in the near future.

The War Cabinet took note, with approval of this declaration.

Winston S. Churchill to Anthony Eden
(*Premier papers, 3/230/1*)

7 July 1941
Action this Day

ARRIVAL OF AMERICAN TROOPS IN ICELAND

Once the American Congress has received the news we should make the most of the event that our Ministry of Information can manage. The papers of Tuesday should carry this as the greatest event for some time, or at any rate for some weeks. We should also exploit it round the world through all agencies open to us.

Please think of this and if you agree concert the matter with Duff Cooper without delay. I do not think the Americans will object to our splashing the news, but you might consult Winant, telling him how important it is to give the people some encouragement at this particularly grim and fateful moment.

[1] In order not to confuse Iceland with Ireland in official documents, Churchill gave instructions for it to be referred to as Iceland (C).

Winston S. Churchill to Admiral Sir Dudley Pound
(Premier papers, 3/230/1)

7 July 1941
Action this Day

BRITISH ADMIRALTY DELEGATION AND SIZE OF UNITED STATES FORCE TO GARRISON ICELAND

The BAD[1] seem to be making heavy weather over this. The only thing that matters is that five or six thousand American troops should reach the Island in question. Whether they are reinforced later, whether they are supplementary or additional to what we have got there, are trifles the discussion of which should not obscure, still less obstruct, the proceedings. Nothing matters in this place in the first instance except the moral effect. Far from being 'nonplussed', or 'more than ever surprised', the BAD should keep quiet and rub their hands.

Winston S. Churchill to President Franklin D. Roosevelt
(Premier papers, 3/460/2)

7 July 1941
8 p.m.
Personal and Secret

1. I was encouraged and relieved to read the documents on Defence Plan No. 3. Putting such a plan into immediate operation would give timely and needed aid.[2] At present the strain upon our resources is far too great.

2. The Battle of the Atlantic continually changes. Owing to the U-boats working ever farther West we have recently been forced to provide A/S escorts for the Eastbound convoys throughout their passage, and instead of dispersing the Westbound convoys when they were about halfway across the Atlantic, we now have to keep these convoys intact and provide A/S escorts for them almost up to Newfoundland.

The effect of this has been that the strength of the escorts is now only about half of what was found necessary when we only had to escort up to 35°W. We are extremely doubtful whether these reduced escorts will be sufficient to protect the convoys enough.

3. We have so far only had one trial of strength over a convoy with this reduced protection, with the result that five ships of the convoy were sunk and

[1] British Admiralty Delegation, Washington.

[2] Under Defence Plan No. 3, which President Roosevelt approved on 4 July 1941, a United States Ocean Escort was established, to consist of 6 battleships, 5 heavy cruisers, 27 destroyers, 27 'old' destroyers and 48 patrol aircraft, plus British Commonwealth forces of escort vessels, plus Canadian aircraft. There was also a United States Striking Force of 3 aircraft carriers, 4 light cruisers, 12 destroyers and 12 patrol aircraft. ('Secret', Serial 00176, 4 July 1941, *Cabinet papers, 127/16*)

two ships damaged and three U-boats were sunk. This was not unsatisfactory as we estimate that during its passage the convoy was attacked by no less than eight U-boats. The result, however, was only achieved by taking away the escorts from two Westbound convoys which happened to be in the vicinity of the Eastbound convoy, and thus reinforcing the Eastbound convoy. Robbing a Westbound convoy of its escort means that the next Eastbound convoy must be inadequately defended, and at this moment we are anxious about the safety of an Eastbound convoy which, from this cause, was left ill-protected.

4. The introduction of Defence Plan No. 3 would also enable us to give better protection to the Gibraltar and Freetown convoys, which at present are poorly escorted or not escorted at all.

5. Our anti-invasion plans would also be considerably strengthened by the introduction of Defence Plan No. 3 as a larger part of our destroyer force which is at present in the Western Atlantic would be available on this side.

6. We have been very lucky in rounding up all the eight enemy supply ships which were out, and we feel that if we can keep the seas clear of them it will not only hamper their U-boat operations but also make it unlikely that they will send warship raiders on to the trade routes. Your striking and task forces with their aircraft carriers would no doubt play a dominating part in keeping the seas clear.

7. I was much concerned at Senator Wheeler's indiscretion or worse. Although he did not give the right date for the sailing of the expedition to Iceland (C) the danger of his statement lay in the fact that if the enemy had become aware that the expedition had sailed from Newfoundland but without knowing where it was going to, its destination was made clear by Wheeler. Had the enemy meant to interfere with this convoy they would have had time to move seven or eight U-boats to a suitable intercepting position. This is based on what we believe to be the present disposition of U-boats as revealed to us by DF bearings and signals and the positions in which convoys and independent ships have been attacked. I pray God your men will get there safely.

Winston S. Churchill to Oliver Lyttelton

(*Cabinet papers, 65/19*)

7 July 1941
8 p.m.
Personal and Secret

1. Very glad you have arrived safely. Have talked to Anthony in Yorkshire about your No. 1, Twist.[1] You will already have received War Office 76097 to

[1] The telegraphic prefix of Lyttelton's telegrams to Churchill.

Commander-in-Chief, Middle East, which crossed yours. Emphasis of these two telegrams is somewhat different, but we accept and, indeed, prefer yours. Proceed accordingly in your relations with Free French.

2. However, you must not overlook the main point, which is to gain the Arab world by establishment and proclamation at earliest of Syrian independence in whatever form is most acceptable. Your paragraph 3 of No. 1, Twist, is far from adequate. Our policy is to give the Syrian Arabs independence. We are quite willing that the Free French should represent the interests of France and prove that among our nations of Europe France is the favoured and privileged Power in Syria. Our only British interests, except ordinary trade, are to keep the Germans out and win the war.

3. From this point of view the Arabs bulk far more largely in our minds than the Free French, and there can be no question of any lengthy delay in negotiating treaties which satisfy them and convince them they have not merely exchanged one set of Frenchmen for another. Catroux's proclamation says 'as soon as possible'. This should mean that within a few days of the Vichy French surrendering, prompt and vigorous negotiations should begin, and be pressed earnestly and swiftly to a conclusion.

4. Nothing in the above, of course, affects British martial law, which we need to defend the country and keep out the Germans.

I have no doubt you have all this in your mind.

War Cabinet, Defence Committee (Operations): minutes
(Cabinet papers, 69/2)

7 July 1941 10 Downing Street
9.45 p.m.

RAIDS

The Prime Minister said that he preferred a large scale raid since otherwise losses were apt to be out of proportion to the moral or material advantages obtained, but since he understood that large scale operations were not possible at present he would be prepared to agree to raids by very small numbers of men.

The Committee agreed to raiding by small parties. The strength of these to be of the order of 10 men.

Winston S. Churchill to the Production Executive
(*Churchill papers, 20/36*)

7 July 1941
Action this Day

PRIORITY FOR TANKS, SPARES, 2-POUNDER AND 6-POUNDER GUNS AND ARMOUR PIERCING AMMUNITION[1]

I consider this most desirable, and hope it can be done without serious derangement of existing priorities. If not, please report to me on the loss involved in other quarters, in order that I may decide. The matter is urgent.

Winston S. Churchill to Lord Woolton
(*Churchill papers, 20/36*)

7 July 1941

I am glad that you are preparing for the American authorities an estimate of our full requirements of pork and dairy products, and that you have asked them for a greatly increased programme for eggs. The total figure of the food imports to be obtained from America will, I trust, be much bigger than the one and a third million tons at present envisaged. With due notice I feel sure that the Americans, without rationing themselves, could produce much more food for export to us. (Pork production in the United States frequently fluctuates by nearly half a million tons from year to year.)

I trust that every effort is made to get our meat from the nearest sources. With due warning and a guarantee perhaps the Argentine could also expand their meat production.

Oil and oil-seeds are no doubt obtained as far as possible from Africa and imported on ships returning from the Middle East; we can ill afford to send ships to India or the Pacific for this purpose now.

Winston S. Churchill to Air Chief Marshal Sir Charles Portal
(*Cabinet papers, 120/300*)

7 July 1941
Most Secret

Here is a very unorthodox proposal. One of our great aims is the delivery on German towns of the largest possible quantity of bombs per night. Surely it would be possible as the nights lengthen to send less-qualified crews to the

[1] This request had been made by Lord Beaverbrook on 4 July 1941.

Ruhr or over nearby places in Germany, and keep the regular trained pilots and crews for the more important sorties. One would suppose they might have a certain proportion of expert leaders and fly very high, aiming simply at large built-up areas. They could work in the dark periods. Thus we might greatly increase our discharges at an earlier date than would otherwise be possible.

Winston S. Churchill to Air Chief Marshal Sir Charles Portal
(*Cabinet papers, 120/300*)

7 July 1941
Action this Day

Two nights out of the last four the main weight of our bombing attack has been on Brest. We were assured that the first of the two nights had been highly successful, yet no less than 108 Bombers were sent last night. This is far too great an emphasis to be put on Brest at a time when the devastation of the German cities is urgently needed in order to take the weight off the Russians by bringing back aircraft.[1]

Winston S. Churchill: Oral Answers
(*Hansard*)

8 July 1941 House of Commons

QUESTIONS TO MINISTERS

Mr Stokes[2] asked the Prime Minister what procedure Members of this House should follow when they wish to put Questions pertaining to the action of the Minister of State newly appointed for residence in the Near East?

The Prime Minister: Such Questions should be addressed to me.

Sir Irving Albery: Does that mean that the Minister of State in the Middle East is acting as deputy to the Prime Minister?

The Prime Minister: No, Sir.

[1] Following Churchill's Minute, there was an intensification of bombing raids on Germany: Hanover was bombed on July 14, 19 and 25; Hamburg on July 16 and 25; Frankfurt-on-Main and Mannheim on July 21, 22 and 23; and Berlin on July 25.

[2] Richard Rapier Stokes, 1897–1957. On active service in the Royal Artillery, 1915–18 (Military Cross and bar). Unsuccessful Labour candidate, 1935. Labour MP from 1938 until his death. Minister of Works, 1950–1; Minister of Materials, 1951. Privy Councillor, 1950.

Winston S. Churchill to General Auchinleck
(*Cabinet papers, 20/23*)

8 July 1941
7.25 p.m.
Personal and Secret
Repeated to Minister of State

I am concerned about the references in your speech as reported here about the need for American man-power in the war against Germany. At this particular moment when the President, having landed Marines in Iceland, is trying to obtain authority from Congress, where he has no certain majority, to allow United States Army troops to be dispatched overseas outside the Western Hemisphere, I fear your remarks will be exploited by the isolationists and will be an impediment to the end we all desire. The American Ambassador, Mr Winant, tells me that Wavell's references a few days ago on the same lines did harm, and that your observations will be unhelpful. They are also contrary to what I have said about our not needing an American Army this year or next year, or any year that I could foresee.

It is a mistake for Generals in High Command to make speeches or give interviews to Press correspondents. There are several other passages in your speech which I would rather you had left out. The very cool and almost disparaging reference to the Russian effort will give offence in some quarters in this country, and I doubt the wisdom of revealing so many of your own thoughts, however sensible they may be, to the enemy. Now that you have broken the ice with the war correspondents, I trust you will not find it necessary to make any further public statements on political or strategic issues, or that if you wish to do so you will consult me beforehand.

Winston S. Churchill to Oliver Lyttelton
(*Churchill papers, 20/40*)

8 July 1941
Personal and Secret

Please see the telegram (T379) I have sent to General Auchinleck. I am sure both he and you will weaken yourselves by making informal speeches or giving interviews to the Press. I shall be defining your duties to some extent tomorrow in answer to a question in the House of Commons. It would be better to leave that sort of thing to me. You can always consult me beforehand. Your appointment has been very well received in all quarters.

Winston S. Churchill to Oliver Lyttelton
(*Churchill papers, 20/40*)

8 July 1941
8.55 p.m.
Personal and Secret

Your telegrams 472 and 473 CXG from Gibraltar.

1. Lord Gort has already agreed to give priority to the work necessary to improve the aerodrome.

2. Other commitments will not allow us for the present to undertake regular operations upon the mainland of the Iberian peninsula nor in Spanish Morocco.

3. Arrangements have recently been made to install a broadcasting transmitter at Gibraltar.

4. Special Operations Executive already have in hand the distribution of propaganda material and leaflets in North Africa. Lord Gort has been asked for further information as to his requirements.

5. We fully agree with the suggestions to appoint an American Liaison Officer at Gibraltar and that American warships should visit Casablanca and Dakar. Foreign Office have taken up these points.

Winston S. Churchill to General Ismay
(*Churchill papers, 20/36*)

8 July 1941
Most Secret

DCO[1] should be asked to consider plans for a raid in the north of Norway on the scale of about three or four thousand men, to stay at least two, and possibly three or four, nights before coming off. Let me have his opinions by tomorrow.

John Colville: diary
(*Colville papers*)

8 July 1941

After lunching with Father at the Turf, I got back to No. 10 and went down to talk to the PM while he was preparing to go to sleep. 'I hear you are plotting to abandon me,' he said, 'You know I can stop you. I can't make you stay with

[1] Director of Combined Operations, Admiral of the Fleet Sir Roger Keyes.

me against your will but I can put you somewhere else.' I said yes, but I hoped he wouldn't; and after I had taken out one of my unfinished contact lenses to show him, he said I might go and agreed that the short, sharp battle of the Fighter Pilot was far better than the long wait of a Bomber crew before they reached their objective. He made a few remarks about how wrong I was to go when I knew the routine of the office (though he clearly thought I was right!) and said he would not have let me if the bombing in London had been heavy but as there was a lull he couldn't say no.

The tropical heat wave, which started more than three weeks ago, continues – at well over 90° in the shade.

Winston S. Churchill: Oral Answers

(*Hansard*)

9 July 1941 House of Commons

MINISTER OF STATE (DUTIES, MIDDLE EAST)

Mr Hore-Belisha asked the Prime Minister whether he will define the duties which the Minister of State will discharge in the Middle East, in particular, his relations with and his authority over the Commander-in-Chief, His Majesty's Ambassador in Cairo, and other representatives of this country in the Middle East, who now receive their instructions through other Government Departments; and whether the responsibilities of the Secretaries of State for Foreign Affairs, War, Air, the Colonies, and the Minister of Information, are in any way qualified by the new appointment?

The Prime Minister (Mr Churchill): The principal tasks of the Minister of State will be, first, to facilitate the conduct of operations by the Commanders-in-Chief in the Middle East by relieving them, so far as possible, of a number of extraneous responsibilities with which they have hitherto been burdened, and, secondly, to settle promptly matters within the policy of His Majesty's Government but which involve several home departments or local authorities. The appointment of the Minister of State will not interfere with the existing relationships between the Commanders-in-Chief in the Middle East and the Service Ministers, or between His Majesty's Ambassador, Cairo, and other representatives of His Majesty's Government in the Middle East, and the Ministers in this country to whom they are responsible. The Minister of State will make reference home whenever necessary on important issues of policy; but it is to be hoped that the presence of a War Cabinet Minister with wide discretionary powers will smooth, hasten, and concert action in the Middle East between the various authorities in that area.

Mr Hore-Belisha: While I thank the Prime Minister for his answer, will he say whether the Minister of State has authority over the Commander-in-Chief and His Majesty's Ambassador, or whether it is entirely a matter for consultation in the smoothing-out of difficulties?

The Prime Minister: The Minister of State has authority in matters which are not concerned with the conduct of operations, but that authority is derived from his position as a member of the War Cabinet, and will no doubt be exercised in harmony with that fundamental principle.

Sir Irving Albery: With reference to the power which the Minister of State has to decide priority questions in the matter of military supplies, will not this be contingent on the operational functions of the Commander-in-Chief?

The Prime Minister: We set up some two months ago a new officer in the Middle East, General Sir Robert Haining, to whom I have applied the somewhat rare title of Intendant-General. His business is to serve the Commander-in-Chief with the largest possible measure of supplies in accordance with the wishes of the Commander-in-Chief and the needs of the Army, and also in accordance with the practical business of handling the great mass of supplies arriving from this country and the United States, and the Minister of State will have the benefit of the advice of Sir Robert Haining in anything which may touch this part of his duty. I would say that the kind of relations which I hope to see between the Minister of State and the Intendant-General on the one hand, and the Commander-in-Chief of the Army on the other, are very largely the sort of relations which prevail in the matter of supplies between the War Office and the Ministry of Supply in this country and General Sir Alan Brooke, commanding the Army in the United Kingdom.

Mr Thorne: Will the Minister of State be armed with plenary powers, or will he be expected to consult with the War Cabinet every now and again?

The Prime Minister: Yes, Sir. Nobody in this country has plenary powers, except in accordance with the constant supervision of Parliament, exercised through the War Cabinet.

Mr Hore-Belisha: Does the area of the Middle East Command remain exactly the same as it was, including Iraq?

The Prime Minister: I am not certain whether it has been announced, but a change has been made in the responsibilities for the defence of Iraq, which have been transferred to the Indian Command, and will be exercised by General Wavell as Commander-in-Chief in India.

Mr Hore-Belisha: Does the Minister of State control that area?

The Prime Minister: No, Sir; he does not control any of these areas. He is in the closest touch with the Government of India, and he can communicate with them direct if he wishes, reporting at the same time to us, and I have no doubt that the closest contact will be arranged by him.

Mr Mander: What will be the relations of the Minister of State with the representatives of the Dominions on the spot? Will he be in close contact and consultation with them?

The Prime Minister: Yes, Sir, the relations will be of close contact with them and continuous courtesy and good will.

MOSLEMS (MOSQUE AND CULTURAL CENTRE, LONDON)

Mr Hannah[1] asked the Prime Minister whether, in view of the urgent need of making friends of Moslem countries all over the East, he will take steps to make better known the gift by the Government of a prominent London site for a mosque and institute worthy of the capital of the Empire?

The Prime Minister: My hon. Friend is right to draw attention to this matter. I am sure that he will be glad to know that our many friends in Moslem countries all over the East have already expressed great appreciation of this gift of a site for a mosque and Islamic cultural centre in London. We shall certainly take any appropriate opportunity to keep the Moslem world informed of the progress of this most interesting project.

Mr Hannah: While thanking the Prime Minister very cordially for that splendid answer, may I ask whether the Government realize that the Japanese, having built a mosque in Tokyo, are booming it throughout the whole Moslem world, and must not we do likewise?

The Prime Minister: I should not always set up the conduct of the Government referred to as a pattern which we must follow with unreasonable care.

ICELAND (UNITED STATES OCCUPATION)

Mr Lees-Smith (by Private Notice) asked the Prime Minister whether he has any information to give the House with regard to the situation in Iceland?

The Prime Minister: The military occupation of Iceland is an event of first-rate political and strategic importance; in fact, it is one of the most important things that has happened since the war began. It has been undertaken by the United States in pursuance of the purely American policy of protecting the Western Hemisphere from the Nazi menace. I understand that in the view of the American technical authorities modern conditions of war, especially air war require forestalling action, in this case especially in order to prevent the acquisition by Hitler of jumping-off grounds from which it would be possible, bound by bound, to come to close quarters with the American Continent. It is not for me to comment on these American views, although I may say they seem fairly obvious to anyone who takes an intelligent interest in what is going on.

The seizure of Iceland by Hitler would be of great advantage to him in

[1] Ian Campbell Hannah, 1874–1944. A schoolmaster in China, 1897–99; in South Africa, 1901. President of King's College, Nova Scotia, 1904–06. Professor of Church History, Oberlin College, Ohio, 1915–25. Among his published books were *Eastern Asia, a History*, *Christian Monasticism*, and *History of British Foreign Policy*. Conservative Member of Parliament for the Bilston Division of Wolverhampton from 1935 until his death.

bringing pressure to bear both on Great Britain and the United States. We have for some time past, with the assent of the Icelandic people and the Legislature, maintained a strong garrison in the Island, and the arrival of powerful United States forces will greatly reduce the danger to Iceland. This measure of American policy is therefore in complete harmony with British interests, and we have found no reason on any occasion to object to it; indeed, I cannot see that we should have had any grounds for doing so in view of the invitation extended to the United States by the Icelandic Government. We still propose to retain our Army in Iceland, and, as British and United States Forces will both have the same object in view, namely, the defence of Iceland, it seems very likely they will co-operate closely and effectively in resistance of any attempt by Hitler to gain a footing. It would obviously be foolish for the United States to have one plan for defending Iceland and for the British Forces to have another.

If any issue of principle arises, it may be safely left to the British and American naval, military and Air Force authorities concerned, who will, I have no doubt, study each other's convenience to the utmost. Looked at from every point of view, I have been unable to find any reason for regretting the step which the United States have taken, and which in the circumstances they have been forced to take; indeed, I think I may almost go so far as to say, on behalf of the House of Commons as well as of His Majesty's Government, that we really welcome it. Whether similar satisfaction will be aroused in Germany is another question, and is one which hardly concerns us this morning.

The second principle of United States policy, which I understand has led them to the occupation of Iceland, has been the declared will and purpose of the President, Congress and people of the United States, not only to send all possible aid in warlike munitions and necessary supplies to Great Britain, but also to make sure we get them. Here again is a course of action for which the United States must take full responsibility. Apart from this, the position of the United States Forces in Iceland will, of course, require their being sustained or reinforced at sea from time to time. These consignments of American supplies for American Forces on duty overseas for the purposes of the United States will, of course, have to traverse very dangerous waters, and, as we have a very large traffic constantly passing through these waters, I daresay it may be found in practice mutually advantageous for the two navies involved to assist each other, so far as is convenient, in that part of the business. I really do not think I have anything further to say about a transaction which appears at every point to be so very plain and simple.

SYRIA (FRENCH ARMISTICE PROPOSAL)

Mr Lees-Smith: Has the Prime Minister any information to give the House regarding the situation in Syria?

The Prime Minister: It is true that we have received a formal application from the French High Commissioner in Syria, General Dentz, for a discussion of terms leading to an armistice. I need hardly say how very glad His Majesty's Government will be to see an end brought to this distressing conflict, in which 1,000 to 1,500 British, Australian and Indian soldiers who volunteered to join the Army in order to defend France have fallen, killed or wounded, under French bullets as the result of the lamentable confusion in which the affairs of so many good people in so many parts of the world have been thrown by the victories of Hitler's Army. I, therefore, should welcome the negotiations, and I trust they may reach a speedy conclusion. Pending any formal arrangement being made, military operations must, of course, continue without abatement.

John Colville: diary
(*Colville papers*)

9 July 1941 Chequers

The PM and most of his family went down to Chequers for the night, for Lady Goony's funeral tomorrow.[1] Being in attendance I drove Diana Sandys there in my car. The sentries refused to let us in, but we forced an entrance by the back door. The Sinclairs also came.

At dinner I sat between Lady Sinclair[2] and Mrs C. The PM talked afterwards of the political future, the conversation arising from his congratulations to Archie Sinclair on his KT[3] and Archie saying that a KG[4] for Anthony Eden would ruin his chances of being PM. Winston said that Eden now had a serious competitor: Oliver Lyttelton, who was *persona grata* to the Conservative Party and who had an opportunity of establishing his reputation in Egypt. Anthony Eden was not supported in the House or in the party though personally he, Winston, admired his great moral and physical courage. 'He would equally well charge a battery or go to the stake for his principles – even though the principles might be wrongly conceived and he might charge the battery from the wrong angle?' Oliver Lyttelton was 'tough and stuffy' – and ready to take responsibility.

[1] The funeral of Lady Gwendeline Churchill (known as Goony), the wife of Churchill's brother Jack. She was buried in the cemetery at Bladon where both Lord Randolph and Lady Randolph Churchill were buried (and where Churchill and his brother were also to be buried).

[2] The former Marigold Forbes, whom Sir Archibald Sinclair married in 1918. She died in 1975. She and her husband lived in Thurso.

[3] Sir Archibald Sinclair had just been made a Knight of the Thistle (an honour reserved for Scotsmen).

[4] Anthony Eden was not made a Knight of the Garter until 1954, during Churchill's second Premiership (and shortly before Eden himself became Prime Minister).

After dinner the PM and Archie talked till 2.00 a.m. while I played the gramophone for them. The PM showed Archie with great glee the parody of 'To be or not to be' written at the time of Napoleon's invasion threat and now hung in the passage at Chequers. They talked of what should be done with the enemy leaders after the war. The PM thought that when the war was over there should be an end to all bloodshed, though he would like to see Mussolini, the bogus mimic of Ancient Rome, strangled like Vercingetorix in old Roman fashion. Hitler and the Nazis he would segregate on some island, though he would not so desecrate St Helena. But we still had a long way to go.[1]

The PM inveighed against defeatism and said it would be better to make this island a sea of blood than to surrender if invasion came. He had been impressed by a letter from Reynaud to Pétain, sent some weeks ago, in which the former recalled how the Generals had said to him that after the Franco-German Armistice England would have 'her neck wrung like a chicken' in three weeks.[2] Reynaud had sent copies of this letter through the American Ambassador at Vichy to the PM and to the President. It is impressive reading.

Finally the PM and the S of S agreed that the French had acted shamefully in demanding more fighter squadrons from us after they knew the battle was lost.

The PM seems reconciled to my joining the RAF and, as he went to bed, said that a Fighter Pilot had greater excitement than a polo-player, big game shot and hunting-man rolled into one. I owe my release largely to Mrs C's spirited intervention on my behalf.

War Cabinet, Battle of the Atlantic Committee: minutes
(*Cabinet papers, 86/1*)

9 July 1941 — 10 Downing Street
5.30 p.m.
Secret

The Meeting had before them a Report by the Ministry of War Transport on Emergency Lighting in Ports (BA (41) 89). This showed a considerable improvement in the position.

The Prime Minister said that plans should be based on the assumption that enemy air attacks next winter would not be such as to prevent night working in the ports generally, notwithstanding attacks from time to time on particular port areas.

[1] On 11 July 1941 Churchill's step father-in-law, Major George Cornwallis-West, wrote to him: 'My great wish is to be allowed to see the end of Hitler and his gang. Before execution they ought to be shewn round the Countries they have devastated in large iron cages!' (*Churchill papers, 1/361*)

[2] It was as a reflection on this remark that Churchill later commented (in Ottawa, on 30 December 1941): 'Some chicken! Some neck!'

The Prime Minister referred to President Roosevelt's announcement that the merchant shipping constructed in the United States of America would amount to 4½ million tons in 1941, 5½ million tons in 1942 and 7 million tons in 1943. He asked the Minister of War Transport to find out urgently from Sir Arthur Salter whether the President's statement referred to deadweight or to gross tonnage.

War Cabinet, Defence Committee (Operations): minutes

(*Cabinet papers, 69/2*)

9 July 1941 Prime Minister's Room
12 noon House of Commons

DEFENCE OF CENTRAL LONDON
POSSIBLE INVASION EXERCISE

Summing up the discussion, the Prime Minister said that, although he felt that the enemy might well attempt some kind of attack of this sort on the centre of London, he did not think that the proposed exercise would give a sufficiently realistic picture of what would occur to justify the very great dislocation and loss which it would occasion. He would like to see it done throughout as a Staff study, starting with the air action and following through all the various processes, such as the posting of cordons to close the routes though without actually stopping the traffic. There might be a separate mobilization of the Home Guard to find out what might be expected of it. He would like every possibility of testing matters out in theory and imagination exhausted before the holding of a full dress exercise was decided upon. He invited the Commander-in-Chief, Home Forces,[1] in consultation with the War Office and the Air Ministry, to study and to make proposals for the holding of a Staff exercise on the lines he had suggested, either to test the whole organization simultaneously or a part at a time. He would be very glad to be associated personally with such an exercise.

[1] General Sir Alan Brooke.

Winston S. Churchill to Anthony Eden
(*Churchill papers, 20/40*)

9 July 1941
2.25 p.m.
Most Immediate
Most Secret

Something like the following should be sent to the Minister of State[1] for his information:

Following from Prime Minister. Personal and Secret. Begins. An agent who we think is sure came a fortnight ago to establish a liaison between us and Vichy. Our talks with him were on the dead level. He now sends us the following, dated 5th July:

'1. The French Government has given the following general instructions to General Dentz:

'When Syria is occupied by the British the French Civil Servants must remain at their posts and carry on with their duties in collaboration with the Free French Forces.

'2. I am requested to beg of you most earnestly to take these instructions into account. Goodwill on your part on this occasion will make the best impression.

'3. Failure to meet this, the first wish expressed by my Government so soon after my return, would have an unfortunate influence on my future actions.'

This must be considered in relation to the formal request for armistice with which you have already been acquainted. We propose replying to the Agent for Pétain and Huntziger[2] to the effect that:

1. England has no interest in Syria except to win the war.

2. Arab independence is a first essential and nothing must conflict with that.

3. De Gaulle must naturally in the circumstances represent French interests in Syria in the interim. He will thus keep alive the fact that, without prejudice to Arab independence, France will have the dominant privileged position in Syria among all European nations.

4. Everything must be done to soften (adoucir) the relations between the De Gaulle and French adherents in the meanwhile. We are all committed to Arab independence, but we think that France could aim at having in Syria after the war the same sort of position as we had established between the wars in Iraq.

[1] Oliver Lyttelton.

[2] Charles Huntziger. The senior French negotiator at the armistice talks at Rethondes and on the French Armistice Commission at Wiesbaden, June 1940. A member of the Vichy Government, as Minister of War, September 1940 to April 1942. In May 1941 he and Darlan negotiated with the Germans the Paris Protocols, whereby Vichy agreed to give assistance to the anti-British rebellion in Baghdad, and to facilitate German air, road and rail links through Syria to Iraq. In November 1941 he was killed in an aircraft while returning from an inspection in North Africa. At the time of the Briare meeting (11–12 June 1940), de Gaulle, as Under-Secretary for War, had been so impressed by Huntziger's coolness under attack by General Guderian's armoured corps that he had wanted him to replace Weygand as Commander-in-Chief, and had gone so far as to inform Huntziger of this.

5. Don't forget that when we win, as we shall, we shall not tolerate any separation of Alsace-Lorraine or of any French colony from France. So try your best to feel your way through the detestable difficulties by which we are both at present afflicted.

Oliver Harvey:[1] *diary*
(*'The War Diaries of Oliver Harvey'*)

9 July 1941

Cripps telegraphed last night to say he had seen Stalin (to whom he had delivered a personal message from PM), who had offered that we should conclude an agreement pledging ourselves (a) to mutual aid and (b) to no separate peace. Winston saw it last night and rang up AE at 2 a.m. to suggest that he came across and talk about it. AE was already in bed and the talk took place today. W already had an enthusiastic reply prepared expressing his personal approval and saying he had summoned the Cabinet tonight to consider it. AE insisted the PM shouldn't reply directly again, and himself produced a draft of acceptance. W is so impetuous though his instinct here was absolutely sound. There must be no hanging back with Russia, but it is after all for the Foreign Secretary to do these things. (A is having some difficulty with the PM who likes to take all the decisions and get all the credit!)

But what is important is not so much these paper undertakings but the action here which we can take to help the Russians. Here the PM is less helpful. The Navy are non-cooperative about operations in the North. The Air Force are doing a lot in the West. The Navy suffer from excessive caution as AE said today – they always want to be safe two moves ahead.

Winston S. Churchill to J. V. Stalin
(*Cabinet papers, 65/19*)

10 July 1941
1 a.m.

Ambassador Cripps having reported his talk with you and having stated the terms of a proposed Anglo-Russian agreed declaration under two heads, namely:

(1) Mutual help without any precision as to quantity or quality; and
(2) Neither country to conclude a separate peace,

I have immediately convened the War Cabinet, including Mr Fraser, Prime Minister of the Dominion of New Zealand, who is with us now. It will be necessary for us to consult with the Dominions of Canada, Australia and

[1] Eden's Principal Private Secretary.

South Africa, but in the meanwhile I should like to assure you that we are wholly in favour of the agreed declaration you propose. We think it should be signed as soon as we have heard from the Dominions and published to the world immediately thereafter.

Winston S. Churchill to Sir Stafford Cripps
(*Cabinet papers, 65/19*)

10 July 1941
1 a.m.

For your own information, what we have in mind is declaration in following terms:

'His Majesty's Government in the United Kingdom and the Government of the USSR have agreed and declare as follows:

'(1) The two Governments mutually undertake to render each other assistance of all kinds in the present war against Germany.

'(2) They further undertake that during this war they will neither negotiate nor conclude an armistice or treaty of peace except by mutual agreement.'

As Dominion Governments have to be consulted, you should not yet communicate actual text to Stalin. But it will help to show you what we mean and to give him any explanations he may require.

Winston S. Churchill to A.V. Alexander and Admiral Pound
(*Cabinet papers, 20/36*)

10 July 1941
Action this Day
Most Secret

It seems absolutely necessary to send a small mixed squadron of British ships to the Arctic to form contact and operate with the Russian naval forces. This should be done in advance of the particular Operation we have in hand. The effect upon the Russian Navy and upon the general resistance of the Russian Army of the arrival of what would be called a British fleet in the Arctic might be of enormous value and spare a lot of English blood.

The advantage we should reap if the Russians could keep the field and go on with the war, at any rate until the winter closes in is measureless. A premature peace by Russia would be a terrible disappointment to great masses of people in our country. As long as they go on, it does not matter so much where the front lies. These people have shown themselves worth backing and we must make sacrifices and take risks even at inconvenience, which I realize, to maintain their morale.

I do not see why the arrival and announced arrival of 'a British fleet in the Arctic' should necessarily be irreconcilable with the Operation you have in mind. The Squadron would no doubt go to Archangel and might well be so moved and handled so as to distract attention from the intended point of contact.

Pray let me know about this at your earliest.

War Cabinet: minutes
(*Cabinet papers, 65/19*)

10 July 1941 10 Downing Street
5 p.m.
Secret

The Prime Minister explained that the Air Ministry, who were responsible for the defence of certain aerodromes of lesser importance which had no troops stationed near them, had made appeals for volunteers, hoping to get men who were too young or too old for ordinary military service. He (the Prime Minister) had felt that it was undesirable to make public appeals for volunteers for aerodrome defence. This had led to the suggestion that the 18-year-old group might be called up, not for service on aerodromes, but in order to increase the number of men available for service in the Army generally. This, however, had only been put forward for consideration as one of the ways in which the shortage of men for the Army might be met. He proposed that the issues involved should be discussed at a special Meeting of Ministers to be presided over by the Lord President.[1] This was agreed.

War Cabinet, Defence Committee (Operations): minutes
(*Cabinet papers, 69/2*)

10 July 1941 Prime Minister's Room
6 p.m. House of Commons

The Prime Minister would send a telegram to Mr Hopkins explaining our need for more rifles and ammunition and urging the necessity for further supplies from America.[1]

The Prime Minister said that he would very much like to see a small Naval force operating with the Russians at Murmansk and he hoped that there would be no delay in making the preparations for sailing such a force when further information had been obtained.

[1] Sir John Anderson.
[2] This conclusion was underlined in the Defence Committee minutes.

Winston S. Churchill to General Ismay
(*Churchill papers, 20/36*)

10 July 1941

In future the expression 'landing' will be applied exclusively to landings from sea. All arrivals from the Air will be described as 'descents', and this terminology will rule throughout official correspondence.

Winston S. Churchill to General Sir Alan Brooke, and to General Ismay for the Chiefs of Staff Committee
(*Premier papers, 3/263/4*)

10 July 1941
Most Secret

PARACHUTE EXERCISE

1. It is said that the attack will be made at dawn. This cannot, however, imply that all the parachute and glider troops will arrive simultaneously at dawn. To move as many as 1,000 troop-carrying 'planes, or their equivalent, from French, Belgian and Dutch bases, would occupy several hours – at least four or five, i.e., almost all the present hours of darkness. Therefore, as the journey is short, they would either be arriving in instalments during the night (in which case zero hour would probably be 1 a.m.), or if the first ones arrived at dawn the rest would straggle out during the remaining hours of daylight. In the latter case, they would be cut to pieces by our Fighters. There can be no question of parachutists arriving in instalments by daylight. It is noticeable that the Germans have never yet tried these descents by night. There are very great difficulties in finding exact points in which to make low altitude descents at night.

The Air Staff must be consulted upon all these vital problems. It is no good starting staff exercises or studies of this kind involving so much dislocation, upon a basis which is unreal and could not possibly occur. It is quite easy to say '12,000 parachutists land at dawn. What would you do?' But this statement is meaningless without a detailed analysis of the movements which I have indicated.

2. A smaller scale attack might well be more dangerous. Five hundred desperadoes, coming out of the blue without the slightest preliminary indication, might descend by day, or at any rate in the half-light of dawn, at or near the centre of government. These, however, would first be picked up by the RDF, and would run serious risk of interception by night and almost certain destruction by day. Nevertheless, surprise has such sovereign virtues in war, that the proposition should be attentively examined. The centres of government and executive control should, at any rate, be made reasonably

secure against such a sudden rush of this kind if upon examination any probability can be attached to it. The first hour is the only hour that matters, and the first ten minutes are the minutes that matter most.

3. I shall be glad if Home Forces will consult with the Air Staff, and hack me out clear-cut answers to the above queries and suggestions. Two or three days should suffice for the study.

Winston S. Churchill to General Sir Alan Brooke, and to General Ismay for the Chiefs of Staff Committee
(*Churchill papers, 20/36*)

10 July 1941

How do we stand at present on the strategic and tactical camouflaging of defences against enemy attacks on airfields? What body is studying the lessons of Maleme and the batteries thereabouts?

Obviously action proceeds on two lines, viz.:

(a) The concealment of the real guns and deceitful presentation of the dummy guns. There might well be two or three dummy guns, or even more, for every real gun.
(b) The best of all camouflage is a confusing variety of positions made in which no one can tell the real from the sham.

The tactics of holding fire from particular batteries during the early phases of an attack are no doubt also being studied.

Pray let me have a report by Saturday next.

Winston S. Churchill to Anthony Eden
(*Churchill papers, 20/36*)

10 July 1941
Most Secret

I think you should be pretty stiff with the Finns. They cannot march with the Germans and expect to have any conveniences from the sea or any immunity for their ships. It is no use their putting up some democratic Tanner[1] camouflage, and doing their dirty work behind it.

The least we ask of them is that they should lie down and keep quiet.

[1] Väinö Tanner became Foreign Minister of Finland on the outbreak of the Russo-Finnish war in November 1939. He was denounced by Molotov as the 'evil genius' of the earlier Soviet-Finnish negotiations, whose emergence as Foreign Minister left 'little hope for an understanding' (*Pravda*). In March 1940 he helped to negotiate a peace treaty with Moscow, under which considerable tracts of Finnish territory, occupied by Soviet troops, were ceded to the Soviet Union (and were still part of the Russian Federation in 1999). Tanner was then replaced as Foreign Minister. He had earlier (11 December 1926 to 18 December 1927) been Prime Minister of Finland.

Winston S. Churchill: Note[1]
(*Premier papers, 3/283*)

11 July 1941
Most Secret

REPORT ON THE ACTION OF THE 2ND ARMOURED DIVISION

This report must be read in its setting. It was never contemplated in London that the dispatch of an army to Greece should lead to a dangerous weakening of the Cyrenaican frontier. The minimum force necessary to hold the Province was to be left there, and in addition Benghazi was to be made a strong naval and air base (Prime Minister's instructions to Mr Eden, paragraph 4 (a), dated February 12, 1941). The main object of the advance to the western frontier of Cyrenaica and the holding of Benghazi was to secure a strong flank for the protection of the Nile Valley and the invaluable aerodromes situated in Cyrenaica.

2. One Brigade Group of the 2nd Armoured Division was sent to Greece. The 7th Armoured Division went back to the workshops in Cairo to refit. It was never reported that this refit of vehicles, instead of taking four or five weeks, would, in fact, take four or five months. Thus the armoured force left to hold the vital flank in Cyrenaica was inevitably reduced to the following formations and units of the 2nd Armoured Division:

3rd Armoured Brigade:
3rd Hussars (Light Tanks)
6th Royal Tank Regiment (re-equipping with Italian tanks).
The Support Group.
The KDG's (Armoured Cars).

To this was added later the 5th Royal Tank Regiment (48 Cruiser Tanks). The deficiencies of this force in transport and the condition of their vehicles are fully set out in the report. (See also General Wavell's addenda to paragraph 6 (black line). No intimation of these weaknesses was made to His Majesty's Government, who were entitled to suppose, in view of the telegrams above cited, that a sufficient armoured force, properly equipped and well-supported by air, had been left to guard the Western flank.

3. Paragraph 8 states that 'the original task of the 2nd Armoured Division was to prevent the enemy occupying El Agheila'. For this purpose the line of the marshes well to the west of the town was the indispensable position. This, it is stated, could not be held for lack of transport. An addition of say 500 lorries would have been sufficient for this, and it seems extraordinary that the whole of this number should not have been supplied at a time when no fewer than 8,800 lorries were being embarked for Greece. For, what were the

[1] Printed as War Cabinet Paper No. 159 of 1941.

consequences foreseen and foreseeable. They were that all intention of holding El Agheila or Marada had to be abandoned and (paragraph 8) 'If the enemy were to advance, a delaying action would be fought in the area of Mersa Brega; and if a serious attack developed *the plan was to withdraw*.'[1] But since withdrawal from El Agheila, and thereafter from Mersa Brega, opened the doors of Cyrenaica to the enemy, entailed the loss of Benghazi and rendered immediately untenable the position of the Australian Division, it is evident that a disaster of major consequence was certain to occur if the enemy advanced in any serious strength. While, therefore, His Majesty's Government were left under the impression that adequate arrangements had been made to hold the essential positions guarding Cyrenaica, the Commander-in-Chief, Middle East, and the General Commanding in Cyrenaica were resigned to disaster should the enemy press hard.

4. It is often necessary in war to make woeful sacrifices in one part of the theatre in order to act in strength in another. But it was certainly wrong in the actual situation on the Cyrenaican frontier to proceed on the basis of withdrawal with all its consequences in the face of attack without making this clear to His Majesty's Government beforehand.

5. Upon the tactical story of the fighting, a few comments may be made:

(a) There is an imperative need for every armoured formation to have attached to it, and working with it, aircraft whose pilots and observers have been for some time in intimate association with the armoured unit, and who have the military knowledge and experience necessary to enable them to report as correctly as possible, in all the difficulties of war, what they see. The General commanding an armoured division should have his own aircraft, however few, attached to him, as much an integral part of his Command as his own divisional communication car.

(b) Attention is drawn to the confusing and unhelpful nomenclature and organization of our armoured units. It is unreasonable and misleading to speak of a unit as an 'armoured division', when in fact it is only an armoured brigade with a support group or some extra details. The expressions '2nd Armoured Division, less one Brigade', there being only two, which occur here as they do later with the 7th Division at Sollum, alone convict the system.

(c) Several important instances are given of the effective use of motorized artillery against hostile Tanks, and it would seem that a larger proportion of artillery should be used with every armoured brigade group and work with them in all circumstances. No fear of losing guns in this kind of warfare should prevent their going about with the Tanks. No Armoured Force should grieve too much about losing some of their

[1] This phrase was italicized in the Note as printed and circulated to the War Cabinet.

guns if they have previously knocked out a number of enemy tanks with them.

(d) It is difficult to base a defensive on armoured forces. It should rather be the aim to employ large armoured formations on the offensive, to keep them concentrated as far as possible for that purpose, to contrive places and opportunities for them to achieve the highest manipulation of their power. The Tank formation is a weapon little concerned with the lines or flanks of its own troops. Its supreme function lies in its impact and progression. Aided by good fortune, as General von Rommel[1] should have taught us, it makes the events by which it lives and thrives.

6. The whole of this account shows how well and faithfully the troops of all units acquitted themselves in the midst of so much order, counter-order and disorder.

Winston S. Churchill to Viscount Halifax
(*Premier papers, 4/69/1*)

11 July 1941
Personal and Private

Glad if you can bring home with you two of the best smallest size wireless sets with plenty of batteries. Treasury agree they may be bought from official funds as I need them for my work.

Winston S. Churchill to Colonel Jacob
(*Churchill papers, 20/36*)

11 July 1941
Action this Day
Secret

Let me have a full statement on one sheet of paper of the present position about Poison Gas, both output and stocks.

[1] Erwin Rommel, 1891–1944. Entered the German army, 1910. On active service in the First World War in France, Italy and Roumania; awarded Germany's highest decoration for bravery, *Pour le Mérite*, at the Battle of Caporetto, 1917. Colonel, commanding Hitler's Headquarters Guard, 1939–40. France, February–June 1940. Commanded the Afrika Korps, February 1941-March 1943. Inspector of Coastal Defences, 1944, with responsibility for preparing France against an Allied assault; wounded by an Allied attack, 17 July 1944 (three days before the anti-Hitler bomb plot). Under suspicion of implication in the bomb plot, he accepted the option of suicide and was given a state funeral.

Winston S. Churchill to David Margesson and Lord Beaverbrook
(*Churchill papers, 20/36*)

11 July 1941

Out of 1,441 Infantry and Cruiser Tanks with the troops, 391 are 'unfit for action'. This is far too high, and I am sure it is capable of reduction if something like the arrangements for repair introduced into the Air Force last year could be provided.

Will you please consult together and make me a proposal for the more prompt handling of these repairs. The number of Tanks out of action ought never to exceed 10 per cent. of those in this country. More especially is this the case in view of the period of maximum preparedness which is now approaching.

Winston S. Churchill to Sir Archibald Sinclair
(*Churchill papers, 20/36*)

11 July 1941

Although radio beam bombing was neutralized last winter by our interference, it seems that the enemy is re-equipping his whole bomber force with improved radio receivers, and hopes to overwhelm our counter-measures next winter by the multiplicity of his beam stations.

No radio methods can of course prevent his finding and bombing targets like Coventry and Birmingham on fine moonlight nights. But it is on these that our normal night defence should be most effective. It is the dark cloudy nights that will be our main danger, and we should make every preparation to deal with the enemy beams whose positions and wave-lengths we now know.

I am informed that the equipment needed is not very remote from that used in ordinary commercial practice, so that it should be possible to obtain it from America even if it cannot be manufactured here. Everything should be ready by the Autumn. Pray let me know what the position is and what measures are in hand to counter enemy developments.

Winston S. Churchill to Lord Cherwell
(*Churchill papers, 20/36*)

11 July 1941
Action this Day

Please bring to luncheon here (Chartwell) tomorrow at 1.30 p.m. all those figures relative to our aircraft programme. I have asked MAP[1] either to make the return or to help you to make one on the following lines:-

Aircraft and engine to have an agreed man-hours figure attached to it, e.g., a Stirling takes, say, 75,000 man-hours, but I suppose a training machine only 5,000 man-hours. There is very little use jumbling them all together. We want to reduce them to man-hour terms, which will give a line of figures[2] showing the actual expenses of the industry between now and the end of next June.

It might be a help if you talked it over with MAP this afternoon. I have spoken to the Minister about it. Then you would perhaps be in a position to tell me, in outline at any rate, what the prospects are.

Winston S. Churchill to General Sikorski
(*Churchill papers, 20/22*)

11 July 1941

My dear General Sikorski,

I wish to thank you most warmly for your letter of July 5, enclosing the sum of £1550.1.11 to be used for the restoration of the Guildhall.

I value more than I can say this further gift from the Poles in Great Britain for an object which commands the sympathies of the British peoples throughout the world.

I have sent your cheque to the Lord Mayor, and I am sure that he and the citizens of London will share my feelings of gratitude. Our children will remember in the future that our ancient Guildhall when rebuilt will through this gift commemorate our alliance with the valiant Polish nation whose sons have shared our perils and will be with us in our victory.

Yours very sincerely,
Winston S. Churchill

[1] Minister of Aircraft Production.
[2] Churchill noted in the margin: 'I prefer a line of figures to a graph'.

On 12 July 1941, in Moscow, the Anglo-Soviet Agreement was signed, pledging mutual assistance between Britain and the Soviet Union, and no separate peace with Germany. That day, the Vichy forces in Syria surrendered, and an armistice was signed at Acre.

Winston S. Churchill to Oliver Lyttelton
(*Churchill papers, 20/40*)

12 July 1941
Personal and Secret

Your Minister of Propaganda must confine himself exclusively to propaganda in the Middle East. There must be no intrusion upon propaganda outside your sphere, whether in foreign countries or at home. We alone must deal with British public opinion. We suffered inconveniences last week from the Wavell-Auchinleck interviews. On the other hand, Cairo should be the centre of all propaganda addressed to the Arab world, the Palestinian Jews, the Egyptians and Abyssinians. For this you surely want someone who knows something about the East. I still think Hubert Young, now Governor of Trinidad, is the best of those mentioned. I know him personally quite well, and can vouch for his ability. He is deeply versed in Eastern problems, and was with me when the Middle East Department was founded, and also at Cairo. He is a most agreeable personality, and would command respect in Cairo.

Winston S. Churchill to Air Chief Marshal Sir Charles Portal
(*Churchill papers, 20/36*)

12 July 1941
Action this Day
Secret

1. I am afraid I cannot possibly agree with the statement in your minute that 90 Blenheims must be kept idle at Takoradi as an additional and intermediate reserve in your supply of Blenheims for the Middle East. There is a reserve here, there is to be another large reserve at Takoradi, and no doubt finally a third reserve in the Middle East. And this at a time of increasing stringency.

2. I cannot believe that this situation at Takoradi has arisen out of policy. It has come simply because of the inadequate arrangements for passing the Blenheims on. It would be far better to get them to the Middle East as quickly as possible.

3. No more Blenheims are to go to Takoradi, apart from those now actually loaded or loading, until the capacity for passing them on from Takoradi has reached 60 a month, and the total number at Takoradi has been reduced from 90 to 50.

Winston S. Churchill to Air Chief Marshal Sir Charles Portal
(*Churchill papers, 20/36*)

12 July 1941

GAP BETWEEN AIRCREWS AND SERVICEABLE AIRCRAFT

I am not at all sure about this. It seems to me that every man ought to have his horse, even if he is not going to ride it on any particular day. Should an emergency come, the full strength of the force will be mounted. I find a difficulty in reconciling the various arguments of the Air Ministry. We are now told that the shortage is to be in machines rather than in pilots. Have these calculations been made on the basis of 16 machines to 26 or 28 pilots? If so, it is difficult to believe in an impending shortage of machines. When the squadron goes into action, or there is Air fighting on a large scale, many more pilots are saved than machines – especially over this country. I can readily believe that a Squadron Leader would like to have a large surplus of pilots on hand in his squadron, but this might easily be explained by a less strenuous effort. What you are doing is developing a principle of spare crews for airplanes, or the half-timer system for personnel. There must be a limit to progression along this road. It is a very odd tendency, especially in relation to emergency. Apart from squadron convenience, there is the public point of view. In order to keep twelve machines fighting you require sixteen or twenty machines with the squadron and 28 pilots. This, apart from all reserves behind. We shall very soon reach the position at this rate where a squadron is a unit which never fights at more than half its effective strength. We are tending to an ever-smaller front-line ratio to the men and machines involved.

Winston S. Churchill to Lord Woolton
(*Churchill papers, 20/36*)

12 July 1941

I am pleased to learn that the amount of food 'requisitioned' in USA is now far above the figure quoted in your May Report. I understand that the programme of our full requirements is much higher than the amount 'requisitioned' so far. I am sure that, given sufficient warning, America can and will produce or in some way provide a very large quantity of the foodstuffs we need so badly. If we can import them on the short haul, shipping for almost all we require should be available.

The only point in doubt is whether you have asked for sufficient pork. America would find it difficult to provide us with beef or mutton, but pork supplies can be rapidly expanded, and if necessary imported in non-refrigerated tonnage.

Winston S. Churchill: Minute[1]

(*Churchill papers, 20/36*)

12 July 1941

1. I was deeply concerned at the new programmes of MAP, which show a static condition for the next twelve or eighteen months in numbers of aircraft. No doubt new production would be bent on in the later phase. I asked that these figures should be subjected to the test of man-hours involved in each type of machine. This certainly shows an improvement of about 50 per cent. in the British field by the twelfth month from now. The American figures improve the calculation both from the number of aircraft and the man-hours standpoint, and one might say that the output for July 1942 would be to the present output as 1 to 1.75.

2. I cannot feel that this is enough. Our estimate of German monthly production by numbers is 2,100, which is the numerical level at which we stand up till July 1942, and indeed thereafter, apart from new projects. We must assume that the Germans also would derive comfort from translating their numbers of aircraft into the man-hours. They may or they may not be making a similar expansion in size and quality. Broadly, from the figures put before me, the impression would be one of equality for the next twelve months, so far as British and German construction is concerned, leaving any increase to be supplied by our share of United States production. Moreover, this takes no count of MAP's caveat that their estimates may be reduced by 15 per cent.

3. We cannot be content with the above situation, which excludes all possibility of decisive predominance indispensable for victory. I wish, therefore, these programmes to be re-examined, and the following three methods of expansion, together with any others suggested, to be explored by the highest authorities concerned. The three methods are:

(a) An improvement in the existing figures by speeding up and working the machine-tools longer, or by any other measures taken in the sphere of MAP production.

[1] Churchill circulated this Minute (Prime Minister's Personal Minute M.733/1) to the Ministry of Aircraft Production, Sir Charles Craven, Sir Archibald Sinclair, Air Chief Marshal Sir Charles Portal, General Ismay ('to implement or report progress in one week') and Lord Cherwell.

(b) By the construction of new factories and assembling plants, or by the reoccupation or full occupation of plants vacated for the sake of dispersion. This may well be justified in view of our increasing command of the British air by day and the improvement in night-fighting devices.

(c) By a reclassification of the Bomber programme so as to secure a larger delivery from well-tried types in that period. Fighter aircraft must continually strive for mastery, and rapid changes of design may be imperative. But a large proportion of the Bomber Force will in the next twelve months be employed under steady conditions and within ranges which are moderate. While all Bombers required for long-distance or great heights or daylight action must be the subject of intensive improvement, a large proportion of the Bombing Force will be carrying their nightly load to (say) the Ruhr or other nearby targets. It would seem that the Air Staff could divide their activities into near and far, and that on this basis some good lines of production, which have not yet reached their maximum, could be given a longer run at the peak, with very definite addition to numbers. This would, for instance, seem to apply to the Blackpool Wellington, which is a new supply, reaching its peak in November, but only running for six months at that level. If it were allowed a twelve months' run at the peak, it may be that a larger delivery would be possible from November on.

4. The criterion of Bomber strength is the weight of bombs deliverable per month on the reasonably foreseeable targets in Germany and Italy. Have the Air Staff plans been applied to the figures of production with this end in view? It may be that a heavier load carried by a new machine would give better results. But a machine which is good enough to carry 2 tons to the Ruhr ought to have a long run in continuous production before it is discarded. There are no doubt other instances. I have asked MAP to review their programmes accordingly, having regard to the grievous loss on too hasty change-overs.

5. The new programme is substantially less than the March figures and far below the October figures. However, many materials have been accumulated on the October basis. A substantial expansion should therefore be possible if all factors are fitted to the optimum. The Air Ministry should show how this latest programme, apart from any expansion, fits in with their pilot production for the next twelve months, having regard, on the one hand, to the reduced scale of losses which has been found operative by experience, and, on the other, to the much more lavish pilot establishment now said to be necessary in proportion to machines. Bombs, explosives, guns and all accessories must be measured in relation both to the existing programme and the necessary expansion. In principle, however, we must aim at nothing less than having an Air Force twice as strong as the German Air Force by the end of 1942. This ought not to be impossible if a renewed vast effort is made now. It is the very

least that can be contemplated, since no other way of winning the war has yet been proposed.

Winston S. Churchill to Ernest Bevin
(*Churchill papers, 20/22*)

13 July 1941
Secret

My dear Bevin,

I do not think you ought to underrate the amount of solid opinion that has gathered against what is thought to be the reluctance of the Ministry of Labour to use any serious pressure against workpeople who fail in their duty. This feeling found repeated expression in the recent Debates on Production. Undoubtedly, many people are vexed by your speeches, in which the blame is always thrown upon the employers.

I should have thought that de-reservation was an obvious and indispensable remedy at the present time. I had myself to use it in the last war in the case of the Coventry Strike, and the mere declaration proved effective. No country engaged in a war like this for life has ever allowed men to escape military service because they are needed in industry, when they are found to be shirking their duty in industry.

The point you make about the Services not wishing to 'find room for industrial delinquents' is wholly inadmissible. Considering they are all short of men, there is no question of finding room.

I do not know whether you would care to discuss the matter point by point with Sir John Wardlaw-Milne. I regret to see he made an attack upon you in the House. As, however, it was couched in moderate terms and contained no personal reproaches, I do not see why that should be an obstacle. The Committee will certainly go ahead with their report, and its publication will be injurious from many points of view.

Apart from this, I feel the issues raised must be discussed in the War Cabinet sitting alone. Perhaps, therefore, you will circulate Wardlaw-Milne's letters and your letters to me, confining circulation to our colleagues alone. Sir Edward Bridges will of course make the circulation at your request. I can do so if you wish, but it seems to me it would better come from you.

I am very loth to do anything that would arouse acute political controversy, but it would be our duty not to flinch from it in a matter which touches so nearly the life of the State.

Yours very sincerely,
Winston S. Churchill

Winston S. Churchill: Minute[1]
(*Churchill papers, 20/36*)

13 July 1941
Action this Day

How are you getting on with torpedo supplies? I am told the monthly output for the coming year only just balances expenditure, leaving nothing for the outfits of new ships. Our stocks of 21-inch seem fairly good, but those of 18-inch leave very little margin. This is particularly serious in view of the increasing use of this weapon by the RAF and FAA.[2] Please report on one sheet!

Winston S. Churchill to Air Chief Marshal Sir Charles Portal
(*Churchill papers, 20/36*)

13 July 1941
Action this Day

I did not understand that the Fighter Command meant to have another Sunday holiday today, and I am assured *roulement* would be instituted to enable squadrons which had not yet been engaged to take part in the offensive. In view of the struggle on the Russian front, it is inadmissible that our effort should stop like this. Out of 90 squadrons, less than 30 seem to me to have been engaged. Even a reduced effort would have been better than complete cessation.

Winston S. Churchill to General Maitland Wilson
(*Churchill papers, 20/41*)

14 July 1941

Hearty congratulations on the skill and tenacity with which you and your troops have conducted this difficult, obstinate Syrian campaign, and have brought it to a highly satisfactory conclusion. We greatly admired here at home your extrication of the British and Empire forces from Greece, and now in Syria you have accomplished an operation of equal complexity with a happier ending. Please convey to all ranks the thanks and appreciation of His Majesty's Government.

[1] Churchill addressed this Minute to the First Lord (A.V. Alexander), the First Sea Lord (Admiral of the Fleet Sir Dudley Pound), and the Controller (Rear-Admiral Bruce Fraser).
[2] Fleet Air Arm.

Winston S. Churchill to General Sikorski
(*Churchill papers, 20/22*)

14 July 1941

My dear General,

The Foreign Secretary has told me of the negotiations which are taking place between yourself and the Soviet Ambassador[1] with the object of reaching an agreement between your two Governments.

I know your difficulties and I greatly appreciate the efforts which you are making to bring about agreement. I hope that you will be successful. A Polish-Soviet understanding is of immense and urgent importance to the common cause.

Yours v sincerely,
Winston S. Churchill

Winston S. Churchill: speech
(*'The Unrelenting Struggle', pages 187–192*)

14 July 1941 Hyde Park
11.30 a.m.

Members of the Civil Defence Forces, it is a good thing that today we should assemble here representatives of the vast army which conducts the civil defence of London, and which is itself typical of all those similar forces which have been called into being and have acquitted themselves with distinction in every city, in every town, and in every village of our land.

I see before me an array of men and women who have just come out of one long, hard battle and may at any moment enter upon another. The defence of London last winter against Hitler's act of terror showed decisively that the assault upon our lives and homes, launched indiscriminately upon men, women, and children, military and civil, old and young alike, failed utterly in its purpose of breaking the British spirit.

The defence of London, in which you bore your part, was the counterpart of the defeat of the German air force by our fighters a few weeks earlier in the Battle of Britain. These two events, which were imitated and rivalled in every part of the country, showed that the weapon of indiscriminate air attack upon

[1] Ivan Mikhailovich Maisky, 1884–1975. Born in Omsk, the son of a Jewish doctor and a non-Jewish mother. A Menshevik, he was exiled by the Tsarist regime in Siberia, but escaped to Germany, and took a degree in economics at Munich University. Lived in London, 1912–17. Returned to Russia during the revolution. Became a Bolshevik, 1922. Counsellor at the Soviet Embassy in London, 1925–7. Soviet Ambassador to Britain, 1932–43. A Deputy Foreign Minister, 1943–5. Soviet member of the Reparations Committee, 1945–8. Arrested during one of Stalin's anti-Jewish purges, 1949. Imprisoned, 1949–53. Released from prison, 1953. Worked at the Soviet Academy of Sciences from 1957 until his death, writing his memoirs, and preparing various historical studies.

these Islands, which had produced such frightful consequences at Warsaw and Rotterdam, could not prevail against British tenacity and resolution.

In this war, so terrible in many aspects and yet so inspiring, men and women who have never thought about fighting or being involved in fighting before have been proud to emulate the courage of the bravest regiments of His Majesty's armies, and proud to find that, under the fire of the enemy, they could comport themselves with discipline and with composure. It is that quality, universally spread among our people, which gives us the foundation from which we shall prosecute to the end this righteous war for the freedom and future of mankind.

We shall not turn from our purpose, but we can only achieve that purpose if we have behind us a nation sound at the core and in every fibre. For the moment there is a lull, but we must expect that before long the enemy will renew his attacks upon us. It is true that some of his forces are away attacking the lives and rights of another vast branch of the human family; but he still has very large forces close at hand, and if he has not come recently to London it is certainly not because he likes us better.

The courage of Londoners, and the organization of our many defence and municipal services under unexampled strain, not only enabled us to come through what many might have thought a mortal peril, but impressed itself in every country, upon the minds of every country in the world, and gained us scores of millions of friends in the United States. I do not hesitate to say that the enormous advance in United States opinion towards making their contribution to British resistance thoroughly effective has been largely influenced by the conduct of Londoners and of the men and women in our provincial cities in standing up to the enemy's bombardments.

We must certainly prepare ourselves to receive other visits in the future. We shall be ready. We shall be more ready than we have ever been before, but whether the enemy comes again here or not will not alter our course of action. We are now bombing him at a heavier rate in discharge of tons of bombs than he has in any monthly period bombed us.

This is only a beginning. We shall continue the process, and upon a growing scale, month after month, until at last we have beaten down this horrible tyranny which has reared itself against our life and against the honour of every free people in the world. Therefore it is of the utmost consequence that you should regard yourselves as constantly in action, that every preparation should be brought to an even higher pitch of efficiency, and that the utmost vigilance should be maintained in all formations.

It has given me great pleasure to see you here this beautiful summer morning, and to thank you in the name of His Majesty's Government not only for the memorable services you have rendered in the past but for the spirit which will enable you to confront and overcome whatever menaces the future may contain.

Winston S. Churchill: speech[1]
(*BBC Written Archives Centre*)

14 July 1941
Noon

County Hall,
London

It seems to be odd that it should have taken the stress of a great world war to bring me for the first time to the County Hall, and I am very glad indeed to find that by the time the call came the hall had not already ceased to exist. You have taken in this building some of the blows and scars which have fallen upon London, but like the rest of London you carry on.

The impressive and inspiring spectacle we have witnessed in Hyde Park this morning displays the vigour and efficiency of the civil defence forces of London. They have grown up in the stress of emergency. They have been shaped and tempered by the fire of the enemy, and this morning we saw them all, in their many grades and classes – the wardens, the rescue and first-aid parties, the casualty services, the decontamination squads, the fire services, the report and control centre staffs, the highways and public utility services, the messengers, the police. All these we have seen on a lovely English summer morning, marching past, men and women in all the pomp and panoply – not of war, though it is war – but of their civic duties. There they marched, and as one saw them passing by no one could but feel how great a people, how great a nation we have the honour to belong to.

How complex, sensitive, resilient, is the society we have evolved over centuries, and how capable of withstanding the most unexpected strain! Those whom we saw this morning were the representatives of nearly a quarter of a million organized functionaries and servants in the defence of London, who, in one way or another, stand to their posts or take an active part in the maintenance of the life of London and Greater London against an attack which, when it began and while it was at its pitch, was unexampled in history.

And what we saw today in Hyde Park was only symbolic of what can be produced, though on a smaller scale, throughout the length and breadth of this country – a competent and embattled Island.

In September last, having been defeated in his invasion plans by the RAF, Hitler declared his intention to raze the cities of Britain to the ground, and in the early days of that month he set the whole fury of the Hun upon London.

None of us quite knew what would be the result of a concentrated and prolonged bombardment of this vast centre of population. Here in the Thames Valley, over 8,000,000 people are maintained at a very high level of modern civilization. They are dependent from day to day upon light, heat, power, water sewerage, and communications on the most complicated scale.

[1] This speech was broadcast live on the BBC.

The administration of London in all its branches was confronted with problems hitherto unknown and unmeasured in all the history of the past. Public order, public health, the maintenance of all the essential services, the handling of the millions of people who came in and out of London every day; the shelter – not indeed from the enemy's bombs, for that was beyond us, but from their blast and splinters – the shelter of millions of men and women, and the removal of the dead and wounded from the shattered buildings; the care of the wounded when hospitals were being ruthlessly bombed, and the provision for the homeless – sometimes amounting to many thousands in a single day, and accumulating to many more after three or four days of successive attacks – all these things, with the welfare and the education amid these scenes of our great numbers of children here – all these presented tasks which, viewed in cold blood beforehand, might well have seemed overwhelming.

Indeed, before the war, when the imagination painted pictures of what might happen in the great air raids on our cities, plans were made to move the Government, to move all the great controlling services which are centred in London, and disperse them about the countryside, and also it was always considered a very great danger that a sudden wave of panic might send millions of people crowding out into the countryside along all the roads.

Well, when you are doing your duty and you are sure of that, you need not worry too much about the dangers or the consequences. We have not been moved in this war except by the promptings of duty and conscience, and therefore we do not need to be deterred from action by pictures which our imagination or careful forethought painted of what the consequences would be.

I must, however, admit that when the storm broke in September, I was for several weeks very anxious about the result. We were then not prepared as we are now. Our defences had not the advantages they have since attained, and again I must admit that I greatly feared injury to our public services, I feared the ravages of fire, I feared the dislocation of life and the stoppage of work, I feared epidemics of serious disease or even pestilence among the crowds who took refuge in our by no means completely constructed or well equipped shelters.

I remember one winter evening travelling to a railway station – which still worked – on my way north to visit troops. It was cold and raining. Darkness had almost fallen on the blacked-out streets. I saw everywhere long queues of people, among them hundreds of young girls in their silk stockings and high-heeled shoes, who had worked hard all day and were waiting for bus after bus, which came by already overcrowded, in the hope of reaching their homes for the night. When at that moment the doleful wail of the siren betokened the approach of the German bombers, I confess to you that my heart bled for London and the Londoners.

All this sort of thing went on for more than four months with hardly any intermission. I used to hold meetings of my Ministerial colleagues and members of the authorities concerned every week in Downing Street in order to check up and see how we stood. Sometimes the gas had failed over large areas – the only means of cooking for great numbers of people; sometimes the electricity. There were grievous complaints about the shelters and about conditions in them. Water was cut off, railways were cut or broken, large districts were destroyed by fire, 20,000 people were killed, and many more thousands were wounded.

But there was one thing about which there was never any doubt. The courage, the unconquerable grit and stamina of the Londoners showed itself from the very outset. Without that all would have failed. Upon that rock, all stood unshakable. All the public services were carried on, and all the intricate arrangements, far-reaching details, involving the daily lives of so many millions, were carried out, improvised, elaborated, and perfected in the very teeth of the cruel and devastating storm.

I am very glad to come here today to pay my tribute and to record in the name of the Government our gratitude to all the civil authorities of London who, first under Sir John Anderson, and through the darkest moments under the courageous and resourceful leadership of Mr Herbert Morrison – so long master of the London County Council, and now acting in an even higher sphere – to all who carried out their duties faithfully, skilfully, and devotedly, so that at last we made our way through the tempest, and came for the time being, at any rate, into a calm spell.

During her long ordeal London was upheld by the sympathy and admiration of the other great cities of our Island – and let us not forget here loyal Belfast, in Northern Ireland – and when after the enemy wearied of his attack upon the capital and turned to other parts of the country, many of us in our hearts felt anxiety lest the weight of attack concentrated on those smaller organisms should prove more effective than when directed on London, which is so vast and strong that she is like a prehistoric monster into whose armoured hide showers of arrows can be shot in vain. But in the event, the staunchness and vigour of London were fully matched by the splendid behaviour of our ports and cities when they in turn received the full violence and frightful cruelty of the enemy's assault; and I say here that, while we are entitled to speak particularly of London, we honour them for their constancy and a comradeship of suffering, of endurance, and of triumph. That comradeship in this hideous, unprecedented, novel pressure has united us all, and it has proved to the world the quality of our Island life.

I have no doubt whatever, as I said to the civil defence forces in Hyde Park this morning, that the behaviour of the British people in this trial gained them conquests in the mind and spirit and sympathy of the United States of America which swept into an ignominious corner all the vilest strokes of Goebbels' propaganda.

We have to ask ourselves this question: Will the bombing attacks of last autumn and winter come back again? We have proceeded on the assumption that they will. Some months ago I requested the Home Secretary and Minister of Home Security and his principal colleagues, the Minister of Health and others, to make every preparation for the autumn and winter war as if we should have to go through the same ordeal as last year, only rather worse. I am sure that everything is being done in accordance with those directions. The shelters are being strengthened, improved, lighted and warmed. All arrangements for fire-control and fire-watching are being perpetually improved.

Many new arrangements are being contrived as a result of the hard experience through which we have passed and the many mistakes which no doubt we have made – for success is the result of making many mistakes and learning from experience. If the lull is to end, if the storm is to renew itself, London will be ready, London will not flinch, London can take it again.

We ask no favours of the enemy. We seek from them no compunction. On the contrary, if tonight the people of London were asked to cast their vote whether a convention should be entered into to stop the bombing of all cities, the overwhelming majority would cry, 'No, we will mete out to the Germans the measure, and more than the measure, that they have meted out to us'. The people of London with one voice would say to Hitler: 'You have committed every crime under the sun. Where you have been the least resisted there you have been the most brutal. It was you who began the indiscriminate bombing. We remember Warsaw in the very first few days of the war. We remember Rotterdam. We have been newly reminded of your habits by the hideous massacre of Belgrade. We know too well the bestial assault you are making upon the Russian people, to whom our hearts go out in their valiant struggle. We will have no truce or parley with you, or the grisly gang who work your wicked will. You do your worst – and we will do our best.' Perhaps it may be our turn soon: perhaps it may be our turn now.

We live in a terrible epoch of the human story, but we believe there is a broad and sure justice running through its theme. It is time that the Germans should be made to suffer in their own homeland and cities something of the torment they have twice in our lifetime let loose upon their neighbours and upon the world.

We have now intensified for a month past our systematic, scientific, methodical bombing on a large scale of the German cities, seaports, industries, and other military objectives. We believe it to be in our power to keep this process going, on a steadily rising tide, month after month, year after year, until the Nazi regime is either extirpated by us or, better still, torn to pieces by the German people themselves.

Every month as the great bombers are finished in our factories or sweep hither across the Atlantic Ocean we shall continue the remorseless discharge of high explosives on Germany. Every month will see the tonnage increase, and, as the nights lengthen and the range of our bombers also grows, that unhappy, abject, subject province of Germany which used to be called Italy will have its fair share too.

In the last few weeks alone we have thrown upon Germany about half the tonnage of bombs thrown by the Germans upon our cities during the whole course of the war. But this is only the beginning, and we hope by next July to multiply our deliveries manifold.

It is for this reason that I must ask you to be prepared for vehement counter-action by the enemy. Our methods of dealing with the German night raiders have steadily improved. They no longer relish their trips to our shores. It is not true to say they did not come this last moon because they were all engaged in Russia. They have a bombing force in the West quite capable of making very heavy attacks. I do not know why they did not come, but, as I mentioned in Hyde Park, it is certainly not because they have begun to love us more. It may be because they are saving up, but even if that be so, the very fact that they have to save up should give us confidence by revealing the truth of our steady advance from an almost unarmed position to a position at least of equality, and soon of superiority to them in the air.

But all engaged in our civil defence forces, whether in London or throughout the country, must prepare themselves for further heavy assaults. Your organization, your vigilance, your devotion to duty, your zeal for the cause must be raised to the highest intensity.

We do not expect to hit without being hit back, and we intend with every week that passes to hit harder. Prepare yourselves, then, my friends and comrades in the Battle of London, for this renewal of your exertions. We shall never turn from our purpose, however sombre the road, however grievous the cost, because we know that out of this time of trial and tribulation will be born a new freedom and glory for all mankind.

Winston S. Churchill: statement

(*Hansard*)

15 July 1941 House of Commons

BUSINESS OF THE HOUSE

(PRODUCTION DEBATE)

The Prime Minister (Mr Churchill): I have a few words to say about the Business of the House. I am somewhat concerned at the effects produced abroad and overseas by the two days' Debate on Production. Statements that our industry is only working 75 per cent. of some unspecified standard and that the Ministry of Aircraft Production is in chaos from top to bottom tend to give a general impression in the United States and the Dominions, particularly

Australia, that things are being very ill-managed here and that we are not trying our best. It is impossible for the newspapers to report our Debates except in a very abridged form, but sensational statements of this kind telegraphed all over the world do serious harm to our cause wherever they go. Moreover, they do not at all represent the immense and well-directed effort which is yielding remarkable results in almost every field of war production, and they do far from justice to the admirable tenure of the Ministry of Supply by my right hon. Friend the present President of the Board of Trade.[1]

I much regret that it was not possible for me, because of the many other things I have to do, to be present in the House except during the closing speeches of that Debate. It is obviously not possible for considered Ministerial answers to be submitted to these charges on the spur of the moment. It is not like ordinary party, peace-time fighting, when any score handed across the Table is good enough for the purposes of the occasion. These are very serious times in which we live. I have, however, read thoroughly the Official Report of the two days' Debate, and I have given directions that all allegations of any serious substance shall be sent to the various Departments concerned in order that the facts may be ascertained. On the Third Sitting Day after 20th July I propose to set up the same Votes as were under discussion last week and to have a third day's Debate, in Public Session. I will myself endeavour to make a full and comprehensive statement on the whole question of production so far as the public interest permits. I hope by this means, which is inspired by the greatest possible respect for the House, to remove any mistaken and evil impression which may be doing us harm in any part of the world.

Mr Shinwell: May I ask the Prime Minister, with reference to the statement he proposes to make on Production, whether he proposes on that occasion to initiate a Debate or merely to make a statement?

The Prime Minister: I propose to have a third day's Debate and to initiate the Debate myself, and it will then be open for anyone to take up the quarrel, if they think there is any public advantage in so doing.

Mr Shinwell: I did not myself participate in last week's Debate and so at least I can put a question with perfect freedom. I gather that the right hon. Gentleman suggested that it was difficult for Ministers to make an impromptu reply to all the points raised in the Debate. Is it not also difficult for hon. Members who are not in the Government to make a reply to my right hon. Friend, and will it not be perhaps even more difficult when he, who is in full possession of all the information, has initiated the Debate? Would it not be more desirable for my right hon. Friend to make a statement which can be read in the Official Report by hon. Members and for us to have a Debate later on?

[1] Sir Andrew Duncan, who had succeeded Oliver Lyttelton as President of the Board of Trade on 29 June 1941.

The Prime Minister: I do not mind, but when statements are made affecting the whole of our production, and the character of our production, perhaps an hour or two before the end of the Debate, it is quite impossible for Ministers to do justice to them in their answers. If we were engaged in ordinary party politics it would be quite easy to throw cheap scores across the House, to the gratification of supporters of a Government who are in a majority; but in time of war time for the preparation of a much more reasoned answer is required. Grave consideration has to be given not only to the actual facts but to what part of those facts can be stated in public, and in what form they can be stated in public, and I certainly could not undertake to answer all the charges that are made in the course of a Debate without having the opportunity of considering the matter maturely and comprehensively beforehand.

Earl Winterton: May I ask the right hon. Gentleman a question about the course of the Debate? I presume that if the right hon. Gentleman makes his opening statement in answer to the points which were made in the course of the previous Debate, other hon. Members will follow him. Will some Minister reply at the end of the Debate, so that there will be, as it were, answers given to the answerers? Some hon. Members may have the temerity to differ from the view put by the right hon. Gentleman.

The Prime Minister: Every endeavour will be made to preserve the general liveliness of our discussions.

Mr Maxton: While appreciating the right hon. Gentleman's difficulty, namely, that it is more difficult to reply in wartime to charges made by his supporters, than it is in peace-time to answer charges made by his opponents, may I ask him this question? Since it is, as he says, the effect created abroad by these statements which is disturbing, will the right hon. Gentleman turn his attention to the fact that he has a Ministry of Information which exercises control over what is to go abroad? If the Government had dealt a little more efficiently with the Debate a week ago, they would not have had any difficulty about the forthcoming Debate.

The Prime Minister: The Ministry of Information places no ban upon full publication all over the world of the public Debates in this House. Anything that is said here goes into these other countries, and that is why great responsibility attaches to what is said here.

Mr Lawson: Is the right hon. Gentleman aware that it is not only people abroad who are disturbed about these statements but people in this country and that there will be great satisfaction that he has undertaken to meet these points? Will he also take note of the fact that whatever the circumstances, it has been a rather too frequent practice on the part of Ministers to evade answering questions and criticisms?

The Prime Minister: I cannot admit that there has been any practice of evasion. I do not see why we should evade. We neither need to evade nor to shrink from dividing if necessary and we are perfectly capable of defending ourselves, but in a time of war when the affairs of the country are very complicated, and when enormous business is divided among a great number of Ministers, it is not possible to give the same answers on every topic that is raised as could be done when the ordinary party fight was in progress. Every prominent politician on both sides is well acquainted with that fact.

Mr Mander: In the forthcoming Debate on Production, would the Prime Minister be good enough to bear in mind the friendly advice given to the Government from all parts of the House last week, in regard to the setting up of a Ministry of Production; and would he be good enough to deal with that in the course of the proceedings?

The Prime Minister: I am always indebted to my hon. Friend for the great quantity of friendly advice which he is always ready to give, but I should like to have the opportunity of preparing my own speech in my own way.

Winston S. Churchill: speech
(*Hansard*)

15 July 1941 House of Commons

WAR SITUATION

Mr Lees-Smith: May I ask the Prime Minister whether he has any information to give the House with regard to the Russian Agreement?

The Prime Minister: Towards the end of last week it became possible to make a solemn agreement between the British and Russian Governments, carrying with it the full assent of the British and Russian people and all the great Dominions of the Crown, for united action against the common foe. Both the British and Russian Governments have undertaken to continue the war against Hitlerite Germany to the utmost of their strength, to help each other as much as possible in every way and not to make peace separately. My right hon. Friend the Foreign Secretary and the right hon. and learned Member for East Bristol (Sir Stafford Cripps), our Ambassador in Moscow, were indefatigable in carrying matters to a swift conclusion. The Agreement which has been signed, the text of which has been published, cannot fail to exercise a highly beneficial and potent influence on the future of the war. It is, of course, an Alliance, and the Russian people are now our Allies. General Smuts has, with his usual commanding wisdom, made a comment which, as it entirely represents the view of His Majesty's Government, I should like to repeat now. He says:

'Let no one say that we are now in league with Communists and are fighting the battle of Communism. More fitly can neutralists and fence sitters be charged with fighting the battle of Nazism. If Hitler, in his insane megalomania, has driven Russia to fighting in self-defence, we bless her arms and wish her all success, without for a moment identifying ourselves with her

Communistic creed. Hitler has made her his enemy and not us friendly to her creed, just as previously he treacherously made her his friend without embracing her Communism.'

My right hon. Friend the Foreign Secretary, in these busy days, has also been instrumental in bringing about a very great measure of agreement between the Russian Soviet State and the Polish Republic. These negotiations have not yet reached their conclusion, but I am very hopeful that, aided by the statesmanship of General Sikorski, another important step will soon be taken in the marshalling of all the peoples of the world against criminals who have darkened its life and menaced its future.

The House will also have read, I have no doubt, the good news from Syria. A military Convention has been signed, in a cordial spirit on both sides, putting an end to a period of fratricidal strife between Frenchmen and Frenchmen, and also between Frenchmen and British, Australian and Indian soldiers, all of whom drew the sword of their own free will in defence of the soil of France. The fact that our relations, such as they are, with the Vichy Government have not been worsened during these weeks of distressing fighting, when the forces on both sides acquitted themselves with so much discipline, skill and gallantry, is a proof of the deep comprehension of the French people of the true issues at stake in the world. It is a manifestation of that same spirit which leads them to wave encouragement to our bombing aircraft, although the bombs have, in the hard fortune of war, to be cast on French territory because it is in enemy hands.

We seek no British advantage in Syria. Our only object in occupying the country has been to beat the Germans and help to win the war. We rejoice that with the aid of the forces of General de Gaulle, led by General Catroux and General Legentilhomme, we have been able to bring to the peoples of Syria and the Lebanon the restoration of their full sovereign independence. We have liberated the country from the thraldom exercised by the German Armistice Commission at Wiesbaden, and from the dangerous German intrigues and infiltration which were in progress. The historic interests of France in Syria, and the primacy of those interests over the interests of other European nations, is preserved without prejudice to the rights and sovereignty of the Syrian races.

The conclusion of this brief Syrian campaign reflects credit upon all responsible – upon General Wavell, who was able to spare the Forces first to put down the revolt in Iraq, and afterwards to act in Syria, while at the same time making vigorous head against the German and Italian Army and its strong armoured elements which have for so many months been attempting unsuccessfully to invade the Nile Valley. The actual conduct of the campaign was in the hands of General Sir Maitland Wilson, who, it will be remembered, was the General who extricated our Forces from the very great dangers by which they were encompassed in Greece. He did not tell us much about what was going on in either case, but in both cases his operations constitute an admirable example of military skill. I hope it will soon be possible to give fuller accounts to the public than they have yet received of the Syrian fighting, marked as it was by so many picturesque episodes, such as the arrival of His Majesty's Lifeguards and Royal Horse Guards, and the Essex Yeomanry, in armoured cars, across many hundreds of miles of desert, to surround and capture the oasis of Palmyra. There are many episodes of that kind, of great public interest, which I trust may soon be made public.

We are entitled to say that the situation in the Nile Valley has for the time being, at any rate, been considerably improved. If anyone had predicted two months ago, when Iraq was in revolt and our people were hanging on by their eyelids at Habbaniya, and our Ambassador[1] was imprisoned in his Embassy at Baghdad, and when all Syria and Iraq began to be overrun by German tourists, and were in the hands of forces controlled indirectly but none the less powerfully by German authority – if anyone had predicted that we should already, by the middle of July, have cleaned up the whole of the Levant and have re-established our authority there for the time being, such a prophet would have been considered most imprudent. The heavy and indecisive fighting at Sollum by our desert Army, and the stubborn defence of Crete in which such heavy losses were inflicted on the enemy's air power, must be judged to have played their part in arriving at the general result.

Winston S. Churchill to Cyril E. Lloyd[2]

(*Churchill papers, 20/22*)

15 July 1941

My dear Mr Lloyd,

The death on active service of Temporary Lieutenant Joel, RNVR[3] adds yet another name to Parliament's tragic but glorious Roll of Honour. The Borough of Dudley loses a faithful friend who has served it loyally and well during the ten years he has been its representative in the House of Commons. It would be only fitting that the seat he left vacant should go uncontested and the electors of Dudley will surely agree with me in deploring the by-election that has been imposed upon them at a time when their whole attention should be focused upon far greater and graver matters.

A year ago an all-party Government was formed under my leadership,

[1] Sir Kinahan Cornwallis.

[2] Cyril Edward Lloyd, 1876–1963. Conservative Member of Parliament for Dudley, 1922–29. Re-elected at the by-election, 1941. Defeated, 1945. President, National Federation of Iron and Steel Manufacturers, 1925. Member of the United Kingdom Sugar Industry Inquiry Committee, 1934–5.

[3] Dudley Jack Barnato Joel, 1904–1941. Racehorse owner. Conservative Member of Parliament for the Borough of Dudley from 1931 until his death in action in May 1941, while serving in the Royal Naval Volunteer Reserve.

having as its first aim the concentration of the nation's energies and resources upon the grim fight for survival. That alliance of parties and the political truce of which it was the outcome have worked admirably, leaving ample scope under our flexible Parliamentary system for constructive criticism by the people's representatives in the House of Commons.

At an hour in our history when we are fighting the most formidable enemy we have ever confronted, the nation has no time for political privateers who sail from constituency to constituency flying fantastic flags of their own designing.[1]

I ask Dudley to give you an overwhelming majority and thus provide the world with yet further evidence that the people of Britain are solid behind their Government in its colossal task of organizing victory over the dark forces of tyranny and treachery.

Yours sincerely,
Winston S. Churchill

Winston S. Churchill to Anthony Eden
(*Churchill papers, 20/36*)

16 July 1941

In view of the obnoxious and aggressive attitude of Finland, I trust we have already seized all the Finnish ships and subjected the Finns to every inconvenience in our power. M. Gripenberg[2] should be made to feel his position acutely. One cannot be on two sides at once.

Winston S. Churchill to Sir Archibald Sinclair
(*Churchill papers, 20/36*)

16 July 1941

Investigations by the Ministry of Home Security into the effect of German high explosive bombs has shown that a far greater amount of damage is done by blast, which destroys buildings, &c., than by splinters, which find very few useful targets, especially at night when most people are under cover.

The higher the proportion of high explosive to bomb-case the greater the blast. If the weight of the metal case is increased, we get more splinters.

[1] The rival candidate at Dudley, N. P. Billing, standing as a National Independent, advocated a policy of aerial reprisals against Germany. He received 4,869 votes, as against 6,234 cast for Lloyd.

[2] George Gripenberg.

Our GP bombs[1] have a charge-weight ratio of about 30-70. The Germans work with a larger ratio about 50-50. These are not only more efficient for destroying cities; they are also cheaper.

In these circumstances the charge-weight ratio of our bombs ought to be reconsidered, especially now that the Air Ministry have asked for such a large expansion in output.

Winston S. Churchill to Anthony Eden, and to General Ismay for the Chiefs of Staff Committee
(*Churchill papers, 20/36*)

16 July 1941
Action this Day
Most Secret

I must repeat my conviction that Japan will not declare war upon us at the present juncture, nor if the United States enters the war on our side. I agree with the views of the Chiefs of Staff that we are in no position to declare war upon Japan without the United States being in on our side. Therefore, I do not consider that a war between Britain and Japan is likely at the present time. If, contrary to the above views, Japan should attack us, I am of opinion that the United States would enter the war as the weight upon us would clearly be too great. Nevertheless, since the threatened Japanese moves in Indo-China are of serious menace to us, further precautions in the Far East should be taken so far as they are possible without condemning us to misfortune in other theatres.

Winston S. Churchill to Anthony Eden, Lord Moyne and Viscount Cranborne[2]
(*Churchill papers, 20/31*)

16 July 1941

I see no reason why the Duke of Windsor should not towards the end of September visit Canada and the United States if he so desires. Such a request would not be denied to any Governor of Nassau. The itinerary must be exactly prescribed and agreed. I presume he would go to New York, where he would stay at a hotel rather than with Society people and do any shopping which the

[1] The General Purpose (as opposed to Anti-Submarine or Armour Piercing) bomb.
[2] The Foreign, Colonial and Dominions Secretaries.

Duchess may require. Thereafter they would go to the EP Ranch[1] of which I expect they would soon get tired and after that return via Washington, where the President has promised to give a luncheon of about 12 to them both on their way south to Miami and so to Nassau. There is no reason why this tour should not be worked out and everything done for the comfort and honour of the former King-Emperor and his wife. But it all must be planned beforehand.

When the arrangements have been made and all the telegrams drafted, please let me have a draft of the telegram I should send him.

Winston S. Churchill to General Sir John Dill
(*Premier papers, 3/283*)

16 July 1941

ACTION OF THE 2ND ARMOURED DIVISION DURING THE WITHDRAWAL FROM CYRENAICA MARCH–APRIL 1941

1. I must retain the right to address my own Cabinet colleagues as I think fit upon such information as is before me at any time. I will, however, circulate CRME – 1709 (G) O.

2. It does not seem greatly to affect my view. See especially paras. 5 and 6. I was never under the impression that the intention was to withdraw without fighting, but with the loss of Ageila the door was open, and only manoeuvres of withdrawal remained should the enemy advance in superior strength. There is no question of General Wavell having 'deceived the Government', and nothing in my paper suggested that. He did not, however, inform us accurately, or sufficiently fully, about the position on his Western flank, nor about the long absence of the 7th Armoured Division.

3. Your remark about 'Officers who were taken prisoner and are therefore unable to state their case' would seem to preclude Ministers and others responsible for the conduct of war from forming any opinion about it until prisoners are released at the peace. One has to form provisional judgments, and my judgment is quite clear, namely, that His Majesty's Government were extremely ill-treated in the want of measures taken for the effective security of this vital Western flank position.

4. You should read again the Chiefs of the Staff's telegrams to you and Wavell before the decision was taken to send the Army to Greece. That

[1] Edward, Prince of Wales: the ranch in Alberta that the Duke of Windsor had bought while Prince of Wales during a visit to Canada in 1919. It consisted of 2,000 acres of cattle-grazing prairie, with the Rockies visible to the West. He had visited it three times after buying it: in 1923, 1924 and 1927. His aim, he wrote, was 'to make available the best English and Scottish blood in Shorthorn cattle, Clydesdale horses and Hampshire sheep to the farming of Canada'. After his visit in 1941, the Duke was not to see his ranch again for more than ten years.

decision was freely taken by the men on the spot, without the slightest pressure from home. Indeed, the whole emphasis of the Chiefs of the Staff was the other way. I have approved the course you took and have defended it successfully in Parliament. But I certainly had no idea our Western flank was to be left in the condition now disclosed. Risks had to be run, no doubt, but the loss of Benghazi should never have been so tamely envisaged, nor the Western flank left so hopelessly under-insured.

War Cabinet, Battle of the Atlantic Committee: minutes
(*Cabinet papers, 86/1*)

16 July 1941 10 Downing Street
6.30 p.m.
Secret

The Prime Minister said that it was clearly desirable that there should be a fast convoy across the North Atlantic, but that for the present the adequacy and economical use of escort vessels was the governing factor.

The Prime Minister said that while the decline in shipping losses was encouraging, there must be no complacency. Nothing should be said in public which could be taken as a boast that the Battle of the Atlantic had been won, since there might well be surprises in store for us.[1]

John Colville: diary
(*Colville papers*)

16 July 1941

The PM apparently wanted to make Duncan Sandys Undersecretary for Foreign Affairs – the most important and responsible of the Undersecretaryships. Eden has tactfully expressed a preference for Richard Law[2] on grounds

[1] In the Battle of the Atlantic the British inability to read many of the German navy Enigma keys had proved a serious setback at the end of 1940 and in the early months of 1941. At the beginning of March 1941 the settings of the German naval Home Water Enigma were broken: during May they were being read with a delay of between three and seven days; by June and July they were being read with a maximum delay of seventy-two hours, and often with a delay of only a few hours. The action this enabled the Royal Navy to take considerably reduced merchant shipping losses.

[2] Richard Kidston Law, 1901–1980. Youngest son of Andrew Bonar Law (two of his brothers were killed in action on the western front). Editorial Staff, *Morning Post*, 1927; *New York Herald-Tribune*, 1928. Conservative MP for Hull South-West, 1931–45; for South Kensington, 1945–50; for Haltemprice, 1950–4. Elected to the Other Club, 1936. Member of the Medical Research Council, 1936–40. Financial Secretary, War Office, 1940–1; Parliamentary Under-Secretary of State, Foreign Office, 1941–3. Privy Councillor, 1943. Minister of State, 1943–5. Minister of Education, 1945. Created Baron Coleraine, 1954. Chairman National Youth Employment Council, 1955–62.

of experience. So Duncan will go to the War Office. Stirred by this example of nepotism John Peck offers me £5 to suggest that the best choice for Minister of Information would be Vic Oliver![1]

Oliver Harvey: diary
(*'The War Diaries of Oliver Harvey'*)

16 July 1941

Continual appeals from Maisky[2] and Cripps for more action to help the Russians. They want some land operations. AE is worried at the lack of support of the Chiefs of Staff and even of the PM who, for all his brave words, is reluctant to agree to raids. He wants either enormous raids with armoured divisions or nothing at all.

Brigadier Stewart Menzies to Winston S. Churchill
(*Secret Service papers, HWI/14*)

17 July 1941
Most Secret

Reference attached. (59/T10)[3]

I am of the opinion that the source would definitely be imperilled if this information was passed to Moscow in its present form, as it would be impossible for any agent to have secured such information regarding operations for the 16th July. I have, however, arranged with the War Office for the gist to be incorporated with other material, a copy of which I enclose.

[1] Churchill's son-in-law.

[2] The Soviet Ambassador in London.

[3] Churchill was pressing 'C' to send as much Enigma-based Eastern Front material as possible to Stalin. The decrypt CX/MSS/59/T10 had been sent at 7.30 p.m. on 15 July 1941 with regard to operations on the Eastern Front on July 16. The summary as submitted to Churchill read: 'Russians threatened by envelopment at Smolensk. Support of 4th Panzer Army (Armee) with main battle front at Smolensk. Russians are to be prevented from withdrawing. Railways in the rear to be bombed.'

I would point out that General Macfarlane[1] was instructed to inform the Russians that we possess a well placed source in Berlin who has occasional access to operational plans and documents. This explanation has been accepted by the Russians. I have, however, refused to furnish them with detailed identifications, which might well arouse their suspicions as to the real origin of the information, for they would appreciate the impossibility of being able to furnish us with any identifications on the Western front.

I enclose a sample of the type of information which has been passed and which should prove of considerable assistance to the Russian General Staff.

C

John Colville: diary
(*Colville papers*)

17 July 1941

At 5.30 Harry Hopkins appeared, having suddenly arrived from America in a bomber, laden with ham, cheese, cigars etc. for the PM . . .

Winston S. Churchill to Sir Edward Bridges
(*Premier papers, 4/85/1*)

17 July 1941

I have a feeling that Parliament does not at all understand the very great advance made in the refinement of priority questions through the development of the allocation principle. Let me have a note on this not exceeding one page. In fact I think we hear very little about priorities now. Here and there there may be a focal point, but speaking generally, am I not right in supposing that all is running smoothly? See, for instance, how well the giving of 1A to the production of tanks on psychological grounds has been adjusted. Priorities now resolve themselves into the opening out of bottle-necks. No one has an absolute priority to the exclusion of all others. There have been no recent clashes. Comment freely on this by Friday.

[1] Frank Noel Mason-MacFarlane, 1889–1953. On active service, 1914–18, France Belgium and Mesopotamia; Afghan War, 1919. Military Attaché, Budapest, Vienna and Berne, 1931–34; Berlin and Copenhagen, 1937–39. Director of Military Intelligence, British Expeditionary Force, France and Belgium, 1939–40; Gibraltar, 1940. Head of British Military Mission to Moscow, 1941–42. Governor and Commander-in-Chief, Gibraltar, 1942–44. Knighted 1943. Chief Commissioner, Allied Central Commission, Italy, 1944. Colonel Commandant, Royal Artillery, 1944. Labour Member of Parliament for North Paddington, 1945–46.

Winston S. Churchill to General Ismay, for the Departments concerned
(*Premier papers, 3/88/3*)

17 July 1941

GAS CONTAINERS

What is the cause of the failure to produce containers in June? A fall from 1,500 to 500 tons is shocking and absolutely contrary to the express instructions of the Cabinet over many months. Who is responsible? The absolute maximum effort must be used with super-priority to make, store, and fill into containers, the largest possible quantities of gas.

Let me know who is responsible for this failure.

At any moment this peril may be upon us. Papers must be prepared for Cabinet discussion next week.

Winston S. Churchill to Lord Cherwell
(*Churchill papers, 20/36*)

17 July 1941

See Wardlaw Milne's statement[1] about 75 per cent. war effort. What datum line does he work from? He does not tell us. It is a pot-shot. The only true datum line is the two or three months following Dunkirk in 1940. This was the maximum intensity of British effort. It could never be maintained at that rate. Some relief is necessary – holidays, &c.

But what are the actual figures? Take, say, May and June, and the first half of July 1940; compare them with the similar outputs of this year; or again compare the three months after Dunkirk with the last three months, for which figures are available. Test the above comparisons by the number of workers employed, the number unemployed, in the country, the output of the five or six principal weapons. Other ideas will occur to you.

My own idea is that we are about 87 per cent. of the peak effort, but have a far larger output. But then the night shift and machine tool position is far from good.

Do your best to find the solid truth.

[1] In the House of Commons on 10 July 1941.

War Cabinet, Defence Committee (Operations): minutes
(*Cabinet papers, 69/2*)

17 July 1941 Cabinet War Room
10.30 p.m.

The Prime Minister said that he proposed to send short telegrams to General Auchinleck to the effect that if a strong offensive could be delivered in the Western Desert before the end of September, we should be prepared to send out 150 of our latest cruiser tanks, leaving the United Kingdom in the first week of August and reaching Egypt by the middle of September. We should also be prepared to scrape up extra shipping for Convoy WS 11 so as to permit the despatch of 60,000 men before the end of August. These reinforcements in men and tanks could be regarded by General Auchinleck as the reserves referred to in his telegram, thus enabling him to engage the whole of his existing armoured forces in the September battle.

It would take three weeks to prepare and load the cruiser tanks. The situation in Russia during that period might have changed drastically to our disadvantage and we might be faced with an imminent threat of invasion. In this event we should be obliged to retain these tanks but the decision would be taken before General Auchinleck had been committed to his offensive.

If on the other hand General Auchinleck found that he could not, even with these reinforcements, stage an offensive before the end of September with reasonable prospect of success, he should inform us accordingly and we should then be spared the decision of further encroaching upon our import programme and of sending away tanks which were needed for armoured divisions at home.

J. V. Stalin to Winston S. Churchill
(*Churchill papers, 20/132*)

18 July 1941

Let me express my gratitude for the two personal messages which you have addressed to me.

Your messages were the starting point of developments which subsequently resulted in agreement between our two Governments. Now, as you have said it with full justification, the Soviet Union and Great Britain have become fighting allies in the struggle against Hitlerite Germany. I have no doubt that, in spite of all the difficulties, our two States will be strong enough to crash our common enemy.

Perhaps it is not out of place to mention that the position of the Soviet forces at the front remains tense. The consequences of the unexpected breach of the non-aggression pact by Hitler, as well of the sudden attack against the Soviet

Union – both facts giving advantages to the German troops – still remain to be felt by the Soviet Armies.

It is easy to imagine that the position of the German forces would have been many times more favourable had the Soviet troops had to face the attack of the German forces not in the region of Kishinev, Lwow, Brest, Kaunas and Viborg, but in the region of Odessa, Kamenez-Podolsk, Minsk and environs of Leningrad.

It seems to me further that the military situation of the Soviet Union, as well as of Great Britain, would be considerably improved if there would be established a front against Hitler in the West (Northern France) and in the North (Arctic).

The front in Northern France not only could divert Hitler's forces from the East, but at the same time would make it impossible for Hitler to invade Great Britain. The establishment of the front just mentioned would be popular with the British Army, as well as with the whole population of Southern England.

I fully realize the difficulties involved in the establishment of such a front. I believe, however, that, in spite of the difficulties, it should be formed, not only in the interests of our common cause, but also in the interests of Great Britain herself. This is the most propitious moment for the establishment of such a front, because now Hitler's forces are diverted to the East, and he has not yet had the time to consolidate the positions occupied by him in the East.

It is still easier to establish the front in the North. Here on the part of Great Britain would be necessary only naval and air operations without the landing of troops or artillery. The Soviet military, naval and air forces would take part at such an operation. We would welcome if Great Britain could transfer to this theatre of war something like the one light division or more of the Norwegian volunteers which could be used in Northern Norway to organize rebellion against the Germans.

Winston S. Churchill to Lord Hankey[1]

(*Churchill papers, 20/22*)

18 July 1941

My dear Maurice,

The changes arising from Duff Cooper's leaving the Ministry of Information make it necessary for me to have the Duchy of Lancaster at my

[1] Maurice Pascal Alers Hankey, 1877–1963. Entered Royal Marine Artillery, 1895. Captain, 1899. Retired, 1912. Secretary to the Committee of Imperial Defence, 1912–38. Lieutenant-Colonel, Royal Marines, 1914. Knighted, February 1916. Secretary to the War Cabinet, 1916–18; to the Cabinet, 1919–38. Created Baron, 1939. Minister without Portfolio, September 1939-May 1940. Chancellor of the Duchy of Lancaster, 1940–1. Paymaster-General, 1941–2. His brother Hugh was killed in action in South Africa in March 1900. His brother Donald was killed in action on the Western Front in October 1916.

disposal.[1] I do not wish to interrupt the valuable work which you have undertaken outside the scope of your official Office. The four important Committees over which you now preside would suffer in any hands but yours. Moreover, Duff Cooper who will succeed you at the Duchy will have to start at once upon a Mission to the Far East to report to the Cabinet upon the desirability or otherwise of concerting more closely the business of the various Departments which centres at Singapore. It is not intended at present to reproduce for him in the Far East conditions resembling those of the Minister of State in Cairo; but something has to be done to improve the celerity of despatch of business out there and a Minister of Duff Cooper's standing will be able, in a few months, to make proposals to that end.

The Paymaster-Generalship is vacant, and I shall be glad if you will take that post while continuing your present extraneous duties. Precedent exists which enables the Paymaster General to receive a salary for work outside his Office. It can therefore be arranged that you receive the same salary as you do at the present time. I can also arrange that as Paymaster General you would be included in the Ministers of Cabinet rank not in the War Cabinet. Thus, should this plan commend itself to you, all that in fact would be changed would be your title.

Yours sincerely,
Winston S. Churchill

Harold Nicolson: diary
(*'Diaries and Letters, 1939-1945'*)

18 July 1941

When I got back to the Ministry after lunch, I got a message from the Prime Minister's Private Secretary to say that he wants to see me at No. 10 at 5.30. I discuss this with Duff. He says that he is to be made Chancellor of the Duchy of Lancaster and to go to Singapore to coordinate. The PM had just mentioned me, and said that the Labour Party wanted a Labour man in my job. Duff thinks that if I am offered something as good, I should accept it, but if something worse, I should refuse and go back to my writing. A later message comes that the interview is cancelled and that I shall receive a communication 'in another form'.

At 5.55 it arrives in the shape of a black box from Downing Street.

[1] Alfred Duff Cooper became Chancellor of the Duchy of Lancaster with special responsibilities for the Far East. He was succeeded as Minister of Information by Brendan Bracken.

Winston S. Churchill to Harold Nicolson
(*Churchill papers, 20/22*)

18 July 1941

My dear Harold Nicolson,

The changes at the Ministry of Information lead me to ask you to place your Office as Parliamentary Secretary at my disposal.

I should be very much obliged if you would give your services to the public as a member of the Board of Governors of the BBC, where I am sure you could make a most effective contribution. This would not entail the vacation of your seat in the House of Commons, nor the renouncement of your salary as a Member. I propose to issue a certificate under the House of Commons Disqualification (Temporary Provision) Act, 1941.

Yours sincerely,
Winston Churchill

Harold Nicolson: diary
(*'Harold Nicolson, Diaries and Letters, 1939-1945'*)

18 July 1941

I realize that this means the end of any political ambitions which I may ever have cherished. I am hurt and sad and sorry. The PM's Secretary telephones to say that he wants a reply at once, and could I send it by taxi. Well, I send it.

Elizabeth Layton: diary
(*Nel papers*)

18 July 1941

He was in a bad temper all this week and every time I went to him he used a new and worse swear word. However, he usually rounded it off by beaming goodnight at me, so one can't bear any malice or even let it worry one.

Winston S. Churchill to Anthony Eden and Lord Moyne
(*Churchill papers, 20/31*)

19 July 1941
Secret

I understood that the Duke of Kent was starting almost immediately, in which case there would be no danger of his clashing with the Duke of Windsor. He should be out of America by the end of August, and the Duke of

Windsor should not be leaving Nassau before the third week in September. Matters had better be arranged on this basis.

I myself saw no reason why the Duke of Kent should not pay a short visit to Washington, if he so desires, after he has finished his visits to the Canadian airfields. But if it is thought that this would clash with the Duke of Windsor's luncheon there, or be too close to it to be comfortable, or be a burden on President Roosevelt, then his visit should be confined to Canada.

Winston S. Churchill to Herbert Morrison
(Churchill papers, 20/36)

19 July 1941

I should like to have my opinion put on record that this sentence[1] is far too heavy for expressions of opinion, however pernicious, which are not accompanied by conspiracy. Nothing in the internal state of the country justifies such unreasonable and unnatural severity. I consider such excessive action defeats its own ends. If this crazy female is to be treated in this way, what is to be done with Captain Ramsay,[2] who was accessory after the fact to the felonies of Tyler Kent and Anna Wolkow,[3] and what is to be done about the Peace Pledge Union?

Winston S. Churchill to Herbert Morrison[4]
(Churchill papers, 20/36)

19 July 1941

I have recently been shown photographs illustrating the methods of concealment which have been adopted, for instance, for RDF stations, and which appear extremely effective. I trust that the possibilities of using methods

[1] Five years penal servitude on Miss Elsie Orrin for saying to two soldiers that Hitler was 'a good ruler, a better man than Mr Churchill'.

[2] Archibald Henry Maule Ramsay, –1955. Educated at Eton and Sandhurst. On active service in France, 1914–16 (severely wounded). British War Mission, Paris, 1918. Invalided out of the Army, 1919. Conservative Member of Parliament for Peebles, 1931–45. Parliamentary Member of the Potato Marketing Board, 1936. Detained at Brixton Prison under Regulation 18b of the Defence of the Realm Act, 23 May 1940–26 September 1944. The eldest of his four sons died on active service, 1943.

[3] Tyler Kent, an employee of the United States Embassy in London, had been arrested, with his colleague Anna Wolkow, on 20 May 1940. In Kent's flat was found thirty folders, containing 1,500 secret documents (including a copy of the important telegram from Churchill to Roosevelt of that day's date, which Kent had stolen from the embassy). His intention was to smuggle the documents back to the United States to help isolationist organizations there. He was sentenced to seven years in prison, and deported back to the United States at the end of the war.

[4] Churchill also marked this Minute: 'First Lord of the Admiralty, Secretary of State for War, Secretary of State for Air, Minister of Supply, Minister of Aircraft Production, and Minister of Works and Buildings'.

of concealment, in all their various applications, as opposed to mere camouflage, has been taken into account for both service and civilian purposes.

John Colville: diary
(*Colville papers*)

19 July 1941 Chequers

General Alexander,[1] C-in-C Southern Command, came to lunch.

At tea-time the Soviet Ambassador arrived bringing a telegram for the PM from Stalin who asks for diversions in various places by English forces. It is hard for the Russians to understand how unprepared we still are to take the offensive. I was present while the PM explained the whole situation very clearly to poor, uninformed Maisky.

Sir Alan Brooke (C-in-C Home Forces), Colonel Bob Laycock[2] (who commanded the SAS battalion in Crete) and Peregrine Churchill[3] came to dine and sleep. Sir Dudley Pound also.

Peregrine S. Churchill: recollection
(*Letter to the author, 10 March 1998*)

19 July 1941 Chequers

The reason I was at Chequers that weekend was that I had been 'summoned' by the Prime Minister to explain to the War Cabinet the Russian technique of using fake armoured vehicles, trucks, boats and even weapons to

[1] Harold Rupert Leofric George Alexander, 1891–1969. Educated at Harrow and Sandhurst (as was Churchill). On active service, 1914–18 (wounded three times, despatches five times, DSO, Military Cross). Lieutenant-General commanding 1st Corps, 1940 (despatches). General Officer Commanding Southern Command, 1940–2; Burma, 1942; the Middle East, 1942–3. Commander-in-Chief, 18th Army Group, North Africa, 1943; Allied Armies in Italy (15th Army Group), 1943–4. Knighted, 1942. Field Marshal, 1944. Supreme Allied Commander, Mediterranean Theatre, 1944–5. Created Viscount, 1946. Knight of the Garter, 1946. Governor-General of Canada, 1946–52. Created Earl Alexander of Tunis, 1952. Minister of Defence (in Churchill's second premiership), 1952–4. Order of Merit, 1959. In 1962 he published *The Alexander Memoirs, 1940–1945*.

[2] Robert Laycock, 1907–1968. Joined the Royal Horse Guards, 1927. Leader of the Commando group known as Layforce which operated behind-the-lines operations from 1940, in North Africa. After high casualties during an attack on Crete in May 1941 it was disbanded. Laycock later led a Commando attempt to assassinate Rommel in the Western Desert. After the attempt failed, only Laycock and one other soldier managed to make their way back to British lines. Active behind the lines in Sicily and Italy, 1942–3. Training Commando groups in Britain, 1943. Chief of Combined Operations from October 1943 including the planning of the D-Day landings.

[3] Peregrine Churchill, the son of Churchill's brother Jack. Born 1913. He was one of three children, the others being his elder brother John and his sister Clarissa (who later married Anthony Eden). An inventor and Company Director.

deceive and confuse the enemy as to the extent of their forces and their position. The Russians were always experts at using camouflage and reproduction to foil the enemy.

As a result of this meeting, Britain went so far as to build camouflage covers for the purposes of hiding military headquarters, weapons stores and even sea ports. For example a realistic 'cover' was created to conceal the boats in the port of Newhaven.

Winston S. Churchill to General Auchinleck

(*Premier papers, 3/291/1*)

19 July 1941

1. Prolonged consideration has been given both by the Chiefs of the Staff and the Defence Committee of the War Cabinet to your telegram No. 1533 of 15/7 in reply to my No. 064 of 6/7. The Chiefs of the Staff now send you their No. 148 of today with which we are in full agreement.

2. It would seem that if you had a substantial further consignment of tanks from here and the United States approaching during the middle of September together with other large reinforcements, this might act as a reserve on which you could count either to press your offensive if successful or to defend Egypt if it failed.

3. The Defence Committee were concerned to see the 50th Division, your one complete, fresh British Division, locked up in Cyprus in what appeared to be a purely defensive role, and wonder whether other troops might not have been found.

4. It did not see how a German offensive could develop upon Syria, Palestine and Iraq from the north before the end of September at the earliest. The Defence Committee felt that Persia was in far greater danger of German infiltration and intrigue and that strong action may have to be taken there. This however is in General Wavell's sphere, and his evident wish to act in Telegram No. 9392/G of 17/7 is receiving urgent and earnest attention here.

5. If we do not use the lull accorded us by the German entanglement in Russia to restore the situation in Cyrenaica, the opportunity may never recur. A month has passed since the failure at Sollum, and presumably another month may have to pass before renewed effort is possible. This interval should certainly give plenty of time for training. It would seem justifiable to fight a hard and decisive battle in the Western Desert before the situation changes to our detriment, and to run those major risks without which victory has rarely been gained.

6. It is difficult to understand on the information we have at present the reasons underlying the plan of the offensive of June 15. Our forces were defeated in detail by the arrival on the 3rd morning of all the enemy tanks

from Tobruk, whose garrison meanwhile stood idle. It would have seemed more consistent with accepted principles of strategy and common sense to have engaged the Tobruk garrison in heavy and continuous action before or during the climax of the attack upon Sollum. There may of course be reasons of which we are not aware which rendered these well-worn principles of war inapplicable. Neither can we judge from here on our present information whether it was right to break off the battle on the third day. There are always excellent reasons in favour of retirements. Victory rewards those whose will-power overcomes these reasons.

7. Thirdly, it seems that the Air Force was used as a mere series of small umbrellas spread over our marching columns, and that its large superiority was frittered away in passive defence by standing patrols, instead of being used in offensive strategic combination with the Army for the general purposes of the battle. No doubt this arose from the earnest desire of the Air Force to protect the Army. This however does not alter the fact of what happened.

8. Before the battle I expressed to your predecessor my doubts whether General Wilson with his vast experience of the Western Desert, would not have been a better choice than General Beresford-Peirse whose standing in the Army was so much less. We still think that Wilson should have the Command of the next offensive if there is to be one unless of course you propose to take personal Command yourself.

9. I should be very much obliged if you will let us know what your general intentions are for the immediate future; and you may be assured that our only desire is to sustain you and furnish you with the means of success.

Winston S. Churchill to Oliver Lyttelton

(*Churchill papers, 20/41*)

20 July 1941
Private and Secret

Please see my telegram No. 69 and that of Chiefs of Staff to Auchinleck, and let me know what you think about the position. Have not had any acknowledgment from Auchinleck of telegram I was forced to send him about his speech. I should be sorry if he were hurt by the absolutely necessary warning which I had to give him about political speeches. My only desire is to help him in every way. Do you see all my telegrams to him? I wish you to do so.

Winston S. Churchill to Oliver Lyttelton
(*Churchill papers, 20/41*)

20 July 1941
Personal and Secret
'To be enciphered in my Private Office'

PROPOSAL THAT RANDOLPH CHURCHILL ACT AS LIAISON OFFICER TO OLIVER LYTTELTON

I still do not think your plan for R is good. Why do I need a liaison with you when we can communicate freely and frequently? It will, I fear, put R in a false position, as everything I say about ME will be attributed to his influence. Much antagonism will be drawn upon him. There would be no harm in his coming home once to explain in detail your present situation, but thereafter, if you have no use for him, it would be more fair to him to let him return to active duty. It will always be to his credit that his telegram played a decisive part in the important and beneficial changes which have been accomplished.

Winston S. Churchill to General Wavell[1]
(*Churchill papers, 20/41*)

20 July 1941
Personal and Private

Your 9392.G. Cabinet will consider Persian situation tomorrow. I am in general agreement with your view, and would like to give Persians an ultimatum from Britain and Russia to clear out the Germans without delay or take the consequences. Question is what forces we have available in case of refusal. Pray let me know your views.

Winston S. Churchill to Admiral Pound, and to General Ismay for the Chiefs of Staff Committee
(*Churchill papers, 20/36*)

20 July 1941
Action this Day

GLEN SHIPS

I strongly deprecate bringing this ship home. We sent these three ships all round the Cape with much heartburning in the hopes of Mandibles[2] and for

[1] Wavell was in New Delhi, as Commander-in-Chief, India. Churchill also sent a copy of this telegram to the Viceroy of India.
[2] The attack on the Dodecanese Islands.

other island attacks. The Commandos have been frittered away, and are now disbanded. The late régime in the Middle East showed no aptitude for combined operations. There was no DCO[1] but only a lukewarm and uninfluential Committee. Nevertheless, we cannot exclude the need of landing operations in the future. The other two Glen ships are being mended and it would be altogether wrong to take this one away. I hope therefore the Chiefs of the Staff will consider the matter in all its bearings.

Winston S. Churchill to J. V. Stalin
(*Premier papers, 3/401/1*)

20 July 1941 Chequers

I am very glad to get your message, and to learn from many sources of the valiant fight and the many vigorous counter-attacks with which the Russian armies are defending their native soil. I fully realize military advantage you have gained by forcing enemy to deploy and engage on forward westerly front, thus exhausting some of the force of his initial effort.

2. Anything sensible and effective that we can do to help will be done. I beg you, however, to realize limitations imposed upon us by our resources and geographical position. From the first day of the German attack upon Russia we have examined possibilities of attacking occupied France and the Low Countries. The Chiefs of Staff do not see any way of doing anything on a scale likely to be of the slightest use to you. The Germans have 40 Divisions in France alone, and the whole coast has been fortified with German diligence for more than a year, and bristles with cannon, wire, pill-boxes and beach-mines. The only part where we could have even temporary Air superiority and Air fighter protection is from Dunkirk to Boulogne. This is one mass of fortifications with scores of heavy guns, commanding the sea approaches, many of which can fire right across the Straits. There is less than five hours' darkness, and even then the whole area is illuminated by searchlights. To attempt a landing in force would be to encounter a bloody repulse, and petty raids would only lead to fiascos doing far more harm than good to both of us. It would all be over without their having to move or before they could move a single unit from your front.

[1] Director of Combined Operations.

3. You must remember that we have been fighting all alone for more than a year, and that, though our resources are growing and will grow fast from now on, we are at the utmost strain both at home and in the Middle East by land and Air, and also that the Battle of the Atlantic, on which our life depends, and the movement of all our convoys in the teeth of the U-boat and Focke Wulf blockade, strains our naval resources, great though they be, to the utmost limit.

4. It is therefore to the North we must look for any speedy help we can give. The Naval Staff have been preparing for three weeks past an operation by seaborne aircraft upon German shipping in the north of Norway and Finland, hoping thereby to destroy enemy power of transporting troops by sea to attack your Arctic flank. We have asked your Staffs to keep a certain area clear of Russian vessels between July 28 and August 2, when we shall hope to strike. Secondly, we are sending forthwith some cruisers and destroyers to Spitzbergen, whence they will be able to raid enemy shipping in concert with your naval forces. Thirdly, we are sending a flotilla of submarines to intercept German traffic on the Arctic coast, although owing to perpetual daylight this service is particularly dangerous. Fourthly, we are sending a minelayer with various supplies to Archangel.

This is the most we can do at the moment. I wish it were more. Pray let the most extreme secrecy be kept until the moment when we tell you publicity will not be harmful.

5. There is no Norwegian light division in existence, and it would be impossible to land troops either British or Russian, on German occupied territory in perpetual daylight without having first obtained reasonable Fighter Air cover. We had bitter experiences at Namsos last year, and in Crete this year, of trying such enterprises.

6. We are also studying as a further development the basing of some British Fighter Air Squadrons on Murmansk. This would require first of all a consignment of anti-aircraft guns, then the arrival of the aircraft, some of which could be flown off carriers and others crated. When these were established, our Spitzbergen Squadron could come to Murmansk and act with your naval forces. We have reason to believe that the Germans have sent a strong group of dive-bombers, which they are keeping for our benefit should we arrive, and it is therefore necessary to proceed step by step. All this, however, will take weeks.

7. Do not hesitate to suggest anything else that occurs to you, and we will also be searching earnestly for other ways of striking at the common foe.

John Colville: diary
(*Colville papers*)

20 July 1941 Chequers

After dinner we had a deplorable American film, *Citizen Kane*, based on the personality of William Randolph Hearst.[1] The PM was so bored that he walked out before the end.

After the film we sat up till 3.00 while the PM talked about food supplies and imports. Hopkins said that the export of finished steel goods, such as knives, and aluminium fishing rods to the US, while of no economic importance, was playing into the hands of the Isolationists, who declared that America was sending us products she could ill afford in order that we might support our exports. Nonsense, of course; but the political issue was quite considerable when vast Lease-Lend appropriations were before Congress. Hopkins also said that the US could and should send us more food.

Finally Attlee and Harriman were yawning so much that Hopkins insisted that the PM, in irrepressible spirits, should go to bed. When Winston started on what he was going to do to the Nazi leaders after the war – and the Nazi cities during it – Hopkins said that he, Winston, only read the bits of the Bible that suited him and that they were drawn from the Old Testament. 'I'm not surprised they all leave you, the way you go on: there's Tommy lost at least two stone, there's Jock going into the Air Corps (beware of the coloured gals in Alabama if you go to be trained there), there's Seal gone to the United States, and you have to give that girl[2] of yours a medal to have her stay.' At that moment everybody started taking out their watches and the PM was forcibly taken to bed.

[1] William Randolph Hearst, 1863–1951. Born in San Francisco, the son of a US Senator. Editor and Proprietor of the *New York American*, the *New York Evening Journal*, the *Boston American*, the *Boston Advertiser*, the *Chicago Herald and Examiner*, the *Chicago American*, the *San Francisco Examiner*, and the *Los Angeles Examiner*. In 1903 he married Millicent Wilson: they had five sons. Unsuccessful candidate for Mayor, New York, 1905. Congressman. Resident at his self-designed castle, the Hearst Ranch, San Simeon, a treasure house of medieval and renaissance European art and furniture which Churchill had visited in 1929 as Hearst's guest. During the 1930s Churchill wrote a number of articles for Hearst's newspapers..

[2] Kathleen Hill (see page 380, note 3).

War Cabinet: minutes
(*Cabinet papers, 65/23*)

21 July 1941
5 p.m.

The Prime Minister said that he would still prefer to postpone sending a communication on the lines proposed.[1] As for a Japanese attack on Singapore, he did not believe that anything of the sort was contemplated. It might well be that, even if Japan encroached on the Dutch East Indies, the right policy would be that we should not make an immediate declaration of war on Japan. Once war had been declared, Japanese cruisers would attack our sea communications, and none of our shipping would be safe unless heavily protected by convoys. At the present moment we were not in a position to send an adequate fleet to the Far East. Several of our capital ships were undergoing repair and would not be available for about three months. For all these reasons, he would much prefer to wait and see how the situation developed, and, if a menacing situation should come about, take steps to strengthen our forces in the Far East. He also thought that it would be wise to allow time for the American situation to develop. In any event, taking a shorter view, he thought it would be right to wait a few days and see the result of the action which it now seemed certain that Japan meant to take in Indo-China, which might well have an effect on United States opinion.

John Colville: diary
(*Colville papers*)

21 July 1941
11 a.m.

On the way back to London we all, in a great cortege of cars, stopped at Northolt to see the new big bombers. A Stirling, a Halifax, a Lancaster, a B17 (Flying Fortress) and a B24 (Liberator) were all drawn up for inspection.

[1] Following Anglo-Dutch-Australian Staff talks in February 1941, and British-Dutch Staff talks in April 1941, the Staffs concerned had proposed the creation of 'a reciprocal Agreement to co-operate to the full extent of their available resources if any of them were forced to take military action to counter armed action by the Japanese forces against its territory or mandated territory'. (*Cabinet papers, 65/23*)

Winston S. Churchill to Air Chief Marshal Sir Charles Portal
(*Churchill papers, 20/36*)

21 July 1941
Action this Day

Under the directions given at the time when the Battle of the Atlantic was declared in March, the Coastal Command received a special flow of reinforcements. I understand that in pursuance of this, all the Flying Fortresses, B24s, that have come from the United States recently, have been sent to Coastal Command. In the United States these machines are considered the ideal bombers for Berlin, &c. Mr Hopkins has been asking me about their use, and seemed to be recording an American impression that they were lying idle because we had no crews wherewith to man them. I am correcting this impression, but I think on the widest grounds it would be a very good thing if these bombers were used against Germany in bombing raids. Furthermore, the Coastal Command have been reinforced by sixty-five Catalinas and many Sunderlands, and the Battle of the Atlantic is very much eased by recent results as well as by the impending developments following upon the United States occupation of Iceland, of which the First Sea Lord will tell you.

Pray let me have your views.

C-in-C Bomber Command says he is very short and not expanding.

War Cabinet, Defence Committee (Operations): minutes
(*Cabinet papers, 69/2*)

21 July 1941 10 Downing Street
9.45 p.m.

The Prime Minister said that he was not at all attracted by the idea of bombing oil targets. If the Germans succeed in getting control of the oil fields in Russia, then all our efforts on oil would be wasted. The best way of helping the Russians was to bring down the heaviest possible scale of attack on German cities. If communications were interrupted at the same time, so much the better. He deplored the fact that the Liberators received from America had been allocated to Coastal Command; now was the time for every heavy bomber to concentrate on Germany.

The Prime Minister asked what progress was being made with the development of the method of attacking tanks by the dropping of clusters of plastic bombs from the air. If the experiments were successful and the bombs were ready, it might be worth while sending some of them by a speedy route to the Middle East.

John Colville: diary
(Colville papers)

22 July 1941

The PM held a meeting on American aircraft, since Harry Hopkins and Averell Harriman think we are not making full use of the B17s and B24s we have received.

Winston S. Churchill to General de Gaulle
(Churchill papers, 20/41)

22 July 1941
Personal and Secret

I am grieved that you do not find the Syrian Convention[1] agreeable to you, and I am glad you are returning to Cairo to talk things over with Lyttelton. I ought to let you know, in all friendly frankness, that the antagonism between the Free French and Vichy is on all sides represented as the cause of the bitter resistance of the Vichy troops, and that the antipathy of the Syrian people to the French, whether Vichy or Free, is strongly marked. Not even the extreme bravery of your forces, headed by the gallant Le Gentilhomme and directed by General Catroux with so much loyalty and skill, could counterbalance these heavy burdens, which are unhappily inherent in the situation. I hope, therefore, you will consider our difficulties as well as your own and will continue to have confidence in my desire to help you in every possible way.

Winston S. Churchill to David Margesson
(Churchill papers, 20/36)

22 July 1941

The Commander-in-Chief[1] should be asked to state his assets and not only his deficiencies as at B. An Army does not consist of deficiencies.

[1] Under the Armistice Convention of 14 July 1941 – 'Putting an end to Hostilities in the Levant' – it was recognized that the Free French Command had a 'pre-eminent interest in all questions affecting the Vichy troops' (Article 1). But the 'alternative of rallying to the Allied cause or of being repatriated will be left to the free choice of each individual' (Article 2). De Gaulle sought in vain to prevent the repatriation of General Dentz' army to Vichy France.

[2] General Sir Alan Brooke, Commander-in-Chief, Home Forces.

Winston S. Churchill to General Auchinleck
(*Churchill papers, 20/41*)

23 July 1941
Personal

All your telegrams to us and ours to you show that we should have a talk. COS[1] greatly desire this. Unless immediate military situation prevents you leaving, hope you will come at once, bringing with you one or two Staff Officers. In your absence, which should be kept secret, Blamey will act for you. CAS[2] is making best arrangements for transport.

Winston S. Churchill to General Ismay, for the Chiefs of Staff Committee
(*Churchill papers, 20/36*)

23 July 1941
Most Secret

I wish the Commandos in the Middle East to be reconstituted as soon as possible. Instead of being governed by a Committee of officers without much authority, General Laycock should be appointed DCO. The three Glen ships and the DCO, with his forces, should be placed directly under Admiral Cunningham, who should be charged with all combined Operations involving sea transport and not exceeding one Brigade. The Middle East Command have indeed maltreated and thrown away this invaluable force.

Winston S. Churchill to Lord Beaverbrook
(*Churchill papers, 20/36*)

23 July 1941

I am informed that some factories working for the Production Departments keep large stocks of materials for munitions production, with the result that others may encounter temporary shortages.

It would seem that something like six months' supply would be ample for any one factory, and that it is perhaps necessary to rationalize the distribution of stocks in the country. I should be glad if you would look into this matter and report to me whether you consider that action of this kind is needed.

[1] The Chiefs of Staff, General Sir John Dill, Admiral of the Fleet Sir Dudley Pound and Air Chief Marshal Sir Charles Portal.

[2] The Chief of the Air Staff, Air Chief Marshal Sir Charles Portal.

Winston S. Churchill to Oliver Lyttelton
(*Churchill papers, 20/41*)

24 July 1941
Personal and Secret

Your telegram No. 8, Limit.[1]

Your attitude towards de Gaulle is strongly approved. There is no real chance of his releasing us from our obligations to him as he would do in persisting in such an ultimatum as you properly rejected. Do not, therefore, allow him to upset or impede our policy in Syria. On this basis you should do your utmost to keep him in a good mood, making full allowance for the difficulties of his position.

War Cabinet: minutes
(*Cabinet papers, 65/19*)

24 July 1941
Noon

Prime Minister's Room
House of Commons

The Prime Minister said that he was most anxious that we should do all we could to help the Russians. He asked whether some of the Tomahawk aircraft assigned to us could be made available.[2]

The Prime Minister said[3] that recent telegrams from General Auchinleck revealed a certain difference in outlook on the situation. General Auchinleck had mentioned the possibility of a German attack through Anatolia early in September. This was surely most unlikely. No serious threat could develop in this direction for some considerable time. He had invited General Auchinleck to pay a short visit to this country, for consultation. It was hoped that he would arrive in the middle of the following week.

The Prime Minister said that it was most important that we should make every endeavour to carry out the plan of basing three squadrons at Murmansk. If this could be done, our ships would be able to go to this port, and it would make the whole difference to our effective cooperation with the Russians in this area.

[1] The telegram sent on 22 July 1941, and received in London the following day, in which Oliver Lyttelton reported, of his strong discussion with De Gaulle in Cairo: 'I told him that he must accept the Prime Minister's assurances, reinforced by my own, that we have undertaken to protect the historical interests of France in Syria, and would see to it that she was predominant European power there.' (Telegram No. 8 Limit, 21 July 1941 *Churchill papers, 20/41*)

[2] Sixty Tomahawk aircraft from the United States were sent on to the Soviet Union immediately upon reaching British ports.

[3] Both this and the subsequent intervention by Churchill were recorded in typescript only in the War Cabinet's Confidential Annex (*Cabinet papers, 65/23*).

Charles Eade: notes of a luncheon[1]
(*Charles Eade papers*)

24 July 1941 No. 10 Annexe

I sat next but one to the Prime Minister, with Lady Ridley[2] on my left and the Hon. Mrs Edwin Montagu[3] on my right.

We started lunch without the Prime Minister who was detained at a Cabinet meeting, but he arrived before the first course was finished. He seemed in particularly good spirits. The lunch party was a little more formal than the previous one, and the ladies left us at the end of lunch in order that the men could continue the conversation.

Mr Churchill addressed one particular remark to me concerning the newspaper reports that there was to be an appointment of a supreme minister of war production. He said that the newspapers had been devoting some space to this question and to prophesying that an appointment was to be made. As a matter of fact, he said, it was not his intention to make any such appointment. If it were possible to find a man of such outstanding qualifications and personality that he could supervise and control Lord Beaverbrook (Minister of Supply), Lt Col. Moore Brabazon (Minister of Aircraft Production), the Admiralty, the War Office, Air Ministry and all the other departments concerned, Mr Churchill would be quite prepared to hand over the conduct of the war to such a super man and be willing to serve under him himself.

I suggested an alternative suggestion and prophecy which had been put up by newspapers that although there might not be a Minister of War Production, there would be a committee or sub cabinet of certain ministers concerned with this problem.

Mr Churchill replied that the machinery for that kind of cooperation already existed, and that everything that was decided regarding war production was referred to him for the final OK and that there was no weakness in this method. Mr Churchill said that this continual criticism about British war production, such as that uttered in the House of Commons recently by Sir John Wardlaw-Milne and Mr Austin Hopkinson,[4] did us very

[1] Those present were Clementine Churchill, Sir William Jowitt (the Solicitor General) and Lady Jowitt, the Dowager Lady Wimborne, Lady Ridley, the Hon. Mrs Edwin Montagu, Sir Henry Strakosch and John Colville.

[2] Churchill's cousin Rosamond Cornelia Gwladys Guest (DBE 1918), the daughter of Churchill's aunt Cornelia and Ivor Bertie, Lord Wimborne. In 1899 she married the 2nd Viscount Ridley.

[3] Beatrice Venetia Stanley, 1887–1948. Clementine Churchill's cousin. The confidante of Asquith from 1912 to 1915, she married Edwin Montagu in July 1915. Her London house was at 62 Onslow Gardens, Kensington, and her country house, Breccles Hall, in Norfolk. Her husband died in 1924.

[4] Austin Hopkinson, 1879–1962. On active service in South Africa (Lieutenant, Imperial Yeomanry), 1900 and 1914–18. Head of an engineering firm. Independent MP, 1918–29 and 1931–45. Lieutenant, Fleet Air Arm, 1940.

great harm in America, and also in this country. It was stupid to talk about our output being only 75 per cent., unless one could say 75 per cent. of what. The facts were that after 22 months of war, our arms output was greater than at any time in the last war. It was true that the output from each individual worker was not as great as it used to be, but that was because of the dilution of labour, so many unskilled workers having been introduced among the skilled craftsmen. He also felt that the sort of food working people were getting is not varied or interesting enough and this also affected their work and output. Mr Churchill felt that these continual complaints about British production being inefficient, badly organized and in a complete muddle must do us very great harm in America because America was sacrificing a great deal of normal peacetime output, such as motor cars, in order to help us in our arms drive.

The fact was, we were producing even more than we were just before the Dunkirk evacuation when workers carried on until they fell asleep at their machines from sheer exhaustion.

I mentioned to the Prime Minister that Mr Willkie was reported in today's evening papers as having criticized President Roosevelt for not being more energetic and more enterprising in swinging American aid to the side of Britain.

The Prime Minister laughed and said: 'I am quite sure that President Roosevelt would not be made angry by such a speech as that.'

There was one piece of really secret information which the Prime Minister let out at lunch, and he glanced at me as he said: 'This is secret.'

It was to the effect that M. Reynaud, the former Prime Minister of France until the collapse a year ago, had sent a letter to the Vichy Government reminding them at the time France surrendered, the French Generals, Weygand and others, had declared that the Germans would wring Britain's neck like a chicken's within three weeks. The Prime Minister added that at the time of the final battle, before the surrender of France, he was asked by the French Government to throw into the battle every available British plane without keeping anything at all in reserve for the defence of this country. He had refused to do so and, as he said at today's luncheon, thank God for that decision, because if we had thrown away those planes in France, we could never have won the Battle of Britain at the end of the Summer and the war might then have been lost.

Mr Churchill also remarked on the way the French had fought against us in Syria and indicated that it was a pity they had not fought with the same courage and spirit against the Germans in France. He deplored the collapse of the French morale and spoke with admiration of the nation's tremendous and courageous efforts in the earlier parts of the last war. He felt that they must have been drained of their best and noblest blood in those terrible campaigns on the Western Front.

I said that when I had visited France in the early months of 1940, I had been depressed by what I had seen of the French people, particularly the French soldiers. They had seemed slack, careless and indifferent. I had the feeling that they were content to take the war casually and sip their aperitifs at the cafes. It seemed to me that they had gone soft and over-civilized. Churchill said:[1]

Mr Churchill said that he had received letters from British Prisoners of War in Germany urging him to continue to fight to the very end and assuring him that bad as the conditions were under which they were living, they could survive them and would suffer them in order that the final battle might end in victory. The Prime Minister was obviously very moved by the sentiments expressed in these letters to him.

Mr Churchill was bitter in his criticism of Japan, which country, as just announced in today's newspapers, has been allowed by the Vichy Government to take over the defence and occupation of French Indo-China. He spoke scornfully of the old honour of Samurai, the code of Japanese chivalry, which, today, had been completely discarded and he felt that attention should be drawn in the papers to the dishonourable actions of the Japanese who, as he said, were willing to abide by their treaties with Germany if it meant that they could do so by taking over territories which they have long coveted. He added that despite their aggressive attitude the Japs were still interested in and sensitive to British newspaper criticism.

The conversation also drifted on to the subject of what we might do to the Germans when the war was won, and one woman, Lady Wimborne,[2] I think, suggested – though probably not seriously – that the race should be exterminated by killing all the babies, and Winston got a laugh by saying: 'Need we wait as long as that?'

Somebody then started to quote some figures showing the length of time necessary to sterilise every person in Germany and Winston brought the lunch party back to reality by observing that if people like his guests, the product of a very high order of civilization, could be capable of discussing such subjects like this and talking of what might be done in this way to the Germans, it must surely give us some idea of what sort of things that the Germans themselves might be ready and willing to do to us if they ever have the chance. The Germans, said Mr Churchill, are great fighters with much courage and determination, but when things are going badly, and they see defeat coming, they are very quick to turn up the book of instructions to the page 'How to surrender', 'How to whine' and 'How to get Merciful Treatment from your Adversary'.

[1] At this point there is a gap in the manuscript, which Charles Eade may have wanted to fill in at a later date.

[2] Alice Katherine Sibell Grosvenor, daughter of the 2nd Baron Ebury. She married Ivor Churchill Guest, Baron Ashby St Ledgers (later 1st Viscount Wimborne) in 1902. They lived at Canford Magna, Dorset. He died in 1939, she in 1948. Lord Wimborne's mother, Lady Cornelia Guest, was Churchill's aunt.

I cannot say that these words were the actual words used by the Prime Minister, but this was the effect of what he said. I remarked that they did all that very successfully last time and the Prime Minister replied: 'Exactly.' The Germans, he said, must never be allowed to have weapons, they could be given anything else, even colonies, but no weapons.

Sir Henry Strakosch[1] said: 'I hope we are not going to give back their colonies,' and Mr Churchill said: 'We are not in a giving mood.'

There was considerable gossip at the table about the broadcast by Cassandra[2] of the *Daily Mirror* in which he attacked P. G. Wodehouse[3] for broadcasting for the Nazis. Although the Prime Minister had not heard this broadcast, he made it quite clear that if it were being attacked merely because it had been a vulgar and bitter assault on Wodehouse, instead of a quiet, refined criticism, then he was in favour of the broadcaster, and against the criticism.

I said that my criticism of the broadcast was not its vulgarity, but merely that the broadcaster had attempted to ape the vigorous attack by American journalist, Quentin Reynolds,[4] on Dr Goebbels, and he had failed lamentably to do so, because his voice was too thin and high pitched.

Speaking of the German attack on Russia, the Prime Minister regarded this as a 'windfall' for us, and he even murmured in a low voice that he thought the Russians would still be fighting 12 months from now. Anything, he felt,

[1] Henry Strakosch, 1871–1943. Entered banking in the City of London, 1891; closely connected with South African industrial development and gold mining from 1895; Chairman of the Union Corporation Ltd, London. Author of the South African Currency and Banking Act, 1920. Knighted, 1921. Represented South Africa at the Genoa Conference, the League of Nations Assembly and the Imperial Conference, 1923. A Trustee of the League of Nations Loan for the Financial Reconstruction of Hungary, 1924. Member of the Royal Commission on Indian Currency and Finance, 1925–6. Member of the Council of India, 1930–7. Delegate of India, Imperial Economic Conference, Ottawa, 1932. Adviser to the Secretary of State for India, 1937–42. Chairman of the Economist Newspaper Ltd. Elected to the Other Club, 1939. In his will, published on 5 February 1944, he left Churchill £20,000.

[2] William Neil Connor, 1909–1967. Advertising copywriter,1929–35. Columnist, under the pen-name Cassandra, *Daily Mirror,* from 1935 until his death. Published *The English At War*, 1940. A columnist for the British Army Newspapers, 1942–46. Knighted, 1966. His memoir, *Cassandra: Reflections in a Mirror*, was published posthumously in 1969.

[3] Pelham Grenville Wodehouse, 1881–1975. Author. Published his first book in 1902; *My Man Jeeves*, 1919; *The Code of the Woosters*, 1938. Captured by the Germans at Le Touquet, 1940. Interned in Upper Silesia; as he was over sixty he was released from internment, but not allowed to leave Germany. Persuaded by an American broadcasting company to broadcast from Berlin to the United States; these wartime broadcasts, although not favouring the Nazis, created considerable hostility in Britain. Lived in Paris after the war, then in the United States: never returned to Britain. Became an American citizen in 1955. Knighted, 1975 (six weeks before he died, at the age of ninety-three).

[4] Quentin James Reynolds, 1902–1965. American writer and journalist. Foreign Correspondent, International News Service, 1928–32. Associated Editor, *Collier's Weekly*, 1933–45. During the war he published *London Diary*, 1940; *Don't Think It Hasn't Been Fun*, 1945, *Only the Stars are Neutral*, 1942; *Dress Rehearsal* (the story of the Dieppe raid), 1943, and *The Curtain Rises*, 1944. Among his books for children was *The Battle of Britain*, published in 1953.

which delayed the German invasion attempt of this country was all to the good, because, although some of our Generals might say that they would welcome an invasion attempt by Germany, he, himself, would not welcome such a move. He did not want the Germans in this country at all alive or dead, and said that even when dead, he did not think they would be very good manure.

Sir Henry Strakosch, who apparently has some inside information about the oil position in Germany, declared that on his knowledge, he would say that the Germans had to beat Russia within 3 months (2 months from the time of speaking) if they were to win the War, because their wastage of petrol during such fierce fighting would eat tremendously into their reserves.

I asked him whether it was a fact that stored petrol, such as the Germans are supposed to have in reserve, would not deteriorate with keeping, and he replied that that was true, but the Germans had it mostly stored in the form of crude oil which did not deteriorate.

At this, the Prime Minister remarked that that was why it was so imperative that we should continue to bomb German refineries.

I asked, then, whether it would not be better to concentrate on the destruction of the lubricating oil rather than petrol and whether that would be a short cut to slowing down the German mechanized forces.

Strakosch replied that a great deal of the German Air Force was flown on the Diesel type of engine which did not require lubricants or high-octane petrol.

The Prime Minister said that this was perhaps true of their bombers, but that their high speed fighters were certainly using high-octane petrol of the very finest quality.

One amusing remark made by Mr Churchill during the course of the lunch was to the effect that this week he had seen the two extremes of human emotion. On the one hand, the joy and gratitude of Mr Duff Cooper, who was leaving his post as Minister of Information, and on the other hand, the misery, dejection and apprehension of Mr Brendan Bracken who had been appointed to the position of Minister of Information.

Somebody mentioned during the general hubbub of conversation the departure of Mr Geoffrey Dawson from the editorship of *The Times*. The Prime Minister commented on this, and I felt certain I heard at the end of his sentence the remark 'the last flick of a Quisling'.

I immediately said: 'What was your comment, Sir, regarding the editor of *The Times*?'

Mr Churchill grinned one of his typically roguish, mischievous grins and said: 'I have not made any comment about the editor of *The Times*', at which there was a little laughter at the other end of the table.

I asked him if he would make a comment, and he laughed again, but said nothing.

The Prime Minister does not dominate his table. No one waits for him to initiate a topic of conversation . Mrs Churchill is much noisier, talks a lot in a loud voice and laughs a great deal. Talk does not centre on Mr Churchill and no one stops talking to hear what he has to say. Mrs Churchill is a charming and friendly personality who does a little leg-pulling at his expense. For instance, she asked him whether he was enjoying his lunch and when he replied that it was very good, she told him that it was rabbit and that he would not have eaten it if he had known. (Certainly, it was a well-dressed-up dish and I had not recognized it as rabbit.) Churchill just grunted and said he 'liked bunny'. Bunny was very good, but he didn't want to eat it all the time.

Other remarks made by Mr Churchill during lunch:

'Anger is a waste of energy. Steam which is used to blow off a safety valve would be better used to drive an engine.'

'Opinions differ. That is why we have check waistcoats.'

War Cabinet: minutes

(*Cabinet papers, 65/23*)

24 July 1941 10 Downing Street
5.30 p.m.
Most Secret

The Prime Minister referred to Operation Puma.[1] The forces for this operation had now been increased to 20,000 by the incorporation of the forces for Operation Thruster.[2] The whole had been placed under the command of General Alexander. The Admiral in charge of the operation was Admiral Hamilton. Provisional arrangements had now been made for this force to leave this country about the 10th August. It would not reach its destination until nine or ten days later. The actual decision as to whether the operation should be carried out must, of course, depend upon the situation at the time, and the operation could be called off any time up to, say, the 20th August. He thought, however, that we must now take General Franco's speech[3] as an indication of hostility to us, and that we should be well advised to make certain

[1] A British plan to seize the Portuguese Azores Islands in the Atlantic in the event of a German move against Spain and Portugal. There are nine islands: Flores, Corvo, Terceira, Sao Jorge, Pico, Faial, Graciosa, Sao Miguel and Santa Maria. The capital of the Azores is Ponta Delgada (on Sao Miguel).

[2] The planned seizure of the Spanish Canary Islands and the Portuguese Cape Verde Islands in the event of a German move against Spain and Portugal.

[3] On 17 July 1941, during a speech on the fifth anniversary of the outbreak of the Spanish Civil War, Franco denounced the United States for putting its economic power behind Britain's war effort. The war itself, he said, had been an 'uninterrupted sequence' of Axis triumphs; the first battle had been 'fought and won' in Spain. Franco also spoke of his contempt for the 'plutocratic democracies' telling his listeners: 'Gold ends by debasing nations as well as individuals, and the exchange of fifty old destroyers for various remnants of an empire is eloquent in this regard'.

of securing the Canary Islands before we were anticipated by the enemy.

There were considerable Spanish forces in the Islands, and there would probably be hard fighting. But the commanders of the forces were satisfied that the operation held a good prospect of success.

The Prime Minister said that the alternative of postponing the operation until September had been considered, but the weather then was much less likely to be favourable. He thought that the course of events in Russia was more likely than anything to have a determining influence on Spain's attitude.

The force proposed was sufficient to enable us if we were successful in capturing the Canary Islands, to deal later with other Atlantic islands.

Winston S. Churchill: recollection
(*'The Second World War, Volume Three'*)

24 July 1941

One afternoon in late July Harry Hopkins came into the garden of Downing Street and we sat together in the sunshine.[1] Presently he said that the President would like very much to have a meeting with me in some lonely bay or other. I replied at once that I was sure the Cabinet would give me leave.

John Colville: diary
(*Colville papers*)

24 July 1941

The PM said that one of the most striking things about this age was 'the lamentable lack of Charlotte Cordays'.[2]

On late duty at No. 10 where future strategy in the Middle East was being discussed. First Harry Hopkins and then the PM spoke to President Roosevelt on the telephone, and the PM, forgetting he was not on the 'scrambler', said some things about a certain rendezvous which he afterwards bitterly regretted!

[1] This was the day on which, at 3 p.m., the War Cabinet Committee on Technical Assistance for the United States held its first meeting, with Ernest Bevin in the Chair, Lord Cherwell and Lord Hankey among the British representatives, and Hopkins, Harriman and Lee among the Americans. The Committee was able to report that the United States Government would arrange for American firms 'to undertake complete responsibility' of various specific areas of the manufacture of military equipment, tasks to be, if possible, the American representatives added, 'of the highest importance' (Technical Assistance from the United States of America Committee, First meeting of 1941, 3 p.m., 24 July 1941: *Cabinet papers 99/36*). The tasks suggested were for the maintenance and repair of aircraft, the assembly and overhaul of tanks, and the maintenance of shipping, both in Britain and in the Middle East.

[2] In 1793 Charlotte Corday murdered the French revolutionary leader, Jean Paul Marat, while he was in his bath. During the Suez Crisis of 1956, when someone at a dinner party in London lamented that there were 'no Charlotte Cordays in Egypt', John Colville's grandmother, the Dowager Marchioness of Crewe, remarked: 'But what makes you think that Colonel Nasser ever takes a bath.'

Winston S. Churchill to King George VI
(*Churchill papers, 20/20*)

25 July 1941

Sir,

I have received an invitation from the President to meet him somewhere off Newfoundland, and I gather the 8th, 9th or 10th of August would be convenient. The Cabinet strongly approve of my going, and if Your Majesty would graciously consent, I should propose to sail from Scapa on the evening of the 4th.

I should like to take with me the First Sea Lord, the CIGS and Air Marshal Freeman,[1] leaving the Chief of the Air Staff and General Ismay to carry on the work of the Chiefs of the Staff's Committee each day. During my absence, which should not be more than twelve days, I should leave the Lord Privy Seal, should Your Majesty approve, with full powers to act for me.

I hope Your Majesty will feel that all this is in accordance with the public interest.

I can of course return by flying-boat from Newfoundland in a few hours, but I cannot foresee any cause likely to make this necessary.

General Auchinleck should be with us on Monday or Tuesday next week, and we can take all the necessary decisions about the Middle East before I leave.

With my humble duty, I remain
Your Majesty's faithful subject and servant,
Winston S. Churchill

Winston S. Churchill to President Franklin D. Roosevelt
(*Churchill papers, 20/41*)

25 July 1941
Personal and Secret

Cabinet has approved my leaving. Am arranging if convenient to you to sail August 4th, meeting you some time 8th-9th-10th. Actual secret rendezvous need not be settled till later. Admiralty will propose details through usual

[1] Wilfred Rhodes Freeman, 1888–1953. Major, Manchester Regiment, on active service in France, 1914–18 (despatches, DSO, MC). Deputy Director of Operations and Intelligence, Air Ministry, 1927–30. Chief Staff Officer, Inland Area, 1930. Air Officer Commanding Palestine and Transjordan, 1930–1. Commandant, Royal Air Force Staff College, 1933–6. Member of the Air Council for Research Development and Production, 1936–40. Knighted, 1937. Air Chief Marshal, 1940. Vice-Chief of the Air Staff, 1940. Chief Executive, Ministry of Aircraft Production, 1942–5. Created Baronet, 1945.

channels. Am bringing First Sea Lord Admiral Pound, CIGS Dill, and Vice-Chief Air Freeman. Am looking forward enormously to our talks which may be of service to the future.

Winston S. Churchill to President Franklin D. Roosevelt
(*Cabinet papers, 65/23*)

25 July 1941
Personal and Secret

I am most grateful for your message about the tank programme.[1] This addition to our tank resources in the coming critical months is splendid. As to the longer term policy, all our experience goes to show that more heavily armed and armoured vehicles are required for modern battle, and we should therefore plan to increase the output of medium tanks at the expense of light tanks, but not, of course, at the expense of your air programme.

2. I am much interested in your suggestion that men for our Tank Corps should be trained in the United States. We are examining it here, and will let you know our views as soon as possible.

3. We have been considering here our war plans, not only for the fighting of 1942, but also for 1943. After providing for the security of essential bases, it is necessary to plan on the largest scale the forces needed for victory. In broad outline, we must aim first at intensifying the blockade and propaganda. Then we must subject Germany and Italy to a ceaseless and ever-growing air bombardment. These measures may themselves produce an internal convulsion or collapse. But plans ought also to be made for coming to the aid of the conquered populations by landing armies of liberation when opportunity is ripe. For this purpose it will be necessary not only to have great numbers of tanks, but also of vessels capable of carrying them and landing them direct on to beaches. It ought not to be difficult for you to make the necessary adaptation in some of the vast numbers of merchant vessels you are building so as to fit them for Tank-landing fast ships.

4. If you agree with this broad conception of bringing Germany to her knees, we should not lose a moment in:

[1] On 12 July 1941 Roosevelt had telegraphed to Churchill: 'We have had a thorough review of our whole tank situation here during the last few days and I can now give you the following results. We plan to increase our peak production of our medium tank from 600 to 1,000 a month reaching that goal by April 1, 1942. We will build 600 medium tanks more than we had planned prior to January 1. We will increase our light tank production by 150 per month so that we will have nine hundred more light tanks prior to January 1 than we had planned. Assuming these schedules are maintained and I believe they will be, it means that we can give you 800 to 1,000 light tanks and 800 to 1,000 medium tanks prior to January 1. I will send you in a few days the exact scheduling of these. We can also as of August 1 start training 500 of your tanks corps men in this country if you think that would be helpful. Will you let me know about this soon so that we can make our plans immediately.' (Secret, Prime Minister's Personal Telegram, T. 401)

(a) Framing an agreed estimate as to our joint requirements of the primary weapons of war, e.g. aircraft, tanks, &c.
(b) Thereafter considering how these requirements are to be met by our joint production.

5. Meanwhile, I suggest that our combined staffs in London should set to work as soon as possible on (a) and that thereafter our technical experts should proceed with (b).

Winston S. Churchill to J. V. Stalin
(*Premier papers, 3/401/1*)

25 July 1941
Most Secret

1. I am glad to inform you that the War Cabinet have decided, in spite of the fact that this will seriously deplete our fighter aircraft resources, to send to Russia as soon as possible 200 Tomahawk Fighter Aeroplanes. One hundred and forty of these will be sent from here to Archangel, and 60 from our supplies in the United States of America. Details as to spare parts and American personnel to erect the machines have still to be arranged with the American Government.

2. Up to two to three million pairs of ankle boots should shortly be available in this country for shipment. We are also arranging to provide during the present year large quantities of rubber, tin, wool and woollen cloth, jute, lead and shellac. All your other requirements from raw materials are receiving careful consideration. Where supplies are impossible or limited from here we are discussing with the United States of America.

Details will, of course, be communicated to the usual official channels.

3. We are watching with admiration and emotion Russia's magnificent fight, and all our information shows the heavy losses and concern of the enemy. Our air attack on Germany will continue with increasing strength.

Winston S. Churchill to General Auchinleck
(*Churchill papers, 20/41*)

25 July 1941
Personal and Secret

Very glad you will come. Looking forward so much to seeing you. Am sure we can settle everything to the best advantage here.

Winston S. Churchill to Air Chief Marshal Sir Charles Portal
(*Premier papers, 3/11/1*)

25 July 1941
Most Secret

This spell of dry weather brings the forest of Nieppe[1] into importance.

It would be good to have an experiment in forest burning, the results of which could be observed close at hand.[2]

Winston S. Churchill to General Ismay, for the Chiefs of Staff Committee
(*Churchill papers, 20/36*)

25 July 1941

TECHNICAL TELEGRAMS FROM THE MINISTER OF STATE, MIDDLE EAST

I always think it is a mistake to stand on ceremony in these matters, and certainly I should not cut myself off from any channel of information and advice. However, I will give directions that telegrams from the Minister of State to me should not be circulated to the Chiefs of the Staff. This one is no more woolly than the others we have received from the most orthodox fountain-heads.

Winston S. Churchill to William Mackenzie King
(*Churchill papers, 20/41*)

25 July 1941
Personal and Secret

I agree with you that it is not practicable to hold a formal Imperial War Conference in the near future. Nor am I entirely convinced of its necessity, though I would of course defer to Dominion wishes. A telegram from Malcolm[3] leads me to hope that perhaps you might be willing to pay a short informal visit here, and nothing would give us greater pleasure. You would be able to see for yourself the temper of the people and judge their ordeal. A great reception would await you, and you would, of course, take part in all our Cabinet proceedings. But I understand fully all your difficulties and do not suppose for a moment that I am pressing you against your better judgment. Kindest regards.

[1] In France, north-west of Lille, a few miles from where Churchill had served as a battalion commander in 1916. The forest is only fifty miles from the Channel coast.

[2] As a prelude to a possible bombing raid to ignite the Black Forest in Germany. The Black Forest was more than four hundred miles from the Channel coast.

[3] Malcolm MacDonald, British High Commissioner to Canada.

General Sir Alan Brooke: diary
(*'Turn of the Tide'*)

25 July 1941

I motored to Tidworth with Martel[1] to meet the PM. He was coming down to see the 1st Armoured Division to say a few words to them to let them know that he realized the losses they had sustained in having to send some hundred and fifty tanks to the Middle East. Everywhere he had an astounding reception. He drove in my car between troops lining both sides of the road, all of them cheering him as he went and shouting, 'Good old Winnie!' His popularity is quite astonishing.

John Martin: diary
(*Martin papers*)

25 July 1941

With PM to Tidworth to inspect armoured division and watch exercise (plus Gen. Lee and Cheney of US).[2] Thence to Chequers. Working late on Production speech. To bed 4.50 a.m.

Elizabeth Layton: letter to her parents
(*Elizabeth Nel papers*)

[25-26 July 1941]

Went down to Chequers Friday 25th, . . . was ready by 7.30 when they arrived. Mr C then went for a sleep. After dinner he seemed very energetic. About 12 he sent me out for a walk on the terrace. It was very dark and the sentries kept asking 'Who goes there?' Then 'Password' (it was FINGER). Came in about 12.30 and listened to records.

At about one a.m. we repaired to a lovely room, sort of library-cum-picture gallery, called the Hawtrey Room, and he shooed everyone else off saying 'Off to bed with all of you, leave me alone with Miss Layton'. I felt like a lamb being led to the slaughter!

He dictated until 4.30 without a break – shorthand this time – and really it was an education to take it down. Some of it was just plain statement, expounding '<u>production</u>' (it is for the Production Debate) but some of it was

[1] Commander of the Royal Armoured Corps.

[2] General J.C. Lee (known to the troops as 'Jesus Christ'), who was later in charge of supply for American troops in the European Theatre; and Major-General James H. Cheney, a senior Army Air Force officer.

real rhetoric. All the gestures and intonations were there. I couldn't help feeling rather thrilled.

Once he stopped for about 5 minutes. Said 'Are you tired?' I assured him I wasn't. Said he 'We must go on and on, like the gun-horses, till we drop'. One phrase made me giggle '. . . and the whole world can cry a dismal cacophonous chorus of stinking fish all round the world'. (Heaven knows what it means) – but you should have heard the fire with which it was delivered.

Mr Martin hadn't gone to bed and we two ended about 4.45 eating old scones which I had burgled from the kitchen and giggling weakly.

Was up by about 10 and on the job about 10.30. Got it all typed out.

Got some sleep in the evening, then after dinner did various small jobs. A telegram from Mr Churchill to the President on the subject of his 'Canadian trip', and a telegram from Mr Hopkins to the same on the subject of his trip to Moscow.

You might think that seeing such a person at close quarters might lessen one's admiration and respect, or make him seem more commonplace. But not so in this case; he is just as amazing and terrific and full of character in his private life as he is over the radio or in the H of C.

He bullies his servants, but then completely makes up by giving a really charming smile. On the rare occasions when a brave soul has expostulated at his treatment he has been told 'Oh don't mind me, it's only my way'. So that is the way one has to look at it. Last week everything I did seemed to be wrong, and there were some truly healthy swear-words flying. I felt a bit upset once, but he afterwards said goodnight so sweetly I couldn't bear any malice! And so he gets away with it!

Winston S. Churchill to General Ismay, and to Colonel Hollis
for the Chiefs of Staff Committee
(*Churchill papers, 20/36*)

26 July 1941

Great importance should be attached to furnishing C-in-C Home Forces with a much larger number of mobile AA Batteries, particularly of low-ceiling guns, to work with the Field Divisions and accompany the troops and armoured columns.

The Germans are quite right in always keeping their flak to the fore. No large body of troops should be assembled or be on the line of march without mobile Bofors batteries to give them protection.

Do I understand that the 218 guns will be employed in this way? If so, I think the arrangement is very sound. If not, I should like the Chiefs of the Staff to consider this point. Otherwise I am in full agreement with the re-deployment proposed.

Winston S. Churchill to Air Chief Marshal Sir Charles Portal
(*Churchill papers, 20/36*)

26 July 1941

In view of the importance of obtaining as much information as possible about the experiences of the German Air Force in Russia, I trust that the evidence to be obtained from intercepted wireless messages of homing aeroplanes has not been overlooked. I hope that we have considered giving the Russians details of the use we make of the call sign information. If necessary, perhaps we should send out trained men and equipment to assist them in collecting and collating it.

Winston S. Churchill to Hugh Dalton
(*Churchill papers, 20/36*)

26 July 1941

MDI[1] has designs of small sabotage weapons with delay action mechanisms. If large quantities of these were dropped in the occupied territories with suitable simple instructions for use some would almost certainly fall into the hands of local inhabitants anxious to undertake offensive action, if not suicidally dangerous.

Apart from the military advantage wide-spread action of this sort would certainly have a considerable effect on morale.

Pray let me have your views on this suggestion.

[1] The defence establishment near Whitchurch, ten miles from Chequers, at which experiments were made throughout the war on bombs and explosives. It came directly under Churchill's authority as Minister of Defence.

Winston S. Churchill to James Stuart,[1] *Sir Douglas Hacking*[2] *and Major Dugdale*[3]
(*Churchill papers, 2/428*)

26 July 1941

Pemberton-Billing[4] is no doubt an exceptional candidate, but it will never do to let these by-elections flop as did the one at Dudley. If there is a fight, strenuous exertions must be made to secure a large poll and bring up all our people. Posters and loud-speakers should be provided from our central organization, and Ministers outside the Cabinet should be asked to speak. The figures at Dudley must be considered damaging, both to the Government and to the war effort. Every effort should be made to produce attractive candidates who represent the Party, and both the official Liberal and Labour Parties should be pressed to cooperate.

Pray in future let me have a report beforehand on the steps you propose to take in any new by-election. A candidate has no right to fight an election in the complacent, easy-going manner of Mr Lloyd. This point should be brought to the notice of other candidates early in the day. I will not send the letter of approval to a candidate who does not make the proper exertions in a contest. I hope you will be able to assure me of this before asking me to send a message.

[1] The Chief Whip.

[2] Douglas Hewitt Hacking, 1884–1950. On active service in France, 1914–16 (despatches, OBE). Conservative MP for the Chorley Division of Lancashire, 1918–45. Parliamentary Private Secretary, Ministry of Pensions, 1920; Admiralty, 1920–1; War Office, 1921–2. Conservative Whip, 1922–5. Parliamentary Under-Secretary of State, Home Office, 1925–7. Secretary, Department of Overseas Trade, Parliamentary Secretary, Board of Trade, and Parliamentary Under-Secretary of State for Foreign Affairs, 1927–9. Government Delegate, League of Nations, Geneva, 1933. Parliamentary Under-Secretary, Home Office, 1933–4; Dominion Affairs, 1935–6. Chairman of the Conservative Party Organization, 1936–42. Created Baronet, 1938; Baron, 1945.

[3] Thomas Lionel Dugdale, 1897–1977. Joined the Royal Scots Greys, 1916. On active service, 1916–18. Captain, 1923; Major, Yorkshire Hussars (Yeomanry), 1927. Conservative Member of Parliament for Richmond, Yorkshire, 1929–59. Parliamentary Private Secretary to Stanley Baldwin (when Prime Minister), 1935–37. A Lord of the Treasury, 1937–40. Deputy Government Chief Whip, 1941–42. Vice-Chairman of the Conservative Party, 1941–42; Chairman, 1942–44. Created Baronet, 1945. Minister of Agriculture and Fisheries, 1951–54. United Kingdom Delegate, Council of Europe and West European Union, 1958–59. Created Baron Crathorne, 1959. Chairman of the Political Honours Scrutiny Committee, 1961–76; of the North of England Advisory Committee for Civil Aviation, 1964–72.

[4] N. Pemberton Billing, 1880–1948. Founder and editor of *Aerocraft*, 1908–10. On active service in the Boer War, 1899–1901 and in the First World War (Royal Naval Air Service). Squadron Commander, 1916. Unsuccessfully contested a by-election at Mile End in support of a strong air policy, 1916. Independent Member of Parliament for East Hertfordshire, 1916–21.

Winston S. Churchill to Sir Kingsley Wood
(*Churchill papers, 20/20*)

26 July 1941

Pray see the attached from the Lord Privy Seal.[1] I have always considered that P. J. Grigg[2] should have the reversion, and I believe he might have obtained it but for his somewhat robust views. I thought of making this change the other day, but David Margesson objected strongly to losing Grigg, whom he declares is invaluable at WO. I did not wish to deprive a new Secretary of State of any assistance till he was firmly in the saddle. He is getting a grip of his work now, and the case for a change is very strong. I had not thought of Street[3] in this connection. Is he not junior to P. J. Grigg, and in any case he is much wanted at the Air Ministry.

The other point raised by the Lord Privy Seal is more general. There is much to be said for it. There is no doubt that the idea that the Permanent Secretary to the Treasury is Head of the Civil Service has been answerable for a very serious cramping effect upon our war preparations, and that the present occupant[4] has a very bad record and is the object of widespread distrust. Pray let me know your view.

[1] Clement Attlee.

[2] Percy James Grigg, 1890–1964. Educated at Bournemouth School and St John's College, Cambridge. Entered the Treasury, 1913. Served in the Royal Garrison Artillery, 1915–18. Principal Private Secretary to successive Chancellors of the Exchequer, 1921–30. Chairman, Board of Customs and Excise, 1930; Board of Inland Revenue, 1930–4. Knighted, 1932. Finance Member, Government of India, 1934–9. Elected to the Other Club, 1939. Permanent Under-Secretary of State for War, 1939–42. Secretary of State for War, 1942. Privy Councillor, 1942. National MP, East Cardiff, 1942–5. British Executive Director, International Bank for Reconstruction and Development, 1946–7. Subsequently chairman of Bass, and a director of Imperial Tobacco, the Prudential Assurance Company and other companies.

[3] Arthur William Street, 1892–1951. On active service, Hampshire Regiment and Machine Gun Corps, 1914–18 (Egypt, Sinai, Palestine; wounded, despatches, Military Cross). Principal Private Secretary. Minister of Agriculture and Fisheries, 1919; First Lord of the Admiralty, 1919–22. Accompanied the First Lord to Constantinople during the Chenak crisis, 1922. Secretary, Royal Commission on Superior Civil Services in India, 1923–24. Second Secretary, Ministry of Agriculture and Fisheries, 1936–38. Deputy Under-Secretary of State for Air, 1938–45. Chairman, Anglo-French Co-ordinating Committee for Aircraft Production and Supply, 1939–40. Knighted, 1941. Permanent Secretary, Control Office for Germany and Austria, 1945–46. Deputy Chairman, National Coal Board, 1946–51. One of his three sons was killed on active service with the Royal Air Force in 1944.

[4] Sir Horace Wilson.

Winston S. Churchill to L. S. Amery
(*Churchill papers, 20/36*)

26 July 1941
Most Secret and Private

APPOINTMENT OF A NEW VICEROY OF INDIA

I cannot settle this appointment yet. I had thought that Cranborne would be far and away the best. I am now worried about his health. I am sure the public would never stand the appointment of Sam Hoare, though he himself would greatly desire it. My own inclination would be to ask Linlithgow to continue for another year. I am not at all sure from his letter that he would refuse if it is put to him as a matter of war-time duty.

Let me know what your ideas are.[1]

Winston S. Churchill to Sir Walter Citrine
(*Churchill papers, 20/22*)

26 July 1941
Private and Confidential

My dear Citrine,

I am fully aware of the force of all you say, but I could not take the responsibility at the present juncture of releasing men from the Armed Forces in the large numbers required. We are approaching the invasion season, and orders have been given for all our arrangements to be at concert-pitch from September 1 onwards. Not until the middle of October will the worst of the danger be passed. The Army already accepted in February a reduction in their demand upon manpower of over 500,000 men. I regret to say that it will be necessary to give them back up to perhaps 100,000 of these, as so many drains have been made upon the Army, and the Units are wilting somewhat through normal wastage. Of course, however, no more coal miners will be called up.

Perhaps you will explain this to your Committee, treating the communication, and especially the figures mentioned, as secret.

Yours v sincerely,
Winston S. Churchill

[1] Lord Linlithgow agreed to remain as Viceroy until October 1943, when he was succeeded by Lord Wavell.

John Martin: diary
(*John Martin papers*)

26 July 1941 Chequers

Harry Hopkins arrived. To bed after 2 a.m., PM saying: 'This is a half holiday: we must work tomorrow.'

John Colville: diary
(*Colville papers*)

27 July 1941

After lunch I sat with the PM and Mrs C in the garden while they told me about a book of Cecil Beaton's[1] – *My Royal Past* – with which they are both delighted. The PM also talked about the long speech on production which he is to make tomorrow and which is eagerly awaited by his growing body of critics. Apparently he has been working on it all the weekend – until 10 to 5 one morning! It is very important from the point of view of informed opinion in the country.[1]

Elizabeth Layton: letter to her parents
(*Elizabeth Nel papers*)

[27 July 1941]

Next day, Sunday, was terrible. First there was lots of the Production Speech to he redone. Then Mr Hopkins' speech (to be postscript to the 9 p.m. Sunday news) to be recopied with alterations (and ten minutes after I had started the 15 pages he was asking 'Have you nearly finished – how much more?').

Then a 20-minute lunch. Then more of Mr Churchill's speech (the bit he had given me was a mere 28 pages). Then Mr Winant arrived and he and Harry corrected the latter's speech, which had to be retyped.

After dinner we did a telegram, then settled down in the Hawtrey Room – Mr C, Prof, Mr Martin and me – to correct his speech and do alterations. It

[1] Cecil Walter Hardy Beaton, 1904–80. Photographer and designer. Held his first exhibition of photographs, and published his first photographic essay, in 1930. Photographer for the Ministry of Information, 1940–5. CBE, 1957. Knighted, 1972.

[2] To prepare his production speech, Churchill asked Lord Cherwell for 'comparisons of output under four or five large heads at the 22nd month of the last war and the 22nd month of this war' (Prime Minister's Personal Minute, S.26/1, 22 July 1941: *Premier papers 4/85/1, folio 344*). He also asked for, and received, detailed factual information from the Admiralty, the Air Ministry, the Ministry of Agriculture and Fisheries, the Ministry of Labour, the Ministry of Supply, the Board of Trade, Lord Woolton, Lord Beaverbrook, Ismay and Bridges.

was an absolute education – the thoroughness with which every detail was turned over and searched. I loved every minute.

Bed about 2 Sunday night.

Winston S. Churchill to Lord Woolton
(*Churchill papers, 20/36*)

27 July 1941

I understand that you have under consideration a flexible coupon system, should it become necessary to ration the secondary foodstuffs, which would make the coupons available for the purchase of a variety of alternative goods and dispense with registration at particular shops. Though rigid rationing might be easier to administer, some system which left the consumer a reasonable freedom of choice would seem much better. Individual tastes have a wonderful way of cancelling out. Besides your power to vary the prices of the different commodities both in money and coupons would enable you to exercise great control over demand.

Should you decide that the extension of rationing is inevitable, it would seem, therefore, that the flexible coupon system has much to commend it. I look forward to hearing your views about this in due course.

Winston S. Churchill to Sir Archibald Sinclair
(*Churchill papers, 20/36*)

27 July 1941

Your reply to my Minute No. M.744/1 suggests that my point has not been fully appreciated.

If we rely on blast effect rather than splinters for destroying buildings there is no need for high penetration, more especially as less than one fifth of the area of most towns is covered with buildings. Hence we should not allow our charge-weight ratio to be reduced by our desire to make a bomb with high penetration.

Small bombs of this type are, of course, useful for destroying services, but it would seem, if the Ministry of Home Security's results are right, that our larger bombs should all aim at a high charge-weight ratio.

Perhaps you could let me have a list showing the tonnage and the charge-weight ratios of the various types of bombs which will be in production six months and twelve months from now.

I am pleased to note that the American bombs have a high charge-weight ratio. Is it really necessary to carry out elaborate tests of their penetrating power before ordering a large number? There seems to be a considerable volume of evidence that destruction is more widespread if the bomb detonates well above the surface.

Winston S. Churchill to J. V. Stalin
(*Foreign Office papers, 954/24*)

28 July 1941

1. Rubber.

We will deliver the goods here or United States by the best and quickest route. Please say exactly what kind of rubber and which way you wish it to come. Preliminary orders are already given.

2. Mr Harry Hopkins has been with me these days. Last week he asked the President to let him go to Moscow. I must tell you that there is a flame in this man for democracy and to beat Hitler. He is the nearest personal representative of the President. A little while ago when I asked him for a quarter of a million rifles they came at once. The President has now sent him full instructions and he leaves my house tonight to go to you. You will be advised of his arrival through the proper channels. You can trust him absolutely. He is your friend and our friend. He will help you to plan for the future victory and for the long-term supply of Russia. You could talk to him also freely about policy, strategy and Japan.

3. The grand resistance of the Russian army in defence of their soil unites us all.[1] A terrible winter of bombing lies before Germany. No one has yet had what they are going to get. The naval operations mentioned in my last telegram to you are in progress. Thank you very much for your comprehension in the midst of your great fight of our difficulties in doing more. We will do our utmost.[2]

[1] Two days earlier, on 26 July 1941, Churchill and the other members of the War Cabinet's Defence Committee were sent an Intelligence forecast that German troops might reach the Caucasus 'by mid-August', and be ready, after a month of organizing an air-striking force, to develop a 'large scale attack' on northern Iraq, or on Britain's 'whole position at the head of the Persian Gulf'. (Defence Committee (Operations) Paper No. 3 of 1941, 25 July 1941: *Cabinet papers, 69/3*)

[2] On the previous day, 27 July 1941, Air Marshal Sir Charles Portal had presented Churchill with the Air Ministry's plan to send two Hurricane squadrons to Murmansk, 'to operate in support of Russian operations' and to 'protect as far as possible' the Murmansk area ('Outline Plan', 'Secret', 26 July 1941: *Premier papers, 3/395/4, folio 93*). 'So proceed,' Churchill noted. 'We must give what help is possible.' (Note of 27 July 1941: *Premier papers, 3/395/4, folio 92*)

War Cabinet: minutes
(*Cabinet papers, 65/19*)

28 July 1941
5 p.m.

10 Downing Street

BLOCKADE POLICY

The Prime Minister emphasized the importance of maintaining the position that the Germans were responsible for the feeding of the people whose countries they had overrun. He was not aware of any great pressure on the matter from the United States of America, and thought that it would be wrong to make any concession at the present time.

UNDERTAKINGS TO THE NETHERLANDS GOVERNMENT[1]

The Prime Minister agreed that the action taken by the United States Government, as the result of Japanese encroachments in Indo-China, rather altered the position. But he still deprecated giving an automatic undertaking to the Netherlands Government that we would go to war with Japan in certain circumstances, irrespective of the attitude of the United States. He thought that the right course would be to concentrate on the practical step of making an approach to the United States Government on the Far Eastern position.

In discussion it was also pointed out that the action taken by the United States Government in restricting oil exports to Japan would almost certainly have the effect of increasing Japanese pressure on the Netherlands East Indies. This was a strong argument which should certainly be put to the United States Government.

Elizabeth Layton: letter to her parents
(*Elizabeth Nel papers*)

28 July 1941

Monday we were in town by lunch-time. Had to do the speech into Speech Form, and believe me, it was a job. They took it away until 5.30, then Mrs Hill and I had the most awful hurroosh to get it done by 9.30. Mr Rowan came in every five minutes, and we had two of the girls helping check, but even so it was only just done in time.

He checked quite a lot that evening, which I retyped, and went over to the Annexe in the big car with Mr Rowan about 3.

When we finished he went off and Mr Martin and I cleared up. We were so hungry I had to go and raid the kitchen, and we ended up in the Great Hall about 4.45 eating some scones . . .

[1] Because of the particular secrecy of this item, it was recorded in the War Cabinet's Confidential Annex. (*Cabinet papers, 65/23*).

One thing about Mr C – he would never be one to take a dislike for no reason – he is a most warm-hearted person and infinitely loyal to his friends. And if one ever managed to gain his regard he'd stand by one to the death.

Elizabeth Layton: letter to her parents[1]
(*Elizabeth Nel papers*)

29 July 1941

Tuesday, Speech Day, was terrific. Got up at 8, was on duty at 9. The whole morning till 11.30 was a series of frantic spurts to get something retyped, then a lull, then another spurt. It was the longest speech he had ever done, 10,000 words. Finally he went off about 11.35, looking simply beaming, attended by Mrs and Mary, 2 PS's, 2 detectives, Sawyers,[2] Mrs Hill and me. He came back for something – smiled at us and apologized for having kept us up so late. It felt worth it, suddenly.

Winston S. Churchill: speech
(*Hansard*)

29 July 1941 House of Commons[3]

The Prime Minister (Mr Churchill): On 22nd January of this year I explained to the House the system of administration and production which it was proposed to adopt. I stated this in detail and at length, and I hope my statement may be studied again by those who have forgotten it, because it is the system we have followed since, and it is the system to which, in general and in principle, I propose to adhere. Changes in personnel are caused from time to time by the march of events and by the duty of continual improvement. Changes in machinery are enjoined by experience, and naturally while we live we ought to learn. Change is agreeable to the human mind and gives

[1] This letter was written between 29 July and 3 August 1941, in the form of a diary.

[2] Frank Sawyers. Churchill's valet both before and during the Second World War. On 7 June 1946 Churchill wrote to a prospective employer: 'Sawyers came everywhere with me in these six and a half tempestuous years, and showed many excellent qualities. He is absolutely honest, capable of attending to a great many personal details as a valet, and always rises to the occasion. In my illnesses he has been very attentive, and he stood up to the bombardment well. He was particularly good in the air journeys which at first had to be made in uncomfortable machines. He waits well at table, and also has an admirable manner with visitors. He has a good memory and always knows where everything is. He is leaving me at his own wish, and I am sorry to lose him.'

[3] This session was held, as had been many previous sessions since the destruction of the Commons chamber, in the chamber of the House of Lords.

satisfaction, sometimes short-lived, to ardent and anxious public opinion. But, if Parliament is convinced, and those to whom it has given its confidence are convinced, that the system is working well and smoothly, then I say change for the sake of change is to be deprecated. In war-time, especially in vast, nation-wide and in some respects world-wide organization, continuity and stability must not be underrated. If we were perpetually to be altering our system or lending ourselves too lightly to that process, we might achieve the appearance of energy and reform only at the expense of the authority of individuals and only to the detriment of the smooth working of the machinery, and at a heavy cost in output, which is the sole objective. Therefore, it is at the point where I left off this subject when I discussed it with the House in January that I take up my theme today.

There are two main aspects in which production must be considered. First, the organization of planning and control, and, secondly the actual conditions present in the factories. Let us see first of all what was, and what is the system upon which the high administrative control of our war effort proceeds. The foundation must, of course, be a single, coordinated plan for the programmes of the three Services based upon our strategic needs. In my capacity as Minister of Defence, without which I could not bear the responsibilities entrusted to me for bringing about a successful outcome of the war, in that capacity, I prepared for the War Cabinet during the first three months of this year a revised general scheme, bringing together the whole of our munition production and import programme, and prescribing the highest reasonable target at which we ought to aim. For this purpose I was furnished with the forward programmes of the various fighting Departments, very much in the same way as the Service Estimates are brought before the Cabinet and the Treasury in the autumn in time of peace. I discussed these programmes orally and in writing with the Ministers and Service Chiefs of those Departments. The programmes were also examined by my own statistical Department under Professor Lindemann, now Lord Cherwell, and through the machinery of the Office of the Minister of Defence which, as the House knows, embodies the peace-time Committee of Imperial Defence organization. The work of these organizations proceeds ceaselessly. The strategic aspect of production is also continually considered by the Chiefs of Staff Committee, which meets every day, to advise or direct the conduct of the war. The general scheme, or War Supply Budget for the year 1941, a series of printed documents agreed with the Service Ministers and comprising a perfectly clear apportionment of resources and tasks, received the final approval of the War Cabinet on 31st March, and thereafter became mandatory on all Departments. There is, of course, no absolute finality in this scheme. Within its general framework revision and adjustment under the pressure of events are continuous.

So much for the framework of the general layout. The execution of this scheme on the military side is confided to the three great Supply Departments, namely, the Controller's Department of the Admiralty, the Ministry of Supply and the Ministry of Aircraft Production. The work had been parcelled out, and it remained for them to do it. The picture so luridly drawn of the chaotic and convulsive struggles of the three Supply Departments, without guidance or design, is one which will no doubt be pleasing to our enemies, but happily has no relation to the facts. The question however arises whether, in their execution of the approved scheme, the three Supply Departments have either been wanting in energy, or, on the contrary, through excess of zeal have quarrelled with each other or have trespassed upon each other's domain. There are no doubt instances of friction at the fringe of these powerful organizations, but I do not believe they bear any proportion worth mentioning to their individual and concerted efforts. It must be remembered that a very high proportion of our war production is carried out in factories working solely for one Department. That is true of aircraft factories, naval shipbuilding firms, ordnance factories, automobile factories and many others. A system has also been worked out for the allocation of the capacity of private engineering firms, either to single Departments, or, in other cases, to two or more Departments in stated proportions. Probably half the factories concerned and certainly more than three-quarters of the men employed are working now, at this time, for one single Department. The Admiralty has its many firms, with their factories dating from long ago and kept alive during our rotten periods by Admiralty orders. The Air Ministry has been striving for a great many years to build up an aircraft industry in this island pending the day when Parliament should decide to have an Air Force equal to any within striking distance of these shores. The War Office, always in time of peace the drudge and starveling of British defence, had its own Ordnance Factories and was at last on the eve of the war accorded a Ministry of Supply and this Ministry of Supply has of course extended over a very large part of the remaining British industry.

At the point which we have now reached in our munitions development almost all firms and factories are working under the complete control of the Government at the fulfilment of the approved and concerted programmes. They are either working directly or indirectly in the sphere of war production, or they are ministering to our domestic and other needs. In this domestic field also, however, a very complete and searching organization under Government control has been instituted. At the present moment, the whole industry of the country with inconsiderable exceptions, which may soon be licked up and absorbed, is assigned its function under Government authority. There are no doubt a number of minor aspects of our national life which have not yet been effectively regimented. When and as they are wanted, their turn will come. We are not a totalitarian State but we are steadily, and I believe as fast as possible, working ourselves into total war organization. When we are given vivid instances of lack of organization or of inter-departmental rivalry in some of the shops and factories, and when these are all bunched together to make an ill-smelling posy, it is just as well to remember that the area of disputation is limited, circumscribed and constantly narrowing.

In order to regulate the imports of commodities from abroad in accordance with the policy prescribed by the War Cabinet, we have, as I explained six months ago, the Import Executive comprising the heads of the Importing Departments, and presided over by my right hon. Friend the President of the Board of Trade, and formerly by him when he was Minister of Supply. This is working very smoothly and I am not aware of any troubles or disputes which have arisen. I should certainly hear of these soon enough if there were any. By the side of this Import Executive we have the North American Supply Committee with its elaborate corresponding organization in the United States. We are always trying to tighten up and make more precise and definite the work of our Purchasing Commissions in the United States. I should certainly not pretend that there is not a great deal of room for improvement and refinement, but it would be a mistake to suppose that the efficiency of our Purchasing Commissions under the supreme control of Mr Purvis has not reached a very high level or that it is not constantly being shaped and sharpened. A year ago, six months ago, there were a lot of troubles and discordances but latterly, although again I should be the first to hear of them, my information is that they have very largely died away.

We have of course to come to very clear-cut agreements with our American friends and helpers. They are making an immense effort for the common cause and they naturally ask for the fullest and clearest information about what is happening to their goods and whether there is waste or misdirection. It is our duty to satisfy them that there is no muddle, or that muddle is reduced to a minimum and that they are getting value for their money. We welcome their criticism because it is at once searching, friendly and well informed. The improvement in the ordering of imports and of the British purchases in the United States, and in the relations of the very large number of competent persons who work night and day on both sides of the ocean, in this sphere is, I am glad to say, steady and progressive.

Now I come to the home scene. What are the relations of the three Supply Departments in the vast fertile production field of this busy island? I have already said that for their chief production each of the Fighting Services through its Supply Department or Ministry to an overwhelming extent commands its own factories and labour. Nevertheless, there is an inevitable region of debatable ground of firms which serve several Departments at once. Many of them are small sub-contracting firms or firms which make components. Besides this, a process of change is continually going forward to meet the rapidly varying demands of the war. A firm is resigned by the Admiralty and can be transferred either to the Ministry of Aircraft Production or to the Ministry of Supply. Particular lines of production acquire special urgency or importance as we gain experience from the fighting or as new ideas come along. One line of production dries up because it is no longer needed; another opens or grows in scale. Obviously there is rivalry in this part of the field between the Supply Departments. There ought to be rivalry and there ought to be zealous competition within the limits of the programme prescribed. It is this zealous competition, limited though it be to a fraction of our industry, which presents the hard cases and sometimes the bad instances of which so much is made.

It is among other things for the purpose of resolving the disputes and rivalries of the Departments in this limited field that the Production Executive was called into being in January. The Minister of Labour, himself a contributory factor as Minister of Labour to the work of the rest of the Executive and himself a Member of the War Cabinet, presides over a committee of six, three of whom are the heads of the Supply Departments, and the other two are the President of the Board of Trade and the Minister of Works and Buildings. As I explained to the House six months ago, all the members of this body have every interest to agree. They may have different interests to advocate because they have different duties to discharge, but it is a delusion to suppose that they do not feel a corporate responsibility and try to work together for the common purpose and for the execution of the approved programmes entrusted to them. If they agree they have the power to act. Each can make his contribution to the common action immediately and the movement of labour and materials can be ordered there and then. If there is a difference which cannot be settled by agreement or compromise, any Minister of Cabinet rank, and they are all such, has the right of appeal to the War Cabinet, or, as between the Service Supply Departments, in the first instance to me as Minister of Defence. During my tenure I have seen some very sharp differences but those differences have never been so sharp as they were, as I well remember having lived through it, in the days of the last war. All I can say now is that for the last four months no question of departmental rivalry or dispute has been brought to me or the War Cabinet from the Production Executive. I give the assurance to the House today that in the high controlling organization there is now no dispute in progress about priorities of labour, raw materials, factory space or machine tools. Do not suppose however that this remarkable fact is the result of inertia or decay. On the contrary, as I shall show before I sit down – I am afraid I shall have to make a somewhat prolonged demand on the patience of the Committee, the subject is of great importance and must be dealt with comprehensively – production in all its forms is gaining steadily and swiftly, not only in volume, but, even at its present high altitude, in momentum.

I may say, while I am on the point, that much of this talk about difficulties of settling priorities is a back number. The whole business of priorities has undergone a complete transformation. We have no more of these arrogant, absolute priorities in virtue of which one Department claimed all that there was of a particular commodity and left nothing for the lesser but indispensable needs of others. Although the 1A priority is still maintained largely for psychological reasons, for certain particular spheres of production such as aircraft, and tanks now, it is no longer exercised in the crude manner of the last war or in the early months of this. The method of allocation of labour, materials, and facilities has modified and to a large extent replaced the scale of priorities. Allocation is the governing principle, and priorities are becoming little more than a stimulus upon its detailed assignments.

It is at this point and in this setting that I will deal with the suggestion that a Ministry of Production should be formed. Several speakers referred to this in the recent Debate, and apparently it is regarded by some of our most important newspapers as an easy and speedy solution of our difficulties. There is however a difference among the advocates of a Ministry of Production. Some ask that there should be a complete merging of the Supply Departments of the Admiralty, the Air Ministry and the War Office, and that there should be one great common shop, or vast Department or emporium serving all fighting needs. That would be very pretty if we were not at war. Others, recoiling from the frightful disturbance and confusion which would accompany the transition and the danger of upsetting so much in the midst of war, are content to ask for one Minister, presumably assisted by a secretarial staff, who should be interposed between the Prime Minister and Minister of Defence and the three Supply Departments. Nothing would be easier than for me to gratify this request by asking one of my colleagues in the War Cabinet to call himself Minister of Production and to duplicate the work of general apportionment which I already do. But, so far from helping me in my task, or helping the Departments in theirs, this would be an additional complication, burden and cause of delay.

Moreover, the relations of this Minister of Production with the three Supply Departments would be most unsatisfactory. He would either have to trust them and use them, as I do, for the purpose of executing the prescribed programmes, or he would be left to break into these Departments, interfere with their work and try to get things done by his personal exertions. The Ministers at the head of these Departments are men of energy, experience and knowledge. They work night and day, and they have powerful, far-reaching, swift-running machinery at their disposal. If, in the sphere assigned to them, they cannot execute the programme with which they are charged, I do not myself see how a super-Minister from outside, with his skeleton staff, could do it for them. If the new Minister's control were nominal, and did not affect the Ministerial responsibility of the heads of the Supply Departments, it would be a farce and a fraud upon the public to which I will not stoop. If, on the other hand, the Minister of Production attempted to lay strong hands on the internal administration and day-to-day work of these Departments, they would confront him with a knowledge superior to his own and far more intimate, and all the resulting differences would have to come to me, with very great friction to the administrative machine and additional burdens upon the head of the Government.

Furthermore, these matters cannot be considered without reference to the personalities involved. I have not been told who is to be this superman who, without holding the office of Prime Minister, is to exercise an overriding control and initiative over the three Departments of Supply and the three Ministers of Supply. Where is the super-personality who, as one of the members of the War Cabinet, will dominate the vast, entrenched, established, embattled organization of the Admiralty to whose successful exertions we owe our lives? Where is the War Cabinet Minister who is going to teach the present Minister of Aircraft Production how to make aircraft quicker and better than they are being made now? Who is the War Cabinet Minister who is going to interfere with Lord Beaverbrook's control and discharge of the functions of Minister of Supply duly and constitutionally conferred upon him? When you have decided on the man, let me know his name, because I should be very glad to serve under him, provided that I was satisfied that he possessed all the Napoleonic and Christian qualities attributed to him. In the conduct of vast, nation-wide administration there must be division of functions, and there must be proper responsibility assigned to the departmental chiefs. They must have the power and authority to do their work, and be able to take a proper pride in it when it is done, and be held accountable for it if it is not done.

Moreover, as I have tried to show, such difficulties as exist are not found at the summit but out in the country in a minority of smaller firms and factories. I do not for a moment deny that there are many things that go wrong and ought to be put right, but does anyone in his senses suggest that this should be the task of the super-Minister, that he should take up the hard cases and breakdowns by direct intervention from above? All he could do would be to refer complaints or scandals that came to his notice to the heads of the three Supply Departments, and, if he did not get satisfaction, he, having no power to remove or change the Ministers involved, would have to come to me, on whom rests the responsibility of advising His Majesty in such matters.

For good or ill, in any sensible organization you must leave the execution of policies already prescribed to the responsible Ministers and Departments. If they cannot do it, no one can. It is to them that complaints should be addressed. It is to them that Members should write. Any case of which full particulars are provided – I must add that proviso – will be searchingly examined. We do not stand here to defend the slightest failure of duty or organization. But let us have the facts. A kind of whispering campaign has been set on foot; there is a flood of anonymous letters. Vague and general charges are made. And all this fills our shop window, greatly to our detriment. It is impossible for me, within the limits of this Debate, to deal with various specific allegations which were made by Members in different parts of the House in the two preceding days of this Debate. Such a treatment of the matter would be entirely out of proportion, and I should have to trespass upon the Committee altogether unduly.

I turn aside, however, for a moment to deal with one particular aspect of the problem of production, namely machine tools. *The Times*, in its leading article this morning, makes the valuable suggestion that a census of machine tools throughout the country be held. There have already been three – in June, 1940, in November, 1940, and a partial census of the principal firms in June, 1941. The Supply Ministers are responsible for the use of machine tools to the best advantage. There is, however, a controller of machine tools, Mr Mills,[1] a business man of the highest repute, whose sole duty is to supervise their employment by all Departments. By the joint agreement and good will of the three Supply Departments, this gentleman has independent powers. He has his own representatives throughout the country. Although he is actually under the Ministry of Supply, he can remove any machine tool that is idle from any Department or factory and transfer it to another, and he is continually exercising these powers. He exercised them on several occasions against the late Minister of Aircraft Production[2] before the recent changes in the Government took place. This functionary is given these powers with good will by people who wish to submit their Departments to his use of them.

There are, however, three limiting factors in the use of machine tools. The first is any shortage that may exist of skilled labour, which we are striving by every method to overcome. The second is the undoubted difficulty we have found in working to the full extent night shifts under conditions of air attack. It is the third limiting factor which gives rise to the complaints which are made. I am not an expert in these matters, but I am told that there are between two and three hundred kinds of machine tools in our census. Their effective use is governed by certain precision machine tools of which there is a shortage. I need not say how intense are the efforts to break down these vexatious bottle-necks. Moreover, the precision tools of which there is a shortage vary sometimes with the varying demands of war production, and sometimes the block is found here and sometimes there. Thus, when people go about the country and see at some garage or factory or in some small firm a number of machine tools of the lower grades, or of peace-time specialized types, lying idle and write to their Member about it, the explanation is not that

[1] Percy Herbert Mills, 1890–1968. Munitions manufacturer. Director, Electrical and Musical Industries Ltd. Chairman, EMI Electronics Ltd. Controller-General of Machine Tools, 1940–44. Knighted, 1942. President of the Economic Sub-Commission, British Element, Central Commission for Germany, 1944–46. President of the Birmingham Chamber of Commerce, 1947–48. Chairman, National Research Development Corporation, 1950–55. Minister of Power, 1957–59. Paymaster General, 1959–61. Created Baronet, 1953; Baron, 1957. Viscount, 1962.

[2] Lord Beaverbrook; he was, more accurately, the 'former' not the 'late' Minister.

the supply of machine tools is not organized to the highest degree, not that the Government do not know about these machine tools, where they are and what they are, not that they do not in general know about them and have them on their census list, it is because, owing to the shortage at key points of special precision types, many of these tools cannot be brought into action, and there would be no sense in crowding out the factories with redundant machinery.

That is a digression which I have made because I have read with some interest the thoughtful article which appears in *The Times* this morning. Hardly any part of our common organization for war production has been more thoroughly and precisely examined than the question of machine tools. No one can be engaged, as my right hon. Friend the member for Carnarvon Boroughs (Mr Lloyd George) knows, in munition production for one day without feeling that this is, as it were, the ganglion nerve, the centre of the whole supply.

I said just now that I cannot go into details of many of the cases which the hon. Members brought up in the Debate. If they will write about them, they will be gone into in detail. There was, however, one charge made by my hon. Friend the Member for North Aberdeen (Mr Garro Jones) which, as it has had wide publicity and as it affects the United States supplies, requires to be answered. My hon. Friend said:

'The sad feature of the United States supply of aircraft is that whereas orders were energetically placed in the last two years or more for airframes and engines, those who placed them forgot at the same time to ensure that supplies of maintenance equipment and ancillary equipment were provided. What is the result? Of one type of aircraft imported from the United States, complete and operationally ready, there are several hundred – or were a few weeks ago – lying unpacked in inland warehouses, in their crates, for the sole reason that those who placed the orders on behalf of the Ministry of Aircraft Production did not order the necessary ancillary equipment.' – [Official Report, 9th July 1941; col. 204, Vol. 373.]

So far as aircraft on British order are concerned, this statement is quite untrue. All British orders for American aircraft have always been placed with spare engines and spares for airframes. There has been no failure or oversight of this kind in ordering British aircraft.

The mistake into which my hon. Friend has fallen arose from an exceptional event. When the French collapsed, all their contracts for aircraft in the United States were taken over immediately, for what they were worth, by the Minister of Aircraft Production. There was not an hour's delay. These aircraft had to be accepted in the condition in which they were prepared for the French, under French orders. This is the case to which I am sure reference was made in this passage of my hon. Friend's speech. They had to be accepted in the condition in which the French had specified them and in which they were delivered by the American manufacturers. This was a windfall, but it had its drawbacks. For instance, the French Tomahawks arrived without spare engines or spares for their airframes, exactly as my hon. Friend pointed out. They were built to take French guns. Their wireless sets did not tune with ours. Their instruments were on the metric system. They were not armoured according to our conditions. They differed in many ways from our methods of control and manoeuvre. Instead of pushing some lever forwards, you had to pull it backwards, which our pilots found most inconvenient.

As swiftly as possible these aircraft have been modified and brought into use. The 'cannibal' system was frequently resorted to of necessity, leaving lots of them partly gutted, but practically all of these French American aeroplanes are in use and have been most satisfactory in operation. Now there is the whole of that story that has been paraded as a typical scandal and example of how we do our business.

Mr Garro Jones (Aberdeen, North): No one would be more delighted than I to feel that British aeroplane orders were complete with operational equipment. My right hon. Friend has told the Committee that the types ordered for the French were not complete with operational equipment. Did I understand him correctly to say that the types ordered for British use were complete with their operational equipment?

The Prime Minister: Yes, I said that as plainly as I could. I said that the suggestion that they had not been ordered with their operational equipment was untrue, and I adhere to it. Everything that has been ordered on British account has been ordered complete. The aeroplanes ordered on French account were lacking in this equipment. An inquiry addressed to the Minister concerned would have elicited an immediate explanation, but when allegations of this sort are given the utmost publicity in Parliament by a Member speaking from the front Bench opposite, uninformed American readers – here is where the serious part comes – must come to the conclusion that there is disorganization and incapacity in the conduct of our munitions business, and this opinion, so damaging to us, would be based entirely on misconception and misunderstanding. It is not, I am glad to say, shared by the American authorities. I presided at a recent meeting attended by Mr Harry Hopkins, the Lease-Lend authority, to whose words we listened with so much comfort the other night. He, with his full knowledge and attended by expert American officers, dwelt upon the trials and difficulties attending the modification of aircraft from the United States on French account and expressed satisfaction with the arrangements we had made to overcome them. But outside this circle, who know all the facts, inside the United States, where there is a vigorous campaign against the policy pursued by the President and the majority, I fear that harm has been done, and it cannot be easily overtaken or healed.

What are the other elements which produce oscillations or discordances in the process of production? They arise, of course, out of the changing conditions of the war. As new needs arise, new directions have to be given, which undoubtedly cause disturbances in the flow of production, but I must say I have the feeling that the British machinery of production, vast and intricate though it be, is capable not only of flexible adaptation but of sustaining successfully a number of inevitable jerks. These take place, for instance, largely in the sphere of aircraft production. The Minister of Aircraft Production explained to the House on the second day of this Debate the constant changes in the design of aircraft which arose from the progress of our aeronautics and our experience of manufacture and war. He showed how it was sometimes inevitable that there should be a break in the continuity of production because one type had failed and another had proved itself, because one type was being faded out and another being worked in, and how this must happen when you run the risk of ordering off the drawing board and carrying out large orders on the basis of the pilot model without having the time to go through all the processes which in peace-time make the completion of the aeroplane from the moment of its conception a matter of five or six years.

It is a difficult question to decide when the mass production of a particular type should be discarded in favour of a new and better type, and to what intensity such a process of transformation should be carried. I think on the whole, at this moment, we have carried it a bit far. Aircraft of a particular type which slowly work up to the peak of production may be discarded after too short a run at the peak level – no doubt for very good reasons, very fine reasons, greater bomb capacity, greater speed and so forth. Simplification and continuity of serial production are, of course, the basic factors necessary in securing the flow of output, and it is a question of balancing between the two sides. All the same, believe me, mastery of the air, leadership and command in design cannot possibly be achieved except by a process of interminable trial and error and the scrapping of old types. Something better comes along. You cannot afford to miss it, even if you have to pay, and pay heavily, in numbers of output or dislocation in a section of the workshops. The struggle for air mastery requires vast numbers, but those vast numbers could not succeed alone unless the forward leading types constantly achieve the highest level of enterprise and perfection. Combat in the air is the quintessence of all physical struggle. To lose primacy in the quality of the latest machines would be incompatible with the attainment of that command of the air in quality and in quantity upon which a large part of our confidence is founded.

I am glad to tell the Committee that our spring and summer fashions in aircraft are this year farther ahead of contemporary German production than they were last year. The enemy borrowed many ideas from our fighter aeroplanes when he felt their mettle a year ago, and we borrowed from him too, but in the upshot we have confronted him in 1941 with fighter aircraft which in performance, speed, ceiling and, above all, gun armaments have left our pilots with the old, and even an added, sense of technical superiority. It would take too long to describe, as I easily could do, some of the smaller causes of oscillation which affect the execution of the Navy and Army Supply programmes. I could show in a way which I think would satisfy the Committee that a certain measure of change, with resulting dislocation, is inevitable under the strenuous conditions of war, but I do not propose to enter upon either of those fields today.

Let me come, on the other hand, to an example of criticism which is helpful and constructive. I have read the Seventeenth Report of the Select Committee on National Expenditure. It deals with the conditions in the filling factories. These are admittedly far from satisfactory. Since the war began great factories have been built in out-of-the-way districts, without time to meet the needs and amenities of the working population. They have not by any means yet reached their full capacity and proper standards. Although we have been making many millions of shells there are still several millions of shells and their components, including fuses, which are not yet filled. But there is no need for alarm, but rather for greater exertion, because in this war we are firing shells at men and not, as in the last war, so largely at the ground. Nor have we a great battlefront continuously engaged. We are making on an enormous scale, but we are not firing on any scale. It is important to remember in the battles in the desert the difficulties of getting ammunition to the places where the guns are, and since the front in France broke down there is no field of fire for our artillery. Therefore, what we have witnessed is not, as in the last war, as I know so well and as did my right hon. Friend before me, the feeling of intense effort to feed the guns from day to day, but we are piling up large and satisfactory reserves with no corresponding outflow to drain them off at the present time. Let me say nothing which would in any way remove from the minds of those engaged in the filling factories the view that catching up with the filling of the already large stores of components, fuses and shell-cases is not a work of prime and high order and of national importance.

Representatives of the Select Committee visited the filling factories in June and they produced a number of extremely shrewd and valuable suggestions dealing with transport, hostels, canteens, Sunday work and piece-work. We agree with nearly all of them. We will adopt almost all of them. We agree with them the more readily and we can adopt them the more speedily because, as I see from the records, on 7th January and on 5th February, in my capacity as Minister of Defence, I presided over two successive meetings of the Supply Committee on this very subject. Almost every one of these proposals had already been ordered to be put into operation months before, and has been or is being carried into effect with very great improvement, in spite of the many difficulties attendant upon the bringing into action of these great new plants in out-of-the-way districts under the conditions which prevailed last winter.

I have here a detailed account of all that had been set on foot or that had been done before the Select Committee visited the factories. I will send it to the Chairman of the Committee for their further observations. It is too long for me to read to the Committee in detail, but it shows that great minds sometimes think alike, and that the Government great minds had a good long start of the great minds of the Select Committee. The Report of the Select Committee is the kind of criticism that one wants – not mere vague abuse and prejudice, in which only bad citizens and bad people indulge in times like these, but helpful and constructive suggestions, many of which were contained in the speeches made from the Front Benches opposite.

I leave the first part of this subject, dealing with discordances and shortcomings alleged to be attributable to faults or weaknesses in the high control, and I come to the more general charges of slackness and inefficiency in the factories themselves, whether due to local lack of management or to lack of zeal in the workpeople. There is a certain class of member of all parties – you can count them on your fingers and toes – who feel, no doubt quite sincerely, that their war work should be to belabour the Government and portray everything at its worst, in order to produce a higher efficiency. I see that a Motion has been put on the Paper calling specifically for the appointment of a Minister of Production. I consider that to be a perfectly proper step for the Members concerned to take. I regret only that the motion cannot be moved in this form today. If the Members who have fathered it do not feel satisfied with the reasons I have given against creating a Minister or Ministry of Production, I hope that they will not hesitate to go to a Division by moving a nominal reduction of one of the Votes we are discussing. That is the straightforward and manly course. No one should be deterred in war-time from doing his duty merely by the fact that he will be voting against the Government or still less because the Party Whips are acting as tellers.

We are often told that 'the House of Commons thinks this' or 'feels that'. Newspapers write: 'The general feeling was of grave uneasiness,' 'There was much disquiet in the Lobby,' etc. All this is telegraphed all over the world and produces evil effects. No one has a right to say what is the opinion of the House of Commons unless there has been a Division. We suffer now from not having Divisions. We have Debates, to which a very small minority of Members are able to contribute because of the time. They express their anxiety and grievances and make our affairs out as bad as they possibly can, and these bulk unduly in the reports which reach the public or are heard abroad. These members do not represent the opinion of the House of Commons or of the nation, nor do their statements give a true picture of the prodigious war effort of the British people. Parliament should be an arena in which grievances and complaints become vocal. The Press also should be a prompt and vigilant alarm bell, ringing when things are not going right. But it is a very heavy burden added to the others we have to bear if, without a vote being cast, the idea should be spread at home and abroad that it is the opinion of the House of Commons that our affairs are being conducted in an incompetent and futile manner and that the whole gigantic drive of British industry is just one great muddle and flop.

People speak of workmen getting £6, £7 or £8 a week and not giving a fair return to the State. It is also asserted, on the other hand, that the workmen are eager to work, but that the mismanagement from the summit is such that they are left for weeks or even months without the raw material, or the particular component or the special direction which they require for their task. We may be quite sure that in an organization which deals with so many millions of people under all the stresses of the present time and in view of the present conditions, as well as the inevitable oscillations of war-time which I have mentioned, there are a great many faults, and we must try sedulously to eradicate those faults and to raise the harmony and cohesion of our whole productive effort. Here again, it is important to preserve a sense of proportion and not to be led away by thinking that hard cases, wrong deeds and minor or local discordances represent more than a very small fraction of our war performance. It is no less important – indeed, in a way it is even more important – not to sum up and condemn the whole effort of the nation as if it were expressed in these discordances and failures. That is my complaint about the recent Debate and the use made of it by certain sections of the Press and the results upon our own self-confidence and still more upon opinion friendly, hostile or balancing in foreign countries.

Mr A. Bevan (Ebbw Vale): Who said that?

The Prime Minister: I am quoting no particular person. I am saying that the effect of the Debate was to give that hostile impression. When I read the Debate, that was the effect it had upon me, and I set myself to present a complete picture to the Committee. I was distressed at this aspect of the matter. I therefore ventured to ask the House to resume the Debate, and I should be glad to have the matter brought to a plain issue.

It is on this footing and with these preliminaries in dealing with the second sphere of my subject, namely, what is going on in the factories, that I come to the remark of my right hon. Friend the Member for Kidderminster (Sir J. Wardlaw-Milne), who said that 'our people are only working up to 75 per cent. of their possible efficiency'. I am well aware that, in making that statement, my hon. Friend did not wish to attack the Government or in any way to embarrass the national defence. In fact, he has been ill-used. This particular sentence has been wrested from its context and from the whole character of his speech. Nevertheless, as Chairman of the Select Committee on National Expenditure, he holds a very responsible position and is credited with exceptional knowledge. A statement like this, coming from him, although uttered with the best of motives, is serious when it is broadcast apart from its context. I have to think of its effect in Australia, for instance, where party politics are pursued with the same robust detachment as was exhibited by our forerunners in this House in the seventeenth and eighteenth centuries. A statement like this, taken out of its context, or in a very summarized version of what was said, becomes the subject of lively discussion out there. Australian troops are bearing with great distinction much of the brunt of the fighting in the Middle East, and it must be very painful to Australians to be told that we are only making a three-quarter effort here at home to put proper weapons in their hands. In America, such a statement is meat and drink to the Isolationist forces. Americans are being asked to pay much heavier taxes, to give up their food, to alter their daily lives, and to reduce their motor-cars, indulgences and pleasures of all kinds, in order to help Britain, and I cannot help being deeply disturbed when they are told on what seems to be high British authority that we are making only a three-quarter hearted effort to help ourselves. My hon. Friend's allegation has been wrested from its context. I have no quarrel with him, but it has gone to all parts of the country and to all quarters of the world; but nothing can be done about that.

What is important is whether it is true; but how difficult to decide because, after all, this is a double expression of opinion – first as to whether it is 75 per cent., or not, and, secondly, 75 per cent. of what? I have tried to find a datum line, and I take as the datum line the three months after Dunkirk. Then, it will be admitted, our people worked to the utmost limit of their moral, mental and physical strength. Men fell exhausted at their lathes, and workmen and working women did not take their clothes off for a week at a time. Meals, rest, and relaxation all faded from their minds, and they just carried on to the utmost limit of their strength. Thus there was a great spurt in June, July and August of last year. Immense efforts were made, and every semi-finished weapon was forced through to completion, very often at the expense of immediate future output, producing an altogether abnormal inflation of production. So let us take those three months as the datum line; you could not have a harder test.

Now is it true that we are only working 75 per cent. of that? There are certainly one or two reasons why we cannot wholly recapture and maintain indefinitely the intense personal efforts of a year ago. First of all, if we are to win this war – and I feel solidly convinced that we shall – it will be largely by staying power. For that purpose you must have reasonable minimum holidays for the masses of workers. There must, as my hon. Friend himself urged in his speech, be one day in seven of rest as a general rule, and there must be, subject to coping with bottle-necks and with emergencies which know no law, a few breaks and where possible one week's holiday in the year. Since what I will call the Dunkirk three months datum period, we have undoubtedly relaxed to that extent. Sunday work is practically eliminated, and brief periods of leisure have been allowed to break the terrible routine strain of continuous employment. I am quite sure that if we had not done so, we should have had a serious crack which would have cost far more in production than these brief periods of rest from labour.

Next, allowance must be made for the very severe change in the diet of the heavy manual worker. It is quite true that no one has gone short of food; there has been no hunger, there has not been the confusion of the last war at some periods, but no one can pretend that the diet of the British people and especially of their heavy workers has not become far less stimulating and interesting than it was a year ago. Except for our Fighting Services, we have been driven back to a large extent from the carnivore to the herbivore. That may be quite satisfactory to the dietetic scientists who would like to make us all live on nuts, but undoubtedly it has produced, and is producing, a very definite effect upon the energetic output of the heavy worker. [Interruption.] The Noble Lord knows I could discuss a great many matters in Secret Session, but he is one of the first to get up and say he would like to have these discussions in public, under conditions where nothing can be said by the Government in answer to the kind of criticism with which he associated himself. We want more meat in the mines and the foundries, and we want more cheese. Why should that gratify Lord Haw-Haw?[1] Lord Haw-Haw should also bear in mind the statement of Mr Harry Hopkins the other day, on the intention of the United States to see that we get our food, and of their intention to keep clear the sea-lanes by which our food will be brought. I know of the great arrangements which have been made to send us food in nourishing, varied and more interesting quantities. Therefore there is no need to tell me I am helping Lord Haw-Haw. If he never gets any more consolation than he gets from me, his lot will be as hard as his deserts. Every effort will be made, and is being made, to supplement this deficiency, and I share the hope of the Minister of Food and the Minister of Agriculture that our rations in 1942 will be more stimulating and more intensely nourishing than in 1941.

That is the second reason. The first is the need for some relaxation; then there is this question of food, which has come upon us gradually and which is serious. I wish it to be known all over the United States that it is serious, because it encourages them in their actions. The third reason is this: Look at all the dilution we have had. It is estimated that one-third more people are working in the war industries than there were a year ago. A great many of these are trainees and newcomers. It would not be wonderful if they failed to preserve the same level of output per pair of human hands as was achieved by

[1] William Joyce, 1906–1946. Born in Brooklyn, New York City: his mother was English and his father Irish. Moved to England, 1921. At the outbreak of war in September 1939 he and his wife moved to Germany, where he offered his services to the Nazis. Broadcast to Britain, with news intended to undermine British morale. Arrested by the British at Flensburg, just after the end of the war. Tried for High Treason in London. His only defence was that he was an American citizen and therefore not legally able to perform acts of treason against Britain. The prosecution however stated that for the first nine months of the war he had a British passport and therefore did owe allegiance to the crown. He was found guilty and sentenced to death. All appeals were turned down and he was executed in 1946.

the skilled craftsmen of a year or 18 months ago. Naturally they will improve. They are improving, but dilution means a reduction in efficiency per pair of human hands in the earlier stages.

Then, fourthly, there has been a great dislocation by reason of the air raids, by which the Germans hoped to smash up our industries and break down our power of resistance last autumn and winter. Air-raid destruction, extraordinary blitzes on our ports and manufacturing centres, the restrictions of the blackout, the interruption and delays of transportation, all played their delaying and dislocating parts. The remedy and counter-measure which was proposed and carried through when possible with such extreme vigour by the Supply Departments, with Lord Beaverbrook and the Ministry of Aircraft Production in the van as the inspiring force, took the form of dispersion. This was a matter of life and death, in the aircraft industry as well as in other key war industries. The great Bristol firm, for instance, was dispersed into nearly 45 sub-centres. I could give you – and the enemy too – a score of instances of the dispersion of firms to 20, 30 or 40 sub-centres. All this has been an obstacle to the smooth running of production. It has placed us, however, in a position in which we are immune from mortal damage from enemy air raids in our aircraft production and other branches of munitions. We may suffer, we may be retarded, we can no longer be destroyed. When a great firm like the Bristol firm is divided and dispersed, consider the trials of the workpeople and the problems of the management. Workpeople by the thousand have to be moved from their homes, plant has to be shifted, ruined factories have to be reconditioned, domestic affairs have somehow or other to be adjusted, often with great sacrifice and hardship, and it is a marvel what has been done to overcome these grievous and novel difficulties. That they should hamper the pace and intensity of production was inevitable.

I have now described to the Committee a number of solid factors which have fallen upon us since the Dunkirk period, all of which have tended to obstruct and reduce output. I should like to give the Committee some facts and figures to show how far we have succeeded, by improved organization and by the smoother running of our expanding machinery, in overcoming these adverse currents which I have set out at length. But here I encounter a new difficulty. I am told we cannot have these Debates in Secret Session, they must be in public. The Germans must read in two or three days every word we say, and therefore I cannot give actual figures. In addition, I am told by my hon. Friends to 'Let us have none of those comparative percentages; let us not be told that we are producing half as much again or double what we produced this time last year, because we were producing nothing last year or something like it.' As my hon. Friend said – it is a Lancashire saying – 'Twice nowt is nowt.' So, according to these critics, I am inhibited from all vindicatory comparisons. I must not say how much better we are than at this time last year when, after all, we had been at war for ten or eleven months, and so were presumably making something. I must not say how much better we are than at the twenty-third month of the last war, nor how our output compares with the peak of the last war, because it is contended conditions have changed. Well, Sir, this is rather easy money for the critics. A handful of Members can fill a couple of days' Debate with disparaging charges against our war effort, and every ardent or disaffected section of the Press can take it up, and the whole can cry dismal cacophonous chorus of stinking fish all round the world. But no answer must be made, nothing must be said to show the giant war effort, the prodigy of national zeal, which excites the astonishment of friend and foe, which will command the admiration of history, and which has kept us alive.

I defy these tyrannical prohibitions. I intend to make comparisons, both with the Dunkirk datum period and with the similar peak periods of the last war. Despite all the troubles I have enumerated, the Ministry of Supply output in the last three months has been one-third greater than in the three months of the Dunkirk period. Though our Navy, Army and Air Force are larger, the Ministry has one-third more people working in its factories. Thus, despite dilution, dispersion, reduced food, the blackout, and all the troubles I have described, each man is turning out, on the whole, each day, as much as he did in that time of almost superhuman effort. Let me present the balance-sheet. One-third more workers and one-third more output is quits. But all the adverse factors I have described have somehow or other been cancelled out by superior development of our machinery and organization. We have made, in the last three months, more than twice the field guns we made in the Dunkirk period. The ammunition we are turning out is half as much again. The combined merchant and naval ship-building now in active progress is bigger, not only in scale but in current daily volume of execution, than it was at any period in the last war, and, of course, the work now is immeasurably more complex than it was then.

In aircraft production it is foolish to calculate only by the number of machines, though these have largely increased, because one machine takes 5,000 man-hours, and another, 75,000 man-hours. Judged, however, either by the test of numbers or man-hours eventuating in aircraft production, the increase even above the spurt period of a year ago is substantial. The increase since this Government took office is enormous, and I should be proud to tell the Committee what it is. I am not going to do so, because the enemy do not tell us their figures, much as we should like to have them. The Committee must, therefore, be content with my assurance that progress and expansion on a great scale are continuous, and are remorselessly spurred on. This progress has been accomplished under the fire of the enemy, under air assault, which Hitler was led to believe would shatter our industries and reduce us to impotence and subjection. It has been done in spite of the difficulties of dispersion, and has been done not only with no sacrifice in quality but with a gain in quality, both actual and relative. Now that the air battles are developing again in scale and intensity we can claim that our fighters are at least as much ahead of the enemy as when we defeated him a year ago. As for the bombers, in the year that has passed, in British production alone, taking no account of the now rapidly expanding United States imports, we have doubled our power of bomb discharge on Germany at 1,500 miles range, and in the next three months, though this time taking account of the American reinforcements, we shall double it again. In the six months after that we shall redouble it. Besides all this we have ploughed the land, and, by the grace of God, have been granted the greatest harvest in living memory, perhaps the greatest we have ever known in these Islands. So much for comparison with the high level of the Dunkirk period.

Now I turn to some comparisons with the last war. That was a terrible war. It lasted 52 months; there was frightful slaughter; there was an immense British effort; there was a complete final victory. We are now in the twenty-third month. We have lost large stocks of equipment on the beaches of Dunkirk, our food has been rationed, our meat reduced, we have been bombed and blacked out, and yet, even in this seventh quarter of the war, our total output of war-like stores has been nearly twice as great as our total output of production in the corresponding seventh quarter of the last war, and has equalled our production in the fourteenth and culminating quarter of the last war. We have rather more workers in the metal industry than we had then. When all those now working to complete and equip our new factories become available, and the Ministry of Labour has completed its task of collecting workers from unessential industries, we shall produce even more. But to reach in two years the level only achieved in the fourth year of the last war is, I venture to submit, an achievement which deserves something better than flouts and jeers.

We are told how badly labour is behaving, and then a lot of people who never did a day's hard work in their lives are out after them. Again I claim to look back to the last war. In that war we had many bitter and devastating strikes, and in the final two years nearly 12,000,000 working days were lost through labour disputes. So far, in the whole 23 months of this war, we have lost less than 2,000,000 days. I was anxious to have the latest information about trade disputes in the country. I received, a few minutes before I rose to speak, a report that at 11 o'clock today there was no stoppage of work of any kind arising from a trade dispute in any part of Great Britain.

It is the fashion nowadays to abuse the Minister of Labour. He is a workman, a trade union leader. He is taunted with being an unskilled labourer representing an unskilled union. I daresay he gives offence in some quarters; he has his own methods of speech and action. He has a frightful load to carry; he has a job to do which none would envy. He makes mistakes, like I do, though not so many or so serious – he has not got the same opportunities. At any rate he is producing, at this moment, though perhaps on rather expensive terms, a vast and steady volume of faithful effort, the like of which has not been seen before. And if you tell me that the results he produces do not compare with those of totalitarian systems of government and society, I reply by saying, 'We shall know more about that when we get to the end of the story.'

I daresay that some of our critics will not like this kind of talk. They call it complacency. Living in comparative idleness, they wish to lash the toilers of body and mind to further exertions. To state facts which are true and encouraging is to be accused of a cheap and facile optimism. Our critics do not like it; neither do the Germans, but for different reasons. But I consider that if, for days on end, the whole national effort is disparaged and insulted, and if, all over the world, we are depicted by our friends and countrymen as slack, rotten and incompetent, we are entitled, nay, it becomes a pressing duty, to restore the balance by presenting the truth.

A number of Votes have been put down as a basis of this Debate. I do not think I shall be out of Order if I place our discussion in its relation to the general aspects of the war before we separate for a short Recess, during which Members will be able to regain contact with their constituents and Ministers to give undivided attention to their work. When I look out upon the whole tumultuous scene of this ever-widening war, I feel it my duty to conclude by giving a very serious warning to the House and to the country. We must be on our guard equally against pessimism and against optimism. There are, no doubt, temptations to optimism. It is the fact that the mighty Russian State, so foully and treacherously assaulted, has struck back with magnificent strength and courage, and is inflicting prodigious and well-deserved slaughter for the first time upon the Nazi armies. It is the fact that the United States, the greatest single Power in the world, is giving us aid on a gigantic scale and advancing in rising wrath and conviction to the very verge of the war. It is the fact that the German air superiority has been broken, and that the air attacks on this country have for the time being almost ceased. It is the fact that the Battle of the Atlantic, although far from won, has, partly through American intervention, moved impressively in our favour. It is the fact that the Nile Valley is now far safer than it was 12 months ago or three months ago. It is the fact that the enemy has lost all pretence of theme or doctrine, and is sunk ever deeper in moral and intellectual degradation and bankruptcy, and that almost all his conquests have proved burdens and sources of weakness.

But all these massive towering facts, which we are entitled to dwell on, must not lead us for a moment to suppose that the worst is over. The formidable power of Nazi Germany, the vast mass of destructive munitions that they have made or captured, the courage, skill and audacity of their striking forces, the ruthlessness of their centralized war-direction, the prostrate condition of so many great peoples under their yoke, the resources of so many lands which may to some extent become available to them – all these restrain rejoicing and forbid the slightest relaxation. It would be madness for us to suppose that Russia or the United States is going to win this war for us. The invasion season is at hand. All the Armed Forces have been warned to be at concert pitch by 1st September and to maintain the utmost vigilance meanwhile. We have to reckon with a gambler's desperation. We have to reckon with a criminal who by a mere gesture has decreed the death of 3,000,000 or 4,000,000 of Russian and German soldiers. We stand here still the champions. If we fail, all fails, and if we fall, all will fall together. It is only by a superb, intense and prolonged effort of the whole British Empire that the great combination of about three-quarters of the human race against Nazidom will come into vehement and dynamic life. For more than a year we have been all alone: all alone, we have had to guard the treasure of mankind. Although there have been profound and encouraging changes in the situation, our own vital and commanding responsibilities remain undiminished; and we shall discharge them only by continuing to pour out in the common cause the utmost endeavours of our strength and virtue and, if need be, to proffer the last drop of our heart's blood.

Harold Nicolson: diary
('Diaries and Letters, 1939-1945')

29 July 1941

At the House today Winston makes a long and careful speech about production. It does not go very well. There is a sense of criticism in the air.

Winston S. Churchill to Oliver Lyttelton
(*Churchill papers, 20/41*)

29 July 1941
Most Immediate
Most Secret

As regards proposed staff conversations, you will have seen instructions already sent to Sir H. Knatchbull-Hugessen in Foreign Office telegram No. 1651 to Angora. The next stage is to hold the conversations, and it seems unnecessary to say anything more to the Turkish authorities for the present. Incidentally, with reference to paragraph 1 of your telegram under reference, while there would be no objection to asking the Turks to send ships to Egypt, it is doubtful whether it can be said that there is grave risk in sending big ships to Alexandretta now that we hold Cyprus. Anyhow, it is essential to get the opinion of the Commander-in-Chief, Mediterranean, on this before deciding what the Turks should be told.

2. As regards the reply to Angora telegram No. 591 to Cairo, the Chiefs of

Staff do not agree that categorical dates and figures, arising from a preliminary study by the Joint Planners and not yet approved by the Commanders-in-Chief or the Chiefs of Staff, should be given to His Majesty's Ambassador, even for his personal information. They might be dangerously misleading and only cause subsequent disappointment. It would be unsafe to bank on no serious German threat before the 15th October, and not only the Turks, but Sir H. Knatchbull-Hugessen must realize that the redemption of any promise now given to the Turks must depend on developments in the Middle East as a whole. But meanwhile it is important that the Turks should be told that, while we agree that the threat to Turkey is real and most serious, our present information does not suggest that it is immediate, and, subject to the concurrence of the Commanders-in-Chief, you should communicate to Sir H. Knatchbull-Hugessen, to be passed to the Turks in whatever manner he thinks best, the information contained in paragraphs 1 and 2 of War Office telegram No. 79993 of the 24th July to the Commander-in-Chief, Middle East, and Commander-in-Chief, India.

3. We shall, of course, be discussing the whole question with Auchinleck and Tedder this week.

Winston S. Churchill to Sir Kingsley Wood
(*Churchill papers, 20/20*)

30 July 1941 10 Downing Street
Most Secret

There are tales that Sir Horace Wilson holds a weekly meeting of Heads of Departments to teach them the way they should go, or not go. This raises well-founded suspicions, but perhaps the rumour is not true. Will you find out discreetly, and let me know.[1]

[1] Sir Kingsley Wood replied that same day: 'There is no truth in this. The last meeting of Heads of Departments was several months ago when a special meeting was held to carry out the Cabinet's decision as to civil servants leave.'

Winston S. Churchill to Clement Attlee
(*Churchill papers, 20/36*)

30 July 1941
Action this Day
Most Secret

Please see letter from Sir Robert Knox.[1] I think it would be a mistake to go forward with this proposal. The Conservative Party might resent strongly the elevation to the Peerage of one who has this record, albeit many years old, of inciting mutiny among His Majesty's troops. Moreover, his Communist and German connections are also open to comment. Elevation to the Peerage is still considered an honour, and much coveted by some people. It would be thought unseemly that The King should be advised, out of so many who are rendering good service, to select Mr Price.[2] Serious injury might be done to the Administration if such a nomination were to be pressed unduly upon The King.

In view of the comments, now for the first time quoted, of the members of the Scrutiny Committee, I could not accept their previous verdict without re-submitting Mr Price's name, together with the secret information. In this case one might expect an adverse opinion, which would be decisive.

I am sorry, too, about Jos Wedgwood, for whom I have a high regard. I do not think the Americans would care one way or the other, but he has made such an arrant fool of himself in the United States, and shown himself so incapable of discharging serious and helpful work that people will ask: 'Why should he be picked out for so high an honour, above all the brave and skilful people who might receive the Royal favour?'

I have been most anxious to meet your wishes, but I hope you will take Macmillan's[3] suggestion and look about for some solid Trade Unionist or Member of your Party. It occurs to me that Citrine might be willing to go to

[1] Robert Uchtred Eyre Knox, 1889–1965. War Office secretariat, 1912–14. On active service 1914–16 (Distinguished Service Order, despatches, severely wounded). War Office, 1918–19; Treasury, 1920; Private Secretary to the Permanent Secretary to the Treasury, 1928–39. Secretary, Coronation Commission, 1936–7. Knighted, 1937. Secretary, Political Honours Scrutiny Committee, 1939–65. Secretary, Coronation Commission, 1952–53.

[2] George Ward Price, 1886–1961. Educated at St Catherine's College, Cambridge. *Daily Mail* War Correspondent, in the first Balkan war. Official War Correspondent at the Dardanelles and with the Salonica army. A Director of Associated Newspapers Ltd and special foreign correspondent for the *Daily Mail* between the wars. War Correspondent in France, 1939; in Tunisia, 1943; in France, 1944.

[3] Hugh Pattison Macmillan, 1873–1952. Advocate, Scottish Bar, 1897. Assistant Director of Intelligence, Ministry of Information, 1918. Lord Advocate of Scotland, 1924. Chairman of several Royal Commissions (including Lunacy and Mental Disorder, 1924) and Courts of Inquiry (including the Mining Industry Dispute, 1925). Created Baron (Life Peer), 1930. A Lord of Appeal in Ordinary, 1930–39 and 1941–47; A Lord of Appeal, 1947–52). Minister of Information, 1939–40. President, Society for the Promotion of Nature Reserves, 1943–47.

the Lords in this connection. He has already accepted a title, much to my surprise, and a Peerage would give him a footing for serious work in Parliament.[1]

Oliver Harvey: diary
(*'The War Diaries of Oliver Harvey, 1941-1945'*)

30 July 1941

RUSSO-POLISH TREATY

Treaty finally signed at 4.30. All very friendly – photographers and films. PM pulled out of his afternoon sleep to come and sign – looked very bleary – eyes very watery in the spotlight.

John Colville: diary
(*Colville papers*)

30 July 1941

Was present at the signing of the Russo-Polish treaty in the S of S's room at the FO. It was signed against a background of spotlights and a foreground of camera-men by the PM, Eden, Sikorski and Maisky, while a bust of the Younger Pitt looked down, rather disapprovingly I thought. Although this treaty abrogates the Soviet-German treaty of 1939, and leaves the frontier question unsettled, it has caused a lot of Polish heart-burning, including, I believe, the resignation of the President. To a Pole, a Russian has no advantages over a German – and History makes this very understandable.

Auchinleck, the new C-in-C Middle East, dined with the PM and I had a conversation with him beforehand. He thought the situation in the Western Desert had been mis-handled – 'not by the High Command, but tactically I mean'.

Winston S. Churchill to J. V. Stalin
(*Premier papers, 3/401/1*)

31 July 1941
Secret and Personal

Following my personal intervention, arrangements are now complete for the despatch of 10,000 tons of rubber from this country to one of your northern ports.

[1] Citrine did not accept a Peerage until 1946.

2. In view of the urgency of your requirements, we are taking the risk of depleting to this extent our metropolitan stocks, which are none too large and will take time to replace.

3. British ships carrying this rubber, and certain other supplies, will be loaded within a week, or at the most ten days, and will sail to one of your northern ports as soon as the Admiralty can arrange convoy.

4. This new amount of 10,000 tons is additional to the 10,000 tons of rubber already allocated from Malaya. Of this latter amount, 2,651 tons have already sailed on the 20th July in SS *Volga* from Port Swettenham for Vladivostok. SS *Arctika* has also sailed from Malaya with 2,500 tons on board. SS *Maxim Gorki*, which left Shanghai on July 25th and SS *Krasny Partisan*, due to sail from Hong Kong on August 1st, should reach Malaya early in August and pick up additional cargoes of rubber, which, added to those carried in the first two ships, will raise the amount to 10,000 tons, in addition to the 10,000 in my paragraph 1.[1]

Daily Telegraph: leading article
(*'Daily Telegraph'*)

31 July 1941

Not seldom a brilliant debating speech forfeits to reflection much of the glamour of its first success. That decidedly is not the case with the Prime Minister's memorable contribution on Tuesday to the long-drawn debate on production. Second thoughts there chime with first impressions. As an intellectual exercise alone it was sufficiently amazing. To hold the rapt attention of an exacting audience for an hour and a half with the exposition of a subject at once so many-sided and so bristling with detail and to do this without any lapse into dullness but with a sustained vigour and good humour to the end, is no common feat. It must be admitted, too, by the critics whom the Prime Minister was answering, that the argument was as cogent, and in some notable directions as disconcerting, as the wit by which it was enlivened was refreshing. Mr Churchill could not have better vindicated his fitness for the leadership for which the nation has learned to look to him.

One caveat that reflection on the event suggests must, however, be entered. The preparation of such an exercise must needs have imposed a heavy strain on the precious time and not inexhaustible energy of a man who is already

[1] On 1 August 1941 General Mason-Macfarlane reported from Moscow what seemed to be the encouraging news that 'Stalin seems absolutely confident of being able to hold up the German attacks this autumn without losing either Leningrad, Moscow or Kiev. He does not think the Germans will penetrate anywhere to a depth of more than 100 kilometres from the present front.' (Letter of 1 August 1941: *War Office papers, 216/124*)

carrying a burden well-nigh not to be borne. His rare gifts and his vitality are not commodities in unlimited supply; and the call upon them should be rationed in the national interests. What is consumed in debate cannot be given to things more urgent and vital. Those who realize the magnitude of Mr Churchill's services to the common cause of which, as he says, we are still the champions should be wary of subjecting his strength to a breaking strain.

John Colville: diary
(*Colville papers*)

31 July 1941

The PM walked back from the House after the Cabinet, a thing he has never done before, and though he was talking to me at the top of his voice about war memorials (a train of thought engendered by the Cenotaph!) hardly anybody in the street recognized him.

On late duty at No. 10. The PM returned from the Other Club, somewhat cantankerous, and dictated voluminous notes about the war until 2.15 a.m.

Winston S. Churchill to General Ismay, for the Chiefs of Staff Committee
(*Churchill papers, 20/36*)

31 July 1941

I cannot feel that this operation, involving war with Persia in the event of non-compliance, has been studied with the attention which its far-reaching character requires. While agreeing as to its necessity, I consider that the whole business requires exploring, concerting, and clamping together, as between the Foreign Office and the War Office, and between the Middle East Command and the Government of India. We must not take such grave steps without having clear-cut plans for the various eventualities. For instance, what happens if the Persian troops around and about the Ahwaz oil fields seize all Anglo-Persian Oil Company employees and hold them as hostages? What attitude is expected from the Bakhtiari and the local inhabitants? What happens to British residents in Teheran? Is there any danger of the oil wells being destroyed rather than that they should fall into our possession? We must be very careful not to commit an atrocity by bombing Teheran. Are our available forces strong enough to occupy the Ahwaz oil fields in the face of local and official Persian opposition? How far north do we propose to go? What aerodromes are available? How is the railway to be worked if the Persians refuse to help?

These and many other questions require to be thought out. It would be well if the Lord President with the Secretaries of State for Foreign Affairs, War and

India reviewed the whole matter and reported to the War Cabinet during the early part of next week. Meanwhile, all necessary action of a preparatory character should proceed. I am in favour of the policy, but it is of a very serious character, and should not be undertaken until the possible consequences and alternative situations have been thoroughly surveyed and careful, detailed plans made and approved.

Winston S. Churchill to General Ismay
(*Churchill papers, 20/36*)

I shall want plenty of photographs of Port Sudan, Massawa, the new port which is being developed in the Red Sea, Asmara, Basra, Tobruk, &c.

War Cabinet: minutes
(*Cabinet papers, 65/19*)

31 July 1941 — Prime Minister's Room
12.15 p.m. — House of Commons

It was also known that a convoy had been attacked on the 29th July in the South Atlantic. Full details had not yet been received. The Germans claimed to have sunk 17 ships, and it was fairly certain that 10 had been sunk, mostly of small tonnage.

The Prime Minister said that this attack on the Southern Atlantic route would almost certainly be followed by others. As soon as American plans matured, we should bring back destroyers and corvettes now based on Halifax to protect this route.[1]

[1] Churchill did not tell the War Cabinet that, as a result of increasingly successful progress at Bletchley in breaking the German naval Enigma, all German U-boat instructions were being read, 'continuously and with little or no delay' (F.H. Hinsley and others, *British Intelligence in the Second World War, Its Influence on Strategy and Operations*, Volume 2, London, 1981, page 163). As a result, trans-Atlantic convoys could be routed away from the U-boat packs. This Intelligence breakthrough came at the very moment when fears had intensified that the rate of sinking of merchant ships would soon overtake the rate of new construction. (In April 1941 more than 70 British merchant ships had been sunk; in May 1941 more than 90; in June the number fell to just under 60 and in both July and August to under 30 a month) Thanks to the decrypts of the naval Enigma, that nightmare was now over, and Churchill could be far more confident that the trans-Atlantic supplies would not be fatally interrupted. The Battle of the Atlantic Committee, which struggled so hard to find new construction and to accelerate the rate of turn-round of ships in port, could meet now in a less fearful atmosphere. For the rest of 1941, one area at least of Churchill's anguish could be reduced. (But only for another six months; at the end of February 1942 a new U-boat Enigma setting remained unbroken for another ten months, and the nightmare returned. From January 1943, however, the decrypting was restored, and safety again assured.)

The Prime Minister said[1] that the Defence Committee would have to study two important problems in the near future –

(1) The reinforcement of the Middle East with heavy bombers, and

(2) A service to carry Air Force personnel from one part of the Middle East theatre to another if the need arose.

In order to carry out (2) it was necessary that as many troop-carrying aircraft as possible should be made available. He asked the Secretary of State for Air to make a report to the War Cabinet on the number of transport aircraft which could be made available in the Middle East within, say, the next two or three months.

The Prime Minister also referred to the extent of the forces now in the Middle East; and to the scale of reinforcements of tanks. He gave directions that General Auchinleck should see a copy of the recent exchange of telegrams between himself and President Roosevelt on this subject.

[1] In view of the particular secrecy of this item, it was not circulated with the War Cabinet Minutes, but it was recorded in the Confidential Annex (*Cabinet papers, 65/23*).

August 1941

Winston S. Churchill to Anthony Eden
(*Churchill papers, 20/36*)

1 August 1941

Could you not tell the Dutch that we have already assumed the duty of safeguarding and restoring their possessions and rights to the best of our ability during the war and at the peace? It follows therefore that an attack upon the Netherlands East Indies would lead us to do the utmost in our power. We must, however, remain the sole judge of what actions or military measures are practicable and likely to achieve our common purposes.

Should the United States be disposed to take supporting action many things would become possible which we cannot undertake now.

Oliver Harvey: diary
(*'The War Diaries of Oliver Harvey, 1941-1945'*)

1 August 1941

PM has finally agreed to our giving the Dutch an assurance in general terms to help them in Dutch East Indies if attacked. Meanwhile the other problems of US co-operation are being referred to Roosevelt.

War Cabinet, Defence Committee (Operations): minutes
(Premier papers, 3/286)

1 August 1941
11 a.m.

Downing Street

IRAN (PERSIA)

The Prime Minister said that, as a result of discussion with the Chiefs of Staff, the previous evening, it was apparent that our proposed action in Iran required a good deal of further examination. He was much in favour of action and did not wish any delay in the preparations, but we must be quite certain what we were letting ourselves in for. The Persians might be induced by the Germans to resist, but even if we got their agreement to expel the Germans, there was then the further demand for passage of supplies to Russia on the railway from the Persian Gulf to the Caspian. Would we have to put many troops in to secure compliance with this? We certainly did not want to let the Russians into Northern Persia if it could be avoided.

THE SITUATION IN THE MIDDLE EAST
THE WESTERN DESERT[1]

The Prime Minister said that the next three months seemed to present a great chance in the Western Desert. The Germans were fully occupied in Russia; they were having great difficulty in keeping their forces in Cyrenaica supplied, so much so that they might have to withdraw. This was unlikely, however, unless they could be caused to fight hard and exhaust their resources. The question for examination was how could this hard fighting be brought about? Very great efforts had been and were being made to pour troops and equipment into the Middle East, and yet we were now told that nothing could be done until the 1st of November and in the intervening period the Germans would be allowed to remain quiescent. It would be a very great reflection on us if, in this vital period when the Russians were bearing the full brunt of the attack, and when conditions were so favourable, we took no action of any kind.

Sir Claude Auchinleck said that the necessity for action was obvious but the means were not so easy. Continual pressure was being kept up on the enemy by light forces both in the Sollum area and at Tobruk. Heavy pressure could only be applied with armoured forces. The Tobruk tanks, for example, could be used to engage the enemy, but they were required as a counter-attack weapon, without which Tobruk might be taken by assault. Short of using our only brigade of Cruiser Tanks for a battle, serious pressure could not be brought on the Germans in the Western Desert. The risk of such a battle could be taken, but it might involve annihilation of the brigade and this would put back our ultimate major offensive perhaps several months.

[1] This discussion was attended by General Auchinleck.

The Committee were informed that the present comparison of forces showed that we had about 230 Cruiser and Infantry Tanks available for operations, including those in Tobruk, and the Germans had about the same number of tanks armed with guns and comparable in power to our Cruiser Tanks.

The Prime Minister inquired whether more energetic steps should not be taken to bring the tanks which were arriving in the Middle East into action earlier than at present forecast. We had been given to understand that there were 10 trained Tank Regiments in the Middle East. Already six weeks had passed since the last battle and surely a good deal of training must be going on even though the units had not their full complement of tanks. It seemed incredible that it should take a month for a brigade of the 1st Armoured Division to be fit for action after its arrival in the Middle East.

Sir Claude Auchinleck said that there were three processes which had be gone through by formations arriving. First they had to be unloaded; secondly the tanks had to be put through the shops to correct any defects and make them fit for the desert; thirdly the formation had to have a short period of desert training. He was advised that it would be most unwise to put the brigade of the 1st Armoured Division into action before the 1st of November.

The Prime Minister again drew attention to the serious supply situation which all our information tended to show existed on the German side in Cyrenaica. The Royal Navy and Royal Air Force would have to intensify their efforts to cut the enemy's communications, but it would be wrong to ask them to take even greater risks if the Army was not prepared to take advantage of the situation by fighting a battle.

Mr Attlee thought that the next two months were vital. If we waited till November the Germans would be able to switch back their forces and our chances would be gone.

Sir Claude Auchinleck pointed out that the last offensive had failed because it had been launched before the Army was ready. If the same kind of thing were repeated we should not only jeopardize our tank forces, but also the whole of Egypt. If we had not at the present moment our brigade of tanks and if the Germans could make adequate arrangements for maintenance there would be nothing to stop them walking straight through to the Delta.

Mr Attlee thought that the failure should be attributed to the fact that everything was not thrown into the battle. In any case how could Egypt be saved if we waited to strike till the Germans had ample time to reinforce. We should also lose Tobruk. Information showed that the Germans were not in a position to launch an offensive in the near future.

Sir Claude Auchinleck said that if an opportunity should occur in which he thought a reasonable chance existed of carrying out an offensive, he would act at once. He did not see such an opportunity at the present moment.

The Prime Minister said that the war could not be waged on the basis of waiting until everything was ready. He thought that it was a frightful prospect that nothing should be done for four and a half months at a time when a small German army was having the greatest difficulty in so much as existing. The Army should establish closer contact with the enemy at Tobruk and in the Western Desert and set to work to make the enemy fight. He was ready to authorize quite exceptional measures if by any means a battle could be brought on earlier than November. But if there was no prospect of such a battle then he must reserve the right to withhold the brigade of the first armoured division.

The Committee then considered the air situation in the Middle East.

The Prime Minister said that there were nearly 50,000 airmen in the Middle East or on their way; there were 2,000 aircraft and 1,500 pilots and yet only 450 machines could be put into battle. This appeared to be much too small an effort.

Air Marshal Tedder said that he regarded the first task of the Air Force to operate against Cyrenaica. If he were given these additional resources he would do his best to provide the Army with the opportunity which they wanted for an offensive, by intensifying his attack on the enemy's lines of communications.

An Army Co-operation Wing, consisting of one Army squadron, one bomber squadron and one fighter squadron, had been formed in the Western Desert and was training with the Army, and perfecting the organization and communications for co-operation. Practical experience had been gained in Syria and he hoped as a result of the steps now being taken, that if an offensive were planned the co-operation of all squadrons would be effective. The operations in Crete had prevented the building up of the air superiority for the recent battle by intense operations over the enemy's forward communications during the preliminary period.

The Prime Minister once more emphasized the vital importance of intensifying the naval and air attacks on the enemy's lines of communications. During the next day or two he would set down the general conclusions which had emerged from the discussions which had been held in the last two or three days.

Oliver Harvey: diary

(*'The War Diaries of Oliver Harvey, 1941-1945'*)

1 August 1941

AE very cross today after again spending 5 hours in Defence Committee – completely wasting time while PM discoursed on strategy to Auchinleck. AE finds PM's views on strategy disastrous: he pressed Auchinleck to undertake an immediate offensive in the Western Desert which Auchinleck refused to do as he hadn't got enough tanks. PM very rude but General very calm and answered well. If Wavell hadn't been made to undertake the offensive at Sollum 2 months ago with inadequate forces which lost us 200 tanks, Auchinleck could have undertaken a proper offensive now with adequate forces. Now however it is necessary to wait till forces are reasonably adequate. The meeting broke up in some confusion, PM grumbling and growling – purple in the face and with streaming eyes. AE is really worried at the PM's management or lack of management – feels he is wearing out the Chiefs of Staff to no purpose.

Winston S. Churchill to Lord Linlithgow

(*Churchill papers, 20/49*)

1 August 1941
Personal and Secret

Leo[1] has shown me your letter about finding a successor.[2] Of course, after all your hard service you must be the judge, but before I look elsewhere I should like to know whether you would not be willing to continue for another year, i.e., till April 1943. I have the greatest confidence in you; the war is moving East, and the approaching period may well be one of the most dangerous in the history of the British trusteeship of India. It would be possible, no doubt, to arrange for a period of three months' leave. Pray let me know your wishes. Kindest regards.[3]

John Colville: diary

(*Colville papers*)

1 August 1941

The PM disappeared to Chequers and I shall not see him for a fortnight as he is very shortly off on a historic journey ('Operation Riviera!'). He is as excited as a schoolboy on the last day of the term. Brendan has persuaded him, against his will, to take two newspaper reporters.

[1] L. S. Amery, Secretary of State for India.
[2] As Viceroy of India, the position Lord Linlithgow had held since 1938.
[3] Lord Linlithgow agreed to remain as Viceroy.

Clementine Churchill to Winston S. Churchill
(*Spencer-Churchill papers*)

1 August 1941 10 Downing Street

I feel very strongly that on this all-important journey you should have a Doctor with you (The Ship's Doctor – no good – merely like Doctor Jones of the *Enchantress*).'[1]

Please take Sir Charles Wilson –

Brendan agrees with me.

Winston S. Churchill to Anthony Eden, Sir Edward Bridges and General Ismay
(*Churchill papers, 20/36*)

2 August 1941

In all correspondence, it would be more convenient to use the word 'Persia' instead of 'Iran', as otherwise dangerous mistakes may easily occur through the similarity of Iran and Iraq. In any cases where convenient, the word 'Iran' may follow in brackets after Persia.

Formal correspondence with the Persian Government should, of course, be conducted in the form they like.

Winston S. Churchill to Oliver Lyttelton
(*Churchill papers, 20/41*)

2 August 1941
11.35 p.m.

I am sorry you are having all this trouble with de Gaulle. Did you hand him the telegram I prepared for your use in certain circumstances, No. 19, Prior? It would be much better if he returned home as soon as possible. We must not on any account allow the peace and safety of Syria to be compromised by the Free French. We have no ambitions there ourselves except to win the war, but we must not allow anything to conflict with this. Should he create any breach or dangerous situation it would affect the whole question of the British relationship with him and his movement, not only in Syria but generally. It might be well if you could let him see the gulf on the edge of which he is disporting himself. I am very glad Spears is of use to you. No one is more capable of standing up to Frenchmen in British interests when required. If you think it desirable, you should give de Gaulle the following message from me:

[1] The *Enchantress* was the First Lord of the Admiralty's official yacht, on which Churchill had spent many months between 1911 and 1914.

'I deeply regret to hear of the increasing friction between you and the British authorities, military and civil, which has arisen in Syria. We could not in any circumstances allow our military security in Syria to be compromised, or our task in fighting the Germans to be made more difficult. It would be of great advantage if your Excellency would return to England as soon as possible in order that I may discuss with you personally the difficulties which have arisen, and which if left unchecked and unadjusted might affect the basis of our relations.'

I do not think the surrender of Jibuti ought to be delayed merely because the Governor will not surrender to the Free French. Military considerations must predominate over points of ceremony. If the surrender were made to us we could install a Free French Administration provided we were satisfied that their attitude would be helpful.

Oliver Harvey: diary
(*'The War Diaries of Oliver Harvey, 1941-1945'*)

[2 August 1941]

AE[1] told me today that he had been over to Chequers on Saturday and – as I had expected – PM was most penitent, apologising for having kept him so long and even saying 'Yes, I'm afraid sometimes I do talk rather a lot. I'm quite ashamed of myself!' AE said at Chequers it was like a Russian play. He arrived at 6 p.m. having motored at speed from Frensham to get there in time for the Defence Committee, to find PM and Auchinleck sitting in two chairs in the garden. PM said, 'I'm afraid you will be very cross with me but I've put off the Defence Committee till after dinner, as I think I'll now go off and have a sleep!!' When dinner came, PM suddenly said, 'I don't want to do any more tonight. I want to see that film again of Nelson and Lady Hamilton!' It was then found that the film unit had already set off back to London. PM said it must be got back and so telephoning went on at intervals through dinner which was very prolonged. 'Put people across the road to stop them!' However the film unit slipped through the net, and there being no cinema the PM finally and reluctantly settled down to work at midnight and they then worked solidly up till 2 a.m.; AE getting back to Frensham at 4 a.m.! PM in the highest spirits at the idea of his jaunt.

[1] Anthony Eden.

General Ismay to General Auchinleck: recollection of a conversation
('*The Memoirs of General the Lord Ismay*')

[2 August 1941] [Chequers]

One week-end, Auchinleck and I were together at Chequers. We had known and kept touch with each other for close on twenty years, and I thought that the best service that I could render to an old friend, for whom I had both admiration and affection, was to try to give him a close-up picture of the remarkable phenomenon who was now his political chief. Here is the gist of what I said. Churchill could not be judged by ordinary standards; he was different from anyone we had ever met before, or were ever likely to meet again. As a war leader, he was head and shoulders above anyone that the British or any other nation could produce. He was indispensable and completely irreplaceable. The idea that he was rude, arrogant and self-seeking was entirely wrong. He was none of these things. He was certainly frank in speech and writing, but he expected others to be equally frank with him. To a young brigadier from Middle East Headquarters, who had asked if he might speak freely, he replied, 'Of course. We are not here to pay each other compliments.' He was a child of nature. He venerated tradition, but ridiculed convention. When the occasion demanded, he could be the personification of dignity; when the spirit moved him, he could be a *gamin.* His courage, enthusiasm and industry were boundless, and his loyalty was absolute. No commander who engaged the enemy need ever fear that he would not be supported. His knowledge of military history was encyclopaedic, and his grasp of the broad sweep of strategy unrivalled. At the same time, he did not fully realize the extent to which mechanization had complicated administrative arrangements and revolutionized the problems of time and space; and he never ceased to cry out against the inordinate 'tail' which modern armies required. 'When I was a soldier,' he would say, 'infantry used to walk and cavalry used to ride. But now the infantry require motor-cars, and even the tanks have to have horse boxes to take them to battle.' He had a considerable respect for the trained military mind, but refused to subscribe to the idea that generals were infallible or had any monopoly of the military art. He was not a gambler, but never shrank from taking a calculated risk if the situation so demanded. His whole heart and soul were in the battle, and he was an apostle of the offensive. Time and again he would quote from Nelson's Trafalgar memorandum:[1] 'No captain can do very wrong if he places his ship alongside that of an enemy.' He made a practice of bombarding commanders with telegrams on every kind of topic, many of which might seem irrelevant and superfluous. I begged Auchinleck not to allow himself to be irritated by these

[1] Written on board HMS *Victory* on 9 October 1805.

never-ending messages, but to remember that Churchill, as Prime Minister and Minister of Defence, bore the primary responsibility for ensuring that all available resources in shipping, man-power, equipment, oil, and the rest were apportioned between the Home Front and the various theatres of war, in the best interests of the war effort as a whole. Was it not reasonable that he should wish to know exactly how all these resources were being used before deciding on the allotment to be given to this or that theatre? He was not prone to harbouring grievances, and it was a mistake to take lasting umbrage if his criticisms were sometimes unduly harsh or even unjust. If I had done so, I should never have had a moment's happiness.

Winston S. Churchill to Oliver Lyttelton

(*Churchill papers, 20/41*)

3 August 1941
Most Secret

1. Very many thanks for your most interesting letter. I have had long talks with Auchinleck, in whom I have the greatest confidence. We have also had meetings of the Defence Committee, at which Turkish and other questions were settled, as you will be informed through the regular channels.

2. I am most grateful to you for all your private and personal telegrams to me, and I hope you will continue to keep me fully informed.

Winston S. Churchill to General Dobbie

(*Churchill papers, 20/41*)

3 August 1941

Now that the convoys have reached you safely with all their stores and reinforcements, I take occasion to congratulate you on the firm and steadfast manner in which you and your devoted garrison and citizens have maintained Malta inviolate against all attacks for more than a year, and to express my confidence that with the help of God our cause will continue to prosper, and that the contribution of Malta to the final victory will add a noble chapter to the famous story of the island.

Winston S. Churchill to Admiral Somerville
(*Churchill papers, 20/41*)

3 August 1941

1. I must not fail to congratulate you upon the skill and resolution with which the extremely difficult and hazardous operations of conducting the troop convoys to Malta were carried out by you and all ranks and ratings under your Command. This is only the latest of a long series of complicated and highly successful operations for which you and Force H have been responsible.

2. Please also convey my compliments and thanks to Admiral Syfret,[1] whose success was especially pleasing to me.

Winston S. Churchill to Sir Edward Bridges, General Ismay, and Private Office
(*Premier papers, 3/485/6*)

3 August 1941
Secret

On or about the 10th, an airplane, possibly carrying Lord Beaverbrook, will come out to us. This must bring, apart from letters and urgent papers, an assortment of the most important Foreign Office telegrams, and if possible an assortment of Boniface,[2] perhaps paraphrased. Competent people must be put to make the assortments, and they must be put in a weighted case, so that they will sink in the sea if anything happens to the airplane.

Pray put this in train.

[1] Edward Neville Syfret, 1889–1972. Entered the Royal Navy, 1904. Captain, 1929. Naval Secretary to the First Lord, 1939–41. Rear-Admiral, 1940. Commanded Force H, 1941–3. Knighted, 1942. Vice-Admiral, 1943. Vice-Chief of the Naval Staff, 1943–5. Commander-in-Chief, Home Fleet, 1945–8. Admiral, 1946.

[2] All material derived from the Enigma intercepted German top secret radio transmissions, as decrypted at Bletchley Park. Churchill instructed BrigadierMenzies ('C') to make the selection for him. Churchill was also to be sent diplomatic decrypts ('BJ') which he instructed Desmond Morton to select. They were mostly intercepted Japanese and Italian, but also neutral diplomatic messages.

John Colville: diary
(Colville papers)

3 August 1941

We raided Berlin heavily last night.

The PM left for the north with a retinue which Cardinal Wolsey might have envied.[1]

John Martin: diary
(John Martin papers)

3 August 1941

Departure from Wendover in PM's special train. PM himself in best form and siren-suit. Rueful disappointment at lunch when Prof, with the aid of the slide rule which always accompanied him, calculated the volume of champagne consumed by the PM throughout his life and found it was less than that of our railway coach.

Sir Alexander Cadogan: diary
(Churchill papers, 4/225)[2]

3 August 1941

Special train left Marylebone at 12.30. Arrived Wendover just before 1.30, where we picked up PM (in his rompers), Dill and Pound. Freeman already aboard the train: also the 'Prof.' Lunched with PM, Pound and Dill. Excellent lunch – unlimited quantities of very good sirloin of beef and delicious raspberry and currant tart.

[1] The 'retinue' included Dill, Pound and Air Chief Marshal Sir Wilfred Freeman; Professor Lindemann (recently ennobled as Lord Cherwell), Sir Alexander Cadogan, Commander C.R. 'Tommy' Thompson, John Martin, and Detective Inspector W.H. Thompson; Colonel Hollis and Lieutenant-Colonel Jacob of the Office of the Minister of Defence, Captain Schofield (Director of the Trade Division, Admiralty), Commander Goodenough (Plans Division, Admiralty), Paymaster Captain Brockman, Brigadier Dykes (Director of Plans, War Office), Captain Nutting (Military Assistant to Sir John Dill), and Group Captain Yool (Staff Officer to the Vice Chief of the Air Staff, Sir Wilfred Freeman) (*Premier papers, 3/485/7, folio 81*).

[2] Sir Alexander Cadogan sent Churchill several diary extracts when Churchill was preparing his war memoirs after the war.

Winston S. Churchill to Queen Elizabeth
(*Churchill papers, 20/20*)

3 August 1941

Madam,

I am most grateful to Your Majesty for the kindness of your letter and for allowing me to see beforehand the script of the broadcast to the women of America. I may say I think it is exactly what is needed, and it is only with great hesitation that I have suggested a few alternatives.

Let me also thank Your Majesty for the very gracious good wishes on my voyage and mission with which your letter ends. I must say I do not think our friend would have asked me to go so far for what must be a meeting of world-wide notice, unless he had in mind some further forward step; in fact the meeting will be a forward step in itself.

With my humble duty I remain
Your Majesty's devoted and faithful servant,
Winston S. Churchill

Winston S. Churchill to General Smuts
(*Churchill papers, 20/41*)

4 August 1941
Personal and Secret

Auchinleck has been with me for the last few days. I have formed the very highest opinion of him. He is looking forward greatly to your arrival at Cairo. I have earnestly pressed upon him the need for an early offensive in Libya, and for wearing down the enemy meanwhile by every means, both on their front and their communications. At present he has not committed himself to anything large before November 1 when our armoured reinforcements will not only have arrived but become desert-worthy and desert-trained. He has promised to try to accelerate by every possible means. Anything you can do in this direction will be most welcome to me. I dread the idea of this long delay, when, as we know for certain the enemy is hard pressed for supplies and would be greatly embarrassed by making exertions. In war one cannot wait to have everything perfect, but must fight in relation to the enemy's strength and plight. I am appalled by the proposal to remain passive all this time, when the golden opportunity may be lost. But you must hear the very strong practical arguments advanced from the other side.

I hope to cable you again later.

Sir Alexander Cadogan: diary
(*Churchill papers, 4/225*)

4 August 1941 Thurso

Arrived Thurso at 9.30. About 10 we drove to the harbour and were taken in a launch to the destroyer *Oribi*. Stayed on the bridge. Flat calm but misty and dull. Interesting going into Scapa through the booms. (Took something over an hour, I suppose). Went on board *Prince of Wales*[1] and saw our cabins, and found Harry Hopkins on board. He was very interesting on his Moscow trip. Lunch on *King George V*.

Back in our ship about 4. Harry H began to retail his Russian story to PM and me, till 4.30. Then we got under way, and I went up on the bridge. We took a long time circling slowly out of the harbour and didn't get clear till about 5.30, with 3 destroyers in escort. Weather cleared, and there was a gleam of sun.

Film after dinner – much too long: Leslie Howard as a modern Scarlet Pimpernel.[2] Not too bad. Bed about 12.15.

Winston S. Churchill to President Franklin D. Roosevelt
(*Churchill papers, 20/49*)

4 August 1941 HMS *Prince of Wales*
sent 6.25 p.m.
Personal and Secret[3]

Harry returned dead beat from Russia, but is lively again now. We shall get him in fine trim on the voyage. We are just off. It is 27 years ago today that Huns began their last war. We must make good job of it this time. Twice ought to be enough. Look forward so much to our meeting. Kindest regards.

[1] Commanded by Captain J.C. Leach, MVO, the *Prince of Wales* had been in action three months earlier against the *Bismarck* when the *Hood* had been sunk. The *Prince of Wales* had obtained the two hits which had slowed down the Bismarck and led to her ultimate destruction. Captain Leach was on the bridge when it was struck by a shell from the *Bismarck*; most of those standing with him were killed.

[2] *Pimpernel Smith* was a modernized version of *The Scarlet Pimpernel*, set in mid-1939, showing preparations for war. An effete academic, Professor Smith leads an archaeological dig trying to disprove the existence of an Aryan country; in fact he and his fellow 'archaeologists' are trying to smuggle anti-Nazi Germans out of Germany. Leslie Howard (who was killed in the plane crash with General Sikorski in 1942) both directed the film and starred in it.

[3] This was Telegram Tudor No. 1, Churchill's first telegram in the Tudor series, which he used throughout this trans-Atlantic journey. Tudor No. 2 was a telegram for Hopkins to Roosevelt, sent that same evening, asking Roosevelt to bring to the meeting with Churchill the full figures of the United States' planned monthly production of munitions for 1942.

Colonel Jacob: diary
(Jacob papers)

4 August 1941 HMS *Prince of Wales*

After dinner we had a cinematograph show in the Ward Room at which the Prime Minister was present wearing the Mess Dress of the Royal Yacht Squadron. The film was *Pimpernel Smith*, which he quite obviously enjoyed very much. He had not done a stroke of work during the day and was in a thoroughly good temper. We all went to bed about midnight, and very soon afterwards the ship began to heave.

Winston S. Churchill: recollection
('The Second World War, Volume Three')

5 August 1941 [HMS *Prince of Wales*]

On the second day the seas were so heavy that we had to choose between slowing down and dropping our destroyer escort. Admiral Pound, First Sea Lord, gave the decision. Thenceforward we went on at high speed alone. There were several U-boats reported, which we made zigzags and wide diversions to avoid. Absolute wireless silence was sought. We could receive messages, but for a while we could not speak except at intervals. Thus there was a lull in my daily routine and a strange sense of leisure which I had not known since the war began.

The sea was rough and the quarterdeck unusable, but I found plenty of exercise in making my way three or four times a day through all the compartments and up and down all the ladders to the bridge. In the evenings we had an excellent cinema, where the latest and best films were presented to our party and to those officers who were off duty.

Oliver Harvey: diary
('The War Diaries of Oliver Harvey, 1941-1945')

5 August 1941

The carefully guarded secret of PM's visit to President Roosevelt (he left on Sunday) has leaked out from German sources at Lisbon. We are having to announce it.

Winston S. Churchill to the four Dominion Prime Ministers[1]
(*Premier papers, 3/485/3*)

6 August 1941 HMS *Prince of Wales*

A little while ago I received an invitation through Mr Hopkins from President Roosevelt to meet him somewhere in Newfoundland. With the approval of The King and the War Cabinet, I thought it my duty to accept, and have accordingly started. The President has expressed lively pleasure, and after the meeting has taken place full publicity will be given at a moment to be fixed by mutual agreement. Till then all is evidently most secret. Although we have long been in intimate correspondence and have spoken over the telephone, I have never had the pleasure of meeting President Roosevelt. I am taking the First Sea Lord, the CIGS and the VCAS, Sir Alexander Cadogan of the Foreign Office, together with various technical officers; and Mr Hopkins, on his way back from Russia, is also coming with me. The President is bringing Mr Sumner Welles,[2] Admiral Stark[3] and the opposite numbers of the Army and Air Chiefs. We expect the meeting will last about three days, during which time the whole field of future action can be explored. I can return at short notice by air if necessary. I hope you will approve of this action, which may be productive of important benefits and can hardly be harmful. Naturally I hope that the President would not have wished for this meeting unless he contemplated some further forward step. I shall keep you informed of what happens. Kindest regards.

John Martin: diary
(*John Martin papers*)

6 August 1941 HMS *Prince of Wales*

A comparatively idle day, PM reading 'Hornblower'[1] and doing no work. Rendezvous with destroyer escort from Iceland. Thick fog.

[1] Of Canada (Mackenzie King), South Africa (Field Marshal Smuts), Australia (Robert Menzies) and New Zealand (Peter Fraser).

[2] Sumner Welles, 1892–1961. Born in New York City. Entered the United States Foreign Service, 1915. A specialist on Central and South America. Under-Secretary of State, 1937–43. Special Representative of President Roosevelt in Europe, 1940. Accompanied Roosevelt to the meeting with Churchill off Newfoundland, 1941.

[3] Harold Raynsford Stark, 1880–1972. Commissioned into the United States Navy, 1905. Served in European waters, 1917–18. Rear-Admiral, 1934. Commanding the Cruisers, Battle Force, 1938–9. Chief of Naval Operations, 1939–42. Commander, US Naval Forces in Europe, 1942–5. Honorary British knighthood, 1945.

[4] By C.S. Forester. It had been recommended to him by Oliver Lyttelton before he left for Cairo as Minister Resident, Middle East.

Winston S. Churchill to Clement Attlee
(*Churchill papers, 20/48*)

6 August 1941 HMS *Prince of Wales*

I don't see much harm in leakage. If asked a direct question questioner should be asked not to put his question; but if he persists the answer should be 'I cannot undertake to deal with rumour.' Telegram to Dominions should go. About *Tirpitz* I fear there will be no such luck. Have no doubt Roosevelt will see us out to sea on the return journey. We have now picked up new destroyer escort.

2. Tell Anthony to be very stiff with de Gaulle, Catroux and the Free French. They cannot be allowed to mess up our Syrian position and spoil our relations with the Arabs. Their pretensions require to be sternly corrected, even the use of force not being excluded. It is important to let them realize in good time that they will be made to obey. I don't see how they can resist.

Sir Alexander Cadogan: diary
(*Churchill papers, 4/225*)

6 August 1941 HMS *Prince of Wales*

We picked up the destroyers from Iceland. They were 3 minutes ahead of time and found us in mid-Atlantic, in a patch of fog – a good show! After lunch, I drafted something for the PM about the Far East. Harry H produced a tub of admirable caviare, given him by Joe Stalin. That, with a good young grouse, made a very good dinner. As the PM said, it was very good to have such caviare, even though it meant fighting with the Russians to get it. When HH refused a second brandy PM said 'I hope that, as we approach the US, you are not going to become more temperate.' Film after dinner, *The Devil and Miss Jones*.[1] Bad.

[1] Made in 1941, directed by Sam Wood. A business tycoon pretends to be a clerk in his own department store in an attempt to put down a labour dispute. The tycoon was played by Charles Coburn.

Ian Jacob; diary
(Jacob papers)

7 August 1941 HMS *Prince of Wales*

The Germans, in their Transozean broadcast, gave a report, said to have emanated from Lisbon, that the Prime Minister and President Roosevelt were going to have a meeting in the near future somewhere in the Western Hemisphere. The Lord Privy Seal[1] asked what he was to do about it. The Prime Minister did not seem to worry in the least, and he is secretly hoping the *Tirpitz* will come out and have a dart at him.

Clementine Churchill to Winston S. Churchill
(Baroness Spencer-Churchill papers)

7 August 1941

I do hope my Darling that this momentous journey besides being an impulse to American resolve will rest & refresh you.

How I would love to be with you in that beautiful ship. I hope you often sip the air on the Bridge.

Tender love my dearest
Clemmie

Winston S. Churchill to Clement Attlee
(Churchill papers, 20/49)

7 August 1941 HMS *Prince of Wales*

It would be a pity if anything happened to lead Mr Mackenzie King to join us in Newfoundland. Please make sure Dominions Office give no encouragement to any such plan. I have no reason to suppose he has any idea of coming. Trust all arrangements will be made to receive him with most cordial welcome if he arrives in England before I get back.

[1] Clement Attlee.

Winston S. Churchill to Lord Beaverbrook
(*Churchill papers, 20/48*)

7 August 1941 HMS *Prince of Wales*

If you feel like coming, which I should greatly welcome, aim at afternoon, eleventh, or morning, twelfth, but please do not run needless risks. It may be advisable for you to stay longer this side.

General Ismay to Oliver Lyttelton
(*Churchill papers, 20/49*)

7 August 1941

Our need for American tanks in the Middle East has been vigorously pressed upon the United States authorities for some time past, and it is recognized by the President himself. The strategic background for this request has been fully explained by the Prime Minister and our Chiefs of Staff to Hopkins and American Service representatives here. No opportunity will be lost of putting the case to the President and the United Chiefs of Staff.

Sir Alexander Cadogan: diary
(*'The Diaries of Sir Alexander Cadogan OM, 1938-1945'*)

7 August 1941 HMS *Prince of Wales*

Bad film after dinner *The High Sierras*.[1] Awful bunk. But the PM loves them and they keep him quiet. After, he played HH[2] at backgammon. I couldn't see that HH was as good as all that. I crept off about 12.30, leaving them at it. PM demanding that we should get in tomorrow evening (which we could quite easily do). 1st Sea Lord equally (but silently) determined that we *shan't!*

[1] A film with Humphrey Bogart, in which a gangster is sprung from prison to carry out a robbery, falls in love with a crippled girl and pays for an operation to help her, but then dies in a shoot out. The *New York Times* said that the film had about it 'that ennobling suggestion of futility which makes for irony and poetry'.

[2] Harry Hopkins.

Sir Alexander Cadogan: diary
(*'The Diaries of Sir Alexander Cadogan OM, 1938-1945'*)

8 August 1941 HMS *Prince of Wales*

Film *Lady Hamilton* after dinner. Quite good. PM seeing it for 5th time, moved to tears. At the close he said 'Gentlemen I thought this film would interest you, showing great events similar to those in which you have been taking part.' Left him and HH playing backgammon. HH ended up a winner of seven guineas.

Winston S. Churchill to John Moore-Brabazon[1]
(*Churchill papers, 20/36*)

9 August 1941 HMS *Prince of Wales*

Your tables of output include trainers, miscellaneous and others, whereas your diagrams are confined to operational types. It would be helpful if the tables were sub-divided, so that the diagram could be immediately reconciled with the table.

The man-hours diagram is disappointing. It shows little rise and is far below the target of 3rd July. Pray let me have figures for the number of men and women working and the hours worked in (a) the main air-frame factories and (b) the main engine factories, showing, if possible, the number of men and women under training. These tables should be carried back for a few months, if possible, so that the rate of progress can be seen.

Winston S. Churchill to Sir John Anderson
(*Churchill papers, 20/36*)

9 August 1941 HMS *Prince of Wales*

I understand there is a proposal to make it a penal offence for any motorist who gets a supplementary ration of petrol not to keep a log book in which every journey is entered.

To create and multiply offences which are not condemned by public opinion, which are difficult to detect and can only be punished in a capricious manner, is impolitic. To make it a penal offence not to keep a log book might

[1] Lord Beaverbrook's successor as Minister of Aircraft Production.

come under this heading, especially as only one twenty-fifth of our oil consumption is involved.

I understand there is an alternative proposal to tell motorists that unless they can produce a log book they will risk having their supplementary ration refused or reduced. Might not this be sufficient?

Winston S. Churchill to Sir Edward Bridges
(*Churchill papers, 20/36*)

9 August 1941 HMS *Prince of Wales*

Complaints were made that I did not answer the detailed criticisms made in the Production Debate. This, indeed, as I explained was impossible in the time. But let us have all the specific points explored, and see what the answers would be. We might then have a White Paper.

Winston S. Churchill to General Ismay
(*Premier papers, 3/4/1*)

9 August 1941 HMS *Prince of Wales*

DEFENCE OF AERODROMES IN THE UNITED KINGDOM

This matter cannot rest where it is left by Secretary of State for War. Somebody must be responsible for seeing that they are effectively obstructed until they are properly guarded. You had better get the Secretaries of State for War and Air together, and concert measures which assure the position. Thereafter you should write to Sir Richard Wells.[1]

Action is most urgent, and Captain Margesson's answer will be no help against the enemy.

Winston S. Churchill to Sir Andrew Duncan[2]
(*Churchill papers, 20/36*)

9 August 1941 HMS *Prince of Wales*

I understand that the Import Executive will shortly consider the arrangements made to provide cargoes for the additional ships to be put at our disposal by the USA in the near future. It is of the first importance that all the

[1] Sydney Richard Wells, 1879–56. Conservative Member of Parliament for Bedford, 1922–45. Knighted, 1938. Created Baronet, 1944. Of his seven sons, three were killed in action in the Second World War. Chancellor of the Primrose League, 1946–48.

[2] Chairman of the Import Executive.

shipping space that becomes available to us (whether from United States sources or from an improvement in the shipping position) is fully utilized to bring in cargoes which will increase our war effort and give the people a healthy and varied diet.

2. Cargoes must be readily available for shipment as opportunity offers, and a report should be prepared at once, showing the steps taken to this end by increasing our orders and by building up reserve stocks close to ports overseas.

3. I see from IE (41) 108[1] that it is proposed to import 748,000 tons of softwood and 422,000 tons of hardwood in the second half of the year. This is far more than the figures mentioned at a recent Battle of the Atlantic Meeting. Is this large import of timber being brought in because no more useful cargoes are available? Has the Minister of Agriculture been given the chance of suggesting any alternatives? For example, half a million tons of maize (which should be obtainable in the United States) would be of great value in keeping our chicken population going.

Winston S. Churchill to Oliver Lyttelton
(*Churchill papers, 20/41*)

9 August 1941 HMS *Prince of Wales*
Secret

Hornblower admirable.[2]

Winston S. Churchill to King George VI
(*Churchill papers, 20/49*)

9 August 1941 HMS *Prince of Wales*
Most Secret

With humble duty I have arrived safely and am visiting the President this morning.

On the morning of 9 August 1941 Churchill left the *Prince of Wales* and crossed by barge to the Augusta. Awaiting him on the upper deck was President Roosevelt, to whom Churchill handed a letter from King George VI, which the King had written six days earlier.

[1] Import Executive paper No. 108 of 1941.

[2] As Churchill's telegram was marked 'Secret', much time was spent by members of the Cairo High Command trying to work out what military operation had been given the code name 'Hornblower'.

King George VI to President Franklin D. Roosevelt
(Roosevelt papers)

3 August 1941

This is just a note to bring you my best wishes, and to say how glad I am that you have an opportunity at last of getting to know my Prime Minister. I am sure that you will agree that he is a very remarkable man, and I have no doubt that your meeting will prove of great benefit to our two countries in the pursuit of our common goal.

John Martin: diary
(John Martin papers)

9 August 1941

Arrived Placentia Bay, Newfoundland, led in through swept channel by USS *McDougal.* When we were about to enter harbour it was discovered that US ships were keeping a zone time 1½ hours ahead of Newfoundland summer time and we were turned around to delay before coming in. We moved slowly into what might have been a Hebridean loch, finally anchoring alongside the President's flagship, USS *Augusta*, about 9 a.m. A Royal Marine band and guard were mounted. The band played the Star Spangled Banner and then across the water came God Save the King in reply. No gun salutes were exchanged as HMS *Prince of Wales* carried no saluting guns.

After the usual naval courtesies the President's Naval ADC called to discuss arrangements for the day (taking Harry Hopkins with him on his return). Then, at 11 o'clock the PM, accompanied by the First Sea Lord, the CIGS, the VCAS, Cadogan, Cherwell and myself) crossed by barge to the *Augusta* to visit the President. Roosevelt met us on the upper deck, supported on the arm of his son, Franklin, accompanied by Gen. Marshall,[1] Admiral Stark, Gen. Arnold, Sumner Welles and Elliott Roosevelt.[2] After shaking hands and introducing his party, the PM handed the President a letter from the King, which I had brought with me. The two then went off to a private luncheon . . .

[1] George Catlett Marshall, 1880–1959. Second Lieutenant, United States Infantry, 1901. On active service in France, 1917–18; Chief of Operations, 1st Army; Chief of Staff, 8th Army Corps. Aide-de-Camp General Pershing, 1919–24. Chief of Staff of the United States Army, 1939–45. Chairman of the newly created Joint Chiefs of Staff Committee to advise the President on strategy, 1941–45. An advocate of the principle of 'Germany First' in Anglo-American military priorities. Representative of the President of China with the rank of Ambassador, 1945–47; Secretary of State, 1947–49; Architect of the Marshall Plan to rebuild the shattered economies of Europe. Secretary of Defence 1950–51. Nobel Peace Price, 1953.

[2] Captain Elliott Roosevelt accompanied his father on several of his wartime journeys, including the meetings with Churchill off Newfoundland, at Casablanca, Cairo and Teheran, 1943. In 1946 he published his memoirs, *As He Saw It.*

Winston S. Churchill: narrative of events
(*Churchill papers, 4/225*)

[10 August 1941]

On Sunday morning, the 10th August, Mr Roosevelt came aboard HMS *Prince of Wales* and, with his staff officers and several hundred representatives of all ranks of the United States Navy and Marines, attended Divine Service on the quarterdeck, conducted by the ship's chaplain, Rev. W. G. Parker,[1] and Rev. R. W. Shrum, Chaplain, United States Navy. This Service was felt by us all to be a deeply moving expression of the unity of faith of our two peoples, and none who saw it will forget the spectacle presented that sunlit morning on the crowded quarterdeck – the symbolism of the Union Jack and the Stars and Stripes draped side by side on the pulpit; the American and British chaplains sharing in the reading of the prayers; the highest naval and military officers of Britain and the United States grouped in one body behind the President and myself; the close packed ranks of British and American sailors, completely intermingled, sharing the same books and joining heartily together in the prayers and hymns familiar to both.

4. The President remained for a luncheon party to which I had invited some 30 British and American guests. Afterwards short but cordial speeches were made by Mr Roosevelt and myself.

John Martin: diary
(*John Martin papers*)

10 August 1941

After the President's departure, the PM, in very genial mood, asked me if I'd like to go ashore with him. We were a small party, pulled to the beach in a whaler (Cadogan, the Prof, Harriman and Tommy). We went about like the first discoverers, with not a soul to meet, the PM collecting a fistful of flowers.

Sir Alexander Cadogan: diary
(*Churchill papers, 4/225*)

10 August 1941

I changed and went ashore on a shingly bay with the PM (in his rompers), Harriman, the 'Prof', John Martin and Tommy Thompson.

[1] Wilfred Graham Parker, 1905-1941. A New Zealander. Chaplain, *Prince of Wales*, from 1939 until his death when the ship was sunk by the Japanese off Malaya on 10 December 1941. His name is on the Plymouth Naval Memorial on Plymouth Hoe (Panel 44, Column 3).

We clambered over some rocks, the PM like a schoolboy, getting a great kick out of rolling boulders down a cliff.

We soon re-embarked and landed on a spit further along, over which we walked and found a turf clearing – an ideal place for a picnic. But it clouded over and we were caught in a short, but extremely violent, shower.

Back about 5.45 and soon changed into a dinner jacket. We gave a dinner on board to American Generals and Admirals, and Sumner Welles.

John Martin: diary
(John Martin papers)

10 August 1941

In the evening I accompanied the PM to dinner with the President, only eleven at table.[1] It was a straightforward American meal of tomato soup, roast turkey with cranberry sauce and apple pie with cheese.

Winston S. Churchill: narrative of events
(Churchill papers, 4/225)

[10 August 1941]

JOINT ANGLO-AMERICAN DECLARATION OF PRINCIPLES

At one of our first conversations, the President told me that he thought it would be good if we could draw up a joint declaration laying down certain broad principles which guide our policies along the same road.

Wishing to follow up this most hopeful suggestion, I gave him, on August 10, a tentative outline of such a declaration. The text was as follows:

The President of the United States of America and the Prime Minister, Mr Churchill, representing His Majesty's Government in the United Kingdom, being met together to resolve and concert the means of providing for the safety of their respective countries in face of Nazi and German aggression and of the dangers to all peoples arising therefrom, deem it right to make known certain principles which they both accept for guidance in the framing of their policy and on which they base their hopes for a better future for the world.

First, their countries seek no aggrandisement, territorial or other;

Second, they desire to see no territorial changes that do not accord with the freely expressed wishes of the people concerned;[2]

[1] The Americans present were the President, Harry Hopkins, Rear-Admiral Ross McIntire, the President's doctor, Edwin 'Pa' Watson, and his aide, Captain Beardall, United States Navy.

[2] For the full text of the Joint Anglo-American Declaration of Principles (later known as the Atlantic Charter), see Churchill's telegram to Attlee of 11 August 1941, printed below.

FAR EAST

Our hope had been to induce the President to give a strong warning to Japan against any further encroachment in the South-West Pacific, and to give to us and the Dutch an assurance that we should have the armed support of the United States in the event of our being attacked by the Japanese.

Accordingly on the 10th August I handed to the President the following short memorandum proposing a system of 'parallel' communications to the Japanese Government:-

Declaration by United States Government that –

1. Any further encroachment by Japan in the South-West Pacific would produce a situation in which the United States Government would be compelled to take counter-measures even though these might lead to war between the United States and Japan.

2. If any Third Power becomes the object of aggression by Japan in consequence of such counter-measures or of their support of them, the President would have the intention to seek authority from Congress to give aid to such Power.

Declaration by His Majesty's Government.

Same as above, *mutatis mutandis*, the last phrase reading:-

'. . . their support of them, His Majesty's Government would give all possible aid to such Power.'

Winston S. Churchill: narrative of events
(*Churchill papers, 4/225*)

[11 August 1941]

On the following morning, the 11th August, I discussed these proposals with the President.

It was clear at once that, on consideration, the President had decided that he would be unable to give an assurance that he would go to Congress for authority to give armed support.

He referred to certain negotiations that had been proceeding with the Japanese Government, culminating in a set of proposals by the latter. The Cabinet will have already seen the telegram in which I summarized these proposals. It is true that they included an assurance that Japan would station no further troops in the South-Western Pacific area except French Indo-China, and a contingent promise of ultimate withdrawal from the latter. But a number of the conditions attached were obviously wholly unacceptable.

The President declared that he was under no illusion as to the value or the sincerity of these proposals, but he thought it would be useful to pursue a discussion of them, if only for the sake of gaining, say, a month's time.

He assured me that the economic measures against Japan would meanwhile be maintained in full force, and he seemed to think that this was the most that he could do. He did not offer to give any further warning to Japan, and I think that in this he may have been under the influence of Mr Sumner Welles, who seemed to be of the opinion that the time for warnings was past.

I pointed out that the Japanese promise to withdraw from Indo-China was conditional on 'the settlement of the China incident'. This plainly indicated that the Japanese intention was to attack Yunnan northward from Indo-China and to cut the Burma Road. It would, therefore, be essential to make it clear that a condition of continuing discussions with the Japanese would be that they should not use Indo-China as a base for operations against China.

The President readily agreed to this. He explained that, when the discussions were resumed, he would renew his proposals for the neutralization of both Siam and Indo-China.

Most important of all, he finally agreed to end his communication to the Japanese Ambassador with a warning in the words which I had given him on the previous day, that any further encroachment by Japan 'would produce a situation in which the United States Government would be compelled to take counter-measures, even though these might lead to war between the United States and Japan'. He proposed to add that it was, of course, obvious that, the Soviet being a friendly Power, the United States Government would be similarly interested in any conflict in the North-West Pacific area.

I authorized the President to inform Japan that in this matter His Majesty's Government were in accord with the United States Government and would cooperate fully with them.

The President said that he would at once telegraph to Mr Cordell Hull to arrange for the Japanese Ambassador to call upon him on his return to Washington, and to tell his Excellency that he would have an important message to deliver. He would see the Ambassador as soon as possible, and would give him the message in writing.

I later asked for a copy of this message, but I was told, at the time of our departure, that it had not yet been drafted.

The President, however, assured me, on more than one occasion, that he would include in it the final words which I have quoted above. Evidently this is the crucial part of the message, and I am confident that the President will not tone it down. He has a copy of the record of our conversation in which this wording is reproduced. Mr Sumner Welles undertook that a copy of the draft of the message would be given as soon as possible to His Majesty's Ambassador in Washington.

Even taken by itself this warning should have a considerable deterrent effect on Japan. And when we remember that the Japanese will already have suffered the shock of the Anglo-American joint declaration, I think we may hope that they will pause before proceeding to further outrage.

1. The North Atlantic and the Caribbean

WESTERN HEMISPHERE DEFENCE PLAN NO. 4

A plan for early assistance by the United States Navy in the Battle of the Atlantic had previously been worked out and, as the President now stated that the United States were ready to implement this plan, the necessary steps to put it into force were agreed upon.

At an early date (it is hoped by the 1st September) the United States Navy will take over the responsibility for the safety of our North Atlantic Convoys to the West of 26° West. They will be assisted by units of the Royal Canadian Navy. With the exception of the occasional escorts necessary for our troop convoys, we shall thereby be enabled to withdraw the majority of the units of the Royal Navy now in the Western Atlantic for employment in other areas.

This unparalleled gesture of friendship by a neutral Power is to be made under the guise of protection for United States communications with Iceland (C).[1] The measures taken will continue to be guided by our own experienced Officers. All details were worked out and agreed in detail by the Naval authorities.

At our meeting on the morning of August 11 the President gave me a revised draft, which we took as a basis of discussion.

Before examining this document the President explained that his idea was that there should be issued simultaneously in Washington and London, perhaps on the 14th August, a short statement to the effect that the President and the Prime Minister had held conversations at sea, that they had been accompanied by members of their respective staffs; that the latter had discussed the working out of aid to the democracies in the Lease and Lend act; that these naval and military conversations had in no way been concerned with future commitments other than as authorized by Act of Congress.

The statement would proceed to say that the Prime Minister and the President had discussed certain principles relating to the civilization of the world and had agreed on a statement of them.

I deprecated the emphasis which a statement on these lines would lay on the absence of commitments. This would be seized on by Germany and would be a source of profound discouragement to the neutrals and to the vanquished. I very much hoped, therefore, that the President could confine the statement to the positive portion which dealt with the question of aid to the democracies, more especially as the President had guarded himself by the reference to the Lease and Lend Act.

The President accepted this.

There followed a detailed discussion of the revised text of the declaration.

Several minor alterations were easily agreed.

The chief difficulties were presented by Points 4 and 7, especially the former.

With regard to this, I pointed out that the words 'without discrimination' might be held to call in question the Ottawa agreements, and I was in no position to accept them. This text would certainly have to be referred to the Government at home and, if it was desired to maintain the present wording, to the Governments in the Dominions. I should have little hope that it would be accepted. Mr Sumner Welles indicated that this was the core of the matter, and that this paragraph embodied the ideal for which the Administration had

[1] Churchill had given instructions for Iceland to be referred to as Iceland (C) in order to differentiate it more clearly from Ireland.

striven for the past nine years. I mentioned the British experience in adhering to Free Trade for eighty years. I said that, if the words 'with due respect for their existing obligations' could be inserted, and if the words 'without discrimination' could disappear, and 'trade' be substituted for 'markets', I should be able to refer the text to His Majesty's Government with some hope that they would be able to accept it.

As regards Point 7, I pointed out that while I accepted this text, opinion in England would be disappointed at the absence of any intention to establish an international organization of peace after the war. I promised to try to find a suitable modification, and later in the day I suggested to the President the addition to the second sentence of the words 'pending the establishment of a wider and more permanent system of general security'.

I telegraphed these amendments for immediate submission to the Cabinet. I had not finished dictating the telegram much before 2 p.m. and that I should have had in my hands within the next 12 hours the Cabinet's most helpful reply reflects the utmost credit on all concerned.

The Cabinet, in their reply, suggested a further variant of Point 4, and desired the insertion of a new paragraph between Points 4 and 5.

Meanwhile, I had heard that the President had accepted all the amendments which I had submitted to him on 11th August.

Record of Conversations between the Prime Minister and the President
(*Premier papers, 3/485/5*)

11 August 1941
Most Secret

On the subject of Operation 'Pilgrim'[1] the President observed that he had indications from certain quarters that a German move might be made into the Peninsula about September 15th. It would be possible for his forces, destined for the Azores, to be ready by approximately the same date; that is to say, it would take three weeks to embark them and five to six days to get the ships there. The President said that in his view the way to proceed would be for His Majesty's Government to intimate to Dr Salazar that they, owing to their pre-occupation elsewhere, would be unable to send him the assistance promised, and would he therefore accept the assistance of the United States. If Dr Salazar agrees he would have to inform the US that he would accept their assistance together with a token contingent from Brazil. The President explained that it was essential for his own purposes that he should have a direct request from Dr Salazar.

[1] The plan to seize the Portuguese and Spanish Island groups in the Atlantic, consisting of Operations 'Thruster' (the Azores), 'Springboard' (Madeira) and 'Puma' (the Canaries and Cape Verde Islands).

The Prime Minister said that we must recognize that the Operation 'Pilgrim' might fire the whole train in the Peninsula. We must therefore have simultaneously a naval force to protect the Azores against forestalling German action pending the entry of American forces. The President pointed out that the US Government would be unable to send forces to the Azores and to the Cape Verde Islands simultaneously. Moreover there was this difference, that the former were in the Western Hemisphere, whereas the latter were east of 26 degrees. He might be able to work them into a scheme but would make no definite promise here and now. He added that unlike Operation 'Pilgrim', the occupation of the Azores could be done in any month of the year.

It was agreed that the first step would be for His Majesty's Government to inform the United States Government that they had informed Dr Salazar of the possibility that they would be precluded from giving Portugal the assistance promised.

FAR EAST

The President handed round copies of the annexed two documents received from the Japanese Ambassador in Washington on August 6th. He proposed to inform the Japanese that the United States Government were interested in the suggestion there made, and that the US Government were ready to begin discussions on them, but that it would be a *sine que non* that during these discussions the Japanese should not extend their occupation of Indo-China and should not make it a base of operations against China. When these discussions were opened he would again put forward his proposals for neutralization both of Indo-China and Siam.

He would add the warning that any further move by Japan would produce a situation in which US Government would be compelled to take certain measures even though this might lead to war between US and Japan.

The Prime Minister said that in addition to the conditions suggested by the President it would be essential to maintain the full pressure of economic measures which the US Government had already adopted in regard to Japan. He suggested also that it would be highly desirable if possible to be able to verify through American observers that Japan observed a standstill arrangement during the course of the talks. The President, however, felt that this would be very difficult.

It was agreed that the President should himself make these communications to the Japanese Ambassador in Washington on his return there. He would telegraph at once to Mr Hull instructing him to make an appointment for him with the Japanese Ambassador, intimating that the President would have an important communication to make. The Prime Minister authorized the President to inform the Japanese Ambassador that His Majesty's Government had been consulted and were acting in this matter in close accord with the US Government.

The President declared that he had every intention of maintaining economic measures in full force.

The question then arose as to the part which the Soviet would play in this procedure. The President suggested that the Soviet Ambassadors in London and Washington should be informed that these negotiations with the Japanese were being entered upon in order to secure a delay and it might be suggested that the Soviet Government should express to the Japanese Government the hope that the plan would be successful and that if so it should apply to the North Pacific Region as a whole. This might be effected by adding to the warning to be given to the Japanese a statement to the effect that it was of course obvious that the Soviet being a friendly Power the US Government would be similarly interested in any conflict in the North West Pacific. The President inquired whether His Majesty's Government would be ready to give an assurance that they had no designs on Siam or Indo-China and sought no alteration in the status quo. The Prime Minister asserted and authorized the President to inform the Japanese that His Majesty's Government were in complete accord with them in this matter and would collaborate fully.

JOINT DECLARATION

The President handed round a revise of the draft declaration which had been submitted to him yesterday.

Before examining this document the President explained that his idea was that there should be issued simultaneously in Washington and London perhaps on Thursday of this week a short statement to the effect that the President and the Prime Minister had held conversations at sea, that they had been accompanied by members of their respective staffs; that the latter had discussed the working out of aid to the democracies in the Lease and Lend Act; that these naval and military conversations had in no way been concerned with future commitments other than as authorized by Act of Congress.

The statement would proceed to say that the Prime Minister and the President had discussed certain principles relating to the civilisation of the world as a whole and had agreed on a statement of principles.

Sumner Welles: memorandum

(*'The White House Papers of Harry L. Hopkins'*)

11 August 1941

As I was leaving the ship to accompany the President back to his flagship Mr Churchill said to me that he had likewise given the President copies of these documents. He impressed upon me his belief that some declaration of the kind he had drafted with respect to Japan was in his opinion in the highest degree important, and that he did not think that there was much hope left unless the United States made such a clear-cut declaration of preventing Japan from expanding further to the south, in which event the prevention of war between Great Britain and Japan appeared to be hopeless. He said in the most emphatic manner that if war did break out between Great Britain and Japan, Japan immediately would be in a position through the use of her large number of cruisers to seize or to destroy all of the British merchant shipping in the Indian Ocean and in the Pacific, and to cut the lifelines between the British Dominions and the British Isles unless the United States herself entered the war. He pled with me that a declaration of this character participated in by the United States, Great Britain, the Dominions, the Netherlands, and possibly the Soviet Union would definitely restrain Japan. If this were not done, the blow to the British Government might be almost decisive.

Winston S. Churchill: Directive
(*Churchill papers, 20/36*)

11 August 1941

THE BRITISH PURCHASING COMMISSION IN THE UNITED STATES

A great mass of orders has already been placed in the United States for British war munitions, etc. These have been harmonized both as between British departments and between British home production and British orders placed in America. Mr Purvis has been made finally responsible, and any discordances should be reported to him for settlement in the office of the Minister of Defence. However, it is now necessary to make further large provision, particularly in respect of shipping, bomber aircraft, and tanks, both for the British account and for the United States' armed forces. Moreover, the arrival of Russia as an active partner against Hitler will require not only certain readjustments of British orders, original and supplementary, but also a very considerable expansion of plants and installations for the longer-term policy.

2. So far as the British supplementary programme is concerned, there need be no trouble about priorities as between heavy bomber aircraft and tanks. We no longer consider priorities as dominated by the time factor, but prefer to deal in simultaneous quantitative allocations.

On this basis, if our American colleagues will state what are the prospects, whether through improved production from existing plants or the preparation of new ones, of greatly increasing production, and will let us know their views about how it is to be divided between British and United States needs, we will do the share-out between our British departments. For instance, we do not think that our need for a supplemental programme of heavy bomber aircraft should exclude all simultaneous expansion in tanks. The ratio for the whole programme as between heavy bomber aircraft and tanks would be, say, 6 to 4, or 6½ to 3½, both types of production proceeding simultaneously as fast as possible. This method of approach is suggested as the most convenient.

3. We greatly welcome a further assignment of 150,000 rifles. Although ammunition is very short, these are absolutely needed to arm the personnel defending the fighter airfields. At least 150,000 of them have at present to rely on pikes, maces, and grenades. Even although .300 ammunition in Great Britain is very short and does not amount to above 80 rounds per rifle, production is now flowing in the United States for our benefit, which will this month be clear of the paying off of the overdrawn 50 million rounds, and should amount to 20 to 25 million rounds per month. Even if only ten rounds could be handed out to the men at certain airfields with their rifles, this would be far better than the makeshifts we now have to employ, and would enable the strictest instructions to be given to all uniformed personnel to fight to the death, which instructions can hardly be given very confidently when no weapon can be placed in the hands of soldiers and airmen concerned.

We hope therefore that the most rapid deliveries possible off 150,000 rifles will be made, as the invasion season is fully operative after September 15. In the event of our reporting to the President that great and active preparations are being made by the enemy in the Dutch, Belgian, and French ports for invasion, of which there is no sign at present, we would ask as a matter of emergency that a further consignment of .300 ammunition should be rushed across, this being recovered later from our monthly quotas of production.

4. It would seem indispensable that the re-equipment of the Russian armies should be studied at once upon the grand scale. After preliminary conferences between the British and United States supply departments, it would seem advisable, and indeed inevitable, that a further conference should be held in Moscow. Both for this purpose and in any preliminary conference that may be necessary the Prime Minister would nominate Lord Beaverbrook, Minister of Supply, who should arrive here today, as the British representative, with power to act for all British departments.

Winston S. Churchill to the Admiralty

(*Churchill papers, 20/49*)

11 August 1941

Utmost strength to be put on decyphering telegrams from here during next 24 hours.

Winston S. Churchill to Clement Attlee
(*Churchill papers, 20/49*)

11 August 1941
Most Secret

Have reached satisfactory settlement about Naval Plan No. 4, as already reported to Admiralty.

Secondly, President is prepared to take very helpful action corresponding with, or consequent upon, operation 'Pilgrim'.[1]

Thirdly, he intends to negotiate with Japan on the basis of a moratorium for, say, a month, during which no further military movements are to be made by Japan in Indo-China and no encroachment upon Siam. He has agreed to end his communication with a very severe warning, which I drafted, that further encroachments either in the South or North of the Pacific will be met by counter-measures which may lead to war between Japan and the United States. With this we should, of course, associate ourselves, and presumably the Dutch Government will do the same. The notification to Japan would be secret.

Fourthly, the President wishes to issue at the moment of general release of meeting story, probably 14th or 15th, a Joint Declaration signed by him and me, on behalf of His Majesty's Government, of the broad principles which animate the United States and Great Britain at this favourable time. I send you herewith his draft of the statement (my immediately following telegram), which you will see is not free from the difficulties attaching to all such Declarations. The fourth condition would evidently have to be amended to safeguard our obligations contracted in Ottawa and not prejudice the future of Imperial Preference. This might fall into its place after the war in a general economic settlement with decisive lowering of tariffs and trade barriers throughout the world. But we cannot settle it now. For the sake of speedy agreement I have little doubt he will accept the following amendments:

After the word 'endeavour' insert 'with due respect to their existing obligations'.

And after the word 'access' omit the words 'without discrimination and'.

Also, leave out the word 'markets' and insert the word 'trade'.

The seventh paragraph is most remarkable for its realism. The President undoubtedly contemplates the disarmament of the guilty nations, coupled with the maintenance of strong united British and American armaments both by sea and air for a long indefinite period.

Having regard to our views about the League of Nations or other

[1] The plan to seize the Portuguese and Spanish Island groups in the Atlantic.

International organization, I would suggest the following amendment after the word 'essential':

'pending the establishment of a wider and more permanent system of general security'.

He will not like this very much, but he attaches so much importance to the Joint Declaration, which he believes will affect the whole movement of United States' opinion, that I think he will agree.

It would be most imprudent on our part to raise unnecessary difficulties. We must regard this as an interim and partial statement of war aims designed to reassure all countries of our righteous purpose and not the complete structure which we should build after victory.

You should summon the full War Cabinet, with any others you may think necessary, to meet tonight, and please let me have your views without the slightest delay. Meanwhile, immediately full accounts are being sent you on the other points, together with Cadogan's report of the conversation. I fear President will be very much upset if no Joint Statement can be issued, and grave and vital interests might be affected.

I had purposed to leave afternoon 12th, but we have both now postponed departure twenty-four hours.

Please let me have your views about the Joint Declaration in advance of those on other points which I have mentioned to you in this skeleton form, and on which I am sending you separate telegram.

Winston S. Churchill to Clement Attlee

(*Premier papers, 3/485/1*)

11 August 1941
Most Secret

JOINT ANGLO-AMERICAN DECLARATION OF PRINCIPLES[1]

The President of the United States of America and the Prime Minister, Mr Churchill, representing His Majesty's Government in the United Kingdom,

[1] The origin of this Declaration of Principles (also known as the Atlantic Charter) was a telegram from Roosevelt to Churchill of 15 July 1941, in which the President referred to a matter 'which might cause unpleasant repercussions over here'. This was the rumour that the British Government had begun to commit itself to various 'trades or deals' with some of the occupied countries. For example, Roosevelt wrote 'the stupid story that you have promised to set up Yugoslavia again as it formerly existed', and another story 'that you promised Trieste to Yugoslavia'. There were, Roosevelt warned, 'certain racial groups' in the United States for whom such promises would cause 'dissension and argument', such as the Czechs and Slovaks or the Walloons and Flemings. 'You will remember,' Roosevelt added, 'that back in early 1919 there was serious trouble over actual and alleged promises to the Italians and to others.' Roosevelt's telegram continued: 'I am inclined to think that an overall statement on your part would be useful at this time, making it clear that no postwar peace commitments as to territories, populations or economies have been given. I could then back up your statement in very strong terms'. (Telegram received on 15 July 1941, 'Secret': *Churchill papers, 20/41*)

being met together, deem it right to make known certain common principles in the national policies of their respective countries on which they base their hopes for a better future for the world.

First, their countries seek no aggrandisement, territorial or other.

Second, they desire to see no territorial changes that do not accord with the freely expressed wishes of the peoples concerned.

Third, they respect the right of all peoples to choose the form of government under which they will live; and they wish to see self-government restored to those from whom it has been forcibly removed.

Fourth, they will endeavour to further the enjoyment by all peoples of access, without discrimination and on equal terms, to the markets and to the raw materials of the world which are needed for their economic prosperity.

Fifth, they hope to see established a peace, after the final destruction of the Nazi tyranny, which will afford to all nations the means of dwelling in security within their own boundaries, and which will afford assurance to all peoples that they may live out their lives in freedom from fear.

Sixth, they desire such a peace to establish for all safety on the high seas and oceans.

Seventh, they believe that all of the nations of the world must be guided in spirit to the abandonment of the use of force. Because no future peace can be maintained if land, sea or air armaments continue to be employed by nations which threaten, or may threaten, to use force outside of their frontiers, they believe that the disarmament of such nations is essential. They will further the adoption of all other practicable measures which will lighten for peace-loving peoples the crushing burden of armaments.[1]

Winston S. Churchill to the Foreign Office
(*Churchill papers 20/49*)

11 August 1941

The position about Japan is as follows:

President proposed to Japan some time ago neutralization of Indo-China and Siam under joint guarantee of United States, Japan, Britain, China and others. Japanese reply, which will be cabled you fully as soon as more urgent messages have been dealt with, agrees to the principle of no encroachment upon Siam and military withdrawal from Indo-China, but adds a number of conditions fundamentally unacceptable.

For instance, the withdrawal to take place after the China incident is settled, meaning thereby after Chiang Kai-shek is strangled, and further requiring

[1] For the final version of the Atlantic Charter, see Churchill's telegram to Attlee of 12 August 1941, beginning 'President and I this morning agreed . . .'

recognition of Japan's preponderant position in these regions; also requiring United States to abstain from all further military preparations in these regions, and seeking lifting of the economic sanctions.

2. President's idea is to negotiate about these unacceptable conditions and thus procure a moratorium of, say, 30 days in which we may improve our position in Singapore area and the Japanese will have to stand still. But he will make it a condition that the Japanese meanwhile encroach no further, and do not use Indo-China as a base for attack on China. He will also maintain in full force the economic measures directed against Japan.

These negotiations show little chance of succeeding, but President considers that a month gained will be valuable. I point out, of course, that the Japanese would double-cross him and would try to attack China or cut the Burma communications. However, you may take it that they consider it right to begin the negotiations on these lines, and in view of what has passed between United States and Japan it will be necessary to accept this fact.

3. In the course of these negotiations, President would renew his proposals for neutralization of Siam as well as Indo-China.

4. At the end of the Note which the President will hand to the Japanese Ambassador when he returns from his cruise in about a week's time, he will add the following passage, which is taken from my draft:

'Any further encroachment by Japan in the South-West Pacific would produce a situation in which the United States Government would be compelled to take counter-measures, even though these might lead to war between the United States and Japan.'

He would also add something to the effect that it was obvious that, the Soviet being a friendly Power, United States Government would be similarly interested in any similar conflict in North-West Pacific.

5. I think this is entirely good and that we should associate ourselves therewith and endeavour to get the Dutch to come in in full agreement, because either the Japanese will refuse the conditions the President prescribes – namely, continuance of the economic sanctions and no movement on the Japanese part and no invasion of Siam – or alternatively, they will go on with their military action while lying about it diplomatically.

In this case the conditions indicated by the final passage just quoted would come into play with great force, and the full effect of parallel declarations could be realized. Soviet Government should also be kept informed. It might be dangerous to tell the Chinese what we are doing for them, though they might be assured in general terms that we have had their security in mind in all that we have done.

6. On all these grounds I consider that we should endorse the proposed course of action, and that the Dominions should be told about it and made to see that it is a very great advance towards the gripping of Japanese aggression by united forces.

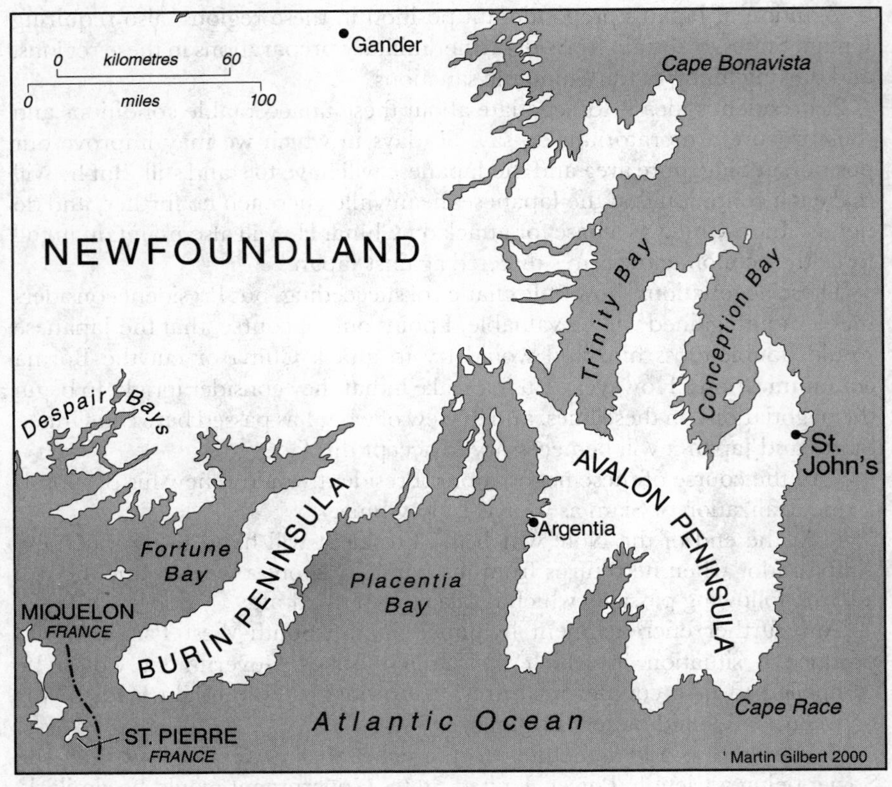

2. Placentia Bay, Newfoundland

Winston S. Churchill: recollection
(*'The Second World War, Volume Three'*)

[11 August 1941] [Placentia Bay]

I had only finished dictating the telegrams about 2 p.m., and that I should have had in my hands within the next twelve hours the War Cabinet's most helpful reply reflects credit on all concerned. I subsequently learned that my telegrams had not reached London until after midnight, and that many of the Ministers had already gone to bed. Nevertheless a War Cabinet meeting was summoned for 1.45 a.m., and there was a full attendance, including Mr Peter

Fraser, Prime Minister of New Zealand, who was in England at the time. As a result of a full discussion they sent me a telegram just after 4 a.m., welcoming the proposal and suggesting a further version of Point 4 (non-discrimination in world trade) and the insertion of a new paragraph dealing with social security. Meanwhile I had heard that the President had accepted all the amendments I had suggested to him on August 11.

War Cabinet: minutes
(*Cabinet papers, 65/19*)

12 August 1941 Cabinet War Room
1.45 a.m.

The War Cabinet met as a matter of great urgency in order to discuss two telegrams which had been received from the Prime Minister (Tudor Nos. 15 and 16). The second telegram contained the draft of a Joint Declaration, prepared by the President of the United States of America, to be signed by him and by the Prime Minister. The former telegram contained the Prime Minister's comments on the draft, and on the discussions generally.

In discussion, the view was expressed that, while the Declaration in certain respects fell short of what the War Cabinet would themselves like to have seen issued, the right course was to accept it in its present form, subject to modification on a limited number of points.

The War Cabinet –

Authoriszed the despatch to the Prime Minister of telegram Abbey No. 31, which was drafted during the Meeting as a first indication of their views, and agreed to consider the matter further at a Meeting to be held later that morning (at 10 a.m.).

Oliver Harvey: diary
(*'The War Diaries of Oliver Harvey, 1941-1945'*)

12 August 1941

I found AE very indignant this morning at having been aroused at 2 a.m. by a telegram from PM marked 'Attend to at once!' containing text of a joint declaration which FDR had proposed that they should both issue as a result of their meeting. A terribly woolly document full of all the old clichés of the League of Nations period. The Cabinet hastily got together and met to consider it. There is obviously no alternative but to accept it, woolly though it is. The Cabinet is considering it again today in the cold light of morning. AE feels that FDR has bowled the PM a very quick one – such a document might well have been communicated in advance.

Winston S. Churchill to Clement Attlee
(*Churchill papers, 20/48*)

12 August 1941
Most Secret

President has accepted all my amendments to joint declaration and is most insistent that it should be issued simultaneously with announcement of meeting. Therefore there may not be time for consultation with Dominions and if Cabinet see no objection I should hope they might agree that I could anticipate Dominion concurrence.

War Cabinet: minutes
(*Cabinet papers, 65/19*)

12 August 1941 10 Downing Street
10 a.m.

Discussion turned mainly on the terms of paragraph 4 of the draft Declaration.

The following text put forward by the Chancellor of the Exchequer:[1]
'Fourth. – They will endeavour, with due respect to their existing obligations (or engagements), to further, within the limits of their governing economic conditions, the progressive attainment of a well-balanced international economy, which would render unnecessary policies of discrimination and other impediments to the freedom of trade.

Winston S. Churchill to Clement Attlee
(*Churchill papers, 20/48*)

12 August 1941
Most Secret

Please thank Cabinet for amazingly swift reply. I put your alternative clause 4 to President, but he preferred to stick to the phrasing already agreed. I do not myself see any real difference. Phrase about 'respect for existing obligations' safeguards our relations with Dominions. We could not see how competition of cheap labour would come in as all countries preserve the right of retaining or imposing national tariffs as they think fit pending better solutions.

[1] Sir Kingsley Wood.

2. The President cordially accepted your new paragraph 5, but you will see that the reference to 'want' comes in where the President originally wished it – at the end of paragraph 6. A few verbal flourishes not affecting substance have been added.

3. We have laid special stress on the warning to Japan which constitutes the teeth of the President's communication. One would always fear State Department trying to tone it down; but President has promised definitely to use the hard language.

4. Arrival Russia as a welcome guest at hungry table and need of large supplementary programmes both for ourselves and the United States forces make review and expansion of United States production imperative. President proposes shortly to ask Congress for another 5 billion dollars Loan-Lease Bill. President welcomes Beaverbrook's arrival at Washington, and I am convinced this is the needful practical step. See also the Roosevelt-Churchill message to dear old Joe. I think they will send Harriman to represent them, and I should propose that Beaverbrook should go for us to Moscow or wherever Russian Government is. We do not wish conference in Russia to start before latter part of September, by when it is hoped we shall know where the Russian front will lie for the winter.

5. They are sending us immediately 130,000 more rifles, and I look for improved allocations of heavy bombers and tanks. I hope they will take over whole ferry service and deliver both in England and in West Africa by American pilots, many of whom may stay for war training purposes with us.

6. Your promptness has enabled me to start home today, 12th. President is sending American destroyers with us, who are not considered escort but will chip in if any trouble occurs. Franklin Junior is serving on one of them and has been appointed Liaison Officer to me during my day in Iceland (C), where there will be a joint review of British and American forces.

7. Lord Beaverbrook is now proceeding with Harriman by air to United States. The joint telegram to Stalin comes out 48 hours after the main story.

8. I trust my colleagues will feel that my mission has been fruitful. I am sure I have established warm and deep personal relations with our great friend.

Winston S. Churchill: recollection
(*'The Second World War, Volume Three'*)

[12 August 1941]

On August 12, about noon, I went to see the President to agree with him the final form of the Declaration. I put to the President the Cabinet's revised version of Point 4, but he preferred to adhere to the phrasing already agreed, and I did not press him further on this point. He readily accepted the insertion of the new paragraph about social security desired by the Cabinet. A number of verbal alterations were agreed, and the Declaration was then in its final shape.

John Martin: diary
(*John Martin papers*)

12 August 1941

Lord Beaverbrook (Minister of Supply), who had arrived in Newfoundland by air the previous day, came aboard HMS *Prince of Wales*. In the morning the PM went over to the USS *Augusta* for his final conference with the President. Cadogan and Sumner Welles joined in the discussion. Agreement was reached on the text of a Joint Declaration ('The Atlantic Charter') and on a joint message to Stalin. The President handed the PM a letter to The King. The PM remained to lunch with the President, after which he and his staff took leave of Mr Roosevelt on the deck of the American flagship.

Sir Alexander Cadogan: diary
(*Churchill papers, 4/225*)

12 August 1941

Went over to *Augusta* with Harry H about 11.30 and fixed up with Sumner Welles drafts of Joint Declaration, announcement of the meeting and a joint telegram to Stalin. Then another meeting with the President, at which Beaverbrook was also present. Went without a hitch. Lasted till after 1, when I had lunch in the Ward Room. Got final texts checked with Sumner Welles and went to take my leave of the President, and back to the ship, where I worked hard on telegrams to London. Sailed at 5. Grey, drizzly weather, but an impressive sight as we sailed down the lines with 2 US destroyers astern. They are coming with us to Iceland. Clocks on 2 hours, so we dined at 9. Film (the world's worst) began not much before 11, so I didn't get to bed before 1 or after.

Winston S. Churchill to Clement Attlee
(*Churchill papers, 20/48*)

12 August 1941
Most Secret

President and I this morning agreed that following statement should be broadcast on Thursday August 14 at three p.m. (It should not repeat not be released before then to Press):

Begins. 'The President of the United States and Prime Minister Mr. Churchill, representing HM Government in United Kingdom, have met at sea.

They have been accompanied by officials of their two Governments, including high-ranking officers of their military, naval and air services.

The whole problem of supply of munitions of war, as provided by Lease-Lend Act, for armed forces of the US and for those countries actively engaged in resisting aggression has been further examined.

Lord Beaverbrook, the Minister of Supply of British Government, has joined in these conferences. He is going to proceed to Washington to discuss further details with appropriate officials of US Government. These conferences will also cover supply problem of Soviet Union.

The President and Prime Minister have had several conferences. They have considered the dangers to world civilization arising from policy of military domination by conquest upon which Hitlerite Government of Germany and other governments associated therewith have embarked, and have made it clear the steps which their countries are respectively taking for their safety in facing those dangers.

They have agreed upon following joint declarations:

The President of USA and Prime Minister, Mr Churchill, representing HM Government in United Kingdom, being met together, deem it right to make known certain common principles in national policies of their respective countries on which they base their hopes for a better future for the world.

First their countries seek no aggrandisement, territorial or other. Second, they desire to see no territorial changes that do not accord with the free express wish of the peoples concerned; third, they respect right of all peoples to choose the form of Government under which they will live; and they wish to see Sovereign rights and self-Government restored to those who have been forcibly deprived of them.

Fourth, they will endeavour, with due respect for their existing obligations, to further enjoyment by all States, great or small, victor or vanquished, of access, on equal terms, to trade and to the raw materials of the world which are needed for their economic prosperity; fifth, they desire to bring about fullest collaboration between all nations in economic field with object of securing for all improved labour standards, economic advancement and social security;

Sixth, after final destruction of Nazi tyranny, they hope to see established a peace which will afford all nations the means of dwelling in safety within their own boundaries, and which will afford assurance that all the men in all the lands may live out their lives in freedom from fear and want.

Seventh, such a peace should enable all men to traverse the high seas and oceans without hindrance.

Eighth, they believe all of the nations of the world, for realistic as well as spiritual reasons, must come to abandonment of use of force. Since no future peace can be maintained if land, sea or air armament continue to be employed by nations which threaten, or may threaten, aggression outside of their frontiers, they believe, pending establishments of a wider and more permanent system of general security, that the disarmament of such nations is essential. They will likewise aid and encourage all other practicable measures which will lighten for peace-loving peoples the crushing burden of armament.

Winston S. Churchill: recollection
(*'The Second World War, Volume Three'*)

12 August 1941

The profound and far-reaching importance of this Joint Declaration was apparent. The fact alone of the United States, still technically neutral, joining with a belligerent Power in making such a declaration was astonishing. The inclusion in it of a reference to 'the final destruction of the Nazi tyranny' (this was based on a phrase appearing in my original draft) amounted to a challenge which in ordinary times would have implied warlike action. Finally, not the least striking feature was the realism of the last paragraph, where there was a plain and bold intimation that after the war the United States would join with us in policing the world until the establishment of a better order.

Sir Alexander Cadogan: diary
(*'The Diaries of Sir Alexander Cadogan OM, 1938-1945'*)

12 August 1941
late afternoon

As I came in he lowered the paper in his hand, took off his spectacles and said 'Thank God I brought you with me.' The simplicity of the seven word tribute and his manner of saying it were proof of its sincerity, and I was deeply moved and puffed up with a great pride.

Winston S. Churchill to Clement Attlee

(*Premier papers, 3/401/1*)

12 August 1941

President and I have agreed on following joint message to M. Stalin. Please instruct His Majesty's Ambassador in Moscow to arrange with his United States colleague to communicate it to M. Stalin as soon as convenient. We propose to publish it in American and British morning papers, Saturday, August 16:[1]

Winston S. Churchill and President Franklin D. Roosevelt to J. V. Stalin

(*Premier papers, 3/401/1*)

12 August 1941

We have taken the opportunity afforded by the consideration of the report of Mr Harry Hopkins on his return from Moscow to consult together as to how best our two countries can help your country in the splendid defence that you are making against the Nazi attack. We are at the moment co-operating to provide you with the very maximum of supplies that you most urgently need. Already many shiploads have left our shores, and more will leave in the immediate future.

We must now turn our minds to the consideration of a more long-term policy, since there is still a long and hard path to be traversed before there can be won that complete victory without which our efforts and sacrifices would be wasted.

The war goes on upon many fronts, and before it is over there may be yet further fighting fronts that will be developed. Our resources, though immense, are limited, and it must become a question as to where and when those resources can best be used to further to the greatest extent our common effort. This applies equally to the manufactured war supplies and to raw materials.

The needs and demands of your and our armed services can only be determined in the light of the full knowledge of the many factors which must be taken into consideration in the decisions that we make. In order that all of us may be in a position to arrive at speedy decisions as to the apportionment of our joint resources, we suggest that we prepare for a meeting to be held at Moscow, to which we would send high representatives who could discuss these matters directly with you. If this conference appeals to you, we want you to know that, pending the decisions of that conference, we shall continue to send supplies and materials as rapidly as possible.

[1] For the text of the joint telegram to Stalin, see the following document.

We realize fully how vitally important to the defeat of Hitlerism is the brave and steadfast resistance of the Soviet Union, and we feel therefore that we must not in any circumstances fail to act quickly and immediately in this matter of planning the programme for the future allocation of our joint resources.

John Martin: diary
(*John Martin papers*)

12 August 1941

At 5 p.m. HMS *Prince of Wales*, with an escort of destroyers, sailed for Iceland, exchanging compliments with USS *Augusta* as she moved away.

Winston S. Churchill to Clement Attlee
(*Churchill papers, 20/48*)

13 August 1941

1. Many thanks for your kind message. I am delighted you will broadcast statement and declaration yourself. Please make a definite break between the preliminary statement and the actual text by saying: 'I will now read the actual text of the Joint Declaration.' I do not consider any comment will be required from me as announcement is itself sufficient to fill the newspapers. I might broadcast on the Sunday night following my return when reaction in United States to our meeting and joint declaration will be apparent.

Any necessary guidance can be given to the Press confidentially, but they will surely see Joint Declaration proposing final destruction of Nazi power and disarmament of aggressive nations while Britain and United States remain armed is an event of first magnitude. It would be well to let this soak in on its own merits on friend and foe.

2. For your secret information President is remaining at sea until end of week in order to cover my return. I told him this was not necessary, but he insisted.

3. We shall be most interested to know how it is all taken.

4. I read with much pleasure your admirable war statement at end of session.

Winston S. Churchill to King George VI
(*Churchill papers, 20/49*)

13 August 1941

Most grateful to Your Majesty for good wishes. Lord Privy Seal will submit full text of all telegrams recording business. I have established with President most cordial personal relations and trust Your Majesty will feel that results justify mission. President has given me personal letter, which I shall hope to deliver to you at luncheon on Tuesday, 19th.

Winston S. Churchill to Clement Attlee
(*Churchill papers, 20/49*)

13 August 1941
Most Secret

I suggest that when joint message to M. Stalin is broadcast it might be prefaced as follows:
'At their recent meeting, the President of the United States of America and the Prime Minister discussed the question of aid to the Soviet Union.
'They drew up together the text of a joint message which has been communicated to M. Stalin by the United States and British Ambassadors in Moscow.
'Here is the text of that message.'

Winston S. Churchill to Clement Attlee
(*Churchill papers, 20/49*)

13 August 1941

Planning arrive Iceland (C) daylight Saturday,[1] leaving at dark. Should be glad of mail and papers.

Secretary of State War is very welcome if he wishes to come by air. Can take him back by sea.[2]

1 Saturday 16 August 1941.
2 David Margesson did not go to Iceland.

John Martin: diary
(John Martin papers)

14 August 1941 HMS *Prince of Wales*

Owing to latest U-boat information, course altered to further north.

Sir Alexander Cadogan: diary
(Churchill papers, 4/225)

14 August 1941 HMS *Prince of Wales*

PM has got one of his untidy colds coming on. Film after dinner. A Donald Duck, and thereafter appalling slapstick by Laurel and Hardy, PM hated it, and thought I had chosen it (as I had!).

Harry Hopkins: memorandum
('The White House Papers of Harry L. Hopkins')

[14 August 1941] HMS *Prince of Wales*

During the trip back on the *Prince of Wales* I played backgammon with the Prime Minister several times for a shilling a game. The enclosed Canadian money was handed me by the Prime Minister on the last day of the Conference, August 11, 1941.[1]

The Prime Minister's backgammon game is not of the best. He likes to play what is known to all backgammon addicts as a 'back game'. As a matter of fact, he won two or three very exciting games from me by these tactics. He approaches the game with great zest, doubling and redoubling freely.

John Martin: diary
(John Martin papers)

15 August 1941 HMS *Prince of Wales*

At sea, joined by relief destroyer and aircraft escorts from Iceland. *Prince of Wales* carried out AA firings at smoke bursts and balloons. In the afternoon we altered course to close a homeward convoy – about 75 ships, heavily laden, with many aircraft visible on deck (described by PM as 'a delectable sight'), keeping their stations in very good order. The *Prince of Wales* and escorting destroyers passed through the columns of the convoy and then turned and came through again on the opposite course. Messages were exchanged with

[1] Thirty-two dollars in Canadian bills and some small change.

the Commodore and we waved to the cheering crews and passengers as we passed near. It was a gallant sight, but the ships of the convoy looked terribly vulnerable in spite of their escort. Then we left them and made course for Iceland.

Winston S. Churchill to Anthony Eden
(*Churchill papers, 20/49*)

15 August 1941

If you think well, please send message in my immediately following telegram to Menzies through Dominions Office and take any preliminary action you may think necessary. When the time comes I should propose myself to tell the Japanese Chargé d'Affaires that, if Japan disregards American warning and becomes involved in war with the United States, we shall range ourselves instantly by the side of the Americans. This might be Tuesday night or Wednesday morning.

2. I told President about our plans in Persia and he seemed to be quite content with them. I presume you are going ahead as arranged.

3. I read your wind-up of the session with much pleasure.[1]

Winston S. Churchill to Robert Menzies
(*Churchill papers, 20/49*)

15 August 1941

Many thanks for your telegram. You have no doubt seen the relevant cables about meeting. I trust you approve of what was accomplished. President promised me to give the warning to Japan in the terms agreed. Once we know this has been done we should range ourselves beside him and make it clear that if Japan becomes involved in war with United States she will also be at war with Britain and British Commonwealth. I am arranging this with Eden, and you will be advised through the regular channels. You should note that the President's warning covers an attack upon Russia, so that perhaps Stalin will line up too and of course the Dutch. If this combined front can be established, including China, I feel confident that Japan will lie quiet for a while. It is, however, essential to use the firmest language and the strongest combination.

[1] On 6 August 1941, the last day of the parliamentary session (which resumed on September 8), Eden recalled the situation a year earlier: 'I can remember a week when I was at the War Office when our trained and equipped forces in this country did not number one division. It is a different story now, but an enormous amount remains to be done . . . During this brief Recess our watchword must be "Production and more production, effort and more effort, until the victory is won."'

2. United States Navy is effectively taking over America–Iceland stretch of Atlantic, thus giving us relief equal to over fifty destroyers and corvettes soon to be available for home waters and South Atlantic.

Winston S. Churchill to Clement Attlee
(*Churchill papers, 20/48*)

15 August 1941

1. Menzies has only recently returned Australia, and I cannot think we should be justified in summoning him half round the world by air for only 3 or 4 days' conference in a fortnight's time. He would no doubt like invitation to join War Cabinet, but this raises many complications about the other Dominions and the size of War Cabinet. Although he is unhappy in Australia, there is no other man of comparable eminence and knowledge there.

2. I doubt whether Smuts can be away from South Africa for so long, and also whether we should press him to dangerous flight through Mediterranean.

3. I hope to see Fraser before he leaves, but I do not think he should be pressed to stay till end of month.

4. Is it not much better to let Mackenzie King have stage to himself, treating him with all the ceremony extended to Menzies?

5. Delay in answering due to difficulty of breaking wireless silence with many U-boats about.

Winston S. Churchill to Brendan Bracken
(*Churchill papers, 20/48*)

15 August 1941
Immediate

1. Unless we had issued by broadcast at 3 p.m. German wireless would have been first to announce to British public news already issued early morning in United States.

2. All film reels and other photographs were ordered to leave us Sunday night, but no plane could be got away from Gander until Tuesday, if then. Responsibility must therefore be divided between rotation of earth and climate of Newfoundland. Cable me whether you have now got them.

3. Martin is sending further details.

4. I am very sorry for your troubles.

Winston S. Churchill to Brendan Bracken
(*Churchill papers, 20/49*)

16 August 1941

Superseding all other telegrams.

I cannot understand how you have not got the films. Tell the Press we have all taken the greatest trouble to help them. Every effort has been made to deliver the films to you. They are incomparably better than anything American cameramen have taken.

In consequence of their premature release, you can publish at earliest possible moment. Make sure there will be no recriminations with the Americans.

Pictures will not be at all stale on date of our return United Kingdom.

On 16 August 1941, while Churchill was returning from his meeting with Roosevelt, an Anglo-Soviet agreement was signed in Moscow by Sir Stafford Cripps and Vyacheslav Molotov, giving the Soviet Union £10 million of British credit, at three per cent interest over five years, to replace lost Soviet war material from British stock. That night, in the continuing effort to divert German fighter aircraft from the Russian front, British bombers struck at Cologne and other Rhineland targets.

Winston S. Churchill: narrative
(*Churchill papers, 4/225*)

[16 August 1941] [Iceland]

HMS *Prince of Wales* reached the island on Saturday morning, the 16th August, and anchored at Hvals Fiord, from which we travelled to Reykjavik in a destroyer. On arrival at the port, I received a remarkably warm and vociferous welcome from a large crowd, whose friendly greetings were repeated whenever our presence was recognized during our stay, culminating in scenes of great enthusiasm on our departure in the afternoon, to the accompaniment of such cheers and hand-clapping as have, I was assured, seldom been heard in the streets of Reykjavik.

I was greeted on the quay by His Majesty's Minister, Mr. C Howard Smith,

CMG,[1] the General Officer Commanding Iceland Force, Major-General H.O. Curtis, CB, DSO, MC[2] and other British and American Officers. After a short visit to the Althinghaus, to pay my respects to the Regent[3] and the members of the Icelandic Cabinet, I proceeded to inspect a joint review of the British and American Forces. I took the salute with the President's son standing beside me, and the parade provided another remarkable demonstration of Anglo-American solidarity.

On return to Hvals Fiord, I visited HMS *Ramillies* (and addressed representatives of the crews of the British and American ships in the anchorage), HMS *Hecla* and HMS *Churchill*. HMS *Prince of Wales* sailed from Iceland that evening.

John Martin: diary
(*John Martin papers*)

16 August 1941 Iceland

Anchored at Hvals Fiord, where several British and American ships were in harbour. Here we transferred to the Canadian destroyer *Assiniboine* for Reykjavik, where we spent the day. There were crowds in the streets and remarkable enthusiasm, with cheering and clapping, said to be unusual among these stolid, undemonstrative people. It was a lovely sunny day and the place looked most attractive, not unlike somewhere in the West Highlands. We were first driven to the Althinghaus, where the PM was received by the Regent and the Icelandic Cabinet. At the Regent's suggestion the PM went out on to the balcony and addressed the crowd in the square, who gave him a tumultuous reception. He then went on to review a big parade of American and British troops, the President's son Franklin standing beside him at the

[1] Charles Howard Smith, 1888–1942. Entered the Foreign Office, 1912. Minister to Denmark, October 1939. *The Times* obituary stated: 'The invasion of Denmark by the Germans in April, 1940, brought his tenure of office to an end. Guided by a Gestapo agent, the Germans with bayonets fixed burst into the Legation and roughly marshalled all the occupants, who were kept under guard while the Chancery was rifled. Mr and Mrs Howard Smith, with bayonets pointed at them, were forced into a car and driven to a barracks. Eventually they were allowed to return to the Legation, and their departure with Legation and consulate staffs was arranged by the American Minister.' Minister to Iceland, May 1940 (he took up his post on 10 May 1940).

[2] Henry Osborne Curtis, 1888–1964. Joined the British Army, 1908. On active service, 1914–18 (France, Salonika, Palestine). Wounded three times. Military Cross, 1917. Distinguished Service Order, 1919. Officer Commanding, British Troops in Palestine, 1934–36. General Officer Commanding 46th Division, Dunkirk, 1940; Iceland Force, 1940–42; Salisbury Plain District 1943; Hampshire and Dorset, 1944; Hampshire and Aldershot, 1948. Two of his four sons were killed in action in the Second World War.

[3] Sveinn Björnsson, 1881–1952. Member of the Reykjavik Town Council, 1912. Special Envoy to the United States (1914) and Britain (1915). Minister to Denmark, 1920–24 and 1926–41. Regent of Iceland three times, 1941–43, assuming all the prerogatives in Icelandic affairs previously held by the Danish King (who was under German occupation). First President of the Republic of Iceland (re-elected twice by acclamation), 1944–52.

saluting base. After lunch with the British Minister we went for a short drive to see something of the country, visiting a transit camp for RAF trainees and hot springs from which it was hoped to provide the capital with central heating. Tea at Force HQ at Artun and left in destroyer at 5.30, seen off by the Icelandic Prime Minister, Mr Hermann Jonasson,[1] and again a demonstrative crowd. After visiting HMS *Ramillies* finally weighed anchor in HMS *Prince of Wales* about 10 p.m. with an escort of destroyers, the American ships taking station ahead.

Ronald Ladbrook[2]*: recollections*
(*Letter to the author, 27 December 1968*)

16 August 1941 Iceland

We moved off to anchor and received sailing orders for midnight. The *Prince of Wales* appeared in the anchorage and that afternoon during a peaceful siesta we were aroused and ordered to change into blues. Lower deck was cleared and we were fallen in on the forecastle deck. The Prime Minister appeared, stumping stolidly forward. He wore a Trinity House jacket and cap, and was followed by a US naval ensign who was Franklin Roosevelt junior. There was a flurry as he suddenly barked 'Bring me a soapbox.' A dais was found and he climbed up on it. He spoke to us for nearly a quarter of an hour, saying that the war would last another three years at least and that hard times lay ahead. He told us that we were carrying out one of the most vital jobs of the war in ensuring that the food and supplies without which Britain could not survive reached us from North America. He would not deny that this was one of the bleakest times in Britain's history, but he was confident that we would survive, and with right on our side and help from allies – a glance to the ensign here – we should win through to a great and glorious victory.

'Three cheers for the Prime Minister', said the Captain. For the first time Winston smiled and with a wave of the hand stalked off the foredeck, followed by the officers. We were dismissed and rushed amidships to cheer him on his way as the launch left the ship's side. It sped away across the fiord and Winston turned and saluted.

I found Taff, a Rhondda Valley pitman, next to me at the rail. 'There goes the bastard,' he said in a voice full of venom, 'back to his bloody brandy.' Startled, I

[1] Hermann Jonasson, 1896–1976. After receiving a legal degree at Reykjavik University he became the city's Chief of Police. Chairman of the Progressive Party. Prime Minister of Iceland 1934–42 and 1956–58. His son Steingrimur Hermannsson was later Governor of the Central Bank of Iceland.

[2] Ronald Edmund Ladbrook, 1920–. Educated at St Olave's School, then Merton College, Oxford (1939–40). Lieutenant, Royal Naval Volunteer Reserve, 1940-45. Returned to Merton College, 1946–49 (BA, History, 1948; Diploma of Education, 1949). Served in the Royal Air Force, 1949–61; Flight-Lieutenant, 1949. Tutor in History, Royal Air Force College, Cranwell, 1949–54. Middle East Air Force, 1954–55. Squadron Leader, 1956. Retired from the RAF, 1961. Assistant Master, Stanbridge School, Romsey, 1962-65, teaching history and economics.

turned and looked at him. Taff whipped round, glared defiantly and turned to the hatchway. 'And the best of bloody luck to him,' he added as he disappeared.

Winston S. Churchill: speech
(*'The Unrelenting Struggle', page 228*)

16 August 1941 Iceland

I am glad to have an opportunity to visit the nation which for so long has loved democracy and freedom. We, and later the Americans, have undertaken to keep war away from this country. But you will all realize that if we had not come others would.

We will do all in our power to make sure that our presence here shall cause as little trouble as possible in the lives of the Icelanders. But at the moment your country is an important base for the protection of the rights of the nations.

When the present struggle is over, we, and the Americans, will ensure that Iceland shall receive absolute freedom. We come to you as one cultured nation to another, and it is our aim that your culture in the past may be joined to your progress in the future as a free people. I have pleasure in wishing you happiness and good luck in time to come.

Winston S. Churchill to Anthony Eden
(*Churchill papers, 20/36*)

16 August 1941

1. I have now had time to read this speech[1] thoroughly. It does not make so hostile an impression upon me as I have derived from the summaries and extract. I do not think it would be a sound deduction from this speech that Franco had given himself over to the Axis. There is much to be said for the suggestion of Ambassador Hoare that Franco was trying:

(a) To put himself at the head of his own movement; and
(b) To reconcile Germany in advance to some arrangement by which Suñer[2] would be restrained or excluded.

2. I do not think that this speech by itself, in the absence of further development, could be taken as a basis for the action contemplated known as 'Puma' or 'Pilgrim'[3] – such action would have to be justified on other grounds. Meanwhile, however, preparations are going and should go forward.

[1] General Franco's speech of 17 July 1941, see page 977, n.3.

[2] Serrano Suñer, the Spanish Foreign Minister, and strong supporter of closer ties between Spain and Germany.

[3] Pilgrim was the planned seizure of the Portuguese island groups in the Atlantic (Madeira, Azores, Canary Islands and Cape Verde). Puma covered the Canary Islands and Cape Verde Islands.

Winston S. Churchill to General Ismay
(*Churchill papers, 20/36*)

16 August 1941

COMMANDOS

1. I settled with General Auchinleck that the three Glen ships were all to remain in the Middle East and be refitted for amphibious operations as soon as possible.

2. That the Commandos should be reconstituted, so far as possible, by volunteers by restoring to them any of their former members who may wish to return from the units in which they have been dispersed, and that Brigadier Laycock should have the command and should be appointed Director of Combined Operations.

3. The DCO and the Commandos will be under the direct command of General Auchinleck. This cancels the former arrangement which I proposed of their being under the Naval C-in-C.

Winston S. Churchill to A. V. Alexander, Admiral Pound and Admiral Fraser
(*Churchill papers, 20/36*)

16 August 1941

1. I am greatly interested in the proposed design of the *Lion* and *Temeraire*. Let me know the exact point which has been reached in the general construction and in the drawings.

2. It is most important not to reproduce in these two ships the faults which are apparent in the 5 KG 5;[1] namely:

(a) The retrogression to the 14-inch gun from our well-tried 15-inch type; and

(b) The marring of the structure by the provision of the aerodrome amidships. Merely for the sake of having a couple of low quality aircraft, the whole principle of the citadel so well exemplified in the *Nelson* and the *Rodney* has been cast aside.

The space of about 40 feet amidships entails a degree of heavy armouring in this vital area, which is improvident having regard to the needs for carrying a lesser protection as far forward and aft as possible. It may well be that 1,000 or 1,500 tons of armour are misplaced through the opening of this hiatus in the citadel of the ship.

[1] The King George V class battleships; they were the largest and most powerful battleships to see active service in the Royal Navy. Their main armament was ten 14-in guns. There were five KGVs in all: *King George V* (completed in October 1940, 42,237 tons deep load), *Prince of Wales, Duke of York, Anson* and *Howe*. There is a comprehensive description of these ships in V.E. Tarrant, *King George V Class Battleships*, Arms and Armour Press, London, 1991.

3. I understand, and hope, that the *Lion* and *Temeraire* will carry nine 16-inch guns in three triple turrets, with six guns firing directly ahead, and the rear turret on the most forward bearing possible. These three turrets should be grouped together as closely as possible to form the central citadel comprising funnels and director tower, and covering with the turret and heaviest armour the magazines and vital machinery spaces. If this were done, it should be possible to give a 6-inch turtle deck carried very far forward, if possible to the bow, thus protecting the speed of the ship from bow damage.

4. Although it looked very progressive to be able to fly two aeroplanes off a battleship, the price paid in the rest of the design was altogether excessive. It might, however, be possible in a ship with a citadel outlined above to arrange to flip off one or two aircraft from the Quarter-deck, but no serious sacrifice of design must be made for this. A Capital ship of the consequence of the *Lion* or *Temeraire* must depend upon having an aircraft carrier working with her, or at the very least a cruiser capable of flying off an aircraft. She should on no account be spoiled for the sake of carrying aircraft.

5. I should very much like to see these two ships pressed forward beyond what is at present approved. Before, however, any final decision is taken upon the design there ought to be a conference of a number of sea officers, including the late and present Commanders-in-Chief who have served in the *King George V* or *Prince of Wales*. The successful design of the *Arethusa* was evolved from a conference of Admirals convened, at my direction, in the Winter of 1911.

Pray let me have your views.

Winston S. Churchill to Admiral Pound, Sir Archibald Sinclair and John Moore-Brabazon

(*Churchill papers, 20/36*)

16 August 1941

1. This is a melancholy story.[1] You will see from reading the Minutes that we were promised 'Grummans', with folding wings, at twenty a month beginning in April. We still have none, and are only promised the schedule set out in the First Lord's Minute of July 26th.

2. I regard the supply of from 6 to 12 'Grummans' to *Victorious* and *Ark Royal* as of first importance; especially is this the case with any carrier operating in the Mediterranean. The surprise which will be effected upon the enemy when these fast Fighters rise to engage them may give considerable easement, almost at once.

[1] When Churchill dictated this sentence to a new stenographer, Peter Kinna, to whom he had not given dictation before, the stenographer thought that the Prime Minister was making a general comment to him on the state of affairs, and replied: 'I am so sorry'.

The cutting down of enemy bomber aircraft attack at sea far exceeds in importance and urgency any other duty which can be performed by a Carrier in the Mediterranean; even if they can only work within 40 to 50 miles of the parent ship they can do all that is necessary. The enemy must be made to feel that to go near a ship convoyed by an aircraft carrier is to incur heavy losses from aircraft almost equal to shore-based fighters.

3. We have now no aircraft carriers in the Eastern Mediterranean. Therefore, there is no point in sending folding-wing 'Grummans' there at present. The August, September and October quotas for 'Grummans' now assigned to the United Kingdom (total 22), and the 24 now assigned to the Middle East in the September and October quotas – total 46 – should all be made available in the United Kingdom for the equipping of our aircraft carriers. Deliveries to the Middle East after October should be considered later.

Let me have a monthly report of the equipment of the aircraft carriers with 'Grummans'.

4. When do we get our next new aircraft-carrier *Indomitable?*

5. Unless there is some reason to the contrary of which I am not aware, the following orders should be given now.

'The September and October batches of 12 Grummans with folding wings should be sent to the United Kingdom and not (repeat not) to the Middle East.

Winston S. Churchill to Lord Halifax and Lord Beaverbrook
(*Churchill papers, 20/41*)

16 August 1941

Loss of Purvis is most grievous.[1] Will you consult together and let me have your individual or joint advice upon successor? Thank you very much for your letter. Trust you are pleased with what we accomplished.

Sir Alexander Cadogan: diary
(*Churchill papers, 4/225*)

17 August 1941 HMS *Prince of Wales*

Foul day. Fairly heavy sea and rain. Spent some time on the bridge. PM paid a round of visits to Gun Room, Ward Room and Warrant Officers. Film again – can't remember what.

[1] Arthur Purvis, Chairman of the British Supply Council in North America, was among a number of passengers killed on the evening of August 14 when an aircraft of Atlantic Ferry Command crashed while taking off. He was on his way back to Washington after a visit to London.

Winston S. Churchill: speech
(*John Martin papers*)

18 August 1941 Scapa Flow

FAREWELL SPEECH TO HMS *PRINCE OF WALES*

Many years ago there was a statesman who came back from a European Conference and said he had brought with him 'Peace with Honour'.[1] We have not sought Peace on this occasion; and as for Honour, we have never lost it. But we have brought back a means of waging more effective war and surer hope of final and speedy victory.

John Martin: diary
(*John Martin papers*)

18 August 1941

Early morning gun practice before coming in to Scapa. Thence by HMS *Tartar* to Thurso, where Lady Sinclair was waiting to receive us (and promised me grouse for our mess) and we boarded our special train.

John Colville: diary
(*Colville papers*)

18 August 1941

Jack Churchill, Desmond[2] and I discussed the rising annoyance in the House of Commons at the PM's personal resentment of criticism – which is meant to be helpful – and the offence which has been given to many people, including Ministers, by his treatment of them. Desmond goes so far as to say that the PM is losing many people's friendship. The PM himself does not expect to retain his popularity if he wins the war for us: he has before him the examples of Wellington and Disraeli amongst others. But that he should lose his personal friends owing to the impatience of his manner is unfortunate – and unfair to one so innately loveable and generous.

[1] On his return from the Congress of Berlin, Benjamin Disraeli told the House of Commons: 'Lord Salisbury and myself have brought you back peace – but a peace I hope with honour.' (*Hansard*, 5 August 1874).

[2] Desmond Morton.

Sir Alexander Cadogan: diary
('The Diary of Sir Alexander Cadogan OM, 1938-1945')

18 August 1941

ON THE TRAIN FROM SCOTLAND TO LONDON

Long lunch. Winston did himself well, finishing up with a Benedictine. 10 min. later he called for a brandy. The attendant reminded him he had had Benedictine. He said: 'I know: I want some brandy to clean it up.'

John Colville: diary
(Colville papers)

19 August 1941

The PM arrived back in London. The Cabinet met him at King's Cross; Leslie Rowan, John Peck and I greeted him on the steps of the Annexe as he emerged from his car, smiling broadly, still dressed in his nautical clothes. Ralph Assheton[1] had brought his wife and child to see the return; nobody else was there.

John Martin told me he had heard Roosevelt say that he did not intend to declare war: he intended to wage it.

War Cabinet: minutes
(Cabinet papers, 65/19)

19 August 1941 10 Downing Street
11.30 a.m.

The Prime Minister gave the War Cabinet an account of his discussions with President Roosevelt and of his short visit to Iceland on the return journey.

The President had been overjoyed at the meeting. The greatest cordiality had prevailed, and the Americans had missed no opportunity of identifying themselves with our cause. The American Naval Officers had not concealed their keenness to enter the war. While he (the Prime Minister) had had discussions with the President on political matters, Staff discussions had

[1] Ralph Assheton, 1901–1984. Conservative Member of Parliament for Rushcliffe, Nottinghamshire, 1934–45; for the City of London, 1945–50; for Blackburn West, 1950–55. Parliamentary Secretary, Ministry of Labour and Ministry of National Service, 1939–42; Ministry of Supply, 1942–43. Financial Secretary to the Treasury, 1943–44. Chairman of the Conservative Party Organization, 1944–46. Created Baronet, 1945. chairman of the Public Accounts Committee, 1948–50; of the Select Committee on Nationalized Industries, 1951–53. A Director of several public companies, including Borax Ltd, Rio Tinto Zinc, and the National Westminster Bank. Created Baron Clitheroe, 1955. Lord Lieutenant of Lancashire, 1971–76. His wife Sylvia was a Fellow of the Royal Institution of Chartered Surveyors and of the Chartered Land Agents' Society. Their son Ralph, born in 1929, was later Chairman of RTZ Chemicals Ltd., and of the Yorkshire Bank.

proceeded simultaneously. These had been most useful, and would be reported on on a later occasion.

The following were the main points dealt with in the Prime Minister's survey:

By the 1st September the American Navy would have a convoy system in full operation between their coasts and Iceland. This would afford great relief to our Naval vessels engaged on convoy duties. This procedure would present the enemy with a dilemma. Either he could attack the convoys, in which case his U-boats would be attacked by the American Naval forces; or he could refrain from attack, which would be tantamount to giving us victory in the Battle of the Atlantic.

The Prime Minister explained how the idea of a Joint Declaration had come about, and how keen the President had been on its immediate publication. The President had been very pleased with the new paragraph dealing with social security, suggested by the War Cabinet, but had been somewhat reluctant to agree to the modifications in the fourth paragraph, which, in its original form, might have ruled out the continuance of Imperial Preference. He (the Prime Minister) had been most grateful to the War Cabinet for having met at 1.45 a.m. on the 12th August in order to furnish him with their comments without delay.

The Prime Minister drew attention to passages in the Declaration which were significant of the changed attitude as compared with that of 1917–18. Instead of saying that there would be no more war, we aimed at adequate precautions to prevent war happening again by effectively disarming our enemies. Again, instead of trying to ruin German trade, we now took the view that the world could not afford to see any large nation unprosperous. It was also important that the President should have agreed to a Declaration which in his (the President's) phrase referred to the 'final destruction of Nazi tyranny'.

These had not been discussed in detail, but would be taken up by Lord Beaverbrook and Mr Harriman.[1] The broad picture was that American production at present was somewhat disappointing. American industry was working to supply their own forces, our forces, and now those of the Russians. There would have to be a review of United States programmes, and measures would have to be taken which would involve restrictions on civil consumption. This was not easy to enforce on a nation not at war.

The Prime Minister gave the War Cabinet information as to the President's reaction to the three matters referred to in the margin.

[1] Details of the discussions at Argentia concerning the Beaverbrook-Harriman mission to Moscow were somehow conveyed to the Japanese, whose Embassy in London telegraphed them to Tokyo (and to the Japanese Embassy in Washington). Churchill was shown a transcript, as decrypted at Bletchley. He sent it to Lord Beaverbrook with the laconic comment in the margin: 'Pretty accurate stuff.' (*Secret Intelligence Service papers*).

The discussion and Conclusions reached are recorded in the Secretary's Standard File of War Cabinet Conclusions.[1]

SECRETARY'S FILE ONLY

The Prime Minister gave some more general information about his visit to the United States President, over and above what is recorded in the Minutes.

The Prime Minister said that he had got on intimate terms with the President. Of the six meals they had had together, five had been on the President's ship. The President had shown great activity, considering his physical disabilities, and on one occasion had walked (every step causing him pain) a considerable distance in front of Marines drawn up on parade, notwithstanding that his own people had advised him against doing this.

The Prime Minister said that the family influence on the President was great. Both his sons were in uniform and clearly urged him that American assistance in money and *matériel* was not enough.

The Prime Minister gave his impression of the President's attitude towards the entry of the United States into the war. He was obviously determined that they should come in. On the other hand, the President had been extremely anxious about the Bill for further appropriations for Lease-Lend, which had only passed with a very narrow majority. Clearly he was skating on pretty thin ice in his relations with Congress, which, however, he did not regard as truly representative of the country. If he were to put the issue of peace and war to Congress, they would debate it for three months. The President had said that he would wage war, but not declare it, and that he would become more and more provocative. If the Germans did not like it, they could attack American forces.

Full agreement had now been reached on the scheme whereby the American Navy would have their convoy system in full operation between their country and Iceland by the 1st September. This would release no less than 52 British destroyers and corvettes now based on Halifax for convoy duty on other routes. Each of our North Atlantic convoys would be escorted by 5 US destroyers, together with a capital ship or a cruiser. The President's orders to these escorts were to attack any U-boat which showed itself, even if it were 200 or 300 miles away from the convoy. Admiral Stark intended to carry out this order literally, and any Commander who sank a U-boat would have his action approved. Everything was to be done to force an 'incident'. This would put the enemy in the dilemma that either he could attack the convoys, in which case his U-boats would be attacked by American Naval forces, or, if he refrained from attack, this would be tantamount to giving us victory in the Battle of the Atlantic. It might suit us, in six or eight weeks' time, to provoke Hitler by taunting him with this difficult choice.

[1] Marked 'Secretary's File Only', and limited to a single uncirculated typescript.

The Prime Minister said that he had thought it right to give the President a warning. He had told him that he would not answer for the consequences if Russia was compelled to sue for peace and, say, by the Spring of next year, hope died in Britain that the United States were coming into the war. The President had taken this very well, and had made it clear that he would look for an 'incident' which would justify him in opening hostilities.

Dealing with supplies for Russia, the Prime Minister said that we might have to make some sacrifices, but this would be well worth while so long as the Russian front remained in being. When Lord Beaverbrook returned to this country he would have to go to Moscow. If the Foreign Secretary also thought of going to Moscow to deal with the more general political issues, he was sure that nothing but good would come out of the visit. The technical aspects of supplies questions should, however, he thought, be handled by Lord Beaverbrook.

BOMBING POLICY[1]

The Prime Minister said that our attacks should not be pressed too hard if the weather was unfavourable. Consideration should also be given to attacking the less heavily defended centres.

The War Cabinet concurred in this view.

CONFIDENTIAL ANNEX[2]

The Prime Minister referred to his Telegram No. 19 Tudor of 11th August, 1941,[3] regarding the position *vis-à-vis* Japan. The President had proposed to Japan some time ago the neutralization of Indo-China and Siam under a joint guarantee of the United States, Japan, Britain, China and others, but there had been a number of conditions which were unacceptable to the Japanese. The President's idea was to negotiate about these unacceptable conditions and thus procure a moratorium of 30 days, during which we might improve our position in Singapore and the Japanese would have to stand still. At the end of the Note which the President proposed to hand to the Japanese Ambassador was a passage to the effect that any further encroachment by Japan in the South-west Pacific would produce a situation in which the United States Government would be compelled to take counter-measures even though this might lead to war between the United States and Japan. The President also proposed to add that the United States Government would be similarly interested in the North-west Pacific and Manchukuo which might make it possible for the Russians to associate themselves with this move.

[1] In night raids over Germany that May, 43 bombers had been shot down or crashed (out of 2,416 sorties). In June the losses had been 91 (out of 3,288 sorties). Between 1 and 18 August a total of 107 bombers had been shot down, the highest rate of loss in the night bombing offensive. In the attack on Berlin on the night of 12/13 August 70 aircraft took part, of which nine were lost.

[2] *Cabinet papers, 65/23.*

[3] Churchill telegram to the Foreign Office beginning 'The position about Japan is as follows' (see the documents for 11 August 1941).

Later in the meeting the Prime Minister read out to the War Cabinet a telegram which had just arrived from President Roosevelt to the effect that the President had seen the Japanese Ambassador who had approached him on the subject of the resumption of the informal conversations which had been taking place regarding the neutralization of Indo-China and Siam. The President said that the statement he had made to the Ambassador was no less vigorous and substantially similar to that already agreed with the Prime Minister. The Japanese Ambassador had asked whether negotiations could be restarted. To this the President had replied that if Japan was prepared to readjust its position the conversations might be resumed, but not before a clear statement had been made by the Japanese of their aspirations and plans.

NAVAL REINFORCEMENT, FAR EAST

Sir Tom Phillips said that whereas the Germans possessed a small, but very modern fleet, the Japanese Navy consisted, like our own, of a mixture of old and modern ships; her oldest battleships were inferior to the R Class ships which it was proposed to send out to the Far East. These four R Class ships together with the *Rodney, Renown* and *Nelson* (when repaired) should, in their own waters, and operating under cover of shore-based aircraft, be a match for any forces the Japanese were likely to bring against them.

Mr Attlee said that apart from the attitude of the Dominion Governments concerned, it seemed sounder to send a modern ship to a new theatre of operations. The arguments put forward by the Vice-Chief of the Naval Staff assumed that we would be prepared to remain on the defensive in Malayan waters even if Japan attacked Russia. We should find such action hard to justify in the circumstances.

The Prime Minister invited the First Lord of the Admiralty to consider the proposal to send as quickly as possible one modern Capital Ship, together with an aircraft carrier, to join up with *Repulse* at Singapore. He would not come to a decision on this point without consulting the First Sea Lord, but in view of the strong feeling of the Committee in favour of the proposal, he hoped that the Admiralty would not oppose this suggestion. The Committee would take its final decision on Monday, 20th October, after which he would reply to the telegram on this question which he had just received from the Government of Australia. In the meantime, no action in the contrary sense should be taken, and such preparations as were possible should be made.

OPERATION 'PILGRIM'

The Prime Minister said that President Roosevelt had been anxious to occupy the Azores, but wanted to receive an invitation from Dr Salazar. Such an invitation, however, was unlikely to be received unless and until a German act of aggression took place against the Iberian Peninsula. He (the Prime Minister) had told President Roosevelt that we might have to carry out Operation Pilgrim in September without waiting for an act of provocation.

Otherwise we should run the risk of being deprived of Gibraltar without obtaining an alternative Naval base. We should not, however, set the Operation in motion without giving most careful consideration to all the factors involved at the last moment: i.e., in about three weeks' time. The President had said that steps would be taken to have in readiness, by about the middle of September, American forces of occupation. We should, of course, keep the Americans informed of our intentions; but they would not misunderstand the position if we decided that the Operation should not take place.

The Secretary of State for Foreign Affairs said that he thought that the President had read a good deal into Dr Salazar's letter to him, which had only referred to the provision of war material.

The Prime Minister said that the President had chosen to read Dr Salazar's letter in this way. He (the Prime Minister) thought that in view of the President's interest in the Azores, we ought to consider a slight change in our policy, namely, that we should now inform Dr Salazar that, owing to our other preoccupations, we were not in a position to supply the Portuguese with armaments for the defence of the Atlantic Islands in the immediate future, and that they should therefore apply to the United States for such assistance.

Winston S. Churchill to John Moore-Brabazon and Sir Archibald Sinclair
(Churchill papers, 20/36)

19 August 1941

NEW AIRCRAFT PRODUCTION PROGRAMME

It is clear that the utmost effort must be made, and that even then results will be short of our requirements. Please report what practical steps you are taking to give effect to my Minute M 733/1 of July 12,[1] as modified by your reply of August 2. Let me have a Progress Report before the month is out. Inform me also of any way in which I can assist you. The table of forecasts should be modified, in red ink, to show the somewhat improved target now being aimed at.

[1] The Minute beginning 'I am not at all sure about this', printed on page 931.

Winston S. Churchill to General Sir John Dill, and to General Ismay, for the Chiefs of Staff Committee
(*Churchill papers, 20/36*)

19 August 1941
Action this Day

The important thing is not so much to reduce our troops in Iceland as to make it a training ground for Alpine Units. Can you not give some mountain guns to the artillery, instead of withdrawing them? Let me have a scheme for providing skis, snow shoes, &c., for the largest number that can be trained in mountain fighting under glacial conditions. The fact that a few more Americans have come should make the training all the easier. I regard the creation of these Alpine Units as a vital feature in our inner organization. I ask that this may be taken up with the utmost vigour.

Winston S. Churchill to Air Chief Marshal Sir Charles Portal
(*Churchill papers 20/36*)

19 August 1941

Thank you very much for your full explanation.[1] Even if the airmen had been in error they would not have been to blame, because it is the system that is at fault. The lack of effective and intimate contact between the air and the ground forces calls for a drastic reform. The needs of the Army should be met in a helpful spirit by the Air Ministry. It is the responsibility of the Air Force to satisfy the Army now that the resources are growing. I hope I may have your assurance that you are striving night and day to end this lamentable breakdown in the war machine. We need not go into the past; but if the Army is not well treated in the future the Air Ministry will have failed in an essential part of its duties.

Print and circulate as you propose.

Winston S. Churchill to David Margesson
(*Churchill papers, 20/36*)

19 August 1941

REPAIR OF TANKS

Your minute of 15th July, 1941, states a number of requirements which, if they could all be met, would make life too easy. Everything practicable should

[1] The Report by Brigadier A.F. Harding and Air Commodore L.O. Brown on certain aspects of the General Headquarters, Middle East Report on the Action of the 2nd Armoured Division during the withdrawal from Cyrenaica, March–April, 1941.

be done to meet the various desiderata, but the main contribution must be a genuine effort and good management. I am shocked to see that a month later we still have 25 per cent. of Infantry Tanks out of order, and that out of 400 Cruiser Tanks no fewer than 157 are unfit for action. I have no doubt there can be made plenty of explanations for such a failure, but failure it remains, none the less.

Pray do not let it be thought that you are satisfied with such a result. If you simply take up the attitude of defending it there will be no hope of improvement.

Winston S. Churchill to Lord Woolton
(*Churchill papers, 20/36*)

19 August 1941

PUBLIC REACTION TO FOOD CONTROL
POSTAL CENSORSHIP REPORT ON HOME OPINION

I do not know whether you have seen the attached report, which I have just read. There is light as well as shade in it. Nevertheless, I very much fear the influence of the official machine when applied to the billion petty transactions of ordinary daily life. I feel very anxious about the state of opinion disclosed.

Winston S. Churchill to Lady Willingdon[1]
(*Churchill papers, 20/22*)

19 August 1941

My dear Lady Willingdon,

I was greatly distressed on returning to England to hear of your irreparable loss.

Freeman's[2] outstanding services to our country and to the Empire were continued to the last moment of his life. He died in harness.

[1] Lady Marie Adelaide (Marie, Marchioness of Willingdon), daughter of the 1st Earl Brassey. Vice-President of the Overseas League. Her husband had died in August 1941. She died in 1960.

[2] Freeman Freeman-Thomas, 1866–1941. Educated at Eton and Trinity College Cambridge. Liberal MP 1900–06 and 1906–10. Junior Lord of the Treasury, 1905–12. Created Baron Willingdon, 1910. Governor of Bombay, 1913–19 and of Madras, 1919–24. Created Viscount, 1924. Governor-General of Canada, 1926–31. Created Earl, 1931. Privy Councillor, 1931. Viceroy of India, 1931–36. Created Marquess, 1936. His elder son, born in 1893, was killed in action on the western front on 14 September 1914.

To you who shared his labours and responsibilities and were his devoted companion and inspirer the separation must be overwhelming. Please accept my deepest sympathy, vain tho' words may be.

Yours very sincerely,
Winston S. Churchill

Winston S. Churchill to L. S. Amery
(*Churchill papers, 20/36*)

20 August 1941

ATLANTIC CHARTER

Any explanation of the general principles referred to in Point 3[1] must be considered first by the Cabinet. The application of such principles would only arise in such cases where transference of territory or sovereignty arose. The expression 'peoples' requires definition. There are at least a dozen races in India, and half a dozen large Provinces as strongly differentiated from one another as the nations of Europe. It would be as absurd to talk about 'the Indian people' as it would be to talk about 'the European people'. No right of secession is admitted in the United States.

Generally speaking, it is silly to make heavy weather about these broad affirmations of principle. I am sure that the Lord Privy Seal in his remarks did not intend to suggest, e.g., that the natives of Nigeria or of East Africa could by a majority vote choose the form of Government under which they live, or the Arabs by such a vote expel the Jews from Palestine. It is evident that prior obligations require to be considered and respected, and that circumstances alter cases.

I look to you to prepare suitable drafts of telegrams to the Viceroy and the Governor of Burma.

John Colville: diary
(*Colville papers*)

20 August 1941

On late duty at No. 10. Just before going down to dress for dinner the PM, nodding his head gloomily, said that the situation was very grim. I suppose he was referring to the German progress in the Ukraine and towards Leningrad;

[1] The third point in the Atlantic Charter, which L.S. Amery (Secretary of State for India and Burma) had queried with regard to India and Burma, read: 'They respect right of all peoples to choose form of Government under which they will live; and they wish to see Sovereign rights and self-Government restored to those who have been forcibly deprived of them.'

or perhaps to certain failures and disappointments in our production. It is an attitude very dissimilar to that of the general public, whose optimism is almost too buoyant at present.

After dinner the PM asked me about the tests I had undergone at Euston House.[1] I described the questions in the Intelligence test and the PM said that if that was the standard, Nelson and Napoleon would have been considered unsuitable. What, he wanted to know, was the use of catering for a lot of 'chess-players who would die young of epilepsy'?

He was incensed by a letter from the cranky, pacifist Duke of Bedford and ended his scathing remarks on the subject by saying he was so glad that when this war was over he would be old enough 'to leave it all: the scorn that I have for them'. By them I think he meant politics. Whatever may in fact happen, he certainly now has the intention of washing his hands of politics after the war and retiring to Chartwell to write a book. But he thinks it will be a long war yet; and can he retain his position until the end of it? There are no signs of his popularity diminishing or authority weakening, and this American journey, coupled with his speech on Russia, has regained any prestige he had lost. But public opinion is fickle.

Winston S. Churchill: memorandum[2]
(*Churchill papers, 4/225*)

20 August 1941
Most Secret

I give below,[3] for the information of the Cabinet, some account of the conversations which took place at my recent meeting with President Roosevelt. This indicates, in broad outline, the course of the discussions and the final results achieved under the various headings. To it is appended, in Annex III, a report on the conversations between the British and American Chiefs of Staff.

I also attach (Annex IV) a diary and record of the personnel of the Mission. I would draw special attention to the holding of Divine Service on the quarterdeck of HMS *Prince of Wales*, attended by President Roosevelt, with his staff of officers and representatives of all ranks of the United States Navy and Marines. All were impressed with this episode.

[1] Colville was persevering in his efforts to enter the Royal Air Force.
[2] Printed for the War Cabinet as War Cabinet Paper No. 202 of 1941.
[3] The account which Churchill printed with this memorandum, and which was largely drafted by Sir Alexander Cadogan, is incorporated in this volume in its relevant places in the document selection as 'Winston S. Churchill : narrative'. Some of it was subsequently used by Churchill in Volume Three of his war memoirs.

War Cabinet, Defence Committee (Operations): minutes
(Cabinet papers, 69/2)

20 August 1941 10 Downing Street
6 p.m.

PERSIA

The Prime Minister said that from the recent telegrams from Teheran we could only regard the Persian attitude to our representations for the eviction of German personnel in Persia as unacceptable. The time had come to take military action however regrettable it might be. Delay in the expulsion of the Germans from Persia would be dangerous, and it was essential that we should have one clear channel by which we could send supplies to Russia. This was in fact one of the few measures we could take to help a country which was making such a stupendous effort against the enemy.

The Prime Minister directed that for publicity purposes our reasons for the action we proposed to take would initially be confined to the need to eliminate German influence in Persia. If, subsequently military operations developed on a considerable scale, our action could be fully justified on the grounds that we were keeping open a line of communication with Russia.

Winston S. Churchill to Sir Archibald Sinclair
(Churchill papers, 20/36)

20 August 1941

I am glad you are equipping our aerodromes with blind-landing apparatus, which may be most important in the coming winter.

I note that all new bomber and GR aircraft[1] made in England, with the exception of a few Blenheims, have standard equipment, but only 30 per cent. of the aerodromes. We should endeavour to complete the rest before March. No doubt you have explored the possibility of getting standard equipment from America. Perhaps extra pressure could be put on through Harriman and Hopkins to this end.

We should press on also with the night-fighter squadrons. You expect to have 17 ready by the end of this year or early 1942. Cannot we get them

[1] General Reconnaissance aircraft, for maritime patrol or anti-submarine work.

completed by the Autumn for the night-bombing season? If the turbin-light[1] proves a success it will be important to be able to use ordinary fighter squadrons to co-operate with the searchlight-carrying aircraft. No doubt you have this in mind.

Winston S. Churchill to Sir John Anderson
(*Churchill papers, 20/36*)

20 August 1941

NEED FOR MOTORISTS IN RECEIPT OF A SUPPLEMENTARY PETROL RATION TO KEEP A LOG BOOK

I am by no means convinced that there are sufficient reasons for imposing this additional obligation on the public. There is a growing and justifiable impatience of multiplying the filling-up of forms, and providing a new foundation upon which further layers of officials may build their homes. If you feel there is no other means of securing your objects, it would be better to bring the matter before the Cabinet.

Winston S. Churchill to Lord Beaverbrook
(*Churchill papers, 20/36*)

20 August 1941
Action this Day

Pray see the attached statement[2] prepared at my direction by Lord Cherwell. We must expect gas warfare on a tremendous scale. It may break out at any moment. Please see the alarming restriction which has had to be imposed on the production of mustard gas – (A). And also the explanation of this at (B). What do the Air Ministry mean by stopping the charging of 250-lb. bombs? This seems most improvident and is contrary to a number of Cabinet decisions, which are to the effect that the maximum possible gas is to be produced and charged into suitable containers, or otherwise stored.

I invite you to give your personal attention to this new aspect. The whole matter is dangerous and urgent in the last degree.

[1] Fighter Command's problem of illuminating parts of the sky was approached through Group Captain W. Helmore's 'Turbinlite' which, fitted in the nose of an aircraft, threw out a strong diffused light in which, it was hoped, a second aircraft would be able to detect and attack a bomber. It was an ingenious idea, full of difficulties of its own, and never properly tested operationally because the German attacks died away in May 1941. Another method of illumination, favoured by Coastal Command, was the use of a naval 24-inch searchlight fitted into the under-turret of a Wellington bomber, (designed by Squadron-Leader H. de V. Leigh, a First World War pilot). By May 1942 five Wellingtons had been fitted with the Leigh Light.

[2] Not printed: on gas and gas weapons.

War Cabinet: minutes
(*Cabinet papers, 65/19*)

21 August 1941 10 Downing Street
11.30 a.m.

The Prime Minister, on behalf of the War Cabinet, extended a warm welcome to the Prime Minister of Canada. He hoped that he would stay as long as possible, and would take the fullest possible part in their deliberations, and would also attend meetings of the Defence Committee (Operations). The whole country had the greatest admiration for the war effort made by Canada under Mr Mackenzie King's leadership.

Reference was made to a protest against British high altitude bombing of places in Occupied France, handed to our Ambassador at Madrid (Telegram No. 1202 from Madrid). The French Embassy had complained that 6 people had been killed at Lille, and 80 at Brest.

The Prime Minister said that the Vichy Government had not complained of our bombing military objectives in Occupied France. He thought it would be desirable that a distinction should be drawn between the latitude given to our bombers when bombing targets in Occupied France as compared with the instructions given to them when bombing targets in Germany.

PROPOSAL TO ASK RUSSIA TO DESTROY CAUCASIAN OIL FIELDS[1]

The Prime Minister said that he thought it was difficult for us, at a time when we were offering so little assistance to the Russians in the operational field, to press them to undertake this work of demolition. Russian agriculture was greatly dependent upon petrol. These oil fields produced 27 million tons a year, and their destruction would condemn large sections of the Russian people to starvation.

Continuing, the Prime Minister said that the amount of help which we could give to the Russians by way of oil imports was so very small that he could not see that we had any effective inducement which we could offer them to destroy their oil fields, if they were not prepared to reach a decision themselves to do it. It was impossible for us to say what M. Stalin would do in regard to this issue. He thought that we must be ready to bomb the oil fields ourselves if the Russians did not destroy them.

[1] This item was included in the War Cabinet Confidential Annex (*Cabinet papers, 65/23*). The Paymaster-General, Lord Hankey, had submitted a proposal that, to avoid the Russian Caucasian oil industry falling into German hands, the Russians themselves should be asked to destroy it.

Winston S. Churchill to Sir John Dill and Ronald Cross
(*Churchill papers, 20/36*)

22 August 1941
Action this Day

Let me have a scheme prepared that we could consider Monday night, for sending two more complete infantry divisions to the Middle East, at the earliest moment.

Let me know what shipping will be required. Some of the lorries can surely go direct from the United States from the great numbers now being landed.

When these figures have been supplied, I will ask President Roosevelt for the loan of his shipping for this particular purpose, and I daresay I can get it.

As a modification of the above, the divisions could go to Halifax or New York, and re-embark there upon American ships. The Minister of Shipping should throw himself into this plan, and let me have a report from all angles.

I am convinced that by the end of November we should have two more divisions in that theatre, though whether they would operate in Persia, Iraq or the Middle East Command must depend upon circumstances.

Let me also have the time-table of the movement of the First Armoured Division to ME.

Winston S. Churchill to Admiral of the Fleet Sir Dudley Pound
(*Churchill papers, 20/36*)

22 August 1941
Action this Day
Most Secret

1. Further to my minute[1] about supplies reaching Tripoli from Italy, will you please consider the sending of a flotilla and, if possible, a cruiser or two to Malta, as soon as possible.[2]

2. We must look back to see how much our purpose has been deflected. There was the plan, considered vital by you, of blocking Tripoli Harbour, for which *Barham* was to be sacrificed. There was the alternative desperate proposal by the C-in-C Med., to bombard it, which was afterwards effected without the loss of a man or a single ship being damaged. There was the melancholy 'Anson' tale. There was the arrival of Mountbatten's flotilla in Malta. All this took place several months ago. It would be well to get out the dates. How is it that the urgency of this matter has declined? How is it that we

[1] Of 20 August 1941: not printed.

[2] This was Force K, the naval striking force which was formed at Malta in October 1941, consisting of two cruisers *Aurora* and *Penelope* and two destroyers, *Lance* and *Lively*.

are now content to watch what we formerly thought unendurable, although it is going forward on a bigger scale against us?

3. The reason why Mountbatten's flotilla was withdrawn from Malta was less because of the danger there, than for the needs of the Cretan affair, in which the flotilla was practically destroyed. We have thus lost sight of our purpose, on which there was such general agreement, and in which the Admiralty was so forward and strong.

4. Meanwhile, three things have happened. First the Malta defences have been markedly strengthened in air and AA guns, and the German air forces have been drawn away to some extent to Russia. Secondly, the Battle of the Atlantic has turned sharply in our favour, we have more AU-boat craft,[1] and we are to expect a substantial relief through American action west of the 26th Meridian affecting our destroyers and corvettes. Thirdly, General Auchinleck is disinclined to move before November.

5. Are we then to wait and allow this ever-growing reinforcement, mainly of Italians and of supplies, to pile up in Libya? If so, General Auchinleck will be no better off when at last he considers himself perfectly ready, than he is now, relatively to the enemy.

6. I shall be glad to hear from you over the weekend, and we could discuss it at the Staff Meeting on Monday night.

Winston S. Churchill to Oliver Lyttelton

(*Churchill papers, 20/42*)

22 August 1941

I have told you repeatedly that de Gaulle's interests or amour-propre must not stand in the way of the effective prosecution of the war, whether in Syria or Jibuti. On August 2, I told you that surrender of Jibuti ought not be delayed merely because Governor will not surrender to Free French. I have never suggested an assault on Jibuti, but only that if the garrison will surrender to us, and not to de Gaulle, you should accept their surrender. I will deal with any complaints de Gaulle may make when he comes home, which I hope will be as soon as possible. I do not understand why removing the Italian civil and military personnel from the blockaded town will accelerate surrender. Surely it will leave more food for those who remain? Please report at once on the simple issue. Will Jibuti surrender to British?[2]

[1] Anti U-boat craft.

[2] Jibuti was still held by forces loyal to Vichy France in May 1942, with de Gaulle still insisting that it should be surrendered in the first instance to Free French troops. In December 1942 it declared for the Free French, and for de Gaulle, without fighting.

Winston S. Churchill to Eduard Beneš

(*Churchill papers, 20/22*)

22 August 1941

My dear Dr Beneš,

Thank you so much for sending me the album of photographs, which I found awaiting me on my return to London. These excellent photographs provide a fine record of the preparation of the Armed Forces of Czechoslovakia for the day when your country can be liberated once again. I hope that it will not be long before this album portraying the training of the Czech Army can be brought to its true and proper end.

Yours very sincerely,
Winston S. Churchill

Winston S. Churchill: Engagement Cards

(*The Forbes Magazine Collection*)

23 August 1941[1]

General Sikorski
Sir Firoz Khan Noon[2] } to lunch

Japanese Ambassador, Berlin, to Foreign Minister, Tokyo: decrypt[3]

(*Secret Intelligence Service papers, HW1/25*)

23 August 1941

When seeing Dietrich[4] on the 9th on other business, he told me he had been at GHQ until the previous day and had just returned to Berlin. While talking

[1] As this is the only day in 1941 for which I have found no documents, I have included Churchill's one engagement for that day. Churchill spent much of the day preparing his broadcast for the following day, 24 August 1941.

[2] Firoz Khan Noon, 1893–1970. Educated in Lahore and Oxford. Advocate, Lahore High Court, 1917–26. Minister for Education and Medical and Public Health, Punjab, 1931–36. Knighted, 1933. High Commissioner for India in the United Kingdom, 1936–41. Member of the Viceroy's Executive Council (for Labour Affairs), 1941–42; (for Defence), 1942–45. Indian Envoy to the British War Cabinet, 1944–45. Member of the All-Pakistan Legislature, 1947–50; Governor of East Pakistan 1950–53. Chief Minister of West Punjab, 1953–55. Foreign Minister of Pakistan, 1956–57; Prime Minister (and Foreign Minister and Member of the Interior), 1957–58.

[3] This Japanese diplomatic message was sent from Berlin to Tokyo on 15 August 1941. It was decrypted at Bletchley and the summary circulated eight days later.

[4] Sepp Dietrich, 1892–1976. One of Hitler's closest colleagues, for whom he acted as bodyguard before 1933. A General in the Waffen SS, 1940–45. Commanded the 1 SS Panzer Corps in the Soviet Union, 1941; the Sixth SS Panzer Army in the Battle of the Bulge, 1944. Sentenced by an American military court to 25 years in prison for the murder of American soldiers in the Ardennes. Released ten years later. Subsequently sentenced by a German Court to 18 months imprisonment for his part in the 1934 'Blood Purge' (the Night of the Long Knives).

about the question of America he said that Hitler had declared that, in the event of a collision between Japan and the United States, Germany would at once open hostilities with America.

In view of the fact that this talk with Dietrich was entirely fortuitous, it is difficult to do other than accept this statement at its face value.

Winston S. Churchill to Anthony Eden and Brigadier Menzies
(*Secret Intelligence Service papers, HW1/25*)

24 August 1941

In view of the fact that the Americans themselves gave us the key to the Japanese messages, it seems probable the President knows this already. But anyhow it is vy desirable he sh'd know it. Propose me action please.[1]

Winston S. Churchill to Admiral Pound
(*Secret Intelligence Service papers, HW1/25*)

24 August 1941

What action will the C in C Mediterranean take on this information?[2] Surely he cannot put up with this kind of thing.

I see on other papers that the mere rumour of his being at sea has disturbed *Ossag* & Co., but is this true? Is he going simply to leave these ships to the chance of a submarine, without making any effort by his surface forces to intercept them?

Please ask specifically what if anything he is going to do. We are still at war.[3]

[1] Brigadier Menzies noted on Churchill's minute: 'The Americans have had this message.'

[2] An Enigma decrypt had revealed German tankers, including the *Ossag*, taking the route down the west coast of Greece and then across the sea to Benghazi.

[3] Admiral Pound replied to Churchill that day that he had asked the Commander-in-Chief, Mediterranean, if it was possible to take action against the tankers. Pound also pointed out to Churchill 'the danger of compromising our source of information, which can easily be done if we send a surface ship out to intercept a ship in an area which our forces do not normally operate in. It is unnecessary to stress what the loss of this information would mean to us.'

Winston S. Churchill to General Ismay, for the Chiefs of Staff Committee
(*Churchill papers, 20/36*)

24 August 1941
Action this Day

In view of the threatened Persian plan to effect demolitions on the railway from the Persian Gulf to the Caspian, what arrangements have been made to follow up our advance with strong force of engineers and railway repair parties? What arrangements have been made to construct blockhouses &c. to guard bridges or deviations? All this ought to have been thought out and prepared for. How does it stand?

Winston S. Churchill to David Margesson and General Sir John Dill
(*Churchill papers, 20/36*)

24 August 1941
Action this Day

Remember, please, that General Wavell is the Officer responsible for the Persian campaign. It seems astonishing that he should leave for England at the very moment when all hangs in the balance. There would of course be no objection to his going to Basra or Cairo, where he would still be in full control. I suppose he realizes that I am holding him responsible for this campaign and for deciding whether the forces involved are adequate or not.

Winston S. Churchill to General Ismay, for the Chiefs of Staff Committee
(*Churchill papers, 20/36*)

24 August 1941

1. See the telegram from Macfarlane[1] about Panfilov's[2] misgivings as to our not having enough strength for Countenance.[3] Also telegram from Military Attaché at Teheran[4] showing evident determination of Persians to resist and also to destroy railway. In these circumstances, it is essential that more

[1] Head of the British Military Mission to Moscow.

[2] General A.T. Panfilov. Staff Officer, Soviet General Staff. Later commander of the 3rd Guards Tank Corps, which on 3 May 1945 linked up with advanced units of the British 2nd Army at Wismar, on the Baltic.

[3] British operations in Persia and the Persian Gulf.

[4] Allan Cholmondeley Arnold, 1893–1962. Entered the Army, 1912. On active service on the Western Front, 1914–15 (Military Cross, despatches thrice); in North Russia, 1919 (despatches, OBE). Colonel, 1938. Military Attaché, Ankara, 1940–45 (CBE). Governor of India, Food Department, 1946–48. Ministry of Food (London), 1949–54.

reinforcements should be set in motion eastwards at once. Is it true that the 10th Indian Division has not got a white battalion to each brigade? If so, three battalions of British troops should be sent to join General Quinan[1] by the fastest possible route. As General Auchinleck proposes to remain inactive for many weeks, he should be directed to move larger forces eastwards than are at present arranged. At least the equivalent of one extra division, including the three British battalions aforesaid, should be set in motion now. If all goes well they can easily be countermanded. Let me know what forces are likely to be available in Egypt. Where is the last brigade of the 50th Division? Surely Cyprus is in no immediate danger.

2. Let a plan be prepared for consideration by which the rest of the 1st Armoured Division could be carried through the Mediterranean to Alexandria. See recent reports that the Germans are moving many of their torpedo aircraft to the Black Sea. Now is the time when they will be busy there for a more daring repetition of Tiger. To make it worth while it would have to be proved that the offensive in the Western Desert could be accelerated by at least three weeks. All the dangers of the delay in the offensive, enabling the Germans to bring back large Air forces to Cyrenaica, must be weighed. Also the wider dangers of our long inactivity. See also General Auchinleck's telegram to which I refer, and General Smut's second telegram to me and my answer. I look to my professional colleagues to make a great effort to accelerate the offensive and solve the problems. If the scheme breaks down in detail, or will not achieve the necessary acceleration, or on final review we do not think it good enough, we shall at any rate have done our best. But let the effort to solve the problem be made with all possible zeal.

We will discuss it all tomorrow night.

Winston S. Churchill to the four Dominion Prime Ministers
(*Churchill papers, 20/42*)

24 August 1941
Most Secret and Personal

You will wish to have full account of my meeting with President Roosevelt. The President was clearly much gratified that the meeting should have been held. The greatest cordiality prevailed and the United States representatives missed no opportunity of identifying themselves with our cause. While I had

[1] Edward Pellew Quinan, 1885–1960. Entered the Indian Army, 1905. Commanded the 9th (Jhansi) Infantry Brigade, 1934–38. Major General, 1937. A District Commander, Waziristan, 1938. Lieutenant-General, 1941. General Officer Commanding Iran and Iraq, 1941. General, 1942. Knighted, 1942. Commander of the North-Western Army in India, 1943. Retired, 1943. Colonel, 8th Punjab Regiment, 1945.

discussions with the President on political matters very useful discussions between the staffs proceeded simultaneously. Some of the results of the meeting have already been communicated to you. It may, however, be helpful if I supplement what you already know.

(a) Convoys – By the 1st September United States Navy will have a convoy system in full operation between American coast and Iceland (C), affording great relief to our naval vessels engaged on convoy duties, and presenting enemy with acute and decisive dilemma. Either he can attack the convoys, in which case his submarines would in turn be attacked by United States naval forces, or he can refrain from attack, which will be equivalent to giving us victory in Battle of Atlantic.

(b) Joint Declaration – Details of the proposal and text as agreed were communicated to you at the time. You will no doubt agree as to the special significance of the sixth and eighth points, which contrast with attitude of 1917–18, in that we now do not simply assume that there will be no more war, but aim at adequate precautions to prevent it by effectively disarming our enemies. Further, instead of trying to ruin German trade, we now take view that it is not to the interest of the world that any large nation should be unprosperous. It is also, in my view, of great importance that President should have agreed to a Declaration which refers to 'final destruction of Nazi tyranny'.

(c) Japan – You have already been informed of United States design to secure a breathing space of a month or so during which we can improve our position in Singapore area, while Japanese will be obliged to hold their hand. The President has since carried out his intention to convey a strong warning to the Japanese as to the action which the United States would take, irrespective of its consequences, if Japan encroaches further in the South-West Pacific. I hope very shortly that it will be possible to give you the President's exact words to the Japanese Ambassador and to let you know what we propose to do by way of matching this warning by the United States. In the meantime, I mean to make it clear in my broadcast that we will stand by the United States if they are attacked by Japan. This, I know, represents your views.

(d) Russia – The joint message to Stalin, on which the President and I agreed, was also communicated to you at the time. I think that the United States will send Harriman to represent them, and I am proposing that Lord Beaverbrook should go for us. We do not wish the conference in Russia to start before the latter part of September, when I hope we shall know where the Russian front will be for the winter.

(e) Supply – These questions were not discussed in detail, but were left for Beaverbrook and Harriman to take up together. The addition of Russian requirements and the need of a large supplementary programme both for our own and United States forces makes a review and expansion of United States production imperative. I am afraid that broad picture at present is that United

States production is somewhat disappointing. It is all on the way, but it is late. Measures, difficult to enforce on a nation not at war, will have to be taken involving drastic restrictions on civil consumption. Meanwhile, however, United States are sending us 150,000 more rifles at once, and I look for improved allocations of merchant shipping, bombers and tanks. I have just heard from Mr Hopkins of an important improvement in the bombers. I hope also that it may be possible to arrange for the Americans to take over the ferry service and delivery of aircraft both here and in West Africa by United States pilots, many of whom may stay for war training with us. They will set up establishments on the West Coast, both at Bathurst and in Liberia.

President sent two United States destroyers with us on our return journey, not officially as escort, but with orders to join in if trouble occurred. As you know, I took opportunity on my way home to pay a short visit to Iceland (C), where I was enthusiastically received, and reviewed large numbers of British, Australian and United States troops.

John Colville: diary
(*Colville papers*)

24 August 1941

After dinner we heard Winston's splendid speech on the wireless, describing his American journey, and containing a spirited message to each of the enslaved countries.

Winston S. Churchill: broadcast
(*Churchill papers, 9/152*)

24 August 1941 Chequers

I thought you would like me to tell you something about the voyage which I made across the ocean to meet our great friend, the President of the United States. Exactly where we met is a secret, but I don't think I shall be indiscreet if I go so far as to say that it was 'somewhere in the Atlantic'.

In a spacious, landlocked bay which reminded me of the West Coast of Scotland, powerful American warships protected by strong flotillas and far-ranging aircraft awaited our arrival, and, as it were, stretched out a hand to help us in. Our party arrived in the newest, or almost the newest, British battleship, the *Prince of Wales*, with a modern escort of British and Canadian destroyers, and there for three days I spent my time in company, and I think I may say in comradeship, with Mr Roosevelt; while all the time the chiefs of staff and the naval and military commanders both of the British Empire and of the United States sat together in continual council.

President Roosevelt is the thrice-chosen head of the most powerful state and community in the world. I am the servant of King and Parliament at present charged with the principal direction of our affairs in these fateful times, and it is my duty also to make sure, as I have made sure, that anything I say or do in the exercise of my office is approved and sustained by the whole British Commonwealth of Nations. Therefore this meeting was bound to be important, because of the enormous forces at present only partially mobilized but steadily mobilizing which are at the disposal of these two major groupings of the human family: the British Empire and the United States, who, fortunately for the progress of mankind, happen to speak the same language, and very largely think the same thoughts, or anyhow think a lot of the same thoughts.

The meeting was therefore symbolic. That is its prime importance. It symbolizes in a form and manner which everyone can understand in every land and in every clime, the deep underlying unities which stir and at decisive moments rule the English-speaking peoples throughout the world. Would it be presumptuous for me to say that it symbolizes something even more majestic – namely: the marshalling of the good forces of the world against the evil forces which are now so formidable and triumphant and which have cast their cruel spell over the whole of Europe and a large part of Asia?

This was a meeting which marks for ever in the pages of history the taking-up by the English-speaking nations, amid all this peril, tumult and confusion, of the guidance of the fortunes of the broad toiling masses in all the continents; and our loyal effort without any clog of selfish interest to lead them forward out of the miseries into which they have been plunged back to the broad highroad of freedom and justice. This is the highest honour and the most glorious opportunity which could ever have come to any branch of the human race.

When one beholds how many currents of extraordinary and terrible events have flowed together to make this harmony, even the most sceptical person must have the feeling that we all have the chance to play our part and do our duty in some great design, the end of which no mortal can foresee. Awful and horrible things are happening in these days. The whole of Europe has been wrecked and trampled down by the mechanical weapons and barbaric fury of the Nazis; the most deadly instruments of war-science have been joined to the extreme refinements of treachery and the most brutal exhibitions of ruthlessness, and thus have formed a combine of aggression the like of which has never been known, before which the rights, the traditions, the characteristics and the structure of many ancient honoured states and peoples have been laid prostrate and are now ground down under the heel and terror of a monster.

The Austrians, the Czechs, the Poles, the Norwegians, the Danes, the Belgians, the Dutch, the Greeks, the Croats and the Serbs, above all the great

French nation, have been stunned and pinioned. Italy, Hungary, Rumania, Bulgaria have bought a shameful respite by becoming the jackals of the tiger, but their situation is very little different and will presently be indistinguishable from that of his victims. Sweden, Spain and Turkey stand appalled, wondering which will be struck down next.

Here, then, is the vast pit into which all the most famous states and races of Europe have been flung and from which unaided they can never climb. But all this did not satiate Adolf Hitler; he made a treaty of non-aggression with Soviet Russia, just as he made one with Turkey, in order to keep them quiet till he was ready to attack them, and then, nine weeks ago today, without a vestige of provocation, he hurled millions of soldiers, with all their apparatus, upon the neighbour he had called his friend, with the avowed object of destroying Russia and tearing her in pieces. This frightful business is now unfolding day by day before our eyes. Here is a devil who, in a mere spasm of his pride and lust for domination, can condemn two or three millions, perhaps it may be many more, of human beings, to speedy and violent death. 'Let Russia be blotted out – Let Russia be destroyed. Order the armies to advance.' Such were his decrees. Accordingly from the Arctic Ocean to the Black Sea, six or seven millions of soldiers are locked in mortal struggle. Ah, but this time it was not so easy.

This time it was not all one way. The Russian armies and all the peoples of the Russian Republic have rallied to the defence of their hearths and homes. For the first time Nazi blood has flowed in a fearful torrent. Certainly, 1,500,000 perhaps 2,000,000 of Nazi cannon-fodder have bit the dust of the endless plains of Russia. The tremendous battle rages along nearly 2,000 miles of front. The Russians fight with magnificent devotion; not only that, our generals who have visited the Russian front line report with admiration the efficiency of their military organization and the excellence of their equipment. The aggressor is surprised, startled, staggered. For the first time in his experience mass murder has become unprofitable. He retaliates by the most frightful cruelties. As his armies advance, whole districts are being exterminated.[1] Scores of thousands – literally scores of thousands – of executions in cold blood are being perpetrated by the German police-troops upon the

[1] Since July 18 German Police messages, decrypted at Bletchley, had revealed details of mass shootings of victims described variously as 'Jews', 'Jewish plunderers', 'Jewish bolshevists' or 'Russian soldiers' in numbers varying from under a hundred to several thousand at a time. On August 7 the SS Cavalry Brigade reported, as one decrypt revealed, that it had carried out 7,819 'executions' to date in the Minsk area, while on the same day a police decrypt revealed 30,000 executions in the central sector since the police had arrived in Russia. In the week following Churchill's speech the shooting of Jews in groups numbering from 61 to 4,200 was reported on seventeen occasions in the southern sector. (F.H. Hinsley and others, *British Intelligence in the Second World War, Its Influence on Strategy and Operations*, volume 2, London, 1981, Appendix 5, page 671). The summaries of these decrypts as circulated are now available in the Secret Intelligence Service papers at the Public Record Office, Kew, series HWI).

Russian patriots who defend their native soil. Since the Mongol invasions of Europe in the sixteenth century, there has never been methodical, merciless butchery on such a scale, or approaching such a scale. And this is but the beginning. Famine and pestilence have yet to follow in the bloody ruts of Hitler's tanks. We are in the presence of a crime without a name.

But Europe is not the only continent to be tormented and devastated by aggressions. For five long years the Japanese military factions, seeking to emulate the style of Hitler and Mussolini, taking all their posturing as if it were a new European revelation, have been invading and harrying the 500,000,000 inhabitants of China. Japanese armies have been wandering about that vast land in futile excursions, carrying with them carnage, ruin and corruption and calling it the 'Chinese Incident'. Now they stretch a grasping hand into the southern seas of China; they snatch Indo-China from the wretched Vichy French; they menace by their movements Siam; menace Singapore, the British link with Australia; and menace the Philippine Islands under the protection of the United States. It is certain that this has got to stop. Every effort will be made to secure a peaceful settlement. The United States are labouring with infinite patience to arrive at a fair and amicable settlement which will give Japan the utmost reassurance for her legitimate interests. We earnestly hope these negotiations will succeed. But this I must say: that if these hopes should fail we shall of course range ourselves unhesitatingly at the side of the United States.

And thus we come back to the quiet bay somewhere in the Atlantic where misty sunshine plays on great ships which carry the White Ensign, or the Stars and Stripes. We had the idea, when we met there – the President and I – that without attempting to draw up final and formal peace aims, or war aims, it was necessary to give all peoples, especially the oppressed and conquered peoples, a simple rough-and-ready wartime statement of the goal towards which the British Commonwealth and the United States mean to make their way, and thus make a way for others to march with them upon a road which will certainly be painful, and may be long!

There are, however, two distinct and marked differences in this joint declaration from the attitude adopted by the Allies during the latter part of the last war; and no one should overlook them. The United States and Great Britain do not now assume that there will never be any more war again. On the contrary, we intend to take ample precautions to prevent its renewal in any period we can foresee by effectively disarming the guilty nations while remaining suitably protected ourselves.

The second difference is this: that instead of trying to ruin German trade by all kinds of additional trade barriers and hindrances as was the mood of 1917, we have definitely adopted the view that it is not in the interests of the world and of our two countries that any large nation should be unprosperous or shut out from the means of making a decent living for itself and its people by its industry and enterprise. These are far-reaching changes of principle upon which all countries should ponder. Above all, it was necessary to give hope and the assurance of final victory to those many scores of millions of men and women who are battling for life and freedom, or who are already bent down under the Nazi yoke. Hitler and his confederates have for some time past been adjuring, bullying and beseeching the populations whom they have wronged and injured, to bow to their fate, to resign themselves to their servitude, and for the sake of some mitigations and indulgences, to 'collaborate' – that is the word – in what is called the New Order in Europe.

What is this New Order which they seek to fasten first upon Europe and if possible – for their ambitions are boundless – upon all the continents of the globe? It is the rule of the Herrenvolk – the master race – who are to put an end to democracy, to parliaments, to the fundamental freedom and decencies of ordinary men and women, to the historic rights of nations; and give them in exchange the iron rule of Prussia, the universal goose-step, and a strict, efficient discipline enforced upon the working class by the political police, with the German concentration camps and firing parties, now so busy in a dozen lands, always handy in the background. There is the New Order.

Napoleon in his glory and his genius spread his Empire far and wide. There was a time when only the snows of Russia and the white cliffs of Dover with their guardian fleets stood between him and the dominion of the world. Napoleon's armies had a theme: they carried with them the surges of the French Revolution. Liberty, Equality and Fraternity – that was the cry. There was a sweeping away of outworn medieval systems and aristocratic privilege. There was the land for the people, a new code of law. Nevertheless, Napoleon's Empire vanished like a dream. But Hitler, Hitler has no theme, naught but mania, appetite and exploitation. He has, however, weapons and machinery for grinding down and for holding down conquered countries which are the product, the sadly perverted product, of modern science.

The ordeals, therefore, of the conquered peoples will be hard. We must give them hope; we must give them the conviction that their sufferings and their resistances will not be in vain. The tunnel may be dark and long, but at the end there is light. That is the symbolism and that is the message of the Atlantic meeting. Do not despair, brave Norwegians: your land shall be cleansed not only from the invader but from the filthy quislings who are his tools. Be sure of yourselves Czechs: your independence shall be restored. Poles, the heroism of your people standing up to cruel oppressors, the courage of your soldiers, sailors and airmen, shall not be forgotten: your country shall live again and resume its rightful part in the new organization of Europe. Lift up your heads, gallant Frenchmen: not all the infamies of Darlan and of Laval shall stand between you and the restoration of your birthright. Tough, stout-hearted Dutch, Belgians, Luxembourgers, tormented, mishandled, shamefully cast-away peoples of Yugoslavia, glorious Greece, now subjected to the crowning insult of the rule of the Italian jackanapes; yield not an inch! Keep your souls clean from all contact with the Nazis; make them feel even in their fleeting hour of brutish triumph that they are the moral outcasts of mankind. Help is coming; mighty forces are arming in your behalf. Have faith. Have hope. Deliverance is sure.

There is the signal which we have flashed across the water; and if it reaches the hearts of those to whom it is sent, they will endure with fortitude and tenacity their present misfortunes in the sure faith that they, too, are still serving the common cause, and that their efforts will not be in vain.

You will perhaps have noticed that the President of the United States and the British representative, in what is aptly called the 'Atlantic Charter', have jointly pledged their countries to the final destruction of the Nazi tyranny. That is a solemn and grave undertaking. It must be made good; it will be made good. And, of course, many practical arrangements to fulfil that purpose have been made and are being organized and set in motion.

The question has been asked: how near is the United States to war? There is certainly one man who knows the answer to that question. If Hitler has not yet declared war upon the United States, it is surely not out of his love for American institutions; it is certainly not because he could not find a pretext. He has murdered half a dozen countries for far less. Fear of immediately redoubling the tremendous energies now being employed against him is no doubt a restraining influence. But the real reason is, I am sure, to be found in the method to which he has so faithfully adhered and by which he has gained so much.

What is that method? It is a very simple method. One by one: that is his plan; that is his guiding rule; that is the trick by which he has enslaved so large a portion of the world. Three and a half years ago I appealed to my fellow countrymen to take the lead in weaving together a strong defensive union within the principles of the League of Nations, a union of all the countries who felt themselves in ever-growing danger. But none would listen; all stood idle while Germany rearmed. Czechoslovakia was subjugated; a French Government deserted their faithful ally and broke a plighted word in that ally's hour of need. Russia was cajoled and deceived into a kind of neutrality or partnership, while the French Army was being annihilated. The Low Countries and the Scandinavian countries, acting with France and Great Britain in good time, even after the war had begun, might have altered its course, and would have had, at any rate, a fighting chance. The Balkan States had only to stand together to save themselves from the ruin by which they are now engulfed. But one by one they were undermined and overwhelmed. Never was the career of crime made more smooth.

Now Hitler is striking at Russia with all his might, well knowing the difficulties of geography which stand between Russia and the aid which the Western Democracies are trying to bring. We shall strive our utmost to overcome all obstacles and to bring this aid. We have arranged for a conference in Moscow between the United States, British and Russian authorities to settle the whole plan. No barrier must stand in the way. But why is Hitler striking at Russia, and inflicting and suffering himself or, rather, making his soldiers suffer, this frightful slaughter? It is with the declared object of turning his whole force upon the British Islands, and if he could succeed in beating the life and strength out of us, which is not so easy, then is the moment when he will settle his account, and it is already a long one, with the people of the United States and generally with the Western Hemisphere. One by one, there is the process; there is the simple, dismal plan which has served Hitler so well. It needs but one final successful application to make him the master of the world. I am devoutly thankful that some eyes at least are fully opened to it while time remains. I rejoiced to find that the President saw in their true light and proportion the extreme dangers by which the American people as well as the British people are now beset. It was indeed by the mercy of God that he began eight years ago that revival of the strength of the American Navy without which the New World today would have to take its orders from the European dictators, but with which the United States still retains the power to marshal her gigantic strength, and in saving herself to render an incomparable service to mankind.

We had a church parade on the Sunday in our Atlantic bay. The President came on to the quarter-deck of the *Prince of Wales*, where there were mingled together many hundreds of American and British sailors and marines. The sun shone bright and warm while we all sang the old hymns which are our common inheritance and which we learned as children in our homes. We sang the hymn founded on the psalm which John Hampden's soldiers sang when they bore his body to the grave, and in which the brief, precarious span of human life is contrasted with the immutability of Him to Whom a thousand ages are but as yesterday, and as a watch in the night. We sang the sailors' hymn 'For those in peril' – and there are very many – 'on the sea'. We sang 'Onward Christian Soldiers'. And indeed I felt that this was no vain presumption, but that we had the right to feel that we were serving a cause for the sake of which a trumpet has sounded from on high.

When I looked upon that densely-packed congregation of fighting men of the same language, of the same faith, of the same fundamental laws and the same ideals, and now to a large extent of the same interests, and certainly in different degrees facing the same dangers, it swept across me that here was the only hope, but also the sure hope, of saving the world from measureless degradation.

And so we came back across the ocean waves, uplifted in spirit, fortified in resolve. Some American destroyers which were carrying mails to the United States marines in Iceland happened to be going the same way, too, so we made a goodly company at sea together.

And when we were right out in mid-passage one afternoon a noble sight broke on the view. We overtook one of the convoys which carry the munitions and supplies of the New World to sustain the champions of freedom in the Old. The whole broad horizon seemed filled with ships; seventy or eighty of all kinds and sizes, arrayed in fourteen lines, each of which could have been drawn with a ruler, hardly a wisp of smoke, not a straggler, but all bristling with cannons and other precautions on which I will not dwell, and all surrounded by their British escorting vessels, while overhead the far-ranging Catalina air-boats soared – vigilant, protecting eagles in the sky. Then I felt that – hard and terrible and long drawn-out as this struggle may be – we shall not be denied the strength to do our duty to the end.

Winston S. Churchill to General Smuts
(*Churchill papers, 20/49*)

24 August 1941
Most Secret and Personal
Of highest degree secrecy decypher yourself.

Most grateful for your general appreciation with which I am in full accord. What do you say about Auchinleck's proposal not to strike until November? Are you convinced so long a delay is inevitable? Ought not wearing-down attacks to be made? If we accumulate for a set-piece battle, will not they do the same in spite of their worse communications?

On 25 August 1941, British forces landed at Spitzbergen. The 2,000 Russian civilians on the island were then taken on board the *Empress of Canada* to Archangel, after which the British forces on Spitzbergen withdrew. Also on 25 August 1941, British and Soviet forces advanced into Persia. Landing that day from Basra, a British infantry brigade occupied the oil refinery at Abadan.

Winston S. Churchill to General Ismay
(*Churchill papers, 20/36*)

25 August 1941

1. This telegram[1] dwells too much on adverse possibilities, and the picture has altered even since it was written. I do not believe that the Germans will reach the Caucasus during the next three weeks. But the Caucasus is a very

[1] A draft reply to Robert Menzies.

large place, and if we are going to look upon the worst side of things it is better to be precise. Where, exactly, are their troops expected to be, and in what numbers, by the latter half of September? What aerodromes will they work from, and is the Batum–Baku railway assumed to be in working order? Is it reasonable to suppose that Tiflis will fall by the end of September? If not, why puzzle and alarm the Australian Party politicians unduly?

2. I do not know how it is possible to calculate so exactly the Air Force which the enemy could use. It might be more, or less. What data are you going on?

3. I do not believe the Turks will give the Germans free passage through their country. This cannot be stated with absolute certainty, but we all know of Marshal Chakmak and the Army indicates the aversion the Turks would have to have large German forces settling down in their midst. It is at least five to one against their doing so, and the emphasis should be cast in this sense.

4. Para. 6 states the case justly, and should be given its reasonable prominence. So should the marked passage in para. 11.

5. The paper would gain substantially if it were shortened, focused and made more decisive in its guidance. I could not assume responsibility for the telegram in its present form.

War Cabinet: minutes
(*Cabinet papers, 65/19*)

25 August 1941 10 Downing Street
5 p.m.

The Prime Minister expressed his anxieties about the position. The United States public was being called upon to put up with all the inconveniences of war without the stimulus of being at war. He sometimes wondered whether the President realized the risk which the United States were running by keeping out of the war. If Germany beat Russia to a standstill and the United States had made no further advance towards entry into the war, there was a great danger that the war might take a turn against us. While no doubt we could hope to keep going, this was a very different matter from imposing our will on Nazi Germany.

The Prime Minister said that he had said this quite definitely to President Roosevelt on several occasions.[1] He had told him that he had rather the United States came into the war now, and that we got no more supplies from the United States for six months, than that supplies from the United States should be doubled but the USA kept out of the war.

[1] The feeling expressed in the War Cabinet that Britain would not be 'able to crush the Nazi regime unless America came into the war'.

Lord Halifax then suggested that the Prime Minister might ask President Roosevelt privately whether he would welcome a public statement being made to this effect by the Prime Minister.

The Prime Minister said that he had in effect already said this publicly. He recalled a declaration that there could be no satisfactory peace unless the United States was a party to it.

In discussion, it was pointed out that American opinion was perhaps apt to attach particular importance to the Prime Minister's statement 'Give us the tools and we will finish the job'.

Lord Halifax added that the Prime Minister's statements had as much, if not more, effect in the United States, as those made by the President.

The War Cabinet were reminded by the Prime Minister of the arrangement whereby the United States was to take over the work of patrol and escorting our convoys as far as Iceland. This might bring about developments which would affect the position materially.

PERSIA[1]

The Prime Minister proposed, and the War Cabinet agreed, that unless more reassuring news was received on the following day, orders should be sent for the immediate despatch of these additional forces to Persia.

Winston S. Churchill to Admiral of the Fleet Sir Dudley Pound
(*Churchill papers, 20/36*)

25 August 1941
Most Secret

Will you please let me have on one sheet of paper a list of the effective Japanese fleet and flotillas, with dates of construction, and the ships which are ready now.[2]

[1] This item was recorded in the War Cabinet's Confidential Annex (*Cabinet papers, 65/23*).

[2] Replying three days later, Admiral Pound revealed that the principal feature of the force, the King George V class battleships, could not in Pound's view be sent out at that time because sixty per cent of the crews consisted of men under twenty-one 'who have never been to sea before', and that as a result it was inevitable 'that mishandling of material should occur at first'. At the same time, the Admiralty review had made clear that no aircraft carrier was then available, as *Illustrious* and *Formidable* had been damaged in action, and *Furious* and *Ark Royal* were receiving 'essential refits' ('Most Secret', 28 August 1941, *Admiralty papers, 199/ 1934*).

Winston S. Churchill to A. V. Alexander and Admiral Pound
(*Churchill papers, 20/36*)

25 August 1941
Most Secret

It should become possible in the near future to place a deterrent Squadron in the Indian Ocean. Such a force should consist of the smallest number of the best ships. We have only to remember all the preoccupations which are caused us by the *Tirpitz* – the only capital ship left to Germany against our 15 or 16 battleships and battle-cruisers – to see what an effect would be produced upon the Japanese Admiralty by the presence of a small but very powerful and fast force in Eastern waters. It may be taken as virtually certain that *Tirpitz* will not sally forth from the Baltic while the Russian Fleet is in being, as she is the only unit which prevents Russian superiority there. Nevertheless, in making dispositions which take some time to alter, we must provide for two 'KGVs' and one 'Nelson' with the C-in-C. This allows for accidents, refits and leave. One aircraft carrier, preferably unarmoured should also be provided for the broad waters.

2. The most economical disposition would be to send *Duke of York*, as soon as she is clear of constructional defects, via Trinidad and Simonstown, to the East. She could be joined by *Repulse* or *Renown* and one aircraft carrier of high speed. This powerful force might show itself in the triangle Aden-Singapore-Simonstown. It would exert a paralysing effect upon Japanese naval action. The *Duke of York* could work up on her long, safe voyage to the East, leaving the C-in-C, Home Fleet, with two 'KGVs' which are thoroughly efficient. It would be, in my opinion, a more thrifty and fruitful use of our resources than to send *Prince of Wales* from regions where she might, though it is unlikely, meet *Tirpitz*.

3. I do not like the idea of sending at this stage the old 'R' Class battleships to the East. The manning problem is greatly increased by maintaining numerically large fleets in remote waters, owing to the greater number of men in transit. Besides this, the old ships are easy prey to the modern Japanese vessels, and can neither fight nor run. They might, however, be useful for convoy should we reach that stage, which is not yet by any means certain or even, in my opinion, probable.

4. I am, however, in principle in favour of placing a formidable fast, high-class Squadron in the aforesaid triangle by the end of October, and telling both the Americans and Australians that we will do so. It seems probable that the American negotiations with Japan will linger on for some time. The Americans talk now of ninety days, and the Japanese may find it convenient to wait and see how things go in Russia.

5. It would always be an advantage, if possible, to change the armoured *Victorious* for the *Ark Royal* for service in the narrow waters of the

Mediterranean, and I suppose you will wish to strengthen Force H with one of the 'Nelsons' as well as either *Repulse* or *Renown*.

6. Naturally, C-in-C Home Fleet will require a first call upon an A/C carrier, preferably *Ark Royal*. Furious will have to do some more work on 'Railway' operations. *Victorious* would be well placed in Force H. This would leave *Illustrious*, *Formidable* and *Indomitable*, as they come to hand, together with *Eagle* and *Argus* for the needs of the Eastern triangle and the Mediterranean. You ought to be very well off by the end of the year.

Pray let me have your thoughts on the above.

Winston S. Churchill to Oliver Lyttelton and General Auchinleck
(*Churchill papers, 20/42*)

25 August 1941

1. The blockade of Jibuti should be pressed with extreme severity.

2. If the Governor wishes to surrender to British troops rather than to Free French, this should be accepted, even if it means the exclusion of Free French from the area thereafter, though this should, if possible, be avoided.

3. The Governor should be told that, if he destroys the port and railway, he and his Frenchmen will be held as internees in Africa or India till the end of the war. Otherwise we are quite willing to repatriate then to France.

Hugh Dalton: diary
(*'The Second World War Diary of Hugh Dalton, 1940-45'*)

26 August 1941

A meeting of Ministers at 5 p.m. at No. 10, when PM gives us an account of recent events. He seems to me to be in extremely good form, very lucid and rationally optimistic.

He says that he felt that his courtship with the President had been carried as far as it could be by correspondence and that now it was necessary to add a personal contact. The President is a tremendous friend of ours and will do all he can, both to help us to win the war and to consolidate peace afterwards. The most important definite result of the Atlantic Talks was naval. Pound and 'Betty' Stark[1] 'fell in love with each other'. Next month the new convoy system will be operating.

So long as one American merchantman is being escorted by one American warship, any number of British merchantmen can join in. There will also be other extensions, e.g. around Iceland, of forbidden zones in which loiterers

[1] Admiral H.R. Stark, US Navy.

with evil intent may be shot up. And so That Man will have to choose between getting into a shooting match with the USA or finally admitting that he has lost the Battle of the Atlantic. (The US sailors, I gather, would much prefer the former!) Apart from these preparations, the Battle of the Atlantic has been going very well for us. The last two months of sinkings have been very low. Our decision not to go on publishing them was taken because, at that time, they were so bad that we did not want to encourage the enemy and depress our own people; now we don't want to publish them because they are so good that they might encourage the Isolationists and hamper our friends in America.

On the other hand, we have been having very great success in our attacks, by air and submarine, on enemy shipping. We have never before had such good opportunities for unrestricted submarine warfare and we have some very good new devices for air attack on enemy ships. We have now completely closed the Channel to them and there are no signs of invasion preparations in any of the West European ports.

The PM still does not think that the Japs will go to war with us. The Americans have been giving them very serious warnings which they may well interpret as meaning that the US will make war on them if they advance any further, e.g. into Thailand. He has said that, if the Americans get involved in the war in the Far East, we shall wholeheartedly go in with them. He has been very rude to the Japs in his broadcast on Sunday – 'All this has got to stop' – and he thinks this will have had the effect of checking them. The Russians also have been very firm to them regarding supplies to Vladivostok from the USA.

Meanwhile, the President is gaining time by conducting what is really rather a humbugging negotiation with the Japs on the conditions on which there could be a general guarantee of the neutrality of Indo-China and Thailand. This might be guaranteed, not only by the US and the Japs and the British Commonwealth, but by France and China and everybody else! The President first hoped to keep this negotiation going on for thirty days; he now hopes he can spin it out to ninety. Long before then we shall be able to put a really strong fleet in the Indian Ocean without denuding the Mediterranean. One of our damaged battleships has nearly completed its repair in the American yards, and a new one is just coming off the stocks.

The PM thinks that the Russians are doing very well indeed, and jeers at all the experts who began by saying it would all be over in a few days or weeks. He is confident that Russian resistance will continue through and beyond the winter, though they may lose more ground. He thinks that Leningrad may fall, but not Moscow. He says the German losses have been prodigious. Never in any nine weeks, either of this war or the last, have the Germans lost anything like these casualties. They are behaving with the most complete brutality towards the Russians, murdering them, soldiers and civilians alike, like rats by tens of thousands behind their advancing lines. Our entry into Iran, which can be powerfully defended on other grounds, will also have the effect of establishing a close link, with a route through a warm water port, and so across the Pacific to the USA, between us and them. This will help particularly in the defence of the Caucasus and the whole Volga Basin. The Russians have a very good fleet on the Caspian Sea, and of course nobody else has.

Returning to the Atlantic Conference, the PM says that there has been a slide back in US opinion since May or June. (Several other people have told me that the President could have brought them right in then, but his health was not good and he could not decide, and so missed that tide, which has not yet returned.) There is a good deal of playing politics and this will only be remedied when they 'unfurl the flag'.

As to Peace Aims, it was the President's suggestion that they should have a statement,; the PM put up the first draft, which the President amended, and which then was further amended by Cabinet consultations. The PM draws attention to two points of sharp difference between this composition and those of 1917. Then we spoke much of a 'war to end war' and of a general organization afterwards in which all were committed equally to disarm. On the other hand, we were full of ideas of making Germans pay enormous reparations and of impoverishing them by seizing their trade.

Now we look at things differently. We must disarm the Germans and their accomplices but give no undertaking, which they can afterwards exploit, that we shall give them within any measurable time any sort of equality as regards arms. On the contrary, we must take care to see that we are sufficiently strongly armed to prevent any repetition, in Europe or the world, of these catastrophes. On the other hand, we now take the view that impoverished nations are bound to be bad neighbours, and we wish to see everyone prosperous, including the Germans. In short, our aim is to make Germany 'fat but impotent'.

As I told several people after listening to his broadcast last Sunday, I think that these ideas are both sense in themselves and will go over very well both with the Right and the Left in this country.

Winston S. Churchill to Anthony Eden

(*Churchill papers, 20/36*)

26 August 1941

I am afraid I have talked to Mr Mackenzie King in the opposite sense, saying that I thought it would be a very good thing for M. Dupuy to stay at Vichy as long as he could, as we greatly needed a window there, and that he might if necessary quote me as being in favour of the reciprocal retention of the Vichy representative in Canada. Mr Mackenzie King himself raised the question, and I was not aware that you had a different view.

Winston S. Churchill to General Wavell
(*Churchill papers, 20/42*)

26 August 1941

You are responsible for the general conduct of the Persian campaign and for estimating the adequacy of the forces required. It is therefore not possible for you to come home on leave until we see exactly how things will go. The newspaper headlines here declare that you are conducting the campaign, and I am sure a shock would be given to public opinion if you were not at the directing centre. So far it looks as if your estimates were right, and that the Persian opposition will not be serious. I have, however, asked that another additional Division should be ready to move Eastward from the Middle East at the shortest possible notice, and that one British Brigade of this division should be ready to come through by desert route to join the 8th Indian Division, which has no British infantry.

Although we have taken action to expel the Germans, our main object is to join hands with the Russians and establish a warm-water through route by which American supplies can reach the Caspian region. Nothing less than this will suffice.

We are looking forward very much to your return, but, if you leave India, you must remain at Basra or Cairo during present crisis in full control of Persian operations.

Winston S. Churchill to the Production Executive
(*Churchill papers, 20/36*)

26 August 1941

I am concerned at the great amount of manpower and raw materials which are still being directed to constructional work. The works and building programme is using 2¼ million tons of imported materials a year (iron, steel and timber) and three quarters of a million men.

Has not the time come to disallow all new projects of factory construction, save in the very exceptional cases? Can we justify further expenditure when so much existing plant is only half employed? Could not building resources be better used in providing hostels and amenities for the labour needed to man extra shifts in the existing plant?

The utmost economy should also be sought in service requirements, which are apt to be on a more lavish scale than the needs of the moment or the available resources justify.

I trust that there is some machinery for preventing designs being accepted which are wasteful of imported material.

Please inform me what safeguards you have to ensure –

(a) That new factories or building undertakings are really essential.

(b) That the plans and designs for such undertakings are of the most economical character.

(c) That building labour is used to the best advantage.

Winston S. Churchill to General Ismay

(*Churchill papers, 20/36*)

26 August 1941
Action this Day
Most Secret

DESPATCH OF TWO INFANTRY DIVISIONS TO THE MIDDLE EAST

Pray make arrangements with Lord Leathers and the War Office Movements Branch to further this reinforcement in the light of our discussion last night. Ingenuity and contrivance must be used to minimize the demand I must make upon the President. The request will be for one round voyage of a certain number of ships from America to this country, to the Middle East, and back to the United States. They ought to have them at their disposal again in January, or February. If *Normandie* could be taken over, transhipment might be possible at Trinidad, which would release earlier some of the smaller liners. Arrangements for reception in the Middle East, involving transhipment to smaller vessels, must also in that case be considered.

Let me have the best plan possible, and focus the outstanding points of difficulty, so that I can myself preside over the final conference. Imports may be cut.

Winston S. Churchill to General Ismay

(*Churchill papers, 20/36*)

26 August 1941
Most Secret

RAILWAY COMMUNICATIONS, MIDDLE EAST

This should be considered by one of the Committees under the COS Committee. What I am principally concerned with is the through route from the Persian Gulf to the Caspian. The other projects mentioned by Mr Amery seem to be more speculative. Alternatively, a motor road might suffice, or be better. It is of the utmost importance that strong railway detachments should be available, and rolling stock of the proper gauge to utilize to the full the supply of the Volga basin by improving the existing railway facilities.

Let me have a report within one week, and a synopsis of the report not exceeding two pages.

John Colville: diary
(*Colville papers*)

27 August 1941

In the morning the PM had a conference with Halifax, who is just back from Washington, Beaverbrook, Sinclair and Eden, about supplies from America and to Russia. Meanwhile Maisky complains that we are in effect doing nothing for Russia: we say we cannot form a 'second front' and we only supply inadequate armaments. Thus the US, in spite of all the fanfares, has only delivered 5 bombers to the USSR. It is difficult to see what we can do: geography, and shortage of trained, equipped men, make a military diversion out of the question. We are sending a lot of fighters and are helping economically. It is no use recriminating, but after all when we were fighting alone and for our lives the Russians were actually supplying Germany with the material means of attacking us.

The military situation is not good today. The Germans are driving south eastwards, behind Kiev, and threaten to cut off the southern armies of the USSR and turn all their positions on the Dnieper.

Winston S. Churchill to General Ismay, for the Chiefs of Staff Committee
(*Churchill papers, 20/36*)

27 August 1941

In several quarters there are indications of a German move against Murmansk. It appears that, though there were no transports found when we made our abortive Air attack, considerable numbers are on the move now. What are we going to do about it now? Is it settled that we can do nothing more in the North? When do our two Squadrons reach Murmansk? Can nothing naval be done to obstruct the movement of German transports?

Winston S. Churchill to Lord Beaverbrook and General Sir John Dill
(*Churchill papers, 20/36*)

27 August 1941
Action this Day
Most Secret

1. We ought to try sometimes to look ahead. The Germans turned up in Libya with 6-pounder guns in their tanks, yet I suppose it would have been reasonable for us to have imagined they would do something to break up the ordinary I tank. This had baffled the Italians at Bardia, &c. The Germans had specimens of it in their possession taken at Dunkirk, also some Cruiser tanks,

so it was not difficult for them to prepare weapons which would defeat our tanks.

2. I now try to look ahead for our side, to have Alpine troops formed in Norway, and to have the power to spring a surprise in tanks on the enemy in Libya. Instantly, everyone tries to make difficulties, so that, in three or four months, should it be desired to take action we shall be confronted with the usual helpless negation. We ought to have it in our power to place at least a 100 A22s in a desert-worthy condition in the field by January or February at latest. To do this it is necessary to get over all the minor modifications for desert warfare. Why should this not go forward at the same time as the final improvements are being made in the tank itself? The people in Egypt will never believe the tank is desert-worthy unless they have tried it on the spot. The various improvements made at home can be flown out or explained by telegram. Instead of this we are to wait till the beginning of 1942, and then send two tanks out which are to be then sniffed at and experimented with, and a whole new lot of faults found by the Nile authorities.

3. What I have asked is this: That two of these tanks shall go out now with a certain number of skilled men and spare parts; that these men shall be kept in close touch with the improvements made here, and shall at the same time deal with the 'desert-worthy' aspect, imparting to us the result of any improvements they make. I would have been willing to have allowed the double process to go on at home, but if it is going to take till 1942 anyhow at home, and then have to be gone over all again in the Middle East, I feel that my original thought was right.

Pray let me have some help in this matter.

Where is it supposed these tanks will fight in the Spring of 1942 except in the Middle East?

Winston S. Churchill to Sir Archibald Sinclair
(*Churchill papers, 20/36*)

27 August 1941

Your minute of 6th August shows that the most promising weapon at present in sight for aerial attack on tanks is the Jefferis bomb, and I am pleased to note that you have ordered 50,000 of these.

As I understand these weapons go into the ordinary light bomb container it should be possible to put them into use at once and I should favour postponing further manufacture of the Sticky Bomb and a part of the Bombard ammunition in order to obtain immediately an adequate supply of these aerial bombs.

It seems likely that when the tactics have been worked out and the pilots have had some practice, considerable improvement in the chance of hitting as shown in the first trials may be expected. We should get immediately a large supply of dummy bombs and give a selected group of pilots plenty of practice against ground targets.

If the expected improvement is achieved we should investigate at once the possibility of sending through the Mediterranean at an early date in a warship an adequate supply with the pilots who have practised with the dummy bombs.

It might also be well to consider whether the Russians might be able to improvise these bombs rapidly, in which case they should be given full details.

General Ismay

General Shearer[1] to be apprised. These might help in ME. Please make proposals for speedy action.

Winston S. Churchill to Air Chief Marshal Sir Charles Portal
(*Churchill papers, 20/36*)

27 August 1941

I have certainly sustained the impression that the Air Ministry in the past has been most hard and unhelpful both to the Army and to the Navy in meeting their special requirements. The Navy succeeded in breaking away before the war, but the Army lies under a sense of having been denied its proper Air assistance. To some extent this can be excused by the plea that the need of increasing the RAF was paramount. Now that that need is no longer so overwhelming, I trust the Army's grievances and complaints will be met.

There is a widespread belief that we have not developed dive-bombers because of the fear of the Air Ministry that a weapon of this kind specially associated with the Army might lead to a formation of a separate Army wing.

All these things happened before your time, but their consequences are with us today.

[1] Eric James Shearer, 1892–1980. Indian Army, 1911. On active service in Europe 1914–18 (despatches, Military Cross). On active service, Iraq rebellion, 1919 (despatches); Malabar rebellion, 1922. General Staff, War Office, 1924–29. Retired, and joined Fortnum and Mason; Joint Managing Director, 1933–38. Returned to the Army, 1939. Director of Military Intelligence, Middle East, 1940–42. Military Spokesman, Cairo, 1941–2. Retired, 1942. Managing Director and Chairman of several trading and transport companies, including London and Overseas Freighters, 1961–66.

Winston S. Churchill to General Ismay, for the Chiefs of Staff Committee
(*Churchill papers, 20/36*)

27 August 1941
Action this Day
Most Secret

Now that it seems that the Persian opposition is not very serious, I wish to know what are the plans for pushing on and joining hands with the Russians, and making sure we have the railway in working order in our hands. We do not simply want to squat on the oil fields, but to get through communication with Russia. We have made certain proposals to the Shah, but these may be rejected, or the Russians may not agree to them. What, therefore, are the plans to join hands with the Russians, and what are the troop movements foreseen in the next week by our different forces?

Winston S. Churchill to General Wavell
(*Churchill papers, 20/42*)

27 August 1941

I entirely agree to your coming over on duty for consultation as C-in-C for India and consider visit will be invaluable. Pray, however, do not go beyond Cairo till situation in Persia can be measured by us as well as by you.

John Colville: diary
(*Colville papers*)

27 August 1941

I was on late duty and most of the time was occupied with De Gaulle, whose attitude is deplorable and whose pronouncements, private and public, are intolerable. The PM is sick to death of him.

Winston S. Churchill to General de Gaulle
(*Churchill papers, 20/42*)

27 August 1941
Personal and Secret

Your note about the movement of Free French Parachutists from England to the Middle East has been placed before me. I greatly regret the tone you have thought fit to adopt in addressing representatives of His Majesty's Government and public departments in London. I trust you will withdraw your note in its present form as otherwise it will be impossible to deal with its subject-matter.

Winston S. Churchill to Oliver Lyttelton
(*Churchill papers, 20/49*)

27 August 1941

Any difficulties you have had with De Gaulle are due to his belief that he has me on his side. It is true I have always supported him against Catroux, but his recent conduct has affected my relations with him. I regret that you did not convey to him, at any rate in your own words, the note of warning which I struck in my two messages. You have not answered my last telegram on this subject. There is, of course, no question of recognizing De Gaulle as the French Government. After the very unfriendly expressions about England which he has used in many quarters, he will have a lot of leeway to make up before he regains his former position in British esteem.

Winston S. Churchill to President Franklin D. Roosevelt
(*Churchill papers, 20/42*)

28 August 1941
Personal and Secret

Operation Pilgrim which I mentioned to you. We have now found a way of being able to execute this if necessary after the month of September has passed, and indeed during the winter months. We shall not, therefore, be forced to move unless provocation has been given beforehand, either by German invasion of peninsula or Spanish connivance in undue infiltration or actual Spanish attack upon Gibraltar. This makes things much easier and also will present a better footing for any action you might take elsewhere. Meanwhile, we are keeping forces at about ten days' notice. Trouble may well arise in latter part of September.

Winston S. Churchill to General Dushan Simovitch[1]
(*Churchill papers, 20/22*)

27 August 1941

My dear Excellency,
Thank you for your letter of August 14 and for the reports on the conditions in Yugoslavia which you enclosed.

[1] Prime Minister of Yugoslavia from March 1941 to January 1942 (in exile from April 1941).

These reports indeed present a terrible picture of the barbarities of the enemy and the sufferings of the Yugoslav people. It is against such tyranny and cruelty that Great Britain, Yugoslavia and their Allies are fighting today. I know that the people of Yugoslavia, though overwhelmed by the first on-rush of the enemy, will not cease to resist him by all the means in their power, thus powerfully contributing to his destruction.

You may be assured that the suggestion that contacts should be made with the patriots of Split will be sympathetically examined, although I cannot say whether the operation will be feasible.

Yours vy faithfully,
Winston S. Churchill

Winston S. Churchill to Hugh Dalton
(*Churchill papers, 20/36*)

28 August 1941

I understand from General Simovitch that there is widespread guerrilla activity in Yugoslavia. It needs cohesion, support and direction from outside.

Please report briefly what contacts you have with these bands and what you can do now to help them.

Winston S. Churchill to General Shearer
(*Cabinet papers, 120/723*)

28 August 1941

CONDITIONS ON CRETE

Please look at this. Is there no possibility of our keeping guerrilla going in Crete instead of merely getting our people out?

War Cabinet: minutes
(*Cabinet papers, 65/19*)

28 August 1941 10 Downing Street
11.30 a.m.

No serious opposition had so far met the advance of our forces in Persia.

Attention was drawn to the importance of making contact with the Russian forces at the earliest possible moment. The Prime Minister said that he proposed to telegraph to M. Stalin on this point.

Heavy rain was now hindering the German movements. The Russians claimed air superiority in the Central Sector; this was attributed to German petrol difficulties. On the Ukraine front the situation had deteriorated, and the German thrust south-east from Gomel had now reached the Bryansk–Kiev Railway, thus endangering the Russian forces in the Kiev Sector. In the Dnieper bend the Germans had seized the west bank of the river and had established a bridge-head at Dniepropetrovsk. The Germans claimed some 85,000 prisoners and 475 guns in the Dnieper salient. In Finland the Finns were approaching the Murmansk Railway, and on the Baltic front the Germans were close to Tallinn. On the Leningrad front the Germans were close to Lyuban, some 50 miles south of Leningrad on the Moscow Railway.

The Prime Minister said that it was important that the Germans should not obtain Russian ships in the Baltic. It was for consideration whether we should give the Russians any undertaking in regard to replacement after the war of any shipping (including naval vessels) which they destroyed in order to prevent its falling into the hands of the enemy.

The Prime Minister said that General de Gaulle's behaviour in recent weeks had been very disturbing. He was now on his way back to this country and had made some extraordinary statements in an interview at Brazzaville, of which a censored version had appeared in that morning's issue of the *Daily Telegraph*.[1] If these statements were confirmed, we might have to modify our attitude to General de Gaulle.

The Secretary of State for Foreign Affairs was invited to circulate the uncensored account of this interview to the War Cabinet, and the Minister for Information to report in what form the interview had appeared in the United States.

In discussion, it was pointed out that the Free French policy in Syria had been, from some points of view, an embarrassing commitment. If we could take a new view of the position in Syria we might be able to reach a general settlement with the Arab countries, including a settlement of the Palestine question, which would bring us increased support throughout the world.

[1] Expressing de Gaulle's opposition to the Atlantic Charter. This opposition was most forcefully expressed in a telegram from de Gaulle to the Free French Delegation in London, sent from Brazzaville on 25 August 1941, in which he declared: 'As regards our position with reference to the Churchill-Roosevelt declaration, known as the "Atlantic Charter" we must show the greatest possible prudence, as to both substance and form, over the first article so far as "aggrandisements" are concerned. Without speaking of the Rhine at present, we must reserve to ourselves the possibility of an extension of our position in the Rhineland districts in case of a collapse of the Reich. For, in this case, given the material and moral destruction which has begun in the Rhineland districts, unforeseen things may happen. The line should be: we seek no extension of territory, but we do not expressly renounce all aggrandisement of a different sort. As for Article 4, it should involve formal reserves on our part. We cannot accept, after the war, access by Germany and Italy to raw materials on the same footing as France whom they have cruelly despoiled.'. (General de Gaulle, *The Call to Honour, 1940–42, Documents*, page 222).

The Prime Minister and the Foreign Secretary explained that our policy in this matter was as follows:

(1) One policy in regard to Syria would be guided by the following two principles:

(a) Syria for the Syrians;

(b) That so far as any European nation had privileges in Syria, that country would be France.

(2) Negotiations in regard to the settlement of Syria would be taken in hand as soon as possible and would not be left over till the end of the war.

(3) The question of a settlement of the Arab question generally raised far more difficult issues, and it would probably be premature to attempt to deal with it at the present time.

The Secretary of State for the Colonies said that the Jews shared the opinion that it would be premature to attempt to deal with these wider issues at the present time, as the Arabs were still of the opinion that we should not win the war.

HEADLIGHTS

The Prime Minister suggested that advantage should be taken of the present period, in which we were almost entirely free from night air attack, to have adequate lighting on vehicles engaged on war work, including, in particular, vehicles used for such purposes as the transfer of workers engaged in filling factories. We might thus secure a considerable improvement in our war effort. If frequent night air attacks started again, we should have to revert to the regulations now in force.

MIDDLE EAST

The Prime Minister said that a plan was being prepared to send two more British Divisions to the Middle East before the end of January, or earlier if possible, if shipping resources permitted. The Chiefs of Staff and the Ministry of War Transport were cooperating in working out the amount of shipping which would be required, and he proposed to make a personal appeal to President Roosevelt. While this demand would, no doubt, involve difficulties for the United States, he felt sure that they should be able to overcome them. We already had 14 Divisions in the Middle East, not counting the Indian Divisions in Persia. Further Indian Divisions were forming in 1942. Work was also being carried out in overhauling communications, and we could reasonably hope to be able to form a front which would hold the enemy forces on the Caspian line.

The Prime Minister said that the extent of the help which we could give to Turkey depended very largely on the situation in Cyrenaica. When that had been cleaned up we might be able to do more. This matter should be examined at a smaller gathering.

Winston S. Churchill to Sir Edward Bridges
(*Cabinet papers, 65/19*)

28 August 1941

BLACK-OUT RESTRICTIONS

1. Mr Harcourt Johnstone[1] will preside over an interdepartmental committee containing representatives of the Offices concerned for the purpose of devising the best possible plan for relaxation of the black-out restrictions during the present comparative lull in the enemy's air attack:

(a) on vehicles required for vital war services; and
(b) or factories and ports.

The object is to secure the maximum production for war purposes.

2. The Committee should consider inter alia –

(a) the categories of vehicles permitted to relax;
(b) the subdued character of the lighting enabling them to proceed at a reasonable speed;
(c) the particular routes over which and areas in which these relaxations may be especially required by the Ministry of Supply, Ministry of Aircraft Production and the Admiralty; and finally,
(d) the means of speedy return to present style if and when this is rendered necessary by enemy action in any district or throughout the country.

3. The Committee is to report in one week to the Prime Minister. All departments are expected to cooperate in the public interest to the utmost. The preparation of the best possible plan must be considered a technical study and does not necessarily commit the ministerial heads of the Departments concerned to its adoption. This may be remitted to a Committee of War Cabinet Ministers on grounds of general policy.

John Colville: diary
(*Colville papers*)

28 August 1941

At lunch time we heard the news that the Persians had ceased to resist.

[1] Harcourt Johnstone, 1895–1945. Known as 'Crinks'. Educated at Eton and Balliol College, Oxford. On active service, 1914–18. Liberal MP for Willesden East, 1923–4. Unsuccessful Liberal Candidate for Eastbourne, 1925. MP, South Shields, 1931–5, and for West Middlesborough, 1940–5. Secretary, Department of Overseas Trade, 1940–5. A member of the Other Club from 1932, and its Joint Honorary Secretary (with Brendan Bracken) from 1937.

Winston S. Churchill to Lord Linlithgow
(*Churchill papers, 20/42*)

28 August 1941
Personal and Secret

I am most grateful to you for undertaking this prolongation of your arduous duties and delighted that your doctor considers you thoroughly fit. I see no difficulty in your having a rest in South Africa during June, July and August 1942, subject, of course, to the exigencies of war. The sooner the announcement is made the better, but early October will be time enough.

You must be pleased with the success of our Persian campaign. We ought to be able to hold the half-circle from the Volga to the Nile and thus make a sure defence which will keep war from the Indian peoples under our care.

Every good wish.

Winston S. Churchill to General Sir John Dill
(*Churchill papers, 20/36*)

28 August 1941
Action this Day

1. General MacFarlane ought not to be out of Russia during these critical days. If he could have flown home quickly, his absence from his post might have been tolerated. No one knows when Lord Beaverbrook will go to Russia.

2. I cannot agree to his coming home by sea unless you consider that he is so much overstrained as to be unable to do his duty. I thought he was a very tough man and sent there for that reason. If he comes home now he will not go back. What is the name of the second-in-command[1] who you say is first class?

Winston S. Churchill to Sir Kingsley Wood
(*Churchill papers, 20/36*)

28 August 1941
Action this Day

ATLANTIC CHARTER: POINT FOUR

Will you please convene sometime tomorrow S of S for Foreign Affairs, S of S for War and Minister of Supply, and consider together, having regard to my suggested amendments, the political issues involved, and advise me. Perhaps my amendments are not necessary. My own view is that there can be no great future for the world without a vast breaking down of tariffs and other barriers. The United States, which will be more than ever the world creditor,

[1] Brigadier (later Major-General) Kenneth Godfrey Exham.

although hitherto the worst offender in tariff matters, seems now disposed to promote a policy of reduction. If this mood were implemented it would be natural that the measures which we have been forced to take should also be thrown into the common pot.

Winston S. Churchill to Harry Hopkins
(*Churchill papers, 20/42*)

28 August 1941
Personal, Secret and Private

I ought to tell you that there has been a wave of depression through Cabinet and other informed circles here about President's many assurances about no commitments and no closer to war, &c. I fear this will be reflected in Parliament. If 1942 opens with Russia knocked out and Britain left alone again, all kinds of dangers may arise. I do not think Hitler will help in any way. Tonight he has 30 U-boats in line from the eastern part of Iceland to northern tip of Ireland. We have lost 25,000 tons yesterday (27th) and today (28th), but he keeps clear of the 26th meridian. You will know best whether anything more can be done. Should be grateful if you could give me any sort of hope. Persia was okay. Kindest regards.[1]

Winston S. Churchill to Robert Menzies
(*Churchill papers, 20/42*)

28 August 1941
Secret and Private

While I scrupulously abstain from all interference in Australian politics I cannot resist telling you with what sorrow I have learnt of your resignation. You have been at the helm during these two terrible years of storm and you were with us here during its most anxious time for Australia. We are all very grateful to you for the courage you showed and the help you gave. I am the gainer by our personal friendship. I went through a similar experience when I was removed from the Admiralty at a moment when I could have given the Anzacs a fair chance of victory at the Dardanelles. It is always a comfort in such circumstances to feel sure one has done one's duty and one's best. My wife and family send their regards.

[1] After talking to Roosevelt about Churchill's telegram, Hopkins told the President, 'that not only Churchill but all the members of the Cabinet and all the British people I talked to believed that ultimately we will get into the war on some basis or other and if they ever reached the conclusion that this was not to be the case, that would be a very critical moment in the war and the British appeasers might have some influence on Churchill.' (Quoted in Robert E. Sherwood, *The White House Papers of Harry L. Hopkins*, Volume l, London, 1948, page 374.)

Winston S. Churchill to Oliver Lyttelton
(*Churchill papers, 20/42*)

28 August 1941

1. The utmost effort will be made to develop your railway projects. I am referring your telegram to the Chiefs of the Staff Committee authorizing maximum priority.

2. If De Gaulle interview with the American Press at Brazzaville is authentic, he has clearly gone off his head. This would be a very good riddance and will simplify our further course.

3. De Gaulle has put himself entirely out of court. I am sorry you did not warn him as I said. Never mind.

Winston S. Churchill to Captain Primrose[1]
(*Churchill papers, 20/22*)

28 August 1941

Dear Captain Primrose,

Thank you so much for sending me an album containing photographs of my visit to Iceland. I have much pleasure in accepting the album, which will remind me of that encouraging and memorable occasion.

The smartness and cheerful appearance of the men in your command contributed greatly to the pleasing impression which I carried away from the island.

Yours very truly,
WSC

[1] William Harold Primrose, 1884-1957. Entered the army, 1903. Transferred to the Royal Flying Corps, 1915. Established the Communications Wing, 1919, to carry people and documents between London and Paris for the Peace Conference. Commanded an armoured car unit, Palestine and Iraq, 1922-26. Air Defence of Great Britain, Air Ministry, 1927-33. Retired, 1933. Air mail adviser, Air Ministry, 1933-36. Recalled to service, 1939. Air Officer Commanding, Iceland, 1940-41; Northern Ireland, 1942-44.

John Colville to Colonel Legh[1]
(*Churchill papers, 1/361*)

28 August 1941

Dear Colonel Legh,

The Prime Minister is very grateful for the four brace of grouse which The King so kindly sent him from Balmoral, and would be glad if you would tell His Majesty how touched he is by his gracious and thoughtful act in sending Mr Churchill so acceptable a present.

Yours sincerely,

Winston S. Churchill to J. V. Stalin
(*Cabinet papers, 65/23*)

29 August 1941

1. I have been searching for any way to give you help in your splendid resistance pending the long-term arrangements which we are discussing with the United States and which will form the subject of the Moscow Conference. Maisky has represented that fighter aircraft are much needed in view of heavy losses. We are expediting the 200 Tomahawks about which I telegraphed in my last. Our two Squadrons should reach Murmansk about 6th September, comprising 40 Hurricanes. You will, I am sure, realize that fighter aircraft are the foundation of our home defence, besides which we are trying to obtain Air superiority in Libya, and also to provide for Turkey so as to bring her on our side. Nevertheless, I could send 200 more Hurricanes, making 440 fighters in all, if your pilots could use them effectively. These would be 8- and 12-gun Hurricanes which we have found very deadly in action. We could send 100 now and two batches of 50 soon afterwards, together with mechanics, instructors, spare parts and equipment to Archangel. Meanwhile, arrangements could be made to begin accustoming your pilots and mechanics to the new type if you will send them to air squadrons at Murmansk. If you feel this would be useful, orders will be given here accordingly, and a full technical memorandum is being telegraphed through our Military Air Mission.

2. The news that the Persians have decided to cease resistance is most welcome. Even more than safeguarding the oil fields, our object in entering Persia has been to get another through route to you which cannot be cut. For

[1] Piers Walter Legh, 1890–1955. Entered the Grenadier Guards, 1910. On active service, 1914–18 (despatches twice). Aide-de-Camp to the Duke of Connaught, Governor-General of Canada, 1914–15. Equerry to the Prince of Wales, 1919–36. Equerry to King George VI, 1936–46. Master of the Household of King George VI, 1941–52. Knighted, 1952. Master of the Household of Queen Elizabeth II, 1952–53.

this purpose we must develop the railway from the Persian Gulf to the Caspian and make sure it runs smoothly with reinforced railway material from India. The Foreign Secretary has given to Maisky for you the kind of terms we should like to make with Persian Government, so as to have a friendly people and not be compelled to waste a number of divisions merely guarding the railway line. Food is being sent from India, and if the Persians submit, we shall resume payment of the oil royalties now due to the Shah. We are instructing our advance guards to push on and join hands with your forces at a point to be fixed by the Military Commanders somewhere between Hamadan and Kasvin. It would be a good thing to let the world know that British and Russian forces had actually joined hands. In our view it would be better at this moment for neither of us to enter Teheran in force as all we want is the through route. We are making a large-scale base at Basra, and we hope to make this a well-equipped warm water reception port for American supplies, which we can thus surely reach the Caspian and the Volga region.

3. I must again express the admiration of the British nation for the wonderful fight the Russian armies and Russian people are making against the Nazi criminals. General MacFarlane was immensely impressed by all he saw at the front. A very hard time lies before us, but Hitler will not have a pleasant winter under our ever-increasing Air bombardment. I was gratified by the very firm warning your Excellency gave to Japan about supplies via Vladivostok. President Roosevelt seemed disposed, when I met him, to take a strong line against further Japanese aggression, whether in the South or in the North-West Pacific, and I made haste to declare that we would range ourselves upon his side should war come. I am most anxious to do more for Chiang Kai-shek than we have hitherto felt strong enough to do. We do not want war with Japan, and I am sure the way to stop it is to confront those people, who are divided and far from sure of themselves, with the prospect of the heaviest combination.

Winston S Churchill to Arthur Fadden

(*Churchill papers, 20/42*)

29 August 1941
Secret

1. Now that you have taken up your great Office[1] I send you my most cordial good wishes for success, and assure you that I and my colleagues will do everything in our power to work with you in the same spirit of comradeship and goodwill as we worked with Mr Menzies, who, we are so glad to see, is serving under you as Minister for the Coordination of Defence.

[1] As Prime Minister of Australia.

2. We have followed attentively the difficulties which have arisen in Australia about your representation over here, and perhaps it will be a help if I let you see our side of the question and how we are situated.

3. Since the declarations of the Imperial Conference of 1926 embodied in the Statute of Westminster all Dominion Governments are equal in status to that of the Mother Country, and all have direct access to the Crown. The Cabinet of His Majesty's Government of Great Britain and Northern Ireland, of which at present I have the honour to be the head, is responsible to our own Parliament and is appointed by The King because they possess a majority in the House of Commons. It would not be possible therefore, without organic changes, about which all the Dominions would have to be consulted, to make an Australian Minister who is responsible to the Commonwealth Legislature a member of our body. The precedent of General Smuts in the last war does not apply, because he was an integral member of the War Cabinet of those days appointed by The King because of his personal aptitudes, and not because he represented the South African or Dominions point of view.

4. In practice, however, whenever a Dominion Prime Minister visits this country – and they cannot visit it too often or too long – he is always invited to sit with us and take a full part in our deliberations. This is because he is the head of the Government of one of our sister Dominions, engaged with us in the common struggle, and has presumably the power to speak with the authority of the Dominion concerned, not only on instructions from home, but upon many issues which may arise in the course of discussion. This is a great advantage to us, and speeds up business.

5. The position of a Dominion Minister other than Prime Minister would be very different, as he would not be a principal, but only an envoy. Many Dominions Ministers other than Prime Ministers have visited us from Australia, Canada, New Zealand and South Africa during the present war, and I am always ready to confer with them or put them in the closest touch with the Ministers of the various Departments with which they are concerned. In the normal course the Secretary of State for the Dominions and the High Commissioner for the Dominion concerned look after them, and secure them every facility for doing any work they may have to do. This arrangement has given satisfaction, so far as I am aware, to all concerned.

6. I have considered the suggestion that each of the Dominions should have a Minister other than the Prime Minister sitting with us in the Cabinet of the United Kingdom during this time of war. I have learnt from the Prime Ministers of the Dominions of Canada, South Africa and New Zealand that they do not desire such representation and are well content with our present arrangements. Some of the Dominion Prime Ministers have, indeed, taken a very strongly adverse view, holding that no one but the Prime Minister can speak for their Government except as specifically instructed, and that they might find their own liberty of action prejudiced by any decisions, some of

which have to be made very quickly in wartime, to which their Minister became a party.

7. From our domestic point of view as His Majesty's Servants in the United Kingdom, there are many difficulties. We number at present eight, and there has been considerable argument that we should not be more than five. The addition of four Dominion representatives would involve the retirement from the War Cabinet of at least an equal number of British Ministers. Dwelling within a parliamentary and democratic system, we rest, like you do, upon a political basis. I should not myself feel able, as at present advised, to recommend to His Majesty either the addition of four Dominion Ministers to the Cabinet of the United Kingdom, which would make our numbers too large for business, or the exclusion of a number of my present colleagues who are the leading men in the political parties to which they belong.

8. If, of course, you desire to send anyone from Australia as a special envoy to discuss any particular aspect of our common war effort, we should, of course, welcome him with the utmost consideration and honour, but he would not be, and could not be, a responsible partner in the daily work of our Government.

9. His relationship with the existing High Commissioner for Australia and with the Secretary of State for the Dominions would be for you to decide. It would seem, however, if such an envoy remained here as a regular institution, that the existing functions of the High Commissioner would to some extent be duplicated, and the relations of the Secretary of State with the High Commissioner generally might be affected. Such difficulties are not insuperable, but they may as well be faced. The whole system of the work of the High Commissioners in daily contact with the Secretary of State for the Dominions has worked well, and I am assured that the three other Dominions would be opposed to any change.

10. We should, of course, welcome a meeting of Dominion Prime Ministers if that could be arranged, but the difficulties of distance and occasion are, as you know, very great. We are also quite ready to consider, if you desire it, the question of the formation of an Imperial War Cabinet. So far-reaching a change could not, however, be brought about piecemeal, but only by the general wish of all the Governments now serving His Majesty.

Winston S. Churchill to David Margesson
(*Churchill papers, 20/36*)

29 August 1941
Action this Day
Secret

I must draw your attention to the state of the Cruiser tanks. This week, out of 408, there are actually more unfit for service than fit. This figure and the system on which it rests require evidently strong handling. The proportion of unfit is getting worse each week.

Let me know who is responsible and what you are going to do about it.

John Colville: diary
(*Colville papers*)

29 August 1941

To Chequers, driving down with Tommy and Mary. Brigadier Shearer, who was formerly managing director of Fortnum and Mason and is now on the Staff of the C-in-C Middle East, was the only guest. Points from the conversation at dinner were:

Jubilation over our success in Persia, which had been very well received all over the world. The PM said that last Sunday morning he had had qualms. We had been doing something for which we had justification but no right. The man in the street, on the other hand, seemed elated that we had at last taken a leaf from Hitler's notebook. In support of this Shearer quoted the liftman at his hotel, a figure who played in his conversation the same recurring role as the schoolboy in Macaulay's essays.

Referring to a certain operation, the PM said he mistrusted set pieces which were rehearsed, like a play, so fully that nothing could go wrong – and then just before the performance the theatre caught fire or the Lord Chamberlain withdrew his licence.

Mr C showed considerable optimism. He compared the situation in the Middle East a year ago, when he had but 80,000 ill-equipped troops, with that today, when apart from a tremendous army, we were in possession of Syria, Iraq, Abyssinia, Eritrea, both Somalilands and Persia, and were confident in the Western Desert.

The Yugoslav revolution, when Prince Paul fled, might well have played a vital part in the war: it caused Hitler to bring back his panzer divisions from the north and postponed for six weeks the attack on Russia.

Winston S. Churchill to Randolph S. Churchill
(*Churchill papers, 1/362*)

29 August 1941

I had hoped to have some letter from you telling me about the changes in your work and position and giving me some news of your life, and I think you might have found time to do this when so good an opportunity was offered you as General Shearer's return. You are very often in my thoughts and it is nice to feel that this process is reciprocated.

General Shearer is at Chequers with me now. He leaves tomorrow. I have had several talks with him and have tried to place him in possession of my views about the campaign. I think you are very fortunate in serving under so highly competent and understanding a chief, and I trust that now you have for the first time got a fine opportunity and can say to yourself, 'You have a responsible job, havenue?', you will take the fullest advantage of it and win the approval of those you serve under and with and the regard of those under your direction.

I had a very interesting and by no means unfruitful meeting with the President in Newfoundland, and in the three days when we were continually together I feel we made a deep and intimate contact of friendship. At the same time one is deeply perplexed to know how the deadlock is to be broken and the United States brought boldly and honourably into the war. There is a very dangerous feeling in America that they need not worry now as all will be well. Hitler will give no help in bringing things to a head by attacking American ships until at least he sees his way through the Russian miscalculation and morass. Meanwhile the larger pay envelopes spreading through the United States and the boom caused by our war necessities is leading to all kinds of consumptions which positively detract from the war effort. Besides this, the American people must now put up with taxation and many other of the inconveniences of war without its commanding stimuli. The President, for all his warm heart and good intentions, is thought by many of his admirers to move with public opinion rather than to lead and form it. I thank God however that he is where he is. You will no doubt in time see the film of our meeting and of my inspection of Iceland, which I am sure you will find very interesting.

Turning to your part of the world, we have certainly been very successful in tidying up the Eastern Flank. Persia, though questionable as taking a leaf out of the German book, has given great pleasure here and enormously improved our situation. We have joined hands with the Russian armies and naval forces on the Caspian and in the Volga Basin, and I hope to make a good through route by which United States supplies can reach these vast regions and massive Russian forces. Compare this with the situation when Iraq was ablaze, Palestine quaking and Syria in the hands of the frogs. I lunched with Maisky today, all the representatives of the Allied defeated powers being present. He sent you friendly messages and enquired after you.

Mackenzie-King is with us now, and stayed here last week. He also sent you messages. He has made himself most friendly and helpful over here, and I am backing him up in every way.

Your mother is much better now. She was very tired, but retired for treatment to a home hard by, which has done her no end of good. She is, I know, sending you a letter by the same hand that bears this. Mary is now a gunner in the Anti-Aircraft Batteries, and is going to learn to work Predictors, etc. I thought it was better for her to do this than go into munitions or hospitals. She begins by being a private, but she has all the qualities to win her way, and is the greatest darling that can be imagined.

Into Battle[1] has yielded much larger profits from the United States than I expected, and I shall be ready to give you £500 more on account of it, provided that you pay the income tax upon it on your appropriate scale when it falls due and also devote £400 of it to the payment of your bills and debts, to the bottom of which we never seem to be able to get. I have not told Pamela about this but I will do so during next week.

I do hope that you will make a success of your important work which may easily broaden as time goes on. I have asked that the Commandos should be reconstituted and that Laycock should go out as DCO and this I understand is being done.[2] I do not wish you to rejoin him, because you are more useful where you are.[3] General Shearer tells me that for the purpose of your present work you are entitled to visit any part of the Front, and therefore you need not feel tied to an office stool when fighting is going on.

Winston S. Churchill to Admiral of the Fleet Sir Dudley Pound

(*Churchill papers, 20/36*)

29 August 1941

1. It is surely a faulty disposition to create in the Indian Ocean a fleet considerable in numbers, costly in maintenance and manpower, but consisting entirely of slow, obsolescent or unmodernized ships which can neither fight a fleet action with the main Japanese force nor act as a deterrent upon his modern fast, heavy ships, if used singly or in pairs as raiders. Such dispositions might be forced upon us by circumstances; but they are inherently unsound in themselves.

[1] *Into Battle*, a volume of Churchill's speeches from May 1938 to November 1940, had been edited by Randolph Churchill, and published in February 1941.

[2] Robert Laycock was about to take up his appointment as Deputy of Combined Operations (and from 1943 was Chief of Combined Operations).

[3] Randolph Churchill had recently been transferred from the Commandos to General Staff I (Information and Propaganda), General Headquarters, Middle East, Cairo.

2. The use of the 4 'Rs'[1] for convoy work is good as against enemy 8-inch cruisers. But if the general arrangements are such that the enemy is not afraid to detach an individual fast, modern battleship for raiding purposes, all these old ships and the convoys they guard are easy prey. The 'Rs' in their present state would be floating coffins. In order to justify the use of the 'Rs' for convoy work in the Indian and Pacific Oceans it would be necessary to have one or two fast heavy units, which would prevent the enemy from detaching individual heavy raiders without fear of punishment. No doubt the Australian Government would be pleased to count the numbers of old battleships in their neighbourhood, but we must not play down to uninstructed thought. On the contrary, we should inculcate the true principles of naval strategy, one of which is certainly to use a small number of the best fast ships to cope with a superior force.

3. The potency of the dispositions I ventured to suggest in my minute M.819/1[2] is illustrated by the Admiralty's own extraordinary concern about the *Tirpitz*. *Tirpitz* is doing to us exactly what a 'KGV' in the Indian Ocean would do to the Japanese Navy. It exercises a vague, general fear and menaces all points at once. It appears, and disappears, causing immediate reactions and perturbations on the other side.

4. The fact that the Admiralty consider that 3 'KGVs' must be used to contain *Tirpitz* is a serious reflection upon the design of our latest ships, which, through being undergunned and weakened by hangars in the middle of their citadels, are evidently judged unfit to fight their opposite number in a single ship action. Bur after making allowances for this, I cannot feel convinced that the proposal to retain 3 'KGVs' in the Atlantic is sound, having regard (a) to the American dispositions which may now be counted upon and (b) to the proved power of Aircraft Carriers to slow down a ship like *Tirpitz* if she were loose. It also seems unlikely that *Tirpitz* will be withdrawn from the Baltic while the Russian fleet remains in being. And further, the fate of *Bismarck* and all her supply ships must surely be present in the German mind. How foolish they would be to send her out, when by staying where she is she contains the three strongest and newest battleships we have, and rules the Baltic as well! I feel, therefore, that an excessive provision is being made in the Atlantic, and one which is certainly incomparably more lavish than anything we have been able to indulge in so far in this war.

5. The best use that could be made of the 'Rs' would be even at this late date to have them re-armoured against aircraft attack and used as a slow-moving Squadron, which could regain for us the power to move through the Mediterranean and defend Malta indefinitely.

[1] Royal Sovereign Class battleships. *The Royal Sovereign*, with eight 15–inch guns, had been launched in 1918. The other battleships in this class were *Ramillies, Resolution, Revenge* and *Royal Oak*.

[2] Churchill's Minute to A.V. Alexander and Admiral Pound of 25 August 1941, printed on pages 1109–10.

6. I must add that I cannot feel that Japan will face the combination now forming against her of the United States, Britain and Russia, while already preoccupied in China. It is very likely she will negotiate with the United States for at least three months without making any further aggressive move or joining the Axis actively. Nothing would increase her hesitation more than the appearance of the force I mentioned in my minute M.819/1 and above all a 'KGV'. This might, indeed, be a decisive deterrent.

7. I should like to talk these matters over with you.

Winston S. Churchill to John G. Winant
(*Churchill papers, 20/22*)

29 August 1941

My dear Ambassador,

Thank you for sending me the gramophone record which is being used in the American Defence Savings Campaign. This seems to me to be an admirable advertising agent and I am passing on the idea with a view to some similar action being taken over here.

I should be grateful if you would convey my thanks to Secretary Morgenthau.

Yours very sincerely
Winston S. Churchill

Winston S. Churchill to Air Chief Marshal Sir Charles Portal
(*Churchill papers, 20/36*)

29 August 1941
Action this Day

The loss of 7 Blenheims out of 17 in the daylight attack on merchant shipping and docks at Rotterdam is most severe. Such losses might be accepted in attacking *Scharnhorst*, *Gneisenau* or *Tirpitz*, or a south-bound Tripoli convoy, because, apart from the damage done, a first-class strategic object is served. But they seem disproportionate to an attack on merchant shipping not engaged in vital supply work. The losses in our Bombers have been very heavy this month, and the Bomber Command is not expanding as was hoped. While I greatly admire the bravery of the pilots, I do not want them pressed too hard. Easier targets giving a high damage return compared to casualties may more often be selected.

Let me have a return showing all bombers written off in August for any cause, including crashes on landing, and also the number of bombers received from MAP and the number manufactured and imported.

Winston S Churchill to Air Marshal Freeman
(*Churchill papers, 20/36*)

30 August 1941

ATTACK ON GERMAN SHIPPING IN ROTTERDAM
MESSAGE TO BLENHEIM PILOTS AND AIRCREW

The devotion and gallantry of the attacks on Rotterdam and other objectives are beyond all praise. The Charge of the Light Brigade at Balaclava is eclipsed in brightness by these almost daily deeds of fame.

Tell the Squadrons and publish if you think well.

Winston S. Churchill to Air Chief Marshal Sir Charles Portal
(*Churchill papers, 20/36*)

30 August 1941
Action this Day

What is being done about increasing the night fighter defence in the Middle East? I gather they are by no means up to date with our devices, yet Alexandria, Suez and the Suez Canal are places of the highest consequence.

Pray let me have a short report. General Pile[1] might be helpful in drawing up a list of an advanced échelon of night-fighting devices, organization and supplies. All this is very important. Speed is vital.

Winston S. Churchill to Lord Beaverbrook
(*Churchill papers, 20/36*)

30 August 1941

I wish you to go to Moscow with Mr Harriman in order to arrange the long-term supply of the Russian armies. This can only be achieved almost entirely from American resources, though we have rubber, boots, &c. A large new installation must be made in the United States. Rate of supply is of course limited by the ports of entry and by the dearth of shipping. When the metre-gauge railway from Basra to the Caspian has been doubled in the Spring, this will be an important channel. It is our duty and our interest to give the utmost possible aid to the Russians, even at serious sacrifices by ourselves. However,

[1] Frederick Alfred Pile, 1884–1976. Entered the Army, 1904. On active service, 1914–18 (despatches, DSO, MC). Colonel, 1928. Succeeded his father as 2nd Baronet, 1931. Major-General, 1937. Commander, 1st Anti-Aircraft Division, Territorial Army, 1938–9. Lieutenant-General, 1939. General Officer, Commanding-in-Chief, Anti-Aircraft Command, 1939–45. General, 1941. Knighted, 1941. Director-General, Ministry of Works, 1945. In 1949 he published *Ack-Ack, Britain's Defence Against Air Attack During the Second World War.*

no large flow can begin until the middle or end of 1942, and the main planning will relate to 1943. Your function will be not only to aid in the forming of the plans to help Russia, but to make sure we are not bled white in the process, and even if you find yourself affected by the Russian atmosphere, I shall be quite stiff about it here. I am sure, however, you are the man for the job, and the public instinct has already endorsed this.

The decision to send Harriman means that Hopkins does not feel well enough himself to go. There is no point in sending Eden at the present time.

As to the date, we are in the hands of the Americans, but we must act in a bona fides spirit and not give occasion for anyone to say we have been fooling the Russians or playing for delay. It will be necessary to settle the date of the Conference in the next few days. I do not think a fortnight one way of the other makes any difference as 90 per cent. of its work must relate to long-term projects.

Winston S. Churchill to General Wavell

(Churchill papers, 20/42)

30 August 1941

I am so glad the Persian adventure has prospered. There is now no reason why you should not return home as you proposed. I am deeply interested in your railway projects which are being sedulously examined here.

Everyone here is delighted you have had another success.

Winston S. Churchill to Anthony Eden

(Churchill papers, 20/36)

30 August 1941

PRISONERS OF WAR, RAILWAYS AND AERODROMES IN PERSIA

War Office telegram 87092 (b). Why should not the military age male Germans be made prisoners of war?

Have you provided in (d) for the control and improvement of the railway line, and above all the establishment of aerodromes?

Winston S. Churchill to General Ismay, for the Chiefs of Staff Committee
(*Churchill papers, 20/36*)

30 August 1941
Most Secret

Although personally I am quite content with the existing explosives, I feel we must not stand in the path of improvement, and I therefore think that action should be taken in the sense proposed by Lord Cherwell and that the Cabinet Minister responsible should be Sir John Anderson.

I shall be glad to know what the Chiefs of the Staff Committee think.[1]

Winston S. Churchill to General Ismay, for the Chiefs of Staff Committee, and to Richard Cross
(*Churchill papers, 20./36*)

PROVISION OF SHIPPING FROM THE UNITED STATES TO CARRY BRITISH REINFORCEMENTS TO THE MIDDLE EAST

Pray see and check the attached draft telegram to the President and meanwhile proceed to perfect our plans on the basis that the answer will be favourable.

As to the extra 25,000 men which have to be spread about the October and November convoys, surely you can contrive something to get round this without seriously injuring the existing lay-out of the convoys. Could not, for instance, the big ships in the Pacific come round to Freetown or St Helena, and thus double the carrying capacity of our existing troop-carrying liners over the shortened route? All this detail must be worked at perseveringly. The arguments are set out in my draft telegram to the President.

Winston S. Churchill to R.H. Morgan[2]
(*Churchill papers, 20/22*)

30 August 1941
Private and Confidential

Dear Mr Morgan

I am afraid I should not be able to give much elucidation of the words I used which, in these matters of foreign affairs, have to be very carefully considered both upon their positive and negative side.

[1] This (Prime Minister's Defence Minute D.246/1) is the first of Churchill's official Minutes to refer to atomic weapons. Sir John Anderson, the Lord President of the Council, was to remain the Cabinet Minister responsible for the rest of the war.

[1] Robert Harry Morgan, 1880–1960. Schoolmaster; headmaster, 1907–31. Served in the Royal Navy during the First World War. Conservative Member of Parliament for Stourbridge, 1931–45. Parliamentary Secretary, National Union of Teachers.

I should have thought however that you would be very pleased with the favourable turn our affairs in the Far East have taken. It is only a month ago that the Japanese seemed about to invade Siam and establish bases from which to attack Singapore, since when the United States, Great Britain and Russia have successively come into line in their various ways and I cannot feel at all sure that serious danger may not be averted.

Far from being disquieted, I think you should be reassured.

Yours sincerely,
Winston S. Churchill

Winston S. Churchill to Arthur Fadden and Peter Fraser
(Churchill papers, 20/42)

30 August 1941
Personal and Secret

Events about Japan seem to have taken a favourable turn in the last month. The Japanese were then threatening to invade Siam as well as make jumping-off grounds in Indo-China on the approaches to Singapore. However, as you will have seen from the telegrams sent you about our Atlantic conference, I persuaded the President to take a hard line against further Japanese encroachments in the South Pacific, and he was also willing to add the North-Western Pacific. You will have seen the notes delivered by the United States Government to Japan. The President and State Department think it a good thing to gain time, be it 30 days or 90 days, so long as there are no further encroachments, and the Japanese seem disposed to parley on this basis. Our interests are served by a standstill, and the Japanese for their part want to know what is going to happen to Russia.

2. As soon as the President had made these declarations I made the statement in my broadcast which conformed to all we had agreed upon with you and other Dominions beforehand and has since been endorsed by all. Encouraged by this, Russia comes along with a very stiff answer to the Japanese complaint about American supplies entering Vladivostok. The Russian Siberian Army has been very little diminished so far, and their Air Force is capable of heavy and much dreaded bombing of Japan. We have thus got very heavy forces, to wit, Great Britain and Russia coming into line with the United States in the van, and in addition Japan is sprawled in China. They would thus have about three-quarters of the human race against them, and I do not wonder they are plunged in deep anxiety and hesitation. I cannot believe the Japanese will face the combination now developing around them. We may therefore regard the situation not only as more favourable, but as less tense.

3. Nevertheless, the growth of our battleship strength, the ravages made in

the German Navy, and the measure we now have of the Italian Navy, which is now reduced, apart from *Tirpitz* and the U-boats, to very modest proportions, will make it possible in the near future for us to place heavy ships in the Indian Ocean. The Admiralty are carefully considering what is the best disposition to make. But I would like to let you know that, as they become available, we contemplate placing a force of Capital Ships including first-class units in the triangle Aden-Singapore-Simonstown before the end of the year. All this will be without prejudice to our control of the Eastern Mediterranean. I can assure you we are giving constant attention to all this, and you may be sure we shall never let you down if real danger comes.

To Prime Minister of Australia only:

4. Private. Whenever I wish to send you some absolutely personal message I will precede by the code word 'Winch' as I did to your predecessor. Such messages will, of course, be for yourself alone. You may communicate the above to your Cabinet.

Winston S. Churchill to Sir Edward Bridges
(*Churchill papers, 20/36*)

30 August 1941

AIRCRAFT PRODUCTION

1. The situation disclosed by Lord Cherwell is of the utmost gravity. In this connection please see my previous minutes after my discussions with Sir Charles Craven[1] and the action taken thereupon. But all this is not enough. We must have at least a 30 per cent. expansion upon what is now projected. 50 per cent. would not be enough. Making allowances for the spurt in the comparable months of last year, our aircraft production is almost static. Great demands will be made upon us for Russia, Turkey and the Middle East. Numbers will be a prime factor. An intense effort must be made.

2. For this purpose please, by my directions, ask the Lord President to convene together the following Ministers or professional Heads of Departments:

The Minister of Supply,
The President of the Board of Trade,
The Minister of Labour,

[1] Charles Worthington Craven, 1884–1944. On active service with the Royal Navy, 1914–16. Chairman and Managing Director of Vickers-Armstrong. Knighted 1934. President of the British Employers' Confederation. Member of the Air Council, 1940. Controller-General, Ministry of Aircraft Production, 1941–42. Created Baronet, 1942. Industrial Adviser to the Minister of Production, 1943–44.

The Secretary of State for Air, or CAS,
The Minister of Aircraft Production,
with power to add to the number should any essential Department be found to be omitted. This Committee should make a plan to propose to me for final approval by the War Cabinet to achieve this great renewed expansion of Air Production, pointing out what will have to be sacrificed in other directions. We cannot win this war unless we get more airplanes. The current losses are very heavy. The great flow of Empire pilots is now coming forward. The American production will only be a make-weight.

I regard this subject as a major factor in the war at the present time.

John Colville: diary
(*Colville papers*)

30 August 1941 Chequers

The PM stayed in bed for lunch, working at his box. He had spent most of the morning composing a long letter to Auchinleck about the future and I all but died of heart failure trying to get hold of it in time to catch Brigadier Shearer at Paddington on his return to the Middle East.

At lunch Mrs Churchill, whose make-up is a mixture of great virtues and glaring defects, was so malicious about the Halifaxes that Tommy and I could hardly believe our ears. She accused them of being very jealous of Winston and exceedingly ambitious.

The Halifaxes arrived at tea-time and Mrs C was all over them. Lord Halifax, whose reputation in this country and the US makes him out a reactionary and an obscurantist, seemed very Liberal in his conversation with the PM over the tea-table in the Long Gallery. He was emphatic that we must 'cough up supplies for Russia', and he said, in discussing the future of the Conservative Party, that secondary schoolboys were on the whole better educated than public schoolboys. To this Winston said: 'They have saved this country. They have the right to rule it.'. He was referring to the RAF pilots, the majority of whom have come from the secondary schools.

The PM considered that the only hope for the Tory party at the next election was to choose young candidates who had won their spurs in the war. To succeed in politics a man should enter the H of C if possible in the twenties.

They discussed the 4th point of the Atlantic Charter, which declares for freedom of trade and access to raw materials. The PM thought that this would in fact be achieved and foresaw a great increase in wealth as a result. Halifax said the Tories would not object, except perhaps Amery.

When he went to bed, after tea, the PM who is always talking about my joining up – with approval! – said, as he unlocked one of his 'buff boxes': 'You will have to forget a great many things. Be wise rather than well-informed. Give your opinion but not the reasons for it. Then you will have a valuable contribution to make.'

The Edens arrived and also the American Ambassador. At dinner I sat next to Mrs Eden, whom I found easy to get on with. Over the brandy, the PM, periodically supported by Halifax and Eden, made an impassioned appeal to Winant to realize the importance of the issues hanging on America entering the war. (Winant, of course, like Roosevelt, is no sufferer from illusions about this.) The PM said that after the joint declaration, America could not honourably stay out. She could not fight with mercenaries. Better she should come in now and give us no supplies for six months than stay out and double her supplies. If she came in, the conviction of an allied victory would be founded in a dozen countries. This was 'a war of science and psychology'. America could not produce men, or the ships to transport them, for years: we did not ask for that, but we must have an American declaration of war, or else, though we cannot now be defeated, the war might drag on for another 4 or 5 years, and civilization and culture would be wiped out. If America came in, she could stop this. She alone could bring the war to an end – her belligerency might mean victory in 1943. (Eden thought 1942.)

Winant said that on the day he was killed, Purvis had told him he thought the US might be in the war next March. This prospect seemed to give Winston little satisfaction. He thought the delay too long. He asked whether he should not commit a calculated indiscretion on the subject. Winant said it was better to leave that to his Government.

Eden said that we had now won the war for existence; we had not yet started the war for victory.

As a less serious epilogue, the PM discoursed on Equalitarianism and the White Ant. He recommended Lord Halifax to read Maeterlinck[1]. Socialism would make our society comparable to that of the White Ant. He also gave an interesting account of the love life of the duck-billed platypus.

After dinner we saw films of the Russian campaign.

[1] Maurice Maeterlinck, the Belgian-French dramatist and poet, whose *Life of the Bee*, based on observations made in his own apiaries, was published in 1901. It was followed by his *Life of the Ant*.

Winston S. Churchill to Oliver Lyttelton
(*Churchill papers, 20/22*)

30 August 1941

My dear Oliver,

I have written a very long letter to General Auchinleck, which I have asked him to show you.[1]

You and I are in such constant telegraphic correspondence that I will not add more, as the plane is leaving, except to say how pleased everyone is here with all your work, and how thankful I am I was inspired to make the momentous changes which have rendered it possible.

Yours ever,
WSC

PS De Gaulle has disavowed his interview and is returning I think with his tail between his legs.

Winston S. Churchill to Brendan Bracken
(*Churchill papers, 20/36*)

31 August 1941

1. How is our big broadcasting station, which is to override foreign broadcasts, getting on? There was a long delay in setting about it, but I understand the fullest priorities have been given. Please give me a short report – half a page.

2. I think it very important that the German films of the invasion sent to Russia should be shown in England, and also that they should be sent to the United States. Mr Winant fully concurs with this last. I sent you a message last week that I thought ten minutes of these German atrocities would be the best possible prelude to the Atlantic Meeting and Iceland films. What has been done about this?

3. Have the Icelanders got a copy of the film about themselves?

Winston S. Churchill to Admiral of the Fleet Sir Dudley Pound
(*Churchill papers, 20/36*)

31 August 1941

If you think fit, and the ships are safely in port, please convey to the Admiralty War Staff, Trade Division, C-in-C, Western Approaches, Coastal

[1] Not traced.

Command and others concerned, my compliments upon the vigilance, ingenuity and flexible organization which has in the last week enabled so great a number of ships to pass safely through the exceptionally heavy U-boat concentration.

Winston S. Churchill to Herbert Morrison
(*Churchill papers, 20/36*)

31 August 1941

Will you please let me have a short report on the Irish immigrants now coming over in considerable numbers, and how your security measures are working upon them.

This would be the best way to get spies and assassins into the United Kingdom and special vigilance is required.

Winston S. Churchill to General Sir James Edmonds[1]
(*Churchill papers, 20/36*)

31 August 1941
Secret

According to the best figures we have been able to obtain, the German losses in the ten weeks of their invasion of Russia approach two millions, killed, wounded and missing. Surely this, if true, is more than they lost in any one year of the last War, and is incomparably greater than in any other ten weeks' period.

I shall be obliged if you will unearth some helpful figures on this point.

[1] James Edward Edmonds, 1861–1956. Educated at King's College School, London. 2nd Lieutenant, Royal Engineers, 1881; Major, 1899. On active service in South Africa, 1901–2, and on the Western Front, 1914–18. British Delegate to the Red Cross Conference, 1907. Colonel, 1909. Deputy Engineer-in-Chief, BEF, 1918 (despatches six times). Officer in charge of the Military Branch of the Historical Section of the Committee of Imperial Defence, 1919–49. Brigadier-General. Knighted 1928. Author of the twelve-volume *Military Operations in France and Belgium*, the first volume of which was published in 1922, the twelfth in 1945. In 1951 he published *A Short History of World War I*.

John Colville: diary
(*Colville papers*)

31 August 1941 Chequers

As it was hot and sunny, the PM got up before lunch and sat in the garden with Halifax, Winant and, when they arrived, Prof and Lord Melchett.[1]

I sat next to Lord Halifax at lunch and talked about links with the past. He made himself very agreeable.

The PM went off to see a 'bombard' display . . .

Lord Gort and Admiral Somerville (Commanding Force 'H') dined. As the conversation, about the defence of Gibraltar, seemed likely to be tedious, I slipped away at the end of dinner and, with Mary, saw a sentimental film about a circus called *Chad Hannah*.[2]

The PM would not stop talking and we did not go to bed until 3.00 a.m. Lord G seems to be enjoying himself as Governor and C-in-C of Gibraltar.

[1] Henry Ludwig Mond, 1898–1949. Educated at Winchester. On active service in France, 1915–18 (wounded, 1916). Liberal MP, Isle of Ely, 1923–4; East Toxteth, 1929–30. Succeeded his father as 2nd Baron Melchett, 1930. Deputy Chairman, Imperial Chemical Industries, 1940–7. Director of the International Nickel Company of Canada. His elder son was killed in a flying accident at sea in April 1945.

[2] A country boy (Henry Fonda) joins a circus in the 1840s and falls in love with the bare-back rider (Dorothy Lamour). Later he falls in love with another circus runaway (Linda Darnell).

September 1941

Winston S. Churchill to Anthony Eden
(Churchill papers, 20/36)

1 September 1941
Secret

It is not intended that all contacts between the Free French in London and our Departments should come to an end, but that the three specific matters mentioned in Major Morton's minute (which I showed you) shall be allowed to rest in deadlock, and that generally a chilling and dilatory attitude should be adopted towards all requests made by the Free French.

No notice will be taken of General de Gaulle's arrival, and it will be left to him to make any overtures. Should he desire an interview, he will be asked for explanations of his unfriendly conduct and absurd statements. If and when these explanations are received, it will be possible to judge whether an interview between him and me is likely to serve any useful purpose.

Winston S. Churchill to President Franklin D. Roosevelt
(Churchill papers, 20/49)

1 September 1941

1. The good results which have been so smoothly obtained in Persia put us in touch with the Russians, and we propose to double, or at least greatly improve, the railway from the Persian Gulf to the Caspian, thus opening a sure route by which long-term supplies can reach the Russian reserve positions in the Volga Basin. Besides this there is the importance of encouraging Turkey to stand as a solid block against German passage to Syria and Palestine. In view of both these important objectives, I wish to reinforce the Middle East armies with two regular British Divisions, 40,000 men, in addition to the 150,000 drafts and units which we are carrying ourselves between now and

Christmas. We cannot, however, manage to find the whole of the shipping by ourselves. Would it be possible for you to lend us 12 United States liners and 20 United States cargo ships manned by American crews from early October till February? These would come carrying cargo to United Kingdom ports under any flag arrangement convenient. If they could arrive here early in October, we would send them forward as additions to our October and November convoys to the Middle East.

2. I know, Mr President, from our talks that this will be difficult to do, but there is a great need for more British troops in the Middle East, and it will be an enormous advantage if we can hold Turkey and sustain Russia, and by so doing bar further advance eastward by Hitler. It is quite true that the loan of these liners would hamper any large despatch of United States forces to Europe or Africa, but, as you know, I have never asked for this in any period we can reasonably foresee in the near future.

3. It is for you to say what you would require in replacements of ships sunk by enemy action. Hitherto we have lost hardly anything in our well-guarded troop convoys. I am sure this would be a wise and practical step to take at the present juncture, and I shall be very grateful if you can make it possible.

Winston S. Churchill to Air Chief Marshal Sir Charles Portal

(*Churchill papers, 20/36*)

1 September 1941
Action this Day
Secret

I was delighted to see in the last return that we have practically 100 Fighter Squadrons (99½) in the Metropolitan Air Force. The vast changes in the war situation arising from the arrival of Russia as a combatant, and the improvement of our position in the Middle East, including Persia, make me inclined to a large further reinforcement of the Middle East to influence Turkey and/or sustain Russia on her southern flank. My thought is turning to the dispatch of as many as 20 Fighter Squadrons complete to the Iraq-Persia and Syrian theatre. It may be these Squadrons would come into action against German bombers and dive-bombers while defending territories under our control or that of our Allies, and that we should then reproduce the favourable conditions of fighting which enabled us to inflict such heavy losses upon the Germans when they made their Air attack upon us last year in the Battle of Britain. This might be a more paying business than the very hard struggles in France, which of course we must continue as occasion serves. This force would have to go by long sea route round by the Cape, and could not come into action till the end of the year. It should take with it the effective organization of one or two Control Centres (like No. 11 Group), so that the full power of the Fighter defence could be manifested. It would not leave the country till the invasion period is over. It is of course, additional to all you have in hand for the East.

I shall be obliged if you will have this situation examined in all its bearings, and let me know about numbers of personnel required, what demands on shipping, and what you think of this important transference of war power. Such forces operating north and south of the Caspian would be a gigantic contribution to Russia's war effort, and allied with bomber forces might long dispute the eastward advance of the Germans. The Indian Air Force would come into action in the same areas.

Winston S. Churchill to Admiral of the Fleet Sir Dudley Pound

(*Churchill papers, 20/36*)

1 September 1941

At the time the attached letter[1] was written, I did not know that a 4-gun 14-inch turret was contemplated. I cannot help grieving that we have not got the 3 triple 16-inch turrets for the five KGVs. The matter is academic and irretrievable. None the less, as my thought has dwelt on these matters for the last thirty years, I should like to know what is known at the Admiralty about the American ships contemporary to KGV. Admiral Stark told me that they were 3 triple turrets of 16-inch. When I asked him whether he had not overrun the 35,000-ton limit, he said: 'No, but they had given up the 500 tons they used to keep to veer and haul upon.'

Please let me have the legend of these American ships as far as you have knowledge of them at the Admiralty.

Let me also know what they do about the hangar and any advantages in strength and structure possessed by *KGV* to compensate for the loss of gun-power.[2]

[1] From Churchill to Sir Samuel Hoare (the First Lord of the Admiralty) written on 3 May 1937. It is published in Companion Volume 5, Part III, of this biography, *The Coming of War, 1936–1939*, pages 665–7.

[2] Admiral Pound replied that the equivalent American ship (the USS *North Carolina*) had a heavier main armament, but somewhat lighter secondary armament. The British ship had heavier protection and slightly higher speed. He preferred the British method of carrying two aircraft in hangars amidships as compared with the American practice of providing two exposed catapults on the quarter-deck.

Winston S. Churchill to General Wavell
(*Churchill papers, 20/42*)

1 September 1941
Personal

I agree with Chiefs of Staff that your presence in Teheran at present time would be helpful to Bullard[1] in dealing with military requirements and for ensuring that Russian influence is kept within reasonable bounds.

Winston S. Churchill to Lord Beaverbrook[2]
(*Churchill papers, 20/36*)

2 September 1941

It is imperative that the campaign now under way in the United States to discredit us and the Administration by alleging that we make insufficient or improper use of American supplies should be promptly and fully countered. All Departments concerned should confer with the Ministry of Information in this matter and should provide the information which the Ministry requires to rebut attacks or promote an effective line of counter-propaganda.

Winston S. Churchill to General de Gaulle
(*Churchill papers, 20/22*)

2 September 1941

Dear Général de Gaulle,

I had until recently been looking forward to seeing you upon your return, but the evidences I have since received of your unfriendly attitude by speech and action towards the British nation have filled me with surprise and sorrow. I have before me a message sent by you through General Spears about the sending of Free French parachutist troops to the Middle East, which is of a character which prevents its consideration. I have also the reports which have

[1] Reader William Bullard, 1885–1976. Acting Vice-Consul, Beirut, 1909–10. Served subsequently in the Consular Service, in Tbilisi, Trebizond, Erzerum and Basra. Civil Adviser, Basra, 1914. Deputy Revenue Secretary, Mesopotamia (Iraq), 1919. Military Governor, Baghdad, 1920. Middle East Department, Colonial Office (under Churchill), 1921. Agent and Consul, Jedda, 1923–25; Consul, Athens, 1925–28; Addis Ababa, 1928; Consul-General, Moscow, 1930. Knighted, 1936. Minister, later Ambassador, Teheran, 1939–46. Director, Institute of Colonial Studies, Oxford, 1951–56.

[2] As well as to the Minister of Supply (Lord Beaverbrook) Churchill sent similar Minutes to the Minister of Aircraft Production (John Moore-Brabazon), the Secretary of State for War (David Margesson), the Secretary of State for Air (Sir Archibald Sinclair), the President of the Board of Trade (Sir Andrew Duncan), the Minister of War Transport (Lord Leathers) and the Minister of Food (Lord Woolton).

appeared in the United States' newspapers of certain remarks and opinions attributed to you by an American correspondent, who is, I am assured, an extremely trustworthy journalist. I understand that you challenge his version of the interview you gave him. In that case I should be glad to know in what respects the reports which have been published are incorrect.

I have instructed Major Morton to bring these reports to your attention. They are, unhappily, representative of a number of other reports which have made a most painful impression upon me and upon the British Cabinet.

Until I am in possession of any explanations you may do me the honour to offer, I am unable to judge whether any interviews between us would serve a useful purpose.

I remain,
Yours very faithfully,
Winston S. Churchill

Winston S. Churchill to Admiral Pound
(*Secret Intelligence Service papers, HW1/43*)

3 September 1941

Admiral Cunningham sh'd feel sorry about this.[1] It is a melancholy failure.

Winston S. Churchill to Air Chief Marshal Sir Charles Portal
(*Churchill papers, 20/36*)

3 September 1941
Action this Day

This is a very serious paper,[2] and seems to require your most urgent attention. I await your proposals for action.

[1] The summary of Enigma decrypt CX/MSS/205/T2 stated: 'Tanker *Ossag* to leave Benghazi evening 3rd September after discharging cargo of aviation fuel.'

[2] A Minute by Lord Cherwell dated 2 September 1941 about the results of bombing raids on Germany in June and July, which showed that two-thirds of the bomber crews failed to strike within five miles of their target. Churchill later wrote in *The Second World War*, Volume Three, page 253: 'Two thirds of the crews actually failed to strike within five miles of it. The air photographs showed how little damage was being done. It also appeared that the crews knew this, and were discouraged by the poor results of so much hazard. Unless we could improve on this there did not seem much use in continuing night bombing.'

Winston S. Churchill to General Ismay
(*Churchill papers, 20/36*)

3 September 1941

I hear there are 1,000 Bombards in existence as well as plenty of practice ammunition. Would it not be well to form at once one or more experimental batteries to practise with this weapon and work out the best tactics for its use?

I have in mind the possibility of sending with the next convoy to the Middle East 100 Bombards and 20,000 rounds of ammunition (about 350 tons) and as many Puff Balls as can be fitted in.

War Cabinet, Defence Committee (Operations): minutes
(*Cabinet papers, 69/2*)

3 September 1941 10 Downing Street
6 p.m.

PERSIA

The Prime Minister said that the time had now come to take a firm line with the Persian Government, and he had drafted a telegram accordingly to the Ambassador in Tehran. We should continue to foster a friendly attitude on the part of the Persians, but at the same time make it clear to them that we and the Russians were in military control of their country and would require facilities and safeguards.

We could not permit the Persians to haggle about turning over to us the German nationals who had taken refuge in the German Legation.

The great prize was the Trans-Persian Railway which had been completed only just before the outbreak of war. Possession of this valuable line of communication would enable us to build up a front behind the natural barrier of the Caucasus Mountains and the Caspian.

Sir Alexander Cadogan: diary
(*'The Diaries of Sir Alexander Cadogan OM, 1938-1945'*)

3 September 1941

6. Meeting at No. 10 of Defence Committee on Persia. Quite plain now that PM is planning grandiose warfare in Persia. Well, A. might stop him if he was here, but as he chooses to be on holiday, I can't keep up a 3-cornered wrangle between Frensham, No. 10 and FO. Got some of his phrases inserted in to the telegram to Teheran. But he won't like it. But would he be able to ride PM off his Persian campaign?

7.30 took draft telegrams (revised) to Teheran to PM. Found him sitting (in rompers) in garden with Max. Joined them for 20 minutes or so. PM approved drafts. (I last sat there with poor old Neville . . .)[1]

Winston S. Churchill to Sir Alexander Cadogan
(*Churchill papers, 20/36*)

3 September 1941
Action this Day

I spoke to the Secretary of State on the telephone,[2] and I do not think it will be necessary to bring him up to London for conference this afternoon.

I should like the attached telegram sent at once to Bullard. He has got a wrong outlook, and wants toning up. Pray send my telegram off unless you have any observations to make.

Winston S. Churchill to Sir Reader Bullard
(*Cabinet papers. 65/23*)[3]

3 September 1941

1. Your various telegrams. Dismiss from your mind any idea of a generous policy towards the Germans to please the Persians or anyone else. We respect diplomatic immunity, but even that is to be subject to a proper treatment of Sir Lancelot Oliphant,[4] now being held by the enemy. You will receive special instructions on this point from the Foreign Office. We have protested against the Turks taking over the care of German or Italian interests, and if they do we shall transact no business with them on such subjects.

2. Your No. 637 referring to War Office No. 87294, the policy set out by the Chiefs of the Staff is approved. Paragraphs 2 and 3 fall under the head of 'facilities' which will be drastically interpreted. We cannot tell how the war in these regions will develop, but the best possible through-route from the Persian Gulf to the Caspian will be developed at the utmost speed and at all

[1] It was two years to the day since Neville Chamberlain had broadcast from 10 Downing Street that Britain was at war with Germany.

[2] Eden was at Frensham, in Surrey, where he had a country home.

[3] A note on this telegram as transmitted to Teheran states: 'This telegram is of particular secrecy and should be retained by the authorized person and not passed on.'

[4] Lancelot Oliphant, 1881–1965. Joined the Foreign Office, 1903. Served in Constantinople and Teheran, 1905–11. Assistant Under-Secretary of State for Foreign Affairs, 1927–36. Knighted, 1931. Deputy Under-Secretary of State for Foreign Affairs, 1936–9. Ambassador to Belgium, 1939. Interned in Germany, June 1940 to September 1941. Ambassador to the Belgian Government (in London), 1941–4.

costs in order to supply Russia. It is very likely that large British forces will be operating in and from Persia in 1942, and certainly a powerful Air Force will be installed.

3. We hope it will not be necessary in the present phase at any rate to have an Anglo-Russian occupation of Teheran, but the Persian Government will have to give us loyal and faithful help and show all proper alacrity, if they wish to avoid it. At the present time we have not turned against the Shah, but, unless good results are forthcoming, his misgovernment of his people will be brought into the account. Although we should like to get what we want by agreement with the Persian Government and do not wish to drive them into active hostility, our requirements must somehow be met, and it ought to be possible for you to obtain all the facilities we require, bit by bit, using the leverage of a possible Russian occupation of Teheran. There is no need to fear undue Russian encroachments, as their one supreme wish will be to get the through-route for American supplies. The fact that the Mufti[1] has escaped from Persian surveillance is much regretted. His capture, dead or alive, is an important object, of which the Persian Government should be made to feel the importance.

Anthony Eden to Sir Reader Bullard
(*Cabinet papers, 65/23*)

3 September 1941
Personal and Secret

The following summary of our eventual naval, military and air requirements is sent for your information. Matter will be discussed with Soviet Government but you should bear in mind that these are the kind of things which we shall have to have:

NAVAL

(i) Occupation, control and use of the naval base and station at Khurramshahr.
(ii) Retention of all captured merchant ships other than those under Persian flag.
(iii) Retention of all captured warships until the end of the war with Axis.

[1] Haj Amin el-Husseini, 1891–1974. Left Palestine after the Arab riots of 1920; sentenced to fifteen years' imprisonment *in absentia* for his part in arousing the Arabs against the Jews. Appointed Mufti of Jerusalem (by Herbert Samuel), March 1921, in succession to his half-brother. A senior member of the Executive Committee of the Supreme Moslem Council, and leader of the anti-Jewish movement among the Arabs of Palestine. Fled Palestine in disguise after the murder of Lewis Andrews in 1937. In exile in Baghdad in 1941, he helped to direct a pro-German uprising. Broadcast from Berlin, 1942; while in Berlin he protested to Hitler when some small exceptions were made to Jewish children being sent to concentration camps. Imprisoned in France, 1945–6. Went to Cairo, 1946; there the Arab League Council transferred to him all funds for Palestinian purposes. In 1948 he urged the total expulsion of all Jews from Palestine. Living in Beirut at the time of his death.

(iv) Facilities for use of all Persian ports and harbours.
(v) Full British control of all navigable Persian rivers at the head of the Persian Gulf.
(vi) Persian navigation lights of Shatt-el-Arab to be placed in British hands.
(vii) The right to acquire local craft as necessary for minesweeping and patrol purposes.

ARMY

(i) Control of the Persian railways in order to ensure the efficient operation and military security of the system.
(ii) The right to free use of all communications including ports, railways, roads and telegraphs, and the right to develop these communications as we deem necessary. We shall require to establish Allied personnel in key positions in these communications.

AIR

(i) The full use of Persian aerodromes, landing grounds and flying boat bases, including the right to carry out constructional work to expand or improve them where necessary.
(ii) Facilities for the establishment and maintenance of air defence systems particularly for the defence of Abadan and the oil fields.
(iii) The use of any aircraft maintenance and workshop facilities in Persia that may be required.

Elizabeth Layton to her parents
(*Elizabeth Nel papers*)

4 September 1941

We started out at 10.30, me in the car with him. It was rather exciting. At first he just read things, and passed them to me to hold, and then he started in on his speech. It was difficult at first trying to write in the joggling car, and several times I almost landed on top of him with a bump. However, he was quite oblivious to any kind of interruption. His right hand was gesturing just as it would (I knew) when the speech was delivered, and his tones were gentle or rasping, according to what he was expressing – in fact the motion and tones were just as expressive as the words themselves. It was a fine speech – I don't think anyone after hearing Mr Churchill composing a speech could possibly doubt his utter single-mindedness and nobility of purpose. When we got up to town it must have been about 11.45, and he was due to reach the Mansion House at 1.15. He jumped out and said 'Now run in and type like hell,' which I did. A few minutes later, however, there was an urgent call 'go to the Cabinet Room with your notebook'. When I got in there were His Lordship[1] and the

[1] Churchill.

Foreign Secretary, and HE said 'I want the FS to hear that bit about this time last year – just read it'. So I fumbled with my notebook, couldn't find the place and must have looked rather embarrassed, for he then said 'Just sit down and take your time. I don't want you to hurry.'

War Cabinet: minutes
(*Cabinet papers, 65/23*)

4 September 1941
11.30 a.m.

10 Downing Street

The Prime Minister said that Persia was now entirely in our hands, and it was clear that we must extend the scope of our original demands. It was important that we should have complete control over Persia during the war, and more especially of the road and railway communications to Russia. The previous day he (the Prime Minister) had discussed the best methods for developing the railway systems in the Middle East, so that they could not only support our Armies but enable us to increase through traffic to Russia. As a result of this discussion, arrangements had been made for increasing the engines and rolling stock available. These arrangements were being supervised by the Ministers of Supply and War Transport. It would seem, therefore, that when our Mission left at the end of the month for Moscow under the Minister of Supply (who would for the time being be in charge of all the non-diplomatic Missions in Russia) we should have something concrete to offer in the way of deliveries over the railway through Persia, as well as deliveries from the United States by Vladivostok.

The Prime Minister read to the War Cabinet a telegram (No. 619) which had been sent to Sir R. Bullard (Teheran) setting out our policy, as summarized above.

Winston S. Churchill: speech
(*BBC Written Archives Centre*)

4 September 1941

Mansion House
London

My Lord Mayor,[1] nothing in your year of office will stand out more vividly in your mind than this entertainment held today of so many military representatives of the Dominions to give a hearty welcome and do all honour to the Prime Minister of Canada, Mr Mackenzie King.

I have, as Mr Mackenzie King has reminded us, known him for a great

[1] Sir George Wilkinson, see page 81, note 1.

many years. I remember, as a young Under-Secretary for the Colonies, negotiating with him the details of some Canadian legislation about which there was some hitch in the days when he was here at the side of that great Canadian, Sir Wilfrid Laurier.[1] That is now thirty-five or thirty-six years ago, and ever since then I have enjoyed the honour and the pleasure of his friendship and have followed with close attention the long, consistent political message which he has delivered to his country, to the Empire, and to the times in which we live.

Today you have listened to a memorable and momentous declaration made here amid our ruins of London, but it resounds throughout the Empire, and is carried to all parts of the world by the marvellous mechanism of modern life and of modern war. You have listened to a speech which, I think, all those who have heard it will feel explains the long-continued authority which Mr Mackenzie King has wielded while, during more than fifteen years, he has been Prime Minister of the Dominion of Canada.

He has spoken of the great issues of the war and of the duty which lies before free men in all parts of the world to band together lest their heritage be wasted. He has spoken of the immense burden we have to bear, of our unflinching resolve to persevere in carrying forward our standard in common, and he has also struck that note, never absent from our minds, that no lasting or perfect solution of the difficulties with which we are now confronted – with which the whole world is now confronted – no diversion of that sad fate by which the whole world is menaced, can be achieved without the full cooperation in every field of all the nations which as yet lie outside the range of the conqueror's power.

In Mr Mackenzie King we have a Canadian statesman who has always preserved the most intimate relations with the great Republic of the United States, and whose name and voice are honoured there as they are on this side of the Atlantic. I had the opportunity of meeting the President of the United States a few weeks ago, and I know from him the great esteem in which Mr Mackenzie King is held and how much he has contributed to joining together in close sympathetic action the Republic of the United States and the Dominion of Canada.

I am grateful to Mr Mackenzie King today for having put in terms perhaps more pointed than I, as a British Minister, would use, that overpowering sense we have that the time is short, that the struggle is dire, and that all the free men of the world must stand together in one line if humanity is to be spared a deepening and darkening and widening tragedy which can lead only, as Mr Mackenzie King has said, to something in the nature of immediate world chaos.

[1] Wilfrid Laurier, 1841–1919. Entered the Canadian Parliament (Ottawa), 1871. Leader of the Liberal Party, 1891. Premier of Canada, 1896–1911 (the first French Canadian to hold the post). Knighted, 1897.

I hope, Mr Mackenzie, during your all too brief visit here, a visit which in a few weeks must draw to its close, you have found yourself able to see with your own eyes what we have gone through, and also to feel that unconquerable uplift of energy and of resolve which will carry this old island through the storm and carry with it also much that is precious to mankind.

You have seen your gallant Canadian Corps and other troops who are here. We have felt very much for them that they have not yet had a chance of coming to close quarters with the enemy. It is not their fault, it is not our fault, but there they stand and there they have stood through the whole of the critical period of the last fifteen months at the very point where they would be the first to be hurled into a counter-stroke against an invader. No greater service can be rendered to this country, no more important military duty can be performed by any troops in all the Allied forces. It seems to me that although they may have felt envious that Australian, New Zealand, and South African troops have been in action, the part they have played in bringing about the final result is second to none.

You have a great knowledge of the flexible organization, a system ever changing and expanding, yet ever growing into a greater harmony, by which the British Commonwealth of Nations is conducted. You have also a knowledge of your own people, and your association with them is so long and so intimate that it has enabled you to realize and express in these hours of trouble a more complete unity of Canada than has ever before been achieved. The war effort of Canada during this war has not happily so far required effusion of blood upon a large scale, but that effort in men, in ships, in aircraft, in air training, in finance, in food, constitutes an element in the resistance of the British Empire without which that resistance could not be successfully maintained.

Canada is the linchpin of the English-speaking world. Canada, with those relations of friendly, affectionate intimacy with the United States on the one hand and with her unswerving fidelity to the British Commonwealth and the Motherland on the other, is the link which joins together these great branches of the human family, a link which, spanning the oceans, brings the continents into their true relation and will prevent in future generations any growth of division between the proud and the happy nations of Europe and the great countries which have come into existence in the New World.

For all these reasons we are all the better that you, my Lord Mayor, have bidden us to come here today. You have had a strange tenure of office. Buildings have fallen about your ears and been laid in ruins, but you carry on; you carry on unflinching and unwearing.

You carry forward the proud traditions of the City of London, always in the van in the struggle for Britain and once again I have no doubt you will, as Lord Mayor of London, have played a worthy part in carrying our latest grievous ordeal to a happy ending.

Winston S. Churchill to Luke Fawcett[1]

(*Churchill papers, 20/22*)

4 September 1941

My dear Sir,

The handsome wallet which you and George Hicks[2] sent me on behalf of the Amalgamated Union of Building Trade Workers has given me real pleasure. I am proud to call myself a builder and still prouder that your Union should recognize me as such.[3] Please accept my grateful thanks.

I am so touched by your kind remarks and can only assure you in reply that I for my part can never forget the support and encouragement which the Trade Unions, themselves in the forefront of the battle, gave in the darkest days in 1940 and are giving with all their heart today.

Yours very faithfully,
Winston S. Churchill

Winston S. Churchill to Sir Stafford Cripps

(*Churchill papers, 20/42*)

4 September 1941

Moore-Brabazon made a remark of the kind you describe[4] in the course of an impromptu speech to a private luncheon of aircraft officials about a month ago. I do not know how he fell into this lapse because on the very first day of the German attack on Soviet Russia he expressed the strongest agreement with what I proposed to say in my broadcast that night. As you know, this kind

[1] Luke Fawcett, 1881–1960. Educated at Elementary school. A building worker. President, Amalgamated Union of Building Trade Workers, 1934–41; General Secretary, 1941–52. Knighted, 1948. Member of the War Damage Commission and Central Land Board, 1948–59. Chairman, Southern Regional Board for Industry, 1952–60. Part-time Member, Atomic Energy Authority, 1954–58.

[2] Ernest George Hicks, 1879–1954. Began work as a general builder at the age of 11; later became a bricklayer. National Organizer for the Bricklayers' Society, 1912. President of the National Federation of Building Trade Operatives, 1919 (and 1936–7); first General Secretary of the Amalgamated Union of Building Trade Workers, 1921–41. President of the Trades Union Congress, 1926–7. Labour MP for East Woolwich, 1931–50. Member of the Central Housing Advisory Committee (which led to the Housing Act, 1935), and the Holidays with Pay Committee. Member of the Anglo-Russian Parliamentary Committee, and of the Empire Parliamentary Association. Parliamentary Secretary, Ministry of Works, throughout Churchill's war-time premiership, 1940–5. CBE, 1946.

[3] Following newspaper publicity in 1928 about the bricklaying work he was doing at Chartwell (building a wall, and two cottages) Churchill was invited, on 4 September 1928 to join the Amalgamated Union of Building Trade Unions. He had accepted, telling Sir Horace Wilson (then Permanent Under-Secretary of State at the Ministry of Labour): 'I am always strongly in favour of organizing workmen for trade purposes.'

[4] John Moore-Brabazon, the Minister of Aircraft Production (from May 1941 to February 1942) had said that he hoped Germany and the Soviet Union would destroy each other.

of opinion has been current in England until the recent attack on the Soviet by Hitler, just in the same way as our Communists have talked about the Capitalist powers wearing themselves out and leaving the Soviet masters of the scene. As soon as his attention was drawn to what he had said Moore-Brabazon withdrew the statement and expressed regret for having made it. Here the matter would have ended, but for the mischievous spirit of Mr Tanner which led him to give it the utmost publicity at the Trades Union Congress.

2. The way to handle this matter is to make the least possible of it, and I should think you would be wise to mention it to Molotov if at all, only in the course of conversation. There is no question of Moore-Brabazon being asked to resign. I shall have to answer questions in the House of Commons which will make it clear that the policy of His Majesty's Government is as I have declared it. You are wrong in thinking Moore-Brabazon is 'a responsible Cabinet Minister'; he is a Minister of Cabinet rank, not a member of the War Cabinet, and without any responsibility except to administer the office with which he has been entrusted, in accordance with the policy prescribed. He has in fact been making extreme personal exertions to get Fighter airplanes to Russia.

3. I am rather surprised not to have had any answer to my telegram to Stalin giving him aircraft which cost us dear, other than the curt remark made to you by Molotov. It is never necessary for you to deliver my telegrams to Stalin personally unless you wish to do so.[1]

Sir Stafford Cripps to Anthony Eden
(Foreign Office papers, 954/24)

4 September 1941
Secret

Vyshinski[2] handed me today Stalin's reply to Prime Minister's message, as Molotov is suffering from influenza. The text of this statement is contained in my immediately following telegrams.

2. Vyshinski rightly termed it a document of the gravest importance. It contains what I am convinced is a perfectly frank statement of the situation and without any exaggeration.

[1] John Peck, who crossed out this last paragraph before the telegram was sent, noted: 'Sir A. Cadogan discussed this with the PM & subsequently despatched it minus the last paragraph.'

[2] Andrei Vyshinski, 1883–1954. Professor of Criminal Law, Moscow, 1923; Deputy State Prosecutor, 1933; State Prosecutor, 1935, and the principal public figure conducting the 'purge trials'. First Deputy Minister for Foreign Affairs, 1940, with particular responsibility for overseeing the incorporation of Latvia and Estonia into the Soviet Union. Foreign Minister, 1949–53. Principal Soviet Delegate at the United Nations, 1953–54.

3. It demonstrates the result of our not being able to do anything to create a diversion, and shows that unless we can now at the last moment make a super-human effort we shall lose the whole value of any Russian front, at any rate for a long period, and possible for good.

4. We have unfortunately considered the war here as no direct responsibility of ours, but merely as a war which we desired to assist in any way that we could, without unduly endangering our own position. I have tried to emphasize how vital it was that we should do our utmost if we wanted to keep this front effectively in being, but I fear it is now almost too late unless we are prepared to throw everything in, in an effort to save this front. I beg that you will consider this point of view with the great seriousness that it deserves, and even now take some action to save a collapse here.

5. From the point of view of supplies you will observe from the message how seriously this has deteriorated in the last three weeks, so that now the task of sending adequate supplies is a very much greater and more difficult one. If we are to do anything effective, it will be necessary to envisage very large and immediate help, otherwise it is doubtful if it is much good doing anything at all.

6. I think that with some immediate relief of pressure and large supplies, the fighting could still be kept going here, and so save our country from an onslaught this winter.

J. V. Stalin to Winston S. Churchill

(*Cabinet papers, 65/23*)

4 September 1941 Kremlin
Personal

I express thanks for promise to sell to Soviet Union a further 200 fighters in addition to the 200 previously promised. I do not doubt that the Soviet aviators will succeed in mastering them and putting them into use.

I have, however, to say that these aeroplanes, which apparently cannot be put into use quickly and at once, but at different periods and in separate groups, will be incapable of effecting serious changes on the Eastern front. They will be unable to effect serious changes, not only because of the large scale on which the war is being waged, which necessitates the continuous supply of a large quantity of aeroplanes, but chiefly because the situation of the Soviet forces during the last three weeks has considerably deteriorated in such important areas as the Ukraine and Leningrad.

As a matter of fact, the relative stabilization at the front which we succeeded in achieving about three weeks ago has broken down during the last week, owing to transfer to Eastern front of thirty to thirty-four fresh German infantry divisions and of an enormous quantity of tanks and aircraft, as well as a large increase in activities of the twenty Finnish and twenty-six Roumanian divisions. Germans consider danger in the west a bluff, and are transferring all their forces to the east with impunity, being convinced that no second front exists in the west, and that none will exist. Germans consider it quite possible to smash their enemies singly: first Russia, then English.

As a result we have lost more than one-half of the Ukraine and, in addition, the enemy is at the gates of Leningrad.

These circumstances have resulted in our losing Krivoi Rog iron-ore basin and a number of metallurgical works in the Ukraine: we have evacuated one aluminium works on Dnieper River and a further aluminium works at Tikhvin, one motor and two aircraft works in the Ukraine, two motor and two aircraft works in Leningrad; and these works cannot be put into operation in the new localities in less than from seven to eight months.

All this has led to a weakening of our defensive capacity and face [? group omitted ?s][1] Union of Soviet Socialist Republics with a mortal menace.

Question arise [?group omitted: ?s] and how to emerge from this more than unfavourable situation.

I think that there is only one means of egress from this situation, viz., to create in the present year a second front somewhere in the Balkans or France, capable of drawing away from the Eastern front thirty to forty divisions and at the same time of ensuring to the Union of Soviet Socialist Republics 30,000 tons of aluminium by the beginning of October next, and a *monthly* minimum of aid amounting to 400 aircraft and 500 tank [? group omitted: ? s] (of small or medium size).

Without these two forms of help Union of Soviet Socialist Republics will either suffer defeat or be weakened to such an extent that it will lose for a long period any capacity to render assistance [two groups undecypherable] by its active operations on fronts of the struggle against Hitlerism.

I realize that present message will cause dismay to your Excellency. But what is one to do? Experience has taught me to look facts in the face, however unpleasant they are, and not to fear to express the truth however undesirable it may be.

The Persian affair has, in fact, turned out pretty well. The joint operations of British and Soviet forces pre-determined [? the omitted] question. So it will be in future so long as our forces act jointly. But Persia is but an episode. The issue of war will not, of course, be decided in Persia.

The Soviet Union, like England, does not desire war with Japan. The Soviet Union does not consider it possible to violate agreements, including the neutrality agreement of Japan. But if Japan violates this agreement and attacks the Soviet Union she will meet with a due rebuff on the part of Soviet forces.

[1] The phrase 'group omitted' in square brackets was inserted by those who decoded the telegram and were unable to decode a group of letters that would normally have indicated a particular word.

Finally, allow me to express thanks for admiration you have expressed at the actions of Soviet forces, which are waging a bloody war with robber hordes of Hitlerite [? group omitted] for our common cause of liberation.

Anthony Eden: recollection
('The Eden Memoirs, The Reckoning')

[4 September 1941]

On the afternoon of September 4th, Sir Alexander Cadogan rang me up to say that Maisky was delivering a message to the Prime Minister from Stalin that evening and Mr Churchill had particularly asked that I should be there, so I drove back again to London. Stalin's message was a cry for help.

Maisky, in delivering this message, spoke sombrely about the seriousness of the situation. The Prime Minister explained to him the various reasons which made it impossible for us to operate on the Continent in such a way as to draw off German forces from the Russian front. He then arranged for the Ambassador to have a meeting with the Chiefs of Staff and myself the next day, in order to receive fuller information.

Mr Churchill and I had some talk after Maisky had left, when Sir John Dill joined us. Dill took a grim view of the Russian military position, especially at Leningrad. Anxious as the Prime Minister and I were to help the Russians, we had to admit that the case against a landing in France was overwhelming, above all because of the power of the German air force, if Portal had estimated it aright.

Winston S. Churchill: recollection
('The Second World War, Volume Three')

[4 September 1941]

The discussion went over the ground already covered in the interchange of telegrams. The Ambassador pleaded for an immediate landing on the coast of France or the Low Countries. I explained the military reasons which rendered this impossible, and that it could be no relief to Russia. I said that I had spent five hours that day examining with our experts the means for greatly increasing the capacity of the Trans-Persian railway. I spoke of the Beaverbrook-Harriman Mission and of our resolve to give all the supplies we could spare or carry. Finally Mr Eden and I told him that we should be ready for our part to make it plain to the Finns that we would declare war upon them if they advanced in to Russia beyond their 1918 frontiers. M. Maisky could not of course abandon his appeal for an immediate second front, and it was useless to argue further.

Anthony Eden to Sir Stafford Cripps
(*Foreign office papers, 954/24*)

4 September 1941
Secret

The Soviet Ambassador asked to see the Prime Minister and myself this evening in order to deliver to the Prime Minister a personal message which his Excellency had received from M. Stalin. The interview lasted for an hour and a half, and the following are the main points made by the Soviet Ambassador during the conversation:

(i) For the last eleven weeks Russia had been bearing the brunt of the German onslaught virtually alone. The Soviet Government calculated that there were 240 German divisions opposed to them with an additional sixty Finnish and Roumanian divisions. The Russian armies were therefore enduring a weight of attack never equalled in history.

(ii) M. Maisky emphasized with great earnestness the seriousness of the present situation. He did not want to use dramatic language, he said, but this may be a turning point in history. He added that, if Soviet Russia were defeated, how could we hope to win the war?

(iii) The Ambassador admitted the difficulties of an opposed landing on the coast of France or the Low Countries and accepted that expert military opinion might condemn such an operation, but he argued that there were occasions in war when the political chiefs must be prepared to accept an overriding responsibility. The Ambassador instanced General Sazonov's attack in 1914 which saved the Allied armies and made final victory possible.

(iv) The Ambassador asked whether, if the proposal to establish a second front were ruled out, fresh efforts could not now be made to meet Russian requirements in respect of munitions and supplies as set out by Stalin. If the Soviet Government knew now what aeroplanes and tanks they could count upon, they could then throw in their last resources. The Ambassador also urged his Government's need for aluminium.

(v) His Excellency asked that we should consider broadening the scope of the Moscow conference to include strategic questions. Each country was pursuing its own plan and so far there had been no attempt to make a joint plan.

(vi) The Ambassador recalled that on a previous occasion he had asked that we should help to put pressure on Finland. Could not we and the United States join in an attempt to force Finland to make peace? Marshal Mannerheim's[1] declaration of today, which indicated the determination to cross Finland's 1918 frontiers and invade Russia, created a new situation in which there was an opportunity for the United States and ourselves to act.

2. The Prime Minister agreed that Russia was bearing the brunt of the present German attack, but this was not through lack of any effort on our part. From the day of the German invasion of Russia he had asked the Chiefs of Staff to examine the possibility of an invasion of the French coast or of the coast of Norway. Military opinion was unanimously against such a course. We did not believe that the Ambassador understood the difficulties of such an operation or the limited forces which were at our disposal to carry it out. The Prime Minister then described to M. Maisky the state of defences on the French coast, gave him our information as to the strength of the German forces and recalled the teaching of this war in respect of operations carried out without sustained air support. He assured the Ambassador that he and every one of his colleagues desired nothing so much as to bring help to Russia by the creation of a second front. But the criterion must be whether any action by us would relieve the pressure on the Russian front. If so, Mr Churchill had always been ready to face the risks and the losses which would be involved in such an operation. If, however, no operation was in our power that would cause the Germans to divert forces at present engaged against Russia, then it would be foolish to delude ourselves. If by our action we could draw the weight of attack off Russia he would not hesitate to take such action, even at the risk of losing 50,000 men.

3. So far as action in the Balkans was concerned, such a task was even more formidable. He reminded M. Maisky that this spring it had taken us seven weeks to land two divisions and an armoured brigade, though there had been no opposition at the ports of landing.

4. The Prime Minister agreed, however, as to the gravity of the communication which the Ambassador had made to him. His Excellency would not expect an answer at once. Mr Churchill would examine the situation afresh with his colleagues and his technical advisers, but he

[1] Carl Gustaf Emil Mannerheim, 1867–1951. Served in the Imperial Russian Army, 1881–1916; Major-General, 1911. On active service in the war against Japan, 1905, and against Austria-Hungary, 1914–16. Returned to Finland, January 1918, and led the war of liberation against Russia as Commander-in-Chief of the Finnish Army (then virtually non-existent). Entered Helsinki at the head of 16,000 men, 16 May 1918. Recalled as Commander-in-Chief, following the Soviet invasion of Finland in November 1939, and in the war against the Soviet Union, 1941–4. President of Finland, 1944.

emphasized again that such an examination had already been made many times with the sole desire of doing everything in our power to help our Russian allies who were fighting so magnificently. As regards winning the war, if the worst came to the worst, we would continue the fight in this island and wherever we could until victory was won.

5. As regards supplies, the Prime Minister said that he understood M. Stalin's request that he should be made aware as soon as possible of the help that we and the United States could give him in aeroplanes, tanks and other material. He had anticipated that these matters would be decided at the meeting in Moscow which Lord Beaverbrook and Mr Harriman were to attend, but it might be that we should now examine the possibility of giving some immediate indication of what we could do. The Prime Minister then explained to M. Maisky the extent of our present production and of the help which we were receiving and could expect to receive from the United States in the near future. As regards a discussion of strategic plans at the Moscow conference, the Prime Minister saw no objection to this. At the same time, our own plans were fairly simple: to hold our position in this island, which was threatened by an enemy operating from Norway to Brest, to improve our communications across the Atlantic with the help of our American friends, and in the Middle East to build up a position of strength from Persia to Libya, from which offensive action might later be possible. The Prime Minister said that he had spent five hours that day examining with his advisers the means for greatly increasing the capacity of the Trans-Persian Railway. If this route could be assured and its capacity greatly increased, Russia would then have an assured warm-water channel for the receipt of American supplies. He saw no alternative but that Russia should hold on through the winter and then maybe in the spring, with the help of our reinforced armies in the Middle East which would be in contact with the Russian armies, some offensive action might be possible, perhaps in conjunction with Turkey, who would be encouraged to join with us as she saw our strength grow. The Prime Minister was convinced that there was no action which it was in our power to take which could affect events in Russia in the next two months.

6. As regards Finland, Mr Churchill said that the Ambassador's suggestion would at once be examined. I explained that action such as M. Maisky had suggested had already been taken and I understood that Mr Welles had spoken to the Finnish Minister in Washington as a result. The Prime Minister added that he was now prepared to send a personal message to President Roosevelt on the matter, and it was agreed that we should be ready for our part to make it plain to the Finns that we would declare war upon them if they advanced into Russia beyond their 1918 frontiers.

Winston S. Churchill to President Franklin D. Roosevelt
(*Churchill papers, 20/42*)

5 September 1941
Personal and Most Secret

The Soviet Ambassador brought the subjoined message[1] to me and Eden last night, and used language of vague import about the gravity of the occasion and the turning-point character which would attach to our reply. Although nothing in his language warranted the assumption, we could not exclude the impression that they might be thinking of separate terms. The Cabinet have thought it right to send the also subjoined reply. Hope you will not object to our references to possible American aid. I feel that the moment may be decisive. We can but do our best.

With kindest regards,

War Cabinet: minutes
(*Cabinet papers, 65/19*)

5 September 1941 10 Downing Street
12.30 p.m.

The Prime Minister informed the War Cabinet that the previous evening the Soviet Ambassador had asked for an interview at which he had communicated a personal message from M. Stalin. The Prime Minister then read to the War Cabinet the message, a copy of which is annexed.

In conversation, M. Maisky had emphasized the salient points of the message and had drawn attention to the great size of the German forces engaged on the Eastern Front and the serious nature of the losses the Russians had incurred both in men and in resources. He had said that the present might be the final turning point of the war and that if Russia were defeated, our own chance of winning might have gone for ever. He had earnestly pressed for action on our part to draw away some of the German forces. Although there was nothing in the actual words which M. Maisky used to justify it, he (the Prime Minister) had the feeling that the possibility of a separate peace could not be altogether excluded.

The Prime Minister said that he had informed M. Maisky that he would carefully consider M. Stalin's message and would reply to it within 24 hours. He had explained the various reasons which made it impossible for us to operate on the Continent in such a way as to draw off forces from the Russian front. We would not hesitate to sacrifice 50,000 men if we thought that by so

[1] Stalin's message to Churchill of 4 September 1941, printed on pages 1160–2 above.

doing we would relieve the pressure on the Russians. All the Military Advisers to the Government were agreed that there was nothing effective which could be done this year. He had also explained that it was physically impossible for a second front to be built up in the Balkans unless Turkey came into the war. He told him that from the start of the invasion of Russia, he had continually pressed the Chiefs of Staff to examine every possible measure which might be taken to assist the Russians. The Chiefs of Staff had done their best but the results had all been negative. He had invited him to see the Chiefs of Staff with the Foreign Secretary the following morning so that he could hear at first hand the arguments on which their opinions were based. This meeting had taken place.

The First Sea Lord gave the War Cabinet an account of the discussion which the Foreign Secretary and the Chiefs of Staff had had with M. Maisky. The formation of a front in France had first been considered and M. Maisky had made great play with the fact that we controlled the sea and could land anywhere we liked. He suggested that we should land a force of fifteen to twenty Divisions so as to draw off thirty or forty from Russia. The Russian Admiral thought this would be a possible operation if diversions were simultaneously made in other directions to confuse the enemy. The Chiefs of Staff had explained that in narrow waters sea power and air power must be considered together and that even if we managed to land fairly considerable forces, the Germans would concentrate their Divisions, of which they still had twenty or thirty in France, much quicker by rail than we could do by sea. The Germans had quite a powerful air force in France, including between 200 and 300 bombers and 500 fighters and would be able to act from a secure position against our landings. The Chiefs of Staff had tried not to harp too much on the difficulties of the operation as they realized that considerable sacrifices would be justified if any good object could be achieved. They had emphasized, however, that nothing that we could do could possibly cause the Germans to draw off appreciable land forces from the Eastern Front this autumn. M. Maisky had suggested that the best way in which we could ensure against invasion would be to engage the Germans in France. The Chiefs of Staff had pointed out the fallacy of this argument. The best opportunity the Germans had had of successfully invading this country was when a feeble front was established on the River Somme; if the Germans had allowed that front to remain, our strength would have been drawn away into France and we should have fallen an easy prey. The Germans could easily recreate that situation if we placed considerable forces in France in the near future. We could pin no hope on a rising in France as the people were quite without arms or organization.

The discussion had then turned on the possibility of a Balkan front and the Chiefs of Staff had explained how impossible it would be to land any appreciable forces in Greece in existing circumstances.

The Prime Minister said that there was no escape from the conclusion reached by the Chiefs of Staff as to the impossibility of any action in Northern France or in the Balkans of a nature to draw forces away from the Russian front and the War Cabinet expressed their agreement with this view.

The Prime Minister then drew attention to a telegram which had been received from Sir Stafford Cripps (No. 1090 from Moscow) in which our Ambassador earnestly begged that we should give consideration to the Russian situation, which seemed most serious and make super-human efforts to draw German forces away. The Prime Minister said that while he fully sympathized with the attitude of mind displayed in this telegram, the views expressed took no account of the hard facts of the situation and he proposed to send a suitable reply. The Prime Minister then read to the War Cabinet a draft which he had prepared in reply to M. Stalin's message. He felt that M. Stalin was worthy of being told the truth and was capable of facing the facts of a situation. He did not think, therefore, that we should make promises which we could not possibly fulfil.

The Minister of Labour and National Service[1] agreed, and said that it would be worth including in the message a statement to that effect. It would be wrong to mislead the Russians by promising to do things which were beyond our power.

The Minister of Supply[2] said that he thought the terms of the telegram were too harsh and depressing. The Russians were asking for 500 tanks and 400 aircraft a month and he favoured an immediate promise that from the time when navigation would reopen, we would provide the Russians with half of this demand from our own resources. We would then press the Americans to supply the other half from their own resources without diminishing our appropriations. This was a promise which he felt that we should fulfil; it would mean a very great effort on our part, particularly in transportation, but to keep the Russian Army in the field would be an objective worthy of every ounce of our energy.

The Minister of Supply inquired whether an immediate attack in Cyrenaica could not be made. A big success in that theatre would have great moral effect even though it might not directly assist the Russians.

The Prime Minister said that he was just as anxious as anyone else for an early success in Libya and had spent several days discussing matters from every angle with General Auchinleck; the latter had promised to strike at the earliest possible moment and it would be unwise to over-ride his judgment. General Smuts had been consulted and had expressed the same view. If we fought too soon, we would not have any remarkable success and our power to

[1] Ernest Bevin.

[2] Lord Beaverbrook.

renew the fight would be put back by many months. If we waited till the right moment, we might achieve great results.

The Home Secretary and Minister of Home Security[1] agreed, and said that there was a potential field of trouble in the activities of various bodies here trying to stir up a campaign against the Government on the issue of help to Russia. If M. Maisky overdid his support of such a campaign, there was a grave danger that it would stimulate a reaction which would defeat his ends.

The Prime Minister said that he was very much alive to this danger, and agreed that M. Maisky should be warned. In the meanwhile he would prepare a re-draft of his reply and would look further into the possibility of making a definite promise to fulfil half the Russian demands from our resources – a course which he was inclined to favour.

Anthony Eden: diary
(*'The Eden Memoirs, The Reckoning'*)

5 September 1941

Maisky was then summoned. First of all Winston spoke to him roundly but kindly, as only he can combine, about Soviet propaganda here in favour of second front, and said only result would be rough reaction and recrimination all would wish to avoid. Maisky said he understood, but pleaded that when asked he could not say that he was satisfied with our help when in fact he was not. All this while final draft was being typed. Maisky was, I think, pleased with it, and we finished up by calling in Max's help to find some aluminium, of which Russians want 30,000 tons, pretty well at once it seems!

To celebrate this, Winston insisted on a restaurant dinner and carried Max and self off to Ritz. Very good dinner, oysters, partridge etc. and good talk.

John Martin: diary
(*John Martin papers*)

5 September 1941

Business over reply to Stalin kept us late, so that PM cancelled departure for Ditchley. Then worked till nearly 3 a.m. He said, 'I feel the world vibrant again.'

[1] Herbert Morrison.

Winston S. Churchill to J. V. Stalin
(*Foreign Office papers, 954/24*)

5 September 1941
Personal and Most Secret

1. I reply at once in the spirit of your message. Although we should shrink from no exertion, there is, in fact, no possibility of any British action in the West, except Air action, which would draw the German forces from the East before the winter sets in. There is no chance whatever of a second front being formed in the Balkans without the help of Turkey. I will, if Your Excellency desires, give all the reasons which have led our Chiefs of Staff to these conclusions. They have already been discussed with your Ambassador in conference today with the Foreign Secretary and the Chiefs of Staff. Action, however well-meant, leading to only costly fiascos, would be no help to anyone but Hitler.

2. The information at my disposal gives me the impression that the culminating violence of the German invasion is already over, and that winter will give your heroic armies a breathing space. This, however, is a personal opinion.

3. About supplies. We are well aware of the grievous losses which Russian industry has sustained and every effort has been and will be made by us to help you. I am cabling President Roosevelt to expedite the arrival here in London of Mr Harriman's Mission, and we shall try even before the Moscow Conference to tell you the numbers of aircraft and tanks we can jointly promise to send each month, together with supplies of rubber, aluminium, cloth, &c. For our part we are now prepared to send you, from British production, one-half of the monthly total for which you ask in aircraft and tanks. We hope the United States will supply the other half of your requirements. We shall use every endeavour to start the flow of equipment to you immediately.

4. We have given already the orders for supplying the Persian railway with rolling stock to raise it from its present capacity of two trains a day each way up to its full capacity, namely, twelve trains a day each way. This should be reached by the spring of 1942, and meanwhile will be steadily improving. Locomotives and rolling stock have to be sent round the Cape from this country after being converted to oil burners and the water supply along the railway has to be developed. The first forty-eight locomotives and 400 steel trucks are about to start.

5. We are ready to make joint plans with you now. Whether British armies will be strong enough to invade the mainland of Europe during 1942 must depend on unforeseeable events. It may be possible, however, to assist you in the extreme North when there is more darkness. We are hoping to raise our armies in the Middle East to a strength of three-quarters of a million before

the end of the present year, and thereafter to a million by the summer of 1942. Once the German-Italian forces in Libya have been destroyed, all these forces will be available to come into line on your southern flank, and it is hoped to encourage Turkey to maintain at the least a faithful neutrality. Meanwhile, we shall continue to batter Germany from the Air with increasing severity and to keep the seas open and ourselves alive.

6. In your first para, you used the word 'sell'. We had not viewed the matter in such terms and have never thought of payment. Any assistance we can give you would better be upon the same basis of comradeship as the American Lease-Lend Bill, of which no formal account is kept in money.

7. We are willing to put any pressure upon Finland in our power, including immediate notification that we will declare war upon them should they continue beyond the old frontiers. We are asking the United States to take all possible steps to influence Finland.

Winston S. Churchill to Sir Stafford Cripps

(*Premier papers, 3/401/1*)

5 September 1941

Your telegram No. 1090.

Your first sentence in paragraph 4 is unjust, but you do not know the practical and technical facts. If it were possible to make any successful diversion upon the French or Low Countries shore which would bring back German troops from Russia we should order it even at the heaviest cost. All our generals are convinced that a bloody repulse is all that would be sustained, or, if small lodgments were effected, that they would have to be withdrawn after a few days. The French coast is fortified to the limit,[1] and the Germans still have more divisions in the West than we have in Great Britain, and formidable air support. The shipping available to transport a large army to the Continent does not exist unless the process were spread over many months. The diversion of our flotillas to such an operation would entail paralysis of the support of the Middle Eastern armies and a breakdown of the whole Atlantic traffic. It might mean the loss of the Battle of the Atlantic and the starvation and ruin of the British Isles. Nothing that we could do or could have done would affect the struggle on the Eastern front. From the first day when Russia was attacked I have not ceased to press the Chiefs of the Staff to examine every form of action. They are united in the views here expressed.

2. When Stalin speaks of a front in the Balkans you should remember that, even with the shipping then available in the Mediterranean, it took us seven

[1] Even larger scale German construction of fortifications on the French coast began in the spring of 1942.

weeks to place two divisions and one armoured brigade in Greece, and that, since we were driven out, the whole of the Greek and many of the island airfields are occupied by the German and Italian Air Force and lie wholly outside the range of our fighter protection. I wonder that the losses sustained by our shipping and the Fleet in the evacuations of Greece and Crete have been forgotten. The conditions are far more adverse now than then, and our naval strength is reduced.

3. When you speak in paragraph 3 of 'a super-human effort' you mean, I presume, an effort rising superior to space, time and geography. Unfortunately these attributes are denied us.

4. The situation in the West would be entirely different if the French front were in being, for then I have no doubt the invasion of Russia would have been impossible because of the enormous counter-attacks that could be immediately launched. No one wants to recriminate, but it is not our fault that Hitler was enabled to destroy Poland before turning his forces against France, or to destroy France before turning them against Russia.

5. The 440 fighter aircraft which we have taken from our seriously diminished reserve are no doubt petty compared to the losses sustained by the Russian Air Force. They constitute, however, a painful and dangerous sacrifice on our part. The attacks by the Royal Air Force both by day and by night are maintained with our utmost strength, and the even character of the fighting above the French coast shows the high degree of air power still possessed by the Germans in the West.

6. Nothing (repeat nothing) that we could do or could have done can effect the terrible battle proceeding on the Russian front. Arrangements can still be made to provide for the campaign of 1942. The route established through Persia will be opened to the full, and whatever can be found and shipped from British resources, and from American resources which would otherwise have come to Britain, will be sent as fast as possible. I am pressing President Roosevelt to send Mr Harriman here at the earliest moment in order that the Russians may know what aid they may expect in 1942 to compensate for the losses sustained by their munitions industry and make their plans accordingly. Meanwhile, I am sending a reply to Stalin's telegram today (see my immediately following telegram), and this present message is solely for your own guidance. I sympathize keenly with your feelings as you watch the agony of Russia at close quarters, but neither sympathy nor emotion will overcome the kind of facts we have to face.

John Martin: diary
(John Martin papers)

6 September 1941

At Ditchley Park, visiting the establishment at Bletchley on the way.[1] Among guests David Niven and wife,[2] Sir Charles and Lady Portal, Mr and Mrs Dick Law.[3]

Winston S. Churchill to Anthony Eden
(Churchill papers, 20/36)

6 September 1941

Please look at this.[4] You have an open door which you should force at the earliest moment. Please consult with the S of S for India so far as may be necessary, and demand as soon as possible and by the best method the expulsion of the Germans and Italians from Afghanistan. If necessary, money should be used to smooth matters, but let us get rid of them now while all this part of the world is under the impression of our Persian success.

Please let me know before Monday what you will do.

Winston S. Churchill to Anthony Eden
(Churchill papers, 20/36)

6 September 1941
Action this Day

Your Minister at Teheran[5] does not seem to be at all at the level of events. We mean to get the Germans in our hands, if we have to come to Teheran and invite the Russians there, too. The same is true about the Italians. The Bulgarian, Roumanian and Hungarian communities need not be brought into the picture at the moment. I feel this business requires your personal grip. It is

[1] The Government Code and Cypher School (GS and CS), where German top secret radio transmissions, including the Enigma messages – having been received at radio stations in Britain and overseas – were decrypted, translated and distributed; and at which high and low grade Signals Intelligence (Sigint) was coordinated.

[2] James David Graham Niven, 1910–1983. Entered the Army, 1929. Resigned Commission, 1932. Actor; among the pre-war films in which he starred was *Wuthering Heights* (after the viewing of which, Churchill commented: 'What terrible weather they have in Yorkshire!'). On active service, 1939–45: Normandy, Belgium, Holland and Germany. His first wife, Primula Rollo, died in 1946.

[3] Mary Virginia Nellis, of Rochester, New York State (Churchill's mother's home town). She had married Richard Law in 1929.

[4] Secret information concerning Afghanistan.

[5] Sir Reader Bullard.

a matter between you and your Officer. Undoubtedly we must acquire complete military control of Persia during the war. Please let me know what action you propose to take.

Winston S. Churchill to General Auchinleck
(*Churchill papers, 20/42*)

6 September 1941
Personal and Secret

Please see telegram No. 584 from Prime Minister Fadden.[1] I am pretty sure they will play the game if the facts are put before them squarely. We do not want either your supply of Tobruk or your other combinations to be hampered. If meeting their demand would do this, let me have the facts to put to them. Australia would not tolerate anything shabby. Of course, if it does not make any serious difference we ought to meet their wishes.

2. I have told the Foreign Office to repeat my most secret correspondence with Stalin to you and Minister of State.

3. President is going to give us the shipping necessary to transport the extra two divisions or their equivalent to the Middle East.

Winston S. Churchill to Arthur Fadden
(*Churchill papers, 20/49*)

6 September 1941

Your telegram No. 584 raises serious issues and you ought to know the facts before you decide. Will cable fully Monday after Chiefs of Staff and Auchinleck have been consulted.

[1] The Australian Prime Minister had asked that all Australian troops in Tobruk be withdrawn.

Summary of a German Enigma message[1]
(*Secret Service papers, HWI/51*)

6 September 1941

GERMAN POLICE

Mopping up operations continuing on Southern sector of Russian Front. The following points are perhaps of interest as throwing light on the activities of either side:

Germans report capture of 'partisans', who had been detailed for blowing-up operations. 20 'partisans', including 4 'gun-women' captured and shot.

Over 3,000 Jews shot by various units.[2]

1. SS Brigade had lost two men, whose lorry had been blown up by a mine.

Winston S. Churchill General Ismay and Private Office
(*Churchill papers, 20/36*)

7 September 1941

Find out what has happened to the 150,000 rifles, promised from the United States. Where are they at the moment? Not more than 25,000 are to be sent in any one ship.

Winston S. Churchill to Sir Kingsley Wood and Viscount Cranborne
(*Churchill papers, 20/36*)

7 September 1941

What has happened about our measures to make Southern Ireland feel the weight of the war? Have you enforced all the steps decided upon by the Cabinet? It does not seem that they have produced any effect.

Please let me have another report.

[1] Among the Enigma summaries sent to Churchill in August and September were twenty-five, decrypted from German Police signals, which referred to the mass murder of Jews on the Eastern Front. On his copy of most of these summaries, including this one, Churchill circled the figure (in this instance '3,000') of those who had been shot. This particular message had been transmitted by the Germans on 31 August 1941.

[2] These figures, although high, did not give the full scale of the slaughter. Other German units, including specially formed SS *Einsatzgruppen*, were murdering ten times as many Jews in massacres – such as at Babi Yar, near Kiev, where more than 33,000 Jews were killed in four days – which were not reported in messages which British Intelligence was able to intercept (ordinary telephone links, and land-line-telegraphic exchanges, were not susceptible to eavesdropping).

Winston S. Churchill to David Margesson and General Sir John Dill
(*Churchill papers, 20/36*)

7 September 1941
Action this Day

INDIAN ARMY

I am astonished that the expression 'dilution' should be used by the War Office in this connection. To say that a brigade of Indians is 'diluted', i.e., rendered less strong by having a British battalian added to it, is surely not what is meant. I insist upon the word being withdrawn at once. The proper word is 'strengthening'.[1]

Winston S. Churchill to Sir John Anderson
(*Churchill papers, 20/36*)

7 September 1941

I have been deeply concerned at the slow expansion of the production of heavy and medium bombers. In order to achieve a first-line strength of 4,000 medium and heavy bombers, the Royal Air Force require 22,000 to be made between July 1941 and July 1943, of which 5,500 may be expected to reach us from American production. The latest forecasts show that of the remaining 16,500 only 11,000 will be got from our own factories. If we are to win the war we cannot accept this position, and, after discussion with the Minister of Aircraft Production and Sir Charles Craven, I have given directions for a plan to be prepared for the expansion of our effort to produce a total of 14,500 in the period instead of 11,000. This can only be done by a great concentration of effort and by making inroads on our other requirements. Materials and machine tools should not present an insuperable difficulty and there will be enough pilots to fly the aircraft. The crux of the matter will be the provision of sufficient skilled labour to set up the machines and to train great numbers of fresh men and women. This skilled labour can only be found at the expense of other projects.

I have asked the Minister of Aircraft Production to draw up a plan for this new programme and to state the demands he must make for its fulfilment. I have also asked him to make suggestions as to how these demands could be met. I have asked the Secretary of State for Air to adjust his programme for

[1] On 10 September 1941 Churchill minuted to General Sir John Dill: 'I have already asked that the word "dilution" should not be used in respect of the addition of a British battalion to an Indian brigade. It was the War Office which instituted this highly derogatory expression about the British Army. A telegram should be sent to the Middle East substituting the word "intermingling" or "strengthening".' (Prime Minister's Personal Minute, M884/1, *Churchill papers, 20/36*).

the expansion of the Royal Air Force to fit the new production programme. This will give some easement in the preparation of airfields, the manufacture and filling of bombs, &c., since the full first-line strength will be achieved rather later than at present planned.

I wish you to take the plan which the Minister of Aircraft Production will produce, to convene such Ministers as may be concerned and to prepare for my consideration proposals for implementing the plan. It will be necessary to show what the effect on our other activities will be. It may be necessary to slow up the Admiralty programme or to reduce the flow of equipment for the Army. Above all, it will certainly be necessary drastically to curtail the building of the great number of new factories which are now in the early stages of construction, or which are about to be started, and which absorb so much labour, not only in their erection but in the fabrication of the materials they require. You should call for a return of all such factories showing the object for which they are intended, the date when they were started and the state of their progress, and the year and month in which they are likely to come into operation. Other long-term projects must give way to the overriding need for more bomber aircraft.

I regard this subject as a major factor in the war at the present time and I should like to receive your preliminary proposals in a fortnight. Thereafter, you must watch over the progress of the scheme and I will hold periodic conferences to stimulate action.

Winston S. Churchill to President Franklin D. Roosevelt
(*Churchill papers, 20/42*)

7 September 1941
Personal and Secret

1. Am indeed grateful for your prompt response to my appeal about Middle East shipping,[1] and very glad you like the policy. I am also planning to send seventeen more squadrons of fighter aircraft to the same theatre.

2. About supply help for Russia I meant to add: 'If they keep fighting it is worth it; if they don't we don't have to send it.' We are hitting ourselves very hard in tanks, but this argument decided me.

[1] In a telegram on 6 September 1941, Roosevelt told Churchill: 'I can now assure you that we can provide transports for 20,000 men. These ships will be United States Navy transports manned by Navy crews. Our Neutrality Act permits public ships of the Navy to go to any port. Maritime Commission is arranging to place 10 or 12 additional ships in the North Atlantic run between American ports and Great Britain so that you could release 10 or 12 of your cargo ships for carrying cargo to the Middle East.' Roosevelt added: 'I am loaning to you our best transport ships. Incidentally I am delighted that you are going to reinforce the Middle East. For your private and confidential information I am planning to make a radio address Monday night relative to the attack on our destroyer and to make perfectly clear the action we intend to take in the Atlantic.' (Prime Minister's Personal Telegram T.552, 6 September 1941, Most Secret, *Churchill papers, 20/42*)

3. We all await with profound interest your promised statement for Monday. I am speaking Tuesday in the House.

Winston S. Churchill to Arthur Fadden

(*Churchill papers, 20/42*)

7 September 1941
Most Secret and Personal

Regret delay in replying to above-quoted telegram,[1] but rapid changes in the situation make a firm appreciation of future possibilities very difficult. Remarks which follow deal only with points raised in the first paragraph of the telegram. Remaining points will be dealt with in a separate telegram.

2. Our position in Syria and Iraq may be threatened by a German advance:
(a) on Syria through Anatolia.
(b) on Iraq through Caucasus and Persia (Iran).
(c) a combination of (a) and (b).

3. Through Anatolia – If Turkey does not grant passage to German forces, the large land and air forces necessary for conquering Turkey could hardly be withdrawn from Russia, refitted and reconcentrated in less than six to eight weeks. Weather conditions in Anatolia virtually preclude operations from 1st December to the end of March. We therefore feel that the concentration by the Germans of sufficient forces on Turkish frontier to overcome that country is now improbable until a date so late that an attack on Syria through Anatolia is not likely before the spring.

4. If, however, contrary to expectations, Turkey were to give passage to German forces, three or four German divisions might arrive on the Syrian frontier before the end of the year and be reinforced at the rate of one division a month. This force might be supplemented if sea routes through Turkish territorial waters were available. A great deal therefore depends on what help the Turks may expect from us. As to this we have instructed our Attachés at Ankara to speak on the following lines:

(a) If Turkey resists, we will come to her aid at once with substantial forces. Our essential object in the Middle East is destruction of German Africa Corps and reconquest of Cyrenaica, but we expect that, at latest by 1st December, we could send to Turkey four divisions and at least one armoured brigade. Air support will be on a considerable scale, and preparations should be made to receive a force of eight fighter, one army co-operation, two heavy, and six medium bomber squadrons.

[1] Of 7 August 1941, in which Arthur Fadden had asked that the Australian troops in Tobruk be withdrawn, and doubted whether the British troops in the Middle East were seriously threatened.

(b) We shall provide a strong force of anti-aircraft artillery for the defence of our own troops and of those aerodromes allotted to us and, in addition, we are sending to the Turks an immediate and special consignment of 100 3.7-inch anti-aircraft guns. These are in addition to the normal allocation of six equipments per month.

5. Through the Caucasus and Persia – Even in the event of an early Russian collapse, a full-scale drive through the Caucasus on Persia and Iraq would not be possible this year. The control we have gained in Persia adds greatly to the security of our right flank in these regions.

6. Turning now to our own action to meet a German advance, whichever way it may come, our first requirement is facilities to operate air forces both offensively and defensively. Steps are accordingly being taken to improve and increase aerodrome facilities throughout this area and by consent of the Turks in Anatolia. These will give flexibility to our air forces in the Middle East.

7. The second requirement is to improve communications, both rail and road, throughout the areas under our control. This is being pushed forward with all despatch.

8. In addition, steps are being taken to develop as rapidly as possible our maintenance arrangements in the Basra area, including construction of additional ports, so that proposed increased forces in Persian Gulf area can be maintained.

9. Western Desert – We must clear Eastern Cyrenaica at the earliest possible moment, not only for the defence of our base in Egypt, but also to retain control of the Eastern Mediterranean. Position is as follows:

10. It is estimated that enemy has at present in Cyrenaica two German divisions (one armoured and one light motorized) and six Italian (including one motorized and one armoured). We do not think that with these forces he could undertake a major offensive against the Delta. He is in considerable difficulties with his supply and is short of mechanical transport. In addition, we are sinking a good proportion of his reinforcements of men and material from Italy. If, however, he were able to establish a firm base on the Halfaya–Capuzzo–Bardia line and to build up the necessary mechanical transport and supplies, it is possible that a limited offensive might be carried out against Sidi Barrani.

11. Our aim is to take the offensive as soon as a favourable opportunity presents itself, but Commander-in-Chief does not wish to risk another setback, such as 'Battleaxe',[1] or to move until he feels he can go right forward. He estimates that for this offensive his armoured force must not be less than two armoured divisions. These will not be ready for action until 1st November, but

[1] The British offensive in the Western Desert, begun on 15 June 1941, under General Wavell's command, in which the British forces, after four days of fighting, were forced to withdraw with the loss of more than a hundred tanks (and 122 British troops killed).

this would not preclude him from attacking sooner if a favourable opportunity were presented to him. Importance of holding Tobruk has been clearly demonstrated. Question of relief of garrison has been dealt with in my telegram of 9th August, No. 556.

War Cabinet, Defence Committee (Operations): minutes
(*Cabinet papers, 69/2*)

8 September 1941 — 10 Downing Street
7 p.m.

The Prime Minister, in summing up, said that we should accept the Persian offer to intern the Germans in Persia, provided that definite action to this end was instituted within forty-eight hours. We should be willing to consider further questions of exchange, and means of allowing non-military personnel to be sent to Germany. In addition to this we should say to the Persians that there were other issues connected with the wellbeing of the Government and to this end there must be reform. At the same time, however, orders should be given to our troops to advance to Tehran, and arrangements should be made with the Russians for them to move forward simultaneously a force of the same size to the capital, the detailed arrangements being made by the local Military Commanders.

Winston S. Churchill to Sir Edward Bridges and General Ismay
(*Churchill papers, 20/36*)

8 September 1941

My intention is that Dr Crow[1] and Colonel Jefferis remain as at present under the office of Minister of Defence, together with all their establishments of Research and Experiment.[2] They will take directions from me, and work exactly as they are working now. If desired by the Minister of Supply, they will

[1] Alwyn Douglas Crow, 1894–1965. On active service, 1914–17 (wounded, despatches, OBE). Joined the Proof and Experimental Establishment, Royal Arsenal, 1917; Director of Ballistics Research, 1919–39; Chief Superintendent, Projectile Development, 1939–40; Director and Controller of Projectile Development, 1940–5. Knighted, 1944. Director of Guided Projectiles, Ministry of Supply, 1945–6. Head of Technical Services, Joint Services Mission, Washington, 1946–53.

[2] The research and experiment establishment under Dr Crow and Colonel Jefferis was at Whitchurch, a few miles north of Chequers.

come under the War Cabinet vote or office of Minister of Defence vote if there is one.

To the Minister of Supply will be entrusted the task of manufacture according to the specifications and quantities approved.

Pray meet together and put this into shape, so that I may send a minute to the Minister of Supply.

Winston S. Churchill to General Sir John Dill
(Churchill papers, 20/36)

8 September 1941
Secret

Please let me have a short report on the present position of Delay-action Fuzes.

At the end of the last war, the Germans used these on a great scale for rendering impossible the use of railway lines, and also for booby-traps, when they retreated in France.

The periods of delay should be varied from a few days to several months, so that uncertainty is never absent and breakdowns on the lines are continual. I understand the method was a small metal box, not much bigger than a cigar case, in which an acid gradually ate through a metal wire, thus establishing a contact or opening an orifice. No doubt many improvements have taken place.

The whole aspect of our lay-out in the East leads me to think that provision of these devices on a very considerable scale should be undertaken. We are making airfields in Anatolia, Syria, Persia, Cyprus, &c., and railways and roads are being improved and pushed forward. We ought to have the means of making them unusable by the enemy for a considerable time, should we have to fall back. The best way of doing this would be to build in the mines beforehand, leaving a small sealed passage through which the appropriate fuze could be passed, should it become necessary to arm these mines. Every airfield should have 20 or 30 mines built into it. Should it be necessary to evacuate, the fuzes could be put in and the surface smothered over. The danger period must certainly last at least six months, and railroads (at any rate in their forward sections) should have at least 3 or 4 mines to the mile, and all bridges and tunnels should be mined. The uncertainty of when a line or road would be out of order is more baffling than even widespread destruction, which is over once and for all.

Pray let me have your thought on this.

Winston S. Churchill to President Franklin D. Roosevelt
(*Churchill papers, 20/42*)

8 September 1941

Pray accept my deep sympathy in your most grievous loss.[1]

Winston S. Churchill to Admiral of the Fleet Sir Dudley Pound
(*Churchill papers, 20/36*)

8 September 1941

My idea was not that the President should build Winettes[2] as such, apart from any ready arranged for, but that, out of the great number of merchant vessels being constructed in the United States for 1942, he should fit out a certain number with brows and side-ports to enable Tanks to be landed from them on beaches, or into Tank-landing-craft which would take them to the beaches.

Please help me to explain this point to him, showing what kind of alteration would be required in the American merchant ships now projected.

John Colville: diary
(*Colville papers*)

8 September 1941

The PM arrived back from Ditchley, his attention divided between his speech in the House tomorrow and supplies for Russia.

[1] The death of Roosevelt's mother. Roosevelt replied by telegram to Churchill: 'Thank you for your kind and friendly message.' Churchill's American-born mother had died almost twenty years earlier, at the age of sixty-eight.

[2] Landing Ship Tank (Mark 1). Following the failure of the Anglo-French Dakar expedition, Churchill had sought, at a meeting of the Joint Planning Staff on 29 October 1940, the construction of landing ships capable of putting tanks ashore. Three light draught tankers, the Maracaibos, were converted into tank carriers – *Thruster*, *Bruiser* and *Boxer*, each able to carry thirteen tanks and twenty-seven three-ton lorries. Designs were then drawn up for purpose-built vessels. The vessels were at first dubbed the 'Winston', later the 'Winnette'. More than a thousand were mass produced in the United States.

War Cabinet: minutes
(*Cabinet papers, 65/19*)

8 September 1941 10 Downing Street
5 p.m.

YUGOSLAVIA

The Prime Minister suggested that the part played by Yugoslavia, and in particular General Simovitch, in delaying the German plan and making the Germans fight for their success should not be overlooked.

Encouraging references about Yugoslavia should be made in the Press from time to time, and we should do everything possible to re-equip Yugoslav forces which were fighting on our side.

MISSION TO RUSSIA

The Prime Minister said that he proposed to state in the House of Commons that no time had been or would be lost in the despatch of our Mission, but that it must await the arrival of the United States delegates. In the meanwhile, important supplies were being despatched to Russia. He would add that the Minister of Supply would take charge of all non-diplomatic Missions in Moscow.

BLACK SEA[1]

The Prime Minister said that a German thrust in Thrace would bring them rapidly to the Bosphorus and the Dardanelles. The Italian Fleet could then enter the Black Sea, engage the Russian Fleet and possibly attack Batum. The only preventive measure open to us would be to send a flotilla of submarines into the Black Sea; we could only do this with Turkish permission, since the currents in the Bosphorus rendered it impossible for a submarine to pass through while submerged.

AUSTRALIAN GARRISON AT TOBRUK

The Prime Minister said that he had received a telegram from the Prime Minister of Australia asking whether we could take steps to relieve the Australian garrison at Tobruk. Mr Fadden was anxious to make a statement in the Commonwealth Parliament on the 15th September. He had telegraphed to Mr Fadden saying that the issue he had raised was a serious one; the views of the Chiefs of Staff and of the Commander-in-Chief, Middle East, would have to be obtained before a reply could be sent. When these views had been received he proposed to place the facts before the Australian Prime Minister. If Mr Fadden still demanded the removal of the Australian

[1] This and the following three items were recorded in the War Cabinet's Confidential Annex (*Cabinet papers, 65/23*).

garrison from Tobruk, they would have to be relieved, irrespective of military considerations.

The War Cabinet concurred.

UNITED STATES

The Prime Minister said that President Roosevelt had offered in a personal telegram to let us have the use of enough US Naval transports (manned by US Naval crews) to carry 20,000 British troops to the Middle East. The President also said that he would provide ten or twelve additional ships on the North Atlantic route which would enable us to release a similar number of cargo ships to carry supplies to the Middle East. The President had added that he was pleased that we had decided to reinforce the Middle East theatre.

Winston S. Churchill to Sir Stafford Cripps

(*Churchill papers, 20/42*)

9 September 1941
Most Immediate

Please inform M. Stalin from Prime Minister that we are arranging to supply 5,000 tons of aluminium from Canada as soon as arrangements for shipment are completed, and 2,000 tons monthly thereafter. First shipments will be via Vladivostok, unless Persian route would be preferable to Russian Government.

Winston S. Churchill: Oral Answers

(*Hansard*)

9 September 1941 House of Commons

Mr Clement Davies: May I ask the Prime Minister this question? If in the course of the statement he proposes to make today he finds himself prevented or hampered from making the fullest statement on the matter which is uppermost in all our minds, namely, the assistance which is being rendered to Russia now, or will be rendered, will he, if he thinks profit would come thereby to the enemy, consider holding part of the proceedings in Secret Session either today or on some other day?

The Prime Minister: The House is rather difficult to please in these matters. When we debate in secret there are demands for a Debate in public, and when we debate in public it is suggested that the Debate should be in secret. I can only say that I shall endeavour to give satisfaction to whichever mood is uppermost.

Mr Davies: May I assume that the statement the right hon. Gentleman will make will be as full in public as it would be in Secret Session?

The Prime Minister: I think it would be very dangerous to make an assumption of that kind. It is rather unnecessary, considering that the hon. and learned Gentleman is about to hear what I have to say.

Winston S. Churchill: speech
(Hansard)

9 September 1941 House of Commons

The Prime Minister (Mr Churchill): Late in July I learned that the President of the United States would welcome a meeting with me in order to survey the entire world position in relation to the settled and common interests of our respective countries. As I was sure that Parliament would approve, I obtained His Majesty's permission to leave the country. I crossed the Atlantic Ocean in one of our latest battleships to meet the President at a convenient place. I was, as the House knows, accompanied by the First Sea Lord, the Chief of the Imperial General Staff, and the Vice-Chief of the Air Staff, together with the Permanent Secretary to the Foreign Office and others. We were, therefore, in a position to discuss with the President and with his technical advisers every question relating to the war and to the state of affairs after the war.

Important conclusions were reached on four main topics: First of all, on the Eight-Point Declaration of the broad principles and aims which guide and govern the actions of the British and United States Governments and peoples amid the many dangers by which they are beset in these times. Secondly, on measures to be taken to help Russia to resist the hideous onslaught which Hitler has made upon her. Thirdly, the policy to be pursued towards Japan in order, if possible, to put a stop to further encroachment in the Far East likely to endanger the safety or interests of Great Britain or the United States and thus, by timely action, prevent the spreading of the war to the Pacific Ocean. Fourthly, there was a large number of purely technical matters which were dealt with, and close personal relations were established between high naval, military and air authorities of both countries. I shall refer to some of these topics in the course of my statement.

I have, as the House knows, hitherto consistently deprecated the formulation of peace aims or war aims – however you put it – by His Majesty's Government, at this stage. I deprecate it at this time, when the end of the war is not in sight, when the conflict sways to and fro with alternating fortunes and when conditions and associations at the end of the war are unforeseeable. But a Joint Declaration by Great Britain and the United States is an event of a totally different nature. Although the principles in the Declaration, and much of the language, have long been familiar to the British and American democracies, the fact that it is a united Declaration sets up a milestone or monument which needs only the stroke of victory to become a permanent part of the history of human progress. The purpose of the Joint Declaration signed by President Roosevelt and myself on 12th August, is stated in the Preamble to be:

'To make known certain common principles in the national policies of our respective countries on which they base their hopes for a better future for the world.'

No words are needed to emphasize the future promise held out to the world by such a Joint Declaration by the United States and Great Britain. I need only draw attention, for instance, to the phrase in Paragraph 6:

'after the final destruction of the Nazi tyranny'.

to show the profound and vital character of the solemn agreement into which we have jointly entered. Questions have been asked, and will no doubt be asked, as to exactly what is implied by this or that point, and explanations have been invited. It is a wise rule that when two parties have agreed a statement one of them shall not, thereafter, without consultation with the other, seek to put special or strained interpretations upon this or that passage. I propose, therefore, to speak today only in an exclusive sense.

First, the Joint Declaration does not try to explain how the broad principles proclaimed by it are to be applied to each and every case, which will have to be dealt with when the war comes to an end. It would not be wise for us, at this moment, to be drawn into laborious discussions on how it is to fit all the manifold problems with which we shall be faced after the war. Secondly, the Joint Declaration does not qualify in any way the various statements of policy which have been made from time to time about the development of constitutional government in India, Burma or other parts of the British Empire. We are pledged by the Declaration of August, 1940, to help India to obtain free and equal partnership in the British Commonwealth with ourselves, subject, of course, to the fulfilment of obligations arising from our long connection with India and our responsibilities to its many creeds, races and interests. Burma also is covered by our considered policy of establishing Burmese self-government and by the measures already in progress. At the Atlantic meeting, we had in mind, primarily, the restoration of the sovereignty, self-government and national life of the States and nations of Europe now under the Nazi yoke, and the principles governing any alterations in the territorial boundaries which may have to be made. So that is quite a separate problem from the progressive evolution of self-governing institutions in the regions and peoples which owe allegiance to the British Crown. We have made declarations on these matters which are complete in themselves, free from ambiguity and related to the conditions and circumstances of the territories and peoples affected. They will be found to be entirely in harmony with the high conception of freedom and justice which inspired the Joint Declaration.

Since we last met the Battle of the Atlantic has been going on unceasingly.

In his attempt to blockade and starve out this Island by U-boat and air attack, and the very formidable combination of U-boat and air attacks, the enemy continually changes his tactics. Driven from one beat, he goes to another. Chased from home waters, driven from the approaches to this island, he proceeds to the other side of the Atlantic. Increasingly hampered by United States patrols in the North Atlantic, he develops his malice in the South. We follow hard upon his track, and sometimes we anticipate his tactics. But it is not desirable to give him too precise or, above all, too early information of the success or failure of each of his various manoeuvres, and it was therefore decided that the publication of our shipping losses at regular monthly intervals should cease. Accordingly, no statement of losses has been published for July and August, and I do not think the time has come to give the actual figures yet. The public, and indeed the whole world, have however derived the impression that things have gone much better in those two months. I cannot deny that this is so.

The improvement in the sea war manifests itself in two directions. In the first place, there is a very great falling off in the sinkings of British and Allied ships, with a corresponding increase in the tonnage of invaluable cargoes safely landed on our shores. The estimates which I made at the beginning of the year of the volume of our importations for 1941, and which I mentioned to the House on another occasion, to which it would be improper to refer,[1] look to me as if they would not only be made good but exceeded. The second improvement is the extraordinary rise during the last three months in the destruction of German and Italian shipping. This has been achieved very largely by the development of new and brilliant tactics by the Coastal Command and the Royal Air Force bombing squadrons, acting with the Coastal Command. To the exploits of the Air Force must be added those of our submarines. The destruction of enemy shipping by both these forms of attack has been enormous. In fact, I may say – and I would like the House to pay attention to this statement because it is really an extraordinary one for anyone to be able to make – the sinkings of British and Allied ships by enemy action in July and August, added together, do not amount to much more than one-third of the German and Italian tonnage which we have sunk by our aircraft and our submarines. How remarkable that statement is may be judged when we remember that we present perhaps ten times, or it may be even twenty times, the target to hostile attack upon the seas as is presented to us by the shipping of the enemy. His ships make short voyages, darting across a narrow strip of water or slinking along the coast from one defended port to another under air protection, while we carry on the gigantic world-wide trade of Britain with, as has often been stated and can hardly be too often repeated, never less than 2,000 ships at sea and never less than 400 in the danger zone.

[1] Churchill's Secret Session speech of 25 June 1941 (see pages 847–58).

I have for some time looked for an opportunity of paying a tribute to our submarines. There is no branch of His Majesty's Forces which in this war has suffered the same proportion of fatal loss as our submarine service. It is the most dangerous of all the Services. That is perhaps the reason why the First Lord tells me that entry into it is keenly sought by officers and men. I feel the House would wish to testify its gratitude and admiration for our submarine crews, for their skill and devotion, which have proved of inestimable value to the life of our country. During 1941 British submarines have sunk or seriously damaged seventeen enemy warships. Some of them were U-boats. Besides the warships, 105 supply ships have fallen to their torpedoes. This is an average of fifteen ships a month, or one ship every two days. The ships which have been torpedoed varied between large liners of 20,000 tons and caiques and schooners loaded with troops and military stores. They also included a considerable number of laden troop transports and tankers, most of which were passing across the Mediterranean, through the British submarine attack, in order to keep alive the enemy's armies in Libya. Submarines of the Royal Netherlands Navy and the Free French Naval Forces have been operating in combination with our submarines and have contributed in a most gallant manner to these results.

There are other perils which have been overcome and other labours of splendid quality which have been performed unknown, or almost unknown, to the public. I mentioned some of these to the House upon a private occasion, and it has been suggested to me that this particular reference should also obtain publicity. The first deals with the anti-mining service. We do not hear much about the mine menace now. Yet almost every night thirty or forty enemy aeroplanes are casting these destructive engines, with all their ingenious variations, at the most likely spots to catch our shipping. The attack, which began in November, 1939 – which began, indeed, when the war opened – with the ordinary moored mine laid by night in the approaches to our harbours, was succeeded before the end of 1939 by the magnetic mine, with all its mysterious terrors, and is now waged continually by the acoustic mine as well as the magnetic in many dangerous combinations. We do not hear much about all this now, because, by the resources of British science and British organization, it has been largely mastered. We do not hear much about it because 20,000 men and 1,000 ships toil ceaselessly with many strange varieties of apparatus to clear the ports and channels every morning of the deadly deposits of the night. You will remember the lines of Kipling:

Mines reported in the fairway,
Warn all traffic and detain.
'Send up *Unity*, *Claribel*, *Assyrian*,
Stormcock, and *Golden Gain*.'

This is going on night after night, day after day, and it may well be imagined, as the service has to be performed in all weathers and constantly under the attack of the enemy, how excellent is the service rendered by the brave and faithful men engaged in it. We do not hear much about them because this work is done in secret and in silence, and we live on. We take it as a matter of course, like the feats of the salvage service, to which I must also refer. The salvage service has recovered, since the beginning of the war, in every circumstance of storm and difficulty, upwards of 1,000,000 tons of shipping which would otherwise have been cast away. These marvellous services of seamanship and devotion and the organization behind them, prove at every stage and step the soundness of our national life and the remarkable adaptiveness of the British mind and the tenacity of the British character by which we shall certainly be saved and save others.

Although, as I have admitted, there has been a very great improvement in our losses at sea in July and August, it would be a very foolish mistake to assume that the grave dangers which threaten us are at an end. The enemy has been employing a greater number of U-boats and a larger number of long-range aircraft than ever before, and we must expect further increases. We have made prodigious exertions and our resources are continually growing. The skill and science of the Admiralty staff and their commanders, working in perfect harmony with the Royal Air Force, have gained these successes, but the Admiralty would be the last to guarantee their continuance as a matter of course, and certainly the slightest relaxation of vigilance, of exertions and of contrivance would be followed swiftly by very serious relapses. It must be remembered also that the Germans are much hampered on the American parts of the Atlantic, which are very extensive, by the fear of trouble with the powerful American Naval forces which ceaselessly patrol the approaches to the Western Hemisphere. This has been a help to us. I could wish it might be a greater help. But here again, the enemy's tactics may change. No doubt Hitler would rather finish off Russia and then Britain before coming to close quarters with the United States. That would be in accordance with his habitual technique of one by one. Hitler has, however, also the greatest possible need to prevent the precious munition supplies, now streaming across the Atlantic, in pursuance of the policy of the United States Government, from reaching our shores. Should he do so the area of the danger zones would again become ocean-wide. In the meanwhile, let us hear no vain talk about the Battle of the Atlantic having been won. We may be content with the successes which have rewarded patience and exertion, but war is inexhaustible in its surprises, and very few of those surprises are of an agreeable character.

It was with great pleasure that on my homeward voyage I visited Iceland, where we were received with the utmost cordiality by the Government and the people, and where I had the honour of reviewing large numbers of the strong British and United States Forces which, no doubt for entirely different reasons and in pursuance of separate duties, happen to be engaged jointly in defending this all-important island and stepping-stone across the Atlantic from Nazi intrusion and attack. Very considerable British and United States Air and Naval Forces are also assembled in Iceland in the harbours and on the airfields. The spacious airfields which we have constructed, and which we are expanding there and in Newfoundland, will play an ever-increasing part, not only in the control of the broad waters, but in the continual flow of that broadening stream of heavy bombers, now attacking Germany night after night, which will play a decisive part, or one of the decisive parts, in the final victory.

Our affairs have also prospered in the Eastern theatre of the war. Our relations with Iraq are governed by the Treaty of Alliance, which in time of war or other emergency accords to us wide powers for the purposes of defence both of Iraqian and British interests. The Germans had, of course, practised their usual methods of building up by infiltration and intrigue a pro-German party in Baghdad, and on 2nd April the pro-German leader, Rashid Ali, carried out a *coup d'état* in Baghdad, forcing the constitutional ruler of the country, the Regent, to fly from the capital. This move did not find us wholly unprepared. We had the right and the duty to protect our lines of communication through Iraq, and orders were at once given to send to the Port of Basra, at the head of the Persian Gulf, an Indian division which was held in readiness for this emergency. This division disembarked at Basra on 18th April, without opposition. Hoping perhaps to secure from us recognition for his illegal regime, Rashid Ali even pretended to welcome the arrival of our troops. Soon, however, instigated by the Germans and lured on by promises of prompt and powerful air support, he resorted to open war against us in utter breach of the Treaty. Our air-training station at Habbaniya, where about 1,500 airmen and soldiers were stationed, was attacked on 2nd May by the Iraqian Army, and the position seemed for some days most critical. Reinforcements were sent through Basra and India by air, and strong mobile columns moved from Palestine to relieve Habbaniya by land. Before they could reach Habbaniya, however, the reinforced garrison, aided by the aircraftsmen in training, turned the tables on its attackers in the most spirited manner, and, in spite of a superiority of three to one, drove the enemy off with heavy losses. By a bold stroke the bridge across the Euphrates was then captured intact, and, in spite of difficulties due to floods, our troops reached Baghdad on 30th May, thus liberating our gifted and resolute Ambassador from his virtual blockade in the British Embassy.

While all this was going on, Rashid Ali appealed constantly to the Germans to make good their promises, but only thirty or forty German aeroplanes arrived from Syria and endeavoured tentatively to instal themselves at Baghdad and also to the North at Mosul. But meanwhile there was an explanation for this failure of the Germans. The German parachute and airborne corps, which no doubt was to have operated in Iraq and would have been assisted on its journey across Syria by the Vichy French, had been largely exterminated in the Battle of Crete. Over 4,000 of these special troops were killed, and very large numbers of carrier aircraft were destroyed. This specialist corps were so mauled in the ferocious fighting that, although they forced us to evacuate Crete, they were themselves in no condition for further operations. We, therefore, suppressed the revolt of Rashid Ali, and he and his partisans fled to Persia – I like to call it Persia, if only out of consideration for my right hon Friend, and I hope the House will permit me to indulge myself in that fashion – and the exiled Regent was able to return and to re-establish a lawful Government in Iraq. With this Government we have been able to return to the basis of friendly co-operation which we have followed for a good many years, and which we propose to follow. The Treaty is now being loyally observed on both sides. Our ground and air forces have been accorded full facilities throughout Iraq, and the situation which in April had appeared so disastrous was fully restored by the end of May. There are still dangers in Iraq which require attention, but which need cause no serious anxiety.

The intrigues of the Germans with the Vichy French in Syria had meanwhile been in full swing, and the Vichy French Governor, General Dentz, in a base and treacherous manner was striving his utmost to further the German interests. We were ourselves hard pressed. Our Armies in Greece had been evacuated, having lost much of their equipment, our Western Front in Cyrenaica had been beaten in by the incursion of General Von Rommel's German Africa Corps, and we had the revolt in Iraq to put down. Nevertheless, we found it possible, in conjunction with the Free French, to invade Syria on 8th June. The six Free French Battalions under General Le Gentilhomme fought gallantly and co-operated with our forces, which ultimately reached the equivalent of about four Divisions. The Australian and Indian troops distinguished themselves repeatedly in action. Although the Vichy French forces in their antagonism to the Free French movement fought with unusual vigour, by 11th July the conquest of Syria was complete and all Germans had been driven out. The occupation of Syria by the Army of the Nile carried with it the means of securing the safety of Cyprus, which until then, as anyone can see, had been in great danger from the air forces which the Germans were trying to build up in Syria in order to cut Cyprus off from naval protection. All this part of the Levant thus came in to a far more satisfactory condition. Our naval and air control over the Eastern end of the Mediterranean became effective, and we obtained direct contact with our Turkish friends, and the control of the pipe line and other resources.

This is the point at which it will be convenient for me to explain our position in Syria. We have no ambitions in Syria. We do not seek to replace or supplant France, or substitute British for French interests in any part of Syria. We are only in Syria in order to win the war. However, I must make it quite clear that our policy, to which our Free French Allies have subscribed, is that Syria shall be handed back to the Syrians, who will assume at the earliest possible moment their independent sovereign rights. We do not propose that this process of creating an independent Syrian Government, or Governments – because it may be that they will not be one Government – shall wait until the end of the war. We contemplate constantly increasing the Syrian share in the administration. There is no question of France maintaining the same position which she exercised in Syria before the war, but which the French Government had realized must come to an end. On the other hand, we recognize that among all the nations of Europe the position of France in Syria is one of special privilege, and that in so far as any European countries have influence in Syria, that of France will be pre-eminent. [Hon. Members: 'Why?'] Because that is the policy which we have decided to adopt. We did not go there in order to deprive France of her historic position in Syria, except in so far as is necessary to fulfil our obligations and pledges to the Syrian population. There must be no question, even in war-time, of a mere substitution of Free French interests for Vichy French interests. The Syrian peoples are to come back into their own. This is fully recognized in the documents which have been exchanged between the Minister of State and the representatives of the Free French.

I was asked a question about our relations with Iraq. They are special; our relations with Egypt are special, and, in the same way, I conceive that France will have special arrangements with Syria. The independence of Syria is a prime feature in our policy.

While all this was going on in the Levant, on the Eastern flank of the Army of the Nile, that Army struck two heavy blows at the German and Italian forces which had recaptured Cyrenaica. These forces found themselves unable to advance upon Egypt, as had been foreseen, without destroying the stronghold of Tobruk, which was firmly held by Australian and British troops. The heavy attacks made by our Forces in the Western Desert in the middle of May and the middle of June, while they did not succeed, as we had hoped, in forcing the enemy to retreat, played a great part in bringing him to a standstill. All the German boasts which they had widely circulated throughout Europe and the East that they would be in Suez by the end of May have thus proved to be vain. Powerful reinforcements have reached the Army of the Nile in the interval, and I feel considerable confidence that we shall be able to defend Egypt successfully from German invasion across the Western Desert. Thus the position both on the Western and on the Eastern flanks of the Nile Valley has been greatly improved. A marked recovery has been made from the unfortunate setback coming after the victories over the Italians which occurred at the beginning of April. Altogether we are entitled to be content with these favourable developments.

Now I turn to a far wider field. The magnificent resistance of the Russian Armies and the skilful manner in which their vast front is being withdrawn in the teeth of Nazi invasion make it certain that Hitler's hopes of a short war with Russia will be dispelled. Already in three months he has lost more German blood than was shed in any single year of the last war. Already he faces the certainty of having to maintain his armies on the whole front from the Arctic to the Black Sea, at the end of long, inadequate, assailed and precarious lines of communication, through all the severity of a Russian winter, with the vigorous counter-strokes which may be expected from the Russian Armies. From the moment, now nearly eighty days ago, when Russia was attacked, we have cast about for every means of giving the most speedy and effective help to our new ally. I am not prepared to discuss the military projects which have been examined. Such a discussion would be harmful to our interests, both for what was said and for what was not said. Nor will it be possible for anyone representing the Government to enter upon any argument on such questions. In the field of supply more can be said. I agreed with President Roosevelt upon the message which was sent to Premier Stalin, the terms of which have already been made public. The need is urgent, and the scale heavy. A considerable part of the munition industry and iron and steel production of Russia has fallen into the hands of the enemy. On the other hand, the Soviet Union disposes of anything from 10,000,000 to 15,000,000 soldiers, for nearly all of whom they have equipment and arms. To aid in the supply of these masses, to enable them to realize their long continuing force and to organize the operation of their supply, will be the task of the Anglo-American-Russian Conference.

There has been no unavoidable delay in arranging for this conference or in choosing the personnel of the British Mission. Some people seem to think nothing has been done, nothing has been sent and nothing is going on. The study of the whole problem has been ceaselessly proceeding, both in the United States and here, and we are waiting the arrival of the American Mission under Mr Harriman, which I trust will soon be here. This Mission contains important representatives of the United States Fighting Services. Our Mission will be headed by Lord Beaverbrook, who has already visited the United States and has been in the closest conference with the President and his advisers and officers. It must be remembered that we already have a Military Mission with officers of high rank in Moscow. Those whom Lord Beaverbrook takes with him will therefore supplement those who are already there, and during the conference he will be in charge of all of them. The names are already selected and will be published in due course. It is obviously undesirable to announce the date when the Mission will start for the conference, but no time will be lost. Meanwhile, many very important emergency decisions are being taken, and large supplies are on the way.

We must be prepared for serious sacrifices in the munitions field in order to meet the needs of Russia. The utmost exertion and energy will therefore be required from all concerned in production in order not only to help Russia but to fill the gaps which must now be opened in our longed-for, and at last arriving supply. It must be remembered that everything that is given to Russia is subtracted from what we are making for ourselves, and in part at least from what would have been sent us by the United States. In terms of finished munitions of war the flow of our own production in this country and the Empire is still rising. It will reach full flood during this third year of our war-time munitions production. If the United States are to fulfil the task they have set themselves, very large new installations will have to be set up or converted, and there will have to be a further curtailment over there, as they fully recognize, of civilian consumption. We must ourselves expect a definite reduction in the military supplies from America on which we had counted, but within certain limits we are prepared to accept those facts and their consequences.

Other limiting factors are also present. There is time, there is distance, there is geography. These impose themselves upon us. There are the limitations of transport and of harbour facilities. Above all, there is the limitation of shipping. Only three routes are open – the Arctic route by Archangel, which may be hampered by the winter ice; the Far Eastern route via Vladivostok, which is scowled upon by the Japanese and operates over only 7,000 miles of railway line; and, finally, the route across Persia, which leads over a 500-mile stretch from the Persian Gulf to that great inland sea, the Caspian, upon which the Russians maintain a strong naval force and which again gives access to the very heart of Russia, the Volga Basin.

The Germans were, of course, busy betimes in Persia with their usual tricks. German tourists, technicians and diplomatists were busy suborning the people and Government of Persia with the object of creating a Fifth Column which would dominate the Government at Teheran and not only seize or destroy the oil fields, which are of the highest consequence, but – a fact to which I attach extreme importance – close the surest and shortest route by which we could reach Russia. We thought it necessary, therefore, to make sure that these machinations did not succeed. Accordingly, we demanded of the Persian Government the immediate expulsion of their Teutonic visitors. When under local duress the Persian Government failed to comply with our request, British and Russian Forces entered Persia from the South and from the North in sufficient and, indeed, overwhelming strength.

The Persian Government, having made such resistance as they thought fit, sued for peace. We must have the surrender into our hands of all the Germans and Italians who are on the premises; we must have the expulsion of the German and Italian Legations, whose diplomatic status we, of course, respect; and we must have the unquestioned control and maintenance of the through communications from the warm-water port of Basra to the Caspian Sea. It is from this point particularly that American and British supplies can be carried into the centre of Russia in an ever-widening flow, and naturally every effort will be made, and is being made, to improve the railway communications and expand the volume of supplies which can be transported over the existing British-gauge railway, which has happily only recently been completed and now requires only large accessions of rolling stock and locomotives to expand it greatly as a line of supply.

The House will, I have no doubt, approve the somewhat drastic measures we thought it right to take to achieve those important objects and the further measures we may have to take. The occupation of Persia enables us to join hands with the Southern flank of the Russian Armies and to bring into action there both military and air forces. It also serves important British objects in presenting a shield which should bar the eastward advance of the German invader. In this the Armies of India, whose military quality has become shiningly apparent, will play an increasing part, and in so doing will keep the scourge of war a thousand miles or more from the homes of the peoples of India. One must, therefore, expect that very considerable deployments of British, Indian, and Dominion Forces, will gradually manifest themselves in these enormous and desolate or ill-developed regions. The Allied front now runs in an immense crescent from Spitzbergen in the Arctic Ocean to Tobruk in the Western Desert, and our section of this front will be held by the British and Empire Armies with their growing strength fed and equipped by ocean-borne supplies from Great Britain, from the United States, from India and from Australasia. I am glad to say that adequate naval power will be at hand in both the Atlantic and Indian Oceans to secure the sea routes against attack.

If we now look back for a moment, we can measure the solid improvement in our position in the Middle East or East which has been achieved since the French suddenly fell out of the war and the Italians made haste so eagerly to come in against us. At that date all we had in those parts was from 80,000 to 100,000 men, starved of munitions and equipment, which had all been sent to the French front, always first to claim the best we had. We had lost our means of safe communication through the Mediterranean and almost all the main bases on which we relied. We were anxiously concerned for our defence of Nairobi, Khartoum, British Somaliland and, above all, of the Nile Valley and Palestine, including the famous cities of Cairo and Jerusalem. None was safe, but, nevertheless, after little more than a year we have managed to gather very large and well-equipped Armies, which already begin to approach 750,000, which are supplied and are being supplied with masses of equipment of all kinds. We have developed an Air Force almost as large as that we had in Great Britain when the war began, an Air Force which is rapidly expanding. We have conquered the whole of the Italian Empire in Abyssinia and Eritrea and have killed or taken prisoner the Italian armies of over 400,000 men by which these regions were defended. We have defended the frontiers of Egypt against German and Italian attack. We have consolidated our position in Palestine and Iraq. We have taken effective control of Syria and provided for the security of Cyprus. Finally, by the swift, vigorous campaign in Persia which has taken place since the House last met we have joined hands with our Russian Allies and stand in the line to bar the further Eastward progress of the enemy. I cannot help feeling that these are achievements which, whatever the future may contain, will earn the respect of history and deserve the approval of the House.

Thus far then have we travelled along the terrible road we chose at the call of duty. The mood of Britain is wisely and rightly averse from every form of shallow or premature exultation. This is no time for boasts or glowing prophecies, but there is this – a year ago our position looked forlorn and well nigh desperate to all eyes but our own. Today we may say aloud before an awe-struck world, 'We still are master of our fate. We still are captain of our souls.'[1]

John Colville: diary
(*Colville papers*)

9 September 1941

The House has reassembled for one week and I went down to hear the PM make a statement on the situation. His speech, which dealt with the US, Persia and Russia, was quite well received although, for the first time, a number of members left while he was still speaking. He himself thought it a very good speech, 'well-designed' as he said to me on the way back in the car.

Winston S. Churchill to Anthony Eden
(*Churchill papers, 20/36*)

10 September 1941

It might be well to bring these Chinese anxieties[2] to United States attention. I am sure the President has no intention of 'selling out China'.

[1] The poet William Ernest Henley (1849–1903) had written, in his poem 'Invictus':

It matters not how strait the gate,
How charged with punishments the scroll,
I am the master of my fate:
I am the captain of my soul.

Another of Churchill's favourite verses was an earlier stanza of this same poem:

In the fell clutch of circumstance,
I have not winced nor cried aloud:
Under the bludgeonings of chance
My head is bloody, but unbowed.

[2] About the talks being conducted between the United States and Japan.

Winston S. Churchill to General Sir John Dill
(Churchill papers, 20/36)

10 September 1941
Action this Day

TRANS-PERSIA RAILWAY

Please see attached from Lord Beaverbrook. In view of the danger to Murmansk and the masses of stuff we are planning to send to Russia and the difficulties of developing the railway through Persia and carrying at the same time, it seems most urgent to explore the full possibilities of road transport. I could cable Mr Hopkins asking for the necessary lorries, drivers and mechanics, if these are necessary, and I have little doubt the United States would ship them to Basra pretty quickly. I know nothing about the roads, but the whole matter must be examined together with a plan for improving the roads while the vehicles are coming from America.

Let me have your views on this, if possible by tomorrow, so that I can act.

Winston S. Churchill to Field Marshal Smuts
(Churchill papers, 20/49)

10 September 1941

I have very carefully considered your telegram No. 1061 of 6th September with my advisers. We do not place any great reliance on current reports of large concentrations in Bulgaria and the Aegean Islands. Two German divisions were recently moved down to Bulgarian coast from Germany or from Czechoslovakia, and it appears possible that a small seaborne expedition against the Crimea or the eastern shores of the Black Sea may be under preparation. But, including these two divisions, total German forces in Bulgaria only about four divisions, and we do not think it at all likely that Germany would attempt attack on Turkey without far greater backing to Bulgarian and Italian forces. Bulgarian concentrations on Turkish frontier remain as they have been for some months at 10 divisions. Italians have, we believe, only 4½ divisions in whole Aegean area, including Dodecanese.

We think that rumours of an attack on Turkey are being deliberately spread by enemy in order to encourage a submissive frame of mind in Turks prior to forthcoming trade negotiations and in pursuance of their usual policy of mystification.

Nevertheless I fully agree that a double threat to our Middle East position still continues, and we are fully alive to the necessity of getting Turkey into a firm and unequivocal alliance. We remain convinced that the Turks will oppose a stubborn resistance to an Axis attack, but nothing we can at present offer will induce them to declare for us before that attack begins. We must therefore make the best we can of their present faint-hearted attachment.

I can tell you for your personal and most secret information that our Military Attaché and Air Attaché[1] in Angora are at present engaged in staff conversations with the Turkish General Staff. You will remember that the initiative for these conversations came from the Turks and that arrangements had been made for the Commanders-in-Chief and the Turkish Marshal to conduct them. An unfortunate leakage of information in Angora, however, made the Turks too nervous to proceed with this plan and we had to be content with conversations on a lower level. From accounts so far received these are making good progress and although the Turks make larger demands than we can yet meet we are prepared to make a firm offer to them of substantial army and air forces, the strength of which would depend on the situation in North Africa, together with as much war material as we can supply over improved communications which we are putting in hand with all expedition. We propose also, if their attitude is sufficiently encouraging, to send them at once 100 3.7-inch AA guns.

Winston S. Churchill to Anthony Eden
(*Churchill papers, 20/36*)

10 September 1941
Most Secret

PEACE OVERTURES

I am sure we should not depart from our policy of absolute silence. Nothing would be more disturbing to our friends in the United States or more dangerous with our new ally, Russia, than the suggestion that we were entertaining such ideas. I am absolutely opposed to the slightest contact. If you do not agree, the matter should be brought before the War Cabinet sitting alone.

[1] Major-General William Archibald Fraser, CB, CBE, MVO,. DSO, MC and Captain George Eric Maxia O'Connell, DSO, RN.

Winston S. Churchill to Arthur Fadden
(*Cabinet papers, 65/23*)

11 September 1941
Most Strictly Secret

1. I send you in its entirety General Auchinleck's private telegram[1] to me about relieving the Australian troops in Tobruk. I do so in complete confidence in your discretion. General Auchinleck's telegram is the result of prolonged consultation with the Naval and Air Commanders in the Middle East.[2]

2. You will see from this telegram that if you insist upon the relief of the Australians in Tobruk it is physically impossible for it to be completed in time for you to make the statement you desire to the Commonwealth Parliament by the middle of this month. In fact only half could be removed during the moonless period of September, and the other half would have to be removed during the latter half of October, which is the very time when all preparations for the offensive will be intense, and when the preparatory work of the Air Force will demand their complete concentration on the enemy's rear areas, dumps and airfields. In no case could you make any statement to the Commonwealth Parliament because any suggestion in public that the reliefs were to take place might lead to heavy air attacks on Tobruk Harbour and along the coast at the time when your troops would be withdrawing. If, however, you insist that the Australian troops must be withdrawn, orders will be issued accordingly irrespective of the cost entailed and the injury to future prospects. I trust, however, that you will weigh very carefully the immense responsibility which you would assume before history by depriving Australia of the glory of holding Tobruk till victory was won, which otherwise by God's help will be theirs for ever.

3. I feel bound again to impress upon you the vital importance of maintaining absolute secrecy about future operations or movements of troops which the question of relief of your forces has compelled the Commander-in-Chief to reveal to us.

[1] In which General Auchinleck warned of the risk of further withdrawal of Australian troops from Tobruk, pointing out that in the recent withdrawal of one Australian Infantry Brigade Group and an Indian Cavalry Regiment 'the naval risks involved were appreciable as nearly all ships were attacked by aircraft' and that 'a continuation of relief would throw an added burden on fleet destroyers at expense of our naval operations'. (Prime Minister's Personal Telegram, T.568, *Cabinet papers, 65/23*).

[2] Admiral Sir Andrew Cunningham and Air Marshal Tedder.

War Cabinet: minutes
(*Cabinet papers, 65/19*)

11 September 1941 Prime Minister's Room
12 noon House of Commons

AID TO RUSSIA

The Prime Minister said that, in view of the inadequacy of other routes, it was important to take all practicable steps to improve routes through Persia. We must not be content with developing the railway, but should also explore the possibilities of improving the roads and getting vehicles from the United States.

AID FROM THE UNITED STATES

The Prime Minister read to the War Cabinet a personal telegram which he had received from Mr Harry Hopkins, and the reply which he had sent. Briefly, the American proposal, which had been accepted, was that a conference should be held in London between high military officials of the United States and corresponding officials of the British Government, for two purposes: First, of stating the amount of material aid, including that already allocated to the British Government, which the United States Government could make available by the 1st July, 1942, and to discuss the allocations to be made therefrom in order to aid Russia. Secondly, of obtaining from British officials complete estimates of British requirements to accomplish victory over the Axis Powers.

It was proposed that this conference, which would last 4 or 5 days, should be held in the following week, and that immediately thereafter the British and United States Missions should proceed to Moscow.

THE UNITED STATES AND THE ATLANTIC

The Prime Minister said that we had now received information as to the areas in the Atlantic in respect of which the United States Navy would assume responsibility for convoys other than troop convoys. The line which had been drawn by the President was far more favourable than had been expected. It ran East of Iceland down the 10th Meridian to the Faroes, and then across to the 26th Meridian to a point just West of the Azores. The area therefore covered nearly three-quarters of the North Atlantic. Any Axis ships West of this line would be attacked by US Naval Forces. Further, the President proposed to convoy ships flying the American or Icelandic flag, and this protection would extend to any of our ships which cared to join these convoys. For the present, the United States proposed to leave the slow convoys (in which there were no ships flying the US or Icelandic flag) to the care of the Canadian Navy, and to confine their protection to the fast Halifax convoys.

The Prime Minister pointed out that the recent attack on one of our convoys in Greenland waters had taken place well within the area for which the United States would be responsible. He thought that the dispositions made by the President must almost certainly lead to conflict with German U-boats, and that such conflict would result in a rise in tempers.

The Prime Minister said that he believed that the President would include in his broadcast that night some details of the above arrangement. It was, however, of the greatest importance that there should be no speculation in the Press indicating any foreknowledge or expectation of a statement on these lines.

Winston S. Churchill: Oral Answers
(Hansard)

11 September 1941 House of Commons

MINISTER OF AIRCRAFT PRODUCTION[1] (REMARKS)

Mr Gallacher asked the Prime Minister whether the remarks in the recent speech of the Minister of Aircraft Production regarding operations between the Russian and German armies on the Eastern Front represent the policy of His Majesty's Government?

The Prime Minister: The versions which have been given to the public of the remarks made at a private gathering at the end of July by the Minister of Aircraft Production bear a construction which represents neither the policy of His Majesty's Government nor the views of my right hon. and gallant Friend. I happen to know what the views of my right hon. and gallant Friend were, because on the day when Hitler attacked Russia I told him on the telephone the line I was going to take that night of wholehearted support for Russia, and he expressed enthusiastic assent. He emphasized these sentiments in a public speech at Chertsey on 9th August. Moreover, my right hon. and gallant Friend has all the while been ardently at work, as I know from daily observation, sending hundreds of fighter aircraft to Russia, many of which have already got there. Therefore, although the phrasing of what he said at the private gathering taken from its context might well be misconstrued, I am satisfied that he was and is in the fullest accord with the policy which His Majesty's Government are earnestly pursuing.

Mr Shinwell: Has my right hon. Friend seen and read the correspondence which passed between the Minister of Aircraft Production, Sir Ernest Salmon and Mr Blackburn, organizer of the Amalgamated Engineering Union, and, if not, may I send him copies of the correspondence? After having perused the correspondence, will he agree that the Minister of Aircraft Production, for his own sake and for the advantage of the Government, should make a personal statement at that Box?

[1] John Moore-Brabazon.

The Prime Minister: I have, of course, read the correspondence, and I was astonished that anybody should have taken the mischievous action of making all this sensation, which does nothing but harm to Russia as well as to Britain and leads to suspicions between those whose fortunes are linked together. As to a statement by my right hon. and gallant Friend, he is, of course, welcome to make a personal statement if he desires, but I have assumed the duty of dealing with this matter.

Mr Shinwell: If my right hon. Friend intends to rebuke those who have raised this matter – as apparently he does – without any hostile intent but merely for the purpose of seeking a reasonable explanation of the statement, will he take exception to a public statement being made quoting the actual statements made by the right hon. and gallant Gentleman the Minister for Aircraft Production and his admission that the statements were made?

The Prime Minister: I think it would be unhelpful to the general interest. That is my view. I have very carefully considered what I should say, because I could easily use arguments which would be quite effective from the point of view of merits for and against but which would tend to give an altogether disproportionate importance and significance to this matter. Therefore, I have forborne from quoting. I would also say that it is very inconvenient, and I think contrary to our way of carrying on our business, to found accusations in public upon reports of what passed at a private gathering at which no written record was taken –

Mr Shinwell: What about the admission?

The Prime Minister: My right hon. and gallant Friend certainly said that he was sorry his words had borne that construction. So he is, but that was not what he meant, and I am satisfied that at the root of the matter he is with us heart and soul.

Mr Gallacher: Is the Prime Minister aware of the deep and bitter feeling that exists among many trade unionists in factories – in almost every factory in the country – as the result of this, and will he not be prepared to assure the workers that he will take every step to clear out of his Government anyone who is not 100 per cent. in cooperation with the Soviet Union?

The Prime Minister: I do not think I should be prepared to seek guidance in matters of policy or conduct from an hon. Gentleman whose attitude has been notorious for his changed opinions whenever he has been ordered to do so by a body outside this House.

Mr Gallacher: On a point of Order. I want to put it to you, Mr Speaker, that as the representative for West Fife I have never taken orders from anyone outside this country at any time. I ask protection from you, Sir, and demand the withdrawal of that insulting remark made by the Prime Minister. The Prime Minister has no right to make such a false statement. It is a dirty, cowardly, rotten action on the part of the Prime Minister, the action of a blackguard. It is a dirty lie, a foul, dirty lie.

Mr Gallacher: Mr Speaker, after very deep reflection about what occurred in the House earlier, I want to apologize to you and to the House for the offensive words I used after I had put to you my point of Order, and to make a complete withdrawal of the offensive remarks directed towards the Prime Minister.

John Colville: diary
(*Colville papers*)

11 September 1941

The PM was dining with Beaverbrook at No. 12. I took them in a large file of papers on gas warfare, about which the PM has sent many instructions and minutes in the last year. I sat with them while they talked about it and reviewed our present much improved position in this respect. Beaverbrook is convinced the Germans will use gas. He says he is certain of it. Winston thinks Hitler's followers may prevent him <u>if</u> they consider they are fighting a losing battle.

The PM worked till 2.00. I sat beside him most of the time and tried to answer his questions. The King has offered him the Lord Wardenship of the Cinque Ports (in succession to Lord Willingdon). The idea was Anthony Bevir's,[1] who suggested it 'sub Rosa' to Alec Hardinge. The PM is much attracted by the historic splendour of the appointment, which was held by Pitt, Wellington and Palmerston, but daunted by the rates, taxes and cost of upkeep of Walmer Castle.[2]

Winston S. Churchill to General Ismay, for the Chiefs of Staff Committee
(*Churchill papers, 20/36*)

12 September 1941
Most Secret

1. It will not be possible for the whole British Army (other than those in the Middle East) to remain indefinitely inert and passive as a garrison of this island against invasion. Such a course, apart altogether from military considerations, would bring the Army into disrepute. I do not need to elaborate this.

[1] Anthony Bevir, 1895–1977. On active service, 1915–18 (despatches twice, badly gassed). Entered the Colonial Office, 1921. Assistant Secretary, War Cabinet Office, 1939. Private Secretary to Neville Chamberlain, 1940; to Churchill, 1940–5; to Clement Attlee, 1945–51; to Churchill, 1951–5, and to Anthony Eden, 1955–6; Secretary for Appointments, 1947–56. CBE, 1944. CVO, 1946. Knighted, 1952.

[2] Churchill accepted the Lord Wardenships of the Cinque Ports. The flag which was a part of his appointment hangs today in his former study at Chartwell.

2. An expeditionary force equivalent to six divisions should be organized for action oversea.

3. Unless unexpected developments open a new theatre in Spain or Morocco, or invasion becomes imminent, we should attempt the liberation of Norway at the earliest suitable moment.

4. A plan should be prepared to act in whatever is thought to be the best place. This plan should be brought before the Defence Committee before the end of the present month.

Winston S. Churchill to Anthony Eden
(*Churchill papers, 20/36*)

12 September 1941

Will you telegraph to Craigie at Tokyo asking him to make sure that the new Foreign Secretary[1] has a chance of reading the warning letter I sent to Matsuoka.[2] It will read better now than it did then.

Winston S. Churchill to the Earl of Athlone[3]
(*Churchill papers, 20/22*)

12 September 1941

My dear Athlone,

How very kind of you to send me the photograph of the statue. I trust it did not deter timid recruits from their original purpose.

Mackenzie King did very well over here, and I think he was pleased with all the arrangements made for his reception and entertainment. I have known him for a great number of years, and we get on very well together. I did not press him on the Conscription issue in Canada. This war is strangely different from the last. In two years' struggle with the greatest military Power, armed with the most deadly weapons, barely 100,000 of our people have been killed, of which nearly half are civilians. It would therefore be hard to argue an immediate necessity for Conscription in Canada.

There was a discreditable incident over here when some of the Canadian soldiers booed the Dominion Prime Minister. Of course they are all 'fed up' with having no fighting and nothing but drill and discipline instead. One can

[1] Matsuoka had been succeeded as Japanese Foreign Minister by Admiral Toyoda.

[2] Churchill's letter of 2 April 1941, printed on pages 439–40.

[3] Prince Alexander of Teck, 1874–1957. Younger brother of the future Queen Mary. In 1904 he married Queen Victoria's granddaughter, Princess Alice. Relinquished his German name, 1917, and created Earl of Athlone (assuming the surname Cambridge). Governor-General of South Africa, 1924–31; of Canada, 1940–46.

easily understand it because at home many of them have farms and businesses of their own to run. Besides there is Party feeling in Canada, and the Government is organized on a Party basis. This cannot be helped.

Very many thanks for all you say so very kindly about me, and I earnestly wish you continued success in your most arduous, responsible task.

Yours very sincerely,
Winston S. Churchill

PS Roosevelt this morning excellent.[1] As we used to sing at Sandhurst, 'Now we shan't be long!?'

Winston S. Churchill and General de Gaulle: discussion[2]
(*Premier papers, 3/120/2*)

12 September 1941 10 Downing Street
12 noon
Most Secret

The Prime Minister said that he had witnessed with very great sorrow the deterioration in General de Gaulle's attitude towards His Majesty's Government. He now felt that he was no longer dealing with a friend. He had received a letter from General de Gaulle on the subject of a recent press interview. Clearly an important person whose utterances carried weight was often in danger of being taken advantage of by newspaper correspondents. But quite apart from this matter, the Prime Minister had received evidence from many sources that General De Gaulle had throughout his recent travels left a trail of Anglophobia behind him everywhere he stepped. This was a most serious matter in all the circumstances, and the Prime Minister had been greatly pained by the accumulation of evidence he had received.

General de Gaulle said that it could not be seriously maintained that he was an enemy of Great Britain. His position and previous record made it inconceivable that he was. He would, however, say frankly that recent events, especially in Syria, had profoundly disturbed him and cast doubts in his mind as to the attitude of many British authorities towards him and the Free French

[1] On 11 September 1941 President Roosevelt broadcast to the United States and to the world, following an unsuccessful torpedo attack on the American destroyer *Greer*, that henceforth any German or Italian vessels of war which entered the Atlantic zone under American protection did so 'at their own peril'. Roosevelt also declared: 'when you see a rattlesnake poised to strike, you do not wait until he has struck before you crush him'. (Broadcast, Washington 11 September 1941: B.D. Zevin (editor), *Nothing to Fear, The Selected Addresses of Franklin Delano Roosevelt, 1932–1945*, London, 1947, pages 287–95.) As well as the *Greer*, on 4 September 1941, a United States merchant ship, the *Steel Seafarer*, had been sunk in the Red Sea on 5 September 1941 by German aircraft, 220 miles south of Suez.

[2] These notes were prepared by the only other person present during the discussion, Captain C.M. Berkeley, of the Offices of the War Cabinet. It was Captain Berkeley who had been Churchill's interpreter during his visits to France in May and June 1940.

Movement. These events, added to the great difficulties of his personal position, to his isolation, and no doubt to the factor of his personal temperament, had led him to utterances which must clearly have been disagreeable to British ears. He wished to express his frank regret for these utterances.

2. Syria.

The Prime Minister said that he had been at great pains before General de Gaulle's arrival in Egypt to make it clear to all concerned that the General was the man he trusted and the man with whom he proposed to work. Everything had been done to smooth the path before General de Gaulle.

No doubt there had been faults on the British side in handling relations, and he could well believe that General de Gaulle had suffered some annoyances. To some extent hitches of this nature were unavoidable, but General de Gaulle knew that he could appeal to the Prime Minister at any moment and that efforts would at once be made to smooth out any difficulty. Instead General de Gaulle had become increasingly antagonistic and had made no communication to the Prime Minister.

General de Gaulle reminded the Prime Minister of his message of the 28th June in which he had stated that any breach over Syria would have the most serious consequences on the Free French Movement. On his arrival in Syria he soon realized that many of the British authorities had no conception of the status of the Free French Movement. He found himself surrounded with political and military authorities who to all appearances had it as their aim to diminish the role of the Free French in Syria. His representatives had endured countless humiliations, and the agreements he had entered into with the Minister of State, apparently to their mutual satisfaction, had remained a dead letter for a whole fortnight.

In normal circumstances difficulties of this sort between two countries would be smoothed out in a moment by their Ambassadors. At a time when France was broken and humiliated, his own efforts to vindicate her must fail if he met with such treatment.

The Prime Minister explained Britain's attitude in regard to Syria. Britain had no ambitions of any sort in that country, and no desire whatever to supplant France. Her one object was the defeat of Hitler, there and everywhere, and nothing must stand in the way of that purpose. Syria was an important unit in the Arab world, as well as one of the military factors in the defence of Egypt. We could not allow a repetition of events in Syria, the repercussions of which in adjacent territories endangered our military position. It followed that we had to be in control in Syria for all purposes connected with the winning of the war. That, he repeated, was the sole purpose that had brought us there.

Clearly the securing of our position in the Arab world involved a transfer of many of the functions previously exercised by France in Syria to the Syrians themselves. The position of France in respect of Syria after the war would be different from that which had obtained before the war, not because Britain would have acquired some of the powers previously exercised by France, but because France would have voluntarily transferred a large part of those powers to the Syrians. That was essential. The Arabs saw no sense in driving out the Vichy French only to be placed under the control of the Free French. They desired their independence, and had been promised it.

Once again Britain sought no selfish advantage, pursued no Imperial ambitions, in Syria. She recognized that France had been preeminent in Syria in the past and that she would still remain preeminent there, as compared with other European countries, after the war, though many of her former powers would have been surrendered. The only British object – and this applied as much to Jibuti as to Syria – was to prosecute the war; but for that purpose we could not tolerate any development which rendered our task more difficult, and which might involve loss of time, effort and even lives.

General de Gaulle denied that he entertained any suspicions of selfish British motives in Syria. Although British and French policies towards the Arab world were not the same, in Syria or elsewhere, there could be no disagreement on the principles laid down by the Prime Minister, and it was he himself who had promised the Syrians their independence.

Similarly he had always recognized the fact that the ultimate military control must rest in British hands. This principle, laid down in the agreements of 7th August, 1940, had been confirmed in his recent negotiations with the Minister of State and had been scrupulously respected – though the British Authorities in Syria had not met this Free French willingness to accept the general authority of their High Command in any helpful or accommodating spirit.

The question was not one of principle – on which there was no disagreement – but one of method, regarding which he maintained that the Free French in Syria had been subjected to constant and unnecessary humiliations.

The Prime Minister said that he would be ashamed to use the British power, which in Syria was overwhelming, for any purpose not essential to the defeat of Hitler. For any such purpose, however, as to assure the necessary degree of security, he would not hesitate to use the full power at our disposal against any one, in the knowledge that he would thus be serving the common cause.

General de Gaulle said that it was natural and good that British forces – whose overwhelming preponderance over the Free French in Syria he did not contest – should be used in all cases where their use would contribute to the defeat of the common foe.

The Prime Minister said that matters now seemed to be going more smoothly in Syria and that the relations between General Catroux and the British Military Authorities were now satisfactory.

He wished to reiterate the point, however, that the British Command could not allow itself to be exposed to dangers which might have been warded off, such as local risings which might spread to adjacent territories. Further, the political situation in Syria must be so handled as to give the Arab world a real measure of satisfaction. He went on to outline the possible course of events in the Middle East in the future, and gave General de Gaulle an estimate of the huge forces we were building up in that area. The British Government were determined to maintain a position which would permit them to hurl the totality of their forces against the enemy when the time came, without having to divert a portion of those forces for the purpose of maintaining the security of the territories upon which we were based. Nothing could be allowed to interfere with the prosecution of the war, and that principle was the touchstone of British policy as far as Syria was concerned.

General de Gaulle said that he fully appreciated what the Prime Minister had said. The Free French would abide by their promises to the Arabs and would play their part in future campaigns, placing their full resources resolutely at the side of the British armies.

The Prime Minister assured General de Gaulle that he was not unmindful of the importance to the common cause of so treating the Free French Movement in Syria as to make the French nation realize that General de Gaulle was the guardian of its interests in Syria, and that those interests were preeminent as compared with those of other European countries. To strengthen General de Gaulle's position in France, he would particularly bear in mind the General's position as defender of the historic connection between France and Syria.

General de Gaulle said that he had much evidence to show that the necessity for the Syrian campaign had been understood in France, and that it had lead to no stirring of anti-British or anti-Free French feeling.

The Prime Minister said that he had been anxious that developments in Syria should not damage General de Gaulle's standing in French eyes. It was no part of British policy to belittle the Free French contribution to the Syrian campaign.

General de Gaulle said that he hoped the Prime Minister had received, together with less welcome reports, echoes of the very deep and sincere admiration for the British Imperial forces which he had repeatedly expressed in the past few weeks.

The Prime Minister then turned to the question of Jibuti. He put the hypothetical case that the Governor might be willing to surrender to the British but not to the Free French, or that he might make it a condition of surrender that the territory would not subsequently be handed over to the Free French. The territory was at present being severely blockaded, but passive resistance might not break down for several months. If such a condition were to be put, would General de Gaulle wish to proceed with this somewhat inconvenient conflict, or would he be prepared to accept the terms and to secure the military use of this important territory for the Allies for the rest of the war?

General de Gaulle said that he attached little importance to the form of the surrender. It might well be that for reasons of prestige, the Vichy Government might impose conditions such as those the Prime Minister had outlined. Those conditions need not, in his judgment, be taken too seriously, and it would be of some importance to avoid giving the enemy an excuse for alleging, as he had done in the case of Syria, that once again British greed had prevailed over the Free French cause. Subject to that proviso, he attached little importance to the actual terms. He asked, however, that the details of the administration of the territory after the surrender should be settled in advance by agreement between the British and Free French Authorities.

In practice the terms of surrender would no doubt leave His Majesty's Government free to make what arrangements they saw fit for the subsequent administration of the territory.

The Prime Minister then turned to the question of the leadership of the Free French Movement. He had come to the conclusion that it would be in the Free French interest if a formal Council were created, which would have an effective voice in shaping the policy of the Movement of which General de Gaulle was the head as the recognized leader of all Free Frenchmen.

General de Gaulle agreed that there would be some advantage in his having about him some body analogous to a government. He had given the matter a good deal of thought, but there were some difficulties. A Council such as the Prime Minister had suggested would only be of value if it consisted of really representative persons. Such representatives would be difficult to find, in view of the profound revolution now in progress in France. Moreover, if the Free French Movement had awakened an echo in the people of France, the reason was largely that it was a movement marked by a very high degree of unanimity. That unanimity had been achieved by avoiding all contact with politics and basing the whole Movement upon the continuance of the struggle against the common foe. The creation of a representative Council would inevitably bring political factors into play, and the unanimity of the Movement might thereby be endangered. He would, however, give the whole question very careful thought. He was already examining the possibility of summoning a Free French Congress of representatives of all the territories which had rallied to the Movement, early next year. Some form of Conseil de Gouvernement might perhaps emerge from that Congress, which would provide the Movement with a democratic basis.

The Prime Minister said that he had a double object in view: to encourage General de Gaulle's supporters in France, and therefore to do nothing which would diminish General de Gaulle's stature as the champion of continued resistance to the enemy; and at the same time to improve relations between His Majesty's Government and the Free French Movement by giving the latter a broader basis. He believed that the latter purpose would be served by the creation of a Council, with whom His Majesty's Government would then deal. He was glad to hear that General de Gaulle proposed to give this matter his earnest attention.

In conclusion, The Prime Minister asked General de Gaulle to realize how important it was to give no ground to the suspicion that he (the General) entertained hostile thoughts towards Great Britain, or even thoughts that might subsequently take on a hostile character. He wished to press this advice upon the General, because already some British figures entertained a suspicion that General de Gaulle had become hostile and had moved towards certain Fascist views which would not be helpful to collaboration in the common cause.

General de Gaulle said that he would give the utmost weight to the Prime Minister's advice. He did not think that the accusation of authoritarian views could be maintained in the light of his most recent statements and of certain further statements he proposed to make. He begged the Prime Minister to understand that the leaders and members of the Free French Movement were necessarily somewhat difficult people; else they would not be where they were. If this difficult character sometimes coloured their attitude towards their great ally, in so far as daily actions and utterances were concerned, he could rest assured that their entire loyalty to Great Britain remained unimpaired.

The Prime Minister said that he would be glad to see General de Gaulle again at some future time if the latter wished. If the Minister of State came home, a meeting *à trois* might be convenient.

Winston S. Churchill to the Duke of Windsor

(*Churchill papers, 20/42*)

13 September 1941
Private and Secret

I am very glad Your Royal Highness's arrangements for visit to United States and Canada are now satisfactorily completed. I also spoke to Mr Mackenzie King about helping your visit to Canada in every possible way. Our dearest wish and greatest need in this country is to have the United States enter the war. It is no use pressing them, but, on the other hand, no word should ever be spoken inconsistent with this object. I hope Your Royal Highness and the Duchess will be most carefully on guard against the manoeuvres of isolationists, who will be eager to entrap you, and would not hesitate to exploit and misrepresent anything you say. I hope, indeed, that your journey will be pleasant and successful. The President is looking forward to seeing you again, and he is our greatest friend. If you require advice on any point, do not hesitate to telegraph personally to me.

Winston S. Churchill to Sir Edward Bridges and General Ismay
(*Churchill papers, 20/36*)

13 September 1941

It is certain that confusion will arise between Bandar Shahpur and Bandar Shah at either end of the Trans-Persian Railway. Therefore for all British official purposes the two places should be called Bandar Caspian and Bandar Gulf. Pray let directions be given in this sense.

Winston S. Churchill to R. A. Butler
(*Churchill papers, 20/36*)

13 September 1941

It would be the greatest mistake to raise the 1902 controversy[1] during the war, and I certainly cannot contemplate a new Education Bill. I think it would also be a great mistake to stir up the public schools question at the present time. No one can possibly tell what the financial and economic state of the country will be when the war is over. Your main task at present is to get the schools working as well as possible under all the difficulties of air attack, evacuation, &c. If you can add to this industrial and technical training, enabling men not required for the Army to take their places promptly in munitions industry or radio work, this would be most useful. We cannot have any Party politics in wartime, and both your second and third points raise these in a most acute and dangerous form. Meanwhile you have a good scope as an administrator.

[1] In 1902, as a young Conservative Member of Parliament, Churchill became involved in the Conservative Government's Education Bill and made a number of speeches expounding its provisions and commending its objects – at the Oxford Union, in Accrington, at Oldham and at Preston. The Education Bill, introduced by A. J. Balfour on March 24, took all secondary and primary education out of the hands of school boards and placed them under the care of county and county borough councils. At the same time, it brought under the control of the local authorities not only the board schools but also the 'voluntary schools' – principally Church schools – whose managers were, however, allowed to retain rights over the appointment of teachers while undertaking to maintain the fabric of the schools. On 21 July 1902 Churchill wrote to his constituency chairman: 'There is, I understand, a very general agreement throughout the party in Oldham, and even in some quarters beyond it, that the Education Bill now before Parliament will in fact effect a real and substantial improvement in the existing system, that it will increase the volume and improve the quality of education, that it gives to Voluntary schools a long-delayed, urgently needed measure of justice, and that for all these reasons it deserves consistent support.'

Winston S. Churchill to Brendan Bracken
(*Churchill papers, 20/36*)

13 September 1941

Surely more stir ought to be made about Hitler shooting the Norwegian Trade Unionists, and sending others for long periods of penal servitude. Ought not the TUC[1] to pass resolutions of sympathy? Why don't you get into touch with Citrine and work up a steady outcry? The names of the two victims should be publicized as martyrs.[2]

Winston S. Churchill to Lord Cherwell
(*Churchill papers, 20/36*)

13 September 1941

Your paper about the Army. It will be necessary to prevent any diminution in the strength of the Army in 1942, and very special measures will have to be adopted to secure this. There can be no question of switching off Army munitions for some time to come. I have asked that an expeditionary force of six divisions, in addition to the two going East, should be prepared. Where it will go must depend on events. What is left will be barely sufficient to give security at home.

The provision of the necessary men will cause great difficulties. I hope, however, that ADGB, ARP,[3] Coastal Defence and the heavy artillery, together with some of the rearward services, may yield two or three hundred thousand men. We shall draw sharply upon reserved occupations. At the present time there is grave danger of several divisions having to be broken up.

Please take the above for your guidance.

[1] The Trades Union Congress, whose General Secretary was Sir Walter Citrine.

[2] On 10 September 1941 the Germans executed two Norwegians prominent in the Trade Union Movement. According to *The Times* two days later, the leading articles of all Swedish newspapers 'expressed disgust at the brutal efforts to subdue a proud Nordic people'. At the same time the funds of all Norwegian trade union and youth organizations were seized and all youth organizations, including the Boy Scouts were made illegal. The two Norwegians arrested and executed on 10 September 1941 were Viggo Hansteen, born in Oslo in 1900, a Supreme Court barrister since 1933, and Senior Legal Adviser to the Norwegian Trade Union Congress; and Rolf Wickstrom, born in Oslo in 1912, a metalworker, and Chief Shop Steward of the Skabo Railway Carriage Works in Oslo. Both men are buried at the Oslo Cathedral Memorial Cemetery. Every May 17 (the National Day) a wreath is laid at the monumental stone erected at their joint burial place.

[3] Air Defence of Great Britain, and Air Raid Precautions.

Winston S. Churchill to General Ismay, for the Chiefs of Staff Committee
(*Churchill papers, 20/36*)

14 September 1941
Action this Day

1. The Air Force demand shows the unbridled use of ground personnel. We are planning to place eighty squadrons in the Middle East by the spring of 1942. There are already 45,000 Air Groundmen there, and it is now proposed to add 40,000 more, making a total of well over 1,000 men to every squadron of sixteen aircraft first-line strength. It is evident that a searching enquiry must be held into these establishments, which on their present scale will ruin our war effort.

In the meanwhile, only 20,000 Air Force personnel can be included in the convoys up to the end of December.

It should be noted that only thirteen Air squadrons are being sent from here, not seventeen, as stated in these papers.

2. The additional divisions should go intact, in accordance with my request to the President. He would never have given me the extra shipping but for the attraction of placing two strong additional divisions in the Middle East. I cannot face him with a demand to use his ships for details and drafts.

3. The above makes a total of 60,000. The troops in para. 3 for India would seem to come next, in view of the four extra divisions we are to get as a result of them. The AT and AA artillery would naturally have precedence over the field and medium, with which ME is already so heavily supplied. 18,000 additional Army Service Corps is a requirement very hard to justify. What particular task is this force, almost equivalent to a division in numbers, needed for?

4. With regard to drafts. The Army of the Nile has not fought lately, and although there is the usual wastage for sickness I cannot feel that drafts to complete the first reinforcements, i.e., 10 per cent. drafts at the base over and above full strength with the units, or drafts to cover estimated additional wastage, should take precedence over organized fighting troops. They should fit in as convenient.

5. Meanwhile, let me have a table showing the present strength of each of the battalions or artillery regiments (British) for which these 31,000 additional drafts are now said to be required. Infantry drafts should receive priority over other branches.

6. Some time ago I had some figures showing the ratio of fighting troops to the rearward services in the Middle East. Could these be brought up to date on the assumption that it was possible to carry the whole 142,000 now asked for?

Winston S. Churchill to Mary Churchill
(Lady Soames papers)

14 September 1941 10 Downing Street

My darling –

Only a line to give you all my love & to tell you how often I think of you & how interested I've been by all y'r cheery letters. Mummie will tell you the rest & the news.

Your ever loving father
Winston S. Churchill

John Martin: letter
(John Martin papers)

14 September 1941

I have had to find a successor to the youngest of the Private Secretaries, Jock Colville, who is being allowed to join the RAF. I have got such a nice boy, whom the PM has accepted, a young captain in the Coldstream Guards.[1]

Winston S. Churchill to Field Marshal Smuts
(Churchill papers, 20/42)

14 September 1941
Personal and Most Secret

I am content with President's action, which can only be judged in relation to actual naval movements concerted at our meeting. His line runs from North Pole down 10th Meridian to about Faroes, then trends away south-west to 26th Meridian, which is followed to the Equator. He will attack any Axis ship found in this vast area. Sixteen U-boats have cut up one of our convoys in the last few days off the tip of Greenland, nearly a thousand miles inside the prohibited zone. When I asked that American destroyers should be sent from Iceland to help our escorts, they went yesterday at once, and, had the U-boats not vanished meanwhile, Anglo-American forces would have been in action together against them. United States assumption of responsibility for all fast British convoys other than troop convoys between America and Iceland

[1] Francis David Wynyard Brown, 1915–67. Third Secretary, Foreign Office, 1938–40. Captain, Coldstream Guards (Brigade Intelligence Officer, 1940–41. Assistant Private Secretary to the Prime Minister, 1941–44; Assistant British Political Adviser, Supreme Headquarters, Allied Expeditionary Force (SHAEF), 1945; Political Division, Central Commission for Germany, 1945–6; First Secretary, British Embassy, Paris, 1949–52; UK Delegate to NATO, Paris, 1952–54; Minister, British Ministry, Ankara, 1959–62. Deputy Minister for the United Kingdom Mission to the United Nations, 1965.

should enable Admiralty to withdraw perhaps forty of the fifty-two destroyers and corvettes we now keep based on Halifax and concentrate them in home waters. This invaluable reinforcement should make killing by hunting groups other than escorts possible for the first time. Hitler will have to choose between losing the Battle of the Atlantic or coming into frequent collision with United States ships and warships. We know that he attaches more importance to starving us out than to invasion. American public have accepted the 'shoot at sight' declaration without knowing the vast area to which it is to be applied, and in my opinion they will support President in fuller and further application of this principle, out of which at any moment war may come. All the above is for your own most secret information.

Winston S. Churchill to Admiral of the Fleet Sir Dudley Pound
(*Churchill papers, 20/36*)

14 September 1941

I obtained the enclosed[1] from C-in-C Fighter Command, and invite your consideration of it. C-in-C Home Fleet would naturally act with any ships he has in the broader waters of the North Sea. Strong flotillas with cruiser support would have to operate against enemy transports in the red shaded area from the Wash to the Isle of Wight. I hope you are adhering to your intention to keep at least one or two heavy ships at Plymouth in the precautionary period. Fighter Command ought to be able to give good protection at times when your ships are working in the red area on definite operations. But we must beware of the waste inflicted upon the Air Force by standing patrol.

Perhaps you will let me have your views at your leisure.

Winston S. Churchill to Arthur Fadden
(*Churchill papers, 20/42*)

14 September 1941
Most Secret and Personal

1. Armoured formations in Middle East excluding Iraq.

(a) Present position. There is one armoured division trained and equipped with British and American cruisers and one Army Tank Brigade equipped with British Infantry tanks.

[1] A letter of 12 September 1941, and map, illustrating the extent to which Fighter Command could protect the Fleet if it were to move southward during a German invasion of Britain.

(b) Future prospects:

(i) By mid-October, there will be another Armoured Brigade completely equipped with British cruisers, and sufficient infantry tanks will have arrived to equip another Army tank battalion.

(ii) Thus, by 1st November, we will have available trained and equipped one armoured division, one armoured brigade, one Army tank brigade and one Army tank battalion.

(iii) By 1st January, 1942, provided present rates of supply of tanks from United Kingdom and United States are maintained, we expect position will be:
2 armoured divisions, trained and equipped.
1 armoured brigade, equipped but not fully trained.
2 Army tank brigades (less one regiment), trained and equipped.

(iv) By April 1942, in addition to (iii), we shall have 1½ armoured divisions organizing and equipping in Middle East and possibly also one Australian armoured brigade, equipped but not fully trained.

(c) Present monthly rates of supply of tanks to Middle East are:

(i) From United Kingdom, 'I' tanks 40, cruisers 30.

(ii) From United States, light cruisers 60, medium cruisers 50.

2. Air strengths. Apparent discrepancy between forecasted and actual figures for bomber and fighter squadrons, as given in my telegrams Nos. 426 and 518, is due in part to figures in latter being exclusive of Malta, whereas those in 426 were not, and in part to forecast in former telegram having proved optimistic. Growth in strength of air force in Middle East (including Malta and Iraq) shown by following comparison of total number of modern types available. Fighters and bombers on 4th April 293, on 18th July 790, and on 1st August 878. Figures include reserves in the command, exclude all aircraft *en route.* Supply of equipment and personnel has kept pace.

3. Present number of squadrons ready for operations and equipped with modern aircraft in Middle East, inclusive of Malta – fighters 18, medium bombers 9, heavy bombers 4, Army co-operation 2, general reconnaissance 3½. These are backed by substantial reserves. There are also a number of squadrons equipped with obsolescent types.

4. Future prospects. Two additional fighter and two additional medium bomber squadrons are due to be formed by end September. Our present aim is to build up to a total of 26 fighter, 17 medium bomber, 2 Beaufort, 5 heavy bomber, 6 Army co-operation, 2½ general reconnaissance and 4 transport squadrons, making total first-line strength of about 1,000 aircraft.

5. Air support of Army. Whole strength of air force is available for support of the Army whenever military situation demands, but at other times air power must be used against enemy as thought best by Air Officer Commanding-in-Chief. At present time, major fighter effort is being

employed to ensure supplies by sea to Tobruk. Need for giving full air support to the Army is entirely recognized, but we consider that the only air units which should be permanently allotted to the Army are those required for tactical reconnaissance. Essence of problem of cooperation between Army and air forces lies in adequate training and good communications, and not in providing numbers of aircraft restricted to one specialized rôle. Advantage is being taken of present lull to perfect intercommunication systems and exercise ground staff and air crews in their use. General Officer Commanding-in-Chief and Air Officer Commanding-in-Chief are working in close conjunction to improve general standard of training in air cooperation.

Winston S. Churchill to Anthony Eden and L. S. Amery
(*Churchill papers, 20/36*)

14 September 1941

This telegram,[1] like all Indian messages, is windy and wordy. The writer's estimate differs from the facts in our possession, and leads to mere procrastination. Pray consider it together and advise upon action.

Why should we suppose things will be better in a month, except that the Russians will be nearer the winter?

In para. 3 he talks about 'Germans marching through Afghanistan to invade India'. This seems to overlook the immense distances they have to travel, and the fact that they must fight their way against both Russian and British forces.

Winston S. Churchill to Colonel Davidson[2]
(*Churchill papers, 20/36*)

14 September 1941

INTELLIGENCE NOTES ABOUT RUSSIA[3]

I don't see the point of reiterating these 'Most Secret' labels. It is sufficient to give the information which you think trustworthy without reference to its source. The document itself should be labelled 'Most Secret – to be burnt', but

[1] Telegram No. 308 from the British Minister, Kabul, Sir Francis Wylie, on the policy to be pursued in Afghanistan.

[2] Francis Henry Norman Davidson, 1892–1973. Entered the Army, 1911. On active service in France and Flanders, 1914–19 (wounded, despatches four times, Military Cross and bar, Distinguished Service Order). Commander Corps Royal Artillery, 1st Corps, British Expeditionary Force, 1939–40. Director of Military Intelligence, War Office, 1940–44. British Army Staff, Washington, 1944–46. Colonel Commandant, Intelligence Corps, 1952–60.

[3] These notes were based upon intercepted German top secret radio signals decrypted at Bletchley Park.

the words 'Most Secret' should in the next few days be dropped gradually from the text.

Winston S. Churchill to Air Chief Marshal Sir Charles Portal
(*Churchill papers, 20/36*)

15 September 1941

1. I thank you for your proposed action, which as you say deals with perhaps the greatest Air operational problem.[1]

2. I hazard this suggestion. Send a stratosphere airplane with a marker bomb of delay-action, and let it fall in the built-up area to be attacked. At the right time in the night this bomb should explode and begin to burn through the orifice, thus guiding the night bombers. Alternatively, can you not drop a bomb, which although buried in the ground will contain a wireless beacon to which our instruments are specially responsive?

3. It is an awful thought that perhaps three-quarters of our bombs go astray. If we could make it half and half we should virtually have doubled our bombing power.

Winston S. Churchill to David Margesson
(*Churchill papers, 20/36*)

15 September 1941
Most Secret

I have had discussions with Sir Alan Brooke and the Adjutant-General[2] on the subject of manpower and the army at home, and I send you my views on the subject.

1. General Brooke has 900,000 men, out of which he forms 20 motorised, 9 County and 6 armoured divisions, together with 10 brigades and other units equivalent to 3 more divisions, total 38 divisions. This works out at under 24,000 men to the division, which is quite a clean lay-out.

2. On no account should any of these divisions be broken up during 1942,

[1] The number of British bomber aircraft which failed to find their targets.

[2] Ronald Forbes Adam, 1885-1982. On active service, France, Flanders and Italy, 1914-18 (despatches, Distinguished Service Order). Succeeded his father, as second Baronet, 1926. Deputy Chief of the Imperial General Staff, 1938-39. General Officer Commanding-in-Chief, Northern Command, 1939-40. Knighted, 1941. Adjutant-General to the Forces, 1941-46. Colonel Commandant, Royal Army Dental Corps, 1945-51. Chairman and Director-General of the British Council, 1946-54. President of the Middlesex Cricket Club (MCC), 1946-47. Member of the Miners' Welfare Committee, 1946-52. Chairman of the National Institute of Industrial Psychology, 1947-52. Principal, Working Men's College, 1956-61. President of the United Nations Association.

or any of the combatant units in these divisions eliminated, except by conversion to other forms of combatant service, i.e., machine-gun regiments into anti-tank regiments, or infantry divisions into armoured divisions. If for any reason at any time shortage of men leads to units being below strength, the cadres should be maintained in spite of the arguments against overheads. Thus if we have need to expand, these cadres can be filled up to full strength. The suppression of combatant cadres cannot be accepted.

3. Outside General Brooke's command the War Office have a million men in Great Britain and 100,000 in Northern Ireland. They also have their annual intake of the nineteen-year-olds, and the 125,000 men I have sanctioned from civil life. It is from these sources in the first place that the means of keeping up the strength of General Brooke's army must be found.

4. The first and largest source is ADGB[1] This is rapidly becoming an abuse. It absorbs 280,000 men and we are confronted with a demand for an additional 50,000 men. No addition of any kind can be allowed to ADGB other than the recruitment of women. We got through last year's Air attacks with a far weaker Home Defence than we now have. All plans involving increased manpower of ADGB should be resisted. If it should be desired to multiply the number of guns, this must be done by producing the number of men from existing guns, and where possible by bringing in Home Guard, who will for this special work receive a fee for attending drills. A certain measure of relaxation of instant readiness may be given in some districts. The increases which we must make in the mobile flak can always be used to reinforce towns which become the subject of special attack. It is not by any means certain that the attack will be on the same scale as before, and unlikely that it will take continuous form.

5. The coast batteries are continually growing and devouring more men. Here, too, an alteration of the relief system, the part employment of Home Guard, an increasing differentiation in the scale of efficiency and readiness in various areas must be made to give relief. No increase in the manpower of Coast Defence can be accepted.

6. Should we get through this winter without increased severity of Air attack, a substantial combing of ARP must be expected, together with ever-increasing dilution of ADGB. Far too much of our strength is being absorbed in passive defence. Only a certain amount of our manpower can be employed on defence against air raiding, whether in batteries, search-lights, smoke apparatus, night-fighter squadrons, or the many forms of radio defence. Every new idea starts a new Service, and all these Services attempt to grow continuously. We cannot accept this if the mobile and offensive character of our field army is to be maintained.

[1] Air Defence of Great Britain.

7. The Adjutant-General has explained to me all the measures which he is taking to comb the rearward Services. Some lowering of the numbers employed in heavy and medium batteries (without destruction of cadres) might perhaps be considered. The troops employed in home defence should have their motor transport narrowly adapted to the rôles they may be expected to play. They should on no account be treated as if they were divisions in the line on a French front with 500 miles communication to the ports. Due consideration must be given to the fact that they live and act in this well-supplied country and in close proximity to its factories and repair shops. Every addition to brigade, divisional, corps, or other staffs should be rigorously criticized and the habit of detaching men from battalions for such a purpose corrected.

8. I am very glad to hear that it will be possible to halve the number of training schools owing to the fact that we now have only to deal with the normal intake. The Royal Army Service Corps repair depots should in every command be merged with those of the Royal Army Ordnance Corps.

9. It is only when all these and many other expedients have been stringently applied that the question of further demands upon the civil population will fall to be considered. I am prepared to face this if I am satisfied that everything in human power has been done to promote the higher combative power of the army from its own existing resources.

10. It will be necessary to form as soon as possible an Expeditionary Force for action either on the Northern or the Southern flank of the enemy's western coasts. This force should consist of not less than the equivalent of two armoured and four motorized divisions, and should be ready to act in the early part of 1942. It should be organized under GHQ, Home Forces, and it seems worthy of consideration whether its actual command, should it come into action, should not also be directed from this centre. As we have also to provide two more British divisions shortly for the Middle East, it will be seen how imperative the upkeep of the Home Army has become.

Pray let me have your thought on all these matters with a view to giving effect to the policy here outlined.

War Cabinet: minutes
(*Cabinet papers, 65/19*)

15 September 1941 10 Downing Street
5 p.m.

The War Cabinet had before them a Memorandum by the Foreign Secretary (WP(41) 219) on the question whether we should declare war on Finland, Hungary and Roumania. In his view, the arguments against declaring war on the last two countries were conclusive. As regards Finland, he recommended that we should neither threaten nor issue a declaration of war unless strongly pressed by the Soviet Government.

General agreement was expressed with the view that we should not declare war on Hungary or Roumania at this juncture, as this would serve no useful purpose.

As regards Finland, the Prime Minister thought that, by a threat of war, we might achieve something. He thought we should indicate to Finland that continued invasion of Russia by Finnish forces must inevitably lead to a declaration of war by us.

The Prime Minister reminded the War Cabinet that in June last the War Cabinet had considered the proposal for a large-scale exercise to test plans for the defence of London against an airborne attack. Doubts had been expressed about the scheme, and a decision had been deferred.

The Chiefs of Staff no longer wished to hold the exercise this autumn, but felt that the project should not be abandoned altogether.

The Prime Minister said that it should be an instruction to all Departments concerned in the preparations against invasion that our defences and preparations should continue throughout the winter, and that Departments should be prepared to carry out a large scale exercise in the early spring. He invited Ministers concerned to give the necessary instructions to their Departments.

The War Cabinet took note, with approval, of this statement.

The Prime Minister said he had had a long talk with General de Gaulle on Friday, the 12th September. He gave the War Cabinet a short account of the interview, a written record of which would be circulated. Perhaps the main point of interest was the proposal to form a Council for the Free French Movement.

There could now be some relaxation in the attitude of caution which had been enjoined upon Departments in their relations with the Free French.

The Prime Minister informed the War Cabinet[1] that the Commonwealth Government had insisted on the withdrawal of the Australian Division from Tobruk. He read out his Most Secret and Personal telegrams to the Prime Minister of Australia and a Most Secret and Personal telegram from the Prime Minister of Australia.

In discussion the view was expressed that the decision was a lamentable one; but that the sooner the operation of withdrawing the Australians from Tobruk was carried out the better. If possible they should all be moved out during the present month. The Chiefs of Staff had already telegraphed to the Commanders-in-Chief to make plans for the withdrawal of the Australian troops from Tobruk.

[1] This, and the remaining War Cabinet discussion printed here, were not circulated to Ministers, but retained in typescript in the War Cabinet's Confidential Annex (*Cabinet papers, 65/23*).

The Prime Minister reminded the War Cabinet of the request which he had made to President Roosevelt to give us the use of Naval transports to carry additional British troops to the Middle East. At the time that he had made this request he had contemplated that we should send out two additional British Divisions to the Middle East. The military authorities now proposed to send out a large number of reinforcements, drafts, and RAF ground personnel. The Prime Minister said that he did not feel able to tell President Roosevelt that we had abandoned the idea of sending two additional Divisions to the Middle East but still wanted the use of the ships.

The Prime Minister added that it now appeared that President Roosevelt would allow the ships to make a second trip.

Winston S. Churchill to Arthur Fadden
(*Churchill papers, 20/42*)

15 September 1941
Most Secret

Orders will at once be given in accordance with your decision. The maintenance of secrecy for the present is of the highest consequence to all.

Winston S. Churchill to J. V. Stalin
(*Churchill papers, 20/42*)

16 September 1941

I am most anxious to settle our alliance with Persia and to make an intimate efficient working arrangement with your forces in Persia. There are in Persia signs of serious disorder among tribesmen and of breakdown of Persian authority. Disorder, if it spreads, will mean wasting our divisions holding down these people, which again means burdening the road and railway communications with movements and supplies of aforesaid divisions, whereas we want to keep the lines clear and improved to the utmost in order to get supplies through to you. Our object should be to make the Persians keep each other quiet while we get on with the war. Your Excellency's decisive indications in this direction will speed forward the already favourable trend of our affairs in this minor theatre.

Winston S. Churchill to Colonel Hollis, for the Chiefs of Staff Committee
(*Churchill papers, 20/36*)

17 September 1941

1. All possible must be done to accelerate the movement and turn-around of the fast American transports in order to secure to us the benefits of a second trip. The sailing of these transports from America must not be delayed for the sake of carrying the Canadian Armoured Troops. To carry them is convenient but not essential. The delay of reloading of these ships in UK ports from October 23 to November 15 cannot be accepted. An evolution should be made of putting No. 1 extra division on board in the shortest time. At least a fortnight should be saved on this if it can be reconciled with convoy movements.

2. The Field State of the Army of the Nile is good. This is not surprising considering they have taken nearly five months' rest from all fighting. The 60 British battalions average 880 and the 45 artillery regiments are only short by 9 per cent. It is inconceivable that more than a quarter of this artillery can be heavily engaged in continuous bombardment during the next four months. Drafts for the artillery cannot therefore have high priority. The six Tank Transporter and sixteen Standard MT Companies deserve a high place. This applies also to the naval relief, to the Indian reinforcements (which are the seed-corn), and to the artillery, &c., for the two new Indian divisions in Iraq. 10,000 to 20,000 drafts for the infantry can be worked in as convenient, and there may be some specialist items in the RASC[1] field which are urgently needed. Let us remember, however, nothing can get there before Crusader.[2] Malaya can wait and West Africa can be fitted in or not as convenient. The problem we have to settle is one of priority.

3. The supreme object to be aimed at is to send British divisions Nos. 1 and 2 to the Middle East in accordance with the proposal made to President Roosevelt. Spreading the movement over another month or two, especially if we get the American second trip, will surely provide for all the desiderata. There is no question of saying that anything *never* goes.

4. I look to the Air Ministry to make the existing squadrons in ME go forward with their expansion to 62½ squadrons by all the methods of improvisation which under great pressure they are now adopting. They should keep the first place in their 20,000 allocation for the 12,000 necessary to sustain the thirteen new squadrons and the backing for the other four from South Africa.

5. I should be grateful if these points could be woven into a revised programme of reinforcements for the Middle East, and I shall be very glad to

[1] Royal Army Service Corps.

[2] Operation planned for the Western Desert, to drive the Germans and Italians from Cyrenaica.

discuss any difficulties outstanding with the COS Committee tonight or tomorrow night.

Winston S. Churchill to General Sir John Dill
(*Churchill papers, 20/36*)

17 September 1941

OPERATIONS IN THE WESTERN DESERT, 14–15 SEPTEMBER 1941

Why do you suppose our troops immediately retreated when they saw the German reconnaissance in force coming towards them? It is true they followed them up later in the day when the Germans had achieved their object and were retiring. But would not this advance by the enemy into the open desert outside all protection from mines, masked A/T batteries &c., have given a fine opportunity for a vigorous counter-stroke and a smart action under equal conditions in the open?

I should be glad if you could enlighten me.

Winston S. Churchill to William Mackenzie King
(*Churchill papers, 20/42*)

17 September 1941
Personal and Most Secret

1. Hitler wants to find out all he can about our convoys, not only in order to try to sink our ships, but also to sabotage their cargoes and to make mischief among their crews. We are doing all we can to defeat him by perfecting security arrangements in our own ports and also in neutral ports, in South America and elsewhere.

2. The United States are taking similar precautions. Their Security Service is working closely with our own.

3. I feel sure you must have been deeply impressed by the report made to the Canadian Chiefs of Staff at the request of the Chief of the Canadian Naval Staff by the British Naval Security Mission under Brigadier Craig,[1] Royal Marines, which has recently toured the Western Hemisphere.

4. We have studied this report carefully here to see what further lessons we could learn for the protection of our end of the Atlantic bridge, and how we

[1] Archibald Maxwell Craig, 1895–1953. Joined Royal Marines, 1912. Staff Officer, Intelligence, Staff of Commander-in-Chief North America and West Indies, 1930–32. Assistant (later Deputy) Director of Naval Intelligence, 1938–40. Second in Command, Portsmouth and Plymouth Divisions, Royal Marines, 1941–42. British Naval Security Mission, 1941. Commanded Chatham Division, Royal Marines, 1942–44. Retired, 1944 with the rank of Major-General. Director, Air Survey Company of Rhodesia, 1948.

might help each other. Halifax and Liverpool or Glasgow are equally important to us both.

5. So technical is security in war, and of such wide application, that I have thought well to appoint Lord Swinton,[1] who is of Ministerial standing, to co-ordinate our own security arrangements and to report direct to me.

6. We have found by experience that there are two prerequisites of security in war:

(a) An efficient Security Service centrally controlled, enjoying wide powers under the law and operating specially in all ports and key places.

(b) A system of 'protected areas' where security measures are rigidly enforced.

7. I should be very grateful if you would give your personal attention to Brigadier Craig's report and offer you any help which it is in my power to give. Would it aid you were I to lend you officers with special training and wartime experience in security to collaborate with the officers of your Government in working out the necessary measures for our common protection?

Winston S. Churchill to General Auchinleck
(*Churchill papers, 20/42*)

17 September 1941
Personal and Most Secret

1. I am grieved at Australian attitude, but I have long feared the dangerous reactions on Australian and world opinion of our seeming to fight all our battles in the Middle East only with Dominion troops. For this reason, apart from desire to reinforce you, I have constantly pressed sending out some British Infantry Divisions. Your decision to put 50th Division in Cyprus was, as you know, painful to us. I know that when you put it there you thought Cyprus was a place of special danger, but situation has been changed by Russian war and I am sure you will continue to review employment of this British division in what looks like a safe defensive rôle.

2. All the more do I feel it necessary to send to the Middle Eastern theatre the two additional British divisions from home. For this large project I felt able to appeal to President Roosevelt, feeling sure it would attract him. In the result he has made a very fine proposal to send six of his finest fast American transports to make one trip or perhaps two between Britain and ME. Apart from actual help in transportation, the arrival of these ships, manned by United States personnel and flying the American flag through the U-boat zone

[1] Then Chairman of the Security Executive (for his biographical note, see page 1241, note 3).

and in British harbours, is another important forward step towards full American action.

3. I was therefore very much disturbed to receive your No. Susan CS/52 making little of the arrival of these divisions and preferring a mass of details and drafts. I cannot approach the President again upon so complete a change in what I proposed to him. One division must go at once in American transports; I hope also to send the other division in British transports. It may be necessary, however, to relegate this other division to the second trip.

4. I cannot agree to assign highest priority to 35,000 more Air-groundmen for the Middle East. This would mean 80,000 to 85,000 Air personnel to keep only a maximum of eighty squadrons in active operations, or 1,000 groundmen to every squadron of sixteen aircraft in action. The Air Ministry have been requested to revise their immediate demands.

5. I have studied attentively your Field States and was relieved to see that your sixty infantry battalions average 880 and your forty-five regiments of artillery are only on the average 9 per cent below strength. It is impossible to imagine a situation in the next four months when you will be using any great mass of artillery in continuous bombardment. Therefore I cannot feel that artillery drafts should have a high priority. Infantry drafts are good whenever they can come, but they must yield priority at the present time. I hope to send you 20,000. High priorities will be given to six Tank Transporter Corps and sixteen Standard MT Corps and to various specialist units of the RASC. Anyhow, nothing material can now reach you before Zero day. In the meantime no cadres are to be destroyed without previous sanction from here. You should notify us of any which have fallen exceptionally low. All deficiencies can be made good early next year. The immediate problem is one of priorities. We are not making an army to conform to conventional establishments, but to achieve definite tactical, strategic and political objectives. Improvisation cannot be excluded from the duties of the Military and Air Staffs.

6. I trust Australian withdrawal will not further delay offensive. The situation has already worsened. The enemy are far better supplied with petrol. African Panzer Corps is now called African Panzer Gruppe.[1] By waiting until you have an extra brigade you may well find you have to face an extra division. Various names of significant places are now creeping in to the Special Information. Your movements of transport and formation of dumps are noted by the enemy. The whole future of the campaign of 1942 in ME and our relations with Turkey and Russia are involved.

[1] Not entirely correct: the Deutsches Afrika Korps, which Churchill incorrectly calls the Afrika Panzer Korps, known to the British as the Africa Corps, had not changed its name. The Panzergruppe Afrika was a new, higher headquarters, almost equivalent to an Army Headquarters and about to become one. Rommel had been appointed to command this new HQ: it consisted of two corps, the Africa Corps and the XX1 (Italian) Corps.

Winston S. Churchill to Oliver Lyttelton
(*Churchill papers, 20/42*)

18 September 1941
Personal and Secret

1. Impossible that Auchinleck should suppose we do not agree with him. My whole series of telegrams, including especially mine of September 11 to Fadden, which was repeated to Auchinleck and is now repeated to you herewith, shows how strongly we deprecate Australian resolve to quit the line at this juncture. Moreover I particularly stimulated Auchinleck when he was at home not to prejudice defence of Tobruk by making a needless relief.

2. I was astounded at Australian Government's decision, being sure it would be repudiated by Australia if the facts could be made known. Allowances must be made for a Government with a majority only of one faced by a bitter Opposition, parts of which at least are isolationist in outlook.

3. It is imperative that no public dispute should arise between Great Britain and Australia. All personal feelings must therefore be subordinated to appearance of unity. Trouble has largely arisen through our not having any British infantry divisions in the various actions, thus leading the world and Australia to suppose that we are fighting our battles with Dominion troops only.

4. I am telegraphing to Auchinleck to assure him of Chiefs of Staff's full agreement with his military views.

Winston S. Churchill to General Auchinleck
(*Cabinet papers, 65/23*)

18 September 1941
Personal and Secret

Minister of State tells me you are distressed by Australian attitude and Blamey's conduct. I therefore assure you that the Chiefs of the Staff entirely endorse the military views expressed in your 1558 of 10.9.41. So do Cabinet and I. We telegraphed this to Australia, feeling confident they would accept it as decisive. Great allowances must be made for a Government with a majority of one playing politics with a bitter Opposition, part of whom at least are isolationist in sentiment. Whatever your and our personal feelings may be, it is our duty at all costs to prevent an open dispute with the Australian Government. Any public controversy would injure foundations of Empire and be disastrous to our general position in the war. Everything must be borne with patience, and in the end all will come right.[1] You have all our sympathy and confidence.

War Cabinet: minutes
(*Cabinet papers, 65/23*)

18 September 1941 — 10 Downing Street
12 noon

The Prime Minister said that he had received a disturbing telegram from the Minister of State saying that General Auchinleck was perturbed by the Australian Government's insistence that their troops should be withdrawn from Tobruk. The General had gone so far as to prepare a telegram asking to be relieved of his command, as the Australian refusal to allow their troops to remain in Tobruk was based on military and not political grounds. It seemed that the telegram from the Australian Government had followed one which they had received from General Blamey, and which the latter had not shown to the Commander-in-Chief. General Auchinleck also thought that perhaps His Majesty's Government endorsed the opposite military view to his own. This view was, of course, erroneous. The Minister of State had persuaded General Auchinleck not to send the telegram.

The Prime Minister then read to the War Cabinet a telegram which he had sent to the Commander-in-Chief to the effect that the Cabinet, himself and the Chiefs of Staff entirely endorsed his military views in this matter and had been confident that the Australian Government would regard them as decisive. He should, however make allowance for the political situation in Australia. The Prime Minister had ended up by assuring General Auchinleck of our sympathy and confidence and asking him to have patience. The Prime Minister added that at the proper time it would be necessary to inform the Australian Government of this difficulty we had had with the Commander-in-Chief. It also might be desirable to find a relief for General Blamey.

USSR

The Prime Minister said that he had sent a telegram to M. Stalin saying that the Harriman Mission and ourselves were now engaged on working out a programme of monthly deliveries to Russia and that the Joint Mission hoped to arrive by the 25th September. In this telegram the Prime Minister said that he had also referred to the importance of the route through Persia and had said that the possibility of military cooperation with the Russians on their

[1] 'All will come right': a phrase Churchill which had first heard forty years earlier, during the Boer War, and which he often used. The Afrikaans, *Ales sal reg kom*, was the motto of Martinius Steyn, the Boer leader and President of the Orange Free State.

southern front were being examined by our Military Advisers. He had also referred to the importance to Turkey.

The Secretary of State for Foreign Affairs said that he had seen M. Maisky on the previous day and he had stated that the Russians were most anxious for help on their southern front.

The Prime Minister said that the possibility of helping them here would have to be examined. The position would, of course, be much easier if the position of our western flank in Libya was cleared. A move in this direction would greatly impress the Turks. The Russians should realize, however, that if there was a large British force in the Caucasus, that would largely occupy the capacity of the Trans-Persian railway, and would diminish the flow of supplies to Russia by that route. It was also important that M. Stalin should realize the importance of our supplying Turkey with as much material as possible. If we sent everything to Russia we might discourage the Turks from coming in on our side.

The Prime Minister said that it must be remembered that until Russia entered the war we had expected to receive ourselves the whole extractable surplus of American supplies. Now that Russia was in the war we should have to make sacrifices. We can only hope that under pressure from us, the Americans would make further efforts to increase their production. He thought it would be good thing if, when final figures had been arrived at as to what the Russians were to receive, they could be presented in a form which showed, broadly, equal contributions from the Americans and from ourselves.

Winston S. Churchill to Colonel Hollis, for the Chiefs of Staff Committee
(*Churchill papers, 20/36*)

18 September 1941

TRANSPORT OF TWO INFANTRY DIVISIONS TO THE MIDDLE EAST

It is our duty to take a view about whether serious fighting will take place or not in the interval before all convoys arrive. It should not be assumed that the risk of this is evenly spread over the whole period, and that at any given moment we must provide the maximum addition of effective fighting strength. It would seem that the only serious fighting to be expected is our long-delayed offensive in the Western Desert, for which nothing more can now arrive in time. However, should this offensive succeed, very great strain will be thrown upon the transport (RASC) services, including specialized RASC units, either to hold the ground gained or to make an ambitious leap forward to the west. In these circumstances I am disposed to meet, if possible the RASC requirements, which at first I thought excessive. 13,500 are provided in the COS minute; 4,000 more could be obtained by delaying the five infantry battalions promised to India in the October convoy. There seems more urgency in the former than in the latter case. India is no doubt very thin, but on this new showing they will still receive 7,900, namely, three battalions plus drafts for expansion. This is a considerable infusion of white troops. Therefore, I wish the five battalions, 4,000, to be delayed till the New Year, and the 4,000 passages saved devoted to reinforcement of the RASC for ME. It should be explained to India that the delay is only a short one and that the expansion programme should proceed.

2. It is difficult to see from what quarter and by what line of advance other 'serious fighting' will develop in the period covered by our convoys to the end of 1941 and their arrival by the end of February 1942. In this five-months period it is not likely that Turkey will open the door to a German invasion of Syria, and still less likely that, if she refuses, a way through Asia Minor can be forced by the enemy. Unless there is a complete collapse of Russia the Germans will be chary of embarking on a major war with Turkey, costing perhaps another million men. Therefore, I cannot see the risk of invasion of Syria, Palestine, &c., from the north as likely to be operative before the winter is over – say, March. This is also the view which has been taken in various COS papers.

3. The only other route by which serious attack can fall upon us is through the Caucasus and across the Caspian. This presupposes the mastery of the Black Sea, in which the Russians have at present an overwhelming naval superiority, involving the capture of Sebastopol and also of Novorossisk, the subsequent traversing of the Caucasus from Batum to Baku, or alternatively a movement north of the Black Sea and through the Caucasus from north to south. This would be a prohibitive winter operation. A third possibility would be a German march round the Caspian, forcing the line of the Volga and destroying the last reserve armies of Russia. This is plainly an operation impossible to complete within the next six months, unless we assume the surrender or collapse of Russia. Unless this happens the Caspian, strongly held by Russian naval forces, must remain a great shield to the northward.

4. Therefore, in order to bring about the 'serious fighting' suggested, Turkey and/or Russia must yield in the period mentioned or the Germans must force their way from Anatolia or through the Caucasus or round the north of the Caspian. A sensible practical view of the admitted uncertainties of war should exclude all these possibilities before the spring of 1942.

5. I cannot therefore accept the theory of continuous even risk from day to day, and I consider that we are justified in relying upon no 'serious fighting' other than in the Western Desert in this theatre till March 1942, unless, of course, we choose to take the offensive. In these circumstances I feel free to give proper weight to the major political-strategic issues involved in the broad decision to send two additional divisions in the van of the reinforcements.

6. What are these considerations? First, the moral need of our having a

substantial, recognizable British stake and contribution in the Middle East, and freeing ourselves from the imputation, however unjust, of always using other people's troops and blood. Secondly, the effect produced upon Turkey by our being able to add two divisions to the forces already mentioned in the Staff conversations, thus appreciably increasing the chances of influencing Turkish action. Thirdly, the basis of my appeal to the President, which I do not wish upset. Fourthly, the possibility that these two divisions may move in by Basra, in order to give an effective right-hand to the Russian reserve forces to the north of the Caspian.

The various alternatives will remain open to us in the three months during which these divisions will be in transit.

7. In deciding, therefore, between A, B and C, I hope full consideration may be given to these arguments. The difference between A and B is only 14,000 men, less 4,000 additional RASC obtained by cutting India, equals 10,000 men. On this difference depends the broad gesture of carrying two complete British divisions to the eastern theatre with a three months' option of where they will be brought into play.

Winston S. Churchill to J. V. Stalin

(*Foreign Office papers, 954/24*)

18 September 1941
Personal and Secret

Many thanks for your message.[1] The Harriman Mission has all arrived and is working all day long with Beaverbrook and his colleagues. The object is to survey the whole field of resources so as to be able to work out with you a definite programme of monthly delivery by every available route and thus help repair so far as possible losses of your munition industries. President Roosevelt's idea is that this first plan should cover up till end of June, but naturally we shall go on with you till victory. I hope the Conference may open in Moscow 25th of this month, but no publicity should be given till all are safely gathered. The routes and method of travel will be signalled later.

2. I attach great importance to opening the through route from Persian Gulf

[1] On 15 September 1941 Churchill had received a telegram from Stalin, stating that the absence of a 'second front simply favours the designs of our common enemy'. Stalin went on to ask, as German forces drove ever further eastwards across the Ukraine, that twenty-five to thirty British Divisions should be sent to Archangel, or transported through Persia, in order to fight in the 'southern regions' of the Soviet Union. This, Stalin added, would constitute 'a serious blow' against German aggression (Personal Message, dated Kremlin, 13 September 1941, received in London, 15 September 1941: *Foreign Office papers, 954/24, folio 403*). Reading this, Churchill later recalled his feelings. It was 'almost incredible', he wrote, that the head of the Russian Government, with all his military experts, 'could have committed himself to such absurdities. It seemed hopeless to argue with a man thinking in terms of utter unreality'. (Winston S. Churchill, *The Second World War*, Volume 3, London, 1950, page 411)

to Caspian, not only by railway but by a great motor road, in the making of which we hope to enlist American energies and organization. Lord Beaverbrook will be able to explain the whole scheme of supply and transportation; he is on the closest terms of friendship with Harriman.

3. All possible theatres in which we might effect military cooperation with you have been examined by the Staffs. The two flanks, North and South, certainly present the most favourable opportunities. If we could act successfully in Norway the attitude of Sweden would be powerfully affected, but at the moment we have neither the forces nor the shipping available for this project. Again in the south the great prize is Turkey; if Turkey can be gained another powerful army will be available. Turkey would like to come with us but is afraid, not without reason. It may be that the promise of considerable British forces and supplies of technical material in which the Turks are deficient will exercise a decisive influence upon them. We will study with you any other form of useful aid, the sole object being to bring the maximum force against the common enemy.

4. I entirely agree that the first source from which the Russian fleet should be replenished should be at the expense of Germany. Victory will certainly give us control of important German and Italian naval vessels and in our view these would be most suitable for repairing losses to the Russian fleet.

Winston S. Churchill to Arthur Colgate[1]

(*Churchill papers, 20/22*)

19 September 1941

Dear Mr Colgate,

The late member for the Wrekin[2] was a victim of the pirates of the Atlantic in peculiarly dastardly circumstances. As much as any man who has died in the fighting line, he gave his life for his country and his name is honoured.

The electors of the Wrekin might well have been spared the worry, trouble and cost of a contested by-election in these fateful days when our whole attention should be concentrated upon the war effort. But your return as the official candidate supporting the National Government has been challenged,

[1] Arthur Colegate, 1884–1956. A Director of Brunner Mond & Co. President of the Industrial Property Committee of the International Chamber of Commerce, 1925–29. Unsuccessful Conservative candidate, Sowerby, 1929. Vice-Chairman, Midland Union of Conservative Associations. Conservative Member of Parliament for Wrekin, 1941–45; for Burton, 1950–55. Knighted, 1955.

[2] James Baldwin-Webb, 1894–1940. On active service, 1914–18 (Battle of the Somme). Retired from the army with the rank of Colonel, 1932. Member of Birmingham City Council from 1925. Conservative Member of Parliament for the Wrekin (Shropshire) from 1931 until his death. While on a mission to Canada, he was drowned in the torpedoing of the *City of Benares* (when eighty-three evacuee children were also drowned).

and I hope and believe that on Friday next the electors will give you a decisive victory. It is a public duty of real importance for every elector to record a vote when called upon to do under our free constitution.

National unity is the foundation of our strength. The country is fighting to overcome the greatest peril which has ever faced the liberties of the world and your return as member for the Wrekin will be still further proof that the nation stands firm and steadfast by the principles of cooperation and mutual help.

Yours sincerely,
Winston S. Churchill

John Martin: diary
(*John Martin papers*)

[19 September 1941]

The house[1] came to life again on Friday for a luncheon the PM gave to the British and American Missions to Moscow. It was quite a triumph for the Government Hospitality Fund and the Ministry of Works, who only received their orders the evening before. One of the big reception rooms upstairs, at present unfurnished, had to be hastily prepared, floors cleaned, tables and chairs brought in and decorations arranged. We had to do without pictures, but the bare walls (and broken window frames) gave an appropriate note of wartime austerity.

War Cabinet, Defence Committee (Operations): minutes
(*Cabinet papers, 120/36*)

19 September 1941
6 p.m.

AID TO RUSSIA

The Prime Minister referred to a telegram he had just received from President Roosevelt in which the President said that he hoped United States production of tanks would rise to 1,400 a month in May, 1942. The Prime Minister enquired what effect this would have upon the results of the recent discussions with the Americans.

Lord Beaverbrook said that the President's figure indicated an increase of about 350 tanks per month in the month of May, but American estimates were most unreliable and too much importance should not therefore be attached to this one. They had, for example, promised us forty medium tanks in September and had only produced six.

[1] 10 Downing Street.

The Prime Minister said he thought that it was not reasonable to disparage the efforts of the Americans who were making such great efforts on our behalf.

The Prime Minister suggested two verbal alterations to Lord Beaverbrook's report. The first to make clear that the promise made by himself to M. Stalin had been done with the full approval of the whole Cabinet. The second to alter the allegation of a 'failure' in the American Production programme to 'retardation'. He thought that the report should be adopted and that Lord Beaverbrook should be authorized to show it to Mr Harriman if he thought such a course advisable.

The Committee then considered a General Directive for the Anglo-American-Russian Conference which had been prepared by the Prime Minister. The Committee were informed that the Chiefs of Staff agreed with the contents of the directive. The question for consideration was how much military information could be communicated to the Russians. For example should they be informed of our strength in the Middle East?

The Prime Minister thought that it would probably be unavoidable that we should tell them of our strength in the course of the discussions which were certain to take place on joint action in the South Eastern Theatre. It would be necessary to make clear to them what a vast effort we were making on sea, in the air, in munitions production and also on land. There were approximately 3,500,000 armed men in the Services, all drawn from the United Kingdom, in addition to the Forces of the Dominions.

Mr Eden said that he had seen M. Maisky earlier in the day who had expressed disappointment that we had not made any specific reply to M. Stalin on the subject of action in South Russia. From what he said, it appeared likely that the Russians would take the line in discussion that we had 600,000 men in the Middle East and could we not, therefore do something to help them. The Russian situation was becoming serious in the Ukraine and there might soon be a threat to the Caucasus. The Russians realized that it would take time for our forces to come into action, but if they knew that help was on its way they could throw in their last reserves. We had stated that a front had been formed from Archangel to Tobruk, but if the Germans reached the Caucasus the position of the Turks would be serious and a break might take place in this front. He had explained to M. Maisky the limitations of transport and the fact that the Trans-Persian railway would be fully occupied in carrying goods to Russia, but M. Maisky had said that the Russians might prefer to have troops.

The Prime Minister said that the time factor would rule out effective help before the winter. We would naturally like to send troops to Baku but the Russians would probably ask us to go to Astrakhan which would be a bad proposition. M. Stalin had quoted the precedent of the last war when Russian troops had been sent to France, but the position was quite different: then the

Russians had had no arms but plenty of men and their men had been sent to join up with the arms which we and the French possessed. The present situation was exactly the reverse: the Russians could not possibly be short of men and we should, therefore, send arms. We could of course study every possible means of helping them in the South East, but he felt it would be much more profitable to do everything to bring Turkey in. In principle we were willing to give them our right hand in the Middle East, but we could not possibly join up with them before the winter.

Lord Beaverbrook said that he agreed with the Prime Minister's directive and proposed to show it to Mr Harriman but not to the Russians.

The Committee then considered what specific offer of army equipment should be made to the Russians from British sources for the period October 1941 to June 1942, and what policy should govern offers beyond the end of this period. There was considerable discussion on this point, the following being the main arguments used:

(a) Lord Beaverbrook said that he was convinced that, unless we could make the Russians exact and substantial offers, they would not continue the struggle. It might turn out that the course of the war or the limitations of transport would prevent us fulfilling these offers in their entirety, but he did not think he could do anything useful in Russia unless he was equipped with an offer on a really attractive scale.

Moreover, he was convinced that we could, if we bent our energies to it, very greatly increase our present plan of production and that it would be well worth our doing so, even at some expense to the size of our own forces, if by so doing we could keep the Russians in the field for a long period.

(b) The Prime Minister realized that Lord Beaverbrook would have a difficult task, but felt that it would be unwise to be too specific in offers for the distant future when the position would be so speculative, and knowing as we did that the war might easily swing back in our direction at any time. If the Russians had a breathing space, that would be the very time they would press for us to fulfil our obligations so that they could re-equip their forces, and we should be unable to carry out our promises. We should guarantee our offers over the short period and tell the Russians that we would work up perhaps to double the quantity in succeeding months.

(c) Sir Archibald Sinclair suggested that, before making any greatly increased offers, we should find out the Russian situation. His opinion was that their output of aircraft was still very large. Furthermore, the Russians might like to have equipment in different proportions to that proposed by us.

The committee then discussed in detail a number of items of army equipment and the amounts which should be offered to Russia.

The Prime Minister pointed out that the Russians had an immense army and, presumably, had a very large output of army equipment. Anything we could offer would appear like a drop in the ocean, though it might mean a great sacrifice on our part. He could never agree to any proposal which would mean cutting down the size of our Army below its present level. We could not build up new factories here and the Russians would have to look to the United States of America for large long-term contracts. America, not ourselves, would have to be the arsenal for the Russian Army. He would draft a statement of what should be offered for the Committee to consider.

The Committee then adjourned, and resumed at 10.30 p.m.

On resumption, the Prime Minister read to the Committee a draft which he had prepared as a guide for Lord Beaverbrook, to cover the offers to be made to the Russians, firstly for the period October 1941 to June 1942 and secondly for the subsequent period.

A number of amendments were suggested and the draft was finally approved, and given to Lord Beaverbrook.

Harold Balfour;[1] *recollection*[2]

(*'Wings Over Westminster'*)

[19 September 1941]

As the designated number two Minister I found myself a very silent member of this high-powered gathering. At once it was clear that Churchill, Eden and Beaverbrook were the only ones on the positive side for aid. The Service Ministers and their Chiefs of Staff were on the negative side. The Air Ministry case was, though invasion danger was past, the air defences of Britain had to be kept up to strength and further expanded to meet the threat of heavier enemy raids. Bomber Command had to be built up. The Middle East was crying out for Hurricanes and Spitfires for the Western Desert. As for the RAF, so for the Army and Navy. Not a rowing boat, a rifle or a Tiger Moth could be spared without weakening and without grave risk. It was soon clear that the division between the positives and the negatives was acute. Discussion and argument went to and fro. After an hour and more Churchill made clear that in his view, an offer – a fair offer – of supplies from all three Services must

[1] Harold Harington Balfour, 1897–1988. A great grandson of Field-Marshal Lord Napier of Magdala. Educated Royal Naval College, Osborne. Joined 60th Rifles, 1914; Royal Flying Corps, 1915–17 (Military Cross and bar). Served in the Royal Air Force, 1918–23. Conservative MP for the Isle of Thanet, 1929–45. Parliamentary Under-Secretary of State for Air, 1938–44. Privy Councillor, 1941. Minister Resident in West Africa, 1944–5. Created Baron Balfour of Inchrye, 1945. A member of the Board of British European Airways, 1955–66. Chairman, BEA Helicopters Ltd. He published *An Airman Marches* in 1935 and *Wings Over Westminster* in 1973. His elder brother, a Lieutenant-Commander, Royal Navy, was killed on active service in 1941.

[2] Captain Balfour, Parliamentary Under-Secretary of State for Air, was present throughout the War Cabinet Defence Committee discussions on September 19; I have printed his published recollection here, as an elaboration and illumination of the official Cabinet Office record.

be forthcoming; that the political and strategic importance of supporting Russia demanded this even at some risk to ourselves. Churchill did not neglect to remind the Service members that there were those in the room who had gone on record as saying that if Russia was attacked, she could not last three weeks against the German forces.

From the time of Churchill's declaration of the policy to be followed, the battle became one of what, and how much. Though the front had been narrowed, stubborn resistance was just as strong, even stronger. At 7.30 p.m. the atmosphere of reason and debate seemed to deteriorate. I detected an acid note creeping into assertion, denial, exhortation. Churchill's shoulders became more hunched. A scowl on his brow deepened. His interjections were more frequent and impatient. On and on we went. Out-of-date aircraft were offered – and rejected. Old guns or tanks were likewise taken and thrown out of the Cabinet window. Unwanted naval craft were sunk without trace.

At around 8 p.m. the Prime Minister entered into the sad, pathetic role. His head sank lower. In a voice more of sorrow than anger, he made his little speech. 'Gentlemen, the role of a Prime Minister must always be difficult. In war it is more so. When his colleagues fail to agree, his role indeed becomes a harsh one. But these matters must be settled. We must stay at our task until we can agree. We will continue, and we will stay here all night if necessary.' As Churchill spoke, a Marine messenger entered unnoticed, came up behind the Prime Minister's chair and when he had finished speaking, bent down and whispered something in the Prime Minister's ear. Churchill turned round like a bulldog ready to growl and snap at an unexpected pat on the shoulder. The poor Marine jumped back about a yard and retreated from the room. It was clear to me what the domestic message had been. It was 8.15 and 'Mrs Churchill wants to know when you are coming to dinner'. Churchill paused; then again he spoke to us. 'Gentlemen, as I said, we have to decide these grave matters. But let us adjourn for a short while to obtain some sustenance. It is now 8.15. Let us meet again at 9 o'clock. Well, perhaps not 9 – let us say 9.30. No, let us make it 10.30.'

As a young officer I had always been taught to be on parade five minutes before time, so at 10.25 I was back on the doorstep of No.10. As I got there, two other Ministers joined me. The door was opened. Before I could walk down the passage to the Cabinet room I saw, coming towards me, a beaming figure in a blue siren-suit. The Prime Minister. He took me by the arm and said, 'Wait, my boy, wait.' I had never been called 'my boy' before by Churchill. 'I have something to show you.' He led me – and the others who had meanwhile arrived – to the little anteroom on the left of the passage. 'See,' he said. 'This has come for me today,' and he pointed to a large imitation Queen Anne-style cabinet, on the top of which was printed this inscription:

To the Rt. Hon. Winston Churchill, PC, MP, Prime Minister of Great Britain. A tribute of admiration from the President and People of Cuba.

'I have had some difficulty today in getting this through the Customs,' he said, as he opened one of the drawers to show lovely bundles of long Havana cigars. Turning to the waiting Ministers, he addressed us thus: 'Gentlemen, I am now going to try an experiment. Maybe it will result in joy. Maybe it will end in grief. I am about to give you each one of these magnificent cigars.' He paused. He continued with Churchillian rolling of sound and digestive enjoyment of spoken words. 'It may well be that these each contain some deadly poison.' Then came the word picture which he alone could paint. 'It may well be that within days I shall follow sadly the long line of coffins up the aisle of Westminster Abbey.' Another pause before finale. 'Reviled by the populace; as the man who has out-Borgia-ed Borgia.' Each of us was presented with a lovely – and in those days, extremely rare – Havana cigar. We lit up. We sailed into the Cabinet room. In half an hour we had settled all we had argued about for hours. Russian aid was safe and firm.[1]

On 20 September 1941, when it became clear through the Enigma decrypts that the Germans planned to launch an all-out assault on Moscow in twelve days' time, Churchill authorized the despatch of a warning to Stalin, through the British Military Mission in Russia. Eight further warnings were sent to Moscow in the following four days, giving the Russian High Command more than a week's notice of German intentions and dispositions.

Winston S. Churchill to Anthony Eden
(Churchill papers, 20/36)

20 September 1941

I think that great value might be obtained at the present time by dropping leaflets on Italy referring particularly to the fact that hundreds of thousands of Italians have been sent from sunny homes to die in the frozen mud of the Ukraine. Pray have this matter considered by the Political Warfare Executive.

I am sending a copy of this Minute to the Secretary of State for Air, in order that the operational aspect also may be considered.

[1] John Colville minuted to Churchill eight days later: 'I am sending one cigar from each box of the cabinet which you received from Cuba, to Lord Rothschild that they may be tested for poison or any other noxious content. Lord Cherwell hopes that you will not smoke any of the cigars until the result of the analysis is known. He points out that there has just been a round-up of undesirable elements in Cuba, which has shown that a surprisingly large number of Nazi agents and sympathizers exist in that country.' (Minute of 23 September 1941: *Churchill papers, 2/434*)

Winston S. Churchill to Field Marshal Smuts
(*Churchill papers, 20/42*)

20 September 1941
Personal and Secret

Your No. 1129.[1] Shipping alone vetoes all large projects suggested. Am sending two divisions and about eighty thousand other reinforcements to Middle East between now and Christmas. To help in this I have had to beg loan of American transports from Roosevelt, which have been kindly given. If we can clear up Cyrenaica we shall have substantial forces to give right hand to Russia in Caspian region and/or influence action Turkey. This last I regard as most immediate prize. Hope at least to procure Turkish resistance to German demands for passage through Anatolia. Meanwhile, Beaverbrook and Harriman leaving for Moscow. We have had to make terrible sacrifices in tanks and aircraft and other munitions so sorely needed. If Russians stay in it is worth it. If they quit we don't have to send it. Hope to reach total of twenty-five divisions from Caspian to Nile during 1942. I doubt very much whether Russians would be wise to press us to cumber the Trans-Persian Railway, which we are rapidly developing, with movement and supply of the few divisions we could actually send into Russia. All these matters will be discussed at Moscow and studied by our Staffs. Will keep you informed.

General Wavell to Winston S. Churchill
(*Churchill papers, 20/30*)

20 September 1941

My dear Prime Minister,

Someone has just sent me a copy of the *National Review* for August and has called my attention to pages 137-8.[2] I am very distressed if this sort of stuff is being written, with no vestige of truth in it. You, I know, and I, as I am sure you know, think of nothing but the national interest and the winning of this

[1] In which Smuts wrote: 'It must be borne in mind that German occupation of Caucasus in coming winter may seriously endanger our position in Persia and Iraq and call for large Indian Forces in that area and for this and other reasons assurance may have to be given to Stalin that supply route through Persia to Russia will be kept open at all costs and large forces for this purpose will be employed.' (Prime Minister's Personal Telegram, T.599, 20 September 1941, *Churchill papers, 20/42*)

[2] The *National Review* ascribed Wavell's dismissal to Churchill's jealousy: 'General Wavell is a national hero, his brilliant campaign in Cyrenaica was only checked by the demands made on him for other campaigns. He spoke his mind on these matters and, while always obeying orders, he pointed out what would happen. It did happen. Wavell's number was up – a more malleable, or, at any rate, a less instructed, soldier must be found. The Commander-in-Chief in the Near East had become a menace, his position was too preponderant, he was devoted, successful and frank. India was further away. He had better go there.'

war and any talk of jealousy is absurd. I am writing to the sender of the magazine to say how much I resent this sort of thing and how harmful it is to our cause, if there is anything else I can do to stop it I would of course do it.

You are carrying the heaviest burden of responsibility any man has ever shouldered, and I am very sorry if the Press add to your burdens in this way.

With my sincerest good wishes to you in your great task.

Yours most sincerely
A. P. Wavell

Winston S. Churchill to General Wavell
(*Churchill papers, 20/20*)[1]

20 September 1941

My dear Wavell,

Thank you so much for your letter. I shall ever be grateful to you for all you have done to win the war, and I look forward with hope to your acting in a still wider field than the Nile valley in the coming year.

It is a profound satisfaction to me to feel – as I have always felt – that you do not misjudge the spirit and motives with which I try to carry my burden. My admiration for your character, conduct and military capacity is constant.

All good wishes,
Believe me,
Yours very sincerely,
Winston S. Churchill

Winston S. Churchill to Anthony Eden and Major Desmond Morton
(*Churchill papers, 20/36*)

20 September 1941
Secret

I regard the attached[2] as most serious. At any moment we may be at war with Japan, and here are all these Englishmen, many of them respectable, two of whom I know personally, moving around collecting information and sending it to the Japanese Embassy. I cannot believe that the Master of

[1] A note by Leslie Rowan on the copy of this letter stated: 'Original in manuscript sent to General Wavell'.

[2] A report on the sources of information available to the Japanese Embassy.

Sempill[1] and Commander McGrath[2] have any idea of what their position would be on the morrow of a Japanese declaration of war. Immediate internment would be the least of their troubles. I consider Lord Swinton[3] should see them all and caution them, and require them to cease their activities, failing which other measures will have to be taken. Meanwhile, none of them must have access to any Government Department. It is impossible for Lord Sempill to continue to be employed at the Admiralty, I do not know in what capacity.

The only one whose position appears to be unexceptionable, because it is open and avowed, is Mr Edwardes.[4] But do the Departments to whom he has access know that he is a salaried servant of the Japanese Government, receiving £4,500 a year? Are there no measures which can be taken to warn the whole circle of Government Departments against men who have these special connections?

Some time ago I directed that the Japanese Embassy were to have no more facilities in London and about the country than, for instance, the American Embassy is accorded at the present time in Berlin. This should certainly carry with it the effectual closing down of the activities of this English nebula.

Pray let me know what action can be taken.

[1] William Francis Forbes-Sempill, 1893–1965. Royal Flying Corps, 1914; Royal Naval Air Service, 1916; Royal Air Force, 1918. Special Technical Mission to the United States, 1918. Retired from the RAF, 1919. Member of the Civil Air Transport Committee, and the Advisory Committee for Aeronautics. Requested by the Imperial Japanese Navy to undertake the organization, equipment and training of the Imperial Japanese Naval Air Service, 1921. A frequent competitor in the King's Cup Air Race, 1924–30. Asked by the Greek Government to report on the reorganization of the Greek Naval Air Service, 1926. President of the Royal Aeronautical Society, 1927–30. President of the British Gliding Association, 1933–42. Succeeded his father, as 19th Baron Sempill, 1934. Rejoined Naval Air Service, 1939; retired, 1941. Among his publications was *The British Aviation Mission to the Imperial Japanese Navy*.

[2] Not traced.

[3] Philip Cunliffe-Lister, 1884–1972. On active service, 1914–17 (Military Cross). Joint Secretary, Ministry of National Service, 1917–18. Conservative MP, 1918–35. President of the Board of Trade, 1922–3, 1924–9 and 1931. Secretary of State for the Colonies, 1931–5. Created Viscount Swinton, 1935. Secretary of State for Air, 1935–8 (when he advocated a larger Air Force expansion than the Government was prepared to accept). Brought back into Government on the outbreak of war as Chairman of the United Kingdom Commercial Corporation, responsible for pre-empting purchases of supplies and materials overseas that were needed by the German war machine. Appointed by Churchill in May 1940 to be Chairman of the Security Executive, concerned with measures against sabotage in Britain and overseas. Organized the supply route to the Soviet Union through the Persian Gulf, 1941–2. Cabinet Minister Resident in West Africa, 1942–4. Minister for Civil Aviation, 1944–5. Minister of Materials, 1951–2. Secretary of State for Commonwealth Relations, 1952–5. Created Earl of Swinton, 1955. His elder son died of wounds received in North Africa in 1943.

[4] Arthur Henry Francis Edwards. In 1903 he entered the Chinese Maritime Customs Service, rising to Officiating Inspector-General in 1927. He resigned from the Service in 1928. Lived subsequently in London.

Winston S. Churchill to Colonel Hollis, for the Chiefs of Staff Committee
(*Premier papers, 3/88/1*)

21 September 1941

COS Minute of September 19, paragraph 2. The particular operation Crusader does not, I believe, contemplate so long a period of heavy fighting to clear the area, and it is to achieve this complete and swift result that we are having to wait so long. Be this as it may, the differences between A and B could not appreciably affect the issue. See tables attached, marked 'X' and 'Y'.[1] By adopting A we should lose the 9,402 drafts in the third column of 'Y', and in addition nine wireless sections, one Army Tank Brigade Signals, two heavy AA regiments, one Reconnaissance Battalion, three Field squadrons RF, totalling 4,508. These are what have to be balanced against two brigades and other elements to complete the whole of No. 2 Division. For the sake then of these details we should have to sacrifice the broad simple policy of carrying two additional complete divisions to the Middle East.

2. There is no need to refer this matter to General Auchinleck. It will be three months before these divisions have reached the scene. We cannot tell where it will be best to use them. They may be needed for Persia, and to give a right hand to the Russians (that is to say, outside General Auchinleck's Command); they may be needed for Syria, to encourage or possibly act with the Turks; or, again, they may be used in the Nile Valley or the Western Desert. These options will remain open to us.

3. I hope, therefore, that after the very full and careful examination that has been given to this matter, and the small margin to which it is reduced, the Chiefs of the Staff will support me in the decision to which I have come, which is taken on the broadest political-strategic grounds, and for which I must bear the final responsibility.

4. If desired, I shall be ready to discuss the points orally at a Staff Meeting on Monday night.

Winston S. Churchill to Air Chief Marshal Sir Charles Portal
(*Churchill papers, 20/36*)

21 September 1941

Do our fighter pilots over France carry a sufficient supply of French money? I am told they are only given 50 francs. In my view, at least 3,000 francs should be carried as part of a pilot's equipment, and passed from hand to hand.

[1] Table X gave two lists of units: Plan A) totalling 18,500 men, and Plan B, 32,500 men. Table Y gave details of drafts under Plan A totalling 10,095 men and under Plan B of 19,587 men.

Winston S. Churchill to General Sir John Dill
(*Churchill papers, 20/36*)

21 September 1941

I am not prepared to let this[1] lapse or be slurred over, or fall into oblivion. More than admonitions are required when 600 German Legionaries are allowed to go back to Vichy France for further use by Germany against us. It might take 600 British lives to deal with these men so casually and incontinently allowed to slip through our fingers. A formal letter should be written by the War Office to the Commander-in-Chief, Middle East, asking for the action taken by him in respect of 'Milpal', and pointing out the gravity of the injury to British interest involved in this supine conduct of the Command in Syria. If a sergeant or a corporal makes a slip, he is punished or reprimanded. The Staff Officers around General Wilson are to blame for not having raised the point and understood what was going on. If General Wilson takes the blame himself, it can be written off against his good services in other directions, but he ought to be left in no doubt of the harm that has been done. The fullest detailed explanation should be provided.

Winston S. Churchill to General Sir John Dill
(*Churchill papers, 20/36*)

21 September 1941

Thank you. I am glad to see by later telegrams that it is proposed to reorganize the forward Area, so that any similar movements of the enemy can be struck at offensively by the forward troops. I understand this readjustment is to be completed about 23rd instant. If this is right now, I still do not see why it was not right earlier. The losses of ten tanks, &c., that the enemy suffered at the hands only of armoured cars without tanks, shows that a pretty good 'cop' could have been staged. However, perhaps we shall get a second chance. P'raps not. Fortune is a jade.

[1] The return of about 600 German members of the French Foreign Legion who were allowed to return to France at the termination of hostilities in Syria.

Winston S. Churchill to J. V. Stalin
(*Premier papers, 3/401/7*)

21 September 1941

My dear Premier Stalin,

The British and American Missions have now started, and this letter will be presented to you by Lord Beaverbrook. Lord Beaverbrook has the fullest confidence of the Cabinet, and is one of my oldest and most intimate friends. He has established the closest relations with Mr Harriman, who is a remarkable American, wholeheartedly devoted to the victory of the common cause. They will lay before you all that we have been able to arrange in much anxious consultation between Great Britain and the United States.

President Roosevelt has decided that our proposals shall, in the first instance, deal with the monthly quotas we shall send to you in the nine-months period from October 1941 to June 1942, inclusive. You have the right to know exactly what we can deliver month by month, in order that you may handle your reserves to the best advantage.[1]

The American proposals have not yet gone beyond the end of June 1942, but I have no doubt that considerably larger quotas can be furnished by both countries thereafter, and you may be sure we shall do our utmost to repair as far as possible the grievous curtailments which your war industries have suffered through the Nazi invasion. I will not anticipate what Lord Beaverbrook will have to say upon this subject.

You will realize that the quotas up to the end of June 1942 are supplied almost entirely out of British production, or production which the United States would have given us under our own purchases or under the Lend-Lease Bill. The United States were resolved to give us virtually the whole of their exportable surplus, and it is not easy for them within that time to open out effectively new sources of supply. I am hopeful that a further great impulse will be given to the production of the United States, and that by 1943 the mighty industry of America will be in full war swing. For our part, we shall not only make substantially increased contributions from our own existing forecast production, but also try to obtain from our people an extra further effort to meet our common needs.

General Ismay, who is my personal representative on the Chiefs of Staff Committee, and is thoroughly acquainted with the whole field of our military policy, is authorized to study with your commanders any plans for practical co-operation which may suggest themselves.

If we can clear our western flank in Libya of the enemy we shall have

[1] That week's British tank production (for the week ending 27 September 1941) was 20% higher than all previous records; all the tanks were sent to Russia.

considerable forces, both air and army, to co-operate upon the southern flank of the Russian front.[1]

It seems to me that the most speedy and effective help would come if Turkey could be induced to resist a German demand for the passage of troops, or, better still, if she would enter the war on our side. You will, I am sure, attach due weight to this.

I have always shared your sympathy for the Chinese people in their struggle to defend their native land against Japanese aggression. Naturally we do not want to add Japan to the side of our foes, but the attitude of the United States, resulting from my conference with President Roosevelt, has already enforced a far more sober view upon the Japanese Government. I made haste to declare on behalf of His Majesty's Government that should the United States be involved in war with Japan Great Britain would immediately range herself on her side. I think that all our three countries should, as far as possible, continue to give aid to China, and that this may go to considerable lengths without provoking a Japanese declaration of war.

Believe me,
Yours sincerely,
Winston S. Churchill

Winston S. Churchill to Lord Beaverbrook
(*Churchill papers, 20/43*)

21 September 1941
'To be put over the Scrambler to him at Scapa via Flagship'

General Wavell proposes to go to Tiflis via Baghdad on his return to India. He speaks Russian, and I contemplate his directing or possibly, if the forces grow large enough, commanding, the right hand we shall give to the Russians in and about the Caspian Basin in the forthcoming campaign. It is therefore important that he should confer with high Russian military authorities on the whole position of their southern flank and in Persia.

You may bring this into your discussions, and see that the most is made of it. Actual dates can be settled later.

[1] This was Operation Velvet.

Winston S. Churchill to Brigadier Menzies, General Brooke and Admiral Pound
(*Secret Intelligence Service papers, HW1/86*)

22 September 1941

MEDITERRANEAN: NAVAL AND SHIPPING[1]

Surely this is a dangerously large circulation. Why sh'd anyone be told but the 3 C-in-Cs. They can give their orders without giving reasons. Why should such messages go to subsidiary HQ's in the Western Desert.

Winston S. Churchill to Lord Beaverbrook and Averell Harriman
(*Churchill papers, 20/43*)

22 September 1941

All good wishes to you both and your colleagues for your memorable journey, on which you carry with you the hope of the world.

Winston

Winston S. Churchill to President Franklin D. Roosevelt
(*Churchill papers, 20/43*)

22 September 1941
Personal and Secret

Your cheering cable about Tanks[2] arrived when we were feeling very blue about all we have to give up to Russia. The prospect of nearly doubling the previous figures encouraged everyone. The Missions have started in great goodwill and friendship.

Kindest regards.

[1] Churchill had been studying a 7 a.m. summary of a series of decrypts on German fuel ship movements in the Mediterranean, from Naples to Bardia.

[2] The tanks available in Britain were 3,994 medium tanks and 1,953 light tanks between October 1941 and June 1942. These were 'minimum figures', Roosevelt explained a week later, 'because I have directed that production during the next nine months be increased by ten or fifteen per cent'.

Winston S. Churchill to Admiral Pound, Admiral Fraser and Sir Stanley Goodall.[1]
(*Churchill papers, 20/36*)

22 September 1941
Secret

1. Naturally, being all for stiff ships, I am very glad we have 1,370 tons more armour, and another 790 tons of weight in the hull. The deeper armour belt and hard nose are good. It is very satisfactory to be able to combine this with superior speed, as has been done. I am still not convinced, however, that the lengthening of the citadel area caused by interpolating the aerodrome amidships instead of aft has not used up a lot of this fine armour without advantage to the 'citadel' principle on which fighting and flotation alike depend. I should like to go further into this on other papers.

2. Our ship is longer, narrower and deeper than the American. I presume this makes for speed.

3. We have exceeded the Treaty[2] limit by 1,750 tons, while the Americans with the 16-inch gun are either within it or only 200 tons over it. Can this be true?

4. There is much to be said for twenty 5-inch guns for AA and A/T armament, as for sixteen 5.52-inch guns; in fact, some people would prefer more numerous gun positions to deal with multiplied Air Attacks.

5. It is when we come to compare nine 16-inch guns and ten 14-inch guns that sorrow rises in the heart, or ought to. Nine 16-inch at 2,700 pounds per round equals 24,300 pounds. Ten 14-inch guns at 1,590 pounds equals 15,900 pounds. Difference 8,400 on the broadside.

6. It is interesting to note that the Germans in the *Bismarck* chose four turrets of two 15-inch, whereas we went to the other extreme of three turrets, of which two were four-gun, but a smaller gun. The Americans coming in between the two may have hit the happy medium, and have as well the biggest punch.

War Cabinet: minutes
(*Cabinet papers, 65/19*)

22 September 1941 — 10 Downing Street
6.15 p.m.

The Prime Minister said that the Soviet Government had responded favourably to a suggestion from the TUC that a TUC delegation should visit

[1] Stanley Vernon Goodall, 1883-1965. Royal Corps of Naval Constructors, 1907. Constructor Commander, Royal Navy, 1917-19. Director of Naval Construction, Admiralty, 1936-44. Knighted 1938. Assistant Controller (Warship Production), 1942-51.

[2] The Washington Naval Treaty (1922), as extended by the London Naval Treaty (1930).

Russia. The TUC wished to send their delegation at once. If so, its visit would coincide with the Meeting with the British and USA Missions. He had suggested to Sir Walter Citrine that it would be a good plan to postpone the TUC visit for a week or so, but the TUC were unwilling to adopt this suggestion. It would be highly inconvenient that the two visits should synchronize, and the Russians might try to play off one British delegation against the other. Further, if the visits coincided, the TUC delegation might not receive the attention which was its due.

The Prime Minister said that, when Parliament met, it might be necessary to disclose in Secret Session the steps taken to send supplies to Russia.

The view was generally expressed that this would be desirable, even if not strongly urged. If the matter was discussed in Secret Session and Members were satisfied with the assurances given, this would have a favourable effect on public opinion generally.

Winston S. Churchill to Air Chief Marshal Sir Charles Portal
(*Churchill papers, 20/36*)

22 September 1941

1. It is not necessary that the Marker apparatus, whatever it is, should be dropped in the actual town to be attacked. It might well be ten miles away, or even more, so long as its position is accurately defined and can be imparted in time to our Bombers. It is not intended to supersede but only to confirm and cross-check other methods of navigation.

2. Suppose a very fast airplane dropped a Marker beacon before dusk in the open country near the target, and then after dark this beacon began to speak, then we could tell our bombers to steer accordingly, like naval ships fire at each other for practice with a deflection on the guns.

3. All this should be pursued night and day by your people.

Winston S. Churchill to King George VI
(*Churchill papers, 20/20*)

22 September 1941

Sir,

I have been deeply touched by Your Majesty's most gracious and kindly wish to honour me with the appointment of Lord Warden of the Cinque Ports. The Lord Chancellor has informed me that Your Majesty had consulted him upon the proprieties and precedents and that he had advised in a favourable sense. I should certainly regard it as an extraordinary compliment, far beyond my deserts, to be included in that long line of Prime Ministers and eminent men who have across the centuries filled that office. The Lord Chancellor assures me that it could be announced that I should not be installed or go into residence at Walmer Castle until the end of the war. This seems most necessary as otherwise I fear its proximity to the enemy's aircraft and indeed artillery might create a need for heavy structural repairs before very long.

The future after the war is so uncertain and I doubt very much whether many private persons will be able to face the expense of living in so large and so fine a house. These however are problems which need not be considered in this precarious stage of our journey. Let me therefore thank Your Majesty for this renewed mark of the confidence and kindness which has been so great a help and encouragement to me in the fateful months during which I have been First Minister of the Crown. It is this that makes Your Majesty's spontaneous intention so agreeable to me.

With my humble duty,
I remain,
Your Majesty's faithful and devoted servant
and subject,
Winston S. Churchill

Winston S. Churchill to the Duke of Windsor
(*Churchill papers, 20/43*)

22 September 1941
Personal and Private

I should say something[1] about your life in the Bahamas and how you felt your work there might help not only the people there from whom you had received so much kindness, but also might promote friendly contacts with the United States. Of course when London was being bombed and Great Britain threatened with invasion you could not help wishing, like every other faithful subject of the King, like every Briton in every part of the world, to share the fortunes of those at home. In war however one serves where one is told. 'Act well thy part, there all the honour lies.' From this you could pass directly to the American bases in the West Indian Islands, one of which is in the Bahamas Group. Say we have not regarded these bases as the purchase price for the very welcome American destroyers, although that was the form in which the

[1] The Duke of Windsor had asked Churchill for guidance as to what he should say in public during his visit to the United States, when he would be seeing President Roosevelt. The Duke replied by telegram to Churchill on 23 September 1941: 'Many thanks for your long and most helpful note, the gist of which I will tell the President. Greatly appreciate your telegraphing in time for me to leave here with some ammunition for Washington.' (Prime Minister's Personal Telegram, T.607, *Churchill papers, 20/43*)

arrangement was made. It is the settled policy of His Majesty's Government to aid the United States to the utmost in providing for the security of the Western Hemisphere. These islands have formidable strategic importance as air bases for attacks upon the United States and their effective defence against all aggressors is an important part of the safety and freedom of the people of the United States. The British nation neither fear nor envy the greatness and the power of the United States. On the contrary they rejoice with every increase because they know that the ideals and principles of humane and law-respecting action which have guided the United States for so many years are the same as those for which the British Commonwealth and Empire are now fighting. One of the dearest wishes in British hearts is that America shall forever remain the land of the free and the home of the brave. After this it would be well to pay a tribute to the President for his generous heart which beats in sympathy with the poor and the oppressed of every land, and whose strong hand is uplifted in wrath against tyranny and aggression. We must not forget how many peoples there are now striving to defend their hearts and homes and their right to live their own life in their own lands. The whole British Empire is as one in its inflexible unwearying resolve to fight against Hitlerism until the Nazi Tyranny has been forever destroyed. The United States have taken a very prudent step from their own point of view in occupying Iceland (C) which was the first of the great stepping-stones by which the dictatorships of the Old World might march to the conquest of the New. Although this far ranging action of the United States was taken for the sake of the safety of the United States it would be silly to pretend that we in Britain were not very glad to see it done. The joint occupation of Iceland by British and United States forces was a proof that the Bridge across the Atlantic Ocean would not be broken down and that the arms and supplies which Congress had resolved should be sent to Britain should reach the hands for whom they were made. Here was another illustration of the saying of the Old Free Traders, whose ideas perhaps have a part to play in the future reconstruction of the world, 'All legitimate interests are in harmony'. It had been decided that the British and United States Mission should be sent to confer in Russia with the leaders of the Russian Government. This was not because the Russians were communists, but because they were brave and were fighting a righteous war to defend their native soil against brutal, unprovoked attack. Lastly, there were the Chinese people for whom the American nation had always felt such warm sympathies and who had rights which were precious not only to the Chinese, but to free men all over the world. You might end by saying that this time of struggle and of sorrow might be long, but it would not last for ever. It would only last till victory of the righteous cause had been won and that thereafter an opportunity would be presented to the English speaking nations of the world to render further service to all mankind in guiding them by their example and by their aid out of the dark valleys of death and destruction into an age more rich in culture and prosperity, more warm, more cheered by security and social justice and more lighted by hope than any which history has known.

Speech notes end.

You would naturally ask the President whether anything in this would embarrass him. I cannot think it would but it is better to be doubly sure. I trust these suggestions may be of some help to Your Royal Highness and I take the responsibility for advising you accordingly to make use of them should you wish to do so. With best wishes to you and the Duchess for a successful and pleasant holiday.[1]

Winston S. Churchill: General Directive[2]
(*Cabinet papers, 69/3*)

22 September 1941
Secret

ANGLO-AMERICAN-RUSSIAN CONFERENCE

1. The position reached as a result of the Beaverbrook-Harriman conversations is set out in Lord Beaverbrook's report of today's date. We must consider ourselves pledged to fulfil our share of the tanks and aircraft which have been promised to Russia, and Lord Beaverbrook must have a considerable measure of discretion as to what quantities of other equipment and of material should be offered at the conversations in Moscow.

2. Assurance must be given to Russia of increased quotas from the 1st July, 1942, to the 30th June, 1943. During this period British war production will be at its height and American ditto in its third year of development. It would be wiser not to be committed to precise figures based on optimistic forecasts of Anglo-American production. There are dangers also in promising the Russians a percentage of British and American output which they may immediately ask should be increased. We should not disclose speculative figures of our joint production when none are given of theirs by the Russians. They should, however, be invited to set forth their remaining resources in accordance with the various rearward lines they may hope to hold. Lord Beaverbrook should be free to encourage the prolonged resistance of Russia by taking a justifiably hopeful view of these more distant prospects.

[1] On 4 October 1941 Lord Halifax telegraphed to Anthony Eden: 'Prime Minister may like to know that the President spoke well to me yesterday on the Windsors after seeing them here. He reported the Duke as being very robust on war and victory and his attitude generally showed a great improvement on the impression the President had formed when he met him a year ago in the Bahamas.' (Secret and Personal, Telegram No. 4551 from Washington, *Churchill papers, 20/31*)

[2] Printed as War Cabinet Defence Committee (Operations) Paper No. 12 of 1941 (Prime Minister's Personal Minute D.259/1).

3. Russian attention should be directed to the limitations of shipping, and still more of transportation from the various ports of access. The rapid destruction of world shipping, the effort required to make it good, and the vital needs of this country, now cut to the bone, should be stressed.

4. Encouragement should be offered, with American approval, to the keeping open of the Vladivostok route and overawing Japan for that purpose. Special emphasis should be laid upon the development on the largest scale and with the utmost energy of the route from the Persian Gulf to the Caspian, both by rail and road. The practical limitations which time enforces both upon working up the traffic on the Trans-Persian railway and upon the motor-road construction should be explained. The conflict between the movement of supplies and of troops and their maintenance at any given period along this route must be pointed out. The Russians will no doubt give their own estimate of the capacity and facilities of Archangel and of its railway connections with Central Russia, having regard to both winter ice and probable enemy action.

5. The Conference must proceed upon the basis that the United States is not a belligerent. The burden upon British man-power is already heavy and the strain will be intense during 1942 and onwards. Apart from the help we get from Dominions, India and the Colonies, our manpower is fully engaged. We have to feed ourselves and keep alive by maintaining vast merchant fleets in constant movement. We have to defend the British Isles from invasion,[1] for which the Germans can at any time gather a superior army, and also from the most dangerous forms of Air attack by the main strength of the enemy Air Force, which can rapidly be transferred from East to West at the enemy's convenience. We have to maintain our armies in the Middle East and hold a line from the Caspian to the Western Desert. We hope to develop on this front during 1942 approximately twenty-five divisions, British, Indian and Dominion, comprising, with all the exceptional rearward services needed in these undeveloped regions and strong proportionable Air Force, about a million men. The strain on shipping of supplying these forces largely round the Cape, and the time taken in the turn-round of available ships, should be explained, if necessary, in detail.

6. For the defence of the British Isles we have an army of slightly over two million men, backed by about one-and-a-half million armed Home Guard. We possess only about three-and-a-half million rifles, and can only get 100,000 more or so in the next year. Of this army of two million men, 900,000 constitute the Field Force, comprising 20 mobile infantry divisions, 9 less mobile county or beach divisions, and 6 armoured divisions, 3 of which are only partly formed, together with five Army tank brigades, of which only one

[1] On the following day, 23 September 1941, Churchill learned that the oil fuel and flame projectors for beaches, the 'F' schemes, had now been successfully tested, and were to be installed in eighteen different British ports, including Poole, Teignmouth, Looe, Yarmouth, Lowestoft, Penzance, Fowey, Padstow, Llanelly, Fishguard and Dartmouth, ('Secret', 23 September 1941: *Admiralty papers, 1/7808*)

is as yet complete. Nearly a million men will be required for the enormous Air Force we are creating; 750,000 are already enrolled. The Navy already absorbs half a million sailors and marines. When to this is added the shipbuilding, Aircraft production and munitions industries, and the need of food production at home and other domestic civilian industries all cut to a minimum, it will be seen that the manpower and available womanpower of a population of 44,000,000 is, or will soon be, engaged to the limit.

7. Out of the eleven hundred thousand men behind the Field Army at home, the Air Defence of Great Britain, the Coastal Defence, the garrison of Northern Ireland, the draft-producing units and training schools, the defence of aerodromes and vulnerable points, leave only a small margin.

8. It will not be possible to increase the Field Army at home beyond the number of divisions – less than forty – already mentioned, and great efforts will be needed to maintain the existing strength at home while supplying the drafts for the Middle East, India and other garrisons abroad, e.g., Iceland, Gibraltar, Malta, Aden, Singapore, Hong Kong.

9. We could not allow the force needed in Great Britain to repel invasion to fall below 25 infantry and 4 or 5 armoured divisions. It must be noted that troops can be transferred by the enemy across the main lateral railways of Europe incomparably quicker than any of our divisions could be recalled from abroad. The number of divisions available for offensive oversea action is therefore small.

10. Apart from the twenty-five British and Imperial Divisions proposed to be built up in the Middle East during 1942, an Expeditionary Force of six or seven divisions including two armoured divisions, is the maximum that can be conceived. This is being prepared. Even if more were available, the shipping does not exist to carry larger forces and maintain them overseas. All ideas of twenty or thirty divisions being launched by Great Britain against the western shores of the continent or sent round by sea for service in Russia have no foundation of reality on which to rest. This should be made clear.

11. We have every intention of intervening on land next spring, if it can be done. All the possibilities are being studied, including action on the northern and southern flanks of the Russian front. In the north an expedition into Norway would raise a serious revolt and might, if it succeeded, win the Swedish Government with its good army to our cause. This has been studied in detail. It is not, however, seen how the Russian forces could help, in fact their intervention would antagonize Sweden beyond all hope; the hostility of Finland is already declared.

12. At any moment we may be called upon to face the hostility of Spain and the penetration of the Germans into Morocco, Algeria and West Africa. Should the French resist in Africa, our available force might be sent to help them there. In both these cases the sea routes are short and not comparable with the vast distance round the Cape.

13. In the Middle East, on the southern flank of Russia, we shall deploy the strong forces mentioned above. Once the Western Desert and Cyrenaica have been cleared of the German and Italian armies now active there, our Middle Eastern forces would have a choice of action. If they increasingly give their right hand to the Russians, either in the Caucasus or east of the Caspian, it must be realized that their supply will choke the rail and road connection from the Persian Gulf. On the other hand Turkey, if she could be gained, is the great prize. Not only would the German road to Syria and Egypt be barred by powerful Turkish armies, but the Black Sea naval defence could be maintained with great advantages, thus helping the defence of the Causcasus. The action of Turkey one way or the other may be determined in the near future by the promises, should she become involved, of help in troops and modern equipment, including especially aeroplanes, tanks, anti-tank and anti-aircraft artillery, &c. It should be made clear to the Russians that much of this equipment and the greater part of the troops would, of course, be withdrawn from the contributions available for Russia which are all we can give. In order, however, to induce Turkey to come in on our side, especially in the near future, it would be well worth Great Britain and Russia revising their arrangements.

14. We are much interested in the development of the Polish and Czech Armies in Russia, the latter being only small, and we should be glad to help in their equipment. It should be pointed out that the Poles and Czechs have influential communities in the United States. If a proportion of our equipment could be earmarked for the Poles and Czechs, it would have a good effect.

15. The Russians will no doubt ask how you propose to win the war, to which our answer should be: 'By going on fighting till the Nazi system breaks up as the Kaiser's system broke up last time.' For this purpose we shall fight the enemy wherever we can meet them on favourable terms. We shall undermine them by propaganda; depress them with the blockade; and, above all, bomb their homelands ceaselessly, ruthlessly, and with ever-increasing weight of bombs. We could not tell last time how and when we should win the war, but by not giving in and not wearying we came through all right. We did not hesitate to face Germany and Italy alone all last year, and the determination of the British masses to destroy the Nazi power is inflexible. The phrases 'Nazi tyranny' and 'Prussian militarism' are used by us as targets rather than any implacable general condemnation of the German peoples. We agree with the Russian Government in hoping to split the Germans, and to isolate the criminal Nazi régime.

16. Of course, we cannot predict what action the United States will take. The measures already sanctioned by President Roosevelt and his Government may at any time in the near future involve the United States in full war, whether declared or undeclared. In that case we might look forward to a general offensive upon Germany in 1943. If German morale and unity were

seriously weakened, and their hold upon the conquered European countries relaxed, it might be possible to land large numbers of armoured forces simultaneously on the shores of several of the conquered countries, and raise widespread revolts. Plans for this are now being studied by the British Staffs.

John Colville: diary
(*Colville papers*)

22 September 1941

I find the PM has been busy with the Missions to Russia and that it has been decided to give large numbers of fighters and supplies of Munitions to the Soviet Government at great expense to ourselves. But, as the PM says, it is worthwhile in order to keep Russia in the war.

The Minister of State (Oliver Lyttelton) returned from Cairo and dined with the PM, who has much to discuss with him.[1]

Oliver Harvey: diary
(*'The War Diaries of Oliver Harvey, 1941-1945'*)

23 September 1941

Lyttelton arrived back from Cairo yesterday on short visit. He dined with PM and AE last night. PM in a mood of deep depression, AE said, very bitter about the constant nagging of the Press against the Government. 'As if they were doing nothing.'

John Colville: diary
(*Colville papers*)

23 September 1941

Francis Brown, my successor at No. 10, arrived. It seems odd to recall the Brigade Intelligence officer of the Coldstream Guards to become an untrained

[1] Unknown to Colville or to any of the members of Churchill's Private Office, for the previous ten days German Enigma decrypts had made it almost certain that some special activity against Tobruk was being planned. On September 12 Panzergruppe Afrika had asked for maps and overlays of the Tobruk defences as a matter of urgency. Nine days later a further German Air Force Enigma decrypt referred to a 'special operation' against Tobruk (OL 1108 of 12 September 1941 and OL 1241 of 21 September 1941: F.H. Hinsley and others, *British Intelligence in the Second World War: Its Influence on Strategy and Operations*, Volume 2, London, 1981, page 301). The date of the operation was unknown. But successive decrypts made it clear that Rommel was planning, not merely to strengthen his own positions around the besieged port's defensive perimeter but to seek to overrun it.

private secretary and to let me go off to become an untrained aircraftsman. Being responsible I feel rather guilty, but nevertheless not repentant.

Back to No. 10 on late duty. The PM spent the time till 2.00 a.m. in discussing the dissensions in the Free French movement. A breach between De Gaulle and Muselier threatens to cause a public rift in the movement. De Gaulle is autocratic and right wing; Muselier is a Liberal (and a very loose-living one) who wants De Gaulle's powers to be delegated to a Council. The PM, who is heartily sick of the Free French, ended by handing the whole matter over to the reluctant Eden.

Winston S. Churchill to Anthony Eden
(*Churchill papers, 20/36*)

23 September 1941

1. We did not want General de Gaulle to create a shadow French Government with offices to individuals at the present stage. Such a development might come after a conference had been held of representatives of Free Frenchmen from all over the world, but this cannot happen for several months. In the meanwhile, the announcement of the kind of Cabinet proposed by General de Gaulle would divide Frenchmen and excite ridicule in France. Therefore, no such announcement should be allowed.

2. As General de Gaulle had repeatedly expressed very unsuitable anti-British sentiments, we have advised him to form a Council by which he should be advised and with whom he should act. This Council should not be composed of office-holders, but of six or seven Frenchmen representative of the Right and Left. The kind of list which the British Government think would be most successful is subjoined.[1]

3. The relations of General de Gaulle to this Council should be those of a Governor, who is the accepted head and has definite executive powers, but who on fundamental issues, as well as broad matters of policy, must be guided by his colleagues. Decisions and decrees, other than those purely administrative or necessitated by war emergency, must issue from the Governor-in-Council and will be altogether of a different order from any such decision emanating from the chief or governor himself. The line of demarcation between the said decisions shall be defined in due course in consultation with His Majesty's Government and the Council.

4. General de Gaulle, having invoked the good offices of the Prime Minister and His Majesty's Government to prevent scandal and division in the Free French movement, is invited to confer with Admiral Muselier and a

[1] The list which Churchill enclosed was: General de Gaulle, Admiral Muselier, General Legentilhomme, Capitaine de Vaisseau d'Argenlieu, M. Plevens, M. Dejean, M. Labarthe and Capitaine de Vaisseau Moret.

representative of His Majesty's Government upon the best methods of giving effect to the above.

5. It must be understood that the control of the Free French Secret Service must be vested in someone acceptable to the new Council and to His Majesty's Government.

6. Admiral Muselier should withdraw the various statements attributed to him which are of a disruptive character. He should do this in accordance with the aide-memoire subjoined, which has been prepared by the Admiralty.

7. In the meanwhile, no statement must be issued by any of the French parties concerned, and none will be allowed to pass the British censorship during the few days necessary to restore harmony and form an instrument.

8. The charge of all these matters is committed to the Secretary of State for Foreign Affairs, who will nominate the British representative and will fill in as necessary the subjoined annexures; not hesitating to use whatever powers may be necessary, including the forcible restraint of individuals.

Winston S. Churchill to Herbert Morrison

(*Churchill papers, 20/36*)

23 September 1941

I have been disturbed by the accounts in the papers of the riotous behaviour of the internees in the Isle of Man. This has evidently made a bad impression on the public. The strictest discipline should now be enforced and punishments of markedly deterrent character should be imposed upon all who took part in the disorders. The ringleaders should be removed to prison. The impression has been created of great weakness and timidity in the authorities. Surely the guard should be armed with buckshot, so that there need be no hesitation in firing when necessary. Are you satisfied with the camp authorities? I presume you will make a report to the Cabinet upon the whole incident. As you know, I am in favour of mitigations to well-disposed prisoners, but all riots and disorders should be sternly repressed.

Winston S. Churchill to Brendan Bracken

(*Churchill papers, 20/36*)

23 September 1941

Why don't you try to arrange for a cinema in the House of Commons, where Members can see the films of the M of I,[1] and German and Russian films, &c.?

[1] Ministry of Information.

Winston S. Churchill to the Reverend J. Scott Lidgett[1]
(*Churchill papers, 20/22*)

23 September 1941

My dear Dr Scott Lidgett,

The question was most carefully considered by the Cabinet, and the decision was taken that exemption from military service could not be granted to Officers of the Oxford Group Movement. This of course in no way deprives individuals of their rights as conscientious objectors. All the circumstances connected with this Movement were weighed, and I much regret I can hold out no hope of any change of policy during the continuance of the present Administration.

Yours very faithfully
Winston S. Churchill

PS Thank you so much for your very kind good wishes.

War Cabinet: minutes
(*Cabinet papers, 65/19*)

24 September 1941
6 p.m.
10 Downing Street

The Prime Minister emphasized the extreme importance of not allowing any public mention in the Press of differences in the Free French Movement. The Movement was of the utmost importance, but its influence might suffer seriously if there was a split.

PALESTINE

The Prime Minister referred[2] to the suggestion that had been made that Ibn Saud should become King of an Arab Federation; and that provision should be made for an autonomous Jewish State, with reasonable room for expansion. This suggestion had been well received by Dr Weizmann, and he (the Prime Minister) would be glad if the Foreign Secretary, the Secretary of

[1] John Scott Lidgett, 1854–1953. Entered the Wesleyan ministry, 1876. Co-founder of the Bermondsey Settlement, 1891. Alderman of the London County Council, 1905–1910; 1922–28. President of the Evangelical Free Churches of England and Wales, 1906–07. Member of the Royal Commission on Venereal Diseases, 1913–15. President of the Free Church Commission, 1912–15. Member of Senate, University of London, 1922; Vice-Chancellor, 1930–32; Member of the Court of the University, 1929–44. Companion of Honour, 1933. Among his many publications were two in 1941, *The Cross Seen from Five Standpoints* and *The Crowns of Jesus*. In 1952, aged ninety-eight, he published *Salvation*. His only son was killed in the First World War.

[2] Because of the particular secrecy of this, and the subsequent item, they were recorded in the War Cabinet's Confidential Annex (*Cabinet papers, 65/23*).

State for India and the Secretary of State for the Colonies would consult with the Minister of State and see whether this suggestion could be carried further.

TURKEY

The Prime Minister said that it was more important to secure that the Turks would resist enemy pressure to give passage to German troops through their country, and would allow us to make preparations on Turkish aerodromes in advance of hostilities, on the lines of what Germany had done in Bulgaria, than to press them to enter the war on our side. The Prime Minister mentioned that General Wavell was going to Tiflis where he would have discussions with the Russians. We were sending out reinforcements to the Middle East which would enable us to act in North Persia and, if necessary, in the Caucasus.

Winston S. Churchill to Lord Linlithgow
(*Churchill papers, 20/43*)

24 September 1941
Personal and Secret

We have good reason to believe that shipping in Indian ports is not being turned round as quickly as possible. See particularly Secretary of State for India's No. 11,300 of September 16. I should be grateful if you would intervene personally and drive the business forward.

John Martin: diary
(*John Martin papers*)

25 September 1941

With PM and Mrs Churchill visited Walmer Castle and PM's Squadron (No. 615)[1] at Manston.

John Colville: diary
(*Colville papers*)

25 September 1941

The new Lord Warden left Victoria at 12.45 to visit his Cinque Ports, travelling in the new railway coach which has been prepared for him and taking with him Mrs C, Jack Churchill, Tommy, John Martin (for today only)

[1] Churchill had been Air Commodore of No. 615 Squadron since before the war.

and me. Walmer Castle disappointed its new owner and Mrs C in particular thought it gloomy and unwieldy. Having a liking for feudal relics I admired the deep moat and the bastions, and was also interested to see the chairs in which Mr Pitt read and the Duke of Wellington died.

We proceeded by car to Manston, saw and had tea with the PM's Fighter Squadron (No. 615) and looked at the Hurricanes. I had a long talk with the Squadron Leader[1] who showed me the cases of maps, food, matches, money etc. carried by all Fighter Pilots in case they should come down in France. We also saw a short film of the Squadron's latest attack on an enemy convoy. I met Air Vice Marshal Leigh-Mallory[2] who succeeded Park[3] in command of No. 11 Group.

We spent the night in a quiet siding, half a mile from a stone marking the centre of England and a few miles short of Coventry.

The PM dictated half of his speech for the House of Commons next Tuesday. It promises to be one of his best.

Squadron-Leader Gillam: recollection
(*Letter to the author, 20 January 1983*)

[25 September 1941] [Manston]

Conditions were uncomfortable and we were having to stay in the dispersal hut for long periods and have our food brought to us. We were very proud to

[1] Squadron-Leader Gillam, AFC (1938) DFC (after the Battle of Britain). Later he was awarded a bar to his DFC and the DSO for shipping attacks in the Channel, and subsequently a bar to his DSO for attacks on V-weapon sites.

[2] Trafford Leigh-Mallory, 1892–1944. On active service, 1914–19 (despatches, Distinguished Service Order). Deputy Director of Staff Duties, Air Ministry, 1931–34. Senior Air Staff Officer, Iraq, 1936–37. Air Officer Commanding No. 12 Fighter Group (defence of the Midlands and the East Coast shipping routes), 1937–40; No.11 Group (south of England), 1940–42. Air Officer Commanding-in-Chief, Fighter Command, 1942. Knighted, 1943. Air Commander in Chief, Allied Expeditionary Force, 1943–44. Put in to effect the Transportation Plan for the sustained bombing of German communications before the Normandy landings (with 9,000 aircraft under his command). Appointed Commander-in-Chief, South-East Asia Command, but killed, with his wife, in an air crash, near Grenoble, while on the way to take up his duties, 14 November 1944. His body, that of his wife, and those of eight others on the flight, were found under several feet of ice-packed snow on 7 June 1945, thirty miles east of Grenoble near the peak known as 'The Devil's Chimney'. All ten bodies were buried in the mountain village cemetery in the presence of a full company of the French Air Force, which had been under the Marshal's command in June 1944. Leigh-Mallory's brother George had died while climbing Mount Everest twenty years earlier: his body was discovered on Everest in 1999.

[3] Keith Rodney Park, 1892–1975. A New Zealander; Private, New Zealand Field Artillery, 1911. New Zealand Expeditionary Force, 1914. Royal Field Artillery, 1915 (on active service at Gallipoli, and in France). Seconded to the Royal Flying Corps, 1916. Captain, Royal Air Force, 1918 (Military Cross and bar; DFC). Senior Air Staff Officer, Fighter Command, 1938. Commanded No. 11 Fighter Group, April–December 1940. Air Officer Commanding No. 23 Group, Training Command, 1941. Commanded RAF Egypt, 1942. Knighted, 1942. Air Officer Commanding Malta, 1942–3; Middle East, 1944. Allied Air Commander-in-Chief, South East Asia, 1945–6. One of his two sons was killed in action in Korea, 1951.

get some cakes a table cloth and several large teapots. All was laid out and Churchill and Lady Churchill arrived and came into the dispersal hut and I proudly showed him our spread and asked if he would like some tea. He replied, 'Good God no, my wife drinks that, I'll have a brandy.'

Needless to say there was no brandy available. We chatted for a time and he asked me to let him have a copy of the monthly operations diary we did for October and November.

War Cabinet: minutes
(*Cabinet papers, 65/19*)

25 September 1941 10 Downing Street
11.30 a.m.

The Foreign Secretary said that on the previous evening he and the First Lord had had long discussions with General de Gaulle and Admiral Muselier. The result had been that the General and the Admiral had agreed to continue in somewhat uneasy association.

The Foreign Secretary added that the Minister of War Transport[1] was disturbed at the proposal that Admiral Muselier should have control of the Free French Navy and Mercantile Marine. He thought that the officers and men of vessels of the French Merchant Navy now working for us would very much dislike being put under Admiral Muselier.

The Prime Minister said that, of course, there was no intention to give the Free French any increased measure of control, over and above what they already possessed, of French merchant ships or crews. If there was any doubt on this point, the Foreign Secretary should take an early opportunity of making this clear to the Free French Headquarters.

Reference was made to the result of the Wrekin by-election in which the Government candidate had had a small majority.

The Prime Minister said that such results might well give an entirely false impression to public opinion abroad of the degree of support which the National Government had in the country. For this reason it was important that the Government case should be strongly represented at by-elections, and that Government speakers should go down to the constituencies in which by-elections were being held.

The War Cabinet endorsed this view.

A short discussion took place in which several Ministers expressed their sense of dissatisfaction with the attitude adopted by certain newspapers which

[1] Lord Leathers.

appeared to seize every opportunity of representing the Government's actions in an unfavourable light. The attitude was probably encouraged by the absence of air attacks on this country.

The Prime Minister said that it was his intention to take a pretty firm line with the Government's critics in his statement in the House of Commons on the following day.

The War Cabinet took note of this statement.

Winston S. Churchill to the Chiefs of Staff

(*Churchill papers, 20/36*)

25 September 1941

I attach a summary of the official correspondence which has passed in the last fifteen months in regard to offensive and defensive measures in chemical warfare, together with a table showing the stock position of the more important gas-filled weapons. Please report whether you are satisfied with the present position and our means of retaliating on the Germans if necessary.

There may be a difficulty in maintaining stocks owing to chemical deterioration. Normally, if there were a consumption, stocks could be replaced. Please let me have your views on this aspect of the matter as well.

Winston S. Churchill to Sir Kingsley Wood

(*Churchill papers, 20/36*)

25 September 1941

We shall certainly be faced with demands to increase the pay of the Army, but I think it would be better to try to give the soldier an equivalent to the nest-egg which the civilian will have at the end of the war for the Income Tax he pays on his wages. The soldier ought to have a bonus or nest-egg equal to that of the average wage-earner.

Will you have this examined, and let me have a scheme which the Cabinet could consider. I believe you would find it less expensive in the long run, and it has the merit of being a novel and original idea which no one has asked for yet. Moreover, it will cost you nothing till the war is over. 5,000,000 men at, say £30 apiece would be £150,000,000. The great thing is to propose a plan and not have it forced upon one.

Winston S. Churchill to Anthony Eden
(*Churchill papers, 20/36*)

25 September 1941

We now know that the Grand Mufti[1] is in the Japanese Legation at Teheran. It seems of the utmost importance to obtain his surrender, and meanwhile I presume all measures are being taken to prevent his getting away. Will you please do whatever is possible.

Winston S. Churchill to David Margesson
(*Churchill papers, 20/36*)

25 September 1941

Many plans are being made for the amusement of troops during the winter. They are allowed to use Government transport, within limits, to get to the nearest sizeable town. Officers are not allowed to have this privilege. It might be possible to arrange for Officers to have reasonable use of available Government transport on paying for petrol. Many of them are too poor to hire any other form of transport, but this would be fair and acceptable. The use might be controlled by the Corps Divisional Staff.

Pray let me have your views on this.

Winston S. Churchill to A. V. Alexander and Admiral Pound
(*Churchill papers, 20/36*)

25 September 1941

Why not give the Graph U-boat,[2] when she is repaired, to the Yugoslav navy? They have a submarine crew which has arrived at Alexandria, but their vessel was in too bad a condition for the Admiral to allow it to go to sea. I rather like the idea of the Yugoslavs working a captured German U-boat.

[1] Haj Amin al-Husseini, Grand Mufti of Jerusalem, (see page 1153, note 1). Churchill knew of the Mufti's presence in Teheran from an intercepted Japanese diplomatic message.

[2] This U-boat had been captured in August 1941 by a Hudson aircraft of the Royal Air Force in the Western Approaches.

Winston S. Churchill to Harry Hopkins
(*Churchill papers, 20/49*)

25 September 1941

Now that our Missions are on their way to Moscow, it may be profitable to survey the field covered by the discussions in London.

2. The offers which we both are making to Russia are necessary and worth while. There is no disguising the fact, however, that they make grievous inroads into what is required by you for expanding your forces and by us for intensifying our war effort. You know where the shoe will pinch most in the next nine months. We must both bend our efforts to making good the gaps unavoidably created. We here are unlikely to be able to expand our programmes much above what is already planned. I earnestly hope that you will be able to raise the general level of yours by an immediate short-term effort.

3. You will have heard that good progress was made in the discussions on overall requirements for victory. A joint memorandum giving estimated eventual requirements, as far as we can foresee them, was drawn up and is being taken back to Washington by General Embick.[1] Further work on this will have to be done in Washington, and an estimate of what is required to maintain Russian resistance will have to be added. Would it be possible to try to reach, in the second half of 1942, the output now planned for the first half of 1943? If such an attempt were successful it would not only lay the foundations for the victory programme, but would help to meet more speedily than otherwise the short-term requirements of us both. It would also enable greater help to be given to the Russians in the second half of 1942.

4. I saw Mr Sherwood[2] yesterday.

All good wishes.

[1] Stanley D. Embick, 1877-1957. On active service as a Second Lieutenant with the United States Army against the Spanish forces, Cuba, 1898; Colonel, Signal Corps, France, 1917, and Chief of Staff, American Section, Supreme War Council, 1917-18. Chief of the War Plans Division, 1939. Retired from the army with the rank of Major-General, 1940. Recalled to active duty, 1941.

[2] Robert Emmet Sherwood, 1896-1955. An American citizen, he enlisted in the Canadian Army in order to fight in France; gassed and wounded at Arras. Editor of *Vanity Fair*, 1919-20. Associate editor of *Life*, 1920-24; editor, 1924-28. Pulitzer Prize winning playwright. Friend and confidant of both President Roosevelt and Harry Hopkins. One of Roosevelt's speechwriters. In October 1941 he was appointed head of the United States Foreign Information Service, charged with co-ordinating anti-Nazi propaganda. In 1948 he published the two-volume *The White House Papers of Harry L. Hopkins, An intimate history*. It was one of the first detailed books about a senior wartime figure and war policy at the centre, preceding the first volume of Churchill's war memoirs; Churchill had sent Sherwood fourteen typewritten pages in answer to Sherwood's questions to him. In 1945 he worked on Samuel Goldwyn's film *The Best Years of Our Lives*, a title, he later wrote, that 'referred hopefully to the future as opposed to the past'.

Winston S. Churchill to Lord Beaverbrook[1]
(Churchill papers, 20/43)

25 September 1941
Absolutely Personal and Secret

I am sure you realize that no one in Russia, including Cripps and all your party, must know about our special sources of information.[2]

John Colville: diary
(Colville papers)

26 September 1941

We arrived at Coventry Platform and the PM was not dressed. He always assumes he can get up, shave and have a bath in quarter of an hour whereas in reality it takes him twenty minutes. Consequently he is late for everything. Mrs C seethed with anger.

Lord Dudley (the Regional Commissioner)[3] and the Mayor[4] met us. We went to the centre of the town, where the PM inspected a parade of the Civil Defence Services, and then to the Cathedral. The German bombers assuredly did their worst at Coventry.

The PM will give the V sign with two fingers in spite of the representations repeatedly made to him that this gesture has quite another significance.

We toured very thoroughly the Armstrong Siddeley factory, where aircraft parts and torpedoes are made; and the PM had a rousing reception. As we entered each work-shop all the men clanged their hammers in a deafening welcome.

I drove with Jack Churchill whom some of the crowd took for Maisky!

The Whitley bomber factory is a hotbed of communism and there was some doubt of the reception the PM would get. But his appearance with cigar and semi-top-hat quite captivated the workers who gave him vociferous applause. We saw the lines of finished bombers and amongst them a rickety biplane built in the same factory during the last war. A new Whitley took off and flew past,

1 Lord Beaverbrook was still on his way to Russia by sea.

2 A reference to the top secret German radio signals decrypted at Bletchley (Enigma, later known as Ultra). Beaverbrook was one of only two dozen members of the inner circle of Government who knew of the existence of this source.

3 William Humble Eric Ward, 1894–1969. On active service 1914–18 (wounded, Military Cross). Conservative Member of Parliament for Hornsey 1921–24 and 1931–32. Succeeded his father as third Earl of Dudley, 1932. President of the Society of British Gas Industry, 1926–27; and the British Iron and Steel Federation, 1935–36; of the Birmingham Chamber of Commerce, 1937–39. Regional Commissioner for Civil Defence, No. 9 (Midland) Region, 1940–45.

4 Alfred Robert Grindley. An engineer. Coventry County Councillor from 1924–64. Mayor of Coventry 1941. An Honorary Freeman, 1962.

a Hurricane pilot did stunts, and No. 605 squadron of Hurricanes flew over in astonishingly tight formation. When we drove away, the men and women of the factory quite forgot their communism and rushed forward in serried ranks to say good-bye. But I was disgusted to hear that their production-tempo had not really grown until Russia came into the war.

We lunched on the train, after visiting the cemetery where Coventry's air-raid dead are buried in one common grave. Lord Dudley lunched with us.

At 2.30 we reached Birmingham and there visited a tank factory, where the enthusiasm was even greater than at Coventry, and the Spitfire works at Castle Bromwich. Last of all we saw a display of aerobatics by two test pilots, one in a Hurricane and the other in a Spitfire. Their performance was so daring as to be positively frightening and we all shuddered as Henshaw, the Spitfire pilot, flew over us upside down, some 40 feet from the ground.

The drive back to the station was a triumphant procession. The crowds stood on the pavements, as thick as for the Opening of Parliament in London, for miles and miles along the route. They waved, they cheered, they shouted: every face seemed happy and excited. I have seen the PM have many enthusiastic receptions, but never one to equal this. It is clear that his name and fame are as great today as they have ever been. He was deeply moved.

We spent the night in a siding. There was a storm cloud owning to the non-arrival of a pouch but after much lightning and many claps of thunder (some of which were telephoned to John Peck at No. 10!), the sky cleared with the advent of dinner and lots of champagne.

The PM finished his speech and I tried laboriously to teach myself mathematics. To bed at 2.00.

Winston S. Churchill to Anthony Eden

(*Churchill papers, 20/36*)

26 September 1941
Action this Day
Secret

This is very unpleasant. Our intention was to compel de Gaulle to accept a suitable Council. All we have done is to compel Muselier and Co. to submit themselves to de Gaulle. I understood you were going to make sure that the resulting government represented what we want. It is evident that this business will require the closest watching, and that our weight in the immediate future must be thrown more heavily against de Gaulle than I had hoped would be necessary.

I am renewing my directions that he is on no account to leave the country.

Winston S. Churchill to Lord Beaverbrook
(*Churchill papers, 20/43*)

26 September 1941
Most Secret and Personal

Nothing sensational has happened since you left. At sea it has been knock for knock. You have heard how our submarines and aircraft have made good dent in Mediterranean pipe-line. In Northern Area our and Russian submarines have sunk four merchant ships between them. Our destroyers got in among some E-boats attacking an East Coast convoy and did good work. Our losses about 70,000 tons since you left. Total for the month about 175,000 tons. One-man submarine got into Gibraltar on Saturday last, damaging two tankers and sinking an oiler. Weather has curtailed air operations. Fairly heavy attack one night on Berlin, Frankfurt and Ostend. Four bombers failed to return and sixteen crashed on landing in fog. Good day on Sunday, when we destroyed twenty-four enemy over Northern France, plus eight probables and thirteen damaged. Our losses fourteen fighters, three pilots safe.

Russian Front

2. In the North, German attacks on Murmansk have been held. Germans have got footing on Oesel and captured Moon and Worms. In Leningrad morale reported high. Russians admit fall of Kiev and German claim to have taken 150,000 prisoners. Bypassed Russian troops seem to be fighting vigorously and making strenuous attempts to break to the East. Germans thrusting Eastwards to Kharkov. In South, all communications with Crimea cut.

3. Lyttelton arrived on Sunday and has given us valuable picture of Middle East situation. He takes optimistic view of our general strategic position. Much depends on Crusader.[1] There is no doubt that Germans are feeling the pinch. I have good hopes of a success. Relief of Australians from Tobruk has progressed smoothly, and if all goes well we may not have to take out the 3rd Brigade by sea.

Turkey

4. We are going all out to impress the Turks by attractive promise of help, which, if followed by victory against Rommel, should stiffen them against German pressure.

Persia.

5. Ex-Shah left for Mauritius. Negotiations for Anglo-Soviet-Persian Alliance now in train.

[1] Operations in the Western Desert to relieve Tobruk, which had been under Axis siege since April 1941.

Caucasus

6. I have told you of Wavell's visit to Tiflis, where he will hold out our right hand to Russians. We aim to build up formidable Anglo-Russian force, which should be in position by the time Germans can arrive in Caucasus. One or both of two additional Infantry Divisions going to Middle East before end of year can be sent to Persia if situation demands.

TUC Delegation to Moscow

7. Citrine wanted to send Delegation to Moscow and Soviet Government agreed. Cabinet thought it undesirable that delegation should reach Moscow within at least a week of arrival of your Mission. Position has been communicated to TUC and Maiksy. Will let you know further developments.

Free French

8. De Gaulle very tiresome. He and Muselier at loggerheads. We shall get an accommodation, and meanwhile nothing is being said about it all.

9. Hope sea voyage is doing you good. Best of luck.

John Colville: diary

(*Colville papers*)

27 September 1941

We reached Liverpool. The PM, in his curious semi-naval garb, toured the new Aircraft Carrier *Indomitable*. After we had climbed up and down endless companions and seen the aircraft on deck, he made a speech to the assembled ship's company. I am always impressed by his skill in suiting his words to his audience. On this occasion he spoke of the man-of-war and his wife, or sweetheart, the Aircraft Carrier who goes out to find his dinner for him and sometimes cooks it or has it done to a turn so that the man-of-war may eat it. It was thus with the *Bismarck*, it might well be the same with the *Tirpitz*.

The docks at Liverpool are a scene of great devastation. Many acres have been entirely cleared of buildings by the bombs.

The PM visited C-in-C Western Approaches[1] at his headquarters, where Lord Derby[2] also awaited him, and then the party returned to the train for lunch.

In the afternoon we slept and I played some backgammon with Mrs Churchill. It was a stiflingly hot day for so late in the year. We reached

[1] Admiral Sir Percy Noble, later Head of the British Admiralty Delegation in Washington.

[2] Edward George Villiers Stanley, 1865–1948. Educated at Wellington College. Lieutenant, Grenadier Guards, 1885–95. Conservative MP for West Houghton, 1892–1906. Postmaster-General, 1903–5. 17th Earl of Derby, 1908. Director-General of Recruiting, October 1915. Under-Secretary of State at the War Office, July–December 1916. Secretary of State for War, December 1916–18. Ambassador to France, 1918–20. Secretary of State for War, 1922–4. Member of the Joint Select Committee on the Indian Constitution, 1933–4. In 1960 Randolph Churchill published *Lord Derby, 'King of Lancashire'*.

Chequers before 6.00. Clarissa[1] was there and Venetia Montagu. We all sat in the garden and the PM played with Mary's dog, Suki, which is a very engaging poodle.

Oliver Lyttelton (the Minister of State) came for the weekend with his son Anthony,[2] a precocious but rather irritating youth who is a private in the Marines.

The PM was in a happy frame of mind at dinner. Having described Mr Granville MP as 'the son of a bitch', he remarked that there must have been a great many bitches in the last generation!

After dinner we saw a bad English film, *Cottage to Let* produced by Anthony Asquith. Later a pouch arrived containing the following telegram:

'*General Catroux à Ld Warden des Cinq Ports. Reçevez je vous prie mes chaleureuses felicitations pour votre elevation a la pairie qui rejouit tous mes camarades Francais Libres. General Catroux.*'[3]

The PM was highly entertained and sent the following reply: '*Mille remerciements mais ce n'est pa si grave que ça. Vive La France Libre.* (signed) Mister Churchill.'

Winston S. Churchill to Lord Reith[4]

(*Churchill papers, 20/36*)

27 September 1941

I doubt very much whether it will ever be possible for me to live at Walmer Castle, or indeed whether anybody will be able to live in such fine houses after the war. I mentioned this to The King when accepting the appointment, which I regard as a compliment. Clearly I cannot attempt to reside there at the present time, as it is well within range of the enemy's batteries on the French coast, and the mere report of my residing there would be sufficient to get the whole place knocked down. In these circumstances I think it would be perfectly proper for the Office of Works to take it over during the war in whatever way they think most conducive to the public interest. I should hope, therefore, that as long as I do not use the castle at all or derive any benefit from it, it and the gardens could be taken care of by the state. After the war the position could be reviewed.

Perhaps you will let me know what you think can be done.

[1] Clarissa Churchill, daughter of Winston Churchill's brother Jack. In 1952 she married Anthony Eden (as his second wife).

[2] Antony Alfred Lyttelton, 1920–1980. Entered the Royal Marines, as a private, 1940. Served on the General Staff, Mediterranean, as an officer, 1942–45 (despatches). Member of the London Stock Exchange, 1950–75. Succeeded his father, as 2nd Viscount Chandos, 1972.

[3] General Catroux was under the impression that, as Lord Warden of the Cinque Ports, Churchill had been elevated to the House of Lords.

[4] Minister of Works and Buildings.

Winston S. Churchill to Sir Archibald Sinclair and Brendan Bracken
(*Churchill papers, 20/36*)

27 September 1941

What is the reason for giving so much publicity to the discreditable behaviour of the six American airmen published in all the newspapers today?[1] The story is one which will be meat and drink to our enemies over there. Surely the matter could have been handled as one of internal discipline?

Who is responsible?

Winston S. Churchill to Air Chief Marshal Sir Charles Portal
(*Cabinet papers, 120/300*)

27 September 1941
Secret

BOMBING POLICY

It is very disputable whether bombing by itself will be a decisive factor in the present war. On the contrary, all that we have learnt since the war began shows that its effects, both physical and moral, are greatly exaggerated. There is no doubt that the British people have been stimulated and strengthened by the attack made upon them so far. Secondly, it seems very likely that the ground defences and night fighters will overtake the Air attack. Thirdly, in calculating the number of bombers necessary to achieve hypothetical and indefinite tasks, it should be noted that only a quarter of our bombs hit the targets. Consequently an increase in the accuracy of bombing to 100 per cent. would in fact, raise our bombing force to four times its strength. The most we can say is that it will be a heavy and, I trust, a seriously increasing annoyance.

[1] The six American airmen had been asked to resign their commissions in the Royal Air Force, having returned to the United States in protest at receiving a lower rate of pay than they said they had been promised. As a result of the dispute they had refused to take part in active operations. The report in the *Manchester Guardian* stated: 'The officers admitted that they signed documents before leaving Canada in which the conditions of service were laid down, but said they did not read the papers before signing them. The number of officers affected is a very small percentage of the American pilots who have come over to serve side by side with British RAF personnel. Many of these, dissociating themselves from the attitude taken up by the six pilots, say it is their unanimous wish to maintain the high standard won by their squadrons.'

Winston S. Churchill to William Mackenzie King
(*Churchill papers, 20/49*)

27 September 1941
Secret

I should be glad if you could give a friendly hand to the Duke of Windsor during his visit to Western Canada.

Winston S. Churchill to Howard Smith
(*Churchill papers, 20/22*)

28 September 1941

Dear Mr Howard Smith,

In my letter of 29 August I said that we would see what could be done about the points you raised in connection with welfare in Iceland.

As regards the pipes for the proposed hot water system at Reykjavik, I fear that the provision of the necessary steel, which is in the neighbourhood of 3,000 tons, is beyond our strength. We have however been able to take some steps in the matter of amenities for the troops in Iceland and you will find details in the enclosed note.

Yours very truly
Winston S. Churchill

NOTE

WELFARE OF TROOPS IN ICELAND

The following steps have been taken by the War Office to fulfil the requirements of the General Officer Commanding, Iceland:

(i) A part-time and well qualified Entertainment Officer has been made available.
(ii) The War Office are making arrangements for a Warrant Officers and Sergeants' Club.
(iii) A larger proportion of draught (as opposed to bottled) beer is being sent to Iceland.
(iv) Two further mobile cinemas are being despatched as soon as arrangements can be made.
(v) 275 specially designed battery radio sets are at the port of shipment and should be despatched shortly.

Winston S. Churchill to Viscountess D'Abernon[1]
(*Churchill papers, 2/417*)

28 September 1941
Personal and Private

My dear Helen,

Thank you so much for your letter. It was very nice to hear from you again. Tell Edgar[2] I often think of him and you, and of all the pleasant days of the past.

I should not bring the furniture back to Morpeth Mansions.[3] Although probably the enemy will not be able to keep up continuous raids as before, we must expect him to save up for some exceptionally heavy efforts, and all the area around Victoria Station is in the very bull's eye.

As you have asked for my advice, dear Helen, I must say I am rather concerned at your both being at Hove. The danger of invasion does not seem immediate, but at any time we might have to order a clearance of the civil population from the coastal towns. There is no intention of doing this at the present time, but we have already discouraged people as much as possible from residing on the coast, especially between the Wash and the Isle of Wight, and it would I think only be prudent to look around during the winter for some resting-place on the other side of the island or farther inland.

Would you mind burning this letter after reading it and let me know you have done so, as it is for your personal information only, and if it got into other people's hands it might excite unnecessary alarm.

Yours ever,

[1] Lady Helen Venetia Duncombe, daughter of the 1st Earl of Feversham. In 1890 she married Edgar Vincent, later 1st Viscount D'Abernon. From 1914 to 1918 she served as a nurse on the Western and Italian Fronts. Their country house was at Stoke D'Abernon in Surrey, their London home at 20 St James's Place (which had been badly damaged by bombs early in the Blitz).

[2] Edgar Vincent, 1857–1941. Served in the Coldstream Guards, 1877–82. Financial Adviser to the Egyptian Government, 1883–9. Knighted, 1887 (at the age of thirty). Governor of the Imperial Ottoman Bank, 1889–97. Conservative MP, 1899–1906. Created Baron D'Abernon, 1914. Chairman, Central Control Board (Liquor Traffic), 1915–20. Mission to Poland, 1920. Ambassador to Berlin, 1920–6. Created Viscount, 1926. Chairman, Medical Research Council, 1929–33. In 1931 he published an account of the battle of Warsaw, *The Eighteenth Decisive Battle of the World.* In 1890 he married Lady Helen Venetia Duncombe, daughter of the 1st Earl of Feversham.

[3] In the decade before the war Churchill, as well as having his home at Chartwell, had also lived and worked in a flat in Morpeth Mansions, Victoria.

John Colville: diary
(*Colville papers*)

28 September 1941

The PM talked to me while he was dressing for dinner. He said that so far the Government had only made one error of judgment: Greece. He had instinctively had doubts. We could and should have defended Crete and advised the Greek Government to make the best terms it could. But the campaign, and the Yugoslav volte-face which it entailed, had delayed Germany and might after all prove to have been an advantage. I was surprised at the PM's assertion that he had doubted the wisdom of going to Greece. I seem to remember his influencing the decision in favour of an expedition and Dill being against it.[1] Incidentally he has now got his knife right into Dill and frequently disparages him. He says he has an alternative CIGS in mind: Sir Alan Brooke, C-in-C Home Forces. He went on to say that we cannot afford military failures. As regards all this talk of a diversion on the Western Front, a landing on the Continent could only have one outcome. The War Office would not do the job properly; indeed it was unfair to ask them to pit themselves against German organization, experience and resources. They had neither the means nor the intelligence. But critics would ask how we were going to win the war and that was difficult to answer. On one or two occasions lately I have heard him say he thinks it will last for several years more in all probability.

Finally he said that he ought really to have procured me a commission in the RAF straight away. There was no advantage in going through the ranks. I disagree and said so, but was squashed!

While the PM was in his bath I was able to persuade him to delete a passage in his speech referring to Persia in which he spoke of the FO 'in all its long and chequered career'.

At dinner there was much good-natured but scathing comment on Hore Belisha, Winterton, Jack Seely[2] and Oliver Stanley[3] (who, said the PM, was really suited to be Dean of a Cathedral, walking round the monastic fish-

[1] On 12 February 1941 Churchill had indeed supported British military help for Greece, with Dill opposing it for fear of 'another Dunkirk'. But two weeks later it was Dill and Eden who, from Athens had strongly urged the sending of a British expedition to Greece, and Churchill who had been hesitant.

[2] John Edward Bernard Seely, 1868–1947. French gold medal for saving life at sea, 1891. On active service in South Africa, 1899–1900 (DSO). Liberal MP, 1900–6, 1906–10, 1910–22 and 1923–4. Secretary of State for War, 1912–14. On active service on the Western Front, 1914–18 (despatches, DSO, Major-General). Deputy Minister of Munitions (under Churchill), 1918. Under-Secretary of State for Air (under Churchill), 1919. Chairman of the National Savings Committee, 1926–43. Created Baron Mottistone, 1938. His eldest son, Frank, was killed in action on the Western Front in April 1917.

[3] Oliver Frederick George Stanley, 1896–1950. Son of the 17th Earl of Derby. Educated at Eton. On active service, France, 1914–18 (Military Cross, despatches). Major, 1918. Called to the Bar, 1919. Conservative MP for Westmorland, 1924–45; for Bristol West, 1945–50. Parliamentary Under-Secretary, Home Office, 1931–3. Minister of Transport, 1933–4; of Labour, 1934–5. Privy Councillor, 1934. President of the Board of Education, 1935–7; of the Board of Trade, 1937–40. Secretary of State for War, January–May 1940; for the Colonies, 1942–5.

ponds and contemplating some academic *mot* which he could bring out next time he was invited to dine with the Fellows of his old College). The PM admitted that he had been responsible for the appointment of Jack Seely as S of S for War: he had suggested it to Asquith during a cruise on the *Enchantress* on the only occasion on which Asquith had mentioned politics, and at the time it had seemed to him to have distinct possibilities. Oliver Lyttelton recalled how just after Munich Crinks Johnstone[1] had told Duff Cooper he had been the worst S of S for War of the century and Duff Cooper had replied: 'How dare you say such a thing in the presence of Jack Seely.'

The PM launched an attack on Shinwell who had refused office in May 1940, because he thought the post offered him was inadequate to his deserts, and now took refuge in talking of the Government as a lot of 'pinchbeck Napoleons'. Then he reminisced about Harrow, where he said he had spent the unhappiest days of his life, and told how he and F. E. Smith had been booed when they went there in 1912. However he was going down again to hear the songs (he repeated several word-perfect by heart) and would recall me from wherever I then might be so that I could accompany him.

After dinner we saw an American film called 'John Doe',[2] which I enjoyed, and the PM then closeted himself with Oliver Lyttelton in the Hawtrey Room and talked so long, as well as dictating telegrams, that I did not get into bed till twenty-five to four. The PM said he supposed I was looking forward to the RAF and lights out at 10.00 p.m.!

War Cabinet: minutes

(*Cabinet papers, 65/23*)

29 September 1941
5 p.m.

The Prime Minister said that he had received a telegram from the Prime Minister of Australia which referred to steps which he had taken to ensure the secrecy of communications passing between the two Governments.

The Prime Minister then read to the War Cabinet the draft of a reply which he proposed to send to Mr Fadden. In this reply he had referred to the difficulty which we had experienced in preventing General Auchinleck from resigning his command on the ground that the Australian Government had no confidence in his military judgment. The draft reply also expressed the hope that Mr Fadden would reconsider the decision to withdraw the remaining two

[1] Harcourt Johnstone.

[2] Made in 1941. Directed by Frank Capra: regarded by many as his finest film. A man who needs money (played by Gary Cooper) agrees to impersonate a non-existent person who said he would be committing suicide as a protest, and a political movement begins. The female lead was played by Barbara Stanwyk.

Australian Brigades now in Tobruk without reference to the great impending operation, and also referred to the pained impression created by the suggestion implied, though not by Mr Fadden, that we had thrown an undue burden on Australian troops.

Winston S. Churchill to Arthur Fadden
(*Cabinet papers, 65/23*)

29 September 1941
Personal and Secret

1. I am very glad to receive your No. 638 and I think I ought to let you know, for your most secret information about Tobruk, that Lyttelton and I only with difficulty prevented General Auchinleck from resigning his command on the grounds that the Australian Government had no confidence in his military judgment. Had your decision been based on political grounds he would not have felt the want of confidence implied.

2. The September relief has been effected successfully. The cost is measured by an indefinite delay in the intermingling of the 6th British Division with the two Indian Divisions in Iraq and Persia, thus making three mixed Anglo-Indian units. I still hope that you will reconsider your decision that the last two Australian Brigades must be pulled out of Tobruk without reference to the great pending operation by which we trust all will be relieved. The exchange of these brigades with others during the October moonless period will certainly handicap the Air Force in their preliminary fight for air superiority before the battle by forcing them to divert their strength to providing fighter cover for the shipping involved. Every day's delay in delivering the attack will make our task more formidable. Everything points to the first days of November, and the period during which the remaining Australian Brigades would be involved is very short. Australian troops have borne the burden of Tobruk, and we should all deeply regret that they should be cut out of the honour.

3. Believe me, everyone here realizes your political embarrassments with a majority of only one. Nevertheless, Australia might think this is a time to do and dare. We have been greatly pained here by the suggestion, not made by you but implied, that we have thrown an undue burden on the Australian troops. The debt to them is immense, but the Imperial Forces have suffered more casualties actually and relatively. Moreover, the British Submarine Service has lost nearly a third killed outright, and I could give you other instances.

Therefore, we feel we are entitled to count upon Australia to make every sacrifice necessary for the comradeship of the Empire. But please understand that, at whatever cost, your orders about your own troops will be obeyed.

Winston S. Churchill to General Auchinleck
(*Churchill papers, 20/43*)

29 September 1941

1. Thank you very much for your telegram No. 1568 Susan of 21st September and also for your full and helpful letter. In addition to the units and details mentioned in my No. 093 Susan of 17th September, I have now arranged to send you 4,000 more RASC, making 18,000 in all. The two divisions will not necessarily go to you. By the time they are round the Cape it may be that Basra rather than Suez will be their port.

2. The CIGS is cabling you details of October and November convoys. The October convoy will make up the full quota of Bofors guns promised, *i.e.*, 250 extra.

3. It is settled that General Riddell-Webster[1] comes to you from India immediately as Principal Administrative Officer over both Q and A.[2] The Intendant-General's functions exercised under the Minister of State will begin only at the line where more than one Service is involved, and their scope will conform broadly to what you have planned with the Minister of State.

4. All now depends upon the battle. It may well be that you will be granted by the enemy the time you have asked. But every day's delay is dearly purchased in the wider sphere. The prize is Turkey, whose action may well be determined by victory in Cyrenaica.

5. I hope to persuade the Australian Government not to hamper you by pulling out their last two brigades from Tobruk in the October moonless period.

All good wishes.

John Martin: diary
(*John Martin papers*)

29 September 1941

Jock Colville's last day. Group photograph with PM on garden steps. I gave a sherry party in our mess, about eighty people.

[1] Thomas Sheridan Riddell-Webster, 1886–1974. Entered the Army, 1905. On active service, 1914–18 (despatches). Deputy Quarter-Master General, 1939–40. General Officer Commanding-in-Chief, Southern India, 1941. Lieutenant-General in charge of Administration, Middle East, 1941–42. Knighted, 1942. Quarter-Master General to the Forces, War Office, 1942–46. President of the British Legion (Scotland), 1949–65.

[2] Quartermaster and Administrative Services.

John Colville: diary
(*Colville papers*)

29 September 1941

At 3.00 p.m. the private secretaries, Barker[1] and Tommy assembled at No. 10 and were photographed with the PM in the garden. 'Well,' said the PM, 'Let me have three copies and put them down to Mr Colville; they are being done in his honour. And by the way, we had better have a photograph of the cabinet. They are an ugly lot, but still.'

John Martin gave a sherry party to say good-bye to me. Brendan's cook, Mrs Norgren, did her very best, with notable results, and she made me a cake with a little aeroplane on it. The whole of Whitehall seemed to be there, from the PM and Mrs Churchill downwards. The PM told me he would not for the world miss an opportunity of seeing me off the premises!

Winston S. Churchill: speech
(*Hansard*)

30 September 1941 House of Commons

WAR SITUATION

The Prime Minister (Mr Churchill): It is, I think, a little more in harmony with Parliamentary custom for Ministerial statements to be made whenever possible in the course of the normal Business of the House rather than upon Adjournment Motions, and, as this course is equally convenient today, I shall follow it. The House will remember that in June last year I deprecated the making of too frequent expositions of Government policy and reviews of the wear situation by Ministers of the Crown. Anything that is said which is novel or pregnant will, of course, be studied attentively by the enemy, and may be a help to home in measuring our affairs. The House will have noticed how very silent the Nazi leaders have fallen. For seven months Hitler has said nothing about his war plans. What he blurted out in January and February certainly proved helpful to us.

'In the spring' (he said) 'our submarine warfare will begin in earnest, and our opponents will find that the Germans have not been sleeping. The Luftwaffe and the entire German defence forces will, in this way or that, bring about the ultimate decision.'

And again:

'In March and April naval warfare will start such as the enemy had never expected.'

[1] Charles Barker, Chief Clerk, 10 Downing Street. Jock Colville wrote: 'Efficient and entertaining, he was popular with the Private Secretaries. An expert on old silver' (*The Fringes of Power*, page 247, note 1).

We were, therefore, led to expect a crescendo of attacks upon our lifeline of supplies. Certainly the Germans have used an ever larger force of U-boats and long-range aircraft against our shipping. However, our counter-measures, which were undertaken in good time on the largest scale, have proved very successful. For reasons which I have explained very fully to the House, we have since June abandoned the practice of publishing statements at regular monthly intervals of our shipping losses, and I propose to continue this salutary practice. But, apart from anything that may happen during this afternoon, the last day of the month, I may make the following statement to the House. The losses from enemy action of British, Allied and neutral merchant ships during the quarter July, August and September have been only one-third of those losses during the quarter April, May and June. During the same period our slaughter of enemy shipping, German and Italian, has been increasing by leaps and bounds. In fact, it is about one and a half times what it was in the previous three months. So we have at one end a reduction in our average monthly losses to about a third and a simultaneous increase in the losses inflicted upon the enemy of half as much again.

These important results enable us to take a more expansive view of our import programme. Very few important ships carrying munitions have been lost on the way. Our reserves of food stand higher than they did at the outbreak of war, and far higher than they did a year or eighteen months ago. My right hon. Friend the Minister of Food, who has a pretty tough job, now finds himself able to make some quite appreciable improvements in the basic rations of the whole country, and in particular to improve the quantities and varieties of the meals available for the heavy worker during the coming winter. There will be better Christmas dinners this year than last, and at the same time more justification behind those dinners. It seems likely now that we shall bring in several million tons more than the import total which I mentioned in private to the House earlier in the year, which total was itself sufficient to keep us going. We are now within measurable distance of the immense flow of American new building, to which, together with our own construction, we look to carry us through 1942 and on progressively till the end of the war.

I deprecate premature rejoicings over these considerable facts, and I indulge in no sanguine predictions about the future. We must expect that the enemy U-boat warfare, now conducted by larger numbers of U-boats than ever before, supported by scores of Focke 'wolves', will be intensified. The U-boats will be beaten, and kept beaten, only by a corresponding intensification of our own measures and also, to put it very plainly, by that assistance which we are receiving in increasing degree from other quarters. We must not, I repeat, relax for an instant; nevertheless, the facts that I have stated must be regarded as not entirely unsatisfactory, and certainly they are most stultifying to Hitler, who so obligingly warned us of his hopes and plans. This is, I think, an apt illustration of the dangers which should prevent those who are engaged in the high conduct of the war from having to make too many speeches about what they think is going to happen or would like to happen or what they intend to try to do. All the more is this habit important when we have to deal not only with our own affairs but with those of other great Allied or associated nations.

Here I may perhaps be pardoned for making an observation of a somewhat encouraging character. We are no longer alone. Little more than a year ago we seemed quite alone, but, as time has passed, our own steadfast conduct, and the crimes of the enemy, have brought two other very great States and nations into most intimate and friendly contact and concert with us. Whether we look to the East or whether we look to the West, we are no longer alone. Whether we look at the devoted battle lines of the Russian Armies or to the majestic momentum of United States resolve and action, we may derive comfort and good cheer in our struggle which, nevertheless, even if alone, we should carry on inflexibly, unwearyingly, and with steadily increasing resources. The fact, however, that at every stage we have to consider the interests of our Russian ally and also the outlook, wishes and actions of the United States, makes it all the more necessary, imperative even, that I and my colleagues should be particularly careful about any pronouncements, explanations or forecasts in which we might otherwise be tempted to indulge.

I feel sure that the House of Commons, which is the solid foundation of the British war effort and which is resolved to prosecute the war as sternly and implacably as did our forerunners in bygone days, will expect and require from the Ministers who are its servants a particular measure of caution and restraint in all their public utterances about the war.

We have climbed from the pit of peril on to a fairly broad plateau. We can see before us the difficult and dangerous onward path which we must tread. But we can also feel the parallel movement or convergence of the two mighty nations I have mentioned, Russia and the United States. We feel around us the upsurge of all the enslaved countries of Europe. We see how they defy Hitler's firing parties. Far away in the East we see the faithful, patient, inexhaustible spirit of the Chinese race, who too are battling for home and freedom. We are marching in company with the vast majority of mankind, all trending, bearing, forgging steadily forward towards a final goal which, though distant, can already be plainly seen.

When we reflect upon the magnitude of modern events compared with the men who have to try to control or cope with them, and upon the frightful consequences of those events on hundreds of millions, the importance of not making avoidable mistakes grows impressively upon the mind.

For these reasons I could not attempt to discuss at the present time questions of future strategy. They are discussed every day in the newspapers, in an exceedingly vivid and often well-informed manner, but I do not think that His Majesty's Government ought to take any part just now in such

Debates. Take, for instance, the question of whether we should invade the Continent of Europe in order to lift some of the weight off Russia, and whether we ought to take advantage of the lull now that Hitler is busy in Russia to strike him in the West. I shall be guilty of no indiscretion if I admit that these are questions which have several times occurred to those responsible for the conduct of the war. But what could I say about them that would be useful? If I were to throw out dark hints of some great design, no one would have any advantage but the enemy. If, on the other hand, I were to assemble the many cogent reasons which could be ranged on the other side, I should be giving altogether gratuitous reassurance to Hitler.

Such confidences are not reciprocated by the enemy. They have told us nothing since Hitler's speech in February. We are in complete ignorance at this moment about what he is going to do. We do not know how far he will attempt to penetrate the vast lands of Soviet Russia in the face of the valiant Russian defence, or how long his people will endure their own calamitous losses, or, again, whether he will decide to stand on the defensive and exploit the territory of immense value which he has conquered. Should he choose this last, we do not know whether he will turn a portion of his vast armies Southwards, towards the Valley of the Nile, or whether he will attempt to make his way through Spain into North-West Africa, or whether, using the great Continental railways of Europe and the immense chains of airfields which are in excellent order, he will shift his weight to the West and assemble an extensive army with all the special craft that he has constructed for an attempted invasion of the British Islands. It would certainly be in his power, while standing on the defensive in the East, to undertake all three of these hazardous enterprises, on a great scale, together, at one time.

The enemy's only shortage is in the air. This is a very serious shortage, but, for the rest, he still retains the initiative. We have not had the force to take it from him. He has the divisions, he has the weapons, and on the mainland of Europe he has ample means of transport. If he does not tell us his plans, I do not see why we should tell him ours. But I can assure the House that we study and ponder over these dangers and possibilities and on how best to dispose our resources to meet them every working day, and all days are working days, from dawn to far past midnight. We also have the advantage of following very closely all the arguments which are used about them in the public Press and of considering every helpful suggestion which reaches us from any quarter. More than that I really cannot say, and I feel sure that the House would reprove me if I were by any imprudence or desire to be interesting to say anything which afterwards was seen to be harmful.

There is, however, one matter upon which I may speak a little more freely, namely, the material assistance in the way of munitions and supplies which we and the United States are giving to Russia. The British and United States Missions are now in conference with the chiefs of the Soviet at Moscow. The interval which has passed since President Roosevelt and I sent our messages from the Atlantic to Premier Stalin has been used in ceaseless activity on both sides of the ocean. The whole ground has been surveyed in the light of the new events, and many important supplies have already been despatched. Our representatives and their American colleagues have gone to Moscow with clear and full knowledge of what they are able to give to Russia month by month from now onward. The Soviet Government have a right to know what monthly quotas of weapons and supplies we can send and they can count upon. It is only when they know what we can guarantee to send, subject, of course, to the hazards of war, that they themselves can use their vast resources and reserves to the best possible advantage. It is only thus that they can best fill the gap between the very heavy losses sustained and the diminution of munitions-making power which they have suffered on the one hand and the arrival of really effective quantities of British and American supplies on the other. I may say at once, however, that in order to enable Russia to remain indefinitely in the field as a first-class war-making power, sacrifices of the most serious kind and the most extreme efforts will have to be made by the British people and enormous new installations or conversions from existing plants will have to be set up in the United States, with all the labour, expense and disturbance of normal life which these entail.[1]

We have just had a symbolic Tank Week for Russia, and it has, I feel – in fact, I know – given an added sense of the immediate importance of their work to the toiling men and women in our factories. The output of Tank Week is only a very small part of the supplies which Britain and the United States must send to Russia, and must send month after month upon a growing scale and for an indefinite period. It is not only tanks, the tanks for which we have waited

[1] The Soviet Air Force was to receive, in nine monthly deliveries, a total of 1,800 British Hurricanes and Spitfires, 900 American fighters and 900 American bombers. The Soviet Navy was sent 150 sets of 'Asdic' submarine detection sets, 1,500 naval guns, 3,000 anti-aircraft machine guns, and eight destroyers 'before the end of 1941'. For the Soviet Army, the 'immediate requirements' included 1,000 tanks a month together with 'a proper complement of accessories and spare parts', 300 anti-aircraft guns a month, 300 anti-tank guns a month, and 2,000 armoured cars a month, together with their anti-tank guns, as well as (from Britain) three million pairs of army boots at once, followed by 400,000 pairs a month, and (from the United States) 200,000 pairs of army shoes a month. More than a million metres of army cloth were to be supplied each month. Other Soviet needs which the British and American Governments supplied included 4,000 tons of aluminium a month, substantial quantities of copper, tin, lead brass, nickel and cobalt, 13,000 tons monthly of steel bars for shells, industrial diamonds, machine tools, rubber, wool, jute and lead; 20,000 tons a month of petroleum products, including lubricating oil for aviation engines, shipping to enable the transport of cargoes of up to half a million tons a month for food, oil and war material imports; and medical supplies on a vast and comprehensive scale, including more than ten million surgical needles and half a million pairs of surgical gloves. ('Medical Supply Committee, Report': *Cabinet papers, 99/7*). The British signatory of this report was Churchill's doctor, Sir Charles Wilson. Other medical supplies sent to Russia included 20,000 amputation knives, 15,000 amputation saws, 100 portable X-ray sets, 4,000 kilogrammes of local anaesthetics, more than a million doses of the recently discovered antibiotics (including M & B 693), sedatives, heart and brain stimulants, 800,000 forceps (including forceps for bone operations), instruments for brain and eye operations, and a million metres of oilcloth for covering wounds.

so long, that we have to send, but precious aircraft and aluminium, rubber, copper, oil and many other materials vital to modern war, large quantities of which have already gone. All these we must send and keep sending to Russia. It is not only the making and the giving of these commodities, but their transportation and reception which have to be organized. It may be that transportation rather than our willingness or ability to give will prove in the end the limiting factor. All this is now being discussed and planned with full authority and full knowledge by our representatives and the American representatives in conclave in Moscow with Premier Stalin and his principal commanders. It would certainly not be right for me in public Session, or even in Secret Session, at the present time to make any detailed or definite statements upon these subjects. The veriest simpleton can see how great is our interest, to put it no higher, in sustaining Russia by every possible means.

There are, however, other interests which have to be remembered at the same time. In some respects the problems we now have to face are similar to those which rent our hearts last year, when we had, for instance, to refuse to send away from this country for the help of France the last remaining squadrons of fighter aircraft upon which our whole future resistance depended; or again, they remind one of the occasion when, rightly judging Hitler's unpreparedness for invasion in the summer of 1940, we took the plunge of sending so many of our tanks and trained troops all round the Cape to the Valley of the Nile in order to destroy the Italian Armies in Libya and Abyssinia. If it is now thought that we solved those problems correctly we should hope that there might be grounds for confidence that in these new problems His Majesty's Government and their professional advisers will not err either in the direction of reckless improvidence or through want of courage. Anyone who, without full knowledge, should attempt to force the hands of those responsible would act without proper warrant and also – I say it with great respect – would not achieve any useful purpose, because in the discharge of the duties which the House has confided to us we are determined to take our own decisions and to be judged accordingly.

Here I must say a few words about the British Army. There is a current of opinion, which finds frequent expression, that the brass hats and Colonel Blimps and, of course, the much abused War Office, are insisting on building up a portentous, distended and bloated mass of soldiers in this island at the expense of the manufacture of those scientific weapons and appliances which are the main-spring of victory in modern war. The truth is far different. We have never had, and never shall have, an Army comparable in numbers to the armies of the Continent. At the outbreak of war our Army was insignificant as a factor in the conflict. With very great care and toil and time, we have now created a medium sized, but very good Army. The cadres have been formed, the battalions, batteries, divisions and corps have taken shape and life. Men have worked together in the military units for two years. Very severe training was carried out all through last winter. It will continue all through this winter. The Army is hardened, nimble and alert. The commanders and staff have had opportunities and are having opportunities of handling large scale movements and manoeuvres.

Our Army may be small compared with the German or Russian armies. It has not had the repeated successful experiences of the German army, which are a formidable source of strength. Nevertheless, a finely tempered weapon has been forged. It is upon this weapon, supported by nearly 2,000,000 of armed and uniformed Home Guard, that we rely to destroy or hurl into the sea an invader who succeeded in making a number of successive or simultaneous lodgments on our shores. When I learned about the absolutely frightful, indescribable atrocities which the German police troops are committing upon the Russian population in the rear of the advance of their armoured vehicles, the responsibility of His Majesty's Government to maintain here at home an ample high-class force to beat down and annihilate any invading lodgment from the sea or descent from the air comes home to me in a significantly ugly and impressive form. I could not reconcile such responsibilities with breaking up or allowing to melt away the seasoned, disciplined fighting units which we have now at last laboriously and so tardily created.

As our Army must necessarily be small compared with European standards, it is all the more necessary that it should be highly mechanized and armoured. For this purpose a steady flow of skilled tradesmen and technicians will be required in order to use the weapons which the factories are now producing in rapidly increasing numbers. There is no question of increasing the numbers of the Army, but it is indispensable that the normal wastage – considerable even when troops are not in contact with the enemy – should be made good, that the tanks should be kept filled and that the battalions, the batteries, and the tank regiments should be at their proper strength. Above all we cannot have the existing formations pulled to pieces and gutted by taking out of every platoon and section trained men who are an essential part of these living entities, on which one of these fine or foggy mornings the whole existence of the British nation may depend.

I hope, indeed, that some of our ardent critics out of doors – I have nothing to complain of here – will reflect a little on their own records in the past, and by searching their hearts and memories will realize the fate which awaits nations and individuals who take an easy and popular course or who are guided in defence matters by the shifting winds of well-meaning public opinion. Nothing is more dangerous in wartime than to live in the temperamental atmosphere of a Gallup Poll, always feeling one's pulse and taking one's temperature. I see that a speaker at the weekend said that this was a time when leaders should keep their ears to the ground. All I can say is that the British nation will find it very hard to look up to leaders who are detected in that somewhat ungainly posture. If today I am very kindly treated by the mass of the people of this country, it is certainly not because I have followed public opinion in recent years. There is only one duty, only one safe course, and that is to try to be right and not to fear to do or say what you believe to be right. That is the only way to deserve and to win the confidence of our great people in these days of trouble.

Our hearts go out to our British Army, not only to those who in the Mediterranean and in the East may soon have to bear the brunt of German fury and organization, but also to that splendid, but not too large, band of men here at home whose task is monotonous and unspectacular, whose duty is a long and faithful vigil, but who must be ready at any hour and on any day to leap at the throat of the invader. It may well be the occasion will never come. If that should be the final story, then we may be sure that the existence of the kind of army we have created would be one of the reasons why once again in a war which has ravaged the world our land will be undevastated and our home inviolate.

Of course we strive to profit from well informed criticism, whether friendly or spiteful, but there is one charge sometimes put forward which is, I think, a little unfair. I mean the insinuation that we are a weak, timid, lethargic Government, usually asleep, and in our waking hours always held back by excessive scruples and inhibitions, and unable to act with the vehemence and severity which these violent times require. People ask, for instance, 'Why don't you bomb Rome? What is holding you back? Didn't you say you would bomb Rome if Cairo were bombed?' What is the answer? One answer is that Cairo has not yet been bombed. Only military posts on the outskirts have been bombed. But, of course, we have as much right to bomb Rome as the Italians had to bomb London last year, when they thought we were going to collapse, and we should not hesitate to bomb Rome to the best of our ability and as heavily as possible if the course of the war should render such action convenient and helpful.

Then there is the case of Persia. I see complaints that we have acted feebly and hesitatingly in Persia. This surprises me very much. I do not know of any job that has been better done than that. With hardly any loss of life, with surprising rapidity and in close concert with our Russian Ally, we have rooted out the malignant elements in Teheran; we have chased a dictator into exile, and installed a constitutional Sovereign pledged to a whole catalogue of long-delayed sorely-needed reforms and reparations; and we hope soon to present to the House a new and loyal alliance made by Great Britain and Russia with the ancient Persian State and people, which will ratify the somewhat abrupt steps we were forced to take, and will associate the Persian people with us not only in their liberation but in the future movement of the war. He must, indeed, be a captious critic who can find a pretext to make a quarrel out of that. The Persian episode, so far as it has gone, would seem to be one of the most successful and well conducted affairs in which the Foreign Office has ever been concerned. It ill deserves the treatment it has received from our natural and professional crabs.

In conclusion, let me once again repeat to the House that I cannot give them any flattering hopes, still less any guarantee, that the future will be bright or easy. On the contrary, even the coming winter affords no assurance, as the Russian Ambassador has candidly and shrewdly pointed out, that the German pressure upon Russia will be relaxed; nor, I may add, does the winter give any assurance that the danger of invasion will be entirely lifted from this island. Winter fog has dangers of its own, and, unlike last year, the enemy has now had ample time for technical preparation. We must certainly expect that in the spring, whatever happens in the meanwhile, very heavy fighting, heavier than any we have yet experienced in this war, will develop in the East, and also that the menace to this island of invasion will present itself in a very grave and sharp form. Only the most strenuous exertions, a perfect unity of purpose, added to our traditional unrelenting tenacity, will enable us to act our part worthily in the prodigious world drama in which we are now plunged. Let us make sure these virtues are forthcoming.

John Colville: diary
(*Colville papers*)

30 September 1941

I packed frantically all the morning. At lunch time, when the PM had returned from the House of Commons after making a highly successful speech, I went in to the Cabinet Room to say goodbye to him. He said it must only be *au revoir* as he hoped I should often come back and see him. He ought not to be letting me go, and Eden had been 'very sour' about it and about recalling a trained officer from the army to take my place; but I had so much wanted to go and he thought I was doing a very gallant thing. He said: 'I have the greatest affection for you; we all have, Clemmy and I especially. Goodbye and God bless you.' I went out of the room with a lump in my throat such as I have not had for many years.

Winston S. Churchill to Colonel Hollis, for the Chiefs of Staff Committee
(*Churchill papers, 20/36*)

30 September 1941
Action this Day

When I visited *Indomitable* last week, I was astonished to learn that the handful of Hurricanes to be allotted to this vital war unit were only of the lower type, Hurricane Ones. I trust it may be arranged that only the finest aeroplanes that can do the work go into all aircraft carriers. All this year it has been apparent that the power to launch the highest class fighters from aircraft carriers may reopen to the Fleet great strategic doors which have been closed against them. The aircraft carrier should have supreme priority in the quality and character of suitable types.

Winston S. Churchill to Anthony Eden

(*Churchill papers, 20/36*)

30 September 1941

Why is it necessary for Duff Cooper to make any speeches or give any interviews except in terms of platitudes?[1] It is his business to work behind the scenes and certainly not to develop a strong policy by declarations in public. DC's views are quite sound but the Ambassador's statement of them is much to be preferred. The less he says and the more he sees the better.

Winston S. Churchill to Herbert Morrison

(*Churchill papers, 20/36*)

30 September 1941

During my visit to Coventry I was told it would give great satisfaction in the city if the status of the Mayor could be raised to that of Lord Mayor. I attach a list which shows that all the heavily bombed towns have Lord Mayors with the exception of Southampton and Swansea, the populations of which are much smaller than that of Coventry.

Will you consider whether this mark of distinction might not be given to Coventry, which was the first large town to suffer heavy bombardment.

Winston S. Churchill to Lord Hankey

(*Churchill papers, 20/36*)

30 September 1941
Action this Day

I hope that our programme of consignments to Russia is being carried out satisfactorily and that all the departments concerned realize the importance of getting the goods shipped before Archangel freezes up.

[1] Alfred Duff Cooper was then in Egypt, on his way to Singapore, as Minister Resident. The Ambassador was Sir Miles Lampson.

Pray inform me if there is anything I could usefully do to expedite the process.

There is great delay in the despatch of the promised A/C.[1]

Winston S. Churchill to J. V. Stalin
(*Churchill papers, 20/43*)

30 September 1941
Personal and Secret

I am most anxious to settle our alliance with Persia and to make an intimate efficient working arrangement with your forces in Persia. There are in Persia signs of serious disorder among tribesmen and of breakdown of Persian authority. Disorder if it spreads will mean wasting our divisions holding down these people which again means burdening the road and railway communications with movements and supplies of aforesaid divisions whereas we want to keep the lines clear and improved to the utmost in order to get supplies through to you. Our object should be to make the Persians keep each other quiet while we get on with the war. Your Excellency's decisive indications in this direction will speed forward the already favourable trend of our affairs in this minor theatre.

Winston S. Churchill to Lord Beaverbrook[2]
(*Churchill papers, 20/43*)

30 September 1941
Most Secret and Personal

About Quentin Reynolds. He cannot surely be a member of the delegation and at the same time write articles for the *Daily Express*. This would cause much anger here and be an impediment to you. Will you also point out to Harriman difficulties the dual capacity will cause with the American Press. Meanwhile, in your own interests we are holding Reynolds's copy. So glad you are arrived safely. Good luck. Many thanks for your telegram just received.

[1] Aircraft.
[2] Lord Beaverbrook had arrived in Moscow.

Winston S. Churchill to Lord Riverdale[1]
(*Churchill papers, 20/22*)

30 September 1941

My dear Lord Riverdale,

I have carefully considered the protest which you forwarded with your letter of September 19, against the removal of men from Sheffield. The Minister of Labour has arranged for representatives to go to Sheffield at once and make an investigation.

I must remind you that the demand for skilled labour is very heavy, and the expansion of our munitions production is dependent upon the Minister of Labour providing the new factories with the nuclei necessary to get production going.

There is no reserve of unemployed skilled labour and the demand can only be met by redistributing the existing skilled labour force and by filling in the gaps in individual firms by upgrading, dilution, and the employment of women.

I understand that, of the firms protesting whose names appear on the list you sent, forty-one are covered by the special iron and steel scheme, and another sixteen are partly so covered. This scheme, if efficiently worked, should give the firms an adequate safeguard against withdrawal of essential labour.

In view of the urgency of the demand for this labour on work of the highest priority, I cannot agree that there should be a standstill on the withdrawal of labour from Sheffield; but the matter will be reconsidered in the light of the report. Meanwhile, the Minister of Labour will take all practicable steps to ensure that key-men are not withdrawn unless it is absolutely necessary.

Yours sincerely,
Winston S. Churchill

[1] Arthur Balfour, 1873–1957. Steel manufacturer. Master Cutler of Sheffield, 1911–12. Member of the Industrial Advisory Committee to the Treasury, 1914–18. Member of the Imperial Mineral Resources Bureau, 1920. Knighted, 1923. Chairman, Government Committee on Industry and Trade, 1924. Created Baronet, 1929. Member of the Economic Advisory Council, 1930. Created Baron Riverdale, 1935. Chairman, Advisory Council for Scientific and Industrial Research, 1937–46. In his *Who's Who* entry he wrote: 'Is a Freemason, a Churchman, and a Conservative'.

Winston S. Churchill to Brendan Bracken
(*Churchill papers, 20/30*)

30 September 1941
Secret

Try to get hold of this man,[1] who was most friendly and helpful in the days before the war, but who now seems to have become disgruntled through having been left out of touch. He used to come to all the luncheons of the Focus.[2] I don't want to quarrel with him needlessly. Let me know what you will do before you do it.[3]

Winston S. Churchill to President Franklin D. Roosevelt
(*Churchill papers, 20/49*)

30 September 1941
Personal and Secret

I am most grateful to you for your encouraging cable about tanks available for export by mid-1942.[4] They more than restore the expectations we had prior to the recent conference.

2. Losses at sea have been heavier towards the end of the month and some convoys have suffered very severely. Actually the quarter ending September is one-third losses of the quarter ending June, but I fear a hard time in October when the balance of light and darkness favours the U-boats.

3. The Harriman-Beaverbrook combination are firmly knit together. I hope for a successful agreement with Stalin. On the whole the last week on the Russian front has been better than we feared. Kindest regards.

[1] Joseph Toole, 1887–1945. Educated at Mount Carmel Roman Catholic School, Salford. Worked first as a newsboy, then as a labourer in an iron foundry and in electrical shops. Labour MP for Salford, 1923–4 and 1929–31. Lord Mayor of Manchester, 1936–7.

[2] A pre-war anti-Nazi grouping, founded in 1937, and spanning all political Parties and professions. It was known formally as the Anti-Nazi Council. It obtained its title from Churchill's remark to fellow opponents of appeasement, 'Let us form a focus . . .'.

[3] When Brendan Bracken offered to use Alderman Toole 'as much as possible on a fee and expense basis' provided Churchill approved, Churchill noted on Bracken's letter: 'Yes please'. (Note of 26 October 1941, *Churchill papers, 20/30*).

[4] Earlier that day Roosevelt had telegraphed to Churchill: 'I have cabled our mission in Moscow today that we can make available from July 1, 1942 to January 1, 1943, 1,200 tanks a month for England and Russia combined; from January 1, 1943 to July 1, 1943, 2,000 tanks a month. I told our mission to make a commitment to Russia of 400 tanks a month beginning July 1, in addition to those already promised and advised them after consultation with your representatives to increase the amount still further if that seemed desirable. We are making commitment to the Russians over and above the commitments made of July 1 of 3,600 combat planes between July 1, 1942 and July 1, 1943. We are going to put the production of tanks to well over 2,500 a month. This large increase in tanks is due to our doubling our whole tank production (Warren Kimball, *Churchill and Roosevelt, the Complete Correspondence*, Volume one, page 243).

October 1941

Winston S. Churchill to Sir Edward Bridges
(*Churchill papers, 20/36*)

1 October 1941

During any period of special danger from invasion and, of course, during invasion it would be desirable that the Home Secretary should attend the meetings of the Defence Committee. Will you make the necessary arrangements and notifications?

Winston S. Churchill to Sir Edward Bridges
(*Churchill papers, 20/36*)

1 October 1941

THE GOVERNMENT OF INDIA'S INVOLVEMENT
IN THE MIDDLE EAST QUESTION

Endeavour to drain this Indian morass and try to let me have a small cup of clear water. The matter should, I think, be settled by agreement between the Secretaries of State for Foreign Affairs and India and the Minister of State, but let me have your paper first.

Winston S. Churchill to Colonel Hollis, for the Chiefs of Staff Committee
(*Churchill papers, 20/36*)

1 October 1941

While I do not disagree with the general lines of this negative paper,[1] I do not see any advantage in being in so great a hurry to close the door. We had

[1] The paper was a Minute by Colonel Hollis, dated 29 September 1941, critical of the concept of a British Trans-Caucasian Front, as suggested by Stalin.

much better hear what our Mission say about Russia when they come back. The matter had better be brought up again then.

Winston S. Churchill to David Margesson and General Sir John Dill
(*Churchill papers, 20/36*)

1 October 1941
Action this Day

1. The danger of our forces being organized on a basis so cumbrous that they will be incapable of effective overseas or amphibious action has now grown very great. The condition of the armoured divisions has recently attracted attention. As new ideas and new requirements come along the tendency to growth is continual. In order to preserve the efficiency of the army a continued process of pruning is indispensable.

2. The dire need of finding men to maintain the fighting units at proper strength makes ceaseless economy in the rearward services imperative. I am doing my utmost to sustain the strength of the army against the growing volume of criticism about its reputed size and obvious enforced passivity. I feel therefore bound to press for assistance from the War Office and I hope I may count upon you to help me.

3. For this purpose a Committee of Officers acquainted with the establishments should be set up with orders to make a plan for a 25 per cent. reduction in the rearward services and non-fighting troops showing how this be done with the least possible injury. This work should be completed by the 15th instant and the Defence Committee will then be able to see what is entailed in the particular cuts proposed. I wish to be consulted about the personnel of this Committee. If it fails, I shall have to ask for an outside Committee, as I know how hard it is for a Department to reform itself.

Winston S. Churchill to Sir Archibald Sinclair
(*Churchill papers, 20/36*)

1 October 1941

I really do not think you need refer to my statements, especially as you agree with them, or go worrying about headlines or anything silly like that.[1] I do not like the passage you propose to use, at all. The plans I mentioned are not 'grandiose' plans. There would be nothing 'grandiose' in Hitler using seventy-

[1] Sir Archibald Sinclair had sent Churchill the notes for a speech he was to make at Middlesbrough, in which he intended to refer to Churchill's speech of 30 September 1941 about German shortages in the Air.

five divisions against Russia, using twenty-five towards the Middle East, sending half a dozen through Spain to stir up trouble at Gibraltar or in Morocco and keeping fifty divisions available for invasion. He would still have one hundred to spare. His difficulty would be shortage in aircraft, for all these campaigns at once, which is what I said. The sentence marked 'A' implies that their current production equals their losses; this is certainly not true when you consider all the crashes and wastage. With far less losses we make very slow headway, in fact our ASUs[1] are drained for the petty expansions made. The striking power of the German long-range bomber force (B) is affected not only by its losses, but by large numbers employed in Russia. I do not therefore think your statement is sound. It certainly would cause lively controversy and force me to make a pretty sharp answer. See also my other notes.

I should have thought it was sufficient to say at this moment that while the German Air Force was engaged so deeply in Russia it was doubtful whether they could maintain the same continuity of attack as last winter, but that they still had a substantial bomber force in the west, and by saving up could make attacks which, though not so continuous, might be as bad as, or worse than, last year. You might mention that tip-and-run attacks on the coast towns were a temptation to them.

Winston S. Churchill to Lord Beaverbrook

(*Churchill papers, 20/49*)

1 October 1941

1. Very glad to receive your second telegram, as Spitfire story would be most difficult. Once you open door to Spitfire with cannon guns everything else will be despised. We are getting fine results from Tomahawks in Middle East. We have already sent 300 Tomahawks and Hurricanes and are shipping a further 100 Hurricanes. We hope to pack October consignment of 200 fighters before end of month. Stringent orders have been given to accelerate despatch. Time-table of departures will be cabled by Air Ministry.

2. Thankful for your and Averell's escape.[2] Things here are very steady.

[1] Aircraft Storage Units.

[2] On approaching Moscow, the plane bringing Lord Beaverbrook and Averell Harriman from North Russia had been shot at by a Soviet anti-aircraft battery.

Winston S. Churchill to Lord Beaverbrook
(*Churchill papers, 20/49*)

1 October 1941

You are right about no copy having been received. Mistake arose through advertisement in *Daily Express* of September 25, as follows:

'Quentin Reynolds goes to Russia for *Daily Express*. He will be sending messages from the war front, from the factories, from the heart of Russia, exclusively for the *Daily Express*.'

This advertisement arose out of a perfectly legitimate contract which Christiansen[1] had made through Colliers with Quentin Reynolds.

2. I do not know why Cripps did not talk it over with you. You can show my present telegram to Harriman.

3. Arrangements for Quentin Reynolds now set forth in your No. 24, Linen, are quite satisfactory.

4. I am sorry for publicity given to your caviare story which exposes me to criticism under rationing regulations.

5. Pay no more attention to any of these trifles.

Winston S. Churchill to Brigadier Menzies
(*Secret Intelligence Service papers, Dir/C Archive, 7706*)

2 October 1941

Are you warning the Russians of the developing concentration? Show me the last five messages you have sent to our missions on the subject.[2]

War Cabinet: minutes
(*Cabinet papers, 65/19*)

2 October 1941 Prime Minister's Room
12.15 p.m. House of Commons

The Prime Minister said that two Papers had been prepared for circulation to the War Cabinet dealing with

(a) Jewish Policy generally.

[1] Arthur Christiansen, editor of the *Daily Express*.

[2] In addition to the German Air Force Enigma decrypts, British Intelligence had just begun to break the German Army Enigma key, code name 'Vulture'. This key was used for communications between armies and army groups on the eastern front, and the Army High Command. Vulture was broken a few times between June and September, and with some regularity from October until mid-December. It was the Vulture decrypts that gave the numbers of German armoured and motorized divisions committed to the drive on Moscow, to be launched on October 2. 'C' was able to assure Churchill that the essential details had indeed been sent to Moscow, including information about German air and ground concentrations in the Smolensk area which had indicated impending major operations there.

(b) Recruitment of Jewish Units for General Service in the British Army.

These papers raised difficult issues, which might involve fairly lengthy consideration. The Papers would be circulated to the War Cabinet and a date fixed for discussion.

In the course of preliminary discussion, the following points were made:

(1) The Prime Minister said that, if this country and the United States emerged victorious from the war, the creation of a great Jewish State in Palestine would inevitably be one of the matters to be discussed at the Peace Conference.

(2) The Colonial Secretary[1] said that Dr Weizmann, and other members of the Zionist organization, were making increasingly large claims as to the possibilities of Jewish immigration after the war. Dr Weizmann had recently suggested that at least 3 million Jews should be absorbed comparatively quickly into Palestine. This was impracticable, and he thought that the time had come when we should say something to prevent our silence being taken as evidence of assent to these increasing claims.

(3) The Prime Minister was disposed to doubt the need for a public reply to these claims, but thought that perhaps a private warning might be given.

(4) The Minister of Labour and National Service[2] said that, if an autonomous Jewish State could be set up, the question of regulating the flow of immigration thereto would be a matter to be settled by the authorities of that State. This would greatly ease our difficulties in the matter.

BRITISH MISSIONS TO RUSSIA

The Prime Minister said that it was most undesirable that members of our missions should talk politics in Russia. He thought that we should tell the Russian Government that the withdrawal of three officers had been requested, but that, as no charges had been formulated against them, it was therefore impossible for us to make any enquiry. It should be added that in this instance we were prepared to withdraw the three officers, but that in any future cases that might arise definite charges must be made so that they could be investigated.

The Prime Minister reminded the War Cabinet that the TUC Delegation had been asked to postpone their visit to Russia so as to avoid clashing with the Moscow Conference. Now that the Conference was almost at its close, there was no objection to the TUC Delegation leaving forthwith. Meantime, however, a report had been received from the pilot of the last Catalina which had done the journey by air, stressing the dangers of the air journey owing to weather conditions. We had undertaken to provide means to enable the

[1] Lord Moyne (who was later assassinated by two Jewish terrorists in Cairo).

[2] Ernest Bevin, who later opposed Jewish emigration to Palestine by the survivors of the Holocaust.

Delegation to visit Russia, whether by air or by sea. He thought that the Secretary of State for Air should consider the matter and decide whether the risks of the air journey were such as should be accepted, and should then see Sir Walter Citrine and inform him of his conclusion. He (the Prime Minister) was disposed to deprecate the party going by air. If a decision was reached against the party going by air, it would then be for the First Lord of the Admiralty to consider what arrangements could be made for the journey in a Naval vessel – for example, in a destroyer.

Lord Beaverbrook to Winston S. Churchill
(*Churchill papers, 20/43*)

2 October 1941

1. The Conference will be concluded at 4 o'clock this afternoon when the memorandum will be signed by Molotov, Harriman and me. It has been unanimously approved by all my colleagues and by the Ambassador, by all of Harriman's colleagues and the American Ambassador.[1]

2. The following, contained in your memorandum to me on my departure, have not, (repeat not) been given: 1025 pounders, bren guns, sten guns, all other minor items where 20% of production was to be expressed in actual figures.

Some latitude has been taken in regard to dates of delivery but this does not apply to tanks and air planes, which we are expecting to deliver monthly and regularly.

3. There has not been any concession in excess of authority conferred on me. There was a long discussion about the types of aircraft. Stalin wanted 300 bombers and 100 fighters and the decision stands at 300 fighters and 100 bombers. Britain's proportion is recorded as 200 fighters and Harriman has not (repeat not) been required to contribute his powers although I think he has conceded everything he was authorized to give.

4. The entire success of the Agreement is due to the enthusiasm which the Russians have shown as the negotiations have turned out to their liking. The eggs for the pudding will steadily increase from night to night culminating in scenes of complete happiness at the Kremlin on Tuesday night followed by plenty of drink on Wednesday night at a dinner party given by Stalin and lasting from six until half past one. The Russians are deeply grateful and absolutely confident. I am satisfied that we have a faithful friend now. We cannot over estimate their enthusiasm now that they believe our promises will be carried out.

[1] Laurence A. Steinhardt.

General Sir Alan Brooke: diary
(*'Turn of the Tide'*)

3 October 1941

At midnight[1] received special messenger from the War Office with orders to carry out examination for attack on Trondheim[2] and preparation of plan of attack. The whole to be in by next Friday! Also that I was to dine tonight at Chequers and spend night there to discuss plans. I motored back to London in the morning and spent most of the afternoon studying details of the plan.

Winston S. Churchill to Lord Beaverbrook
(*Churchill papers, 20/43*)

3 October 1941
Action this Day
By Private Code
Personal and Secret

Heartiest congratulations to you all. The unity and success proclaimed is of immense value. No one could have done it but you. Now come home and make the [one group undecypherable][3] stuff. Impossible to restrain the feeling of optimism here.

Winston S. Churchill to Field Marshal Smuts
(*Churchill papers, 20/49*)

3 October 1941

Would earnestly advise against public assumptions that United States will be in war. They say to me: 'Do let us declare war for ourselves.' With patience, Alles sal reg kom.[4]

[1] Midnight, 2 October 1941.
[2] Churchill's coded adjective was lost in transmission.
[3] Operation Ajax.
[4] All will come right: a phrase Churchill had first heard forty years earlier, during the Boer War, and which he often used as an exhortation.

Winston S. Churchill to Colonel Hollis, for the Chiefs of Staff Committee
(Churchill papers, 20/36)

3 October 1941
Action this Day

TANK LANDING CRAFT FOR USE AS FLOATING ANTI-AIRCRAFT BATTERIES

These vessels must be hurried forward with the highest priority and special exertions. The guns, crews and battery organizations should be assembled forthwith on shore, and should be exercised in battery in a space conforming to the deck space and with every other circumstance necessary to resemble the conditions at sea. Thus when the vessels are ready, the crews will be integral units and largely worked up. They should have plenty of target practice.

Let me have proposals.

Winston S. Churchill to the Prime Ministers of Australia and New Zealand[1]
(Churchill papers, 20/43)

3 October 1941

1. You will, I am sure, be glad to hear about the most recent form of help to us from the President of the United States.

2. I have been eager to send to Eastern theatre two complete infantry divisions over and above the normal reinforcements which reach there regularly in our routine convoys. Shipping was the difficulty.

3. President Roosevelt has responded promptly to my appeal, and has offered to lend us transports with United States naval crews and also fast cargo vessels to be manned by British personnel, sufficient to carry half this force with full equipment.

4. These ships with one division will leave England early in November, and United States have undertaken to assist in providing the escort for part of the way. This is a great step forward.

Winston S. Churchill to William Mackenzie King
(Churchill papers, 20/49)

3 October 1941

I think that we may well congratulate ourselves on the most recent form of help which the President of the United States is giving us.

By now I hope that your technical representatives and ours will have largely

[1] Arthur Fadden and Peter Fraser.

completed arrangements with United States representatives for the transport across the Atlantic in United States vessels, with their own naval crews, of the bulk of personnel of your Armoured Division, with United States escort over a large part of the way.

I have been very eager to send Auchinleck two complete infantry divisions over and above the normal reinforcements which reach him regularly in our routine convoys, but shipping has been the difficulty. President Roosevelt's agreement to allow us the use of the same transports with their crews, when they have completed their work for you, and also fast United States cargo vessels manned by our personnel, sufficient to carry half this force for the Middle East with full equipment, is going to be of the greatest assistance.

Winston S. Churchill to Lord Beaverbrook

(*Churchill papers, 20/43*)

3 October 1941
Secret

Following is an extract from a recent telegram from Washington:

'Bucharest, 26th September, CO. No attempt was made by Russians before evacuating Nikolaevsk to destroy 35,000 [ton] battleship, the two cruisers, and two submarines and other craft under construction there.'

The following are extracts from signals received from the British Naval Liaison Officer, Black Sea:

BNLO's Signal 1804/21. Russian COS (Intelligence), BSF states that 'hulls of all new ships at Nikolaev, including battleships under construction, have been removed together with most of the machinery and armament, for completion in other ports.'

BNLO's 1828/24. 'Unofficially informed hull of battleship was blown up before evacuation of Nikolaev. This is contrary to official notification.'

This information was confirmed in BNLO's recent letter and he is of the opinion that the information in the second telegram is more likely to be correct. The hulls of the others were towed, apparently to Mariupol and Kerch. The Germans claim to have captured many hulls, particularly the battleships and some submarines, and have published some rather dubious photographs in substantiation.

Please impress on Stalin strongly the importance we attach to destruction of ships liable to fall into the hands of the enemy and to the 'scorched earth' policy.

If you consider it injudicious to make this communication at the close of your Mission, please pass this on to Cripps.

John Martin: diary
(*John Martin papers*)

3 October 1941

To Chequers in afternoon. Three Chiefs of Staff and Sir Alan Brooke there. Discussion of 'Ajax'.[1]

General Sir Alan Brooke: diary
(*'Turn of the Tide'*)

3 October 1941

At 6 p.m. picked up Dill at the War Office and drove to Chequers discussing details[2] with him on the way. Dudley Pound, Portal and Attlee formed the party. We sat up till 2.15 a.m. discussing the problem, and I did my best to put the PM off attempting the plan. Air support cannot be adequately supplied and we shall fall into the same pitfall as we did before.

General Sir Alan Brooke: diary
(*'Turn of the Tide'*)

4 October 1941 Chequers

Resumed discussion at 11 a.m. and went on till 1 p.m. I think PM was beginning to weaken on the plan. Returned to London and made arrangements for conference on Monday to start discussing plan. Finally motored home in time for dinner. Very weary after hard week short of sleep.

Winston S. Churchill to David Margesson and General Sir John Dill
(*Churchill papers, 20/36*)

4 October 1941
Action this Day

I was greatly disturbed by the statement of C-in-C, Home Forces,[3] that he would have to reduce his standard divisional formations to eleven fully mobile divisions, apart from three in Ireland, by the Spring. This destruction of more than half our Army would be intolerable, and the Cabinet should certainly

[1] The code name for a possible attack on the Norwegian port of Trondheim. The attack did not take place.
[2] Of Operation Ajax.
[3] General Sir Alan Brooke.

have been warned by you before any such situation even approached the limits of discussion.

2. There is no sort of warrant or necessity for such mutilation of the Army. Apart from active operations, the impending losses in the winter through normal wastage cannot exceed 60,000 men, and an intake of more than that number has been arranged. The twenty-six standard divisions and the nine county divisions and the seven armoured divisions, including the Guards (forming), are not on any account to be reduced. If new units are required, easement may be found in the four or five independent brigades and the twelve unbrigaded battalions.

3. Please investigate the Commander-in-Chief's statement at once, and give me your report upon it. In the meantime, the following rule must be observed: No existing divisional formation is to be reduced in standard or converted to a different form without my express authority obtained in each case beforehand in good time. I must also be informed of any new units you wish to create in substitution for existing units, and any important changes in the establishments, whether in personnel or equipment. Let me have a list of any that are now in progress or in prospect.

Winston S. Churchill to Colonel Hollis, for the Chiefs of Staff Committee
(*Churchill papers, 20/36*)

4 October 1941
Action this Day

The enclosed No. 39, Linen,[1] should be circulated to the members of the Defence Committee, including the Ministers concerned.

I attach the utmost importance to 'A.'[2] It is vital that delivery should begin at once. Pray let proposals and preparations for this be made forthwith, and let me have a report on Monday evening. A special convoy will probably be necessary.

I cannot too strongly emphasize the vital importance and extreme urgency of this transaction.

[1] The final telegram sent on 4 October 1941, from Lord Beaverbrook about the military supplies to be sent by Britain to Russia.

[2] Tanks and aircraft to reach Archangel early in October.

Winston S. Churchill to President Franklin D. Roosevelt
(*Churchill papers, 20/43*)

4 October 1941
Personal and Most Secret

1. I have heard from Halifax of his talks with you and Harry about the Middle East. I take a favourable view of the near future there. I am sending Mr. Attlee, the Lord Privy Seal, to represent us at the International Labour Office Convention to be held on the 27th instant, at which I understand you will be present. He will bring you a long letter from me dealing with matters of the utmost secrecy and importance, which I cannot trust to the cables. He will also be able to give you full information about our organization in Cairo. Meanwhile, you should know that I arranged some time ago that General Auchinleck should have complete authority over the air as well as over the army whenever major operations are impending or in progress. The Lord Privy Seal will start by air around 23rd, and I trust you will be able to see him on arrival. I can only spare him for a fortnight on account of parliamentary business.

2. Max and Averell seem to have had a great success at Moscow, and now the vital thing is to act up to our bargain in early deliveries. Hitler evidently feels the draught. We made almost exactly 2,000 aircraft in September, and I think our first-line strength tonight is slightly ahead of the Germans. Besides this, the Russian Air Force is still very formidable.

3. All my best wishes and kindest regards. How I wish we could have another talk.

Winston S. Churchill: message to the National Foreign Trade Council[1]
(*Churchill papers, 20/49*)

4 October 1941

In the grim business in which we are engaged we have not forgotten that the material welfare of mankind must still depend upon trade. We regret that preoccupations in other fields prevent us from taking as full a part in your present deliberations as we should wish, but we shall follow them with keen interest and we have no doubt that they will contribute to the establishment of the better order to which we all look forward, and for which the close co-operation of the English-speaking peoples will be so vital. Meanwhile, I know that I speak for all my countrymen when I express the deepest gratitude for what the manufacturers and the business community of the United States have done, and are doing, for the cause to which we are devoted.

[1] The meeting was held in Washington. Churchill sent this message through Lord Halifax (in Prime Minister's Personal Telegram. T.649A).

John Martin: diary
(*John Martin papers*)

5 October 1941 Chequers

Chequers. Two escaped airmen (Sq.Ldr. Gibbs[1] and P/O Rennie[2]) to lunch. Gen Paget[3] for the night.

Winston S. Churchill to David Margesson
(*Churchill papers, 20/36*)

5 October 1941
Action this Day

I do not approve the idea of using the Army to dig land drains or for other work of this character during the winter. It is not the case that the Air Force have a similar scheme. Their proposal is to send 8,000 skilled technicians of the RAF, in uniform, on loan to the factories for about six months. Their case is entirely different from that of the Army, and I think their plan is a good one.

2. The statements made by the C-in-C, Home Forces, the other night require your first attention, and no question can arise of using our Army as you propose if anything like the C-in-C says is true. I am sure it is not true. But get on with this before anything else. Military considerations should rule your thoughts, and you should not yield to the weak elements in the country who do not understand that quality, efficiency, smartness of bearing, high discipline, are the vital characteristics of an armed force that may have to meet the Germans.

[1] Edward Philip Patrick Gibbs. Born in Singapore, 1910. Educated in Britain. Commissioned in the RAF, 1932. Served in Aden, 1935. Squadron Leader, January 1941. Commanded No. 130 Squadron. Attacked by four German fighters near Calais, January 1941, he shot down one of them. After being shot down over France on 9 June 1941 he evaded capture, crossing into Spain on 26 August 1941 and returning to the United Kingdom by flying boat from Gibraltar, 17 September 1941. Returned to active service. Destroyed a Messerschmitt during a raid on Brest, December 1941. Awarded the Distinguished Flying Cross, 27 January 1942; mentioned in despatches, 11 June 1942.

[2] Basil John Allan Rennie. Pilot Officer. Shot down near Belgium while on a raid against Aachen, 9 July 1941. Reached Spain, 9 August 1941. Returned to active duty after his successful evasion. Awarded the Military Cross, 13 March 1942. Promoted Flight-Lieutenant. While serving as a Pilot Instructor in Britain he contracted toxic hepatitis and died, 15 October 1942.

[3] Bernard Charles Tolver Paget, 1887–1961. Son of Francis Paget, Bishop of Oxford. Entered the Army, 1907. On active service, 1914–18 (wounded twice, despatches, DSO, MC). Major-General, 1937. Commander the 18th Division, and in Norway, 1940, where he extracted two brigades from the Dombaas-Aandalsnes area during a seven-day action that won specific praise from Churchill in the House of Commons. CB, 1940. Chief of the General Staff, Home Forces, 1940–1. Commander-in-Chief, South Eastern Command, 1941. Commander-in-Chief, Home Forces, 1941–3. Knighted, 1942. General, 1943. Commander-in-Chief, 21st Army Group, 1943. Commander-in-Chief, Middle East Force, 1944–5. His younger son died of wounds received in action in Germany in 1945 (posthumous DSO).

3. In any emergency like heavy air raids or the harvest, the Army should, of course, give immediate and generous aid. But we shall want all our men in the Spring and every unit in the highest state of readiness. There may even be operational demands before the Spring. Your responsibility is to have them all ready like fighting cocks, in accordance with the directions which I give as Minister of Defence. Parades, exercises and manoeuvres, the detailed development of the individual qualities of sections, platoons and companies, continual improvement and purging of the officers of middle rank, courses and competitions of all kinds, should occupy all ranks. There should be plenty of marching with bands through towns and industrial districts. The monotony should be relieved by more generous leave being granted both to officers and men. Facilities for transport to the towns for amusement should be elaborated, as a little fun is the counterpart of the hard training which must be exacted. We need regular units of the highest type, and not a mud-stained militia that is supposed to turn out and take a hand in the invasion should it come. I pointed out to the House last week the dangers of yielding to soft, easy and popular expedients, and the dark places into which we have been led thereby. There is no need to bring the matter before the Lord President's Committee.

Winston S. Churchill to A. V. Alexander
(*Churchill papers, 20/36*)

5 October 1941
Secret

Is there no possibility of helping the Air Force on the Tripoli blockade with some surface craft, including a cruiser or two?

We seem to leave it all to the Air Force and the submarines.

Winston S. Churchill to Peter Fraser[1]
(*Churchill papers, 20/43*)

5 October 1941
Most Secret and Personal

Date of operation uncertain, owing to Australian demand to release all their troops from Tobruk, which complicated our plans. Hope these difficulties will be overcome. Will cable you later.

[1] Prime Minister of New Zealand.

Winston S. Churchill: message for the Viceroy's Defence Council
(*Churchill papers, 20/43*)

5 October 1941

I was deeply interested by all you reported to me about India's war effort. In the first year of the war it was impossible to find the weapons and equipment necessary for the Indian Army. In the second year something was done. In the third year large supplies of the most deadly modern war apparatus will come in a steady flow to the expanding formations of the Indian Army. The sons of India have already in this war shown themselves worthy of the highest respect and honour among military men. Wherever they have fought – in Cyrenaica, in the Sudan, in Eritrea, in Abyssinia, in Syria, and now latest of all in Persia – the Indian divisions have played an important and distinguished part. During 1942 the armies of India, with their British comrades, will be fighting on the long front from the Caspian to the Nile. By so doing they will be barring the eastward progress of the war, and thus keeping the horrors of Nazi invasion thousands of miles away from the plains of Hindustan and the homes of their dear ones. This is a highly honourable task, and also, as anyone can see, the best strategy. This is equally true whether applied to the interests of India herself or to the fortunes of the World Cause now being fought out.

Winston S. Churchill to Ernest Bevin
(*Churchill papers, 20/22*)

5 October 1941
Private

My dear Bevin,

Citrine and the others are now on their way to Russia, and I am having them taken good care of by the Admiralty. They will certainly not be back for a month. Meanwhile, no action seems necessary.

When I spoke to Citrine on the telephone, he told me that he did not want to quarrel with you, that the TUC were worrying about the Beveridge Committee, and that he hoped I would go into the question when he came back. He also promised to try to get the *Daily Herald* put right, and suggested that you and I and he should have a talk with the Management. He said that you thought he was behind the attacks in the *Daily Herald* on the Ministry of Labour policy, but that this was not true.

About the Man Power Debate. My line is that we shall be very glad to hear what the House has to say on the subject, and will then decide whether we wish to make a considered Statement on another day. This would not preclude you from answering any minor point that might crop up, or any violent attack. But do not get drawn into anything like a general debate or important speech. We want to know more clearly where we are before we try anything of that kind.

Yours very sincerely,
Winston S. Churchill

Winston S. Churchill to Lady Willingdon
(*Churchill papers, 20/22*)

5 October 1941

My dear Lady Willingdon,

I meant to thank you before for your very kind letter about my appointment to the Lord Wardenship.

Clemmie and I went down to see Walmer one afternoon and were shown round by the Ministry of Works people. It was a perfect day and the Castle (even though most of the rooms were without furniture) and the garden were looking their best. We so much admired all you had done to improve and beautify the place. I am afraid it must have been a sad wrench to leave it.

We shall look forward to hearing more from you about it some day. We shall have a great many questions to ask.

Yours very sincerely,
Winston S. Churchill

Winston S. Churchill to Lord Halifax
(*Churchill papers, 20/43*)

5 October 1941
Personal and Secret

You will see from my last speech in the House that I deprecated any attempt by British Ministers to discuss in public possibilities of action by us on the Continent. I am sure it is better to keep off these topics.

War Cabinet: minutes
(*Cabinet papers, 65/23*)

6 October 1941
5 p.m.

The Prime Minister said that the War Cabinet would now have seen the reply to the telegram which he had sent to Mr Fadden on the 30th September.

Mr Fadden had persisted in his refusal to reconsider the evacuation of the remaining Australian troops from Tobruk.

Since this telegram had been sent, Mr Fadden's Government had fallen, and he had been succeeded by Mr Curtin.[1] The Prime Minister said that he proposed to put to Mr Curtin the same question that he had put to Mr Fadden, as soon as relations had been established with him. It did not, however, seem that there would be any prospect that the Australian Government would change their mind.

Winston S. Churchill to David Margesson
(*Churchill papers, 20/36*)

6 October 1941

PROPOSAL TO FORM AN IRISH BRIGADE[2]

I shall be glad to have an expression of opinion from the War Office on this suggestion. We have Free French and Vichy French, so why not Loyal Irish and Dublin Irish?

War Cabinet: minutes
(*Cabinet papers, 65/19*)

6 October 1941 10 Downing Street
5 p.m.

The Prime Minister read a telegram from the Minister of Supply giving the results of the Moscow Conference, which must be regarded as highly satisfactory. It was clear that, from the Russian point of view, the only thing which counted was the early arrival in Russia of supplies under the Agreement. A meeting of the Defence Committee (Supply) had been held the previous afternoon under the Chairmanship of the Lord Privy Seal to set in motion the despatch of supplies under the Agreement. As a result, he (the Prime Minister) had been able to send a telegram to M. Stalin, which he read to the War Cabinet, explaining the action taken to ensure the regular delivery of supplies.

[1] John Curtin, 1885–1945. Member of the Australian House of Representatives, 1928–31 and 1934–45. Leader of the Opposition, 1935–41. Prime Minister of Australia, 1941–45 (and Minister of Defence, 1942–45). Chairman of the Advisory War Council, Canberra, 1941–44.

[2] This proposal had been put forward in *The Times* in a letter from Sir Hubert Gough, then a Home Guard Zone Commander, formerly (1916–18) Commander of the Fifth Army on the Western Front. Several Irish Regiments had been part of his command.

Winston S. Churchill to David Margesson
(*Churchill papers, 20/36*)

6 October 1941
Action this Day

I feel some anxiety regarding the scheme conducted by the new Army Bureau of Current Affairs. The test must be whether discussions of such matters conducted by Regimental Officers will weaken or strengthen that highly tempered discipline without which our armies can be no match for the highly trained forces of Germany. The qualities required for conducting discussions of the nature indicated in paragraph 8 of the attached pamphlet[1] are not necessarily those which fit for command in the field. Will not such discussions only provide opportunities for the professional grouser and agitator with a glib tongue? They seem to be in a different category from educative lectures by trained teachers or experts.

Pray consider this matter and let me have your personal views. Meanwhile please suspend action.

Winston S. Churchill to General Sir John Dill
(*Churchill papers, 20/32*)

6 October 1941

I should be glad if this[2] could be brought up-to-date, showing exactly what was effected in the relief. I doubt myself whether the enemy has the batteries and artillery ammunition for a sustained assault of this kind. I do not believe the Italian troops are capable of such efforts. It is surely not to be conceived that the forces mentioned in paragraph 5 could all be engaged at Tobruk for a fortnight without any attempt to profit by the situation on the desert front.

Winston S. Churchill to Anthony Eden
(*Churchill papers, 20/36*)

6 October 1941

Do you think this is a good plan?[3] The Foreign Office will never know whether the document has in fact been burnt or not. Is there any register kept of these documents, and whether they are returned or notified 'Burnt'? What

[1] The pamphlet was entitled *Current Affairs in the Army. The outline of a new idea.*
[2] 'A Short Appreciation of the Situation at Tobruk', dated 29 September 1941, by General Sir John Dill.
[3] Foreign Office instructions on certain documents that they were either to be burnt or returned to the Foreign Office.

is the proportion of 'burnings' to 'returnings'? Within what period has the document to be burnt or returned? How many documents are there outstanding now neither burnt nor returned? Would not a time limit of one week be better, and all documents asked for back after this period? Would it not be better to have all documents returned and not give the option of burning? This would not, of course, apply to my Private Office. I expect you will find there are a good many of these documents attached to files in circulation in other Departments. Anyhow, I should be glad if you would give some direction in the matter.

Winston S. Churchill to Lord Beaverbrook[1]
(*Churchill papers, 20/43*)

6 October 1941
Action this Day
Personal and Secret

We have not lost an hour in making good your undertakings. I have sent the following telegram to Stalin.

Winston S. Churchill to J. V. Stalin
(*Churchill papers, 20/43*)

6 October 1941
Personal and Secret

I am glad to learn from Lord Beaverbrook of the success of the Tripartite Conference at Moscow. '*Bis dat qui cito dat.*'[2] We intend to run a continuous cycle of convoys leaving every ten days. Following are on the way and arrive Archangel, October 12th:

20 heavy tanks.
193 fighters (pre-October quota).

Following will sail October 12th, arriving October 29th:

140 heavy tanks.
100 Hurricanes.
200 bren carriers.
200 anti-tank rifles and ammunition.
50 2-pounder guns and ammunition.

[1] Lord Beaverbrook was returning to Britain from Russia by sea.
[2] He gives twice who gives quickly. The phrase is attributed to the first century Roman author Publius Syrus.

Following will sail October 22nd:

200 fighters

120 heavy tanks.

Above shows that total of the October quota of aircraft and 280 tanks will arrive Russia by November 6th. The October quota of bren carriers, anti-tank rifles and 2-pounder anti-tank guns will all arrive in October. Twenty tanks have been shipped to go via Persia and fifteen are about to be shipped from Canada via Vladivostok. The total tanks shipped will therefore be 315, which is nineteen short of our full quota. This number will be made up in November. The above programme does not take into account supplies from United States.

2. In arranging this regular cycle of convoys we are counting on Archangel to handle the main bulk of deliveries. I presume this part of the job in hand.

Good wishes.

Harold Nicolson: diary
(*'Diaries and Letters, 1939-45'*)

6 October 1941

Rab says that he was dining the other night with Winston, Eden and Beaverbrook, and that Winston spoke with deep sympathy of Baldwin.[1] Winston has no capacity of meanness, and that it why we love him so. A great soul in a great crisis.

Winston S. Churchill to Anthony Eden
(*Churchill papers, 20/36*)

7 October 1941

Mr Palmer[2] is only thirty-seven. He has a safe seat. The Americans are shy of young Englishmen of military age who arrive in their midst to stir them into the war. I am extremely reluctant to multiply the certificates I have to give to Members of Parliament who take offices of profit. My view is that, in the absence of any altogether exceptional aptitudes for some particularly important work, he ought either to fight or vote.

[1] When Churchill was invited in 1945 by Clement Attlee to join a message of greeting to Baldwin on his eightieth birthday, he declined to do so, and explained, privately: 'I wish Stanley Baldwin no ill, but it would have been better for our country if he had never lived.'

[2] Gerald Eustace Howell Palmer, 1904–1984. Farmer, forester and iconographer. Conservative Member of Parliament for Winchester, 1935–45. On active service, Royal Artillery, 1939–45 (despatches). A Forestry Commissioner, 1963–65.

Winston S. Churchill to General Auchinleck
(*Churchill papers, 20/43*)

7 October 1941
Action this Day

The following appears in the *Daily Herald* of today:

BIG MOVES ON WAY IN LIBYA
By A. B. Austin,[1] War Correspondent

Britain is nearing air mastery over the Mediterranean.

As a result, we are on the eve of big events in the Libyan desert.

Our Air Staff believes the Russian campaign has proved such a strain on the Luftwaffe that Hitler is now hundreds of planes short of the strength he would like to have on the North African front.

Meanwhile, the Middle East strength of the RAF has been growing and its losses have been relatively small.

I have several times noticed this kind of statement, and have been informed that it is in accordance with the wishes of your Intelligence Department. I now wish to hear from you whether this is, in fact, the way you wish the hand played. Otherwise, I can have the Press asked privately to abstain from all further speculation.

Winston S. Churchill to Harry Hopkins
(*Churchill papers, 20/43*)

7 October 1941
Personal and Secret

Lyttelton is needed back at his post in Cairo and is already on the way. No doubt you have seen my telegram of 4.10.41 to President. Attlee will bring a most important and secret letter from me. Meanwhile, you are justified in feeling confident about our position in Egypt. We do not feel like being turned out at all. Averell and Max will soon be back. There is a big crunch on for Moscow. They tell me opinion has gone much better on your side in the last

[1] Alexander Berry Austin, 1903–1943. Journalist. Joined the *Morning Post*, 1925, first as assistant librarian, then as a reporter and finally as a Parliamentary Sketch Writer. Joined the *Daily Herald* as a reporter, 1937. Press Section, Fighter Command, 1939–40. Daily Herald Air Correspondent, 1940–41. In training with the Commandos, 1941; took part with the Commandos in the Dieppe Raid, 1942, as the representative of the whole British Press. Reporter with the First Army, Tunisian Campaign, 1943; with the Fifth Army, Salerno Landings, 1943. Author of *Fighter Command* (the story of the Battle of Britain), *We Landed at Dawn* (Dieppe) and *The Birth of an Army* (the First Army's campaign in Tunisia). His last despatch, on the road to Camerelle with the British infantry, began: 'Along the Road of Death we are driving to the plain of Naples.' This report was published in the *Daily Herald* the day before the news broke of his death under fire.

month. Is this so? Hope your health is better. Come over and see us soon. We are still alive and kicking. Kindest regards from everyone here.

Winston S. Churchill: Note[1]
(*Cabinet papers, 69/3*)

7 October 1941
Secret

Renown awaits the Commander who first in this war restores Artillery to its prime importance upon the battlefield, from which it has been ousted by heavily armoured tanks. For this purpose three rules are necessary:

(a) Every field gun or mobile AA gun should carry a plentiful supply of solid armour-piercing tracer shot: thus every mobile gun will become an anti-tank gun, and every battery possess its own anti-tank protection.

(b) When guns are attacked by tanks they must welcome the occasion. The guns should be fought to the muzzle. Until the approaching tanks are within close range batteries should engage them at a rapid rate of fire with HE[2]. During this phase the tracks of the tanks are the most vulnerable target. At close quarters solid AP[3] shot should be fired; this should be continued so long as any of the detachments survive. The last shot should be fired at not more than ten yards' range. It may be that some gun crews could affect to be out of action or withhold their fire, so as to have the superb opportunity of firing AP at the closest range.

(c) It may often happen as a result of the above tactics, especially when artillery is working with tanks, that guns may be overrun and lost. Provided they have been fought to the muzzle, this should not at all be considered a disaster, but, on the contrary, the highest honour to the battery concerned. The destruction of tanks more than repays the loss of field guns or mobile AA guns. The Germans have no use for our captured guns, as they have a plethora of their own types, which they prefer. Our own supplies are sufficient to make good the deficiencies.

The principle must be established by the Royal Artillery that it is not good enough for tanks to attack a group of British batteries properly posted, and

[1] Printed for the War Cabinet as Defence Committee (Operations) Papers No. 17 of 1941.
[2] High Explosive.
[3] Armour Piercing.

that these batteries will always await their attack in order to destroy a good proportion of tanks. Our guns must no more retreat on the approach of tanks than Wellington's squares at Waterloo on the approach of hostile cavalry.

2. The Germans made a practice from the beginning of their invasion of France, and have since developed it consistently, of taking what they call 'flak' artillery with their most advanced parties and interspersing all their armoured and supply columns with it. We should do the same. The principle should be that all formations, whether in column or deployed, should be provided with a quota of AA guns for their protection. This principle is applicable to columns of all kinds, which should be freely supplied with machine-guns, as well as with Bofors as the supply of these weapons becomes more plentiful.

3. 250 Bofors are now being sent to General Auchinleck for him to use in the best possible way with all his columns, and at all the assembly points of his troops or refuelling stations required in the course of offensive operations.

Nevermore must the Army rely solely on aircraft for its protection against attack from the air. Above all, the idea of keeping standing patrols of aircraft over moving columns should be abandoned. It is unsound to 'distribute' aircraft in this way, and no air superiority will stand any large application of such a mischievous practice.

4. Upon the Military Commander-in-Chief in the Middle East announcing that a battle is in prospect, the Air Officer Commanding-in-Chief will give him all possible aid irrespective of other targets, however attractive. Victory in the battle makes amends for all, and creates new favourable situations of a decisive character. The Army Commander-in-Chief will specify to the Air Officer Commanding-in-Chief the targets and tasks which he requires to be performed, both in the preparatory attack on the rearward installations of the enemy and for air action during the progress of the battle. It will be for the Air Officer Commanding-in-Chief to use his maximum force for these objects in the manner most effective. This applies not only to any squadrons assigned to Army Co-operation permanently, but also to the whole air force available in the theatre.

5. Bombers may, if required, be used as transport or supply machines to far-ranging or outlying columns of troops, the sole object being the success of the military operation. As the interests of the two Commanders-in-Chief are identical it is not thought that any difficulty should arise. The Air Officer Commanding-in-Chief would naturally lay aside all routine programmes and concentrate on bombing the rearward services of the enemy in the preparatory period. This he would do not only by night, but by day attacks with fighter protection. In this process he will bring about a trial of strength with the enemy fighters, and has the best chance of obtaining local command of the air. What is true of the preparatory period applies with even greater force during the battle. All assembly or refuelling points or marching columns of the enemy should be attacked by bombers during daylight with strong

fighter protection, thus bringing about air conflicts not only of the highest importance in themselves, but directly contributing to the general result.[1]

Winston S. Churchill to Air Chief Marshal Sir Charles Portal
(*Churchill papers, 20/36*)

7 October 1941
Secret

We all hope that the air offensive against Germany will realize the expectations of the Air Staff. Everything is being done to create the bombing force desired on the largest possible scale, and there is no intention of changing this policy. I deprecate, however, placing unbounded confidence in this means of attack, and still more expressing that confidence in terms of arithmetic. It is the most potent method of impairing the enemy's morale we can use at the present time. If the United States enters the war, it would have to be supplemented in 1943 by simultaneous attacks by armoured forces in many of the conquered countries which were ripe for revolt. Only in this way could a decision certainly be achieved. Even if all the towns of Germany were rendered largely uninhabitable, it does not follow that the military control would be weakened or even that war industry could not be carried on.

2. The Air Staff would make a mistake to put their claim too high. Before the war we were greatly misled by the pictures they painted of the destruction that would be wrought by air raids. This is illustrated by the fact that 750,000 beds were actually provided for air raid casualties, never more than 6,000 being required. This picture of air destruction was so exaggerated that it depressed the statesmen responsible for the pre-war policy, and played a definite part in the desertion of Czechoslovakia in August 1938. Again, the Air Staff, after the war had begun, taught us sedulously to believe that, if the enemy acquired the Low Countries, to say nothing of France, our position would be impossible owing to the air attacks. However, by not paying too much attention to such ideas, we have found quite a good means of keeping going.

3. It may well be that German morale will crack and that our bombing will play a very important part in bringing the result about. But all things are always on the move simultaneously, and it is quite possible that the Nazi warmaking power in 1943 will be so widely spread throughout Europe as to be to a large extent independent of the actual buildings in the homeland.

[1] Churchill later commented, in Volume Three of his war memoirs: 'General Montgomery was not one of those to whom the paper was sent, and it was not till after I met him in Tripoli in 1943, after the victory of the Eighth Army at Alamein eighteen months later, that I chanced to show him a copy. "It is as true now," he wrote, "as when it was written." Renown by then had certainly attended his restoration of artillery to its position upon the battlefield.'

4. A different picture would be presented if the enemy's air force were so far reduced as to enable heavy accurate daylight bombing of factories to take place. This, however, cannot be done outside the radius of fighter protection, according to what I am at present told. One has to do the best one can, but he is an unwise man who thinks there is any certain method of winning this war, or indeed any other war between equals in strength. The only plan is to persevere.

I shall be delighted to discuss these general topics with you whenever you will.

Winston S. Churchill: Directive[1]

(*Churchill papers, 23/9*)

8 October 1941
Secret

AIR DEFENCE OF GREAT BRITAIN

1. We cannot state how severe the air raids will be this winter or what the danger of invasion will be in the spring. These two vultures will hang above us to the end of the war. We must be careful that our precautions against them do not unduly weaken our Mobile Field Army and other forms of our offensive effort.

2. It would seem reasonable to fix the total of ADGB personnel at its present figure of 280,000 plus any additional recruitment of women that they can attract. This will give them at least 30,000 more than what we got through the air raids with last year. The proposed addition of 50,000 to a total of 330,000 cannot be supplied. Many more high and low-ceiling guns are coming to hand now. Some of these might be mounted in additional batteries, but unless ADGB can contrive by praiseworthy thought and ingenuity to man them within the limits of the personnel mentioned they will have to be kept in Care and Maintenance.

3. Having regard to the parity now existing between the British and German Air Forces and the Russian factor, it is unlikely that the enemy would make heavy and continuous air attacks on Great Britain in combination with or as a prelude to invasion. He would need to save up for that. We should feel a major air onslaught on this island as it developed. We should discern the assembly in the river mouths of invasion craft and shipping. There would thus be a short but effective period of time in which to adjust ourselves to the particular form of attack.

4. ADGB must therefore become as flexible as possible and keep static defence at a minimum. For this purpose as large a proportion as possible of

[1] Printed for the Chiefs of Staff as Chiefs of Staff Paper No. 612 of 1941.

ADGB should be in a mobile form. General Pile should prepare schemes for giving the utmost reinforcement of mobile flak to General Brooke's Army. Sometimes they must take their guns from the site. In other cases a duplicate set of mobile guns may be made available. Thus we can shift the weight from one leg to the other as the need requires.

5. A similar kind of shuttle service is required for coastal defence. No more men (other than normal wastage) can be provided for the coast batteries. A detailed study must be made of the coast to economize manpower in the batteries according to the strategic danger. This can be done either by reducing the personnel per gun in certain sectors, and thus reducing the degree of readiness, or by reducing the number of guns for which crews are provided. The demand for 9,000 additional coast defence gunners cannot be met. These must be used in the mobile and offensive spheres. However, should invasion threaten, ADGB must not only liberate to the utmost its mobile forces, but must also be ready to provide additional gunners to bring the coast batteries up to the highest level.

6. Above all, we cannot go on adding gun to gun and battery to battery as the factories turn them out and so get an ever larger proportion of our limited trained manpower anchored to static and passive defence.

7. General Pile should be assisted in every way to prepare schemes for increasing the mobile flak of the Army and reinforcing the coast batteries, while at the same time without any addition (apart from women) to his numbers, 280,000, maintaining the indispensable minimum which served us so well last year.

8. The Chiefs of the Staff Committee is requested to advise and consider what proposals should be made to give effect to the foregoing principles.

Winston S. Churchill to David Margesson and Sir Archibald Sinclair

(*Churchill papers, 20/36*)

8 October 1941

I think now the time is ripe to form an Irish Brigade, also an Irish Wing or Squadron of the RAF. If these were taken in hand they would have to be made a great success of. The pilot Finucane[1] might be a great figure.

[1] Churchill noted in Volume Three of his war memoirs: 'Wing-Commander "Paddy" Finucane, DSO, DFC and two bars, was killed at the age of twenty-one in July 1942, when, after continuous exploits, he was leading a fighter wing in a mass attack on enemy targets in France. It was always said that the Luftwaffe would never get him, and it was actually a ground shot from an unusual single machine-gun post which hit his Spitfire. He flew slowly out to sea, talking calmly to his comrades. Finally, when ten miles from the French coast, he sent his last message, spoken probably as his engine stopped: 'This is it, chaps.' He crashed from about ten feet above the sea, and his machine sank at once. Finucane had always vowed not to be taken prisoner, and it was probably this that made him fly out to sea rather than inland, where he would have had a good chance of survival.'

Pray let me have proposals. The movement might have important political reactions later on.

President Franklin D. Roosevelt to Winston S. Churchill
(*Churchill papers, 20/43*)

8 October 1941

I deeply regret, at this very late date, the necessity of re-opening with you what had been agreed upon in regard to American Flag Navy operated transports going to England for the proposed troop movement to the Near East.

I do so with utmost confidence that you will consider the problem (sympathetically) and my frank statement of it.

I have determined to send a message to Congress in the immediate future, recommending sweeping amendments to our Neutrality Act. I am convinced that that Act is seriously crippling our means of helping you. I want not only to arm all our ships but I want to get the authority from Congress to send American Flagships directly into British ports. After long conferences with Congressional Leaders, I have reached the conclusion that it would be disastrous to this legislation if one of our transports, proceeding to or from Britain and in British waters or in a British port, were to be sunk when manned by US Navy Officers and men. Such an event might jeopardize our lend-lease and other aid.

I appreciate to the full of your dilemma of rearranging plans for transfer of men to the Near East.

I have given careful study to other means of accomplishing the same ultimate objective.

I suggest, as a first alternative, that you send here or transfer from your ships under repair, here, enough officers and men to man our transports. This would make a total of about three thousand officers and men. The ships would then sail from Canadian ports, under British Flag and with British crews under lend-lease arrangements.

The second alternative would be for us to continue manning these six transports, send them to Halifax, you to send the troops to board the transports in Halifax. We would then transport the expedition through Western Hemisphere waters and thence to the Near East destination. We believe, if considered advisable by the Navy Department and the Admiralty, we could escort this fast convoy all the way.

I feel that one of the two foregoing alternatives is necessary in order not to jeopardize the legislation to eliminate the restrictions under which we are operating or to break down the growing public sentiment for the policy of additional aid and cause this sentiment to reverse itself. Of the two alternatives offered, I prefer the first – namely, your using your crews to man the transports.

I have directed Admiral Stark to acquaint Admiral Little[1] with the foregoing.

F. D. Roosevelt

Winston S. Churchill to President Franklin D. Roosevelt
(*Churchill papers, 20/43*)

8 October 1941

Fully understand situation which can quite well be coped with here. We definitely prefer your second alternative of sending our troops to Halifax for transhipment and onward passage to Near East in United States transports with United States escorts so far as needful. This plan lessens greatly dislocation of complex escort programmes and delay in subsequent convoys. Furthermore, your valuable fast ships would not run any appreciable risk from U-boat attack by having to run in and out of the danger zones. If you agree our experts can make a firm programme whereby nine British liners arrive at Halifax with 20,800 men comprising the 18th Division and start transhipment to your transports on 7th November.

John Curtin to Winston S. Churchill
(*Churchill papers, 20/43*)

8 October 1941

I take the occasion of the commencement of my work as Prime Minister of the Commonwealth of Australia to assure you of the desire of my Government to cooperate fully with you and with the Governments of other Dominions in all matters associated with the welfare of the Empire. In particular, we will devote our energies to the effective organization of all our resources so that we may play our part in bringing victory to the Empire and our Allies.

Winston S. Churchill to John Curtin
(*Churchill papers, 20/49*)

8 October 1941

I thank you for your telegram on assuming the direction of Commonwealth affairs, and cordially reciprocate the good wishes it contains. You may be sure we shall work with you on a basis of most intimate confidence and comradeship.

[1] Admiral Sir Charles Little, former Second Sea Lord and Chief of Naval Personnel (1938–41), who was Head of the British Admiralty Delegation in Washington.

Winston S. Churchill to Anthony Eden
(*Churchill papers, 20/36*)

8 October 1941
Action this Day

I have a feeling I might make a short broadcast Sunday night on German atrocities in these many lands; the cheating about the exchange of prisoners; and cognate topics. You could, I dare say, give me a pretty good dossier.[1] What do you think?

Winston S. Churchill to President Franklin D. Roosevelt
(*Churchill papers, 20/43*)

8 October 1941

After discussion with Ambassador Winant I send you this note setting out the result of our Cabinet discussion on the matter which has been causing us some difficulty.

We have been considering carefully what should be the next step regarding the Conference upon Wheat which is due to resume its deliberations next week. I feel a certain amount of concern as to the repercussions on the war situation of the proposed Wheat Agreement in its present form. The draft seems to give the impression that it is contemplated to force on the wheat-importing countries of Europe, as a condition of immediate post-war relief, a series of obligations, including a drastic restriction of their wheat production, which would vitally affect their agricultural systems. This is to touch a tender spot in the policy of many countries. Any Wheat Agreement capable of this construction would, in our view, be dangerous in the extreme. It would supply Nazi propaganda with a weapon which it would not be slow to use. It would arouse widespread suspicions as to the spirit in which the United States and the United Kingdom mean to use their power when the war is over and would confuse and dishearten the elements in Europe now hoping and working for the defeat of Germany. We regard it as essential, therefore, to remove from the draft agreement all provisions implying Anglo-American interference in European Agricultural policy.

The relation of Russia to any Agreement also raises a difficulty. Russia was still a neutral at the time when the arrangements for the Wheat Conference were made. But, as things are now, it appears to us virtually out of the question either to conclude an Agreement which may seriously affect her interests without consulting her, or to approach her on such a matter at a time when

[1] Churchill had just read a letter of 7 October 1941 from the Greek Prime Minister, in exile, Emmanuel Tsouderos, on German atrocities in Greece.

she is engaged in a life-and-death struggle, and when her richest wheatfields are in the battle area.

We have been considering what instructions we can give to our delegates, who are now on their way to Washington, with a view to meeting these difficulties, but we have not been able to find a really satisfactory solution consistent with the present framework of the draft agreement. Considerable revision would certainly be required; and we are alive to the danger which we are anxious to avoid, of protracted negotiations which might lead to a breakdown. For our part, we welcome the proposals for establishing a pool of wheat for post-war relief. There are other important features of the Agreement, which do not prejudice, or which could easily be given a form which would not prejudice, the interests of unrepresented countries, e.g., the agreement of the four exporting countries represented as to the ratios of their respective export quotas, and the provisions for an 'ever-normal' granary.

The other issues of policy might usefully be explored by the Conference with a view to preparing the ground for later decisions; but it seems to me that we should be ill-advised to attempt to reach definite conclusions about these now. Apart from the fact that important countries not represented at the Conference are affected, there seems to be advantage in trying to fit these questions into the larger discussions on Anglo-American collaboration in regard to post-war economic problems generally which, as Lord Halifax will be able to explain more fully, we hope to be able to begin at an early date.

If you agree generally with my view, I will instruct our delegation accordingly.

Winston S. Churchill to Josiah Wedgwood

(*Wedgwood papers*)

8 October 1941 10 Downing Street

My dear Jos,

Thank you so much for your letter of October 4, which I was very glad to get.[1]

Do you really imagine I never think about these things? How do you suppose I pass my life?

Yours vy sincerely,
Winston S. Churchill

[1] This paragraph of Churchill's letter was typed. The subsequent paragraph was added by Churchill in his own hand. Wedgwood had written in his letter: 'Do you remember in the Boer War how Captain Vandeleur refused to surrender? Do you remember how you dared to escape, oh! many times? For heaven's sake tell your "technical advisers" where they get off, and use the Army to fight Germans. The men won't let you down if you give a lead – unless you wait too long. Don't get old and lazy. I enclose one letter from a couple of dozen but I don't agree that you are not a strategist – only soft-hearted.' (*Churchill papers 20/30*)

Oliver Harvey: diary
(*'The War Diaries of Oliver Harvey, 1941-1945'*)

9 October 1941

AE dined with PM last night. They had a long and intimate evening. 'I regard you as my son,' Winston said – 'I do not get in your way nor you in mine.' He said he wished AE were back again at WO where Margesson, though good in H of C was making no headway. Both PM and AE very anxious and eager about forthcoming desert campaign. The soldiers are very confident.

War Cabinet: minutes
(*Cabinet papers, 65/19*)

9 October 1941 10 Downing Street
12.15 p.m.

SPAIN

Reference was made to a recent article in the *Daily Mirror* which contained a violent attack on Spain.

The Prime Minister said that it was clearly contrary to the national interest that articles which increased the risk of Spain coming into the war against us should be published. If persuasion was useless, we must arm ourselves with the necessary powers.

SOUTHERN IRELAND

The Prime Minister said there were indications that public opinion in Ireland would be gratified if some action was taken which acknowledged the considerable help which we were receiving by the enlistment in our forces of volunteers from Southern Ireland. He had asked the Secretary of State for War to consider the formation of an Irish Brigade. He would be grateful if the Home and Dominions Secretaries would examine, from their points of view, the position of men from Southern Ireland, who enlisted in this Brigade.

The Prime Minister referred[1] to President Roosevelt's offer to make United States transports available to take troops to the Middle East. He had now asked that this plan might be changed, since he was afraid that if any of these ships came to this country and was sunk, it might endanger his efforts to repeal the Neutrality Act. The President had submitted two alternative proposals. The matter had been fully considered the day before by the Chiefs of Staff, who had decided to accept the second proposal, namely, that the troops

[1] Because of its exceptional secrecy, this item was recorded only in the War Cabinet's Confidential Annex (*Cabinet papers, 65/23*).

concerned should go to Halifax, from which port the Americans would send them in their own vessels, and under United States escort, to the Middle East.

Winston S. Churchill to General Auchinleck
(*Churchill papers, 20/43*)

9 October 1941
Personal

Making allowances for drafts and units despatched up to and including convoy WS 12, War Office now calculate your infantry battalions at following strengths on assumption figures given in your paragraphs 3 and 5 include officers: Rifles, 796; Motor, 838; Machine Gun, 843; Reconnaissance, 810; Regiments, Royal Horse Artillery and Field, 560; Medium, 577; Anti-Tank (36-gun), 426; Anti-Tank (48-gun), 558.

Although these figures do not contain the ideal war establishments, which after all are arbitrary, they nevertheless give you very solid units.

Winston S. Churchill: Directive[1]
(*Churchill papers, 23/9*)

9 October 1941
Most Secret

ARMY STRENGTHS

We have now in the United Kingdom (including Northern Ireland) twenty-six standard motorized infantry divisions and the Polish division, total twenty-seven, well equipped with guns and transport, with an average strength of about 15,500 men, with ten Corps organizations and Corps troops (61,000). There are eight county divisions for work on the beaches, averaging about 10,000, without artillery other than coast artillery and with little transport. We have five armoured divisions and four Army Tank brigades; the whole comprising fourteen armoured brigades (with 5 divisional elements); four Brigade Groups with artillery and transport; seven infantry brigades and twelve un-brigaded battalions: furthermore, eight aerodrome defence battalions and the 100,000 men in the Home Defence and Young Soldiers' battalions.

2. It is proposed to transform this organization into twenty-seven standardized divisions (hereinafter to be called Field Divisions), plus the Polish Division (which will have an armoured element), total twenty-eight; and to

[1] Circulated to the War Cabinet as Defence Committee (Operations) Paper No. 18 of 1941.

increase the armoured forces to seven armoured divisions with eight Army Tank brigades, the whole comprising twenty-two armoured brigades (with seven divisional elements). The four Brigade Groups are to remain. Instead of the eight county divisions and other units mentioned above, there will be thirteen brigades, plus the equivalent of two Ally brigades, and eight 'Detached Battalions'; the foregoing constituting the Home Field Army, which can thus be reckoned the equivalent of forty-five divisions. In addition, there will still be the eight aerodrome battalions and the Home Defence and Young Soldiers' battalions.

3. The object of these changes is to increase the war-power of the army, particularly in armoured troops; and to provide additional field, anti-tank and flak artillery, including that required for five additional Indian divisions, to be formed during 1942. For this last purpose also it will be necessary to provide up to seventeen British battalions for the Indian Army.

4. No reduction in the force mentioned in para. two is compatible with our war needs. To maintain it during the next nine months. i.e., to July 1, 1942; and also to maintain the drafts for the army of the Middle East, for India and for our garrisons in Iceland, Gibraltar, Malta and Hong Kong, &c., with a normal wastage of 50,000 a quarter there must be provided an intake to the army of 278,000 men. Measures are being taken to provide this. The army also requires at least 142,000 more women above the 63,000 already recruited.

5. In my directive on ADGB I have proposed that the personnel should be fixed at 280,000 men and that the suggested increase of 50,000 be disallowed: also that the suggested increase of 9,000 in the Coast batteries should be disallowed. The savings thus provided will be applied towards strengthening the Field Army. Finally ADGB will continually endeavour to develop for the service of the Home Field Army the largest amount of mobile flak possible, and also a transferable force available to strengthen the coastal batteries should the Emergency Period of Invasion be instituted. As it is unlikely that the enemy could afford prolonged and widespread bombing of our towns in the advent of Invasion, a shuttle arrangement of this kind should be possible, enabling us to meet according to events either a sustained air attack or Invasion. The Anti-Aircraft force is formed into twelve Divisions.

6. The Army of the Nile now consists of the 50th and 70th (formerly 6th) British Divisions, the 1st, 2nd and 7th Armoured Divisions with the Cavalry Armoured Division (forming) and two Army Tank Brigades; the three Australian Divisions; one New Zealand; two South African, one Polish and Foreign equivalent, and the 4th and 5th Indian Divisions, total sixteen Divisions. It is intended to reinforce the Middle East with two British Divisions, the 18th and 2nd, from the United Kingdom as convenient.

7. Apart from the two divisions mentioned above, India has in action in Persia and Iraq the 6th, 8th and 10th Indian divisions, and General Wavell

proposes to send the 17th by the end of the year. During 1942, four extra Indian divisions and one Indian armoured division will also take the field; total nine.

8. For the defence of India, there will remain the equivalent of three British divisions and five Indian divisions, over and above those which will operate outside India.

9. There remain our garrisons abroad, to wit:

Iceland (C) – the equivalent of 1 division.
Gibraltar and Malta – that of 2.
Singapore – that of 3.
Aden, Hong Kong and other minor garrisons – that of 1.
Total division-equivalent of garrisons, 7.

10. If we estimate our Army in divisions or their equivalent, the general layout for 1942 is as follows:

United Kingdom	45
Anti-Aircraft divisions	12
Army of the Nile	16
Army of India in Iraq and Persia	9
Army of India at home	8
Fortress Garrisons	7
Native African Divisions	2
	—
Grand total	99

11. It is our duty to develop, equip and maintain all these units during 1942.

Winston S. Churchill to Sir Edward Bridges and General Ismay
(*Churchill papers, 20/36*)

10 October 1941
Action this Day

A scheme must be prepared for the evacuation of civilians from the coastal areas from the Wash to the Isle of Wight and also of nodal points like Colchester, Ipswich and Canterbury. This scheme will be put into operation in successive pre-arranged stages from the moment when the Invasion Emergency Period is instituted. This might be between zero minus 21 and a shorter date. It is expected that the assembly of the shipping and invasion craft in the river mouths or their movements into the basins, together with other symptoms, will give something like this warning.

2. The Lord Privy Seal will convene and preside over a small committee of the essential high authorities in order that this scheme may be elaborated. Thereafter, C-in-C, Home Forces, will take it as a basis upon which to work

and will be free at any time to ask the Defence Committee for its application.

3. Sir Edward Bridges and General Ismay will arrange the Committee for the approval of the Lord Privy Seal.

Winston S. Churchill to Anthony Eden
(*Churchill papers, 20/36*)

10 October 1941
Action this Day

GENERAL CATROUX'S DESIRE TO PROCLAIM MARTIAL LAW IN SYRIA

General Auchinleck ought not to be cluttered up with this sort of stuff when all his mind should be turned in other directions. I presume that the Minister of State is already on the spot, and it is clearly his business to take all this off the shoulders of the Commander-in-Chief. If the Minister of State thinks imposition of martial law justifiable we should certainly support him. Perhaps you will draft me a suitable answer or show me what you will send yourself.

Winston S. Churchill to David Margesson
(*Churchill papers, 20/36*)

10 October 1941

I see some odd court-martial cases mentioned in the papers. First, a sergeant who told a Home Guard lieutenant 'So what?' and 'Put a sock in it' in the presence of troops, but who was merely reprimanded. He should surely have been reduced to the ranks. Second, some soldiers who were heard calling the sergeants 'Bastards with three stripes' but who apparently were honourably acquitted on the grounds that this was a word of common use in the Army. The major giving evidence said he had often turned a deaf ear to it when used about himself.

In sharp contrast, two Canadians who deserted in Canada and made their way over here after great adventure in order to fight received sixty days.

All this seems to require very clear guidance from you and the Army authorities.

Winston S. Churchill to Harry Hopkins
(*Churchill papers, 20/43*)

10 October 1941

We want Mountbatten over here for a very active and urgent job.[1] Please explain to the President how disappointed he was not to be able to fulfil the invitation to the White House, with which he had been honoured. He will seek an audience before leaving.

Winston S. Churchill to Lord Louis Mountbatten
(*Churchill papers, 20/43*)

10 October 1941

We want you home here at once for something which you will find of the highest interest.

Anthony Eden: diary
(*'The Reckoning'*)

10 October 1941

Max returned in morning and Winston and I heard his account. Very lively and entertaining and, he clearly maintains, satisfactory. He believes that Stalin will fight on, come what may, and that he hates Hitler, which he certainly did not in 1935, with cold fury…

Motored to Chequers in the afternoon, Russian news looking bad…

Party was only Max, Harriman and self. We had much gossip about Moscow. Harriman told me privately that Stalin had spoken of an alliance after the war and proposed it to Max. He thought S would be offended if we did not return some reply.

After an interlude for films, more talk about Russia and plans to aid, our production and American etc.

[1] To succeed Admiral of the Fleet Sir Roger Keyes as Director of Combined Operations. The culmination of Mountbatten's tenure of the post was the Dieppe Raid in 1942.

Winston S. Churchill to John Curtin
(*Churchill papers, 20/43*)

10 October 1941
Most Secret and Personal

Since my message of 3rd October was sent, President has asked for an alteration in method of transporting the extra divisions. This is due to his resolve to seek from Congress the revision of the Neutrality Law, thus becoming empowered to arm all American merchant ships and with the prospect of sending them direct to British ports. He did not wish any incident, such as an attack on American transports in British waters, to prejudice consideration by Congress of this further legislation. I have therefore arranged with him to carry the leading division 20,800 men to Halifax in British ships, and he will carry them in American ships all the rest of the way to Suez. This slows up our programme by about a month, but the amendment of the Neutrality Act outweighs all other considerations.

2. I presume you are aware that our growing Naval strength in capital ships will presently enable us to place a strong Squadron of battleships and a battle cruiser in the Indian Ocean, cruising as far as Singapore.

Elizabeth Layton: letter to her parents
(*Elizabeth Nel papers*)

12 October 1941

Not in a very good temper this morning. He suddenly said 'Gimme t–gr–spts–pk.' Interpreting this as 'Give me a toothpick' I leapt up, looked round and then started rummaging in the bag in which such necessities should be kept. After less than 30 seconds he said, very bored and superior 'now Miss Layton, just stop playing the bloody ass and ask Sawyers.'[1]

I couldn't help feeling amused. Presently, after having dictated something, he found I'd put 'Somehow I think it right' (which was what I thought he'd said). So, fairly patient, he said 'no, no, I said *now the time* is right' (with accents like that).

So I did it again. Gave it back. There was a roar of rage. 'God's teeth, girl, can't you even do it right the second time. I said *ripe ripe ripe–P P P.*'

[1] Churchill's valet.

I should, perhaps, have realized, but he hadn't mentioned that 'right' was 'wrong'. However he forgave me and was very amiable for the rest of the day. I can't help feeling rather fond of him – he is a loveable person, in spite of his impatience.[1]

Winston S. Churchill to Lord Beaverbrook
(*Churchill papers, 20/36*)

12 October 1941

ANTI-AIRCRAFT WEAPONS AND AMMUNITION

During your absence I have considered the questions you raised with me about the UP weapon and its subsidiary variants of the proximity fuze, viz., PE and radio. The great need is the manufacture of AD ammunition for the 50 batteries which are already deployed.[2] PE and radio are in the sphere of research and experiment; but these researches should be pressed to the utmost because of the immense strategic advantages to the Navy which would flow from their effective solution.

Up to the present time I take full responsibility for all that has been done. You wish as Minister of Supply to have full control of both the manufacture and research, and I shall be very glad if you will assume it as from the date of this minute. As the three Services are concerned, you will no doubt arrange for the necessary consultations.

General Sir Alan Brooke: recollection
(*'Turn of the Tide'*)

12 October 1941

After having made all arrangements to go to Chequers and for special train to collect me at Wendover station at 1.45 a.m., I suddenly received message during afternoon that PM wanted us at 10 Downing Street instead. Went there at 6.30 p.m. All Chiefs of Staff, Tovey, Sholto, Paget and I attended. PM

[1] Peter Kinna later recalled being present during moments of impatience: 'If you had the temerity to ask him to repeat a word, Kinna later recalled, 'he nearly killed you with words. It upset his train of thought. He never paused.' But with Churchill's 'slight impediment' – pronouncing the letter 's' as 'sh' – Kinna noted, it was not always easy to hear what he said. There was another problem for those who took Churchill's dictation – the fascination of his remarks. 'Sometimes I just wanted to listen and not take it down,' Kinna remembered. 'I found myself listening instead of taking it down.' (Conversation with the author, 24 August 1982). John Martin later recalled how it was sometimes 'difficult to interpret' Churchill's oral instructions. 'One didn't always understand what he said,' Martin explained. 'He just grunted or said "get me my minute" – and you had to know which one he had in mind.' (Conversation with the author, 15 October 1982)

[2] The Unrotated Projectile anti-aircraft rocket; the PE fuze anti-aircraft device; and AD anti-aircraft ammunition.

very dissatisfied with our Appreciation.[1] Told me that he was expecting a detailed plan for the operation, and instead of that I had submitted a masterly treatise on all the difficulties. He then proceeded to cross-question me for nearly two hours on various items of the Appreciation, trying to make out that I had unnecessarily increased the difficulties. However, I was quite satisfied that there was only one conclusion to arrive at. Finally left at 8.30 p.m., dined at club and embarked on train at 11 p.m.

At 6.30 p.m. we assembled at 10 Downing Street. The PM was already in the Cabinet Room, and I saw at once from his face that we were in for the hell of a storm! He had with him what he used to classify as some of his 'colleagues', usually Anthony Eden, Attlee, Leathers on this occasion, and possibly a few others. On my side of the table I had the various Naval and Air Commanders-in-Chief who had collaborated with me, Paget, who was nominated as commander of this Expedition, and some of my staff.

When we were all assembled he shoved his chin out in his aggressive way and, staring hard at me, said: 'I had instructed you to prepare a detailed plan for the capture of Trondheim, with a commander appointed and ready in every detail. What have you done? You have instead submitted a masterly treatise on all the difficulties and on all the reasons why this operation should not be carried out.' He then proceeded to cross-question me for nearly two hours on most of the minor points of the appreciation. I repeatedly tried to bring him back to the main reason – the lack of air-support. He avoided this issue and selected arguments such as: 'You state that you will be confronted by frosts and thaws which will render mobility difficult. How can you account for such a statement?' I replied that this was a trivial matter and that the statement came from the 'Climate Book'. He at once sent for this book, from which it at once became evident that this extract had been copied straight out of the book. His next attack was: 'You state that it will take you some twsenty-four hours to cover the ground between A and B. How can you account for so long being taken? Explain to me exactly how every hour of those twenty-four will be occupied?' As this time had been allowed for overcoming enemy resistance on the road, removal of road-blocks and probable reparation to demolition of bridges and culvers, it was not an easy matter to paint this detailed picture of every hour of those twenty-four. This led to a series of more questions, interspersed with sarcasm and criticism. A very unpleasant gruelling to stand up to in a full room, but excellent training for what I had to stand up to on many occasions in later years.

The meeting finished shortly after 8.30 p.m. and for the second time Winston had been ridden off Trondheim.

[1] Of the proposed amphibious landing at Trondheim, in northern Norway.

Winston S. Churchill to J. V. Stalin
(*Churchill papers, 20/43*)

13 October 1941
Personal and Secret

I thank you for your letter of 3rd October. I have given incessant directions to accelerate by every means the deliveries at Archangel as reported to you in my telegram of the 6th October. Your request for 3,000 lorries will be met immediately from our Army stock, but deliveries must not impede the flow of tanks and aircraft. We are asking Harriman to arrange a larger long-term programme from the United States.

2. About Persia. Our only interests there are: first, as a barrier against German penetration eastward; and, secondly, as a through route for supplies to the Caspian Basin. If you wish to withdraw the five or six Russian divisions for use on the battlefront, we will take over the whole responsibility of keeping order and maintaining and improving the supply route. I pledge the faith of Britain that we will not seek any advantage for ourselves at the expense of any rightful Russian interest during the war or at the end. In any case, the signing of the Tripartite Treaty is urgent to avoid internal disorders growing, with consequent danger of choking the supply route. General Wavell will be at Tiflis on the 18th October, and will discuss with your generals any questions which you may instruct them to settle with him.

3. Words are useless to express what we feel about your vast, heroic struggle. We hope presently to testify by action.

Winston S. Churchill to Clement Attlee
(*Churchill papers, 20/36*)

13 October 1941

I shall be glad if you will let me have the Party and political background of Admiral Evans's[1] career. I was not aware that he had had any previous associations with the Labour Party, at any rate I know of nothing of a formal or public character. It would, I think, expose both him and me to very serious criticism if it could be suggested that he had been induced to join the Labour Party by the prospect of a Peerage. There are many Officers of higher standing in the Navy to whom the honour of a Peerage has not been accorded.

[1] Edward Ratcliffe Garth Russell Evans, 1881–1957. Entered the Royal Navy, 1897. Second-in-Command, British Antarctic Expedition, 1909; returned in command of the expedition after the death of Captain Scott. On active service, 1914–18 (despatches twice). Rear-Admiral commanding the Royal Australian Navy, 1929–31. Knighted, 1935. Commander-in-Chief, the Nore, 1935–9. London Regional Commissioner for Civil Defence, 1939–45. Created Baron Mountevans, 1945.

The Navy would watch this point very narrowly, and their opinion about it might be very adverse. The Service would know quite well whether he had in fact been Socialist in political opinion. I should think it likely that he knows little or nothing about politics. He has certainly expressed in public no vigorous opinion showing knowledge or conviction of your Party's programme.

Winston S. Churchill to Herbert Morrison
(*Churchill papers, 20/36*)

13 October 1941

RECRUITMENT OF WOMEN

Something very much more powerful than a meeting in the Albert Hall is required. I think the Cabinet will have to consider in the near future as a major issue the compulsory service of women. This is being brought forward as a result of the Lord President's Committee.

Winston S. Churchill to Emanuel Shinwell
(*Churchill papers, 20/22*)

13 October 1941

Dear Mr Shinwell,

The delay in answering your letter of October 7 has been due to the fact that I referred it to the Admiralty. The First Lord will be quite willing to see you on the subject, and will show you the Memorandum he has prepared at my request.

Meanwhile, I can only say that I entirely agree with you that the size of the convoys should be reduced, that they should be graded according to speed, and that much stronger escorts should be provided. The difficulty is that all our escorts are already strained to the utmost in bringing in the large volume of shipping on which our war effort depends. Therefore we have to do the best we can with the numbers we have got. The results achieved during the last Quarter and in the first part of the present month are remarkable in view of the difficulties and the great and increasing number of U-boats operating. Indeed I feel that what has been accomplished constitutes one of the greatest feats ever performed by the Admiralty. But of course things may turn worse again in the future.

With regard to the convoy system, this was searchingly reconsidered in February, and experiment was tried of releasing from convoys ships of a speed between 12 and 15 knots, and letting them find their own way as do those over 15 knots. The results were immediately unfortunate, and the experiment has been discontinued. I know of no responsible person acquainted with the facts who would advocate the abandonment of the convoy system.

Winston S. Churchill to General Auchinleck
(Churchill papers, 20/43)

14 October 1941
Personal

Many thanks for your letter of 30th September, just received. In view of your statement that it would be a great help to you if the relief of the remaining Australians could be postponed until after 'Crusader', I sent this morning the attached telegram to the Australian Government. I now see in current telegrams that 'Cultivator'[1] has begun. It may be that the new Government will be willing to give you the easement you desire. I should be glad for the sake of Australia and history if they would do this. I do not know exactly what stage 'Cultivator' has reached, and you should certainly not interrupt any movement ordered. In a day or two I shall hear what they decide and will advise you.

2. The Russian news is increasingly grave.[2] All now hinges on you.

Winston S. Churchill to John Curtin
(Churchill papers, 20/43)

14 October 1941
Personal and Secret

I feel it right to ask you to reconsider once again the issue raised in my telegram Winch No.1 to your predecessor. I have heard again from General Auchinleck that he would be very greatly helped and convenienced if the remaining two Australian brigades could stay in Tobruk until the result of the approaching battle is decided. I will not repeat the arguments which I have already used, but I will only add that if you felt able to consent it would not expose your troops to any undue or invidious risks and would at the same time be taken very kindly as an act of comradeship in the present struggle.

[1] A convoy from Alexandria to Tobruk bringing troops to relieve the Australian units there.

[2] On 12 October 1941 the Germans captured Kaluga, 100 miles south-west of Moscow, and in the Bryansk pocket took 660,000 Russian soldiers prisoner. On October 13 the Russians evacuated Vyazma, and there were heavy German bombing raids on railway communications around Moscow. On October 14 the Russians evacuated Kalinin, on the Moscow–Leningrad railway, and evacuated Mariupol on the Sea of Azov.

Winston S. Churchill to Peter Fraser
(*Churchill papers, 20/44*)

14 October 1941
Most Secret and Personal

The long delay in striking has been caused by the need to gather ample air and tank strength. This has, we believe, now been achieved in full measure. I do not think the enemy will be able to alter these conditions before the day comes. I will cable you more fully early next week.

Winston S. Churchill: Oral Answers
(*Hansard*)

14 October 1941 House of Commons

WAR SITUATION (RUSSIA)

Mr Shinwell asked the Prime Minister whether he will make a statement on the war situation on the Eastern front?

The Prime Minister (Mr Churchill): No. Sir. This must obviously be left to the Russian High Command, who are conducting their great battle. I should not presume to add anything to their communiqués at this juncture.

Mr Shinwell: Is my right hon. Friend aware that there is considerable disquiet throughout the country about the form, the substance and the speed of the assistance rendered to Russia, and in the circumstances will he provide facilities for an early Debate on the subject?

The Prime Minister: The hon. Member should not suppose that he has a monopoly of anxieties in these times.

Winston S. Churchill to Anthony Eden and Lord Beaverbrook
(*Churchill papers, 20/36*)

14 October 1941
Most Secret

This file is really worth looking through in view of the statement that Stalin made to Lord Beaverbrook about not remembering when he was warned. This was the only message before the attack that I sent Stalin direct.[1] It had to be somewhat cryptic in view of the deadly character of the information contained. Its brevity, the exceptional character of the communication, the

[1] Churchill's message to Stalin of 3 April 1941. Several other warnings were sent to Stalin between April and June 1941 through the British Foreign Office via the Soviet Ambassador, Ivan Maisky.

fact that it came from the Head of the Government and was to be delivered personally to the Head of the Russian Government by the Ambassador were all intended to give it special significance and arrest Stalin's attention. It was astonishing that the Ambassador should have had the effrontery to delay this message for sixteen days, and then merely to hand it to Vyshinsky. It may very well never have reached Stalin at all, or merely have been put casually before him. That Sir Stafford Cripps should think the fact that he had been writing a long personal letter about the war to Vyshinsky, and that this would be more likely to make an impression than a direct message from me, only shows his lack of sense of proportion. Sir Stafford Cripps has a great responsibility for his obstinate, obstructive handling of this matter. If he had obeyed his instructions, it is more than possible that some kind of relationship would have been constructed between me and Stalin.

Let me have this back.[1]

War Cabinet, Defence Committee (Operations): minutes
(*Cabinet papers, 69/2*)

15 October 1941
10 p.m.

CYRENAICA

The Prime Minister referred to a telegram he had received from Mr Fraser asking for an assurance that adequate air support would be provided for the New Zealand Division in the forthcoming operations. He had been about to answer this telegram and give the necessary assurance when a telegram from the Commanders-in-Chief in the Middle East had come giving figures which seemed to show that we should be inferior in the air to the German and Italian air forces. The Chief of the Air Staff had taken a different view and was confident that we should be superior, basing his opinion on the wider information available at home. The matter was of such importance, however, that it had been decided, subject to the approval of the Defence Committee, to send Sir Wilfrid Freeman out to the Middle East to clear up the facts. He would also see in what way the air forces for the battle could be strengthened, and make proposals for any assistance which could be given from here.

The Committee expressed their approval of this proposal.

[1] Anthony Eden replied to Churchill that same day, 14 October 1941: 'It should be borne in mind that at this time the Russians were most reluctant to receive messages of any kind; and, even if Stalin did receive your message, he now probably prefers to forget the fact. Only thus, to some extent, can he exonerate himself. The same attitude was adopted towards the later messages which, with your permission, I gave to Maisky, beginning several weeks before the attack. These have never been acknowledged or referred to, to this day.' (Churchill papers, 20/36)

STRATEGIC OPTIONS

The Prime Minister said that he had been equally anxious to take advantage of the Russian situation to get a footing in Norway, and he had given instructions for Commander-in-Chief, Home Forces, and General Paget, to make a plan; but instead of a plan a Paper had been produced showing all the insuperable objections to any action. He had been disappointed in this result but, in face of the disinclination of General Paget (who had practical experience of the country and who had proved his mettle in difficult circumstances) to undertake the operation, he had not felt he could press it much further. He had nevertheless given orders that preparations should go on though without steps being taken which would dislocate our convoys. The essential point, he thought, was that we should place ourselves in the position to strike with a force of up to three divisions and one armoured division in November. This was all the more necessary in view of the possibility that favourable opportunities might present themselves in the Mediterranean. If General Auchinleck won a victory and cleared Cyrenaica, he might then be able to push on to Tripoli. This, in turn, might lead Germany to press the French to give them the use of Bizerta, a request which Weygand might decide to refuse. We might find ourselves invited to send forces to Casablanca. If this contingency arose, it would be necessary for us to be prepared immediately to put forward proposals on the following lines. We would undertake to restore France to her former greatness but in return the French would have to promise forthwith concessions in Morocco to the Spaniards, and thus fortify the latter in their resistance to a German advance through their country. In order to put forward such proposals, however, we required to know exactly what these concessions should be and the Foreign Office should work out concrete proposals.

SICILY

The Prime Minister said he would favour operations against Sicily if a plan could be made. The Norwegian operations could be used as cover and our force could be prepared ostensibly for that. He would like to have a plan worked out with an estimate of the shipping required and the interruption which would be caused to our Middle East convoys. The Committee could then decide whether to authorize active preparations for the operation.

The Committee agreed with this proposal.

THE CAUCASUS

The Prime Minister proposed that instructions should be sent to General Wavell in the following terms. While we did not know what instructions General Kozlov[1] had received from his own Government, our own attitude

[1] General D.T. Kozlov. Commander of the Transcaucasian Front, August to December 1941; of the Caucasus Front, December 1941 to January 1942; and of the Crimea Front, January to May 1942.

was that the five Russian divisions now in Persia should be freed to return and take part in the defence of the Caucasus, leaving a symbolic force behind. At the same time we should offer to send a symbolic force to help in the defence of the Caucasus and should notify our willingness to be responsible for maintaining Russian interests in Persia and for safeguarding the route for Russian supplies.

A telegram in the above sense was drafted and approved by the Prime Minister subsequent to the Meeting.

Winston S. Churchill to Averell Harriman
(*Churchill papers, 20/22*)

15 October 1941

My dear Averell,

Thank you so much for your letter of October 14, giving me the message sent today by the President to Monsieur Stalin. I am glad to have this early and encouraging account of your deliveries to Russia.

The caviare has arrived, and it was very kind of you to send it to me.

Yours very sincerely,
Winston S. Churchill

PS I hope indeed you are better. Let us meet soon.[1]

Winston S. Churchill: Note[2]
(*Churchill papers, 23/9*)

15 October 1941
Secret

SUPPLIES TO RUSSIA AND THE PERSIAN GULF AREA

The Moscow Conference has laid down a programme of supplies to Russia. It remains to give effect to it. This calls for a revision of the present organization for dealing with these matters. Since some supplies to Russia will go through the Persian Gulf area, it is necessary that there should be a single co-ordinating authority to deal with supplies (a) to Russia by whatever route, and (b) to the Persian Gulf Area.

[1] Churchill saw Harriman that night. According to Harriman's own recollection, Churchill told him that he was 'satisfied the Russians would continue to fight no matter where the front might be', although he had not put out of his mind the thought that Hitler still might attempt an invasion of the British Isles. Harriman, who was about to leave for Washington, asked Churchill how he saw the war developing. 'Well,' the Prime Minister replied, 'Hitler's revised plan undoubtedly is now – Poland, '39; France, '40; Russia, '41; England, '42, and, '43, maybe America.' W. Averell Harriman and Elie Abel, *Special Envoy to Churchill and Stalin, 1941–1946*, London, 1976)

[2] Circulated to the War Cabinet as War Cabinet Paper No. 111 of 1941.

2. The first essential is to lay down clear lines of Departmental responsibility.

Departmental Responsibilities

The primary responsibility for all arrangements to improve and administer road and rail transport in the Persian Gulf Area and for port development in this area must rest with a single Department, namely, the War Office. To avoid confusion, all communications on these matters should pass through this single channel. The War Office will, no doubt, keep in close touch with the Foreign Office representative in regard *e.g.*, to negotiations with the Persian Government on transport matters.

3. The Ministry of War Transport's prime responsibility is, of course, the arrangement and programming of shipments. The Ministry will maintain representatives in the Persian Gulf and Russian ports, to watch over port arrangements, and to improve port administration, in cooperation with the national authorities.

4. The Ministry of Supply is responsible for obtaining locomotives and other stores as requested by the War Office, in connection with the improvement of land communications and port development in the Persian Gulf Area.

5. The United Kingdom Commercial Corporation, in dealing with supplies for Russia, will act as agents for the Ministries of Supply and Food. In running local road transport services, they will be under the control of the local military authorities.

6. In order to reduce the number of separate bodies concerned in these matters, the work hitherto performed by the Section of the Ministry of Economic Warfare dealing with Russian trade will be transferred to the Ministry of Supply.

Ministerial Executive

7. The necessary coordination of Departmental activities, and the settlement of disputed points, will be entrusted to a Ministerial Executive, which will take the place of the present Committee for the Co-ordination of Allied Supplies. This body, which will be known as the Allied Supplies Executive, will be composed as follows:

Chairman

The Minister of Supply.

Members

The Secretary of State for War (or his representative).

The Parliamentary Secretary to the Ministry of War Transport.

Representatives of the Foreign Office, and other Departments, will be summoned to attend when required.

Secretariat

8. The Executive will have a small liaison Secretariat (part of the War Cabinet Secretariat), which will maintain close contact with

(a) The Section of the Ministry of War Transport which deals with supplies to Russia and the Persian Gulf Area.

(b) The staff of the North American Supply Committee.

Lieutenant-Colonel Jacob will be attached to the Executive as representing the Office of the Minister of Defence.

Terms of Reference

9. The Terms of Reference to the Executive will be as follows:

(1) To determine questions relating to military and civil supplies to Russia and the Persian Gulf Area, including the improvement of communications in that area, and the settlement of general priorities. The broad strategic issues as to the scale of military supplies will be reserved for the Defence Committee.

(2) The Executive will also deal with miscellaneous questions remitted to them as to military and civil supplies to other Allied or friendly countries; e.g., Turkey and the Netherlands East Indies, and, if necessary, settle priorities of civil supplies when the Middle East area is also involved.

Civil Supplies

10. It will be open to the Executive to appoint a subsidiary body in the place of the present Sub-Committee on Civil Supplies, to deal with the large number of detailed administrative problems which arise in regard to the dispatch of civil supplies to the Middle East and Persian Gulf Areas.

Franklin D. Roosevelt to Winston S. Churchill

(*Churchill papers, 20/20*)

15 October 1941 The White House
Washington

Dear Winston,

Mountbatten has been really useful to our Navy people & he will tell you of his visit to the Fleet in Hawaii. The Jap situation is definitely worse & I <u>think</u> they are headed North – however in spite of this you & I have two months of respite in the Far East.

Dicky will tell you of a <u>possibility</u> for your people to study – to be used only if Pétain goes & Weygand plays with us.[1]

I wish I could see you again!

As ever yours
Franklin D. Roosevelt

[1] An American amphibious landing, by invitation, in French North Africa, in co-ordination with a British advance from Cyrenaica to Tripoli.

Winston S. Churchill to H. G. Wells[1]

(*Churchill papers, 20/30*)

15 October 1941
Private

My dear Wells,

Many thanks for your letter and its enclosure, which I had already read in the *Sunday Dispatch*.[2] It is quite impossible, as I am sure you realize, for me to discuss these matters outside the secret circle, for the reasons which I gave in the House of Commons a little while ago.

I hope however you will not suppose that we do not face squarely all the issues, and will not too readily abandon the confidence you have hitherto expressed in

Yours very sincerely,
Winston S. Churchill

Sir Alexander Cadogan: diary

(*'The Diaries of Sir Alexander Cadogan OM, 1938-1945'*)

16 October 1941

Cabinet at 12.15. Cabinet lasted till 1.40. Boxes meanwhile piling up. On Abyssinia PM took wise line that we must not saddle ourselves with a Protectorate – and all the responsibility that implies. Perhaps the Emperor can't govern well, but we can't keep everyone on apron-strings. 'The grant of self-government implies the grant of mis-government. I mean, otherwise there wouldn't be any fun in it at all'!

[1] Herbert George Wells, 1866–1946. A prolific writer, author of more than seventy books, he published one of his best-known works, *The Time Machine*, in 1895. In his book *Men Like Gods*, published in 1925, Churchill appears thinly disguised as Rupert Catskill, whose 'wild imaginings had caused the deaths of thousands of people'.

[2] In an article in the *Sunday Dispatch* on 12 October 1941, H.G. Wells wrote that 'the only forces that are fighting the Germans wholeheartedly are the British Air Force, the Russian people, the British Fleet, some American ships, and a miscellany of British-led forces in the Near East. We have considerable accumulations of troops in the Near East, but they are not yet fighting Germans.' Wells added: 'I still detect a considerable resistance to fighting all out with Russia as an Ally; a tendency to delay and find excuses for unhelpfulness. The common British people have to overcome that reluctance. It is the way to disaster. We cannot afford to half-help our stoutest Ally. Evidently they feel that intensely now.'

War Cabinet: minutes
(*Cabinet papers, 65/19*)

16 October 1941
12.15 p.m.

Prime Minister's Room
House of Commons

The Secretary of State for Foreign Affairs said that the Dutch Minister[1] had complained of the heavy casualties to the Dutch population caused by our bombing of Rotterdam on the night of the 3rd/4th October. Our aircraft had evidently bombed the town in mistake for the harbour.

The Prime Minister instructed the Chief of the Air Staff to give directions that the greatest care was to be taken in carrying out night attacks on objectives in enemy-occupied countries friendly to ourselves.

The Prime Minister said[2] that he had had a telegram from General Auchinleck about the relief of the Australian troops from Tobruk. General Auchinleck said that it was essential that the first half of the relief should be completed, but that it would be a help if the second half of the operation could be cancelled. A definite decision must be given by the 19th October.

The Prime Minister said that it was greatly to be hoped that the Australian Government would agree to leave a Brigade in Tobruk. If they did not agree to this course, he feared that the effect on the prestige of the Australian troops would be very great when the full facts and the correspondence became known. He had already addressed a further request to the Australian Government on the matter, although he had little hope that they would reverse the decision taken by their predecessors.

The Prime Minister said1 that if Japan declared war on Russia, the latter would certainly press us to declare war on Japan. We were, of course, already committed to go to war with Japan if Japan was at war with the United States. But we ought not to commit ourselves to any action which would involve us in war with Japan unless the United States was also at war with that country.

More generally, the Prime Minister said that the Far Eastern situation had undoubtedly changed, and that the United States Government was nearer to a commitment than they had been in the past. We ought to regard the United States as having taken charge in the Far East. It was for them to take the lead in this area, and we would support them.

[1] Edgar van Verduynen (see page 227, note 1).

[2] This, and the subsequent War Cabinet discussions of 16 October 1941 printed here, were recorded only in the War Cabinet's Confidential Annex (*Cabinet papers, 65/23*).

Winston S. Churchill to General Auchinleck
(*Churchill papers, 20/20*)

16 October 1941
Private and Secret

My dear General Auchinleck,

Tedder's estimate of strength actual and relative, is so misleading and militarily untrue that I found it necessary at once to send Air Chief Marshal Freeman to Cairo. Only in this way can the facts be established, we here be properly informed and you yourself reassured as to the Air strength at your disposal. The Air Staff here know just as much and in some ways more than the Air Intelligence in Egypt. Their conviction is that you will have a substantial numerical superiority in the battle zone, even if all Italian planes are counted as if they were equal to German or British. Moreover, Tedder's telegram assumed, on the basis of an estimate of September 7, that the Russian front would be stabilized by October 15, thus permitting reinforcement to begin. It will certainly not be stabilized for some weeks, if then, and thereafter several more weeks must elapse before any effective transference can be made of German Air units already battered and worn.

I thought it very wrong that such mis-statements should be made by the Air authorities in Cairo on the eve of a decisive battle and I shall not conceal from you that such conduct has affected my confidence in their quality and judgment.

You will find Freeman an officer of altogether larger calibre and if you feel he would be a greater help to you and that you would have more confidence in the Air Command if he assumed it, you should not hesitate to tell me so. The time has now come when for the purposes of the major operation impending, the Air is subordinated to you. Do not let any thought of Tedder's personal feelings influence you. This is no time for such considerations. On the other hand I am very glad to see that you and Tedder are in accord upon the tactical employment of the Air Force and that there is no danger of its being parcelled out among the various divisions, thus losing its power to make the characteristic contribution of its arm.

I am very glad you are sending an officer home to tell me and the CIGS something more of your plans. Upon 'Crusader' and the use made of it, issues affecting the whole immediate future of the war depend. Turkey, French North Africa and Spain will pick their steps accordingly. The struggling Russian armies will feel that our long period of inaction has been at last broken and that they are not the only people engaging the enemy. Feeling here has risen very high against what is thought to be our supine incapacity for action. I am however fully in control of public opinion and of the House of Commons. Nevertheless it seems to me, on military grounds alone, that everything should be thrown into this battle that can be made to play its part. This is also the view of the Defence Committee, both political and expert Members. God has granted us this long breathing space and I feel sure that if all is risked all may be won.

We have been considering how to help you exploit success, should it be granted to us. Any long delay after a victory in Cyrenaica in pushing on to Tripoli would seem fatal to that extension of your plan. It is rather a rapid dash forward, while the shock of the battle still reigns and before the enemy can bring new forces into Africa or into Italy, that seems alone possible. Directions have been given here to prepare an expedition to Norway and shipping for about four divisions, including one armoured division, is being gathered. Winter clothing is being issued to the troops assigned. This forms a real cover. However, from about the middle of November or perhaps even a little earlier I shall be holding a substantial force which can as easily steer south as north. Should your operation change the attitude of Weygand we could enter by Casablanca at his invitation; or alternatively action against Sicily in conjunction with your army may be taken. This last plan[1] is now being studied by the Chiefs of the Staff and the Defence Committee. The situation in Italy, and particularly in Sicily, gives grounds for hope and audacity on our part. On this you will presently receive details.

This letter is evidently most private and secret, but I should be pleased if you would show it to the Minister of State to whom I have not had time to write separately.

With every good wish,
Believe me,
Yours sincerely,
Winston S. Churchill

PS I sent, your account of the American light cruiser tanks exercising to the President by Mr Harriman yesterday.

Winston S. Churchill to L. S. Amery
(*Churchill papers, 20/36*)

17 October 1941

GOVERNORSHIPS OF BOMBAY AND MADRAS

There is no objection to moving a good man from Madras to Bombay, which is a more difficult parish. There would then be a vacancy for Madras. Pray let me have your list of names.

[1] Operation Whipcord.

The Duke of Sutherland[1] is available. He has held various minor offices and seems in many ways qualified.

You promised me that you would let me have epitomes of the Indian telegrams. I am sorry not to have had one in the case of the Viceroy's telegram of 10th October.

I cannot resist drawing your attention in your own letter to 'try and think'. Mr Welldon[2] taught me this was wrong, and that 'try to think' was right. He suggested that the vulgar error, of which I rejoice to convict you, probably arose from the scriptural phrase 'try and prove', the two verbs in this case being of independent value. So what!

Winston S. Churchill to David Margesson

(*Churchill papers, 20/36*)

17 October 1941

DISCUSSION ON CURRENT AFFAIRS IN THE ARMY

I do not approve of this system of encouraging political discussion in the Army among soldiers as such. The material provided for the guidance of the Officers in the short notes is hopelessly below the level of that available in the daily Press. Discussions in which no controversy is desired are a farce. There cannot be controversy without prejudice to discipline. The only sound principle is 'no politics in the Army'.

I hope you will wind up this business as quickly and as decently as possible and set the persons concerned in it to useful work.

[1] George Granville Sutherland-Leveson-Gower, 1888–1963. Known as 'Geordie'. Succeeded his father as 5th Duke of Sutherland, 1913. Served with the British Military Mission to Belgium, 1914–15. Commanded Motor Boat Flotillas, Egypt and Adriatic, 1915–17. Represented the Colonial Office in the House of Lords, 1921–2. Under-Secretary, Air Ministry, 1922–4. Paymaster-General, 1925–8. Parliamentary Under-Secretary of State for War, 1928–9. Lord Steward of the Household, 1936–7.

[2] James Edward Cowell Welldon, 1854–1937. Headmaster of Harrow School, 1885–98, while both Churchill and Amery were there. Bishop of Calcutta, 1898–1902. Canon of Westminster, 1902–6. Dean of Manchester, 1906–18. Dean of Durham, 1918–33. On 28 September 1896, while Churchill was on his way to India, Welldon wrote to him: 'I implore you not to let your wild spirits carry you away to any action that may bring dishonour on your school or your name. It is impossible that I should not hear of your follies and impertinences if you are guilty of them, and you will recognize that you put a severe strain upon my friendship if you ask me to treat you as a friend when other people speak of you with indignation or contempt.'

Winston S. Churchill to Tom Williams[1]
(*Churchill papers, 20/22*)

17 October 1941
Personal

My dear Tom Williams,

I had a talk with Sir Charles Wilson, and was glad to find from him that he thought you were in very good hands and receiving the best treatment. Do not hesitate to take a month or six months off while you are having the teeth out and the cause of the trouble removed. I am sure you will find it shorter in the end to take the necessary rest, and give yourself the best chance.

All good wishes.

Yours vy sincerely,
Winston S. Churchill

Winston S. Churchill to Major Stuart Black[2]
(*Churchill papers, 2/416*)

17 October 1941

My dear Sir,

I thank you for your letter of October 12, and I am complimented by your wish to have a tablet placed on the wall of your house recording the fact that I made my first political speech at a garden party at Claverton Manor.

I gladly consent to your proposal.

Yours very faithfully,
Winston S. Churchill

[1] Tom Williams, 1888–1967. The tenth child of a coal miner who had been blinded in a mining accident. Worked in the coalmines: a checkweigher, 1916–22. Labour Member of Parliament for Don Valley, 1922–59. Parliamentary Private Secretary, Minister of Agriculture, 1924; Minister of Labour, 1929–31; Ministry of Agriculture, 1940–45. Privy Councillor, 1941. Minister of Agriculture and Fisheries, 1945–51. Responsible for the Agriculture Act (1947) which was designed to protect the interests of both farmers and consumers. Created Baron (Life Peer) as Lord Williams of Barnburgh. Member of the Political Honours Scrutiny Committee from 1961 until his death. He published his autobiography, *Digging for Britain*, in 1965.

[2] Major Black was the owner of Claverton Manor near Bath. On 12 October 1941 he had written to Churchill: 'Dear Prime Minister, In last week's *Sunday Times* it is stated you made your first political speech at a garden party near Bath and I believe it was at this house. Bath is noted, as you may be aware, for the tablets on the walls of houses which have been associated with the lives of famous men. I would be greatly honoured if you would permit me to have an inscription, approved by you, carved on the wall beside the front door of my house recording your visit here on such a memorable occasion, as it would be of the greatest interest to future generations. Yours admiringly, A.A. Stuart Black' (*Churchill papers*, 2/416).

War Cabinet, Defence Committee (Operations): minutes
(*Cabinet papers, 69/2*)

17 October 1941

NAVAL REINFORCEMENTS, FAR EAST

The Committee had before them a minute which the Foreign Secretary had addressed to the Prime Minister on the possibility of sending Capital Ship reinforcements to the Far East.

The Prime Minister said that he had been considering the Admiralty's proposals to send to the Far East a fleet consisting of half a dozen of our older and slower Capital Ships. Although the Far East could at present still be regarded as a secondary theatre, it seemed to him wrong to send a squadron of Capital Ships that were neither strong enough to engage the weight of the Japanese Navy, nor yet fast enough to avoid action except in circumstances of their own choosing.

We had before us the example of the battleship *Tirpitz* which now compelled us to keep on guard a force three times her weight in addition to the United States forces patrolling the Atlantic. The presence of one modern Capital Ship in Far Eastern waters could be calculated to have a similar effect on the Japanese Naval Authorities, and thereby on Japanese foreign policy.

The *Repulse* had already reached the Indian Ocean. No time should now be lost in sending the *Prince Of Wales* to join up with her at Singapore. We could afford to accept some risk of the *Tirpitz* breaking out into the Atlantic in the knowledge that we ought by air action from aircraft carriers to be able to slow her up to become a prey for the heavy metal of our Capital Ships.

Mr Alexander agreed that there were strong arguments in favour of the Prime Minister's proposal, but pointed out that whereas the *Tirpitz* was a threat to our trade convoys in the Atlantic, our dispositions in the Far East would be governed more by the need to protect our own trade routes than to raid Japanese shipping. A strong reason for keeping three King George's in home waters was the need to have modern ships to take part in important operations in the Western Mediterranean.

Mr Eden said that from the point of view of deterring Japan from entering the war, the despatch of one modern ship, such as the *Prince Of Wales*, to the Far East would have a far greater effect politically than the presence in those waters of a number of the last war's battleships. If the *Prince Of Wales* were to call at Cape Town on her way to the Far East, news of her movements would quickly reach Japan and the deterrent effect would begin from that date.

Sir Tom Phillips said that whereas the Germans possessed a small, but very modern fleet, the Japanese Navy consisted, like our own, of a mixture of old and modern ships; her oldest battleships were inferior to the R Class ships which it was proposed to send out to the Far East. These four R Class ships together with the *Rodney*, *Renown* and *Nelson* (when repaired) should, in their own waters, and operating under cover of shore-based aircraft, be a match for any forces the Japanese were likely to bring against them.

Mr Attlee said that apart from the attitude of the Dominion Governments concerned, it seemed sounder to send a modern ship to a new theatre of operations. The arguments put forward by the Vice-Chief of the Naval Staff assumed that we would be prepared to remain on the defensive in Malayan waters even if Japan attacked Russia. We should find such action hard to justify in the circumstances.

The Prime Minister invited the First Lord of the Admiralty to consider the proposal to send as quickly as possible one modern Capital Ship, together with an aircraft carrier, to join up with *Repulse* at Singapore. He would not come to a decision on this point without consulting the First Sea Lord, but in view of the strong feeling of the Committee in favour of the proposal, he hoped that the Admiralty would not oppose this suggestion. The Committee would take its final decision on Monday, 20th October, after which he would reply to the telegram on this question which he had just received from the Government of Australia. In the meantime, no action in the contrary sense should be taken, and such preparations as were possible should be made.

Mr Alexander agreed to communicate with the First Sea Lord at once on this proposal, and to make recommendations to the Defence Committee early the following week.

MILITARY SUPPORT TO RUSSIA

Lord Beaverbrook thought that we should do much more to help the Russians and should immediately send a large force either to Murmansk or to Archangel. If Murmansk were lost Archangel would immediately be threatened. It is essential to encourage the Russians at this time.

The Prime Minister said that he was averse to spreading our forces unduly with the probability of a heavy attack on this country looming in the Spring. Nevertheless, he thought that further examination should be given to the possibility of sending a small force to Murmansk.

It must, however, be a guiding principle that no resources which were required to make 'Whipcord'[1] a success should be diverted elsewhere.

[1] The planned invasion of Sicily. It did not finally take place until July 1943.

Rear-Admiral T.S.V. Phillips to Admiral Sir Dudley Pound
(*Captain Stephen Roskill papers*)

17 October 1941

My dear First Sea Lord,

In the three days since you left, two developments have been taking place, on neither of which I felt it was necessary yet to suggest your return, but I feel they are of such importance that I am sending Griffiths[1] from Plans Division up with this letter so as to put you in the picture.

The two developments are:

(1) Proposals and plans for following up a success in Operation 'Crusader'.

(2) The proposals for sending heavy ships to the Far East have been given new life by the change in the Japanese Cabinet yesterday.

(2) The change in the Japanese Cabinet naturally started everybody thinking about the Far East again, and the Foreign Secretary put in a paper to the Defence Committee raising the question of sending capital ships to the Far East. Simultaneously a telegram was received from the Australian Government (who have apparently been told by the Prime Minister of the intention to send a capital ship force to the Far East) asking for information about this force, and in particular on the inclusion in it of certain modern units. This telegram was read out at the DO meeting but I have not seen a copy of it.

The Prime Minister at once raised the old question of sending out the *Prince of Wales* and gave the Defence Committee all the arguments that he has used before. He was also most scathing in his comments on the Admiralty attitude to this matter.

The First Lord and I defended the position as well as we could, but the Prime Minister led the other members of the Defence Committee to the conclusion that it was desirable to send the *Prince of Wales* to join the *Repulse* and go to Singapore as soon as possible. The Admiralty expressed their dissent.

The Prime Minister, however, of course said that he could take no final decision on this matter without consulting you. He asked the First Lord to put the matter before you (which I intended to do in any case) and he said that he wants to take a decision on Monday.

[1] Commander R.W. Griffiths.

Winston S. Churchill to General Auchinleck
(*Churchill papers, 20/44*)

17 October 1941
Personal and Secret

1. Australians have sent an obdurate reply and relief must proceed.

2. I am disquieted by your phrase that retardation 'of date of "Crusader" now depends on other factors'. I have never so far heard of any of these other factors or any whisper of retardation. On the contrary, I was encouraged by Shearer to hope for an earlier date. I hope you will be able to reassure me at once.

3. I am looking forward to arrival of your Staff Officer.

4. I am sending a letter by Freeman, who should be with you on Sunday morning.

Winston S. Churchill to Major-General Sir Alfred Knox
(*Churchill papers, 20/22*)

18 October 1941
Private

My dear General,

There is no question of our sending rifles to Russia. On the contrary, we suggested to them that they might let us have a quarter of a million from their very large stocks. They were mildly surprised.

Please let me have a statement of the equipment of your Home Guard in Bucks. I do not know what you mean by saying 'they could at present only last four minutes in action.' A good soldier husbands his ammunition and makes every shot tell, and the time he can stay in action is not measured by how long it will take to fire it all off. Ammunition for the .300 is now coming through better from the United States.

Many thanks for writing,

Yours very sincerely,
Winston S. Churchill

Winston S. Churchill to General Auchinleck
(*Churchill papers, 20/44*)

18 October 1941
Most Secret
Most Immediate
Personal and Secret

Your CS 139 confirms my apprehensions. Date was mentioned by you to Defence Committee, and though we felt the delay most dangerous we accepted it, and have worked towards it in our general plans. It is impossible to explain to Parliament and the nation how it is our Middle East Armies have had to stand for 4½ months without engaging the enemy while all the time Russia is being battered to pieces. I have hitherto managed to prevent public discussion, but at any time it may break out. Moreover, the few precious weeks that remain to us for the exploitation of any success are passing. No warning has been given to me of your further delay, and no reasons. Your DDO[1] may easily take a week on homeward journey. I must be able to inform War Cabinet on Monday number of days further delay you now demand.

Moreover, the Lord Privy Seal leaves Monday for United States, carrying with him a personal letter to the President, which I did not wish to entrust to the Cables or Cipher Department. In this letter, which would be handed to the President for his eye alone, and to be burnt or returned thereafter, I was proposing to state that in the moonlight of early November you intended to attack. It is necessary for me to take the President into our confidence, and thus stimulate his friendly action. In view of the plans we are preparing for 'Whipcord'[2] I am in this letter asking him to send three or four United States Divisions to relieve our troops in Northern Ireland, as a greater safeguard against invasion in the spring. I fixed the date of the Lord Privy Seal's mission in relation to the date you had given us. Of course, if it is only a matter of two or three days, the fact could be endured. It is not, however, possible for me to concert the general movement of the war if important changes are made in plans agreed upon, without warning or reason. Pray therefore telegraph in time. Am repeating this to Minister of State.

[1] John Francis Martin Whiteley, 1896–1970. 2nd Lieutenant, Royal Engineers, 1915. On active service, 1915–18 (despatches, Military Cross). General Staff Officer, War Office, 1935–38. On active service, 1939–45 (despatches five times). Major-General, 1943. Commandant, National Defence College and Canadian Army Staff College, Canada, 1947–49. Deputy Chief of the Imperial General Staff, London, 1949–53. Knighted, 1950. Chairman, British Joint Services Mission, Washington, and British Representative on the Standing Group of the Military Committee of the North Atlantic Treaty Organization (NATO), 1953–56.

[2] The proposed invasion of Sicily.

Winston S. Churchill to Oliver Lyttelton
(Churchill papers, 20/44)

18 October 1941
In Private Cypher
Personal and Secret

See my 108 Susan (MO 5) of 18.10[1] to Auchinleck. We were staggered to learn of further delays proposed for 'Crusader', and I rely upon you to do your utmost to abridge them. I had hoped to hear from you before now. Have you not been kept fully informed?

Winston S. Churchill to David Margesson
(Churchill papers, 20/36)[2]

18 October 1941
Action this Day

1. During my visit to the Richmond AA Mixed Battery I learned, with much surprise, that the present policy of the ATS is that ATS personnel in mixed batteries should not consider themselves part of the battery, and that no 'battery *esprit de corps*' was to be allowed. This is very wounding to the ATS personnel, who have been deprived of badges, lanyards, &c., of which they were proud. Considering that they share the risks and the work of the battery in fact, there can be no justification for denying them incorporation in form.

2. In present circumstances it is possible also that the whole efficiency of a battery could be upset by an order from the War Office, ATS Headquarters moving one of a predictor team to another unit. The AA Command has no say in such matters. Obviously, this cannot continue when we are relying upon these mixed batteries as an integral part of our defence.

3. I found a universal desire among all ranks that the women who serve their country by manning guns should be called 'Gunners', and 'Members of the Royal Regiment of Artillery'. There would be no objection to the letters 'ATS' being retained.

[1] The previous document.
[2] This was Churchill's thousandth numbered Minute (in the series of Prime Minister's Personal Minutes).

Winston S. Churchill to Harry Hopkins
(*Churchill papers, 20/49*)

19 October 1941
Personal and Secret

I was rather worried about Averell, whose health really wants looking after.[1] Presume you are taking care of this. Kindest regards.

Winston S. Churchill to Sir Francis Wylie[2]
(*Churchill papers, 20/44*)

19 October 1941

AFGHANISTAN

I have been much pleased with the way in which you have handled the question of turning out the Germans and Italians, but I think you ought to know that from 11th September, when this task was entrusted to you, to 17th October, you have sent 6,639 cipher groups. The labour and cost of this profuse telegraphing and the choking effect of such lengthy messages upon the higher administration ought never to be forgotten. Clarity and cogency can, I am sure, be reconciled with a greater brevity.

Winston S. Churchill to General Ismay, for the Chiefs of Staff Committee
(*Churchill papers, 20/36*)

20 October 1941
Action this Day

How was it that we did not think it worth while to remain in occupation of Spitzbergen when the Germans evidently do? How is it that the *Harrier* has insufficient fuel to complete her task? Why was it necessary to burn all the valuable coal stores, and quit the Island?

[1] After a visit to Northern Ireland, where he had been billeted in a country house of a retired army officer, Harriman had become 'gravely ill' – in the words of his biographer, Elie Abel – and 'was forced to spend three weeks in bed, feverish and at times delirious, with what the doctors believed to be a form of paratyphoid, probably traceable to drinking water from the Irishman's old well'.

[2] Francis Verner Wylie, 1891–1970. Entered the Indian Civil Service, 1915. Served in the Indian Army, 1915–19. Indian Political Service, 1920–38. Knighted 1938. Governor of the Central Provinces and Berar, 1938–40. Minister to Afghanistan, 1941–43. Governor of the United Provinces, 1945–47

The whole Operation has a half-hearted air.[1] What is it proposed to do about Spitzbergen now?[2]

Winston S. Churchill to Lord Cherwell
(*Churchill papers, 20/36*)

20 October 1941

I have not seen for some time the shipping curve of gains and losses. Please send it along.

Winston S. Churchill to President Franklin D. Roosevelt
(*Churchill papers, 20/20*)

20 October 1941
For yourself alone

PART I

My dear Mr President,

1. Sometime this Fall, General Auchinleck will attack the German and Italian armies in Cyrenaica with his utmost available power. We believe his forces will be stronger than the enemy's in troops, in artillery, in aircraft, and particularly in tanks. His object will be to destroy the enemy's armed and, above all, armoured forces, and to capture Benghazi as quickly as possible.

2. Should this operation prosper, the plans which have been prepared for a

[1] The Spitzbergen operation had been decided by the Defence Committee on 7 August 1941. In Churchill's absence (he was then on his way across the Atlantic to meet Roosevelt), Attlee presided at the meeting, during which the Committee agreed to Stalin's request for a British naval landing at Spitzbergen, to evacuate some two thousand Russians working at the mining settlements and wireless and meteorological stations. At the Defence Committee it was pointed out 'that the Spitzbergen expedition had been originally decided on for purely political reasons'. The Russians had asked 'for much that we could not do, e.g. an expedition of 22–25 divisions on the continent, the supply of 5,000 fighters, 5,000 bombers and 10,000 anti-aircraft guns, and so forth'. It had, therefore, been decided 'to accede to the request that Spitzbergen and Bear Island should be occupied'. The Russians hoped for a permanent British presence at Spitzbergen. But the Admiralty felt that such a permanent presence would serve 'no useful purpose'. (Defence Committee (Operations) No. 55 of 1941 7 August 1941: *Premier papers 3/410, folio 50*)

[2] On 22 October 1941 Colonel Hollis wrote to Churchill: 'The Spitzbergen operation of August was designed and carried out to ensure that the enemy derives no benefit from the Island, i.e. from the coal mines or from meteorological and wireless stations there. The Island is icebound in winter, the only access being by air during the limited hours of twilight and when flying conditions permit. The Navy do not require the use of the Island as a refuelling base. It was therefore considered unnecessary and, in fact, undesirable, to establish a British garrison in the Island and to expect it to live throughout the winter in arctic conditions and in wooden buildings, which could easily be set alight by incendiary air attack. Our immediate object was achieved by destroying the coal stocks and the facilities for mining coal and by putting out of action the wireless and meteorological stations.' (*Churchill papers, 4/240*).

further rapid advance upon Tripoli may be carried out. Should success attend this further effort, important reactions may be expected which it is provident to study in advance.

3. General Weygand may be stirred into joining in the war, or the Germans may make demands upon him or Vichy for facilities in French North Africa which may force him into the war.

4. To profit by these contingencies, we are holding a force equivalent to one armoured and three field divisions ready with shipping from about the middle of November. This force could either enter Morocco by Casablanca upon French invitation, or otherwise help to exploit in the Mediterranean a victory in Libya.

5. In order to cover effectively these preparations, we have prepared large-scale plans for a descent upon the Norwegian coast; and also for a reinforcement of the Russians in Murmansk. There is substance as well as shadow in these plans.

6. It seems therefore probable that we shall have to send away from Great Britain four or even five divisions besides the 18th Division which will arrive at Halifax on November 7 on its journey round the Cape to Suez. We must expect that as soon as Hitler stabilizes the Russian front, he will begin to gather perhaps fifty or sixty divisions in the west for the invasion of the British Isles. We have had reports which may be exaggerated, of the building of perhaps 800 craft capable of carrying eight or ten tanks each across the North Sea, and of landing anywhere upon the beaches. Of course there will be Parachute and Airborne descents on a yet unmeasured scale. One may well suppose his programme to be: 1939 – Poland; 1940 – France; 1941 – Russia; 1942 – England; 1943 — ? At any rate, I feel that we must be prepared to meet a supreme onslaught from March onwards.

7. In moving four or five divisions, including one armoured division, out of the United Kingdom in these circumstances, we are evidently taking risks. Should events happily take the course assumed in the earlier paragraphs of this letter, and should we in fact reduce our forces at home to the extent mentioned, it would be a very great reassurance and a military advantage of the highest order if you were able to place a United States Army Corps and Armoured Division with all the Air Force possible, in the North of Ireland (of course at the invitation of that Government as well as of His Majesty's Government), thus enabling us to withdraw the three divisions we now have in Northern Ireland besides the troops in Iceland (now being relieved), for the defence of Great Britain.

8. We should feel very much freer to act with vigour in the manner I have outlined if we knew that such a step on your part was possible. Moreover, the arrival of American troops in Northern Ireland would exercise a powerful effect upon the whole of Eire, with favourable consequences that cannot be measured. It would also be a deterrent upon German invasion schemes. I hope this may find a favourable place in your thoughts. I do not suggest that

any decision should be taken until we see the result of the approaching battle.

Personal and Secret

PART II

9. A decisive success in the Mediterranean theatre would also, I hope, allay the doubts and anxieties of some of your Generals about the wisdom of our trying to hold the Middle East, and particularly the Nile Valley. The organization of the rearward services is steadily improving, but we welcome all helpful and constructive criticism. I had a long talk with General Brett,[1] who lunched with me, and have carefully noted various suggestions which he made. He is of course a strong partisan for keeping the Air Force subordinate to the Army, and not having any independent strategic Air service. This may be sound so far as the United States is concerned, but over here we have needed to emphasize the dominance of the Air Arm in its independent aspect, and from this it follows that the parts of our Air Force associated with the Navy or the Army should only be subsidiary to the parent Service.

10. In the Middle East, as I told you in a recent telegram, I have ruled that whenever a major military operation is in hand, the Air Force should be effectively subordinated to General Auchinleck.

In practice, no difficulty has arisen between him and the Air Commander except the difficulty, so often present in war, of finding out what is the right thing to do. At the last action on June 15–18, our Air was so anxious to serve the Army that it allowed itself to be parcelled out among the various columns, affording a number of local umbrellas and losing its decisive power to strike at the enemy's Air force. We hope to profit by our previous mistakes.

11. 'Unity of Command' could not be extended to cover the Navy. The Admiral, who invariably leads the Fleet to sea, must be at Alexandria or within an hour or two of it. In combined operations, of which we have a long and variegated experience, we have never followed the practice of subordinating the Navy to the Army, or vice versa. The very best relations prevail between the Naval and Military Commanders-in-Chief, and I do not know of any inconvenience that has arisen except of course that when the Admiral is fighting at sea, his Deputy cannot speak with the same authority. This coming battle will be entrusted on land to General Cunningham, and on sea to his brother, Admiral Cunningham, and, by an odd coincidence, the Commander of all the Air forces which are to be engaged is also named Coningham.[2] Let

[1] Of the United States Army Air Force (see page 1703, note 1).

[2] Arthur Coningham, 1895–1948. Born in New Zealand. On active service with the New Zealand forces, Samoa and New Zealand, 1914–16; with the Royal Flying Corps, Europe, 1916–19 (Military Cross, Distinguished Service Order, Distinguished Flying Cross); in Kurdistan, 1923 (despatches). Bomber Command, 1939–45; with the 8th Army in North Africa. Knighted, 1942. Formed the 1st Tactical Air Force, French North Africa, 1943; operations against Sicily and Italy, 1943. Air Officer Commanding-in-Chief, 2nd Tactical Air Force, 1944–45. Air Marshal, 1946. Air Officer Commanding-in-Chief, Flying Training Command, 1945–47.

us hope that the firm of Cunningham, Cunningham and Coningham[1] will flourish.

12. The idea of having One Man in complete command of everything is more attractive in theory than in practice. No sooner has all power been placed in one hand, than it has to be divided up again. I have described the arrangements of the Command on which we are working. In organization we draw the line between the Q services[1] of the Army (which are under the Military Commander-in-Chief), and those of the rear (which are under the Minister of State and his Officer, the Intendant-General) at the point where more than one Service is involved. This solution, which has been reached after other alternatives have been tried, leaves the field workshops and factories in the Delta under the Army, but assigns all common services, ports, landing facilities, rearward communications and long-term projects to the sphere of the Minister of State.

13. All my information goes to show that a victory in Cyrenaica of the British over the Germans will alter the whole shape of the war in the Mediterranean. Spain may be heartened to fight for her neutrality. A profound effect may be produced upon the already-demoralized Italy. Perhaps most important of all, Turkey may be consolidated in her resistance to Hitler. We do not require Turkey to enter the war aggressively at the present moment, but only to maintain a stolid, unyielding front to German threats and blandishments. As long as Turkey is not violated or seduced, this great oblong pad of poorly-developed territory is an impassable protection for the Eastern flank of our Nile Army. If Turkey were forced to enter the war, we should of course have to give her a great deal of support which might be better used elsewhere, either in French North Africa or in the Caucasus. We are making promises of support to Turkey (contingent on the military situation) which amount to between four and six divisions, and twenty or thirty Air Squadrons, and we are actively preparing, with them the necessary airfields in Anatolia. But what Turkey requires to keep her sound is a British victory over Germans, making all promises real and living.

14. Those dispositions as I have set them out, do not allow us in the next six months to make any serious contribution to the Russian defence of the Caucasus and Caspian Basin. The best help we can give the Russians is to relieve the five Russian Divisions now crowded into Northern Persia. If these are brought home and used in the battle, I have pledged the faith of Britain to Stalin that no rightful Russian interest shall suffer, and that we will take no advantages in Persia at their expense. I do not however see how, in the period mentioned, we can put more than a symbolic force into the Caucasus, and the

[1] Admiral Sir Andrew B. Cunningham, Lieutenant General Sir Alan G. Cunningham and Air Vice Marshal Sir Arthur Coningham.

[2] Quartermaster services.

Russians retain a similar representation in Persia. The Russians much disturb Persia by their presence, their theories and their behaviour, and the outbreak of disorders would mean that we should have to spread three or four British-Indian divisions to keep open the communications from the Persian Gulf to the Caspian. These communications, which are a vital part of our joint Aid to Russia policy, would thus be largely choked by the need of supplying the extra forces. I have been trying to get the Russians to see this point.

15. In my telegram of July 25, 1941, which I sent you before our Atlantic meeting, I spoke of the long-term project for 1943 of the simultaneous landing of say 15,000 tanks from hundreds of specially-fitted ocean-going ships on the beaches of three or four countries ripe for revolt. I suggested that the necessary alterations could easily be made at this stage to a proportion of your merchant ships now building on so vast a scale. I now send you the drawings prepared by the Admiralty, which illustrate the kind of treatment the vessels would require. You will see that it is estimated only to add about £50,000 to their cost, and I suppose a proportionate delay. It seems to me that not less than 200 ships should be thus fitted. There is sufficient time, as we cannot think of such a plan before 1943. But the essential counterpart of the Tank programme you have now embarked upon, is the power to transport them across the oceans and land them upon unfortified beaches along the immense coastline Hitler is committed to defend. I trust therefore Mr President, that this will commend itself to you.

16. I send you a short note which I have made upon the use of artillery, both Field and Flak. This has its bearing upon the approaching offensive in Part I, as well as upon the organization of our Home Army to meet invasion. All the authorities are agreed upon the principles set forth, and you are very welcome to show this paper, should you think it worth while, to your Officers.

17. I also send, for your own personal information, a note I have made on the structure, present and future of the British and Imperial Armies which we are endeavouring to organize in 1942. Of course the figure of about 100 divisions does not, as is fully explained, mean 100 mobile standard Field Divisions. Some are Garrison; some are Anti-Aircraft; and some are equivalents in Brigade groups. Broadly speaking, however, it represents a much more considerable deployment of military strength than we had planned at the outbreak of the war. This has been rendered possible by the fact that we have not been engaged to any serious extent since the losses of Dunkirk, and that munitions and reserves have accumulated instead of being expended on a great scale.

18. I have not referred to the Japanese-menace, which has seemed to grow so much sharper in the last few days, nor to the splendid help you are giving us in the Atlantic, because we discussed these great matters so fully at our meeting, and events are now telling their own tale in accordance with our anticipations. I still think, however, that the stronger the action of the United

States towards Japan, the greater the chance of preserving peace. Should however peace be broken and the United States become at war with Japan, you may be sure that a British declaration of war upon Japan will follow within the hour. We hope to be able before Christmas to provide a considerable Battle-squadron for the Indian and Pacific Oceans.

19. Lastly, Mr President, let me tell you how I envy the Lord Privy Seal in being able to fly over to the United States and have a good talk with you. My place is here, and therefore I have taken this opportunity of writing you so long a letter. Might I ask that all reference to the forthcoming operations[1] shall be kept absolutely secret, and for yourself alone? For this purpose I have separated the first part of the letter from the rest in the hopes that after reading it you will speedily consign it to the flames.

With kindest regards and every good wish,

Believe me, Mr President,
Your sincere friend,

Winston S. Churchill: speech
(Hansard)

21 October 1941 House of Commons

MEMBERS OF PARLIAMENT: VISITS TO IRELAND[2]

The Prime Minister (Mr Churchill): May I bring this discussion to a close? There was a suggestion today when the Rule was suspended that it would finish at about this time.

Mr Maxton: I regret that owing to the fact that the Scottish train was three hours late in arriving today, no one of the three of us was present and heard of that tacit arrangement. Otherwise, I should not have intervened. This is my first intimation.

The Prime Minister: I am not complaining, because I think that the whole character of the Debate has been upon a high level and has been of value and importance. I do not think there are such very great differences between us. Certainly I must say, as I have been referred to in the Debate, that there is no part of the powers conferred on His Majesty's Government in this time of trial that I view with greater repugnance than these powers of exceptional process against the liberty of the subject without the ordinary safeguards which are inherent in British life. Those high-sounding familiar phrases like *Habeas Corpus*, 'petitioner's right', 'charges made which are known to the law', and 'trial by jury' – all these are part of what we are fighting to preserve. We all

[1] Operation Crusader.

[2] Herbert Morrison had visited both Northern and Southern Ireland, in connection with the imminent internment in Brixton Jail of Cahir Healy, former MP for Fermanagh and Tyrone, and since 1925 an MP in the Northern Parliament.

care about them and understand them, and we are determined that they shall not be in-roaded upon by anything except the need of self-preservation which arises in time of war.

I recognize that this legislation and the Regulations which are based upon it were passed at a moment of great danger. It is possible that if in this lull – and it is only a lull – the matter were considered, the house would be in a different temper. I must say that I should feel very proud and happy if I could come down to the House, even while the war was going on, and say, 'Our position is now so good and solid, we now see the path before us so firm and clear, that even in time of war we can of our own free will give back these special powers.' Unhappily that is not the case at present. The time may come, but not at present. In the meanwhile, I cannot conceive how Parliament can better keep control of the exercise of these abnormal powers than by insisting upon their being exercised in the discretion of a Minister present in the House and accountable to the House. The Minister has been made accountable to the House. He has come down today and has explained in the greatest detail his use of the powers in a particular case. I should think it was a most objectionable thing to have this discretionary power conferred upon him, but it must be a discretionary power, and there must be a choosing between this and that. The House has given the power, and I am bound to say that the manner in which my right hon. Friend has explained the whole position has given the House the feeling, first, of the submissiveness of the Executive to the Parliamentary institutions, and, second, of the care with which these Powers are exercised.

For my part, I hope that the day may come as speedily as possible, even before the end of the war, when we may be able to relieve ourselves of these exceptional powers, or some of them. In the meanwhile, I feel that we are entitled to ask from the House a general measure of support for the Minister charged with executing them. There can be no question of going behind the powers of the House. The powers of the House are overriding and inalienable and everything that is done is done on the responsibility of the House, be it right or be it wrong. The House has power to wreck that action provided, of course, that it is confident that it is representing the country in the course which it is taking. Therefore, I hope the Debate may come to an end with a feeling that it has in no way derogated from the authority and freedom of Parliamentary institutions. I particularly resent the suggestion that we are adopting the methods of Fascist States. We are not. Why, Sir, we are the servants of the House. It may be true that the House will support their servants, but if they do not the powers in their hands are without effect, and while that fact is established it is absolutely improper, as well as unhelpful, to place us upon the level of totalitarian Governments which have no corrective legislature, no law but their own wills and the enforcement of their own particular doctrines in any way they choose.

Winston S. Churchill to General Auchinleck
(*Churchill papers, 20/44*)

21 October 1941
Personal

OPERATION CRUSADER

1. Your 1581 Susan. We have no choice but to accept your new proposal.[1] I will not therefore waste further words upon it.

2. Your paragraph 5. The War Office Movements Branch state that the three MT ships and two out of the three personnel ships arrived on 2nd October, and the remaining personnel ship two days later. We do not understand why, when every day was of measureless consequence, it took nearly a fortnight to unload these 150 vehicles from three separate ships.

3. Your paragraph 6 raises technical issues upon which War Office are telegraphing separately.

4. Your paragraph 7. It seems misleading to calculate in divisions when ours are wholly different from those of the enemy. Our latest information is that you have 658 medium Tanks including Infantry Tanks, Cruisers and American Cruisers, as against 168 comparable German and Italian Tanks of 15 tons and upwards, plus, of course, 234 German and Italian light Cruiser Tanks of the 9-tonner type.

5. Paragraphs 9 and 10. Your new date has been withheld from the Defence Committee. It was never intended that dates or details should be given even to President, and the phrase I am now using is, 'some time during the fall'.

Winston S. Churchill to Oliver Lyttelton
(*Churchill papers, 20/44*)

21 October 1941
Personal and Secret

All here were astonished we were not informed in good time of proposed further delay from which the very greatest dangers may arise. According to War Office and Ministry of Supply the axle story is without substance. The fact that a fortnight was taken to unload the 150 tanks of the 22nd Brigade is a scandal. Tedder's alarmist figures about our Air inferiority have now been corrected by Freeman, and it is agreed by Tedder that we have a large superiority at present even counting Italians as equals. When did you first learn of the proposed retardation? Are you being kept properly informed? Keep in touch with Freeman.[2]

[1] For the date of Operation Crusader.

[2] After further enquiries, Freeman increased his figures of German air strength substantially, while Tedder lowered his.

Winston S. Churchill to General Ismay
(*Churchill papers, 20/36*)

21 October 1941
Action this Day

Please check and point this up for me in time for tonight's meeting:

1. Clarification is needed about the telegrams from ME. General Auchinleck says that the 150 tanks which he had expected in September only *arrived* the 4th to 14th October. Actually they arrived the 2nd October, or only one day later than he had expected. Twelve days were taken in unloading the whole of these tanks. What happened to them then? We are told they had to be stripped down to be made desert-worthy and have their front axles strengthened. We now know this was not necessary so far as the axles were concerned and that the desert-worthy additions could all have been executed at the unit in a day or two. We do not know, however, what ME has done. Have they, in fact, already pulled these tanks to pieces and begun splicing the axles? If so, the three weeks' delay of which they speak may be unavoidable, even though the process was unnecessary. How was it no one went out with the tanks to tell the people out there about them?

2. By other telegrams and discussions it is known that an armoured brigade or division requires to be a month with its new vehicles to fire the guns and perform combined exercises. How far does this apply to the 22nd Armoured Brigade, who were fully trained with these very tanks when they went out? I suppose they would say they must have some additional desert practice, which seems reasonable.

3. But if these 150 tanks only cleared arrival on the 14th October and then there is a three weeks' period to make them desert worthy, this would carry us to the 7th November. What then happens to the necessary month, or perhaps somewhat shorter period, for them to be practised in the hands of troops and work in the desert with their commanders? They story we have been told, as now pieced together, does not hold water, even on the revised programme. We have got to find out (1) what has been or is being done mechanically and what is the existing state of each of the 150 tanks; (2) what changes will be made in their treatment as a result of the War Office telegram about the axles, and will any shortening up of the date be possible; (3) what about the desert training period of the 22nd Armoured Brigade?

Have this all cleaned up and the necessary telegram drafted for my consideration tonight.

War Cabinet, Defence Committee (Operations): minutes
(Cabinet papers, 69/2)

21 October 1941
10 p.m.

The Prime Minister referred to a telegram from the Minister of State to the Secretary of State for Foreign Affairs requesting guidance on how the defence of the Caucasus was likely to affect the general strategic scheme in the Middle East theatre during the next three or four months.

Our commitments in the Middle Eastern theatre were becoming widespread, and although we could now afford some dispersion of our forces with the object of misleading the enemy as to our real intentions, we must maintain the power to achieve timely concentrations in the vital theatre.

A general discussion ensued during which the Prime Minister reviewed possible enemy moves during the Winter and Spring and the various courses of action open to us. It was clear that we could not be strong in all the areas in which we should like to show strength, i.e. in the Mediterranean, North Africa and Libya, on the Turkish border and in the Caucasus, while retaining at Home the minimum strength required to meet possible German invasion in the Spring. Splitting our forces into penny packets would be most unsound.

The Prime Minister suggested that a plan should be worked out for establishing the 50th Division (ex Cyprus) and the 18th Division on the southern shore of the Caspian Sea by the end of February, 1942. This should enable the Russians to withdraw their five Divisions from Northern Persia, and we could, if necessary, add this British Corps to their forces on the Caucasian front. The problem of maintaining these forces in Northern Persia without undue interference with the passage of supplies to Russia over the line of communication from the Persian Gulf should be further examined.

Mr Eden said that he would much like to offer the support of these two Divisions to the Russians. Without some bribe of this nature he doubted whether we should be able to persuade the Russians to move their forces from Northern Persia to defend the Caucasus. Much would depend on whether our line of communication across Persia would be adequate to maintain this British force in addition to a steady supply of equipment and material to Russia.

The Committee:

(a) Invited the Naval Staff to examine and report on the full naval implications of Operation 'Whipcord'.[1]

(b) Invited the War Office to draw up a programme for moving the 50th and 18th Divisions to Northern Persia by the end of February, 1942.

[1] The planned invasion of Sicily.

RUSSIA: THE BATTLE FOR MOSCOW

The Prime Minister drew attention to the German armoured thrust which was developing in the direction of Vologda. This must mean either that the Germans had more than sufficient forces to invest Moscow, or that they had decided to abandon the direct assault on Moscow and rely on depriving Russia of her lifeline to Archangel by cutting the railway at Vologda.

It was hard to reconcile the first alternative with the anxiety of the German High Command concerning the serviceability of the armoured forces in the Moscow area. It appeared more likely that the Germans had decided to strike north and south and thus to isolate Russia by cutting communications with Archangel and by a drive to the Caucasus.

The Committee:

Invited the Chief of the Imperial General Staff to submit to the Prime Minister a report (with maps) on the Russian railway system and on the implications of the German thrust north-east of Moscow on Russian communications.

JIBUTI

The Prime Minister took a serious view of the situation of the 60,000 Italian civilians who, according to reports, would be very short of food by the New Year. Now that the monsoon was over, the use of the railway to Jibuti was not essential for the evacuation of these people, and a plan should be worked out, in consultation with General Platt for getting these 60,000 Italians out of the country as soon as possible. Owing to their shipping losses in the Mediterranean we could no longer expect the Italians to carry these people away for us. The possibility of evacuating them in our own ships to India or elsewhere should be considered.

HOME DEFENCE

The Prime Minister asked what progress had been made on the proposal to incorporate units of the Home Guard into mobile formations for Home Defence in emergency. He hoped that at least one Home Guard Brigade would be available in each Corps Area. Once the Russians had been reduced to the level of a second-rate military power, the Germans could quickly mount an invasion of this country. It was vitally important, in view of the forces and material which would be leaving this country in the next few months, that we should have some flexibility to expand our Home Defence forces.

Sir John Dill said that he had discussed the proposal to embody some of the Home Guard with the Director General, and it was hoped that it would be possible to mobilize a force of six Home Guard Brigades in emergency.

Sir Charles Portal emphasized the importance of aerodrome defence measures. He thought it very probable that the Germans would attempt to beat our Air Forces on the ground instead of engaging in another Battle for Britain. The best way to defeat an attempt at invasion would be to break up the invasion forces before they could be launched.

The Prime Minister agreed with these views and stressed the importance of continuing photographic reconnaissance of the invasion ports. The Germans would attempt to camouflage their concentrations of light craft and we might fail to penetrate their disguises unless photographs at all stages of their preparations were available.

Oliver Harvey: diary
(*'The War Diaries of Oliver Harvey, 1941-1945'*)

21 October 1941

Beaverbrook put in a paper to the Defence Committee which was considered last night in which he attacked the Government for failure to help Russia. The PM at once tackled him about it and asked what more he thought the Government could do – the Norway operation regarded as technically impossible had been superseded in favour of Sicily operation which would take effect only four days later than the former. B. blustered and growled and finally acquiesced. PM told AE he didn't think he meant to go out – but if he did, it would mean war to the knife against him.

Winston S. Churchill to John Curtin
(*Churchill papers, 20/44*)

22 October 1941
Most Secret

Your telegram 18th October. Petrol stocks. I fully appreciate your anxiety to strengthen Australian stocks in view of general position in Pacific.

The question of augmenting stocks of petrol in Australia has been constantly before my Government, and I note your recognition that an improvement has already been effected from July position. Fact that it was not possible to rebuild stocks more rapidly has, as you will realize, been due to shortage of tankers, and as soon as additional tankers became available from United States we took immediate steps to increase the number of ships in Eastern waters. It is, however, impossible to satisfy as fully and as speedily as we should like all competing claims that we have to meet. There is need for compromise and the help we have had from Australia in the matter is much appreciated.

When the Petroleum Department told High Commissioner of our expectation of raising stock of motor spirit to 300,000 tons by the end of the year, the figure was quoted after careful examination of position and in light of a considered programme. Additional demands for aviation spirit in Middle East have had to be met, and we are asking United States to let us keep some tankers in United Kingdom programme to allow diversion of British-controlled tankers to aid position in Indian and Pacific Oceans. Provided consumption does not exceed 52,000 tons a month we expect to secure stock of 300,000 tons at end of year and will endeavour to improve further thereafter.

Your paragraph 2. Would earnestly ask you to continue reduced motor spirit consumption till end year and then not to exceed 70,000 tons a month.

Your paragraph 5. We hope to retain such of above additional shipping in Indian and Pacific Oceans as is necessary to maintain stock position in future, but you will appreciate that ability to do so depends on Atlantic losses and extent of future United States tanker assistance.

Your paragraph 6. We shall build up aviation stock to figure stated as soon as possible, and make utmost endeavour to maintain it.

I have given instructions that in arranging allocation of available tankers over next few months every effort should be made to secure the progressive building-up of Australian stocks as rapidly as possible.

Winston S. Churchill to General Ismay

(*Churchill papers, 20/36*)

22 October 1941

Wait upon the Secretary of State with this minute and inform him that the Prime Minister and Minister of Defence cannot agree to the retirement of Sir Hugh Dowding. In a matter of this importance affecting an officer who commanded in the decisive 'Battle of Britain', the Prime Minister should have been consulted beforehand.

2. The enforced retirement from the Active List of Sir Hugh Dowding cannot be accepted. The *Gazette* must be cancelled in this respect, and the form of the announcement must be settled forthwith.

3. No important decisions about the appointment of Commanders-in-Chief or the retirement of officers of the highest consequence are to be taken by any of the Service Departments without consultation with the Prime Minister. This principle is fully recognized by the other Service Departments.

Winston S. Churchill: Written Answer
(*Hansard*)

21 October 1941 House of Commons

STANDARD OF LIVING

Mr MacLaren[1] asked the Prime Minister whether, from the data in possession of its various Departments, the Government will ascertain and publish what is necessary in food, housing accommodation, clothing and other essentials to maintain a person, whether pensioner or dependant, in a good state of health and comfort?

The Prime Minister: I am afraid that what constitutes a good state of health and comfort is so much a matter of opinion that no good purpose would be served by such a publication as the hon. Member proposes.

Winston S. Churchill to Anthony Eden
(*Churchill papers, 20/36*)

23 October 1941

The King of Greece came to see me yesterday. He was unhappy because apparently Lyttelton was lending himself to the idea of a new Constitution for Greece, and he pointed out the difficulties of a Government in exile doing that without power to make contact with the will of the people. I did not know Lyttelton had expressed such opinions. If so, he should be asked to desist. We alone here will deal with the Greek King and Government.

2. He complained that Monsieur Tsouderos,[2] when giving a short broadcast, was told to cut the minutes down from four to three, and the part selected to be cut out by the BBC was the compliment he intended paying to the King – 'Oh we don't want that in.' I am referring this point also to M of I.

3. There were six obnoxious persons in Egypt whom we had promised to remove five months ago, but nothing has happened about it. They were all Greeks.

4. Could instructions be given to prevent our minor officials in Egypt advocating Republicanism in Greece?

5. Could he have a Liaison Officer attached to him to facilitate contact with the British Government? He mentioned Mr Butler, formerly Equerry to the Duke of Kent.

[1] Andrew MacLaren, 1883–1975. Educated at Technical College and School of Art, Glasgow. Labour Member of Parliament for Burslem, 1922–23, 1924–31 and 1935–45.

[2] Emmanuel Tsouderos, 1882–1956. A banker from Crete, and a republican. Prime Minister, Foreign Minister and Finance Minister of Greece, 20 April 1941 to 13 April 1944, fleeing with the King to London after the Greek surrender on 23 April 1941. Also served as Minister of the Interior, May 1942–April 1944.

6. I think all these points should be sympathetically attended to. Our policy is to support the Greek King and Government, and not to allow them to be undermined or ill-used. I showed the King the letter I was writing to Monsieur Tsouderos at your request, and he was very pleased with it.

Winston S. Churchill to Anthony Eden
(Churchill papers, 20/36)

23 October 1941

Would it not be a good thing to give Sir Samuel Hoare a GCB before he returns to Madrid? Let me know your views.[1]

Winston S. Churchill to Lord Beaverbrook
(Churchill papers, 20/36)

24 October 1941
Action this Day

I should like a demonstration of the following to be given for me by the staff of MD[2] at the Princes Risborough range, at 11 a.m. on Saturday, 25th October, if possible, or alternatively at 11 a.m. on Monday, 27th October.

1. Two bombards will fire practice ammunition at a moving target approaching from 200 yards to 75 yards and receding to 150 yards.
2. Six practice rounds will be fired at a 6-foot target at 200 yards to observe grouping.
3. Three bombards will fire live rounds at 2-inch mild steel plates at 10°, 25° and 45° at a distance of 75 yards.
4. ST grenades Mark 1 and 2 will be demonstrated statically on 1-inch steel plate.
5. Any other item.

[1] Sir Samuel Hoare, who had already received the GBE (in 1927) for the first civil flight to India, was not created GCB in 1941, but was raised to the Peerage three years later, as Viscount Templewood.

[2] The Ministry of Defence establishment based just outside Whitchurch in Buckinghamshire, ten miles from Chequers. It was the scene of intensive rocket and bomb research throughout the war.

Winston S. Churchill to General Auchinleck

(*Churchill papers, 20/44*)

24 October 1941
Personal and Secret

I have seen Brigadier Whiteley and also received your letter 11th for which I thank you.

2. I was naturally shocked by Tedder's misleading figures, but I will take your advice about him and am reassuring him accordingly. I am telling Air Ministry Freeman may come home.

3. I am now telegraphing to Prime Minister of New Zealand. There is no need for you to send a Staff Officer thither.

4. War Office contend that axles 22nd Brigade did not need your special strengthening. Their full argument will be telegraphed separately. But now we must look only to the future.

5. While disappointed and alarmed by retardation I fully accept your new arrangements. Enemy is now ripe for sickle. I trust this condition will continue. Anyhow I do not see how they can get more armour in time, and that is what it all turns on. Should success attend your armour battle the rest of them will be in the bag.

6. You should not hesitate to press on to Tripoli hot foot upon success if granted. Any lengthy delay will almost certainly close this prospect. You will be justified in running extraordinary risks with your available fast forces while the going is good. Do not exclude help from Malta while on the way. We are studying this.

7. 'Whipcord' will be fitted in so as to act if all goes well. All is being prepared to sail 23rd, arriving 9th December. Up to about 2nd December we can turn them back, but we cannot keep them hanging about indefinitely. We are concerting all this with Whiteley.

8. Russians are resisting very strongly in front of Moscow and winter is near. This is the moment for us to strike hard. I have every confidence you will do so. Throw all in and count on me.

9. Please show this telegram to Minister of State.

Winston S. Churchill to Peter Fraser

(*Churchill papers, 20/44*)

24 October 1941
Most Secret

1. Your Pefra No. 2. In order to make quite sure of the relative Air figures I send Air Chief Marshal Freeman, VCAS., to Cairo to confer with Air

Marshal Tedder. Following are agreed figures of Home and Middle Eastern Staffs British Air Forces 660, Axis Forces 642. Probable serviceability of these forces Day 1, British Forces 528, Axis Forces 385. Of these latter little more than 100 are German. Moreover, all Axis forces are in shop window. We expect to have about 50 per cent. reserves behind the counter. Germany has also in Aegean and Crete 156 all types, excluding all short-range fighters. In Malta we have 64 bombers. Serviceability 72 and 48 respectively. No doubt is entertained by Commanders that, unless the situation alters markedly, we shall have good air superiority.

2. General Auchinleck assures me that New Zealand Division will have all proper protection. We must not, however, repeat mistake of action 15th to 18th June by frittering away superiority to put up small local umbrellas over each unit and detachment, thus losing chance of beating main enemy Air Force out of the sky.

3. Much has been risked in delay in order to gather sufficient armoured forces. It is unlikely that enemy can reinforce his armour before battle. We shall have 658 infantry tanks, cruiser tanks and American cruisers of 12 tons or upwards against 168 comparable Axis vehicles. Axis has in addition 234 9-ton light tanks which play a serious part. The armoured battle is what matters and we hope to force enemy to it. Destruction of his armoured force would bring ruin to the rest.

4. Infantry are limited only by transport, but are declared to be superior in numbers to enemy. General Auchinleck hopes to deploy 450 field guns and over 500 anti-tank guns with 325 Bofors and over 100 heavy mobile AA guns, the last named exclusive of those in Tobruk. Our columns will therefore be protected by their own flak to an extent never known by us before.

5. All the above is of fateful secrecy. War Cabinet here have declined to be informed of date of offensive. Unless situation alters in interval, we are justified in sober confidence. Kindest regards.

Winston S. Churchill to Air Marshal Tedder
(*Churchill papers, 20/44*)

24 October 1941
Personal and Secret

I am sure you now have a great opportunity. Nothing matters but the battle. I wish you all success.

Winston S. Churchill to Lord Moyne
(*Churchill papers, 20/22*)

24 October 1941

My dear Walter,

I was quite sure your remarks in the House of Lords upon strategic policy would involve you in widespread unfavourable comment, and I see by the Press that these fears are confirmed. Parliament is quite prepared to be guided by the advice which I gave, namely that Ministers should not embark upon strategical discussions. The difficulty of doing this with any effect has shown itself self-evident. Either such statements are jejeune and pointless, or they touch secret matters, Moreover, the statements of one Minister are contrasted maliciously with those of another. I know how difficult your work is in the House of Lords, and greatly admire your success in it, but please take the advice of an old friend.

Yours v sincerely
Winston S. Churchill

Winston S. Churchill to Air Chief Marshal Sir Charles Portal
(*Churchill papers, 20/36*)

24 October 1941

I am not content with the arrangements made for the two Squadrons in Murmansk. I thought they were to take their aircraft and move to the south of the front where they might have come into action with the Russian air force. Instead of this, the personnel only is being sent. When is it expected that these two Squadrons will again come into action, and where? The most serious mistake we have made about the Russians was in not sending eight Air Force Fighter Squadrons, which would have gained great fame, destroyed many German aircraft, and given immense encouragement all along the front. This is the only criticism among the many that have been made which I feel strikes home.

Winston S. Churchill to Colonel Davidson[1]
(*Churchill papers, 20/36*)

24 October 1941

My general impression is that the scale of the fighting has diminished on both sides, and that many fewer divisions are engaged each day than a month ago. What do you say to this?

[1] Director of Military Intelligence.

What date is the winter expected to set in in earnest in the Moscow region?
Is there any sign of digging in on any part of the front?
What, in your opinion, are the chances of Moscow being taken before the winter? I should be inclined to put it evens.

Winston S. Churchill to Sir Stafford Cripps[1]
(*Churchill papers, 20/44*)

25 October 1941

You were, of course, right to say that the idea of sending 'twenty-five to thirty divisions to fight on the Russian front' is a physical absurdity. It took eight months to build up ten divisions in France, only across the Channel, when shipping was plentiful and U-boats few. It is only with the greatest difficulty that we have managed to send the 50th Division to the Middle East in the last six months. We are now sending the 18th Division only by extraordinary measures. All our shipping is fully engaged, and any saving can only be made at the expense of our vital up-keep convoys to the Middle East or of ships engaged in Russian supplies. The margin by which we live and make munitions of war has only narrowly been maintained. Any troops sent to Murmansk now would be frozen in darkness for the winter.

2. Position on the southern flank is as follows: Russians have five divisions in Persia, which we are willing to relieve. Surely these divisions should defend their own country before we choke one of the only supply lines with the maintenance of our forces to the northward. To put two fully armed British divisions from here into the Caucasus or north of the Caspian would take at least three months. They would then only be a drop in the bucket.

Winston S. Churchill: statement
(*'The Times'*)

25 October 1941

His Majesty's Government associate themselves fully with the sentiments of horror and condemnation expressed by the President of the United States upon the Nazi butcheries in France.[2] These cold-blooded executions of innocent people will only recoil upon the savages who order and execute them.

[1] Sir Stafford Cripps was then in Kuibyshev, to which Stalin, the Soviet Government, and the diplomats in Russia, had withdrawn as German forces drew closer to Moscow.

[2] On 20 October 1941 the German Military Commander of the Nantes region, Lieutenant-Colonel Hotz, had been assassinated by members of the French resistance. Two days later fifty hostages were shot in Nantes as a reprisal. Today, one of the main streets in the city is named in their honour.

The butcheries in France are an example of what Hitler's Nazis are doing in many other countries under their yoke. The atrocities in Poland, in Yugoslavia, in Norway, in Holland, in Belgium, and above all behind the German fronts in Russia, surpass anything that has been known since the darkest and most bestial ages of mankind.

They are but a foretaste of what Hitler would inflict upon the British and American peoples if only he could get the power. Retribution for these crimes must henceforward take its place among the major purposes of the war.

Winston S. Churchill to Oliver Lyttelton
(*Churchill papers, 20/44*)

25 October 1941

1. Your 0/18188, paragraph 3. No one can assume that Germany will 'continue to be inextricably engaged in Russia during the winter'. It is far more probable that in a month or so the front in Russia, except in the south, will be stationary. Russia, through loss of munition capacity, will have been reduced to a second-rate military power, even if Moscow and Leningrad are held. At any time Hitler can leave, say, one-third of his Armies opposite Russia and still have plenty to threaten Great Britain, to put pressure upon Spain, and to send reinforcements to discipline Italy as well as pushing on in the East.

2. No one must suppose, therefore, that things will be better for us next year or in the Spring. On the contrary, for 'Whipcord'[1] it is probably a case of 'now or never'. In my view, by the end of December these prospects will he indefinitely closed.

3. Hitler's weakness is in the air. The British air force is already stronger than his, and with American aid increasing more rapidly. The Russian air force is, perhaps, two-thirds of the German, well organized in depth and quite good. Even when the Italian air force is counted for what it is worth, Hitler has not enough air for the simultaneous support of the operations open to his armies. However, the main part of the British air force has to be kept at home against invasion, and is largely out of action.

4. It is therefore of importance to us to seek situations which enable us to engage the enemy's air force under favourable conditions in various theatres at the same time. Such an opportunity is presented in a high degree by 'Whipcord'.

5. If we can before January secure the combination of airfields – Tripoli, Malta, Sicily and Sardinia – and can establish ourselves upon them, a heavy and possibly decisive attack can be made upon Italy, the weaker partner in the

[1] The planned invasion of Sicily.

Axis, by bombers from home based on the above system of airfields. The lack of aerodromes in Italy, north of Sicily, should make this possible. All air fighting in this new theatre is a direct subtraction from the enemy's normal air effort against Great Britain, against the Nile Valley, and in support of his South-Eastward advance.

6. Other advantages would be gained from British air predominance in the Central Mediterranean. Subject to what is said in paragraph 9, the sea route from the Mediterranean would be opened to strongly-escorted convoys with all the savings in shipping accruing therefrom, as well as the stronger support of Eastern operations.

7. The reaction upon France and French North Africa following such achievements, including the arrival of British forces on the Tunisian border, might bring Weygand into action, with all the benefits that would come from that.

8. The foundation of the above is, of course, a victorious 'Crusader'.[1] You ought to welcome the very powerful diversion of enemy strengths, particularly air strengths, which 'Whipcord'[2] would bring, provided it runs concurrently with 'Acrobat'.[3] Nothing gives us greater safety or baffles the enemy more than the sudden simultaneous upspringing of a great variety of targets. This applies particularly in the few weeks which remain while the enemy is disentangling his surplus air forces from the Russian theatre and re-equipping them for action elsewhere. As I am sure you realize slow advance in Libya by gradual stages after full preparation, making everything sure as you go, while nothing else happens anywhere, ensures the maximum of opposition and certainly gives the time for it to be brought to bear. Such a course would certainly give ample time for the strong German reinforcement of Sicily and for further domination of Italy by German troops. I hope you feel, as I do,[4] the fleeting character of the opportunity presented and how short is the breathing-space which now remains before Germany, having tidied up her front against Russia, can redispose her forces in other theatres. It is, as you truly say, 'a question of timing'.

9. What will be the enemy's reaction to our attempt to gain a zone of air predominance in the Central Mediterranean and thus to open the passage? To bring superior air power to bear will take him time in view of the disposition of the airfields which will remain to him in Italy. Therefore, he will need to put pressure on Spain to procure the closing of the Straits of Gibraltar. We are led to believe that the Spaniards will resent and resist any invasion of

[1] Churchill deleted, in the telegram as finally sent, the words he had dictated after 'a victorious "Crusader"': 'the long delay in which has imposed so grievous a strain upon our affairs'.

[2] The planned invasion of Sicily.

[3] The plan for the British 8th Army to advance into Tripolitania from Cyrenaica.

[4] Churchill had originally written: 'It astonishes me that you do not understand'.

their country by the Germans, who are hated by the morose and hungry Spanish people. A British victory in 'Crusader' will powerfully affect the mood of the Spanish Government. Hitler no doubt can force his way through Spain, just as he can dominate Italy. His deterrent is found in the political sphere. His aim is to establish a United States of Europe under the German hegemony and the New Order. This depends not only upon the conquest, but even more upon the collaboration, of the peoples. Nothing will more effectively destroy such hopes than the continuance of the murders and reprisals, slaughter of hostages, &c., which is now going on in so many countries. It will be a very serious step for him to take to add Spain and Italy to the already vast subjugated and rebellious areas over which his troops are spread.

10. For all the above reasons the close synchronization of 'Crusader' and 'Whipcord' and their intimate connection seem highly desirable. On the other hand, it must be realized that we shall not be able to[1] remain inactive except for the advance in Libya. I am confronted with Russian demands for a British force to take its place in the line on the Russian left flank at the earliest moment. It will not be possible in the rising temper of the British people against what they consider our inactivity[2] to resist such demands indefinitely. If, therefore, it were decided to abandon 'Whipcord' or alternative action in French North Africa at French invitation, as mentioned in Chiefs of Staff paper, it would be necessary to make preparations soon for moving a substantial force into Russia.

11. Your further comments should reach us by Monday night, when Defence Committee will meet.

Winston S. Churchill to John Curtin
(*Churchill papers, 65/23*)

25 October 1941
Most Secret

1. Your 682. Tobruk. Relief is being carried out in accordance with your decision, which I greatly regret.

2. Your 686. I am still inclined to think that Japan will not run into war with ABCD[3] Powers unless or until Russia is decisively broken. Perhaps even then they will wait for promised invasion of British Isles in Spring. Russian resistance is still strong, especially in front of Moscow, and winter is now near.

[1] Churchill had originally written: 'do nothing except a leisurely advance'.
[2] Churchill had originally written: 'our military incapacity for action'.
[3] America, Britain, China and the Dutch East Indies.

3. Admiralty dispositions had been to build up towards the end of the year *Rodney, Nelson* and four Rs[1] based mainly on Singapore. This, however, was spoiled by recent injury to *Nelson*, which will take three or four months to repair.

4. In the interval, in order further to deter Japan, we are sending forthwith our newest battleship, *Prince of Wales*, to join *Repulse* in Indian Ocean. This is done in spite of protests of Commander-in-Chief, Home Fleet,[2] and is a serious risk for us to run. *Prince of Wales* will be noticed at Cape Town quite soon.

In addition, the four R Battleships are being moved as they become ready to Eastern waters. Later on *Repulse* will be relieved by *Renown*, which has greater radius.

5. I agree with you that *Prince of Wales* will be the best possible deterrent, and every effort will be made to spare her permanently. I must, however, make it clear that movements of *Prince of Wales* must be reviewed when she is at Cape Town because of danger of *Tirpitz* breaking out and other operational possibilities before *Duke of York* is ready in December.[3]

Lord Beaverbrook to Winston S. Churchill
(*Churchill papers, 20/20*)[4]

25 October 1941

Prime Minister

It is necessary for me to retire from the Defence Committee. But I will say nothing unless you wish to make a statement.

My decision is of course, entirely due to continuing & violent attacks of asthma, particularly when I am confined for long periods.

B

Lord Beaverbrook to Winston S. Churchill
(*Churchill papers, 20/20*)

25 October 1941

This is not a complaint. It is not a grievance.

It is, I believe, an important communication.

Two things have been made manifest to the enemy:

(1) Our intention not to attack in the West.

(2) Our intention to attack in Libya.

[1] The Royal Sovereign Class battleships. The *Royal Sovereign*, with eight 15–inch guns, had been launched in 1918. The other battleships in this class were *Ramillies, Resolution, Revenge* and *Royal Oak*.

[2] Vice-Admiral Sir John Tovey.

[3] Six days later Churchill sent an almost identical telegram to Peter Fraser (New Zealand) and Field Marshal Smuts (South Africa).

[4] Churchill wrote on Beaverbrook's letter: 'Put in sealed envelope and keep in locked box'.

Now whatever may be the policy of the government, mayn't we have uncertainty, doubt, anxiety and concern in the hearts of the enemy?

Nothing would be involved save only secrecy, duplicity, deceit and camouflage.

Here let me say that nothing will ever separate me from your policy. Right or wrong, I follow you. But I am the victim of the Furies.

On the rockbound coast of New Brunswick, the waves beat incessantly. Every now and then comes a particularly dangerous wave that breaks viciously on the rocks. It is called the 'Rage'.

That's me.

B

Winston S. Churchill to Lord Beaverbrook

(*Churchill papers, 20/20*)

26 October 1941
Secret

My dear Max,

Your two notes of the 25th. I am surprised you have not realized the enormous extent and elaboration of the deceptive measures which are being taken to make the enemy believe we are going to do an Ajax.[1] General Ismay will be able to inform you of it in detail if you can spare the time.

I was not aware that our intention to attack in 'Crusader' had been made manifest to the enemy. There have been a good many articles in the papers suggesting this, but I cannot help that. Everything in my power is done to conceal 'Crusader' and to let 'Ajax' become manifest. That is I gather what you wish.

2. I am very sorry to read what you say about your asthma, and of course there is no need for you to attend the night meetings of the Defence Committee during these winter months. I could not however view your retirement from the Defence Committee at this juncture as anything but a mark of want of confidence in me. It would certainly become public, and lead to recriminations of a character fatal to any form of collaboration between us. We can talk about this tomorrow driving back from the demonstration to luncheon if you like. You know I am expecting you tomorrow, both to give me the bombard demonstration and to bring your party to the Machine Tools luncheon at No. 10.

WSC

[1] The amphibious landing at Trondheim, as a preliminary to the attempt to drive the Germans from Norway.

Winston S. Churchill to Herbert Morrison
(*Churchill papers, 20/36*)

26 October 1941
Secret

Pray look at the Stuart Campbell[1] article in today's *Sunday Pictorial* and let me know whether this does not constitute a further foundation for the suppression of this paper.[2]

General Sir Alan Brooke: diary
(*'Turn of the Tide'*)

26 October 1941

At 6 p.m. left for Chequers where I arrived about 7.45 p.m. I found that the only other guest was Lindemann. Dinner lasted on till about 11 p.m. by the time we had finished having snuff, etc. After dinner the PM sent for his dressing-gown to put over his 'siren suit'. The dressing-gown is a marvellous garment, rather like Joseph's many-coloured robe. We then proceeded upstairs where he had a small cinema. There we watched Russian and German films till about midnight. We then came down and spent from midnight to 1 a.m. with an explanation of 'Bumper'[3] Exercise which I had to give.

The PM then dismissed Lindemann and told him he wanted to speak to me. He proceeded to discuss impending operations in North Africa and Mediterranean and all the hopes he attached to them. From that he went on to discuss defence of this country against invasion and the strength of the

[1] Editor of the *Sunday Pictorial*, 1940–46.

[2] In an attack on the House of Commons on 26 October 1941, headed 'second-raters', Stuart Campbell wrote: 'Well, there it is. The news from Russia gets darker every hour; the exhortations to Britain for harder work grow more tempestuous every day – and the House of Commons goes on holiday again. Hardly concealing their blushes, the elected representatives of the people have folded their bags like the burglars and quietly stolen away. They have need to blush, for since August 7 these guardians of our liberties, charged with the task of quickening the nation's war effort, have been away from the job for one month and nineteen days. And now they can find so little to do for us that they have all been sent packing again. Traditional though this latest break may be, the plain man will be justified in thinking that this is yet another sign that the politicians are letting the people down'. The article went on to attack Churchill for not sacking the 'bulk' of Members of Parliament, 'this tuneless chorus'. In Stuart Campbell's words: 'That mystery has now turned into a canker. A canker that has eaten deep into this nation's capacity to organize for total war. For it has become as clear as day that we cannot pick a government of eighty-four – and that is precisely the number – out of Mr. Baldwin's second-rate stable and expect to be ahead of Hitler at the finishing post. Mr. Churchill has proved that himself. His only starters who look like lasting the course – his Beaverbrooks, his Bevins and his Wooltons – were not running around trying to buy up safe political seats six years ago.'

[3] One of a number of anti-invasion exercises which General Brooke, as Commander-in-Chief, Home Forces, had organized.

forces left for this purpose. I told him of the forces I had, of being very short of tanks if we went on sending them to Russia as proposed. He assured me that I should have some 4,000 tanks in this country by the spring. Finally at 2.15 a.m. he suggested we should proceed to the hall to have some sandwiches, and I hoped this might at last mean bed. But no! We went on till ten to three before he made a move for bed. He had the gramophone turned on, and in the many-coloured dressing-gown, with a sandwich in one hand and watercress in the other, he trotted round and round the hall, giving occasional little skips to the tune of the gramophone. On each lap near the fireplace he stopped to release some priceless quotation or thought. For instance he quoted a saying that a man's life is similar to a walk down a long passage with closed windows on either side. As you reach each window, an unknown hand opens it and the light it lets in only increases by contrast the darkness of the end of the passage.[1]

Winston S. Churchill to General Simovitch
(*Churchill papers, 20/22*)

26 October 1941
Secret

My dear Prime Minister of Yugoslavia,

In reply to your letter of October 20, I have to inform you that immediately after my interview of October 13 with the King of Yugoslavia, the whole question of assistance to your brave compatriots in Yugoslavia was closely examined by the appropriate authorities in this country. The conclusion was reached that, owing to the difficulties imposed upon us by geography, it was impossible for us to send any assistance to Yugoslavia from this country, and a telegram was therefore despatched to the authorities in the Middle East, instructing them to send as much help as possible as quickly as possible to Yugoslavia. As you know, our authorities in the Middle East are already in touch with the Serbian patriots.

I remitted your letter of October 21 to the Chiefs of Staff, and they have sent a further telegram to the authorities in the Middle East, impressing upon them the need for immediate help to Yugoslavia on as large a scale as transportation facilities will permit.

Yours sincerely,
Winston S. Churchill

[1] General Brooke later recalled, 'Considering the burden of responsibility he was bearing his lightheartedness was unbelievable.' On the following morning Brooke accompanied Churchill to a demonstration of the 'Bombard', mortar. 'It was a good example of the interest he took in all sorts of details,' Brooke later wrote 'I think it was on this occasion that the Bren-gun he carried in his car was pulled out so that he could practise with it. He would certainly have sold his life dearly if it had ever come to that.' ('*Turn of the Tide*')

Winston S. Churchill to Admiral of the Fleet Sir Roger Keyes
(*Churchill papers, 20/22*)

26 October 1941
Personal and Secret

My dear Roger,

I have your letter and memorandum of October 21, and I can assure you that all the considerations personal to yourself were present to my mind in the decisions which I had to take.[1] I am quite sure you have not been the victim of intrigue, although of course there is a widespread Service prejudice against bringing back retired Officers to Executive positions or retaining them there when they are verging upon, or have already reached, their seventieth year. Your very high rank and personal association with me also caused embarrassment and friction.

I am extremely sorry to tell you that the proposals which I had made to Mr Andrews[2] about Northern Ireland were rejected by him in the most decisive manner. They wish to keep the existing Officer as long as possible, and to make no change at present. I was so surprised at this that I asked Mr Andrews to come over and see me, but his attitude remained unchanged. I could not of course override his wishes, which have been a disappointment to me, but I have done my very best.

In regard to what you say on Page 2 of your letter about people begging you to 'continue to fight for the prosecution of offensive warfare', I can only say that I am sure you will most scrupulously respect the many secret matters with which you have been brought into contact, as the slightest leakage may cause disaster and loss of life in the various Operations which are impending.

Yours sincerely
Winston S. Churchill

Winston S. Churchill to John Curtin
(*Cabinet papers, 65/23*)

26 October 1941
Most Immediate

Our new fast minelayer, *Latona*, was sunk and the destroyer *Hero* damaged by air attack last night in going to fetch the last 1,200 Australians remaining in Tobruk. Providentially, your men were not on board. I do not yet know our casualties. Admiral Cunningham reports that it will not be possible to move

[1] To replace Keyes by Lord Louis Mountbatten.
[2] The Prime Minister of Northern Ireland.

these 1,200 men till the next dark period, in November. Everything in human power has been done to comply with your wishes.

Winston S. Churchill to John Curtin
(*Churchill papers, 20/44*)

27 October 1941
Immediate

Fortunately, HMS *Latona* was only carrying thirty-eight other ranks to Tobruk; remainder, to number of about a thousand men, were in three accompanying destroyers. About fifteen low bombing attacks between 19.00 and 22.30. Casualties: HMS *Latona* – Naval officers, four missing, one wounded; ratings, twenty-five missing, seventeen wounded. Army officers, six wounded; other ranks, seven missing, one wounded. HMS *Hero* – No casualties. We must be thankful these air attacks did not start in the earlier stages of the relief.[1]

Oliver Harvey: diary
(*'The War Diaries of Oliver Harvey, 1941-1945'*)

27 October 1941

PM is disquieting AE by giving very evident signs of anti-Bolshevik sentiment. After his first enthusiasm, he is now getting bitter as the Russians become a liability and he says we can't afford the luxury of helping them with men, only with material. No one stands up to him but AE – not even the Labour Ministers who are as prejudiced as the PM against the Soviets because of their hatred and fear of the Communists at home.

[1] In Volume Three of his war memoirs, Churchill wrote: 'It has given me pain to have to relate this incident. To suppress it indefinitely would be impossible. Besides, the Australian people have a right to know what happened and why. On the other hand, it must be remembered that, apart from the limitations of their rigid party system, the Australian Governments had little reason to feel confidence at this time in British direction of the war, and that the risks their troops had run when the Desert Flank was broken, and also in the Greek campaign, weighed heavily upon them. We can never forget the noble impulse which had led Australia to send her only three complete divisions, the flower of her manhood, to fight in the Middle East, or the valiant part they played in all its battles.'

War Cabinet: minutes
(*Cabinet papers, 65/19*)

27 October 1941 10 Downing Street
5 p.m.

The War Cabinet had before them a Memorandum by the Foreign Secretary circulating a draft telegram to Lord Halifax and the Dominion Governments on the proposal that we should declare war on Finland, Hungary and Roumania, and asking for their observations.

In the course of discussion, the Prime Minister said that, if we declared war on these three countries, this would lend colour to the suggestion that Hitler was at the head of a vast coalition of European States. This was another strong reason against the course proposed.

The Prime Minister drew the War Cabinet's attention[1] to telegram No. 22, dated 26th October, from Sir Stafford Cripps at Kuibyshev. In this telegram Sir Stafford said that relations between this country and Russia, as reflected at his post, were getting worse, and that if we could not open a second front the only way in which we could improve matters was to send troops to Russia, and he urged the despatch of a force not less than a corps, with an adequate proportion of RAF, to either the northern or southern extremities of the Russian battle front. The Prime Minister said that on the previous day, after consulting the Foreign Secretary, he had sent a telegram to Sir Stafford Cripps pointing out the reasons why we could not send troops to Russia.

At a later stage in the discussion the Prime Minister referred to the proposal that British troops should be sent to the Caucasus, or to the southern Russian front in the Ukraine. It was clear that it would take a very long time, probably two or three months, to get a British corps into action on this front. It would be extremely difficult to build up a supply line. There was the further point that it would certainly be difficult to get the Australian Government to agree to their troops fighting on this front, and it would be very difficult to make a force available without drawing on the Australians. There was the further consideration that if we sent British troops to the Caucasus, we should require the full use of the Persian railways, and it would be impossible to send in supplies to Russia by this route. This proposal was one which we should not entertain.

Reference was made to the two British fighter squadrons which had been sent to Murmansk.

The Prime Minister said that he wished that a larger force had been sent. In any case he greatly regretted the arrangement entered into, that the

[1] Because of the particular secrecy of this item, it was recorded only in the War Cabinet's Confidential Annex (*Cabinet papers, 65/23*).

machines with which these squadrons had been equipped should be handed over to the Russians and that our personnel should return to this country. It would be a great encouragement to the Russians if the arrangements made in this matter could now be modified and the two British fighter squadrons, complete with personnel and equipment, could be sent south from Murmansk or Archangel, to take part in the air fighting on the main Russian front. It would, of course, be necessary to ask the Russians to give an undertaking that proper arrangements would be made for these squadrons to receive their supplies. This course would also involve some reduction in the increase in the air forces to be sent to the Middle East.

The Prime Minister said that since Mr Curtin's Government had taken up office they had made three requests:

(1) They adhered to the request of the previous Government for the relief of the Australians at Tobruk.

(2) They had made a request for an increase in the petrol supplied to Australia.

(3) They had requested that a first-class battleship should be sent to the Pacific.

The Prime Minister read to the War Cabinet a telegram which he had sent to the Prime Minister of Australia, on the 25th October, dealing with the first and third of these matters.

The Prime Minister added that since that telegram had been despatched it had been reported that the minelayer *Latona* and the destroyer *Hero* had been damaged by air attack when going to fetch the last 1,200 Australians at Tobruk. As a result it would not now be possible to move these 1,200 men until the next dark period. He read to the War Cabinet a copy of the telegram to the Prime Minister of Australia reporting these facts.

Winston S. Churchill to Emanuel Tsouderos

(*Churchill papers, 20/22*)

27 October 1941

My dear Prime Minister,

Through Your Excellency I wish, on this fateful anniversary of Mussolini's crime,[1] to express once more the gratitude of the British people to the Hellenes for all they have done, and are doing, for the Allied cause. To the fame already earned by the Greek people when they thrilled the world by their Albanian victories and their undaunted resistance to Nazi might, new lustre is being

[1] In the early hours of 28 October 1940 Mussolini had delivered an ultimatum to Greece, followed three hours later by the invasion of Greece by Italian troops based in Albania. The Italian troops were repulsed. After the war, October 28 was declared a Greek national holiday.

added. The campaign of resistance to the German and Italian domination which is now being waged in Greece itself; and the warfare in which the Greek forces of the Middle East will be engaged when their preparations are complete will have proved the unquenchable spirit of Greece anew.

I wish, at the same time, to take this opportunity once more to reaffirm to Your Excellency that your Government, now declared to be a democratic Government under the beloved constitutional Monarchy, enjoys the full confidence and support of His Majesty's Government and the British people.

The glory of Greece shines not only in her antiquity, but even brighter in these tragic years. It is vindicated by the constancy of her people in cruel bondage. Their martyrdom will be avenged by the Panhellenic Army of Liberation. The unity of all her sons and daughters behind their King and Government in the cause of their Fatherland will bring its sure reward.

Yours very sincerely,
Winston S. Churchill

War Cabinet, Defence Committee (Operations): minutes
(*Cabinet papers, 69/2*)

27 October 1941
10 p.m.

ASSISTANCE TO RUSSIA

The Prime Minister said that there was no doubt a strong case for sending some troops to fight with the Russians, but there was also a great deal to be said against it. The 50th Division might be moved to the Causasus front in a month and it might be joined in three months by the 18th Division. These formations would form a small body on a large front; they would be armed with different arms to the Russians and would be certain in the end to be overwhelmed. Great labour would be involved in getting them to the front, in the course of which the supply route to Russia would be choked. A more promising project might be to send some air squadrons. We had sent two to Murmansk and he had felt that we should have sent more. He had intended that the two squadrons should be moved by the Russians to a more Southerly part of the front, but they had now handed over their aircraft to the Russians and the question was what to do with the personnel. The best thing might be to bring them away by sea, but this might greatly discourage the Russians. It would probably be better that they should take over forty British aircraft and be joined by four or five further squadrons. We could say to the Russians that this was the only force which could reach them within the next two months and we could offer it on the understanding that it would be moved to a part of the line where operations would be possible.

The question then arose how best to explain the position to the Russians.

One way to do this might be to tell the President of the United States of these telegrams from Sir Stafford Cripps and of our views upon them. He would fully appreciate the difficulties of our position and he might telegraph to Stalin and show him how impossible it was for us to contemplate moving any large number of divisions to the Russian front.

Sir John Dill said that two of the routes through the Caucasus would be almost impassible in winter and very easy to defend, but one route – that running near the Caspian to Baku – was through open country. We might be able to send two divisions from the Middle East. If, when they arrived, the Russians were still resisting at Rostov, these divisions could join them on that front. Failing that, they would at any rate get to the Caucasus. It was impossible to say what rate of movement could be achieved without consulting the Commander-in-Chief, Middle East, as it depended upon the transport available. If it were decided to employ air forces on the Russian front, the best thing to do would be to send them in to support our own troops.

Sir Charles Portal agreed and pointed out that, unless the Royal Air Force squadrons operated at one end or the other of the Russian front, they would find themselves in great difficulties over maintenance.

The Prime Minister thought that the Russians would insist on these divisions going to Astrakhan. He was not at all inclined to favour the idea of sending them. The forces would not be of a size which would in any way affect the march of events on the Eastern Front and the Russians would not think much of so small a reinforcement. He hoped that a more profitable line of action would be open to us in the Mediterranean.

Sir Alexander Cadogan: diary

(*The Diaries of Sir Alexander Cadogan, OM, 1938-1945*)

27 October 1941

Defence Committee at 10. Old Pound heavily and convincingly killed 'Whipcord'[1] and we buried it and put up a little headstone. Poor Winston very depressed.

[1] The proposed invasion of Sicily.

Winston S. Churchill to General Ismay, for the Chiefs of Staff Committee
(*Churchill papers, 20/44*)

28 October 1941
Most Secret

1. In view of the Mid-East latest telegram No. ME 0/19301 and of your own decisive abandonment of the project 'Whipcord', which you advocated and which I espoused, I now consider that plan at an end.

2. A force equivalent to two divisions and one armoured division should, however, stand ready to exploit 'Crusader' and 'Acrobat' should they be successful. There is no reason, unless hope be a reason, to expect that General Weygand will invite us into Bizerta or Casablanca as the result of our impending operations. Should he do so, we must be ready to profit by so great a turn of fortune. The same Commanders should study this case forthwith, and it should be concerted with Mid-East HQ and especially with Admiral Cunningham.

3. The situation might arise either through the effect of a British victory, if gained, on French morale or, which is not to be excluded, by a German demand on Pétain for the use of this theatre in consequence of the loss of Tripoli, actual or probable.

4. The name of this operation will be 'Gymnast'.

5. It is important to know at once what orders should be issued to convert 'Whipcord' into 'Gymnast', so as to make the least possible inroads upon shipping, and secondly, what the demands upon shipping would be and their full effect.

6. I have received advices from America that our friends there are much attracted by the idea of American intervention in Morocco, and Colonel Knox talked to Lord Halifax about 150,000 United States troops being landed there. We must be ready, if possible, with a simultaneous offer, or anyhow a British offer, to General Weygand at any moment which seems timely after a success in 'Crusader'. This might turn the scale in our favour. The offer should therefore be couched in the most effective terms. I will not myself address the President on the subject until after results of 'Crusader' are apparent.

7. I have had a letter from him by Lord Louis Mountbatten, in which he expresses lively interest in Tangier. This should also be examined, but it evidently raises very great complications with the Spaniards and the French, and it would be wrong to sacrifice the chance of French cooperation for the sake of it.

8. As soon as the decisions in respect of tidying up the remains of 'Whipcord' and preparing for 'Gymnast' have been taken, the minor operations on the 'Ajax' coast[1] should begin. Let me know what is proposed.

[1] The coast of Norway.

Winston S. Churchill to Sir Stafford Cripps
(*Churchill papers, 20/44*)

28 October 1941
Immediate

I fully sympathize with you in your difficult position, and also with Russia in her agony. They certainly have no right to reproach us. They brought their own fate upon themselves when, by their pact with Ribbentrop, they let Hitler loose on Poland and so started the war. They cut themselves off from an effective second front when they let the French Army be destroyed. If prior to June 22 they had consulted with us beforehand, many arrangements could have been made to bring earlier the great help we are now sending them in munitions. We did not however know till Hitler attacked them whether they would fight, or what side they would be on. We were left alone for a whole year while every Communist in England, under orders from Moscow, did his best to hamper our war effort. If we had been invaded and destroyed in July or August 1940, or starved out this year in the Battle of the Atlantic, they would[1] have remained utterly indifferent. If they had moved when the Balkans were attacked much might have been done, but they left it all to Hitler to choose his moment and his foes. That a Government with this record should accuse us of trying to make conquests in Africa or gain advantages in Persia at their expense or being willing to 'fight to the last Russian soldier' leaves me quite cold. If they harbour suspicions of us it is only because of the guilt and self-reproach in their own hearts.

2. We have acted with absolute honesty. We have done our very best to help them at the cost of deranging all our plans for rearmament and exposing ourselves to heavy risks when the spring invasion season comes. We will do anything more in our power that is sensible, but it would be silly to send two or three British or British-Indian divisions into the heart of Russia to be surrounded and cut to pieces as a symbolic sacrifice. Russia has never been short of manpower, and has now millions of trained soldiers for whom modern equipment is required. That modern equipment we are sending, and shall send to the utmost limit of the ports and communications.

3. Meanwhile we shall presently be fighting ourselves as the result of long-prepared plans, which it would be madness to upset. We have offered to relieve the five Russian divisions in Northern Persia, which can be done with Indian troops fitted to maintain internal order but not equipped to face Germans. I am sorry that Molotov rejects the idea of our sending modest forces to the Caucasus. We are doing all we can to keep Turkey a friendly neutral and prevent her being tempted by German promises of territorial gain

[1] Churchill originally wrote at this point: 'only have laughed'. Churchill deleted the phrase at Anthony Eden's suggestion.

at Russia's expense. Naturally we do not expect gratitude from men undergoing such frightful bludgeonings and fighting so bravely, but neither need we be disturbed by their reproaches. There is of course no need for you to rub all these salt truths into the Russian wounds, but,[1] I count upon you to do your utmost to convince Russians of the loyalty, integrity, and courage of the British nation.

4. I do not think it would be any use for you and Macfarlane to fly home now. I could only repeat what I have said here, and I hope I shall never be called upon to argue the case in public. I am sure your duty is to remain with these people in their ordeal, from which it is by no means certain that they will not emerge victorious. Any day now Hitler may call a halt in the East and turn his forces against us.

Winston S. Churchill to Air Chief Marshal Sir Charles Portal
(*Churchill papers, 20/36*)

28 October 1941

We are making great efforts to increase the production of bombers, using a high proportion of our resources to do so. It is therefore vital that we should press on with all measures to increase the number of them that bomb their targets. I am glad to see that you are making good progress with the radio marker bombs, but I have not been informed how you are getting on with the other steps described in your Minute of 11th September. Have results, as shown by the night photographs or other information, in the last three months been any better than in June and July? Have we any means, such as photographs taken from similar heights, of comparing the damage we have done to the enemy and the damage they have done to us?

Winston S. Churchill to A. V. Alexander
(*Churchill papers, 20/36*)

28 October 1941

1. This is a bad story. The design of the offending fuze was made by the Admiralty and approved by the DNO.[2] They were not referred to Dr Crow.

[1] Churchill originally wrote 'you must have a robust constitution'. He deleted the phrase at Eden's suggestion, replacing it with: 'I rely upon you to do your utmost to convince the Russians'.

[2] William Rudolph Slayer, 1896-1971. On active service in the Royal Navy, 1914-18 (despatches, Distinguished Service Cross). Director of Naval Ordnance, Admiralty, 1938-41. Chief of Staff, Home Fleet, 1943; Captain, HMS *Excellent*, 1945 (despatches twice, Distinguished Service Order). British naval representative, Military Staff Committee, United Nations, 1946. Admiral, Commanding the Reserves, 1950-52. Knighted, 1952. Commander-in-Chief, East Indies Station, 1952-54.

I am now informed that the first 3,000 fuzes for issue are expected early in December and about 16,000 will be ready by the end of the year.

2. When is *Conqueror* going to get to work again? Surely she has other weapons besides UP and other projectiles besides those operated by the defective Admiralty fuze.

3. You say 'an opportunity has been taken for *Conqueror* to undergo boiler cleaning and refit'. Considering she has done absolutely nothing all these months, it is very disappointing. I asked for a weekly report of her activities. Let me know exactly what weapons she carries and when she will begin again 'trailing her coat'. So much depends upon finding out what these weapons can do and how to keep off air attack that a greater effort should be put behind these vital experiments.

Winston S. Churchill to General Ismay and Sir Edward Bridges
(*Churchill papers, 20/36*)

28 October 1941

There must be an enquiry into the responsibility leading to the delay about the front axles of the Cruiser tanks. I propose that Mr Justice Singleton should undertake this, and report to me. Before fetching any witnesses from the Middle East, he must see whether he can arrive at a conclusion from the documentary evidence from that quarter and the examination of War Office and M of S[1] witnesses here. You should ask Lord Beaverbrook and the Secretary of State kindly to concur in this procedure. Letters should be drafted to the Judge, and also to the Lord Chancellor.[2]

We must know where we are, and make sure no similar breakdown occurs in future.

Winston S. Churchill: speech
(*Harrow School Archive*)

29 October 1941 Harrow School

Head Master,[3] Ladies and Gentlemen, Harrow boys:[4]

Almost a year has passed since I came down here at your Head Master's kind invitation in order to cheer myself and cheer the hearts of a few of my friends by singing some of our own Songs. The ten-months that have passed

[1] Ministry of Supply.

[2] Viscount Simon.

[3] Arthur Paul Boissier, headmaster from 1940 to 1942.

[4] Among the boys who heard Churchill speak were a future Assistant Secretary of the Treasury (Michael Stuart); a 1948 Olympic Pentathlon competitor (John Lumsden); a Grenadier Guardsman, mentioned in despatches in Cyprus in 1958 (Peter Ratcliffe); a Conservative Whip, 1967–70 (Anthony

have seen very terrible, catastrophic events in the world – ups and downs – misfortunes – but can anyone sitting here this afternoon, this October afternoon, not feel deeply thankful for what has happened in the time that has passed and for the very great improvement in the position of our country and of our home. Why, when I was here last time we were quite alone, desperately alone, and we had been so for five or six months. We were poorly armed. We are not so poorly armed today; but then we were very poorly armed. We had the unmeasured menace of the enemy and their air attack still beating upon us, and you yourselves had had experience of this attack; and I expect you are beginning to feel impatient that there has been this long lull with nothing particular turning up!

But we must learn to be equally good at what is short and sharp and what is long and tough. It is generally said that the British are often better at the last. They do not expect to move from crisis to crisis; they do not always expect that each day will bring up some noble chance of war; but when they very slowly make up their minds that the thing has to be done and the job put through and finished, then, even if it takes months – if it takes years – they do it – but they do it.

Another lesson I think we may take, just throwing our minds back to our meeting here ten months ago and now, is that appearances are often very deceptive, and as Kipling well says:

'. . . meet with triumph and disaster
And treat those two imposters just the same'.

You cannot tell from appearances how things will go. Sometimes imagination makes things out far worse than they are; yet without imagination not much can be done. Those people who are imaginative see many more dangers than perhaps exist, certainly many more than will happen; but then they must also pray to be given that extra courage to carry this far-reaching imagination. But for everyone, surely, what we have gone through in this period – I am addressing myself to the School – surely from this period of ten months this is the lesson: never give in, never give in, never, never, never, never – in nothing, great or small, large or petty – never give in except to convictions of honour and good sense. Never yield to force: never yield to the apparently overwhelming might of the enemy. We stood all alone a year ago,

Royle, later Baron Fanshawe); a Vice-President of the Society of British Aerospace Companies, 1966 (Michael Clark); a marine engineer with Swan Hunter (Ian Pease); a merchant in Buenos Aires (Norman Powell); the leader and Surveyor of the Trans-Antarctic Expedition, 1955–58 (David Stratton); the Chief Constructor, Submarines, Ministry of Defence, Navy, 1968 (David Henry); and a Conservative Member of Parliament for Woking, 1964 (Cranley Onslow, later Baron Onslow). Michael Stuart later recalled: 'He left me in no doubt that we were going to win the war'. Stuart added: 'He was visibly moved to tears by the songs'. (*Letter to the author, 22 May 1999*). Michael Clark recalled: 'He had no need to look at his school songbook to remember the words, as he knew them all by heart – which greatly impressed us all.' (*Letter to the author, 25 May 1999*).

and to many countries it seemed that our account was closed, we were finished. All this tradition of ours, our songs, our School history, this part of the history of this country, were gone and finished and liquidated.

Very different is the mood today. Britain, other nations thought, had drawn a sponge across her slate. But instead our country stood in the gap. There was no flinching and no thought of giving in; and by what seemed almost a miracle to those outside these islands, though we ourselves never doubted it, we now find ourselves in a position where I say that we can be sure that we have only to persevere to conquer.[1]

You sang here a verse of a School Song; you sang that extra verse written in my honour, which I was very greatly complimented by and which you have repeated today; but there is one word in it I want to alter – I wanted to do so last year but I did not venture to. It is the line –

Nor less we praise in darker days.

Do not let us speak of darker days; let us speak rather of sterner days. These are not dark days: these are great days – the greatest days our country has ever lived: and we must all thank God that we have been allowed, each of us according to our stations, to play a part in making these days memorable in the history of our race.

Winston S. Churchill to David Margesson

(*Churchill papers, 20/36*)

29 October 1941

1. All this seems to make many difficulties out of fairly simple things. Women should be enlisted in the ATS[2] and should always wear that badge. This ensures that their special needs in treatment, accommodation, &c., are kept up to a minimum standard wherever they may be by the women influences organizing the ATS. When, however, they are posted to a combatant unit and share in practice with the men the unavoidable dangers and hardships of that unit, they should become in every respect members of it. They should wear, in addition to the ATS badge, all regimental insignia appropriate to their rank. Although their well-being is still supervised by the ATS authorities, they should be considered as detached from the ATS and incorporated in the combatant unit. This does not imply any alteration in

[1] In a widely-acclaimed speech at the Guildhall, London, on 4 September 1914, Churchill declared: 'You have only to persevere to save yourselves, and to save all those who rely upon you.'

[2] The Auxiliary Territorial Service. Formed in 1939, and initially composed of volunteers, these women in khaki made a significant contribution to the work of Anti-Aircraft Command, participating in all the tasks except firing the guns.

their legal status, nor need it involve any Parliamentary discussion (although Parliamentary authority could easily be obtained were it necessary).

2. Considering the immense importance of having a large number of women in AA Batteries and that the efficiency of the Batteries depends upon carefully organized gun teams, it is imperative that these women should not be moved without reference to the Battery Command. The idea that there is an army of ATS under its own Commander-in-Chief, part of which lives alongside particular batteries and gives them a helping hand from time to time, is contrary to our main interest, namely, the maintenance of a larger number of AA Batteries with a smaller number of men.

3. You are good enough to say that I have been misinformed on various points. I should like to go further into this. I shall be glad to have a meeting at 5 p.m. on Tuesday, the 4th November, at which General Pile and other Officers of the ADGB,[1] as well as representatives of the ATS are present, and I trust you and the Adjutant-General will also come.

Winston S. Churchill to Field Marshal Smuts
(*Churchill papers, 20/44*)

29 October 1941
Most Secret and Personal

Many thanks for your message.[2] Fully agree importance of heavy and concentrated attacks on vital targets. Recent dispersal of our bombing has been due mainly to prolonged spell of exceptionally bad weather, which has restricted areas of possible operations and greatly increased normal difficulties of navigating and identifying targets by night. This has been a bitter disappointment at a time when we wanted to strike our heaviest blows. Navigational aids are being developed which give higher hopes for the future. We will make a great effort to achieve concentrated attacks on largest scale while operations in Libya are in progress.

[1] The Air Defence of Great Britain.

[2] Smuts had telegraphed to Churchill (received 28 October 1941): 'I wish to express my personal thanks and thanks of South African War Supplies Organization for great personal trouble you have taken in elucidating forward position of primary and augmenting cartridges for 10 lb. mortar bombs. Your detailed telegram has now placed matter very clearly in front of us and we wish you to know that we are deeply grateful for efforts that have been made to meet our demands in this matter.'

Winston S. Churchill to André Labarthe[1]
(*Churchill papers, 20/22*)

29 October 1941

Dear Monsieur Labarthe,

I congratulate you and your colleagues on the journal *La France Libre* which has now published its first anniversary number.

French literature, which all the world of culture has known and loved for centuries, today in France is twisted to serve the enemies of France who are trying to stifle and destroy French thought, French culture and French freedom.

On the soil of England *La France Libre* keeps the bright flame alive for that sure coming day when all good Frenchmen will once again be free to think and write the truth as they see it.

In wishing your venture all success for the future
Believe me,
Yours very truly,
Winston S. Churchill

Winston S. Churchill to Lord Beaverbrook
(*Churchill papers, 20/20*)

30 October 1941 10 Downing Street
3.45 a.m.
Private and Secret

My dear Max,

Yr mission to Moscow, so well discharged, and yr speeches about it, have made you an International figure. You ought not to have put out yr rumours about retiring on grounds of ill health (wh the public wd not accept) without considering this large, grave aspect. You must not let petty departmental squabbles vex you unduly. You know that in all that is essential to the success of our Supply you can count on me to see you get fair play. I feel sure of your friendship and loyalty which I have always reciprocated. I am vy sorry indeed for yr asthma. But you are knocking things about now in a good many directions at the same time, and this reacts heavily upon me. There is no question of a cabal by yr colleagues against you, & I sh'd not allow it if there

[1] André Labarthe, 1902–1967. Scientific adviser, Department of Research, Air Ministry, Paris, 1934. Mission to England and to the United States, 1934. Private Secretary to the Technical Director, Under-Secretary's Department for Air, 1939. Left France, June 1940. Director-General of French Armament and Scientific Research at General de Gaulle's headquarters, London, July–September 1940. Founder and Editor *La France Libre*, from November 1940. Secretary of Information, North Africa, 1943. Editor of the monthly magazine *Tricolor*, New York, 1943–45.

were. You ought not to wear yourself out by yr furies – you need all yr strength, & I need all mine, to beat the only enemy who matters – Hitler.

As you know I am not afraid of any crisis Parliamentary or others because I am only doing my duty without thought of self. My trouble is to restrain my combative instincts, amid the gad flies of criticism. Try to be as good an adviser to yrself as you are so often to me.

Your sincere friend
Winston S. Churchill

PS I am dealing with the specific points you have raised separately.

Winston S. Churchill to Major Randolph S. Churchill
(Churchill papers, 1/362)

30 October 1941

Brigadier Whiteley brings you these few lines to thank you for your letter which the Air Marshal brought back. He has done very well here and has been a help in several ways.

Your sisters have chosen the roughest roads they could find. Mary is Acting Temporary Unpaid Lance Bombardier and will in five or six weeks probably be promoted Sergeant. I hope she will presently be posted to a mixed battery in one of the parks near London so that we shall be able to see something of her on her leave. These two months of Amazonian Sparta have made a man of Judy[1] and also contrariwise improved her looks. Sarah,[2] casting aside about £4,000 of contracts, is undergoing austerities with the WAAF. We think they are very heroic. They are certainly braver than the lady in *The Black Mousquetaire* who 'did not mind death, but couldn't stand pinching'.

Things are pretty hard here now that the asthma season has come on and Max fights everybody and resigns every day. The Communists are posing as the only patriots in the country. The Admirals, Generals and Air Marshals chant their stately hymn of 'Safety First'. The Shinwells, Wintertons and

[1] Judy Montagu, Randolph's cousin, the daughter of Edwin and Venetia Montagu.

[2] Sarah Millicent Hermione Spencer Churchill, 1914–1983. Born while her father was returning from the siege of Antwerp, 7 October 1914. Edward Marsh was her godfather. She married Vic Oliver on 25 December 1936 (divorced, 1945). On stage in Birmingham, Southampton, Weston-Super-Mare and London, 1937–9; on tour with Vic Oliver in the play *Idiot's Delight*, 1938. Playing on the London stage in *Quiet Wedding*, 1939; in J.M. Barrie's *Mary Rose*, 1940. Appeared in the film *Spring Meeting*, 1940. Entered the Women's Auxiliary Air Force, October 1941; Assistant Section Officer (later Section Officer) at the Photographic Interpretation Unit, Medmenham, 1941–5. Accompanied her father (as ADC), to the Teheran Conference, November 1943, and to Yalta, February 1945. In 1949 she married Anthony Beauchamp, who died in 1957. In April 1962 she married the 23rd Baron Audley, MBE, who died in July 1963. In 1951 she appeared on the stage in the United States in *Grammercy Ghost*. She published *The Empty Spaces* (poems) in 1966, and *A Thread in the Tapestry* (recollections) in 1967, *Collected Poems* in 1974 and *Keep on Dancing* (further recollections) in 1981.

Hore-Belishas do their best to keep us up to the mark. In the midst of this I have to restrain my natural pugnacity by sitting on my own head. How bloody!

Winston S. Churchill to General Auchinleck
(*Churchill papers, 20/22*)

30 October 1941
Most Secret

My dear General,

Brigadier Whiteley has been a great help over here and will be able to give you a full account of our affairs. I have also to thank you for your three most interesting letters which were a real pleasure to read and to receive.

Everything seems perfect now and I can only hope and pray that the weather will not change in the interval. For us that interval is trying as we have nothing to say to Russia, to the United States or to many enquirers here. However, it may be that the luck will hold and certainly the destruction of the enemy armour will open the door to many possibilities.

At present we have scarcely any military credit and it is little use talking to the United States, to Russia, to Spain, to Turkey or to Weygand. Should success attend your efforts, I shall try my utmost to win the last-named factor by the offer of a substantial force and I am not without hopes of obtaining American support. I fully agree with Middle East that the acquisition of Bizerta, and all that would imply, would be the best of all. But we have no right to count upon it.

I was very sorry to give up 'Whipcord'.[1] Chiefs of Staff were so keen upon it and so were the appointed Commanders. It was, however, perhaps 'a task beyond the compass of our stride'. For the reasons I gave in my telegram to you, I do not think the opportunity will remain open.

Whiteley will tell you of my talk with him. You need not worry about the last 1,000 Australians in Tobruk or let their relief complicate your future plans. They can come out by the front door instead of the back. I also think that you ought to make sure of having some refreshment from Malta during 'Acrobat'.[2] Whiteley is going into this with Dobbie on his return. Even if you look at it as no more than an extra insurance, it would be prudent.

I am going to have an enquiry for my personal information into the tragical lack of contact between the War Office and the Ministry of Supply on the one hand and Middle East reception on the other about the front axles of the 22nd Armoured Brigade. This is not so much for the purpose of fixing responsibility

[1] The proposed invasion of Sicily.
[2] The planned advance from Cyrenaica into Tripolitania.

as for avoiding a recurrence of such break-downs. Considering the many months over which tanks have been passing from us to you, it is astonishing that no one at your end thought of saying 'We distrust all your axles and are fitting our slabs to strengthen them thus taking (so many) days'; or that no one from our end arrived with the tanks able to answer all your questions and to give a good warrant. On such mishaps the fates of battles and of empires turn.

I am greatly cheered by what the Brigadier has told me of the way in which you are concentrating all your power upon the destruction of the enemy's armour and of his armed force generally. Here is the true principle. '. . . seek ye the kingdom of God; and all these things shall be added unto you',[1] or, as Napoleon put it, '*Frappez la masse et tout le reste vient par surcroit.*'[2]

With all good wishes,
Believe me,
Yours very sincerely,
Winston S. Churchill

Winston S. Churchill to General Sir John Dill
(*Churchill papers, 20/36*)

31 October 1941
Secret

1. I am very glad to see the 50th Division moving out of Cyprus, and am glad that it can be relieved by elements of the 5th Indian Division. No decision has, however, yet been taken about moving the 50th Division to the Caucasus. Where will it wait in the interval?
2. Nothing in these moves is on any account to interfere with 'Crusader'. Pray reassure me on this.

Winston S. Churchill to Sir Edward Bridges
(*Churchill papers, 20/36*)

31 October 1941

I see an announcement that all Civil Servants affected by the comb at Whitehall will have their wages made up to their present salaries. This seems to be a very important decision of principle. When was it taken, and by whom? I do not seem to remember it being brought before the Cabinet. Why should the Civil Servant be favoured in this respect? No one looks after the grocer whose business is ruined or the professional man who is called up for the Army.

[1] St Matthew, chapter 6, verse 33.
[2] Strike at the main body of troops, and the others will be yours.

2. Nothing must be done to impair the efficiency of the Whitehall staffs, but if people can be spared they ought not to receive exceptional favours. Let me have a report.

Winston S. Churchill to Sir Archibald Sinclair and Air Chief Marshal Sir Charles Portal
(*Churchill papers, 20/36*)

31 October 1941

1. I saw Sir Hugh Dowding this afternoon and he accepted your proposal for reinstatement on the active list and for his taking charge of the Committee on Establishments. He asked for a fortnight in which to complete the small book he has written during his unemployment. I have undertaken to read the book myself at the week-end. I cannot think it will affect technical matters in any way.

2. In the meanwhile he will read up any papers on the subject and prepare his mind for his new duties. Pray let me have your other names for the Committee, which should not exceed three. There is no need to publish his reinstatement in the *Gazette* until this book trouble is cleared up, but let me see the form which the announcement will take.

Winston S. Churchill to General Ismay, for the Chiefs of Staff Committee[1]
(*Churchill papers, 20/36*)

31 October 1941

There is no need yet to tell the President or Mr Mackenzie King about movements of *Prince of Wales*. In about a week or ten days, I will do so. Now that 'Whipcord' is defunct it seems very likely she will go the whole way. But there is no need for us to make up our minds about this yet.

[1] Churchill also sent a copy of this Minute to the Secretary of State for the Dominions, Viscount Cranborne.

Winston S. Churchill to Harold Laski[1]

(Neville Laski papers)

31 October 1941 10 Downing Street

My dear Harold Laski,

I have but now found an opportunity of expressing to you my sorrow and deep sympathy on your father's death. I know how much you and your brother[2] will feel his loss. It is for you the severance of a link with childhood which can never be replaced. He was a very good man whose heart overflowed with human feeling and whose energies were tirelessly used for other people and large causes.

I feel I have lost a friend, and all my memories of Manchester and Cheetham are veiled in mourning.

Once more, accept my sympathy
Yours sincerely
Winston S. Churchill

[1] Harold Joseph Laski, 1893–1950. Political philosopher and historian; the son of Nathan Laski (an influential member of the Jewish community in North-West Manchester, Churchill's former constituency). Lecturer in History, McGill University, Montreal, 1914–16; Harvard University, 1916–20. Vice-Chairman of the British Institute of Adult Education, 1921–30. Member of the Fabian Society Executive, 1922. Lecturer in Political Science, Magdalene College, Cambridge, 1922–5. Professor of Political Science, London, 1926–50. Member of Executive Committee of Labour Party, 1936–49.

[2] Neville Jonas Laski, 1890–1969. On active service in Gallipoli, 1915, Sinai, 1917 and France 1918. Barrister. King's Counsel, 1930. President of the London Committee of Deputies of British Jews, 1933–40. Recorder of Liverpool, 1956–63. A Judge of the Crown Court. Author of *Jewish Rights and Jewish Wrongs* (1939).

November 1941

Winston S. Churchill to Anthony Eden
(*Churchill papers, 20/36*)

1 November 1941
Action this Day

ANGLO-RUSSIAN MILITARY CONSULTATIONS

I was not aware that we had ever taken the line that there should be no consultation on military matters. On the contrary, did we not tell them definitely we would consult on military matters? Certainly, I wrote a paper for Lord Beaverbrook's guidance which dealt entirely with the military situation apart from that of supply. General Ismay was sent to Russia for the purpose of embarking on the military discussion. It could have made no difference in fact, as there is no practical step which can at present be taken of any serious importance. He might have explained by facts and figures how very foolish and physically impossible was the suggestion that we should send 'twenty-five or thirty' divisions to the Russian front. He could have explained how even moving two or three divisions in at either end of the Russian front would choke the communications needed for Russian supplies. On the other hand, I do not see why these conversations did not take place, at some time or other, in the Conference. Undoubtedly, Lord Beaverbrook and Stalin touched upon the military issue.

All this should be cleared up and discussed at Cabinet on Monday. Perhaps you will draft a reply to Cripps for us to consider. He is evidently preparing his case against us.

General Wavell has already been to Tiflis without finding anyone in authority to speak to him. He speaks Russian well, and it might well be that he should undertake a journey to Moscow. It is only by the southern flank that we could enter for many months to come.

Anyhow, let us get the facts straightened out.

PS You should see Wavell's telegram (16495G cipher, 31/10) just received, showing how even two divisions at or north of Tabriz will completely choke the Trans-Persian Railway.

Winston S. Churchill to Admiral Sir Dudley Pound
(*Churchill Papers, 20/36*)

1 November 1941
Most Secret

1. The Duty Captain tells me that the *Prince of Wales* will not reach Capetown before the 17th. Considering she started four or five days ago, this seems a very long time. What speed is she making? It would be a very good thing if she arrived a few days earlier.

2. What has been done about the *Anson*? If it is decided that *Prince of Wales* should go on to Singapore, it would be very good if *Anson* arrived in the offing of Simonstown before dark on the night *Prince of Wales* sailed eastward, and that they should sail in company, thus favouring the idea that two of this class were in the Indian Ocean. What steps can be taken to enable the presence of *Prince of Wales* at Capetown to be reported to the enemy? She would stay there, I suppose, four or five days. After that, there might be danger from U-boats as there is no net.

3. When and where would *Prince of Wales* meet *Repulse*? Assuming we go on eastwards, when would they both turn up at Singapore?

Please let me know what plans you have.

Winston S. Churchill to John Curtin
(*Churchill papers, 20/44*)

1 November 1941

WITHDRAWAL OF AUSTRALIAN TROOPS FROM TOBRUK

Every effort will be made to carry out your wishes during next dark period.

Winston S. Churchill to President Franklin D. Roosevelt
(*Churchill papers, 20/44*)

1 November 1941
Triple Priority
Personal and Secret

1. As your Naval people have already been informed we are sending that big ship you inspected into the Indian Ocean as part of the Squadron we are

forming there. This ought to serve as a deterrent on Japan. There is nothing like having something that can catch and kill anything. I am very glad we can spare her at this juncture. It is more than we thought we could do some time ago. The firmer your attitude and ours the less chance of their taking the plunge.

2. I am grieved at the loss of life you have suffered with *Reuben James*[1]. I salute the land of unending challenge.

Winston S. Churchill to General Ismay, for the Chiefs of Staff Committee
(*Churchill papers, 20/36*)

2 November 1941

While fully understanding General Wavell's point of view, we have definitely decided to play the sequence 'Crusader', 'Acrobat', 'Gymnast'.[2] There can be no going back on this.

Winston S. Churchill to John Curtin
(*Churchill papers, 20/44*)

2 November 1941
Personal and Most Secret

I am very glad you are pleased about the big ship. There is nothing like having something that can catch and kill anything. I am increasingly hopeful she will be able to go right on towards Malaya. Will advise you about publicity when the moment comes.

2. Blamey will no doubt tell you about far-reaching plans we have in the Desert. War Cabinet here expressed desire not to be informed of dates or details. We hope to be well off for air, tanks and flak. We seem to have pretty well cut off the traffic from Italy to Tripoli, and they are now trying to send their stuff round to Benghazi direct.

[1] On 31 October 1941 the United States Navy destroyer, the *Reuben James*, was torpedoed in the North Atlantic, while escorting the British trans-Atlantic convoy HX 156 for Halifax; 115 of her crew, including all her officers, were drowned.

[2] The relief of Tobruk; the advance into Tripolitania, and the planned landing in French North-West Africa.

3. Earle Page[1] has arrived and we had a very pleasant meeting of the Cabinet with him. He is going to make a statement to us on Thursday next, and I am taking him round inspecting the north-east coast cities and defences Friday and Saturday.

4. Give my regards to Menzies. I am so glad he is on your War Council.

Winston S. Churchill to Field Marshal Smuts
(*Churchill papers, 20/44*)

2 November 1941
Personal and Secret

In that big ship now on its way to you is Admiral Tom Phillips, who will command in the Indian Ocean. He is a great friend of mine and one of our ablest admirals. He has been all this war Vice-Chief of the Naval Staff and knows the whole story back and forth. He has a great desire to have the honour of meeting you, and it would give me pleasure if you would accept this as a personal introduction from me. I hope you will also have a look at the ship.

Winston S. Churchill to Peter Fraser
(*Churchill papers, 20/44*)

3 November 1941

Nothing is so good as having something that can catch and kill anything. It keeps them bunched. Good wishes.

War Cabinet: Confidential Annex
(*Churchill papers, 65/24*)

3 November 1941
5 p.m.

The Prime Minister thought that the next act of Japanese aggression was likely to be against Yunnan, and saw no evidence of any early intention on their part to attack the Netherlands East Indies. Our policy in the Far East

[1] Earle Christmas Grafton Page, 1880–1961. Born and educated in Australia. On active service with the Australian forces, France and Egypt, 1914–18. Acting Prime Minister of Australia, 1923–24, 1926–27. Minister of Commerce and Deputy Prime Minister, 1934–39. Minister of Health, 1937–38. Knighted 1938. Prime Minister, 1939. Minister of Commerce, 1940–41. Special Australian Envoy to the British War Cabinet, 1941–42. Companion of Honour, 1942. Member of the Australian War Council, 1942–45, Minister of Health, Australia, 1949–56.

should be to persuade the United States to cover our weak position in that area. We should not run the risk of finding ourselves at war with Japan without American support. We should therefore press the United States Government to declare that they would take up arms against Japan if she committed any further act of aggression. Such a declaration would be in line with the policy which President Roosevelt had developed orally at the Atlantic Meeting. No doubt the President would find it necessary to use such language as that in such-and-such circumstances he would find it necessary to seek the support of Congress for the measures required by national security for the United States.

The War Cabinet:

Invited the Prime Minister in the meantime to send a Personal telegram to President Roosevelt. This telegram should make it plain that we would support any action which the United States saw fit to take to restrain Japanese aggression in the Far East, but that we could not take the lead; and would urge strongly that the President should make a public declaration that the United States would take measures for their national security if Japan made any further encroachments in the Far East.

(The Foreign Secretary undertook to submit a draft to the Prime Minister on these lines.)

Winston S. Churchill to General Sir John Dill

(*Churchill papers, 20/36*)

3 November 1941
Action this Day

AVAILABILITY AND REQUIREMENTS OF ARMOURED FORMATIONS

All experience shows that all Commanders-in-Chief invariably ask for everything they can think of, and always represent their own forces at a minimum. I do not therefore consider there is any inherent virtue in the sweeping claims put forward by C-in-C, Home Forces. He would like to have them met, and so should I, but I do not admit that the need can be expressed in this form. It is only a few months ago that I saw with pleasure that we might have a thousand tanks available to meet an autumn invasion. Now we have got two thousand or more, and at least another fifteen hundred should be available by the Spring, making 3,500.

General Brooke should organize these in the best possible way, bearing in mind that for Home Defence against invasion the utmost possible should be put in the front line of formations, and that the reserve need not be on the scale required in the Middle East.

2. While I am calling for the most vigorous measures to resist invasion in the Spring, I am, of course, very sceptical of the stories that are told about its scale. The evidence which supports the tale of the 800 flat-bottomed vessels, each carrying eight or ten Tanks, rests on the flimsiest foundation, viz.: an agent saw some of these vessels being made at one place, and he thought others were being made at other places to the number of 800. If there is any other evidence behind this story, let me have it.

3. With the improvements in photography and the increased power in the air, very formidable resistance should be made to the assemblies of large numbers of vessels in the river mouths of the Low Countries. Now that we have the command of the air over the Pas de Calais, it is not seen how Dunkirk, Calais and Boulogne can be used for the purposes of invasion. All shipping gathered in these harbours and the smaller ones could be bombed by daylight under Fighter cover. This was not the case last year.

4. There can be no question of our going back on our promises to Russia. If, of course, Archangel freezes up, we must do our best by other routes. But it is far too soon to raise any such issues now when the ink is hardly dry on our promise, and we have been unable to do anything else to help the Russians.

5. The only external demands which General Brooke will suffer from are, first, possible Armoured Division or two Operational Brigades for 'Gymnast', but this is very hypothetical; and, secondly, wastage in the Middle East according to normal scale of replacement. If we win the battle, the wounded tanks will be repairable. Besides the loss of the enemy is as good as a gain to us.

6. General Auchinleck has the 1st, 2nd, 7th and Yeomanry Armoured formations, and two extra Tank Brigades. These should all be in good order by the Spring. We should try to get him as many as possible from the United States.

7. It seems a pity to withdraw any Valentines from the 6th and 8th Divisions. I agree with your paras. (d) and (e), but it is essential to try to give India a larger proportion. Let me see the JIC[1] report referred to in para. 4.

8. I have asked Lord Beaverbrook for a forecast of tank production in the next six months.

9. Let us have a meeting on Wednesday night at 10 p.m. to thrash this out. Lord Beaverbrook and C-in-C, Home Forces, should be asked. Let me have other names.

[1] The Joint Intelligence Committee (headed by Victor Cavendish-Bentinck). Its reports were based upon the widest range of Intelligence information including the Enigma decrypts and diplomatic intercepts.

Winston S. Churchill to General Auchinleck
(*Churchill papers, 20/44*)

3 November 1941
Personal

Two of the A22 Tanks called Churchills are in WS 12[1] due at Suez about 25th November. They are sending some expert technical people with them. My object in sending you these is that you shall be able to test them for Desert work and suggest in good time any improvements or changes necessary. The tank was only ordered fifteen months ago and is, of course, in its teething stage. It is, however, very likely the strongest and best available for 1942. Its existence should be kept most secret and it should be kept out of all danger of falling into enemy hands. I shall be glad if you will take this under your own wing and report to me about it at your leisure.

War Cabinet: Confidential Annex
(*Cabinet papers, 65/24*)

3 November 1941
5 p.m.

The Prime Minister said that several telegrams had been exchanged with Sir Stafford Cripps on the question whether we should have discussions with the Russians regarding military cooperation. There had been little or no discussion on military cooperation during the Moscow Conference, which, of course, had been arranged to deal with Supply matters. Since, however, the point had been raised, the Prime Minister said that he thought the best plan would be that he should telegraph to M. Stalin and offer to send General Wavell to Russia to discuss the question of military cooperation. On the whole, he thought it would be a good plan that General Paget[2] should visit Russia at the same time as General Wavell, and assist him in the discussions. General Paget would be fully instructed before he left this country, and would be able to put General Wavell into the picture as seen from here.

Some discussion followed as to whether it would be desirable that General Paget should join General Wavell. It would, in any event, be desirable to warn Stalin that General Paget's impending appointment as Commander-in-Chief in the Far East should not be disclosed.

[1] The twelfth convoy to the Middle East that went round the Cape of Good Hope and through the Red Sea to Suez City, at the southern end of the Suez Canal.

[2] Paget was Commander-in-Chief designate in the Far East, in succession to Air Chief Marshal Sir Robert Brooke-Popham.

General Wavell (and General Paget, if he joined him) would be able to explain to M. Stalin the limited possibilities of sending a British force to Russia. Quite apart from the time involved, if either the Archangel or the Persian route was to be used to maintain any considerable British force, this would make it impossible to send any appreciable volume of supplies to Russia over these routes.

Later in the meeting, the War Cabinet were informed that – through no fault of their own – two of the three senior members of our Military Mission in Moscow had not established really close relations with the Russian Government. It was suggested that there might be advantage in making changes in these appointments when a suitable opportunity offered.

The War Cabinet:

1. Invited the Prime Minister to telegraph to M. Stalin and suggest that General Wavell and General Paget should go to Russia in order to discuss with the Russian authorities the possibilities of military cooperation.

2. Took note that, in connection with this visit, consideration would be given to changes in the personnel of the Military Mission in Moscow.

Winston S. Churchill to J. V. Stalin
(*Cabinet papers, 65/24*)

4 November 1941
Personal and Secret

1. In order to clear things up and to plan for the future I am ready to send General Wavell, Commander-in-Chief in India, Persia and Iraq, to meet you in Moscow, Kuibishev, Tiflis or wherever you will. Besides this, General Paget, our new Commander-in-Chief secretly designated for the Far East, will come with General Wavell. General Paget has been in the centre of things here and will have with him the latest and best opinions of our High Command. These two officers will be able to tell you exactly how we stand, what is possible and what we think is wise. They can reach you in about a fortnight. Do you want them?[1]

2. We told you in my message of 6th September that we were willing to declare war on Finland. Will you, however, consider whether it is really good business that Great Britain should declare war on Finland, Hungary and Roumania at this moment? It is only a formality, because our extreme blockade is already in force against them. My judgment is against it because,

[1] Stalin replied that he would only receive Wavell and Paget if they could include an understanding 'on war aims and on plans of the post-war organization of peace' and an agreement 'on mutual military assistance in Europe'. ('Personal Message', 8 November 1941: *Premier papers, 3/170/l, folios 73-5*)

first, Finland has many friends in the United States and it is more prudent to take account of this fact. Secondly, Roumania and Hungary; these countries are full of our friends; they have been overpowered by Hitler and used as a catspaw. But if fortune turns against that ruffian, they might easily come back to our side. A British declaration of war would only freeze them all and make it look as if Hitler were the head of a grand European alliance solid against us. Do not, pray, suppose it is any want of zeal or comradeship that makes us doubt the advantage of this step. Our dominions, except Australia, are reluctant. Nevertheless, if you think it will be a real help to you and worth while, I will put it to the Cabinet again.

3. I hope our supplies are being cleared from Archangel as fast as they come in. A trickle is now beginning through Persia. We shall pump both ways to our utmost. Please make sure that our technicians who are going with the tanks and aircraft have full opportunity to hand these weapons over to your men under the best conditions. At present our Mission at Kuibishev is out of touch with all these affairs. They only want to help. These weapons are sent at our peril and we are anxious they shall have the best chance. An order from you seems necessary.

4. I cannot tell you about our immediate military plans any more than you can tell me about yours, but rest assured we are not going to be idle.

5. With the object to keeping Japan quiet we are sending our latest battleship *Prince of Wales*, which can catch and kill any Japanese ship, into the Indian Ocean, and are building up a powerful battle squadron there. I am urging President Roosevelt to increase his pressure on the Japanese and keep them frightened so that the Vladivostok route will not be blocked.

6. I will not waste words in compliments because you know already from Beaverbrook and Harriman what we feel about your splendid fight. Have confidence in our untiring support.

7. I should be glad to hear from you direct that you have received this telegram.

Winston S. Churchill to Sir John Anderson

(*Churchill papers, 20/36*)

4 November 1941
Action this Day

I am concerned at certain passages in your Report on Manpower (WP (41) 247), which seem to assign to the Production Executive inquisitorial and discretionary powers over the Supply Departments which it was never intended that it should have.

In paragraph 12 you propose the appointment by the Production Executive of a permanent Inspection Commission on the use of Labour, whose function it would be to carry out continuous investigation into the possibilities of securing manpower economies in industry. I realize that, until demands for labour have been the subject of a thorough investigation (corresponding to the check of Service requirements carried out by the Defence Committee), such demands cannot be finally accepted. Nevertheless, may there not perhaps be a risk that such a Commission would cut across the responsibilities of the Departmental Ministers on which depend our system of Cabinet government, with Parliamentary supervision? Clearly, however, there is no objection to such inquiries being carried out by a body appointed jointly by the Supply Ministers (or one of their number) and the Minister of Labour, if the Ministers concerned agree to this course, and report is made to them. But the proposal as at present drafted may, I think, be open to some misconception.

The second point I wish to raise is the last sentence of paragraph 9(d), where it is stated that 'Any dispute on this point' (broadly, the Ministry of Labour's obligation to make substitute labour available) 'between the Ministry of Labour and the Supply Department concerned will be referred to the Production Executive <u>for decision</u>' (my underlining).

The Production Executive was set up to enable the Ministers concerned to meet together and to lay down by agreement certain general rules to prevent undercutting or over-bidding between the Supply Departments, and to secure a broad measure of unity of practice between them. But if agreement cannot be reached on the Production Executive, that body has no power by itself to overrule the Departmental Chief. Nothing can deprive him of his right to come to the Cabinet.

If there is any likelihood that there will be a number of labour disputes which cannot be settled on the Production Executive, and which are not of sufficient importance to be brought to the Cabinet, them some other tribunal will have to be set up to settle them. There can be no question of making the Minister of Labour, as Chairman of the Production Executive, judge in any disputes on labour questions to which his Department is a party.

At the meeting on Manpower on Thursday afternoon (DC (S) (41) 11th Meeting) certain decisions were reached which affect the figures given in the earlier part of your memorandum (WP (41) 247). I think it would be to the convenience of the Cabinet if you would arrange for a revise of your memorandum to be issued to include these alterations of figures and also modifications of the two paragraphs to which I have drawn attention in the Minute.

Winston S. Churchill to the Marquess of Salisbury[1]
(*Churchill papers, 20/22*)

4 November 1941

My dear Salisbury,

Thank you for your letter of October 21 informing me of the Watching Committee's views on the Coal situation.

Your Committee rightly show their anxiety that our war effort shall not suffer for lack of coal, and I should like to assure both you and them that this vital matter is being kept constantly under review. With the larger stocks accumulated during recent months and the better spread of supplies and stocks, there is now every prospect that we shall be able this winter not only to meet all our war needs, but to provide a fair standard of comfort for the civilian population as well. The problem is now therefore rather the long-term one of equating production to growing needs as the demands upon our man-power from every quarter steadily increase.

To provide for these growing needs, as well as to make good the natural wastage in the mining industry, we have, as you know, found it necessary to bring back a large number of ex-miners to the pits from other industries and this process is still going on. We have for the present been able to equate output to our transport possibilities at this time of the year, and I trust we may be able to continue to do so.

I cannot disturb or weaken the Army in view of the onslaught which may be made upon us in the Spring. I am sure your Committee will realize that our defence against invasion and keeping open the Atlantic lifeline are the first of my responsibilities. We have a good tale to tell about the second, but only the event can prove the first.

Yours v sincerely,
Winston S. Churchill

[1] Lord James Edward Hubert Gascoyne-Cecil, Viscount Cranborne, 1861–1947. Son of the 3rd Marquess of Salisbury (Prime Minister, 1885–86, 1886–92 and 1895–1902). Conservative Member of Parliament for Darwen, 1885–92; for Rochester, 1893–1903. Succeeded his father, as 4th Marquess, 1903. Lord President of the Council, 1922–24. Lord Privy Seal, 1924–29. Leader of the House of Lord, 1925–29.

Winston S. Churchill to the Chairman,
Peebles and Southern Midlothian Unionist Association
(*Churchill papers, 20/22*)

4 November 1941

My dear Sir,

Very careful consideration has been given to your letter of October 1st, in which you inform me that the Peebles and Southern Midlothian Unionist Association wishes the Government to consider whether it should ask the House of Commons to take such steps as may be expedient, if necessary by Act of Parliament, to declare vacant the seat at present held by Captain A. H. Maule Ramsay, MP.

After full consideration of the position of the Government and of the lines of action which might be adopted by any Government in order to declare a seat vacant, and of precedents which might bear upon this particular case, I am satisfied that it is not possible for the Government to proceed either by legislation or by Motion in the House of Commons to carry out the wishes of your Association.

Captain Ramsay is detained under Defence Regulation 18B, but has not been convicted of any offence which would lead to his expulsion from the House of Commons. In your letter to Captain Ramsay you base your request for his resignation in the main on his withdrawal of support from the Government which he was returned to support. You may have had other circumstances also in mind, but you will I am sure realize how dangerous a precedent might be established if the Government legislated in order that a seat might be declared vacant because a Member had, even in wartime, withdrawn his support from it. I am convinced that the House of Commons would be very critical if any such action was suggested.

The above observations would arise equally on procedure by motion, but I have had investigations made as to this procedure and am satisfied that there are no precedents in modern times which bear any relation to the present case.

It is regrettable that the Unionist Association of Peebles and Southern Midlothian should find itself faced with these unusual difficulties but I am sure it will be realized that it is not possible for the Government to take action on the lines advocated by the Association.

Yours faithfully,
Winston S. Churchill

Anthony Eden: diary
(*'The Reckoning'*)

4 November 1941

Meeting at 10 p.m. with Winston and Chiefs of Staff. Dickie[1] appeared in his new role. Then talk about Far East, Russia and other plans. Altogether a useful evening. Winston said he was off tomorrow evening until Monday[2] and would I mind the shop and call together Chiefs of Staff if need be. Later we talked over whiskies in his room, particularly of Wavell and Paget's projected visit to Moscow. I suggested it might be useful if I went sometime. Winston agreed. Both thought it better after results of 'Crusader'[3] were visible. Timetable thus a little difficult. Depends upon how long Stalin takes to reply.

Hugh Dalton: diary
(*'The Second World War Diary of Hugh Dalton, 1940–45'*)

4 November 1941

Summons for Juggery,[4] first for 10 p.m., afterwards put to 10.45. I arrive at CWR taking Glenconner[5] with me, though it is most unlikely that he will either be wanted, or allowed, in the inner room. We find Cranborne also waiting in the Mess-Anteroom. I do not get in till 11.45. PM in a good mood. We have a useful discussion. All possible is to be done to help the guerrillas. A further conference on lower level with the Admiralty tomorrow.

Winston S. Churchill to General Ismay, for the Chiefs of Staff Committee
(*Premier papers, 3/395/3*)

5 November 1941
Action this Day

We do not know when the Germans will arrive in the Caucasus, nor how long it will be before they come up against the mountain barrier. We do not know what the Russians will do, how many troops they will use, or how long

[1] Lord Louis Mountbatten, who had just been appointed Commodore, Combined Operations (CCO) in place of Admiral of the Fleet Sir Roger Keyes, the former Director of Combined Operations (DCO).

[2] Monday 10 November 1941.

[3] General Auchinleck's forthcoming offensive in Cyrenaica.

[4] Yugoslav business: Yugoslav partisans under General Draja Mihailovitch had been fighting the Germans since September south-west of Belgrade. The Yugoslavs were known colloquially as 'Jugs'.

[5] Christopher Grey Tennant, 1899–1983. Midshipman, Royal Navy, November 1914; later Sub-Lieutenant. Succeeded his father, as 2nd Baron Glenconner, 1920.

they will resist. It is quite certain that if the Germans press hard, neither the 50th nor the 18th British Divisions could be on the spot in time, and the British Indian Divisions in Persia and Iraq would not be good enough to send. We are held in a grip by the delay in 'Crusader' and it is not possible to see beyond that at the present moment. I cannot feel any confidence that the Germans will be prevented from occupying the Baku oil fields, or that the Russians will effectively destroy these fields. The Russians tell us nothing, and view with great suspicion any inquiries we make on this subject.

The only thing we have it in our power to do is to base four or five heavy Bombing Squadrons in Northern Persia to aid the Russians in the defence of the Caucasus, if that be possible, and if the worst happens, to bomb the Baku oil fields effectively and try to set the ground alight. These squadrons will, of course, require Fighter protection. Neither the Bombers nor the Fighters can be provided till after 'Crusader' and its consequences can be judged. A plan should, however, be made based on a large transference of Air from Libya to Persia, so as to achieve the denial of the oil fields to the enemy as long as possible. Pray let this be done during the next week, so that we can see what is involved. One cannot tell how long the Russians will retain the command of the Black Sea, although with their forces it is inexcusable they should lose it.

Winston S. Churchill to A. V. Alexander and Admiral Pound
(*Churchill papers, 20/36*)

5 November 1941

I much regret that the number of U-boat prisoners taken by us should have been published. I commented unfavourably upon this publication six months ago. The figure is so small that it advertises to the world the failure of all our efforts against them. There was absolutely no need to make such a disclosure, gratuitously encouraging the enemy and discouraging our friends.

Were you aware beforehand that this was going to be done?

Winston S. Churchill to Sir Archibald Sinclair
(*Churchill papers, 20/36*)

5 November 1941

Your reply to my Minute M 1024/1.[1]

I do not think you should dismiss a matter like this so lightly. I am told it is

[1] Churchill's suggestion that the Royal Air Force should introduce a system, such as obtained in civil airway companies before the war, whereby mechanics and fitters worked for certificates of competence in each different make of engine.

the explanation of the far higher economy reached by the Germans in maintaining their Air Force.

I must beg you to have the matter more searchingly examined.

Winston S. Churchill to William Mackenzie King
(*Churchill papers, 20/44*)

5 November 1941
Most Secret

In view of the threatening situation in the Far East, and the need for doing all we can to make Japan understand what she might be faced with if she persists in going to war, we have decided to place a force of capital ships before the end of the year in the triangle Aden-Singapore-Simonstown.

Our original idea had been to send the battleships *Rodney* and *Nelson* and the four R battleships (*Royal Sovereign, Revenge, Resolution* and *Ramillies*) based mainly on Singapore. This scheme, however, became impossible in its entirety owing to the recent injury to the *Nelson*.

What we have now decided is to send forthwith our newest battleship the *Prince of Wales* to join the battle-cruiser *Repulse*, which is already in the Indian Ocean. The *Prince of Wales* will be at Capetown quite soon. In addition, the four R battleships are being moved as they become ready to Eastern waters, and later the *Repulse* will be relieved by the *Renown* which has greater radius.

We shall have to review the movements of the *Prince of Wales* when she is at Capetown in the light of the danger of the *Tirpitz* breaking out and of other operational possibilities before the *Duke of York* is ready in December. We shall, however, make every effort to spare the *Prince of Wales* permanently, and I am sure that you will agree that she will be the best possible deterrent to Japan.

Sir Alexander Cadogan: diary
(*'The Diary of Sir Alexander Cadogan OM, 1938-1945'*)

5 November 1941

Cabinet at 12.15 . . . PM produced his redraft to telegram to Roosevelt but he had left out the guts – proposal for a fresh warning. So I scribbled a para for insertion and he accepted it.

Winston S. Churchill to President Franklin D. Roosevelt
(*Churchill papers, 20/44*)

5 November 1941
Personal and Secret

1. I have received Chiang Kai-shek's attached appeal addressed to us both for air assistance. You know how we are placed for air strength at Singapore. None the less, I should be prepared to send pilots and even some planes if they could arrive in time.

2. What we need now is a deterrent of the most general and formidable character. The Japanese have as yet taken no final decision, and the Emperor appears to be exercising restraint. When we talked about this at Placentia you spoke of gaining time, and this policy has been brilliantly successful so far. But our joint embargo is steadily forcing the Japanese to decisions for peace or war.

3. It now looks as if they would go into Yunnan cutting the Burma Road with disastrous consequences for Chiang Kai-shek. The collapse of his resistance would not only be a world tragedy in itself, but it would leave the Japanese with large forces to attack north or south.

4. The Chinese have appealed to us, as I believe they have to you, to warn the Japanese against an attack in Yunnan. I hope you might think fit to remind them that such an attack, aimed at China from a region in which we have never recognized that the Japanese have any right to maintain forces, would be in open disregard of the clearly indicated attitude of the United States Government. We should, of course, be ready to make a similar communication.

5. No independent action by ourselves will deter Japan because we are so much tied-up elsewhere. But, of course, we will stand with you and do our utmost to back you in whatever course you choose. I think myself that Japan is more likely to drift into war than plunge in. Please let me know what you think.

War Cabinet: Confidential Annex
(*Cabinet papers, 65/24*)

5 November 1941
12.15 p.m.

The Prime Minister referred to a telegram from Chungking, reporting that General Chiang Kai-shek believed that the Japanese meant to make an attack on Yunnan in about a month's time. The Prime Minister read to the War Cabinet the draft of a personal telegram from himself to President Roosevelt dealing with the Far Eastern situation.

Referring to the suggested air reinforcements for Singapore the Prime Minister said that the development of our Air Force had not proceeded as fast as we had hoped. We had now to meet the demands of Russia to whom we had promised to send 200 machines a month. Further, it was essential to obtain and keep air superiority in the Middle East. Above all we had to keep a sufficient air force in this country to assist in repelling any invasion Germany might make next spring. Hitler had great need to invade this country. It would be possible for him to contain the Russian front, and to move sufficient forces to the West and stage an operation on such a scale as had never been attempted before, and regardless of losses. The key to repelling such an attempt lay in fighter superiority over the enemy. Once the fighter command of the air was lost, Germany could invade this country.

The Prime Minister, continuing, said that to send bombers to Singapore at this present moment, when they could be more usefully employed on attacking targets in Germany and Northern France, would be a waste of effort.

As regards our naval strength in the Pacific and Indian Oceans, we had taken some risk in detaching the *Prince of Wales* from the Home Fleet. The *Prince of Wales* was now on her way to Cape Town and likely to proceed to Singapore. Whether she would remain there permanently could not yet be decided, but it was hoped to keep her in Eastern waters until the *Nelson* and *Rodney* were available. In any case, her appearance at Cape Town would have a deterrent effect on Japan. It was intended to build up a battle squadron, based on Singapore, which could be used for the protection of the vital supply lines between Australia and the Middle East.

The Prime Minister then referred to Telegram No. 714 from the Australian Government which suggested that Japan should be warned that any attack by her on Russia would be resisted by force by this country. The suggestion was somewhat alarming, for the one situation he was anxious to avoid was that we should be at war with Japan without the assistance of the United States. It must be remembered that a great step forward had taken place at the Atlantic Conference when President Roosevelt had agreed to tell Japan that if she took further steps in pursuance of a policy of domination by force, the United States would have to take steps to safeguard her security and interests.

As for the safety of Australia herself, for which this country took supreme responsibility, he could not emphasize too strongly that if this question arose then we should be prepared to abandon our position in the Middle East in order to go to her assistance. The essential task was to determine the right disposition of our forces. In this matter, risks could not be avoided. We had to balance up the danger of finding ourselves too short of forces in this or that area at a crucial moment. All these questions were the subject of continuous, almost hourly, review by the Staffs concerned.

The Prime Minister said that he would be glad to discuss this matter further with Sir Earle Page and in the meantime Sir Earle Page might discuss the naval, military and air force aspects of the position individually with each Chief of Staff.

Winston S. Churchill to Sir Robert Brooke-Popham[1]
(*Churchill papers, 20/44*)

5 November 1941

You will shortly be receiving an official telegram informing you that it has been decided, in view of developments in the Far East, that the duties of Commander-in-Chief, Far East, should be entrusted to an army officer with up-to-date experience.

Meanwhile, I wish to congratulate you on the fine work which you have done, and I propose, if it would be agreeable to you, to submit your name to The King for the award of a baronetcy in recognition of your distinguished services.

Winston S. Churchill to Sir Patrick Hannon[2]
(*Churchill papers, 20/22*)

5 November 1941

My dear Sir

I am in full agreement with the National Union of Manufacturers about the vital importance which our export trade will have in the period after the War, and I share their anxiety that no unnecessary obstacles shall be put in the way of its maintenance while the War lasts. But it is not correct to attribute the drastic cuts in our exports to deference to the USA. The reduction of exports is due to our increasing pre-occupation with warlike measures. The Lease-Lend undertaking is a declaration of our understanding that, while the US is willing to stint its own citizens in order that we may be able to prosecute the

[1] Henry Robert Moore Brooke-Popham, 1878–1953. Entered the Army, 1898. Royal Flying Corps, 1912. On active service, 1914–18. Director of Research, Air Ministry, 1919–21. Commandant, Royal Air Force Staff College, 1921–26. Knighted, 1927. Air Officer Commanding Fighting Area Air Defence of Great Britain, 1926–28; Iraq Command, 1928–30. Air Officer Commanding-in-Chief, Air Defence of Great Britain, 1933–35. Inspector-General Royal Air Force, 1935–36. Retired list, 1937. Governor and Commander-in-Chief, Kenya, 1937–39. Recalled to the RAF, as Commander-in-Chief, Far East, 1940–1. Reverted to the retired list, 1944. He declined the baronetcy.

[2] Patrick Hannon, 1874-1963. Director of the Irish Agricultural Wholesale Society, 1901-04; of the Agricultural Organization, Cape Colony, 1905-09. Unsuccessful Conservative candidate, East Bristol, 1910. Member of Council, National Service League, 1911-15. Editor of *The Navy*, 1911-18. Conservative Member of Parliament, Moseley, 1921-50. President of the Industrial Transport Association, 1927-37. President of the National Union of Manufacturers, 1935-53. Knighted, 1936.

War effectively, it should not be expected to do so in order that we shall escape necessary sacrifices even in our export trade. The difficulties with which we have to deal are inherent in our own situation. Our problem is to balance the merits of the various demands which are made upon the resources under our control. There may well be two opinions about the wisdom of any particular decision which the Government has reached, and I shall be glad to see that any representations which the National Union may care to make receive the most careful consideration. But there is no difference between us about our object.

Yours very faithfully
Winston S. Churchill

Winston S. Churchill to Air Chief Marshal Sir Hugh Dowding
(*Churchill papers, 20/22*)

5 November 1941

My dear Dowding,

I have looked through some part of your proofs and have had the book carefully read for me by Brendan Bracken. We both agree that for various reasons it would not be a good thing for you to publish the book at this time. The Air Ministry are moreover anxious about the technical aspects.

I have asked you to do a very important work which will be a real service to the country, and for which I believe you are specially fitted. I would suggest to you that this duty should come first, and that you should defer the publication till after you have discharged it.

Yours very sincerely,
Winston S. Churchill

Winston S. Churchill to General Auchinleck
(*Churchill papers, 20/44*)

6 November 1941
Personal

I presume you are watching the constant arrival of anti-tank guns upon your front, both as observed by road and as reported in our most secret by air.

Winston S. Churchill: Memorandum[1]
(*Cabinet papers, 66/19*)

6 November 1941
Secret

MANPOWER

It may be a convenience to my colleagues if I set out the provisional views which I have formed on some of the major issues which we have to settle.

1. The age of compulsory military service for men should be raised by ten years, to include all men under 51. While this might not make very many men available for an active fighting role, it would assist the Minister of Labour in finding men for non-combatant duties in the Services.

The possibility that the age should be raised again later on need not be excluded; but it would seem that an increase of ten years in the upper limit would be sufficient at the moment.

2. The case for calling up young men at 18½, instead of 19, seems fully established. Indeed, I would go further, and call them up at 18 if this would make any substantial contribution.

3. On the whole, I am not yet satisfied, in view of the marked dislike of the process by their service men folk, that a case has been established for conscripting women to join the Auxiliary Services at the present time. Voluntary recruitment for these Services should, however, be strongly encouraged. For the present, the advertising campaign to get women to join the Auxiliary Services should be confined to the ATS.[2]

4. Should the Cabinet decide in favour of compelling women to join the Auxiliary Services, it is for consideration whether the method employed should not be by individual selection, rather than by calling up by age groups. The latter system would inevitably discourage women from joining up until their age group was called.

5. The campaign for directing women into the munitions industries should be pressed forward. The existing powers should be used with greater intensity. This should be closely linked with measures to secure the utmost practicable degree of concentration in the less essential industries and in such services as banking, insurance and various types of commercial agencies.

6. Employers might well be encouraged, in suitable cases, to make further use of the services of married women to industry. This would often have to be on a part-time basis, and means must be found to ease the burden on women who are prepared to perform a dual role.

[1] Printed for the War Cabinet as War Cabinet Paper No. 258 of 1941.
[2] The (women's) Auxiliary Territorial Service.

Winston S. Churchill: speech
(*'The Unrelenting Struggle'*, *pages 277-9*)

7 November 1941 Hull

I wanted very much to see this city which has suffered by the malice of our assailants. I can see that it has had many of its fine buildings shattered and gutted. But I also see that it has not had the heart of its people cast down.

The resolution of the British people is unconquerable. Neither sudden nor violent shocks, nor long, cold, tiring, provoking strains and lulls, can or will alter our course. No country made more strenuous efforts to avoid being drawn into this war, but I dare say we shall be found ready and anxious to prosecute it when some of those who provoked it are talking vehemently about peace. It has been rather like that in old times.

I am often asked to say how we are going to win this war. I remember being asked that last time very frequently, and not being able to give a very precise or conclusive answer. We kept on doing our best; we kept on improving. We profited by our mistakes and our experiences. We turned misfortune to good account. We were told we should run short of this or that, until the only thing we ever ran short of was Huns. We did our duty. We did not ask to see too far ahead, but strode forth upon our path, guided by such lights as led us, and then one day we saw those who had forced the struggle upon the world cast down their arms in the open field and immediately proceed to beg for sympathy, mercy and considerable financial support.

Now we have to do it all over again. Sometimes I wonder why. Having chained this fiend, this monstrous power of Prussian militarism, we saw it suddenly resuscitated in the new and more hideous guise of Nazi tyranny. We have to face once more the long struggle, the cruel sacrifices, and not be daunted or deterred by feelings of vexation. With quite a little forethought, a little care and decision, and with rather a greater measure of slow persistency, we need never have had to face this thing in our lifetime or in that of our children.

However, we are all resolved to go forward. We were equally resolved when a year and three months ago we found ourselves absolutely alone, the only champion of freedom in the whole world that remained in arms. We found ourselves with hardly any weapons left. We had rescued our Army, indeed, from Dunkirk, but it had come back stripped of all its accoutrements. Every country in the world outside this island and the Empire to which we are indissolubly attached had given up on us, had made up their minds that our life was ended and our tale was told. But by unflinchingly despising the manifestations of power and the threats by which we were on all sides confronted, we have come through that dark and perilous passage, now once again masters of our own destiny.

Nor are we any longer alone. As I told the House of Commons, our own steadfast conduct and the crimes of the enemy have brought other great nations to our side. One of them is struggling with Herculean vigour and with results which are profoundly significant. The other, our kith and kin across the Atlantic Ocean, is straining every nerve to equip us with all we need to carry on the struggle regardless of cost to them or of risk to their sailors and ships. They are driving forward with supplies across the ocean and aiding us to strike down and strangle the foe who molests the passage of those supplies. Therefore we find ourselves today in a goodly company, and we are moving forward and we shall move forward steadily, however long the road may be.

I have never given any assurances of a speedy or easy or cheap victory. On the contrary, as you know, I have never promised anything but the hardest conditions, great disappointments, and many mistakes. But I am sure that at the end all will be well for us in our island home, all will be better for the world, and there will be that crown of honour to those who have endured and never failed which history will accord to them for having set an example to the whole human race.

Winston S. Churchill to Admiral Pound

(*Churchill papers, 20/36*)

7 November 1941

1. The 20 Assault Landing Craft, the 20 Heavy Support Craft and 127 Tank Landing Craft seem to me insufficient. This programme must be carefully concerted with the Army. Very large operations may be required in 1943.

2. What are 'Z' Craft?[1]

3. If a small floating dock is constructed in India, how long will it take and what alternative construction will it displace?

4. In view of the sad tale of the King George V class, it would be wrong to proceed with the construction of the *Lion*, let alone the later ones, without the whole design being examined by a conference of Sea Officers who have either commanded or used these ships. I favour the principle of three triple 16-inch gun turrets. What are your armour demands for 1942? If the question of design were satisfactorily settled, I would support making a beginning upon the turrets and mountings, provided of course that the tank programme is not interfered with.

5. Let me have the legend of the 100 Convoy Escort vessels to be built in the United States.

[1] A special type of naval vessel that I have also been unable to identify.

6. Let me have the list of the eleven new or modernized capital ships attributed to Germany, Italy or Japan at the end of 1943, and the list of our eleven. It seems probable that the war will be finished before any new capital ships can be built, i.e. 1947. If we win the war we shall disarm the enemy. If we lose it he will disarm us. The question cannot therefore be considered in the somewhat alarmist spirit of paragraph 9.

7. The new aircraft carrier must be weighed against other demands for armour and ship-building labour. How long will she take to make?

8. I agree to the three 6-inch cruisers and to the triple 8-inch turrets of one 8-inch gun cruiser.[1]

9. Let me have the brief legend for the 'Heavy Support Craft'.

10. You do not mention destroyers in your programme. I suppose this is because all the yards are fully booked up with them. Let me have a return showing what you have got building, dividing them into three classes and showing the rates at which each class can be built.

Winston S. Churchill: speech
(*'The Unrelenting Struggle', pages 280-1*)

8 November 1941 Town Hall
Sheffield

This great city so intimately interwoven with our war effort has undergone this storm of fire and steel and come through with many scars, but with the conviction that however hard may be the trial, and whatever the future may bring, Sheffield will not be unequal to it.

This foul war, forced on us by human wickedness, has now gone on for more than two years. None of us can say at what moment the bugles will sound the 'Cease Fire', but of this we may be sure that, however long and stern it may be, the British Nation and the British Commonwealth of Nations will come through united, undaunted, stainless, unflinching.

When we look back over the time that has passed since world peace was broken by the brutal assault upon Poland, we see the ups and downs through which we have gone. Many disappointments have occurred, very often many mistakes, but still when we look back to fifteen months ago and remember that then we were alone and almost unarmed, and we now see our armed forces developing their strength with modern weapons; when we look across the wide stretches of European land and see that great warrior Stalin at the head of his valiant Russians; when we look westward across the ocean and see the Americans sending their war vessels out to rid the seas of pirate vermin, in

[1] The 8-inch gun cruiser was never built.

order that they may carry to the fighting front line here, without regard to the opposition they may encounter, the weapons, munitions and food we require, it is a message of inspiration, because we are sure that before we get to the end of the road we shall all be together.

I urge you to continue your labours. The work of everyone is of vital importance. This is a struggle for life, a struggle in which every man and woman, old and young, can play a hero's part. The chance of glory and honour comes now here, now there, to each and every one. However hard the task may be I know you will all be ready for that high moment. God bless you all.

Winston S. Churchill: speech
(*'The Unrelenting Struggle', page 281*)

8 November 1941

James Neil and Company,
Munitions Factory
Sheffield

I give you my compliments and congratulate you on the way you are getting on with the war effort. The work you are doing plays a vital part in the war. Everyone who keeps his time is doing his best to rid the world of this curse of war and Hitlerism. I am proud to come among you because I am told you have lost only 4½ hours' time during air raids, although since January there have been 120 alerts. This is the way to stand up to it as the Artillery men do with their guns, as the sailors stand on watch, as the airmen do in cutting the enemy down from the high air. You are doing your bit in the same way. Their work cannot begin until yours is finished. We have only to hold together to go safely through the dark valley, and then we will see if we can make something lasting of our victory.[1]

[1] A report on Churchill's visit in the *Sheffield Telegraph and Independent* for 10 November 1941 began: 'The long cherished hope that Mr. Winston Churchill would see Sheffield in wartime was realised on Saturday, when, during two and a half hours' unheralded visit, he witnessed varied examples of the city's vital manufacturing processes in two factories, met municipal leaders and civil defence officials, and received an overwhelming ovation wherever he went. The people's welcome of the great national leader lacked nothing in warmth and spontaneity. It seemed that their joy at seeing him was all the greater because it was unexpected. He came amongst them as the grim, dour, determined Winston of popular conception. As they rushed out of side streets to greet him with cheers and hand-waving when he rode by in an open car beside the Lord Mayor, he repeated his old trick of holding aloft his hat on the end of his walking stick. Then to vary the form of acknowledgment, he gave the V sign, evoking waves of cheering.'

John Martin: diary
(*John Martin papers*)

8 November 1941

To Chequers. PM arrived back from tour of Hull, Sheffield etc. Heavy RAF losses last night and today.

Winston S. Churchill to H. G. Wells
(*Churchill papers, 20/30*)

8 November 1941
Private and Confidential

My dear Wells,

I have received your letter of November 2 sending me a copy of an article 'Raids and Raids' which you hope to publish shortly. I have read the article and I am grateful to you for having sent it to me.

Available shipping, sufficiency of escorts, preoccupations of our surface ships, distances in relation to surprise-approach, potential applicability of Air power on both sides, fate of friendly populations compromised but not defended, are all among the points which require and receive consideration.

Yours very sincerely,
Winston S. Churchill

Winston S. Churchill to Averell Harriman
(*Churchill papers, 20/44*)

8 November 1941
Private and Secret

Thank you so much for news about Harry.[1] Trust he will soon be better. Give him my kindest regards. I hope you have been taking care of yourself. Every good wish.

[1] Harry Hopkins. Earlier that day Averell Harriman had telegraphed to Churchill: 'You will be anxious, I am sure, to know about Harry. He has been working too much and his strength is literally exhausted. He is at the hospital for rest and treatment. I believe confidently there are no further complications and that in a couple of weeks he will be back on his feet. He is being kept away from his work in the meantime.' (Prime Minister's Personal Telegram T. 790, *Churchill papers, 20/44*)

Harry Hopkins to Winston S. Churchill
(*Churchill papers, 20/44*)

8 November 1941
Secret

I am not too sick to tell you that our tank production is exceeding our expectations and we are in the process now of planning a very substantial increase in our tanks for you and the Middle East.[1]

Winston S. Churchill to Harry Hopkins
(*Churchill papers, 20/44*)

9 November 1941
Personal and Secret

Delighted to hear from you, also to hear your news. Averell and Watson[2] have kept me well informed of your progress. Happy days will come again.

Winston S. Churchill to General Ismay, for the Chiefs of Staff Committee
(*Churchill papers, 20/36*)

9 November 1941
Action this Day

Let us hurry up the arrangements for sending volunteer pilots and airplanes to join Chennault's party.[3] Let me know what is proposed.

[1] Churchill sent copies of Hopkins' telegram to the Minister of Supply (Lord Beaverbrook), the Secretary of State for War (David Margesson) and the Secretary of State for Foreign Affairs (Anthony Eden).

[2] General Edwin Watson, Secretary and Personal Assistant to President Roosevelt. Known in the White House as 'Pa'. Roosevelt's biographer, James MacGregor Burns, wrote of him as 'another Southerner, genial, bluff, adept at letting the right people see his chief and mollifying the disappointed'. (*Roosevelt: The Soldier of Freedom*). He died in Algiers on the way back from the Yalta Conference, February 1945.

[3] The International Air Force in China, commanded by Major-General Claire L. Chennault, an American officer who had been a pilot in the First World War. Since 1937, having retired from the United States Army Air Force because of hearing problems, he had trained Chinese pilots in Chiang Kai-shek's air force. In 1941 he set up an American Volunteer Group – the Flying Tigers – of some 200 aircraft, which fought against the Japanese in China, and later in Burma. From July 1942 he commanded the China Air Task Force, and from March 1943 the Fourteenth United States Army Air Force.

Winston S. Churchill to President Franklin D. Roosevelt
(*Churchill papers, 20/44*)

9 November 1941
Personal and Secret

The destruction of the two Axis convoys destined for Benghazi, between Italy and Greece, is highly important both in itself and in its consequences.[1] It is also noteworthy that the two Italian heavy cruisers would not face our two 6-inch light cruisers, nor their six destroyers our two.[2]

I have also an increasingly good impression of the Moscow front.[3]

Winston S. Churchill to Field Marshal Smuts
(*Premier papers, 3/476/3*)

9 November 1941
Most Secret

Your Nos. 1339[4] and 772. I entirely agree with all you wish, but I do not think it would be any use for me to make a personal appeal to Roosevelt at this juncture to enter the war. At the Atlantic Meeting I told his circle that I would rather have an American declaration of war now and no supplies for six months than double the supplies and no declaration. When this was repeated to him he thought it a hard saying. We must not underrate his Constitutional difficulties. He may take action as Chief Executive, but only Congress can declare war. He went so far as to say to me, 'I shall never declare war; I shall make war. If I were to ask Congress to declare war they might argue about it

[1] Nine out of ten supply ships were sunk and the tenth was left burning. There were no British casualties or damage. Three Italian destroyers were sunk and two damaged.

[2] The destruction of the convoy had only been possible because of intercepted messages which, when decyphered, had given in advance the precise route and timing of the convoys and their escorts. Churchill was worried lest the secrecy of Britain's signals intelligence had been endangered. 'C' was asked about a signal from Malta giving details of the convoy, and replied reassuringly: 'The Malta signal was sent out as the result of an aircraft sighting, which quite naturally corresponded with our own Most Secret information. The signal, however, was based on the aircraft sighting and not on our material. No security, therefore, was disregarded.' ('Most Secret', C/8035, 12 November 1941: *Cabinet papers, 120/766*)

[3] German troops had been considerably slowed down in their advance towards Moscow. But on the Leningrad front the town of Tikhvin was captured, and Leningrad effectively besieged.

[4] On 4 November 1941 Churchill had received a discouraging telegram from General Smuts. 'I am struck,' wrote Smuts, 'by the growth of the impression here and elsewhere that the war is going to end in stalemate and thus fatally for us.' Smuts believed that the principal need and urgency was the entry of the United States into the war, which, he believed, 'may decisively warn off Japan and do more than anything else in keeping Russia in the war'. It was essential, Smuts argued, for Churchill to intervene personally with Roosevelt. 'I trust you are on the lookout,' Smuts added, 'for the right moment and manner of appeal to him for action.' (Telegram No. 1339, 'Secret', 4 November 1941: *Premier papers, 3/476/3, folio 35*)

for three months.' The draft Bill without which the American Army would have gone to pieces passed by only one vote. He has now carried through the Senate by a small majority the virtual repeal of the Neutrality Act. This must mean, if endorsed by the other House, constant fighting in the Atlantic between German and American ships. Public opinion in the United States has advanced lately, but with Congress it is all a matter of counting heads. Naturally, if I saw any way of helping to lift this situation on to a higher plane I would do so. In the meanwhile we must have patience and trust to the tide which is flowing our way and to events.

2. Your 772. I have sent you in my telegram No. 1259 a message I sent the President some days ago about Chiang Kai-shek. So far I have received no answer.

Winston S. Churchill to C. E. Thomas[1]

(*Churchill papers, 20/22*)

9 November 1941

Dear Mr Thomas,

Thank you for forwarding me the cigar which was sent you by the Secretary of the 'Fox and Geese' Comforts Fund, Ickenham, Middlesex.

I thank you also for your kind expressions. It gives me pain to read the bitter, vitriolic articles and propaganda in which the *Daily Mirror* and *Sunday Pictorial* specialize. It is remarkable that they do not do more harm in the Services and workshops. Considering their great ability your writers are playing a poor part in this long struggle and certainly one which adds to my load.

Yours very truly,
Winston S. Churchill

Winston S. Churchill: speech

(*BBC Written Archives Centre*)

10 November 1941 — Mansion House
London

Alike in times of peace and war the annual Civic Festival we have observed today has been by long custom the occasion for a speech at the Guildhall by the Prime Minister upon foreign affairs.

This year our ancient Guildhall lies in ruins, our foreign affairs are shrunken and almost the whole of Europe is prostrate under Nazi tyranny.

[1] Cecil Thomas, Editor of the *Daily Mirror* from 1934 to 1948. During his editorship the circulation doubled to 1,700,000 and it was recognized as the newspaper of the Forces.

The war which Hitler began by invading Poland and which now engulfs the European continent has broken into the north-east of Africa; may well involve the greater part of Asia; nay, it may soon spread to the remaining portions of the globe. Nevertheless, in the same spirit in which you, my Lord Mayor,[1] have celebrated your assumption of office with the time-honoured pageant of Lord Mayor's Day, so I, who have the honour to be your guest, will endeavour to play, though very briefly – for in wartime speeches should be short – the traditional part assigned to those who hold my office.

The condition of Europe is terrible in the last degree. Hitler's firing parties are busy every day in a dozen countries. Norwegians, Belgians, Frenchmen, Dutch, Poles, Czechs, Serbs, Croats, Slovenes, Greeks, and above all in scale Russians, are being butchered by thousands and by tens of thousands after they have surrendered, while individual and mass executions in all the countries I have mentioned have become a part of the regular German routine. The world has been intensely stirred by the massacre of the French hostages. The whole of France, with the exception of the small clique whose public careers depend upon a German victory, has been united in horror and indignation against this slaughter of perfectly innocent people. Admiral Darlan's tributes to German generosity fall unseasonably at this moment on French ears, and his plans for loving collaboration with the conquerors and the murderers of Frenchmen are quite appreciably embarrassed. Nay, even the arch-criminal himself, the Nazi ogre Hitler, has been frightened by the volume and passion of world indignation which his spectacular atrocity has excited. It is he and not the French people who have been intimidated. He has not dared to go forward with his further programme of killing hostages.

This, as you will have little doubt, is not due to mercy, to compassion, to compunction, but to fear, and to a dawning consciousness of personal insecurity rising in a wicked heart.

I would say generally that we must regard all these victims of the Nazi executioners in so many lands, who are labelled Communists and Jews – we must regard them just as if they were brave soldiers who die for their country on the field of battle. Nay, in a way their sacrifice may be more fruitful than that of the soldier who falls with his arms in his hands. A river of blood has flowed and is flowing between the German race and the peoples of nearly all Europe. It is not the hot blood of battle where good blows are given and returned. It is the cold blood of the execution yard and the scaffold, which leaves a stain indelible for generations and for centuries.

Here then are the foundations upon which the New Order of Europe is to be inaugurated. Here then is the house-warming festival of the *Herrenvolk*. Here then is the system of terrorism by which the Nazi criminals and their quisling accomplices seek to rule a dozen ancient famous States of Europe and

[1] Sir John Dawson Laurie, 1872–1954. A contemporary of Churchill at Harrow.

if possible all the free nations of the world. In no more effective manner could they have frustrated the accomplishment of their own designs. The future and its mysteries are inscrutable. But one thing is plain. Never to those blood-stained accursed hands will the future of Europe be confided.

Since Lord Mayor's Day last year some great changes have taken place in our situation. Then we were alone, the sole champion of freedom. Then we were ill-armed and far outnumbered even in the Air. Now a large part of the United States Navy, as Colonel Knox has told us, is constantly in action against the common foe. Now the valiant resistance of the Russian nation has inflicted most frightful injuries upon the German military power, and at the present moment the German invading armies, after all their losses, lie on the barren steppes exposed to the approaching severities of the Russian winter. Now we have an Air Force which is at last at least equal in size and numbers, not to speak of quality, to the German Air Power.

Rather more than a year ago I announced to Parliament that we were sending a battle fleet back into the Mediterranean. The destruction of the German and Italian convoys – and the Admiralty brings today the news of the destruction of another Italian destroyer – the passage of our own supplies in many directions through that sea, the broken morale of the Italian navy, all these show that we are still the masters there.

Today I am able to go further. Owing to the effective help we are getting in the Atlantic from the United States, owing to the sinking of the *Bismarck*, owing to the completion of our splendid new battleships and aircraft carriers of the largest size, as well as to the cowing of the Italian navy already mentioned, I am able to go further and announce to you here at the Lord Mayor's annual celebration that we now feel ourselves strong enough to provide a powerful naval force of heavy ships, with its necessary ancillary vessels, for service if needed in the Indian and Pacific Oceans. Thus we stretch out the long arm of brotherhood and motherhood to the Australian and New Zealand peoples and to the peoples of India, whose armies and troops have already been fighting with so much distinction in the Mediterranean theatre. And this movement of our naval forces, in conjunction with the United States Main Fleet, may give a practical proof to all who have eyes to see that the forces of freedom and democracy have not by any means reached the limits of their power.

I must admit that, having voted for the Japanese alliance nearly forty years ago, in 1902, and having always done my very best to promote good relations with the Island Empire of Japan, and always having been a sentimental well-wisher to the Japanese and an admirer of their many gifts and qualities, I should view with keen sorrow the opening of a conflict between Japan and the English-speaking world.

The United States' time-honoured interests in the Far East are well known. They are doing their utmost to find ways of preserving peace in the Pacific.

We do not know whether their efforts will be successful, but should they fail I take this occasion to say, and it is my duty to say, that, should the United States become involved in war with Japan, the British declaration will follow within the hour.

Viewing the vast sombre scene as dispassionately as possible, it would seem a very hazardous adventure for the Japanese people to plunge quite needlessly into a world struggle in which they may well find themselves opposed in the Pacific by States whose populations comprise nearly three-quarters of the human race. If steel is the basic foundation of modern war, it would be rather dangerous for a power like Japan, whose steel production is only about 7 million tons a year, to provoke quite gratuitously a struggle with the United States, whose steel production is now about 90 millions; and this would take no account of the powerful contribution which the British Empire can make. I hope therefore that the peace of the Pacific will be preserved in accordance with the known wishes of Japan's wisest statesmen. But every preparation to defend British interests in the Far East, and to defend the common cause now at stake, has been and is being made.

Meanwhile, how can we watch without emotion the wonderful defence of their native soil and of their freedom and independence which has been maintained single-handed, all alone, for five long years by the Chinese people under the leadership of that great Asiatic hero and Commander, General Chiang Kai-shek? It would be a disaster of the first magnitude to world civilization if the noble resistance to invasion and exploitation which has been made by the whole Chinese race were not to result in the liberation of their hearths and homes. That, I feel is a sentiment which is deep in all our hearts.

To return for a moment before I sit down to the contrast between our position now and a year ago, I must remind you, I do not need to remind you here in the City, that this time last year we did not know where to turn for a dollar across the American exchange. By very severe measures we had been able to gather and spend in America about £500,000,000 sterling, but the end of our financial resources was in sight – nay, had actually been reached. All we could do at that time a year ago was to place orders in the United States without being able to see our way through, but on a tide of hope and not without important encouragement.

Then came the majestic policy of the President and Congress of the United States in passing the Lend and Lease Bill, under which in two successive enactments about £3,000,000,000 sterling were dedicated to the cause of world freedom without – mark this, for it is unique – the setting up of any account in money. Never again let us hear the taunt that money is the ruling thought or power in the hearts of the American democracy. The Lend and Lease Bill must be regarded without question as the most unsordid act in the whole of recorded history.

We for our part have not been found unworthy of the increasing aid we are receiving. We have made unparalleled financial and economic sacrifices ourselves, and now that the Government and people of the United States have declared their resolve that the aid they are giving shall reach the fighting lines, we shall be able to strike with all our might and main.

Thus we may, without exposing ourselves to any change of complacency, without in the slightest degree relaxing the intensity of our war effort, give thanks to Almighty God for the many wonders which have been wrought in so brief a space of time, and we may derive fresh confidence from all that has happened and bend ourselves to our task with all the force that is in our souls and with every drop of blood that is in our bodies.

We are told from many quarters that we must soon expect what is called a 'peace offensive' from Berlin. All the usual signs and symptoms are already manifest, as the Foreign Secretary will confirm, in neutral countries, and all these signs point in one direction. They all show that the guilty men who have let Hell loose upon the world are hoping to escape with their fleeting triumphs and ill-gotten plunders, from the closing net of doom.

We owe it to ourselves, we owe it to our Russian Ally, and to the Government and people of the United States, to make it absolutely clear that whether we are supported or alone, however long and hard the toil may be, the British nation and His Majesty's Government in intimate concert with the Governments of the great Dominions will never enter into any negotiations with Hitler or any party in Germany which represents the Nazi régime. In that resolve, we are sure that the ancient City of London will be with us to the hilt and to the end.

Winston S. Churchill to General Ismay, for the Chiefs of Staff Committee
(*Churchill papers, 20/36*)

10 November 1941
Action this Day
Most Secret

1. Middle East HQ are still toying with 'Whipcord'[1] for the spring. We cannot afford to send any landing craft from here round the Cape, as they would be out of action at both ends for three months. While studying the diversion raid against 'Truncheon'[2] an alternative against 'Yorker'[3] must also be considered, as this would lead to something, whereas the former is only an episode.

2. Let me have a report of progress of preparations for 'Gymnast'.[4]

[1] The planned British invasion of Sicily.
[2] The British plan for a landing at Livorno (Leghorn) in north-west Italy.
[3] The planned capture of Sardinia: this was postponed until 1943.
[4] The planned landing in French North Africa.

Winston S. Churchill: Oral Answers
(*Hansard*)

11 November 1941 House of Commons

MONTENEGRO (ITALIAN ATROCITIES)

Commander Sir Archibald Southby:[1] asked the Prime Minister whether his attention has been called to the atrocities being committed against the civilian population by Italian punitive expeditions into Montenegro; and why military objectives in Rome have not been bombed as a reprisal?

49. Sir T. Moore[2] asked the Prime Minister whether there is any technical political or other objection to the bombing of Rome by our Air Forces?

The Prime Minister (Mr Churchill): While I have no information of any particularly brutal Italian atrocities in Montenegro – I mean nothing out of the ordinary compared with their usual behaviour – I have recently made it clear that retribution for crimes of such a nature must henceforward take its place amongst the major purposes of the war. As regards the bombing of Rome, I have nothing to add to the statement in my speech to this House on 30th September.

Sir A. Southby: Will my right hon. Friend say why Rome has not been bombed; is he aware of the propaganda now being carried on in this country with the object of abolishing night bombing; and will he consider the significance of this agitation arising just at the moment that our position of being able to bomb our enemy objectives is getting better and better?

The Prime Minister: I do not see what the last part has to do with the Question on the Paper, which is fully covered by my Answer.

Sir T. Moore: Does my right hon. Friend really think it is wise to provide a hide-out for this rat Mussolini?

The Prime Minister: I thing it would be as well to have confidence in the decision of the Government, whose sole desire is to inflict the maximum amount of injury on the enemy.

ATLANTIC CHARTER (PRIME MINISTER'S ADVISERS)

Sir W. Smithers[3] asked the Prime Minister the names of the personal advisers who accompanied him on his recent voyage in a British battleship when he met the President of the United States of America; and what were their duties?

[1] Conservative Member of Parliament for Epsom, see page 274, note 2.

[2] Thomas Cecil Russell Moore, 1886–1971. Educated at Trinity College Dublin. Entered the Army, 1908. On active service in France, 1914–15. General Headquarters, Ireland, 1916–18. On active service in Russia, 1918–20; Ireland, 1920–23 (OBE, 1918, CBE, 1919, despatches twice). Retired with the rank of Lieutenant-Colonel, 1925. Conservative MP for Ayr Burgh, 1925–50; Ayr, 1950–64. Knighted, 1937. Created Baronet, 1956.

[3] Waldron Smithers, 1880–1954. Member of the London Stock Exchange. Conservative Member of Parliament for Chislehurst, 1924–45; for Orpington, 1945–54. Knighted, 1934.

The Prime Minister: I am circulating in the Official Report the names of those who accompanied me on my recent voyage when I met the President of the United States of America.

Sir W. Smithers: If Lord Cherwell was one of the members of the party, does not my right hon. Friend think it unwise – [Interruption].

Mr Kirkwood:[1] Seeing that the Prime Minister has met President Roosevelt, when is he to meet Mr Joseph Stalin?

Following are the names:[2]

Henry Channon: diary

('Chips')

11 November 1941

In the Commons the Prime Minister was in a bellicose mood; he answered Questions ungraciously, especially one about the 'Prof', Lord Cherwell.

I went to the smoking-room and ordered brandy and ginger ale. Nearby sat Sir Waldron Smithers, an ass of a man, alone. Suddenly the Prime Minister, attended by Harvie-Watt,[3] entered and they, too, sat down. Suddenly the Prime Minister saw Smithers, and rose, and bellowing at him like an infuriated bull, roared: 'Why in Hell did you ask that Question? Don't you know that he (Lord Cherwell) is one of my oldest and greatest friends?' – the unfortunate Member for Chislehurst tried to defend himself – but the Prime Minister, still shaking, refused to listen or be pacified, and went on 'You make protestations of loyalty – I won't have it. President Roosevelt was most impressed by him.' And so forth – It was an extraordinary scene. The 'Prof' otherwise 'Baron Berlin', or, correctly, The Lord Cherwell, has long since been a subject of speculation to the House, and from time to time there have been questions and veiled innuendos reflecting on his Teutonic origin. But Winston's almost blind loyalty to his friends is one of his most endearing qualities.

[1] David Kirkwood, 1872–1955. Trained as an engineer on the Clyde. Active in the Trade Union movement, Clydeside. Deported from the Clyde, 1916, for organizing a protest against an increase in house rents. A Member of the Glasgow Town Council, 1918–22. Labour MP for Clydebank Dumbarton Burghs, 1922–50; for Dumbartonshire, 1950–1. Privy Councillor, 1948. Created Baron, 1951. In 1935 he published *My Life of Revolt* (with a foreword by Churchill).

[2] Churchill then read out the names, including Lord Cherwell, of those who had accompanied him to the meeting with Roosevelt.

[3] George Steven Harvie-Watt, 1903–89. Called to the Bar, 1930. Conservative MP, 1937–59. Assistant Government Whip, 1938–40. Lieutenant-Colonel commanding the 31st Battalion, Royal Engineers, Territorial Army, 1938–41; Brigadier, 6th Anti-Aircraft Brigade, 1941. Parliamentary Private Secretary to the Prime Minister (Churchill), July 1941 to July 1945. Created Baronet, 1945. He published his memoirs, *Most of My Life*, in 1980.

Colonel George Harvie-Watt: recollection
(*'Most of my Life'*)

[11 November 1941] [House of Commons]

On 11th November 1941 Waldron Smithers, a bumbling sort of chap with his heart in the right place, asked some critical questions in the House about Lord Cherwell and hinted that he was an alien. The PM was livid, rightly so, and said in an aside to me 'Love me, love my dog, and if you don't love my dog you damn well can't love me.' Afterwards Winston left the Chamber of the House with me and went to the Smoke Room. I've never seen him in such a temper before. Later Waldron Smithers came up with his tail between his legs and started grovelling to Winston who told him to get the hell out of here and not to speak to him again. Poor Smithers got the shock of his life.

Anthony Eden: diary
(*'The Reckoning'*)

11 November 1941

Winston told me that he had had a difficult morning in House, fifteen questions and many supplementaries. He felt resentful. Maisky came to see us both at noon, to give Stalin's answer. This was sharp and critical, though I believe the presentation to be worse than the substance. Anyway Winston was, excusably, very angry and pretty rough with Maisky.

J. V. Stalin to Winston S. Churchill
(*Cabinet papers, 65/24*)

Handed to the Prime Minister by Ambassador Maisky[1]
11 November 1941

Your message received on 7th November.

1. I fully agree with you that clarity should be established in the relations between the USSR and Great Britain. Such a clarity does not exist at present. The lack of clarity is the consequence of two circumstances:

(a) There is no definite understanding between our two countries on war aims and on plans of the post-war organization of peace.

(b) There is no agreement between the USSR and Great Britain on mutual military assistance against Hitler in Europe.

[1] This telegram had been sent from the Kremlin, Moscow, on 8 November 1941; Churchill sent copies to the King, Anthony Eden, Lord Beaverbrook, Sir Edward Bridges and Major Morton.

As long as there is no accord on both these questions there can be no clarity in the Anglo-Soviet relations. More than that: to be quite frank, as long as the present situation exists there will be difficulty to secure mutual confidence. Of course, agreement on military supplies to the USSR has a great positive value, but it does not settle, neither does it exhaust, the whole problem of relations between our two countries. If the General Wavell and the General Paget, whom you mention in your message, will come to Moscow with a view to conclude agreement on two fundamental questions referred to above, I naturally would be happy to meet them and to discuss with them these questions. If, however, the mission of the Generals is confined to the questions of information, and to the consideration of secondary matters, it would not be, I think, worth while to intrude upon the Generals. In such a case, it would be also very difficult for me to find time for the conversations.

2. It seems to me an intolerable situation has been created in the question of the declaration of war by Great Britain to Finland, Hungary and Roumania. The Soviet Government raised this question with the British Government through the secret diplomatic channels. Quite unexpectedly for the USSR the whole problem – beginning with the request of the Soviet Government to the British Government and ending with the consideration of this question by the United States Government – received wide publicity. The whole problem is now being discussed at random in the Press – friendly as well as the enemy. And after all that, the British Government informs us of its negative attitude to our proposal. Why is all this being done? To demonstrate the lack of unity between the USSR and Great Britain?

3. You can rest assured that we are taking all the necessary measures for speedy transportation to the right place of all the arms coming from Great Britain to Archangel. The same will be done with regard to the route through Iran. In this connection, may I call your attention to the fact (although this is a minor matter) that tanks, planes and artillery are arriving inefficiently packed, that sometimes parts of the same vehicle are loaded in different ships, that planes, because of the imperfect packing, reach us broken?

Oliver Harvey: diary

(*'The War Diaries of Oliver Harvey, 1941-1945'*)

11 November 1941

Maisky brought the PM and AE this morning Stalin's reply to the message about Wavell. It was pretty stiff and Stalin is evidently feeling out in the cold. He complained that there was no real confidence or cooperation between the two countries because there had been no discussion about future military strategy or post-war cooperation. If the British generals could discuss both these problems, they would be welcome, if not, Stalin wouldn't have time for them. Finally, Stalin said our attitude in refusing to declare war on Finland etc. after his repeated requests was 'intolerable'.

PM bit Maisky and said that it was not our fault that there had been no planning before Russia came into the war when coordination of plans would have made the whole difference.

War Cabinet: Confidential Annex
(*Cabinet papers, 65/24*)

11 November 1941
5 p.m.

The Prime Minister read to the War Cabinet a copy of the telegram which (in accordance with the conclusion of the War Cabinet on 3rd November) he had sent to Premier Stalin on the 4th November, dealing with –

(a) the proposal to send Generals Wavell and Paget to Moscow:
(b) the proposed declaration of war on Finland, Hungary and Roumania:
(c) the despatch of the *Prince of Wales* to the Far East,
and other matters.

He also read the reply, dated the 8th November which had been handed to him that day (11th November) by M. Maisky.

When M. Maisky had handed him the telegram, he had said that a telegram of this kind could not be answered. There had been some frank speaking, in which he explained that if Russia had only let us know that they were coming into the war on our side, matters might have been different. As regards the suggestion in M. Stalin's telegram of the 8th November that we should now reach a definite understanding on war aims and on plans for the post-war organization of peace, he had said that we could not go beyond the Atlantic Charter now. At the end of the meeting, he (Prime Minister) had said that he would consult the Cabinet.

The Prime Minister said that he was strongly convinced that the right course was not to send any reply for, say, a week, more especially as it was clear that the Russians did not wish for a visit from Generals Wavell and Paget.

The Foreign Secretary said that he would like to tell M. Maisky that M. Stalin's message was such that the Prime Minister and the War Cabinet could not be expected to reply to it immediately. He thought that this might lead to M. Maisky saying that we had taken the message in the wrong way, and that this might lead to some improvement in the atmosphere.

The Prime Minister said he felt sure that the right course was to leave the letter unanswered for a week or so. Only harm would come for an attempt to answer points in a message such as had now been received.

After further discussion, the War Cabinet agreed as follows:

(1) When the Foreign Secretary saw M. Maisky on the following day, he should inform him that it was not possible to send any reply for the present to M. Stalin's telegram of the 8th November, since it raised such very large issues. He could add that the Prime Minister and the War Cabinet were pained and surprised at the tone and contents of the message. He would also say that the Minister of Supply proposed to discuss with M. Maisky the points about the package of tanks, planes and artillery, which should have been brought directly to his notice;

(2) The Foreign Secretary was authorized to send to Sir Stafford Cripps a copy of the message received from M. Stalin, and to inform him of our attitude in regard to it.

Arising out of the above, some further discussion took place in regard to the proposed declaration of war by Great Britain on Finland, Hungary and Roumania. The disadvantages of this course, more particularly in regard to Finland, had become increasingly strong during the last week or so. But it was fair to point out that we had gone a long way towards telling the Russians that if they pressed the point strongly we would declare war on Finland.

Nevertheless, the general view of the War Cabinet was that we should not take this step at the moment.

The Prime Minister pointed out that the step was one we could always take, but, once taken, it was irrevocable. If the matter was raised in Parliament, we should say that the issues were complicated and would take time to settle. If there was any risk of discussion of the matter in the House, it would be necessary to go into Secret Session at once.

FAR EAST

The Foreign Secretary referred to a letter received by the Prime Minister from the Dutch Government which raised again the question of giving a guarantee to the Dutch in the event of an attack by Japan on the Dutch East Indies. Mr Eden said that we might be criticized for promising to declare war on Japan in the event of her attacking the United States whilst withholding such a promise from the Dutch if the Dutch East Indies was attacked.

The Prime Minister said that a serious situation would arise if we were committed to declare war on Japan and were not assured that the United States would come in too. Should the Japanese land in the Dutch East Indies the temperature in America would immediately rise. It would therefore be wiser to see how the situation developed as a result of such an event than that we should be committed to such action beforehand.

Winston S. Churchill to Admiral Pound
(*Churchill papers, 20/36*)

11 November 1941
Action this Day
Secret

I should like to talk over with you again the idea of *Prince of Wales* being entirely separated from her two destroyers. I do not quite see what all this haste is to arrive at Singapore for a pow-wow. This is one of those cases where I am for 'Safety First'.

Winston S. Churchill to General Chiang Kai-shek
(*Churchill papers, 20/44*)

11 November 1941
Secret

I have been earnestly considering your message. I am very sensible of the grave dangers to which you draw attention and admire the spirit in which you face this new threat to China.

2. My information also suggests that South China may be Japan's next objective. But I am not sure that Japan has finally made up her mind to attack Kunming. My military advisers consider that for so difficult an enterprise Japanese will need to assemble at least four to five divisions. Their forces in Tongking do not yet appear to have reached half that strength. Nevertheless, I fully appreciate the serious consequences if they were to succeed in taking Kunming.

3. While, therefore, I cannot disregard the possibility that Japan may yet intend in the near future to strike elsewhere against territories where she would hope to obtain the materials of which our embargo is depriving her, I am examining with all speed in what way we could, with the resources at our disposal, help to strengthen the International Air Force and to enable it to give you as expeditiously as possible support in personnel and material. Our Commander-in-Chief in the Far East reports that Chennault will be ready to move into China with three squadrons in about a fortnight, and he has sent a staff officer to learn Chennault's exact state and how we can best help him. I will keep in touch with you, and hope to be able to tell you soon more definitely what we may be able to do to help.

I have, of course, communicated with the President of the United States, doing all I could.

Winston S. Churchill to Sir Archibald Sinclair
and Air Chief Marshal Sir Charles Portal
(*Churchill papers, 20/36*)

11 November 1941
Action this Day

1. The losses sustained both by the night bombers and day fighters have been lately very heavy.[1] There is no need to press unduly the offensive by the fighters over France; about two sweeps a month instead of four should be sufficient combined with a continuance of the attacks on shipping. While the degree of attack may be lightened, the impression of its continuance should be sustained.

2. I have several times in Cabinet deprecated forcing the night bombing of Germany without due regard to weather conditions. There is no particular point at this time in bombing Berlin.[2] The losses sustained last week were most grievous. We cannot afford losses on that scale in view of the failure of the American bomber programme. Losses which are acceptable in a battle or for some decisive military objective ought not to be incurred merely as a matter of routine. There is no need to fight the weather and the enemy at the same time.

3. It is now the duty of both Fighter and Bomber Command to re-gather their strength for the spring.

4. Let me have a full report about the heavy losses of bombers on the night of the last heavy raid on Berlin.

Winston S. Churchill to Oliver Lyttelton
(*Churchill papers, 20/45*)

11 November 1941

I could find no answer but silence to your and Auchinleck's telegrams about 'Crusader'. No view can be taken of the future until we know how this goes. A battle is a veil through which it is not wise to peer.

[1] On the night of 7–8 November 1941, on the heaviest British bombing raid of the war over Berlin, of 169 aircraft taking part, 21 had been lost, most of them owing to freak severe weather. That same night, of 55 bombers that bombed Mannheim, seven were lost, again largely because of the bad weather. On the night of November 8–9 on a bombing raid on Essen by 54 aircraft, six were lost.

[2] No subsequent major bombing raid took place over Berlin until January 1943.

Anthony Eden: diary
(*'The Reckoning'*)

11 November 1941

In evening before dinner Winston and I and Max discussed whole business, Max and I being the men of peace. Meanwhile there will surely be more trouble with Cripps, whose idea is to come home and play a part here.

Dined with Winston, Brendan only other present. W talked of future and suddenly said that if anything happened to him I should have to take over. Brendan approved. Announcement was repeated later when Chief Whip and P.J.[1] came in. I am unhappy that Jack Dill is to be moved.[2] I am convinced that Winston underrates him. He did not consult me on this, merely remarking that he had taken his decision and adding: 'I know that you will not agree.'

Winston S. Churchill: speech
(*Hansard*)

12 November 1941 House of Commons

DEBATE ON THE ADDRESS

I have heard many Debates upon occasions like this in the years off and on – mostly on – during which I have been in Parliament, and I know well that it is a ceremonial occasion on which the foils have the buttons securely fastened to their tips and complimentary exchanges are made. I think there was a note of warm kindliness in both the speeches which came from the leaders representative of the two parties opposite. I am particularly grateful for the appreciation and encouragement which those two right hon. Gentlemen gave to His Majesty's Government. We have had two speeches from the Mover and Seconder of the Address which everyone will feel were adequate to the occasion – very excellent speeches from a Member who has in this war already gained the Military Cross[3] and also from my hon. Friend the Member for the Brightside Division (Mr Marshall)[4] who in Sheffield has not been far from the fighting front.

It has been aptly remarked that Ministers, and indeed all other public men,

[1] James Stuart, and P.J. Grigg, Permanent Under-Secretary of State for War.

[2] Churchill had decided to replace General Sir John Dill as Chief of the Imperial General Staff by General Sir Alan Brooke, Commander-in-Chief, Home Forces. Brooke was to remain CIGS until the end of the war.

[3] Captain Richard Pilkington, Conservative Member of Parliament for Widnes (1935–45), and a member of the Coldstream Guards Reserve of Officers, who appeared in the debate wearing his army uniform. From 1942 to 1945 he was Civil Lord of the Admiralty.

[4] Fred Marshall, 1883–1962. Educated at Elementary School. Member of the Sheffield City Council, 1919; Alderman, 1926. Lord Mayor, City of Sheffield, 1933–34. Labour Member of Parliament for Sheffield Brightside, 1930–31 and 1935–50. Parliamentary Secretary, Ministry of Town and Country Planning, 1945–47.

when they make speeches at the present time have always to bear in mind three audiences: first, our own fellow countrymen; secondly, our friends abroad; and thirdly, the enemy. This naturally makes the task of public speaking very difficult. Yet under our Parliamentary and democratic system, Government Ministers are frequently called upon to make speeches in both Houses of Parliament and in the country at war savings meetings and the like. We have over eighty Ministers in the Government and they cannot all be equally informed about the general course of affairs and military operations.

It is not possible for me with my other duties to read all the Ministerial speeches, and of course many of our Ministers are natural orators and speak entirely extemporaneously and on the spur of the moment. In those circumstances, as anyone can see, one may easily find discrepancies arising. These discrepancies when they occur immediately attract the attention of our faithful and vigilant Press and are paraded as examples of ministerial discordance, or at any rate lack of concert. I hope therefore that those who feel that their war work lies especially in the direction of criticism will make allowances for these difficulties inherent in the situation. I hope they will also remember that no sensible person in war-time makes speeches because he wants to. He makes them because he has to and to no one does this apply more than to the Prime Minister. I have repeatedly called attention to the disadvantages of my having to give too frequent reviews of the war, and I have always declined to be drawn into discussions about strategy or tactics so far as they may have relation to current or pending events. The House has shown me great indulgence in this matter, but I feel that I should be excused today from entering upon discussion of the war position, to which I referred in a speech I made only a month ago. Most of all shall I refrain from making any prediction about the future. It is a month ago that I remarked upon the long silence of Herr Hitler, a remark which apparently provoked him to make a speech in which he told the German people that Moscow would fall in a few days. That shows, as everyone I am sure will agree, how much wiser he would have been to go on keeping his mouth shut.

Even I, in my modest way, run great risks of giving dissatisfaction when I speak. Some people are very hard to please. It is impossible to please everybody; whatever you say, some fault can be found. If, for instance, I were to pay – as I should like to pay – strong tribute to the splendid heroism and undaunted gallantry of our Russian Allies, I should immediately be answered, 'Let us have deeds, not words.' If I were to omit all reference to Russian bravery, it would, on the other hand, be said, 'Not even one kindly word was spoken to cheer on these heroes.' If I were to describe the help in detail which we are giving to Russia, that might be very interesting but it would give away to the enemy secrets which are Russian as well as British. Again, if I gave an appreciation of the fighting on the Russian front, I should get hit either way. If my account were favourable, I should be accused of fostering complacency.

On the other hand, if it were grave, I should be accused of spreading needless despondency and alarm, and the Russians would not thank me for underrating or disparaging their giant strength. I must mention these facts merely as illustrations of the difficulties and dangers of making too many speeches about the war at times like these, and to give a respectful explanation to the House of why, with one fleeting exception, I am not going to refer today to any of the changing phases of this tremendous struggle.

I am, however, able to give some information about the war at sea. The house will remember the very good reasons which were given for leaving off publishing monthly figures of sinkings by enemy action and how these precise periodical statements, made at too frequent intervals, gave the enemy valuable information as to how his varying tactics were succeeding; but there is no objection to giving exact figures for longer periods, and I take this occasion to give figures of the last four months, ending with October, without dividing them into months, and compared with the figures, already published, of the four preceding months, ending with June. They are certainly well worthy of mention. I am speaking in round numbers. In the four months ending with June, we lost just over 2,000,000 tons, or an average of 500,000 tons per month. In the last four months, ending with October, we lost less than 750,000 tons, or an average of 180,000 per month. 180,000 contrasts very favourably with 500,000 tons. I see opposite me my right hon. Friend, the Member for Carnarvon Boroughs (Mr Lloyd George). We shared, I in a very humble position but with full knowledge, the terrible anxieties of 1917. We saw the figures mount, but we also saw the sudden fall. However, we must not count at all that the danger is past, but the facts are more favourable than are represented by the reduction on the four-monthly period from 500,000 to 180,000, because, from the point of view of keeping alive our power to wage war at sea and of increasing it, you have to take account not only of what is lost but of new building. You have to deduct the new building and see how the position stands. I do not intend to give exact figures about new building, but, making allowance for new building, the net loss of our Mercantile Marine, apart altogether from captures from the enemy and United States assistance, has been reduced in the last four months to a good deal less than one fifth of what it was in the previous four months. That is an impressive fact. This has been done in spite of the fact that there were never more U-boats or more long-range aircraft working than there are now. While that fact should lead us to increase our successful exertions and should in no way favour an easy habit of mind, it does, I think, give solid and sober assurances, as was mentioned by my right hon. Friend earlier, that we shall be able to maintain our seaborne traffic until the great American shipbuilding promised for 1942 comes into service. The United States are, of course, building new merchant ships on a scale many times what we are able to do in this Island. Having regard to the many calls upon us, our new shipbuilding is confined to a certain proportion of our resources, but the United States are embarking on an output of ships incomparably greater than what we can produce and far surpassing the enormous efforts they successfully made in the last war. If we are able to get through this year, we shall certainly find ourselves in good supply of ships in 1942. If the war against the U-boats and the enemy aircraft continues to prosper as it has done – about which there can be, of course, no guarantee – the Freedom Powers will be possessed of large quantities of shipping in 1943, which will enable oversea operations to take place utterly beyond British resources at the present time.

Meanwhile, the destruction of enemy shipping is proceeding with even greater violence that before. During the four months ended October, there were sunk or seriously damaged nearly 1,000,000 tons. In the Mediterranean, the enemy's losses have been particularly severe, and there is evidence that he has found it very difficult to reinforce, or even to supply, his armies on the African shores. This last convoy was a particularly valuable one, and its total destruction, together with the devastation being wrought by our submarines in the Mediterranean, is certainly very much to be rejoiced over. There are at least 40,000 Italian women, children and non-combatants in Abyssinia. Some time ago, guided by humanitarian instincts, we offered to let the Italian Government take these people home, if they would send under the necessary safeguards their own shipping to the ports on the Red Sea. The Italian Government accepted this proposal, and agreement was reached on all the details, but they have never been able so far to send the ships specified, because the destruction of their ships has proceeded at such a high rate and to such a serious extent. All this makes me hopeful – although, of course, I will not prophesy – that the German and Italian boasts that they will take Suez by the end of May last, will very likely remain unfulfilled at Christmas. That is much more than we had any right to expect when the Italian Government declared war upon us and the French deserted us in the Mediterranean eighteen months ago.

The fact that our shipping losses have so remarkably diminished, and diminished at the very time when Hitler boasted that his sea war would be at its height, must be taken in conjunction with our greatly increased production of food at home. I have always held the view that the British people, especially the heavy workers, must be properly fed and nourished if we are to get the full results from our war effort, and at the beginning of the year, when it looked as if we should have to choose to some extent between food and munitions imports, I asked the Cabinet to approve a minimum of food imports to be maintained, if necessary, even at the expense of munitions materials. There is no doubt that the dietary of our people has been severely curtailed and has become far less varied and interesting. Still, at the rate we are now going, it is sufficient for our physical health, although I am hoping that we shall be able to give a somewhat larger share of the available supplies to the workers who need it most. This will be done by a rapid expansion of canteens, which will supply meals off the ration to the workers they serve at places where those workers are actually gathered. I am glad to say that the figure which we prescribed for minimum food imports will now probably be achieved, and even a little surpassed, and that the Minister of Food has now been able to make certain minor relaxations during the winter months in the severity of his restrictions. As a precaution, we have amassed stocks of bulky articles of our diet which amount to double what we had in September, 1939. We are going to make a job of this war, and those who are working on the job must have their strength fully maintained, because although much has been asked of them in the past, we are going to ask them for more as the struggle deepens.

The agricultural Ministers for England and Scotland are also to be congratulated upon the very great expansion they have made of our home food production. In the short space of two years, the area under crops has been increased by no less that 45 per cent. Although the corn harvest that was gathered was not quite so good as we had hoped it would be before I left for the Atlantic meeting – and here I must say that in future I shall be as careful in abstaining from prophesy in agricultural matters as I am in military matters – nevertheless, the cereal crop was 50 per cent. greater than in 1939. We should also have very large crops of potatoes, sugar beet, fodder roots and other fodder crops this year. Despite the lack of imported feeding stuffs we have well maintained our head of cattle, both dairy cows and beef cattle, and I hope – I say this on the spur of the moment and shall perhaps get into trouble – that my right hon. and Noble Friend will see if he can do something with the hens. All who have to do with the land, farmer and farm worker alike, have played a worthy part in this achievement. But satisfactory as are the results to date, there must be no relaxation of our efforts. Despite all difficulties, we must go on to produce still more, not only because of the ever-present menace to our importation from abroad, but because it is possible that as the war develops our military operations will make much more extensive demands on our shipping.

I mention these facts at the risk of being accused of complacency. When I spoke a month ago I mentioned the fact that our people would have better Christmas dinners this year than last year, and dinners which would be more justified by the food position. For this I incurred a rebuke from the *Daily Herald,* which wrote, with a spartan austerity which I trust the editorial staff will practise as well as preach, that we were 'making war not wassail'. It is a poor heart that never rejoices.

The House may rest assured that we shall not err on the side of over-indulgence. The building-up of reserves is continuous, and I trust that we shall not be blamed for stoking up those fires of human energy and spirit upon which our victory in this long struggle depends.

Some months ago we were anxious about the coal position for this winter, and it still gives cause for concern. I am glad to say that, thanks to the exertions of the President of the Board of Trade and of the Secretary of the Mines Department –

Mr Gallacher (Fife, West): And the miners.

The Prime Minister: I am coming to that – the situation is better than appeared likely a few months ago. Our stocks of coal are now between 2,000,000 and 3,000,000 tons larger than they were a year ago and are far better distributed, and the men, who have responded most nobly to the appeal made, are working a longer working week than before. There has been great concern on the part of some of the younger miners at not being allowed to go to the Army. We have had some very hard cases of young men who wished to go and serve in the Fighting Forces, and we all understand how they feel. But they can really best help the war effort at the moment by staying where they are, although at the same time, as things develop, we must endeavour to meet the wishes of individuals as far as possible in regard to the form of service they give. I know how tremendous was the contribution which the miners made in the last war, when we had the same difficulty in holding the men at the pits. What the position will be if this country becomes the scene of actual strife I cannot tell, but I sympathize entirely with their feelings, and if we have to ask them to make the sacrifice, it is because of the vital necessity of coal to our whole production. Against this improved situation we have to bear in mind the steadily increasing demand which is coming as our war industries expand, and it is necessary that all efforts for the production of and economy in fuel should continue. There are good grounds for the belief that we shall come through the winter all right, and that, without having deranged our Army by withdrawing thousands of coal miners from their platoons, the regular process of our coal supply will be maintained.

There is nothing that Hitler will dislike more than my recital of these prosaic but unassailable facts. There is nothing that he and his Nazi régime dread more than the proof that we are capable of fighting a prolongued war and the proof of the failure of their efforts to starve us into submission. In the various remarks which the Deputy Führer, Herr Hess, has let fall from time to time during his sojourn in our midst, nothing has been more clear than that Hitler relied upon the starvation attack more than upon invasion to bring us to our knees. His hopes were centred upon starvation, as his boasts have made the world aware. So far as 1941 at least is concerned, those hopes have been dashed to the ground. But this only increases his need to come at us by direct invasion as soon as he can screw up his courage and make his arrangements to take the plunge. Therefore, we must have everything working forward for the improved weather of the spring, so that we are well prepared to meet any scale of attack that can be directed upon us. Although we are infinitely stronger that we were a year ago, or even six months ago, yet at the same time the enemy has had ample time for preparations, and you may be sure that if an invasion of this country is attempted by the Germans, it will be upon a plan which has been thought out in every detail with their customary ruthlessness and thoroughness.

I now come, on what I hope is a fairly solid foundation, to the criticism of the Government. My right hon. Friend the Member for South-West Bethnal Green (Sir P. Harris) spoke of criticism as being the life-blood of democracy. Certainly we are a very full-blooded democracy. In war it is very hard to bring about successes and very easy to make mistakes or to point them out after they have been made. There was a custom in ancient China that anyone who wished to criticize the Government had the right to memorialize the Emperor, and, provided he followed that up by committing suicide, very great respect was paid to his words, and no ulterior motive was assigned. That seems to me to have been, from many points of view, a wise custom, but I certainly would be the last to suggest it should be made retrospective. Our universal resolve to keep Parliamentary institutions in full activity amid the throes of war has been proved. That is a feat of enormous difficulty, never accomplished in any such complete perfection in history. His Majesty's Government base themselves upon the House of Commons. They look to the House for aid and comfort, in the incalculable perils by which we are beset. We are entitled to seek from the House from time to time the formal renewal of their confidence. The Debate on the Address furnishes the signal outstanding Parliamentary opportunity of the year. It is the Grand Inquest of the nation. The fact of passing the Address in reply to the Gracious Speech without any Amendment is the proof to the nation and to the whole world that the King's Ministers enjoy the confidence of Parliament. This is essential to any Government in times of war, because any sign of division or any suspicion of weakness disheartens our friends and encourages our foes. We shall therefore give the fullest facilities to the Debate on the Address, either upon the general Debate or upon Amendments.

I should like to point out to people outside this House and to countries abroad which do not realize the flexibility and potency of our Parliamentary institutions, nor how they work, that any Amendment, however seductive, however misleading, however tendentious, however artful, however sober, or however wide, which the wit or other qualities of men may devise, can be placed upon the Paper, can be fully debated by the arrangement of calling particular Amendments. None shall be individiously excluded. If a Division takes place, it is a matter of confidence, which, nevertheless, enables everyone to see exactly where we stand and how far we can call upon the loyalty of this House. If such Amendment should be moved and pressed to a Division – I say this for the information of countries abroad – those who vote against the Government will not be assaulted with rubber truncheons, or put into concentration camps, or otherwise molested in their private lives. The worst that could happen might be that they might have to offer some rather laborious explanations to their constituents. Let it not be said that Parliamentary institutions are being maintained in this country in a farcical or unreal manner. We are fighting for Parliamentary institutions. We are endeavouring to keep their full practice and freedom, even in the stress of war.

In order that there may be no misunderstanding about the basis on which this Debate takes place, I must state that the Government stand united as a corporate body, as a band of men who have bound themselves to work together in special faith and loyalty. There can be no question of any individual Ministers being singled out, by intrigue or ill-will or because of the exceptional difficulties of their tasks, and being hounded down in any Government over which I have the honour to preside. From time to time the force of events makes changes necessary, but none are contemplated at the present moment. Neither do I consider it necessary to remodel the system of Cabinet government under which we are now working, nor to alter in any fundamental manner the system by which the conduct of the war proceeds, nor that by which production of munitions is regulated and maintained.

The process of self-improvement is, of course, continuous, and every man and woman throughout the land, in office or out of office, in Parliament or in the cities and municipalities of our country – everyone, great and small, should try himself by his conscience every day to make sure he is giving his utmost effort to the common cause. Making allowance for the increase of population, we have reached, in the 26th month of this war, and in some ways have surpassed, the deployment of national effort at home, which after all the slaughter, was not reached until the 48th month of the last war. We cannot rest content with that, and if Parliament, by patriotic and constructive counsel, and without unduly harassing those who bear the load, can stimulate and accelerate our further advance, the House of Commons will be playing its part, unyielding, persevering, indomitable, in the overthrow of another Continental tyranny as in the olden times.

War Cabinet: Confidential Annex
(*Cabinet papers, 65/24*)

12 November 1941
5.30 p.m.

The Prime Minister thanked Sir Earle Page very cordially for his statement which would be most fully considered by the Chiefs of Staff. The United Kingdom were resolute to help Australia if she were menaced with invasion. But Sir Earle Page would recognize that it would be a grave strategical error to move forces to the Far East – possibly to remain inactive for a year – which were now actively engaged against Germany and Italy. Our correct strategy was to move our strength from theatre to theatre as the situation changed. At the present time the theatre in which forces could be most profitably employed was the Middle East. A policy of spreading our resources to guard against possible but unlikely dangers, might be fatal.

What was the best deterrent to employ against the Japanese? In his view the answer was to maintain a stiff attitude towards her but not to become involved in war with her unless we had the assurance of United States participation. There were four situations which we had to contemplate in the Far East:

(i) The United States at war with Germany and Japan neutral.
(ii) The United States in the war with us and Japan in the war against us.
(iii) Both countries out of the war.
(iv) The United States out of the war but Japan in against us.

The fourth possibility was clearly the most unfavourable and the one which we should at all costs avoid. But the whole position was too complex to be dealt with on the basis of any rigid formula and he hoped that they might be allowed some latitude in handling the matter. We had to watch the situation from week to week, and from month to month, and to deal with it as best we could.

The Prime Minister said that he was not one of those who believed that it was in Japan's power to invade Australia. Nevertheless, he would renew his assurance that if Australia were gravely threatened, we should cut our losses in the Middle East and move in great strength to Australia's assistance. Such a decision, however, was not one to be taken lightly.

The Prime Minister went on to refer to the difficulties which faced President Roosevelt as a result of the slow development of American opinion and the peculiarities of the American Constitution. Nobody but Congress could declare war. It was, however, in the President's power to make war without declaring it. President Roosevelt was a great leader. In the last twelve months American opinion had moved under his leadership to an extent which nobody could have anticipated. They had made immense credits available to us; they had made immense resources available to us under the Lease-Lend Act; their Navy was escorting the Atlantic convoys; and finally they were taking a firm line with the Japanese.

The Prime Minister then referred to the series of personal telegrams which President Roosevelt and he had exchanged since the beginning of the war. This exchange of views continued down to the present moment, but it would be a great error on his part to press President Roosevelt to act in advance of American opinion.[1]

The difference between the two countries in a nutshell was that he, the Prime Minister, had it in his power with the approval of the War Cabinet to go to the Mansion House and say 'Should the United States become involved in war with Japan, the British declaration will follow within the hour'. The

[1] John Peck later recalled a remark by Churchill at this time: 'The American Constitution was designed by the Founding Fathers to keep the United States clear of European entanglements – and by God it has stood the test of time.' (Conversation with the author, 18 August 1982)

American President had no such power, and it remained possible, though unlikely, that the United States would disinterest themselves if we were to declare war on Japan.

Very likely developments in America might become more rapid after the repeal of the Neutrality Act.

The Prime Minister said[1] that we were in the difficulty that the RAF expansion programme fell short both of our expectations and our needs.

Winston S. Churchill to Lord Linlithgow
(*Churchill papers, 20/45*)

12 November 1941
Strictly personal and secret

1. I was startled to learn how far you had gone about the release of the remaining Satyagrahi prisoners. As you know, I have always felt that a man like Nehru[2] should be treated as a political *détenu* and not as a criminal, and have welcomed every mitigation of his lot. But my general impression of this wholesale release is one of a surrender at the moment of success. Undoubtedly the release of these prisoners as an act of clemency will be proclaimed as a victory for Gandhi's party.[3] Nehru and others will commit fresh offences, requiring the whole process of trial and conviction to be gone through again. You will get no thanks from any quarter. The objections of Hope[4] and Hallett[5] should not be lightly turned aside.

[1] In answer to a suggestion by the Australian representative, Sir Earle Page, that the 'air forces at Singapore be used as a "fire break" against an attack on the Burma Road' by Japan.

[2] Jawaharlal Nehru, 1889–1964. Like Churchill, educated at Harrow. Barrister-at-Law, Inner Temple, 1912. Member of the All-India Congress Committee, 1918–47. President, Indian National Congress, 1929. Imprisoned several times, for his political activities, and calls for non-co-operation. Vice-President, Interim Government of India, 1946. Prime Minister of India from 1947 until his death. (Both his daughter Indira Gandhi, and his grandson, Rajiv Gandhi, were subsequently Prime Ministers of India; and both were assassinated.)

[3] In August, Lord Linlithgow had offered to enlarge his Executive Council by bringing in more Indians, and also to set up a War Advisory Council of leading Indians. At the same time he promised that after the war a body would be set up 'representative of the principal elements in Indian national life' to frame a constitution. The offer was rejected by the Indian National Congress, which demanded an immediate guarantee that India would be 'completely freed' after the war from the British connection. When Linlithgow declined to make such a pledge, Gandhi initiated a pacifist campaign and urged Congress to stir up popular feeling against the war effort. Linlithgow had thereupon ordered the arrest of several Congress leaders, including Jawaharlal Nehru (who, like Churchill, was an Old Harrovian).

[4] Arthur Oswald James Hope, 1897–1958. On active service, 1914–18, Coldstream Guards (Military Cross). Conservative Member of Parliament for Nuneaton, 1924–29, for Aston, 1931–39. Governor of Madras, 1940–46. Succeeded his father as 2nd Baron Rankeillour, 1949.

[5] Maurice Garnier Hallett, 1883–1969. Joined the Indian Civil Service, 1907. Magistrate and Collector, 1916. Secretary to the Government of Bihar, 1920–24. Chief Secretary, Bihar and Orissa, 1930–32. Secretary to the Government of India, Home Department, 1932–36. Knighted, 1937. Governor of Bihar, 1937–39; Governor of the United Provinces, 1939–45. One of his two sons was killed in action in the Second World War.

2. The Cabinet, to whom I mentioned it this evening, felt they must have more time to consider the matter after they have received your official advice. It will not be possible for us to send an answer before Monday at earliest, so I asked the Secretary of State to desire you to postpone the motion on the 17th for a few days. We often do this in the House of Commons when replies from other Governments have to be awaited.

3. Kindest regards.[1]

Winston S. Churchill: Business of the House
(*Hansard*)

13 November 1941 House of Commons

The House will, I am sure, admit that there have been a great many opportunities for raising matters of general interest. We have had a very large number of Debates on almost all the important aspects of our life in present conditions. There is no reason why such facilities should not be provided in the coming Session. It is the desire of the Government that they should be continued – at any rate until we get to some point in the Session where, in order to wind up our affairs, Government Business must monopolize the whole time. I have made it clear that the rights of Members to criticize the action of the Government will remain unimpaired by the Motion. I am sorry that Private Members have not the facilities of bringing forward their legislative proposals, but the present time is not appropriate for the consideration of such Measures, and if any suggestions are made to Ministers, they will receive careful consideration. If Members feel that something needs to be done, they should have recourse to the Ministers upon the subject, and then the Government could, of course, initiate legislation.

The remaining provisions in the Motion I am moving continue the arrangements that were in operation last Session in regard to the sending in of Amendments to Bills and notices of Questions on days when the House is not sitting, the handing in of Amendments to Bills before the Second Reading and the dispensing with the usual notice for new Clauses to be moved on the

[1] Lord Linlithgow replied on 15 November 1941: 'The sentences of these satyagrahis are mostly due to expire within four months, so we are not giving them much. My new colleagues tell me that they have no hope that Congress will respond and I agree. They are anxious to impress moderate opinion outside Congress and to enhance their own prestige by showing that they can get things done. Including Moslems they were unanimous in their advice. I think that they may be right, though I confess that if left to myself I would not have favoured release, but I am quite definite that it would not be wise to resist them. I can assure you that there is no surrender about it, and that all my colleagues are to be relied upon to protect our war effort. You may count upon me to dig my toes in if I think they are going too far. Rumour reaches me that you hate long telegrams so I must rely upon Amery to give you further particulars. Best messages. We are in great heart here and full of fight.' (Prime Minister's Personal Telegram, T. 813, 'Personal', 'No circulation', *Churchill papers, 20/45*)

Report stage. We took those steps under the conditions of war, and I think they were found generally convenient, and the House would like to have the some flexibility in the present Session. We also ask the House to continue the power by which the suspension of the Rule may be moved without notice. This power was used only on a few occasions last Session, and we feel that it should not become a practice to move such a Motion without due notice. We cannot foresee with accuracy in these times of trial the course of events, but we feel that the Government should have this power which might occasionally be required to meet the general convenience of the House and to obtain essential Government Business.

Winston S. Churchill to James Stuart and Sir Douglas Hacking
(*Churchill papers, 20/36*)

13 November 1941
Action this Day

I do not understand how a Member[1] who uses the language at A[2] could wish to receive a Government Whip from 'the most incompetent Government in modern times'. I think the Whip should be withdrawn and the reason published. First, however, I should like to know what would be the expected reaction in his constituency of Croydon, and, secondly, whether he holds some position in the Party as an organizer. As a large-scale guinea-pig and salaried representative of various business interests whose Parliamentary work he does, he is not at all in a strong position.

His remarks about the Government are not criticism but mere abuse, and he would be a good subject for an example.

[1] Sir Herbert Williams (see page 670, note 1).
[2] On 13 November 1941 the *Daily Mirror* reported Sir Herbert Williams telling Croydon Conservatives on the previous day: 'I believe the splendid British people will win, however incompetent the Government, but an incompetent Government will add greatly to the cost in life and treasure. The present Government is not only incompetent; it is in many respects the most incompetent Government of this country in modern times. Mr. Churchill possessed a most amazing capacity of speech in inspiring the people of the Empire and the friendly neutrals. In that respect he is a wonderful asset. He is not so good as a manager of our war effort, and most unfortunately he has failed to gather round him a team capable of the efficient production of the Departments of State'.

Winston S. Churchill to Air Marshal Tedder
(*Churchill papers, 20/45*)

13 November 1941
Most Secret

I am very glad to see from most secret sources good effects of your attacks. I hope it will be 'Crescendo'.[1]

Winston S. Churchill to the Earl of Derby
(*Churchill papers, 20/22*)

13 November 1941
Private

My dear Eddie,

Thank you for your letter recommending Alderman Shennan[2] for an honour.

The great merits of the good people of Lancashire have not been unrewarded, nor have you been backward in singing their praises. There are ten knights on the Lancashire County Council as against nine on the London County Council, though the financial responsibilities of the latter body alone are more than five times greater. Essex, a thickly populated county and comparable in size, has only two, and the West Riding of Yorkshire, about a third smaller, has only three.

It is difficult to make a hard and fast division between towns and counties, but as far as Liverpool itself is concerned there are two other recommendations before me for knighthoods besides the name which you put forward, though these of course may not be successful. I think perhaps that you ought to know that there have been the following civil defence awards for that town given this year, 43 British Empire Medals and a bar, 2 MBEs, 29 George Medals, 1 OBE.

Nevertheless, I will see that your recommendation has consideration, but if it is not successful I hope you will not feel in view of what I have said that either Liverpool or Lancashire are neglected.

Forgive me for having to make these points.

Yours ever
W

[1] In replying to Churchill's telegram later that day, Tedder wrote: 'Thank you for your message. Real crescendo begins tomorrow'. ('Immediate', 'Most Secret', 13 November 1941, 11.41 a.m. (received 3.35 p.m.): *Churchill papers 20/45*)

[2] Alfred Ernest Shennan, 1887–1959. A Chartered Architect. Alderman, Liverpool, 1934–59; Leader of the Conservative Party in the City Council. Chairman of the Civil Defence Committee. Knighted, 1952.

Winston S. Churchill to Lord Beaverbrook
(*Churchill papers, 20/22*)

13 November 1941

My dear Max,

Your letter of November 10. As I have told you several times there is no question of the creation of a Production Ministry with Mr Bevin at its head. The possibility of a Production Ministry or Ministry of Munitions faded when a year ago you felt unable to take MAP as well as M of S,[1] both of which I had managed to have vacant simultaneously. Since then I have committed myself by reasoned argument in Parliament against it, and I do not propose to stultify myself publicly at the present time, or to make an altogether unsuitable appointment.

2. There has never been any question of putting the Ministry of Supply under the Production Executive. The Production Executive is a clearing-house for over-lapping interests among the various Supply Departments. It also affords an opportunity to the minor Departments which are consumers having a chance of asking for what they want. I do not understand why in one breath you object to the Production Executive under Mr Bevin, who you yourself proposed for the Chair, and do not like attending its meetings, and at the same time advocate as a Production Minister the same Mr Bevin of whom you would be a direct subordinate. The Production Executive has no power to overrule you against your will, because you can at once carry the matter to the Cabinet or to me. On the other hand, for the sake of a quiet life one would hope that a good many matters would be discussed and cleared up there.

3. Since you invite me to say what I want, I should be glad if you would either attend the Production Executive yourself, or send someone who has power to settle for you in accordance with the discussions, or appeal to me or to the Cabinet if agreement is impossible. If there is any serious disagreement, or you have an objection to sitting on the Production Executive under Mr Bevin or with Lord Reith and Sir Andrew Duncan, I am willing in the hopes of making things more agreeable to you, to preside over the meetings of the Executive myself, when the points in dispute can be thrashed out. I have a fairly heavy load to carry as you know, but I would certainly do this in any particular case rather than you should be upset.

4. There is no question of interfering in any way with your authority over the Iron and Steel or Machine Tool Controls. I presume that you do not claim the right yourself to decide the allocation of steel and machine tools. This is a matter on which the user Ministers stand on an equal footing. It should therefore continue to be settled by consultation between the Ministers

[1] The Ministry of Aircraft Production and the Ministry of Supply.

concerned. This has given rise to no difficulty in the past, and there is no reason to suppose that it would do so in the future.

Yours ever,
Winston S. Churchill

General Sir Alan Brooke to his wife
(*'The Turn of the Tide'*)

[13 November 1941][1] [Chequers][2]

He then went on to say that he wanted me to take over . . .[3] and asked me whether I was prepared to do so. It took me some time to reply, as I was torn by many feelings. I hated the thought of old Dill going and our very close association coming to an end. I hated the thought of what this would mean to him. The magnitude of the job and the work entailed took the wind out of my sails. The fact that the extra work and ties would necessarily mean seeing far less of you tore at my heart strings. And finally a feeling of sadness at having to give up Home Forces after having worked them up to their present pitch.

The PM misunderstood my silence and said: 'Do you not think you will be able to work with me? We have so far got on well together.' I had to assure him that these were not my thoughts, though I am fully aware that my path will not be strewn with rose petals. But I have the greatest respect and real affection for him, so that I hope I may be able to stand the storms of abuse which I may well have to bear frequently.

He then went on to explain the importance he attached to the appointment, and the fact that the Chiefs of Staff Committee must be the body to direct military events over the whole world. He also stated that his relations with me must from now on approximate to those of a Prime Minister to one of his Ministers. Nobody could be nicer than he was, and finally, when we went to bed at 2 a.m., he came with me to my bedroom to get away from the others, took my hand and looking into my eyes with an exceptionally kind look, said: 'I wish you the very best of luck'.

1 General Brooke set out this recollection in a letter to his wife on 16 November 1941.

2 Among Churchill's guests at Chequers that weekend were Sir Hugh Dowding, Captain Hillgarth and General Ismay, who dined and slept on the Friday night; General Nye, Sir James Grigg and General Sir Alan Brooke, who dined and slept on the Saturday night; and Lord Louis Mountbatten and Lord Cherwell, who dined and slept on the Sunday night. Churchill's daughter Sarah dined on the Saturday night.

3 As Chief of the Imperial General Staff, in succession to General Sir John Dill.

General Sir Alan Brooke: recollection
(*'Turn of the Tide'*)

[13 November 1941] [Chequers]

There is no doubt that I was temporarily staggered by the magnitude of the task I was undertaking. Let it be remembered the situation we were in at that time . . . We were faced with a possible invasion across the Channel, with increasing difficulties in the Middle East, a closed Mediterranean, dark clouds growing in the Far East and a failing Russia driven back to the very gates of Moscow. The horizon was black from end to end with only one shaft of light in the possible entry of America into the war. To pick up the strategic reins at the War Office at such a moment was sufficient to cause the deepest anxiety. Added to that was the certain trial of working hand in hand with Winston in handling the direction of war. I had seen enough of him to realize his impetuous nature, his gambler's spirit, and his determination to follow his own selected path at all costs, to realize fully what I was faced with.

I can remember clearly that after he had taken me away to his study and had offered me this appointment, he left me alone temporarily to rejoin the others. I am not an exceptionally religious person, but I am not ashamed to confess that as soon as he was out of the room my first impulse was to kneel down and pray to God for guidance and support in the task I had undertaken. As I look back at the years that followed I can now see clearly how well this prayer was answered.

Lord Camrose[1] *to Seymour Berry*[2]
(*Camrose papers*)

14 November 1941

Dear Seymour,

I sat next to our friend last night. He seemed to be quite optimistic and thought things were going along rather well for us. On his advices, Moscow is

[1] William Ewart Berry, 1879–1954. Newspaper proprietor. Founder of *Advertising World*, 1901. Editor-in-Chief of the *Sunday Times*, 1915–36. Chairman, Financial Times Limited, 1919–45; Allied Newspapers Limited, 1924–36. Created Baron Camrose, 1929. Chief Proprietor and Editor-in-Chief of the *Daily Telegraph and Morning Post*, 1936–54. Principal Adviser, Ministry of Information, 1939. Advanced to a Viscountcy, 1941. One of Churchill's close friends (he was elected to the Other Club in 1926), and from 1945 a principal financial adviser; in 1946 he negotiated both the sale of Churchill's war memoirs, and also the purchase of Chartwell by a group of Churchill's friends and its conveyance to the National Trust (Camrose himself contributing £15,000 and sixteen other friends £5,000 each).

[2] John Seymour Berry, 1909–1995. Elder son of the 1st Baron (later Viscount) Camrose. Educated at Eton and Christ Church, Oxford. Conservative MP for Hitchen, 1941–5. On active service in North Africa and Italy, 1942–5 (despatches). Vice-Chairman of the Amalgamated Press Ltd., 1942–59. Succeeded his father, as 2nd Viscount, 1954. Subsequently Chairman of Daily Telegraph Ltd.

not likely to fall and, in any case, the Russians have made, and are making, large preparations for munition works well to the East. He had nothing much to say about the South but did not seem to view it as too critical.

He feels that the country has settled down and is no longer resentful about the absence of the second front. One of the things which influenced him here was evidently the attitude of the Sunday papers as he told me twice that the Sunday papers were now calmer and nothing like so critical.

I had a talk with him about his own position at the end of the war. His present decision is to retire immediately we have what he called 'turned the corner'. By this, of course, he means achieved victory. If he were 50 or 55 he would still be looking forward to a political career and would be planning his future; but as he was now nearing 70 he viewed his own future in quite a different way. He was fully determined not to make the ghastly error that LG had made, but he felt, in any case, that his age precluded him from planning to be a big figure in the long and complicated negotiations which the peace would involve.

While he did not say so, I am sure he also had in mind the idea that he should make provision for his family. To do this he would have to be able to write. I ventured to say to him that in all probability the country would demand that he continued in power in the absence of anybody arising of the same quality to take his place. He agreed that this might be the case, but maintained that he himself could not view such a thing with satisfaction having regard to his age.

I arranged for the *Telegraph* to send me a message immediately they received the result of the Neutrality Act vote at Washington. I passed it across the table to Fred Lawson[1] (who was in the Chair) to announce. Needless to say, it was received with great enthusiasm and Winston was highly delighted. He said he did not care a damn about the smallness of the majority.[2] The thing was that the President now had power to act and the size of the majority would soon be forgotten. He anticipated great things from this new decision and I could see he feels that it cannot now be many days before America is finally in the war.[3]

[1] Edward Frederick Lawson, 1890–1961. Member of the Levy-Lawson family, owners of the *Daily Telegraph*. On active service in Palestine, 1917 (Distinguished Service Order, Military Cross, despatches three times). Colonel, 1918. Worked under his uncle, Viscount Burnham, on the *Daily Telegraph*, 1919–39; General Manager, 1928–39. Vice-Chairman, Newspaper Proprietors' Association, 1934. Brigadier-General, in charge of the final defence perimeter around Dunkirk, May 1940. Major-General commanding the Yorkshire Division, 1941. Director of Public Relations, War Office, 1942–45. Succeeded his father, as 4th Baron Burnham, 1943. Managing Director of the *Daily Telegraph*, 1945–61. In 1955 he published *Peterborough Court* (the story of the *Daily Telegraph*).

[2] On the question of arming United States merchant ships, after a Senate vote of 50 to 37, the vote in the House of Representatives was 212 to 194. This gave Roosevelt less support from his own Democrats than he had obtained on Lend-Lease.

[3] Churchill continued to make time to receive visitors from the United States. On November 21 Bebe Daniels and Ben Lyon brought him five special thumbs up badges which were being sold in New York by Mayor La Guardia on behalf of the British War Relief Society in the United States. Four days later he received John B. Snyder, Chairman of the Military Appropriations Sub-Committee of the House of Representatives.

Winston S. Churchill to A. V. Alexander and Admiral Pound
(*Churchill papers, 20/36*)

14 November 1941
Action this Day

U-BOATS SUNK

1. I am much disquieted by these facts. We are sinking less than two a month. They are increasing by nearly twenty. The failure of our methods about which so much was proclaimed by the Admiralty before the war, is painfully apparent. I presume we have lost a far higher proportion of British submarines placed in service since the beginning of the war than the enemy.

Let me have the actual figures.

2. I regard the whole position as so serious that I wish to have a special meeting in the near future to survey the whole problem and consider whether anything can be done beyond the present measures.

Let me know what increases are to be expected month by month in our anti-U-boat hunting-craft. Let all the considerations about the German difficulty of training crews and other aspects be assembled and reviewed. Let me know when you will be ready.

Winston S. Churchill to the 'Jewish Chronicle'
(*'Jewish Chronicle', 14 November 1941*)[1]

14 November 1941

On the occasion of the centenary of the *Jewish Chronicle*, a landmark in the history of British Jewry, I send a message of good cheer to Jewish people in this and other lands. None has suffered more cruelly than the Jew the unspeakable evils wrought on the bodies and spirits of men by Hitler and his vile régime. The Jew bore the brunt of the Nazi's first onslaught upon the citadels of freedom and human dignity. He has borne and continued to bear a burden that might have seemed to be beyond endurance. He has not allowed it to break his spirit; he has never lost the will to resist. Assuredly in the day of victory the Jew's sufferings and his part in the struggle will not be forgotten. Once again, at the appointed time, he will see vindicated those principles of righteousness which it was the glory of his fathers to proclaim to the world. Once again it will be shown that, though the mills of God grind slowly, yet they grind exceeding small.[2]

Winston S. Churchill

[1] A facsimile of this message is reproduced in Joan Comay, *The Diaspora Story, The Epic of the Jewish People Among the Nations*, Weidenfeld and Nicolson, London, 1981, page 99.

[2] In his poem *Retribution*, Longfellow wrote: 'Though the mills of God grind slowly, yet they grind exceeding small; Though with patience He stands waiting, with exactness grinds He all.'

Winston S. Churchill to the London Editor, 'Birmingham Gazette'
(*Churchill papers, 20/22*)

14 November 1941

My dear Sir,

I gladly send my tribute of congratulations to the *Birmingham Gazette* on its 200th anniversary. Since 1741 it has fought for and witnessed many great reforms in the living conditions of the people of this country, and it has never ceased to uphold the principles of democratic freedom. It survives today in all its robust vigour.

Only as part of the free Press of a free country could this journal have lived so vigorously and survived so long. Now it is by victory in arms alone that the freedom which it holds dear will be preserved.

The other day I visited your city and met there citizens of strong courage and sound sense. It was with no small pride that I talked to these men and women who are labouring hard to send from this industrial battlefront the reinforcements which will stem and turn the tide of conflict.

These are the worthy inheritors of a tradition in the building of which the *Birmingham Gazette* has taken a notable part.

Yours very faithfully,
Winston S. Churchill

Winston S. Churchill to Flying Officer Charles Challen[1]
(*Churchill papers, 20/22*)

14 November 1941

My dear Challen,

As leader of the Government, which is supported by the Conservative, Labour and Liberal parties, I call on the electors to support you at the poll. Your return will be an endorsement of the country's unshakable loyalty to the principle of national unity, which we regard as the foundation of our strength in prosecuting the war to a victorious conclusion.

The people of Hampstead will surely be proud to be represented in Parliament by a Hampstead man with your splendid record of achievement. You lost an arm in the service of your country in the last war and today, in the honoured uniform of the Royal Air Force, you are once again serving the

[1] Charles Challen, 1894–1960. On active service, Royal Field Artillery, 1914–18, in France and Egypt. Called to the Bar, Gray's Inn, 1922. Member of the Hampstead Borough Council, 1931–45. Chairman of the Hampstead Conservative and Unionist Association, 1937–42. Flight-Lieutenant, Royal Air Force, September 1939 to December 1945. Conservative Member of Parliament for Hampstead, 1941–50.

nation. Not only this, but, as a member of the Hampstead Borough Council, you have for ten years past taken a prominent part in the municipal affairs of your borough.

Your personal qualifications apart, you are standing as a supporter of the Government of National Unity which, despite the cavilling of impatient and uninformed critics, has during the past year and a half developed an ever-increasing concentration of the nation's effort to organize victory. Their work goes on and must go on until victory is made secure.

I look to Hampstead to make a special point of going to the poll – and going early in the day – to vote for you and so register their confidence in the Government that represents the nation's inflexible will to vindicate free democracy against totalitarian tyranny.

Yours sincerely,
Winston S. Churchill

Winston S. Churchill to James Stuart, Sir Douglas Hacking and Colonel Harvie-Watt
(*Churchill papers, 20/36*)

15 November 1941

I see no reason to write a special assurance to this man.[1] His candidature is only splitting the dissident vote.

I suggest an answer in the 3rd person that the Prime Minister has nothing to add at present to his various public statements on the subject.

Winston S. Churchill to General Auchinleck
(*Churchill papers, 20/45*)

15 November 1941
Personal and Secret

I have it in Command from The King to express to all ranks of the Army and Royal Air Force in the Western Desert, and to the Mediterranean Fleet, His Majesty's confidence that they will do their duty with exemplary devotion in the supremely important battle which lies before them. For the first time, British and Empire troops will meet the Germans with an ample equipment in modern weapons of all kinds. The battle itself will affect the whole course of the war. Now is the time to strike the hardest blow yet struck for final victory,

[1] Arthur Dolland, the Non-Party All-out for Russia Candidate at the Hampstead by-election.

home and freedom. The Desert Army may add a page to history which will rank with Blenheim and with Waterloo. The eyes of all nations are upon you. All our hearts are with you. May God uphold the right.

You should use this message if, when and as you think fit.

Winston S. Churchill to Herbert Morrison
(*Churchill papers, 20/36*)

15 November 1941
Secret

I shall be glad to know what action you have taken about enabling the twelve couples of married internees to be confined together. Now that order has been restored in the Isle of Man, there should be no particular reason against their going there. If not, there must surely be some prisons in England in which arrangements could be made for reasonable association of husband and wife.

Is it true that when aliens are interned, husband and wife are interned in one place? If so, it seems invidious to discriminate against those of British nationality.

Feeling against 18B is very strong, and I should not be prepared to support the Regulation indefinitely if it is administered in such a very onerous manner. Internment rather than imprisonment is what was contemplated.

Sir Oswald Mosley's wife[1] has now been eighteen months in prison without the slightest vestige of any charge against her, and separated from her husband.

Has the question of releasing a number of these internees on parole been considered, or on condition of their finding sureties for good behaviour, &c.?

I should be glad if you would make proposals to the Cabinet before the debate in the House takes place.

[1] Diana Mitford, 1910– . Third daughter of the 2nd Baron Redesdale. A cousin by marriage of Clementine Churchill, she married Oswald Mosley in 1936, was arrested with him in 1940, and imprisoned for the duration of the war. Her sister Unity, like her an admirer of Hitler, tried to commit suicide on the outbreak of war. Her brother, Tom Mitford, was killed in action in Burma in 1945.

Winston S. Churchill to Sir Stafford Cripps
(*Premier papers, 3/170/1*)

15 November 1941
Personal and Secret

I have read all your telegrams and I know how hard it must be to watch events at a distance and have time idle on your hands when so much is going on. All the same I am sure it would be a mistake from your point of view to leave your post and abandon the Russians and the Soviet cause with which you are so closely associated while all hangs in the balance at Leningrad, Moscow and in the south. Your own friends here would not understand it. I hope you will believe that I give you this advice not from any fear of political opposition which you might raise over here by making out we had not done enough, etc. I could face such opposition without any political embarrassment, though with much personal regret. The Soviet Government, as you must see upon reflection, could never support you in an agitation against us because that would mean that we should be forced to vindicate our action in public which would necessarily be detrimental to Soviet interests and to the common cause. Force of circumstances would compel them to make the best of us. After all, we have wrecked our Air and Tank expansion programmes for their sake, and in our effort to hold German Air power in the west we have lost more than double the pilots and machines lost in the Battle of Britain last year. You must not underrate the strength of the case I could deploy in the House of Commons and on the broadcast, though I should be very sorry to do so. The Government itself was never so strong or unchallenged as it is now. Every movement of the United States towards the war adds to that strength. You should weigh all this before engaging in a most unequal struggle which could only injure the interests to which you are attached. I have taken full note of your wish to come home. Indeed you told me about it before you returned last time. You may be sure I will tell you when to come at the right moment for you and for the cause. It may not be for some months yet.

Sir Alexander Cadogan: diary
(*'The Diaries of Sir Alexander Cadogan, OM, 1938-1945'*)

16 November 1941

These week-ends are awful. Ministers get time to 'think', which I think they do on country walks, in the course of which they lash themselves into a frenzy – about nothing much. Then, on returning home, they seize the telephone receiver like a drunkard seizes the bottle, and the whole place flares up. *That* shows you what would happen if we had a Cabinet of 'non-Departmental'

Ministers. And the PM sits somewhere in the country, like a spider in the middle of his web, and tickles them all up.[1] I don't believe it produces much beyond frayed nerves and tempers.

Winston S. Churchill: Minute[2]
(*Churchill papers, 20/36*)

16 November 1941
Action this Day

I see in the Press that there is to be a debate on Manpower on the Address. It would be more convenient for the Government to make a statement on the subject in about a fortnight. We do not want a debate to go off at half-cock. I had even thought of making a preliminary statement myself when the time comes. It will be quite easy to persuade the House to wait for a short time.

Winston S. Churchill to David Margesson
(*Churchill papers, 20/36*)

17 November 1941
Most Secret

I saw General Nye[3] on Saturday night, and told him that we had in mind his appointment as VCIGS and that Sir John Dill was retiring on reaching the age limit. I was thus, for the first time, in a position to invite him to talk with freedom. I was much impressed by the clarity and range of his views. I have no doubt this appointment will be widely acclaimed by the public, and will conduce greatly to the smooth working in the War Office.

2. On Sunday night I saw Sir Alan Brooke, and told him that the CIGS would be vacant, that we intended to appoint General Nye as VCIGS and that we wished, on this basis, that he should become CIGS. He seemed quite glad to accept these responsibilities, and I feel very sure that we shall be able to work together in harmony. He is a combination of wisdom and vigour which I have found refreshing.

[1] Churchill was spending that day, a Sunday, at Chequers.

[2] Addressed to the Lord President of the Council (Sir John Anderson), the Minister of Labour (Ernest Bevin) and the Chief Whip (James Stuart). It was Churchill's 1,050th numbered Minute since the summer of 1940.

[3] Archibald Edward Nye, 1895–1967. On active service, 1914–18, enlisting as a private soldier. Lieutenant, 1916. Major-General, 1940. Director of Staff Duties, War Office, 1940. Lieutenant-General, 1941. Vice-Chief of the Imperial General Staff, 1941–46. Knighted, 1944. Governor of Madras, 1946–48. High Commissioner for the United Kingdom in India, 1948–52; in Canada, 1952–56.

3. I asked him to express his opinion about his successor as C-in-C, Home Forces. He rather surprised me by saying that he thought General Paget was a Staff Officer rather than a Commander; but upon consideration he came down decidedly in favour of General Paget becoming Commander-in-Chief. He did not think General Alexander would quite fill that post, nor, indeed, the command in the Far East. He saw great advantage, in keeping General Alexander here, as an Army Commander able to take command of some excursion such as we have talked about.

4. We then considered General Pownall for the Far East, and this project seemed to be well worthy of consideration. General Pownall has a very fine brain, and is a highly-trained Officer. There is an advantage in a man going to such a post after he has had the opportunity of seeing how things work at the centre and the summit. I hope you will consider this.

5. The question of General Macready, who will be by-passed by General Nye, at present serving under him, was mentioned. I have an admiration for General Macready and his work, but I do not think that in time of war a personal difficulty like this can be allowed to obstruct the right solution. It would seem natural and desirable that General Montgomery should succeed General Paget in the command of the vacant South-Eastern Army, where he already commands a Corps.

6. I have arranged with the India Office and the Government of India for Sir John Dill to be appointed Governor of Bombay. The Viceroy, while welcoming his appointment to an Indian Governorship, had been inclined to think Madras more suitable, but both the Secretary of State and I take the opposite view, as Dill's proved capacity is far above Hope's.[1]

7. In order that the announcements here and in India shall be synchronized, it is necessary to wait till Wednesday morning. It is advantageous that the whole of this series should come out together, thus leaving no uncertainties. Perhaps you will let me see the draft announcement, which should state *inter alia* that Sir John Dill is retiring under the age limit at the end of the year.

8. With regard to his baton, I hear that the Duke of Connaught[2] is not expected to live much longer, which would give us another vacancy, and it would be natural to take that occasion to promote Sir John Dill to Field Marshal. However, if necessary, I could ask The King and Treasury to allow us another additional, making two, pending absorption. The former course is preferable.[3]

[1] Arthur Hope, Governor of Madras (see page 1446, note 4).

[2] Prince Arthur William Patrick Albert, (1850–1942). Seventh child and third son of Queen Victoria. Created Duke of Connaught, 1874. Married, 1879, Princess Luise Margarete of Prussia (who died in 1917). On active service in Egypt (1882). Field Marshal, 1902. Governor-General of Canada, 1911–16. He died on 16 January 1942.

[3] Sir John Dill was promoted to Field Marshal on 19 November 1941. The next two promotions to Field Marshal were Lord Gort and Lord Wavell, on 1 January 1943.

Winston S. Churchill to Norman Bower[1]
(*Churchill papers, 20/22*)

17 November 1941

My dear Bower,

As leader of the Government, which is supported by the Conservative, Labour and Liberal parties, I call on the electors to support you at the poll. I await, with especial eagerness, the verdict that, through you, Harrow will deliver, for my associations with the town and the school on the hill go back to my early youth and have always been very close and cordial.

I hope and believe that Harrow will seize the opportunity given by this by-election to express its unflinching support of the national effort as reflected in the National Government. We are engaged upon the Herculean labour of rescuing Europe and saving ourselves from the unspeakable 'New Order' and all the abominations that go with it.

Against totalitarian thoroughness we have to oppose the total effort of a free and united nation. Any vote not given to you in this election will be a vote for party strife and divided counsels. Constructive criticism is good for all Governments, but in the midst of the grave crisis that threatens us from without, it is idle to pretend that political sniping is an asset to the national effort.

Your return will be an endorsement of the country's unshakable loyalty to the principle of national unity, which we regard as the foundation of our strength in prosecuting the war to a victorious end.

I trust that the electors of Harrow, so far from assuming that the result of the election is a foregone conclusion, will appreciate the importance of going early to the poll and giving you not only a substantial but an overwhelming majority.

Yours sincerely,
Winston S. Churchill

War Cabinet: Confidential Annex
(*Cabinet papers, 65/24*)

17 November 1941
12.30 p.m.

The Prime Minister indicated to the War Cabinet the scope and date of impending operations in Cyrenaica. If these were successful, they would have

[1] Norman Bower, 1907–1990. Called to the Bar, Inner Temple, 1935. Member of the Westminster City Council, 1937. Unsuccessful Conservative candidate, West Bermondsey, 1931; North Hammersmith, 1935. Member of Parliament, Harrow, 1941–51.

a profound effect on our relationship with other countries. In regard to Russia, we should no longer be in the position that they were fighting and we were not, except in the air.

War Cabinet, Defence Committee (Operations): minutes
(*Cabinet papers, 69/2*)

17 November 1941
10 p.m.

TANKS[1]

The Prime Minister then referred to the fact that the requirements in the various theatres of the war were all set out to include 50% reserves, as if these must be regarded as part of the necessary equipment and be maintained indefinitely intact. It would naturally be desirable to have large reserves, but the showing of the figures in this way gave a wrong impression and caused inflated demands.

Sir John Dill said that if such a large number were given to Russia we should not have enough Valentines to replace the 170 which had just been withdrawn from the troops to be sent to the Middle East, and at the same time to provide the training requirements of India and New Zealand. The Matilda was a very good tank but it was not suitable for use with armoured divisions on account of its slow speed and small range. As far as he knew, we had not made any promise to the Russians to provide one type of tank rather than another and from what was known of the Russian tactics the Matilda would admirably serve their purpose. Matildas were not suitable for sending to India.

Considerable discussion took place on this question, in the course of which it was observed that Lord Beaverbrook's proposal would mean sending, in the period from December to March, 115 more Valentines than was proposed by the War Office.

Finally, the Prime Minister directed as follows:

(a) Efforts should be continued to produce the maximum number of tanks between now and next March.

(b) No reserve of tanks should be permitted at Home until formations overseas were fully equipped.

(c) A more generous allowance of tanks should be made available for India, the reserves of the Middle East over and above 25% being drawn upon for the purpose.

[1] It was twenty-six years earlier that Churchill, then First Lord of the Admiralty, had taken the initiative, and provided the funds for the research into, and experimental trials of, what within two years was to become the first operational Tank.

(d) Further discussion should take place between Lord Beaverbrook and the War Office on the proportion of Valentines to be included in the monthly quota for Russia, some delay in the completion of the equipment of the armoured divisions in the Home Forces being accepted to enable this proportion to be raised.
(e) A further statement should be furnished to the Committee by the War Office within a week to show the amended distribution resulting from these decisions.

Winston S. Churchill to Lord Cherwell, Sir Edward Bridges and General Ismay
(Churchill papers, 20/36)

17 November 1941

It is my wish before the end of the year to have fully planned the War Production Budget of 1942 and to submit this for approval to the Cabinet. For this purpose the programmes of the Navy, Army and Air Force, which are already far advanced, must be settled and the resulting tasks of the Supply Department set forth.

At the same time the Import Programme already completed on a basis of 33 million tons and the Home Production should be surveyed. I should propose that of the extra 2 million tons import available, half a million tons should go to food or feeding-stuffs and the other 1½ million tons to munitions in order to make up for their heavy cut this year. But this does not mean that needless imports, like timber, should be allowed undue expansion. The emphasis must be placed on a sharper war effort.

The third major element is manpower, now under Cabinet discussion but far advanced towards settlement.

It should be possible to state the above in broad outlines in a directive to be circulated about December 15. Perhaps you will let me have a preliminary study. The directive should not exceed one of my white square double sheets and should follow the model of last year.

Winston S. Churchill to James V. Forrestal
(Churchill papers, 20/45)

17 November 1941

Thank you so much for your most kind letter. We are still going strong here and I am cheered by all that is happening on your side.

Winston S. Churchill to President Franklin D. Roosevelt
(*Churchill papers, 20/45*)

18 November 1941
Personal and Secret

1. We are immensely encouraged by your Neutrality Amendment.[1]
2. Words in my letter 'sometime during the fall'[2] mean now. Kindest regards.

John Martin: diary
(*John Martin papers*)

18 November 1941

Battle in Libya began. I'm very impatient at absence of news of its progress.[3]

General Auchinleck to Winston S. Churchill
(*Churchill papers, 20/45*)

18 November 1941
Private
Most Secret
Most Immediate
despatched 10.30 p.m.
received 11.10 p.m.

Wireless silence is being maintained by Crusader and weather is hampering air observation consequently we have no definite news of progress made but we assume it to be satisfactory. We are refraining from disclosing real scope of operation as we think it more than likely that Rommel may not (repeat not) even yet have realized this hence our reference to patrols.

[1] On 13 November 1941, allowing American merchant ships to be armed, and to sail into war zones.

[2] For the launch of Crusader in the Western Desert.

[3] On the night of November 17, as what had been intended as a spectacular start to the Crusader offensive, a British commando force landed from the sea two hundred miles behind German lines, to attack Rommel's headquarters at Apollonia. Rommel, however, their target, was absent in Rome, and Lieutenant-Colonel Keyes, son of Admiral of the Fleet Sir Roger Keyes, was killed in the fighting inside one of the headquarter's houses, wrongly believed to be Rommel's. An Enigma decrypt disclosing that Rommel, having flown to Rome on November 1, would not return to North Africa until the evening of November 18, was sent to the Middle East in an emergency signal (OL 2008 of 17 November 1941), but must have arrived too late to stop the Commando Attack (F.H. Hinsley and others, *British Intelligence in the Second World War: Its Influence on Strategy and Operations*, Volume 2, London, 1981, page 303). Colonel Keyes was awarded a posthumous Victoria Cross for his part in the raid.

Winston S. Churchill to General Auchinleck
(*Churchill papers, 20/45*)

18 November 1941
Personal and Secret

Your 0/27464. As soon as I received your ME 0/19301 of 27th October Lemon, I moved the Chiefs of the Staff to consider exploitation of possible success in 'Crusader' and 'Acrobat',[1] by endeavouring to bring the French in North Africa out on our side, thus giving us Bizerta. In consequence an operation is being fully mounted by which the equivalent of two and a half divisions can be rapidly moved into Tunis, Algiers or Morocco at French invitation. I now send you full particulars of this in following telegram from Chiefs of Staff.

2. I have always thought it possible that 'Crusader' if successful, even apart from 'Acrobat', might lead to a German demand for facilities in Bizerta or Tunis generally. There is a possibility that Pétain and/or Weygand would resist, in which case operation in paragraph 1 would follow.

3. Whether Germans make demands or not, the moment success in 'Crusader' should become apparent, I am appealing to Roosevelt to put all possible pressure on Weygand, including sending American troops, and will, of course, offer Weygand the aid mentioned in paragraph 1. One of my reasons for fearing delay 'Crusader' was risk Weygand might be removed by German pressure. He is in Vichy now and a worse man may replace him. Anyhow, you may be sure we shall exploit to the full in the political strategic field any success you may gain.

Winston S. Churchill: Oral Answers
(*Hansard*)

18 November 1941 House of Commons

GOVERNMENT DEPARTMENTS: CO-ORDINATION

Mr De la Bère: Does the right hon. Gentleman realize how little has been done, and how much remains to be done, in the way of coordination? Surely he is aware that real coordination has never existed?

The Prime Minister: I am certainly not accepting any of those sweeping statements.

Mr De la Bère: Nevertheless, they are true.

[1] The follow-up to the conquest of Cyrenaica (Crusader) was to be an advance from Cyrenaica into Tripolitania (Acrobat). A third Operation in prospect if Crusader and Acrobat succeeded was a British landing in French North Africa with the tacit support of the Vichy French authorities there (Gymnast).

GREAT BRITAIN AND RUSSIA (CO-OPERATION)

Mr Wedgwood asked the Prime Minister whether the cooperation between the war executives of Great Britain and the Soviet are yet as close as they were between Great Britain and France when France was free and an Ally?

The Prime Minister: Yes, Sir, so far as geography and other conditions allow.

Winston S. Churchill to Sir Archibald Sinclair
(*Churchill papers, 20/29*)

18 November 1941

Please see attached.[1] It is astonishing that Mr Roberts[2] should have formed the impression described at 'A' as a result of working under you in the Air Ministry, and also that, while enjoying confidential views of our affairs in his relations with you, he should make such statements in public. I do not think such behaviour is compatible with his position as your PPS. No sort of apology is contained in his letter. There would be no objection to his making criticisms of this kind from an independent position, and I do not think he should be hampered by being retained in quasi-confidential circles. By all means let him go outside and abuse us to his heart's content, so long as he does not reveal any of the secret matters which he has picked up in your office.

It would do him no harm to improve his spelling.[3]

Winston S. Churchill to Oliver Lyttelton
(*Churchill papers, 20/45*)

18 November 1941
Secret

We must get to the bottom of the delay caused by the front axles of the cruiser tanks. I propose to appoint Mr Justice Singleton to hold an enquiry into this delay, with some such terms of reference as the following:

To ascertain what delay was caused to the readiness of the 22nd Armoured Brigades to start offensive operations by the need for strengthening the axles of its cruiser tanks.

[1] A letter of 17 November 1941 from Wilfred Roberts, MP to Churchill's Parliamentary Private Secretary, Colonel Harvie-Watt, about a critical speech Roberts had made at Carlisle two days earlier, in which he had said (in a passage marked 'A' by Harvie-Watt, on a *Daily Mirror* cutting): 'In the face of inefficiency and muddle he did not believe in sitting back, folding one's arms and saying: This is the sort of thing one can expect in a war.'

[2] Wilfrid Hubert Wace Roberts, 1900– . Labour Member of Parliament for North Cumberland, 1935–50. A Justice of the Peace for Cumberland from 1938.

[3] Churchill has twice circled the word 'speach' in Roberts's letter to Colonel Harvie-Watt.

To determine whether any such delay could have been avoided, to assign responsibility therefor, and to make any recommendations to ensure the fullest liaison and concert between the Home Departments involved and the Middle East authorities, so as to avoid such accidents in future deliveries.

It is clearly undesirable to bring any witnesses from the Middle East if it can possibly be avoided, and I would therefore be glad if, as a first step, you would arrange for a full statement of the matter to be drawn up and sent home. This statement should give dates and should state on whose authority the crucial decisions were made. I shall, of course, call for full statements of the case as seen from this end from the Ministry of Supply and the War Office, and when all three statements are available I should hope to be in a position to decide how the matter should be further handled.

Winston S. Churchill to General Sir Alan Brooke
(*Churchill papers, 20/22*)

18 November 1941
Private

My dear Brooke,

Thank you for your kind letter. I did not expect that you would be grateful or overjoyed at the hard anxious task to which I summoned you. But I feel that my old friendship for Ronnie and Victor,[1] the companions of gay subaltern days and early wars is a personal bond between us, to which will soon be added the comradeship of action in fateful events.

Yours very sincerely,
Winston S. Churchill

[1] Of Brooke's brother Victor, Churchill later wrote: 'Victor was a subaltern in the 9th Lancers when I joined the 4th Hussars, and I formed a warm friendship with him in 1895 and 1896. His horse reared up and he fell over backwards, breaking his pelvis, and he was sorely stricken for the rest of his life. However, he continued to be able to serve and ride, and perished gloriously from sheer exhaustion whilst acting as liaison officer with the French Cavalry Corps in the retreat from Mons in 1914.' Of Ronald Brooke, Churchill wrote: 'In the Boer War he was Adjutant of the South African Light Horse, and I for some months during the relief of Ladysmith was Assistant Adjutant, the regiment having six squadrons. Together we went through the fighting at Spion Kop, Vaal Krantz, and the Tugela. I learned much about tactics from him. Together we galloped into Ladysmith on the night of its liberation. Later on, in 1903, although I was only a youthful Member of Parliament, I was able to help him to the Somaliland campaign, in which he added to his high reputation. He was stricken down by arthritis at an early age, and could only command a reserve brigade at home during the First World War. Our friendship continued till his premature death in 1925.' (Winston S. Churchill, *The Second World War*, Volume 2, London, 1949, page 233, note 2)

Winston S. Churchill to Fiorella La Guardia[1]
(*Churchill papers, 20/22*)

18 November 1941

My dear Mr La Guardia,

Thank you so much for your kind letter of October 14, sending me the 'Thumbs Up' pins of the British War Relief Society. I was keenly stirred by receiving such a message of friendship and encouragement from the great warm-hearted City of New York.[2]

May I in return, Mr Mayor, send to you and to those who support this endeavour the sincere gratitude we in Britain feel for all the fine work you in America are doing to aid us in the common cause.

With all good wishes,

Yours very sincerely,
Winston S. Churchill

Winston S. Churchill to General Auchinleck
(*Churchill papers, 20/45*)

19 November 1941
11.30 a.m.
Personal and Secret

I have forbidden all mention in Press of big offensive, but this cannot surely be necessary or possible for long. We are puzzled at hearing nothing from you.

Winston S. Churchill to General Auchinleck
(*Churchill papers, 20/45*)

19 November 1941
12.30 p.m.
Secret and Personal

Presume you have read special information[3] about flood disaster to enemy in Derna region.

[1] Fiorello Henry La Guardia, 1882–1947. Born in New York of Jewish Italian parentage. On active service in Italy with the United States Army Air Force, commanding a bomber squadron, 1917–18. Republican member of the House of Representatives, 1919–21 and 1923–33. Mayor of New York, 1933–45. Director of the United Nations Relief and Rehabilitation Agency (UNRRA), 1946.

[2] Churchill had first visited New York in 1895, shortly before his twenty-first birthday. 'What an extraordinary people the Americans are!' he wrote to his mother. 'Their hospitality is a revelation to me and they make you feel at home and at ease in a way that I have never before experienced.'

[3] Based on Enigma decrypts of the German Army's own top secret messages.

Winston S. Churchill: statement
(Hansard)

19 November 1941 House of Commons

MR SPEAKER'S GOLDEN WEDDING[1]

The Prime Minister: I rise to commit an irregularity, and I will venture to ask the indulgence of the House. The intervention which I make is without precedent, and the reason for that intervention is also without precedent, and the fact that the reason for my intervention is without precedent is the reason why I must ask for a precedent for my intervention. We have searched the records of Parliament back, generation after generation, century after century, at any rate until we have reached the time of Mr Speaker Rous in 1653, before which time the occupants of the Chair held their tenure for shorter and more precarious periods, and in all this long range of Parliamentary history, there has been no occasion when a Speaker of the House of Commons has celebrated his golden wedding while occupying the Chair.

This unique event demands a procedure of its own, and I would like to assure you, Sir, that you are generally beloved throughout the House of Commons and that this affection extends to your home and your family. I would like to assure you that we have in thirteen years gained complete confidence in your impartiality, in the manner in which you vindicate and champion the rights of the House of Commons, in the way in which you protect minorities and their interventions in discussion, and in the kindliness and courtesy with which you treat all Members when they have access to you. I know I shall be expressing the sentiment of the whole House – all of them, everyone – when I say that we wish to share with you in this joyous event, and we wish that our expression shall be borne upon the records of the House and shall stand as a precedent for future times, should any such extraordinary but happy occurrence arise in the cycles of the future.

I must add that it has been arranged to make a presentation to you later today and that my right hon. Friend the Member for Carnarvon Boroughs (Mr Lloyd George), the Father of the House, will bring a considerable delegation to meet you. For the convenience of Members, it would be a good thing if our Debate could end a little earlier than usual so as to enable this ceremony to take place. I thank the House for having indulged me in this manner. I trust that my action may be condoned on account of the general unanimity in the sentiments which I have expressed.

[1] Captain Fitzroy, who had become Speaker in June 1928 (when Churchill was Chancellor of the Exchequer), had married Muriel Douglas-Pennant in 1891. He had entered the House of Commons in 1900, in the same year as Churchill.

Charles Eade: notes of a luncheon
(*Charles Eade papers*)

19 November 1941 10 Downing Street[1]

Although Mr and Mrs Churchill are still living at Storey's Gate Buildings, they usually lunch at Downing Street where Mr Churchill does his work, Mrs Churchill told me.

The others present were Mr A. P. Herbert, MP[2] and Mrs Herbert, the Hon. Mrs Edwin Montagu, a relative of Mrs Churchill's (who was also at the second luncheon) and Major General Sir Reginald Barnes.[3] Barnes was, until recently, Colonel of the 4th Hussars in which position he had just been succeeded by Mr Churchill.

When Mr Churchill first left Sandhurst and joined the 4th Hussars in 1895, Barnes was a fellow subaltern and he was Mr Churchill's companion on the trip to Cuba when they were with the Spanish army in the fighting against the Cuban rebels. He has retained Mr Churchill's friendship throughout life. Mr Churchill called him 'Reggie' and Barnes called Churchill either 'Winston' or 'Old Dear'.

I sat next to Mr Churchill on his left, with Mrs Montagu on my left. Mrs A.P. Herbert was the other side of the Prime Minister.

The luncheon consisted of a sort of fishcake, small cutlets of beef and a simple baked jam pudding. Drinks were sherry before lunch, then white wine, Port, Brandy and coffee. When the baked jam pudding was served, Mr Churchill remarked: 'This is the sort of thing which helps Lord Woolton,' and expressed great satisfaction at seeing it on the table; then went on to say to the agreement of everybody present, that Lord Woolton was doing a very fine job as Minister of Food.

Mr and Mrs Churchill talked about their two daughters, Sarah and Mary, who are in the WAAF and ATS respectively. Mr Churchill said that it was very good evidence of the democratic days in which we live that it frequently

[1] This luncheon was held in the Garden Room of 10 Downing Street, an area at the back of the building and below the ground level of the street. It was here that Churchill held his weekly luncheons with the King.

[2] Alan Patrick Herbert, 1890–1971. Educated at Winchester and New College, Oxford. Humorist; began writing for *Punch*, 1910. On active service with the Royal Naval Division, Antwerp, Gallipoli and France (wounded), 1914–18. Called to the Bar, 1918. Joined the staff of *Punch* 1924. Independent MP for Oxford University, 1935–50 (when the University seats were abolished). Petty Officer, River Thames Naval Auxiliary Patrol, June 1940. Knighted, 1945. A Trustee of the National Maritime Museum, 1947–53. Author of more than sixty works of prose and verse, including a novel about Gallipoli, *The Secret Battle*. In 1914 he married Gwendolen Quilter: they had four children.

[3] Reginald Walter Ralph Barnes, 1871–1946. Entered the Army, 1890. Lieutenant, 4th Hussars, 1894, and one of Churchill's close Army friends. Went with Churchill to Cuba, 1895. Captain, 1901. Lieutenant-Colonel commanding the 10th Hussars, 1911–15. Colonel, 1914. Brigadier-General, commanding the 116th Infantry Brigade, and the 14th Infantry Brigade, 1915–16. Commanded the 32nd Division, 1916–17 and the 57th Division, 1917–19. Major-General, 1918. Knighted, 1919.

happened at his dining table that he had two women privates sitting down with generals, without any embarrassment on either side. He spoke very proudly of his daughters and said that they were working very seriously and were not going out for quick commissions, but wished to be sergeants first. Mary is now a corporal in the ATS and it is frequently her duty to reprimand other girls she catches in the quiet parts of the camp cuddling with soldiers. The idea of his daughter performing such a duty seemed highly amusing to the Prime Minister. Apparently, Mary had told her father that it very often happens that the right sort of girls are not put into the operational units.

Mr Churchill said that he had just come from a most interesting ceremony in the House of Commons, where it had been his pleasure to make a speech on the occasion of the Speaker's golden wedding. He was obviously very pleased to have taken part in such a ceremony.

The Prime Minister joked about Mr Herbert's appearance in the uniform of a Petty Officer in the Navy and asked whether Herbert was a Chief Petty Officer. Herbert replied that he was only an ordinary Petty Officer in charge of a boat which he himself had previously owned.

Somebody mentioned Mr Stanley Baldwin and Mr Churchill said that his information was that Mr Baldwin was today a haunted man. Apparently, even his own family treated him with but scant respect. Mrs Churchill chipped in to say that she had heard recently of one occasion where Mr Baldwin in his own house murmured a mild complaint because the wireless was playing too loudly, and the only effect was that someone turned it on even louder. She also said that Baldwin was sent about the house to get things when somebody else was perhaps too tired or lazy to do it. Winston said to his wife: 'Well, I hope you are never going to treat me like that!'

The Prime Minister amused the table by talking about some of his visitors from America and told how he was repeatedly pressed to meet a certain US Bishop. He could not understand why there was so much eagerness to get him to meet this Bishop so quickly. However, at last, he saw him for a few minutes. Later, it turned out that this particular bishop, although of some use to us in America, was rather frowned upon by the Methodists in this country, because he had previously been suspected of burning down his church, presumably in order to collect the insurance money and it seemed to be only a matter of time before this would come out.

Another question discussed was the new military changes. It was announced this morning that General Sir John Dill CIGS is being retired on reaching the age limit of 60, and being replaced by Sir Alan Brooke, with Major-General Nye, aged 45, as vice-chief. Mr Churchill made it very clear to me that the retirement of Dill was not entirely due to the question of age. He did not explain what the trouble was, but I certainly got the impression that there was a good reason, apart from the age limit, for Dill's departure from the head of the army. He also made it very clear that he has the highest opinion of Major-General Nye, who, the Prime Minister said, had a very good grasp of affairs and was able to express himself well and clearly, and was a coming man. Nye is the son of a Sergeant-Major and went to a school for the sons of NCOs. He is, therefore, not a representative of the old school tie tradition. Mr Churchill said that he had the highest regard possible for the 'old school tie' man, but he did feel in the present conditions, there might be a very good reason for the big promotion for a man representative of a more democratic education. On the other hand, this did not mean Nye had been promoted merely because he was not 'old school tie'. The promotion which had been rapid, was due to his ability. The Prime Minister also spoke with warm approval of the manner in which Dill had taken his retirement 'like a gentleman' and commented on the fact that Admiral Sir Roger Keyes had made such a fuss about his retirement, revealed four days ago, from his position as Organizing Officer and Director of Operations of the Commandos used as shock troops for our raids on the continent. Churchill felt, however, that Keyes' protest and public statements about his retirement were really caused by Lady Keyes,[1] a very formidable woman, and the Prime Minister said that he wished he could recruit Lady Keyes for active service.

Sir Reginald Barnes spoke about his position with the Home Guard from which he would have to retire owing to the age limit. The Prime Minister spoke about the importance of the Home Guard and said that the plan for defence was that in the event of an invasion, the first line of defence along the coast would be by the Home Guard, so that regular troops could be kept mobile in the rear to go to the necessary positions when called upon. Mr Churchill added that if the worst came to the worst, we would certainly use gas against the invader, and, he said, 'we have plenty of that'.

An interesting example of how the great man's mind can be in confusion about some ordinary piece of general knowledge was revealed when Sir Reginald Barnes mentioned that he was due to retire from the Home Guard on January 31. Mr Churchill laughed and said: 'Not January 31, January 30.'

Barnes replied: 'No, January, 31,' and Churchill said: 'No, it cannot be. There are only 30 days in January.' Then he paused and said doubtfully: 'Aren't there?'

At the other end of the table, Herbert started muttering under his breath: 'Thirty days hath September, etc' and I said: 'No, January has 31 days,', which the Prime Minister agreed was the case.

Continuing the point about retirement owing to age limits, Mr Churchill said that politics was almost the only profession left in which no age limit operated; then he paused for a moment and added that of course the Church came into the same class and Herbert chipped in to say that the law also did not set an age limit.

[1] Eva Bowlby. She married Keyes in 1906. In the First World War she served in the Voluntary Aid Detachment (VAD), in the Second World War in Civil Defence.

Discussing the retirement of Dill and Keyes, and in response to my enquiry about whether it was always wise to operate on an age limit, Mr Churchill murmured under his breath: 'Sometimes it is kinder that way.'

Another point at the luncheon was that Mr Churchill said that he had been reading a memorandum, presumably from someone in the War Office,[1] who pointed out that there was fame and honour waiting for the General who could bring back artillery into its old position of importance in warfare, a position from which it had been ousted by the tanks. He told Barnes he would let him read that report, if he promised to return it.

Mr Churchill also mentioned, in reply to a question from A. P. Herbert, about Commando raids on occupied territory. Herbert said that there was much discussion about these raids, but he did not know what to say about them. The Prime Minister said that he did not think it was a good thing to discuss. I pointed out that a lot of this discussion arose from the fact that these raids had been well reported in the American Press, particularly the *Christian Science Monitor*, and that such stories as I had lifted had been stopped by the censor.

Mr Churchill said that he had given instructions that we could not have stories about these raids, and that the best attitude to adopt was that the public might well be told that more was going on than could be talked about. He particularly did not want the name of Keyes' successor to be printed. I said I had had the name passed to me last Saturday and that I had put it up to censorship and it had been killed. I added that I was not asking Mr Churchill whether the name I had was the right one, but that I thought it probably was. Mr Churchill then said he assumed the name I got was Lord Louis Mountbatten and added that that was the right name, but he did not want attention drawn to it and did not want the name revealed. There was no good purpose served in publishing stories of raids by twenty or thirty men in which we perhaps took one prisoner and left behind three of our own men. At the same time, things would be happening, and were happening, and he then dropped a remark which indicated to me that although it was very secret and nothing must be published about it or even spoken, we were on the verge of a big attack by our army in Libya.

Another question discussed was that of the activities of the Oxford Group which Mr Herbert had been attacking in Parliament. Beyond general antagonism, Mr Churchill did not say very much, but I gathered a great deal of support for it which had been expected when the matter was raised in Parliament had failed to materialize. Among the supporters, apparently, was the Marquis of Salisbury, but when it came to the point, he did not do anything about it.

[1] In fact, Churchill's own memorandum of 7 October 1941.

Mr Churchill spoke to me about the shortage of paper and asked how the *Sunday Dispatch* was getting on for paper. I told him we were in the same position as others. Our circulation had reached its permitted maximum and that it had increased from 700,000 to 1,060,000 since I took over the editorship three and a half years ago. He said, with a grin, that he was amazed that his articles had continued to run for so long. He had thought it might be possible to extract a few articles from his old published writings, but had no idea it would be possible to go on for over a hundred weeks.

I told him I also was very surprised, but also very happy that that was the situation. He said he was also happy. I told him I always handled the articles myself, because I realized that some of the old articles written years ago might have unfortunate implications if published now and that any doubtful passages were eliminated by me. He said that there had been one article which had rather worried him, but that everything had turned out all right and he would not tell me what the point was.

We also talked about the question of Japan and I raised the point that there was no other country in the world which was in the extraordinary position of having two voices, both apparently speaking with authority. On one side, we have the representatives of Japan's economic interests who appeared anxious to reach a peace and understanding with the English-speaking races. On the other side, we had militarist parties who appeared to be determined on war at any price. Mr Churchill said that this was so, and that same extreme party had even gone to the extent of assassinating members of the Government who were not prepared to be as aggressive as the fanatics felt that they should be. Discussing the question of the Japanese war strength, Mr Churchill said no one knew the fighting capacity of the Japanese Navy, but so far as their aeroplanes were concerned, we were of the opinion that they were not good, certainly, they have not performed remarkably well against the Chinese.

As for the possibility of America entering the war, either against Japan or against Germany, he felt it was most likely he would land the second of four possible prizes. The first prize would be the entry of the US into the war without involving Japan. The second prize would be the entry of the US on our side with Japan on the side of the enemy. The third prize would be that neither would enter the war at all and the fourth prize would be Japan in the war against us, but with the US still staying neutral.

Mr Churchill spoke with great appreciation and gratitude of what America has sent us and is sending. He told us that long before the Lend and Lease Act had been passed, he had told the purchasing agents to go ahead with any sort of orders and they would be paid for somehow. I said that probably the Americans realized that they would probably not be paid for what they were sending us. Churchill said, with a flash of vigour, 'They will be paid: they will be paid with victory.' Referring to the influx of planes from America, Mr Churchill said that it was absolutely essential that any fighting planes must be the best of their type and that anything else but the best was useless for the fighter. On the other hand there were many modifications we could have in the case of bombing planes. Refinements could be cut out of planes which could fly to Germany last year and drop bombs and could still fly and bomb this year, even though there may be other and better bombers in existence.

Mr Churchill spoke of the vast output we should be having in 1942 and 1943. He said, with a grin, even he was a little startled when he heard that the Americans were planning for 1948 and 1949. Mr Herbert questioned whether it would be to our interest to have America in the war or whether it would be better if America continued to supply us with arms. The point was that if America entered the war, she would be so busy equipping her own army that she would not have anything to spare for us. Mr Churchill, who had dealt with this point, I remember, at the first luncheon, said at once, if America entered the war it would be such a development of war fever, such an impetus in war production, that it would be very much greater than it could be with America remaining technically neutral.

Speaking of arms production, not only of this country and America, but of all countries, he said that one could take it as a general rule that in the first year of the war, arms output was nothing; in the second year, there was very little; in the third year 'quite a lot' and America was in the second year 'very little'. The new aeroplanes coming over from America, said Mr Churchill, were very good. American experts had been over our factories and had learned much from us and by their frankness we had learned much from them. He had been tremendously impressed by the experts the US had sent to this country with one exception. That was a general named Embick who had come over here, and, having seen the defences at Dover, proclaimed that nothing could save England from invasion, and that was the story he had carried back with him to the US.

On the other hand, there was General Marshall who had been very helpful to us when he had stripped the US army of its weapons in order to send them to Britain. This, remarked Mr Churchill, was a very grave step because nothing could be worse for the morale of an army, newly recruited from the citizens of America, than to find that they had no weapons with which to train.

I remarked that there had been many articles recently in American papers and magazines about the poor morale of the American army, about the soldiers being discontented and low spirited because they felt they were probably wasting their time and I added that the only way of keeping up their spirits was by America's entry into the war. Mr Churchill said that was true because otherwise, it was like a football team being in constant training, knowing they will not be called upon to play a match.

We also discussed Russia. Speaking of the magnificent resistance the Russians have shown to the Germans, Mr Churchill said that it would be inconceivable in the last war that the Russians could have withstood the onslaught of the Germans for five months. He felt that it was due not only to the improvement of the Russians, but also to a certain deterioration of the Germans, and added that while the shock troops, the panzer divisions and so on of the Germans, were remarkable, once we could pierce through that 'outer crust', the masses behind were not so formidable.

The Russians were excellent at handling the tanks, planes and other machines we sent them. They were so anxious to use them that they had little patience in listening to instructions – they just wanted to get them into action. Mr Churchill made some remarks praising very highly the ordinary Russian soldiers, although he made it clear he deplored the Russian system. He spoke with appreciation of the ability and efficiency of Russian engineers and skilled workmen generally, who were, he said, the aristocracy of the new system. Turning to me, he said that there would be no room for people of my job in the Communist system, but I said I could not agree as *Pravda* and *Izvestia* are two very prominent and successful papers.

Mr Churchill remarked on the difficulty of dealing with the Russians, because they were not prepared to tell us everything. I suggested that they were suspicious of us. He said yes, that was probably true, but at any rate we had never signed a pact with Germany. He then said he wished to tell a story, but stressed that if we ever re-told it, we must not attribute it to him. He said that a British representative went to Russia and was shown round the sights. He was taken round by a guide who said at one point: 'This is Winston Churchill Square.' A little further on, the guide said: 'This is Eden Hotel, and late Marshal Goering Hotel,' and proceeding on their way a little further, the guide said: 'This is Beaverbrook Street, late Himmler Street.' At this point, the guide offered his English visitor a cigarette and the Englishman, taking it, said: 'Thank you comrade, late bastard!'

At this point, Mrs Churchill, who had retired to the adjoining room with the ladies, put her head in through the door to say that we must join the ladies now, because she and the Hon. Mrs Edwin Montagu were going out to do some work in connection with Mrs Churchill's 'Aid for Russia Fund'[1] and that she and Mrs Montagu were working women and that it was all right for people like her husband and others who had no work to do, to sit around and talk, but she had to get going; so we went into the adjoining room, and said good bye to these two ladies and sat round with Mrs Herbert, Mr Herbert and Sir Reginald Barnes for further conversation with the Prime Minister.

[1] By the end of October 1941, Clementine Churchill's Aid to Russia Appeal had raised (in twelve days), £370,000, and had already sent to Russia 53 emergency operating outfits, 30 blood-transfusion sets, 70,000 surgical needles, half a ton (one million doses) of the painkiller phenacetin (now known to be potentially damaging to the liver and the kidney, and largely discontinued) and seven tons of absorbent cotton-wool.

Barnes commented on the excellent cigar he was smoking and said: 'Winston, is this one of those you got from Havana?' Mr Churchill said that it was, and Barnes said, 'You know, when I was in Cuba, I brought back a box of these cigars for Old Brab and I think that was the best thing I ever did for the Army!'

Old Brab referred to Colonel Brabazon who was colonel of the 4th Hussars when Barnes and Churchill were in it as subalterns in 1895.

Churchill scoffed at Barnes' remark and said: 'You know you would have got the job anyway. You were obviously the man for it.'

Talking of the war in general, Mr Churchill likened himself to a dead cat, floating on the sea, but would eventually be washed up on the shores of victory. I commented on this to the effect that he would very strongly resent it if anybody else likened him to a dead cat, and from the way in which he laughed, I am quite sure he agreed with me.

I managed to bring up the question of Mr Shinwell, the Socialist MP for Seaham. He is one of Mr Churchill's bitterest critics and Mr Churchill spoke of him quite heatedly as an objectionable man and he appeared to have strong feelings against him. He said that when he formed his government, and the Labour Party came into it, it was up to the Labour Party to nominate some of the people for places in the ministries. They nominated Shinwell among others and he was offered the position of Parliamentary Secretary to the Ministry of Food. The Minister is Lord Woolton, who sits in the House of Lords. The Parliamentary Secretary was a position of considerable dignity in the House of Commons and it is now held by Major Lloyd George,[1] but Shinwell refused it, presumably because he thought that as a former Minister of Mines, he was entitled to a bigger post.

Mr Churchill said that great attention was frequently paid abroad to criticism by private members. For instance, a recent speech by Edgar Granville, who said that there should be some changes in the Cabinet, was cabled to America and given great prominence which would never have been attached to it in this country.

As we left, Mr Herbert tried to draw Mr Churchill into a discussion about the Merchant Navy and some improvement for the men who served in it. He said that he had been asked, if he got the opportunity, to mention this to the Prime Minister, but Winston quickly brushed this aside and obviously did not wish to discuss it at this point.

[1] Gwilym Lloyd George, 1894–1967. Second son of David Lloyd George. Educated at Eastbourne College and Jesus College, Cambridge. On active service in France, 1914–19 (Major, Royal Artillery; despatches). Liberal MP for Pembrokeshire, 1922–4 and 1929–50; for Newcastle North, 1951–7. Assistant Liberal Whip in the House of Commons, 1924. Parliamentary Secretary to the Board of Trade, 1931 and 1939–41. Parliamentary Secretary, Minister of Food, 1941–2; Ministry of Fuel and Power, 1942–5; Ministry of Food, 1951–4. Secretary of State for the Home Department and Minister for Welsh Affairs, 1954–7. Created Viscount Tenby, 1957.

On our way out, Mrs Herbert peeped into the Cabinet Room, and Winston, who had gone in there by another door, saw her, and invited us all in. He marched up to one end of the room where there was a big map of the world. Pointing to it, he drew our attention to the vast area covered by the British Empire, Soviet Russia and China. Pointing to the British Isles, he said how much of that Empire would collapse if these small islands are overwhelmed. Then he added, twirling a ruler around Central Europe, it did not matter so much what was happening there in these countries under Hitler's rule, compared to the great immensity of the globe as a whole.

He then turned to me and commented with approval on the fact that I was carrying my gasmask, but I honestly told him I did not usually carry it. I only had it on because I was lunching with him in Downing Street. At that, he gave a short laugh, but made no comment. Then I shook hands and left.

Air Marshal Tedder and General Auchinleck to Winston S. Churchill
(*Churchill papers, 20/45*)

19 November 1941
Most Secret
despatched 2.22 p.m.
received 4 p.m.

Situation Crusader afternoon 18th satisfactory and although no contact has been obtained with enemy other than by patrols operating well in advance of main bodies our armoured troops are now well positioned on enemy's southern flank. Rain in Cyrenaica has been very heavy and may have impeded our advance slightly besides limiting air action on both sides. Probability is that enemy more seriously affected by bad weather than ourselves. Absence of enemy air activity in forward areas was remarkable. In spite of great extent of front covered by our mechanized forces it still seems doubtful if Rommel may not yet have appreciated scale of our operations in the air and on the land. For this reason we are most repeat most anxious not repeat not to disclose this in our communications or by any other means for the present.

General Auchinleck to Winston S. Churchill
(*Churchill papers, 20/45*)

19 November 1941
Private
Most Secret
Most Immediate
despatched 8 p.m.
received 10 p.m.

1. Owing to weather and atmospheric news from front coming in very slowly. We are doing all we can to rectify this but you realize distances are great.

2. Now seems certain that enemy was surprised and unaware of imminence and weight of our blow. Indications, though these remain to be confirmed, are that he is now trying to withdraw westward from area Bardia-Sollum. Until we know area reached by our armoured troops today it is not possible to read the battle further at moment. I myself am happy about situation and will telegraph immediately we get news of Cunningham's dispositions.

3. A communiqué is being issued 2100 hours GMT disclosing that major offensive is in progress so need for concealing this no longer obtains.

Winston S. Churchill to General Auchinleck
(*Churchill papers, 20/45*)

19 November 1941
Personal
Most Secret

I am glad things have opened well. We scrupulously observed your wishes about no indication of scale of offensive being published. I would rather you had not released a communiqué from Cairo in these circumstances, as we have to deal with Press and public here. Communiqué itself is perhaps precipitate in praising at so early a stage the skill and deception employed. It is much better to let events tell their own tale. For the next few days all your communiqués should be issued through London and not through Cairo. Send all here at earliest. We shall be most careful to help you in every way.

Lord Camrose to Winston S. Churchill
(*Churchill papers, 2/417*)

20 November 1941

Dear Winston,

Herewith I am sending you a biography of yourself by Lewis Broad,[1] published today.

Mr Broad is the Night Editor of the *Daily Telegraph*.

If you should have time to look at the work I think you will like it.

Yours sincerely,
Wm Camrose

War Cabinet: Confidential Annex
(*Cabinet papers, 65/24*)

20 November 1941
12 noon

The Secretary of State for Foreign Affairs said that information had been received to the effect that Marshal Pétain had been forced to dismiss General Weygand from his post in North Africa. In these circumstances, the Prime Minister had sent an urgent message to President Roosevelt.

The Prime Minister outlined the salient points in the message which had been despatched. He had told President Roosevelt that our operations in Cyrenaica had started and that the prospects were favourable. He had asked the President to do all he could to preserve General Weygand in his Command. If not, we hoped that he would try to get some friendly figure from retirement appointed, as, for example, General Georges.[1]

The Prime Minister added that he thought nothing more could be done, until we knew the upshot of the battle which was now raging in Cyrenaica. If we could say that we had won an important victory, we should then ask President Roosevelt to say to Marshal Pétain that now or never was the time

[1] Lewis Broad, 1901-1976. A journalist and author who spent twenty years on the staff of the *Daily Telegraph*, which he joined in 1924. Night editor during the London Blitz, 1940-41, and during the flying bomb attacks on the capital, 1944. His 1941 biography, *Winston Churchill: Man of War*, was reissued in 1947. In 1955 he wrote a biography of Anthony Eden, and in 1961 *The Abdication 25 Years After: a Reappraisal*. In 1969 he published *Women of Number Ten*.

[2] Joseph Georges, 1875–1951. Entered the French Infantry, 1897. Chief of Staff to Marshal Foch, 1918. Head of the French Economic Service in the Ruhr, 1923. Chief of Staff to Marshal Pétain, 1925–6. Chef de Cabinet in the Maginot Government, 1929. Commanded the 19th Corps in Algeria, 1931. Wounded in Marseille at the time of the assassination of King Alexander of Yugoslavia, 1934. Created Generalissimo, 1934. Commander of the Forces and Operations in the North East, 1939–40. A member of the French Committee of National Liberation, 1943.

when he should tell North Africa to assert its independence and freedom, and that we would give all the aid in our power.

The Prime Minister said that if the Germans asked for access to Bizerta, the line to take with the French would be that, if they agreed, the United States would never help them again, and we would put on a merciless blockade. If they refused to concede facilities at Bizerta we should offer them the military aid for which preliminary arrangements had already been made.

The Foreign Secretary said that, while he entirely agreed with the view put forward by the Prime Minister, he was a little anxious about the time-table.

The Prime Minister said that the matter had better be considered again on the following day, in the light of the military situation in Cyrenaica.

Winston S. Churchill to President Franklin D. Roosevelt

(*Cabinet papers, 65/24*)

20 November 1941
Personal and Secret

The approach and deployment of our forces in Libya has been most successful, and the enemy was taken by surprise. Only now does he realize the large scale of our operations against him. Heavy fighting between the armoured forces seems probable today. Orders have been given to press what is now begun to a decision at all costs. The chances do not seem to be unfavourable.

2. It would be disastrous if Weygand were to be replaced by some pro-Hun officer just at the moment when we are likely to be in a position to influence events in North Africa both from the East and from home. I hope you will try your utmost at Vichy to preserve Weygand in his command. If this cannot be achieved some friendly figure from retirement, like General Georges, might be agreed upon. I have not seen Georges since the collapse, but I have reason to believe his heart is sound. I knew him very well. Anyhow, Mr President, Tunis and all French North Africa might open out to us if we gain a good victory in Libya, and we must be ready to exploit success. I am afraid, on the other hand, lest Hitler may demand to occupy Bizerta in view of possible danger to Tripoli. It is now or never with the Vichy French and their last chance of redemption.

3. Very glad to get Averell back here.

Winston S. Churchill: Business of the House
(Hansard)

20 November 1941 House of Commons

Mr Bevan . . . The Prime Minister is correct in saying that the usual channels arrange these things, which means, in fact, that the Government arrange these things. The House has not had any opportunity to express its voice on the policy of the Government except through the limited opportunities provided by the gerrymandering of Debate through the usual channels.

The Prime Minister: I think that is a very unfair suggestion. The representatives of the three parties, it is quite true, do support the Government, but those who are outside and take an independent view get their chance of expressing their views through their respective parties as to the course decided upon. I do not think that can be called gerrymandering, except by those who have a predilection for using offensive terms.

Mr Bevan: That is a predilection in which we follow the Prime Minister. We shall have an opportunity of pointing out how offensive some of his references have been in the very recent past. It was entirely unnecessary and unprecedented to have used yesterday's Debate for the discussion of very small matters for which ample opportunity would be provided in future.

LIBYAN OFFENSIVE

Mr Pethick-Lawrence: Has the Prime Minister any statement to make on the situation in the Middle East?

The Prime Minister: The House will, I am sure, have been interested to learn from the Cairo communiqué that an offensive against the German and Italian armies on the Libyan front has begun. This offensive has been long and elaborately prepared, and we have waited for nearly five months in order that our Army should be well equipped with all those weapons which have made their mark in this new war. There is nothing in the world quite like the war conditions prevailing in the Libyan desert, in which swift and far-ranging movements are only possible by an extraordinary use of armour, air-power and mechanization. The conditions are in many respects like those of sea war. The principal units involved keep wireless silence while preparing or making their rapid and extensive movements. The encounter, when it is achieved is like a clash of fleets or flotillas, and, as in a sea battle, all may be settled one way or the other in the course of perhaps two hours. If, in this case, the enemy armour is destroyed or seriously defeated, and his air power is dominated, the plight of his infantry and artillery, crowded in the coastal regions, would evidently become serious in some respects.

The object of the British and Empire offensive is not so much the occupation of this or that locality but the destruction of the army, and primarily of the armoured forces, of the enemy. For this purpose the Army of the Western Desert took up its preliminary situations on a broad front from the sea to the Giara ut oasis, and all was in readiness by nightfall on the 17th. At dawn on the 18th the general advance began. Very heavy and exceptional rains hampered the movements of our forces, which had great distances to cover. These rains, however, appear to have been far more heavy in the coastal regions than in the desert, and may well prove more harmful to the enemy than to us. During the 18th, our Armies came into contact with the enemy outposts at many points, and it seems certain that the enemy were taken completely by surprise.

The Desert Army is now favourably situated for a trial of strength. I do not know, up to the present, whether this trial has actually begun, or taken place, between the heavy armoured forces, but evidently it cannot be long delayed. It is far too soon to indulge in any exultation. General Auchinleck and General Cunningham, in command, under him, of the Eighth Army, have made a brilliant and successful strategic approach and obtained positions of marked advantage. All now depends upon the battle which follows. It is evident that the next few days will see developments which will include many highly interesting features. One thing is certain, that all ranks of the British and Empire troops involved are animated by a long-pent-up and ardent desire to engage the enemy and that they will fight with the utmost resolve and devotion, feeling as they all do that this is the first time we have met the Germans at least equally well-armed and equipped and realizing the part which a British victory in Libya will play upon the whole course of the war.

Winston S. Churchill to General Sikorski

(*Churchill papers, 20/45*)

20 November 1941

I welcome your Excellency's message from Tobruk and your generous tribute to the work of the British forces in the Middle East. We, too, are proud that Polish troops are now fighting by our side in the African desert. Under their gallant commander, they have already shown themselves worthy comrades of those who fought so well in Poland and in France. They are playing a notable part in the common struggle for final victory and so for the liberation of Poland and the establishment of a lasting peace.

All good wishes for your journey to Russia.

Winston S. Churchill to Brendan Bracken
(*Churchill papers, 20/36*)

20 November 1941

1. GHQ, ME,[1] will issue its own communiqués to the world through London, and only through London. These communiqués can be either joint or from the Services individually. Only in very exceptional circumstances will any amendment be made. Special arrangements will be made to ensure no delay. There is no need to encypher communiqués. A special staff to be organized at WO.

2. No newspaper material is to emanate directly from Cairo. Whether Dominion or foreign, it is to come through here. There is no intention to censor or delay any Press matter passed by the Middle East censor. It will merely pass through our nozzle so as to ensure uniform delivery to the world. Only in very exceptional cases will any alteration be made here. Special arrangements are being made to ensure almost instantaneous release. Everything put out by Cairo should be sent *en clair* to us.

General Auchinleck to Winston S. Churchill
(*Churchill papers, 20/45*)

20 November 1941
Most Secret
Personal
despatched 5.54 p.m.
received 7.40 p.m.

Regret our communiqué seemed unsuitable to you. Reference to success of secrecy measures was put in for a definite purpose. Entirely agree as to desirability of letting events speak for themselves, a view to which I am naturally strongly inclined personally. It is, however, inconsistent with pressure put on us to be more communicative. I submit that the editing of our communiqués in London as proposed in your telegram is likely to prove dangerous and unworkable. In this connection I ask you to refer to your personal telegram No. 61626 (MO5) of 15/4/41 to General Wavell. In my opinion a communiqué is a weapon which can be used against the enemy and conversely against us unless controlled absolutely by the Higher Command on the spot. It will not (repeat not) be possible for anyone in London to appreciate the immediate effect on the enemy in this theatre of any alteration in the wording of communiqués drafted here and I request therefore that you will not insist on the procedure laid down in your telegram. I will ensure that

[1] General Headquarters, Middle East.

communiqués issued from here are confined to bald statements and not embroidered in any way. As there will not be time for me to receive your reply to this telegram before this evening we shall send today's communiqué to London for issue but I strongly urge that it be published as drafted here and not altered. In any event it seems as if we must release this communiqué here tonight so that something can appear in the Egyptian press tomorrow. Failure to issue a comminqué here is certain to cause undue alarm and despondency locally.

Winston S. Churchill to General Auchinleck
(*Churchill papers, 20/45*)

21 November 1941
Personal
Most Secret
Most Immediate
despatched 5.30 p.m.

1. You may return to procedure in my No. 61626 (MO5) of 15/4 quoted by you. Naturally we are inconvenienced here when first news for publication of long awaited important events reaches us through your Cairo communiqués issued to the World. You promised to keep me properly informed. Pray remember we have a Parliament, Press and public here at least as important as your Cairo audience. Moreover, I have to deal with President Roosevelt whose action at Vichy about Weygand or his successor is of the highest consequence.

2. From what I learn from special sources which you know,[1] I have formed a favourable impression of our operations. I should be glad to have your own appreciation.

Winston S. Churchill to General Auchinleck
(*Churchill papers, 20/45*)

21 November 1941
10.10 p.m.

Your communiqué just received. Admirable. Presume you have already received my 125 Susan despatched this morning, authorizing you to issue future publications without reference to me.

[1] That is, Enigma.

Winston S. Churchill to General Auchinleck and Air Marshal Tedder
(*Churchill papers, 20/45*)

21 November 1941
11 p.m.
Private

Thank you very much for your 1597 and AOC, ME 376,[1] which are both most encouraging.

Winston S. Churchill to J. V. Stalin
(*Churchill papers, 20/45*)

21 November 1941
11 p.m.
Personal and Secret

Many thanks for your message just received.[2] At the very beginning of the war I began a personal correspondence with President Roosevelt, which has led to a very solid understanding being established between us and has often helped in getting things done quickly. My only desire is to work on equal terms of comradeship and confidence with you.

2. About Finland. I was quite ready to advise the Cabinet to declare war upon Finland when I sent you my telegram of 5th September. Later information has made me think that it will be more helpful to Russia and the common cause if the Finns can be got to stop fighting, and stand still or go home, than if we put them in the dock with the guilty Axis Powers by a formal declaration of war and make them fight it out to the end. However, if they do not stop in the next fortnight and you still wish us to declare war on them, we will certainly do so. I agree with you that it was very wrong any publication should have been made. We certainly were not responsible.

3. Should our offensive in Libya result, as we hope, in the destruction of the German-Italian Army there, it will be possible to take a broad survey of the war as a whole, with more freedom than has hitherto been open to His Majesty's Government.

4. For this purpose, we shall be willing in the near future to send the Foreign Secretary, Mr Eden, whom you know, via the Mediterranean to meet you at Moscow or elsewhere. He would be accompanied by high military and other experts and will be able to discuss every question relating to the war, including the sending of troops not only into the Caucasus but into the fighting line of

[1] About the course of the 'Crusader' battle.
[2] Stalin's telegram to Churchill of 11 November 1941, printed on pages 1431–2.

your armies in the south. Neither our shipping resources nor the communications will allow large numbers to be employed, and even so you will have to choose between troops and supplies across Persia.

5. I notice that you wish also to discuss the post-war organization of peace. Our intention is to fight the War in alliance with you and in constant consultation with you to the utmost of our strength, and however long it lasts, and when the War is won, as I am sure it will be, we expect that Soviet Russia, Great Britain and the United States will meet at the Council table of the victors, as the three principal partners and agencies by which Nazism will have been destroyed. Naturally, the first object will be to prevent Germany, and particularly Prussia, breaking out upon us for the third time. The fact that Russia is a Communist State and Britain and the United States are not, and do not intend to be, is not any obstacle to our making a good plan for our mutual safety and rightful interests. The Foreign Secretary will be able to discuss the whole of this field with you.

6. It may well be that your defence of Moscow and Leningrad, as well as the splendid resistance to the invader along the whole Russian front, will inflict mortal injuries upon the internal structure of the Nazi régime. But we must not count upon such good fortune, but simply keep on striking at them to the utmost with might and main.

Winston S. Churchill to President Franklin D. Roosevelt

(*Churchill papers, 20/45*)

22 November 1941
1.05 p.m.
Personal and Secret

1. News of first three days' operations in Libya indicates that our armoured forces have been successfully engaged with bulk of German armoured forces in area Sidi Rezegh–Capuzzo.

2. On 19th November first action of Fourth Armoured Brigade (all American tanks) resulted in withdrawal Twenty-first German Armoured Division with loss of twenty-six tanks against twenty of our own. Action was resumed the following morning and enemy again withdrew with additional losses.

3. On afternoon 20th November our Seventh Armoured Brigade inflicted casualties estimated at seventy tanks, thirty-three armoured cars and several hundred prisoners on detachment Fifteenth German Armoured Division east of Sidi Rezegh, where we captured nineteen aircraft and crews complete.

4. The Italian Armoured Division which our troops successfully engaged on 18th November has taken no further part in battle.

5. On afternoon 20th November our armoured forces were concentrating to engage enemy tanks and MT[1] in area Capuzzo–Bardia.

6. Air battle is developing favourably. Enemy bomber effort has been reduced by low-flying attacks on enemy aerodromes, and fourteen Ju. 87s were burnt out yesterday on ground. Little enemy air interference has been experienced so far with our land operations.

7. Our fighter sweeps have been active and on 20th November knocked down four Me. 110s, three Me. 109s, two Ju. 87s and one Ju. 88 certain, at cost of four fighters. RAF is flying ammunition up for Fourth Armoured Brigade.

8. This shows that our operations in Western Desert have made a very encouraging start.

Winston S. Churchill to General Auchinleck

(*Churchill papers, 20/45*)

22 November 1941
Personal

1. Thank you for the very full information now flowing. I might perhaps broadcast Sunday night if it seems expedient, so please let me have anything that comes to hand. What I say will, of course, be on most general lines, like my statement in the House of Commons. I am anxious, however, to make any success tell fully all over the world, and especially with the French. The moment we can really claim a victory I propose to address the President about an offer to Vichy. I fear very much the Germans may get hold of Bizerta unless we can rouse the French to a last effort. This can only be done through Roosevelt. It is not impossible he might offer troops.

2. Let me know for my most secret information how your mind is moving towards extensive exploitation westwards. It may be things will go with a run, in which case I presume you will run considerable risks with your light forces.

3. Everything seems to have gone splendidly so far.

[1] Motor transport.

General Auchinleck to Winston S. Churchill
(Churchill papers, 20/45)

22 November 1941
Most Secret
Private

1. Thank you for your permission to issue communiqués from here. Great care will be taken in their drafting.

2. From latest information situation seems to be as follows. About sixty German tanks some fifteen miles north east Bir El Gubi surrounded by our three armoured brigades which are attacking them. Fighting here likely to be heavy and casualties severe but chances of totally destroying this enemy force which probably contains bulk of his remaining German tanks seems good.

3. There are almost certainly some German tanks of 15 Armd. Div., and German lorried infantry units in area El Adem–Bir El Gubi co-operating with Italian 132 Armd. Div. which may now be withdrawing north west from El Gubi in contact with South African Armd. Cars and 1 South African Inf. Bde.

4. It seems that enemy's main object yesterday was to break through to the west with his main tank force and effect junction with these western detachments. This attempt seems to have been frustrated by our armd. forces.

5. Tobruk sally is proceeding satisfactorily though slowly owing opposition by German infantry and minefields. Sally was preceded by successful feint attack by Poles and British infantry in west sector.

6. New Zealand Div. moved yesterday to Sidi Azeiz ten miles north west Capuzzo and today is to move Bir Chenrit A Adar ten miles west north west Bardia and cut pipe line between Bardia and Capuzzo. One brigade NZ Div. with infantry tanks is to move west today along Trigh Capuzzo from Sidi Azeiz under orders 30th Corps HQ for action as required towards Gambut and Tobruk.

7. 4 Ind. Div. is planning attack on Sidi Omar from north with view of shortening our line of supply from railhead to forward troops.

8. Support group 7 Armd. Div. and 5 South African Infantry Brigade are in vicinity Sidi Rezegh protecting rear and flank our armoured brigades surrounding German tanks already mentioned and co-operating with Tobruk sally.

9. Force of South African armd. cars and Indian infantry from Jarabub is reported to be attacking Jalo 180 miles west of Jarabub.

10. To sum up prospects of achieving our immediate object namely destruction German armoured forces seem good. Once achieved seems unlikely that such German and Italian Armoured forces as may remain will be able to offer effective resistance our further advance though they may have delaying power.

PART TWO

11. German troops in Capuzzo and Halfaya estimated two battalions infantry likely to resist strongly but their capture should only be matter of time especially if water supply can be cut off.

12. Italian and German troops investing Tobruk east of El Adem should be destroyed or rounded up by our troops advancing from south and Tobruk garrison. Same applies to enemy MT and troops still in Gambut area. Remainder Italian troops investing Tobruk namely three divisions will probably try to withdraw towards Derna but they are believed short of transport and may be unable to get away.

13. Italian and German armoured and motorized troops now in area El Adem – El Gubi – Bir Hacheim will it is thought retire on Mechili and fight there or withdraw on Jedabya. Here again transport difficulties may hamper movement.

14. Cunningham's intentions as soon as enemy armour has been destroyed are to push on westwards with all speed raise siege Tobruk and pursue enemy. It may (repeat may) be possible for our light motorized forces to press on towards Agheila and Benghazi but maintenance difficulties are considerable. Every effort will be made to continue envelopment and destruction of enemy.

15. This brief appreciation is you will realize highly conjectural but not I think beyond the bounds of possibility. Would like to add that forecasts and deductions by Brigadier Shearer and his Intelligence Staffs have to date proved extraordinarily accurate and farseeing. I am more than pleased with them. The success of the American light tanks seems to have been remarkable.

Winston S. Churchill to President Franklin D. Roosevelt

(*Churchill papers, 20/45*)

22 November 1941

Following appreciation by General Auchinleck has just reached me. I send it for your personal and most secret information:

2. About sixty German tanks some fifteen miles north-east of Bir El Gubi are surrounded by our three armoured brigades, which are attacking them. Fighting will probably be heavy and casualties may be severe, but chances of total destruction of enemy force, which includes the bulk of his remaining German tanks, seem good.

3. It appears that his main object yesterday was to break to the west with this main tank force and join up with the remainder of his army. This attempt seems to have been foiled.

4. There are some German tanks of Fifteenth Armoured Division and German motorized infantry in area El Adem–Bir El Gubi. These are co-operating with Italian Ariete Division (Armoured), which may now be

withdrawing north-west from El Gubi. One South African Infantry Brigade and South African Armoured cars are in contact with them.

5. The sortie from Tobruk is going slowly but satisfactorily. It is being opposed by German infantry, and there are a lot of minefields. The feint attack by British and Polish infantry which preceded the sortie was successful.

6. One South African Brigade and the Support Group of the Seventh Armoured Division are protecting the flank and rear of our Armoured Brigades (see paragraph 2 above).

7. In summary, prospects of destroying German forces seem good. If we are successful in this, such German and Italian armoured forces as may escape us may delay, but are unlikely to offer, effective resistance to our further advance.

8. There are about two battalions of German infantry in Capuzzo and Halfaya. These are likely to resist strongly, but their destruction or capture seems likely in time. The same applies to the Italian and German troops which have been investing Tobruk, and also to the enemy forces which are still near Gambut. The Italian forces amounting to three Divisions opposite Tobruk will probably make an attempt to retire in the direction of Derna. They are, however, short of mechanized transport and may be unable to escape.

9. Those German and Italian armoured and motorized troops which are referred to in paragraph 4 may try to retreat on Mechili, where they may fight. Alternatively, they may retire further on Jedabya, but transport difficulties may hamper them.

10. You will realize that this brief appreciation is highly conjectural. Our Intelligence has been extraordinarily accurate and far-seeing. The American light tanks seem to have achieved remarkable success.

Winston S. Churchill to R. A. Butler

(*Churchill papers, 20/36*)

22 November 1941

Let me have a short note showing the number of boys who leave the public elementary schools at 15 years and over, under the war conditions of 1941.

How many of these go into any form of industry and employment? How many are there in munitions between the ages of 15 and 18½ years? How many go into Cadet Corps of various kinds? How many pursue their education in secondary schools or go on to the Universities?

I am anxious that the educational and disciplinary aspects of these boys' lives shall rank as prominently in our minds as the need to find considerable numbers for ARP, AA Batteries, &c.

Winston S. Churchill to General Auchinleck
(*Churchill papers, 20/45*)

23 November 1941

1. Most grateful for your appreciation, which I realize is given under necessary reserve. Personally I like the look of things and share your confidence. Prolongation of battle must wear down enemy with his limited resources. I shall not broadcast Sunday night, as decision is not immediately in sight. I have sent an epitome of your last message to President. Remember I am waiting for moment to appeal to President to tell Vichy France it is now or never and to make the boldest offer for aid in French North Africa from United States and Britain. I hope this moment may come within the next week.

2. If you think well, tell troops: 'Enthusiasm for magnificent fighting and manoeuvres of desert army rising high here at home and throughout the Empire. Your countrymen and comrades in the British army, RAF and Royal Navy are watching from hour to hour. We are sure you will shake the life out of the enemy in this famous battle.'

Winston S. Churchill to General Auchinleck
(*Churchill papers, 20/45*)

23 November 1941

C is sending you daily our special stuff.[1] Feel sure you will not let any of this go into battle zone except as statements on your own authority with no trace of origin and not too close a coincidence. There seem great dangers of documents being captured in view of battle confusion. Excuse my anxiety.

[1] Information derived from Enigma decrypts of German top secret radio signals, including summaries of actual German messages.

Winston S. Churchill to General Auchinleck
(*Churchill papers, 20/45*)

23 November 1941
Personal and Most Strictly Secret

I asked C to emphasize to you the importance of our No. MK. 96,[1] repeated WD/68 of 23rd, to Shearer. When one sees the invaluable cargoes of fuel now being directed upon Benghazi, and the enemy air concentration at Benina, it would seem that quite exceptional risk should be run to sterilize these places, even for three or four days. The enemy's fear of this operation is obviously well founded. The only time for such a venture is while he is in the throes of the battle. Chance of success will diminish as soon as he has been able to reinforce with troops withdrawing or escaping from the battle zone. There is a lot to be picked up cheap now, both at Benghazi and west of Agheila, which will rise in price enormously once the main battle is over. I am sure you will be considering this. Please remember how much they got by brass and bluff at the time of the French collapse. What is the mission of the Oasis force?

Winston S. Churchill to Admiral Cunningham
(*Churchill papers, 20/45*)

23 November 1941

I asked the First Sea Lord to wireless you today about the vital importance of intercepting surface ships bringing reinforcements, supplies and, above all, fuel to Benghazi. Our information here[2] shows a number of vessels now approaching or starting. Request has been made by enemy for air protection, but this cannot be given owing to absorption in battle of his African air force. All this information has been repeated to you. I shall be glad to hear through Admiralty what action you propose to take. The stopping of these ships may save thousands of lives, apart from aiding a victory of cardinal importance.

[1] A decrypt sent from Bletchley Park to GHQ Cairo, 8th Army, and to the Naval and Air Commanders-in-Chief. This decrypt gave details of the air fuel cargo on board two oil transports, *Maritza* and *Procida*, destined for Benghazi and the German airfield at Benina. Within twenty-four hours of Churchill's telegram *Maritza* and *Procida* had been sunk and the fuel supplies for Rommel's air support drastically curtailed. A digraph (two capital letters, in this case MK) was chosen to give any eavesdropper the idea that it was an individual British agent (usually indicated by such a digraph) rather than the German army and air force's own most secret radio signals (believed by the Germans to be unbroken and unbreakable).

[2] Again, information derived directly from the German top secret Enigma messages, decrypted at Bletchley and studied by Churchill and the Chiefs of Staff on a daily (and at times hourly) basis.

Winston S. Churchill to Sir Edward Bridges
(*Churchill papers, 20/36*)

23 November 1941
Most Secret and Personal

I propose to define the scope of the Production Executive by the consequences of the series of events rather than by a paper constitution. The consequences of these events will be restrictive. First, the War Production Budget being settled will remove altogether the idea that the Production Executive is a general planning authority. Secondly, the agreements reached between the Supply Ministers will be encouraged in every way. This was the core of the original plan of the Production Executive, to which the additional Ministers were only added later on. Thirdly, the autonomy of the various Ministries and the responsibility of their Departmental Chiefs will be strongly insisted upon. Thus there will remain for the Production Executive:

(a) The carrying into effect of such modifications which the course of the war may require in the approved War Production Budget if these cannot be settled at a lower level.
(b) The adjustment of differences between the three Supply Ministers.
(c) To provide a forum on which the minor consumers can be represented.

Pray bear all this in mind as particular points came up for decision. The Production Executive is like the governor of an engine and not like the governor of a province.

The above is for your own private guidance.

Winston S. Churchill to General Ismay, for the Chiefs of Staff Committee
(*Churchill papers, 20/36*)

23 November 1941
Most Secret

1. 'A'[1] is a better paper than I thought General Embick was capable of writing or helping to write. It proceeds on the assumptions of the strength of invasion which have been adopted here as a basis for our preparations. These were no doubt imparted to General Embick, but I must make it clear that though these data may be accepted in order to keep our defence up to the mark, they do not rest on any solid basis other than that of prudent apprehension.

2. In Para. 4 of 'A' the nine County Divisions are unduly disparaged. These troops are among the best in the Army and are not in any sense 'second-line'.

[1] A report on the British defence system by General Embick.

They differ from the Field Divisions only in lacking one artillery regiment out of three and two field RE[1] companies and the highest scale of transport. Confusion is wrought in our affairs by the writing down of these divisions because of these minor deficiencies, and I have asked on other papers for measures to be taken to place them on a level with the other divisions. Meanwhile, it is clear that General Embick was misled in thinking them to be in contrast with the 'regular divisions with which they are associated'.

3. The two criticisms of the arrangements for beach defence by Corps should be carefully examined, and I should be glad to see the answers.

4. The great fault of this paper, as of many studies about invasion, is that it ignores the time sequence of events. An invasion on so vast a scale could not be prepared without detection. Not only 800 alleged landing craft, but many other vessels and large ships, would have to be assembled in the river mouths and harbours. Aerial photography would reveal this process, and the Air Force would subject them to the heaviest bombing during what might well be a fortnight or more. From Dunkirk to Dieppe our air strength is now sufficient to enable us to make daylight attacks under fighter air cover. When the difficulties of embarkation have been surmounted, it will still be necessary to marshal these ships and bring them across the sea. By that time it is reasonable to expect that naval resistance will be available in a very high form. General Embick assumes that there will be no warning, and that all our small craft will be engaged in the Battle of the Atlantic. But this is absurd, once the scale of the invasion is raised above the level of heavy raids. Let me have a time-table (on one sheet of paper) of what the Navy will do on each day from the alert on Day 1 to Day 20, and what forces will be in hand.

5. The whole of this preliminary but indispensable phase plays no part in General Embick's thought, yet in it is comprised the main and proved defence of the island from invasion. Wishing to train our Army and keep it keen, we have, naturally, stressed what happens after the enemy lands, but the Royal Navy and Royal Air Force are responsible for shattering the assembly of the armada and for cutting it down, striking into it decisively *en passage*. There must be no lifting of this obligation off these two forces.

6. Para. 9 (a) of Document 'A' is mere assertion. Our view has been based on the closest possible study of the relative strengths. We know our fighter force is actually and relatively far stronger than it was last year, when it was enough. The perfecting of air control, which was the foundation of the Battle of Britain, has also made great strides since then. The assumption 'Given sustained local air superiority' is very hard to accept when it is remembered how much more powerful our fighter force is, and that we could attack by day any lodgments under fighter protection at our selected moment, while the enemy would be driven into trying to maintain standing patrols.

[1] Royal Engineer.

7. In Para. 9, sub-para. (5), the usual American point about putting the Air under the Army is stressed.

8. I understand we are soon to have the report of the new Committee on Invasion, which is being prepared. There is no reason why the gist of this document, without saying where it comes from, should not be given to the officers concerned on both sides. It will be very wrong if an attempt is made to work up the unduly alarmist possibilities of invasion. First, the resources of the enemy in shipping and the facts relating to their alleged construction of invasion craft must be examined with the same attention as the Air Intelligence brings to bear upon the air production in Germany. Secondly, the time factor necessary for the assembling and marshalling of the armada and the action of the Royal Air Force during this period. Thirdly, the use of gas by us upon the invasion ports, either at the moment of embarkation or against lodgments. Fourthly, the action of the Royal Navy, having regard to the probability of due warning being received.

All the above must be studied as features of equal importance to the resistance which will be offered by our military forces once the enemy has landed.

Winston S. Churchill to David Margesson
(*Churchill papers, 20/36*)

23 November 1941

1. It is thought that the invasion danger will manifest itself gradually by the assembly in the ports and river mouths of large numbers of ships and landing craft, and also by troop movements on a great scale. At a certain stage in these proceedings, which may conceivably take months and after all may only be a blind, we should have to proclaim the alert. If this moment were rightly chosen it should be about a fortnight before zero day. It is not intended that the whole of the Home Guard should thereupon cease their civilian occupations, but only that a special section of them should be called out and embodied, like the militia used to be.

2. The rest of the Home Guard would not be called out until a few days before zero hour, as far as we could tell, or perhaps only when the embarkation of the invaders had already begun. They would, however, increase their vigilance between the alert and the alarm.

3. The special section I have in mind would of course consist not, as your minute suggests of persons under 18 and over 60 years, but of the great mass of hefty manhood now in reserved occupations who may not join the Army but have volunteered for the Home Guard. This class would attend additional drills, and would be paid for attendance at these drills. They would not come out whole-time till the alert. There is no need to make heavy weather of the

proposal by forming brigades with the War Office standards of equipment. They would be armed with rifles, machine guns and Bren carriers. They can be organized in battalions. They would not alter their characteristic civilian and voluntary status until the alert.

4. This proposal is of course quite separate from the employment of the Home Guard in relief of ADGB[1] and Coastal Defence.

Pray let me have definite proposals on the scale of four battalions in each Corps area.

Winston S. Churchill to Admiral Pound
(*Churchill papers, 20/36*)

23 November 1941
Most Secret

What is the present plan about the distribution of the aircraft carriers? Since these telegrams[2] were received, we have lost the *Ark Royal*,[3] but we still have four good new ones. I do not want to waste any one of them by sending it all round the Cape, unless such a voyage coincided with an inevitable working up period. At present I am waiting to see what will happen in the Mediterranean. Of course if Admiral Cunningham is going to take station in the Central Mediterranean, or if we get Tripoli or perhaps French North Africa comes out, it would be worth putting at least two aircraft carriers there. We cannot see ahead clearly enough at present. I suppose you will give one of the older ones to the Indian Ocean and Pacific.

Please let met have a short note.

Winston S. Churchill to Sir Edward Bridges
(*Churchill papers, 20/36*)

23 November 1941
Secret

No man has more need to fear investigation of his record than Lord Chatfield, who shamefully failed to state the naval case against giving away the

[1] Air Defence of Great Britain.

[2] Two telegrams, of 1 November and 2 November 1941, from the Commander-in-Chief, Mediterranean (Admiral Cunningham) requesting extra aircraft carriers for the Mediterranean.

[3] On 12 November 1941 the aircraft carrier *Ark Royal* was returning to Gibraltar having taken aircraft to Malta, when it was struck by a U-boat torpedo twenty-five miles from Gibraltar. It sank the following day. Of its ship's complement of 1,600 there was only a single death.

Irish bases.[1] Moreover, he was a sailor who prolonged his official life after he had left the Navy by building up credit with the advocates of appeasement. If it comes to a fight, he is going to get pretty well knocked about. But this is the very reason why a controversy of this kind should not be allowed. I therefore agree with the proposal that you put forward in paragraph 11.[2]

After the War a far wider latitude in the disclosure of official information can be given. There are only a few things which should never be mentioned.

Mr Eden should see your memorandum and my minute.

Winston S. Churchill to Josiah Wedgwood
(*Churchill papers, 20/22*)

23 November 1941
Private

My dear Jos,

There is nothing you could tell me about the Palestine question that I do not probably know, and very little you would be likely to say with which I am not in general agreement.

But I cannot undertake to cut into one of my days in the way that would be involved if I were to see your deputation. I have a very heavy burden to carry, especially just now. Please have mercy.

Yours ever,
Winston S. Churchill

Winston S. Churchill to Lewis Broad
(*Churchill papers, 2/416*)

23 November 1941

Dear Mr Broad,

Thank you so much for sending me an inscribed copy of your biography of myself, which my Secretary acknowledged a few days ago.

[1] At the beginning of 1939, when Lord Chatfield was Minister of the Co-Ordination of Defence, and the Cabinet (of Neville Chamberlain) agreed to transfer the sovereignty of the Irish naval bases to Ireland. This sovereignty had been secured by Churchill during the Irish Treaty negotiations in 1922. In 1939 he was a leading Parliamentary opponent of the transfer of the sovereignty of the bases to Eire.

[2] For refusing Lord Chatfield permission to quote official documents in his memoirs.

I have only just been able to peer into the book, and it seems to be only too kind and generous. All the same, it looks very readable. I am very grateful to you for all you say in your preface.[1]

Yours very truly,
Winston S. Churchill

Winston S. Churchill to Anthony Eden
(*Churchill papers, 20/36*)

23 November 1941
Secret

My own feeling is that we might give Hull[2] the latitude he asks. Our major interest is: no further encroachments and no war, as we have already enough of this latter. The United States will not throw over the Chinese cause, and we may safely follow them in this part of the subject. We could not of course agree to an arrangement whereby Japan was free to attack Russia in Siberia. I doubt myself whether this is likely at the present time. I remember that President Roosevelt himself wrote in, 'There must be no further encroachment in the North', at the Atlantic Conference. I should think this could be agreed. The formal denunciation of the Axis Pact by Japan is not in my opinion necessary. Their stopping out of the war is in itself a great disappointment and injury to the Germans. We ought not to agree to any veto on American or British help to China. But we shall not be asked to by the United States.

Subject to the above, it would be worth while to ease up upon Japan economically sufficiently for them to live from hand to mouth – even if we only got another three months. These, however, are only first impressions.

I must say I should feel pleased if I read that an American-Japanese agreement had been made by which we were to be no worse off three months hence in the Far East than we are now.

[1] At the end of his preface to *Winston Churchill, Man of War* (in the Hutchinson 'Leaders of Britain in the War' series), Lewis Broad wrote: 'His elevation to the Premiership after eight months of war was acclaimed by the people's voice. Never, in modern times at any rate, has the choice of Prime Minister been made with such national unanimity, transcending all thoughts of party. It was because the people recognized in him the incarnation of the nation fighting the most decisive war in its history. The purpose of the pages that follow is to unfold the developments and achievements of this man of war.'

[2] Cordell Hull, Secretary of State from 1933 to 1944.

Oliver Harvey: diary
(*'The War Diaries of Oliver Harvey, 1941-1945'*)

24 November 1941

Hull has told us of the results of his talks with the Japs. The latter have put forward a series of specious proposals in return for which they require relaxation of freezing. Hull is considering a slight lifting of freezing in return for reduction of Jap forces from Indo-China as a temporary measure. PM is rather in favour as he wants present situation in Far East to endure and not get worse. FO feel that this is a thin edge of wedge, that Japs have no intention of letting up themselves but are seriously pinched by blockade. If US is firm, our experts believe Japs will give way further rather than fight. Meanwhile our heavy ships are on the way to reinforce Singapore.

War Cabinet; Confidential Annex
(*Cabinet papers, 65/24*)

24 November 1941
5.30 p.m.

The Prime Minister said that we could rely upon the United States not to abandon the cause of China. He thought that any measure of relaxation of our blockade should be done on the basis of giving the Japanese enough to live on from hand to mouth. If we could maintain the present position in the Far East for another three months, it would be greatly to our advantage.

The Prime Minister then read to the War Cabinet a telegram which he had despatched to M. Stalin on 21st November, in reply to a message received from him on the same date. This telegram referred to the proposed visit of the Foreign Secretary to Moscow.

The Prime Minister said that he thought that the Foreign Secretary should be accompanied on his visit by General Wavell and Sir Henry Pownall, and also by transport experts who could explain the limitations on the amount of goods which we could send into Russia, and on the forces which we could maintain, over the same communications. It might also be an advantage if Mr Harriman accompanied Mr Eden, in order to deal, not with the political aspects, but with questions of supplies to Russia from this country and from the United States.

Winston S. Churchill to President Franklin D. Roosevelt
(*Churchill papers, 20/45*)

24 November 1941
For your personal and secret information

I have received a message in following sense from General Auchinleck, dated 10.20 a.m., 23rd November, at Cairo. He thinks that the battle is moving to a climax. It now appears that some at any rate of the German tanks yesterday reported being attacked by our forces north of Bir-el-Gubi succeeded breaking out in a north-easterly direction. At Sidi Rezegh our troops were being strongly pressed on 22nd November from west and east by reported forces of 100 enemy tanks. Our resistance, as far as is known, is successful. Situation appears to be that enemy, having failed to break out towards Bir-el-Gubi, now attempts to go west through Sidi Rezegh through narrow ravine which still exists between Tobruk troops and 30 Corps. At time of message battle is proceeding on Sidi Rezegh, where 30 Corps is concentrating troops. Evening of the 22nd November one brigade Australian division reported south of Gambat. Tobruk report more prisoners taken, but no other news. 132nd Italian Armoured division is reported to have moved west to Bir-Hacheim, and is being watched.

Winston S. Churchill to General Auchinleck
(*Churchill papers, 20/45*)

24 November 1941
Personal

I see remainder of 1st Armoured Division reaches Suez today. I send you subjoined report I have received as to state of their equipment. This division was the best-trained regular tank division in the Army and has been sent you with many heart-searchings from here. It should play its part in the battle if prolonged or in the exploitation if success is gained. Apart from 160 tanks there is an excellent support group, which surely could go into battle now. Let me know what use you propose to make of these units and, if possible, the time-table of their disembarkation, assembly and movement to the front.

The following is the composition of the part which arrives today:
Divisional Headquarters and Divisional Troops.
2nd Armoured Brigade:

The Bays
9th Lancers
10th Hussars } Tank Regiment, each armed with about one-third M.3 Light and two-thirds Crusader Tanks.

1st Rifle Brigade – Motor Battalion.

1st Support Group:
11th Regiment RHA
76th Anti-Tank Regiment
61st Light AA Regiment.

The above contains sixty M.3 Light and 106 Crusader tanks. Except for sixty of the Crusaders, all are completely ready for the desert. The sixty are short of some desert equipment, which is in the shipments with the tanks, and it should be possible to fit it in a week.

Winston S. Churchill to General Ismay
(*Churchill papers, 20/36*)

24 November 1941
Most Secret

Let me have your full report about the remainder of the 1st Armoured Division. When did they arrive and what is the condition of their tanks? How far are they desert-worthy? What about their axles? How far are they trained? Can anything be done to speed them up or to speed up their unloading?

Winston S. Churchill to General Ismay, for the Chiefs of Staff Committee
(*Churchill papers, 20/36*)

24 November 1941
Most Secret

1. Although 'Crusader' is still undecided, it is prudent to take a forward view on the assumption of success.

2. The importance of pressing on with 'Acrobat'[1] while the effects of a victory are still operative and before the Germans can effectively establish themselves in Bizerta, is recognized by all. Nevertheless, this operation turns mainly upon the speed with which it can be executed. A delay of two or three weeks would probably close all prospects. We have not yet taken a final decision about beginning 'Acrobat'; but this must be ripe for settlement during the present week.

3. As soon as 'Crusader' is successful and in the event of a rapid 'Acrobat' being ordered, I propose to address President Roosevelt on the following lines:[2]

[1] The planned advance from Cyrenaica into Tripolitania.
[2] Printed as the next document.

4. No one can tell yet how 'Crusader' will finish, nor when or whether 'Acrobat' will begin, nor what Pétain's reaction or any independent reaction in French North Africa will be. If all these three go well we shall be fighting along the whole North African shore, and we shall have to send not only drafts but reinforcements, particularly of armoured troops, as the North African campaign develops. We shall have to do this in face of an invasion threat which will be mounted against us, probably only as a threat, in the Spring. We must therefore bring the nine Beach or County Divisions up to full strength, because the equivalent of three or four divisions, including armour, will have to go into Africa through Morocco or Algiers. Then will be the time to ask President Roosevelt to send over some extra divisions, even though not fully trained or equipped, for Northern Ireland.

5. Should the African war develop towards the west in this way, the greatest possible effort will have to be made to open the Mediterranean to our ships and transport, as the sole lateral communication must be by sea along the African coast. Admiral Cunningham would from time to time take station in the Central Mediterranean. It might be found easier and cheaper in men and materials to carry the war into 'Whipcord'[1] than to try to maintain a 2,000 mile front defensively along the North African shore. We might hope if worthy of good fortune to retain the initiative.

6. Should events take the course outlined above, General Auchinleck would have charge of Northern Africa and everything west of the Suez Canal inclusive, and General Wavell would have charge of everything east of the Canal. Wavell's Command would comprise Palestine, Syria, anything that happens in Turkey or Persia and anything that we become concerned with in the Caucasus or further north in Russia. He would at the same time continue to be Commander-in-Chief, India, which is the great base from which a large proportion of the supplies for the Eastern Command will be drawn. He would be provided with a Deputy of the highest order for purely Indian work.

7. On this layout it would seem more reasonable to leave Burma in the Far Eastern Command.

8. On the other hand, we may not win 'Crusader'; we may not decide to embark on 'Acrobat': we may fail in 'Acrobat': Pétain may go even more rotten than he is now; French North Africa may pass under German control; an Anglo-American effort may be made to take Dakar;[2] Gibraltar harbour may be rendered untenable and we may have to carry out the island projects. These must be considered the bad developments in the West. Should they occur, the emphasis of our efforts in 1942 will be upon the Eastern Front. In that case the arrangements for the Commands now proposed by the Chiefs of

[1] The planned British invasion of Sicily.

[2] British support for a Free French effort to take Dakar in September 1940 (Operation Menace) had failed.

the Staff would be more applicable, and will be at once considered. I am not, however, at all convinced that the greatest efforts would be got out of India by those arrangements.

Winston S. Churchill to President Franklin D. Roosevelt
(*Churchill papers, 20/45*)

24 November 1941

In view of our victory in 'Crusader', we propose to press on to Tripoli and the frontiers of Tunis. We also hold ready in Great Britain the forces assigned to 'Gymnast'.[1] The chance to get French North Africa in our hands is 'now or never'. For this purpose Vichy should be offered the choice between blessings and cursings. Will you therefore instruct Admiral Leahy to tell Pétain what we British are willing to do, and will you make the greatest possible offer to him on behalf of the United States? We remember that Colonel Knox spoke some time ago of the possibilities of American troops and marines being landed in Morocco if invited by the French. The number of 150,000 was mentioned. I have also your message by Lord Louis Mountbatten about Tangier. But we must be specially careful not to antagonize the Spaniards at this moment. Can you not authorize Admiral Leahy to promise Pétain the support (a) of an American Expeditionary Force, and (b) supplies, both military and civil, escorted by American warships provided North Africa resists the German penetration now beginning? If so, everything possible will be done by the United States and British peoples to sustain the French Empire and to re-establish France when the victory is won.

This is the blessings side of the story.

On the other hand (says Leahy), if you do not take this last chance of saving French greatness and honour, and if you collaborate directly or indirectly with Germany, United States will cut off all supplies and blot you out of the book of the elect. Should the Toulon fleet be handed over to the Germans the British will retaliate by air bombardment of Toulon, and should this lead to France becoming an ally of Germany the British will, of course, hunt the Vichy Government with perpetual bombing wherever it moves. Moreover, every French ship within the prohibited zones will be sunk at sight, and the most complete blockade of France in our power immediately established.

This is the cursing side of the story.[2]

[1] A possible British landing in French North Africa, ideally with the tacit support of the Vichy authorities there.

[2] 'Behold, I set before you this day a blessing and a curse,' (Deuteronomy, chapter 11, verse 26). 'And it shall come to pass, when the Lord thy God hath brought thee in unto the land whither thou goest to possess it, that thou shalt put the blessing upon Mount Gerizim, and the curse upon Mount Ebal' (Deuteronomy, chapter 11, verse 29).

Winston S. Churchill to Sir Walter Monckton[1]
(*Churchill papers, 20/45*)

24 November 1941

Broadcast tonight by an Australian speaking from battle headquarters referred four times to prowess of American tanks. It is quite right to pay these compliments, but proportion should be observed, remembering that four out of five tanks in the battle are of British manufacture. By overdoing a good thing you may create reaction and cause ill-feeling in our tank factories, which are working night and day.

Winston S. Churchill to General Ismay, for the Chiefs of Staff Committee
(*Churchill papers, 20/36*)

24 November 1941

1. See other telegrams on the subject of the change of command in the Far East. Australia complains of relief of Brooke-Popham, which was made on advice of Governor, Burma,[2] and confirmed by Mr Duff Cooper. I do not think precedents show that we have ever consulted Australia on this appointment. Did we do so in the case of Brooke-Popham? We certainly did not in the change from Wavell to Auchinleck. I feel this Australian Government is out to make the most trouble and give the least help. For that reason we have to be particularly careful.

2. Since Paget was appointed and they were no doubt informed we have changed to Pownall, keeping Paget at home, which will give them the impression we are sending a second choice. The whole matter must be carefully considered.

3. See particularly 238/6 from Commander-in-Chief, Far East, paragraph 8, which is exactly the opposite to what I was advised, namely, that it was essential to have a soldier on account of American susceptibilities re independent air.

4. There is no need to answer them in a hurry, as we are in the battle and they are not, but the whole situation must be reviewed and tidied up in the course of the present week.

[1] Sir Walter Monckton was then in Cairo, in charge of information services under the Minister of State, Oliver Lyttelton.

[2] Reginald Dorman-Smith, 1899–1977. Educated at Harrow and Sandhurst. 2nd Lieutenant, Indian Army, 1918; served in the 15th Sikhs. Major, Queen's Royal Regiment (Territorial Force), 1930; honorary Colonel, 1937. A County Alderman, Surrey, 1931–5; Justice of the Peace, 1932. Conservative MP for Petersfield, 1935–41. President of the National Farmers Union, 1936–7. Knighted, 1937. Minister of Agriculture and Fisheries, January 1939 to May 1940. Privy Councillor, 1939. Governor of Burma, 1941–6. High Sheriff of Hampshire, 1952. A Justice of the Peace for Hampshire, 1960.

Winston S. Churchill to General Auchinleck
(*Churchill papers, 20/45*)

25 November 1941
Personal

1. Your 1606 of 24th instant.[1] I cordially endorse your view and intentions and His Majesty's Government wish to share your responsibility for fighting it out to the last inch, whatever may be the result. It is all or nothing, but I am sure you are the stronger and will win.

2. You have no doubt had my message about the rest of the 1st Armoured Division landing Suez today. Ram it in if useful at earliest without regard for future. Close grip upon the enemy by all units will choke the life out of him.

3. Am immensely heartened by your magnificent spirit and will-power. Say 'Bravo' to Tedder and RAF on air mastery.

4. We sent *Aurora* and *Penelope* out from Malta last night and duly sank the two vital oil transports *Procida* and *Maritza*.[2] The Admiral is after the others.

5. Please burn all special stuff and flimsies while up at the Front.

Winston S. Churchill: Oral Answers
(*Hansard*)

25 November 1941 House of Commons

PEACE AIMS

Mr Mander asked the Prime Minister whether he will make it clear to the enemy that, in any settlement of peace terms, full restoration will have to be made of machinery and other property removed from an occupied country and arrangements made for the reconstruction of property destroyed, furthermore that any Germans settled in territory outside Germany must be removed?

The Prime Minister: We must not count our chickens before they are hatched.

[1] In which Auchinleck told Churchill: 'In his attack yesterday evening enemy used Italian tanks which I take as evidence that he is running short of his own. I am convinced that he is fully stretched and desperate and that we must go on pressing him relentlessly. We may immobilize temporarily at least practically all our tanks in process but that does not (repeat not) matter if we destroy all his. Fact that he has abandoned Sidi-Omar and Sollum garrisons to their fates and that we have already taken over 3,000 (repeat 3,000) prisoners (including 1,000 (repeat 1,000) Germans) at Tobruk and Sidi-Omar is significant. I have accordingly ordered General Cunningham to attack with all available resources regain Sidi-Rezegh and join hands with Tobruk garrison which is to co-operate by attacking enemy to its front.'

[2] An Enigma decrypt (MK 191 of 25 November 1941) revealed that the sinking of these two ships and their air fuel cargo had placed the German Air Force operations in Cyrenaica in 'real danger'.

Winston S. Churchill to Oliver Lyttelton
(*Churchill papers, 20/45*)

26 November 1941
12.45 a.m.
Most Immediate
Personal and Secret

General Auchinleck's authority over all Commanders is supreme and all his decisions during the battle will be confirmed by us.[1] Your action and attitude highly approved. Communicate to General Auchinleck.

Oliver Harvey: diary
(*'The War Diaries of Oliver Harvey, 1941-1945'*)

26 November 1941

I was woken up in the night by the arrival of a telegram from Auchinleck and Lyttelton saying that they had decided to remove Cunningham from command of the battle because he was badly shaken. He had been replaced by a General Ritchie.[2]

What a business! We really don't run to good Generals. But the battle is reported to be going fairly well in spite of the General, and A and L are confident that it may yet be won.

We also had another shock in the night in the shape of a message from Roosevelt to the PM and another from Hull thro' Halifax showing that they proposed to appease Japan by falling in with the last Jap offer subject to very insufficient safeguards.[3] I have never seen anything like it since Munich. But the Americans want to gain more time in the Far East and believe this is the

[1] General Auchinleck had replaced General Sir John Cunningham by General Ritchie.

[2] Neil Methuen Ritchie, 1897–1983. On active service, 1914–18 (France, Mesopotamia, Palestine; despatches, Distinguished Service Order, Military Cross). On active service in Palestine, 1938–39 (despatches). Brigadier, General Staff, 1939. Commander, 51st Highland Division, 1940. Deputy Chief of Staff, Middle East, 1941. Commander of the 8th Army, Libya, 1941 (rank of Lieutenant-General). Commander of 52nd Lowland Division, 1942–43. General Officer Commanding-in-Chief, Scottish Command, and Governor of Edinburgh Castle, 1945–47. Knighted, 1945. Commander-in-Chief, Far East Land Forces, 1947–49. Commander, British Army Staff, Washington, 1950–51.

[3] On 25 November 1941 Roosevelt had informed Churchill by telegram of Japanese proposals for a *modus vivendi*, put forward by the Japanese Ambassador in Washington to Cordell Hull. Even America's demand for a withdrawal of Japanese troops from Indo-China had been held out to Hull as a possibility. Nor did Roosevelt dismiss the Japanese approach out of hand; instead, he suggested to Churchill a possible modification of the Anglo-American economic embargo on Japan, permitting the renewal of certain exports from the United States to Japan, and suggesting to Churchill that Britain, Australia and the Dutch East Indies do the same for a trial period of three months. Roosevelt ended his telegram however: 'I am not very hopeful and we must all be prepared for real trouble, possibly soon.' (Telegram received 25 November 1941: *Premier papers, 3/156/5, folios 64-5*)

way to do it. I'm afraid it is not and it will only serve to get the Japs round a difficult corner at the expense of the Chinese. It will also convince them that we won't fight if pressed. We have sent an urgent message to say we hope they'll give further consideration to our views.

Winston S. Churchill to President Franklin D. Roosevelt
(*Churchill papers, 20/45*)

26 November 1941
3.20 a.m.
Immediate
Secret

Your message about Japan received tonight. Also full accounts from Lord Halifax of discussions, and your counter-project to Japan on which Foreign Secretary has sent some comments. Of course, it is for you to handle this business and we certainly do not want an additional war. There is only one point that disquiets us. What about Chiang Kai-shek? Is he not having a very thin diet? Our anxiety is about China. If they collapse, our joint dangers would enormously increase. We are sure that the regard of the United States for the Chinese cause will govern your action. We feel that the Japanese are most unsure of themselves.[1]

Winston S. Churchill to General Auchinleck
(*Churchill papers, 20/45*)

26 November 1941
4.40 p.m.
Personal

You are no doubt constantly considering the movement forward of reserves towards the battle zone. I am well aware that this is conditioned by transport and how important it is for you to do the work with the minimum mouths to feed. I should be glad, however, to know what you have in reserve; suppose you need another division, or two or three brigades, where would you get them from? You could, I suppose, if necessary, bring a brigade of the 50th Division back from Baghdad.

Please let me know your resources and ideas.

[1] In addition to his own sources of Intelligence, Roosevelt also received Intelligence material direct from Churchill, who used regularly to minute to 'C', on Enigma decrypts and interpretations, especially those referring to the Far East: 'Make sure the President knows this,' or 'Make sure the President sees this.' Unknown to either Washington or London, however, on 26 November 1941 a Japanese naval force set sail from the Kurile Islands, north of Japan, through fogs and gales, towards the Pearl Harbor naval base at Hawaii.

Winston S. Churchill to Admiral Pound
(*Churchill papers, 20/36*)

26 November 1941
Action this Day
Secret

1. A large-scale movement of U-boats to the Eastern Mediterranean in an attempt to dominate that sea, as you think seems intended by the enemy, should not be unsatisfactory to us. We have very little traffic there and will obtain relief on the Atlantic route. It may indeed be a confession that the Battle of the Atlantic is adverse to the enemy. The German U-boats will not prevent British submarines or aircraft from taking their toll of Axis shipping going to Africa.

2. We should of course follow the U-boats into the Mediterranean with our flotillas. Sixteen or twenty destroyers and corvettes should make a great difference to the Mediterranean fleet. As we are so largely unencumbered by the need to protect merchant ships, we can afford to have some good U-boat hunting.

3. One must expect, however, that when the stress of battle in Libya dies down the German Air Force in Greece and Crete will help their U-boats by attacking our hunters. What can the Air Ministry do to meet this situation? Evidently as soon as we are free from the battle crisis they must attack both the U-boat bases and the airfields. This is the kind of campaign we ought to be able to manage fairly well.

4. I could if necessary, when your plans are complete, ask the President for any additional help you may require in the Atlantic.

Winston S. Churchill to Lord Linlithgow
(*Churchill papers, 20/45*)

26 November 1941
Personal, Private and Secret

I am sure it would be a mistake to make a flag-day out of this very small unwelcomed gesture of conciliation.[1] I had hoped the matter could be dealt with by smooth administration through your personal influence upon and contact with provincial governors. Your own convictions were against the policy on merits. Hallett's and Hope's grave arguments remain unanswered. The extraordinary powers accorded to the Central Government to deal with war emergencies are now to be used to override the independence of the

[1] The release by the Viceroy of the Indian national leaders, headed by Jawaharlal Nehru, who had been imprisoned for urging a public campaign against the war effort.

provinces in their responsibility for law and order. This is a sad contrariety, and I wish I had been kept better informed before you reached the position now disclosed. If you consider a statement inevitable, it would be better couched in a modest tone, something like this:

> In view of the complete failure and collapse of the Satyagrahi movement and the expiry of the great bulk of the sentences imposed, the Government of India hold the view that throughout India it should be possible to expedite the release of prisoners whose offences have been merely of a formal character and without serious harmful intent. Although in some provinces like the United Provinces the numbers concerned and local conditions may cause some delay, it is hoped that practically all the ordinary demonstrators may be released by the end of the year.

Let me know by return whether this sort of announcement would meet your difficulty, and please suggest any alteration in the wording which you may think necessary.

Winston S. Churchill to Philip Guedalla[1]
(*Philip Guedalla papers*)

26 November 1941

Thank you so much for your kindness in sending me a copy of your biography of myself.[2] I have as yet only been able to glance at the book, which seems all too complimentary and generous. I have heard good accounts of it, and I am sure it is most readable.

I am very glad to know that you are now recovered from your recent illness.

Yours vy sincerely,
Winston S. Churchill

[1] Philip Guedalla, 1889–1944. Educated at Rugby and Balliol College Oxford. President of the Oxford Union, 1911. Barrister, 1913. Legal Adviser, Contracts Department, War Office and Ministry of Munitions, 1915–17. Organizer and Secretary, Flax Control Board, 1917–20. A friend of Lloyd George. Unsuccessful Liberal candidate, 1922, 1923, 1924, 1929 and 1931. Historian; author of *Mr Churchill: A Portrait*, 1941. Squadron-Leader, RAF, 1943.

[2] This was *Mr Churchill: A Portrait* (London, Hodder and Stoughton). Also published in 1941 were Lewis Broad's *Winston Churchill: Man of War* (London, Hutchinson); Cecil Roberts, *A Man Arose* (poem, London, Hodder and Stoughton); Phyllis Moir, *I Was Winston Churchill's Private Secretary* (New York, Wilfred Funk); Paul Manning and M. Bronner, *Mr England: The Life Story of Winston Churchill* (Chicago, John Winston); E.W.D Chaplin, *Winston Churchill and Harrow* (Harrow, Harrow School Bookshop); John Collingwoode Read, *Winston Spencer Churchill: Man of Valour* (Toronto, Canadian Association of Broadcasting); Stanley Nott, *The Young Churchill* (New York, Coward McCann), and Richard Harding Davis, *The Young Winston Churchill* (New York, Scribner).

Winston S. Churchill to Commander Agnew[1]
(*Churchill papers, 20/45*)

27 November 1941

Many congratulations on your fine work since you arrived at Malta, and will you please tell all ranks and ratings from me that the two exploits in which they have been engaged, namely, the annihilation of the enemy's convoys on 8th November, and of the two oil ships on Monday last, have played a very definite part in the great battle now raging in Libya.[2] The work of the Force has been most fruitful, and all concerned may be proud to have been a real help to Britain and our cause.

Winston S. Churchill to John Curtin
(*Churchill papers, 20/45*)

27 November 1941

1. Mr Evatt,[3] your Minister of External Affairs, is reported as criticizing in public our not yet having declared war on Finland, Hungary and Roumania. The question of Finland is very difficult because a formal declaration of war will bind them to the Germans, lead to greater pressure on the Russian northern front, and greatly disturb our friends in Sweden and to a lesser extent in Norway, whereas by other methods we may induce them simply to stop fighting and send a large portion of their soldiers back home. I have had correspondence with Stalin on the point and have told him that, unless there is 'a cessation of military operations and the *de facto* exit of Finland from the war' to use his own words, within a fortnight from 21st November, we shall declare war upon Finland. Stalin is satisfied with this and our relations have become extremely cordial. The point is now being put in a most severe form by the Foreign Office to the Finnish Government, and we shall see with what

[1] William Gladstone Agnew, 1898-1960. On active service, Royal Navy, 1914-18. Commander Force K, based on Malta, 1941-44 (his force consisted of two light cruisers, *Aurora* and *Penelope*, and two destroyers; its first operation were carried out from Malta on 21 October 1941). Distinguished Service Order (1943) and bar (1944). Deputy Director of Personnel Services, Admiralty, 1947-49. General Secretary, National Playing Fields Association, 1950-53.

[2] Force K, a naval striking force comprising the cruisers *Aurora* and *Penelope* and the destroyers *Lance* and *Lively*, had been formed in October 1941, based on Malta.

[3] Herbert Vere Evatt, 1894–1965. Born in Australia. Member of the New South Wales Legislative Assembly (Labour), 1925–9. King's Counsel, 1929. Justice of the High Court of Australia, 1930–40. Attorney-General and Minister for External Affairs, 1941–9; Deputy Prime Minister, 1946–9. Member of the Advisory War Council, 1941–5; of the Australian War Cabinet, 1941–6. Australian Representative in the UK War Cabinet, 1942 and 1943. Australian Member of the Pacific War Council, 1942–3. Leader of the Australian Delegation of the UN General Assembly, 1946 and 1947. Chairman of the United Nations Palestine Commission, 1947. In 1945 he received the Freedom of the City of Athens for defending the interests of small nations. Leader of the Parliamentary Labour Party, Australia, 1951–60.

result. If we have to declare war on Finland, we shall, of course, do the same to Hungary and Roumania. The arguments about this also are evenly balanced, especially in the case of Roumania, which has been made a cat's-paw by Germany. I will let you know what happens.

2. It would be a great pity if, while these delicate and highly disputable matters are in the balance, your Ministers should start criticizing our policy in public. We have never said a word in public about Australian Government's insistence upon the withdrawal of all troops from Tobruk, which cost us life and ships, and added appreciably to General Auchinleck's difficulties in preparing his offensive; and no one here, or, I presume, in Australia, outside the circles of Government has the slightest inkling of the distress which we felt. I am sure it is far better that all these inevitable divergences should be kept secret, and that we should try so far as possible to understand each other's difficulties. Surely the sending of the *Prince of Wales* into eastern waters in face of the very grave misgivings of the Admiralty about the undoubted risks of a break-out by the *Tirpitz* in the next few weeks should convince you of our wish to act towards your Government in true comradeship and loyalty.

3. Accept my deepest sympathy in the feared loss of the *Sydney* so close to Australian shores. We also have had a grievous blow this week in the loss of the *Barham*, which blew up as a result of a U-boat torpedo, involving the death of about seven hundred men.[1] This is being kept strictly secret at present as the enemy do not seem to know, and the event would only encourage Japan.

4. General Auchinleck is in good heart about the battle in Libya, although it will be hard, long and bloody.

Winston S. Churchill to Oliver Lyttelton

(*Churchill papers, 20/45*)

27 November 1941
Secret and Personal

Following is text of message I have received from the President:

In view of growing importance of operations Middle East and Libya, I am sending my old friend, Bill Bullitt,[2] as my personal representative to visit the area, to report to me and to be of what assistance he can to your supply and similar problems. He leaves by Clipper, the southern route, about 1st December.

[1] More than 500 men were drowned when the battleship *Barham* (built in 1915) was sunk on 25 November 1941 by a German U-boat off Sollum. Shortly afterwards (on 19 December 1941) the cruiser *Neptune* (1934) struck a mine off Tripoli: more than 700 men were drowned.

[2] William Christian Bullitt, 1891–1967. Entered the State Department, 1917. President Wilson's special emissary to Russia, 1919. United States Ambassador to the Soviet Union, 1933–6; to France, 1936–41. President Roosevelt's special representative in the Far East, 1941. Special Assistant Secretary of the Navy, 1942–3. Served as a Major in the French armed forces, 1944.

I would be grateful if you personally would ask your civilian and military authorities out there to put at Bullitt's disposal such information as you and they think proper. If there is any person in the area whose opinions you would wish Bullitt to seek, or if there is any special problem you think Bullitt should devote special attention to, please let me know.

Following is text of my reply:

We shall be very glad to see Bullitt in the Middle East, and I hope matters will be tidied up there by the time he arrives. I am telling Oliver Lyttelton to see he has all facilities and to look after him.

War Cabinet: Confidential Annex
(*Cabinet papers, 65/24*)

27 November 1941
5 p.m.

The second suspicion which the Foreign Secretary thought we must exorcise from M. Stalin's mind was '. . . That we should be prepared to make peace with a Germany controlled by the Army, if they were to overthrow the Party.'

The Prime Minister said that we had made a public statement that we would not negotiate with Hitler or with the Nazi *régime*; but he thought it would be going too far to say that we should not negotiate with a Germany controlled by the Army. It was impossible to forecast what form of Government there might be in Germany at a time when their resistance weakened and they wished to negotiate.

Winston S. Churchill to General Auchinleck
(*Churchill papers, 20/45*)

27 November 1941
6.27 p.m.
Personal and Most Secret

CIGS and I both wonder whether, as you saved the battle once, you should not go up again and win it now. Your presence on the spot will be an inspiration to all. However, this is, of course, entirely for you to judge.

Winston S. Churchill to Averell Harriman
(*Churchill papers, 20/22*)

27 November 1941

My dear Averell,

I understand that Lord Beaverbrook has discussed with you the shortage of .30-inch ammunition. Our need for it is great and our stocks are low. I realize that the Russian requirements must be heavy but if there is anything you can do to obtain increased supplies for us from the United States during the coming months I should be very grateful.

Yours very sincerely,
Winston S. Churchill

P.S. The razor is a joy diurnal.
WSC

Randolph S. Churchill to Winston S. Churchill
(*Churchill papers, 1/362*)

[27 November 1941]

You know that I am far from fanciful. On the night of 27 Nov I was lying awake in my bed at Battle HQ 7 Armoured Div: & the moon & the clouds combined to give the effect of your face on an enormous scale brooding over the battlefield. It was the most remarkable phenomenon I have ever seen.

Winston S. Churchill: Memorandum[1]
(*Churchill papers, 23/9*)

27 November 1941
Secret

BUILDING PROGRAMMES

The Lord President, at my request, has reviewed building programmes and, as a result of his report, the following directions are now issued for the guidance of all Departments:

[1] Printed for the War Cabinet as War Cabinet Paper No. 141 of 1941.

A. LIMITATION

1. (a) The total numbers of insured adult workers in the building industry should be progressively reduced from 920,000 to 792,500 during the first three months of 1942.

Departments should aim at making this reduction effective very soon after the 1st January, 1942.

(b) Our general manpower policy assumes that the building industry will be able to make a further contribution by the end of June 1942. By then the total numbers should be reduced to 770,000; and Departments should aim at getting down towards that figure soon after March.

(c) Our further objective should be to secure that, after the end of the 1942 building season, the numbers employed on new building are reduced to 250,000. The total labour force in the industry should then be about 600,000.

Departments should plan their programmes on this basis.

(d) Further reductions will be possible on the completion of the programmes for aircraft factories and aerodromes, which in their last phase will be employing about 150,000 men.

For the time being Departments should proceed on the basis that by mid-1943 the labour force of the industry will be reduced to 500,000.

2. Departments whose allocations have been reduced or who are now employing numbers in excess of their allocations should submit reports to the Minister of Works and Buildings by the 15th December next, showing how they propose to modify their existing programmes in order to get down to their new allocations by the 1st January next.

B. SUPERVISION

3. The existing machinery for scrutinizing the Departmental building programmes under the Ministry of Works and Buildings will continue to operate under the authority of the Production Executive. As and when necessary the Minister can consult a military officer in the War Cabinet Secretariat in order to preserve close contact with the Defence Committee. The Minister will be responsible for determining – subject to appeal, in the event of disputes, to the Production Executive, and if necessary to higher authority – the allocation of building labour between the Departments within the total laid down from time to time by the Prime Minister's Directives.

4. The Minister's policy will be based on the following considerations, subject of course to existing ministerial responsibilities:

(a) In any clash between the requirements of different projects, the bias should be to give precedence to those which tend towards the improvement of the striking power of our forces, e.g., the essential munitions of war are of more importance than the ARP: the bomber programme takes precedence over food storage.

(b) Even for the most urgent requirements every effort must be made to make do with existing premises rather than build new factories or extensions.

(c) No new factory should be constructed unless it can be shown that the fullest practicable use is being made of all existing capacity, including double-shift working.

(d) The standards of construction demanded must be reduced to the lowest efficient level.

(e) Departments must exercise the greatest possible economy of building labour, and do all in their power to avoid wasteful use of labour by insistence on uneconomically early dates of completion.

(f) The sites of new factories and extensions must, wherever possible, be so chosen as to reduce the demand for hostels or housing to a minimum. Full use must be made of compulsory billeting and every other practical expedient before recourse is had to building.

(g) The standards of storage must be the lowest that are consistent with avoiding serious waste.

(h) The force of building labour available for maintenance, air-raid precautions and air-raid damage must be reduced to the minimum required on the assumption that any stricken area will be able to obtain the maximum aid from all neighbouring sources, including labour employed on Government building work.

(i) When the present programme for providing static water is completed, any further constructional work in connection with air-raid precautions (including hospitals and shelters) must be limited to that which can be carried out during lull periods by this minimum maintenance force.

Clare Sheridan[1] *to Winston S. Churchill*

(*Churchill papers, 1/361*)

27 November 1941

My dear Winston,

I expect you feel as we all do about birthdays after the age of forty – nevertheless my greetings go to you on the day and – since your friends seem

[1] Clare Consuelo Frewen, 1885–1970. Churchill's cousin. Daughter of Moreton Frewen and Clara Jerome. Educated in Paris and Germany. Sculptress and writer. European correspondent of the *New York World*, 1922. Her husband, Wilfred Sheridan, whom she married in 1910, was killed in action in France in September 1915 (his elder brother had been killed in action in the Boer War). Of her two daughters, Margaret married Comte Guy de Renéville, and became an authoress under the name 'Mary Motley'; Elizabeth Anne Linley, died in 1913 of tuberculosis, aged thirteen months. Her son Richard was five days old when his father was killed in action. At the age of 21 he would inherit 6,000 acres which his father had inherited when his own elder brother had been killed in the Boer War (since the reign of Henry VIII no first-born son had lived to inherit them). Richard Sheridan came of age on 20 September 1936. On 17 January 1937 he died of peritonitis in a hospital in Algeria. In 1939 Clare Sheridan published a memoir of her son, *Without End*.

bent on showering you with the Jerome past, let me add this small contribution a lithograph of your Mother and mine![1] Yours as usual carrying off the palm for looks and character!

I shall be in London from Sunday night to Wednesday or Thursday staying at 46 Upper Grosvenor Street (Mayfair 8323). I have hardly any hope that you will have a spare moment for me. However, as you told me to let you know when I pass through London I am taking you at your word.[2]

Love and best wishes
from
Clare

Robert Utting[3] to Winston S. Churchill
(*Churchill papers, 2/423*)

28 November 1941

Dear Sir,

Allow me to wish you very many happy returns of the day, with good health, good luck and all the best.

I still remember, which is fifty years ago, when you brought Lady Churchill[4] to see the horses, you told Lady Churchill how these horses were bred, without looking at a calendar. Old Trainer Sherwood's[5] words after you left were: 'That young Gentleman will one day make a great man.' How right he was! Let me thank you for your great work. God Bless you.

I remain, Dear Sir,
Yours obediently,
Robert Utting

[1] Churchill's mother Lady Randolph Churchill (who died in 1921) and Clare Sheridan's mother Clara Frewen (who died in 1935) were sisters.

[2] Churchill invited Clare Sheridan to lunch at 10 Downing Street on Wednesday 3 December 1941.

[3] A Minute by Lord Beaverbrook of 28 November 1941, stating disagreement with the decision reached at a Defence Committee (Supply) Meeting the previous day about the bomber programme.

[4] That is, Lady Randolph Churchill, Churchill's mother.

[5] Robert Sherwood, 1835–1894. As a young jockey he brought off the double in the French Derby and the French Oaks in 1853, and won the Epsom Derby in 1855. In Hong Kong as a trainer, 1863–75. Opened a small stable at Newmarket, 1880. Among his patrons was Lord Randolph Churchill, for whom in 1889 he won the Oaks with L'Abesse de Jouarre (known to the bookmakers, and to Winston and Jack Churchill, as 'Abcess on the Jaw').

Lady Violet Bonham Carter[1] *to Winston S. Churchill*
(*Churchill papers, 2/416*)

28 November 1941

Dearest Winston,

I send you for your birthday this dictionary of quotations – partly because it may 'come in handy' – & partly because I think it is a rather amusing browsing-ground for a fallow moment – (if you ever have one!) – I sometimes dip into it as a bridge to sleep – when the show on this side is too exciting to leave behind.

(It is interesting to see how many obscure & forgotten unknown men have endowed the language with immortal phrases – 'fit as a fiddle' etc.)

All my love to you on your birthday – my gratitude for your creation – & my prayers for your preservation.

Ever your true & bloody Duck –
Violet

I should love to see you someday –

Winston S. Churchill to Lord Beaverbrook
(*Churchill papers, 20/36*)

28 November 1941

This[2] does not represent the facts. The decision taken last night was that the proposal was to be printed in a final form together with the contributions to be made by the Air Ministry, which would enable us to form a final estimate of the cost in other directions, and whether we could meet it. I am hopeful there will be enough for both bombers and tanks. I do my best.

[1] Helen Violet Asquith, 1887–1969. Elder daughter of H.H. Asquith. Educated in Dresden and Paris. Married, 1915, Sir Maurice Bonham Carter (who died in 1960). President of the Women's Liberal Federation, 1923–5 and 1939–45; President of the Liberal Party Organization, 1945–7. A Governor of the BBC, 1941–6. Member of the Royal Commission on the Press, 1947–9. Unsuccessful Liberal candidate, 1945 and 1951. DBE, 1953; created Baroness Asquith of Yarnbury, 1964. Published *Winston Churchill as I Knew Him*, 1965.

[2] A complaint by Beaverbrook about the allocation of raw materials; part of his continuing dispute with the Air Ministry which had begun when he was Minister of Aircraft Production, and had simmered (and sometimes boiled over) throughout the year.

Winston S. Churchill to Admiral Pound
(*Churchill papers, 20/36*)

28 November 1941

I cannot help feeling that the estimate of 36[1] operating in the North Atlantic by December 15 is worse than it will be. I hope you will consider the possibility of reinforcing the Mediterranean with at least a dozen destroyers. They need not necessarily be there very long, as the situation may change with the decision in Libya. Numbers are, however, the essence of successful hunting, and we ought to get good results.

Pray let me know whether anything more can be done.

2. Is it not possible to advance the date of 'Anklet'?[2] The delays in taking action seem endless.

3. Let me have U-boat sinkings for November.

Winston S. Churchill to Anthony Eden
(*Churchill papers, 20/36*)

28 November 1941
Action this Day

You seem to be taking it for granted that war will be declared on all three Powers[3] on December 3rd. I did not wish this decision to be taken till we know what Finland will do. Moreover, the 3rd is too soon. The 5th is a fortnight after my telegram to Stalin. I am only tonight sending my telegram to Mannerheim. We must leave reasonable time for a reply.

My opinion about the unwisdom of this measure remains unaltered, and I still have hopes that the Finns will withdraw. I was not aware that this step would be taken at this juncture.

[1] The estimated number of U-boats operating in the North Atlantic. Churchill noted in his war memoirs: 'Post-war figures show that the average daily number of U-boats operating in the North Atlantic during December 1941 was eight. In addition, on any given day many others were on outward or homeward passages. The shipping losses by U-boats during November 1941 were 61,700 tons, the lowest figure recorded for any month since May 1940.

[2] A British plan for intercepting German coastal traffic along the coast of northern and southern Norway.

[3] Finland, Roumania and Hungary.

Winston S. Churchill to Field Marshal Mannerheim
(*Churchill papers, 20/45*)

28 November 1941
Personal, Secret and Private

I am deeply grieved at what I see coming, namely, that we shall be forced in a few days out of loyalty to our Ally Russia to declare war upon Finland. If we do this, we shall make war also as opportunity serves. Surely your troops have advanced far enough for security during the war and could now halt and give leave. It is not necessary to make any public declaration, but simply leave off fighting and cease military operations, for which the severe winter affords every reason, and make a *de facto* exit from the war. I wish I could convince your Excellency that we are going to beat the Nazis. I feel far more confident than in 1917 or 1918. It would be most painful to the many friends of your country in England if Finland found herself in the dock with the guilty and defeated Nazis. My recollections of our pleasant talks and correspondence about the last war lead me to send this purely personal and private message for your consideration before it is too late.

Winston S. Churchill to General Ismay, for the Chiefs of Staff Committee
(*Churchill papers, 20/36*)

28 November 1941

HELP FOR THE GUERRILLA FIGHTERS IN YUGOSLAVIA

Everything in human power should be done. Please report what is possible.[1]

[1] 'The morale of the insurgents as a whole is now reported to be high,' Hugh Dalton informed Churchill. This was 'in spite of the occupation by the Germans of the upper Morava valley' in which many of the partisans had been operating. There was little doubt, Dalton added, that the partisans 'are immobilizing not less than 7 German and 12 Italian Divisions. It seems, therefore, absolutely essential to keep the revolt going if we possibly can, and to regard it as an extension of the Libyan front.' ('Yugoslav Revolt', letter dated 11 December 1941: *Cabinet papers 69/3*)

Winston S. Churchill to the Duke of Windsor
(*Churchill papers, 20/31*)

28 November 1941

I greatly regret incident in the House of Commons last Tuesday.[1] Attack was delivered in Supplementary Questions, which Under-Secretary of State for the Colonies could not have foreseen and for which he was unprepared. Sloan[2] had, of course, no support in the House of Commons and I have seen little or no reference to the incident in the British Press beyond the bare report.

I would strongly advise leaving the matter alone. I heard from Lord Halifax of the success of your visit. He reported that on the whole the Press, with the exception of one or two rags, had behaved all right.

F. D. W. Brown to A. S. Hodge[3]
(*Churchill papers, 20/31*)

28 November 1941

Dear Hodge,

The Prime Minister has approved the following broadcasts about which you have written to me recently:

(1) Mr Amery's broadcast this Saturday in the German Service about the Prime Minister. (I have informed Mr Harrison[4] and suggested two small amendments.)

[1] In a question to the Under-Secretary for the Colonies (George Hall), Alexander Sloan asked whether the visit of the Duke of Windsor to the United States 'was undertaken with the consent' of the Government, to which Hall replied: 'Yes. Sir.' In his supplementary question, which had not been on the Order Paper, Sloan asked: 'Is my hon. Friend aware of the bitter comment that is being made in United States newspapers and elsewhere in regard to the ostentatious display of jewellery and finery at a period when the people of this country are strictly rationed', and if so would he make representations to the Prime Minister 'to have this gentleman and his wife recalled, since their visit is doing a certain amount of harm and certainly no good.' When another Member of Parliament, Gerald Palmer, interjected to say that the hostile Press reports were 'by no means representative of the general welcome given in the United States to the Duke and Duchess', Sloan commented that 'there are literally scores of thousands of these Press cuttings, not filtering into this country but flooding the country'. If Hall was not aware of this 'he cannot be paying attention to the Press cuttings'. Hall made no further comment.

[2] Alexander Sloan. Secretary of the National Union of Scottish Mineworkers. Labour Member of Parliament for South Ayrshire from 1939 until his death in 1945.

[3] Alan Hodge, 1915–1979. Assistant Private Secretary to the Minister of Information, 1941–45. Editor of The Novel Library, 1946–52. Joint Editor of *History Today*, 1951–79. Churchill's principal research assistant on his four volume *A History of the English-speaking Peoples* from 1953.

[4] Geoffrey Wedgwood Harrison, 1908–1990. Entered the Foreign Office, 1932. Served in Tokyo, 1935–37; in Berlin, 1937–39. First Secretary, Foreign Office, 1941–45. Counsellor of Embassy, Brussels, 1945–47. Minister in Moscow, 1947–49. Head of the Northern Department, Foreign Office, 1941–51; Assistant Under-Secretary of State, 1951–56. Knighted, 1955. Ambassador to Brazil, 1956–58; to Persia, 1958–63; to Moscow, 1965–68.

(2) On December 23rd, by Lord Moyne about the Colonial Empire in the Empire Service.

(3) On December 24th, by Mr R. A. Butler on Education, in the Overseas Service.

(4) At a date not yet fixed, by Mr Geoffrey Shakespeare,[1] in the North American Service.[2]

(5) On Christmas Eve, by Mr Geoffrey Shakespeare, to evacuated children in Australia, New Zealand and South Africa.

Ian Malcolm[3] *to Winston S. Churchill*
(*Churchill papers, 2/420*)

28 November 1941

My dear Winston

This letter is to wish you a very happy birthday, with long life and health to support the great undertaking which rests almost entirely upon your shoulders. I had no idea that you were born on the Feast of St Andrew, our Scottish Patron Saint; who, I feel sure, will make time to protect all your undertakings, as well as to look after the fortunes of Russia and our Scottish selves.

I can't tell you with how much interest and devotion I follow your great career. I wait for every broadcast speech of yours with the utmost eagerness, and am never disappointed. These speeches have become my primary interest in the Highland fastness that now contains me, after having been so close to the front line in the last war, and then, during the past twenty years, helping to prepare the defence of the Suez Canal for the present one. One feels very

[1] Geoffrey Hithersay Shakespeare, 1893–1980. Served in the Great War, at Gallipoli and in Egypt. President of the Cambridge Union, 1920. Private Secretary to Lloyd George, 1921–3. Called to the Bar, 1922. National Liberal MP for Wellingborough, 1922–3. Liberal MP for Norwich, 1929–31; Liberal National MP for Norwich, 1931–45. Liberal-National Chief Whip, 1931–2. Parliamentary Secretary at the Ministry of Health, 1932–6; and at the Board of Education, 1936–7. Parliamentary and Financial Secretary, Admiralty, 1937–40. Parliamentary Under-Secretary of State, Dominions Office, 1940–2. Created Baronet, 1942.

[2] To the United States and Canada, where the writer of this footnote, one of more than four thousand British evacuees sent to Canada and the United States in the summer of 1940, had just celebrated his fifth birthday.

[3] Ian Zachary Malcolm, 1868–1944. Attaché, British Embassy, Berlin, 1891–93; Paris, 1893–96. Attached to the Embassy in St Petersburg for the Coronation of the Emperor, 1896. Conservative Member of Parliament for Stowmarket, 1895–1906; for Croydon, 1910–19. Parliamentary Private Secretary to the Chief Secretary for Ireland, 1901–03. In 1902 he married Jeanne Langtry, the daughter of Lady de Bath (Lily Langtry, the actress). British Red Cross Officer, France, Switzerland, Russia and North America, 1914–17. Private Secretary to A.J. Balfour, 1919. Created Baronet, 1919. British Government Representative on the Suez Canal Board, 1919–39. Among his books were *Indian Pictures and Problems* (1907), *War Pictures Behind the Lines* (1915), and *Highland Lore and Legend* (1938).

useless; but I am sure that an old man is of more value looking after his own farmyard at home than touting for work when he knows he is over age.

I enclose a humble birthday present for you. Please hand it to Mrs Churchill for her Russians. They are doing splendidly, and far better than I ever thought possible after all I saw of them in 1915.

Dear Winston, God-speed to you, and may you have all the support you require from every quarter to help you in your tremendous work.

Yours ever,
Ian M

Winston S. Churchill to Ian Malcolm
(*Churchill papers, 2/420*)

29 November 1941

Thank you so much. I am encouraged by your most kind letter from a brother Hooligan.[1]

Winston

Harry Hopkins to Winston S. Churchill
(*Churchill papers, 2/416*)

29 November 1941

Dear Winston. Happy birthday. How old are you anyway?[2] I hope to celebrate the next one with you. Love to all the family.

Harry

[1] In the summer of 1901 Churchill had joined a group of young Conservative MPs who, like himself, were dissatisfied with Party policy. Calling themselves 'Hooligans' or 'Hughligans' after one of their leading members, Lord Salisbury's son Lord Hugh Cecil, they dined every Thursday in the House of Commons, inviting a distinguished guest to dine with them. A former and a future Liberal Prime Minister – Lord Rosebery and H.H. Asquith – were among their guests. In the spring of 1902, after a debate initiated by the Liberals in which the Conservative Government was accused of abusing its powers under martial law in South Africa, Churchill and seven other 'Hooligans' voted against the government. Their dinner guest that night, Joseph Chamberlain, asked them: 'What is the use of supporting your own Government only when it is right? It is just when it is in this sort of pickle that you ought to have come to our aid.'

[2] Churchill was about to be sixty-seven.

R. F. Meiklejohn[1] *to Winston S. Churchill*
(*Churchill papers, 2/420*)

29 November 1941

Dear Prime Minister,

I am sending you every good wish for your birthday as one who met & served with you 43 years ago, though you will not, I imagine, remember me.

We met up the Nile, and had quite a long conversation the night before Omdurman. I was sitting up with my Company of the Royal Warwickshire, behind the zariba, & we speculated on the chances of a night attack, and the morrow. I rather think you brought in the first news next morning that the Dervishes were attacking.

We met again in S. Africa (Durban) early in 1900. I was on the Hospital ship *Maine* – & you had escaped from the Boers. I was invalided home under your mother's charge.[2]

Do not trouble to answer this – but when this war ends I may write again, for I personally know only one other survivor of the 1898 campaign, and if you then are taking a well-earned rest & cared to talk over times of very long ago we might have a chance of doing so.

I still preserve relics of Omdurman.

Yours sincerely
R. F. Meiklejohn

Lady Desborough to Winston S. Churchill
(*Churchill papers, 2/417*)

29 November 1941

Dear dear Winston,

Just one hug for your Birthday – never to be answered, but soon to be returned!

Ettie[3]

[1] Ronald Forbes Meiklejohn, born 1876. Educated at Rugby. Joined the Royal Warwickshire Regiment, 1896. Lieutenant, 1898. Nile Expedition 1898; in action at Atbara and Khartoum. Served in the South African War, 1899–1900 (relief of Ladysmith; operations in Cape Colony; Distinguished Service Order). Captain, 1900. Staff Captain, Naval Base, Cape Colony, 1904. Staff Officer, Coastal Defence, Scotland Command, 1910–14. Major, 1914. Employed at the Admiralty, 1914. General Staff Officer, Intelligence, North Russia Expeditionary Force, 1919. Lieutenant-Colonel, 1919. General Staff Officer, British Military Mission to Finland, 1919–20.

[2] During the Boer War, Lady Randolph Churchill had organized the financing and running of a hospital ship, the *Maine*. Among the soldiers whom she tended was her own son Jack, who had been lightly wounded in the foot. The *Maine* had been bought and equipped by an Anglo-American group; Churchill's mother was the Executive Committee's representative on board.

[3] Churchill replied by telegram: 'Thank you so much dear Ettie. Winston'.

Desmond Morton to Winston S. Churchill
(*Churchill papers, 20/420*)

29 November 1941
Personal

Dear Winston,

On your last birthday the great battle of the Air was won, though we hardly knew it.

On this birthday the great battle of the Atlantic is won, though we hardly dare own it.[1]

By next birthday may the great battle of the Land be won under your Leadership, is the prayer of yours most sincerely

Desmond Morton

General Auchinleck to Winston S. Churchill
(*Churchill papers, 2/429*)

29 November 1941

The Army of the Nile wishes you a happy Birthday and many more of them.

General de Gaulle to Winston S. Churchill: telegram
(*Churchill papers, 2/429*)

29 November 1941

VOTRE ANNIVERSAIRE EST AUJOURDHUI CELUI DE LESPERANCE STOP IL SERA DANS LAVENIR UNE FETE DE LA VICTOIRE STOP JE VOUS ADRESSE MES VOEUX LES PLUS SINCERES =

C. DE GAULLE

[1] Morton's optimism was misplaced. Although the British use of the German Naval Enigma decrypts had substantially reduced U-boat attacks on trans-Atlantic merchant ships in the autumn and winter of 1941, a new Enigma machine for U-boats was instituted in February 1942 and not broken for ten months, during which time there were numerous sinkings in the Atlantic, and especially in United States coastal waters.

Winston S. Churchill to Anthony Eden
(*Churchill papers, 20/36*)

29 November 1941
Action this Day

Finland and Co. I don't want to be pinched for time if there is a chance of Finland pulling out of the big war. See Mallet's[1] telegram of today. See also my telegram to Stalin No. 188, which says, 'If they do not stop in the next fortnight and you still wish us to declare war on them . . .' Procedure therefore should be as follows. If we have not heard by the 5th that the Finns are not going to pull out, or have heard they are contumacious, we then telegraph to Stalin saying that 'if he still wishes it' we will declare war forthwith. The Roumanian and Hungarian declarations will follow, also in accordance with whatever he may desire.

Winston S. Churchill to Air Chief Marshal Sir Charles Portal
(*Churchill papers, 20/36*)

29 November 1941

I see statements in the Press that RAF, ME,[2] are making 200 sorties per day. As they have well over 500 aircraft in action, this figure should be nearly 1,000 if, as is stated, they are making two sorties per day per squadron.

I am bound to say my impression is that the GAF[3] are doing marvels, outnumbered four to one as they are.

Why is it we cannot turn Derna into a Namsos?[4] I feel much concerned at the way in which the enemy endure our air superiority.

Winston S. Churchill to General Auchinleck
(*Churchill papers, 20/43*)

29 November 1941
Personal and Most Secret

CIGS and I do not intend to suggest that you should in any way supersede Ritchie. What we still think would be wise is for you to visit the battlefield

[1] Victor Louis Mallet, 1893–1969. 2nd Lieutenant, 1914. On active service, 1914–18. Entered the Diplomatic Service, 1919. Counsellor at Washington, 1936–9. Minister at Stockholm, 1940–5. Knighted, 1944. Ambassador at Madrid, 1945–6; at Rome, 1947–53.

[2] Royal Air Force, Middle East.

[3] German Air Force.

[4] A reference to the ability of the Germans in April 1940 to force the British troops to withdraw from Namsos in Norway, as a result of superior German air power.

should a new impulse be clearly needed. Coming fresh to the scene with your drive and full knowledge of the situation, you will put new vigour into the troops and inspire everyone to a supreme effort. Nevertheless, as I said before, this must be a matter for your judgment.

John Curtin to Winston S. Churchill
(*Churchill papers, 20/43*)

29 November 1941
Most Secret

I have your Most Secret telegram of 28th November Winch No. 6 and very greatly regret that you have had distress of mind from any attitude taken by this Government. In Australia, we are endeavouring to educate the public to a realization of, and as a Government to assume, our share of the burden associated with foreign policy. We have many difficulties which I need not detail here but of which you will be aware. We assume that your Government welcomes our independence of thought and advice rather than that we should wait on you for guidance and support. The latter would be most unhelpful to you and would be equally unhealthy from an Australian national viewpoint. Consequently, sometimes it is inevitable that the Commonwealth Government will formulate a policy at variance with yours. You know that often only a narrow distinction may exist between the expression of a policy and criticism of some other view but we will be at great pains to see to it here that no criticism of your policy in respect of the war and foreign affairs is given publicity.

Actually, it would be difficult to construe what Dr Evatt said with regard to Finland, Hungary and Roumania as criticism of your Government. The reference is as follows:

> Begins.
> It is a strange feature of the present struggle that, while we are Allies of Russia in the fight against Germany, we are still at peace with these three eager satellites and accomplices of Germany. Ends.

This reference included a recital of the facts and could be made by any one without any suggestion of blame.

I appreciate the dilemma you have been in with regard to these countries particularly Finland. I have noted from your telegram under reply and from telegrams received today from the Secretary of State, the present position of the matter and realize that you are doing everything possible to help our cause.

I greatly appreciate your expression of sympathy in the loss of the *Sydney* –

it is a heavy blow to us. The sinking of HMS *Barham* is another shock and we feel for you deeply in this loss of life and material. It is all a terrible (? group omitted) but must be borne. I am glad to read your comment that General Auchinleck is hopeful. Naturally, we follow this campaign very carefully and with hope for a happy conclusion.

Finally, may I say that we do not need any concrete demonstration, such as you instance, to make us aware of your comradeship and goodwill towards us. We know that your great work is not only for Great Britain but for all of us and we are doing and will continue to do everything in our power to give you practical assistance.

Kindest regards and I take the opportunity of adding Many Happy Returns of Sunday's anniversary.

Curtin

Winston S. Churchill to Anthony Eden
(*Churchill papers, 20/36*)

30 November 1941
Secret

I think it most important that the United States should continue their relations with Vichy and their supplies to North Africa and any other contacts unostentatiously for the present. It would be a great mistake to lose any contacts before we know the result of the battle in Libya and its reactions. There is always time to break, but it is more difficult to renew contacts.

Winston S. Churchill to General Auchinleck
(*Churchill papers, 20/46*)

30 November 1941
Personal and Secret

1. Although I have no news from the front later than your No. 1626, I cannot help feeling that we are forging steadily ahead against a resourceful and determined foe. Thank you so much for your full accounts and for your kind good wishes.

2. I may have to make a statement to House on Tuesday on information received to that date, especially if events continue to take a favourable turn. I think it would then be proper, unless you see objection, to disclose the change

in command, which will by then be more than a week old, and the reason. Statement would be laconic and something like the following:

On 23rd November General Auchinleck repaired to General Cunningham, Advance Headquarters, where he remained for three days. On 26th November he became convinced that General Cunningham's proposed dispositions were not in accord with the principle of relentless offensive at all risks and at all costs on which General Auchinleck's conception of the battle was founded. General Auchinleck therefore removed General Cunningham from the Command of the 8th Army and replaced him by Major-General Ritchie. This decision was immediately approved and confirmed by the Minister of State and by me. Since 26th November, therefore, General Ritchie has conducted the battle with skill and resolution under the general supervision of the Commander-in-Chief.

Winston S. Churchill to the Dominion Prime Ministers[1]
(Cabinet papers, 65/24)

30 November 1941
sent at 2.30 a.m.
Most Secret
Personal

1. There are important indications that Japan is about to attack Thailand and that this attack will include a seaborne expedition to seize strategical points in the Kra Isthmus.

2. The Royal Air Force are reconnoitring on an arc of 180 miles from Kota Bharu for three days commencing the 29th November and Commander-in-Chief Far East has requested Commander-in-Chief United States Asiatic Fleet at Manila to undertake air reconnaissance on the line Manila–Camranh Bay on the same days. Commander-in-Chief Far East has asked for permission to move into Kra Isthmus if reconnaissance establishes the fact that escorted Japanese ships are approaching the Isthmus, and he is pressing for an immediate decision on this point. Time is the essence of this plan particularly at this season of the year when the Kra Isthmus is water-logged. Consequently great tactical advantage lies with the side which gets there first.

3. Our Military Advisers fear that operation might lead to a clash which might involve us in war and they have always emphasized that unless our vital interests were immediately threatened this should be avoided so long as we

[1] John Curtin (Australia), Peter Fraser (New Zealand), William Mackenzie King (Canada) and Field Marshal Smuts (South Africa).

have no certainty of United States support. In view however of United States Government's constitutional difficulties any prior guarantee of such support is most unlikely.

4. In these circumstances His Majesty's Ambassador at Washington has been instructed to explain the position at once to the United States Government and to take following line. To allow the Japanese to establish themselves so near the Malay frontier would be an obvious threat to Singapore, even though at present season it might not develop at once. We have also to bear in mind the encouragement which Japanese success would give to their extremists. Japanese appetite would inevitably grow and other Far Eastern peoples would be correspondingly depressed. It looks therefore as though, to ensure the defence of Singapore and for wider reasons, we might have to take proposed action to forestall the Japanese.

5. Lord Halifax is to ask for an urgent expression of the United States Government's views and has been reminded of the importance of ensuring ourselves of United States support in the event of hostilities.

6. We should be grateful for your views by most immediate telegram.

War Office Note

(*War Office papers, 208/3043*)

30 November 1941
Secret

FAR EAST: GENERAL PRINCIPLES OF POLICY AND STRATEGY

The effect of war with Japan on our main war effort might be so severe as to prejudice our chances of beating Germany. Our policy must therefore be – and is – avoidance of war with Japan.

Winston S. Churchill to President Franklin D. Roosevelt

(*Premier papers, 3/469*)

30 November 1941
Action this Day
Personal and Secret

It seems to me that one important method remains unused in averting war between Japan and our two countries, namely, a plain declaration, secret or public as may be thought best, that any further act of aggression by Japan will lead immediately to the gravest consequences. I realize your constitutional difficulties, but it would be tragic if Japan drifted into war by encroachment without having before her fairly and squarely the dire character of a further aggressive step. I beg you to consider whether, at the moment which you judge right which may be very[1] near, you should not say that 'any further Japanese aggression would compel you to place the gravest issues before Congress', or words to that effect. We would, of course, make a similar declaration or share in a joint declaration, and in any case arrangements are being made to synchronize our action with yours. Forgive me, my dear friend, for presuming to press such a course upon you, but I am convinced that it might make all the difference and prevent a melancholy extension of the war.[2]

General Auchinleck to Winston S. Churchill
(*Churchill papers, 20/46*)

30 November 1941

Our supply column reached Tobruk morning of 29th. The commander of XIII Corps'[3] birthday message to you is, 'Corridor to Tobruk clear and secure. Tobruk is as relieved as I am.'

Winston S. Churchill to General Godwin-Austen
(*Churchill papers, 20/46*)

30 November 1941
Personal

I am highly complimented by your message. 13 Corps have fought a great fight in this astounding battle.[4]

[1] Churchill added the word 'very' at the last moment, when this telegram was ready for despatch.

[2] Churchill wrote in his war memoirs: 'On the 30th, shortly after noon (American time), Mr Hull visited the President, who had on his desk my cable of the same date, sent overnight. They did not think my proposal of a joint warning to Japan would be any good. Nor can we be surprised at this when they had already before them an intercept from Tokyo to Berlin, also dated November 30, telling the Japanese Ambassador in Berlin to address Hitler and Ribbentrop as follows: "Say very secretly to them that there is extreme danger that war may suddenly break out between the Anglo-Saxon nations and Japan through some clash of arms, and add that the time of the breaking out of this war may come quicker than anyone dreams."'

[3] Alfred Reade Godwin-Austen, 1889–1963. 2nd Lieutenant, 1909. On active service, Gallipoli and Mesopotamia, 1915–19 (Military Cross). Commanded the 14th Infantry Brigade, Palestine (Arab revolt), 1938–9 (despatches). Major-General, 1939. Commanding the 8th Division, on active service in East Africa and Abyssinia (for which he was awarded the CB), 1940. Principal Administrative Officer, India Command, New Delhi, 1945–6. Knighted, 1946. General, 1946. Chairman, South-Western Division, National Coal Board, 1946–8.

[4] On 29 November 1941, as Auchinleck's supply columns entered Tobruk, the 8th Army announced the capture of General von Ravenstein, General Officer Commanding the 21st Panzer Division, and 600 of his men.

King George VI and Queen Elizabeth to Winston S. Churchill: telegram
(*Churchill papers, 1/361*)

30 November 1941 Buckingham Palace

MANY HAPPY RETURNS OF THE DAY FROM US BOTH

GEORGE R I

Winston S. Churchill to King George VI and Queen Elizabeth: telegram
(*Churchill papers, 1/361*)

30 November 1941

I AM DEEPLY GRATEFUL TO YOUR MAJESTIES FOR THE GRACIOUS MESSAGE WHICH HAS REACHED ME ON MY BIRTHDAY

WINSTON CHURCHILL[1]

Lord Beaverbrook to Winston S. Churchill
(*Chuchill papers, 2/416*)

30 November 1941

My Dear Winston,

This letter carries Birthday greetings of a difficult colleague & a devoted follower.

What you mean to our people in this crisis is beyond reckoning, beyond any figure in our history.

But one who has worked intimately with you in the dark days & in the gleams of wintry sunshine, can measure the inspiration with which you sustain your people.

And this knowledge gives me the right to say that the victory, when it comes, will all be yours.

For those who have served with you it will be sufficient glory to be known as Churchill's man.

Yours affectionately
Max

[1] A note by Leslie Rowan on the final draft of this telegram stated: 'No. 10 asked to send off – also "variations of this theme" to Queen Mary, Queen Wilhelmina, Grand Duchess of Luxembourg and Prince Bernhard'. Leslie Rowan added that this was done by Anthony Bevir.

Sir Samuel Hoare to Winston S. Churchill
(*Churchill papers, 2/419*)

30 November 1941
Private and Personal

British Embassy,
Madrid

Dear Winston,

I have just heard that it is your birthday and on that account I am putting this letter in the bag to wish you many happy returns of the day. What a year you have had! In some respects it has been like 1758, but far more dangerous to the British people. Today, with Rostov[1] and the Libyan battle it looks as if your next year may follow its predecessor as 1759 – a year of victories – followed 1758 – a year of peril. May this be so. In any case you can look back with patriotic pride to many great achievements.

I will not burden these good wishes with any remarks about Spain and myself, except to say that since I came back from England I have been the centre of every kind of approach and enquiry, both from Spaniards and foreign diplomats. This shows that the wind is going in our favour. If this is so, it is a further sign of the good effects that the last year has had upon our fortunes.

On no account trouble to acknowledge this,[2]

Yours ever
Samuel Hoare

Charles Balaam[3] to Winston S. Churchill
(*Churchill papers, 2/416*)

30 November 1941

Dear Mr Churchill,

It is probable that Hercules having, in turn, passed on to you the burden Atlas foisted on him, you will have forgotten the name of the present writer. You will, perhaps, recall it, however, when I mention Ventnor and the butterflies.

[1] On 28 November 1941, at the start of their winter counter-offensive, Russian troops had driven the Germans from Rostov-on-Don, forcing General von Kleist to retreat to Taganrog. This was the Germans' first major set back on the Eastern Front.

[2] Churchill replied by telegram: 'Thank you for your letter. Winston'.

[3] Charles John Balaam, 1873-1944. A youthful friend of Churchill when they were both staying at Ventnor on the Isle of Wight in the 1880s (Churchill was then staying with his nanny, Mrs Everest). Entered the London and County Bank, 1892. Subsequently a civil servant; in 1918, as Acting Divisional Officer for London and South Eastern Division, Employment Department, Ministry of Labour, he was appointed an Officer of the Order of the British Empire (OBE) and in 1935, as Divisional Controller, South Eastern Division, Ministry of Labour, he was promoted Commander of the Order (CBE). He died on 18 January 1944.

So much has come true since those days that, greatly daring, I venture to write to remind you of the prophetic instinct you possessed & which you may have forgotten.

When you were ten years of age you told me that, in years to come, you were going to design a mighty gun, a mile in length, for the defence of New York Harbour.

Now, you and another, have forged a weapon which spans the Atlantic.

When you were twelve I heard you tell my mother that one day you would become Prime Minister.

What you did not know when you aided History to anticipate Herself was that you would be greater than the greatest.

A little while ago you coined an epigram which will not die – 'Never before did so many owe so much to so few.'

You did not know that its terms could be still further reduced. Of you it may be said with equal truth – 'never before have all owed so much to one.'

– and now how do I dare to write such things?

As I write I have before me a letter dated 4 January 1895.

It was written to me & ended, 'your affectionate friend Winston S. Churchill'.

These lines may, in the stress of things, never meet your eye.

But the writing of them has given me great joy & pride & the wealth of all the world could never filch my letter from me.

That the God of War may continue to gird you until the God of Peace shall give you the Peace which passeth understanding is the fervent wish of one,

Charles Balaam

Alice, Viscountess Wimborne to Winston S. Churchill

(*Churchill papers, 2/423*)

30 November 1941 Ashby St Ledgers

Dearest Winston,

My loving felicitations for your birthday join the legions you will receive,[1] making one more of such messages inspired by affection, gratitude, admiration and love. I hope that good news may illuminate the day like a shaft

[1] Kathleen Hill prepared a list for Churchill 'to see at leisure' of all those who had sent him birthday telegrams and letters, all of which, she noted, had been acknowledged. Those who had written were: King George VI and Queen Elizabeth, Queen Mary, the Grand Duchess and the Prince of Luxembourg, the Queen of the Netherlands and Prince Bernhard, the Maharajahs of Bikaner and Nepal, Desmond Morton, Lord Beaverbrook, each of the three Chiefs of Staff, Ernest Bevin, General Paget, Anthony Eden, Sir Kingsley Wood, Clement Attlee, A.V. Alexander, Leo Amery, Harold Balfour, Major General Sir Reginald Barnes, the Duchess of Buccleuch, the Marquess of Camden, Lord Carnarvon, Lord Ivor Churchill, Mary Churchill, Judy Montagu, HMS *Churchill*, Sir Kenneth Clark, Sir Bede and Lady Clifford, Lady Desborough, Reginald Fellowes and his wife, Sir Ian

of light, that some special cause for rejoicing may distinguish it for you. Your heart will be with those fighting to the death in Libya up and at the throats of the German beasts at last. Were I one of them, when my moment came I would say 'For England and Churchill', and God would defend the right.

God bless you dearest Winston and all happiness to you, and love,

from
Alice

Lady Leslie[1] *to Winston S. Churchill*
(*Churchill papers, 1/361*)

30 November 1941

Many happy Returns full of Victory – of your dear Birthday – Darling Winston – How grateful the whole world seems to be – that you were born! Seymour[2] will be giving you from me the two small Chinese Fish – you may remember them on yr Mother's dinner table years ago – I thought it could be like a message from her. I always hope she knows all you have been able to

Hamilton, Kathleen and Averell Harriman, Harrow School (Headmaster), George Harrap, the Boys of Harrow School, George Hicks, Captain Hillgarth, Harry Hopkins, Lord Iliffe, Sir Stanley Jackson, the Countess of Kimberley, Lord Leathers, Marjorie Leslie, Lionel and Leonie, Jack Leslie, Lord and Lady Lytton, Lord McGowan, Captain Margesson, the Duchess of Marlborough, Sir Edward Marsh, Colonel Moore-Brabazon, Lord Moyne, Vic Oliver, Alfred J. Salisbury, Julian and Edwina Sandys, Sir Archibald Sinclair, the Speaker of the House of Commons, Brigadier Frank Spencer, Sir Henry Strakosch and Lady Strakosch, the Duke of Sutherland, the editor of the *Essex Chronicle*, Ronald and Nancy Tree, Alice, Viscountess Wimborne, Gilbert Winant, 'all at Chartwell and Tango', the Household Staff at No. 10, Sir Harry Brittain, Sir Francis Whitmore (Lord Lieutenant of Essex), Alice Lady Avebury, 'Jim' (unidentified!), General Wavell, General Auchinleck, William Mackenzie King, General Smuts, Robert Menzies, the Governor-General of New Zealand, Peter Fraser, Regis Oliveira, Ivan Maisky, General de Gaulle, Count Raczynski, Dr. Beneš, The Netherlands Prime Minister, Virgil Tilea, Vincent Massey, the Norwegian Prime Minister, Hubert Young (Governor of Trinidad), Eugene Ramsden MP, Captain Morris, RA, Sir Henry MacGeagh, Vice-Admiral Swirski, the Turkish Ambassador, the Chilean Ambassador, the Greek Prime Minister, the Luxembourg Foreign Minister, M. Quotaichi, Hubert Ripka (Czechoslovakian Government), General Simovich, the Brazilian Ambassador, the Belgian Prime Minister and the Belgian Ambassador, Sir John Laurie (as Lord Mayor), Sir John Laurie (personal), Mrs V. Laughton Mathews (WRNS), Charalambos Simopoulos, Anti-Aircraft Command, Dr Chaim Weizmann, General Kukiel (Polish Forces), the Officer Commanding the 239th Light AA Battery, Lord Halifax, Sir G. Ogilvie-Forbes, V.C.W. Forbes, General Sikorski, Lady Colefax, Sir Eustace Tennyson d'Eyncourt, Alexandre Bogomolov, Colonel Mihailovic, the Staff of the Offices of War Cabinet, Marshal Stalin, Sir Ian Malcolm, Leonard Plugge, W. Leach, Sir Robert Lynn, and Geneviève Tabouis.

[1] Leonie Blanche Jerome, 1859–1943. Sister of Lady Randolph Churchill. She married Colonel John Leslie in 1884. Their younger son Norman was killed in action on 18 October 1914.

[2] William Seymour Leslie, 1889–1979. Churchill's cousin. Second son of Sir John and Leonie Leslie (Churchill's aunt). Secretary of Queen Charlotte's Maternity Hospital, Hammersmith. After his retirement he lived near Dublin.

achieve. How pleased and surprised old General Brab[1] wd have been had he known you wd one day be Colonel of the 4th Hussars.

Bless you Dearest – Jack[2] and the family here send you all good wishes.

Yr devoted, admiring and loving
Venerable Aunt Leonie[3]

Randolph S. Churchill to Winston S. Churchill
(*Churchill papers, 1/362*)

30 November 1941 North Africa

Many Happy Returns and all my love and deepest admiration
Randolph,

Battle Headquarters 8th Army

L.S. Amery: radio broadcast
(*Churchill papers, 2/416*)

30 November 1941

EXTRACT

He is today the spirit of old England incarnate, with its unshakeable self-confidence, its grim gaiety, its unfailing sense of humour, its underlying moral earnestness, its unflinching tenacity. Against that inner unity of spirit between leader and nation the ill-cemented moral fabric of Hitler's perversion of the German soul must be shattered in the end.

[1] Brigadier-General Sir John Brabazon, 1843–1922. Churchill's first commanding officer (in 1895).

[2] John Leslie (known as Jack), 1857–1944. Lieutenant, Grenadier Guards, 1877. On active service in Egypt, 1882. Married Churchill's Aunt Leonie (Lady Randolph Churchill's sister), 1884. On active service in Egypt, 1882; South Africa, 1900. Lieutenant-Colonel Commanding the 5th Royal Irish Fusiliers, 1900–08; retired with the rank of Colonel. Succeeded his father as 2nd Baronet, 1916. A Justice of the Peace for County Monaghan.

[3] Churchill replied by telegram: 'Thank you so much dearest Leonie for your lovely letter and gift. Am writing. Winston'.

December 1941

Winston S. Churchill to General de Gaulle
(*Churchill papers, 2/429*)

1 December 1941

Thank you so much for your charming message which I have received and read with the greatest pleasure.

Winston S. Churchill

General Auchinleck to Winston S. Churchill
(*Churchill papers, 20/46*)

1 December 1941
Private

Summary. Enemy attempts to encircle and destroy New Zealand Division were badly co-ordinated and have not (repeat not) so far succeeded. Enemy attempt to reconcentrate 15 and 21 Panzer Divisions and Ariete Division has not (repeat not) so far succeeded. Enemy tank strength seems definitely at low ebb while ours appears relatively good. Our Infantry tanks with New Zealand Division will be most valuable in event of renewed enemy attack. Difficult to forecast but seems possible that enemy may now try and stabilize front east of El Adem with his German infantry covered by his remaining tanks on their south flank. Plans to deal with this contingency are in hand. Alternatively he may fling everything into renewed attack which should result in his becoming weaker than he already is. Enemy has been sending all operation orders in clear for last two days which is significant of haste and disorganization. Nothing will make me unduly optimistic but I am absolutely confident.

Ritchie has grasped battle completely and is thinking far ahead. Our Air Force continues to do magnificently and had most successful action today.

Propose to go forward myself tomorrow.

Robert Barrington-Ward:[1] *diary*
(Barrington-Ward papers)

1 December 1941

Brendan first. Then Winston from a War Cabinet, looking (at 67) very fresh and young and spry. He is a different man altogether from the rather bloated individual whom I last saw (close to) before the war. His cheerful, challenging – not to say truculent – look is good to see just now; but it covers up a great deal of caution, even vacillation at times. Perhaps instinctively acquired. Anyway it is good to see, and the public thinks so too, and it is the right 'face' to put to the vast responsibilities which he is discharging. A lack of the finer perceptions, no doubt! But no doubt either about vigour and purpose. He might and does contradict his appearance by hesitation over risks to be taken, but he would not be found wanting in the last ditch.

War Cabinet: Confidential Annex
(Cabinet papers, 65/24)

1 December 1941
6 p.m.

The Prime Minister said that, as the result of a report that Japanese forces were moving southwards, possibly with the intention of committing an act of aggression against Siam, there had been an exchange of telegrams with the Dominion Governments. The Australian Government thought that if Japan committed an aggression against Siam, we should at once take warlike measures. Field Marshal Smuts had thought that we could assume that the United States would support us, once we became involved in the Far East. Even if we took the initiative in advancing to the Kra Isthmus, it would be manifest that we were acting defensively in forestalling a Japanese landing. Mr Mackenzie King, on the other hand, had warned us in strong terms of the dangers of becoming involved with Japan with no assurance of United States cooperation. The Chiefs of Staff, having considered the telegrams from the four Dominions, had not departed from the view which they had previously expressed, that –

[1] Robert Robin McGowan Barrington Ward, 1891–1948. Joined the staff of *The Times*, 1913. Brigade Major, 1914–18 (Military Cross, Distinguished Service Order, despatches thrice). Assistant Editor, *Observer*, 1919–27. Assistant Editor and Chief Leader Writer, *The Times*, 1927–34; Deputy Editor, 1934–41. Supported Neville Chamberlain and appeasement, writing in his diary at the time of Munich: 'Most of this office is against Dawson and me!' Succeeded Geoffrey Dawson as Editor of *The Times*, 1 October 1941. Retired due to ill-health, 1947, travelling by sea to South Africa with hope of restoring his health. Died on board ship in the harbour of Dar-es-Salaam, where he was buried.

(a) Until we were assured of American military support, we should take no action, save in defence of our vital interests, which was likely to precipitate war with Japan:
(b) An occupation by Japan of the Kra Isthmus could only be with the object of attacking Singapore. Nevertheless, it would not by itself be an attack on our vital interests.

The Prime Minister said that he was still of opinion that we ought not to assume that the outbreak of war between England and Japan would necessarily precipitate the entry of the United States into the war. There was a strong party in the United States who would work up prejudice against being drawn into Britain's war.

The Prime Minister added that with the Dominions Secretary and the Chiefs of Staff, he had had a meeting that morning with Sir Earle Page and Mr Bruce; the Foreign Secretary had joined them shortly before the close of the meeting. He (the Prime Minister) had explained that, in his view, we should not resist or attempt to forestall a Japanese attack on the Kra Isthmus unless we had a satisfactory assurance from the United States that they would join us should our action cause us to become involved in war with Japan. The same would apply, with even more force, in the event of a Japanese attack on Russia, or aggression in the Netherlands East Indies. He had conveyed this view to Mr Bruce, and had authorized the despatch to Mr Curtin of a copy of his telegram of the 30th November to President Roosevelt.

Winston S. Churchill to Captain Pim[1]
(*Churchill papers, 2/416*)

1 December 1941

My dear Pim

Thank you so much for the charming souvenir I have received from the Officers of the Upper War Room. It will always recall one of my most vivid nights among your maps.

Thank you also for your good wishes.

Yours sincerely,
Winston S. Churchill

[1] Richard Pike Pim, 1900–1987. Served in the Royal Volunteer Reserve, 1914–18. Commander, RNVR Ulster Division, 1929. Joined Royal Irish Constabulary, 1921. Assistant Secretary, Ministry of Home Affairs, Northern Ireland, 1935. In charge of Churchill's War Room at the Admiralty, 1939–40; at Downing Street, No. 10, Annexe, and on Churchill's war-time travels (from Newfoundland 1941 to Potsdam 1945), 1940–5. Knighted, 1945. Inspector-General, Royal Ulster Constabulary, 1945. Member of Council of the Winston Churchill Memorial Trust, 1965–9.

Winston S. Churchill: speech
(*Hansard*)

2 December 1941 House of Commons

MAXIMUM NATIONAL EFFORT

The Prime Minister (Mr Churchill): I beg to move,

'That, in the opinion of this House, for the purpose of securing the maximum national effort in the conduct of the war and in production, the obligation for National Service should be extended to include the resources of womanpower and manpower still available; and that the necessary legislation should be brought in forthwith.'

We have to call upon the nation for a further degree of sacrifice and exertion. The year 1941 has seen the major problems of creating war production capacity and manufacturing equipment largely solved or on the high road to solution. The crisis of equipment is largely over, and an ever-broadening flow is now assured. The crisis of manpower and womanpower is at hand and will dominate the year 1942. This crisis comes upon us for the following reasons. The great supply plants have largely been constructed; they are finished; they must be staffed, and they must be fully staffed. We must maintain the powerful mobile army we have created with so much pains both for Home Defence and for Foreign Expedition. We must maintain our armies in the East and be prepared for a continuance and an extension of heavy fighting there. We must provide for the expansion of the Air Force in 1942 and the far greater expansion which it will take in 1943. We must face a continuous growth of the Navy to man the great numbers of warships of all kinds coming steadily into service. We must provide modern equipment for the large armies which are being raised and trained in India.

Apart from our own needs, we must keep our engagements to send a substantial supply of tanks, aeroplanes and other war weapons or war commodities to Russia in order to help make good the loss of munition-making capacity which Russia has sustained by the German invasion. We have had also to forgo very important supplies we had expected from the United States but which have now, with our consent, been diverted to Russia. We have also to recognize that United States production is only now getting fully under way and that the quotas we had expected will in many respects be retarded. This is only too often the case in munitions production. The House will remember how I have several times described to them in the last five or six years the time-table of munitions production. First year, nothing at all; second year, very little; third year, quite a lot; fourth year, all you want. We are at the beginning of the third year. The United States is getting through the second year. Germany started the war already well into the fourth year. If one does not prepare before a war, one has to prepare after and be very thankful if time is given. But all this disparity of production will rectify itself in the passage of time. All comes even at the end of the day, and all will come out yet more even when all the days are ended.

We have been hitherto at a disadvantage in having to fight a well-armed enemy with ill-armed or half-armed troops. That phase is over, and in the future the Hun will feel in his own person the sharpness of the weapons with which he has subjugated an unprepared, disorganized Europe and imagined he was about to subjugate the world. In the future our men will fight on equal terms in technical equipment, and a little later on they will fight on superior terms. We have to make arrangements for all this, and we have to make arrangements in good time. A heavy burden will fall upon us in 1942. We must not be found unequal to it. We shall not be found unequal to it.

It has not been necessary, nor would it indeed have been helpful, to make the demands upon the nation which I am about to set forth until now. These demands will intimately affect the lives of many men and women. They will also affect the life of the nation in the following way. There will be a further very definite curtailment of the amenities we have hitherto been able to preserve. These demands will not affect physical health or that contentment of spirit that comes from serving great causes, but they will make further inroads upon the comfort and convenience of very large numbers and upon the character and aspect of our daily life. Much has already been done. Luxury trades have been virtually abolished by cutting off raw materials. The compulsory concentration of industry has reduced labour used in making up what is left. This is passing away rapidly. It must not be supposed that there are large reserves of idle people leading a leisurely existence who can now be called to the national ranks. The entire adult British race, with very few exceptions, gets up in the morning, works all day and goes to bed tired out at night. In our form of society people have been accustomed to find their own jobs to a very large extent, thus saving a vast Government machinery. If all the efforts of everyone were really devoted solely to making war, there would be no food or fuel, no transport or clothes. We have to recognize the fact that a very large proportion of the population, particularly women, is occupied in ministering to the needs of the more actively engaged population and that that number has increased since the last war with the increase of population who have to be ministered to. The process which is now to be applied – and has indeed been continuously applied – much more vigorously is not the calling of idle people to work, but the sharpening and shifting forward of a proportion of their effort into work which is more directly related to the war. It is a general moving up nearer the front which will affect a large block of the people. What we have to make is a definitely harder turn of the screw. I promised eighteen months ago 'blood, tears, toil and sweat'. There has not yet been, thank God, so much blood as was expected. There have not been so many tears. But here we have another instalment of toil and sweat, of inconvenience and self-denial, which I am sure will be accepted with cheerful and proud alacrity by all parties and all classes in the British nation.

The severity of what is required must not be under-rated. The population of Great Britain today is about 46,750,000. Of this, 33,250,000 – 16,000,000 men and 17,250,000 women – are between 14 and 65 years of age. Making allowance for the increase of population which I have just referred to, we have already reached, at the 27th month of this war, the same employment of women in industry, the Services and the Forces as in the 48th month of the last war. The munitions industries in Great Britain have increased in the first two years of this war more rapidly than in four years of the last war. We have 1,000,000 more men in munitions industries at this moment than we had at the end of the last war. What we have now to do is something more than that. I am not at all disguising the seriousness of the proposals which I submit to the House of Commons. On the other hand, it must also be remembered that the changes in our life which will take place, although severe, will not be violent or abrupt. They will be gradual, and gradually increasing in intensity. I propose to give today only the broad outlines and the principal features of the changes which we now propose. My right hon. Friend the Minister of Labour and National Service, who has devoted an immense amount of time to the proposals which are now put forward, and who has been assisted in his task by very strong Cabinet Committees and by repeated conferences on every aspect, will, in winding up the Debate on the next Sitting Day, expound the policy in more detail and also reply to any points which may be raised today. I am not attempting in my speech to state with precision the legal form of the new obligations. There are many verbal refinements, for example, as between Forces and Services, which would be necessary in a Bill or a Defence Regulation. My words are intended to convey the general aspect and prospect to the House. A White Paper will be presented before the Second Reading of the Bill, which will give definitions. Still, I imagine that what I will say is pretty nearly related to the actual facts. But I cannot cover every detail without preventing the House from seeing the picture as a whole.

I deal first with men. There will be three important changes in the case of males. Hitherto reservation from military service has been by occupational blocks. It is now proposed to change over gradually from this system of block reservation to a system of individual deferment. The method of block reservation under the Schedule of Reserved Occupations was a sufficiently good and flexible instrument so long as there was not an acute shortage of manpower. It avoided the waste of ardent men with highly specialized attainments which so disastrously characterized the opening years of the last war. There has been a very careful and steady husbanding of those who possessed specialized attainments of every kind, either in knowledge or in skill. The system of block reservation has already been modified by introducing protected work, which provides a rough test of the importance to the war effort of the work upon which the persons in particular shops are engaged; that is to say, a factory would be given protection, which meant that it was so directly connected with the war effort that its personnel would not be called up until a somewhat later age than in the non-protected factory. This has already been a refinement upon the system of block reservation by trades. The situation now demands that there should be a further refinement of the system so that men should no longer be reserved by virtue of their occupation, but that the sole test should be the importance to the war effort of the work upon which they are engaged. For instance, a carpenter may be doing work of direct importance to an aeroplane or to a ship, but he may also be making a piece of furniture. It is clear that there must be a discrimination at the point which we have now reached. The test will always be the relation to the war effort.

How is this transition to be accomplished? We propose to raise the age of reservation by one-year steps at monthly intervals, commencing on 1st January, 1942. That is to say, every month the reserved age will rise by one year, thus bringing a new quota into the area of those more searching, individual, detailed examinations. In this process individual deferment will be granted only to men engaged on work of national importance. Services such as the Merchant Navy and Civil Defence will, of course, be excluded from this scheme. Special arrangements will also be made for certain industries where particular problems arise, for instance, the mining and agricultural industries, and the building industry with its special system of allocation, although I must say that we look to a very considerable reduction in the building industry as the great works and plants come gradually to completion.

To cope with all these new complications, the existing deferment machinery of the Ministry of Labour will be developed by further decentralization of 45 districts and the setting-up of 45 District Boards on the composition of which my right hon. Friend will say more when he speaks. In order that these District Boards may, with full knowledge, be able to give decisions, the object held in view will be twofold; first, to transfer men from less essential work to work of greater importance in the war effort, and also to obtain men to keep up the Armed Forces. Men in the munitions and other vital war industries and services who become de-reserved under the new scheme and in respect of whom deferment is not granted will, in general, be recognized as available for transfer to work of higher priority in those same industries, and a redistribution of labour within the munitions and other essential industries will be secured. This will, of course, affect only a fraction, but a very important fraction. Men in other industries, not war industries, not granted deferment, will be called up to the Forces. I am trying to keep the munitions clear of the new requirements of the Armed Forces as far as possible.

Mr Bellenger (Bassetlaw): Up to what age limit?

The Prime Minister: I shall come to that presently. Those not granted deferment will of course retain their individual rights under the National Service Act concerning conscientious objection, postponement of calling-up on account of exceptional hardship, and other mitigations. They will have the full protection and rights which are enjoyed by those called up by the National Service Act.

I come now to the point which the hon. Member opposite very rightly raised. The second great change affecting men is the raising of the age for compulsory military service from 41 to 51. Men called up over the age of 41 will not be posted for the more active duties with the Forces. They will be used either for static or sedentary duties to liberate younger men. It is not intended to call upon anybody to do tasks for which he is physically unfitted, but there are a great many tasks in the modern Armed Forces which can be discharged by men whom one would not expect to march with the troops. Very large numbers have volunteered already. The newcomers over 41 will all set free fighting men already in the Services for active mobile jobs. In other cases men between 41 and 51 will be directed into non-military tasks more closely concerned with the war effort than those which they are already discharging.

In raising the age of legal obligation from 41 to 51, we bring under review nearly 2,750,000 more men, the vast majority of whom are already in useful employment, but a portion of whom will now where necessary be directed forward into more direct forms of war effort. We may later have to advance another decade; in the last war, we went to 57. It is not necessary, however, to do this at the present time, because mercifully the slaughter has so far been much less. Of course, as you mount the age groups the effective yield even for indirect war purposes diminishes very rapidly, and it is more than ever desirable in these advanced groups to leave persons belonging to them in those useful occupations, which they have so often naturally found for themselves. But at the point we have reached in mobilizing the national war effort, the avoidance of needless friction and disturbance becomes an increasingly important factor. Although you may say that by shifting A and B, from this job to that, you will get some improvement in the more direct war effort, unless it is a very marked improvement, the friction may rob you on the one hand of what you gain on the other. We must endeavour to administer the whole of this process with very great care and discrimination in the public interest and with the sole object of bringing the utmost volume of war effort out of this vast and varied community.

The third change is to the side of youth. It is proposed to lower the age of military service to 18½, thus bringing in an additional 70,000 recruits to the Armed Forces during the year 1942. I must explain that the wastage from the Army, apart from battle casualties, is very considerable. It has been greatly reduced by the fact that instead of moving men out of the Army when they are not fit as marching troops, they are now moved into those same sedentary occupations that I have been mentioning. But the wastage is very considerable, and it has to be made good, and the first half of the 1923 class – I said it would bring in 70,000 recruits in the year 1942 – will be registered on

Saturday, 13th December, and their calling-up will commence in January, 1942. The second half of the 1923 class will be registered early in the New Year. Assurances were given to Parliament that no one brought into the Army under the National Service Act would be sent abroad younger than 20. This did not apply, I may point out, and has not in practice applied either to the Navy or to the Air Force or to the many volunteers who have joined the Army, and there is no reason why it should apply to the Army above the age of 19. In case particular units have to be sent abroad at short notice, one does not want to pull perfectly fit young men of 19 and upwards out of their sections and platoons, and they themselves would be very much offended if they were to be so treated and if they had to see all their comrades going away while they were left, as if they were unfit, on the shore. It is not thought that any large use is likely to be made of this power in the near future, but none the less we ask the House to release us from this restrictive pledge.

Mr Shinwell (Seaham): I am sorry to interrupt my right hon. Friend, but it is desirable that there should be no misunderstanding upon this point, which is one of great substance. Are we to understand that the pledge previously given will be removed as regards youths of 19 and that youths of 19 can now be despatched overseas?

The Prime Minister: If the House releases the Government from its undertaking, that would follow, but it is entirely in the hands of the House.

I must now speak about the Home Guard. It is our great prop and standby against invasion and particularly that form of invasion by airborne troops carried in gliders or crashable aircraft. Today we have nearly 1,700,000 men, the bulk of them well-armed, spread about the whole country. I say that the bulk of them are well-armed. Although we have a good many million rifles in this country, we have not got rifles for all. We have several million men who will fight to the death if this country is invaded but for whom we have not been able to manufacture the necessary number of rifles, although our rifles are now numbered by a good many million. Therefore we supplement them with machine-guns, tommy-guns, pistols, grenades and bombards, and, when other things fail, we do not hesitate to place in the citizen's hands a pike or a mace, pending further developments. After all, a man thus armed may easily acquire a rifle for himself. At any rate that is what they are doing in Russia in defending their country. Although they have vast supplies of rifles, they are fighting with everything, and that is what we shall certainly do, if we are assailed in our Island.

The Home Guard is therefore, as I say, the great prop and standby against invasion. Because of this being spread out all over the country, it is particularly adapted to meet an airborne descent. In the summer of last year we were an unarmed people, except for the few regular troops we had. Now, wherever he comes down the parachutist comes down into a hornet's nest, as he will find. The Home Guard was formed and founded in the passionate emotion of the summer of 1940. It has become a most powerful, trained, uniform body, which plays a vital part in our national defence. We must make sure that this great bulwark of our safety does not deteriorate during the inevitably prolonged and indefinite waiting period through which we have to pass or may have to pass. Power must now be taken by Statute to direct men into the Home Guard in areas where it is necessary and to require them to attend the drills and musters indispensable to the maintenance of efficiency. Liability for service in the Home Guard will be defined by Regulation. We do not propose to exercise this power until that Regulation has been subject to a special discussion in the House of Commons, apart altogether from the discussions of this Bill. I do not want to delay the passage of the Bill when it comes on next week by a too detailed discussion on that point. We will have a separate discussion of it at a later period.

There is another change which applies to both boys and girls. It is proposed to register boys and girls between the ages of 16 and 18. This will be done by Defence Regulation. We must be careful particularly that our boys do not run loose during this time of stress. Their education, their well-being, their discipline, and the service they can render must all be carefully supervised. All boys and girls in these age groups will be registered and subsequently interviewed under arrangements made by the Youth Committees of the education authorities, who will thus be able to establish and maintain direct contact with all of them. We have to think of the future citizens as well as of the business of carrying on the defence of the country. Those who are not already members of some organization or doing useful work of some kind, will be encouraged to join one or other of the organizations through which they can obtain the training required to fit them for National Service. There are fine opportunities for helping in the war open to strong, lively boys of 16 to 18. They can serve in the various Youth Organizations, such as the Cadets and the Junior Training Corps, the Air Training Corps, the Sea Cadets and in voluntary organizations on the civil side. Boys of 17 may already join the Home Guard, and we hope to be able to take some of the 16 year class – like the 'powder-monkeys' in Nelson's day – in some areas where the Home Guard will be entrusted with anti-aircraft and coast defence duties. However, in all these fields the well-being and training of the boys will be the prime consideration.

Mr Stephen (Glasgow, Camlachie): Does the right hon. Gentleman mean that compulsion is going to be applied?

The Prime Minister: No. I have not said so. I said they would be encouraged.

Viscountess Astor (Sutton, Plymouth) rose –

The Prime Minister: I am coming to the point which the Noble Lady has uppermost in her mind – the subject of women. In order to put as many minds at rest as possible, let me begin by saying two things. First, we do not propose at the present time to extend compulsion to join the Services to any married women, not even childless married women. They may of course volunteer, but they will not be compelled. Secondly, as regards married women and industry, we have already the power, and my right hon. Friend has already been given the power and has been frequently reminded of it, to direct married women into industry. This power will continue to be used with discretion. The wife of a man serving in the Forces or Merchant Navy will not be called upon to work away from her home area; nor will women with household responsibilities be moved from their home area. But there are some married women without children or other household responsibilities whom we may have to call upon to go to another area where their industrial services are needed.

Women are already playing a great part in this war, but they must play a still greater part. The technical apparatus of modern warfare gives extraordinary opportunities to women. These opportunities must be fully used, and here again the movement must be towards the harder forms of service and nearer to the fighting line. All women above 18 years are already liable to be directed by the Ministry of Labour and National Service into industry, but we have not the power at present, according to our reading of the law, to require women to serve in the uniformed Auxiliary Forces of the Crown or Civil Defence. We propose to ask Parliament to confer that power upon us. We seek it and take it, subject of course to the rule that all affected will have exactly the same rights and safeguards as men subject to compulsory military service. The new power will be applied in the first instance, and probably for some time to come, only to unmarried women between the ages of 20 and 30. The power is general, but the new power will be applied only to the age group between 20 and 30. The number in this class is 1,620,000. Of course the vast majority of them are already usefully employed, and only perhaps a quarter or one-third will be affected and will be required to exchange their present employment for one more effective in the war effort. Those so required will have the option to choose, first, the Auxiliary Forces, secondly, Civil Defence and, thirdly, such industrial work as may be specified by the Ministry of Labour as requiring workers. This work comprises primarily filling factories and also a certain number of factories in places where it is difficult to obtain the necessary woman labour by the ordinary processes; also certain other bottlenecks and industries where there is a need for exceptionally speedy reinforcement. Those women who choose to join the Auxiliary Forces will not be free to decide which force they join. The Wrens[1] and the Waafs,[2] to use terms which have passed into the commonplace of our daily speech, both have waiting lists, and although the increasing requirements of the WAAF may at a later date outstrip their waiting lists, it is to the ATS[3] that this special movement of young women must be directed.

1 The Women's Royal Naval Service (WRNS).
2 The Women's Auxiliary Air Force (subsequently the Women's Royal Air Force, WRAF).
3 The Women's Auxiliary Territorial Service.

Why is it that we have to make this demand on women for the Army? Here I will make a digression. Two vultures hang over us, and will hang over us until the end of the war. We do not fear them, but we must be constantly prepared against them. The first is Invasion, which may never come, but which will only be held off by our having large, well-trained, mobile forces and many other preparations in a constant high state of readiness, which has to go on month after month at the same pitch of readiness. Moreover, if we are to use the striking forces overseas at any period in the war, we must be sure that those that remain at home are of sufficient strength, because upon this island the whole fortune and fate of the world depend. Here is a case where the saying, 'Better to be sure than sorry' deserves a larger measure of respect than it usually does in war. We do not want the horrors which are perpetrated by the Germans wherever they go in so many countries to be thrust upon us here, to the utter ruin not only of ourselves but of the world cause. It is absolutely necessary that not only the armies in the East should be maintained and reinforced continually, but that we should constantly stand in this island with a very powerful and perfectly equipped Army ready to leap at the throat of any invader who might obtain a lodgment from the sea or the air. Anyone can see that to maintain this readiness over a long and indefinite period is a great burden and strain and a first charge upon our military effort, but, in order to do our full duty in the war, we must always be trying to discharge that task with the highest economy of manpower, drawing as little from munitions as necessary and keeping as few people in sedentary or static situations if they are capable of acting with the mobile forces. That is the process we are applying – exactly the same process in the military forces as in industry – a move on to a more active form of employment.

What is the other vulture for whom we must be ready? It is our old acquaintance the Air Raider, whom we already know so well. We have had a very easy time for the last six months, because the enemy has been occupied in Russia, but at any time Hitler may recognize his defeat by the Russian Armies and endeavour to cover his disaster in the East by wreaking his baffled fury upon us. We are all ready for him and will receive him when he comes, by day or night, with far greater forces and every modern improvement. But we have always to be ready. Great quantities of anti-aircraft equipment are now coming out of the factories. Behind them are the range-finders and predictors and a host of elaborate appliances of a highly delicate and highly secret character which it is not necessary to specify. Besides these there are the searchlights and balloons, to which many new adaptations and complications are attached. We cannot afford to keep so many scores of thousands of trained soldiers, many of whom who are fit for the mobile field forces, standing about at these static defences. We must reduce the number in order to keep the field armies up to strength and to prevent our having to draw upon the munition factories for the maintenance of the field armies. This great Service called

ADGB, Air Defence of Great Britain, must yield a substantial proportion of its manpower to the field troops and mobile anti-aircraft artillery. Just at the time when it is receiving larger numbers of guns for which it has waited long, it has not only to manage to use these guns and bring them into service, but it has also to yield up a large proportion of the manpower it has. I must say that it has adapted itself to the task with great skill and ingenuity. It happens that all these new appliances, which so vastly increase the power of anti-aircraft artillery, require no great physical strength to handle. They are appliances which trained women can handle just as well as men, and every woman who serves in the Air Defence not only renders a high service herself, but releases a man – actually four-fifths of a man – for the active troops.

Over 170,000 women are needed for the ATS, and of these over 100,000 are required for the Air Defence forces. The mixed batteries which have been already formed have been a great success. They have been several times in action. There are more women than men in these establishments, which are as healthy, happy and honourable a community as anyone has ever seen.

We are asking the House to give us compulsory powers to call up single women. We propose to apply these powers to women between 20 and 30. We do not propose, when once they have joined the ATS, to compel them to serve in the lethal or combatant branches. Women will have the right to volunteer, but no women in the ATS will be compelled to go to the batteries. It is a matter of quality of temperament, of feeling capable of doing this form of duty, which every woman must judge for herself and not one in which compulsion should be used. I want to make it clear that a woman may be compelled to join the ATS, but only volunteers from within the ATS will be allowed to serve with the guns. I have no doubt we shall get the response which is required.

As I stated earlier, we do not propose to extend compulsion to join the Services or Forces to any married women at the present time. Nevertheless it is in this great field of married women or women doing necessary household work, comprising about 11,000,000 persons, that we see our largest reserves for industry and home defence for the future. The part-time employment of women in industry has already been developed, but on nothing like the scale which must be reached in the months which lie before us. This is a matter to which employers would be wise to give their immediate attention. They should consider whether and to what extent they can adapt their businesses, particularly smaller businesses and industries, to a part-time system. An immense variety of arrangements are possible to enable women to divide up domestic tasks and then be free to work close at hand in the factory or the field. The treatment of this problem must be flexible. In some cases women will arrange to 'Box and Cox'. In others a group of five or more may arrange for each to cook a day in turn, or again the development of crêches and public nurseries or combined nurseries may free, or partially free, mothers of families from domestic duties. Whenever practicable, work will be brought as near to the homes as possible. Some further spreading of components may be possible, which I need not refer to in detail. The whole of this process needs to be developed with the greatest energy and contrivance, and Government Departments here and in the provinces must take a share. I am very anxious that the smooth running of the great Departments, upon which so much of our life and war effort depends, should not be upset by pulling people out of the routine to which they have become accustomed. Nevertheless, a substantial contribution will have to be made from the young unmarried women in the 20 to 30 group by the public Departments.

Such are the new burdens which the hard course of our fortunes compels us to invite the nation to assume. Nothing less than these will suffice at the present time, and even more may be required by the ordeals of the future. We shall welcome Parliamentary discussion and the focusing of public opinion upon the details of a measure so intimately affecting the homes of our country. We desire to fit the knapsack with its extra load upon the national shoulders in the least galling and most effective manner. The aid of the House is required in this process, but that the load must be picked up now, and carried on henceforward to the end, embodies, we are sure, the resolve of the British people.

•

Oliver Harvey: diary
('*The War Diaries of Oliver Harvey, 1941-1945*')

2 December 1941

Tête-à-tête lunch with AE. He began at once that he was very perturbed over Far East and at PM's reaction to it. It looks pretty certain now that Japs mean war. But we've had a much better telegram from Halifax saying that he had seen Roosevelt on his return and that he was in fact ready to support us in whatever action we thought necessary if Japs attacked. This is the contrary of the line PM has assumed and is pressing, viz. that we must wait for the Americans to act. AE wants to send a good forthcoming telegram in reply, saying we mean to occupy Kra and help Dutch, and presume USA will support us. But PM is defeatist and appeasing where Far East is concerned and so, as usual, are the Chiefs of Staff.

AE is even more perturbed at PM himself who is again showing increasing signs of weary and dictatorial behaviour. His eye is getting watery again as before the Atlantic Meeting. He says he won't go to Cabinet any more!

Winston S. Churchill to Anthony Eden
(*Cabinet papers, 69/2*)

2 December 1941

1. Lord Halifax's 5519. Paragraph 6.[1] Our settled policy in (a), (b) and (c) is not to take forward action in advance of the United States. Except in the case of a Japanese attempt to seize the Kra isthmus (which is unlikely), there will be time for the United States to be squarely confronted with a new act of Japanese aggression. If they move, we will move immediately in support. If they do not move, we must consider our position afresh.

2. An attack on the Kra isthmus would not be helpful to Japan for several months. In any case we should not take forestalling action without a definite guarantee of United States support.

3. A Japanese attack upon the Dutch possessions may be made at any time. This would be a direct affront to the United States following upon their negotiations with Japan. We should tell the Dutch that we should do nothing to prevent the full impact of this Japanese aggression presenting itself to the United States as a direct issue between them and Japan. If the United States declares war on Japan, we follow within the hour. If, after a reasonable interval, the United States is found to be incapable of taking any decisive action, even with our immediate support, we will nevertheless, although alone, make common cause with the Dutch. Having regard to the supreme importance of the United States being foremost, we must be the sole judge of timing the actual moment.

4. Any attack on British possessions carries with it war with Great Britain as a matter of course.

Winston S. Churchill to General Fowkes[2]
(*Churchill papers, 20/46*)

2 December 1941

War Cabinet were today given an account of your victory at Gondar.[3] The operations appear to have been brilliantly conceived and brilliantly executed,

[1] In which Lord Halifax wrote that President Roosevelt wished him 'to ask you what His Majesty's Government would do in the event of (a) Japanese reply being unsatisfactory, reinforcements not yet having reached Indo-China; and (b) Japanese attack on Thailand (Siam) other than attack on Kra Isthmus, attack covering, in his mind, such Japanese pressures on Thailand as to force concessions to the Japanese dangerously detrimental to the general position.'

[2] Charles Christopher Fowkes, 1894–1966. 2nd Lieutenant, 1914. On active service, 1914–15 (France, Belgium, Egypt, North Russia). Military Cross. Colonel, 1938. Acting Major-General, 1941. On active service, Middle East and Abyssinia, 1941–42 (despatches, Distinguished Service Order).

[3] On 29 November 1941 General Guglielmo Nasi, commander of the Italian garrison at Gondar, the last remaining Italian-controlled town in Abyssinia, surrendered.

and the War Cabinet have asked me to convey to you and all ranks under your command an expression of their warm appreciation.

Winston S. Churchill to General Wetherall[1]
(*Churchill papers, 20/46*)

2 December 1941
Personal

On the victorious conclusion of the campaign in Abyssinia, the War Cabinet have asked me to send you and all under your command their warmest congratulations. The gallantry, tenacity and devotion to duty which have been so consistently shown by all ranks and units of the Imperial Forces have richly deserved the victory they have won.

Winston S. Churchill to Sir Archibald Sinclair
(*Churchill papers, 20/36*)

2 December 1941

How did this person[2] become a Squadron Leader? Why is he selected to put out this squalid stuff?

After this exhibition I cannot allow him to broadcast.

Winston S. Churchill to General Ismay, for the Chiefs of Staff Committee
(*Churchill papers, 20/36*)

3 December 1941
Most Secret

1. It is too soon to decide how 'Crusader' will go. It seems that a decision will be reached before either the 50th (less one brigade) or the 18th Division is involved.

[1] Harry Edward de Robillard Wetherall, 1889–1979. On active service, 1914–18 (wounded, despatches, Military Cross). General Staff Officer, Weapon Training, Scottish Command, 1930–34. Commander of the 19th Infantry Brigade, 1938–40. Commander of the 11th African Division, Abyssinia, 1941. General Officer Commanding-in-Chief, East Africa, 1941–42; Ceylon, 1943–45. Commander-in-Chief, Ceylon, 1945–66. Knighted 1946.

[2] Henry Hector Bolitho, 1898–1974. Born in New Zealand. Travelled through New Zealand with the Prince of Wales 1920, and wrote his first book, *With the Prince in New Zealand*. Went to England, 1922. Novelist and biographer. Specialized in books about the Royal Family, including *Victoria, the Widow and her Son* (1934). Biographer of King Carol of Roumania (1939). Served as a Squadron Leader in the Royal Air Force Volunteer Reserve, 1940–45: Editor of *RAF Journal*, and author of *Task for Coastal Command*. In 1954 he published *Jinnah, Creator of Pakistan*, and in 1962 a volume of memoirs, *My Restless Years*.

2. Until 'Crusader' is decided there is no use thinking about 'Acrobat', still less about 'Gymnast'.[1]

3. Should 'Crusader' succeed, apart from mopping up, before the middle of this month 'Acrobat' might be attempted provided (a) it is immediate, (b) it is carried through with light forces which may be sacrificed, and (c) there is reasonable hope of favourable Vichy reactions about 'Gymnast'. In no case will the 50th or 18th Division be employed in 'Acrobat'.

4. If we are beaten in 'Crusader', the enemy will also be severely mauled and we can revert to our defensive positions about Mersa Matruh and in Tobruk, without danger of immediate disaster. His difficulties of supply and the toll he pays will continue. In this case also the destination of the 50th and 18th Divisions would be open.

5. There is, therefore, no reason to withdraw from our project of placing the 50th and 18th Divisions, plus an Indian Division, upon the Russian southern flank wherever it may rest, when the transportation difficulties have been overcome; provided always that Stalin prefers troops to supplies.

War Cabinet: Confidential Annex
(*Cabinet papers, 65/24*)

3 December 1941
12.30 p.m.

FINLAND

The Prime Minister said that the position was that if we received a wholly unsatisfactory reply, or if it was clear that we were to receive no reply, further reference to M. Stalin would be unnecessary. It might well be, however, that a reply would take one of several possible intermediate forms, and in this event consultation with M. Stalin would be appropriate.

The Prime Minister added that he wishes it to be on record that in his view this declaration of war on Finland (and also on Hungary and Roumania) would not assist either our cause or that of the Russians. The sole justification for it was that it was necessary in order to satisfy the Russian Government.

The Prime Minister referred in this connection to the statement made by the Hungarian Under-Secretary of State for Foreign Affairs to the United States Minister at Budapest when informed of our intended action: 'Now we no longer have two roads, but only the one we do not want to follow.'

[1] The planned advance into Tripolitania, and the planned landing in French North-West Africa.

Winston S. Churchill to David Margesson
(*Churchill papers, 20/36*)

3 December 1941

All quotations from this document[1] must be read in their context. The view set forth expresses the opinions of most decent Englishmen and certainly my own. It was not, however, written for the enemy's eyes. But the inconvenience of capture occurred two months ago. It would be silly to stir up the matter again. The paper was, I am sure, written by my son, and General Shearer told me when he was over here how good he thought it was. Obviously it is not attuned to the present mood, but much the best thing is to leave the matter alone. It would be unfortunate if these sentiments were publicly connected with me. This would indeed get them a widespread vogue.

If the officer in question is not fit for his duties, a change should be made by his immediate superiors. There could be no question of disciplinary action about a document which was approved by high authority both at the time of and after its publication.

I question whether it is wise to make a stir about calling-in this document which the enemy has already exploited to the full. But certainly no more should be printed, and the defects of the document should be pointed out to the Intelligence Department in the Middle East.

Oliver Harvey: diary
('*The War Diaries of Oliver Harvey, 1941-1945*')

3 December 1941

On Far East PM wishes to wait for Americans and see a Jap-American war start (which we would immediately enter) rather than a Jap-British war which the Americans might or might not enter. He fears that anti-British and isolationist opinion in America would react unfavourably to a Jap war if we were first in it. We here feel that this is the wrong way round and that Roosevelt has given us a straight undertaking to support us and he can't and won't do more, and American opinion is more likely to be impressed unfavourably if, when we or our Allies are attacked or threatened, we then wait for the Americans.

[1] A document issued by General Staff I Branch (Information and Propaganda), General Headquarters, Middle East, dealing with Russia, and critical of Soviet Communism. The document, of which Randolph Churchill was the author, had been captured by the Germans and published by them.

War Cabinet, Defence Committee (Operations): minutes
(*Cabinet papers, 69/2*)

3 December 1941
5.30 p.m.

FAR EAST

The Committee then considered whether it would now be advisable to make a more definite statement to the Dutch that we would support them if attacked.

The Prime Minister read to the Meeting a Minute he had addressed to the Foreign Secretary dealing with this question. He did not think that we could pursue any other course than that set out therein.

Sir Dudley Pound said that he was not entirely happy with the latter part of part 3 of the Prime Minister's Minute. We had always held the view that a decision whether or not to declare war in any particular circumstances would have to be judged in the light of the situation at the time. It would be very awkward if we had to declare war on behalf of the Dutch without the support of the United States.

The Prime Minister thought that we were now bound to go a bit further with the Dutch than we had done up to the present. If the Japanese attacked the Dutch, the impact of the event should be allowed to strike the United States and we should give them a short period in which to make up their minds what to do. If they failed to do anything, then we should face a very awkward situation in this country if we did not act. All he wanted to avoid was being landed in an automatic declaration of war and also he did not wish to step in in front of the United States and give the anti-British party cause for saying that the United States were again being dragged into a British war.

Mr Eden thought that there would, in practice, be no doubt as to the American action if only on account of the vital importance to their defence programme of the rubber and tin which they received from the East Indies. On the other hand, there was a slight danger that the Americans might say that if we were not prepared to act, then why should they? It might possibly be better to tell the President definitely that we were prepared in any event to stand by the Dutch.

Lord Cranborne questioned whether we could afford to wait after an attack on Dutch possessions before taking action. We would find ourselves in a very unfortunate position if Dutch resistance collapsed while we were making up our minds whether to come to their assistance or not.

Sir Earle Page said that the Australian Government were keenly concerned in the safety of the Netherlands East Indies. He thought the best thing would be to include a sentence in the reply to Lord Halifax's telegram drawing attention to, and endorsing, the President's statement that in the case of a direct attack on the Dutch we were all in it together.

There was general agreement with this view and a sentence on the lines suggested by Sir Earle Page was approved for inclusion in the draft.

Sir Dudley Pound explained the situation regarding an entry into the Kra Peninsula and pointed out that the Commander-in-Chief, Far East, was not authorized to advance without specific orders from London.

The Prime Minister said that he was prepared to take any action that might be necessary, provided he was quite sure of American support. With regard to the suggestion that had been made by the Australian Government that we should promise to declare war in the event of a Japanese attack on Russia provided a reciprocal assurance could be obtained, he did not think there was any immediate likelihood of such an attack. Moreover, there was not the slightest chance of obtaining a reciprocal assurance. If this remote contingency should arise, we would attune our attitude to that of the United States of America.

ASSISTANCE TO RUSSIA

The Prime Minister explained for the benefit of Sir Earle Page the present situation in Cyrenaica and the various projects which were in view for the exploitation of success in the battle. At present the battle was very evenly balanced and the time was drawing near when the Foreign Secretary would have to go to Russia to see M. Stalin. He would have to explain to him our general war situation and the reasons why it was quite impossible for a large army to be sent either to the north or the south of the Russian front. The question then arose whether he was to make a definite pledge for the sending of a small token force of some two divisions and ten squadrons RAF to co-operate with the Russians on the Don. We had at one time hoped to be able to offer two British and one Indian division, though the late CIGS, in pressing this matter, had the mental reservation that by the time these troops reached the Caucasus the Russian front would be back on the mountains and our troops would be well placed to deal with the Baku oil fields. Now the Chiefs of Staff were strongly in favour of keeping everything for the Libyan Battle. He was inclined to doubt, however, whether by the time the 18th Division arrived in January it could possibly be required in the desert.

Sir Earle Page enquired what the relative numerical strength in Cyrenaica was.

The Prime Minister said that the Germans and Italians were believed to have about 150,000 men. We had 100,000, but had superiority in air force and tanks over the Germans. The size of our forces were limited partly by the difficulties of maintenance and partly by what was available. For example, we were unable to use the three Australian divisions because the Australian Government had insisted that they should be used together. The 50th Division could come gradually into the battle, and in January the 18th Division would arrive. He enquired whether the Australian Government would agree to one of their divisions being put into Cyprus to relieve the 5th Indian Division there.

The Prime Minister said that he thought M. Stalin attached importance to having British troops on the Russian front. He (the Prime Minister) had never liked the idea of sending troops through the Caucasus, and he felt it was like taking coals to Newcastle. He had preferred the idea of giving the Russians as much equipment as possible. No tanks sent round the Cape would avoid being caught up in the Libyan battle, so that anything we offered to the Russians would have to go in through Archangel, which he understood might not be open for more than another three weeks.

Lord Beaverbrook said that the only way of getting out of sending divisions to the Russian Front was to make an offer of equipment in lieu.

The Prime Minister suggested that the statement of our policy which we should lay before the Russians should be as follows:

(i) We would press on the Libyan offensive with all the means at our disposal;

(ii) We did not propose, therefore, to send troops north of Persia because it would mean diverting them from the Libyan battle and would at the same time choke the Persian supply line to Russia;

(iii) We felt that the Russian cause would best be served by our engaging the Germans in the manner proposed while sending to Russia the utmost that we could spare in the way of equipment;

(iv) We were making good the promises which we had made in Moscow but now we were prepared to run a greater risk in the United Kingdom in the Spring and would send, in addition, as fast as the capacity of the North Russian ports would allow, a further 500 tanks and 500 aircraft.

If the Committee were in general agreement with a policy on these lines, he thought that it should be examined in detail by the Chiefs of Staff with a view to its being submitted to the War Cabinet the following day.

Field Marshal Mannerheim to Winston S. Churchill

(*Churchill papers, 20/46*)

4 December 1941

Personal, Secret and Private

I had yesterday the honour to receive through the intermediary of the American Minister at Helsinki your letter of November 29, 1941, and I thank you for your courtesy in sending me this private message. I am sure you will realize that it is impossible for me to cease my present military operations before my troops have reached positions which in my opinion would give us the security required. I would regret if these operations, carried out in order to safeguard Finland, would bring my country into a conflict with England, and I will be deeply grieved if you will consider yourself forced to declare war upon Finland. It was very kind of you to send me a personal message in these trying days, and I have fully appreciated it.[1]

Winston S. Churchill to General Auchinleck
(*Churchill papers, 20/46*)

4 December 1941
Personal

1. Very glad to get your resolute telegram. Although sudden swift success was desirable, a prolonged wearing-down battle in Libya is useful and advantageous to us and unduly costly to enemy upon sea communications.

2. German retreat from Rostov and Taganrog gives you important easement on your eastward flank, and, as long as you are closely locked with the enemy, the Russians cannot complain about no second front. Destination of 50th and 18th Divisions need not be finally settled yet, but clearly the battle in Libya would have first claims.

3. Please let me know about your reinforcements. Naturally, you will use the whole of the 50th Division as and when you require it, and I hope the brigade you have already diverted will soon be on the scene. I could, if necessary, ask Australia either to send an Australian division forward, or to relieve the 5th Indian Division in Cyprus for the time being. Let me know more about the 1st Armoured Division, which landed on 24th, namely: 1 Armoured Brigade, Divisional Headquarters and Support Group. This ought to be very important quite soon. What other reinforcements have you got moving? I should like to feel that you had plenty queueing up, and I am glad 18th Division will be arriving in January in addition to your regular convoys.

4. The only thing that matters is to beat the life out of Rommel and Co.

[1] Churchill wrote in his war memoirs: 'This reply made it clear that Finland was not prepared to withdraw her troops to her 1939 frontiers, and the British Government therefore went ahead with the arrangements to declare war. Similar action followed in regard to Roumania and Hungary.'

Lord Halifax to Anthony Eden
(*Premier papers, 3/156/5*)

4 December 1941
Most Immediate, Most Secret
received 11 a.m.

I saw the President with Under-Secretary of State,[1] this evening and read to him your telegram. The President agrees with your second paragraph that the first two hypotheses are in practice indistinguishable. Before giving definite reply on your suggestion of simultaneous warning, he wished to be clear on the following points.

Do you mean by the words 'if she uses Indo-China as a base for further aggression', some actual act of jumping off by Japan, or building up of a base which clearly must be intended for further aggression?

2. I said that I read your telegram to mean the first, although it was plain that building up of a base would *pro tanto* diminish the Japanese dependence on vulnerable supply lines.

The President was much alive to this, but I think that his own mind leant in favour of making a warning if given conditional on actual jumping off.

3. The point also arose in the discussion whether your wording 'as a base for further aggression' was or was not intended to cover the hypothesis of intensified attack on Burma Road from Thailand (Siam).

The President, however, said that he thought the point was academic as concentration of troops in southern Thailand could hardly be intended for attack on the Burma Road by land, except through Thailand, in which case the issue would be clear. The only practicable alternative in his view would be for the Japanese to bomb Rangoon, when again the issue would be clear.

4. The President assented to the interpretation of support as recorded in paragraph 8 of my telegram No. 5519 as meaning armed support. Character of this armed support must be decided by the Staffs.

5. In the circumstances of hypothesis C, the President indicated assent to our putting Kra Isthmus plan into operation in this eventuality, and I have no doubt in this case you can count on armed support of the United States.

6. I read the President your third paragraph, to which he gave assent.

In this connection, he said their information led them to think it probable that the Japanese attacks might be directed against the Netherlands East Indies, particularly against some island north of Sumatra.

He made comment on this that any action of the kind would prove more easy of presentation to United States public opinion on the ground of threat to the Phillipines by encirclement.

7. He recognized the force of your paragraphs 4 and 5 concerning the proposed guarantee to Thailand and the intimation at the present moment to

[1] Sumner Welles.

the Thai Prime Minister[1] of our intention. He thought, however, that you might consider two other suggestions. The first, that we should make private communication to Thailand that we had no intention of invading them, but that if the Japanese with or without Thailand's agreement went in, we should immediately do the same in our own self-defence.

Second, that in view of the Japanese inspired propaganda intimating that we intended to invade Thailand, you might make public statement now to the effect that His Majesty's Government had no intention of committing aggression against Thailand and were only concerned to see her sovereignty and independence preserved.

War Cabinet: Confidential Annex
(*Cabinet papers, 65/24*)

4 December 1941
6 p.m.

The following points were made in discussion on Telegram 5577.[2]

Paragraph 6 recorded the President's assent to the statement in paragraph 3 of telegram 6672 that in the event of any direct attack on ourselves or the Dutch, we should obviously all be in it together.

The Prime Minister said that, in the light of this assurance, we could now say to the Dutch that if any attack was made on them by Japan, we should at once come to their aid, and that we had every confidence that the United States would do so also.

The First Lord of the Admiralty suggested that it might be wise to tell President Roosevelt that, in view of what he had said, we were proposing to make a statement on these lines to the Dutch.

The Foreign Secretary, however, pointed out that this would need to be very carefully phrased, since President Roosevelt was probably under the impression that we had already given an assurance on these lines to the Dutch.

The Prime Minister said that he thought that further steps could now be taken to concert Staff plans with the Dutch.

The Prime Minister thought that, in view of the assurances given in paragraphs 4 and 5, instructions could now be given to the Commander-in-

[1] Pibul Songgram, Prime Minister of Thailand, 1938–44. While a student in France in the early 1920s he came to admire Fascism in general, and Mussolini in particular. Facilitated the Japanese invasion of Thailand, December 1941, enabling Japanese troops to pass through Thailand on their way to Malaya and Burma. As a reward, Thailand received two of the Shan States of Burma. Forced from power, 1944, by a political rival (Pridi Phanomyong) who had made secret contact with the British Special Operations Executive (SOE) and the American Office of Strategic Services (OSS).

[2] Lord Halifax's telegram from Washington, received at 11 a.m. that morning.

Chief, Far East, to put Operation 'Matador'[1] into effect, if the circumstances made this necessary.

It was clear that President Roosevelt was anxious to make some communication to the Government of Siam in order to stiffen their resistance to Japanese aggression. Some objection, however, was seen to the first suggestion in paragraph 7, on the ground of probable leakage of our intention to Japan; while neither suggestion was hardly consistent with our proposal to carry out a forestalling operation in certain circumstances.

The position in regard to Siam would require further consideration. The suggestion favoured was an offer of help from both ourselves and the United States in the event of attack by Japan, without, however, indicating very precisely what form that help would take.

The Prime Minister summing up the discussion, suggested that the War Cabinet should take the following provisional decisions:

(a) That we could now say to the Dutch that in the event of attack on them by Japan we should at once come to their aid.

(b) That instructions should now be given to our Commanders to put Operation 'Matador' into effect either as a forestalling measure, if a Japanese attack on the Kra Isthmus was plainly imminent, or if Japan invaded Siam.

(c) That we should give some joint assurance with the United States to the Government of Siam.

The decisions taken would have to be embodied in telegrams:

(1) To our Ambassador at Washington:

(2) To our Minister at Bangkok:[2]

(3) To the Commander-in-Chief in the Far East:

(4) To Admiral Phillips, Commander-in-Chief, Eastern Fleet, who was now at Manila, to acquaint him with the position.

(5) To the Prime Ministers of the Dominion Governments acquainting them with the position.

These telegrams would require careful drafting, and the drafts should be submitted to him (the Prime Minister).

The War Cabinet agreed to this procedure.

[1] The planned advance by British forces in Malaya to occupy the area of Singora and Patani in southern Thailand, should the Japanese move into Thailand. The plan had been devised by Air Chief Marshal Sir Robert Brooke-Popham, Commander-in-Chief, Far East.

[1] Josiah Crosby, 1880–1958. Entered the Diplomatic Service as a student interpreter, Siam, 1904; Vice-Consul, Siam, and Travelling District Judge, 1907; Vice-Consul, Bangkok, 1911; Consul, for French Indo-China, at Saigon, 1917–19; retiring Consul-General, Bangkok, 1919–20. Consul-General, Saigon, 1920; Batavia (Dutch East Indies), 1921–34; Siam, 1934–41. Retired from the Diplomatic Service, 1943. Author of *Siam: The Crossroads* (1945). After his retirement he lived in Kenya and the Seychelles.

ASSISTANCE TO RUSSIA

The Prime Minister said that a discussion had taken place at the Meeting of the Defence Committee on the previous evening, as to the military assistance which we could give to Russia. At that meeting the view taken had been that we should lay the following policy before the Russians:-

(i) We would press on the Libyan offensive with all the means at our disposal:[1]

The Chiefs of Staff had been invited to examine this policy and to submit definite proposals for the additional equipment which might be offered to the Russians, together with the implications of such an offer.

The Chief of the Air Staff said that we could not spare any British machines, but he thought it might be possible to find 300 aircraft from America. It must be remembered that we had only about 100 more fighters of the Hurricane and Spitfire types (i.e. excluding night fighters) in this country than at the time of the Battle of Britain last year. It was very difficult to make an accurate forecast of the number of British machines that would be available between now and June next, owing to the impossibility of assessing the effect of possible bombing attacks on production and the amount of reinforcements that would be necessary for the Middle East.

After a careful survey of the situation, he suggested that we should offer the Russians 300 United States aircraft, on the condition that these machines were duly delivered to us by the United States.

The Prime Minister said that he was clearly of opinion that it would be wrong for us to send two Divisions to the Southern Russian front, the result of which would be to clog the communications to Russia through Persia. While we had fulfilled our deliveries to Russia, the American deliveries had lagged behind their undertakings, and they now proposed to divert to Russia, shipping which had previously been allocated to sustain the Import Programme to this country.

Reference was made to the telegrams exchanged with M. Stalin. In his telegram of the 21st November to M. Stalin, the Prime Minister had said that 'Mr Eden would be accompanied by high military and other experts, and would be able to discuss every question relating to the war, including the sending of troops, not only into the Caucasus, but into the fighting line of your armies in the South'. It was true that this was only an offer to discuss, but in his reply of the 23rd November M. Stalin had said 'I believe our joint consideration and acceptance of an agreement concerning the common military operations of the Soviet and British forces at our front, as well as speedy realization of such an agreement, would have a great positive value'.

[1] This, and the further three areas of assistance to Russia, were set out at the end of the Defence Committee minutes of 3 December 1941 (pages 1556–7).

The Foreign Secretary said that there was no doubt that M. Stalin expected that he (the Foreign Secretary) would arrive with a definite proposal to make British troops available to fight in South Russia.

The Prime Minister said that when this offer had been made, the late Chief of the Imperial General Staff, in recommending the despatch of two Divisions to South Russia, had made a mental reservation that by the time our troops reached the Caucasus the Russian front would almost certainly have moved back to meet us, and that these Divisions would not in fact get beyond the Caucasus, where they would be of great value in assisting to hold the gap between the mountains and the Caspian. All this, of course, was altered by the success of the Russians at Rostov.

The suggestion was made that the Foreign Secretary might postpone his visit, giving as a reason the difficulties of the international situation, particularly in the Far East.

The Prime Minister thought that a postponement would be disastrous. There was no certainty that the Foreign Secretary would be in a better position if he made his visit at a later date.

Summing up the discussion, the Prime Minister said that he thought it was generally accepted that it would be a mistake for us to send two Divisions into South Russia. Our troops would be better employed elsewhere, and he felt sure that M. Stalin would recognize this. He still wished, however, that at an earlier stage in the Russian campaign we had found it possible to send 10 squadrons of fighters to the Moscow front.

The question whether the Foreign Secretary should be authorized to make some further offer of military supplies, e.g., tanks and aircraft, was a matter which must be further studied.

Sir Alexander Cadogan: diary

('*The Diaries of Sir Alexander Cadogan OM, 1938-1945*')

4 December 1941

Cabinet at 6. We had had very good telegram from Roosevelt about Far East, which removed many PM's doubts, and he said we could now guarantee Dutch. Discussed Russian trip. Appears now that we shall not even have material to offer to Russians – in place of Divisions. A – rightly – made a stink about this, but agreed to go. PM again stamped on A Sinclair for suggesting postponement.

Dined at home. Back to FO by 9.45 to draft telegrams. Went over to see PM at 11, and eventually got drafts passed. Home about 12.30 – rather tired.

Winston S. Churchill to John Curtin
(*Churchill papers, 20/46*)

5 December 1941

Forthcoming attitude of President described in Dominions Office telegram M No. 421 enables us at last to move forward with greater security. We have authorized forestalling action at Kra Isthmus if necessary, and are about to assure Dutch that we will help them at once if they are attacked. This meets your wishes in most respects. Please treat President's attitude with utmost secrecy.

On 5 December 1941, Hitler ordered the transfer of an Air Corps from the Russian Front to the Sicily-Tripolitania area.

Winston S. Churchill to General Ismay, for the Chiefs of Staff Committee[1]
(*Cabinet papers, 66/20*)

5 December 1941

1. It is necessary that the Foreign Secretary should be authorized to inform M. Stalin as follows:

The prolongation of the battle in Libya, which is drawing in so many Axis resources, will probably require the use both of the 50th and 18th Divisions which we had hoped might be available for the defence of the Caucasus or for action on the Russian front. In the near future therefore these divisions cannot be considered available. The best form which our aid can take (apart from supplies) is the placing of a strong component of the Air Force, say ten Squadrons of fighters and bombers, on the southern flank of the Russian armies, where among other things they can help protect the Russian naval bases on the Black Sea. These squadrons will be withdrawn from the Libyan battle at the earliest moment when success has been gained. The movement of their ground personnel and stores will not unduly choke the trans-Persian communications, as would be the case if Infantry Divisions were sent. The High Command in the Middle East have been ordered to make plans for this movement.

2. The attitude of Turkey becomes increasingly important both to Russia and to Great Britain. The Turkish army of 50 Divisions requires air support.

[1] This Minute was circulated, on Churchill's instructions, for the information of the War Cabinet, as War Cabinet Paper No. 298 of 1941, headed: 'To be kept under lock and key. It is requested that special care may be taken to ensure the secrecy of this document.'

We have promised a minimum of 4 and a maximum of 12 squadrons to Turkey in the event of Turkey being attacked. In this event we might require to withdraw some of the squadrons proposed to be sent into action on the Russian southern front. The best use of our aircraft on both shores of the Black Sea requires to be decided according to circumstances by consultation between the British and Russian Governments.

Winston S. Churchill to David Margesson and General Dill
(*Churchill papers, 20/36*)

5 December 1941
Secret

1. By all means send an officer to meet General Cunningham on arrival, as you propose in your paragraph 1. There is no reason why there should be any immediate publicity. Generals Wavell and Auchinleck have both visited this country without a word being said. The usual D notice would be issued to the Press. We do not want the change of command made public until the operation is successful, or in a fair way to be.

2. If you look at General Auchinleck's No. 1609 Susan, you will see that the reason he gave for superseding General Cunningham on November 24 was: 'I have reluctantly concluded that Cunningham, admirable as he has been up to date, has now begun to think defensively, mainly because of our large tank losses.' See also the Minister of State's Nocop No. 3724, which says that 'Cunningham, it appears, is shaken and now thinking in terms of withdrawal and defence. All the subordinate commanders are in great heart and full of aggressive spirit.' The statement, such as is proposed in General Auchinleck's No. 1629 Susan, that General Cunningham 'became indisposed on November 24 and was admitted to hospital' is not true. I do not think that I ought to become a party to statements which are not true, although meant kindly. It was only 'much against his will' that General Cunningham on the 27th and 28th 'agreed to go to hospital'. The rule of the Service is that a man is either sick or fit. If he is sick, he should report sick or be removed from duty for that cause. If he is fit, he must be held accountable for his actions. Soldiers and subordinate officers would be treated according to this rule, and I do not think a general should have special favour. General Auchinleck's reputation will gain greatly from the truth being known, and on the other hand we shall all be liable to censure if we lend ourselves to a pious fraud. The truth is bound to come out.

3. I will, however, if you wish, bring the matter before the Cabinet, but I have not much doubt what their opinion will be or what Parliament would expect.

Sir Alexander Cadogan: diary
(*'The Diaries of Sir Alexander Cadogan OM, 1938-1945'*)

5 December 1941

5.30 went to see PM who gave me instructions about declarations of war this midnight on Finland, Hungary, and Roumania. I shall have to ring him at midnight. He off to Chequers.

War Cabinet, Defence Committee (Operations): minutes
(*Cabinet papers, 69/1*)

5 December 1941 Cabinet War Room
9.30 p.m.

OPERATION 'WORKSHOP'[1]

The Prime Minister regretted that the Operation did not commend itself to the Chiefs of Staff. There was, of course, no absolute guarantee of success in war nor was it ever possible during a campaign to provide what could be regarded as fully adequate forces for any particular battle or operation. Many of the greatest battles of history had been won with forces which, before the event, would have been considered hopelessly inadequate. It was quite out of the question to denude Home Waters to the extent contemplated and, at the most, two additional destroyers might be added to the eight already proposed.

If, in the Staff view, 'Workshop' was too difficult and hazardous an operation, then on this basis Operation 'Mandibles'[2] could be ruled right out of court.

He had always regarded 'Workshop' as a worth-while Operation which we could take in our stride with a good reasonable chance of success and a very fair dividend in proportion to the risks involved.

Mr Eden said that he was impressed with the view of the Commander-in-Chief, Mediterranean, who regarded 'Workshop' as being an insufficient prize; nevertheless he was anxious to hit the Italians and to make use of the special Service troops for this purpose. In his view there were other places which would give greater profit such as raids on the Italian coast at particularly important localities.

There was general agreement that whether Operation 'Workshop' was carried out or not, every effort should be made to plan and carry out raiding operations either against the Italian coast or in North Africa. There was also agreement that 'Mandibles' should be held in abeyance for the time being.

The Prime Minister said that he would like the Chiefs of Staff to see how the plan could be improved and to make a further report to the Committee.

[1] The planned capture of Pantellaria Island.
[2] The planned capture of the Dodecanese Islands.

Sir Dudley Pound said that if it was so important to score a success with this Operation that the risks of carrying it out with inadequate forces were accepted, the Chiefs of Staff would make every endeavour to see that the forces available were put to the best use and given every assistance possible.

Sir Alexander Cadogan: diary
(*'The Diaries of Sir Alexander Cadogan OM, 1938-1945'*)

5 December 1941

Dined at home, worked and prepared packing.[1] But an awful night, as Finn reply came in about 11.30 and a telegram from Washington (a good one) with messages from President about Far East. Spent about 1½ hours telephoning to A, PM and FO. Finally fixed up decision to declare war on Finland, H and R,[2] and got PM's approval to reply to President. Bed about 1. Very tired.

Winston S. Churchill to F. C. Watt[3]
(*Churchill papers, 20/22*)

5 December 1941

My dear Watt,

As Leader of the Government which is supported by the Conservative, Labour and Liberal Parties, I call on the electors of Central Edinburgh to support you at the poll on the 11th December. Your election by a large majority will demonstrate the country's determination to maintain unity in the face of an evil and barbarous foe. Unity is essential to our victory.

Central Edinburgh will have in you as a representative a man who in the last war enlisted and served in the Argyll and Sutherland Highlanders and in the King's Own Scottish Borderers. You were wounded in France in the service of your country. For some time now you have taken a deep interest in the problems of the constituency and your experience of affairs will constantly be at the service of your constituents.

You are standing as a supporter of the Government of National Unity, which is developing with ever-increasing effect, the nation's determination and effort to win the victory which is so necessary for our liberty and our very existence.

[1] Sir Alexander Cadogan was to accompany Anthony Eden to Moscow.

[2] Hungary and Roumania.

[3] Francis Clifford Watt, 1896–1971. On active service, 1914–18 (wounded). Called to the Scottish Bar, 1925. Junior Counsel to Treasury for Scotland, 1940–46. Conservative Member of Parliament for Edinburgh Central, 1941–45. Sheriff of Caithness, Sutherland, Orkney and Zetland, 1952–61; of Stirling, Dunbarton and Clackmannon, 1961–71.

I know that all the voters of Central Edinburgh will, at whatever personal inconvenience, exercise their privilege and do their duty by going to the poll on the 11th December. By voting for you and by registering in this way their confidence in the Government they will encourage it in its task of vindicating freedom and the rule of law against injustice, cruelty and crime.

Yours sincerely,
Winston S. Churchill

Winston S. Churchill to Anthony Eden
(*Churchill papers, 20/36*)

6 December 1941
Secret

The First Sea Lord has made arrangements to bring the eleven Russian Trade Union delegates back on your ship. This is the only chance in the near future. The difficulties of accommodation on the ship will be considerable. There will certainly not be room for the Russian delegates and your party, including M. Maisky, to be accommodated in the captain's quarters astern. It is proposed that the warrant officers' mess should be cleared and placed at the disposal of the Russian delegates, the warrant officers crowding into the wardroom. You must judge for yourself whether this will cause embarrassment on class-social lines.

I may say that in the *Prince of Wales* we found the vibration was so bad aft that we all went to the warrant officers' mess amidships, which was cleared for us. I daresay on the voyage out you will find this convenient. In that case you might allocate the quarters aft to the Russians, which would give them honour at the price of discomfort.

I strongly advise you to sleep on the bridge if there is a cabin available. There is no doubt whatever that the warrant officers' mess is the most comfortable place in the ship.

Winston S. Churchill to Air Chief Marshal Sir Charles Portal
(*Churchill papers, 20/36*)

6 December 1941

The following are the main conclusions which we reached in our talk last night:

1. 'Gee'[1] is to be started on 1st February, 1942, unless examination shows

[1] 'Gee' was the name given to a radio device by means of which British bombers could fix their positions when operating over Germany.

that the weather conditions over the last ten or twelve years prove that March is likely to be far more favourable than February. In that event the matter should be referred to me again for decision.

2. Every effort is to be made to broaden the front of the fighter force. To this end reserves of pilots and machines should be disposed in squadrons, and thus allow *roulement* to be extended in the event of protracted fighting.

3. As an experiment a night fighter wing is to be issued with day fighting machines with a view to introducing a system of dual purpose fighter squadrons, if the experiment proves successful.

Winston S. Churchill to Lord Woolton
(*Churchill papers, 20/36*)

6 December 1941

Amid your many successes in your difficult field, the Egg Distribution Scheme seems to be an exception. I hear complaints from many quarters, and the scarcity of eggs is palpable.

I send you a note which the Minister of Agriculture has furnished on his side of the problem.

Will you please give me a very short statement of your plans and policy.

Winston S. Churchill to Lord Beaverbrook
(*Churchill papers, 20/36*)

6 December 1941

I hope to be able to go to Shoeburyness on the afternoon of Thursday, 11th December, and would be grateful if you would arrange for a demonstration of the following types of UP weapons:

1. Type K.
2. Apparatus AD, Type L.
3. Apparatus AD, Type J.
4. Rocket U, 5-inch.
5. Rocket U, 3-inch.[1]

[1] The Unrotated (or Unrifled) Projectile weapons concerned were: Type K: anti-aircraft rocket; Apparatus AD, Type L and Apparatus AD, Type J: rocket for defence of aerodromes and similar places against low flying aircraft; Rocket U, 5-inch: original design was for delivering chemical warfare charge, but subsequently became area barrage weapon; and Rocket U, 3-inch: anti-aircraft barrage weapon.

Before coming to a decision on the priority proposals set out in your minute of 2nd December, it is desirable, I think, to see these various weapons and decide their relative merits. I hope, therefore, that you will be able to accompany me.

Of course, if cloudy it must be cancelled.

Sir Alexander Cadogan: diary
(*'The Diaries of Sir Alexander Cadogan OM, 1938-1945'*)

6 December 1941

Found report of reconnaissance of Japanese armada moving west, south of Cambodia point.[1] Rang up A. Brooke into meeting of C of S, who didn't seem to know quite where they were. Informed Winant. Later saw Dutch and told them what had been planned about a warning, and asked them to get ready. But all may be now in melting-pot if the monkeys are going for Kra Isthmus. Later heard that they had gone into west coast of Indo-China. This gives us more time. We may yet get a joint warning. PM has approved message to Thai PM.

Winston S. Churchill: recollection
(*'The Second World War, Volume Three'*)

[6 December 1941]

On December 6 it was known both in London and Washington that a Japanese fleet of about thirty-five transports, eight cruisers, and twenty destroyers was moving from Indo-China across the Gulf of Siam. Other Japanese fleets were also at sea on other tasks.

[1] One of those working at Bletchley, Malcolm Kennedy, wrote in his diary on 6 December 1941 that Churchill 'is all over himself at the moment for latest information and indications re Japan's intentions and rings up at all hours of the day and night, except for the 4 hours in each 24 (2 to 6 am) when he sleeps'. Quoted in David Stafford, *Churchill and Secret Service*, page 234.

Winston S. Churchill to General Ismay
(*Churchill papers, 20/36*)

6 December 1941
Action this Day

MIRI OIL[1] DENIAL SCHEME

So long as the oil plant is effectively denied to the enemy, the question of time and method may be left to the Commander-in-Chief on the spot. The danger must be considered imminent, and, if the Colonial Office wish to put their seven-day scheme into force, they should not be prevented, it being understood that the more drastic method would be used to finish it up in case of emergency.

The details should be settled by COS Committee.

Averell Harriman to Harry Hopkins
(*'Special Envoy to Churchill and Stalin, 1941-1946'*)

6 December 1941

The President should be informed of Churchill's belief that in the event of aggression by the Japanese it would be the policy of the British to postpone taking any action – even though this delay might involve some military sacrifice – until the President has taken such action as, under the circumstances, he considers best. Then Churchill will act 'not within the hour but within the minute'. I am seeing him again tomorrow. Let me know if there is anything special you want me to ask.

Averell Harriman: recollection
(*'Special Envoy to Churchill and Stalin, 1941-1946'*)

[6 December 1941] [Chequers]

As Kathleen Harriman's birthday fell on the weekend, she was asked to Chequers along with her father and Ambassador Winant. Her actual birthday was Sunday, but it was mistakenly celebrated Saturday evening at dinner. When the birthday cake was carried in, the Prime Minister offered an appropriate toast and gave Kathleen an autographed copy of his book *The River War*.[2]

1 Miri, in Sarawak, just across the border from Brunei, on the South China Sea.

2 Churchill's account of the war in the Sudan in 1898, first published in two volumes by Longmans Green, London, in 1899. A revised one-volume edition was published in 1902, and a cheap one-volume edition in 1915 (reprinted in 1933). In the book Churchill described his part in the cavalry charge at the Battle of Omdurman.

William Mackenzie King to Winston S. Churchill
(*Churchill papers, 20/46*)

6 December 1941
sent 5.44 p.m.
received 2.30 a.m., 7 December 1941

I desire to inform you personally that a proclamation by His Majesty, on the advice of His Privy Council for Canada has been issued at this moment in Ottawa declaring and proclaiming that a state of war with Roumania, Hungary and Finland exists and has existed in Canada as from the 7th day of December.

Winston S. Churchill to General de Gaulle
(*Churchill papers, 20/22*)

7 December 1941
Most Secret

My dear General de Gaulle,

I have just heard from General Auchinleck that he is most anxious to use a Free French Brigade immediately in the Cyrenaican operations. I know this will be in accordance with your wishes, and how eager your men will be to come to grips with the Germans.

We are looking forward to seeing you and Madame de Gaulle at luncheon on Wednesday next.

Yours sincerely,
Winston S. Churchill

Winston S. Churchill to the Honorary Secretary of the Welsh Parliamentary Party
(*Churchill papers, 20/22*)

7 December 1941

Mr dear Sir,

I thank you for your letter of December 3 regarding the Welsh Language Petition.

Much as I should like to meet the deputation of the Welsh Parliamentary Party, I regret that, owing to the many tasks which fall to my lot at this time, it is impossible for me to arrange a date when I might meet your deputation.

I am however asking the Home Secretary to arrange a meeting with you at some time mutually convenient.

Yours faithfully,
Winston S. Churchill

George Rennie[1] *to Winston S. Churchill*
(*Churchill papers, 2/416*)

7 December 1941

Dear Churchill,

I wonder if you would like to be reminded of 2, I think rather famous remarks you made to me when lunching or dining with me soon after the battle of Spion Kop.[2] One was you said you were going to be the first Chancellor of the Exchequer to wear a row of medals on your robes. The other was, you said, at present I am only known by being the son of my father, some day my father will be known by being my father. We first met at the crammer James.[3] Congratulations & best of luck.

Yours sincerely,
George A. P. Rennie

John Martin: diary
(*John Martin papers*)

7 December 1941 Chequers

Duchess of Marlborough and Lord Blandford[4] to lunch. Winant[5] to lunch and dinner.

Winston S. Churchill to the Prime Minister of Thailand
(*Hansard*)

7 December 1941

There is a possibility of imminent Japanese invasion of your country. If you are attacked, defend yourself. The preservation of the full independence and

[1] George Arthur Paget Rennie, 1872–1951. Entered the Army, 1898. On active service in South Africa, 1899–1902 (despatches twice, Distinguished Service Order) and in Europe, 1914–18 (despatches six times, CMG). Colonel, 1918 (acting Brigadier-General).

[2] A battle during the Boer War. 'The scenes on Spion Kop were among the strangest and most terrible I have ever witnessed,' Churchill wrote to his friend Pamela Plowden on 28 January 1900. Seventy British officers and 1,500 men had been killed 'to little purpose'. He himself had been 'for five very dangerous days continually under rifle and shell fire and once the feather in my hat was cut through by a bullet'. (*Lady Lytton papers*)

[3] In March 1893 Churchill had begun studying for his army examination (which he had twice failed earlier) at Captain James's establishment in Lexham Gardens, West London. He retook the army exam that July, and passed.

[4] Mary, Duchess of Marlborough (Mary Cadogan, daughter of Viscount Chelsea), who married the 10th Duke of Marlborough in 1920; and their eldest son, John George Vanderbilt Henry Spencer-Churchill, Marquess of Blandford, born in 1926 and subsequently 11th Duke of Marlborough. In 1945 Lord Blandford became a Second Lieutenant, Life Guards.

[5] John G. Winant, the United States Ambassador.

sovereignty of Thailand is a British interest, and we shall regard an attack on you as an attack on ourselves.

John G. Winant: recollections
(*'A Letter from Grosvenor Square'*)

[7 December 1941] [Chequers]

The Prime Minister was walking up and down outside the entrance door – the others had gone in to lunch twenty minutes before. He asked me if I thought there was going to be war with Japan. I answered 'Yes.' With unusual vehemence he turned to me and said:

'If they declare war on you, we shall declare war on them within the hour.'

'I understand, Prime Minister. You have stated that publicly.'

'If they declare war on us, will you declare war on them?'

'I can't answer that, Prime Minister. Only the Congress has the right to declare war under the United States Constitution.'

He did not say anything for a minute, but I knew what was in his mind. He must have realized that if Japan attacked Siam or British territory it would force Great Britain into an Asiatic war, and leave us out of the war. He knew in that moment that his country might be 'hanging on one turn of pitch and toss'.

Nevertheless he turned to me with the charm of manner that I saw so often in difficult moments, and said, 'We're late, you know. You get washed and we will go in to lunch together.'

Winston S. Churchill to General Auchinleck
(*Churchill papers, 20/46*)

7 December 1941
6.25 p.m.

1. Your 1640. Glad indeed to receive all your news, which certainly gives me the impression we are wearing them down. Do whatever you please about the reinforcements. Meanwhile, I will not address Australian Government. I am telling De Gaulle you will use the Free French Brigade, which will relieve a somewhat tense situation.

2. Your CGS 1636 puzzled us a good deal, especially para. 5, but this is now explained. The War Office are replying about the defective wireless sets and Fordson trucks and contend their case is good.

3. Please give me best estimate possible of losses South African and New Zealand troops, as, if they are very heavy, I ought to send telegrams to their respective Governments.

4. Most Secret – for yourself alone. President has now definitely said that United States will regard it as hostile act if Japanese invade Siam, Malaya, Burma or East Indies, and he is warning Japan this week, probably Wednesday. We and the Dutch are conforming. This is an immense relief, as I had long dreaded being at war with Japan without or before United States. Now I think it is all right.

5. Also for yourself alone. Russian news continues to be good, and a Russian success north of Black Sea will react favourably on Turkey, as will a victory in Libya. There is good deal of evidence of rising anti-German feeling in French North Africa resulting from Weygand's dismissal. So we may still have hopes of 'Gymnast',[1] which remains all set.

6. Although General Cunningham is arriving home almost immediately, and there will certainly be much talk behind the scenes, I do not intend to make any announcement until your news is decidedly good. Let me know the moment when you feel the tide has definitely turned. I should find it difficult to make out that he was superseded on health grounds, because that was not the reason which you gave me in your original telegram, which I imparted to Cabinet. I could, however, when the time comes, say something like this:

'General Auchinleck proceeded to battle headquarters on November 24th, and on the 26th he decided to relieve General Cunningham and appoint Major-General Ritchie to the Command of the 8th Army in his place. This action was immediately endorsed by the Minister of State and by me. General Cunningham had rendered brilliant service in Abyssinia and is also responsible for the planning and organization of this present offensive in Libya, which began with surprise and success and is steadily progressing. He has since been reported by the medical authorities to be suffering from serious overstrain and has been granted sick leave.'

It would seem to me wrong in the interests of the Army that the classical severity of your action, which was greatly admired here, should be marred by the explanations which many people know would not square with the actual facts.

7. I hope progress of your operations will enable statement to be made some time this week. Let me know your views.

[1] The planned British landing in French North Africa.

Averell Harriman: recollections
(*'Special Envoy to Churchill and Stalin, 1941-1946'*)

[7 December 1941] [Chequers]

The Prime Minister seemed tired and depressed. He didn't have much to say throughout dinner and was immersed in his thoughts, with his head in his hands part of the time.

Winston S. Churchill: recollection
(*'The Second World War, Volume Three'*)

[7 December 1941] [Chequers]

It was Sunday evening, December 7, 1941. Winant and Averell Harriman were alone with me at the table at Chequers. I turned on my small wireless set shortly after the nine o'clock news had started. There were a number of items about the fighting on the Russian front and on the British front in Libya, at the end of which some few sentences were spoken regarding an attack by the Japanese on American shipping at Hawaii, and also Japanese attacks on British vessels in the Dutch East Indies. There followed a statement that after the news Mr Somebody would make a commentary, and that the Brains Trust programme would then begin, or something like this. I did not personally sustain any direct impression, but Averell said there was something about the Japanese attacking the Americans, and, in spite of being tired and resting, we all sat up.[1] By now the butler, Sawyers, who had heard what had passed, came into the room, saying, 'It's quite true. We heard it ourselves outside. The Japanese have attacked the Americans.' There was a silence. At the Mansion House luncheon on November 11, I had said that if Japan attacked the United States a British declaration of war would follow 'within the hour'. I got up from the table and walked through the hall to the office, which was always at work. I asked for a call to the President. The Ambassador followed me out, and, imagining I was about to take some irrevocable step, said, 'Don't you think you'd better get confirmation first?'

In two or three minutes Mr Roosevelt came through. 'Mr President, what's this about Japan?' 'It's quite true,' he replied. 'They have attacked us at Pearl Harbor. We are all in the same boat now.' I put Winant on to the line and some interchanges took place, the Ambassador at first saying, 'Good,' 'Good' – and then, apparently graver, 'Ah!' I got on again and said, 'This certainly

[1] The actual wording of the announcement was: 'The news has just been given that Japanese aircraft have raided Pearl Harbor, the American naval base in Hawaii. The announcement of the attack was made in a brief statement by President Roosevelt. Naval and military targets on the principal Hawaiian island of Oahu have also been attacked. No further details are yet available.'

simplifies things. God be with you,' or words to that effect. We then went back into the hall and tried to adjust our thoughts to the supreme world event which had occurred, which was of so startling a nature as to make even those who were near the centre gasp. My two American friends took the shock with admirable fortitude. We had no idea that any serious losses had been inflicted on the United States Navy. They did not wail or lament that their country was at war. They wasted no words in reproach or sorrow. In fact, one might almost have thought they had been delivered from a long pain.

John G. Winant: recollections

(*'A Letter from Grosvenor Square'*)

[7 December 1941] [Chequers]

We looked at one another incredulously. Then Churchill jumped to his feet and started for the door with the announcement, 'We shall declare war on Japan.' There is nothing half-hearted or unpositive about Churchill – certainly not when he is on the move. Without ceremony I too left the table and followed him out of the room.

'Good God,' I said, 'you can't declare war on a radio announcement.'

He stopped and looked at me half-seriously, half-quizzically, and then said quietly, 'What shall I do?' The question was asked not because he needed me to tell him what to do, but as a courtesy to the representative of the country attacked.

I said, 'I will call up the President by telephone and ask him what the facts are.'

And he added, 'And I shall talk with him too.'

We got through to the White House in a few minutes and the President told me very simply the story of the attack – so tragic in itself and yet the final mistake that was to end the power of the Axis. He could not, however, over the open transatlantic telephone, tell the extent of the crushing losses sustained by the fleet, or the heavy casualties. I said I had a friend with me who wanted to speak to him. I said, 'You will know who it is, as soon as you hear his voice.'

John Martin: recollection

(*Letter to the author, 3 September 1982*)

[7 December 1941] [Chequers]

Soon after the first excitement I was able to obtain on the telephone from the Admiralty news of the Japanese attack on Malaya.

Admiral Layton[1] *to the Admiralty*
(*John Martin papers*)[2]

7 December 1941

Report from Kota Bharu.[3] An attempt is being made to land from 3 or 5 (? Transports). One landing craft is already approaching mouth of river.

Anthony Eden: recollection
(*'The Reckoning'*)

[7 December 1941]

I set out from Binderton on my Arctic journey to Russia on the morning of December 7th. I had chosen a strong delegation from the Foreign Office to accompany me, including Sir Alexander Cadogan, the Permanent Under-Secretary, Mr Oliver Harvey, who had again become my invaluable private secretary, and the resourceful and tireless Mr Frank Roberts[4] of the Central Department. Mr Maisky travelled with us to take part in the talks. As Permanent Under-Secretary and therefore my principal official adviser, Cadogan was at all times wise and thorough. These qualities, and his exceptional experience, enabled him to take much of the burden off me.

I left Euston on a lovely afternoon, but during the long journey northward I began to feel chilled and sick. When I reached Invergordon at 8 o'clock the next morning I saw a doctor, who diagnosed gastric influenza, the only time I was ill during the war in Europe. Soon after, a naval officer said that the Prime Minister wanted to speak to me on the telephone; this, he explained, meant going to his headquarters. I was reluctant, for I felt miserable and wanted to get straight on to the destroyer and make for Scapa and my cruiser. I thought

[1] Geoffrey Layton, 1884–1964. Entered the Royal Navy, 1903. On active service, 1914–18. (Commander, 1916. Distinguished Service Order, 1918). Rear-Admiral, 1935. Vice-Admiral Commanding the 1st Battle Squadron and Second-in-Command, Home Fleet, 1939–40. Knighted, 1940. Commander-in-Chief, China Station, 1940–42; Ceylon, 1942–45; Portsmouth, 1945–47.

[2] This is the message in the form that John Martin took it down over the telephone and handed it to Churchill.

[3] Japanese troops brought by sea from Indochina, landed at Kota Bharu at 12.25 a.m. on 8 December 1941 local time, 4.55 p.m. 7 December 1941 Greeenwich Mean Time. This was almost two hours before the attack on Pearl Harbor which took place at 6.30 p.m. 7 December 1941 Greenwich Mean Time (8 a.m. December 7 local time). Kota Bharu lay on the east coast of Malaya near the border with Thailand. Simultaneously with the Kota Bharu landings the Japanese attacked Singora in Thailand.

[4] Frank Kenyon Roberts, 1907–1998. Entered the Foreign Office in 1930. Desk Officer, Central Department, dealing with Germany and issues connected with Germany, 1937–40; subsequently Deputy Acting Head, Central Department, with responsibility for the Allied Governments in London, also for Spain and Portugal. United Kingdom Deputy High Commissioner in India, 1949–51. Knighted, 1953. Ambassador to Yugoslavia, 1954–7; to the Soviet Union, 1960–2; to the Federal Republic of Germany, 1963–8.

it would need all my strength anyway. However, ill as I was, I felt that I must take the call, the more so when I was told that the United States Ambassador was with the Prime Minister. Mr Churchill told me what he knew of the Japanese attack on Pearl Harbor. He was quite naturally in a high state of excitement. I could not conceal my relief and did not have to try to. I felt that whatever happened now, it was merely a question of time. Before, we had believed in the end but never seen the means, now both were clear.

Mr Churchill began laying plans. He said he must go to the United States at once. I saw the force of this, but I did not imagine we could both be away and was not sure that the Americans would want him so soon. I felt that my visit to the Russians was important and that they would be resentful if it were postponed. Reluctantly I asked what Mr Churchill wanted me to do. He replied at once that I must carry on with my journey, while he crossed the Atlantic. I demurred, saying that I did not see how we could both be away at once. He said we could. The emphasis of the war had shifted, what now mattered was the intentions of our two great allies. We must each go to one of them. I should repeat every telegram from Moscow to him and he would do the same at his end. After some more exchanges, Mr Churchill added: 'Wait a minute, someone else wants to speak to you. Gil Winant came on the line. It was good to hear the relief in his voice as he acclaimed our decisions and wished me God speed. I knew that in his heart he was acclaiming something else too. The United States and Britain were now allies in the war against Japan.

Winston S. Churchill to General Chiang Kai-shek
(Churchill papers, 20/46)

8 December 1941
Most Immediate
despatched 12.20 a.m.

British Empire and United States have been attacked by Japan – Always we have been friends: now we face a common enemy.

Winston S. Churchill to Eamon de Valera
(Churchill papers, 20/46)

8 December 1941
Most immediate
despatched 12.20 a.m.

Now is your chance. Now or never. 'A nation once again'. Am very ready to meet you at any time.

Winston S. Churchill and Averell Harriman to Harry Hopkins
(*Churchill papers, 20/49*)

8 December 1941
1.35 a.m.
Most Immediate

Thinking of you much at this historic moment – Winston, Averell

President Franklin D. Roosevelt to Winston S. Churchill
(*Churchill papers, 20/46*)

8 December 1941

The Senate passed the all-out declaration of war 82 to nothing, and the House has passed it 382 to 1. Today all of us are in the same boat with you and the people of the Empire and it is a ship which will not and can not be sunk.

Winston S. Churchill: reflection
(*'The Second World War, Volume Three'*)

[8 December 1941]

Silly people, and there were many, not only in enemy countries, might discount the force of the United States. Some said they were soft, others that they would never be united. They would fool around at a distance. They would never come to grips. They would never stand blood-letting. Their democracy and system of recurrent elections would paralyse their war effort. They would be just a vague blur on the horizon to friend or foe. Now we should see the weakness of this numerous but remote, wealthy, and talkative people. But I had studied the American Civil War, fought out to the last desperate inch. American blood flowed in my veins. I thought of a remark which Edward Grey[1] had made to me more than thirty years before – that the United States is like 'a gigantic boiler. Once the fire is lighted under it there is no limit to the power it can generate'. Being saturated and satiated with emotion and sensation, I went to bed and slept the sleep of the saved and thankful.

[1] Foreign Secretary from 1905 to 1916, while Churchill was successively Under-Secretary of State for the Colonies, President of the Board of Trade, Home Secretary, First Lord of the Admiralty and Chancellor of the Duchy of Lancaster.

Harold Nicolson: diary
(*'Diaries with Letters, 1939-1945'*)

8 December 1941

The House has been specially summoned. Winston enters the Chamber with bowed shoulders and an expression of grim determination on his face. The House had expected jubilation at the entry of America into the war and are a trifle disconcerted. He makes a dull matter-of-fact speech. He has a great sense of occasion. The mistake he makes is to read out his message to the Siamese Prime Minister. The Siamese are bound to capitulate, and it was a mistake to expect them to do anything else.

Henry Channon: diary
(*'Chips'*)

8 December 1941

The House of Commons, so quickly summoned, was crowded. There was an immense queue and I rescued Pam Churchill and led her into the inner lobby. Coming back I actually collided with her father-in-law, Winston, who closely followed by Clemmie and Harvie-Watt, was pushing his way through the crowd. And after Prayers the Prime Minister rose and made a brief and well-balanced announcement that the Cabinet had declared a state of war to exist at 1 o'clock with Japan. Nobody seems to know whether this recent and dramatic development is helpful to the Allied cause or not. It means immense complications, but will probably bring about America's immediate entry into the war . . .

Geoffrey Lloyd whispered to me how lucky Winston was. Now Libya will be forgotten. Russia saved the Government in July; now Japan will do likewise . . .

Winston S. Churchill: speech
(*Hansard*)

8 December 1941 House of Commons

WAR WITH JAPAN

PRIME MINISTER'S DECLARATION

The Prime Minister (Mr Churchill): As soon as I heard, last night, that Japan had attacked the United States, I felt it necessary that Parliament should be immediately summoned. It is indispensable to our system of government that Parliament should play its full part in all the important acts of State and at all the crucial moments of the war; and I am glad to see that so many

Members have been able to be in their places, despite the shortness of the notice. With the full approval of the nation, and of the Empire, I pledged the word of Great Britain, about a month ago, that should the United States be involved in war with Japan, a British declaration of war would follow within the hour. I, therefore, spoke to President Roosevelt on the Atlantic telephone last night, with a view to arranging the timing of our respective declarations. The President told me that he would this morning send a Message to Congress, which, of course, as is well known, can alone make a declaration of war on behalf of the United States, and I then assured him that we would follow immediately.

However, it soon appeared that British territory in Malaya had also been the object of Japanese attack, and later on it was announced, from Tokyo, that the Japanese High Command – a curious form; not the Imperial Japanese Government – had declared that a state of war existed with Great Britain and the United States. That being so, there was no need to wait for the declaration by Congress. American time is very nearly six hours behind ours. The Cabinet, therefore, which met at 12.30 today, authorized an immediate declaration of war upon Japan. Instructions were sent to His Majesty's Ambassador at Tokyo,[1] and a communication was despatched to the Japanese Chargé d'Affaires at 1 o'clock today to this effect:

Foreign Office, December 8th.

Sir,

On the evening of December 7th His Majesty's Government in the United Kingdom learned that Japanese forces, without previous warning, either in the form of a declaration of war or of an ultimatum with a conditional declaration of war, had attempted a landing on the coast of Malaya and bombed Singapore and Hong Kong.

(2) In view of these wanton acts of unprovoked aggression, committed in flagrant violation of international law, and particularly of Article I of the Third Hague Convention, relative to the opening of hostilities, to which both Japan and the United Kingdom are parties, His Majesty's Ambassador at Tokyo has been instructed to inform the Imperial Japanese Government, in the name of His Majesty's Government in the United Kingdom that a state of war exists between the two countries.

I have the honour to be, with high consideration,

Sir,
Your obedient servant,[2]
(Sgd.) Winston S. Churchill

[1] Sir Robert Craigie.

[2] Churchill later wrote, in his war memoirs: 'Some people did not like this ceremonial style. But after all when you have to kill a man it costs nothing to be polite.'

Meanwhile, hostilities have already begun. The Japanese began a landing in British territory in Northern Malaya at about 6 o'clock – 1 a.m. local time – yesterday, and they were immediately engaged by our Forces, which were in readiness. The Home Office measures against Japanese nationals were set in motion at 10.45 last night. The House will see, therefore, that no time has been lost, and that we are actually ahead of our engagements.

The Royal Netherlands Government at once marked their solidarity with Great Britain and the United States at 3 o'clock in the morning.

The Netherlands Minister informed the Foreign Office that his Government were telling the Japanese Government that, in view of the hostile acts perpetrated by Japanese forces against two Powers with whom the Netherlands maintained particularly close relations, they considered that, as a consequence, a state of war now exists between the Kingdom of the Netherlands and Japan.

I do not yet know what part Siam, or Thailand, will be called upon to play in this fresh war, but a report has reached us that the Japanese have landed troops at Singora, which is in Siamese territory, on the frontier of Malaya, not far from the landing they had made on the British side of the frontier. Meanwhile, just before Japan had gone to war, I had sent the Siamese Prime Minister the following message. It was sent off on Sunday, early in the morning:

'There is a possibility of imminent Japanese invasion of your country. If you are attacked, defend yourself. The preservation of the full independence and sovereignty of Thailand is a British interest, and we shall regard an attack on you as an attack on ourselves.'

It is worth while looking for a moment at the manner in which the Japanese have begun their assault upon the English-speaking world. Every circumstance of calculated and characteristic Japanese treachery was employed against the United States. The Japanese envoys, Nomura and Kurusu, were ordered to prolong their mission in the United States, in order to keep the conversations going while a surprise attack was being prepared, to be made before a declaration of war could be delivered. The President's appeal to the Emperor, which I have no doubt many Members will have read – it has been published largely in the papers here – reminding him of their ancient friendship and of the importance of preserving the peace of the Pacific, has received only this base and brutal reply. No one can doubt that every effort to bring about a peaceful solution had been made by the Government of the United States, and that immense patience and composure had been shown in face of the growing Japanese menace.

Now that the issue is joined in the most direct manner, it only remains for the two great democracies to face their task with whatever strength God may give them. We must hold ourselves very fortunate, and I think we may rate our affairs not wholly ill-guided, that we were not attacked alone by Japan in our period of weakness after Dunkirk, or at any time in 1940, before the United States had fully realized the dangers which threatened the whole world and had made much advance in its military preparation. So precarious and narrow was the margin upon which we then lived that we did not dare to express the sympathy which we have all along felt for the heroic people of China. We were even forced for a short time, in the summer of 1940, to agree to closing the Burma Road. But later on, at the beginning of this year, as soon as we could regather our strength, we reversed that policy, and the House will remember that both I and the Foreign Secretary have felt able to make increasingly outspoken declarations of friendship for the Chinese people and their great leader, General Chiang Kai-shek.

We have always been friends. Last night I cabled to the Generalissimo assuring him that henceforward we would face the common foe together. Although the imperative demands of the war in Europe and in Africa have strained our resources, vast and growing though they are, the House and the Empire will notice that some of the finest ships in the Royal Navy have reached their stations in the Far East at a very convenient moment. Every preparation in our power has been made, and I do not doubt that we shall give a good account of ourselves. The closest accord has been established with the powerful American forces, both naval and air, and also with the strong, efficient forces belonging to the Royal Netherlands Government in the Netherlands East Indies. We shall all do our best. When we think of the insane ambition and insatiable appetite which have caused this vast and melancholy extension of the war, we can only feel that Hitler's madness has infected the Japanese mind, and that the root of the evil and its branch must be extirpated together.

It is of the highest importance that there should be no under-rating of the gravity of the new dangers we have to meet, either here or in the United States. The enemy has attacked with an audacity which may spring from recklessness but which may also spring from a conviction of strength. The ordeal to which the English-speaking world and our heroic Russian Allies are being exposed will certainly be hard, especially at the outset, and will probably be long, yet when we look around us over the sombre panorama of the world, we have no reason to doubt the justice of our cause or that our strength and will-power will be sufficient to sustain it. We have at least four-fifths of the population of the globe upon our side. We are responsible for their safety and for their future. In the past we have had a light which flickered, in the present we have a light which flames, and in the future there will be a light which shines over all the land and sea.

Winston S. Churchill to King George VI
(*Churchill papers, 20/20*)

8 December 1941
Most Secret

Sir,
I have formed the conviction that it is my duty to visit Washington without delay, provided such a course is agreeable to President Roosevelt, as I have little doubt it will be. The whole plan of the Anglo-American defence and attack has to be concerted in the light of reality. We have also to be careful that our share of munitions and other aid which we are receiving from the United States does not suffer more than is, I fear, inevitable. The fact that Mr Eden will be in Moscow while I am at Washington will make the settlement of large-scale problems between the three great Allies easier.

These reasons were accepted by my colleagues in the Cabinet unanimously today, and I therefore ask Your Majesty's permission to leave the country. I should propose to start quite soon, in a warship, and to be absent altogether for about three weeks. I shall take with me a staff on the same scale as I took to the Atlantic meeting.

During my absence the Lord Privy Seal will act for me, assisted by the Lord President of the Council, the Chancellor of the Exchequer, and other members of the War Cabinet. I would propose that during this period the three Service Ministers should temporarily sit with the War Cabinet. While I am away the Foreign Office will report to the Lord President, and the Defence Committee to the Lord Privy Seal. I shall of course be constantly in touch by wireless with all that goes on, and can give decisions whenever necessary. I should propose to take with me the First Sea Lord and the Chief of the Air Staff, as the concert of all our arrangements with the Americans on a high level is all-important.

I hope I may receive Your Majesty's approval of this course. I am, of course, keeping my intention secret.

With my humble duty,

I remain Your Majesty's most devoted, faithful servant and subject,

Winston S. Churchill

PS – I am expecting that Germany and Italy will both declare war on the United States, as they have bound themselves by treaty to do so. I shall defer proposing my visit to the President until this situation is more clear.

Oliver Harvey: diary
(*'The War Diaries of Oliver Harvey, 1941-1945'*)

8 December 1941

Arrived at Invergordon about 8 a.m. and drove to Naval Commander's office where we proceeded to get through to No. 10. AE has developed a chill during the night and is already rather under the weather. AE spoke to PM who was in highest spirits at America and Japan and blandly announced that he was going off to America himself! AE who thus first heard of it, asked when and was told 'next Thursday'. Wouldn't it be a bad thing for both to be away at once? Oh no! Alec[1] and I who were with AE were horrified. We both felt he would not be wanted in America at such a moment and there was nothing for him to do there if he went. But I am aghast at the consequence of both being away at once. The British public will think quite rightly that they are mad. AE saw this too and telephoned to Winant who had only understood the PM's visit was for later on, he didn't favour it now. We felt it most important to try and stop PM especially as it would be fatal to put off AE's visit to Stalin to enable PM to visit Roosevelt. It would confirm all Stalin's worst suspicions. AE decided to speak to Attlee too. The latter knew nothing of the project but entirely agreed with AE that it ought at least to be postponed. He promised to urge this in Cabinet today. Finally, AE spoke again to PM to communicate his fears, but PM would have none of them.

Really the PM is a lunatic: he gets in such a state of excitement that the wildest schemes seem reasonable. I hope to goodness we can defeat this one. AE believes the Cabinet and finally the King will restrain him, but the Cabinet are a poor lot for stopping anything.

We embarked on destroyer at 11.30 for Scapa to join our ship. We are to telephone PM.

Winston S. Churchill to Sir Horace Wilson
(*Churchill papers, 20/36*)

8 December 1941

I approve the recommendations for Honours in the New Year List enclosed in your minute of November 28, subject to the following notes:

[1] Sir Alexander Cadogan.

1. Sir Auckland Geddes[1] should be recommended for a Barony. The Committee say that it is not thought that the time has yet arrived for the consideration of Regional Commissioners. I do not, however, think of Sir Auckland as a Regional Commissioner, but rather in the light of his services as Minister during the last war and His Majesty's Ambassador at Washington. The Home Secretary should be informed of the proposal.

2. 'C' (Brigadier Menzies) should be recommended for a CB. If, as I assume, a Military Award would be more suitable. I shall be glad if you will take up with the Secretary of State for War his inclusion in the Service List on the present occasion.[2]

3. Major-General E. L. Spears should be recommended for a KBE. If it would be more appropriate to include this in the Foreign Office List, the matter should be taken up with that Department. Mr Eden has informed me of his concurrence in the proposed award.[3]

4. Mr Alvar Liddell[4] (in List for MBE) should be omitted; but Mr Val Gielgud[5] (also of the BBC) should be added to the List for an OBE.

Winston S. Churchill to Alfred Duff Cooper

(*Churchill papers, 20/46*)

9 December 1941
Personal and Secret

1. You are appointed Resident Cabinet Minister at Singapore for Far Eastern affairs. You will serve under, and report directly to, the War Cabinet,

[1] Auckland Campbell Geddes, 1879–1954. A distant relative of Lord Haldane. On active service in South Africa, 1901–2. Doctor of Medicine, Edinburgh, 1908. Professor of Anatomy, Royal College of Surgeons, Dublin, 1909–13. Professor of Anatomy, McGill University, Canada, 1913–14. Major, Northumberland Fusiliers, 1914. Assistant Adjutant-General, GHQ, France, 1915–16. Director of Recruiting, War Office, with the rank of Brigadier-General, 1916–17. Knighted, 1917. Conservative MP, 1917–20. Minister of National Service, 1917, 1918 and 1919. President of the Local Government Board, 1918. Minister of Reconstruction, 1919. President of the Board of Trade, 1919–20. Ambassador to Washington, 1920–24. Chairman of the Rio Tinto Company, 1925–47. Created Baron, 1942.

[2] Brigadier Menzies was made a Companion of the Order of the Bath in 1942, and was knighted a year later.

[3] General Spears did receive his knighthood in the 1942 New Year's Honours List.

[4] Alvar Lidell, 1908-1981. The son of Swedish parents who emigrated to Britain a decade before his birth. A BBC announcer in Birmingham, 1931; transferred to London, 1933. Announced the abdication of Edward VIII in 1936 and Neville Chamberlain's broadcast on 3 September 1939 that Britain was at war with Germany. A wartime news reader of whom *The Times* wrote in his obituary (9 January 1981) that he created 'a kind of confidence among his hearers so that they felt what he was saying was copperbottomed and A1 at Lloyd's'.

[5] Val Henry Gielgud, 1900–1981. Joined the Radio Times, 1928. Head of Sound Drama, BBC, 1929–64. Author of novels, stage plays and broadcast plays. His books included *Outrage in Manchukuo*, 1937; *Beyond Dover*, 1940; and *Confident Morning*, 1943. OBE, 1942; CBE, 1958. Among the recreations which he listed in *Who's Who* were 'reading (especially Military History)' and 'enjoys the society of Siamese cats'.

through its Secretary. You are authorized to form a War Council, reporting first its composition and the geographical sphere it will cover. This will presumably coincide with the geographical sphere of the military Commander-in-Chief. Your principal task will be to assist the successful conduct of operations in the Far East (a) by relieving the Commanders-in-Chief as far as possible of those extraneous responsibilities with which they have hitherto been burdened; and (b) by giving them broad political guidance.

2. Your functions will also include the settlement of emergency matters on the spot, where time does not permit of reference home. You will develop a local clearing-house for prompt settlement of minor routine matters which would otherwise have to be referred to separate Departments here. On all matters on which you require special guidance you will, provided there is time, refer the matter home. You will, in any case, report constantly to His Majesty's Government.

3. When Captain Oliver Lyttelton was appointed Minister of State at Cairo it was laid down that this did not affect the existing responsibilities of His Majesty's Representatives in the Middle East, or their official relationships with their respective Departments at home. The same will apply in the Far East. The successful establishment of this machinery depends largely on your handling of it in these early critical days.

4. You had no reason to assume that you did not possess the confidence of the Foreign Secretary, and he was astonished that you should have conceived such an idea. With your knowledge of the various Public Departments and of Cabinet procedure, it should be possible for you to exercise a powerful, immediately concerting influence upon Far Eastern affairs. Telegraph to me at once your concrete proposals and the form in which you would like your appointment and its scope to be defined and published. All good luck and kindest regards. We must fight this thing out everywhere to the end.

Winston S. Churchill to Sir Hughe Knatchbull-Hugessen
(*Churchill papers, 20/46*)

9 December 1941
Personal and Secret

1. Your No. 2840. I hope you will not feel it necessary to be apologetic if confronted with Turkish criticism of our operations in Libya. You should remind Turkish critics how they pressed their good offices upon us to secure an appeasement in Iraq and another in Syria, when with a little patience the whole situation was restored. There is no justification for complaining about the confident character of the Cairo pronouncements. We believe that confidence will prove well-founded. Although the battle has been protracted,

it has been all the more costly to the enemy, and we have good reason to expect that we shall become their masters.

2. You should certainly adopt a robust tone in dealing with cavillers who are so obviously playing for safety themselves. The turn of world events is vastly in our favour. The Germans have had another heavy blow, this time in front of Moscow. The United States is in the war up to the neck. I have never reproached the Turks with the attitude they have adopted since the outbreak of war, because I feel their own consciences prick them and because I hope they will redeem their character as allies when events become more clear.

3. Always please be very careful not to send unduly lengthy telegrams about trifling matters. These cumber the wires and exhaust the cyphering staff. A highly selective process should be applied to the transmission of mere background gossip. Cogency and brevity are the tests of diplomatic correspondence.

Winston S. Churchill to Lord Woolton
(*Churchill papers, 20/36*)

9 December 1941

You say that you would have preferred to bring sweets and chocolates within the Points scheme and hope to do so subsequently.

Would it not be better to postpone rationing until you are able to do so? If you introduce a sweets ration now, all the forces of conservatism and arguments of administration economy will be arrayed against any subsequent proposal to alter matters.

I gather that it was admitted in the Lord President's Committee that a sweets ration would lend itself to irregularities more easily than our other rations. Anything which diminishes respect for the rationing regulations is objectionable; if we create artificial illegalities that are neither enforceable nor condemned by public opinion, the habit of evasion may spread to cases where it would be injurious.

We have done without a sweets and chocolate ration for so long that a small further delay may be tolerated. We should avoid allowing exceptions to the principle that any rationing of the secondary foods which you feel compelled to introduce should be incorporated in the Points system.

Winston S. Churchill to the Chairman of the Forestry Commission[1]
(*Churchill papers, 20/36*)

9 December 1941

I see reports in the papers that timber-felling companies are ruthlessly denuding for profit many of our woodlands. What arrangements have you got to make sure that some of the finest trees are left and that due consideration is given to the appearance of the countryside. I know we have got to cut down very severely, but there is no reason why a certain number of trees should not be left.

Let me know in a few lines what you are doing to replant. Surely you are replanting two or three trees for every large one you cut down.

Winston S. Churchill to Peter Fraser
(*Churchill papers, 20/49*)

9 December 1941

NEW ZEALAND DIVISION

I am deeply grieved about the severe losses your heroic division has suffered in the forefront of the battle. All the accounts I have received pay the highest tribute to their brilliant work. The war is going well in Libya and in Russia and on the Atlantic and in the United States. Every good wish and kindest regards.

Winston S. Churchill to Field Marshal Smuts
(*Churchill papers, 20/46*)

9 December 1941
Personal and Secret

Your 829. All this has been carefully studied, but campaign in Africa will not be finished before it is necessary to announce arrival of Eden Mission at Moscow. We are wearing them down steadily in Libya, and the Russians have had another marked success on the Moscow front. I am well content with

[1] Roy Lister Robinson, 1883–1952. Born in Australia. Came to Britain as a Rhodes Scholar. Assistant Inspector for Forestry, Board of Agriculture and Fisheries, 1909; Superintending Inspector, 1914. Head of the Timber Supplies Department, Ministry of Munitions, 1916–18 (while Churchill was Minister of Munitions) Appointed a Forestry Commissioner when the Commission was established, 1919; Chairman from 1932 until his death. (Knighted, 1931). After the Second World War he was largely responsible for two white Papers which led to the considerable expansion of forestry after the war. He was the only man to attend all six Empire and Commonwealth Forestry Conferences (taking the Chair in South Africa, 1937, and in England, 1947). Created Baron, 1947. It was while acting as Britain's chief delegate to the 1952 Conference in Canada that he died. His only son was killed in action in 1942.

Sunday's developments in the Far East. I think it almost certain that Germany and Italy have promised Japan to declare war on the United States. Every good wish.

Winston S. Churchill to David Margesson
(*Churchill papers, 20/36*)

9 December 1941
Personal and Secret

I have considered carefully your minute to me of 3.11.41 about the ATS,[1] and I am willing that the principles you propose should have a trial. It is up to you to make these Batteries attractive to the best elements in the ATS and those who are now being compelled to join the ATS. I fear Mrs Knox[2] has a complex against women being connected with lethal work. She must get rid of this. Also there is an idea prevalent among the ladies managing the ATS that nothing must conflict with loyalty to the ATS and that Battery *esprit de corps* is counter to their interest or theme. No tolerance can be shown to this. The prime sphere of the women commanders is welfare, and this should occupy their main endeavours.

The conditions are very bad and rough, and I expect will get worse now that large numbers are being brought into the War Office grip by compulsion or the shadow of compulsion. A great responsibility rests upon you as Secretary of State to see that all these young women are not treated roughly. Mrs Knox and her assistants should be admirable in all this, but do not let them get in the way of the happy active life of the Batteries or deprive women of their incentives to join the Batteries and to care as much about the Batteries as they do about the ATS.

I shall be very glad to have a further report from you on how the principles enunciated in your minute are, in fact, being applied. Every kind of minor compliment and ornament should be accorded to those who render good service in the Batteries.

[1] The (women's) Auxiliary Territorial Service.

[2] Jean Marcia Knox, 1908–1993. Daughter of G.G. Leith Marshall. Temporary Chief Controller, and War Substantive Controller, Auxiliary Territorial Service, 1941–43. CBE, 1943. Wife of Squadron-Leader G.R.M. Knox. In 1945 she married the 3rd Baron Swaythling (Stuart Albert Samuel Montagu).

Winston S. Churchill to President Franklin D. Roosevelt
(*Premier papers, 3/458/5*)

9 December 1941
Most Secret

I am grateful for your telegram of December 8. Now that we are, as you say, 'in the same boat', would it not be wise for us to have another conference? We could review the whole war plan in the light of reality and new facts, as well as the problems of production and distribution. I feel that all these matters, some of which are causing me concern, can best be settled on the highest executive level. It would also be a very great pleasure to me to meet you again, and the sooner the better.

2. I could, if desired, start from here in a day or two, and come by warship to Baltimore or Annapolis. Voyage would take about eight days, and I would arrange to stay a week, so that everything important could be settled between us. I would bring Pound, Portal, Dill and Beaverbrook, with necessary staffs.

3. Please let me know at earliest what you feel about this.

General Ismay: recollection
(*Churchill papers, 4/233*)

[9 December 1941] [Cabinet War Room]
[10 p.m.]

Hollis and I clearly remember the meeting to which you refer, but I think you might have summoned it unexpectedly and, for some reason or another, there is no record of what was said.[1]

[1] At ten o'clock on the night of 9 December 1941, an emergency meeting was summoned in the Cabinet Room at 10 Downing Street to consider the future movements of the *Prince of Wales* and *Repulse*, and their four attendant destroyers. Churchill put forward two suggestions. One, Ismay later recalled, in a letter to Churchill on 6 August 1948 – while Churchill was writing his war memoirs – was that the ships 'should vanish into the ocean wastes and exercise a vague menace', acting as 'rogue elephants'. The other was that they should go across the Pacific 'and join the remnants of the American fleet'. Ismay told Churchill that no suggestion had been made that night that the ships should remain in the war zone, or go on the offensive; nor was any final decision reached, except to 'reconsider the problem in the morning light'.

Winston S. Churchill to Anthony Eden
(*Churchill papers, 20/49*)

10 December 1941
sent at 5.35 a.m.
Most Immediate
Personal and Secret

1. Since you left much has happened. United States have sustained a major disaster at Hawaii, and have now only two battleships effective in Pacific against ten Japanese. They are recalling all their battleships from Atlantic and have laid embargo on all exports of munitions for the time being. This is for your own information alone. Secondly, we are going to be heavily attacked in Malaya and throughout Far East by Japanese forces enjoying command of the sea. Thirdly, Italy and Germany are about to declare war on United States. German navy has already been ordered to attack American ships and a tripartite declaration of implacable war against British Empire and United States is expected either 10th or 11th. Fourthly, magnificent Russian successes at Leningrad, on whole Moscow front, at Kursk and in south; German armies largely on defensive or in retreat, complaining of terrible winter conditions and ever-strengthening Russian counter-attacks. Fifthly, Auchinleck reports tide turned in Libya, but much heavy fighting lies ahead on this our second front. Sixthly, urgent necessity to reinforce Malaya with aircraft from Middle East.

2. In view of above you should not offer ten squadrons at present time. Everything is in flux with United States supplies and I cannot tell where we are till I get there.

3. Hope you are better. We are having a jolly time here. Will start Thursday if invited.

Winston S. Churchill: recollection
(*'The Second World War, Volume Three'*)

[10 December 1941]

I was opening my boxes on the 10th when the telephone at my bedside rang. It was the First Sea Lord. His voice sounded odd. He gave a sort of cough and gulp, and at first I could not hear quite clearly. 'Prime Minister, I have to report to you that the *Prince of Wales* and the *Repulse* have both been sunk by the Japanese – we think by aircraft. Tom Phillips is drowned.' 'Are you sure it's true?' 'There is no doubt at all.' So I put the telephone down. I was thankful to be alone. In all the war I never received a more direct shock. The reader of these pages will realize how many efforts, hopes, and plans foundered with these two ships. As I turned over and twisted in bed the full horror of the news sank upon me. There were no British or American capital ships in the Indian Ocean or the Pacific except the American survivors of Pearl Harbor, who were hastening back to California. Over all this vast expanse of waters Japan was supreme, and we everywhere were weak and naked.

Kathleen Hill: recollection
(*Conversation with the author, 15 October 1982*)

[10 December 1941]

I sat in the corner silently and unobtrusively. When he was upset I used to try to be invisible. When the two ships went down I was there. That was a terrible moment. 'Poor Tom Phillips,' he said.

Admiral Pound: reflection[1]
(*Churchill papers, 20/59*)

[10 December 1941]

Let us suppose for a moment that Kota Bharu aerodrome had been held by the Army and therefore not captured by the Japanese, and that the fighter protection asked for by Admiral Phillips had been available. Under these conditions there was a very fair chance of these battleships shooting up the invasion forces at Kota Bharu and Singora. If this had occurred the Army were in a position to drive those forces which had landed into the sea and we should then have been given the time required to put reinforcements into Malaya before the Japanese could have remounted their expeditions.

If this had occurred, it is a fair assumption that Malaya, Sumatra and Java would still be in our hands today and that we should be in a far better position to deal with Japan than we are at the present moment.

[1] Pound set down this reflection in a letter to Churchill on 8 March 1942 (marked 'Most Secret').

General Auchinleck to Winston S. Churchill
(*Churchill papers, 20/46*)

10 December 1941
received 12.25 a.m.
Most Immediate
Private

Enemy is apparently in full retreat towards the west but his remaining tanks are still covering withdrawal. El Adem is in our hands. South Africa and Indian troops joined hands there with British troops from Tobruk and I think it now permissible to claim that siege of Tobruk has been raised. We are pursuing vigorously and pressing enemy hard at all points with fullest and most effective cooperation with RAF.[1]

Viscount Halifax to Winston S. Churchill
(*Churchill papers, 20/46*)

10 December 1941 Washington DC
received 12.50 a.m.
Most Secret

President most warmly welcomes suggestion of meeting. But on security grounds as regards return he does not at all like idea of your coming here. He would like Bermuda which would be secret and save you time. In view of Congress exigencies he would find it very difficult to leave before night of January 5th reaching Bermuda January 7th.

Winston S. Churchill to President Franklin D. Roosevelt
(*Premier papers, 3/458/5*)

10 December 1941
Secret

We do not think there is any serious danger about return journey. There is, however, great danger in our not having a full discussion on the highest level about the extreme gravity of the naval position, as well as upon all the production and allocation issues involved. I am quite ready to meet you at Bermuda or to fly from Bermuda to Washington. I feel it would be disastrous to wait for another month before we settled common action in face of new adverse situation particularly in Pacific. I had hoped to start tomorrow night,

[1] Patrick Kinna noted on this telegram: 'Copy sent to the King'.

but will postpone my sailing till I have received rendezvous from you. I never felt so sure about the final victory, but only concerted action will achieve it. Kindest regards.

Winston S. Churchill: statement
(*Hansard*)

10 December 1941 House of Commons

The Prime Minister (Mr Churchill): I have bad news for the House, which I think I should pass on to them at the earliest possible moment. A report has been received from Singapore that His Majesty's Ship *Prince of Wales* and His Majesty's Ship *Repulse* have been sunk while carrying out operations against a Japanese attack on Malaya. No details are yet available except those contained in the Japanese official communiqué, which claims that both ships were sunk by air attack. I may add that on our next Sitting Day I shall take occasion to make a short statement on the general war situation, which has, from many points of view, both favourable and adverse, undergone important changes in the last few days.

King George VI to Winston S. Churchill
(*Churchill papers, 20/20*)

10 December 1941 In the Train
South Wales

My dear Prime Minister,

The news of the loss of the *Prince of Wales* & *Repulse* came as a great shock to the Queen and I when we were on our tour in S. Wales today. For all of us it is a national disaster, & I fear will create consternation in Australia. The lack of details makes the fact harder to bear, coming as it does on top of yesterday's bad news re. the US battleships. I thought I was getting immune to hearing bad news, but this has affected me deeply as I am sure it has you.

There is something particularly 'alive' about a big ship, which gives one a sense of personal loss apart from considerations of loss of power.

I understand you are not undertaking your journey just now, for which I am very thankful.

Believe me
Yours very sincerely
George R.I.

War Cabinet: Confidential Annex
(*Cabinet papers, 65/24*)

10 December 1941
6 p.m.

The Prime Minister said that the United States was now moving her Atlantic Fleet to the Pacific. Even so, she would not have as strong a Fleet in that ocean as Japan. For the moment we could not send more ships to the Pacific, and we should have to develop a different kind of warfare until more ships were available.

Sir Earle Page said that Australia was anxious that the best possible use should be made of the forces available to us. He suggested that it might be possible, by the use of aircraft and submarines, to keep the Japanese out of the Indian Ocean.

He added that if we could give help to China to continue in the war, this might well be one of the determining factors. He suggested that Russia might be able to give material aid to China and thus tide over the immediate position.

The Prime Minister said that he had little doubt that Russia would continue to give aid to China.

Sir Earle Page then suggested that a special appeal should be made to M. Stalin that Russia should come into the war against Japan. He referred to the use which might be made of shore-based aircraft in the neighbourhood of Vladivostok against the Japanese mainland, and to the valuable help which could be obtained from the large number of submarines which Russia possessed in Far Eastern waters.

The Prime Minister said that, in view of the enormous service which Russia was giving to us by hammering the German Army on her Western front, he did not wish to ask Russia to declare war on Japan. To do so would make it impossible for Russia to bring Divisions from Siberia which might be of incalculable value on her Western front. It was perhaps relevant that, in view of the changed situation, he had had to telegraph to the Foreign Secretary that he could not now offer the Russians to make ten squadrons available for service on their Southern front. It was, of course, open to the United States, if they wished, to urge Russia to declare war on Japan.

Winston S. Churchill to Ernest Bevin
(*Churchill papers, 20/36*)

10 December 1941
Action this Day

I see it reported that you say Members of Parliament are liable to be called up equally with others. The rule, I have made which was followed in the last war, and must be followed in this, was that service in the House of Commons ranks with the highest service in the State. Any Member of Parliament or Peer of Parliament has a right to decide at his discretion whether he will fulfil that service or give some other form. Members of either House are free, if at any time they consider their political duties require it, and reasonable notice is given, to withdraw from the Armed Forces or any other form of service in order to attend Parliament.

I could not possibly agree to any smirching of this principle.

Winston S. Churchill to Sir Orme Sargent[1] *and General Ismay*
(*Churchill papers, 20/36*)

10 December 1941
Action this Day

This most foolish remark at the end of paragraph 3[2] must be immediately cancelled. We want to get the Poles armed as soon as possible. Why then should we tell the Russians that it will only be at their expense?

Let me know who drafted this. He evidently does not understand the general situation.

Henry Channon: diary
(*'Chips'*)

10 December 1941

A dreadful day of despair and despondency. The Prime Minister stalked into the House and seemed anxious to speak. After a preliminary parley and

[1] Orme Garton Sargent, 1884–1962. Educated at Radley. Entered Foreign Office, 1906. Second Secretary, Berne, 1917; 1st Secretary, 1919. At the Paris Peace Conference, 1919. Counsellor, Foreign Office, 1926. Head of the Central Department of the Foreign Office, 1928–33. Assistant Under-Secretary of State for Foreign Affairs, 1933. Knighted, 1937. Deputy Under-Secretary of State, 1939; Permanent Under-Secretary, 1946–9. Known in the Foreign Office as 'Moley'.

[2] In a telegram from the War Office (London) to No. 30 Military Mission (the British Military Mission to Russia) about arming Poles who were being evacuated from Russia, many of them having been prisoners in Siberia and Central Asia labour camps since the occupation of eastern Poland by Russia in September 1939.

getting up and sitting down twice, he announced the sinking of both the *Prince of Wales* and the *Repulse* at Malaya. A most shattering blow for our Pacific fleet and Naval prestige . . . A wave of gloom spread everywhere. The House was restive, the Government suddenly unpopular . . . Dejected I came home and gave luncheon to the Iveaghs[1] who had been at the Lords. They, too, were depressed. I could have cried.

At dinner Mrs Greville[2] said, 'If only the Prime Minister could have permanent laryngitis we might win the war.' An allusion to his unfortunate reference on Monday to the menacing presence in the Pacific of our battleships at this convenient moment. A heart-breaking remark viewed in the light of subsequent events. Thousands of lives lost[3] – it is terrible.

Henry Channon: diary
(*'Chips'*)

11 December 1941

Just before twelve o'clock the Prime Minister, looking worn, entered the Chamber and announced that Members of Parliament would be allowed a free choice between entering the Armed Services or attending to their Parliamentary duties. I was relieved, for I know how utterly hopeless I should be in uniform, although at times I hanker for it. I am too old, too flat-footed, too unfit and too temperamentally hopeless – besides, I am gun-shy. Then he made a perhaps over-long statement, a spirited yet slightly defensive explanation, of the recent Cairene communiqués which were, everyone now realizes, over-enthusiastic and misleading. By putting too much emphasis on this feature of this extraordinary week the Prime Minister increased the very suspicions which he wished to allay, and I watched Members shift uneasily as they do when they are irritated, and think that they are being imposed upon. Then he turned to the larger theatre of war and he had his usual exhilarating effect on the House.

[1] Rupert Edward Cecil Lee Guinness, Second Earl of Iveagh, 1874–1967. Conservative Member of Parliament, 1908–10 and 1918–27. Succeeded his father as Earl, 1927. His wife Gwendolen (Countess of Iveagh) succeeded her husband as Member of Parliament for Southend, 1927–35. Their only son was killed in action on active service on 8 February 1945.

[2] Margaret Helen Anderson McEwan, daughter of a Conservative Member of Parliament. She was married to Captain, the Hon. R. Greville, who had died in 1908. In 1922 she was created a Dame of the Order of the British Empire. A society hostess, famous for her fine jewellery. Henry Channon wrote of her in his diary on 4 August 1939: 'She was vituperative about almost everyone'. During the war she lived at the Dorchester Hotel. She died in September 1942. She left many of her jewels to Queen Elizabeth.

[3] In fact, 513 men lost their lives on *Repulse* and 327 on *Prince of Wales* (including Admiral Phillips), a high toll, but less than feared. More than 1,285 men were saved.

Harold Nicolson: letter to his wife
('Diaries with Letters, 1939-1945')

11 December 1941

Winston this morning was very grim and said we must expect 'heavy punishment'. I like him best when he makes that sort of speech. I am full of faith. We simply can't be beaten with America in. But how strange it is that this great event should be recorded and welcomed here without any jubilation. We should have gone mad with joy if it had happened a year ago.

Winston S. Churchill: Oral Answers
(Hansard)

11 December 1941 House of Commons

NATIONAL SERVICE ACTS
(MEMBERS OF PARLIAMENT)

Sir P. Harris (by Private Notice) asked the Prime Minister whether he has any statement to make about the position of Members of Parliament under the National Service Acts?

The Prime Minister (Mr Churchill): Yes, Sir. I am glad to take this opportunity of explaining the position of Members of Parliament under the National Service Acts.

In the view of His Majesty's Government it would not be appropriate to confer on Members of Parliament a statutory exemption from the obligations which they share in common with everyone else. Members of Parliament have, however, also the high duty of service in the Legislature, and they must themselves be the judges of how that duty can best be performed. They are therefore given a free choice by virtue of their position as Members of Parliament and not as a favour. This was the position in the last war, and has always been maintained in the present war. Furthermore, if a Member of Parliament joins the Armed Forces of the Crown, and later decides that he wishes to devote his whole time to Parliamentary duties, arrangements are made for his release from military service for that purpose, provided, of course, that reasonable notice is given to arrange for his relief.

Considering the very large number of Members serving with the Forces, and the many questions that may arise in the combining and reconciling of their duties, it is very satisfactory that there has been so little difficulty in practice.

Mr Bernays:[1] While I thank my right hon. Friend for his reply, which has done so much to clarify the situation, can he say whether, as a result of these National Service Acts, anything has been done to alter the ancient rights and Privileges of Parliament?

The Prime Minister: I think I can safely reassure my hon. Friend on that point.

Mr Gallacher: In view of the favoured position occupied by Members of Parliament in relation to the ordinary citizen, could it not be made a condition that, where Members of Parliament choose Parliament rather than the Forces, they attend Parliament every day and do their duty by their constituents?

The Prime Minister: I do not think the question is one of favour, but rather of the discharge of important duties. Those duties, as I have several times pointed out, are sometimes better discharged by silence than by speech.

Mr Gallacher: It is not a question of silence or speech, but it is notorious that while there is –

Mr Speaker: The hon. Member is giving information, not asking for it.

Mr Gallacher: I will ask for information. I wish to ask the Prime Minister whether he is not aware of the feeling of discontent that exists in the country because of the absenteeism in this House in comparison with the lack of absenteeism in the industries of the country. Will he not see to it that Members attend the House and do their duty? It is not necessary for them to make speeches to do their duty.

The Prime Minister: Some people, by their absence, contribute as much to the progress of our affairs as by their presence.

Winston S. Churchill: speech

(*Hansard*)

11 December 1941 House of Commons

The Prime Minister: A great many things of far-reaching and fundamental importance have happened in the last few weeks. Most of them have happened in the last few days, and I think it opportune, in reply to my right hon. Friend, to give the House the best account I can of where we stand and how we are.

I will begin with the Battle of Libya. A lot of people in easy positions have

[1] Robert Hamilton Bernays, 1902–1945. Educated at Rossall and Worcester College, Oxford. President, Oxford Union, 1925. *News Chronicle* leader-writer, 1925; correspondent in India, 1931; in Germany and Austria, 1934. Liberal MP for Bristol North, 1931–45 (Liberal National after 1936). Parliamentary Secretary, Minister of Health, 1937–9; Ministry of Transport, 1939–40. Deputy Regional Commissioner, Southern Civil Defence Region, 1940–2. Sapper, Royal Engineers, 1942; 2nd Lieutenant, 1943; Captain, 1944. Author of *Naked Fakir: a Study of Gandhi* and *Special Correspondent*. Killed in an aeroplane accident while flying from Italy to Greece, March 1945.

been very much down upon the Military Spokesman in Cairo.[1] They accuse him of having taken unduly favourable views of our position at different dates. I am not going to apologize for the Military Spokesman in Cairo.[1] I have read every day the statements he has made, and I have also read all the reports which come continually from the front. I think the Military Spokesman in Cairo has been pretty well justified in what he has said, having regard to how things stood, or seemed to stand, at each moment when he said it. Of course, it is quite a difficult thing to have a Military Spokesman at all. It would be much more convenient to the military Commander to remain quite silent. But then it is said, 'Are we to know nothing of what is going on? Is it to be kept to a small secret circle? Is nothing to be told to the public, is nothing to be told to the Empire, is nothing to be told to the Army?' Remember, there is a very great army in the Middle East. Only a small part of it is able to fight in this Battle of Libya, but all are watching with very great interest what occurs. I do not think that you could go on the basis of fighting for three weeks or a month with no information being given by our side except in very guarded communiqués, and the only stories being told coming out from the enemy, who are not always entirely truthful in their accounts. Therefore, I am in favour of the Military Spokesman in Cairo, and I think he has discharged an extremely difficult task wisely and well. Also, if anybody based their hopes on what he said, that man would find today that he has not been misled. There might be ups and downs, there might be disappointments, there would certainly be the ebb and flow of battle, but, in the main, news founded upon the daily output of the Military Spokesman would be found to be thoroughly in accordance with where we are at the present time.

It must be remembered that although here at Westminster, and in Fleet Street, it has been sought to establish the rule that nothing must be said about the war and its prospects which is not thoroughly discouraging, and although I must admit that the British public seem to like their food cooked that way, the Military Spokesman, addressing a large Army, might do more harm than good if he always put things at their worst and never allowed buoyancy, hope, confidence and resolve to infect his declarations. There ought to be a fair recognition of the difficulties of a task of that kind. This defence also applies to the admirable official communiqués which have been issued by General Auchinleck's headquarters, which have given a very informing and effective picture of the confused struggle which has been proceeding.

The Libyan offensive did not take the course which its authors expected, though it will reach the end at which they aimed. Very few set-piece battles that have to be prepared over a long period of time work out in the way they are planned and imagined beforehand. The unexpected intervenes at every

[1] Brigadier Shearer. Many Members of Parliament believed that Churchill was talking about his son Randolph.

stage. The will-power of the enemy impinges itself upon the prescribed or hoped-for course of events. Victory is traditionally elusive. Accidents happen. Mistakes are made. Sometimes right things turn out wrong, and quite often wrong things turn out right. War is very difficult especially to those who are taking part in it or conducting it. Still, when all is said and done, on 18th November General Auchinleck set out to destroy the entire armed forces of the Germans and Italians in Cyrenaica, and now, on 11th December, I am bound to say that it seems very probable he will do so. The picture that was made by the Commanders beforehand was of a much more rapid battle than has actually taken place. They had the idea which I expressed to the House, that the whole German armoured forces would be encountered by our armour in a mass at the outset, and that the battle would be decided one way or the other in a few hours. This might have been the best chance for the enemy. However, the sudden surprise and success of our advance prevented any such main trial of strength between the armoured forces. Almost at the first bound we reached right up to Sidi Rezegh, dividing the enemy's armoured forces and throwing them into confusion. In consequence of this, a very large number of fierce, detached actions took place over an immense space of desert country, and the battle, though equally intense, became both dispersed and protracted. It became a widespread and confused battle of extremely high-class combatants, mounted upon mechanized transport and fighting in barren lands with the utmost vigour and determination. The commander of the 21st German Armoured Division, General von Ravenstein, whom we captured, expressed himself very well when he said, 'This warfare is a paradise to the tactician but a nightmare to the quartermaster,'

Although we have large armies standing in the Middle East, we have never been able to apply in our desert advance infantry forces which were numerically equal to those which the enemy had gradually accumulated on the coast. We have always been fighting with smaller numbers pushed out into the desert than he has been able to gather there, over a course of months, in his coastal garrisons. For us the foundation of everything was supply and mechanized transport, and this was provided on what hitherto had been considered a fantastic scale. Also, we have to rely upon our superiority in armour and in the air. But most of all in this struggle everything depended for us upon an absolutely unrelenting spirit of the offensive, not only in the generals but in the troops and in every man. That has been forthcoming; it is still forthcoming. All the troops have fought all the time in every circumstance of fatigue and hardship with one sincere, insatiable desire, to engage the enemy and destroy him if possible, tank for tank, man to man and hand to hand. And this is what has carried us on. But behind all this process working out at so many different points and in so many separate combats has been the persisting will-power of the Commander-in-Chief, General Auchinleck. Without that will-power we might very easily have subsided to the defensive and lost the precious initiative, to which, here in this Libyan theatre, we have for the first time felt ourselves strong enough to make a claim.

The first main crisis of the battle was reached between 24th and 26th November. On the 24th General Auchinleck proceeded to the battle headquarters, and on the 26th he decided to relieve General Cunningham and to appoint Major-General Ritchie, a comparatively junior officer, to the command of the 8th Army in his stead. This action was immediately endorsed by the Minister of State and by myself. General Cunningham has rendered brilliant service in Abyssinia and is also responsible for the planning and organization of the present offensive in Libya, which began, as I have explained, with surprise and with success and which has now definitely turned the corner. He has since been reported by the medical authorities to be suffering from serious overstrain and has been granted sick leave. Since 26th November, therefore, the 8th Army has been commanded, with great vigour and skill, by General Ritchie, but during nearly the whole time General Auchinleck himself has been at the battle headquarters. Although the battle is not yet finished, I have no hesitation in saying that for good or ill it is General Auchinleck's battle. Watching these affairs, as it is my duty to do, from day to day, and often from hour to hour, and seeing the seamy side of the reports as they come in, I have felt my confidence in General Auchinleck grow continually, and although everything is hazardous in war, I believe we have found in him, as we have also found in General Wavell, a military figure of the first order.

The newspapers have given full and excellent accounts of the strangely interspersed fighting in which the British Armoured Corps, the New Zealand Division, the South African Divisions, an Indian Division, the British 70th Division and the rest of the Tobruk garrison, including the Poles, all played an equally valiant and active part.

At the beginning of the offensive I told the House that we should for the first time be fighting the Germans on equal terms in modern weapons. This was quite true. Naturally there have been some unpleasant surprises, and also some awkward things have happened, as might be expected beforehand. Those who fight the Germans fight a stubborn and resourceful foe, a foe in every way worthy of the doom prepared for him. Some of the German tanks carried, as we knew, a six-pounder gun which, though it of course carries many fewer shots, is sometimes more effective than the gun with which our tanks are mainly armed. Our losses in tanks were a good deal heavier than we expected, and it may be that at the outset, before it was disorganized, the enemy's recovery process for damaged vehicles worked better than ours. I am not so sure of it, but it may be so. It is very good at that. However, we had a good superiority in numbers of armoured vehicles, and in the long rough and tumble we gradually obtained mastery so far as the first phase of the battle is concerned.

Our Air Force was undoubtedly superior throughout in numbers and quality to the enemy, and although the Germans have drawn in the most extravagant manner upon reinforcements from many quarters, including the Russian front, that superiority has been more than maintained. The greatest satisfaction is expressed by the troops and by the Military Authorities about the way in which they have been helped and protected by the action of the Royal Air Force. None of the complaints in the previous enterprises have reached us here upon that score. Like other people concerned, I had hoped for a quick decision, but it may well be that this wearing down battle will be found in the end to have inflicted a deeper injury upon the enemy than if it had all been settled by manoeuvre and in a few days. In no other way but in this Libyan attack could a second front have been brought into action under conditions more costly to the enemy and more favourable to ourselves. This will be realized when it is remembered that about a half, and sometimes more than a half, of everything, men, munitions and fuel, which the enemy sends to Africa is sunk before it gets there, by our submarines, cruisers and destroyers, and by the activities of our Air Force, acting both from Libya and from Malta. In this way, the prolongation of the battle may not be without its compensations to us. From the point of view of drawing weight from the vast Russian front, the continuance of the fighting in its severity is not to be regarded as an evil.

The first stage of the battle is now over. The enemy has been driven out of all the positions which barred our westward advance, positions which he had most laboriously fortified. Everything has been swept away except certain pockets at Bardia and Halfaya, which are hopelessly cut off, and will be mopped up, or starved out, in due course. It may be definitely said that Tobruk has been relieved – or, as I prefer to state it, has been disengaged. The enemy, still strong but severely mauled and largely stripped of his armour, is retreating to a defensive line to the west of the Tobruk forts, and the clearance of the approaches to Tobruk, and the establishment of our air power thus far forward to the west in new airfields, enables the great supply depots of Tobruk, which have been carefully built up, to furnish support for the second phase of our offensive, with great economy in our lines of communication. Substantial reinforcements and fresh troops are available close at hand. Many of the units which were most heavily engaged have been relieved and their places taken by others, although we have to keep the numbers down strictly to the level which our vast transportation facilities permit. The enemy, who has fought with the utmost stubbornness and enterprise, has paid the price of his valour, and it may well be that the second phase will gather more easily the fruits of the first than has been our experience in the fighting which has taken place so far. As the House knows, I make it a rule never to prophesy, or to promise, or to guarantee future results, but I will go so far on this occasion as to say that all danger of the Army of the Nile not being able to celebrate Christmas and the New Year in Cairo has been decisively removed.

Before I leave the purely British aspect of the war, I must report to the House the progress of the Battle of the Atlantic. When I last spoke on the subject, I said that in the four months ending with October, making allowance for new building but not for sea captures or United States assistance, the net loss of our Mercantile Marine had been reduced to a good deal less than one-fifth of what it was in the four months ending in June – a tremendous saving. As these were the very months when Hitler had boasted that his strangulation of our seaborne supplies would be at its height, we were entitled to rest with some solid assurance upon that fact. The House was right to treat the fact as of great importance, because these matters of sea power and sea transport involve our lives. The month of November has now gone by, and, without revealing actual figures, I am glad to say that it fully maintained the great recovery of the previous four months. In the first 10 days of this month, we have also found that the progress and position have been well maintained. These are the foundations upon which we live and carry forward our cause.

Now I turn to Russia. Six weeks or a month ago people were wondering whether Moscow would be taken, or Leningrad in the north, or how soon the Germans would overrun the Caucasus and seize the oil fields of Baku. We had to consider what we could do to prepare ourselves on the long line from the Caspian Sea to the Mediterranean. Since then a striking change has become evident. The enormous power of the Russian Armies, and the glorious steadfastness and energy with which they have resisted the frightful onslaught made upon them, have now been made plain. On the top of this has come the Russian winter; and on the top of that, the Russian Air Force. Hitler forced his armies into this barren and devastated land. He has everywhere been brought to a standstill. On a large portion of the front he is in retreat. The sufferings of his troops are indescribable. Their losses have been immense. The cold snow, the piercing wind which blows across the icy spaces, the ruined towns and villages, the long lines of communications, assailed by dauntless guerrilla warriors, the stubborn unyielding resistance with which the Russian soldiers and the Russian people have defended every street, every house, every yard of their country – all these facts have inflicted upon the German armies and the German nation a bloody blow, almost unequalled in the history of war. But this is not the end of the winter; it is the beginning. The Russians have now regained definite superiority in the air over large parts of the front. They have the great cities in which to live. Their soldiers are habituated to the severity of their native climate. They are inspired by the feeling of advance after long retreat and of vengeance after monstrous injury.

In Hitler's launching of the Nazi campaign upon Russia we can already see, after less than six months of fighting, that he made one of the outstanding blunders of history, and the results so far realized constitute an event of cardinal importance in the final decision of the war. Nevertheless, we must remember the great munitions capacities which have been lost to Russia by the German invasion, and our pledges to the Russians for the heavy monthly quotas of tanks, aeroplanes and vital raw materials which we have made. Although, as we can all see, our position has changed in various important ways not all in a favourable direction, we must faithfully and punctually fulfil the very serious undertakings we have made to Russia.

A week ago the three great spheres, Libya, the Atlantic and Russia, would almost have covered the scene of war with which we were concerned. Since then it has taken an enormous and very grave expansion. The Japanese Government, or ruling elements in Japan, have made a cold-blooded, calculated, violent, treacherous attack upon the United States and ourselves. The United States have declared war upon their assailants, and we and the Royal Netherlands Government have done the same. A large part of the Western hemisphere, State after State, Parliament after Parliament, is following the United States. It is a great tribute to the respect for international law and for the independence of less powerful countries which the United States has shown for many years, particularly under the Presidency of Mr Roosevelt, that so many other States in Central and South America and in the West Indies, powerful, wealthy, populous communities, are in the process of throwing in their lot with the great Republic of North America.

It will not stop here. It seems to me quite certain that Japan, when she struck her treacherous and dastardly blow at the United States, counted on the active support of the German Nazis and of the Italian Fascists. It is, therefore, very likely that the United States will be faced with the open hostility of Germany, Italy and Japan. We are in all this too. Our foes are bound by the consequences of their ambitions and of their crimes to seek implacably the destruction of the English-speaking world and all it stands for, which is the supreme barrier against their designs. If this should be their resolve, if they should declare themselves resolved to compass the destruction of the English-speaking world, I know that I speak for the United States as well as for the British Empire when I say that we would all rather perish than be conquered. And on this basis, putting it at its worst, there are quite a lot of us to be killed.

The Generalissimo, Chiang Kai-shek, has sent me a message announcing his decision to declare war against Japan and also against Japan's partners in guilt, Germany and Italy. He has further assured me that the whole of the resources of China are at the disposal of Great Britain and the United States. China's cause is henceforth our cause. The country which has faced the Japanese assault for over four years with undaunted courage is indeed a worthy Ally, and it is as Allies that from now on we will go forward together to victory, not only over Japan alone, but over the Axis and all its works.

The Japanese onslaught has brought upon the United States and Great Britain very serious injuries to our naval power. In my whole experience I do not remember any naval blow so heavy or so painful as the sinking of the *Prince of Wales* and the *Repulse* on Monday last. These two vast, powerful ships constituted an essential feature in our plans for meeting the new Japanese danger as it loomed against us in the last few months. These ships had reached the right point at the right moment and were in every respect suited to the task assigned to them. In moving to attack the Japanese transports and landing-craft which were disembarking the invaders of Siam and Malaya at the Kra Isthmus or thereabouts, Admiral Phillips was undertaking a thoroughly sound, well-considered offensive operation, not indeed free from risk, but not any different in principle from many similar operations we have repeatedly carried out in the North Sea and in the Mediterranean. Both ships were sunk by repeated air attacks by bombers and by torpedo-aircraft. These attacks were delivered with skill and determination. There were two high-level attacks, both of which scored hits, and three waves of torpedo-aircraft of nine in each wave which struck each of our ships with several torpedoes. There is no reason to suppose that any new weapon or explosives were employed or any bombs or torpedoes of exceptional size. The continued waves of attack achieved their purpose, and both ships capsized and sank, having destroyed seven of the attacking aircraft.

The escorting destroyers came immediately to the rescue and have now arrived at Singapore crowded with survivors. There is reason to believe that the loss of life has been less heavy than was at first feared. But I regret that Admiral Sir Tom Phillips is among those reported missing. He was well known to us at Whitehall, and his long service at the Admiralty in a central position as Vice-Chief of the Naval Staff made him many friends, who mourn his loss. Personally, I regarded him as one of the ablest brains in the naval Service, and I feel honoured to have established personal friendship with him. On his way out I was most anxious that he should see General Smuts, and so was he, and a long interview was arranged between that great statesman and a Naval Officer whose long service at or near the summit of the Admiralty had made him acquainted with every aspect of the war. It is a very heavy loss that we have suffered. I hope that in a short time it will be possible to inform the relatives of the many who have safely arrived at Singapore from both these great ships. Still, the loss of life has been most melancholy.

Naturally, I should not be prepared to discuss the resulting situation in the Far East and in the Pacific or the measures which must be taken to restore it. It may well be that we shall have to suffer considerable punishment, but we shall defend ourselves everywhere with the utmost vigour in close cooperation with the United States and the Netherlands. The naval power of Britain and the United States was very greatly superior – and is still largely superior – to the combined forces of the three Axis Powers. But no one must underrate the gravity of the loss which has been inflicted in Malaya and Hawaii, or the power of the new antagonist who has fallen upon us, or the length of time it will take to create, marshal and mount the great force in the Far East which will be necessary to achieve absolute victory.

We have a very hard period to go through, and a new surge of impulse will be required, and will be forthcoming, from everybody. We must, as I have said, faithfully keep our engagements to Russia in supplies, and at the same time we must expect, at any rate for the next few months, that the volume of American supplies reaching Britain and the degree of help given by the United States Navy will be reduced. The gap must be filled, and only our own efforts will fill it. I cannot doubt, however, now that the 130,000,000 people in the United States have bound themselves to this war, that once they have settled down to it and have bent themselves to it – as they will – as their main purpose in life, then the flow of munitions and of aid of every kind will vastly exceed anything that could have been expected on the peace-time basis that has ruled up to the present. Not only the British Empire now but the United States are fighting for life; Russia is fighting for life, and China is fighting for life. Behind these four great combatant communities are ranged all the spirit and hopes of all the conquered countries in Europe, prostrate under the cruel domination of the foe. I said the other day that four-fifths of the human race were on our side. It may well be an under-statement. Just these gangs and cliques of wicked men and their military or party organizations have been able to bring these hideous evils upon mankind. It would indeed bring shame upon our generation if we did not teach them a lesson which will not be forgotten in the records of a thousand years.

Admiral of the Fleet Sir Roger Keyes: May I first of all express my grief at the loss of an old friend, Admiral Sir Tom Phillips? May I ask the Prime Minister whether, in view of the very grave anxiety in this House and throughout the country at the loss of His Majesty's Ship *Prince of Wales* and His Majesty's Ship *Repulse*, and in view of the erroneous deductions which appear to have been drawn from that misfortune, he can given an assurance that his expert advisers are still of the opinion that the battleship is still the foundation of sea power, and that they are confident that the *Prince of Wales* was as well protected against under-water and air attack as the *Bismarck*.

Mr Speaker: I do not think this is the occasion to discuss that.

Sir R. Keyes: With all respect to you, Mr Speaker, I am asking the question in order to allay the anxiety of the people.

Mr Speaker: I think the hon. and gallant Member is raising a quite different issue. The Prime Minister has made a statement, and what the hon. and gallant Member now wishes to raise would mean a prolonged discussion, and we could hardly go into that.

Sir R. Keyes: I accept your Ruling, Mr Speaker, but I would like to ask the Prime Minister whether it is a fact that these ships were acting without the support of land-based or seaborne fighters?

The Prime Minister: I will give a fuller account when full reports have been received, but I do not think my hon. and gallant Friend ought to be in too great a hurry to assume that the friend to whom he has just paid a tribute –

who was a most skilful naval officer – acted otherwise than on sound naval lines.

Sir R. Keyes: I am not suggesting for one moment that he did.

Sir Hugh O'Neill: Is the Prime Minister satisfied that these great ships had sufficient air protection escort, and can he say whether the seven aircraft destroyed were destroyed by anti-aircraft or by our own aeroplanes?

The Prime Minister: They were destroyed by anti-aircraft fire.

Major-General Sir Alfred Knox: Have we adequate aircraft for the Navy?

The Prime Minister: We have only a certain amount of aircraft to meet the many engagements which we have to face. We certainly sent as many reinforcements as we could many months ago to the waters where we anticipated this new danger. I cannot say that our Air Force anywhere is as strong as I would like to see it. Although I had not intended to go into details, it is early days to form an opinion of this episode. I understand it was not possible for shore-based aircraft to give the support to the ships that had been hoped for, because of the attack which had been made on their aerodromes. The Admiral proceeded on the basis that clouds which were very low afforded effective protection for the offensive stroke that was made. For a certain period in the operation a rift in the clouds enabled the ships to be discerned, and on the way back conditions became favourable to air attack. I cannot, however, give any undertaking that occasions may not arise when ships may not have to engage without having either carrier support or being so close to the land that they can have effective shore-based air support. That is a matter which has to be judged on the spot by the responsible officers, and my opinion, on expert authority, is that what was done was rightly and wisely done and risked in the circumstances.

Mr Bellenger: May I ask for your guidance, Mr Speaker? The Prime Minister has made a statement, with much of which the House will have great sympathy and perhaps be in agreement, but with certain features of which some hon. Members may disagree. Although I do not ask for the possibility of debating that statement, if the Prime Minister makes controversial statements, as, for example, when he discussed the Cairo spokesman, is there not to be some opportunity for hon. Members to express their opinions and perhaps to offer a few observations to the Prime Minister on the matter?

Mr Speaker: I am now concerned only with the question before the House. Other occasions arise when there can be full Debate, but this is not the occasion for that.

The Prime Minister: With the leave of the House, may I say that I thought I was meeting the wishes of the House in making this statement? I thought I was being respectful to the House and following a course which it approved. I could quite easily have made the statement on the broadcast, and then I should not have been exposed to questions. I am always in the hands of the

House. If hon. Members wish me to make these statements to them, I shall be delighted to do so, but if hon. Members think I had better not, I will wait until some other time.

Mr Bellenger: I should have liked to put one or two points to the Prime Minister. I submit to you, Mr Speaker, that this is an important matter. The fortunes of our country are at stake. I suggest to you that in future, although we would welcome statements by the Prime Minister, they should be put on a regular basis so that other Members may have an opportunity of expressing their views briefly on what the Prime Minister has said.

Winston S. Churchill to President Franklin D. Roosevelt
(Churchill papers, 20/46)

11 December 1941

I see reports that Admiral Leahy is to leave Vichy. Am most anxious to discuss with you offering Vichy blessings or cursings on the morrow of a victory in Libya. Trust your link with Pétain will not be broken meanwhile. We have no other worthwhile connection.

President Franklin D. Roosevelt to Winston S. Churchill
(Churchill papers, 20/46)

11 December 1941
Personal

Delighted to have you here at the White House. Impossible for me to leave country during intensive mobilization and clarification naval action in Pacific.

I know you will bear in mind that the production and allocation problems can and will be worked out with complete understanding and accord. We shall have to use allotted planes for about three weeks but hope to resume schedule of shipments to you and Russia by January first. Practically all other Lease-Lend articles are continuing to be shipped. Details of production and allocation can be handled at long range.

Naval situation and other matters of strategy require discussion.

My one reservation is great personal risk to you. Believe this should be given most careful consideration for the Empire needs you at the helm and we need you there too.

The news is bad but it will be better.

Warm regards,
Roosevelt

Winston S. Churchill to Clement Attlee and Lord Woolton
(*Churchill papers, 20/36*)

12 December 1941

POSSIBLE REDUCTION IN RATIONS

It would be a mistake, in my opinion, to announce these restrictions now. It would savour of panic. Our position has immeasurably improved by the full involvement of the United States. The reserves are good. We have no longer any need to strike attitudes to win United States' sympathy, we are all in it together, and they are eating better meals than we are.

I trust no announcements of this character will be made in the immediate future, and I hope I may be consulted before any final decision is taken by the War Cabinet.

Winston S. Churchill to President Franklin D. Roosevelt
(*Churchill papers, 20/46*)

12 December 1941
Most Secret and Personal

1. We feel it necessary to divert 18th Division now rounding the Cape in your transports to Bombay to reinforce army we are forming against Japanese invasion of Burma and Malaya. I hope you will allow your ships to take them there instead of to Suez. Route is both shorter and safer.

2. Our previous telegrams. Thank you so much. Hope rendezvous will be about 21st. I am enormously relieved at turn world events have taken.

Winston S. Churchill to King George VI
(*Churchill papers, 20/20*)

12 December 1941

Sir,

I realized how deeply Your Majesty would feel the loss of your two splendid ships. Quite apart from personal sorrow it is a very heavy blow, and our combinations formed in the Far East with so much difficulty from limited resources are disrupted.

I shall look forward to discussing the new situation with Your Majesty at luncheon today.

Taking it altogether, I am enormously relieved at the extraordinary changes of the last few days.

I remain
Your Majesty's devoted servant,
Winston S. Churchill

Winston S. Churchill to Field Marshal Smuts
(Churchill papers, 20/46)

12 December 1941
Most Secret

1. I must express to you my admiration for the brilliant part played by the South African Divisions in the Libyan battle, and with you I grieve for the serious losses they have suffered. It looks now as if this battle is working out all right.

2. Pacific situation is most serious. We are doing all in our power to restore it. Entry of United States makes amends for all and makes the end certain. Am doing utmost to concert action with them.

3. I am so glad you saw Tom Phillips before he met a sailor's death.

Kindest regards,

Winston S. Churchill to John Curtin
(Churchill papers, 20/46)

12 December 1941
Secret and Personal

1. No one will realize better than you how grievous the loss of our two ships is to me. It has temporarily ruptured our whole scheme of naval deterrence, and we are now making other plans with straitened resources. We think Japanese will go for Philippines, Burma and Singapore, and we are doing our best to reinforce at all points.

2. Accession of United States as full war partner makes amends for all and makes the end certain. Am taking all possible measures to concert action with them.

All good wishes,

Winston S. Churchill to General Wavell
(*Churchill papers, 20/49*)

12 December 1941

1. You must now look east. Burma is now placed under your command. You must resist the Japanese advance towards Burma and India and try to cut their communications down the Malay Peninsula. We are diverting 18th Division, now rounding Cape, to Bombay, together with four fighter squadrons of the RAF, now *en route* for Caucasus, Caspian theatre. We are also sending you a special hamper of AA and AT guns, some of which are already *en route*. You should retain 17th Indian Division for defence against the Japanese. Marry these forces as you think best and work them into the eastern fighting front to the highest advantage.

2. It is proposed at a convenient moment in the near future by arrangement between you and Auchinleck to transfer Iraq and Persia to the Cairo Command. The Russian victories and Auchinleck's Libyan advance have for the time being relieved danger of German irruption into the Syrian-Iraq-Persian theatre. The danger may revive, but we have other more urgent dangers to meet.

3. I hope these new dispositions arising from the vast changes in the world situation of the last four days will commend themselves to you. I shall endeavour to feed you with armour, aircraft and white personnel to the utmost possible, having regard to the great strain we are under. Pray cable me fully your views and needs. All good wishes.

Winston S. Churchill to Anthony Eden
(*Churchill papers, 20/46*)

12 December 1941
Personal and Most Secret

The loss of the *Prince of Wales* and *Repulse* together with United States losses at Pearl Harbor gives Japanese full battle-fleet command of Pacific. They can attack with any force overseas at any point. Happily area is so vast that the use of their power can only be partial and limited. We think they will go for Philippines, Singapore and the Burma Road. It will be many months before effective superiority can be regained through completion of British and American new battleships. The United States, under shock of Pacific disaster and war declaration, have embargoed everything for the present. I hope to loosen this up, but in present circumstances with a Russian victory and our new dangers we cannot make any promises beyond our agreed quota of supplies. You should point out what a grievous drain the airplanes are to us with all these demands for fighters in the East. On the other hand, accession of United States makes amends for all and with time and patience will give certain victory.

We telegraphed to you yesterday Chiefs of Staff's opinion, with which I concur, about asking Russia to involve herself with Japan. This can only be done when Russia feels strong enough. Victory on the European battlefield must have priority in our minds. This view, however, does not bind United States.

Am just off.

Winston S. Churchill to Anthony Eden
(*Churchill papers, 20/46*)

12 December 1941

Add to my last:

In view of evident strong wish of United States, China, and I expect Australia, that Russia should come in against Japan, you should not do anything to discourage a favourable movement if Stalin feels strong enough to do so. All I meant was that we should not put undue pressure upon him, considering how little we have been able to contribute.

Winston S. Churchill to the Governor[1] and defenders of Hong Kong
(*Churchill papers, 20/49*)

12 December 1941

We are all watching day by day and hour by hour your stubborn defence of the port and fortress of Hong Kong. You guard a link between the Far East and Europe long famous in world civilization. We are sure that the defence of Hong Kong against barbarous and unprovoked attack will add a glorious page to British annals.

All our hearts are with you in your ordeal. Every day of your resistance brings nearer our certain final victory.

[1] Sir Mark Young, a Colonial civil servant who had served in Ceylon, Sierra Leone, Palestine, Barbados, and Trinidad and Tobago. From 1938 to 1941 he had been Governor and Commander-in-Chief of the Tanganyika Territory. Taken prisoner by the Japanese in Hong Kong, he remained in Japanese captivity until 1945.

Winston S. Churchill to General Auchinleck
(*Premier papers, 3/290/1*)

12 December 1941
Personal and Secret to you and Minister of State
To be decyphered by General Auchinleck's Personal Staff

1. The great changes in world situation during last four days require a review of our affairs.[1] I must ask you to spare 18th Division now rounding Cape for diversion to Bombay. This seems justified by improved prospects of your battle, and even more by very decided Russian successes, which relieve our immediate anxieties in Caucasus and south of Caspian. It is required by grievous need of strengthening long-starved India and enabling a stronger resistance to be made to Japanese advance against Burma and down Malay Peninsula. Easement in Persia and Iraq makes you freer to use remainder of 50th Division from Baghdad or 5th Indian Division in Cyprus if you need them. Nothing must, of course, prejudice 'Crusader', and I hope that even with this diversion of 18th Division you will be able to pursue 'Acrobat' and keep 'Gymnast' in mind dependent on Vichy or French North African reactions to a Libyan victory.

2. It is proposed that your command should be extended eastwards to cover Iraq and Persia, thus giving local unity of command in event of Turkish and Caucasus danger reviving. This change will only be effected as convenient between you and Wavell.

3. Wavell must now look east. He will be given command of the Burma front. He will be reinforced by 18th Division, which he can work to eastward to best advantage as he chooses and will keep 17th Indian Division. Four aircraft squadrons, now rounding Cape for the Caucasus will go to India.[2] We are also sending a special hamper of AA and AT guns, some of which are already *en route*.

4. Japanese war having broken out and American and British battleship strengths being so gravely reduced, Hong Kong is isolated and must fight to the end. We cannot tell how America will fare at Manila, observing that Japanese have battle-fleet command of all these waters, though they cannot do everything at once. Brooke-Popham's command is therefore reduced to Malay Peninsula, Singapore and Borneo.

5. Pownall is with you in Cairo. We think that, in view of impending

[1] Churchill originally dictated at this point, but crossed out in the telegram as sent: 'I am going to Washington with Pound, Portal and others to confer with President on general layout of Anglo-American plans and our own allocations.' (Draft Telegram, *Churchill papers, 20/46*)

[2] Churchill originally dictated at this point, but crossed out in the telegram as sent: 'probably at Karachi, for offensive action against Japanese approach'.

extension of your command, he might relieve General Arthur Smith[1] as your CGS. Would this accord with your views? This depends upon whether he is needed for Singapore, on which we are enquiring.

6. Disclosure of Cunningham supersession passed off very well here, being, in fact, submerged by larger events. Please continue to send me your personal appreciations, which I greatly value. I am so glad things are going well in your grand campaign. Try increasingly to mention names of regiments about which enemy is already informed. It gives so much satisfaction here.

Winston S. Churchill: Note[2]

(*Churchill papers, 23/9*)

12 December 1941
Secret

SUPPLIES TO RUSSIA AND THE PERSIAN GULF

I understand there has been doubt on the interpretation of the respective responsibilities of the Allied Supplies Executive and of the War Office regarding the development and maintenance of supply routes in the Persian Gulf area. These were stated in paragraphs (2) and (9) of my previous Note (WP (G) (41) 111).

In order to clear this doubt it should be understood that the War Office have complete control of the railways and roads in the Persian Gulf area. The Allied Supplies Executive may at any time ask for the allocation of capacity on these routes for carrying supplies to Russia, but the responsibility for the development and maintenance of the routes rests entirely with the War Office.

[1] Arthur Francis Smith, 1890–1977. Joined the Coldstream Guards, 1910. On active service, 1914–18 (wounded thrice, Distinguished Service Order, Military Cross, Croix de Guerre). Brigadier, General Staff, British Troops in Egypt, 1938–39). Chief of the General Staff, Middle East, 1940–41. Knighted, 1942. General Officer Commanding London District, 1942–44. General Officer Commanding-in-chief, Persia and Iraq Command, 1944–45; Eastern Command, India, 1945–46. Chief of the General Staff, India, 1946; Deputy Commander-in-Chief, India, 1947. Commander of the British forces in India and Pakistan, November 1947. Lieutenant of the Tower of London, 1948–51.

[2] Circulated to the War Cabinet as War Cabinet Paper No. 153 of 1941.

Winston S. Churchill: Memorandum
(*Churchill papers, 23/9*)

12 December 1941
Secret

THE FUNCTIONS OF THE CHANCELLOR OF THE DUCHY OF LANCASTER AS RESIDENT MINISTER OF CABINET RANK AT SINGAPORE FOR FAR EASTERN AFFAIRS

1. The Chancellor of the Duchy of Lancaster has been appointed Resident Minister of Cabinet rank at Singapore for Far Eastern Affairs. He will serve under and report directly to the War Cabinet, through its Secretary.

2. The Chancellor of the Duchy will preside over a War Council, which will consist of –[1]

The Officer Commanding Australian Troops will be invited to attend when he is in Singapore, and will be informed when matters affecting Australia are to be discussed.

(The addition of other members to the Council may later be found necessary).

3. The limits of the geographical sphere within which the Chancellor of the Duchy will operate will coincide with the geographical sphere of the Military Commander-in-Chief. In practice, however, in the present situation the Chancellor of the Duchy's activities are likely to be mainly confined to Malaya.

4. The principal task of the Chancellor of the Duchy will be to assist the successful conduct of operations in the Far East –

(a) by relieving the Commanders-in-Chief as far as possible of those extraneous responsibilities with which they have hitherto been burdened, and

(b) by giving them broad political guidance.

5. The Chancellor of the Duchy's functions will also include the settlement of emergency matters on the spot, where time does not permit of reference home. He will develop a local clearing-house for the prompt settlement of minor routine matters which would otherwise have to be referred to separate Departments at home. On all matters on which he requires special guidance he will, provided there is time, refer the matter home. He will in any case report constantly to His Majesty's Government.

6. Similarly, while expenditure remains the responsibility of the appropriate Minister at home and departmental representatives on the spot concerned with expenditure will work under existing delegated powers, referring home

[1] The Governor of the Straits Settlements, The Commander-in-Chief, Far East, The Naval Commodore, The Air Officer Commanding, The General Officer Commanding, The Director of Propaganda for the Far East.

to their Departments as may be necessary, the Chancellor of the Duchy is authorized to act at his own discretion by giving overriding authority to departmental officers to incur expenditure when satisfied that urgent action is necessary and that there is no time to refer home. He will then immediately report the action which has been taken. Such action will rarely be necessary where large financial commitments are involved.

7. The appointment of the Chancellor of the Duchy does not, of course, in any way impair the existing responsibilities of the Commanders-in-Chief, or His Majesty's Representatives in the Far East, or their official relationships with their respective Departments at home, with whom they will continue to correspond direct.

8. The Chancellor of the Duchy will take steps to establish liaison with the Governments of the Commonwealth of Australia and of New Zealand.

9. The Chancellor of the Duchy is being asked to submit a report as soon as sufficient experience of the working of the system has been gained. In particular he will report on the scope and geographical sphere of the functions which he can usefully perform in present circumstances.

Winston S. Churchill to Anthony Eden

(*Churchill papers, 20/46*)

12 December 1941

Before you left you asked for views of COS on the question whether it would be to our advantage for Russia to declare war on Japan. COS considered views are as follows:

(a) Russian declaration of war on Japan would be greatly to our advantage provided, but only provided, that the Russians are confident that it would not impair their western front either now or next Spring.

(b) Considerations which have weighed with us are as follows:

(c) Advantages:

(i) Extension of ABCD[1] to include Russia would lower morale, complicate strategy, and hasten exhaustion, of Japan;

(ii) Japanese are known to dread air attacks from Vladivostok area on their towns, which are particularly vulnerable naval bases and industry. United States Under-Secretary of State has suggested use by Americans of Russian air bases, though not necessarily expressing the views of the American Chiefs of Staff or appreciating the maintenance and supply difficulties entailed since the Vladivostok supply route would be closed;

[1] America, Britain, China and the Dutch East Indies.

(iii) Russia possesses in the Pacific about 100 submarines (about half of which are suitable for long-distance patrols), which would contain substantial proportion of Japanese destroyers;

(iv) Russia should be able to engage Japan the more easily now that there are concrete signs that Germany is beginning to stabilize on the Russian front, except possibly in the south, and pressure is likely to weaken.

(v) Japanese, by operations based on Siam, may cut the Burma Road. This would result in a serious weakening of Chinese resistance and would lead eventually to the release of Japanese forces for employment against Russia. By striking now the Russians would anticipate this threat.

(d) Disadvantages:

(i) We have not sufficient information about Russian resources to be certain that war with Japan would not prejudice Russia's ability to –

(a) interfere with German efforts to stabilize during the winter, and

(b) prepare for full-scale operations in the spring;

(ii) We do not know whether Russia would be strong enough to withstand such land and air attacks as Japan would be bound to launch against Maritime Provinces if bombing attacks on Japan from Russian bases were proving effective;

(iii) Vladivostok supply route would be closed (whereas Japan, if wishing to avoid a *casus belli*, might have hesitated to interfere with Russian and neutral shipping using it).

2. If your discussions lead you to the opinion that the Russians would be prepared to declare war on Japan, it is for consideration whether the exercise of any pressure required should be by the Americans rather than ourselves. It may be that the Russians would attempt to secure some *quid pro quo* which it might be more expedient for the Americans to concede.

3. This appreciation raises the following questions:

(a) What air and land forces have the Russians in the Far East and what is the Russian estimate of the Japanese forces against which they would have to contend?

(b) How high do the Russians assess their ability as regards both trained personnel and equipment to maintain a war on two fronts, as the Vladivostok route would be closed?

(c) Have the Russians plans for striking at the mainland of Japan by air?

(d) Would the Russians welcome or facilitate the use of their bases in the Far East by the Americans.

Colonel Harvie-Watt to Winston S. Churchill
(Harvie-Watt papers)

12 December 1941

There has been a certain amount of 'Lobby talk' regarding your broadcast on Monday night last. It was generally felt that you had been ill-advised to undertake that task, as it appeared to Members – and they had received similar expressions of opinion from constituents – that you were very tired,[1] and in consequence, your speech did not have the full effect it might have had.

Your speech on the War Situation on Thursday was first-class, and the House was delighted with what you said. There has, however, been some discussion as to why in your survey of the world situation you referred at such length to the Cairo Spokesman. Members considered it would have been better to have left this point alone, as it tended to strengthen the rumour which has been prevalent in the House for some time, that the Cairo Spokesman is the Junior Member for Preston.[2] There was also some expression of regret about your remark that you could well have made your statement on the broadcast, when you would not have been exposed to questions.

Ian Jacob: diary
(Ian Jacob papers)

12 December 1941

Once again we found ourselves setting out in the Prime Minister's special train, this time at 10.30 p.m. from Euston. The party was larger than last time when we went to the Atlantic Meeting, but in essentials it was the same. The main addition was Lord Beaverbrook and his retinue. Lord Beaverbrook has his private saloon on the train, and had a dinner party there before the train started. We got the luggage all stowed away before the Prime Minister arrived. It was generally given out that the party was to be headed by Lord Beaverbrook and that the Prime Minister was going to see him off. So well was this fiction maintained, that after we sailed Sharpe[3] was amazed when I told him that the Prime Minister was on board. Lance Bombardier Mary Churchill of the ATS came up in the train to see us off, and she and Mrs Hill the stenographer were the last to leave the ship when we sailed.

[1] Churchill put a circle around the words 'very tired' and noted in the margin: 'Well, who forced me? & why am I not allowed a gramophone record of a statement in the House.'

[2] Churchill's son Randolph. Churchill noted in the margin: 'This is not true. A question sh'd be put to S of S for War who sh'd give the lie or at best deny the rumour. Luckily they will all soon be going home.'

[3] Group Captain A.C.H. Sharp, one of the four Air Ministry personnel, accompanying Sir Charles Portal.

Winston S. Churchill to Sir Edward Bridges
(*Churchill papers, 20/36*)

12 December 1941
Most Secret

PRIME MINISTER'S VISIT TO THE UNITED STATES

Nothing should be published or admitted till we get to the other side. I thought that in about a week we would give you the OK to tell the Dominion Prime Ministers. Meanwhile, if the rumours become tiresome, the Minister of Information should tell the editors why we are absent from London. He should scrupulously avoid any mention of dates, landing-points or method of travel.

Winston S. Churchill to James Stuart and David Margesson
(*Churchill papers, 20/36*)

13 December 1941

I understand there is no truth whatever in the rumour that my son was the Military Spokesman at Cairo. If this is so, as I am sure it is, a question should be arranged to be asked next week: 'Who is the Military Spokesman?' to which the answer should be given. I believe it is Brigadier Shearer. As I have defended him most whole-heartedly there is no reason why his name should not be known. The occasion should be taken to pay a compliment to his abilities, which are altogether exceptional.

Winston S. Churchill to Anthony Eden
(*Churchill papers, 20/46*)

13 December 1941
Secret

Possibility of asking Russian Government to lend us portion of their Far Eastern submarine fleet has been considered, but rejected owing to impossibility of finding crews. If, however, Russians would lend us both submarines and crews to sail under British flag and orders, this would be different.

Winston S. Churchill to Anthony Eden
(*Churchill papers, 20/46*)

13 December 1941
Personal and Secret

It may well be that recent successes on the Russian front may make Stalin more willing to face a war with Japan. The situation is changing from day to day in our favour and you must judge on the spot how far and how hard it is wise to press him.

Winston S. Churchill to General Ismay
(*Cabinet papers, 69/3*)

13 December 1941

Reference your minute of December 12.[1]

I am hoping to make an offer, blessing or cursing, to Pétain in the names of Great Britain and United States. I do not think this prospect would be marred by a Free French descent upon Miquelon and St Pierre. It would be more convenient if it happened after an Anglo-American ultimatum has been delivered and rejected, but if you feel that it is better to unmuzzle Muselier now, I am prepared to consent.

Winston S. Churchill to Clement Attlee, and to General Ismay for the Chiefs of Staff Committee
(*Churchill papers, 20/36*)

13 December 1941

We have assumed responsibility for the defence of Malaya, Burma and India. Hitherto they have not been menaced, and we have not had the resources.

Pray do all in your power to get men and materials moving into India, and reinforce with air from the Middle East as soon as the battle in Libya is decided in our favour. An effort should be made to send armoured vehicles at the earliest moment after a Libyan decision.

[1] About authorization for Admiral Muselier to rally St Pierre and Miquelon to Free France.

Winston S. Churchill to Lord Linlithgow[1]
(*Churchill papers, 20/49*)

13 December 1941

1. You will have seen my various telegrams to Wavell, Duff Cooper and Dorman-Smith.[2]

2. We shall do everything in our power to support you, though you will realize how much our resources are strained. Hope 18th Division with all its modern equipment will give Wavell something in hand to use as is thought best, alone or intermingled with Indian forces.

3. This is no time, when Japanese armies are approaching Burma and India, to embark on constitutional changes, and I hope you will give no countenance to any proposals without giving the Cabinet full notice beforehand. Mr Rajagopalachari[3] ought to take up his duties as Premier of Madras if he wants to have 'real power'. At present he has deserted his post at caucus bidding, in the face of the enemy. I could not be responsible for constitutional changes involving legislation in the present crisis.

All good wishes,

Winston S. Churchill to L. S. Amery and Sir Edward Bridges
(*Churchill papers, 20/36*)

13 December 1941

The Viceroy should be warned that no change in our policy can be made without full Cabinet discussion beforehand, and that he should in no way lend himself to any of these overtures at this stage.

The ex-Premier of Madras had the whole Government of that vast province in his hands. At the order of the Congress caucus, he threw it down and deserted his post in the heat of war. The dangers of bombardment and invasion are now very near India. The Japanese are at the gates. Let Mr Rajagopalachari resume his responsible duties before prating about 'real power'.

Personally I would rather accord India independence than that we should have to keep an army there to hold down the fighting races for the benefit of the Hindu priesthood and caucus.

I do not see any prospect of changing the declared policy on which we have

[1] Viceroy of India.

[2] Governor of Burma.

[3] Shrinivas Prasonna Rajagopalachari, 1883–1963. Advocate, High Court, Madras, 1906. Joined the Mysore Civil Service, 1906; Assistant Private Secretary to the Maharaja of Mysore, 1919–27. First Member of Council, 1935. Home Minister and Vice-President, Executive Council, Gwalior State. Knighted 1945. Government Director, Central Board, Imperial Bank of India, 1949–53.

agreed during the war, and I should not be myself prepared to take the responsibility of throwing India into confusion or of burdening the House of Commons with legislation of a highly controversial character.

Winston S. Churchill to Reginald Dorman-Smith
(*Churchill papers, 20/49*)

13 December 1941
Personal and Secret

Wavell has been placed in charge of military and air defence of Burma. We have diverted 18th Division, four fighter squadrons and AA and AT guns, which were rounding the Cape, to Bombay for him to use as he thinks best. The battle in Libya goes well, but I cannot move any air from there till decision is definitely reached. All preparations are being made to transfer four to six bomber squadrons to your theatre the moment battle is won.

Every good wish,

Winston S. Churchill to Alfred Duff Cooper
(*Churchill papers, 20/49*)

13 December 1941
Personal and Secret

Deprecate publicity till Pownall arrives. Meanwhile, you have Percival,[1] whom you may put in charge temporarily if need be.

2. We are sending 18th Division, now rounding Cape, and four fighter Squadrons and some AA and AT[2] guns to Wavell to use to best advantage. Libyan battle goes well, but till we have a definite decision I cannot withdraw anything from there. All arrangements are being made to transfer four to six bomber squadrons to your theatre at earliest possible moment thereafter.

3. The German armies have sustained what is already little short of a disaster in front of Moscow and to the south, and Russian counter-attacks and winter conditions may produce a military catastrophe for Hitler. Entry of United States as full partner seems to me decisive on final result.

[1] Arthur Ernest Percival, 1887–1966. A clerk in a City office in London, 1907–14. On active service, 1914–18 (DSO, Military Cross, wounded). Served in North Russia, 1919 (bar to DSO), and in Ireland, 1920–2 (OBE, despatches twice). General Staff Officer, Malaya, 1936–8. Brigadier, General Staff, 1st Corps, British Expeditionary Force, France, September 1939 to February 1940. Assistant Chief of the Imperial General Staff, 1940. General Officer Commanding 44th (Home Counties) Division, 1940–1. CB, 1941. General Officer Commanding, Malaya, May 1941. Surrendered to the Japanese, 15 February 1942. Released from captivity in Manchuria, August 1945. Present on board USS *Missouri* for the Japanese surrender. In 1947 he published *The War in Malaya*.

[2] Anti-aircraft and Anti-tank guns.

4. Am very glad you are where you are, and I am sure there will be a record defence pending re-establishment of naval power.

Give my love to Diana.[1]

Winston S. Churchill to Lord Halifax
(*Churchill papers, 20/47*)

13 December 1941
Personal and Secret

I see no objection to full publicity once we have arrived. Indeed, there are great advantages in it on both sides of the ocean. I have no doubt quite good plans can be made for return either by sea or by air with a wide choice of ports and islands. Don't worry about it at all.

Give my regards to Harry. Looking forward to seeing you.

Winston S. Churchill to Admiral Pound[2]
(*Churchill papers, 20/36*)

13 December 1941
Secret

No doubt, now that you have the two aircraft carriers coming to you, you will use the whole crew of the *Ark Royal* to man one of them. Thus a perfect organization of men, thoroughly versed in the carrier work, will take over a brand-new ship. Up to the present they have been having their leave. They could move on board wholesale. This ought to save you time in getting the carrier efficient. You would begin with a perfectly trained ship's company.

2. What will be done about the crews of the *Prince of Wales* and *Repulse*, the bulk of whom are at Singapore? Is it true there is a cruiser, the *Capetown*, in Ceylon from which all the men have been taken for other necessary purposes? If so, here is a means of manning the *Capetown*.

3. Should not these ideas, especially the first, be sent to the Second Sea Lord?[3] Perhaps it has all been done already.

[1] Lady Diana Olivia Winifred Maud Manners, 1892–1986. Daughter of the 8th Duke of Rutland. In 1919 she married Alfred Duff Cooper (later Viscount Norwich). After her husband's death in 1954 she was known as Lady Diana Cooper.

[2] This was Churchill's first Minute dictated on board ship, while on his way to the United States. It was given the designation M(A) 1.

[3] William Jock Whitworth, 1884–1973. On active service in the First World War (DSO). Vice-Admiral, Commanding Battle Cruiser Squadron, 1939–41. In command of HMS *Warspite* at the Battle of Narvik, 1940. Knighted, 1941. Second Sea Lord, 1941–44. Admiral, 1943. Commander in Chief, Rosyth, 1944–46.

Winston S. Churchill to Admiral Pound
(*Churchill papers, 20/36*)

13 December 1941
Secret

1. I approve the proposal to form a force of four aircraft carriers, namely: *Indomitable, Illustrious, Formidable* and *Hermes*, as soon as possible for action in the Indian Ocean. I agree that Admiral Somerville should come home to organize this form of warfare, and that Admiral Syfret shall take his place, commanding Force H at Gibraltar. What cruisers do you propose to attach to the carriers? When is it expected they will be able to act together? Where will they be based? What part are the *Revenge, Royal Sovereign*, and *Ramillies* to play? Do you still intend to send *Resolution* to join them?

2. It seems of highest consequence to try to hold positions on each side of the Straits of Malaya, and if this is impossible at least on each side of the Straits of Sunda. Where should these troops come from, and how can they be moved?

3. It is most important to have control of Madagascar and the Mozambique Channel. I do not think 'Truncheon'[1] should be used for that purpose. It would take too long for 'Truncheon' to get there, and it may be needed elsewhere. It would be natural to use the South African troops now in Egypt or Libya. One of the divisions needs a rest after their hard fighting. They would be employed near South Africa in an island of great South African interest. They could recuperate there, and be relieved later on by some brigades of KAR, which are or will be spare. Empty shipping returning from Suez could easily carry this expedition. The date of occupation could be advanced by the shortening of the voyage. I could urge this upon General Smuts, if desired.

When you have got the base in Madagascar, how do you propose to use it? Are you going to base cruisers or destroyers upon it? Is your main object the freeing of the Mozambique Channel from U-boats?

Best of all would be if Vichy could be persuaded to throw in their lot with us, and hand over this base.

4. This is one of the main points I wish to put to the President. I hope we may make together a joint offer of blessing or cursing to Vichy, or failing Vichy, to French North Africa.

We cannot tell yet how France will have been affected by the American entry. There are also the hopes of favourable reactions from a Libyan victory. Above all, the growing disaster of the German armies in Russia will influence all minds. It may well be that an American offer to land an American Expeditionary Force at Casablanca, added to the aid we can give under

[1] A combined Operations raid, planned for January 1942, on the Italian port of Livorno (Leghorn).

'Gymnast', would decide the action of French North Africa (and incidentally Madagascar). At any rate, it is worth trying. I don't want any changes in our dispositions about 'Gymnast' or 'Truncheon' until we know what the reply of Vichy will be.

It must be borne in mind that the United States would be generally favourable to North and West Africa as a major theatre of American operations.

John Martin: diary
(*John Martin papers*)

14 December 1941 [HMS *Duke of York*]

At sea. Southerly gale. Unpleasant motion; but I survived the day. Making poor progress in these unhealthy 'Bloody Foreland' waters.

Sir Charles Wilson: notes
(*Contemporary Medical Archives Centre*)

14 December 1941 [HMS *Duke of York*]

The men went to action stations in the morning but it turned out to be one of our own aircraft.

John Martin: diary
(*John Martin papers*)

15 December 1941 [HMS *Duke of York*]

At sea. Still stormy and impossible to get on deck. Only half our proper speed.

Winston S. Churchill to J. V. Stalin
(*Churchill papers, 20/50*)

15 December 1941

Am proceeding to confer with President Roosevelt on our joint plans. From Washington I will cable you fully on situation. I will establish contact with M. Litvinov,[1] assuming this to be your wish.

It is impossible to describe the relief with which I have heard each successive day of the wonderful victories on the Russian front.[2] I have never felt so sure of the outcome of the war.

Winston S. Churchill to John Curtin
(*Churchill papers, 20/47*)

15 December 1941
Personal and Most Secret

Fullest opportunity for knowing all the essential facts and putting forward suggestions and views will be afforded to Page. You will realize that decisions have to be taken rapidly.

2. We have diverted 18th Division plus four fighter air squadrons plus AA and AT guns, which were rounding the Cape for Middle East, to Bombay. We have placed defence Burma under Wavell. General Pownall is relieving Brooke-Popham, who is not up to the job at Singapore.

3. We are organizing a force of four aircraft carriers with cruisers for action in the Indian Ocean in a form of novel warfare designed to repair our lack of modern capital ships. The four R battleships will be available for convoy escorts.

[1] Maxim Litvinov (born Meier Wallakh), 1876–1952. Born in Bialystok, then Tsarist Russia, of Jewish parentage. A revolutionary, he was in exile in France and Britain from 1902 to 1917. Married an Englishwoman, Ivy Low. The first Bolshevik representative in London, November 1917 to September 1918 (when he was deported). In effective control of Soviet foreign policy, as Deputy Commissar for Foreign Affairs, 1926–30. Commissar for Foreign Affairs, 1930–39 (when Stalin dismissed him in favour of Molotov). Soviet Ambassador in Washington, 1941–43. Neither purged nor exiled, he lived his final years in quiet retirement. After his death, his widow returned to live in England.

[2] On 13 December 1941 the Russian forces in front of Moscow continued to push the Germans away from the city. On December 14 reports from Berlin admitted that there had been a substantial loss of materials through the freezing of vehicles, tanks and guns stuck in deep mud. On December 15, north of Moscow, the Russians drove the Germans out of Klin and advanced towards Kalinin (which was retaken on the following day). South of Moscow, the near-siege of Tula was broken. In the Ukraine, the Germans were being pushed back to within thirty miles of Orel.

4. Am on my way to confer with President Roosevelt on general concerted war effort. Will keep in touch with Casey.[1] Please keep this last paragraph especially secret until I arrive.

Winston S. Churchill to General Ismay, for the Chiefs of Staff Committee
(*Churchill papers, 20/50*)

15 December 1941

Beware lest troops required for ultimate defence Singapore Island and fortress are used up or cut off in Malay Peninsula. Nothing compares in importance with fortress. Are you sure we shall have enough troops for prolonged defence? Consider with Auchinleck and Commonwealth Government moving 1 Australian Division from Palestine to Singapore. Report action.

Winston S. Churchill to Clement Attlee and Private Office
(*Churchill papers, 20/50*)

15 December 1941

THE FOUR LABOUR PEERS[2]

These names, and the explanation which accompanies them, may be published in the morning papers of 22nd December. There should thus be a ten-day interval between their publication and the regular New Year's *Gazette*, and effort should be made by the Minister of Information to secure a favourable reception from the Press. I trust that you will yourself make sure that the *Daily Herald* is not hostile.[3]

It will not be possible for me to sign the letters offering the gentlemen concerned the Peerages, and they should be told from my Private Office in the third person without giving any reason.

[1] Richard Gardiner Casey, 1890–1976. Born in Australia. Educated in Australia and at Trinity College, Cambridge. On active service at Gallipoli and in France (DSO, MC). Active in Australian politics between the wars. Australian Minister for Supply and Development,1939–40. Australian Minister to the United States, 1940–2. Minister of State Resident in the Middle East, and Member of the British War Cabinet, 1942–3. Governor of Bengal, 1944–6. Minister of External Affairs, Australia, 1951–60. Created Baron, 1960. Governor-General of Australia, 1965–9.

[2] The four new Labour Peers were Captain Wedgwood Benn MP (who became a Viscount), and Commander R.H. Fletcher, MP, Charles Latham (leader of the London County Council) and Josiah Wedgwood, MP, who became Barons.

[3] The *Daily Herald* commented: 'These are not political honours or rewards, but a special measure of State policy. The idea is to strengthen Labour in the House of Lords, where the Party's present strength is insufficient to carry out all the duties which fall upon the Party.'

Text of draft statement follows:

Draft Statement not to be published in the *Gazette*, but issued as a Press Notice through No. 10 Downing Street.

The King, on the advice of the Prime Minister and His Majesty's Government, has been graciously pleased to confer Peerages upon four Members of the Labour Party as announced today.

These creations are not made as political honours or rewards, but as a special measure of State policy. They are designed to strengthen the Labour Party in the Upper House, where its representation is disproportionately weak, at a time when a Coalition Government of the three Parties is charged with the direction of affairs.

Sir Charles Wilson: notes
(*Contemporary Medical Archives Centre*)

16 December 1941 [HMS *Duke of York*]

After being under hatches for two days we were allowed on deck this morning. It was quite mild and the PM appeared. 'This,' he said, 'is a new war with Russia victorious, Japan in and America in up to the neck.'

John Martin: diary
(*John Martin papers*)

16 December 1941 [HMS *Duke of York*]

At sea. Much less rough. Increased speed and again possible to walk on deck. Making south towards Azores.

Winston S. Churchill to Brigadier Hollis
(*Churchill papers, 20/36*)

16 December 1941
Secret

BEVERIDGE REPORT ON SKILLED MANPOWER FOR THE SERVICES

I should be obliged if you would study this Report and the file and, together with Mr Martin and Mr Brown, try to prepare the material for a short (two pages) Directive by me.

2. In doing this it should be remembered: first, that Parliament has now risen till the middle of January, so that there is plenty of time for the War Office to act; secondly, the general principle of the points made by Lord Cherwell carrying out my minute. But a much more effective and precise reply should be made by the War Office than has been produced up to the present.

3. The great point to bring out is, as stated by the Secretary of State for War,

'. . . the duty of the War Office is to make an efficient fighting machine rather than a well-conducted industrial establishment.' It is quite impossible to make sure that no technical skill is wasted in the Army. Nothing must be done seriously to break up the cohesion of sections, platoons and companies. No general disturbance of the Army system can be tolerated in view of the danger of invasion in the spring.

4. The question of non-commissioned officers who are still tradesmen raises many difficulties. A man should not be made to feel that he is kept back from promotion because he possesses technical skill. The details require more thought than I am able to supply.

5. This Report should be sent back with my Directive from Bermuda by airplane. After it gets back a War Office committee, such as I outline, should be set up to draft an effective answer for the War Office, showing their difficulties and promising amendment. This committee might consist of the Financial Secretary,[1] Mr Duncan Sandys, Sir James Grigg and General Nye, who will be back from Russia by then. I should like this to be submitted to me about the 10th January and the matter can then, if necessary, be brought before the Cabinet.

6. Sir William Beveridge[2] is a clever fussy fellow, without any comprehension of army life, but very good at paper schemes which commend themselves to the Press.

Winston S. Churchill to Clement Attlee

(*Churchill papers, 20/50*)

16 December 1941

INFORMING HOUSE OF COMMONS AND DOMINION PRIME MINISTERS ABOUT 'ARCADIA'[3]

Do whatever you think necessary after hearing Admiralty on security aspect. Personally, I see no harm. You are justified in being firm with the

[1] Harry Frederick Comfort Crookshank, 1893–1961. On active service, 1914–18; Captain, 1919. Foreign Office, 1919–24 (Constantinople and Washington). Conservative MP, 1924–56. Secretary for Mines, 1936–9. Financial Secretary, Treasury, 1939–43. Postmaster-General, 1943–5. Minister of Health, 1951–2, and Lord Privy Seal, 1952–5 (Churchill's second premiership). In 1954 and 1955 he was one of the Conservative Cabinet Ministers most determined that Churchill should retire. Created Viscount (by Anthony Eden), 1956.

[2] William Henry Beveridge, 1879–1963. Civil servant at the Board of Trade, 1908–16, when first Lloyd George and then Churchill gave him considerable responsibilities in connection with the creation of a scheme of compulsory state-aided national insurance; Ministry of Munitions, 1915–16; Ministry of Food, 1917–18 (Permanent Secretary, 1919). Knighted, 1919. Director of the London School of Economics and Political Science, 1919–37. Member of the Royal Commission on the Coal Industry, 1925. Master of University College, Oxford, 1937–45. Chairman, at Churchill's suggestion, of the Interdepartmental Committee of Social Insurance, 1941–2. Liberal MP, 1944–5. Baron, 1946. Author of more than twenty books on politics and political science; and of the Beveridge Report.

[3] The code name for Churchill's visit to the United States.

House when Auchinleck is advancing, Russia is victor and United States of America an ally.

We are making better speed now.

Winston S. Churchill for the Chiefs of Staff Committee[1]
(*Cabinet papers, 69/4*)

16 December 1941
Most Secret

MEMORANDUM ON THE CONDUCT OF THE WAR
PART I – THE ATLANTIC FRONT

Hitler's failure and losses in Russia are the prime fact in the war at this time. We cannot tell how great the disaster to the German Army and Nazi régime will be. This régime has hitherto lived upon easily and cheaply won successes. Instead of what was imagined to be a swift and easy victory, it has now to face the shock of a winter of slaughter and expenditure of fuel and equipment on the largest scale.

Neither Great Britain nor the United States have any part to play in this event, except to make sure that we send, without fail and punctually, the supplies we have promised. In this way alone shall we hold our influence over Stalin and be able to weave the mighty Russian effort into the general texture of the war.

2. In a lesser degree the impending victory of General Auchinleck in Cyrenaica is an injury to the German power. We may expect the total destruction of the enemy force in Libya to be apparent before the end of the year. This not only inflicts a heavy blow upon the Germans and Italians, but it frees our forces in the Nile Valley from the major threat of invasion from the west under which they have long dwelt. Naturally, General Auchinleck will press on as fast as possible with the operation called 'Acrobat', which should give him possession of Tripoli, and so bring his armoured vanguard to the French frontier of Tunis. He may be able to supply a forecast before we separate at Washington.

3. The German losses and defeat in Russia and their extirpation from Libya may of course impel them to a supreme effort in the spring to break the ring that is closing on them by a south-eastward thrust either through the Caucasus or to Anatolia, or both. However, we should not assume that necessarily they will have the war energy for this task. The Russian armies, recuperated by the winter, will lie heavy upon them from Leningrad to the Crimea. They may easily be forced to evacuate the Crimea. There is no reason at this time to

[1] This was the first of five memoranda which Churchill wrote for the Chiefs of Staff during the trans-Atlantic voyage. The other three were written on December 17, 18, 20 and 22.

suppose that the Russian Navy will not command the Black Sea. Nor should it be assumed that the present life-strength of Germany is such as to make an attack upon Turkey and a march through Anatolia a business to be undertaken in present circumstances by the Nazi régime. The Turks have fifty divisions; their fighting quality and the physical obstacles of the country are well known. Although Turkey has played for safety throughout, the Russian command of the Black Sea and the British successes in the Levant and along the North African shore, together with the proved weakness of the Italian Fleet, would justify every effort on our part to bring Turkey into line, and are certainly sufficient to encourage her to resist a German inroad. While it would be imprudent to regard the danger of a German south-west thrust against the Persian-Iraq-Syrian front as removed, it certainly now seems much less likely than heretofore.

4. We ought therefore to try hard to win over French North Africa, and now is the moment to use every inducement and form of pressure at our disposal upon the Government of Vichy and the French authorities in North Africa. The German setback in Russia, the British successes in Libya, the moral and military collapse of Italy, above all the declarations of war exchanged between Germany and the United States, must strongly affect the mind of France and the French Empire. Now is the time to offer to Vichy and to French North Africa a blessing or a cursing. A blessing will consist in a promise by the United States and Great Britain to re-establish France as a Great Power with her territories undiminished. It should carry with it an offer of active aid by British and United States expeditionary forces, both from the Atlantic seaboard of Morocco and at convenient landing-points in Algeria and Tunis, as well as from General Auchinleck's forces advancing from the east. Ample supplies for the French and the loyal Moors should be made available. Vichy should be asked to send their fleet from Toulon to Oran and Bizerta and to bring France into the war again as a principal.

This would mean that the Germans would take over the whole of France and rule it as occupied territory. It does not seem that the conditions in the occupied and the hitherto unoccupied zones are widely different. Whatever happens, European France will inevitably be subjected to a complete blockade. There is of course always the chance that the Germans, tied up in Russia, may not care to take over unoccupied France, even though French North Africa is at war with them.

5. If we can obtain even the connivance of Vichy to French North Africa coming over to our side we must be ready to send considerable forces as soon as possible. Apart from anything which General Auchinleck can bring in from the east, should he be successful in Tripolitania, we hold ready in Britain (Operation 'Gymnast') about 55,000 men, comprising two divisions and an armoured unit, together with the shipping. These forces could enter French North Africa by invitation on the twenty-third day after the order to embark

them was given. Leading elements and air forces from Malta could reach Bizerta at very short notice. It is desired that the United States should at the same time promise to bring in, via Casablanca and other African Atlantic ports, not less then 150,000 men during the next six months. It is essential that some American elements, say 25,000 men, should go at the earliest moment after agreement, either Vichy or North African, had been obtained.

6. It is also asked that the United States will send the equivalent of three divisions and one armoured division into Northern Ireland. These divisions, could, if necessary, complete their training in Northern Ireland. The presence of American forces there would become known to the enemy, and they could be led to magnify their actual numbers. The presence of United States troops in the British Isles would be a powerful additional deterrent against an attempt at invasion by Germany. It would enable us to nourish the campaign in French North Africa by two more divisions and one complete armoured division. If forces of this order could be added to the French Army already in North Africa, with proper air support, the Germans would have to make a very difficult and costly campaign across uncommanded waters to subdue North Africa. The North-West African theatre is one most favourable for Anglo-American operations, our approaches being direct and convenient across the Atlantic, while the enemy's passage of the Mediterranean would be severely obstructed, as is happening in their Libyan enterprise.

7. It may be mentioned here that we greatly desire American bomber squadrons to come into action from the British Isles against Germany. Our own bomber programme has fallen short of our hopes. It is formidable and is increasing, but its full development has been delayed. It must be remembered that we place great hopes of affecting German production and German morale by ever more severe and more accurate bombing of their cities and harbours, and that this, combined with their Russian defeats, may produce important effects upon the will to fight of the German people, with consequential internal reactions upon the German Government. The arrival in the United Kingdom of, say, twenty American bomber squadrons would emphasize and accelerate this process, and would be the most direct and effective reply to the declaration of war by Germany upon the United States. Arrangements will be made in Great Britain to increase this process and develop the Anglo-American bombing of Germany without any top limit from now on till the end of the war.

8. We must however reckon with a refusal by Vichy to act as we desire, and on the contrary they may rouse French North Africa to active resistance. They may help German troops to enter North Africa; the Germans may force their way or be granted passage through Spain; the French fleet at Toulon may pass under German control, and France and the French Empire may be made by Vichy to collaborate actively with Germany against us, although it is not likely that this would go through effectively. The overwhelming majority of the

French are ranged with Great Britain, and now still more with United States. It is by no means certain that Admiral Darlan can deliver the Toulon fleet over intact to Germany. It is most improbable that French soldiers and sailors would fight effectively against the United States and Great Britain. Nevertheless, we must not exclude the possibility of a half-hearted association of the defeatist elements in France and North Africa with Germany. In this case our task in North Africa will become much harder.

A campaign must be fought in 1942 to gain possession of, or conquer, the whole of the North African shore, including the Atlantic ports of Morocco. Dakar and other French West African ports must be captured before the end of the year. Whereas however entry into French North Africa is urgent to prevent German penetration, a period of eight or nine months' preparation may well be afforded for the mastering of Dakar and the West African establishments. Plans should be set on foot forthwith. If sufficient time and preparation are allowed and the proper apparatus provided, these latter operations present no insuperable difficulty.

9. Our relations with General de Gaulle and the Free French movement will require to be reviewed. Hitherto the United States have entered into no undertakings similar to those comprised in my correspondence with him. Through no particular fault of his own his movement has created new antagonisms in French minds. Any action which the United States may now feel able to take in regard to him should have the effect, *inter alia*, of re-defining our obligations to him and France so as to make these obligations more closely dependent upon the eventual effort by him and the French nation to rehabilitate themselves. If Vichy were to act as we desire about French North Africa, the United States and Great Britain must labour to bring about a reconciliation between the Free French (de Gaullists) and those other Frenchmen who will have taken up arms once more against Germany. If, on the other hand, Vichy persists in collaboration with Germany and we have to fight our way into French North and West Africa, then the de Gaullists' movement must be aided and used to the full.

10. We cannot tell what will happen in Spain.[1] It seems probable that the Spaniards will not give the Germans a free passage through Spain to attack Gibraltar and invade North Africa. There may be infiltration, but the formal

[1] Early in December 1941, Churchill learned of the success in Spain of the Naval Attaché, Captain Hillgarth, in continuing to seek out and encourage Spaniards who were opposed to any direct Spanish commitment to Germany. Three plans were evolved, as the Defence Committee were told at the beginning of December, 'for stimulating Spanish resistance in the event of a German invasion of Spain' ('SOE Plans for Spain', December 1941: *Cabinet papers, 69/3*). The first plan was to supply and store automatic weapons and ammunition for anti-Franco groups in Navarre, the second was to bring a number of Spaniards to London 'for training in wireless telegraph communications'. The third was to train in Britain seventy former Spanish Republicans 'to enable them to be landed in Spain and used for demolitions etc. in the event of a German invasion'.

demand for the passage of an army would be resisted. If so, the winter would be the worst time for the Germans to attempt to force their way through Spain. Moreover, Hitler, with nearly all Europe to hold down by armed force in the face of defeat and semi-starvation, may well be chary of taking over unoccupied France and involving himself in bitter guerrilla warfare with the morose, fierce, hungry people of the Iberian peninsula. Everything possible must be done by Britain and the United States to strengthen their will to resist. The present policy of limited supplies should be pursued.

The value of Gibraltar harbour and base to us is so great that no attempts should be made upon the Atlantic islands until either the peninsula is invaded or the Spaniards give passage to the Germans.

11. To sum up, the war in the West in 1942 comprises, as its main offensive effort, the occupation and control by Great Britain and the United States of the whole of the North and West African possessions of France, and the further control by Britain of the whole North African shore from Tunis to Egypt, thus giving, if the naval situation allows, free passage through the Mediterranean to the Levant and the Suez Canal. These great objectives can only be achieved if British and American naval and air superiority in the Atlantic is maintained, if supply lines continue uninterrupted, and if the British Isles are effectively safeguarded against invasion.

John Martin: diary
(John Martin papers)

17 December 1941 [HMS *Duke of York*]

At sea. Our destroyers left us in the afternoon.

Ian Jacob: diary
(Ian Jacob papers)

17 December 1941

There has been some talk of our flying on from Bermuda to save time. Our progress during the first few days has been so slow on account of the bad weather that the Prime Minister is eager to press on. However, the project has been dropped. The saving was found on examination to be only one day, and the arrangements would have been so difficult, that it would not have been worth while.

Winston S. Churchill to Lord Halifax
(*Churchill papers, 20/49*)

17 December 1941
Please decypher yourself
Most Secret and Personal

Prime Ministers of Australia, South Africa, New Zealand and Canada have now been informed that I am on my way to confer with President on matters relating to concerted war effort, and requested to keep this information especially secret until my arrival is announced. Dominion Ministers in Washington should, therefore, not inform their Governments direct.

Winston S. Churchill to William Mackenzie King
(*Churchill papers, 20/47*)

17 December 1941
Decypher yourself
Most Secret and Personal

Planning arrive Washington around 22nd, staying a week. Hope to see you. Please tell no one.

Winston S. Churchill to Lord Halifax
(*Churchill papers, 20/47*)

17 December 1941
Secret

Please thank President for most kind invitation to stay at the White House, which I am delighted to accept. I propose my party there should consist only of myself, Thompson, Martin, valet[1] and two detectives. Accommodation will be required in Mayflower Hotel for Sir Charles Wilson, Brown, two stenographers and Royal Marine orderlies.

Please also reserve two rooms and sitting-rooms for Harriman at the Mayflower (type of rooms to which he is accustomed there).

[1] Frank Sawyers.

Winston S. Churchill for the Chiefs of Staff Committee
(*Cabinet papers, 69/4*)

17 December 1941
Most Secret

MEMORANDUM ON THE CONDUCT OF THE WAR
PART II – THE PACIFIC FRONT

1. The heavy losses inflicted by Japan upon the United States and British Forces in the Pacific theatre have given the Japanese, for the time being, superiority in these vast waters. There are at present few points in the East Indies to which they cannot transport a superior land force. By insulting the western seaboard of Canada and the United States, or the shores of Australia, with attacks of individual cruisers or seaborne aircraft they may seek to cause alarm and the dispersion of our forces. However, on account of the great number of objectives open to them – far more than they can possibly devour simultaneously they must be expected, if they act wisely, to concentrate upon securing their military position in the East Indies. On this principle they would do their utmost to capture Manila while making their longer advance overland towards Singapore. At the same time they would strike at Burma and the Burma Road thus isolating China. No relief is possible for Hong Kong. The Japanese must be expected to establish themselves on both sides of the Straits of Malacca and in the Strait of Sunda, to take a number of islands in the Malaysian Archipelago and to endeavour to occupy various parts of the Dutch East Indies.

The above, if stubbornly resisted, will involve the employment of very large numbers of Japanese troops, and their supply and maintenance will strain Japanese sea transport.

We should ask the United States authorities what is their view about a Japanese attempt to take and occupy Hawaii by an expedition. With the knowledge at present available to us, it seems it would be an ill-judged and therefore unlikely enterprise.

2. We do not know what estimate of time the United States authorities place upon the resistance of Manila and other key points in the Philippines. We expect, however, that Singapore island and fortress will stand an attack for at least six months, although meanwhile the naval base will not be usable by either side. A large Japanese army with its siege train and ample supplies of ammunition and engineering stores will be required for their attack upon Singapore. Considerable Japanese forces also will be needed for the attack on Burma and the Burma Road. The line of communication between the Malaysian Archipelago and Japan is nearly 2,000 miles in length and dangerously vulnerable. The Japanese armies landed in the Malay Peninsula or in Indo-China, Siam and Burma, will soon constitute immense commitments which would be immediately imperilled by the recovery by the United

States of major sea control in the Pacific. This process should be aided by Great Britain. In the meanwhile an attack upon Japanese sea communications by United States and Dutch submarines and other vessels constitutes a grievous danger to the enemy.

3. How then is the superiority of Anglo-American sea power to be regained? The two new 45,000 ton Japanese battleships are dominating factors, and it is not seen how a superior line of battle can be drawn out against Japan in the Pacific theatre for some time. It may well be that this will not be achieved until the two new American 16-inch gun battleships join the Pacific Fleet. The date of May has been mentioned, but it is not known to us whether this is the date of commissioning of these ships or of their being fully worked up. It would seem unjustifiably hazardous to fight a general fleet action until these two ships at least have joined the United States Pacific Fleet. Diversions and enterprises by United States aircraft carriers escorted by fast cruisers against the exposed cities of Japan constitute a form of interim offensive action which will presumably be earnestly studied.

4. The British naval contribution to the war against Japan has been crippled by the sinking of the *Prince of Wales* and the *Repulse*. We have to base on Scapa Flow the five Capital ships, viz., *King George V, Duke of York, Rodney, Nelson* (ready at the end of February) and *Renown*, together with one modern aircraft carrier, *Victorious*. We contemplate basing on Gibraltar (while it is available) the *Malaya* and a second modern aircraft carrier, probably *Formidable*. These forces should be sufficient to assure the ultimate control of the Atlantic in the event of a sortie by the *Tirpitz* (probably the most powerful vessel afloat), supported by *Scheer* and also by the *Scharnhorst, Gneisenau* and *Prinz Eugen*, if at any time they can be repaired at Brest. We hope by frequent air bombing to keep these last three ships out of action. We therefore concur with the United States Naval Authorities in their transference of all American Capital Ships from the Atlantic to Hawaii or elsewhere in the Pacific. We ask, however, that as many United States destroyers as possible shall be left to guard the vital supply line between America and the British Isles.

5. In the meanwhile we propose to organize in the Indian Ocean a force of three armoured carriers, viz., *Indomitable, Illustrious* and *Hermes*, together with suitable cruiser escort. At a later stage *Furious* will be available. This force, based on Trincomalee and ranging as far as Port Darwin, should be formed and in action from the end of February. The four 'R' Class battleships, *Ramillies, Revenge, Royal Sovereign* and *Resolution* will be available as they arrive upon the scene for convoy or other duties between the Cape, Australia and Egypt. It is thought by the Admiralty that the three aircraft carriers, working in combination, may exercise a very powerful deterrent effect upon the movement of Japanese heavy ships into the Indian Ocean or in the waters between Australia and South Africa, and may to some extent repair the loss of battleship strength. We presume the United States will make their numerous

and powerful aircraft carriers play a similar part in the northern Pacific. We are ready to concert action with the United States fleet, and we should welcome the study of the combined use of all important units in the Pacific for any major offensive operation which may be deemed practicable. It would be only in the last resort that we should withdraw the *Queen Elizabeth* and *Valiant* from the Mediterranean. If adequate air forces were available on the Egyptian and Libyan shores this would not necessarily expose North East Africa to German overseas invasion. The withdrawal of these two battleships from the Eastern Mediterranean would, however, make the victualling of Malta far more difficult, and would exercise a disastrous effect upon Turkey, whose confidence it is so important to maintain. Only if Australia were to be threatened with imminent invasion on a large scale could we contemplate such a step. We therefore propose that *Warspite*, when repaired in February, should join Admiral Cunningham's fleet at Alexandria. It may, however, be observed that in supreme emergency or for a great occasion, these three fast modernized ships united to the three aircraft carriers aforesaid, and with the 'R' Class battleships, constitute a respectable force.

6. This is the best we can do until the completion and working up of the *Anson* and the *Howe*. The original dates for these were May and September 1942, plus two months working up in each case. Since the Japanese Declaration of War, extreme priority has been given to these vessels, and 24-hour shifts are being worked upon them. It is hoped that the *Howe* may be advanced from September, perhaps to July. Unless some serious losses have been suffered in the interval, as is always possible, or unless the two Italian 'Littorio' battleships have been taken over effectively and manned by the Germans, these two ships might be considered available to reinforce the Allied fleets in the Pacific either themselves or by setting free their two consorts. If they were added to the two new United States 16-inch gun battleships they should give a good margin of superiority, even if in the judgment of the United States Naval Authorities that has not been achieved earlier. We may, therefore, look to the Autumn of 1942 as the period when we shall have recovered superior naval control of the Pacific. From that moment all the Japanese overseas expeditions will be in jeopardy, and offensive operations on the largest scale may be set on foot either against their country, their possessions or their new conquests. These again should be the subject of immediate planning.

The questions which remain open are how much injury we shall have to suffer in the interval, how strongly the Japanese will fortify themselves in their new positions, and whether the Philippines and Singapore can hold out so long. It is of first importance for us to bridge this waiting period by every conceivable means.

John Martin: diary
(*John Martin papers*)

18 December 1941 [HMS *Duke of York*]

At sea. Gale at night.

Winston S. Churchill for the Chiefs of Staff Committee
(*Cabinet papers, 69/4*)

18 December 1941
Most Secret

MEMORANDUM ON THE FUTURE CONDUCT OF THE WAR
PART III – 1943

If the operations outlined in Parts I and II should prosper during 1942 the situation at the beginning of 1943 might be as follows:

(a) United States and Great Britain would have recovered effective naval superiority in the Pacific, and all Japanese overseas commitments would be endangered both from the assailing of their communications and from British and American expeditions sent to recover places lost.
(b) The British Isles would remain intact and more strongly prepared against invasion than ever before.
(c) The whole West and North African shores from Dakar to the Suez Canal and the Levant to the Turkish frontier would be in Anglo-American hands.

Turkey, though not necessarily at war, would be definitely incorporated in the American-British-Russian front. The Russian position would be strongly established, and the supplies of British and American material as promised would have in part compensated for the loss of Russian munitions-making capacity. It might be that a footing would already have been established in Sicily and Italy, with reactions inside Italy which might be highly favourable.

2. But all this would fall short of bringing the war to an end. The war cannot be ended by driving Japan back to her own bounds and defeating her overseas forces. The war can only be ended through the defeat in Europe of the German armies, or through internal convulsions in Germany produced by the unfavourable course of the war, economic privations, and the Allied bombing offensive. As the strength of the United States, Great Britain, and Russia develops and begins to be realized by the Germans an internal collapse is always possible, but we must not count upon this. Our plans must proceed upon the assumption that the resistance of the German Army and Air Force will continue at its present level and that their U-boat warfare will be conducted by increasingly numerous flotillas.

3. We have therefore to prepare for the liberation of the captive countries

of Western and Southern Europe by the landing at suitable points, successively or simultaneously, of British and American armies strong enough to enable the conquered populations to revolt. By themselves they will never be able to revolt, owing to the ruthless counter-measures that will be employed, but if adequate and suitably equipped forces were landed in several of the following countries, namely, Norway, Denmark, Holland, Belgium, the French Channel coasts and the French Atlantic coasts, as well as in Italy and possibly the Balkans, the German garrisons would prove insufficient to cope both with the strength of the liberating forces and the fury of the revolting peoples. It is impossible for the Germans, while we retain the sea-power necessary to choose the place or places of attack, to have sufficient troops in each of these countries for effective resistance. In particular, they cannot move their armour about laterally from north to south or west to east; either they must divide it between the various conquered countries – in which case it will become hopelessly dispersed – or they must hold it back in a central position in Germany, in which case it will not arrive until large and important lodgments have been made by us from overseas.

4. We must face here the usual clash between short-term and long-term projects. War is a constant struggle and must be waged from day to day. It is only with some difficulty and within limits that provision can be made for the future. Experience shows that forecasts are usually falsified and preparations always in arrear. Nevertheless, there must be a design and theme for bringing the war to a victorious end in a reasonable period. All the more is this necessary when under modern conditions no large-scale offensive operation can be launched without the preparation of elaborate technical apparatus.

5. We should therefore face now the problems not only of driving Japan back to her homelands and regaining undisputed mastery in the Pacific, but also of liberating conquered Europe by the landing during the summer of 1943 of United States and British armies on their shores. Plans should be prepared for the landing in all of the countries mentioned above. The actual choice of which three or four to pick should be deferred as long as possible, so as to profit by the turn of events and make sure of secrecy.

6. In principle, the landings should be made by armoured and mechanized forces capable of disembarking not at ports but on beaches, either by landing-craft or from ocean-going ships specially adapted. The potential front of attack is thus made so wide that the German forces holding down these different countries cannot be strong enough at all points. An amphibious outfit must be prepared to enable these large-scale disembarkations to be made swiftly and surely. The vanguards of the various British and American expeditions should be marshalled by the spring of 1943 in Iceland, the British Isles, and, if possible, in French Morocco and Egypt. The main body would come direct across the ocean.

7. It need not be assumed that great numbers of men are required. If the

incursion of the armoured formations is successful, the uprising of the local population, for whom weapons must be brought, will supply the corpus of the liberating offensive. Forty armoured divisions, at 15,000 men apiece, or their equivalent in tank brigades, of which Great Britain would try to produce nearly half, would amount to 600,000 men. Behind this armour another million men of all arms would suffice to wrest enormous territories from Hitler's domination. But these campaigns, once started, will require nourishing on a lavish scale. Our industries and training establishments should by the end of 1942 be running on a sufficient scale.

8. Apart from the command of the sea, without which nothing is possible, the essential for all these operations is superior air power, and for landing purposes a large development of carrier-borne aircraft will be necessary. This however is needed anyhow for the war in 1942. In order to wear down the enemy and hamper his counter-preparations, the bombing offensive of Germany from England and of Italy from Malta, and if possible from Tripoli and Tunis, must reach the highest possible scale of intensity. Considering that the British first-line air strength is already slightly superior to that of Germany, that the Russian Air Force has already established a superiority on a large part of the Russian front and may be considered to be three-fifths the first-line strength of Germany, and that the United States resources and future development are additional, there is no reason why a decisive mastery of the air should not be established even before the summer of 1943, and meanwhile heavy and continuous punishment inflicted upon Germany. Having regard to the fact that the bombing offensive is necessarily a matter of degree and that the targets cannot be moved away, it would be right to assign priority to the fighter and torpedo-carrying aircraft required for the numerous carriers and improvised carriers which are available or must be brought into existence.

9. If we set these tasks before us now, being careful that they do not trench too much upon current necessities, we might hope, even if no German collapse occurs beforehand, to win the war at the end of 1943 or 1944. There might be advantage in declaring now our intention of sending armies of liberation into Europe in 1943. This would give hope to the subjugated peoples and prevent any truck between them and the German invaders. The setting and keeping in movement along our courses of the minds of so many scores of millions of men is in itself a potent atmospheric influence.

Ian Jacob: diary
(*Ian Jacob papers*)

18 December 1941 [HMS *Duke of York*]

A fine but muggy morning, with a moderate swell. The Chiefs of Staff had a long meeting this morning with the Prime Minister and Lord Beaverbrook in the Admiral's Bridge. The discussion was mainly about the way to handle the forthcoming talks in Washington, and was satisfactory from our point of view provided we got our ideas adopted. The Admiral's Bridge makes quite a good meeting place, not very roomy, but quiet and warm. On a sunny day it is rather like meeting in a greenhouse! The view up there is superb, especially when the waves are dashing over the bow.

This evening's film was the best we have had, namely, *The Private Lives of Elizabeth and Essex*. Bette Davies, who took the part of Queen Elizabeth, is a fine actress, and gave a really good performance, though some of the scenes between her and Errol Flynn, who was Essex, were rather long drawn out.

Winston S. Churchill to Lord Beaverbrook
(*Churchill papers, 20/36*)

18 December 1941
Secret

I had not intended that the Regional Boards should be under the Production Executive. I suppose this became necessary because the Ministry of Aircraft Production and the Ministry of Supply are no longer under one head as in the days when I was at the Ministry of Munitions. Then we had the Area Organization which was felt to be a great help to the Minister of Munitions. The memory of that Area Organization gives weight to the volume of opinion in favour of Regional Boards. We also had our own Labour Department, so there was no danger of a different labour policy being followed in the Ministry of Supply and in the air production. Under present arrangements the Minister of Labour and National Service must inevitably co-ordinate labour policy between Ministry of Supply, Ministry of Aircraft Production and the Admiralty. I do not see how this is to be avoided as it is not intended to remodel the functions of the Minister of Labour.

2. Will you please explain to me exactly what the Regional Boards now do? Do they cover the same work as the old Area Organization, except that they report to the Production Executive instead of to the Minister of Supply; or do they do different work?

3. As you know, I am steadily restricting the functions of the Production Executive. First, by framing the War Budget of 1942. This should have been achieved this month, but our journey has postponed it till January, and developments may well have affected previous calculations. Secondly, by supporting all processes by which the three Supply Ministers settle matters between themselves in accordance with the aforesaid War Budget. This relegates the Production Executive in practice to three main functions:

(a) Adjusting outstanding disputes between Supply Ministers, if any arise;

(b) Dealing with changes in the approved War Budget which are caused by the movement of events; and

(c) Giving some place where the minor consumer can have his claims considered apart from the interests of the three Supply Ministers.

It is not my intention that the Production Executive should have any functions other than these. As you know, I have given instructions to Sir Edward Bridges in that sense.

4. Let me have your further observations giving fair recognition to the facts set out above.

Winston S. Churchill to Sir Alan Brooke[1]

(*Churchill papers, 20/36*)

18 December 1941
Secret

POSSIBLE FORMATION OF A POLISH DIVISION IN BRITAIN

I do not consider that the issue of tanks to the Poles should be delayed until all the British Armoured Divisions have not only been completed but have a large reserve of tanks standing behind them. I thought it was agreed that, in the first place, the Divisions were to be given their initial equipment and the reserve built up afterwards as more tanks come to hand. The Poles should be treated on this footing equally with the British divisions. I do not see how the date of April 1, 1943, could possibly be accepted as a fair treatment of the problem by General Sikorski. I hope, therefore, you will let me have proposals on the basis I have indicated.

2. It should surely be possible to give a good outfit of tanks to the Poles and yet enable them to work together as a corps. It is convenient, but not indispensable, that every unit in the army should have exactly the same organization. It is not necessary that the Poles should have the identical equipment, i.e., the whole 3,500 vehicles to which the British armoured divisions have been expanded. A practical solution would be to let them have a couple of hundred more tanks during the next six months, and work up to the full usual formation later. It should surely be possible to use the Polish force together and not to separate the tank component from the rest.

I hope you will let me have further proposals.

[1] This was Churchill's first Minute to General Brooke after his appointment as Chief of the Imperial Staff (in succession to General Dill).

Winston S. Churchill to Admiral Pound
(*Churchill papers, 20/36*)

19 December 1941
Secret

GERMAN SUBMARINES

You might care to see my marginal notes on the Admiralty paper. Perhaps you will take some opportunity of seeing me about it.

I think the estimates of properly manned German U-boats coming into service are on the high side. I doubt the 36 in the Atlantic now, and as usual I assert my view that our sinkings are judged very conservatively by the Admiralty. I should have had a meeting on this but for our present voyage. It will be necessary to impress upon the United States authorities the extreme need for increasing the programme for destroyers and other anti-submarine craft. Our own programme – 136 by this time next year – is pretty good.[1]

We had better keep the file with us, and have the meeting on return.

Winston S. Churchill to General Auchinleck
(*Churchill papers, 20/49*)

19 December 1941

For yourself and Minister of State alone.

I rejoice in your continued victorious advance and pursuit. I am on my way to the United States to confer with President Roosevelt about the future conduct of the war. Please continue to send me your admirable accounts, which will help me in convincing American doubters of the wisdom of our Middle Eastern campaign. When will 2nd Armoured Brigade strike, and where?

Every good wish,

Winston S. Churchill to General Ismay, for the Chiefs of Staff Committee
(*Churchill papers, 20/49*)

19 December 1941

1. Your Taut No. 59. First three paragraphs from Duff Cooper express same anxieties as I conveyed to you in my Grey No. 8 beginning 'Beware'.

[1] That day, unknown to Churchill when he wrote this Minute, the cruiser *Neptune* struck a mine off Tripoli. Of its crew of more than 700, only one survived (he survived as a prisoner of war, having been picked up by the Germans from a raft on which, during four days of drifting, the ship's Captain, R.C. O'Connor, and thirteen others, perished).

Duff Cooper's proposal to concentrate on defence of Johore for the purpose of holding Singapore conforms exactly to view taken by Dill here.

2. After naval disasters to British and American sea-power in Pacific and Indian Oceans we have no means of preventing continuous landings by Japanese in great strength in Siam and the Malay Peninsula. It is therefore impossible to defend, other than by demolitions and delaying action, anything north of the defensive line in Johore, and this line itself can only be defended as part of the final defence of Singapore Island fortress and the naval base. This is not a matter, as General Brooke's telegram suggests, for the Commander-in-Chief, Far East. It is for His Majesty's Government to assign to the Commander-in-Chief, Far East, the task he is to perform

3. He should now be told to confine himself to defence of Johore and Singapore, and that nothing must compete with maximum defence of Singapore. This should not preclude his employing delaying tactics and demolitions on the way south and making an orderly retreat.

4. Your Taut No. 59 does not say who is now Commander-in-Chief, Far East. Has Pownall got there? If not, where is he? He should fly there at earliest moment.

5. Your Taut No. 46. It was always intended that all reinforcements diverted from the Cape to India should be used by Wavell for defence of Burma or sent forward to Far East Command as situation requires. Your proposal, paragraph 3, sub-section (c), also your action in diverting the anti-aircraft guns and Fighter squadrons in paragraph 5, are fully approved.

6. 18th Division can similarly be used by Wavell either for his own needs or to help Far East Command; but why stop there? If 18th Division is sent eastward it would seem wise to get at least one Australian Division moving into India to replace it.

7. Please say what you are doing and how you propose to overcome the growing difficulties of sending reinforcements into Singapore. Also what has been done about reducing number of useless mouths in Singapore Island? What was the reply about supplies?

Clementine Churchill to Winston S. Churchill

(*Baroness Spencer-Churchill papers*)

19 December 1941 10 Downing Street

My darling,

You have been gone a week & all the news of you is of heavy seas delaying your progress – plans to change into planes at Bermuda, so as to arrive in time, & then those plans cancelled.

I hope you are able to rest in spite of wind & weather and the anxiety in the Far East. How calm we all are – Hong Kong threatened immediately,

Singapore ultimately? perhaps not so ultimately Borneo invaded – Burmah? to say nothing of the blows to America in the Pacific.

Here I am bound to my Russian Fund. We have passed the Million Pound target & that without what will come in from the Flag Days, held not only in London but all over the country. I visited many depôts all over London from dawn till dusk – The people came running everywhere – They are so good & sweet especially the old & they all asked about you. Yesterday Mary's leave came to an end; I took her & Judy[1] in your car & deposited them as night was falling at their new camp near Enfield.

Well my beloved Winston. May God keep you and inspire you to make good plans with the President. It's a horrible world at present. Europe overrun by the Nazi hogs & the Far East by yellow Japanese lice.

I am spending Christmas here at the Annexe & going to Chequers on Saturday the 27th.

Tender love & thoughts,
Clemmie

Winston S. Churchill to Clement Attlee
(Churchill papers, 20/49)

19 December 1941

I deeply regret the loss of Lees Smith.[2] He was a good man and true.

Please send me some account of what passed in Secret Session.

We have gone on ahead of our escort for the last three days and have thought it better to maintain wireless silence. Fully agree with your proposal in your Taut No. 56 for release of information. All necessary steps will be taken from our end.

Winston S. Churchill for the Chiefs of Staff Committee
(Cabinet Papers, 69/4)

20 December 1941
Most Secret

MEMORANDUM ON THE FUTURE CONDUCT OF THE WAR
PART IV – NOTES ON THE PACIFIC

The Japanese have naval superiority, which enables them to transport troops to almost any desired point, possess themselves of it, and establish it for

[1] Judy Montagu the daughter of Clementine Churchill's cousin Venetia Montagu (formerly Venetia Stanley).

[2] The Rt. Hon Hastings Bertrand Lees-Smith, MP, died on 18 December 1941, aged sixty-three.

an air-naval fuelling base. The Allies will not have for some time the power to fight a general fleet engagement. Their power of convoying troops depends upon the size of the seas, which reduces the chance of interception. Even without superior sea-power we may descend by surprise here and there. But we could not carry on a sustained operation across the seas. We must expect therefore to be deprived one by one of our possessions and strong-points in the Pacific, and that the enemy will establish himself fairly easily in one after the other, mopping up the local garrisons.

2. In this interim period our duty is one of stubborn resistance at each point attacked, and to slip supplies and reinforcements through as opportunity offers, taking all necessary risks. If our forces resist stubbornly and we reinforce them as much as possible, the enemy will be forced to make ever larger overseas commitments far from home; his shipping resources will be strained, and his communications will provide vulnerable targets upon which all available naval and air forces, United States, British, and Dutch – especially submarines – should concentrate their effort. It is of the utmost importance that the enemy should not acquire large gains cheaply; that he should be compelled to nourish all his conquests and kept extended, and kept burning up his resources.

3. The resources of Japan are a wasting factor. The country has long been overstrained by its wasteful war in China. They were at their maximum strength on the day of the Pearl Harbor attack. If it is true, as Stalin asserts, that they have, in addition to their own Air Force, 1,500 German aeroplanes (and he would have opportunities of knowing how they got there), they have now no means of replacing wastage other than by their small home production of 300/500 per month. Our policy should be to make them maintain the largest possible number of troops in their conquests overseas, and to keep them as busy as possible, so as to enforce well-filled lines of communication and a high rate of aircraft consumption. If we idle and leave them at ease they will be able to extend their conquests cheaply and easily, work with a minimum of overseas forces, make the largest gains and the smallest commitments, and thus inflict upon us an enormous amount of damage. It is therefore right and necessary to fight them at every point where we have a fair chance, so as to keep them burning and extended.

4. But we must steadily aim at regaining superiority at sea at the earliest moment. This can be gained in two ways: first, by the strengthening of our capital ships. The two new Japanese battleships built free from Treaty limitations must be considered a formidable factor, influencing the whole Pacific theatre. It is understood that two new American battleships will be fit for action by May. Of course, all undertakings in war must be subject to the action of the enemy, accidents, and misfortune, but if our battleship strength should not be further reduced, nor any new unforeseen stress arise, we should hope to place the *Nelson* and the *Rodney* at the side of these two new American

battleships, making four 16-inch-gun modern vessels of major strength. Behind such a squadron the older reconstructed battleships of the United States should be available in numbers sufficient to enable a fleet action, under favourable circumstances, to be contemplated at any time after the month of May. The recovery of our naval superiority in the Pacific, even if not brought to a trial of strength, would reassure the whole western seaboard of the American continent, and thus prevent a needless dissipation on a gigantic defensive effort of forces which have offensive parts to play. We must therefore set before ourselves, as a main strategic object, the forming of a definitely superior battle fleet in the Pacific, and we must aim at May as the date when this will be achieved.

5. Not only then, but in the interval, the warfare of aircraft carriers should be developed to the greatest possible extent. We are ourselves forming a squadron of three aircraft arriers, suitably attended, to act in the waters between South Africa, India, and Australia. The United States have already seven regular carriers, compared with Japan's ten, but those of the United States are larger. To this force of regular warship aircraft carriers we must add a very large development of improvised carriers, both large and small. In this way alone can we increase our sea power rapidly. Even if the carriers can only fly a dozen machines, they may play their part in combination with other carriers. We ought to develop a floating air establishment sufficient to enable us to acquire and maintain for considerable periods local air superiority over shore-based aircraft and sufficient to cover the landing of troops in order to attack the enemy's new conquests. Unless or until this local air superiority is definitely acquired, even a somewhat superior fleet on our side would fight at a serious disadvantage. We cannot get more battleships than those now in sight for the year 1942, but we can and must get more aircraft carriers. It takes five years to build a battleship, but it is possible to improvise a carrier in six months. Here then is a field for invention and ingenuity similar to that which called forth the extraordinary fleets and flotillas which fought on the Mississippi in the Civil War. It must be accepted that the priority given to seaborne aircraft of a suitable type will involve a retardation in the full-scale bombing offensive against Germany which we have contemplated as a major method of waging war. This however is a matter of time and of degree. We cannot in 1942 hope to reach the levels of bomb discharge in Germany which we had prescribed for that year, but we shall surpass them in 1943. Our joint programme may be late, but it will come along. And meanwhile the German cities and other targets will not disappear. While every effort must be made to speed up the rate of bomb discharge upon Germany until the great scales prescribed for 1943 and 1944 are reached, nevertheless we may be forced by other needs to face a retardation in our schedules. The more important will it be therefore that in this interval a force, be it only symbolic, of United States bombing squadrons should operate from the British Isles against the German cities and seaports.

6. Once the Allies have regained battle fleet superiority in the Pacific and have created a seaborne air power sufficient to secure local supremacy for certain periods, it will be possible either to attack the Japanese in their overseas conquests by military expeditions or to attack them in their homeland. It may well be the latter will be found the better. We must imagine the Japanese Air Force as being steadily and rapidly reduced and having no adequate power of replenishment. The approach to the shores of Japan near enough for seaborne air power to ravage their cities should be freed from its present prohibitive cost and danger. Nothing will more rapidly relieve the Japanese attacks in the East Indian theatre. Under the protection of the superior battle fleet and the seaborne air power aforesaid, it should be possible to acquire and regain various island bases, enabling a definite approach to be made to the homeland of Japan. The burning of Japanese cities by incendiary bombs will bring home in a most effective way to the people of Japan the dangers of the course to which they have committed themselves, and nothing is more likely to cramp the reinforcing of their overseas adventures.

7. The establishment of air bases in China or Russia from which attacks can be made upon the Japanese cities is in everyone's mind. It is most desirable that Russia should enter the war against Japan, thus enabling her own and Allied aircraft to bomb all the main cities in Japan from a convenient distance and would also make available a force of about seventy Russian submarines to cut the Japanese lines of communications with their overseas commitments, especially at the time of departure from Japan. However, this is not a point upon which we can press the Russians unduly at the present time. They have withstood and are withstanding the giant assault of the German Army. They have achieved undreamed of success. If their resistance to the German Armies were to bring down or even if their pressure upon them were to be relaxed, all the problems the Caucasus, Syria, Palestine and Persia would resume the menacing shape they have only lately lost, entailing immense diversions of force upon Great Britain and offering no satisfactory assurance of success. The influence of the German losses, and defeats against Russia upon the German people must be depressing, and if this is prolonged it may provoke stresses within the German régime of the utmost hopeful consequence. M Stalin has indicated that perhaps in the spring he may be able to act against Japan. If he does not feel able, or willing to do so now, it would be a mistake to press him unduly. Russia has more than rowed her weight in the boat, and she alone must judge when to take on more burden. The question of whether air bases in Russia could be acquired without entailing war between Japan and Russia is worth while studying. It would certainly not be in Japan's interest, any more than that of Russia, to open up this new front of war. It might mean that an attitude of non-belligerance might be adopted by Russia at a period before she would be willing to come in to the war. Such an attitude of non-belligerency might permit aircraft, based in China, to refuel in Siberia before and after bombing Japan.

8. The danger of the Japanese using their numerous cruisers to raid shipping between Australia and the Middle East, and even to assail our convoy route round the Cape, will require to be met by the provision of battleship escort. We propose to use the four 'R' Class battleships for this purpose if we need to. It is to be hoped that United States will also be ready to help in convoying work against cruiser attacks in the Pacific.

9. Lastly, there is the question of whether we should ask the United States to base her battle-fleet in Singapore, or perhaps make such a movement conditional on our adding our two battleships from the Atlantic. I am in much doubt about this. When we see what happened to the *Prince of Wales* and the *Repulse* in these narrow waters soon to be infested with aircraft based at many places we cannot feel that they would offer an inviting prospect to the United States. It would be represented as a purely British conception. One is not sure the work they could do when they got there, and whether they would not suffer unduly heavy losses. It would redouble the anxieties and waste of force upon the whole of the Pacific seaboard of America. It would put out of the way all possibility of a seaborne offensive against the homelands of Japan. It is conceivable that the United States authorities would agree to it at any time which can at present be foreseen.

10. We cannot tell what will happen in the Philippines, and whether or not how long United States troops will be able to defend themselves. The defence and/or recapture of the Philippines cannot be judged upon theoretical principles. Wars of the present scale are largely wars of attrition and a wise choice of a particular battle-field is not necessarily the only criterion. The Philippines will undoubtedly appear to the United States as an American battle ground which they are in honour bound to fight for. The Japanese will have to expend war power and aircraft in this conflict, and even if it does not proceed in the best heatre the process of exhaustion and wearing down of the weaker country by the stronger is of very great advantage and relief to us in the Pacific.

11. For these reasons it would not be wise to press the Americans to move their main fleet to Singapore.

12. We need not fear that this war in the Pacific will, after the first shock is over, absorb an unduly large proportion of United States forces. The numbers of troops that we should wish them to use in Europe in 1942 will not be so large as to be prevented by their Pacific operations, limited as these must be. What will harm us is for a vast United States Army of ten millions to be created which for at least two years while it was training would absorb all the available supplies and stand idle defending the American continent. The best way of preventing the creation of such a situation and obtaining the proper use of the large forces and ample supplies of munitions which will presently be forthcoming is to enable the Americans to regain their naval power in the Pacific and not to discourage them from the precise secondary overseas operations which they may perhaps contemplate.

Patrick Kinna: recollection
(*Letter to the author, 10 October 1984*)

[20 December 1941] HMS *Duke of York*

I well remember one morning when I was taking dictation from WSC in his cabin, feeling none too well because of the very rough seas, my feelings being aggravated by the PM's cigar-smoke, I could hear some matelots whistling and I knew only too well from experience that the PM could not bear whistling at any time. I hoped he couldn't hear it – but he did! Suddenly he angrily told me to go and tell those sailors to stop whistling. I had a shrewd idea what they would say to me! However, I hastily left his cabin, not knowing quite what to do. I think I said a few hurried prayers and the whistling miraculously ceased. I returned to continue taking dictation, the Prime Minister obviously believing that I had quietened the ship's company!

Clement Attlee to Winston S. Churchill
(*Churchill papers, 20/23*)

20 December 1941 11 Downing Street

My dear Prime Minister,

I was sorry to hear that you had had a stormy voyage. I hope you have had a better time in the later part of the journey.

Events in the Far East have rather disturbed public, Press and MPs most of whom seem to have been oblivious of the danger of which we have been conscious for months. House, was, therefore fractious and difficult. Contrary to the information of the Whips it became clear that there was great opposition to adjourning for a month. To press it would have meant a division with a substantial minority so there was no option but to accept January 7th which had been proposed unfortunately by Shinwell.

In secret session there was general tendency to blame the Government for alleged unpreparedness in the Far East with special reference to Air strength and defence of aerodromes while the question of the sending out into action of the capital ships was much stressed. There was an undercurrent of opposition to the Government generally and some organized interrupting of Alexander[1] mainly from a group of Conservatives.

Winterton led off pretty reasonably though critical of you under the guise of saying that the responsibility must be placed on the right shoulders. He was rather truculent at the end with threats of what should be done if we had not provided Indian troops with Air Support. I spoke next in order to announce

[1] A. V. Alexander, First Lord of the Admiralty.

your and Anthony's visits, the former appeared already to have become widely known. I dealt generally with allied cooperation and indicated the general considerations which ought to be taken into account in making criticisms of the sufficiency of our armaments in any given area. Keyes followed with a recital of his grievances and qualities from Dunkirk to date. Others followed all more or less critical. Alexander gave a very good account of the whole position in the Far East and of the battleship business and of the whole circumstances as to air support so far as known but was interrupted a lot. In the last few minutes Margesson said a word about defence of aerodromes. The House ended in rather an uneasy mood due, I think, largely to apprehension rather than to anything definite. There are of course a number of trouble makers on both sides of the House who are now fishing in these disturbed waters.

There is also a good deal of apprehension about the defence of India with which is connected anxiety as to the political situation. This cannot be ignored as it transcends Party divisions. The *Evening Standard* and the *Mail* and other papers have now joined the *Herald* in demanding action of some kind on the Indian political position.

We have reviewed the Far Eastern position in the Defence Committee and have done our utmost to reinforce. Earle Page has been very persistent and the tone in Australia is very critical. I think that I have demonstrated to him that we are doing our utmost in the circumstance, but he harps on the past.

The Russian Front and Libya are bright spots in a rather gloomy landscape, but we none of us have been under any delusions as to what Japan's entry into the war meant. The general public will gradually appreciate the position.

With all good wishes for Christmas to you and the party.

Yours ever,
Clement R. Attlee

Sir Archibald Sinclair to Winston S. Churchill
(*Churchill papers, 20/29*)

20 December 1941

Air Ministry,
Whitehall

We are anxiously following your progress and I hope all goes well with you. I am afraid you have had rather a rough passage.

It was a bit rough too in the House of Commons yesterday, but not as bad as I had been led to expect. Roger Keyes made a very emotional and largely irrelevant speech (including a long account of his failure to persuade you to abandon the Weygand plan for closing the gap between the French and British Armies), but it caught the mood of the House and must be rated a success. Alexander made a good speech in winding up, but, although the debate had been quiet up till then (as I had observed to Kingsley Wood, who agreed with me), the House did not give him a very good hearing. Nobody complained of your absence – indeed, I am sure that everybody approved the reason for it. Nevertheless, it seemed to me that the House could not get over their disappointment that you were not there to hear their complaints and answer them with your unique authority. David[1] said a few sentences at the end on the defence of aerodromes, and that went well. They are restive and anxious and it is important that you should be there before we have another debate.

The daylight attack on Brest was successful yesterday. The telegrams will give you the main facts. Let me only add that Peirse tells me that the squadrons who took part in the attack are very pleased with the result. The operation was well planned and for once we were favoured by the weather. The defence of the heavy bombers proved remarkably effective. One Stirling, indeed, on the way back had the insolence to break formation and dive after four Messerschmitts, shooting down one! The latest figures of casualties suffered and inflicted are:

Casualties suffered:
4 Stirlings and 1 Manchester missing.
1 Manchester crashed, crew killed.
1 Halifax down in the sea, crew rescued.
1 Long Range Hurricane missing.
Enemy casualties claimed:
10 Me.109s certain.
3 Me.109s probable.
6 Me.109s damaged.

The Stirlings alone claim six Messerschmitts. One Stirling claims to have beaten off an attack by nine of them. It always takes some time thoroughly to sift the reports, and these figures may be later and more accurate than those which you will have received in your signals. The photographs which I have seen show that both battle cruisers were damaged but that the *Prince Eugen* was not hit.

Good luck to you in the conversations in America, on which so much depends for all of us and especially for the Royal Air Force.

Archie

[1] David Margesson, Secretary of State for War.

Winston S. Churchill to Lord Halifax
(*Churchill papers, 20/47*)

20 December 1941
Hush
Most Secret

1. I am, of course, leaving arrangements for forthcoming conference entirely in hands of President and his advisers. Nevertheless, you might like to have a few suggestions, gist of which you could pass to President in appropriate form.

2. On first evening (Monday) we should like to comply with general practice by an exchange of views informally, I with President, and Chiefs of Staff with Joint Staff Mission. Chiefs of Staff would be glad of your views and advice early.

3. After hearing views of Joint Staff Mission, Chiefs of Staff will complete Tuesday morning a short paper they have prepared on Allied strategy. After tea Tuesday I suggest Joint United States – British Staff Conference. We think it essential this should be on highest level with President in the (? chair). I shall have already given President my views on general situation and am prepared to develop them at the Conference.

4. Unless American Chiefs of Staff would prefer to table paper of their own on Joint strategy, suggest our Chiefs of Staff paper should form basis of our first formal discussion. Joint strategy must be settled and agreed at the outset before we can decide dispositions and programme.

5. Subsequently, Joint Conference might meet daily in the morning. I should hope we can limit the numbers attending as far as possible, say, to maximum of eight on our side and ten on the American side.

6. Once strategy has been agreed, Staffs can get down to dispositions and supply experts can go fully into action.

7. I am attracted by the idea of holding a Supreme Allied War Council meeting towards the end of the Conference, to which Monsieur Stalin's and General Chiang Kai-shek's representatives would be invited.

If President favours this proposal, I should like to sound Moscow and Chungking at once.

Winston S. Churchill to Clement Attlee
(*Churchill papers, 20/50*)

20 December 1941

Stalin's demand about Finland, Baltic States and Roumania are directly contrary to the first, second and third articles of the Atlantic Charter, to which Stalin has subscribed. There can be no question whatever of our making such an agreement, secret or public, direct or implied, without prior agreement with the United States. The time has not yet come to settle frontier questions, which can only be resolved at the Peace Conference when we have won the war.

2. The mere desire to have an agreement which can be published should never lead us into making wrongful promises. Foreign Secretary has acquitted himself admirably and should not be downhearted if he has to leave Moscow without any flourish of trumpets. The Russians have got to go on fighting for their lives, anyway, and are dependent upon us for very large supplies, which we have most painfully gathered, and which we shall faithfully deliver.

3. I hope the Cabinet will agree to communicate the above to the Foreign Secretary. He will no doubt act with the necessary tact and discretion, but he should know decisively where we stand.

4. Later. Cabinet answer to Eden now received. I fully concur.

Winston S. Churchill to Sir Orme Sargent
(*Churchill papers, 20/50*)

20 December 1941

MESSAGE TO ADMIRAL DARLAN

Amended answer suggested:

At present time the British, if victorious, would refuse to treat or meet at a Peace Conference any French Government which contained men who had actively hampered our efforts to win war. War will be certainly won by Britain, United States and Russia, but it is not won yet, and there may be time for entire new chapter to be written. If French fleet at Toulon were to sail for North and West African ports and be prepared to resist German attack, that would be an event of the first order. Whoever commanded or effected such a great stroke of policy and strategy would have made a decisive contribution to Allied Cause, which carries with it restoration of France as one of leading Powers in Europe. Such a service would entitle the author to an honourable place in Allied ranks and terrible difficulties in which we were all placed in the previous period would appear in their true light or fade away. The moment for such an action may be very near. General Auchinleck will soon complete destruction of all German and Italian forces in Libya. The United States are known to take a deep interest in French North Africa. We hold strong forces in Great Britain capable of giving that aid. We should be prepared to discuss the plan in detail arranged by anyone who possessed the power and the will to take this invaluable step towards the salvation of France.

You may add if you think fit: 'The above comes from Churchill himself.' These are my suggestions only, and you should, of course, discuss with the Lord President and the Lord Privy Seal as well as with COS Committee.

Winston S. Churchill to Viscount Cranborne
(*Churchill papers, 20/50*)

20 December 1941

CONVERSATIONS WITH MR DE VALERA

Your conduct of negotiations approved. I will, of course, discuss the whole matter with the President and bring it before the Cabinet on my return. We must give time for the American pressure to work. If, as I hope, United States forces arrive in Northern Ireland in the near future, this will be a potent factor. Meanwhile, do not give them any arms.

Winston S. Churchill to Anthony Eden
(*Churchill papers, 20/47*)

20 December 1941
Secret

Naturally you will not be rough with Stalin. We are bound to United States not to enter into secret and special pacts. To approach President Roosevelt with these proposals would be to court a blank refusal and might experience lasting trouble on both sides.

2. The strategic security of Russia on her western border will be one of the objects of peace conference. The position of Leningrad has been proved by events to be of particular danger. The first object will be the prevention of any new outbreak by Germany. The separation of Prussia from South Germany, and actual definition of Prussia itself, will be one of the greatest issues to be decided.[1] But all this lies in a future which is uncertain and probably remote. We have now to win the war by a hard and prolonged struggle. To raise such issues publicly now would only be to rally all Germans round Hitler.

3. Even to raise them informally with President Roosevelt at this time would, in my opinion, be inexpedient. This is the sort of line I should take thus avoiding any abrupt or final closing of interviews. Do not be disappointed if you are not able to bring home a joint public declaration on lines set forth in your Cabinet paper. I am sure your visit has done utmost good and your attitude will win general approval.

This voyage seems very long.

[1] The separation of Prussia from South Germany was to remain Churchill's aim until the end of the war. It disregarded the fact that many of the most extreme Nazis were South Germans, and some of the most dedicated and daring anti-Nazis were Prussians.

Winston S. Churchill to J. V. Stalin
(*Churchill papers, 20/50*)

20 December 1941

I send you sincere good wishes for your birthday[1] and hope that future anniversaries will enable you to bring to Russia victory, peace and safety after so much storm.

J. V. Stalin to Winston S. Churchill
(*Churchill papers, 20/47*)

21 December 1941

Thank you very much indeed for your good courtesy on occasion of my birthday. I take this opportunity to express to you and to the friends British Army my sincere congratulations in connection with your recent victories in Libya.

Winston S. Churchill to David Margesson
(*Churchill papers, 20/36*)

21 December 1941

Your minute of 3rd December about the Beveridge report.[2]

1. The memorandum to be published by the War Office at the same time as the Beveridge report on the use of skilled men in the services must be both more effective and more precise than that at present proposed.

2. The War Office should also take their stand on the grounds that it is their duty to make an efficient fighting machine rather than a well-conducted industrial establishment. Nothing must therefore be done seriously to break the cohesion of section, platoon and company, and no general disturbance of the army system can be tolerated in view of the danger of invasion in home ports.

3. It must, however, be clearly shown how skilled men in units, as they at present exist, are being used and how still better use will be made of them. The memorandum should thus firmly rebut those suggestions in the Beveridge report which would affect the cohesion and military efficiency of the army.

4. This does not mean that the War Office can use the excuse of military efficiency to cover over the grave defect brought to light by the report. The memorandum should not appear merely to be a whitewashing document, but

[1] It was Stalin's sixty-second birthday; he was born in 1879, five years after Churchill.

[2] On the use of skilled men in the armed Services.

should show that a really serious effort is being made to rectify short-comings. Parliament and the public will only be reassured if the War Office can state in concrete, rather than in abstract, how amendment is being made. The memorandum should therefore deal specifically and in a manner readily understood by the layman with the main points in the report.

5. These are:

(a) That the reservoir of unused skill in the army is sufficient to cover all future demands for skilled men, except armament artificers.

(b) That economy in skilled men could be secured by review of the establishment of many field units.

(c) That more effective steps could be taken to utilize the skill of those men whose units will be required at the front but which at present are not engaged.

(d) That great improvements are possible in the machinery for testing, remuster and transfer of skilled men.

(e) That a special corps of mechanical engineers should be formed to put an end to present duplication.

(f) That men should be enlisted into the army as a whole and not into specific corps or units.

6. The War Office reply will have to be carefully drafted if it is to be effective. You should set up a small committee which I suggest might consist of the Financial Secretary, Sir James Grigg and the Adjutant-General,[1] to prepare it. I should like the reply to be submitted to me about 10th January so that the matter can, if necessary, be brought before the Cabinet in good time.

Winston S. Churchill to Private Office, 10 Downing Street
(*Churchill papers, 20/50*)

21 December 1941

Following message from the Prime Minister to the Commander-in-Chief and Governor, Hong Kong,[2] should be despatched in cypher if this is still practicable:

(Secret.)

We were greatly concerned to hear of the landings on Hong Kong Island which have been effected by the Japanese. We cannot judge from here the conditions which rendered these landings possible or prevented effective counter-attacks upon the intruders. There must, however, be no thought of surrender. Every part of the island must be fought and the enemy resisted with the utmost stubbornness.

[1] Lieutenant-General Sir Ronald Forbes Adam, Adjutant-General to the Forces, 1941-46.
[2] Sir Mark Young.

The enemy should be compelled to expend the utmost life and equipment. There must be vigorous fighting in the inner defences and, if the need be, from house to house. Every day that you are able to maintain your resistance you help the Allied cause all over the world, and by a prolonged resistance you and your men can win the lasting honour which we are sure will be your due.

If cypher message cannot be sent, following shorter message should be despatched *en clair*:

The eyes of the world are upon you. We expect you to resist to the end. The honour of the Empire is in your hands.

In either case the shorter message may be given to troops.

Winston S. Churchill to Field Marshal Smuts

(*Churchill papers, 20/47*)

21 December 1941
Most Secret
Personal

I thought it my duty to cross the Atlantic again, and hope in a few days to confer with President Roosevelt on the whole conduct of the war. I hope of course to procure from him assistance in a forward policy in French North Africa and in West Africa. This is in accordance with American ideas, but they may well be too much preoccupied with the war with Japan. I will keep you informed.

Kindest regards.

Winston S. Churchill to Clementine Churchill

(*Baroness Spencer-Churchill papers*)

21 December 1941 'At sea'

My darling,

Yesterday, Saturday, finished the longest week I have lived since the war began. We have had almost unceasing gales. For a long time going round the Bloody Foreland in the worst part of the U-boat and Focke Wulf areas we could not make more than six knots unless we threw off our destroyer escort. For thirty-six hours we were within 5- or 600 miles of Brest, with its bomber squadrons, and it was very fortunate that no Focke Wulf spotted us through the gaps in the clouds. Three days ago we left our destroyers behind as they could not keep up in the rough sea, and in half an hour we hope to meet the American destroyer escort just North of Bermuda. The weather has again turned so rough that we shall no doubt leave them behind too and press on, but even so we now speak of Tuesday afternoon as the likely time for reaching Annapolis. If this is realized, the voyage will have taken ten days, which is a big slice in times like these.

I am very well and have not suffered from seasickness at all, though I took two doses of Mothersill the first day. These ships literally cannot go more than 17 or 18 knots in a really heavy sea. No one is allowed on deck, and we have two men with broken arms and legs. I have a lovely cabin in the bridge structure as well as my apartments aft. These latter are unusable owing to the noise and vibration. Here it is cool and quiet and daylight. I spend the greater part of the day in bed, getting up for lunch, going to bed immediately afterwards to sleep and then up again for dinner. I manage to get a great deal of sleep and have also done a great deal of work in my waking hours. We have been very well supplied with official telegrams and secret news.

We have twenty-seven cypherers on board for this service alone, and all my telegrams from Auchinleck and others are coming through, but of general news one knows but little except what the wireless says, and oddly enough we have got practically nothing from the United States wireless. I do not, therefore, know the situation I shall find on arrival. I feel I ought to go to Canada while I am over this side, but I do not quite know when or how I shall come back. I shall certainly stay long enough to do all that has to be done, having come all this way at so much trouble and expense.

We make a very friendly party at meal times, and everyone is now accustomed to the motion. The great stand-by is the cinema. Every night we have a film. I have seen some very good ones. The one last night, *Blood and Sand*,[1] about bull-fighters, is the best we have seen so far. The cinema is a wonderful form of entertainment, and takes the mind away from other things.

About these other things. The worst that has happened is the collapse of the resistance of Hong Kong; although one knew it was a forlorn outpost, we expected that they would hold out on the fortified island for a good many weeks, possibly for several months, but now they seem on the verge of surrender after only a fortnight's struggle. Not very good news has also come in from Malaya. Owing to our loss of the command of the sea, the Japanese have an unlimited power of reinforcement, and our people are retreating under orders to defend the Southern tip and the vital Fortress of Singapore. I have given a good many instructions to move men, guns and aircraft in this direction. We must expect to suffer heavily in this war with Japan, and it is no use the critics saying 'Why were we not prepared?' when everything we had was already fully engaged. The entry of the United States into the war is worth

[1] Directed by Rouben Mamoulian (1941), with Tyrone Power, Linda Darnell and Rita Hayworth in the leading roles. A technicolour film about a bullfighter (played by Tyrone Power) who falls in love with a socialite (Rita Hayworth), turning away from his faithful Carmen (Linda Darnell) who stands by him when he faces real danger in the bull ring.

all the losses sustained in the East many times over. Still these losses are very painful to endure and will be very hard to repair.

On the other hand there is good news. We made a fine kill of U-boats round Gibraltar, about seven altogether in a week. This is a record. There has never been such a massacre, and it should dunch the spirits of the survivors when they get home to see how many of their companion vessels have been sent to the bottom. But the best of all is Auchinleck's continuous victorious advance. Before the end of the year he will be at Benghazi and well on the road farther West. No doubt there will still be pockets of resistance to mop up, but there is every hope that the whole armed force of the enemy, which amounted to 100,000 Italians and 50,000 Huns, will be dead or captured. That, at any rate, would be a clean job, and gives relief as well as encouragement at an anxious juncture. It is very important for the Americans that we should have proofs that our soldiers can fight a modern war and beat the Germans on even terms, or even at odds, for that is what they have done. This lends weight to our counsels and requests.

I had been hoping till an hour ago to dine with the President tomorrow, Monday, night – and this is not yet impossible – but it is still blowing hard and from my porthole I can see, every minute, tremendous seas pouring over the bows of the ship, while down below can be heard the crash of them striking the sides. We are running obliquely across the waves and sometimes the ship rolls very heavily. However, once you get used to the motion, you don't care a damn.

You can imagine how anxious I am to arrive and put myself in relation to the fuller news and find out what is the American outlook and what they propose to do. Long and not free from risk as the voyage has been, I am glad I did not try to fly, although they make you fine stories of how you can cover the Atlantic in twelve or fourteen hours. In the Winter time this is very rare. There are all kinds of difficulties and dangers, and sometimes you are kept waiting six, eight or ten days for favourable weather, so that the tortoise may still beat the hare. Everything is being kept open for the return journey, as I, particularly, do not wish to make up my mind; nor does anyone know how it will be accomplished. As soon as I get established in the White House I will ring you up on the trans-Atlantic cable. I wish particularly to know the length of your stockings, so that I can bring you a few pairs to take the edge off Oliver Lyttelton's coupons.

I had a telegram from Randolph asking for a message for his paper *Parade*. You should ask Brendan to show you one of these. It is quite a fine publication, and I have sent them a Christmastide greeting.

They seem to have kept Anthony's visit to Russia very secret up to the present, but I suppose it will be out at the same time as mine, i.e. tomorrow or the day after. I look forward so much to talking to you over the telephone, but we shall have to be careful as, of course, it is not secret.

I have read two books, *Brown on Resolution*[1] and *Forty Centuries Look Down*. You would like both of them, particularly the opening part of *Brown on Resolution*, which is a charming love story most attractively told. The other is a very good account of Napoleon's relations with Josephine, and his excursions of various kinds to and in Egypt. I will bring them both back for you.

I am frightfully fed up with the idea of an extra day being tacked on to all these others, but one has to accept the inevitable. Being in a ship in such weather as this is like being in a prison, with the extra chance of being drowned.[2] Nevertheless, it is perhaps a good thing to stand away from the canvas from time to time and take a full view of the picture. I find it has clarified my ideas, although for the first few days one was numb and dull and stupid. That process may have proved restful and preparatory for the busy days that are to come.

I hope the Fund is getting on well, and I daresay before I return it will have reached the million mark. I hope you brought off your camouflage trick of publishing the photograph of me buying the badge on your Flag Day on the 17th.

Anthony Eden to Winston S. Churchill
(*Churchill papers, 20/47*)

22 December 1941 Moscow

Thank you for your heartening message. Our work has ended on a friendly note. Final discussions with Stalin were the best and I am sure that the visit has been worth while. We have allayed some at least of the past suspicions. Stalin, I believe, sincerely wants [grp. undec. ?military] agreements but he will not sign until we recognize his frontiers and we must expect continued badgering on this issue. Meanwhile our position and that of America is completely safeguarded. Banquet lasted until 5 this morning, Stalin's birthday. We drank your health and some others. Stalin spoke very warmly of you.

Timoshenko,[3] who was present, was most confident of the Russian

[1] *Brown on Resolution* by C.S. Forester (1899–1966) was published in 1929. It is a story of individual courage and resistance, set in the First World War.

[2] A reference to Dr Johnson's remark: 'No man will be a sailor who has contrivance enough to get himself into jail; for being in a ship is being in a jail, with the chance of being drowned.' (*Journal of a Tour to the Hebrides*, 3rd edition, page 126, 31 August 1773)

[3] Semyon Timoshenko, 1895–1970. A friend of Stalin since the 1920 campaign against Poland. Participated in the occupation of eastern Poland, 1939; in the invasion of Finland, 1940. Commissar of Defence, in charge of reorganizing the Soviet forces (with special reference to the training and discipline of recruits), May 1940–June 1941. Chairman of the Soviet High Command Higher Committee, 23 June 1941; Commander of the Western Front, June–September 1941; of the South-Western Front, September–May 1942. His forces were driven back at the Battle of Kharkov, May 1942, after which he was transferred to the (quieter) North-Western Front. Subsequently Representative of the Soviet High Command in the Battle of the Balkans.

prospects in the south. Both he and Stalin emphasized the fall in German morale.

We leave tomorrow.

Winston S. Churchill to General Paget[1]
(*Churchill papers, 20/36*)

22 December 1941

This is a most admirable paper,[2] and I agree with every word of it. I am glad to think that in your new great sphere you will have an opportunity of putting into force the many wise and stimulating principles it contains. You may count on my assistance in every way. I have already done all in my power to prevent sections and platoons from being disturbed needlessly, or the infantry used for civil purposes other than in emergencies or the harvest. While I greatly admire the conception of a well-armed infantry battalion working with the élan and combined individualism of a pack of hounds, I am also anxious about the smart side of things. I hope there are going to be no fussy changes in the Manual Exercises and that 'spit and polish' will not be incompatible with effective field training.

2. Pray let me have a further note to show how you are applying the ideas of this paper and return it to me. I have been very much pleased by it.

Winston S. Churchill to Lord Woolton
(*Churchill papers, 20/36*)

22 December 1941

EGG DISTRIBUTION SCHEME

The fact that 370,000 small producers have enough gumption to keep chickens is a matter for congratulation; under this head the only complaint I have heard is that this practice is not sufficiently encouraged. After all, the backyard fowls use up a lot of scrap and so save cereals.

I quite recognize your difficulties, with your imports cut to one-third, but I hope that you will get in the quantity which you had planned, so that this important animal protein which is so essential in the kitchen should not be deficient.

[1] General Brooke's successor as Commander-in-Chief, Home Forces.

[2] On the Training of Infantry by Major General John Utterson-Kelso, sent to Churchill on 15 November 1941 by General Paget.

Winston S. Churchill to Lord Moyne
(Churchill papers, 20/50)

22 December 1941

I am distressed at tragedy of Federated Malay States. As you know, we cannot give any effective protection north of the defensive line in Johore. They have always stood by us so well in the past and now we can do nothing for them. Please let me know what is happening and what they say about it. I presume that all assurances have been given that we will see them righted in the final victory. What is being done about destroying stocks and plant, as well as communications?

Winston S. Churchill to President Franklin D. Roosevelt
(Churchill papers, 20/49)

22 December 1941

Impossible reach mouth Potomac before 6.30 p.m., which would be too late for plan you have so kindly made for us. Can anchor Hampton Roads at 4.15 p.m. I should like to come on by airplane to Washington airfield, reaching you in time for dinner. If weather prevents this could I have a train to Washington from whatever is most convenient starting point in the vicinity of Hampton Roads? Please on no account come out to meet me either way. Looking forward so much to seeing you at White House.

White House itinerary
(Commander C. R. Thompson papers)

22 December 1941

The Prime Minister and party arrived Hampton Roads, Va., aboard HMS—,[1] late afternoon Dec. 22. A special train had been assembled at Phoebus[2] to bring party to Washington. The PM decided to fly to Washington with his immediate party. This flight handled by the Navy. Remaining members of party boarded the special train at Phoebus and arrived Washington just before midnight, Dec. 22. The PM landed Anacostia Naval Air Station.

[1] Left blank for secrecy.
[2] A small town near Hampton Roads.

Sir Charles Wilson: diary[1]
(*'Winston Churchill, The Struggle for Survival, 1940-65'*)

22 December 1941 Washington DC

Before we anchored in Chesapeake Bay the PM was talking about steaming up the Potomac to Washington. Now he was like a child in his impatience to meet the President. He spoke as if every minute counted. It was absurd to waste time; he must fly. Portal, Harriman, Max and I came with him. The rest of the party followed by train.[2]

Our Lockheed was over the lights of Washington in three-quarters of an hour. It gave me a sense of security; we were a long way from the war and the London black-out. On landing I let the PM have a start before I got out. Looking around, I noticed a man propped against a big car, a little way off. The PM called and introduced me. It was President Roosevelt. Even in the half-light I was struck by the size of his head. I suppose that is why Winston thinks of him as majestic and statuesque, for he has no legs to speak of since his paralysis. He said warmly that he was very glad to welcome me. I was a doctor, and he immediately began to speak of the casualties at Pearl Harbor, many of them with very bad burns. He made me feel that I had known him for a long time. Halifax took me in his car to the Mayflower Hotel, while Max went with the PM to the White House.

Sir Charles Wilson: diary
(*'Winston Churchill, The Struggle for Survival, 1940-65'*)

22 December 1941

It was nearly midnight and I had gone to my room when a page brought a message from the PM to say that he wanted to see me at the White House. I went in one of the President's cars, but when we arrived at the gate the guards ran out from the lodge and flashed their torches on the driver's pass. They looked at me doubtfully before they allowed the car to enter the grounds. A black servant opened the door with a friendly smile.

I was taken up some stairs to the PM's bedroom, which I found deserted. It smelt of cigar smoke and I tried to open the window. The crumpled bed-clothes were thrown back, and the floor was strewn with newspapers, English

[1] The diary of Sir Charles Wilson (later Lord Moran) has been the object of controversy. Those who are its custodians have informed me that it is 'not a diary in the accepted sense of the word'. It would appear that Lord Moran used his short contemporary notes and jottings as the basis for a substantial elaboration several years later. This document is therefore offered to the reader with the admonition *Caveat Lector*. It is essentially a post-war memoir, an exercise in reconstruction. The first two diary entries quoted here, for 14 and 16 December 1941, came from Lord Moran's briefer, more contemporary, but almost certainly also post-war, notes.

[2] In Sir Charles Wilson's original notes this paragraph appears as follows: '5.30 p.m. Arrive Chesapeake Bay after nine long days racket. The PM with Portal, Harriman, the Beaver & me are to fly to Washington. The rest of the party will come in by trains'.

and American, just as the PM had thrown them away when he had glanced at the headlines; it would have been the first thing he would have done when they took him to his room, for he always wants to know what the papers are saying about him. I had plenty of time to catch up with the news, for it was an hour and a half before the PM came out of the President's room. He looked at me blankly; he had forgotten that he had sent for me.

'I am sorry I have kept you waiting.'

'Is there anything wrong?' I asked.

'The pulse is regular,' he said with a whimsical smile.

He wanted to know if he could take a sleeping pill. He must have a good night. No; there was nothing else he needed. Already his thoughts were back in the President's room. When I left him I said he could take two reds,[1] for I could see he was bottling up his excitement. Max took me down in the lift.

'I have never seen that fellow in better form. He conducted the conversation for two hours with great skill.'

Max, too, was agog; he lives on his nerves. The PM had been able to interest the President in a landing in North Africa. Indeed, according to Max, the President was very forthcoming; he said he would like to send three American divisions to Ulster. That had gone down well.

Winston S. Churchill: Press Conference
(Roosevelt papers)

23 December 1941 Washington DC

The President: And so I will introduce the Prime Minister.

(to the Prime Minister): I wish you would stand up for one minute and let them see you. They can't see you.

(applause greeted the Prime Minister when he stood up, but when he climbed on to his chair so that they could see him better, loud and spontaneous cheers and applause rang through the room)

The President: (to the Press) Go ahead and shoot.

Q What about Singapore, Mr Prime Minister? The people of Australia are terribly anxious about it. Would you say to be of good cheer?

The Prime Minister: We are going to do our utmost to defend Singapore and its approaches until the situation becomes so favourable to us that the general offensive in the Pacific can be resumed.

Q Thank you, sir.

Q Mr Minister –

Q (interposing) Mr Prime Minister, isn't Singapore the key to the whole situation out there?

[1] Barbiturate sleeping pills.

The Prime Minister: The key to the whole situation is the resolute manner in which the British and American Democracies are going to throw themselves into the conflict. As a geographical and strategic point it obviously is of very high importance.

Q Mr Minister, could you tell us what you think of conditions within Germany – the morale?

The Prime Minister: Well, I have always been feeling that one of these days we might get a windfall coming from that quarter, but I don't think we ought to count on it. Just go on as if they were keeping on as bad as they are, or as good as they are. And then one of these days, as we did in the last war, we may wake up and find we ran short of Huns.

(laughter)

Q Do you think the war is turning in our favor in the last month or so?

The Prime Minister: What?

Q Do you think the war is turning in our favor in the last month or so?

The Prime Minister: I can't describe the feelings of relief with which I find Russia victorious, the United States and Great Britain standing side by side. It is incredible to anyone who has lived through the lonely months of 1940. It is incredible. Thank God.

Mr Godwin:[1] Mr Prime Minister, there have been suggestions from various sources that possibly the German retreat – or the Russian success – has some element of trickery in it, that the Germans are not particularly routed. In other words, a bit of camouflage. Can you throw any light on that, or do you care to?

The Prime Minister: Well, of course, it is only my opinion, but I think that they have received a very heavy rebuff. Hitler prophesied that he would take Moscow in a short time.

Mr Godwin: (interjecting) Yes.

The Prime Minister: (continuing) Now his armies are joggling backwards over this immense front, wondering where he can find a place to winter. It won't be a comfortable place. They have had immense losses. And the Russians have shown a power of resiliency, a gift of modern warfare under their leader, Stalin, which has rendered immense service to the world cause.

Q Mr Minister, can you tell us when you think we may lick these boys?

The Prime Minister: What?

Q About what year –

[1] Earl Godwin, political writer and special correspondent, including *Washington Star* and *Montreal Star*, 1908–17. Lieutenant, United States Army, 1918–19. Chairman of publicity at the inaugural of President Wilson, and at President Roosevelt's third inaugural. White House correspondent, *Washington Times-Herald*, 1933–40. Radio broadcaster and news analyst, from 1934, including 'Watch the World Go By' from 1942. President of the Radio Correspondents Association, 1939–45.

Mr Early:[1] (interposing) (to the Prime Minister) When they might lick these boys?

Q How long will it take them to lick them?

The President: (aside) Oh.

The Prime Minister: If we manage it well, it will only take half as long as if we manage it badly. (loud laughter)

Q How long, sir, would it take if we managed it badly?

The Prime Minister: That has not been revealed to me at this moment. We don't need to manage it badly.

Q How long if we manage it well, sir?

The Prime Minister: What?

Q How long if we manage it well?

The Prime Minister: Yes?

Q How long if we manage it well?

The Prime Minister: Well, it would be imprudent to indulge in a facile optimism at the moment.

Q Do you favor a personal conference of yourself, Mr Roosevelt, Stalin, and Chiang Kai-shek?

The Prime Minister: In principle, Yes. (loud laughter)

Q Do you think it is important, Mr Prime Minister, that our American war materials continue to go, to some extent at least, through the Middle East and to Russia during this particular period?

The Prime Minister: My feeling is that the military power and munitions power of the United States is going to develop on such a great scale that the problem will not so much be the – whether to choose between this and that, but how to get what is available to all the theatres in which we have to wage this World War.

Q Mr Prime Minister, in one of your speeches you mentioned three or four of the great climacterics. Would you now add our entry into the war as one of those, sir?

The Prime Minister: I think I may almost say, 'I sure do.' (loud laughter)

Q Mr Prime Minister, during your talks here, will you take up economic, and diplomatic, and post-war problems?

The Prime Minister: I hope not too much on them. Well, really, we have to concentrate on the grim emergencies, and we – when we have solved them, we shall be in a position to deal with the future of the world in a manner to give the best results, and the most lasting results, for the common peoples of

[1] Stephen T. Early, 1889–1951. Joined the United Press as a reporter, at the age of 19. Joined the Associated Press, 1913. On active service, infantry Captain, 1917–18 (Silver Star for 'meritorious service'). Washington representative of Paramount News, 1927–33. Secretary to President Roosevelt, 1933–45. President of the Pullman Standard Car Manufacturing Company, 1945–48; Under-Secretary of Defence, 1948–9; Deputy Secretary of Defence, 1949–50.

all the lands. But one has only a certain amount of life and strength, and only so many hours in the day, and other emergencies press upon us too much to be drawn into those very, very complicated, tangled and not in all cases attractive jungles.

Q Mr Prime Minister, can you say anything now about the prospect of an anti-Axis command on those discussions?

The Prime Minister: I think it would be – it would be very difficult to arrange. What you require is the broad blocking in of the main plans by the principal personages in charge of the action of the different States, and then the release of that to the highest military expert authorities for execution. But this is a war which is absolutely – literally world-wide, proceeding at the same time from one end of the globe to the other, and in the air, on the land, and on the sea. I do not think there has ever been a man born – even if he were Napoleon, he wouldn't know anything about the air – who could assume the functions of world commander-in-chief for the – I would say associated powers. (laughter)

Q Mr Prime Minister, are you giving consideration to creation of an Allied supplies command, whereby materials of the anti-Axis powers would be allocated under a central agency?

The Prime Minister: Well, there is the very closest liaison between our people over here and the United States officers. Lord Beaverbrook is here with an executive staff, and we have, I believe, quite a large staff here, and they are in the closest accord. Then at the summit of the problem is a fairly simple one of allocation in accordance with the emergency. And of course, the rule we have got to follow is to – to see how much we can help each other. It should be a rivalry in mutual helpfulness, and that is the only one.

Q (interposing) Mr Minister, do you anticipate a German offensive on a new front in the near future?

The Prime Minister: There is a lot of talk about their coming along – coming along and making an attack in the Mediterranean. There is a lot of talk about their getting ready for an invasion of England next year. We have heard a lot of this, and I expect something will come of it, but where, I can't tell. I will be very glad to be informed. Gentlemen, if you have got any information, it will be thankfully received. (laughter)

Q Mr Minister, have you any information as to whether the Germans have lost more *matériel* in Russia than they can replace by spring?

The Prime Minister: I should think that they have got ample *matériel*, because they not only have their own vast factories – which were running at full war speed when the war broke out – they have a great accumulation, and they have what they captured from so many other countries. I shouldn't think that was where they would run short. But of course, the quality of the *matériel*, as we move on each year into new and better times, they might not have the power to keep in the race with that.

Q Thank you, Mr Minister.

Q (interposing) Mr Prime Minister, what are the materials that Germany is most likely to run short of? What are the materials of which they are most short?

The Prime Minister: I did hear something about oil and other things, but it is rather technical for me.

Q Mr Prime Minister, can you interpret any of the recent events in Germany as possible internal collapse – symptomatic of an internal collapse?

The Prime Minister: Don't let us bank on that. We have got to bank on an external knockout. If the internal collapse comes, so much the better.

Q Mr Minister, have you any doubt of the ultimate victory?

The Prime Minister: I have no doubt whatever.

Q Thank you, Mr Prime Minister.

Q (interposing) What about a Christmas Message for the American people?

The Prime Minister: I am told I have to do one on Christmas Eve, but I won't give it away beforehand.

Winston S. Churchill to William Mackenzie King
(*Churchill papers, 20/49*)

23 December 1941 Washington DC

INVITATION TO OTTAWA

Thank you so much. I will certainly come. Let us arrange it later.

Winston S. Churchill to Clement Attlee, for the War Cabinet
(*Churchill papers, 20/50*)

23 December 1941

War Cabinet and Defence Committee circulation only.

President handed me following alternative drafts for a declaration of common purpose:

1. Draft of Joint Declaration by United States, Great Britain, China, the Netherlands, and other Governments

The Government of the United States of America, Great Britain, Australia, Canada, the Union of Soviet Socialist Republics, the Union of South Africa, New Zealand, China and the Netherlands,

Having subscribed to a common program of purposes and principles embodied in the Joint Declaration of the President of the United States of America and the Prime Minister of Great Britain dated 14th August, 1941, known as the Atlantic Charter,

Being convinced that complete and world-wide victory of all of them is essential to defend and preserve life, liberty, independence as well as the righteous possibilities of human freedom and justice not only in their own lands but everywhere, and, that the struggle in which they are now engaged is a common defense of human decencies everywhere against savage and brutal force seeking to subjugate the world,

Declare:

(1) Each Government pledges itself to employ its full resources against the Axis forces of conquest and to continue such employment until these forces have been finally defeated;

(2) Each Government pledges itself to the other Governments associated in this declaration to effect full co-ordination of military effort and use of resources against the common enemies;

(3) Each Government pledges itself to continue war against, and not to make a separate peace with, the common enemies or any of them.

Other Governments desirous of associating themselves in this declaration are hereby privileged to adhere to this declaration.

2. Joint Declaration by the United States of America, China, Great Britain, the Union of Soviet Socialist Republics and other signatory Governments

The Governments signatory hereto,

Having subscribed to a common program of purposes and principles embodied in the Joint Declaration of the President of the United States of America and the Prime Minister of Great Britain dated 14th August, 1941, known as the Atlantic Charter,

Being convinced that complete victory over their enemies is essential to defend life, liberty and independence, and to preserve human freedom and justice not only in their own lands but everywhere, and that the struggle in which they are now engaged is a common defense against savage and brutal forces seeking to subjugate the world,

Declare:

(1) Each signatory Government pledges itself to employ its full resources against the Government or Governments which signed the Tripartite Pact on 27th September, 1940, with which it is or may be at war, and to continue such employment until that Government or those Governments have been finally defeated;

(2) Each signatory Government pledges itself to co-operate with the others to the entire extent of its capacity to effect full co-ordination of military effort and use of resources against the common enemies or any of them.

I think this of utmost importance, and consider either draft or a combination would do, but should be glad to have your views leaving me latitude to choose.

Things are moving very quickly here. They are willing to give me everything I have asked for, including four divisions for Northern Ireland and air squadrons based on British Isles for immediate bombing attacks on Germany.

Will send you further report later.

Percy Chubb[1]*: recollection*

(*Letter to the author, 1 March 1977*)

23 December 1941

I remember that the invitation said 'dress informal', but fortunately we found out that at The White House informal dress meant black tie. Our taxi got us to The White House gate five minutes early, so we waited outside until the proper time. On arrival, we were put all by ourselves in the Blue Room for a few minutes and then ushered into the Red Room, where the group was gathering. As I remember it, the party consisted of the President and Mrs Roosevelt, Churchill and his staff, Harry Hopkins, and a cousin of Mr Roosevelt (Mrs Robbins ?)[2] who was staying at The White House. We were the only outsiders. The President himself shook up whiskey sour cocktails for all of us, and just as he was finishing Churchill bustled in. We then moved to the small dining room with a long thin table. The President sat on one side in the middle, with Mrs Roosevelt opposite him. Churchill was on her right. Commander Thompson, Churchill's aide, was on the President's left. I sat next to him with Harry Hopkins on my left at the end of the line.

The conversation was dominated by the President and the Prime Minister, discussing of all things, the Boer War. Churchill was subdued and looked tired. After all, he had just arrived across the Atlantic and had faced a press conference on his arrival that day. In contrast, the President was in a buoyant mood and kept needling Churchill for having been on the wrong side in the Boer War. (FDR had been part of an informal group of Boer sympathizers at Harvard.) When he felt crowded too far, Churchill would take a puff of his cigar and counter attack with a verbal sally and then settle back again into his chair. The conversation then got round to the question of the food supply we were shipping to England – 'too many powdered eggs' said Churchill, 'the only good thing you can make with them is Spotted Dick.' 'Nonsense' said FDR, 'You can do as much with a powdered egg as with a real egg.' I opened my mouth for the only time all evening to ask how you could fry a powdered egg.

[1] Percy Chubb, 1909-1982. Grandson of Thomas Caldecott Chubb, marine insurance underwriter. Assistant Deputy Administrator for Fiscal Affairs, War Shipping Administration, 1941-45. Chairman of Chubb and Son, insurance underwriters. President of the American Institute of Marine Underwriters. His wife was a grandniece of President Theodore Roosevelt.

[2] If it was Mrs Robbins, she was not a cousin of the President, but the wife of his Protocol Officer, Warren Robbins. She was notorious for having, on one official occasion at least, dyed her hair purple.

My most vivid recollection is of a moment when FDR said that he had had an unhappy childhood. His ambitions at Harvard had not been fulfilled and he hadn't even been asked to join the right Club. Churchill took a puff at his cigar and growled: 'When I hear a man say that his childhood was the happiest time of his life, I think (puff) my friend you have had a pretty poor life.' I was also delighted when he used a favourite saying of my father's: 'There is no use having a dog and barking yourself.'

Patrick Kinna: recollection
(*Letter to the author, 10 October 1984*)

[24 December 1941] The White House

One morning the Prime Minister wanted to dictate while he was in his bath – not a minute could be wasted – He kept submerging in the bath and when he 'surfaced' he would dictate a few more words or sentences. Eventually he got out of the bath when his devoted valet, Sawyers, draped an enormous bath-towel around him. He walked into his adjoining bedroom, followed by me, notebook in hand, and continued to dictate while pacing up and down the enormous room. Eventually the towel fell to the ground but, quite unconcerned, he continued pacing the room dictating all the time.

Suddenly President Roosevelt entered the bedroom and saw the British Prime Minister completely naked walking around the room dictating to me. WSC never being lost for words said 'You see, Mr President, I have nothing to conceal from you.'[1]

Winston S. Churchill to the War Cabinet and Chiefs of Staff Committee
(*Churchill papers, 20/50*)

24 December 1941

(i) The President and I discussed the North African situation last night. Mr Hull, Mr Welles, Mr Hopkins, Lord Beaverbrook and Lord Halifax also took part in the discussion.

(ii) There was general agreement that if Hitler was held in Russia he must try something else, and that the most probable line was Spain and Portugal en route to North Africa. Our success in Libya and the prospect of joining hands with French North African territory was another reason to make Hitler want, if he could, to get hold of Morocco as quickly as possible. At the same time, reports did not seem to suggest threat was imminent, perhaps because Hitler had enough in hand at the moment.

[1] For a similar incident, see Colonel Ian Jacob's diary entry for 28 December 1941.

(iii) There was general agreement that it was vital to forestall the Germans in North-West Africa and the Atlantic islands. In addition to all the other reasons, the two French battleships, *Jean Bart* and *Richelieu*, were a real prize for whoever got them. Accordingly, the discussion was not whether, but how.

(iv) Various suggestions were made:

(a) The United States Government might speak in very serious and resolute terms to Vichy, saying that this was final chance for them to reconsider their positions and come out on the side that was pledged to restoration of France. As a symbol of this Pétain might be invited to send Weygand to represent him at an Allied conference in Washington.

(b) An approach might be made to Weygand in the light of a North African situation fundamentally changed by British advance and by United States entering into war and their willingness to send a force to North Africa.

(v) It was suggested, on the other hand, that the effect of such procedure might be to extract smooth promises from Pétain and Weygand, the Germans meanwhile being advised of our intentions and that, accordingly, if these approaches were to be made, it would be desirable to have all plans made for going into North Africa, with or without invitation. I emphasized immense psychological effect likely to be produced both in France and among French troops in North Africa by association of United States with the undertaking. Mr Hull suggested that it might well be that a leader would emerge in North Africa as events developed.

The President said that he was anxious that American land forces should give their support as quickly as possible wherever they could be most helpful, and favoured the idea of a plan to move into North Africa being prepared for either event, i.e., with or without invitation.

(vi) It was agreed to remit the study of the project to Staffs on assumption that it was vital to forestall the Germans in that area and that the Libyan campaign had, as it was expected to do, achieved complete success. It was recognized that the question of shipping was plainly a most important factor.

(vii) I gave an account of the progress of fighting in Libya, by which the President and other Americans were clearly much impressed and cheered.

(viii) In course of conversation the President mentioned that he woul propose at forthcoming conference that United States should relieve our troops in Northern Ireland, and spoke of sending three or four divisions there. I warmly welcomed this, and said I hoped that one of the divisions would be an armoured division. It was not thought that this need conflict preparations for a United States Force for North Africa.

(ix) There was also some talk about the relation of the present discussions between representatives of Great Britain and the United States to a possible meeting including all Dominions and all other Allies. The general conclusion was that it was important to bring them all in, but not to establish any permanent body that would limit the action or capacity to take prompt decision of United States, Great Britain and Russia.

Winston S. Churchill to Clement Attlee
(*Churchill papers, 20/50*)

24 December 1941

A. – In view of the question which Admiral Darlan asked as to attitude of British Government if he took Pétain's place, the report that Pétain has resigned and Darlan taken his place seems quite possible.

B. – This may well result in a revolt in North Africa, and as it is essential we should be in a position to take immediate advantage of it, all preparations for operation 'Gymnast'[1] should be put in hand forthwith.

Winston S. Churchill to Clementine Churchill
(*Baroness Spencer-Churchill papers*)

24 December 1941 'but now White House'[2]

I have not had a minute since I got here to tell you about it. All is very good indeed: and my plans are all going through. The Americans are magnificent in their breadth of view.

Tender love to you and all. My thoughts will be with you this strange Christmas eve.

Your ever loving husband
W

[1] A possible British landing in French North Africa, ideally with the tacit support of the Vichy authorities there.

[2] Churchill dictated this letter to his wife on 21 December 1941 on 10 Downing Street notepaper. In his own handwriting he wrote at the top of the first page, 'At Sea'; but that night he added 'but now White House' and added – entirely in his own handwriting – the sentences printed here.

Winston S. Churchill: broadcast
(BBC Written Archives Centre)

24 December 1941 Washington DC

I spend this anniversary and festival far from my country, far from my family, yet I cannot truthfully say that I feel far from home. Whether it be the ties of blood on my mother's side, or the friendships I have developed here over many years of active life, or the commanding sentiment of comradeship in the common cause of great peoples who speak the same language, who kneel at the same altars and, to a very large extent, pursue the same ideals, I cannot feel myself a stranger here in the centre and at the summit of the United States. I feel a sense of unity and fraternal association which, added to the kindliness of your welcome, convinces me that I have a right to sit at your fireside and share your Christmas joys.

This is a strange Christmas Eve. Almost the whole world is locked in deadly struggle, and, with the most terrible weapons which science can devise, the nations advance upon each other. Ill would it be for us this Christmastide if we were not sure that no greed for the land or wealth of any other people, no vulgar ambition, no morbid lust for material gain at the expense of others, had led us to the field. Here, in the midst of war, raging and roaring over all the lands and seas, creeping nearer to our hearts and homes, here, amid all the tumult, we have tonight the peace of the spirit in each cottage home and in every generous heart. Therefore we may cast aside for this night at least the cares and dangers which beset us, and make for the children an evening of happiness in a world of storm. Here, then, for one night only, each home throughout the English-speaking world should be a brightly-lighted island of happiness and peace.

Let the children have their night of fun and laughter. Let the gifts of Father Christmas delight their play. Let us grown-ups share to the full in their unstinted pleasures before we turn again to the stern task and the formidable years that lie before us, resolved that, by our sacrifice and daring, these same children shall not be robbed of their inheritance or denied their right to live in a free and decent world.

And so, in God's mercy, a happy Christmas to you all.

Winston S. Churchill to Peter Fraser[1]
(*Churchill papers, 20/49*)

24 December 1941

Best Christmas and New Year wishes from Washington. We have seen many changes since you left England and I know how your anxieties have increased. There is, however, much to cheer us at this season. No longer alone, but aided by the immense resources of this great country now fully aroused to war, I look forward with confidence to whatever the future may hold.

General Sir Alan Brooke: diary
(*'Turn of the Tide'*)

24 December 1941
London

Another hard day. Chiefs of Staff meeting in the morning. The situation beginning to become difficult. Winston, arrived in Washington far from the war, pushing for operation by USA and ourselves against North Africa and banking on further success of Middle East offensive towards Tripoli. On the other side Duff Cooper in Singapore by his demands inspiring the Australians to ask for more and more for the Far East. In the middle Auchinleck struggling along with the forces at his disposal and sending optimistic personal and private messages to PM, little knowing that his activities must shortly be curtailed owing to transfer of air and sea reinforcements from Middle East to Far East.

At 3 p.m. Defence Committee meeting to settle aerodrome defence and 'scorched earth' policy in Malay peninsula.

General Auchinleck to Winston S. Churchill
(*Churchill papers, 20/47*)

24 December 1941
Western Desert
Personal

Royal Dragoons repeat Royal Dragoons occupied repeat occupied Benghazi this morning.

The Army of the Nile send you hearty greetings for Christmas.

[1] Prime Minister of New Zealand.

Winston S. Churchill to General Auchinleck
(Churchill papers, 20/49)

25 December 1941

My heartiest congratulations to you, Ritchie, Army and Air Force of the Nile, on re-entry of Benghazi and on the great victory won by so much hard fighting and skill which is now manifesting itself in Cyrenaica.

2. I have a hard request to make to you. We concentrated everything on your battle, with the result that we are now desperately short in the new theatre which the Japanese attack has opened. I think, without compromising 'Acrobat,'[1] you should be able to spare at once for Malaya and Singapore:

(a) A force of American tanks, even if its full strength only amounted to one hundred.

(b) Apart from the Blenheims, &c., already on the way, four squadrons of Hurricanes are needed urgently in Singapore. Our ability to bring in further reinforcements depends on our getting a sufficient air force there,in good time so as to protect the sea approaches. At present our old-quality aircraft are knocked about by Japanese sea-borne fighters. Only air power at Singapore and Johore can keep the door open, and if the door is shut the fortress will fall, and this would take the bloom off our Libyan successes. We are examining sending *Indomitable* to pick up these four squadrons at Massawa, by which means they could be flown off her deck to Singapore before the end of January. Pray ask Air Marshal Tedder from me to study this most earnestly.

3. It has occurred to me that you might send some of your damaged tanks to India for repair, thus relieving your workshops, which must be congested, and could not in any ease cure these tanks for some months. In India, however, when repaired they will form the training nucleus for the armoured units we are forming. Please explore this idea with General Wavell.

4. Most secret for yourself and Minister of State alone. I have obtained here three important decisions:

Firstly, to the sending of four American divisions immediately into Northern Ireland, thus liberating at least two fully-trained British divisions for overseas.

Secondly, American bomber squadrons will come over to attack Germany from the British Isles.

Thirdly, and most important for you, the Americans are very ready to come in on a vigorous application of 'Gymnast,' so that if you can arrive at, the frontiers of Tunis we will put such a screw on Vichy or on French North Africa as will give us the best chance of bringing them out on our side. Not only

[1] The planned advance from Cyrenaica into Tripolitania.

British 'Gymnast' forces, but some highly-trained American divisions may be thrown into the scale.

5. Naturally, you must not divest yourself of anything that would prevent 'Acrobat,' but I am sure you will feel that all our successes in the West would be nullified by the fall of Singapore.

6. Every possible step will be taken to reinforce you and the Admiral with Air Force from home, and the Metropolitan bombing strength against Germany must be drawn upon as necessary.

7. You will receive official and detailed messages on these subjects. Meanwhile, all good wishes for Christmas and the New Year.

Winston S. Churchill to General Macready
(*Churchill papers, 20/36*)

25 December 1941
Secret

This is really disgraceful.[1] Let me see draft telegram which you will send, making sure disciplinary action is taken against persons guilty of this carelessness.

Winston S. Churchill to the Chiefs of Staff Committee
(*Churchill papers, 20/50*)

25 December 1941

1. President agrees.[2] Commander *Vernon* proceeding direct to Malaya and action should be taken accordingly.

2. Telegram will follow shortly with further proposal for reinforcing Malaya, including important measure now being discussed with United States authorities here.

[1] A telegram from General Auchinleck about the two Churchill tanks which arrived in the Middle East in an unserviceable state owing to being shipped on the well deck unsheeted and unlocked and exposed therefore to bad weather.

[2] That an American troop transport, the *Mount Vernon*, containing personnel of 53rd Brigade Group, should join the Singapore convoy.

Winston S. Churchill to Major Randolph Churchill
(*Churchill papers, 20/33*)

25 December 1941 Washington DC

All best wishes for a Happy Christmas. Tender love. Papa.

King George VI to Winston S. Churchill
(*Churchill papers, 20/59*)

25 December 1941
Private and Personal

The Queen and I send our warmest Christmas wishes to the President and Mrs Roosevelt as well as to yourself and the members of your delegation.

You, and the vital work in which you are all engaged, are much in my thoughts, and I pray that the success of your conversations may bring us nearer to happiness in the New Year.

George R.I.

Winston S. Churchill: recollection
(*'The Second World War, Volume Three'*)

[25 December 1941]

The President and I went to church together on Christmas Day, and I found peace in the simple service and enjoyed singing the well-known hymns, and one, 'O little town of Bethlehem', I had never heard before. Certainly there was much to fortify the faith of all who believe in the moral governance of the universe.

It was with heart-stirrings that I fulfilled the invitation to address the Congress of the United States. The occasion was important for what I was sure was the all-conquering alliance of the English-speaking peoples. I had never addressed a foreign Parliament before. Yet to me, who could trace unbroken male descent on my mother's side through five generations from a lieutenant who served in George Washington's army, it was possible to feel a blood-right to speak to the representatives of the great Republic in our common cause. It certainly was odd that it should all work out this way; and once again I had the feeling, for mentioning which I may be pardoned, of being used, however unworthy, in some appointed plan.

I spent a good part of Christmas Day preparing my speech.

General Sir Alan Brooke: diary
('Turn of the Tide')

25 December 1941

I had to prepare wire to PM with reference to his desire to carry out 'Gymnast' operation (i.e. reinforcements to French North Africa in event of being called in). Problem complicated by the fact that it does not look as if we are likely to be called in, and secondly that PM now is toying with the idea of carrying out such a plan against resistance, and finally owing to the fact that shipping available does not admit of both occupying North Africa at request of French and reinforcing Far East sufficiently to secure Singapore, Burma, and Indian Ocean communications. We have laid down that first of all in importance comes security of this country and its communications and after that Singapore and communications through Indian Ocean. This is correct, as, if the latter go, the Middle East or possibly India may follow suit. Committee lasted till 6 p.m. News received this evening that Hong Kong had fallen on Xmas Eve.

Garrison Norton[1]*: recollections*
(Letter to the author, 27 December 1964)

25 December 1941 [White House]

All the guests drank champagne, but WSC drank whisky. Roosevelt made a short speech and WSC responded. Both speeches were brief. After dinner all the guests went to a film showing of *Oliver Twist*.[2] It was a bad and boring film. After perhaps half an hour the reel had to be changed. WSC rose rapidly and excused himself with the words: 'I must go and do some homework'. He disappeared, leaving Roosevelt and his family at the film. The 'homework' was, apparently, his speech to the Senate and Congress, delivered on the following day.

[1] Garrison Norton, 1900-1994. Assistant to the Chairman of the Civil Aeronautics Authority, 1934. Subsequently Director of the Office of Transport and Communications, State Department, and (1940-41) an Assistant Secretary of State. On active service in the navy. Assistant Secretary of State in charge of policies on international transportation and communications, 1947-49. Assistant Secretary of the Navy, 1956-59. President of the Institute of Defense Analyses, 1959-65. His mother was a descendant of the abolitionist William Lloyd Garrison.

[2] A 1933 version of the Dickens' story, starring Dickie Moore as Oliver Twist. In 1942, Moore, a leading child and then juvenile actor, gave the 14-year old Shirley Temple her first screen kiss (in 'Miss Annie Rooney').

Winston S. Churchill: speech[1]
(*BBC Written Archives Centre*)

26 December 1941 Washington DC

JOINT SESSION OF CONGRESS

I feel greatly honoured that you should have invited me to enter the United States Senate Chamber and address the representatives of both branches of Congress. The fact that my American forebears have for so many generations played their part in the life of the United States, and that here I am, an Englishman, welcomed in your midst, makes this experience one of the most moving and thrilling in my life, which is already long and has not been entirely uneventful. I wish indeed that my mother, whose memory I cherish across the vale of years, could have been here to see. By the way, I cannot help reflecting that if my father had been American and my mother British, instead of the other way round, I might have got here on my own. In that case, this would not have been the first time you would have hear my voice. In that case I should not have needed any invitation, but if I had, it is hardly likely it would have been unanimous. So perhaps things are better as they are. I may confess, however, that I do not feel quite like a fish out of water in a legislative assembly where English is spoken.

I am a child of the House of Commons. I was brought up in my father's house to believe in democracy. 'Trust the people' – that was his message. I used to see him cheered at meetings and in the streets by crowds of working men way back in those aristocratic Victorian days when, as Disraeli said, the world was for the few, and for the very few. Therefore I have been in full harmony all my life with the tides which have flowed on both sides of the Atlantic against privilege and monopoly, and I have steered confidently towards the Gettysburg ideal of 'government of the people by the people for the people'. I owe my advancement entirely to the House of Commons, whose servant I am. In my country, as in yours, public men are proud to be the servants of the State and would be ashamed to be its masters. On any day, if they thought the people wanted it, the House of Commons could by a simple vote remove me from my office. But I am not worrying about it at all. As a matter of fact, I am sure they will approve very highly of my journey here, for which I obtained the King's permission in order to meet the President of the United States and to arrange with him all that mapping-out of our military plans, and for all those intimate meetings of the high officers of the armed services of both countries, which are indispensable to the successful prosecution of the war.

I should like to say first of all how much I have been impressed and en-

[1] This speech was broadcast live from Washington.

couraged by the breadth of view and sense of proportion which I have found in all quarters over here to which I have had access. Anyone who did not understand the size and solidarity of the foundations of the United States might easily have expected to find an excited, disturbed, self-centred, atmosphere, with all minds fixed upon the novel, startling, and painful episodes of sudden war as they hit America. After all, the United States have been attacked and set upon by three most powerfully-armed dictator States. The greatest military power in Europe, the greatest military power in Asia, Germany and Japan, Italy, too, have all declared, and are making, war upon you, and a quarrel is opened, which can only end in their overthrow or yours. But here in Washington, in these memorable days, I have found an Olympian fortitude which, far from being based upon complacency, is only the mask of an inflexible purpose and the proof of a sure and well-grounded confidence in the final outcome. We in Britain had the same feeling in our darkest days. We, too, were sure in the end all would be well. You do not, I am certain, underrate the severity of the ordeal to which you and we have still to be subjected. The forces ranged against us are enormous. They are bitter, they are ruthless. The wicked men and their factions who have launched their peoples on the path of war and conquest know that they will be called to terrible account if they cannot beat down by force of arms the peoples they have assailed. They will stop at nothing. They have a vast accumulation of war weapons of all kinds. They have highly-trained, disciplined armies, navies, and air services. They have plans and designs which have long been tried and matured. They will stop at nothing that violence or treachery can suggest.

It is quite true that, on our side, our resources in manpower and materials are far greater than theirs. But only a portion of your resources is as yet mobilized and developed, and we both of us have much to learn in the cruel art of war. We have, therefore, without doubt, a time of tribulation before us. In this time some ground will be lost which it will be hard and costly to regain. Many disappointments and unpleasant surprises await us. Many of them will afflict us before the full marshalling of our latent and total power can be accomplished. For the best part of twenty years the youth of Britain and America have been taught that war is evil, which is true, and that it would never come again, which has been proved false. For the best part of twenty years the youth of Germany, Japan and Italy have been taught that aggressive war is the noblest duty of the citizen, and that it should be begun as soon as the necessary weapons and organization had been made. We have performed the duties and tasks of peace. They have plotted and planned for war. This, naturally, has placed us in Britain and now places you in the United States at a disadvantage which only time, courage, and strenuous, untiring exertions can correct.

We have indeed to be thankful that so much time has been granted to us. If Germany had tried to invade the British Isles after the French collapse in June,

1940, and if Japan had declared war on the British Empire and the United States at about the same date, no one could say what disasters and agonies might not have been our lot. But now at the end of December, 1941, our transformation from easy-going peace to total war efficiency has made very great progress. The broad flow of munitions in Great Britain has already begun. Immense strides have been made in the conversion of American industry to military purposes, and now that the United States are at war it is possible for orders to be given every day which a year or eighteen months hence will produce results in war power beyond anything that has yet been seen or foreseen in the dictator States. Provided that every effort is made, that nothing is kept back, that the whole manpower, brain-power, virility, valour, and civic virtue of the English-speaking world with all its galaxy of loyal, friendly, associated communities and States – provided all that is bent unremittingly to the simple and supreme task, I think it would be reasonable to hope that the end of 1942 will see us quite definitely in a better position than we are now, and that the year 1943 will enable us to assume the initiative upon an ample scale.

Some people may be startled or momentarily depressed when, like your President, I speak of a long and hard war. But our peoples would rather know the truth, sombre though it be. And after all, when we are doing the noblest work in the world, not only defending our hearths and homes but the cause of freedom in other lands, the question of whether deliverance comes in 1942, 1943, or 1944 falls into its proper place in the grand proportions of human history. Sure I am that this day – now – we are the masters of our fate; that the task which has been set us is not above our strength; that its pangs and toils are not beyond our endurance. As long as we have faith in our cause and an unconquerable will-power, salvation will not be denied us. In the words of the Psalmist, 'He shall not be afraid of evil tidings; his heart is fixed, trusting in the Lord.' Not all the tidings will be evil.

On the contrary, mighty strokes of war have already been dealt against the enemy; the glorious defence of their native soil by the Russian armies and people have inflicted wounds upon the Nazi tyranny and system which have bitten deep, and will fester and inflame not only in the Nazi body but in the Nazi mind. The boastful Mussolini has crumbled already. He is now but a lackey and serf, the merest utensil of his master's will. He has inflicted great suffering and wrong upon his own industrious people. He has been stripped of his African empire, Abyssinia has been liberated. Our armies in the East, which were so weak and ill-equipped at the moment of French desertion, now control all the regions from Teheran to Benghazi, and from Aleppo and Cyprus to the sources of the Nile.

For many months we devoted ourselves to preparing to take the offensive in Libya. The very considerable battle, which has been proceeding for the last six weeks in the desert, has been most fiercely fought on both sides. Owing to the difficulties of supply on the desert flanks, we were never able to bring numerically equal forces to bear upon the enemy. Therefore we had to rely upon a superiority in the numbers and quality of tanks and aircraft, British and American. Aided by these, for the first time, we have fought the enemy with equal weapons. For the first time we have made the Hun feel the sharp edge of those tools with which he has enslaved Europe. The armed forces of the enemy in Cyrenaica amounted to about 150,000, of whom about one-third were Germans. General Auchinleck set out to destroy totally that armed force. I have every reason to believe that his aim will be fully accomplished. I am glad to be able to place before you, members of the Senate and of the House of Representatives, at this moment when you are entering the war, proof that with proper weapons and proper organization we are able to beat the life out of the savage Nazi. What Hitler is suffering in Libya is only a sample and foretaste of what we must give him and his accomplices, wherever this war shall lead us, in every quarter of the globe.

There are good tidings also from blue water. The life-line of supplies which joins our two nations across the ocean, without which all might fail, is flowing steadily and freely in spite of all the enemy can do. It is a fact that the British Empire, which many thought eighteen months ago was broken and ruined, is now incomparably stronger, and is growing stronger with every month. Lastly, if you will forgive me for saying it, to me the best tidings of all is that the United States, united as never before, have drawn the sword for freedom and cast away the scabbard.

All these tremendous facts have led the subjugated peoples of Europe to lift up their heads again in hope. They have put aside for ever the shameful temptation of resigning themselves to the conqueror's will. Hope has returned to the hearts of scores of millions of men and women, and with that hope there burns the flame of anger against the brutal, corrupt invader, and still more fiercely burn the fires of hatred and contempt for the squalid quislings whom he has suborned. In a dozen famous ancient States now prostrate under the Nazi yoke, the masses of the people of all classes and creeds await the hour of liberation, when they too will be able once again to play their part and strike their blows like men. That hour will strike, and its solemn peal will proclaim that the night is past and that the dawn has come.

The onslaught upon us so long and so secretly planned by Japan has presented both our countries with grievous problems for which we could not be fully prepared. If people ask me – as they have a right to ask me in England – why is it that you have not got ample equipment of modern aircraft and Army weapons of all kinds in Malaya and in the East Indies, I can only point to the victories General Auchinleck has gained in the Libyan campaign. Had we diverted and dispersed our gradually growing resources between Libya and Malaya, we should have been found wanting in both theatres. If the United States have been found at a disadvantage at various points in the

Pacific Ocean, we know well that it is to no small extent because of the aid you have been giving us in munitions for the defence of the British Isles and for the Libyan campaign, and, above all, because of your help in the Battle of the Atlantic, upon which all depends, and which has in consequence been successfully and prosperously maintained. Of course it would have been much better, I freely admit, if we had had enough resources of all kinds to be at full strength at all threatened points; but considering how slowly and reluctantly we brought ourselves to large-scale preparations, and how long such preparations take, we had no right to expect to be in such a fortunate position.

The choice of how to dispose of our hitherto limited resources had to be made by Britain in time of war and by the United States in time of peace; and I believe that history will pronounce that upon the whole – and it is upon the whole that these matters must be judged – the choice made was right. Now that we are together, now that we are linked in a righteous comradeship of arms, now that our two considerable nations, each in perfect unity, have joined all their life energies in a common resolve, a new scene opens upon which a steady light will glow and brighten.

Many people have been astonished that Japan should in a single day have plunged into war against the United States and the British Empire. We all wonder why, if this dark design, with all its laborious and intricate preparations, had been so long filling their secret minds, they did not choose our moment of weakness eighteen months ago. Viewed quite dispassionately, in spite of the losses we have suffered and the further punishment we shall have to take, it certainly appears to be an irrational act. It is, of course, only prudent to assume that they have made very careful calculations and think they see their way through. Nevertheless, there may be another explanation. We know that for many years past the policy of Japan has been dominated by secret societies of subalterns and junior officers of the Army and Navy, who have enforced their will upon successive Japanese Cabinets and Parliaments by the assassination of any Japanese statesman who opposed, or who did not sufficiently further, their aggressive policy. It may be that these societies, dazzled and dizzy with their own schemes of aggression and the prospect of early victories, have forced their country against its better judgement into war. They have certainly embarked upon a very considerable undertaking. For after the outrages they have committed upon us at Pearl Harbor, in the Pacific Islands, in the Philippines, in Malaya, and in the Dutch East Indies, they must now know that the stakes for which they have decided to play are mortal.

When we consider the resources of the United States and the British Empire compared to those of Japan, when we remember those of China, which has so long and valiantly withstood invasion and when also we observe the Russian menace which hangs over Japan, it becomes still more difficult to reconcile Japanese action with prudence or even with sanity. What kind of a people do they think we are? Is it possible they do not realize that we shall never cease to persevere against them until they have been taught a lesson which they and the world will never forget?

Members of the Senate and members of the House of Representatives, I turn for one moment more from the turmoil and convulsions of the present to the broader basis of the future. Here we are together facing a group of mighty foes who seek our ruin; here we are together defending all that to free men is dear. Twice in a single generation the catastrophe of world war has fallen upon us; twice in our lifetime has the long arm of fate reached across the ocean to bring the United States into the forefront of the battle. If we had kept together after the last War, if we had taken common measures for our safety, this renewal of the curse need never have fallen upon us.

Do we not owe it to ourselves, to our children, to mankind tormented, to make sure that these catastrophes shall not engulf us for the third time? It has been proved that pestilences may break out in the Old World, which carry their destructive ravages into the New World, from which, once they are afoot, the New World cannot by any means escape. Duty and prudence alike command first that the germ-centres of hatred and revenge should be constantly and vigilantly surveyed and treated in good time, and, secondly, that an adequate organization should be set up to make sure that the pestilence can be controlled at its earliest beginnings before it spreads and rages throughout the entire earth.

Five or six years ago it would have been easy, without shedding a drop of blood, for the United States and Great Britain to have insisted on fulfilment of the disarmament clauses of the treaties which Germany signed after the Great War; that also would have been the opportunity for assuring to Germany those raw materials which we declared in the Atlantic Charter should not be denied to any nation, victor or vanquished. That chance has passed. It is gone. Prodigious hammer-strokes have been needed to bring us together again, or if you will allow me to use other language, I will say that he must indeed have a blind soul who cannot see that some great purpose and design is being worked out here below, of which we have the honour to be the faithful servants. It is not given to us to peer into the mysteries of the future. Still, I avow my hope and faith, sure and inviolate, that in the days to come the British and American peoples will for their own safety and for the good of all walk together side by side in majesty, in justice, and in peace.

Winston S. Churchill to Clement Attlee

(*Churchill papers, 20/50*)

26 December 1941

Things are moving so well here that I am sure it is my duty to prolong my stay till we get the main line straightened out. We are making plans both for

'Gymnast' and for Australian and Singapore defence. COS feel that they need more time. I propose therefore to go to Ottawa for two or three days at the beginning of next week and then return here for an equal period. Considering time and trouble it took us to get here it would be a pity not to make a good job of it.

I am avoiding being precise about date but I shall certainly not be back for one-day meeting of Parliament on 8th January.

Will you commend this to Cabinet and mention it formally to the King.

Winston S. Churchill to Peter Fraser

(*Churchill papers, 20/50*)

26 December 1941

I will send you a full telegram shortly about all the measures we are taking in conjunction with the United States to cope with the Japanese in the Pacific.

I profoundly admire the courage and composure with which New Zealand is facing the new situation, so full of immediate danger and of ultimate safety.

Sir Charles Wilson: diary

(*'Winston Churchill, The Struggle for Survival, 1941–65'*)

27 December 1941

When I got back to the hotel at ten o'clock, after a stroll through the streets, I found an urgent message. I was wanted at the White House. Would I go at once. I took a taxi.

'I am glad you have come,' the PM began.

He was in bed and looked worried.

'It was hot last night and I got up to open the window. It was very stiff. I had to use considerable force and I noticed all at once that I was short of breath. I had a dull pain over my heart. It went down my left arm. It didn't last very long, but it has never happened before. What is it? Is my heart all right? I thought of sending for you, but it passed off.'

There was not much to be found when I examined his heart. Indeed, the time I spent listening to his chest was given to some quick thinking. I knew that when I took the stethoscope out of my ears he would ask me pointed questions, and I had no doubt that whether the electro-cardiograph showed evidence of a coronary thrombosis or not, his symptoms were those of coronary insufficiency. The textbook treatment for this is at least six weeks in bed. That would mean publishing to the world – and the American newspapers would see to this – that the PM was an invalid with a crippled heart and a doubtful future. And this at a moment when America has just come into the war, and there is no one but Winston to take her by the hand. I felt that the effect of announcing that the PM had had a heart attack could only be disastrous. I knew, too, the consequences to one of his imaginative temperament of the feeling that his heart was affected. His work would suffer. On the other hand, if I did nothing and he had another and severer attack – perhaps a fatal seizure – the world would undoubtedly say that I had killed him through not insisting on rest. These thoughts went racing through my head while I was listening to his heart. I took my stethoscope out of my ears. Then I replaced it and listened again. Right or wrong, it seemed plain that I must sit tight on what had happened, whatever the consequences.

'Well,' he asked, looking full at me, 'is my heart all right?'

'There is nothing serious,' I answered. 'You have been overdoing things.'

'Now, Charles, you're not going to tell me to rest. I can't I won't. Nobody else can do this job. I must. What actually happened when I opened the window?' he demanded. 'My idea is that I strained one of my chest muscles. I used great force. I don't believe it was my heart at all.'

He waited for me to answer.

'Your circulation was a bit sluggish. It is nothing serious. You needn't rest in the sense of lying up, but you mustn't do more than you can help in the way of exertion for a little while.'

There was a knock at the door. It was Harry Hopkins. I slipped away. I went and sat in a corner of the secretaries' room, picking up a newspaper, so that they would not talk to me. I began to think things out more deliberately. I did not like it, but I determined to tell no one.[1]

[1] Dr Michael Dunnill, Consultant Pathologist, John Radcliffe Hospital, Oxford, writes: 'The description that Moran gives is fairly typical of an attack of angina pectoris. This is caused by a deficiency of blood supply to the heart muscle due to the narrowing of the coronary arteries, that is the arteries supplying the heart muscle, by atheroma. This pain is typically in the chest but radiates down the left arm and is brought on by excessive effort such as the use of considerable force to open the window. If the patient persists in the effort, shortness of breath due to failure of the left ventricle and consequent waterlogging of the lungs often occurs and I see that Churchill said that he was in fact short of breath.' Dr Dunnill adds: 'The symptoms described should have acted as a warning that the Prime Minister's heart was not a hundred per cent fit but a great many people have attacks of angina pectoris like this and live for many years. In fact the course adopted by Moran on this occasion was quite correct. To have ordered bed rest for six weeks would not have been good therapy as there is no evidence that this does the patient any good and only tends to make them neurotic.' (Letter to the author, 15 October 1984)

Winston S. Churchill to the Earl of Athlone[1]
(Churchill papers, 20/47)

27 December 1941

Thank you so much for your invitation to visit Canada, which I gladly accept.

I propose leaving here Sunday, 28th, to arrive Ottawa 9 a.m. Monday, 29th, leaving Ottawa on the afternoon of Wednesday, 31st, so as to be back here early on morning of Thursday, 1st January.

The following will accompany me:

Commander Thompson (Personal Assistant) and one Private Secretary.

Two detectives, one male stenographer and valet.

I am also bringing:

Air Chief Marshal Sir Charles Portal (CAS);

Sir Charles Wilson, President Royal College of Physicians;

Brigadier Hollis (Secretary, COS Committee);

Wing Commander Oulton,[2] acting as ADC to CAS;

One Clerical Officer, one male and one female stenographer; and

One Royal Marine orderly.

It would be very convenient if arrangements can be made for Sir Charles Wilson and my personal staff to be accommodated with me and remainder of the party together somewhere handy.

I have taken the opportunity of Mr Mackenzie King's presence here to discuss with him some details of the programme which he is communicating to Ottawa for your consideration.

Arrangements are being made by BAD,[3] Washington, with Naval Authorities, Ottawa, for dealing with cypher traffic for me.

[1] Governor-General of Canada.

[2] Wilfrid Ewart Oulton, 1911-97. Pilot Officer, Royal Air Force, 1931. Ministry of Aircraft Production, 1940-41. Posted to Washington, 1941, as adviser on navigational training for British and Commonwealth air crew at American flying schools. Aide-de-Camp to the Chief of the Air Staff, during Churchill's visit to Washington, 1941. Commanded a Halifax bomber, 1943, sinking two U-boats and sharing in the destruction of a third. Established and commanded a Flying Fortress squadron in the Azores, 1943. Three times mentioned in despatches; Distinguished Flying Cross and Distinguished Service Order. Deputy Director, Maritime Operations, Northern Ireland, 1945. Deputy Director, Flying Control (later Air Traffic Control), Air Ministry, when he helped set up the early systems at Heathrow. Commander of the Joint Task Force 'Operation Grapple', the Christmas Island nuclear tests, 1956-58. Senior Air Staff Officer, RAF Coastal Command, 1958-60. Subsequently worked for EMI Electronics, with responsibility for military and aviation projects.

[3] British Admiralty Delegation, Washington.

Winston S. Churchill to Clement Attlee
(*Churchill papers, 20/50*)

27 December 1941

At meeting today it was provisionally decided that every possible expedient to accelerate the following moves was to be adopted by both nations:

(i) Reinforcements for Middle East to Far East and consequent replacements.

(ii) Relief of Iceland (C) and despatch American troops to Northern Ireland.

(iii) Moves of American air (?)[1] reinforcements to United Kingdom.

2. At same time it was laid down that we must be ready to take every possible advantage of an opportunity in French North Africa. United States could send 1 Marine Amphibious Division Combat (? to) assist, but on very (? light) scale of transport to open door, arriving at Casablanca about D.21. British would have to provide air and A/A initially.

3. If such revised Anglo-American 'Gymnast' were ordered obvious other movements must suffer, but no stream must dry up altogether.

4. Above plans are of such great importance that we must satisfy ourselves that British ships (? are) being used to further this end as economically as humanly possible. Small drafts living hard in (? stowage) must be accepted. Risks may have to be taken with monster liners and use made of armed merchant cruisers. This will involve review of all our shipping movements and resources to ensure we call as (? economically) as possible upon Americans, who are already asking us to help them in the troop ship class.

5. Please inform us as soon as possible:

(a) Assuming British undertake all Middle and Far East movements envisaged above, what assistance can we offer on trans-Atlantic moves and at what cost to normal commitments?

(b) Roughly, at what rate will British move from Middle East to Far East and replacements from United Kingdom be carried out?

(c) Cutting 'Gymnast' to the bone, when could advance parties arrive Casablanca, assuming 'Pilgrim' and 'Bonus' cancelled?[2]

(d) To what extent can we maintain a flow of Eastern reinforcements, accepting some risk in arrival of remainder of 'Gymnast'?

[1] The items before the question marks were unclear in the telegram as decoded in London: the supposed words were inserted by the decoding clerks.

[2] The British plan to take over the Portuguese island groups in the Atlantic Ocean if the Germans were to move against Portugal; and the British plan for an amphibious operation against the Vichy-held island of Madagascar in the Indian Ocean.

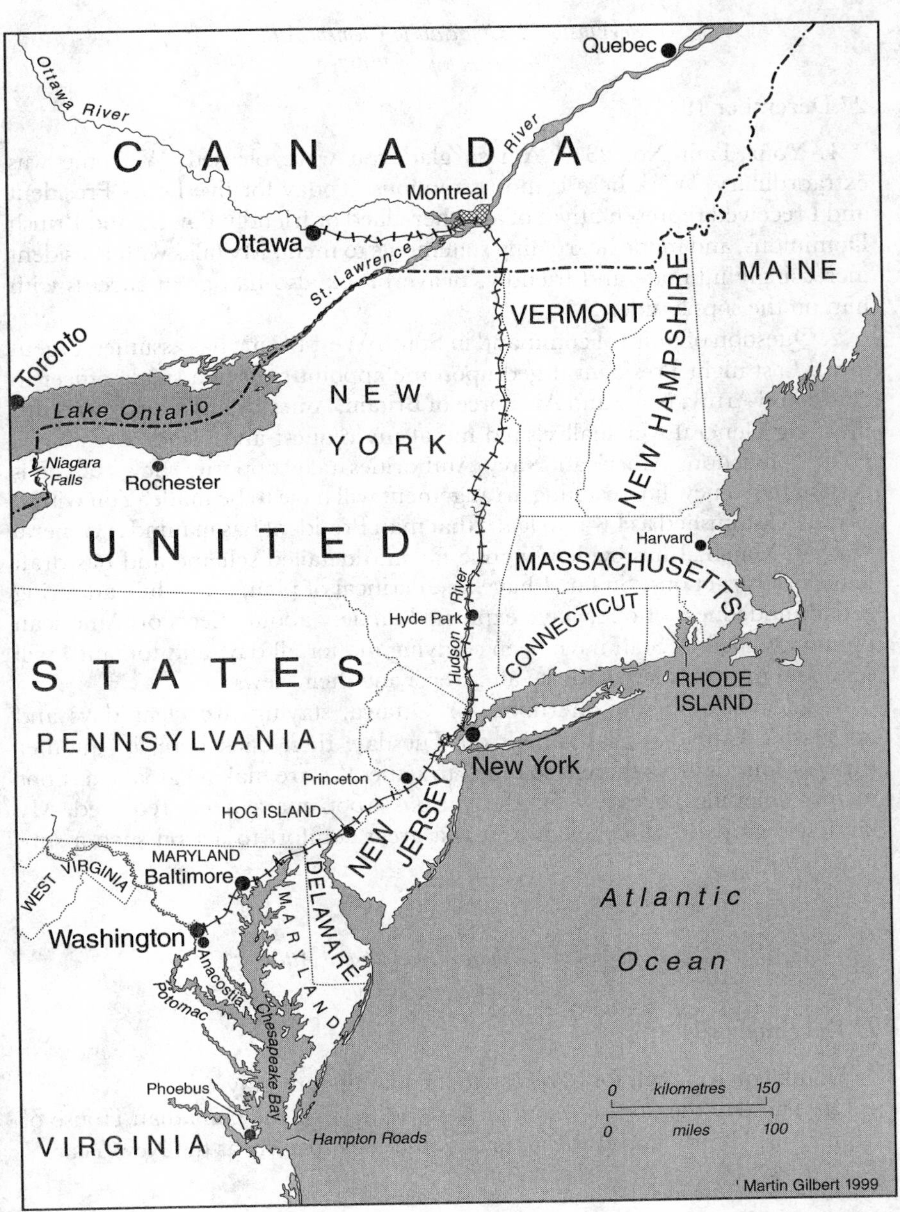

3. The Eastern Seaboard of the United States:
Churchill's journey from Washington to Ottawa

Winston S. Churchill to Clement Attlee
(*Churchill papers, 20/47*)

27 December 1941

1. Your Taut No. 231.[1] Am so glad you were pleased. Welcome was extraordinary. Work here is most strenuous. Today for five hours President and I received representatives of all other allied or friendly Powers and British Dominions, and made heartening statements to them. My talks with President increasingly intimate and friendly. Beaverbrook also had great success with him on the supply side.

2. Question of unity of command in South-West Pacific has assumed urgent form. Last night President urged upon me appointment of a single officer to command Army, Navy and Air Force of Britain, America and Dutch, and this morning General Marshall visited me at my request and pleaded case with great conviction. American Navy Authorities take opposite view, but it is certain that a new far-reaching arrangement will have to be made. You will be as much astonished as I was to learn that man President has in mind is General Wavell. Marshall has evidently gone far into detailed scheme and has draft letter of instructions. So far, I have been critical of plan, and while admiring broadmindedness of offer have expressed anxiety about effects on American opinion. Chiefs of Staff have been studying matter all day, and tonight I will send you my considered advice after receiving their views.

3. I leave tomorrow afternoon for Ottawa, staying two clear days and addressing Canadian Parliament on Tuesday, then back here for another three or four days, as there is so much to settle. We are making great exertions to find shipping necessary for the various troop movements required. My kindest regards to all colleagues. It is a great comfort to act on such a sure foundation.

Winston S. Churchill to Clement Attlee
(*Churchill papers, 20/50*)

27 December 1941

Thank you so much for agreeing to lengthening my stay.

On Tuesday the 30th December I am addressing the Canadian House of Commons. Utterly impossible to lay another egg so early as the New Year.

[1] Attlee's telegram to Churchill congratulating him on his speech to Congress.

Winston S. Churchill to John Curtin
(Churchill papers, 20/47)

27 December 1941
Personal and Most Secret

1. On Japan's coming into war we diverted at once 18th British Division, which was rounding Cape in American transports, with President's permission, to Bombay and Ceylon, and Mr Roosevelt has now agreed that leading Brigade in United States transport *Mount Vernon* should proceed direct to Singapore. We cancelled move of 17th Indian Division from India to Persia and this Division is now going to Malaya. A week ago I wirelessed from the ship to London to suggest you recall one Australian Division from Palestine either into India to replace other troops sent forward or to go direct, if it can be arranged, to Singapore. I have impressed upon military authorities importance of not using up forces needed for defence of Singapore and Johore approaches in attempting to defend northern part of Malay Peninsula. They will fall back slowly, fighting delaying actions and destroying communications.

2. The heavy naval losses which United States and we have both sustained give Japanese power of landing large reinforcements, but we do not share the views expressed in your telegram to Mr Casey, No. 1106 of 24th December, that there is danger of early reduction of Singapore fortress, which we are determined to defend to the utmost tenacity.

3. You have been told of the air support which is already on the way. It would not be wise to loose our grip on Rommel and Libya by taking away forces from General Auchinleck against his judgment just when victory is within our grasp. We have instructed Commanders-in-Chief, Middle East, to concert a plan for sending fighters and tanks to Singapore immediately situation in Libya permits.

4. I and the Chiefs of Staff are in close consultation with the President and his advisers, and we have made most encouraging progress. Not only are they impressed with the importance of maintaining Singapore, but they are anxious to move a continuous flow of troops and airplanes through Australia for the relief of the Philippines, if that be possible. Should the Philippines fall, President is agreeable to troops and airplanes being diverted to Singapore. He is also quite willing to send substantial United States forces to Australia, where the Americans are anxious to establish important bases for the war against Japan. General Wavell has been placed in command of Burma as well as India, and instructed to feed reinforcements arriving in India to the Malaya and Burmese fronts. He, like everyone else, recognizes the paramount importance of Singapore. General Pownall has now arrived. He is a highly competent army officer.

5. You may count on my doing everything possible to strengthen the whole front from Rangoon to Port Darwin. I am finding the greatest co-operation from our American Allies. I shall wire more definitely in a day or two.

6. Your 819 (Taut 147) about Russia.

It was not possible to reach any agreement on post-war territorial arrangements with Stalin, but Mr Eden's conferences ended in goodwill. I do not think it useful or even prudent to press the Russians to get into the war with Japan, when they have so much need of their Siberian forces to beat the German army, and when the defeats of that army are the dominant military factor in the world war at this moment.

However, as soon as he feels strong enough, I have very little doubt Stalin will take a stronger line with Japan. I hope you realize that it would be quite impossible for His Majesty's Government to make a bargain with Stalin involving the forcible transfer of large populations against their will into the Communist sphere. Articles 2 and 3 of the Atlantic Charter clearly forbid any such act on our part, and by attempting it we should only vitiate the fundamental principles of freedom which are the main impulse of our cause.

From my tentative informal soundings of the President I am sure that his views would be as strong as mine.

Ian Jacob: diary
(*Ian Jacob papers*)

[27 December 1941] Washington

Throughout the time of our visit to Washington the Prime Minister received a series of most exasperating telegrams from Mr Curtin, the Prime Minister of Australia. The Australian Government have throughout the war taken a narrow, selfish, and at times a craven view of events; in contrast to New Zealand who, though at times naturally critical of failures, has throughout been a tower of strength. 'That dear old man', as the Prime Minister calls Mr Fraser, the Prime Minister of New Zealand,[1] is as honest and straight-forward as you make them.

The Prime Minister has been most forbearing in his replies to Mr Curtin, realizing that an exchange of abuse and recrimination gets no one anywhere, and knowing that the Australians have at last some real cause for alarm. It is sad to see no sign of gratitude, or understanding of world problems even, in the Australian mind. They are only too ready to turn and bite us.

I fear that the Prime Minister's treatment of Mr Menzies is somewhat to blame. He has never really understood the Far East problem and has deliberately starved Singapore in favour of home and the Middle East, without paying enough attention to the feelings of Australia. His policy was undoubtedly right, but he should have taken great pains to make Australia understand what was being done, and give them the impression that he was

[1] Fraser was ten years younger than Churchill.

really taking them into his confidence. I am afraid we shall have a lot of bother with Australia as a result.

Winston S. Churchill to John Curtin
(*Churchill papers, 20/50*)

28 December 1941

Matters have moved with great speed here and I send you the text of the sub-joined agreement which has been reached between the President and myself with the approval of His Majesty's Government. The President is sure the Dutch will agree. I trust I may receive the assent of your Government to these arrangements designed so largely for your interest and safety. The President and the American staffs regard this decision as of the utmost urgency. The initiative has come from them, and the President proposes to state publicly that the appointment of General Wavell has been, at his direct suggestion, endorsed by his advisers. It is desired to make a public statement by January 1st at latest.

Ian Jacob: diary
(*Ian Jacob papers*)

28 December 1941

After breakfast, Jo[1] had gone down to see the Prime Minister at the White House, and had had to ring Jones[2] quite genuinely to bring a paper down which he wanted urgently for the Prime Minister. Jones rushed off in the car, and got successfully into the White House, and delivered the paper to Jo in the little room off the Prime Minister's bedroom where the Private Secretaries had their abode. He noticed that the Prime Minister was in the bath. Jones then came out into the central passage and stood looking about for a few moments, when what should he see coming towards him but the President in his wheeled chair, unaccompanied by anyone. Jones stood rooted to the spot, and the President addressed him saying:

'Good morning. Is your Prime Minister up yet?'

'Well, Sir,' said Jones. 'it is within my knowledge that the Prime Minister is at the present moment in his bath.'

'Good,' said the President, 'then open the door.'

Jones accordingly flung open the bathroom door to admit the President, and there was the Prime Minister standing completely naked on the bath-mat.

[1] Colonel Hollis.
[2] Personal Assistant to Colonel Hollis.

'Don't mind me,' said the President, as the Prime Minister grabbed a towel, and the door closed.

Jones' day was made. Not only had he seen the inside of the White House, but he had spoken to the President and seen a meeting between him and the Prime Minister in unique circumstances.[1]

Winston S. Churchill to Clement Attlee
(*Churchill papers, 20/50*)

28 December 1941

Things have moved very quickly. The President has obtained the agreement of the American War and Navy Departments to the arrangement proposed in my last telegram, and the Chiefs of Staff Committee have endorsed it. I therefore anxiously await your approval. As soon as it is given, pray send the sub-joined telegrams to Australia, New Zealand and South Africa. The President will address the Dutch the moment I tell him you agree. Foreign Office should follow suit.

2. You should also despatch the following telegram to General Wavell. 'Staffs here are working on details both by themselves and with Americans. Position of Duff Cooper's consent requires to be reviewed, and in any case must not complicate these larger solutions. Please give me your ideas.'

3. Deeply shocked by Curtin's insulting speech[2] and vexed by his hectoring telegrams. Speech made bad impression here and the worst in Canada. We must not allow the Australian Government to impede the good relations we have with the United States. It may be that I shall have to make a broadcast to the Australian people.

4. Cannot help feeling very anxious about the convoys we are putting into Singapore without sufficient protection against air or surface attack. The risk must be run. I am sure Admiralty will do utmost possible.

5. I must rely on you to keep The King informed at every angle and obtain his approval.

[1] But not truly unique, see Patrick Kinna's earlier recollection (see page 1676).

[2] In a broadcast on 27 December 1941, Curtin said that the Australian government had 'never been satisfied with the air position', and that the representations made by his government in the previous few days were a 'restatement of those made over a long period'.

Winston S. Churchill to Major Randolph Churchill[1]
(*Churchill papers, 20/47*)

28 December 1941

The Prime Minister thinks it would be better to add separate short paragraphs at end about Mediterranean Fleet and Royal Air Force. The message is therefore as follows:

'From all over the Empire and from the bottom of our hearts we send to the Armies of the Nile and the desert every good wish for the New Year. These Armies have behind them a glorious record of victory.

'Deserted by their Allies in June 1940, left only with small and ill-equipped forces, with their communications through the Mediterranean virtually cut, these Armies, representing not only the Motherland but all parts of the Empire, have grown ceaselessly in strength and will still grow with every month that passes.

'They have marched forward steadfastly upon the path of victory which was forward to the path of Liberation. All defeats and set-backs have been repaired and repaid with interest. Egypt, the Sudan and East Africa were first of all successfully defended against heavy odds. Abyssinia has been freed and her Emperor restored to his Throne and Country from which he had been wrongly expelled.

'British Somaliland has been regained and Italian Somaliland and Eritrea conquered. Palestine has been defended, Syria freed of German intrigue, Iraq and Persia brought into effective military alliance. Latest of all is the famous victory manifesting itself more plainly every day in Cyrenaica.

'More than a quarter of a million prisoners have been taken. This proud record of achievement has won the lasting gratitude of the British Nation and Commonwealth of Nations and takes its place among the memorable campaigns of History.

'At one time you had deep anxiety for loved ones at home to endure the bombardment last winter.

'They have watched your toils and triumphs with glistening eyes. The task is not yet finished. Even greater days may lie ahead. In all these, rest assured of love and honour of those who sent you forth and long for the day of your victorious return.

'To the Mediterranean Fleet we send every good wish. The great victories over the Italian Navy, the constant interruption of the enemy's supplies, and the continual flow of supplies to our Armies have testified to their magnificent work, and constitute a noble page in Naval History.

[1] Randolph Churchill had asked his father for a Christmas message that he could publish in *Parade*, the magazine for troops in the Middle East. The first message, sent telegraphically on 21 December 1941, arrived too corrupt for publication at Christmas, and was superseded by this version, identical with the original one, with the exception of the added final paragraph.

'The Royal Air Force has made a vital contribution during all this time. Their determination and devotion to duty have overcome all difficulties, and we have watched with admiration their victorious assaults upon the enemy. We are proud of them and wish them all well.'

Winston S. Churchill to Peter Fraser
(*Churchill papers, 20/47*)

28 December 1941
Most Secret and Personal

I send you the sub-joined all-important agreement between the President and myself, which has been approved by the Cabinet. The President proposes to announce that it was at his suggestion, endorsed by his advisers, that General Wavell was chosen. I have the fullest confidence in General Wavell, who has unique experience in handling three or four separated theatres simultaneously. It is necessary that the announcement should be made by January 1 at latest, and I hope I may have your early agreement to an arrangement designed to be a help and security for New Zealand and to enable the war against Japan to be prosecuted with the utmost vigour.

Winston S. Churchill to Field Marshal Smuts
(*Churchill papers, 20/47*)

28 December 1941
Most Secret and Personal

I hope you will approve of the arrangement which is sub-joined. The President will announce publicly that the appointment of General Wavell was at his suggestion, endorsed by his advisers. I am sure myself this is a good arrangement, and events are moving on such a scale and at such a speed here that it would be most injurious to obstruct them.

2. I read your reply to my telegram No. 1436 to the President. You must not overlook the immense changes which air-power introduced into sea-war. Besides that, it will be some months before the arrival of the new American battleships giving plurality in the Pacific.

Winston S. Churchill to John Curtin, Peter Fraser and Field Marshal Smuts
(*Churchill papers, 65/20*)

28 December 1941
Most Secret and Personal

Text of Agreement begins:

(a) That unity of command shall be established in the South Western Pacific. Boundaries are not yet finally settled, but presume they would include Malay Peninsula, including the Burmese front to the Philippines and southward to the necessary supply bases, principally Fort Darwin, and supply lines in Northern Australia.

(b) That General Wavell should be appointed Commander-in-Chief, or, if preferred, Supreme Commander, of all United States, British, British Empire and Dutch forces of the land, sea and air who may be assigned by the Governments concerned to that theatre.

(c) General Wavell, whose Headquarters should in the first instance be established at Surabaya, would have an American officer as Deputy Commander-in-Chief. It seems probable that General Brett[1] would be chosen.

(d) That the American, British, Australian and Dutch naval forces in the theatre should be placed under the command of an American admiral, in accordance with the general principles set forth in paragraphs (a) and (b).

(e) It is intended that General Wavell should have a staff in the sort of proportion as Foch's High Control Staff was to the great staffs of the British and French armies in France. He would receive his orders from an appropriate joint body, who will be responsible to me as Minister of Defence and to the President of the United States, who is also Commander-in-Chief of all United States forces.

(f) The principal Commanders comprised in General Wavell's sphere will be C-in-C, Burma; C-in-C, Singapore and Malaya, C-in-C, Netherlands East Indies; C-in-C, Philippines; and C-in-C, of the southern communications via the south Pacific and North Australia.

(g) India, for which an Acting Commander-in-Chief will have to be appointed, and Australia, who will have their own Commander-in-Chief, will be outside General Wavell's sphere, except as above mentioned, and are the two great bases through which men and material from Great Britain and the Middle East on the one hand and the United States on the other can be fed into the fighting zone.

[1] George H. Brett, 1886–1963. Second Lieutenant, United States Cavalry, 1911; United States Air Force, 1915. Brigadier-General, 1936; Major-General, 1940; Lieutenant-General, 1942. Among his many decorations and honours were the Distinguished Service Medal with Oak Leaves Cluster, the Distinguished Flying Cross, and an honorary knighthood (KCB).

(h) United States navy will remain responsible for the whole of the Pacific Ocean east of the Philippines and Australasia, including the United States approaches to Australasia.

(i) A letter of instructions is being drafted for the Supreme Commander safeguarding the necessary residuary interests of the various Governments involved and prescribing in major outline his task. This draft will reach you shortly.

Winston S. Churchill to General Wavell
(*Churchill papers, 20/47*)

28 December 1941
Most Secret and Personal

The President and his military and naval advisers have impressed upon me the urgent need for a unified command in the South-West Pacific, and it is the unanimous desire, pressed particularly by the President and General Marshall, that you should become the supreme Commander of the Allied Forces by land, air and sea assigned to that theatre. The attached agreement, which is substantially in its final form, has been agreed to by the President and by His Majesty's Government. The letter of instructions referred to is being drafted, the terms of which will be issued shortly. While I hope these terms will set your mind at ease on the various unprecedented points involved, I should, of course, be ready to receive your observations upon them.

2. I feel sure you will value the confidence which is shown in you, and I request you to take up your task forthwith. Matters are so urgent that the details which are being studied by the Chiefs of Staff Committee must not delay the public announcement, which must be made at latest on 1st January.

3. You are the only man who has the experience of handling so many different theatres at once, and you know we shall back you up and see you have fair play. Everyone knows how dark and difficult the situation is. The President will announce that your appointment has been made by his desire.

4. Pray let me know your ideas as to staff, which will be essentially a super-staff rather than an actual handling body. If you like to take Pownall as your Chief of Staff, Percival might discharge the duties of Singapore and Malaya Commander.

White House itinerary
(*Commander C. R. Thompson papers*)

28 December 1941

The Prime Minister and small party left Washington by special train 2.15 p.m.

Winston S. Churchill to W. M. Hughes[1]
(*Churchill papers, 20/47*)

29 December 1941
Private, Personal and Secret

You are reported as saying that removal of Brooke-Popham was belated. As you know, this was decided upon by us before Japan began her sudden war. If you will look at Commonwealth telegrams on this subject you will see that the Government of which you are a member protested against removal of Brooke-Popham without their being previously consulted, and also they sent most fervently eulogistic letter to him assuring him of their utmost confidence.

2. In these circumstances, whatever other reproaches you cast upon us in this time of stress, I do not see how the epithet 'belated' can be used.

3. Speaking to you as a comrade of the last war and remembering how you faced the far worse shocks of the Dardanelles, I cannot help expressing my wonder and sorrow at some of the things that are said. I am labouring for your interests night and day, and I feel sure that you will never fall out of the line.

Winston S. Churchill to General de Gaulle
(*Churchill papers, 20/50*)

29 December 1941

I have received your telegram and you may be sure I pleaded your case strongly to our friends in United States. Your having broken away from agreement about Miquelon and St Pierre raised a storm which might have been serious had I not been on the spot to speak to the President. Undoubtedly, result of your activities there has been to make things more difficult with United States, and has, in fact, prevented some favourable developments which were occurring. I am always doing my best in all our interests.

[1] William Morris Hughes, 1864–1952. Educated in Wales and London. Emigrated to Australia, 1884. A Labour MP in the 1st Federal Australian Parliament. Prime Minister of Australia, 1915–23. Australian Delegate to the Paris Peace Conference, 1919. Minister for External Affairs, 1921–3; for Health and Repatriation, 1934–7; for External Affairs, 1937–9; for Industry, 1939–40. Attorney-General, 1939–40. Minister for the Navy, 1940–1.

Clementine Churchill to Winston S. Churchill
(*Baroness Spencer-Churchill papers*)

29 December 1941 10 Downing Street

My darling Winston,

I have been thinking constantly of you and trying to picture and realize the drama in which you are playing the principal – or rather it seems – the only part. I pray that when you leave, that the fervour you have aroused may not die down but will consolidate into practical & far-reaching action.

The news from Malaya is disquieting; & now I see that the Japanese have reached Medan in the north eastern corner of Sumatra just opposite Penang. This is one of the places I visited with Walter[1] on the East Indies cruise. Medan is a lovely clean commercial town with a fine harbour – its outskirts full of rich Dutch villas with glorious gardens.

In the midst of their own preoccupations Malaya 2 days ago cabled me £25,000 for my Russian Fund. I was much moved.

Sir Charles Wilson: notes
(*Contemporary Medical Archives Centre*)

29 December 1941

He slept well in the train & seems in better heart this morning. On arriving at the station in Ottawa the big fur-hatted Canadian Mounted Police kept back with difficulty the vast enthusiastic crowd which pushed good naturedly towards him & soon engulfed him.

J. Pierrepoint Moffat:[2] *'Notes on Mr Churchill's visit to Ottawa'*[3]
(*Randolph Churchill papers*)[4]

[29 December 1941]

Mr Churchill spent three days in Ottawa. The Canadians, who are by nature undemonstrative, let themselves go and found in their complete

[1] Lord Moyne.

[2] Jay Pierrepont Moffat, 1896–1943. Graduated from Harvard, 1917, when he entered the United States Diplomatic Service. Served in Warsaw, Tokyo, Constantinople, Ottawa (1925–27) and Berne. Consul-General, Sydney, 1935–37. United States Minister in Ottawa from 13 June 1940 until his death; also, from February 1941, Minister in Ottawa to the exiled Luxembourg Government. Died unexpectedly at his home in Ottawa on 24 January 1943, of a phlebitis from which he was thought to be recovering. He married Lilla Cabot Grew in 1927.

[3] This document was found among Randolph Churchill's papers after his death in 1968; I have been unable to find who sent it to him, or its archival origin.

[4] These notes, for both December 29 and December 30, were written on 31 December 1941, marked 'Strictly confidential'.

enthusiasm a vent for all their 'pent up' feelings. People travelled from all over the country to get just a glimpse of him in his car as he drove by.

The first time I saw him was at the station. In addition to the Cabinet Mr King had asked the Speaker,[1] Malcolm Macdonald, Mayor Lewis[2] and myself to be on the station platform. (Although we were the only four announced by the press, most of the other foreign representatives came.) At the proper hour the train backed in. There was Mr Churchill standing on the back platform in characteristic pose, puffing a newly lit cigar and holding up his right hand making the sign of V. As the temperature was about zero introductions on the platform were made on the double quick and he hastened away to Government House.

The next time I saw Mr Churchill was at a luncheon at the Chateau Laurier given by Mr King, with just the Cabinet and the foreign representatives present. As I was seated, in defiance of protocol, ahead of the other Ministers I found myself immediately opposite Mr Churchill, about three feet across a narrow table. I thus had a very good chance to observe him and to listen to the general tenor of his conversation. I had the impression that the session of the War Cabinet, from which he had just come, could not have been entirely without incident. For the first three or four minutes neither Mr Churchill nor his two neighbors, Mr King and Mr Crerar[3], spoke at all, and it was only later on that conversation grew easy and ended up in a love feast. Mr Churchill kept coming back to the situation of man power and woman power on the British Isles. He commented on the fact that with the Empire at war for two and one-half years with the greatest military power in the world there had been only one hundred and twenty thousand deaths, including civilians in the air raids. It might be argued that Britain was over-insured in the number of armed men kept on the British Isles, but he felt it was better to be safe than to be sorry and if one had any worries as to the safety of the home front it would be doubly hard to work out a strategy abroad. The loss of the *Prince of Wales* and the *Repulse* had been a terrible blow. Many of his advisers wanted the British to keep silent on this but his immediate instinct had been to tell the truth and give the people confidence in the Government's honesty, and everyone now recognized that he was right.

At the end of the lunch there were three short speeches. This first was by Mr King, in which he vowed that Canada would give everything it possessed

[1] James Allison Glen, 1877-1950. Born in Scotland. Educated at Glasgow University. Emigrated to Canada, 1911. A lawyer. Entered the Candian House of Commons, 1926;, Speaker of the House, 1940-45.

[2] Stanley Lewis, 1888–1970. An electrician by trade. Secretary-Treasurer of the Dominion Electric Co. Mayor of Ottawa, 1936–1948, the longest serving Mayor in the history of Canada's capital.

[3] Thomas Alexander Crerar, 1876–1975. Born in Ontario. Lived in Manitoba: a farmer and grain buyer. Elected to the Canadian House of Commons, 1917. Minister of Immigration and Colonization, 1936–38. Minister of Mines and Resources, 1939–45. Senator, 1945–66.

in the way of men and money, – a complete dedication of effort. Senator Dandurand,[1] saying a few words in French, referred to the magnificent effort which Quebec has made 'voluntarily', and then expressed the hope that in his big speech before Parliament the next day Mr Churchill would say a few words in French. Mr Churchill then arose and said that the reason he was acclaimed and the reason he had been chosen as a leader during this crisis was two-fold. The first was that he could put into words what every Briton felt, and thus give expression to what he wanted said; the second was that he was not afraid of assuming responsibility. He then referred to the black hours in the past when only faith had brought the British through. He talked of the bettering military situation, said that even though the Germans might next spring drive back the Russians nonetheless the grievous, if not mortal, wound that the Russians had given to the German Army was an unexpected help that could not have been counted on. He paid tribute to the United States and said that although one could not peer too far in the future, it would be up to the English speaking nations to give guidance to a distracted world.

The next time I saw Mr Churchill was at dinner at Government House. The dinner was quite small, just the Governor General,[2] Princess Alice[3] and their staff; Mr Churchill and his staff; the Chief Justice of Canada[4] and Miss Duff; the Chiefs of the Canadian Army, Navy and Air Staffs[5] and their wives; Mrs Harry Crerar, Silvercruys,[6] Lilla and myself. This time Lilla sat immediately opposite him at table and much of the time the conversation was general back and forth between the Earl of Athlone and himself. At first his voice was rather thick and he was none too communicative, but he gradually became his usual self and toward the end full of jokes and humor. He enthused about the President and said that every time he had an opportunity to be with him he put off everything else, even to the point of virtually ignoring Lord Halifax. He grumbled about having to make another oration in Parliament on the morrow and said that he was not a hen to lay an unlimited number of eggs.

[1] Raoul Dandurand, 1861–1942. A Liberal; called to the Canadian Senate, 1898. Privy Councillor, Canada, 1909. Leader of the Government in the Senate, 1921–30 and 1935–42. Privy Councillor (United Kingdom), 1941.

[2] The Earl of Athlone.

[3] Alice Mary Victoria Augusta Pauline, 1883–1981. Only daughter of Prince Leopold, Duke of Albany, Queen Victoria's youngest son. In 1904 she married Prince Alexander of Teck, the future Queen Mary's youngest brother. Princess Alice was active in war work, 1914–18; then accompanied her husband to South Africa (1924–31) and Canada (1940–46) while he was Governor-General. She was Chancellor of the University College of the West Indies. In 1966 she published her memoirs, *For My Grandchildren.*

[4] Lyman Poore Duff, 1865–1955. Born in Ontario. A Judge of the Supreme Court of Canada, 1906. Chief Justice of Canada from 1933 until his retirement in 1944, Knighted, 1934.

[5] Vice Admiral Percy W. Nelles, CB, Chief of the Naval Staff, 1934-44; Air Marshal L.S. Bredner, CB, DSC, Chief of the Air Staff, 1940-43; and Lieutenant-General K. Stuart, CB, DSO, MC, Chief of the General Staff (Army), December 1941 to December 1943.

[6] Baron Robert Silvercruys, Belgian Minister to Canada and Doyen of the Diplomatic Corps.

After dinner some one hundred or more high Canadian officials were invited. He stood in line and shook hands with the first fifty or so who came and then disappeared upstairs, never coming down to greet the other guests or even to stand in the doorway and let them see him. He handles a crowd extremely well but he handles a small group badly. Frequently he does not even look into the eye of the people who are passing in line. He makes no attempt to carry on a desultory conversation – I actually saw him walk away once in the middle of some polite remarks that were being made to him – and he makes no attempt to convey an impression of pleasure or interest in shaking someone's hand – a customary compliment to the handshaker, even though all concerned know that such interest would be merely window-dressing.

Sir Charles Wilson: diary
(*'Winston Churchill, Struggle for Survival, 1941-65'*)

29 December 1941 Ottawa

Whenever we are alone, he keeps asking me to take his pulse. I get out of it somehow, but once, when I found him lifting something heavy, I did expostulate. At this he broke out:

'Now, Charles, you are making me heart-minded. I shall soon think of nothing else. I couldn't do my work if I kept thinking about my heart.'

The next time he asked me to take his pulse I refused point-blank.

'You're all right. Forget your damned heart.'

He won't get through his speech tomorrow if this goes on.

Winston S. Churchill: speech
(*BBC Written Archives Centre*)

30 December 1941 Ottawa

It is with feelings of pride and encouragement that I find myself here in the House of Commons of Canada, invited to address the Parliament of the senior Dominion of the Crown. I am very glad to see again my old friend Mr Mackenzie King, for fifteen years out of twenty your Prime Minister, and I thank him for the too complimentary terms in which he has referred to myself. I bring you the assurance of good will and affection from every one in the Motherland. We are most grateful for all you have done in the common cause, and we know that you are resolved to do whatever more is possible as the need arises and as opportunity serves. Canada occupies a unique position in the British Empire because of its unbreakable ties with Britain and its ever-growing friendship and intimate association with the United States. Canada is a potent magnet, drawing together those in the New World and in the Old whose fortunes are now united in a deadly struggle for life and honour against the common foe. The contribution of Canada to the Imperial war effort in troops, in ships, in aircraft, in food, and in finance has been magnificent.

The Canadian Army now stationed in England has chafed not to find itself in contact with the enemy. But I am here to tell you that it has stood and still stands in the key position to strike at the invader should he land upon our shores. In a few months, when the invasion season returns, the Canadian Army may be engaged in one of the most frightful battles the world has ever seen, but on the other hand their presence may help to deter the enemy from attempting to fight such a battle on British soil. Although the long routine of training and preparation is undoubtedly trying to men who left prosperous farms and businesses, or other responsible civil work, inspired by an eager and ardent desire to fight the enemy, although this is trying to high-mettled temperaments, the value of the service rendered is unquestionable and I am sure that the peculiar kind of self-sacrifice involved will be cheerfully or at least patiently endured.

The Canadian Government have imposed no limitation on the use of the Canadian Army, whether on the Continent of Europe or elsewhere, and I think it is extremely unlikely that this war will end without the Canadian Army coming to close quarters with the Germans, as their fathers did at Ypres, on the Somme, or on the Vimy Ridge. Already at Hong Kong, that beautiful colony which the industry and mercantile enterprise of Britain has raised from a desert isle and made the greatest port of shipping in the whole world – Hong Kong, that Colony wrested from us for a time until we reach the peace table, by the overwhelming power of the Home Forces of Japan, to which it lay in proximity – at Hong Kong Canadian soldiers of the Royal Rifles of Canada and the Winnipeg Grenadiers, under a brave officer whose loss we mourn, have played a valuable part in gaining precious days, and have crowned with military honour the reputation of their native land.

Another major contribution made by Canada to the Imperial war effort is the wonderful and gigantic Empire training scheme for pilots for the Royal and Imperial Air Forces. This has now been as you know well in full career for nearly two years in conditions free from all interference by the enemy. The daring youth of Canada, Australia, New Zealand, and South Africa, with many thousands from the homeland, are perfecting their training under the best conditions, and we are being assisted on a large scale by the United States, many of whose training facilities have been placed at our disposal. This scheme will provide us in 1942 and 1943 with the highest class of trained pilots, observers, and air gunners in the numbers necessary to man the enormous flow of aircraft which the factories of Britain, of the Empire and of the United States are and will be producing.

I could also speak on the naval production of corvettes and above all of merchant ships which is proceeding on a scale almost equal to the building of the United Kingdom, all of which Canada has set on foot. I could speak of many other activities, of tanks, of the special forms of modern high-velocity cannon and of the great supplies of raw materials and many other elements essential to our war effort on which your labours are ceaselessly and tirelessly engaged. But I must not let my address to you become a catalogue, so I turn to less technical fields of thought.

We did not make this war, we did not seek it. We did all we could to avoid it. We did too much to avoid it. We went so far at times in trying to avoid it as to be almost destroyed by it when it broke upon us. But that dangerous corner has been turned, and with every month and every year that passes we shall confront the evil-doers with weapons as plentiful, as sharp, and as destructive as those with which they have sought to establish their hateful domination.

I should like to point out to you that we have not at any time asked for any mitigation in the fury or malice of the enemy. The peoples of the British Empire may love peace. They do not seek the lands or wealth of any country, but they are a tough and hardy lot. We have not journeyed all this way across the centuries, across the oceans, across the mountains, across the prairies, because we are made of sugar candy.

Look at the Londoners, the Cockneys; look at what they have stood up to. Grim and gay with their cry 'We can take it', and their war-time mood of 'What is good enough for anybody is good enough for us'. We have not asked that the rules of the game should be modified. We shall never descend to the German and Japanese level, but if anybody likes to play rough we can play rough too. Hitler and his Nazi gang have sown the wind; let them reap the whirlwind. Neither the length of the struggle nor any form of severity which it may assume shall make us weary or shall make us quit.

I have been all this week with the President of the United States, that great man whom destiny has marked for this climax of human fortune. We have been concerting the united pacts and resolves of more than thirty States and nations to fight on in unity together and in fidelity one to another, without any thought except the total and final extirpation of the Hitler tyranny, the Japanese frenzy, and the Mussolini flop.

There shall be no halting, or half measures, there shall be no compromise, or parley. These gangs of bandits have sought to darken the light of the world; have sought to stand between the common people of all the lands and their march forward into their inheritance. They shall themselves be cast into the pit of death and shame, and only when the earth has been cleansed and purged of their crimes and their villainy shall we turn from the task which they have forced upon us, a task which we were reluctant to undertake, but which we shall now most faithfully and punctiliously discharge. According to my sense of proportion, this is no time to speak of the hopes of the future, or the broader world which lies beyond our struggles and our victory. We have to win that world for our children. We have to win it by our sacrifices. We have not won it yet. The crisis is upon us. The power of the enemy is immense. If we were in any way to underrate the strength, the resources or the ruthless savagery of that enemy, we should jeopardize, not only our lives, for they will be offered freely, but the cause of human freedom and progress to which we have vowed ourselves and all we have. We cannot for a moment afford to relax. On the contrary we must drive ourselves forward with unrelenting zeal. In this strange, terrible world war there is a place for everyone, man and woman, old and young, hale and halt; service in a thousand forms is open. There is no room now for the dilettante, the weakling, for the shirker, or the sluggard. The mine, the factory, the dockyard, the salt sea waves, the fields to till, the home, the hospital, the chair of the scientist, the pulpit of the preacher – from the highest to the humblest tasks, all are of equal honour; all have their part to play. The enemies ranged against us, coalesced and combined against us, have asked for total war. Let us make sure they get it.

That grand old minstrel, Harry Lauder[1] – Sir Harry Lauder, I should say, and no honour was better deserved – had a song in the last War which began, 'If we all look back on the history of the past, we can just tell where we are'. Let us then look back. We plunged into this war all unprepared because we had pledged our word to stand by the side of Poland, which Hitler had feloniously invaded, and in spite of a gallant resistance had soon struck down. There followed those astonishing seven months which were called on this side of the Atlantic the 'phoney' war. Suddenly the explosion of pent-up German strength and preparation burst upon Norway, Denmark, Holland, and Belgium. All these absolutely blameless neutrals, to most of whom Germany up to the last moment was giving every kind of guarantee and assurance, were overrun and trampled down. The hideous massacre of Rotterdam, where 30,000 people perished, showed the ferocious barbarism in which the German Air Force revels when, as in Warsaw and later Belgrade, it is able to bomb practically undefended cities.

On top of all this came the great French catastrophe. The French Army collapsed, and the French nation was dashed into utter and, as it has so far proved, irretrievable confusion. The French Government had at their own suggestion solemnly bound themselves with us not to make a separate peace. It was their duty and it was also their interest to go to North Africa, where they would have been at the head of the French Empire. In Africa, with our aid, they would have had overwhelming sea power. They would have had the recognition of the United States, and the use of all the gold they had lodged

[1] Harry MacLennan Lauder, 1870–1950. As a boy, worked in a flax mill and then, for ten years, in a coal mine. Made his career as comedian and songwriter. First appeared on the Scottish stage in 1882; in London 1900. Organized concerts for charitable purposes, 1914–18; he also gave concerts on the western front. Knighted, 1919. His songs included 'I love a lassie' and 'Stop yer tickling, Jock'. His only son, Captain John Lauder, was killed in action on the western front in December 1916.

beyond the seas. It they had done this Italy might have been driven out of the war before the end of 1940, and France would have held her place as a nation in the counsels of the Allies and at the conference table of the victors. But their generals misled them. When I warned them that Britain would fight on alone whatever they did, their generals told their Prime Minister and his divided Cabinet, 'In three weeks England will have her neck wrung like a chicken.' Some chicken! Some neck!

What a contrast has been the behaviour of the valiant, stout-hearted Dutch, who still stand forth as a strong living partner in the struggle! Their venerated Queen and their Government are in England, their Princess and her children have found asylum and protection here in your midst. But the Dutch nation are defending their Empire with dogged courage and tenacity by land and sea and in the air. Their submarines are inflicting a heavy daily toll upon the Japanese robbers who have come across the seas to steal the wealth of the East Indies, and to ravage and exploit its fertility and its civilization. The British Empire and the United States are going to the aid of the Dutch. We are going to fight out this new war against Japan together. We have suffered together and we shall conquer together.

But the men of Bordeaux, the men of Vichy, they would do nothing like this. They lay prostrate at the foot of the conqueror. They fawned upon him. What have they got out of it? The fragment of France which was left to them is just as powerless, just as hungry as, and even more miserable, because more divided, than the occupied regions themselves. Hitler plays from day to day a cat-and-mouse game with these tormented men. One day he will charge them a little less for holding their countrymen down. Another day he will let out a few thousand broken prisoners of war from the one-and-a-half or one-and-three-quarter millions he has collected. Or again he will shoot a hundred French hostages to give them a taste of the lash. On these blows and favours the Vichy Government have been content to live from day to day. But even this will not go on indefinitely. At any moment it may suit Hitler's plans to brush them away. Their only guarantee is Hitler's good faith, which, as everyone knows, biteth like the adder and stingeth like the asp.

But some Frenchmen there were who would not bow their knees and who under General de Gaulle have continued to fight on the side of the Allies. They have been condemned to death by the men of Vichy, but their names will be held and are being held in increasing respect by nine Frenchmen out of every ten throughout the once happy, smiling land of France. But now strong forces are at hand. The tide has turned against the Hun. Britain, which the men of Bordeaux thought and then hoped would soon be finished, Britain with her Empire around her carried the weight of the war along for a whole long year through the darkest part of the valley. She is growing stronger every day. You can see it here in Canada. Anyone who has the slightest knowledge of our affairs is aware that very soon we shall be superior in every form of equipment to those who have taken us at the disadvantage of being but half armed.

The Russian armies, under their warrior leader, Josef Stalin, are waging furious was with increasing success along the thousand-mile front of their invaded country. General Auchinleck, at the head of a British, South African, New Zealand and Indian army, is striking down and mopping up the German and Italian forces which had attempted the invasion of Egypt. Not only are they being mopped up in the desert, but great numbers of them have been drowned on the way there by British submarines and the RAF in which Australian squadrons played their part.

As I speak this afternoon an important battle is being fought around Jedabya. We must not attempt to prophesy its result, but I have good confidence. All this fighting in Libya proves that when our men have equal weapons in their hands and proper support from the air they are more than a match for the Nazi hordes. In Libya, as in Russia, events of great importance and of most hopeful import have taken place. But greatest of all, the mighty Republic of the United States has entered the conflict, and entered it in a manner which shows that for her there can be no withdrawal except by death or victory.

[Churchill then spoke in French]:

Et partout dans la France occupée et inoccupée (car leur sort est égal), ces honnêtes gens, ce grand peuple, la nation française, se redresse. L'espoir se rallume dans les coeurs d'une race guerrière, même désarmée, berceau de la liberté révolutionnaire et terrible aux vainqueurs esclaves. Et partout, on voit le point du jour, et la lumière grandit, rougeâtre, mais claire. Nous ne perdrons jamais la confiance que la France jouera le rôle des hommes libres et qu'elle reprendra par des voies dures sa place dans la grande compagnie des nations libératrices et victorieuses.

Ici, au Canada, où la langue française est honorée et parlée, nous nous tenons prêts et armés pour aider et pour saluer cette résurrection nationale.

[Translation: And everywhere in France, occupied and unoccupied, for their fate is identical, these honest folk, this great people, the French nation, are rising again. Hope is springing up again in the hearts of a warrior race even though disarmed, cradle of revolutionary liberty and terrible to slavish conquerors. And everywhere dawn is breaking and light spreading, reddish yet, but clear. We shall never lose confidence that France will play the role of free men again and, by hard paths, will once again attain her place in the great company of freedom-bringing and victorious nations.

Here in Canada, where the French language is honoured and spoken, we are armed and ready to help and to hail this national resurrection.]

Now that the whole of the North American continent is becoming one gigantic arsenal, and armed camp; now that the immense reserve power of Russia is gradually becoming apparent; now that long-suffering, unconquerable China sees help approaching; now that the outraged and subjugated nations can see daylight ahead, it is permissible to take a broad forward view of the war.

We may observe three main periods or phases of the struggle that lies before us. First there is the period of consolidation, of combination, and of final preparation. In this period, which will certainly be marked by much heavy fighting we shall still be gathering our strength, resisting the assaults of the enemy, and acquiring the necessary overwhelming air superiority and shipping tonnage to give our armies the power to traverse, in whatever numbers may be necessary, the seas and oceans which, except in the case of Russia, separate us from our foes. It is only when the vast shipbuilding programme on which the United States has already made so much progress, and which you are powerfully aiding, comes into full flood, that we shall be able to bring the whole force of our manhood and of our modern scientific equipment to bear upon the enemy. How long this period will take depends upon the vehemence of the effort put into production in all our war industries and shipyards.

The second phase which will then open may be called the phase of liberation. During this phase we must look to the recovery of the territories which have been lost or which may yet be lost, and also we must look to the revolt of the conquered peoples from the moment that the rescuing and liberating armies and air forces appear in strength within their bounds. For this purpose it is imperative that no nation or region overrun, that no Government or State which has been conquered, should relax its moral and physical efforts and preparation for the day of deliverance. The invaders, be they German or Japanese, must everywhere be regarded as infected persons to be shunned and isolated as far as possible. Where active resistance is impossible, passive resistance must be maintained. The invaders and tyrants must be made to feel that their fleeting triumphs will have a terrible reckoning, and that they are hunted men and that their cause is doomed. Particular punishment will be reserved for the quislings and traitors who make themselves the tools of the enemy. They will be handed over to the judgment of their fellow-countrymen.

There is a third phase which must also be contemplated, namely, the assault upon the citadels and the home-lands of the guilty Powers both in Europe and in Asia. Thus I endeavour in a few words to cast some forward light upon the dark, inscrutable mysteries of the future. But in thus forecasting the course along which we should seek to advance, we must never forget that the power of the enemy and the action of the enemy may at every stage affect our fortunes. Moreover, you will notice that I have not attempted to assign any time-limits to the various phases. These time-limits depend upon our exertions, upon our achievements, and on the hazardous and uncertain course of the war.

Nevertheless I feel it is right at this moment to make it clear that, while an ever-increasing bombing offensive against Germany will remain one of the principal methods by which we hope to bring the war to an end, it is by no means the only method which our growing strength now enables us to take into account. Evidently the most strenuous exertions must be made by all. As to the form which those exertions take, that is for each partner in the grand alliance to judge for himself in consultation with others and in harmony with the general scheme. Let us then address ourselves to our task, not in any way underrating its tremendous difficulties and perils, but in good heart and sober confidence, resolved that, whatever the cost, whatever the suffering, we shall stand by one another, true and faithful comrades, and do our duty God helping us, to the end.

A few minutes after Churchill's speech of 30 December 1941, he was led into the Speaker's Chamber where the photographer Yousuf Karsh had set up his camera and lights.

Yousuf Karsh:[1] *recollection*

(*Jean Nicol, 'Meet me at the Savoy'*)

[30 December 1941]

He only gave me a few minutes, and he sat scowling with a huge cigar clenched in his teeth. I begged him to remove the cigar as it was spoiling the wonderful line of his jaw, but he refused and told me to hurry. So I got everything ready, and just as I was about to take the photograph I dashed forward and snatched the cigar from his mouth, and look at the good result.[2]

[1] Yousuf Karsh, born in Armenia, 1908. Educated in Canada. Studied photography in Boston. Portrait photographer from 1932. Among his subjects were George Bernard Shaw, H.G. Wells, Einstein, and Picasso. His first one man exhibition (of many) was held at the World Pavilion of Canada, Expo '67, Montreal. He published his autobiography, *In Search of Greatness*, in 1962.

[2] The 'good result' was the frowning face subsequently used in innumerable books, articles and magazines, and also used on the British stamps issued shortly after Churchill's death in 1965. After the cigar incident was over, Karsh took another photograph, known in the Churchill family as the 'smiling' photograph: I have used it on the front cover and spine of this volume. For many of those who knew Churchill, the smiler was a truer likeness than the frowner.

Winston S. Churchill to Clement Attlee and Lord Cranborne
(*Churchill papers, 20/50*)

30 December 1941

Curtin article in the *Melbourne Herald* has made a very bad impression in high American circles, and, of course, excited lively scorn in Canada. I think you should call Earle Page to account in Cabinet for it and ask him what is the meaning of this sort of language. By placing their relations with Britain after those with Russia, Dutch and China, and by saying they rely on United States of America unhampered by any pangs of traditional friendship for Britain, they must be taken as relieving us of part of our responsibility in pursuance of which we have sacrificed His Majesty's Ships *Prince of Wales* and *Repulse*. Once again, to get better understanding you should take a firm stand against this misbehaviour, which certainly does not represent the brave Australian nation. I hope, therefore, there will be no weakness or pandering to them at this juncture, while at the same time we do all in human power to come to their aid.

In the same way a very firm attitude should be adopted in the House of Commons to snarlers and naggers who are trying to make trouble out of the Japanese attack on us in the Far East. I hope you will endeavour to let all issues stand over successively until I return so that I may face any opposition myself.

Winston S. Churchill to the Chiefs of Staff
(*Churchill papers, 20/50*)

30 December 1941

ACCOUNT OF CARRYING OUT OF 'ANKLET' AND 'ARCHERY'[1]

What was the point of doing 'Anklet' at all if not to try to interrupt north and south enemy coastal traffic? I understood 'Archery' was to be a baffle to cover real 'Anklet'. But it is only baffling that seems to have come off. I cannot understand why on threat of dive-bombers arriving Bodo the operation 'Anklet' should have been turned into 'Raid of short duration'. After all these elaborate preparations you have certainly made a very hasty departure. Pray let me have full explanation of what appears to be a complete abandonment of the original plans.

[1] 'Anklet': to interrupt German coastal traffic along the northern and southern coasts of Norway. 'Archery': a cover for 'Anklet'.

Winston S. Churchill to Clement Attlee
(*Churchill papers, 20/50*)

30 December 1941

I do not think we ought to remove Brooke-Popham's name from New Year's Honours List for a Baronetcy. It was decided to remove him before war began, and the Baronetcy was awarded for his good service. It would be most unfair to make him a scapegoat. If Malay Peninsula has been starved for sake of Libya and Russia no one is more responsible than I, and I would do exactly the same again. I hope, therefore, his name will be restored to the list, and Brendan Bracken should be able to explain position to editors and place decision squarely upon me. Should any questions be asked in Parliament I should be glad if it could be stated that I particularly desire to answer it myself on my return.[1]

Winston S. Churchill to General Auchinleck
(*Churchill papers, 20/68*)

31 December 1941

I have a feeling that it would be well if you could arrange it to finish up the Bardia, Sollum, Halfaya pockets as soon as possible, and that some sacrifice might well be made to this end. Have you no siege batteries available? Every one here is delighted with the progress made towards the West.

Churchill left Ottawa by train at 3 p.m. on 31 December 1941, reaching Washington at noon on 1 January 1942. He thus spent New Year's Eve travelling; the New Year began as his train was travelling southward along the Hudson River. At midnight, as 1942 began, it would have been in the region of Roosevelt's house at Hyde Park.

[1] Despite Churchill's telegram, Air Chief Marshal Sir Robert Brooke-Popham did not receive a Baronetcy. He had been knighted in 1927.

Appendices

Appendix A: Members of the Cabinet, 1941

WAR CABINET

Prime Minister and Minister of Defence
Winston S Churchill
Lord President of the Council
Sir John Anderson
Lord Privy Seal
Clement Attlee
Secretary of State for Foreign Affairs
Anthony Eden
Minister without Portfolio
Arthur Greenwood
Minister for Aircraft Production
Lord Beaverbrook (until 1 May 1941)
Minister of State
Lord Beaverbrook (from 1 May 1941)
Oliver Lyttelton (from 29 June 1941)
Minister of Supply
Lord Beaverbrook (from 29 June 1941)
Chancellor of the Exchequer
Sir Kingsley Wood
Minister of Labour and National Service
Ernest Bevin

MINISTERS NOT IN THE WAR CABINET, 1941

First Lord of the Admiralty
A. V. Alexander

Minister of Agriculture and Fisheries
Robert Hudson
Secretary of State for Air
Sir Archibald Sinclair
Minister for Aircraft Production
J. Moore-Brabazon (from 1 May 1941)
Secretary of State for Colonial Affairs
Lord Lloyd
Lord Moyne (from 8 February 1941)
Secretary of State for Dominion Affairs
Viscount Cranborne
Minister for Economic Warfare
Hugh Dalton
President of the Board of Education
H. Ramsbotham
R.A. Butler (from 20 July 1941)
Minister of Food
Lord Woolton
Minister of Health
Malcolm MacDonald
Ernest Brown (from 8 February 1941)
Secretary of State, Home Office, and Home Security
Herbert Morrison
Secretary of State for India and Burma
L. S. Amery
Minister of Information
Alfred Duff Cooper
Brendan Bracken (from 20 July 1941)
Minister of Labour and National Service
Ernest Bevin
Chancellor of the Duchy of Lancaster
Lord Hankey
Alfred Duff Cooper (from 20 July 1941)
Lord Chancellor
Viscount Simon
Paymaster-General
Lord Hankey (from 20 July 1941: office vacant before then)
Minister of Pensions
Sir W. Womersley
Postmaster-General
W. S. Morrison
Minister, Scottish Office
Ernest Brown

Tom Johnston (from 8 February 1941)
Minister of Shipping
Ronald Cross
Minister of Supply
Sir Andrew Duncan
President of the Board of Trade
Oliver Lyttelton
Sir Andrew Duncan (from 29 June 1941)
Minister of Transport
J. Moore-Brabazon
Secretary of State for War
David Margesson
Minister of War Transport
Lord Leathers (from 1 May 1941: when the Ministry was established)

Appendix B

BRITISH CODE NAMES

Abigail: bombing reprisal raids against German cities (see also Delilah, Jezebel and Rachel)
Abstention: the seizure of the Dodecanese island of Castelorizzo
Acrobat: advance from Cyrenaica into Tripolitania
Ajax: planned military landing at the Norwegian port of Trondheim, intended to help Russia by dislodging the Germans from northern Norway, and possibly inducing Sweden to join the Allies
Anklet: interception of German coastal traffic along the cost of northern and southern Norway.
Appearance: landings east and west of Berbera, British Somaliland, March 1941.
Arcadia: First Washington Conference, December 1941
Archery: Combined Operations raid on Vaagso area, Norway, December 1941
Argentia: the Churchill-Roosevelt meeting off Newfoundland, August 1941
Ballast: plan to establish a British military force in Spanish North Africa
Battleaxe: offensive operations in the Sollum, Tobruk, Capuzzo area, June 1941 'to wipe out the enemy operation in Libya and to seize aerodromes in Cyrenaica'. It was halted after four days, having failed in its objective.
Blackthorn: assistance to Spain in the event of the German occupation of Spain
Bonus: British plan for an amphibious operation against Vichy-held Madagascar, in the Indian Ocean

Brisk: British plan to take the Portuguese Azores to provide air and naval bases for closing the 'Atlantic gap' in which German U-boats could operate with little threat of British air attack.
Bruiser: early name for Battleaxe (above)
Bumper: anti-invasion exercise
C: Iceland (during Churchill's visit, in August 1941)
Claymore: operation against the Lofoten Islands
Colorado: Crete
Countenance: British and Indian operations in Persia and the Persian Gulf to protect oil installations
Crusader: Operations in the Western Desert, November 1941, to clear the Germans and Italians from Cyrenaica
Cultivator: convoy from Alexandria to Tobruk and the relief of the Australian troops besieged there, October 1941
Delilah: bombing reprisal raid against Düsseldorf
Demon: the evacuation of Greece
Double Winch: aircraft taken by aircraft carrier in convoy from Gibraltar to a point in the Mediterranean from which they could fly more safely to Malta, Suda Bay (Crete) and Alexandria (Egypt), April 1941
Dunlop: air re-inforcements for the Middle East
Exporter: British campaign to take Syria from Vichy French control. The operation, using British, Australian, Indian, Free French and Palestinian (Jewish) forces, was begun on the morning of 8 June 1941
F scheme: oil fuel and flame projectors for potential invasion beaches near British ports
Goldeneye: British liaison delegation for Spain, based in Gibraltar
Gymnast: the British plan to land in French North-Africa in the spring of 1942 (later developed into the Torch, landings of November 1942)
Influx: British occupation of Sicily
Jaguar: the transfer of 140 fighter aircraft through the Mediterranean to Malta and Egypt on board the aircraft carriers *Ark Royal*, *Argus*, *Furious* and *Victorious*.
Jezebel: bombing reprisal raid against Bremen
K Force: a naval striking force to intercept German supply ships on their way to Tripoli. The force, which was formed at Malta, consisted of two cruisers and two destroyers
Lancelot: the visit of a senior Vichy officer to London.
Lustre: military aid to Greece (infantry divisions from Egypt to Thrace)
Mandibles: the seizure of the Italian Dodecanese Islands
Marie: Free French plan to take Jibuti from Vichy France, with British assistance
Matador: planned British advance from Malaya into southern Thailand, and occupy Singora, before the Japanese arrived. It was 33 hours sailing from Japanese held Saigon to Singora

Menace: the attempt to seize Dakar in September 1940
Mutton: aerial mines used against incoming bombers
Pilgrim: British plan to take the Portuguese island groups in the Atlantic, combining 'Thruster' (the Azores), 'Springboard' (Madeira) and 'Puma' (Canaries and Cape Verde)
Puma: planned seizure of the Spanish Canary Islands, and the Portuguese Cape Verde Islands; using a force of 20,000 men, to be commanded by General Sir Harold Alexander (later Field Marshal Earl Alexander of Tunis)
Rachel: bombing reprisal raid against Mannheim
Railway: reinforcements of aircraft to Malta from Gibraltar
Ration: food for Vichy France
Retribution: the German attack on Yugoslavia (April 1941)
Riviera: Churchill's journey across the Atlantic to see President Roosevelt at Argentia Bay, Newfoundland (August 1941)
Rubble: Norwegian merchant ships based in the Swedish port of Gotenburg, running the German naval blockade, escorted by the Royal Navy
Salient: passage of two ships to Egypt through the Mediterranean
Scorcher: British plans for the defence of Crete
Shrapnel: a plan to seize the Cape Verde Islands from Portugal
Smeller: Air Interception radar equipment
Springboard: plans for the seizure of Madeira
Thruster: seizure of the Azores Islands if Germany moved against Spain and Portugal
Tiger: tank reinforcements to Egypt through the Mediterranean
Truncheon: a British combined operations raid on Livorno (Leghorn) in north-west Italy, palnned for January 1942
Velvet: British air and military aid to the southern flank of the Russian front
Victor: a military exercise in Britain, as a practise against invasion
Whipcord: the planned British invasion of Sicily
Winch: the despatch of fighter aircraft to Malta by aircraft through the Mediterranean from Gibraltar
Workshop: the planned apture of Pantellaria Island
Yorker: the planned capture of Sardinia

Appendix C

ABBREVIATIONS

AA: anti-aircraft
ABC: American-British Conversations
ABCD Powers: America, Britain, China and the Dutch East Indies

A/C: aircraft carrier
ACIGS: Assistant Chief of the Imperial General Staff
AD: anti-aircraft ammunition
ADGB: Air Defence of Great Britain
AFV: Armoured Fighting Vehicle
AI: Air Interception radar equipment (codename 'Smeller')
ARP: Air Raid Precautions
AS: anti-submarine
ASU: Air Storage Units, aircraft in storage
AT: Anti-Tank
ATS: Auxiliary Territorial Service
ASV: Air-to-Surface Vessel, an airborne radar device
AU-boat: anti-U-boat
BAD: British Admiralty Delegation, Washington
BBC: British Broadcasting Corporation
BEF: British Expeditionary Force
C: the head of the Secret Intelligence Service (Brigadier Menzies)
CCO: Commodore Combined Operations (Lord Louis Mountbatten)
CAS: Chief of the Air Staff (Air Chief Marshal Sir Charles Portal)
CD: Coastal Defence
CGS: Chief of the General Staff (of an army command)
CIGS: Chief of the Imperial General Staff (General Sir John Dill; later General Sir Alan Brooke)
COS: Chiefs of Staff
CWR: Cabinet War Room (also known as the Central War Room)
DC(O): Defence Committee (Operations)
DCO: Director of Combined Operations (Admiral of the Fleet Sir Roger Keyes)
DF: directions finding (tracking radio signals)
EA: enemy aircraft
FAA: Fleet Air Arm
FOP: Future Operations (Planning)
FS: Foreign Secretary
GAF: German Air Force
Gee: aircraft course-fixing device
GHQ, ME: General Headquarters, Middle East (Cairo)
GOC: General Officer Commanding
GOC-in-C: General Officer Commanding-in-Chief
GR: general reconnaisance aircraft (martime patrol and anti-submarine work)
H of C: House of Commons
HE: His Excellency
HE: High Explosive
HQ: headquarters

HQ ME: Headquarters Middle East (Cairo)
HX: transatlantic convoys from Halifax, Nova Scotia, to British ports
ICI: Imperial Chemical Industries
IE: Initial Equipments, for Royal Air Force crews
IE: Import Executive
ILP: Independent Labour Party
JIC: Joint Intelligence Committee
JPS: Joint Planning Staff
Ju: Junker (German aircraft)
KGV: King George V class battleships
LAM: Long Aerial Mine
L of C: Lines of Communication
LC bomb: Light Case (thin casing) bomb
LCF: Landing Craft (Flak)
LSI: Landing Ship (Infantry)
LST: Landing Ship (Tank)
M of I: Ministry of Information
MAP: Ministry of Aircraft Production
ME: Middle East
Me: Messerschmidt
MEW: Ministry of Economic Warfare
MI5: Military Intelligence 5 (a branch of the Secret Intelligence Service)
MoS: Ministry of Supply
MP: Member of Parliament
MT: motor transport
MV: merchant vessel
OL: messages sent to the Commander-in-Chief in the Middle East containing information based upon decrypts of German top secret (Enigma) radio messages
OTC: Officers Training Corps
PAC: Parachute and Cable device, an anti-aircraft rocket
PBY: Catalina twin-engined flying boat
PE fuzes: an anti-aircraft device, for ground fire against attacking aircraft
PIAT: Projectile Infantry Anti-Tank gun
PM: Prime Minister
PRU: Photographic Reconnaisance Unit
Q services: Quartermaster services
R battleships: *Royal Sovereign*, *Revenge*, *Resolution*, *Ramilles*
RAF: Royal Air Force
RASC: Royal Army Service Corps
RDF: Radio Direction Finding (later Radar)
RE: Royal Engineers
RNVR: Royal Naval Volunteer Reserve

SAA: small arms ammunition
SIS: Secret Intelligence Service
SO: Special Operations
SOE: Special Operations Executive
SS: steamship
ST grenade: Sticky-bomb Type, anti-tank grenade
TLC: Tank Landing Craft
TUC: Trades Union Congress
UP: Unrotated projectile (also unrifled projectile): an anti-aircraft rocket
VCIGS: Vice Chief of the Imperial General Staff
WAAF: Women's Auxiliary Air Force
WC: War Cabinet
WP: War Cabinet Paper
WS: Convoys from Britain to Egypt that went via the Cape of Good Hope, the Indian Ocean and the Red Sea
WSC: Churchill's initials: appearing at the bottom of each of his many thousands of minutes

Maps

LIST OF MAPS

In the text:

Between pages 1728 and 1745

4. Central and Eastern Europe, and the Balkans

0 kilometres 100
0 miles 75
North Sea
Flensburg
Baltic Sea
Kiel Canal
Kiel
Wismar
Hamburg
Emden
HOLLAND
River Elbe
Bremen
Berlin
Hanover
Potsdam
GERMANY
RUHR
Gelsenkirchen
Essen
Duisberg
G ttingen
D sseldorf
Leipzig
Cologne
Aachen
Buchenwald
River Rhine
Black Forest
RHINELAND
Wiesbaden
Frankfurt-on-Main
SUDETENLAND
Plzen
(Pilsen)
Mannheim
Nuremberg
LORRAINE
FRANCE
Nancy
Strasbourg
Stuttgart
River Danube
ALSACE
BAVARIA
' Martin Gilbert 1999

5. Germany

6. Yugoslavia, Greece, and the Aegean Sea

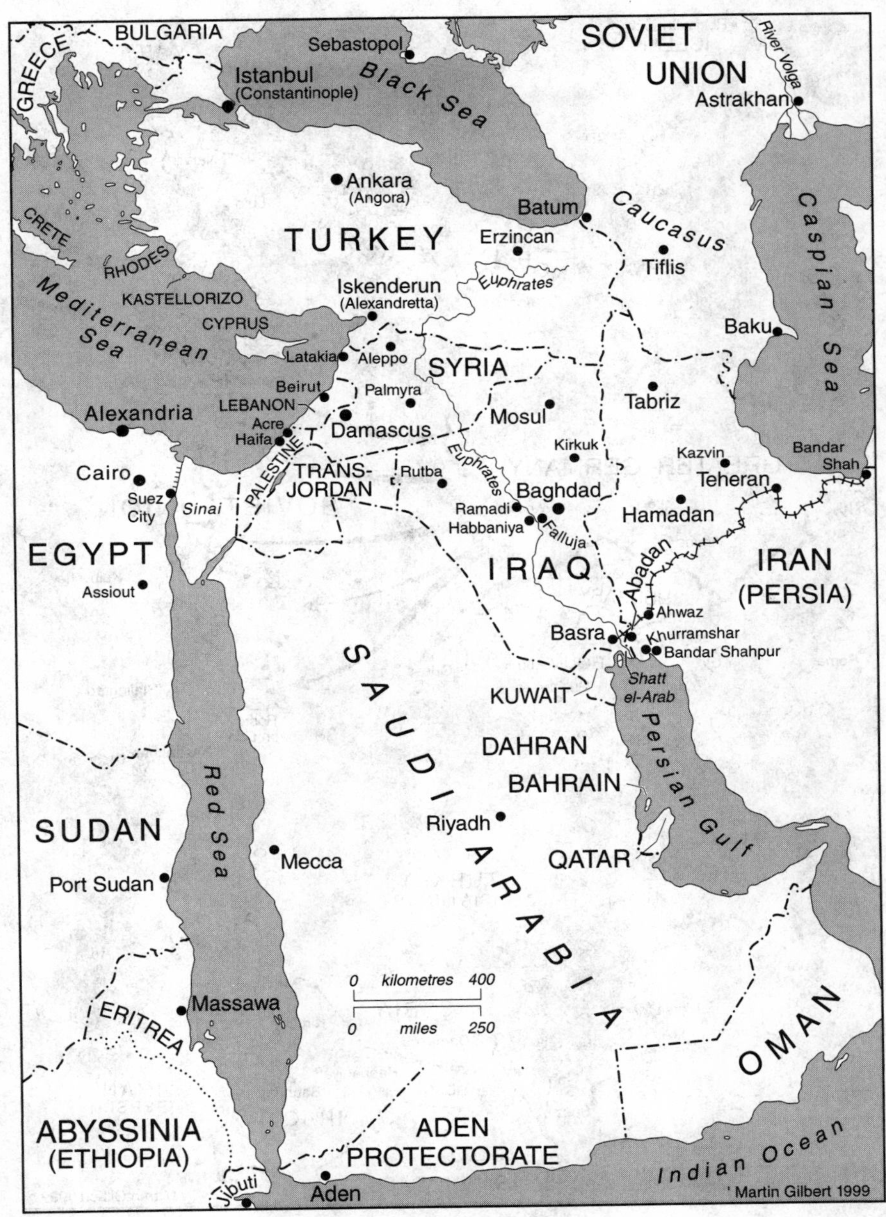

7. The Middle East and Iran

8. Europe and the Middle East at the time of the German invasion of the Soviet Union

9. The German invasion of the Soviet Union, June to December 1941

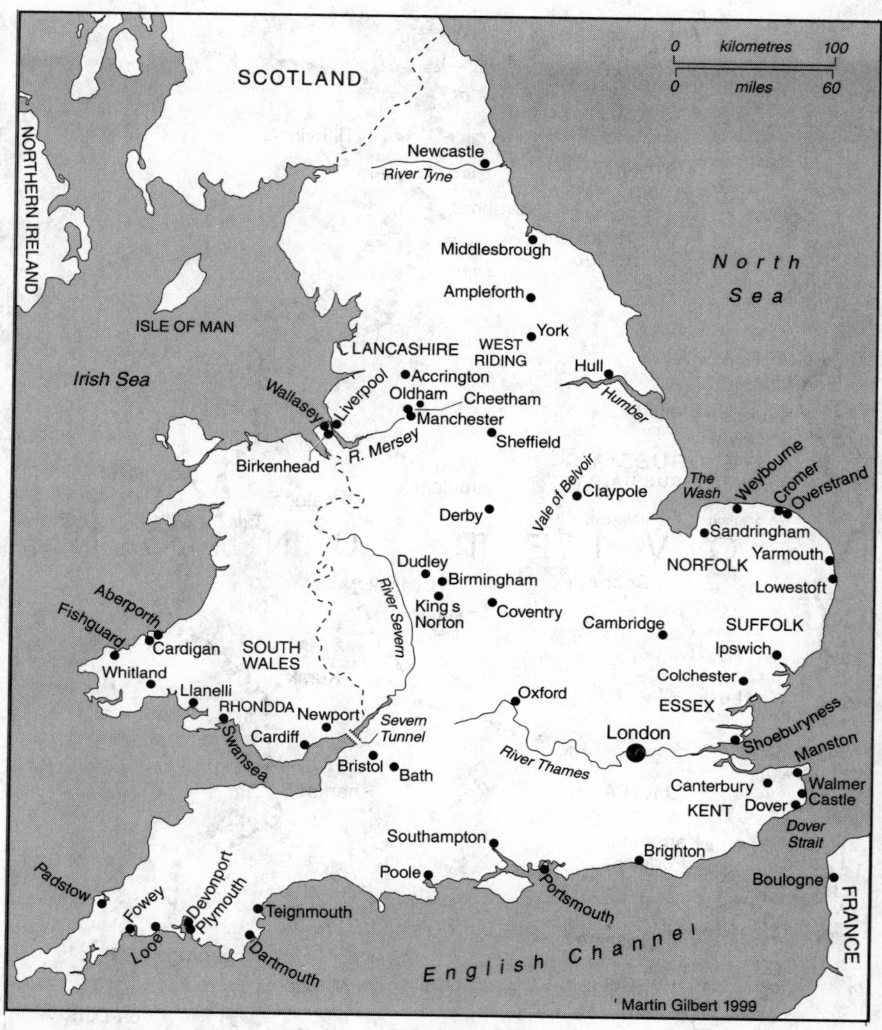

10. England and Wales

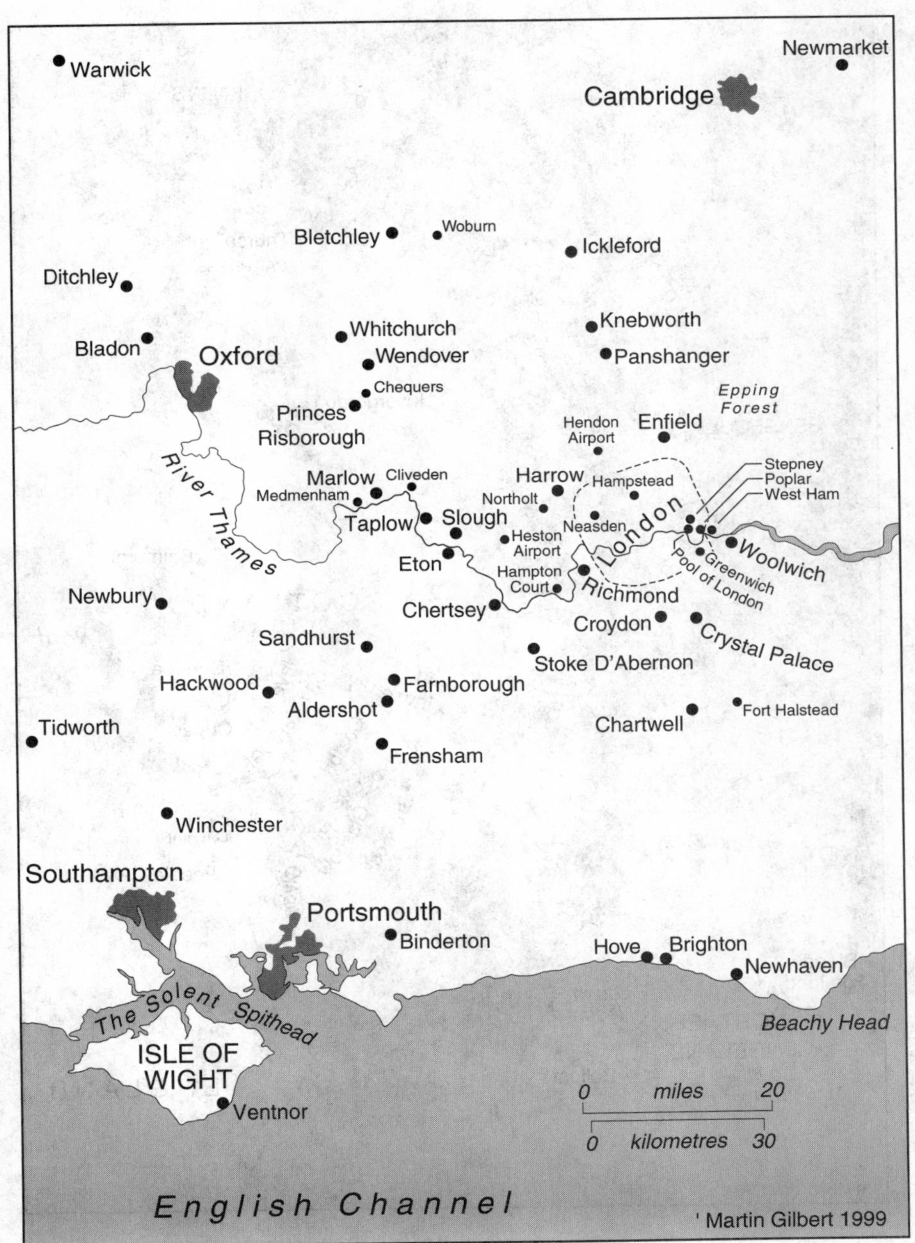
Warwick
Newmarket
Cambridge
Bletchley
Woburn
Ickleford
Ditchley
Knebworth
Whitchurch
Bladon
Oxford
Wendover
Panshanger
Chequers
Epping Forest
Princes Risborough
Hendon Airport
Enfield
River Thames
Marlow
Cliveden
Harrow
Hampstead
Stepney
Poplar
West Ham
Medmenham
Northolt
Taplow
Slough
Neasden
London
Heston Airport
Woolwich
Eton
Hampton Court
Greenwich
Pool of London
Richmond
Newbury
Chertsey
Croydon
Sandhurst
Crystal Palace
Stoke D'Abernon
Hackwood
Farnborough
Aldershot
Fort Halstead
Tidworth
Chartwell
Frensham
Winchester
Southampton
Portsmouth
Binderton
Hove
Brighton
Newhaven
The Solent
Spithead
Beachy Head
ISLE OF WIGHT
Ventnor
0 miles 20
0 kilometres 30
English Channel
' Martin Gilbert 1999

11. Southern England

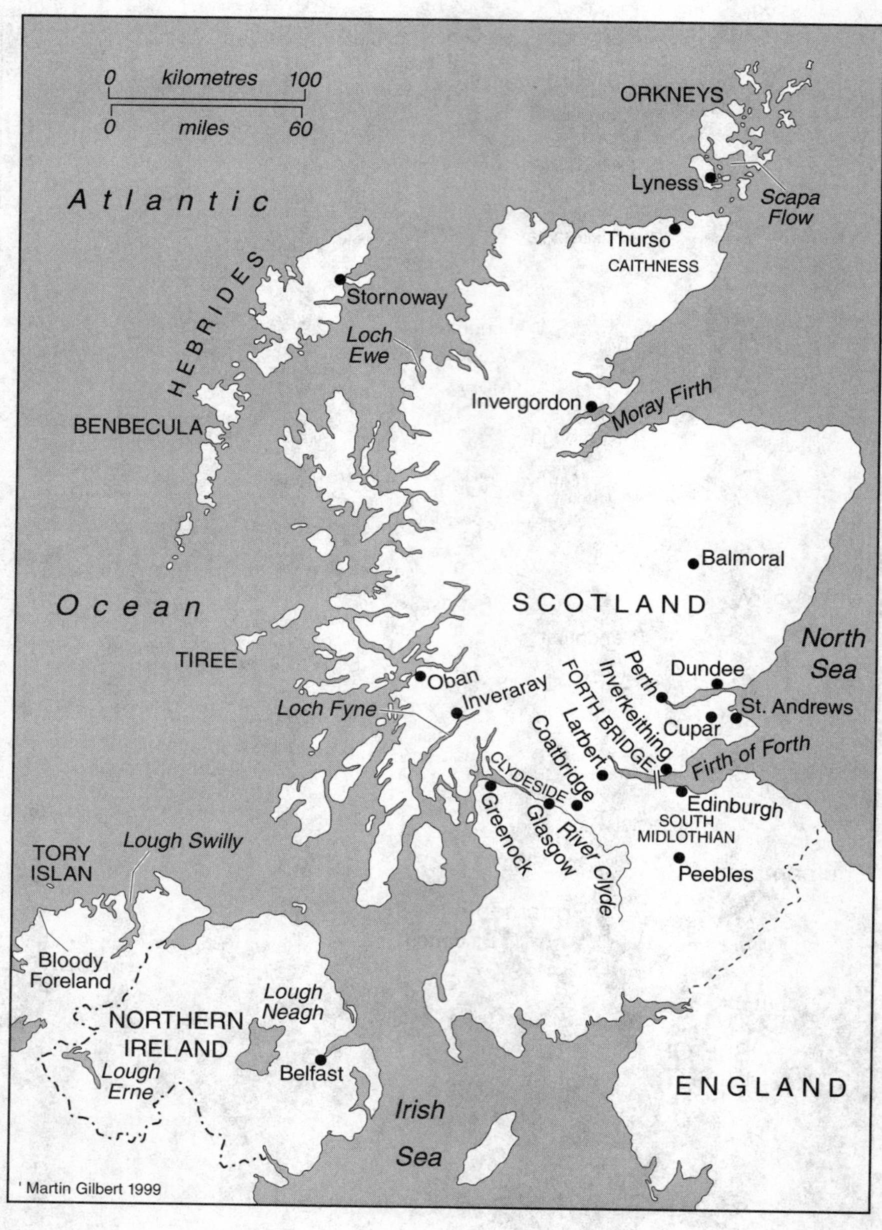

12. Scotland and Northern Ireland

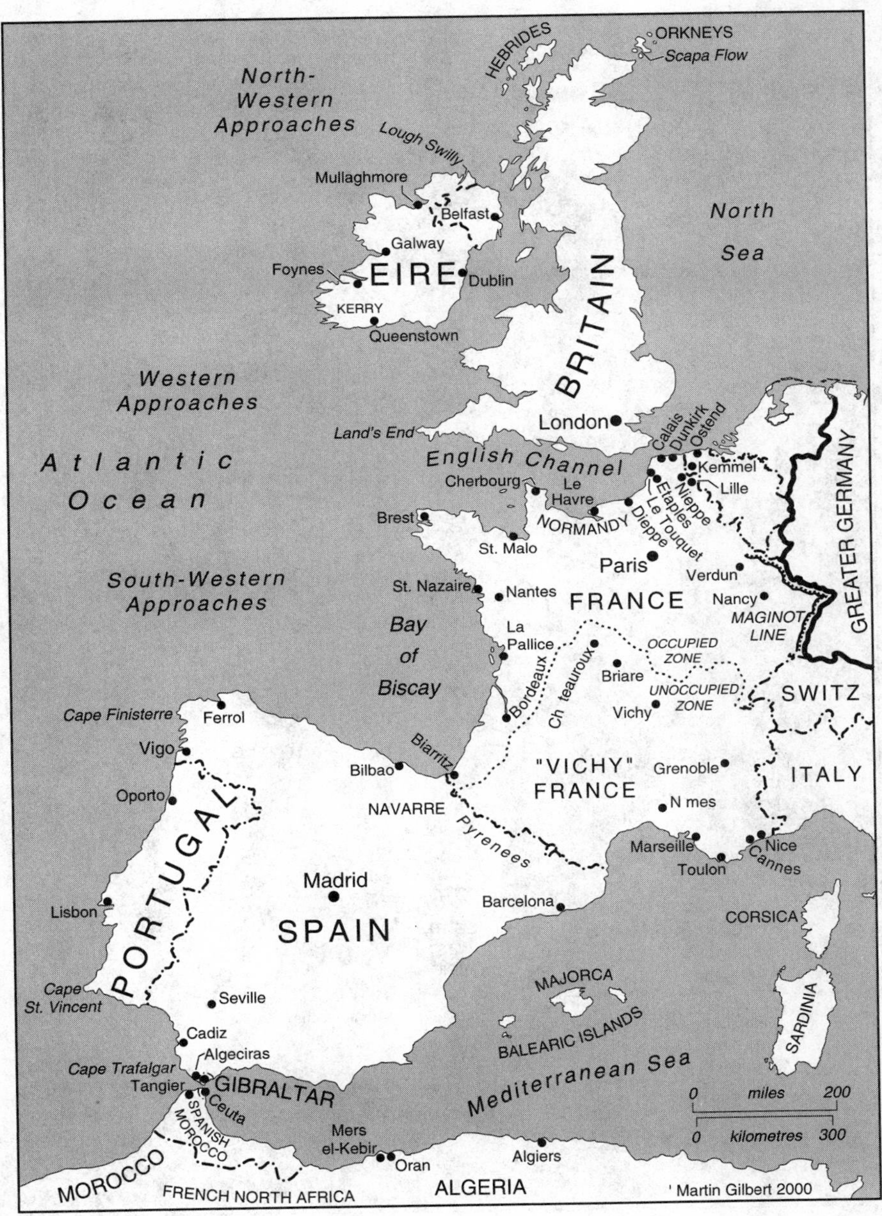

13. Western Europe from Scapa Flow to Cape St Vincent

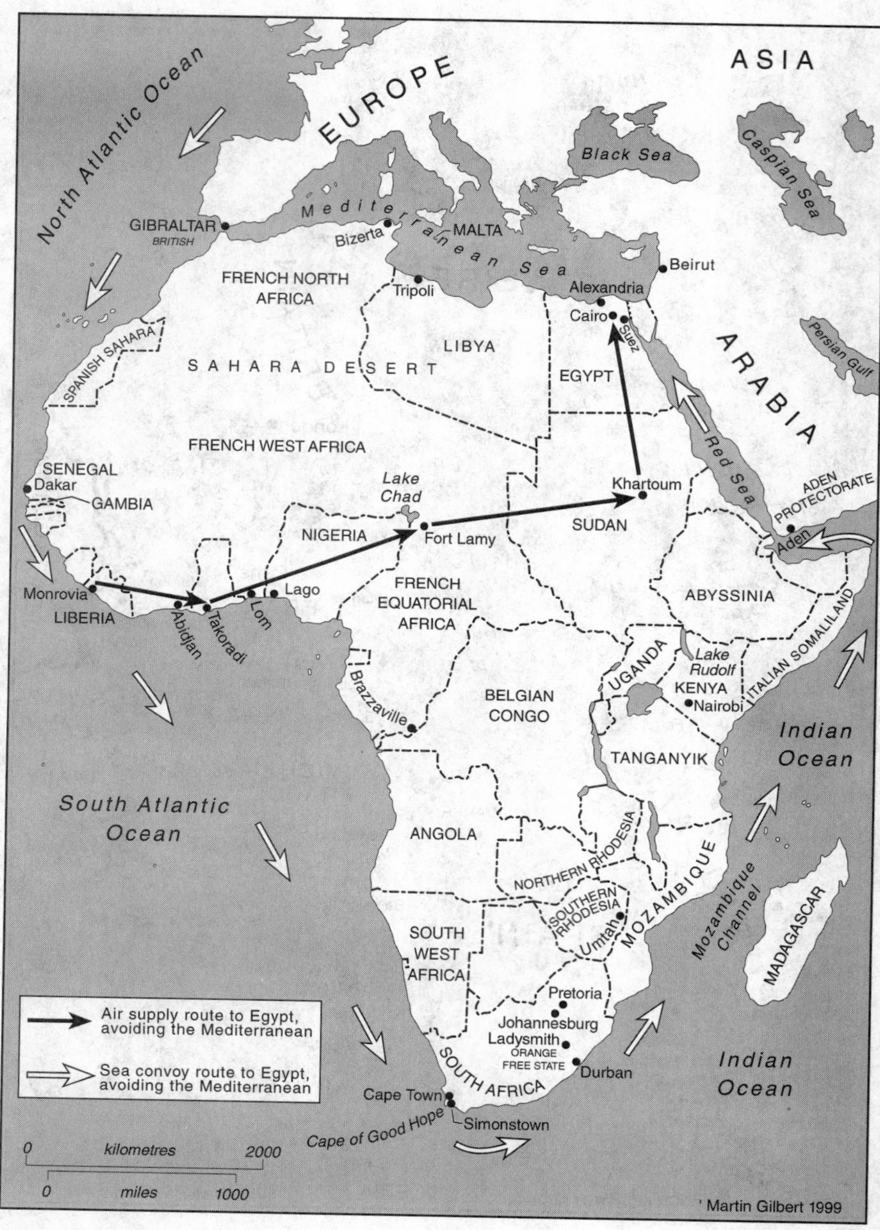
ASIA
EUROPE
North Atlantic Ocean
Black Sea
Caspian Sea
Mediterranean Sea
GIBRALTAR
BRITISH
Bizerta
MALTA
Beirut
FRENCH NORTH AFRICA
Tripoli
Alexandria
Cairo
Suez
SPANISH SAHARA
LIBYA
Persian Gulf
SAHARA DESERT
EGYPT
ARABIA
Red Sea
FRENCH WEST AFRICA
SENEGAL
Dakar
GAMBIA
Lake Chad
Khartoum
ADEN PROTECTORATE
NIGERIA
Fort Lamy
SUDAN
Aden
Monrovia
LIBERIA
Abidjan
Takoradi
Lom
Lago
FRENCH EQUATORIAL AFRICA
ABYSSINIA
UGANDA
Lake Rudolf
KENYA
Nairobi
ITALIAN SOMALILAND
Brazzaville
BELGIAN CONGO
Indian Ocean
TANGANYIK
South Atlantic Ocean
ANGOLA
NORTHERN RHODESIA
MOZAMBIQUE
Mozambique Channel
SOUTHERN RHODESIA
Umtah
MADAGASCAR
SOUTH WEST AFRICA
Pretoria
Johannesburg
Ladysmith
ORANGE FREE STATE
Durban
Air supply route to Egypt, avoiding the Mediterranean
Sea convoy route to Egypt, avoiding the Mediterranean
Indian Ocean
SOUTH AFRICA
Cape Town
Simonstown
Cape of Good Hope
0 kilometres 2000
0 miles 1000
' Martin Gilbert 1999

14. Africa

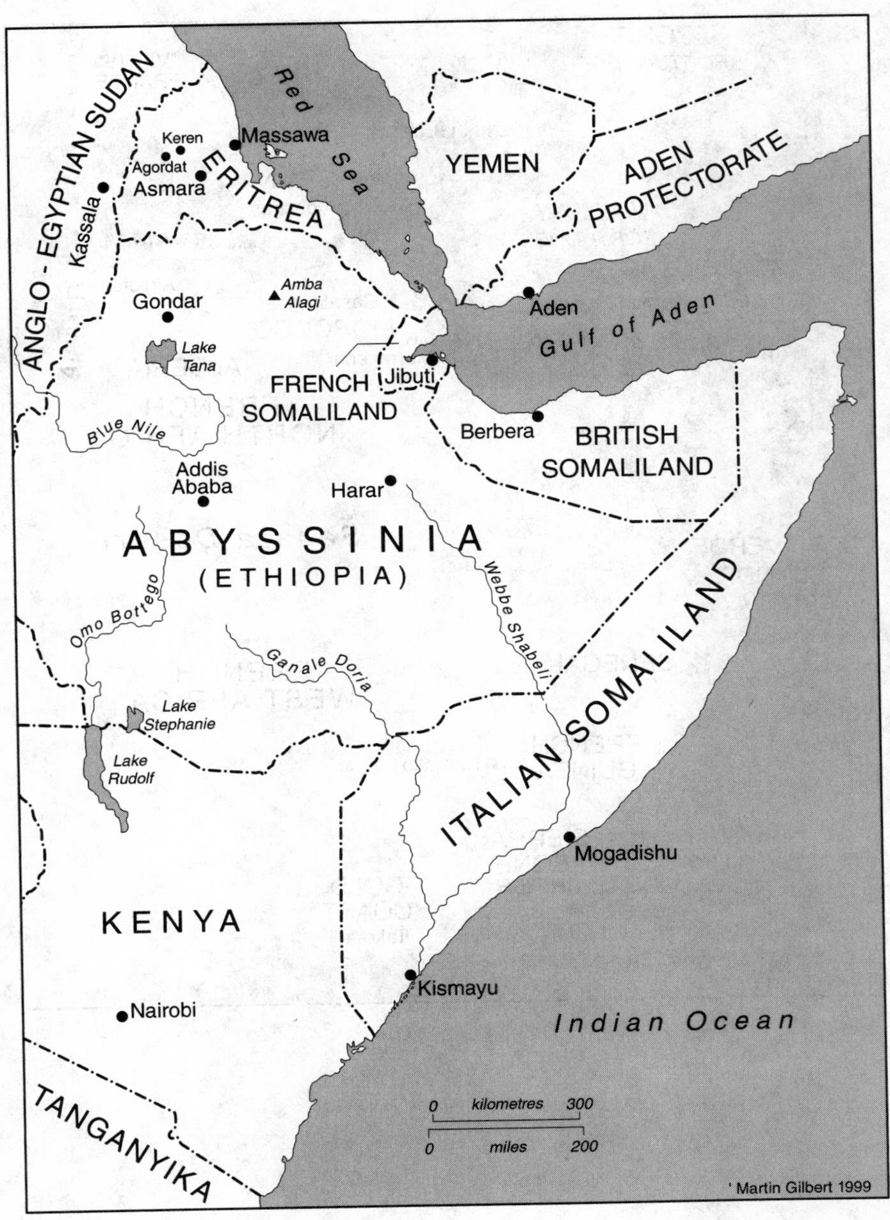

15. East Africa

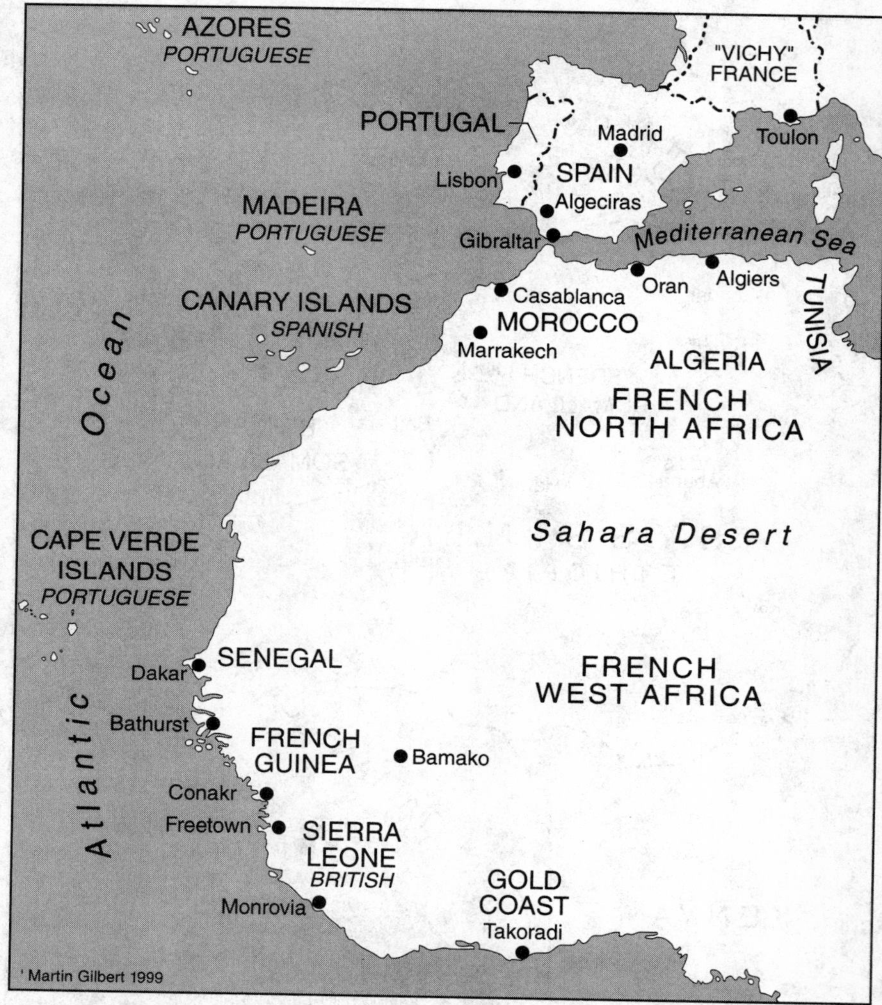

16. The Iberian Peninsula, French North Africa and West Africa

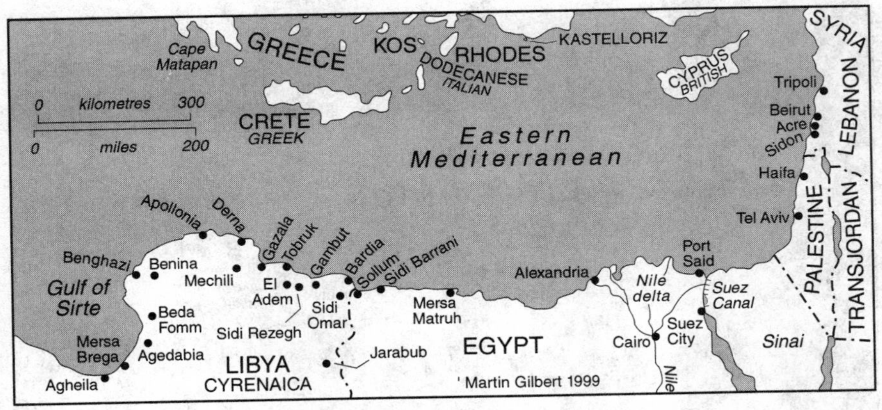

17. The Eastern Mediterranean

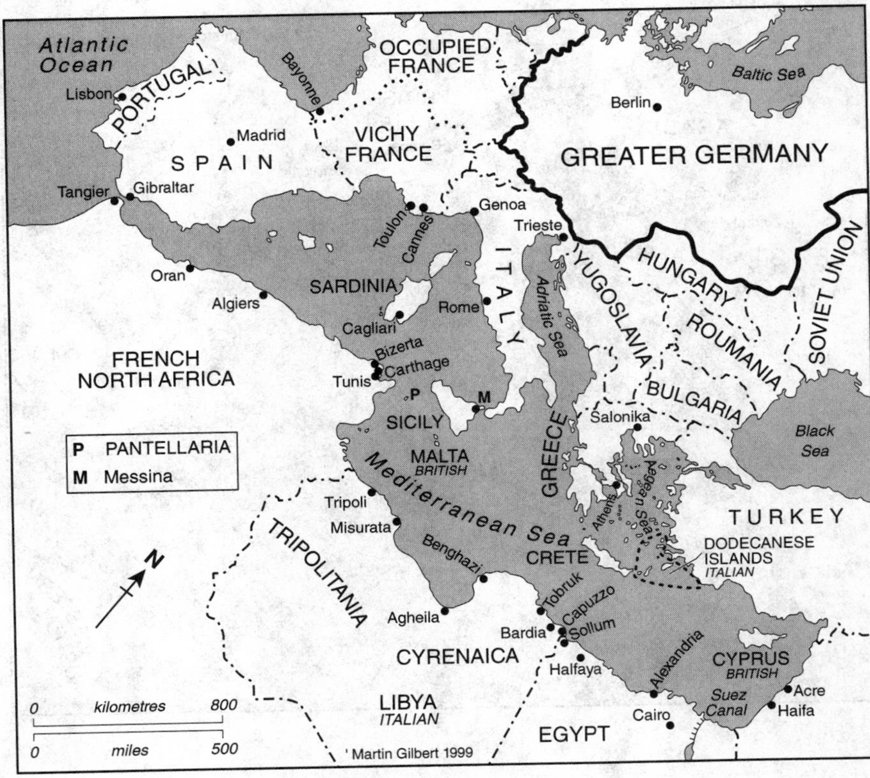

18. The Mediterranean

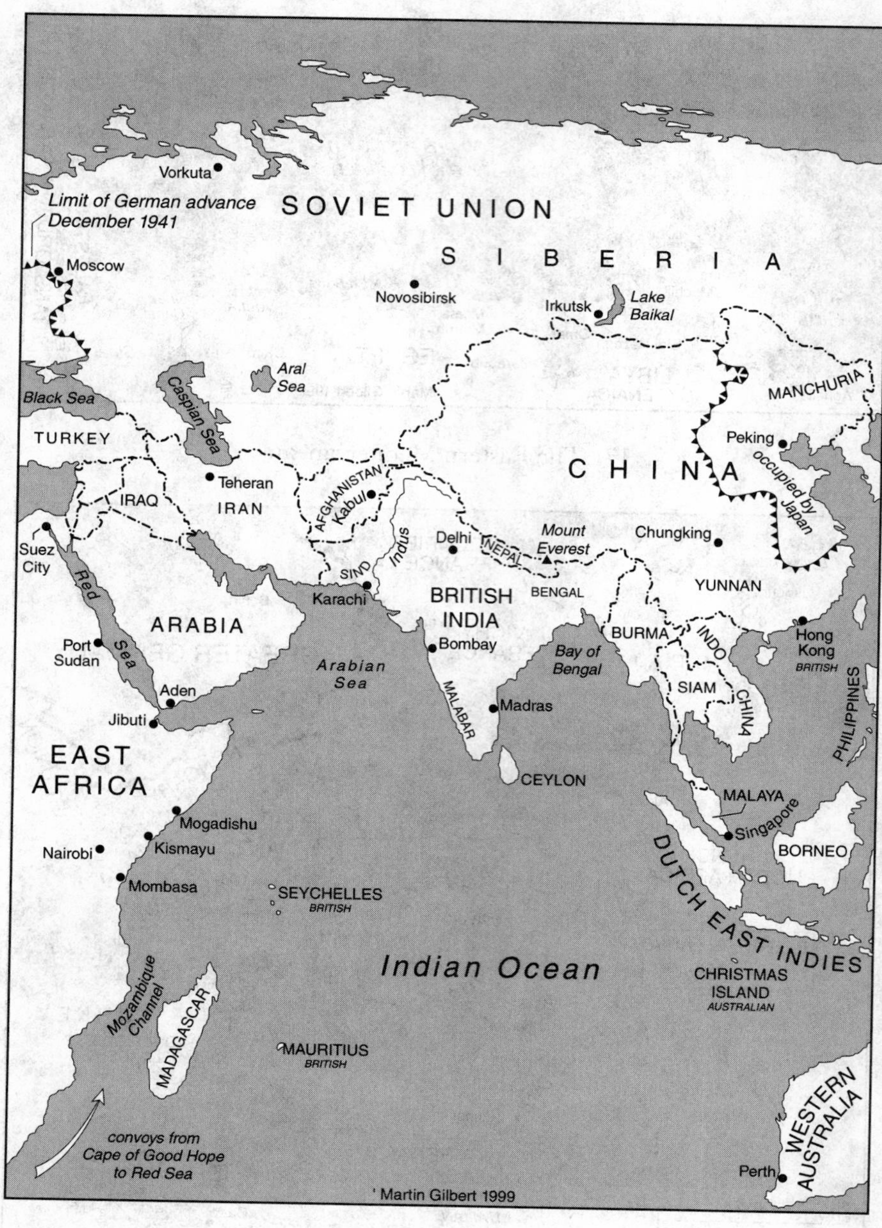
Vorkuta
Limit of German advance December 1941
SOVIET UNION
S I B E R I A
Moscow
Novosibirsk
Irkutsk
Lake Baikal
Aral Sea
Caspian Sea
Black Sea
TURKEY
MANCHURIA
Peking
occupied by Japan
C H I N A
Teheran
AFGHANISTAN
Kabul
IRAQ
IRAN
Suez City
Indus
Delhi
NEPAL
Mount Everest
Chungking
SIND
Karachi
BRITISH INDIA
BENGAL
YUNNAN
Red Sea
ARABIA
Port Sudan
Bombay
Bay of Bengal
BURMA
INDO CHINA
Hong Kong
BRITISH
Arabian Sea
SIAM
Aden
Jibuti
MALABAR
Madras
PHILIPPINES
EAST AFRICA
CEYLON
MALAYA
Singapore
BORNEO
Mogadishu
Kismayu
Nairobi
Mombasa
DUTCH EAST INDIES
SEYCHELLES
BRITISH
Indian Ocean
CHRISTMAS ISLAND
AUSTRALIAN
Mozambique Channel
MADAGASCAR
MAURITIUS
BRITISH
WESTERN AUSTRALIA
convoys from Cape of Good Hope to Red Sea
Perth
' Martin Gilbert 1999

19. The Indian Ocean

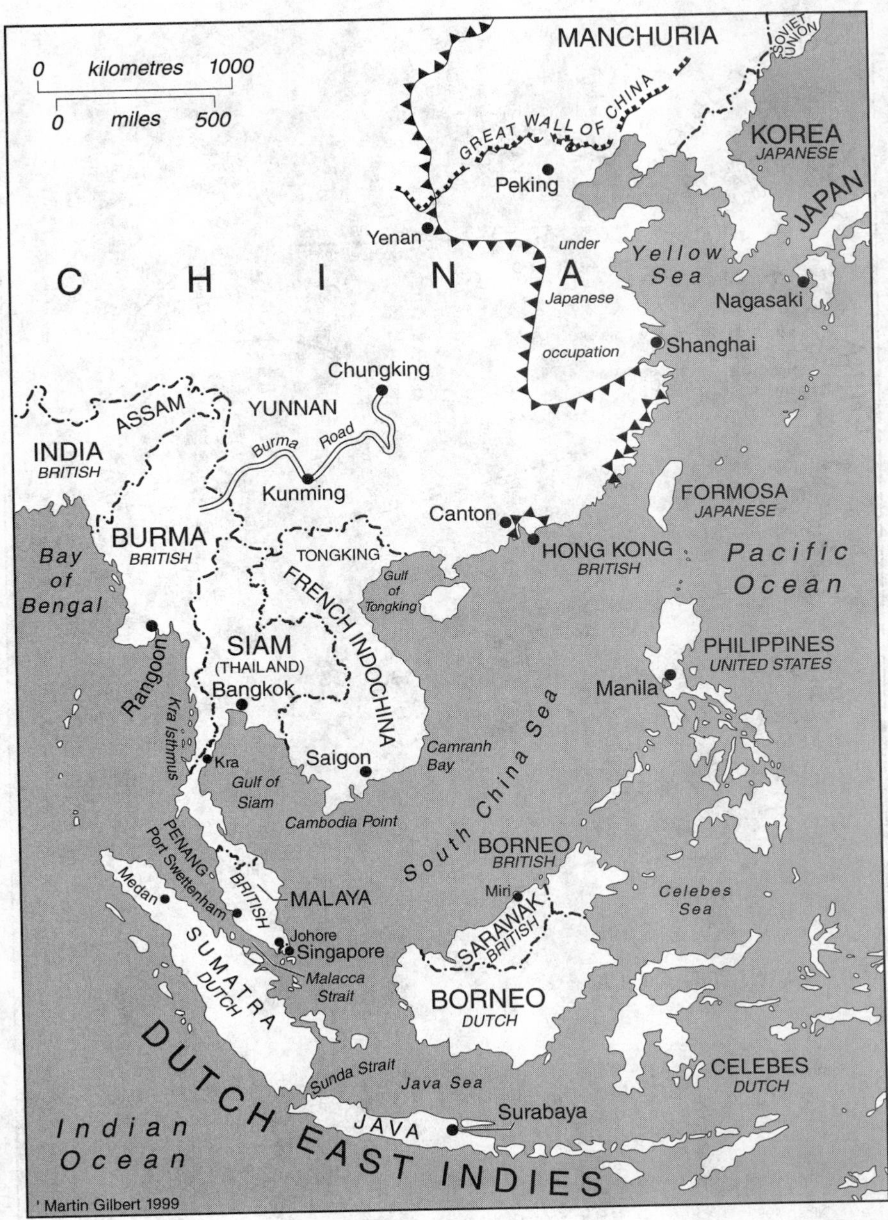

20. The Far East

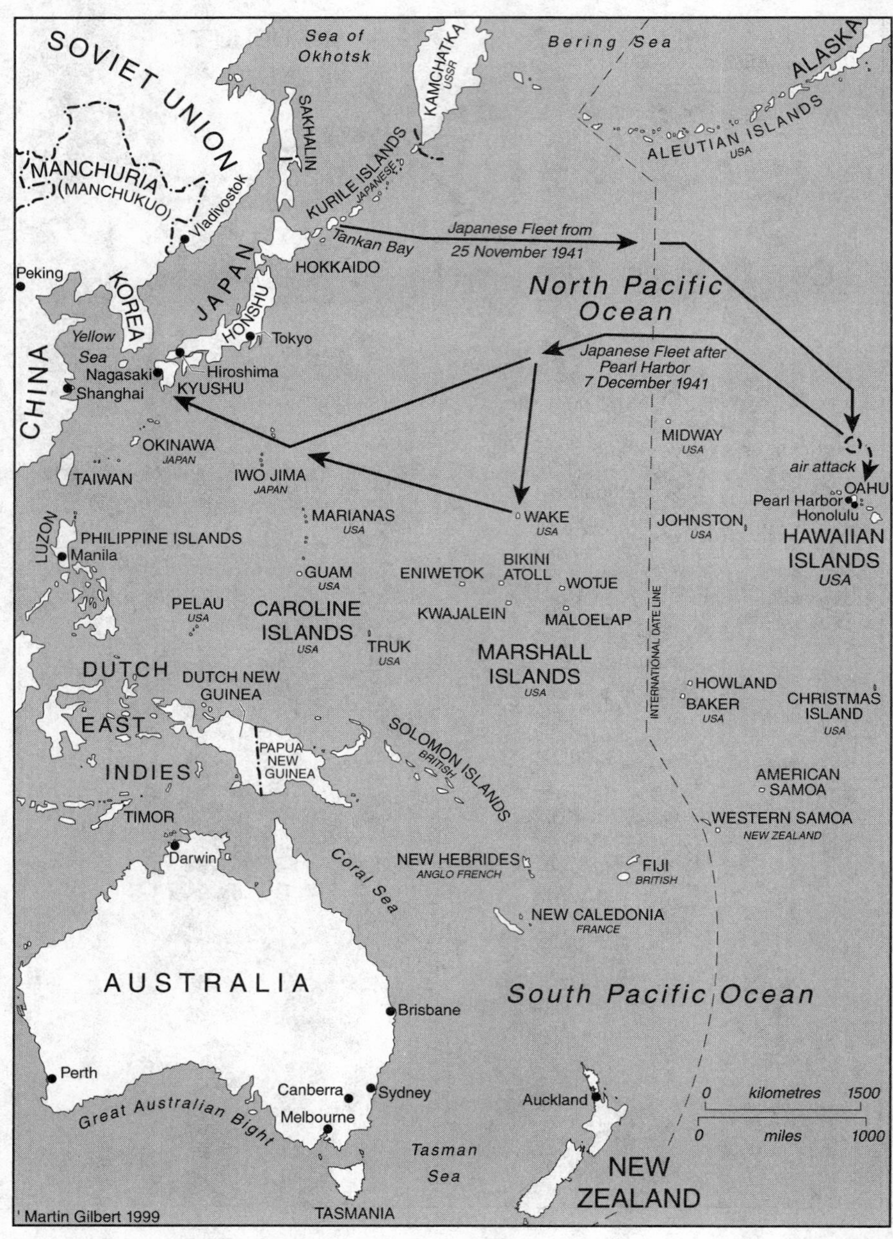

21. The Pacific Ocean

22. Hitler's plan, 11 June 1941

Index

Compiled by the Author

The Churchill Center

With its headquarters in Washington, D.C., and active internationally, the Churchill Center works to encourage study of the life and thought of Sir Winston Churchill; to foster research about his speeches, writings and deeds; to advance knowledge of his example as a statesman; and, by programmes of teaching and publishing, to impart that learning to men, women and young people around the world. The Center has an active membership in the United States, and also in Great Britain, Canada and Australia through the associated International Churchill Societies. Together, the Center and Societies publish a quarterly journal, *Finest Hour*, the bi-annual *Churchill Proceedings*, and other publications. They also sponsor annual international conferences, arrange Churchill tours which have visited Britain, Australia, France and South Africa, and have an internet website (www.winstonchurchill.org).

The Churchill Center has helped bring about the re-publication of more than twenty of Churchill's long-out-of-print books, and launched the campaign to support the completion of the Churchill War Papers by Martin Gilbert – of which this volume is the third – an endeavour generously supported by Mrs Wendy Reves. The Center has sponsored three academic conferences in the United States and Britain; several seminars where students and scholars discuss Churchill's books; scholarships for Churchill Studies at the University of Edinburgh and the University of Dallas; and a number of reference works. In 1998 it launched the Churchill Lecture Series, in which world figures seek to apply Churchill's experience to the world today.

Members of The Churchill Center and Societies have contributed a substantial sum to a permanent endowment which will supplement member subscriptions and donations, and enable the creation of a headquarters building, a Churchill library, computer facilities linked to the major Churchill archives, video programmes for schoolchildren, college and graduate level courses on Churchill's career, fellowships to assist graduate students, visiting professorships and academic appointments. The overall aim is to impress the qualities of Churchill's leadership on the new leaders of the 21st Century.

Membership in the Churchill Center and Societies is available for a small subscription, with discounts to students. For further information please contact:

- USA: The Churchill Center, PO Box 385-W, Hopkinton, NH 03229; toll-free telephone: (888) WSC-1874

- UK: International Churchill Society, PO Box 1257, Melksham, Wiltshire, SN12 6GQ

- Canada: International Churchill Society, 3256 Rymal Road, Mississauga, Ontario, L4Y 3C1

- Australia: International Churchill Society, 181 Jersey Street, Wembley, WA 6014.